The Law Book Price Guide:

A Market Value Reference for Antiquarian, Out-of-Print and Rare Law Books and Documents and Other Law-Related Materials.

Compiled with a Preface and Bibliography

by Richard Adamiak

Published by:
Richard Adamiak
1545 East 60th Street
Chicago, Illinois 60637

Published in the United States of America

ISBN 0-9610650-0-1

CONTENTS

SINCERE THANKS TO THE FOLLOWING COLLEAGUES FOR PERMISSION TO USE MATERIAL FROM THEIR CATALOGUES

Blackwell's Rare Books
Fyfield Manor, Nr. Abingdon
Oxon OX13 5LR, England
Tel: 0865-390692

D & E Lake Ltd.
106 Berkeley Street
Toronto, Canada M5A 2W7
Tel: 416-863-9930

Frognal Rare Books
18 Cecil Court, Charing Cross Rd.
London WC2N 4HE, England
Tel: 240-2815

Meyer Boswell Books
982 Hayes Street
San Francisco, CA 94117
Tel: 415-346-1839

Professional Books Ltd.
46 Milton Trading Estate
Abingdon, Oxfordshire OX14 4 SY
England
Tel: 235-834821

Robert H. Rubin Books
P.O. Box 558
Stoughton, Mass. 02072
Tel: 617-344-0740

If you are not already on their mailing lists you certainly should be. See the last page of the preface for instructions.

Preface

The purpose of this guide is to present the recent market values of rare, antiquarian and out-of-print law books and cognate materials. It makes available the recent catalogues of major specialist dealers in that area and this format provides the maximum information in a conveniently accessible form. For a work of its type its coverage is extensive, although not comprehensive. Many books are sold by these dealers either off the shelf or by quotation which do not appear in their catalogues; the sample is certainly representative.

The guide is designed to be useful to a wide variety of users, among them collectors, general booksellers, institutional law librarians, law firm librarians, scholars, other specialist law book dealers, special collection and reference librarians in academic and public libraries, appraisers and auctioneers. The substantial and diversified response to its publication has confirmed the assumption that the need for such a work would be recognized.

There do exist works which provide some information regarding the value of law materials, but their utility is limited by their highly selective content; for example, auction records do contain some law material, but their coverage is highly selective, usually limited to the most valuable variety. Other price guides also contain some law material but this is usually presented as falling within another area of the booktrade, such as Americana.

The object of this preface is to clarify the process by which prices are established by enumerating the factors whose interaction constitutes the process of evaluation, and by explaining how those factors interact.

Like other commodities, law materials are subject to the law of supply and demand. According to that law strict-applied, the purchase of a book is proof of its value at that time. A somewhat broader construction, however, is in order here. The prices in this work are anything but capricious, despite the fact that they may vary considerably. They are the result of the considered judgment of experienced professionals, all of whom exhibit a high degree of expertise. The fact that a book did not sell is not cogent evidence that it was "not worth" the price. Effective demand can be very much a matter of chance, varying greatly from place to place and time to time. Thus, these prices can be taken as indicators of "fair market value." On the other hand, the data should not be applied mechanically; the prices should be taken as indicators of price ranges.

The several variables which are considered by the dealers in law materials when pricing their stock are the same variables considered when evaluating rare books generally. These are the following: 1) intrinsic importance, including influence; 2) availability, both in the recent past and in the distant past; 3) the physical condition of the volume; 4) recent sale and auction records; 5) the fluctuation of the currency; 6) effective demand.

The first is the most salient variable. Few works are so well known that their importance is obvious; most require recourse to reference works to ascertain their significance. There are few books or authors about which no substantive information can be found, although some may require considerable time and effort. Naturally, the greater the authority of the source, the more reliable the opinion will be.

The second variable is availability. Should it be necessary to explore beyond this guide it is probable that more than one source will have to be consulted. The more rare a work appears from the perusal of the major reference works, the more works will have to be consulted to establish genuine rarity. To verify an unrecorded edition, the reference materials must be virtually exhausted. The fact that a work may be genuinely rare is no guarantee that another copy will not appear in the near future. So long as proper procedures have been followed, the appearance of another copy should not reflect badly on the integrity or expertise of the dealer.

The number of copies reported held in institutional collections is also relevant to the matter of availability. This is also determined by consultation of the proper references. This factor is only of significance when just one or two copies are reported.

The physical condition of the volume is always important and can be of critical importance. With very few exceptions the most valuable condition of any book is its original published state. This presents no problem with books published since the advent of standard publisher bindings in the nineteenth century. Before that, most books were sold in binder's boards, buff blue or grey, known simply as "boards." As a rule, books in this state are also "uncut," i.e., the margins of the leaves have not been trimmed. Sometimes they are also "unopened," which means precisely that. An "unopened" book is necessarily "uncut." The degree to which this uncommon state affects value can vary greatly; it greatly increases the value of works of signal importance but has no appreciable effect on those of modest significance. Such bindings were meant to be temporary; purchasers were expected to have the books bound to suit their taste. Leather of one sort or another was the popular choice, calf usually, sometimes sheep (also called roan), or vellum. For American books sheep was the rule, calf the exception. The use of morocco (goatskin) did not become widespread until the early nineteenth century. A book bound at, or very near, the time of publication in such materials is called a book in "contemporary" binding. This is the most common state in which old law books are found. Due to the nature of the materials, books in contemporary bindings are rarely free of external defects, are rarely "fine." The defects may be minor (slight rubbing, traces of wear, slight dampstain), moderate (hinges cracked or worn, extremeties worn, chipped spines, moderate dampstain) or serious (serious wear generally, heavy dampstain, covers detached or missing). The latter results in a considerable decrease of value. All external defects can be rectified to some degree, but no book should be restored until its importance has been determined. Works of little importance have been restored at a cost far beyond their value and works of great importance have been permanently devalued by improper procedures and materials. Library markings decrease value, can be costly to remove, and can render some books difficult to sell at any price. Signatures should be checked.

Procedures and costs vary considerably; the options are generally either complete rebinding or restoration. The latter procedure, which usually means rebacking the volume in leather which matches the covers, is most desirable but also more expensive than rebinding. But it is advisable if the volume is of significant value. The initial cost of acquisition and the cost of restoration must always be weighed against the anticipated price and effective demand.

For books of considerable value which cannot be restored, and for those of lesser value, rebinding is the most appropriate procedure. Rebinding a significant work always entails some devaluation but this can be minimized by the proper choice of style and materials. In all cases the result should duplicate or approximate the original, but there are standard exceptions. Books originally bound in full leather may be rebound in half-leather of the appropriate kind. Mistakes can be costly and consultation with an expert is advisable. I once saw a first edition of Adam Smith's Wealth of Nations (1776) rebound in standard grain morocco, a material which would never have been used at that time. The resulting incongruity greatly devalued the book and rendered it difficult to sell at any price.

Most frequently encountered in the law book trade are books of modest value, to be somewhat arbitrary, those worth less than $100.00. And frequently these are the books most in need of some work; they were published to be used by the legal profession and show signs of that use. Rebinding in cloth, if necessary, is most appropriate for these and linen is the best material. It is inexpensive, easy to work with and has a pleasant appearance and texture. For more hefty volumes starched buckram is appropriate. Dark colors are best because neither material is moisture or soil resistant.

Binders can vary greatly in price and expertise and it is advisable to secure more than one estimate.

Internal defects can also vary in seriousness, ranging from minor (loose leaves or signatures and slight dampstain or soil) to severe (missing text due to trimming, tearing or worming, very heavy dampstain and missing leaves). The last named may result in a total devaluation.

Odd volumes from multi-volume sets, with few exceptions, have no value. The exceptions are those from works of great importance. Dealers may hold these in the hope of completing the set and will pay a good price for the last volume.

When one is selling books they should be described as accurately as those in this guide. When shipping them, each volume should be wrapped tightly in paper and taped and ample packing should be added.

The next to be considered are price and auction records. Dealers are always interested in these but use them in different ways. A previous record is always relevant but any number of legitimate reasons may cause a dealer to price a comparable copy of the same book differently or a different copy similarly. For example, the effective demand for a particular book may be much greater for one dealer than another. This in my experience will not cause the dealer with the greater demand to price a book more than it is worth, but it may well cause the dealer with the lesser demand to price it less than it is worth. This partly accounts for the fact that dealers within this specialized area frequently buy from each other at no great discount. These dealers do not price their books mechanically on the basis of records and the user should again be cautioned against this error. No two books are identical; and effective demand is always decisive.

A similar admonition is in order regarding auction records. Because dealers comprise most of the audiences at auctions their records usually represent wholesale prices. Exceptions to this are usually conspicuous when several records for a book are available.

Because the value of books is always to some degree relative to the values of other books, no sale or auction record is ever completely irrelevant, however dated it may be. A record from fifty years ago may be the only information available for a book, but it will tell the user something if compared with the contemporary records of books whose current market values are readily accessible. However, such information must be used with great care.

The value of the currency is of course of considerable importance. In the past ten years or so the prices of law materials have risen both relatively, due to inflation, and absolutely, because of increased demand.

The foregoing are the variables considered by professionals when pricing their stock. Should the user find it necessary to look beyond this guide, a prudent consideration of these variables will enable him to establish an accurate price range for almost any law material encountered.

A question frequently asked is, where do dealers get their stock? The answer is, from a variety of sources, among them, private collections, institutional duplicates, public sales and auctions and finally, from general booksellers. Books tend to gravitate toward the dealers who specialize in them. Prices for law materials can vary considerably both within and beyond the specialized trade. Such materials appear on the shelves and in the catalogues of more general bookdealers of whose stock they constitute but a fraction. Among high-priced general bookdealers whose clientele is not particularly cost-conscious, prices for some materials, usually the better known, can range considerably beyond those found among specialists. On the other hand, prices among general bookdealers whose trade tends to be more of a local nature may be considerably below specialist prices. Here again, effective demand is the major determinant. By great effort and at considerable cost the specialist has expanded the sphere of effective demand. It may be nesessary to mail one thousand catalogues to locate the one recipient who not only wants to buy a particular book but who is willing and able to pay for it.

All the dealers specializing in law have established lines of supply of long standing with more general book-dealers, and these relations are based on mutual trust and mutual advantage.

With exceptions, specialized law book dealers will pay from ten percent to fifty percent of their anticipated retail price for materials they are interested in purchasing. A great deal of variation can be expected here and it is not at all attributable to suspicious practices. For example, one dealer may place a great premium on condition and will pay a higher price for a book in fine condition than another dealer for whom condition is less important. But the second may pay more than the first for an average copy. A dealer will pay more for a book if there is already a back-order for it or if this particular dealer has a client anxious to purchase the book. The overhead is lower because it won't be necessary to store and catalogue the book. Some dealers have a great demand for particular authors while other dealers may have found it almost impossible to sell those same authors. Timing can also play a part. A dealer may tend to pay more for a book if a catalogue is impending and if it is not only a book which will sell but which will also make the catalogue more interesting. There can be a great many variations in this matter.

It might seem from the foregoing that this business is quite lucrative. In my experience this is not the case. A brief enumeration of the costs which are not readily visible should demonstrate that the margin of profit is far less than one might expect: travel, reference works, printing, postage, advertising, rent, packing materials and in some cases salaries are the major expenses, but there are many minor ones. Also, the amount of time required is enormous. Moreover, the reader should bear in mind that a catalogue which sells 50% is regarded as a successful one. Still, it is profitable and interesting, and sometimes rewarding in other ways.

This guide can be kept current without much cost or difficulty, by getting on the mailing lists of the dealers whose catalogues were used for it. Simply write to them and ask to be added. And the best way to stay on a mailing list is to buy; so I would suggest an order, however modest, from each catalogue, to indicate continued interest. The information in these catalogues, as the user can readily see, is quite valuable, well worth the modest cost of keeping it up to date.

If the user is a dealer and does not intend to buy but would like the catalogues for pricing purposed only, it is best to say so. Send the dealer a check for $5.00 and ask to be added to the mailing list for a year. I'm sure that my colleagues will be happy to accommodate you.

It might interest the user to know that although we are competitors, the relations among the dealers in the specialist law book trade have always been quite cordial.

I would be happy to receive any comments or criticisms of the guide from any interested parties.

The following currency conversion table will be useful.

1975	1 pound sterling	= $2.22
1976		= $1.81
1977		= $1.75
1978		= $1.92
1979		= $2.12
1980		= $2.28
1981		= $2.02
1982		= $1.75

BIBLIOGRAPHY

This bibliography is rather extensive, perhaps too extensive, but the proper use of the works listed in it will enable any user conveniently to evaluate the factors which are the main determinants of value. Sometimes one source will be sufficient; but other times several will have to be consulted. The sources are categorized but of course there may be considerable overlapping.

AUCTION RECORDS.

American Book Prices Current. NY, current volumes.
Book Auction Records. Dawson (U.K.) current volumes.

(Streeter Sale) *The Celebrated Collection of Americana Formed by the Late Thomas W. Streeter*. NY, 1966.
Jahrbuch der Auktionspreise. Hamburg. current volumes.

For notes on the use of auction records see the preface to the guide.

GENERAL REFERENCE.

ADAMS, H. M., *Catalogue of Books Printed on the Continent of Europe, 1501-1600, in Cambridge Libraries*. 1967. strictly bibliographic.
Encyclopedia of the Social Sciences, 1936; an excellent reference for the importance of authors from all times and places.
Encyclopedia Britannica, 11th Edition, 1910; another excellent reference of similar scope.
CARTER, John, and MUIR, Percy (eds.), *Printing and the Mind of Man*, 1967; includes only the most important law materials but is worth consulting if in doubt; inclusion in this work significantly increases the value of a book.
National Union Catalogue: Pre-1956 Imprints, 1968ff; contains reliable bibliographic information and reliable records of holdings in institutional libraries.
British Museum General Catalogue of Printed Books to 1955, strictly bibliographic but should be consulted if a book is not listed in the previous entry, i.e., *Pre-1956*.
BRUNET, J-C., *Manuel du Librairie*. 5th ed., rev. 1860; contains not only sound bibliographic data, but some availability data and useful evaluations of individual works.
SABIN, Joseph, *A Dictionary of Books Relating to America*. 1868 (Reprinted in 1961); bibliographic data with selective holding information which is now unreliable.
SABINE, George, *A History of Political Theory*. 3rd ed., 1961, a fine and convenient reference.

ANGLO-AMERICAN LAW AND LEGAL HISTORY

The Annotated Eberstadt Catalogues of Americana. NY, 1965. Valuable annotations with price and availability data which, though dated, may still be of some use.

FRIEND, William J., *Anglo-American Legal Bibliographies: An Annotated Guide*. DC, 1944. (Reprint available from Rothman) of obvious importance.

HOFFMAN, David, *A Course of Legal Study*, 2nd ed., enl., Balto, 1836. valuable evaluations of the importance of individual works. (Reprint available from Hein & Co.)

MARVIN, J. G., *Legal Bibliography*. Philadelphia, 1847. Simply indispensable; extensive coverage and replete with the most useful annotations. (Reprint available from Meyer Boswell)

RADIN, Max, *Handbook of Anglo-American Legal History*. St.P., 1936. Extensive coverage in a very convenient format.

WALLACE, John W., *The Reporters, Arranged and Characterized with Individual Remarks*. 4th ed., rev. & enl. Boston, 1882. also indispensable. (Reprint available from Professional Bks)

BRITISH LAW AND LEGAL HISTORY

ABBOTT, L. W., *Law Reporting in England, 1485-1585*, C, 1973; Far more restricted in scope than Wallace but more extensive in the examination of the few reporters it does include.

BEALE, Joseph Henry (ed.), *A Bibliography of Early English Law Books*, Harvard, 1926; ANDERSON, Robert R. (ed), *A Supplement to Beale's Bibliography* (1943); bibliographic data only but valuable because of its unusual detail; the collations could not be more complete. (Reprint of both books bound together available from Professional Books)

COWLEY, John D., *A Bibliography of Abridgements, Digests, Dictionaries and Indexes of English Law to the Year 1800*; bibliographic data only but useful and the only work on the subject (Reprint available from Professional Books)

The Dictionary of National Biography, 1921-22. Standard; if nothing can be found about a particular book something can still usually be learned about the author and this is the first place to look.

HOLDSWORTH, Sir William, *The History of English Law*. 1903-66, (Reprinted, 1966), indispensable and of great authority.

LOWNDES, William T., *The Bibliographer's Manual of English Literature*, rev. & enl. ed., 1890. Very selective in law content but provides in convenient form very useful information for major works by major authors,for example, a listing of all the editions of Blackstone's *Commentaries*.

MAXWELL, W. Harold, and Leslie F., *A Bibliography of English Law to 1650, Including Books Dealing with that Period Printed from 1480 to 1925*. London, Sweet & Maxwell, 1925. Volumes one and two are the most important; bibliographic data and some short annotations of major works; this work, like the following entry, is frequently cited but I've never found it particularly useful.

MAXWELL, W. Harold and Leslie F., *A Legal Bibliography of the British Commonwealth of Nations*. 2nd ed., 1955ff. Volumes one and two "English Law to 1800" are the most relevant.

POLLARD, A. W., & REDGRAVE, G. R., A Short Title Catalogue of Books Printed in England, Scotland and Ireland....1475 1640. 2nd ed., rev. & enl. by W. A. Jackson et al. London, 1976. Comprehensive, with brief bibliographic data and some availability information in the form of locations of copies.

WING, David, Short-Title Catalogue of Books Printed in England Scotland, Ireland....1641-1700. 2nd ed., rev. & enl; the bare essentials of bibliographic data with some notice of the location of copies.

WINFIELD, Percy, The Chief Sources of English Legal History. Harvard, 1925. An excellent and convenient reference.

AMERICAN LAW AND LEGAL HISTORY

FRIEDMAN, Lawrence, History of American Law. NY, 1973. Reliable and convenient.

HOWES, Wright, U.S.IANA (1650-1950), rev. & enl. ed., NY, 1962. For many years a standard work: always worth consulting even though its law content, if that area is narrowly construed, is very selective; bibliographic data with price ranges which, although out of date, are still very valuable.

JOHNSON, Allen, Dictionary of American Biography. NY, 1928ff, Authoritative but selective.

KEITT, Lawrence, An Annotated Bibliography of Bibliographies of Statutory Materials of the United States. Harvard, 1934. Very useful for some of the materials most commonly encountered.

National Cyclopedia of American Biography. NY, 1898ff., Most comprehensive coverage; here many figures of lesser importance may be found.

POUND, Roscoe, The Formative Era of American Law. Boston, 1938. Covers the essentials and is very authoritative.

SHAW, Ralph R. and SHOEMAKER, Richard (eds.), American Bibliography: A Preliminary Checklist. NY, 1958ff, bibliographic data and location of copies. (for works from 1801-1835)

WARREN, Charles, A History of the American Bar. Boston, 1911. Extensive and authoritative. (Reprint available from Hein)

EVANS, Charles, American Bibliography, 1639-1800, 1903 (Reprinted 1963), bibliograpical data, select auction records and very limited location data, now unreliable.

MEDICAL JURISPRUDENCE

GARRISON, Fielding, A Medical Bibliography, 3rd ed. rev. by Leslie Morton. Philadelphia, 1970.

GARRISON, Fielding, An Introduction to the History of Medicine. 4th ed., rev. & enl., Philadelphia, 1929. Both works are authoritative and very useful.

ROMAN LAW, CANON LAW AND CONTINENTAL LEGAL HISTORY

These are frequently the areas in which reliable information is difficult to find. If the Encyclopedia of the Social Sciences and the 11th edition of the Britannica yield nothing, something can usually be found in one or more of the following.

ALLEN, J. W., History of Political Thought in the Sixteenth Century. London, 1928 (Reprinted 1960)

GIERKE, Otto, *Natural Law and the Theory of Society, 1500-1800*, translated with an Introduction by Ernest Barker. Cambridge, 1958; Contains a very useful extensive annotated bibliography.

GIRARD, Paul F., *A Short History of Roman Law, Being the First Part of His "Manuel Elementaire de Droit Romain"* translated by A. H. Frazer. Toronto, 1906. Contains a short but splendid bibliographical essay noting the major editions of the *Corpus Juris Civilis* and a sketch of the evolution of the civil law in Europe with estimates of the major figures in that evolution.

GROSS, Hanns, *Empire and Sovereignty: A History of the Public Law Literature in the Holy Roman Empire, 1599-1804*. Univ. of Chicago, 1973, Very useful and readily available.

JÖCHER, Christian, *Allgemeines Gelehrten Lexicon*.(General Directory of Scholars), 1750 (Reprinted 1960), 11vols. very valuable, both comprehensive and detailed.

LAROUSSE, Pierre, *Grand Dictionnaire Universel du XIX Siècle*. Paris, 1866ff.; Not as comprehensive as Jöcher but still very extensive in coverage; quite useful

SANDYS, John Edwin, *A History of Classical Scholarship*, 3rd ed., rev., Cambridge, 1920, 3vols., (Reprinted 1967). Because of its ambitious range it is frequently wanting in details but it can be useful in come cases.

The following two references are also quite useful:

BAKER, J. H., *Maunal of Law French*. (Available from Professional Books)

HORTON, Carolyn, *Cleaning and Preserving Bindings and Related Materials*, 2nd ed., rev. Chicago, American Library Association, 1969. A small amount of time and effort in the area of preservation can help to avoid costly restorations. This book is an excellent introduction to the subject and is available from the ALA, 50 E. Huron St., Chicago, Ill. 60611, at a very modest price.

ADDENDA

HOLDSWORTH, W. S. *The Historians of Anglo-American Law*. NY 1928.

HOLDSWORTH, W. S. *Sources and Literature of English Law*. Oxford 1925.

THE FROGNAL BOOKSHOP LTD.

68 LYMINGTON ROAD LONDON NW6 1JB ENGLAND
Tel: (01) 435 9757 Telex: Finresbook NW6

CATALOGUE 45

LAW AND LEGAL HISTORY OF THE BRITISH ISLES

(1975)

1. **[ACTS relating to PROPERTY].** Anno quadragesimo tertio Georgii III. Regis [etc.] 1803-5 & n.d. **4 items in 1 vol.** Folio. Contemp. ½ cf./mbld. sides; worn. **£15.00**
The items are 43 G.III. c.99 (re-organizing the collection of duties), 43 G.III. c.122 (establishing a property tax) with a Bill modifying it, & 45 G.III. c.49 (also altering the property tax).

2. **ANDREWS, W.** Old-time Punishments. 1890. 1st. Fp. plate (after Cruikshank) & many illus. Index. x, 251pp. Orig. decd. b'ram; very sl. fdd. **£15.00**

3. **ANNESLEY, Alexander.** A Compendium of the Law of Marine Insurances, Bottomry, Insurance on Lives, and of Insurance against Fire. 1808. 1st. Indices. xvi, 198 [ii] pp. Contemp. diced cf., jts. & corners worn; head of sp. defective. **Kress P.5294. £25.00**

4. **[ANSTEY, John].** The Pleader's Guide: a Didactic Poem ... containing the Conduct of a Suit at Law. New ed. 1803. xvi, 212, [i] pp. Later cf., uncut; sp. sl. rbbd. **£10.00**
A comic poem full of mockery of writs, fees, pleadings, and "the law's delay" in general.

5. **ASHBY, Matthew, & William WHITE (litigators).** Ashby and White: or, the Great Question, Whether an Action Lies ... for an Elector, who is Deny'd his Vote ... Resolved ... with other Cases. 1705. 1st. Index. [ii], 257, [iii] pp. Mod. ½ cf./mbld. sides. **Not in S. & M. £30.00**
Ashby brought & won an action against White for refusing to allow him to vote in an election. The Commons, being sole arbiters of elector's rights, took cognizance of the case & voted Ashby guilty of breach of privilege.

6. **ATKYNS, J.T.** Reports of Cases ... in ... Chancery, in the Time of ... Lord Hardwicke. 1765[-7]. Folio. **3 vols.** Indices. First advert. leaf to vol. 1. Vol. 3 lacks title & B_2 (fly-title). Mod. b'ram. **S. & M. ii. 104. £40.00**

7. **The ATTORNEY'S COMPLEAT POCKET-BOOK.** Containing ... Choice and Approved Precedents in Law, Equity, and Conveyancing. The Second Edition ... with large Additions. 1743. 12mo. Index. Final advert. leaf. [iv], 298, [xxvi] pp. Contemp. cf., lacks label; sl. rubbed. Bk-pl. **S. & M. ii. 70. £20.00**
This work (a collection of formulae for documents, without the remarks on court procedure & fees on which Powell (q.v.) lays such stress) was reprinted throughout the century.

8. **BACON, John (ed.).** Liber regis, uel thesaurus rerum ecclesiasticarum. 1786. 4to. Appendix. Index. [x], xviii, 1391pp. Contemp. annots. Contemp. cf., re-backed. **S. & M. ii. 36. £40.00**
An account of the value & income of all the benefices in Britain, based on the survey of Henry VIII's time; with remarks on the law concerning presentation to livings.

9. **[BACON, Matthew].** A New Abridgement of the Law. 1736[-1740]. 1st. **Vols. 1-3 (A – Piracy) only** (all published until 1759). Folio. Indices. [xxii], 692/[xx], 687, [i]/[xxii], 823, [i] pp. Two leaves in vol. 1 repeated. Contemp. cf.; sl. rbbd. **S. & M. ii. 2. £35.00**
This long-standing work was completed in five volumes in 1759. Its comprehensiveness, and still more the logical system of sub-division employed within each title, placed it far above all previous compendia of its kind.

10. **BARLOW, Theodore.** The Justice of Peace; a Treatise containing the Power and Duty of that Magistrate. 1745. 1st. Folio. Index. xxii, 592, [cxxxvi] pp. Contemp. cf.; rbbd. **S. & M. ii. 54. £30.00**
Barlow gains an advantage over Dalton & other predecessors, and anticipates Burn, by his use of an alphabetical method.

11. **BARRINGTON, Daines (1728-1800).** Observations on the More Ancient Statutes, from Magna Charta to the Twenty-first of James I. cap. XXVII, with ... a Proposal for New Modelling the Statutes. 1769. 3rd ed., rev. 4to. Index. xii, 516pp. Contemp. cf., re-backed; corners worn. **£40.00**
A work written in a liberal spirit, which condemns many savage punishments & other injustices which had been founded (sometimes without authority, as Barrington shows in regard to "peine forte et dure") on the ancient statutes, & calls for an annual committee of lawyers to recommend obsolete acts for repeal. This edition includes much new material drawn from Petyt's MSS. in the Inner Temple Library.

12. **BATEMAN, Joseph.** The Auctioneer's Guide; containing a Practical Treatise on the Law of Auctions ... Rules for Valuing ... Law of Distress ... Forms, Tables and Precedents. N.d. [1846]. 3rd ed., rev. Index. Publisher's cat. & cat. of Waterlow & Sons (printers), with fine lith. trade-card, at end. xxiv, 358, 16, [iv] pp. Orig. cl., re-backed with part of orig. spine; sl. rbbd. **S. & M. iii. 15. £10.00**

13. **BATEMAN, Thomas.** A Treatise of Agistment Tithe ... as Settled in Pursuance of a Decree of ... Exchequer. 1778. 2nd ed., rev. xxiv, 102pp. Lacks last (blank or advert.), leaf. **S. & M. ii. 44.** – **EVERY MAN his OWN PROCTOR;** containing Instructions ... to obtain Probate of Wills and Letters of Administration. 1786. 1st. 72pp. **S. & M. ii. 158.** – **LOVELASS, P.** The Law's Disposal of a Person's Estate who Dies without Will or Testament. 1790. 6th ed., rev. Index. xxii, 258, [x] pp. **S. & M. ii. 148** – **3 works in 1 vol.** Contemp. ½ cf./mbld. sides, rbbd. **£40.00**
Bateman's work explains a form of tithe exacted on the cost of pasturage of sheep & cattle, which was for long neglected, but suddenly (& most inexplicably, since much pasture-land was being converted to arable uses at the time) began to be widely demanded by clergymen in the late eighteenth century.

14. **BLACKHAM, Robert J.** Wig and Gown; The Story of the Temple, Gray's & Lincoln's Inn. N.d. [c.1932]. 1st. Illus. Index. xii, 240, [iv] pp. Orig. cl., sl. fdd.; d.w. **£7.50**

15. **BLACKSTONE, Henry.** Reports of Cases ... in ... Common Pleas and Exchequer Chamber. 1791[-6]. 1st. **2 vols.** Folio. Indices. [xvi], 526, [ii], 527-694, [xxii]/[x], 626, [xxii] pp. Sl. browned. Mod. b'ram. **S. & M. ii. 87.**
£25.00

16. **BLACKSTONE, Sir William (1723-1780).** Commentaries on the Laws of England. Dublin, 1771. First uniform ed. in 8vo. **4 vols.** Two engr. tables in vol. 2. Appendices. Index. Vol. 1 lacks final blank, vol. 4 first & last blanks. Sig. 2G (vol. 3) mis-signed 2H. Sm. hole in E, (vol. 4) aff. three letters. Sl. spotted. Contemp. cf., new labels; head of sp. & upper cvr. of vol. 2 repaired; jts. rbbd. **S. & M. ii. 5. £80.00**
With Blackstone the law of England, hitherto despised by the universities & confined within the crabbed exclusive circle of the Inns, achieved a rational basis which entitled it to the rank of a liberal & humane study. This accomplishment far outweighs the flaws of the work, its expedient generalities and its too-ready acceptance that "whatever is is right".

17. ——————— Commentaries ... with Notes and Additions by Edward Christian. 1809. **4 vols.** Engr. fp. port., & fldg. engr. table in vol. 2. Index. Orig. cl., uncut fdd. & sl. stnd. **S. & M. ii. 5.**
£70.00

18. ——————— Commentaries ... Barron Field's Analysis ... Notes, and a Life ... by George SHARSWOOD. Philadelphia. 1876[-7]. **2 vols.** Fp. port. Index. 8, xl, 485, 531/xx, 368, 443, [xci] pp. Mod. cl. **£30.00**
Sharswood's ed. dates from 1859 & illustrates the respect still accorded to the work in the U.S.A., where it need not be distorted by the revisions necessary to maintain it as a manual of current law (which indeed it was never intended to be), and so can be read in its original purity.

19. ——————— Commentaries ... in the Order, and comprising the whole Substance, of ... Blackstone. 1819. 1st thus. Index. xii, 838, xviii, [xxxi] pp. Contemp. cf., sl. rubbed. Bk-pl. Sir Robert Peel [the younger], & one other bk-pl. **£20.00**
A revision & re-arrangement, as well as abridgement, of Blackstone's work.

20. **BOHUN, William.** Institutio Legalis: or, an Introduction to the Study and Practice of the Laws of England, as now Regulated and Amended. 1724. 3rd ed. rev. Index. Advert. leaves, xvi, 572, [xiv], [vi] pp. I_4 & T_4 torn without loss. Contemp. cf., fine. **S. & M. ii. 7. £50.00**
Avoiding historical & philosophical excursions (except for one, in which he asserts that the Court of Common Pleas existed before Magna Charta), Bohun digests in one body the various guides to K.B. & C.P. practice, actions, pleas etc.

21. **[BOOTH, William].** The Compleat Sollicitor Performing his Duty: and Teaching his Clyent. By Ja. Cotterel, 1672. 4th ed., rev. Index. [xxiv], 488pp. Sl. stnd. at end. Contemp. sheep, head of sp. sl. torn. **Wing B. 3738D. S. & M. ii. 70. £40.00**
The title of solicitor was then to the courts of equity what that of attorney was to those of law, but in effect the two were often combined. The author, after some very quaint general remarks, proceeds to the writs, actions, forms etc. of each court.

22. **BORTHWICK, W.M.** Letters to Sir William Rae ... Lord Advocate of Scotland. Edinburgh, 1825. 1st. [ii], 22pp. Mod. mbld. wraps. **£6.00**
Complaints of "the law's delay" & of persecution by a high officer, Sir John Hope, Deputy Advocate. Borthwick, a journalist, implies a political motive behind his sufferings.

23. **BOSANQUET, J.B. & C. PULLER.** Reports of Cases ... in ... Common Pleas, and Exchequer Chamber, and in the House of Lords. **Vol. 2 (1799-1801), of 3, only.** Folio. Index. xii, 614, [xx] pp. Mod. cl. **S. & M. ii. 87. £8.00**

24. **BOYD, Robert.** The Office, Powers, and Jurisdiction of His Majesty's Justices of the Peace, and Commissioners of Supply. Edinburgh, 1787. 1st. **2 vols.** 4to. Index. xxvi, 510/[ii], 513-1028, [xx] pp. Short tear in 2F, , without loss. Contemp. cf., sl. rbbd. **Not in S. & M.**
£50.00
Boyd's work differs from those of Burn & his predecessors in that, while they expound the particular duties of a J.P. for his own instruction, Boyd explains the character & scope of the magistrature (especially in Scotland) to the layman. His observations on legal history are curious & wide-ranging.

25. **[BRADY, Robert].** A Full and Clear Answer to a Book ... by William Petit ... Animadversions upon a Book, called Jani Anglorum Facies Nova. For Samuel Lowndes, 1681. 1st. [viii], 252, [ii], 40, [ii], 134pp. Contemp. cf., jts. sl. worn. **Wing B. 4188-9. S. & M. i. 100.**
£50.00
Opposes Petyt's theory that the parliamentary system was already advanced in development before the reign of Henry III.

26. ——————— An Historical Treatise of Cities, and Burghs or Boroughs. Shewing their Original ... also ... when they first sent their Representatives to Parliament. 1704. 2nd ed. Folio. Index. Cancel (variant preface) bound after title. 3 unsigned leaves after M_2. Irregularly paged. Title sl. browned. Mod. ½ cf./mbld. sides. Bk-pl. **S. & M. i. 259.**
£40.00

27. ——————— Anr. copy, without extra cancel leaf. Contemp. panelled cf., later label; sl. rubbed. **£40.00**

28. **BRIBERY, CORRUPTION & INTIMIDATION** in the Election of Members ... an Abridgement of the Evidence ... before the Select Committee. 1837. 1st thus. viii, 148pp. Re-bound wraps; sl. fdd. **£8.00**

29. **BROOKE, Sir Robert (?–1558).** La Graunde Abridgement· [–La Secounde Part.] In aedibus Richardi Tottell, 12th Oct. 1576. [4th ed.] **2 pts. in 1.** French text. Black letter. 4to. Woodcut title-border to each part (McKerrow 196). Blank 2X, (final) to pt. 1. Index. [iv], 351, [i]/328 leaves. Some marginal stains & few worm-holes, but a fine copy in contemp. English cf. blind lines & central stamp, initialled W.P., lacks ties, upper jt. neatly restored at head & foot. **Beale R.471-2. S.T.C. 3828. Sweet & Maxwell i. 187. £250.00**
Based on the similarly-titled work of Fitzherbert, but enriched with much new material from the Year Books of the last two Henries & from Brooke's own experience on the bench. With the signature & note of purchase, dated 1650, of Roger Twysden (1597-1672), Kentish antiquary, student of mediaeval history, & steadfast Royalist.

30. **BROWN W[illiam].** Privilegia Parliamentaria Senatûs consensu sublata. Being Remarks upon the Acts ... for preventing any Inconveniencies that may Happen by Privilege of Parliament ... How to commence & prosecute ... Suits ... against any Peer, Member ... or other Privileged Person. 1704. 1st. Index. [viii], 147, [xiii] pp. Final advert. leaf. Contemp. sheep, rbbd. **S. & M. ii. 18.**
£25.00
By the acts of 1692 & 1704 members of the two houses were laid open to private prosecution, though not to arrest. An appendix, "Curiosities in Clerkship", includes one of the last cases of a Wager of Law (vadium legis), whereby one was discharged of a debt alleged against him on producing six witnesses to swear that it did not exist: a procedure whose name (to wage or wag = to carry, carry out, perform) & character seem to mark it as a Saxon survival.

31. ——————— Praxis almae curiae Cancellariae ... a Collection of Precedents, by Bill and Answer, Plea and Demurrer, in Causes (wherein Equity hath been allowed) ... in ... Chancery. 1714. 3rd ed., rev. **2 vols.** Index. Two final advert. leaves to vol. 2. [viii], 576/[viii], 484, [xii] pp. Contemp. cf., sl. rbbd. **S. & M. i. 218. £30.00**
Vol. 1 is a collection of bills, with an appendix of orders; vol. 2 contains answers, demurrers etc. Many actual proceedings of the previous thirty years are transcribed.

32. **BRUNTON, George & David HAIG.** An Historical Account of the Senators of the College of Justice, from ... M.D.XXXII. Edinburgh, 1836. 1st. Index. xlviii, 567pp. **44 autographs** (incl. some duplicates) tipped in or mounted on back e-p's. Inscribed by Mrs. Haig on e-p. Contemp. ¼ roan/cl. sides; front hinge broken. Bk.-pl. **S. & M. v. 16.**
£50.00
The autographs include David Hume, James Boswell, Alexander Wight, William Robertson, Lord Kames, & other notables of Scottish law & literature.

33. **BUNBURY, William.** Reports of Cases in the Court of Exchequer. Ed. Geo. Wilson. 1755. 1st. Index. Table of Barons of the Exchequer, etc. Privilege leaf before title. [vi], 348, [xlviii] pp. Signed by Wilson at end of preface. Few annots. Mod. ¼ cf./mbld. sides. **S. & M. ii. 100. £25.00**

34. **BURN, Richard.** A New Law Dictionary: Intended for General Use ... Continued ... by John Burn. 1792. 1st. **2 vols.** Fp. port. Final advert. leaf, viii, 442/[ii], 446, [ii] pp. S_1 (vol. 2) torn without loss. Contemp. cf., sl. rbbd. **S. & M. ii. 2. £30.00**
Burn deletes many Latin & French definitions which became obsolete when writs & pleadings were ordered to be given in English, & so finds room to make the larger articles (Judgement,

Jury, Purchase, Will, etc.) more detailed & better arranged than before.

35. ———— The Justice of the Peace, and Parish Officer. Twenty-third ed., ed. George Chetwynd. 1820. **5 vols.** Index. Orig. bds., uncut; rbbd; sps. defective. **S. & M. ii. 56.** £30.00

36. **BYNG, John, Admiral.** The Trial . . . at a Court Martial. 1757. 1st. Folio. Appendix. 130, 19pp. Mod. wraps. £35.00

Byng was found guilty of disobeying orders in an action off Minorca. This sacrifice of a brave & popular officer to a doubtful principle was widely resented, & prompted Voltaire's remark that the English thought it proper to shoot an occasional admiral "pour encourager les autres".

37. **[CARTER, Samuel].** Lex Vadiorum. The Law of Mortgages . . . Payment of the Mortgage-Money . . . Assignments . . . Redemption . . . Cases of Pawns and Pledges Adjudged. 1706. 1st. Index. [xvi], 224, [xxiv] pp. Contemp. sheep, later label; sl. rbbd. **S. & M. ii. 150.** £30.00

Gives special attention to precedents in equity upon various branches of the subject.

38. **CAY, John.** An Abridgment of the Public Statutes in Force and Use from Magna Charta. 1739. 1st. **2 vols.** Folio. Index. [xxxvi], [674]/[ii], 742, [xliv] pp. Errata leaf. $6O_{3-4}$ in vol. 1 (pp. 509-512) inverted. Contemp. cf., rubbed. **S. & M. ii. 177.** £40.00

The first uniform abridgment since Pulton's (q.v.). Includes at length the two books of customs-rates (Grimston's & Compton's), & a table of sheriff's fees.

39. **CHANCELLOR, E.B.** The Romance of Lincoln's Inn Fields and its Neighbourhood. N.D. [c.1930]. 1st. Illus. Index. Orig. cl.; sl. mkd. £5.00

40. **CLARK, George.** The Penal Statutes Abridged, and Alphabetically Arranged. 1777. 1st. xii, 206pp. **S. & M. ii. 113.** – **A DIALOGUE** between a Country Gentleman and a Lawyer, upon the Doctrine of Distress for Rent. 1772. 1st. Index. xii, 72pp. **S. & M. ii. 143.** – **EVERY MAN'S POCKET COMPANION:** or, Hints upon the Law respecting Landlord and Tenant. 1778. 1st, [ii], 38pp. **S. & M. ii. 143. 3 works in 1 vol.** Contemp. cf., sl. rubbed. £35.00

The first work is a guide to penalties for magistrates, the second explains the laws of distress & how it is affected by the type of tenure, & the third contains remarks on notices to quit & ejectments.

41. **CLARKE, Thomas J. (1857-1916).** Glimpses of an Irish Felon's Prison Life, introd. P.S. O'Hegarty. Dublin, 1922. 1st. xx, 104pp. Orig. cl.; fdd. & sl. stnd. £6.00

Prison memories of 1883-98 by an emissary from the "blood-dyed Clan-na-Gael" executed as a rebel in 1916.

42. **COKE, Sir Edward.** The First [-Fourth] Part of the Institutes of the Lawes of England. By M.F., I.H. & R.I. [etc.], 1639 [1642, 1648, 1644]. **Four parts in three vols.** Pt. 1, fourth ed.; pt. 3, second ed.; pts. 2 & 4, **first eds.** Folio. Black letter. Fp. ports to pts. 1 & 3 (wanting from 2, not issued in 4). Woodcut title-borders (McK. 283). Indices. Port. of Littleton in pt. 1. Final blanks to pts. 1, 3 & 4. Contemp. cf., later labels; jts. of pt. 2 sl. worn. **S.T.C. 15787, Wing C.4948, 4961 & 4929; S. & M. i. 286, 345, 224 & 176.** £500.00

The most valuable part of Coke's work (& by several years the first to appear, whence the discrepancy of edition numbers) was the first, the Commentary on Littleton's Tenures, a precious compendium of the rights of property in law & history. The rest is diffuse & discursive, & the task of producing true Institutes (in Justinian's sense) of English law was reserved for Blackstone; but if the design is faulty, the weight & authority of Coke's observations cannot be impugned.

43. ———— The Compleat Copyholder . . . Antiquity and Nature of Mannors ai ' Copy-holds . . . CALTHROP, C., 'lation between the Lord of a Manno. .d the Copy-holder . . . Forme of Keeping a Copy-hold Court. For W. Lee, and D. Pakeman, 1650. 1st collected. **3 pts. in 1 vol.** 4to. Index. [viii], 76, [iv]/[ii], 52/[ii], 180pp. Mod. ¼ cf./mbld. sides; fine. **Wing C.4914. S. & M. i. 246.** £60.00

The seignorial courts (courts leet & courts baron), which decided disputes between the lord of the manor & his tenants, were incoherent & unregulated survivals from the feudal age. This work of Coke imposed order & the authority of the central judicial system on these local jurisdictions, & established as fact the old dictum of Bryan, that the court-leet was only a necessary extension of King's Bench.

44. ———— The Reports . . . faithfully rendred into English. For W. Lee, M. Walbanck, D. Pakeman, and G. Bedell, 1658. 1st Eng. Folio. Indices. Final leaf with table of judges. [viii], 1131, [iii] pp. Several names on title. Lower margins damp-stained throughout. Title sl. frayed. New ¼ cf./mbld. sides; red label. **Wing C.4944. S. & M. i. 196.** £65.00

First English edition of the complete series of Reports as published in French in eleven volumes. An English abridgment had appeared in 1650. Coke's Reports revived a tradition which had been neglected since the cession of the Year Books, & prepared the way for the innumerable volumes of reports which began to appear under the Commonwealth & are continued in the semi-official series of to-day.

45. ———— The Reports . . . exactly Translated . . . to which are now Added the Respective Pleadings. 1738. **13 pts. in 7 vols.** Indices. Some browning. New cl., leather labels. **S. & M. i. 196.** £75.00

The pleadings had been given in Latin in an ed. of 1727.

46. ———— [HAWKINS, William]; An Abridgment of the First Part of My Ld. Coke's Institutes. 1719. 3rd ed. Index. Advert. leaf before title. [vi], 495, [xcii] pp. Index sl. browned. Contemp. cf., jts. sl. rbbd. **S. & M. i. 288.** £30.00

Hawkins fuses Coke & Littleton into one, & adds some observations from writers who lived subsequent to Coke's day.

47. **COLERIDGE, [John Duke Coleridge, Baron]. (Chief Justice 1880-94).** Speech . . . in the . . . Lords . . . upon the Bill to prevent Cruelty to Animals. Soc. for the Protection of Animals, 1876. 1st. 8pp. Disbound. £5.00

Coleridge supports the Bill, but allows (in deference to public opinion) some indulgence to blood-sports.

48. ———— COLERIDGE, E.H. Life, 1904. 1st. **2 vols.** Illus. Index. xiv, 306/[vi], 451pp. Orig. cl., uncut, worn; lib. labels on cvrs. £5.00

49 **COLQUHOUN, Patrick (1745-1820).** A Treatise on the Police of the Metropolis, explaining the Various Crimes and Misdemeanors . . . and suggesting Remedies. 1796. 1st. Foldg. table. xiv, 5-369, [ii] pp. A_1 cancelled; quire A contains only three leaves. Final errata leaf. Lacks front e-p; otherwise a fine copy in orig. mbld. bds., paper label, uncut., sl. worn. **S. & M. ii. 128.** £65.00

50. ———— Sixth edition. 1800. ½ title. Index. [xiv], xvi, 655, [xxxii] pp. New ¼ cf./mbld. sides. £35.00

51. ———— Seventh ed. 1806. ½ title. Index. [xiv], xvi, 655, [xxxii] pp. Contemp. tree cf. £35.00

Colquhoun was among the first to see the need for an organized police-force designed to prevent rather than to punish crime; he clarified the relation between police, magistrates & judges, opposed the multitude of capital penalties, and showed the benefits of an exact registration of buildings & tradesmen.

52. **REPORT from the COMMITTEE.** Appointed to Examine into . . . the Late Obstructions to the Execution of the Orders of this House. N.d. [1772]. 1st. Folio. Appendix. 12pp. Disbound. £7.50

A privilege case, in which the Commons decided that a House messenger (W. Whittam) was authorized to arrest a man in his home on the Speaker's orders. The Lord Mayor and Corporation had released the prisoner.

53. **CORONATION of King GEORGE IV.** Ceremonies and Ancient Customs . . . at the Coronations of the Kings of England. 1820. 1st. 3 fold'g etched plates by I.R. Cruikshank. 48pp. – DENNIS, J.; A Key to the Regalia. 1820. 1st. iv, 122pp. – Collections relative to Claims at the Coronations . . . beginning with King Richard II. 1820. 1st. viii, 96pp. – The Queen's Claim to Coronation Examined. 1821. 1st. 32pp. (Disallows Q. Caroline's claim, on precedent). – Considerations on the Coronation Oath. 1821. 1st. 107pp. (Anti-Established Church). **Four items in one vol.** Lib. stamp on each title. Mod. cl. £20.00

54. **COWEL[L], John (1554-1611).** A Law Dictionary: or, the Interpreter of Words and Terms, used either in the Common or Statute Laws . . . Improved by the Addition of many Thousand Words. [Ed. T. Manley & others] 1708. Folio. Index. [xii], [327], [xii] pp. First advert. leaf. Contemp. cf., edges sl. rbbd. **S. & M. i. 4.** £50.00

Cowell was a university civilian, & adverted on certain doctrines of common law (notably the restriction of royal prerogative) in the contemptuous spirit of his order; a licence which, seized upon by the peevish Coke, came near costing him his liberty. Notwithstanding these licences, his work (first published in 1607) was generally held in high regard.

55. **CRAIG of Riccartoun, Sir Thomas (1548-1608).** The Right of Succession to the Kingdom of England . . . against the Sophisms of Parsons the Jesuite, who assumed the . . . Name of Doleman. [Tr. J.G.] 1703. 1st. Folio. Index. [xxxiv], 230, 245-432, [xviii] pp. Pagination & signatures irregular (231-244, i.e. $2N_1$-$2P$, omitted); nothing missing. Contemp. panelled cf., sp. gilt; rbbd. **S. & M. i. 92.** £50.00

Parsons opposed hereditary monarchies, & chose the decay of Elizabeth I as a fit occasion to resist the impending succession of James VI of Scotland. Craig (author of the Ius Feudale) composed his reply in 1602, & the peaceful accession of the King rendered its issue unnecessary; but Parsons's reasonings were afterwards taken up by the English Republicans & even by the anti-Catholic conspirators against Charles II. A Scottish legal document of 1691, on paper (deed of settlement by a minister's widow, Agnes Douglas of Cullen, of her estate on her son) is inserted.

56. **CREECH, William.** An Account of the Trial of William Brodie and George Smith . . . for Breaking into, and Robbing, the General Excise Office of Scotland. Edinburgh, 1788. 2nd ed., rev. Two etched ports. by John Kay. xxiv, 288pp. **Inscribed** by author on ½ title. Fp. & ½ title loose. Contemp. cf., rbbd.; jts. worn. £15.00

Remarkable trial of a highwayman (Brodie, alias Dixon) who lived a double life as a worthy citizen. The reporter was not a lawyer but a juryman. The portraits and an account of the hanging were added for this edition.

57. **CROMARTIE or CROMERTY, George [Mackenzie, 1st] Earl of (1631-1714).** An Historical Account of the Conspiracies by the Earls of Gowry and Robert Logan . . . against . . . James VI . . . Vindication of Robert III . . . from the Imputation of Bastardy. Edinburgh, 1713. 1st. **2 pts. in 1.** ½ title. Red & black title. A_4 blank. xvi, 127, [i]/80pp. Sl. browned. Contemp. panelled cf.; re-backed. £25.00

Written by a Royalist veteran of the Commonwealth days to disprove the idea (frequently used to stir up sedition in Scotland) that Gowry etc. were victims of injustice.

58. **CROMPTON, R[ichard].** L'Authorite et Iurisdiction des Courts de la Majestie de la Roygne. In aedibus Caroli Yetsweirt, 1594. 1st. Sm. 4to. French text. Black letter. [iv], 232 leaves. Many early marginal annots. (few cropped). Names on title. 18th-cent. ¼ sheep/mbld. sides, jts. worn. Bk-pl. Thomas Hamilton, 6th Earl of Haddington (d.1735). **S.T.C. 6050, S. & M. i. 176.** £125.00

A guide to all the courts then existing, from Star Chamber & Court of Wards (which did not endure for the study of a more scientific generation) down to Assize of Bread; dedicated (in the French of Paris, not of Westminster) to Sir John Puckering, Keeper of the Great Seal.

59. **CUNNINGHAM, T.** A New and Complete Law-Dictionary, or General Abridgement of the Law. 1764[-5]. 1st. **2 vols.** Folio. Unpaged. Sm. lib. stamps at intervals. Last leaf of vol. 2 sl. defective, aff. few words of three lines. Recent cl., fdd., sl. mkd.; lib. labels. **S. & M. ii. 3.** £40.00

By including frequent summaries of cases, precedents in equity, & statutes, Cunningham fairly accomplished his promise to combine the matter of an abridgement with that of a dictionary. In the latter aspect he drew largely on Cowell.

60. **CURSON, H[enry].** The Law concerning Estates Taile, and Remainders and Reversions expectant thereupon. 1703. 1st. Index. 341, [iii] pp. Mod. cl. Bk-pl. **S. & M. ii. 147.** £20.00

61. **DALTON, Michael (1554–c.1640).** The Country Iustice, conteyning the Practise of the Iustices of the Peace out of their Sessions. For the Societie of Stationers, 1618. 1st. Folio. Woodcut title-border. Index. First blank. [xvi], 370, [xii] pp. **Interleaved** throughout, with some contemp. MS. notes, incl. special orders on the poor, Catholics, etc. for the county of Norfolk. Two further leaves of notes (one in 18th-cent. hand) inserted. Fine copy in contemp. cf., re-backed; new e-p's; corners worn; remains of silk ties. **S.T.C. 6205 (none in U.S.A.)** £100.00

A popular work in its day, more detailed in points of practice than Lambard or Crompton, & reprinted as the standard work until 1746.

62. **DANBY, Thomas, Earl of.** Memoirs relating to the Impeachment of. 1711. 2nd ed. Advert. leaf before title. [vi], 234, 110pp. A_{3-4} loose. Contemp. panelled cf., sl. worn. £20.00

Danby's case is important for the relation between King & Parliament. As Lord Treasurer & a favourite of the King, he was impeached for raising an army & arranging a peace with France without reference to Parliament. These transactions, which led to the shameful Dutch war, were exposed in 1674, & the consequent revulsion in favour of Holland & against the Stuarts' Catholic leanings cleared the way for the events of 1688.

63. **DAWSON, George.** Origo Legum: or a Treatise of the Origin of Laws, and their Obliging Power: as also of their Great Variety. For Richard Chiswell, 1694. 1st. ½ title. Red & black title. [xxvi], 168, 220pp. Sl. stnd. at end. Contemp. mottled cf., sp. gilt; rbbd. **S. & M. i. 16. Wing D.459.** £40.00

64. **The DECISIONS of the COURT of SESSION** . . . Abridged . . . in Form of a Dictionary. Edinburgh, 1741. **2 vols.** Folio. Red & black titles. Indices. Errata leaf. [iv], viii, [xxxvi], 601/[xxxii], 555, [i], [xxxii] pp. Contemp. cf., sps. gilt; two sm. holes in upper cvr. of vol. 2. Bk-pl. Forbes Leith of Whitehaugh. **S. & M. v. 57.** £60.00

This work is far more than the compilation it appears to be; for much of the material used (ranging from Sinclair's MS. of 1540-48 to Forbes's of 1698-1718) was previously unpublished. The editor was the celebrated Lord Kames. Lord Woodhouselee added two more volumes in 1797.

65. **DEGGE, Sir Simon.** The Parsons Counsellor, with the Law of Tithes or Tithing. By the Assigns of Richard and Edward Atkins . . . for Henry Twyford, 1681. 2nd ed. rev. **2 vols. in 1.** Index. Errara leaf. [xxxii], 212/-408, [xxxviii] pp. Contemp. sheep, sp. sl. rbbd. **Wing D.853, S. & M. ii. 13.** £25.00

66. ———— Anr. ed. (3rd). 1681. **2 vols. in 1.** Index. [xxxii], 212/-422, [xxxiv] pp. Contemp. sheep, sp. rbbd. **Wing D.854.** £25.00

67. **D[ISNEY], W[illiam].** Nil dictum quod non dictum prius; or, a Transcript of Government . . . in the State of Nature or Religion. By A.B. for F.T., 1681. 1st. [viii], 38, 49-196pp. Sigg. C_4 to C_8 omitted by printer; pagination irregular accordingly; nothing missing. Contemp. cf., jts. rbbd. **Wing D.1672c; S. & M. ii. 11.** £40.00

Disney's outline of the British constitution anticipates Blackstone in its doctrine that in the legislature, or "Parliament", the King, Lords & Commons are equal partners, each acting as a check on the others. He condemns all theories of divine right, & deprives them even of their customary Scriptural support.

68. **DODSON, John (ed.).** A Report of the Judgment . . . by . . . Sir William SCOTT . . . in the Case of Dalrymple the Wife, against Dalrymple the Husband. 1811. 1st. viii, 96, iv, cclxxvipp. Contemp. cf., re-backed; sl. rubbed. £15.00

An important test case to determine what constituted a legal marriage under Scots law. The Chancellor's decision was that three papers (a "sacred promise" & two declarations) given by J.W.H. Dalrymple to Johanna Gordon sufficed to establish her as his legal wife.

69. **DUNCOMBE, Giles.** Trials per Pais: or, the Law of England concerning Juries by Nisi Prius, &c. with a . . . Treatise of the Law of Evidence. 1739. 7th ed., rev. First advert. leaf. Index. [xxii], 527, [xli] pp. Contemp. cf., sl. rbbd. Bk-pl. (early "Chippendale" style) of D. Pigott, 1744. **S. & M. i. 237.** £45.00

70. **ERSKINE of CARDROSS, John.** The Principles of the Law of Scotland: in the Order of Sir George Mackenzie's Institutes. Edinburgh, 1791. 7th ed., rev. ½ title. Index. [vi], 519, [i], 29pp. Contemp. tree cf., edges sl. rbbd. £15.00

First published in 1754, revised for a century and a half, and still recognized as an authority.

71. **EVERY MAN his OWN LAWYER:** or, a Summary of the Laws now in Force in Ireland. Dublin, 1755. 1st. Index. [iv], 348, [x] pp. Final blank. Several cancels in sigg. D & E, mounted on stubs. F_4 defective at head, with damage to head-line & 4 lines of text. Contemp. cf., sl. rubbed. **S. & M. ii. 189.** £20.00

72. **F., G.** The Touchstone of Precedents, relating to Judicial Proceedings at Common Law. For Awnsham Churchill, 1682. 2nd imp. Title (a cancel) loosely inserted. Index. [vi], 379, [xxi] pp. Signatures jump from I_8 to M_1; nothing missing. Some other minor mis-signing & mis-pagination. Three leaves loose. Contemp. cf.; head of sp. torn; rbbd. **Wing F.22; S. & M. ii. 75.** £30.00

An alphabetical Abridgment on a small scale; the author hints timidly at the obsoleteness of style & matter of the standard work on his subject, meaning no doubt Fitzherbert's Natura Brevium. Wing records no copies in the U.S.A.

73. **FIELDING, Henry.** An Enquiry into the Causes of the Late Increase of Robbers, &c. with some Proposals for Remedying this Growing Evil. Dublin, 1751. 1st thus. [xvi], 96pp. Mod. ¼ cf./mbld. sides. Cf. Kress 5112-3. £50.00

Fielding's renown as a novelist obscures the fact that he was as distinguished a magistrate as his brother, the blind Sir John. He blames the profusion of luxurious amusements, the failure to find employment for the poor under the existing laws, and the uncertainty of detection & arrest.

74. **FIGGIS, Darrell.** A Chronicle of Gaols. Dublin (Talbot Pr.), 1917. 1st. [vi], 130pp. Orig. printed wraps, sl. frayed. £10.00

Prison diary of a writer interned for republican sympathies in 1916.

75. **FINLASON, W.F.** A Treatise on Martial Law: as Allowed by the Law of England, in Time of Rebellion: with Practical Illustrations Drawn from the . . . Jamaica Case. 1866. 1st & only ed. Index. lii, 452pp. Orig. cl., fdd., corners stnd. £20.00

Martial law as an element of the constitution faded away after 1689, & before this book was written there was not even a satisfactory definition of it available. The Jamaica rebellion of 1865 (many interesting details of which are given) drew attention to the deficiency.

76. FITZGERALD, Percy. Chronicles of the Bow Street Police-Office. 1888. 1st. **2 vols.** Illus. viii, 332, 40/[vi], 380pp. Orig. dec'd cl., jts. sl. rubbed. £15.00
Anecdotes of the court in Sir John Fielding's time & afterwards.

77. FITZGIBBONS, John. The Reports of . . . Cases . . . in . . . King's Bench . . . with some special Cases in . . . Chancery, Common Pleas and Exchequer. 1732. Folio. Mostly black letter. Index. [iv], 321, [xv]pp. Mod. ¼ cf./mbld. sides. **S. & M. ii. 90.** £20.00

78. FITZHERBERT, [Sir] Anthony (d.1538). The New Natura Brevium. 1704. Index. [lxiv], 600pp. Contemp. cf., jts. sl. rubbed. £35.00
This long-standing source-book for common law consists of a commentary on the writs & actions listed in the Register as printed in 1531. Fitzherbert says that the old Natura Brevium had been corrupted by translation & interpolation.

79. FORTESCUE, Sir John (fl. 1430-1471). De laudibus legum Angliae . . . Hereto are ioind the two Summes of Sir Ralph de Hengham . . . never before publisht. [Ed. John SELDEN]. For the Companie of Stationers, 1616. 1st thus. **3 pts. in 1.** Latin & Engl. text. First blank. [x], 132, [iii] leaves, 56, [xii], 160pp. Contemp. vellum, detached at front hinge; lacks ties. S.T.C. 11197. **S. & M. i. 17.** £90.00

80. ———— Anr. ed. By John Streeter [etc.], Sold by G. Sawbridge [etc.]. 1672. Latin & Engl. text. [vii], 132, [iii] leaves, 52, [xii], 140pp. Contemp. sheep, rbbd. **Wing F.1613.** £60.00
Fortescue's work, written for the instruction of the future King Edward IV, is a summary for the layman containing the first outline of the peculiarly English scheme of constitutional monarchy, with many interesting comparisons between English & Roman methods. The two works of Hengham are thirteenth-century notes on King's Court procedure, including texts of writs, remarks on the jurisdiction of sheriff's & baron courts, etc.

81. ———— WATERHOUS[E], Edward; Fortescutus Illustratus, or a Commentary on that nervous Treatise De laudibus legum Angliae. By Tho. Roycroft for Thomas Dicas, 1663. 1st. Folio. Index. [xx], 593, [vi]pp. Last two leaves sl. torn at inner margin with loss of few letters. Mod. ½ cf./bds. **Wing W. 1046. S. & M. i. 171.** £90.00
Erudite, incoherent, strangely adulatory of King James I, and chiefly valuable for its large & compendious quotation of original materials.

82. FULLER, H. Julian. "Old Q" and the Apothecary; being the Record of a Framous Trial. 1913. 1st. Privately printed. 4to. Illus. 47pp. **Inscribed by the author.** Contemp. ½ mor./cl. sides; sl. rbbd. £10.00
A test case (Fuller v. Executors of the Duke of Queensberry) which gave an apothecary the right to recover payment for attendance; previously he could charge only for medicines. The new order was recognized by statute (55. Geo. III, cap. 194) in 1815.

83. G[ARDINER] R. Instructor Clericalis, The First[-Fourth] Part. 1707 [1705, 1706]. 4th [3rd, 2nd, 1st] ed. **4 vols.** Indices. Sm. ink-stain on M, (vol. 1) aff. two letters. Contemp. cf., sps. sl. rbbd. **S. & M. ii. 75.** £50.00
This series of instruction-books for clerks consisted largely of works previously published under separate titles. The volumes present cover (1) abbreviations & forms for writs, (2) forms for declarations, (3 & 4) forms for bars & pleadings. Two more volumes (further pleadings, & demurrers) were added in 1713-14.

84. GIFFORD, John. The Complete English Lawyer; or, Every Man his Own Lawyer. 9th ed. 1824. **2 pts. in 1.** Fp. port. (Sir Charles Abbott, C.J.). Index. 688/[iv], 148pp. Orig. bds., uncut; sp. torn. £10.00

85. GILMOUR of Craigmiller, Sir John, and Sir David FALCONER of Newton. A Collection of Decisions of the Lords of Council and Session . . . from July 1661 . . . to January 1686. Edinburgh, 1701. 1st. **3 vols. in 1.** 4to. General & individual titles. Indices. 10, [ii], 136, [xviii]/[ii], 80, [xvi]/[ii], 32, 15, [i]pp. Contemp. mottled cf., sp. gilt; rbbd. **S. & M. v. 46.** £40.00
Includes an appendix of Acts of Sederunt of the Lords of Session 1681-1696.

86. GLANVILL, Ranulf de (fl. c. 1185). De legibus et consuetudinibus regni Angliae, ed G.E. Woodbine. Yale U.P./O.U.P. (Yale Historical Publications, no.13), 1932. 1st thus. Latin text & Engl. introd. & notes. Index. xii, 306pp. Orig. ¼ canvas/ bds.; sl. mkd. £20.00
A sound critical text, with a comprehensive though not fully-detailed collation, of the most important of mediaeval English law-books. Glanvill's work, clearly & simply written, was the foundation of the treatises of Bracton & "Fleta", & even of the Scottish "Regiam Maiestatem" (see SKENE).

87. [HALE, Sir Matthew] (1609-1676). The History of the Common Law of England. 1713. 1st. Advert. leaf before title. Engr. table. [vi], 264, [xii]pp. Contemp. cf., jts. & edges rbbd. **S. & M. i. 168.** £40.00

88. ———— Anr. variant imp. (History and Analysis of the Common Law). 1713. Advert. leaf. Errata leaf (not included in collation) before B_1. [viii], 264, [xii]pp. Contemp. cf., sp. & lower cvr. rbbd. £40.00
Notwithstanding the title, this like the former is bound without the Analysis.

89. ———— The History of the Common Law of England. 1716. 2nd ed. **2 pts. in 1.** Index. First & last advert. leaves. [vi], 261, [xi]/[xiv], 148, [xxviii]pp. Contemp. cf., sp. sl. rbbd. **S. & M. i. 168.** £30.00
Like Hale's Pleas of the Crown, this was left without its final revision at his death; but it is marked with his usual truth & diligence, & was the foundation of the subject for more than a century from its publication. The Analysis forms the second part of the 1716 edition.

90. ———— A Short Treatise touching Sheriffs Accompts . . . to which is added, a Tryal of Witches, at . . . Bury St. Edmonds . . . before the said Sir Matthew Hale. [–Discourse touching Provision for the Poor.] 1716. **3 pts. in 1 vol.** Engr. fp. table. 143, [i]pp. Old ½ cf./mbld. sides, sl. rbbd. **S. & M. ii. 54.** £40.00
Hale deduces the history of revenue-collection at county level from the Conquest to his own time, with remarks on coinage. The witch-trial at Bury (very much on the Salem pattern, complete with "afflicted children") ended in the hanging of two old women. Hale's proposals on the poor include a work-house system.

91. ———— Historia Placitorum Coronae. The History of the Pleas of the Crown . . . Published from his . . . Original Manuscript. Ed. Sollom Emlyn. 1736. 1st. **2 vols.** Folio. Fine engr. fp. ports. by George Vertue. Index. [iv], xx, [viii], 710/[vi], 414, [cxcvi]pp. Two extra leaves (signed *2P^2 & *2R^2) in each vol. **S. & M. i. 58.** And:–
FLETA, seu commentarius juris Anglicani . . . Liber primus [all published] [Ed. Sir S. Clarke.] 1735. 1st thus. Latin text. Folio. [viii], 98pp. **S. & M. i. 39.**
Two works in one vol. Contemp. cf., worn. £75.00
Hale's work, although only an unfinished third portion of his proposed corpus of crown law, is a precious guide to capital offences. Emlyn's large notes correct some references & bring the statute law down to date. Clarke's Fleta (bk. I only) collates this author with Glanvill & Bracton, & is altogether more thorough & correct than Selden's old text.

92. HALLIFAX, Samuel, Bp. of St. Asaph. An Analysis of the Civil Law, in which a Comparison is . . . made between the Roman Laws and those of England. Ed. J.W. Geldart. Cambridge U.P., 1836. 1st thus. Indices. Advert. leaves tipped in at end. Errata slip. xxxvi, 228pp. Corner of front e-p. torn away. Orig. cl.; sp. fdd. **S. & M. ii. 64.** £15.00
Last edition of the last attempt to maintain the civil law in its pre-eminent position as an object of study in the universities. It is noteworthy that Hallifax no longer ventures to denigrate the law of England.

93. HAMILTON, A.H.A. Quarter Sessions from Queen Elizabeth to Queen Anne: Illustrations . . . Drawn from Original Records (Chiefly of . . . Devon). 1878. 1st in book form. Index, xii, 364, 30pp. Orig. cl., sl. rbbd. £8.00

94. HARRIS, Richard. Her Majesty's Judges and their Relation to Advocacy. 1899. 1st. Sm. 4to. 122pp. Orig. printed bds.; sp. defective, edges worn. £10.00
Includes (with much light-hearted matter) some important remarks on the definition of murder, & on some alleged misdirection of the jury by judges in murder trials.

95. HAWKINS, Sir Henry (Baron Brampton). Reminiscences, ed. Richard Harris. 1904. 1st. **2 vols.** Fp. ports. & other illus. x, 331/viii, 310, 16pp. Orig. dec'd cl., uncut; sl. mkd. £10.00

96. HAWKINS, William. A Treatise of the Pleas of the Crown: or a System of the Principal Matters relating to that Subject. 1724[-6]. 2nd ed., rev. **2 vols. in 1.** Folio. Indices. [xiv], 266, [xliv]/[viii], 464, [lxxvi]pp. Contemp. cf., rbbd. **S. & M. ii. 116.** £35.00
The first comprehensive work on the subject, piecing out the imperfections & omissions of Stanford, Coke (Inst. III), Hale, & the various books on Justices of the Peace.

97. HERBERT, William. Antiquities of the Inns of Court and Chancery . . . with a concise History of English Law. 1804. 1st. Index. 24 copper-engr. plates. xii, 378, [x]pp. Sl. spotted. Contemp. grained cf., re-backed. £50.00

98. HOPE of Craighall, Sir Thomas (?–1646). Minor Practicks, or, a Treatise of the Scottish Law . . . BAYNE, Alexander; a Discourse on the Rise and Progress of the Law of Scotland. Edinburgh, 1726. 1st. **2 vols. in 1.** Index. viii, 148, ii/[ii], ii, 151-245pp. Contemp. sprinkled cf., sp. gilt; sl. rbbd. **S. & M. v. 51.** £50.00
Like Hale's corresponding work on common law (q.v.), this important collection of notes & questions was posthumously published, by Bayne, from the author's remains. Besides his "Discourse", the editor has added an alphabetical summary of the Acts of Sederunt from 1661 to his own time.

99. HUTCHESON, Gilbert. Treatise on the Offices of Justice of Peace, Constable, Commissioner of Supply, and Commissioner under Comprehending Acts, in Scotland. Edinburgh, 1806[-8]. 1st. **2 vols. & Supplement.** Index. Orig. bds., uncut; heads of sps. frayed; edges worn. **S. & M. v. 53.** £30.00
Includes many interesting historical references & extracts.

100. INGRAM, T.D. Compensation to Land and House Owners: being a Treatise on the Law of the Compensation . . . payable by Railway and other Public Companies. 1864. 1st. Index. Publisher's cat. xii, 300, 36pp. Orig. cl. paper label; sl. fdd. **S. & M. iii. 114.** £10.00
An illustration of the pressure thrown on the existing law, & on the whole principle of the sanctity of private property, by the rapid extension of railways & their attendant property transactions.

101. IRELAND. General Prisons Board. First Report. Dublin (H.M.S.O.), 1879. 1st. 133pp. Title-page partially pasted to e-p.; text not aff. Few inner margins affected by crude sewing. Old ½ cf./mbld. sides; worn; lower cvr. defective. £5.00

102. IRELAND, Samuel. Picturesque Views, with an Historical Account of the Inns of Court. 1800. 1st. 21 aquatint plates. Errata leaf. ½ title. xvi, 254; [i]pp. Contemp. diced cf., re-backed; corners worn. £60.00

103. J., W. The Common and Statute Law of England, concerning Trials in High-Treason, Misprision of Treason, and in all other Crimes and Offences relating to the Crown. 1710. 1st. Index. [viii], 406, [xxvi]pp. Contemp. cf., sl. rbbd. **S. & M. ii. 34.** £20.00
Brief & at times dangerously over-simplified (whence a note on the fly-leaf "ubi bene nemo melius, ubi male nemo peius") but more concise & convenient than the wiser & more deeply read Hist. Placitorum Coronae of Hale (q.v.).

104. JACOB, Giles (1686-1744). Lex Constitutionis: or, the Gentleman's Law . . . Statutes relating to the King . . . Nobility . . . Commons . . . Justices of Peace . . . Introduction to . . . Tenures of Land, Descents . . . Estates . . . Trials of Offenders, Courts . . . etc. 1719. 1st. Index. xiv, 360, [xii]pp. Contemp. cf., sl. rbbd. **S. & M. ii. 11.** £20.00

105. ———— City-Liberties: or, the Rights and Privileges of Freemen. Being a Concise Abridgment of all the Laws, Charters, By-laws, and Customs of London. 1732. 1st. Index. viii, 168, [viii]pp. Contemp. sheep, edges rubbed. **S. & M. i. 277.** £25.00
A useful alphabetical digest of the laws & customs of the city as then existing, with ordinances relating to trade, elections, special courts & their jurisdiction, etc. Apparently the only edition; a new work, giving the charters at length, appeared in 1765.

106. ———— The Common Law Common-Plac'd: containing, the Substance and effect of all the Common Law Cases . . . Terms of the Law . . . Writs and Processes . . . with an Abstract of Statutes. 1733. 2nd ed. rev. Folio. Index. [iv], 388, v-vi, [viii]pp. Preface leaf conjugate with 5I$_4$ (pp. 387-8) in error, & therefore misbound. Contemp. cf., sl. rbbd. **S. & M. ii. 64.** £30.00

107. ———— The Student's Companion: or, the Reason of the Laws of England. 1734. 2nd ed., rev. Index. [xi], ix, 282, [vi]pp. Contemp. cf., sl. rubbed. **S. & M. i. 8.** £15.00
An attempt to supply the law with that logical background whose want is so much felt in all the older "institutes" and hand-books. The prolific Jacob declares this his favourite work.

108. ———— A New Law-Dictionary . . . Fifth Edition, with great Additions . . . and the Law-Proceedings done into English. 1744. Folio. [viii], [811], [v]pp. Sl. browned. Contemp. cf., rbbd.; jts. worn. **S. & M. i. 6.** £30.00
This edition includes many new citations of Chancery cases, & gives the new English versions of writs as provided for by the act of 1731.

109. ———— Anr. (seventh) ed. 1756. Folio. Index. [viii], [826], [iv]pp. Lower margins sl. wormed. Contemp. cf., rbbd.; head of sp. torn. £30.00

110. JEAFFRESON, John Cordy. A Book about Lawyers. 1867. 1st. 2 vols. Index. viii, 384/viii, 431pp. Contemp. ½ roan/mbld. sides; rbbd. £20.00
Historical & biographical anecdotes in fourteen sections; The Great Seal, Loves of the Lawyers, Houses & Householders (including the Inns), etc.

111. JONES, Sir William. Les Reports de . . . un des Justices del' Banck le Roy . . . del . . . Common Banck d'Ireland. By T.R. and N.T. for Thomas Basset and Richard Chiswell, 1675. 1st. Folio. French text. Black letter. Index. [xii], 463, [i], [xxi]pp. Final errata leaf. Few leaves sl. soiled. Large copy. Contemp. sprinkled cf., jts. & edges rbbd. **Wing J.1003; S. & M. i. 199.** £30.00

112. [JUSTICE, Alexander]. A General Treatise of the Dominion of the Sea, and a Compleat Body of the Sea-Laws . . . Laws of the Rhodians and Romans . . . France . . . Customs of Merchants [etc]. 1732. 3rd ed., rev. 4to. Folding engr. fp. & plate of flags. Appendix. Index. [xxvi], 378, 421-684, 108pp. Sigg. 3C$_3$-3Z$_4$ (pp. 379-420) omitted in printing; nothing missing. Sm. hole in 3H$_3$ aff. few letters. Contemp. cf., re-backed; sl. rbbd. **S. & M. ii. 326.** Not in **Kress.** £120.00
For this edition the chapter on the laws of Oleron (a French maritime code of the thirteenth century, ratified for English use in 1375) was revised according to Cleirac's text & notes (Les . . . Coûtumes de la Mer, 1671) & a new appendix on the history of the English navy added. A section on insurance is also included.

113. KEBLE, Joseph. Reports in . . . King's Bench . . . from the XII to the XXX Year of . . . King Charles II. By W. Rawlins [etc.] for Thomas Dring [etc.], 1685. 1st. **3 vols.** Folio. Black letter. Indices. First privilege leaves to vols. 1 & 3 (wanting in vol. 2). Lacks two blanks. Contemp. cf.; sl. rbbd, one cvr. sl. torn. **Wing K.116; S. & M. ii. 91.** £50.00

114. KELHAM, Robert. Domesday Book Illustrated . . . an Account . . . as also of the Tenants in Capite or Serjanty. 1788. 1st. Index. ½ title. viii, 399, [i]pp. Orig. blue bds., uncut; paste-downs detached; sp. & jts. worn. **S. & M. i. 75.** £20.00

115. KELYNG, Sir John. A Report of Divers Cases in Pleas of the Crown . . . in the Reign of . . . King Charles II. 1708. Folio. Black letter. Index. [iv], 138, [xiv]pp. First privilege leaf. Contemp. cf., re-backed. Bk-pl. **S. & M. ii. 91.** £20.00

116. KNAPP, Andrew, and William BALDWIN (eds.). Criminal Chronology; or, the New Newgate Calendar; being . . . Memoirs of Notorious Characters . . . Convicted of Outrages on the Laws. 1809-11 & n.d. **4 vols. & supplementary vol.** Engr. fp. to each vol., title, & 43 plates. Indices. Extra sheet (K^4) between O$_2$ & O$_3$ of vol. 3. Some browning. Contemp. ¼ cf./mbld. sides; rbbd; jts. worn. Cf. **S. & M. ii. 119 (4 vols.).** £80.00

117. LAMB, Charles. The Old Benchers of the Inner Temple, ed. Sir F.D. Mackinnon. O.U.P., 1727. 1st thus. 4to. Illus. xxvii, 78pp. H-m. paper. Orig. b'ram, uncut; sl. fdd. £12.00
Mackinnon's large notes give biographies of the benchers of Lamb's time, among whom Daines Barrington is the most notable.

118. LANE, Richard. Reports in the Court of Exchequer . . . in . . . the Raign of . . . King James . . . being the first Collections in that Court hitherto extant. For W. Lee, D. Pakeman, and G. Bedell, 1657. 1st. Black letter. Sm. folio. Index, [iv], 119, [v]pp. Mod. ½ cf./mbld. sides. Bk-pl. **Wing L.340; S. & M. i. 212.** £35.00
Lane shows a special interest in questions of royal prerogative.

119. The LAWS concerning the ELECTION of MEMBERS of PARLIAMENT; with the Determinations of the . . . Commons . . . and all their Incidents. 1774. Index. Publisher's cat. xx, 392, [xii], 6pp. Contemp. cf., re-backed. **S. & M. ii. 25.** £20.00
Originally published (as "Determinations" alone) in 1741.

120. A LETTER to a NOBLE LORD; containing some Remarks on . . . Two Acts . . . for Vesting in his Majestie the Estates of Certain Traitors, &c. And . . . for . . . Abolishing the Heritable Jurisdictions in . . . Scotland. 1748. 1st. ½ title. [ii], 28pp. Disbound. £10.00
Condemns these acts as unconstitutionally adding to the wealth of the crown.

121. LEWORTHY, William, & the GLOBE INSURANCE COMPANY. Trial between . . . before Mr. Baron Graham. 1810. 1st. xvi, 180pp. Contemp. tree cf.; jts. rubbed. £15.00
The company refused to pay Leworthy's claim for fire-insurance, suspecting him of fraud. He sued for payment, but the jury found for the company. The trial illustrates the public prejudice against insurance companies at the time; the verdict was clearly exceptional.

122. LILLY, John. The Practical Register: or, a General Abridgment of the Law, as it is now Practised in the several Courts . . . The Second Edition . . . brought down to this present Year. 1735. **2 vols.** Folio. Indices. [iv], 882, [iv]/[xviii], 880, [vi]pp. Contemp. cf., rbbd. **S. & M. ii. 78.** £50.00
Successor to Styles's Register of 1657. The Table of Statutes is misbound, being transferred from vol. 1 to vol. 2.

123. LITTLETON, Sir Thomas (?–1481). Tenures in English. Lately perused and amended. By Iane Yetsweirt, 1597. Black letter. 142 leaves. Title v. frayed (aff. L of Littleton) & backed. Margin of last leaf defective, not aff. text. Few corners frayed. New ¼ calf/mbld. sides. **Beale T.60. S.T.C. 15776. S. & M. i. 293.** £120.00

124. ———— Tenures, in French and English. By John Streater [etc.], Sold by George Sawbridge [etc.], 1671. 12mo. French & Engl. text. First blank. [xxii], 436, [ii]pp. Two sm. marginal defects. Contemp. sheep, rbbd. **Wing L.2588. S. & M. i. 293.** **£30.00**
First bilingual edition. "Not the name of a lawyer, but of the law itself" (Coke). Littleton's account of the laws of property, as they stood immediately before the economic revolutions of the Tudor period, has always been admired for its clarity & judiciousness.

125. LIVES and EXPLOITS of the Most Noted HIGHWAYMEN, ROBBERS and MURDERERS . . . Brought Down to the Present Time. Hartford (Conn.), 1851. (Rev. ed.). Wood-engr. illus. 287pp. Sl. stnd. New cl., leather label. **£12.50**
The last case included, that of James Porter, is of American origin.

126. LUTWYCHE, Sir E. Un Livre des Entries: contenant auxi un Report des Resolutions . . . sur . . . Exceptions prises as Pleadings; et sur autres Matters. 1704. 1st. **2 vols.** Folio. Black letter. Fp. port. Privilege leaves. Indices. General & volume-titles to vol. 1. [xiv], 849pp., 850-912 [i.e. 910] leaves/[ii], 912-1668, [civ]pp. Contemp. cf., re-backed; rbbd. **S. & M. ii. 46.** **£35.00**

127. MACKENZIE of Rosehaugh, Sir George (1636-1691). Idea eloquentiae forensis hodiernae: una cum actione forensi ex unaquaque juris parte. Edinburgh, excudebat haeres Andreae Anderson, 1681. 1st. Latin text. [xii], 182, [ii]pp. Final blank. A_1 torn without loss; fore-margin of E_4 defective. Contemp. sheep, rbbd. **Wing M.164; S. & M. v. 74.** **£40.00**
Mackenzie justly laments that the eloquence of Scots advocates (he might have added English counsel) is never preserved as an example to the student. In the hope of endowing modern oratory with the dignity attaching to a Cicero, he gives Latin versions of six of his own speeches, with general remarks on the duties & qualifications for speaking at the bar.

128. ———— The Laws and Customs of Scotland, in Matters Criminal. Edinburgh, for Mr. Andrew Symson, 1699. "2nd" (actually 4th) ed. Folio. 4 pts. in 1. Red & black title. Index. [viii], 292, [iv], [ii], 30, [ii], 31-66 [actually 70], [iv], 62pp. Lacks final blank. Some irregular signing & pagination. Main- & fly-title of "Mutilation" reversed; one corner torn from the former. Contemp. cf., sl. rubbed. **Wing M.168. S. & M. v. 74.** **£60.00**
At a time when the approaching Union threatened the independence of Scottish law, Mackenzie's work asserted the antiquity & merit of the national system. Sir A. Seton's Treatise of Mutilation & Demembration is added to this edition as an appendix.

129. ———— Observations upon the XVIII Act Parliament XXIII. K. James VI against Dispositions made in Defraud of Creditors, &c. Edinburgh, by the Heirs and Successors of Andrew Anderson . . . for Mr. Andrew Symson, 1699. Second ed. Folio. [iv], 62pp. Lacks final blank. Several contemp. corrections. Title-border cropped at head. Mod. cl. **Wing M.189 (none outside U.K.). Aldis 3866.5.** **£40.00**

130. ———— Pleadings, in some . . . Cases, before the . . . Courts of Scotland, since . . . 1661. Edinburgh, 1704. 16mo. [viii], 296pp. Margins of F_1 & G_1 sl. defective, aff. one line. Fore-margins short; one sl. cropped. Old cf., re-backed; sides rbbd. **S. & M. v. 74.** **£20.00**

131. ———— The Institutions of the Laws of Scotland. Edinburgh, 1757. 8th ed. 12mo. Index. [viii], 296, [xxiv]pp. Contemp. cf., sp. rbbd. **£10.00**

132. MADOX, Thomas (?–1735). The History and Antiquities of the Exchequer of the Kings of England . . . Taken from Records, 1769. 2nd ed. **2 vols.** 4to. Index. [viii], xxx, 802/[iv], 478, [ccxc]pp. $3E_4$ (vol. 2) torn without loss. Contemp. cf., sl. rbbd. **Kress 6656; S. & M. i. 210.** **£50.00**
Madox's great history of the oldest of our courts of record until the time of Edward II is founded on a large knowledge of ancient documents, especially the Great Roll ascribed to the fifth year of Stephen (but perhaps of the preceding reign) which is treated of in a distinct dissertation, and the Dialogus de Scaccario (c.1170) which is printed in full. The detailed index, embracing a glossary, is new to this edition.

133. MAGNA CHARTA and Antiqua Statuta. Magna charta, cum statutis quae Antiqua vocantur . . . quibus accesserunt nonnulla nunc primum typis edita. Apud Richardum Totelum, 12. Iun. 1556. **2 pts. in 1.** Latin & French text. Black letter. Woodcut initials. Index. [viii], 170, [ii]/72 leaves. Corner of A_1 torn away, without loss of text. Contemp. name on title & few annots. Otherwise a fine copy in mod. calf. **S.T.C. 9278; Beale S.16; S. & M. i. 350.** **£250.00**
The volumes issued under the title Magna Charta, from Pynson's of 1508 onward, acquired an accumulation of other ancient statutes & other pieces. This edition is distinguished by a fresh application to the original rolls of Parliament (undertaken to eclipse the version printed by Marsh in the same year) which yields the Capitula Itineris (a guide to pleas determined by the circuit judges), Edward I's Statutes of Wales with many readings unknown to Owen (q.v.), an old summary of Kentish local law, two acts against Piers Gaveston, and some lesser pieces, besides corrected readings in the statutes previously published.
Here, as in all the old texts, "Magna Charta" is not John's of 1215 but Henry III's of 1224.

134. MANUSCRIPT. [Precedents, maxims & definitions]. N.p., n.d. [1615-28]. Folio. French text. 514, [xiv], 515-44pp. Last few leaves sl. frayed & soiled. Early names of John Whittacre & John Stockman on last leaf. Contemp. blind-stamped cf., MS. guards (Missal, early 15th cent.); paste-downs & upper cvr. detached. **£120.00**
A volume of observations digested alphabetically under subjects from the Yearbooks, Stanford's Plees del Coron, Fitzherbert's Abridgment, and the reports of Plowden, Dyer, and Coke; closely written in a single though variable hand showing italic influence, & ruled in red. A few headings, as Pape & Surrender, are left blank; others cover twenty or more items, each with a reference. The book illustrates the want of a general guide to law & equity before the publication of Coke's Institutes. John Stockman was admitted to the Middle Temple on 10 Nov. 1611 & John Whitacres (sic) to Lincoln's Inn on 24th Oct. 1612.

135. ———— LYNDESAY, H. Ane Epitome of . . . Practices . . . containing the Mater and Substance of the haill Practices contained in the Prin[cip]le (sic) Books be [sic] Sr. John NISBET. N.p. [Edinburgh?], n.d. [c.1700]. Sm. 4to. Index. [ii], 424, [96]pp. Contemp. sheep, clasps & ends of sp. defective; rbbd. **£80.00**
An alphabetical digest from the works of the celebrated Nisbet of Dirleton. The last 96pp. are blank except for a few acts of convention of Edinburgh (1717) & a resolution of Kirkcudbright justices concerning the poor (1725) in a second hand.

136. ———— MEDLYCOTT, James (Master in Chancery?) Report and Schedule of Accounts in the case Waller v. Southwell. 1716. Folio. 92pp. Upper margins repaired throughout, few words obscured; marginal defects towards end aff. few lines of c.20 leaves. Fore-margins shaved. Later bds., sp. defective. Phillipps Ms. 20108. **£30.00**
After four years' debate, Edward Southwell, steward to the late James Waller (an Irish landowner) is cleared of the charge of embezzlement brought by Waller's executors.

137. MANWOOD, John. A Treatise of the Laws of the Forest . . . Original and Beginning of Forests . . . Treatise of the Pourallee . . . Statutes of the Forest. For the Company of Stationers, 1665. 3rd ed. 4to. Black letter. Index. [xxiv], 552pp. Contemp. cf., re-cased, head of sp. repaired. **Wing M.554; S. & M. i. 299.** **£50.00**
Includes many extracts from ancient records & charters, beginning with the Carta de Foresta ascribed to King Canute.

138. MARGAROT, Maurice (?–1816). RAMSEY, – (ed.); The Trial . . . before the High Court of Justiciary, at Edinburgh, on the 13th and 14th of January, 1794, for Sedition. Edinburgh, n.d. [1794]. 1st complete. Etched fp. port. by John Kay. Contemp. MS note in pencil on A_2. Orig. calico-bkd. mbld. bds., uncut; worn; sp. sl. torn; fp. & title loose. **£15.00**
Margarot was one of many in Scotland (cf. MUIR) who were influenced by the new ideas from France; his crime was his association with a "Convention" to promote universal suffrage. He was transported. The annotator, clearly an eyewitness, records how the broad Scots of Lord Justice-Clerk Craufurd led Margarot to say that, while needing no counsel, he would welcome an interpreter.

139. MERITON, George. Land-Lords Law . . . being a Collection of Several Cases in the Law concerning Leases . . . Distresses, Replevins, Rescous and Waste, and several other Matters. For John Place . . . and Thomas Basset, 1669. 3rd ed. 12mo. Index. [xii], 258, [xv]pp. Sm. rust-hole in H_4. Back e-p. defective. Contemp. sheep, ends of sp. worn. **Wing M.1804. S. & M. ii. 144.** **£25.00**
Amusing "character" of a speculator ("mony is the god he adores . . . he's an excellent chymist, transmutes all into gold and silver") in contemp. hand on e-p.

140. ———— Anr. ed. (4th). For Thomas Basset . . . and John Place, 1681. Index. [viii], 257, [i], [xviii]pp. Lacks last blank. Some leaves soiled. Old ½ cf./mbld. sides; sl. worn. **Wing M.1805. S. & M. ii. 144.** **£25.00**

141. MILLER, John. An Inquiry into the Present State of the Statute and Criminal Law of England. 1822. 1st. viii, 332pp. Contemp. cf., gilt arms on upper cvr.; jts. worn; rbbd. **S. & M. iii. 153.** **£35.00**
Miller complains of the profusion & confusion of statutes & reports, & of the leniency of penal reformers, especially those who attempt to withdraw all capital punishment. From the library of the Hudson's Bay Company, *with their arms on the cover.*

142. MODERN REPORTS. The Third Part . . . being . . . Special Cases in King's-Bench in . . . the Reign of Charles II . . . James II., and . . . William & Mary. 1725. 3rd ed. Folio. Black letter. Indices. [xx], 338, [xxxvi]pp. Contemp. cf., jts. worn. **£20.00**
One of a series of twelve volumes covering all the courts of record from 1674 to 1725, & intended to form an up-to-date body of precedents.

143. MORTIMER, Thomas (1730-1810). Lectures on the Elements of Commerce, Politics, and Finances; Intended as a Companion to Blackstone's Commentaries. 1801. 1st. List of subscribers. xxviii, 442pp. Final blank. Orig. bds., uncut; sp. sl. worn. **Kress B.4422. £25.00**

144. MUIR, Thomas (1765-1798). MACKENZIE, Peter: Life . . . with a Full Report of his Trial. Glasgow, 1831. 1st. Engr. fp. port. ½ title. viii, 160pp. Uncut. Mod. cl. **£15.00**
Muir, an enthusiast for Parliamentary reform and French democracy (cf. MARGAROT) was transported for sedition in 1794 after a discreditable trial. An American ship, sent for that very purpose by sympathizers in New York, rescued him from Sydney; after a shipwreck he was taken on board a Spanish vessel, was wounded in an exchange with two English ships, & died in France, where he had been made an honorary citizen.

145. [NEEDHAM, Marchamont] (Fl. 1640-78). The Excellencie of a Free-state; or the Right Constitution of a Common-wealth [ed. Sir Henry VANE]. For Thomas Brewster 1656. 1st in bk. form. 12mo. [viii], 246, [v]pp. **Long inscription by the author** on e-p. & around title. Few text corrections. 18th.-cent. black mor. gilt; jts. worn. **Wing N.388.** **£100.00**
Needham – physician, turncoat, & the first of our political journalists – tells us in his inscription that the book was compiled (by the fanatic Vane) from the editorials to his newsbook, Mercurius Politicus. He adds that his doctrine of a regularly elected assembly displeased the masters of the Rump, "and for this excuse the Council of State did a[w]hile suspend my pension; which sheweth, how little mind they had to rise." This "pension" paid by the supposed enemies of corruption to a vulgar scribbler, & his consequent vast idea of his own importance, throws a singular light on the history of the English Republic.

146. NELSON, William. Lex Maneriorum: or, the Law and Customs of England, relating to Manors and Lords of Manors, their . . . Tenants, and others. 1733. 2nd ed., rev. Index. Appendix of pleadings. [xvi], 272, [viii], 168, [viii]pp. Contemp. cf., re-backed; rbbd. **S. & M. ii. 125.** **£15.00**

147. NICOLAS, Sir Harris. A Treatise on the Law of Adulterine Bastardy, with a Report of the Banbury Case. 1836. 1st. Index. xvi, 588pp. Few margins sl. torn. mod. bds., leather label. **S. & M. i. 310.** **£30.00**
A chronological arrangement of reported cases (some previously unpublished) from Foxwell's of 1284 to Gardner's of 1824, preceded by remarks on Bracton's & Britton's views on the subject.

148. NOY, [Sir] William. Reports and Cases . . . now translated. By F.L. for Matthew Walbancke . . . and T. Firby, 1656. 1st. Folio. Black letter. Index. [xii], 185, [xi]pp. $2C_4$ blank. Some browning throughout. Mod. cl. **Wing N.1449; S. & M. i. 200.** **£20.00**

149. OKE, George C. The Synopsis of Summary Convictions: showing . . . the Penalties, &c. for 1300 Offences . . . Forms and Notes . . . List of Indictable Offences . . . Abstract of the Juvenile Offenders Act. 1848. 1st. Index. Publisher's cat. xiv, 398, 16pp. Sl. spotted. Orig. cl., fdd., sp. frayed. **S. & M. iii. 163.** **£12.00**
Written for the use of J.P.s. The idea of a list of penalties & other circumstances for each offence likely to be tried by a magistrate originated with Barlow (q.v.).

150, OLDFIELD, T.H.B. An Entire and Complete History . . . of the Boroughs of Great Britain [–together with the Cinque Ports] . . . Sketch of Constitutional Rights. 1792. 1st. **3 vols.** Errata slip pasted in vol.1. Title of vol.3 repaired at inner margin. New cl. **£35.00**
An interesting contribution to parliamentary history, designed to show the abuses of the constituency system & the need for reform.

151. ———— History of the Original Constitution of Parliaments, from the Time of the Britons to the Present Day. 1797. 1st. ½ title. [viii], 548pp. Contemp. ½ cf./mbld. sides; sl. worn. **£20.00**

152. OWEN, Aneurin (ed.). Ancient Laws and Institutes of Wales. Public Records Commission, 1841. 1st. Folio. Welsh, Latin & English text. Wood-engrs. in text. Index. [iv], xvi, [viii], 1006pp. Orig. cl., paper label; sl. shaken; fdd. **£60.00**
The first comprehensive edition of the Welsh laws, from the three local codes (erroneously fused into one by previous editors) supposedly ratified by the tenth-century King Howel Dda, or the Good, to Edward I's Statute of Ruddlan, or Statuta Walliae, which settled the form of Welsh jurisprudence under direct English sovereignty.

153. OWEN, Thomas. The Reports of . . . one of the Justices of the Common Pleas. By T.R. for H. Twyford, T. Dring, and J. Place, 1656. Folio. Black letter. Index. [xii], 158, [viii]pp. Two sm. worm-holes throughout. Old annots. Contemp. sheep, re-backed; worn. **Wing O.832. S. & M. i. 201.** **£25.00**

154. PARKER, John. Notes on the Law of Arbitration in Scotland. Edinburgh, 1830. 2nd ed. Index. xxxvi, 341pp. Few sl. stns. Orig. calico-bkd. bds., edges worn. **S. & M. iii. 167.** **£15.00**
Revised ed., with new cases, of a work first issued in 1820.

155. PARKES, Samuel (1759-1825). Thoughts on the Laws relating to Salt: with Arguments for the Repeal of those Laws. 1817. 1st. Index. Adverts. at end. 229, [ii]pp. Orig. bds., uncut; sp. defective; jts. worn. **Kress B.7014.** **£30.00**
The heavy salt-duty prevented the use of that mineral in many industrial & agricultural processes, which in consequence had to be laid aside or maintained with expensive materials from abroad. Parkes's facts & figures, in which even farmers could learn that protective duties were doing them no good, carried all the weight of his high reputation as a chemist.

156. PARTRIDGE, S.G. Prisoner's Progress. N.d. [1935]. 1st. Illus. Index. 288, 24pp. Orig. cl., sl. fdd. **£12.00**
A study of prisons & prisoners, crime detection & prevention, trials, & executions in the early nineteenth century.

157. PEARCE, Robert R. A Guide to the Inns of Court and Chancery: with Notices of their Ancient Discipline . . . Eminent Men . . . Regulations of the Four Inns. 1855. 1st. Publisher's cat. at end. xii, 440, [xl]pp. Orig. cl., sl. fdd. **£15.00**

158. PELHAM, Camden. The Chronicles of Crime; or, the New Newgate Calendar. 1841. 1st. **2 vols.** Illus. (etched plates) H.K. Browne. Indices, xii, 592/viii, 636pp. Few plates sl. stnd. Mod. ¼ cf./cl. sides. **£35.00**

159. PETYT, William (1636-1707). The Antient Right of the Commons of England Asserted. For F. Smith, T. Bassett, J. Wright, R. Chiswell, and S. Heyrick, 1680. 1st. Lacks first leaf (blank or privilege). [x], 76, 184pp. Some contemp. pencil annots. Name cut from head of title. 19th-cent. ½ cf./mbld. sides; worn. **Wing P.1945. S. & M. ii. 116.** **£50.00**
After the Restoration, some loyal but thoughtful persons could not reconcile their respect for the Commons with their devotion to the Throne. To calm their scruples, Petyt suggests that Parliament was not the offspring of sedition against Henry III, but coeval & integral with the Saxon & even the mythical British monarchy. This led to the conclusion that the term "Parliament" included the King & his powers (see DICKENS, & BRADY for a contrary view).

160. ———— Miscellanea Parliamentaria: containing Presidents. 1. Of Freedom from Arrests. 2. Of Censures . . . for Misdemeanours. By N. Thompson, for T. Bassett, and J. Wickins. 1680. 1st. Blank before title (mounted). [xxvi], 220, [lxiv]pp. Mod. cf. **Wing P.1948. S. & M. i. 106.** **£50.00**
An important study of the origins of parliamentary privilege. Petyt was the Tower Archivist & a notable benefactor to the Middle Temple library, where he deposited his collection of state papers (see BARRINGTON).

161. P[HILIPOT], J[ohn], Somerset Herald. The Catalogue of the Lord Chancellors of England, the Lord Keepers . . . and the Lord Treasurers. By Tho. Cotes . . . Sold by Andrew Crooke, 1636. Sm. 4to. Woodcut arms (Howard) on A_4V. [viii], [ii], 93 [actually 82], 79-82, 85pp. Two quires signed M, the second of two leaves only. Corner of $[2]M_2$ defective without loss of text, & catch-word shaved. Mod. ½ cf./mbld. sides. **S.T.C. 19846.** **£45.00**

162. P[HILLIPS], H[enry]. The Grandeur of the Law; or, an exact Collection of the Nobility and Gentry . . . whose Honors and Estates have . . . by . . . their Ancestors been acquired or . . . augmented by the Practice of the Law. For Arthur Jones, 1684. 1st. Fp. port. (Lord Guildford, Keeper of the Seal). Index. Lacks final blank. [viii], 276pp. Mod. ¼ mor./mbld. sides; fine. **Wing P.2022. S. & M. ii. 49.** **£30.00**

163. POPHAM, Sir John. Reports and Cases . . . now faithfully Translated. By Tho. Roycroft for Henry Twyford and John Price, 1656. 1st. Folio. Black letter. Index. [viii], 212, [viii]pp. Some old annots. Sl. browned. Title sl. frayed. Lib. stamp on title. Mod. cl. **Wing P.2942. S. & M. i. 201.** **£20.00**

164. POWELL, Thomas. The Attourneys Academy: or, the Manner and Forme of Proceeding Practically, upon any Suite, Plaint or Action . . with . . .

Fees of the Officers. For Benjamin Fisher, 1630. 3rd ed., rev. 4to. Index. [xii], 88, 16, 89-230. [lxi] pp. Few sl. marginal defects. Contemp. sheep, v. rbbd. **S.T.C. 20164. S. & M. i. 184.** **£85.00**
Dedicated to Sir Francis Bacon, with some quaint verses. Powell compares himself to a navigator tracing new paths through the mysteries of legal bureaucracy and its emoluments; he calls for a formal recognition & regulation of counsel's fees, so that a dissatisfied client may sue for repayment & damages. The sixteen inserted leaves contain a new chapter on the Verges Court.

165. PRIESTLEY, Joseph, & others. An Interesting Appendix to ... BLACKSTONE's Commentaries on the Laws of England. Philadelphia, 1773. 1st collected. General & individual title-pages. [iv], iv, 5-119, [i], xii, 155, [i] pp. Sl. browned. Inner margins wormed at beginning & end, just affecting text of last few leaves. Contemp. sheep, sl. worn. **Evans 12684.** **£60.00**
Blackstone supported the penal statutes which defended the authority of the Church of England. The volume contains Priestley's "Remarks" opposing this attitude, Blackstone's reply, & Priestley's counter-attack; further arguments against Blackstone in the "Letters" of Philip Furneaux; & speeches (one by Lord Mansfield) from a case of 1767 bearing on the subject. Blackstone's reflections on John Wilkes's case (1769) also appear.

166. PRISONS, Parliamentary Reports on. Report ... on the ... Gaols of the City of London. 1814. 1st. Folio. Evidence & appendices. 107pp. – Report [on] the Condition and Treatment of Prisoners ... in Lincoln Castle. 1812. 1st. Folio. Two engr. fold'g plans. Appendix. 103pp. – Reports ... on the Laws relating to Penitentiary Houses. 1811. 1st. **3 pts.** Folio. Two engr. fold'g plans of hulks. Appendices. [ii], 187pp. – Papers relating to the Convict Establishment at Portsmouth, Sheerness, and Woolwich. 1816. 1st. Folio. 20pp. **Four items in one vol.** Mod. b'ram. **£75.00**
Includes in the first report on penitentiary houses several pages of evidence & a letter by Jeremy Bentham.

167. RALEIGH, Sir Walter. The Perogative [sic] of Parliaments in England. Proved in a Dialogue betweene a Counsellour of State, and a Iustice of Peace. Printed 1640. 4to. [viii], 66pp. Lacks final blank. Disbound. **S.T.C. 20650. S. & M. i. 70.** **£25.00**
Raleigh's Justice offers in support of constitutional government many dire warnings against irresponsible favourites and unauthorized taxes; remarks for which Sir Walter, had he lived, might have claimed the merit of prophecies, and whose fulfilment doubtless promoted the present reprint.

168. REPORTS of CASES Taken and Adjudged in the Court of CHANCERY, in the Reign of ... Charles I [– William and ... Mary] ... Arguments relating to ... the said Court, its Dignity, Power & Jurisdiction. By the Assigns of Richard and Edward Atkins ... for John Walthoe, 1693[-4]. 1st. **2 vols.** Indices. [xlvi], 288, 88/[xvi], 304, 353-437, [xix] pp. Sigs. in vol. 2 jump from U to 2A, with corresponding gap in pagination; nothing missing. Some browning. Vol. 1 mod. cl.; vol. 2 contemp. cf., rbbd. **Wing R.1090; S. & M. i. 219.** **£35.00**
The reports are generally brief, & uninformative on the arguments used but vol. 1 contains an important discussion of the relation, then still in a formative state, between Chancery and other courts. Against Coke, & notwithstanding two old statutes alleged to the contrary, the author supports a personal decision of James I that judgments in King's Bench etc. could be modified in the courts of equity.

169. ——— The Third Part of Reports of Cases ... in Chancery. 1716. 1st. Index. [xxx], 224pp. Contemp. cf., sl. rbbd. **S. & M. i. 219.** **£15.00**
Successor to the preceding item, including a group of cases heard by Sir W. Cowper (later Lord Chancellor), more fully & clearly reported than the rest.

170. REYNOLDS, John. The Triumphs of Gods Revenge against the ... Sinne of (Wilful and Premeditated) Murther. For William Lee, 1635. [Third ed.] Folio. Engr. title. **6 parts (some dated 1634) in 1.** [xxviii], 464pp. Anti-Papal reference on p.180 inked out. Few marginal tears. Contemp. cf., re-backed cl.; sl. rbbd. **S.T.C. 20944** (var. imprint to bk. 1). **£70.00**
Fictional narratives, whose style is that of the French romances, but whose content that of the older tragedies. The moral element (although attested by the Archbishop of Canterbury) vanishes after the preface.

171. ROMILLY, Sir Samuel (1757-1818). Observations on the Criminal Law of England, as it Relates to Capital Punishments. 1810. 1st. [ii], ii, 76pp. Mod. ¼ b'ram/bds. **S. & M. iii. 196.** **£20.00**
Romilly's important declaration against the multitude of capital offences was adapted from his speech in Parliament, 9th Feb. 1810. He added remarks on the folly of Paley (in his Moral Philosophy), who defended the system of maintaining a quantity of crimes punishable in theory by death, & allowing juries to save the prisoner's life by perverting the facts.

172. ROSE, John. A Constitutional Catechism ... with copious Notes, Principally Extracted from the Commentaries of the late Judge BLACKSTONE, Bristol, 1795. 1st. viii, 87pp. Contemp. ½ cf./mbld. sides; rbbd. **Not in S. & M.** **£10.00**

173. [SAINT GERMAN, Christopher] (?–1540). The dyaloges in Englishe, betwene a Doctour of divinitie, and a Student in the lawes of England. [Aedibus Richardi Totteli; an. 1554]. [Second English collected ed.] Black letter. Woodcut title-border, inverted (McK. 48) & initials. Index. 176, [iv] leaves. Sl. stnd. towards end; sm. marginal worm-holes in last two leaves; but a fine copy in mod. calf. **Beale T.473; S.T.C. 21571; S. & M. i. 23.** **£250.00**
A work always valued for its clear exposition of technical points. St. German disputed the questions of royal & Papal prerogative (both touched on in the "Additions" to these dialogues) with Sir Thomas More, in a temperate spirit which earned general respect.

174. SAYER, Joseph. The Law of Costs. Dublin, 1768. 1st thus. [xvi], 280pp. Contemp. cf., sl. rbbd.; lower jt. cracked. **S. & M. ii. 83.** **£15.00**
Reprinted from the London ed. of the same year.

175. SELDEN, John (1584-1654). Titles of Honor. By William Stansby for John Helme, 1614. 1st. Sm. 4to. Glossary of oriental names. Index. [xxxviii], 391, [xlii] pp. Lacks blanks A_4 & $3K_2$. Two leaves sl. mkd. Sm. hole in C_2 aff. few letters. Contemp. cf., head of sp. repaired; edges rubbed. **S.T.C. 22177.** **£120.00**
The first of Selden's great historical works, displaying his deep & various reading & the wide-ranging comparison between the customs of diverse races & ages which raises him to the rank of a valuable social historian. Ben Jonson contributes a long eulogy in verse.

176. ——— Titles of Honor. William Stansby for Richard Whitakers, 1631. Second ed. Sm. folio. Red & black title. Text woodcuts & engrs. Old annots. Sm. hole in $4D_3$ aff. two lines of text. [xxxvi], 941, [i] pp. Lacks final blank. Contemp. sprinkled cf.; jts. weak. Bk-pl. Alexander Thomson. **S.T.C. 22178. S. & M. i. 151.** **£95.00**

177. ——— Anr. copy. Final blank. Old cf.; worn; re-backed. **£95.00**
This edition was greatly enlarged.

178. ——— Tracts ... Jani Anglorum Facies Altera ... [tr. & ed.] Redman Westcot ... England's Epinomis ... Original of Ecclesiastical Jurisdiction ... Administration of Intestates Goods. For Thomas Basset and Richard Chiswell, 1683. 1st collected. Lacks port. [ii], [xxxii], 132, [viii], 40, [iv], 24pp. Title sl. frayed. Mod. ¼ cf./mbld. sides. **Wing S.2441a.** **£60.00**

179. SHEPPARD, William. The Court-keepers Guide ... Useful for the ... Keeping of Law Days, or Courts Baron. By W.G. for Gabriel Bedel, and Thomas Collins, 1662. 5th ed., rev. Index. [iv], 254, [iv], [xiv] pp. Title-border shaved. Contemp. sheep, two sm. holes in sp., sl. worn. **Wing S.3181. S. & M. i. 250.** **£50.00**
Replaced the obsolete & uninformative works of the "modus tenendi curiam" type, the only guides to the subject up to then in print.

180. ——— Actions upon the Case for Deeds, viz. Contracts, Assumpsits, Deceipts, Nusances, Trover and Conversion, Delivery of Goods, and for other Male-feasance and Misfeasance. For S.S. ... Sold by William Jacob, and Nicholas Cox, 1675. 2nd ed. Black letter. Index. [viii], 822, [xxii] pp. $2C_4$ sl. defective aff. few letters. Sl. wormed. Contemp. cf., sl. rbbd.; head of sp. sl. torn. **Wing S.3175. S. & M. ii. 19.** **£40.00**
A compilation from the reports, with a brief definition of Action on the Case by way of preface.

181. [SHOWER, Sir Bartholomew] (?–1701). Cases in Parliament Resolved and Adjudged, upon Petitions, and Writs of Error. For A. and J. Churchill, 1698. 1st. Folio. [xii], 224, [ii] pp. Lacks final blank. Contemp. cf., sp. & edges rbbd. **Wing S.3650; S. & M. ii. 22.** **£35.00**
The first collection of its kind: cases expounding the jurisdiction of the House of Lords in a wide variety of cases.

182. ——— The Second Part of the Reports of Cases and Special Arguments ... in ... King's Bench. 1720. Folio. Mostly black letter. Fp. port. Index. [xii], 519, [xxi] pp. Lacks final blank. Some browning. Mod. b'ram. **S. & M. ii. 96.** **£25.00**
This part was posthumously published from a fair copy corrected by the author.

183. ——— The Compleat English Copyholder: or, a Guide to ... the ... Law of England, together with the Adjudged Cases relating to Manors, Copyhold Estates, Courts-Leet and Courts Baron. 1735. 1st & only ed. **2 vols.** Index. [viii], 384/[ii], 385-598, [lxxiv] pp. Fine copy in contemp. cf., sp. of vol. 2 sl. rbbd. **S. & M. i. 246.** **£50.00**
Shower's posthumous work completed the rationalization of the seignorial courts & the tenures subject to their jurisdiction which Coke (q.v.) had begun.

184. SIDERFIN, Thomas. Les Reports des divers special Cases ... en le Court del Bank le Roy. By W. Rawlins [etc.] for Samuel Keble, 1683. French text. Folio. Indices. [iv], 467, [lxxxv]/[viii], 179, [xi] pp. Contemp. MS. glossary inserted in vol. 1, which includes blank $2K_4$ but lacks final blank. Few annots. Contemp. cf.; sl. rubbed. **Wing S.3757-8. S. & M. ii. 96.** **£40.00**

185. ——— Anr. set. 19th-cent. ½ cf./mbld. sides; sps. rubbed; lacks one label. **£38.00**

186. SKENE of Curriehill, Sir John (tr. & ed.). Regiam Majestatem. The Auld Lawes and Constitutions of Scotland ... fra the Dayes of King Malcolm the Second, untill ... James the First. Edinburgh, 1774. [2nd Engl. ed.] 4to. Index. [xii], 464, 124pp. Sl. soiled. Two sm. ink-stains on $2K_1$ verso. Contemp. cf., re-backed; sides rbbd. **S. & M. V. 106.** **£40.00**
Skene's translation of the old Scots laws appeared concurrently with his Latin collection in 1609. The English contains three extra items; an anonymous treatise on courts baron, & two summaries (probably Skene's own) on the form of process before the Lords of Session & on criminal causes.

187. SPELMAN, Sir Henry (1562-1641). Reliquiae Spelmannianae ... Posthumous Works. Oxford (Clarendon Pr.), 1698. 1st. Folio. Device on title. Two fold'g tables. Index. [xxxii], 214, [xii] pp. Lacks final blank. Inner margin of A_1 defective; text not aff. Contemp. mottled cf.; sp. rbbd. & frayed. **Wing S.4391.** **£70.00**
Consists largely of the treatise on Feuds and Tenures by Knight-Service, together with the Apology for Abp. Abbot (convicted of manslaughter by chance-medley in a test case for a clergyman's rights under such circumstances). remarks on wills, coinage, & the rank of knight, etc.

188. SPOTTISWOOD, John. An Introduction to the Knowledge of the Stile of Writs, Simple and Compound, Made Use of in Scotland. Edinburgh, 1765. 5th ed., rev. 12mo. Index. [iv], 588, [xx] pp. Few leaves sl. stnd. Contemp. cf., sl. rubbed. **£15.00**

189. STATUTES. Acts for Making Provision for the Effectual Performance of Quarantine; with Orders in Council, &c. 1817. 1st collected. 4to. Index. 86, [lx], [ii], 149-216pp. Interleaved throughout. Contemp. diced cf., rbbd; lacks spine. **£20.00**

190. ———. An Act for the Amendment and Better Administration of the Laws relating to the Poor. N.d. [1834]. Index. xxiv, 104pp. Orig. wraps, sp. torn. **£5.00**
A convenient edition of the Poor Law act of 1834.

191. ——— **Ireland.** A Collection of the Several Acts relating to Game. Dublin, 1829. 1st collected. [iv], 170pp. Contemp. cf.; fine. **£10.00**

192. ——— A Collection of Acts relating to the Criminal Law of Ireland. Dublin, 1834. [– Supplement, 1838]. 1st collected. Indices. [viii], 364/[iv], 349-476pp. Contemp. cf., sl. mkd. **£10.00**

193. ——— A Collection of Miscellaneous Acts relating to Ireland. Dublin, [1833-]1838. 1st collected. General & individual titles. Indices. [iv], [iv], 160, 32, 120, 64, 18pp. Contemp. cf., sl. rbbd. **£10.00**
Consists largely of acts relating to the administration of justice.

194. ——— A Collection of Miscellaneous Acts relating to Ireland. Dublin, [1829-]1838. 1st collected. General & individual titles. Individual pagination. Contemp. cf., sl. rbbd. **£10.00**
Acts against the wilful burning of agricultural land, on the recovery of small debts, etc.

195. ——— **Scotland.** The Laws and Acts of Parliament made by King James the First [– Queen Anne]. Edinburgh, 1682-3 & 1731. **3 vols.** 12mo. Indices. Vol. 2 lacks final blank. [viii], 1018/640/875pp. Old cf., re-backed; sl. rbbd. Bk-pls. **Wing S.1266; S. & M. v. 116-7.** **£40.00**

196. ——— Anr., vol. 3 (James VII – Anne) only. 1731. 875pp. Some fore-margins shaved. Sl. browned. Contemp. cf., re-backed. **£8.00**

197. The STATUTES at LARGE concerning Elections of Members to Serve in the House of Commons. 1734. 1st. Index. [vi], 109 [i.e. 119], [xv], 10pp. **S. & M. ii. 26 – ORDERS & RESOLUTIONS of the ... COMMONS** on Controverted Elections and Returns. 1736. 2nd ed., rev. 12mo, Index. viii, 209, [vii] pp. **S. & M. ii. 26. – COWLEY, J.;** The Candidates Guide: or the Electors Rights Decided ... Resolutions ... concerning the Rights of Elections. 1734. 1st. [ii], 30pp. This ed. not in **S. & M.** **Three works in one vol.** Contemp. cf., lower cvr. rbbd. **£35.00**

198. ——— concerning Bankrupts. 1765. [2nd ed.]. Index. [iv], 144, [xxxvi], 4pp. Sl. stnd. Mod. cl. **S. & M. ii. 216.** **£20.00**
Includes obsolete acts (from 34-35 Hen. VIII. c.4) as well as those in force.

199. STATUTES relating to the SEWERS, within Westminster, and Part of Middlesex. 1809. vi, 70pp. Contemp. ¼ roan/mbld. sides; red labels on sides; spine defective. **£10.00**
Published by the Commissioners of Sewers, who were established by the first act in the book (23 H. VIII. c.5).

200. STEUART or STEWART of GOODTREES, Sir James. An Index or Abridgement of the Acts of Parliament and Convention, from ... King James the First ... to the Ninth Session of the Current Parliament. Edinburgh, 1702. (2nd ed., rev.). 12mo. Index. [xii], 330pp. Lacks U_5 (pp. 237-8) (cancel, not bound in). Two similar cancel leaves loosely inserted. Contemp. cf., worn. **S. & M. v. 117.** **£10.00**

201. ——— The Index or Abridgement, from ... 1424 to ... 1707 ... with the Act Ratifying ... the Treaty of Union of the Two Kingdoms. Edinburgh, 1707. (3rd ed., rev.) [xii], 298, [ii] pp. Final blank. Tear in X_3 without loss. And – **BRUCE, Alexander;** The Index ... of such Acts ... as ... concern the whole United Kingdom, or particularly ... Scotland ... to ... 1726. Edinburgh, 1726. 1st. 12mo, [ii], viii, 106, [ii] pp. Final blank. **2 works in 1 vol.** Contemp. cf., rbbd. **S. & M. v. 117.** **£20.00**

202. STIRLING, Family of. RIDDELL, John: Comments in Refutation of Pretensions ... in a Recent Work "The Stirlings of Keir and their Family Papers". Privately printed. Edinburgh, 1860. 4to. Limited 300. xx, 260pp. Orig. cl., paper label; sl. worn. Bk-pl. **£15.00**
A striking example of a Scottish family feud. The bone of contention was the heritage of the extinct Cadder Stirlings, which had been disputed by the Drumpellier (represented by Riddell) & Keir branches ever since 1541.

203. STUART, Gilbert (1742-1786). Observations concerning the Public Law, and the Constitutional History of Scotland. Edinburgh, 1779. 1st. Appendices. Errata leaf. xxiv, 396pp. Sl. spotted. Contemp. cf., rbbd.; jts. weak. **S. & M. v. 118.** **£20.00**
Desultory but learned remarks on feudal laws & tenures, the position of the king & nobles, the Scots parliament, etc., including the first blows in the quarrel with Robertson which Stuart afterwards pursued in his History.

204. SWINTON, John. An Abridgment of the Public Statutes in Force and Use Relative to Scotland, from the Union ... to the Twenty-Seventh Year of his present Majesty. Edinburgh, 1788. 1st. **2 vols.** 4to. Index. ½ titles. xii, [652]/[ii], [528], [xxx] pp. Contemp. sheep, rbbd. **S. & M. v. 119.** **£40.00**
Replaces the work of the elder Swinton (1755). Schedules of customs & excise are given in full.

205. TENANTS LAW: or, the Laws concerning Landlords, Tenants and Farmers. 1750. 13th ed., rev. 12mo. Index. 314, [xxxiv] pp. Contemp. cf., sl. stnd.; sp. sl. rbbd. **S. & M. ii. 144.** **£15.00**

206. THREE PATENTS concerning the Honourable Degree and Dignitie of BARONETS. By Robert Barker, 1617. Sm. 4to. 39pp. A_1 blank except for large signature within border. Some stns. Mod. wraps. **S.T.C. 9238.** **£15.00**
The rank of baronet was created in 1611 as a reward for landowners who cultivated estates in Ulster. This pamphlet gives the terms of the patent for creating a baronet, & defines his place in the scale of precedence.

207. TOLLER, Samuel. The Law of Executors and Administrators. 1800. 1st. Index. xvi, 414, [ii] pp. Contemp. cf., sl. rbbd. **S. & M. ii. 160.** **£15.00**

208. ——— Third ed., rev. Appendices. Index. xvi, 516, [lxxxii] pp. Some spotting. Contemp. cf., re-backed; sides worn. **£10.00**
Replaces the 160-year-old work of Wentworth (q.v.).

209. TOWNSEND, William C. The Lives of Twelve Eminent Judges of the Last and of the Present Century. 1846. 1st. **2 vols.** Index. xii, 474/viii, 527pp. Contemp. cf.; sps. rbbd. **Not in S. & M.** **£20.00**
Just & spirited studies, enlarged from the Law Magazine, of Buller, Eldon, Erskine, Kenyon, Redesdale, etc.

210. TUCKER, A.G.C. Supplement to the Observations intended to Prove that the Judgement ... in the ... Cause ... Cholmondeley and ... Damer Versus ... Clinton is Unfounded in Law. Exeter, 1818. 1st. [ii], 39pp. Disbound. **£5.00**
The case concerned the ambiguously-worded will of Samuel Rolle; the family of Horace Walpole was involved.

211. VAUGHAN, Sir J. The Reports and Arguments of ... late Chief Justice of ... Common Pleas. Ed. Edward Vaughan. By Thomas Roycroft for Richard Marriott [etc.], 1677. 1st. Folio. Mostly black letter. Fp. port.

Indices. [xiv], 420, [lv]pp. Mod. ¼ cf./mbld. sides. Wing V.130. S. & M. ii. 96. £30.00

212. VENTRIS, Sir Peyton. The Reports ... Third impression ... with ... several Thousands of References, never before Printed. 1716. **2 pts. in 1.** Folio. Black letter, Privilege leaf before title. Indices. [xii], 430, [xxiv]/[xviii], 368, [xx]pp. Some browning and spotting. First leaf partially backed. Mod. cl. **S. & M. ii. 97.** £25.00
The new references were contributed by one Richardson, serjeant at law.

213. VERNON, Thomas. Cases Argued and Adjudged in ... Chancery. 1726. 1st. **2 vols.** Folio. Fp. port. (Vertue after Kneller). Indices. First privilege leaf to vol. 1. [xiv], 490, [lxii]/[xii], 767, [cix]pp. Vol. 2 lacks first blank. Contemp. annots. Fine mod. ½ cf./mbld. sides. **S. & M. ii. 106.** £45.00

214. WALKER, Thomas (1784-1836). The Original. 1836. Second ed. iv, 444pp. Contemp. cf., sl. worn. Bk-pls. £15.00
Published as a periodical (Nos. 1-29) in May-Dec. 1835. Walker was a magistrate, & reforms in local government & the local courts occupy much of his attention; but with these are interspersed reflections on manners, politics, & (most particularly) diet & health.

215. WASHINGTON, Joseph [& Henry (BOULT)] (eds.). An Exact Abridgment of all the Statutes of King William and Queen Mary, and of King William III and Queen Anne. 1704. Rev. ed. Index. [lxxxii], 662 [actually 678], [lxxxvi]pp. Extra sig., (I)[8], inserted between sigs. I & K. Contemp. cf., rbbd. **S. & M. ii. 178.** £20.00
Continuation of Wingate's Abridgment (q.v.).

216. WENTWORTH, Thomas. The Office and Duty of Executors ... Now Enlarged with a Supplement ... by H. CURSON. 1728. 1st thus. Index. Final advert. leaf. [iv], vi, [x], 468, [lxxii]pp. Mod. cl. **S. & M. i. 318.** £20.00
Wentworth on Executors first appeared in 1641, & was found worthy to be revised & reprinted as late as 1829.

217. [WHITELOCKE, Sir Bulstrode (1605-1676)]. Monarchy Asserted, to be the Best ... Form of Government, in a Conference ... with Oliver late Lord Protector and a Committee of Parliament. "London" [Amsterdam or the Hague], "John Redmayne for Philip Chetwyn", 1660. 1st. [vi], 112pp. Lacks first blank. 19th-cent. cf., sp. gilt; sl. rbbd. Bk-pl. **Wing W.1988.** £40.00
Report of an attempt by Parliamentarians desirous to curb military influence, at persuading Cromwell to ascend the throne. Like Caesar he refused, professing respect for the constitution; Whitelocke believes that fear of the army was his true reason.

218. WIGHT, Alexander. An Inquiry into the Rise and Progress of Parliament, Chiefly in Scotland. Edinburgh, 1784. 1st. 4to. Index. Errata leaf. xiv, 609pp. Few contemp. annots. (corrections to documents). Orig. bds., uncut; edges & jts. worn. **S. & M. v. 126.** £50.00

219. WILKINS, David (ed.). Leges Anglo-Saxonicae ... leges Edvardi ... Guilielmi conquestoris ... et Henrici I. Latine ... Henrici SPELMANNI codex legum veterum. 1721. 1st thus. Folio. Old English, Latin & French text. List of subscribers. Index. [xvi], xxiv, 434, [xviii]pp. Contemp. Dutch blind-stamped vellum, upper jt. sl. worn. Fine copy. **S. & M. i. 30.** £70.00
Wilkins extended his collection to the year 1224, where the old editions of "Ancient Statutes" (see MAGNA CHARTA) began, & corrected the text from Rochester, Canterbury, & Cottonian MSS. His Latin versions have been attacked.

220. WINGATE, Edmund [& Joseph WASHINGTON] (eds.). An Exact Abridgment of all the Statutes in Force and Use from ... Magna Charta ... to the year 1689. 1704. Rev. ed. Index. First blank. [ii], 726, [lxiv]pp. Sl. wormed at end. Contemp. cf., sp. sl. rbbd. **S. & M. ii. 178.** £20.00
Continued by the work of Washington (q.v.).

221. WOOD, Thomas. An Institute of the Laws of England ... in their Natural Order. 1722. 2nd ed. Fp. port. Index. xii, 663, [xxxiv]pp. Contemp. cf., rubbed & worn. **S. & M. ii. 65.** £20.00
An attempt (superseded by Blackstone, who preserves much of Wood's arrangement) at a methodical digest of English law.

222. ———— Anr. (eighth) ed. 1754. Index. [ii], x, 692, [xxxvi]pp. Contemp. cf., rbbd. **S. & M. ii. 65.** £20.00

223. WOODFALL, William (c.1773-1806). The Law of Landlord and Tenant. 1802. 1st. Index. Errata leaf. xii, 716, [ii]pp. One leaf of contents misbound. Mod. ½ cf./mbld. sides. **S. & M. iii. 250.** £20.00
First edition of a work whose successive revisions, in which something of the original method can still be traced, have carried its name down to the present day. Woodfall ended his life as Chief Justice of Cape Breton, Nova Scotia.

224. WORSFOLD, T.C. Staple Inn and its Story. 1906 [1903 on title.] Second ed. Illus. Index. 128, [iii]pp. Orig. cl.; fdd. £5.00

225. WRIGHT, Andrew. Court Hand Restored; or, the Student's Assistant in Reading Old Deeds, Charters, &c. ... Ancient Names of Places ... Ancient Surnames. 1778. 2nd ed. 4to. List of subscribers. 20 engr. plates. [viii], 100pp. Old ½ cf./mbld. sides; jts. & edges rbbd. **S. & M. i. 10.** £50.00

226. ———— Anr. (sixth) ed. 1822. 23 engr. plates. xvi, 60, [ii]pp. Title cut round & mounted. Later ½ mor./mbld. sides; sp. sl. fdd. **S. & M. i. 10.** £40.00
Written to cure the decay of paleographical knowledge which followed the abolition of law-Latin by the acts of 1731-3, Wright's work was standard until this century. The later ed. includes transcripts of the quotations in the plates, & three additional plates of charter hands from 1100 to 1591.

227. Court Hand Restored. 8th ed. 1846. 4to. 23 plates. Facs. of charter of Thomas la Warre, 1422, with partial MS. translation, loosely inserted. Orig. cl., re-backed. Sl. stnd. £20.00

228. WYATT, John (ed.). The Practical Register in Chancery. 1800. 1st thus. Index. ½ title. viii, 492pp. Contemp. cf., sl. rubbed. **S. & M. ii. 105.** £15.00
Greatly enlarged from the edition of 1714, about half the material being newly added by Wyatt.

229. YATE, Walter Honywood. Political, Historical, and Analytical Arguments, proving the Necessity of a Parliamentary Reform, and Pointing Out the Means of Effecting that ... Measure. 1825. 2nd ed. **2 vols.** xcviii, 252/xii, 240pp. Orig. bds., paper labels; uncut & unopened; sps. sl. torn. £35.00
The author's plan includes secret ballots, abolition of parliamentary privilege, & triennial elections at which three members (only one of whom, chosen annually by the voters of his constituency, actually sits in the Commons) are elected for each seat.

230. [YORKE, H.C.]. Some Considerations on the Law of Forfeiture, for High-Treason. 1746. 2nd ed., rev. & enlarged. Engr. fold'g table. viii, [vi], 180, [ii]pp. **S. & M. i. 277.** And:– **[ROBINSON, R.].** A Discourse concerning the Law of Inheritances in Fee, and ... the Several Degrees of Consanguinity. 1736. 1st. Engr. fold'g table. Index, xiv, 74, [vi]pp. **S. & M. ii. 148.** **Two works in one vol.** Sl. browned. Contemp. cf., rubbed. £30.00
Yorke argues strongly for the doctrine that a traitor's hereditaments revert to the Crown & justifies it on grounds both logical (notably that property like government is an institution of civil society, & that he who has outraged the latter loses his right to the former) & historical. Robinson attempts to restore the genealogical structure postulated in Bracton & Britton.

THE FROGNAL BOOKSHOP LTD.
68 Lymington Road, London NW6 1JB
Telephone: (01)-435 9757
Cables: Finresbook, London NW6

THE FROGNAL BOOKSHOP LTD.

68 LYMINGTON ROAD LONDON NW6 1JB ENGLAND
Tel: (01) 435 9757 Cables Finresbook NW6

CATALOGUE 46

LAW AND LEGAL HISTORY

(1976)

CATALOGUE 46
LAW AND LEGAL HISTORY

All books are published in London and of octavo size, except where stated.

Prices are NET, postage and insurance extra. No conversion charge for foreign currency.

Please confirm all telephoned orders in writing, stating number of catalogue and item, author, title and price.

Customers not previously known to us are requested **not to send payment with their orders**, but either to give two trade references or to pay on our pro-forma invoice.

For details of current and future catalogues see inside back cover.

NOTES

An index of subjects may be found at p.51.

Minor inscriptions & book-plates which cause no disfigurement to the volume are omitted from the description.

European jurists are listed under the Latin form of the surname (e.g. Grotius) except where such form consists only in the addition of a suffix (e.g. Schulting-ius) or does not exist in common usage.

BIBLIOGRAPHICAL REFERENCES

BEALE BEALE, J.H.; A Bibliography of Early English Law Books. Harvard U.P., 1926.
B.M.C. Catalogue of Books Printed in the XVth Century Now in the British Museum. 9 vols.
———— **(Fr., Ger., It.)** Short-Title Catalogue of French [German, Italian] Books Printed between 1501 & 1600 in the British Museum.
KRESS Kress Library of Business and Economics; Catalogue. Harvard U.P., 1940-1967. 4 vols.
S.T.C. POLLARD, A.W., & G.R. REDGRAVE; Short-Title Catalogue of Books Printed in England, Scotland and Ireland ... 1475-1640. 1926.
S. & M. MAXWELL, L.F., etc.; Legal Bibliography of the British Commonwealth. Sweet & Maxwell, 1955-1964. 7 vols.
WING WING, D.M., Short-Title Catalogue of Books Printed in England, Scotland, Ireland, Wales ... 1641-1700. 1972 & 1945. 3 vols.

1. An ACCOUNT of the PROCEEDINGS of the HOUSE of PEERS upon the . . . Publick Accounts. 1702. 1st. Folio. Fold'g tables. 86pp. – **ACCOUNT of the PROCEEDINGS** . . . in Relation to the . . . Act for Preventing Occasional Conformity. 1702. 1st. Folio. 28pp. – **The BILL entituled, an ACT for PREVENTING OCCASIONAL CONFORMITY**, with the Amendments made by the Lords . . . Reports of the Conferences. 1702. 1st. Folio. 64pp. **Three works in one vol.** contemp. mottled cf., sp. gilt; sl. rbbd. **£50.00**
With the establishment in 1688 of a more responsible scheme of government, corruption & negligence in the administration of public funds became a lively & persistent issue. The first item here contains evidence & arguments on irregularities in collecting & recording various branches of the revenue.

2. ADDINGTON [Sir] William. An Abridgment of Penal Statutes, which Exhibits . . . the Offences, and the Punishments . . . to which are Subjoined . . . Adjudged Cases. 1786. 3rd ed. 4to. Index. [iv], 694, [iv], [xcii]pp. Contemp. cf., sl. rbbd. **S. & M. i. 358.** **£50.00**
Addington succeeded his friend Sir John Fielding at Bow Street in 1780.

3. ADSHEAD, Joseph. Prisons and Prisoners. 1845. 1st. Etched fp. by George Cruikshank, & other illus. xviii, 13-320pp. Orig. cl., fdd., ends of sp. frayed. **Cohn 6. Not in S. & M.** **£75.00**
The work is a defence of the solitary-confinement system, and gives up a whole chapter to refuting Dickens's attacks on that system as applied in Philadelphia & Boston. Other contents include studies of prisons old (Newgate) & new (Pentonville), with French & American comparisons.

4. ALEXANDRO, Alexander ab (Alessandro Alessandri) (?-1494). Genialium dierum libri sex, varia ac recondita eruditione referti. Ed. Giovanni Ferrari. Paris, apud Ioannem Roigny, 1550. 1st thus. Latin text. Sm. folio. Device on title (printing-press, after Dürer's design for Badius) & woodcut initials. Index. [lxxvi], 370pp. Blank f8. Sl. stnd. Last leaf sl. browned & frayed. Later vellum, ties. **£100.00**
This work of miscellaneous learning on Greek & Roman life, law & letters, modelled on the Noctes Atticae of Gellius, was a fruitful source for compilers of quotation-mongers for some centuries; more significantly, it marks the beginning of the study of Roman law from a historical rather than merely practical point of view. The typography is excellent work of the Parisian golden age.

5. An ALPHABETICAL ABRIDGEMENT of the First Parliament of King James the VII . . . and of the Convention of Estates . . . and . . . Sessions of . . . King William and Queen Mary. Edinburgh, by the Heirs and Successors of Andrew Anderson, 1698. 1st. 12mo. 132pp. Contemp. panelled cf., sp. & edges worn. **Not in S. & M. Wing A.2898 (Nat. Lib. Scot. only).** **£30.00**

6. AMBLER, Charles (Attorney-General) (c. 1720-1794). Reports of Cases Argued and Determined in the High Court of Chancery. 1790. 1st. Folio. ½ title. Index. [xvi], 784, [xxiv]pp. Lacks last two leaves of index. Mod. cl. **S. & M. i. 344.** **£15.00**
Pearne v. Lisle *(p.75) contains an interesting judgment of Lord Hardwicke L.C.; he denies that Holt C.J.'s decision in* Gould v. Smith *(2 Salk. 666) leads to the conclusion that a human being cannot legally be a chattel – in other words that English law does not recognize a state of slavery; and he pours scorn on Holt's dictum that there is no such thing as a slave in English law.*

7. An ANALYTICAL DIGEST of ALL the CASES REPORTED. 1838-1841. 4 **vols. (16 issues) in 1.** Index to each quarter. Contemp. ½ cf./mbld. sides; rbbd.; jts. worn. **S. & M. ii. 212.** **£15.00**
The series ran from 1830 to 1845.

8. ANCIENT LAWS of IRELAND. Ed. W.N. Hancock & others. Dublin, H.M.S.O., 1865-79. 4 vols. 1st. English & Irish text. ½ titles. Indices. Folding lith. facss. Orig. ¼ roan/bds.; spines rubbed & worn. Lib. stamps & labels. **S. & M. iv. 3.** **£75.00**
Produced as a result of a Royal Commission formed in 1852. Includes the Senchus Mor (the Pandects of Irish law, compiled at the instance of St. Patrick), the Book of Aicill (decisions in criminal law), & certain tracts of the Brehons or judges. A supplementary volume of texts & a glossary appeared in 1901.

9. ANDREAS or ANDREAE, Johannes. Processus iudiciarius . . . et [GERARDI Monachi] juris defensorium una cu[m] p[ro]curator[um] manuali. [Nuremberg (impressum per . . . Joannem Weyssenburger), 16th April 1510.] Sm. 4to. Schwabacher letter. Large woodcut on title (partially coloured.) index. [iv], 34, [4] leaves. Some errors in foliation. Several head-margins cropped affecting running-titles and (in last quire) first line of text. Mod. ½ calf/mbld. sides. **No. ed. in B.M.C.** **£90.00**
A small treatise (which, from its style, seems to be two hundred or more years older than the date of printing) on the method of holding a court, with two

similar handbooks, one a guide to the rights & privileges of accused persons. The author does not appear to be identical with the canon lawyer Andreae (13th cent.), nor the work with the much larger Processus of Auerbach, frequently printed in the fifteenth century.

10. ARNISAEUS, Henningius. Doctrina politica in genuinum methodum, quae est Aristotelis, reducta. Amsterdam (L. Elzevir), 1651. Rev. ed. 12mo. Engr. title. Index. 584,[cxlvi]pp. Contemp. vellum. **Willems 1121.** **£30.00**
A survey according to the rules of Aristotelian logic of every possible relationship between human beings, with a multitude of historical examples.

11. ARNOT, Hugo. A Collection and Abridgment of Celebrated Criminal Trials in Scotland from A.D. 1536 to 1784. Edinburgh, 1785. 1st. 4to. Appendix of documents. Index. xxiv, 400pp. Sl. spotted. Contemp. tree cf., sp. gilt; rbbd.; jts. worn. Bk-pl. Marquess of Lansdowne (subscriber.) **S. & M. v. 6.** **£50.00**
Written to present to English readers a picture of regal, judicial & (especially) religious tyranny gradually overborne by the power of reason. William Fitzmaurice, 1st Marquess of Lansdowne, was Prime Minister from 1782 to 1785 under the title of Earl of Shelburne.

12. ATH (town of Hainault, 13 miles N.E. of Mons). Chartes, Statuts, et Ordonnances de Polities. Mons, 1760. French text. [ii], 92[i.e. 114]pp. Contemp. cf., sp. & upper cvr. worn. Bk-pl. **£20.00**
An interesting group of trade regulations, many dealing with the local breweries, & some surviving from the Spanish occupation. The code (if it deserves the name) of Ath was assembled in 1612, & later revised. Leaves G_{1-3} have been cancelled.

13. ATKYNS, J.T. (Baron). Reports of Cases . . . in . . . Chancery, in the Time of . . . Lord Hardwicke. 1765[-7]. Folio. **3 vols.** Indices. First advert. leaf to vol. 1. Vol. 3 lacks title & B_2 (fly-title). Mod. b'ram. **S. & M. i. 344.** **£40.00**
Atkyns arranges his cases by subjects, not chronologically; his design (echoed in the modern case-book) is to produce a "system or digest" of equity by way of case law.

14. AUFRÉRI, Estienne (fl. c. 1483) (ed.). Decisiones materiaru[m] quotidianaru[m] . . . in capella sedis archiep[iscop]alis Tholose decise . . . additiones . . . co[n]cordate . . . cum decisionibus Rote et parlamenti delphinalis. [Lyons, A. du Ry, 4th Sept.] 1527. Rotunda letter. Red & black title within woodcut border. Woodcut inits. & final device. Index. [xxiv], 192 leaves. Commentary on four sides of text. Few early annots. Damp-stained throughout, severely towards end. Mod. ¼ vellum/mbld. sides. **No. ed. in B.M.C.** **£90.00**
Five hundred decisions in the archiepiscopal court of Toulouse, edited (from the papers of one Jean de Coursier) & annotated by Aufréri between 1483 & 1503. This ed. includes many new references.

15. BACKUS, Joseph. A Digest of Laws relating to the Office and Duties of Sheriff, Coroner and Constable. N.Y., 1812. 1st. **2 vols.** Indices, [x], 490/[vi], 478pp. Sl. browned. Mod. cl. **£20.00**

16. BACON, John (ed.). Liber regis, uel thesaurus rerum ecclesiasticarum. 1786. 4to. Appendix. Index. [x], xviii, 1391pp. Contemp. annots. Contemp. cf., re-backed. **S. & M. i. 164.** **£40.00**
An account of the value & income of all the benefices in Britain, based on the survey of Henry VIII's time; with remarks on the law concerning presentation to livings.

17. ———— Anr. copy. Contemp. cf., jts. worn, head of sp. defective. **£35.00**

18. BARBARO, Antonio. Pratica criminale. Venice, 1739. 1st. 4to. Ital. text. [iv], 282pp. Old mbld. bds., sp. worn. **£20.00**
A simple account of Venetian criminal law, freed from the Roman veneer that often obscures Italian jurisprudence. Moneylending is still unconditionally described as a crime.

19. BARNARDISTON, Thomas (Serjeant-at-Law) (c.1700-1752). Reports of Cases . . . in . . . King's Bench. 1744. 1st. **2 vols.** Folio. Indices. [xiv], 470, [xxviii]/[xii], 470, [xxiv]pp. Contemp. cf., rbbd., ends of jts. torn. **S. & M. i. 292.** **£30.00**

21. BAYLEY, [Sir] John (1763-1841). A Summary of the Law of Bills of Exchange, Cash Bills, and Promissory Notes. 1813. 3rd ed., ed. W.E. Barnes. Index. [xvi], 256pp. Mod. ½ cf./mbld. sides. **S. & M. ii. 23.** **£15.00**

22. BEATSON, Robert. A Political Index to the Histories of Great Britain and Ireland; or, a Complete Register of the Hereditary Honours, Public Offices, and Persons in Office. 1788. 2nd ed. rev. xii, 482, [ii], 16/viii, 392, 20, [iv]pp. Contemp. sprinkled cf., sl. rbbd. **Not in S. & M.** **£40.00**
Includes (e.g.) Chief Justices, puisne judges, Chief Barons & Barons, & Masters of the Rolls from the beginning, & serjeants-at-law & masters in Chancery

from 1660. Vol. 2 contains Scots, Irish & colonial lists.

23. BEAWES, Wyndham. Lex Mercatoria Rediviva: or, the Merchant's Directory . . . Trading Companies and Colonies . . . Laws subsisting about Aliens . . . Traffick of the Whole World . . . European Coins, Weights, and Measures, Dublin, 1773. 6th ed. 4to. List of subscribers. Fold'g table of currencies (mounted). [viii], 776pp. Some browning. Few leaves sl. frayed. Names on title. Mod. cl. **Kress 6920. S. & M. i. 518.** **£80.00**
This useful work is laid out in two parts. The first is in the form of a law-abridgment, especially full in the article (not well documented up to that time) of insurances; the other is a regional survey of commerce, including the Americas. Sweet & Maxwell records this as the third edition.

24. [BECCARIA, Cesare Bonesana, Marchese di] (1735-1793). An Essay on Crimes and Punishments . . . with a Commentary, attributed to M. de Voltaire. Edinburgh, 1778. 12mo. x, 11-192pp. Contemp. sheep, rbbd. **£15.00**
Beccaria's theory of law anticipates the watchword & the principles of the Utilitarians. Like his editor, he was strongly influenced by English rationalism.

25. BECKERS, Wilhelm. Synopsis iuris imperii Romano-Germanici. Cologne, 1649. 3rd ed. Latin & German text. 12mo. Engr. title. Appendix. [x], 512, [xxxvi]pp. Sl. browned. Last two gatherings wormed, aff. text of last three leaves. Vellum, sl. soiled; lower cvr. wormed. Bk-pl. **£15.00**
The constitution & laws of the Holy Roman Empire, with (in the Appendix) a statement of its revenues.

26. BELL, George Joseph. Commentaries on the Laws of Scotland, and on the Principles of Mercantile Jurisprudence. 1816[-19]. 3rd ed. **2 vols.** 4to. Index. xl, xvi, 496, xlii, [viii]/[xxvi], 568, [lx]pp. Sl. spotted. Mod. cl. **S. & M. v. 10. Not in Kress.** **£60.00**
Scots commercial law had been brought to a highly advanced condition by its practisers, who drew their ideas from France, but no general statement of it had been set down. Bell corrects this want in great detail; his especial purpose is to reconcile Scots law with that of England as expounded by Lord Mansfield, and (in this edition) to examine & promote international co-operation in the law of trade.

27. BENTHAM, Jeremy. Defence of Usury; shewing the Impolicy of the Present Legal Restraints on . . . Pecuniary Bargains . . . Letter to Adam Smith. Dublin, 1788. [Second ed.] ½ title. [vi], 232pp. Lower corner of H_3 restored, with few words in pen facsimile. Contemp. tree cf., sl. worn. **Kress B.1368.** **£40.00**
First published in London in the preceding year. Bentham finds inconsistencies in Blackstone's maintenance of the existing laws, and argues against Adam Smith that "cheap money", instead of making loans accessible to worthy applicants to the exclusion of speculators, would effectively paralyse solid & valuable industrial schemes because all available capital had been drawn off by frivolous hands.

28. BENTON, Thomas H. (1782-1858). Thirty Years' View; or, a History of the Working of the American Government for Thirty Years . . . with Historical Notes . . . and . . . Notices of Eminent Deceased Cotemporaries [sic.] N.Y., 1854-6. 1st. **2 vols.** Engr. fp. to each vol. First & final advert. leaves. x, 740, [xvi]/788, [iv]pp. Few leaves sl. mkd. & stnd. Mod. ½ cf./cl. sides. **£50.00**
The author sat for Missouri in the Senate throughout the period of these memoirs. Although he showed the inevitable bias of the Southerner (ill dissembled in this work by a ponderous assumption of indifference), he was always honourably opposed to any disruptive tactics or wanton denigration of legitimate Northern interests; and this sense of justice rendered him one of the most respected men in Congress until he carried it too far for his party, & went like Peel into the wilderness.

29. BERLICHIUS, Burchardus. De novercarum iure, statu et affectu novus et utilis tractatus . . . Accessit in fine dissertatio de novercarum, praesertim durarum & iniustarum, usu & encomio. Leipzig (apud Eliam Rehefeld, & Johan. Gros), 1628. 1st. 4to. Red & black title. Index. [viii], 376, [xiv]pp. Some browning. Contemp. vellum. **£50.00**
The laws of stepmotherhood in relation to descent, nobility & clergy, children by previous marriage, etc. A vein of bovine & pedantic humour, apparently endemic among Teutonic jurists (cf. KORNMANN) breaks out in several places; for example, there are 79 anagrams on NOVERCA (stepmother), mostly in the traditional spirit of hostility.

30. BILLINGHURST, George, & Henry CURSON. Arcana Clericalia: or, the Mysteries of Clerkship Explained; declaring the . . . Parts of Deeds and their Nature. 1705. Rev. ed. Final advert. leaf. [xvi], 590, [ii]pp. Lib. perforation on title. Mod. cl. **S. & M. i. 489.** **£30.00**
This manual of conveyancing was originally Billinghurst's; Curson revised the arrangement of the work, & added an analysis.

31. BIRD, G. The Practising Scrivener, and Modern Conveyancer: being a Collection of All Sorts of Choice Presidents. 1729. 1st. Folio. Index. [iv], 720, [xliv]pp. Contemp. cf., sl. rbbd. **S. & M. i. 479.** **£50.00**
Includes a large number of forms for shipping & other commercial transactions, many of them involving American, West Indian or Russian interests. Real property is represented here only by leases; other assurances were destined for three further volumes which never appeared.

32. BLACKSTONE, [Sir] William (1723-1780). Commentaries on the Laws of England. Oxford (Clarendon Press), 1766 [1767, 1768, 1769]. **Vols. 1 & 2** 2nd ed.; vols. 3 & 4 1st. **4 vols.** 4to. Two engr. tables (one fold'g) Index. [iv], viii, 486, [ii]/[viii], 520, [xx]/[viii], 456, xxviii/[viii], 436, viii, [xl]pp. Final blank to vol. 1. Contemp. cf., sl. rbbd.; upper jt. of vol. 4 worn & hole in spine. **S. & M. i. 27. Printing & the Mind of Man 212.** **£500.00**
When he became the first professor of common law in the old universities, Blackstone held it his duty to justify the ways of the law to the intelligent layman. This he accomplished with a lucidity of explanation, a coherence of arrangement, and an ingenuity in finding rational support for the most obscure eccentricities of the law, which have never been surpassed. Only in his tendency to appoint himself defending counsel for the existing law, in place of sitting in judgment on it as compared with possible reforms, has he provoked dissent from Bentham (q.v.), Furneaux, & a few others.

33. ———— Another set. Oxford, 1768[-69]. Vols. 1 & 2, 3rd ed.; Vols. 3 & 4, 1st. **4 vols.** 4to. Two engr. tables in vol. 2. Appendix to vol. 2 bound before text. Few worm-holes in vol. 3, Vols. 1, 2 & 4 contemp. cf., later labels, sides rbbd.; vol. 3 mod. ¼ cf./cl. sides, jts. rbbd. **£500.00**

34. ———— Anr. (18th) ed., ed. John Williams. 1823. **4 vols.** Fp. port. & two engr. tables. Index. Contemp. ½ cf./mbld. sides; sl. rbbd. **S. & M. i. 28.** **£60.00**

35. ———— An Analysis of the Laws of England. Oxford, 1759. 4th ed. Appendix. Two engr. tables. Index. lxx, [vi], 190, [xiv]pp. Contemp. cf., sl. rbbd. **S. & M. i. 27.** **£40.00**
The Commentaries grew from this work, followed its order, and incorporated some material directly from it – notably the tables of descents, the appendix of deeds, & the introductory discourse.

36. ———— Tracts, Chiefly Relating to the Antiquities and Laws of England. Oxford, Clarendon Press, 1771. 4to. Engrs. of seals in text. Engr. table. Index. 356, lxxx, [xx]pp. Few leaves sl. spotted. Contemp. cf., sl. rbbd., upper jt. sl. worn. **S. & M. i. 30.** **£180.00**
This third edition is the first to include the Analysis (which is revised so as to agree with the Commentaries as published) and the Observations on the Oxford Press. Of the other contents, the less controversial part of the essays on Consanguinity & on Copyholds went into the Commentaries; the texts of & introduction to Magna Charta & its confirmations are an independent work.

37. ———— Anr. copy. Contemp. cf., edges rbbd., jts. sl. worn. **£180.00**

38. B[LOUNT], T[homas] (1618-1679). Fragmenta Antiquitatis. Antient Tenures of Land, and Jocular Customs of some Mannors. By the Assigns of Richard and Edward Atkins . . . for Abel Roper[etc.], 1679, 1st. Index. First privilege & final errata leaf. [vi], 176, [xvi]pp. Later ½ roan/cl. sides. **S. & M. i. 398. Wing B.3333** **£40.00**
This popular collection of curious tenures (mostly petty serjeanty or copyhold) was for many laymen a light-hearted introduction to the mysteries of feudalism.

39. BÖCKELMANN, Johann Friedrich (1632-1681). Compendium Institutionum Justiniani, sive elementa iuris civilis. Amsterdam, 1710. Red & black title. Index. [xxxii], 282, [xxii], 102, [xviii]pp. Contemp. vellum. **£30.00**
Böckelmann's preface complains of the complexity of formlessness of law-studies, & the practice among doctors of pouring out thesis after thesis on half-a-dozen unvarying titles of the Institutes or Code instead of clarifying the law as a whole.

40. BOSANQUET, J.B. & C. PULLER. Reports of Cases . . . in . . . Common Pleas and Exchequer Chamber, and in the House of Lords. **Vol. 2 (1799-1801), of 3, only.** 1802. 1st. Folio. Index. xii, 614, [xx]pp. Mod. cl. **S. & M. i. 293.** **£8.00**

41. BOSSIUS, Aegidius. Tractatus varii, qui omnem ferè criminalem materiam . . . complectuntur. Venice, apud Franciscum Laurentinum, 1562. 3rd ed. 4to. Index [lxviii], 300 leaves. Few contemp. annots. Contemp. blind-tooled cf.; corners worn; spine defective. **£60.00**
Posthumously edited by the author's son Francesco. The work contains a large

chapter on the rights & duties of a ruler, with an interesting emphasis on the latter ("The Pope can depose a prince who oppresses his subjects", "A prince in all his actions stands in place of a god, & must therefore adhere strictly to truth in all his decisions, since God is truth"), and several chapters on the principles of taxation.

42. BOTT, Edmund. Decisions of the Court of King's Bench, upon the Laws relating to the Poor. 1793. 3rd ed., ed. Francis Const (1st thus). **2 vols.** Index. [lxviii], [cxciv], 680, [iv]/[lviii], 893, [iii], [iv]pp. Two extra titles (for use when the work was bound in 4 or 6 parts) at end of each vol. Contemp. cf., rbbd., re-backed. **S. & M. i. 386.** **£50.00**
This massive work did all that could be done to clarify the laws of settlement & relief, whose intricacy confounded even Blackstone. The text is preceded by a valuable alphabetical digest embracing both case & statute law.

43. [BOWMAN, E.] The English Pleader. Being . . . Precedents of Declarations . . . Pleas and Issues . . . Recoveries and Concords of Fines. 1734. 1st. Index. Two advert leaves before title. [iv], 400, [xvi]pp. Lib. perforation on title. Mod. cl. S. & M. i. 264. **£30.00**
One of a number of works produced to satisfy doubts about the correct terminology of pleadings following the statutory introduction of the English language in these documents.

44. BOYDEN, Roland W. (Overseer of Harvard, member Versäilles Reparation Comm.; 1863-1931).
ELIOT, S.A.; In Memory of. Boston Bar Ass., 1933. 1st. Port. 38pp. Orig. b'ram, fine. **£5.00**

45. BOYER, Abel (1667-1729). The History of the Reign of Queen Anne, Digested into Annals. 1703[-1713]. 1st. **11 vols. in 10.** Engr. port. & maps (lacks one map). Two leaves in vol. 6 in facs. Two leaves in vol. 1 misbound. Sl. browned. Mod. cl. **£80.00**
A history, well supplied with documents, by one of the most respected of the French Protestant refugees who adopted a literary career in London.

46. ———— The Political State of Great Britain . . . Proceedings in Parliament [etc.] Feb., 1711. 1st. [iv], 77-174 [i.e. 200]pp. First leaf of text signed L_1; pagination irreg. accordingly. Three extra quires ($r^* - r^{****}$) between R & S. Sl. browned. Mod. ¼ cf./mbld. sides. **£15.00**
No. 2 of 60 monthly newsbooks.

47. BRADFORD (Yorks.) The Acts relating to the Transfer of the Bradford Waterworks to the Corporation of Bradford . . . New Works [etc.] Bradford, 1856. 1st. Index. [iv], 246, [iv], xliipp. Orig. cl., sl. worn & fdd. Not in S. & M. **£10.00**

48. BRADLEY, Joseph P. (1813-1892). LEWIS, W.D. & A.Q. KEASBEY (eds.); Miscellaneous Writings . . . Review of his Judicial Record. Newark, N.J., 1901. 1st. Engr. fp. port. xii, 436pp. Mod. cl. **£20.00**
As Associate Justice of the U.S. Supreme Court (appointed by President Grant in 1870) Bradley presided over the "Legal Tender" case of 1870 and the Electoral Commission of 1876, both of which vindicated the President's authority against the claims of Congress. This book refutes the charge that he was a mere mouthpiece for Grant. His writings are essays on political, religious, moral & scientific subjects.

49. BRADY, Robert (?-1700). A Complete History of England . . . unto the End of the Reign of King Henry III. By Tho. Newcomb for Samuel Lowndes, 1685. 1st. Folio. Engr. fp. port. Imprimatur leaf. Red & black title. Index. [x], lxviii, [viii], 676, 254, [lxviii]pp. Contemp. mottled sheep, rbbd., jts. & corners worn. Bk-pl. Wing B. 4186. S. & M. i. 125. **£75.00**
A partisan work in which Brady marshalled his extensive knowledge of records to support his theories on the constitution, namely that Parliament was a creation of the thirteenth century & that its rights were therefore inferior in priority (& hence, according to the logic of the day, in importance) to those of the crown.

50. BRERETON, C.D. Observations on the Administration of the Poor Laws in Agricultural Districts. Norwich, 1824. 3rd ed. Lacks ½ title. [ii], 119, [vi]pp. Mod. cl. **Kress B. 6642.** **£10.00**
Under the "allowance system" created by some Norfolk magistrates in the 1790s, magistrates could make orders for payment of unconditional outdoor relief to the able-bodied unemployed, overriding the authority of the local vestry. Brereton complains of the perjury, malingering & waste of public money that ensued.

51. BRISSON, Barnabas (1548-1591). De formulis et solennibus [sic] populi Romani uerbis libri VIII. ex recensione Francisci Caroli Conradi. Halle & Leipzig, 1731. Latin text. Folio. Engr. fp. port. Red & black title. Indices. [xl], 728, [liv]pp. Genealogical table of Burgundian & Merovingian kings (unrelated to this work) bound in before K_1. Sl. browned. Contemp. Dutch blind-stamped vellum. **£30.00**
A compendium (first pubd. 1582) of the language, customs & ordinances of Roman law, religion & government, by a French jurist who lost his life in defence of his master Henri IV. The title-page promises a life of the author, but this was evidently never included in the impression.

52. The BRISTOL RIOTS, their Causes, Progress and Consequences. Bristol, 1832. 1st. Lith. fp. Appendix. [iv], 404pp. Few leaves loose. Orig. cl., fdd.; head of sp. sl. torn. **£50.00**
In October 1831 Sir Charles Wetherell, a judge & a notorious enemy of reform, arrived in Bristol to hold the assizes. At this a mob, stirred up over the previous 18 months by trade-union agitation, poured into the street & burned down a great part of the city. Four of the leaders were hanged for arson, & two officers who had neglected to fire on the people were court-martialled. This Tory account throws all the blame on Lord Grey's Government for allying itself with Radicals & maddening the mob with a glimpse of power.

53. BROWN, William. Modus transferendi status per recorda: a Compleat Collection of Choice Precedents for Fines upon Writs of Covenant, and Common Recoveries upon Writs of Entry in the Post . . . Nature and Operation of, and the Use and Practice relating to, Fines and Recoveries. By the Assigns of Richard and Edward Atkins [etc.], 1698. 1st. Index. [viii], 398, [xxvi]pp. Some browning. Contemp. panelled cf., re-backed. S. & M. i. 489. **Wing B.5092.** **£40.00**
Originally conceived as a volume of precedents supplementary to Browne's Treatise of Fines & Recoveries (1678), this book is nonetheless converted into an independent work by the addition of definitions of the actions themselves & of their components, with some general instructions.

54. BROWN, William (barrister-at-law). Reports of Cases . . . in the High Court of Chancery. 1785. 1st. **Vol. 1 (of 4) (1778-1785) only.** Folio. Index. [iv], iv, [x], 496, [xvi]pp. Contemp. ¼ cf./mbld. sides; head of sp. defective. **S. & M. i. 345.** **£10.00**

55. BRUNTON, George & David HAIG. An Historical Account of the Senators of the College of Justice, from . . . M.D. XXXII. Edinburgh, 1836. 1st. Index. xlviii, 567pp. **44 autographs** (incl. some duplicates) tipped in or mounted on back e-p's. **Inscribed** by Mrs Haig on e-p. Contemp. ¼ roan/cl. sides; front hinge broken. Bk.-pl. S. & M. v. 16. **£50.00**
The autographs include David Hume, James Boswell, Alexander Wight, William Robertson, Lord Kames, & other notables of Scottish law & literature.

56. BRYDGES, Sir [Samuel] Egerton (1762-1837). Arguments in Favour of the Practicability of Relieving the Able-bodied Poor, by Finding Employment for them. "Pamphleteer", 1817. 1st. 133-163pp. Disbound. **£5.00**
Proposes to create agricultural & highway jobs, farmers etc. being compelled by law to take on a quota of poor labourers.

57. BURN, Richard (ob. 1789). The Justice of the Peace, and Parish Officer. 1758. 5th ed. Folio. Index. xviii, 792, [viii]pp. Cancel leaf (*293-4) inserted after $4F_1$. Few marginal worm-holes. Contemp. cf., upper cvr. worn, head of sp. frayed. **S. & M. i. 226.** **£65.00**

58. ———— Anr. (11th) ed. 1770. **4 vols.** Index. Contemp. cf., rbbd. **S. & M. i. 226.** **£60.00**
Includes an appendix on the jurisdiction of magistrates in Scotland, & a revision the title "Poor" on the authority of Burrow's Settlement Cases (q.v.).

59. ———— Ecclesiastical Law. 1797. 6th ed., ed. Simon Fraser, **4 vols.** Index. Contemp. cf., sl. rbbd. **S. & M. i. 166.** **£30.00**

60. BULLINGBROOKE, Edward. The Duty and Authority of Justices of the Peace and Parish Officers for Ireland. Dublin, 1788. New ed., ed. J.G. Butler. 4to. Index. xx, 912, [xx]pp. Margins sl. wormed. Contemp. cf., sl. rbbd., upper jt. worn. **S. & M. iv. 11.** **£25.00**

61. BUNBURY, William. Reports of Cases in the Court of Exchequer. Ed. Geo. Wilson. 1755. 1st. Index. Table of Barons of the Exchequer etc. Privilege leaf before title. [vi], 348, [xlviii]pp. Signed by Wilson at end of preface. Few annots. Mod. ¼ cf./mbld. sides. **S. & M. i. 322.** **£25.00**

62. BURROW, [Sir] James. A Series of the Decisions of . . . King's Bench upon Settlement cases. 1768. 1st. **2 vols.** 4to. Indices. Advert. leaf before title of vol. 2. xvi, 364/xviii, [xxxiv], 629-654, 365-626pp. Contemp. cf., rbbd. **S. & M. i. 386.** **£40.00**
A short treatise on punctuation (Thoughts upon Pointing), intended to be placed at the end of vol. 2, has been bound before the text of that volume. The Reports are a striking commentary on Blackstone's complaint that the diverse means of gaining a settlement in a parish, so as to be supported in poverty out of the rates of that parish, had disastrously confounded the working of the old poor law.

63. ———— Anr. ed. Dublin, 1790. ½ title. Index. [xiv], 846, [xviii]pp. $2K_4$ & $2P_4$ torn without loss. Piece torn from head-margin of $2Q_1$.

Two leaves of index shaved. Contemp. cf., rbbd.; jts. worn. **S. & M. i. 386.** **£15.00**

64. BYNKERSHOEK, Cornelius van (1673-1743). Opera omnia. Leyden, 1767. Folio. **2 vols. in 1.** ½ titles. Engr. fp. port. Indices. [iv], 459, [i]/[ii], 532pp. Occasional light damp-stains; otherwise a fine large copy in contemp. vellum, gilt; lacks ties; sl. soiled. **£150.00**
Bynkershoek, by his knowledge & application of the civil law, liberated Dutch jurisprudence from a confusion of statutes & ill-founded decisions. This edition includes both sides of his controversies with Noodt on the legal status of unwanted children, & with Pagenstecher on the origin of the Authenticae.

65. C., J. Thesaurus Brevium. Or, a Collection of Approved Forms of Writs, and Pleadings to those Writs, and Entries. By W. Rawlins [etc.] for T. Basset [etc.], 1687. 2nd ed., rev. Folio. Black letter. First privilege leaf, Index. [xxiv], 310, [lxxxii]pp. Contemp. cf., rbbd., corners worn. **Wing C.76; S. & M. i. 265.** **£50.00**
A short-cut to practical knowledge of writs, giving exemplifications drawn from the previous hundred years of the most important of them, with related matter.

66. CABALA, sive Scrinia Sacra, Mysteries of State . . . in Letters of Illustrious Persons. For G. Bedell, and T. Collins, 1663. [2nd ed., enlarged]. Folio. Red & black title. First privilege leaf. Index. [xiv], 416, [x]pp. sl. Stnd. Mod. ¼ cf./mbld. sides. **Wing C.185.** **£50.00**
Includes many letters by Sir Francis Bacon, with some of Sidney, Raleigh, & the Earl of Essex.

67. CALTHROP, Sir Henry (1586-1637). Reports of Special Cases touching several Customs and Liberties of the City of London . . . whereunto is annexed divers Ancient Customs . . . Reprinted from the Edition of 1670. 1872. [viii], 244pp. Library perforation on title. Mod. cl. **S. & M. i. 437.** • **£6.00**

68. CAMPBELL, John, Lord. The Lives of the Chief Justices of England. 1849 [-1857]. 1st. **3 vols. in 6.** Additional printed title to the second part of each vol. **Extra-illus.** with 93 copper- or steel-engr. & two mezzotint plates. Index. Contemp. ½ cf./mbld. sides; jts. & edges rbbd. **£85.00**
The plates are for the most part portraits of the Chief Justices & other judges, with a few of other public characters, and three views of buildings. They include a fine early portrait of Lord Suffolk by Elstracke (c. 1630), & a rare contemporary print of the parties to the Gunpowder Plot; the rest are mostly of the period 1780-1840.

69. CARDOZO, B.N. (1870-1938). Selected Writings, ed. M.E. Hall. N.Y. 1947. 1st collected. Fp. port. Index. xxiv, 456pp. Orig. cl.; sp. fdd. **£6.00**

70. CAREW, Bampfylde Moore (1693-c. 1770), King of the Gypsies. The Life. Bath, 1802. [New ed.]. Fp. port. Glossary of underworld slang. [ii], 124pp. First three leaves wormed, affecting port. & one word of title. Contemp. sheep, rubbed; jts. worn. **£10.00**

71. CARTER, A.G.W. The Old Court House: Reminiscences and Anecdotes of the Courts and Bar of Cincinnati. Cincinnati, Ohio, 1880. 1st. Steel-engr. fp. & other illus. 466pp. Orig. cl., gilt: re-cased; ends of sp. frayed. **£15.00**
Recollections of the Ohio Supreme Court & the Court of Common Pleas from 1819 onwards, including complete lists of the judges & court officers and Cincinnati lawyers at various periods.

72. CASES and RESOLUTIONS of CASES . . . in . . . King's Bench, concerning Settlements and Removals. 1742. 4th. ed. Index. [xxiv], 418, [xxx]pp. Mod. cl. **S. & M. i. 387.** **£20.00**
Cases in the time of Lord Parker C.J., preceding & complementing Burrow (q.v.).

73. CATHERINE II, Empress (1729-1796). The Grand Instructions to the Commissioners Appointed to Frame a New Code of Laws for the Russian Empire. Tr. Michael Tatischeff. 1768. 1st Engl. 4to. [xxiv], 258pp. Sl. spotted. Contemp. stained cf., sl. rbbd. **£120.00**
The Instructions, a lively image of benevolent & self-respecting despotism, consist of 655 articles of precept & example on the ethics of justice & government. The Empress, enlightened by an acquaintance with many of the greatest thinkers of the time, herself composed the work & added a scheme for the code itself.

74. CHANCELLOR, E. Beresford. The Romance of Lincoln's Inn Fields. N.d. [c.1930]. 1st. Illus. Index. 318pp. Orig. cl.; sl. fdd. **£5.00**

75. CHINA, [Nationalist] Republic of. Civil Code, tr. Ching-lin Hsia & others, introd. Foo Ping-Sheung. N.p. [Shanghai], 1931. 1st Engl. Index. xxxii, 382pp. Orig. wraps, sp. frayed. **£15.00**

76. ———— Criminal Code, tr. Ching-lin Hsia & Boyer P.H. Chu. Shanghai, 1936. 1st Engl. Index. xvi, 162pp. Fine in frayed d.w. **£15.00**
The civil code was promulgated in 1930, the criminal in 1935; intended to give expression to Sun Yat-Sen's ethical & sociological ideas, they are remarkable for their simplicity & rigidity.

77. CLARENDON, Edward [Hyde], Earl of (1609-1674). Miscellaneous Works. 1751. 2nd ed. Folio. Red & black title. [iv], 348, [ii], 369-770pp. Signatures jump from $4U^1$ to $5B^2$; pagination irreg. accordingly. Mod. ¼ cf./mbld. sides. **£40.00**
The most substantial item here is the Vindication against a charge of high treason (1667).

78. ———— the Life . . . Written by Himself. Oxford (Clarendon Pr.), 1759. 1st. Folio. Engr. fp. port. & vignettes. Index. [iv], 134, [ii], 523pp. Contemp. cf., re-backed; jts. & edges worn. **£50.00**

79. CLARKE, Thomas J. (1857-1916). Glimpses of an Irish Felon's Prison Life, introd. P.S. O'Hegarty. Dublin, 1922. 1st. xx, 104pp. Orig. cl. fdd. & sl. stnd. **£6.00**
Prison memories of 1883-98 by an emissary from the "blood-dyed Clan-na-Gael" executed as a rebel in 1916.

80. COCKBURN, Sir Alexander (1802-1880). Nationality: or the Law relating to Subjects and Aliens, Considered with a View to Future Legislation. 1869. 1st. [ii], 218pp. Orig. cl., sl. mkd. **S. & M. iii. 70.** **£15.00**
The Lord Chief Justice condemns the bearing of dual nationality & the practice of varying the treatment & status of aliens according to that allotted in their native lands to British citizens; it may be remembered that the latter doctrine (robustly interpreted by Palmerston) had led to several shameful incidents in the previous decade, notably that of Don Pacifico through which Cockburn himself rose to fame.

81. COKE, Sir Edward (Chief Justice) (1551-1633). The Reports . . . faithfully rendred into English. For W. Lee, M. Walbanck, D. Pakeman, & G. Bedell, 1658. 1st. Engl. Folio. Indices. Final leaf with table of judges. [viii], 1131, [iii]pp. Names on title. Lower margins stnd. Title sl. frayed. New ¼ cf./mbld. sides. **Wing C.4944. S. & M. i. 296.** **£80.00**
Coke's Reports were published in eleven volumes between 1600 & 1615. They were so highly regarded by the old lawyers as to be cited simply as "Reports", without the author's name; and Coke's profusion of observation & comment, however confounding to one who wishes merely to ascertain facts, arguments & judgment in each case, add much to the permanent value of the work.

82. ———— The Reports . . . exactly Translated . . . to which are now Added the Respective Pleadings. 1738. **13 pts. in 7 vols.** Indices. Some browning. New cl., leather labels. **S. & M. i. 296.** **£80.00**
The pleadings had been given in Latin in an ed. of 1727.

83. ———— The Third Part of the Institutes of the Laws of England: concerning High Treason, and other Pleas of the Crown, and Criminall Causes. By M. Flesher, for W. Lee, and D. Pakeman, 1644. 1st. Folio. Black letter. Engr. fp. port. Woodcut title-border. [xii], 244, [ii]pp. Few leaves sl. mkd. Contemp. cf., jts. & edges worn. tail of sp. defective. **Wing C.4960. S. & M. i. 360.** **£180.00**
The third Institute centres on criminal statutes, as the second does on civil. Many of the now accepted principles of interpretation of statutes were settled by Coke; he pays particular attention to the "mischief" rule, namely the rule that the words of the statute are to be construed in reference to the specific wrong (either as stated in the preamble or as deduced from history) which the statute was intended to cure. In an Epilogue of rare eloquence, Coke deplores the excess of capital punishments, and declares his belief that the highest justice is to prevent and not to punish; twentieth-century jurisprudence can scarcely say more.

84. ———— [HAWKINS, William.] An Abridgment of the First Part of My Lord Coke's Institutes; with some Additions . . . shewing in what Points the Law has been Altered. 1719. 3rd ed., rev. 12mo. First advert. leaf. [vi], 496, [civ]pp. Mod. ½ cf./mbld. sides. **S. & M. i. 452.** **£30.00**
This useful abbreviation outlived its rivals & was last reprinted in 1822.

85. ———— TROTMAN, Edward; Epitome undecim librorum relationum. Excus. per assignat. J. More, 1640. 1st. French text. Index. [x], 580pp. **S.T.C. 5527; S. & M. i. 297.** – Un Exact Table de Tout l'Principal Matteires . . . Conteynns en le Abridgment. For W. Lee . . . and H. Twyford, 1664. 1st. [xxxvi] pp. **Wing T.2305; S. & M. i. 297. 2 items in 1 vol.** Mod. ¼ cf./mbld. sides. **£40.00**

86. COLER, William N. A Practical Treatise on the Law of Municipal Bonds. N.Y., 1873. 1st. **2 vols.** Index. 468/498 [ii]pp. Trade card of printers at end of vol. 2. Contemp. sheep, rbbd., jts. worn. **£25.00**
Surveys this peculiarly American contribution to the theory & practice of taxation as applied in each state, & endeavours to dispel the confusion

into which the subject had been thrown by attempts to define the legal position of state governments in terms of the English law of corporations. The name of Luke Hansard, one of the family of parliamentary printers, is written in each volume.

87. COLERIDGE, [John Duke Coleridge, Baron]. (Chief Justice 1880-94.) Speech . . . in the . . . Lords . . . upon the Bill to prevent Cruelty to Animals. Soc. for the Protection of Animals, 1876. 1st. 8pp. disbound. £5.00
Coleridge supports the Bill, but allows (in deference to public opinion) some indulgence to blood-sports.

88. COLIGNY, Gaspard de, Admiral (1517-1572). La Vie . . . Mémoires sur ce qui se passa au Siège de S. Quentin. Leyden (B. & A. Elzevir), 1643. 1st French. **2 pts. in 1.** 12mo. [viii], 144/88pp. Contemp. vellum. **Not in Willems.** £30.00
The murder of Coligny, a distinguished soldier who turned Protestant in 1561, stood out among the events of St. Bartholomew's Day 1572. The Life is translated from an anonymous Latin work; the account of the action before St. Quentin, where Coligny was captured by the Spaniards, is his own.

89. A COLLECTION of All the TREATIES of Peace, Alliance, and Commerce, between Great-Britain and other Powers, from . . . 1648 to . . . 1783. 1785. 1st collected. **3 vols.** viii, xlviii, 400/[iv], 5-414, [ii]/[iv], 5-434, [iv]pp. Orig. bds., uncut; sps. defective. **S. & M. i. 604.** £40.00
Includes Charles Jenkinson (Lord Liverpool)'s "Conduct of . . . Great-Britain in Respect to Neutral Nations" (first pubd. 1757), & some related material such as the treaty of 1778 between France & the U.S.A.

89a. ———— Treaties . . . from the Revolution in 1688. 1772. 1st collected. Vol. I (of 2) only (1688-1727). viii, 404, [iv]pp. **S. & M. i. 603.** £10.00

90. A COLLECTION of the DEBATES and PROCEEDINGS in PARLIAMENT . . . upon the Inquiry into the Late Briberies and Corrupt Practices. Printed . . . 1695. 1st. 4to. iv, 63pp. Mod. ½ cf./mbld. sides. **Wing E.1281.** £30.00
Some petty malversations of an army agent led the Commons to inquire into several suspicious transactions. It emerged that Sir John Trevor, Speaker of the Commons, had accepted £1,000 from the City of London to promote a bill, & that the Governor of the East India Company had paid out £157,000 to the Duke of Leeds & others.

91. A COLLECTION of the LAWS relating to the ORDNANCE, 1774. 1st. 4to. Index. ½ title. [ii], 200, [viii]pp. Contemp. cf., rbbd. lower jt. worn. **Not in S. & M.** £30.00
Includes the Articles of War.

92. A COLLECTION of STATE TRACTS, Publish'd on Occasion of the Late Revolution . . . and during the Reign of King William III. 1705 [-7]. 1st collected. **3 vols.** Folio. Red & black titles. Indices. [viii], 712, [xvi]/[vi], 788, [xiv]/[vi], 774, [xxxii]pp. $4M_{1-4}$ (vol. 3) misbound after quire N. Vols. 2 & 3 lack two blanks each. Some sl. browning. Contemp. cf., sl. rbbd. Re-backed. £100.00
Consists largely of pamphlets exposing the Catholic leanings & unconstitutional dealing of Charles II & his brother.

93. COLLINS, Arthur (1682-1760) (ed.). Proceedings, Precedents, and Arguments, on Claims and Controversies concerning Baronies by Writ, and other Honours. 1734. 1st. Index. Errata leaf. [ii], 4, [ii], 415, [xiii]pp. Few sl. stns. Contemp. sprinkled cf., jts. & edges worn. **S. & M. i. 204.** £50.00
Collins devoted more than half a century to the study of the peerage. This book contains records of disputes & questions arising out of peerages, drawn from the MSS. of Dugdale & others.

94. COLQUHOUN, Patrick (1745-1820). A Treatise on the Police of the Metropolis, Explaining the Various Crimes and Misdemeanors . . . and Suggesting Remedies. 1800. 6th ed., rev. ½ title. Index. [xiv], xvi, 655, [xxxii]pp. New ¼ cf./mbld. sides. **S. & M. i. 438.** £35.00

94a. ———— Seventh ed. 1806. ½ title. Index. [xiv], xvi, 655, [xxxii]pp. Contemp. tree cf., v. sl. rbbd. £35.00
Conservative & authoritarian by temperament, Colquhoun nonetheless pointed the way to many social reforms of the Victorian & later periods. There is something new in his attack on drunkenness, given as it is from a practical rather than moral point of view, & in his condescending but honest efforts to see how "the poor" live & think & to provide accordingly. He perceives that crime is better prevented than punished, & that the multitude of capital penalties is barbarous in theory & obsolete in practice.

95. COMMITTEE Appointed to Consider the . . . LAND FORCES & MARINES. Report. 1746. 1st. Folio. Appendix. [ii], 75-212pp. Mod. mbld. wraps. £15.00

96. ———— **to whom the PETITION of the MERCHANTS . . . of LINEN, THREADS, & TAPES . . . was Referred.** Report. 1744. 1st. [ii], 67-72pp. Mod. wraps. **Kress 4731.** £6.00

97. ———— **Appointed to Examine . . . the . . . PETITIONS of the MANUFACTURERS of . . . [CHEQUED & STRIPED] LINEN.** Report. 1751. 1st. Folio. [ii], 289-316pp. Mod. wraps. **Kress 5156.** £10.00

98. ———— **to whom the PETITIONS concerning the HARBOURS of RYE and DOVER were Referred.** Report. 1757. 1st. Folio. [ii], 387-404pp. Mod. wraps. £8.00

99. ———— **Appointed to Inquire into the . . . WEIGHTS and MEASURES.** Report. 1758. 1st. Folio. Appendix. [ii], 413-464pp. Mod. wraps. £10.00

100. ———— **to whom the . . . REPORT . . . for FORTIFYING MILFORD HAVEN . . . was Referred.** Report. 1758. 1st. Folio. Large fold'g map. [ii], 407-410pp. Mod. wraps. £8.00

101. ———— **Appointed to Inquire into the MANAGEMENT and APPLICATION of MONEY, COLLECTED . . . for REPAIRING . . . ANY . . . HIGH-WAY.** Report. 1765. 1st. Folio. [ii], 467-8pp. Mod. wraps. £5.00

102. ———— **to Enquire into . . . the ASSAY OFFICES.** Report. 1773. 1st. Folio. Appendix. [ii], 61-98pp. Mod. wraps. £10.00
Includes a list of all the gold- & silversmiths whose marks were registered with the London assay office.

103. [COOKE, E.] Argumentum Anti-Normannicum: or an Argument Proving . . . that William, Duke of Normandy, Made No Absolute Conquest of England by the Sword. By John Darby, 1682. Engr. fp. [x], 164pp. Early lib. stamp of the Inner Temple (before 1730) on title & three other leaves. **William Petyt's** copy, signed on title & with two long extracts from Ms. chronicles transcribed into margins. 19th-cent. ½ cf./mbld. sides; rbbd. **Wing C.4907a. S. & M. i. III.** £80.00
Carelessly ascribed to Sir Edward Coke by Wing. The "foolish dispute" (Gibbon) whether William "conquered" England or received it by consent was a part of the question, how far the constitution of England was pre-Norman in its origin & principles. Cooke espoused the Saxonist party, of which Petyt was of course the leader. This copy was probably bequeathed by Petyt to the Inner Temple, where he once held the treasurership & where his manuscript collection was deposited.

104. COOKE, G.W. (1814-1865). The Acts for Facilitating the Inclosure of Commons in England & Wales; with a Treatise on the Law of Rights of Commons. 1855. 2nd ed., rev. Index. Supplement bound in. vi, xii, 504, [ii], 507-528pp. Contemp. cf., rbbd. **S. & M. ii. 76.** £20.00
The inclosure movement was one of the first cases in which the law was forced to set aside established rights of property in the public interest. Cooke describes the old law in detail before setting out the new.

105. COOTE, R.H. A Treatise on the Law of Mortgage. 1821[-3]. 1st. **2 vols. in 1.** Indices. viii, 372/[viii], 373-712pp. Contemp. cf., rbbd. **S. & M. ii. 78.** £20.00

106. CORNISH ELECTIONS. Four pamphlets.

1. Motion for a New Writ for . . . St. Mawes. 1817. 1st. 23pp. Disbound. [Speeches by Canning, Sir S. Romilly, etc.].
2. RASHLEIGH, J.C. Letter to the Freeholders of Cornwall. St. Austell, 1826. 1st. 40pp. Orig. blue wraps; loose. [Disguised manifesto for Tremayne, the incumbent M.P.].
3. BOASE, W.M. Hints on the Exercise of the Elective Franchise. Falmouth, 1835. 1st. 42pp. Disbound. [Warning to new voters against bribery etc.].
4. The Banner of Blue, an Oration. N.p. [Liskeard], n.d. [c.1830]. 1st. 15pp. Orig. blue wraps. [Satirical poem on Cornish pocket boroughs.]

Four items £25.00

107. CORPUS IURIS CANONICI . . . a Petro Pithoeo, et Francisco fratre, iurisconsultis, ad veteres codices manuscriptos restitutum, et notis illustratum. N.p. [Frankfurt?], 1695. **2 vols. in 1.** Folio. Ports. on title. Engr. tables of consanguinity & affinity. Index. [lxiv], 492/[xii], 488, [lxxxii], [vi], 86, [xii], 87-140pp. Sl. stnd. Contemp. sprinkled cf., sp. gilt; rbbd. £40.00
The Corpus of 1590, with the seventh book of Matthaeus & Lancelotto's Institutes of Canon Law, reprinted from a Paris edition of the previous year.

108. CORVINUS van BELDEREN, Arnold. Iurisprudentiae Romanae summarium: seu codicis Iustinianei methodica enarratio. Amsterdam (L. & D. Elzevir), 1655 [-60]. 1st. **2 pts. in 1.** 4to. Red & black title. Index. [viii], 792, [viii]/[xvi], 302, [ii]pp. Final blank. Sl. browned. Sm. rust-hole in $3G_2$. Contemp. cf., sp. gilt; sp. & corners sl. worn. £60.00
A body of law based on the Code, very rich in collateral illustration. Corvinus is especially well informed on the later Imperial administrative system.

109. COX, Sir E.C. Police and Crime in India. N.d. [c.1910]. 1st. Illus. 328, [16]pp. Orig. b'ram, gilt; sl. rbbd. & fdd. £7.50

110. COWEL, John (1554-1611). The Interpreter: or Booke containing the Signification of Words. Cambridge, by John Legate, 1607. 1st. 4to. Device on title. [viii], [576]pp. Lacks A_1 (first leaf of text) (supplied in facs.) $3L_1$ defective with loss of last line of text. Some old scoring. Contemp. cf., corners worn, upper jt. weak. **S.T.C. 5900. S. & M. i. 7.** £80.00
Cowel was a university civilian who approached the common law as an interested, learned & respectful outsider. Unfortunately he allowed himself the licence of repeating some contemptuous expressions thrown out against Littleton by Hottoman, and also insinuated into his sketch of the monarchy the Roman doctrine of imperator legibus solutus. *The farmer provided a reason, the latter an excuse, for an attack on him which ended in the suppression of his book by royal proclamation in 1610. Nonetheless, the law-lexicographers of the following century found Cowel's work essential to their purpose.*

111. ———— Institutiones Iuris Anglicani, ad methodum et seriem Institutionum Imperialium compositae. N.p. [Frankfurt?] (cura et impensis Guilielmi Fitzeri), 1630. [2nd ed.] Latin text. Index. 348, [xxii]pp. Title sl. frayed. Sl. browned. Mod. ½ cf./mbld. sides. **S. & M. i. 21.** £50.00
A summary of English law adapted to the scheme, & even to the individual titles, of Justinian. This quaint idea has some beneficial consequences; thus the necessity of saying something under the heads de Obligationibus, de Divisione Stipulationum, etc. forces Cowel to attempt a system of the law of contract, two hundred years before English lawyers generally recognized it as an independent subject.

112. CROKE, Sir George (Justice, C.P. & K.B.) (c.1560-1641). The Reports of . . . Select Cases . . . Adjudged . . . the Time that he was Judge. By R. Hodgkinsonne . . . Sold by William Leak [&] Thomas Firby. 1657. 1st. Folio. Black letter. Engr. fp. port & vignette. Cancelland title bound between privilege & errata leaves. [xxviii], 670pp. $3Q_1$ misbound before $3Q_2$. Contemp. cf., sl. rbbd; one corner worn. **Wing C.7014** (var. imp.) **S. & M. i. 298.** £40.00
English version by Sir H. Grimston (preceding the publication of the French) of the third & last series of Croke's valuable reports, covering the years 1625-1640.

113. CROMARTIE, George [Mackenzie], Earl of (1631-1714). An Historical Account of the Conspiracies by the Earls of Gowry, and Robert Logan . . . against . . . James VI. Edinburgh, 1713. 1st. **2 pts. in 1.** ½ title. Red & black title. A_8 blank. xvi, 127, [i]/80pp. Sl. browned. Contemp. cf.; re-backed. £25.00
Written by a Royalist veteran of Commonwealth days to disprove the idea (frequently used to stir up sedition in Scotland) that Gowry etc. were unjustly condemned.

114. CROMPTON, R[ichard]. L'Authorite et Iurisdiction des Courts de la Majestie de la Roygne. In aedibus Caroli Yetsweirt, 1594. 1st. Sm. 4to. French text. Black letter. [iv], 232 leaves. Many early marginal annots. (few cropped). Names on title. 18th-cent. ¼ sheep/mbld. sides, jts. worn. Bk.-pl. Thomas Hamilton, 6th Earl of Haddington (d.1735). **S.T.C. 6050. S. & M. i. 259.** £200.00
A guide to all the courts then existing, from Star Chamber & Court of Wards (which did not endure for the study of a more scientific generation) down to sheriff's, hundred, & pie-powder courts; dedicated (in the French of Paris, not of Westminster) to Sir John Puckering, Lord Chancellor. The work is laid out like an abridgment, with the names of the courts as general heads.

115. CURRAN, J. Philpot (Master of the Rolls for Ireland; 1750-1817). CURRAN, W.H.; Life. 1819. 1st. **2 vols.** Fp. port. Facs. Appendix. viii, 448/viii, 532pp. Sl. spotted. New ½ cf./mbld. sides. £30.00
Curran distinguished himself as a brilliant orator and as the patriotic defender of those exposed to the rigours of the law by the failure of the 1798 rebellion.

116. DALRYMPLE, David (afterwards Lord Hailes) (1726-1792) (ed.). Memorials and Letters relating to the History of Britain in the Reign of James the First. Glasgow, 1762. 1st. Sm. 8vo. [xx], 152pp. Contemp. cf., sl. rbbd. **Not in S. & M.** £50.00
This unassuming work, printed from MSS. in the Advocates' Library, vividly shows how the King's pedantic interference in matters of law – assisted by Bacon among others – grew into a tyrannous violation of judicial independence. Several ridiculous letters to James from his beloved Duke of Buckingham also appear.

117. DALRYMPLE, John. An Essay towards a General History of Feudal Property in Great Britain. 1757. 2nd ed., rev. 12mo. [xii], 276pp. Contemp. cf., jts. worn. **S. & M. v. 29.** £20.00
A useful survey for the cultivated layman, embracing (as matters naturally arising out of the incidents of real property) the history of jurisdictions & the evolution of parliaments. The preface calls for a reconciliation of English & Scots law as a help to commerce.

118. DAREAU, F. Traité des Injures dans l'Ordre Judiciaire . . . Jurisprudence du Petit-Criminel. Ed. – Fournel. Paris, 1785. 1st thus. **2 vols.** French text. Index. Mod. cl. £20.00
A practical treatise on French criminal law, untouched by the spirit of metaphysical theorization which possessed many European jurists of the day.

119. DARLING, Charles J. [afterwards Sir Charles]. Scintillae Juris. 1879. 3rd ed., rev. 12mo., 112pp. **Short A.L.s.** from the author to Sir Henry Hawkins (later Lord Brampton) inserted, referring to one of Hawkins's jokes which is included in the book; also inscribed on d.w. Orig. parchment, sl. fdd.; printed d.w. (repaired at spine). £15.00
A little book of humorous reflections, evidently privately printed for circulation within the Bar. Mr. Justice Hawkins, a great sportsman & story-teller, may be assumed to have contributed the "father-in-law" pun on p.25. Darling was raised to the bench & became celebrated as a wit in his turn.

121. De CORAS, Jean. Arrest Mémorable du Parlement de Tholose, contenant une Histoire Prodigieuse d'un Supposé Mary. Paris (pour Galliot du Pré), 1572. 1st. French text. Woodcut title-border. Index. [xvi], 160pp. Fore-margins sl. wormed. Later ¼ cf./mbld. sides; jts. & edges worn. £50.00
This is a petty Tichborne Case of old France. A poor soldier named Arnauld du Tilh extracted some confidential information from a sick man, Martin Guerre; trading on this & on an accidental resemblance, he visited Guerre's home & tricked the law into putting Guerre's wife (utterly against her will) & property into his hands. He was finally attacked, exposed by the real Guerre when on the point of winning his case, & hanged.

122. De FERRIÈRE, Claude-Joseph. The History of the Roman or Civil Law . . . DUCK, [A.]; Treatise of the Use and Authority of the Civil Law in England. Tr. J. B[eaver]. 1724. 1st Engl. Index. [x], iv, 170, xxxviiipp. A_8 torn without loss. **S. & M. i. 612.** – **ARGOUT [or ARGOUX], [Gabriel];** History of the Origine of the French Laws, tr. J. Beaver. 1724. 1st. Engl. Index. [xvi], 105, [vii]pp. **Two works in one vol.** Contemp. cf., rbbd. £30.00
These works were probably issued together, & constitute an attempt to encourage the study of the civil law in England – no longer with a view to its adoption, though Duck may have had some such object in mind in 1653, but in order to broaden the mind of the common lawyer.

123. La DEFFAITE des TROUPES HUGUENOTTES et POLITIQUES, en Champagne; par le Sieur de Saint-Paul. Paris (chez Didier Millot), 1589. 1st. French text. 14, [ii]pp. Final blank. Mod. ¼ cl./mbld. sides. £40.00
An early news-book recording the defence of Château Landré, near Chalons, by Vandi (an old servant of the murdered Duke of Guise) & Tourteron, & the repulsion of the Protestants under d'Inteville & de Thermes.

124. DEGGE, Sir Simon. The Parsons Counsellor, with the Law of Tithes and Tithing. By the Assigns of Richard and Edward Atkins . . . for Henry Twyford. 1681[-1677]. 3rd ed. rev. **2 vols. in 1.** Index. [xxxii], 212/[ii], 215-408, [xxvi]pp. Sl. wormed. $2F_{3-4}$ (advert. leaves) defective (lower half of each leaf torn out). Lib. stamp on title & A_2. **Wing D.854. S. & M. i. 167.** £30.00
This, as the date of pt. 2 shows, is the ed. of 1677 with a cancel title.

125. De LOLME, Jean-Louis (1745-1807). The Constitution of England; or, an Account of the English Government. 1821. New ed. Engr. fp. port. Index. [vi], xvi, 518, [xvi]pp. Sl. spotted. Old ½ roan/cl. sides; rbbd. **S. & M. i. 100.** £15.00

126. De LUGO, Joannes. Disputationum de iustitia et iure, tomus primus [–secundus]. Lyons, 1652. New ed. **2 vols. in 1.** Folio. Red & black titles. [xiv], 606, [xiv]/[xvi], 624, [xx]pp. sl. stnd. Contemp. cf., sl. rbbd.; head of sp. torn. £50.00
Although this work is conceived as a commentary on the Secunda Secundae of Aquinas, the legal connotations of the title give a true idea of its subject. It consists of discussions of the moral aspects of the rights of property, personal injuries, punishment, self-defence, and contracts. The author (a Spanish cardinal) is in general quite mediaeval in style & thought, but he offers some interesting remarks on exchanges, & seems disposed to find exceptions to the Church's general prohibition of usury.

127. De MALTE, Herman François. Les Nobles dans les Tribunaux, Traité de Droit . . . où les Questions qui conviennent aux Nobles sont . . . agitées. Liège, 1680. 1st. French text. Folio. Red & black title. Index. [xxiv], 416pp. Few

leaves sl. stnd. Contemp. mottled cf., gilt; sl. rbbd. £40.00
A compendium of all that concerns the nobility in civil jurisprudence; their rights & duties in marriage, dress & arms, laws of the chase, laws of servants, etc. of a proposed second part, treating of nobility in criminal law, the author completed only a single title which determined that a noble was not authorized to execute summary justice on his adversary.

128. De THERAMO, Jacobus [Palladinus], Archdeacon of Aversa (1349-?). Compendium p[er]breve Consolatio peccatorum nuncupatu[m]. Et apud nonnullos Belial vocitatu[m]. N.p. [Strassburg, Heinrich Knoblochtzer], 1484. Folio. Latin text. Gothic (rotunda) letter. Double column. 42 lines. Capital spaces with guide letters. 92 (of 94) leaves, lacking first & last blanks. Capitals & rubrications supplied in red, crudely heightened in blue & gold in later hand. Few margins sl. wormed. 19th-cent. ¼ mor./mbld. sides; sl. rbbd. **Goff J.70; B.M.C. i. 89.** £500.00
This work is an allegory, a celebration of the Aquinate philosophy with its union of divinity & Aristotelian logic, and a manual of practice for advocates. The devils, through their proctor Belial, bring an actio spolii *against Jesus for violating the confines of hell. God, not wishing to try a cause in which his son is party, relegates the jurisdiction to Solomon, with Augustus, Isaiah, Aristotle, & Jeremiah as assessors. Moses (appearing for Jesus) is induced to waive his right of objection to Belial as one excommunicated; the cause is tried with all the forms of civil law, & judgment given against the demons.*

129. De TOCQUEVILLE, Alexis. Democracy in America. Tr. Henry Reeve, introd. J.C. Spencer. N.Y., 1841. 4th Engl. (following 8th French) ed., rev. Fold'g map. Index. xvi, 494/xx, 386pp. Some spotting. Orig. cl.; vol. I re-backed with part of orig. spine; fdd. £20.00
In general De Tocqueville sees the Americans as they wish to see themselves, a perfect union of freedom & government; but he sounds a wise & solemn warning, that the sheer number & influence of the people at large, driving their representatives beyond what is just or holding them back from it, poses a serious threat for the future.

130. DIAMOND, A.S. Primitive Law. 1935. 1st. Index. x, 452pp. **Inscribed** by the author. Orig. cl., sl. mkd. & fdd. **S. & M. ii. 99.** £6.00
Considers the ground over which Sir Henry Maine had travelled in the light of recently-found historical & anthropological evidence.

131. DIGGES, Sir Dudley (1583-1655) (ed.). The Compleat Ambassador; or two Treaties of the Intended Marriage of Qu. Elizabeth ... in ... Letters of ... Sir Francis Walsingham ... Lord Burleigh ... and others. By Tho. Newcomb, for Gabriel Bedell and Thomas Collins, 1655. 1st. Folio. Engr. title (bound as fp). Red & black printed title. Index. [vi], 442, [xiv]pp. Lacks final blank. Leaf D, mis-signed C_1; I_1 signed I_2. New ¼ cf./mbld. sides. **Wing D.1453.** £150.00
A picture, in original documents, of Elizabeth's juggling with her suitors. The first was the future Henri III of France (a connection which might have drawn England into the violent scenes of 1572), & the other the Spanish Duke of Alençon, whom the Queen called her Frog, & kept on a chain for some years.

132. DODD [or DOD], Charles R. [& others] (ed.). The Parliamentary Companion. 1847. 15th year. 16mo. 260pp. Orig. limp cl., sp. sl. frayed. £8.00

133. ———— 1867. 35th year. 16mo. 320pp. Orig. limp cl., sp. sl. frayed. £8.00

134. ————1874. 42nd year. 16mo. 336pp. Sl. spotted. Orig. limp cl., sp. worn. £6.00

135. ———— 1880 (2nd parliament). 48th year. 16mo. 336pp. Orig. limp cl., sl. worn. £6.00

136. DOMAT, Jean (1625-1696). Les Loix Civiles dans leur Ordre Naturel, Suivies du Droit Public. The Hague, 1703. New ed., rev. Folio. **2 vols. in 1.** Red & black titles. Engr. table of consanguinity. Index. [x], xxxvi, 548/[xx], 272, [xxxvi]pp. Contemp. blind-stamped vellum, sl. stnd. £40.00
Domat began public life as the friend & literary executor of Pascal. His great work, founded on a scheme which he had made for the use of his own children, was published between 1689 & 1697; this edition includes his addresses to the Clermont assizes, over which he presided for many years.

137. DRING, Thomas. A Catalogue of the Lords, Knights, and Gentlemen, that have Compounded for their Estates. Chester, 1733. [2nd ed., rev.] [xvi], 130pp. Last five leaves in photostatic facs. Few leaves wormed. Mod. ¼ cl./mbld. sides. **Not in S. & M.** £10.00
A record (slightly enlarged from the London edition of 1655) of Royalists who were obliged to pay large sums in order to redeem their estates from confiscation under the Protectorate.

138. DUANE, William J. Sampson against the Philistines, or the Reformation of Lawsuits ... Agreeably to the Principles of the Ancient Trial by Jury. Philadelphia, Pa., 1805. 2nd ed. Appendix. 96pp. Browned. Orig. wraps, uncut & unopened; sl. worn. £15.00
Abolish the rapacious breed of lawyers (says the author), and the hierarchy of courts which the hypocrite Washington imported from tyrannous old England; and let all cases be decided by a tribunal of honest citizens as in the days of good King Alfred. Britain never beheld such a flight of visionary Saxonism in jurisprudence as this from the new world.

139. DUARENUS, Franciscus (1509-1559). Omnia quae quidem hactenus edita fuerunt opera ... plurimis in Digesta ... & Codicem commentariis ... locupletata. Ed. Nicolas Cisner. Lyons (apud Guliel. Rouillium), 1584. (2nd complete ed.) Folio. **2 vols. in 1.** Index. Red & black title with device. [xx], 1127, [i]/[iv], 1129-1632, [xxvii]pp. Sl. wormed at end. 18th-cent. cf., rubbed. £90.00
After the Italian Alciat had pointed the way, Duarenus became the first native Frenchman to raise the civil law from its confined & barren state to a liberal study in which philosophy, poetry & history were summoned in aid. His commentaries on the Pandects were his most important work; among the lesser treatises is one which takes up the cause (neglected between the times of Gerson & of Jansen) of French ecclesiastical liberty. Cisner's edition of 1579 included much unpublished material, & this re-issue adds some more in an appendix.

140. DUGDALE, [Sir] William (1605-1686). Origines Juridiciales, or Historical Memorials of the English Laws. By F. & T. Warren, 1666. 1st. Folio. Red & black titles. Many plates of arms. First imprimatur leaf. [viii], 332, [iv], 116, [ii]pp. L_2 torn without loss. $2B_1$ (plate) repaired affecting border. One shield cut from plate at $3A_2$. Mod. ½ cf./mbld. sides. **S. & M. i. 20. Wing D.2488. £60.00**
Dugdale is our best & often our only authority for the manners & customs of the old lawyers, and most especially of the Inns. The edition is reported to have been seriously damaged in the Fire of London, and this no doubt explains why many copies, including this, omit the five portraits. The work also includes a legal bibliography.

141. ———— Another copy. Fine-paper edition, issued (apparently) without the title-page & imprimatur leaf. Five fine engr. ports. (often omitted). [iv], 332, [iv], 116, [ii]pp. Fly-title to Chronica Series misbound before index. Contemp. cf., rbbd., jts. worn. £80.00
Three of the portraits are the work of Hollar.

142. DUKER, Carl Andreas, or DUCKER (ed.). Opuscula varia de Latinitate jurisconsultorum veterum. Leyden, 1711. 1st thus. Index. Final errata leaf. [xxviii], 490, [xxxii]pp. Contemp. vellum, blind-stamped. Bk-pl. Sir John Martin-Harvey (actor). £25.00
The argument over the merits of the ancient lawyers' Latin style began in France in the sixteenth century, & was a part of the larger question, how far Justinian's compilers had preserved the sense & spirit of the older texts. Duker, following a hint of Bynkershoek's, collected the writings of Valla, Hottoman, Alciat, & others on the subject. The controversy was sufficiently alive to promote a reprint in Leipzig as late as 1783.

143. Du MAY, Lous, Sieur de Sallettes. The Estate of the Empire: or, an Abridgement of the Laws and Government of Germany. [Tr. anon.] By J. Macock for Richard Royston, 1676. 1st Engl. Index. [xiv], 333, [xix]pp. Lacks fp. port. Lib. perforation on title. Mod. ½ cf./mbld. sides. **Wing D.2522.** £20.00
Du May is a German Fortescue, his work being a dialogue between a prince and his teacher. He maintains the dignity & authority of the emperor (with the electors as constitutional checks) against those who see Germany as a mere confederation.

144. ———— Discours Historiques et Politiques sur les Causes de la Guerre de Hongrie, et ... de la Paix entre Léopold I ... et Mahomet IV. Lyons, 1665. 1st. French text. 12mo. a_4 blank. [viii], 184pp. Book-plate with cardinal's arms & initials U.J.C.G., printed in three colours. Contemp. vellum, sp. defective. £20.00
Traces the internal troubles of Hungary & their effect on foreign interests from the fourteenth century.

145. DUNLOP, Alexander. Letter to the Freeholders of the County of Dumbarton, on Parliamentary Reform. Edinburgh, 1830. 1st trade. [iv], 46pp. Mod. mbld. wraps; fine. £7.50
Advocates the extension of voting rights among proprietors of their own land. Previously printed as an election manifesto.

146. Du PONCEAU, Peter S. A Dissertation on the Nature and Extent of the Jurisdiction of the Courts of the United States. Philadelphia, 1824. 1st. Appendix. Errata leaf. xxxviii, 254, [i]pp. Orig. bds., uncut; sp. torn; fine modern folding cloth case & mor.-backed slip-case. £60.00
An important examination, by the Provost of the Philadelphia Law Academy, of a serious problem in U.S. jurisprudence: how the scope & privilege of each court, founded on & enlarged by the vague term "common law", was to be reconciled with the dictates of the Constitution. The Vice-Provost, Thos. Sargeant, contributes a section on the American judicial system before 1789.

147. EXTRACTS from the TREATIES between Great-Britain and other ... States, of such Articles as relate to the Duty and Conduct of the Commanders of ... Ships of War. 1792 [-1801]. 2 pts. in 1. 4to. Index. lx, 380/[ii], 383-406pp. Contemp. cf., sl. rbbd. **Not in S. & M.** £40.00
A revision of Edmunds's collection (1741; S. & M. i. 603). The second part is a supplement embracing treaties with Russia, Sweden & Denmark.

148. FABER, Johannes. Syntagma triplex iuris civilis et criminalis, canonici, et feudalis. Geneva, 1679. Folio. Indices. [xliv], 336, [xxiv], 24, [viii], 16, [iv], 58, [xiv], 8, 8, 28, 24, [viii]pp. Contemp. vellum. £50.00
A reduction of the law to catechistic form, embracing first the general civil, canon & feudal law, & afterwards the particular subject of substitutions (contingent future interests) & some points of court procedure.

149. FABER (le Fèvre), Petrus. Ad tit. de diversis regulis iuris antiqui ... commentarius: ex repetita eiusdem auctoris praelectione ... auctus. Paris, apud Dionysium Duvallium, 1585. Folio. Device on title. Index. Inscription on title, "In labore solatium. – Ant. Schultingii". [xii], 780, [xix]pp. Sl. stnd. Contemp. limp vellum; lacks ties. **B.M.C. (French) p.160.** £90.00
Edition revised by the author, a jurist of Toulouse, who dedicated it to Cujas. A note by the publishers illustrates printing practice of the time; Faber's MS had to be transcribed into a fair copy for the printers, & the copyist abandoned his work in time of plague, delaying the edition for two years. Anton Schulting (1659-1734) (q.v.) is best known as the editor of the ante-Justinianean laws.

150. FACHINEUS, Andreas. Controversiarum iuris libri decem ... nunc primum in Italia excusi ... adiecto decimo libro nunquam antehac edito. Venice, apud Societatem Venetam, 1602. Folio. Bird's-eye view of Venice on title-page. Index. [lx]pp., 1372 columns. Lacks final blank. Sm. hole in title. Last leaf sl. soiled. Contemp. sheep, rubbed; paste-downs detached. £70.00
The author, a native of Forli, shows himself a jurist of the old type, apparently ignorant of all that lies outside the strict limits of his subject. He falls heavily on Hottoman as a "heretic" for doubting the authenticity of a letter of Justinian inserted in the Code (de summa Trinitate) asserting the pre-eminence of the popes; yet elsewhere he speaks respectfully of the French school & condescends to cite Cujas & Budé.

151. FENWICK, Sir John. The Proceedings ... upon a Bill of Attainder for High Treason. Printed ... 1698. 1st. Index. [ii], 348, [ix]pp. Contemp. cf., jts. sl. worn. **Wing P.3545.** £30.00
Fenwick was executed for plotting on behalf of the former King James II. His trial raised the question whether the parliamentary bill of attainder was subject to the rules applicable to indictments, requiring precise specification of the offence.

152. FEUERBACH [Paul Johann] Anselm, Ritter von (1775-1833). Aktenmässige Darstellung merkwürdiger Verbrechen. Giessen, 1828 [-9]. 1st. **2 vols.** German text. xviii, 604, [ii]/vi, 698pp. Sl. spotted. Contemp. ¼ sheep/cl. sides; rbbd. £85.00
Feuerbach was a pioneer of criminal psychology. There is a romantic – almost Dickensian – floridity in his studies of murderers & frauds from birth to execution; but a serious purpose emerges in his narratives & in his exposure of the subsequent legal proceedings. The Bavarian state penal code embodies his views on criminal justice.

153. ———— Narratives of Remarkable Criminal Trials, tr. & ed. Lady Duff Gordon. 1846. 1st Engl. xii, 368pp. Orig. cl., sl. mkd. & shaken. £20.00
Fourteen cases selected from the German original (see previous item).

154. FIENNES, Nathanael [Lord] (1608-1669). Speech ... before ... Parliament ... 20th of January, 1657. By Henry Hills and John Field, 1657. 1st. Sm. 4to. [ii], 26pp. **Wing F.881** – Speech ... concerning Bishops and ... London Petition. Printed ... 1641. 1st. Sm. 4to. [ii], 28pp. Lacks final blank. **Wing F.880.** Two works in one vol. Blanks bound in at end. Mod. ¼ cf./mbld. sides. £30.00
A pompously Biblical declamation for the opening of Parliament & an attack on episcopal suffrage by the second son of the first Viscount Saye & Sele, an active Cromwellian like his father.

155. FINCH, [Sir] Henry (?-1625). Nomotechnia (graecè) cestascavoir, un Description del Common Leys Dangleterre solonque les Rules del Art. For the Societie of Stationers, 1613. 1st. French text. Folio. [v], 22, [ix], 23-150 leaves. Lacks first blank. Twelve extra leaves (d-e[4]) between D_3 & D_4. One line deleted in ink on N_8 verso, & another on Q_4 verso. Contemp. cf., re-backed & corners repaired. **S.T.C. 10870. S. & M. i. 238.** £120.00
If any man could be said to have written the true Institutes of English Law before Blackstone, his name was not Coke, but Finch. As printed here the work is principally a survey of crown law & of courts with some remarks on writs; each chapter has an appendix showing how the King's prerogative bears on the subject – a compliment no doubt to King James, to whom the work is dedicated. Later in the same year, Finch produced a much-adapted English version, "Law or a Discourse thereof", which was widely read & highly valued.

156. [FIOCCO, Domenico]. L. Fenestellae de magistratibus sacerdotiisque libellus ... Pomponii Laeti itidem de magistratibus & ... legibus. Lyons (L. Cloquemin), 1581. 16mo. Device on title. Index. 162, [x]pp. Sl. stnd. Few margins sl. frayed. Mod. ¼ cf./mbld. sides. £50.00
The ancient work of Fenestella on the Roman magistracies is mentioned by Lactantius & others, but what is printed here is a fifteenth century forgery; a similar work by Pomponio Leti, the notorious devil-worshipper, is subjoined.

157. FITZGERALD, Percy. Chronicles of the Bow Street Police-Office. 1888. 1st. **2 vols.** Illus. viii, 332, 40/[vi], 380pp. Orig. dec'd cl.; jts. sl. rubbed. SOLD
Anecdotes of the court in Sir John Fielding's time & afterwards, & of London crime in general.

158. FITZGIBBONS, John. The Reports of ... Cases ... in ... King's Bench ... with some special Cases in ... Chancery, Common Pleas and Exchequer. 1732. Folio. Mostly black letter. Index. [iv], 321, [xv]pp. Mod. ¼ cf./mbld. sides. **S. & M. i. 300.** £20.00

159. [FOGGI, Francesco]. Saggio sopra l'Impunità legitima o l'Asilo. Leghorn, 1774. 1st. 4to. 212pp. Contemp. bds., sl. worn. £20.00
By a strange fatality, the new Anglo-French liberalism (with Locke, Hume & Voltaire frequently quoted) is employed to defend the mediaeval system of asyla & places of immunity. The ascription is from a note on the title.

160. FORTESCUE, Sir John (fl. 1430-1471). De laudibus legum Angliae ... The two Sums of Sir Ralph de HENGHAM ... with Notes. For Abel Roper, 1660. Latin & Engl. text. [viii], 132, [iii] leaves; 52, [xii], 140pp. Some old annots. Contemp. cf., jts. & corners worn. **Wing F.1612. S. & M. i. 22.** £65.00

161. ———— Anr. ed. By John Streeter [etc.], 1672. Collation as above. Contemp. sheep, rbbd. **Wing F.1613.** £60.00
Fortescue's work, a manual of English government written for the future Edward IV, presents a surprisingly advanced theory of constitutional monarchy. The two Summae of Hengham are accounts of procedure in the primitive King's Court (c.1300), throwing interesting light on the relation between the lord's & the sheriff's (county) jurisdiction.

162. ———— De laudibus legum Angliae ... Translated into English ... Notes of Mr. Selden ... Summs of Sir Ralph de Hengham. 1737. 1st thus. Folio. Latin & Engl. text. Engr. fp. Index. [iv], lxiv, 130, [xiv], [ii], ii, 36, [ii], iv, 42, [ii]pp. Contemp. cf., rbbd., jts. worn. £50.00
Translated by Francis Gregor; to Selden's notes he has added a few selected from the Fortescutus Illustratus *of Waterhouse, & some of his own.*

163. FULBECK, William (1560-?). A Parallele or Conference of the Civil Law, the Canon Law, and the Common Law of this Realme of England. For the Company of Stationers, 1618. 2nd ed. 4to. [xii], 104, [8] leaves. **S.T.C. 11416. S. & M. i. 179** – The Second Part of the Parallele. By Thomas Wight, 1602. 1st. 4to. [viii], 74, [viii] leaves. **S.T.C. 11415a. S. & M. i. 179.** – The Pandectes of the Law of Nations. By Thomas Wight, 1602. 1st. 4to. [iv], 90 leaves. **S.T.C. 11414. S. & M. i. 595.** Three works in one vol. Contemp. cf., rbbd., head of sp. & corners worn. Bk-pl. Sir Lucius O'Brien & another. £200.00
Fulbeck was purely a common lawyer, & approached the civil law from the opposite side to Cowel (q.v.). His design in the Parallel (a series of 22 dialogues) was to show that the best elements of each type of law all pointed the same way, common law having the pre-eminence; the Pandects (the first English statement of international law) carry this tendentious idea much farther, producing a diversity of historical examples from all known nations in support of monarchic rule, privileged nobility & religious intolerance, & also (more pleasingly) against trade restriction & ideological warfare.

164. FULLER, H. Julian. "Old Q" and the Apothecary; being the Record of a Famous Trial. 1913. 1st. Privately printed. 4to. Illus. 47pp. **Inscribed** by the author. Contemp. ½ mor./cl. sides; sl. rbbd. SOLD

A test case (Fuller v. Executors of the Duke of Queensberry) which gave an apothecary the right to recover payment for attendance; previously he could charge only for medicines. The new order was recognized by statute (55 Geo. III, cap. 194) in 1815.

165. FULLER, Nicholas. The Argument ... in the Case of Thomas Lad, and Richard Maunsell. N.p. [Amsterdam?], 1607. 1st. Sm. 4to. [iv], 32pp. 19th-cent. ½ mor./mbld. sides. S.T.C. 11460. S. & M. i. 186. **£75.00**
Argues that in claiming the power to fine & imprison for criminal offences the Church Commissioners had exceeded their statutory authority, & that the common-law rule "nobody may be condemned out of his own mouth" rendered illegal their practice of putting their "prisoners" upon oath & interrogating them. Lad & Maunsell were so treated on charges arising from a dissenting meeting. We learn from Coke (12 Rep. 19, 26, 44) that the vengeful divines managed to fix a charge of heresy on Fuller for his writings, but that he carried all his points notwithstanding. So discredited, the powers of the Commission died an unlamented death after the Restoration.

166. G[ARDINER], R. Instructor Clericalis. The First [-Fourth] Part. 1707 [1705, 1706]. 4th [3rd, 2nd, 1st] ed. **4 vols.** Indices. Sm. ink-stain on M, (vol. 1) aff. two letters. Contemp. cf., **sps. sl. rbbd. S. & M. i. 269. £50.00**
This series of instruction-books for clerks consisted largely of works previously published under separate titles. The volumes present cover (1) abbreviations & forms for writs, (2) forms for declarations, (3 & 4) forms for pleadings, especially in case & covenant. Two more volumes (further pleadings, & demurrers) were added in 1713-14.

167. GARROWAY, [Sir Henry] (1575-1646). A Speech ... at a Common-Hall ... upon a Speech ... by Mr. Pym. Printed ... 1642. 4to. [ii], 14pp. Title & last leaf repaired. Mod. wraps. Wing G.280. **£20.00**
An alderman who boldly stood up for his King against the strong Parliamentary party on the Common Council accuses the Commons of stirring up riots to disturb the King when he visited the City.

168. GASPARRO, Francesco Maria. Institutiones juris civilis. Venice, 1755. 1st. 4to. ½ title. Index. [x], 252pp. Q_{1-4} (pp. 245-8) misbound in reverse order after A_5 = Institutiones juris canonici. Venice, 1755. 1st. 4to. ½ title. Index. [xiv], 360pp. **2 works in 1 vol.** Few margins sl. wormed. Contemp. limp vellum, shaken. **£25.00**

Elementary works for the Rome University, based on the Institutes & Gratian respectively.

169. GASTIER, René. Le Nouveau Praticien Français. Paris, 1667. 3rd ed., rev. **2 pts. in 1.** French text. 4to. Engr. fp. port. Red & black title. [xlv], 500, 488pp. Lib. stamp on verso of fp. & e-p. Contemp. sprinkled cf., sp. gilt; sl. rbbd. **£60.00**
The first part almost amounts to the institutes of French law; the second explains the revenue system of France at that desperate time when Colbert vainly attempted to restore the economic health of the nation.

170. "GIFFORD, John" (A. Whellier). English Lawyer; or, Every Man his Own Lawyer. 1830. 17th ed. Engr. fp. port. (Lord Eldon.) Index. Supplement bound in. 688/51, 12-13, 12-204pp. (pagination irreg. owing to cancels.) Contemp. ½ cf./cl. sides; sl. rbbd. S. & M. ii. 377. **£20.00**
The most durable of all the popular instructors. The supplement contains chapters on insurance, customs & excise, & taxes.

171. GILMOUR of Craigmiller, Sir John, and Sir David FALCONER of Newton. A Collection of Decisions of the Lords of Council and Session ... from July 1661 ... to January 1686. Edinburgh, 1701. 1st. **3 vols. in 1.** 4to. General & individual titles. Indices. 10, [ii], 136, [xviii]/[ii], 80, [xvi]/[ii], 32, 15, [i]pp. Contemp. mottled cf., sp. gilt; rbbd. S. & M. v. 46. **£40.00**
Includes an appendix of Acts of Sederunt of the Lords of Session 1681-1696.

172. GLADSTONE, William Ewart. Speeches on Parliamentary Reform. 1866. 1st. Appendix of letters. iv, 336, 32pp. Orig. cl., sl. fdd. **£10.00**
Speeches on the early stages of the bill which was to become the second Reform Act in the following year.

173. [GLASSE, S.]. The Magistrate's Assistant; or, a Summary of those Laws which Immediately Respect the Conduct of a Justice of the Peace. Gloucester, 1788. 2nd ed. Appendix of forms. Fold'g table (sl. torn). xvi, 544, lxviii, xxivpp. Sl. stnd. Contemp. cf., sl. rbbd. **S. & M. i. 228. £25.00**
A compilation intended to be more convenient for quick reference than the larger work of Burn.

174. GNEIST, Rudolf (ed.). Institutionum et regularum iuris Romani syntagma. Leipzig, 1880. 2nd ed., rev. xxviii, 390, [ii]pp. Many pencil annots. (suggested translations) by J. F. Hobson of New College, Durham. Title sl. stnd. Contemp. ½ roan/cl. sides, rbbd. **£20.00**

Parallel texts of Gaius & Justinian, together with critical texts of the 12 Tables, Ulpian & Paulus.

175. GODOLPHIN, John. Synêgoros thalassios [Gr.] A View of the Admiral Jurisdiction ... Laws, Customes, Rights, and Privileges of the High Admiralty ... Extract of the Ancient Laws of Oleron. By W. Godbid for Edmund Paxton ... and John Shirley, 1661. 1st. Index. [iii], 208, [xvi]pp. Mod. ½ mor./cl. sides. S. & M. i. 351. **£70.00**
The great improvement in British naval power under Cromwell created a demand for works dealing with the law of the subject. Godolphin's is the first treatise on this question apart from Rowghton's pamphlet of about 1540.

176. GOMEZ, Antonio. Commentariorum, variarumque resolutionum iuris ... tomi tres. Ed. Manuel Soarez de Ribeira. Frankfurt, 1597 (colophon 1607). Folio. Red & black title in border incorporating large woodcut (Judgment of Solomon). Index. [viii], 564, [xvi]pp. Two blanks. – **DIEZ de MENA, Flores:** Recentiorum practicarum quaestionum iuris canonici ... libri tres. Frankfurt, 1605. Red & black title with device. Index. [xii], 308, [xvi]pp. Final blank. **Two works in one vol.** Sl. browned & stnd. **Inscribed** by David Dalrymple of Hailes (?grandfather of Lord Hailes), 1712. Contemp. vellum, corners worn. **£80.00**
The first work deals with wills, contracts & criminal law, the second with canon law (which of course includes all testamentary questions, & extends far into the region of contractual obligations); both are examples of the old style of Spanish jurisprudence, which gives everything to authority & nothing to invention.

177. GREENLEAF, Simon. A Collection of Cases Overruled, Doubted, or Limited in their Application, taken from American and English Reports. Portland, Maine, 1821. 1st. Index. Fourfold interleaving throughout. 128pp. Few MS. additions. Contemp. cf., worn. **£15.00**
Includes the Rules of the U.S. Supreme Court & Circuit Court.

178. GREENWOOD, William. Bouleutêrion [Graecè] or, a Practical Demonstration of County-Judicatures. Wherein is Amply Explained the Judicial and Ministerial Authority of Sheriffs and Coroners. For John Place, 1685. 6th ed., rev. Index. [xvi], 418, [xxii], 22pp. Sl. stnd. Contemp. cf., re-backed; corners rbbd. S. & M. i. 390. **Wing G.1874 (Lincoln's Inn & Yale Law Lib. only). £50.00**
Includes forms of writs & pleadings appropriate to the county courts, with an appendix of documents in the case Carew Pearse v. Cox & others, *a leading case for annulling county-court decisions on matters arising outside their territory.*

179. GRIFFIN-STONESTREET, G.S. Letters to a Man of Rank upon the Impolitic Tendency of a Motion by Col. Williams, M.P., to Repeal the Royal Marriage Act. 1834. 1st. Errata leaf. [ii], 72pp. Disbound. **£10.00**
The Act prohibited any descendant of George II. from marrying under 25 or without consent of Parliament; but the real issue between Williams & the author was whether parental interference in marriage was in general worthy of legislative support.

180. GROTIUS, Guilielmus (Willem de Groot). Vitae jurisconsultorum quorum in Pandectis exstant nomina. Leyden, 1690. 1st. 4to. Engr. port. Index. [x], 200, [xiii]pp. Final errata leaf. Contemp. vellum. **£40.00**
A bold attempt to trace the lives of the jurisconsults from "Papirius" (as compiler of the Leges Regiae) to Hermogenian, including not only the forty-odd who are quoted in the Pandects, but many who are only named. The author was brother to Hugo Grotius, & left the book to be issued posthumously by his son.

181. GROTIUS, Hugo (Huig de Groot) (1583-1645). De iure belli ac pacis libri tres ... cum annotatis auctoris, ex postrema eius ... cura. Accesserunt annotata ... & libellus ... de aequitate ... nec non Ioann. Frid. Gronovii V.C. notae. Hague, 1680. 1st collected. Engr. port. & title. Red & black printed title. Index. [viii], xx, 680, [xiv], 32, [10], 216, [cviii]pp. Contemp. cf., re-backed; sides worn. **£40.00**
Includes the Mare Liberum (the occasion of Grotius's dispute with Selden), a small posthumous treatise on equity, dispensation & waiver of right, & some lesser items.

182. ———— Anr. ed. Amsterdam, 1689. Engr. fp. port. & title. Index. [x], xxxiv, 904, [8], [viii], 32, [10], [xcvi]pp. Contemp. vellum, gilt, arms on sides of Charles Spencer, 3rd Earl of Sunderland (d.1722). Lacks ties. Re-backed. **£50.00**
Similar contents to the previous item. Lord Sunderland, great-uncle of the Duke of Marlborough (& thus an ancestor of Winston Churchill), was one of the most celebrated book-collectors of his time.

183. ———— De jure belli ac pacis libri tres, cum ... J.F. Gronovii notis, & J. Barbeyracii animadversiones; commentariis insuper ... Henr. L.B. de Coceii ... **observationibus Samuelis L.B. de Cocceii ... Grotii dissertatio de mari libero, ac libellus ... de aequitate.** Lausanne, 1751. 1st collected. **5 vols.** Latin text. 4to. Engr. fp. ports. Indices. Some sl. browning. Contemp. cf., sl. rbbd. **£90.00**
A fine variorum edition assembled by C.G.F. Dumas & W.P. Kellinger. Besides the well-known annotations of Gronovius & Barbeyrac there are present those of the two Cocceii, Polish jurists who held high office at the Prussian court.

184. ———— **Institutiones iuris naturalis et gentium, ex ... Grotii de iure belli ac pacis libris excerptae.** Cambridge, 1703. 2nd ed. 12mo. First errata leaf. [vi], 152pp. Contemp. sprinked cf., sl. rbbd. **£20.00**
An abridgment by question & answer of Grotius's great work.

185. GUTHRY, Henry, Bp. of Dunkeld (?-1676). Memoirs ... wherein the Conspiracies and Rebellion against King Charles I. are ... Narrated. Ed. Geo. Crawfurd. Glasgow, 1748. 12mo. Index. [viii], xii, [iv], 304, [xxxiv]pp. Contemp. cf., sp. gilt; sl. rbbd. **£20.00**
Guthry resisted English interference in the Scots liturgy, but when the revolution came to a head he held by the lawful government, even to the loss of his benefice. He covers the years 1573 to 1649.

186. HALE, Sir Matthew (1609-1676). The Analysis of the Law; being a Scheme, or Abstract, of the Several Titles and Partitions of the Law. 1739. 3rd ed. Engr. fp. table. Index. [xiv], 148, [xxvi]pp. Mod. wraps. **This ed. not in S. & M. £30.00**
Blackstone confesses his indebtedness to this early reconciliation of law & logic, which is sometimes found issued with Hale's History of the Common Law.

187. HAMILTON, A.H.A. Quarter Sessions from Queen Elizabeth to Queen Anne; Illustrations ... Drawn from Original Records (Chiefly of ... Devon). 1878. 1st in book form. Index. xii, 364, 30pp. Orig. cl. sl. rbbd. S. & M. i. 393. **£8.00**

188. HAMILTON, Duke of, & others, v. STEWART. Proof in the Conjoined Processes ... Pursuers Proof ... Condescendence of Facts. N.p. [Edinburgh], 1766. 1st. 4to. French & Engl. text. Index. Pagination irregular through cancellation. Appendix. Many corners creased. Orig. wraps, frayed, sp. defective; sewing weak. **£50.00**
Evidence collected in France & England to prove that Archibald Stewart, supposed heir to the Duke of Douglas, was not the son of Sir John & Lady Douglas but had been bought by them in France after the real son had been stillborn. Diderot is a witness, & swears that French letters corroborative of Stewart's case betray themselves by their style as English forgeries. The Lords of Session decided against Stewart, but in 1769 this judgment was reversed in the English House of Lords.

189. HANCOCK, B.F. The Law, Without the Advice of an Attorney ... containing the Laws of Pennsylvania relative to Bonds ... Deeds, Mortgages ... Leases ... Jurors ... Interest, Landlord and Tenant ... Stage Drivers [etc.] Norristown, Pa., 1831. 1st. Index. 136pp. Spotted. Contemp. ¼ roan/mbld. sides; worn. **£20.00**
This is a less disreputable work than the title implies, being in fact a miniature abridgment centred on the statutes of the state.

190. HARRISON, Joseph. The Accomplish'd Practiser in the High Court of Chancery. 1767. 5th ed. **Vol. 2 (of 2) only.** Index. [ii], 426, [xx]pp. Mod. cl. **S. & M. i. 339. £8.00**
Includes most of the practical information, vol. 1 being devoted to historical matters & to the offices of the court.

191. HATSELL, John (1743-1820). Precedents of Proceedings in the House of Commons, with Observations. Dublin, 1786. **3 vols.** Indices. [xiv], 240, [xvi]/[x], 306, [l]/[xvi], 361, [xxx]pp. Contemp. tree cf., sps. gilt; lacks some labels; vol. 2 sl. stnd. S. & M. i. 176. **£50.00**
Cases & records collected from the Commons Journals & other MSS. Some of the observations are ascribed by Hatsell to Arthur Onslow, whose long speakership gave the office the dignity & probity which has ever since attached to it.

192. HAWKINS, Sir Henry (Baron Brampton). Reminiscences, ed. Richard Harris. 1904. 1st. **2 vols.** Fp. ports. & other illus. x, 331/viii, 310, 16pp. Orig. dec'd cl., uncut; sl. mkd. **£10.00**

193. HEATH, Sir Robert. Maxims and Rules of Pleading; in Actions Real, Personal and Mixt. [Ed. W. Brown.] For Abel Roper, 1694. 1st. Index. [vi], 332, [xxvi]pp. Lib. perforations on title & E, . Sl. browned. Mod. ½ cf./mbld. sides. **S. & M. i. 271. Wing H.1340. £50.00**
Earlier works, including even that of Euer (q.v.), tended to assume that the reader knew the theory of pleading & only required correction in detail; Heath makes some attempt to explain "why" as well as "how".

194. HEINECCIUS, Johann Gottlieb (1681-1741). Elementa iuris civilis secundum ordinem Institutionum, Amsterdam, 1728. Red & black title. xx, 418pp. Many old annots. Title repaired at inner margin. Contemp. vellum. **£20.00**
Revised by the author to overshadow a German piracy.

195. ———— Anr. (6th) ed. Leyden, 1751. Red & black title. Indices. xvi, 418, [xxviii]pp. Contemp. cf., sl. rbbd. **£15.00**

196. ———— **Historia iuris ciuilis Romani ac Germanici.** Leyden, 1740. 6th ed. Red & black title. Index. Folding tables. [xl], 414, 112, [lvi]pp. Contemp. cf., jts. worn; spine frayed. **£15.00**
Edition revised by the author, with a new preface.

197. ———— **Praelectiones academicae in Hugonis GROTII de Iure Belli et Pacis libros III.** Geneva, 1748. 3rd ed., rev. 4to. iv, 616pp. Sl. browned. Contemp. ½ vellum/mbld. sides. **£25.00**

198. HENDEN, E., W. NOY, R. MASON, & H. FLEETWOOD. The Perfect Conveyancer: or, Severall Select and Choice Presidents ... not formerly ... Printed. By F.L. for Matthew Walbancke ... Sold by Abel Roper, 1655. 2nd ed. 4to. Index. [xii], 548pp. Margins of M_1 & $2L_1$ defective, affecting side-notes. Few leaves soiled. Some weakening of paper through damp; few leaves frayed at beginning & end, slightly affecting text of $3Z_4$ & $4A_1$. Last leaf repaired. Mod. ½ cf./mbld. sides. **Wing P.1479; S. & M. i. 485. £60.00**

199. HERBERT, William. Antiquities of the Inns of Court and Chancery ... with a concise History of English Law. 1804. 1st. Index. 24 copper-engr. plates. xii, 378, [x]pp. Sl. spotted. Contemp. grained cf., re-backed. **Not in S. & M. £50.00**

200. HERBERT, William, M.P. A Letter to the Chairman of the Committee of the House of Commons, on the Game Laws. 1823. 1st. 16pp. Sl. browned. Sewn as issued. **Kress C.1073. £5.00**
Proposes a registry of persons licensed to sell game; this would put the poacher out of business, & so prevent both his activities & the necessity of punishing him.

201. HIGHMORE, Anthony. A Succinct View of the History of Mortmain; the Statutes relative to Charitable Uses; and ... the Last Mortmain Act. 1787. 1st. Index. [vi], viii, 186, [vi]pp. Contemp. cf., lacks spine. **S. & M. i. 497. £15.00**

202. HILL, Constance. Good Company in Old Westminster and the Temple. 1925. 1st. Illus. Index. [x], 206, [ii]pp. Orig. cl., sl. mkd. **£8.00**
Based on the recollections (1808-1834) of Anne Rickman, daughter of the Speaker's secretary; Lamb, Wordsworth, Queen Caroline, the burning of Parliament in 1834, etc.

203. HINDE, Robert. The Modern Practice of the High Court of Chancery. Dublin, 1786. Index. [iv], 622, [xviii]pp. Lib. perforation on title. Mod. cl. S. & M. i. 339. **£20.00**

204. HOBBES, Thomas. Tracts ... containing I. Behemoth, the History of the Causes of the Civil Wars ... II. An Answer to Arch-bishop Bramhall ... III. An Historical Narration of Heresie ... IV. Philosophical Problems. For W. Crooke, 1682. [2nd ed.] **3 pts. in 1.** General & individual titles. [ii], [iv], 339, [v]/[iv], 160/[viii], 84, [ii]pp. Few margins frayed. First two leaves repaired. Sl. wormed. Mod. ¼ cf./mbld. sides. **Wing H.2265. £50.00**
"Behemoth", a dialogue in defence of Charles I & in condemnation of his enemies, his allies & most of his apologists, is the most important item in this collection; it also includes replies to criticisms on "Leviathan" & questions on gravity, the nature of heat, & other scientific subjects.

205. HOBHOUSE, John Cam[Lord Broughton] (1786-1869). Reform of Parliament ... Speech ... on Mr. Lambton's Motion. 1821. 1st. 32pp. Disbound. **£5.00**
Argues that wider suffrage would not open the House to demagogues, but rather close it to ambitious placemen – he points to Canning as an example.

206. HODGSON, E. The Trials at Large of the Capital and other Convicts, on the King's Commission ... for the City of London and ... County of Middlesex. 1791-2. 1st. **8 numbers (17 parts) in one vol.** 470, 467-472pp. One leaf torn without loss. Few pencil scribbles. Contemp. ¼ sheep/mbld. sides; worn. **Not in S. & M. £40.00**
A complete year's proceedings in the Middlesex county court before the Lord Mayor, Recorder, Common Sergeant, etc. These cases are in general unknown to the regular reports, from which Hodgson's accounts differ in that he reports the evidence and specifies the sentence. They show how the obsolete criminal laws were applied (how, for example, the jury would falsify the value of stolen goods to save a thief's neck) and are full of interesting details of language & society.

207. HOLY ROMAN EMPIRE. Der erst [-ander] Theyl aller des heyli. röm. Reichs Ordnungen, gehaltener Reichstäge unnd Abschiedt, sampt der gülden Bullen. Besonderlich auch der Artikel Policey, Constitutionen, das Keyserlich Regiment [etc.] ... new mit Fleisz zusamen getragen. Mainz (F. Behem), 1560. **2 vols. in 1.** German text. Folio. Red & black titles. Woodcut arms on title, text woodcuts of coins, & woodcut of Diet of 1356 on A_1. Index. [xxii], 334, [i]/243, [ix] leaves. First title re-margined; 17 leaves at beginning & end repaired at inner margin; lacks blank $2K_8$; sm. holes in $3S_6$ & $3T_1$; marginal defects to three leaves. Margins stnd. Some old annots. Contemp. blind-stamped pig; sp. & upper jt. repaired; lacks clasps. **£300.00**
Second collected ed. of the imperial laws & acts of the Reichstäge of the Holy Roman Empire, beginning with the Golden Bull of 1356, & here extended to the monetary edict of Ferdinand I (1559). Most of the contents are attempts to impose coherence on the innumerable independent lords, ecclesiastics, & city governments of the Empire, and to reconcile their claims & powers; and there are many incidental references to the troubles of the Reformation.

208. HOMES, J.A. The Act to Amend the Law of Insolvency, Bankruptcy, and Execution ... Act for the Relief of Insolvent Debtors ... Act for Facilitating Arrangements between Debtors and Creditors. 1844. 1st. Index. viii, 136pp. Orig. printed bds., sp. defective. **Not in S. & M. £10.00**

209. HOPE of Craighall, Sir Thomas. Practical Observations upon Divers Titles of the Law of Scotland, Commonly called ... Minor Practicks. Ed. John Spottiswood. Edinburgh, 1734. 1st thus. viii, 554pp. Contemp. cf., sl. rbbd., sp. sl. frayed. **S. & M.v. 52. £30.00**
Includes as an appendix an account of religious houses in Scotland, extracted by Spottiswood's son from among his father's papers.

210. HOPKINSON, Francis. Miscellaneous Essays and Occasional Writings. Philadelphia, 1792. 1st collected. **3 vols.** Two fold'g engr. plates. vi, 384/iv, 288, 305-422/iv, 216pp. Signatures of vol. 2 jump from S_7 to U_1; pagination irregular accordingly. Lib. perforations on titles. Mod. cl. **£50.00**
Periodical essays, scientific experiments, remarks on the contribution, and (vol. 3) decisions in the Penna. Admiralty, by an author evidently comparable, in both his political & his private character, with Franklin. Hopkinson's signature is pasted to the second leaf of vol. 1.

211. HORSMAN, Gilbert, & others. Precedents in Conveyancing. 1757. 2nd ed. **2 vols.** Folio. Index. [xxiv], 580/[xvi], 581-1135, [xxix]pp. Contemp. cf., rbbd.; heads of sps. sl. torn. **S. & M. i. 482. £60.00**
Gives a comprehensive view of the many commercial matters into which the conveyancer's province had been extended since the Statute of Frauds.

212. H[UTTON], Sir R. The Young Clarks Guide: or an Exact Collection of Choice English Presidents ... of Indentures. Letters of Atturney, Releases, Conditions &c. By T.R. and M.D. for Ambrose Isted ... and Samuel Herick, 1670. 12th imp. **Pt. 1 (of 3) only.** Index. [xvi], 336pp. Sm. hole in F_8 aff. few letters. Few leaves sl. soiled. Mod. ½ cf./cl. sides. **S. & M. i. 483. £30.00**
The fullest collection of forms then available. This volume covers indentures, assignments, releases, letters of attorney, covenants, bills, wills & conditions.

213. INDIAN STATUTORY COMMISSION. Report. H.M.S.O., 1930. 1st. **Vol. 1** (Survey) only. Fold'g. maps. xxvi, 409pp. Orig. wraps; fdd. **£7.50**
Vol. 2 contained the recommendations of the Commission; there were fifteen further vols. of memoranda.

214. IRELAND. General Prisons Board. First Report. Dublin (H.M.S.O.), 1879. 1st. 133pp. Title-page partially pasted to e-p.; text not aff. Few inner margins affected by crude sewing. Old ½ cf./mbld. sides; worn; lower cvr. defective. **£5.00**

215. JACOB, Giles. The Statute-Law Common-Plac'd: or, a Second General Table to the Statutes. 1719. 1st. Index. [xi], v, 220, [iv], 4pp. Two advert. leaves at end. Contemp. cf., rbbd. **S. & M. i. 548. £20.00**

216. ———— A New Law-Dictionary. 1762. 8th ed. Folio. Unpaged. Lacks final leaf (index to references to Holt C.J.'s decisions). Mod. ½ cf./mbld. sides. **S. & M. i. 9. £20.00**

217. [JANE, Joseph]. Eikôn Aklastos [Gr.] The Image Unbroken ... The Impudence, Falshood, Vanitie, and Prophannes ... in a Libell entitled Eikonoclastes [Gr.] N.p. [Netherlands?] Printed ... 1651. 1st. Sm. 4to. 71, 56-267pp. Sigg. & pagination of quires H & I repeated. Some contemp. MS. corrections. Mod. ¼ cf./mbld. sides. **Wing J.156; Almack p.74. £60.00**
A reply, section by section, to Milton's strictures on the Eikon Basilike; sometimes ascribed to John Earle, the Latin translator of the Eikon.

218. JENKS, Edward. Law & Politics in the Middle Ages. N.Y., 1912. 3rd imp. (following 1st London ed.) Index. Table of sources. xiv, 352pp. Orig. cl., sl. fdd. **Not in S. & M. £6.00**

219. JONES, Sir William (C.J. [Ireland]) (1566-1640). Les Reports de ... un des Justices del' Banck le Roy ... del ... Common Banck d'Ireland. By T.R. and N.T. for Thomas Bassett and Richard Chiswell, 1675. 1st. Folio. French text. Black letter. Index. [xii], 463, [i], [xxi]pp. Final errata leaf. Few leaves sl. soiled. Large copy. Contemp. sprinkled cf., jts. & edges rbbd. **Wing J.1003; S. & M. i. 199. £35.00**

220. JUSTINIAN I, Emperor. Corpus juris civilis ... cum notis ... Dionysii GOTHOFREDI ... PAULI receptae sententiae cum selectis notis J. CUJACII ... Antonii ANSELMO ... observationes. Amsterdam (Blaeu, L. & D. Elzevir), Leyden (Hacke), 1663. Bound in 2 vols. Folio. Engr. & printed titles. Indices. [xx], 796/[x], 388, [xii], 300, 92, [xxxix]pp. Sigg. 3L-3Q in vol. 2 consolidated into three signatures each of six leaves. Sl. stnd. Final leaf backed & with long narrow hole aff. 12 lines of index. Contemp. mottled cf., sps. gilt; sl. rubbed. Bk-pl. **£80.00**
This splendid edition, which was twenty years in the making, applies to the Corpus the principles of the familiar Dutch variorum classics. The standard commentary of Godefroy is attached to an improved text, & enriched with the notes of many doctors, from Baldus to Barthius: & to the usual constituents of Godefroy's editions are added a consular list, the fragments of the Twelve Tables & of Ulpian, the Sententiae of Julius Paulus, & the original Greek of the Novellae. The general editor was Simon van Leeuwen of Leyden.

221. ———— Another copy. Reference tags (defective, some torn away) on fore-edges. $2L_4$ (vol. 1) & R_4 (vol. 2) torn without loss. Sl. mkd. Contemp. cf., rubbed. **£75.00**

222. ———— Anr. ed. Amsterdam (Blaeu, Elzevir & Hackius), 1664. **2 vols. in 1.** Engr. title. Index. [xxii], [ii], 1038, [ii]/820, [ii]pp. Thumb-tags pasted to fore-margins (some torn away). Contemp. blind-stamped vellum, lacks ties. **£25.00**
A handy version of the previous item, without the notes.

223. ———— Corpus iuris civilis ... Notae ... Dionysio Gothofredo IC. auctore. N.p. [Geneva], (J. Vignon), 1619. **4 vols. in 1.** 4to. Red & black title in border. Index. Numbered in columns. $2H_4$ (vol. 2) blank. Sl. browned & soiled. Reference-tags on fore-margins. Many annots. by Sir Francis Grant (Baron Grant of Nova Scotia); signed by him & dated 1705 on title. Contemp. black mor., rbbd., head & tail of sp. worn. **£30.00**

224. ———— Corpus iuris civilis ... cum summariis, argumentis, epitomis, & indicibus cl. v. Dionysii Gothofredi. Geneva (J. Vignon), 1620. 4to. Index. Numbered in columns. Vellum thumb-tag at fore-margin at beginning of each book. Sl. wormed. Contemp. cf., rbbd., head of sp. frayed. **£25.00**

225. ———— Anr. ed. Amsterdam, 1700. **2 vols. in 1.** General engr. title. 7 blank leaves (2 with annots.) bound before vol. 2. Index. [xx], [ii], 1038/821pp. Vellum tabs on fore-edges. Contemp. cf., sp. gilt; tail of sp. broken. Bk-pl. **£15.00**

226. ———— Institutionum ... libri IIII. Ed. Gregorius Haloander. Paris (ex officina Roberti Stephani), 1534. 1st thus. Device on title. Index. [viii], 296, [viii]pp. Final colophon leaf. Table of consanguinity sl. cropped. **Not in B.M.C. – MELANCTHON, Philip (1497-1560);** De legibus oratio ... de gradibus oratio (–Praefatio in Aeschinis et Demosthenis orationes). Paris (ex officina Roberti Stephani), 1534. 1st collected. Device on title. Final blank. 62, [ii]pp. **B.M.C. (French) p.309. Two works in one vol.** Faintly ruled in ink throughout. 18th-cent. cf., gilt; upper jt. worn; sl. rbbd. **£90.00**
Two fine examples of Parisian printing at the beginning of its most splendid era. The speeches of Melancthon, most refined & accomplished of the early Lutherans, seem to date from his youthful studies at Tubingen; although as yet unknown to Luther, he already complains of religious tyranny & of the hatred shown to the jurists (who were beginning to connect themselves with the spirit of the Renaissance) by the petty pedants (doctorculi) of the old theology.

227. ———— Institutiones ... Fr. Accursii glossis illustratae, Geneva [G.S. du Bois & G. Guéroult], 1555. Device on title & last leaf. Index. [lxiv], 600pp. Sl. stnd. 19th-cent. cf., sp. rbbd. **Not in B.M.C. £60.00**
An edition in the mediaeval style, with the old Vita Justiniani of Gilles Perrin, the rambling commentary of the second Accursius, & some additional notes by Porchus (q.v.) on descents. Some fragments of the Leges Romuli & the Twelve Tables are included.

228. ———— Institutionum ... libri ... ex antiquissimis exemplaribus repraesentati, per Ant. Contium. [–Enchiridion titulorum ... de

verborum ac rerum significatione ... de regulis iuris (etc.)] Paris, 1560. **2 pts. in 1 vol.** 1st thus. Indices. 136 [i.e. 134], [ii]/79 leaves. Lacks final blank. Old annots. Sl. stnd. 19th-cent. cf., re-backed. **£40.00**
An early annotated edition, collated with the Greek of Theophilus.

229. ———— Institouta Theophilou antikensôros [sic] [Gr.] Institutiones, Theophilo ... interprete ... Paratitla et notae ... Dionysio Gothofredo I.C. authore. N.p. [Paris], 1587. 1st thus. 4to. Gk & Lat. text. Index. [viii], 308, 329, [v]pp. Sl. stnd. Contemp. vellum. **Not in B.M.C. £80.00**
Theophilus's Greek version of the Institutes, made for the many "Romans" who knew no Latin, is often a valuable guide to the construction of the original. This edition of Gothofredus, or Godefroy (1549-1622) includes not only the original Latin but also the Latin version made from the Greek by J. Curtius.

230. ———— Institutiones ... typis variae, rubris nucleum exhibentibus [ed. A. Corvinus]. Paris, 1676. 16mo. Engr. & printed titles. Text in red & black throughout. Glossary [iv], 391, [cii]pp. Final blank. Sl. stnd. Contemp. cf., rubbed; jts. worn. **£15.00**
The little edition of Corvinus (first pubd. Leyden, 1661) has one novelty; the most important passages are printed in red to form a summary or abridgment.

231. ———— Digestorum seu pandectarum libri quinquaginta ex Florentinis pandectis repraesentati. Florence (in officina Laurentii Torrentini), 1553. 1st thus. Folio. **3 vols. in 5.** Devices on title & last leaf. Many woodcut initials. Five blanks (m_4, C_4, $2S_4$, $3a_4$ & $4d_4$) as called for. Sm. marginal holes in four leaves; occasional spotting; but a fine large copy in 18th-cent. sheep. rbbd. **Adams J.578. Brunet III. 615. £350.00**
This splendid edition was conceived as a type-facsimile of the famous MS. of the Pandects, brought to Amalfi (according to the old but not undisputed account) early in the twelfth century & finally deposited in Florence in 1406, which revived the study of the Pandects after centuries of neglect. The editors, Lelio Torelli & his son Francesco (assisted by Pietro Vettori), spent ten years in the collation.

232. KEBLE, Joseph. Reports in ... King's Bench ... from the XII. to the XXX. Year of ... King Charles II. By W. Rawlins [etc.] for Thomas Dring [etc.], 1685. 1st. **3 vols.** Folio. Black letter. Indices. First privilege leaves to vols. 1 & 3 (wanting in vol. 2). Lacks two blanks. Contemp. cf., sl. rbbd., one cvr. sl. torn. **Wing K.116; S. & M. i. 302. £60.00**
Keble was one of the first to publish his own reports (as opposed to translating other men's) in English. The tables, sometimes bound separately, are included in the appropriate volumes.

233. KELLER, F.L. Ueber Litis Contestation und Urtheil nach classischem Römischen Recht. Zurich, 1827. 1st. German text. Index. [ii], xxiv, 614pp. Mod. cl. **£10.00**
Examination of civil proceedings in the light of the Institutes of Gaius & other sources recently discovered or examined.

234. KILBURN, Richard. Choice Presidents upon All Acts of Parliament, relating to the Office and Duty of a Justice of Peace ... Cases ... Method of Making Up Court-Rolls. By the Assigns of Rich. and Edw. Atkins ... for Richard Tonson, 1681. 2nd ed. 12mo. Index. [iv], 418pp. Some side-notes shaved. F_{12} sl. torn. New ¼ cf./mbld. sides. **Wing K.429 (Bibl. Nationale, Paris, only). S. & M. i. 229. £50.00**

235. KING, Sir Robert. A Vindication of [his] Designs and Actions, in Relation to the Late, and Present Lord Kingston. Printed ... 1699. 234pp. Contemp. black mor. gilt; a.e.g.; fine contemp. bk-pl. Sir Robert Southwell, Clerk to the Privy Council. **Not in Wing. £30.00**
King's enemies represented him as the conventional wicked uncle, oppressing his nephews out of spite at not being appointed guardian to them & in the hope of getting an estate in which the elder nephew had a prior interest, & persuading the old lord to disinherit the youth. He claims to have acted (with authority from Tillotson, Stillingfleet, & other noted divines) because the actual guardian had married the boy to an Irish Catholic.

236. KIRWAN & SHERIDAN, Rex v. RIDGEWAY, William; Proceedings in the Cases of. Dublin, 1811. 1st. 293pp. Last leaf sl. frayed. Mod. cl. **£10.00**
Trial of Catholics who held a meeting to campaign for representation in Parliament.

237. KITCHIN, John. Jurisdictions; or, the Lawful Authority of Courts Leet, Courts Baron, Court of Marshallseys, Court of Pypowder, and Ancient Demesne ... Tenures, and all their Incidents ... Writs, with their Severall Returnes, in English. By T: Roycroft, for M: Walbancke ... and H: Twyford, 1651. 1st Engl. Index. [iv], 602, [xxvi]pp. Sm. holes in G_3, $2I_1$, & $2O_8$ aff. few letters. U_2 torn without loss. Twelve leaves of English writs (signed 2P*³-2Q*⁴) between $2P_1$ & $2P_2$. Few leaves browned. Mod. ½ cf./mbld. sides. **Wing K.656. S. & M. i. 401. £60.00**
The hastily-produced supplement appears to be the first attempt to provide precedents of writs in English as demanded by the republican government.

238. KORNMANN, Heinrich. De virginitatis iure tractatus novus et iucundus. [–Linea amoris, sive commentarius in versiculum gl. Visus, colloquium, convictus, oscula, factum.] "Virginopoli" [Frankfurt?] 1631. [2nd ed.] 24mo. **2 pts. in 1.** [ii], 290, 233 [i.e. 133], [xix]pp. Several irregularities in signing. Contemp. vellum. **£40.00**
The author handles virgins in the language & style of his calling (he was a respectable jurist from Kirchhain), but scarcely in its spirit; "what colour hair best suits a virgin" (he prefers blondes) is among the most innocent of his questions.

239. LAMBARD, William (1536-1601). Eirenarcha: or of the office of the Justices of Peace, in two Bookes. By Ra: Newbery, and H. Bynneman, 1581. 1st. Black letter. Woodcut title-border, arms on verso of title, & initials. Table of statutes. Final device leaf. [viii], 512, [xvi]pp. First & last leaf, just aff. title-border. One sm. worm-hole in text. Old annots. Slip with additional side-note pasted on E_6. 19th-cent. cf., jts. rbbd. **Beale T.387. S.T.C.15163. S. & M. i. 229. £200.00**
Lambard's work was the first practical & comprehensive English manual for magistrates, & set new standards of clarity & simplicity in law-writing. The author was ahead of his time in combining the study of law (he was a bencher of Lincoln's Inn) with that of lay history; his Perambulation of Kent (1576) is the earliest published work on English local history.

240. ———— Fourthly ... enlarged. By Thomas Wight, and Bonham Norton, 1599. Black letter. **2 pts. in 1.** Woodcut inits. & head-pieces. Indices. [ii], 607, [77]/80pp. Inscribed on title "To the right worshypfull knight Syr Thomas Walsingham W Lambarde". First eight words cancelled but legible. Few annots. in two early hands; later name of Hen[ry] King on title & e-p. Sm. piece torn from one fore-margin. Contemp. cf., central gilt lozenge, gilt & blind lines; lacks ties; re-backed. **Beale T.395; S.T.C.15169; S. & M. i. 229. £200.00**
The author's final revision, inscribed in his own hand to Sir Thomas Walsingham (1568-1630), his companion on the Kent commission & a notable patron of his researches into the antiquities of the county. We have verified the handwriting by collation with a letter of 1594 (MS. Harl. 6996).

241. LANE, Richard (Attorney-General & Lord Keeper) (1584-1650). Reports in the Court of Exchequer ... in ... the Raign of ... King James ... being the first collections in that Court hitherto extant. For W. Lee, D. Pakeman, and G. Bedell, 1657. 1st. Black letter. Sm. folio. Index. [iv], 119, [v]pp. Mod. ½ cf./mbld. sides. Bk-pl. **Wing L.340. S. & M. i. 212. £40.00**
Lane shows a special interest in questions of royal prerogative. A notable case is R. v. Earl of Nottingham & others (1610), a very early example of a man's conveying away an estate on trust in order to save it for his family should his real property become amenable to forfeiture. The settlor here was Sir Robert Dudley (1573-1639), the traveller, engineer & scientist, of Italian fame.

242. LECKIE, Gould Francis. Essay on the Practice of the British Government; distinguished from the Abstract Theory on which it is Supposed to be Founded. 1812. 1st. Errata slip. xx, 176pp. Review (from the Edinburgh Review no.40, Nov. 1812) pasted on extra blanks at end. Contemp. ½ cf./mbld. sides; sp. defective; corners worn. **£10.00**
Leckie's "abstract theory" is of an active monarchy restrained, but not dominated, by Parliament. The angry reviewer accuses him of fashioning the Constitution in his own image.

243. ———— Anr. ed. "Pamphleteer", 1817. 49-105pp. Disbound. **£5.00**

244. A LETTER to a NOBLE LORD; containing some Remarks on ... Two Acts ... for Vesting in his Majestie the Estates of Certain Traitors, &c. And ... for ... Abolishing the Heritable Jurisdictions in ... Scotland. 1748. 1st. ½ title. [ii], 28pp. Disbound. **Not in S. & M. £10.00**
Condemns these acts as unconstitutionally adding to the wealth of the crown.

245. A LETTER to the PUBLIC ADVERTISER. 1764. 1st. 51, [i]pp. Disbound. **Not in Kress. £15.00**
Sarcastic remarks, by a partisan of John Wilkes, on the conduct of his enemies before & during his trial.

246. LEVINZ, Sir Creswell (Justice, C.P.). Les Reports. 1702. 1st. **Vol. 3 (1682-1696) only.** Folio. French text. Black letter. Index. [xxii], 440, [xii]pp. Mod. cl. **S. & M. i. 303. £10.00**
Probably the last book written in law-French.

247. LEY, Sir James, Earl of Marlborough. Reports of Divers Resolutions ... upon Cases in the Court of Wards,

and other Courts at Westminster. By Tho. Roycroft for H. Twyford, Tho. Dring, and Jo. Place, 1659. 1st. Folio. Black letter. Index. [iv], 84, [viii], 28pp. Margins sl. wormed. Contemp. cf., re-backed. **Wing M.688. S. & M. i. 357.** **£50.00**
The Court of Wards took cognisance of the king's rights over crown lands during the minority or lunacy of the tenant; a fruitful source of corruption & oppression, it was abolished in 1661. Ley's treatise on Wards & Liveries is included. This is the only published volume of reports in the Court of Wards.

248. LEYDEN, University of. Collection of 73 juridical disputations, or notices of theses to be maintained in public debate by the candidate for the licenciate or doctorate of laws. Leyden, 1600-1632. All 1st. 4to. 8, 12 or 16pp. One title wanting; two defective; one item lacks two leaves of text. Contemp. MS. table on e-p. Contemp. vellum head of sp. defective. **£250.00**
These documents were printed immediately before the debate, and contain the texts of the theses which the student had to defend in oral discussion before the faculty; some of them give a summary of the authorities & reasons to be used. (Luther's "Wittenburg Theses" consisted of a notice of much the same kind.) Among the authors we observe Willem de Groot (Grotius), a fellow-townsman & so presumably a relative of Hugo. Four items were printed by the Elzevirs. A complete list of contents is available on request.

249. LINDENBROGIUS, Fridericus (c.1560-1638) (ed.). Codex legum antiquarum ... quibus accedunt formulae solennes [sic] ... nunc primum editae: et glossarium. Frankfurt (apud Iohannem et Andream Marnios), 1613. 1st. Folio. Index. Final errata leaf. [xxiv], 1570, [ii]pp. Sl. browned. Fine copy in contemp. vellum. **£150.00**

250. ———— Anr. copy. Some browning. Old sprinkled sheep, sp. gilt; jts., edges & foot of sp. worn. **£140.00**
This was for two hundred years the standard collection of the Teutonic codes & other enactments, civil & ecclesiastical, of the dark & early middle ages.

250a. LINDWOOD, William (Bishop of St. Davids, c. 1365-1446). Provinciale seu Constitutiones Anglie Cum summariis atq; iustis annotationibus [etc.] ... [Explicitu ... accuratione ... Andree BOCARD ... In ... parisiana academia ... anno ... Millesimo quingentesimoprimo] Paris, A. Bocard for J. Badius Ascensius, 28th May 1501. Folio. Tables; index. Gothic (rotunda) letter, printed in red & black. Woodcut initials. [2], 192, [xix] leaves. Lacks final blank. Contemp. & later annotations (some cropped). Some damp-stains in first three & last two quires. Title & last leaf repaired, sl. aff. text. Early blind-tooled English calf; central stamp & triple lines; re-backed; sl. rubbed. **S.T.C.17107. S. & M. i. 181; Beale T.403.** **£200.00**
Lindwood's collection of decrees issued by successive Archbishops of Canterbury, from Stephen Langton to Henry Chichele, is to English canon law what the Code is to the civil law. It was first printed by Rood & Hunt, Oxford, 1483-5; this is the first annotated edition, edited by André Bocard (who also printed it) & issued jointly by Joost Bade, or Badius (afterwards celebrated for his association with the great classical scholars of France) and a syndicate of English booksellers.

251. LITTLETON, Sir Thomas (?-1481). Tenures in English. For the Companie of Stationers, 1616. Index. 142, [ii] leaves. Title frayed. Sl. stnd. at end. Few old annots. Mod. cf. **S.T.C.15781. S. & M. i. 457.** **£75.00**
"Not the name of the author only, but of the law itself" (Coke). Littleton's account of the law of real property, as it stood immediately before the economic revolutions of the Tudor age, set a rare example of thoroughness, brevity & judgment among the early law-writers.

252. ———— Tenures, in French and English. By John Streeter [etc.] Sold by George Sawbridge [etc.], 1671. 12mo. Index. [xxii], 436, [ii]pp. P_2 torn without loss. One fore-margin shaved. Contemp. cf., rbbd. **Wing L.2588. S. & M. i. 459.** **£35.00**
The first, & for some centuries the only, bilingual edition.

253. LIVES and EXPLOITS of the Most Noted HIGHWAYMEN, ROBBERS and MURDERERS ... Brought Down to the Present Time. Hartford (Conn.), 1851. (Rev. ed.) Wood-engr. illus. 287pp. Sl. stnd. New cl., leather label. **£15.00**
The last case included, that of James Porter, is of American origin.

254. The LIVES and EXPLOITS of the MOST CELEBRATED ROBBERS & BANDITTI. Philadelphia, Pa. (G.G. Evans), n.d. [c.1860]. Hand-col'd lith. fp. & wood-engr. plates. 284, 22pp. Orig. cl., gilt; fdd.; jts. & corners rbbd. **£20.00**

255. LOUTHIAN, John. The Form of Process before the Court of Justiciary in Scotland; containing the Constitution of the Sovereign Criminal Court and ... Circuit Courts. Edinburgh, 1732. 1st. vi, 302, [ii]pp. Final errata leaf. Contemp. cf., sp. rbbd. **S. & M. v. 71.** **£30.00**
A short manual of criminal court practice & the rules of evidence, written for the layman & reflecting the dangerous imbalance between the Lord Advocate, who himself or by deputy managed all prosecutions, & the ignorant pannel (prisoner) defended on the equivalent of a dock brief.

256. [LOVELASS, Peter]. [The Law's Disposal] of a Person's Estate who Dies without Will or Testament ... Disposal ... by Will and Testament. Dublin, 1787. 2nd ed. Appendix. Index. xvi, 256, [x]pp. Strip cut from head of title, with loss of three words. Lib. perforation & stamp on title. Sl. browned. Mod. cl. **S. & M. i. 492.** **£15.00**

257. LUSON, Hewling (1743-?). Inferior Politics; or, Considerations on the ... Poor ...: Plan for the Reduction of the National Debt. 1786. 1st. Errata leaf. Sm. repair to B_8. – Comparative View of Mr. Gilbert's Bill. 1787. 1st. – Conciliation; or, Considerations on the ... War. 1797. 1st. – Case and Vindication. 1803. 1st. **Inscribed** to R. Reeve. – Appendix to the Case. 1812. 1st. **Five items in one vol.** (bound in reverse order). MS table. Contemp ½ vellum/mbld. sides; rbbd. **£30.00**
Arguments connecting the rise of crime with the industrial revolution, with a Bill in which L.'s ideas were embodied by a M.P.; a pamphlet against continued war with France; & two items on the author's dismissal from a post in Sheerness dockyard after (as he says) he had found corruption in the clerks & excess of authority in the Commissioner.

258. MACKENZIE of Rosehaugh, Sir George (1636-1691). Idea eloquentiae forensis hodiernae: una cum actione forensi ex unaquaque juris parte. Edinburgh, excudebat haeres Andreae Anderson, 1681. 1st. Latin text. [xii], 182, [ii]pp. Final blank. A_3 torn without loss; fore-margin of E_4 defective. Contemp. sheep, rbbd. **Wing M.164; S. & M. v. 74.** **£40.00**
Mackenzie justly laments that the eloquence of Scots advocates (he might have added English counsel) is never preserved as an example to the student. In the hope of endowing modern oratory with the dignity attaching to a Cicero, he gives Latin versions of six of his own speeches, with general remarks on the duties & qualifications for speaking at the bar.

259. ———— The Laws and Customes of Scotland in Matters Criminal. Edinburgh, by Thomas Brown, 1678. 4to. Red & black title. First privilege leaf. [xiv], 582pp. S_4 repaired. Sl. browned. Contemp. cf., worn, re-backed. **Wing M.167 (Nat. Lib. Scot. only). S. & M. v. 74.** **£50.00**
In these institutes of Scots crown law, Mackenzie offers his famous justification of torture. Inspection of the passage reveals that he is not pursuing a crotchet of his own, but re-stating in English a common-place of civil law. Three editions appeared in 1678.

260. ———— Another edition ("2nd", i.e. 4th). Edinburgh, for Mr. Andrew Symson, 1699. Folio. **4 pts. in 1.** Red & black title. Index. [viii], 292, [iv], [ii], 30, [ii], 31-66 [i.e. 70], [iv], 62pp. Lacks final blank. Some irregular signing & pagination. General & fly-title of "Mutilation & Demembration" reversed; one corner torn from the former. Contemp. cf., sl. rbbd. **Wing M.168. S. & M. v. 74.** **£60.00**
Includes Sir A. Seton's "Treatise of Mutilation and Demembration" as an appendix.

261. ———— Observations upon the XVIII. Act Parliament XXIII. K. James VI. against Dispositions made in Defraud of Creditors, &c. Edinburgh, by the Heirs and Successors of Andrew Anderson ... for Mr. Andrew Symson, 1699. Second ed. Folio. [iv], 62pp. Lacks final blank. Several contemp. corrections. Title-border cropped at head. Mod. cl. **Wing M.189 (none outside U.K.) Aldis 3866.5. S. & M. v. 74.** **£40.00**

262. ———— Pleadings, in some ... Cases, before the ... Courts of Scotland, since ... 1661. Edinburgh, 1704. 16mo. [viii], 296pp. Margins of F_1 & G_1 sl. defective, aff. one line. Fore-margins short; one sl. cropped. Old cf., re-backed; sides rbbd. **S. & M. v. 74.** **£20.00**

263. MACKENZIE, Lord. Studies in Roman Law, with Comparative Views of the Laws of France, England and Scotland. Edinburgh, 1865. 2nd ed., rev. Index. xxxvi, 404, [40]pp. Last leaf of publisher's cat. defective. Orig. b'ram, mkd. & sl. fdd.; lacks front e-p. **S. & M. v. 138.** **£8.00**

264. MacNALLY, Leonard (1752-1820). The Justice of the Peace for Ireland: Containing the Authorities and Duties of the Various Conservators of the Peace; Sheriff ... Coroner [etc.] Dublin, 1812. 2nd ed. **4 vols.** Index. Contemp. sheep, flap covering fore-edge; two ties defective; otherwise fine. **S. & M. iv. 56.** **£30.00**
MacNally is supposed to have written the words of the song "Sweet Lass of Richmond Hill".

265. [MACPHERSON, James]. The Rights of Great Britain Asserted against the claims of America. 1776. 4th ed., rev. Fold'g table. [iv], 104pp. Final advert. leaves. **Kress 7226** (3rd ed.) – **WESLEY, John**: Some Observations on Liberty. Edinburgh, 1776. 1st. Lacks ½ title. 36pp. cf. **Kress 7275.** – **SERIOUS ENQUIRIES** into the Motives & Consequences of our Present Armament against Russia, 1791. 1st. Fold'g table. [ii], 60pp. **Kress B.2194.** – **A SERIES of LETTERS** containing a Particular Account of the Massacres of Paris, 1793. 1st collected. [ii], 178pp. **Four works in one vol.** **SOLD**
The authors of "Ossian" & of Methodism have a common theme, that liberty and independence are not synonymous; Wesley takes this ground in refuting Price's "Observations on Civil Liberty".

266. MAITLAND, [F.W.]. Selected Essays, ed. H.D. Hazeltine, G. Lapsley, & P.H. Winfield. C.U.P., 1936. 1st collected. Index. x, 264pp. Orig. cl., fdd. & sl. mkd. **S. & M. ii. 230.** **£6.00**
Includes the introd. to the Rolls Series ed. of Memoranda de Parliamento *& some essays from periodicals.*

267. MANUSCRIPT. [Precedents, maxims & definitions.] N.p., n.d. [1615-1628.] Folio. French text. 514, [xiv], 515-544pp. Last few leaves sl. frayed & soiled. Early names of John Whittacre & John Stockman on last leaf. Contemp. blind-stamped cf., MS. guards (Missal, early 15th cent.); re-backed with orig. spine. **£120.00**
A very thorough & detailed common-place book in alphabetical order, written in a single though variable semi-italic hand & ruled in red. The sources are the Year-books of Edward IV (with occasional cases from other reigns), reports from Plowden to Coke, & (very rarely) Fitzherbert's Natura Brevium & "Doctor & Student". John Stockman was admitted to the Middle Temple on 10th Nov. 1611, & John Whitacres (sic) to Lincoln's Inn on 24th Oct. 1612.

268. ———— Alphabetical digest of cases (titles "Administration" to "Coppyhoulds" only). N.d. (c. 1610). Folio. French text. [412] leaves, many blank. Two leaves containing notes on perjury etc., of similar date but in English, inserted. Uncut. Contemp. vellum, lacks ties; frong hinge broken. **£150.00**
This volume differs from the usual common-place book in that it consists for the most part of full-length reports, many of them without references & therefore presumably not taken from any published source. The long period of time covered (1553-1607) & some variations of style suggest that the compiler has used the papers of more than one reporter; but activity is concentrated on the Court of Queen's Bench in the last twenty years of the reign of Elizabeth I, a fact which suggests that for this period the source is the note-book of a serjeant. Particular interest is shown in copyholds, which occupy more than half the space used.

269. ———— **De la SERNA, Diego.** Re[col]lectio de servitutibus pr[a]edialibus ... ad explicat[ion]em t[itu]li ff. de Servitutibus. N.p., n.d. [Spanish, late 17th cent.] Sm. 4to. 71 leaves, the last two blank. Closely written in a neat hand, with calligraphic headings & colophon. Contemp. vellum, ties sl. defective; sl. mkd. **Phillipps MS.4526.** **£50.00**
Probably arranged by one Guerra, whose name is on the title in the same hand as the rest, from a course of lectures; however, it is not a collection of detached notes, but a coherent treatise with full references. We cannot identify it with any published work.

270. ———— Lex Terr[a]e explained by a Digest of the Matt[er]s in Litt[leton's] Tenures & Ld. Cokes Comentaries ... illustrated by the application of most of the Cases to some Maxime & recd. Rule of Law. N.d. [after 1676]. MS. on paper in a degenerate chancery hand. 206pp. First & last leaves mounted. Purchase note on e-p. of W.H. Black (1808-72) of the Public Record Office. Some margins wormed; few head-lines cropped. Mod. ¼ mor./cl. sides; bk-pl. **£60.00**
With an appendix of 206 maxims & a leaf of abbreviations.

271. ———— LYNDESAY, H; Ane Epitome of Duries Practices ... containing the Mater and Substance of the haill Practices contained in the Prin[cip]le (sic) Books be [sic] Sr. John NISBET. N.p. [Edinburgh?], n.d. [c. 1700]. Sm. 4to. Index. [ii], 424, [96]pp. Contemp. sheep, clasps & ends of sp. defective; rbbd. **£80.00**
An alphabetical digest from the works of Sir A. Gibson (Lord Durie) & the celebrated Nisbet of Dirleton. The last 96pp. are blank except for a few acts of convention of Edinburgh (1717) & a resolution of Kirkcudbright justices concerning the poor (1725) in a second hand.

272. ———— [Maxims, precedents, & definitions.] N.d. [c.1718.] Sm. 4to. 7 blank leaves/490pp. 28 blanks cut out at end. Contemp. vellum; sl. fdd. **£50.00**
The emphasis of this work is on London & Middlesex county court forms & practice, and also those of King's Bench.

273. ———— **MEDLYCOTT, James (Master in Chancery, apptd. 1706).** Report and Schedule of Accounts in the case Waller v. Southwell. 1716. Folio. 92pp. Upper margins repaired throughout, some words obscured; marginal defects towards end aff. few lines of c.20 leaves. Last leaf soiled. Fore-margins shaved. Mod. ½ cf./mbld. sides. **£40.00**
After four years' debate, Edward Southwell, steward to the late James Waller (an Irish landowner) is cleared of the charge of embezzlement brought by Waller's executors. This volume digests the statements of the witnesses as to the translations involved.

274. ———— Notes on Contingent Remainders & Executory Devises, and on Uses. C.1817. 4to. 175 leaves, 87-9 blank; four more blanks at end. Neatly written in copperplate hand, with side-notes in left-hand & references in right-hand margin. Several slips inserted. Contemp. vellum, soiled; sp. defective. **£20.00**
Derived largely from Charles Fearne's book on Remainders (ed. Butler) & F.W. Saunders's on Uses; but the writer has alleged several new cases, some of which alter the reasoning of the original work; thus he quotes the case Gulliver v. Wickett, which applies the Purefoy v. Rogers rule (treating future interests disposed by will as remainders whenever possible) in circumstances where Fearne had held it irrelevant.

275. ———— **LAMBERT & SON, James (solicitors);** Letter-book, 1823-1828. Folio. Alphabetical index in prelims. [xxv], 528pp. Last leaf loose. Orig. green vellum, sl. shaken. **£60.00**
James Lambert (succeeded in the practice by his son G.J. Lambert during the currency of this volume) worked from Hastings, but evidently had Yorkshire connections; much of the correspondence relates to transactions in land near Settle. There are a number of interesting side-lights on the price of land & of agricultural materials.

276. MANUTIUS, Paulus (1512-1574). Antiquitatum Romanarum ... liber de legibus. Venice, 1569. New ed. Italic letter. Device on title. Index. [xii], 13-304, [lxxii]pp. Contemp. vellum, later labels. **£75.00**
Paolo Manuzio, perhaps a better scholar than his father Aldus, wrote this elegant commentary on the laws of the Roman republic (one of a series of works on Roman antiquities) in 1557.

277. MARANTA or MARANTE, Roberto. Tractatus de ordine iudiciorum ... intitulatus Speculum Aureum et Lumen Aduocatorum. Venice [apud Cominum de Tridino], 1549. Device on title. Woodcut initials. Index. 172, [xl]pp. Some worming of inner margin; few holes in text in quires L-Q. Sl. frayed. Contemp. limp vellum, soiled & worn; loose in covers; lacks ties. **Not in B.M.C.** **£60.00**
Revised edition, with summaries & an index by Giambattista Ziletti, of a treatise on jurisdiction written in 1520-5. The author touches on usury ("a species of rapine"), the use of torture ("may be resorted to without evidence, if only used to gain an answer 'Yes' or 'No'") and the thousand-year-old struggle between the Lombardic & Roman codes for mastery in Italy.

278. MARCH, Joseph. Actions for Slander and Arbitrements. Ed. W. B[rown]. For Elizabeth Walbanck, 1674. 1st thus. Index. 320, 410-476, [xviii]pp. Foremargin of title defective, aff. border & one letter. Contemp. cf., sl. rbbd. **Wing M.573. S. & M. i. 247.** **£30.00**
First published in 1648, an early date for a monograph of this kind; its existence illustrates the extreme need for guidance through the absurdly over-refined criteria as to what words were or were not actionable.

279. MARCULFUS (fl. c. A.D.700). Marculfi monachi aliorumque auctorum formulae veteres ... Accessit liber legis Salicae. Ed. Jérome & Théodore Bignon. Paris (S. Cramoisy), 1665. 1st thus. 4to. **2 pts. in 1.** Index. [lx], 368, [xvi], 270pp. Lacks engr. port. Contemp. sprinkled cf., sp. gilt; sl. rbbd. **£50.00**
The formulae (or precedents of deeds) of Marculf are the most ancient records of French law in practice, and important guides to the social system of the time. They are here accompanied by two other collections of similar character, & by the laws of the Salic Franks, inhabitants of the Low Countries whence the Frankish nation drew its origin.

280. MARESCOTTO, Ercole. Variarum resolutionum liber primus, & secundus. Rome, 1614. 1st. **2 vols. in 1.** Folio. Red & black title. Indices. [xx], 224/[iv], 307, [cxliii]pp. Some browning. Contemp. vellum, re-backed; lacks ties; corners v. worn; sp. defective. **£40.00**
Observations founded on proceedings in the Vatican & Neapolitan courts, by a member of a celebrated Roman family.

281. MARINE SOCIETY. Bye-Laws and Regulations, 1809. 5th ed. Engr. fp. 180pp. Marginal repair to I_5. Contemp. tree cf., sp. gilt; sl. rbbd. **£20.00**
This ed. includes an account of the Society, which was formed by Sir John Fielding (the blind magistrate), Jonas Hanway, & others, to improve the mental & bodily health of boys & men in the Navy. It seems to have been the first recognition of the British sailor as a being possessed of human rights.

282. MARTINI, Fridericus. De Iure censuum, seu annuorum redituum ... commentarius. Freiburg im Breisgau, 1604. 1st. 4to. Red & black title. Index. [xlviii], 544, [lxxvi]pp. Final blank. Some browning. Tear in lower margin of V_4. Sm. hole in X_1. Contemp. vellum, paste-downs detached. £50.00
In Germany & Austria, it had become common for ecclesiastical bodies to sell the revenues of their estates to private persons for a lump sum. Papal intervention to prevent the abuse led to deep questioning on the nature of rents & revenues in general; this book is a contribution by a professor of canon law in the Freiburg University.

283. MASCOV, Johann Jakob (1689-1761). Principia iuris publici imperii Romano-Germanici ex ipsis legibus ... eruta. Leipzig, 1759. 5th ed. Index. [viii], 464, [xii]pp. Contemp. vellum, sl. soiled. Bk-pl. £15.00

284. MAZZEI, Francesco. De legitimo actionis spolii usu commentarius. Rome, 1773. 1st. 4to. Red & black title. Index. viii, 156pp. One quire loose. Later wraps; sp. torn. £20.00
The scope of the Actio spolii, or civil action to regain stolen property, had been obscured by a passage in the canon law which had lately been exposed as spurious.

285. MECKEN, Bodo Heinrich. Disputatio juridica de chirographo, praecipuè verò eo, quod per vim extortum esse dicitur. Jena, 1673. 1st. 4to. [40]pp. Mod. bds. £20.00
Doctoral thesis on the cases in which a deed was rendered invalid by duress of the signatory.

286. MELVILLE, Henry [Dundas], Viscount (1740-1811). The Trial by Impeachment. 1806. Engr. fp. port. Appendix of tables. iv, xcvi, 8, 3-230, 131-378, [viii]pp. Several irregularities caused by insertion of cancel leaves. Mod. ½ mor./bds. £15.00
Melville was acquitted (on a point of law only) of charges of converting public money to his own use while he was Treasurer to the Navy & a favoured colleague of the younger Pitt. The case, in which Sir Samuel Romilly led for the Crown, was a memorable revival of the half-forgotten system of impeachment.

287. METROPOLITAN RAILWAY CO. & METROPOLITAN DISTRICT RLY. CO. v. BURROW & BURROW. Petition of Appeal. N.d. [1884]. 1st. 4to. [ii], 10, 6, 288pp. Orig. cl., sl. mkd. & fdd. £10.00
A case touching on assessment of compensation for land purchased for railway purposes, taken before the Lords by the company. This volume (consisting largely of documents) was prepared jointly by the solicitors in the case, probably for the use of the Law Lords who were to hear it. It seems to be unreported.

288. MIDDLETON, Conyers (1683-1750). A Treatise on the Roman Senate. 1747. 1st complete. First advert. leaf. [ii], 196pp. – Remarks on Two Pamphlets ... against [the] Introductory Discourse. 1748. 1st. ½ title. [ii], xl, 128pp. – [STEBBING, Henry] Observations on ... An Introductory Discourse. 1747. 1st. 34pp. Three works in one vol. Mod. ¼ cf./mbld. sides. £40.00
The second part of the Treatise, being a discussion of the authority & procedure of the senate, is here added to an earlier publication. The rest of the collection is concerned with Middleton's attack on belief in the miraculous powers of the early Christians.

289. MILL, Job. The Present Practice of Conveyancing: or Select Precedents of Conveyances ... from ... Original Draughts. 1746. 1st. Lge. 4to. Index. [iv], 686, [xiv]pp. Sl. stnd. Advert. leaf before title. Contemp. cf., sp. sl. frayed, jts. rubbed. S. & M. i. 484. £30.00

290. MILLAR, John. Elements of the Law relating to Marine Insurances. Edinburgh, 1787. 1st. Index. xii, 560, [viii]pp. Lib. perforations on title & G_1. Quires 3G & 3H bound in reverse. Mod. cl. S. & M. i. 525. £25.00
Great advances in the law of insurance, as a branch of contract, were made under the jurisdiction and by the personal influence of Lord Mansfield; it is Millar's design to take account of these, and to keep abreast with the recent extension of insurance far beyond its marine origins.

291. MITFORD, John (Lord Redesdale). A Treatise on the Pleadings in ... Chancery, by English Bill. Dublin, 1789. 2nd ed. ½ title. Index. [xxii], 264, [xii]pp. Sl. stnd. Lib. perforation on title. Mod. cl. S. & M. i. 340. £15.00

292. MODERN REPORTS: or, Select Cases Adjudged ... since the Restoration. 1720[-25]. 3rd ed.. 3 vols. (1661-90). Folio. Indices. [xii], 314, [xxii]/[x], 322, [xx]/[xx], 338, [xl]pp. Vol. 1. sl. browned. Mod. cl. S. & M. i. 304. £50.00
The Modern Reports, which were finally (1682-1738) extended to twelve volumes of which these are the first three, are notoriously an incoherent & irregular series; but they are important as a hesitant step towards the codification of case law & the throwing-off of superannuated precedents. They also revived the principle (neglected since the collapse of the year-books) of reporting arguments as well as facts & judgments.

293. ——— Anr. copy. Pt. 3 (1682-1690) only. Folio. Index. [xx], 338, [xxxviii]pp. Contemp. cf., rbbd. £15.00

294. MOLLOY, Charles. De jure maritimo et navali; or, a Treatise of Affairs Maritime and of Commerce. For John Bellinger ... and John Walthoe, 1688. 4th. ed. Copper-engr. fp. & title. Index. [xxiv], 434, [xiv]pp. Sl. spotted. Mod. mottled cf., old upper cvr. preserved. S. & M. i. 511; Kress 1677. £95.00
The first of the three books treats of international law and naval administration, the second of commerce, the third of the law of aliens, merchants & colonization. "Policies of Assurance" are the subject of bk. 2 chap. 7.

295. MONACELLI, Francesco. Formularium legale practicum fori ecclesiastici. Rome, 1703. 1st. Folio. ½ title. Red & black title. Index. [lviii], 376pp. Stnd. at end; last seven leaves frayed without loss of text. Contemp. vellum, head of sp. defective, upper jt. cracked. £30.00
A book of precedents relating to ecclesiastical jurisdiction, with large annotations.

296. MONTESQUIEU, Charles de Secondat, Baron de (1689-1755). The Spirit of Laws ... Translated from the Edition published in Edinburgh in 1750. Aberdeen, 1756. 2 vols. 12mo. xxviii, 346, [ii]/xiv, [ii], 388pp. Name on titles. Few leaves of vol. 2. sl. stnd. Contemp. cf., spines gilt; jts. worn; labels defective. £20.00

297. MORGAN, John. Essays. Dublin, 1789. Vol. 3 (of 3) only. Narrow strip cut from title. Sl. browned. Mod. cl. S. & M. i. 379. £10.00
The bulk of Morgan's work dealt with the law of evidence; this volume includes the essays on special verdicts, trials at bar & repleaders, with part of that on new trials.

298. MOORE, Sir Francis, Serjeant-at-Law. Cases ... ore primierment Imprime. Ed. Sir Geoffrey Palmer. By R. Norton for Robert Pawlet, 1663. 1st. Folio. French text. Black letter. Engr. fp. port. (repaired.) Index. [xx], 918, [lxxiv]pp. Mod. ¼ cf./mbld. sides. Wing M.2535. S. & M. i. 305. £35.00
Moore gives cases in all four superior courts, many of them touching the application of Henry VIII's revolutionary land laws. These Reports are still of considerable authority.

299. ——— Anr. copy. Lacks port. Mod. cl. £30.00

300. MORONIUS, Nicolaus. Tractatus aureus de fide, Treugua, et pace. Venice (apud Damianum Zenarum), 1574. Second ed., rev. by the author. Index. Device on title. [xcvi], 426pp. Occasional light staining. Contemp. limp vellum; worn. Not in B.M.C. or Adams. £40.00
A treatise on oaths, obligations & feudal responsibilities, including much information on civil actions & commercial contracts. The author attended on the Vatican court, & his jurisprudence was of the old quibbling breed.

301. MORTIMER, Thomas (1730-1810). Lectures on the Elements of Commerce, Politics, and Finances; Intended as a Companion to Blackstone's Commentaries. 1801. 1st. List of subscribers. xxviii, 442pp. Final blank. Orig. bds., uncut; sp. sl. worn. Kress B.4422. Not in S. & M. £25.00

302. MOSAYCARUM ET ROMANARUM LEGUM COLLATIO, ex integris ... veterum juris auctorum libris ... desumpta ... Iustiniani Novellae ... Iuliani Antecessoris ... de Consiliariis [et] de Contutoribus. Heidelberg (S. Broun), 1656. Index. [xii], 241, [x]pp. Sm. piece cut from head of title. Mod. ¼ cf./mbld. sides. £20.00
These sources for the study of Roman jurisprudence before Justinian, & for the ancient laws regarding the guardianship of minors, were printed from MSS. collected by Pierre Pithou (1539-96), whose notes are included.

303. MURRAY of Glendook, Sir Thomas (ed.). The Laws and Acts of Parliament made by King James the First [to] King Charles the Second. Edinburgh, 1681. 1st. Engr. title. Red & black title. Engr. plate of arms & nine ports. Index. Pagination irregular. Leaf K_1 in dictionary defective with loss of half a column; blank margin of final attestation leaf defective; hole in margin of plate of arms. Mod. ¼ cf./mbld. sides. S. & M. v. 116. £50.00
Includes Skene's "De verborum significatione" (a dictionary of Scots law-terms), & an abridgment of the statutes.

304. NELSON, W[illiam] (c.1650-1730). The Office and Authority of a Justice of Peace ... shewing also the Duty of Constables, Commissioners of Sewers, Coroners, Overseers [etc.] 1724. 8th ed. First advert. leaf. [vi], 708pp. Sl. stnd. Contemp. cf., lower cvr. rbbd., re-backed. S. & M. i. 48. £30.00
In this edition Nelson professes to have taken particular care to insert all authoritative resolutions of the superior courts touching statutes; by this it was intended both to relieve magistrates from the labour of studying the statutes themselves and to prevent them from mistaking their statutory powers through misinterpretation.

305. NEVILE, Christopher. The New Poor Law Justified: with Suggestions for ... Insurance Offices for the Poor. 1838. 2nd ed. ii, 18pp. Stitching broken. Disbound. Not in Kress. £5.00
Defence of the "lesser eligibility" doctrine, apparently on the grounds that nobody ever gets into the "House" unless he is too lazy or thoughtless to keep himself out.

306. NONIUS, Tobias. Interpretationes in nonnullos Institutionum titulos. Venice (apud Dominicum Farreum), 1579. Device on title. Index. [xxiv], 310 leaves. L_{1-4} & L_{5-8} bound in reverse order. First quire sl. wormed. Sl. stnd. Contemp. vellum, worn & wormed. Not in B.M.C. or Adams. £50.00
Dissertations on wills & contracts, given in the author's youth in the law-school of Perugia. The preface is dated 1557, but we can find no record of any other edition before 1584.

307. NOODT, Gerard (1647-1725). Opera omnia, ab ipso recognita, aucta, emendata. Leyden, 1724. 1st collected. 2 vols. in 1. Folio. Red & black titles. Indices. [vi], 644, [xxiv]/[iv], 590, [xvi]pp. Few contemp. MS. corrections (not listed in errata). Fine copy in contemp. blind-stamped vellum. £90.00
Although superseded by Barbeyrac's two folios of 1735, this edition has the merit of embracing the first publication of Noodt's very influential commentary on books 1-27 of the Pandects, which he wrote between the ages of 68 & 77.

308. NOY, [Sir] William (Attorney-General) (1577-1634). Reports and Cases ... now translated. By F.L. for Matthew Walbancke ... and T. Firby, 1656. 1st. Folio. Black letter. Index. [xii], 185, [xi]pp. $2C_4$ blank. Some browning throughout. Mod. cl. Wing N.1449. S. & M. i. 200. £30.00
The editor represents that Noy's analysis of the pleadings is above that of any reporter since Plowden, & casts sidelong aspersions on the prolixity of Coke. This is probably a gesture of defiance against the republic; Noy was an unmitigated King's man, the real begetter of the disastrous ship-money legislation.

309. OBSERVATIONS on the Last Session of P–RL–M–NT. in a Letter from a Member to a Nobleman of Distinction. 1749. 1st. ½ title. 48pp. New grey bds. £10.00
Accuses the Ministry of irregularly dissolving Parliament, to avoid exposure of their negotiations with the Emperor Charles VII. at Hanau & their subservience to a military cabal.

310. ODGERS, W. Blake, & others. Six Lectures on the Inns of Court and of Chancery. 1912. 1st. Fold'g map. Index. [viii], 272pp. Lib. stamp on e-p. Orig. bds., sl. mkd. & fdd. £4.00

311. OKEDEN, D.O.P. A Letter to the Rev. Harry Farr Yeatman, on his Inquiry. Salisbury, 1833. 1st. 12pp. Sewn as issued. £4.00
An Asst. Poor Law Commissioner replies to a supporter of the old system. See YEATMAN.

312. The ORIGIN, OBJECT & OPERATION of the APPRENTICE LAWS. Pamphleteer, 1814. 1st. 217-242pp. Disbound. Title detached. £5.00
Arguments by a committee of London manufacturers against restrictive practices in trade.

313. OWEN, Aneurin (ed.). Ancient Laws and Institutes of Wales. Public Records Commission, 1841. 1st collected. 2 vols. Welsh, Latin & Engl. text. ½ titles. [xliv], 904/[xvi], 1128pp. Orig. cl., paper lables; sps. rbbd. Lib. labels; S. & M. i. 577. £60.00
This important edition supersedes that of Wotton (1730) in scope as well as in accuracy; it includes Edward I's Statuta Walliae, and distinguishes between the three provincial variants of the so-called Laws of Howel Dda, or the Good.

314. OWEN, Thomas. The Reports of ... one of the Justices of the Common Pleas. By T.R. for H. Twyford, T. Dring and J. Place, 1656. Folio. Black letter. Index. [xii], 158, [viii]pp. Pagination jumps from 76 to 81. Two sm. worm-holes throughout. Old annots. Contemp. sheep, re-backed; worn. Wing O.832. S. & M. i. 306. £35.00

315. OXFORD UNIVERSITY. A Catalogue of all Graduats [sic] in Divinity, Law, and Physick; and of all Masters of Arts & Doctors of Musick ... between October 10th 1659, and October 10th ... 1727. [Oxford], Clarendon Pr., 1727. 1st. [viii], 256pp. Sm. piece torn from A_2, affecting signature. Contemp. panelled cf., jts. sl. worn. Bk-pl. £20.00
A useful biographical source-book quoting the college, degree, & exact date of graduation. University officials from 1659, & M.P.s from 1603, are listed in an Appendix.

316. PARIS, J.A., & J.S.M. FONBLANQUE. Medical Jurisprudence. 1823. 1st. 3 vols. Appendix. Index. [iv], l, xvi, 440/[iv], 472/[iv], 154, [ii], 372pp. Mod. cl. S. & M. ii. 265. £50.00
The accent of this work is on medicine (and some wider science, notably relating to poisons) for the lawyer, rather than on law for the physician; it was one of the first publications of its kind, & provided much of the material from which the science of crime-detection was to grow.

317. The PARISH and the UNION; or, the Poor ... under the Old System and the New ... Evidence ... in the Reports of the Select Committee. 1837. 1st. Appendix, viii, 246pp. Orig. cl., fdd. Not in S. & M. £20.00
Charles Knight, the arch-purveyor of "useful knowledge", presided over this collection of evidence for and against the new poor law given before the Fazakerley Committee.

318. PARK, James Allan. A System of the Law of Marine Insurance. Philadelphia, 1789. 1st Amer. Index. [xxiv], xliv, 530, [xlvi]pp. Sl. spotted. Lib. perforation on title. Mod. cl. S. & M. i. 512. £20.00
Includes chapters on fire & life insurance.

319. PARKES, Samuel (1759-1825). Thoughts on the Laws relating to Salt: with Arguments for the Repeal of those Laws. 1817. 1st. Index. Adverts at end. 229, [ii]pp. Orig. bds., uncut. sp. defective; jts. worn. Kress B.7014. £30.00
The heavy salt-duty prevented the use of that mineral in many industrial & agricultural processes, which in consequence had to be laid aside or maintained with expensive materials from abroad. Parkes's facts & figures, by which even farmers could learn that protective duties were doing them no good, carried all the weight of his high reputation as a chemist.

320. PARTRIDGE, S.G. Prisoner's Progress. N.d. [1935.] 1st. Illus. Index. 288, 24pp. Orig. cl., sl. fdd. £12.00
A study of prisons & prisoners, crime detection & prevention, trials, & executions in the early nineteenth century.

321. PAUL, John. A Digest of the Game Laws ... with Notes. 1806. 4th ed., ed. J.I. Maxwell. [xviii], 138, [ii]pp. Final advert. leaf. Orig. wraps, uncut; sp. defective. S. & M. i. 466. £15.00

322. PEAKE, Thomas. A Compendium of the Law of Evidence. Philadelphia, Pa., 1807. 1st Amer. Vol. 2 (of 2) only. Index. [vi], viii, 428, [xvi]pp. Sl. spotted. Mod. cl. S. & M. i. 379. £8.00
Pleadings, actions in tort, bankruptcy, disputed wills, & actions against officers of law & of the church.

323. PEARS, Edwin (ed.). Prisons and Reformatories at Home and Abroad; being the Transactions of the International Penitentiary Congress ... July 3-13, 1872. 1872. 1st. xx, 796pp. xx, Orig. cl., fdd.; jts. worn; sl. shaken. £40.00
The congress was held at the instance of the U.S. government, Dr. E.C. Wines (q.v.) serving as commissioner to arouse European interest. Half the volume consists of reports from throughout Europe, Russia, & the U.S.A., & the rest of discussions, papers (including one by Edwin Chadwick) & a life of John Howard.

324. PEERE WILLIAMS, William. Reports of Cases Argued and Determined in ... Chancery, and of some Special Cases ... in ... King's Bench. 1768. 3rd ed. 3 vols. Folio. Indices. [xii], 788, [lxxxiv]/[viii], 756, [lxxiv]/[xvi], 504, [cxviii]pp. Contemp. cf., rbbd. jts. sl. worn. S. & M. i. 348. £50.00

325. ——— Anr. ed. (1st). 1740-49. Vols. 2 & 3 only (1722-1735). Privilege leaves. Indices. Mod. cl. £20.00

326. PECKIUS, P. Tractatus de amortizatione bonorum, a principe impetranda. Cologne, apud Ioannem Gymnicum, 1582. 1st. Index. [viii], 183, [v]pp. Margin of title repaired. Sl. stnd. Lacks e-p's. Contemp. vellum, lacks ties; sp. sl. defective. B.M.C. (Ger.) p.680. £70.00
An essay on the acquisition of real property by those bodies (especially churches & monasteries) which were reckoned under the heading of Manus mortuae. The subject was raised into prominence at the Reformation; to allow such acquisitions was injurious to the state, to forbid them disagreeable to the church; & the author, although a Catholic in the Spanish service, concludes that ecclesiastical bodies must continue, as was customary, to seek special permission for such proceedings.

327. PELHAM, Camden. The Chronicles of Crime; or, the New Newgate Calendar. 1841. 1st. 2 vols. Illus. (etched plates) H.K. Browne. Indices. xii, 592/viii, 636pp. Few plates sl. stnd. Mod. ¼ cf./cl. sides. £35.00

328. PELLEGRINO, Marcantonio. Tractatus ... de fideicommissis praesertim universalibus ... compluribus additamentis illustratus. Lyons, A. de Harsy, 1606. 4to. Red & black title with device; index. [viii], 1510, [xc]pp. Some browning throughout; sm. pieces torn from lower corners of three leaves; text not affected. Occasional tiny marginal worm-holes. 18th-cent. calf, gilt; re-backed & re-cornered. £50.00
The author of this treatise on trusts, wills & descents held official posts in Venice & Padua.

329. PEREZ, Antonio. Praelectiones in duodecim libros Codicis Iustiniani ... Editio nova, ab Auctore recognita & aucta. Amsterdam, Elzevir, 1661. 4to. 2

pts. in 1. Red & black title. Index. [xvi], 694/665, [lix]pp. Some early scoring & few annots. Contemp. (or orig.) blind-stamped vellum; sl. worn; sp. detached along upper joint. £60.00
The design of the author (a Spaniard who obtained a chair at Louvain) was to embrace all ages & to provide for all degrees of scholarship; he preserves many details of current French, German & Spanish practice. From a MS. note on the title-pages, it appears that the book was issued bound: "Available at 2 florins 20 stivers with the binding; bought at Leyden".

330. ———— **Institutiones imperiales erotematibus distinctae, atque ex . . . principiis, regulisque iuris, explicatae.** Leyden. 1689. New ed. 12mo. Engr. title. Index. 556, [iv]pp. Sl. stnd. towards end. Contemp. cf., jts. weak, ends of sp. torn. Bk-pl. £15.00
Intended to strike a medium between the barren summary of Wolfius & the learned commentaries, unfit for elementary use, of Cujacius & others.

331. P[HILIPOT], J[ohn], Somerset Herald. The Catalogue of the Lord Chancellors of England, the Lord Keepers . . . and the Lord Treasurers. By Tho. Cotes . . . Sold by Andrew Crooke, 1636. Sm. 4to. Woodcut arms (Howard) on A_4v. [viii], [ii], 93 [actually 82], 79-82, 85pp. Two quires signed M, the second of two leaves only. Corner of [2]M_2 defective without loss of text, & catchword shaved. Mod. ½ cf./mbld. sides. **S.T.C.19846. S. & M. i. 219.** £45.00

332. PHILLIMORE, Sir Robert (1810-1885). The Ecclesiastical Law of the Church of England. 1873. 1st. **2 vols.** Index. lxxx, 1074/[ii], 1075-2386pp. Sl. spotted. orig. cl., jts. & sps. worn; hinges repaired; fdd. **S. & M. ii. 279.** £20.00
Successor to Burn's work (q.v.). With the decline in scope & importance of ecclesiastical law, subsequent writers have been very much less copious than Phillimore; as Judge of the Admiralty Court (the last before the amalgamation) & Dean of Arches, he kept alive the old Doctors' Commons tradition.

333. PIGNORIO, Lorenzo (1591-1631). De servis, et eorum apud veteres ministeriis, commentarius. Padua, 1656. Second ed. Fp. port. Woodcuts in text. Indices. [ii], [xvi], 280, [viii], [xii]pp. Old ¼ parchment/mbld. sides; fdd. £35.00
A miscellaneous work, full of quotations & facsimiles of ancient coins, instruments, & sculptures relating to slaves & slavery in the ancient world.

334. PITTS, John W. Eleven Numbers against Lawyer Legislation and Fees at the Bar. N.p. [Athens, Ga?], 1843. 1st in bk. form. 48pp. Orig. printed wraps. sl. mkd. & stnd.; plastic folder. **Not in Sabin.** £50.00
Like Cato (or Theodore Roosevelt), Pitts desires that the horny-handed sons of toil, & not the doctors & drunkards (he evidently thinks these words synonymous) of the Bar & the colleges, should give laws to the nation; he wishes to exclude lawyers from Congress & prohibit their taking money for their work. Nos. 1-6 are reprinted from the Georgia "Southern Recorder"; the rest are new.

335. POLL-BOOK. [Poll for the County of Leicester.] N.p., n.d. [1720]. 1st. viii, 160pp. Title supplied in 19th-cent. MS. facs. Sl. browned. Later ½ cf./mbld. sides, sl. rbbd. £30.00
Candidates were Lord William Manners (elected, maj. 17) & F. Mundy. This copy belonged to one of Manners's agents, who has written "to be spoke to" or "sold" against the names of several men (tenants, no doubt) who voted for Mundy.

336. ———— A Copy of a Poll taken for the County of Derby . . . 1734. Nottingham, n.d. [1734]. 1st. [ii], 56, 38pp. Sl. browned. Later ½ cf./mbld. sides; sl. rbbd. £40.00
Lord Charles Cavendish & Sir Nathaniel Curzon (both in the Duke of Devonshire's interest) elected.

337. ———— The Poll for a Knight of the Shire, to Represent the County of Leicester . . . 1775. Leicester, 1775. 1st. 4to. Two fold'g tables. [vi], 132pp. Later ½ cf./mbld. sides; sp. defective. £25.00

338. ———— The Poll at the Electing of Two Knights of the Shire to Represent the County of Leicester . . . 1830. Leicester, 1830. 1st. 4to. Index. [viii], 132pp. Contemp. ½ cf./mbld. sides; jts. rbbd. £20.00
First contested election since 1775 (see above).

339. POPHAM, Sir John (C.J.) (c.1531-1607). Reports and Cases . . . now faithfully Translated. By Tho. Roycroft for Henry Twyford and John Price, 1656. 1st. Folio. Black letter. Index. [viii], 212, [viii]pp. Some old annots. Sl. browned. Title sl. frayed. Lib. stamp on title. Mod. cl. **Wing P.2942. S. & M. i. 305.** £30.00
Includes a description of the coifing of ten Serjeants in 1594, with Popham's speech on that occasion.

340. PORCHUS, [Johannes] Christophorus. Lectura . . . super primo secundo & tertio institutionum cu additionibus . . . Jasonis de Mayno. [Arte & industria . . . Andree parmeñ. de soziis Venetijs . . . Mccccl xxxiiii.] [Venice, A. de Soziis, 24th Dec. 1484.] Folio. Latin text. Gothic (rotunda) letter. Double column. 66 lines. 136 leaves. Final register leaf with device. Leaf a_1 in red & black, preceded by gathering of two leaves (1 with printer's advertisement on verso, 2 blank) within two conjugate blanks. Leaf f_1 signed k_1. **Hain 13293. Goff P.398 (2 copies only). B.M.C.V. 398. – SANCTO BLASIO, Baptista de.** Tractatus de actionibus et natura earum: super arbore Johãnis actionum. [Impensa et diligentia . . . Erhardi ratdolt . . . Venetijs . . . [m.cccc.] lxxxj.] Venice, E. Ratdolt, 5th May 1481. 1st. Folio. Latin text. Gothic (rotunda) letter. 61 lines. 26 leaves including first blank. Woodcut initials. First quire (preface and "tree", or table, of actions) printed on vellum in red & black, with a small woodcut. **Hain 3237. Goff S.126. B.M.C.V.284. – MAYNO, Jason de.** De iure emphiteotico. [Impressum . . . in . . . bononia per Ugonem de rugerijs . . . 1481.] Bologna, Ugo de Rogeriis, 27th Mar. 1481. 1st. Folio. Latin text, Gothic (rotunda) letter. Double column. 66 lines. Index. 66 leaves, incl. first & final blanks. Capital spaces. Signature-holes in fore-margins. Sl. wormed at end. **Hain 10960; not in Goff or B.M.C. Three works in one volume.** Large copies. Occasional marginal browning. Lib. stamp on a_1 of first work. Ownership inscription of Johann Schrenk (after 1482), with annots. by him & another. Contemp. oak bds., wormed, lacking clasps, one corner damaged; newly re-backed pigskin. £1,500.00
Three commentaries on civil law by professors in the Pavia university, where Johann Schrenk tells us that he attended Jason de Mayno's morning lectures in 1482. The first work contains a printer's advertisement (omitted from the Register, & therefore not intended to be bound in), where Andreas de Soziis boasts (evidently out of chagrin at having to grant priority to a German) that the improver of the art of printing, i.e. himself, deserves at least as much credit as the originator. The second item (a commentary on actions at law with a schematic table ascribed to "Johannes", which doubtless means the great 13th-century jurist Johannes Andreae) is generally found issued with other tracts by the same author; but it has its own colophon.

341. POSTIUS, Ludovicus. De subhastatione tractatus . . . Huic editioni accesserunt eiusdem auctoris additamenta. Coloniae Allobrogum [Geneva] (J.A. & S. de Tournes), 1671. Folio. 3 pts. in 1. Red & black title. ½ title. Index. [vi], 446, 72, [xvi], [iv], 93-284, [xxxii]pp. Some browning. Inner margins of about 30 leaves wormed, slightly affecting text. New ¼ cf./mbld. sides. **Not in Kress or Goldsmith.** £60.00
Revised ed. of an early work on auction sales, first published in 1644. The author, assisted by his nephew Gianfrancesco, adapted his method from the practice of Rome, Perugia, Bologna, & Macerata; and there is an appendix of relevant test cases in the Roman courts.

342. PREVOTIUS (Prévost), Claudius. Commentarius de magistratibus pop. Rom. ex variis authoribus collectus. Lausanne (F. le Preux), 1579. 1st. Latin text. [viii], 188, [iv]pp. Final blank. Contemp. English cf., central blind-stamp; head of sp. defective; lower corners worn. **Not in B.M.C.** £40.00
A simple summary, posthumously edited by the municipal printer of Berne from his Lausanne office.

343. PRIDEAUX, Humphrey. The Original and Right of Tithes . . . Truly stated. To which is Annex'd the Draught of a Bill . . . for the Restraining of Pluralities of Benefices. 1736. 2nd ed., rev. [xvi], 256pp. Sl. stnd. Mod. tree cf., sp. sl. rbbd. Bk-pl. Lord Selborne L.C. **S. & M. i. 193.** £20.00
Although a bigot in many ways, Prideaux abandons the position of divine right & argues the case on historical & rational grounds.

344. PRINCIPLES of the LAWS of ENGLAND . . . and Practice of the Superior Courts: in . . . Question and Answer. 1839. 1st. iv, 384pp. Orig. cl., mkd. & fdd. **S. & M. iii. 186.** £10.00
Designed to instruct articled clerks for the examinations lately instituted.

345. PRIVY COUNCIL. Printed form of summons to a meeting of the Privy Council at Whitehall, with date & subject of discussion filled in by hand. 9th. July, 1778. Single leaf. £10.00
The recipient was probably William de Grey, 1st Baron Walsingham (formerly Chief Justice C.P.). The subject of debate was "plantation affairs"; in other words, the Council was to exercise its judicial powers in respect of offences committed & actions disputed in the colonies, which doubtless included America.

346. PROPOSALS Concerning the CHANCERY, wherein is set forth the Desires of Divers Well-affected-Persons, for the Regulating of the High-Court of Chancery . . . and Abolishing the Severall Fees, Offices and Officers. By William Ellis . . . Sold by George Badger, 1650. 1st. Sm. 4to. Fold'g table of fees. [ii], 28pp. Catchword subjoined to last leaf in reference to the table, which is in fact bound before. Mod. ¼ cl./mbld. sides. **Wing P.3718. S. & M. i. 344 (title inaccurately cited).** £50.00
The Six Clerks' Office, its inflated fees and its incompetent officers, is the author's particular ground of objection; in general he condemns the isolation of the Court, whereby monopolists & placemen are shut in & accomplished lawyers shut out.

347. PRUSSIA, Constitution of. Die Reform der preussischen Verfassung. Leipzig, 1870. 1st. German text. x, 273pp. **Inscribed** by the author to Prince Christian of Schleswig-Holstein, with the book-plate of the latter. Mod. ½ cf./mbld. sides. £30.00
The author's purpose is to strengthen the Prussian-led North German Confederation against French pressure, & to speed the union of Germany, by creating a constitutional monarchy on the English pattern. Schleswig-Holstein, a recent bone of contention between Austria & Prussia, inevitably had a deep interest in such a scheme.

348. PUFENDORF, Samuel (1632-1694). Elementorum iurisprudentiae universalis libri II. The Hague (A. Vlacq), 1660. 1st. [xii], 384, [ii]pp. Errata leaf. Fine copy in contemp. vellum. £60.00
Pufendorf's first work. He investigated the nature of right & wrong, in principle & action, according to the logical scheme of his old master, the geometrician Weigel; embraced all that he had learned from Grotius, from Hobbes, & from his own experience of human conduct in wartime (Dano-Swedish hostilities condemned him to custody & so gave him leisure to write), & established his reputation for ever. The publisher Adrian Vlacq was a noted mathematician, & shares with Henry Briggs the merit of establishing the first substantial tables of logarithms.

349. ———— De jure naturae et gentium libri octo, cum annotatis Joannis Nicolai Hertii. Amsterdam, 1715. 4to. Engr. fp. port. Red & black title. Index. [x], 929, [vii], 142pp. $V_{1\text{-}4}$ bound before $V_{1\text{-}2}$. Contemp. sprinkled cf., rbbd., ends of sp. & corners worn. £40.00
In his youth Pufendorf was an assiduous student of Hobbes. Without following his master to every cynical & splenetic conclusion, he applied his methods of mathematical precision to dispel the visionary clouds which had previously enveloped the subject, and have often done so since. This edition of Hertius (first printed in 1706) appears to have been the first with annotations.

350. ———— Of the Law of Nature and Nations. Eight Books. Ed. Jean Barbeyrac; tr. Basil Kennett. 1729. 4th ed., enlarged. Folio. Index. [xxiv], [iv], 88, 878, [xxii]pp. Title & last leaf cut round & mounted. New ¼ calf/mbld. sides. £40.00
This edition includes Barbeyrac's Historical Account of Morality, translated by Thos. Carew.

351. ———— **De officio hominis & civis,** juxta legem naturalem, libri duo. Cambridge, ex officina Joan. Hayes, 1682. [xxii], 164, [ii]pp. Final advert. leaf. Mod. ½ cf./cl. sides. **Wing P.4174.** £25.00
Pufendorf's own digest of his great work.

352. ———— Anr. ed. Cambridge, 1701. [xxiv], 162, [iv]pp. Copious contemp. annots. (complete transcript of treatise **de Moribus,** attr. to Seneca.) Title ruled. Contemp. cf., later label; jts. rbbd. £20.00

353. PULTON, Ferdinando (ed.). A Kalender, or Table, comprehending the Effect of all the Statutes . . . beginning with Magna Charta . . . whereunto is annexed an Abridgement of all the Statutes. For the Company of Stationers, 1608. [2nd ed., rev.] Folio. Black letter. Index. [vii], 449, [iii] leaves. Lacks first blank. $3U_{1\text{-}4}$ reversed, & the latter mis-signed $3S_4$. 19th-cent. ½ vellum/mbld. sides; sl. rbbd. **S.T.C. 9548. S. & M. i. 565.** £100.00
An abridgment in two parts, the usual subject-classification being preceded by a chronological summary (the "Kalender" proper) which helpfully includes repealed, expired, private, & standing but unenforced statutes, each with a distinguishing mark.

354. RAMSEY, William. The Whole Proceedings on the King's Commission of the Peace, Oyer and Terminer, and Gaol Delivery for . . . London, and also the Gaol Delivery for . . . Middlesex . . . in the Mayoralty of . . . Sir Richard Carr Glyn. 1798-9. 1st. **8 pts. in 1 vol.** 4to. Index. 668pp. Sl. browned & spotted. Mod. cl. **Not in S. & M.** £40.00
See HODGSON for a note on the Old Bailey reports.

355. RASTELL, William [later Sir William] (1508-1565) (ed.). Natura brevium. The olde tenures. Lyttylton tenures. The new talys. The articles uppon the new talys. Diversyte of courtes. Justyce of peace. The chartuary. Court baron. Court of hundrede. Returna brevium. The ordynaunce for takynge of fees in the escheker. [By W. Rastell . . . 1534.] 1st collected. Gothic (rotunda) letter. Index. [xxviii], 424pp. Few old annots. Sm. hole in $2H_2$ with loss of few letters (supplied in contemp. MS.); otherwise a fine copy in old calf, re-backed, panels of 16th-cent. French binding (blind-stamped with two medallion-busts & border) set into sides. Edges worn. **Beale T.1. S.T.C.18394. S. & M. i. 183.** £750.00
A collection of twelve law-treatises, being in effect almost all the text-books then in use. "New Talys" is "Novae Narrationes", a fourteenth-century collection of statements of claim on sundry writs; the Chartuary is a collection of forms of deeds showing how conveyancing was done before the Statute of Uses; the rest are familiar or self-evident. John Rastell and his son William brought a welcome element of scholarship to English law-printing. Both were barristers, and William, who abandoned his trade after printing this book, lived to be a justice of Common Pleas; but as a staunch Catholic (his father married the sister of St. Thomas More) he was forced into exile in 1558, & died in Louvain.

356. RAYMOND, Robert, Lord (Chief Justice, K.B.). Reports of Cases . . . in . . . King's Bench and Common Pleas. 1743. 1st. **Vol. 1 (of 2) only.** Folio. Index. [xiv], 746, [xlvi], [ii]pp. Mod. cl. **S. & M. i. 307.** £10.00
Cases 1689-1702, many of them preserving judgments & dicta of Holt C.J.

357. REPORTS of CASES Taken and Adjudged in the Court of CHANCERY, in the Reign of . . . Charles I[-William and . . . Mary] . . . Arguments relating to . . . the said Court, its Dignity, Power & Jurisdiction. By the Assigns of Richard and Edward Atkins . . . for John Walthoe, 1693[-4]. 1st. **2 vols.** Indices. [xlvi], 288, 88/[xvi], 304, 353-437, [xix]pp. Sigs. in vol. 2 jump from U to 2A, with corresponding gap in pagination; nothing missing. Some browning. Vol. 1 cf., re-backed; vol. 2 contemp. cf., rbbd. **Wing. R.1090; S. & M. i. 348.** £35.00
The reports are generally brief, & uninformative on the arguments used; but vol. 1 contains an important discussion of the relation, then still in a formative state; between Chancery and other courts. Against Coke, & notwithstanding two old statutes alleged to the contrary, the author supports a personal decision of James I, that judgments in King's Bench etc. could be modified in the courts of equity.

358. REYNOLDS, John. The Triumphs of Gods Revenge against the . . . Sinne of (Wilful and Premeditated) Murther. For William Lee, 1635. [Third ed.] Folio. Engr. title. **6 parts (some dated 1634) in 1.** [xxviii], 464pp. Anti-Papal reference on p.180 inked out. Few marginal tears. Contemp. cf., re-backed.; sl. rubbed. **S.T.C.20944** (var. imprint to bk.1). £85.00
Fictional narratives, whose style is that of the French romances, but whose content that of the older tragedies. The moral element (although attested by the Archbishop of Canterbury) vanishes after the preface.

359. ROALFE, Matilda. Law Breaking Justified. Edinburgh, 1844. 1st. 16pp. Disbound. £6.00
The author, an agitator for atheism, argues vigorously from ancient precedent against the blasphemy laws, & condemns the early Socialists for selling out to Christianity.

360. ROBERTS, Samuel. A Digest of Select British Statutes . . . which, according to the Report of the Judges . . . appear to be in Force in Pennsylvania. Pittsburgh, Pa., 1817. 1st. Index. xx, 442, [ii]pp. Sl. stnd. Lib. perforation on title. Mod. cl. £20.00

361. ROBINSON, Christopher. Reports of Cases Argued and Determined in the High Court of Admiralty. 1806[-8.] Vol. 1 3rd ed., vol. 2 2nd ed., remainder 1st. **5 vols. (of 6.)** Indices. Lib. stamps at intervals. Mod. cl., sl. fdd. **S. & M. i. 355.** £40.00
The Admiralty Court, a placid nest of sinecures for the most part, enjoyed a vast access of business arising from the war at sea against Napoleon. These volumes cover the greater part of this period (1798-1804); a sixth vol. appeared in 1808.

362. [ROLLE, Sir Henry]. [Abridgment des Plusieurs Cases et Resolutions. 1668. 1st.] **Vol. 2 (of 2) only.** Folio. French text. Black letter. Without title, as issued. 836, [viii]pp. Contemp. sheep, sp. sl. worn. **S. & M. i. 19.** £20.00
Rolle's Abridgment follows the pattern of Brooke by adding fresh material from the records of Parliament & from the author's own experience to the existing structure.

363. ROPER, R.S. Donnison. A Treatise upon the Law of Legacies. 1804. 2nd ed., rev. **2 vols.** Index. xvi, 522/[ii], 598, [xxxii], [ii]pp. Sl. spotted. Contemp. cf., rbbd. **S. & M. ii. 306.** £20.00

364. ROSCOE, Henry. Eminent British Lawyers. (Cabinet Cyclopaedia, Biography.) 1833. Engr. title (sl. stnd.) [ii], 428, [ii]pp. Strip torn from printed title aff. first word. Orig. cl., mkd. & fdd. **Not in S. & M.** £6.00
Fourteen judges & jurists from Coke to Romilly.

365. ROSE, John. A Constitutional Catechism . . . with copious Notes, Principally Extracted from the Commentaries of the late Judge BLACKSTONE, Bristol, 1795. 1st. viii, 87pp. Contemp. ½ cf./mbld. sides; rbbd. **S. & M. i. 106.** £10.00

366. RUGGLE, George (c.1575-1622). Ignoramus, comoedia ... cum notis historicis et criticis ... accurante Johanne Sidneio Hawkins. 1787. 1st thus. Latin text with English annots. Engr. fp. Woodcuts in text. viii, cxxii, [ii], 320pp. H_2 torn without loss. Mod. ¼ cf./mbld. sides. **S. & M. i. 241. £30.00**
Ruggle's Ignoramus, written in about 1612, is a quaint by-product of the ancient enmity between the academics & the common lawyers; it holds up the language & style of the law to ridicule in a framework derived from Terence & the Italian comedy. Hawkins's edition includes a copious life of the author, notes, and a glossary.

367. SACHEVERELL, Henry (1672-1724). The Tryal ... before the House of Peers, for High Crimes and Misdemeanors. 1710. 1st. Folio. First privilege leaf. 328pp. MS. index of counsel etc. on e-p's. Contemp. panelled cf., sp. gilt; jts. worn. **£50.00**
Sacheverell was impeached for preaching against the toleration of dissenters, the justice of the revolution of 1688, & the conduct of the government. He suffered a mild sentence, and became a national hero for his supposed defence of Church & people against tyranny & corruption.

368. [SADLER, J.]. Rights of the Kingdom: or, Customs of our Ancestors, Touching the Duty, Power, Election or Succession of our Kings and Parliaments. For J. Kidgell, 1682. 4to. [viii], 200, 209-320pp. Signatures jump from 2C to 2E through change of printer; pagination correspondingly irregular. Strip torn from $2G_3$ aff. few letters of seven lines. Corner of title torn away. Mod. ½ cf./cl. sides. **Wing S.279. S. & M. i. 106. £50.00**
Amid much folly (e.g. that the Lords had no right to legislative power but usurped it in Stephen's time, that Gildas is an authority for the origin of Parliament, & that the end of the world is near) Sadler offers some good sense on the rights of the Commons – most especially in their judicial capacity – & the contractual obligations (which he treats as explicit in the Coronation oath) of King & people. His theory of the constitution was admired by Locke.

369. [SAINT GERMAN, Christopher] (?-1540)]. The dyaloges in Englishe, betwene a Doctour of divinitie, and a Student in the lawes of Englande. [Aedibus Richard Totteli, an. 1554.] [2nd English collected ed.] Black letter. Woodcut title-border, inverted (McK.48), & initials. Index. 176, [iv] leaves. Sl. stnd. at end, but a fine copy in mod. cf. **Beale T.473; S.T.C.21571; S. & M. i. 23. £250.00**

370. ——— Anr. ed. By the Assignes of John More, 1638. 176, [iv] leaves. Later sheep, rbbd., jts. worn. **S.T.C.21582; S. & M. i. 25. £60.00**

371. ——— Anr. ed. 1721. 12mo. Index. [xii], 366, [xl]pp. Contemp. cf., re-bkd., rbbd. **S. & M. i. 25. £30.00**
St. German, the modest & judicious adversary of St. Thomas More, is the most philosophical of our early lawyers; much of his work is devoted to reconciling common law with the law of nature & the dictates of ethics, & he discusses many points of land law & ecclesiastical law from this point of view. His arguments on the doctrine of consideration in contract (ii.24) are of particular interest; he suggests (in anticipation of Lord Mansfield) that moral obligations ought to suffice to make a good contract, & tells us that in the ecclesiastical courts they would in fact support an action – a fact which seems to have escaped the notice of Lord Wright & others who have discussed the subject.

372. ST. MARY-LE-BONE, Parish of (Middlesex). Acts of Parliament for Regulating the Affairs of the Parish. 1841. 1st collected, Index. 518pp. Opinions of the Solicitor-General & Attorney-General on the election of vestrymen under the Metropolis Management Act 1855 in view of the decision in *R.v. Churchwardens of St. Pancras* (1855, folio; 2 printed & 1 blank leaf, folded) inserted. Contemp. cf., rbbd., sp. & jts. worn. Ex-St. Mary-le-Bone Vestry Lib. **£20.00**
Comprehensive view of Mid-Victorian local government, including poor-law administration.

373. SALKELD, William (Sergeant-at-law.) (1671-1715.). Reports of Cases Adjudged in ... King's Bench, with some Special Cases in ... Chancery, Common Pleas, and Exchequer. 1718. 1st. **Vol. 2 (of 2)** (L-W and Pleadings) only. Folio. Index. [xii], 411-794, [cx]pp. Contemp. cf., re-backed, rbbd. **S. & M. i. 308. £10.00**

374. ——— Reports ... in One Volume Complete. Ed. George Wilson. 1773. 1st thus. Lge. 4to. Indices. First privilege leaf. [xii], [250], [x], [238], [viii], [232], [lxx]pp. Contemp. cf., rbbd., jts. worn. **S. & M. i. 308. £20.00**

375. SCHIEFER, J.F. An Explanation of the Practice of Law containing the Elements of Special Pleading ... Elements of a Plan for Reform. Dublin, 1793. Index. xxxii, 340pp. A_8 sl. rbbd. Margin torn from D_7, just touching text. Sl. stnd. throughout. Lib. perforation on title. Mod. cl. **S. & M. ii. 83. £20.00**
A sarcastic exposure of the law's delay, with proceedings on the part of plaintiff and of defendant arranged on opposite pages to show the waste of time & money on each hand.

376. SCHILTER, Johannes (1632-1705). Thesaurus antiquitatum Teutonicarum ... castigavit ... notas ... addidit Joannes Georgius SCHERZIUS. Ulm (D. Bartholomaeus), 1727[-8.] 1st Folio. **3 vol.** Latin & Old & Middle High German text. General title & fp. bound with vol. 3, as issued. Individual titles, some dated 1726. Indices. Few plates after ancient MSS. Few lib. stamps. Title of vol. 1 backed. Contemp cf., sps. & edges rubbed & worn. **Brunet V.212. £120.00**
A collection of immense importance for early German history, language & literature. Among the contents are the metrical gospels of Otfridus, the earliest monuments of the German tongue; the Salic Law, corrected from a MS. in the royal library of Paris; the Alemannic Landrecht, falsely ascribed to Charlemagne, collated from twelve MSS.; and a number of early poems, Biblical paraphrases, & translations. Vol. 3 is a dictionary of early German.

377. SCHOTANUS, Bernardus. Animadversiones in Julii Pacii analysin institutionum imperialium. Utrecht, 1706. New ed., rev. Red & black title. Index. [xvi], 1080pp. Folding table. Some browning. Contemp. vellum. **£35.00**
This book, which forms a general ground-work to the civil law, was a minor battery in the struggle which Cornelius Bynkershoek was then waging to establish in Holland a rational code on the Roman pattern. This is clear from Schotanus's preface, which laments the licence given to the caprice of individual judges in the existing confusion.

378. SCHULTING, Anton (1659-1734) (ed.). Jurisprudentia vetus ante-Justinianea. Leyden, 1717. 1st collected. 4to. Red & black title. Index. [lviii], 941, [lxxxi], [ii]pp. Lacks blank*******$_2$. Final blank. Fine copy in contemp. mottled cf., sp. gilt; sl. rubbed; head of sp. sl. torn. **£100.00**
The standard collection of Roman law before Justinian until the nineteenth century, when Mai's discoveries transformed our knowledge of the Institutes of Gaius. Schulting offers the remains of Gaius, Julius, Paulus, Ulpian, Dositheus, Papinian, the Gregorian & Hermogenian Codes, etc.

379. ——— Anr. ed. Editio nova ... Praefatus est D. Georgius Henricus Ayrer. Leipzig, 1737. 4to. Index. Engr. vignette on *$_2$. [lxxxvi], 941, [lxxix]pp. Lacks blank a_1. Some browning. Contemp. tree cf., gilt, arms of Nijmegen (Noviomagus) on sides; sl. rubbed. **£70.00**
Includes variants in the texts of Gaius, Julius Paulus, & the two early Codes, from Würzburg & Gotha MSS. Nijmegen was the home town of Schulting's family.

380. SCOTLAND. The Actis of Parliament of the maist hie, maist excellent, and michtie Prince ... James the sext ... King of Scottis, begun and haldin at Edinburgh, the xv. day of Decemb. the 3eir ... ane thousand, fyve hundretth lxvii. [Edinburgh, R. Lekprevik, 1568.] 1st. Sm. Folio. Black letter. Large woodcut (cropped) on title. 23 [of 25] leaves. Lacks F_1 & F_4 (final leaf). One corner of C_1 repaired; text not affected. 16th-cent. MS. notes pointing out the two missing leaves. Some staining. Mod. ¼ cf./mbld. sides. **S.T.C.21880 (B.L. & Huntington only.) S. & M. v. 110. £150.00**
In this first Parliament of James VI. (James I of England) the unfortunate queen Mary, then held prisoner at Lochlevin Castle, surrendered her throne to the infant James; the Romish religion which she had chosen was forever extinguished in the land; and the Earl of Murray, as regent, laid a path towards the restoration of order by enactments for reform of the coinage & for the suppression of Border bandits.

381. ——— Registrum magni sigilli regum Scotorum in archivis publicis asservatum. A.D. MCCCVI-A.D. MCCCCXXIV. Ed. T. Thomson. 1814. 1st. Folio. Latin text. Index. Five engr. facs. plates. xiv, 256, 48pp. Mod. ½ cf./mbld. sides. **S. & M. v. 96. £50.00**
Texts of charters granted under the Great Seal of the Scottish kings from 1306 to 1424, illustrating the nature of tenancy in chief, the position of religious houses, etc. under Robert Bruce & his successors. The series was extended as far as 1668 over the next hundred years.

382. SELDEN, John (1584-1654). Titles of Honor. By William Stansby for John Helme, 1614. 1st. Sm. 4to. Glossary of oriental names. Index. [xxxviii], 391, [xlii]pp. Lacks blanks A_4 & $3K_2$. Two leaves sl. mkd. Sm. hole in C_2 aff. few letters. Contemp. cf., head of sp. repaired; edges rubbed. **S.T.C. 22177. £120.00**
The first of Selden's great historical works, displaying his deep & various reading & the wide-ranging comparison between the customs of diverse races & ages which raises him to the rank of a valuable social historian. Ben Jonson contributes a long eulogy in verse.

383. ——— Titles of Honor. William Stansby for Richard Whitakers, 1631. Second ed. Sm. folio. Red & black title. Text woodcuts & engrs. Old annots. Sm. hole in $4D_3$ aff. two lines of text. [xxxvi], 941, [i]pp. Lacks final blank. Contemp. sprinkled cf.; jts. weak. Bk-pl. Alexander Thomson. **S.T.C. 22178. S. & M. i. 208. £100.00**

384. ——— Anr. copy. Final blank. Old cf., worn; re-backed. **£100.00**
This edition was greatly enlarged.

385. ——— The Historie of Tithes. 1618. 1st published. Sm. 4to. Red & black title. [vi], xxii, 491, [vi]pp. Marginal repair to last leaf. 19th-cent. ½ cf./mbld. sides. Bk-pl. Earl of Selborne. **S.T.C.22172. S. & M. i. 94. £100.00**
Selden designed an impartial history; but his great learning (& his natural bias towards the civil side) exposed so many irregularities in the theory & ancient practice of tithes that he was accused as a blasphemer by the church, & acclaimed as a prophet by the Quakers & dissenters. He was obliged to clear himself before the church authorities. Lord Selborne, the Lord Chancellor responsible for the revolutionary Judicature Acts of the 1870s, himself wrote a book on tithes in 1888.

386. ——— Anr. copy. Some head-lines cropped. Light stns. at end. 18th-cent. ¼ sheep/mbld. sides, jts. worn. Bk-pl. Thomas, Earl of Haddington (d.1735). **£90.00**

387. ——— De dis Syris syntagmata II. **Adversaria** nempe de numinibus ... in Veteri Instrumento memoratis. Leyden (Elzevir), 1629. 2nd ed., rev. Latin text. Red & black title. [xl], 373, [i]pp. Title sl. browned. 19th-cent. cf., rbbd., head of sp. torn. **Willems 322. £60.00**
This edition was greatly enlarged, partly to satisfy the request of the Elzevirs & partly to silence the partisans of a German jurist, Faber, who had written on the same subject. Milton drew many names & attributes of the heathen gods in "Paradise Lost" bk. II from this work.

388. ——— The Priviledges of the Baronage of England, when they Sit in Parliament. By T. Badger for Matthew Walbanck, 1642. 1st. [vi], 168pp. Publisher's cat. printed on back pastedown. Contemp. (orig.?) sheep, re-backed, edges rbbd. **Wing S.2434. S. & M. i. 208. £70.00**
This little work is a parergon from Selden's study of the parliamentary records. The publisher's catalogue is by far the earliest example known to us of a list printed separately, as opposed to the common type which forms a part of the collation of the book; its position seems to indicate that the book was bound by the printer.

389. ——— Vindiciae secundum integritatem existimationis suae, per convitium de scriptione Maris Clausi ... laesae. Apud Cornelium Bee, 1653. 1st. [iv], 64pp. **Wing S.2444.**
EUTYCHIUS, Patriarch of Alexandria. Ecclesiae suae origines. Excudebat Richardus Bishopus. 1642. 1st. Latin & Arabic text. [ii], xxxviii, 184pp. **Two works in one vol.** Contemp. vellum; lib. stamp & labels. **£120.00**
Selden denies suggestions made by Grotius's defenders that he had written the Mare Clausum as flattery to Charles I., hoping for a pardon when he was in prison. The other work (bound first) is a tenth-century Church history, valuable for its information on the eastern sects from their own point of view.

390. ——— Uxor Ebraica, seu de nuptiis et divortiis ex iure civili ... Ebraeorum, libri tres. Frankfurt am Oder, 1673. New ed. 4to. **2 pts. in 1.** Index. [xxiv], 456 [i.e. 464], [xvi], 248, [viii]pp. Sl. browned. Contemp. vellum; lib. stamps & labels. **£80.00**
Edited by J.C. Beckmann. Also includes the works De successionibus ... in bona defunctorum, & De successionibus in pontificatum.

391. ——— De synedriis et praefecturis juridicis veterum Ebraeorum, libri tres. Amsterdam, 1679. 4to. New ed. ½ title. [xii], 361, [viii], 428, [xii], 266, [xii]pp. Contemp. vellum; lib. labels. **£60.00**
A work on the civil laws & government of the Jews, begun as early as 1638, but never completed.

392. ——— Tracts ... Jani Anglorum Facies Altera ... [tr. & ed.] Redman Westcot ... England's Epinomis ... Original of Ecclesiastical Jurisdiction ... Administration of Intestates Goods. For Thomas Basset and Richard Chiswell, 1683. 1st collected. Lacks port. [ii], [xxxii], 132, [viii], 40, [iv], 24pp. Title sl. frayed. Mod. ¼ cf./mbld. sides. **Wing S.2441a. £60.00**
First ed. of all except the first item.

393. ——— Opera omnia, tam edita quam inedita ... collegit ac recensuit ... David Wilkins. 1726. 1st collected. **3 vols.** Folio. Latin & Engl. text. Lacks fp. port. Few text engrs. Contemp. cf., rbbd.; two jts. sl. torn. **S. & M. i. 36. £120.00**
This edition by the learned editor of the Leges Anglo-Saxonicae is not yet superseded for reference; it is furthermore a monument of typography, for which William Caslon cut his roman & other types.

394. ——— Anr. copy. **Vol. 3 only (in 2 pts.)** Few copper-engrs. & woodcuts in text. Index. Contemp. cf., worn, jts. weak. **£20.00**
Includes all the English works, notably the History of Tithes, Titles of Honour, & Table Talk.

395. SELECT COMMITTEE on POOR RATE RETURNS. Report. 1822. 1st. Folio. 44pp. – Supplemental Appendix. 1822. 1st. Folio. 240pp. – **A BILL** to Amend the Laws regarding ... the Poor. N.d. [1822]. 1st. Folio. 26pp. **Two works (three parts) in one vol.** Mod. ½ cf./cl. sides. **£20.00**
All this material relates to the attempt to take an accurate account of money received for, & actually spent on, the poor. The Appendix gives returns from every parish from 1816 to 1821, & the Bill proposes to make vestrymen responsible for disbursing the poor-rate.

396. SERJEANTS' INN. Old Serjeants' Inn, Chancery Lane. Law Union & Rock Insurance Co., 1912. 1st. Privately printed. Five col. plates of arms, & other illus. 54pp. orig. b'ram, t.e.g.; sl. fdd. **£8.00**

397. [SHELFORD, Leonard (1795-1864)]. [The Law relating to the Probate, Legacy and Succession Duties. 1861. 2nd ed.] Appendix. Index. xxii, 668, [iv], 24pp. Lacks title. Orig. cl., paper label; fdd. & sl. stnd. **S. & M. ii. 324. £8.00**

398. SHEPPARD, William (?-1675). Of Corporations, Fraternities, and Guilds ... with Forms and Presidents, of Charters of Corporation. For H. Twyford, T. Dring, and J. Place, 1659. 1st. **2 pts. in 1.** [vi], 130/-188pp. Lacks first & last blanks. First few leaves sl. wormed. Fore-margins of last two leaves defective, affecting one side-note. Contemp. sheep, corners worn. **S. & M. i. 533. £50.00**
Sheppard is the most authoritative of our early monograph-writers. This is the most ancient work upon the law of incorporations; before this zealous republican, none had ventured to set his hand to a matter so immediately touching the royal prerogative. In our copy all references to Cromwell as Lord Protector have been altered to "King" or deleted; a sign perhaps that the book was not on sale until after the return of King Charles.

399. SHOWER, Sir Bartholomew (1658-1701). The Second Part of the Reports of Cases and Special Arguments ... in ... King's Bench. 1720. Folio. Mostly black letter. Fp. port. Index. [xii], 519, [xxi]pp. Lacks final blank. Some browning. Mod. b'ram. **S. & M. i. 309. £25.00**
This part was posthumously published from a fair copy corrected by the author.

400. SIDERFIN, Thomas. Les Reports des divers special Cases ... en le Court del Bank le Roy. By W. Rawlins [etc.] for Samuel Keble, 1683. French text. Folio. Indices. [iv], 467, [lxxxv]/[viii], 179, [xi]pp. Contemp. MS. glossary inserted in vol. 1, which includes blank $2K_4$ but lacks final blank. Few annots. Contemp. cf.; sl. rubbed. **Wing S.3757-8. S. & M. i. 309. £50.00**

401. ——— Anr. set. 19th-cent. ½ cf./mbld. sides; sps. rubbed; lacks one label. **£45.00**

402. SMITH, James Walter. A Handy Book on the Law of Private Trading Partnership. 1871. Index. 96, 24pp. Orig. limp cl., worn. **Not in S. & M. £5.00**

403. SOUTH AFRICA. Report on the Natives of South-West Africa and their Treatment by Germany. H.M.S.O. (ed.9146), 1918. 1st. Folio. Illus. photos (scenes of hangings, etc.). Appendices. 212pp. Orig. blue wraps, fdd.; spine defective. **£20.00**

404. SPELMAN, Sir Henry (1562-1641). Reliquiae Spelmannianae ... Posthumous Works. Oxford (Clarendon Pr.), 1698. 1st. Folio. Device on title. Two fold'g tables. Index. [xxxii], 214, [xii]pp. Lacks final blank. Inner margin of A_1 defective; text not aff. Contemp. mottled cf.; sp. rbbd. & frayed. **Wing S.4391. S. & M. i. 37. £70.00**
Consists largely of the treatise on Feuds and Tenures by Knight-Service, together with the Apology for Abp. Abbot (convicted of manslaughter by chance-medley in a test case for a clergyman's rights under such circumstances), remarks on wills, coinage & the rank of knight, etc.

405. SPOTTISWOOD, John. An Introduction to the Knowledge of the Stile of Writs, Simple and Compound, Made Use of in Scotland. Edinburgh, 1765. 5th ed., rev. 12mo. Index. [iv]. 588, [xx]pp. Few leaves sl. stnd. Contemp. cf., sl. rubbed. **S. & M. v. 108. £15.00**

406. SPRY, Thomas (c.1620-1685). LEWIS, J.F. ... Lawyer & Physician; The First Attorney ... in the Delaware River Settlements. Philadelphia, Pa., 1932. 1st. Illus. Index. x, 126pp. Orig. cl., uncut; fine. **£15.00**
Privately printed for distribution among the city lawyers. Includes many extracts from New York, Virginia, New Jersey & Penna. records.

407. STANFORD, Sir William (1509-1558). Les Plees del Coron: divisees in plusiours Titles & Common Lieux ... dernieremt corrigee [sic] avecques un Table ... iammais per cy devant imprimee. In aedibus Richardi Tottell, 1560. [Second ed.] French text. Sm. 4to. Black letter. Woodcut title-border (Beale 49) & initials. Indices. [xiv], 198 leaves. ¶$_{3-4}$ (table of chapters) misbound after ¶$_{4}$. Old ink scoring & few annots. 18th-cent. cf., re-backed; sl. rbbd. **Beale T.487. S.T.C.23220. S. & M. i. 365.** £250.00
The most ancient monograph on our criminal law, distinguished by the historical sense which led the author to draw frequently on the authority of Bracton & other early writers.

408. ——— Anr. ed. In aedibus Richardi Tottelli, 1574. Sm. 4to. French text. Black letter. Woodcut title-border (Beale 47) & initials. Index. [xiv], 193 [i.e. 198] leaves. **Beale T.489. S.T.C. 23222. S. & M. i. 365.** – An Exposition of the Kinges Prerogative, Collected out of ... Fitzherbert, and other Olde Writers. By Richard Tottel, n.d. [1577]. [5th ed.]. 4to. Black letter. 85 leaves. **Beale T495. S.T.C.23216. S. & M. i. 119.** Two works in one vol. Contemp. cf., rbbd., re-backed. £300.00
The King's Prerogative (a commentary on 17 Ed. II.) is ahead of its time in several ways. Stanford boldly wrote it in 1548 when he was still a barrister & could not invoke his authority as a judge to justify his action; it is full of intelligent historical references; and it seems to be the earliest monograph on statutory interpretation.

409. STATE TRACTS: being a Collection of Several Treatises relating to the Government. Printed ... 1689. 1st collected. Folio. [iv], 240, 367-468pp. Signatures jump from 3D to 5B; pagination irreg. accordingly; nothing missing. 5H & 5I each a single leaf. Contemp. sprinkled cf., sp. rbbd. **Wing S.5329.** £50.00
Includes Andrew Marvell's "Account of the Growth of Popery", & a number of items illustrating the dying struggles of arbitrary & irresponsible government incarnate in King Charles & his "cabal".

410. STATUTES. A Collection ... relating to High Treason, and Misprision of High Treason. 1709. [2nd ed.] 12mo. Privilege leaf before title. Index. 114, [xiv]pp. **S. & M. i. 367. – A FORM and METHOD** of Trial of Commoners, in Cases of High Treason and Misprision of High Treason. 1709. 1st. 12mo. 44, [iv]pp. **S. & M. i. 367. Two works in one vol.** Contemp. sprinkled cf., royal arms on sides, gilt; lacks label; sl. rbbd. £30.00

Presentation inscription from David Dalrymple, advocate, to W. Forbes, 31st July 1710. Comparison with the inscription in item 176 shows that this Dalrymple was the grandfather of the celebrated Lord Hailes.

411. ——— Anno regni Georgii II. regis ... duodecimo. [–An Act for Prohibiting the Importation of Books Printed Abroad.] 1739. 1st. Folio. Black letter. [ii], 691-694pp. Mod. wraps. £15.00
This Act (12 Geo. II. cap 36) forbade the importation of foreign editions of books which had been published in Britain within the previous 20 years. The Irish reprints, many of which can be seen in this catalogue, must have escaped through not being regarded as "foreign" according to the intent & meaning of the Act.

412. ——— Anno regni ... Georgii II ... decimo octavo. [–An Act for Punishing Mutiny and Desertion.] 1744. **3 pts. in 1.** Woodcut arms on title. 116, [ii], 119-172, [vi], 48pp. Contemp. cf., sl. rbbd. £10.00
The annually-renewed Mutiny Act (in fact a complete code of military law) with an act concerning recruitment for regiments serving abroad, and the Articles of War for 1745.

413. ——— Anno quadragesimo tertio Georgii III. Regis [etc.] 1803-5 & n.d. **4 items in 1 vol.** Folio. Contemp. ½ cf./mbld. sides; worn. £20.00
The items are 43. G.III. c.99 (re-organizing the collection of duties), 43 G.III. c.122 (establishing a property tax) with a Bill modifying it, & 45. G.III. c.49 (also altering the property tax).

414. ——— Acts for Making Provision for the Effectual Performance of Quarantine; with Orders in Council, &c. 1817. 1st collected. 4to. Index. 86, [lx], [ii], 149-216pp. Interleaved throughout. Contemp. diced cf., rbbd., lacks spine. £20.00

415. ——— An Act fot the Amendment and Better Administration of the Laws relating to the Poor. N.d. [1834]. Index. xxiv, 104pp. Orig. wraps., sp. torn. £5.00
A convenient edition of the Poor Law Act of 1834.

416. ——— Statutes of the United Kingdom ... 54 George III. 1814. 1st collected. Index. xxxviii, [ii], 1138, [vi]pp. Orig. bds., uncut; sp. defective; edges worn. £20.00

417. ——— A Collection of the Public General Statutes, Passed in the Tenth and Eleventh Year of ... Queen Victoria. H.M.S.O., 1847. 1st. 4to. Index. xxxviii, [xii], 1056pp. Contemp. cf., rbbd. £8.00

418. ——— **Ireland.** A Collection of Acts relating to the Criminal Law of Ireland. Dublin. 1834. [–Supplement. 1838.] 1st collected. Indices. [viii], 364/[iv], 349-476pp. Contemp. cf., sl. mkd. £10.00

419. ——— A Collection of Miscellaneous Acts relating to Ireland. Dublin, [1833-] 1838. 1st collected. General & individual titles. Indices. [iv], [iv], 160, 32, 120, 64, 18pp. Contemp. cf., sl. rbbd. £10.00
Consists largely of acts relating to the administration of justice.

420. ——— **Scotland.** The Laws and Acts of Parliament made by King James the First [-Queen Anne]. Edinburgh, 1682-3 & 1731. **3 vols.** 12mo. Indices. Vol. 2 lacks final blank. [viii], 1018/640/875pp. Old cf., re-backed; sl. rbbd. Bk-pls. **Wing S.1266; S. & M. v. 116-7.** £40.00

421. ——— Anr., vol. 3 (James VII-Anne) only. 1731. 875pp. Some foremargins shaved. Sl. browned. Contemp. cf., re-backed. £8.00

422. The STATUTES at LARGE concerning Elections of Members to Serve in the ... Commons. 1734. 1st. Index. vi, 109 [i.e. 119], [xv], 10pp. **S. & M. i. 152. – ORDERS & RESOLUTIONS** of the ... Commons on Controverted Elections and Returns. 1736. 2nd ed., rev. 12mo. Index. viii, 209, [vii]pp. **S. & M. ii. 26. – COWLEY, J.;** The Candidates Guide: or the Electors Right Decided ... Resolutions ... concerning the Rights of Elections. 1734. 1st. [ii], 30pp. **This ed. not in S. & M. Three works in one vol.** Contemp. cf., lower cvr. rbbd. £40.00

423. ——— concerning Bankrupts. 1765. [2nd ed.]. Index. [iv], 144, [xxxvi], 4pp. Sl. stnd. Mod. cl. **S. & M. ii. 543.** £20.00
Includes obsolete acts (from 34-35 Hen. VIII. c.4) as well as those in force.

424. STATUTES relating to the ADMIRALTY, NAVY, SHIPS of WAR, and INCIDENTAL MATTERS. 1768. 4to. Blank with engr. vignette before title. Index. 8, 1018pp. Leaf 6N$_2$ (index) defective with loss of 2/3 text. Contemp. cf., rbbd., jts. sl. worn. **S. & M. i. 351.** £50.00

425. STATUTES relating to the SEWERS, within Westminster, and Part of Middlesex. 1809. vi, 70pp. Contemp. ¼ roan/mbld. sides; red labels on sides; spine defective. **This ed. not in S. & M.** £10.00
Published by the Commissioner of Sewers, who were established by the first act in the book (23 H.VIII. c.5).

426. STEPHEN, Henry John. New Commentaries on the Laws of England. (Partly Founded on Blackstone). Third ed., ed. James Stephen. 1853. **4 vols.** Indices. Contemp. cf., two labels; sl. rubbed. Fine set. **S. & M. ii. 339.** £30.00
After the extensive reforms of the early nineteenth century, Blackstone's text could no longer be kept up to date by notes & supplements. Stephen's replacement retained many of Blackstone's definitions & remarks, but abandoned the distinction between rights of persons & of things.

427. STEUART or STEWART of GOODTREES, Sir James. An Index or Abridgement of the Acts of Parliament and Convention, from ... King James the First ... to the Ninth Session of the Current Parliament. Edinburgh, 1702. (2nd ed., rev.) 12mo. Index. [xii], 330pp. Lacks U$_3$ (pp. 237-8) (cancel, not bound in). Two similar cancel leaves loosely inserted. Contemp. cf., worn. **S. & M. v. 117.** £10.00

428. ——— The Index or Abridgement ... from ... 1424 to ... 1707 ... with the Act Ratifying ... the Treaty of Union of the Two Kingdoms. Edinburgh, 1707. (3rd ed., rev.) [xii], 298, [ii]pp. Final blank. Tear in X$_2$ without loss. And: – **BRUCE, Alexander;** The Index ... of such Acts ... as ... concern the whole United Kingdom, or particularly ... Scotland ... to ... 1726. Edinburgh, 1726. 1st. 12mo. [ii], viii, 106, [ii]pp. Final blank. **2 works in 1 vol.** Contemp. cf., rbbd. **S. & M. v. 117.** £20.00

429. ——— Dirleton's Doubts and Questions ... Resolved and Answered. Edinburgh, 1715. 1st. Folio. Red & black title. [iv], 340, 16pp. Contemp. cf., sl. rubbed. **S. & M. v. 117.** £60.00
There was a proverb in Scotland, "Doubting with Dirleton and resolving with Steuart", that is not resolving at all. Too much of Steuart's work consists of Dirleton's words repeated with approving comments; yet his eighteen years' experience as Lord Advocate provided him with the matter of some more solid observations.

430. STRANGE, Sir John (M.R.) (1696-1754). Reports of Adjudged Cases in ... Chancery, King's Bench, Common Pleas, and Exchequer. Ed. John Strange. 1755. 1st. **2 vols.** Folio. Engr. fp. port. Index. [ii], 714/[ii], 1272, [c]pp. Contemp. cf., rbbd. **S. & M. i. 309.** £40.00
Strange includes an unusual number of cases turning on points of criminal law.

431. ——— Anr. copy. Lacks port. Contemp. annots., probably by William de Grey. Mod. cl. £45.00
Sir William de Grey, afterwards Baron Walsingham, held both the law-offices & afterwards became Chief Justice of Common Pleas. He has corrected the reports at several points, & occasionally amplified them. The volumes contain the book-plate of his son Thomas.

432. STRANGE, Sir Thomas. Hindu Law; principally ... such portions ... as concern the Administration of Justice, in ... India. [2nd ed., rev.] 1830. **2 vols.** Appendices. Index. xxxii, 32, 344/viii, 488pp. Supplement bound after prelims. of vol. 1. Few leaves sl. spotted. Orig. cl.; paper labels; uncut; sp. fdd. £30.00
Vol. 1 is a general account drawn from the Smritis (text-books), their later commentaries which exemplify provincial varieties of law, & the recent Digest of Jagannatha. Vol. 2 is an annoted case-book.

433. The STUDENT'S LAW-DICTIONARY; or Compleat English Law-Expositor .... Table of the Most Usual Latin Contractions. 1740. 1st. [iv], [438], [xvi]pp. Mod. cl. **S. & M. i. 12.** £30.00
Intended to fill the space between the compact but obsolete Termes de la Ley & the accurate but ponderous Law Dictionary of Cowel.

433a. STURCH, Christoph. In titulum Pandectarum de Diversis Regulis Iuris Antiqui commentarius: curâ Henrici Hahnii ... editus. Helmstadt (J. Heitmüller), 1658. 1st thus. 4to. [xxiv], 644pp. Sl. browned. Contemp. blind-stamped vellum, new label. £40.00
The editor gives this Polish jurist especial praise for explaining the reasons behind the law. The work was first published in 1590; it occasionally touches on the conflict of civil law & town laws, & has the curious feature of paraphrasing each maxim in verse.

434. SUGDEN, Edward Burtenshaw (later Lord St. Leonard's). A Practical Treatise of the Law of Vendors and Purchasers of Estates. 1808. 3rd ed. Indices. lx, 664pp. Sl spotted. Contemp. cf., rbbd. Upper jt. weak. **S. & M. ii. 346.** £15.00
Sugden revised this standard work single-handed for nearly sixty years. By a strange fatality, disputes over his own estate formed a cause célèbre of the 1870s.; his will was lost, & his daughter was allowed to reconstruct it from memory.

435. SULLIVAN, Francis Stoughton (1719-1776). Lectures on the Constitution and Laws of England ... on Magna Charta, and ... the English Statutes. Second edition, [with] a Discourse ... by Gilbert STUART. 1776. 4to. ½ title. Index. xvi, xxxii, 415pp. Few contemp. ink or pencil annots. Some spotting. Large copy in old ½ mor./cl. sides, rubbed, jts. worn. Lib. labels. **S. & M. i. 108.** £50.00
Lectures delivered in the University of Dublin where, in the author's opinion, circumstances required a more detailed & precise historical work than that of Blackstone. The annotator severely criticizes Stuart's discourse & often doubts the relevance of his quotations.

436. SURTEES, W.E. A Sketch of the Lives of Lords Stowell and Eldon. 1846. 1st. viii, 180pp. Inscribed by the author to William Aldam, M.P. Sl. spotted. Orig. cl., sl. mkd. £15.00
Surtees's grandfather was related to both the subjects, & provided much of the material for this volume. Some unpublished letters are included. Lord Eldon was of course an old-fashioned but upright & influential Lord Chancellor; his brother turned to the civil law, & became Judge of the Consistory Court.

437. SWINTON, John. An Abridgment of the Public Statutes in Force and Use Relative to Scotland, from the Union ... to the Twenty-Seventh Year of his present Majesty. Edinburgh, 1788. 1st. **2 vols.** 4to. Index. ½ titles. xii, [652]/[ii], [528], [xxx]pp. Contemp. sheep, rbbd. **S. & M. v. 119.** £50.00
Replaces the work of the elder Swinton (1755). Schedules of customs & excise are given in full.

438. SZEGEDI, Joannes. Tripartitum juris Hungarici tyrocinium, iuxta ordinem titulorum operis tripartiti. Tirnovo, 1767. Indices. Red & black title. 856, [xl]pp. Lib. stamps on ½ title & title. Old annots. on e-p's. £50.00
The Opus Tripartitum (somewhere between Institutes & Pandects in scope) was compiled by Stefan Werbocz at the instance of King Ladislas II, & was the first of the five volumes of the Hungarian corpus. This commentary is the work of a Jesuit priest.

439. TABLES showing the NUMBER of CRIMINAL OFFENDERS. Committed ... or Bailed ... in the Year 1842. H.M.S.O., 1843. Folio. 8, 66, 106pp. Mod. wraps. £20.00
Figures for the year show a great increase in offences against property in the manufacturing districts.

440. TAYLOR, John (1704-1756). Elements of the Civil Law. Cambridge [University Press], n.d. [1755]. 1st. 4to. Three errata leaves. Engrs. of coins in text. Index. x, 589, [i]pp. Contemp. cf., sp. gilt; sl. rubbed. £50.00
Taylor, who adapted this work from his tutorial lectures to the grandsons of Lord Granville, wrote with the idea of presenting Roman law as a basis for a gentleman's conduct of life; in consequence it is uncritical & ill-arranged, but spirited in style & observation, & useful in its task of removing the civil law from the schools to the polite world.

441. ——— Anr. (2nd) ed. N.d. [1756]. 4to. [x], 584, [xii]pp. Contemp. cf., jts. worn. **S. & M. v. 143.** £40.00

442. TENANTS LAW: or, the Law concerning Landlords, Tenants and Farmers. 1753. 14th ed. 12mo. Index. 314, [xxxiv]pp. Contemp. cf., jts. worn. **S. & M. i. 461.** £15.00

443. ——— Anr. ed. (16th). 1768. 12mo. Index. [ii], 320, xxviiipp. Contemp. sheep, rbbd., jts. worn. **S. & M. i. 461.** £15.00

444. THOMAS, Ernest C. Leading Cases in Constitutional Law. 1901. 3rd ed., ed. C.L. Attenborough. Index. xiv, 136, 32pp. Orig. limp. cl., sl. worn. **S. & M. ii. 355.** £6.00

445. THREE PATENTS concerning the Honourable Degree and Dignitie of BARONETS. By Robert Barker, 1617. Sm. 4to. 39pp. A$_1$ blank except for large signature within border. Some stns. Mod. wraps. **S.T.C.9238.** £20.00
The rank of baronet was created in 1611 as a reward for landowners who cultivated estates in Ulster. This pamphlet gives the terms of the patent for creating a baronet, & defines his place in the scale of precedence.

446. TIBET and the CHINESE PEOPLE'S REPUBLIC. A Report to the International Commission of Jurists. Geneva, 1960. 1st. Appendices. xiv, 344pp. Orig. wraps; fine. £6.00

447. TILLESLEY, Richard. Animadversions upon M. Seldens History of Tithes, and his Review thereof. By Iohn Bill, 1619. 1st. Sm. 4to. First leaf blank except for signature in woodcut frame. Royal arms on title verso. [xl], 236pp. Some light staining; last leaf very sl. frayed; few sm. worm-holes in fore-margins; otherwise a fine copy in contemp. vellum, ties (one broken), paste-downs detached. **S.T.C.24073** (Huntingdon copy only in U.S.A.). **S. & M. i. 196.** £90.00
Tillesley, although wanting much of Selden's reading & learning, attempts to meet him on his own ground of quotation & legal authority. He crowns all with an anagram; SELDEN reversed is NEDLES, needless.

448. ——— Anr. copy. Lacks first blank. Fore-margins sl. stnd. – **GAUDEN, John:** The Case of Ministers Maintenance by Tithes. By Thomas Maxey, for Andrew Crook, 1653. 1st. 4to. [iv], 46pp. Lacks A$_2$ (dedication?) & first leaf of text. Last line of most pp. cropped. Sl. stnd. **Wing G.344. Not in S. & M. – [STEPHENS, J.]:** An Apology for the Ancient Right ... of the Bishops to Sit ... in Parliaments. By W. Godbid, for Richard Thrale, 1660. 1st. 4to. [viii], 120pp. Lacks C$_2$ (pp. 9-10). Corner torn from last leaf. **Wing S.5446. Not in S. & M. – An ANSWER to the RECTORS LIBEL.** Dublin, by Richard Wilde, 1694. 1st. 4to. [ii], 22pp. Sl. browned. **Wing A.3440 (not in B.L., none in U.S.A.) Four items in one vol.** 19th-cent. ½ roan/mbld. sides, rbbd. £120.00
Gauden has often been cited as author of the Eikon Basilike. The last item alleges that a parson cannot on his own authority, & on hearsay evidence, suspend a parishioner from communion.

449. TIMOUR, or Tamerlane, Prince of the Mongols (c.1335-1406). Institutes, Political and Military ... Translated into Persian by Abu Taulib Alhusseini; and thence into English ... by Major [William] DAVY. Ed. Joseph White. Oxford, Clarendon Pr., 1783. 1st. Persian & English text. 4to. Engr. port. & diagram. Index. lii, 408, lxpp. Mod. ¼ cf./mbld. sides. £50.00
Notwithstanding the title, this work is rather a history of the civil & military administration of Timour than a legal code; it appears to be genuinely his work, & was originally written in the Mongol language, a form of Turkish. Davy translated it from a MS. in the Hunterian library.

450. TOWER, Charlemagne. The Charlemagne Tower Collection of American Colonial Laws. Philadelphia, Pa. (Historical Society, privately printed), 1890. 1st. 4to. Engr. fp. port. 300pp. Orig. cl., uncut; sl. mkd. £20.00
Bibliog. of nearly 1000 editions of statutes to 1799, with an appendix of miscellaneous Americana.

451. A TREATISE on the LAW of the DESCENT of an INTESTATE'S REAL ESTATE; comprising the Alterations made therein by ... 3 & 4 W. IV. c.106, with ... Notes; and on the Distribution of an Intestate's Personal Estate. 1834. 1st. IV, 38pp. Sl. spotted. Orig. bds.; sp. defective. **Not in S. & M.** £15.00

452. TRIALS. William Earl of Kilmarnock, George Earl of Cromertie, and Arthur Lord Balmerino. 1746. 1st. – Simon Lord Lovat. 1747. 1st. Lacks 2T^2 (pp. 161-4). – Lawrence Earl Ferrers. 1760. 1st. – Admiral John Byng. 1757. 1st. Appendix. – William Lord Byron.

1765. 1st. – Thomas Earl of Macclesfield. 1725. 1st. Last leaf browned. **Six items in one vol.** Folio. [ii], 40/[ii], 188/[ii], 56/130 [i.e. 134], 20/[ii], 48/[ii]. 284pp. Contemp. ½ cf./bds., sl. rbbd. **£90.00**
The trial of Lord Macclesfield, L.C., is remarkable as the most extreme (since mediaeval times) among the few cases of corruption in judges; that of Adml. Byng, for the sympathy aroused on his behalf at home & abroad; & those of Lords Byron (predecessor of the poet) & Ferrers as rare examples of the process of trying a peer for felony (murder in each case) before the Lords.

453. TUCKER, A.G.C. Supplement to the Observations intended to Prove that the Judgement . . . in the . . . Cause . . . Cholomondeley and . . . Damer versus . . . Clinton is Unfounded in Law. Exeter, 1818. 1st. [ii], 39pp. Disbound. **£5.00**
The case concerned the ambiguously-worded will of Samuel Rolle; the family of Horace Walpole was involved.

454. Van ECK, Cornelius. Theses juris controversi. Utrecht, 1694. 1st. xx, 176pp. – **BOCKELMANN, J.F.** Tractatus . . . de differentiis juris civilis, canonici et hodierni. Ed. C. van Eck. Utrecht, 1694. 1st. Index. [ii], 30, 153, [vii]pp. – **FORNERIUS, G., & A. CONTIUS.** Tractatus de Feudis . . . HOTTOMANNUS, F. Elementa iuris feudalis . . . opusculum . . . nunc primun [sic] editum. Ed. C. van Eck. Leeuwarden, 1694. 1st thus. Index. [viii], 221, [vi]pp. **Three works in 1 vol.** Contemp. MS. contents & other notes on e-p's. Contemp. vellum; sl. stnd. **£60.00**
536 disputed points of law collected by Van Eck out of his lectures, with two other volumes (one including an unpublished treatise on feudal law by the great French jurist Hottoman) edited by him.

455. Van LEEUWEN, Simon. Censura forensis theoretico-practica, id est, totius iuris civilis Romani, usuque recepti, & practici methodica collatio. Amsterdam, 1685. 3rd ed., rev. **2 pts. in 1.** Folio. Red & black title. Indices. Engr. tables in text. [xxxvi], 558, [xxxiv]/[xii], 218, [xxii]pp. Contemp. vellum. **£80.00**
When Holland emerged from beneath the shadow of conquest, her jurists at last had leisure to consider the absurdity of giving up the lives of hundreds of learned citizens to the study of Roman law, while the practical jurisprudence of the state was based on a confusion of local codes & customs & Spanish enactments. Van Leeuwen therefore attempted to set forth the institutes of Dutch Law, based on the civil law (he anticipates Bynkershoek in this), & with precedents & examples from the laws of every European nation.

456. VANTIUS, Sebastianus. Tractatus de nullitatibus processuum ac sententiarum causarum. Venice (apud Hieronymum Cavalcalupum), 1559. 1st. Device on title. Index. [viii], 275, [lvi] leaves. *8 blank. Lacks $2L_{3-4}$. Few ink annots. Sl. marginal worming at end. Few light stains. Title worn. Contemp. vellum, soiled. **Not in B.M.C. or Adams. £30.00**
According to the preface, legal tricks for annulling judgments & cancelling cases were a standing abuse in the courts of the time. In writing a treatise to correct their abuse, the author professes to have been aided by a vision.

457. VAUGHAN, Sir John, Chief Justice (C.P.) (1603-1674). The Reports and Arguments. Ed. Edward Vaughan. By Thomas Roycroft for Richard Marriott [etc.], 1677. 1st. Folio. Mostly black letter. Fp. port. Indices. [xiv], 420, [lv]pp. Mod. ¼ cf./mbld. sides. **Wing V.130, S. & M. i. 310. £30.00**
Vaughan was a firm royalist, & would neither sit in Parliament nor practise at the bar while the republican government was in office.

458. VENTRIS, Sir Peyton (Justice, C.P.) (1645-1691). The Reports . . . Third impression . . . with . . . several Thousands of References, never before Printed. 1716. **2 pts. in 1.** Folio. Black letter. Privilege leaf before title. Indices. [xii], 430, [xxiv]/[xviii], 368, [xx]pp. Some browning and spotting. First leaf partially backed. Mod. cl. **S. & M. i. 310. £30.00**
The new references were contributed by one Richardson, serjeant at law. Includes Sir M. Hale's speech in Atkyns v. Clare *(Exchequer, 1672) in which he protested against the franchise of* retorna brevium *which gave some lords an element of private jurisdiction within their demesnes, a serious cause of obstruction & delay in county-court matters.*

459. VERNON, Thomas (1654-1721). Cases Argued and Adjudged in . . . Chancery. 1726. 1st. **2 vols.** Folio. Fp. port. (Vertue after Kneller). Indices. First privilege leaf to vol. 1. [xiv], 490, [lxii]/[xii], 767, [cix]pp. Vol. 2 lacks first blank. Contemp. annots. Fine mod. ½ cf./mbld. sides. **S. & M. i. 349. £50.00**
Vernon's clear & concise reports preserve many cases from the seminal Chancellorship of Lord Nottingham. The annotator has collated these with the Chancery Cases (see item 357) & added several interesting remarks.

460. VIDOCQ, Eugène-François (1775-1843). FROMENT, –; Histoire de Vidocq . . . d'après Lui-même. Paris 1829. 1st. **2 vols. in 1.** French text. 12mo. **Engr. fp. port. viii, 316/356pp.** Vol. 2 lacks title, probably as issued. Sl. browned. Central stain to some leaves in vol. 1. Contemp. vellum. **£25.00**
Vidocq began his career as one of the most notorious thieves & forgers in France, but changed his cloth and became chief of the Paris Bureau de Sûreté, founder of the science of detection, and the original of most of the detective fiction of the century.

461. VINNIUS, Arnold (1588-1657). In quattuor libros Institutionum imperialium commentarius. Amsterdam (D. Elzevir), 1665. 4th ed., rev. 4to. Red & black title. Index. [xii], 888, [xx]pp. Lacks front e-p. Contemp. vellum, sl. soiled. **£50.00**
The commentary of Vinnius, undertaken with the honest intention of clarifying the Institutes rather than of burying them under an accumulation of aimless pedantry, is printed from an annotated copy found among the author's papers; some further remarks by Prof. Johan Schulting of Nijmegen (father of Anton, q.v.) are inserted.

462. ——— **Commentarius** . . . editio ultima . . . aucta indicibus decisionum et constitutionum. Leyden, 1709. 4to. Engr. dedication leaf. [vi], 828, [xxiv]pp. Mod. ½ red mor./cl. sides. **£40.00**

463. ——— **In quatuor libros Institutionum imperialium commentarius** . . . Jo. Gottl. Heineccius j.c. recensuit. Lyons, 1747. **2 vols.** Latin text. 4to. Red & black title to vol. 1. Index. Engr. table. [xvi], 568/[ii], 571-998, [xlii], [vi], 194pp. Blank $6P_4$. Lacks final blank. Contemp. cf.; upper cvrs. sl. worn. **£40.00**
This edition includes the author's Selectae juris quaestiones.

464. ——— **Institutionum, sive elementorum, libri quatuor, notis perpetuis** . . . illustrati. Leyden, 1709. 12mo. Engr. title & fold'g engr. dedication. Index. [xxii], 632, [xxiv]pp. Contemp. vellum, later label. **£20.00**
A different work from the last, retaining the notes on the Prooemium, but thereafter much briefer.

465. VOET, Johannes (?-1714). Commentarius ad Pandectas, in quo praeter Romani juris principia . . . jus etiam hodiernum, & praecipuae fori quaestiones excutiuntur. Leyden, 1698. 1st. **Vol. 1 (books 1-22) (of 2) only.** Latin text. Folio. Index. [xvi], 980, [lxx]pp. Final blank. Contemp. mottled cf., sp. gilt; rbbd. **£20.00**
Voet's influential commentary, whose second volume (Pandects bks. 23-50) appeared in 1704, pays special attention (as the title promises) to current problems, especially those (naturally important to a Dutchman) of maritime law.

466. Von der RECK, Mordius. Disputatio juridica de piscatione. Strassburg (J. Städel), 1662. 1st. 4to. [iv], [20]pp. Some head-margins shaved. 19th-cent. ½ mor./mbld. sides. **Westwood & Satchell 175. £60.00**
This thesis on the definition, rights, uses, & penalties of fishing (with some reference to hunting & hawking) reflects the high importance which these sports still assumed in the life & thought of the German nobility.

467. VULTEIUS, Hermannus. Jurisprudentia Romana. Abr. & ed. J.A. Corvinus. Amsterdam (Elzevir), 1658. 2nd ed. 24mo. Engr. title. Index. [xii], 358pp. Contemp. vellum, sp. sl. wormed. **£30.00**
Distils the essence of Institutes, Code, Digest & later authority into a space no larger than that of the Institutes alone.

468. WAGNER, Georg Wilhelm. De mutatione successionis in familiis illustribus. Giessen, 1740. 1st. Sm. 4to. [x], 50pp. Mod. wraps. **£10.00**
Thesis for a doctorate in the University of Giessen, one of the three centres (with Jena & Franeker) for the study of the law in Germany.

469. WALKER, Clement (?-1651) [& another]. The Compleat History of Independency upon the Parliament. For Henry Brome, 1661 [-1660]. 1st collected. **4 pts. in 1.** Red & black general title (mounted on cancel stub). [vi], 18, [viii], 27-174, [ii], 18/[viii], 262, [ii]/[ii], 58/[viii], 124pp. Many side-notes cropped in pt. 2. Last few leaves frayed. Mod. ½ cf./mbld. sides. **Wing W.324. £50.00**
Walker was an M.P. of the Presbyterian belief, but his vivid, garrulous, vulgar history of the civil war shows all factions – Presbyterians, Independents, & soldiers – in an equally bad light. Cromwell took notice of the work by consigning Walker to the Tower.

470. WALKER, Thomas (1784-1836). The Original. 1836. Second ed. iv, 444pp. Contemp. cf., sl. worn. Bk-pls. **£15.00**
Published as a periodical (Nos. 1-29) in May-Dec. 1835. Walker was a magistrate, & reforms in local government & the local courts occupy much of his attention; but with these are interspersed reflections on manners, politics, & (most particularly) diet & health.

471. [WARD, Leslie] ("Spy") (illus.). The Book of the Bench. 1909. 1st collected. 4to. 39 mounted col. plates. Orig. cl., gilt; edges sl. worn. **£50.00**

Portraits (reproduced from Ward's original water-colours, not from the published lithographs) & biographies of judges from "Vanity Fair"

472. [WARNER, John, Bishop]. Church-Lands Not to be Sold. Or, a Necessary and Plaine Answer to the Question of a Conscientious Protestant. Printed . . . 1648. 1st. Sm. 4to. [iv], 82pp. Sl. stnd. Sm. marginal hole in L_3. Lacks final blank. 19th-cent. annots. on e-p. & title. Old ¼ cf./mbld. sides, sl. rbbd. S. & M. i. 166. **Wing W.900. £30.00**
A "ghost" edition is ascribed to 1640 by Sweet & Maxwell & to 1646 by some others; the annotator here concludes that it does not exist, & Wing does not record it.

473. WARREN, Charles. History of the Harvard Law School and of Early Legal Conditions in America. N.Y., 1908. 1st. 3 vols. Illus. Appendices. Index. Orig. ¼ roan/cl. sides; sl. rubbed. **£30.00**
Includes a complete roll of students.

474. ——— The Story-Marshall Correspondence. N.p. [Williamsburg, Va.], 1941. 1st separate. 21pp. **Inscribed** by Warren. Orig. wraps, fine. **£5.00**
Extracts from letters between Joseph Story & John Marshall, Chief Justice, 1819-1831. Rep. from "William & Mary College Quarterly".

475. WASHINGTON, Joseph [& Henry (BOULT] (eds.). An Exact Abridgment of all the Statutes of King William and Queen Mary, and of King William III, and Queen Anne. 1704. Rev. ed. Index. [lxxxii], 662 [actually 678], [lxxxvi]pp. Extra sig., (l)[8], inserted between sigs. 1 & K. Contemp. cf., rbbd. **S. & M. i. 566. £20.00**
Continuation of Wingate's Abridgment (q.v.).

476. ——— Anr. ed. (William & Mary only). By the Assigns of R. Atkins [etc.], 1694. 1st. Index. [viii], 232pp. Contemp. cf., two sm. worm-holes on spine. **Wing E.913 (var. imprint). £15.00**

477. WELLS, John C. & H.T. Wells's Lawyer and United States Form-book . . . Property Exempt from Execution . . . Laws of Contracts . . . Constitution of the United States . . . and Forms . . . System of Book-keeping. N.p. [N.Y.], n.d. [1849]. 300pp. Orig. ¼ roan/printed bds., corners worn. **£7.50**

478. WESEL, Abraham van. Commentarius ad novellas constitutiones Ultrajectinas . . XIV. Aprilis – M.D.C.LIX. promulgatas. Utrecht, 1666. 1st. Sm. 4to. Index. [viii], 326, [xxiv]pp. Final blank. Contemp. vellum; paste-downs detached. Sl. soiled. **£30.00**
An explanation of some recent statutes of the province of Utrecht relating to the transfer of property between man & wife, the age & privileges of majority, the position of second marriages, & the rights of usury.

479. WESEMBECK, Mathias (1531-1581). Paratitla in Pandectas . . . ab auctore recognita. Basle (per Eusebium Episcopium & Nicolai fr. haeredes), 1572. 4th ed. Folio. Device on title & last leaf. Index. 427, [i], [xx]pp. Title cut round & mounted. Last four leaves sl. frayed. Later cf., sp. gilt; head & tail of sp. defective. **£60.00**
The author was a Belgian jurist exiled for his religious opinions and protected by the Saxon court. This ed. includes his Prolegomena on the study & sources of the law.

480. ——— **In Pandectas iuris civilis et Codicis Iustiniani lib. IIX [sic] commentarii.** Basle (per Eusebium Episcopium, & Nicolai fr. haeredes), 1575. Folio. Device on title. Index. [viii], 386, [xviii], [ii], 82, [viii]pp. Strip torn from foot of title. Contemp. sheep, rbbd. **£80.00**
Fifth edition of the Paratitla, with a commentary (never before printed) on books 1-8 of the Code.

481. ——— **Commentarii in Pandectas . . . et Codicem . . ., aucta ab Arnoldo Vinnio, cum notis . . . Reinhardi Bachovii.** Amsterdam, 1665. 4to. Red & black title. Index. [viii], 854, [xxviii]pp. Sm. worm-holes in leaves 3 & 4 of each gathering. Contemp. sprinkled cf., sp. gilt; jts. sl. rbbd. **£40.00**
The augmented edition of Vinnius first appeared in 1648. Wesembeck's treatise de Feudis is included.

482. ——— **RAUCHBAR, Andreas;** Oratio de vita et obitu. Wittemberg (Z. Lehmann), 1587. 1st. Italic letter. Errata leaf. [75]pp. Sl. browned. Mod. wraps. **Not in B.M.C. £30.00**
Commemorative oration on Wesembeck delivered at the enrolment ceremony of three licenciates (Nicholas Claudius, Johann Müller, & Liberius Hoffmann).

483. WHITELOCKE, [Sir Bulstrode] (1605-1676). Notes upon the King's Writt for Choosing Members of Parliament, XIII. Car. I. being Disquisitions of the Government of England. Ed. Charles Morton. 1766. 1st. **2 vols.** 4to. Index. 1_F 518/[iv], 452, [xiv]pp. Contemp. cf., rbbd. **S. & M. i. 140. £60.00**
Whitelocke was inclined to the party, & admitted to the friendship of Cromwell; but he abhorred & attempted to mitigate the extravagance of the republicans. This work (printed from the author's MS.) is a conciliatory scheme of parliamentary government dedicated to Charles II; a discursive work suggesting the manner of Selden (from whose papers Whitelocke drew many of his illustrations) & Coke, & in which the intention of explaining the duty, purpose & practice of elective representation is almost lost in a sea of comment & example.

484. WIGHT, Alexander. An Inquiry into the Rise and Progress of Parliament, Chiefly in Scotland. Edinburgh, 1784. 1st. 4to. Index. Errata leaf. xiv, 609pp. Few contemp. annots. (corrections to documents.) Orig. bds., uncut; edges & jts. worn. **S. & M. v. 126. £50.00**
Includes 180pp. of documents. In recognizing that Saxon or Norman references to the King's council, probi homines, barones etc. do not prove the existence of anything agreeable to the established definition of a parliament, Wight places himself on much surer ground than the polemists of the previous century.

485. WILLCOCK, J.W. The Law of Municipal Corporations; Together with . . . a Treatise on Mandamus and Quo Warranto. Philadelphia, Pa., 1836. 1st. Amer. Index. xx, 306pp. A_1 torn without loss. See S. & M. ii. 381. – **WARREN, S.** Popular and Practical Introduction to Law Studies. Philadelphia, Pa., 1836. 1st. Amer. Index. x, 242pp. Sl. spotted. See S. & M. ii. 371. **Two works in one vol., as issued,** with general title. Contemp. cf., sl. rbbd. **£25.00**

486. WILLIAMS, E. Staple Inn; Customs House, Wool Court, and Inn of Chancery. 1906. 1st. Appendix (incl. list of admissions 1716-1881). Index. xii, 210pp. orig. dec'd cl., sp. fdd. **Not in S. & M. £10.00**

487. WILLIAMS, John. Special Report of the Speech . . . in Support of Mr. Fitzhardinge Berkeley's Motion, in Favor of . . . Voting by Ballot. N.d. [1849]. 1st. 8pp. Sewn as issued. **£4.00**
Reports the case of a man whose landlord gave him notice to quit for voting the wrong way.

488. WILLIAMS, Joshua. Principles of the Law of Real Property. 1849. 2nd ed. Index. xx, 432pp. Some old ink annots. Contemp. ½ cf./mbld. sides; rbbd. **S. & M. ii. 383. £10.00**
With interesting appendices on the effect of the intestacy provisions in the Wills Act 1837 on coparcenary tenure & tenure by the curtesy (not in the first edition).

489. WILLIAMS, T. Every Man his Own Lawyer, or, a Complete Law Library. 1818. 2nd ed., rev. Appendix of forms. Index. xii, 573, [viii], [iii]pp. Few leaves loose. Contemp. cf., sl. rbbd. **S. & M. ii. 384. £15.00**
Follows a suggestion of Sir William Jones's for a digest, in the order of Blackstone, of all the law which the layman might need to know in ordinary life or in the unskilled offices (so to speak) of juryman, constable, churchwarden, etc.

490. WILLIS, Browne. Notitia Parliamentaria; or, an History of the Counties, Cities, and Boroughs . . . what Boroughs were . . . Parliamentary, but now Disus'd; What do at this day return to Parliament . . . etc. 1715-16. 1st. **2 vols. (of 3). Indices; appendices.** [ii], [vi], xl, 183, [i], 10/[ii], [iv], xii, 558pp. Contemp. panelled cf., sps. gilt, jts. sl. rubbed. Bk-pls. ("book-stack" style) Thos. Percival. **£30.00**
The author intended to survey all the counties of Britain alphabetically, listing Members past & present & other items of local history; but want of support truncated his design, which was never completed. Vols. 1-2 extend as far as Durham.

491. WILSON, George (Serjeant-at-Law). Reports of Cases . . . in the King's Courts. 1770 [-75]. 1st. **3 pts. in 2 vols.** Folio. Indices. [xviii], 342, 424, [xliv]/[x], 564, [xxvi]pp. Mod. cl. **S. & M. i. 310. £30.00**
Pt. 2 includes R. v. Wilkes *(John Wilkes committed to the Tower for seditious libel; released, & breach of Parliamentary privilege found) and a similar case,* Entick v. Carrington & others *(King's messengers broke into & searched a bookseller's shop on a warrant from the Secretary of State; warrant held illegal, & messengers liable for trespass).*

492. WINES, E.C. Commentaries on the Laws of the Ancient Hebrews. Philadelphia, Pa., n.d. [1853]. 1st. xvi, 17-640pp. Lib. stamp on title. Orig. cl., sl. fdd.; ends of sp. frayed. **£15.00**
With an introductory essay on government, which ingeniously portrays the covenant between God & the Israelites as a perfect "social contract", with the result that the Biblical authorities commonly cited in favour of divine right etc. are turned into precedents for democracy.

493. WINGATE, Edmund. An Exact Abridgment of All Statutes in Force and Use, from the Beginning of Magna Charta, until 1641 . . . Continued . . . to . . . 1681. By the Assigns of J. Bill [etc.], Sold by G. Sawbridge [etc.], 1681. Addenda on A_2. Indices. [iv], 688, [lxiv]pp. Final errata leaf. Contemp. cf., rbbd. **Wing E.909. S. & M. i. 566. £25.00**

494. ——————— Anr. ed. rev. 1700. [ii], 726, [lviii], 8pp. Contemp. cf., sp. sl. frayed, upper jt. worn. Wing E.912. **£20.00**

495. ——————— Anr. ed. 1704. First blank, [ii], 726, [lxiv]pp. Sl. wormed at end. Contemp. cf., sp. sl. rbbd. **£20.00**

496. WISHEART, George, Bp. of Edinburgh (1609-1671). A Complete History of the Wars in Scotland; under the Conduct of the Illustrious James Marquis of Montrose. N.p. [Edinburgh], 1720. 1st complete. **3 pts. in 1.** [xiv], 132/[ii], 135-200/lvi, 24pp. Pt. 3 lacks leaf A_3 (pp. 5-6). Contemp. panelled cf., rbbd., paste-downs detached. **£20.00**
The second part of Wisheart's Royalist history (together with several original letters of Lord Montrose, a description of the King's death by Alexander Henderson, & other documents) is here printed for the first time.

497. WISSENBACH, Johann Jakob (ed.). Exercitationum ad quinquaginta libros Pandectarum partes duae. Franeker, 1661. 3rd ed., rev. 4to. **2 pts. in 1.** Red & black title. Engr. port. on *4 verso. Index. [xvi], 16pp., 17-624 columns, [iv]pp. 625-1132 cols., [lvi]pp., 279 cols., [xx]pp., 232 cols., [xxii]pp. Margins sl. wormed. Contemp. blind-stamped vellum, ties. Bk-pl. **£50.00**
Wissenbach conceived the excellent scheme of reviving 97 theses from the German & Dutch universities, and arranging them as a perpetual commentary on the Pandects.

498. WOODDESON, Richard (1745-1823). Elements of Jurisprudence treated of in the Preliminary Part of a Course of Lectures on the Laws of England. Dublin, 1792. ½ title. 208pp. Contemp. mottled cf., sp. gilt; sl. rbbd. **S. & M. i. 599.** **£20.00**
Reprinted from the London ed. of 1783. Succeeding Blackstone in the Vinerian professorship, Wooddeson endeavoured to go more deeply than his predecessor into the ethical & theoretical aspects of his subject.

499. WOOLLGAR, J.W. Suggestions to Overseers, with Reference to the Making, Collecting, and Accounting for Poor Rates. 1839. 1st. Sm. 4to. 27pp. 2 tables. Sewn as issued. **Not in Kress.** **£5.00**

500. WRIGHT, Andrew. Court Hand Restored; or, the Student's Assistant in Reading Old Deeds, Charters, &c. . . . Ancient Names of Places . . . Ancient Surnames. 1778. 2nd ed. 4to. List of subscribers. 20 engr. plates. [viii], 100pp. Old ½ cf./mbld. sides; jts. & edges rbbd. **S. & M. i. 14.** **£50.00**

501. ——————— **Anr. (sixth) ed.** 1822. 23 **engr. plates. xvi,** 60, [ii]pp. Title cut round & mounted. Later ½ mor./mbld. sides; sp. sl. fdd. **S. & M. i. 14.** **£40.00**
Written to cure the decay of palaeographical knowledge which followed the abolition of law-Latin by the acts of 1731-3, Wright's work was standard until this century. The later ed. includes transcripts of the quotations in the plates, & three additional plates of charter hands from 1100 to 1591.

502. ——————— Anr. (fourth) ed. 1815. 4to. 24 engr. plates. Indices. xii, 56pp. Sl. spotted. Few old annots. Mod. cl. **£35.00**

503. ——————— Anr. (8th) ed. 1846. 4to. 23 engr. plates. xiv, 62pp. Lithographic facs. of deed of Thomas de la Warr (1422) inserted. Orig. cl., re-backed. **£20.00**

504. ——————— Anr. (9th) ed., ed. C.T. Martin, 1879. 4to. 23 engr. & 7 lith. plates. xviii, 100pp. Orig. cl., fine. **£20.00**

505. WYATT, John (ed.). The Practical Register in Chancery. 1800. 1st thus. Index. ½ title. viii, 492pp. Contemp. cf., sl. rubbed. S. & M. i. 348. **£20.00**
Greatly enlarged from the edition of 1714, about half the material being newly added by Wyatt so as to form a complete abridgment of Chancery practice.

506. YATE, Walter Honywood. Political, Historical, and Analytical Arguments, proving the Necessity of a Parliamentary Reform, and Pointing Out the Means of Effecting that . . . Measure. 1825. 2nd ed. **2 vols.** xcviii, 252/xii, 240pp. Orig. bds., paper labels; uncut & unopened; sps. sl. torn. **£35.00**
The author's plan includes secret ballots, abolition of parliamentary privilege, & triennial elections at which three members (only one of whom, chosen annually by the voters of his constituency, actually sits in the Commons) are elected for each seat.

507. YEATMAN, H.F. A Letter to D.O.P. Okeden . . . with an Inquiry into the Merits of his Poor Law Report. Sherborne, 1833. 1st. 63, 26pp. Orig. ¼ cl./bds.; fine. **Not in Kress.** **£8.00**
Answer to Okeden's charges that the Sherborne magistrates had been meddling with the administration, & subsidising idleness, in the manner complained of by Brereton (q.v.) See OKEDEN for a reply.

FROGNAL RARE BOOKS

18 Cecil Court, Charing Cross Road
London WC2N 4HE, England.
Tel. (01) 240 2815. Cables Finresbook London WC2

CATALOGUE 49

LAW AND LEGAL HISTORY

(1977)

For an index of subjects see p. 31.
For details of current and future catalogues see inside back cover.

1. ACHERLEY, Roger. The Britannic Constitution: or, the Fundamental Form of Government . . . Demonstrating, the Original Contract entered into by King and People. 1727. 1st. Reasons for Unity in the State . . . Supplement to the Britannic Constitution. 1741. 1st. **2 parts in 1. Folio.** [viii], 5-696, [x]/[iv], 24pp. Two sm. marginal holes. One page ink-spotted. Mod. ½ cf./cl. sides, sl. rbbd. **S. & M.i.98.** **£70.00**
In his first chapter Acherley supposes that the first British king was appointed, the rights of monarch, peers & commons allotted, and the principles of parliament laid down at an assembly held some few centuries after the Flood. It is only fair to add that his theory – that the Revolution of 1688 was no revolution but an example of the normal working of the constitution – is better conceived, & in the main better argued, than this grotesque illustration of it would suggest.

2. ADDINGTON, (Sir) William. An Abridgment of Penal Statutes. N.d. [1779]. 2nd ed., rev. 4to. Indices. **Signed by the Author** on title (to prevent piracies). [iv], 658, [lxiv]pp. Contemp. cf., sp. rbbd. & head worn. **S. & M.i.358.** **£75.00**
As Bow Street magistrate Addington continued the good work of his predecessors the brothers Fielding: he also shared their literary interests, being known as an associate of stage-folk & something of an author in his own right.

3. ADDISON, C.G. A Treatise on the Law of Contracts and Rights and Liabilities ex Contractu. 1856. 4th ed. Index. lxx, 1264pp. Few margins soiled & sl. frayed. Mod. cl. **S. & M.ii.3.** **£15.00**

4. ALLEN, John. Inquiry into the Rise and Growth of the Royal Prerogative in England. 1830. 1st. viii, 170pp. Sl. spotted. Contemp. cf., sp. gilt; rbbd. **S. & M.i.111.** **£20.00**
Argues, from the early history of the Teutonic peoples, that all prerogatives which are not vouched for by statute or recognized as customary must be rejected as alien to the spirit of the constitution.

5. ARCHBOLD, John Frederick. A Collection of the Forms and Entries . . . in the Courts of King's Bench & Common Pleas. 1828. 2nd ed. Index. xvi, 628pp. Mod. cl. **S. & M.ii.10.** **£10.00**

6. ———————. The Justice of the Peace, and Parish Officer; with the Practice of Country Attornies. 1846. 4th ed. **3 vols.** Indices. Contemp. cf., sl. rbbd. **S. & M.ii.9.** **£30.00**
Vol. 3 is a self-contained treatise on the Poor Law. This continued to be revised & reprinted long after "Stone's Justice" had taken over from the first two volumes.

7. The ARGUMENTS upon the WRIT of HABEAS CORPUS . . . whereunto is annexed, the Petition of Sir John Elliot. By M.F. for W. Lee, M. Walbancke [etc]. 1649. 1st. Sm. 4to. [ii], 96pp. Title torn without loss & sl. frayed. Browned. Fore-margin uncut. Mod. wraps. **Wing A.3649. S. & M.i.154.** **£45.00**
Elliot & others were imprisoned on a special warrant from the Privy Council; their counsel (including Selden) used the writ of Habeas Corpus, in anticipation of the status which it took later in the century, to test the validity of this detention. The deep discussion on the subject of imprisonment without trial which ensued is perhaps the first legal argument on this sensitive question.

8. ARNOT, Hugo. A Collection and Abridgement of Celebrated Criminal Trials in Scotland, from A.D. 1536, to 1784. 1st. 4to. List of subscribers. Appendix. xiv, [ii], xv-xxiv, 400pp. Sl. spotted. Sl. stnd. at end. New ¼ cf./mbld. sides. **S. & M.v.6.** **£50.00**
Arnot writes largely for English readers, to whom he shows forth Scots criminal law as a chaos of royal, ecclesiastical & judical tyranny, slowly dispelled by the light of reason. Notwithstanding this view, & despite some strong remarks against the anti-Catholic laws, work was heavily subscribed for among the Scots.

9. The ASSERTION is, that the Title of the House of Hanover to the Succession . . . is a Title Hereditary. 1710. 1st. Final advert. leaf. 38, (ii)pp. Disbound. **£15.00**
A counterblast both to those who held that property in the crown was vested in the Stuarts in perpetuity, & to those who imagined that the constitution had been turned into some form of elective monarchy; with a glancing blow at the opposite fancy, that the monarch was above all laws.

10. AUSTIN, John. Lectures on Jurisprudence. 1873. 4th ed., ed. Robert Campbell. **2 vols.** Index. xxiv, 524/xiv, 525-1170, [ii], 20pp. Orig. cl., sl. mkd. & fdd. **S. & M.ii.15.** **£25.00**
John Stuart Mill attended Austin's original course of lectures, & the notes which he took at the time furnished some corrections to this edition. Austin & his wife Sarah (who was responsible for the former edition) were notable associates of Bentham & the Mills.

11. BAGENAL, Philip Hope. Crime in Ireland. The Winter Assizes in Ulster, Munster, Leinster, and Connaught. Dublin, 1880. 1st. Appendix. 88pp. Mod. cl. **£10.00**
Land League terrorism as seen in the courts.

12. [BAILEY, Samuel] (1791-1870). The Rationale of Political Representation. 1835. 1st. viii, 436pp. Sl. spotted. Contemp. cf., gilt, rubbed, lacks label. Bk-pl. Lord Belper. **£30.00**
Bailey, a wealthy Sheffield manufacturer, was sometimes called the Bentham of the North. His endeavour to bring science to a question formerly divided between precipitous idealism & placid acceptance of the status quo lends colour to the comparison.

13. BALFOUR of PITTENDREICH, Sir James (?-1583). Practicks: or, a System of the more ancient Law of Scotland. Edinburgh, 1754. 1st. Folio. Index. [ii], xviii, 684, [x]pp. Lib. stamp on e-p's, title & a_1. Contemp. cf., re-backed, worn. **S. & M.v.8.** **£50.00**
Balfour, governor of Edinburgh Castle & President of the Court of Session, was instrumental in bringing about the downfall of the regent Earl of Morton. This abridgment of Scots law from statutes & decisions is of his time, but not definitely from his hand.

14. [BALLOW, Henry.] A Treatise of Equity. Dublin, 1756. [2nd ed.] [xxii], 258pp. Margins of last few leaves defective through damp. Contemp. cf., jts. & edges worn. **S. & M.i.255.** **£25.00**
The earliest known monograph on equity; as edited by Gilbert & later by Fonblanque, it remained until 1820 the standard to which the various imprints of the "Chancellor's foot" (Selden's famous description of equity) were reduced.

15. BARRINGTON, Daines (1728-1800). Observations on the More Ancient Statutes, from Magna Charta to the Twenty-first of James I. 1769. 3rd ed., rev. 4to. Index. xii, 516pp. Sl. spotted at end. Contemp. cf., newly re-backed. **S. & M.i.546** **£75.00**
Barrington, who is best remembered as a naturalist & for his critical examination of the young Mozart's genius, strikes a flood of various and picturesque learning from these apparently barren materials. His work, here enriched with many additions (some drawn from Petyt's papers) gave a strong impulse to the historical study of the law.

16. BATEMAN, Joseph. Auctioneer's Guide; containing a Practical Treatise on the Law of Auctions. N.d. [1846]. 3rd ed. Index. Adverts. of Waterlow & Sons, with fine lithographed trade card, at end. xxiv, 358, 14, [ii] [iv]pp. Few press-cuttings pasted in. Orig. cl., sl. worn & shaken. **S. & M.ii.22.** **£25.00**
One of the press-cuttings reports a case (Ellis v. Colley) which must surely be the last example of tenure by elegit (conveyance of freehold land to the creditors until the debt is paid out of its rents & profits); it was argued before the Under-Sheriff of Denbighshire in about 1850, & is therefore most probably unreported.

17. BENTHAM, Jeremy. Traités de Législation Civile et Pénale. tr. & ed. Étienne Dumont. Paris, 1820. 2nd ed. **3 vols.** French text. Lacks ½ titles. xl, 368/[ii], iv, 380/viii, 456pp. Sl. spotted. Sm. worm-hole in last four leaves. Contemp. ½ cf./mbld. sides, re-backed; corners rubbed. **£75.00**
Digested from the General Principles of Legislation, Principles of the Civil & Penal Codes, Panopticon, & some other treatises. Dumont's preface gives a criticism of Bentham & an account of his own methods as editor.

18. ———————. A Treatise on Judicial Evidence, ed. E. Dumont, tr. anon. 1825. 1st Engl. Lacks ½ title. xvi, 366pp. Few leaves at beginning & end stained. Mod. ½ cf./mbld. sides. **S. & M.ii.27.** **£75.00**
This, the first English appearance of Bentham's most important legal work is not the author's own text but a back-translation from the French of Dumont.

19. SOLD.

20. [BETHELL, Slingsby.] The Interest of Princes and States. For John Wickins, 1680. 1st. First blank. 2 advert. leaves at end. [xiv], 354, [iv]pp. Contemp. calf, worn. **Wing B.2064.** **£100.00**
Includes a chapter on the Protestant movement in France, & another on the parliament summoned by Richard Cromwell in 1658. The whole work, based on French models but drawn from the author's own experience, is a most curious political Survey of Europe.

21. BLACKSTONE, Sir William. An Analysis of the Laws of England. Oxford (Clarendon Press), 1762. 5th ed. Index. [lxxxiv], 190, [xiv]pp. Few contemp. annots. Lib. stamp on verso of title. Contemp. calf, spine & edges rubbed. **S. & M.i.27.** **£40.00**
The outline on which Blackstone's Vinerian lectures, & the Commentaries which grew from them, were built.

22. ———————. Commentaries on the Laws of England, ed. Edw. Christian. 1803. 14th ed. Engraved fp. port. & 2 engr. tables. Indices. 2 leaves of addenda after A_4 of vol. 1. Contemp. calf, sl. rubbed., jts. worn. **S. & M.i.28. 4 vols.** **£85.00**

See also under Robert Malcolm KERR*

23. BLACKWOOD, Adam (1539-1613). Adversus Georgii Buchanani dialogum, de iure regni apud Scotos, pro regibus apologia. Poitiers (apud Franciscum Pagaeum), 1581. 1st. Sm. 4to. Final errata leaf. [xii], 342, [ii]pp. Title defective & repaired with loss of text, mostly on verso (privilege). L_2 repaired with sl. loss. Wrong imposition in sig. C; correct order of page noted in early MS. Old calf, re-backed, edges sl. worn. S. & M.v.17. £95.00
Defence of Mary's right to reign in Scotland, by a fine scholar & lawyer who owed to her his place in the local administration of Poitiers. He does not seem able to distinguish between Queen & Crown; he has too much respect for the one to emulate Buchanan in the accuracy of his discussion of the other.

24. ————. Martyre de la Royne d'Escosse . . . contenant le Vray Discours des Traisons à elle faictes à la Suscitation d'Élizabet Angloise. Antwerp (chez Gaspar Fleysben), 1588. [2nd ed., enlarged]. French text. [viii], 660pp. Lacks final blank. Sl. stained. 17th-cent. mottled calf, spine gilt, worn. This edition not in B.M.C. £120.00
Blackwood received many favours from Queen Mary & repaid her with the best efforts of his pen. This furious denunciation of her executioners is anonymous but was printed among Blackwood's works in 1644; so also were the virulent declamations & verses against Elizabeth which are added to this edition.

25. ————. Opera omnia. Paris (apud Sebastianum . . . et Gabrielem Cramoisy), 1644. 1st collected. Sm. 4to. Engraved device on title. Lacks engr. port. Index. [xliii], 735, [xxiii]pp. Paper flaw in 4K$_3$, affecting last line. Contemp. calf, spine gilt, jts. & edges worn. Not in S. & M. £90.00
Blackwood displayed his gratitude to Queen Mary as the champion of her rights while she lived, & of her memory after her death. His most important work is a reply to Buchanan, asserting the legitimacy & authority of the Scottish Kings; he is also responsible for an angry exposure, in French, of Mary's trial & execution. Gabriel Naudé (1600-1653), the discoverer of the true authorship of the Imitatio Christi, contributes a life of Blackwood.

26. BLOUNT, Thomas (1618-1679). Nomo-lexikon (Graece): a Law-Dictionary. By Tho. Newcomb, for John Martin and Henry Herringman, 1670. 1st. Folio. Errata leaf. [xiv], [272]pp. Contemp. calf, sp. & jts. worn. Wing B.3340. S. & M.i.6. £85.00
Blount was a Catholic & therefore excluded from practice; he was also (as his well-known "Ancient Tenures" shows) a diligent researcher among records. His work was thus principally antiquarian & so it did not establish itself alongside the improved editions of Cowell's Dictionary as a source for lawyers.

27 B[LOUNT], T[homas]. Fragmenta Antiquitatis. Antient Tenures of Land, and Jocular Customs of some Mannors. By the Assigns of Richard and Edward Atkyns [etc.], 1679. 1st. First imprimatur leaf. Index. Final errata leaf. [vi], 176, [xvi]pp. Contemp. sheep, re-backed; edges rubbed. Wing B.3333. S. & M.i.398. £50.00
Light-hearted though it is, Blount's collection of singular copyhold & petty serjeanty tenures was for many a useful introduction to the mysteries of mediaeval land-holding. We owe to him our knowledge of the Dunmow Flitch, the Black Ram of Enborne, the Tutbury Bull, & other curiosities of feudalism.

28 BODIN, Jean (1530-1596). De republica libri sex Latine ab auctore redditi. Frankfurt (sumptibus Jonae Rosae viduae, typis Anthoni Hummi), 1641. Index. [xiv], 1222, [lxxxii]pp. Blank 4H$_4$. 2I$_1$ torn without loss. Browned. Contemp. calf, worn, lacks label. £30.00
Bodin was the earliest writer to attempt a theory of government on comparative principles. His Latin version, like Hobbes's of the Leviathan, is accounted superior to the original.

29. BÖCKELMANN, Johan Friedrich. Synopsis iuris publici imperii Romano-Germanici, ed. Alexander Arnold Pagenstecher. Groningen, 1698. 1st thus. [viii], 296pp. Lacks P$_8$ & Q$_1$ (pp 239-242) in Pagenstecher's life of Böckelmann. Browned. Contemp. calf, spine defective, corners worn. £15.00

30. BOOTE, Richard. An Historical Treatise of an Action or Suit at Law, 1781. 2nd ed., rev. Appendix. Advert. leaves at end. xxxii, 268, [iv]pp. Contemp. calf, rubbed; spine sl. worn. S. & M.i.298. £20.00
Boote points out many abuses in procedures; he is so far ahead of his time as to suggest that special pleading is an anachronism – pointing the moral by printing two pleadings of thirty pages each – & that the diversity of original writs is unnecessary.

31. BRIERLY, James Leslie. LAUTERPACHT, Sir H.; Brierly's Contribution to International Law. 1955. 1st separate (rep. from "British Year Book of International Law".) Fp. port. 20pp. **Presentation copy.** Orig. wraps, fine. £10.00

32. BROUGHAM, [Henry Peter] (afterwards Lord) (1778-1868). Speech . . . on his Motion, that an Humble Address be Presented . . . To Issue a Commission for Inquiring into . . . the Laws of this Realm. 1828. Index. xii, 126, [ii], 8pp. Mod. bds., orig. wraps bound in; uncut; fine. S. & M.ii.45. £35.00
With Brougham a reforming spirit, hitherto the preserve of laymen, not only made entrance to the legal profession but was carried to its highest offices. This is his manifesto, in which redundancy in pleading, restrictions on advocacy, obsolete forms of action, incongruities in the law of evidence, & other faults & flaws are successively held up to the light. This "Authentic Edition" has the advantage of Brougham's corrections.

33. ————. Speech in the House of Lords . . . upon the Eastern Slave Trade. 1838. 1st. 4to. **Limited 20** on large paper. **Signed** by Sir Edward Burtenshaw Sugden (Afterwards Lord St. Leonards, Lord Chancellor.) [vi], 66pp. Few marginal worm-holes. Disbound. £30.00
Angry condemnation of an Order in Council enabling Guiana planters to import black "apprentices" on terms amounting, in Brougham's view, to a revival of slavery in the colony. The Duke of Wellington's government had narrowly evaded a vote of censure moved by Brougham on the day before he made this speech. The appearance on this copy of the name of Sugden, a confirmed Tory, does honour to the impartiality of giver & receiver alike.

34. BURN, Richard. The Justice of the Peace, and Parish Officer. Ed. John Burn, 1788. 16th ed. **4 vols.** Index. R$_4$ (vol. 1) sl. mkd. Contemp. cf., rbbd., jts. & ends of sps. worn. S. & M.i.226. £50.00

35. ————. The Justice of the Peace, and Parish Officer, ed. G. Chetwynd. 1820. **5 vols.** 23rd ed. Index. Errata slips. in vols. 2-5. Contemp. calf, rubbed. S. & M.ii.50. £30.00

36. BURTON, Walter Henry. An Elementary Compendium of the Law of Real Property. 1845. 6th ed., ed. E.P. Cooper. Index. 8pp. adverts. before title. xxxvi, 728pp. Some ink scoring. Mod. cl. S. & M.i.51. £15.00

37. BRITISH LIBERTIES, or the Free-born Subject's Inheritance: containing the Laws that form the Basis of those Liberties . . . Essay on Political Liberty . . . View of the Constitution. 1766. 1st. [xii], lxxx, 396pp. Contemp. cf., rbbd. S. & M.i.154. £30.00
Based on the similarly-titled collection of Care (1684), this work makes little pretence to originality; but it has the merit & interest of invoking the words & ideas of Montesquieu, & even of Rousseau, to illustrate the theory of freedom under law.

38. CAMPBELL, John (afterwards Lord, L.C.) (1779-1861). Reports of Cases determined at Nisi Prius in . . . King's Bench and Common Pleas, and on the Home Circuit. Vols. 1-3, 1818, 2nd ed.; vol. 4 1816, 1st. **4 vols.** Indices. Contemp. cf., sps. sl. defective, jts. worn. S. & M.ii.54. £40.00
The future Lord Chancellor & biographer is one of several lawyers who undertook, about 1800, to explore the field of Nisi Prius cases. All these are important for the history of commercial law. Most of Campbell's cases embody decisions of Lord Ellenborough.

39. CANISIUS, Henricus (?-1610). Summa iuris canonici in quatuor institutionum libris contracta . . . Accessit commentarius in regulas iuris lib. VI. Decretal. Antwerp (apud Hieronymum Verdussium), 1619. 4th ed. Index. [xxiv], 666, [xlvi]pp. Corner of T$_3$ defective, two lines of side-note affected. Contemp. vellum. £40.00
A simple handbook of canon law, including by way of appendix the text of the concordat between the emperor Frederick III & Pope Eugenius IV (1447) relating to ecclesiastical jurisdiction within the Empire.

40. CHITTY, Edward. An Index to All the Reported Cases, Statutes, and General Orders, in or relating to . . . Equity and Bankruptcy. 1837. 2nd ed. **4 vols.** (1-3 text; 4 addenda & indices) Sl. spotted. Contemp. cf., rbbd.; vol. 4 re-backed; vol. 3 jts. worn. S. & M.ii.63. £30.00

41. CHITTY, Joseph (1776-1841). A Treatise on the Game Laws, and on Fisheries. 1826. 2nd ed. Appendix (statutes, & forms of proceedings). Index. xx, 878pp. Old cl., fdd., lower cvr. stnd. S. & M.ii.63. £20.00

42. COKE, Sir Edward. (Chief Justice) (1551-1633). His Speech and Charge With a Discoverie of the Abuses and Corruption of Officers. For Nathaniell Butter, 1607. [2nd imp.] [xiv], [48]pp. Lacks first blank. Sm. hole in E$_1$ aff. few letters. Running titles & one side-note cropped. Blanks bound in at end. Mod. ¼ cf./mbld. sides. S.T.C.5497. S. & M.i.575. £95.00
Coke's charge to the jury at the opening of the Norwich assizes (August 1606) contained an account of the duties of judge & jury, followed by a history of Catholic plots from Ridolfi to Fawkes – this last prompted by a resurgence of recusant activity. Robert Pricket, a poor soldier, transcribed this speech from memory (as he says) & dedicated it to the Earl of Exeter. Coke was furious at the misrepresentation of his ideas (see his account in 7 Reports, preface) & the book was quickly put down; but there is no justification for Maxwell's suggestion that the speech was altogether a forgery.

43. ————. The First Part of the Institutes of the Lawes of England: or, a Commentary upon Littleton. By M.F., I.H. and R.Y., 1639. 4th ed. Folio. Engr. fp. port. Woodcut title-border. Fold'g table. Index. [v], 395, [xxx] leaves. Ink-stain on 2F$_1$ & 2F$_2$. Corner of 2I$_1$ sl. defective. Mod. ½ cf./mbld. sides. S.T.C. 15787. S. & M.i.449. £130.00
"Coke Littleton" far overshadows the rest of the Institutes; and despite innumerable reforming statutes & decisions, it cannot be called obsolete until English law itself is obsolete. This is the last edition produced during Coke's lifetime.

44. ————. The First Part of the Institutes . . . or, a Commentary upon Littleton. 1703. 10th ed., rev. Folio. Two engr. ports. Fold'g table (torn without loss). Index. [x], 88, [ii]pp., 395, [xxxi] leaves. Contemp. cf., re-backed, edges worn. S. & M.i.450. £75.00
First edition to include the Complete Copyholder (published separately in 1630), a landmark in the history of the suppression by the King's courts of the old irregular feudal jurisdictions. Also included are Coke's readings on Fines & on Bail & Mainprize.

45. ————. The Reports, ed. J.H. Thomas & J.F. Fraser. 1826. 1st thus. 13 parts in 6 vols. Index. ½ titles. Mod. ½ calf/cloth sides. S. & M.ii.297. £80.00
The last edition, incorporating (besides the editors' work) notes from the papers of Lord Ellesmere L.C., a contemporary (& enemy) of Coke and principal architect of the Court of Chancery. Head-notes, such as now appear in all reports, are a useful feature of this edition.

46. (————). A Little Treatise of Baile and Maineprize. For William Cooke, 1637. 2nd ed. Sm. 4to. [iv], 34pp. Sm. repair at inner margin of A$_4$. Last leaf repaired on verso. Disbound. S.T.C. 5490. S. & M.i.575. £50.00
After this edition, this treatise vanished into obscurity for fifty years; it was included with the First Institute from the 1680s onward, but was never reprinted separately.

47. ————. The First Part of the Institutes of the Laws of England; or, a commentary upon Littleton. Ed. Francis Hargrave & Charles Butler. 1794. 15th (1st octavo) edition. **3 vols.** Index. Fold'g table in vol. 1. Unpaged. B$_7$ (vol. 1) sl. torn without loss. 2H$_3$ (vol. 3) defective at one corner with loss of few letters. Mod. cl. S. & M.i.451. £50.00
Hargrave began work on a critical edition of Coke-Littleton – the first ever made – in about 1780. Five years later, Butler took over the uncompleted task. Their united labours were brought to light in 1788 & have remained unsuperseded. Observations by Sir Matthew Hale & Lord Nottingham are included. Some of Butler's notes are new to this edition.

48. A COMPLEAT COLLECTION of the STANDING ORDERS of the House of Lords in England. 1748. Index. [ii], 118, [viii]pp. Later boards, spine sl. rubbed. S. & M.i.143. £20.00
Published as a supplement to one of the "Parliamentary Histories", of which several versions appeared in the 1740s.

49. [COOKE, E.] Argumentum Anti-Normannicum: or, an Argument proving . . . that William, Duke of Normandy, made no Absolute Conquest of England. By John Darby, 1682. 1st. Engr. fp. [x], 164pp. Contemp. cf., later label, rbbd. Wing C.4907a. S. & M.i.645. £120.00
Cooke (not Sir Edward Coke, in spite of Wing's careless attribution) supports Petyt's Saxonist theory of the origin of Parliament; his argument is that the "Conquest" was merely an incident in the development of the constitution, & not the beginning of a new order. The Evelyn library copy, with modern book-label & press-mark in a seventeenth-century hand.

50. COOKE, George Wingrove (1814-1865). The History of Party; from the Rise of the Whig and Tory Factions . . . to the Passing of the Reform Bill. 1836-7. 1st. **3 vols.** xii, 612/viii, 498/viii, 628pp. Sl. spotted. Contemp. ½ cf./mbld. sides, sps. gilt, sl. rbbd. & fdd. £50.00
Cooke was an early student of University College (London) where he fell under the influence of John Austin & Andrew Amos, & through them of Bentham.

51. CRAIG of RICCARTOUN, Sir Thomas (1548-1608). Ius feudale tribus libris comprehensum, quibus . . . consuetudines feudales & praediorum iura . . . continentur. Impensis societatis stationariorum, 1655. 1st. Folio. [xii], 384pp. Few sm. marginal worm-holes & other defects. Contemp. vellum. Wing C.6802. S. & M.v.26. £120.00
Craig studied for several years in France; afterwards coming to England for negotiations connected with the Union, he became a close friend of Camden. In him, and through this work in particular, Scotland at last produced a jurist fit to represent her in the European republic of letters. The editor, Robert Burnet, gives in his preface an interesting survey of Scots legal literature.

52. ————. Ius feudale, tribus libris comprehensum. Ed. James Baillie. Edinburgh, 1732. 1st thus. Folio. Engr. fp. port. Index. xxii, 524, [lii]pp. Contemp. panelled cf., rbbd., jts. worn. Bk-pl. Lord Camden. S. & M.v.26. £70.00
Baillie's edition, besides its useful index & summaries, is the first to present a reasonably correct text. Sir Charles Pratt, Viscount Bayham & Earl Camden (1713-1794) was the Chief Justice who in 1762 established the illegality of the warrant for the arrest of Wilkes; he was a close friend of the elder Pitt's, whose disgust at the oppressive methods invoked for the taxation of the Americans he shared.

53. CROMPTON, George. The Practice of the Courts of King's Bench and Common Pleas, ed. Baker John Sellon. 1798. 2nd ed., rev. **2 vols.** Index. xx, lxxx, 548, [lii]/xii, 544pp. Corner of F$_1$ (vol. 1) defective without loss of text. Vol. 2 sl. wormed at end. Contemp. cf., sps. sl. rbbd., one jt. sl. split. S. & M.i.267. £40.00
This book might serve as an exceedingly useful companion to Fielding's novels, Dickens's "Pickwick", & other works of the time in which the law plays an important part.

54. CRUISE, William. A Digest of the Laws of England respecting Real Property. 1824. 3rd ed. **6 vols.** Index. Contemp. cf., rbbd., lacks one label. S. & M.ii.87. £75.00

55. CUMBERLAND, Richard (Bp. of Peterborough). De legibus naturae disquisitio philosophica . . . Elementa philosophiae Hobbianae. Dublin, 1720. Latin text. Cancel title mounted on stub. [lxvi], 426pp. Contemp. cf., later label; sl. rbbd. £30.00
Originally published in 1672. Cumberland, in refuting Hobbes's principles, shows himself a pioneer Utilitarian; for he replaces Hobbes's central law of self-preservation with one of "benevolence to all rational beings", or in other words of the good of humanity as a whole.

56. DALTON, Michael (c.1554-1630). Officium Vicecomitum. The Office and Authority of Sherifs [– An Appendix or Supplement]. By John Streater [etc.], 1670. Folio. **2 parts in 1. BLACK LETTER.** Index. [iv], 500/[iv], 501-564, [xxviii]pp. Sm. hole in 3E$_1$ aff. few letters. Few old annots. Contemp. cf., sp. defective, jts. & corners worn. Wing D.152. S. & M.i.222. £120.00
Includes an appendix of new statutes & cases, supposed by S. & M. not to have been included until 1682.

57. DAVIDSON, Robert, and David DOUGLAS. Decisions of the Court of Session, from November 1793 to July 1794. Edinburgh, 1795. Folio. Index. [iv], 159-292pp. Orig. wraps, uncut, lacks sp. Not in S. & M. £15.00
These reports, sponsored by the Faculty of Advocates & so anticipating by 70 years the English semi-official pattern, often show the highly advanced Scots commercial law of the time in action.

58. ————. Decisions of the Court of Session, from Nov. 1796 to July 1797. Edinburgh, 1800. 1st. Folio. Index. [ii], 102, [ii]pp. Orig. wraps, uncut, spine defective. Not in S. & M. £15.00

59. A DECLARATION of the COMMONS. Assembled in Parliament, concerning the Jurisdiction of the Admiralty. For Edward Husband, 1648. 1st. Sm. 4to. 6, [ii]pp. Final blank. Wing E.2556. S. & M.i.351. **Boards.** £40.00
Instructions to the newly organized Court of Admiralty for dealing with arrears of maritime & commercial cases.

60. De LOLME, J.-L. (1745-1807). The Constitution of England or an Account of the English Government. 1781. 3rd ed. Index. Contents bound after introduction. [vi], iii-xvi, 480, [xxiv]pp. Final errata leaf. Contemp. calf, edges sl. worn. S. & M.i.100. £35.00
Includes four new chapters, one of them (II.20) prompted by a conversation with Franklin & dealing with the American question. The Preface, containing a spirited account of de Lolme's struggles with booksellers & patrons, is also new.

61. ————. Another copy. same. upper jt. worn. £35.00

62. ————. The Constitution of England. Halifax (Yorks.), 1822. Engr. fp. port. Index. xvi, 516pp. Contemp. calf blind-tooled & gilt, corners & ends of spine rubbed. S. & M.ii.98. £25.00

63. ————. The Constitution of England. Ed. John MacGregor. 1853. 1st thus. Index. Publisher's cat. at end. xx, 376, 32pp. Single wormhole through text; few more in e-p's. Orig. cl., sl. wormed & faded. £10.00
Macgregor's short but diligent Life of de Lolme throws out the theory that the English version of the "Constitution" was made by Francis Maseres.

64. DICKINSON, William. A Practical Guide to the Quarter Sessions and Other Sessions of the Peace. Ed. T.N. Talfourd.

1838. 4th ed. Index. lxvi, 986pp. Sl. spotted. Contemp. calf, worn, re-backed. S. & M.ii.100. £15.00

65. DIGGES, Sir Dudley (1583-1639) (ed.). The Compleat Ambassador: or two Treaties of the intended Marriage of Qu: Elizabeth. By Tho: Newcomb, for Gabriel Bedell and Thomas Collins, 1655. 1st. Folio. Engraved fp. by W. Faithorne. Red & black title. Index. [xiv], 442, [vi] pp. Sm. piece torn from inner margin of G_4. Contemp. sprinkled calf, spine gilt, worn. **Wing D.1453.** £150.00

Diplomatic correspondence recording attempts to draw England into an alliance with France by the marriage of Elizabeth with a French potentate – the future King Henri III in 1572, & the Duke of Alençon in 1581. Warned by the sad example of Queen Mary, Elizabeth & her counsellors, Walsingham & Burleigh, escaped with honour from these dangerous involvements; the machinations by which they did so, outwitting in the process the best brains of France, were justly displayed as an example to the next age.

66. DIXON, W. Hepworth. The London Prisons: with an Account of the Most Distinguished Persons ... Confined in them. 1850. 1st. Wood-engraved fp. Appendix. xx, 426, [ii] pp. Final advert. leaf. Mod. ½ calf/mbld. sides. £35.00
Enlarged from papers written for Dickens's newspaper, the "Daily News".

67 DOUBLEDAY, H.A. The Mar Case. 1866 to 1885 & After. 1936. 1st. separate (reprint from "Complete Peerage"). 4to. [ii], 100pp. Orig. wraps, uncut & unopened; fine. £5.00
A dispute (which ascended to the House of Lords) between Lords Kellie & Mar over the right to the latter title.

68. The DUTIES and POWERS of PUBLIC OFFICERS, and Private Persons, with Respect to Violations of the Public Peace. N.p., n.d. [c.1780]. 1st. 16pp. Head-margin of title cut away. Sewn as issued. Not in S. & M. £8.00
Evidently published soon after the "Gordon riots"; proceedings arising from these are cited as authority for the punishment of magistrates who are lax in conserving the peace.

69. [ELLIS, W.] A Summary of the Roman Law, taken from Dr. Taylor's Elements of the Civil Law ... Dissertation on Obligation. 1772. 1st. ½ title. [vi], lxx, 328, [xxxii] pp. Contemp. calf, spine gilt, edges rubbed, jts. worn. £25.00
The Dissertation on Obligation is an original work of the abbreviator, and a very sensible one; treating the subject in its moral rather than commercial sense, he postulates a natural law of obligation founded on the instinct whereby men find it agreeable to their own interest to care for their neighbours – the definition of "neighbour" expanding as civilization increases. In other words, he traces the natural law of self-love & the civil law of responsibility for one's fellows to a single source.

70. ERVIN, Spencer. Henry Ford vs. Truman H. Newberry; the Famous Senate Election contest. N.Y., 1935. 1st. Index. xviii, 616pp. Fine in sl. frayed d.w. £15.00
Newberry, senator for Michigan, was convicted at first instance of having violated the U.S. Corrupt Practices Act during the primary election for the Republican candidate. On appeal, however, it was held that the Act itself was unconstitutional, Congress having no authority to regulate primary elections by statute. The conviction was quashed & the Act altered. On Ford's side especially, strong personal feelings (racial & otherwise) were engaged in this constitutional question.

71. An EXACT COLLECTION of the DEBATES of the House of Commons ... at Westminster. October 21. 1680 ... and ... at Oxford ... March 21. 1680. For R. Clavel ... and A. Churchil, 1689. 1st. [viii], 144 [i.e. 136], 145-464pp. Names of members inserted in contemp. MS. Sl. spotted. Mod. bds. **Wing E.2574.** £40.00
Proceedings in the last Parliament of Charles II's reign. In order to prevent a Catholic revival, the Commons (as once before) passed a Bill to exclude the pro-Roman Duke of York (James II) from the throne; the angry king dissolved Parliament & set about priming the electorate so that future Houses could be compounded of his nominees. In the event his puppet-Parliament was never summoned, but those who were to sit in it became the Tory party of the next age; the older parliamentarians formed the Whig faction.

72. EXTRACTS from the INFORMATION RECEIVED by Her Majesty's Commissioners, as to the Administration and Operation of the Poor-Laws. 1833. 1st. Index. xii, 432pp. Orig. printed cloth, sl. worn. £20.00
A selection from the as yet unpublished evidence brought before the Commission, showing the desperate state of poor relief under the 1601 system.

73. FITZHERBERT, Sir Anthony. The New Natura Brevium ... to which is added a Commentary, supposed to be written by the late Lord Chief Justice Hale. 1794. 9th ed., rev. **2 vols.** Index. Unpaged. Contemp. cf., jts. of vol. 1 worn, vol. 2 re-backed. **S. & M.i.269.** £50.00
From its first publication in about 1532 until the passing of the Common Law Procedure Act, 1852, Fitzherbert's commentary on the writs was one of the most authoritative books in the law. The English version of the text is that of Hughes (1652); that of the writs themselves is by George Wilson, the reporter (1755). Hale's "Commentary", like most of his works, is compounded of detached observations.

74. FONBLANQUE, Albany (1793-1872). England under Seven Administrations. 1837. 1st in bk. form. **3 vols.** Engr. fp. ports. Index. Fps. & titles spotted. Contemp. cf., gilt, sps. rbbd. Bk-pl. Lord Belper. £30.00
Leading articles from the "Times", "Morning Chronicle" etc. by an outstanding political journalist.

75. FOX, Charles James. "PHILOPATRIS WARWICENSIS" (Samuel Parr, 1747-1825). Characters of the Late Charles James Fox. 1809. 1st. **2 vols.** Final errata leaf. xii, 312/[ii], 313-834, [ii] pp. Vol. 2 spotted at end. Contemp. stained cf., gilt, sps. rbbd., lacks labels. Bk-pl. Lord Belper. £25.00
Parr was called the Johnson of the Whigs, although his emulation was confined to the most ephemeral of the Doctor's qualities, namely his genius for conversation & controversy.

76. ——————— TROTTER, John Bernard; Memoirs of the later Years of. 1811. 3rd ed. xl, 552pp. Sl. spotted. Contemp. stnd. cf., gilt; jts. worn. Bk-pl. Lord Belper. £15.00
Written by Fox's private secretary, & including an appendix of letters.

77. FRACCHETTA, Girolamo (1560-1620). Il Prencipe. Venice (appresso Gio. Battista Ciotti), 1599. Rev. ed. Italian text. Index. [lx], 350pp. Lacks final blank. Few leaves sl. browned. Few old annots. Contemp. vellum; lacks ties. B.M.C. (It.) p.276. £75.00
Fracchetta has none of the cynicism of Machiavelli or Aretino; his Prince is a philosopher-king bound by no obligation to his subjects, but voluntarily submitting himself to the dictates of God & reason. This book (here revised by himself) arose out of study for his larger works, the Seminario de'Governi.

78. FRIEDRICH II, King of Prussia (Frederick the Great). The Frederician Code; or, a Body of Law for ... Prussia. Edinburgh, 1761. 1st Engl. **2 vols.** [ii], xlviii, 490/viii, 506pp. Lib. stamps on titles. Contemp. calf, spines & edges worn. £40.00
The plan for this code was drawn up by Frederick himself & is still to be seen among his works. As the German language was then about as well known in Britain as the Sanscrit, the translator followed the French edition drawn up under the supervision of the younger Cocceius, Frederick's chancellor.

79. FURNEAUX, Philip (1726-1783). Letters to the Hon. Mr. Justice Blackstone, concerning his Exposition of the Act of Toleration, and some Positions relative to Religious Liberty, 1771. 2nd ed. rev. **Presentation** copy. xxiv, 284pp. Mod. cloth. S. & M.i.29. £50.00
Furneaux, a dissenting minister, objected to Blackstone's harsh construction of the Act of Toleration & to his general support of the principle that those who dissent from the established religion deserve to suffer the animadversion of the law. This edition includes among other improvements Lord Mansfield's speech in Chamberlain of the City v. Evans *(1767, House of Lords) wherein it was held that a dissenter elected to an office for which affirmation of the Anglican faith was required was immune from the statutory penalties imposed on those who refused to serve.*

80. GABBETT, Joseph. A Digested Abridgment, and Comparative View, of the Statute Law ... in the Order of ... Blackstone's Commentaries. Dublin, 1812. 1st. **Vol. 2 (of 4)** (Private Wrongs & Criminal Law) only, in 2 parts. Indices. [ii], 900/[ii], 901-1252, 156, lxviiipp. T_4 (part 2) torn without loss. Contemp. calf, rubbed. S. & M.ii.132. £10.00

81. GALE, C.J. & T.D. WHATLEY. A Treatise of the Law of Easements. 1839. 1st. Index. xvi, 464pp. Mod. cloth. S. & M.ii.132. £15.00
An early example of the citation of an American case as authority for English law appears at page 131 (judgment of Story J. on appropriation of running water in Tyler v. Wilkinson.*)*

82. A GENERAL SYSTEM of the LAWS concerning Bankrupts. 1761. 1st & only edition. 2 volumes in 1. Index. (xxiv), 291/[ii], 292-494. [xcii] pp. Sm. lib. stamp on title & 14 other leaves. Contemp. calf, sl. rubbed. Lib. bk-pl. S. & M.i.542. £35.00
Includes a large appendix of precedents.

83. SOLD.

84. GLAMORGAN, County of. Broadsheet giving notice of the courts to be held by Alexander Pulling & William Mills, revising barristers, for revising the electoral registers of Cardiff, Caerphilly, Swansea, etc. according to the provisions of the Reform Act, 1867. Cardiff, 1867. Tall folio. Folded. Margins sl. frayed. £10.00

85. GLANVILLE, John. Reports of Certain Cases, Determined ... by the Commons in Parliament, in the Twenty-first and Twenty-second Years of ... James the First ... Historical Account of the ancient Right of determining Cases upon controverted Elections. 1775. 1st. [iv], cxiv, 145-154, 144pp. Index misbound before text. Title spotted. Contemp. cf., sp. & edges worn. S. & M.i.151. £35.00
Glanville was chairman of a Select Committee appointed in 1623 to hear election cases & to rationalize the law concerning them; Coke, Noy & Selden were also members. Glanville's reports, covering that & the following year, are important for the history of the jurisdiction of the Commons; for the Glanville Committee did much to render obsolete the King's claim, through the Lord Chancellor, to be competent to judge election cases.

86. GLEN, W. Cunningham. The General and other Consolidated Orders of the Poor Law Commissioners and the Poor Law Board. 1868. 6th ed. Index. Advert. leaves at end. xxiv, 594, 40pp. Orig. cl., fine. **S. & M.ii.139.** £10.00

87. ———————. The Elementary Education Acts, 1870 & 1873, 3rd ed. (first incl. 1873 Act.) Index. Fold'g table. xl, 332pp. Orig. cl., sl. fdd. S. & M.ii.139. £10.00

88. GONZALEZ, Tomas. Documents from Simancas relating to the Reign of Elizabeth (1558-1568). Transl. & introd. Spencer Hall. 1865. 1st Engl. Index. xxiv, 112pp. Orig. cloth, spine faded. £10.00
A historical account based by Gonzalez on Spanish state papers of the sixteenth century.

89. [GORDON, Thomas]. A Collection of Papers, all written some of them published, during the late Rebellion. Dublin, 1748. 12 mo. xxiv, 248pp. Sl. spotted. Contemp. calf, jts. worn, edges rubbed. £30.00
Anti-Jacobite tracts by a Whig journalist, some of them suggesting Papal involvement in the Scottish troubles. Papers 28-30 contain some vigorous arguments for the strong punishment of public libels.

90. GOTHOFREDUS [Godefroy], Jacobus (1587-1652). Novus in titulum Pandectarum de Diversis Regulis Iuris Antiqui, commentarius. Geneva (sumptibus Petri Chouet), 1653. 1st. 4to. Red & black title with device. Index. [xxx], 804, [lxviii] pp. Sl. wormed & browned. 19th-cent. ½ calf/mbld. sides, rubbed; upper jt. worn. £60.00
Godefroy, greatest of a remarkable dynasty of jurists, brought an exceptional historical & critical knowledge to this subject; he was unequalled in his acquaintance with the ante-Justinianean law.

91. [GREENE, John]. The Privileges of the Lord Mayor and Aldermen of the City. The Advantages of the Freemen ... Usage of the Mayor's Court [etc.] 1708. 1st. [xvi], 216pp. Later ½ cf./mbld. sides, re-backed, edges worn. S. & M.i.439. £40.00

92. SOLD.

93. GROTIUS, Hugo. (1583-1645). De jure belli ac pacis libri tres ... Annotata in epistolam Pauli ad Philemonem, Dissertatio de mari libero, & Libellus ... de aequitate, indulgentia, & facultate. Amsterdam, 1689. Latin text. Engraved & printed titles. Index. [x], 904, [8], [viii], 32, [10], [xcviii] pp. S_7 torn without loss. Lower margins sl. stained throughout. Contemp vellum, spine torn. £50.00
The Libellus de Aequitate (a brief but searching account of the ways in which the rigours of the law might be relaxed) was posthumously published by Blancard in 1680. The notes of Gronovius are included.

94. ———————. De origine gentium Americanarum dissertatio altera. Paris (S. Cramoisy), 1643. 1st. Device on title. 36pp. **Sabin 38561** –
De LAET, Jan (?-1649). Notae ad dissertationem Hugonis Grotii de origine gentium Americanarum. **Paris,** 1643. 2nd ed. 224pp. **Sabin 38561.** –
———————. Responsio ad dissertationem secundam ... Grotii. Amsterdam (Jean Maire for L. Elzevir), 1644. 1st. Index. [iv], 116, [viii] pp. **Sabin 38562. Willems 1007. 3 works in 1 volume.** Contemp. calf, spine & corners worn. £380.00
Grotius imagined, from some accidental likeness of names, that the original inhabitants of central America were Norsemen, other parts being colonised by Africans & Chinese. In this he presumed too highly on his reputation as a universal savant, and the much larger "Notae" of Jan de Laet (author of the "Elzevir Republics") very fairly correct him. This work includes the whole text of Grotius's first dissertation. It is followed in our collection by Grotius's petulant & unworthy riposte & then by de Laet's final word; in this (apart from the main question) the author counters Grotius's theory that the Chinese knew nothing of printing until it was shown them by the Portuguese. Sabin wrongly calls for a map in de Laet's Responsio.

95. HALE, Sir Matthew (1609-1676). Historia placitorum coronae. The History of the Pleas of the Crown. Ed. Sollom Emlyn. 1736. 1st. **2 vols.** Folio. Engr. fp. port. Index. [iv], xxviii, 146, 143-710/[vi], 156, 149-414, [ccxxviii] pp. **S. & M.i.362.**
Bound with.
FLETA, seu commentarius iuris Anglicani. [ed. Sir S. Clarke]. 1735. 1st thus. **Book 1 only (all published).** Folio. [viii], 98pp. **S. & M.i.53.** Contemp. calf, spine gilt, rubbed, jts. worn. £120.00
Being professedly a history, Hale's work is scarcely fit for the part of a current text-book which was forced upon it by the want of other materials; nonetheless it adds to its learning of the past many judicious illuminations of the present & reforming suggestions for the future, so that as a monument of criminal jurisprudence it cannot be rated too highly. Clarke's incomplete "Fleta" depends for its considerable merit on a Cotton MS. & on his collation of the text with that of Glanville.

96. HANSENIUS, Johannes Baptista. De iureiurando veterum liber. Toulouse (typis Raymundi Colomerii), 1614. 1st. 4to. Device on title. Index. Blank ¶4. [xvi], 164, [x] pp. Sl. browned. Contemp. vellum. £50.00
Observations on the nature & incidents of an oath in antiquity. The author resembles his contemporary Selden both in his general manner & in his remarkable knowledge of Byzantine & mediaeval Latin literature.

97. HARCOURT, Francis Vernon. Hints to Young Officers, on the Principles of Military Law, and ... Courts Martial. 1833. 1st. xii, 182pp. Orig. cl., paper label, fdd. **Not in S. & M.** £10.00

98. HARE, Thomas. A Treatise on the Election of Representatives, Parliamentary and Municipal. 1859. 1st. Presentation copy. xxxiv, 338pp. Sl. spotted. Contemp. ½ cf./mbld. sides, sl. rbbd., upper jt. sl. worn. Bk-pl. Lord Belper. S. & M.i.156. £20.00
This important work anticipates many of the modern objections to the "first-past-the-post" system, rigid party divisions, & other faults in the British electoral structure.

99. HARVARD LAW SCHOOL. The Centennial History ... 1817-1917. N.p., 1918. 1st. Photogravure fp. & other illus. Index. Appendices (bibliog. of works by teachers, list of staff, etc.) x, 412pp. Orig. cl., sl. rbbd & fdd. £15.00

100. HAWKINS, Williams. A Treatise of the Pleas of the Crown: 1724. 2nd ed. 2 vols in 1. Folio. First advert. leaf. Index. [xiv], 266, [xliv]/[viii], 464, [lxxvi] pp. Vol. 2 sl. spotted. Contemp. cf., rbbd., jts. worn. S. & M.i.362. £50.00
In order & completeness & in his attempt to explain the reasons of the law Hawkins surpasses all his predecessors even Hale, whose great "History" was in any event unpublished at the time.

101. [HAWLES, Sir John]. The Englishman's Rights ... 1763. 12mo. [viii], 60pp. Head-margin of title repaired. Lib. label & stamps on three leaves. Mod. wraps. £15.00

102. HAYES, W. & T. JARMAN. Concise Forms of Wills, with Practical Notes. 1838. 2nd ed. Index. xxiv, 360pp. Contemp. annotations. Sl. dust-stained. Mod. cloth. S. & M.ii.160. SOLD.

103. HEALES, Alfred. The History and Law of Church Seats, or Pews. 1872. 1st & only edition. 2 vols. Indices. xxiv, 216/xii, 180pp. Contemp. ½ calf/mbld. sides, jts. weak. S. & M.ii.162. £25.00
This subject was rendered surprisingly complex by the Victorian religious revival & by the conflict between the claims of the clergy & the common law relating to easements. Heales's work (whose first volume is entirely historical) is the last of five 19th-century monographs on the subject.

104. HILL, Frederic. Crime: its Amount Causes and Remedies. 1853. 1st. Appendix. Index. xvi, 444pp. Lib. stamp on title-verso. Orig. dec'd cloth, sp. fdd. & sl. defective at foot. Upper jt. torn. S. & M.ii.166. £30.00
This work by a former Inspector of Prisons in Scotland expresses the honest Victorian conviction that bad education, bad homes & bad laws, rather than innate depravity, make the hardened criminal.

105. HEINECCIUS, Johannes Gottlieb (1681-1741). Elementa iuris civilis secundum ordinem Institutionum. Amsterdam, 1738. 4th ed. Red & black title. Index. xvi, 418, [xxviii] pp. Quire 2C of seven leaves only. Many contemp. annots. sl. browned. Lacks e-p's. Contemp. calf, worn. £15.00

106. HEINECCIUS, Johannes Gottlieb. Elementa iuris civilis secundum ordinem Pandectarum. Amsterdam, 1740. 4th ed. 2 vols. Engr. fold'g fp. port. (sl. torn at fold.) Red & black title. Index. xxviii, 552/350, [xlvi] pp. O_3 & O_4 misbound before O_1, O_7 & O_8 before O_5 (vol. 1). Lib stamps on title-verso (vol. 1) & A_2 (vol. 2). Few contemp. annots. Contemp. cf., sp.s & edges worn. £30.00

107. ———————. A Methodical System of Universal Law: or, the Law of Nature and Nations. Tr. & ed. George

Turnbull. 1763. 1st Engl. Final errata leaf. [x], 324/[ii], 244, [ii], 247-326, [ii]pp. 2 vols. Lacks ½ titles & front e-ps. Titles sl. browned. Contemp. sheep, rbbd., jts. worn. S. & M.i.596. £25.00
Includes Turnbull's own Discourse on Moral and Civil Law; this is an interesting attempt to draw the image of a truly natural law – one which uses beneficially, in place of suppressing or constraining, the instincts of human nature.

108. HEWART, Lord (L.C.J.). The New Despotism. 1929. 1st. Index. viii, 9-308pp. Orig. cl., sl. fdd. S. & M.ii.164. £10.00
Lord Hewart, author of the most famous of all dicta, expresses opinions similar to those more recently elaborated by the Master of the Rolls in reference to Parliament.

109. HODY, Humphrey (1659-1706). A History of English Councils and Convocations, and of the Clergy's Sitting in Parliament. 1701. 1st. Advert. leaves at end. [xiv], 432, 288, [iv]pp. Fore-margins of A_2 & B_1 frayed. Sl. wormed, esp. at end. Cancel-stub between B_7 & B_8. Contemp. panelled cf., sl. rbbd, sp. sl. wormed. S. & M.i.132. £25.00
The rising controversy regarding the clergy's part (individually & collectively) in temporal government moved Hody to publish these memoirs, closely based on the records, of the ancient organization of the English Church. In some copies page 288 (here partially given up to a publisher's catalogue) is re-set & a short appendix added.

110. HOPE, Sir Thomas (?-1646). Minor Practicks; or, a Treatise of the Scottish Law. Ed. Alexander Bayne. Edinburgh, 1726. 1st. viii, 148, [ii], [ii], 151-246pp. Contemp. cf., worn, sm. hole in lower cvr. S. & M.v.51. £50.00
Hope's work, like Hale's History of the Common Law, is an incomplete composition brought to light after the author's death. The editor has added a short history of Scots law & a summary of Acts of Sederunt from 1660-1726.

111. HUBER, Ulrich (1636-1694). Praelectionum iuris civilis tomi III ... Accedunt Christiani Thomasii ... additiones ... et Luderi Menckenii ... remissiones ad ius Saxonicum. Frankfurt & Leipzig, 1749. 4th ed. 3 vols. 4to. Engr. fp. port. Red & black title. Index. Sl. spotted. Contemp. mottled calf, very worn. Lib. labels. £50.00
A continuous exposition of the civil law, following the order of the Institutes & the Pandects & developed from Huber's lectures in the Leipzig university. His purpose was to present his work as an organic whole & not as a succession of unrelated observations.

112. JARMAN, Thomas. A Treatise on Wills. 1855. 2nd ed., ed. E.P. Wolstenholme and S. Vincent. 2 vols. Index. Publisher's cat. inserted in vol. 1. Last 36pp. of table of cases misbound after p.32. Sl. spotted. Orig. cloth, faded. Vol. 1 re-cased, vol. 2 shaken. S. & M.ii.185. £20.00
Like Mr. Spenlow, the author of this immense standard work never found time to make a will of his own.

113. [JOHNSON, Rev. Samuel]. A History and Defence of Magna Charta ... with an Introductory Discourse ... Bill of Rights ... Essay on Parliaments. Dublin, 1769. 1st Irish. [ii], xl, 278pp. Contemp. cf., corners sl. worn. S. & M.i.550. £40.00
The author's theme is that the Charter was (in modern language) a declaratory, not an innovatory statute – a confirmation of the ancient laws, not a reformation. Dr. Johnson was taxed with the authorship but denied it, & in truth the style is not his; a namesake, a country clergyman, has been reasonably suggested as the author.

114. JUSTICE, Alexander. A General Treatise of the Dominion and Laws of the Sea. 1705. 1st. 4to. Fold'g engr. fp. & plate of flags. Index. [vii], vi, 660, 40, [viii]pp. Sl. browned. Some contemp. corrections. Mod. ½ cf./mbld. sides. This ed. not in Kress. S. & M.i.509. £120.00
This useful work includes a well-documented historical section, texts of the most important codes, a collection of treaties, suggestions for the future of British shipping, forms of charter-party etc., & an appendix on insurance.

116. JUSTINIAN I. Emperor. Digestorum seu pandectarum pars tertia [-quarta.] Paris, 1562. Pts. 3 & 4 (of 6) only, in 1 vol. Devices on titles. 372/400pp. Ownership inscription "Foy pour devoir – E. Hartford" (Edward Seymour, 2nd Earl of Hertford, c.1540-1621) on title of pt.3. Contemp. cf., sp. gilt; lacks ties, rbbd. upper jt. worn. £35.00
This Earl of Hertford was son to the Duke of Somerset, the ambitious and unfortunate Lord Protector of Edward VI's time, & brother-in-law to Lady Jane Grey. He spent the years 1561-1567 in the Tower; if he had the book when it was new, he must have followed his sister-in-law in making study the comfort of his solitude. A genealogy by the historian T.A. Walker & a note on the binding by Lord Belper are pasted inside the covers.

117. ———— [Corpus iuris civilis, ed. Dionysius Gothofredus. Geneva, 1619.] 2 vols. in 1. 4to. Lacks first title. Indices. 16pp., 17-126 columns, [i]p, 2018 columns, [xvi]pp. 972 columns, [x]pp, 568 columns. Last leaf frayed. Contemp. annots. old ¾ cf./mbld. sides, re-backed, sides worn. £25.00

118. ————. Institutionum libri quatuor. The Four Books of Justinian's Institutions. Tr. & ed. George Harris. Oxford, 1811. 3rd ed. 4to. Latin & English text. Engr. table. 370, [ii]pp. Lib. stamps on title. Sl. spotted. Few pencil annots. Contemp. ½ cf./mbld. sides, re-backed. rubbed. S. & M.v.135. £20.00

119. KEBLE, Joseph. An Assistance to Justices of the Peace. By W. Rawlins, S. Roycroft, and H. Sawbridge ... for Ch. Harper, 1683. 1st. Folio. BLACK LETTER. First privilege leaf. Index. [vi], 140, 137-430, 457-720, [viii]pp. Several irregularities in pagination etc. caused by change of printer. Few sm. marginal worm-holes. Contemp. cf., tail of sp. sl. torn, some leaves loose. Wing K.113. S. & M.i.229. £40.00
Keble's work was designed as a supplement to the standard justices' manuals, whose provision it abridges alphabetically. In a preliminary section, everything in the statute-book which concerns justices is set out at length.

120. KELHAM, Robert. Domesday Book Illustrated ... Tenants in Capite or Serjanty therein mentioned ... Translation of the Difficult Passages. 1788. 1st. viii, 400pp. S_3 a cancel. Orig. bds., uncut, re-backed cl.; worn. S. & M.i.92. £30.00
The first general commentary on Domesday Book, which had been made available for study in Farley's great type-facsimile edition in 1783.

121. KERR, Robert Malcolm. (Judge, London Sheriff's Court) (1821-1902) (ed.). BLACKSTONE, Sir William; Commentaries on the Laws of England ... Adapted to the Present State of the Law. 1862. 3rd ed. 4 vols. 2 fold'g tables in vol. 2. Index. Orig. cl., uncut & unopened; fdd. S. & M.i.28. £50.00

122. ———— PITT-LEWIS, G.; Commissioner Kerr – an Individuality. 1903. 1st. 2 ports. Index. x, 396, [viii]pp. Orig. cl., t.e.g., uncut, mark of lib. label on upper cover. £10.00

123. SOLD.

124. KYD, Stewart (c.1760-1811). A Treatise on the Law of Bills of Exchange and Promissory Notes. Albany, N.Y., 1800. 2nd Amer. (from 3rd London) ed. Index. xii, 284, [iv]pp. Sl. browned & stnd. Mod. cl. Not in Kress. This ed. not in S. & M. £20.00
Kyd, a Scotsman like most commercial-law specialists, was associated with Thomas Paine, Horne Tooke, & other radicals.

125. LAMB, Charles. The Old Benchers of the Inner Temple. Ed. Sir F.D. Mackinnon. O.U.P. 1927. 1st thus. 4to. 7 collotype plates. Index. Limited 600. Orig. b'ram. £15.00

126. LANGFORD, John Alfred. Prison Books and their Authors. 1861. 1st. Wood-engr. ports. xii, 358pp. Orig. dec'd cloth, rubbed, spine faded. £15.00
Boethius, Raleigh, Cervantes, Bunyan etc.

127. The LAW-FRENCH DICTIONARY. Alphabetically Digested ... to which is added, the Law-Latin Dictionary. Ed. F.O. 1701. 1st. [iv], [152], [iv], [496]pp. Group of worm-holes in text throughout. First two leaves frayed. Sl. stained. Contemp. cf., re-backed, rubbed. Lib. label. S. & M.i.9. £25.00
The Latin section is by far the more curious & comprehensive; it is drawn (the author says) from thirty years' study of writs, entries & pleadings.

128. The LAW of ERRORS and Writs of Errors ... wherein is contained the Nature and End of the Writ of Error ... Errors in Law and in Fact ... Pleadings ... Statutes of Jeofails [etc.] 1703. 1st. Index. [xxxii], 336, [xxiv]pp. Few sl. stains. Contemp. calf, jts. & corners worn. S. & M.i.276. £40.00
The first, & for nearly 80 years the only, monograph on the subject. The Author's preface dares to insinuate that the Statutes of Jeofail, designed to piece out the imperfections of the old writ de errore corrigendo as an engine for reversing faulty decisions, had not fully served their purpose.

129. LAWS concerning the ELECTION of MEMBERS of PARLIAMENT: with the Determinations of the ... Commons. 1780. 6th ed., rev. Index. Final advert. leaf. Contemp. calf, jts. & edges rubbed. S. & M.i.151. £25.00
Includes a new preface embodying remarks prompted by Douglas's (Lord Glenbervie's) lately-published History of Contested Elections. The advertisement is a curiosity; originally bound (as the offsetting shows) between pages 140 & 141, it looks at first like a law-report, but at length reveals itself as a puff for Owen's "Nevil Holt" mineral water.

130. LESSIUS, Leonardus (1554-1623). De iustitia et iure caeterisque virtutibus cardinalibus libri quatuor. Antwerp (ex officina Plantiniana), 1612. 3rd ed., rev. Folio. Engr. title. Index. Final device leaf. [xvi], 804, [lxviii]pp. One leaf sl. stained. Contemp. calf, 18th-cent. re-backing & re-cornering, tail of spine & edges worn. £120.00
This work is conceived as a commentary on the Secunda Secundae of Aquinas, with one book devoted to each of the cardinal virtues – Prudence, Justice, Fortitude, & Temperance. However, book 2 (Justice), which extends far beyond the sphere of Aquinas, occupies four-fifths of the entire work. Enjoying all the precision of the Aristotelian method without its mediaeval triviality, the work is a remarkable contribution to jurisprudential literature.

131. ————. De iustitia et iure ceterisq; virtutibus cardinalibus libri quatuor ... cum appendice de monte pietatis. Antwerp (ex officina Plantiniana), 1626. 6th ed., rev. Folio. Fine engr. title (Galle after Rubens.) Index. [xvi], 826, [lxviii]pp. Ownership inscr. on title, "Monasterii Cantinipratensis in bellinghen". Lib. stamp on $*_2$. Contemp. blind-stamped calf over wooden boards (probably a monastery binding); spine & corners repaired, jts. cracked. £120.00
In 1619 the Austrian rulers of Belgium, wishing to break the power which Italian money-lenders held over the nation's capital, established a system of monts-de-piété. Some prelates, impelled perhaps by a misguided spirit of nationalism, condemned this institution as contrary to the Church's teaching on usury. Lessius proves in his appendix that the Bull of Leo X., which was appealed to by the malcontents, did not apply to the Belgian scheme.

132. A LETTER concerning the DISABLING CLAUSES lately offered to the House of Commons, for regulating Corporations. By Randal Taylor, 1690. 1st. Sm. 4to. 22, [ii]pp. Final blank. Disbound. Wing L.1531. £20.00
In an exaggerated reaction against Charles II's attempt to manufacture a friendly House of Commons by doctoring the charters of the municipal corporations, there had lately been added to a pending Bill, in a very underhanded fashion, two clauses disabling all mayors, aldermen etc. who had connived at this work from afterwards holding office. The author condemns this extravagant act of revenge against men whose motives were generally honest & who might still do good service to their country.

133. A LETTER from a FRENCH LAWYER to an English Gentleman, upon the Present Revolution. For Ric. Chiswell, 1689. 1st. Sm. 4to. [ii], 18pp. Disbound. Wing L.4. £20.00
Argues that France will not be impelled by zeal for Rome to assist the Stuarts in any attempt to recapture the English crown. If King Louis has any such inclination (says the author) the Estates both can & will suppress it – a statement so naive in its ignorance of the farce that was the French assembly as effectively to prove that "French lawyer" is a fiction.

134. LEVI, Leone (1821-1888). The Law of Nature and Nations, as Affected by Divine Law. 1855. 1st. xii, 116, [ii]pp. Orig. cl., fdd., head of spine sl. defective. £20.00
In this work the distinguished economist notices an anomaly which his own time could scarcely conceive, but which has been painfully brought to the notice of the present age – that while science advances morality & humanity do not necessarily keep pace, but may be static or even decline.

135. LEY, Sir James (Earl of Marlborough) (1552-1629). Reports of divers Resolutions in Law, arising upon Cases in the Court of Wards, and other Courts at Westminster. By Tho. Roycroft for H. Twyford, Tho. Dring, and Jo. Place, 1659. 1st. Folio. Black letter. Index. [iv], 84, [viii], 28pp. Sl. marginal worming. Contemp. calf, re-backed, edges rubbed. Wing M.688. S. & M.i.357. £50.00
The only early collection of reports in the Court of Wards, where Ley was King's attorney from 1609 to 1617. They preserve some interesting specimens of conveyance to uses. Ley's Treatise on Wards & Liveries included.

136. LOCCENIUS, Johannes (1599-1677). Dissertationum politicarum syntagma. Amsterdam (apud Joannem Ianssonium), 1644. 2nd ed. 12mo. Engr. title. [xxii], 540pp. Sl. stained. Fly-title sl. defective with loss of one letter. Contemp. vellum. £30.00
The most important item in this collection by a prominent Swedish jurist & historian is the first, De ordinanda republica, a study of the causes of civil strife. The other works include an essay on the popular theme of the comparison between the p·lity of bees & that of man.

137. LUMLEY, W.G. The Rating Act, 1874 ... Addendum to the Law of Parochial Assessments. 1874. 1st. Index. [ii], 52pp. – CIRCULAR of the LOCAL GOVERNMENT BOARD. 1874. 1st. 12pp. Two works in one volume, as issued. 24pp. adverts. Orig. cloth, sl. faded. Not in S. & M. £5.00

138. MAGNA CHARTA, cum statutis, tum antiquis, tum recentibus, maximopere animo tenendis. By Richard Tottel, 1576. Black letter. French, English and Latin text. Woodcut initials. Indices. [viii], 247 leaves. Blank $¶_8$. Names of three members of the Waller family on title & e-p. Few old annots. Scribbles on verso of last leaf; lacks final blank; otherwise a fine copy in 19th-cent. green mor., gilt. a.e.g. Beale S.19. S.T.C.9281 (reading "March" in colophon.) S. & M.i.350. £300.00
The Magna Charta printed in the early editions is that of Henry III, issued ten years after John's. Many other ancient statutes had been added to it over the years; but this edition is designed rather as a current handbook of statute law, including the Statute of Uses & many other recent enactments.

139. MARTENS, Georg Friedrich von. The Law of Nations, founded on the Treaties and Customs of ... Europe. Tr. William Cobbett. 1803. Appendix. xxxii, 454pp. Sl. spotted. Contemp. diced cf., rubbed. £20.00
This version was commissioned from Cobbett by the U.S. Government. For this London edition he added a new preface & brought the list of treaties down to date.

140. MARY, Queen of Scots. SCOTUS, Romualdus (pseud.?) Summarium rationum, quibus cancellarius Angliae et prolocutor Puckeringius ... persuaserunt occidendam esse ... Mariam. N.p. [Ingolstadt], 1588. 1st. Sm. 4to. 37 leaves. Some browning. 19th-cent. brown mor., sl. rubbed. £120.00
Latin version of the prosecutors' arguments at the trial of Mary, with a detailed but bigoted & rhetorical confutation by a Scottish Catholic, & some memorial epigrams. Ownership inscription on title of the Jesuits' college in Brussels.

141. MAY, Thomas Erskine (afterwards Lord Farnborough) (1815-1886). A Treatise upon the Law, Privileges, Proceedings and Usage of Parliament. 1844. 1st. Index. xvi, 496pp. Contemp. ½ calf/mbld. sides, sl. rubbed. Sp. faded. Bk-pl. Lord Belper. S. & M.ii.238. £25.00
The first comprehensive work on the subject. The humble Assistant Librarian to the House of Commons has impressed his name on the subject even to our own day.

142. ————. A Treatise on the Law, Privileges ... 1868. 6th ed. Index. xxvi, 808, 36pp. Orig. cloth, sl. fdd. £15.00

143. ————. The Constitutional History of England since the Accession of George the Third. 1873. 4th ed., rev. Index. xx, 460/xii, 420/xiv, 500pp. 3 vols. Contemp. polished tree calf, gilt, arms on upper covers (Wellington College prize); spines sl. worn. £30.00
Includes a new chapter covering the years 1861-1871.

144. MEREWETHER, Henry Alworth, & Archibald John STEPHENS. The History of the Boroughs and Municipal Corporations of the United Kingdom. 1835. 1st. 3 vols. ½ titles. Index. Mod. ½ calf/cloth sides. Gross 79. S. & M.i.417. £50.00
The exaggerated notions of the antiquity, purity & equality of the English local government system which were promulgated by Sharpe & adopted by Oldfield, still inform Merewether's far more scholarly compilation with a partial & tendentious spirit; but the solid foundation of documents on which it rests ensures that it shall not fall below a certain level of accuracy.

145. The MODERN CONVEYANCER: or Conveyancing Improv'd. Being a Choice Collection of Presidents. By the Assigns of Richard and Ed: Atkyns ... for John Walthoe, 1695. 1st. Index. ½ title. [ii], 52, 466, [xxii]pp. Final advert. leaf. Contemp. calf, sl. worn. Wing M.2336. S. & M.i.484. £85.00
Marriage-settlements, which were still something of a novelty, play a large part in this work.

146. MOLLOY, Charles. De jure maritimo et navali: or, a Treatise of Affairs Maritime and of Commerce. 1707. 6th ed., rev. Engr. fp. & title. Index. [iv], xx, 293, 278-476, [xvi]pp. Pagination & signing irregular. Sl. browned & spotted. Contemp. calf, rubbed. Kress 2566. S. & M.i.511. £60.00

147. MONTESQUIEU, Charles de Secondat, Président & Baron de (1689-1755). The Spirit of Laws. 1777. 2 vols. 12mo. xx, 334/xii, 386pp. Lib. stamp on verso of each title. Contemp. cf., worn. £20.00
Includes a translation of the Life by Maupertuis.

148. ————. The Spirit of Laws. Glasgow, 1793. 2 vols. 12mo. xxiv, 382/xiv, 428pp. Contemp. mottled cf., re-backed, corners sl. worn. £20.00

149. ————. The Spirit of Laws. 1794. 2 vols. xxii, 352/xii, 386pp. Contemp. mottled cf., sps. gilt; one label defective; sps. & edges rubbed. £20.00

150. MOORE, Sir Francis (1558-1621). Cases, ed. Sir Geoffrey Palmer. By R. Norton for Robert Pawlet, 1663. 1st. Folio. French text. Black letter. Lacks engr. fp. port. Index. [xx], 918, [lxxiv]pp. Mod. cloth. Wing M.2535. S. & M.i.305. £30.00
Many of Moore's cases turn on the Statute of Uses & the earliest attempts made by conveyancers to adapt their

science to it; for example, The Earl of Bedford's Case *(p.718, no.1006) shows how conveyance to uses began to break free from the strict law governing remainders. Also included is the speech of Lord Ellesmere L.C. to Sir Henry Montagu, the new Chief Justice of King's Bench – the character of a good judge, with several very plain hints against Coke as an example to be avoided.*

151. MOORE, John Bassett. A Digest of International Law as embodied in Diplomatic Discussions, Treaties ... Decisions ... Writings of Jurists [etc.] Washington, D.C. (Govt. Printing Office), 1906. 1st. **8 vols.** Including index volume. Orig. cloth, (vol. 4 not uniform), sl. faded & frayed, vol. 6. stained. £80.00
This work was the result of an Act of Congress of Feb. 1897 ordering the production of a Digest to replace that of Wharton (1887).

152. MURPHY, W.F., & C.H. PRITCHETT. Courts, Judges, and Politics: an Introduction to the Judicial Process. N.Y., 1961. 1st. Index. xviii, 708pp. Lib. label, & stamp on title. Orig. cl., sl. fdd. £5.00

153. MACKENZIE, Sir George (1636-1691). The Laws and Customes of Scotland, in Matters Criminal. Edinburgh (by Thomas Brown), 1678. 4to. Red & black title. First privilege leaf. [xiv], 582pp. Contemp. sheep, spine gilt, rubbed. **Wing M.167. S. & M.v.75.** £85.00
Like much Scottish legal writing, this work puts its English contemporaries (Hale not excepted) to shame in point of order & exactitude. His remarks on witchcraft in particular show such an admirable spirit of reason that it is clearly unjust to accuse him of barbarity on account of his defence of torture; indeed, it appears that on this point he merely followed his authorities in the civil law. Three editions appeared in 1678.

154. MACLAURIN, [John] (later Lord Dreghorn). Arguments and Decisions, in Remarkable Cases, before the High Court of Justiciary and other Supreme Courts, in Scotland. Edinburgh, 1774. 1st. 4to. xvi, [ii], xvii-xl, 776, [viii] pp. Final advert. leaf. Sl. spotted. Contemp. cf., re-backed, rubbed; edges worn. **S. & M.v.76.** £40.00
A far more learned work than Arnot's more famous collection. Maclaurin's cases, in some of which he himself took part, include R. v. Maclauchlan *(1737) (interesting questions of the definition of treason & the effect of drunkenness on liability, arising from the Porteous riots) &* Macintosh v. Dempster *(1767)*

(a deep discussion of the extent of Parliamentary privilege in regard to arrest & prosecution.)

155. NASMITH, David. Outline of Roman History ... with Special Reference to ... Jurisprudence. 1890. 1st. Map. Table. Indices. xx, 618, [ii] pp. Orig. b'ram, sp. & upper cvr. marked. **S. & M.v.139.** £5.00
Includes versions of the Institutes of Gaius & Justinian.

156. NEILD, James, (1744-1814). An Account of the Rise, Progress, and Present State of the Society for the Discharge and Relief of Persons Imprisoned for Small Debts. 1808. 3rd ed. Two engr. ports.: fold'g plan of Newgate Prison. Final errata leaf. [ii], 602pp. Contemp. tree calf, gilt, jts. & corners worn. **Kress B.5407.** £75.00
The Society was founded in 1772. Its policy was generally to relieve the individual, not to reform the law; however Neild (the treasurer) does suggest some innovations. The bulk of the work is a complete catalogue of British prisons, with details of their provision for debtors.

157. NELSON, William (fl. 1684-1726). The Laws concerning Game ... together with the Forest Laws. 1751. 4th ed. 12mo. First & last advert. leaves. Index. xviii, 255, [xxxviii] pp. Contemp. calf, rubbed, upper jt. cracked. **S. & M.i.465.** £20.00

158. NEUMAYR, Johann Wilhelm. Von der Neutralitet und Assistentz oder Unpartheylichkeit und Partheylichkeit in Kriegszeiten. Erfurt (Johann Birckner), 1622. 2nd ed. Sm. 4to. German text. Engr. title-border. [viii], 398, [ii] pp. Browned throughout. Contemp. vellum, sl. wormed, lacks ties. £85.00
A remarkable work for its time in many ways – in its subject, its use of the vernacular, and its bold reliance on modern history in preference to ancient authority for its examples. It is clear from Neumayr's prefatory address to Duke Johann Ernst of Saxony that the awful & unprecedented spectacle of a pan-European conflict, with the new moral & practical problems which it raised for those states not yet directly engaged in the war, called the work into being; it does not inquire into the ethics of the case, but attempts to lay down a path of safety for unaligned governments.

159. NEVILE, C(hristopher). The Justice and Expediency of Tenant-Right Legislation Considered. 1848. 1st. vi, 34pp. Sewn as issued. **Kress C.7511.** £6.00
A protest against a Bill intended to give agricultural tenants a right to claim compensation at fixed rates from their landlords for improvements carried out by themselves. The Bill, which did not pass, would have been an early example of State encroachment on property rights.

160. NICOLAS, Nicholas Harris (ed.) The Privy Purse Expences of King Henry the Eighth, from November MDXXIX, to December MDXXXII. W. Pickering, 1827. 1st. Index. xlvi, 372pp. Orig. cloth, paper label, uncut & unopened; faded. £20.00
Printed from a MS. formerly in the collection of Harley, Earl of Oxford.

161. NICHOLLS, George. Poor Laws – Ireland. Three Reports. H.M.S.O., 1838. 1st. viii, 172pp. Orig. cloth, marked & faded, pastedowns detached. £30.00
Recommends the extension of the English system to Ireland, where there was then no central administration of the poor at all. The third report examines the Dutch & Belgian systems.

162. NOLAN, Michael. A Treatise of the Laws for the Relief and Settlement of the Poor. 1805. 1st. 2 vols. Index. xl, 390/xxxii, 384, 188, [xlviii] pp. Contemp. calf, spines sl. rubbed. **S. & M.ii.258.** £35.00
Nolan boldly attempts to form a coherent system from the multitude of decisions, using them (according to the principle later enunciated by Stephen & Pollock) with more general application than the ratio *of each case, read strictly, would imply.*

163. NOODT, Gerard (1647-1725). Opera omnia ... Accessit v.cl. Joannis Barbeyracii historica . vitae auctoris narratio. Leyden, 1735. 2 vols. Folio. Engr. fp. port. Red & black titles. Index. [xx], 648, [xx]/[iv], 590, [xvi] pp. 20_1 & 20_4 (vol. 1) & $3L_{1-3}$ (vol. 2) reversed. Few sm. marginal tears. Contemp. boards, uncut; sl. worn. £80.00
The best edition of Noodt's works, corrected by an anonymous but learned hand, & with a Life translated & enlarged by Barbeyrac from one which he had formerly written in French. Noodt's masterpiece, his commentary on books 1-27 of the Pandects (begun when was past seventy), occupies vol. 2.

164. NORTON-KYSHE, J.W. (ed.) The Dictionary of Legal Quotations. 1904. 1st. Index. xxiv, 344pp. Orig. b'ram, spine faded. **S. & M.ii.259.** £10.00

165. OKE, George C. A Handy Book of the Game and Fishery Laws. 1861. 1st. Index. xiv, 212, 28pp. Orig. cloth, sl. faded. **S. & M.ii.261.** £10.00

166. OLDFIELD, T.H.B. The Representative History of Great Britain and Ireland. 1816. 1st. 6 vols. Appendices. Contemp. calf, gilt, m.e., re-backed; sides rubbed. **S. & M.i.152. Gross 304.** £95.00
Taking up the doctrine of Granville Sharpe that universal suffrage (at least among householders) was essential to the original constitution of England & had merely been overlaid by the institution of close boroughs & bought & sold franchises, Oldfield traces the progress of corruption, first in general & afterwards seat by seat. The works (the third & last of Oldfield's Parliamentary writings) is at once a symptom & a cause of rising discontent with the electoral system.

167. ————. Another set. ½ calf/mbld. sides, spines gilt; jts. worn; spine of vol. 1 frayed. Bk-pl. Lord Belper. £95.00

168. OWEN, Hugh, Jr. (afterwards Sir Hugh). The Elementary Education Act, 1876 ... Provisions of Factory Acts. 1876. 1st. Index. xxiv, 118pp. Orig. cl. sp. fdd. **Not in S. & M.** £5.00

169. PALMER, William. The Law of Wreck, Considered with a View to its Amendment. 1843. 1st. [iv], 54pp. Autograph note, initialled, on title. **S. & M.ii.265.**
———— **An ACT** for Consolidating and Amending the Laws relating to Wreck. 1846. 1st. 4to. 957-982pp. **2 works in 1 vol.** Contemp. calf, gilt, sl. rubbed. £25.00
Proposes that shipwrecked property should be held by the Crown for six years on trust for the owner, with other strong provisions against the wreckers & plunderers who were still active in Cornwall & elsewhere. The statute (9 & 10 Vict. c.99) met some of the author's demands.

170. PAPERS relative to the RUPTURE with SPAIN, Laid before Both Houses of Parliament. 1762. 1st. 4to. [ii], 72pp.
———— **PRELIMINARY ARTICLES of PEACE,** between his Britannick Majesty, the Most Christian King, and the Catholic King. 1762. 1st. French & English text. 4to. 24pp. **2 works in 1 vol.** First title repaired at inner margin & partially guarded. Mod. cloth. £40.00
Diplomatic correspondence of the elder Pitt & Lord Bristol (the ambassador to Spain), & a treaty, recording the beginning & end of the quarrel whose dilatory prosecution caused the resignation of Pitt & the downfall of the Newcastle government.

171. [PARSONS, Robert] (c.1550-1610). An Answere to the Fifth Part of Reportes lately set forth by Syr Edward Cooke ... concerning the ... Lawes ... which do apperteyne to Spirituall Power & Jurisdiction. N.p. [St.-Omer], 1606.

1st. Sm. 4to. Index. [lxxii], 387 [i.e. 386], [xii] pp. Lacks last leaf of index. Sl. browned. Mod. ½ calf/mbld. sides. **S.T.C.19352. S. & M.i.126.** £85.00
The famous English Jesuit, who at one time came near to raising a civil war in England, here offers his reply to Coke's contention (in his observations on Caudrey's Case*) that the statute I Eliz.I, which confirmed the monarch as head of the Church, was a declaratory, not an innovatory law – that the King had always held that position. The Pope never.*

172. PARSONS, Theophilus (Chief Justice of Massachusetts) (1750-1813). PARSONS, Theophilus, Jnr.; Memoir ... with Notices of some of his Contemporaries. Boston. Mass., 1859. 1st. Engr. fp. port (sl. stained). Publisher's cat. at end. viii, 476, 12pp. Orig. cloth, head of spine & upper cvr. sl. stained; sl. faded. £25.00
As a young man Parsons took a notable part in settling the Massachusetts state constitution. He was a man of wide interests with a leaning towards mathematics, & as a judge he won high repute. This copy is inscribed by the author to Levi Parsons.

173. PAUL, John. Every Landlord or Tenant his Own Lawyer, ed. Geo. Wilson. 1778. 4th ed. [iv], 180pp. Contemp. ¼ sheep/mbld. sides, rubbed. **S. & M.i.461.** £15.00

174. PEARSON, Anthony. The Great Case of Tithes ... to which is added, a Defence of some other Principles held by the ... Quakers. 1730. 1st collected. viii, 292, [viii] pp. Contemp. panelled cf., jts. & edges sl. worn. **S. & M.i.193.** £30.00
Pearson's arguments against the legal establishment of tithes include the bold but reasonable suggestion that the Biblical injunctions, however they may weigh in themselves, had nothing to do with the institution as he found it. First published in 1657, the work is here augmented with an elaborate justification of women's preaching & other features of Quakerism.

175. PEREZ, Antonio. Praelectiones in duodecim libros Codicis ... Editio ultima, ab auctore recognita. Antwerp & Amsterdam (Wetstein), 1695. **2 vols. in 1.** 4to. Red & black title. Index. [xvi], 690/662, [liv] pp. Contemp. blind-stamped vellum. £80.00
Among older works on the Code, the commentary of Perez is at once the fullest & the most practical.

176. ———— another copy ... pars altera. Amsterdam (D. Elzevir), 1671. 3rd ed. 4to. **Vol. 2 (of 2)** (books 8-12) only. Index. 665, [lix] pp. Signature of William Salkeld, 18th-cent. English serjeant & law-reporter, on title. Contemp. vellum. **Willems 1457.** **£15.00**

177. PERKINS, John. A Profitable Booke ... treating of the Lawes of England. Apud Richardum Tottell, 14th December 1576. French text. Black letter. Index. [xx], 168 leaves. Corners sl. stnd. sm. ink-stains on H, & U, . Mod. calf. **Beale T.422. S.T.C.19636. S. & M.i.485.** £250.00
Perkins explains, in an unusually logical style, the law of real property so far as it relates to the transference of land by purchase. He was the conveyancer's Mentor for three hundred years. He seems to have been a pupil or protegé of Littleton's; his expression "mon master Littleton" may imply nothing more than the average lawyer's reverence for the great authority, but as it is peculiar to Perkins one may fairly infer some special & personal attachment from it.

178. PERKINS, John. A Profitable Booke ... treating of the Lawes of England. For the Company of Stationers, 1621. 16mo. French text. Index. [xxiv], 168 leaves. Contemp. calf, blind-tooled & gilt, central design of small tools on sides; lacks ties; upper jt. rubbed. **S.T.C.19644. S. & M.i.485.** £100.00
See previous item.

179. PHILLIPS, Charles (1787-1859). Curran and his Contemporaries. 1851. 4th ed., rev. Engr. fp. port. (John Philpot Curran, Master of the Rolls for Ireland). Index. viii, 596pp. Sl. spotted. Orig. dec'd cloth; sp. fdd., sl. worn. **Not in S. & M.** £15.00
Reminiscences of some Irish characters, especially of the patriots of "ninety-eight" – Curran, Emmett, Wolfe Tone, Grattan, Flood etc. This edition includes remarks on the life of the Duke of Wellington.

180. P[HILIPPS], H. The Grandeur of the Law: or, an exact Collection of the Nobility and Gentry ... whose Honors and Estates have by some of their Ancestors been ... augmented by the Practice of the Law. For Arthur Jones, 1684. 1st. [viii], 276, [x] pp. Later calf, re-backed. **Wing P.2022. S. & M.i.207.** £50.00
An essential though unreliable source for any student of legal biography.

181. PHILIPPS, J.T. The Fundamental Laws and Constitutions of Seven Potent ... States ... viz. Denmark, Sweden, Germany, Poland, England, Holland and Swisserland. 1752. 1st. Appendix. [xii], 428pp. Presentation copy. Corner cut from front e-p. Contemp. mottled calf, spine gilt, gilt border & central lozenge on sides; upper jt. worn; edges rubbed. **S. & M.i.105.** £45.00
A selection of charters basic to the respective constitutions of the states listed. The appendix includes (among other interesting items) Manasseh ben Israel's petition to Cromwell on behalf of the Jews, and an epistle in praise of Grotius addressed by Philipps to a most unpromising pupil, William "the Butcher", Duke of Cumberland.

182. POLLOCK, [Sir] Frederick, (1845-1937). A Digest of the Law of Partnership. 1877. 1st. Index. xxxvi, 136pp. Contemp. calf, spine rubbed, jts. worn. **S. & M.ii.284.** £20.00
Pollock's Introduction is of durable interest. He explains his method of using decided cases not merely to lay down the law for the identical circumstances if they should recur, but as material out of which general legal positions may be evolved; a device which (he says) may put an end to the dichotomy between general *statutes &* particular *cases, and enable both to be wrought together into a single codified body of law.*

183. ————. Essays in Jurisprudence and Ethics. 1882. 1st collected. Index. xii, 384pp. Contemp. polished cf., gilt, m.e., Edinburgh Univ. prize label & arms; jts. worn. **S. & M.ii.284.** £15.00

185. POWELL, John Joseph (c.1755-1801). An Essay upon the Learning of Devises, from their Inception by Writing, to their Consummation by the Death of the Devisor. 1788. 1st. Index. xii, 727, [xxv] pp. Q, & U, cancels. Some stains throughout. Corner of title defective without loss of text. Contemp. calf, rubbed. **S. & M.i.493.** £20.00
The author was a pupil of Charles Fearne, of Contingent Remainder fame.

186. POWELL, Thomas. The Attourneys Academy: or, the Manner and Fourme of Proceeding Practically, upon any Suite. For Benjamin Fisher, 1630. 3rd ed. Indices. [xii], 88, 16, 89-230, [lx] pp. Sl. wormed & stnd.
———— [AGARD[E], Arthur] The Repertorie of Records: remaining in the 4 Treasuries ... the Exchequer ... Index of the Records of the Chancery and Tower ... Calendar of ... Records of the Tower. For B. Fisher, 1631. 1st. First blank. [vi], 218 [i.e. 216] pp. sl. wormed & stnd.
———— [POWELL, T.] The Attornies Almanacke ... for ... such as shall have occasion to remove any Person, Cause, or Record ... to ... the higher Courts. For Ben: Fisher, 1627. 1st. First leaf blank except for signature. [vi], 72pp. **Three works in 1 vol.** 4to. Contemp. sprinkled calf, sl. rbbd. **S.T.C.20164/194/20165. S. & M.i.275/75/275.** £350.00
Agard's work (a first attempt at a guide to the national archives, written in about 1610 & completed by Powell) is dedicated to an Unknown Patron, "Mercury", whose "wings were sicke" and who has retired "to hide him from the great incensed Jove". This has sometimes been taken as a reference to Bacon in his disgrace; and from its mysterious tone, in combination with certain typographical peculiarities in the text, some observers have deduced allusions to Bacon's authorship of the Shakespearean plays. But this dedication is clearly Powell's own; it therefore dates from about 1630, when Bacon was not in retirement but in his grave. Furthermore, many indications in these verses point to Coke. Having defied Jove (the king) on the issue of prerogative, he retired in 1628 from public life and presently issued his commentary on Littleton, which established him as the supreme interpreter of the law (Mercury is the god of interpreters); furthermore, he had a favourite phrase in his hours of triumph, that he had "got upon his wings again". Students of Shakespeare must therefore be content with the clear echoes of "King Lear" on p.217 of the Academy, & of Mercutio's Queen Mab speech in the preface to the Almanac.

187. POWELL, Thomas Reed. The Logic and Rhetoric of Constitutional Law. 1918. 1st separate (rep. from "Journal of Philosophy".) **Inscribed** by the author. 645-658pp. Orig. wraps, sl. frayed. £5.00

188. PRACTICAL INSTRUCTIONS on the PASSING of PRIVATE BILLS through both Houses of Parliament. Containing the Standing Orders. 1825. 1st. Index. viii, 294pp. Fore-margins stnd. & damp-weakened. Few old annots. & some ink scoring. Contemp. ½ cf./mbld. sides, worn. **S. & M.ii.287.** £20.00
Written by a Parliamentary Agent with the laudable design of rendering solicitors entrusted with the management of private bills independent of his fraternity. The appendix (forms of petitions) includes examples for gas-lighting schemes and even for railways.

189. PRICE, Richard (1723-1791). Observations on the Nature of Civil Liberty, the Principles of Government, and the Justice and Policy of the War with America. 1776. 3rd ed. [vi], 128pp. Mod. cl. £20.00
In addition to exposing the moral injustices & commercial dangers of the war, Price strikes at the very root of the doctrine that one "state" or "country"

(he neglects to define these terms) could lawfully be subject to another. This prefigurement of the Commonwealth was hardly less admired at home than in America.

190. ——————— Another copy. 1776. 4th ed. Mod. cloth. £20.00

191. PRYNNE, William (1600-1669). Brief Animadversions on, Amendments of, and Additional Explanatory Records to, the Fourth Part of the Institutes . . . by . . . Sir Edward Cooke. By Thomas Ratcliffe [etc.] for A. Crooke [etc.], 1669. 1st. Folio. Indices. Final errata leaf. [xvi], 424, [lxviii] pp. Contemp. calf, re-backed, corners sl. worn. Bk-pl. Duke of Westminster. **Wing P.3905. S. & M.i.261.** £120.00
In the easy task of improving on Coke's knowledge of records, Prynne found a fair & open field for his immense though far from impartial reading in the documents then committed to his care.

191a. PUFENDORF, Samuel. (1632-1694). De officio hominis et civis, iuxta legem naturalem. Ed. Gershom Carmichael. Edinburgh, 1724. 1st thus. Latin text. Index. [xlii], xii, 536pp. Single worm-hole in few leaves. Contemp. cf., sl. rubbed. £30.00

192. PULTON, Ferdinando. De pace Regis et Regni, viz. a Treatise declaring which be the great and generall Offences of the Realme. For the Companie of Stationers. 1623. [4th ed.] Folio. Black letter. Index. [v], 324. [i.e. 243], [xvii] leaves. Lacks first blank. Few margins sl. soiled. Contemp. cf., later label, rubbed; upper jt. worn, head of sp. sl. defective. **S.T.C.20498. S. & M.i.365.** £120.00
A useful summary of criminal law, far more accessible than the crabbed work of Stanford (Pulton's only predecessor) & very modern in its inclusion of such matters as the law of principal & accessory, private prosecution (then called "appeal") of felonies, evidence, etc. A Catholic, & as such excluded from the inner circles of the law, Pulton writes clearly & intelligently for the layman.

193. RALEIGH, Sir Walter. The Perogative [sic] of Parliaments in England. Proved in a Dialogue betweene a Counsellour of State, and a Justice of Peace. Printed 1640. Sm 4to. [viii], 66pp. Gatherings C.G.H. & I set up by a different printer from the rest. Mod. mbld. boards. **S.T.C.20650. S. & M.i.137.** £50.00
Foreseeing the disasters that must ensue from "taxation without representation", Sir Walter by the mouth of his Justice urges King James to summon a parliament, to trust in the loyalty & good faith of the representatives, & not to be persuaded by false counsellors that it would be a compromise of his dignity to refuse the advice & consent of the members.

194. [RASTELL, John]. Les Termes de la Ley: or Certaine Difficult and Obscure Words and Termes of the Common Law and Statutes . . . Expounded. By the Assignes of John More, 1636. French & English text. [viii], 302 leaves. Title frayed & with lib. perforation. Sl. browned. New ½ cf./mbld. sides. **S.T.C.20718. S. & M.i.11.** £90.00

195. RASTELL, John. Another edition. 1721. French & English text. [iv], 592pp. Corner of title repaired, border affected. Sl. browned. Lib. perforation on title. Mod. cloth. £30.00

196. RAYNER, John. Cases at Large concerning Tithes . . . Introduction, comprehending a . . . View of the Whole Law of Tithes . . . Acts of Parliament. 1783. 1st. 3 vols. Contemp. cf., sps. sl. worn. **S. & M.i.194.** £60.00
No part of Rayner's work is of more durable value than his 36-page index of Authorities; by adding critical remarks on each work, he converted it into a legal bibliography in miniature.

197. RECUEIL de QUELQUES DISCOURS POLITIQUES escrits sur diverses Occurrences des Affaires et Guerres Estrangères depuis quinze Ans en ça. N.P. [Brussels?], 1632. 1st collected. French text. [iv], 698, [ii] pp. Final blank. Sl. stained. Contemp. vellum, lacks ties, sl. rodent damage to fore-edges. £65.00
A collection of twelve anonymous pamphlets of the years 1617-1629, illustrating French attitudes to the Thirty Years' War up to the time of their intervention.

198. REGULA PLACITANDI. A Collection of Special Rules for Pleadings, from the Declaration to the Issue . . . Directions for Laying of Actions . . . Precedents. By the Assigns of R. & E. Atkyns [etc.], 1694. 2nd ed. Index. [viii], 310, [xxvi] pp. Contemp. sheep, new label; sl. rbbd. **Wing R.759. S. & M.i.277.** £60.00
The author represents, with some justice, that the other books of pleading merely bombard the student with precedents without explaining how they are made & what dictates their contents.

199. REGULATIONS and INSTRUCTIONS relating to his Majesty's Service at Sea. 1772. 11th ed. 4to. Engr. title-vignette & ornaments. Lacks ½ title. Fold'g schedule at end. [ii], 232pp. Sl. spotted. Contemp. mottled cf., worn. £40.00

200. ——————— another edition. 1808. 4to. Appendices. Index. viii, 286, [ii], 287-440, [cxcviii], xxxiv, [ii] pp. Final errata leaf. Signatures irregular. Contemp. sprinkled cf., jts. & edges rbbd. £40.00

201. REPORT from the SELECT COMMITTEE of the House of Lords, on the Present State of Discipline in Gaols . . . Minutes of Evidence [etc.] [H.M.S.O.], 1863. 1st. Folio. Appendices. xxx, 512pp. b_3 torn without loss. Contemp. ½ cf./cl. sides, re-backed, rbbd. £40.00
The Earl of Carnarvon's Committee recommended an extension of the solitary-confinement system, stricter application of statutory directions on diet & hard labour with the more general use of treadmills & similar exercises for the latter, & the adoption of photography for the future identification of prisoners.

202. [RIDPATH, George]. An Historical Account of the Antient Rights and Power of the Parliament of Scotland. N.P., 1703. 1st. xxxii, 160pp. Contemp. sprinkled cf., jts. v. sl. rbbd.; fine copy. Bk-pl. John Hay, 1st Marquess of Tweeddale. **S. & M.v.51.** £85.00
Written on the near prospect of a union of the two kingdoms, in the bold hope that the new order, instead of increasing the subordination of Scotland, might rescue the Scots parliament from the depression into which it had been cast under the arbitrary government of James VI.

203. ———————. Parliamentary Right Maintain'd, or the Hanover Succession Justify'd. N.p. [Edinburgh?], 1714. 1st. Errata leaf *5. [x], 262pp. Contemp. panelled cf., upper jt. partially split, lower cvr. markd. £45.00
A judicious work which undermines the Scriptural authorities for "divine right", & asserts the historical continuity of checks & limitations on the British monarchy, while at the same time arguing that the Act of Union serves as an adequate bar to further & less justifiable interferences with the succession on the part of Parliament.

204. ROLT, Sir John (1804-1871) (Lord Justice of Appeal) Memoirs, ed. C.T. le Quesne. Inner Temple, 1939. 1st. Collotype plates. Index. [vi], 216pp. Orig. cl., uncut. Fine. £8.00

205. RUDDIMAN, Thomas (1674-1757). An Answer to the Reverend Mr. George Logan's late Treatise on Government. Edinburgh, 1747. 1st. Engr. fp. Lacks final blank. Q_4 a cancel. x, 402pp. Contemp. cf., sp. gilt; rubbed, upper jt. worn. Bk-label. **S. & M.v.100.** £30.00
Logan argued in general that the Scottish throne partook of an elective quality; in particular, that Robert III, second King of the Stuart line (1390-1406) was a bastard, so that the entire Stuart succession was vitiated. Ruddiman produces weighty authorities to the contrary.

206. ———————. An Introduction to . . . Anderson's Diplomata Scotiae. Edinburgh, 1773. 1st Engl. [xii], 232pp. British Museum duplicate stamp. Old ½ cf./boards, uncut, worn. **S. & M.v.100.** £20.00
A learned dissertation on the Scottish charters, with some very accurate critical remarks on those whose authenticity was in doubt; also including chapters on the Scottish coinage.

207. RUGGLES, Thomas. The Barrister: or, Strictures on the Education Proper to the Bar. 1818. 2nd ed., rev. xvi, 269, [iii] pp. Orig. cloth, uncut, faded. **S. & M.ii.310.** £20.00
Ruggles's preface expresses the growing desire of lawyers to mingle with & be accepted by the polite world.

208. RUSSELL, Sir William Oldnall. A Treatise on Crimes and Misdemeanours. 1877. 5th ed., ed. Samuel Prentice. 3 vols. Indices, lxxii, 1062/lii, 1020/liv, 810pp. Contemp. calf, sps. & edges rubbed. **S. & M.iv.312.** £30.00
Mid-Victorian editions of this work were so highly regarded in the U.S.A. that C.S. Greaves, editor of the fourth edition, was invited to participate in the compilation of the New York Criminal Code.

209. [St. GERMAIN, Christopher (?-1540.)] Two Dialogues in English, between a Doctor of Divinity, and a Student in the Laws of England. By the Assigns of Rich. and Edw. Atkins . . . Sold by Charles Harper, William Crook, and Richard Tonson, 1687. Cancel title. [ii], 366, [viii] pp. S_3 sl. ink-stnd. Worm-hole in last four leaves (contents.) Contemp. sheep, head of sp. sl. torn & wormed. **Wing S.318 (var. imprint) S. & M.i.25.** £70.00
St. Germain, the modest & judicious adversary of Sir Thomas More, undertook to square the law of England with that of natural justice; he discusses many particular points of ecclesiastical, constitutional & property law in this light. Alone among our legal writers he is able to consider such questionable matters as legal fictions, the denial of meat & drink to the jury while considering their verdict, & the refusal of counsel to those indicted of felony, both in a rational spirit & with direct knowledge of the historical circumstances which lie behind them.

210. [SALMON, Thomas (1679-1767) (ed.)]. Tryals for High-Treason, and Other Crimes. With proceedings on Bills of Attainder, and Impeachments. 1720. 1st. 6 vols. Index. Advert. leaf f_4 in vol. 1. Errata leaf in vol. 3. Q_1 (vol. 5) torn without loss. Contemp. panelled calf, two jts. worn. **S. & M.i.371.** £160.00
This work is adapted from Salmon's folio "State Trials" 1717, with some reports abridged but including a few new cases. The period 1635-1690 – the fall of Charles I's counsellors & that of his own person, the struggles between the Rump & those who were too republican for the Republic, the royalists' revenge, the rise & fall of Titus Oates, & the Abdication – naturally occupies the bulk of the work. The last trial in vol. 5 is that of Captain Kidd the pirate.

211. SANDYS, Charles. The Vindication, whereinne ye Practices of a Countrie-Atturney been notablie Displaied. 1847. 1st. 64pp.
——————— A Letter to Messrs. Kingsford, Son & Wightwick. 1848. 1st. 6pp. 2 works in 1 vol. Contemp. ½ cf./mbld. sides, sl. rbbd. £10.00
An extraordinary quarrel between Sandys & a fellow-attorney, Henry Kingsford of Canterbury, over alleged misdealing with a client's property, preceded by some vigorous remarks on the manners & morals of attorneys in general.

212. [SAUNDERS, Sir Edmund. (C.J., K.B.) (?-1683)]. Summus Angliae Seneschallus: or, a Survey of the Lord High-Steward of England . . . Manner of Arraigning a Peer. Printed . . . 1680. 1st. Sm. 4to. 36pp. Few page-numerals cropped. Disbound. **Wing S.745. S. & M.i.218.** £25.00
Saunders, a man of the lowest origin, made himself known in the law by his diligence & good sense despite his ill-fashioned manners & repulsive habits. He was appointed Chief Justice of King's Bench in 1683 to be the King's tool in his attempt to corrupt the electoral system, but died within six months. This pamphlet was addressed to Lord Stafford & others, Catholics whom Saunders was about to defend on their trial for high treason. It is a quaint assembly of patently second-hand learning.

213. SAUNDERS, John Simcoe. The Law of Pleading and Evidence in Civil Actions . . . with Practical Forms: and the Pleading and Evidence to support them. 1828. 1st. 2 vols. Index. xii, 560/[ii], 561-1036, [iv] pp. Final advert. leaves to vol. 2. Sl. spotted. Contemp. calf, rbbd. **S. & M.ii.315.** £20.00
A good manual of the art of special pleading as practised in the last years of its existence.

214. SAYLE, R.T.D. Notes on the South-East Corner of Chancery Lane. 1929. 1st. Sm. 4to. Illus. Index. vi. 70pp. Orig. cloth, sl. fdd. £5.00
Brief history of Messrs. Sweet & Maxwell & their predecessors.

215. SCHÜTZ, Johann Christian. Specimen iuris consolidationis pertinentiarum, vulgo von Einlösung der abgesplissenen Pertinentien zur Sohlstatt. Cologne, sumptibus Wilhelmi Metternich, 1718. 1st. German & Latin text. Fraktur letter. Index. [xii], 108, [xx] pp. Final errata leaves. Some browning. Ownership inscr. of Ignaz Nüppeney von Welling, prefect of Eschweiler (1719) & W. Baumeister, Aulic counsellor, of Düsseldorf, with the latter's bk-label. Contemp. parchment, sl. rubbed & shaken. £95.00
In the absence of any system of primogeniture, many German estates were so often divided & subdivided among a plurality of heirs as to become inconvenient to the fiscal authorities & uneconomical to the owners. The jus consolidationis *was designed to provide a means of restoring such estates to their pristine unity; but its application, which was greatly expanded after 1700, was hindered by the great diversity of municipal laws. Schütz's work examines the origin, nature, & operation of the system in an attempt to reduce it to uniformity.*

216. SCHWEDER, Gabriel. Introductio in jus publicum imperii Romano-Germanici novissimum. Tübingen, 1722. Rev. ed. Engr. fp. Index. [xxiv], 1014, [lxiv] pp. Sl. spotted. Contemp. vellum. £25.00
First published 1682, but continually revised by the author, who opposes the theory that the German empire is an absolute monarchy.

217. SELDEN, John. (1584-1654). Opera omnia, tam edita quam inedita . . . collegit ac recensuit . . . David Wilkins. 1st collected. 3 vols. in 6. Folio. Latin & Engl. text. Fp. port. Index. Contemp. calf, worn. **S. & M.i.36.** £180.00
This edition by the learned editor of the Leges Anglo-Saxonicae is not yet superseded for reference; it is furthermore a monument of typography, for which William Caslon cut his roman & other types.

218. SEYSSEL, Claude de (?-1520), Joannes TILIUS, & others. Respublica, sive status regni Galliae. Leyden (ex officina Elzeviriana), 1626. 1st thus. 16mo. Engr. title. 613, [xi] pp. Contemp. cf., initials R.G.[rosvenor] on upper cover; clasps; sp. rbbd. Bk-pl. Hugh, 2nd Duke of Westminster. **Willems 259.** £25.00

219. SHAFTESBURY, [Anthony Ashley Cooper], Earl of (1621-1683). Some Observations concerning the Regulating of Elections for Parliament. By Randall Taylor, 1689. 1st. Sm. 4to. [ii], 5-18pp. Disbound. **Wing S.2899/4534** (duplicate listing). £20.00
Lacks the text of a Bill embodying some of Shaftesbury's idea (pp.1-4). They include a uniform qualification for voters throughout the kingdom, and an annual review of the electorate to prevent voters from lapsing into irresponsibility – the latter an idea far ahead of our own time, much more of the seventeenth century.

220. SHAW, James. The Parochial Lawyer; or, Churchwarden's and Overseer's Guide . . . Law, Practice, and Proceedings of Vestries . . . Hints . . . for the Management . . . of the Poor. 1835. 4th ed. Index. xii, lxviii, 252pp. Sl. spotted. Contemp. ½ parchment/mbld. sides, sp. gilt, sl. mkd. **S. & M.i.322.** £15.00
Written to help local government officials adapt themselves to the new poor law, this work enjoyed a brief but very lively circulation.

221. SHAW, Joseph (1671-1733). Parish Law: or, a Guide to Justices of the Peace, Ministers, Churchwardens, Overseers [etc.] 1748. 6th ed., rev. Index. [xvi], 378, [xxii] pp. Contemp. cf., sp. sl. wormed, sl. rbbd. **S. & M.i.382.** £25.00
The principal revisions in this edition are those occasioned by the Vagrancy Act of 1744 (17 Geo.II.cap.25); the editor tells us of an enormous increase in the vagrant population during the preceding five years, a significant social movement whose effects were soon afterwards felt in the capital.

222. SHEPPARD, William (fl. 1620-1675). The Touch-Stone of Common Assurances. For W. Lee, M. Walbancke, D. Pakeman, & G. Bedell, 1651. [3rd ed.] 4to. Index. [xii], 530 [i.e. 626], [iv] pp. Few sm. marginal tears. Old ink annots. Occasional sl. browning. Contemp. cf., re-backed & re-cornered, lower cover worn. **Wing S.3215 (var. imprint) S. & M.i.487.** £120.00
This manual of conveyancing was found to be of such value that the lawyers of Charles II's time, chagrined at the thought of being so deeply indebted to the determined Republican Sheppard, supposed that the Touchstone was a work of Sir John Doderidge's which he had appropriated. It was last printed in 1826 & continues to be highly regarded from a historical point of view.

223. SIDERFIN, Thomas. Les Reports des divers Special Cases . . . en le Court del Bank le Roy. By W. Rawlins [etc.] for Samuel Keble, 1683. 1st. 2 vols. Folio. Black letter. Indices. [iv], 467, [lxxxv]/[viii], 179, [xi] pp. 19th-cent. ½ cf./mbld. sides, rbbd., heads of sps. frayed. **Wing S.3757-8. S. & M.i.309.** £50.00
Most of Siderfin's cases are trifling actions in debt, assumpsit, or "case for words" – inconsiderable, though sometimes (especially the last) amusing. Manby v. Scott *(vol. 1 p.109) is however a curiosity, containing arguments by all the judges on the extent to which a husband is bound by his wife's contracts for necessaries. A Gibbonian sarcasm on p.72 is worth quoting; three regicides are convicted of the murder of Charles I., "esteant del High Court d'Injustice que luy condemne".*

224. SIDNEY, Algernon (1621-1683). Discourses concerning Government . . . to which is added, the Paper he deliver'd to the Sheriffs . . . before his Death. 1704. 2nd ed. Folio. Engr. fp. port. Index. [viii], 424, [xlviii] pp. Few lib. stamps. Corner of N_2 torn away without loss of text. Signature of Henry Edward, Cardinal Manning (1819-1901) inside cover. Few marginal worm-holes. Contemp. panelled cf., later label, jts. worn. **S. & M.i.107.** £75.00
Sidney, who served as ambassador to Sweden under Cromwell, laid the foundation of theory for English-speaking republicanism. His work (written, like Locke's, in answer to Filmer's "Patriarcha") has at its centre the doctrine of a natural justice & order of government from which all human institutions (including kingship) vary at their peril; an idea calculated to appeal to the Age of Reason in both England & America.

225. A SKETCH of the HISTORY and PROCEEDINGS of the DEPUTIES appointed to Protect the Civil Rights of the Protestant Dissenters . . . Laws affecting . . . Dissenters. 1813. 1st. Appendix of statutes etc. Index. xii, 262pp. $(A)_4$ a cancel. Later cloth, fdd. £15.00
In the late 18th century the influence of & alliance with the powerful Methodist body gave the old-established dissenting communities the will to press for relief from the seventeenth-century statutes which disabled them.

226. SMITH, Josiah W. A Compendium of the Law of Real and Personal Property. 1877. 5th ed. 2 vols. Index.

cvi, 654, [iv], 32/[ii], 655-1374, 32pp. Few leaves of vol. 2 frayed & sl. soiled. Vol. 1 orig. cl., fdd.; vol. 2 new cloth, orig. spine laid down. S. & M.ii.331. **£20.00**

227. SMITH, Sir Thomas (1414-1577). The Commonwealth of England: and the Manner and Government thereof. By R. Young for J. Smethwicke, 1640. 12mo. Final device leaf. [xii], 272, [ii]pp. Lacks engr. fp. port. Contemp. sheep, sp. defective, worn & sl. wormed. **S.T.C.22867. S. & M.i.107. £40.00**
Smith travelled widely on the continent, at first as a student of civil law (which he learned at Pavia & taught at Cambridge), & later as a respected diplomat. This wide experience makes his work an admirable successor to that of Fortescue. Despite his classical & civilian training, he writes of the English institutions (especially of Parliament) with sympathy & understanding.

228. [SOMERS, John, Lord (L.C.) (1650-1716.)] Jura Populi Anglicani: or the Subject's Right of Petitioning set forth. Occasioned by the Case of the Kentish Petitioners. 1701. 1st. Sm. 4to. xiv, 15-64pp. Title sl. torn without loss. Disbound. S. & M.i.159. **£35.00**
The petitioners, magistrates & gentlemen of Kent, had urged the Commons to withdraw their opposition to the King's maintenance of a standing army. They were immediately taken into the custody of the Serjeant-at-Arms. Somers examines the legality of this imprisonment & the justice of the Whiggish policies deplored by the petitioners; he delicately, or cunningly, omits to mention that his own opposition to these same policies had led to his dismissal & impeachment.

229. SOMNER, William. A Treatise of Gavelkind, both Name and Thing. By R. & W. Leybourn, for the Authour, 1660. 1st. Sm. 4to. Index. [xiv], 216, [viii]pp. Lacks first blank. Mod. wraps. **Wing S.4668. S. & M.i.477. £95.00**
Somner was an academic rather than a lawyer, a pupil of the great scholar Meric Casaubon; the accent of his book is accordingly philological in the main, although he includes a chapter on the place of gavelkind in the history of the law of descents & prints several ancient charters showing it in action.

230. SPEECHES and PASSAGES of this Great and Happy Parliament: from ... November, 1640 to ... June, 1641. For William Cooke, 1641. 1st collected. Sm. 4to. Pagination & signing irregular through changes of printer. Fore-margin of K_1 defective without loss of text. Mod. ½ cf./mbld. sides. **Wing E.2309. £85.00**
Speeches of the King, Waller, Vane, Pym, Strafford (on his impeachment) & others, with the texts of several petitions & their answers.

231. SPENCE, George. An Inquiry into the Origin of the Laws and Political Institutions of Modern Europe. 1826. 1st. Index. xxxvi, 600pp. Contemp. cf., sp. gilt, re-backed; jts. rbbd.; lib. labels on & within upper cvr. **S. & M.i.37. £40.00**
Spence endeavours to derive a large proportion of the Teutonic institutions (including the Anglo-Saxon) directly from the Romans. Conjecture, as may be imagined, patches many a flaw in his arguments.

232. SPOTTISWOOD of SPOTTISWOOD, John. An Introduction to the Knowledge of the Stile of Writs, Simple and Compound, made Use of in Scotland. Edinburgh, 1765. 5th ed. 12mo. Index. [iv], 588, [xx]pp. Contemp. cf., sp. & edges worn. **S. & M.v.108. £30.00**
A collection of annotated precedents for bonds, charters-party, policies of insurance, & other commercial contracts. The new appendix includes further precedents, with rules of civil & criminal practice & tables of fees.

233. STAIR, Sir James Dalrymple, Viscount. The Institutions of the Laws of Scotland. Ed. John Gordon & William Johnstone. Edinburgh, 1759. 1st thus. Folio. Index. [xii], 802, [xlvi]pp. Contemp. cf., jts. & lower cover worn. **S. & M.v.108. £40.00**
Learned & judicious though it is, Stair's work suffers in a measure from its dependence on the order & content of the original Institutes, which leads to many omissions especially in the field of criminal law. His hope to be "pleasant and useful to all persons of honour" was clearly not fulfilled, since this is the only edition called for between 1693 & 1824; but among lawyers his merits were always recognized

234. ——————. Another copy. Lib. stamp on title. Sl. spotted at end. Contemp. cf, re-backed, rbbd, front hinge broken. **£40.00**

235. STATUTE. Anno regni Georgii ... nono. (An Act ... to put ... customs under the Management of ... Commissions, and for ... ascertaining the Duties on Tobacco.) 1723. 1st. Folio. [ii], 595-602pp. Sl. stnd. Disbound. **£10.00**

236. ——————. An Act of Parliament for Repairing the Highways from Counter's Bridge in ... Middlesex ... to ... the Powder Mills [etc.] O.U.P., 1769. 1st. fold'g fp. map (repaired on verso.) Index. [ii], 106, [xxxvi]pp. Mod. ½ roan/mbld. sides, sl. rbbd. **£15.00**

237. ——————. A Collection of the Public General Statutes, Passed in the Tenth and Eleventh Year of ... Queen Victoria. 1847. 1st collected. Lg. 8vo. Index. 1,1056pp. Last leaf sl. soiled. Contemp. cf., rbbd. **£15.00**
Suspension of the Poor Laws, alteration of the Canadian constitutions, promotion of settlement in New Zealand, & enclosure of land were among the most prominent objects of legislation.

238. STEPHEN, Henry John. New Commentaries on the Laws of England (Partly Founded on Blackstone.) 1841. 1st. **4 vols.** Index. Contemp. cf., sps. gilt; rbbd. **S. & M.ii.339. £65.00**
More free than Kerr's edition in its adaptation of Blackstone, & yet still retaining the spirit & much of the language of its great original, Stephen's work worthily closes the succession of general abridgments of English law.

239. STEPHEN, [Sir] James Fitzjames. Liberty, Equality, Fraternity. 1873. 1st. viii, 350pp. Sl. spotted. Orig. cl., uncut, sl. fdd. **Not in S. & M. £30.00**
Stephen takes an authoritarian view of criminal law; opposing Mill's view that self-protection is the only valid excuse for the coercion of one human being by another, he postulates certain universal principles of morality which may justifiably be enforced by law. It is a rare testimony to his merits that, notwithstanding this unfashionable view, his work continues to be cited with respect.

240. STEUART of GOODTREES, Sir James. The Index of Abridgement of the Acts of Parliament and Convention, from ... 1424 to ... 1707. Edinburgh, 1707. 1st. Final blank. [xii], 298, [ii] pp. **S. & M.v.117.**
—————— **BRUCE, Alexander.** The Index or Abridgment of such Acts of the British Parliament ... as ... concern ... Scotland ... from ... 1707, to ... 1726. Edinburgh, 1726. 1st. 12mo. First final blanks. [ii], viii, 106, [ii]pp. **S. & M.i.17. 2 works in 1 vol.** Few sl. stns. Contemp. cf., later label, rbbd, edges worn. **£25.00**

241. —————— Dirleton's Doubts and Questions in the Law of Scotland, Resolved and Answered. Edinburgh, 1715. 1st. Folio. Lacks engr. port. Red & black title. [iv], 340, 16pp. Contemp. panelled cf., rbbd., upper jt. & edges worn. S. & M.v.117. **£50.00**
A Scots proverb characterizes Steuart's performance; "to doubt with Dirleton and resolve with Steuart" is to resolve ineffectually or not at all. He makes many questions far too simple, & never gives an authority; but his 18 years' experience as Lord Advocate undoubtedly afforded him the matter of some solid observations.

242. STORY, Joseph (1779-1845). STORY, William W.; Life and Letters. 1851. 1st. **2 vols.** Engr. fp. port. Index. xii, 574/viii, 676pp. Sl. spotted. Two leaves loose in vol. 2. Orig. cl., uncut, sl. worn & shaken. **£20.00**
Together with John Marshall, Story bore a noble part in laying down a tradition of judicial uprightness & moral courage amid the corruption of American public life. His many writings on commercial law, & his close relations with Lord Stowell, made him known & respected in England & helped to cement the bond between the American & English judicatures.

243. ——————Commentaries on the Law of Agency as a Branch of Commercial and Maritime Jurisprudence. Boston, Mass., 1869. 7th ed., ed. I.F. Redfield & W.A. Herrick. Index. xxxvi, 674pp. Orig. cl., sl. fdd., upper cvr. stnd. **S. & M.ii.343. £10.00**

244. STRANGE, Sir John (1696-1754). Reports of Adjudged Cases in ... Chancery, King's Bench, Common Pleas, and Exchequer. Ed. John Strange. 1755. 1st. **2 vols.** First privilege leaf to each vol. Index. Lacks fp. port. [ii], iv, 714/[ii], 715-1272, [c]pp. Several annots. to the earlier cases by Sir William de Grey, L.C.J. (later Lord Walsingham) (1719-1781) Mod. cloth. Bk-pl. Thomas de Grey (the Judge's father) **S. & M.i.309. £50.00**
De Grey has several times added information concerning counsel & occasionally abbreviated a point of law, concentrating on cases tried previous to his call to the Bar in 1742. He was Chief Justice of Common Pleas for ten years, & Lord Eldon bears witness to his great learning & power of memory.

245. STUART, Gilbert (1742-1786). Observations concerning the Public Law of Scotland – with Occasional Remarks concerning English Antiquity. Edinburgh, 1779. 1st. Appendix of documents, charters, etc. xxiv, 396pp. Sl. spotted. Some pencil annots. Contemp. sprinkled cf., jts. & edges worn. **S. & M.v.118. £45.00**
Stuart designs to show that the characteristic institutions of Scotland – feudal, parliamentary, & juridical – of Scotland are more ancient & more purely national than Robertson & others supposed, He is not, however, an uncritical patriot; for example, he condemns the arbitrary jurisdiction (nobile officium) of the Court of Session.

246. ——————. Another copy. Old calf, gilt, rubbed. **£45.00**

247. STUART, James. Trial ... before the High Court of Justiciary. Edinburgh, 1822. 2nd ed. Appendix. [iv], 186, [ii], 20pp.
—————— Trial ... for Murder. (Different report.) Edinburgh 1822. 2nd ed. 44pp.
—————— **MACKINTOSH, Sir James.** Debate ... on a Motion made by ... to consider ... the Punishment of Death. Edinburgh, 1819. 56pp.
—————— **BOWDLER, C.** On the Punishment of Death, in the Case of Forgery, 1819. 3rd ed. 60pp.
—————— **BUXTON, T.F.** Speech ... in the ... Commons ... on the Bill "for Mitigating ... Punishment". 1821. 1st. [ii], 70pp.
Five works in one vol. Contemp. annots. on e-p. Contemp. ½ cf./mbld. sides. sl. worn. **£50.00**
Stuart's case was one of the sensations of its day; having fought a duel with & shot dead a baronet who had insulted him in the press, he was acquitted of murder. The other works exemplify the growing revulsion against capital punishment; those of Mackintosh (still a liberal in this respect) & Buxton are speeches in favour of an abortive Bill to remove forgery from the list of capital offences.

248. SUTTON, Robert. A Complete Guide to Landlords, Tenants, and Lodgers. N.d. [1799]. 1st. [iv], 104pp. **This ed. not in S. & M.**
—————— **MARRIOT, W.** The Country-Gentleman's Lawyer; and the Farmer's Complete Library. N.d. [1795]. 1st. [iv], 122, [ii]pp. Final advert. Leaf. **S. & M.i.460.**
—————— **WHITTAKER, S.** The Law of Bankrupts. 1801. 1st. Index. [iv], 100, [viii] pp. **S. & M.ii.309.**
—————— **CLAVERING, H.** The New Complete Parish Officer. N.d. [1796]. 1st. [iv], 130pp. **This ed. not in S. & M.**
—————— **TOMLINS, T.E.** A Familiar Explanation of the Law of Wills. 1801. 6th ed. ½ title. Index. xvi, 171, [v]pp. **S. & M.i.494.**
Five works in one vol. Contemp. tree sheep, sl. rbbd. **£75.00**

249. TAIT, George. A Treatise on the Law of Evidence in Scotland. Edinburgh, 1834. 3rd ed. Ed. Adam Urquhart. Appendix of forms. Index. xxxii, 516pp. Upper margin of ½ title cut away. Orig. boards, paper label, uncut; jts. & sp. worn. **S. & M.v.120. £20.00**
First pub'd 1824. The next edition was a literal reprint; this, however, is largely revised to include new rules concerning admissibility, which had been formulated as a result of an expansion in the use of juries in Scotland.

250. TAYLOR, J.O. The Law affecting River Pollution. Edinburgh, 1928. 1st. Index. xii, 5-102pp. Orig. bds., sl. mkd. **S. & M.ii.353. £5.00**

251. TAYLOR, (John) Pitt (1811-1888). A Treatise on the Law of Evidence. 1885. 8th (Taylor's last) ed. **2 vols.** Indices. cxxvi, 834/[ii], 835-1810pp. Contemp. cf., sps. rbbd. **S. & M.ii.353. £20.00**
One may spare a smile for the 73-year-old author's dignified complaint at the "embranglements" introduced into the subject by the Judicature Act & its aftermath, & his innocent self-congratulation for continuing to labour at his task in the ensuing confusion.

252. THORPE, Francis (1595-?). Charge, as it was delivered to the Grand-Jury at Yorke Assizes. By T.W. for Mathew Walbancke, and Richard Best, 1649. 1st. Sm. 4to. [ii], 30pp. Mod. wraps. **Wing T.1071. S. & M.i.208. £50.00**
Opening the York assizes as circuit judge, Thorpe took occasion for a loud triumph over the King's dead body before proceeding to explain the duties of the jury. For this he was rewarded with a place on the Exchequer bench; but liking the tyrant Cromwell no better than the tyrant Charles, he retired in 1655. Apart from its interest as a republican manifesto, this speech is curious as showing with what boldness, & with what impunity, a judge could fill out his addresses with irrelevancy & political bias.

253. TO the PEOPLE of GREAT BRITAIN and NORTH of IRELAND, against ... Alms-giving for the Payment of Union Rates. 1849. 1st. 8pp. Disbound. **£5.00**

254. TREGONY, Pocket Borough of (Cornwall). Collection of MSS. & Ephemera relating to the **ELECTIONS,** on the Earl of Darlington's nomination, of G. Wentworth & Col. Callaghan (1806) & of Gore Langton (1808) & to disputes raised by the first election. Includes 3 A.l.ss. from Darlington to his agent Edw. Coode, one instructing him to operate on the voters; list of voters with remarks ("Paid", "Oppositionist", "Turn him out" etc.); opinion of two counsel, incl. Sir Vicary Gibbs (later Attorney-General) on the first election, with advice as to how to escape the consequences of allowing the Mayor of St. Austell to sit illegally as Returning Officer; issue of "Royal Cornwall Gazette", 8.xi.1806, reporting first election; several notices to quit, printed or MS. served on refractory tenants; semi-literate A.l.s. from Mary Allen, tenant's wife, appealing for 6 weeks' stay of rent; etc. **About 50 items.** Mod. 4to. album. **£150.00**
A very explicit portrait of proceedings in a country election before Reform. The second Earl of Darlington (later created Duke of Cleveland) bought the estate in 1806 from a Mrs. Barwell, & was soon plunged into the turmoil of election life. His first election was nearly overthrown by a technicality; but his London attorney Tippet, strenuously accusing the opposition of bribery before a Commons Committee, & hastily applying (on Gibb's advice) for a writ to suppress the obnoxious Mayor, evidently contrived to "catch them napping" & "keep all snug" (his own words), for Wentworth is found still sitting in 1808. Another curious incident is the buying out of an independent householder named Jacob, who in obliging his Lordship breaks a previous contract, & gets into Chancery. It is notable that the names of parties are never once mentioned; evidently in so remote a borough, elections could be conducted entirely by candidates who represented nobody but themselves & their patrons.

255. TURNER, Sir Llewelyn (Welsh judge & prison reformer, 1823-1903). Memories, ed. J.E. Vincent. 1903. 1st. **Author's copy,** with his book-plate & some MS. corrections. Photogravure fp. & other plates. xviii, 492pp. Orig. cl., t.e.g., sl. fdd. **£12.00**

256. ULPIAN (-Domitius Ulpianus). Fragmenta libri singuli regularum, et incerti auctoris collatio legum Mosaicarum et Romanarum. Ed. Johann Cannegieter. Utrecht, 1768. 1st thus. 4to. Red & black title. Index. [vi], 142, [xxx], 173-540pp. Sl. browned. Contemp. ¼ cf./mbld. sides; sides worn. **£40.00**
These two works are among our best sources for the texts of the older jurists, who are otherwise preserved only by the imperfect faith of the Pandects. Cannegieter includes a treatise of his own on abbreviations & their influence on textual corruption, with a supplement of miscellaneous observations.

257. VENATORIUS, Daniel. CORVINUS, Arnoldus; Venatorius illustratus ... Venatorii ... methodica Codicis Justinianei enarratio ... emendata. Leyden (H. Verbiest) 1656. 1st thus. 12mo. Red & black title with engr. device. Index. [xxiv], 636pp. Contemp. vellum. **£30.00**

258. VENTRIS, Sir Peyton (1645-1691). The Reports. 1716. 3rd ed., rev. **2 parts in 1.** Folio. Black letter. Indices. First privilege leaf (repaired) General & individual titles. [x], 430, [xxiv]/[xviii], 368, [xx]pp. Sl. spotted. Some old annots. Mod. cl. **S. & M.i.310. £30.00**
Ventris sat on the bench for only two years; the bulk of his admirable Reports is explained by his having begun them in 1668, less than a year after his call to the Bar. Smith's Case *(p.66; commissioners of sewers guilty of contempt of court for trying a cause themselves in defiance of a writ to remove it into King's Bench) might be found useful authority by judicial champions of the common man against the bureaucratic tribunals of to-day.*

259. WALPOLE, Sir Robert. A Short History of that Parliament which committed [him] to the Tower. For J. Almon ... and J. Williams, 1763. 1st. xii, 62, [ii]pp. Lib. stamp on first three leaves. Sl. frayed. Sewn as issued; uncut; loosely inserted in mod. wraps. **£25.00**
Walpole's account of the venial parliament which contrived his impeachment. The satirical dedication to the Earl of Oxford is ascribed to William Pulteney, then Walpole's ally, afterwards his greatest enemy.

260. WARD, Robert. An Enquiry into the Foundation and History of the Law of Nations in Europe, from the ... Greeks and Romans, to ... Grotius. 1795. 1st. **2 vols.** Index. cviii, 396/[iv], 628pp. Sl. spotted. Contemp. sprinkled cf., re-backed; edges sl. worn. **£40.00**
This work began as the preface to a body of international law, directed against the fashionable doctrine of a natural or absolute law of nations applicable to all times, places & peoples; but Ward's historical examples & observations grew at such a rate that he at last made a separate work of them.

261. WARREN, Samuel. A Popular and Practical Introduction to Law Studies. 1835. 1st. Appendix. Index. xvi, 522pp. Few leaves spotted. Contemp. ½ cf./mbld. sides, rubbd. **S. & M.ii.371. £30.00**
Warren, author of "Ten Thousand a Year", was a genial & epicurean luminary of the Northern Circuit.

262. WATSON, William. The Clergyman's Law: or, the Complete Incumbent. 1725. 3rd ed. Folio. Index. [xii], 652, [lxii]pp. Contemp. cf., worn, ends of sp. defective. **S. & M.i.176. £30.00**

263. WEBSTER, Daniel. Speeches and Forensic Arguments. Boston, Mass., 1848. 8th ed. 3 vols. Engr. fp. port. viii, 25-520/20, 17-482/564pp.
———— Diplomatic and Official Papers. N.Y. 1848. 1st. Engr. fp. port. Fold'g map. 392pp. Altogether 4 vols. Sl. spotted. Contemp. diced cf., gilt, jts. rbbd., lacks some labels. £75.00

264. ———— HARVEY, Peter: Reminiscences and Anecdotes of. Boston. Mass, 1877. 1st. 2 steel-engr. & 2 wood-engr. plates. Index. xvi, 480pp. Press-cutting ("Evening Transcript" review of Lodge's Life of Webster, 1883, with contemptuous reference to Harvey's work) pasted on e-p. Orig. b'ram, sl. mkd. & fdd. £15.00

265. WEST, William. The First [-Second] Part of Symboleography ... Newly Augmented with divers Presidents touching Marchants Affaires. For the Companie of Stationers, 1605[-6]. **2 parts in 1 vol.** 4to. Partly black letter. Index. [vi], [318]/[ii], 304, [viii] leaves. Final blank. Contemp. MS. inscr. (metrical "Rules for Purchasing Land") on e-p. Contemp. cf., worn, re-backed. Pt. 1 not in S.T.C. (cf. 25271, listed as 8vo); pt. 2 S.T.C.25279. (Huntington only.) S. & M.i.487. £250.00
The growth of English commerce & the application of the Statute of Uses caused a revolution in the science of conveyancing, & presented a challenge to the profession which West was the first to meet at all worthily. He takes a commendably wide view of his subject, embracing commercial agreements, indictments, Chancery bills & answers, & general remarks on contract & on equity. Part 2 is dedicated to Coke.

266. ———— The First [-Second] Part of Symboleographie. By Miles Flesher, 1647 [- By Miles Flesher and Robert Young, 1641.] **2 parts in 1.** 4to. Partly black letter. Index. [vi], [306]/[ii], 350, [viii] leaves. Final blank. Publisher's cat. pasted inside lower cover; imprint at head torn away, four lines of text also affected. Sm. hole in Y_6 (pt.1) with loss of few letters. Sl. browned & stnd. Some contemp. annots. Contemp. cf., jts., sp. & corners worn. Wing W.1394. S. & M.i.487. £150.00
Includes a new appendix of bills & answers in Exchequer, Wards & Liveries, & Star Chamber, with a short account of each court. There are also some new precedents in the body of the work. Publisher's cat. printed separately, as opposed to those included in the collation, are of extremely rare occurrence before 1790.

267. WESTERN, Thomas George. Commentaries on the Constitution and Laws of England, Incorporated with the Political Text of ... de Lolme. 1841. 3rd ed., rev. Index. xviii, 476, civpp. Some spotting. Orig. cl., paper label, uncut; fdd.; edges worn. S. & M.ii.375. £15.00

268. [WHELLIER, A.] "John Gifford". The Complete English Lawyer, or, Every Man his Own Lawyer. 1824. **2 parts in 1.** Engr. fp. port. (Sir C. Abbott, L.C.J.) Index. 289, 298-688/iv, 148pp. Sl. spotted. Mod. ½ cf./mbld. sides. S. & M.ii.377. SOLD.
First edition to include the supplement containing the law of insurance, taxes, customs etc.

269. WIELING, Abraham (ed.) Iurisprudentia restituta, sive index ... in ... Corpus ... Accesserunt ... I. Usus Pandectarum per Iac. Labittum ... II. Henrici Hahnii oratio de usu chronologiae ... III. Henrici Brencmanni dissertatio de legum inscriptionibus. IV. Bern. Henrici Reinoldi oratio de inscriptionibus legum. Amsterdam, 1727. 1st thus. Red & black title. Engr. dedication leaf. [xvi], xcvi, 400, 200, 278pp. Contemp. vellum. £60.00
A collection of particular value to those desirous to use the Corpus, Novellae & Edicts as historical sources.

270. WIENER, Leo. Commentary to the Germanic Laws and Mediaeval Documents. Harvard U.P./O.U.P., 1915. 1st. Index. lxii, 255pp. Orig. cl., uncut; corners sl. rbbd. £18.00
A philological study of Teutonic legal language.

271. WILKES, John. KIDGELL, J.: A Genuine and Succinct Narrative of a Scandalous, Obscene, and Exceedingly Profane Libel, entitled, an Essay on Woman. 1763. 1st. 4to. 16pp. Several blanks bound in at end. **Signed by the author on title.** Mod. ½ cf./mbld. sides. £80.00
Wilkes printed a few copies of the scurrilous "Essay" on his private press simultaneously with the subscription issue of the "North Briton". One of his printers acts in collusion with Kidgell (a miserable family chaplain) & others in bringing the "Essay" to the notice of the authorities; & Wilkes's enemies very cunningly made this indefensible work, rather than the more sensitive "North Briton", the apparent fulcrum of their operations both in court & in the press.

272. ————. A Letter to a Noble Member of the Club in Albemarle-Street. 1764. 1st. 4to. title. [ii], 20pp. Disbound. £45.00
The Club was intended as a social rallying-point for members of the opposition party; but having nothing in common except their enemies, they soon desisted from this association. Wilkes, writing from Paris, offers suggestions for their conduct in a sneering tone which suggests that he augurs no private or public good from these fair-weather friends, who use his name as a cloak for party intrigues with which he has no sympathy.

273. ————. A LETTER to the COMMON COUNCIL of the City of London. With Remarks on Lord Chief Justice Pratt's Letter to ... Exeter. 1764. 2nd ed. [ii], 38pp. Disbound. £30.00
Pratt, who declared the illegality of Wilkes's arrest, was rewarded by the city of Exeter for his "defence of liberty" by being declared a Freeman. The writer attacks Pratt for implying, by his acceptance, that he was not unwilling to be seen as having acted on behalf of Wilkes, not on behalf of abstract justice. The Common Council, who offered a vote of thanks to the City members who had supported Wilkes, also receive some abuse.

274. ————. ENGLISH LIBERTY: being a Collection of Interesting Tracts ... containing the Private Correspondence, Public Letters, Speeches, and Addresses, of ... Wilkes. For T. Baldwin, n.d. [1769]. 1st collected. **2 parts in 1 vol.** Folio. Engr. fp., preceded by explanation leaf. xviii, 236/-392pp. Last leaf backed. Contemp. ¼ cf./mbld. sides, worn. £180.00
The most elaborate of Wilkes's propaganda collections, published when he was a prisoner & a public hero. The earlier part (covering the false warrant, the Talbot & Martin duels, etc.) largely follows the "Paris" collection of 1767; but there is plenty of new material relating to Wilkes's electioneering activities and to the "St. George's Fields massacre", in which a clash between constables & "Wilkites" led to the death of one of the latter. Some letters from Churchill (with unpublished verses) & the novelist Smollett are also included.

275. ———— [ALMON, John] (1738-1805). The History of the Late Minority ... during the Years 1762, 1763, 1764 and 1765. 1766. 3rd ed., rev. [xii], 9-332pp. Some pencil scoring. Contemp. red sprinkled mor., sp. gilt, gilt border & arms of **John Earl of Bute,** on sides. Autograph of the first & last Baron Carlingford, Lord Privy Seal (1823-1898) on e-p. Sl. rubbed. & stnd. £90.00
Written by Wilkes's publisher & foremost partisan, & including a detailed account of his activities. A remarkable association copy *from the library of the man whom Wilkes drove out of the Premiership.*

276. WILLIAMS, David. The Laws relating to the Clergy. 1822. 2nd ed., rev. Index. [iv], viii, 682, [viii]pp. Sl. spotted. Contemp. ½ cf./mbld. sides, jts. sl. worn. S. & M.ii.381. £20.00

277. WILLIAMS, Joshua. Principles of the Law of Real Property. 1855. 4th ed. Fold'g table of descents. Appendix. Index. xxii, 442pp. Orig. cl., sl. fdd. S. & M.ii.383. £10.00

278. ————. Another edition ... intended as a First Book for the Use of Students in Conveyancing. 1875. 11th ed. Index. xxxii, 570pp. Orig. cl., sl. fdd., sp. sl. frayed. £10.00

279. WILLIAMS, Thomas Walter. A Digest of the Statute Law. 1791. 3rd ed. **2 vols.** 4to. Index. iv, 714/[ii], 755, [vii]pp. Contemp. cf., rbbd., jts. worn, lacks labels. S. & M.i.567. £40.00

280. ————. The Whole Law relative to the Duty and Office of a Justice of the Peace. Ed. H.N. Tomlins. 1812. 3rd ed. **4 vols.** Fold'g table. Index. Contemp. cf., sl. stnd., one jt. sl. split. S. & M.ii.384. £50.00
Last edition of this rival of Burn.

281. WOODFALL, William. Practical Treatise on the Law of Landlord & Tenant, ed. S.B. Harrison, 1837. 3rd ed. (of Harrison's version). Indices. liv. 1040pp. Contemp. cf., rbbd. S. & M.ii.391. £15.00
Book 4 of Harrison's Woodfall is a brief collection of conveyancing & pleading precedents.

282. ———— & S.B. HARRISON. Another ed. ed. Henry Horn. 1856. 7th ed. Index. Advert. leaves before title. [xvi], lxiv, 1048pp. Some margins frayed towards end. Mod. cl. S. & M.ii.391. £15.00
First edition to take account of the great changes in forms of action – notably the abolition of "Doe and Roe" ejectments – wrought by the Common Law Procedure Act, 1852.

283. WOOLRYCH, Humphrey W. A Treatise on the Law of Ways. 1829. 1st. Appendix of forms & precedents. Index. xxxvi, 396pp. Contemp. cf., rbbd., sp. defective. S. & M.ii.392. £15.00
The road-building boom of the 1820s gave rise to a number of legal works; most of these confined themselves to highways, but Woolrych takes a wider scope. This edition preserves the law as it stood immediately before the Prescription Act.

284. WOOLSEY, Theodore D. Introduction to the Study of International Law. 1874. 4th ed. Index, 488, 40pp. Orig. cl. fdd. & sl. worn. S. & M.ii.392. £10.00

285. WORDSWORTH, Charles F.F. The Law and Practice of Elections (for England and Wales) as Altered by the Reform Acts. 1835. 2nd ed. Appendix of statutes. Index. xl, 336pp. Mod. cl. S. & M.i.392. £15.00

286. WROTTESLEY, F.J. The Examination of Witnesses in Court. 1931. Rep. Index. viii, 178pp. Orig. ¼ cl./bds., sl. fdd. S. & M.i.394. £3.00

287. WYNNE, Edward. Eunomus: or, Dialogues concerning the Law and Constitution of England. With an Essay on Dialogue. 1809. 3rd ed. **2 vols.** xxiv, 288/[ii], 337, [iii]pp. Orig. bds., uncut, sl. worn. S. & M.i.110. £25.00
In these dialogues, written in the 1720s, law & letters pleasantly if inconclusively join hands almost for the first time.

288. YELVERTON, Sir Henry (1566-1630). The Reports ... of divers Special Cases in ... King's Bench. 1735. "3rd" (1st English) ed. Index. First privilege leaf. [xii], 228, [xxiv]pp. Sl. browned. Contemp. cf., rbbd., jts. sl. torn. S. & M.i.310. £30.00
Yelverton was a lawyer in the best tradition; as Attorney-General & judge, hated by Buckingham & distrusted by the King, he proved at last that while honesty & just dealing might be objectionable, they were also indispensible. His reports are of an admirable if at times confounding brevity.

289. ————. The Reports. Dublin, 1792. "Fourth" (1st Dublin & 1st 8vo) ed. Index. [xvi], 228, [xxxii]pp. Contemp. cf., rbbd., jts. worn. S. & M.i.311. £30.00

290. YORKSHIRE. The Year Book for the Use of the Justices of the West Riding ... 1901-2 [-1912-13]. **12 vols.** Fold'g tables. Orig. b'ram, fdd. fore-margins of cvrs. stnd. Not in S. & M. £40.00
In addition to lists of personnel & sundry matters similar to those found in the standard justices' manuals, these year-books contain interesting statistics, financial & otherwise, of the Yorkshire police.

291. BARING, Daniel Eberhard (1690-1753) (ed.). Clavis diplomatica, specimina veterum scripturarum tradens ... Praemissa est bibliotheca scriptorum rei diplomaticae. Hanover, 1754. 2nd ed., rev. 4to. 74 copper-engraved plates (misbound at end & out of order.) Index. [xiv], 616, [xx]pp. Fly-title to plates misbound after preface. First & last leaves repaired at inner margins. Some spotting. Contemp. ¼ calf/mbld sides, rubbed, jts. worn. Not in Besterman. £95.00
A useful compendium of palaeographical knowledge, with an annotated bibliography of writers on all subjects connected with the study of historical documents. The rest of the text is drawn from Mabillon, Struvius (their contributions are new to this edition), Goebel, Ruddiman, & others, with a new appendix of ancient German & Latin charters. The plates illustrate old book-hands, contractions, seals, & scribes' marks.

292. LAUTERBECK, Georg. Regentenbuch ... allen Regenten und Oberkeiten zu Anrichtung und Besserung erbarer und guter Policey, christlich und nötig zu wissen. [Leipzig, durch Jacobum Berwald], 1559. Folio. German text. Schwabacher letter, woodcut device on final leaf, & initials. [xii], 224, [ii] leaves. Two blanks at end. Blank piece cut from title. First quire sl. frayed. sl. stained. ... **MEURER, Noe.** Von forstlicher Oberherrligkeit unnd Gerechtigkeit, was die Recht, der Gebrauch, die Billigkeit deszhalben vermög. [Pforzheim, bey Georg Raben], 1560. 1st. Folio. German text. Fraktur letter. Hohenzollern arms on verso of title. Final device. 100 leaves. Margins sl. stained. **2 works in 1 volume.** Some ... old annots. Contemp. blind-stamped pig, clasps, v. worn. £350.00
Lauterbeck's work (dedicated to the Counts of Mansfield, ten brothers, in whose service he was) is a treatise of government in which the authentic spirit of primitive German liberty speaks through a cloud of Roman illustration; he asserts the responsibility of a ruler to the law, the sanctity of an oath, and the beauties of peace, with chapters on education, currency, & other matters of municipal law. At the end he translates a fragment of Musonius, the Stoic philosopher, on a similar subject. Meurer, author of several law-books, discusses the rights of the forest – hunting, fishing, possession of timber & wild beasts, etc. – in the light of civil & canon law.

293. RYMER, Thomas, & Robert SANDERSON (ed.). Foedera, conventiones, literae, et cujuscunque generis acta publica inter reges Angliae, et alios quosvis imperatores, reges, pontifices [etc.] The Hague (Jean Neaulme), 1739-45. 3rd ed., ed. George Holmes. **10 vols.** Folio. Indices. 10 engraved plates in vol. 9. "Avertissement" leaf (signed $*_2$) bound before A_1 of vol.1. Contemp. MS. transcript of Anglo-French truce of 1325 (from a Bodleian MS.) & five engravings of Great Seals from an 8vo ed. of Blackstone's Law Tracts, inserted in vol.1. Two leaves loose in vols. 4 & 9. Vol. 5 lacks $5*_2$ blank$_1$ & N_{2-3} (pt.3) reversed. L_2 [illegible] torn without loss. Contemp. marbled boards, uncut, worn, ends of sps. defective, jts. weak. S. & M. i.604. £250.00
Last edition, including some new items – an account of the English constitution in French, written by an unknown ambassador in 1565, and le Clerc's Historical Abridgment of the Foedera which forms vol.10.

294. SELVA, Johannes de. Tractatus de beneficio. [Paris], Francois Regnault, n.d. [c.1520]. 4to. Gothic (rotunda) letter. Red & black title with device (cf. Renouard 943). Index. 299, [xiii] leaves. Final blank. Few sl. stns. Some head-lines shaved. Title sl. soiled. Contemp. sheep, MS. guards (legal document dated 1480); lacks ties, tails of sp. repaired. **Adams 879. Not in B.L. or Lib. of Congress.** £150.00
In this work on ecclesiastical appointments the author, a jurist of Limoges, takes frequent occasion to limit the powers of the Pope to dispense with the normal rules of preferment. He is equally unfriendly to the pretensions of the French crown to an independent right of appointment. The absence of a colophon is unusual; however, there is no doubting the genuineness of the blank, which would have born the imprint if one were required.

295. The LAW QUARTERLY REVIEW. Vol.59 no.1 – vol.90 no.4 (Jan. 1943–Oct. 1974) lacking only vol.60 no.3 (July 1944). Orig. wraps, early issues faded, some spines sl. torn. 127 **issues.** £200

296. The MODERN LAW REVIEW. Quarterly (bi-monthly from vol.17) Vol.9 no.1 – vol.37 no.6 (Jan. 1946 – Nov. 1974) lacking four issues (16/3; 20/6; 22/3; 30/2) & vol.33. Orig. cloth fine. Remainder orig. wraps. early years faded., some sl. worn. 148 issues in 143. £200

Open Mon.-Fri. 10.00 am.-6.00 p.m.
FROGNAL RARE BOOKS
Telephone 01-240-2815
18 Cecil Court, Charing Cross Rd
London WC2N 4HE
Catalogues issued on Law. Economics. Caricature

(1977)

C A T A L O G U E 51

H I S T O R Y

and

C O N S T I T U T I O N A L L A W

BACON, Sir Francis (Viscount St. Alban's, Baron Verulam)
The two Bookes...of the Proficience and Advancement of Learning, Divine and Humane. Sm.4to. Oxford: I.L. Printer to the University for Thomas Huggins. 1633. 3rd ed. (i),335pp. Old vellum, later e-ps, sl. browned, light pencilling in margins, t-p sl. worn & dusty. STC 1166. GIBSON 83. £120

BARCLAY, Family of.
Quarto volume containing transcripts of five 18th-cent. collections of documents relating to the Barclays of Matheris and Ury, copied by a Miss Barton in 1856-8. 256 leaves of which 221 onwards are blank. Contemp. mor. gilt, arms of Hudson Gurney on sides; faded & sl. mkd. £50

The immediate sources seem to have been two 18th-cent. MSS. (one folio, one quarto) preserved at Ury; but these in turn included many charters etc. of much earlier date.

BARWICK, John, Dean of St. Paul's (1612-1664)
BARWICK, Peter; The Life. 1724. 1st English. 2 engraved ports. Appendix of documents. Index. Title browned. Book-plate Thomas, Earl of Strafford.(dated 1712) Contemp. calf, spine gilt, rubbed. £25

Biography written by the Dean's brother (originally in Latin).

BATTY, Lieut.-Colonel (illus.)
The Eventful History of the Mutiny and Piratical Seizure of H.M.S. Bounty: its Cause and Consequences, J. Murray, 1831. 6 etched plates. Orig. cloth, sp. rbbd. £25

No.25 in the Family Library series.

BEATSON, Robert.
A Political Index to the Histories of G.B. and Ireland; or, a Compleat Register of the Hereditary Honours. Public Offices, and Persons in Office. 1788. 2nd ed. rev. Contemp. sprinkled calf, sl. rubbed. £40

BÈGUE, or Le Bègue, -
The History of the Campagnes 1548 and 1549. (transl. anon.) N.p. (Edinburgh ?), 1707. 1st Engl. Browned. Contemp. calf, jts. & corners worn. £20

A 16th-cent. French account of Anglo-Scots hostilities, translated with a long preface to remind the Scots, on the eve of Union, how their courage had once safeguarded their independence.

BENTON, Thomas H. (1782-1858)
Thirty Years' View; or, a History of the Working of the American Government for Thirty Years...with Historical Notes...and...Notices of Eminent Deceased Contemporaries N.Y. 1854-6. 1st edition. 2 vols. Engraved fp. to each volume. First & final advert. leaves. A few leaves sl. stained. Modern ½ calf. £50

The author was a Senator for Missouri throughout the period of these memoirs.

(BETHELL, Slingsby)
The Interest of Princes and States. For John Wickins, 1680. 1st edition. First blank. 2 advert. leaves at end. (xiv),354,(iv)pp. Modern calf. WING B.2064. £120

Includes a chapter on the Protestant movement in France & another on the parliament summoned by Richard Cromwell in 1658. The whole work, based on French models but drawn from the author's own experience, is a political Survey of Europe.

BIOGRAPHICAL SKETCHES
of Eminent Persons, whose Portraits form Part of the Duke of Dorset's Collection at Knole. 1795. 1st edition 2 copper-engraved plates (views of Knole). Final advert. leaves. xxiv,164,(iv)pp. Contemp. sprinkled calt, jts. & corners sl. worn. £30

BLACKWOOD, Adam (1539-1613)
Adversus Georgii Buchanani dialogum, de iure regni apud Scotos, pro regibus apologia. Poitiers (apud Franciscum Pagaeum),1581. Sm.4to. 1st edition. Final errata leaf. (xii),342,(ii)pp. Title defective & repaired with loss of text, mostly on verso (privilege). I_2 repaired with sl. loss. Wrong imposition in sig. C; correct order of pages noted in early MS. Old calf, rebacked, edges sl. worn. S. & M. v.17. £80

Defence of Mary's right to reign in Scotland, by a fine scholar & lawyer who owed to her his place in the local administration of Poitiers.

BOETHIUS (Boece or Boyce),Hector (c.1470-1550)
Scotorum historiae a prima gentis origine...libri xix.. Continuatio per Ioannem Ferrerium Pedemontanum...scripta. Paris (a Jacobo du Puys), 1574. 1st complete edition Folio. Latin text. (vi),(xxii),402,(xviii) leaves. Some sl. browning. Contemp. Italian ½ blind-tooled calf, oak boards, clasps (defective) elaborate label on lower cover; spine & one corner worn; sl. wormed. GRAESSE I.467 £180

This great history of Scotland was first published in Paris in 1527; mediaeval in content but Renaissance in style, it was instrumental in putting Scotland in touch with the main stream of European scholarship. This edition by Giovanni Ferrerio (a fine scholar with strong associations with Aberdeen, though his origin was Italian) includes the two books which Boethius added after 1527, together with a continuation by the editor.

(BOLINGBROKE Henry St. John, Viscount)(1678-1751)
Remarks on the History of England. 1743. 1st collected. Index. xvi,328,(vi)pp. Contemp. mottled calf, sp.gilt; head of sp. defective, cvrs. worn. £30

A series of letters originally contributed to the anti-Walpole periodical "The Craftsman", & reprinted here. The long dedication to Walpole is new to this edition.

H13) BOSSUET,(Jacques Benigne)(1627-1704)
Oraisons funèbres...avec les Observations de Voltaire...de Chateaubriand (etc) Paris,1824. ½ title. 310pp. Old ½ calf; spine gilt; FINE. £20

First one-volume collection of these memorial addresses on Queen Henrietta Maria, the Prince de Condé, etc.

H14) BOYER, Abel. (1667-1729)
The History of the Reign of Queen Anne, digested into Annals. 1703 (-1713). 1st edition. 11 volumes in 10. Engraved port. & maps (lacks one map). Two leaves in vol.6 in facs. Two leaves in vol.1 misbound. Sl.browned. Modern cl. FINE SET. £80

A history well supplied with documents, by one of the most respected of the French Protestant refugees who adopted a literary career in London.

H15) .....The Political State of G.B....Proceedings in Parliament (etc.) Feb.1711. 1st edition. (iv),77-174 (i.e.200pp) First leaf of text signed L_1; pagination irreg. accordingly. Three extra quires (r* r***4) between R. & S. Sl. browned. Modern ½ calf. £20

No.2 of 60 monthly newsbooks.

H16) BREE,John.
The Cursory Sketch of the State of the Naval, Military and Civil Establishment and Domestic Oeconomy of this Kingdom During the 14th Century; Account of the Campagin of King Edward the Third in Normandy and France. 1791. 1st edition. 4to. Index. Contemp. calf. Book-plate William Henry Hyett. FINE COPY. £45

Although this was to be the first volume of a series, the remaining volumes were never printed.

H17) BROUGHAM,H.P.,Baron Brougham & Vaux)(1778-1868)
An Inquiry into the State of the Nation. 1806. 1st edition. Lacks ½ title. KRESS B.5018.(3rd ed.)

H17) BROUGHAM...cont.
...An ANSWER to the INQUIRY. 1806. 1st edition. Lacks ½ title. KRESS B.5001. Two works in 1 volume. Browned. Contemp. ½ roan. Sp. faded. Lib. label. £35

In this early work Brougham reproaches the late Ministry for neglecting their opportunity of restraining Napoleon by presenting a United Austrian, Spanish, Russian & British front against him, & for submitting the nation to dangerous suspense between peace & war. It is in fact a party manifesto for the new government, & the second writer fairly exposes it as such.

H18) BROWNE, Sir Thomas.
Essai sur les Erreurs Populaires...Traduit de l'Anglois. Paris, 1733. 1st French edition. 3 vols. in 2. 12mo. Index. Blank T_4 (vol.1). Lacks title to vol.2.,perhaps as issued. E3 (vol.1) torn without loss. Sm.defect at corner of $2A_2$ (vol.2) Signatures in vol.2 jump from $2F_1$ to 2H. Contemp. sprinkled calf, spines gilt, jts. & corners sl. worn. Bk-pl. KEYNES 87-88. £150

Browne's "Pseudodoxia", is dedicated in this French version to the then Duc de Richelieu.
The title-page to vol.2 was probably cancelled when it was decided to print pp.431 onward as a separate "suite" & bind them with the second volume.

H19) (CENTORIO degli ORTENSI, Ascanio.)
Mémoires de la Guerre de Transilvanie & de Hongrie, entre l'Empereur Leopold I. & le Grand Seigneur Mehemet IV. Amsterdam (chez Daniel Elsevier),1680. 1st French edition. 2 volumes in 1. 12mo. Final blank to each vol. Four leaves repaired at inner margin. Later vellum. Etched bk-pl. Harald Wiens. WILLEMS 1584. £50

A narrative (originally in Italian) of a war in which Poland, Russia, Sweden & the Ottoman & Holy Roman Empires became involved in attempts by the Rakoczy princes of Transylvania to extend the principality at Polish expense.

H20) CHARLES I., King.
Eikon Basilike (graece) vel Imago Regis Caroli. In illis suis Aerumnis et Solitudine...Hague, ex officina Samuelis Broun, 1649. 12mo. Latin text. Lacks first leaf (blank?) Fp. double-page etching by HOLLAR inserted. (xv),272pp. Modern ½ calf. FINE. ALMACK 52. MADAN 41. £40

The second impression of Johan Earle's Latin version.

H21) CHARLES II, King.
An Account of the Preservation...after the Battle of Worcester...Letters to Several Persons. (Ed. Sir David Dalrymple) Glasgow (Foulis),1766. 1st edition. viii,190pp. Lacks final blank. Sl. spotted. Contemp. sprinkled calf. Sl. rubbed. £40

This lively narrative was dictated by the King to Samuel PEPYS, who added his own comments in places - his first appearance in print, the Diaries being then undeciphered.

H22) CLARENDON,Edward Earl of. (Lord High Chancellor of England & Chancellor of the University of Oxford)(1609-1674)
The Life of. Containing:
1. An account of the Chancellor's life..to the Restoration in 1660.
2. ...and of his History of the Grand Rebellion..to his banishment in 1667.
Written by Himself. Oxford (Clarendon Press) 1759. Folio. 1st edition. Engraved fp. port. & vignettes. Indices. Contemp. panelled calf; sl worn. £70

H23) CLAIRAC, Chevalier de.
L'Ingenieur de Campagne, ou Traité de la Fortification Passagère. Paris, 1749. 1st edition. 4to. 36 FOLDING COPPER ENGRAVED PLATES. xxiv,248pp. Single marginal worm-hole at beginning and end. Occasional sl. stains. Contemp. sprinkled calf, spine gilt, worn. £150

H24) CLARKSON, Thomas.(1760-1846)
Abolition of the African Slave-Trade, by the British Parliament. Abridged from Clarkson. Together with a brief view

H24) CLARKSON,T. cont.
...of the present state of the Slave-Trade and of Slavery. Sm.8vo. 2 vols. AUGUSTA, P.A.Brinsmade 1830. 1st thus. Bds. paper labels; uncut. E-ps. sl. browned. FINE COPY of this scarce edition. KRESS C.2474. £55

First published in 1808 in London.

H25) COCHIN(-) &(-)BELLICARD.
Observations upon the Antiquities of the Town of Herculaneum discovered at the Foot of Mount Vesuvius. 1756. 2nd edition. 42 engraved plates by Bellicard. Index. Modern calf-backed boards. £60

Includes a description of the Antiquities in the Neighbourhood of Naples.

H26) (COLBERT,Jean-Baptiste,Marquis de Torcy)(1665-1746)
Mémoires...des Négociations depuis le Traité de Ryswick jusqu' à la Paix d'Utrecht. The Hague,1756-7. 1st edition. Vols. 1-3 (of 5) only. French text. Contemp. sheep, worn. £20

H27) COOKE, George Wingrove.(1814-1865)
The History of Party; from the Rise of the Whig and Tory Factions...to the Passing of the Reform Bill. 1836-7. 1st edition. 3 vols. Sl. spotted. Contemp. ½ calf, spines gilt, sl. rubbed & faded. £80

Cooke was an early student of University College (London), where he came under the influence of John Austin & Andrew Amos, & through them of Bentham.

H28) COPE, Sir John (?-1760).
The Report of the Proceedings and Opinion of the Board of General Officers on their Examination into the Conduct, Behaviour and Proceedings. 1749. 1st edition. 4to. Appendix. Final errata leaf. Sl. spotted. Contemp. ½ calf; edges worn. £30

Cope commanded the royal forces which were defeated at Prestonpans in 1745. This inquiry clears him from all charges of incompetence & negligence.

H29) CORNISH ELECTIONS: Four pamphlets.
1. Motion for a New Writ...St. Mawes. 1817. 1st edition. 23pp. Disbound. (Speeches by Canning, Sir S.Romilly etc.)
2. RASHLEIGH,J.C. Letter to the Freeholders of Cornwall. St. Austell. 1826. 1st edition. 40pp. Orig. wraps; loose. (Disguised manifesto for Tremayne, the incumbent M.P.)
3. BOASE,W.M. Hints on the Exercise of the Elective Franchise, Falmouth,1835. 1st edition. 42pp. Disbound. (Warning to new voters against bribery etc.)
4. The Banner of Blue, an Oration. N.p.(Liskeard), n.d. (c.1830) 1st edition. 15pp. Orig. wraps. (Satirical poem on Cornish pocket borough)

4 items: £60

H30) CRAUFURD LINDESAY, John Lindesay,Earl of (1702-1749)
ROLT, Richard; Memoirs of the Life of. 1753. 1st edition.4to. Etched fp. port. & five etched folding plans. List of subscribers. Final errata leaf. Some spotting. 19th-cent. ½ mor. sp. gilt, jts. & corners worn. £40

This Earl was a distinguished soldier, who fought in Russia, Tartary & Hungary before returning to help in the suppression of the Jacobites.

H31) CROMWELL, Oliver.
CROMWELLIANA. A Chronological Detail of Events in which... Cromwell was Engaged, from 1642 to his Death. Westminster 1810. 1st edition. Folio. ½ title. Red & black title. Index. Four engraved plates, folding facs. Sl. spotted. Contemp. ½ calf. sp. & corners rubbed. £20

Consists entirely of extracts from contemporary news-sheets.

H32)...... A SHORT CRITICAL REVIEW of the Political Life. 1747. 3rd edition, rev. 12mo. Engraved fp. port. Appendix of documents. Tears in P9-Q6 repaired affecting one to four lines on verso of each. Fore-margin of A_2 shaved. Contemp. calf, sp. & jts. sl. worn. £20

H33) CROMARTIE, George (MacKenzie), Earl of: (1631-1714)
An Historical Account of the Conspiracies by the Earls of Gowry, and Robert Logan...against...James VI. Edinburgh, 1713. 1st edition. 2 parts in 1. ½ title. Red & black title. A8 blank. Sl. browned. Contemp. calf; rebacked. £40

Written by a Royalist to disprove the idea that Gowry etc., were unjustly condemned.

H34) CULLODEN PAPERS:
comprising an Extensive and Interesting Correspondence from the Year 1625 to 1748...Letters from...Lord Lovat...State Papers. 1815. 1st edition. 4to. Engraved title, two ports., and one facs. Last leaf repaired on blank verso. Sl. spottd. Contemp. calf, rebacked, corners sl. worn. £30

After long neglect, these documents were discovered in the possession of the Forbeses of Culloden.

H35) CURTIUS, Quintus Marcus.
De Rebus Gestis Alexandri Magni...cum omnibus Supplementis, Variantibus Lectionibus, Commentariis ac Notis perpetuis... curavit & digessit Henricus Snakenburg, Delft & Leyden, A. Beman etc. 1724. Sm.4to. Edited H. Snakenburg. FINE ENGRAVED ADDITIONAL TITLE after Van der My by F. Bleswyck; title in red & black. Folding engraved map & 16 engraved plates of medals, portraits, classical scenes etc., (three folding) Index. Contemp. blind-stamped vellum. £150

A VERY FINE COPY of this, the standard history of the life and death of Alexander the Great, including accounts of the wars and with an extensive index.

H36) De LOLME, Jean-Louis, (c.1745-1807)
The Constitution of England, or an Account of the English Government; in which it is compared with the Republican Form of Government, and occasionally with the other Monarchies in Europe. T. Spilsbury 1775. 2nd edition. Contemp. calf, sp. gilt, label. Sl. rubbed. FINE COPY. £40

In fact the first English ed., an enlarged and improved transl. by the author of his first French ed. pub'd in Holland in 1772.

H41) DIGGES, Sir Dudley: The Compleat Ambassador cont.
...with a French potentate - the future King Henri III in 1572, & the Duke of Alencon in 1581.

H42) .....Memoires et Instructions pour les Ambassadeurs ou Lettres et Negotiations de Walsingham, Ministre & Secretaire de'Etat, sous Elisabeth Reine d'Angleterre. Amsterdam, G. Gallet. 1700. Sm.4to. 1st French, transl. Louis Boulesteis de la Contie. Title in red & black. Index. A few lower margins sl. dampstained & with one or two sl. tears. Contemp. vellum; sp. defective & worn. £120

The first translation of "The Compleat Ambassador", 1655, edited by Sir Dudley Digges, Master of the Rolls, etc; a work which describes the machinations of Elizabeth's suitors.

H43) A DISSERTATION upon PARTIES;
In Several Letters to Caleb d'Anvers. 1743. 6th ed. Engr. fp. Index. Contemp. calf. £40

Halkett and Laing give the author as Henry St. John, Viscount Bolingbroke.

H44) DIXON, W. Hepworth.
The London Prisons: with an Account of the Most Distinguished Persons...Confined in them. 1850. 1st edition. Wood-engraved fp. Appendix. Final advert. leaf. Modern ½ calf. £35

Enlarged from papers written for Dickens's newspaper, the "Daily News."

H45) DODINGTON, George Bubb (1691-1762)
The Diary, ed. Henry Penruddocke Wyndham. Salisbury 1784. "New edition" (actually 1st) ½ title. Final advert. leaf. Appendix of documents. Contemp. sprinkled calf; sp. gilt; lacks label, jts. worn. £40

This diary by Dodington, an Irishman, is a chronicle of political intrigues & society notorieties.

H37) De LOLME, J-L.
The Constitution of England...1781. 3rd edition. Index. Contents bound after introduction. Final errata leaf. Contemp. calf, edges sl. worn. S. & M.i.100. £35

Includes four new chapters, one prompted by a conversation with Franklin & dealing with American questions and the position of her colonies, another on the important question on the right of taxation etc. The preface, containing an account of de Lolme's struggles with booksellers & patrons, is also new.

H38) ......Another copy; same edition. Contemp. cf; sl. worn. £35

H38) ..... Another copy. 1807. new edition. Engraved fp. port. Index. Sl. stained at beginning and end. Modern cl. S. & M. ii.98. £25

De Lolme died in the year this edition was printed, & it includes a short anonymous biography & some additional notes.

H39) .....Another copy. Halifax (Yorks.) 1822. Contemp. cf., blind-tooled & gilt, sl. rubbed. £25

H40) .....Another copy. Ed. John Macgregor. 1853. 1st thus. Index. Publisher's cat. at end. Single worm-hole through text; few more in e-ps. Orig. cl., worn. £15

Macgregor's short Life of de Lolme disproves the theory that the English version of the "Constitution" was made by Francis Maseres.

H41)
DIGGES, Sir Dudley (1583-1639)(ed.)
The Compleat Ambassador: or two Treaties of the Intended Marriage of Qu: Elizabeth. By Tho: Newcomb, for Gabriel Bedell and Thomas Collins, 1655. 1st edition. Folio. Engr. fp. by W. FAITHORNE. Red & black title. Index. Sm. piece torn from inner margin of G4. Contemp. sprinkled calf, worn. WING D.1453. £180

Diplomatic correspondence recording attempts to draw England into an alliance with France by the Marriage of Elizabeth

H46) DRING, Thomas.
A Catalogue of the Lords, Knights and Gentlemen, that have Compounded for their Estates. Chester 1733, 2nd ed., rev. Last five leaves in photostatic facs. Few leaves wormed. Modern ½ calf. £20

A record (slightly enlarged from the London edition of 1655) of Royalists who were obliged to pay large sums in order to redeem their estates from confiscation under the Protectorate.

H47) Du BARRY, (Marie-Jeanne Gomard de Vaubernier) Comtesse. (1741-1793) Letters to and from...History of that Favourite...Anecdotes of the Court of Versailles. 1779. 1st Engl. Corner torn from R4, text not affected. U1 torn without loss Contemp. mottled calf, gilt. £15

H48) DUNLOP, Alexander.
Letter to the Freeholders of the County of Dumbarton; on Parliamentary Reform. Edinburgh 1830. 1st trade ed. Mod. wraps. FINE. £10

Advocates the extension of voting rights among proprietors of their own land. Previously printed as an election manifesto.

H49) (ELLIS, George.)
History of the Late Revolution in the Dutch Republic. 1789. 1st edition. Contemp calf, ARMS of Sir James HARRIS, 1st Baron Malmesbury, on sides; jts. & edges worn. £35

In 1785 a party of French sympathisers, playing on anti-British feeling in Holland, attempted to get up a revolution against the pro-British Stadtholder William V. They were defeated, & the Dutch constitution was afterwards adapted to strengthen the Stadtholderate.

H50) EUGÈNE, (Francois), Prince of Savoy (1663-1736)
The Life and Military Actions of...with an Account of his Death and Funeral. 1739. 1st edition. Final blank. Contemp. sheep, jts. & edges worn. £20

This great soldier became one of the most popular men in Britain as a result of his share in Marlborough's campaigns.

H51) **EWALD, Alex Charles.**
Our Public Records, a brief Handbook to the National Archives, 1873. 1st edition. Orig. cloth, label worn, corner cut from e-p. **£10**

list of the most important documents among the Public Records, incl. State Papers etc. and a Glossary.

H52) **An EXACT COLLECTION of the DEBATES**
of the House of Commons...at Westminster. October 21,1680... and...at Oxford...March 21. 1680. For R. Clavel...and A. Churchil, 1689. 1st edition. Names of members inserted in contemp. MS. Sl. spotted. Mod. boards. WING E.2574. **£60**

Proceedings in the last Parliament of Charles II's reign.

H53) **FERNE,(Sir) John (c.1550-1610)**
The Blazon of Gentrie: devided into Two Parts. The first named the Glorie of Generositie. The second, Lacyes Nobilitie. By John WINDET, for Andrew Maunsell, 1586. 1st edition, 2nd issue. Z4 & 2K2 (final leaf) blanks, the latter repaired. Three unsigned leaves of tables (two shaved) between 2D1 & D2. Piece torn from margin of T6 without loss of text. (xx), 41/130pp. Numerous woodcut arms in text and tables of desent. A FINE COPY in OLD VELLUM, lacking ties. STC 10825. **£350**

Ferne, a fashionable student of the Inner Temple, collected the material of this book for the Polish adventurer Albert, Count Lasky, who laid claim against the name & fortunes of the Lacy family. When Lasky vanished under a cloud, Ferne published his book to clear himself of complicity. It is a dialogue between a herald, a knight, a comic rustic (often very informative on the changing social & religious order), & others, "full of curious information, & far above the level of the early heraldic writers" (D.N.B.)

H54) **FIENNES,Nathaniel (Lord)(1608-1669)**
Speech...before...Parliament...20th of January 1657. By Henry Hills and John Field 1657. 1st edition. Sm.4to. (ii),26pp. WING F.881.
...Speech...concerning Bishops and...London Petition,Printed

H54) **FIENNES, Nathaniel...cont.**
...1641. 1st edition. (ii),28pp. Lacks final blank. WING F.880. Two works in 1 volume. Blanks bound in at end. Mod. ½ calf. **£30**

Biblical declamation for the opening of Parliament & an attack on episcopal suffrage.

H55) **FONBLANQUE, Albay (1793-1872)**
England under Seven Administrations. 1837. 1st in book form. 3 vols. Engraved fp. ports. Index. Fps. & titles spotted. Contemp. calf, gilt, sps. rubbed. Bk-pl. LORD BELPER. **£30**

Leading articles from the "Times", "Morning Chronicle" etc. by an outstanding political journalist.

H56) **FOX, Charles James.**
"PHILOPATRIS WARWICENSIS" (Samuel Parr, 1747-1825) Characters of the Late Charles James Fox. 1809. 1st edition. 2 vols. Final errata leaf. Vol.2 spotted at end. Contemp. cf, gilt, sps. rubbed, lacks labels. Bk-pl. LORD BELPER. **£40**

Parr was called the Johnson of the Whigs.

H57).....TROTTER, John Bernard; Memoirs of the Later Years of. 1811. 3rd edition. Sl. spotted. Contemp. calf, gilt, jts. worn. Bk-pl. LORD BELPER. **£20**

Written by Fox's private secretary, & including an appendix of letters.

H58) **FRACCHETTA, Girolamo (1560-1620)**
Il Prencipe. Venice (appresso Gio Battista Ciotti),1599. Rev. edition. Italian text. Index. (lx),350pp. Lacks final blank. Few leaves sl. browned. Few old annots. Contemp. vellum; lacks ties. B.M.C.(It.) p.276. **£95**

Fracchetta's Prince is a philosopher-king bound by no obligation to his subjects, but voluntarily submitting himself to the dictates of God & reason. This book (here revised by himself) arose out of study for his larger work, the Seminario de' Governi.

H59) **FRIEDRICH II. (Frederick the Great). King of Prussia.**
Oeuvres posthumes. Berlin (Voss et Fils/Decker et Fils),1788. 1st collected. 15 vols. Engr. fp. port. Contemp. ½ sprinkled calf; sp. of vol. 1. sl. defective; edges rubbed. **£150**

Includes the Histoire de Mon Temps, Histoire de la Guerre de Sept Ans, poetical works, many letters to Voltaire & d'Alembert (with some from the latter), & some other pieces.

H60) **FROUDE, James A.**
The Divorce of Catherine of Aragon. 1891. Orig. cl. fdd. **£10**

H61) **GARROWAY,(Sir Henry)(1575-1646)**
A Speech...at a Common-Hall...upon a Speech...by Mr. Pym. Printed...1642. 4to. (ii),14pp. Title & last leaf repaired. Modern wraps. WING G.280. **£20**

Garrow accuses the Commons of stirring up riots to disturb the King when he visited the City.

H62) **GLADSTONE, William Ewart. (1809-1898)**
Speeches on Parliamentary Reform. 1866. 1st edition. Appendix of letters. Orig. cloth, sl. faded. **£20**

Speeches on the early stages of the bill which was to become the second Reform Act in the following year.

H63) .....Vaticanism: An Answer to Replies and Reproofs. John Murray. 1875. 1st edition. 128pp. Disbound. **£10**

Gladstone was not only a magnificent leader of Victorian Liberalism but also a High Churchman with a strong taste for theology.

H64) **GONZALEZ,Tomas.**
Documents from Simancas relating to the Reign of Elizabeth (1558-1568) Transl. & introd. Spencer Hall. 1865. 1st Engl. index. Orig. cloth, sp. faded. **£10**

Historical account based by Gonzalez on Spanish state papers of the 16th century.

H65) **GORGES, Family of**
YATE, Henry Gorges Dobyns; Anecdotes of the Gorges Family. 1785. MANUSCRIPT on paper. 268pp., the first 130 written on recto only, the rest blank. Contemp. stained calf, gilt, worn, upper jt. weak. Author's book-plate. **£40**

Includes interesting facts & documents relating to Sir Ferdinando Gorges (1566-1647) pioneer American colonist and at one time lord of the Province of Maine.

H66) **(GRANT, William, Lord Prestongrange)**
The Occasional Writer: containing an Answer to the Second Manifesto of the Pretender's Eldest Son. 1745. 1st edition. Lacks ½ title. (ii),54pp. Later boards, uncut, sewing weak, spine defective. **£20**

An important anti-Jacobite tract. The author (identified in contemp. MS. on the title) was a Lord of Session.

H67) **GREEN,J.R.**
A Short History of the English People. 1892. 4 vols. Illus. Orig. cloth, gilt, t.e.g. **£20**

H68) .....& Miss Kate NORGATE. Another edition. Newnes.1907. 4 vols. Orig. dec'd cloth, gilt. FINE SET. **£20**

H69) **GREVILLE, Charles Cavendish Fulke.**
The Greville Diary, including Passages hitherto Withheld from Publication. Ed.P.W.Wilson. 1927. 2 vols. Illus. Index. Orig. b'ram, gilt, FINE. **£20**

Reprint of Wilson's Longman edition, consisting of selected passages with a connecting commentary.

H70) **GUEVARA,Antonio de. Bp. of Mondonedo (ob.1544)**
The Familiar Epistles...Transl. from the Spanish by Edward Hellowes. For Ralph NEWBERRIE 1577 (3rd Engl. edition) Sm.4to Black letter. (viii)402,(vi)pp. Index. Few old annots. 19th century ½ calf, sl. rubbed. STC 12434. **£220**

The author, a Spanish bishop, was historiographer to Charles He offers observations on ancient & modern history etc. PP 293-521 contain twelve letters of advice to those about to marry.

H71) GUICCIARDINI, Francesco (1482-1540)
Histoire des Guerres d'Italie, transl. Jerome Chomedey, ed. François de la Noue. Geneva (heritiers d'Eustache Vignon), 1593. 1st thus. 2 vols. French text. Indices. Vol.1 lacks final blank. Occasional ink scoring.
Modern ½ calf. £150

First edition with the observations of de la Noue (1531-1591) a Breton soldier in the service of the Dutch republic; he compiled them during a period of imprisonment.

H72) GUISCHARDT, Karl Gottlieb (1724-1775)
Memoires militaires sur les Grecs et les Romains. The Hague (P.de Hondt), 1758. 1st edition. 2 vols. in 1. 4to. French text. Red & black titles; folding engraved plates. FINE COPY in contemp. mottled calf, rebacked, sl. rubbed. £150
BRUNET pp 1826/7.

Guischardt, a practical soldier, with the learning & judgement of a scholar is the author of this study of the ancient art of war. Frederick the Great placed a high value on his services & dubbed him Quintus Icilius after one of Caesar's officers.

H73) GUTHRY, Henry, Bp. of Dunkeld (?-1676)
Memoirs...wherein the Conspiracies and Rebellion against King Charles I are...narrated. Ed. Geo. Crawfurd. Glasgow 1748. 12mo. Index. Contemp. calf, sp. gilt, sl. rubbed. £30

Guthry resisted Scotch interference in the Scots liturgy, but when the revolution came to a head, he held by the lawful government, even to the loss of his benefice. He covers the years 1573 to 1649.

H74) HAILES, Sir David Dalrymple, Lord (1726-1792)
Annals of Scotland, from the Accession of Malcolm III...to the Accession of Robert I (- To the Accession of the House of Stewart.) Edinburgh, 1776 (-1779) 1st edition. 2 vols. 4to. ½ titles. Errata leaf in vol.1. Lacks final blanks. Contemp. calf, jts. worn. £60

The major work of a great Scots lawyer & antiquary.

H80) (HENDERSON, Andrew) The History of the Rebellion cont.
.....STEWART, Charles Edward Louis Philip Casimir "Prince". The YOUNG CHEVALIER: or, a Genuine Narrative of All that Befell that Unfortunate Adventurer. N.d.(c.1747) 1st edition. Tear repaired in D_1. Last leaf defective without loss of text. Some spotting. Two works in 1 vol. Later ½ calf, worn. Upper jt. weak. £25

H81) HEYLYN, Peter (1600-1662)
A Help to English History with Additions to 1773; with the coats of arms of the nobility. Lists of the extinct Viscounts and Barons. The Praetorian Banner Displayed and a list of the said Magistrates. 1773. Appendix. 54 COPPER-ENGRAVED PLATES. Contemp. calf. FINE COPY. £40

H82) HODY, Humphrey (1659-1706)
A History of English Councils and Convocations, and of the Clergy's Sitting in Parliament. 1701. 1st edition. Advert. leaves at end. Fore-margins of A_5 & B_1 frayed. Sl. wormed, esp. at end. Cancel-stub between B_7 & B_8. Contemp. panelled calf, sl. rubbed. S. & M. i,132. £30

In some copies page 288 (here partially given up to a publisher's catalogue) is re-set & a short appendix added.

H83) HUME, David.
Essays and Treatises on Several Subjects. 1758. New edition. 4to. Index. viii,540pp. Contemp. signature on e-p of Edward Williams (a clergyman attached to the See of St. Asaph) with pencil annots. in his hand. Contemp. calf, rebacked, corners worn. £150

This is the first edition to include the dissertation on the Passions and some other items which had been published separately.

H84) .....The History of England from the Invasion of Julius Caesar to the Revolution in 1688. 1789. New edition with the author's last corrections and improvements. 8 vols. Approx. 50 engraved plates. Index. Contemp. tree calf. Some joints worn, part. vol.1. £30

H75) HALFORD, Sir Henry.
Essay and Orations, Read and Delivered at the Royal College of Physicians; also, an Account of the Opening of the Tomb of King Charles I. 1831. 1st edition. An essay on the treatment of gout is appended. Fp. port & facs. Contemp ½ calf, gilt. FINE. £25

H76) HARRAL, Thomas.
Henry the Eighth and George the Fourth; or, the Case fairly stated. 1820. 1st edition. fp. ports. Calf. £15

Divided into four parts: The English Law of Divorce; Sketch of the Trials of Henry the Eight's Queens; Proceedings against Caroline Amelia Elizabeth, whilst Princess of Wales; and a parallel between the lives and characters of Henry the Eighth and George the Fourth.

H77) HARRIS, William (1720-1770)
An Account of the Life and Writings of Charles I. 1758. 1st edition. Appendix. Contemp. calf. £15

H78) HAY of DRUMBOOTE, Richard.
An Essay on the Origine of the Royal Family of the Stewarts. Edinburgh 1793. 2nd edition. Sm.4to. MS note on e-p. "Chas. Stuart 1793. Only thirty copies of this printed." Appendix of charters. (iv),42pp. Later ½ mor., sl. rubbed & faded. £20

H79) HELVICUS, Christophorous (1581-1616)
Theatrum Historicum et Chronologicum, Aequalibus ...Intervallis...Digestum. Ed. & enlarged J. BALTHASAR. Oxford 1662. 6th edition. 4to. Latin text. Black and red title. Index. Contemp. calf. Lacks e-ps; sl. rubbed. £70

Chronological tables with lists of rulers, important events etc.

H80) (HENDERSON, Andrew)
The History of the Rebellion,1745 and 1746...Character of the Highlanders...Declarations of the Pretender, and the Journal of his Marches (etc) 1748. 2nd edition. Some spotting.

H85) An IMPARTIAL ACCOUNT of the AFFAIRS of SCOTLAND from the Death of King James the Fifth, to the Tragical Exit of the Earl of Murray, Regent of Scotland. 1705. 1st Engl. ½ title. Sl. stained. Contemp. panelled calf, rebacked & recornered; rubbed. £25

A 16th century work taken from the Latin.

H86) JOHNSTONE, (James) Chevalier de (1719-c.1800)
Memoirs of the Rebellion in 1745 and 1746. (transl. anon.) 1820. 1st Engl. 4to. 2 engraved ports. & 1 plan. Sl. spottd. Contemp. calf, rebacked. £30

The author was one of the Young Pretender's aides-de-camp. He takes his memoirs to 1759, when as a mercenary in the French service he fought against the British in Canada.

H87) JENKINS, James.
The Martial Achievements of G.B. and Her Allies; from 1799 to 1815. Large 4to. 1814-5. (plates water-marked 1812-20). Engraved title, hand-coloured dedication leaf and 52 hand-coloured AQUATINT PLATES including the plate with the legend "Martial Achievements vol.1". Lacks portrait. Modern ½ calf, uncut. ABBEY: Life 365. FINE. £850

Some copies carry a portrait of the Duke of Wellington: this was not issued during part publication, but is a later insertion and is therefore mostly missing in these early copies.

H88) JOPP, James.
Historical Reflections on the Constitution and Representative System of England. 1812. 1st edition. Appendix (chronological table of constituencies) Final errata leaf. Contemp. polished calf, gilt. FINE COPY. £45

Written to counteract Sharp's, Pitt's & Burdett's doctrine that the original electoral system of England provided for universal suffrage, Jopp argues that only a slight redistribution of constituencies, & a strict enforcement of existing laws against bribery, is needed.

H89) KILMARNOCK,(William Boyd), Earl of (1704-1746)
FOSTER, James; An Account of the Behaviour...after his Sentence, and on the Day of his Execution. For J. Noon...and A. Millar 1746. 1st edition. Appendix (petitions & other letters of the Earl) 51,(iii)pp. Sl. spotted. Later ½ calf, faded. £20

H90) KIRKTON, James (c.1620-1699)
The Secret and True History of the Church of Scotland, from the Restoration to the Year 1678...Account of the Murder of Archbishop Sharp, by James Russell. Ed. Charles Kirkpatrick Sharpe. Edinburgh 1817. 1st thus. 4to. Three etched plates, (two ports.) & vignettes. Some browning. Later ½ calf, rbbd. £20

Kirkton was a popular preacher of extreme presbyterian views.

H91) LABAUME, Eugene.
A Circumstantial Narrative of the Campaign in Russia, embellished with plans of the Battles of the Moskwa and the Malo-Jaroslavitz 1815. 2nd edition, considerably improved. Tr. from the French. 2 folding engraved plans, one frayed at edges; lacks fp. map. Contemp. calf, rebacked. £20

H92) LECKIE,Gould Francis.
Essay on the Practice of the British Government; distinguished from the Abstract Theory on which it is Supposed to be founded. 1812. 1st edition. Errata slip. Review (from Edinburgh Review) pasted on extra blanks at end. Contemp. ½ calf. spine defective, corners worn. £20

H93) .....Another copy. "Pamphleteer", 1817. 49-105. disbound. £9

H94) A LETTER from a FRENCH LAWYER
to an English Gentleman, upon the Present Revolution. For Ric. Chiswell, 1689. 1st edition. Sm.4to. (ii),18pp. Disbound. WING L.4. £20

H95) LLOYD,(Henry) (1739-1783)
A Political and Military Rhapsody, on the Invasion and Defence of Great Britain and Ireland..(with) a Supplement by the Editor. 1798. 5th ed., rev. Two folding maps (one col'd in outline) & one foldingplate (showing the Pike and the Pikemen and military formations) Modern ½ calf. £70

Among the many schemes presented for the defence of England under the threat of French invasion, this of Lloyd (posthumously published) stands out for the wide experience of the author; born in Wales, he was by turns a novice in a monastery, a military engineer in France, an officer in Prussia, and a general in the Russian service. A large part of the supplement consists of powerful arguments against Pitt's schemes of finance & "sinking funds" in general.

H96) LOUIS XVIII,(Louis Stanislaus Xavier), King of France.
Mémoires, ed. Duc de D--. Paris 1832. 1st edition. 12 vols. French text. Sl. spotted. Contemp. ½ mottled calf, spines gilt, two labels. sps. rubbed; jts. sl. worn. Book-plate Viscount Eversley. £120

The last Louis, was twice a fugitive & twice a king. Lord Eversley was better known as Charles Shaw Lefevre, Speaker of the Commons.

H97) LOVAT, Lord Simon Fraser (1676-1747)
Memoirs of the Life...Written by Himself, in the French language; and now first translated, from the original Manuscript. 1797. 1st edition. Sl. spotted. Title repaired in inner margin. Contemp. calf, rebacked. £35

Lovat,whose actions as a Jacobite traitor & rebel were perhaps the least discreditable of his life, is best known through Hogarth's vivid portrait. The French text was unpub'd.

H98) MACKINTOSH, James (Sir)(1765-1832)
Vindiciae Gallicae. Defence of the French Revolution and its English Admirers, against the accusations of the Rt. Hon. Edmund Burke; including some strictures on the late production of Mons. de Calonne. G.G.J. and J. Robinson 1791. Second ed., corrected. Advert. leaf. Modern ½ calf. £70

H98) MACKINTOSH, James. Vindiciae Gallicae cont.
.....Published the same year as the first edition.
This work introduced Mackintosh to Sheridan, Grey, Whitbread, Fox and the Duke of Bedford and eventually to Edmund Burke himself, to whose arguments he soon professed himself a convert, and for whose genius he entertained a chivalrous admiration.

H99) (MACQUEEN, Daniel)
Letters on Mr. Hume's History of G.B. Edinburgh 1756. 1st ed. ½ title. Contemp. calf, jts. worn, sl. rubbed. £35

A temperate reply to Hume's assertion that the early reformers were as much blinded & corrupted by fanaticism as were the Roman Catholics by superstition & servility.

H100) MALLING, Ove.
Great and Good Deeds of the Danes, Norwegians and Holsteinians. Transl. anon. 1807. 1st Engl. 4to. Index. Some spotting. Contemp. ½ calf, worn. £20

H 101) MARGARET of ANJOU, consort of King Henry VI (1429-1482)
BAUDIER, Michel: A History of the Memorable and Extraordinary Calamities of. (transl. anon.) 1737. 1st edition. Some spotting. Later ½ calf; jts. & edges worn. £15

The original French of this 17th century biography was not yet published.

H 102) MASSON, Frédéric.
Cavaliers de Napoléon. Paris n.d. (1895) 1st edition. 4to. Illus. (22 mounted photogravure plates, one hand-coloured & vignettes) Édouard Detaille. Few margins sl. marked. One guard sl. torn. Contemp. ¾ mor.,t.e.g.,uncut, orig. wraps bound in; sp. faded, jts. & corners sl. worn. £75

H 103) MATTHAEUS, Antonius (1635-1710)
De Rebus Ultrajectinis et imprimis de bello cum Covordensibus ...olim gesto...Narratio historica..Hague 1740. 4to. Red & black title. Index. Title-page repaired in fore-margin. Some

H 103) MATTHAEUS, Antonius, De Rebus...cont.
.....browning. Old ½ parchment/limp boards (worn) £50

The Annals of Utrecht from 1138-1233, by an unknown writer of the 13th century. Matthaeus edited the work from a MS in the Utrecht church library, and added a mass of learned notes quoting many episcopal proclamations & other contemporary documents. His edition first appeared in 1690.

H 104) MAZZINI, Joseph.
Royalty and Republicanism in Italy; or, Notes and Documents relating to the Lombard Insurrection, and to the Royal War of 1848. Charles Gilpin. 1850. 1st edition. ½ title, adverts. Orig. cloth, sl. rubbed & sl. wear on top of spine otherwise FINE. £30

H 105) MENNECHET, Édouard.
Histoire de France depuis la Fondation de la Monarchie. Paris 1843. 2nd edition. 4 vols. French text. Sl. spotted. Contemp. ½ calf, sl. rubbed. £20

H 106) MILTON, John.
Letters of State...to most of the Sovereign Princes and Republicks of Europe. From...1649 till..1659. To which is added an account of his life. Together with several of his Poems; and a catalogue of his works never before printed. 1694. 12mo 1st Engl. edition. Transl. Edward Phillips. Title repaired at foot with sl. loss of printed margin. Contemp. calf, rebacked hinges sl. worn. Bk-pl. WING M.2126. £270

The first publication of a life of Milton. Edward Phillips, the translator, was Milton's youngest nephew.

H 107) MONK, George. Duke of Albemarle.
SKINNER, Thomas: The Life, edited & introd. William Webster. 1724. 2nd edition. Engraved fp. port. Contemp. panelled calf, spine gilt; jts. & edges worn. £20

Webster's Preface contradicts Clarendon's hostile view of Monk's character.

H 108) MONTRÉSOR, Comte de.
Mémoires...durant le Ministère du Cardinal de Richelieu. Relation de Monsieur de Fontenailles...(- autres Pièces curieuses) "Leyden" (Brussels, F. Foppens), 1665. 1st collected. 2 vols. 12mo. Few contemp. annots. in vol. 1. Contemp. vellum. WILLEMS 2015. FINE. £95

Montrésor took a leading part in the struggle against Richelieu, whom he describes in surprising terms; " a very lucky man, who in the difficulties which he encountered owed far more to the assistance of fortune than to that of the prudence with which he is commonly supposed to have been endowed." The Mémoires proper (vol.1) appeared in 1663; vol.2, of which this is the first edition, is a supplement containing miscellaneous pieces from the time of the Fronde.

H 109) MORAY, Bishopric of
Registrum episcopatus Moraviensis. Edinburgh (Bannatyne Club), 1837. 1st edition. 4to.12 lith. or engr. facs. plates, some folding; 1 map. Index. Plates sl. stained. Contemp. full brown mor., gilt panels on sides, spine & inside borders gilt, t.e.g.; jts. sl. rubbed. FINE COPY. £40

A collection of ancient documents relating to the see of Moray, including (besides the register itself) a separate register of the Dean & chapter and a 16th century statement of revenues

H 110) The NAVAL HISTORY
of G.B. with the Lives of the most illustrious Admirals and Commanders. 1768. 4 vols. 11 engraved portraits & 4 folding engraved maps, 2 of them hand-coloured. Contemp. calf, rbbd. £40

H 111) (NEWTON, Richard, D.D.)(1676-1753)
Pluralities Indefensible - a Treatise...to the Consideration of the Parliament of G.B. By a Presbyter of the Church of England. J. Osborn & J. Rivington 1743. 1st edition. Contemp. sprinkled calf, gilt spine, label. Sl. rbbd, bk-pl. FINE COPY £30

This is an answer to Bishop Wharton on pluralities. Newton was the founder of Hertford College, Oxford and became Canon of Christ Church. He is better known for his work on"University Education."

H 112) NICOLAS, Nicholas Harris (ed.)
The Privy Purse Expences of King Henry the Eighth, from Nov. MDXXIX, to Dec. MDXXXII. W. Pickering 1827. 1st edition. Index. Orig. cloth, paper label, uncut & unopened; faded. £20

Printed from a MS. formerly in the collection of Harley, Earl of Oxford.

H 113) NIEUHOF, Jan.
Die Gesantschaft der ost-indischen Geselschaft in den vereinigten Niederländen an den tartarischen Cham und nunmehr auch sinischen Keyser verrichtet. Amsterdam (durch Jacob Mörs),1669. 2nd edition, enlarged. Folio. Red & black title. Engraved port. & 33 (of 34) DOUBLE-PAGE PLATES. Lacks plate 32 (pagoda) & folding map. 109 copper-engravings in text. (vi),420,(xii)pp. Two text leaves (*3-4) & three plates repaired, the latter on versos; text engr. on p. 72 pasted over another engraving which had been repeated in error from p. 70. Several plates loosely inserted. Contemp. ½ roan/boards, very worn, hinges broken. £300

This second German edition is the first in that language to include the text engravings.

H 114) NORTH, Roger
Examen: or, an Enquiry into the Credit and Veracity of a Pretended Complete History; shewing the perverse and wicked design of it and the many falsities and Abuses of Truth...; to vindicate the Honour of the late King Charles. 1740. 1st ed. 4to. Engraved port. Modern calf-backed boards. £60

A Vindication of Charles II in response to Dr. White Kennett's "History of England", by the Attorney-General to James II, valuable for the many original anecdotes it contains and the view it presents of party politics.

H 115) (ORRERY) Charles Boyle, Earl of.
Dr. Bentley's Dissertations on the Epistles of Phalaris, and the Fables of Aesop, Examin'd. For Tho. Bennet, 1698. 2nd ed. Lacks 1st blank. Index. Contemp. calf. Lacks fp. WING O.470. £15

H 116) PANMURE, Fox Maule, Baron (Earl of Dalhousie)1880-1874)
The Panmure Papers...Selection from the Correspondence, ed. Sir G. Douglas & Sir G.D. Ramsay. 1908. 2nd edition. 2 vols. Photogravure fp's. Index. Orig. b'ram, uncut & unopened, FINE. £20

Correspondence of the Crimean War period between Panmure (then Secretary for War) & the Queen, Palmerston, Raglan, etc. Queen Victoria's active participation in affairs is clearly seen in these letters.

H 117) PAPERS relative to the RUPTURE with SPAIN,
Laid before Both Houses of Parliament. 1762. 1st edition. 4to. .... PRELIMINARY ARTICLES of PEACE,between his Britannick Majesty, the Most Christian King, and the Catholic King. 1762. 1st edition. French & Engl. text. 4to. 2 works in 1 vol. First title repaired at inner margin & partially guarded. Mod.cloth. £40

Diplomatic correspondence of the elder Pitt & Lord Bristol (the ambassador to Spain), & a treaty, recording the beginning end of the quarrel whose dilatory prosecution caused the resignation of Pitt & the downfall of the Newcastle government.

H 118) PATTEN, Robert.
The History of the Rebellion: with Original Papers, and the Characters of the Principal Noblemen and Gentlemen Concern'd in it. 1717. 2nd edition, rev. 2 parts in 1. Advert. leaf before 2K,; pagination interrupted at this point. Contemp. panelled calf, sp. & jts. rubbed. £25

An eye-witness account from the Hanoverian point of view.

H 119) PEREFIXE, Hardouin de, Bishop of Rodez (1605-1676)
Histoire du roy Henri le Grand...augmentée par l'Auteur. Paris, 1662. 4to. 1st French. Engraved fp. port. 18th-cent. calf, rebacked, corners sl. worn. £95

Perefixe, a distinguished prelate who had formerly written anti-Jansenist pamphlets, wrote this life of Henri IV for his pupil Louis XIV. This edition (preceded by two Elzevir impressions) includes a new collection of anecdotes of Henri's wit and wisdom.

H 120) PUFENDORF, Samuel.(1632-1694)
An Introduction to the History of the Principal Kingdoms & States of Europe. 1719. 8th ed. corrected and improved. With an appendix...introduction to the History of the Principal Sovereign States of Italy, part. Venice, Modena, Mantua,Florence and Savoy. Index. Calf, rubbed; jts. sl. worn. £35

H 121) (PULLEN, Tobias)
A Vindication of Sir Robert King's Designs and Actions, in Relation to the Late and Present Lord Kingston. 1699. FINE contemp. black morocco, gilt panels with cornerpieces on sides, spine panelled in six compartments; a.e.g. BOOK-PLATE SIR ROBERT SOUTHWELL (Clerk to the Privy Council.)WING P.4169. £60

H 122) PUNT, Jan (1711-1779)
Lijk-staetsie van zyne Doorluchtigste Hoogheid den Heere Willem Carel Hendrik Frisco, Prince van Orange. The Hague (P.Gosse & N. van Daalen) 1755. 1st edition LARGE FOLIO. French & Dutch text. 41 FINE DOUBLE-PAGE COPPER ENGRAVED PLATES. 40pp. List of subscribers. Signed at end of text by Gosse. Plate 1, sl. browned & with marginal tears repaired on verso; otherwise A VERY FINE COPY IN CONTEMP. ½ VELLUM/ Marbled sides, sl. rubbed. £600

Brunet lists a French edition printed at the Hague of the same date and with the same plates.
Scenes from the funeral procession of the Prince of Orange, culminating in a fine view of the market-place & cathedral of Delft. Punt, who engraved the plates from drawings by P. van Cuyk, was a theatrical designer & picture engraver of some note; he preserves many instructive details of military & other costumes, musical instruments, etc.

H 123) RALEIGH, Sir Walter.
The Perogative of Parliaments in England: Proved in a Dialogue (pro & contra) betweene a Councellour of State and a Justice of Peace. "Midelburge" 1628. 1st edition. Sm.4to. viii,66pp. Lacks final blank. Fore-margins sl. stained. Later wraps. STC 20648a. S. & M.i.137. £160

Foreseeing the disasters that must ensue from "taxation without representation", Sir Walter, with the help of his Justice, urges King James to summon a parliament, to trust in the loyalty & good faith of the representatives, & not to be per-

H 123) RALEIGH, Sir Walter. The Perogative of Parliaments cont.
....suaded by false councellors that it would be a compromise of his dignity to refuse the advice & consent of the members. This issue with variant catchword "Couns" on B_1, recto.

H 124) ....Another copy. Printed 1640. Gatherings C.G.H & I set up by a different printer from the rest. Modern marbled boards. STC 20650. £90

H 125) RAY of WHITEHAVEN, James.
A Compleat History of the Rebellion....to its total Suppression at the Glorious Battle of Culloden. 1757. 1st edition. 12mo. Engraved fp. port. (William, Duke of Cumberland) 2 engraved plans (shaved at one margin). Sl. browned. Later sheep, sl. rubbed. £30

An eye-witness account by a volunteer in "Butcher" William's forces.

H 126) RECUEIL de DIVERSES PIÈCES,
servans à l'Histoire de Henry III."Cologne" (The Hague, Adriaan Vlacq), 1662. 12mo. Final blank. 462,(ii)pp. Contemp. vellum. WILLEMS 868. £80

This collection of a contemporary diary & three other documents was published by the Elzevirs in 1660; Vlacq, the mathematician-publisher, produced two copies - one of 1660 & the present.

H 127) RERESBY, Sir John, (1635-1689)
Travels and Memoirs. 1813. 1st thus. 39 portraits & other plates (some hand-coloured) and extra-illustrated with 15 further plates. Index. Contemp. red mor., gilt, a.e.g, sl. rubbed. Bk-pl. £60

Reresby, a noted Royalist, spent the years of Cromwell's government travelling in Europe. This is the first publication of the travels. Most of the illustrations are printed from original plates of the 17th and 18th centuries.

H 128) RICHER,A.
Great Events from Little Causes, or, a Selection of...Stories, Drawn from the Histories of Different Nations. (Tr. anon. from the French) Dublin, 1768. 12mo. Sl. spotted. Contemp. calf, sl. rubbed. £15

H 129) RIDPATH, George (c.1717-1772)
The Border-History of England and Scotland, Deduced from the Earliest Times, to the Union of the Two Crowns. Ed. Philip Ridpath. 1810. New edition. 4to. Index. Sl. browned. One marginal repair, text not affected. Later ½ calf, rebacked, with orig. spine, jts. rubbed. £20

First published 1776.

H 130) RIMIUS, Heinrich.
Memoirs of the House of Brunswick from the most Early Accounts ...to the End of the Reign of King George the First. 1750. 1st edition. 4to. Eight folding or double-page tables. Index. List of subscribers. Contemp. mottled calf, spine gilt, jts. & corners worn. £40

H 131) ROHAN,(Henri) Duc de (1579-1638)
Mémoires. (Amsterdam L. Elzevir) 1644. 1st edition. 12mo. Sphere device on title. First blank & blank K_8. A_1 frayed & with sm. hole affecting few letters. Contemp. vellum. WILLEMS 1016. £60

Rohan succeeded his friend & master Henri IIII as leader of the French Protestants. His brilliance as a soldier was displayed in the Thirty Years' War, where Venice at first, & then France found him an invaluable servant. This edition gives books 1-3 of the Memoirs, with a supplement containing proceedings at the Conference of French Reformed Churches held at Saumur in 1611.

H 132) RUDDIMAN, Thomas (1674-1757)
An Answer to the Reverend Mr. George Logan's late Treatise on Government. Edinburgh 1747. 1st edition. Engraved fp. Lacks final blank as a cancel. Contemp. calf, spine gilt; rubbed, upper jt. worn. Bk-label. S. & M.v.100. £30

H 133) RUDDIMAN, Thomas.
An Introduction to...Anderson's Diplomata Scotiae. Edinburgh 1773. 1st Engl. British Museum duplicate stamp. Old ½ calf, uncut, worn. S. & M.v.100. £30

A dissertation on the Scottish charters, with some critical remarks on those whose authenticity was in doubt; also including chapters on the Scottish coinage.

H 134) RUSSELL, Lord John.
An Essay on the History of the English Government and Constitution. 1823. 2nd edition, revised. PRESENTATION COPY. Modern cloth. Bk-pl. Diana Russell (later member of the author's family) £20

H 135) SANDERSON, Robert, Bishop of Lincoln.
Episcopacy (as established by Law in England) not Prejudicial to Regal Power written in the time of the Long Parliament, by the Special Command of the late King. For Robert Pawlett 1673. Engraved portrait by W. HOLLAR. Title in red & black. Edges of title & portrait sl. frayed & browned. Publishers' catalogue. Modern marbled boards. WING S.600. £20

H 136) SAXE,(Maurice), Marshal (1696-1750)
Reveries or Memoirs upon the Art of War. (Transl. Sir Wm. Fawcett) 1757. 1st Engl. 4to. 34 COPPER-ENGRAVED PLATES (mostly folding) numbered as 40, bound at end. Dedication misbound before contents. Contemp. calf, rebacked. Edges worn. £150

In addition to his great achievements in the field, Saxe was one of the first scientific soldiers since Roman times. His ideas include many improvements in dress, equipment & discipline designed to advance the health, comfort & education of the private soldier. A short tract at the end is concerned with the falling birthrate and suggests remedies.

H 137) The SEAT of the WAR in HUNGARY...
being an Historical and Geographical Account of the Ancient Kingdom of Hungary, and Provinces adjoining to it. 1717. 1st edition. 12mo. Engraved folding map. Sl. wormed, mostly at end.

H 137) The SEAT of the WAR in HUNGARY...cont.
....L_4 sl. torn without loss. Catchword on last leaf of prelims. incorrect ("The" for "An"), probably as a result of a last minute change of title.Contemp. panelled calf, top edge of upper cover worn. SOLD

Written to illustrate the campaigns of Prince Eugene against the Sultan.

H 138) SHAFTESBURY, (Anthony Ashley Cooper),Earl of (1621-83)
Some Observations concerning the Regulating of Elections for Parliament. By Randall Taylor, 1689. 1st edition. Sm.4to. (ii),5-18pp. Disbound. WING S.2899/4534 (duplicate listing) £25

Lacks the text of a Bill embodying some of Shaftesbury's ideas (pp1-4). They include a uniform qualification for voters throughout the kingdom, and an annual review of the electorate to prevent voters from lapsing into irresponsibility.

H 139) SPEECHES and PASSAGES
of this Great and Happy Parliament: from...November,1640 to...June,1641. For William Cooke,1641. 1st collected ed. Sm.4to. Pagination & signing irregular through changes of printer. Fore-margin of K_1 defective without loss of text. Modern ½ calf. WING E.2309. £85

Speeches of the King, Waller, Vane, Pym, Strafford (on his impeachment) & others, with the texts of several petitions & their answers.

H 140) (STEWART, James Francis Edward,"The Old Pretender") (1688-1766)
The Pretender's Declaration English'd...with a Postscript... in relation to Dr. Lesley's Letter. Transl. -. Asgill.1715. 1st English edition. 24pp. Spotted. Later ½ calf, worn. £15

The "Declaration" commands King George peaceably to depart the Kingdom.

H 141) (SWIFT, Jonathan)(1667-1745)
The Publick Spirit of the Whigs: Set Forth in their Generous Encouragement of the Author of the Crisis. For John Morphew, 1714. 1st edition. 4to. (i),45pp. Lacks last blank. Title sl. soiled. Modern calf backed marbled boards, handwritten label. TEERINCK 596. GOLDSMITH CAT.5185 (2nd edition) £55

The scarce first edition. Owing to objections raised by the Scots Lords the next issue was censored and five paragraphs had to be omitted.
"The Crisis", by Sir Richard Steele, was a pamphlet casting doubt on the legitimacy of Queen Anne's succession. Swift returned from his new living in Ireland to deal with it; and, as the Tory party was troubled by internal quarrels, he seized the opportunity of denigrating the Whigs, Steele's masters.

H 142) .....The Historical Works. Glasgow R. Urie 1769. 1st thus. 3 vols. Index. No half titles, none called for. Contemp. calf, spines sl. rubbed. TEERINCK 105 £50

H 143) TANNER, Thomas.
Notitia Monastica, or a short History of the Religious Houses in England and Wales. Oxford, At the Theatre,1695.1st. Engraved title vignette & five engraved plates of arms. Contemp. annots. in the hand of a knowledgeable scribe, includes many additional references. Indices. Modern calf backed boards. WING T.144. £50

H 144) TIMOUR, or TAMERLANE, Prince of the Monguls (c.1335-1406)
Institutes, Political and Military...transl. into Persian by Abu Taulib Alhusseini; and thence into English...by Major W. Davy. Edited Joseph White. Oxford, Clarendon Press. 1783. 1st edition. Persian & English text. 4to. FINE ENGRAVED PORT. of the AUTHOR & two ENGRAVED PLATES demonstrating MILITARY MANOEUVRES. Index. Modern calf backed boards. £60

Historical sources cite this as the best account of Timour's life and civil and military rule; apparently written by himself in the Mongul language. Translated by Davy from a MS in the Hunterian Library.

H 145) (TOLAND, John)(1670-1722)
The Art of Governing by Partys: Particularily in Religion, in Politics, in Parliament, on the Bench and in the Ministry. For Bernard Lintott 1701. 1st edition. Final errata leaf. Later ½ calf; edges worn. £150

The suggestions include shorter parliaments, more even distribution of the suffrage & a uniform qualification.

H 146) De TOCQUEVILLE, Alexis.
Democracy in America. Transl. Henry Reeve; introd. J.C. Spencer. N.Y. 1841. 4th Engl. edition (following the 8th French ed.). Folding map. Index. 2 vols. Some spotting. Orig. cloth; vol. 1 rebacked with orig. spine. Faded. £30

H 147) TORCY, Jean-Baptiste Colbert, Marquis de (1665-1746)
Memoirs...containing the History of the Negotiations from the Treaty of Ryswic to the Peace of Utrecht. (Transl.anon.) 1757. 1st Engl. 2 vols. Lacks final blank. Vol.2 wrongly paged & signed due to changes of printer. Sl. spotted. Contemp. ½ calf; sps. & edges worn. Bk-pl. EARL of GUILDFORD. £20

Torcy, nephew of the finance-minister Colbert, was Secretary of State during Louis XIV's last years. He is our best authority for the French side of the long struggle for the Spanish crown.

H 148) TREVELYAN, George Otto.
The Life and Letters of Lord Macaulay. 1876. 1st edition. 2 vols. Engraved portrait; half titles. E-ps sl. spotted. Contemp. ½ calf, gilt, t.e.g., sl. rubbed; sl. tear head of vol.1. £30

H 149) TULKET, Marmaduke.
A Topographical, Statistical & Historical Account of the Borough of Preston...Origin of the Guild Merchants' Fete... Directory for 1821. Preston 1821. 1st edition. Six COPPER ENGRAVED PLATES. Fp. sl. spotted. Contemp. boards; jts. & ends of spine rubbed. £50

H 150) TURENNE, Henri de la Tour d'Auvergne, Vicomte de, Marshal (1611-1675)
RAMSAY, (Andrew Michael, Chevalier de)(1686-1743); History of...Turenne. (Transl. anon.) 1735. 1st Engl. 2 vols. Index. $2B_4$ (vol.1) sl. defective at one corner. Contemp. calf, lacks labels, jts. & corners worn. £25

Turenne was one of the great commanders of his age. Ramsay, likewise a soldier, was a Scotsman who turned Catholic & settled in France. Vol.2 consists of documents, including the whole text of Turenne's own memoirs.

H 151) TURPIN,-.
Histoire de l'Alcoran. "Londres" (Paris),1775. 1st edition. 2 vols.12mo. French text. Vol.1 lacks ½ title. Marginal repair to last leaf of vol.1. Contemp. tree calf, sps. rubbed, jts. worn. £30

H 152) VARILLAS, (Antoine)(1624-1696)
Histoire de Henri Second. Abraham Wolfgang Amsterdam,1693. 1st separate edition. 2 vols. in 1. 12mo. French text. Final blank. Sl. browned. Contemp. vellum. £45

Originally published together with the life of Francois II in the previous year.

H 153) VITALIS, Janus.
In Coronatione Caroli Caes. Imp. Max.Panaegyris. No paging. (Rome S. Guileretus) n.d. (1519) 1st edition. 4to. FINE WOODCUT on TITLE. Six leaves. MODERN CRIMSON MOROCCO, GILT. Fine. B.M.C.(It.) p.734. £250

Commemorative Latin verses on the Coronation, as Charles V of the Holy Roman Empire, of the youthful but already active Spanish King; a last attempt by the Romans to associate themselves with "their" Emperor, who had not shown his face in Rome since 1354. The piece ends with an exhoration to Charles against the Turks, which he took up twelve years later. Several other panegyrical pieces were published by Vitalis, a native of Perugia, but he attracted more attention for the erotic verses recorded by Brunet & others.

H 154) WALKER, Clement,(& another) (-1651)
The Compleat History of Independency upon the Parliament. For Henry Brome 1661 (-1660). 1st collected edition. 4 parts in 1 volume. Red & black general title (mounted on cancel stub). Some side-notes cropped in part 2. Last few leaves frayed. Modern ½ calf. WING W.324. £50

Walker, an M.P. of the Presbyterian belief. His work on the civil war resulted in his banishment to the Tower by Cromwell.

H 155) (WALLACE, Robert)(1697-1771)
Characteristics of the Present Political State of G.B. A. Millar 1758. 1st edition. Errata, t.e.g. First 18 pages of this work are an advertisement for it. Modern calf. KRESS 5763. HIGGS 1618. McCULLOCH p.257. GOLDSMITH LIB.9325. £150

The work embraces sundry speculations, on matters connected with the condition and prospects of society, the influence of public debts and taxes, the increase of riches etc.
It has been alleged that Malthus was under considerable obligation to some of Wallace's speculations (McCulloch).

H 156) WALPOLE, Horace.
Historic Doubts on the Life & Reign of Richard III.1768. 2nd edition. 4to. Two etched plates (Grignion after Vertue) Early restoration to one corner of fp. Several pencil annots. & ink notes on e-ps.,by Richard & John Paget (1794-7). Contemp. ½ calf; sp. & jts. worn. £25

The annotators, besides deleting several hostile references to the Stuarts, quote the Croyland Chronicle in evidence against Walpole's parallel between the accession of Richard & that of William III.

H 157)....Another copy. Same. Contemp. calf, rebacked;worn. £30

H 158) WATSON, R (ichard).(1737-1816)
An Address to the People of G.B. R.Faulder 1798. 2nd ed. (i),42,(i)pp. Disbound. Fine. KRESS B.3752. £12

Watson was Lord Bishop of Landaff. He wrote many sermons and religious tracts, his most famous in 1796 "an Apology for the Bible" in a Series of Letters addressed to Thomas Paine. The above pamphlet is an energetic appeal in support of the war against France, which excited great attention. Fourteen regular editions were sold besides many pirated ones.

H 159) WELLINGTON, Arthur Wellesley, Duke of.
MAXWELL,W.H. Life of. 1845. 4th edition. 3 vols. STEEL-ENGRAVED FRONTISPIECE, TITLES & 22 PLATES; 19 PLANS & MAPS, some hand-coloured. Some extra portraits bound in. Wood-engraved text illustrations. Appendix. FINE MODERN ½ green calf/marbled sides; spines gilt; 2 labels. £50

H 160) WHITELOCKE, (Sir Bulstrode) (1605-1676)
Memorials of the English Affairs, from...Expedition of Brute to this Island, to the end of the Reign of King James the First. Published from his Original Manuscript, with some account of his Life and Writings by William Penn and a Preface by James Welwood. J. Pemberton. 1709. 1st edition. Folio. Index. Copyright permission leaf before t-p. Contemp. panelled calf, gilt; corners & spine sl. rubbed. FINE COPY. £60

Sir Bulstrode Whitelocke was the only son of the Judge Sir James Whitelocke, became a lawyer and was appointed a commissioner of the Great Seal in 1648. He was intimate with Cromwell but in later years fell out of favour.

H 161) .....Notes upon the King's Writ for Choosing Members of Parliament,XIII. Car.I being Disquisitions of the Government of England. Edited Charles Morton. 1766. 1st edition. vols. 4to. Index. Contemp. calf, rubbed. S. &M.i.140. £60

This work (printed from the author's MS.) is a conciliatory scheme of parliamentary government dedicated to Charles II with illustrations taken from Selden and Coke.

H 162) WILKES, John.
English Liberty: being a Collection of Interesting Tracts... containing the Private Correspondence, Publick Letters, Speeches and Addresses of...Wilkes. For T. Baldwin, n.d.(1769) 1st collected edition. 2 parts in 1 vol. Folio. Engraved fp. preceded by explanation leaf. xviii,236/-392pp. Last leaf backed. Contemp. ½ calf. Worn. £180

The most elaborate of Wilkes's propaganda collections pub'd when he was a prisoner & a public hero. The earlier part (covering the false warrant, the Talbot & Martin duels,etc) largely follows the "Paris" collection of 1767; but there is plenty of new material relating to Wilkes's electioneering activities and to the "St. George's Fields massacre", in which a clash between constables & "Wilkites" led to the death of one of the latter. Some letters from Churchill (with unpublished verses) & the novelist Smollett are also included.

H 163) ..... A LETTER to the COMMON COUNCIL of the City of London. With Remarks on Lord Chief Justice Pratt's letter to...Exeter. 1764. 2nd edition. (ii),38pp. Disbound. £30

Pratt, declared the illegality of Wilkes's arrest, was rewarded by the City of Exeter for his "Defence of liberty" by being declared a Freeman. The writer attacks Pratt for implying,by his acceptance, that he was not unwilling to be seen as having acted on behalf of Wilkes, not on behalf of abstract justice. The Common Council, who offered a vote of thanks to the City members who had supported Wilkes, also receive some abuse.

H 164) .....(ALMON, John)(1737-1805). The History of the Late Minority...during the Years 1762-5. 1766. 3rd edition, rev. Some pencil scoring. Contemp. red sprinkled morocco, sp.gilt, gilt borders & ARMS of John, EARL of BUTE, on sides. Autograph of the first and last Baron Carlingford, Lord Privy Seal (1823-1898) on e-ps. Later bookplate Francis Fortesque Urquhart, Balliol College. Sl. rubbed. £90

Almon, influential bookseller & journalist, was Wilkes's publisher & foremost partisan, and this work includes a detailed account of Wilkes's activities. A remarkable association copy from the library of the man (Earl of Bute) whom Wilkes drove out of the Premiership.

H 165) WILLIAMS, John.
Special Report of the Speech...in Support of Mr. Fitzhardinge Berkeley's Motion, in Favour of...Voting by Ballot. N.d.(1849) 1st edition. 8pp. Sewn as issued. £10

H 166) WILLIS, Browne (1682-1760)
Notitia Parliamentaria; or, History of the Counties, Cities and Boroughs in England and Wales with a Series of Lists of the Representatives in the several Parliaments from 1541 to 1660. 1750. 4th edition. 2 parts in 1 vol. Index. Contemp. calf., rubbed; sp. sl. torn. S.&M.i.418.35. £60

An alphabetical list of historical summaries of the cities, towns and boroughs in England and Wales. Also the list of representatives and an appendix.

H 167) ŽATOCIL, Jan Norbert. (1630-1691)
Leto-a Denno-pis, to jest: celeho kratovskeho stareho a noveho mest Prazskych, leta 1648. PRAGUE 1685. 1st edition. CZECH text. Gothic letter. Engraved armorial frontispiece portrait of the patriot Jiri Plachy, & four other plates (one folding). (xvi)90pp. Title, a2 & o1 supplied in old MS. facsimile. All plates except fp. laid down & repaired, one with slight loss at fold.
New ½ calf/marbled sides. HORAK 17.159. £45

A record of the defence of Prague against the Swedes by a handful of citizens, one of the last actions of the Thirty Years' War. The author was present as a student leader.

++++++++++++++++++++++

All books are published in London and of octavo size, except where stated.
Prices are NET, postage and insurance extra. No conversion charge for foreign currency.
Please confirm all telephoned orders in writing.

++++++++++++++++++++++

Our shop at 18 Cecil Court, Charing Cross Road, London WC2N 4HE, is open Monday to Friday 10 a.m. - 6 p.m. Books from catalogues can generally be inspected by arrangement.

FROGNAL RARE BOOKS

18 Cecil Court, Charing Cross Road
London WC2N 4HE, England.
Tel. (01) 240 2815. Cables Finresbook London WC2

CATALOGUE 51

LAW AND LEGAL HISTORY
(1978)

CATALOGUE 51
LAW AND LEGAL HISTORY

All books are published in London and of octavo size, except where stated.

Prices are NET, postage and insurance extra. No conversion charge for foreign currency.

Please confirm all telephoned orders in writing, stating number of catalogue and item, author, title and price.

Customers not previously known to us are requested **not to send payment with their orders**, but either to give two trade references or to pay on our pro-forma invoice.

1. An **ACCOUNT of the PROCEEDINGS of the HOUSE OF PEERS** upon the ... Publick Accounts, 1702. 1st edition. Folio. Fold'g tables. 86pp.
ACCOUNT of the PROCEEDINGS ... in relation to the ... Act for Preventing Occasional Conformity. 1702. 1st edition. Folio. 28pp.
The BILL entituled, an ACT for PREVENTING OCCASIONAL CONFORMITY, with the Amendment made by the Lords ... Reports of the Conferences. 1702. 1st edition. Folio. 64pp.
Three works in one vol. Contemp. calf, sp. gilt; sl. rubbed. £50.00
With the establishment in 1688 of a more responsible scheme of government, corruption & negligence in the administration of public funds became a lively & persistent issue. The first item here contains evidence & arguments on irregularities in collecting & recording various branches of the revenue.

2. **ADDINGTON, (Sir) William.** An Abridgment of Penal Statutes, n.d. (1779) 2nd edition, revised. 4to. **SIGNED by the Author** on title (to prevent piracies). (iv), 658, (lxiv)pp. Indices. Contemp. calf, sp. rubbed & head worn. S. & M. i.358. £75.00
As Bow Street magistrate Addington continued the good work of his predecessors the brothers Fielding; he also shared their literary interests, being known as an associate of stage-folk & something of an author in his own right.

3. **ADSHEAD, Joseph.** Prisons and Prisoners. 1845. 1st edition. **PRESENTATION COPY** "To the Governor of Bridewell, with the author's compliments". Etched fp. by George Cruikshank, one folding (of Pentonville Prison), & one tinted plate. xviii, 13-320pp. Orig. cloth, sl. soiled; shaken; a few leaves loose. **Cohn 6. Not in S. & M.** £90.00
The work is a defence of the solitary confinement system, and gives up a whole chapter to refuting Dickens's attacks on that system as applied in Philadelphia & Boston. Other contents include studies of prisons old (Newgate) & new (Pentonville), with French and American comparisons.

4. ————. Another copy. Contemp. ½ morocco, sp. gilt, upper board detached, name on front free e-p & verso of fp. £75.00

5. **ALEXANDRO, Alexander ab (Alessandro Alessandri) (?-1494).** Genialium dierum libri sex, varia ac recondita eruditione referti. Ed. Giovanni Ferrari. Paris, apud Joannem Roigny. 1550. 1st thus. Latin text. Sm. folio. Device on title (printing press, after Dürer's design for Badius) & woodcut initials. (lxxvi), 370pp. Index. Blank f_8. Sl stained. Last leaf sl. browned & frayed. Later vellum ties. Fine copy. £150.00
This work of miscellaneous learning on Greek & Roman life, law & letters, modelled on the Noctes Atticae of Gellius, was a fruitful source for compilers of quotation-mongers for some centuries; more significantly, it marks the beginning of the study of Roman law from a historical rather than merely practical point of view. The typography is excellent work of the Parisian golden age.

6. **AMOS, M.S.** The Legal Mind. 1931. 1st separate (offprint from "Law Quarterly Review"). **INSCRIBED PRESENTATION** to J.M.R. Butler by the author. 27-42pp. Stapled as issued. £5.00

7. **ANDRES, John.** Precedents of Leases, with Practical Notes. 1878. 2nd edition. xvi, 328pp. Indices, includ. index of cases. Some pencil annotations. Orig. cloth, label chipped. £4.00

8. **ANDREWS, William.** Old-Time Punishments. 1890. 1st edition. Fp. (Bank Restriction Note, after Geo. Cruikshank) & text illus. x, 252pp. Index. Orig. dec'd b'ram, t.e.g., sp. fdd. Sl. rubbed. £20.00

9. **ARGYLL, Duke of.** The Reign of Law. 1872. 16th ed. 4 engr. plates of birds. xxx, 462, 4pp. Index, notes, advert. leaves. E-ps. sl. browned. **INSCRIBED:** W. Robertson, 1931. Contemp. blue boards with gilt bird on recto. £5.00
This is a general discussion of law, both natural and civil, in the popular "people's edition".

10. **ARMOUR-HANNAY, S.B.** Valuation for Rating. 2nd ed. by the author and John CARMONT. Edinburgh. 1912. lii, 456pp. Orig. cl. stained. £10.00

11. **ARNOT, Hugo.** A Collection and Abridgement of Celebrated Criminal Trials in Scotland from A.D.1536 to 1784. Edinburgh. 1785. 1st edition. 4to. xxiv, 400pp. Index, appendix of documents. Sl. spotted. Contemp. tree calf, sp. gilt, rubbed, jts. worn. Bk-pl. Marquis of Lansdowne (subscriber). **S. & M. v.6.** £70.00
Written to present to English readers a picture of regal, judicial & religious tyranny gradually overborne by the power of reason. William Fitzmaurice, 1st Marquis of Lansdown, was Prime Minister from 1782-1785 under the title of the Earl of Shelbourne.

12. **The ASSERTION** is, that the Title of the House of Hanover to the Succession ... is a Title Hereditary. 1710. 1st edition. Final advert. leaf. 38, (ii)pp. Disbound. £15.00
A counterblast both to those who held that property in the crown was vested in the Stuarts in perpetuity, & to those who imagined that the constitution had been turned into some form of elective monarchy; with a hint that the monarch was not above all laws.

13. **ATKYNS or ATKINS, Sir Robert (1621-1710).** Parliamentary and Political Tracts. 1741. 2nd edition. (ii), 429, (iii)pp. Contents leaf before title, half title, final advert. leaf. Contemp. calf, rubbed, lower jt. cracked, lacks label. **S. & M. i.128.6.** £45.00
Includes a tract on the power, jurisdiction and privilege of Parliament, and the antiquity of the House of Commons asserted, another on the Ecclesiastical Jurisdiction, and an argument concerning the election of members to Parliament.
Atkyns wrote these tracts between 1680 and 1689, when his resistance to royal encroachments caused him to be forced off the Bench. They are expressive of his high opinion of both the rights & the duties of Parliament. In particular he limits the King's power to dispense with penal laws, & considers how far the courts may take cognizance of questions arising out of elections.

14. **ATKYNS, J.T. (Baron).** Reports of Cases ... in ... Chancery, in the Time of ... Lord Hardwicke. 1765(-7). Folio. **3 vols.** Indices; first advert. leaf to vol. 1. Vol. 3 lacks title & B_1 (fly-title). Mod. b'ram. **S. & M. i.344.** £40.00
Atkyns arranges his cases by subjects, not chronologically; his design (echoed in the modern case-book) is to produce a "system or digest" of equity by way of case law.

15. **(ATWOOD, William).** A True Account of the Unreasonableness of Mr. Fitton's Pretence against the Earl of Macclesfield. N.p., n.d. (1685). 1st edition. Folio. 8pp. Sl. soiled. Folded as issued. Sp. repaired. **Wing A.4183A (B.L. & Bodleian only).** £50.00
Fitton took possession of the Macclesfield estates under the Commonwealth on the strength of an alleged deed of settlement. Atwood, author of several legal & constitutional works, later became Chief Justice of the Province of New York.

16. **BACON, Sir Francis (Viscount St. Alban's, Baron Verulam).** The Essayes or Counsels, civill and morall. By J. Haviland. 1632. Newly enlarged (3rd edition). Sm. 4to. [vi], 338, [ii], 339-40, [xxxviii]pp. Title page & last leaf a little brittle with age & browned at edges. One or two pen notes. Wanting first & last blank. Two-leaf table misbound as usual before last leaf of text. Calf, jnts. neatly repaired. **STC 1150; Gibson 16.** £150.00

17. ————. Law Tracts, (containing) 1) Proposition for compiling an amendment of our laws. 2) Offer of a digest of the laws. 3) Elements of the common law of England. 4) Use of the law. 5) Cases of treason, etc. 6) Arguments in law in certain great and difficult cases. 7) Ordinances in Chancery. 8) Reading on the Statute of Uses. Lintot. 1741. 2nd ed. ½ title, booklist, (ii), 356, (xvi)pp. Index. Modern calf. Sm. corner of last leaf of index torn off with some loss of text. **S. & M. i.20.1. Gibson 255.** £95.00
The second edition was published from the unsold sheets of the first with half-title added and a new title page substituted.
Most of the small treatises have been separately published. The Elements of the common law (no. 3) was one of the earliest, if not the first, published collection of maxims of the English Law.

18. ————. MALLET, (David); The Life. 1740. 1st edition. ½ title. Red & black title with engraved vignette. viii, 197, (iii)pp. Contemp. cf., sl. worn, recased & corners repaired. £30.00
Mallet, who was Pope's literary executor, promises impartiality; but in general he exonerates Bacon at the expense of Coke and King James.

19. **BACON, Nathaniel (?-1660).** An Historical and Political Discourse of the **Laws** & Government of England ... with a Vindication of the Ancient Way of Parliaments in England, collected from some Manuscript Notes of John Selden. 1689: for John Starkey. 4th edition. **2 parts in 1 vol.** fol. Index. (ii), (xviii), 204/(iv), 188, (vi)pp. Advert. leaf. Bk-pl.: **Watkin Williams** superimposed on Richard Mostyn's. Some damp-stain. in lower rt. corners, end-papers sl. browned. Contemp. clf, sp. rbbd. & sl. torn at head. **S. & M. i.99/9. Wing S.2428.** £150.00
"The first edition having become so rare a second edition was secretly printed in 1672 which was suppressed. It was again secretly reprinted in 1682 and the publishers were prosecuted." "The 1682 edition appears to have been reissued in 1689 with the 1682 imprint." (S. & M.).

20. **BARLOW, Theodore.** The Justice of the Peace: A Treatise Containing the Power and Duty of the Magistrate. 1745. By Henry Lintot. 1st ed. folio. Appendix. Index. xxii, 492, (cxxxvi)pp. A little worming sl. aff. text. Bk-pl.: W.W.G. Wynne. Contemp. clf. sl. torn and spotted; otherwise a fine copy. **S. & M. i.224/6.** £230.00
Barlow gains an advantage over Dalton and other predecessors and anticipates Burn, by his use of an alphabetical method.

21. **BARNARDISTON, Thomas (Serjeant-at-law) (c.1700-1725).** Reports of Cases ... in ... King's Bench. 1744. 1st. **2 vols.** Folio. Indices. (xiv), 470, (xxviii)/(xii), 470, (xxiv)pp. Contemp. cf. rbbd., end of jts. torn. **S. & M. i.292.** £30.00

22. **BARNES, Henry.** Notes and Cases in Points of Practise: taken in the Court of Common Pleas ... with a Table containing the Names of the Cases. 1754. 1st edition. **2 vols.** Index. ii, xl, 352/lvi/xxxvi, 392, xxxvi pp. Advert leaves. Sm. hole in first leaf of vol. 1, ownership signature on title. Contemp. calf. Bookplates. Worn, joints cracked. **S. & M. i.292.5.** £45.00
Henry Barnes was one of the Secondaries of the Court of Common Pleas.

23. **BARRINGTON, The Hon. Daines (1728-1800).** Observations on the More Ancient Statutes from Magna Charta to the Twenty-first of James I. With an appendix ... a proposal for new modelling the Statutes. 4to. W. Bowyer & J. Nichols. 1769. 3rd edition, revised. Index. xii, 516pp. Sl. spotted at end. Contemp. calf, newly rebacked. Fine copy. **S. & M. i.546.3.** £95.00
Barrington was a lawyer and writer in natural history and English antiquities; these observations were his first publication. It is a book full of curious information on the state of English society in the middle period with many additions (some drawn from Petyt's papers) and of some importance to the impetus it brought to the historical study of the law.

24. **BATEMAN, Joseph.** Auctioneer's Guide; containing a Practical Treatise on the Law of Auctions. N.d. (1846). 3rd ed. xxiv, 358, 14, (ii), (iv)pp. Index. Adverts. of Waterlow & Sons, with fine lithographed trade card, at end. Few press-cuttings pasted in. Orig. cloth, sl. worn & shaken. **S. & M. ii.22.** £25.00
One of the press-cuttings reports a case (Ellis v. Colley) which must surely be the last example of tenure by elegit (conveyance of freehold land to the creditor until the debt is paid out of its rents & profits); it was argued before the Under-Sheriff of Denbighshire in about 1850, & is therefore most probably unreported.

25. **(BECCARIA, Cesare Bonesana, Marchese di) (1735-1793).** Traité des Délits et des Peines, Traduit de l'Italien, d'après la troisième Édition. (Transl. André Morellet) Lausanne, 1766. 1st French. 12mo. xxiv, 242, xxv-xxxii pp. Corner torn from L_1 without loss of text. Contemp. sheep, rebacked calf, edges sl. worn. £70.00

26. **(BECCARIA, R. de).** An Essay on Crimes and Punishments, transl. from the Italian; with a Commentary attributed to M. de Voltaire transl. from the French. Edinburgh, Bell & Murray for Gordon and Creech. 1778. A new edition. x, 11-191pp. Contemp. calf, rubbed, joints weak. **S. & M. i.358.5.** £65.00
Beccaria's work, influenced by Locke & Addison, is one of the foundation stones of criminal jurisprudence. The French version from which this is a translation, was by Morellet, a Jesuit of pronounced revolutionary inclinations.

27. **BELL, George Joseph.** Commentaries on the Laws of Scotland, and on the Principles of Mercantile Jurisprudence. Ed. John McLaren. 1870. 7th ed. 2 vols. 4to. Index. xxviii, 796/xvi, 740pp. Contemp. bds worn; sp. sl. torn & frayed. **S. & M. v.10.** £95.00
Bell's purpose is to reconcile Scot's Law with that of England as expounded by Lord Mansfield and, in this edition, to examine and promote international cöoperation in the law of trade.

28. **BELL, Henry Nugent.** The Huntingdon Peerage; comprising a detailed Account of the Evidence and Proceedings connected with the recent Restoration of the Earldom; together with ... a Genealogical History of the House of Hastings, Baldwin, Cradock & Joy, 1820. 1st Edition. 4to. 2 engr. portraits, engr. dedication. Copiously annotated. [ii], viii, 404pp. Modern boards, buckram spine, paper label. £30.00
Bell, a young lawyer, made it his business to investigate cases of "disputed or confused pedigree". He instigated and pressed Hans Francis Hastings' claim to the defunct Earldom. This copy of his work belonged to John Mammot, Steward to the first Marquis of Hastings, who was closely affected by the Restoration. Many marginal notes, some very amusing (Bell is referred to as "Grand Puffer and Chief Transporter of his own lies") proclaim that Bell was a rogue and the claim spurious.

29. **BENTHAM, Jeremy (1748-1832).** Elements of the Art of Packing, as Applied to Special Juries. Effingham Wilson, 1821. 1st edition. viii, 270, (ii)pp. Final advert. leaf. Contemp. ½ calf, gilt; sl. wear. **S. & M. ii.27.** Bookplate Viscount Birkenhead. £250.00
A classic in the history of free speech. Bentham explains how the jury in the Court of King's Bench had come increasingly to consist of "special jurymen" chosen from a roster of faithful slaves of the ministry, & liberally & openly paid for their verdicts; how the Libel Act of 1792, designed to protect those charged with criminal libel from manipulation of the law by the State prosecutors, had by this means been shamefully evaded; how the protests of a courageous Sheriff of London, Sir Richard Philips, had been shuffled off by Chief Baron Macdonald; & how amid these abuses the impartiality of the judges had become as insecure as in the black days of Charles II & Jeffreys.

30. ————. Elements of the Art of Packing ... 1821. 1st edition. Contemp. cf., sp. gilt, jts. & edges sl. rubbed. ... as above. £250.00

31. ————. The Book of Fallacies: from Unfinished Papers of Jeremy Bentham. By a Friend. (Pregrine Bingham ?) John and H.L. Hunt, 1824. 1st edition. xii, 411pp. ½ calf; sl. wear. Scarce work. £250.00
The substance of this treatise, one of the most unfinished of all Bentham's Manuscripts, was published first in French by M. Dumont. However as it was aimed at continental circulation it omitted Bentham's considerations to British Institutions and interests, which have been published in this work, edited, but not re-written, by Bingham.

32. ————. Traités de Législation Civile et Pénale, transl. & edited Étienne Dumont. Paris, 1820. 2nd edition. 3 **vols.** French text. Lacks ½ titles. Sl. spotted; sm. worm-hole in last four leaves. Contemp. ½ calf; rebacked, corners sl. rubbed. £180.00
Digested from the General Principles of Legislation, Principles of the Civil & Penal Codes, Panopticon, & some other treatises. Dumont's preface gives a criticism of Bentham & an account of his own methods as editor.

33. **BILLINGHURST, George (of Gray's Inn).** Arcana Clericalia or the Mysteries of Clerkship As to the Sure Settlements of Estates by Deeds, Fines, Recoveries &c. With the Forms of All Manner of Charterparties in Maritime Cities, Towns and Corporations. 1674: for Henry Twyford. 2nd edition. Mostly black letter. 16mo. Engr. fp. torn at edges. Indices. (xvi), 240, (ii), 179-352, (xvi), 68, (ii), 58pp. E-p's sl. torn & browned. Contemp. clf. sl. worn & torn, v. weak jts. **S. & M. i.489/3. Wing B. 2905.** £200.00
A compendium of many different subjects relating to clerkship with an analytical table of conveyancing. There is a section on the forms of instruments relating to merchants & traders and another section of directions for the sueing out of recoveries.

34. ———— **& Henry CURSON.** Arcana Clericalia: or, the Mysteries of Clerkship Explained; declaring the ... Parts of Deeds and their Nature. 1705. Rev. ed. Final advert. leaf. (xvi), 590, (ii)pp. Lib. perforation on title. Mod. cl. **S. & M. i.489.** £150.00
This manual of conveyancing was originally Billinghurst's: Curson revised the arrangement of the work, & added an analysis.

35. **BLACKSTONE, (Sir) William (1723-1780).** Commentaries on the Laws of England. Oxford (Clarendon Press). 1766(-9). Vols. 1 & 2: 2nd edition; 3 & 4: 1st edition. **4 vols.** 4to. Two engraved tables (one folding). Index. FINE COPY in contemporary calf, two labels, rubbed; sm. hole in spine of vol. 4. **S. & M. i.27. Printing & the Mind of Man 212.** £750.00
When he became the first professor of common law in the old universities, Blackstone held it his duty to justify the ways of the law to the intelligent layman. This he accomplished with a lucidity of explanation, a coherence of arrangement, and an ingenuity in finding rational support for the most obscure eccentricities of the law, which have never been surpassed. Only, in his tendency to appoint himself defending counsel for the existing law, in place of sitting in judgment on it compared with possible reforms, has he provoked dissent from Bentham, Furneaux, & a few others.

36. ————. Another set. Same. Contemp. calf. FINE SET. £750.00

37. ————. Commentaries on the Laws of England. A new edition, with practical notes by Joseph CHITTY. Large 8vo. **4 vols.** William Walker (etc) 1826. Portrait, two tables (1 fold'g). ½ calf; worn & rubbed. Vol. 1 spine loose; vol. 2 spine rehinged; sl. spotting of e-ps. **S. & M. i.28. Yale Law Lib. Cat. C.S. Eller p. 18-19.** £120.00
The fp. port. of Blackstone is by Sir Joshua Reynolds engraved by Edward Scriven and this is the only edition which contains this particular one. Portraits in other editions are after Gainsborough.
The notes are by Joseph Chitty with the exception of "notes upon the law of descents" which are by his son Henry Chitty. This is the only edition which Chitty edited; although a selection of his notes is included in most American editions of the Commentaries.

38. ————. **KERR, Robert Malcolm (ed.).** Commentaries on the Laws of England ... adapted to the present State of the Law. 1862. 3rd edition. **4 vols.** 2 folding tables in vol. 2. Index. Orig. cloth, uncut & unopened, faded. £60.00
The editor was Judge in London

Sheriff's court and lived from 1821-1902.

39. ——————. The Great Charter and Charter of the Forest, with other authentic instruments: to which is prefixed an introductory discourse containing The History of the Charters. Oxford, Clarendon Press, 1759. Copper plate engrs. 1st. Large 4to. (4), lxxvi, (4), 86pp. Illustrations. Contemp. calf, gilt ornamental borders, rubbed, ends of outer hinges sl. worn. Marbled end-papers. Fine wide margins, **a very fine copy. S. & M. 550.3. Higgs 2105.** **£500.00**

Concerning this quarto edition, Richard Thomson in An Historical Essay on the Magna Charta of King John, 1829, says: "This beautiful and rare edition of the English cartae, is usually supposed to have been executed under the direction of the celebrated Baskerville; but was actually produced under the superintendence of Dr. Prince, and constituted one of these volumes, which afforded him most pleasure in having printed."

Verso of title page reads: "Imprimatur; Westmorland, canc. Universitatis Oxon. . ." Half-title page read: "Magna carta, Carta de foresta, etc." Engraved dedication to the Earl of Westmorland is surmounted with his armorial ensigns.

Following this is the "introduction" (i) = lxxvi; a half-title (1 l.) and the "Tabula", 1 l. There are 14 initials in text ornamented with engravings of "various public buildings in Oxford", two fine tailpieces are two historical vignettes. Other tail-pieces are ten engravings of the royal seals which are attached to the original instruments.

On p. ii Blackstone says that these charters are "carefully printed from the originals themselves, or (where those are not at present in being) from contemporary inrollments and records".

40. ——————. Law Tracts. Oxford (Clarendon Press), 1762. 1st collected. 2 vols. 8 engraved plates of seals; 2 engraved tables, one folding. Index. (iv), 258, (vi)/(iv), cxx, 136, (vii)pp. Book-plate in each vol. Contemp. calf; hinges sl. weak and sl. rubbed. **Fine set. S. & M. i.30.** **£200.00**

Blackstone's work on Magna Charta & related documents – the first historical & critical study of these pieces – fills volume 2. The other items are the Treatise on Consanguinity, written to extricate the university of Oxford from a series of disputes caused by uncertainty as to the extent of blood-relation; considerations on copy-holders, in which those tenants were held not to be freeholders for electoral purposes – an opinion presently confirmed by statute; and an essay on the Law of Descents.

41. ——————. Law Tracts. 1762. 1st collected. 2 vols. Another copy as above. Titles & last leaves sl. browned. Front e-p removed from each vol. Sm. lib. stamps on title-verso, & labels inside covers. Contemp. mottled calf, jts. worn, edges rubbed. **£180.00**

42. ——————. Tracts, Chiefly Relating to the Antiquities and Laws of England. Oxford, Clarendon Press, 1771. 3rd edition. 4to. Engravings of seals in text. Engraved table. Index. Contemp. calf, label, sl. rubbed, jts. weak, corners worn. **£150.00**
Contains: An Analysis of the Laws of England; An Essay on Collateral Consanguinity; Considerations on Copy-holders; Observations on the Oxford Press; Introduction to the Great Charter, etc.; Magna Carta, Carta de Foresta, etc.

43. ——————. Tracts . . . 1771. 4to. Another copy as above. **£150.00**

44. —————— (Foreign edition/abstract). COYER, M. L'Abbe. Commentaire sur le code criminel d'Angleterre, tr. de l'anglais, de Guillaume Blackstone. Paris, Knapen, 1776. 1st thus. French text. 2 vols. 288/259, (iii)pp. ½ calf. E-ps of vol. 2 browned; bottom of front cover sl. worn. Eller 180. **£45.00**
This is a translation of Blackstone's Commentaries, book IV, "Of public wrongs". Blackstone's appendix to book IV and the index are omitted. The translator, Gabriel Francois Coyer, is designated on title pages "l'abbe Coyer, des Academies de Nancy de Rome & de Londres". In the footnotes, Coyer's notes are marked with the letter "T" to distinguish them from Blackstone's notes.

45. ——————. CURRY, William: The Commentaries . . . Carefully Abridged . . and Continued. 1796. 1st edition. (xvi), 566, (ii)pp. Index. Final advert. leaf. Orig. boards, paper label, uncut; sp. & edges worn. S. & M. i.29. **£60.00**

Curry's abridgment, which consists entirely (except for the notes) of Blackstone's own words, is the first comprehensive re-working of the Commentaries. An earlier attempt by Trusler is far more limited in scope.

46. **BLOUNT, Thomas (c.1619-1679).** Fragmenta Antiquitatis; or, Antient Tenures of Land, and Jocular Customs of some Manors. Edited Josiah Beckwith. York, 1784. 1st thus. Index. xx, 364pp. Modern ½ calf. S. & M. i.398.7. **£65.00**

First edition since 1679 of Blount's collection of copyhold tenures (classified here according to their nature, with extensive revisions by Beckwith).

47. ——————. Fragmenta Antiquitatis; or, Antient Tenures of Land and Jocular Customs of some Manors . . . with explanatory notes . . . by Josiah Beckwith. York, 1784. Sm. ex lib. stamps; cloth-backed boards, rubbed and dust-stained. S. & M. i.398.7. **£65.00**

48. **BOCKELMANN, Johann Friedrich (1632-1681).** Compendium Institutionum Justiniani, sive elementa iuris civilis. Amsterdam, 1710. Red & black title. Index. (xxxii), 282, (xxii), 102, (xviii)pp. Contemp. vellum. **£30.00**
Bockelmann's preface complains of the complexity of formlessness of law-studies & the practice among doctors of pouring out thesis after thesis on half-a-dozen unvarying titles of the Institutes or Code instead of clarifying the law as a whole.

49. **BODIN, Jean (c.1530-1596).** The Six Bookes of a Common-weale . . . out of the French and Latine Copies . . . by Richard Knolles. 1606: Adam Islip, Impensis G. Bishop. 1st English edition. Fol. Title within woodcut border, sl. torn at corners. (x), 794. Notes in contemp. hand insert. as e-ps, front e-p. detached. Notation on various leaves in contemp. hand. Stub of inserted blank between A2 and A3. Few other leaves defective. Dampstained. 17th cent. clf., sp. sl. rbbd., jt. of recto loose & torn. **S. & M. i.606/9. Kress 18/269. STC 3139.** **£250.00**

Bodin was the earliest writer to attempt a theory of government on comparative principles.

50. **BOHUN, W.** The Law of Tithes. 1744. 3rd ed. corrected. 8vo. Index. (iv), iv, 492, (xii). Contemp. clf., fine. S. & M. i.190/4. **£45.00**
Pub's cat. included at end.

51. **BuLTON, Sir Richard (Chief Baron of H.M.'s Court of Exchequer in Ireland).** A Justice of Peace for Ireland; consisting of two books, the first declaring the exercise of that office by one or more Justices of the Peace out of sessions. The second setting forth the form of proceedings in Sessions, and the matter to be enquired of and handled there-in. Whereunto are added many presidents of Indictments of Treason, Felonies, Misprisions, Premunires; and Finable Offences of Force, Fraud, Omission and other misdemeanours. 4to. Dublin, J. Leathley & T. Moore etc. 1750. Enlarged edition by Michael TRAVERS. xiv, 586, 292pp. **2 parts in 1 vol.** Contemp. calf, raised bands, sl. rubbed. A fine copy. S. & M. iv.8-9. **£150.00**
The first edition was published in 1638.

52. **BOSANQUET, J.B. & C. PULLER.** Reports of Cases . . . in . . . Common Pleas and Exchequer Chamber, and in the House of Lords. Vol. 2 (1799-1801), of 3, only. 1802. 1st. Folio. Index. xii, 614, (xx)pp. Mod. cl. S. & M. i.293. **£15.00**

53. **(BOSCAGER, Jean) (1601-1689).** Institution du Droit Romain et De Droit François. Divisee' en IV. Livres. Paris, Jean Guignard 1686. 4to. (xvi), 800, (96)pp. Fp. port. Index. Contemp. mottled calf, gilt. Spine ends worn, lacking small portion; hinges sl. fragile. **£75.00**
Jean Boscager was a Professor of Law at Paris. At the age of 86, he fell in a ditch one evening, was not pulled out until next morning, and only survived a few days.

54. **BOSCAWEN, William.** Convictions on Penal Statutes, with approved Precedents in a variety of Cases (1735-83); particularly under the Game Laws, the Revenue Laws, and the Statutes respecting manufactures. (viii), 212, (xii)pp. 1792. 1st edition. Index. Contemp. ½ cf/marbled sides, sl. rubbed. Book-plate. **S. & M. i.359.7.** **£45.00**
Designed for the information of Justices of the Peace, as a supplement of Burn's work.

55. **BOSSIUS, Aegidius.** Tractatus varii, qui omnem fere criminalem materiam . . . complectuntur. Venice, apud Franciscum Laurentinum, 1562. 3rd ed. 4to. Index. (lxviii), 300 leaves. Few contemp. annots. Contemp. blind-tooled cf.; corners worn; spine defective. **£60.00**
Posthumously edited by the author's son Francesco. The work contains a large chapter on the rights & duties of a ruler, with an interesting emphasis on the latter ("The Pope can depose a prince who oppresses his subjects", "A prince in all his actions stands in place of a god, & must therefore adhere strictly to truth in all his decisions, since God is truth"), and several chapters on the principles of taxation.

56. **de BOULAINVILLERS, Count.** An Historical Account of the Antient Parliaments of France, or States-General of the Kingdom. In Fourteen Letters. Translated by Charles Forman. 1739. (1st ed.). 2 vols. Red-letter titles. Indices. xxxviii, (ii), 332, (viii)/(iv), 364, (xiv). Contemp. clf. gilt, sl. rbbd. **£75.00**

57. **(BOWMAN, E.).** The English Pleader. Being . . . Precedents of Declarations . . . Pleas and Issues . . . Recoveries and Concords of Fines. 1734. 1st. Index. Two advert leaves before title. (iv), 400, (xvi)pp. Lib. perforation on title. Mod. cl. **S. & M. i.264.** **£30.00**
One of a number of works produced to satisfy doubts about the correct terminology of pleadings following the statutory introduction of the English language in these documents.

58. **BOYDEN, Roland W.** (Overseer of Harvard, member Versailles Reparation Comm.; 1863-1931).
ELIOT, S.A.: In Memory of Boston Bar Ass. 1933. 1st. Port. 38pp. Orig. b'ram, fine. **£5.00**

59. **BRACTON or BRETTON, Henry de (fl.1245-1267).** De legibus et consuetudinibus Angliae libri quinq; in varios tractatus distincti . . . Apud Richardum Tottellum, 1569. 1st edition. FOLIO. Index. (xvi), **444** leaves. Last leaf sl. spotted on lower margin, but **A VERY FINE COPY** in contemporary calf, re-backed & edges repaired. **BEALE T.323. S.T.C. 3475. S. & M. i.51.** **£1,200.00**

Bracton's work is the most important early English law treatise and the first to expound the common law in a mature & independent form. This edition, handsomely printed and edited with a creditable degree of judgement for the time, was not superseded until the publication of Woodbine's critical text early in this century.

60. **(BRADLEY, Ralph) (1717-1788).** Practical Points, or, Maxims in Conveyancing. Ed. Joseph Ritson & another. 1804. 1st edition. Interleaved throughout. viii, 148pp. Contemp. MS. note (method of rectifying faulty leasehold title by a new grant to a trustee) opposite E_1, & one other note. Contemp. ½ calf, sides worn. **S. & M. ii.39.** **£55.00**

Although his practice lay in the remote territory of County Durham, Bradley was recognized as one of the first draftsmen of his age. Ritson – critic, folk-song collector, spelling reformer, vegetarian, and tireless ink-duellist – added observations on the Parts of a Deed (pp. 113-148).

61. **BRADY, Robert (?-1700).** A Complete History of England . . . unto the End of the Reign of King Henry III. By Tho. Newcomb for Samuel Lowndes, 1685. 1st. Folio. Engr. fp. port. Imprimatur leaf. Red & black title. Index. (x), lxviii, (viii), 676, 254, (lxviii)pp. Contemp. mottled sheep, rbbd., jts. & corners worn. Bk-pl. Wing B.4186. **S. & M. i.125.** **£150.00**

A partisan work in which Brady marshalled his extensive knowledge of records to support his theories on the constitution, namely that Parliament was a creation of the thirteenth century & that its rights were therefore inferior in priority (& hence, according to the logic of the day, in importance) to those of the crown.

62. **[BRETT, Thomas (1667-1743)].** An Account of Church-Government and Governours, 1701. 1st. viii, 260pp. Contemp. panelled calf, worn, jnts. weak. **£25.00**
A discussion of Church Power and the King's supremacy by an eminent divine and controversial writer.

63. **A BRIEFE DECLARATION** for what Manner of Speciall Nusance concerning Private Dwelling Houses, a Man may have his Remedy by Assise, or other Action. By Tho. Cotes, for William Cooke, 1639. (2nd edition). Sm. 4to. (ii), 46pp. Disbound. **STC 6454. S. & M. i.244.** **£50.00**
A man by the name of Hales wished to bring an action for obstruction of the light & air of his dwelling-house. Four eminent counsel (including Edmund Plowden & Roger Manwood) were consulted as to whether this action would lie, & replied in their discursive fashion with miscellaneous remarks on real-property rights & liabilities. Also included are a series of resolutions of the judges of assize concerning the authority of magistrates.

64. **The BRISTOL RIOTS,** their Causes, Progress and Consequences. Bristol, 1832. 1st. Lith. fp. Appendix. (iv), 404pp. Few leaves loose. Orig. cl., fdd.; head of sp. sl. torn. **£50.00**
In October 1831 Sir Charles Wetherell, a judge & a notorious enemy of reform, arrived in Bristol to hold the assizes. At this a mob, stirred up over the previous 18 months by trade-union agitation, poured into the street & burned down a great part of the city. Four of the leaders were hanged for arson, & two officers who had neglected to fire on the people were court-martialled. This Tory account throws all the blame on Lord Grey's Government for allying itself with Radicals & maddening the mob with a glimpse of power.

65. —————— their Causes . . . Bristol. 1832. 1st edition. As above. **£50.00**

66. **BRITISH MUSEUM ACTS.** Anno Regni Georgii II . . . at the Parliament begun . . . the Tenth day of November, Anno Domini 1747 . . . and from thence continued . . . to the Eleventh Day of January 1753; being the sixth Session of this present Parliament, 1794. (General title for 1st 2 Acts.)
(i) An Act for the Purchase of the Museum or Collection of Sir Hans Sloane, and the Harleian Collection of Manuscripts and for providing one general Repository for the Better Reception and more convenient Use of the said Collection and the Cottonian Library. 5-102pp
(ii) An Act for making perpetual several Laws for Punishment of Persons destroying Turnpikes, Locks and other Works erected by Authority of Parliament. 7pp.
(iii) Anno Septimo Georgii III. An Act to enable the Trustees of the British Museum to exchange sell, or dispose of and duplicates of printed Books, Medals, Coins or other Curiosities. 7pp.
(iv) Statutes and Rules relating to the Inspection and Use of the British Museum and for the better Security and Preservation of the same, 1768. 74pp.
4 items in one vol., contemp. speckled calf, rebacked. **£35.00**

67. **(BROWN, William).** The Clerks Tutor in Chancery . . . Precedents how to draw Affidavits, Petitions, Interlocutory Orders, Reports before Masters, Bills, Answers, Pleas or Demurrers, and Appeals in Parliaments . . . Collection of Special Writs. 1705. 3rd edition. (viii), lxxiv, 397, (xv)pp. Index. Fore-margins wormed at beginning affecting few side-notes. Some browning. Mod. cloth. S. & M. i.337. **£40.00**
Brown covered the entire field of clerkship in all the courts.

68. ——————. Reports of Cases . . . in the High Court of Chancery. 1785. 1st edition. Vol. 1 (of 4) (1778-1785) only. Folio. Index. Contemp. ¼ calf. Head of sp. defective. S. & M. i.345. **£15.00**

69. **BRUNTON, George & David HAIG.** An Historical Account of the Senators of the College of Justice, from . . . M.D. XXXII. Edinburgh. 1836. 1st. Index. xlviii, 567pp. 44 autographs (incl. some duplicates) tipped in or mounted on back e-p's. Inscribed by Mrs. Haig on e-p. Contemp. ¼ roan/cl. sides; front hinge broken. Bk-pl. S. & M. v.f6. **£50.00**
The autographs include David Hume, James Boswell, Alexander Wight, William Robertson, Lord Kames & other notables of Scottish law & literature.

70. **BRYCE, James.** Studies in History and Jurisprudence. 1901: Oxford U.P., New York. (1st ed.). 2 vols. 8vo. Index. xxiii, 462/(ii), 463-926pp. Inscribed: Cyril J. Radcliffe, New College, 1921. Both vols. stamped at end: Printed in U.S.A. Blue cloth with gilt device on covers. A fine copy. S. & M. ii.47. **£25.00**

71. **BULLINGBROOKE, Edward.** The Duty and Authority of Justices of the Peace and Parish Officers for Ireland. Dublin, 1788. New ed., ed. J.G. Bulter. 4to. Index. xx, 912, (xx)pp. Margins sl. wormed. Contemp. cf., sl. rbbd., upper jt. worn. S. & M. iv.11. **£45.00**

72. **BURGES, Cornelius (?-1655).** A New discovery of personal Tithes: or the tenth part of mens cleere gains proved due by the Lawes of this Kingdome. 12mo. J. L(egate) for W. Sheffard 1625. 1st edition. Title in black and red lettering (xii), 81pp. Black borders. Title to A_1 bottom margin cropped with sl. loss. Mod. calf. Fine copy. S.T.C. 4112. S. & M. i.190.6. **£65.00**
Burges, a non-conformist divine, became a powerful advocate for the principles which overthrew church and state and particularly directed his attacks against the revenues of deans and charters and bishops. He procured, however, that St. Paul's cathedral might be opened, and himself appointed lecturer there, with a salary of £400. He also purchased church lands and wrote the above in vindication of such purchases. On the Restoration, however, he lost all this plunder and died in extreme poverty. He wrote several devotional tracts and some controversial ones.

73. **BURLAMAQUI, Jean-Jacques (1694-1748).** The Principles of Natural Law: translated by Mr. Nugent. 1748. 1st Eng. ed. 2 vols. 8vo. xvi, (xxvi), 312/(viii), 372. Contemp. clf. S. & M. i.592/6. **£120.00**
First English edition. Assembled by Burlamaqui from his own notes for lectures delivered in the university of Geneva between 1723 and 1740, this work propounds a theory of law as founded on the nature of mankind and regulated by the mutual obligations of society; the dependence of price on rarity and utility etc. Burlamaqui's work made an immediate appeal to the spirit of the age.

74. ——————. The Principles of Natural Law: translated by Mr. Nugent. 1752. 2nd Eng. ed. 2 vols. 8vo. xvi, (xxiv), 312/(viii), 372. Contemp. clf. S. & M. i.592/6. **£80.00**
Second English translation.

75. ——————. The Principles of Natural and Politic Law, tr. Tho. Nugent. 1763. 2 vols. Contemp. calf, sps. gilt, 2 labels, sl. worn. **£65.00**

76. ——————. The Principles of Natural and Politic Law . . . 2 vols. 1784. 3rd ed., revised & corrected. Contemp. mottled calf, newly rebacked. **£55.00**

77. **BURN, Richard (?-1789).** Ecclesiastical Law. 1763. 1st ed. 2 vols. 4to. Addenda. (vi), xxii, (xviii), 686/(ii), 784. Contemp. clf. S. & M. i.166/22. **£120.00**

78. ——————. The Ecclesiastical Law. ed. Robert Phillimore. 1842. 9th ed. 4 vols. 8vo. Index. Advert. leaves before title of vol. 1. pagination varies. Orig. bds., sl. torn, esp. jt. vol. 1. S. & M. i.166/22. **£80.00**
Last edition of Burn. Phillimore later produced an Ecclesiastical Law under his own name.

79. ——————. The Justice of the Peace, and Parish Officer. (11th) ed. 1770. 4 vols. Index. Contemp. cf., rbbd. S. & M. i.226. £60.00
Includes an appendix on the jurisdiction of magistrates in Scotland, & a revision on the title "Poor" on the authority of Burrow's Settlement Cases.

80. ——————. The Justice of the Peace, and Parish Officer. 1785. 15th ed. 4 vols. 8vo. Index. Three items of ephemera connected with Northumberland justices are inserted; 2 blank forms of mittimus (commitment to gaol for want of sureties) & a form of statement by a pauper woman that she had been got with child, filled & signed with a cross. xxviii, 540/(ii), 624/(ii), 640/(ii), 452, (lxxxiii). Contemp. sheep, sl. worn & frayed. £50.00

81. ——————. The Justice of the Peace. Ed. John Burn. 1788. 16th edition. 4 vols. Index. 3 contemp. printed forms for informations before Northumberland justices inserted in vol. 1. Contemp. calf, sl. rubbed & frayed. £50.00

82. ——————. The Justice of the Peace ... 1793. 17th ed. ed. John Burn. 4 vols. Index. Final errata leaf to vol. 2. Appendix. Few leaves in vol. 4 sl. soiled. Contemp. calf, rubbed. £50.00

83. ——————. The Justice of the Peace ... 1820. 5 vols. 23rd edition. Index. Errata slips in vols. 2-5. Contemp. calf, rubbed. S. & M. ii.50. £40.00

84. —————— (& continued by his son John BURN). A New Law Dictionary: intended for General Use as well as for Gentlemen of the Profession. Dublin, Brett Smith and others. 1792. 1st Dublin edition same year as first English. vii, 739pp. Contemp. calf, rubbed; corner torn from M, without loss of text. S. & M. i.7.13. £48.00

85. **BURROW, (Sir) James (1701-1782).** A Series of the Decisions of ... King's Bench upon Settlement Cases. 1768. 1st. 2 vols. in 1. 4to. Indices. Advert. leaf. Continuation (1768)-72. xv, 364, (ii), ix-xv, 365-625, xxxvi, iv, 627-718, vi, 629-653. Contemp. calf, sl. rubbed. Fine copy. S. & M. i.386. £70.00
With the rarely found "continuation" which contains Decisions of the Court of King's Bench upon Settlement-Cases, for Four additional years, ending in July 1772: to which is added a complete Abridgment of each Case.
The Reports are a striking commentary on Blackstone's complaint that the diverse means of gaining a settlement in a parish, so as to be supported in poverty out of the rates of that parish, had disastrously confounded the working of the old poor law.
Also includes a short treatise on punctuation (thoughts upon pointing).

86. ——————. A Series of the Decisions of ... King's Bench upon Settlement Cases. 1768. 1st. 2 vols. 4to. Indices. Advert leaf. xvi, 364/365-625, ix-xvi, (xxxvi), 629-652pp. Contemp. calf, sl. rbbd. S. & M. i.386. Fine copy. £50.00
Irregular pagination; we have had 3 copies of this work, each a different issue. In this copy errata printed at foot of 2f2 instead of P.653 in others.

87. ——————. Reports of Cases ... in ... the Court of King's Bench. (1756-1758). 1766. 1st ed. 4 vols. Fol. (vi), x, (viii), 652, (1)/(vii), 653-1234, (lxxviii)/(xviii), 1235-1924, (lxxxvi)/(xiv), 1925-2584, (lvi). Indices. Mod. cl. S. & M. i.294/20. £100.00
He retained the mastership of the Crown-office until his death. From many years attendance in court he evolved a meticulous style of reporting which is exact but includes much circumstantial detail.

88. **BURTON (John Hill).** Narratives from Criminal Trials in Scotland. 1852. 1st edition. 2 vols. iv, 310(ii), 320pp. Lib. stamp on first two leaves of each vol. Few sl. stains. Modern cloth. S. & M. v.18. £30.00
Burton, a historian & book-collector as well as a practising lawyer, draws on a number of manuscript sources.

89. **BURTON, Walter Henry.** An Elementary Compendium of the Law of Real Property. 1845. 6th edition, edited E.P. Cooper. Index. 8pp. adverts. before title. xxxvi, 728pp. Some ink scoring. Mod. cloth. S. & M. i.51. £15.00

90. **BUTLER, Charles.** Horae Juridicae Subsecivae: a Connected Series of Notes respecting the Geography, Chronology, and Literary History ... of the Grecian, Roman, Feudal and Canon Law. 1804. 1st. PRESENTATION COPY. Appendix. xvi, 136pp. Orig. boards, spine defective, edges worn. S. & M. 31-23. £25.00
Contains useful information upon the subjects of which it treats and refers the student to authorities to assist him in a further prosecution of each head of inquiry.

91. **BYNKERSHOEK, Cornelis van (1673-1743).** Opera omnia. Geneva, 1761. 4th edition, edited Philippe Vicat. 2 vols. in 1. Folio. ½ title to vol. 1. Red & black titles with devices. Index. xvi, 428/xvi, 480pp. Leaves of gathering 3D bound out of order in each volume. Modern ½ calf/marbled sides. Fine copy. £200.00
A fine edition of the works of one of the greatest Dutch jurists, the great reformer of Roman-Dutch law & a still valuable writer on diplomatic privilege, the rights of war, & other matters of international law.

92. **CABALA.** Sive Scrinia Sacra, Mysteries of State ... in Letters of Illustrious Persons. For G. Bedell, and T. Collins. 1663. (2nd ed. enlarged). Folio. Red & black title. First privilege leaf. Index. (xiv), 416, (x)pp. Sl. stnd. Mod. ¼ cf./mbld. sides. Wing C.185. £50.00
Includes many letters by Sir Francis Bacon, with some of Sidney, Raleigh & the Earl of Essex.

93. **CALENDARIUM INQUISITIONUM POST MORTEM** sive Escaetarum, Hen. III-Ric. III (1217-1485) cum appendice de quamplurimis aliis Inquisitionibus a regno Hen. III useque Jac. I nuper repertis. Edited by J. CALEY and J. BAYLEY. 4 vols. Folio. Printed by Command of H.M. King George III. in pursuance of an address of The House of Commons G.B. 1806-28. ½ calf. Sl. rubbed. Fine set. S. & M. i.82.11. £185.00
These records were taken by virtue of writs, directed to the escheators of each county or district, to summon a jury on oath, who were to inquire what lands any person died seised of, and by what rents or services the same were held, and who was the next heir, and of what age the heir was, that the King might be informed of his right of escheat or wardship; they also show whether the tenant was attained of treason, or was an alien, in either of which cases and value of the lands of which each tenant died seised, etc., and they are the best evidences of the descents of families and of property. (S. & M.). There is a later up-to-date edition in 14 vols. (1904-52).

94. **CALTHORPE, or CALTHROP, Sir Henry (1536-1637).** Reports of Speciall Cases touching severall Customs and Liberties of the City of London ... Divers Ancient Customs and Usages of the City. For Abel Roper, 1655. 1st edition. 2 parts in 1. (viii), 126, (iv), 131-180pp. Sl. frayed at beginning & end. Title & A_2 lack one corner each, without loss of text. Modern ¼ calf. WING C.310. S. & M. i.437. £150.00
Small though it is, Calthorpe's collection stands almost alone in showing the customs of the City in action. It includes his treatise on "Ancient Customs & Usages", an abridgment of the 15th century work known as the Liber Albus, printed separately in 1642.

95. **CALVERT, E. Roy.** Capital Punishment in the Twentieth Century. Introd. Lord Buckmaster. 1930. 4th ed. xviii, 210pp. Index, bibliography, appendix. Includes a small pamphlet of an address to the International Youth Camp of the Fellowship of Reconciliation 1928 entitled "Overcoming evil". £8.00

96. **CAMPBELL, Lord John.** Lives of the Lord Chancellors. 1846-7. Vols. I-III 2nd edition; IV-VII first edition. 7 vols. Contemp. cloth, gilt, spines sl. faded. Fine set. £80.00

97. **CANISIUS, Henricus (?-1610).** Summa iuris canonici in quatuor institutionum libris contracta ... Accessit commentarius in regulas iuris lib. VI. Decretal. Antwerp (apud Hieronymum Verdussium), 1619. 4th ed. Index. [xxiv], 666, [xlvi]pp. Corner of T_2 defective, two lines of side-note affected. Contemp. vellum. £40.00
A simple handbook of canon law, including by way of appendix the text of the concordat between the emperor Frederick III & Pope Eugenius IV (1447) relating to ecclesiastical jurisdiction within the Empire.

98. **CARTER, A.G.W.** The Old Court House; Reminiscences and Anecdotes of the Courts and Bar of Cincinnati. Cincinnati, Ohio. 1880. 1st. Steel-engr. fp. & other illus. 466pp. Orig. cl., gilt; re-cased; ends of sp. frayed. £25.00
Recollections of the Ohio Supreme Court & the Court of Common Pleas from 1819 onwards, including complete lists of the judges & court officers and Cincinnati lawyers at various periods.

99. **CASES in Chancery (1661-1678).** 1707, 1701, 1702. Pt. 1, 2nd ed., Pt. 2, 1st ed., Pt. 3, 1st ed. 3 parts in 1 vol. Folio. Indices. (viii), 312, (xxiv)pp. + (viii), 252, (xx)pp. + (viii), 136, with end-papers. Mod. cl., sl. wtr. st. S. & M. i.345/11. £35.00

100. **CASES IN EQUITY. During the Time of the late Lord Chancellor Talbot.** (1730-37). 1741. 1st ed. 1 vol. fol. vi, 286, (xx). Index. Lacks end-papers. Uncut, mod. cl. S. & M. i.345/12. £45.00

101. **CHAND, Hukm.** Principles of the Law of Consent with special reference to Criminal Law, including the Doctrines of Mistake, Duress, and Waiver. BOMBAY, 1897. 4to. xviii, 581, 12pp. a.e.g., full blue morocco, gilt extra; silk doublures. Fine copy. Also 12pp. catalogue of extracts from the Press etc. on Chand's legal works. £40.00
Mr. Chand who wrote a remarkable work on "Res Judicata" has produced a valuable work on an important branch of law. The nature, operation, scope, and effect of consent are fully discussed in turn but the important plan adopted in this work has been to utilise the decisions of foreign Courts, and the opinions of foreign Jurists for the elucidation of questions on this subject which may come before the Indian Courts. The legal writings of France, Italy and Germany are freely quoted as well as those of England, India, and America.

102. **CHINA, (Nationalist) Republic of.** Criminal Code, tr. Ching-lin Hsia & Boyer, P.H. Chu. Shanghai, 1936. 1st. Engl. Index. xvi, 162pp. Fine in frayed d.w. £15.00
The civil code was promulgated in 1930, the criminal in 1935; intended to give expression to Sun Yat-Sen's ethical & sociological ideas, they are remarkable for their simplicity & rigidity.

103. **CLARENDON, Edward (Hyde), Earl of (1609-1674).** Miscellaneous Works. 1751. 2nd ed. Folio. Red & black title. (iv), 348, (ii), 369-770pp. Signatures jump from $4U^1$ to $5B^2$; pagination irreg. accordingly. Mod. ¼ cf./mbld. sides. £40.00
The most substantial item here is the Vindication against a charge of high treason. (1667).

104. **CLARKE, Thomas J. (1857-1916).** Glimpses of an Irish Felon's Prison Life, introd. P.S. O'Hegarty. Dublin, 1922. 1st. xx, 104pp. Orig. cl. fdd. & sl. stnd. £8.00
Prison memories of 1883-98 by an emissary from the "blood dyed Clan-na-Gael" executed as a rebel in 1916.

105. **CLERK of PENNYCUIK, Sir John & John SCROPE (Barons of Exchequer).** Historical View of the Forms and Powers of the Court of Exchequer in Scotland. Edinburgh, 1820. 1st. 4to. Appendices. (x), 342, (ii)pp. Appendix leaf (Order of Court dated 1822) tipped in at end. Contemp. ¼ morocco, uncut & unopened; edges. rubbed. S. & M. v.22. £60.00
Written by two Barons who were appointed to the Scots Exchequer in 1708, when it was reorganized on the English pattern. The appendices, added by the anonymous editor, contain rules & minutes of the court.

106. **(COKE, Sir Edward (1551-1633)).** A Book of Entries: Containing of Presidents of Counts, Declarations, etc. John Streater, James Flesher, etc.: 1671. 2nd edition. (xviii), 713 leaves, (viii)pp. Lacks end-papers. Mod. cl. S. & M. i.266/43: W. 4908. £150.00
Selden, Rolle, and others, refer to this as New Entries, and New Book of Entries in contradistinction to Rastell's book and the older books, just as Rastell's book before had obtained that distinction. Coke says in his preface that none of the entries in his book had been previously published. Winfield: 306-307.
Winfield, Percy H. The Chief Sources of English History. Cambridge, Harvard U. Press, 1925. 374pp.

107. ——————. The Compleate Copy-Holder; Wherein is contained a Learned discourse of the Antiquity and Nature of Manors and Copy-Holds, with the forme of keeping a Copy-Hold Court and Court-Baron. 1644: for Matthew Walbanck and Richard Best. 3rd edition. Sm. 8vo. Woodcut devices. A contemp. hand has added an index on the final blanks. (iv), 203pp. Lacks final blank. Some marginal notes in early hand. Bk-pl. James Clitheron. Marginal worm. aff. text on 7 leaves; sl. damp-stained. Contemp. calf, rubbed; sp. sl. frayed. S. & M. i.399.13. Wing C.4913. £180.00
"Although the Order of Keeping a Court and Court Baron is called for by the Title of the 1644 edition, it is not to be found in all copies. It was absent from four copies examined." (S. & M.) It is absent from this copy also.
"The publication of this book marks the final triumph of the King's Courts over the feudal courts which virtually put an end to feudal jurisdiction in England. It is a 'book of first class importance'." (Jenks, H.E.L., 73, 82.)

108. ——————. The First Part of the Institutes of the Laws of England. 1664. 6th edition, corrected. For the Company of Stationers. Mostly black letter. Fol. Fp. port. engr., folding table, title in woodcut border. Indices. (x), 395 leaves, (lxii)pp. Errata slip. Fold. table sl. torn aff. one marg. note; a few leaves browned and marked; fol. 144 torn at corner w. piece pinned on; no loss of text, a few marg. notes. S. & M. i.449/7. Wing 4925. £150.00
"Coke-Littleton" far overshadows the rest of the Institutes; and despite innumerable reforming statutes and decisions, it cannot be called obsolete until English law itself is obsolete.

109. ——————. The First Part of the Institutes of the Laws of England. Also Three Tracts: The Statute of Levying Fines (His Reading upon the 27th of Edward the First); Of Bail and Mainprize; Complete Copyholder; also, The Old Tenures of the Laws of England. 1719. 11th edition, corrected. Printed by Eliz. Nutt and R. Gosling. Black letter. Folio. Fp. port. by M. VanderGucht. Folding table. Indices. (xviii), 100, 402 leaves, (lxxiv)pp. Unsigned port. of Littleton insert. before fol. section. Some pages sl. browned. A fine copy. S. & M. i.450/7. £120.00
This first part is a commentary on land law to which is appended the Complete Copyholder (a landmark in the suppression by the King's courts of the old irregular feudal jurisdictions), and other important commentaries.

110. ——————. The First Part of the Institutes of the Laws of England. Ed. Francis Hargrave and Charles Butler. 1794. 15th (Hargrave & Butler's 3rd) ed. 3 vols. Indices. Vol. 1 lacks blank d_4. Vol. 3 lacks title and blank $(a)_8$. Table of consanguinity (from an older edition) inserted in vol. 1. Modern cloth. S. & M. i.451. £85.00
Hargrave began work on a critical edition of Coke-Littleton – the first ever made – in about 1780. Five years later, Butler took over the uncompleted task. Their united labours were published in 1788 & have not been superseded. Observations by Sir Matthew Hale and Lord Nottingham are included. Some of Butler's notes are new to this edition, which is the first in octavo.

111. ——————. An Abridgment of the First Part (of the Institutes) with Some Additions explaining many of the difficult Cases. 1736. Ed. William Hawkins. 6th ed. 8vo. vi, 501, (ci)pp. Advert. leaf. Mod. ½ clf. S. & M. i.452. £70.00
This useful abbreviation outlived its rivals and was last reprinted in 1822.

112. —————— La Neuf^{me} Part des Reports. 1627: For the Societie of Stationers. 3rd edition. Mostly black letter. Woodcut devices. Fol. Index. (xxxiv), 143 leaves. Sl. worm not aff. text. Some early MS, notes. Sl. dampstain. Contemp. clf., rbbd. One gathering loose. S. & M. i.296/31. STC 5517. £200.00
Contains cases such as Dowmans and Pinchons with a general preface delineating the various courts and the functions of those courts. It is particularly useful that the preface has been translated into English and is included with the original.

113. ——————. La Vnz^{me} Part des Reports. 1631: by the Assignes of John More. 5th edition. French text. Fol. Black-letter. Woodcut devices. (x), 100 (101) leaves. Sl. marg. worm. not aff. text; some marg. notes in early hand; sl. dampstain. and brown. Contemp. clf. rbbd.; head of sp. torn. S. & M. i.296/31. STC 5524. K3 & K4 loose. £200.00
This part contains the famous Magdalen College case, a case concerning monopolies and others from Ann. 39. Reg. Eliz. to Trin. 13. Iacobi Regis.

114. (——————). A Little Treatise of Baile and Maineprize. For William Cooke, 1637. 2nd edition. Sm. 4to. (iv), 34pp. Sm. repair at inner margin of A_4. Last leaf repaired on verso. Mod. calf. STC 5490. S. & M. i.575. £90.00
After this edition, this treatise vanished into obscurity for fifty years; it was included with the First Institute from the 1680s onward, but was never reprinted separately.

115. **COLERIDGE, Lord Chief Justice of the Common Pleas.** Speech in the House of Lords. In the Committee upon the Bill to Prevent Cruelty to Animals. 1876: Society for Protection of Animals Liable to Vivisection. 1st ed. 8pp. loose. Wood-engraving of the Society's emblem on the title-page. £12.00
One of the few sound arguments for partial legislation, i.e. allowing most blood sports, since cruel sports do not make cruel men. Rare.

116. **A COLLECTION of All The TREATIES** . . from the Revolution in 1688. 1772. 1st edition, collected. Vol. 1 (of 2) only. (1688-1727). viii, 404, (iv)pp. Contemp. calf, sl. worn. S. & M. i.603. £25.00

117. **A COLLECTION of the DEBATES and PROCEEDINGS in PARLIAMENT** ... upon the Inquiry into the Late Briberies and Corrupt Practices. Printed ... 1695. 1st. 4to. iv, 63pp. Mod. ½ cf./mbld. sides. Wing E.1281. £30.00
Some petty malversations of an army agent led the Commons to inquire into several suspicious transactions. It emerged that Sir John Trevor, Speaker of the Commons, had accepted £1,000 from the City of London to promote a bill & that the Governor of the East India Company had paid out £157,000 to the Duke of Leeds & others.

118. **A COLLECTION of the LAWS relating to the ORDNANCE** 1774. 1st. 4to. Index. ½ title. (ii), 200, (viii)pp. Contemp. cf., rbbd., lower jt. worn. Not in S. & M. £30.00
Includes the Articles of War.

119. **A COLLECTION of SEVERAL TREATISES** concerning the Reasons and Occasions of the Penal Laws. For Richard Royston, 1678. (3rd edition). Sm. 4to. (viii), 132pp. Some worming, mostly in fore- & head-margins. Some running titles cropped. Modern calf-backed boards. This edition not in Wing (cf. c.5192B-C, 1675 & 1677) nor S. & M. £75.00
The first item intended to prove that the civil power was competent to take account of religious opinions, was written in 1583 by the great Lord Burleigh. It is printed with two others, both answers to Catholic protestations against the penal laws.

120. **COLLINS, Arthur (1682-1760).** Proceedings, Precedents, and Arguments, on Claims and Controversies, concerning Baronies by Writ, and other Honours. 1734: for Thomas Wotton. 1st edition. Fol. Index. An MS. index of the "Pedigrees contained in this Work" appended in an early hand. 416pp. Some pp. sl. browned; a few ink marks; some dampstain. 19th cent. ½ vellum bds., rbbd. and soiled; uncut. £150.00
Collins devoted more than half a century

to the study of the peerage. These cases of disputed titles preserve arguments of Bacon, Selden, Lord Nottingham and others.

121. A COMPLETE COLLECTION of the STANDING ORDERS of the House of Lords in England. 1748. (ii), 118, (viii)pp. Index. Later boards, sp. sl. rubbed. **S. & M. i.143.** £20.00
Published as a supplement to one of the "Parliamentary Histories", of which several versions appeared in the 1740s.

122. COMYN, Robert Buckley. A Treatise on the Law of Landlord and Tenant. 1821. 1st edition. xxxii, 586, (ii)pp. Index. Final addenda leaf. Appendix of precedents. Sl. spotted. Contemp. calf, sl. rubbed. **S. & M. ii.74.** £35.00
Comyn's work has some advantages in point of arrangement. It reached a second edition in 1830, but was then superseded by the revised "Woodfall".

123. CONRAD von Lichtenau, Abbot of Ursberg (fl.c.1230). Chronicon . . . cui annexa sunt paraleipomena rerum memorabilium . . . usq; ad annum 1537 . . . Annales Rheginonis abbatis Brumiensis & Lamberti Schaffnaburgensis monachi, Strassburg (sumptibus Lazari Zetzneri), 1609. 1st collected. **3 parts in 1 vol.** Folio. Devices on titles. (viii), 370, (ii), 373-540, (lvi)pp. Index. Many old annots. Contemp. calf, sl. rubbed; head of sp. sl. worn. £150.00
These three mediaeval chronicles are all reprinted from editions produced within Philip Melanchthon's circle. That of Conrad was edited, & continued down to his own time (1537) by an unknown protegé of Philip's; this continuation becomes towards its end an eye-witness account of the Reformation. Rhegino, who lived in the tenth century, was published in 1521 by Sebastian von Rotenhahn; Melanchthon himself edited Lambert, who gives a wearisome but extremely detailed account of the years 1050-1076.

124. The CONVEYANCER'S ASSISTANT and DIRECTOR: being a Treatise containing Tables to all sorts of Conveyances, By the Assigns of Rich. and Edw. Atkyns, 1702. 1st. viii, 443, xx pp. Table. Publisher's Catalogue. Contemp. panelled calf, lower cover repaired, new morocco label, sl. rbbd. **S. & M. i.480.20.** £60.00
An extensive guide to conveyancing which in the words of the author is "not only very useful for Clerks and Practisers of the Law, but also for Inquisitive Country Gentlemen who by the References and Directions hereof in a short time, and for a small Charge, may attain the Art of Drawing neatly and properly upon any Occasion".

125. (COOKE, E.). Argumentum Anti-Normannicum: or, an Argument proving . . . that William Duke of Normandy, made no Absolute Conquest of England. By John Darby, 1682. 1st edition. Engr. fp. (x), 164pp. Modern calf. **From John Evelyn's Library with his bookplate. WING C.4907a. S. & M. i.645.** £150.00
Cooke (not Sir Edward Coke, in spite of Wing's attribution) supports Petyt's Saxonist theory of the origin of Parliament; his argument is that the "Conquest" was merely an incident in the development of the constitution, & not the beginning of a new order.

126. ————. Argumentum Anti-Normannicum or, an Argument Proving, etc. John Darby, 1682. As previous copy. Early lib. stamp of the Inner Temple (before 1730) on title & three other leaves. **William Petyt's copy, signed** on title & with two long extracts from MS. chronicles transcribed into margins. 19th-century ½ calf, rubbed. £120.00

127. ————. Argumentum Anti-Normannicum . . . 1682. Another copy as above. Late 18th-century ½ calf; bookplate of **Edward Duke.** £100.00

128. CORBIN, Jacques (ed.). Le Code Louis XIII . . . Ordonnances et Arrests de ses Cours, Paris (Pierre Billaine), 1628. 1st edition. **2 vols. in 1.** Folio. French text. Red & black title. (xlviii), 792/600, (xxxvi)pp. Index. Vol. 2 lacks title as issued. Sl. browned in parts. Contemp. calf, worn; head & tail of spine defective. £120.00
Corbin claims to be the first general editor to give the complete & genuine text of the enactments contained in his sixteen books. He includes Gilles Bourdin's Latin paraphrase of Francois I's Perpetual Edict for the administration of justice, & in other places adds comments of his own.

129. CORVINUS van BELDEREN, Arnold. Iurisprudentiae Romanae summarium: seu codicis Iustinianei methodica enarratio. Amsterdam (L. & D. Elsevier). 1655(-60). 1st edition. 4to. **2 parts in one volume.** Red and black title. (viii), 792, (viii)/viii, viii, 302pp. Index for part II placed before work. Final blank. Sl. browned. Sm. rusthole in 3G,. Contemp. calf, gilt decorated spine. Corners sl. worn. **WILLEMS 1183.** £150.00
A body of law based on the Code, very rich in collateral illustration. Corvinus is especially well informed on the later Imperial administrative systems.

130. CORVINIUS, Joh. IC. Jurisprudentia Romana H. Vulteii contracta. Sm. 12mo. Amsterdam, ex officina Elzeviriana. 1658. 2nd edition. (xii), 358pp. Engraved title, half title, last blank. Contemp. vellum, sl. stained; bottom edge and hinge of sp. rubbed & worn. **WILLEM 1227.** £45.00

131. COWEL, John (1554-1611). Collected by. The Interpreter: or Booke Containing the Signification of Words. Wherein is set foorth the true meaning of all, or the most part of such Words and Termes, as are mentioned in the Law Writers, or Statutes of this victorious and renowned Kingdome. . . . William Sheares 1637. Not paged, 4to. Contemp. hand-written notes on endpapers. Embossed calf, rubbed. **STC 5900. S. & M. i.7.** £250.00
The first edition was published in Cambridge in 1607. Cowel was a University civilian who approached the common law as an interested, learned & respectful outsider. He repeated some expressions thrown out against Littleton by Hottoman, and also allowed into his sketch of the monarchy the Roman doctrine of Imperator Legibus Solutus. The former provided a reason, the latter an excuse, for an attack on him which ended in the suppression of his book by Royal proclamation in 1610. Nonetheless the law lexicongraphers of the following century found Cowel's work essential to their purposes.

132. COWELL, John. A Law Dictionary: or the Interpreter of Words and Terms, Used either in the Common or Statute Laws. 1727. Folio. Unpaged. Sl. stained at ends. Contemp. calf, sl. worn. **S. & M. i.7-8.** £120.00
First published in 1607 but quickly suppressed on account of some constitutional heresies, Cowell's work was expurgated & enlarged in 1708 & remained the foundation of law-lexicography for a century.

133. CRAIG of RICCARTOUN, Sir Thomas (1548-1608). Ius feudale tribus libris comprehensum, quibus . . . consuetudines feudales & praediorum iura . . . continentur. Impensis societatis stationariorum, 1655. 1st edition. Folio. (xii), 384pp. Few sm. marginal wormholes & other defects. Contemp. vellum. **WING C.6802. S. & M. v.26.** £150.00
Craig studied for several years in France; afterwards coming to England for negotiations connected with the Union, he became a close friend of Camden. In him, and through this work in particular, Scotland produced a jurist able to represent her in the European republic of letters. The editor, Robert Burnet, gives in his preface an interesting survey of Scots legal literature.

134. ————. Ius feudale, tribus libris comprehensum. Ed. James Baillie. Edinburgh, 1732. 1st thus. Folio. Engraved fp. port. xxii, 524, (lii)pp. Index. Contemp. panelled calf, rubbed, jts. worn. **Bookplate of Lord Camden.** £90.00
Baillie's edition, besides its useful index & summaries, is the first to present a reasonably correct text. Sir Charles Pratt, Viscount Bayham & Earl Camden (1713-1794) was the Chief Justice who in 1762 established the illegality of the warrant for the arrest of Wilkes.

135. CROMPTON, R(ichard). L'Authorité et Jurisdiction des Courts de la Majestie de la Roygne. In aedibus Caroli Yetsweirt, 1594. 1st edition. Sm. 4to. French text. Black letter. (iv), 232 leaves. Many early marginal annots. (a few cropped). Names on title. 18th-century ¼ sheep. Jts. worn. Book-plate: Thomas Hamilton, 6th Earl of Haddington (d.1735). **STC 6050. S. & M. i.259.** £200.00
A guide to all the courts then existing, from Star Chamber & Court of Wards down to Sheriff's Hundreds & Pie-powder courts; dedicated (in the French of Paris, not of Westminster) to Sir John Pickering, Lord Chancellor. The work is laid out like an abridgement, with the names of the courts as general heads.

136. (CRUISE, William). An Essay on the Nature and Operation of Fines. 1783. 1st edition. (xii), 236pp. Contemp. ink annots. Mod. cloth. **S. & M. i.489.** £30.00
Unlike his competitors Cruise omits the traditionally parallel subject of recoveries, preferring to treat the present question with more fullness and on a better system.

137. CUNNINGHAM, T. A New and Complete Law-Dictionary, or General Abridgment of the Law. **2 vols.** 1764(-5). 1st edition. Folio. Unpaged. Blanks sl. torn. Contemp. calf, rubbed & torn in places. Otherwise a FINE COPY. **S. & M. i.8.22.** £200.00
By including frequent summaries of cases, precedents in equity & statutes, Cunningham fairly accomplished his promise to combine the matter of an abridgement with that of a dictionary. In the latter aspect he drew largely on Cowell.

138. ————. A New Treatise on the Laws concerning Tithes. 1748. 3rd edition. (ii), 298, (viii)pp. Index. Lacks ½ title. Final blank. Mod. cloth. **S. & M. i.191.** £35.00
Cunningham seems to have succeeded to Giles Jacob's reputation as the factotum of legal literature.

139. CURRAN, J. Philpot (Master of the Rolls for Ireland) (1750-1817). CURRAN, W.H. Life. 1819. 1st. **2 vols.** Fp. port. & facs. viii, 448/viii, 532pp. Appendix. Sl. spotted. New ½ calf. £30.00
Curran distinguished himself as a brilliant orator and as the patriotic defender of those exposed to the rigours of the law by the failure of the 1798 rebellion

140. DALRYMPLE, David (afterwards Lord Hailes) (1726-1792) (ed.). Memorials and Letters relating to the History of Britain in the Reign of James the First. Glasgow. 1762. 1st edition. Sm. 8vo. (xx), 152pp. Contemp. calf, sl. rubbed. £60.00
This work, printed from MSS, in the Advocates' Library, shows how the King's interference in matters of law – assisted by Bacon among others – grew into a tyrannous violation of judicial independence. Several letters to James from his beloved Duke of Buckingham also appear.

141. DALTON, Michael (1554-c.1640). The Countrey Justice, containing the Practice of the Justices of the Peace out of their Sessions: . . . Laws of this Realm. Folio. For the Company of Stationers, 1661. Enlarged, with many Precedents and Resolutions of the Quaeres contained in the former Impressions. (ix), 502, (x)pp. Later calf, corners and spine rubbed; hinges weak & sl. frayed at ends. **WING D.145. S. & M. i.227.24.** £120.00
A popular work in its day, more detailed in points of practice than Lambard or Crompton, & reprinted as the standard work until 1746.

142. ————. Officium Vicecomitum; The Office and Authority of Sherifs. 1670. 3rd edition. Folio. Index. (iv), 564, (xxviii)pp. Modern ½ calf. Black letter. **S. & M. i.222.6. WING D.152. A VERY FINE COPY.** £120.00
"It continued to be a standard authority until the beginning of the 18th century." Holdsworth, H.E.L.iv.119.

143. ————. Officium Vicecomitum. The Office and Authority of Sherifs. (– An Appendix or Supplement.) By John Streater (etc.), 1670. Folio. 2 parts in 1. Black letter. Index. Sm. hole in BE_1 aff. few letters. Few old annots. Contemp. calf, sp. defective, jts. & corners worn. **WING D.152. S. & M. i.222.** £120.00
Includes an appendix of new statutes & cases, supposed by S. & M. not to have been included until 1682.

144. DAMHOUDERIUS, Jodocus. Praxis rerum civilium . . . in quacunque republica forensem administrationem assumentibus apprime utilis & necessaria. Antwerp (apud Ioannem Bellerium), 1569. 1st edition. 4to. **Woodcut portrait on *7, arms on title-verso & last leaf, & 14 other full-page woodcuts.** Index. (lxiv), 532, (xxxvi)pp. Title soiled; corner of this & next three leaves repaired without loss of text. Few sl. stains. Contemporary vellum, re-backed. **Graesse II.322.** £300.00
The author was principal minister of finances in Belgium to the Emperor & afterwards to the King of Spain. His two works (he had published a Praxis Rerum Criminalium some years previously) are accounts of the law applicable to Flanders, which he attempts to express in formal language & to reconcile with the civil law. The fine woodcuts *show various aspects of daily life – an auction-sale in the street, court scenes, a lawyer's office, etc.*

145. DARLING, Charles J. (afterwards Sir Charles). Scintillae Juris. 1879. 3rd ed., rev. 12mo., 112pp. **Short A.l.s.** from the author to Sir Henry Hawkins (later Lord Brampton) inserted, referring to one of Hawkins's jokes which is included in the book; also inscribed on d.w. Orig. parchment, sl. fdd.; printed d.w. (repaired at spine). £20.00
A book of humorous reflections, privately printed for circulation within the Bar. Darling was raised to the bench & became celebrated as a wit.

146. DART, J. Henry. A Compendium of the Law and Practice of Vendors and Purchasers of Real Estate. 1851. 1st. Index. Advert leaves before title. lii, 684pp. Modern cloth. **S. & M. ii.91.** £25.00

147. DAVIES, R. Rice. A Handy Book of the Land, Assessed, and Income Tax Laws. 1864. 1st edition. x, 416pp. Indices. MS. form of tax-assessor's oath written inside back cover. Sl. browned. Orig. cloth, faded; jts. & corners worn. **S. & M. ii.93.** £20.00

148. DEGGE, Sir Simon. The Parsons Counsellor, with the Law of Tithes and Tithing. By the Assigns of Richard and Edward Atkins . . . for Henry Twyford. 1681-1677. 3rd edition, revised. **2 vols. in 1.** Index. Sl. wormed. $2F_{3-4}$ (advert. leaves) defective (lower half of each leaf torn out. Lib. stamp on title & A_2. **WING D.854. S. & M. i.167.** £50.00
This, as the date of part 2 shows, is the edition of 1677 with a cancel title.

149. ————. The Parson's Councellor, with the Law of Tythes or Tything. **2 books in 1 vol.** Richard and Edward Atkins, Henry Twyford etc. 1685. Fourth edition corrected and enlarged with a table etc. Catalogue of Monasteries: table & booklist (of Judges etc. of Inner Temple, Grays Inn, Middle Temple and Lincolns Inn). **WING D.855. S. & M. i.167.45.** Bookplate; inner hinges worn, contemp. calf, rebacked. **KRESS 1620.** £65.00
First published in 1676.

150. De LUGO, Joannes. Disputationum de Institia et Iure, tomus primus (-secundus). Lyons, 1652. New ed. 2 vols. in 1. Folio. Red & black titles. Sl. stnd. Contemp. cf., sl. rbbd.; head of sp. torn. £80.00
Although this work is conceived as a commentary on the Secunda Secundae of Aquinas, the legal connotations of the title give a true idea of its subject. It consists of the rights of property, personal injuries, punishment, self-defence, and contracts. The author (a Spanish cardinal) offers some interesting remarks on exchanges, & finds exceptions to the Church's general prohibition of usury.

151. DICKINSON, William. A Practical Guide to the Quarter Sessions and Other Sessions of the Peace. Ed. T.N. Talfourd. 1838. 4th edition. lxvi, 986pp. Index. Sl. spotted. Contemp. calf, worn, rebacked. **S. & M. ii.100.** £20.00

152. DOUBLEDAY, H.A. The Mar Case. 1866 to 1885 & After. 1936. 1st separate (rep. from "Complete Peerage"). 4to. (ii), 100pp. Orig. wraps, uncut & unopened. Fine. £10.00
A dispute (which ascended to the House of Lords) between Lords Kellie & Mar over the right to the latter's title.

153. ————. The Mar Case. Another copy. Orig. wraps, uncut & unopened. Fine. £10.00

154. DUNDAS, John. An Abridgment of the Acts of the General Assembly of the Church of Scotland. Edinburgh, 1721. 1st edition. (xvi), 288, (xx)pp. Index. Final list of presbyteries. Contemp. sheep, sp. & edges rubbed. **S. & M. v.32.** £30.00

155. DYER, Sir James, Chief Justice (1511-1582). Les Reports del Ley des divers select matters et Resolutions. 1688: by W. Rawlins, S. Roycroft and M. Flesher. 6th edition. French-law; black letter. Folio. Woodcut devices. Index. (xvi), 377 leaves, (lii)pp. Sl. browned at marg. otherwise a fine copy. Mod. ½ cf. **S. & M. i.299/47.** £120.00
"He reported the most remarkable cases that came before the Court of Common Pleas, together with those which, on account of their difficulty, were adjourned into the Exchequer Chamber before all the judges. They are valuable records of the history of English jurisprudence and English manners." (Wallace Rep.)

156. ELDON, John Scott, 1st Earl of (1751-1838). TWISS, Horace; the Public and Private Life . . . with Selections from his Correspondence. 1844. 1st edition. 3 **vols.** 5 engraved portraits, 1 facs., & 4 tinted lith. plates. Plates sl. spotted. Orig. decorated cloth, uncut. Fine set. £40.00
Lord Chancellor Eldon is remembered for his oppressive & obstructive Toryism; but Twiss preserves the true record of him as a learned, diligent & upright judge.

157. ————. TWISS, Horace; Public and Private Life . . . With Selections from his Correspondence. 1844. 1st edition. **3 vols.** 5 engraved portraits, 1 facs. & 4 tinted lithograph plates (spotted). Plates spotted. Contemp. ½ calf, spines rubbed. £35.00

158. ELLESMERE, Thomas Egerton, Baron (Viscount Brackley) (1540-1617). The Speech . . . in the Eschequer Chamber touching the Post-nati. For the Societie of Stationers, 1609. 1st edition. Sm. 4to. (x), 118, (ii)pp. Final leaf blank except for rules. Lacks first blank. 18th-century sheep, spine & edges rubbed. **S.T.C. 7540; S. & M. i.156.** £180.00
As Lord Chancellor, Ellesmere took a notable part in the development of equity as a moderating influence on the common law, successfully maintaining the jurisdictional rights of the Chancery against the assaults of Coke. This is his judgment in Calvin's case, where he held that Scottish citizens born after 1603 were entitled to all the rights of Englishmen; a point of great importance during the next hundred years, when the political relation of the two kingdoms was a matter of infinite dispute.

159. ELLIS, Havelock. The Revaluation of Obscenity. THE HOURS PRESS, Paris, 1931. LIMITED 200 copies on Vidalon Paper and SIGNED by the author. No. 55. Uncut. ½ morocco, cloth sides. Spine ends sl. rubbed; cloth sl. faded. E-p's sl. yellowed. With fine book-plate of Sir Lionel Lawson Faudel-Phillips. £40.00

160. ERSKINE, John of Carnock. An Institute of the LAW of SCOTLAND, in Four Books. In the order of Sir George Mackenzie's Institutions of that Law. **2 vols.** Folio. Edinburgh, Bell & Bradfute, 1828. A new edition with additional notes by James IVORY. Appendix, 80pp. index and publisher's booklist. Modern ½ calf. **S. & M. v.40.** £60.00

161. ————. An Institute of the Law of Scotland. Ed. James Badenach Nicolson. 1871. 8th ed. **2 vols.** 4to. Indices. Orig. cl., paper labels. Corners and sp. end frayed, fdd., label of vol. 1 worn & ex. library stamps. **S. & M. v.40.** £45.00

First published in 1754, revised for a century and a half and still recognised as an authority.

162. ERSKINE, Thomas, Lord (1750-1823). Speeches . . . when at the Bar, on Subjects connected with the Liberty of the Press, and against Constructive Treasons (– on Miscellaneous Subjects) 1810(-1820). 1st collected. 5 vols. Engraved fp. port. to Vol. 4. ½ title in vol. 1 only, as called for. Contemp. stained calf, spines gilt, 2 labels. Sps. rubbed, some jts. worn. **£80.00**
Erskine maintained an unvarying reputation, during his 28 years at the Bar, as a champion of the liberty of the subject. Lord George Gordon & Thomas Paine are among those on whose behalf his eloquence was maintained.

163. L'ÉSPRIT de la COUTUME de NORMANDIE, avec un Recueil d'Arrets Notables du meme Parlement. Rouen, 1720. 4to. 3rd & newly revised edition. Indices. Privilege leaf at end. Sm. hole on title-page. Contemp. mottled calf, spine gilt. Hinges worn and sl. rubbed. Fine copy. French text. **£90.00**
A collection, edited for this edition, of arrests and rules concerning tithes & other ecclesiastical cases.

164. E(UER), S(ampson). Doctrina Placitandi ou l'Art & Science de Bon Pleading. By the Assigns of R. & E. Atkins . . . for Robert Pawlet, 1677. 1st edition. 3 vols. 4to. French text. Index. Name on title of **Robert KELHAM** (law-lexicographer & commentator on Domesday Book); interleaved throughout, with continuous annots. in another hand. Few sl. marginal worm-holes & repairs. 18th-century ½ calf; worn. **WING E.3409. S. & M. i.268. £150.00**
Euer's system of pleading remained in high authority until procedure was reformed in the 1850s. The annotations amount to an independent abridgment of pleading, following Euer's order; they were written in about 1780, for the latest authority cited (4 Burrow) dates from 1776. A few unpublished cases are cited.

165. FACHINEUS, Andreas. Controversiarum iuris libri decem . . . nunc primum in Italia excusi . . . adiecto decimo libro nunquam antehac edito. Venice, apud Societatem Venetam, 1602. Folio. Bird's eye view of Venice on title-page. (lx)pp. 1372 columns. Index. Lacks final blank. Sm. hole in title. Last leaf sl. soiled. Contemp. sheep; rubbed; paste-downs detached. **£120.00**
The author, a native of Forli, was a jurist of the old type, keeping strictly to the limits of his subject. He criticises Hottoman as a "heretic" for doubting the authenticity of a letter of Justinian inserted in the Code (de summa Trinitate) asserting the pre-eminence of the Popes; yet elsewhere he refers respectfully of the French school & cites Cujas & Bude.

166. FENWICK, Sir John. The Proceedings . . . upon a Bill of Attainder for High Treason. Printed . . . 1698. 1st edition. ii, 348, ix pp. Index. Contemp. calf; jts. sl. worn. **WING F.3545. £50.00**
Fenwick was executed for plotting on behalf of the former King James II. His trial raised the question whether the parliamentary bill of attainder was subject to the rules applicable to indictments requiring precise specification of the offence.

167. FEUERBACK, Paul Johann. Narratives of Remarkable Criminal Trials, transl. & edited Lady Duff Gordon. 1846. 1st Engl. xii, 368pp. Orig. cloth; sl. shaken. **£20.00**
Fourteen cases selected from the German original.

168. FIELD v. McGLUMPHY. In re Petition for Mandamus. Affidavits and Exhibits. N.p. (Philadelphia, Pa.), 1899. 1st edition. Lithographed table. 154pp. SIGNED on endpaper by Dr. (Montague) R. Leverson (the most important of the medical witnesses), with many textual corrections in his hand. Additional paragraph inserted on a typed slip at p. 72. Contemp. roan, rebacked, with original wraps bound in. **£30.00**
This extraordinary case in the U.S. Court of Common Pleas arose out of attempts by the New York legislature to enforce compulsory vaccination in a poor part of Brooklyn. As a weapon against this intention the plaintiff, Charles Field, collected these depositions from qualified doctors; most of them are prepared to swear not only that they have seen men killed by vaccination, but that vaccination itself is worthless.

169. FIELDING, Sir John (?-1780). Extracts from such of the Penal Laws, as Particularly Relate to the Peace and Good Order of this Metropolis: with Observations. 1769. 2 vols. New edition, revised. x, (xiv), 426pp. Index. Few leaves sl. spotted. Contemp. calf; jts. & edges sl. worn. **S. & M. i.439. £150.00**
The brothers Fielding, Henry the great novelist & John, the blind magistrate, were among the first to make sensible propositions for the control, as well as punishment, of urban crime. This digest of criminal statutes, with remarks on their grounds, their faults, their abuses & the consequences of their neglect, shows the author's experience as Bow Street Magistrate. His comments on social conditions are acute & often prophetic. A Treatise on the Office of Constable, edited from Henry's MSS., is included.

170. ————. Extracts from such of the Penal Laws . . . 1769. 2 vols. . . . another copy. Contemp. calf, edges & jts. rubbed & sl. worn. **£150.00**

171. FINETT, Sir John. Finetti Philoxenis: Some Choice Observations . . . touching the Reception, and Precedence, the Treatment and Audience, the Puntillias and Contests of Forren Ambassadors in England. By T.R. for H. Twyford and G. Bedell. 1656. 1st edition. Index. (xiv), 250, (x)pp. Lacks first & final blanks. FINE MODERN CALF. **Wing F.947. S. & M. i.599. £180.00**
The author was Master of Ceremonies under James I and Charles I. His book, edited by James Howell, throws important light on the blundering diplomacy of James, the machinations of the Spaniards, & the career of the Duke of Buckingham.

172. FINLASON, W.F. The Judgment of the Judicial Committee in the Folkestone Ritual Case. 1877. 1st edition. 72, 32pp. Publisher's cat. at end. Title detached. Orig. cloth, faded. Not in **S. & M. £10.00**
Finlason disagrees with the principles followed by the Privy Council in considering an appeal by a Folkestone vicar, Charles Ridsdale, against an Arches Court decree barring him from the use of some Romanish observances which he had introduced in his church.

173. (FIOCCO, Domenico). L. Fenestellae de magistratibus sacerdotiisque libellus . . . Pomponii Laeti itidem de magistratibus & . . . legibus. Lyons (L. Cloquemin), 1581. 16mo. Device on title. Index. 162, (x)pp. Sl. stnd. Few margins sl. frayed. Mod. ¼ cf./mbld. sides. **£60.00**
The ancient works of Fenestella on the Roman magistracies is mentioned by Lactantius & others, but what is printed here is a fifteenth century forgery; a similar work by Pomponio Leti, the notorious devil-worshipper, is sub-joined.

174. FIRST REPORT of the COMMISSIONERS appointed to Enquire into the Best Means of Establishing an Efficient CONSTABULARY FORCE in the Counties of England and Wales. Folding graph. xii, 416pp. Orig. cloth, soiled, some dampmarking to prelims, spine split. **HMSO 1839. £40.00**

175. FITZHERBERT, Sir Anthony. La nouvelle Natura Brevium . . . auecques un Table . . . iammais per cy deuaunt imprimee. In aedibus Richardi Tottelli, 1567 (4th ed.). French text. Black letter. Woodcut title-border. Index. (xxxii), 271 leaves. Ink-stains on C_1. Marginal defect to F_4 with loss of few words of last line. Corner torn from D_1. Lacks final colophon leaf. Some early annots. Title frayed. Contemp. calf, worn, rebacked & re-cornered. S.T.C. 10961. **Beale T.347. S. & M. i.269. £180.00**
Fitzherbert's commentary on the writs as printed in Rastell's Register (1531) was one of the most authoritative works in English law from 1534, when it was first printed, until 1852 when the forms of action which it illustrates were abolished.

176. FORSYTH, William. Cases and Opinions on Constitutional Law, and various points of English Jurisprudence. 1869. Index, tables of Cases; Statutes etc. Title-page frayed, modern cloth, label. **S. & M. ii.127. £20.00**

177. FORTESCUE, Sir John (fl.1430-1471). A Learned Commendation of the Politique Lawes of England . . . newly translated . . . by Robert Mulcaster. (By Richarde Tottell. 1573.) Latin & English text. Black & Roman letter. Index. (iii), 132, (iii) leaves. Sl. stnd. Old ink names & annots. on title & blank verso of last leaf, & few in margins. Contemp. cf., re-backed; rbbd. **Beale T.358; S.T.C. 11195; S. & M. i.17. £240.00**
Third edition of Fortescue, & second of Mulcaster's version. The work, written for the instruction of the future King Edward IV is a summary for the layman containing the earliest outline of the peculiarly English scheme of constitutional monarchy, with many interesting comparisons between English & foreign practice.

178. ————. A Learned Commendation of the Politique Laws of England . . . Translated . . . by Robert Mulcaster. By Thomas Wight & Bonham Norton, 1599. Latin & English text. Black & Roman letter. (ii), 3-132, (iii) leaves. Title sl. browned. Contemp. vellum, worn, lacks ties. **Beale T.359; S.T.C. 11196; S. & M. i.17. £200.00**
Fourth edition of Fortescue, & third of Mulcaster's versions. Fortescue had travelled in Europe during the late wars & this enabled him (alone among our early law-writers) to illustrate his remarks by reference to the civil law & the systems of several European states.

179. ————. De laudibus legum Angliae . . . Hereto are joined the two Summes of Sir Ralph de Hengham. (Ed. John Selden.) For the Companie of Stationers 1616. 1st thus. 2 parts in 1. Index. Latin & English text. Index. Lacks first blank, (xvi)pp. 132 leaves, (vi), 56, (xii), 160, (ii)pp. Final blank. 18th-century calf, joints & corners sl. worn. S.T.C. 11197. S. & M. i.22. **£300.00**
Chief Justice Fortescue, the devoted follower of Henry VI in all the troubles of the age, wrote this dialogue between himself & the crown-prince to instruct the latter in the laws of England. It gives a vivid picture of our constitutional monarchy in its primitive state & of the life of the law. The summae of Hengham (Chief Justice, K.B., fl.1274-1309) are accounts of practice showing the relation between the King's courts at various levels. They are published by Selden for the first time & both these & Fortescue are enriched with his notes.

180. FOSTER, Sir Michael. A Report of Some Proceedings . . . for the Trial of the Rebels in the Year 1746 . . . and of other Crown Cases . . . Discourses upon a Few Branches of the Crown Law. Oxford (Clarendon Press), 1762. 1st edition. Folio. (iv), viii, (iv), 412, (xx)pp. Index. Sl. spotted. Contemp. calf, rebacked; sl. rubbed. **S. & M. i.367. £95.00**
The exceptional precision of Foster's reports, & the judiciousness of his Discourses, cause this work (published by his son) to rank as a major authority on criminal law.

181. (FREEMAN, K.). Repertorium Juridicum; an Index to all the Cases in the Year Books, Entries, Reports and Abridgements in Law and Equity: Beginning with Edward I. By a Barrister of the Middle Temple. 1742. 1st edition. 2 parts in 1 vol. Fol. (x), var. pag. An index to each part. **£60.00**

182. FULLER, Nicholas. The Argument . . . in the Case of Thomas Lad, and Richard Maunsell. N.p. (Amsterdam?), 1607. 1st. Sm. 4to. (iv), 32pp. 19-cent. ½ mor./mbld. sides. **S.T.C. 11460. S. & M. i.186. £75.00**
Argues that in claiming the power to fine & imprison for criminal offences the Church Commissioners had exceeded their statutory authority, & that the common-law rule "nobody may be condemned out of his own mouth" rendered illegal their practice of putting their "prisoners" upon oath & interrogating them. Lad & Maunsell were so treated on charges arising from a dissenting meeting. We learn from Coke (12 Rep. 19, 26, 44) that the vengeful divines managed to fix a charge of heresy on Fuller for his writings, but that he carried all his points notwithstanding. So discredited, the powers of the Commission died an unlamented death after the Restoration.

183. FURNEAUX, Philip. (1726-1783). Letters to the Hon. Mr. Justice Blackstone, concerning his Exposition of the Act of Toleration and some Positions relative to Religious Liberty. 1771. 2nd edition, rev. PRESENTATION COPY. xxiv, 284pp. Mod. cloth. **S. & M. i.29. £50.00**
Furneaux, a dissenting minister, objected to Blackstone's harsh construction of the Act of Toleration & to his general support of the principle that those who dissent from the established religion deserve to suffer the animadversion of the law. This edition includes among other improvements Lord Mansfield's speech in Chamberlain of the City v. Evans (1767, House of Lords) where it was held that a dissenter elected to an office for which affirmation of the Anglican faith was required was immune from the statutory penalties imposed on those who refused to serve.

184. GAIUS (fl. 2nd cent. A.D.). The Institutes . . . and Rules of Ulpian. Transl. & ed. James Muirhead. Edinburgh, 1895. Latin and Engl. text. Index. Orig. cloth, sl. worn & fdd. **S. & M. v.139. £10.00**
Gaius is edited from a type-facsimile of the unique MS. (codex Veronensis), produced by Studemund in 1866-74. The second week is a fourth-century epitome of the Liber Regularum of Ulpian.

185. GASPARRO, Francesco Maria. Institutiones juris civilis. Venice, 1755. 1st. 4to. ½ title. Index. (v), 252pp. Q_{4-} (pp. 245-8) misbound in reverse order after A_1 – Institutiones juris canonici. Venice, 1755. 1st. 4to. ½ title. Index. (xiv), 360pp. 2 works in 1 vol. Few margins sl. wormed. Contemp. limp vellum, shaken. **£40.00**
Elementary works for the Rome University, based on the Institutes & Gratian respectively.

186. GENTILIS, Alberico (1551-1611?). De Jure Belli, Libri tres. Hanover: 1598. Excudebat Guilielmus Antonius. 1st German edition. Latin text. 8vo. Woodcut devices. (viii), 716pp. Bk-pl.: Augustus Thorndike. Sl. marg. worm not aff. text. 18th cent. clf. A fine copy. **S. & M. i.601/11. £450.00**
This work contains very correct views upon the science of international law. Gentilis was the first writer who endeavoured to introduce a system of jurisprudence amidst the din of arms. The first edition was printed in Oxford in 1588. (S. & M.).

187. "GIFFORD, John" (A. Whellier). English Lawyer; or, Every Man his Own Lawyer. 1830. 17th ed. Engr. fp. port. (Lord Eldon). Index. Supplement bound in 688/51, 12-13, 12-204pp. (pagination irreg. owing to cancels). Contemp. ½ calf, sl. rbbd. **S. & M. ii.377. £25.00**
The most durable of all the popular instructors. The supplement contains chapters on insurance, customs & excise, & taxes.

188. GILBERT, Sir Geoffrey (1674-1726). The Law of Tenures, including the Theory and Practice of Copyholds. With an Historical Introduction on the Feudal System and Notes by Charles Watkins. 1796: for J. Butterworth. 4th edition, corrected. 8vo. Index. viii, xxviii, 520, (ii)pp. Errata leaf. E-p's & title sl. browned. Mod ½ b'ram. & cl. A fine copy. **S. & M. i.453/20. £75.00**
"Gilbert's treatise contains explanations of many points of the feudal law which are not as fully displayed by any other writer. The author uniformly traces principles to their origin." (Marvin, Leg. Bib.).

189. (————). The Law of Uses and Trusts: collected . . . from the Reports of adjudg'd Cases, in the Courts of Law and Equity, and . . . together with a Treatise of Dower . . . with a complete table . . . Henry Lintot for J. Stagg and others. 1741. 2nd edition. (v), 437, (79)pp. ½ title, adverts, errata. Bookplate: Tho. de Grey. Contemp. calf, rubbed; rebacked. Fine copy. **S. & M. i.256.14. £45.00**

190. ————. A Treatise of Tenures. 1757. 3rd edition, with additions. ii, vi, 338, xxxviii pp. Advert leaf. Index. Contemp. cf. worn, jnts. cracked. **S. & M. i.453. £35.00**
"Gilbert's treatise contains explanations of many points of feudal law which are not as fully displayed by any other writers. The author uniformly traces principles to their origin." (S. & M.).

191. GLANVILLE, Ranulph de (fl.1164-1190). Tractatus de legibus et consuetudinibus Angliae . . . cum diversis manuscriptis nuper examinatis. In aedibus Thomae Wight, 1604. (2nd edition). Index. Lacks first blank & blank A_1; (vii), 116, (xvii)pp. **S.T.C. 11906. S. & M. i.54.**
– ST. GERMAN, Christopher (?-1539). Dialogus de fundamentis legum Angliae et de conscientia. In aedibus Thomae Wight, 1604. (2nd Latin edition). Index. (iv), 73, (ii)pp. Lacks final blank. **S.T.C. 21560. S. & M. i.29.** 2 works in 1 volume. FINE COPY bound in modern calf. **£300.00**
Glanville, the oldest of our general law writers, is collated here with the Scots "Regiam Maiestatem" by a learned though anonymous editor. St. German, an equal adversary to Sir Thomas More, was a pioneer in reconciling the law of England with natural justice; he does this in the three dialogues commonly called "Doctor & Student", of which only the first (printed here) exists in Latin.

192. (GLASS, S.). The Magistrate's Assistant; or, a Summary of those Laws which Immediately Respect the Conduct of a Justice of the Peace. Gloucester, 1788. 2nd ed. Appendix of forms. Fold'g table (sl. torn). Sl. stnd. Contemp. cf., sl. rbbd. **S. & M. i.288. £40.00**
A compilation intended to be more convenient for quick reference than the larger work of Burn.

193. GNEIST, Rudolf (ed.). Institutionum et regularum iuris Romani syntagma. Leipzig, 1880. 2nd ed., rev. Many pencil annots. (suggested translations) by J.F. Hobson of New College, Durham. Title sl. stnd. Contemp. ½ roan/cl. sides. rbbd. **£20.00**
Parallel texts of Gaius & Justinian, together with critical texts of the 12 Tables, Ulpian & Paulus.

194. GOODENOUGH, Erwin R. The Jurisprudence of the Jewish Courts in Egypt. Legal Administration by the Jews under the early Roman Empire as described by Philo Judaeus. Yale University Press. 1929. 1st edition. vii, (i), 268pp. Index. Orig. cloth. Fine. **£30.00**

195. GOTHOFREDUS (Godefroy), Jacobus (1587-1652). Novus in titulum Pandectarum de Diversis Regulis Iuris Antiqui, commentarius. Geneva (sumptibus Petri Chouet), 1653. 1st edition. 4to. Red & black title with device. (xxx), 804, (lxviii)pp. Index. Sl. wormed & browned. 19th-century ½ calf; rubbed; upper jt. worn. **£90.00**
Godefroy, greatest of a remarkable dynasty of jurists, brought an exceptional historical & critical knowledge to this subject; he was unequalled in his acquaintance with the ante-Justinianean law.

196. GRASWINCKEL, Theodore (1600-1666). Dissertatio de iure praecedentiae inter serenissiman Venetam rempubl. & sereniss. Sabaudiae ducem. Leyden, Elzevir, 1644. 1st edition. Latin text. LARGE PAPER (200 mm.). Red and black title. (xii), 356pp. Few head-margins wormed. Some sl. browning. Fine contemp. vellum. **WILLEMS 573** (one L.P. copy at Univ. of Utrecht only recorded). **£300.00**
A legal commentary on claims of the Duke of Savoy against Venice by one of the greatest lawyers of his time, a cousin of Grotius who helped him with the manuscript of "De Jure Belli ac Pacis". He adds many observations on mediaeval history & on international law.
Both Willems and the Rahir catalogue say that ordinary copies are only about 160 mm in height.

197. GRAY'S INN. The War Book of Gray's Inn; preface Viscount Birkenhead. Pub'd by the Masters of the Bench for Butterworth. 4to. 1921. 1st edition. xxxiv, 155pp. index, 7 photogravure plates of Gray's Inn, Gardens, Square and Chapel & portrait of Lord Birkenhead. Cloth. Sl. marked. **£12.00**

198. THE GREEN BAG. 1889-1914. Boston. (monthly) Vols. 1 & 2. 1889 & 1890. (pub'd in 26 vols.). **£40.00**
An entertaining magazine for lawyers. Presenting the humorous side of the law. It features legal antiquities, curious cases, causes celebres, legal anecdotes, etc.

199. (GREENE, John). The Priviledges of the Lord Mayor and Aldermen of the City. The Advantages of the Freemen ... Usage of the Mayor's Court (etc.). 1708. 1st edition. (xvi), 216pp. Later ½ calf; rebacked, edges worn. **S. & M. i.439.** **£40.00**

200. GREENLEAF, Simon. A Collection of Cases Overruled, Doubted, or Limited in their Application, taken from American and English Reports. Portland, Maine, 1821. 1st. Index. Fourfold interleaving throughout. 128pp. Few MS. additions. Contemp. cf., worn. **£30.00**
Includes the Rules of the U.S. Supreme Court & Circuit Court.

201. GREENWOOD, William. Bouleuterion (Graece) or, a Practical Demonstration of County-Judicatures. Wherein is Amply Explained the Judicial and Ministerial Authority of Sheriffs and Coroners. For John Place, 1685. 6th ed., rev. Index. Sl. stnd. Contemp. cf., re-backed; corners rbbd. **S. & M. i.390. Wing G.1874. (Lincoln's Inn & Yale Law Lib. only).** **£60.00**
Includes forms of writs and pleadings appropriate to the county courts, with an appendix of documents in the case Carew Pearse v. Cox & others, *a leading case for annulling county-court decisions on matters arising outside their territory.*

202. GRIFFIN-STONESTREET, G.S. Letters to a Man of Rank upon the Impolitic Tendency of a Motion by Col. Williams, M.P., to Repeal the Royal Marriage Act. 1834. **1st. Errata leaf.** (ii), 72pp. Disbound. **£10.00**
The Act prohibited any descendant of George II. from marrying under 25 or without consent of Parliament; but the real issue between Williams & the author was whether parental interference in marriage was in general worthy of legislative support.

203. GROTIUS, Hugo. De origine gentium Americanarum dissertatio altera. Paris (S. Cramoisy), 1643. 1st edition. Device on title. 36pp. **Sabin 38561.**
– **De LAET, Jan (?-1649).** Notae ad dissertationem Hugonis Grotii de origine gentium Americanarum. Paris, 1643. 2nd edition. 224pp. **Sabin 38561.**
– Responsio ad dissertationem secundam ... Grotii. Amsterdam (Jean Maire for L. Elzevir), 1644. 1st edition. (iv), 116, (viii)pp. Index. **Sabin 38562. Willems 1007.**
3 works in 1 vol. Contemp. calf. Spine & corners worn. **£600.00**
Grotius imagined, from some accidental likenesses of names, that the original inhabitants of central America were Norsemen, other parts being colonised by Africans & Chinese. In this he presumed wrongly and the much larger "Notae" of de Laet (author of the "Elzevir Republics") corrects him. This work includes the whole text of Grotius's first dissertation. It is followed in our collection by Grotius's answer & then by de Laet's final word. Apart from the main question, de Laet counters Grotius's theory that the Chinese knew nothing of printing until it was shown them by the Portuguese.
Sabin wrongly calls for a map in de Laet's Reponsio.

204. GUNDLINGIANA. Darinnen allerhand zur Jurisprudenz, Philosophie, Historie, Critic, Litterature und Ubrigen Gelehrsamkeit ... Halle im Magdeburgischen ... Rengerischen Buchhandlung 1715-1717. **Erstes = Zehndes Stück.** (xiv), 503, (43), 508, (30)pp. Engraved fp. port., indices, separate title-page for each part with printer's device (woodcut), headpieces & initials. Contemp. vellum, soiled.
– **Ein und dreyssigstes Stück (31st part) = Viertigstes Stück** (40th part). 1723-1727. 545, (23), 514, (28)pp. Contemp. vellum, Fine. Indices. Woodcut headpieces and initials.
– **Ein und viertzigstes Stück-Fünf und viertizigstes und letzes Stück** (41st-45th & last part). 1728-1732. (2), 366, (7), 195, (19)pp.
together with:
BÜCHOVIO, Cordato: Die Hoffnung besserer Zeifen aus den Klag-Liedern ... Mangel am Geld ... Frankfurth am Mayn for Johann Friederich Fleischern 1730. (8), 198pp. Contemp. ½ vellum. **£130.00**
Each part complete in itself. See Wilhelm Engelmann "Bibliotheca Juridica", p. 148.

205. (GURDON), Thornhagh. The History of the High Court of Parliament, its antiquity, preeminence and authority, and the History of Court Baron and Court Leet, with the Rights of Lords of Manors in Common Pastures and the growth of the privileges the tenants now enjoy there. Knaplock & J. Tonson, 1731. 1st. **2 vols. in 1 vol.** xviii (xxviii), 254/-645, (viii)pp. Indices, errata. Fine engr. tailpieces at end of prefaces & at end of volumes. Later ½ calf/cloth, corners rubbed, cloth dull. **£45.00**
Interesting index of the books and manuscripts used in the writing of this important historical work.

206. HAI ben SHERIRA, Gaon (fl.988-1038). Sépher hammiqach wehammimcar (The Book of Purchase & Sale, tr. Yischaq ben Reüven). Venice (Moshè Levi Minz), 5362 (1602). 1st. Sm. 4to. Hebrew text. Rabbinic letter. Woodcut title-border. Diagram in text. Final colophon leaf. 96, (1) leaves. Few worm-holes at beginning. Few marginal stains. Later vellum, re-backed. **Zedner p. 278.** **£950.00**
This classic of commercial literature laid down a code of practice for Jewish merchants at a time when Judaism & commerce were almost synonymous. The author, Hai Gaon, was the last of the great Geonim (arbiters of secular law) of Mesopotamia; a thinker of a practical rather than mystical cast, he devoted particular attention to the problems of Jews in foreign parts, & they in turn received his authority with great eagerness; the present text, for example, is a Hewbrew translation from the Arabic made in Spain in the year 1078. Thus the high organization & equally high standards of commercial Jewry in the middle ages & afterwards can be referred to this source as much as any other.
A brief formulary for contracts, probably the most ancient in existence, is printed as an appendix; it includes a Sepher Mashcon (Contract of loan), showing the methods of Jewish money-lenders.
THE EARLIEST CLASSIC OF COMMERCIAL LAW.

207. HAILES, Sir David Dalrymple, Lord (1726-1792). Tracts relative to the History and Antiquities of Scotland. Edinburgh, 1800. 1st collected. 4to. Each tract separately paged. Mod. cloth. **£60.00**
These items (including a catalogue of the Lords of Session from 1532, remarks on "Regiam Maiestatem", etc.) were published between 1768 & 1799. The publisher Constable bought up the remainders & added preliminary leaves to make the present volume.

208. HAKEWEL, William. Modus tenendi Parliamentum: or, the old Manner of Holding Parliaments in England ... and the Manner how Lawes are there enacted by passing of Bills. For Abel Roper, 1660. 12mo. vi, 120pp. A_2 excised leaving stub, possibly contents leaf. **WING H.216. S. & M. i.131.43.**
– The Manner how Statutes are enacted in Parliament by Passing Bills. For John Benson. 1659. 12mo. 121-220pp. **WING H.212. S. & M. i.153.4. 2 works in 1 vol.** Modern calf. **£40.00**
The first work by Hakewel of Lincoln's Inn, is a discussion on the liberty of the subject and the manner of holding Parliaments. The second part is a personal collection showing the way in which statutes are enacted by Bills over a period of 30 years.

209. HALE, Sir Matthew (1609-1676). The Analysis of the Law: being a Scheme or Abstract, of the several Titles and Partitions of the Law. 1716. 2nd edition. First blank. Index. Contemp. calf, jts. sl. worn. **S. & M. i.239.** **£55.00**
Hale's logical system of law, the first of its kind, had a great influence on Blackstone.

210. ——————. Historia Placitorum Coronae. The History of the Pleas of the Crown, with notes by Sollom Emlyn. 1736. **1st edition. 2 vols.** 4to. Engr. folding fp. port. Index. Sl. marg. worming. Contemp. calf, gilt; sl. rubbed. FINE COPY. **£70.00**
Hale's work, although only an unfinished portion of his proposed corpus on crown law, is an important guide to capital offences. Emlyn's large notes correct some references and bring the statute law down to date.

211. ——————. Historia placitorum coronae . . 1736. 1st edition. 2 vols. as above.
bound with:
FLETA, seu commentarius iuris Anglicani. (Ed. Sir Samuel Clarke.) 1735. 1st thus. **Book 1 only (all published).** Folio. **S. & M. i.53.** Contemp. calf, sps. gilt, rubbed, jts. worn. **£150.00**
Clarke's incomplete "Fleta" depends for its considerable merit on a Cotton MS & on his collation of the text with that of Glanville.

212. ——————. The History of the Common Law of England. 1716. 2nd edition. First advert. leaf. Engraved table on R_4 verso. Index. **S. & M. i.239.18.**
– The Analysis of the Law: being a Scheme, or Abstract of the Several Titles and Partitions of the Law. 1716. 2nd edition. First advert. leaf. Index. **S. & M. i.239/16. Two works in 1 volume.** Sl. spotted. Modern ½ calf. **£95.00**
The History, brief though it is, is the most finished & among the most valuable of Hale's works. The Analysis had a considerable influence on Blackstone.

213. ——————. The Judgment of the late Lord Chief Justice of the Nature of True Religion the Causes of its Corruptions ... Additions and Violences: with the desired Cure. In three Discourses, written by himself at several times. Dedicated to the Hon. Judges and Learned Lawyers ... by the faithful Publisher, Richard Baxter. ... annexed the Judgment of Sir Francis Bacon and Dr. Isaack Barrows on the same subject. B. Simmons, 1684. 1st

edition. Sm. 4to. (x), 64pp. Disbound, sewn. Title-page dust-stained. Sm. ex lib. label on bottom of t-p. **Wing 247.** **£25.00**

214. (——————). The Original Institution, Power and Jurisdiction of Parliaments. **2 parts in 1.** Jacob Tonson, 1707. 1st edition. (viii), 240pp. Contemporary panelled calf. Fine copy. **S. & M. i.131.44.** **£90.00**
This work is ascribed as "being from a Manuscript of the late Judge Hales" on the title-page, but according to a ms. note in Mr. Hargrave's copy in the British Museum, appears not to have been written by him.

215. ——————. BURNETT, Gilbert; Life. S.P.C.K. 1823. iv, 68pp.
HAMMOND, H. FELL, John; Life. S.P.C.K. 1823. iv, 80pp.
2 works in 1 vol. Orig. tree calf, rebacked; sl. rubbed. **£15.00**

216. HALHED, Nathaniel Brassey (transl. & edited). A Code of Gentoo Laws, or Ordinations of the Pundits, from a Persian Translation. 1776. 1st. 4to. 8 engraved plates of Shancrit characters & poetry. lxxiv, 322pp. Modern cloth, gilt lettering on spine. Fine. **£60.00**
In 1773 a Committee of eleven Pandits, or Hindu juriconsults, was appointed at the instance of Warren Hastings to compile & translate into the Persian tongue a system of their traditionary laws. This was translated by Halhed, who added an introductory account of Sanscrit literature & Hindu religion & customs.

217. ——————. A Code of Gentoo Laws, or Ordinations of the Pundits, from a Persian Translation. 1777. 2nd ed. 8vo. 8 engraved plates (some folding) of Shancrit characters & poetry. Contemp. ½ calf, rubbed. Some sl. off-setting from 2 or 3 of the plates. **£40.00**
This is the same translation as the 1st 4to. edition.

218. HALLIFAX, Samuel (1733-1790). An Analysis of the Roman Civil Law, Compared with the Laws of England: being the Heads of a Course of Lectures, Publickly Read in the University of Cambridge. CUP 1774. 1st edition. Index. (iv), xxx, 3-160pp. Contemp. calf, newly rebacked. **S. & M. i.612.8.** **£80.00**
Hallifax's simple summary asserts the importance of civil law to the Englishman without proposing, as his predecessors in the 17th century had done, that common law should give way to it.

219. HAMILTON, Duke of, & others, V. STEWART. Proof in the Conjoined Processes ... Pursuers Proof ... Condescendence of Facts. N.p. (Edinburgh), 1766. 1st. 4to. French & Engl. text. Index. Pagination irregular through cancellation. Appendix. Many corners creased. Orig. wraps, frayed, sp. defective; sewing weak. **£50.00**
Evidence collected in France & England to prove that Archibald Stewart, supposed heir to the Duke of Douglas, was not the son of Sir John & Lady Douglas ... had been bought by them in France after the real son had been stillborn. [illegible] is a witness & swears that French letters corroborative of Stewart's case betray themselves by their style as English forgeries. The Lords of Session decided against Stewart, but in 1769 this judgement was reversed in the English House of Lords.

220. (HARBIN, George). The Hereditary Right of the Crown of England Asserted; the History of the Succession since the Conquest Clear'd; and the True English Constitution Vindicated. 1713. 1st edition. Folio. Appendix of documents. Sl. browned; sl. marginal worming. Contemp. panelled calf, rubbed. **S. & M. i.115.** **£75.00**
One of many attempts after the revolution of 1689 to reconcile the subject's liberty with the need for a stable succession. Harbin argues, in opposition to Highden's View of the English Constitution, that the crown is & always was hereditary. His efforts to fit William I, Henry IV etc. into this scheme are curious enough.

221. HARDY, W.J. & W. PAGE (eds.). A Calendar to the Feet of Fines for London & Middlesex. Vol. I: Richard I to Richard III. 1892: Hardy & Page (1st edition). 8vo. Index. Some marg. notes in pencil & ink. Sl. ink st. on final e-p's. Contemp. cvr. sl. worn. Lib. stamp: A. Bonner on title. **£20.00**

222. HARE, Thomas. A treatise on the Election of Representatives, Parliamentary and Municipal. 1859. 1st edition. **PRESENTATION COPY.** xxxiv, 338pp. Sl. spotted. Modern ½ calf. Bk-pl. Lord Belper. **S. & M. i.156.** **£35.00**
This important work anticipates many of the modern objections to the "first-past-the-post" system, rigid party divisions, & other faults in the British electoral structure.

223. HARRISON, S.B. An Analytical Digest of the Reported Cases Determined in the House of Lords, the Several Courts of Common Law, ... and the Court of Bankruptcy ... from Mich. Term. 1756, to Easter Term, 1836 ... Selection of Equity Cases. 1835. 2nd edition. Addenda to the ... Digest. 1837. 1st edition. **4 vols.** Indices. Contemp. ½ calf; rubbed; two vols. rebacked with orig. spines. **S. & M. ii.158.** **£40.00**
Includes a digest of statutes. Some of the cases are otherwise unreported.

224. ——————. An Analytical Digest of the Reported Cases determined in the House of Lords, the several Courts of Common Law, ... and the Court of Bankruptcy ... from Mich. Term 1756 to Easter Term, 1836 ... Selection of Equity Cases. 1837. 2nd edition. **3 vols.** Indices. Sl. spotted. Modern cloth. **S. & M. ii.158.** **£30.00**
Includes a digest of statutes.

225. (HAWARDE, John). Les Reports del Cases in Camera Stellata 1593-1609. From the original MS. Edited by W.P. BAILDON. London 1894. Privately printed by Alfred Morrison. 4to. **Limited to 250 copies.** lxxv, 502pp. uncut & unopened. Appendix & index. Fp. and several plates and text illus. A duplicate quire of pp. 17-32 bound in introduction between pp. xlviii & lxv. Orig. buckram, gilt lettering; covers rubbed. **S. & M. i.291.9.** **£120.00**
The official transcripts of the Court of the Star Chamber under Elizabeth I.

226. HAWKINS, Sir Henry (Baron Brampton). Reminiscences, ed. Richard Harris. 1904. 1st. **2 vols.** Fp. port. & other illus. Orig. dec'd cl., uncut; sl. mkd. **£10.00**

227. HAWKINS, William. A Treatise of the Pleas of the Crown. 1762. 4th edition. **2 vols. in 1.** Folio. Index. Sl. stained. Modern cloth. **S. & M. i.362.** **£60.00**
The fulness, judgment & order of Hawkins's works makes this an important work. – Hale's great "History" was still unpublished when Hawkins's work appeared.

228. HAWLES, Sir John. The Englishman's Right; a Dialogue between a Barrister at Law and a Juryman. 1763. 12mo. (viii), 60pp. Head-margin of title repaired. Lib. label & stamps on three leaves. Modern wraps. **S. & M. i.376.** **£20.00**
The dialogue is a statement of the rights and duties of the jury and its members.

229. HEATHCOTE, Ralph. I. The Irenarch; or, the Justice of the Peace's Manual. II. Miscellaneous Reflections upon Laws, Policy, Manners, &c. in a Dedication to William Lord Mansfield. III. An Assize-Sermon, preached at Leicester, 12 Aug. 1756. 1781. 1st. **3 parts in one vol.** x, 256pp. Contemp. calf. **S. & M. 228/33.** **£50.00**
Ralph Heathcote, writer and divine, was appointed Justice of the Peace for Leicester. His enthusiasm and interest in the task led him to write this guide for J.P.s which includes the history, powers and operations of that appointment and draws on Blackstone, Lambard, Barrington, etc.

230. HEINECCIUS, Johannes Gottlieb (1681-1741). Antiquitatum Romanarum jurisprudentiam illustrantium syntagma. Strassburg, 1755. New edition. **2 vols.** Engraved fp. Index. Folding table. Lib. stamps on versi of titles. & bk-labels. Contemp. calf, worn & sl. stained. **£30.00**
The standard work on Roman legal history throughout the 18th century.

231. ——————. Elementa juris civilis secundum ordinem Pandectarum. Amsterdam, 1740. 4th edition. **2 vols.** Engraved folding fp. port. (sl. torn at fold). Red & black title. Index. A few pages misbound. Some lib. stamps on title-verso. Few contemp. annots. Contemp. calf, sl. worn. **£30.00**

232. HERBERT, William, M.P. A Letter to the Chairman of the Committee of the House of Commons, on the Game Laws. 1823. 1st. 16pp. Sl. browned. Sewn as issued. **Kress C.1073.** **£15.00**
Proposes a registry of persons licensed to sell game; this would put the poacher out of business, & so prevent both his activities & the necessity of punishing him.

233. HEWART, Lord (L.C.J.). Essays and Observations. 1930. 1st. viii, 312pp. Orig. b'ram. **£8.00**

234. HINDE, Robert. The Modern Practice of the High Court of Chancery. Dublin, 1786. Index. Lib. perforation on title. Modern cloth. **S. & M. i.339.** **£30.00**

235. HODGSON, Christopher. Instructions for the Use of Candidates for Holy Orders, and of the Parochial Clergy, as to Ordination, Licences ... Endowment ... Mortgages (etc.). 1845. 6th ed. Appendix of statutes. Index. Orig. ¼ cloth, uncut; faded; sl. worn. **£10.00**

236. HODGSON, E. The Trials at Large of the Capital and other Convicts, on the King's Commission ... for the City of London and ... County of Middlesex. 1791-2. 1st. **8 numbers (17 parts) in one vol.** 470, 467-472pp. One leaf torn without loss. Few pencil scribbles. Contemp. ¼ sheep/mbld. sides; worn. **Not in S. & M.** **£40.00**
A complete Year's proceedings in the Middlesex county court before the Lord Mayor, Recorder, Common Sergeant, etc. These cases are in general unknown to the regular reports, from which Hodgson's accounts differ in that he reports the evidence and specifies the sentence. They show how the obsolete criminal laws were applied (how, for example, the jury would falsify the value of stolen goods to save a thief's neck)

and are full of interesting details of language & society.

237. **HOLWORTHY, John.** An Act for vesting the Sum of Two Thousand Pounds in Trustees . . . for the payment of the Debts of. N.d. (c.1710). 1st edition. Folio. 4pp. Folded as issued. Sl. stained. **£20.00**
Holworthy was bankrupt, & this act made a sum of money previously bound up in his mother's settlement available to pay his debts.

238. **HOMES, J.A.** The Act to Amend the Law of Insolvency, Bankruptcy, and Execution . . . Act for the Relief of Insolvent Debtors . . . Act for Facilitating Arrangements between Debtors and Creditors. 1844. 1st edition. Index. viii, 136pp. Orig. printed boards, sp. defective. **£15.00**

239. **HOOPER, W. Eden.** The History of Newgate and the Old Bailey, and a Survey of the Fleet Prison. 1935. 1st edition. Illus. xvi, 176pp. Orig. cloth. Fine. **£10.00**

240. **HOPE of Craighall, Sir Thomas.** Practical Observations upon Divers Titles of the Law of Scotland. Commonly called . . . Minor Practicks. Ed. John Spottiswood. Edinburgh, 1734. 1st thus. viii, 554pp. Contemp. cf., sl. rbbd. S. & M. v.52. **£50.00**
Includes as an appendix an account of religious houses in Scotland, extracted by Spottiswood's son from among his father's papers.

241. **HORSMAN, Gilbert, & others.** Precedents in Conveyancing. 1757. 2nd ed. 2 vols. Folio. Index. Contemp. cf., rbbd.; heads of sps. sl. torn. S. & M. i.482. **£80.00**
Gives a comprehensive view of the many commercial matters into which the conveyancer's province had been extended since the Statute of Frauds.

242. **HOTTOMAN (HOTMAN), Francois (1524-1590).** De legibus populi Romani liber. Basle (apud Episcopium iuniorem), 1557. 1st edition. Device on title, & another on verso of last leaf. Index. (xvi), 86, (ii)pp. Early ownership inscription of Georges Grillot & others. Contemporary calf, re-backed, sides worn. **£200.00**
Hottoman's reputation as a lawyer has no rival except his reputation as a controversialist. This aspect, however, has no place in the present work; it is a dictionary of Roman Republican laws, with a short account of the contents of each & of the source from which we know it.

243. **HUGHES (W.).** Queries; or Choice Cases for MOOTS, containing several Points of Law, not resolved in the books. Being very useful for the Students of the Common Lawes. Collected by William Hughes. 12mo. George Dawes, 1675. Partly black letter. Publishers' book list at end. Lacks A_1 (blank ?). Modern calf. S. & M. i.23:22. Wing H. 3329. **£55.00**

244. **HUNT, Arthur Joseph.** The Law relating to Fraudulent Conveyances, under the Statutes of Elizabeth and the Bankrupt Acts . . . Law relating to Bills of Sale. 1872. 1st edition. Index. xxiv, 256, 48pp. Publisher's cat. at end. Lib. stamp on title. Orig. cloth, faded. S. & M. ii.176. **£20.00**
Second of two works on the subject published in 1871-2 as a result of changes in the bankruptcy laws.

245. **HURST, Sir Gerald.** A Short History of Lincoln's Inn. 1946. 2nd imp. Illus. Index. viii, 86pp. Orig. cloth, fine in d.w. **£5.00**

246. **H(UTTON), Sir R.** The Young Clarks Guide; or, an Exact Collection of English Presidents . . . of Indentures. Letters of Attorney, Releases, Conditions &c. By T.R. and M.D. for Ambrose Isted . . . and Samuel Herick, 1670. 12th imp. Pt. 1 (of 3) only. Index. (xvi), 336pp. Sm. hole in F_5 aff. few letters. Few leaves sl. soiled. Mod. ½ cf./cl. sides. S. & M. i.483. **£30.00**
The fullest collection of forms then available. This volume covers indentures, assignments, releases, letters of attorney, covenants, bills, wills & conditions.

247. **HUTTON, W(illiam).** Courts of Requests; their Nature, Utility, and Powers Described, with a Variety of Cases, Determined in that of Birmingham. Birmingham, 1787. 1st edition. ½ title. xvi, 430pp. Some spotting. Contemp. ½ calf; rebacked; sides worn. S. & M. i.391. **£60.00**
Courts of Requests (tribunals for the adjustment of minor disputes on broadly equitable lines) were set up in a few towns from the 16th century onwards. Hutton, a Commissioner of the Birmingham Court for fifteen years, gives an amusing account of its personalities & proceedings & the cases that passed before it.

248. **IBBETSON, James.** Three Dissertations. I. On the Folclande and Boclande of the Saxons. II. On the Judicial Customs . . . III. On the National Assemblies under the Saxon and Norman Governments. 1782. 2nd edition. (ii), 170pp. Lacks final blank. Some spotting. Contemp. calf, rebacked, edges worn. S. & M. i.41. **£40.00**
Ibbetson ranks himself with those who believed that both the feudal and the constitutional system were highly developed before the Conquest.

249. **IMPEY, John.** The Practice of the Office of Sheriff and Under Sheriff . . . Practice of the Office of Coroner. 1812. 3rd edition. First advert. leaf. Index. xiv, 600, 8pp. Contemp. calf, rebacked, sl. rubbed. S. & M. ii.179. **£25.00**

250. **INDERWICK, F.A. (edited & introduced).** The Inner Temple: its early history, as illustrated by its Records. 1505-1603. Pub'd by the order of the Masters of the Bench and sold by Henry Sotheran and others. 4to. 1896. 1st edition. xcviii, 536pp. Index, glossary, fp., uncut. Orig. cloth backed boards, uncut. Boards faded. **£20.00**
F.A. Inderwick also wrote a History of the Law Courts in 1895.

251. **INDIAN STATUTORY COMMISSION.** Report. H.M.S.O. 1930. 1st edition. Vol. 1 (Survey) only. Folding maps. Orig. wraps; faded. **£10.00**
Vol. 2 contained the recommendations of the Commission; there were fifteen further volumes of memoranda.

252. **INNER TEMPLE.** Catalogue of the Paintings, Engravings, Serjeants' Rings, Plate, Stained Glass, Sculpture, etc. belonging to the Hon. Society of the Inner Temple. Folio. Printed by order of the Masters of the Bench 1915. (Chiswick Press.) Revised edition of the 1891 list of the Portraits and Prints. ix, 159pp. Uncut. t.e.g. Fine fp. port. of Sir Edward Coke and other ports. and plates. Morocco backed cloth, lacking spine. **£25.00**

253. **INNES, Cosmo.** Lectures on Scotch Legal Antiquities. Edinburgh, 1872. 1st. Appendix. Index. xvi, 326pp. Contemp. panelled calf; t.e.g., rebacked. FINE COPY. S. & M. v.53. **£40.00**
Originally delivered in the Advocates' Library, 1868-9. Innes (a great student of records), argues that the old writers (notably Skene) had distorted not only the history but the character of Scots law by using Roman parallels to piece out the imperfections of their own knowledge, thus making the law as a whole appear far nearer to the civil law than in fact it was.

254. ————. Lectures on Scotch Legal Antiquities. Edinburgh, 1872. Another copy. Orig. cloth; spine faded, sl. shaken. **£35.00**

255. **IRELAND, General Prisons Board.** First Report. Dublin (H.M.S.O.) 1879. 1st edition. 133pp. Title-page pasted to e-p. Few inner margins affected by crude sewing. Old ½ calf; worn. **£10.00**

256. **IVES, George.** The Classification of Crimes. 1904. 1st edition PRIVATELY PRINTED. 4to. INSCRIBED by the Author. (ii), 66pp. Contemp. MS. annots. & additional references. Contemp. ½ calf; rebacked with orig. spine. **£30.00**
A chapter from an unpublished work on "The History of Penal Methods", in which the author distinguishes between "crimes of circumstance" which are punishable as deliberate offences, & "crimes of impulse" which should be viewed as symptoms of disease.

257. **JACOB, Giles (1686-1744).** The Complete Court-Keeper; or, Land-Steward's Assistant: Containing, Courts Leet and Courts Baron, etc. 1741: by Henry Lintot. 4th ed. enlarged. 8vo. Index. Some marg. worm. sl. aff. text of a few pages. A sm. hole in A_3. Bk-pl.: Wm. Wynne. Contemp. cf. rbbd. Sp. sl. torn at tail. Blind-stamped. S. & M. i.400/26. **£50.00**
A compendium covering a diverse range of duties from the manner of holding Courts Leet and Courts Baron to precedents of contracts and leases.

258. ————. A New Law-Dictionary. 1736: by E. and R. Nutt. 3rd ed., enlarged. Fol. Index. Unpaged. Bk-pl.: Watkin Williams. Contemp. cf. worn, sp. torn & pt. of head missing. Otherwise, a fine copy. S. & M. i.9/33. **£130.00**
Jacob's law Dictionary, based on Cowell's is the standard work of the 18th century. This edition is the first to incorporate English forms for law-proceedings, pursuant to the late statute.

259. ————. A New Law-Dictionary: containing, the Interpretation and Definition of Words and Terms Used in the Law. 1736. 3rd edition. Folio. Sm. holes in $5Q_1$ & $7M_1$, affecting few letters. Sl. stained & sl. wormed at inner margin. Modern cloth. S. & M. i.9. **£115.00**

260. ———— A New Law-Dictionary: containing the Interpretation and Definition of Words and Terms used in the Law; and also the Whole Law and the Practice thereof . . . Henry Lintot and others 1756. Folio. The seventh edition, the law proceedings being done into English with great additions and improvements. Some sl. worming at lower margin in first few pages, not affecting text. No paging. Contemp. calf. Hinges worn and some sl. wear of spine ends. A very fine copy. S. & M. i.9.33. **£95.00**

261. ————. The Statute-Law Common-Plac'd: or, a Second General Table to the Statutes. 1719. 1st. Index. Two advert leaves at end. Contemp. cf., rbbd. S. & M. i.548. **£30.00**

262. ————. The Student's Companion: or, the Reason for the Laws of England. 1734. 2nd edition, corrected. Index. Some ink marks on inside of cvr. Contemp. cf. sl. rbbd. S. & M. i.34/46. **£60.00**
An attempt to supply the law with that logical background the want of which is so much felt in all the older "institutes" and hand-books. The prolific Jacob declares this his favourite work.

263. **(JANE, Joseph).** Eikon Aklastos (Gr.) The Image Unbroken . . . The Impudence, Falsehood, Vanitie and Prophannes . . . in a Libell entitled Eikonoclastes (Greek). N.p. (Netherlands). Printed . . . 1651. 1st edition. Sm. 4to. 71, 56-267pp. Sig. & pagination of quires H & I repeated. Some contemp. MS. corrections. Modern ¼ calf. WING J.156. Almack P.74. **£60.00**
A reply, section by section, to Milton's strictures on the Eikon Basilike; sometimes ascribed to John Earle, the Latin translator of the Eikon.

264. **JARMAN, Thomas.** A treatise on Wills. 1855. 2nd edition, edited E.P. Wolstenholme and S. Vincent. 2 vols. Index. Publisher's catalogue inserted in vol. 1. Last 36pp. of table of cases misbound after p. 32. Sl. spotted. Orig. cloth, faded; vol. 1 recased; vol. 2 shaken. S. & M. ii.185. **£30.00**
Like Mr. Spenlow, the author of this immense standard work never found time to make a will of his own.

265. **JENKINS, David.** The Works . . . upon divers Statutes concerning the King's Prerogative and the Liberty of the Subject. By Samuel Roycroft, for Samuel Heyrick. n.d. (1681). (6th edition). 12mo. Engraved fp. port. Index. (xvi), 94pp. Lower margins sl. wormed. Contemp. sheep, worn. WING J.579. S. & M. i.157. **£50.00**
Jenkins, a Welsh judge wrote this while in prison in Newgate, on the Rump's orders. The principal thesis is that the King cannot be deposed by Parliament because he is part of Parliament himself.

266. **JENKS, Edward.** Law & Politics in the Middle Ages. N.Y. 1912. 3rd imp. following the 1st London edition. Index. Table of sources. xiv, 352pp. Orig. cloth, sl. faded. **£8.00**

267. **JUSTINIAN I, Emperor.** Corpus iuris civilis cum summariis, argumentis, epitomis, & indicibus cl. v. Dionysii Gothofredi. Geneva (J. Vignon), 1620. 4to. Index. Numbered in columns. Vellum thumb-tag at fore-margin at beginning of each book. Sl. wormed. Contemp. cf., rbbd., head of sp. frayed. **£40.00**

268. ————. Corpus juris civilis . . . cum notis . . . Dionysii Gothofredi . . . Pauli receptae sententiae orum selectis notis J. Cujacii . . . Antonii Anselmo . . . observationes. Amsterdam (Blaeu, Elzevir & Hackius), 1664. 2 vols. in 1. Engr. title. Index. Thumb-tags pasted to fore-margins (some torn away). Contemp. blind-stamped vellum, lacks ties. **£35.00**
Without Notes.

269. ————. Corpus iuris civilis . . . cum summariis, argumentis, epitomis, & indicibus cl. v. Dionysii Gothofredi. Amsterdam, 1700. 2 vols. in 1. General engr. title. 7 blank leaves (2 with annots.) bound before vol. 2. Index. Vellum tabs on fore-edges. Contemp. cf., sp. gilt; tail of sp. broken. Bk-pl. **£25.00**

270. ————. Institutionum . . . libri IIII. Ed. Gregorius Haloander. Paris (ex officina Roberti Stephani), 1534. 1st thus. Device on title. Index. Final colophon leaf. Table of consanguinity sl. cropped. Not in B.M.C., Melanthon, Philil (1497-1560); De legibus oratio . . . de gradibus oratio (-Praefatic in Aeschinis et Demosthenis orationes). Paris (ex officina Roberti Stephani), 1534. 1st collected. Device on title. Final blank. 62, (ii)pp. B.M.C.: (French) p. 309. Two works in one vol. Faintly ruled in ink throughout. 18th-cent. cf., gilt; upper jt. worn; sl. rbbd. **£150.00**
Two fine examples of Parisian printing at the beginning of its most splendid era. The speeches of Melanthon, most accomplished of the early Lutherans, seem to date from his youthful studies at Tubingen; although as yet unknown to Luther, he already complains of religious tyranny & of the hatred shown to the jurists (who were beginning to connect themselves with the spirit of the Renaissance).

271. ————. Institutionum . . . libri . . . ex antiquissimis exemplaribus repraesentati, per Ant. Contium. (-Enchiridion titulorum . . . de verborum ac rerum significatione . . . de regulis iuris (etc.)). Paris, 1560. 2 pts. in 1 vol. 1st thus. Indices. Lacks final blank. Old annots. Sl. stnd. 19th-cent. cf., rebacked. **£60.00**
An early annotated edition, collated with the Greek of Theophilus.

272. ————. Institouta Theophilou antikensoros (Greek) Institutiones, Theophilo . . . Interprete . . . Paratitla et notae . . . Dionysio Gothofredo I.C. authore. N.p. (Paris), 1587. 1st thus. 4to. Gk. & Latin text. Index. Sl. stnd. Contemp. vellum. Not in B.M.C. **£80.00**
Theophilus's Greek version of the Institutes made for the many "Romans" who knew no Latin, is often a valuable guide to the construction of the original. This edition of Gothofredus, or Godefroy (1549-1622) includes not only the original Latin but also the Latin version made from the Greek by J. Curtius.

273. ————. Institutiones . . . typis variae, rubris nucleum exhibentibus (ed. A. Corvinus). Paris, 1676. 16mo. Engr. & printed titles in red & black throughout. Glossary. Final blank. Sl. stnd. Contemp. cf., rubbed; jts. worn. **£25.00**
The little edition of Corvinus (first pubd. Leyden, 1661) has one novelty; the most important passages are printed in red to form a summary or abridgement.

274. **KEBLE, Joseph.** An Assistance to Justices of the Peace. By W. Rawlins, S. Roycroft, and H. Sawbridge . . . for Ch. Harper, 1683. 1st edition. Folio. Black letter. First privilege leaf. Index. Several irregularities in pagination etc. caused by change of printer. Few sm. marginal worm-holes. Contemp. calf, tail of sp. sl. torn, some leaves loose. WING K.113. S. & M. i.229. **£60.00**
Keble's work was designed as a supplement to the standard justices' manuals, whose provisions it abridges alphabetically. In a preliminary section, everything in the statute-book which concerns justices is set out at length.

275. ————. Reports in . . . King's Bench . . . from the XII. to the XXX. Year of . . . King Charles II. By W. Rawlins (etc.) for Thomas Dring (etc.), 1685. 1st. 3 vols. Folio. Black letter. Indices (complete). Lacks end-papers. Mod. Wing K.116. S. & M. i.302. **£120.00**
Keble was one of the first to publish his own reports (as opposed to translating other men's) in English. The tables, sometimes bound separately, are included in the appropriate volumes.

276. **KELHAM, Robert.** Domesday Book Illustrated . . . Tenants in Capite or Serjanty therein mentioned . . . Translation of the Difficult Passages, 1788. 1st edition. viii, 400pp. S_1 a cancel. Orig. boards, uncut, rebacked, worn. S. & M. i.92. **£30.00**
The first general commentary on Domesday Book, which had been made available for study in Farley's great type-facsimile edition in 1783.

277. **KELLER, F.L.** Ueber Litis Contestation und Urtheil nach classischem Romischen Recht, Zurich 1827. 1st edition. German text. Index. Modern cloth. **£20.00**
Examination of civil proceedings in the light of the Institutes of Gaius & other sources recently discovered or examined.

278. **KILBURN, Richard.** Choice Presidents upon All Acts of Parliament, relating to the Office and Duty of a Justice of Peace . . . Cases . . . Method of Making up Court Rolls. By the Assigns of Rich. and Edw. Atkins . . . for Richard Tonson. 1681. 2nd edition. 12mo. Index. (iv) 418pp. Some side-notes shaved. F_{11} sl. torn. New ¼ calf. WING K.429. (Bibl. Nationale, Paris only). S. & M. i.229. **£80.00**

279. ————. Choice Presidents upon all Acts of Parliament . . . as above. Ed. G.F. For Mary Tonson, 1700. 6th edition. ½ title. Index. Final blank. Some spotting. Contemp. calf, sl. worn. WING K.433. S. & M. i.229. **£60.00**

280. **LANGFORD, John Alfred.** Prison Books and Their Authors. 1861. 1st edition. Wood-engraved portraits. xii, 358pp. Orig. dec'd cloth, rubbed, faded. **£20.00**
Boethius, Raleigh, Cervantes, Bunyan etc.

281. **LAUTERBECK, Georg.** Regentenbuch . . . allen Regenten und Oberkeiten zu Anrichtung und Besserung erbarer und guter Policey, christlich und nötig zu wissen (Leipzig, durch Jacobum Berwald), 1559. FOLIO. German text. Schwabacher letter. Woodcut device on final leaf, & initials. (xii), 224, (ii) leaves. Two blanks at end. Blank piece cut from title. First quire sl. frayed; sl. stained.
– **MEURER, Noe.** Von forstlicher Oberherrligkeit unnd Gerechtigkeit, was die Recht, der Gebrauch, die Billigkeit deszhalben vermöq. (Pforzheim, bey Georg Raben), 1560. 1st edition. FOLIO. German text. Fraktur letter. Hohenzollern arms on verso of title. Final device. 100 leaves. Margins sl. stained. 2 works in 1 volume. Some old annotations. Contemp. blind-stamped pig, clasps, very worn. **£400.00**
Lauterbeck's work (dedicated to the Counts of Mansfeld, ten brothers in whose service he was) is a treatise of government in which the authentic spirit of primitive German liberty speaks through a cloud of Roman illustration; he asserts the responsibility of a ruler to the law, the sanctity of an oath, and the beauties of peace, with chapters on education, currency, & other matters of municipal law.
At the end he translates a fragment of Musonius, the Stoic philosopher, on a similar subject. Meurer, author of several law-books, discusses the rights of the forest – hunting, fishing, possession of timber & wild beasts etc. – in the light of civil and canon law.

282. **A LAW GRAMMAR;** or, an Introduction to the Theory and Practice of English Jurisprudence. 1791. 1st edition. ½ title. Index. B_1 and B_2 cancels. Last leaf sl. wormed. Contemp. calf, sl. worn. S. & M. i.34. **£60.00**
A better-documented & more scientific work than Jacob's of the same title, which however it failed to supersede.

283. The LAW of SEWERS; or, Office and Authority of Commissioners of Sewers, (with) the Laws relating to Rumney Marsh and other marshes and fens. 1732. 2nd edition. Contemp. calf, newly re-backed label. Fine copy. **S. & M. i.471.10.** **£40.00**
Author unknown.

284. The LAW QUARTERLY REVIEW. Vol. 59 no. 1 – vol. 90 no. 4 (January 1943-October 1974) lacking only vol. 60 no. 3 (July 1944). Orig. wraps, early issues faded & some spines sl. torn. **127 issues.** **£200.00**

285. LESSIUS, Leonardus (1554-1623). De iustitia et iure caeterisque virtutibus cardinalibus libri quatuor. Antwerp (ex officina Plantiniana), 1612. 3rd edition, revised. Folio. Engraved title. Index. Final device leaf. (xvi), 804, (lxviii)pp. One leaf sl. stained. Contemp. calf, 18th-cent. rebacking & cornering; tail of sp. & edges sl. worn. **£150.00**
This work is a commentary on the Secunda Secundae of Aquinas, with one book devoted to each of the cardinal virtues – Prudence, Justice, Fortitude, & Temperance. However, book 2 (Justice), which extends far beyond the sphere of Aquinas, occupies four-fifths of the entire work. Written with the precision of the Aristotelian method, the work is a remarkable contribution to jurisprudential literature.

286. ——————. **De iustitia et iure** ceterisq; **virtutibus cardinalibus libri** quatuor ... cum **appendice de monte** pietatis. Antwerp (ex officina Plantiniana), 1626. 6th edition, revised. Folio. Fine engraved title (Galle after Rubens). Index. (xvi), 826, (lxviii)pp. Ownership inscription on title, "Monasterii Gantinipratensis in bellinghen". Lib. stamp on *2. Contemp. blind-stamped calf over wooden boards (probably a Monastery binding); sp. & corner repaired, jts. cracked. **£150.00**
In 1619 the Austrian rulers of Belgium, wishing to break the power which Italian money-lenders held over the nation's capital, established a system of monts-de-pieté. Some prelates condemned this institution as contrary to the Church's teaching on usury. Lessius proves in his appendix that the Bull of Leo X., which was appealed to, did not apply to the Belgian scheme.

287. LEVINGE, Edward P. The Justice's Manual. Dublin, 1857. 2nd edition. Index. xii, 352pp. Few sm. worm-holes at end. Few leaves sl. creased. Modern cloth. **£25.00**
Afterwards expanded as "The Justice of the Peace for Ireland", & so reprinted for thirty years.

288. LEVINZ, Sir Creswell. Reports of ... Cases ... in the Court of King's Bench, (and Common Pleas) during the Time that Sir Robert Foster, Sir Robert Hyde, and Sir John Kelyng were Chief Justices ... 1722. 2nd. **1 vol.** (3 parts bound together). Folio. An index to each part. Mod. cl. **S. & M. i.303/81.** **£40.00**
Translated into English by Serjeant Salkeld et al. *with the original and translation in double columns. Probably the last book written in law-French.*

289. LINDENBROGIUS, Fridericus (c.1560-1638) (ed.). Codex legum antiquarum ... quibus accedunt formulae solennes (sic) ... nunc primum editae; et glossarium. Frankfurt (apud Iohannem et Andream Marnios), 1613. 1st edition. Folio. Index. Final errata leaf. (xxiv), 1570, (ii)pp. Some browning. Old sprinkled sheep, spine gilt; jts. edges & foot of spine worn. **£140.00**
This was for 200 years the standard collection of the Teutonic codes & other enactments, civil & ecclesiastical, of the early middle ages.

290. LITTLETON, Sir Thomas (fl.1445-1481). Les Tenures ... ovesque certeine Cases addes per auters de puisne Temps. For the Companie of Stationers, 1608. 12mo. French text. Black letter. Index. (i), 170, (xxiv) leaves. Lacks final blank. Few old annotations. 18th-century sheep, spine gilt, rubbed. **S.T.C. 15775. S. & M. i.455.** **£150.00**
The original text of the old Testament of English land law. The name of William West, author of the excellent book of precedents called "Symboleography", is subjoined to the Index. A scarce edition of which only three copies are recorded.

291. LIVES and EXPLOITS of the Most Noted HIGHWAYMEN, ROBBERS and MURDERERS. Brought Down to the Present Time. Hartford (Conn. U.S.A.), 1851. Revised edition. Wood-engravings. 287pp. Sl. stained. Mod. cloth. **£10.00**
The last case included is that of James Porter and is of American origin.

292. The LIVES and EXPLOITS of the MOST CELEBRATED ROBBERS & BANDITTI. Philadelphia, Pa. (G.G. Evans), n.d. (c.1860). Hand-col'd lith. fp. & wood-engr. plates. 284, 22pp. Orig. cl., gilt; fdd.; jts. & corners rbbd. **£20.00**

293. LOUTHIAN, John. The Form of Process before the Court of Justiciary in Scotland; containing the Constitution of the Sovereign Criminal Court and ... Circuit Courts. Edinburgh, 1732. 1st. vi, 302, (ii)pp. Final errata leaf. Contemp. cf., sp. rbbd. **S. & M. v.71.** **£35.00**
A short manual of criminal court practice & the rules of evidence, written for the layman & reflecting the dangerous imbalance between the Lord Advocate, who himself or by deputy managed all prosecutions, & the ignorant pannel (prisoner) defended on the equivalent of a dock brief.

294. LUMLEY, W.G. The Rating Act, 1874 ... Addendum to the Law of Parochial Assessments. 1874. 1st edition. Index. (ii), 52pp.
CIRCULAR of the LOCAL GOVERNMENT BOARD. 1874. 1st edition. 12pp. **Two works in 1 vol.** As issued. 24pp. Adverts. Orig. cloth, sl. fdd. **£10.00**

295. LYCKLAMA, Van NIJHOLDT, Marc. Membranarum libri septem, in quibus ... de rebus ... per sectas nostrorum temporum maxime controversis commentarii. Leeuwarden (apud Joannem Jansonium), 1644. 2nd edition. 4to. Index. (xvi), 354, (xvi)pp. FINE COPY in contemporary vellum. **£150.00**
This Frisian jurist discusses numerous controverted questions in the Corpus, with a few from other writers, with the intention of resolving the disputes of over-zealous scholars, whose effect had often been (as he says) that "what was certain in the law is made uncertain".

296. (LYTTELTON, George, Lord) (1709-1773). Considerations upon the Present State of our Affairs ... in a Letter to a Member of Parliament. 1739. 1st edition. First line of title sl. cropped. Modern cloth. **KRESS 443.** **£10.00**
Chiefly concerned with the event of the war with Spain, & with suggested reforms of the jury system.

297. MACCLESFIELD, Earl of v. Countess of. Further Considerations for the Earl of Macclesfield's (sic) Bill. n.d. (c.1700). 1st edition. Folio. 4pp. Sp. & first leaf repaired with sl. damage. Sl. frayed. **£20.00**
Maintains that Lady Macclesfield's adultery operated so effectively to dissolve her marriage that she could lay no claim to dower thereafter.

298. (——————). Bishop Cozens's Argument, Proving that Adultery works a Dissolution of the Marriage ... Substance of Several ... Speeches. n.d. (c.1700). 1st edition. Folio. 4pp. Sp. repaired. **£20.00**
In this celebrated divorce case, the Bishop's contribution was to argue, on the authority of canon law, that the marriage & all the wife's rights depending on it were extinguished by her misconduct.

299. MACKENZIE, of Rosehaugh, (Sir), George (1636-1691). Idea eloquentiae forensis hodiernae: una cum actione forensi ex unaquaque juris parte. Edinburgh, excudebat Haeres Andreae Anderson, 1681. 1st. Latin text. (xii), 182pp. Final blank. A_3 torn without loss; fore-margin of E_4 defective. Contemp. sheep, rubbed. **Wing M.164. S. & M. v.74.** **£60.00**
Mackenzie laments that the eloquence of Scots advocates is never preserved as an example to the student and he gives Latin versions of six of his own speeches, with general remarks on the duties & qualifications for speaking at the bar.
An English edition of this work under the title "Idea of the Modern Eloquence of the Bar"; together with a Pleading out of every part of Law, was published in 1711.

300. ——————. Idea eloquentiae forensis hodiernae: una cum actione forensi ex unaquaque juris parte. Edinburgh, excudebat Haeres Andreae Anderson, 1681. 1st. Latin text. (xii), 182pp. Final blank. Contemp. calf, sl. rubbed; jts. sl. cracked; last few pages sl. browned. **£60.00**

301. ——————. Idea eloquentiae ... 1681. 1st. Another copy. A_3 torn without loss; fore-margin of E_4 sl. defective. Contemp. sheep rubbed. **£60.00**

302. ——————. Observations upon the XVII. Act Parliament XXIII. K. James VI. against Dispositions made in Defraud of Creditors, etc. Edinburgh, by the Heirs and Successors of Andrew Anderson ... for Mr. Andrew Symson. 1699. Second ed. Folio. (iv), 62pp. Lacks final blank. Several contemp. corrections. Title-border cropped at head. Mod. cl. **Wing M.189 (none outside U.K.). Aldis 3866.5. S. & M. v.74.** **£60.00**

303. ——————. Pleadings, in some ... **Cases,** before the ... Courts of Scotland, since ... 1661. Edinburgh, 1704. 16mo. (viii), 296pp. Margins of F_1 & G_1 sl. defective, aff. one line. Fore-margins short; one sl. cropped. Old cf., re-backed, sides rbbd. **S. & M. v.74.** **£35.00**

304. MACLAURIN, (John) (later Lord Dreghorn). Arguments and Decisions, in Remarkable Cases, before the High Court of Justiciary, and other Supreme Courts, in Scotland. Edinburgh, 1774. 1st edition. 4to. Index. Final advert. leaf. Contemp. calf, spine gilt, label. Sl. rubbed. Front e-p loose. Fine Copy. **S. & M. v.76.** **£60.00**
A far more learned work than Arnot's more famous collection. Maclaurin's cases, in some of which he himself took part, include R. v Maclauchlan *(1737) (interesting questions of the definition of treason & the effect of drunkenness on liability, arising from the Porteous riots) &* Macintosh v. Dempster *(1767) (discussion of the extent of Parliamentary privilege in regard to arrest & prosecution).*

305. ——————. Arguments and Decisions ... 1774. Another copy. Modern cloth. **£60.00**

306. MAINE, Sir Henry Sumner. Dissertations on Early Law and Custom. 1883. 1st edition. Index. Orig. cloth, faded. **S. & M. i.597.** **£15.00**
With the aid of recently-circulated knowledge of Sanskrit jurisprudence – which he collates with that of the Romans, Franks & other Teutons, & above all of the Irish – Maine continues the studies initiated by his "Ancient Law".

307. MALE, Arthur. A Treatise on the Law and Practice of Elections. 1820. 2nd edition. Appendix of forms, statutes, etc. Index. (xxiv)pp. Modern ½ calf. **S. & M. ii.231.** **£25.00**
Includes a list of constituencies, with notes of their governing bodies, their returning officer, & the qualifications of their electors.

308. MANUSCRIPT. CHAMBERS, Robert (Barrister). Notices of some of the most Useful Manuscripts in the British Museum arranged alphabetically with a View to facilitate Searches as to Title and Descent of Lands, 1830. Manuscript on paper; black ink, ruled in red. 218pp. Contemp. calf, upper cover & spine detached. **£20.00**
Neatly written on every other page, this manuscript notebook gives ms. reference numbers and some indication of what they contain.

309. ——————. Lex Terr(a)e explained by a Digest of the Matt(er)s in Litt(leton's) Tenures ... Cokes Commentaries ... illustrated by the application of most of the Cases to some Maxime & recd. Rule of Law. N.d. (after 1676). MS. on paper in a chancery hand. 206pp. First & last leaves mounted. Purchase note on e-p. of W.H. Black (1808-72) of the Public Record Office. Some margins wormed; few head-lines cropped. Mod. ¼ mor. Bk-pl. **£60.00**
With an appendix of 206 maxims & a leaf of abbreviations.

310. ——————. **LYNDESAY, H.:** An Epitome of Duries Practices ... containing the Matter and Substance of the ... Practices contained in the Prin(cip)le (sic) Books by Sir John NISBET. N.p. (Edinburgh), n.d. (c.1700). Sm. 4to. Index. (ii), 424, (96)pp. Contemp. sheep; clasps & ends of sp. defective; rbbd. **£80.00**
An alphabetical digest from the works of Sir A. Gibson (Lord Durie) & the celebrated Nisbet of Dirleton. The last 96pp. are blank except for a few acts of convention of Edinburgh (1717) & a resolution of Kirkcudbright justices concerning the poor (1725) in a second hand.

311. ——————. (Maxims, precedents, & definitions). n.d. (c.1718). Sm. 4to. 7 blank leaves/490pp. 28 blanks cut out at end. Contemp. vellum; sl. faded. **£50.00**
The emphasis of this work is on London & Middlesex county court forms & practice and also those of King's Bench.

312. ——————. **(PHILLIPS 20108). MEDLYCOTT, James** (Master in Chancery, appointed 1706). Report and Schedule of Accounts in the case Waller v. Southwell. 1716. Folio. 92pp. Upper margins repaired throughout, some words obscured; marginal defects toward end aff. few lines of c.20 leaves; last leaf soiled; fore-margins shaved. Modern ½ calf. **Phillips MS.20108.** **£60.00**
After four years' debate, Edward Southwell, steward to the late James Waller (an Irish landowner) is cleared of the charge of embezzlement brought by Waller's executors. This volume digests the statements of witnesses as to the translations involved.

313. ——————. (Precedents, maxims & definitions.) N.p. n.d. (1615-1628). Folio. French text. Last few leaves sl. frayed & soiled. Early names of John Whittacre & John Stockman on last leaf. Contemp. blind-stamped cf., MS. guards (Missal, early 15th cent.) re-backed with orig. spine. **£120.00**
A very thorough & detailed commonplace book in alphabetical order, written in a single though variable semi-italic hand & ruled in red. The sources are the Year-books of Edward IV (with occasional cases from other reigns). Reports from Plowden to Coke & (very rarely) Fitzherbert's Natura Brevium & "Doctor & Student". John Stockman was admitted to the Middle Temple on 10th Nov. 1611, & John Whittacres (sic) to Lincoln's Inn on 24th Oct. 1612.

314. ——————. **De la SERNA, Diego.** Re(col)lectio de servitutibus pr(a)edialibus ... ad explicat(ion) em t(itu)li ff. de Servitutibus. N.p., n.d. (Spanish, late 17th cent.). 4to. 71 leaves, the least two blank. Closely written in a neat hand, with calligraphic headings & colophon. Contemp. vellum, ties sl. defective; sl. mkd. **Phillips MS.4526.** **£50.00**
Probably arranged by one Guerra, whose name is on the title in the same hand as the rest, from a course of lectures; however, it is not a collection of detached notes, but a coherent treatise with full references. We cannot identify it with any published work.

315. MARANTA or MARANTE, Roberto. Tractatus de ordine iudiciorum ... intitutlatus Speculum Aureum et Lumen Aduocatorum. Venice (apud Cominum de Tridino), 1549. Device on title. Woodcut initials. Index. 172, (xl)pp. Some worming of inner margin; few holes in text in quires L-Q. Sl. frayed. Contemp. limp vellum, soiled & worn; loose in covers; lacks ties. Not in BMC. **£70.00**
Revised edition, with summaries & an index by Giambattista Ziletti, of a treatise on jurisdiction written in 1520-5. The author touches on usury ("a species of rapine"), the use of torture ("may be resorted to without evidence, if only used to gain an answer 'Yes' or 'No' ") and the thousand-year-old struggle between the Lombardic & Roman codes for mastery in Italy.

316. MARCH, John. Reports: or, New Cases; Taken in the 15, 16, 17 and 18 Years of King Charles the First. By J.C. for Samuel Heyrick, 1675. 2nd edition. 4to. First blank. Blank $2F_2$. Index. Two sm. marginal defects in $2G_1$ each aff. one letter. Modern ½ calf. **WING M.577. S. & M. i.304.** **£40.00**
Reprinted from the edition of 1648, March revived the old year-book habit of quoting the exact words of judges & counsel.

317. MARESCOTTO, Ercole. Vaviarum resolutionum liber primus, & secundus. Rome, 1614. 1st. **2 vols. in 1.** Folio. Red & black title. Indices. Some browning. Contemp. vellum, re-backed; lacks ties; worn. **£40.00**
Observations founded on proceedings in the Vatican, & Neapolitan courts, by a member of a celebrated Roman family.

318. MAZZEI, Francesco. De Legitimo actionis spolii usu commentarius. Rome, 1773. 1st edition. 4to. Red & black title. Index. viii, 156pp. One quire loose. Later wraps; sp. torn. **£20.00**
The scope of the Actio spolii, or civil action to regain stolen property, had been obscured by a passage in the canon law which had lately been exposed as spurious.

319. MECKEN, Bodo Heinrich. Disputatio juridica de chirographo, praecipue vero eo, quod per vim extortum esse dicitur. Jena, 1673. 1st. 4to. (40)pp. Mod. bds. **£20.00**
Doctoral thesis on the cases in which a deed was rendered invalid by duress of the signatory.

320. MEREWETHER, Henry Alworth, & Archibald John STEPHENS. The History of the Borough and Municipal Corporations of the United Kingdom. 1835. 1st edition. **3 vols.** ½ titles. Index. Modern ½ calf. **Gross 79. S. & M. i.417.** **£80.00**
The notions of the antiquity, purity & equality of the English Local Government system which were promulgated by Sharpe & adopted by Oldfied, are still apparent in Merewether's scholarly compilation, but the solid foundation of documents on which it rests bring this work to a high level of accuracy.

321. MIDDLETON, Conyers (1683-1750). A Treatise on the Roman Senate. 1747. 1st complete edition. First advert. leaf. (ii), 196pp. Remarks on two Pamphlets ... against (the) Introductory Discourse. 1748. 1st edition. ½ title. (ii), xl, 128pp. (STEBBING, Henry) Observations on ... an Introductory Discourse. 1747. 1st edition. 34pp. **Three works in 1 vol.** Mod. ¼ calf. **£40.00**
The second part of the Treatise, being a discussion of the authority & procedure of the senate, is here added to an earlier publication. The rest of the collection is concerned with Middleton's attack on belief in the miraculous powers of the early Christians.

322. MINOT, George Richards. The History of the Insurrections in Massachusetts, in 1786. Boston, James W. Burditt, 1810. 2nd edition. iv, 5-192pp., uncut. Orig. boards, backstrip frayed and loose. With the book-plate of The Lucius M. Boltwood Historical and Genealogical Collection, in the Jones Library Inc. Amherst, Mass including a portrait of Lucius M. Boltwood. Pages spotted mainly at edges of some quires. **£40.00**
History of Shay's Rebellion which was thought to have influenced Constitutional Convention to write "Conservative" constitution.

323. The MIRROR (led & mainly edited by Henry MACKENZIE). Nos. 1-110. January 23, 1779-May 27, 1780. **3 vols.** 1781. 3rd ed., corrected. Full calf, sl. rubbed. All published. **£35.00**
First appeared in Edinburgh & appeared twice weekly with contributions from well known men of the day. It was written by its "Society (of Gentlemen)" which consisted of six young advocates who wrote most of the papers. Altogether 39 essays by Mackenzie who assisted with several others; William Craig 16; Alexander Abercromby probably 11; George Horne (a clerk in the Court of Session) 16; William McLeod Bannatyne 5 & Robert Cullen 3. Other contributions came from Prof. William Richardson of Glasgow; Lord Hailes; Dr. William Beattie; David Hume (nephew of the historian); Prof. Frazer Tytler, Alexander Craig & Baron Jordan of the Exchange of Scotland. The essays were, for the most part, serious and well written, and the "Mirror's" popularity in book form was so great that by 1783 5 editions had been published.

324. The MODERN LAW REVIEW. Quarterly (bi-monthly from vol. 17) Vol. 9 no. 1-vol. 37 no. 6. (January 1946-November 1974) lacking four issues (16/3; 20/6; 22/3; 30/2). Vol. 33 orig. cloth; fine; remainder original wraps, early years faded and sl. worn. 148 issues in 143. **£200.00**

325. MODERN REPORTS: Cases in the Courts of King's Bench (vol. XII), (1690-1702). 1769. 3rd edition. Folio. Index. Modern cloth. **S. & M. i.305.88. £30.00**

326. ——————: or Cases in Law and Equity. (1702-10). 1769. 2nd edition. Folio. Supplement. Index. Lacks e-p's. Modern cloth. **S. & M. i.305.88. £25.00**
Contains supplement of Cases, adjudged in the reign of Queen Anne; and now first published from the MS of Mr. T. Lutwych.

327. ——————: **COLQUIT, H.** or, Select Cases Adjudged ... since the Restoration. 1720(-25). 3rd edition. 3 vols. (1661-1690). Folio. Indices. Vol. 1 sl. browned. Modern cloth. **S. & M. i.304. £60.00**
The Modern Reports, which were finally (1682-1738) extended to twelve volumes – of which these are the first three – are a slightly incoherent & irregular series. They are however important as a step towards the codification of case law & the discarding of superannuated precedents. They also revived the principle – neglected since the collapse of the year books – of reporting arguments in addition to facts & judgments.

328. ——————: or, Select Cases in the Courts of King's Bench, Chancery, Common Pleas and Exchequer. (1669-1699). 1769. 4th edition. 5 vols. Folio. Indices. Modern cloth. **S. & M. i.304.88 £120.00**

329. ——————: or, Modern Cases in Law and Equity. (1721-6/1712-24). 1769. 2nd edition. Folio. **2 parts in 1 vol.** Part 1. (vol. 8). Cases in the King's Bench; Part 2. (vol. 9). Cases in Chancery An index to each part. Unpaged. **£40.00**

330. MONACELLI, Francesco. Formularium legale practicum fori ecclesiastici. Rome, 1703. 1st edition. Folio. ½ title. Red & black title. Index. Stained at end; last 7 leaves frayed without loss of text. Contemp. vellum; worn. **£30.00**
A book of precedents relating to ecclesiastical jurisdiction with large annotations.

331. MOORE, John Bassett. A Digest of International Law as embodied in Diplomatic Discussions, Treaties ... Decisions ... Writings of Jurists (etc.). Washington, D.C. (Govt. Printing Office), 1906. 1st edition. **8 vols.** Index volume included. Orig. cloth, sl. faded & frayed, vol. 6 stained; vol. 4 not uniform. **£80.00**
This work was the result of an Act of Congress of February 1897 ordering the production of a Digest to replace that of Wharton (1887).

332. MORGAN, John. Essays. Dublin, 1789. **Vol. 3 (of 3) only.** Narrow strip cut from title. Sl. browned. Mod. cl. **S. & M. i.379. £10.00**
The bulk of Morgan's work dealt with the law of evidence; this volume includes the essays on special verdicts, trials at bar & repleaders, with part of that on new trials.

333. MORONIUS, Nicolaus. Tractatus aureus de fide, Treugua, et pace. Venice (apud Damianum Zenarum). 1574. Second ed., rev. by the author. Index. Device on title. Occasional light staining. Contemp. limp vellum; v. worn. Not in **B.M.C. or A lams. £60.00**
A treatise on oaths, obligations & feudal responsibilities, including much information on civil actions & commercial contracts.

334. MOSAYCARUM et ROMANARUM LEGUM COLLATIO ex integris ... veterum juris auctorum libris ... desumpta ... Justiniani Novellae ... Juliani Antecessoris ... de Consilariis (et) de Contutoribus. Heidelberg (S. Broun), 1656. Index. (xii), 241, (x)pp. Sm. piece cut from head of title. Modern ¼ calf. **£30.00**
These sources for the study of Roman jurisprudence before Justinian, & for the ancient laws regarding the guardianship of minors, were printed from MSS. collected by Pierre Pithou (1539-96), whose notes are included.

335. NALSON, John (1638-1686). An Impartial Collection of the Great Affairs of State, from the Beginning of the Scotch Rebellion ... to the Murther of King Charles I. For S. Mearne, T. Dring, B. Tooke, T. Sawbridge, and C. Mearne, 1682. 1st edition. **2 vols.** Folio. Engraved frontispiece to vol. 1 (wanting in vol. 2), engraved port. with "Mind" leaf. Index. Signatures & pagination irregular in vol. 1. In vol. 2, N_4 torn without loss. Few sm. lib. stamps in vol. 1. Contemp. calf (not uniform), rubbed, corners worn. **WING N.106-7. £120.00**
A collection of documents with a connecting narrative, royalist in tendency & designed to counteract Rushworth's collection with its republican leanings. Despite the claim of the title, Nalson ends in 1641; he published a Trial of Charles I as a separate work.

336. NELSON, William (1684-1726). The Office and Authority of a Justice of Peace ... Duty of Constables, Commissioners of Sewers, Coroners, Overseers of the Poor (etc.). 1711. 4th edition. Contemp. calf, lacks label, sl. worn. **S. & M. i.230. £40.00**

337. NONIUS, Tobias. Interpretationes in nonnullos Institutionum titulos. Venice (apud Dominicum Farreum), 1597. Device on title. Index. (xxiv), 310 leaves. L_{1-4} & L_{5-8} bound in reverse order. First quire sl. wormed. Sl. stnd. Contemp. vellum, worn & wormed. Not in **B.M.C. or Adams. £50.00**
Dissertations on wills & contracts, given in the author's youth in the law-school of Perugia. The preface is dated 1557, but we can find no record of any other edition before 1584.

338. NOODT, Gerard (1647-1725). Opera omnia ... Accessit v. cl. Joannis Barbeyracii historica vitae auctoris narratio. Leyden, 1735. **2 vols.** Folio. Engraved fp. port. Red & black titles. Index. 20_4 & 20_4 (vol. 1) & $3L_3$ & $3L_4$ (vol. 2) reversed. Few sm. marginal tears. Contemp. boards, uncut; sl. worn. **£80.00**
The best edition of Noodt's works, corrected by an anonymous hand, & with a Life translated & enlarged by Barbeyrac from one which he had formerly written in French. Noodt's most important work, his commentary on books 1-27 of the Pandects (begun when he was past seventy) occupies vol. 2.

339. NOY, (Sir) William (Attorney General) (1577-1634). Reports and Cases ... now translated. By F.L. for Matthew Walbancke ... and T. Firby, 1656. 1st edition. Folio. Black letter. Index. $2C_4$ blank. Some browning throughout. Mod. cl. **Wing N.1449. S. & M. i.306/92. £50.00**
The editor contends that Noy's analysis of the pleadings is above that of any reporter since Plowden. Noy was a King's man and advised in favour of the ship-money legislation which was passed without consent of Parliament.

340. OKEDEN, D.O.P. A Letter to the Rev. Harry Farr Yeatman, on his Inquiry. Salisbury, 1833. 1st edition. 12pp. Sewn as issued. **£6.00**
An Assistant Poor Law Commissioner replies to a supporter of the old system.

341. OLDFIELD, T.H.B. The Representative History of Great Britain and Ireland. 1816. 1st edition. **6 vols.** Appendices. Contemp. calf, gilt, m.e., rebacked; sides rubbed. **S. & M. i.152. Gross 304. £120.00**
Oldfield takes up the doctrine of Granville Sharpe that universal suffrage (at least among householders) was essential to the original constitution of close boroughs & bought & sold franchises. He traces the progress of corruption, first in general & afterwards seat by seat. This is the third and last of Oldfield's Parliamentary writings and his dicontent with the electoral system.

342. ——————. The Representative History of Great Britain and Ireland. 1816. 1st edition. **6 vols.** Appendices. Contemp. ½calf; spines gilt; jts. worn; sp. of vol. 1 frayed. Bk-pl. Lord Belper. **S. & M. i.152. Gross 304. £120.00**

343. ORDONNANCE de LOUIS XIV ... donnée a Saint Germain en Laye au mois d'Avril 1667. Paris, 1667. 1st edition. 4to. Index. Final privilege leaf. (vi), 222, (1)pp. Contemp. ownership inscription of Alexandre de Fougy du Chêneauloup, with many annots. in his hand. Sm. piece cut from margin of T_3. Contemp. mottled calf, spine gilt, lacks front e-p's, jts. & edges worn. **£120.00**
As an essential element in the restoration of order after the civil wars, Louis promulgated this law to improve & regularize the administration of Justice; the same act served to strengthen the authority of the central government over the many & varied tribunals of France.

344. ORDONNANCES ROYAUX sur le Faict de la Justice et Authorite d'icelle, Lyons, Chez Claude Castellard, 1625-24. **2 vols. in one.** 12mo. Inner margin of gathering D wormed, affecting a few letters of text. Index. Contemp. vellum, sl. soiled. Bookplate of Sir A. Grant. **£60.00**
An early collection of the Royal Ordonnances made by Henry II, Francis II, Charles IX, Henry III, Henry IV & Louis XIII.

345. The ORIGIN, OBJECT & OPERATION of the APPRENTICE LAWS. Pamphleteer, 1814. 1st. Disbound. Title detached. **£8.00**
Arguments by a committee of London manufacturers against restrictive practices in trade.

346. OWEN, Thomas. The Reports of ... one of the Justices of the Common Pleas. By T.R. for T. Twyford, F. Dring and J. Place, 1656. Folio. Black letter. Index. Pagination jumps from 76 to 81. Two sm. worm-holes throughout. Old annots. Contemp. sheep rebacked; worn. **Wing O.832. S. & M. i.306. £35.00**

347. OWEN, Hugh, Jr. (afterwards Sir Hugh). The Elementary Education Act, 1876 ... Provisions of Factory Acts. 1876. 1st edition. Index. Orig. cloth; sp. faded. **£5.00**

348. OXFORD UNIVERSITY. A Catalogue of all Graduats (sic) in Divinity, Law, and Physick; and of all Masters of Arts & Doctors of Musick ... between October 10th 1659, and October 10th ... 1727. 1st. Sm. piece torn from A_1 affecting signature. Contemp. panelled cf., jts. sl. worn. Bk-pl. **£20.00**
A useful biographical source-book-quoting the college, degree, & exact date of graduation. University officials from 1659, & M.P.s from 1603, are listed in an Appendix.

349. PALMER, John. The Attorney and Agent's New Table of Costs in the Courts of King's Bench, Common Pleas, and Exchequer of Pleas. 1818. 8th edition. 4to. Index. Sl. spotted. Contemp. calf, sl. rubbed. **S. & M. i.284. £30.00**

350. PARK, James Allan (afterwards Sir James, J.) (1763-1838). A System of the Law of Marine Insurances: with three Chapters, on Bottomry, on Insurances on Lives, on Insurances against Fire. 1802. 5th edition. Index. Some ink annots. Modern cloth. **KRESS B.4580. S. & M. i.512. £30.00**
This work, first published in 1787, was the foundation of Park's fame and remained as the standard text until the 1840s.

351. PARKER, Sir Thomas. Reports of Cases concerning the Revenue, Court of Exchequer. 1743-67, with appendix (of) cases (1678-1717). Folio. 1776. 1st. Book-plate of Thos. Grey. **S. & M. i.323.11.** Calf, sl. rubbed, spine gilt. Front cover loose. Fine copy. **£35.00**

352. PARKES, Samuel (1759-1825). Thoughts on the Laws relating to Salt: with Arguments for the Repeal of those Laws. 1817. 1st. Index. Adverts at end. Orig. bds. uncut. Sp. defective; jts. worn. **Kress B.7014. £30.00**
The heavy salt-duty prevented the use of that mineral in many industrial & agricultural processes, which in consequence had to be laid aside or maintained with expensive materials from abroad. Parkes's facts & figures, by which even farmers could learn that protective duties were doing them no good, carried all the weight of his high reputation as a chemist.

353. (PARSONS, Robert) (c.1550-1610). An Answere to the Fifth Part of Reportes lately set forth by Syr Edward Cooke ... concerning the ... Lawes ... which do apperteyne to Spirituall Power & Jurisdiction. N.p. (St. Omer) 1606. 1st edition. Sm. 4to. Index. Lacks last leaf of index. Sl. browned. Modern ½ calf. **STC 19352. S. & M. i.126. £150.00**
The famous English Jesuit, who at one time came near to raising a civil war in England, here offers his reply to Coke's contention (in his observations on Caudrey's Case) that the statute I Eliz. I, which confirmed the monarch as head of the Church, was a declaratory, not an innovatory law – that the King had always held that position, the Pope never.

354. PARSONS, Theophilus (Chief Justice of Massachusetts) (1750-1813). PARSONS, Theophilus, Jnr. Memoir ... with Notices of some of his Contemporaries. Boston, Mass, 1859. 1st. PRESENTATION COPY. Engr. fp. portait. Sl. stained. Publisher's cat. at end. Orig. cl. Spine & upper cvr. sl. stnd. **SABIN 58910. £40.00**
As a young man Parsons took a notable part in settling the Massachusetts state constitution. He was a man of wide interests with a leaning towards mathematics & as a judge he won high repute. This copy is inscribed by the author on the endpaper to Levi Parsons.

355. PARTRIDGE, S.G. Prisoner's Progress. N.d. (1935). 1st. Illus. Index. Orig. cl., sl. fdd. **£12.00**
A study of prisons & prisoners, crime detection & prevention, trials, & executions in the early nineteenth century.

356. PECKIUS, P. Tractatus de amortizatione bonorum, a principe impetranda. Cologne, apud Joannem Gymnicum, 1582. 1st. Index. Margin of title repaired. Sl. stnd. Lacks e-p's. Contemp. vellum, lacks ties; **B.M.C. (Ger.) p. 680. £70.00**
An essay on the acquisition of real property by those bodies (especially churches & monasteries) which were reckoned under the heading of Manus mortuae.

357. PEERE WILLIAMS, William. Reports of Cases Argued and Determined in ... Chancery, and of some Special Cases ... in ... King's Bench. (1st). 1740-49. Folio. **Vols. 2 & 3 only** (1722-1735). Privilege leaves. Indices. Mod. cl. **£20.00**

358. PELHAM, Camden. The Chronicles of Crime; or, the New Newgate Calendar. 1841. 1st. **2 vols.** Illus. (etched plates) H.K. Browne, Indices. Few plates sl. stnd. Mod. ¼ cf. **£40.00**

359. PEREZ, Antonio. Institutiones imperiales erotematibus distinctae, atque ex ... principiis, regulisque iuris, explicatae. Leyden, 1689. New ed. 12mo. Engr. title. Index. Sl. stnd. towards end. Contemp. cf., jts. weak, sp. worn. Bk-pl. **£25.00**
Intended to strike a medium between the barren summary of Wikflus & the learned commentaries.

360. ——————. Praelectiones in duodecim libros Codicis Justiniani ... Editio nova, ab Auctore recognita & aucta. Amsterdam. Elzevir 1661. 4to. **2 parts in 1.** Red & black title. Index. Some early scoring & few annots. Contemp. blind-stamped vellum. **WILLEMS 1273. £60.00**
Perez, a Spaniard, was a professor at Louvain. This work embraces many details of current French, German & Spanish practice.

361. ——————. Praelectionum in duodecim libros Codicis ... pars altera. Amsterdam (D. Elzevir), 1671. 3rd edition. 4to. **Vol. 2 (of 2) (books 8-12) only.** Index. Signature of William Salkeld, 18th-century English serjeant & law-reporter, on title. Contemp. vellum. **WILLEMS 1457. £20.00**

362. ——————. Praelectiones in duodecim libros Codicis ... Editio ultima, ab auctore recognita. Antwerp & Amsterdam (Wetstein), 1695. **2 vols. in 1.** 4to. Red & black title. Index. (liv)pp. Contemp. blind-stamped vellum. **£120.00**
Among older works on the Code, the commentary of Perez is the fullest & the most practical.

363. PERKINS, John. A Profitable Booke ... treating of the Lawes of England. For the Company of Stationers 1621. 16mo. French text. Index. xxiv, 168 leaves. Contemp. calf, central lozenge of small tools, borders and cornerpieces on sides; lacks ties. Joints neatly repaired. **STC 19644. S. & M. i.485. FINE COPY. £200.00**
Perkins explains the law of real property, as it relates to the transference of land by purchase. He was the Conveyancer's mentor for 300 years.

364. ——————. A Profitable Booke, treating of the Lawes of England, translated out of French into English. R.B. for M. Wallbanke. 1642. (31), 388pp. Black letter, table. Later calf, spine ends & corners sl. rubbed, first blank upper part cut away; contemp. annotations and notes on ½ blank and next page. **WING P.1543. S. & M. i.485.57. £185.00**

365. ——————. A Treatise of the Laws of England on Conveyancing. 1757: by Henry Lintot. 14th edition, corrected. 16mo. Index. Advert. leaf. Star-paged. Lib. stamp: E-p's sl. browned, otherwise a fine edition. Contemp. calf. sp. sl. torn at tail. **S. & M. i.485/58. £70.00**

366. PETYT, William (1636-1707). Jus Parliamentarium: or, Ancient Power, Jurisdiction, Rights, and Liberties of the Most High Court of Parliament revived and asserted. 1739. 1st ed. Folio (xxii), xxiv, 400pp. Contemp. calf worn; red-letter title; lib. stamp. **S. & M. i.136/82. £150.00**
An important study of the origins of parliamentary privilege Petyt was the Tower Archivist & a notable benefactor to the Middle Temple library, where he deposited his collection of state papers.

367. PHILLIPS, Charles (1787-1859). Curran and his Contemporaries. 1851. 4th edition, revised. Engraved fp. port. (John Philpot Curran, Master of the Rolls for Ireland). Index. Sl. spotted. Orig. decorated cloth; sp. faded, sl. worn. **£20.00**
Reminiscences of some Irish characters, especially of the patriots of "ninety-eight" – Curran, Emmett, Wolfe Tone, Grattan, Flood etc. This edition includes remarks on the life of the Duke of Wellington.

368. ——————. Vacation Thoughts on Capital Punishments. 1858. 4th edition, revised. Final advert. leaf. Contemp. calf, a.e.g., spine rubbed. **£20.00**
An Irish nationalist & poet in his youth, and afterwards one of the most brilliant of advocates, Phillips here stands out for the abolition of capital punishment.

369. P(HILPOT), J(ohn), Somerset Herald. The Catalogue of the Lord Chancellors of England, the Lord Keepers ... and the Lord Treasurers. By Tho. Cotes ... Sold by Andrew Crooke, 1636. Sm. 4to. Woodcut arms (Howard) on A_4 (viii), (ii), 93 (actually 82), 79-82, 85pp. Two quires signed M_1, the second of two leaves only. Corner of (2)M, defective without loss of text, & catchword shaved. Mod. ½ cf. **STC 19846. S. & M. i.219. £60.00**

370. PITTS, John W. Eleven Numbers against Lawyer Legislation and Fees at the Bar. N.p. (Athens, Ga?), 1843. 1st in bk. form. 48pp. Orig. printed wraps sl. mkd. & stnd.; plastic folder. Not in **Sabin. £50.00**
Like Cato (or Theodore Roosevelt), Pitts desires that the sons of toil, & not the doctors of the Bar & the colleges, should give laws to the nation; he wishes to exclude lawyers from Congress & prohibit their taking money for their work. Nos. 1-6 are reprinted from the Georgia "Southern Recorder", the rest are new.

371. POINTS in LAW and EQUITY, selected for the information, caution, and direction of all persons concerned in Trade and Commerce, with references to the statutes, reports, and other authorities. DUBLIN, John Rice 1793. Sm. 8vo. viii, 208pp. Sm. wormholes beginning and end quires. Bookplate "John Fenton". Contemp. sheep.

rubbed, spine ends worn. S. & M. i.525.73. Author unknown. £25.00

372. POPHAM, Sir John (C.J.) (c.1531-1607). Reports and Cases ... written with his own Hand in French, and now faithfully Translated. By Tho: Roycroft for John Place 1656. 1st edition. Folio. Black letter. Index. (viii), 212, (viii)pp. Few old annots. Last leaf sl. frayed. Sm. lib. stamp on title. Later calf, sl. rubbed. **WING P.2942. S. & M. i.305. RARE.** £120.00
Includes a description of the coifing of ten Serjeants in 1594, with Popham's speech on that occasion. Pp. 125-212 contain anonymous Reports of a later date.

373. POSTIUS, Ludovicus: AUCTION SALES. De subhastatione tractatus ... Huic editioni accesserunt eiusdem auctoris additamenta. Coloniae Allobrogum (Geneva) (J.A. & S. de Tournes), 1671. Folio. **3 pts. in 1.** Red & black title. ½ title. Index. Some browning. Inner margins of about 30 leaves wormed, slightly affecting text. New ¼ calf. sides. **Not in Kress or Goldsmith.** £80.00
Revised ed. of an early work on auction sales, first published in 1644. The author, assisted by his nephew Gianfrancesco adapted his method from the practice of Rome, Perugia, Bologna, & Macerata, and there is an appendix of relevant test cases in the Roman courts.

374. POWELL, Thomas. The Attourney's Academy-or, the Manner and Forme of Proceeding ... in any Court of Record. For Benjamin Fisher, 1630. 3rd edition. Sm. 4to. Index. (xii), 230, (lxii)pp. Some headlines sl. cropped. Modern calf, gilt. A FINE COPY. **STC 20164. S. & M. i.119.** £130.00
Powell was a Welshman, an occasional playwright, & a facetious writer; but his remarks on the jurisdiction of Parliament (partly drawn from Smith's Republic), on the Chancery, on Star Chamber etc. are of historical value. Powell had theatrical connections and often breaks out in the midst of his legal instructions with allusions to Shakespeare (twice in this work). This work is dedicated to Bacon.

375. PRECEDENTS in Chancery, from the Year 1689 to 1722. 1733. 1st ed. 1 vol. Folio. Index. mod. cl. uncut. **S. & M. i.368/36.** £35.00

376. ——————, from 1689 to 1722. 1750. 2nd ed., by a Late Careful and Judicious Hand. 1 vol. Folio. Index. prelims., A, sl. torn at marg. w/out loss of text. Mod. cl. **S. & M. i.348/36.** £30.00

377. PRESTON, Richard. An Essay in a Course of Lectures on Abstracts of Title. 1824. 2nd edition. **3 vols.** Index. Many pencil annots. in vol. 1. Contemp. limp calf, sps. & corners worn. **S. & M. ii.289.** £50.00
The great conveyancer designed this work as a practical introduction to the law of real property in general.

378. PREVOTIUS (Prevost), Claudius. Commentatius de magistratibus pop. Rom. ex variis authoribus collectus. Lausanne (F. le Preus), 1579. 1st edition. Latin text. (viii), 188, (iv)pp. Final blank. Contemp. calf, blind-stamped; head of sp. defective; lower corners worn. £50.00
A simple summary, edited after Prevotius' death by the municipal printer of Berne from his Lausanne office.

379. PRIDEAUX, Humphrey (1648-1724). The Original and Right of Tithes, for the Maintenance of the Ministry in a Christian Church, Truly Stated ... Draught of a Bill .. for the Restraining of Pluralities. Norwich 1710. 1st edition. **2 parts in 1.** Contemp. panelled calf; jts. & edges worn. **S. & M. i.193.** £80.00
Prideaux makes the case for tithes on grounds of natural justice rather than Biblical precedent. His Bill, drawn up in 1691, was a courageous attempt to reform abuses in the Church.

380. ——————. The Original and Right of Tithes ... Truly stated. To which is Annex'd the Draught of a Bill ... for the Restraining of Pluralities of Benefices. 1736. 2nd edition, revised. (xvi), 256pp. Sl. stained. Modern tree calf. Bk-pl. Lord Selborne. **S. & M. i.193.** FINE COPY. £70.00

381. PRIVY COUNCIL. Printed form of summons to a meeting of the Privy Council at Whitehall, with date & subject of discussion filled in by hand. 9th July 1778. Single leaf. £10.00
The recipient was probably William de Grey, 1st Baron Walsingham (formerly Chief Justice C.P.). The subject of debate was "plantation affairs", i.e. the Council was to exercise its judicial powers in respect of offences committed & actions disputed in the colonies, which doubtless included America.

382. PROAL, Louis, Political Crime. 1898. 1st. Orig. cl. faded. £5.00
This book relates the crimes committed by political systems, based on craft and violence and tries to prove by facts that loyal and honest policies are the best and that politics where they part company with morality are not the instruments of good government. It gives historical examples starting with Machiavelli.

383. THE PROCEEDINGS IN THE HOUSE OF COMMONS, Touching the Impeachment of Edward Late Earl of Clarendon, Lord High-Chancellour of England, Anno 1667. 1700. (1st ed.) 8vo. Contemp. calf., rebacked & sl. worn. B_{2-3} repaired without loss of text. £20.00

384. PROPERTY ACTS & STATUTES. George III Regis. Anno Quadragesimo Tertio. An Act for consolidating certain of the Provisions ... for the Affairs of Taxes ... 1803. (1049-1078pp.).
—————— An Act for granting to H.M. ... after the Ratification ... Treaty of Peace, a Contribution on the Profits arising from Property, Professions, Trades and Office. 1803. (129-1343pp.).
—————— Quinto. An Act to repeal certain parts of an Act ... for granting a Contribution on the Profits arising from Property, Professions, Trades, and Offices; and to consolidate ... the Provisions for collecting the said Duties. 1805. (813-926pp.).
—————— A Bill (as amended on re-Commitment) For granting to H.M. further Additional Rates and Duties on Profits arising from Property, Professions, Trades, and Offices in G.B. (110pp.). n.d. **4 items in 1 vol.** Folio. Contemp. ½ calf. Corners rubbed. £40.00

385. PUFENDORF, Samuel (1632-1694). The Divine Feudal Law: or, Covenants with Mankind Represented. Translated from the Latin by Theophilus Dorrington. 1703. 1st. Eng. ed. Index. Contemp. calf., sp. sl. torn. £60.00
According to the translator, this is the last work written by Pufendorf and was published posthumously. It is an essay on the nature and development of religion with the emphasis on issues concerning the Reformation.

386. ——————. Of the Law of Nature and Nations, Eight Books. (Transl. Basil Kennett & others) Oxford 1710 (altered to 1714 in ink) 2nd edition, revised. **Folio.** Index. Spotted at beginning & end. Contemp. panelled calf, worn. £60.00
This edition incorporates Barbeyrac's notes.

387. ——————. Of the Law of Nature and Nations, Eight Books. Transl. Basil Kennett & others. 1729. 4th edition, rev. Folio. Index. Some irregularities in signatures. Contemp. calf, edges worn, rebacked. £80.00
Includes a version of Barbeyrac's Account of the Science of Morality, together with his notes to Pufendorf in their fullest form.

388. ——————. Of the Law of Nature and Nations. Eight Books. Ed. Jean Barbeyrac; tr. Basil Kennett. 1729. 4th ed. corr. & enlarged. FOLIO. Index. Barbeyrac's Historical Account of Morality appended. Contemp. calf rbbd., hinges loose, sp. ends frayed. Bk-pl. **S. & M. i.597/72.** £80.00

389. ——————. De officio hominis & civis, juxta legem naturalem, libri duo. Cambridge, 1701. Copious contemp. annots. (complete transcript of treatise **de Moribus,** attr. to Seneca.) Title ruled. Contemp. cf., later label; jts. rbbd. £40.00

390. ——————. De officio hominis & civis juxta legem Naturalem. Ed. Tho. Johnson. Cambridge, 1735. Latin text. Index. 2 leaves of Publisher's adverts. Contemp. cf., sl. rbbd. Ex-libris stamp. £40.00

391. ——————. De officio hominis et civis juxta legem naturalem libri duo. Selectis variorum notis, maximeq; propriis illustravit ... Tho. Johnson. 1737. 2nd edition, revised. Engraved fp. port. Red & black title with vignette. Index. Contemp. sprinkled calf; jts. & edges worn. £35.00
Johnson produced this edition for the students of Magdalen College, Cambridge, of which he was a Fellow. It includes the Historia Iuris Civilis (A survey of ancient & modern schools of thought on the subject) of Johannes Buddeus of Jena.

392. ——————. De officio hominis et civis juxta legem naturalem libri duo. Selectis variorum notis, maximeq; propriis illustravit ... Tho. Johnson. 1737. 2nd edition, rev. Engr. fp. port. Red & black title with vignette. Index. Sl. stained. Contemp. panelled calf, upper jt. & corners worn. £35.00

393. PULLING, Alexander (Serjeant at Law). The Order of the Coif. 1884. 1st edition. 4to. Chromolith. fp. & seven wood-engraved plates, some folding. Index. A.l.s. from John Hamer Jones to Mr. Serjeant Russell, 23rd Dec. 1896, offering the book as a present; with Russell's bk-pl. Orig. b'ram, gilt, t.e.g.; sl. shaken. £60.00
A splendid chronicle of the Serjeants, ending with a plea for their retention, by one of the last of the order.

394. PULTON, Ferdinando. De Pace Regis et Regni, viz. a Treatise declaring which be the great and generall Offences of the Realme. For the Companie of Stationers. 1623. (4th edition). Folio. Black letter. Index. (v), 324, (i.e. 243) (xvii) leaves. Lacks first blank. Few margins sl. soiled. Contemp. calf, later label; rubbed & sl. worn. S. & M. i.365. £150.00
A useful summary of criminal law, & very modern in its inclusion of such matters as the law of principal & accessory, private prosecution (then called "appeal") of felonies, evidence, etc.

395. RAMSEY, William. The Whole Proceedings on the King's Commission of the Peace, Oyer and Terminer, and Gaol Delivery for ... Middlesex ... in the Mayoralty of ... Sir Richard Carr Glyn. 1798-9. 1st. 8 pts in 1 vol. 4to. Index. 668pp. Sl. browned & spotted. Mod. cl. Not in S. & M. £40.00
See HODGSON for a note on the Old Bailey reports.

396. (RASTELL, John). Les Termes de la Ley: or, Certain Difficult and Obscure Words and Terms of the Common Laws and Statutes. (Ed. Thomas Blount) By John Streater, James Flesher, and Edward Atkyns, 1667. 1st thus. Woodcut arms on leaf before title. Final advert. leaf. (xiv), 614, (ii)pp. Few patches of worming mostly at inner margin. Sl. stained at end. Contemp. calf, sl. worn, rebacked. **WING R.290. S. & M. i.10.** £150.00
Rastell's is the first English law-dictionary, published in Latin in 1527. This is Blount's first edition; he afterwards produced a law-dictionary of his own, but he is better known for his "Ancient Tenures".

397. RAYMOND, Robert, Lord (Chief Justice, K.B.). Reports of Cases ... in ... King's Bench and Common Pleas ... 1765. 2nd. **3 vols.** Folio. Indices (complete). Mod. cloth. **S. & M. i.307.** £95.00
Cases 1694-1732, many of them preserving judgments and dicta of Holt, C.J. Volume III contains the Entries or Pleadings reported by George Wilson for the cases in the first two vols.

398. RAYNAL, Abbe. The History of the Parliament of England. Trans. into English. 1751. 1st Engl. ed. 8vo. Index. Contemp. ¼ calf. sl. rbbd. **S. & M. i.137/95.** £30.00

399. RAYNER, John. Cases at Large concerning Tithes ... Introduction, comprehending a ... View of the Whole Law of Tithes ... Acts of Parliament. 1783. 1st edition. **3 vols.** Contemp. calf, rebacked; sl. worn. **S. & M.i.194.** £120.00
Rayner's comprehensive work includes a 36-page annotated list of authorities – a useful contribution to legal bibliography.

400. ——————. Cases at Large concerning Tithes ... Introduction, comprehending a ... View of the Whole Law of Tithes ... Acts of Parliament. 1783. Another copy. **3 vols.** Contemp. calf; sps. sl. worn. **S. & M. i.194.** £120.00

401. READING, Nathaniel. Letter to Mr. Recorder, about the Sword, Mace, and Pictures at Guild-Hall. 1702. 1st edition. Folio broadsheet. Ms. direction on verso, "For ye Honrd. Mr. Atwood. Inner Temple", with traces of seal. One sm. marginal defect. £20.00
In this amusing case one William Thomas (who counsel Reading was) seized the regalia of the City of London by way of distress, the Corporation being in debt to him. William Atwood later went out to New York & became Chief Justice there.

402. REDDIE, John. Historical Notices of the Roman Law, and of the Recent Progress of its Study in Germany. Edinburgh, for W. & C. Tait and others. 1826. 1st edition. 136pp. uncut and partly unopened. Orig. boards, dust-stained. Not in S. & M. £22.00

403. REDDIE, James. Inquiries Elementary and Historical in the Science of Law. Longman, Orme, Brown (etc.). 1840. 1st edition. Some spotting of e-p's and lower margins of first few pages. Presentation copy "from the Author to J. Fisher, Glasgow 1840". Orig. boards, sl. stained, newly rebacked. **S. & M. i.598.77.** £30.00
Reddie was the legal assessor to the City of Glasgow.

404. RICIUS, Paulus (fl. 1500-1540). De coelesti agricultura ... de communi sacramentorum ratione ... de anima coeli ... de Talmudeorum codice (etc.) Augsburg (per Henricum Stayner). 1541. 1st edition. Folio. Latin text. Full-page woodcut on title. Woodcut initials. (iv), 210 leaves. Verso of title repaired at head. Sl. wormed at end. Some marginal fraying of last 10 leaves. Few stains. Some old annotations. Contemp. blind-stamped pig, lacks one clasp, re-backed. FINE COPY. £350.00
The author was a Jew of Pavia who turned Christian. Writing on Christian religious and philosophical subjects, he retained a deep Hebraic scholarship and the imagery and allegory of the rabbis. He was a pantheist who maintained that the universe had a living soul; the treatise de Anima Coeli which deals with this idea includes many points of reference to Talmudic law. As a rare acquisition to the Christian faith, he was favoured by kings e.g., Charles V (to whom this work is dedicated) and Maximilian (who brought him to Germany); but his friendship with Erasmus is more truly indicative of his character and learning.

405. RIDDELL, John. Tracts, Legal and Historical, with other Antiquarian Matter chiefly relative to Scotland. Edinburgh, 1835. 1st edition. Orig. boards, uncut, sp. & edges worn. **S. & M. v.97.** £30.00
Observations & documents on the death of Richard II, on the Scots law of legitimation (especially as relating to Robert III of Scotland & his Stewart successors), and on certain Scots families.

406. RIDLEY, Sir T. View of the Civile and Ecclesiastical Law, and wherein the Practise of them is streitned and may be relieved within this Land. Oxford, W. Hall for John Forrest. 1662. 3rd edition edited by J. G(regory). Mispagination of pp. 239-270 (mentioned in errata) index. Contemp. calf, rubbed; lacks spine and gathering broken. **S. & M. i.175.** £40.00
One of the earliest books on this subject. Ridley was a Cambridge D.D., an Oxford D.C.L. and an advocate of Doctors' Commons. He had held the post of master in Chancery, chancellor of the Diocese of Winchester and vicar-general for Archbishop Abbot. He wrote this book because "men meanly esteemed the divine and ecclesiasticall law of the land", and in order to protest against the increase of writs of prohibition which prevented its regular enforcement. The book deals mainly with ecclesiastical law.

407. (RIDPATH, George). An Historical Account of the Antient Rights and Power of the Parliament of Scotland. N.p., 1703. 1st edition. xxxii, 160pp. Contemp. sprinkled calf; Bk-pl. John Hay, 1st Marquess of Tweeddale. **S. & M. v.51.** £120.00
Written on the near prospect of a union of the two kingdoms in the hope that the new order, instead of increasing the subordination of Scotland, might rescue the Scots Parliament from the depression into which it had been cast under the arbitrary government of James VI.

408. ——————. Parliamentary Right Maintain'd, or the Hanover Succession Justify'd. N.p. (Edinburgh?) 1714. 1st edition. Errata leaf *5. (x), 262pp. Contemp. panelled calf, upper jt. partially split, lower cover marked. £45.00
This work asserts the historical continuity of checks & limitations on the British monarchy, undermining the Scriptural authorities for "divine right", while at the same time arguing that the Act of Union serves as an adequate bar to further & less justifiable interferences with the succession on the part of Parliament.

409. ROBINSON, Christopher. Reports of Cases Argued and Determined in the High Court of Admiralty. 1806(-8). Vol. 1: 3rd ed., vol. 2: 2nd ed., remainder 1st. **5 vols. (of 6)** Indices. Lib. stamps at intervals. Mod. cl., sl. fdd. **S. & M. i.355.** £40.00
The Admiralty Court enjoyed a vast access of business arising from the war at sea against Napoleon. These volumes cover the greater part of this period (1798-1804); a sixth vol. appeared in 1808.

410. ROLT, Sir John. (1804-1871) (Lord Justice of Appeal). Memoirs, ed. C.T. le Quesne. Inner Temple, 1939. 1st edition. Collotype plates. Index. Orig. cloth, uncut. Fine. £8.00

411. ROSCOE, Henry. Eminent British Lawyers. (Cabinet Cyclopaedia, Biography.) 1833. Engr. title (sl. stnd.) Strip torn from printed title aff. first work. Orig. cl., mkd. & fdd. £10.00
Fourteen judges & jurists from Coke to Romilly.

412. ROSE, John. A Constitutional Catechism ... with copious Notes, Principally Extracted from the Commentaries of the late Judge **BLACKSTONE,** Bristol, 1795. 1st. Contemp. ½ cf. rbbd. **S. & M. i.106.** £10.00

413. RUGGLE, George. (c.1575-1622). Ignoramus, comoedia ... cum notis historicis et criticis ... accurante Johanne Sidnei Hawkins. 1787. 1st. thus. Latin text with English annots. Engr. fp. Woodcuts in text. H_3 torn without loss. Mod. ¼ cf. **S. & M. i.241.** £30.00
Ruggle's Ignoramus, written in about 1612, is a by-product of the ancient enmity between the academics & the common lawyers; it holds up the language & style of the law to ridicule in a framework derived from Terence & the Italian comedy. Hawkins's edition includes a copious life of the author, notes and a glossary.

414. RYMER, Thomas, & Robert SANDERSON (ed.). Foedera, conventiones, literae, et cujuscunque generis acta publica inter reges Angliae, et alios quosvis imperatores, reges, pontifices (etc.) The Hague (Jean Neaulme), 1739-45. 3rd edition, edited George Holmes. **10 vols.** FOLIO. Indices. 10 engraved plates in vol. 9. "Advertissement" leaf (signed *2) bound before A_1 of vol. 1. Contemp. MS. transcript of Anglo-French truce of 1325 (from a Bodleian MS.) & five engravings of Great Seals from an 8vo edition of Blackstone's Law Tracts, inserted in vol. 1. Two leaves loose in vols. 4 & 9. Vol. 5 lacks 5*, blank, & N_{2-3} (part 3) reversed. l_2 (vol. 7. pt. 1) torn without loss. Contemp. marbled boards, uncut, worn, ends of spines defective. **S. & M. i.604.** £300.00
Last edition, including some new items – an account of the English constitution in French, written by an unknown ambassador in 1565, and le Clerc's Historical Abridgment of the Foedera which forms vol. 10.

415. SACHEVERELL, Henry. (1672-1724). The Tryal . . . before the House of Peers, for High Crimes and Misdemeanors. 1710. 1st edition. Folio. First privilege leaf. 328pp. MS index of counsel etc. Contemp. panelled calf, sp. gilt; jts. worn. £50.00
Sacheverell was impeached for preaching against the toleration of dissenters, the justice of the revolution of 1688, & the conduct of the government. He received a mild sentence and became a national hero for his defence of Church & People against tyranny & corruption.

416. (SAINT GERMAN, Christopher) (?-1540). Two Dialogues in English, between a Doctor of Divinity, and A Student in the Laws of England of The Grounds of the said Laws, and of Conscience. Richard and Edward Atkins, 1709. Newly revised and reprinted. 366, 8pp. tables. Modern ¼ calf. Partly black letter. S. & M. i.25.35. £80.00
The first edition in English of the Two Dialogues appeared in 1668 but the original Latin version goes back to 1528. St. German, an adversary of St. Thomas More, was a philosophical lawyer and much of his work is devoted to reconciling common law with the law of nature & the dictates of ethics. He discusses many points of land law & ecclesiastical law from this point of view. In contrast his arguments on the doctrine of consideration suggest (in anticipation of Lord Mansfield) that moral obligations ought to suffice to make a good contract – a fact which would be supported in the ecclesiastical courts.

417. ————. The dyaloges in Englishe, betwene a Doctour of Divinitie, and a Student in the Lawes of Englande. 1721. 12mo. Index. Contemp. calf, rebacked, rubbed. S. & M. i.25. £70.00

418. SALKELD, William (Serjeant-at-law) (1671-1715). Reports . . . Edited George Wilson. 1773. 1st thus. Folio. Indices. First privilege leaf. Contemp. calf, rubbed & jts. worn. S. & M. i.308. £30.00
This is complete in one volume.

419. (SALMON, Thomas) (1679-1767) (ed.). Tryals for High-Treason, and Other Crimes. With proceedings on Bills of Attainder, and Impeachments. 1720. 1st edition. 6 vols. Index. Advert. leaf f_6 in vol. 1. Errata leaf in vol. 3. Q_1 (vol. 5) torn without loss. Contemp. panelled calf, two jts. worn. S. & M. i.371. £160.00
This work is adapted from Salmon's folio "State Trials" of 1717, with some reports abridged but including a few new cases. The period 1635-1690 – the fall of Charles I's counsellors & that of his own person, the struggles between the Rump & those who were too republican for the Republic, the royalists' revenge, the rise & fall of Titus Oates & the Abdication – occupies the bulk of the work. The last trial in vol. 5, is that of Captain Kidd the pirate.

420. SAUNDERS, Sir Edmund. (C.J., K.B.) (?=1683). Les Reports des Divers Pleadings et Cases en le Court del Bank Le Roy en le Temp del Reign de le Roy Charles II. 2 vols. Folio. 2nd edition with the addition of the Reports transl. into English, 1722. 1-84 of vol. II are bound into vol. I. Mod. cl., labels. S. & M. i.308/112. In spite of the modern cloth binding, a very fine set. £90.00
These reports, printed after Saunders's death, extend from 1666-1672, and are esteemed for their simplicity and precision. They are composed in so dramatic a form that Lord Mansfield called him the Terence of Reporters.

421. ————. Summus Angliae Seneschallus: or, a Survey of the Lord High-Steward of England . . . Manner of Arraigning a Peer. Printed . . . 1680. 1st edition. Sm. 4to. 36pp. Few page-numerals cropped. Disbound. WING S.745. S. & M. i.218. £25.00
Saunders was appointed Chief Justice of King's Bench in 1683 to be the King's tool in his attempt to corrupt the electoral system, but died within six months. This pamphlet is addressed to Lord Stafford & others, Catholics whom Saunders was about to defend on their trial for high treason.

422. SCHULTES, Henry. An Essay on Aquatic Rights; intended as an Illustration of the Law relative to Fishing, and to the Propriety of Ground or Soil produced by alluvion and dereliction in the Sea and Rivers. W. Clarke, 1811. 1st edition. Index, errata. Modern ¼ cf./marbled sides. Not in S. & M. £45.00
Henry Schultes was best known for an important pamphlet on early municipal customs.

423. SCHULTING, Anton. (1659-1734) (ed.). Jurisprudentia vetus ante-Justinianea. Leyden 1717. 1st collected. 4to. Red & black title. Index. Lacks blank ***2. Final blank. FINE COPY in contemp. mottled calf, spine gilt; sl. wear on sp. £100.00
The standard collection of Roman law before Justinian until the 19th century, when Mai's discoveries transformed our knowledge of the Institutes of Gaius, Julius, Paulus, Ulpian, Dositheus, Papinian, the Gregorian & Hermogenian Codes, etc.

424. ————. Jurisprudentia vetus ante-Justinianea. New edition. Praefatus est D. Georgius Henrius Ayrer. Leipzig 1737. 4to. Index. Engraved vignette on *2. Lacks blank a_1. Some browning. Contemp. tree calf, gilt, **ARMS OF NIJMEGEN (NOVIOMAGUS)** on sides; sl. rubbed. FINE COPY. £80.00
Includes variants in the texts of Gaius, Julius Paulus, & the two early Codes from Wurzburg & Gotha MSS. Nijmegen was the home town of Schulting's family.

425. SCHÜTZ, Johann Christian. Specimen iuris consolidationis pertinentiarum, vulgo von Einlösung der abgesplissenen Pertinentien zur Sohlstatt. Cologne, sumptibus Wilhelmi Metternich, 1718. 1st edition. German & latin text. Fraktur letter. Index. (xii), 108, (xx)pp. Final errata leaves. Some browning. Ownership inscr. of Ignaz Nüppeney von Welling, prefect of Eschweiler (1719) & W. Baumeister, aulic counsellor, of Düsseldorf, with the latter's bk-label. Contemp. parchment, sl. rubbed & shaken. £150.00
In the absence of any system of primogeniture, many German estates were so often divided & subdivided among a plurality of heirs as to become inconvenient to the fiscal authorities & uneconomical to the owners. The jus consolidationis was designed to provide a means of restoring such estates to their pristine unity; but its application, which was greatly expanded after 1700, was hindered by the great diversity of municipal laws. Schütz's work examines the origin, nature, & operation of the system in an attempt to reduce it to uniformity.

426. SCHWEDER, Gabriel. Introductio in jus publicum imperii Romano-Germanici novissimum. Tübingen, 1722. Revised edition. Engraved fp. Index. Sl. spotted. Contemp. vellum. £25.00
First published in 1682, but continually revised by the author, who opposes the theory that the German Empire is an absolute monarchy.

427. SCOTLAND. The Actis of Parliament of the maist hie, maist excellent, and michtie Prince, and our Souerane Lord James the sext . . . King of Scottis, begun and haldin at Edinburgh, the xv day of Decemb. The Yeir . . . ane thousand, five hundreth lxvii, yeir. (Edinburgh R. Lekprevik, 1658) 1st edition. Sm. Folio. Black letter. Large woodcut (cropped) on title, 23 (of 25 leaves. Lacks F_1 & F_4 (final leaf). One corner of C_1 repaired; 16th century MS notes point out the two missing leaves. Some sl. staining. Modern ¼ calf. STC 21880 (B.L. & Huntington only) S. & M. v.110. £150.00
In this first Parliament of James VI (James I of England) the unfortunate Queen Mary, then held prisoner at Lochlevin Castle, surrendered her throne to the infant James. The Earl of Murray as Regent, laid a path towards the restoration of order by enactments for reform of the coinage & for the suppression of Border bandits.

428. SCOTT, George Ryley. The History of Capital Punishment. Including an Examination of the Case for and Against the Death Penalty. 1950. 1st. Index. Numerous plates and text illus. orig. cl. fine. £6.00

429. SELDEN, John (1584-1654). De dis Syris syntagmata II. Adversaria nempe de numinibus . . . in Veteri Instrumento Memoratis. Leyden (Elzevir), 1629. 2nd edition, revised. Latin text. Red & black title. (xl), 373, (i)pp. Title sl. browned. Modern full calf. **WILLEMS 322.** £120.00
This edition was greatly enlarged, partly to satisfy the request of the Elzevirs & partly to silence the partisans of a German jurist, Faber, who had written on the same subject. Milton drew many names & attributes of the Heathen Gods in "Paradise Lost" book II from this work.

430. ————. De Synedriis & Praefecturis Juridicis Veterum Ebraeorum. Jacobi Flesher, prostant apud Cornelium Bee, 4to. 1650. 1st edition. Errata, title page in red and black. Lacks first blank (A_1) WING 2425. Contemp. calf, worn & rubbed; hinges weak, spine ends sl. frayed. £120.00
A work on Hebraic law with comparisons to other legal systems. It was begun as early as 1638, but never completed.

431. ————. De Synedriis et Praefecturis Juridicis Veterum Ebraecorum, libri tres. Amsterdam. 1679. 4to. New edition. ½ title. Contemp. vellum; lib. labels. A very fine copy. £120.00

432. ————. The Historie of Tithes. The Practice of Payment of them. The Positiue Laws made for them. The Opinions touching the Rights of them (with) a Review of it . . . which both Confirmes it and directs in the Use of it. Sm. 4to. 1618. Modern ½ calf. A FINE COPY. New STC 22172. Variant issue of the first edition. S. & M. i.194-5. £180.00
There are several distinct editions dated 1618 and the New STC lists five of them; however, it seems probable that there were at least three separate printings and that some sheets of the various printings were bound together. It is therefore possible that there may be more than the five variants listed in STC. The above copy fulfils only two of the four points under the STC no. 22172.
Selden designed an impartial history, but his great learning & his natural bias towards the civil side exposed so many irregularities in the theory & ancient practice of tithes that he was accused as a blasphemer by the church, & acclaimed as a prophet by the Quakers & dissenters. For writing this treatise Selden was summoned before the High Commission Court, and he wrote a vindication of it which was never printed.
This work also contains examples of printing in Hebrew, Greek & Anglo-Saxon.

433. ————. The Historie of Tithes. 1618. Sm. 4to. Red & black title. Marginal repair to last leaf. 19th-century ½ calf. Bookplate of the Selborne Library. New STC.22172.3. S. & M. i.194. £180.00

434. ————. The Historie of Tithes. 1618. Sm. 4to. Red & black title. Some headlines cropped. Light stains, at end. 18th century calf-backed boards, joints sl. worn. Bookplate of Thomas, Earl of Haddington (d.1735). New STC 22172.5. £160.00

435. ————. The Historie of Tithes . . . Sm. 4to. 1618. Red and black title. No paging. Signature Bbb is incorrectly imposed (or folded). A few sl. damp-stains in lower margin. Old panelled calf, rebacked. New STC 22172.7. £150.00
Fourth issue of the 1st edition.

436. ————. The History of Tythes . . . Sm. 4to. 1618 (1680). Title page sl. stained. Modern ¼ calf-backed boards. Fine copy. New STC 22173 does not list this edition. £120.00

437. ————, of the Judicature in Parliaments, a Posthumous Treatise: wherein, the Controversies and Precedents belonging to that Title, are Methodically handled. Joseph Lawson (1681) n.d. (8), 188pp. Modern calf, label. Fine copy. S. & M. i.139.110. Wing 2433. £60.00
This work has been attributed to Sir S. D'Ewes.

438. ————. The Priviledges of the Baronage of England, when they Sit in Parliament. By T. Badger for Matthew Walbanck, 1642. 1st edition. (vi), 168pp. Publisher's catalogue printed on back paste-down. Contemp. sheep, rebacked, edges rubbed. WING S2434. S. & M. i.208. £120.00
This little work is a paragon from Selden's study of the Parliamentary records. The publisher's catalogue is by far the earliest example known to us of a list printed separately, as opposed to the common type which forms a part of the collation of the book; its position seems to indicate that the book was bound by the printer.

439. ————. Titles of Honor. Folio. William Stansby for Richard Whitakers. 1631. 2nd edition. Red & black title. Text woodcuts & engravings. (xxxvi), 941, (i)pp. Old annotations. Final blank. Old calf, sl. worn, rebacked. **STC 22178. S. & M. i.208.** £150.00
The first of Selden's great historical works, displaying his deep & various reading & the wide ranging comparison between the customs of diverse races & ages which raises him to the rank of a valuable social historian. Ben Jonson contributes a long eulogy in verse.
This second edition was greatly enlarged.

440. ————. Titles of Honor. Folio. William Stansby for Richard Whitakers. 1631. 2nd edition. Red & black title. Text woodcuts & engravings. (xxxvi), 941, (i)pp. Old annotations. Sm. hole in 4D3 affecting two lines of text. Lacks final blank. Contemp. sprinkled calf, joints weak. Bookplate Alexander Thomson. **STC 22178. S. & M. i.208.** £150.00

441. ————. Tracts . . . Jani Anglorum Facies Altera . . . (transl. & edited) Redman Westcot.
———— England's Epinomis.
———— Of the Original of Ecclesiastical Jurisdictions of Testaments.
———— Of the Disposition or Administration of Intestates Goods. 4 Tracts in 1 volume. Folio. For Thomas Basset and Richard Chiswell. 1683. 1st collected. Lacks portrait. Title sl. frayed. Modern ¼ calf. **WING S.2441a.** £120.00
First editions of all except the first item.

442. ————. Uxor Ebraica, seu de nuptiis ed divortiis ex iure civili . . . Ebraeorum, libri tres. Frankfurt am Oder, 1673. New ed. 4to. 2 pts. in 1. Index Sl. browned. Contemp. vellum; lib. stamps & labels. £120.00
Edited by J.C. Beckmann. Also includes the works De successionibus . . . in bona defunctorum, & De successionibus in pontificatum.

443. ————. Table Talk, edited & introd. Sir Frederick Pollock. Selden Society 1927. 1st thus. Sm. 4to. Four photogravure plates. Index. Orig. cloth backed boards, uncut, sl. worn. £20.00
Edited by Pollock from a MS in the library of Lincoln's Inn, supposed to be a very indirect copy of the original in the possession of Selden's friend Richard Milward, but nonetheless superior to the printed text of 1689.

444. SELVA, Johannes de. Tractatus de beneficio. (Paris), François Regnault, n.d. (c.1520) 4to. Gothic (rotunda) letter. Red & black title with device (cf. Renouard 943) Index. 299, (xiii) leaves. Final blank. Few sl. stains. Some head-lines shaved. Title sl. soiled. Contemp. sheep, MS guards (legal document dated 1480), lacks ties, tail of spine repaired. **Adams 879. Not in B.L. or Lib. of Congress.** £200.00
In this work on ecclesiastical appointments the author, a jurist of Limoges, limits the powers of the Pope to dispense with the normal rules of preferment. He is equally critical of the pretensions of the French crown to an independent right of appointment.
The absence of a colophon is unusual; however the blank appears to be genuine and would have carried the imprint if one were required.

445. SHAW, James. The Parochial Lawyer; or, Churchwarden's and Overseer's Guide . . . Law, Practice, and Proceedings of Vestries . . . Hints . . . for the Management . . . of the Poor. 1835. 4th edition. Index. Sl. spotted. Contemp. ½ parchment; sp. gilt, sl. marked. S. & M. i.322. £20.00
Written to help local government officials adapt themselves to the new poor law, this work enjoyed a very lively circulation.

446. SHEPPARD, William. (1620-1675). Epitome of all the Common and Statute Laws of this Nation in force; wherein more than 1,500 words or terms of the Law are explained. With an Alphabetical Table. Published by His Highness's Special Command. W. Lee, D. Pakeman etc. 1656. 1st edition. Folio. (xxiv), 1131pp. Contemp. calf, rubbed; spine ends frayed and sl. torn. Fine clean copy. S. & M. i.19.19. WING 3184. £280.00
"This methodical Abridgment of both the laws, as well as that called Common, as the Statute Law (now in force) wherein I have at once perform'd two things, viz., My utmost ability in collecting the dispersed Cases and particular conclusions of law under the general entituling, my commanded duty in faithfully rendering them into English, according to the prescription of the Act of Parliament in that cases provided." Preface.

447. ————. The Touch-Stone of Common Assurances: or a plain and familiar treatise, opening the learning of the common assurances or conveyances of the Kingdome. W. Lee, M. Walbancke, est. 1648. 4to. (vi), 529 (i.e. 525), (vii)pp. Errors in paging, including numbers 349-352 omitted. Mod. ¼ clf. Pages sl. spotted, e-p's trn. **WING S.3215. KRESS S.946. S. & M. i.487/71.** £220.00
The Touchstone is one of the most esteemed old treatises, a copious fountain of the law, relating to the transfer of real property. "For the soundness of its propositions, its succinct method, and its excellent arrangement, this book is not surpassed by any work on the law. To the period of its date it was a complete summary of the existing law on the methods of assurance and on various subjects connected with titles." Mr. Preston in his preface to the 7th edition.

448. ————. The Touch-Stone of Common Assurances: or a plain and familiar treatise, opening the learning of the common assurances or conveyances of the Kingdome. W. Lee, M. Walbancke etc. 1651. Sm. 4to. (12), 529, (6)pp. Errors in paging, including numbers 349-352 omitted. Contemp. sheep, rubbed. **WING S.3215. KRESS S.1050. S. & M. i.487.71.** £200.00

449. ————. The Touch-Stone of Common Assurances. For W. Lee, M. Walbancke, D. Pakeman, & G. Bedell, 1651. (3rd, edition). 4to. Index. (xii), 530 (i.e. 528), (iv)pp. Few sm. marginal tears. Old ink annots. Occasional sl browning. Contemp. clf., re-backed & re-cornered, lower cvr. worn. **Wing S.3215 (var. imprint). S. & M. i.487.** £180.00

450. ————. The Touch-Stone of Common Assurances: or A plain and familiar Treatise, opening the Learning of the Common Assurances, or Conveyances of the Kingdom. E. & R. Brooke, Whieldon & Butterworth, etc. 1791. 6th edition. Notes and additional references by Edward Hilliard. 4to. xxviii, Variant pagination, (xx). Mod. cloth. S. & M. i.487/71. £65.00

451. SHOWER, Sir Bartholomew (1658-1701). The Second Part of the Reports of Cases and Special Arguments . . . in . . . the King's Bench. 1720. Folio. Mostly black-letter. Fp. port. Index. Lacks final blank. Some browning. Mod. b'ram. S. & M. i.309. £25.00
This part was posthumously published from a fair copy corrected by the author.

452. SIDNEY, Algernon. (1621-1683). Discourses concerning Government . . . to which is added, the Paper he deliver'd to the Sheriffs . . . before his Death. 1704. 2nd edition Folio. Engraved fp. port. Index. Few lib. stamps. Corner of N_2 torn away without loss of text. Signature of Henry Edward, Cardinal Manning (1819-1901) inside cover. Few marginal worm-holes. Contemp. panelled calf, later label, [illegible]orn. S. & M. i.107. £80.00
Sidney, who served as ambassador to

Sweden under Cromwell, laid the foundation of theory for English-speaking republicanism. His work (written, like Locke's, in answer to Filmer's "Patriarcha") has at its centre the doctrine of a natural justice & order of government from which all human institutions (including kingship) vary at their peril.

453. SKENE of CURRIEHILL, Sir John (c.1543-1617) (ed). Regiam maiestatem. Scotiae veteres leges et constitutiones. Edinburgh, excudebat Thomas Finlason, 1609. 1st edition. Folio. Index. (x), 172 leaves, 16pp. 17-123 leaves. Final errata leaf. Sl. stained. Contemp. calf; rebacked. STC 22623. S. & M. v.106. £150.00
Skene was an important pioneer of Scots legal studies. This volume contains the Regiam Maiestatem itself (an ancient manual of Scots Law, related to Glanville's work on English law), statutes of the mediaeval kings & of the boroughs and other items.

454. ——————. Regium Majestatem. The Auld Lawes and Constitutions of Scotland ... fra the Dayes of King Malcolm the Second, untill ... James the First. Edinburgh, 1609. 1st. Eng. ed. 4to. Index. Pagination varies. Lacks C2 (fol. 12) & C5 (fol. 15). Mod. ¼ calf. Water stains lower margin of leaf 99-100. £150.00
Skene's translation of the old Scot's laws appeared concurrently with his Latin collection in 1609. The English contains three extra items: an anonymous treatise on court's baron, & two summaries (probably Skene's own) on the form of process before the Lord's in session & on criminal causes.

455. A SKETCH of the HISTORY and PROCEEDINGS of the DEPUTIES appointed to Protect the Civil Rights of the Protestant Dissenters ... Laws affecting ... Dissenters. 1813. 1st edition. Appendix of statutes etc. Index. (A)4 a cancel. Later cloth, faded. £20.00
In the late 18th century the influence of & alliance with the powerful Methodist body gave the old-established dissenting communities the will to press for relief from the 17th century statutes which disabled them.

456. SMITH, James Walter. A Handy Book on the Law of Private Trading Partnership. 1871. Index. Orig. limp cl., worn. £5.00

457. SMITH, Josiah W. A Compendium of the Law of Real and Personal Property. 1877. 5th edition. 2 vols. Index. Few leaves of vol. 2. frayed & sl. soiled. Vol. 1 orig. cloth, faded; vol. 2 new cloth, orig. spine laid down. S. & M. ii.331. £20.00

458. SOLORZANO PEREIRA, Juan de. Politica Indiana, sacada en lengua Castellana de los dos tomos del derecho i govierno municipal de las Indias Occidentales ... por el mesmo autor. MADRID: (por Diego Diaz de la Carrera). 1648 1st Spanish edition. FOLIO. Engraved title. Engraved portrait after '"5. Index. (xliv), 1040, (cii)pp. Sm. hole in $3^{\prime}{}_{4}$ affecting border. Some slight occasional browning. Contemporary limp vellum, lacks ties. Sm. tear in upper cover. A VERY FINE COPY. Sabin 86534. Medina BHA.1130. Heredia IV.7886. Ternaux Bib. Amer, 664. Leclerc 3537. Stevens Historical Nuggets 2549. Goldsmith S.427. Maggs: Spanish Books 992. £1,400.00
The work of Solorzano, a jurist of Salamanca and member of the Councils of Castille & the Indies, is a code of law for the Spanish Americas in six books; the last of these, containing an account of the administrative establishment, was newly added by the author to this Spanish version. (The work first appeared in Latin, but the Spanish contains many other revisions.) It is the most valuable published work on the law of the Spanish colonies.

459. (SOMERS, John, Lord (L.C.) (1650-1716). Jura Populi Anglicani: or the Subject's Right of Petitioning set forth. Occasioned by the Case of the Kentish Petitioners. 1701. 1st edition. Sm. 4to. Title sl. torn without loss. Disbound. S. & M. i.159. £20.00
The petitioners, magistrates & gentlemen of Kent had urged the Commons to withdraw their opposition to the King's maintenance of a standing army. They were immediately taken into the custody of the serjeant-at-Arms. Somers examines the legality of this imprisonment & the justice of the Whiggish policies deplored by the petitioners; he omits to mention that his own opposition to these same policies had led to his dismissal & impeachment.

460. SOMNER, William. A treatise of Gavelkind, both Name and Thing. By R.U.W. Leybourn, for the Authour, 1660. 1st edition. Sm. 4to. Index. Lacks first blank. Modern wraps. WING S.4668. S. & M. i.477. £120.00
Somner was an academic rather than a lawyer, a pupil of the scholar Meric Casaubon; the accent of his book is accordingly philological in the main, although he includes a chapter on the place of gavelkin in the history of the law of descents & prints several ancient charters showing it in action.

461. SPELMAN, Sir Henry. (1662-1641). The Larger Treatise concerning Tithes ... with some other Tracts of the same Authour. And a Fragment of Sir Francis Bigot Knight, all touching the same Subject. Edited Jeremy Stephens. By M.F. for Philemon Stephens, 1647/6. 1st edition. Sm. 4to. 2 parts in 1. Final blank. Head of title and a few side notes sl. shaved. A_2 sl. torn without loss. WING S.4928. S. & M. i.195.54.
—————— De non temerandis ecclesiis. Churches not to be Violated. Oxford, by Henry Hall, 1646. Third edition. (32) 40pp. WING S.4921, MADAN 1858. S. & M. i.195.53. 2 works in 1 vol. Modern calf. Fine. £95.00

462. ——————. Reliquiae Spelmannianae ... Posthumous Works. Oxford (Clarendon Pr.), 1698. 1st. Folio. Device on title. Two fold'g tables. Index. Lacks final blank. Inner margin of A_1 defective – text not aff. Contemp. mottled cf.; sp. rbbd. & frayed. WING S.4391. S. & M. i.37. £70.00
Consists largely of the treatise on Feuds and Tenures by Knight-Service, together with the Apology for Archbishop Abbot (convicted of manslaughter by chance-medley in a test case for a clergyman's rights under such circumstances), remarks on will, coinage & the rank of knight etc.

463. SPENCE, George. An Inquiry into the Origin of the Laws and Political Institutions of Modern Europe. 1826. 1st edition. Index. Contemp. calf, sp. gilt; rebacked; jts. rubbed; lib. label. S. & M. i.37. £50.00
Spence derives a large proportion of the Teutonic institutions (including the Anglo-Saxon) directly from the Romans.

464. SPOTISWOODE, (Sir R.). Practicks of the Laws of Scotland, also abstracts out of the ancient records of this Kingdom, whereby is declared the manner of administering Justice on Civil Causes before the College of Justice was erected, and propositions and questions in law, with memoirs of his life and trial, at St. Andrews, December, 1645, and January, 1646. (4), xli, (3), 372. FOLIO. 1706. 1st edition. Panelled calf sl. rubbed. A fine copy. S. & M. v.108. £150.00
Sir Robert Spotiswood was the son of the Archbishop of St. Andrews but was put to death for adhering to the Marquis of Montrose. Lord Clarendon called him "a worthy, honest, loyal gentleman and as wise a man as the Scottish nation had at that time".

465. SPRY, Thomas (c.1620-1685). LEWIS, J.F. ... Lawyer & Physician; The First Attorney ... in the Delaware River Settlements. Philadelphia, Pa., 1932. 1st. Illus. Index. Orig. cl., uncut; fine. £15.00

Privately printed for distribution among the city lawyers. Includes many extracts from New York, Virginia, New Jersey & Penna. records.

466. STAIR, Sir James Dalrymple, Viscount. (1619-1695). The Institutions of the Laws of Scotland, Deduced from its Originals, and Collated with the Civil, Canon and Feudal Laws. Edinburgh, by the Heir of Andrew Anderson, 1693. 2nd edition, rev. Folio. Index. (iv), ii, 780, (xl)pp. Signatures 2L & 2M each a single leaf, conjugate & separated by another gathering signed L^2. Contemp. panelled calf, spine gilt, worn. Bk-pl. George Rose (1744-1818); Treasurer of the Navy etc. under Pitt) WING S.5178. S. & M. v.108. £100.00
The supreme classic of Scots jurisprudence. Stair has been called the Littleton of Scotland – an allusion to the reverence in which he is held for his work which is in fact a digest of jurisprudence with special reference to Scots law. This is the author's final text; no further edition appeared until 1832.

467. ——————. The Institutions of the Laws of Scotland. Ed. John Gordon & William Johnstone. Edinburgh, 1759. 1st thus. Folio. Index. Lib. stamp on title; sl. spotted at end. Contemp. calf, rebacked, front hinge broken. S. & M. v.108. £40.00
This is the only edition called for between 1693 & 1824.

468. ——————. The Institutions of the Law of Scotland, Deduced from its Originals, and Collated with the Civil, Canon, and Feudal Laws. Edited John S. More. Edinburgh 1832. 1st thus. 2 vols. 4to. Index. Sl. spotted. Lib. stamps on titles. Contemp. ½ calf, rebacked, rubbed. S. & M. v.108. £60.00
More regarded Stair's work as a digest of general jurisprudence rather than merely of Scots law, & his 500 pages of notes are designed to extend its usefulness in this way.

469. STANFORD, Sir William (1509-1558). An Exposition of the Kinges Prerogative, Collected out of the great Abridgement of Justice Fitzherbert, and other olde Writers. By Richard Tottel, 1577. Black letter. 85 leaves. Mod. ½ cf. Beale T495. STC 23216. S. & M. i.119. £220.00
This commentary on the statute 17 Edw. II (de praerogativa regis) is the earliest extant monograph on statutory interpretation & is further remarkable for being written in English. It shows the wide reading & historical knowledge which was characteristic of the author.

470. ——————. Les Plees del Coron, diuisees in plusors titles & comon lieux ... dernierment corrigee avecques un table ... In aedibus Richardi Tottelli, 1574. Sm. 4to. French text. Black letter. FINE woodcut title-border (BEALE 47) & Initials. Index. (xiv), 193 (i.e. 198) leaves. BEALE T.489. STC 2322. S. & M. i.365.
——————. An exposition of the Kinges Prerogatiue, collected out of the great Abridgement of Justice Fitzherbert, and other olde writers of the lawes of England. Richard Tottel. n.d. (1577) (5th edition) 4to. Black letter. 85 leaves. BEALE T.495. STC 23216. S. & M. i.119. Two works in 1 volume. Contemp. calf; rubbed; rebacked. A VERY FINE COPY. £400.00
The King's Prerogative (a commentary on 17 Ed. II), written by Stanford in 1548 before he became a judge, is a work of great historical importance and far ahead of its time. It is considered to be the earliest monograph on statutory interpretation.

471. STATE TRACTS: Being a Collection of Several Treatises Relating to the Government. 1689. 1st edition. Folio. (ii), 468 (341)pp. Pagination varies. Contemp. calf; sl. rubbed & worn; first blank loose. Bk-pl. WING S.5329. £150.00
A contemporary hand has indicated some of the authors as being Settle, Shaftesbury, Blount, etc.

471A. ——————: Being a Collection of Several Treatises relating to the Government. Printed ... 1689. 1st collected. Folio. Signatures jump from 3D to 5B; pagination irreg. accordingly; nothing missing. 5H & 5I each a single leaf. Contemp. sprinkled calf, spine rubbed. Wing S.5329. £50.00
Includes Andrew Marvell's "Account of the Growth of Popery" & a number of items illustrating the dying struggles of arbitrary & irresponsible government of King Charles & his "cabal".

471B. ——————: A collection. Published on the Occasion of the Late Revolution ... during the Reign of King William III. 1705 (-7). 1st collected. 3 vols. Folio. Red & black title. Indices $4M_{3-4}$ (vol. 3) misbound. Vols. 2 & 3 lack two blanks each. Calf; rebacked. £100.00
Consists largely of pamphlets exposing the Catholic leanings & unconstitutional dealing of Charles II & his brother.

472. STATUTES concerning Bankrupts. 1765. (2nd ed.) Index. (iv), 144, (xxxvi), 4pp. Sl. stnd. Mod. cl. S. & M. ii.543. £20.00
Includes obsolete acts (from 34-35 Hen. VIII. c.4) as well as those in force.

473. STATUTES. Ireland. The Statutes of Ireland, beginning the Third Yere of K. Edward the Second. Dublin, by the Societie of Stationers, 1621. Folio. BLACK LETTER. Woodcut title-border, & arms on first leaf & title-verso. Index. (xxx), 446pp. Lacks final blank. Contemp. polished calf, large gilt Royal Arms & initials of James I & corner ornaments on each side; re-backed in 18th century & corners repaired; joints & edges worn; lacks ties. Book-plate Signet Library. New STC 14130. S. & M. iv.87. £750.00
This style of binding is also found on books printed by Robert Barker, the King's Printer in London, who would presumably have been the English distributor for this book. Despite the "good authority" mentioned in an 18th-century note on the title, it does not appear that the book was the King's own property. This edition of Richard Bolton is the second collection of Irish Statutes.

474. ——————. A Collection of Miscellaneous Acts relating to Ireland. Dublin, (1833-) 1838. 1st collected. General & individual titles. Indices. (iv), (iv), 160, 32, 120, 64, 18pp. Contemp. cf., sl. rbbd. £10.00
Consists largely of acts relating to the administration of justice.

475. ——————. Statutes of the United Kingdom ... 54 George III. 1814. 1st collected. Index. Orig. bds., uncut; sp. defective; edges worn. £20.00

476. ——————. Acts for Making Provision for the Effectual Performance of Quarantine; with Orders in Council, &c. 1817. 1st collected. 4to. Index. Interleaved throughout. Contemp. diced cf., rbbd., lacks spine. £20.00

477. STATUTES. SCOTLAND. The Laws and Acts of Parliament made by King James the First (-Queen Anne). Edinburgh, 1682-3 & 1731. 3 vols. 12mo. Indices. Vol. 2 lacks final blank. Old cf., re-backed; sl. rbbd. Bk-pls. WING S.1266. S. & M. v.116-7. £40.00

478. ——————. The Laws and Acts of Parliament made by King James the First (-Queen Anne). Edinburgh. Vol. 3 (James VII-Anne) only. 1731. 875pp. Some foremargins shaved. Sl. browned. Contemp. cf., re-backed. £10.00

479. ——————. The Laws and Acts of Parliament made by King James the First, and his Royal Successors. Edinburgh, by Josua van Solingen (etc.), 1682 (1683, 1731) – An Index or Abridgment to the Acts. Edinburgh, by John Reid, 1685. 1st collected. 4 parts in 3 vols. 12mo. Two leaves before title of vol. 1. Lacks blank Z_5 (vol. 2), but includes three other blanks. Some stains in vol. 2. Occasional worming. Contemp. calf; spines gilt, those of vols. 1 & 2 defective at head & foot. EING S.1266 & ALDIS 2326/2364 (vols. 1 & 2). S. & M. v.115-6. £60.00

480. The STATUTES at LARGE concerning Elections of Members to Serve in the ... Commons. 1734. 1st edition. Index. vi, 109 (i.e. 119), (xv), 10pp. S. & M. i.152 ... ORDERS & RESOLUTIONS of the ... Commons on Controverted Elections and Return. 1736. 2nd edition, rev. 12mo. Index. viii, 209, (vii)pp. S. & M. ii.26.
—————— COWLEY, J.: The Candidates Guide: or the Electors Right Decided ... Resolutions ... concerning the Rights of Elections. 1734. 1st edition. (ii), 30pp. This edition not in S. & M. Three works in 1 vol. Contemp. calf, lower cover rubbed. £40.00

481. STEUART or STEWART of GOODTREES, Sir James. An Index or Abridgement of the Acts of Parliament and Convention, from ... King James the First ... to the Ninth Session of the Current Parliament, Edinburgh; 1702. 2nd ed., rev. 12mo. Index. Lacks U_4 (pp. 237-8) (cancel, not bound in). Two similar cancel leaves loosely inserted. Contemp. cf., worn. S. & M. v.117. £10.00

482. ——————. The Index or Abridgement ... from ... 1424 to ... 1707 ... with the Act Ratifying ... the Treaty of Union of the Two Kingdoms. Edinburgh, 1707. (3rd ed., rev.) Final blank. Tear in X_1 without loss. And: – BRUCE, Alexander; The Index ... of such Acts ... as ... concern the whole United Kingdom, or particularly ... Scotland ... to ... 1726. Edinburgh, 1726. 1st. 12mo. Final blank. 2 works in 1 vol. Contemp. cf., rbbd. £20.00

483. ——————. Dirleton's Doubts and Questions ... Resolved and Answered. Edinburgh, 1715. 1st. Folio. Red & black title. Contemp. cf., sl. rubbed. S. & M. v.117. £60.00
There was a proverb in Scotland, "Doubting with Dirleton and resolving with Steuart"; Too much of Steuart's work consists of Dirleton's words repeated with approving comments; yet his eighteen years' experience as Lord Advocate provided him with the matter of some more solid observations.

484. (STILLINGFLEET, Edward, Bp. of Worcester) (1635-1699). The Grand Question, concerning the Bishops Right to Vote in Parlament in Cases Capital, Stated and Argued. For M.P. and Sold by Richard Ramball, 1680. 1st edition. (iv), 188pp. Contemp. mottled calf, spine gilt, jts. sl. worn. Bk-pl. Richard Jones (1707) WING S.5594. S. & M. i.142. £40.00
In answer to Denzil, Lord Holles, who expelled the bishops from the jurisdiction of the upper house.

485. STONE, John. The Practice of the Petty Sessions; to Which Is Added an Appendix to Practical Forms. 1839. 3rd ed. 8vo. Index. Contemp. cloth. £15.00

486. (STRACHEY, –.). An Index to the Records, with Directions to the Several Places where they may be Found ... List of the Latin Sir-Names, and Names of Places. 1739. 1st edition. Final advert. leaf. Contemp. sprinkled calf, rubbed, jts. sl. worn. S. & M. i.78. £25.00

487. STRANGE, Sir John (1696-1754). Reports of Adjudged Cases in ... Chancery, King's Bench, Common Pleas, and Exchequer. Ed. John Strange. 1755. 1st edition. 2 vols. First privilege leaf to each volume. Index. Lacks fp. port. Several annots. to the earlier cases by Sir William de Grey, L.C.J. (later Lord Walsingham) (1719-1781). Modern cloth. Bk-pl. Thomas de Grey (the Judge's father). S. & M. i.309. £80.00
De Grey has several times added information concerning counsel and occasionally abbreviated a point of law, concentrating on cases tried previous to his call to the Bar in 1742. He was Chief Justice of Common Pleas for ten years, & Lord Eldon praises him for his great learning & power of memory.

488. ——————. Reports of Adjudged Cases in ... Chancery, King's Bench, Common Pleas, and Exchequer. Ed. John Strange. 1755. 1st. 2 vols. Folio. Engr. fp. port. Index. Contemp. cf., rbbd. S. & M. i.309. £60.00
Strange includes an unusual number of cases turning on points of criminal law.

489. ——————. Reports of Adjudged Cases in ... Chancery, King's Bench, Common Pleas and Exchaquer. Ed. by John Strange. 1755. 1st. 2 vols. Folio. Engr. fp. port. (laid down). Index. Mod. cl. S. & M. i.309. £60.00

490. STUART, Gilbert (1742-1786). Observations concerning the Public Law of Scotland: with Occasional Remarks concerning English Antiquity. Edinburgh 1779. 1st edition. Appendix of documents etc. xxiv, 396pp. Sl. spotted. Some pencil annots. Contemp. sprinkled calf, jts. & edges sl. worn. S. & M. v.118. £50.00
Stuart shows that the feudal, parliamentary & juridical institutions of Scotland are more ancient & more national than Robertson & others supposed. He does, however, condemn the arbitrary jurisdiction (nobile officium) of the Court of Session.

491. ——————. Observations concerning the Public Law, and the Constitutional History of Scotland with occasional remarks concerning English Antiquity. Edinburgh, William Creech & J. Murray 1779. 1st edition. Contemp. calf; gilt spine, label. Fine copy. S. & M. v.118. £50.00

492. ——————. Observations concerning the Public Law, and the Constitutional History of Scotland. Edinburgh 1779. 1st edition. Appendix of Charters. Errata leaf. Old calf, gilt, rubbed. S. & M. v.118. £50.00

493. STUART, James. Trial ... before the High Court of Justiciary. Edinburgh, 1822. 2nd edition. Appendix. (iv), 186, (ii), 20pp.
... Trial ... for Murder. (Different report) Edinburgh 1822. 2nd. 44pp.
... MACKINTOSH, Sir James. Debate ... on a Motion made by ... to consider ... the Punishment of Death. Edinburgh, 1819. 56pp.
... BOWDLER, C. On the Punishment of Death, in the Case of Forgery. 1819. 3rd edition. 60pp.
... BUXTON, T.F. Speech ... in the ... Commons ... on the Bill "for Mitigating ... Punishment." 1821. 1st edition. (ii), 70pp.
Five works in 1 vol. Contemp. annots. on e-p's. Contemp. ½ calf. Sl. worn. £50.00
Stuart's case was one of the sensations of its day; having fought a duel & killed a baronet who had insulted him in the press, he was acquitted of murder. The other works show the growing revulsion against capital punishment; those of Mackintosh & Buxton are speeches in favour of an abortive Bill to remove forgery from the list of capital offences.

494. A SUMMARY OF THE ROMAN LAW, Taken from Dr. Taylor's Elements of the Civil Law. To Which is Prefixed a Dissertation on Obligation. 1772. 1st ed. Index. Mod. ¼ calf. S. & M. v.142. £25.00
Said to be written by the Rev. W. Ellis, this abridgement is aimed primarily at the student.

495. SWINTON, John. An Abridgement of the Public Statutes in Force and Use Relative to Scotland, from the Union ... to the Twenty-Seventh Year of his present Majesty. Edinburgh. 1788. 1st. 2 vols. Index. ½ titles. Contemp. sheep, rbbd. S. & M. v.119. £50.00
Replaces the work of the elder Swinton (1755). Schedules of customs & excise are given in full.

496. TAYLOR, John (1704-1736). Elements of the Civil Law. Charles Bathurst (1756) 2nd edition. 4to. Index. Contemp. calf, joints weak & worn. S. & M. v.143. £40.00
Taylor, who adapted this work from his tutorial lectures to the grandsons of Lord Granville, wrote with the idea of presenting Roman law as a basis for a gentleman's conduct of life.

497. TAYLOR, (John) Pitt (1811-1888). A Treatise on the Law of Evidence. 1885. 8th (Taylor's last) edition 2 vols. Indices. Contemp. calf; sl. rbbd. S. & M. ii.353. £20.00

498. TENANTS LAW or, the Law concerning Landlords, Tenants, and Farmers. 1753. 14th ed. 12mo. Index. 314, Contemp. cf., jts. worn. S. & M. i.461. £15.00

499. —————— or, the Law concerning Landlords, Tenants and Farmers. (16th) ed. 1768. 12mo. Index. Contemp. sheep, rbbd., jts. worn. S. & M. i.461. £15.00

500. TIBET and the CHINESE PEOPLE'S REPUBLIC. A Report to the International Commission of Jurists. Geneva, 1960. 1st. Appendices. Orig. wraps; fine. £6.00

501. TIDSWELL, Richard Thomas & Ralph D.M. LITTLER. The Practice and Evidence in Cases of Divorce and other Matrimonial Causes. 1860. 1st & only edition. Appendices of fees and forms. Index. First advert leaf. Orig. cloth, lacks front e-p. Sl. frayed & ink-stained. S. & M. ii.358. £20.00

502. TILLESLEY, Richard. Animadversions upon M. Selden's History of Tithes, and his Review thereof. By John Bill. 1619. 1st edition. Sm. 4to. First leaf blank, except for signature in WOODCUT FRAME. ROYAL ARMS ON TITLE VERSO. (xl), 236pp. A few sm. worm-holes in fore-margins and occasional light staining, otherwise A FINE COPY in contemp. vellum, ties (one broken); paste-downs detached. STC 24073. (Huntington copy only) S. & M. i.196. £150.00
Tillesley, fond of anagrams, attempts to compete with Selden in the quotation of legal authority.

503. ——————. Animadversions upon M. Selden's History of Tithes, and his review thereof. By John Bill, 1619. Lacks first blank. Fore-margins sl. stained.
... GAUDEN, John. The Case of Ministers Maintenance by Tithese. By Thomas Maxey, for Andrew Crook, 1643. 1st edition. 4to. (iv), 46pp. Lacks A_2 (dedication) & first leaf of text, Last line of most pages cropped. Sl. stained. WING G.344.
... (STEPHENS, J.) An Apology for the Ancient Right ... of the Bishops to Sit ... in Parliaments. By W. Godbid, for Richard Thrale, 1660. 1st edition. 4to. (viii), 120pp. Lacks C_1 (pp. 9-10) Corner torn from last leaf. WING S.5446.
... An ANSWER to the Rectors Libel. Dublin, by Richard Wilde, 1694. 1st edition. 4to. (ii), 22pp. Sl. browned. WING A.3440.
Four items in one vol. 19th century ½ roan., rubbed. £120.00
Gauden has often been cited as author of the Eikon Basilike. The last item alleges that a Parson cannot on his own authority, & on hearsay evidence, suspend a parishioner from communion.

504. TOLLER, Sir Samuel. The Law of Executors and Administrators. Ed. Francis Whitmarsh. 1818. 4th ed. corrected w. additions. Indices. E-p's sl. spotted; some pages creased. Contemp. bds. sp. torn. S. & M. i.494/36. £20.00

505. TOMLINS, (Sir), T.E. The Law Dictionary, Defining and Interpreting the Terms or Words of Art ... Abstracted from the Last Quarto Edition. 1810. 1st thus. 2 vols. Unpaged. Final advert. leaf to vol. 2. Contemp. calf, rebacked. S. & M. ii.359. £90.00

506. TOWNESEND, George. Tables to most of the Printed Presidents of Pleadings, Writs, and Reform (sic) of Writs. By John Streater, James Flesher, and Henry Twyford, 1667. 1st edition. Mostly black-letter. Folio. Index. (viii), 554pp. Contemp. calf. S. & M. i.279/151. WING T.1984. £75.00
This work serves as a copious index to the precedents contained in the standard reports, the Registers, & the two Naturae Brevium. Sixty-one different works are cited by the author, who compiled the book for exercise while evacuated during the plague.

507. A TREATISE on the LAW of the DESCENT of an INTESTATES REAL ESTATE. Comprising the Alterations made therein by ... 3 & 4 W.IV.c.106. with ... Notes; and on the Distribution of an Intestate's Personal Estate. 1834. 1st. Sl. spotted. Orig. bds.; sp. defective. £15.00

508. TRIALS. William Earl of Kilmarnock, George Earl of Cromertie, and Arthur Lord Balmerino. 1746. 1st. – Simon Lord Lovat. 1747. 1st. Lacks $2T^3$ (pp. 161-4). – Lawrence Earl Ferrers. 1760. 1st. – Admiral John Byng. 1757. 1st. – Thomas Earl of Macclesfield. 1725. 1st. Last leaf browned. Six items in one vol. Folio. Contemp. ½ cf. sl. rbbd. £90.00
The trial of Lord Macclesfield was the most extreme (since mediaeval times) among the few cases of corruption in judges; that of Admiral Byng's was noted for the sympathy aroused on his behalf at home & abroad; & those of Lords Byron (predecessor of the poet) & Ferrers are rare examples of the process of trying a peer for felony (murder in each case) before the Lords.

509. TUCKER, A.G.C. Supplement to the Observations intended to Prove that the Judgement ... in the ... Cause ... Cholomondeley and ... Damer versus ... Clinton is Unfounded in Law. Exeter, 1818. 1st. Disbound. £5.00
The case concerned the ambiguously-worded will of Samuel Rolle; the family of Horace Walpole was involved.

510. TYTLER, Alexander Fraser (Judge-Advocate). An Essay on Military Law, and the Practice of Courts Martial. Edinburgh, 1800. 1st edition. Errata leaf before b_1. Appendices. Index. Modern cloth. S. & M. i.603. £30.00
The Author offers several criticisms of Blackstone, whose pronouncements on military law had been accepted as authority in his time.

511. Van ECK, Cornelius. (ed.). Guilielmi Forneri et Antonii Contii tractatus de feudis. Ut & constitutio Caroli III. Imp. olim edita & exposita a Marquardo Frehero ... Elementa iuris feudalis Francisci Hottomanni. Utrecht, 1698. 1st collected. WOODCUT DIAGRAMS in text. Index. Final blank. Contemp. calf, sp. sl. rubbed. £70.00
A collection of old & scarce tracts on feudal law, including an unpublished summary of the subject by Hottoman, drawn by van Eck from a MS. in the hand of Hottoman's son.

512. VANTIUS, Sebastianus. Tractatus de nullitatibus processuum ac sententiarum causarum. Venice (apud Hieronymum Cavalcalupum), 1559. 1st. Device on title, Index. (viii), 275, (lvi), leaves *8 blank. Lacks $2L_{1-4}$. Few ink annots. Sl. marginal worming at end. Few light stains. Title worn. Contemp. vellum, soiled. Not in B.M.C. or Adams. £30.00
According to the preface, legal tricks for annulling judgements & cancelling cases were a standing abuse in the courts of the time. In writing a treatise to correct their abuse, the author professes to have been aided by a vision.

513. VIDOCQ, Eugene-Francois (1775-1843). FROMENT, -; Histoire de Vidocq ... d'apres Lui-meme. Paris 1829. 1st. 2 vols in 1. French text. 12mo. Engr. fp. port. Vol. 2 lacks title, probably as issued, Sl. browned. Central stain to some leaves in vol. 1, Contemp. vellum. £25.00
Vidocq began his career as one of the most notorious thieves & forgers in France, but changed his cloth and became chief of the Paris Bureau de Surete, founder of the science of detection, and the original of most of the detective fiction of the century.

514. ——————. Memoirs of: Principal Agent of the French Police, until 1827; and now proprietor of the Paper Manufactory at St. Mande. Written by himself. Transl. from the French. 4 vols. sm. 8vo. Whittaker, Treacher & Arnot 1829. Orig. cloth, faded & sl. rubbed. Vols. 25-28 in a pocket edition of famous biographies. £20.00
A fascinating picture of the French underworld.

515. VINNIUS, Arnold (1588-1657). In quattuor libros Institutionum imperialium commentarius. Amsterdam (D. Elzevir). 1665. 4th edition revised. 4to. Red & black title. Index. Lacks front e-p. Contemp. vellum, sl. soiled. WILLEM. £50.00
This commentary was undertaken to clarify the Institutes and is printed from an annotated copy found among the author's papers. Some further remarks by Prof. Johan Schulting of Nijmegen (Father of Anton) are inserted.

516. ——————. In quatuor libros Institutionum imperialium commentarius ... Jo. Gottl. Heineccius j.c. recensuit. Lyons. 1747. 2 vols. Latin text. 4to. Red & black title to vol. 1. Index. Engr. table. Blank $6P_4$. Lacks final blank. Contemp. cf.; upper cvrs. sl. worn. £40.00
This edition includes the author's Selectae juris quaestiones.

517. ——————. Commentarius ... editio ultima ... aucta indicibus decisionum et constitutionum. Leyden, 1709. 4to. Engr. dedication leaf. Mod. ½ red mor. £40.00

518. ——————. Institutionum, sive elementorum, libri quatuor, notis perpetuis ... illustrati. Leyden, 1709. 12mo. Engr. title & fold'g engr. dedication. Index. Contemp. vellum, later label. £30.00
A different work from the last, retaining the notes on the Prooemium, but thereafter much briefer.

519. Von der RECK, Mordius. Disputatio juridica de piscatione. Strassburg (J. Stadel), 1662. 1st. 4to. (iv), (20)pp. Some headmargins shaved. 19th-cent. ½ mor. Westwood & Satchell 175. £60.00
This thesis on the definition, rights, uses, & penalties of fishing (with some reference to hunting & hawking) reflects the high importance which these sports assumed in the life & thought of the German nobility.

520. WAGNER, Georg Wilhelm. De mutatione successionis in familiis illustribus. Giessen, 1740. 1st. Sm. 4to. Mod. wraps. £10.00
Thesis for a doctorate in the University of Giessen, one of the three centres (with Jena & Franeker) for the study of the law in Germany.

521. (WARNER, John, Bishop). Church-Lands Not to be Sold. Or, a Necessary and Plaine Answer to the Question of a Conscientious Protestant. Printed ... 1648. 1st. Sm. 4to. Sl. stnd. Sm. marginal hole in L_1. Lacks final blank. 19th-cent. annots. on e-p. & title. Old ¼ cf. Sl. rbbd. S. & M. i.166. WING W.900. £30.00
A "ghost" edition is ascribed to 1640 by Sweet & Maxwell & to 1646 by some others.

522. WASHINGTON, Joseph (& Henry (BOULT) (eds.)). An Exact Abridgement of all the Statutes of King William and Queen Mary, and of King William II, and Queen Anne. 1704. Rev. ed. Index. (lxxxii), 662, (actually 678), between sigs. I & K. Contemp. cf., rbbd. S. & M. i.566. £25.00
Continuation of Wingate's Abridgement.

523. WATKINS, Charles. Treatise on Copyholds. 1797: for R. Pheney. 1st edition. 2 vols. Indices. xl, 408, (ii)/xvi, 272pp. Lib. stamps, e-p's. browned. Contemp. calf., rbbd; hinges worn & repaired with cellotape; Vol. 1 with plastic wrap. S. & M. i.406/72. £80.00
This work covers many different subjects from the Doctrine of Manors to Courts, Customs and the "doctrine of Free-Bench".

524. WEBSTER, Daniel. Speeches and Forensic Arguments. Boston. Mass. 1848. 8th edition. 3 vols. Engraved fp. port. ... Diplomatic and Official Papers. N.Y. 1848. 1st edition. Engraved fp. port. Folding map. Altogether 4 vols. Sl. spotted. Contemp. diced calf, gilts, jts. rubbed. £80.00

525. ——————. HARVEY, Peter: Reminiscences and Anecdotes of Boston, Mass., 1877. 1st edition. 2 steel-engraved & 2 wood-engraved plates. Index. Press-cutting ("Evening Transcript" review of Lodge's Life of Webster, 1883, with contemptuous reference to Harvey's work) pasted on e-p. Orig. b'ram, sl. marked & faded. £15.00

526. WELLS, John C. & H.T. Wells' Lawyer and United States Form-book ... Property Exempt from Execution ... Laws of Contracts ... Constitution of the United States ... and Forms ... System of Book-keeping, N.p. (N.Y.), n.d. (1849). Orig. ¼ roan/printed bds., corners worn. £10.00

527. WESEMBECK, Mathias (1531-1581). In Pandectas iuris civilis et Codicis Iustinianei lib. IIX (sic) commentarii. Basle (per Eusebium Episcopium, & Nicolai fr. haeredes), 1575. Folio. Device on title. Index. Strip torn from foot of title. Contemp. sheep, rbbd. £80.00
Fifth edition of the Paratitla, with a commentary (never before printed) on books 1-8 of the Code.

528. ——————. Paratitla in Pandectas ... ab auctore recognita. Basle (per Eusebium Episcopium & Nicolai fr. haeredes), 1572. 4th ed. Folio. Device on title & last leaf. Index. Title cut round & mounted. Last four leaves sl. frayed. Later cf., sp. gilt; head & tail of sp. defective. £60.00
The author was a Belgian jurist exiled for his religious opinions and protected by the Saxon court. This edition includes his Prolegomena on the study & sources of the law.

529. ——————. RAUCHBAR, Andreas; Oratio de vita et obitu. Wittenberg (Z. Lehmann) 1587. 1st. Italic letter. Errata leaf. (75)pp. Sl. browned. Mod. wraps. Not in B.M.C. £30.00
Commemorative oration on Wesembeck delivered at the enrolment ceremony of three licenciates (Nicholas Claudius, Johan Muller, & Liberius Hoffmann).

530. WEST, William. The First (-Second) Part of Symboleography ... Newly Augmented with divers Presidents touching Marchants Affairs. For the Companie of Stationers. 1605(-6). 2 parts in 1 vol. 4to. Partly black letter. Index. (vi), (318)/(ii), 304, (viii) leaves. Final blank. Contemp. MS. inscr. (metrical "Rules for Purchasing Land") on e-p. Contemp. calf, worn, rebacked. Part 1 not in STC (cf.25271, listed as 8vo) Part 2. STC 25279. (Huntington only). S. & M. i.487. £250.00
The growth of English commerce & the application of the Statute of Uses caused a revolution in the science of conveyancing, & presented a challenge to the profession which West was the first to meet. He takes a wide view of his subject embracing commercial agreements, indictments, Chancery bills & answers, & general remarks on contract & on equity. Part 2 is dedicated to Coke.

531. ——————. The First (-Second) Part of Simboleography. For the Companie of Stationers. 1610(-11) 2 parts in 1 vol. 4to. Black letter. Index. Final blank. '3-4 (vol. 1) frayed without loss of text. Contemp. calf, sl. worn, head of spine defective. STC 25272. S. & M. i.487. £200.00

532. ——————. The First (-Second) Part of Symboleographie. By Miles Flesher, 1647 (By Miles Flesher and Robert Young, 1641) 2 parts in 1. 4to. Partly black letter. Index. Final blank. Publisher's catalogue pasted inside lower cover; imprint at head torn away, four lines of text also affected. Sm. hole Y_1 (pt. 1) with loss of few letters. Sl. browned & stained. Some contemp. annots. Contemp. calf, worn. WING W.1394. S. & M. i.487. £150.00
Includes a new appendix of bills & answers in Exchequer, Wards & Liveries, & Star Chamber, with a short account of each court. There are also some new precedents in the body of the work. Pub's cat. printed separately, *as opposed to those included in the collation,* are extremely rare *before about 1790.*

533. WIELING, Abraham (ed.). Iurisprudentia restituta, sive index ... in ... Corpus ... Accesserunt ... I. Usus Pandectarum per Iac. Labittum ... II. Henrici Hahnii oratio de usu chronologiae ... III. Henrici Brencmanni dissertatio de legum inscriptionibus. IV. Bern. Henrici Reinoldi oratio de inscriptionibus legum. Amsterdam, 1727. 1st thus. Red & black title. Engraved dedication leaf. Contemp. vellum. £60.00
A collection of particular value to those interested in the Corpus, Novellae & Edicts as historical sources.

534. WILLCOCK, J.W. The Law of Municipal Corporations; Together with ... a Treatise on Mandamus and Quo Warranto. Philadelphia, Pa., 1836. 1st. Amer. Index. A_1 torn without loss. See S. & M. ii.381. – WARREN, S. Popular and Practical Introduction to Law Studies. Philadelphia, Pa., 1836. 1st. Amer. Index. Sl. spotted. See S. & M. ii.371. Two works in one vol., as issued, with general title. Contemp. cf., sl. rbbd. £30.00

535. WILLIAMS, Joshua. Principles of the Law of Real Property, intended as a First Book for the Use of Students in Conveyancing. 1875. 11th edition. Index. Orig. cloth, sl. faded; sp. sl. frayed. S. & M. ii.383. £10.00

536. WILLIAMS, Montagu, Q.C. Leaves of a Life, being the Reminiscences of a Criminal Lawyer. 1890. 1st edition. 2 vols. Orig. cloth, uncut. Fp. port. ... The further reminiscences, Later Leaves. 1891. 1st edition. fp. port. Orig. cloth, uncut, fp. port. Altogether 3 vols. covers marked. Ex Mudie's Library labels on cover. £20.00

537. WILLIAMS, Thomas Walter. The Whole Law relative to the Duty and Office of a Justice of the Peace. Edited H.N. Tomlins. 1812. 3rd edition. 4 vols. Folding table. Index. Contemp. calf, sl. stained, 1 joint sl. split. S. & M. ii.384. £50.00
Last edition of this rival to Burn.

538. WILLIAMSON, J. Bruce. The History of the Temple, London 1925. 2nd edition. Illus. Appendices. Index. Orig. cloth, sl. spotted. £15.00

539. **WILSON, George** (Serjeant-at-Law). Reports of Cases . . . in the King's Courts . . . (1742-1769). 1779. 2nd. ed. corrected. **2 parts in 1 vol.** Folio. Index. Mod. cl. w/out end-papers. **S. & M. i.310/131.** £40.00
Pt. 2 includes R. v. Wilkes *(in which there was a case of a breach of parliamentary privilege when John Wilkes was sent to the Tower for seditious libel) and a similar case,* Entick v. Carrington & others.

540. ————. Reports of Cases . . . in the King's Courts. 1770(-75). 1st. **3 pts in 2 vols.** Folio. Indices. Mod. cl. **S. & M. i.310.** £50.00

541. **WILTON, George Wilton.** Fingerprints; History, Law and Romance. Introd. Robert Heindl. 1938. 1st edition. Illus. Folding table. Index. d.w. Fine. £10.00
The discovery of the forensic value of fingerprints is ascribed to Dr. Henry Faulds (1843-1930) who saw them used in Japan for identification purposes in the 1870s.

542. **WINES, Frederick Howard.** Punishment and Reformation. An Historical Sketch of the Rise of the Penitentiary System. 1895. 1st. Index. Orig. cl. fine. £10.00

543. **WINGATE, Edmund.** An Exact Abridgement of All Statutes in Force and Use, from the Beginning of Magna Charta, until 1641 . . . Continued . . . to . . . 1681. By the Assigns of J. Bill (etc.), Sold by G. Sawbridge (etc.), 1681. Addenda on A_2. Indices. Final errata leaf. Contemp. cf., rbbd. **Wing E.909. S. & M. i.566.** £25.00

544. ————. An Exact Abridgement of All Statutes in Force and Use, from the Beginning of Magna Charta, until 1641 . . . Continued . . . to . . . 1681. rev. 1700. Contemp. cf., sp. sl. frayed, upper jt. worn. **Wing E.912.** £20.00

545. ————. An Exact Abridgement of All Statutes in Force and Use, from the Beginning of Magna Charta, until 1641 . . . Continued . . . to . . . 1681. 1704. First blank, Sl. wormed at end. Contemp. cf., sp. sl. rbbd. £20.00

546. **WISSENBACH, Johann Jakob** (ed.). Exercitationum ad quinquaginta libros Pandectarum partes duae. Franeker, 1661. 3rd ed., rev. 4to. **2 pts. in 1.** Red & black title. Engr. port. on *4 verso. Index. Margins sl. wormed. Contemp. blind-stamped vellum, ties. Bk-pl. £60.00
Wissenbach conceived the excellent scheme of reviving 97 theses from the German & Dutch universities, and arranging them as a perpetual commentary on the Pandects.

547. **WOOD, Thomas.** An Institute of the Laws of England: or, the Laws of England in their natural order, according to common use . . . in four books. Folio. In the Savoy, E. & R. Nutt & R. Gosling . . . for Bernard Lintot etc. 1734. The fifth edition with additions. To which is prefixed, Some Thoughts concerning the Study of the Laws of England in a Letter to the Reverend . . . For E. & R. Nutt, & R. Gosling for D. Midwinter & others. 1734. 4th edition. Table, publisher's adverts. Lacks portrait. Contemp. calf, rubbed; spine frayed & fragile. Fine clean copy. **S. & M. i.38.88.** £85.00
An attempt (superseded by Blackstone, who preserves much of Wood's arrangement) at a methodical digest of English Law.

548. **WOOLRYCH, Humphrey W.** The New Inclosure Act, 8 & 9 Vict. c. CXVIII. 1846. 1st edition. Index. Contemp. annots. (abstract of the statute 9 & 10 Vict. c. LXX, amending the above) on back e-p's. Modern cloth. £10.00

549. **WOOLSEY, Theodore D.** Essay on Divorce and Divorce Legislation. With special reference to the U.S. N.Y. Scribner . . . 1869. 1st edition. Index, appendix, booklist. Orig. cloth; sp. ends sl. frayed. £25.00
The essay is a reprint of articles which appeared in the New Englander for 1867 & 1868 with a number of changes and additions. The author felt that the Divorce Laws of the State at that time were too lax.

550. **WRIGHT, Andrew.** Court Hand Restored; or, the Student's Assistant in Reading Old Deeds, Charters, &c. . . . Ancient Names of Places . . . Ancient Surnames. (fourth) ed. 1815. 4to. 24 engr. plates. Indices. Sl. spotted. Few old annots. Mod. cloth. £35.00

551. ————. Court Hand Restored; or, the Student's Assistant in Reading Old Deeds, Charters, &c. . . . Ancient Names of Places . . . Ancient Surnames. (sixth) ed. 1822. 23 engr. plates. Title cut round & mounted. Later mor. sp. sl. fdd. **S. & M. i.14.** £40.00

552. **(WYNNE, E., 1734-1784).** Eunomus: Or, Dialogues Concerning the Law and Constitution of England. 1774. 2nd ed. **4 vols.** Contemp. calf. S. & M. i.110/128. £90.00
"This work treats incidentally of the character and authority of the several law writers, and more professedly on the origin and progress of the most important subjects and branches of the law, and their connexion with the history and constitution of England." – Harg. Co. Litt. 115b.

553. ————. Eunomus: or, Dialogues concerning the Law and Constitution of England. With an Essay on Dialogue. 1809. 3rd edition. **2 vols.** Orig. boards, uncut, sl. worn. **S. & M. i.110.** £35.00
These dialogues were first writtein in the 1720s.

554. **YELVERTON, Sir Henry (1566-1630).** The Reports . . . of divers Special Cases in . . . King's Bench. 1735. "3rd" (1st English) edition. Index. First privilege leaf. Sl. browned. Contemp. calf; rubbed; jts. sl. torn. **S. & M. i.130.** £30.00
Yelverton as Attorney-General & judge, hated by Buckingham & distrusted by the King, proved that honesty & just dealing were indispensible.

555. **YORKSHIRE.** The Year Book for the Use of the Justices of the West Riding . . . 1901-1902 (-1912-13) Wakefield, 1902 (-13). **12 vols.** Folding tables. Orig. b'ram, faded. Fore-margins of covers stained. £120.00
In addition to lists of personnel & sundry matters similar to those found in the standard justices' manuals, these year-books contain interesting statistics, financial & otherwise, of the Yorkshire police.

FROGNAL RARE BOOKS

18 Cecil Court, Charing Cross Road
London WC2N 4HE, England.
Tel. (01) 240 2815. Cables Finrarebook London WC2

(1979

CATALOGUE 54
LAW AND LEGAL HISTORY

1) AARON, B. & K.W. WEDDERBURN.
Industrial Conflict. A comparative legal survey. 1972. 1st edition. xv,396pp. Index. d.w. £10

Contains articles by Xavier Blanc-Jouvan, Gino Giugni, the editors and other. Research of the legal aspects of labour relations in various parts of the world.

2) ACTS of SEDERUNT
of the Court of Session. Folio. Vol.1 (1628-1739). Edinburgh, 1st edition. (i),307,(viii)pp. Index. Contemp. calf, rubbed, rebacked. S. & M.v.3. £45

A second volume was published in two parts covering 1739-62.

3) ADDINGTON,(Sir) William
An Abridgment of Penal Statutes (covering) the offences - punishments or penalties - mode of recovery - application of penalties etc. - number of witnesses....4to. W. Strahan & M. Woodfall. n.d. (1779) 2nd edition, revised. 657,(lxiv)pp. Indices. SIGNED by the author. S. & M.i.358/2. Some edges of margins sl. stained. Modern cloth, label. £90

Addington was a Bow Street magistrate and continued the good work of his predecessors, the brothers Fielding; he also shared their literary interests, being known as an associate of stage-folk and something of an author in his own right.
The signature by the author on the title was to prevent piracies.

4) .....Another copy. Printed for the author, 1795. 4th edition, with additions and annotations (and) many new adjudged cases. Numbered (260) and SIGNED by the author. 4to. 861,(xc)pp. Index. Some sl. occasional spotting. Contemp. Calf, sl. rubbed, sl. wear on joints. S. & M.i.358/2. £90

5) AMERICAN COLONIAL LAWS.
The Charlemagne Tower Collection of American Colonial Laws. Privately printed for the Historical Society of Pennsylvania.1890. 4to. 298pp. Uncut; fp. port. Orig. buckram. Fine copy. £35

A useful bibliographical tool for American laws and Americana.

6) ANSTRUTHER, Alexander.
Reports, of Cases... in the Court of Exchequer (1792-97). A. Strahan. 1796/8. 3 vols. Contemp. calf, spines sl. rubbed, vol.2 sl torn at head of spine. Very good set. S.&M.i.321. £60

First collection of Exchequer Reports since Bunbury.

7) (ARBUTHNOT, Dr. John)(1675-1734/5.)
Law is a Bottomless-Pit; exemplify'd in the case of the Lord Strutt, John Bull, Nicholas Frog, and Lewis Baboon, who spent all they had in a Law-Suit. Printed from a MS. found in the Cabinet of the famous Sir Humphry Polesworth. John Morphew, 1712. 1st edition. 24pp.
....The Second Part. 1712. 2nd edition. 24pp.
....The Third Part (by the author of the New Atalantis. 1712. 1st edition. 47,(i)pp. Publishers' booklist.
....The Fourth Part. (Lewis Baboon turned honest, and John Bull Politician) 1712. 1st edition. 37,(ii)pp. booklist.
....An Appendix to John Bull still in his Senses: or, Law is a Bottomless-Pit. Edinburgh, James Watson. 1712. 1st edition.22pp
....The Story of the St. Albans Ghost or the Apparition of Mother Haggy. Collected from the best MSS. 1712. 3rd edition. 16pp.
....A Complete Key to the Three Parts of Law is a Bottomless-Pit, and the Story of the St. Alban's Ghost. 1713. 1st edition.8pp.
....A Complete Key to the Four Parts of Law is a Bottomless-Pit and the Story of the St. Alban's Ghost. 1713. 4th edition. 8pp.
Seven parts in modern cloth box. S.&M.i.26/3. £150.

A political - not - legal pamphlet of great merit and full of wit and humour. The Law Suit was the French war. This satirical brochure first applied the name of John Bull to the English people. Arbuthnot dealt with the events of the previous year and brought to light the doings of Spain, Lewis XIV, Holland and England, the last-named represented by John Bull. The work was a great success at the time and went into several editions. A translation of it in French by the Abbé Velly, was printed in 1753.

8) ARGYLL, Duke of.
The Reign of Law. 1872. xxx,462,(iv)pp. Index, notes, 4 engraved plates of birds, advert. leaves. Endpapers sl. browned. Contemp. boards. £5

A general discussion of natural and civil law.

9) ARMSTRONG, J.W.S.
Yesterday. 1955. 1st edition. 191pp. Index, plates. Orig. cloth. Lib. no. on spine. £4

10) ARNOT, Hugo.
A collection and abridgement of Celebrated Criminal Trials in Scotland, from 1536-1784. With historical and critical remarks. 4to. Edinburgh. Printed for the author. 1785. 1st edition. xxiv, 400pp. Index, appendix of documents. Contemp. tree calf, worn, joints sl. split. S. & M.v.6. £70

11).....Another copy. Published in Glasgow. Cloth. Some sl. spotting of prelims. and some margins. £70

12) ARONS, H.G.
Arons' Notes on Proof. The Probative Law. A Commentary on Evidence, Trial Procedure and Practice and Judicial Proof generally...affecting Real Property, Suits in Equity... Criminal Prosecutions and Actions, involving the Police Power...N.Y.1932. 1st edition. xxiv, 561pp. Index. Orig. cloth. Fine. £15

Presentation copy from the author.

13) ATIYAH, P.S.
An Introduction to the Law of Contract. Oxford.1961. 1st edition. xii,246pp. Index. Front endpaper torn out. Orig. cloth. d.w. £6

14) The ATTORNEY'S COMPLEAT POCKET-BOOK.
Containing above four Hundred of such choice and approved Precedents in Law, Equity and Conveyancing as an Attorney might have occasion for, when absent from his Office...By the author of the Attorney's Practise Epitomized. 1764. 4th edition, to which are now added the proper Stamps to the various kinds of Precedents & other useful additions. 2 vols. Index & table. iv,326,xxx/iv,297, xipp. Mod. morocco-backed boards. S.&M.i.263/17. Fine. £110

15) BACON,Sir Francis.(Viscount St. Alban's,Baron Verulam)(1560-1626)
Law Tracts: containing 1) Proposition for compiling an amendment of our Laws; 2)Offer of a Digest of the Laws; 3) Elements of the Common Law of England;4) Use of the Law; 5) Cases of Treason etc.; 6) Arguments in Law in certain great and difficult Cases; 7) Ordinances in Chancery; 8) Reading on the Statute of Uses. Henry Lintot. 1741. 2nd edition. (i),356,(xvi)pp. Half title, booklist. S. &M. i.20/1. GIBSON 255. Contemp. calf, sl. rubbed. Fine. £120

The second edition was published from the unsold sheets of the first, with the half title added and a new title substituted. Most of the small treatises have been separately published. The "Elements of the Common Law" (No.3) was one of the earliest, if not the first, published collection of maxims of the English law.

16) .....MALLET, David: The Life. 1740. 1st edition. viii,197, (iii)pp. Half title, red & black title with engraved vignette. Contemp. calf, sl. worn; recased and corners repaired. £20

Mallet, who was Pope's literary executor, promised impartiality; but in general he exonerates Bacon at the expense of Coke and King James.

17) BALFOUR, Sir James of Pettindreich.(?-1657)
Practicks: or, a System of the more ancient Law of Scotland. Published from several MSS. Folio. Edinburgh. T. & W. Ruddimans. 1754. 1st edition. (ii),xvii,684pp. Index. Ex. lib. bookplate. Endpapers stained, otherwise a sound clean copy. Contemp. calf......

21) BARRY, Rev. E...The Present Practice..Justice of the Peace cont. spotted. Orig. calf, rubbed, spines sl. fragile. S. & M.i.225/7. £60

Contains the Statutes and adjudged Cases down to 1790 (showing) the duty of J.P.s., Sheriffs, Clergymen, Church Wardens, Overseers, Constables etc. The frontispiece is of Lord Thurlow, Lord High Chancellor of Great Britain.

22) BARTON, Charles.
An historical Treatise of a Suit in Equity; a scientific deduction of proceedings used on the Equity sides of the Courts of Chancery and Exchequer, (with) discourse on the rise and progress of Equitable Jurisdiction of those Courts. W. Clarke. 1796. 1st edition. (42),227,(14),(ii)pp. Index. Contemp. calf, sl. rubbed. Very good. S. & M.i.255/6. £80

A useful historical treatise, admirable for its clear and judicious arrangement, though it contains little more than the outlines of practice.

23) BATEMAN,J. (editor)
The General Turnpike Road Act, 3 Geo.IV.CAP.126. With an appendix of forms...(with) an index and notes. A. Maxwell. 1823. 2nd edition. xvi,190,(ii)pp. Adverts. Orig. boards, uncut; heads and labels sl. chipped. S. &M.ii.22. £15

24) BATEMAN, Thomas.
A Treatise on Agistment Tithe; the Nature Right, objects, Mode of payment and Method of ascertaining the value of each species of it...as settled in pursuance of a Decree of the Court of Exchequer. 1774 (with) appendix, containing copies of the Bill, Answers, and Decree in the Court of Exchequer. 1774, in the cause of Bateman against Aistrup and others....1808. 4th edition. xii,101, (i),134pp. Half title; with section giving detailed accounts of Bills of cost. Orig. boards, rubbed, sl. stained, sl. frayed. S. & M.i.190/3. £30

25) BATES, Sanford.
Prisons and Beyond. N.Y.1938. Index. Orig. cloth, sp.fdd. £6

Covers the whole question of prisons, treatment of prisoners, After care and reform.

26) (BATHURST,H. Second Earl, later First Baron Apsley)(1714-1794)
An introduction to the law relative to trials at Nisi Prius. 4to. H. Woodfall & W.Strahan. 1767. 1st edition. (iv),(iv),312pp. Contemp. calf, rubbed, joints worn, stained. Some underlining. Engraved bookplate of Edw. King. S. & M.i.335/1. £80

Bathhurst was Lord Chancellor and a Judge of the Court of Common Pleas.

17) BALFOUR, Sir James..Practicks...cont.
rubbed, spine ends frayed. S. & M.v.8. £95

A collection from the books of law, acts of Parliament and decrees of the Session compiled in the 16th century, and traditionally ascribed to Balfour.
Balfour an eminent Scottish antiquary was Lord President of the Court of Session. His learning and research helped Sir William Dugdale on Scottish ecclesiastical antiquities for his work "Coenobia Scotia" which he published in his Monasticon Aglicanum. Balfour himself published one volume with additions under the title "Monasticon Scoticum".

18) BALFOUR-BROWNE,J.H.
Forty Years at the Bar. 1906. 1st edition. Plates. Orig. cloth, spine sl. faded. £6

BANKRUPT LAWS & BANKRUPTCIES see Parliamentary Reports.

19) BARING, Daniel Eberhard.(1690-1753).
Clavis diplomatica, specimina veterum scripturarum tradens...Praemissa est bibliotheca scriptorum rei diplomaticae. Hanover. 1754. 2nd edition. 4to. (xiv),616,(xx)pp. 74 copper-engraved plates,(misbound at end & out of order) Fly-title to plates misbound after preface. Index. First & last leaves repaired at inner margins. Some spotting. Contemp. boards, rebacked. BRUNET 30187 (p.656). £95

A useful compendium of palaeographical knowledge, with an annotated bibliography of writers on all subjects connected with the study of historical documents. The rest of the text is drawn from Mabillon, Struvius (their contributions are new to this edition), Goebel, Ruddiman, & others, with a new appendix of ancient German & Latin Charters. The plates illustrate old bookhands, contractions seals & scribes' marks.
The first edition of 1737 is far less complete.

20) BARNES, Henry.
Notes and Cases in Points of Practise: taken in the Court of Common Pleas...with a table containing the names of the cases. 2 vols. 1754. 1st edition. ii,xl,352/lvi,xxxvi,392,xxxvipp. Index. Advert. leaves. Sm. hole in first leaf of vol.1, ownership signature on title. Contemp. calf; worn, joints cracked. Bookplates. S. &M.i.292/5. £45

Henry Barnes was one of the Secondaries of the Court of Common Pleas.

21) BARRY, Rev. Edward.
The Present Practice of a Justice of the Peace; and a complete library of Parish Law...1790. 1st edition. 4 vols. Fp. port.,sl.

27) BECCARIA, Cesare Bonesana, Marchese di)(1735-1793)
An Essay on Crimes and Punishments. Transl. from the Italian with a commentary attributed to Voltaire. The English edition is transl from the French. J.Almon. 1767. 1st English edition. xii,179,(i) lxxix,(1)pp. Contemp.sprinkled calf, rubbed, sm. hole in spine & sl. frayed. S.&M.i.358.5. HIGGS 4208. GOLDSMITH 10357. PMM 209. £150

First published in 1764 in Italian, this work was an immediate success and went into 6 editions in 18th months and was translated into 22 languages. Beccaria's work, influenced by Locke and Addison laid the foundations of criminal jurisprudence and its principles have been incorporated into the criminal practice of all civilised countries and its impact on the reform of criminal justice can hardly be exaggerated.
This translation is from the French version by Morellet.

28).....Edinburgh. Bell & Murray. 1778. A new edition. x,11-191pp. Contemp calf, rubbed, joints weak. £65

29) .....E. Hodson. 1801. The fifth edition, revised. iii,(ii), 170,lxxvii,(i)pp. Contemp. sprinkled calf, gilt. Bookplate. Fine. £60

30) BENEMY,F.W.G.
Constitutional Government and West Africa.1968.1st. Orig.cl. £3

31) BERGTHEIL,L.M.
Bankruptcy: its causes and remedy. 1879. 20,(iv)pp. Sample pages of Schedule A bookkeeping statement. Disbound. £12

32) BILLINGHURST, G. & H. CURSON.
Arcana Clericalia: or, the mysteries of clerkship explained. 1705. (xvi),590,(ii)pp. Advert. leaf. Lib. perforations on title. Modern cloth. S. & M.i.489. £45

33) BIRKENHEAD, Earl.
Fourteen English Judges. 1926. 1st edition. x,383pp. 15 plates, index & index of cases. Orig. cloth, worn, half title loose. £10

Includes Francis Bacon, Sir E. Coke, Sir M. Hale, the Earls of Hardwicke & Mansfield, Sir W. Blackstone and others.

34) .....Life by his Son, the Earl of Birkenhead. Frwd. to vol. 2 by Lloyd George and an appreciation by Sir Austen Chamberlain. 2 vols. 1936/1935. 2nd imp./1st edition. Coloured fp. port. in vol. 1 and many other plates. Orig. cloth, sl. faded & marked. £8

35) .....Walter Monckton: the life of. 1959. 1st edition. plates. Orig. cloth. £10

36) BIRON, Sir Chartres.
Without Prejudice. Impression of Life and Law. 1936. 1st edition. Fp. port. and numerous plates. Orig. cloth. £6

37) BLACKSTONE, Sir William.(1723-1780).
An Analysis of the Laws of England. To which is prefixed an introductory Discourse on the study of the law. Oxford, printed at the Clarendon Press. 1759. 4th edition. lxx,(vi),189,(14)pp. 2 tables, 1 folding, index & appendix. Sl. worming in lower margin of last few sections. Contemp. calf, label. Very good copy. S. & M.i.27/6. ELLER 220. £80

The first edition (1756) was anonymous and it was only with the third edition that the author's name appeared. All editions were octavo. The Analysis was the outline for Blackstone's "Commentaries". The preface for the 4th edition is dated as in the third & the arrangement of the text is the same.

38) .....Oxford, Clarendon Press. 1762. 5th edition. lxxvii,(vi), 189,(14)pp. Index, appendix. Front two blanks sl. frayed at edge, ex lib. bookplate on verso of cover. Contemp. calf, gilt, label. Sl. rubbed and spine ends sl. frayed. S. & M.i.27/6. ELLER 221. £75

The preface, dated 2 Nov. 1758, is amended in this edition by footnotes on p.(iii), and ix, to conform to the present edition. The two tables found the in the first four editions of the Analysis are omitted in the 5th; a note on p.ix refers the reader to the author's Law Tracts, which contains these tables. "Postscript" p. (lxxii) - lxxvii, concerns the statutes relative to the Vinerian professorship, fellowships and scholarships at Oxford University.

39) .....Oxford, Clarendon Press. 1771. 6th edition. xi,(iv),230, (14)pp. 2 folding tables, appendix, index. Contemp. calf, label. Fine copy. S. & M. i.27/6. ELLER. 223. £80

This revised edition is the last issued by Blackstone. In the undated preface, he states: "The Commentaries... (of which this work is the outline or abstract) have since (the publication of the 5th edition of the Analysis, 1762) been made public, with a few alterations and improvements... principally in point of subdivision and method. This edition is therefore accommodated to those alterations and improvements; and will be found to correspond as exactly with the printed Commentaries, as the former impressions were calculated to answer to the lectures then read by the professor".

40) .....Commentaries on the Laws of England. DUBLIN, for John Exshaw, Henry Saunders and others. 1766-70. 8vo. Half title to vol.1, appendices, two tables in vol.2. Signatures on titles, solicitor's sm. ownership stamp on endpapers. Marginal repair to

BLACKSTONE, Sir E. An interesting Appendix..1772 cont.
42) ..is a Dublin reprint of the first four tracts from which Bell borrowed his title.

43) .....Title as in previous item. Robert Bell. Philadelphia. 1773. Pagination as in previous item. Special title of part IV reads "By the author of Commentaries on the laws of England". ELLER. 256. £85

This reprint like the previous item is eccentric in format.

43a) .....PRIESTLEY, Joseph (1733-1804)
Remarks on some paragraphs in the fourth volume of Dr. Blackstone's Commentaries...relating to the dissenters. By J.Priestley.
.....A Reply to Dr. Priestley's remarks on the fourth volume of the Commentaries...By the author of the Commentaries.
.....Priestley's Answer to Dr. Blackstone's Reply to remarks on the fourth volume of the Commentaries...
.....The Case of the Late Election for the County of Middlesex, considered on the Principles of the Constitution, and the Authorities of Law.
4 Tracts. Dublin, printed for James Williams. 1770 for the first three tracts and 1769 for the fourth. S. & M.i.29-30/ 13 & 14. ELLER. 263a. £150

Each tract has a special title. Page 34 incorrectly numbered 24. Bound separately in modern marbled wraps. FINE.
This Dublin reprint of the four separately published tracts,were originally issued in London and are the source from which Robert Bell (of Philadelphia) borrowed his title "An interesting Appendix to Sir W. Blackstone's Commentaries..", for his 1772(-3) reprint.

43b) BLACKSTONE, Sir William.
Reports of Cases determined in the several courts of Westminster-Hall from 1746 to 1779. With a preface containing memoirs of his life (by James Clitherow). Folio. 2 vols. H.M.'s Law Printers. 1781. 1st edition. xxxi,(12),iv),679,387(xx),681-1333,46pp. Indices. Bookplate T. Partington. Modern cloth. S.&M.i.293/11. ELLER 225. £200

These reports, with one exception (report of the case of Burgess v.Wheate in vol1 which was reported by Mr. Fazakerly) were compiled entirely by Blackstone from his own notes, prepared for the press, even to an index and a table. They comprise a selection from cases decided in vol1 1746-69 & vol.2 1770-79. Blackstone's "literal errors or omissions" were corrected by the editor, James Clitherow, Blackstone's brother-in-law and executor.

43c) BLACKSTONE, Henry.
Reports of Cases argued and determined in the Courts of Common Pleas and Exchequer Chamber from 1788-1796. With Tables. A.Strahan.1793-96. 2 vols. Folio.Contemp. calf worn.S.&M.i.293/10. £80

BLACKSTONE, Sir. W. Commentaries. Dublin 1766-70 cont.
40)...p.449, new morocco labels. S. & M. i.27/8. ELLER 3. PMM 212, (1st ed.), ROTHSCHILD 407/8.(1st ed.)Contemp. calf, neat repair to 2 joints. £400

The first octavo edition, 1st Dublin, pirated and, with the exception of the misprint of "Willaim" for "William" on title of vol.1, follows the text of the first Oxford edition (1765-69), reproducing in full Blackstone's undated preface, wherein he anticipates a "surreptitious impression".
The "Commentaries" are included in the Grolier Club list of one hundred famous books. It was a "best seller" in the author's lifetime and also provided a good income for the Dublin printers and booksellers with this pirated edition.

41) .....A new Edition with, additions and index. Printed at the revived Apollo Press by John Bell. 1813 (i.e. 1814) 4 vols. in 8. Fp. in vol.1 Gainsborough portrait of Blackstone, engraved by James Godby. Bookplate of Wm. Sampson Hodgkinson. Contemp. calf, gilt panelled sides decorated, a.e.g., gilt panelled spines rebacked with orig. spines, neatly laid down. S. & M.i.28/8. ELLER p.16. An unusual 8 vol. set in a most attractive binding. £200

This is an 1814 reprint from the same setting of type as the 4 vol. edition of 1813, but contains notes by an anonymous editor, called the "Bell's legal classics" edition. No indication of series appears on this copy. The life of Blackstone in vol. 1 is signed James Clitherow and dated Feb. 20, 1781 and is an extract from his preface to B's Reports of Cases, 1781. The above 1814 reprint uses the original 1813 title pages of the respective volumes. Eller mentions an additional special dedication leaf to Princess Charlotte of Wales which is not present in this set.

42) .....An interesting Appendix to Sir William Blackstone's Commentaries....Containing I. PRIESTLEY'S remarks on some paragraphs in the 4th vol. of B's Commentaries, relating to the dissenters. II. B's reply to Priestley's remarks. III. Priestley's answer to B's reply. IV. The case of the late election of the County of Middlesex considered on the principles of the constitution & the authorities of law. V. Furneaux's letters to B. concerning his exposition of the Act of toleration....religious liberty...VI.Authentic copies of the argument of the late Justice Foster in the Court of Judges Delegates, and of the speech of Lord Mansfield in the House of Lords, in the cause between the City of London and the dissenters. America: printed for the subscribers, by Robert Bell...Philadelphia. 1772. (iv),iv,(5)-119,xii,155pp. Parts I-IV have continuous paging, with separate title for each part; parts V-VI have continous paging and a single title. P.155 is an advert. leaf; p. 123 is incorrectly numbered 113. Contemp. calf, label, rubbed. Several marginal wormholes in sections at front & end; the last few pages affect. text. This edition not in S.&M. ELLER 255. £90

This copy (like most) is numbered 5 on binding. The Appendix was published by Robert Bell as vol.5 of the first American edition of B's Commentaries. Philadelphia 1771-2. No British edition of this collection as a whole is known to have been published. There

44) BLOM-COOPER, L. & E. JACKSON.
The Language of the Law. An Anthology of Legal Prose. 1965. 1st ed. xxiv,397pp. Orig. cloth. d.w. £6

See also Terence MORRIS.

45) BLOUNT, Thomas. (c.1619-1679)
Fragmenta Antiquitatis: or, Antient Tenures of Land, and jocular customs of some Manors. Edited by Josiah Beckwith. York. 1784. xx, 364pp. Index. Modern half calf. S. &M. i.398/7. £65

First edition since 1679 of Blount/s collection of Copyhold Tenures (classified here according to their nature, with extensive revisions by Beckwith).

46) .....A Law-Dictionary and Glossary, interpreting such difficult and obscure Words and Terms as are found either in our Common or Statute, ancient or modern Laws. (with) near 3000 words, collected from all the Laws of the Saxon, Danish and Norman Kings.... and an explanation of all the ancient names of the Inhabitants, Cities, Towns, Villages and Rivers of Great Britain. Collected formerly by Mr. Camden and others by W.Nelson. Folio. Eliz. Nutt etc. 1717. 3rd edition. n.p. Paper sl. yellowed. Modern calf-backed cloth. Good copy. S. & M.i.6/8. £95

47) BOHUN, William.
Privilegia Londoni: or, the Rights, Liberties, Privileges, Laws and Customs of the City of London. For John Walthoe. 1723. 3rd edition, with large additions. xvi, 1-296, 273-498p(mistakes in pagination and signatures, but no repeat of the text). Table. Modern morocco-backed boards, gilt. S. & M.i.436/27. £80

Includes the duties, rights, elections etc. of the magistrates & officers of the City; the nature, jurisdiction, and practice of the several Courts and Statutes and Charters relating to the City.

48) BOLTON, Sir Richard.
A Justice of Peace for Ireland; consisting of two books. 1) Declaring the exercise of that office by one or more Justices of the Peace out of Sessions. 2) Setting forth the form of proceedings in Sessions, etc. (with) many presidents of Indicments of Treason, Felonies, Misprisions, Premunires; and Fineable Offences of Force, Fraud, Omission and other misdemeanours. 4to. Dublin. J. Leathley & T. Moore etc. 1750. Enlarged edition by Michael TRAVERS. xiv,586,292pp. 2 parts in 1 vol. Contemp. calf, raised bands. Sl. rubbed. Fine copy.S. & M.iv.8/9. £150

Bolton was Chief Baron of H.M's Court of Exchequer in Ireland. The first edition was published in 1638.

49) .....Another copy. Contemp. calf, rubbed. Some sm. marginal stain in first and last few leaves of pert I. £120

50) BOWKER, A.E.
Behind the Bar. 1947. 1st edition. 323pp. plates, index. £6

51) BRACTON.
GUTERBOCK, Carl: Bracton and his relation to the Roman Law. Contribution to the history of the Roman Law in the Middle Ages. Translated by Brinton Coxe. Philadelphia, J.B. Lippincott. 1866. 1st edition. x,183pp. Index, appendix, errata. Orig. cloth boards, label chipped, endpapers sl. dust-stained. £20

52) BRANDEIS, Louis. (1856-1941)
MASON,A.T. Brandeis: A free man's life. N.Y.Viking Press. 1946. 1st edition. xiii,713pp. Index, appendices, bibliographical notes, numerous illustrations. Orig. cloth, sl. faded. £10

A most detailed and important biography of this famous lawyer, and Justice of the United States Supreme Court.

53) The BRISTOL RIOTS,
their Causes, Progress, and Consequences. By a Citizen. Bristol, Gutch and Martin. 1832. 1st edition. (iv),404pp. Lith. fp.,appendix. Modern cloth, label.
.....Trial of Charles Pinney, Esq., in the Court of King's Bench on an information field by H.M.'s Attorney-General, charging him with neglect of Duty, in his office as Major of Bristol during the Riots. Bristol, Gutch and Martin. 1833. 1st edition. xxxviii,(i), 432pp. Some marginal pencil annots. Modern cloth, label.
2 vols. £120

In October 1831 Sir Charles Wetherell, a judge & a notorious enemy of reform, arrived in Bristol to hold the Assizes. At this a mob, stirred up over the previous 18 months by trade-union agitation, poured into the street & burned down a great part of the city. Four of the leaders were hanged for arson & two officer who had neglected to fire on the people were court-martialled.
This Tory account throws all the blame on Lord Grey's Government for allying itself with Radicals and maddening the mob with a glimpse of power.
The volume of the trial and in particular the preface (an article from Blackwood's Magazine for December 1832 under the title of "Trial of the Bristol Magistrates - Reaction among the Operatives") forms a valuable & judicious commentary on the subject.

54) The BRITISH YEAR BOOK of INTERNATIONAL LAW 1944.
Royal Institute of International Affairs/OUP 1944. Orig. cl. £6

55) BROOKE, Sir Robert. (--1558)
1573. La Graude Abridgement, Collect & Escrie per le Judge tres Reverend Syr Robert Brooke
....(La Secounde Part du Grand Abridgement). In aedibus Richardi Tottell, 5th Jan. 1573. 2 parts in one vol. French text. Mostly

BROOKE, Sir Robert. (--1558) La Graunde Abridgement cont.
55)...Black Letter. Ornamental woodcut title border & initals. Contemp. marginalia & underlining, often in red ink; title with ownership inscriptions & occasional inking over of letters & shapes. (viii),360/338 leaves. Title & last leaf sl. soiled and frayed at edges, a few leaves at end lightly dampstained. Insignificant marginal worming through one or two leaves at end. Fine modern calf. Bookplates of T. Thornton and R.B. Finlay. BEALE R.469-470. STC 3827. S. & M.i.187. McKERROW 196 (title border). £500

Based on the similarly titled work of Fitzherbert, but enriched with much new material from the Year Books of the last two Henries & from Brooke's own experience on the Bench.

56) BRUCE, Alexander.
The Decisions of the Lords of Council and Session 1714-5. With an alphabetical abridgment and the Acts of Sederunt. Folio. Edinburgh John Moncur. 1720. vi(iv),178,287,xxpp. Endpapers dust-stained, otherwise a very good copy. Contemp. calf, rubbed, outer hinges worn. S. & M.v.16. £45

57) BULLER, Sir Francis.
An introduction to the Law relative to Trials at Nisi Prius. A. Strahan. 1793. 6th edition. Contemp. calf, rubbed & sl. torn, top of spine sl. frayed. S. & M.i.335/3. £20

58) BULLINGBROOKE, Edward.
An Abridgment of the Publick Statutes of Ireland now in Force and of general use: and also of such English and British Statutes as relate to and bind Ireland, from Magna Charta to the 6th year of the reign of King George III. (1765-6). 4to. Dublin. Boulter Grierson. 1768. 2 (thick) vols. n.p. With an alphabetical Table.
(with)
An Appendix to the Abridgment of the Statutes of Ireland with a table of the titles of the Statutes. 1768. 3 vols. in 1. 4to.
(with)
An Appendix to the Abridgment of the Statutes of Ireland by Francis VESEY.
George III: 7th - 11th & 12th years (1766-1722) 1776.
13th & 14th years (1772-1774) 1774.
15th & 16th years (1774-1776) 1776.
16th - 18th years (1775-1778) 1778.
19th & 20th years (1778-1780) 1781.
4to. Dublin. David Hay. 5 vols. in 1.
The whole 8 volumes bound uniformly in 2 thick volumes: 4to. Contemp. calf, raised bands, labels. Very sl. rubbed. FINE SET. S.& M.iv.11. (lists no appendix for Bullingbrooke & only four for Vesey.) SCARCE £450

59) BULLINGBROOKE, Edward.
The Duty and Authority of Justices of the Peace and Parish Officers for Ireland: containing the Statutes which give jurisdiction to such Magistrates; and authorities from the best and latest Reports (with) Precedents ...of the Acts of Parliament (with) an alphabetical table of the titles and a chronological table of the Statutes...4to. Dublin. Boulter Grierson. 1766. 1st edition. xviii,(18), 816pp. Some marginal worming, mainly at beginning and end; endpapers & blanks spotted and frayed at margins. Contemp. calf with hand-written titling on spine. Sl. rubbed with sm. tear top of spine. S. & M.iv.11. £120

60) .....Another copy. Contemp. calf, raised bands, label. £120

61) BUNBURY, Shirley.
Bourdin's exposition of the Land Tax, including the recent judicial decisions and the incidental changes in the law effected by the Taxes Management Act. 1885. 3rd edition. xii,182,32pp. Index. Title sl. spotted, lib. stamp on verso. Orig. cloth, lib. stamp on spine. £10

62) BUNBURY, William.
Reports of Cases in the Court of Exchequer (1713-41). Edited by George Wilson. Henry Lintot. 1755. 1st edition. Folio. Index, table of Barons of the Exchequer etc., privilege leaf before title. Signed by the editor at the end of the preface. Contemp. calf, worn, joints cracked. S. & M.i.322/3. £60

63) BURGES, Cornelius. (--1655)
A new discovery of personal Tithes: or the tenth part of Mens Cleere Gains proved due by the Lawes of this Kingdome. 12mo. J.L(egate) for W. Sheffard. 1625. 1st edition. Title in black and red. (xii),81pp. Black borders. Bottom margin of title to A5 cropped with sl. loss. Modern calf. STC 4112. S.& M.i.190/6. £85

Burges, a non-conformist divine, who attacked the principles of revenues received by Deans, Chapters and Bishops, purchased church lands himself and wrote the above in vindication.

64) BURGUS, Petrus Baptista.
De dominio serenissimae Genuensis republicae in mari Ligustico. (Rome excudebat Dominicus Marcianus)(1641). 1st edition. 4to. (x),258,(ii)pp. Fine engraved title and final device leaf. Latin text. Contemp. calf with Arms of Président Pierre Henequin on sides. Rebacked, raised bands, gilt. Bookplate. Endpapers sl. spotted. Fine copy. £150

Working quite independently of Selden (whom however he occasionally quotes) the author proves that the Sea may be subject to every aspect of ownership, and that the ownership of Ligurian waters is logically & historically vested in the Genoese.

65) (BURLAMAQUI, Jean-Jacques)(1694-1748)
Principes Du Droit Politique. Amsterdam. Zacharie Chatelain. 1751. 2 vols. bound in 1. Uncut. Sm. tear in leaf 163. Modern calf-backed boards. HIGGS 229. £75

Original edition was published in 1747.
Burlamaqui was born in Geneva and distinguished himself by being appointed honorary professor of jurisprudence at the age of 26. He lectured with such success that the University of Geneva ranked high as a school of law.

66) BURN, Richard. (--1789)
Ecclesiastical Law. 1763. 1st edition. 2 vols. 4to. Addenda with tables and indices, dedication leaves. Contemp. calf, edges rubbed S. & M.i.166/22. £90

67) .....Another set. Addenda but without tables. £80

68) .....Edited by Robert Phillimore. 1842. 9th edition. 4 vols. Index, advert. leaves before title of vol.1. Orig. boards, sl. torn, esp. joint of vol.1. S.&M. i.166/22. £60

Last edition of Burn. Phillimore later produced an Ecclesiastical Law under his own name.

69) .....The Justice of the Peace and Parish Officer. Ed. John Burn. 16th edition. 4 vols. Index. Three contemp. printed forms, for information, before Northumberland justices inserted in vol.1. Contemp. calf, sl. rubbed & frayed. S.& M.i.226/15. £50

70) .....Another edition. Edited by John King. 1814. 22nd edition. 5 vols. Indices. Contemp. calf, worn and covers broken. £30

71) .....& (continued by his son John BURN).
A New Law Dictionary; intended for general use as well as for Gentlemen of the profession. 2 vols. 1792. fp. port. in vol. 1, half titles. 1st edition. Contemp. tree calf, rubbed. Modern labels and inner hinges repaired. S. & M.i.7/13. £50

72) BURNET, Gilbert.
Lives, Characters, and an address to posterity. (with) two prefaces to the Dublin editions. Edited with introduction & notes by John Jebb. James Duncan. 1833. (iv),lxx,(ii),386pp. Mod.b'ram. £15

Life of Sir Matthew Hale and Baxter's appendix, life of the Earl of Rochester with the preface and appendices of Robert Parsons & letters by Anne, Countess Dowager of Rochester,characters of Archbishop Leighton, Nairn and Charteris, eminent Clergymen, Queen Mary II and the Hon. Robert Boyle.

73) BURNETT, John.
A Treatise on various branches of the Criminal Law of Scotland. 4to. Edinburgh. George Ramsay and others. 1811. 1st edition. viii, (1),612,lxxviii,xvpp. Appendix, index to the Cases. Contemp. calf, edges rubbed, recased. A very good copy. S. &M.v.18. £95

74) BURNS, John. (Writer to the Signet)
The Conveyancing Guide...explanations and forms relative to the Conveyancing (Scotland) Act 1924. Edinburgh. 1925. Orig. cloth, rubbed, shaken. £2

75) BURROW, Sir James. (1701-1782)
Reports of Cases...in...the Court of King's Bench (1756-1758). 1766. 1st edition. 4 vols. Folio. Indices. Modern cloth. S. &M.i.294/20. £100

Burrow retained the mastership of the Crown-office until his death. From many years attendance in Court he evolved a meticulous style of reporting which is exact but includes much circumstantial detail.

76) .....A Series of the Decisions of...King's Bench upon Settlement Cases. 1768. 1st edition. 2 vols. 4to. Indices. Contemp calf sl. rubbed. S. &M. i.386. £50

Irregular pagination as usual.
The Reports are a striking commentary on Blackstone's complaint that the diverse means of gaining a settlement in a parish, so as to be supported in poverty out of the rates of that parish, had distastrously confounded the working of the old Poor Law. Also includes a short treatise on punctuation: "Thoughts upon Pointing".

77) (BURTON, P.)
Cases, with Opinions of Eminent Counsel, in matters of Law, Equity and Conveyancing, alphabetically arranged and digested under distinct heads. (1700-75). 2 vols. W.Clarke & Sons. n.d. 1st edition. Contemp. calf, sl. rubbed. Very good set. SCARCE. S. & M.i.285/2. £70

78) CABALA.
Sive Scrinia Sacra, Mysteries of State...in Letters of Illustrious Persons. For G. Bedell & T. Collins. 1663. 2nd edition, enlarged. Folio. Red & black title. First privilege leaf. (xvi), 416,(x)pp. Index. Modern calf, gilt. WING C 185. £90

Includes many letters by Sir Francis Bacon, with some of Sidney, Raleigh & the Earl of Essex.

79) .....Another copy. Sl. stained. Modern calf-backed boards. £80

80) CALLIS, Robert (fl. 1634)
The Reading of the famous and learned Robert Callis..upon the Statute of 23 H.8. cap.5 of SEWERS; ..at Gray's Inn in August 1622. 4to. M. Flesher for Thomas Basset. 1685. Second edition (with) several Judgments & Resolutions of the reverend Judges upon the Laws of Sewers, ...not before published. With a new and exact table to the whole. (iv),291,(72)pp. Title & prelims. sl. dust-stained at margins. Modern morocco-backed boards. Very good. S.&M.i.470/2. WING C 305. £95

Callis, a Sergeant-in-Law of Gray's Inn was Commissioner of Sewers in his native Lincolnshire.

81) .....Joseph Butterworth. 1824. 4th edition with additions and corrections by William John Broderip. viii,400pp. Calf-backed boards, rubbed. S. & M.i.471/2. £60

82) CALVERT, E.R.
Capital Punishment in the 20th century. Introd. Lord Buckmaster. 1930. 4th edition. Index, bibliography, appendix. £5

83) CAMPBELL, John (Lord).(1781-1861)
The Lives of the Chief Justices of England. From the Norman Conquest till the death of Lord Mansfield. 3 vols. John Murray.1849-1857. Index, publishers' catalogue, adverts. Orig. cloth, gilt, spines faded. Very good set. £50

This set includes the third volume (not always prsent) which is a supplement to the first two.

84) .....Another set. From the Norman Conquest till the death of Lord Tenterden. 3 vols. John Murray. 1858/7. 2nd edition for vols. 1 & 2 and first edition of vol.3. Contemp. embossed pictorial cloth, spines faded, hinges sl. fragile. Good Set. With the engraved bookplate of "John Birkbeck" in each volume. £45

85) ....Lives of the Lord Chancellors. 1848-50. 3rd edition. 7 vols. Contemp. calf, gilt spines, sl. rubbed. Trinity College Prize binding, gilt embossed on covers. FINE SET. S.&M.i.591/1. £120

See also #291. The Lives of all the Lord Chancellors.

86) CARDOZO, Benjamin N.
The Growth of the Law. Yale U.P./OUP 1934. 5th ed. Orig. cl. £4

87) C(arew),G(eorge).
Fraud & Oppression detected and arraigned or An Appeal to the Parliament of England...by the creditors of Sr. William Courten, Sr. Paul Pyndar, Sr. Edward Littleton etc. (with) some necessary advertisements concerning the improvement of Navigation and Trade.

CAREW, George ..Fraud & Oppression..cont.
87)...n.i. 1676. Folio. 1st edition. (iv),(ii blanks)44pp. Uncut. Edges sl. dust-stained & frayed. Modern Wraps. WING C546. S. &M. i.520/22. £35

A narrative of several actions at law in the Courts of Holland between Dutch and English subjects.

88) CARTER,A.T.
A history of English legal Institutions. 1910.4th ed. Orig. cloth, sl. stained and rubbed. £10

89) CAY, John.
An Abridgment of the Publick Statutes in force from Magna Charta, in 9th year of Henry III to 11th year of George II inclusive. 2 vols. Folio. 1739. 1st edition. n.p. Contemp. calf, rubbed, spines sl. worn. Two bookplates of different owners in each volume. S. &M.i.567/38. Good clean set. £100

The first uniform abridgement since Pulton's, it includes at length the two books of custom rates (Grimston's & Compton's), & a table of Sheriff's fees.

90) CHAMBERLAIN, D.H.
The doctrine of Stare Decisis, its reasons and its extent. Prize essay of the N.Y.State Bar Ass., awarded Jan. 10,1885. N.Y. Baker, Voorhis & Co. 1885. 1st published edition. 31pp. Orig. cloth, sl. rubbed & frayed. Presentation copy from the author. £20

91) CHANCELLOR, Beresford E.
The Romance of Lincoln's Inn Fields and its Neighbourhood. n.d. (c.1930). Plates. Orig. yellow cloth, sl. marked. £6

92) CHESHIRE, G.C.
The Modern Law of Real Property. 1962. 9th edition. With the parts on Registered Conveyancing and Town and Country Planning by J.B. Butterworth. Orig. cloth, sl. stained. £8

93) .....Private International Law. Oxford, Clarendon Press. 1961. 6th edition. Index. Orig. cloth, d.w. (sl. frayed) £9

94) .....& C.H.S.FIFOOT.
Cases on the Law of Contract. 1959. 3rd edition. Orig. cloth. Sm. stain on cover. £8

95) .....Another copy. 1960. 5th edition. Orig. cloth. £8

96) (CHILD, David L. & Stephen BATES)
PROCEEDINGS of the Citizens of Boston favorable to a revision of the Laws in relation to Debtor and Creditor. At a meeting held at

(CHILD,D.L. & S.BATES) Proceedings cont.
96)...the Exchange Coffee House, Boston..April 29, 1829, of those citizens who are desirous of devising some measures for the relief of honest and fair debtors, for the punishment of fraudulent ones and for the just and impartial distribution of the property of a failing or insolving debtor, among all his creditors, in proportion to their respective claims. (Boston). 12pp uncut and partly unopened, title & edges dust-stained, sewn as issued. (with) Constitution of a newly formed "Society for the Promotion of the Rights and Interests of bona fide Creditors, and the benefit and relief of honest Debtors" unanimously accepted at a meeting at the Exchange Coffee House on June 3, 1829 with the Hon. Daniel Webster as President. Not in Sabin. £45

97) CHITTY, Edward.
The Commercial and General Lawyer...of the law of England...with consideration...which relate to Commerce, Trade and Manufactures. 1840. xxiv,1224pp. Appendix. Modern cloth. S. & M. see ii,63. £30

98) CHITTY, Joseph. (1776-1841)
Observations on The Game Laws, with proposed alterations for the protection and increase of Game, and the decrease of Crimes. n.d. 1816. 171-204pp. Disbound. Pamphleteer edition. KRESS B.6196. Not in S. & M. £20

99) .....A Treatise on the Game Laws, and on Fisheries; with an Appendix (of) all the Statutes and Cases on the subject. 2 vols. W. Clarke etc. 1812. xii,702b/(i),(i),703-1436,(ii)pp. Uncut. Index, publishers' booklist of lawbooks. Orig. grey boards,dust-stained, rebacked. S.&M.i.462/6. KRESS B.5965. £60

A treatise, with an Appendix of reported cases from 1293-1811.

100) .....Same title, same edition. Vol.2 only. Uncut, orig. boards. rebacked. £20

Contains only the appendix of reported cases from 1293-1811 and the index.

101) CHORIER, Nicolas.
La Jurisprudence du célèbre conseiller et Jurisconsulte Guy-Pape dans ses décisions, avec plusieurs remarques importantes. Grenoble et Paris. 1769. 2nd edition, corrected by a Parliamentary lawyer. 4to. French text. lii,406,(ii)pp. Index. Sl. browned, three wormholes throughout. Modern cloth. BRUNET pp.1812. £80

Guido-Pape, a 15th century jurist of Grenoble, was the first to introduce an element of Roman reason & coherence into the confusion of French International law. Chorier extracted the points of law from Pape's decisions in the Parliament. This edition includes many new annotations, the first being published in 1692.

102) CHRISTIAN, Edward.
The Origin, Progress, and present Practice of the Bankrupt law, both in England and in Ireland. W.Clarke & Sons. 1818. 2nd ed. 2 vols. Contemp. calf, rubbed, lacks label to vol.1, joints weak. S.& M.i.541/10. £80

Every Statute and General Order of the Chancellor is considered chronologically, and an abridgment of each material decision is subjoined to the section or order upon which it immediately depends.

103) CIRCUIT TRAMP.
"Pie-Powder" being dust from the Law Courts. Collected and recollected on the Western Cricuit. 1911. 1st edition. Orig. cloth, edges stained and front lower hinge sl. split. £3

104) CLARK, George.
The Penal Statutes abridged, and alphabetically arranged. Calculated to serve as an alphabetical Common Place Book of the Penal Laws. (with) a collection of Maxims and Rules for proper exposition of Statutes...Fielding & Walker. 1772. 2nd edition, enlarged. By George WILSON. xii,315,(1)pp. Contemp. calf, label. Sl. rubbed, top of spine sl. frayed, some sl. spotting. S.&M. i.359/13. £60

A guide to penalties for magistrates.

105) CLERKE, William.
The Triall of Bastardie: that part of the Second Part of Policie, or Manner of Gouernement of the Realme of England: so termed, Spirituall, or Ecclesiasticall. Annexed, a Table of the Leuitical English and Positiue Canon Catalogues, their Concordance and Difference. Sm.4to. Adam Islip. 1594. 1st and only edition. (xvi),82, (xxii)pp. Four folding tables. Printer's devices on titles; woodcut ornaments and initials. Modern half calf, marbled sides, newly re-backed with gilt lettering on spine. BEALE T.327. STC 5411. S. &M.i.475/8. A fine copy with wide margins. £380

Adam Islip printed in London from 1591 to 1640. He was an apprentice to Hugh Jackson. See BEALE p.181.

107) The CODE NAPOLEON.
or, the French Civil Code. Translated from the original and official edition published at Paris in 1804. By a Barrister of the Inner Temple. Charles Hunter. 1824. xix,628pp. Uncut. Orig. boards, stained, corners rubbed, re-backed. £30

The first translation of one of the most important codes in modern history.

COKE, Sir Edward. The First Part of the Institutes..cont.
112)...to the 8th editions are reprints without essential alterations from the second edition (1629) which was the last edition produced during Coke's lifetime and revised & corrected by the author.This first part of the Institutes is a commentary on Land Law.

113) .....The First Part of the Institutes...Also Three Tracts. Folio. Eliz. Nutt & R. Gosling. 1719. 11th edition, corrected,with the Treatise of the Old Tenures of the Laws of England, with two new Tables, and many references to the modern Law cases..BLACK Letter. (xviii),100pp 402,37 leaves. Engraved frontispiece port. by M. Vander Gucht, folding table, indices. Bookplate. Contemp. calf, rubbed & worn, rebacked. S.&M.i.449-50/7. £150

The three tracts are: Reading upon the Statute of levying fines; Bail and Mainprize; and Compleat Copy-holder.

114) .....Another copy. Same edition. Has an additional unsigned portrait of Littleton inserted before the second section. Some pages sl. browned. Fine copy. £150

115) .....Another copy. T.Wright, for E. Brooke. 1788. Folio. (xxii),xxpp 395,33 leaves. Table. 13th edition with tables by Francis HARGRAVE & Charles BUTLER (with) an Analysis of Littleton by an unknown hand in 1658-9. Modern calf-backed boards. Very good. £150

Hargrave planned a new and elaborate edition and began to publish it in separate parts but abandoned it in 1785 after having completed nearly half of it. It was finished by Butler in 1787.

116) .....Another copy. 3 vols. E. & R. Brooke. 1794. 15th edition with tables by Francis HARGRAVE & Charles BUTLER, including the notes of Chief Justice Hale and Chancellor Nottingham, and an Analysis of Littleton. n.p. Contemp. calf, rubbed, spine sl. frayed & repaired on hinges. S. & M.i.451. £90

The united labours of Hargrave and Butler on the critical edition of Coke-Littleton (the first ever made) first published in 1788 (see previous item) have not been superseded. Some of Butler's notes to this edition are new, which is the first in octavo.

117) .....The Second Part of the Institutes of the Lawes of England, containing the exposition of many ancient and other Statutes. Folio. A. Crooke, W. Leake and others. 1669. 3rd edition. (x),(1),745,(40)pp. Table. Contemp. calf, labels. Covers sl. rubbed, spine ends sl. frayed sl. split. WING C4950. S.&M.i.546/4. £300

No portrait called for, it includes one leaf of an index of Maxims and Rules not called for in S. & M.
This second Institute was published after the author's death by order of the House of Commons. Coke's commentary upon Magna Charta, and particularly on the celebrated 29th is still of great interest to the lawyers of the present age, as the spirit of justice and of civil liberty which pervades and animates the work.

108) CODEX IURIS CANONICI.
PII X Pontificis Maximi iussu digestus Benedicti Papae XV...Praefactione emi Petri Card, Gasparri et Indice Analytico-Alphabetico Auctus. Rome. Typis Polyglottis Vaticanis. 1918. Latin text. xliv, 852pp. Half morocco/cloth sides. Name & address of former owner on first blank. Fine. £12

109) (COKE, Sir Edward)(1551-1633)
A BOOK of ENTRIES: containing...Presidents of Counts, Declarations, Information, Pleints, Indictments, Barres...Folio. John Streater, James Flesher and others. 1671. 2nd edition, corrected. (9),713, (9) leaves. BLACK LETTER, engraved chapter headings, initials and end devices. Reversed calf, rebacked. From the library and with the bookplate of the EARL of LONSDALE. S.&M.i.266/43. WING W.4908. A few sl. spots in the last few leaves of the index. A Fine Copy. £180

Selden, Rolle and others refer to this as New Entries, and New Book of Entries in contradistinction to Rastell's book and the older books, just as Rastell's book before had obtained that distinction. Coke says in his preface that none of the entries in his book had been previously published.

110) .....Another copy. Modern cloth, lacks end-papers. £150

111) .....The COMPLEATE COPY-HOLDER: Wherein is contained a Learned discourse of the Antiquity and Nature of Manors and Copy-Holds, with the forme of keeping a Copy-Hold Court and Court-Baron. Matthew Walbanck and Richard Best. 1644. 3rd edition. Sm.8vo. (iv), 203pp. Woodcut devices. A contemp. hand has added an index on the final blanks. Lacks last blank. Some marginal notes in early hand. Bookplate. Marginal worming aff. text on 7 leaves, sl. damp-stnd. Contemp. calf, rubbed, spine sl. torn. WING C 4913. S. & M.i.399/13. £180

"Although the Order of Keeping a Court and Court Baron is called for by the Title of the 1644 edition, it is not to be found in all copies. It was absent from four copies examined" S.&M. It is absent from this copy also.
The publication of this book marks the final triumph of the King's Courts over the Feudal Courts which virtually put an end to feudal jurisdiction in England. It is a book of first class importance.

112) .....The FIRST PART of the INSTITUTES of the Lawes of England: or, a Commentary upon Littleton. Folio. M.F.I.H. & R.Y. 1639. Fourth edition, corrected. Woodcut title-border, folding table. (v),393,(32) leaves. Lacks fp. port. Title laid down. Contemp. calf, lacks front endpaper, top of spine sl. split, hinges rubbed. STC 15787. S.& M.i.449/7. A very good copy. £400

"Coke Littleton" far overshadows the rest of the Institutes, and despite innumerable reforming statutes & decision, it cannot be called obsolete until English law itself is obsolete. The third

COKE, Sir Edward.
118) .....The Second Part of the Institutes... Folio. W. Rawlins. 1681. 6th edition. (x),744,(40)pp. Fp. portrait, index. Blanks & portrait loose, edges sl. frayed, lower margins stained throughout. Modern cloth. WING C4953. S. &M. i.546/4. £120

119) .....The Third Part of the Institutes...concerning High Treason, and other Pleas of the Crown, and Criminal Causes. A.Crooke etc. 1669. 4th edition. Folio. (viii),243,(xviii)pp. Index. WING C 4963. S. & M.i.360/15.
Coke's Third Institute is a treatise of great learning and having run over all criminal matters and their legal punishments, he concludes with the nature of pardons and restitutions, showing how far, in each of these, our Kings can proceed alone, and where they want the assistance and joint power of their Parliaments. (with)
.....The Fourth Part of the Institutes...concerning the Jurisdiction of Courts. A. Croke etc. 1669. 4th edition with alphabetical table not heretofore printed. Folio. (x),364,(ii),(34)pp. Table. WING C 4931. S. & M.i.258/6.
Coke's posthumous works have been severely criticised, and never received the high homage of his first Institute and Reports. They did not receive the finishing corrections of their author. William Prynne wrote a Folio of Brief Animadversions upon the 4th Institute in which he charges Lord Coke with piracy and numberless errors; but the virulence and spleen manifested in his criticisms and his disposition to magnify trifles, detracts very much from the value of his animadversions.
2 parts bound in 1 vol. Some sl. marginal staining towards the end of the third and the beginning of the fourth Institute. Contemp. sprinkled calf, re-backed. £280

120) .....Another copy. The Third Part...4th edition. Engraved fp. portrait. Index. John Streater. WING C4964.
..... The Fourth Part.... John Streater etc. 1671. 5th ed. Engraved fp. portrait. Index. WING C4932
2 parts bound in 1 vol. Contemp. calf, rubbed, upper hinge broken and split. £250

121) .....The Fourth Part of the Institutes. Folio. M. Flesher. 1648. second edition. (xiii),364,(ii)pp. Fine engraved title & fp. portrait. The collation according to S. & M. is that of the first edition (1644) in that there are only 4 pages (Epilogue) at end and not 35 as called for for the second edition. Endpapers stained, some sl. staining of corners of first few leaves, contemp. signatures & notes on blanks (one dated 1703) and signature only on title. WING C4930. S. &M. i.258-9/6. Contemp. sheep, rubbed, corners and spine ends very frayed. £150

122) .....The Second Part of the Institutes. 2 vols. 1817. n.p.
.....The Third Part..................... 1817.
.....The Fourth Part.................... 1817.
3 vols. in 4. Contemp. calf, rubbed, spines worn. Bookplates of the Soc. of Advocates, Aberdeen. £80

COKE, Sir Edward..cont.
122) .....Many of the mistakes of reference and misquotations in the folio editions of the last three Institutes (2nd - 4th) were corrected in the octavo editions.

123) .....Les Reports de Eduard Coke l'Attorney Generall Le Roigne Folio. Thomae Wight. n.d.(1600). 1st edition. STC 5493. Engr.title.
..........Le Second Part..Thomae Wight.(1602) 1st edition.STC 5495.
..........Le Tierce Part..Thomae Wight.(1602) 1st edition.STC 5499.
..........Le Quart Part...Thomae Wight.(1604) 1st edition.STC 5502.
Four parts, all 1st editions bound in 1 vol. S.&M.i.295/31. BLACK LETTER. French text. Contemp. calf, rubbed, rebacked. End-papers sl. frayed and dust-stained. VERY GOOD SET. £450

Coke's Reports were published in 11 volumes between 1600 and 1615 and were so highly regarded by the old lawyers as to be cited simply as "Reports", without the author's name. Coke's profusion of observations, comments, arguments and judgments in each case, add much to the permanent value of the work.

124) .....Les Reports. Part 1. The Companie of Stationers. 1609. Folio. 5th edition. Engraved title, case headings and initials. Partly BLACK letter, French and Latin text, preface in English. Bookplate. Signature of Ja:Medlycott (Master in Chancery c.1710) on front blank. Contemp. calf, rubbed, spine sl. frayed and split at ends. STC 5497. S.&M.i.295/31. Very good copy. £200

Part I. contains Shelley's case (fol.88 verso).

125) .....The Fift Part of the Reports...Folio. For the Companie of Stationers. 1605. 1st edition. Engraved title with double column (Latin/English description). BLACK letter, French text, preface in Latin and English. Engraved case headings & initials. A few contemp. marginal notes and 4 pages of hand-written index on endpapers and blank before title. Uncut. A few sl. wormholes in margin of last two leaves, last blank stained. Modern buckram, leather label. STC 5504. S.&M. i.295/31. £200

126) .....The Fift Part... 1624. 5th edition. Folio. Contains an additional section of 41 leaves with additional title "Of the King's Ecclesiasticall Law" in two columns: the right-hand being in BLACK letter and in English, with the left one in Latin. The rest of the Reports are in French text. Engraved title, case headings and initial letters. Uncut, front blank. STC 5508. Modern calf-backed marbled boards, raised bands, gilt lettering. Some sl. fraying of margins of first 3 leaves and some sl. marginal staining of last 20 leaves, a very good copy. £180

127) .....La Sept Part...Folio. Societie of Stationers. 1629. 2nd edition. Engraved title, case headings & initials. Some sl. worm'g in lower inner margin, not af. text. Contemp. marginal annotations and some underlining. STC 5512. Contemp. calf, rubbed & top of sp. sl. frayed, sl. loose in binding but with the blanks at each end. Black letter, French text, preface in English. £180

COKE, Sir Edward...cont.
128) .....La Neuf^{me} Part des Reports. Folio. For the Societie of Stationers. 3rd edition. Mostly BLACK letter. Woodcut devices. (xxxiv),143 leaves. Index. Sl. wormed not aff. text, some early MSS notes,sl. dampstained. Contemp. calf, rubbed, one gathering loose. STC 5517. £200

Contains cases such as Dowmans and Pinchons with a general preface delineating the various Courts and the functions of those Courts. It is particularly useful that the preface has been translated into English and is included with the original.

129) .....La Unz^{me} Part...Folio. John More. 1631. 5th edition. (x),100,(101) leaves. French text. BLACK letter. Woodcut devices. Sl. marg. worming not aff. text, some marginal notes in early hand; some sl. dampstaining. Contemp. calf, rubbed, head of spine torn. STC 5524. £200

This part contains the famous Magdalen College case, a case concerning monopolies and others.

130) .....The Life of the Lord Chief Justice of England in the reign of James I with memoirs of his contemporaries by Cuthbert William JOHNSON. 2 vols. 1837. 1st edition. Index, fp. port., Half morocco, sl. rubbed. £60

A most thorough biography of the great English lawyer, long familiar to the legal profession, but to the general reader principally known as the pleader who so rancorously conducted the prosecution of Sir Walter Raleigh.

131) COLERIDGE, Stephen.
Quiet Hours in the Temple. 1924. 1st ed. fp. Orig. cloth. £3

132) A COLLECTION of several TREATISES.
concerning the reasons and occasions of the PENAL LAWS.
1) Execution of Justice in England not for Religion but for Treason: 17 Dec.1583. (By William Cecil, Baron Burleigh).
2) Important considerations by the Secular Priests. 1601. (By William WATSON).
3) Jesuits Reasons unreasonable. 1662. (By Edward STILLINGFLEET)
4to. Richard Royston. 1675. 1st edition. (viii),132pp. Contemp. calf, very rubbed, endpapers stained, some sl. marginal worming in last few leaves. WING C5192B. S. &M.i.360/16. £85

Three tracts against religious toleration, especially as extended to Catholics. The first was written by Lord Burleigh in 1583 & demonstrates that submission to Rome means a spirit of subversion against the temporal government too.

133) COLLYN, Nicholas.
A Briefe Summary of the LAWES and STATUTES of England, so far forth as the same do Concerne the Office of JUSTICES of PEACE,

COLLYN, Nicholas. ..Lawes and Statutes...cont.
133) .....SHERIFFS etc. By T.L. for Mathew Walbancke. 1655. 4th edition. 12mo. xxii,192pp. Sm. piece of blank margin of title torn away. A few sm. wormholes running through first portion, affec. an occasional letter of text. Ownership signatures on title. Modern calf. WING C 5397. S. & M.i.226/21. £250

134) COLUMBIA, Supreme Court of the District.
Daniel SHERWOOD, vs. Andrew B. SEARLES. no.4027. Argument for Appellee by T.H.N. McPHERSON. Washington. D.C.W.H. Moore. n.d. (c.1868) 39pp. Presentation copy by McPherson with his signature on title. Orig. printed wraps. sl. frayed. £15

135) COMBER, Thomas. (1644-1699)
An Historical Vindication of the Divine Right of Tithes...to supply the omissions, answer the objections, and rectifie the mistakes of Mr. Selden's History of Tithes. S. Roycroft. 1682. 1st edition. 4to. (xxviii),247pp. Contemp. calf, rubbed, joints and spine ends worn. Bookplates of Lord SELBORNE. WING C 5472. £40

An answer to those passages in Selden's work which were intended or represented to imply that the payment of tithes was not divinely prescribed or universally practised.

136) The COMPLETE JURYMAN,
or, a Compendium of the Laws relating to Jurors. 12mo. Dublin. John Murphy. 1774. 225,(xiv),(i)pp. Index, publishers' booklist. Signature on title. Contemp. calf, label., sl. stained. S. & M.iv.18. (1752 edition only). £40

Covers Grand and Petit Juries, qualifications of Jurors, various methods of trial, evidence, witnesses, verdicts etc.

137) COOKE, William.
A Compendious System of the Bankrupt Laws. Edward Brooke.1785. viii,(viii),iv,372,(viii),ccxxxiii,(22)pp. With the cases and determination of the Courts of Law and Equity. Appendix of Precedents and index. Modern cloth. S.&M. i.541/16. £40

138) CORVINUS, Arnoldus, (van Belderen).
Jus Feudale per Aphorismos strictum explicatum. Leyden. Ex Officina Moyaert. 1655. (vi),21,(iv)pp. (with)
GEISLERIUS, Joannes Tobias. De Statu Politico, secundum praecepta taciti formato. Amsterdam. Apud J. Janssonium. 1661. 212pp. (with)
BOXHORNIUS, Marcus Zuerius. Institutionum Politicarum. Libri Duo. Leyden. Apid N. Herculis. 1657. 215.
3 works in 1 vol. 12mo. Contemp. vellum. Bookplate. £90

139) COTTON, Sir Robert (Bruce)(1570-1631)
An exact Abridgement of the Records in the Tower of London, from the reign of Edward II to Richard III, of all the Parliaments holden in each King's reign, and the several Acts in every Parliament; revised by William PRYNNE (1600-1669). Folio. William Leake. 1679. 2nd edition. (xxxviii),716,(138)pp. Index. Reversed calf, rebacked. Sl. rubbed. S. &M. i.75/5. WING C 6490 £120

The abridgment records the substance of Acts of Parliament and other particulars, that are not extant in print, among the Statutes of the Parliamentary Rolls and supplies the purpose of a useful index to the Rolls of Parliament. Prynne's revision improved the edition and is considered amongst his important works.

140) COWEL, John, (collected by) (1554-1611)
The Interpreter: or Booke containing the signification of Words. William Sheares. 1637. n.p. 4to. Modern calf-backed boards. Title laid down, some sl. damp-staining and sl. worming throughout. STC 5903. S. &M.i.7/20. £200

The first edition was published in Cambridge in 1607. Cowel's insinuations against Littleton brought an attack against him which ended in the suppression of his book by Royal proclamation in 1610. However the law lexicographer of the following century found his work essential to their purpose and it was held in high regard.

141) .....Another copy. Folio. J. Place & A. & J. Churchill.1701. n.p. Prefaces, appendix containing the ancient names of places in England; Contemp. calf, rebacked. S.&M. i.7/20. £150

This much augmented edition was continued by Tho. MANLEY and took the work to 1684.

142) .....The Institutes of the Laws of England, digested into the method of the Civill or Imperiall Institutions. Transl. by W.G. 1651. 1st edition. (x),283pp. Index. Title & T_{2-6} repaired at corners. Some annots. in early hand. Book-plates of Robert WALPOLE & Charles George Milnes. WING C 6641. S. & M.i.21/8. £200

A summary of English law adapted to the scheme and even to the individual titles of Justinian. Cowell attempts a system of the law of contract 200 years before English lawyers generally recognized it as an independent subject in this work.

143) .....A Law Dictionary; or, Interpreter of words and terms used in the Common or Statute Laws of England...and in Tenures and Jocular Customs. With an appendix. D. Browne etc. 1708. Folio.n.p. Index, advert. leaf. Fine contemp. panelled calf, sl. spotted. Bookplate. Fine copy. S. &M. i.7/21. £150

The work is an enlargement of "Les Termes de la Ley". Until the publication of Jacob's Law Dictionary this was considered to be the best.

144) CRAIGIE, John. (edited by)
Conveyancing Statutes from the 13th century to the present time. Edinburgh. 1895. 1st edition. xvi,763pp. £15

The work is in chronological order and collects the Statutes, repealed and unrepealed, relating chiefly to the conveyance of land and other real rights in Scotland.

145) CROKE, Sir G. (1560-1642)
Les Reports of Cases in King's Bench and Common Bench (1582-1641). Written in French & revised and published in English by Sir Harbottle Grimston. Folio. 3 vols. A. Roper etc. 1669. Engraved fp. ports, indices. Piece cut from upper blank of vol.2. Modern cloth. WING C 7012,7017,7019. S. & M. i,298/37. £180

The three parts comprehend a period of 60 years, Elizabeth, James and Charles. They are quoted with respect for their learning and accuracy and were not published till after his death by his son-in-law Sir Harbottle Grimston (Master of the Rolls).

146) .....Another copy. 1683. Folio. 3 vols. WING C 7013. £30
Contemp. calf, worn & torn. Binding set.

147) CUNNINGHAM, T.
A New and Complete Law-Dictionary, or, General Abridgment of the Law. 1764(-5). 1st edition. Folio. 2 vols. n.p. A few marginal wormholes at end of vol.2. Orig. publishers' adverts. (8vo) loosely inserted. Contemp. calf, spines sl. rubbed, joints of vol.1. weak. S. &M. i,82/22. £200

Cunningham includes summaries of cases, precedents in equity & statutes and combines an abridgement with that of a dictionary. For the part of the dictionary he largely draws on Cowell.

148) (.....) A new Treatise on the Laws concerning Tithes. By a Gentleman of the Middle Temple. W. Griffin. 1766. 2nd edition, enlarged with the addition of several cases never before printed. (iv),298,(viii)pp. Half-title. Bookplate. Contemp. calf, rubbed; spine sl. frayed and hinges weak, sl. spotting of endpapers and prelims. in margins. S. &M. i,191/17. £35

Contains all the Statutes, adjudged Cases, Resolutions and Judgments relative to Tithes.

149) CURIAE, Amicus.(John Payne COLLIER, 1789-1883)
Criticisms on the Bar, including strictures on the principal counsel practising in the Courts of King's Bench, Common Pleas etc. 1819. 1st in book form. (ii),ix,ii,308pp. Modern cloth-backed bds. £30

J.P. Collier is mainly known for his literary work. These papers appeared originally in the "Examiner" during the autumn of 1818.

150) DALRYMPLE, John.
An Essay towards a General History of Feudal Property in Great Britain. Dublin. Sarah Cotter. 1759. 4th edition. vii,(v),344,(iv)pp. subscribers' list, dedication and advert. leaves. Contemp. calf., rubbed. S. &M.i.44/5. £45

A work inspired by the "Esprit des Loix" of Montesquieu, first published in Edinburgh in 1757.
The fourth (Dublin) edition was printed from the first edition.

151) DALTON, Michael. (1554-1640)
The Countrey Justice, containing the Practice of the Justices of the Peace out of their Sessions...Laws of this Realme. John More. 1635. 5th edition, revised, corrected and much enlarged. Folio. (x),410,(x)pp. Minor worming in a few leaves in lower margins. Prelims. sl. stained. Contemp. sprinkled calf, rebacked & repaired. Lower joint torn at foot. STC 6210. S. &M. i,227/24. £150

A popular work in its day, more detailed in points of practice than Lambard or Crompton, and reprinted as the standard work until 1746.

152) .....The Office and Authoritie of Sherifes. Abridged by the former author. Companie of Stationers. 1628. 1st edition of this version. 24mo. (iv),260,(iv) leaves. Device on title, table, dedication leaves. Some sl. staining on last few leaves. Very good. Contemp. calf, rebacked. STC 6213. S. &M.i,222/7. £200

Although better known for his "Office of Justice of the Peace", this work was also held in high repute and continued to be a standard authority until the beginning of the 18th century.

153) DARK, Sidney.
Twelve Bad Men. n.d.(c.1920). 288pp. Orig. cloth, some sl. spotting of prelim. pages. £8

The histories of Louis XI, Cesare Borgia, Cellini, Cromwell, Mazarin, Judge Jeffreys and others.

154) DAVENPORT, Rufus.
The Petitions of Rufus Davenport to the 24 States, for the adoption of the FREE DEBT RULES. Extracted from Gov. Giles' Speech to the Legislature of Virginia. Both dated. 1828, Dec. 1st. (Boston 1839. Jan. 24) 8pp. sewn as issued. Title & edges sl. dust-stnd. Signature "Daniel P. Parker Esq" on title. SABIN 18717.KRESS C2263. £30

Governor William Branch Giles (1763-1830) was Governore of his native State of Virginia from 1826-29; earlier he had been a Representative in Congress, United States Senator and member of the Legislature.

155) DAWSON, Thomas.
The Law of the Press. 1947. 2nd ed.Table of cases. Index.cl. £6

156) The DECISIONS of the ENGLISH JUDGES (Court of Session), during the Usurpation, from 1655-61. Folio. Edinburgh. G. Hamilton etc. 1762. 1st edition. (iv),243pp. Uncut. Index. Bookplate. Orig. grey boards, stained & rubbed with new spine.S.&M.v,29. £80

Taken from the MS of this collection of decisions from the only copy found in the Library of the Faculty of Advocates.

157) DICKINSON, William.
A Practical Guide to the Quarter Sessions and other Sessions of the Peace....J. & W.T.Clarke. 1820. 2nd edition, much enlarged. viii, 901,(ix)pp. Index, booklist. Contemp. calf, sl.rubbed. S.&M.ii,100 £35

158) DIRLETON, Sir J. Nisbet of.
Some Doubts & Questions, in the Law, esp. of Scotland..also some Decisions of the Lords of Council and Session. Folio. Edinburgh. G. Mosman.1698. 1st edition. (xii),228,226,(xvi)pp. Engraved fp. port. by R. White after D. Paton, index, separate title to "Decisions". Corners of last few leaves sl. dampstained. Contemp. calf, neatly rebacked, morocco labels. Bookplate. WING N 1170. S. &M.v,31. ALDIS 3767. £150

According to Lord Hardwicke, Dirleton's Doubts are better than most people's certainties. The inadequacy of Steuart's answer to this work produced a Scots proverb, "Doubtin' with Dirleton & resolving with Steuart".

....See also (STEUART). Sir J.

159) DOBIE, Wm. Jardine.
Manual of the Law of Liferent and Fee in Scotland. Edinburgh.1941. 1st edition. xxvi,335pp. Index and tables of cases. Orig.cl. £12

160) DOUGLAS, N.
An Address to the Judges and Jury, in a case of Alleged Sedition, on 26th May 1817, which was intended to be delivered before passing sentence. Glasgow. D. Mackenzie. 1817. 1st edition. 40pp. Modern marbled wraps. S. &M.v,32. £20

161) (DUCPETIAUX, Edouard)
De la Mission de la Justice Humaine et de l'Inustice de la Peine de Mort. (and) De le Justice de Repression, et particulierement de l'Inutilité et des Effets Pernicieux de la Peine du Mort. Brussels. Cauterts. 1827. xiv,16,105pp. Orig. printed wraps. Removed from a bound volume. £60

Ducepetiaux was a leading Belgian social reformer, official Inspector of prisons and charities and active for prison reform. He refers to the work of Lucas, Mackintosh and others.

162) EAST, Edward Hyde.
Reports of Cases argued and determined in the Court of King's Bench, with tables of the name of cases and principal matters. 6 vols. (of 16) 1800-1805. A. Strahan. 1801-5. Contemp. calf, sl. rubbed. £60

163) ECTON, John.
Thesaurus Rerum Ecclesiasticarum, being an account of the valuations of all the Ecclesiastical Benefices in the several Dioceses in England and Wales...(with) directions and precedents relating to Presentation, etc. T. Osborne etc. 1763. 3rd edition. 4to. With numerous additions by Browne WILLIS. xl,696pp. Index. Contemp. sprinkled calf, gilt panelled spine, sl. rubbed, upper joint weak. KRESS 6094. S. & M.i,168/49. £80

The best edition of Ecton's work.

164) ELCHIES (Lord) Patrick Grant.
Court of Session Cases, from 1733-54; collected and digested into the form of a Dictionary. Edited from the original MSS by W.M. Morison. 2 vols. 4to. Edinburgh. Archibald Constable. 1813. 1st ed. n.p. Contemp. calf, head of spine of vol.2 chipped. PRESENTATION copy from the editor. Very good. S. &M.v,39. £120

Consists of more than 1600 cases, many of which, although ascertaining important points in law and practice, had not been noticed before and in several instances, Lord Elchies throws new light on cases reported by Lord Kilkerran and Lord Kames. Lord Elchies kept a daily record of the cases he considered to be important and compiled the Dictionary from these.

165) ENGLAND, Church of.
Iniunctions giuen by the Queenes Maiestie. 1559. The first yeere of the Raigne of our Soveraign Lady Queene Elizabeth, cum Privilegio Regiae Maiestas. (Assigns of R. Barker)(1600). 32pp. Fine woodcut title. STC 10110. (with)
...Articles to be enquired of in the Visitation, in the first Yeere of the Raign of our most dread Soueraign Ladie Elizabeth...1559. R. Barker. 1600. Title mounted. 12pp. STC 10133.
...Articles whereupon it was agreed by the Archbishops and Bishops ...in the Convocation holden at London..1562. R. Barker.1605. 24pp. One or two headlines shaved. STC 10047.
...Constitutions and Canons Ecclesiastical, treated upon by the Bishop of London. R. Barker. 1604. 172pp. STC 10069.
4 items in 1 vol. Woodcut initials. sm.4to. 17th century vellum-backed boards, sl. rubbed. £100

An interesting collection of four injunctions and articles relating to the Church. The first item is very rare and together with the second item are good examples of BLACK letter printing.

166) ENSOR, R.C.K.
Courts & Judges in France, Germany and England. OUP 1933. 1st ed. Orig. cloth, sl. marked. With A.L. 1 page.* £6

*The author discusses the book and mentions that the Nazis rise in Germany occured after the book had gone to the publishers and he hoped for a second publication to deal with it.

167) (ERSKINE, John of Carnock).
The Principles of the Law of Scotland. In the order of Sir George Mackenzie's Institutions of that law. Edinburgh. John Balfour. 1764. Third edition, revised by the author. (viii),509,(xxvi)pp. Some sl. staining of last few leaves at top of margin. Contemp. sprinkled calf, some wear on back cover. S.&M.v.40. £40

First published in 1754 this work was revised for a century and a half and is still recognised as an authority.

168) ERSKINE, Thomas, Lord. (1750-1823)
Speeches..when at the Bar, on Subjects connected with the Liberty of the Press, and gainst Constructive Treasons (--on Misc. Subjects 1810(-1812). 1st collected edition. 5 vols. Engr. fp. port. to v.4. Half title in vol.1 only, as called for. Contemp. stained calf, spines rubbed, some joints worn. Not in S. & M. £80

After 28 years at the Bar, Fox raised his friend to the woolsack. Erskine maintained an unvarying reputation as a chamption of the liberty of the subject.

169) ESPINASSE, Isaac.
A Digest of the Law of Actions and Trials at Nisi Prius. With 3 chapters on the Law of Corporations and Evidence. 2 vols. 1793. 2nd edition. Contemp. calf, rubbed. S. &M.i.335/6. £45

170) .....Reports of Cases argued and ruled at Nisi Prius.(1796)-(1804). 4 vols. (of 6). A. Strahan. 1796-1804. Index for each vol. Contemp. calf, sl. rubbed. S. &M. i.335/5. £60

Espinasse's Reports are the first substantial body of Nisi Prius cases. As historical sources for the law of obligations & of personal injuries, they have a value often denied to better reports in more traditional fields. They were published at long intervals, ending in 1811.

171) L'ESPRIT de la COUTUME de NORMANDIE,
avec un recueil d' arrets notables du meme Parlement. Rouen.1720. 4to. Third and new revised edition. Indices, privilege leaf. Sm. hole on title. Contemp. Mottled calf, hinges worn & sl. rubbed. French text. £60
A collection, edited for this edition, of arrests and rules concerning tithes & other ecclesiastical cases.

172) EVERITT, Nicholas.
Shots from a Lawyer's Gun. 1901. xix,308,(viii)pp. Pictorial cloth, sl. faded. Publishers' presentation copy with inscription on half title. S. &M.ii.116. £25

S. & M. give the first edition as 1900 and do not mention this 1901 edition.
Instructive elucidation of the law affecting the English sportsman and his gamekeeper. It was still being reprinted in 1927.

173) The FARMER'S LAWYER,
or, every Country Gentleman his Counsellor. By a Gentleman of Lincoln's Inn. W.Strahan & M. Woodfall. 1772. 2nd edition (with) the Law concerning Landlords and Tenants. iv,331,(i)pp. Bookplate. Contemp. calf, repair on front cover. S.&M.i.444/6. (2nd ed.) £30

Contains all the Acts of Parliament, and adjudged Cases thereon, relative to Cattle..Timber and other Trees, Butter and Cheese...

174) FARNSWORTH, Richard Ashley.
Productivity and Law. USA/London. 1975. 1st edition. xii,364pp. Index. Orig. cloth. Sm. ex lib. stamps. £10

Farnsworth was Solicitor of the Supreme Court of Judicature in England and Wales and Director General of the European Institute for Industrial Relations.

175) FAVELL, Samuel.
A Speech on the Propriety of revising the Criminal law, delivered Dec. 10,1808 before the Corporation of the City of London.1819. 1st edition. vii,72pp. Uncut. Disbound,sewn as issued. £20.

176) FERRIERE, M. Claude Joseph de.
The History of the Roman or Civil Law, transl. into English by J(ohn) B(eaver) to which is added Dr. Duck's Treatise of the Use and Authority of the Civil Law in England. S. &M.i.612/6. (with) ...The History of the Origin of the French Laws, transl. from the French by J.B. With preface and notes shewing the analogy of the Laws of the Antient Gauls and Britons. D. Browne. 1724. 1st English edition. Half title to the first work and index for the second. 2 works in 1 volume. Contemp. panelled calf, spine darkened and hinges worn. £80

Ferriere's work was first published in Paris in 1718.
Dr. Duck's treatise was originally published in Latin and was translated into French by Guignard in 1689 and later into English by Dr. Beaver and appended to the above work.
The second work by by M. Gabriel ARGOU, an advocate in the Parliament of Paris and was his only publication.

177) FIELDING, Sir John.(d.1789)
Extracts from such of Penal Laws, as Particularly Relate to the Peace and Good Order of this Metropolis: with Observations. 1769. New edition, revised. Index. Few leaves sl. spotted. Contemp. calf, joints & edges sl. worn. S. &M.i.439. HIGGS 4769. £150

Sir John, brother of Henry the great novelist, was a blind magistrate at Bow Street. Both brothers were among the first to make sensible propositions for the control, as well as punishment, of urban crime. This digest of criminal statutes, with remarks on their faults and abuses together with his comments on social conditions are acute and often prophetic.
A Treatise on the Office of Constable, edited from Henry's MSS, is included.

178) FINCH, Sir Henry.
Law, or, a Discourse thereof..written in French..and done into English by the same author. R. & E. Atkins, etc. 1678. viii,506,(xvi)p Index. Publishers' cat. of law books. Signatures on title, one deleted. Modern morocco-backed boards. WING F932 (with duplicate entry under Heneage Finch, Earl of Nottingham WING N 1405). S.&M.i. 238/10. £150

"Finch's Law" was considered the best elementary book for law students, until the publication of Blackstone's Commentaries. It is one of the few attempts to reduce the common law into a system. His definitions were exact, his style concise and his illustrations clear and authentic.
Many of Finch's valuable parts are incorporated in Blackstone's Commentaries.

179) FINDLAY, John.
A Treatise on the Law of Tithes in Ireland, and Ecclesiastical Law connected therewith. Dublin. John Cumming. 1828. xiv,592,xxxiipp. Uncut, index. Modern boards. S.&M. iv.31. £60

180) FITZHERBERT, Sir Anthony. (1470-1538)
La Nouvelle Natura Brevium..auecques un Table...iammais per cy deuaunt imprimée. In aedibus Richardi Tottelli. 1567. 4th edition. French text. (xxxii),271 leaves. Woodcut title-border, index, BLACK letter. Ink-stains on C_5, marginal defect to F_8 with loss of few words of last, corner torn from D_1, lacks final colophon leaf.Some early annots. Title frayed. Contemp. calf, worn, rebacked & recornered. STC 10961. BEALE T.347. S. &M.i.269. £180

Fitzherbert's commentary on the writs as printed in Rastell's Register (1531) was one of the most authoritative works in English law from 1534, when it was first printed, until 1852 when the forms of action which it illustrates were abolished.

181) .....The New Natura Brevium...the Authorities in Law and some other cases and notes collected by the translator out of the Year-

FIZHERBERT, Sir Anthony..New Natura Brevium..cont.
181)..Books and Abridgments. (with) a Table. 12mo. R. & E. Atkins. 1704. (64),600pp. Contemp. panelled calf, rubbed, sm. tear in sp. & edge frayed. Signatures on title and endpapers. Very good copy. S. &M. i.269/67. £95

Fitzherbert was a Judge of the Common Pleas and is principally known for his famous Abridgment of the Year Books. The above, in spite of its technical character, enjoyed a great reputation. Coke, in his Report, Hale, Willes all quote is as a book of great authority and Blackstone gives it the honour of a place in his work. The translation is by William Hughes.

182) (FITZPATRICK, Hugh).
Statement of the Penal Laws, which aggrieve the Catholics of Ireland, with commentaries. 2 parts in 1 vol. Dublin. 1812. 1st ed. xxvi,xii,13-138/(ii),139-370pp. Title to part 1 laid down and "statement" supplied in MS; title of part 2 has part of top torn off. Contemp. calf, worn & rubbed, hinges loose. S.&M.iv.32. £45

Deals with laws which affect the "Catholic Clergy,....School-Houses and other Charitable foundations" and those that "deny to the Catholics the Right of sitting and voting in either Houses of Parliament" and similar disqualifications.

For reprint see D. SCULLY.

183) FLETA,
seu Commentarius Juris Anglicani sic nuncupatus...accedit tractatulus vetus de agendi excipeindique formulis Gallicanus. Fet Assavoir dictus; subjungitur etiam Joan. Seldeni ad Fletam dissertatio historica. 4to. S.R.Prostant apud H. Twyford etc. 1685. 2nd edition, corrected. Latin text. (viii),553pp. Embossed panelled calf, edges & corners sl. rubbed, rebacked, sm. inkstains on 2 pages. WING F.1291. S.&M. i.53/20. £200

"Fleta" so-called, because the author was confined in the debtors' prison of the Fleet, is a summary of English law which adds new developments in Statutes & forms of action to the older work of Bracton. "Fet Assavoir" belongs to the previous century; it is a manual of King's Court procedure illustrating the relation between that Court & the local jurisdictions & the primitive state of legal representation. Selden's dissertation treats largely of the influence of Roman Law and its professors in England.

184) .....partim e Codice MS. to COTTONIANO; partim ex antiquis Rotulis, veterrimis tam historia quam legum Angliae Scriptoribus emendatus, illustratus, et in integrum restitutus. Fletcher Gyles. 1735. Folio. (vii),97pp. Latin text. Uncut in orig. grey wraps. Wraps dust-stained and sl. frayed, corner of end leaves sl. stnd. S.&M.i.53/20. Lacks backstrip. £45

This edition was edited by Sir Samuel Clarke.

185) FLEURY, Claude. (1640-1723)
Institution au Droit Francois, edited by Edouard Laboulaye & Rodolphe Dareste. Paris. 1858. 1st edition. 2 vols. xxviii,464/ii, 408pp. Lib. stamps on half titles, titles & final leaves. Some spotting. Contemp. morocco-backed boards, edges sl. rbbd. £30

Written by the great ecclesiastical historian in about 1665, this work remained unknown until Laboulaye discovered the MS in the 1830s.

186) FONBLANQUE, John.
A Treatise of Equity. (with) marginal references & notes. 2 vols. Dublin. 1793-5. xiii,(i),449,(xiv)/xxiii,495,62pp. Index for each volume. Endpapers sl. stained. Contemp. calf, sl. rubbd. S.&M.i. 256/12. £60

Henry Ballow or Bellewe published the first monograph on Equity in 1737 which was later edited by Gilbert in 1792 and then by Fonblanque as above. This remained until 1820 the standard to which the various imprints of the "Chancellor's Foot" (Selden's famous description of equity) were reduced.

187) FORBES, William.
A Treatise of Church-lands & Tithes: In two parts. (with) an historical account of ecclesiastical revenues...Edinburgh.1705. 1st edition. (xvi),450,(xii)pp. Index. S.&M.v.43. (with)
...A few remarks by William Forbes on a scurrilous, erroneous, and pedantick pamphlet, entitled...Some Charitable Observations on his late treatise of Church-Lands...Edinburgh,1706.1st ed. 36pp. (with)
...A letter from William Forbes to a Gentleman in the Country, concerning the Parson of Banchory, and his late Pamphlet, entituled Some Just Reflections on a Pasquil against him...Edinburgh. 1706. 44pp. Followed by 1 page of supplement to the Index.
3 works in 1 vol. Contemp. calf, rubbed and worn. ex lib.label. Only the first item in S. & M. £85

The author, a Scottish advocat, based this work on his researches for which he used the Law tracts relating to benefices and tithes, Mackenzie's Observations, Dirleton on Steuart and particularly Dalrymple.

188) .....Another copy of the main work. Contemp. calf, rebacked. £75

189) FORD, Paul Leicester.
List of some Briefs in Appeal Causes which relate to America tried before the Lord Commissioners of Appeals of Prize Causes of H.M.'s Privy Council 1736-58. Brooklyn. N.Y.1889. LIMITED to 250 copies. rep. from the proceedings of the Mass. Historical Society. 20 leaves, printed on one side only. Uncut & partly unopened. Orig. printed wraps, sl. faded. £20
Ford was the author of a bibliography in the field of the history & literature relating to the adoption of the Constitution of theU.S.

190) FORMS of WRITING,
used in the most common Cases in Scotland with such part of the Principles of the Law as appear connected therewith. (with) a Table of Stamp Duties. Edinburgh. 1784. 1st edition. xx,449pp. Contemp. calf, rubbed, spine frayed, hinges worn.S.&M.v.43. £45

191) FORTESCUE, Sir John.(1424-1476)
De laudibus legum Angliae..hereto are joind the two Summes of Sir Ralph de Hengham. (edited by John Selden) Companie of Stationers. 1616. 1st thus. 2 parts in 1 vol. (xvi)pp 132 leaves,(vi),56, (xii),160,(ii)pp. Final blank, lacks first blank. Index. Latin & English text. 18th-century calf, joints & corners sl. worn. STC 11197. S. & M. i.22. £300

Chief Justice Fortescue, wrote this dialogue between himself & the Crown Prince to instruct the latter in the laws of England.
The summae of Hengham (Chief Justice (1274-1309)) are accounts of practice showing the relation between the King's courts at various levels. They are published by Selden for the first time and both works contain his notes.

192) .....The Difference between an Absolute and Limited Monarchy, (with) a learned preface concerning the Laws of England, with remarks, and an index, by Fortescue Alland. W.Bowyer. 1719. 2nd ed. (xvi),lxxxii,(iv),148,(xiv)pp. Title in red & black, engraved vignettes for chapter headings, initial letters and tail-pieces,index, bibliography, dedication and preface. Contemp. panelled & embossed calf, spine gilt. Edges sl. rubbed, inner hinges strengthened. Fine Copy. S.&M.i.114/32. £150

Written between 1471 & 1476, but published for the first time in 1714 it is mainly an English version of Fortescue's famous work "De Laudibus" with the addition of a number of observations meant for the service of King Edward.

193) .....A Learned Commendation of the Politique Laws of England ...newly translated...by Robert Mulcaster. Richarde Tottell.1573. (iii),132,(iii) leaves. Black & Roman letter. Latin & English text. Old ink names & annots. on title & blank verso of last leaf & a few in margins. Contemp. calf, rebacked, rubbed. BEALE T.358. STC 11195. S. &M. i.17. £200

Third edition of Fortescue and the second of Mulcaster's version. The work, written for the instruction of the future King Edward IV it is a summary for the layman containing the earliest outline of the peculiarly English scheme of constitutional monarchy, with many interesting comparisons between English & foreign practice.

194) .....Another copy. Thomas Wight & Bonham Norton.1599.(ii), 3-132,(iii) leaves. Black & Roman letter. Latin & English text. Title sl. browned. Contemp. vellum, worn, lacks ties. BEALE T.359. STC 11196. S. &M. i.17. £180

Fourth edition of Fortescue & third of Mulcaster's version.

195) FOSTER, Sir Michael. (1689-1763)
A Report of some proceedings on the commission of Oyer and Terminer and Goal Delivery for the Trial of the Rebels in the Year 1746 in the County of Surrey and of other Crown Cases (with) discourses on branches of the Crown Law. Folio. Oxford. Clarendon Press. 1762. 1st edition. (iii),viii,(iv),412,(xvii)pp. Index, adverts.,booklist (before title). Contemp. calf, top edge of spine sl. worn, sl.rbbd. Very good copy. S.&M.i.367/11. £120

Foster, a Judge for the King's Bench for 18 years, distinguished for his learning, integrity and independence, and the exceptional precision of his Reports, ranks as major authority on criminal law.

196) .....Another copy. (with) discourses on High Treason, Homicide,...and observations on the writings of Lord Hale. E. & R.Brooke 1792. 3rd edition (with) appendix of new cases and edited by his nephew Michael Dodson. b3-2 misbound before 2F4. Contemp. calf, sl. rubbed. Very good large copy. £60

197) FRANCILLON, James.
Lectures, elementary & familiar on English Law. 1860. 1st series. Orig. cloth, rubbed & stained, frayed. S.&M.ii.129. £10

198) GABBETT, Joseph.
A Digested Abridgment, and comparative view of the Statute Law of England and Ireland to 1811..analytically arranged in the order of Sir W. Blackstone's Commentaries (with) chronological table of the Statutes and an index. 4 vols. Dublin. 1812-18. Gilt dec'd calf with marbled sides. Edges sl. rubbed. S.&M.ii.132. £60

199) GARDINER, Gerald & Andrew MARTIN (editors)
Law Reform Now. 1963.1st edition. Orig. cloth. £8

Contributions by specialist lawyers on each branch of the law.

200) A GENERAL COLLECTION of TRETYS, DECLARATIONS of WAR, etc.
1732. 2nd edition. 4 vols. Contemp. calf, gilt. Sl. worming throughout, affec. letters in a few sections. £90

A compendium containing treaties in Europe from 1648-1731 including "Manifestos, Declarations of War, and other Publick Papers," In vol.4 there is an index of all the treaties.

201) GENTILIS, Alberico. (1551-1611)
De Jure Belli. Libri tres. Hanover. 1598. Excudebat Guilielmus Antonius. 1st German edition. Latin text. (viii),716pp. Woodcut devices. Bookplate. Sl. marginal worming not affec. text. 18th-century calf. Fine copy. ADAMS 424. S.&M.i.601/11. £450

First edition was printed in Oxford in 1588. One of the first works upon the science of International Law.

202) GIFFORD, John.(Pseud)(WHELLIER,A.)
The Complete English Lawyer; or, Every Man his own Lawyer...containing a summary of the Constition of England and its Laws and Statutes...including Laws relating to Trade, Manufacturers, and Commerce...also the Criminal Law of England..with an appendix. 1819. Third edition. (with)
...Supplement to the Complete English Lawyer..containing the Acts of the 59 Geo. III, the Laws of Excise and Customs, the Assessed Taxes and Stamp Duties of all denominations...1819.
2 works in 1 vol. iv-688/iv-148pp. Index, portraits in part 1. Contemp. calf, rubbed, rebacked. Sm.corner torn from front endpaper. Not in S.&M. £35

203) (GILBERT, Sir G. later Lord Chief Baron)(1674-1726)
An Historical View of the Court of Exchequer and of the King's Revenues there answered; by a late Learned Judge. E.&R. Nutt.1738. 1st edition. (xxii),151,(xvii)pp. Advert. leaf (not mentioned in S. & M) torn out. End leaves browned and sl. spotted. Bookplate & signatures. Contemp. calf, rubbed & stained, lower hinge sl. split. S. &M.i.320/15 & 19. £45

204) .....The Law of Evidence. Considerably enlarged by Capel Lofft ..with some account of the author; his abstract of Locke's Essay and his argument in case of Homicide in Ireland. 4 vols. 1791-6. Engraved fp. port.,& 1 other, folding tables, indices. Occasional ink scoring. Contemp. calf, spine rubbed, sl. frayed at ends & lower joint of vol.1 worn. S. &M. i.379/5. £95

Gilbert's work on Evidence was perhaps the most valuable of all his many law writings. About four-fifths of this edition, distinguished by inverted commas & including almost all the case law, is from the editor's pen.

205) .....The Law of Tenures, including the theory and practice of Copyholds. With an historical introduction on the Feudal System & notes by Charles Watkins. 1796. 4th edition, corrected. Index. Errata leaf. Endpapers & title sl. browned. Modern half buckram. S.&M.i.453/20. £75

Contains explanations of many points of the feudal law which are not as fully displayed by any other writer, & traces principles of their origin.

206) GILMOUR, Sir John & Sir David FALCONER.
A Collection of Decisions of the Lords of Council and Session. In two Parts. 1. Decisions: 1661-6 observed by Gilmour. 2.1681-6 by Falconer. Likeways the Acts of Sederunt,1681-91 and continued to 1696. 3 parts in 1 vol. 4to. Edinburgh. James Watson.1701. 1st edition. Privilege leaf, tables to first two parts, indices to all three parts. Main title and separate titles for each part. Ex lib. bookplate. Contemp. panelled calf, rubbed, ends of spine sl. split. S. &M.v.46. £120

207) GLANVILLE, R. de.
A translation of Glanville by John BEAMES, with notes. A.J.Valpy. 1812. 1st English edition. xl,362,(17),(i)pp. Index, sl. spotted. Contemp. calf-backed boards, rubbed, spine worn. S.&M.i.54/28. £30

Translation by Beames of Glanville's famous treatise on the laws and customs of the Kingdom of England, written in 1187-9 and 1st printed in 1554. There is some doubt whether Glanvil wrote it himself and the author was probably Hubert Walter.

208) (GLASS,S.)
The Magistrate's Assistant, or, a summary of those Laws which immediately respect the conduct of a Justice of the Peace. Gloucester. 1788. 2nd edition. xvi,544,lxviii,xxivpp. Appendix, folding table, sl. torn. Contemp. calf, sl. rubbed & stained. S. &M.i.288. £30

A more convenient and quick reference than the larger work of Burn.

209) GODWIN,E.W.
Temple Bar. Illustrated. From the British Architect, Oct.19,1877. 4to. 22pp. 2 plates. Orig. cloth, loose in boards. £10

210) (GOGUET, Antoine Yves)(1716-1758)
The Origin of Laws, Arts and Sciences, and their progress among the most ancient nations. Transl. from the French. 3 vols. Edinburgh. 1761. 1st English. 9 folding copper-engraved plates, folding table for each vol. Vol.2 & 3 bookplate "Lavington" and "Wilberforce Lib. Backsettown". Contemp. calf, gilt on spines. Lacks 1 label on vol.1. Corners & spines rubbed, endpapers sl. browned. S. &M. i.15/6.(1775 edition only).KRESS 5934. HIGGS 2433. £80

The work written by A.Y.Goguet, aided by A.C.Fugere. Vol.1 transl. by Robert Henry; vol.2 by Dr. Dunn and vol.3 by Alexander Spearman.

211) GOLDASTIUS Haiminsfeldius, M. (1576-1635)
Collectio Constituionum Imperialium...recessus, ordinationes, decreta, rescripta, mandata, et edicta...jurisdictions imperii et ecclesiae...Frankfurt-am-Main. Johannis Adami Jungii.1713. Folio. 4 vols. Engraved title with black and red lettering (vol.1). Vols. 2 & 3 engraved publisher's device on title. Index, errata. Contemp. mottled calf, gilt dec'd spines, rubbed & hinges weak. £80

Goldastius's knowledge of the public law of the empire and his acquaintance with the affairs of Germany together with his study of scarce books and old MSS is worthy of the praise accorded him.

212) GOTHOFREDUS, Jacobus.(1587-1652)
Manuale Juris seu parva Juris mysteria...juris civilis Romani. 1. Historia. 2. Bibliotheca. 3. Florilegium..4. Series librorum & titulorum in digestis & in codice. Leyden. J. Verbessel. 1784. 9th edition .12mo.(viii),591pp.Contemp. vellum. Bookplate. £60

213) (GRANGE, Lord, the Hon. James Erskine)
Extracts from the Diary of a Senator of the College of Justice, 1708-18. Edinburgh. 1843. 1st edition. xvi,iv,156pp. With preface by J.M. on Lord Grange. Orig. cloth, sl stained. (with)typed letter by W.R.D. Macmillan, Procurator Fiscal of Ayr to "Strachan" attemting to sell the book on behalf of Allan MacDonald (signature on front endpaper) of Skye. £20

Sidelights on the General Assembly.

214) A Member of GRAY'S INN.
The Law Student's Guide, containing an historical treatise on each of the Inns of Court, with their rules and customs respecting admission, keeping terms, call to the Bar, Chambers etc. (with) remarks on the jurisdiction of the Benchers etc. 1827. 1st edition. viii,159,(i)pp. Orig. cloth, sl. faded. Not in S. & M. £16

215) GROTIUS, Hugo (Huig de Groot)(1583-1648)
Annales et historiae de rebus Belgicis. Folio. Amsterdam. Joannis Blaeu. 1657. 1st edition. Latin text. (xiv),569,(xxiii)pp. Woodcut device on title. Index. Lacks **4 (portrait). Contemp. calf, rebacked, rubbed. £150

Edited by Cornelis & Piet de Groot.
The History of the Low Countries' War of Independence against the power of Spain was published after the great jurist's death by his sons.

216) GUETERBOCK, Karl Eduard.
De Iure Martimo quod in Prussia saeculo XVI et ortum est et in usu fuit. Königsberg. 1866. 1st edition. 4to. 36pp. Latin text. Modern cloth. Bookplate. £20

A University thesis arguing that the 16th century maritime law of Prussia was derived from the Dutch-Flemish code.

217) GWILLIM, Henry.
A Collection of Acts and Records of Parliament, with Report of Cases argued and determined in the Courts of Law and Equity, respecting Tithes. 4 vols. A. Strahan. 1801. 1st edition. Contemp. calf, labels. Some sl. spotting of leaves at each end, lacks label on vol.3 and some signs of wear on hinges. S.&M. i.192/29. £75

218) HAGGARD, John. (edited)
A Report of the judgment in Dew v.Clark and Clark, delivered by Sir John Nicholl in the Prerogative Court of Canterbury, 1826. 1826. 1st edition. (iv),99,(i)pp. Half title, errata. Orig. boards, spine sl. frayed. Presentation copy from the editor. See S.&M.ii.150 (collection of his Reports in the High Court of Admiralty) £30

Edited by Haggard by permission from the Judges's notes.

219) HALE, Sir Matthew. (1609-1676)
The Analysis of the Law: being a scheme or abstract, of the several title and partitions of the Law. 1716. 2nd edition. (xiv),148,(xxvi)p First blank, index. Contemp. calf, joints sl. worn. S.&M.i.239. £55

Hale's logical system of law, the first of its kind, had a great influence on Blackstone.

220) .....The history of the Common Law of England. 1716.2nd edition corrected. (with)
.....The Analysis of the Law: 1716. 2nd edition with alphabetical table.
2 works in 1 vol. Later 18th century calf, gilt. Fine copy. £95

221) .....Historia Placitorum Coronae. The history of the Pleas of the Crown, with notes by Sollom Emlyn. Folio. 2 vols. 1736. 1st edition. Engr. folding fp. port. Index. Sl. marginal worming. Contemp. calf, sl. worn. Very good copy. S.&M.i.362/36. £120

Hale's important work, although only an unfinished portion of his proposed corpus on crown law, is a guide to capital offences. Emlyn's notes correct some references and bring the statute law to date.

222) .....BURNETT, Gilbert: The life and death of Sir Matthew Hale, sometime Lord Chief Justice of H.M. Court of King's Bench. 1682. 2nd edition. Fp. port. (xx),218pp. Errata. Contemp. panelled blind-stamped calf, gilt. Joints sl. weak, endpapers sl. browned. Bookplate. WING B.5828. £48

With a 23 page catalogue of Hale's books printed by William Shrowbury & mss. to be published; and a catalogue of the books given by Hale to Lincoln's Inn according to his will.

223) ....The Life of Sir Matthew Hale. (with)
The Life of the Rev. H. Hammond (1605-1660) by John Fell. A new edition. Oxford. Clarendon Press. 1806. xv,315pp. Contemp. calf, gilt. Sl. rubbed and hinges sl. weak with some sl. worming in lower margins throughout. 2 works in 1 vol. £20

224) ....Another copy. S.P.C.K. 1823. 2 works in 1 vol. Orig. tree calf, rebacked, edges rubbed. £15

224) HALLIFAX, Samuel. (1733-1790)
An Analysis of the Roman Civil Law, compared with the laws of England....course of lectures..read in the University of Cambridge. CUP 1774. 1st edition. Index. Contemp calf, newly rebacked. S. &M.i.612/8. £80

A simple summary which asserts the importance of civil law to the Englishman without proposing, as his predessors in the 17th century had done, that common law should give way to it.

225) HARDRES, Sir Thomas.
Reports of Cases...in the Court of Exchequer (1655-69). Folio. R. & E. Atkins..1693. 1st edition. (xii),512,(444),(xx)pp. Privilege leaf before tile, index. Modern cloth. WING H 703. S. & M.i.322/6. £80

Hardres was a member of Gray's Inn & Serjeant at Law to Charles II. There is a chasm in all the copies of the first edition (pp 233-300) This is one of the scarcer Reports.

226) (HARDWICKE Earl, Philip Yorke) (1720-1790)
Miscellaneous State Papers from 1501 to 1726. 4to. 2 vols. W.Strahan. 1778. Index, engr. fp. in vol. 1. Contemp. half calf, sl. rubbed, tops of spines sl. frayed. Fine set. £150

227) HARGRAVE, Francis (1741-1821)
A complete Collection of State Trials and Proceedings for High Treason...commencing with the 11th year of Richard II..1793. Dublin. 5th edition. 4to. Tables, appendices. 3 vols. Contemp. half calf, joint of vol.1 weak. S. &M. i.369/8. £90

This is the second edition edited by Hargrave and one of the most important and complete compendiums.

228) HART, H.L.A. (Professor of Jurisprudence, Oxford University)
The Morality of the Criminal Law. Two lectures. Jerusalem. Hebrew University/OUP 1965. 1st published edition. 54pp. Orig. cl.dw. £8

229) HARVEY, C.P.
The Advocate's Devil. Frwd. Viscount Monckton of Brenchley.1958. 1st edition. Orig. cloth. £3

230) HARVEY, James.
A collection of English Precedents relating to the Office of a Justice of the Peace; with reference to Statutes. Henry Lintot.1751. 3rd edition, enlarged. vi.371,(xxxi)pp. Addenda. Contemp. calf, rebacked, corners sl. frayed. S. &M.i.228/32. £65

An alphabetical summary of procedure and statute precedents with other related material.

231) HATCHELL, George. (compiled)
Abstract of the Patent and Miscellaneous Rolls of Chancery, inrolled during the reign of William IV,1830-7. Compiled from the original inrolments in the Rolls Office. 4to. Dublin. 1838. (iv),114pp. Indices (nominum & locorum). Calf-backed cloth, stained & spine worn. £35

232) HAWKINS, William.
A Treatise of the Pleas of the Crown. Folio. E. & R. Nutt..1739. 3rd edition. 2 vols. in 1. Index. Contemp. blind-stamped calf, joints weak, sl. stained & spotted. S. & M.i.363. £60

The first comprehensive work on the subject, piecing out the imperfections & ommissions of Stanford, Coke, Hale and the various books on Justices of the Peace.

233) .....Another set. 2 vols. 1777-8. 6th edition. Edited by Thomas Leach. Indices, $3C_6$ in vol. 2 torn without loss, two cancel leaves inserted between $3I_{3-4}$, the cancelled leaf remaining in the text. Contemp. calf, rubbed, one joint worn. S.&M.i.363. Very good. £60

234).....Another set. Thomas Leach. 4 vols. 1795. 7th edition. Indices. Contemp. calf, rubbed. Very good set. £80

This edition includes a new summary of statutory offences & major revisions of the sections on offences against coinage, piracy and some other points.

235) HEINECCIUS, Jo. Gottl. (1681-1741)
Elementa Juris Civilis secundum ordinem Pandectarum commoda auditoribus methodo...edited by Christian Gottlob Richter. 2 vols. Leipzig. 1797. 2nd edition. Index. Some sl. spotting. Latin text. Fine full calf. Bookplate. £40

236) HEUSTON, R.F.V.
Salmond on the Law of Torts. 1961. 13th edition. Index. Tables of Statutes and Cases. Orig. cloth. £5

237) HIGHMORE, A. jur.
A succinct view of the history of Mortmain; the Statutes relative to charitable uses and a full exposition of the last Mortmain Act, comprising the law as it now stands relative to devises, bequests, taxes, leases, visitation and direction of public charities. 1787. 1st edition. Index, half-title. Fine full calf, gilt, label. Bookplate. S. &M. i. 497/11. £60

238) HOBART, Sir Henry (—1625)
Reports in reign of James I with some few Cases in the reign of Queen Elizabeth (King's Bench 1603-25). Folio. R. & W. Leybourn. 1658. Fine engr. fp. port., table, index. Title sl. creased. Modern cloth. WING H2207. S. & M.i.301/63. £80

Hobart was Lord Chief Justice of the Court of Common Pleas & Chancellor to Henry & Charles, Princes of Wales.
The above Reports were published after his death (1st edition in 1641) and were considered of high repute, passing through several editions.

245) HUME-WILLIAMS, Sir Ellis.
The World, the House and the Bar.1930.2nd imp. Orig.cl.rubbed. £5

246) HUNT, Arthur Joseph.
The Law relating to Fraudulent Conveyances, under the Statutes of Elizabeth and the Bankrupt Acts...Law relating to Bills of Sale. 1872. 1st edition. xxiv,256,48pp. Index, publisher's cat. Lib. stamp on title. Orig. cloth, faded. S.&M.ii.176. £20

Second of two works on the subject published in 1871-2 as a result of changes in the bankruptcy laws.

247) HURST, Sir Gerald.
A Short History of Lincoln's Inn. 1946. 1st edition. plates from engravings and paintings. List of Benchers etc. d.w. £6

248) .....Lincoln's Inn Essays.1949. 1st edition. Orig. cl.dw. £5

249) HUTCHESON, Gilbert.
Treatise on the Offices of Justice of Peace, Constable, Commissioners of Supply etc., in Scotland...(with) appendices, ..Statutes, forms of proceedings and writs..2 vols. Edinburgh. W.Creech. 1806. 1st edition. xiv,xx,477,cclxxxvi/xxiii,740,lxxii,li,(iii)pp. Contemp. tree calf, sl. rubbed, lower edges of spines sl. frayed. Bookplates. S.&M.v.53 £80

Includes many historical references and extracts.

250) INDERWICK, F.A.(edited)
The Inner Temple, its early history, as illustrated by its Records. 1505-1603. 4to. 1896. 1st edition. xcviii,536pp. Index, glossary, fp.,uncut. Orig. cloth, faded. £20

Inderwick also wrote a History of the Law Courts in 1895.

251) INDIA & EAST-INDIA COMPANY.
The Law relating to India and the East-India Company with notes & appendix. 1842. 4th edition. 4to. xiv,844pp. Modern buckram. £90

A revised work of the 1840 edition bringing the enactments of the British Parliament down to the end of the previous Session and contains all the latest Acts of the Government of India to Dec. 1842.

252) INGS, Edward.
The Act for the abolition of Arrest on Mesne Process in Civil Actions, ...(with) rules, orders, and cases as..decided in all the Courts, with an appendix of forms. 1840.1st edition. x,272,(iv)pp. Index, booklist. Orig. boards, sl. rubbed. S.&M.ii.181. £12

239) HOOKER, Richard (1554-1600)
Of the Lawes of Ecclesiastical Politie. Eight Bookes. By Will. Stansby. n.d. (1611). With separate title to the 5th Book. W. Stansby, by W. Lowndes 1611. 5 Books altogether. Engraved first title by W. Hole. (iii),453pp. Prelims. sl. stained. STC 13714. S. & M.i.170/69. (with) ....MASON, Francis. Of the Consecration of the Bishops in the Church of England: with their Succession, jurisdiction and other things incident to their Calling. By Robert Barker. 1613. 5 parts. 270pp. STC 17597. 2 works in 1 vol. Contemp. calf, central gilt lozenge with fleur-de-lys on sides. Spine worn, upper joint cracked. £120

In attempting to mediate in the rising dispute concerning church ceremonial & church-government, Hooker was led on to consider the authority & responsibility of the Church in general & from there to examine the nature of human as well as divine laws. The result is one of the masterpieces of English jurisprudence, in fact the first adequate presentation in the English language of the abstract theory of the law.

240) .....Another copy. Will. Stansby..By M. Lowndes. 1617. 6 parts, including Certayne Divine Tractates, H. Fetherstone. 1618. Separate title to 5th book, dated 1616. Folio. the first 4 books 4th edition. Engraved 1st title by W. Hole (mounted & outer margin cropped). (iv) 453pp. Two sermons in 6th part lacks $K_{2\&5}$. Clean tear & sm. stain on E_6. Minor marginal worming to a few leaves. 19th century calf, sl. rubbed. STC 13716. S.&M.i.170/69 (stating that each part should have a separate title, though the collation belies this). £50

241) .....The Works...in Eight Books of Ecclesiastical Polity, compleated out of his own Manuscripts. With several other treatises by the same author and an account of his life and death. For Robert Scot, etc. 1682. (x),553pp. Fine engr. fp. port and additional title for Ecclesiastical Politie by Faithorne & Hole. Red & black printed title. Contemp. mottled calf, gilt panelled spine, joints cracked. Fine crisp copy. WING H2633. S. &M.i.170/68. £160

242) .....Another copy. With the life of the author by Isaac Walton. J. Walthoe, etc. 1723. Folio. lxxxviii,518,(viii)pp. Engr. fp. & additional engr. title to Ecclesiastical Politie. Fine crisp copy. Contemp. panelled calf, gilt spine, joints cracked. Bookplate of Lord Viscount Lymington. £160

243) HOOPER, W. Eden.
The History of Newgate and the Old Bailey, and a Survey of the Fleet Prison. 1935. 1st edition. xvi,176pp. Illus. Orig. cl. £10

244) HUGHES, William.
An Exact Abridgement of all the Statutes in force and use..beginning where Mr. Wingate ends...from Statutes and with an alphabetical table. J. Starkey. 1663. (viii),246,(ii)pp. Advert. leaf. Modern morocco-backed boards. S. &M.i.566/31. £60

253) INNES, C. & James T.Gibson CRAIG.
Memoirs of Thomas Thomson (1768-1852). Edinburgh 1854. 1st edition, privately printed. xi,251pp. Fp. port., list of members of the Bannatyne Club for 1854 and list of works published by Thomson. Orig. boards, sl. chipped. £20

Thomson was a constitutional lawyer, reformer of the Conveyancing & of the registers of Scotland and great scholar of Parliamentary Records. He published many works of importance for Scottish history and law for the Commissioners on the Public Records, mostly privately & historical works for the Bannatyne Club.

254) An INQUIRY into the POLICY of the PENAL LAWS,
affecting the Popish Inhabitants of Ireland....the history and constitution...the rights of Colonies and Planters (with) observations on the laws that restrain the trade of Ireland & some hints respecting America. G.Robinson. 1775. (ii),151pp. Contemp. calf, label. Bookplate. Very good copy. S.&M.iv.43. HIGGS 6248. £185

Higgs lists an edition of 1774.

255) INTERNATIONAL FISCAL ASSOCIATION.
Cahiers de Droit Fiscal International..studies on International Fiscal Law. Vol.61a. Lisbon.1966. 330pp. Multi-lingual. Wraps. £3

256) .....Vol.65b. On the national and esp. international Tax problems arising from the merger of enterprises. Rotterdam. 1970. £3

257) IRONS, J.Campbell.
The Scottish Justices' Manual. Edinburgh/London.1900. 1st. Orig. buckram. Sl. faded. S.&M.v.54. £8

258) IRVING, H.B.
The Life of Judge Jeffreys (1648-1689). 1898. 1st edition. Engr. fp. port., and two other plates. Orig. cloth, rubbed & stained. £15

Judge Jeffreys was Chief Justice of England, Recorder of London and Lord Chancellor.

259) JACOB, Giles.(1686-1744)
The Complete Court-Keeper, or, Land-Steward's Assistant. Containing Courts Leet and Courts Baron, etc. Henry Lintot. 1741. 4th edition, enlarged. viii,522,(xxii)pp. Index. Some marginal worming, sl. affec. text on pp 271-336, sm. marginal hole in A_2. Bookplate. Contemp. calf, rubbed, spine end sl. torn. S. &M.i.400/26. £50

A compendium covering the manner of holding Courts Leet, Courts Baron to Precedents of Contracts and Leases.

260) .....Another copy. J.Worrall.1764. 6th edition with additions from Lord Raymond, Comyns etc. Contemp. calf, rubbed,hinges worn..£40

JACOB, Giles. (1686-1744) cont.
261) The Grand Precedent: or, the Conveyancer's Guide and Assistant. Eliz. Nutt. 1716. 1st edition. Table, publisher's booklist. Marginal worming in last 23 leaves, not affec. text. Modern buckram. S. &M.i.483/37 (only this one edition). £55

262) .....A New Law-Dictionary: containing the interpretation and definition of words and terms used in the law. 1736. 3rd edition.Folio. Sm. holes in 5Q2 & 7M1 affec. few letters. Sl. stained & sl. wormed at inner margin. Modern cloth. S.&M.i.9/33. £90

263) .....Another copy. Folio. H.Lintot etc. 1756. 7th edition. Some sl. worming at lower margin in first few pages not affec. text. n.p. Contemp. calf, hinges worn & some sl. wear of spine ends. Very good. £90

264) JARDINE, David.
Criminal Trials...illustrations of the important periods of English history during the reigns of Queen Elizabeth and James I.(1554-1605) (with) narrative of the Gunpowder Plot, with historical prefaces & notes. 2 vols. 16mo. A. Nattali. 1847. Index, fp. Modern cloth. S.&M.i.370/14 (1832-5 edition) £45

JENKINS, Sir Leoline...see William WYNNE.

265) JENKS, Edward.
The Book of English Law.1932.3rd edition. xx,460pp. Bibliography, index. Orig. cloth, sl. faded. £6

266) ....Another copy. 1912. 1st edition. Orig. cloth, sl.fdd. £6

267) JEREMY, Henry.
An Analytical Digest of the Reports of Cases decided in the Courts of Common Law and Equity, Appeal and Nisi Prius in 1819. 1820. .....1822. 1823. 2 vols. Orig. printed boards, spines darkened & sl. frayed, title sl. spotted. Uncut and unopened. See S.&M.ii.187. £30

S. & M. lists only a later edition covering 1817-23 & 1838-49 in 4 volumes published in 1849-50.

268) JONES, Edward.
Index to Records called the Originalia and Memoranda on the Lord Treasurer's Remembrancer's Side of the Exchequer..extracted from records & mss. of Mr. Tayleure, Mr. Madox & Mr. Chapman..containing all the Grants of Abbey Lands, and other Property, granted by the Crown (1509-1714), also Inrollments of Charters...to several religious Houses, to Cities, Boroughs etc. (with) Pleadings and proceedings relative to the Tenures and Estates of the Nobility and Gentry ...Folio. 2 vols. in 1. Printed for the Editor 1793-5. Index for each volume, subscribers lists. Contemp. half, rubbed, upper cover loose, spine worn.S.&M.i.86/19. GROSS 125. £95

269) The JUSTICE of the PEACE'S GUIDE,
being a Collection of Precedents, relating to the Office of a Justice of Peace...(with) a copy of the Commission of the Peace...12mo. Dublin. Peter Hoey. 1796. 1st edition. v.201,(xiv)pp. Name of owner in gilt letters across front cover & signature with date 1797 on title. Some marginal worming. Contemp. calf, sl. rubbed.S.&M.iv.47. £30

270) JUSTINIAN I, Emperor.
Corpus Juris Civilis, Pandectis..Institutiones, Codice et Novellis.. 1663. Apud Joannem Blaeu. L. & D. Elzevirios. 1st edition. Folio. 2 vols. Latin text. Engr. half title, woodcut device on title & initials in text. Index tabs, wax stamps on endpapers. Contemp. calf, worn. WILLEMS 1299. £75

A fine edition of the commentaries on Justinian it includes other works by him.

271) .....Institutiones sive Elementa...Accesserunt ex Digestis Tituli de Verborum Significatione & Regulis Juris. Amsterdam. ex officina Weststeniana. 1710. 12mo. Edited by Arnoldus Corvinus. Printed in red & black. Index. Contemp. vellum, sl. soiled. Bookplate. £40

272) (KAMES, Lord H. Home.) (1696-1782)
Essays upon Several Subjects:
I. Introduction of the Feudal Law into Scotland.
II.Constitution of Parliament.
III.Honour. Dignity.
IV. Succession or Descent.
With an appendix upon hereditary and indefeasible Right. Edinburgh. A. Kincaid. 1747. 1st edition. S.&M.v.56. Contemp. boards, later reback, new endpapers. Fine copy. £150

Conducted upon a very judicious system of investigating the natural principles of some of the most important objects of judicial science, and tracing the application of them in the laws of Rome of Scotland.

273) KEBLE, Joseph.
An Assistance to Justices of the Peace. W.Rawlins etc. 1683. 1st ed. Folio. BLACK letter. Index. Several irregularities in pagination caused by a change of printers. Few sm.marginal worm-holes. Contemp. calf, tail of spine sl. torn, some leaves loose.WING K 113.S&M.i.229 £60

Keble's work was designed as a supplement to the standard justices' manuals, whose provision it abridges alphabetically. In a preliminary section, everything in the statute-book which concerns justices is set out at length.

274) .....Reports in..King's Bench..from the XII. to the XXX. Year of..King Charles II. W.Rawlins etc. 1685. 1st edition. 3 vols.Folio. BLACK letter. Indices. Lacks end-papers. Modern cloth. WING K 116 S.&M.i.302. £120

275) KEETON, G.W.
Cases on Equity and Trusts.1959. 1st ed. Orig. cloth. £10

276) .....An Introduction to Equity.1965.6th ed. Orig. cloth. £10

277) .....The Law of Trusts.1964. 8th ed. Orig. cloth. £8

278) .....Social Change in the Law of Trusts.1958.1st.Cl.sl.mkd. £5

279) KEIR, D.L. & F.H. LAWSON.
Cases in Constitutional Law. Oxford. 1954. 4th ed. Tables.Index. £8

C.KENNY see under J.W. TURNER.

280) KINGSTON, Charles.
Remarkable Rogues. The careers of some notable criminals of Europe and America. Illus. 1921. 2nd ed. Orig. cloth, faded, sl. stnd. £8

281) LAMBARD, William. (1536-1601)
Eirenarchia, or the Office of the Justices of Peace in foure Bookes. Company of Stationers. 1607. revised, corrected and enlarged. Mostly BLACK letter. 2 parts in 1 vol. (ii),621,(74),80pp. Typographical title border, woodcut initials. Indices. Contemp. calf with blind initials "F.G." on sides, head and foot of spine neatly repaired. STC 15171. S.&M.i.229/43. £280

Lambard's work was the first practical & comprehensive English Manual for magistrates, and set new standards of clarity and simplicity in law-writing. The author was ahead of his time in combining the study of law (he was a benefactor of Lincoln's Inn) with that of lay history; his Perambulation of Kent (1576) is the earliest published work on local history.

282) LANE, Richard.(1584-1650)
Reports in the Court of Exchequer..third to ninth year of King James. With two alphabetical tables. Folio. W.Lee etc. 1657. 1st edition. Lacks last page of index (w-z). BLACK letter. Contemp. calf, rubbed, rebacked. WING L 340. S.&M. i.323/10. £55

Lane shows a special interest in questions of Royal Prerogative. A notable case is Rex v. Earl of Nottingham & others (1610), an early example of a man's conveying away an estate on trust in order to save it for his family should his real property become amenable to forfeiture.

283) LAUTERPACHT, H.
An International Bill of the Rights of Man. Columbia U.P.N.Y.1945. 1st edition. Index. Orig. cloth. £8

284) LAW of TESTAMENTS and LAST WILLS
containing all that is necessary to be known and practised by....

LAW of TESTAMENTS and last WILLS cont.
284) .....Testators, their Executors and Administrators...Compiled by a gentleman of the law for his own private instruction. H.Lintot.1744 1st edition. vii,(xxiv),488,(xii),(ii)pp. Table of cases, index & publisher's booklist. Bookplate. Sm. sl spotting of endpapers & prelims. Contemp. calf, rubbed & frayed, hinges weak. S. &M. i.492/19. £25

285) (LAWRENCE, William)
Marriage by the Morall Law of God Vindicated against all Ceremonial Laws of Popes and Bishops destructive to Filiation Aliment and Succession and the Government of Familyes and Kingdomes. (London) 1680. 1st edition. 4to. (i),(iii),(iv),422pp. Curious, but finely engraved title with six vignettes "the Morall Law, "the Ceremonial Law", "Religion", "Liberty", "Justice" and "Property". WING L 690.
.....The Right of Primogeniture in succession to the Kingdoms of England, Scotland, and Ireland..for the author. 1681. 1st edition. 4to. (i),(xiv),(vi),199,37pp. Index. WING L 691. S.&M.i.476/19.
.....The Two Great Questions...the Peace & Safety of His Maiestie's Person, and of all his Protestant Subjects in His Three Kingdoms... for the author. 1681. 1st edition. 4to. (i),14pp. WING L 693. Three works in 1 vol. Contemp. mottled calf, repaired & rebacked. £200

The first item is said to have been written upon a discontent arising from Lawrence's wife, whom he esteemed dishonest to him. The second was written in support of the Duke of Monmouth's claim to the succession.

286) The LAWS and LIBERTIES of MASSACHUSETS.
Reprinted from the copy of the 1648 edition in the Henry E. Huntington Library. With an introduction by Max Farrand. Cambridge (USA), Harvard U. P.1929. No.140 of a limited edition of 300. Folio. ix, (iv),59pp. Facs. plate of original title. Cloth, frayed d.w.Fine. £35

This was the first attempt at a comprehensive reduction into one form of a body of legislation of an English-speaking country and stands as the basis of all subsequent Massachusetts legislation.

287) LEACH, Thomas.
Cases in Crown Law, determined by the Twelve Judges, by King's Bench and by Commissioners of Oyer and Terminer and General Gaol Delivery. 1730-1800. 2 vols. 1800. 3rd edition. Contemp. calf, very rubbed, spine ends frayed. S.&M.i.303/78. £60

288) LEEWIUS, S.
De Origine & Progressu Juris Civilis Romani Authores & Fragmenta Veterum Jurisconsultorum, cum Notis Arn. Leyden. A. Doude. 1672. (xiv),850,(x)pp. Sl. dampstained at end. Contemp. vellum, sl. soiled Bookplate. £40

289) LEWIS, W.J.
Sheriff Court Practice. With appendices containing the Sheriff Courts (Scotland) Act 1907, the Sheriff Courts (Scotland) Act 1913 and Forms of Writs. Edinburgh 1939. 8th edition. Orig. cloth. Indices. £10

290) LIPSIUS, Justus (1547-1606)
Politicorum sive Civilis Doctrinae libri sex. Qui ad Principatum Madime spectant. Amsterdam. J. Blaeu. 1632. 16mo. 3 parts in 1 vol. 308/85/53pp. Separate titles. Front endpapers partially torn off. Contemp. vellum, sl. soiled. Bookplate. £30

291) The LIVES of all the LORDS CHANCELLORS,
Lord Keepers, and Lords Commissioners, of the Great Seal of England; from William, the Conqueror, to the present time: but more at large of those two great opposites, Edward Earl of Clarendon, and Bulstrode Lord Whitlock. (with) an appendix of many rare and valuable speeches, letters....2 vols. R. Burrough & J. Baker. 1708. 1st edition. (xxiv), 202,(vi)/(ii),520pp. Half-title in vol.2. Modern morocco-backed boards, gilt dec'd spines. S. & M.i.591/8. (2nd edition of 1712 only) £140

Fine set of this rare source book.

See also *85. CAMPBELL'S Lives of the Lord Chancellors.

292) LLOYD, Dennis.
Introduction to Jurisprudence with selected texts. 1960. 2nd imp. xxiii,482pp. Index. Orig. cloth. £10

293) LOVELASS, Peter.
The Law's Disposal of a Person's Estate who dies without Will or Testament. The disposal of estates by will. Printed for the author, P. Uriel. 1786. 2nd edition, revised, enlarged. xiii,247pp. appendix, preface. Contemp. half calf, rubbed, label replaced with hand-written paper one. S. & M.i.492/21. £45

294) .....Another copy. 1787. 4th edition. With an alphabetical index. Bookplate. Contemp. calf, spine sl. darkened. S.&M.i.492/21 (not this edition). £45

295) .....Another copy. 1792. 7th edition.Contemp. half calf,rubbed. £45

296) .....Another copy. 1798. 9th edition.Contemp. calf. sl. rubbed. £45

297) LYNCH, William.
A view of the Legal Institutions, honorary hereditary offices, and feudal Baronies, established in Ireland during the reigh of Henry II ..From Court Rolls, Inquisitions and other original records. 1830. 1st edition. 4to. xxiv,360,(iv),16pp. Booklist.Orig. boards, worn, stained & rubbed. S.&M.iv.54. £45

MACKENZIE, Sir George of Rosehaugh. ..cont. The Institutions..Scotland
305)....Another copy. 12mo. Edinburgh. James Watson. 1706. 4th edition (viii)253,(iv)pp. Index, adverts, dedication leaves. Bookplate. Lacks blanks. Contemp. calf, rubbed, spine sl. frayed. S.&M.v.73. £60

This new edition has Lord Whitlaw's short marginal notes & revised by William Forbes; also includes corrections and additions in the Scots law since the author's time.

306) .....The Laws and Customes of Scotland, in matters criminal.. & how the civil law and laws and customs of other nations do agree with, and supply ours. Edinburgh. Thomas Brown. 1678. Sm.4to. (xiv), 582pp. Title in red and black lettering. Margins repaired in first four leaves. Fine modern calf with gilt dec'd spine & label. WING M 167. S. &M.v.74. £160

In these Institutes of Scots' Crown Law, Mackenzie offers his famous justification of torture. It also includes 28 pages on witchcraft. There were three editions of this date by different printers.

307) .....Pleadings, in some remarkable Cases, before the Supreme Courts of Scotland, since the year 1661..with Decisions. Sm.4to. Edinburgh. George Swintoun etc. 1673. 1st edition. (viii),232,(iv)pp Lacks blanks. Bookplate Soc. of Procurators, Perth.Modern cloth. WING M 191. S. &M.v.93. ALDIS 1949. £95

308) .....Another copy. 1704. 16mo. Margins of F_1 & G_1 sl. defective affec. one line. Fore-margins short, one sl. cropped. Old calf, rebacked, sides rubbed. £60

309) MACMILLAN, Rt. Hon. Lord.
A Man of Law's Tale. 1952. 1st edition. illus. Orig. cloth. £4

310) (MAITLAND,J.)(edited)
The Court of Session Garland. Edinburgh, printed for private circulation. 1871. (with) the supplements and appendix. viii,331pp. Orig. cloth, sl. faded, corners sl. rubbed. S.& M.v.25. Very good. £35

311) MAJORIBANKS, Edward.
The life of Sir Edward Marshall Hall. 1933. 12th ed.Orig. cl. £5

312) MANUDUCTIO ad UNIVERSUM JUS CIVILE et CANONICUM.
Frankfurt/Leipzig. 1677. 12mo. Title in red & black. Sl. stained. Corner torn from front endpaper. Contemp. vellum, sl. soiled. £30

Contains:B.Dn. B.Carpzivius' Methodium de studi Juris: D. Keyser's Historiam Juris Civilis: Nucleum Institutionum: G. Brucksulbergius' Memoriale Juridicum: J.Serpilius' Juris Cononici & Civilis etc.

298) (MACDOUALL, A. Lord Bankton.)
An Institute of the Laws of Scotland in Civil Rights..and the laws of England. In four books. 3 vols. Folio. Edinburgh. R. Fleming. 1751-3. Appendix, table, indices. Bookplates: Society of Procurators, Perth. Contemp. calf, rubbed, spine ends sl. frayed & weak. Endpapers spotted, blank loose in vol.1. S. &M. v.72. £150

299) McGREGOR, O.R.
Divorce in England. 1957. 1st edition. Tables, appendix, index. Orig. cloth, d.w. £6

300) McKENNAN, Judge.
Decree dismissing complainants' bills, in the cases of Francis & Loutrel v.Mellor & Rittenhouse...trading as Godfrey & Co. in the U.S. Circuit Court, Eastern District of Pennsylvania. 8 page pamphlet. Disbound as issued. £10

301) MACKENZIE, of Rosehaugh, Sir George. (1636-1691)
Idea eloquentiae forensis hodiernae: una cum actione forensi ex unaquaque juris parte. Edinburgh. A. Anderson. 1681. 1st edition. Latin text. (xii),182pp. Final blank. Contemp. sheep, rubbed. WING M 164. S. &M.v.74. £60

Mackenzie laments that the eloquence of Scots advocates is never preserved as an example to the student and he gives Latin versions of six of his own speeches, with general remarks on the duties & qualifications for speaking at Bar. An English edition of this work under the title "Idea of the modern eloquence of the Bar", together with a pleading out of every part of law, was published in 1711.

302) ...Another copy. Same edition. Contemp. calf, sl. rubbed, joints sl. cracked, last few pages sl. browned. £60

303) .....The Institutions of the Law of Scotland. 12mo. Edinburgh. John Reid..1688. 2nd edition, corrected & enlarged by the author. (xii),407pp. Lacks 1st blank, tear in last leaf, contemp. annots. Modern calf. WING M159. S. &M.v.73. ALDIS 2768. £70

304) .....Another copy. 12mo. Edinburgh. Thomas Broun 1699. "third" edition corrected, with an alphabetical table of hard words. (x), 263,(ix)pp. Interleaved with blanks and several at each end, some contemp. annotations. Sm.square cut out of last two leaves, affec. 1 letter. (with)
BAYNE, Alexander. Notes, for the use of the students of the Municipal Law in the University of Edinburgh. Being a supplement to Sir G. Mackenzie's Institutions. Edinburgh W. Cheyne. 1754. 2nd edition. iv,156pp. Lacks three leaves of the index. Contemp. calf, rebacked. WING M 161. S. &M. v.74. £120

This third edition is not in Aldis's list. The folio, 2nd edition is number 3866 in that list of the same year but a different printer. The interleaved pages are all blank there are copious contemporary MS. notes.

313) MANWOOD, John.
A Treatise of the Lawes of the Forrest: wherein is declared not onely those Lawes, as they are now in force, but also the originall and beginning of Forests...a Treatise of the Pourallee...Collected of the Common Lawes and Statutes of this land...also out of sundrie learned ancient authors and out of the Assises of Pickering and Lancaster... the Statutes of the Forest, a Treatise of the seuverall offices of Verderors, Regardors and Foresters...Courts of Attachments, Swanimore & Justice seat of the Forest....Societie of Stationers. 1615. 4to. 2nd edition. (xv),258(259) leaves. Sm.hole in blank before title. 17th century inscription on fly-leaf. Contemp. calf, rebacked. STC 17297. S.&M.i.465.38. KRESS 345. £300

First published in 1598 under the title "A Treatise and Discourse of the Lawes of the Forrest". This edition is much enlarged. Manwood was an eminent law writer in the reigns of Elizabeth and James I. He was also a barrister of Lincoln's Inn, game-keeper of Waltham Forest and Justice of the New Forest.
This compendium continued in use as late as 1741.

314) .....Another copy. 1665. 3rd edition. (xxx),552pp. Title-page repaired. Modern calf-backed boards. WING M 554. S.&M.i.465/38. KRESS 1161. GOLDSMITH 1755. £200

315) ..... Another copy. The whole digested under proper titles in an alphabetical order. E. Nutt. 1717. The fourth edition, corrected and enlarged by William NELSON. (v),435,34pp. Bookplate and long hand-written inscription on end-papers from a deputy ranger of Richmond Park. Modern calf-backed boards. £95

The contents and arrangement of Nelson's edition differ very much from the original work. This is the first edition edited by Nelson but he went on revising this until 1741.

316) .....Another copy. 4th edition. 1717. Later calf, spine with raised bands, label. Spine rubbed. Some sl. worm-holes at lower margin, inscription on back end-papers. £90

317) .....An Abridgment of Manwood's Forrest Laws. And of all the Acts Parliament made since; which relate to Hunting, Hawking, Fishing, or Fowling. Nath. Rolls. 1696. 1st and only edition. (i),101, (i)pp. Modern calf-backed boards. WING M 553. S.&M.i.465/39. £80

318) MARSHALL, John. (1755-1835)
The Life by Albert J. Beveridge. 4 vols. Boston/NY. Riverside Press, Cambridge. 1916. Index. Orig. cloth. Very good. £35

319) MARTENS,G(eorg),F(riedrich) von.
The Law of Nations: being the science of national law, covenants, power etc. founded upon the treaties and customs of modern nations in Europe. Transl. from the French by Wm.Cobbett. (with) principal treaties, declarations and other public papers from 1731-38, by the author, continued by the translator down to Nov.1815. William Cobbett,

MARTENS, G.F. The Law of Nations..cont.
319)....1829. 4th edition. xxxii,468pp. Half calf, some sl. spotting. Bookplate. S.&M.i.597/68. £60

The first few editions were printed in Philadelphia as Cobbett was commissioned by the U.S. government for the translation. For the London edition (the first was published in 1803) Cobbett added a new preface & brought the list of treaties down to date.

320) .....Another copy. Same edition. Orig. cloth, faded, spine ends sl. frayed. Bookplate. £60

321) MARWICK, Sir James D.
Sketch of the history of the High Constables of Edinburgh with notes on the early.......Police arrangements of the City. 4to. Privately printed. Edinburgh. 1865. 1st edition. LARGE PAPER COPY. (x),300,60, lxxxivpp. Wood-engravings in text, appendix, index. Contemp. half roan. Rubbed. S. &M.v.79. (octavo copy only) £40

322) MATHEW, Theobald.
For Lawyers and Others. 1938. rep. Illus. Orig. cloth. £6

323) MEGARRY, R.E.
A Manual of the Law of Real Property. 1962. 3rd ed.Tables of cases and statutes, glossary, index. Orig. cloth. £5

324) .....Miscellany-at-Law. A diversion for lawyers and others. 1956. 2nd edition, revised. Orig. cloth. £6

325) MOLLOY, Charles.
De Jure Maritimo et Navali: or, a Treatise of Affairs Maritime and of Commerce. 2 vols. T. Waller. 1769. 9th edition with many additions. xxvi,(ii),404/(iv),344,(52)pp. Index, publisher's booklist. Contemp. calf, sl. rubbed, front hinges repaired. Good set. S. &M.i.511/64. KRESS 6659. GOLDSMITH 10542. HIGGS 4616. £180

The first edition appeared in 1676 but this edition has many additions. It continued to be the best English work on maritime law down to the publication of the work of Lord Tenterden in 1802.

326) MONTESQUIEU, Charles de Secondat,Baron de:(1689-1755)
The Spirit of the Laws. Transl. from the French by Thomas Nugent. (with) corrections and additions. 2 vols. J. Nourse & P. Vaillant. 1750. 1st English edition. Index for both volumes at end of vol.1. Printer's device on each title. Contemp. sprinkled calf, gilt.,sl. rubbed. Very good set. S. &M.i.104/68 (Edinburgh editions only) KRESS 5057. £120

The work is based on Montesquieu's study of the English Constitution and was one of the most influential treatise of the 18th century.

MONTESQUIEU, Charles...The Spirit of the Laws...cont.
327) .....Another copy. 1752. 2nd edition. 2 vols. Some worming,mostly marginal, but affec. one or two letters of text. Contemp. calf, sl. rubbed, spines dry & joints weak. £80

328) .....Another copy. 1802. 2 vols. 1st American edition, from the 5th London edition. xvi,17-368/viii,9-392pp. Translated by Isaiah Thomas, printed in Worcester. U.S.A. Some light uniform browning. Contemp. calf, gilt, recased, inner hinges strengthened, new morocco labels. Fine set. £90

329) MONTGOMERY, Leslie Sydney.
Edward Parkyns Levinge. The Justice of the Peace for Ireland,a treatise on summary jurisdiction and preliminary proceedings as to indictable offences...appendix. Dublin. 1872. 3rd edition, revised and enlarged. xxxiv,1048pp. Index. Bookplate. Contemp. calf, rubbed, sm. split on hinge & spine sl. frayed. S.&M.iv.60; also under iv.52. £25

330) MOORE, John Bassett.
A Digest of International Law as embodied in Diplomatic Discussions, Treaties..Decisions...Writings of Jurists etc. Washington.D.C.1906. 1st edition. 8 vols., including the index volume. Orig. cloth, sl. faded & frayed. Vol.4 not uniform, vol.6 stained. £60

This work was the result of an Act of Congress of February 1897 ordering the production of a Digest to replace that of Wharton (1827).

331) MORRIS, Terence & Louis BLOM-COOPER.
A Calendar of Murder. Criminal homicide in England since 1957. 1964. 1st edition. xvi,413pp. Statistical tables, bibliography, indices. Orig. cl. d.w. £10

332) NELSON, William. (1684-1726)
The Laws concerning Game. Of Hunting, Hawking, Fishing and Fowling etc. with Precedents and (with) the Forest Laws, English forms of convictions, declarations, indictments, justifications, licences, Mittimus's, pleas, warrants etc. in alphabetical order. E. Richardson...1762. 6th edition with all the Acts of Parliament..cases.... xvii,255,(xvii),viiipp. Index, appendix. Contemp. calf, rubbed, corners sl. frayed. S. &M.i.465/41. £45

333) .....The Office and Authority of a Justice of Peace...Duty of Constables, Commissioners of Sewers, Coroners, Overseers of the Poor etc. 1711. 4th edition. (viii),619,(v)pp. Contemp. calf, lacks label. Sl. worn. S. &M. i.230. £40

334) NICOLAS, Sir Harris.
A Treatise on the Law of Adulterine Bastardy, with a report of the Banbury Case, and of all other cases bearing upon the subject. Wm. Pickering 1836. 1st edition. xvi,588,9pp. Index, publisher's cat..

NICOLAS, Sir Harris. A Treatise..law of Adulterine Bastardy..cont.
Modern boards. Fine. S.&M.i.500/29. £60

The first attempt which has been made to collect all the authorities and decisions on the law of Legitimacy in this country and to deduce from them the history and present state of the law.
Sixty cases are reported, ranging from the 13th to the 19th century. Four of the cases are not reported elsewhere.

335)(NICOLSON, William)(Lord Bishop of Carlile.)
Leges Marchiarum, or Border-Laws..(with) original articles and treaties...of England and Scotland for the better preservation of peace and commerce....(with) charters and records. Tim Goodwin. 1705. 1st edition. (8),lvi,388,(iv)pp. Half-title, dedication leaves, publisher's booklist. Contemp. panelled calf, rebacked, sl. rubbed. Fine large copy with wide margins. S.&M.v.83/4. £120

The Bishop published these mediaeval documents to prove that the kingdoms had always treated with each other as equals and without any legal assumption of superiority by England and further the want of a stable political connection.

336) .....Another copy. Same edition. Lacks the half-title. Contemp. calf, rebacked, sl. rubbed. £110

337) .....Another copy. 1747. (iv)xxxiv,262pp. 16mo.Modern calf-backed boards. £65

338) NOY, William. (1577-1634)
The Compleat Lawyer, or, a treatise concerning Tenures and Estates in lands of inheritance for life and other hereditaments and chattels, real and personal. John Benson. 1661. 3rd edition. 16mo. (ii),124, (122)pp. Signature on title. S.&M.i.458/123. WING N 1444. £200

Noy was the Attorney General to King Charles I and this catechism of procedure neatly outlines the different aspects of the law which is then discussed in an essay.

339) NUN, Richard & John Edward WALSH.
The Powers and Duties of Justices of the Peace in Ireland, and of Constables as connected therewith...with a collection of statutes and forms. 2 vols. Dublin. 1844.
...J.E.WALSH. The Statutes 12,13, Vict., chap. 69,70 & 16, relating to the Duties of Justices of the Peace...Dublin 1850. 1 vol. Together 3 vols. Calf, leather labels. Sl. rubbed. S.&M.iv.63. £80

The first two volumes are the second edition. The first edition was published in 1 volume in 1841.

340) OBSERVATIONS on the MARRIAGE LAWS,
particularly in reference to the case of Desertion, or a fraudulent and violated Contract in which the right of the injured party is supported by religious, moral & historical evidence, demonstrating the necessity of Legislative Interference. J. Hatchard etc. 1815.1st edition. 408pp. (with)
H.V.TEBBS Essay on the Scripture Doctrines of Adultery and Divorce and on the criminal character and punishment of Adultery by the Ancient Laws of England and other countries. xvi,254pp.S.&M.i.502/40. 2 works in 1 vol. Embossed, gilt dec'd spine, hinges weak & loose. Fine copy. £95

341) PARK, James Allan (later Sir)(1763-1838)
A system of the Law of Marine Insurances, with three chapters, on Bottomry, on Insurances on Lives, on Insurances against Fire.1802. 5th edition. xx,xlviii,512 (i.e.576)pp. Some ink annots. Modern cloth. S. & M.i.512. KRESS B.4580. £30

This work, first published in 1787, was the foundation of Park's fame and remained as the standard text until the 1840s.

342) PARKER, Herbert.
Courts and Lawyers of New England. 4to. 4 vols. American Hist. Soc., N.Y.1931. 1st edition. Index, numerous portraits. Orig. buckram,labels. Some sl. marks on covers. Fine set. £70

A review of the sources from which the New England system of law, as established by State and Federal Constitutions and Statutes and the Adjudication of the Courts. This documented compilation contains a significant contribution to the legal and historical literature of New England.

343) PARKER, Sir Thomas.
Reports of Cases concerning the Revenue, Court of Exchequer.1743-67, with appendix 1678-1717. Folio. 1776. 1st edition.v,(ii),283,xi)pp. Bookplate of Thos. Grey. S.&M.i.323/11. Calf,sl. rubbed, upper cover loose. £30

344) PARKINSON, C. Northcote.
The Law and the Profits. 1960.1st edition. Illustrations by Osbert Lancaster. Orig. cloth. £6

345) .....Parkinson's Law or the Pursuit of Progress. 1958. 3rd imp. Illus. by Osbert Lancaster. Orig. cloth. £5

PARLIAMENTARY REPORTS.
346) BANKRUPTCIES. Returns to an order of the House of Commons. 18 May 1838 previous to the Act of Parliament 1831, appointing official Assignees to take possession of the Estates. H.o.C.26 April 1839. Folio. 153pp. Orig. blue wraps. £20

PARLIAMENTARY REPORTS...cont.
347) BANKRUPT LAW. Minutes of evidence taken before the Select Committee appointed to consider the Bankrupt Laws and of the operation thereof. Reported 16 March 1818. Folio. H.o.C. 1818. 106pp. Orig. blue wraps, sl. frayed. S.&M. ii.257. £20

348) .....Declarations in lieu of Oaths. Report from the Select Committee of the House of Lords appointed to inquire into the expediency of substituting Declarations in lieu of Oaths in certain cases..... together with the minutes of evidence taken before the Committee and an appendix and index..H.o.C. 19 June 1837. Folio. 126pp. Index. £20

349) .....Report of the minutes of evidence taken in a Committee of the whole House on the Bill for the preventing of Bribery and Corruption in the election of Members to serve in Parliament for the Borough of Penryn, in the County of Cornwall. H.o.C. May 1819. Folio. (ii) 61pp. Orig. blue wraps. £12

350) .....The Second Report: Committee on Scotch Entails. 1828. From the select Committee. H.o.C. 9 June 1828. Folio. 60pp. Orig. blue wraps. S. &M.v.87. £10

351) PASCHALIUS, Carolus.
Legatus...Regii Consiliarii, et in Normaniae Senatu Aduocati generalis distinctum in capita septem et septuaginta. Rouen, apud Raphaelem Parvivallium. 1598. With the collation as called for by ADAMS 368. Early 18th century calf, raised bands on spine, rubbed & spine repaired. Bookplate. £180

352) PAUL, John.
Every Landlord or Tenant his own Lawyer, or, the whole Law respecting Landlords, Tenants, and Lodgers...revised and corrected by an eminent Counsellor at Law. Dublin. W.Gilbert. 1782. (iv),223,(i)pp. Contemp. notes and figures on endpapers. Contemp. sheep, neatly repaired. Not in S.&M. but see 461/12 for other editions. £25

353) PEAKE, Thomas.
Cases determined at Nisi Prius in the Court of King's Bench, from Easter term 30 Geo.3 to Michaelmas 35 Geo.3. A. Strahan. 1795. 1st edition. xii,244,(xxiv)pp. Half title, index. Contemp. calf, sl. rubbed. S.&M. i.335/8. £35

Nisi Prius reports at this period are few in number, their accent is on contractual & tortious offences, whereas the other series generally adhered to the ancient preference for Real Property Cases.

354) PEERE WILLIAMS, William (collected by)
Reports of Cases argued and determined in the High Court of Chancery and on some Special Cases...Court of King's Bench..Folio. Vols 2 & 3 only. 1740-9. 1st edition. Modern cloth. S.&M.i.347/33. £30

PHILIPPS, Fabian...Tenenda non tollenda..cont.
359) ...Philip(p)s was the author of several books relating to ancient customs and privileges in England.
When the Civil War broke out he zealously supported the Royal cause, and two days before the execution of Charles printed and published a protestation against the intended murder.

360) PHILLIPS, O Hood.
A First book of English Law.1960. 4th edition. Orig. cloth. £6

361) PICKERING'S STATUTES at LARGE,
from Magna Charta to the end of 1761. Edited by Danby Pickering. Cambridge. Joseph Bentham. 1762-69. 1st thus. 24 vols. in 25. Vol.24 being in 2 parts, the Index, inverleaved. MS. annotations in vol.1 Sl. marginal worming in vol.1. CONTINUED
.....To the end of 1761. Vols. 25-41. (of 46)(46 George III) 1762-97 under Pickering's editorship. Vol.38 being an index from 1-33 Geo.III. Few contemp. annots. MS. note on interpretation pasted in vol. 26. Folding tables. Contemp. calf, rubbed, some heads of spines sl. frayed, some labels. defective. A very good, sound and clean set. S.&M. Guide to Law Reports and Statutes, Toronto,1929. p.69. £400

Pickering's edition, being in a small format, was and remains one of the most convenient sources for historically valuable material which is not inserted in the modern "Halsbury". This set includes the original series extending to 1761 (24 vols in 25) and 17 of the 22 vols. afterwards added to extend the scope to 1806.

362) PLAYFAIR, Giles & Derrick SINGTON.
The Offenders, Society and the Atrocious Crime. 1957. 1st edition. x,278pp. Appendix, bibliography. Orig. cloth. d.w. £6

Details of six criminal trials and also discusses capital punishment.

363) PLOWDEN, Francis.
Church and State, being an enquiry into the origin, nature and extent of Ecclesiastical and Civil Authority with reference to the British Constitution. 4to. 1795. 1st edition. xvi,620pp. Index. Modern b'ram. S.&M. i.174/100. £60

364) .....A short history of the British Empire during the last twenty months, i.e. May 1792-end of 1793. Dublin. P. Byrne. 1794. 1st ed. 290pp. Contemp. sprinkled calf. One corner & spine end sl. frayed. Very good copy. £30

Plowden is best known for his work "Native Rights of British Subjects" and "Jura Anglorum".

365) PLUCKNETT, Theodore F.T.
A Concise History of the Common Law. 1956. 5th edition. xxvi,746,56pp. Index. Orig. cloth. £10

PEERE WILLIAMS, W. (collected by) cont.
355) .....Reports of Cases...High Court of Chancery...Court of King's Bench. 1695-1735. 3 vols. Folio. 1768. 3rd edition, corrected with many additional references...and notes; two tables to each volume by his son, W. Peere Williams. Contemp. calf, rubbed, some sl. wear on hinges. S.&M.i.347/33. £60

356) .....Another set. 3 vols. 1793. 5th edition with additional references to the proceedings in the Court and to later cases by Samuel Compton Cox. Contemp. calf, sl. rubbed. £45

357) PELLEGRINO, Marcantonio. (PEREGRINUS, Marcus Antony)
Tractatus...de fideicommissis praesertim universalibus...compluribus additamentis illustratus. Lyons. A. de Harsy. 1606. 4to. (viii),1510, (xc)pp. Red & black title with device, index. Some browning throughout, sm. pieces torn from lower corners of three leaves, text not affec., occasional sm. marginal wormholes. 18th century calf, gilt. Rebacked and recornered. FINE. £120

The author of this treatise on Trusts, Wills and Descents held official posts in Venice & Padua.
B.M. lists two editions only Frankfurt 1599 and Venice 1603.

PENRYN BRIBERY BILL see Parliamentary Reports.

358) PETERSDORFF, Charles.
Practical and elementary abridgment of the Common Law as altered & established by the recent Statutes, Rules of Court and modern decisions....a full abstract of all the Cases..in the Courts of Common Law and on Appeal with the rules of Court from 1824-1840 and with the Statutes. With connecting and illustrative references to the earlier authorities and explanatory notes. 5 vols. H. Bond. 1844. Uncut and unopened. Orig. boards, dust-stained.S.&M.ii.277. £80

The supplement to the 15 volume work published in 1825 which took the work to 1824. The interval between 1824-40 was most prolific in important variations in the system of jurisprudence and in the practical administration of the law than any previous period of judicial and legislative history. Although there were many elementary works & digests no publication comprises, as the above, under a connected yet alphabetical arrangement, the then modern law as established by changes that occurred then. The above is a comprehensive consolidation of the whole of the Modern Cases, Statutes & Rules of Court.

359) PHILIPPS, Fabian. (1601-1690)
Tenenda non tollenda, or the necessity of preserving tenures in capite and by Knights-Service, which according to their first Institution were, and are yet, a great part of the Salus Populi and the safety and defence of the King, as well as of his people....Sm.4to. Thomas Leach for the author. 1660. 1st edition. (xiii),276pp. Contemp. calf, rubbed, top of spine & inner hinges worn. Bookplate. WING P 2019. S.&M.i.459/126. KRESS 1037. Fine copy. SCARCE. £150

366) POLLAND, A.J.
Digest of Law of Contract and Tort. 1959. 1st ed. Orig.cloth. £5

367) POLLARD, Robert S.W.
An A B C of War-Time Law. Legal edition. 1940. orig. cloth. £2

368) POTHIER, Robert Joseph. (1699-1772)
Oeuvres de R-J Pothier, contenant les traités du Droit Français. Edited & introduced by M. Dupin. Brussles. J.P.Jonker/Amsterdam. Les Frères Diederichs. 1829-34. 8 vols. Index, lith. fp. ports. French text Some sl. spotting. Contemp. half sheep, marbled sides, rubbed, heads of two spines sl. defective and some joints worn. This edition not in Brunet. £110

Besides his rationalisation of the Pandects (not included here), Pothier wrote a number of French treatises which did great work in releasing his country's laws from the shallow rhetoric of the advocates & the barbarity of the ancient coûtumes. His work on the law of obligations is among the most valuable of these and has had the rare honour of being quoted in an English court of law.

369) POWELL, Tho(mas).
The Attourney's Academy, or, the Manner and Forme of Proceeding... in any Court of Record. Benjamin Fisher. 1630. 3rd edition. Sm.4to. Woodcut ornaments and initials. (xii),230,(lxii)pp. Sl. soiled & dampstained. Last 2 leaves with some blank areas torn away. Contemp. limp vellum, soiled, sm. hole in lower cover. STC 20164. S.&M.i.119. £250

Powell was a Welshman, an occasional playwright & an amusing writer. His remarks on the jurisdiction of Parliament,(partly drawn from Smith's Republic,) on the Chancery, on Star Chamber, etc. are of considerable historical value.

370) PRECEDENTS in CHANCERY,
being Cases argued and adjudged in the High Court of Chancery... 1689-1722. H. Lintot. 1750. The second edition. Folio.(By a late careful and judicious Hand), with a new and more correct table... not printed in any other book of Reports. (viii),598,(40)pp. Modern cloth. S.&M. i.348/36. £45

371) PRIDEAUX, Frederick.
The Hand-Book of Precedents in Conveyancing adapted to the modern law and practice, with notes. 1852. 1st edition. xiv,(i),359pp. Index. Endpapers sl. spotted. Orig. cloth, faded and sl. marked. S.&M. ii.290. (only edition) £16

372) PRIDEAUX, Humphrey. (1648-1724)
The Original and Right of Tithes, for the maintenance of the Ministry in a Christian Church, truly stated...draught of a Bill...for the

PRIDEAUX, Humphrey. (1648-1724)...Right of Tithes..cont.
372)...restraining of Pluralities. Norwich. 1710. 1st edition. 2 parts in 1 vol. Contemp. panelled calf, joints & edges worn. S.& M.i.193. £60

This Bill, drawn up in 1691, was a courageous attempt to reform abuses in the Church and Prideaux makes the case for tithes on grounds of natural justice rather than biblical precedent.

373) .....Another copy. 1736. 2nd edition, revised. Modern tree calf, sl. stained. Bookplate of Lord Selborne. £60

374) PRYNNE, William. (1600-1669).
Brevia Parliamentaria Rediviva. In 13 sections, ...catalogues of the numbers, dates of all bundles of original Writs of Summons & Elections newly found, or formerly extant in the Tower of London...Sm.4to. Printed for the author. 1662. 1st edition. (xxiv),398,(i)pp. Title in ornamental border, dedication, errata leaf. Contemp. sheep, rubbed, spine ends sl. frayed, pages sl. browned & dust-stained in margins of first few leaves. WING P 3902. £150

These writs, of which there are 95, were found by Prynne after the publication of his "Second Part of a Brief Register..." in 1659.

375) .....The Opening of the Great Seale of England...brief historical and legal observations....in respect of Charters, Patents, Writs etc. 4to. Michael Spark. 1643. 1st edition. 32,(i)pp. Disbound. S. &M.i.118/71. £28

376) .....The Soveraigne Power of Parliaments and Kingdomes: divided into Foure Parts together with an Appendix wherein the superiority of our owne and most foraine Parliaments, States, Kingdomes, Magistrates, over and above their lawfull Emperours, Kings, Princes, is evidenced...4to. Michael Sparke. 1643. 1st edition. Modern calf, sl. rubbed. S. &M. i.91/136. £150

Part 1 has a special title "Treachery and Disloyalty of Papists to the Soveraignes, etc." 2nd edition.
Prynne is said to have written more than two hundred books and pamphlets, most of which are fugitive controversial pieces on religious and political subjects. His work is based on the best evidence and this gives his writings a lasting value. He attacked what he considered the great enormities of the age and against the doctrines & disciplines of the Church, was imprisoned for his writings on several occasions, appeared before the Star-Chamber and in addition suffered the loss of his ears and having to stand in the pillory.

377) PUFENDORF, Samuel. (1632-1694)
De Jure Naturae et Gentium. Libri octo. Amsterdam. J. Wolters. 1704. Sm.4to. Revised & corrected. Red & black title with vignette, sl.

384) PULTON, Ferdinando.
An Abstract of all the Penall Statutes which be Generall, in force and use: ...the effect of all those Statutes which do threaten to the Offenders...is also added in their apt Titles, the effect of all other general Statutes...Sm.4to. Thomas Wight. 1600. (xvi),405pp. Title and prelims. sl. stained. Modern calf-backed boards. BEALE S.79 (imperfect copy only). STC 9532. S.&M. i.364/58. £220

First edition was published by Tottell in 1560. This edition has been corrected and amended.
Pulton was a learned barrister of Lincoln Inn who was employed for several years in the consideration of the Statute Law and published two useful books upon that subject. The first was the above work and afterwards The Calendar or Abstract of all the Statutes in use, chronologically arranged with an alphabetical abridgement of them in the manner of Rastell's collection.

385) .....A Collection of Sundry Statutes, frequent in use , with notes in the margent and references to the book cases and books of Entries and Registers. (with) an abridgement of the residue which be expired...also a table or Kalendar. Folio. M. Flesher & R. Young. 1640. (vi),1464,(84)pp. Last leaf (catalogue of certaine Ordinances) laid down, margins of last section and some others carefully repaired, some general marginal staining. First few leaves cut short with some sl. loss of marginal notes on p.2. Fine engraved title with contemp. signature in margin. Contemp. calf, edges sl. rubbed, rebacked and corners repaired. A very good and sound copy. S.&M. i.555-6/37. STC 9331. £280

386) .....De Pace Regis et Regni, viz. A Treatise declaring which be the great and generall Offences of the Realme, and the chiefe impediments of the peace of the King and the Kingdome, as Treasons, Homicides, and Felonies etc...which being reformed or duly checked, Florebit Pax Regis & Regni. Collected out of the Reports of the Common Lawes...and of the Statutes...and out of the painefull workes of the Reverend Judges, Sir Anthnie Fitzharbert, Sir Robert Brooke, Sir W. Stanford, Sir James Dyer, Sir Edward Coke, Knights, and other learned Writers of our Lawes. The Companie of Stationers. 1615. Folio. BLACK letter, engraved chapter heading & initials, index. Contemp. calf, rubbed, spine ends sl. worn & frayed, hinges weak, endpapers sl.stnd. STC 20497. S. & M.i.365/58a. £220

This treatise was a more comprehensive and up-to-date book than Staunford's Pleas of the Crown and was first published in 1609. A comparison between its 41 chapters and Staunford's work shows the effect of the additions to the criminal law made during the 16th century by the Legislature, the Common Law Courts, and the Star Chamber. But it is not only a useful summary of criminal law but very modern in its inclusion of such matters as the Law of Principal & Accessory, Private Prosecution (then called "Appeal") of Felonies, Evidence, etc.

387) .....Another copy. 1623. 4th edition. Folio. Lacks first blank. Few margins sl. soiled. Contemp. calf, later label, rubbed & sl. worn. STC 20498. £150

PUFENDORF, Samuel. De Jure Naturae et Gentium..cont.
377)...browned. viii,929,(vii)pp. Index. Latin text. Contemp. calf, sl. rubbed. Bookplate. £120

First published at Lund in 1672 this is the 2nd edition with the author's emendations.
In this celebrated thesis Pufendorf took up in great measure the theories of Grotius and sought to complete them by means of the doctrines of Hobbes and of his own ideas...He combatted Hobbes's conception of the state of nature and concluded that this is not one of war but of peace....limiting also the authority of the supreme power to what the citizens have acquired under its protection.

378) .....De Officio Hominis et Civis juxta Legem Naturalem. Libri duo. Cambridge. J. Knapton/D. Paul. London, 1715. (xxiv),164,(iv)pp. Blanks, final advert. leaves. Modern cloth. S.&M.i.597/73. £30

379).....Another copy. Edited by Thomas Johnson. Cambridge. 1735. xvi,380,(iv)pp. Advert. leaves, index. Contemp. calf, sl. rubbed. Ex lib. stamp. £30

380) .....Another copy. Tho. Johnson. 1737. 2nd edition, revised. Engraved fp. port., red & black title with vignette. (ii),xvi,510pp. Index. Contemp. calf, joints & edges worn. Not in S. &M. £35

Johnson produced this edition (the previous *379) for the students of Magdalen College, Cambridge, of which he was a Fellow. It includes the Historia Juris Civilis (A survey of ancient & modern Schools of thought on the subject) of Johannes Buddeus of Jena.

381) .....Another copy. as above. 1758. 4th edition, revised. Red & black title with vignette. (ii),xvi,513pp. Index. Bookplate. Contemp. signature on blank. Contemp. calf. Fine copy. £35

382) .....Le Droit de la Nature et des Gens, ou Systeme General...de la Morale la Jurisprudence, et de la Politique. Transl. into French by Jean Barbeyrac. 2 vols.4to. Amsterdam. Pierre de Coup. 1712. 2nd edition, revised, with notes and a preface by the translator & with his "Oratio inauguralis de dignitate et utilitate juris ac historiarum..." Indices, fine engr. fp. port., titles in black & red with vignettes. French text, the oration by Barbeyrac in Latin. Contemp. calf, sl. rubbed, gilt dec'd spines, labels. Fine set. Signature " Dalrymple 1732" on both titles. £120

383) .....Of the Law of Nature and Nations in Eight Books. Edited by Jean Barbeyrac and translated into English by Basil Kennett. Folio. 1729. 4th edition. Chapter heading vignettes and tailpieces. Modern calf-backed boards. S.&M. i.597/72. £120

This,the fourth edition,is edited by Mr. Carew. It includes a version of Barbeyrac's Account of the Science of Morality, together with his notes to Pufendorf in their fullest form.

388) (PURLEWENT, S.)
A Dialogue between a Lawyer and a Country Gentleman, upon the Subject of the Game Laws, relative to hares, partridges and pheasants.(with) three tables showing the offences, the statutes....With a letter to John Glynn upon the Penal Laws of this Country. By a Gentleman of Lincolns Inn. J. Wilkie. 1771. 1st edition. xv,40pp. 3 folding tables, half title. Orig. boards with label. Fine copy. GOLDSMITH 10741. HIGGS 5180. Not in KRESS or S. & M. (both refer only to the second edition apparently published in the same year.) £38

389) RADCLIFFE, G.R.Y. & Geoffrey CROSS.
The English Legal System. 1954. 3rd edition. Orig. cl.,sl. mkd. £3

390) RANKINE, John.
The Law of Land ownership in Scotland. A treatise on the rights and burdens incident of the ownership of lands and other heritages in Scotland. 1879. 1st edition. xliv,957pp. Index. Orig. cloth, faded & rubbed, hinges weak & shaken. S. &M.v.95. £20

391) (RASTELL, John)(—1536)
Les Termes de la Ley, or Certaine difficult and obscure Words and Termes of the Common Lawes and Statutes of this Realme now in Use expunded and explained. John More. 1636. Newly imprinted and much enlarged and augmented with a new addition of above 250 words. xvi, 303pp. Title and last leaves sl. browned and with ms. notes in pen. Contemp. sheep, repaired. STC 20718. S. &M.i.11/48. £180

Rastell published the first English Law-Dictionary in Latin in 1527.

392) .....Another copy. John Streater etc. 1671. Newly corrected... with an addition of more than 100 words. (ii),(xiv),613,(i)pp. Partly BLACK letter. Royal Arms on leaf before title. Contemp. signatures on endpapers. STC R 291. S. &M.i.11/48 (attributes this to William Rastell.) Contemp. sheep, sl. rubbed, final leaf sl. torn. £120

John Rastall or Rastell was one of our early printers. He married the sister of Sir Thomas More and through his friendship became knowledgable in various sorts of learning. He wrote various religious tracts and later took a hand in composing compiling some law books. In 1517 he published his Tables to Fitzherbert's Abridgment and a Table to the Book of Assizes.
The above is the 23rd edition of his English-Law-Dictionary in French and English.

393) RAYMOND, Robert, Lord (Chief Justice)(1626-1683)
Reports of Cases...in...King's Bench and Common Pleas...1765. 2nd ed. 3 vols. Folio. Complete indices. Modern cloth. S.&M.i.307. £95

Cases 1694-1732.

394)..... Reports...as above and Exchequer. 1660-83. Folio.1696.1st edition. 2 tables. Contemp calf,sl. rubbed, joints weak.WING R 417.

RAYMOND, Robert. Reports of Cases...cont.
394).....S. & M. i.308/106. £60

395) .....Another copy. 1743. 2nd edition, corrected with many additional references and 3 tables. Sl. spotted. Contemp. calf, worn, joints cracked. £40

396) RAYNER, John.
Cases at Large concerning Tithes...introduction...view of the whole law of Tithes...Acts of Parliament. 1783. 3 vols. 1st edition. Contemp. calf, rebacked, sl. worn. S.&M.i.194. £90

Rayner's comprehensive work includes an annotated list of authorities - a useful contribution to legal bibliography.

397) REPORTS of CASES in the COURT of CHANCERY.
Part 2 only. Charles II to the 1st year of William & Mary, being special Cases..referring to the Register-Books....R. & E. Atkyns. 1694. 1st edition. xvi,437,(xviii)pp. Table, preface. Endpapers spotted, sl. browned throughout. Contemp. siganture on front e-p. Contemp. calf, sl. rubbed, spine & hinges sl. frayed. S.&M.i.348/38. £25

This volume is complete in itself but there was an earlier part in 1693 which covered the reign of Charles I.

398) RIDDELL, John.
Tracts, legal and historical, with other antiquarian matter, chiefly relative to Scotland. Edinburgh. 1835. 1st edition. x,224pp. Orig. boards, uncut, rubbed, inner hinge loose, dust-stained. Ex lib. bkpt. S. &M. v.97. £30

Observations & documents on the death of Richard II, on the Scots Law of legitimation and on certain Scottish families.

399) ROLLE, Sir Henry. (1589-1656)
Les Reports de divers Cases, Banke le Roy (1614-16) Folio. A.Roper 1675. 1st edition. Engraved fp. port. (loose), index. Contemp. calf. joints cracked, upper cover detached. WING R 1875. S.&M.i.308/109. £45

Rolle was Chief Justice of the King's Bench and a member of the Council of State and under Cromwell was appointed in 1654 as one of the Commissioners of the Exchequer. Cromwell however soon became dissatisfied with his Chief Justice as too honest a man to be relied upon in the impositions he attempted to raise without the consent of Parliament. Rolle retired in 1655 to avoid further resistance to the ruling powers.

400) RÖMER, Carl Heinrich von.
Staatsrecht und Statistik des Churfürstenthums Sachsen und der dabei

406) RUFFHEAD.(Owne). THE STATUTES at LARGE.
From Magna Charta to 4 Geo. III (end of last Session of Parliament). 9 vols. 1762-5. 1st edition. 4to. Modern cloth, labels. (vol.8, corner of cloth & end-papers sl. stained & buckled). Fine uncut set.
With a table of the titles of all the Publick and Private Statutes during that time and a copious index and appendix consisting of obsolete and curious Acts, some of which were never before printed. ....
....Vol.10 & 11. From Geo.III (5th-13th year).1771-4.
....Vol.17 & 18. From Geo.III (35th-41st year)1798-1800.
All with table of titles and copious indices. 4to. Uniform with above. 14 vols. Modern cloth, uncut, very good set. £300

Ruffhead does not include, the text of the statutes in the Second Institute, but prints the old translations & makes marginal emendations when the translation is incorrect. Ruffhead's text is superior in accuracy to Cay's.

407) RUSSELL, Sir Alison.
Legislative Drafting and Forms.1931. 3rd ed. Orig. cloth,sl.rbbd. £5

408) RYMER, Thomas & Robert SANDERSON.(eds.)
Foedera, conventiones, literae, et cujuscunque generis acta publica inter reges Angliae, et alios quosvis imperatores, etc...The Hague. (Jean Neaulme). 1739-45. 3rd edition, edited by George Holmes. 10 vols. Folio. Indices, 10 engraved plates in vol.9. Advert. leaf vol.1. Contemp. MS transcript of Anglo-French truce of 1325, from a Bodleian MS, & 5 engravings of Great Seals from an 8vo edition of Blackstone's Law Tracts, inserted in vol.1. Two leaves loose in vols. 4 & 9, vol.5 lacks 5*2 blank 1 & N2-5 (part 3) reversed. L2 (vol.7. part 1) torn without loss. Contemp. marbled boards, uncut, worn, ends of spines defective. S. &M. i.604. £300

The last edition, including some new items - an account of the English constitution in French, written by an unknown ambassador in 1565 and Le Clerc's historical abridgment of the Foedera which forms vol. 10.

SACHEVERELL, Henry...see TRIALS.

409) SALKELD, William. (1671-1715)
Reports of Cases....in the Court of King's Bench, with some special cases in the Courts of Chancery, Common Pleas and Exchequer 1689-1712. 2 vols. Folio. Nutt..1717/8. 1st edition. With 2 tables. Privilege leaf, loose, sl. frayed & laid down, corners of prelims. stained & frayed, some browning & sl. staining throughout. Modern cloth. S. &M. i.308/111. £45

410) .....Another set. 2 vols. in 1. Folio.(1689-1712). 1721-2.2nd ed. ....Vol.3. 1724. 1st edition. Altogether 3 vols. Contemp. calf, rubbed, sl. frayed, vol.3 edges touched with damp, joints cracked. S. &M. i.308/111. £90

411) .....Complete in 1 vol.1773. 1st thus.Folio. £30

RÖMER, C.H.von. Staatsrecht und Statistik..cont.
400) ...befindlichen Lande. 2 vols.Halle. Joh. Jac. Curts Wittwe. 1787/8. 1st edition. (xv),608,(iii)/(xv),843pp. Several folding tables, including genealogical. Engraved device on titles & end-pieces of each volume, errata leaf. Contemp. half calf, spines rubbed & worn. Very good. £95

A third volume was published in Wittenburg in 1792.
Römer was a practising State lawyer and in this work he felt that with the help of statistics he could illustrate the political situation of the electoral State Laws of Saxony, show how they work and how they could be improved.

401) (ROSCOE,Henry)(1800-1836)
Westminster Hall: or, professional relics and anecdotes of the Bar, Bench and Woolsack. 1825. 3 vols. Engraved titles with vignettes, folding frontispiece to each volume. (sm. tear at fold of the one in vol.2). 11 engraved portraits, index. Imprint in vol.2. partially obliterated by sm. adhesion in paper. Modern morocco-backed boards. S. &M. ii.306. Fine set. £85

A compilation of scattered curiosities of law books and from collections of legal biography and anecdote but also includes some original papers on subjects connected with the law.
Roscoe was the author of Lives of Eminent British Lawyers in Lardner's Cylopaedia, the editor of North's Lives and a Life of his father, the historian and poet.

402) .....Eminent British Lawyers. 1833. Engraved title, sl. stained. (ii),428,(ii)pp. Strip torn from printed title affec. first work. Orig. cloth, marked & faded. £10

In the Cabinet Cyclopaedia series the work covers fourteen judges & jurists from Coke to Romilly.

403) ROSE, George.
Cases in Bankruptcy...Reports of Cases decided by Lord Chancellor Eldon. 1810-16, and contemporaneous cases in other Courts. 2 vols. 1813-6. 2nd edition. Indices. Contemp. calf, rubbed, top of spine sl. frayed. S. &M. ii.307. Very good. £60

404) ROVERE, Richard H.
Howe & Hummel. 1948. 2nd imp. With drawing by Reginald Marsh (from the New Yorker). Orig. cloth. £3

The story of the two glorified New York "shysters"; Bon vivants, boulevardiers, barristers extraordinary.

405) ROYAL INSTITUTE OF INTERNATIONAL AFFAIRS.
The British Year Book of International Law, 1963. OUP. 1965. 1st ed. Ed. by Prof. Sir H.Waldock & R.Y.Jennings. viii,557pp.Index.dw. £10

412) SANDYS, Charles.
Consuetudines Kanciae. A history of Gavelkind and other remarkable Customs in the County of Kent. 1851. 1st edition. xvi,352,12,12pp. Genealogical table (folding),browned, 3 folding facss., title in black and red lettering, list of subscribers, glossary, table of recent statutes relating to Real Property and general index. Two interesting 12 page booklists: 1 of general titles and 1 of books relating to the counties of Kent, Sussex and Surrey: all published by J. Russell Smith. Orig. embossed cloth, top of spine sl. frayed. From the SIGNET Library. S. & M. 2.315. £50

413) SAUNDERS, Sir Edward. (—1683)
Les Reports des Divers Pleadings et Cases en le Court del Bank le Roy en le Temp del Reign de le Roy Charles III. 2 vols. in 1. Folio. W. Rawlins. 1686. Privilege leaves and indices for each vol.,advert. leaf at end of vol.2, tables. Contemp. calf, rubbed. Very good. S.&M. i.308/112. WING S743/4. £90

Saunders's reports were greatly valued for their learning and industry as is shown by their being mentioned in the Reports of Dyer and Plowden.

414) .....Another set. 2 vols. Folio. 1722. 2nd edition with the addition of the translation into English. Pages 1-84 of vol. 2 are bound at the end of vol.1. Modern cloth. Fine set. £90

These reports, printed after Saunders's death, extend from 1666-1672. They are valued for their simplicity and precision.

415) .....Summus Angliae Seneschallus, or, a Survey of the Lord High-Steward of England...manner of arraigning a Peer. 1680. sm.4to. 1st edition. 36pp. Few page numerals cropped. Disbound. WING S 745. S. &M. i.218. £25

This pamphlet is addressed to Lord Stafford & others, Catholics whom Saunders (a catholic himself) was about to defend on their trial for high treason.

416) SAYLE, R.T.D.
Notes on the South-East Corner of Chancery Lane. 1119-1929. 4to. 1929. Plates & facss. v,70pp. Index. Orig. buckram, gilt. Fine. £10

The premises of the original law publishers' Stephen and Sweet, later Sweet & Maxwell. Names of occupants and biographical notices.

417) SCHMIDT, Dr. Karl.
Jus Primae Noctis. Eine geschichtliche Untersuchung. Freiburg im Breisgau (Germany). 1881. 1st edition. xlxxx,397pp. Index & 42 page bibliography. Orig. cloth, spine sl. faded, title sl. browned. German text. £15

418) SCHMITTHOFF, Clive M. The Sale of Goods. 1951. 3rd imp. dw. £3

419) SCHULTING, Anton. (1659-1734)
Dissertationes, de recusatione Judicis, pro rescriptis Imperatorum Romanorum, de transactione super controversiis, quae ex ultimis voluntatibus proficiscuntur....Accedit oratio de jurisprudentia Marci Tullii Ciceronis. Frankfurt. Ex officina Francisci Halmae...1708.4to. (i),(xxiv),294,(i)pp. Engraved vignette on title, tailpieces & initials. Fine copy with wide margins, most probably a large paper copy. Contemp. vellum. Latin text. £120

Schulting was a learned jurist who studied law at Leyden under Voet and Noodt. Together with Bynkershoek, van Eck and Voet he was considered one of the most important and influential jurist in North-west Europe of his time.

420) .....Jurisprudentia vetus Ante-Justinianea. New edition with a preface by Georgius Henrius Ayrer. Leipzig 1737. 4to. (lxxxvi),941, (lxxix)pp. Index, engraved vignette on *2. Lacks blank a_1. Some browning. Contemp. tree calf, gilt, sl. rubbed. Arms of Nijmegen (Noviomagus) on sides. Fine copy. Latin text. £80

This was considered his principal work and includes variants in the texts of Gaius, Julius Paulus and the two early codes from the Wurzburg & Gotha Mss.
Nijmegen was the home town of Schulting's family.

SCOTCH ENTAILS...see Parliamentary Reports.

421) SCOTT, Sir Harold.
Scotland Yard. 1954. 1st edition. Orig. cloth, sl. faded. £3

Sir Harold was Commissioner of the Metropolitan Police 1945-53.

422) SCOTT, John.
Digests of the General Highway and Turnpike Laws, with the Schedule of Forms, as directed by Act of Parliament...also an appendix on the construction and preservation of Roads. E. &C. Dilley. 1778. 2nd ed. xxix,352,(xvi),(i)pp. Uncut, index, postscript, booklist, half-title. Tear in 1 index leaf and 1 other. Orig. boards, sl. rubbed & stained, new spine. S. &M. i.385. £60

423) SEA LAW.
Regulations and Instructions relating to his Majesty's Service at Sea. 4to. 1772. 11th edition. In 5 parts, with appendix, forms of books or accounts, additional regulations...(ii),232pp. Half-title, fine engraved title-vignette & ornamental headings and tail-pieces to each part, folding schedule at end. Endpapers sl. spotted. Contemp. sprinkled calf, rubbed, hinges weak. £70

424) .....1808. 4to. viii,286,(1),287-440,(198),xxxiv,(ii)pp. Appendices, index to the general naval instructions for this edition, final errata leaf. Signatures irregular. Contemp. calf, rubbed, upper hinge repaired. £40

SHEPPARD (or SHEPHARD), William. The Faithfull Councellor..cont.
431) ....WING S 3186. S. &M. i.142 (listed in index but not found in text). £150

Sheppard was an industrious and one of the most authoritative of our early writers on law and a whole hearted supporter of the Commonwealth.

432) .....The Justice of Peace, his Clerks Cabinet, or, a Book of Presidents, or Warrants.....D. Maxwell...1660. 2nd edition. (xvi), 127pp. 4 pages of endpapers with copious contemporary ms notes, much of it relating to the County Court of Cumberland and some to the duties of constables and justices of the peace. Ownership signature on title. Modern boards, calf spine. WING S 3190. S.&M.i.231/65. £200

Sheppard best known for his work The Touchstone of Common Assurances was the author of a large number of legal treatises. He is said to have owed his fortune to Cromwell, who made him one of the Clerks of the Upper Bench. He later became Serjeant-at-Law and prepared the charters granted to certain corporations.

433) .....A Sure Guide for His Majesties Justices of Peace....John Streater...1663. Third edition. (viii),524,(viii)pp. Index. Fine engraved frontispiece. Contemp. calf, rebacked. Fine copy. WING S 3211 (give it as the first edition). S.&M. i.232/67. £200

434) .....The Touch-Stone of Common Assurances....W. Lee etc. 1648. 4to. (vi),529 (i.e.525),(vii)pp. Errors in paging, including 349-352 omitted. Modern calf-backed boards. Pages sl. spotted. WING S 3215. KRESS S 946. S. &M. i.487/71. £220

The Touchstone is one of the most esteemed treatises, a copious fountain of the law, relating to the transfer of real property. To the period of its date it was a complete summary of the existing law on the methods of assurance and on various subjects connected with titles.

435) .....Another copy. Sm.4to. 1651. (xii),529,(vi)pp. Errors in paging as above. Contemp. sheep, rubbed. WING S 3215. KRESS S 1050. £200

436) .....Another copy. 1651. Third edition variant imprint. Contemp. calf, rebacked and corners repaired, lower cover worn. £200

This manual of conveyancing was of such value that the lawyers of Charles II's time, chagrined at the thought of being so deeply indebted to the determined Republican Sheppard, supposed that the Touchstone was a work of Sir John Doderidge's,which he had appropriated. It was last printed in 1826 and continues to be highly regarded from an historical point of view.

437) SMITH, J.C. & Brian HOGAN.
Criminal Law. 1965. 1st edition. Orig. cloth, faded. £8

425) SELDEN, John. (1584-1654)
Mare Clausum, seu de Dominio Maris Libri duo. Leyden. J. & T.Maire. 1636. Sm.4to. 1st continental edition. xii,244pp. 2 wood-engraved Maps of England, 2 plates & text illustrations. Title in red & black. A few leaves with minor damp-staining. Contemp. vellum, sl. stained. Bookplate. Latin text. S. &M. i.514/91. £300

The Mare Clausum is a full exposition of the claims of England to the sovereignty of the Seas, and was written in answer to the Mare Liberum of Grotius.

426) .....Titles of Honor. By the late famous and learned antiquary John Selden of the Inner Temple. Folio. E. Tyler & R. Holt for Thomas Dring. 1672. Third edition, carefully corrected with additions and amendments by the author. (i),(32),756pp. Fine engraved fp. portrait by R. White, some engraved text illustrations of medals, coins etc., chapter headings and initials. Contemp. mottled calf, sl. rubbed, rebacked. A very fine copy. WING S 2440. S.& M.i.208/50. £150

This third much enlarged edition of Selden's first great historical work which raised him to the rank of a valuable social historian. Ben Jonson contributes a long eulogy in verse.

427) SHAW, T.H.
The Law of Tithes. 1794. 1st edition. (i),vi,587,xviipp. Uncut in orig. boards, new spine. S. &M. i.195/51. £50

428) SHELFORD, Leonard.
A Practical Treatise on the Law concerning Lunatics, Idiots and Persons of unsound mind. With an appendix of the Statutes of England, Ireland and Scotland...and Precedents and Bills of Costs. 1833. 2nd edition. lxxxiii,866pp. Index. (with) A Supplement...1834. 1st ed. xxvpp. Uncut, orig. boards, sl. rubbed. S. &M. ii.324. £30

429) SHEPPARD, (or SHEPHARD) (1620-1675)
The Court-Keeper's Guide: or, a plaine and familiar treatise, needful and usefull for the helpe of many that are imployed in the keeping of Law-dayes or Courts Baron. ....jurisdiction of these Courts. J.G.... 1656. 4th edition. (iv),254,(iv),(viii)pp. Index, publishers' cat. Ownership signature on title. Contemp. sheep, neatly repaired. WING S 3180. S. &M. i.405/62. £250

Replaced the obsolete & uninformative works of the "modus tenendi curiam" type, the only guides on the subject up to then in print.

430) ....Another copy. 1662. 5th edition with additions by the author. (iv),254,(iv),(xiv)pp. Index, publishers' cat. for 1662. Contemp. calf, lacking endpapers. Bookplate. WING S 3181. £150

431) .....The Faithfull Councellor: or, the Marrow of the Law in English. In two parts. Sm.4to. R.W....1651. 1st edition.(vi),703, (xii)pp. Alphabetical table. Contemp. calf, rubbed, rebacked...

438) SOMERVILLE, Thomas. (1741-1830)
The history of Political Transactions and of Parties from the Restoration of Charles II to the death of William. A. Strahan. 1792. 1st edition. 4to. xxiv,595,xivpp. Index. Occasional minor spotting. Contemp. sprinkled calf, neatly rebacked. £60

Somerville began this work in 1782 and it took him 10 years to complete it. It covers all aspects of the revolution of 1688.

439) SPELMAN, Sir Henry. (1562-1641)
De non Temerandis Ecclesiis, Churches not to be Violated. A Tract of the Rights and Respects due unto Churches. Written to a Gentleman... Written and first published 30 years earlier and with a new Epistle by his son, Clement Spelman. Oxford. H. Hall..1668. 4th edition. (xiii),52,53-128pp. Lacks first blank. Contemp. sheep, rubbed, spine ends sl. frayed, margins sl. browned. WING S 4922. MADAN 2811. S. &M. i.195/53.(1646, 1st ed. only) Thomason Tracts i.436.(3rd ed.) £60

This scarce treatise concerning Tythes shows Spelman's profund regard for the Church and displayed his learning in spite of his advanced years, when he wrote the tract.

440) .....The Larger Treatise concerning Tithes ...with some other Tracts of the same Author. And a fragment of Sir Francis Bigot Knight, all touching the same subject. Edited by Jeremy Stephens. M.F. for Philemon Stephens. 1647/6. 1st edition. Sm. 4to. 2 parts in 1. (40), 190,28,34pp. Final blank. Head of title and a few side notes sl. shaved. A_2 sl. torn without loss. WING S 4928. S &M. i.195/54. (with) .....De non temerandis ecclesiis. Churches not to be Violated. Oxford. 1646. Third ed. (32),40pp. WING S 4921. MADAN 1858. S. &M.i.195/53. 2 works in 1 vol. Modern calf. Fine. £95

441) .....Reliquiae Spelmannianae. The Posthumous works of Sir Hen. Spelman, relating to the laws and antiquity of England. Folio. Oxford, printed at the Theater for Awnsham and John Churchill...London 1698. (xxxii),214,(xii)pp. 1st edition. Leaves 211/2 & 213/4 misbound. Fine engraved fp. port. by R. White, title vignette of Oxford theater, privilege leaf, dedication, preface, folding charts, index. Contemp. sprinkled, embossed calf. Sl. rubbed, some tears in cover repaired, spine worn & split. A handsome copy. WING S 4930. S. &M.i.37/79. £95
Sl. marginal worming in last few leaves.
Spelman was an eminent antiquary, descended from an ancient family. The above work was published by Bishop Gibson. It consists largely of the treatise on Feuds and Tenures by Knight-Service, together with the apology for Abp. Abbot, (convicted of manslaughter by chance-medley in a test case for a clergyman's rights under such circumstances), remarks on Wills, Coinage & the Rank of Knights etc.

442) SPILSBURY, William Holden.
Lincoln's Inn, its ancient and modern buildings with an account of the Library. William Pickering. 1850. fp. xvi,324pp. Modern cl. £35

W.H. Spilsbury was librarian of Lincoln's Inn.

443) STAIR, Sir James Dalrymple (First Viscount)(1619-1695)
The Decisions of the Lords of Council & Session in the most important Cases debated before them with Acts of Sederunt. 1661-81. With an alphabetical compendium of the decisions. Folio. 2 vols. Edinburgh. A. Anderson. 1683/7. 1st edition. Index for each vol. Contemp. calf, badly rubbed, spine ends sl. frayed, binding sound except for front blanks in vol.1. Contemp. annots. WING S 5175/6. S.&M.v.108. £95

Stair was one of the judges at the Court of Session later becoming president, created a Baronet in 1664. However on account of his conduct of the Test Act, he was superseded and found it necessary to retire to Holland. He was later re-instated and raised to the peerage as Viscount Stair and became Lord-Advocate and one of the principal Secretaries of State. He was again driven from office upon the Parliamentary inquiry into the massacre of Glenco.

444) .....The Institutions of the Law of Scotland, deduced from its originals and collated with the Civil, Canon and Feudal-Laws and with the customs of neighbouring Nations. Folio. 2 parts in 1 vol. Edinburgh. A. Anderson. 1681. 1st edition. (xxii,444/(ii),192pp. WITH .....Modus Litigandi, or Form of Process observed before the Lords of Council and Session in Scotland. Folio. Edinburgh. A. Anderson.1681. 1st edition. 44pp. Title and last two leaves browned, otherwise a very good copy. Bookplate. Contemp. calf, rubbed. 2 works in 1 vol. WING S 5177 & 5179. S. &M.v.108. £180

The supreme classic of Scots jurisprudence. Stair has been called the Littleton of Scotland - an allusion to the reverence in which he is held for his work which is a digest of jurisprudence with special reference to Scots law.

445) .....Another copy. 1693. Folio. 2nd edition, revised. (iv),ii, 780,(xl)pp. Index. Signatures 2_L & 2_M each a single leaf, conjugate & separated by another gathering signed L^2. Contemp. panelled calf, spine gilt, worn. Bookplate George Rose. WING S 5178. £120

This is the author's final text and no further edition appeared until 1832.
George Rose (1744-1818) was Treasurer of the Navy etc. under Pitt.

446) .....Another copy. Edited John Gordon & William Johnstone. Edinburgh 1759. Folio. (xii),802,(xlvi)pp. Index. Lib. stamp on title, sl. spotted at end. Contemp. calf, rebacked, hinge broken. £40

This is the only edition called for between 1693 & 1824.

447) STANFORD, Sir William. (1509-1558)
Les Plees del Coron, divisees in plusors titles & comon lieux. R... Tottelli. 1574. Sm.4to. (xiv),198 leaves. Index, Black Letter,Woodcut title-border (BEALE 47) & initials. French text. BEALE T 489. STC 23222. S. & M. i.365. WITH
.....An Exposition of the Kinges Prerogative, collected out of the great Abridgement of Justice Fitzherbert, and other olde writers of the lawes of England. R.Tottel. (1577). (v),6-85 leaves. Black letter. Sm.4to. Contemp. annots., covering most of A5 margins & over some text.

STANFORD, Sir William. Les Plees del Coron...cont.
447) .....a few leaves sl. cropped & some a little stained. 2 works in 1 vol. Modern half calf. BEALE T 495. STC 23216. S.&M.i.119. £350

Stanford's great abridgment of criminal law is followed here by his English commentary on 17. Ed.II, one of the earliest monographs on statutory interpretation. Both works are of great historical importance.

448) .....Another copy as above. Contemp. calf, rubbed, rebacked. A very fine copy. £350

449) .....Another copy. ...dernierment corrigee avecques un Table... corigee...1583. (xii),196 (i.e.198) leaves. Fine woodcut title-border & initials, Black Letter, French text. BEALE T 490. STC 23223. WITH '.....An Exposition of the Kinges Prerogative...1590. BEALE T 496. STC 23217. Does not contain the dedications to Nicholas Bacon (A_{ii-iv} in 1577 edition) i.e. title is on A_i, summary on verso (A_v in 1577 ed) A_{ii} is "Prerogativa" and on verso Cap.I continuing as in 1577 edition as A_{iii} (leaf 6).
2 works in 1 vol. Fine contemp. calf with device on both covers, rebacked, endpapers browned & not attached to boards, first blank laid down. Armorial bookplate of Lord Halifax, 1702. Fine copy. £300

450) STARKIE, Thomas.
A treatise on Criminal Pleading, with Precedents of Indictment. Special Pleas etc. W. Clarke. 1814. 3rd edition. 2 vols. Annots. on endpapers. Contemp. calf, sl. rubbed, top of spine of vol.1. frayed. S. &M. ii.336. £60

451) STATUTES.
A collection of the several Statutes and parts of Statutes now in Force, relating to High Treason and Misprison for High Treason. By Charles BILL. 1709. 2nd edition. 113,(xiv)pp. S. &M. i.367/6. WITH ...A Form and method of Trial of Commoners in cases of High Treason ......1709. 1st edition. 44,(iii)pp. S. & M. i.367/10.
2 works in 1 vol. 12mo. Contemp. sprinkled calf, gilt, with cornerpieces and central arms of Queen Anne on sides. Rebacked, original spine laid down. £60

452) ..... Magna Carta in F. wherunto is added more statut(es) than ever was imprynted in any one boke before this tyme/with an Alminacke. By me Robert Redman. M.CCCCC.XXIX (for 1539) Narrow 12mo. Gothic (rotunda) letter, title, colophon &almanac printed in red & black. Indices. (viii),5-148,(iv),59,64-74,(iii) leaves. Lacks 8 leaves of text (A_{1-4}, S_{9-12}) Final blank. Early ownership inscription of Morgan Lloyd & Thomas & William Meredith. 19th-century calf, sl. rubbed. BEALE S 8 (wrong collation, omitting part 2) STC 9270. S.& M.i.552/1. £200

The unusual format of this edition indicates that it was designed for easy carriage in a lawyer's bag or Hood. This is the last edition to be provided with a calendar. The two parts are continously printed, though separately paged. Part I ends with dates of the Kings of England, names of Counties, lists of Writs, & moral verses.

STATUTES...cont.
453) ...Scotland. The Laws and Acts of Parliament made by James I and his Royal Successors. Edinburgh. J. van Solingen..1682.(1683, 1731). WITH
An Index or Abridgment to the Acts. Edinburgh. J. Reid. 1685. 1st collected edition. 4 parts in 3 vols. 12mo. Occasional worming, some stains in vol.2. Contemp. calf, gilt, spines of vols. 1 & 2 defective. WING S 1266. ALDIS 2326/2364 (vols. 1 & 2) S.&M.v.115/6. £60

454) .....The Statutes at Large concerning Elections of members to serve in the...Commons. 1734. 1st edition. Index. S.&M.i.152.
....Orders & Resolutions of the...on Controverted Elections and Return. 1736. 2nd edition. S. &M.ii.26.
....J. COWLEY. The candidates guide, or the Electors right decided.. resolutions......1734. 1st edition. Not in S. & M.
3 works in 1 vol. Contemp. calf, lower cover rubbed. £40

SEE ALSO under PICKERING, RUFFHEAD & TOMLINS & RAITHBY.

455) STENTON, Doris M.
English Justice between the Norman Conquest and the Great Charter. 1066-1215. Philadelphia. 1964. 1st published. xii,238pp. Index, bibliography. £10

Jayne Lectures for 1963 and published by the American Philosophical Society.

456) ST(E)UART, Sir James (of Goodtrees).
Dirleton's Doubts and Questions in the Law of Scotland resolved and answered. Folio. Edinburgh. James Watson. 1715. 1st edition. (iv),340, 16pp. Title in black and red, engraved fp. port., index. Some sl. spotting, mainly title & index. Bookplate. Contemp. calf, rubbed and spine worn, upper hinge loose. S. &M.v.117. £60

There was a proverb in Scotland, "Doubting with Dirleton and resolving with Steuart", that is - not resolving at all. Too much of his work consists of Dirleton's words repeated with approving comments. Sir James Steuart was Lord Advocate for 18 years.

457) .....Another copy as above. No portrait (not called for in S.&M) Modern cloth. £60

458) .....The Index or Abridgement..from ...1424-1707...with the Act ratifying...the Treaty of Union of the Two Kingdoms. Edinburgh. 1707. 3rd edition, revised. Tear in X_2 without loss. WITH
'....Alexander BRUCE. The Index...of such Acts...as...concern the whole U.K. or particularly...Scotland..to...1726. Edinburgh. 1726. 1st edition. 12mo. 2 works in 1 vol. Contemp. calf, rubbed.S.&M.v. 117. £20

459) STONE, Julius.
Recent trends in English Precedent with a comparative introduction on the Civil Law. Sydney, Australia. 1945. 1st pub'd edition. Index, bibliography. Orig. printed stiff wraps, edges frayed. £10

460) STRANGE, Sir John. (1696-1754)
Reports of adjudged Cases in...Chancery, King's Bench, Common Pleas, and Exchequer. 2 vols. Folio. Index, first privilege leaf to each vol. Lacks fp. port. Several annots. to the earlier cases by Sir William de Grey (later Lord Walsingham - 1719-81). Modern cloth. Bkpl. Thomas de Grey (the judges's father). S. &M. i. 309. £80

De Grey has several times added information concerning counsel & occasionally abbreviated a point of law, concentrating on cases tried previous to his call to the Bar in 1742. He was Chief Justice of Common Pleas for 10 years & Lord Eldon praises him for his great learning & power of memory.
Strange includes an unusual number of cases turning on points of criminal law.

461) ....Another set. as above. With engraved fp. port. laid down. Modern cloth. £80

462) STREET, Harry.
The Law of Torts. 1963. 3rd edition. Orig. cloth. £5

463) STRYKIUS, S.
Examen Juris Feudalis. (Frankfurt). Jeremiae Schrey. 1692. 12mo. Engraved frontispiece. (xxii),436,(lxiv)pp. Index. Contemp. vellum, spine sl. soiled. £50

464) STUART, Gilbert. (1742-1786)
Observations concerning the Public Law of Scotland....Edinburgh.1779. 1st edition. xxiv,396pp. Appendix of documents etc., sl. spotted,some pencil annots. Contemp. sprinkled calf, joints & edges sl. worn. S. &M. v.118. £50

Stuart shows that the feudal, parliamentary & juridical institutions of Scotland are more ancient and more national than Robertson & others supposed. He does, however, condemn the arbitrary jurisdiction of the Court of Session.

465) .....Another copy as above. Contemp. calf, gilt. Fine. £50

466) STUBBS, W. & G. TALMASH.
The Crown Circuit Companion, containing the Practice of the Assised on the Crown Side, and of the Courts of General and General Quarter Sessions of the Peace...(with) the Clerk of Assise's Circuit Companion. J. Worrall. 2 vols. 1762. Third edition. Index, booklist. Contemp. calf, sl. rubbed. Very good. S.&M.i.360/18. £65

Includes a collection of useful and modern precedents of indictments in criminal cases as well as common law and as those created by Statute...with references to the printed authorities.

467) .....Another set as above. Contemp. calf, very rubbed, spine & corners frayed. 2 vols. bound in 1. Title of vol.2 before p.325. £60

468) STYLE, W.
Narrationes Modernae, or Modern Reports begun in the now Upper Bench Court at Westminster (1646)-55, as well on the Criminall as on the Pleas side. Folio. F.L. for W. Lee etc. 1658. 1st edition. (xix),483, (xxxv)pp. Table, errata. Contemp. calf, sl. rubbed, hinges weak. WING S 6099. S. &M. i.310/125. £80

469) SUBSTANCE of the SPEECHES
delivered by some members of the Faculty of Advocates, at the meeting on 28th Feb. adjourned to the 2nd March, and at the meeting held on the 9th March, 1807, for considering the Bill entitled, "An Act for better regulating the Courts of Justice in Scotland, and the administration of justice therein, and establishing trial by jury in certain civil cases." Edinburgh. James Ballantyne. 1807. (iv),195pp. Half title. Contemp. cloth, faded. £30

With speeches by David Hume, Walter Scott, Jeffrey, Ferguson, Mathew Ross, John Murray, Colquhoun and others.

470) SUGDEN, Edward Burtenshaw.
A Practical Treatise of the Law of Vendors & Purchasers of Estates. 1813. 4th edition. lxviii,643,115pp. Appendix & index. Contemp. calf, sl. rubbed, joints sl. split. Few contemp. annots. £25

471) .....Another copy. 1826. 7th ed. Modern cloth. Sl. spotted. £25

472) .....Another copy. 3 vols. 1839. 10th edition. Modern cloth. Very good set. £55

473) SULLIVAN, Francis Stoughton. (1719-1776)
An Historical Treatise on the Feudal Law, and the Constitution and Laws of England, with a commentary on Magna Charta and illustrations of many English Statutes. 4to. J. Johnson. 1772. 1st edition. xiv, 449pp. Index, half-title. Contemp. sprinkled calf, sl. rubbed, re-backed. Very good copy. S. & M. i.16/25. £90

Lectures delivered in the University of Dublin where, in the author's opinion, circumstances required a more detailed & precise historical work than that of Blackstone.

474) .....Lectures on the Constitution and Laws of England..2nd ed. by Gilbert Stuart with a discourse concerning the laws and government of England. 4to. E. & C. Dilly. 1776. xvi,xxxii,415pp. Index, half title. Contemp. panelled calf, rebacked. Very good copy. S.&M.i.108/113. £80

475) .....Another copy as above. Some sl. marginal spotting. Modern cloth. £75

476) SURREBUTTER, John (John ANSTEY).
The Pleader's Guide, A didactic Poem, in two books, containing the Conduct of a Suit at Law, with the arguments of Councellor Bother'um

482) TAYLOR, John. (1704-1756)
Elements of the Civil Law. Charles Bathurst. 1756. 2nd edition. 4to. (x),584,(xii)pp. Index. Contemp. calf, joints weak & worn. S.&M.v.143. £40

Taylor, who adapted this work from his tutorial lectures to the grandsons of Lord Granville, wrote with the idea of presenting Roman law as a basis for a gentleman's conduct of life.

483) TIDSWELL, Richard Thomas & Ralph D.M.LITTLER.
The Practice and evidence in Cases of Divorce and other Matrimonial causes. 1860. 1st & only edition. (ii),232,cxpp. Appendices of fees and forms, index, advert. leaf. Lacks front endpaper. Sl. frayed orig. cloth, ink-stained. S. &M.ii.358. £20

484) TILGHMAN, Richard A. vs. Roland S. MITCHELL.
In the Circuit Court of the United States for the Southern District of New York. Argument for Complainant on exceptions to Master's Report. Edited by George Harding, July 1871. 35pp. Orig. printed wraps. Top of spine sl. frayed. £15

485) TOLLER, Sir Samuel.
The Law of Executors and Administrators. Ed. Francis Whitmarsh. 1818. 4th edition, corrected with additions. xvi,624pp. Indices. Endpapers sl. spotted, some pages creased. Contemp. boards, spine torn. S.& M. i.494/36. £20

486) TOMLINS & RAITHBY'S STATUTES at LARGE. (U.K. of G.B. and Ireland) Volumes 1-19. 1804-1849. Quarto. From 41 George III to Victoria XIII (1801-1849. With copious indices. All in modern cloth, with labels. A very good set. £300

Every Public Act, that has not been repealed, or was not expired, is given at length. Local and Personal Acts are omitted, the Title only being printed. No Act from which it was conceived any national information could be gathered by the historian, the antiquary, or the lawyer is omitted.
The whole of the copy for the printer was formed of Ruffhead's edition and the proofs read by Cay up to the end of 7 George II and the continuation by Hawkins. The first volume was edited by Mr. Tomlins one of the editors of the Statutes of the Realm. It contains such Statutes antecedent to the reign of Henry VIII as had appeared in any collection of Statutes hitherto published and is said to be the best edition (with the exception of the Statutes of the Realm) covering that period. The later Statutes were edited by Tomlins, Raithby, Simons & Richards.

487) TOWNSEND, William C.
The Lives of Twelve Eminent Judges of the last and of the present Century. 2 vols. 1846. 1st in book form. Index. Contemp. half calf. Spine & edges rubbed. Bookplate. Not in S. & M. £40
Biographies of Kenyon, Gibbs, Ellenborough, Erskine, Redesdale, Eldon etc. reprinted from the Law Magazine.

SURREBUTTER, John (John ANSTEY).
476) .....and Counsellor Bore'um, in an action betwixt John-a-Gull, and John-a-Gudgeon, for assault and battery, at a late contested election. T. Cadell etc. 1796. 1st edition. (Book 1). viii,79,(1)pp. Advert. leaf. Stiff marbled wraps, spine worn. Annots. on endpapers. S. &M. i.262/5. £30

A second part was issued in the 4th edition of 1802.

477) SURTEES SOCIETY.
Testamenta Eboracensia or Wills registered at York illustrative of the history, manners, language, statistics, of the Province of York from the year 1800 downwards. Part I. J.B. Nichols/Surtees Soc. 1836. xii,425pp. With a 12page addition of the rules of the Surtees Society established in 1834. Index. Publishers' cloth, stained & faded. £8

478) T.,R.
The Tenants Law: a Treatise very Useful for Tenants & Farmers of all Kindes, and all other Persons whatsoever...also Parish Law, as to Poor Apprentices, Bastardy etc. fit for all persons to know. For Samuel Speed. 1666. 1st edition. 12mo. (xii),181,(vi)pp. With 6 page publishers' cat. Ownership signatures on title. Copious contemp. MS notes relating to a case about land on verso of last leaf. Contemp. sheep, neatly repaired. WING lists 3rd & 4th edition only. S. & M.i.461/13. £300

479) TABRAM, R.
The Law of Landlord and Tenant,(wherein of Lodgings) with an introductory view of the origin and foundation of Property in Land, and of the different Estates into which it is now divided. (with) an appendix,of requisite forms of notice etc. Stamford. printed for the author by Drakard and Wilson/London. Baldwin etc. 1823. 1st edition. xxvii, 217pp. Disbound in modern wraps. S. &M.ii.350. £30

480) TAIT, George.
A Summary of the Powers and Duties of a Justice of the Peace in Scotland, in alphabetical order, with forms of proceedings etc. in Public and Private Cases and those of a Private Person in Criminal Cases. Edinburgh. J.Anderson. 1815. 2nd edition. viii,373,(1),54pp. Some sl. spotting in prelims. and at end. Contemp. calf, rubbed. S.&M.v.120.£20

481) "TANNER" Car Brake Patent.
U.S. Circuit Court, Northern District of Illinois, in Equity. Thomas Sayles v. the Chicago and North Western Railroad Company. Opinion of his Honor Judge Drummond, sustaining the validity of the "Tanner" Car Brake Patent against the so-called Millholland Brake, and other Defences. N.Y. Baker & Godwin. 1866. 12pp. Orig. printed wraps. Fine. £12

TRIALS.
488) SACHEVERELL, Henry. (1672-1724)
The Tryal...before the House of Peers, for High Crimes and Misdemeanors. 1710. 1st Edition. Folio. 328pp. First privilege leaf. MS index of counsel etc. Contemp. panelled calf, spine gilt, joints worn. £50

Sacheverell was impeached for preaching against the toleration of dissenters, the justice of the revolution of 1688, & the conduct of the government. He received a mild sentence and became a national hero for his defence of Church & People against tyranny & corruption.

489) .....Another copy. As above, but with
...The Bishop of Salisbury's and the Bishop of Oxford's Speeches in the House of Lords on the First Article of Impeachment of Dr. S.... John Morphew. 1710. 12pp.
...The Bishop of Lincoln's and Norwich's Speeches....12pp.
...The Lord's Protest; the names of Right Hon. Peers, who protested against some Proceedings...with their Reasons...1710.(ii)8pp.
Contemp. calf, sl. rubbed, lacking label. Very good copy. £60

490) .....Another copy as *488,but printed by Jacob Tonson and with
...COKE, Arundel alias COOKE & John Woodburne LABOURER.
The Tryal and condemnation of..for Felony, in slitting the nose of Edward Crispe Gent. Folio. John Darby. 1723. 1st edition. 38pp. privilege leaf, copy of indictment.
...LAYER, Christopher. The whole proceeding upon the Arraignment, Tryal, Conviction and Attainder of..for High Treason in compassing and imagining the death of the King. Folio. S. Buckley. 1722. 1st edition. (iv),152pp. Privilege leaf.
.....A True and Exact Copy of the Paper delivered by Christopher Layer, Esq.; at the place of Execution, to the Under-Sheriff of Middlesex on Friday the 17th of this instant May. Folio. James Roberts. 1723. 5pp. Last half page are adverts.
4 items in 1 vol. Contemp. panelled calf, rubbed, spine frayed and joints split and weak. £70

491) TRIALS & HISTORICAL PAPERS.
LAYER, Christopher..the whole proceeding upon the arraignment, Tryal ..of...for High Treason..in the Court of King's Bench. Folio. 1722. 1st edition. (ii),152pp. Privilege leaf.
.....A report from the Committee appointed by..the House of Commons to examine Christopher Layer...Reported...by the Hon. William Pulteney. Folio. Jacob Tonson. 1722. 1st edition. (iv),76pp. Privilege leaf.
.....Appendixes referr'd to in the report from the Committee...Folio. Jacob Tonson. 1722. 1st edition. (iv),31pp. Privilege leaf.
Papers relating to: 1) Captain Charles Halstead. 10pp. 2) Christopher Layer. 64pp. 3) an Intended Insurrection. (iv)pp. 4) John Plunket.44p. 5) the Bishop of Rochester. 32pp. 6) George Kelly.(iv),58pp. 7)Dennis Kelly. 20pp. 8) John Sample. 10pp. 9) the Duke of Norfolk and others. 20pp. 10) to Scotland. 16pp. 11) to Ireland.(ii),2pp.
All 1723, with fly-titles only. 14 items in 1 vol. Contemp. panelled calf, gilt dec'd spine, spine frayed and joints weak. £80

492) TURNER, Edward F.
Legal T. Leaves...1903. 1st edition. Orig. pictorial cloth, rubbed £3

493) TURNER, E.S.
May it please your Lordship. 1971. 1st edition. Plates. dw. £3

494) TURNER, J.W.C.
KENNY'S outlines of Criminal Law. CUP 1962. 18th edition. Orig. cloth, sl. faded. £10

This work first appeared in 1902 and it is characteristic of Kenny's work which has won its most lasting distinction, that he saw the connection between criminal law and all the social sciences more clearly than any English legal writer before him had done, and he thus laid the foundation for the conception of criminal science as one composite subject of which criminal law is a part.

495) .....Another copy. CUP 1966. 19th edition. Orig. cl. sl. marked. £10

496) TYTLER, Alexander Fraser.
An Essay on Military Law, and the Practice of Courts Martial. Edinburgh. 1800. 1st edition. xii,428pp. Index, appendices. Modern cloth S. &M. i,603. £30

The author, who was Judge-Advocate, offers several criticisms of Blackstone, whose pronouncements on military law had been accepted as authority in his time.

497) U.S. PATENT OFFICE.
July 29, 1869. In the matter of Interference. Tal. P. Shaffner vs. Geo. M. Mowbray, manufacture of Nitro-Glycerine. n.d. U.S.A. H. Polkinhorn & Co. 7pp. Orig. printed wraps. Fine. £15

498) UNITED STATES SUPREME COURT.
December Term, 1870. Seymour & Morgan vs. D.M. Osborne et al. Harvester Patents. Opinion by Mr. Justice Clifford. n.d. 17pp. Orig.printed wraps. Presentation copy to Prof. B.S.Fredrick from...Baldwin.£15

499) .....Another copy. No presentation inscription. £12

500) VACHER, Thomas B.
A Pocket Digest of Stamp Duties, and of judicial decisions thereon, with directions on stamped instruments and an appendix of Stamp Acts, tables of duties etc. 1865. 6th edition. Orig. cloth faded & sl. rbbd. £8

501) VALLANCE, Aylmer.
Very Private Enterprise;an anatomy of fraud and high finance. 1955. 1st edition. Orig. cloth. £6

502) VAUGHAN, Sir John. (1603-1674)
Reports and Arguments in the Common Pleas, being all of them Special Cases and to which is added a Tract concerning process out of the Courts at Westminster into Wales, pub'd by his son Edward Vaughan

VAUGHAN, Sir John. Reports and Arguments..cont.
502) ....(1665-74). Folio. Thomas Roycroft...1677. 1st edition. (xiv), 420,(55)pp. Fine engraved fp. port. by R. White, table, partly Black letter. Contemp. calf, rubbed, top of spine sl. worn & frayed. Very good clean copy. WING V 130. S. &M. i,310/126. £95

In 1654 Vaughan acted as one of Selden's executors and shared in the bequest of his estate with Sir Matthew Hale and Roland Jewkes. They preserved his valuable collection of books, amounting to 8000 volumes, by presenting it to the Bodleian Library, where it was deposited in a noble room, later known by the name of the Selden End.

503) VERNON, Thomas. (1654-1721)
Cases argued and adjudged in the High Court of Chancery. (1681-1720) 2 vols. Folio. E. &R. Nutt etc. 1726/8. 1st edition. Engraved fp. port., privilege leaf before title in both vols., indices. Contemp. calf, worn, joints cracked. S. &M. i,349/42. £90

Vernon's clear & concise reports preserve many important cases from Lord Nottingham's Chancellorship.

504) VICARS, John. (1582-1652)
Magnalia dei Anglicana. Or, Englands Parliamentary- Chronicle. Containing a full and faithfull Series, and Exact Narration of all the most memorable Parliamentary Mercies, and mighty (if not miraculous) deliverances, great and glorious Victories, and admirable successes, of the Counsels and Armies of this present Parliament both by Sea and Land...from 1640..to this present yeer. 1646. Compiled in 4 Parts... and to our most renowned Generall, Sir Thomas Fairfaxes late famous Actions, in the West, and the happy (because unbloody) rendition of Oxford...Imprinted in London. J. Rothwell & Tho. Underhill. 1646. 1st collected edition. 3 vols. Sm.4to. Later calf, rebacked.Fine. WING V 319 £120
Vicars was a fanatic who in the rebellion distinguished himself as a zealot for the Presbyterian cause, and wrote against the king,bishops, and independents.
The above is a collection of three of his works.

505) VINNIUS, Arnold. (1588-1657)
Commentarius...editio ultima..aucta indicibus decisionum et constitutionum. Leyden. 1709. 4to. Engraved dedication leaf. (iv),828,(xxiv)pp Modern half red morocco. Fine. £40

506) .....In quattuor libros institutionum Imperialium Commentarius. Amsterdam. D. Elzevir. 1665. 4th edition, revised. 4to. Red & black title. (xii),888,(xx)pp. Index. Lacks front endpaper. Contemp. vellum. Sl. soiled. WILLEMS 1367. £50

This commentary was undertaken to clarify the Institutes and is printed from an annotated copy found among the author's papers. Some further remarks by Prof. Johan Schulting of Nijmegen (father of Anton) are inserted.

VINNIUS, Arnold..cont.
507) ...Institutionum, sive elementorum, libri quatuor, notis perpetuis...illustrati. Leyden. 1709. 12mo. Engraved title & folding engraved dedication. (xxii),632,(xxiv)pp. Index. Contemp. vellum, later label. £30

508) .....Jurisprudentiae Contractae sive Partitionum Juris Civilis libri IV..Adjectus est huic editioni Tractatus de Jurisdictione, Pactis, Transactionibus & Collationibus. Rotterdam. A. Leers. 1664. 3rd edition, corrected. xxx,1096,(xx)pp. Index. Contemp. vellum, sl. soiled. Bookplate. £60

509) VOET, Johannes. (—1714)
Commentarius ad Pandectas, in quo praeter Romani juris principia... jus etiam hoiliernum, & praecipuae fori quaestiones excutiuntur. 1698/1704. Leyden, apud Abrahamum de Hondt. 1st edition. 2 vols.Folio. (xvi),980,(lxx)/(viii),980,(lxxviii)pp. Latin text. Woodcut devices on title, index, final blanks. Later vellum. Spine in vol.1 frayed. A fine set. £120

Voet's influential commentary, whose second volume appeared six years later, is much concerned with current problems and especially those of maritime law.

510) ....Another set, as above. Contemp. vellum. Covers torn & spine repaired in vol.2., also some browning of text. £120

511) ....Volume 1 of the above work only. Folio. 1698. 1st edition. Contemp. calf, rubbed & worn. £50

512) .....De Jure Militari. Amsterdam. Apud. J. Waesbergio. 1706. New edition, revised & corrected. (iv),347,(xvii),19pp. Index, errata, appendix. Contemp. vellum. Bookplate. £50

513) VON der RECK, Nordius.
Disputatio juridica de piscatione. Strassburg. J. Stadel. 1662. 1st edition. 4to. (iv),20pp. Some head-margins shaved. 19th century half morocco. Westwood & Satchell 175. £60

This thesis on the definition, rights, uses, & penalties of fishing (with some reference to hunting & hawking) reflects the high importance which these sports assumed in the life & thought of the German nobility.

514) WADE, E.C.S. & G. Godfrey PHILLIPS.
Constitutional Law. An outline of the law and practice of the constitution, including central and local government and the constitutional relations of the British Commonwealth. 1961. 6th ed. by E.C.S.Wade. Orig. cloth, faded and marked. £4

515)(WADE, J.)
The Cabinet Lawyer or Popular Digest of the Laws of England..also a Dictionary of Law Terms....16mo.1829. 5th edition. xxviii,676,(ii)pp. Calf-backed boards, rubbed & hinges worn & weak.S.&M.ii.368. £18

516) WARD, Leslie ("Spy") illustrations.
The Book of the Bench. 4to. 1909. 1st collected. LARGE PAPER COPY, Limited edition. 39 mounted coloured plates. Orig. vellum, sl. soiled. Foot of spine neatly repaired, lacks ties. £120

Portraits (reproduced from Ward's original water-colours, not from the published lithographs) and biographies of judges from "Vanity Fair".

517) WATKINS, Charles.
Treatise on Copyholds. 2 vols. 1797/9. 1st edition. Indices. Lib. stamps, endpaper browned. Modern cloth. S.&M.i.406/72. £80

Covers many different subjects from the doctrine of Manors to Courts, Customs and the "Doctrine of Free-Bench".

518) .....Another copy. Vol.1 only. 1797. Complete in itself. Contemp. calf, rebacked. £35

The second volume was published in 1799.

519) WELSH LAW.
WOTTON, W. Cyfreithjeu Hywel Dda ac eraill, seu Leges Wallicae Ecclesiasticae & Civiles Hoeli boni et aliorum Walliae Principum....Notes & glossary illustrated by G. Wotton....preface by William Clarke. Welsh & Latin text. G.Bowyer. 1730. 1st and only edition. Folio. (iv), 40,586,(20)pp. Index. Engraved vignette on dedication page and two others. Modern cloth, rebacked. S. &M.i.581/49. £150

520) WHITE, F.T. & O.D.TUDOR.
A Selection of Leading Cases in Equity with notes. A. Maxwell.1849. xxiv,640,8pp. Index, publisher's cat. Endpapers spotted & dust-stnd. Orig. cloth, paper label, inner hinges repaired. S.&M.ii.377. £20

A further volume appeared in 1850 and there are editions up to 1928.

521) WHITEHEAD, Benjamin.
Church Law: a concise Dictionary of Statutes, Canons, Regulations & decided Cases affecting the Clergy and Laity. 1899. 2nd edition. Orig. cloth, sl. rubbed & stained. S.&M.ii.379. £10

522) WILLARD, Joseph A.
Half a century with judges and lawyers. Boston and N.Y. Riverside P. Cambridge. 1895. 1st edition. iv,(i),371pp. Index, fp. port. Orig. cloth, sl. marked. Very good copy. £20

523) WILLIAMS, Glanville.
Criminal Law. The General Part. 1961. 2nd edition. liv,929pp. Tables of cases, statutes, subordinate legislation, index. Orig. cloth. £5

524) WILLIAMS, Montagu.
Leaves of a Life. 1890. 1st edition. 2 vols. Fp., facss letters. Appendix, index. Orig. cloth, sl. stained. £10

525) WILLIAMS, T.
Every Man his Own Lawyer, or a complete Law Library...with an appendix. 1812. 1st edition. viii,632,(viii)pp. Index, adverts. Contemp. panelled calf, sl. rubbed & faded, lacking label on spine. Fine. £65

526) WILLIAMS, T.W.
The Whole Law relative to the Duty and Office of a Justice of the Peace. Edited by H.N.Tomlins. 1812. 3rd edition. 4 vols. Folding table, index. Contemp. calf, sl. stained, 1 joint sl. cracked. S.&M. ii,384. £50

Last edition of this rival to Burns.

527) WILLIAMSON, J. Bruce.
The History of the Temple. 1925. 2nd edition. Illustrations, appendices, index. xiv,690pp. Orig. cloth, sl. spotted. £15

528) WILTON, George Wilton.
Fingerprints, history, law and romance. Introd. Robert Heindl. 1938. 1st edition. xx,318pp. Illustrations, folding table, index. Orig. cloth. d.w. Fine. £10

529) WINES, Frederick Howard.
Punishment and Reformation. An historical sketch of the rise of the penitentiary system. 1895. 1st edition. xi,339pp. Index. Orig. cloth. £10

Sketches originally delivered before the State University of Wisconsin in 1893.

530) WISSENBACH, Johan Jacob.
In Libros VII. Priores Codicis de Justiniani, repetitae praelectionis, commentationes Cathedrarie...2 vols. Sm.4to. Franeker ex typographia Jacobi Horrei. 1701. (x),364/(vi),371-760pp in two columns. Fine engraved fp. port., title of vol.1 in red & black, both titles with vignettes. Contemp. sprinkled calf. One corner and spines sl. rubbed and faded. Fine set. £80

531)(WOOD, Thomas)
A New Institute of the Imperial or Civil Law, with notes shewing in some principal cases....how the Canon Law, the Laws of England, and the Laws and Customs of other Nations differ from it. 12mo. W.B. for Richard Sare. 1704. 1st edition. (2),xvii,(7),361,(8),(2)pp. Table, preface, publisher's advert. leaf. Contemp. panelled calf, gilt, hinges weak, spine ends sl. frayed. Very good. S.&M.i.613/16. £75
Superseded by Blackstone's work who considered it a "valuable performance."

537) YARDLEY, D.C.M.
Introduction to British Constitutional Law. 1960. 1st edition. cl. £3

538) YORKSHIRE.
The Year Book for the use of the Justices of the West Riding..1901-2, (1912-3). Wakefield, 1902(-13). 12 vols. Folding tables. Orig. buckram, faded, fore-margins of covers stained. £90

In addition to lists of personnel & sundry matters similar to those found in the standard justices' manuals, these year-books contain intresting statistics, financial & otherwise, of the Yorkshire police.

539) YOUNG, Walter A.
A Vade Mecum, or Table, containing the substance of such Statutes, ...wherein...Justices of the Peace are inabled to act..in the Sessions and out...with an epitome of Mr. Stamford's Pleas of the Crown. John Streater. 1663. 7th edition. 12mo. (xxii),186,(ii)pp. Long contemp. MSS instructions on front blank, telling the foreman of an Inquest what he may and may not do. Ownership signature on title. Mod. calf. WING Y 96. S. &M. i. 233/82. £180

ADDENDA

540) ANCIENT LAWS and INSTITUTES of ENGLAND,
comprising Laws enacted under the Anglo-Saxon Kings from Aethelbirht to Cnut, with an English translation of the Saxon, the Laws called Edward the Confessor's; the Laws of William the Conqueror and those ascribed to Henry I; also Monumenta Ecclesiastica Anglicana from the 7th to 10th century, and the ancient Latin version of the Anglo-Saxon Laws, with a glossary. Edited by B. Thorpe. Folio. 1840. x,(vi), 548,79pp. Additional remarks, concordance, glossary and indexes. Endpapers spotted, otherwise fine clean copy. Orig. embossed cloth, stained and spine worn, split at ends. S. &M. i.39/1. £90

541) A DIGEST of the LAWS of ENGLAND,
being a continuation of Lord Chief Baron COMYNS's Digest (5 vols. 1762-7) brought down to the present time. By a Gentleman of the Inner Temple. Folio. 1776. (iv),623pp. Uncut, fine paper, original grey boards, marked, corners & edges rubbed, backstrip frayed. Fine clean copy. See S. & M.i.17/5 (under Comyns). £50

542) WALLACE, George.
A System of the Principles of the Law of Scotland. Edinburgh. Folio. A. Millar etc. 1760. 1st edition. Vol. 1, no more published. (iv), xxiv,592pp. Uncut. Half morocco, marbled sides. Sl. stained & rubbed. Some sl. browning & two ink stains on p.29. Very good. S.&M.v.123. £80

543) WELSH LAW
Ancient Laws and Institutes of Wales, comprising Laws supposed to be

(WOOD, Thomas) A New Institute...cont.
532) ....Another copy. In four Books....as an introduction, a treatise of the first principles of laws in general, of their nature and design, and of the interpretation of them. 1721. Third edition, corrected. (ii),144,xvi,414,(x)pp. Index. Modern calf-backed boards. S.&M.i.613/16. £55

This third edition contains the treatise of the First Principles of Laws in General for the first time.

533) WOOLSEY, Theodore D.
Essay on Divorce and Divorce Legislation. With special reference to the United States. N.Y. 1869. 1st edition. 308,4pp. Index, appendix, booklist. Orig. cloth, spine sl. frayed. £25

The essay is a reprint of articles which appeared in the New Englander for 1867 & 1868 with a number of changes and additions. The author felt that the divorce laws of the State at that time were too lax.

534) WRIGHT, Andrew.
Court-Hand Restored, or, the Student's Assistant in reading Old Deeds, Charters, Records etc. With an appendix...ancient names of places in G.B. and Ireland...C.T.Martin. 1879. 4to. 9th edition, corrected and enlarged with 7 new plates by C.T.Martin. Fine modern half calf. S. &M. i.14/20. £40

535) WRIGHT, Cecil A.
Cases on the Law of Torts. 1963. 3rd edition. Orig. cloth. £10

Prof. Wright was Dean and professor of law at the Faculty of Law of the University of Toronto.

536) WYNNE, William. (1734-1784)
The Life of Sir Leoline JENKINS (1623-1685), judge of the High Court of Admiralty and prerogative Court of Canterbury etc., Ambassador & Plenipotentiary for the general peace at Cologne and Nimeguen and Secretary of State to Charles II. With a complete series of letters... Folio. 2 vols. Joseph Downing. 1724. Fine engraved fp. port., in vol.1. Endpapers and blanks browned otherwise a Fine copy. Contemp. calf, very rubbed at edges and spine. Joints weak & sl. frayed. S.&M.i.355/9. £180

Wynne was a law writer and is also supposed to be the author of "Lives of eminent Lawyers", but is better known for his work "Eunomus". The want of professional reports of cases decided in these times in the High Court of Admiralty and Prize Appeal Court of England, is in some measure supplied by the very judicious reports and letters which, in the intervals between 1663 and 1680, Sir Leoline was called upon to address to King Charles II and his Privy Council & to the Lords Commissioners of Prizes.
This work is considered a rich collection of precedents on the maritime law of nations.

WELSH LAW...cont.
543)....enacted by Howel the Good modified by subsequent Regulations under the Native Princes prior to the Conquest by Edward I and Anomalous Laws consisting principally of Institutions which by the Statute of Ruddlan were admitted to continue in force; with an English translation of the Welsh text. With indexes and glossary. Edited by A. Owen. Folio. Issued by the Record Commissioners. 1841. (iv)xv,(viii), 1005pp. Some text illus. Orig. embossed cloth, sl. marked and spine ends frayed. Very good. S. &M. i.577/2. £120

See also *519.

A fine collection of STATUTES of BAREBONES PARLIAMENT, passed by the Government of the English Commonwealth between the dismissal of the Long Parliament in April 1653 and Cromwell's assumption of the title of Lord Protector in the following December.
Cromwell prepared the way for his protectorship by means of these statutes, most of which appoint or regulate Committees of one kind or another. It was his design to convey all the effective powers of government to bodies whose faith was assured and whose want of number promised ease of management in any emergency and his provisions concerning the Admiralty & the Tax system outlived his time, even though all his enactments were annulled at the Restoration & excluded from subsequent collections.
The Statutes are here arranged chronologically and they follow the usual format of the 17th century, whereby all the statutes of any one session were regarded as a single volume, with continuous pagination and signatures. Most early statutes now extant have at some time been bound in larger volumes & subsequently removed; but these (although repaired)are in their original form, which incidentally proves that even those which have no title-pages are genuinely separate issues & should be listed as such by works of references. They are all extremely scarce, having been made objects of destruction by triumphant monarchists after 1660.
There are also a selection of BROADSHEETS on which certain statutes were presented in abridged form for public display.

Details on application. The collection £1,200

We have a large stock of LAW BOOKS not listed in this catalogue and we are always happy to quote individual items to customers.
We also search for BOOKS WANTED and try and obtain out-of-print titles.

We buy most titles of law books printed before 1850 for stock and are always interested to hear of collections and duplicates from individuals or institutions.

FROGNAL RARE BOOKS

18 CECIL COURT CHARING CROSS ROAD LONDON WC2N 4HE ENGLAND

01-240-2815

(1982)

LAW AND LEGAL HISTORY

CATALOGUE 55

1) ACTS and LAWS of the STATE of CONNECTICUT, in AMERICA.
Folio. New-London: Timothy Green; Printer to the Governor and Company of the State of Connecticut. 1784. 1st edition. 8,6,(ii),311pp. Printers' device on title. Some staining of lower half in first 40 pages, sl. browned. Disbound as issued with marbled stiff wraps, repaired. SABIN 15760. BATES 245, 253. INTERESTING ASSOCIATION COPY. With the bookplate "Hoar" Attorney General F. Hoar.
ALSO JONATHAN TRUMBULL'S COPY with his signature on title; portait of Trumbull loosely inserted. Trumbull is the well-known Poet & Jurist. £300

This is the first edition of compilation of 1784 and first supplement., of the BLUE LAWS of Connecticut; a collection of the earliest statistics and judicial proceedings of that Colony; being an exhibition of the rigorous morals and legislation of the Puritans.

2) AMAYA, Francisco de.
Observationum Juris libri tres. Last edition revised by the author. 4to. Geneva. Apud Johannem de la Planche. 1633. (xvi),459,(xxiv)pp. Publishers' device on title, fine engraved chapter headings and initial letters. Contemp. vellum, sl. stained. FINE COPY. DULCET'S Manual del Librero Hispano-Americano 10872. Latin text. £200

Amaya was a Spanish jurist, native of Antequera from the province of Granada and lived in the first half of the 17th century. He was a professor at Salamanca. He wrote and edited several legal works but the above is his most important, first published in 1625, and several editions after 1633.

3) AMERICAN BAR ASSOCIATION.
Official Report of the UNIVERSAL CONGRESS of LAWYERS and JURISTS held at St. Louis, Missouri, U.S.A., Sept. 1904. Under the auspices of the Universal Exposition and the American Bar Association. 4to. St. Louis. 1905. xix,423pp Index. Some sl. spotting. FINE MORROCCO BINDING, gilt decorated, inner dentelles, raised bands, gilt lettering, t.e.g. FINE COPY. £40

4) .....VISIT to ENGLAND, SCOTLAND and IRELAND, 1924.
Memorial Volume. N.Y. Feb. 1926. 4to. (viii),444,(i),55pp. LIMITED EDITION of 250 COPIES, no.41. Numerous portraits and illustrations, appendix. Half morocco, gilt decorated spine with raised bands and gilt lettering, t.e.g. Upper part sl. faded. FINE COPY. £60

5) ANDREWS, William, (Edited by)
Legal Lore: Curiosities of Law & Lawyers. 1897. 1st ed. (vi),280,(vi)pp. Index, booklist, fp., Orig. ribbed cloth, t.e.g., Fp. loose. Fine. £20

A collection of essays by a variety of authors on all aspects of laws, trials etc.

6).....Old-Time Punishments.1890. 1st. Fp (Bank restriction note after Cruikshank) & text illus. x,252pp. Index. Orig. b'ram, t.e.g. Faded. £20

7) ANGLESEY, First Earl (Arthur Annesley)(Late Lord Privy-Seal)
Privileges of the House of Lords and Commons argued and states in two Conferences between both Houses. 1671. (with) a discourse wherein the Rights of the House of Lords are asserted, (also) Precedents touching the Right and Manner of Impeachment in Parliament, collected by Sir W.W. 16mo. (xxiv),179,(4)pp. J. Nutt. 1702. 1st edition. Interesting publishers' booklist. FINE PANELLED & EMBOSSED CALF, newly rebacked with raised bands, label. S. & M.i.140/1. £120

8) ARCHBOLD, John Frederick. (Editor)
Dr. Robinson's Magistrate's Pocket Book, or an epitome of the duties and practice of a Justice of the Peace, out of Sessions, alphabetically arranged... with an index. John Richards...1837. 2nd editions with alterations & additions. xx,466,(40)). Endpaper sl. spotted. Contemp. half calf. S.&M.ii.303. £30

Dr. Robinson's second edition, but the first with Archbold as editor.

9) AUSTRALIAN ORDINANCES of SYNOD.
The Constitutions and Ordinances of Synod of the Diocese of Sydney (1866-19 08) Published by the Authority. Sydney. W.M.Madgwick...1908. 736pp. Index. Orig. cloth, paper label, sl. faded, sm. ex lib. stamps. £18

10) BENTHAM, Jeremy. (1748-1832)
Theory of Legislation. Translated from the French of Etienne Dumont, by R. Hildreth. 1871. 2nd edition. xv,472pp. Uncut & unopened. Modern cloth, label. S. &M.ii.27. £35

First published in French as "Traites de Legislation Civile et Penale" in 1802 in 3 volumes. Dumont had been sent some of Bentham's manuscripts by Romilly & was greatly impressed by their originality and edited them, for many years acting also as a sort of official interpreter, between the great jurist and the world at large.

11) BLACKSTONE, Sir William. 1723-1780)
An Analysis of the Laws of England..Oxford. Clarendon Press. 1762. 5th edition. lxxvii,(vi),189,(14)pp. Index. Front 2 blanks sl. frayed in margin, ex lib. bookplate on verso of cover. Contemp. calf, gilt dec'd spine, label. Rubbed. S & M.i.27/6. ELLER 221. £75

The preface, dated 2 Nov. 1758, is amended in this edition by footnotes on p.(iii), and (iv), to conform to the present edition. The two tables found in the first four editions of the "Analysis" are omitted in the 5th; a note on p.(ix) refers the reader to the author's Law Tracts, which contain these tables. Postscript p. lxxii, concerns the Statutes relative to the Vinerian professorship, fellowships and scholarships at Oxford University.

12) ..... Another copy. 1771. 6th edition. xi,(iv),230,(14)pp. 2 folding tables, appendix, index. Contemp. calf, label. FINE COPY. S. & M.i.27/6. ELLER 223. £80

This revised edition is the last issued by Blackstone. In the undated preface, he states "The Commentaries...- of which this work is the outline or abstract - have since the publication of the 5th edition been made public, with a few alterations and improvements...principally in point of subdivision and method. This edition is therefore accommodated to those alterations and improvements; and will be found to correspond as exactly with the printed Commentaries, as the former impressions were calculated to answer to the lectures then read by the professor".

13) ....Commentaries on the Laws of England. Oxford Clarendon Press. 1765-9. FIRST EDITION, including the RARE SUPPLEMENT at the end of VOLUME 1. 4 vols. 4to. FINE MODERN ANTIQUE CALF, RAISED BANDS, LABELS ON SPINES. S. & M.i.27. ROTHSCHILD 407/8. PRINTING and the MIND of MAN 212. ELLER 1. £2,500

14) .....Another set. Volumes 1 & 2: second edition; volumes 3 & 4 1st edition. 1766-9. Contemp. calf, sl. rubbed. £800

15) .....Another edition. 1766-70. DUBLIN. 4 vols. 8vo. The first octavo edition published; this Dublin edition was pirated and, with the exception of the misprint of "Willaim" for "William" on title of vol.1, follows the text of the first Oxford edition, reproducing in full Blackstone's undated preface, wherein he anticipates a "surreptitious impression". ELLER 3. £400

....Other fine octavo edition in stock.

16) BLACKSTONE, Sir William cont.
Reports of Cases determined in the several Courts of Westminster-Hall from 1746-1779. With a preface containing memoirs of his life (by James Clitherow) Folio. 2 vols. H.M. Law Printers. 1781. 1st edition. xxl,(12),iv,679,38/(xx), 681-1333,46pp. Indices. Bookplate T. Partington. Modern cloth. S.&M.i.293/11. ELLER 225. £200

These reports, with one exception (report of the case of Burgess v. Wheat in vol.1, which was reported by Mr. Fazakerly) were compiled entirely by Blackstone from his own notes, prepared for the Press, even to an index and a table. They comprise a selection from cases decided in 1746-69 (Vol.1) & 1770-79 (Vol.2). Blackstone's "literal errors or omissions" were corrected by the editor, James Clitherow, Blackstone's brother-in-law and executor.

17) .....Tracts, chiefly relating to the Antiquities and Laws of England. Oxford, Clarendon Press. 1771. 3rd edition. 4to. (vi),(iii)-vii,(4),(13)-353,(ii),lxxx,(18),(ii)pp. Illustrations, table. Illustrations consist of tail-pieces, engravings of royal seals, in the tract The Great Charter. The "table of consanguinity" is also engraved and faces p.139. There are three indices. In this copy the error on p.xxi, line 2/3 of "The Great Charter" which appears as a misprint in some copies has been corrected by a reprinted leaf. Contemp. tree calf, gilt, fine marbled endpapers. Sl. rubbed, front lower hinge sl. worn. S. & M.i.30/20. ELLER 240. FINE COPY. £200

The first edition was published with the title "Law Tracts" in two 8vo vols. in 1762. No "second edition" appears to have been published. One tract found in the 1762 edition is omitted in this, and two tracts are included which do not appear in that edition. All the tracts were previously published as separate works, Blackstone subsequently revised the text.
This quarto edition contains the following tracts:
An Analysis of the Laws of England, reprinted from the 6th edition;
An Essay on Collaterial Consanguinity, the tract known as Considerations on Copyholders; Observations on the Oxford Press and the Great Charter of the Forest, with historical introduction.

18) .....FURNEAUX, Philip (1726-1783); Letters to the Hon. Mr. Justice Blackstone, concerning his exposition of the Act of Toleration, and some positions relative to religious liberty. 1771. 2nd edition, revised. PRESENTATION COPY. xxiv,284pp. Modern cloth. S. & M.i.29. ELLER 254. £50

This second edition is with additions and an appendix, containing authentic copies of the argument, prefaces to the first and second editions, and an "advertisement to the first edition" which is the note of apology "for a form of address, which is not suitable ...." Blackstone was appointed a Justice of the Court of Common Pleas on February 9th, 1770.
Furneaux, a dissenting ministery, objected to Blackstone's harsh construction of the Act of Toleration and to his general support of the principle that those who dissent from the established religion deserve to suffer the animadversion of the law. This edition includes among other improvement, Lord Mansfield's speech in Chamberlain of the City v. Evans (1767, House of Lords) wherein it was held that a dissenter elected to an office for which affirmation of the Anglican faith was required was immune from the statutory penalties imposed on those who refused to serve.
See also, 137. SEDGWICK.

19) B(LOUNT), T(homas), (1618-1679)
Fragmenta Antiquitatis. Antient Tenures of Land, and jocular Customs of some Mannors. Richard & Edward Atkins. 1679. 1st edition. (viii),175,(15)pp. Imprimatur leaf before title, index, final errata leaf. WING B 3333. S.&M.i.399/7 Contemp. calf, spine & corners sl. rubbed. Bookplate. £95

19) B(LOUNT), T(homas), cont.
Blount's collection of Singular Copyhold & Petty Serjeanty Tenures was a useful introduction to the mysteries of mediaeval land-holding. We owe to him our knowledge of the Dunmow Flitch, the Black Ram of Enborne, the Tutbury Bull & other curiosities of feudalism.

20) BODIN, Jean. (c.1530-1596)
The Six Bookes of a Common-Weale...out of the French and Latine Copies...by Richard Knolles. 1606. Adam Islip, Impensis G. Bishop. 1st English edition. Folio. (x),794. Title within woodcut border, sl. torn at corners. Notes in contemp. hand inserted as endpapers, front endpaper detached. Notation on various leaves in contemp. hand. Stub of inserted blank between A_2 & 3. Few other leaves sl. defective, sl. dampstained. 17th century calf, spine sl. rubbed and joint of recto loose & torn. S.&M.i.606/9. KRESS 269/18.STC 3139. £250

Bodin was the earliest writer to attempt a theory of government on comparative principles.

21) BOHUN, William.
Privilegia Londoni: or, the Rights, Liberties, Privileges, Laws and Customs of the City of London. John Walthoe. 1723. 3rd edition, with large additions. xvi,498,22pp. Table. Modern calf. S.&M.i.436/27. VERY GOOD COPY. £90

Includes the duties, rights, elections etc., of the magistrates & officers of the City; the nature, jurisdiction and practice of the several courts and statutes and charters relating to the City.

22) THE BOKE for a JUSTYCE of PEACE
Neuer soo wel and diligently set forthe. Londini in aedibus Tho. Berthel regii impress. excus. 1534. FACSIMILE REPRINT Bracebridge Press 1942. LIMITED to 180 copies (149 only actually bound), No.112. PRESENTATION COPY from the printers. Sm.folio, hand set in Venezia type, this book printed in 1942 on paper made prior to the outbreak of war. Half calf, sl. rubbed. FINE. £20

This work was described as the "Stone's Justices Manual" of the 16th century and it preceded the publication in 1579 of Rastell's "Collection of all the statutes from the beginning of Magna Charta".

23) BOUTARIC, F. de.
Traité de Droits Seigneuriaux, et des Matieres Feodales. Toulouse. Gaspard Henault. 1765. (i),(iv),(ii),303,(42)pp. Index. Prelim. pages browned, some marginal worming in some pages towards the end. Contemp. French binding, full calf, gilt dec'd spine; spine ends sl. frayed. French text. £35

Boutaric was professor of French law at the University of Toulouse and a Parliamentary lawyer.

24) BRACTON or BRETTON, Henry de.(died c.1273)
De legibus et consuetudinibus Angliae libri quinq; in varios tractatus distincti...Apud Richardum Tottellum, 1569. 1st edition. Folio. (xvi),444 leaves. Index. Last leaf sl. spotted on lower margin, but a VERY FINE COPY in contemp. calf, rebacked & edges repaired. BEALE T.323. STC 3475. S.&M.i.51/6 £1,200

Bracton's work is the most important early English law treatise, and the first to expound the common law in a mature & independent form. This edition, handsomely printed and edited with a creditable degree of judgement for the time,

24) BRACTON...De legibus...cont.
was not superseded until the publication of Woodbine's critical text early in this century.

25) .....Another copy. 4to. M. Flesher & R. Young. 1640. 2nd edition. (xvi), 444 leaves. Index. Engraved vignette on title & colophon at end. A_6 (index leaf) supplied in fine photographic facsimile; title sl. spotted, some ink annotations; extensive contemp. marginal annotations throughout. Modern dark calf-backed boards. S.&M.i.51/6. STC 3476. £550

The 1640 edition is an unchanged reprint of the first.

26) BRITISH MUSEUM ACTS.
Anno Regni Georgii II...at the Parliament begun...the tenth day of November, 1747...and from thence continued..to the eleventh day of January 1753; being the 6th Session of this present Parliament,1794. General title for first 2 Acts.
i) An Act for the Purchase of the Museum or Collection of Sir Hans Sloane, and the Harleian Collection of Manuscripts and for providing one general repository for the better reception and more convenient use of the said Collection and the Cottonian Library. 5-102pp.
ii) An Act for making perpetual several Laws for Punishment of Persons destroying Turnpikes, Locks and other Works erected by Authority of Parliament. 7pp.
iii) Anno Septimo Georgii III. An Act to enable the Trustees of the British Museum to exchange, sell, or dispose of and duplicates of printed Books, Medals, Coins or other Curiosities. 7pp.
iv) Statutes and Rules relating to the inspection and use of the British Museum and for the better security and preservation of the same. 1768. 74pp.
4 items in 1 volume. Contemp. speckled calf, rebacked. £35

27) BROOKE, Sir Robert. (? - 1558)
1573. LA GRAUNDE ABRIDGEMENT, Collect & Escrie per le Judge tres reverend Syr Robert Brooke...(- La Secounde Part du Grand Abridgement). In aedibus Richardi Tottell, 5th Jan. 1573. 2 parts in 1 volume. French text. Mostly Black Letter. Ornamenttal woodcut title border with ownership inscriptions & occasional inking over of letters and shapes (contemporary). Woodcut initials. Contemporary marginalia & underlining often in red ink. (viii),360/338 leaves. Title & last leaf sl. soiled & frayed at edges, a few leaves at end lightly dampstained. Insignificant marginal worming through one or two leaves at end. Modern calf. Bookplate of T. Thornton (on verso of title) & of R.B. Finlay. BEALE R.469-470. STC 3827. S.&M.i.17/4.McKERROW 196 (title border). £500

Based on the similarly titled work of Fitzherbert, but with new material from the Year Books of the last two Henries & from Brooke's own experience on the Bench.

28) (BRUNSKEL, Percival).
Vindic(ation) of the Case re(lating) to the Greenwax-Fines shewing how the rights and prerogatives of the Crown are diminished, officers enriched and the subjects oppressed by the mismanagement of that revenue. 1684. 2nd edition. Upper outer corners of title and dedication torn and repaired with sm. loss of text (see above). Pagination trimmed. (xvi),100pp. Later calf-backed boards. WING B 5238. S.& M.i.248/5. £50

29) BULLER, (Sir) Francis.
An Introduction to the Law relative to Trials at Nisi Prius. A. Strahan. 1790. 5th edition, corrected with additions to the present time. (xvi),336, (44)pp. Index. A SPECIALLY BOUND COPY INTERLEAVED with NUMEROUS MANUSCRIPT NOTES, including several pages at beginning and end by JOHN MITFORD (First Baron Redesdale, 1748-1830)(Lord Chancellor of Ireland and a member of the Privy Council) with his signature on title and his bookplate. Full calf with two labels (1 lettered J. Mitford's Copy). Sl. rubbed. FINE COPY. £95
S. & M.i.335/3.

See also MITFORD'S own copy of his work "A Treatise on the Pleadings..".

30) CARE, Henry.
English Liberties: or, the Freeborn Subject's Inheritance. Containing Magna Charta, Charta de Foresta. The Statute de Talla gio non concedendo. The Habeas Corpus Act, and several other Statutes; with comments on each of them. Likewise proceedings in appeals of murder, of ship-money, parliaments etc. 16mo. Benj. Harris. 1703. (viii),240pp. Contemp. calf, rubbed, sm. wormhole on upper cover; spine ends sl. frayed. S. & M.i.154/5-8. £60

31) (CHILD, David L. & Stephen BATES)
PROCEEDINGS of the Citizens of Boston favorable to a revision of the Laws in relation to Debtor and Creditor. At a meeting held at the Exchange Coffee House, Boston, on Wednesday evening April 29, 1829, of those citizens who are desirous of devising some measures for the relief of honest and fair debtors for the punishment of fraudulent ones and for the just and impartial distribution of the property of a failing or insolving debtor, among all his creditors, in proportion to their respective claims. Putnam & Hunt. Boston. 12pp. uncut and partly unopened, edges and title sl. duststained. Sewn as issued. Not in Sabin. £45

It includes the constitution of the newly formed "Society for the Promotion of the Rights and Interests of bona fide Creditors, and the benefit and relief of honest Debtors" which was unanimously accepted at a meeting at the Exchange Coffee House on June 3, 1829 with the Hon. Daniel Webster as President.

32) CLERKE, William.
The Triall of Bastardie: that Part of the Second Part of Policie, or manner of Gouernement of the Realme of England: so termed, spirituall, or ecclesiasticall. Annexed, a table of the Leuitical, English and Positiue Canon Catalogues, their concordance and difference. Sm.4to. Adam Islip. 1594. 1st and only edition. (xvi),82,(xxii)pp. 4 folding tables, printers' devices on titles, woodcut ornaments and initials. Moder half calf, rebacked with gilt lettering on spine. FINE COPY with wide margin. STC 5411. BEALE T 327. S. & M. i.475/8. £380

Adam Islip printed in London from 1591 to 1640. He was an apprentice to Hugh Jackson, see Beale p.181.

33) COKE, Sir Edward. (1551-1633)
The Compleate Copy-Holder; wherein is contained a Learned discourse of the antiquity and nature of Manors and Copy-Holds, with the forme of keeping a Copy-Hold Court and Court Baron. Matthew Walbanck etc. 1644. 3rd edition. (iv), 203pp. Woodcut devices. 1st and final blank. Contemp. calf, rebacked. WING C 4913. S. & M.i.399/13. Foot of title (imprint date) shaved. £150

Collates with S. & M.'s 1644 edition, but they state "although the order of keeping a Court and Court Baron is called for by the title of the 1644 edition, it is not to be found in all copies. It was absent from 4 copies examined".

33) COKE, Sir Edward...cont.
It is absent from this and any other copy we have seen.
The publication of this work marks the final triumph of the King's Courts over the feudal Courts which virtually put an end to feudal jurisdiction in England. It is a book of first class importance.

34) .....Of all the long line of Judges who have rendered England famous among the nations for the excellence and impartiality of the administration of Justice, the chief place has been unhesitatingly awarded to Coke. His stand for the independence of judges and the rule of law made him famous among his contemporaries; his skill in propounding and maintaining legal proportions was a potent factor in restating the common law as it had developed in mediaeval precedents, so that it became a system capable of congrouous expansion, a body of rules apt for the settlement of the affairs of a great nation. His Institutes and Reports became classics.
REPORTS. These were published in 11 volumes between 1600-15. They were so highly regarded by the old lawyers as to be cited simply as "Reports" without the author's name. A COMPLETE SET, nearly all in FIRST EDITIONS. Uniformly bound in CONTEMPORARY CALF, newly rebacked. All volumes with the contemporary signature on title "Rich. Hickes...1680". One or two of the earlier volumes have some slight staining but no spotting, a few marginal annotations in the hand of the owner of the signature; all with first and last blanks. Preliminary "Lectori" in Latin, prefaces in English, Text in French, Black Letter. S. & M. i.295-6/31. The 11 volume set £2,000

PART 1. Thomae Wight. 1601. Engraved title, (iii),177,(i) leaves.
S. & M. gives 1600 as the first edition, an undated edition and then this as the third... STC 5493 , although giving the date as 1600, makes this the entry for the first edition.

Le SECOND PART. Thomae Wight.1602. 1st edition. (vi),94 leaves. Printer's device on title, engraved chapter headings. STC 5495.

Le TIERCE PART. Thomae Wight 1602. 1st edition. (variant) (xviii),91 leaves. Printer's device on title, engraved chapter heading. (first 9 leaves stained) STC 5499. (Variant edition published by the Companie of Stationers STC 5500)

Le QUART PART. Thomae Wight. 1604. 1st edition. (x),128 leaves. Device, engraved headings. STC 5502.

QUINTA PARS. the FIFT PART. Latin/English title. Companie of Stationers. 1607. 3rd edition. (iii),127,(i) leaves. Device & vignette on title, engraved chapter headings. STC 5504.

La SIZE PART. Societie of Stationers. 1607. 1st edition. (variant). (ix),80, (1) leaves. Device, vignette on title, engraved headings. STC 5509. Both variants are published by the Societie of Stationers.

La SEPT PART. Societie of Stationers. 1608. 1st edition. (variant). (v),45, (i) leaves. Device & vignette on title; engraved chapter headings, some staining . STC 5511.

La HUICTME PART. Societie of Stationers. 1611. 1st edition (variant) No device, but "London". (xv),173 leaves. Vignette on title, engr. headings.STC 5513

LA NEUFME PART. Societie of Stationers. 1627. 3rd ed. (xvi),143 leaves. Vignette, device, engr. headings. STC 5517.

La DIXME PART. Societie of Stationers. 1629. 3rd ed. (not in S. & M) (xxv), 145 leaves. Vignette, device, engr. headings. STC 5520 (give 1627-no 1629)

La UNZME PART. Asignes of John More Esquire.1631. 5th ed. (v),100(for 101) leaves. Vignette....STC 5524.

35) A COLLECTION of the several STATUTES, and parts of STATUTES, now in force, relating to High Treason, and misprision of High Treason together with a form and method of Trial of Commoners in cases of High Treason... 16mo. R. Gosling. 1723. 44,(iii)pp. Contemp. notes on endpapers, table, priviledge leaf before title. Contemp. calf, rubbed, rebacked. This edition not in S. & M. but see i.367/6 for earlier editions. £65

36) COLLYN, Nicholas.
A Briefe Summary of the Lawes and Statutes of England, so far forth as the same do concern the Office of Justices of the Peace, Sheriffs etc. By T.L. for Mathew Walbancke. 1655. 4th edition. 12mo. xxii,192pp. Small piece of blank margin of title torn away, one or two wormholes running through first portion. Ownership signatures on title. Modern calf. WING C 5397. S.&M.i. 226/21. £250

37) (COOKE,E.)
Argumentum Anti-Normannicum: or, an Argument proving...that William, Duke of Normandy, made no Absolute Conquest of England. By John Darby. 1682. 1st ed. Engraved frontispiece. (x),164pp. Contemp. calf, later label, rebacked. WING C 4907a.S. & M.i.111/1.FROM THE LIBRARY OF EVELYN. £150

Cooke (not Sir Edward Coke, in spite of Wing's attribution) supports Petyt's Saxonist theory of the origin of Parliament; his argument is that the "Conquest" was merely an incident in the development of the constitution, and not the beginning of a new order.

38) CORPUS JURIS CIVILIS. (INSTITUTIONUM D. JUSTINIANI)
recognoverunt adnotationibusque criticis instructum. Edited by D. Albertus, D. Mauritius Fratres Kriegelii, D. Aemilius Herrman & D. Eduardus Osenbrueggen. Lipsiae. (Leipzig) sumtibus Baumgaertneri. 1865. 4to. 3 vols. (iv),992/xxvi,799/(iv),viii,(ii),893,(2)pp. Half calf, sl. rubbed. £50

39) COVERT, Nicholas.
Scrivener's Guide; Forms of Precedents of all sorts of business. Charles Harper. 1695. 1st edition. (xxxviii),447,(i)pp. Table, licence leaf before title, booklist. Signature of previous owner "Thomas Carew", his bookplate and long 5 page hand-written letter signed by Mary Carew a later member of the family. Contemp. calf, rebacked. FINE COPY. S.&M.i.267/54. WING C 6632. £90

Nicholas Covert: one of the Attorneys of the Court of Common Pleas.
Thomas Carew was a lawyer in the Middle Temple and wrote a notebook of cases & legal diary 1720-60; also a book on elections in 1755, mentioned in Mrs. Carew's letter.

40) COWEL, John. (1554-1611)
The Institutes of the Lawes of England, digested into the method of the Civill or Imperiall Institutions. Useful for all Gentlemen who are studious, and desire to understand the customes of this nation. Translated by W.G. Tho: Roycroft for Jo: Ridley. 1651. 1st edition. (x),283pp. Table before text. 24mo. Modern calf. FINE COPY. WING C 6641. S. & M.i.21/8. £300

This work is founded upon the old Feudal Tenures, such as the law of wards & liveries, tenures "in capite", and knight service which Cowel has treated with considerable ability. It was so highly esteemed during the Commonwealth, as to have had the honour of being translated into English by order of Parliament. It also attempt a system of the law of contract, 200 years before English lawyers generally recognized it as an independent subject.

41) COWELL, John. (1554-1611) cont.
Institutiones Juris Anglicani, ad methodum et seriem Institutionum Imperialium compositae & digestae. Oxford. H.H., F. Oxlad, sen. & Ed. Forrest. 16mo. 1676. 4th edition. (xiv),248,(xxii) last leaf blank, table. Table bound out of order. Modern calf-backed boards. FINE COPY. WING C 6643. TCI 238. MADAN 3100.S. & M.i.21/7. £250

The Oxford printer H.H. was Hen. Hall.
This work is a summary of English law adapted to the scheme and even to the individual titles of Justinian.

42) DALTON, Michael. (1554—)
The Office and Authoritie of Sherifes. Abridged by the former author. Printed for the Companie of Stationers. 1628. 24mo. 1st edition of this version. (iv),260,(iv) leaves. Device on title; table, dedication leaves. Some sl. staining on last few leaves, other VERY GOOD COPY. STC 6213. S.&M.i.222/7. Contemp. calf, rebacked. £200

Although better known for his "Office of Justice of the Peace", this work was also held in high repute and continued to be a standard authority until the beginning of the 18th century.

43) A DIALOGUE on the PRINCIPLES of the CONSTITUTION and Legal Liberty, compared with Despotism; applied to the American Question; and the probable events of the war with observations on some important law authorities. W. Owen. 1776. 1st & only edition. (iv),92pp. Halftitle. Modern cloth. Not in KRESS, GOLDSMITH or S. & M. SABIN c.19944. £45

"This dialogue is judiciously conducted, and exhibits a perpicuous, sober and rational defence of the Colonies". Review in the Monthly Review LV.63. Obviously written by a lawyer as in the addenda and even in the dialogue itself, notes and quotations of very ancient law authorities are quoted, both in the original and in translations.

44) ELLESMERE, Thomas Egerton, Baron(Viscount Brackley)(1540-1617)
The Speech...in the Eschequer Chamber touching the Post-nati. For the Societie of Stationers. 1609. 1st edition. Sm.4to. (x),118,(ii)pp. Final leaf blank except for rules. Lacks first blank. 18th century sheep, spine & edges rubbed. STC 7540; S. & M.i.156/19. £180
This is Ellesmere's judgment in Calvin's case, where he held that Scottish citizens born after 1603 were entitled to all the rights of Englishmen

45) AN ESSAY for a GENERAL REGULATION of the LAW, and the more easy and speedy advancement of justice. Address'd to the Rt. Hon. Peter Lord King, Lord High Chancellor of G.B. By a Gentleman of the West Riding of the County of York. Stephen Austen. 1727. 1st and only edition. (iv), 239,(i),8pp. Advert. before title, booklist for Stephen Austen and book cat. for Daniel Midwinter (8 pages). Contemp. calf, rubbed, hinges sl. weak. S. & M.i.249/13 £40

46) FEARNE, Charles.
The Posthumous Works; consisting of a Reading on the Statute of Inrolments, Arguments in the case of General Stanwix, and cases and opinions. Selected by T.M.Shadwell A. Strahan. 1797. 2nd edition. (viii),(xviii),468,(12)pp. Margins at beginning and end sl. browned, sl. frayed in the end part. Contemp. calf, label; upper hinge sl. split at lower end. S.& M.i.338/22. £40

47) FERNE, (Sir) John. (c.1550-1610)
The Blazon of Gentrie: devided into Two Parts. The first named the Glorie of Generositie. The second, Lacyes Nobilitie. By John Windet, for Andrew Maunsell, 1586. 1st edition, 2nd issue. Z_4 & $2K_2$ (final leaf) blanks, the latter repaired. Three unsigned leaves of tables (two shaved) between $2D_1$ & 2; piece torn from margin of T_6 without loss of text. (xx),341/130pp. NUMEROUS WOODCUT ARMS in text and table of descent. A FINE COPY in old vellum, lacking ties. STC 10825. £350

Ferne, a fashionable student of the Inner Temple, collected the material of this book for the Polish adventurer Albert Count Lasky, who laid claim against the name & fortunes of the Lacy family. When Lasky vanished under a cloud, Ferne published his book to clear himself of complicity. It is a dialogue between a herald, a knight, a comic rustic (often very informative on the changing social & religious order) & others, "full of curious information & far above the level of the early heraldic writers". DNB
It is also said that the book was known to Shakespeare, and Dallaway calls it the best epitome then extant on the subject.
Certain of these armorial woodcuts were used by Halliwell-Philipps to illustrate Shakespeare's "The Merry Wives of Windsor".

48) FIDELL, Thomas. (Collected by)
A Perfect Guide for a Studious Young Lawyer: both delightfull and profitable for any Gentleman. Being presidents for conveyances, and other businesse of the like kinde: collected and gathered together out of the most studious, carefull, and learned labours of the Rev. and Learned Sages of the Law: the Lord Coke, the Lord Hobart, the Lord Richardson, Justice Haughton, Justice Reve, Justice Bacon, Sir William Denny, Master Godfrey and Master Jermy. Also divers Copyhold entries in Courts-Barons, with Justice of Peace businesse, very usefull for them and their Clerks, with an addition of Indictments and Fines. 12mo. Tho. Roycroft. 1654. 1st edition. (vi),279,22pp. Fp. port., & table. WING F 849. S.& M.i.481/24. Fine modern calf. £250

49) FIELD v. McGLUMPHY.
In re Petition for Mandamus. Affidavits and exhibits. n.p. (Philadelphia, Pa.) 1899. 1st edition. Lithographed table. 154pp. SIGNED on endpaper by Dr. (Montague) R. Leverson (the most important of the medical witnesses), with many textual corrections in his hand. Additional paragraph inserted on a typed slip at p.72. Contemp. roan, rebacked, with orig. wraps bound in. £30

This extraordinary case in the U.S. Court of Common Please arose out of attempts by the New York legislature to enforce compulsory vaccination in a poor part of Brooklyn. As a weapon against this intention the plaintiff, Charles Field, collected these depositions from qualified doctors; most of them are prpared to swear not only that they have seen men killed by vaccination, but that vaccination itself is worthless.

50) FILANGIERI, Gaetano. (1752-1788)
La Scienza della Legislazione del Cavalier Gaetano Filangieri. VENICE. 1782/6. (Giovanni Vitto). 7 volumes. FINE CONTEMP. MOTTLED CALF, raised bands on spines, gilt, labels, gilt embossed armorial device on both covers of all volumes, marbled endpapers, ties. Italian text. FIRST VENICE EDITION. Vol.1 sl. rubbed, vol.2 cover marked with holes, probably insects. OTHERWISE an EXTREMELY FINE SET IN CONTEMPORARY ITALIAN BINDING of this RARE EDITION. Both the British Library and Kress only mention the volume "delle Leggi Politiche ed Economiche" (vol. 2 in this set) in the series "Scrittori classici Italiani 1803-16. B.M. has a later edition. £300

The work is divided into 4 books:

50) FILANGIERI, Gaetano...cont.

Book I. "Delle regole generali della scienza della legislazione".	Vol. 1.
Book II. " Delle leggi politiche ed economiche".	Vol. 2.
Book III."Delle leggi criminali".	Vols. 3 & 4.
Book IV. "Delle leggi, che riguardano l'educazione, costumi, et l'istruzione pubblica". In three parts.	Vols. 5-7.

Vols. 1 & 2 "The science of legislation" appeared first in 1780 published in Naples; vols. 3 & 4 in 1783 and the last 3 vols. in 1785. An 8th volume was published after Filangieri's death in 1789. The present first Venice edition was corrected & revised by the author.
Filangieri's work is the most comprehensive attempt in these pre-revolutionary decades to apply the general spirit and method of Montesquieu to the requirements of social and political reform. He was styled the Montesquieu of Italy, and Janet and other French critics tried to prove that he owed most of his leading doctrines to Montesquieu. Yet it can be seen that the Italian developed and applied them in a new spirit. He was very sensitive to the intellectual influences making for far-reaching reform. In his enthusiasm he conceived that the human mind had reached a stage in its grasp of social phenomena that warranted a definite code of laws covering all the larger aspects of politics and government. As Montesquieu had revealed the spirit of the laws, Filangieri would set forth the specific content of the laws, as reason and experience dictated.
The volume "Delle legge politiche ed economiche" makes Filangieri one of the most important writers on economics of his period and although he had considerable acquaintance with economical studies of his time, it appeared, however strange, that he knew nothing of Adam Smith, whom he never refers to. He stood between the physiocratic and mercantile theories, was a zealous partisan of free-trade and the single tax, while believing in the balance of trade. He sustains the principle of the balance of trade but argues for a system of liberty both for exportation and importation, tempered only by the opinion that laws ought to be different in countries differently circumstanced - his works are thus the prelude to a historical system of social legislation.

51) ......William KENDALL: The Science of Legislation. Translated from the Italian. G.G. & J. Robinson & R.Treman. London/Exeter. n.d. (1792) 1st Engl. edition. (i-iii),iv-viiii,210pp. Contemp. panelled calf, rebacked. Bookplate of Fullerton of Carstairs. Not in Goldsmith or Kress. £120

First published in Naples in 1780, this is the first English translation of this volume of Filangieri's important work. See KRESS B 4730 for the Italian first edition "Delle leggi politiche ed economiche".

52) .....The Science of Legislation, from the Italian translated by (Sir Richard Clayton). Thomas Ostell. 1806. 1st English edition of the works as far as those related to political and economical laws. 2 vols. xviii,309,(i)/(vi),292,(i)pp. Errata leaf for each volume. With the bookplates of James Barratt, Lymm Hall & Charles J. Bewlay, Carleton Hall. Half calf, sl. rubbed. FINE. GOLDSMITH 19174. Not in KRESS. £120

This is the first English translation of this eminent political writer from Naples of his 7 volume work published between 1780 and 1785.

53) FINCH, Sir Henry.
Law, or a Discourse thereof...written in French...and done into English by the same author. By the Assignes of Richard and Edward Atkins, etc. 1678. viii,506,(xvi)pp. Index, publishers' catalogue of law books. Ink signatures on title one of them deleted. Modern morocco-backed boards. WING F 932 with apparent duplicate entry under Heneage Finch, Earl of Nottingham. WING N 1405. S. & M.i.238/10. £150

53) FINCH, Sir Henry..cont.
"Finch's Law", till the publication of Blackstone's Commentaries was regarded as the best elementary book to be placed in the hands of law students. It is one of the few attempts that have been made to reduce the common law into a system; and the author prided himself, upon having accomplished so difficult a task, as appears from the dedication to King James. His definitions were exact, his style concise and his illustrations clear and authentic. Most of the valuable parts of Finch are incorporated in Blackstone's commentaries.

54) FINETT, Sir John.
Finetti Philoxenis: som Choice Observations...touching the reception, and precedence, the treatment and audience, the puntillias and contests of Forren Ambassadors in England. T.R. for H. Twyford and G. Bedell. 1656. 1st edition. (xiv),250,(x)pp. Index. Lacks first and final blank. Fine modern calf. WING F 947. S.& M.i.599/3. £180

The author was Master of Ceremonies under James I and Charles I. His book, edited by James Howell, throws an important light on the blundering diplomacy of James, the machinations of the Spaniards, and the career of the Duke of Buckingham.

55) FITZHERBERT, Sir Anthony. (1470-1538)
La Nouvelle Natura Brevium...auecques un Table...iammais per cy deuaunt imprimee. In aedibus Richardi Tottelli. 1567. 4th edition. French text. Black Letter. Woodcut title-border. (xxxii),271 leaves. Index. Ink-stains on C_5. Marginal defect to F_8 with loss of few words of last line. Corner torn from D_1. Lacks final colophon leaf. Some early annotations, title frayed. Contemp. calf, rebacked & recornered. STC 10961. BEALE T 347. S.&M.i.269/66 £180

Fitzherbert's commentary on the writs as printed in Rastell's Register (1531) was one of the most authoritative works in English law from 1534, when it was first printed, until 1852 when the forms of action which it illustrated were abolished.

56) FORTESCUE, Sir John.
A Learned Commendation of the Politique Laws of England...newly translated... by Robert Mulcaster. Richarde Tottell. 1573. Latin & English text. Black & Roman Letter. (iii).132,(iii) leaves. Index. Sl. stained. Old ink names and annotations on title & blank verso of last leaf and a few in margins. Contemp. calf, rebacked. BEALE T 358. STC 11195. S. & M.i.22/15 £200

Third edition of Fortescue, and second of Mulcaster's version. The work, written for the instruction of the future King Edward IV is a summary for the layman containing the earliest outline of the peculiarly English scheme of constitutional monarchy, with many interesting comparisons between English & foreign practice.

57) FREEMAN, Samuel, Esq. (Registrar of Probate for the County of Cumberland.)
The Probate Auxiliary, or a Director and Assistant to Probate Courts, Executors....Being the Laws of the Commonwealth of Massachusetts, respecting the Estate of Testators, Intestates and Wards (with) alphabetical index. ....PORTLAND (MASS.) printed by Benjamin Titcombe. 1793. 1st edition. xi,(i), 156,(iv)pp. Paper browned throughout, title frayed at edges with tear in margin and loss of sm. part of upper corner, no loss of text. Modern calf-backed boards. £95

Interesting imprint of Portland in Mass, as that time Maine was part of Mass.

57) FREEMAN, Samuel ...cont.
The printer, Benjamin Titcomb was the first printer in Maine.
Freeman was Judge of Probate of Portland, Maine. EVANS 25512.

58) GENTILIS, Alberico. (1552-1611)
De Jure Belli, libri tres. Hanover: 1598. Excudebat Guilielmus Antonius. 1st German edition Latin text. Woodcut devices. (viii),716pp. Sl. marginal worming not aff.text. Bookplate of Augustus Thorndike. 18th century calf. FINE COPY. S. & M.i.601/11. ADAMS 424. £450

This work contains very correct views upon the science of international law. Gentilis was the first writer who endeavoured to introduce a system of jurisprudence amidst the war-like attitudes.
The first edition was printed in Oxford in 1588.

59) GLANVILLE, Ranulph de. (—1190)
Tractatus de legibus et consuetudinibus Angliae...cum diversis manuscriptis nuper examinatis. In aedibus Thomae Wight. 1604. 2nd edition. (vii),116, (xvii)pp. Index. Lacks first blank & blank A_1. STC 11906. S. & M.i.54/25 .....St. GERMAN, Christopher (—1539). Dialogus de fundamentis legum Angliae et de conscientia. In aedibus Thomae Wight.1604. 2nd Latin edition. (iv),73, (ii)pp. Index. Lacks final blank. STC 21560. S. & M.i.24/29
2 works in 1 volume. FINE COPY. Modern calf. £300

Glanville, the oldest of our general law writers, is collated here with the Scots "Regiam Maiestatem" by a learned though anonymous editor. St. German, an equal adversary to Sir Thomas More, was a pioneer in reconciling the law of England with natural justice; he does this in the three dialogues commonly called "Doctor & Student", of which only the first (printed here) exists in Latin.

60) GRANT, James.
A Practical Treatise on the Law of Corporations in general as well aggregate as sole; including municipal corporation, railway banking, canal etc., universities, colleges, schools, hospitals etc. 4to. 1850. 1st edition. xvi, 749pp. Contemp calf, gilt dec'd spine. Bookplate. FINE. S. & M.ii.144. £30

61) GRASWINCKEL, Theodore. (1600-1666)
Dissertatio de iure praecedentiae inter serenissiman Venetam rempubl. & sereniss. Sabaudiae ducem. Leyden Elzevir. 1644. 1st edition Latin text. LARGE PAPER (200 mm.) Red and black title. (xii),356pp. Few head-margins wormed, some sl. browning. Fine contemp vellum. WILLEMS 573. (1 L.P. copy at Univ. of Utrecht only recorded). £300

A legal commentary on claims of the Duke of Savoy against Venice by one of the greatest lawyers of his time, a cousin of Grotius who helped him with the manuscript of "De Jure Belli ac Pacis". He adds many observations on mediaval history & on international law.
Both Willems and the Rahir catalogue say that ordinary copies are only about 160 mm in height.

62) GUYMIER, Cosmas. (d.1503)
FRANCE: PRAGMATICA SANCTIO. Cosmas Guymier ad notulas ser associando priores. Codicis interpres cognitus huius erit. Paris. Johannen Barbier. 14. Jan.1514. Sm.4to. 205,(41) leaves. Black Letter. Printed in two columns throughout. Table. First and last blank. Title in black and red lettering with PRINTERS' DEVICE. One sm. hole in margin of title, sm. tear on title repaired. Sm. hole in margin of E_{111}. Lacks E1 & 8 of table. Some light underlining and some

62) GUYMIER, Cosmas..Pragmatica Sanctio..cont.
contemporary marginal notes in small neat hand in Latin. Full speckled late 18th century calf. BRUNET, vol.4 p. 855. Bibliotheque Nationale lists editions of 1503,4,7,10,14,30,38 et seq. but their 1514 edition is not printed by Barbier and none of those listed are edited by Cosmas Guymier. British Museum lists copies of 1497, 99 & 1513 but none edited by Barbier or edited by Guymier. Library of Congress does not list a copy of Pragmatica Sanctio during this period. £400

Guymier, a president in the Parliament of Paris, edited this work with the assistance of Peter Cambafort.
Pragmatic Sanctions meant an enactment made respecting the Gallican Church. They existed in the legislation of France and this one was promulgated by Charles VII in 1438 & 1439 and known as the Basilien and Bituricentian decrees. It was abrogated by Francois I at the intercession of Pope Leo X and the celebrated Concordat of 1516 was made in its stead.

63) HALE, Sir Matthew. (1609-1676)
BURNETT, Gilbert: The life and death of Sir Matthew Hale, sometime Lord Chief Justice of H.M. Court of King's Bench. W. Shrowbery. 1682. 2nd edition. (xx),128pp. Engraved frontispiece portrait of Hale. Contemp. ink annotations, on endpapers, first few edges sl. frayed. Modern calf-backed boards.
WING B 5828. £50

Contains a 23 page "catalogue of Hale's books"printed & to be sold by William Shrowbery; manuscripts to be published (Folio in bundles & quarto) and a "catalogue of the books given by Hale to Lincoln's Inn" (according to his will).

64) HERBERT, William.
Antiquities of the Inns of Court and Chancery; containing historical and descriptive sketches...(of) original foundations, customs, ceremonies,..... with a concise history of the English Law. Large 8vo. Vernor. 1804. 1st ed. xii,377,(ix)pp. Index, with 24 COPPER-ENGRAVED PLATES. Fp. foxed, some sl. marginal browning of first few leaves,otherwise fine. Contemp. calf, sl. rubbed and spine and lower edge faded. Inscription and notes on endpapers.
S. & M.i.212/20. £80

Fine copper plates of the various Inns of Court.

65) HERNE, John.
The Law of Charitable Uses, wherein the statute of 43 Eliz. Chap.4 is set forth and explained; with direction how to sue out and prosecute commission grounded upon that statute. J.S.Twyford. 1663. 2nd edition, much enlarged & amended. 12mo. (vi),271,(iii)pp. Table at end. A few headlines sl. shaved. Contemp. sheep rubbed, rebacked with ORIGINAL MS. fore-edge label.
WING H 1569. S. & M.i.497/10. £180

66) HEUMAN, Jo. (von Teutschenbrunn)(1711-1760)
Commentarii de Re Diplomatica Imperatricum Augustarum...Reginarum Germaniae.. (with) 2 appendices: de diplomatibus nonnullis cum augustarum et reginarum Italiae tum Imperatricum Constantinopol. disseritur. 4to. Norimbergae (Nurnberg) Johanni Georgii Lochneri 1749. (xii),493,(27)pp. Index, appendices, errata, 2 FINE COPPER ENGRAVED FOLDING PLATES with 19 FIGURES,(Armorial devices); engraved vignette on title, 2 more on preliminary page and printers' device at end of index. Title sl. browned at top margin. Contemp. morocco-backed boards, gilt decorated. £80

67) HIGHMORE, Anthony.
A Succint View of the History of Mortmain....the statutes relative to Charitable Uses...the last statute of Mortmain. (9 Geo.II.c.36)...Public Charities. J. Butterworth. 1809. 2nd edition with many additional cases, and several not hitherto reported. xxix,(i),592pp. Index. Contemp. speckled calf, gilt dec'd spine, label. S. & M. i.497/11 £60

68) HISTORICUS pseud. (Sir W.V. HARCOURT).
Letters by Historicus on some questions of International Law. Reprinted from "The Times" with considerable additions. London/Camrbidge. Macmillan.1863. 1st and only edition. (xii),(i),212pp. Orig. cloth, marked and faded, pencil annotations, and hand-written index of cases cited on endpaper. S. & M.ii.168. £15

69) The HISTORY and ANTIQUITIES of the FOUR INNS of COURT;
namely, The Inner Temple, Middle Temple, Lincoln's Inn, and Gray's Inn; and of the nine Inns of Chancery; to wit, Clifford's Inn, Clement's Inn, Lion's Inn, New Inn, Strand Inn, Furnival's Inn, Thavies Inn, Staple Inn and Barnard's Inn; also of Serjeant's Inn in Fleet Street and Chancery Lane and Scroop's Inn...(with) an appendix containing several modern orders made by the Society of Lincoln's Inn...(with) lists of the present Benchers of the four Inns of Court. G. Kearsly. 1780. xx,251pp. With the printed card of Rev. J.H. Lupton, St. Paul's School inside cover, some few neat ink annotations in margins. Half calf, fine gilt dec'd spine with label.Scarce. £60

70) HOBLER, Francis, Esq.
Familiar Exercises between an Attorney and his Articled Clerk, on the general principles of the Laws of Real Property: being the first book of Coke upon Littleton reduced to the form of questions. (with) original text and commentary and an appendix. James S. Hodson. 1838. 2nd edition. xvi,342pp. Appendix, folding facsimiles. Orig. cloth., sl. stained, spine faded. £30

71) HUGHES, William, of Gray's Inn.
An Exact Abridgment of all the Statutes in force and use, made in the 16th, 17th & 18th years of the reign of King Charles I and in the 12th,13th & 14th years of the reign of King Charles II. Beginning where Mr. Wingate ends..the 4th of January 1642 and continued the 18th of February 1663. J. Starkey & T. Basset. 1663. (iv),246,(ii),72,321-336pp. Privilege leaf & advert. leaf. Some sl. marginal worming. Ownership signature on title. Modern calf-backed boards. S. & M.i.566/31 gives this title as a reprinted version of WING H 3320 also dated 1663. £150

72) HURST,C.J.B. & F.E. BRAY.(Editors)
Russian and Japanese Prize Cases being a collection of translations and summaries of the principal cases decided by the Russian and Japanese Prize Courts arising out of the Russo-Japanese War, 1904/5. HMSO 1912/13. 2 vols. Vol.1 Russian Cases. Vol.2 Japanese Cases. xi,382/xxvi,475pp. Index for each volume, appendices, digests of cases for each volume. Buckram with leather labels. Sl. faded, particularly spine of vol.2. FINE SET. £60

The publication of these Reports was undertaken by HMSO at the request of the Admiralty and the Foreign Office but the editors alone were responsible for the text of the decisions as they appear. The original decisions were pronounced in Russian and Japanese and the editors had to rely on the translations made rather hurriedly by the Foreign Office. To keep the judgments in the traditional form of English Reports, headnotes have been added and introductory statements of the facts either derived from the statements in the case or

72) HURST & BRAY..Russian & Japanese Prize Cases cont.
...taken directly from the judgment of the Courts. The cases reported in Vol. 1 (Russian cases) relate to neutral ships only, no enemy ships appear to have been the subject of proceedings in the Russian Prize Courts as the superiority of the Papanese Naval Forces at an early stage of the war, reflects this. NOT in S. & M. £60

73) INSTITUTIONS, or PRINCIPAL GROUNDS of the LAWES and STATUTES of ENGLAND.
Newly and very trwely corrected and amended, with many new and good additions ...printed for the Companie of Stationers. 1607. 16mo. 66(ii) leaves. Mostly Black Letter. Title with engraved border. Modern calf. S.&M.i.446/17.STC 9298. £150

This edition appears to be only in the Huntington Library.
First published n.d. (c.1538) by Byddell and then by Myddylton in 1543.
It is almost entirely concerned with Land Law.

74) (JACOB, Giles) (1686-1744)
The Compleat Parish Officer: containing:
1. The authority and proceedings of High Constables...
2. Of Churchwardens...
3. Of Overseers of the Poor, and their Office...
4. Of Surveyors of the Highways and Scavengers...
(with) the Statutes relating to Hackney Coaches and Chairs...
12mo. Eliz. Nutt & R. Gosling. 1720. 2nd edition with additions. (iv),138, (x)pp. Table. Modern calf-backed boards. FINE. S.&M.i.234/8 lists the first edition of 1718 and several editions from the 3rd of 1723 onwards, but not this second edition. £60

According to S. & M. Part 1 "The Office of Constables" was written by Sir Francis Bacon in 1610.

75) JENKINS, David. (1586-1667)
Jenkinsius Redivivus: or the Work of that grave, learned, truly lawyer and courageous Judge Jenkins, whilst a Prisoner in the Tower, and Newgate, by command of the rebellious-Long-Parliament, began at Westminster, Nov.3.1640. Wherein is plainly set forth, the just power and prerogative of the King, the priviledge of Parliament, the liberty of the subject, and what is treason according to the laws of the land...Jo.Hindmarsh. 1681. (xxxii),213pp. No portrait called for, tables before text. Sm.repair on title affec. 3 letters, sm. stain on front blank. Contemp. calf, sl. stained, rebacked. FINE.
WING J 592. TCI 439. S. & M.i.157/31. £150

First and only edition under this title.

76) .....The Works of the eminent and learned Judge Jenkins, prisoner in Newgate, upon divers statutes, concerning, the liberty, and freedome of the subject. With a perfect table thereto annexed. 16mo. J. Gyles. 1648. (xxiv),199pp Frontispiece portrait and table before text. The work is divided and page 190 has the an additional title "Judge Jenkin's Remonstrance to the Lords and Commons of the two Houses of Parliament at Westminster....Feb.1647. By David Jenkins......1648". Pagination is continous after that until page 199. S. & M give 7 pages less for the 1648 editions. Later embossed calf. WING list 4 editions for 1648 all printed by J. Gyles J 574-7. S.&M.i.157/29.Sl. rubbed & fp. port loose. FINE COPY. £150

There were 4 edition all published in 1648.
Jenkins, a Welsh judge, was amongst those whose sense of law & liberty was outraged by the proceedings of King & commons alike. He opposed ship-money as an

76) JENKINS, David..The Works..cont.
unconstitutional impost and though imprisoned for his opposition to the King's authority, he continued to condemn those who denied that authority existed.
The principal thesis of this work is that the King cannot be deposed by Parliament because he is part of Parliament himself.

77) ..... Another copy. 16mo. Samuel Roycroft, for Samuel Heyrick. n.d. (1681). (xvi),94pp. Engraved fp. port. Some sl. worming in lower margin. Contemp. sheep, rubbed, rebacked. WING J579. S.&M.i.157/30. £90

This is the 6th edition. (4 in 1648 & 1 in 1661).

78)
JUSTINIAN. BOCKELMANN(US). Johannis Fridericus. (1633-1681)
Commentariorum in Digesta Justiniani Imp. Libri XXVII. 4to. 2 vols. Trajecti-ad-Rhenum. (UTRECHT). Antonium Schouten. 1694. (xxvi),686,(38)/(i),264pp. Index in vol. 1. Title of Vol. 1 in red and black lettering; both volumes with printers' device on title, engraved chapter headings, tailpieces and initial letters. Contemp. vellum, vol.1 sl. stained. Latin text. FINE COPIES £120

The introduction to the Commentarii contains information about earlier writers.

79) ....Sacratissimi principis, Institutionum, sive elementorum, libri quator, notis perpetuis multo, quam hucufque, diligentius illustrati, cura & studio Arnoldi Vinnii J.C. Edition postrema ab auctore recognita. Amstelodami. (Amsterdam) Ex Officina Elzeviriana.1669 (engraved title 1663). (i), (xxii),643pp. The Elzevier Minerva device (for Amsterdam printing) on printed title and colophon device at end. First and last blank. 12mo. Contemp. vellum. FINE COPY. WILLEM 1408 & see 1310. £80

This is the 5th Elzevir edition and there are two distinct variants. The engraved title of the first is dated 1663 (the previous edition Willem 1310); in the second variant the engraved title is dated 1679.

80) KELHAM, Robert.(1717-1808)
A Dictionary of the Norman or Old French Language...collected from Acts of Parliament, records, law books, manuscripts etc. (with) the laws of William the Conqueror. Edward Brooke. 1779. 1st edition. viii,259,(i),xii,88pp. Contemp. calf, sl. rubbed, rebacked with orig. spine. S.&M.i.9/35 £60

The laws of William are improved from Selden's text and the Latin and English versions revised. Although condemned as incorrect & uncritical, Kelham's work is certainly a great advance over Rastell's "Termes de la Ley".

81) KLANG, Heinrich. (editor)
Kommentar zum Allgemeinen Bürgerlichen Gesetzbuch. Osterreichischen Staatsdruckerei. Vienna. 1933-5. 4 vols. in 6. Indices to each volume. With an appendix on Czechoslovakia. German text. Orig. cloth, sl. faded, some joints frayed. Ownership stamp on endpapers. £80

82) LAMBARD, William. (1536-1601)
The Duties of Constables, Borsholder, Tythingmen and such other law and lay Ministers of the Peace. Whereunto bee adjoyned the severall Offices of Church-Ministers, and Church-Wardens and Overseers of the Poore, Surveyors of the High-wayes and Distributers of the provision against noysome fowle and vermine. Miles Flesher & R. Young.1640. New edition, carefully corrected and profitably augmented. Mostly Black Letter. 103pp. 4 blank leaves inserted between E_{4-5} &

82) LAMBARD, William cont.
F_{4-5}. Ownership inscription on title. Contemp. mottled sheep. STC 15162.7. (lists two copies). S.& M.i.234/9. RARE. £400

83) LAUTERBECK, Georg.
Regentenbuch...allen Regenten und Oberkeiten zu Anrichtung und Besserung erbarer und guter Policey, christlich and nötig zu wissen. (Leipzig, durch Jacobum Berwald). 1599. Folio. German text. Schwabacher letter. (xii),224, (ii) leaves. Woodcut device on final leaf and initials. Two blanks at end. Blank piece cut from title. First quire sl. frayed & stained.
.....MEURER, Noe. Von forstlicher Oberherrligkeit und Gerechtigkeit, was die Recht, der Gebrauch, die Billigkeit deszhalebn vermög. (Pforzheim, bey Georg Raben). 1560. 1st edition. Folio. German text. Fraktur Letter. Hohenzollern Arms on verso of title. Final device. 100 leaves. Margins sl. stained.
2 works in 1 volume. Some old annotations. Contemp. blind-stamped pig, clasps, very worn. £400

Lauterbeck's work (dedicated to the Counts of Mansfeld, ten brothers in whose service he was) is a treatise of government in which the authentic spirit of primitive German liberty speaks through a cloud of Roman illustration; he asserts the responsibility of a ruler to the law, the sanctity of an oath, and the beauties of peace, with chapters on education,currency,& other matters of municipal law. At the end he translated a fragment of Musonius, the stoic philosopher, on a similar subject.
Meurer, author of several law-books, discusses the rights of the forest - hunting, fishing, possession of timber & wild beasts etc., in the light of civil and cannon law.

84)(LAWRENCE,William)
Marriage by the Morall Law of God Vindicated against all Ceremonial Laws of Popes and Bishops destructive to filiation aliment and succession and the Government of Familyes and Kingdomes. n.p. (London). 1680. 1st edition. 4to. (i),(vi),(iv),422pp. Errata leaf (loose, curious, but finely engraved title with six givnettes "The Morall Law", "The Ceremonial Law", "Religion", "Liberity", "Justice" & "Property". WING L 690.
.....The Right of Primogeniture in succession to the Kingdoms of England, Scotland & Ireland...For the author. 1681. 1st edition. 4to. (xxiv),199,(37)pp Index. WING L 691. S. & M.i.476/19.
....The Two Great Questions...the peace and safety of His Maiestie's Person, and of all his Protestant Subjects in his three Kingdoms...For the author. 1681. 1st edition. 4to. (i),14pp. WING L 693.
Three works in 1 volume. Contemp. calf, rubbed & top of spine sl. frayed, errata leaf loose. £200

The first item is said to have been written upon a discontent arising from Lawrence's wife, whom he deemed dishonest to him. The second was written in support of the Duke of Monmouth's claim to the succession.

85) The LAWS and LIBERTIES of MASSACHUSETTS.
Reprinted from the copy of the 1648 edition in the Henry E. Huntington Library. With an introduction by Max Farrand. Cambridge. Harvard U.P. 1929. No.140 of a LIMITED EDITION of 300. Folio. ix,(iv),59pp. Facs. plate of title of original. Folio. Cloth. Dust jacket, frayed. FINE COPY. £35

This was the first attempt at a comprehensive reduction into one form of a body of legislation of an English-speaking country and stands as the basis of all subsequent Massachusetts legislation.

86) LAWS of the STANNARIES of CORNWALL,
made at the Convocation of Parliament of Tinners, at Truro, Sept.13, Anno 27° Geo. II. (with) the Laws made at Truro, 2°, annae reg. Printed by order of the Convocation. n.d. (c.1700). (i),7,(i),126pp. Contemp. speckled calf, rubbed. S. &M.i.468/10. £220

S. & M. do not mention the seven pages of contents and the errata leaf before text.
This present copy bears the Armorial bookplate of James Pascoe and his signature, dated 1768. Some passages are underlined and there are a few mss. notes (including "Common Costs on the...Warden's Court"and the "Method of Proceeding against a person for costs who lives out of the Stanneries" on the two blank endpapers, in the same contemporary hand, presumably Pascoe's.

87) ....Another copy. With notes, references to authorities...(with) several Acts of Parliament, schedule of Fees, Resolution of the Judges and a copious index. Truro. J. Tregoning...1808. 130,(9)pp. Contemp. inscription on first blank. FINELY BOUND MOROCCO, upper cover & spine with gilt decorations. S. & M.i.468/11. £150

88) LITTLETON,Sir Thomas (d.1481)
Littleton Tenures in Englishe. Richard Tottyl. 1576. 24mo. 142,(ii) leaves. Black Letter. A few marginal notes, some sl. marginal worming. 20th century embossed morocco, gilt lines, gilt decorated spine. FINE COPY. STC 15770.
S. &M.i.457/92. £400

Coke says about this work "Not the name of a lawyer, but of the Law itself". Littleton's account of the laws of property, as they stood immediately before the economic revolutions of the Tudor period, have always been admired for their clarity & judiciousness.

89) .....Littleton's Tenures in French and English. With an alphabetical table of the principal matters therein contained. John Streater & others. 1671. 24mo. French & English text. (xxii),436,(ii)pp. First and last blank. First blank partly loose, worn. Contemp. calf embossed on corners,rubbed. Contemp. signature on top of title "f lib. f John Ludford". In folding cloth box, lined, with gilt letters on spine. WING L 2588. S.&M.i.458/119. £200

First and only bilingual edition, for some centuries.

90) .....Another copy. Same edition. Contemp. calf, rubbed. Top of spine sl. frayed. £180

91) LYCKLAMA, Van Nijeholdt, Marc.
Membranarum libri septem, in quibus...de rebus...per sectas nostrorum temporum maxime controversis commentarii. Leeuwarden (apud Joannem Jansonium),1644. 2nd edition. 4to. (xvi),354,(xvi)pp. Index. FINE COPY in contemp vellum. £150

This Frisian jurist discusses numerous controverted questions in the Corpus, with a few from other writers, with the intention of resolving the disputes of over-zealous scholars, whose effect had often been (as he says) that "what was certain in the law is made uncertain".

92) M.P.S.D.A.D.S.M.L.R.D.P.E.D.S.
Abrégé Chronologique de l'Histoire et du Droit Public d'Allemagne,contenant les Guerres, les Traités de Paix, les Loix...Paris. Jean-Thomas Herissant.1754. (xii),721,(i)pp Index, halftitle, errata leaf. French text. From the library of

92) M.P.S.D.A/D.S.M.L.R.D.P.E.D.S. cont.
John Rutherford of Edgerston with his bookplate. Fine contemp. mottled calf, gilt dec'd spine, French binding. Corners & spine ends sl. rubbed. £45

93) MACKENZIE, Sir George. (1636-1691)
Jus Regium: Or, the Just and Solid Foundations of Monarchy. In general; and more especially of the monarchy of Scotland: maintain'd against Buchannan, Naphtali, Dolman, Milton, etc. R. Chiswel. 1684. (vi),210,(iv)pp. Fine engraved frontispiece portrait of Charles II by P.H. van Hove, 2 advert. leaves at end. WING M 164-4 (3 editions same date) either 163 or 4 both same printer. S.&M.i.117/85. Fine modern calf-backed boards. £120

Written as a defence of the Crown against Buchanan etc., this work examines the relationship between Parliament and the King and the history of that relationship, mixing references from legal and biblical authorities.

94) .....The Science of Herauldry, treated as part of the Civil Law, and Law of Nations: wherein Reasons are given for its Principles and Etymologies for its harder terms. Folio. Edinburgh...the Heir of Andrew Anderson. 1680. 1st edition. (i),(vi),98 (i.e. 102),(v)pp. 30 engraved plates, including portrait and half title, table, index of chapter headings with ms. paging in margin. Errors in pagination; some sl. cropping of a few top edges including half title. S.&M.i.206/27.
.....Observations upon the Laws and Customs of Nations, as to Precedency. Edinburgh, the Heir of Andrew Anderson. 1680. 1st edition. (xvi),(i),96pp. Errata & advert. page. S.&M.i.206/28.
2 works in 1 vol. Bookplates. Sprinkled calf, gilt lines, rebacked. Ink ms. notes on endpapers. £180

Mackenzie, was the founder of the Advocat's Library of Edinburgh now the National Library of Scotland.

95) MACLAURIN.(John) (later Lord Dreghorn).
Arguments and Decisions, in Remarkable Cases, before the High Court of Justiciary, and other Supreme Courts, in Scotland. Edinburgh.1774. 1st edition.4to. xvi,(ii),xvii-xl,776,(viii)pp. Index, final advert. leaf. Contemp. calf, spine gilt, label. Sl. rubbed, front endpapers loose. S. &M.v.76. £60

A far more learned work than Arnot's more famous collection. Maclaurin's cases, in some of which he himself took part, include R.v.Maclauchlan (1737) (interesting questions of the definition of treason & the effect of drunkenness on liability, arising from the Porteous Riots) & Macintosh v. Dempster (1767) (a discussion of the extent of Parliamentary privilege in regard to arrest & prosecution.)

96) MAGNA CHARTA and ANTIQUA STATUTA...
Magna Charta, cum statutis quae Antiqua vocantur...quibus accesserunt nonnulla nunc primum typis edita: Apud Richardum Tottelum. 12.Jun.1556. 2 parts in 1 vol. (viii),170,(ii)/72 leaves. Latin & French text. Black Letter. Woodcut initials. Indices. STC 9278. BEALE S 16. S. & M.i.552/1. Fine modern antique calf, raised bands on spine, gilt lettering. A very fine clean copy with wide margins. Name of former owner on title. £450

The volumes issued under the title Magna Charta, from Pynson's of 1508 onwards, acquired an accumulation of other ancient statutes & other pieces. This edition is distinguished by a fresh application to the original Rolls of Parliament (undertaken to eclipse the version printed by Marsh in the same year) which yields the Capitula Itineris (a guide to Pleas determined by the Circuit Judges), Edward I's Statutes of Wales with many readings unknown to Owen, an old

96) MAGNA CHARTA and ANTIQUA STATUTA...cont.
...summary of Kentish local law, two acts against Piers Gaveston and some lesser pieces, besides corrected readings in the statutes previously published.
Here, as in all the old tests, "Magna Charta" is not John's of 1215 but Henry III's of 1224.

97) MAITLAND, Frederic William. (1850-1906)
The Letters. Edited by C.H.S.Fifoot. Published in association with the Selden Society. CUP. 1965 1st edition. xxiv,397pp. Fp. port., & facsimiles, index. Orig. cloth. d.w.,fine. £12

This edition contains all of Maitland's known extant letters except for notes of business engagements or agenda. There are 501 letters printed here for the first time and filled with the wide variety of interests that characterized the distinguished lawyer, historian and medieval scholar.

98) MALE, George Edward.
An Epitome of Juridical or Forensic Medicine; for the use of medical men, coroners, and barristers. T.& G. Underwood. 1816. 1st edition. viii,199,(i)pp Errata, halftitle, uncut. Some sl. spotting. Modern cloth, label. S.&M.ii.231. £35

99) MANLEY, Thomas.
The Clerks Guide, leading into three Parts...to which is added a fourth Part. John Streater etc. 1672. 1st edition. 4 Parts in 1 vol. First blank leaf pasted to front cover with ROYAL ARMS. (vi),655,(i),(iv)661-730,(viii)pp. Lacks last 3 leaves. Index (complete). Fore-margin of last leaf shaved. Contemp. calf, rubbed, spine & edges worn. WING M 443. S.&M.i.43. £60

First and only edition.
A useful collection of precedents in conveyancing & pleading; part 4 concerns fines & recoveries. Part 2 includes a settlement of great complexity & advanced development, made by the celebrated Herbert of Cherbury.

100) MARTENS, G(eorg). F(riedrich) von.
The Law of Nations: being the Science of National Law, Covenants, Power etc. founded upon the Treaties and Customs of Modern Nations in Europe. Translated from the French by Wm. Cobbett. (with) a list of the principal treaties, declarations, and other public papers, from 1731 to 1738, by the author; and continued by the translator down to Nov. 1815. William Cobbett. 1829. 4th ed. xxxii,468pp. Half morocco, gilt spine. FINE COPY. S. &M. i.597/68. £85

The first editions of this work were printed in Philadelphia as the translation was commissioned from Cobbett by the U.S. Government. For the London edition (the first was published in 1803) Cobbett added a new preface & brought the list of treaties down to date.

101) .....Another copy. Same edition. Orig. cloth, faded; spine ends sl. frayed. Bookplate. £75

102) MINOT, George Richards.
The History of the Insurrections in Massachusetts, in 1786. Boston. James W. Burditt. 1810. 2nd edition. iv,5-192pp, uncut. Orig. boards, backstrip frayed & loose. With the bookplate of the Lucius M. Boltwood Historical and Genealogical Collection in the Jones Library Inc. Amherst. Mass. including a portrait of Boltwood. Pages spotted mainly at edges of some quires. £40
History of Shay's Rebellion which was thought to have influenced Constitutional Convention to write "Conservative" constitution.

103) MITFORD, John.(First Baron Redesdale)(1748-1830)
A treatise on the Pleadings in Suits in the Court of Chancery by English Bill. Tall 8vo. W. Owen. 1787. 2nd edition. (viii),(xiv),263,(12)pp. Uncut, index, errata. MITFORD'S OWN COPY WITH HIS BOOKPLATE AND ANNOTATIONS. A FINE COPY in contemp. full calf, raised bands and two labels (1 lettered "Mitford's own copy). S.&M. i.340/39. £90

An exceptionally fine copy. The author was Lord Chancellor of Ireland, a member of the Privy Council etc.

104) ....Another copy. W. Clarke..1814. 3rd edition, with additions. xvii, 268,(24)pp. MITFORD'S OWN COPY SPECIALLY BOUND INTERLEAVED WITH HIS ANNOTATIONS and his SIGNATURE "Redesdale" on title. Calf, sl. rubbed. FINE COPY. £80

See also #29. BULLER. Mitford's copy with his annotations.

105) ....Another copy. V.R.Stevens. 1847. 5th edition, comprising a large body of additional notes by Josiah W. Smith. liv,477pp. Index, table of cases. Embossed calf, gilt, sl. rubbed. FINE COPY. £40

106) MOLLOY, Charles.
De Jure Maritimo et Navali: or, a Treatise of Affairs Maritime, and of Commerce. 2 vols. T. Walker. 1769. 9th edition with many additions. xxvi,(ii),404/(iv),344,(52)pp. Index, publishers' booklist. Contemp. calf, sl. rubbed, rebacked. Very good set. S.& M.i.511/64. KRESS 6659. GOLDSMITH 10542. HIGGS 4616. £180

The first edition appeared in 1676 but this edition has many additions. It continued to be the best English work on maritime law down to the publication of the work of Lord Tenterden in 1802.

107) (MONIPENNIE, John)
The Abridgement or summarie of the Scots Chronicles: With a short description of their original, from the coming of Gathelus, their first Progenitour, out of Grecia into Egypt and their coming into Poringal and Spain: and of their Kings and Governours in Spain, Ireland and Albion, now called Scotland... their reigns, deaths, and burials...and a true description and division of the whole Realm of Scotland...16mo. Edinburgh. George Swintoun and James Glen. 1671. (iv),289,(i)pp. Folding geneological table (repaired), top margin sl. cropped in places. Bookplate of Charles Steurat. Marbled boards, rebacked. WING M 2422. ALDIS 1917. £80

108) N(ELSON),W(illiam). (c.1650-1730)
The Office and Authority of a Justice of Peace, also the Duty of other Parish Officers (with) presidents of indictments and warrants, and judgments and resolutions. Rich & Edw. Atkins. 1707. 2nd edition, corrected and continued to the end of the last Session of Parliament, 1706 and enlarged with many 100 cases not found in other books printed on the subject. (viii),599,(i)pp. Pages evenly browned, reversed calf, some sl. rubbed, later label. S.&M.i.230/48. £90

109) The NEW POCKET CONVEYANCER;
or, Gentleman, Tradesman, Lawyer and Attorney's Magazine of Law, being a choice approved precedents etc. Compiled from the best Authors who have written on these subjects with the addition of many excellent original precedents. By a GENTLEMAN of LINCOLN'S INN. 2 vols. in 1. 12mo. Dublin. Elizabeth Watts. 1765. 1st Dublin edition. vi,(viii),182/(xii),186,(i)pp. Table of contents for each volume, booklist. Sl. worming top of margin in last few leaves. Contemp. calf, raised bands, label FINE. This edition not in S.&M. see i.486/63 for 1st Engl. ed. of 1760 in 1 volume and the second edition in 2 volumes 1773. £60

110) (NICOLSON,William)(Lord Bishop of Carlile.)
Leges Marchiarum, or Border-Laws: containing several Original Articles and Treaties, made by the Commissioners of the Kings of England and Scotland for the better preservation of Peace and Commerce upon the Marches of both Kingdomes, from the reign of Henry III to the Union of the two Crowns in James 1 with preface and appendix of Charters and Records. Tim Goodwin. 1705. 1st ed. (viii),lvi,388,(4)pp. Halftitle and four pages of dedication, appendix in Black Letter, 4 page booklist. Contemp. calf, rebacked. S. & M.v.83/4. £120

During the currency of the Commission appointed to prepare a scheme for an Anglo-Scottish Union, many questions were raised as to the value & necessity of such a union. The Bishop (long respected as a student of Scots & Irish history) published these mediaeval documents to prove that the kingdoms had always treated with each other as equals and without any legal assumption of superiority by England and further the want of a stable political connection had been a cause of constant misery & strife on the border.

111) NORTH, The Hon. Roger. (1653-1734)
The Life of ..Francis North, Baron of Guildford (1637-1685), Lord Keeper of the Great Seal, under King Charles II and King James II, wherein are inserted the characters of Sir Matthew Hale, Sir George Jeffries, Sir Leoline Jenkins, Sidney Godophin, and others the most eminent Lawyers and Statesmen of that time. 4to. John Whiston. 1742. 1st edition.
.....The Life of the Hon. Sir Dudley North, Commissioner of the Customs, and afterwards of the Treasury to H.M. King Charles II and of the Hon. Dr. John North, Master of Trinity College, Cambridge and Greek Professor, Pret-end of Westminster and sometime Clerk of the Closet to the same King Charles II. 4to Printed for the Editor & sold by John Whiston. 1744. 1st edition.
2 volumes in 1. vii,-333,x/vi,288,viipp. Engraved frontispiece portraits to each volume, and indices. Contemp. calf, rubbed, rebacked. £90

Roger North was the younger brother of Francis North, Chief Justice of the Common Pleas 1675-1680, frequently acted as speaker of the House of Lords during Lord Chancellor Nottingham's illness. He was made Lord of the Great Seal in 1682 and became Lord Guilford in 1683.

112) NOVAE NARRATIONES
Herein is contained the Booke called Novae Narrationes, the Booke called Articuli ad Novas Narrationes, the Booke of Dievirsities of Courtes. Newly imprinted 1561. In aedibus Richardi Tottell. Cum privilegio. A-P in 8's. (i),ii-120 leaves. Colophon "Imprinted at London in Fletestrete within Teple-barre at the signe of the hande & Starre by Richarde Tottil, the first daye of Aprill. An.do 1561. French text. First two blank leaves contain hand-written (contemp.) index for first 76 leaves. One hand-written marginal note on verso of fo.54; engraved ornamental initial letter to new chapter on fo.75. Contemp. calf, repaired, rebacked in contemp. style with matching new end-papers. Index leaves sl. browned and frayed, otherwise A FINE COPY WITH WIDE MARGINS. £400

Beale lists two folio copies (1 lacking the title) which makes this the third edition T 110; New STC 18363. S. & M.i.275/112.
It comes from the early years of Edward III's reign and consists of precedents of pleadings upon a number of writs, presumably those which were most commonly used....For the most part the pleadings are given without comment; but here and there throughout the book there are short notes.

113) NOY, William. (1577-1634)
The Compleat Lawyer; or, a treatise concerning tenures and estates in lands of inheritance for life, and other hereditaments and chattells real and personal.

113) NOY, William. The Compleat Lawyer cont.
And how any of them may be conveyed in a legal form by fine, recovery, deed or word, as the case shall require. John Benson. 1661. 3rd edition. 16mo. (ii),124,(122)pp. Modern calf-backed marble boards. FINE COPY. Former owner's signature top of title. S. &M.i.458/123. £200

Noy was the Attorney General to King Charles I and this catechism of procedure neatly outlines the different aspects of the law which is then discussed in an essay.

114) .....The Principal Grounds and Maxims, with an analysis and a dialogue and treatise of the Laws of England; and on tenures, estates etc. (with) a treatise of estates, ascribed to Sir John Doderidge, and observations on a deed of Feoffment. S. Sweet. 1821. 9th edition. With a sketch of the author's life, corrections, notes and references by W.M.Bythewood. 16mo. (xxxvi),431,(i)pp. Index. Contemp. calf, spine darkened, top sl. frayed. S.&M.i.243/8. £18

Noy was known as a "King's man" and advised in favour of the ship-money legislation which was passed without consent of Parliament.

115) .....Reports and Cases taken in the time of Queen Elizabeth, King James and King Charles (1559-1649). Containing...matter of exceptions to all manner of declarations, pleadings, and demurrers...with two tables of cases and contents. Folio. T.R. for Samuel Heyrick.1669. 2nd edition, corrected and amended. (iv),185,(xv)pp. Contemp name on title. Sl. browned at edges. Modern half calf. S. &M.i.306/92. WING N 1450. Black Letter. £120

The first English translation appeared in 1656.The editor in his introduction contends that Noy's analysis of the pleadings is above that of any reporter since Plowden.

116) PERKINS, John.
A Profitable Booke...treating of the Lawes of England. For the Company of Stationers.1621. French text. xxiv,168 leaves. Index. Contemp. calf, central lozenge of small tools, borders and corner pieces on sides; lacks ties. Joints neatly repaired. STC 19644. S. & M.i.485/57. FINE COPY. £200

Perkins explains the law of real property, as it relates to the transference of land by purchase. He was the Conveyancer's mentor for 300 years.

117) .....Another copy. translated out of French into English. R.B. for M. Wallbanke. 1642. (xxxi),388pp. Black Letter. Table. Later calf. Spine ends & corners sl. rubbed, first blank, upper part cut away. With contemp. annotations and notes on half blank and next page. WING P 154. S.&M.i.485/57. £85

118) P(ETYT),G(eorge).
Lex Parliamentaria: or, a Treatise of the law and custom of Parliaments... with an appendix of a case in Parliament between Sir Francis Goodwyn and Sir John Fortescue...J.Stagg. n.d.(1690). 2nd edition. (x),434,(i)pp. Halftitle & advert. leaf before title, booklist at end. WING P 1944. S.&M.i.132/54. £120

First edition published in the same year (1690).
A summary of the rights & procedure of Parliament. The appendix gives a test case for parliamentary privilege; one Sir Francis Goodwin was in 1603 elected for Buckinghamshire while outlawed for debt; and Parliament upheld his right to sit, in face of pressure from James I and the 12 judges.

119) .....Another copy. Henry Lintot. 1798. 3rd edition. (x),434,(i)pp. Fine modern panelled calf, gilt dec'd spine. Margins of first few pages sl. frayed and stained. £120

120) PLACITA GENERALIA & SPECIALIA.
In an Exact Collection of the most usefull and necessary Presidents of Declarations, Plaints, Demurrers...together with the Stiles and Forms of Entring Pleadings as well in superiour Courts, as inferiour, and limited jurisdiction. Charles Harper & John Amery. 1674. 1st and only edition. (vi),685,33,(i)pp. Table, booklist. Contemp. calf, rubbed, hand-written paper label. Endpapers sl. browned. Fine copy. WING P 2334. S. & M.i.275/117. £180

121) POTHIER, Robert Joseph. (1699-1772)
Councillor at the Présidial, a Court of Justice, Professor of law at the University of Orleans. A studious and highly gifted jurist, who worked for 12 years at the correction and co-ordination of the text of the Pandects. Some years earlier he published the Coutume d'Orleans.
Thoroughly acquainted with French law, he wrote a long series of learned monographs on all its various branches which has been of invaluable assistance to the authors of the Code Civil. Writing with great simplicity and extreme clearness, he was accustomed to examine every question under the double aspect of the "for interieur" and the "for exterieur", natural equity and positive law. His works have often been republished in a collected form, from 1773 to the present time.
The following are from the 28 volume set in 12mo, issued and sold separately. All in FINE CONTEMPORARY FRENCH BINDINGS, speckled calf, gilt decorated spines, raised bands, labels, ties. Sl. rubbed. French text with the bookplate of "Me Bonjour, Avocat". Except for the last volume, they are published anonymously as "par l'Auteur du Traité des Obligations".
All volumes published Paris. chez Debure pere. Orleans. La Veuve Rouseau-Montaut.

I. TRAITE du CONTRAT de VENTE selons les regles tant du for de la conscience que du for exterieur. Et le Traite des Retraits, pour servir d'appendice au Traite du Contrat de Vente. 2 vols. in 1. 1765. New edition revised & corrected. xvi,480/vi,208pp. Separate title for vol.2. Sm. tear in last blank.

II. TRAITE du CONTRAT de CONSTITUTION de RENTE;avec le Traite du Contrat de change, de la negociation qui se fait par les lettres-de-change, des billets de change & autre billets de commerce. 2 vols. in 1. 1763. 1st edition. viii,275/viii,258,(i)pp. Indices, separate title for vol.2.

III. TRAITE des CONTRATS de BIENFAISANCE,ou l'on trouve le Traite du Pret a usage, & du precaire; & le Traite du Contrat de Pret de consomption; & le TRAITE du CONTRAT de DEPOT & de MANDAT;un appendice du quasi-contrat negotiorum gestorum; & le Traite du Contrat de Nantissement. 2 vols. 1766/7. 1st edition. x,360,(ii)/xvi,457,(i)pp. Indices, errata.

IV. TRAITE du CONTRAT de MARIAGE,auquel est jointe une Observation generale sur les precedens Traites de l'Auteur. 2 vols.1768. 1st edition. xvi,475/xvi,419,16pp. Index, halftitles.

V. TRAITE de la COMMUNAUTE,auquel on a joint un Traite de la Puissance du Mari sur les personne & les biens de la Femme. 2 vols. 1770. (1st edition 1769). xii,592/xvi,638,(iv),4pp. Index, errata, halftitles.

VI. TRAITE du DROIT D'HABITATION,pour servir d'Appendice au Traite du Douaire. Traite des Donations entre mari & femme, Traite du Don mutuel, auquel on a joint une interpretation de l'article 68 de la Coutume de Dunois. 1771. 1st edition. xxiv,362,70pp. Index, appendix, halftitle.

VII. TRAITE du DROIT de DOMAINE de PROPRIETE,auquel est join un TRAITE du DROIT de POSSESSION. 2 vols. 1772. (1st edition 1771/2) x,484,(i)/xxxix,448pp. Vol.1 is 2 parts in 1. with separate indices, and one for vol.2. Vol.2. is the only volume where Pothier's name appears as the author. This volume also contains a life of Pothier and a bibliography of his works before text.
13 volumes in 11 £250

122) POWELL, Thomas.
The Attourney's Academy- or, the Manner and Forme of Proceeding...in any Court of Record. Benjamin Fisher. 1630. 3rd edition. Sm.4to. Index. (xii),230,(lxii)pp. Some headlines sl. cropped. Modern calf, gilt. FINE COPY. STC 20164. S. & M.275/119. Woodcut ornaments & initials. £200

Powell was a Welshman, an occasional playwright and an amusing writer. His remarks on the jurisdiction of Parliament (partly drawn from Smith's Republic), on the Chancery, on Star Chamber, etc. are of considerable historical value.

123) .....Another copy. Same edition. Sl. soiled and dampstained, last 2 leaves with some blank areas torn away. Contemp. limp vellum, sl. soiled, hole in lower cover.

124) The PRACTICE of the HIGH COURT of CHANCERY UNFOLDED,
with the Nature of the several Offices belonging to that Court, and Reports of many Cases wherein relief has been had and denied. (Choyce Cases in Chancery). 12mo. A. Miller for Abel Ropers. 1652. (viii),(iv),188,(11)pp. Table, 4 page booklist (Abel Roper). Engraved chapter headings & initials. Modern calf. FINE COPY. WING P 3156. S. &M. i.341/47. £220

First edition (London, Dublin & Harvard only). S. & M. do not mention the booklist.

125) The PRACTICK PART of the LAW:
shewing the Office of an Attorney, and a Guide for Solicitors...in all Courts ...(with) the Practice of the Court of Exchequer...(with) the Practice of the Courts in the City of London... Henry Twyford. 1676, revised, corrected and much enlarged with an exact Table...(i),(vi),480,95,(i),(14)pp. Contemp. calf, carefully recased with orig. spine. Cover sl. marked. S.&M.i.276/122. £90

First edition published in 1652. Does not appear to be in WING.

126) PRYNNE, William. (1600-1669)
An Humble Remonstrance against the TAX of SHIP-MONEY lately imposed: laying open the illegality, injustice, abuses, and inconveniences thereof. Written during Prynne's imprisonment in the Tower of London to free his Countrey from that heavy Tax...since that printed without his privity, by an imperfect Copy, An 1641 so full of Non-sense errors, and mistakes almost in every line, as makes it altogether uselesse, yea ridiculous: but now set out by a true Copy, agreeing with the originall; to right the Author, and promote the publique good. (with) some BRIEFE OBSERVATIONS touching the GREAT SEALE of ENGLAND. 4to. Imprimatur: Setp. 1. 1643. John White. Printed for Michael Sparke senior..1643. (ii),34/(ii),32,(i)pp. Titles in engraved borders, some engraved headings & initials. 2 works in 1 vol. FINE LARGE COPY. This edition not in S.&M, but see 1641 edition 329/68. Similarily not in WING; P 3983 for 1641 edition. The second work. WING P 4026. Fine modern calf. £150

It is reckoned that the number of books and pamphlets written by Prynne exceeded 200. He attacked what he considered the great anormities of the age & against the doctrines and disciplines of the Church. He was imprisoned for his writings on several occasions.

127) PUTNAM,B.H. (edited by)
Proceedings before the Justices of the Peace in the 14th & 15th centuries. Edward III to Richard III. With a commentary by T.F.T.Plucknett. The work was published for the Ames Foundation. 1938. 4to. clxi,590,(ii)pp. Analytical index to the indictments and index of persons and places, loose errata leaf inserted. Orig. printed buckram; gilt lettering spine. Fine. £40

128) (RASTELL, John)
An Exposition of Certaine difficult and obscure words, and Termes of the Lawes of this Realme. Newly amended and augmented, both in French and English, for the helpe of such young Students are are desirous to attaine to the knowledge of the same. (A. Islip) Printed for the Company of Stationers. 1609. (iv),196 leaves. Printed in two columns. English (Black Letter) and French. Top edge of margin sl. cropped. Modern calf. New STC 20714. S. &M.i.10-11/47. Table before text. £180

It appears that only two perfect copies exist in this country, 1 at St. John's College, Cambridge and 1 at Liverpool University. The British Library has the title only (Harl. 5937/284); the Bodleian and University Library, Cambridge have imperfect copies only. There are 5 copies in the U.S.A.
This is the first English law dictionary, originally published in French alone, (c.152[illegible]

129) .....Les Termes de la Ley: or, certain difficult and obscure words and terms of the Common and Statute Laws of this Realm, now in use, expounded and explained. Eliz. Nutt and R. Golling. 1721, corrected and enlarged, with the addition of many other words; particularly of those that have been lately introduced into the Statute Law of G.B., never printed in any other impression. (iv),592pp. Printed in two columns, French and English. Contemp. calf, spine ends sl. frayed and rubbed. S.&M.i.11/48. £80

Rastell printed this as the first English law dictionary, originally published in 1527 in Latin.

130) REPORT of the COMMITTEE on the JUDICIARY.
Adverse Report of the Committee on the Judiciary on a Bill to Reorganize the Judicial Branch of the Government (of the U.S.A.) 4to. Stamford. Connecticut. The Overbrook Press 1937. Reprinted from the Senate Calendar: Number 734 Report No.711. June 7th, 1937. LIMITED to 1000 copies for private distribution. 46,(i)pp. Fine hand-made paper, printed in red borders with wide margins, uncut. Presentation slip. Orig. canvas with red lines. Fine. £20

131) RYMER, Thomas & Robert SANDERSON (editors)
Foedera, conventiones, literae, et cujuscunque generis acta publica inter reges Angliae, et alios quosvis imperatores, reges, pontifices (etc). The Hague. Jean Neaulme. 1739-45. 3rd edition, edited George Holmes. 10 vols. FOLIO. Indices. 10 engraved plates in vol.9. "Advertissement" leaf (signed *2) bound before A_1 of vol.1. Contemp. MS. transcript of Anglo-French truce of 1325 (from a Bodleian MS.) ... 5 engravings of Great Seals from an 8vo edition of Blackstone's Law Tracts, inserted in vol.1. Two leaves loose in vols. 4 & 9. Vol.5 lacks 5*2, blank $_1$ & N_{2-3} (part 3) reversed. L_2 (vol.7 part 1) torn without loss.
Contemp. marbled boards, uncut, worn, ends of spines defective. S.&M.i.604/14 £300

Last edition, including some new items - an account of the English constitution in French, written by an unknown ambassador in 1565, and le Clerc's Historical Abridgment of the Foedera which forms volume 10.

132) "RYMER'S FOEDERA".
Thomas Duffus Hardy (Deputy Keeper of the Public Records). Syllabus (in English) of the documents relating to England and other Kingdoms contained in the collection known as "Rymer's Foedera". Vol.1 1869. 1066-1377. Vol.2 1873. 1377-1654. 2 vols. 4to. Full calf, 2 leather labels. Fine. S.&M.i.604/16. £90

A third volume was published in 1885.

133) SACHEVERELL, Henry. (1672=1724)
The Tryal...for High Crimes and Misdemeanors; upon an Impeachment. Jacob Tonson. 1710. Imprimatur leaf before title. 456,(viii)pp. Index. Two leaves of index frayed, in lower margin.
.....The BISHOP of SALISBURY'S...Oxford's...Lincolns and ...Norwich's Speeches, on the Impeachment of Dr. Henry Sacheverell. 1710. 1st edition. 16,16, 33=64pp.
2 works in 1 vol. Contemp. calf, sl. rubbed, spine ends sl. frayed, new label. £30

Sacheverell was impeached for preaching against the toleration of dissenters & other policies which had prevailed since 1689. He received a mild sentence and his supposed defence of the Church against administrative tyranny made him a national hero. The four Bishops voted against him.

134)(St, GERMAN, Christopher)(—1540)
The Dialogue in English, betweene a Doctor of Divinitie, and a Student in the Lawes of England. Newly corrected and imprinted, with new additions.(A.Islip) Printed for the Company of Stationers. 1613. 16mo. 176,(iv) leaves. Table. Signatures of previous owners in ink on margins of title & first leaf; sm. tear repaired on title and last leaf, marginal repair. Modern calf. New STC 21580. S. & M.i.25/34. Mostly Black Letter; title with engraved border. £120

St. German's book, published in Latin in 1523, was important in establishing the relationship between Church & State in English Law. Using the threefold division of laws proposed by Aquinas (divine, natural & human) he discusses the reconcilement of moral & legal duty, the place of equity, & many particular points of land & property law. His views on the rights of the Church were answered in several pamphlets by Sir Thomas More.

135) .....Doctor and Student: or Dialogues between a Doctor of Divinity and a Student in the Laws of England...Eliz. Nutt & R. Gosling. 1721. 12mo. (xii), 366,(xl)pp. Index. Mostly Black Letter. Contemp. calf, rebacked, endpapers sl. spotted. S. & M.i.25/36. £70

The first edition in English appeared in 1668 but the original Latin version goes back to 1528.

136) SALTERN, George.
Of the Antient Lawes of Great Britaine. Sm.4to. John Iaggard. 1605. 1st and only edition, n.p. (86)pp. Sm. repair on title, top margin sl. cropped, sl. aff. engraved heading, some ink underlining. Engraved device on title in addition to heading. Modern calf=backed boards. New STC 21635. S.&M.i.41/29. £60

137) SEDGWICK, James.
Remarks Critical and Miscellaneous on the Commentaries of Sir William Blackstone. 4to. G.G. & J. Robinson etc. 1800. 1st edition. x,(ii),304pp. Halftitle. Tear in halftitle. Modern half calf. S. &M.i.30/15. ELLER 264. £120

An Answer by W.H. Rowe in vindication of Blackstone's commentaries from some strictures contained in Sedgwick's remarks appeared in 1806.

138) (SEGAR, Sir William)
Honor: Military, and Ciuill, contained in foure Bookes. I. Justice, and Jurisdiction Military. II. Knighthood in generall, and particular. III. Combats for life, and triumph. IV. Precedencie of great Estates, and others. Folio. Robert

138) SEGAR, Sir William cont.
Barker. 1602. 1st edition. (iv),256pp. Engraved title with printers' device, royal arms on verso. Engraved chapter headings & initials throughout. Lower corner of title repaired, title and last leaf browned otherwsie FINE. New STC 22164 (calls for portrait). S. &M.i.208/47. £150

Neither Lowndes nor S. & M. mention a portrait and there is none in this copy. The work is dedicated to the Queen and woodcut on the verso of title is of the Royal Arms and supporters. Lowndes says "this work has great merit = viging a comprehensive view of the origin and progress of military institutions and ceremonies.

139) SELDEN, John. (1584=1654)
De dis Syris syntagmata II. Adversaria nempe de numinibus...in Veteri Instrumento Memoratis. Leyden. Elzevir. 1629. 2nd edition, revised. Latin text. Red & black title. (xl),373,(i)pp. Title sl. browned. Later calf, rebacked. FINE. WILLEMS 322. £120

Signature T.J.Mathias on first blank, that of Jo Brown on title. Mathias was the learned author of the "Pursuits of Literature" and editions of Gray's works. This edition was greatly enlarged, partly to satisfy the request of the Elzevirs & partly to silence the partisans of a German jurist, Faber, who had written on the same subject. Milton drew many names & attributes of the Heathen Gods in "Paradise Lost" from this work.

140) .....Mare Clausum seu dominio maris libri duo: I. Mare, ex Jure Naturae seu Gentium...II. Serenissimum Magnae Britanniae Regem Maris circumflui... accedunt M.Z. Boxhornii apologia pro navigationibus Hollandorum adversus Pontum Heuterum, et tractatus mutui commercii & navigationis inter Henricum VII & Philippum archiducem Austriae. Londini (i.e. Amsterdam) iuxta exemplar W. Stanesbeii pro R. Meighen. 1636. An enlarged edition.(same year as the first continental edition published in Leyden). (xxiv),504,61pp. Latin text. 2 wood=engraved maps of England and 2 plates, text illustrations. New STC 22176. WILLEM 449 (states that it is definitely an Elzevier as it has the small vignette "Non Solus" on the title and is cited in the official catalogue for 1638 & 1644). S. &M.i.514... FINE CONTEMP. VELLUM. Contemp. notes in Greek lettering on first blank £400

Selden wrote this work at the time when Charles I was pursuing a highly ambitious maritime policy and tried to show that the Seas round England had been "maria clausa" from very early times. His arguments in support are a striking testimonial to his stupendous erudition. The case as presented by Selden has since been refuted, and it has been shown that there is no reliable evidence that prior to the Stuart dynasty there was any attempt on England's part to prohibit navigation or fishing in the Seas round England, or to demand tribute or tolls from foreign ships for making use of these waters. (Ludovic J. Grant: The King's Chambers.)
Selden's Mare Clausum was published as an answer to Grotius's Mare Liberum.

141) .....The Priviledges of the Baronage of England when they sit in Parliament. 24mo. T.Badger for Matthew Wallbanck. 1642. 1st edition. (vi)167pp. Engraved chapter headings & initials. Contemp. calf, rebacked. WING S 2434. S. & M.i.208/49. £120

Selden's study of the Parliamentary records which he later expanded under "Judicature in Parliaments" in his "Opera Omnia".

142) .....Tracts. Jani Anglorum Facies Altera, rendered into English with notes by Bedman Westcot. England's Epinomis; Original of Ecclesiastical Jurisdictions of Testaments; Disposition of Intestates & Goods. Folio. 4 Tracts in 1 vol. For Thomas Basset & Richard Chiswell to be sold by Robert Clavell. 1683. 1st

142) SELDEN, John...Tracts..cont.
collected English edition. Lacks portrait (though not mentioned in either WING or S. & M) (xxxiii),131,(7),39,(4),(24)pp. Title sl. frayed. Engraved chapter headings, printers' device on titles. Modern calf=backed boards. WING S 2441a. S. & M.i.42/33. £120

143) SELVA, Johannes de.
Tractatus de beneficio. (Paris), Francois Regnault, n.d. (c.1520). 4to. Gothic (rotunda) Letter, red & black title with device (see Renouard 943). 299,(xiiii) leaves. Index, final blank. Few sl. stains, some head=lines cropped, title sl. soiled. Contemp. sheep, MS guards (legal document dated 1480) lacks ties, tail of spine repaired. ADAMS 879. Not in B.L. or Lib. of Congress. £200

In this work on ecclesiastical appointments, the author, a jurist of Limoges, limits the powers of the Pope to dispense with the normal rules of preferment. He is equally critical of the pretensions of the French Crown to an independent right of appointment.
The absence of a colophon is unusual; however the blank appears to be genuine and would have carried the imprint if one were required.

144) SHARP, Granville (1734=1813)
An Account of the Ancient Division of the English Nation into Hundreds and Tithings: An Appendix to several Tracts on National Defence etc. Galabin and Baker. 1784. 1st and only separate edition. 370pp. Uncut. Orig. boards with original printed paper label. A little rubbed & some sl. fraying of spine. AN EXCEPTIONALLY FINE COPY IN THE ORIGINAL CONDITION. Contemp. ink annotations on top of title "A great deal of good matter well worth reading J.Call". GOLDSMITH 12[illegible]i. Not in KRESS. S. &M.i.42/34. £150

145) .....A Declaration of the People's Natural Right to a Share in the Legislature which is the fundamental principle of the British Constitution of State. B.White. 1775. 2nd edition. (iv),xl,244pp. Half title. Modern calf=backed bds. SABIN 79817. GOLDSMITHS' 11368. HIGGS 6484. S.&M.i.148/24. FINE COPY. £150

Sharp believed that a more or less universal suffrage was basic to the British constitution, pocket boroughs & the like being merely corruptions of a later date. He has much to say on the legal position of the American Colonies, where in his opinion the Law of England applies exactly as it does on English soil.

146) .....The Just Limitation of Slavery in the Laws of God,compared with the unbounded claims of the African Traders and British American Slaveholders... with a copious appendix. B.White & E.&C.Dilly. 1776. 1st edition. (ii),68,108, (ii)pp. Advert. leaf. SABIN 79823. KRESS 7255. GOLDSMITH 11499.
....The Law of Passive Obedience...wherein is shewn that...Scripture...cannot ...justify the Claims of Modern Slaveholders...B.White & Dilly. (1776) 1st ed. Index, final errata leaf. 102.(ii)pp. SABIN 79825. KRESS 7257. GOLDSMITH 11501.
....The Law of Liberty, or, Royal Law, by which all mankind will certainly be judges! Earnestly recommended to the serious consideration of all slaveholders and slavedealers...White & Dilly. 1776. 1st edition. 56pp. Index,halftitle. SABIN 79824. KRESS 7256. GOLDSMITH 11500.
....The Law of Retribution: or, a Serious Warning to G.B. and her Colonies, founded on unquestionable examples of God's temporal vengeance against tyrants, slaveholders, and oppressors...W.Richardson for White & Dilly.1776. 1st edition. (ii)358,(ii)pp. Half title, index, final advert. leaf. SABIN 79826. KRESS 7258 GOLDSMITH 11502. 4 works in 2 volumes. Fine contemp. sprinkled calf, gilt. FINE BINDING = FINE COPIES. £450

Sharp was the founder of the anti=slavery movement. It was he who engineered the test case of James Somersett, in which it was established that slavery was not recognized by English law: and in 1787 he founded the first Abolitionist Society. These 4 important pamphlets represent the beginning of public agitation on the subject.

147) SHEPPARD, William. (--1675)
The Justice of Peace, his Clerks Cabinet: or, a Book of Presidents, or Warrants, fitted and made ready to hand for every Case that may happen within the Compass of his Masters Office. For...the Justice of Peace...D. Maxwell, for William Lee. 1660. 2nd edition. FOUR PAGES (of endpapers) covered with COPIOUS CONTEMPORARY MS. NOTES, much of it relating to the County Court of Cumberland, & some of it to the Duties of Constables and Justices of the Peace. (xvi),127pp. Ownership signature on title. Calf=backed boards. WING S 3190. S.& M.i.231/65. £200

Sheppard best known for his work "The Touchstone of Common Assurances" was the author of a large number of legal treatises. He is said to have owed his fortune to Cromwell, who made him one of the Clerks of the Upper Bench. He later became Serjeant=at=Law, and prepared the Charters granted to certain Corporations. He also replaced many of the obsolete guides to the subject up to then in print.

148) ....The President of Presidents. Or, one General President for all Common Assurances by Deeds: being a perfect abstract of the general learning & forms of Presidents, touching or ...relating to ...Conveyances now in use. Illustrated with many excellent cases in the law..Richard and Edward Atkins etc. 1704. Third edition with additions by W. Brown. (xi),400,(8)pp. Table, priviledge leaf before title. Contemp. calf, rubbed, sl. wear on spine. With the bookplate of John Toke, Esq. of Godinton, Kent. S. &M.i.487/70. £60

149) ....The Second Part of the Faithfull Councellour: or, the Marrow of the Law in English....with an alphabeticall table of the most materiall things therein contained. Tho. Roycroft for Hen.Twyford etc. Sm.4to. 1654. (iv),364, (15)pp. Not in S. & M. WING S 3209c (1 copy only at University of Illinois) Modern calf=backed boards. Title and throughout all browned. £80

An edition in two parts first appeared in 1651.
Sheppard was an industrious writer of many law books, and a whole=hearted supporter of the Commonwealth. This doubtless had something to do with the obscurity into which most of his books fell after the Restoration.

150) SIMS, Richard.
A Manual for the Genealogist, Topographer, Antiquary, and Legal Professor, consisting of descriptions of Public Records, Parochial and other Registers, Wills, County and Family Histories....John Russell Smith.1841. 2nd edition. xx,526,(i)(32)pp. Index, errata, 32 page booklist. Orig. embossed cloth, faded, corners sl. rubbed. £40

Richard Sims worked at the British Museum and was the compiler of the "Index to the Heralds' Visitation" and the "Handbook to the Library of the British Museum".

151) SKENE, Sir John. (c.1543-1617)
Regiam Majestatem; the Auld Lawes and Constitutions of Scotland collected furth of the Register and other bukes, fra the dayes of Malcome, the Second untill the time of James the First, translated out of Latine in Scottish language. (with) twa treatises, the ane, anent the Order of Proces observed before the Lords of Counsell and Session, the other, of Crimes and Judges in Criminal Causes. Folio. Edinburgh. Thomas Finlason. 1609. 1st edition. (vi), 158,(i),181,(2) leaves. Numerous engraved headpieces, initials & tail=pieces. First and last blank. Sl. holes in first blank, title sl. browned at edge & lower corner of title, some sl. spotting of first few leaves. With a Scottish Armorial bookplate. Contemp. speckled calf, rubbed & sl. worn. SCARCE. S. &M. v.106. STC 22626. £250

Skene was an important pioneer of Scots legal studies and his translation of

151. SKENE, Sir John. Regiam Majestatem,.cont.
the old Scot's laws appeared concurrently with his Latin collection of the same year in 1609.
The Regiam Majestatem is a Scotch version of Glanvill, compiled in the first half of the 13th century. The two works are collated in Acts of the Parliament of Scotland.

152) SOCIETY of GENTLEMEN PRACTISERS.
The Records in the Courts of Law and Equity called the Law Society. Compiled from Manuscripts in the possession of the Incorporated Law Society of the United Kingdom. 4to. Published by the Society. 1897. cxiii,360pp. Index. Frontispiece plate and 2 other plates of facsimiles. Uncut, buckram, leather label, t.e.g. Fine. £40

The history of the Law Society.

153) SOLORZANO PEREIRA, Juan de.
Politica Indiana, sacada en lengua Castellana de los dos tomos del derecho i Govierno Municipal de las Indias Occidentales...por el mesmo autor. Madrid Por Diego Diaz de la Carrera. 1648. 1st Spanish edition. Folio. Engraved title. Engraved portrait after ??? 5. (xliv),1040,(cii)pp. Index. Sm. hole in 3?4 aff. border. Some slight occasional browning. CONTEMPORARY LIMP VELLUM, lacks ties. Sm. tear in upper cover. A VERY FINE COPY. SABIN 86534. MEDINA BHA 1130. HEREDIA IV,7886. TERNAUX BIB. AMER. 664. LECLERC 3537. STEVENS HISTORICAL NUGGETS 2549. GOLDSMITH S 427. MAGGS: SPANISH BOOKS 992. £1,500

The work of Solorzano, a jurist of Salamanca and member of the Councils of Castille & the Indies, is a Code of Law for the Spanish Americas in six books; the last of these, containing an account of the administrative establishment, was newly added by the author to this Spanish versions.
The work first appeared in Latin, but the Spanish contains many other revisions. It is the most valuable published work on the Law of the Spanish Colonies.

154) (SOMERS, John Lord (L.C.) (1650-1716.)
The Security of English-mens lives, or the trust, power, and duty of the Grand Jurys of England. Explained according to the fundamentals of the English Government, and the declarations of the same made in Parliament by many Statutes. 16mo. Benj. Alsop. 1682. 2nd edition. 168pp. Contemp. calf, rubbed & sl. stained. WING S 4644. S. &M.i.378/34. £85

Published for the prevention of Popish designs against the lives of many Protestant Lords and Commoners, who stand firm to the religion and ancient Government of England.

155) SOMNER, William.
A Treatise of Gavelkind, both name and thing. By R.U.W.Leybourn, for the authour. 1660. 1st edition. Sm.4to. (xiv),216,(viii)pp. Index. Lacks first blank. Modern wraps. WING S 4668. S. & M.i.477. £120

Somner was an academic rather than a lawyer, a pupil of the scholar Meric Casaubon; the accent of his books is accordingly philological in the main, although he includes a chapter on the place of Gavelkin in the history of the law of descents & prints several ancient charters showing it in action.

156) (STANFORD or STAUNFORD, Sir William)(1509-1558)
An Exposicion of the Kinges Prerogative collected out of the Great Abridgement of Justice Fitzherbert and other olde writers of the Lawes of Englande ....1568. (i),(5),6-85 leaves. Black Letter. Colophon: Imprynted at London in flete strete within temple Barre at the signe of the hand and starre by Rychard Tottel. 1568. Cum privilegio. BEALES T 492. New STC 23214. S. & M.i.119/79. Modern antique calf binding. FINE COPY WITH WIDE MARGINS. £400

The King's Prerogative (a commentary on 17 Edward II) was written by Stanford in 1548, before he became a judge, is a work of great historical importance and far ahead of its time. It is considered to be the earliest monograph on statutory interpretation and is further remarkable for being written in English. It shows the wide reading and historical knowledge which was characteristic of the author.

157) ....Les Plees del Coron, diuisees in plusors titles & comon lieux... dernierment corrigee avecques un table...In aedibus Richardi Tottelli.1574. Sm.4to. French text. Black Letter. FINE WOODCUT TITLE-BORDER (BEALE 47) & INITIALS. (xiv),193,(i.e. 198) leaves. Index. BEALE T 489. New STC 23222. S. & M.i.365/68
.....An Exposition of the Kinges Prerogatius, collected out of the great Abridgement of Justice Fitzherbert, and other olde writers of the Lawes of England. Richard Tottel. n.d. (1577)(5th edition). 4to. Black Letter. 85 leaves. BEALE T 495. New STC 23216. S. & M.i. 119/79.
Two works in 1 volume.Contemp. calf, rubbed, rebacked. FINE COPY. £350

Les Plees del Coron is Stanford's great abridgment of criminal law.

158)....Les Plees del Coron.....1583. Richardi Tottelli. Sm.4to......
Fine woodcut title-border (BEALE 47) & initials (xii),196,(i.e.198) leaves. BEALE T 490. NEW STC 23223. S. & M.i.365.
.....An Exposition of the Kinges Prerogative.....Richard Totthil. 1590. BEALE T 496. New STC 23217. S. &M.i.119/79. Does not contain the dedications to Nicholas Bacon (A_{ii-v} in 1577 edition), i.e. Title is on A_i; on verso summary (A_v in 1577 edition) A_{ii} is "Prerogativa" and on verso Cap.I continuing as in 1577 edition as A_{iii} (leaf 6).
2 works in 1 vol. FINE CONTEMP. CALF WITH DEVICE on BOTH COVERS; rebacked; endpapers browned and not attached to boards; first blank laid down. ARMORIAL BOOKPLATE of the Rt. Hon Charles LORD HALIFAX, 1702 on verso of title. A VERY FINE COPY. £300

159) STATUTES
Magna Charta cum statutis, tum antiquis, tum recentibus, maximopere animo tenendis nunc demum ad unum, tipis aedita, per Richardum Tottell. 1576. Black Letter. French, English & Latin text. Woodcut initials,indices. (viii), 247 leaves. Blank ?8. Head-margin of title & fore-margins of last two leaves renewed. Many contemp. annotations (some cropped), ink scribbles on title, few sl. stains. Modern calf, raised bands. BEALE S 19. STC 9281 (reading "March" in colophon) S.&M.i.552/9. £350

A greatly modernised successor to the old "Antiqua Statuta", more than half the volume consisting of enactments dated between 1422 & 1571 & never before published in this form. The annotator preserves three observations on the statutes of Merton & Marlborough, made by Thomas Egerton (later Lord Ellesmere L.C.,the founder of the modern Court of Chancery) in his unpublished Lenten readings in Lincoln's Inn.

160) STATUTES, IRELAND.
The Statutes of Ireland beginning the Third Yere of King Edward II. Dublin. The Societie of Stationers. 1621. Folio. (xxx),446pp. Black Letter. Woodcut title-border, & arms on first leaf & title-verso. Index. Lacks final blank. Contemp. polished calf, LARGE GILT ROYAL ARMS & INITIALS of JAMES I & CORNER ORNAMENTS on each SIDE, rebacked in 18th century & corners repaired. Joints & edges sl. worn, lacks ties. Book-plate SIGNET LIBRARY. New STC 14130. S. & M.iv.87. £750

This style of binding is also found on books printed by Robert Barker, the King's Printer in London, who would presumably have been the English distributor for this book. Despite the "good authority" mentioned in an 18th century note on the title, it does not appear that the book was the King's own property. This edition of Richard Bolton is the second collection of Irish Statutes.

161) STAUNTON, Sir George Thomas.
Ta Tsing Leu Lee; being the Fundamental Laws, and a selection from the Supplementary Statutes, of the PENAL CODE of CHINA; originally printed and published in Pekin, in various successive editions, under the sanction, and by the authority, of the several Emperors of the Ta Tsing, or Present Dynasty. Translated from the Chinese; and accompanied with an Appendix, consisting of authentic documents, and a few occasional notes, illustrative of the subject of the work by Sir George Thomas Staunton. 4to. T.Cadell & W. Davies. 1810. lxxvi, 581,(i)pp. Appendix, index, errata & fp. facsimile of the title of the latest edition of the Ta Tsing Leu Lee of 1805. Half calf, label. Spine sl. darkened & hinges sl. rubbed, sl. wear on top of front hinge. GOOD COPY WITH WIDE MARGINS. £280

162) (STEPHEN, Sir George) (1794-1879)
Adventures of an Attorney in search of Practice, or a delineation of professional life. Saunders and Otley. 1840. 2nd edition. xlii,450pp. Half calf, sl. rubbed. Two bookplates. £15

First edition published in 1839.
Lawyer and author. Formed plan for "Agency Committee" of Anti-Slavery Society; solicitor under act for relieving imprisoned pauper debtors, emigrated to Melbourne, Australia in 1855. Besides the above, he published "Adventures of a Gentleman in search of a Horse by Caveat Emptor", 1835, "Anti-salvery recollections" 18[illegible] and other works.

163) STYLE'S PRACTICAL REGISTER,
begun in the reign of King Charles I consisting of rules, orders and the principal observations concerning the practice of the Common Law in the Courts at Westminster, particularly the Kings Bench, as well in matter criminal as civil. Alphabetically digested under several titles. With a table..C. Harper etc. 1707. 4th edition with large additions. (xiv),682,(6)pp. Advert. leaf before title. Some sections sl. browned. Contemp. calf, label, rubbed spine & hinges worn. S. &M. .279/145. £35

164) SUPREME COURT of JUDICATURE.
Rules of the Supreme Court. 1883. (Presented pursuant to an Act of Parliament) Ordered, by the House of Commons, to be printed 11 July 1883. 4to. Henry Hansard. 417pp. Paper sl. browned. Half calf, rubbed & worn, binding sound. £25

Earl of Selborne was Lord High Chancellor of G.B. at that time and the dedication appointed Lord Justice Lindley, Mr. Baron Pollock, Mr. Justice Manisty & Mr. Justice [illegible] to be the four Judges of the Supreme Court of Judicature.

165) SWAN, Joseph R. (—1884)
A Treatise on the Law relating to the Powers and Duties of Justices of the Peace, and Constables in the STATE of OHIO, with practical forms etc... Columbus (USA) Isaac N. Whiting. 1837. 1st edition. xviii,(i),582pp. Index. Paper sl. browned, endpapers sl. stained. Contemp. calf, rubbed. £95
SABIN WRNS 94012.

Swan was president of the 12th Judicial Circuit; an ardent abolitionist and active in the anti-slavery movement. After 1859 he never again accepted a judicial office or engaged in active legal practice but devoted his time to wide reading and to civic and business enterprises. He also rendered much aid to legislative committees, which habitually called on him to help in drafting important legislation.
It is upon his work as a legal writer, however, that his fame most depends. The above work gave him his greatest renown and has been called "probably the most useful book every published in Ohio". Swan himself prepared 12 editions and up to 1930 27 editions had appeared.

166) THOMAS, A.H. (edited by)
Calendar of Early Mayor's Court Rolls preserved among the Archives of the Corporation of the City of London at the Guildhall a.d. 1298-1307. Cambridge. University Press 1924. xlv,304pp. Indices of names and subjects. PRESENTATION COPY. Orig. cloth, sl. marked. £25

167) TILLESLEY, Richard.
Animadversions upon Mr. Selden's History of Tithes, and his Review thereof. John Bill. 1619. 1st edition. Sm.4to. (xl),236pp. First leaf blank, except for signature in WOODCUT FRAME. ROYAL ARMS on TITLE VERSO. A few sm. wormholes in fore-margins and some occasional light staining, a FINE COPY in CONTEMP. VELLUM, ties (one broken) paste-downs detached. STC 24073 (Hungtington copy only) S. &M. i.196/56 £150

Tillesley, fond of anagrams, attempts to compete with Selden in the quotation of legal authority.

168) VIOLET, Tho.
Narrative of some Remarkable Proceedings concerning the Ships Samson, Salvador, and George, and several other Prize-ships depending in the High Court of Admiraltie: most humbly presented to the Parliament of the Common-wealth of England, and to the Rt. Hon. the Council of State by Authoritie of Parliament,... the Council Officers, of...the Lord General. Sm.4to. (William Du-Gard) 1653. 1st edition. (xviii),114,(4)pp. Index. Half-title with FINE ENGRAVED VIGNETTE and dedication bound before main title & text. WING 593. S.&M.i.354/47.(1659 edition only). Folding chart of list of all such ships as the Fleet of the Parliament of England have brought into this Common-wealth as Dutch-Prizes.. Modern half calf, very sl. cropped at top margin. FINE COPY. RARE. £300

169) WALSH, Robert, Jr. (1784-1859)
An Appeal from the Judgments of G.B. respecting the U.S.of America. Part first containing an historical outline of their merits and wrongs as Colonies; and strictures upon the calumnies of the British writers. Philadelphia: Mitchell, Ames and White. 1819. 2nd edition. lvi,512pp. Uncut, with the orig. boards, detached, some pages loose. WITH BIBLIOGRAPHICAL NOTES. IN CLOTH-MADE SLIPCASE with morocco label on spine. 7 leaves of the notes, 3 leaves of the preface and a few leaves in the browned, some sl. staining and spotting of a few others, but overall a FINE CLEAN COPY in the ORIGINAL STATE. No errata slip. Bookplate of Herman Wm. Kapp. THIS COPY FORMERLY BELONG TO MAHLON DICKERSON, Governor of New Jersey, Secretary of the Navy and U.S. Senator, with his SIGNATURE "M. Dickerson" on fly-leaf. SABIN 101158. HOWES:U.S.IANA W67. £300
The second edition has the same imprint, date & collation as the first but should have an errata slip, not present in this copy.

170) WASHINGTON, J[illegible]eph.
An exact Abridgm[illegible] of all the Statutes of King William and Queen Mary, and of King William III and Queen Anne, in force and use., revised & continue to 3 April, 1704. With two new tables. R.& E. Atkyns. 1704. (82),661,(86pp. Contemp. calf rubbed. S. &M.i.566/35. £30

171) WEST, William.
The First (-Second)Part of Symboleography...newly augmented with divers presidents touching Marchants Affaires. Companie Stationers. 1605(-6) 2 parts in 1 vol. 4to. [illegible],(318)/(ii),304,(viii) leaves. Index, partly Black Letter, final blank. Contemp. MANUSCRIPT INSCRIPTION (metrical "rules for purchasing land") on endpapers. Contemp. calf, worn, rebacked. S. & M.i.487/74. Part I. New STC 25271. Part II. New STC 25279. (4to in 8's). £250

The growth of English commerce & the application of the statute of uses caused a revolution in the science of conveyancing, & the presented a challenge to the profession which West was the first to meet. He takes a wide view of his subject embracing commercial agreements, indictments, Chancery bills & answers, & general remarks on contract & on equity. Part 2 is dedicated to Coke.

172) .....Another copy. ...Symboleography..Companies of Stationers. 1610(-11). 2 parts in 1 vol. 4to. Same collation as above. 1 leaf in vol. sl. frayed. Contemp. calf, sl. worn, head of spine worn. New STC 25272/25279.3. £200

173).....Another Copy. Miles Flesher. 1647. (Flesher & Robert Young 1641) 2 parts in 1. 4to. Partly Black Letter. (vi),(306)/(ii),350,(viii) leaves. Index, final blank. Publishers' catalogue pasted inside lower cover. Imprint at head torn away, 4 lines of text also aff.,sm. hole Y8 (part 1) with loss of few letters. Sl. browned. Some contemp. annotations. Contemp. calf, worn. WING W 1394. £150

Includes a new appendix of bills and answers in Exchequer, Wards & Liveries & Star Chamber, with a short account of each Court. There are also some new precedents in the body of the work. PUBLISHERS' CATALOGUE PRINTED SEPARATELY as opposed to those included in the collation, ARE EXTREMELY RARE before about 1790.

174) WHEATON, Henry.
Elementos de Derecho Internacional. Transl. by Jose Maria Barros. 2 vols. Mexico. J.M. Lara 1854/5. Coleccion de Tratados con las Naciones Estranjeras, Leyes, Decretos Y Ordenes que forman el Derecho Internacional Mexicano. Appendix Al Derecho Internacional by Wheaton. Mexico. 1854. 1 vol. Altogether 3 vols. Contemp. calf-backed boards; corners rubbed, spines faded. SPANISH TEXT. £200

Barros translated Wheaton's Elements of Internation Law (1st American and English editions appeared in 1836).In the third volume he added an important collection of Mexican treaties relating to Aliens and concluded prior to 1854, together with the pertinent laws, degrees, etc.

175) WILKINSON, John.
A Treatise collected out of the statutes of this Common-wealth, and according to common experience of the Lawes, concerning the Office and Authorities of Coroners and Sheriffs. Together with an easie and plaine method for the keeping of a Court-leet, Court-baron and Hundred-Court. (with) the return of Writts by John Kitchin, now all published in English. Company of Stationers..1657. (iv)378,(iii),(i)pp. With the signature of "Henry Rutter his book 1676" on first and last blank; two other signatures. Contemp. calf, rebacked. WING W 2246. S. & M.i.221/8. £120

176) WRIGHT, Rt. Hon. Lord of Durley.
Legal Essays and Addresses. Cambridge. At the University Press. 1939. 1st ed. xxxv,442pp. Index, table of statutes & cases. LORD WRIGHT'S OWN COPY with his ARMS on BOTH COVERS. Calf, gilt dec'd spine & sides. Very sl. rubbed. £40

177) (YORKE, H.C.)
Some Considerations on the Law of Forfeiture, for High Treason, occasioned by a clause in the late act, for making it treason to correspond with the Pretender's sons, or any of their agents, etc. with an appendix concerning Estates-Tail in Scotland. J.J. Rivington. 1748. 3rd edition,further corrected & enlarged. viii,(vi),190pp. LARGE PAPER COPY with vignette on title and small device at end. Contemp. calf, gilt lines, rubbed & spine sl. worn. S. & M.i.368/23. £80

Yorke argues for the doctrine that a traitor's hereditaments revert to the Crown and justifies it on grounds that property like government is an institution of civil society and that he who has outraged the latter loses his right to the former; he adds a variety of historical illustrations.

Blackwell's Rare Books
Catalogue A7

ANTIQUARIAN LAW & HISTORY

(1980)

Antiquarian Law & History

PLEASE QUOTE CATALOGUE NO. A7 WHEN ORDERING

Codeword: "GOLAFRE"

I. LAW

1 **[Anon]** The Law of Evidence; wherein all the Cases that have yet been printed in any of our Law Books or Trials, and that in any wise relate to Points of Evidence, are collected and methodically digested under their proper Heads . . . Third Edition. *Printed by E. and R. Nutt, and R. Gosling (Assigns of E. Sayer), for R. Gosling,* 1739, *with considerable marginalia in contemp. hand,* ix[+xiii+]287[+lix] pp., 8vo, *contemp. tan calf, leather label* **£30.00**

2 **Arnot** (Hugo) A Collection and Abridgement of Celebrated Criminal Trials in Scotland. from A.D. 1536 to 1784, with historical and critical Remarks. *Edinburgh, Printed for the Author by William Smellie,* 1785, xxiv+400 pp., 4to, *contemp. calf, rubbed, rebacked, leather label* **£30.00**

3 **Bateman** (Tho.) A Treatise on Agistment Tithe, in which the Nature, Right, Objects, Mode of Payment, and Method of ascertaining the Value of Each Species of it, are fully Stated and Explained, as settled in Pursuance of a Decree of the Court of Exchequer, made in Easter Term m.dcc.lxxiv. Second Edition. *Printed and sold by Richardson and Urquhart, T. Cadell, and W. Tesseyman,* 1778, [and] An Appendix to the Treatise on Agistment Tithe . . . 1779, *wanting hf. titles,* xxiv+102:xvi+133[+i] pp., 8vo, *contemp. hf. calf, marb. bds., leather label* **£30.00**

4 **Blount** (Thomas) *Νομο-λεξικον*: A Law-Dictionary, interpreting such difficult and obscure Words and Terms, as are found either in our Common or Statute, Ancient or Modern Lawes. With References to the several Statutes, Records, Registers, Law-Books, Charters, Ancient Deeds, and Manuscripts, wherein the Words are used: and Etymologies, where they properly occur. *In the Savoy, Printed by Tho. Newcomb, for John Martin and Henry Herringman,* 1670, FIRST EDITION, *errata lf. present, most margins very fragile through damp, a few sl. defective at corners,* [x+272+i] pp., folio, *contemp. calf, newly rebacked, unlettered* (Wing B3340) **£50.00**

5 **Britton** (John) [on the Laws of England]. The Second Edition, faithfully corrected according to divers ancient Manuscripts of the same Booke, by Edm. Wingate. *Printed by the assignes of John Moore,* 1640, **Black Letter,** *light browning throughout, one lower corner torn away, edges heavily cropped with frequent partial or whole loss of headlines, lacking sig. U,* [xvi+]287(shd. read 291)[+xxi] ff., sm. 8vo, 18*th cent. tan calf, lettered, gilt and blind tooling, sprinkled edges* (STC 3804: Maxwell p. 38/9) **£60.00**

¶This work owes its origin to the project of Edward I. to produce a digest of the English Law somewhat after the manner of the Institutes of Justinian. It was probably written soon after 1290 and is the oldest English law book in the French language'. (Brunner)

6 —— Containing the Antient Pleas of the Crown, Translated; and Illustrated with References, Notes, and Antient Records, by Robert Kelham. *Printed by H. Woodfall and W. Strahan, for J. Worrall,* 1762, [xii+]168[+xxiv] pp., 8vo, *contemp. sheep, leather label* **£20.00**

7 **Burn** (Richard) The Justice of the Peace, and Parish Officer, Thirteenth Edition, 4 Vols. *Printed by W. Strahan and M. Woodfall, for T. Cadell,* 1776, 8vo, *contemp. calf, leather labels, little rubbed* **£35.00**

8 —— The Justice of the Peace, and Parish Officer, continued to the Present Time by John Burn, Sixteenth Edition, to which is added an Appendix, including the Statutes of the last Session of Parliament (28 Geo.3.), 4 Vols. *Printed by A. Strahan and W. Woodfall, for T. Cadell,* 1788, 8vo, *contemp. calf, leather labels* **£30.00**

9 **Burrow** (Sir James) Reports of Cases adjudged in the Court of Kings Bench, since the Death of Lord Raymond . . . Part the Fourth, 2 Vols., Michaelmas Term 30 Geo. 2. 1756 to Trinity Term 1 Geo. 3. 1761 (inclusive). *Dublin, Printed by R. Moncrieffe*, 1785, xviii+1-53[54-607+lxx]:[xii+548+lxxii] pp., 8vo, *contemp. tan calf, leather labels* **£35.00**
¶Vol. i. Fourth Edition: vol. ii. Third Edition.

10 **C[arter]** (S[amuel]) Lex Custumaria: or, a Treatise of Copy-hold Estates, in respect of the Lord—Copy-holder. Wherein the Nature of Customs in general, and of particular Customs, Grants and Surrenders, and their Constructions and Expositions in reference to the thing granted or surrendered, and the Uses or Limitations of Estates are clearly Illustrated . . . *Printed by the Assigns of Richard and Edward Atkins for John Walthoe*, 1696, [xxiv+]384[+xxiv] pp., 8vo, *contemp. calf, panelled in blind, unlettered* (Wing C665) **£35.00**

11 **Cobbett** (William) and T. B. **Howell.** Cobbett's Complete Collection of State Trials and Proceedings for High Treason and other Crimes and Misdemeanors from the Earliest Period to the Present Time. Vols. 1-15 (AD. 1163 to 1719), 15 Vols. *Printed by T. C. Hansard*, 1809-1812, 8vo, *contemp. diced tan calf, gilt, backstrips sl. faded, otherwise in excellent condition* **£250.00**

12 **Convicts, Prisons, etc.** A Collection of 68 Acts of Parliament, 1800-1850, relating to Convicts, Prisons, Courts, etc. bound into 1 volume. Folio, *contemp. hf. morocco, marb. bds. rubbed, sometime crudely rebacked with marb. paper, now split at joint* **£185.00**
¶A list of the contents will be sent on request.

13 **Corporis Ivris Civilis,** quo continentur Institvtionvm libri qvatvor, et Digestorvm sive Pandectarvm libri qvinqvaginta [et] D. Ivstiniani Codicis, libri xii . . . 2 Vols. in 1. *Amstelaedami, apud viduam Danielis Elservirii* . . . 1681, *engr. title*, [xviii+]904:754 pp., 8vo, *contemp. calf, corners little worn, newly rebacked, leather label* **£35.00**

14 **Craig** (Thomas) Jus Feudale tribus Libris comprehensum, quibus non solum Consuetudines Feudales & Praediorum Iura, quae in Scotia, Anglia, & plerisque Galliae locis obtinent, continentur; sed Universum Ius Scoticum, et omnes fere Materiae Iuris clare & dilucide exponuntur, et ad sontes Iuris Feudalid & Civilis singula reducuntur. *Edinburgi, Impressum Anno Dom.* 1655, *considerable marginalia in several hands, edges browned throughout, title soiled*, [xii+]383 pp., folio, *new qtr. calf, leather label, marb. bds.* (Wing C6801—variant imprint) **£65.00**
¶Once the property of John Dalrymple—Stair and of Hugo Dalrymple.

15 —— The Right of Succession to the Kingdom of England, in Two Books; against the Sophisms of Parsons the Jesuite, who assum'd the Counterfeit Name of Doleman; by which he endeavours to overthrow not only the Rights of Succession in Kingdoms, but also the Sacred Authority of Kings themselves . . . now Faithfully Translated into English [by James Gatherer] . . . *Printed by M. Bennet, for Dan. Brown* . . . 1703, pp. [xxxiv+]1-230:245-431[+xvi], folio, *contemp. sprinkled calf, corners worn, newly rebacked, leather label* **£65.00**
¶'This work was originally written in 1602, and dedicated to James the Sixth of Scotland, the legality of whose succession to the crown of England, on the death of Q. Elizabeth, it was intended to prove'. (Lowndes)

16 **Croke** (Sir George) The First Part of the Reports . . . of such select Cases as were adjudged in the said Courts [King's Bench and Commons-Bench], from the 24th to the 44th/45 of the late Queen Elizabeth, . . . rev. and published in English by Sir Harbottle Grimston. *Printed by and for John Field and Tho. Newcomb* . . . 1661, FIRST EDITION, *portrait, some early annotations throughout*, [xi+]920(shd. read 926)[+lxiv] pp., folio, *contemp. crimson morocco, royal arms, on sides, sometime rebacked, backstrip lettered upside down* (Wing C7011) **£65.00**

17 —— The Second Part of the Reports . . . as were adjudged in the said Courts, during the whole Reign of the late King James: . . . revised and published in English by Sir Harbottle Grimston, with an Exact Table of the principal Points of the Law, argued and resolved therein. *Printed by T. Newcomb and W. Godbid* . . . 1559, FIRST EDITION, *portrait, a few pp. soiled, final blank present*, [xxvi+]700[+xxii] pp., folio, *contemp. crimson morocco, royal arms on sides, sometime rebacked and lettered* (Wing C7016) **£65.00**

18 —— The Third Part of the Reports . . . of such select Cases, as were adjudged in the said Courts, the time that he was a Judge in either of them . . . Revised and published in English, by Sir Harbottle Grimston. *Printed by and for Tho, Newcomb* . . . 1661, *portrait*, [xxii+]669[+i] pp., folio, *contemp. crimson morocco, royal arms on sides, sometime rebacked and lettered* (Wing—not recorded) **£75.00**

19 **Cumberland** (Richard) De Legibus Naturae Disquisitio Philosophica, in qua earum Forma, summa Capita, Ordo, Promulgatio, & Obligatio e rerum Natura investigantur; quinetiam Elementa Philosophiae Hobbianae, cum Moralis tum Civilis, considerantur & refutantur. *Typis E. Flesher, prostat verò apud Nathanaelem Hooke*, 1672, FIRST EDITION, *title in red and black, some browning throughout, imprimatur lf. present*, [lxv+]421[+i] pp., sm. 4to, *contemp. sprinkled calf, leather label, upper cover rubbed, head of backstrip sl. defective, joints beginning to crack* (Wing C7580) **£65.00**

20 —— De Legibus Naturae Disquisitio Philosophica . . . *Typis E. Flesher, prostat verò apud Nathanaelem Hooke*, 1672, FIRST EDITION, *title in red and black, imprimatur lf. present, marginal notes and markings in ink and pencil by various hands, signature of James H. Todd, Trin. Coll. Dublin at head of dedication page*, [lxv+]+421[+i] pp., sm. 4to, *contemp. calf, blind tooled, rubbed and corners worn, sometime rebacked, old leather label retained* (Wing w7580) **£60.00**

21 [**Cunningham** (Timothy)] The Law of Bills of Exchange, Promissory Notes, Bank-Notes, and Insurances: containing all the Statutes, Cases at large, Arguments, Resolutions, Judgements, Decrees, and Customs of Merchants concerning them, methodically digested . . . by a Gentleman of the Middle Temple. *Printed for W. Owen*, 1760, FIRST EDITION, xxvi+451 pp., 8vo, *contemp. tan calf, leather label* **£25.00**

22 —— A New Treatise on the Laws concerning Tithes, containing all the Statutes, Adjudged Cases, Resolutions and Judgments relative thereto . . . Third Edn., corr. and enl. *Printed for W. Griffin*, 1748, *some staining throughout, pen trials on title and elsewhere, lacks A^1*, [ii+]304[+viii] pp., 8vo, *contemp. calf, unlettered, corners sl. worn, shelf marks on backstrip* **£15.00**

23 [**Egerton** (Sir Thomas, *Baron Ellesmere and Viscount Brackley*)] The Speech of the Lord Chancellor of England, in the Eschequer Chamber, touching the Post-nati. *Printed for the Societie of Stationers*, 1609, FIRST EDITION, *A^1 & [Q^4] both present, with double printed line borders*, [xii+]118[+ii] pp., sm. 4to, *qtr. crushed maroon morocco, lettered cloth sides* (STC 7540) **£140.00**
¶From the Phillipps collection.
The most important of Lord Ellesmere's judgments. The *Post-nati* were Scots born after the accession of James vi. of Scotland to the English throne. It was ruled that the *Post-nati* were natural-born subjects and therefore entitled to hold land in England.

24 [——] The Speech of the Lord Chancellor of England in the Eschequer Chamber, touching the Post-nati. *Printed for the Societie of Stationers*, 1609, FIRST EDITION, *A^1 and [Q^4], blanks, both present, a prayer in contemporary hand on A^1r*, [xii+]118[+ii][+28 pp. binder's blanks] pp., sm. 4to, *modern hf. calf, leather label, cloth sides* (STC 7520) **£105.00**

25 **Feilding** (Robert) The Arraignment, Tryal, and Conviction of . . . for Felony, in Marrying Her Grace the Dutchess of Cleaveland; his first Wife Mrs. Mary Wadsworth, being then Alive . . . *Printed for John Morphew*, 1708, *browning throughout, several margins repaired*, 27 pp., folio, *disbound* **£15.00**

26 **Fell** (Walter Wm.) A Treatise on the Law of Mercantile Guaranties, and Engagements in the Nature of Guarantie. *Printed for J. Butterworth and J. Cooke*, 1811, *inscribed 'from the Author'*, xxxii+311 pp., 8vo, *orig. drab bds., paper label, all edges untrimmed* **£35.00**

27 **Fitzherbert** (Anthony) La Grande Abridgement collected par le Judge tres reuerend monsieur Anthony Fitzherbert, dernierment Conferre anesq la Copy Escript, et per ceo Correct: Aueques le nombre del fueil, per quel facilement poies trouer les Cases cy Abrydges en les Lyuers dans, nouelment annote: iammais deuaunt imprimee. Auxi vous troues le residuums delauter liuer places ivy in ceo liuer en le fyne de lour apte titles. *In Aedib Ricardi Tottell, duodecimo Nouembris*, 1565, **Black Letter,** *in Anglo-Norman, divisional ti some marginalia, some margins cut close, titles within woodcut borders (McKerrow 122) titl part one supplied in photo-facsimile*, thick folio, 18*th cent. dark brown calf, gilt panelling, n rebacked to match* (STC 10956; Cowley 55: Beale 463/4) **£120.**

28 **Fortescue** (Sir John) De Laudibus Legum Angliae . . . Hereto are ioind the two Summes of Sir Ralph de Hengham L. Ch. Iustice to K. Edward I. commonly calld Hengham Magna and Hengham Parua. Never before publisht [Preface and Notes by John Selden] both on Fortescve and Hengham are added. *For the Companie of Stationers*, 1616, *partly* **Black Letter,** *Latin and English in parallel, some headlines and side notes cropped or shaved, lacks A^1 (blank) but Q^8 (final blank) present*, [viii+]132[+3] ff., 56[+xii+]159 pp. (STC 11197)
[with]
Glanville (R. de) Tractatvs de Legibus & Consuetudinibus regni Angliae, tempore Regis Henrici secundi compositus, Iusticiae gubernacula tenente . . . Et illas solem Leges continet & consuetudines secundum quas placitatur in Curia Regis ad Scaccarium & coram Iusticiis vbicunque suerint. Qui nunc imprimatur post 50. annos a priori & prima Impressione, quia in pluribus concordat cum antiquo libro Legum Scotie vocato Regiam Maiestatem . . . *In aedibus Thomae Wight*, 1604, [x+]116[xvii] ff., *leaf with signature, before title, present* (STC 11906)
[and]
Saint German (Christopher) Dialogvs de fundamentis Legum Angliae et de conscientia . . . *In aedibus Thomae Wight*, 1604, [iv+]73[+ii] ff., *lacks final blank* (STC 21560)
Three items bound together, sm. 8vo, *early sprinkled calf, backstrip originally gilt, now rather rubbed, lacks label, upper joint cracked* **£225.00**

29 **Godolphin** (John) The Orphans Legacy: or, a Testamentary Abridgment. In Three Parts. I. Of Last Wills and Testaments. II. Of Executors and Administrators. III. Of Legacies and Devices. Wherein the most Material Points of Law relating to that Subject, are succinctly Treated, as well according to the Common and Temporal, as Ecclesiastical and Civil Laws of this Realm . . . Second Edition much augmented and enlarged. *Printed for Chr. Wilkinson*, 1677, *some notes in margins and on rear paste-down*, [viii+]478(shd. read 474)[+xx] pp., sm. 4to, *contemp. calf, unlettered, sl. rubbing* (Wing G947) **£45.00**

30 **Grey** (Richard) A System of English Ecclesiastical Law. Extracted from the Codex Juris Ecclesiastici Anglicani . . . for the Use of Young Students in the Universities, who are designed for Holy Orders. Second Edition. *In the Savoy, Printed by E. and R. Nutt, and R. Gosling, for C. King*, 1732, *some discolouration*, [xvi+]448[+lxxxiv] pp., 8vo, *contemp. panelled calf, lacks label, joints cracked, upper cover almost detached* **£15.00**

31 **Grosvenor Divorce.** See item 48.

32 **Hale** (Sir Matthew) The Original Institution, Power and Justification of Parliaments. In two parts . . . with a Declaration of the House of Commons, concerning their Privileges, drawn up by a Select Committee . . . *Printed for Jacob Tonson, Benjamin Barker, and Charles King*, 1707, [x+]240 pp., 8vo, *contemp. tan calf, backstrip and joints rubbed* **£30.00**

33 [**Holles** (Denzil, *First Baron Holles of Ifield*)] A Letter of a Gentleman to his Friend, shewing that the Bishops are not to be Judges in Parliament in Cases Capital. *Printed in the Year*, 1679, [ii+]119 pp., sm. 8vo, *contemp. sprinkled sheep, unlettered, a sound copy* (Wing H2461) **£35.00**

34 **Institutes of Hindu Law:** or, the Ordinances of Menu, according to the Gloss of Cullúca. Comprising the Indian System of Duties, Religious and Civil. Verbally translated from the original Sanscrit, with a Preface, by Sir William Jones. *Calcutta: London, reprinted for J. Sewell*, 1796, *lacks Aa^8 (?final blank)*, xvi[+ii+]366 pp., 8vo, *orange buckram, lettered* **£35.00**

35 **Jacob** (Giles) The Complete Court-Keeper: or Land-Steward's Assistant . . . Seventh Edition . . . *Printed by His Majesty's Law Printers* . . . 1731, *two outer margins defective, some browning throughout*, viii+538[+xxv] pp., 8vo, *contemp. calf, leather label, head of backstrip sl. defective* **£15.00**

36 **Justinian.** Jurisprudentia Philologica, sive Elementa Juris Civilis, secundum Methodum et Seriem Institutionum Justiniani . . . per Robertum Eden. *Oxonii, e Theatro Sheldoniano*, 1744, *engr. portrait, a few fore-margins damp stained*, xx+307 pp., 4to, *tan calf, leather label, upper joints cracked, r.e.* **£45.00**

37 **The Law of Ejectments:** shewing the Nature of Ejectione Firme; the Difference between it and Trespass, and how to be brought or removed where the Lands lie in Franchises . . . as also, Who are good Witnesses or not in the Trial on Ejectment . . . together with the Learning of Special Verdicts at large, relating to Titles of Land and Estates . . . Second Edition . . . In the Savoy, *Printed by J. Nutt* . . . 1713, *generally discoloured*, [ii+]iv[+xi+]328[+xvi] pp., 8vo, *contemp. sheep, little rubbed, small splits in joints, unlettered* **£25.00**

38 **The Law of Evidence;** or, the Attorney and Solicitor's Necessary Assistant, by a Society of Gentlemen. *Printed for W. and J. Stratford*, [1796/7], *date trimmed from title*, [iv+]109(shd. read 99) pp.:
[with]
Rural Law. Being a Digest of the Laws which relate principally to Country Affairs, by a Society of Gentlemen. *Printed for W. and J. Stratford*, 1797, [iv+]119 pp.:
[and]
The Counsellor's Magazine; or, a Complete Law Library for Barristers . . . and Others, who would wish to acquire a competent Knowledge of the Law . . . by a Society of Gentlemen, of the Middle Temple. *Printed by W. and J. Stratford*, 1796, iv+148 pp.:
Three pieces bound together, 8vo, *contemp. qtr. calf, leather label, vellum corners, marb. bds.* **£35.00**

39 **Levinz** (Sir Creswell) A Collection of Select and Modern Entries of Declarations, Pleadings, Issues, Verdicts, Judgments, &c. referring to the Cases in Sir Creswell Levinz's Reports; the Judgment of the Court being added to each President, with Notes and References to the Reports and Entries of the Law, also some Entries in the 10th, 11th and 12th Years of the Reign of the late King William III. *Printed by the Assigns of Richard and Edward Atkins for D. Browne, T. Benskin and J. Walthoe*, 1702, *Knoller's portrait of the author, contents exceptionally clean*, [iv+]223[+xx] pp., folio, *contemp. calf, leather label, upper cover surface damaged by worn* **£75.00**

40 **Lyndwood** (William) Provinciale, (seu Constitvtiones Angliae), continens Constitutiones Provinciales, quatuordecim Archiepiscoporum Cantuariensium, viz. a Stephano Mangtono ad Henricum Chichleium; cum Summariis atque eruditis Annotationibus, summa accuratione denuo revisum atque impressum . . . *Oxoniae, excud. H. Hall, imp. Ric Davis*, 1679, [lxiv+]360+155[+xx+]77[+i] pp., folio, *contemp. calf, sides little rubbed, small crack in lower joint, lacks label* (Wing L3565: Madan 3221) **£85.00**

41 **Manutius** (Paulus) Antiqvitatvm Romanarvm, Liber de Legibvs. Index rerum memorabilium. *Venetiis [Aldus]* 1557, EARLY ISSUE, *with 5 lines on fol. lxxx*, [see Ebert 12990], [iv+lxxx+ii] ff. (Adams M473):
[with]
Sigonius (Carolus) Fasti Consvlares, ac triumphi acti a Romulo Rege vsqve ad T. I. Caesarem. eivsdem in Fastos, et Trivmphos, idest in vniversam Romanam Historiam Commentarivs. Eiusdem de Nominibus Romanorum liber. *Venetiis, ex. Off. Stellae Giordanis Zileti*, 1556, *last lf. creased*, 16+169[+i] ff. (Adams S1115):
Two works bound together, folio, *contemp. vellum, leather label vellum peeled away from cords, lacks ties* **£120.00**

42 **Montesquieu** (Charles Louis de Secondat, *Baron*) The Spirit of Laws. Translated from the French. 2 Vols. *Glasgow, Printed by David Nivan*, . . . 1793, xxiv+381:xiv+427 pp., 12mo, *contemp. marb. sheep, leather labels, backstrips little rubbed* **£45.00**

43 **N[elson]** (William) The Office and Authority of a Justice of Peace, collected out of all the Books, whether of Common or Statute-Law, hitherto written on that Subject . . . Second Edition. *Printed by the Assigns of Rich. and Edward Atkins, for Charles Harper*, 1707, [viii+]599[+i] pp., 8vo, *contemp. calf, paper label, one corner of upper cover damaged, lacks front free end-paper* **£25.00**

44 **The newe greate abredgement** brefly conteynynge, all the actes and statutes of this Realme of England, untyll the xxxv. yere of the reigne of our late noble Kynge of moste worthye and famous memorye Henry the viii. (whose soule God pardone) newly reuysed trulye corrected & amended to the greate pleasure and commoditе of all the readers thereof. *Excusum Londiniin officina Thomas Gaultier, [Imprynted at London by Richard Kele]*, 1551, **Black Letter,** *title within ornamental border* (McK. 101), *some occasional staining in upper margins, lacks final blank*, [viii+]381[+x] ff., thick sm. 8vo, *late 18th cent. dark brown calf, lettered, gilt backstrip, sides bordered with 'Greek-key' ornament, with blind-tooled lozenges, each containing a cross-shaped floral ornament, m.e., small split in one joint* (STC 9525: Cowley 45) **£130.00**

45 **Noble** (Richard) The True Copy of the Original Paper . . . designed for his last Speech . . . *Printed for Samuel Keble, and sold by John Morphew*, 1713, 6 pp., folio, *sewed* **£15.00**

46 —— The Case of Mr. Richard Noble Impartially Consider'd: abstractly from the Man, or Crime, but meerly as to the Law, in relation to the Motion by him made . . . by a Student of the Inner Temple. *Printed and are to be sold by J. Morphew*, 1713, *all outer margins repaired*, [ii+]9 pp., folio, *disbound* **£16.00**

47 **N[oye]** (W[illiam]) A Treatise of the Principall Grounds and Maximes of the Lavves of the Kingdome. Very usefull and commodious for all Students, and such others as desire the Knowledge and Understanding of the Lavves. *Printed for W. Cook*, 1642, *divisional titles, some discolouration*, [viii+]179[+ii] pp., sm. 8vo, *early sprinkled calf, lacks label, joints beginning to crack* (Wing N1452) **£75.00**
¶Includes *A Treatise of Particular Estates* by Sir John Doddridge and *Certaine Observations concerning a Deed of Feoffament* by T.H.

48 **Obscurities and Defects** of the Mercantile Law considered, in an Essay on Bills of Exchange. *Printed for S. Crowder, and sold by W. Wardlaw*, 1769, *some soiling*, vii+57 pp.:
[and]
Grosvenor. Copies of the Depositions of the Witnesses examined in the Cause of Divorce . . . between Richard Lord Grosvenor . . . and Henrietta Lady Grosvenor . . . *Printed for J. Russel*, 1771, *embrowned*, viii+307 pp.:
Two pieces together, 8vo, *contemp. qtr. calf, leather label, marb. bds., little rubbed, upper joint cracking* **£85.00**

49 **The Practick Part of the Law:** shewing the Office of an Attorney, and a Guide for Solicitors in all the Courts of Westminster . . . With the exact Table of Fees of all the said Courts at Westminster . . . Fourth Edition . . . *Printed by John Nutt, Assigne of Edward Sayer, for John Walthoe*, 1711, [vii+]599[+xxv+vii+]120+16 pp., 8vo, *contemp. calf, paper label, chipped, some rubbing* **£21.00**

50 **Prison Reform.** HOWARD (John) The State of the Prisons in England and Wales, with Preliminary Observations, and an Account of some Foreign Prisons and Hospitals, Fourth Edition. *Printed for J. Johnson, C. Dilly, and T. Cadell*, 1792, *wirh 22 engraved plates, (19 folding), Directions to Bookbinder placed after Index, some light foxing*, [vi+]540 pp., 4to, *contemp. marbled calf, sometime rebacked, corners and edges rubbed* **£85.00**

51 **The Resolutions of the House of Commons,** for the Impeachment of Sir William Scroggs Knt. Chief Justice of the Court of King's Bench; Sir Thomas Jones . . . Sir Richard Weston . . . relating to the Arbitary and Illegal Proceedings of the said Judges. *Printed for John Wright, and Richard Chiswell*, 1680, *some margins repaired*, [iv+]27 pp., folio, *disbound* **£20.00**

52 **Sacheverell.** The Tryal of Dr. Henry Sacheverell, before the House of Peers, for High Crimes and Misdemeanors; upon an Impeachment by the Knights, Citizens and Burgesses in Parliament Assembled, in the Name of themselves, and of all the Commons of Great Britain . . . *Printed for Jacob Tonson*, 1710, [iii+]335 pp., *embrowning throughout*:
[and]
Proceedings . . . containing the Reasons of those Lords that Enter'd their Protest in Dr. Sacheverell's Case . . . *Printed, and sold by J. Baker*, 1710, 8 pp.:
2 works bound together, folio, *contemp. panelled calf, rubbed, corners worn* **£30.00**

53 **Salkeld** (William) Report of Cases adjudged in the Court of King's Bench; with some Special Cases in the Courts of Chancery, Common Pleas and Exchequer, from the First Year of K. William and Q. Mary, to the Tenth Year of Queen Anne . . . 2 Vols. in 1. Second Edition carefully Corrected . . . *In the Savoy, Printed by Eliz. Nutt, and R. Gosling, (Assigns of Edw. Sayer) for J. Walthoe and J. Walthoe, jun.*, 1721, *repair to upper margin of title*, [xiii+]793[+cviii] pp., folio, *contemp. tan calf, leather label, corners wearing, sides rubbed* **£45.00**

54 **Scott** (John) Digests of the General Highway and Turnpike Laws; with the Schedule of Forms, as Directed by Act of Parliament; and Remarks. Also, an Appendix, on the Construction and Preservation of Roads. *Printed for Edward and Charles Dilley*, 1778, [xxxi+]352[+xix] pp., 8vo, *contemp. calf, leather label* **£45.00**

55 **Selden** (Ioannes) De Iure Naturali & Gentium, iuxta Disciplinam Ebraeorum, libri septem. *Excud. Richardus Bishopius*, 1640, FIRST EDITION, *title in red and black, hf. title with imprimatur on verso present*, [xl+]847 pp., folio, *contemp. rough calf, leather label, backstrip sl. defective at head and tail* (STC 22168) **£375.00**

56 —— Uxor Ebraica, seu de Nuptiis et Divortiis ex Jure Civili, id est Divino & Talmudico, veterum ebraeorum, Libri Tres, ejusdem de Successionibus ad Leges Ebraeorum in bona Defunctorum, liber singularis: in Pontificatum, libri duo. Editio Nova. *Francofurti ad Oderam, sumptibus Jeremiae Schrey'l, excud. Andr. Becmanus*, 1673, *title in red and black, divisional title*, [xxiv+]456[+xvi+]248[+viii] pp., 4to, *contemp. vellum*, scarce **£55.00**

57 **Shower** (Sir Bartholomew) Cases in Parliament Resolved and Adjudged, upon Petitions, and Writs of Error. Third Edition, newly revised and carefully corrected . . . *In the Savoy, Printed by E. and R. Nutt, and R. Gosling (Assigns of Edward Sayer) for Henry Lintot*, 1740, [xiv+]224[+x] pp., folio, *contemp. calf, leather label, little rubbed and corners worn, small split in upper joint* **£55.00**

58 **Strafford.** RUSHWORTH (John) The Tryal of Thomas Earl of Strafford . . . upon an Impeachment for High Treason by the Commons then Assembled in Parliament . . . to which is added a short Account of some other Matters of Fact transacted in both Houses of Parliament, precedent, concomitant and subsequent to the said Tryal: with some Special Arguments in Law relating to a Bill of Attainder. *Printed for John Wright and Richard Chiswell*, 1680, *engraved portrait by R. White*, [x+]786 pp., folio, *contemp. calf, leather label, all surfaces rubbed, joints cracked, lacks free endpapers* (Wing W2333) **£75.00**

59 **Stanford** (Sir William) Les Plees del Coron, diuisees in plusiours titles et common lieux, per queux home plus redement et plenairement trouera, quelq. chose que il quira, touchant les dits plees . . . *In aedibus Richardi Tottelli* [1567—colophon], *title within woodcut border* [McKerrow & Ferguson 59], *some) worming in upper margins sl. affecting a few letters, general browning throughout with some soiling*, [xiv+]198 ff. (STC 23221):
[and]
An exposcicion of the kings prerogatiue collected out of the great abridgement of Iustice Fitzherbert and other olde writers of the lawes of Englande, whereunto is annexed the Proces to the same Prerogatiue appertaining, 1568 [Col.—*Imprynted . . . by Richard Tottell*, *mostly* **Black Letter,** *staining and some soiling*, [i+]85 ff. (STC 23214):
Two works bound together, sm. 4to, *17th cent. sheep, blind tooled, upper joint cracked, backstrip and label defective* **£250.00**
¶Contemporary ownership inscription of Peter Bancroft, and John Lowe, with the latter's record of purchase at Warrington, and his initials in gilt on both covers.

60 **Sugden** (Edward Burtenshaw) A Practical Treatise of the Law of Vendors and Purchasers of Estates. Second Edition. *Printed for J. Butterworth and J. Cooke*, 1806, li+609 pp., 8vo, *contemp. tan calf, leather label, sides sl. scuffed* **£25.00**

61 **Sullivan** (Francis Stoughton) An Historical Treatise on the Feudal Law, and the Constitution and Laws of England; with a Commentary on Magna Charta, and necessary Illustrations of many of the English Statutes . . . *Dublin, Thomas Ewing*, 1772, *worm hole in lower margin of first 17 gatherings*, xvi+448 pp., 8vo, *contemp. calf, leather label* **£30.00**

62 **Toller** (Samuel) The Law of Executors and Administrators. Second Edition corrected and enlarged. *Printed by A. Strahan, for J. Butterworth and J. Cooke*, 1806, xvi+521[+xci] pp., 8vo, *orig. blue paper bds., backstrip fragmenting and lettered by hand* **£40.00**

63 **Treason.** DE LA MARE (Henry, *Lord*) The late Lord Russel's Case, with Observations upon it. *Printed for Awnsham Churchill*, 1689, [ii+]15 pp., folio, *disbound* (Wing D878) **£15.00**

64 —— THE WHOLE PROCEEDING to Judgment upon the Articles of Impeachment of High Treason . . . against James Earl of Derwentwater, William Lord Widdrington, William Earl of Nithisdale, Robert Earl of Carnwath, William Viscount Kenmuir, and William Lord Nairn . . . *Printed for Jacob Tonson*, 1716, [iv+]20 pp., folio, *disbound* **£20.00**

65 **W.** (T.) The Office of the Clerk of Assize, containing the Form and Method of the Proceedings at the Assizes, and general Gaol-delivery, as also on the Crown and Nisi Prius side, together with the Office of the Clerk of the Peace . . . 2nd Edition, corr. and amended. *Printed for Henry Twyford*, 1682, *some browning throughout, lacks A^1 (? blank)*, [vi+]254[+x] pp., sm. 8vo, *18th cent. hf. calf, marb. bds., newly rebacked, leather label* (Wing W126) **£60.00**

66 **Weare.** JONES (George Henry) Account of the Murder of the late Mr. William Weare, of Lyon's Inn, London. Including the Circumstances which first led to the Discovery of the Murder and the Detection of the Murderers . . . John Thurtell, Jos Hunt, and Wm. Probert. *Printed by J. Nichols and Son, for Sherwood, Jones, and Co.*, 1824, *with folding map, plan and 4 engravings*, [iv+]344 pp.:
[with]
The Horrid Murder of W. Weare, Esq. . . . 1823, *drop title*, 32 pp.:
The Trial of John Thurtell and Joseph Hunt . . . 1824, *drop title, cuts on title*, 8 pp.:
The Hoax Discovered: or, Mr. Weare alive . . . *Published by W. Chubb*, N.D., 8 pp.:
II. of the Hoax Discovered. Wear's Resurrection Explored. Defence of John Thurtell, and his Innocence Authenticated. *Published by W. Chubb*, N.D., *cut on title*, 8 pp.:
[and]
The Medical Adviser . . . Phrenological Appearances of Thurtell's Head. 1824, *cut on title*, pp. 97-112:
Six works bound together, 8vo, *contemp. hf. crimson morocco, rubbed, marb. bds., split in upper joint, lettered* **£50.00**

67 —— The Fatal Effects of Gambling exemplified in the Murder of Wm. Weare, and the Trial and Fate of John Thurtell, the Murdered and his Accomplices . . . to which is added, the Gambler's Scourge; a complete exposé of the whole System of Gambling in the Metropolis . . . *Published by Thomas Kelly*, 1824, *title and 11 engr. plates, all foxed, one torn at fore margin*, xv+512 pp., 8vo, *hf. calf, marb. bds., worn, newly rebacked, leather label* **£20.00**

68 **Wilkins** (David) Leges Anglo-Saxonicae Ecclesiasticae & Civiles, accedunt Leges Edvardi Latinae, Guilielmi Conquestoris Gallo-Normannicae, et Henrici I. Latinae. subjudgitur Domini Henr. Spelmanni (Codex Legum Veterum Statutorum Regni Angliae, quae ab ingressu Guilielmi I. usque ad Annum Nomum Henr. III. edita sunt. Toti Operi praemittitur Dissertatio Epistolaris admodum Rev. Dom. Guilielmi Nicholsoni . . . De Jure Feudali Veterym Saxonum . . . *Typis Guil. Bowyer, imp. Ros. Gosling*, 1721, *some marginalia at beginning*, [xvi+]xxiv+434[+xviii] pp., folio, *contemp. calf, worn, sometime rebacked canvas, orig. backstrip mounted* **£70.00**

69 **Wintoun** (George Seton, *Earl of*) The Tryal of . . . upon the Articles of Impeachment of High Treason . . . together with several Orders of the House of Peers in course of Time preparatory to the said Tryal. *Printed for Jacob Tonson*, 1716, *browning throughout, some margins repaired*, [iv+]69[+i] pp., folio, *disbound* **£20.00**

70 [**Womock** (Laurence, *bp.*)] An Answer to the Gentleman's Letter to his Friend: shewing that Bishops may be Judges in Causes Capital. *Printed by Tho. Braddyll for Robert Clavell*, 1680, *some margins repaired, last lf. soiled*, [ii+]21 pp., folio, *disbound* (Wing W3333) **£25.00**

71 **Zasius** (Ioannes Ulrichus) Catalogvs Legvm Antiqvarum una cum adiuncta summaria Interpretatione. *Argentorati apud Vuolfium Cephalaeum*, 1551, *soiling and staining throughout, margins fragile through damp, some strengthened, pin-hole worming in lower margins and sl. elsewhere*, [viii+]121[+iii] ff., sm. 8vo, *maroon roan, rubbed, backstrip defective, unlettered*, scarce (Adams Z81) **£140.00**

II. HISTORY

72 **Abjuration Oath.** The Case of the Abjuration Oath endeavoured to be Cleared, to the Satisfaction of those who are required to take it. *Printed for J. Nutt*, 1702, [ii+]20 pp., sm. 4to, *disbound* **£15.00**

73 **An Account** of the Proceedings of the Lords Spiritual & Temporal in Parliament Assembled, in Relation to a Bill, intituled, An Act for Preventing Occasional Conformity. *Printed by Charles Bill, and the Executrix of Thomas Newcomb*, 1702, 28 pp., folio, *buckram, lettered* **£15.00**

74 **An Act** for quiet Enjoying of Sequestred Parsonages and Vicaridges by the present Incumbent. [*Printed by Hen. Hills and John Field*, 1657—colophon], *drop title, some browning*, 4 pp., folio, *grey bds.* (Wing E1051) **£20.00**

75 **Adam** (Alexander) Roman Antiquities: or, an Account of the Manners and Customs of the Romans . . . designed chiefly to illustrate the Latin Classics, by explaining words and phrases, from the rites and customs to which they refer. 5th Edition, corrected. *Printed by A. Strahan* . . . 1801, xv+616 pp., 8vo, *tree calf, leather label, little rubbed, bookplate of Fitzherbert* **£15.00**

76 **Adams** (John, *of the Inner Temple*) Index Villaris: or, an Alphabetical Table of all the Cities, Market-Towns, Parishes, Villages and Private Seats in England and Wales. *Printed by A. Godbid and J. Playford, for the Author*, 1680, FIRST EDITION, *title in red and black, lacks folding map, some damp staining*, folio, *contemp. calf, newly rebacked, leather label, new free end-papers* (Wing A479) **£65.00**

77 **Agriculture.** AN ADDITIONAL Act for the Improvement of Tillage. [*Reprinted by Charles Bill* . . . 1691], *drop title*, 5 pp., folio, *disbound* **£12.00**

78 **Alfred.** SPELMAN (Sir John) The Life of Alfred the Great, from the Original Manuscript in the Bodlejan Library: with considerable Additions and several historical Remarks, by the Publisher Thomas Hearne. *Oxford, Printed at the Theater for Maurice Atkins*, 1709, *engraved portrait, shelf marks on title, considerably embrowned, MS. note on St. Neots on front inner fly lf.*, [vi+]238[+ix] pp., 8vo, *18th cent. panelled calf, newly rebacked, joints strengthened, g.e.* **£150.00**
¶Inscribed on one front blank: 'Viro ingenioso et in re antiquaria versatissimo Radulpho Thoresby libellum hunc Amicitiae ergo D.D. Tho. Hearne. xvi Kal. Septembr. m:dcc:ix'

79 **Algarotti** (Count Francis, *Chamberlain to the King of Prussia*) Letters Military and Political. From the Italian, 2nd Edition. *Printed for T. Egerton*, 1783, *hf. title present*, xxviii+319[+i] pp., 8vo, *orig. paper bds., little soiled, edges untrimmed* **£35.00**

80 **America.** [PHILIP V., *King of Spain*] His Catholick Majesty's Manifesto, justifying his Conduct in relation to the late Convention [at the Pardo]. With his Reasons for not Paying the Ninety-Five Thousand Pounds. *Printed for Robert Amey and A. Dodd*, 1739, *text in parallel French and English, some browning*, [iv+]53 pp., sm. 8vo in 4's, *qtr. sheep, marb. bds., lettered* (Sabin 62443: Kress 4439) **£40.00**
¶Concerned mainly with trading, navigational rights and plantation matters in Florida, Carolina and the West Indies.

81 —— POPULAR PREJUDICES against the Convention and Treaty with Spain, Examin'd and Answer'd. With Remarks on a Pamphlet, Entituled, Considerations upon the Present State of our Affairs at Home and Abroad. *Printed for T. Cooper*, 1739, FIRST EDITION, *title little soiled, final blank present but creased*, sm. 4to, *modern hf. sprinkled calf, marb. bds., all edges untrimmed*, scarce (Sabin 64143) **£50.00**

82 —— STAMP ACT. A List of the Minority in the House of Commons, who voted against the Bill to Repeal the American Stamp Act. *Paris, chez J.W.*, 1766, 8 pp., sm. 8vo, *recent tan calf over earlier marb. bds.*, rare (Sabin 41453) **£75.00**

83 —— STAMP ACT. Protest against the Bill to repeal the American Stamp Act, Last Session. *Paris, chez J.W.*, 1766, *title sl. soiled*, 16 pp.:
[and]
Second Protest, with a List of Voters against the Bill to repeal the American Stamp Act, of Last Session. *Paris, chez J.W.*, 1766, 15 pp.:
Two items bound together, 8vo, *recent qtr. calf over earlier marb. bds.*, rare (Sabin 66103—2 pts.) **£100.00**

84 —— STAMP ACT. The Rights of Parliament Vindicated, on Occasion of the late Stamp-Act. In which is exposed the Conduct of the American Colonists. Addressed to all the People of Great Britain. *Printed for J. Almon*, 1766, *sl. discolouration of paper*, 44 pp., sm. 8vo, *binders' cloth, old leather label mounted on upper cover* (Sabin 71374) **£70.00**

85 —— TREATY OF PEACE, Good Correspondence & Neutrality in America, between the most Serene and Mighty Prince James II. by the Grace of God, King of Great Britain, France and Ireland, Defender of the Faith, &c. and the most Serene and Mighty Prince Lewis xiv. the Most Christian King: concluded the 6/16 Day of Novemb. 1686. *Printed by Thomas Newcomb*, 1686, *some discolouration*, 19[+i] pp.+*binder's blanks*, sm. 4to, *hf. calf, marb. bds. lettered* (Wing J393—variant imprint: see Sabin 96532) **£150.00**
¶'The Most Christian King's Subjects shall have full Liberty to Fish for Turtles in the Islands of Cayman'. [Article xvi]

86 **Anne** (Queen). SWIFT (Jonathan) The History of the Four last Years of the Queen. Published from the last Manuscript copy, corrected and enlarged by the Author's own Hand. *Printed for A. Millar*, 1758, xvi+392 pp., 8vo, *contemp. sprinkled calf, rubbed, joints cracked* £75.00

87 **Anne** (Princess) Flos Britannicvs Versis Novissimi Filiola Carola & Marjea nata xvii Marti Anno m.dc.xxxvi. *Oxoniae Typis Leonardi Lichfield*, 1637, *title within typographical border, fore-edge strengthened, 2 ll. repaired at upper/inner margins, sl. dampstaining*, [50] ll., sm. 4to, *recent hf. crimson morocco, marb. bds., lettered* (STC 19037: Madan 804) £300.00
¶Congratulatory poems to celebrate birth of princess Anne (ob. 1640). Contributors included Robert Burton, Abraham Woodhead and Richard Meade.

88 [**Arbuthnot** (John, *M.D.*)] Law is a Bottomless-Pit. Exemplify'd in the Case of the Lord Strutt, John Bull, Nicholas Frog, and Lewis Baboon. Who spent all they had in a Law-Suit. 4th Edition. *Printed for John Morphew*, 1712, *little soiled*, 24 pp.:
[and]
John Bull in His Senses: being the Second Part of Law is a Bottomless-Pit, 3rd Edition. *Printed for John Morphew*, 1712, *little soiled*, 26 pp.:
2 items, sm. 8vo, *sewed, untrimmed* £45.00
¶'An ingenious and lively attack upon the War policy of the whigs; and, if it wants the force of Swift's profounder satire it is an admirably effective and still amusing party squib'. (D.N.B.)

89 **Articles of Peace,** Union, and Confederation, Concluded and Agreed between his Highness Oliver Lord Protector . . . and . . . the United Provinces of the Netherlands . . . *Printed by William du-Gard and Henry Hills*, 1654, [ii+]18 pp., folio, *disbound* £18.00

90 **Australia.** AN ACT to enable His Majesty to establish a Court of Criminal Judicature on the Eastern Coast of New South Wales, and the Parts adjacent. *Printed by Charles Eyre and Andrew Strahan*, 1787, *title dust soiled*, [ii+]5 pp., folio, *unbound* £25.00

91 **Aylmer** (John, *bp. of London*). STRYPE (John) Historical Collections of the Life and Acts of . . . John Aylmer . . . wherein are explained many Transactions of the Church of England; and what Methods were then taken to preserve it, with respect both to the Papist and Puritan. *Printed by W. Bowyer for Brabazon Aylmer*, 1701, *some discolouration*, [xxx+]330[+vi] pp., 8vo, *new qtr. calf, marb. bds., leather label* £30.00

92 **Bacon** (Sir Francis) Cases of Treason. *Printed by the Assigns of John More, and are sold by Matthew Walbancke, and William Coke*, 1641, FIRST EDITION, *some staining and soiling, title and* A^2 *sl. damaged in lower margin, two words in text damaged by adhesion*, [iv+]35 pp. [p. 26 misprinted 62], sm. 4to, *modern hf. citron morocco, cloth sides, lettered in gilt* (Wing B272: Gibson 198) £175.00

93 **Bacon.** MALLET (David) The Life of Francis Bacon, Lord Chancellor of England. *Printed for A. Millar*, 1740, *title in red and black with portrait in vignette*, viii+197[+iii—catalogue] pp., 8vo, *contemp. sprinkled calf, sl. rubbed, newly rebacked, leather label* £45.00
¶From the library of the late R. W. Chapman, with his label. Of this work Bp. Warburton remarked 'that Mallet, in his Life of Bacon, had forgotten that he was a philosopher; and if he should write the life of the Duke of Marlborough, which he had undertaken to do, he would probably forget that he was a general'. (Lowndes)

94 **Balliols.** SCOTT (Benjamin J.) The Norman Balliols in England, compiled in part from Mr. Wentworth Huyshe's *Harold and the Balliols*, with illustrations and additional matter, including two introductory and two concluding chapters and a pedigree. 1914, *profusely illust.*, xx+467 pp., 8vo, *full green niger morocco, gilt panels and fillets, inner dentelle borders, lettered, by Riviere backstrip v. sl. sunned, otherwise an excellent copy* £85.00

95 **Barbary Pirates.** DUNTON (John) A Trve Iovrnall of the Sally Fleet, vvith the Proceedings of the Voyage. Whereunto is annexed a List of Sally Captives names, and the places where they dwell, and a Description of the three Townes in a Card. *Printed by Iohn Dawson for Thomas Nicholes*, 1637, *with the large folding plate of Sally, neatly strengthened at two corners and with two short tears skilfully repaired, faint discolouration throughout*, [iv+]26[+xviii] pp., sm. 4to, *full crushed red morocco, lettered, two single fillets inside borders, book labels of Boies Penrose, of Old East India House, and Alexander Smith, Writer, replaced on endpapers by Sangorski and Sutcliffe* (STC 7357: Hazlitt ii:187) £220.00
¶Collates A-F^4. Catchword on p. 14 (C^1v) is under (incorrect). Pages measure 170×132 mm.

96 —— A Trve Iovrnall of the Sally Fleet, . . . *Printed by Iohn Dawson for Thomas Nicholes*, 1637, *with large folding plan of Sally*, [iv+]26[+xviii] pp., sm. 4to, *19th cent. polished tan calf, leather label, inner borders gilt, marbled endpapers, t.e.g.* (STC 7357: Hazlitt ii:187) £230.00
¶Collates A-F^4. Slightly larger copy than preceeding item, i.e. 180×128 mm. (difference due to binders). This is probably a later printing with catchword on p. 14 (C^1v) now corrected to *the*: the catchword *Lynn* of F^3r is missing (?dropped out) and there are at least three instances of dropped or worn letters.

97 [**Bassett** (Robert)] The Lives of all the Roman Emperors, being exactly Collected, from Iulius Caesar, unto the now reigning Ferdinand the second, with their Births, Governments, remarkable Actions, & Deaths. *Printed by N. and I. Okes, and are to be sold by George Hutton*, 1636, *engr. title by Wm. Marshall*, 156 *heads of Emperors in text, some marginal notes in ink, few side notes just touched, one margin roughly repaired, several frayed, some pp. in centre damp stained and embrowned, minute worm holes in some margins*, [xvi+384] pp., sm. 8vo, *dark green morocco, backstrip, sides & inner borders gilt, g.e. by Eedy of Tavistock, incorrectly titled as Braithwait* (STC 1558) £160.00

98 **Bede** (Venerable) Historiae Ecclesiasticae Gentis Anglorum, libri quinque, . . . cura et studio Johannis Smith. *Cantabrigiae, typis Academicis*, 1722, *with 3 plates and folding map, small snag in fold, occasional light staining*, [xv+]823[+xiii] pp., folio, *sprinkled calf, leather label, gilt, m.e. and end-papers* £100.00

99 **Belgium.** GROTIUS (Hugo) Annales et Historiae de Rebus Belgicis. *Amstelaedami, ex Typog. Joannis Blaeu*, 1657, [xiv+]569[+xxii] pp., folio, *contemp. vellum, leather ties, upper joint cracked* £75.00

100 **Belsham** (W.) History of Great Britain, from the Revolution to the Commencement of the Year 1799. 5 Vols., Second Edition. *Printed for Vernor and Hood*, 1805, 4to, *contemp. diced calf, backstrips tooled and lettered in gilt, a few small stains on sides* £75.00

101 **Bernardi** (John, *Major*) A Short History of the Life of Major John Bernardi, written by himself in Newgate, where he has been for near 33 Years a Prisoner of State, without any Allowance from the Government, and could never be admitted to his Tryal. To which is added by Way of Appendix, a true copy of the Diploma, or Patent of Count of the Empire, granted to the Author's Grand-Father in the Year 1629, and a Translation of it into English, as also Copies of the Major's several Commissions, &c. *Printed by J. Newcomb, for the Benefit of the Author*, 1729, *engr. port. by Van der Gucht, errata lf. present, a skilfully washed copy*, [ii+]135+62[+i] pp., 8vo, *recased in contemp. mottled calf, and carefully rebacked, gilt, new marbled endpapers, armorial bookplate* £45.00

102 **Bernier** (Francois) The History of the Late Revolution of the Empire of the Great Mogol: together with the most considerable Passages, for 5 Years following in that Empire . . . [and—A Continuation] English'd out of the French [by H. Oldenburg]. Parts 1, 3 & 4 only (ex 4). *Printed and sold by Moses Pitt* . . . 1671/2, *folding map torn in inner margin, but repaired, some discolouration throughout*, [xvi+]358:[xvi+]173:[ii+]178+39[+i] pp., sm. 8vo, *contemp. calf, panelled in blind, unlettered* (Wing B2043/2) £65.00
¶There is no evidence that this volume ever contained part ii. From the library of the late Graham Pollard.

103 **Bisselius** (Joannes) Medulla Historica, Septennium II. ab anno m.dc.viii. usque ad anno m.dc.xiv. inclusivè [and] Appendix anni m.dc.xiv. Mariae Stuartae, viventis, ac morientis acta. 2 Vols. in 1. *Ambergae, apud Joannem Burger*, 1675, *titles in red and black, engr. title and 8 fine portraits including 2 of Mary Stuart*, [ii+]511:[ii+]362 pp., sm. 8vo, *contemp. stamped pig-skin, clasps intact, remains of MS. label* £70.00

104 **Blondel** (David) A Treatise of the Sibyls, so Highly Celebrated, as well by the Antient Heathens, as the Holy Fathers of the Church, giving an Accompt of the Names, and Number of the Sibyls, of their Qualities, the Form and Matter of their Verses . . . Englished by J.D. *Printed by T.R. for the Authour*, 1661, *one lf. torn across (? paper fault), title soiled*, [iv+]293[+vi] pp., folio, *new qtr. tan calf, cloth sides, leather label* (Wing B3220) £50.00

105 **Bocalini** (Trajano) Iragguagli di Parnasso: or, Advertisements from Parnassus: in Two Centuries, with the Politick Touchstone. Written Originally in Italian, and now put into English by the Rt. Hon. Henry, Earl of Monmouth. Third Edition, Corrected. *Printed; and are to be sold by Peter Parker*, 1674, *some staining at edges, last lf. laid down*, [xvi+]291 pp., folio, *contemp. sprinkled calf, corners worn, recently rebacked, leather label* (Wing B3384) £35.00

106 [**Bolingbroke** (Henry St. John, *viscount*)] Good Queen Anne vindicated, and the Ingratitude, Insolence, &c. of her Whig Ministry and the Allies detected and exposed, in the Beginning and Conducting of the War . . . *Printed for and sold by W. Owen*, 1748, *some soiling*, [iv+]72 pp., sm. 8vo, *disbound* £21.00

107 —— Letters on the Study and Use of History (to which are added, two other Letters, and Reflections upon Exile). 2 Vols. *Printed for A. Millar*, 1752, FIRST PUBLISHED EDITION, [iv+]315:[iv+]286[+iv] pp., *some foxing throughout*, 8vo, *contemp. sprinkled calf, gilt, leather labels, joints beginning to crack, armorial ex libris of Sir Abraham Hume* [1749-1838—*director of the British Institute, naturalist and collector*] £45.00

108 —— Letters on the Study and Use of History . . . 2 Vols. *Printed for A. Millar*, 1752, FIRST PUBLISHED EDITION, *occasional light foxing*, [ii+]315:[ii+]286[+iv] pp., 8vo, *contemp. mottled calf, bacstrips gilt, rubbed and lacking labels, joints cracking, y.e.* £35.00

109 —— [MALLET (David)] Memoirs of the Life and Ministerial Conduct, with some free Remarks on the Political Writings, of the late Lord Visc. Bolingbroke. *Printed for R. Baldwin*, 1752, FIRST EDITION, *stitching sl. strained*, [xvi+]352 pp., sm. 8vo, *contemp. sprinkled calf, gilt, leather label, head of backstrip sl. defective* £30.00

110 [**Bolton** (Edmund)] Nero Caesar, or Monarchie Depraved. An Historical Worke, by the Translator of Lvcivs Florvs. *Printed by T.S. for Thomas Walkley*, 1624, FIRST EDITION, *engr. title dated* 1623, *contemp. names and inscriptions in ink on both titles*, [xviii+]288 pp., folio, *contemp. limp vellum, front hinge detached, fragments of ties still present* (STC 3221) £50.00

111 **Bonfinius** (Antonius) Rerum Vngaricvm Decades tres, nunc demvm indvstria martini Brenneri Bistriciensis Transsyluani in lucem aeditae, antehac numquam excusae . . . *Basileae, ex Roberti VVinter*, 1543, *title in facsimile, sl. worming in some margins, small piece torn from one corner, one lf. misbound, large device*, [xii+]536[+lvii] pp. (Adams B2415):
[with]
Rhenanus (Beatus) Rervm Germani Carvm libti tres. Adiecta est in Calce Epistola ad D. Philippi Puchaimerū, de loci Plinii per St. Aquaeum attactis . . . *Basileae, in off. Frobeniana*, 1531, *device on title and verso of last lf.*, 194[+ii] pp. (Adams R438):
[and]
Bartelius (Marinus) De Vita Moribus ac Rebvs Praecipve adversvs Tvrcas, Gestis, Georgii Castrioti . . . *Argentorati, apud Cratonem Mylivm*, 1537, *devices on title and verso of last lf., upper margin of last lf. repaired*, [xii+]ccclxxi[+i] pp. (Adams B217):
Three works bound together, folio, *contemp. sprinkled calf, rubbed, corners worn, joints beginning to crack, leather label, gilt crest on backstrip, ex libris label* £210.00

112 **Boyle** (Roger, *Earl of Orrery*) A Treatise of the Art of War: dedicated to the Kings most Excellent Majesty. *Printed by T.N. for Henry Harringman*, 1677, *portrait of Charles ii. and 6 double-page plans, small paper fault in one margin*, [xvi+]206 pp., folio, *contemp. mottled calf, corners worn, some cracking of joints* (Wing O499) £260.00

113 **Brady** (Rob.) An Historical Treatise of Cities, and Burghs or Boroughs. Shewing their Original, and Whence, and from Whom they Received their Liberties, Privileges, and Immunities; what they were, and what Made and Constituted a Free Burgh, & Free Burgesses. As also shewing when they first sent their Representatives to Parliament with a Concurrent Discourse of most Matters and Things Incident, or Relating thereto. Second Edition. *Printed for A.L. and sold by John Nutt*, 1704, [iv+]iv+88[+ii+]38[+v] pp., folio, *contemp. panelled calf, leather label* £45.00

114 **Brand** (John) Observations on Popular Antiquities, including the Whole of Mr. Bourne's Antiquitates Vulgares, with Addenda to every Chapter of that Work, as also an Appendix containing such Articles on the Subject as have been omitted by that Author. *Printed for William Baynes, sold also by W. Blackwood*, 1810, *engr. title*, [ii+]xvi+424 pp., 8vo, *contemp. tan calf, tooled in blind and gilt, leather label, sl. scuffing on sides* £35.00

115 **Bristol** (George Digby, *Earl of*) August 5. Two Letters, the one from the Lord Digby to the Queens Majestie, the other from Mr. Thomas Elliot, to the Lord Digby, with Observations upon the same Letters, also a Noat of such Armes as were sent for by His Maiestie out of Amsterdam, under his owne Hand. *Printed by R.O. and G.D. for John Bartlet*, 1642, *sl. foxing*, 8 pp., sm. 4to, *marb. wrappers* (Wing B4783) £30.00

116 **Buckingham.** M[ATTHIEU] (P[ierre]) The Povverfvl Favorite, or the Life of Aelivs Seianvs. *Printed at Paris*, 1628, *early inscriptions in ink on title, and a small hole in title lf. (not touching letters), several contemp. small ink blots on* K^3 *and* [K^4], *corroded through with loss of a few letters, several page numerals shaved*, [ii+]154 pp., sm. 4to, *qtr. tan morocco, linen sides, lettered* (STC 17664) £140.00

117 **Brooke** (Raphe) A Catalogve and Succession of the Kings, Princes, Dukes, Marquesses, Earles, and Viscounts of this Realme of England, since the Norman Conquest, to this present yeare, 1619. Together with their Armes, Wiues, and Children: the times of their deaths and burials, with many their memorable Actions. Discouering and Reforming many Errors committed, by men of other Profession, and lately published in Print; to the great wronging of the Nobility, and preiudice of his Maiesties Officers of Armes . . . *Printed by William Iaggard*, 1619, FIRST EDITION, *title within wood-cut border, one corner torn away, generally soiled, with tear in lower margin, woodcut arms of monarchs, all other shields left blank, lacks* 4¶$^{3/4}$ *(dealing with Qs. Mary and Elizabeth), lacks* A^1 *(blank), contemp. signatures and writing on front paste-down and verso of errata lf.*, [liv+]276[+iii] pp., folio, *contemp. calf, leather label* (STC 3832) £75.00

118 **Burke** (Edmund) Reflections on the Revolution in France and on the Proceedings in certain Societies in London, relative to that Event. In a Letter intended to have been sent to a Gentleman in Paris. *Printed by J. Dodsley*, 1790, SECOND EDITION, FIRST IMPRESSION, *some discolouration throughout, title and last few ll. heavily stained, upper margin of last 3 ll. sl. defective*, iv+356 pp., 8vo, *qtr. calf, grey bds., leather label, unpressed and untrimmed copy* (Todd 53b) £65.00

119 —— Reflections on the Revolution in France . . . *Printed for J. Dodsley*, 1790, SECOND EDITION, FIRST IMPRESSION, *sl. foxing*, iv+356 pp., 8vo, *contemp. tree calf, lacks label, rubbed, joints beginning to crack* (Todd 53c) £60.00

120 —— Reflections on the Revolution in France . . . *Printed for J. Dodsley*, 1790, SECOND EDITION, FIRST IMPRESSION, *sl. foxing*, iv+356 pp., 8vo, *contemp. calf, sometime rebacked and repaired at corners* (Todd 53c) £60.00
¶With the 'ex-libris' of R. B. Adam and R. W. Chapman, and a pencil note R.W.C. from R.B.A. Apr. 1929 in Dr. Chapman's holograph.

121 —— Reflections on the Revolution in France . . . Fifth Edition. *Printed for J. Dodsley*, 1790, *sl. foxing, few ll. snagged in lower margin*, iv+364 pp., 8vo, *contemp. hf. calf, marb. bds., recently rebacked, leather label* £30.00

122 —— Speech . . . on presenting to the House of Commons (on the 11th of February, 1780) a Plan for the better Security of the Independence of Parliament, and the Oeconomical Reformation of the Civil and other Establishments. *Printed for J. Dodsley*, 1780, FIRST (AUTHORIZED) EDITION, *sl. browning*, [iv+]99 pp., 8vo, *disbound* (Todd 33b) £35.00
¶From the library of the late Graham Pollard.

123 —— Speech . . . on presenting to the House of Commons (on the 11th of February, 1780), a Plan for the better Security of the Independence of Parliament, and the Oeconomical Reformation of the Civil and other Establishments, a New Edition. *Printed for J. Dodsley*, 1780, AUTHORIZED REPRINT, *hf. title soiled*, [iv+]76 pp., 8vo, *sewed, an unopened copy* (Todd 33g) £40.00
¶From the library of the late Graham Pollard.

124 **Burnet** (Gilbert, *bp. of Sarum*) Some Letters. Containing, An Account of what seemed most remarkable in Switzerland, Italy, &c. . . . to T. H. R. B. Rotterdam. *Printed by Abraham Acher*, 1686, 307 pp., *errata lf. present*, 8vo, *contemp. mottled calf, paper label, upper side sl. scuffed, small split in head and tail of upper joint* (Wing B5914) £45.00

Burnet—*continued*

125 [—— (Thomas, *of Charterhouse*)] The Theory of the Earth: containing an Account of the Original of the Earth, and of all the General Changes which it hath already undergone, or is to undergo, till the Consummation of all Things. The Two First Books concerning The Deluge, and concerning Paradise. *Printed by R. Norton for Walter Kettilby*, 1684, FIRST EDITION, *frontis., 2 double plates and text figures, some worming in upper margins, general discolouration*, [xviii+]327 pp., folio, *contemp. mottled calf, joints cracked, lacks label* (Wing B5950) **£50.00**

126 [——] The Theory of the Earth . . . The two last Books, concerning the Burning of the World, and concerning the New Heavens and New Earth. *Printed by R. Norton, for Walter Kettilby*, 1690, LARGE AND THICK PAPER COPY, *frontis., heavily foxed and embrowned throughout*, [xiv+]224:[ii+]52[+i] pp., folio, *contemp. crimson morocco, sometime neatly rebacked and lettered* (Wing B5954) **£75.00**

¶From the library of Gilbert Burnet, bp. of Salisbury, with his armorial bookplate on verso of title.

127 **Burton** (John) Monasticon Eboracense: and the Ecclesiastical History of Yorkshire. Containing an Account of the first Introduction and Progress of Christianity in that Diocese, until the End of William the Conqueror's Reign. Also the Description of the Situation, Fabric, Times of Endowments of all Churches, Collegiate, Conventual, Parochial, or of peculiar Jurisdiction . . . *York, Printed for the Author, by N. Nickson*, 1758, *with 3 folding plates, snags in some folds, lacks last lf. of Index*, xii+448[+xxxii] pp., folio, *contemp. tan calf, tooled in blind and gilt* **£90.00**

128 **Busbec** (Ogier Ghislain de) Omnia quibus accessit Epitome De Moribus Turcarum, indice auctiore. *Ex off. R. Danielii*, 1660, *main title in red and black*, [viii+]386[+xiv] pp., 12mo, *contemp. mottled calf, corners sl. worn, sprinkled edges* (Wing B6217) **£35.00**

129 **Butter.** AN ACT for reforming of Abuses committed in the Weight and false Packing of Butter. *Printed by John Bull and Christopher Barker*, 1662, [ii+]8 pp., folio, *disbound* **£12.00**

130 **Caesar** (C. Julius) The Commentaries . . . of his Wars in Gallia; and the Civil Wars betwixt him and Pompey. Translated into English; with many Excellent and Judicious Observations thereupon. As also the Art of our Modern Training, or Tactick Practice. By Clement Edmonds. Whereunto is adjoyned the Eighth Commentary of the Wars in Gallia; with some short Observations upon it. Together with the Life of Caesar, and an Account of his Medals; revised, corrected, and enlarged. *In the Savoy, Printed by Tho. Newcomb, for Jonathan Edwin*, 1677, *frontis. portrait and 14 plates (of which 9 are folding), a few sl. frayed at fore-edge, divisional titles*, [l+]332 pp., folio, *contemp. mottled calf, corners little worn, sometime rebacked, gilt, leather label* (Wing C200) **£150.00**

131 **Camden** (William) Remaines concerning Britaine: their Languages, Names, Surnames, Allusions, Anagrammes, Armories, Monies . . . Fift Impression, with many rare Antiquities never before imprinted, by the industry and care of Iohn Philipot. *Printed by Thomas Harper, for John Waterson*, 1637, *engr. port. of Camden following title, lacks (A2)*, [v+]420[+ii] pp., sm. 4to, *new qtr. sprinkled calf, marb. bds., leather label* (STC 4526: Hazlitt ii/79) **£50.00**

132 **Canada. Newfoundland.** A REPORT from the Committee of Secrecy, appointed by Order of the House of Commons to examine several Books and Papers laid before the House, relating to the late Negotiations of Peace and Commerce, &c. Reported on the Ninth of June, 5, by the Right Honourable Robert Walpole, Chairman of the said Committee. T her with an Appendix, containing Memorials, Letters, and other Papers referred to in the said Report. *Printed for Jacob Tonson, Timothy Goodwin, Bernard Lintot, and William Taylor*, 1715, *tear in last lf. repaired, staining to some lower margins*, [iv+]94 pp., folio, *modern qtr. calf, marb. bds., unlettered* (Sabin 69729: Kress 2973) **£85.00**

¶Relates in part to the rights of fishing in Newfoundland, with an Appendix of letters etc., dealing with trade and commerce of Britain in various parts of the world.

133 **Carleton** (George, *bp. of Chichester*) A Thankfvll Remembrance of Gods Mercie. In an Historicall Collection of the great and mercifull Deliuerances of the Church and State of England, since the Gospell beganne here to flourish, from the beginning of Queene Elizabeth. 4th Edition revised. *Printed by Aug. Math. for Robert Mylbourne and Humphrey Robins*, 1630, *portrait and 20 engravings in text, a washed copy, lacking engr. title*, [viii+]292 pp., sm. 4to, *19th cent. full crimson morocco, gilt extra, gilt inner borders, g.e. by J. MacKenzie* **£250.00**

134 **Carpenter** (Edward) *ed.* Chants of Labour, A Song Book of the People, with Music, with 2 designs by Walter Crane. *Swan Sonnenschein*, 1880, xii+99[+i] pp., 8vo, *orig. buff cloth, decorated and lettered in red, a little dulled by age, scarce* (Sheffield cat. p. 12) **£35.00**

¶In spite of Walter Crane's leaning towards socialism, this piece is not mentioned by Konody.

135 **Chaloner** (Thomas) De Rep. Anglorvm Instavranda libri decem, hvc accessit in Lavdem Henrici Octaui Regis quondam Angliae praestantis, carmen panegyricum. Item, de Illvstrivm qvorvndam Encomiis Miscellanea, cvm Epigrammatis, ac Epitaphiis nonnullis, eodem authore. *Excud. Thomas Vautrollerius*, 1579, *divisional titles, errata on verso of last lf. head of title neatly remargined, two small holes in one lf, a few marginal notes, stubs of two blanks before title still present*, sm. 4to, *contemp. limp vellum, gilt lines and ornaments, lacks ties, a very clean and large copy, at sometime carefully recased* (STC 4938) **£300.00**

¶The title carries the signature of William Malim, a friend of the author and responsible for the commendatory verses. There is also another inscription at the foot on the title in a neat Chancery hand 'Malim mori; quam cedere amori . . . qth G.B.' The grandsons of Chaloner were among King Charles I's judges.

136 [**Chamberlayne** (Edward)] Angliae Notitia sive Praesens Status Angliae Succincte Enuncleatus. *Oxonii, Typis Leon. Lichfield, Imp. Henric. Clements*, 1686, [xii+]355[+i] pp., 12mo, *contemp. sprinkled calf, unlettered, sprinkled edges* (Wing C1845) **£35.00**

137 [**Charles I.**] His Majesties Declaration, concerning His Proceedings with His Subjects of Scotland, since the Pacification in the Camp neere Berwick. *Printed by R. Young and R. Badger*, 1640, *title heavily soiled and repaired, portrait pasted to verso, some margins frayed, staining throughout, last lf. defective but text intact*, [ii+]63 pp., sm. 4to, *hf. brown buckram, marb. bds., leather label* (STC 22006) **£50.00**

138 [——] His Maiesties Declaration concerning the Treaty: and His Dislike of the Armies Proceedings. Delivered by His Majesty to one of His Servants at His departure from the Isle of VVight . . . *Printed in the Yeare*, 1648, *sl. cropping of head margins, two letters of title just touched, soiled*, 5 pp., sm. 4to, *disbound* (Wing C2288) **£35.00**

139 [——] Restitution to the Royal Author or a Vindication of King Charls the Martyr's most Excellent Book; Intituled *ΕΙΚΩΝ ΒΑΣΙΛΙΚΗ* from the False, Scandalous, and Malicious Reflections lately Published against it. *Printed for Samuel Ceble*, 1691, 8 pp., *little soiled*, folio, *disbound* (Wing R1175) **£25.00**

140 —— GOSTELO (Walter) Charls Stuart and Oliver Cromvvel United, or, Glad tidings of Peace to all Christendom, to the Jews and Heathen, Conversion, To the Church of Rome, certain downfall: The Irish not to be Transplanted . . . *Printed for the Author*, 1655, *engr. portrait laid down, some discolouration throughout*, [xv+]312 pp., sm. 8vo, *contemp. sprinkled calf, backstrip gilt, leather labels, joints beginning to crack* (Wing G1318) **£60.00**

141 —— MALVEZZI (Virgilio, *Marquesse*) Il Davide Perseguitato. David Persecuted. Written in Italian, and done into English by Robert Ashley. *Printed for Humphrey Mosely, portrait of King Charles as David by Marshall*, [ii+]163 pp., 12mo, *new hf. sprinkled calf over early marb. bds.* (Wing M357) **£40.00**

¶From the library of the celebrated book collector James Bindley, with his signature on front paste-down.

142 —— —— Il Davide Perseguitato. *Printed for Humphrey Mosely*, 1647, *engr. frontis., title torn with part loss of one letter, some staining throughout*, [ii+]163 pp., 12mo, *19th cent. hf. calf, crudely rebacked with grey paper, corners rubbed* (Wing M357) **£30.00**

143 —— [w. (C.)] A Perfect Narrative of the whole Proceedings of the High Court of Iustice in the Tryal of the King in Westminster Hall . . . with the several Speeches of the King, Lord President, and Solicitor General . . . [with the Continuations, 3 numbers together]. *Printed for John Playfair*, 1648, *general staining throughout, some edges trimmed*, 16:8:15 pp., sm. 4to, *disbound* (Wing W9) **£40.00**

144 **Charles** (II.) *Ειχων βασιλιχη δευτερα.* The Pourtraicture of His Sacred Majesty King Charles II. with his Reasons for turning Roman Catholick; published by K. James. Found in the Strong Box. *Printed in the Year*, 1694, FIRST EDITION, *frontis., tear in inner margin of title repaired*, xvi+320 pp., 8vo, *19th cent. maroon roan, gilt, g.e., armorial book label* (Wing E312: Madan 132) **£65.00**

Charles—*continued*

145 —— [EGLESFIELD (Charles)] Monarchy Revived; being the Personal History of Charles the Second, from his earliest Years to his Restoration to the Throne. Reprinted from the Edition of 1661. *Printed for Charles Baldwyn*, 1823, *with 14 portraits, all sl. foxed, hf. sheet list of plates tipped in*, [ii+]262 pp., 8vo, *contemp. tan calf, gilt extra, leather label, marb. edges and end-papers* **£25.00**

146 —— GENETHLIACUM Illustrissimorum Principum Caroli & Mariae a Musis Cantabrigiensibus celebratum. *Excusum Cantabridiae, R. Daniel*, 1631, *lacks blank before title, some headlines cut into, 2 catchwords defective, F3 recto shaved at fore-edge*, sm. 4to, *modern qtr. blue morocco, lettered, cloth sides, g.e.* **£95.00**

¶Congratulatory verses from Cambridge University on the birth of the future Charles II., in Latin and Greek, including contributions by Thomas Randolph, Thomas Fuller and Edward King.

147 **Charles iv.** *of Lorraine.* BEAUVAU (Marquis de) Memoires, pour servir a l'Histoire de Charles iv. Duc de Lorraine & de Bar [with—Historie de l'Imprisonnement de Charles iv. Duc de Lorraine . . .]. *Amsterdam, chez Pierre Brunel*, 1711, [xiv+]456[+xviii]:132 pp., 12mo, *new qtr. calf, grey bds., leather label, sprinkled edges* **£25.00**

148 —— Political and Military Observations, Remarks and Maxims, of Charles V. late Duke of Lorrain, General of the Emperor's Forces, from a MS. left by him, and never before printed. *Printed for J. Jones and W. Hawes*, 1699, *foxing throughout*, [xvi+]277[+viii] pp., 8vo, *new qtr. calf, grey bds., leather label* (Wing C3650*) **£45.00**

149 **Charles Louis.** The Manifest of the Most Illustrious, and Soveraigne Prince, Charles Lodowick, Count Palatine of the Rhine . . . concerning the Right of His Succession both in the Princedome, Lands and Palatinate; as also in the Dignity, Voice, Session and Function of the Electorship-Palatine thereunto annexed. Translated . . . *Printed by A. G[riffin] for I. N[orton] and R. W[hitaker]*, 1637, FIRST EDITION IN ENGLISH, *lacks lf. before title (? blank), small piece torn from top outer corner of 2nd ff.*, [vii+77] ff., sm. 4to, *modern qtr. dark green crushed morocco, cloth sides, raised bands and lettered* (STC 5046) **£90.00**

150 **Chatham** (Earl of) Letters written to his Nephew Thomas Pitt, Esq. (afterwards Lord Camelford) then at Cambridge. *Printed for T. Payne, by T. Bensley*, 1804, xxxii+104 pp., sm. 8vo, *contemp. hf. crimson morocco, marb. bds., lettered* **£15.00**

151 **Chichele.** DUCK (Arthur) Vita Henrici Chichele Archiepiscopi Cantvariensis svd Regibvs Henric. v. et vi. *Oxoniae, Excud. Iosephus Barnesius*, 1617, FIRST EDITION, *final lf. of errata present, some soiling by use*, [ii+]108[+iii] pp., sm. 4to, *18th cent. panelled calf, leather label, little rubbed, joints cracking* (STC 7278: Madan 451) **£120.00**

¶Formerly Narcissus Luttrell's copy with his stamped monogram on verso of title and MS. date 1707.

152 —— —— Vita Henrici Chichele Archepiscopi Cantvariensis . . . *Oxoniae, Excud. Iosephus Barnesius*, 1617, FIRST EDITION, *final lf. of errata present*, [ii+]108[+iii] pp., sm. 4to, *new qtr. cf., marb. bds., leather label* (STC 7278: Madan 451) **£95.00**

153 **China.** LE COMPTE (Louis, *Jesuit*) Memoirs and Observations, Topographical, Physical, Mathematical, Mechanical, Natural, Civil and Ecclesiastical, made in a late Journey through the Empire of China and Published in several Letters . . . Translated from the Paris Edition, and illustrated with figures. *Printed for Benj. Tooke and Sam. Buckley*, 1697, *frontis. port. and 3 plates (2 folding), folding chart, small tear in one margin, occasional foxing throughout, sig. [R] present*, [xxiv+]527[+i] pp., [225-240 foliated], 8vo, *new qtr. calf, marb. bds., leather label* (Wing L831) **£155.00**

154 **Churchill** (Sir Winston) Divi Britannici: being a Remark upon the Lives of all the Kings of this Isle, from the Year of the World 2855. unto the Year of Grace 1660. *Printed by Tho, Roycroft, to be sold by Francis Eglesfield*, 1675, *title in red and black, port. of William and Mary inserted as frontis., embellished throughout with cuts of arms*, [vi+]362[+ii] pp., folio, *contemp. mottled calf, surface pock-marked, stitching working loose, otherwise sound* (Wing C4275) **£25.00**

155 **Civil Government.** A POLITICAL CONFERENCE between Aulicus, a Courtier; Demas, a Countryman; and Civicus, a Citizen: clearing the Original of Civil Government, the Powers and Duties of Soveraigns and Subjects in a Familiar and Plain Way, which may be understood by every Ordinary Capacity. *Printed for J.L. and are to be sold by Richard Baldwin*, 1689, [ii+]50 pp., sm. 4to, *modern hf. pale blue morocco, cloth sides, lettered* (Wing P2765) **£35.00**

156 **Civil War.** HAMPDEN. GRENVILLE (George Nugent, *Baron*) Some Memorials of John Hampden, his Party, and his Times. 2 Vols. *John Murray*, 1832, *with 7 engr. plates, some off-setting*, xxvi+402+[i]:v+467 pp., *lacks the publisher's catalogue*, 8vo, *contemp. hf. calf, marb. bds., leather labels* **£25.00**

157 **Clergy.** AN ACT for Confirming of Four Subsidies, Granted by the Clergy. *Printed by John Bill and Christopher Barker*, 1663, [ii+]32 pp., folio, *disbound* **£12.00**

158 **Coal Trade.** GARDINER (Ralph) Englands Grievance Discovered, in relation to the Coal Trade, with the map of the River of Tine, and Situation of the Town and Corporation of Newcastle: the tyrannical Oppression of those Magistrates, their Charters and Grants; the several Tryals, Depositions, and Judgements obtained against them; with a Breviate of several Statutes proving repugnant to their Actings; with Proposals for reducing the excessive Rates of Coals for the Future; and the Rise of their Grants appearing in this Book. *Newcastle, reprinted by D. Akenhead and Sons*, 1796, *folding map and 20 plates*, viii+216 pp., 8vo, *hf. calf, marb. bds. joints cracking* (Upcott p. 1043) **£50.00**

¶Originally published in 1655. A MS. note on front fly-leaf reads 'This is a reprint of a very scarce work. Many of the plates to the original work are preserved in this, from an old batter'd copy which fell in my way'. There are 12 such plates.

159 **Cobbett.** [ANON] The Life of William Cobbett, dedicated to his Sons, *F. J. Mason*, 1835, *portrait and engr. title, both foxed, general marginal soiling*, xvi+422 pp., sm. 8vo, *new qtr. tan calf, grey bds., leather label* (Pearl 217) **£35.00**

160 **Cochrane** (Thomas, *Earl of Dundonald, Admiral of the Red*) The Autobiography of a Seaman. 2 Vols., 2nd Edition. *Richard Bentley*, 1860/61, *with 4 charts*, xxiii+428:xv+488 pp., 8vo, *contemp. hf. calf, leather labels, joints beginning to crack, backstrips little worn* **£30.00**

161 **Columbus.** THE DISCOVERY of America by Christopher Columbus. *Dublin, Printed by P. Dixon Hardy*, [ca. 1820], *with 9 woodcuts (6 full-page)*, 177[+i] pp., 18mo, *orig. marb. sheep, backstrip sl. defective, cracking in back joint* **£22.50**

162 **Comazzi** (John Baptista, *Count*) The Morals of Princes: or, an Abstract of the most Remarkable Passages contain'd in the History of all the Emperors who reign'd in Rome. With a Moral Reflection drawn from each Quotation. Done into English by William Hatchett. *Printed for T. Worrall*, 1729, *engr. frontis., title in red and black*, xvi+391[+i] pp., 8vo, *contemp. panelled calf, unlettered, in fine condition* **£25.00**

163 **Comines** (Philippe de) Memoires, contenans l'Histoire des Rois Louis xi. & Charles viii. depuis l'an 1464 jusques en 1498. Edition nouvelle, . . . augmentee de plusieurs Traittez, Contrats, Testamens & autres Pieces nouvelles. 5 Vols. *Brusselle, chez Francois Foppens*, 1723, *with engr. frontis., 11 portraits and 2 folding tables*, sm. 8vo, *contemp. sprinkled calf, gilt, edges rubbed, sprinkled edges, leather labels* **£185.00**

164 —— Memoirs. Containing the History of Lewis xi. & Charles viii. Kings of France, with the most Remarkable Occurrances in their particular Reigns from the Year 1464 to 1498. Revised and Corrected from divers MSS. and Antient Impressions by Denys Godefroy . . . Faithfully Translated into English. *Printed for John Starkey*, 1674, *engr. frontis., one lf. remargined, some soiling of prelims.*, [xxxviii+]611[+iv] pp., 8vo, *contemp. calf, rubbed, corners worn, joints cracking, lacks label* (Wing C5543) **£25.00**

165 **Conspiracy.** AN ACT for Impowering His Majesty to Apprehend and Detain such Persons as He shall find Just Cause to Suspect are Conspiring against the Government. *Printed by Charles Bill and Thomas Newcomb*, 1689, [ii+]2 pp., folio, *disbound* **£15.00**

166 —— AN ACT for Impowering Their Majesties to Commit without Bayl, such Persons as They shall find Just Cause to suspect of Conspring against the Government. *Printed by Charles Bill and Thomas Newcomb*, 1689, [ii+]2 pp., *disbound* **£15.00**

167 **Constitvtions and Canons Ecclesiasticall,** treated vpon by the Bishop of London, President of the Conuocation for the Prouince of Canterbury, and the rest of the Bishops and Clergie of the said Prouince: and agreed vpon with His Maiesties Licence in their Synode begun at London Anno Dom. 1603 . . . *Imprinted by Robert Barker*, 1604, *considerable damp staining with some fragility of paper, last lf. repaired in inner margin, lacks* A^1 *(blank)*, [xi+74] ff., sm. 4to, *modern full calf, leather label* (STC 10070—catchword on D^1 'cars') **£85.00**

168 **Cope** (Antony) The history of tvvo the most noble Captaynes of the worlde, Anniball and Scipio, of their diuers battayles and victoryes, excedynge profitable to reade, gathered and translated into English oute of Titus Livius, and other authores. *Imprinted by Thomas Marshe*, 1561, *printed in* **Black Letter** *throughout, has blank before text and i(of 2) before table, title and ff. lf. repaired in lower fore-margin, browned and soiled throughout*, [vii+]292(shd. read 300)[+iv] ff., *erratic*, sm. 8vo, *new dark brown calf, leather label* (STC 5720) rare **£320.00**

169 **Coronation.** TAYLOR (Arthur) The Glory of Regality: an Historical Treatise of the Anointing and Crowning of the Kings and Queens of England. *Printed by and for R. and A. Taylor* . . . 1820, *woodcut vignettes, some foxing*, xvi+424(shd. read 428) pp., 8vo, *contemp. hf. calf, marb. bds., corners worn, recently rebacked and lettered* **£25.00**

170 **Cost of Living.** AN ACT for Punishing of such Persons as live at High Rates, and have no visible Estate, Possession or Calling Answering thereunto. [*Printed by Henry Hills and Iohn Field*, 1657—colophon], *drop title*, 4 pp., folio, *grey bds.* (Wing E1049) **£21.00**

171 **Cotton** (Sir Robert) The Antiquity and Dignity of Parliaments (that the Kings of England have been pleased, usually to Consult in the Great Council of Marriage, Peace and War, with their Peers and Commons in Parliament. *Printed Anno Domini*, 1679, *a few margins neatly repaired, contemp. writing on title*, [ii+]13 pp., folio, *disbound* (Wing C6481) scarce **£35.00**

172 [**Courtilz de Sandras** (Gatien de)] The French Spy: or, the Memoirs of John Baptist de la Fontaine, Lord of Savoy and Fontenai, late Brigadier and Surveyor of the French King's Army, now a Prisoner in the Bastile. Containing many secret Transactions relating both to England and France. Translated from the French Original, printed at Cologn in the Year 1699. *Printed for R. Basset*, 1700, FIRST EDITION IN ENGLISH, *upper corner of A[2] and A3 torn away with no loss, a few outer margins ragged*, [xvi+]371[+xiii] pp., 8vo, *contemp. sprinkled calf, leather label, joints beginning to crack, lacks rear free endpaper* (Hazlitt iii/p. 87: Wing C6597A, *6597C) **£55.00**

173 **Cromwell.** [STACE (Machell)] Cromwelliana. A Chronological Detail of Events in which Oliver Cromwell was engaged; from the year 1642 to his Death 1658: with a Continuation of other Transactions, to the Restoration. *Westminster, printed for Machell Stace*, 1810, *with the original 5 plates and* EXTRA-ILLUSTRATED *by the insertion of 11 tinted plates by Woodburn, 17 sepia plates by Smeeton and 54 other portraits and views*, 6+186[+x] pp., folio, *contemp. crimson straight grain morocco, wide borders in gilt and blind, lettered, scuff marks on sides* **£110.00**

174 [**Crouch** (Nathaniel)] England's Monarchs: or, a Compendious Relation of the most Remarkable Transactions, and Observable Passages, Ecclesiastical, Civil, and Military, which have hapned during the Reigns of the Kings and Queens of England, from the Invasion of the Romans to this present . . . by R.B. *Printed for Nath. Crouch*, 1685, *with 25 woodcut portraits, some worming at end with sl. loss*, [iv+]234[+ii] pp., 12mo, *19th cent. hf. tan calf, marb. bds., sprinkled edges* (Wing C7314) **£45.00**

175 [——] The History of the Two Late Kings, Charles the Second and James the Second . . . *Printed by Nath. Crouch*, 1693, *frontis., corner torn away, laid down, writing on verso of title, embrowned throughout*, [iv+]176[+xii] pp. (Wing C7340):
[with]
The Wars in England, Scotland, & Ireland, containing an Account of all the Battles . . . during the Reign of King Charles the First . . . Sixth Edn., rev. and corr. *Printed for Nath. Crouch*, 1697, *woodcuts, foremargin of title repaired, embrowned throughout*, 184[+viii] pp. (Wing C7359A):
2 items bound together, *all margins of both works cropped or cut close, with some loss of letters*, 12mo, *new qtr. calf, marb. bds., unlettered* **£30.00**

176 **D[aniel]** (S[amuel]) The Collection of the History of England: [to the end of Edward iii.]. *Printed for Simon Waterson*, 1626, *title within woodcut border, general browning with some marginal staining, one outer margin repaired*, [v+]222 pp., folio, *new qtr. tan calf, grey bds., leather label* (STC 6251) **£60.00**

177 —— T[RUSSELL] (I[ohn]) A Continvation of the Collection of the History of England, beginning where Samvel Daniell Esquire ended, with the Raigne of Edvvard the third, and ending where the honourable Viscount Saint Albones began, with the life of Henry the seventh, being a compleat History of the beginning and end of the dissention betwixt the two houses of Yorke and Lancaster. With the Matches and issue of all the Kings, Princes, Dukes, Marquesses, Earles, and Viscounts of this Nation, deceased, during those times. *Printed by M. D[awson] for Ephraim Dawson*, 1636, *general soiling throughout, last lf. defective in upper margin and repaired, with some loss, a few fore-margins frayed*, folio, *contemp. calf, rebacked and repaired, leather label* (STC 24297) **£95.00**

178 [**Defoe** (Daniel)] A Speech for Mr. D---sse Younger of Arnistown, if he should be impeach'd of H--- T---n for what he said and did about the Pretender's Medal, lately sent to the Faculty of Advocates at Edinburgh. *Printed for J. Baker*, 1711, FIRST EDITION, *text sl. dust-soiled*, 15[+i—advert. of Sacheverelliana] pp., sm. 8vo, *modern marb. bds., paper label* (Moore 212: Rothschild 748) **£95.00**
¶Published on 30th of August, the Speech is in Scots dialect.

179 **Denmark.** AN ACCOUNT of Denmark, Ancient and Modern. Containing its History, from Swain, the First Christian King, to the Present Time . . . also, the Geography of Denmark . . . *Printed for J. Almon*, 1768, 128 pp., 8 pp. catalogue at end, *with finely engraved portraits of Christian vii. and Caroline Matilda and a genealogical table appended*, 8vo, *contemp. sprinkled tan calf, leather label, red sprinkled edges* **£65.00**

180 —— THE PRESENT STATE of Denmark, in relation to its Government and Laws, its Trade and Manufactures, its Revenues and Forces. Compiled from the Present Archives, and other authentic Materials. Being an exact Description of that Kingdom, as it now exists, and different from any Account hitherto published in the English Language. In a series of letters, mostly written by Monsieur Roger. *Printed for Tho. Osborne*, 1762, xvi+338 pp., 8vo, *qtr. calf, grey bds., recently rebacked, leather label* **£50.00**

181 **Dodington** (George Budd) Diary, from March 8, 1749, to February 6, 1761; with an Appendix, containing some Curious and Interesting Papers . . . by H. P. Wyndham. Fourth Edition. *Printed for G. Wilkie and J. Robinson*, 1809, xvi+472 pp., 8vo, *tan calf, gilt, leather label, little rubbed* **£25.00**

182 **D'Orleans** (J.) The History of the Revolutions in England under the Family of the Stuarts, from the Year 1603, to 1690, in three books; wherein are contain'd many Secret Memoirs relating to that Family, and the last Great Revolution, Anno 1688. Transl. from the French Original Printed at Paris. To which is Prefix'd an Advertisement concerning this History. *Printed for E. Curll and R. Gosling*, 1711, *some staining at beginning*, [xxiv+]328[+xvi+]44 pp., 8vo, *contemp. sprinkled calf, lacks label, joints beginning to crack* **£35.00**

183 **Doyle** (James E.) A Chronicle of England, B.C. 55-A.D. 1485. *Longman, Green* . . . 1864, *with 81 designs by the author, engraved and printed in colours by Edmund Evans*, viii+462 pp., 4to, *full crimson straight grained morocco, gilt extra, lettered, joints rubbed* **£60.00**

184 **Dudley.** [JOBB (Samuel)] The Life of Robert, Earl of Leicester, the Favourite of Queen Elizabeth . . . *Printed for Woodman and Lyon, and C. Davis*, 1727, *lacks the portrait, some soiling*, xvi+289[+lxxvii] pp., 8vo, *hf. russia, upper joint cracked, rubbed, lettered* **£21.00**

185 —— (Lady Jane [Grey]). FLORIO (Michaelangelo) Historia de la vita e de la morte de l'illustriis Signora Giovanna Graia, gia Regina eletta e publicata d'Inghilterra: e de la cose accadute in quel Regno dopo la morte del Re Edoardo vi. Nella quale secondo la Diuina Scrittura si tratta de i principali articoli de la Religione Christiana. Con l'aggiunta d'una dottis, disputa Theologica fatta in Ossonia, l'anno 1554 . . . [*Middelburg*], *Stampato appresso Ricardo Pittore*, 1607, *printed throughout in italic, some damp staining*, pp. 1-208:281-328: 313-378[+xxix+i(blank)], sm. 8vo, *19th cent. straight grained calf, joints tender, g.e.* **£140.00**

186 **Dugdale** (William) The History of Imbanking and Drayning of divers Fenns and Marshes, both in Forein Parts and in this Kingdom; and of the Improvements thereby. Extracted from Records, Manuscripts, and other Authentick Testimonies. *Printed by Alice Warren*, 1662, FIRST EDITION, *with 11 folding maps, title in red and black, text printed in double column, some discolouration of text, few paper faults, but not serious, does not have the five extra leaves containing a note on certain 'Surrounding Grounds'*, [viii+]424[+ii] pp., folio, *18th cent. crimson morocco, gilt and blind tooling, g.e., inner joints cracked, edges rubbed* (Wing D2481: Maddison, Styles and Wood 28) **£300.00**

187 —— Monasticon Anglicanum: A History of the Abbies and other Monasteries, Hospitals, Frieries, and Cathedral and Collegiate Churches, with their Dependences in England and Wales; also of all such Scotch, Irish and French Monasteries, as were in any Manner connected with Religious Houses in England, together with a particular Account of their respective Foundations, Grants, and Donations, and a full Statement of their Possessions, as well temporal as spiritual. 6 Vols. in 8. *James Bohn*, 1846, *with 231 plates, of which 51 are double page, 27 are seals, 14 are habits and 2 are coats of arms, one double plate is inverted, 8 plates are creased, text of one volume badly creased also*, folio, *contemp. hf. dark purple morocco, t.e.g., some vols. lightly scuffed, 4 hinges started, otherwise a very sound set* **£325.00**

188 —— A Short View of the Late Troubles in England; briefly setting forth, their Rise, Growth, and Tragical Conclusion . . . to which is added, a Perfect Narrative of the Treaty at Uxbridge in an. 1644. *Oxford, Printed at the Theater for Moses Pitt*, 1681, FIRST EDITION, *engraved portrait of Charles i.*, [$4B^2$] *a cancel, Advertisement lf. present before title, 5 pp. catalogue of books printed at the Theatre at end*, pp. [vi+]1-136:185-294:361-439:449-488:553-650: 733-959[+vi], folio, *contemp. calf, carefully rebacked to match, leather label* (Wing D2492) **£55.00**

189 [——] A Short View of the Late Troubles in England; . . . *Oxford, Printed at the Theater for Moses Pitt*, 1681, FIRST EDITION, *portrait*, [$4B^2$] *a cancel, piece torn from corner on a divisional title*, [vi+]959[+xi] pp., folio, *hf. calf, brick red bds. sl. rubbed, lettered (incorrectly)* (Wing D2492: Maddison 45) **£48.00**
¶From the library of the late Philip Styles. Extensive marginalia, in pencil, of additions and corrections taken from the *Gough* copy.

190 —— A Short View of the Late Troubles in England . . . *Oxford, Printed at the Theater for Moses Pitt*, 1681, FIRST EDITION, *engraved portrait of Charles i., title supplied from another copy, lacks the Advertisement lf.*, [$4B^2$] *a cancel, 5 pp. Catalogue present*, pp. [vi+1-136:185-294: 361-439:449-488:553-650:733-959[+vi], folio, *contemp. calf, rebacked and lettered, corners worn, new endpapers* (Wing D2492) **£40.00**

191 **East Indies.** [FEYNES (Henri de, *sieur de Monfart*) An Exact and Cvriovs Svrvey of all the East Indies, euen to Canton, the chiefe Cittie of China: All duly performed by land, by Monsieur de Monfart, the like whereof was neuer hetherto, brought to an end. VVherein also are described the hugh Dominions of the great Mogor, to whom that honourable Knight, Sir Thomas Roe, was lately sent Ambassador from the King. Newly translated out of the Trauailers Manuscript. *Printed by Thomas Dawson, for VVilliam Arondell*, 1615, FIRST EDITION, *woodcut initials, title margined and restored with pen-facsimile to a few letters, side notes on 4 pp. just shaved*, [ix+]40 pp., sm. 4to, *19th cent. tan roan, gilt extra, lettered, by W. Pratt for John Bellingham Inglis* (STC 10840) **£500.00**

192 **Edgeworth** (Richard Lovell and Marie) Essays on Irish Bulls. Second Edition corrected. *Printed for J. Johnson*, 1803, *with 2 engraved vignettes, some marginal staining and sl. browning*, iv+303 pp., sm. 8vo, *contemp. sprinkled calf, leather label, joints beginning to crack* **£30.00**

193 **Edward Prince to Wales.** LELAND (John) Genethliacon illustrissimi Eäduerdi Principis Cambriae, Ducis Coriniae, et Comitis Palatini: libellus ante aliquot annos inchaotus, nunc uero absolutus & editus . . . *Londini: (Colophon): Renerum Vuolfium* . . . 1543, FIRST EDITION, *partly italic, woodcut of badge of Prince of Wales within the sun in its splendour on verso of title, one large historiated woodcut initial, printer's woodcut device* (McKerrow 96) *on verso of final lf., some staining or discolouration of first few ll.*, [30] ff., sm. 4to, *18th cent. marbled bds., rebacked modern brown morocco, unlettered, endpapers faintly stained, collation mark of Thomas Rawlines on front free endpaper, ownership stamp (initials) of Albert Ehrmann and Broxbourne Library bookplate* (STC 15443: Hazlitt iii/p. 139) **£325.00**

194 **Elizabeth.** ACADEMIAE OXONIENSIS Pietas erga Serenissimvm et Potentissimvm Iacobvm Angliae Scotiae Franciae et Hibernie Regem, fidei defensorem, Beatissimae Elisabethae nuper Reginae legitime & auspicatissime succedentem. *Oxoniae, Excud. Iosephus Barnesius*, 1603, *title soiled & repaired in fore-margin, the final p. is blank, i.e. the issue without the 'Votum Typographi . . .'*, [iv+]207 pp. (STC 19019: Madan 56/7):
[with]
FUNEBRE OFFICIUM in Memoriam Honoratissimam Serenissimae & Beatissimae Elisabethae nuper Angliae, Franciae, & Hiberniae Regina. *Oxoniae, Excud. Iosephus Barnesius*, 1603, [iv+]182 pp. (STC 19108: Madan 57/9):
[and]
Carleton (George) Heroici Characteres ad Illvstrissimvm Eqvitem Henricum Nevillum. *Oxoniae, Excud. Iosephus Barnesius*, 1603, [vi+]48 pp., *lacks final blank* (STC 2436: Madan 55/3):
Three works bound together, sm. 4to, *hf. blue morocco, gilt, cloth sides, lettered, t.e.g.* **£400.00**

195 —— DIGGES (Sir Dudley, *the Elder*) The Compleat Ambassador: or two Treaties of the Intended Marriage of Qu. Elizabeth of Glorious Memory; Comprised in Letters of Negotiation of Sir Francis Walsingham, her Resident in France, together with the Answers of the Lord Burleigh, the Earl of Leicester, Sir Tho. Smith, and others. Wherein, as in a clear Mirror, may be seen the Faces of the two Courts of England and France, as they then stood, with many remarkable passages of State, not at all mentioned in any History. *Printed by Tho. Newcomb, for Gabriel Bedell and Thomas Collins*, 1635, *engraved frontis. by Faithorne, title in red and black, some damp staining throughout*, [xiv+]441[+iv] pp., folio, *contemp. calf, newly rebacked, leather label, corners worn* (Wing D1453) **£85.00**

196 **Enghein** (Duke d') French Murder! A Circumstantial Account of the Conspiracy against Buonaparte, First Consul of France, with the Particulars relative to the Apprehension and Examination of the accused Persons, viz. General Moreau, Pichegru, Georges, &c. &c. with the cruel Treatment experienced by them, in the various Places of their Confienment. Likewise, an authentic Detail of the Murder of the Duke d'Engehin . . . *Printed and published by A. Kemmish* . . . N.D. [ca. 1804], *folding plate, one margin repaired*, 24 pp., sm. 8vo, *qtr. roan, pink bds., stained, lettered* **£35.00**

197 **Estienne** (Charles) Dictionarium Historicum Geographicum Poeticum: Gentium, Hominum, Deorum, Gentilium, Regionum, Insularum . . . ad incudem vero revocatum, innumerisque pene locis auctum & emaculatum per Nicolaum Lloydium, editio novissima . . . *Imp. B. Tooke, T. Passenger, T. Sawbridge, A. Swalle & A. Churchill*, 1686, *lacks front free endpaper*, [x+107+xii] pp., folio, *contemp. mottled calf, arms in backstrip compartments, unlettered* (Wing E3349: L2664A) **£75.00**

198 **Excise.** AN ADDITIONAL ACT for the better Improvement and Advancing the Receipts of the Excise and New-Impost. *Printed by Henry Hills and Iohn Field*, 1657, *embrowned*, [ii+]61 pp., folio, *grey bds.* (Wing E1171) **£25.00**

199 **Fanshawe** (Lady [Anne]) Memoirs . . . wife of . . . Sir Richard Fanshawe, Bart., Ambassador from Charles the Second to the Court of Madrid in 1665. To which are added, Extracts from the Correspondence of Sir Richard Fanshawe. *Henry Colburn*, 1829, [lxiii+]395[+i] pp., *port., sl. foxed*, 8vo, *contemp. hf. russia, rebacked recently, leather label* **£20.00**

200 **Favine** (Andrew) The Theater of Honour and Knight-hood. Or a Compendious Chronicle and Historie of the whole Christian World. Containing the Originall of all Monarchies, Kingdomes, and Estates, with their Emperours, Kings, Princes, and Gouernours; Their Beginnings, Continuance, and Successions, to this present Time. The First Institution of Armes, Emblazons, Kings, Heralds, and Pursuiuants of Armes: With all the Ancient and Moderne Military Orders of Knight-hood in euery Kingdome . . . written in French [now transl. into English]. *Printed by William Iaggard*, 1623, *with 12 plates and 85 cuts in the text, some staining, last lf. remargined, pagination erratic*, [xviii+]572 (shd. read 574):538 pp., folio, *18th cent. diced calf, gilt, little rubbed* (STC 10717) **£165.00**
¶". . . comprises the most valuable treatise we have in English upon the Foreign orders of knighthood." (Moule cxi)

201 [**Ferguson** (Robert)] The Design of Enslaving England Discovered in the Incroachments upon the Powers and Privileges of Parliament, by K. Charles II. being a New corrected Impression of that Excellent Piece, intituled, A Just and Modest Vindication of the Proceedings of the Two Last Parliaments of King Charles the Second. *Printed for Richard Baldwin*, 1689, [ii+]48 pp., sm. 4to, *new blue wrappers* (Wing F734) **£40.00**

202 **Fire of London.** BROOKS (Thomas) London's Lamentations: or, a Serious Discourse concerning that late fiery Dispensation that turned our (once renowned) City into a ruinous Heap. Also the several Lessons that are incumbent upon those whose Houses have escaped the consuming Flames. *Printed for John Hancock and Nathaniel Ponder*, 1670, *embrowned throughout, name on title, which is fragile at edges, lacks blank before text*, [xxx+]168: 271[+viii] pp., sm. 4to, *contemp. hf. calf, marb. bds., leather label, joints beginning to crack* (Wing B4950) **£65.00**

203 **Fish.** AN ACT giving Licence for Transporting Fish in Forreign Bottoms. [*Printed by Henry Hills and Iohn Field*, 1657—colophon], *drop title*, 3 pp., folio, *grey bds.* (Wing E1138) **£20.00**

204 **Fishing.** AN ACT for Preservation of Fishing in the River of Severn. *Printed by John Bill* . . . 1679, [ii+]5 pp., folio, *disbound* **£15.00**

205 **Flagellants.** [DELOLME (Jean Louis)] The History of the Flagellants, or the Advantages of Discipline; being a Paraphrase and Commentary on the *Historia Flagellantium* of the Abbé Boileau, by Somebody who is not Doctor of the Sorbonne. *Sold by M. Hingeston, Yeats and Robinson, and Fielding and Walker*, 1777, *with engr. title, 4 plates, and head and tail pieces, some off-setting*, [vi+]340 pp., 4to, *qtr. tan calf, marb. bds., vellum corners, new end-papers, leather label* **£55.00**

206 **Forestry Commission.** INSTRUCTIONS agreed upon in Parliament for Commissioners, for Surveying the Forest of Sherwood; The Forest, or Chase of Needwood; The Forest, or Chase of Kingswood; the Forest, or Chase of Ashdown . . . *Printed by Henry Hills and John Field*, 1657. *embrowned*, [ii+]14 pp., folio, *grey bds.* (Wing E1592) **£20.00**

207 **Fosbrooke** (Thomas Dudley) British Monachism; or, Manners and Customs of the Monks and Nuns of England. To which are added; i. Peregrinatiorum Religiosum . . . ii. The Consuetudical of Anchorets and Hermits. iii. Some account of the Continentes . . . iv. Four select Poems, in various styles. A New Edition. *Printed by and for John Nichols, Son, and Bentley*, 1817, *14 plates, some sl. foxed*, viii+560 pp., lge. 4to, *qtr. parchment, marb. bds., corners worn, paper label defective* **£20.00**

208 —— British Monachism; . . . Third Edition, with Additions. *M. A. Natali*, 1843, *with engr. title, portrait and 11 plates, some foxing*, 428 pp., lge. 8vo, *calf, gilt, leather label, rubbed* **£25.00**

209 **France.** BAINES (Edward) History of the Wars of the French Revolution, from the Breaking out of the War in 1792, to the Restoration of a General Peace in 1815, comprehending the Civil History of Great Britain and France, during that Period. 2 Vols. *Printed for Longman* . . . 1817, *with portraits, maps, plans and charts*, [iv+]539:[iv+]595 pp., 4to, *contemp. calf, gilt extra, lettered on backstrips* **£55.00**

210 —— [BESONGUE (N.)] *ed.* L'Etat de la France, ou l'on tous les Princes, Ducs & Pairs, Marêchaux de France & autres Officiers de la Courone: les Evêques, les Cours qui jugent en denrier ressort, les Gouvernours des Provinces, les Chevaliers des trois Ordres du Roy, &c. . . . 3 Vols. *Paris, chez Charle Osmont*, 1698, *with 61 wood cuts of arms and occasional culs-de-lampe, single worm hole through outer margin of last 10 signatures of vol. ii.*, [xxiv+]659[+iv]: [viii+]517:[xii+]448 pp., 12mo, *contemp. sprinkled calf, leather labels, gilt backstrips, vol. i. recently rebacked with orig. backstrip, sl. defective head of backstrip vol. ii.* **£45.00**

211 —— NOLAC (Pierre de) Marie Antoinette. *Arthur L. Humphreys*, 1905, *printed on Arnold paper*, vii+268 pp., sm. 4to, *green crushed morocco, backstrip and edges, browned by sun, t.e.g., lettered* **£25.00**

212 —— PRIOLO (Benjamin) The History of France under the Ministry of Cardinal Mazarine, containing all the remarkable and curious Passages in the Government of that State from the Death of King Louis xiii. to the Death of the Cardinal . . . done into English by Christopher Wase. *Printed for J. Starkey*, 1671, *portrait, lacks* A^1. *title sl. defective in inner margin, some discolouration throughout, some early annotations*, [xxii+]434[+xxiv] pp., sm. 8vo, *early hf. calf, head and tail of backstrip chipped, upper joint cracked, but firm, leather label* (Wing P3506A) **£85.00**

213 —— [VOLTAIRE (F. M. Arouet de)] Le Siecle de Louis xiv. publié par M. [Joseph du Fresne] de Francheville. 2 Vols., Seconde Edition. *Londre, chez R. Dodsley*, 1752, *worming in upper fifth through first vol. with occasional loss to letter-press, three margins torn, no loss, last lf. of index missing*, [xii+]488:[ii+]464 pp., 12mo, *contemp. tan calf, lacks labels, rubbed* **£21.00**

214 **French Parliament.** L'HISTOIRE du Temps, ou le veritable Recit de ce qui s'est passé dans le Parlement depuis le mois d'aoust 1647. jusques au mois de Novembre 1648, avec les Harangues & les Advis differends qui ont esté proposez dans les affairs u'on y a solmnellement traittées. *Rouen, chez David du Petit Val & Jean Viret* . . . 1649, *has sig. m* inserted, damp staining throughout, few ll. wormed in upper margin*, [iv+]240 pp., sm. 4to, *contemp. limp vellum, soiled* **£21.00**
¶The dedication epistle is signed L.P.R. (see Barbier).

215 **Frederick Louis** (*Prince of Wales and son of George II*) Letters, in the Original, and Translation, and Messages, that passed between the King, Queen, Prince, and Princess of Wales; on Occasion of the Birth of the young Princess [Augusta]. *Printed and sold by J. Roberts*, 1737, *some fore-margins creased, some staining*, 30 pp., 8vo, *stitched and untrimmed, enclosed in grey cloth flap-over case, leather label on upper cover* (Rothschild 140) **£55.00**
¶Due to his conduct over the lying-in of his wife, the Prince was ordered to leave St. James and took up residence at Kew, where he gathered together the heads of the opposition. (D.N.B.)

216 **Fuller** (Thomas) A Pisgah-Sight of Palestine and the Confines thereof, with the History of the Old and New Testament acted thereon. *Printed by J.F. for John Williams*, 1650, *with engraved title, plate of arms and 26 (ex 28) maps, plans and other plates, lacks the general map of Palestine and that of the Tribe of Zebulun, staining throughout, most plates creased, 2 with splits at folds, one plate misbound and 2 margins of text repaired, 18th century writing on endpapers*, [viii+]435+202[+xvii] pp., folio, *early vellum, soiled, sometime rebacked* [Wing F2455: Gibson 28] **£130.00**
¶Dedicated to Esme Stuart, Fuller's Patron, aged under one year. Esme died in Paris in 1660, aged 11.

217 [**Fulman** (W.) and J. **Fell**] Rerum Anglicarum Scriptorum Veterum, Vol. i. quorum Ingulfus nunc primum integer, caeteri nunc primum prodeunt. *Oxoniae, e Theatro Sheldoniano*, 1684, [xxviii+ii](blank)+598[+i] pp., folio, *contemp. calf, little rubbed, joints cracking, lacks label* (Wing F2525) **£15.00**

218 **Galtruchius** (P.) The Poetical Histories: being a Compleat Collection of all the Stories necessary for a Perfect Understanding of the Greek and Latin Poets and other Ancient Authors. Now Englished . . . Third Edition, corrected and amended by Marius D'Assigny. *Printed by W.G. and are to be sold by M. Pitt*, 1674, *sl. worming in some lower margins*, [xvi+]111:[ii+]131-453[+xviii] pp., sm. 8vo, *contemp. sprinkled sheep, joints beginning to crack* (Wing G386) **£45.00**

219 **George III.** George the Third, his Court and Family. 2 Vols. *Printed for Henry Colburn and C.*, 1820, *with 18 engraved plates, some foxing throughout*, xvi+431:[iv+]424 pp., 8vo, *finely bound in contemp. green straight grained morocco, leather labels, gilt backstrips, sides panelled and bordered with wide gilt design, inner gilt borders, g.e.* **£65.00**

220 **George iv.** An interesting collection of pamphlets, dealing in part with some of the debts of the Prince of Wales, later George iv., at the beginning of the 19th century. The pamphlets are all dated, or ascribed to, 1806, and centre for the most part on the claims of the Prince's jeweller, Nathaniel Jefferys, who was at one time owed as much as £90,000.00. Mrs. Fitzherbert is, of course, dragged in: Jefferys writes to her in his open letter: *Have the public then, in your opinion, no feelings? They Have: and their's can be no other than feelings of* EXTREME DISGUST. *When the Prince of Wales was married to the Princess, it was agreed that you should retire from that* intimacy of friendship *you had so long enjoyed* . . .
The ten pamphlets 8vo, *all (except one in grey wrappers) in modern marbled wrappers, in good condition apart from occasional sl. dampstaining* **£85.00**

¶ i. JEFFREYS (Nathaniel) A Review of the Conduct of H.R.H. the Prince of Wales in the various transactions with Mr. Jeffreys, during a period of more than twenty years, containing a detail of many circumstances relative to their Royal Highnesses the Prince and Princess of Wales, Mrs. Fitzherbert, &c. Second Edition with additions. *Printed for, and published by, Mr. Jeffreys*, 70 pp.

George iv—*continued*

ii. [GILLILAND (Thomas)] Diamond Cut Diamond; or, Observations on a Pamphlet entitled "Review of the Conduct . . ."; comprising a Free and Impartial View of Mr. Jefferys, as a Tradesman, Politician, and Courtier, during the period of twenty years. By Philo-veritas. *Printed by B. McMillan . . . for C. Chapple*, 1806, [iv+]67[+i] pp.

iii. JEFFERYS (Nathaniel) A Letter addressed to Mrs. Fitzherbert, in answer to a complaint, that her feelings have been hurt by the mention of her name in the Review of the Conduct of the Prince of Wales, with observations on the influence of Example, &c. Second Edition. *Printed for, and published by, Mr. Jefferys, lacking hf. title*, pp. [3]-19.

iv. [GILLILAND (Thomas)] The Diamond New Pointed; being a Supplement to Diamond Cut Diamond: containing Three Letters which Mr. Jefferys sent to the Earl of Moira, with a view to Extort Money from H.R.H. the Prince of Wales, with observations thereon, in a Letter to Mr. Jefferys; including Remarks on his letter to Mrs. Fitzherbert, and many facts never before published. By Philo-veritas. *Printed by B. McMillan . . . for C. Chapple*, [ii+]50 pp.

v. JEFFERYS (Nathaniel) A Refutation of the Positive Falsehoods and Gross Misrepresentations contained in the several publications professing to be in reply to the Review of the Conduct . . . To which is added the Report of the Proceedings upon the Trial before Lord Kenyon, in 1796, for the recovery of the money due to Mr. Jefferys for jewels and plate sold to the Prince of Wales. *Printed for Mr. Jefferys by J. H. Hart*, 62 pp.

vi. AN ADMONITORY Letter to H. R.H. the Prince of Wales, on the subject of the late Delicate Inquiry; containing anecdotes never before Published which may probably lead to the Detection of the real Authors of the late scandalous Attempt to sully the Purity of an illustrious Personage. Sixth Edition. *Printed by Dewick and Clarke for Tipper and Richards*, 30 pp.

vii. AN ANTIDOTE to Poison: or, a Full Reply to Mr. Jefferys' attack upon the Character and Conduct of H.R.H. the Prince of Wales: containing several important particulars derived from Authentic Sources of Information. By Claudio. Second Edition. *Printed by W. Clowes for Matthews and Leigh*, [iv+]94 pp.

viii. A COMPLETE VINDICATION of H. R. H. the Prince of Wales, relative to his Creditors; but not quite so complete a Vindication of the Right Hon. W. Pitt, relative to H.R.H. By the Lion and Unicorn. *Printed for and published by E. Greenland and W. Norris*, [iv+]25 pp.

ix. A LETTER to Nathaniel Jeffreys, late goldsmith and jeweller to H.R.H. the Prince of Wales, late Member of Parliament for the City of Coventry, on the subject of his Extraordinary Pamphlet . . . with an examination into the motives of his publication and its probable consequences. [Second Edition]. *Printed by W. Flint for J. Mawman*, 48 pp.

x. A LETTER to the Right Hon. the Earl of Moira, on the Accusations against H.R.H. the Prince of Wales, by Mr. Paull. With Notes Critical and Admonitory, in which the Character and Principles of Mr. Paull and Sir Francis Burdett, are examined, and their origin and tendency briefly elucidated. [By Theophrastus Junior]. *Printed for Messrs. Jordan and Maxwell, lacking hf. title*, pp. [3]-102.

221 —— A Further collection of pamphlets on the debts of the Prince Regent. 1806, five pamphlets bound together, 8vo, *contemp. qtr. calf, leather label, vellum corners, marb. sides* **£50.00**
¶Comprising:

1. JEFFERYS (Nathaniel) A Review of the Conduct of the Prince of Wales . . . Seventh Edition, N.D., 76 pp.
2. [GILLILAND (Thomas)] Diamond cut Diamond . . . Fifth Edition, 1806, viii+75[+i] pp.
3. [GILLILAND (Thomas)] The Diamond New Pointed . . . 1806, [ii+]50 pp.
4. JEFFERYS REFUTED!! A Letter to Nathaniel Jefferys . . . on the Subject of his extraordinary Pamphlet . . . 1806, 48 pp.
5. AN ANTIDOTE to Poison . . . by Claudio. Second Edition, 1806, [iv+]94[+i] pp.

222 **Gold and Silver refining.** AN ACT to Repeal the Statute made in the Fifth Year of King Henry the Fourth, against the Multiplying Gold and Silver. *Printed by Charles Bill and Thomas Newcomb*, 1689, [ii+]3 pp., folio, *disbound* **£20.00**

223 **Goldsmith** (Oliver) The Grecian History, from the Earliest State to the Death of Alexander the Great. 2 Vols. *Printed by J. and F. Rivington* . . . 1774, FIRST EDITION, *lacking the preliminary blanks*, [iii+]399:[i+]284[+lxiv] pp., 8vo, *newly bound in qtr. tan calf, marb. bds., leather labels* **£50.00**

224 —— The Grecian History, from the Earliest State, to the Death of Alexander the Great. To which is added, a summary Account of the Affairs of Greece from that Period, to the Sacking of Constantinople by the Othomans. New Edition, 2 Vols. *Printed for G. and J. Robinson* . . . 1805, iv+452:375[+lxv] pp., 8vo, *contemp. diced calf, lettered, tooled in blind and gilt, joints sl. rubbed* **£30.00**

225 [——] An History of England, in a Series of Letters from a Nobleman to his Son. 2 Vols. *Printed for W. Osborne and T. Griffin, and J. Mozley*, 1787, 312:280 pp., 12mo, *contemp. mottled sheep, leather labels, joints of vol. i, cracked, y.e.* **£25.00**
¶First published in 1764 and variously ascribed to the Earl of Orrery, Lord Lyttleton, and the Earl of Chesterfield.

226 —— The Roman History, from the Foundation of the City of Rome, to the Destruction of the Western Empire. Second Edition, 2 Vols. *Printed for S. Baker and G. Leigh, T. Davies and L. Davis*, 1770, *one lf. torn, no loss*, [ii+]x+487[+xvi]:[ii+]vi+501+[xi] pp., 8vo, *contemp. hf. tan calf, lettered, marb. bds.* **£36.00**

227 —— The Roman History . . . Fourth Edition, 2 Vols., *Printed for C. Bathurst* . . . 1781, x+487[+xii]:viii+501[+xi] pp., 8vo, *contemp. sprinkled calf, lacks labels* **£35.00**

228 [**Gordon** (Thomas)] A Modest Apology for Parson Alberoni, Governor to King Philip, a Minor; and Universal Curate of the whole Spanish Monarchy: . . . 9th Edition. *Printed for J. Roberts*, 1719, *dust soiled*, 36 pp., sm. 8vo, *disbound* **£15.00**

229 [**Grant** (James)] Random Recollections of the House of Commons, from the Year 1830 to the Close of 1835, including Personal Sketches of the leading Members of all Parties. 2nd Edition. *Smith, Elder, & Co.*, 1836, ix+382 pp., sm. 8vo, *hf. purple calf, little rubbed, leather label* **£35.00**

230 [——] Random Recollections of the House of Lords, from the Year 1830 to 1836, including Personal Sketches of the leading Members. *Smith, Elder & Co.*, 1836, viii+408 pp., 8vo, *orig. qtr. cloth, drab bds. paper label, faded* **£30.00**

231 **Grotius** (Hugo) De Jure Belli ac Pacis, libri tres, in quibus Jus Naturae & Gentium, item Juris Publici praecipua explicantur . . . Joann. Frid. Gronovii. Editio Nov. *Amstelaedami, apud Janssonio Waesbergios*, 1712, *port. and engr. title, printed title in red and black*, [xii+]xxxiv+946[+xciv] pp., 8vo, *contemp. sprinkled calf, leather label, backstrip chipped at base* **£40.00**

232 **Guicciardini** (Francesco) The Historie . . . containing the Warres of Italie and other Partes, continved for manie yeares vnder sundrie Kings and Princes, together with the variations and accidents of the same: and also the Arguments, with a Table at large expressing the principall matters through the whole historie. Rendered into English by Geffray Fenton. *Imprinted by Richard Field*, 1599, *lacks first but has final blank, some damp staining throughout*, [viii+]943[+x] pp., folio, *contemp. sprinkled calf, corners wearing, joints cracking and backstrip defective, but sound* (STC 12459) **£85.00**

233 **Guion** (J. M. B. de la Mothe) La Vie de . . . escrite par Elle-même, 3 Vols. *Cologne, chez Jean de la Pierre*, 1720, *engr. portrait, some embrowning throughout*, xlviii+296:xii+274: xii+298[+iv] pp., sm. 8vo, *contemp. polished calf, gilt, leather labels, edges little rubbed, heads and tails of backstrips sl. worn* **£50.00**
¶A French 'Quietist' author, Madame Guyon 'taught complete indifference, even to eternal salvation, and that in contemplation all distinct ideas should be repulsed, even of the attitudes of God and the mysteries of the life of Christ'. (Cross)

234 **Gunpowder.** AN ACT against the Importation of Gunpowder, Arms, and other Ammunition, and Utensils of War. *Printed by the Assigns of John Bill, deceas'd* . . . 1685, [ii+]3 pp., folio, *disbound* **£18.00**

235 **Gunpowder Plot.** [BARLOW] (William, *bp. of Rochester* [*and later of Lincoln*]) The Sermon Preached at Paules Crosse, the tenth day of November, being the next Sunday after the Discoverie of this late Horrible Treason. *Printed for Mathew Lawe*, 1606, [A^1] *blank, present, tear in lower margin of* D^3, [v+31] pp., sm. 4to, *19th cent. hf. brown calf, marb. bds., leather labels* (McAlpin i/193) **£130.00**
¶Does not have initials 'J.W.' in imprint as in STC 1455. Signatures etc. of 18th/19th cent. owners on blanks etc.

236 [**Gutch** (John)] *ed.* Collectanea Curiosa: or, Miscellaneous Tracts, relating to the History and Antiquities of England and Ireland, The Universities of Oxford and Cambridge and a Variety of other Subjects, chiefly collected, and now first published, from the MSS. of Archbishop Sancroft . . . 2 Vols. *Oxford, at the Clarendon Press* . . . 1781, *sl. foxing*, lxiv+xix+448:[xiv+]468 pp., 8vo, *hf. crimson straight grain morocco, marb. bds., rubbed, backstrips lettered and dulled by dust* **£45.00**
¶From the collection of the late Graham Pollard.

237 [——] Collectanea Curiosa; or Miscellaneous Tracts . . . 2 Vols. *Oxford, at the Clarendon Press* . . . 1781, lxiv+xix+448:[xiv+]468 pp., 8vo, *an uncut and unpressed copy, newly bound in hf. tan calf, marbled bds., leather labels* **£50.00**

238 [**Halifax** (George Savile, *Marquis of*)] The Anatomy of an Equivalent, [1688], *drop title, some staining*, 16 pp., sm. 4to, *disbound* (Wing H291) **£30.00**

239 [——] Observations upon a late Libel, called A Letter from a Person of Quality to his Friend, concerning the Kings Declaration, &c. *Printed for C.M.*, 1681, *drop title*, 8 pp., folio, *disbound* (Wing H316) **£45.00**
¶Hugh Macdonald writes 'I believe *Observations upon a late Libel* to have been written by Halifax, but hastily and for immediate purpose. It is witty and effective and, if I am right in ascribing it to him, it is worth rescuing and adding to the small body of his work.'

240 **Hamilton** (Antoine) Memoires du Comte de Grammont, edition ornée de lxxii portraits, gravés d'apres les tableaux originaux. *Londres, chez Edwards* [1793], *with 75 (ex 78 called for in 'Directions for the Binder'), plates*, [v+]313+77[+ii] pp., 4to, *contemp. tree calf, backstrip gilt, joints cracked, leather label* **£30.00**

241 The **Harleian Miscellany;** or, a Collection of Scarce, Curious, and Entertaining Pamphlets and Tracts, as well in Manuscript as in Print, found in the late Earl of Oxford's Library, interspersed with historical, political, and critical Notes. [Ed. by J. Malham], 12 Vols. *Printed for Robert Dutton*, 1808/11, *all hf. titles present*, 8vo, *contemp. hf. russia, gilt spines, lettered, y.e.* **£375.00**

242 [**Harley** (Richard)] A Supplement to the Faults on Both Sides: containing the Compleat History of the Proceedings of a Party ever since the Revolution . . . *Printed for J. Baker*, 1710, [ii+]76 pp., *soiled*, 8vo, *disbound* **£18.00**

243 **Harrington** (James) The Oceana and other Works, collected, methodiz'd, and review'd, with an Exact Account of his Life prefix'd, by John Toland. To which is added, an Appendix, containing all the Political Tracts wrote by this Author, omitted in Mr. Toland's Edition. *Printed by A. Millar*, 1737, *with engraved portrait and plate, title in red and black, a few marginal tears, discolouration throughout*, xlvi+632 pp., folio, *contemp. calf, corners worn, newly rebacked, leather label* **£60.00**

244 **Hastings.** BARNARD (Thomas) An Historical Character relating to the holy and exemplary Life of the Rt. Hon. the Lady Elisabeth Hastings: to which are added I. One of the Codicils of her last Will . . . II. Some Observations resulting therefrom. III. A Schedule of her other Perpetual Charities; with the principal Rules for their Administration. *Leeds, Printed by James Lister, for John Swale; and sold by S. Birt and T. Martin*, 1742, *embrowned throughout*, xxviii+191 pp., 12mo, *contemp. tan calf, sometime rebacked, old backstrip mounted* **£20.00**

245 **Hearne** (Thomas) *ed.* A Collection of Curious Discourses written by Eminent Antiquaries upon several Heads in our English Antiquities. Together with Mr. Thomas Hearne's Preface and Appendix to the former Edition. To which are added a great Number of Antiquary Discourses written by the same Authors. 2 Vols. *Printed for Benjamin White*, 1775, *folding engr. frontis.*, viii[+v+]lxxi+354:[vi+]449[+xiv] pp., *19th cent. calf, panelled in gilt and blind, leather labels, sl. rubbed* **£45.00**

246 **Henry vii.** BACON (Sir Francis) The Historie of the Reigne of King Henry the Seventh. Whereunto is now added a very useful and necessary Table. *Printed by R.Y. and R.H. and are to be sold by R. Meighen*, 1641, *engr. portrait by Marshall cut down and tipped onto front blank, small paper fault in one margin, sl. discolouration at edges*, [xiv+]248 pp., folio, *contemp. calf, rubbed, upper joint split at head and tail, leather label* (Wing B298: Gibson 120) **£45.00**

247 **Henry, Prince of Wales** (ob. 1612). FELL (Samuel) *ed.* Ivsta Oxoniensivm. *Londini Imp. Iohannis Bill*, 1612, *title within woodcut border, title strengthened at top and fore margins, three successive ll. strengthened at fore margins, some damp staining throughout*, [62 ll.], sm. 4to, *recent hf. crimson morocco, marb. bds. lettered* (STC 19021: Madan 345) **£300.00**
¶Poems by members of the University of Oxford, on the death of Prince Henry, including Isaac Casaubon, William Laud, Robert Burton and Henry King.

248 —— LVCTVS POSTHVMVS sive Erga Defvnctvm Illvstrissimvm Henricvm Walliae Principem, Collegii Beatae Mariae Magdalenae apud Oxonienses Mecaenatem longe indulgentissimum, Magdalenensium officiosa Pietae. *Oxoniae, Excud. Josephus Barnesius*, 1612, *fore-margin of title repaired, some sl. staining, 2 ll. soiled*, [ii+]62[+vii] pp., sm. 4to, *modern hf. crimson morocco, marb. bds., lettered* (STC 19047: Madan 80/7) **£300.00**
¶Poems by Members of Magdalen College, on the Death of Prince Henry, who was connected with the College through his tutor John Wilkinson.

249 —— NETHERSOLE (Sir Francis) Memoriae Sacra Illustriss. Potentiss. Principis Henrici Walliae Principis, Ducis Cornubiae &c. Laudatio Funebris. *Cantebrigiae, ex off. Cantrelli Legge*, 1612, *small tear in fore margin of title repaired, general browning, lacks 1st and final blanks*, [ii+]23[+iii] pp., sm. 4to, *modern qtr. crimson morocco, cloth sides, lettered* (STC 18473) **£110.00**

250 **Henry iv. of France.** HARDOUIN DE PEREFIXE (*bp. of Rodez*) The History of Henry iv. surnamed the Great, King of France and Navarre, written originally in French, and made English by J[ohn] D[avies]. *Printed for John Martyn and Henry Herringman*, 1672, *a few marginal stains*, [xvi+]400 pp., sm. 8vo, *contemp. sheep, unlettered, a sound copy* (?Wing H701—entry cancelled) **£40.00**

251 —— MATHIEU (Pierre, *historiographer of France*) The Heroyk Life and Deplorable Death of the most Christian King Henry the fourth. Adressed to his Inmortall Memory. Translated by Ed. Grimestone. *Printed by George Eld*, 1612, FIRST EDITION IN ENGLISH, *woodcut portrait on* A^4*v., later engr. port. (partly coloured) before title, sl. damp staining at beginning*, [viii+]190:170:[29] pp., sm. 4to, *contemp. calf, edges little rubbed, sometime rebacked, leather label, front paste-down lifted, substitute rear paste-down, lacks free endpapers* (STC 17661) **£180.00**
¶Part iii. *The Tropheis of the Life and Tragaedie of the Death . . . Prince Henry* . . . is is a verse translation by Joseph Sylvester.

252 —— —— Elogue sur les Actions les plus signalees et immortelles de Henry de Grand, dressé en Francois & traduit en Henrieu, Grec & Latin par trois Peres de la Compagne de Iesvs. *Lyon, par Nicolas Iullieron*, 1619, *some staining throughout*, 14 *pp* (lacking D^2—probably blank), sm. 4to, *hf. brown roan, marb. bds. lettered* **£25.00**

253 **Henry of Lorrain, Duke of Guise.** Memoires, relating his Passage to Naples, and heading there the Second Revolt of that People, Englished. *Printed by T.N. for H. Herringman*, 1669, pp. [xiii+]1-390:353-590[+i], sm. 8vo, *contemp. calf, unlettered, small piece missing from lower edge of front cover* (Wing G2226) **£45.00**

254 **Heraldry.** [DOBSON (Mrs. Susannah)] Historical Anecdotes of Heraldry and Chivalry, tending to shew the Origin of many English and Foreign Coats of Arms, Circumstances and Customs. *Worcester, Printed by Holl and Brandish* . . . 1795, *with 5 engr. plates, light staining throughout*, 3+316 pp., sm. 4to, *hf. calf, newly rebacked, leather label* **£15.00**

255 [**Herries** (J. C.)] A Reply to some Financial Mistatements, in and out of Parliament. *Printed for J. Hatchard*, 1803, *folding table*, viii+68[+i] pp., 8vo, *disbound* (Kress B4680; Goldsmith 18706) **£20.00**

256 **Heylyn** (Peter) A Help to English History; containing a Succession of all the Kings of England, the English, Saxons, and the Britons . . . continued with great additions to the First Day of November 1773 . . . now first published by Paul Wright. *Printed for the Editor* . . . 1773, *with 55 engraved plates of arms*, xxii+560[+ii] pp., 8vo, *contemp. sprinkled calf, newly rebacked, leather label* **£25.00**

Heylyn—*continued*

257 —— *MIKPOKOEMOE* A Little Description of the Great World, Augmented and revised. *Oxford, Printed by John Lichfield and William Turner, and are to be sold by W. Turner and T. Huggins*, 1625, *the folding 'Table of Climes' at* A^4, *short tear (paper fault) in* [$3D^6$] *with no loss, damp staining in final sections*, [xvi+]812[+ii] pp., sm. 4to in 8's, *contemp. calf, leather label and head of backstrip sl. defective* (STC 13277: Madan 557: Sabin 31656) **£90.00**
¶The Americas are covered from p. 774 to the end.

258 —— *MIKPOKOEMOE* A Little Description of the Great World. Fourth Edition, Revised. *Oxford, Printed by W. T[urner] for William Turner and Thomas Huggins*, 1629, *title within wood cut border (McKerrow and Ferguson 277), the folding 'Table of Climes' at* A^4, *early owners' inscriptions on last lf. and occasional marginal scoring by them, outer edge of* ¶¶^{3}*r, cropped with part loss of figures*, [xx+]807[+ii] pp., sm. 4to in 8's, *contemp. calf, worn, sometime rebacked, leather label, new antique pastedowns, lacks rear end-paper* (STC 13279: Madan 639: Sabin 31656) **£80.00**

259 **Hohenlohe Schillingsfuerst** (Prince Chlodwig) Memoirs, ed. by Friedrich Curtius, translated from the first German edition and supervised by George W. Chrystal. 2 Vols. *William Heinemann*, 1906, *with 6 plates*, xii+406:vi+502 pp., lge. 8vo, *hf. crimson morocco, gilt, t.e.g., cloth sides, with arms, sl. faded* **£21.00**

260 **Hurault** (Jacques, *French Privy-Councellor*) Politicke, Moral, and Martial Discourses, written in French . . . and translated into English by Arthur Golding. *Printed by Adam Islip*, 1595, FIRST EDITION IN ENGLISH, *large woodcut device on title, woodcut initials, some worming to lower fore-margins throughout, with no loss*, [xvi+]494 pp., sm. 4to in 8's, *contemp. limp vellum, lacking ties, sometime recased with antique rear end-paper, orig. paste-downs worn, front hinge strained, lettered by hand* (STC 14000: Hazlitt ii.p 297) **£450.00**
¶The front free endpaper carries the signature of Sir Philip Mainwaring, sometime secretary for Ireland, and the purchase price of 3s.

261 **Hutchinson** (Colonel John) Memoirs . . . with Original Anecdotes of many of the most distinguished of his Contemporaries, with a summary Review of Public Affairs: written by his widow Lucy . . . Second Edition. *Printed for Longman, Hurst, Rees and Orme*, 1808, *with 2 portraits, 3 other plates and a folding genealogical table, some off-setting*, vi+xiv+452 pp., 4to, *contemp. hf. calf, marb. bds., corners worn, newly rebacked, leather label* **£35.00**

262 —— HUTCHINSON (Lucy) Memoirs of the Life of Colonel Hutchinson, Governor of Nottingham, edited from the Original MS. by the Rev. Julius Hutchinson, to which are added the Letters of Colonel Hutchinson and other Papers. Revised with Additional Notes by C. H. Firth. 2 Vols. *John C. Nimmo*, 1885, *Ltd. to 500 copies with 10 etched portraits of eminent personages*, xxviii+392:[iv+]421 pp., 8vo, *full dark brown morocco, lettered, inner gilt borders, vellum pastedowns and free end-papers, g.e., by Morley of Oxford* **£50.00**

263 **Import Duty.** AN ACT for Granting an Aid to His Majesty by an Imposition on all French Linnens, and all East-India Linnen and several other Manufactures of India . . . *Printed by the Assigns of John Bill deceas'd* . . . 1685, *most corners dog-eared*, [ii+]14 pp., folio, *disbound* **£21.00**

264 **Import Taxes.** AN ACT for Appropriating certain Duties for paying the States General of the United Provinces their Charges for His Majesties Expedition into this Kingdom, and for other Uses. *Printed by Charles Bill, and Thomas Newcomb*, 1689, [ii+]4 pp., folio, *disbound* **£15.00**

265 **Imports.** CONSIDERATIONS on the Bill for prohibiting the Importation of the Growth and Commodities of Spain, now depending in the House of Lords. [*s.l.n.p.* ca. 1707/8], drop title, *strengthened in fold*, 3[+i] pp., folio, *disbound* **£15.00**

266 **Indian Mutiny.** THOMSON (Capt. Mowbray) The Story of Cawnpore. *Richard Bentley*, 1859, *folding chart and 3 plates*, xii+262 pp., 8vo, *orig. crimson cloth, faded* **£30.00**
¶The author was one of two survivors of the massacre.

267 **International Commerce.** A LETTER to the Honourable A-----r M-----re, Com---ner of Trade and Plantation. *Printed for James Roberts*, 1714, *large folding table, small split in fold*, 39 pp., 8vo, *modern hf. calf, marb. bds.*, scarce (Sabin 40480: Kress 2912) **£75.00**
¶Economist and Politician, Arthur Moore was of lowly birth, but by his own efforts became a Member of Parliament and a director of the South Sea Company, which later censured him for 'being privy to a clandestine trade to the prejudice of the corporation'. (DNB)

268 **Ireland.** AN ACT for the Attainder of the Rebels in Ireland. *Printed by Henry Hills and John Field*, 1657, *some browning*, [ii+]24 pp., folio, *grey bds.* (Wing E1092) **£18.00**

269 —— AN ACT for Relief of the Protestant Irish Clergy. *Printed by Charles Bill and Thomas Newcomb*, 1689, [ii+]3 pp., folio, *disbound* **£12.00**

270 —— THE PETITION of the Lords and Commons, Presented to His Majestie [concerning his journey to Ireland] . . . April 18. 1642. Together with His Majesties Answer thereunto. *Printed by Robert Barker, and by the Assignes of John Bill*, 1642, *damp stained and soiled*, [ii+]14 pp., sm. 4to, *new blue wrappers* (Wing E2179) **£35.00**

271 —— THE PRESENT STATE of Ireland: together with some Remarques upon the Antient State thereof. Likewise a Description of the Chief Towns: and a Map of the Kingdome. *Printed by M.D. for Chr. Wilkinson and T. Burrell*, 1673, *folding map, creased and frayed in outer margin, one lf. torn, upper margin of title cut away, some outer margins cropped with sl. loss of side notes, some browning throughout*, [xxiv+]280 pp., 12mo, *early 19th cent. calf, leather label chipped*, very scarce (Wing P3267) **£325.00**

272 —— WALKER (George) A Vindication of the True Account of the Siege of Derry in Ireland. *Printed for Rob. Clavel*, 1689, *some discolouration, a few margins cut close, lacks* A^1, 33[+i] pp., sm. 4to, *modern hf. calf, cloth sides, lettered* (Wing W354) **£75.00**

273 **Isaacson** (Henry) Satvrni Ephemerides sive Tabvla Historico-Chronologica, containing A Chronological Series or Succession of the foure Monarchyes, with an Abridgment of the Annual Memorial Passages in them, as also a Succession of the Kings and Rulers ouer most Kingdomes and Estates of the World, with a Breife Chorographical Description of them, & theire Seueral Storyes Epitomized, with a Compend of the History of the Church of God from the Creation . . . lastly as Appendix of the Plantation and Encrease of Religion in this Monarchy of Britayne . . . *Printed by B. A[lsop] and T. F[awcet] for H Seile and Humphrey Robinson*, 1633, *engraved title by Will. Marshall, "The Frontispiece Explained" facing title, many outer corners worn and fragile, a few pp. torn with some damage of letter press*, [xix+]494[+xvi] pp., lge. folio, *contemp. calf, corners and edges worn, due to worming, backstrip defective, lacks label* (STC 14269) **£50.00**

274 **James I.** [WELDON (Sir Anthony)] The Court and Character of King James, written and taken by Sir A.W., being an eye and eare witnesse. *Printed by R.I. and are to be sold by John Wright*, 1650, *portrait, last 3 blank ll. present, one lower margin repaired, some discolouration throughout*, [viii+]197 pp., sm. 8vo, *20th cent. hf. sheep, marb. bds., unlettered* (Wing W1273) **£42.00**
¶A Collection of scandalous gossip about the King, his ministers and favourites. Heylyn dismisses it as an infamous libel. (DNB)

275 **James II.** An Account of the Private League betwixt the Late King James the Second, and the French King . . . *Printed for Ric. Chiswell*, 1689, [iv+]15[+i] pp., *soiled*, folio, *disbound* (Wing A344) **£20.00**

275A—— —— *Another copy lacking hf. title*, [ii+]15[+i] pp., folio, *disbound* (Wing A344) **£15.00**

276 —— AN ACT for settling the Revenue on His Majesty for His Life, which was settled on His late Majesty for His Life. *Printed for Charles Bill* . . . 1687, [ii+]2 pp., folio, *disbound* **£12.00**

James II—*continued*

277 —— Ducis Eboracensis Fasciae a Musis Cantabrigiensibus raptim contextae. *Cantabrigiae, E Typog. Th. Buck, & R. Daniel*, 1633, *L1v. cut into at foot, several margins cut close, staining at end*, 84 pp., sm. 4to, *qtr. blue morocco, cloth sides, lettered and g.e.* (STC 4480: Case 71) **£90.00**
¶From the Phillipps collection.
Congratulatory poems on the birth of the future James II., including contributions by Cardellus Goodman, adventurer & actor (later forgiven by James II. for highway robbery), Richard Sterne, later Archbishop of York and great grandfather of Laurence Sterne, and Richard Crashaw.

278 —— A REMONSTRANCE and Protestation of all Good Protestants of this Kingdom, against Deposing their Lawful Soveraign King James II. *Printed in the Year*, 1689, *embrowned*, [ii+5] pp., sm. 4to, *marb. wrappers* (Wing R969) **£32.00**

279 —— FOX (Charles James) A History of the Early Part of the Reign of James the Second; with an Introductory Chapter, to which is added an Appendix. *Printed for William Miller*, 1808, *portrait, hf. title present, but heavily soiled, some foxing, throughout*, li+277+clviii pp., 4to, *'Roxborough' binding, little rubbed, cloth faded* **£35.00**

279A—— —— Another copy, *lacks hf. title*, 4to, *hf. calf, marb. bds. leather label* **£35.00**

280 **Justin.** History of the World from the Assyrian Monarchy down to the Time of Augustus Caesar; being an Abridgment of Trogus Pompeius's Philippic History, with Critical Remarks upon Justin. Made English by Mr. T. Brown. Third Edition carefully revised . . . *Printed for D. Midwinter and H. Clements* . . . 1719, *title in red and black, embrowned throughout*, xxiv+408 pp., 12mo, *contemp. sprinkled sheep, corners and backstrip worn* **£21.00**

281 **Kotzebue** (Augustus von) The most Remarkable Year in the Life of . . . containing an Account of his Exile into Siberia, and of the other extraordinary Events which happened to him in Russia, transl. from the German by the Rev. Benjamin Beresford. 3 Vols. *Printed for Richard Phillips, by T. Gillet*, 1802, *port. and 2 plates, sl. stained*, 279:271:228 pp., 12mo, *hf. crimson morocco, lettered, marb. bds.* **£45.00**

282 **Land Tax.** AN ACT for appointing Commissioners for putting into Execution an Act of this Session of Parliament, intituled, An Act for granting an Aid to His Majesty by a Land Tax, to be raised in Great Britain, for the Service of the Year One thousand seven hundred and seventy-five. *Printed by Charles Eyre and William Strahan*, 1775, pp. [ii+] 619-1096, folio, *contemp. hf. calf, unlettered, marb. bds.* **£25.00**

283 —— AN ACT for granting an Aid to His Majesty by a Land Tax, to be raised in Great Britain, for the Service of the Year One thousand seven hundred and seventy-five. *Printed by Charles Eyre and William Strahan*, 1776, [ii+114] pp., folio, *hf. calf, marb. bds. little rubbed* **£15.00**
¶The text of the Oaths of Allegiance, Supremacy and Abjuration has been written out in a neat contemporary copper-plate hand on one of the free end-papers.

284 **Laud** (William, *archb. of Canterbury*) Speech: or His Funerall Sermon, preacht by himself on the Scaffold on Tower-Hill on Friday the 10. of January, 1644. Also, the Prayers which he used at the same time and place before his execution . . . *Printed by Peter Cole*, 1644, pp. [ii+]5-19, *lacks A1 (? blank), general browning throughout*, sm. 4to, *disbound* (Wing L599) **£21.00**

285 **Leeds** (Thomas Osborn, *Earl of*) An Account at Large of . . . the Earl of Danby's Arguments at the Court of King's-Bench at Westminster, upon his Lordship's Motion for Bail . . . together with the Judges Answers and the Earl's Replyes . . . 2nd Edition. *Printed for Charles Mearne*, 1682, *A1 (blank) present, some soiling, sm. worming in inner margins*, [ii+]28 pp., folio, *disbound* (Wing L919) **£18.00**

286 —— The Arguments of the Rt. Hon. the Earl of Danby the Second Time, at the Court of King.s-Bench at Westminster, upon his Lordship's Motion for Bail . . . as they were then exactly taken. *Printed for Richard Tonson*, 1682, *some soiling*, [ii+]15 pp., folio, *disbound* (Wing L922) **£15.00**

287 [——] An Impartial State of the Case of the Earl of Danby, in a Letter to a Member of the House of Commons. *Printed in the Year*, 1679, *some soiling*, 20 pp., folio, *disbound* (Wing I88) **£15.00**

296 **Louis xiv.** The French King's Edict upon the Declaration made by the Clergy of France, of their Opinion concerning the Ecclesiastical Power . . . together with the said Declaration of the Clergy, as they were Registered in the Parliament of Paris, the 23 of March 1682. *Printed in the Year* 1682, *corner of inner top margin torn away*, 8 pp , folio, *disbound* (Wing L3122) **£35.00**

297 **Lucan** (M. Annaeus) De Bello Civili, cum Hug. Grotii, Farnabii notis integris & Variorum selectiss, acc. Corn Schrevelio. *Amstelodami, ex off. Elzeviriana*, 1669, *engr. title, folding map, neat inscr. on title*, [xviii+]614[+cxlvi] pp., 8vo, *19th cent. calf, gilt, leather label, r.e.* **£35.00**

298 **Ludlow** (General Edmund, *Regicide*) A Letter from Major General Ludlow to Sir E[ward] S[eymour] comparing the Tyranny of the first four Years of King Charles the Martyr, with the Tyranny of the four Years Reign of the Late Abdicated King . . . *Amsterdam*, 1691, [ii+]30 pp. (Wing L1489):
[with]
A Letter from General Ludlow to Dr. Hollingworth . . . defending his former Letter to Sir E. S. . . . *Amstdrdam*, 1692, viii+72 pp. (Wing L1468):
[and]
[**Bethel** (Sligsby)] Ludlow no Lyar, or a Detection of Dr. Hollingworth's Disingenuity in his second Defence of King Charles I . . . *Amsterdam*, 1691, xx+63[+i] pp. (Wing B2068):
[and]
Truth brought to Light, or the Gross Forgeries of Dr. Hollingworth, in his Pamphlet Intituled The Character of King Charles the First from the Declaration of Mr. Alexander Henderson, etc. detected . . . *London*, 1693, 40 pp. (Wing T3153):
Four pamphlets bound together, *some browning throughout*, sm. 4to, *tan calf, gilt, coronetted monogram on both covers (? baron Paulet) rubbed at edges, newly rebacked, leather label* **£65.00**

299 **Mackenzie** (Sir George) Jus Regium: or, The Just and Solid Foundations of Monarchy in General; and more especially of the Monarchy of Scotland: Maintain'd against Buchannan, Naphtali, Dolman, Milton, &c. *Printed for Richard Chiswell*, 1684, *lacks front pastedown, rear pastedown lifted and defective, lacking also A1 (? blank), title soiled and creased, some damp staining throughout*, [vi+]209[+v] pp., 8vo, *contemp. sprinkled sheep, backstrip partly defective, back cover damaged* (Wing M163) **£45.00**

300 [**Mackworth** (Humphrey)] A Vindication of the Rights of the Commons of England, by a Member of the Honourable the House of Commons. *Printed, and are to be sold by J. Nutts*, 1701. *title and last lf. soiled, small hole in latter, with sl. loss*, [xii+]40 pp., folio, *qtr. tan calf, lettered, marb. bds.* **£25.00**

301 **Macky** (John) Memoirs of the Secret Services of . . . during the Reigns of King William, Queen Anne, and King George I. including, also, the true Secret History of the Rise, Promotions, &c. of the English and Scots Nobility . . . published from his Original MS.; as attested by his Son Spring Macky. *Printed in the Year* 1733, *sl. browning throughout*, [viii+]lvi+254[+i+]xxxvii[+ix] pp., 8vo, *new qtr. tan calf, leather label, marb. bds.* **£25.00**

302 **Margaret of Anjou.** PREVOST (Antoine Francois) The History of Margaret of Anjou, Queen of England. Translated from the French. 2 Vols. *Printed for J. Payne*, 1755, 288:302 pp., 12mo, *contemp. hf. crimson roan, lettered, rubbed, joints cracked* **£30.00**

303 **Marines.** A LETTER to a Member of Parliament concerning the four Regiments commonly called Mariners. *Printed by A. Bladwin*, 1699, *3 final blank ll. present, stained throughout, small chip from lower margin of 2 ll.*, 14 pp., sm. 4to, *new qtr. tan calf, lettered, cloth sides* (Wing L1670) scarce **£30.00**
¶An anonymous and virulent attack on the Marine regiments, calling for their immediate disbandment.

304 **Mary Stuart.** [BUCHANAN (George)] De Maria Scotorum Regina, totáque eius contra Regem coniuratione, foedo cum Bothuelio adulterio, nefaria in maritum crudelitate & rabie, horrendo insuper & deterrimo eiusdem parricidio: plena, & tragica planè Historia. [*J. Day*, 1572], [ii+]122[+iii] pp., sm. 8vo, *early calf, gilt, leather label, some rubbing, upper joint cracked* (STC 3978) **£375.00**

288 **Leigh** (Edward) Select and Choyce Observations, containing all the Roman Emperours. The first eighteen by Edward Leigh, the others added by his Son Henry Leigh. Certain Choyce French Proverbs, alphabetically disposed and Englished . . . *Printed by Roger Daniel, for John Williams*, 1637, *lacks A1/2, a few headlines cut close, some staining*, [xi+]277 pp., sm. 8vo, *modern panelled calf, leather label, marb. endpapers* (Wing L1003) **£75.00**

289 **Letters** written by eminent Persons in the Seventeenth and Eighteenth Centuries: to which are added, Hearne's Journeys to Reading, and to Whaddon Hall, the Seat of Browne Willis, Esq. and Lives of eminent Men, by John Aubrey. The Whole now first published from the Originals in the Bodleian Library and Ashmolean Museum, with biographical and literary illustrations. 2 Vols. in 3. *Printed for Longman, Hurst* . . . 1813, *sl. discolouration*, pp. xxiii+304:[ii+]1-352:[ii+]353-668, 8vo, *contemp. marbled calf, gilt extra, sprinkled edges, sl. rubbed* **£125.00**
¶*Brief Lives*, in this, its first appearance, was edited by Philip Bliss.

290 **Leycesters** Common-wealth, conceived, spoken and pvblished with the most earnest protestation of all Dutifull good will and affection towards the Realm, for whose good onely, it is made common to many. *Printed*, 1641, *title and last lf. heavily soiled and margins frayed and tender, some other soiling throughout*, [viii+]182 pp., sm. 4to, *contemp. sprinkled calf, recently rebacked and repaired at corners, lettered* (Wing L968) **£85.00**
¶Walsingham, in a letter to Leicester, 29 Sept. 1584 states that the libel was written by Thomas Morgan, a Welsh Catholic, agent to the Queen of Scots, in France. [L. Hotson in *the Listener* 16.3.50]

291 **The Lives** of all the Lords Chancellors, Lords Keepers, and Lords Commissioners, of the Great Seal of England; from William the Conqueror to the Present Time: but more at large of those Two Great Opposites, Edward Earl of Clarendon, and Bulstrode Lord Whitlock. With a Parallel of their Actions, to which is added, an Appendix of many Rare and Valuable Speeches, Letters, &c. referring to the said Lives. 2 vols. in 1. By an Impartial Hand. Second Edition, with Additions. *Printed, and sold by R. Bonwicke, W. Freeman* . . . 1712, [xxv+]336(shd. read 319):216[+viii] pp., 8vo, *dark brown calf, tooled in blind and gilt, lettered* **£45.00**

292 **The Lives** of those eminent Antiquaries John Leland, Thomas Hearne, and Anthony à Wood; with an authentick Account of their respective Writings and Publications, from Original Papers . . . 2 Vols. *Oxford, Printed at the Clarendon Press, for J. and J. Fletcher, and Joseph Pote*, 1772, *engravings, some foxing throughout*, vii+111+iv+139[+cxviii+]20[+ii]: vi+404+58 pp., 8vo, *contemp. mottled calf, corners worn, newly rebacked, leather labels* **£40.00**
¶Once the property of Thomas Arnold the 18th cent. physician and writer on insanity, with his bookplate.

293 [**Lloyd** (David)] State Worthies, or, the States-men and Favourites of England since the Reformation their Prudence and Polciies, Successes and Miscarriages, Advancements and Falls; during the Reigns of King Henry viii, King Edward vi, Queen Mary, Queen Elizabeth, King James, King Charles i. Second Edition, with Additions. *Printed by Thomas Milbourn for Samuel Speed*, 1670, *engr. frontis., title in red and black, one lf. torn, browning throughout*, [xvii+]680:721-1051[+v] pp., sm. 8vo, *19th cent. calf, gilt, leather label, m.e.* (Wing L2646) **£85.00**

294 **Lloyd** (Lodowick) The Stratagems of Ierusalem: with the martiall lawes and militarie discipline, as well of the Iewes, as of the Gentiles. *Printea by Thomas Creede*, 1602, *title heavily soiled and laid down, A2 remargined, heavy staining in most upper margins, one lf. torn with sl. loss of text, last blank present*, [viii+]352[+xiii] pp. (STC 16630):
[with]
A Briefe Conference of Divers Lawes: diuided into certaine Regiments. *Printed by Thomas Creede*, 1602, *general discolouration throughout, fore-margins of Table strengthened, last lf. very defective*, [iv+]143[+vi] pp. (STC 16616):
Two works bound together, sm. 4to, *new qtr. dark brown calf, leather label, marb. bds.* **£75.00**

295 **The London Gazette,** numbers 1368-1375, Dec. 26 to Jan. 20, 1678/[9], 8 issues. *Printed by Tho. Newcomb*, 1678, 8 broadsides, *extended and sometime sewn together, one margin repaired*, folio, *disbound* **£15.00**

305 — — [TYTLER (William)] An Inquiry, historical and critical, into the Evidence against Mary Queen of Scots. And an Examination of the Histories of Dr. Robertson and Mr. Hume, with respect to that Evidence. 3rd Edition, with additions and a postscript. *Edinburgh, Printed for W. Drummond* . . . 1772, xiv+385+29 pp., 8vo, *contemp. calf, leather label, small split in upper joint* **£35.00**

306 **Matthew of Westminster.** Flores Historiarvm: praecipve de Rebvs Britannicis: ab exor dio mundi usque ad annum Domini mcccvii. et Chronicon ex chronicis ad initio mundi vsqve ad annum Domini mcxviii. deductum: auctore Frorentio Wigorniensi monacho. Cui accessit Continvatio vsqve ad annvm Christi mcxli. per quendam eiusdem coenobii eruditum. . . . *Francoforti, typis Wechelianis apud Claudium Marnium & heredes Ioannis Aubrij*, 1601, *embrowning throughout, name rubbed from title leaving small hole*, [viii+] 696[+xxiv] pp., folio, *19th cent. brown sprinkled calf, leather label, greek-key" borders in gilt, m.e., sl. cracking of upper joint* **£135.00**

307 **Matthieu** (Pierre) Aelius Seianus. Histoire romaine, rec. de diuers Autheurs. 3e Ed. *Rouen, chez Iacques Besongne*, 1619, [iv+]304 pp.:
[with]
Histoire des Prosperitez malhevrevses, d'vne femme cathenoise . . . *Rouen, chez Iacques Besongne*, 1619, 199 pp.:
[and]
Remarqves d'estat et d'histoires, sur la vie et les seruices de Monsieur de Villeroy. *Rouen, chez Iacques Besongne*, 1619:
Three works bound together, 12mo, *contemp. vellum, lettered by hand, r.e.* **£45.00**

308 **Memoirs British and Foreign,** of the Lives and Families of the Most Illustrious Persons who dy'd in the Year 1711. more Particularly of The Emperor Joseph, the Dauphin, the Prince of Friesland . . . the Lord Willoughby of Brooke, Monsieur Boileau, Anthony Henley, Esq., Mr. Dodwell, &c. To be continued Yearly [only one further volume in 1714]. *Printed by S. Holt, for Andrew Bell* . . . 1712, viii+557[+x] pp., 8vo, *new qtr. tan calf, leather label, marb. bds.* **£35.00**

309 **Merlin.** [HEYWOOD (Thomas)] The Life of Merlin, Sirnames Ambrosivs. His Prophesies, and Predictions Interpreted; and their truth made good by our English Annals. Being a Chronographicall History of all the Kings, and memorable passages of this Kingdome, from Brute to the Reigne of our Royall Soveraigne King Charles. A Subject never published in this kind before, and deserves to be knowne and observed by all men. *Printed by J. Okes, and are to be sold by Jasper Emery*, 1641, *engr. frontis. (attrib. to Hollar), lower sixth remargined, some foxing throughout*, [lxx+]376 pp., sm. 4to, *19th cent. tan calf, leather label, sprinkled edges* (Wing H1786) **£160.00**

310 **Military.** AN ACT for an Assessment . . . for Three Years; for a Temporary Supply towards the Maintenance of the Armies and Navies of this Commonwealth . . . *Printed by Henry Hills and Iohn Field*, 1657, *embrowned*, [ii+]28 pp., folio, *grey bds.* (Wing E998) **£21.00**

311 —— AN ACT for Distribution of Threescore thousand pounds amongst the truly Loyal and Indigent Commission-Officers, and for Assessing of Offices, and Distributing Moneys thereby raised for their further Supply. *Printed by John Bill and Christopher Barker*, 1662, [ii+]36 pp.:
[with]
AN ACT to explain and supply a former Act for distribution of Threescore thousand pounds . . . [*Printed by John Bill and Christopher Barker*, 1663—col.], 6 pp.:
Two Acts together, folio, *disbound* **£21.00**
¶A benefit for those officers loyal to Charles I.

312 —— AN ACT for the Relief of poor and maimed Officers and Souldiers, who have faithfully served His Majesty, and His Royal Father in the late Wars. [*Printed by John Bill and Christopher Barker*, 1662—col.], *drop title*, 6 pp., folio, *disbound* **£15.00**

313 —— [CHESTERFIELD (Philip Dormer Stanhope, *Earl of*) and Edmund WALLER] The Case of the Hanover Forces in the Pay of Great Britain, impartially and freely examined, with some Seasonable Reflections on the Present Conjuncture of Affairs. *Printed for T. Cooper*, 1743, FIRST EDITION, *hf. title present*, [iv+]83 pp., 8vo, *marb. wrappers* (Gulich *301) **£50.00**

Military—*continued*

314 —— [DELAMARE (Henry Booth, *Earl*)] An Impartial Enquiry into the Causes of the Present Fears and Dangers of the Government, being a Discourse between a Lord Lieutenant, and one of his Deputies, Summoned to hold a Lieutenancy, for Raising the Militia. *Printed in the Year*, 1692, *printed in double column, pagination incorrect*, [ii+]20(shd. read 18) pp., sm. 4to, *modern hf. tan crushed morocco, lettered, cloth sides* (Wing D877) **£35.00**

315 —— [GLEIG (G. R.)] A Narrative of the Campaigns of the British Army at Washington and New Orleans, under Generals Ross, Pakenham, and Lambert, in the years 1814 and 1815; with some Account of the Countries visited. Second Edition. *John Murray*, 1826, [iv+]377 pp., 8vo, *contemp. calf, rubbed, newly rebacked, leather label* (Sabin 27568) **£50.00**

316 —— HISTOIRE DES ORDRES MILITAIRES ou des Chevaliers, des Milices Seculaires & Regulaieres de l'un & de l'autre Sexe, qui ont été établies jusques a present. Contenant leur Origine, leurs Fondations, leurs Progrès, leur maniere de Vie, leur Decadence, leurs Reformes, & les evenemens les plus considerables qui y sont arrivez. Nouvelle Edition, tirée de l'Abbé Giustiniani, du R. P. Bonanni . . . et un Traité Historique de Mr. Basnage sur les Duels. 5 Vols. *Amsterdam, chez Pierre Brunel*, 1721, *with* 187 *engraved plates*, 23 *of which are of regalia, lower margins of* 2 *plates sl. torn, a few water stains*, 8vo, *contemp. calf, gilt, leather labels, most covers sl. rubbed, joints of vol. i tender* **£175.00**

317 —— [RICH (Barnaby)] Vox Militis: foreshewing what Perils are procvred where the people of this, or any other kingdome liue without regard of Marshall discipline, especially when they stand and behold their friends in apparent danger, and almost subuerted by there enemies vniust persecution, and yet with hold their helping hand and assistance. Divided into two parts . . . *Printed by B.A. for Thomas Archer*, 1625, *small area of lower margins damaged with loss of date on title and few words in dedications, small hole in A3 with loss of a few words on verso, final blanks present, one laid down, side notes cut into*, [xiv+]56(shd. read 54) [+binders' blanks] pp., sm. 4to, *new qtr, calf, marb. bds., lettered in gilt* (STC 20980: Cockle 105) **£70.00**
¶Attributed by Lowndes to Gervase Markham, but, according to Cockle, was purloined by George Marcelline from Barnaby Rich's 'Allarme to England'.

318 —— [SEGAR (Sir William)] Honor, Military, and Ciuill, contained in foure Bookes, viz. 1. Justice and Iurisdiction Military, 2. Knighthood in general and particular, 3. Combats for life and Triumph, 4. Precedencie of great Estates, and others. *Imprinted by Robert Barker*, 1602, *with* 8 *engraved plates, hand-coloured, plates* 1 & 2 *conjugate with text, others tipped in, initial letters also coloured, woodcuts in text*, [iv+]256 pp., folio, *new hf. calf, leather label, grey bds.* (STC 22164: Gockle 75) **£180.00**

319 —— TURNER (Sir James) Pallas Armata. Military Essayes of the Ancient Grecian, Roman, and Modern Art of War. Written in the Years 1670 and 1671. *Printed by M.W. for Richard Chiswell*, 1683, *title in red and black, engraved portrait by R. White, small snag in lower margin of prelim. ll.*, [xviii+]372 pp., folio, *contemp. mottled calf, backstrip gilt, leather label, corners worn* (Wing T3292) **£185.00**

320 **Mill** (John Stuart) Autobiography. Second Edition, 1873, vi+323[+ii] pp., 8vo, *orig. green cloth, little worn, hinges started* **£30.00**

321 —— Considerations on Representative Government. *Parker, Son, and Bourn*, 1861, FIRST EDITION, *slight browning, one outer margin sl. torn*, viii+340+4—(cat.) pp., 8vo, *orig. buff cloth, worn and very shabby* **£40.00**

322 **Monstrelet** (Enguerrand de) The Chronicles; containing an Account of the cruel Civil Wars between the Houses of Orleans and Burgundy; of the Possession of Paris and Normandy by the English . . . transl. by Thomas Johnes. 2 Vols. *William Smith*, 1840, *with many cuts in the text*, xxxvi+640:xvi+552 pp., lge. 8vo, *contemp. diced calf, gilt, leather labels* **£25.00**

323 **Montagu** (Edward Wortley) Reflections on the Rise and Fall of the Antient Republicks. Adapted to the present State of Great Britain. *Printed for A. Millar*, 1759, [v+]384 pp., 8vo, *an excellent copy in contemp. mottled calf, leather label, y.e.* **£25.00**

335 [**Oldfield** (Thomas Henton Burnley)] An Entire and Complete History, political and personal, of the Boroughs of Great Britain; to which is prefix'd, an original Sketch of Constitutional Rights . . . 2 Vols. *Printed for G. Riley* . . . 1792, *errata slip present*, xvi+219 +323:vii+547 pp., 8vo, *contemp. tree calf, leather labels, backstrips heavily gilt, corners rubbed, y.e., marb. end-papers* **£40.00**
¶A third volume included the Cinque Ports.

336 —— History of the Original Constitution of Parliaments, from the Time of the Britons to the present Day; . . . to which is added, the present State of the Representation; . . . *Printed for G.G. and J. Robinson*, 1797, viii+548 pp., 8vo, *contemp. tan calf, gilt and blind tooling on sides and backstrip, lettered, armorial crest on sides, marb. edges and end-papers* **£45.00**

337 **Orleans** (Philip, duc d') Memoirs of the Regency of His Royal Highness the late Duke of Orleans, during the Minority of his Present Most Christian Majesty Lewis the xvth. containing the Publick Treaties, State Instruments, and Principal Matters of the Court of France . . . *Printed for R. Montagu* . . . 1732, *portrait, some discolouration*, 2 *pp. catalogue at beginning*, xxxiv+428 pp., 8vo, *contemp. mottled calf, gilt faded, joints cracked, rubbed* **£21.00**

338 **Osborn** (Francis) Advice to a Son. Or Directions for your better Conduct, through the various and most important Encounters of this Life . . . 6th Edition. *Oxford, printed by H.H. for Tho. Robinson*, 1658, [viii+]188[+vii] pp. (Wing O513):
[with]
Advice to a Son. The Second Part. *Oxford, Printed for Tho, Robinson*, 1658, [xii+]189 [+iii] pp. (Wing O514):
[and]
A Miscellany of sundry Essayes, Paradoxes, and Problematicall Discourses, Letters and Characters . . . *Printed by John Grismond*, 1659, [xxxvi+]260 pp. (Wing O515):
[and]
Historical Memoires on the Reigns of Queen Elizabeth, and King James. *Printed for J. Grismond, and are to be sold by T. Robinson*, 1658, [xxi+]108[+xx+]148 pp., *divisional titles* (Wing O515):
[and]
Politicall Reflections upon the Government of the Tvrks. Nicolas Machiavel: The King of Sweden's Descent into Germany . . . Martin Luther: 3rd Edition. *Oxford, Printed by Hen: Hall, for Tho: Robinson*, 1662, [viii+]194(shd. read 196) pp. (Wing O520):
5 works bound together, *a few marginal snags and a few minute rust holes, some marginal staining*, 12mo, *contemp. sprinkled calf, rather worn, head of backstrip sl. defective, ex libris labels* **£210.00**

339 [——] Political Reflections upon the Government of the Tvrks. Nicolas Machiavel: the King of Sweden's Descent into Germany: the Conspiracy of Piso and Vindex against Nero: the Greatnesse and Corruption of the Court of Rome: the Election of Pope Leo the XI: the Defection from the Church of Rome: Martin Luther. *Printed by J. G[rismond] for Thomas Robinson in Oxford*, 1656, FIRST EDITION, *small tear in one margin neatly repaired, a few 'rust' spots*, [viii+]194(shd. read 196) pp., 12mo, *modern tan calf, lettered* (Wing O518) **£190.00**

340 —— The Works; Divine, Moral, Historical, Political. In Four several Tracts. Viz. 1. Advice to a Son, in two parts. 2. Political Reflections on the Government of the Turks, etc. 3. Memoirs on Queen Elizabeth and K. James. 4. A Miscellany of Essays, Paradoxes, Problematical Discourses, Letters, Characters, &c. The Seventh Edition. *Printed for R.D. and are to be sold by Allen Brooke*, 1763, FIRST COLLECTED EDITION, *divisional titles, lacks one*, [xii+]408[+xvii+]409-465[+xv+]467-547[+xxiii+]549-698 pp., sm. 8vo, *contemp. calf, corners worn, backstrip defective, joints beginning to crack, lacks label* (Wing O505) **£65.00**
¶'A conceited fellow. Were a man to write so now, the boys would throw stones at him'. (Samuel Johnson—Lowndes)

341 **Oxford.** AN ACCOUNT of the Visit of His Royal Highness the Prince Regent and Their Imperial and Royal Majesties the Emperor of Russia and the King of Prussia to the University of Oxford, in June 1814. *Oxford, at the Clarendon Press*, 1815, *with* 2 *engr. plates and a folded Broadsheet*, [ii+]77 pp., 4to, *contemp. tan calf, gilt, leather label* **£45.00**

324 **Monteth** (Robert, *of Salmonet*) The History of the Troubles of Great Britain: containing a particular Account of the most remarkable Passages in Scotland, from the Year 1633 to 1650, with an exact Relation of the Wars carried on, and the Battles fought by the Marquis of Montrose . . . Translated into English by Captain James Ogilvie. *Printed for G. Strahan and R. Williamson*, 1735, viii+557+xxii pp., folio, *contemp. sprinkled calf, rubbed, corners worn, covers almost detached* **£28.00**

325 **Nalson** (John) An Impartial Collection of the Great Affairs of State. From the Beginning of the Scotch Rebellion in the Year mdcxxxix. to the Murther of King Charles I. wherein the first Occasions, and the whole Series of the late Troubles in England, Scotland, & Ireland, are faithfully Represented. Taken from Authentick Records, and Methodically Digested. 2 Vols. *Printed for S. Mearne, T. Dring, B. Tooke, T. Sawbridge, and C. Mearne*, 1682/3, *with* 2 *engr. frontis. and the 'Mind' placed opposite, worming in some margins of vol. ii.*, [vi+]lxxix+817[+xv]:[vi+]xii+920[+xxii] pp., folio, *contemp. mottled calf, gilt, lacks one label* (Wing N106/7) **£45.00**

326 **Napoleon.** MAITLAND (Capt. F. L.) Narrative of the Surrender of Buonaparte and of his Residence on Board H.M.S. Bellerophon, with a Detail of the principal Events that occurred in that Ship between the 24th of May and the 8th of August, 1815. *Published by Henry Colburn*, 1826, *folding chart, small tear in margin*, vi+248 pp., 6 pp. catalogue, 8vo, *diced calf, leather label, rubbed at joints* **£21.00**

327 —— [WALDIE (Jane)] Narrative of a Residence in Belgium during the Campaign of 1815; and of a Visit to the Field of Waterloo. By an Englishwoman. *Printed for John Murray*, 1817, *some foxing throughout*, vii+351 pp., 8vo, *drab bds., stained, backstrip and paper label defective, edges untrimmed* **£25.00**

328 **Newcastle.** CAVENDISH (Margaret, *Duchess of Newcastle*) The Life of the Thrice Noble, High and Puissant Prince William Cavendish, Duke, Marquess, and Earl of Newcastle . . . who had the honour to be Governour to our most Glorious King and Gracious Soveraign, in his Youth, when He was Prince of Wales . . . *Printed by A. Maxwell*, 1667, *lacks the engraved portrait*, [xxvi+]199 pp., folio, *contemp. mottled calf, newly rebacked, leather labels* (Wing N853) **£60.00**

329 **Noorthouck** (John) An Historical and Classical Dictionary: containing the Lives and Characters of the most eminent and learned Persons, in every Age and Nation, from the earliest period to the present time. 2 Vols. *Printed for W. Strahan and T. Cadell*, 1776, FIRST EDITION, *sl. worming in some lower fore-margins*, [xi+379]:[i+364] pp., 8vo, *contemp. sprinkled calf, leather labels, little rubbed* **£40.00**

330 **Northampton.** A True Account of the Presentment of the Grand Jury for the last General Assizes held for the County of Northampton, at the Town of Northampton aforesaid. [*Printed by E.M.*, 1683—col.], *drop title*, 2 pp. folio sheet (Wing T2388a) scarce **£25.00**

331 **Northumberland Household Book.** PERCY (Thomas, *bp.*) *ed.* The Regulations and Establishment of the Household of Henry Algernon Percy, the fifth Earl of Northumberland, at his Castles of Wresill and Lekinfield in Yorkshire. Begun anno domini M.D.XII. *Printed* 1770, [xxvi[+ii+]x+464[+iv] pp., 8vo, *contemp. tan calf, gilt, arms on sides, upper joint cracked, lacks leather label* **£45.00**

332 **Oath of Allegiance.** AN ACT to Regulate the Administration of the Oaths required to be taken by Commission or Warrant Officers Employed in Their Majesties Service by Land . . . *Printed by Charles Bill and Thomas Newcomb*, 1689, [ii+]2 pp., folio, *disbound* **£15.00**

333 **Oaths.** AN ACT for the Abrogation of the Oaths of Supremacy and Allegiance and Appointing other Oaths. *Printed by Charles Bill* . . . 1691, [ii+]14 pp., folio, *disbound* **£15.00**

334 **Oldcastle.** [BLACKBOURNE (John, *nonjuror*)] *ed.* A Brefe Chronycle concerynge the Examynacyon and Death of the Blessed Martyr of Christ Syr Johan Oldcastell, the Lorde Cobham, collected togyther by Johan Bale . . . *Printed for C. Davis*, 1729, *frontispiece, small tear in one margin*, viii+157[+i] pp., 8vo, *contemp. panelled calf, newly rebacked, leather label (incorrect)* **£35.00**

342 —— CARMINA QUADRAGESIMALIA ab Aedis Christi Oxon. Alumnis composita et ab ejusdem aedis Baccalaureis Determinantibus in Schola Naturalis Philosophiae publice recitata. 2 Vols. *Oxonii, e Theatro Sheldoniano*, 1723/48. FIRST EDITIONS, *some worming in gutters of vol. i*, [iv+]168:[viii+]151[+iii] pp., 8vo, *contemp. panelled calf, leather labels, joints beginning to crack* (Case 325 (1 & 2)a: Clary 769: Cordeaux & Merry, Univ. 7083) **£25.00**

343 —— THE DEBATES in the House of Commons assembled at Oxford the Twenty first of March, 1680. The Three first Days geing spent in Choosing their Speaker, the Confirming of him, and taking the Oaths as the Law directs . . . [*Printed for R. Baldwin*, 1681—col.], *names of debators inserted in MS. but foremargin trimmed with some loss*, 20 pp., folio, *disbound* (Wing E2546) **£21.00**

344 —— A DECLARATION of the Lords and Commons assembled in Parliament, concerning His Majesties Proclamation for adjourning the Terme to Oxford. Ordaining that no Judge, Minister, or other person belonging to the Chancery, His Majesties Exchequor, or any other Court, shall presume to repair to the said City of Oxon, or doe, or execute any thing belonging to their said Office and imployments, but in the places usuall for doing thereof. *Printed for John Wright*, 1642, **Black Letter,** [ii+]6 pp., sm. 4to, *grey bds. vellum backstrip, unlettered* (Wing E1374) **£35.00**

345 —— [LANGBAINE (Gerard, *the Elder*)] The Ansvver of the Chancellor, Masters and Scholars of the University of Oxford, to the Petition, Articles of Grievance, and Reasons of the City of Oxon. Presented to the Honourable Committee for Regulating the University of Oxford the 24. of July 1649. Second Edition. *Oxford, Printed by H. Hall and are to be sold by Ric. Davis*, 1678, *generally soiled, upper margins cropped with some loss of pagination, lacks final blank*, 46 pp., sm. 4to, *19th cent. hf. calf, rubbed, lettered* (Wing L364: Madan 3184) **£40.00**
¶The City of Oxford sought to deprive the University of some of its privileges, such as the rights of the Chancellor's Court, licensing of ale-houses, discommoning and fining citizens, the ceremony of St. Scolastica's day, priviledged tradesmen and enclosure rights over Port Meadow.

346 **Papists.** AN ACT for Rectifying a Mistake in a certain Act of this present Parliament, For the Amoving Papists from the Cities of London and Westminster. *Printed by Charles Bill and Thomas Newcomb*, 1689, [ii+]2 pp., folio, *disbound* **£12.00**

347 **Paris** (Matthew) Angli, Historiae Maior, a Guilielmo Conquestore, ad vltimum annum Henrici tertii [edited by Archbishop Matthew Parker], cum Indice locupletissimo. *Londini*, 1571, [colophon—(latin motto) *Londini excusum apud Reginaldum Vuolsium* . . . 1570], FIRST EDITION, SECOND ISSUE, *title within woodcut border, soiled and extended, worming in 1st gathering, with no serious loss*, [ii+]1349[+xxxi] pp., folio, *new qtr. tan calf, leather label grey bds.* (STC 19209A) **£200.00**

348 **Parliament.** AN ACT for Removing and Preventing all Questions and Disputes concerning the Assembling and Sitting of this present Parliament. *Printed by Charles Bill and Thomas Newcomb*, 1688, 7 pp., folio, *disbound* **£12.00**

349 —— CHARLES II. His Majesties Declaration to all his Loving Subjects, touching the Causes & Reasons that moved Him to Dissolve the Two last Parliaments. *Printed by the Assigns of John Bill* . . . 1681, 10[+i] pp., folio, *disbound* (Wing C300) **£18.00**

350 —— COBBETT (William) The Parliamentary Debates: forming a continuation of the work entitled—'The Parliamentary History of England from the earliest period to the year 1803'. Published under the superintendence of T. C. Hansard. New Series; commencing with the accession of George iv [and termination with the close of his reign]. 25 Vols. *Printed by T. C. Hansard* . . . 1820-1830, *in double-column throughout*, 8vo, *uniformly bound in 19th cent. hf. purple cloth, marbled bds., backstrips faded, an ex-library set with labels on front covers and pastedowns, but in sound condition* **£250.00**

351 —— A COLLECTION of Loyal Songs written against the Rump Parliament, between the Years 1639 and 1661, containing a great Variety of Merry and Diverting Characters of the Chief Secretaries, who were the Principal Actors in that whole Scene of Affairs. With an Historical Introduction to the Whole. 2 Vols. *Printed for J. Stone* . . . 1731, *discolouration of paper*, [xiv+]264:[v+]288 pp., 12mo, *contemp. sprinkled calf, backstrips gilt, but lacking title labels, surface of lower cover of vol. i badly scuffed, some joints beginning to crack* (Case 128 1d & 2d) **£80.00**

Parliament—*continued*

352 —— [DRAKE (Sir William)] The Long Parliament Revived: or, an Act for Continuation, and the not Dissolving the Long Parliament (call'd by King Charles the First, in the year 1640) but by an Act of Parliament. With Undeniable Reasons deduced from the said Act to prove that that Parliament is not yet Dissolved. Also, Mr. William Pryn his five Arguments fully answered: Whereby he endeavours to prove it Dissolved by the Kings Death, &c. by Tho. Philips. *Printed for the Author*, 1661, *dust soiling throughout, top margins cut close*, [ii+]22 pp., sm. 4to, *grey bds. faded, paper label* (Wing D2136) **£40.00**

353 —— ENGLANDS GLORY in her Royall King, and Honorable Assembly in the high Court of Parliament, above her former usurped Lordly Bishops Synod. With a discourse betwixt Mr. Iohn Calvin and a prelaticall Bishop, whereunto is added the Bishop of Canterburies Dreame. *Printed in the Yeare*, 1641, *most lower margins cropped, some with loss of last line of text*, [vi+]18 pp., sm. 4to, *hf. calf, lettered, marbled bds., rubbed* (Wing E2969) **£45.00**

354 —— THE HISTORY and Proceedings of the House of Commons from the Restoration to the Present Time. Containing the most remarkable Motions, Speeches, Resolves, Reports and Conferences to be met with in that Interval . . . together with a large Appendix containing exact Lists of every Parliament, the Names of the Speakers, their several Posts under the Government; and other valuable, Supplemental Pieces. 14 Vols. *Printed for Richard Chandler*, 1742/44, 8vo, *contemp. sprinkled calf, corners worn, newly rebacked, leather labels* **£220.00**

355 —— A PERFECT DIURNALL of the Passages in Parliament: from the twenty five of July, to the first of August: 1642. *Printed for Robert Wood*, (1642), *drop title, some discolouration, lower margins trimmed*, 8 pp., sm. 4to, *unbound* **£30.00**

356 **Parliamentary Debates.** An Exact Collection of the Debates of the House of Commons, held at Westminster, October 21, 1680 . . . with the Debates of the House of Commons at Oxford, Assembled March 21. 1680. Also a Just and Modest Vindication of the Proceedings of the said Parliament. *Printed for R. Baldwin*, 1689, *inner margin of title repaired, some embrowning throughout*, [viii+]464(shd. read 456) pp., 12mo, *contemp. sprinkled sheep, edges and corners worn, recently rebacked and lettered* (Wing E2674) **£35.00**

357 **Paruta** (Paolo) The History of Venice, in the Times of . . . Henry the 8th, Edward the 6th. Q. Mary, Q. Elizabeth . . . written originally in Italian, Likewise, the Wars of Cyprus, by the same Authour. Wherein the famous Sieges of Nicossia, and Famagosta, and Battel of Lepanto are contained. Made English, by Henry Earl of Monmouth. *Printed for Abel Roper and Henry Herringman*, 1568, *title in red and black, upper fore-corner of last few ll. torn away, upper margin of penultimate lf. torn away with no loss to text, upper and fore-corner of last lf. torn away with some loss of text, this lf. laid down*, pp. [xxii+ii(blank)+]1-444 (shd. read 452), 553-650:1-205, folio, *new qtr. dark blue calf, leather label, marb. bds.* (Wing P636) **£110.00**

358 **Paston Letters.** FENN (John) Original Letters, written during the Reigns of Henry vi. Edward iv. and Richard iii. by various Persons of Rank or Consequence; containing many curious Anecdotes, relative to that turbulent and bloody, but hitherto dark, Period of our History . . . with Notes, Historical and Explanatory . . . by John Fenn. 2 Vols. in 1. *Printed for G.G.J. and J. Robinson*, 1787, *with 3 plates in colour and 14 of facsimiles, folding genealogical table, small tear repaired*, xxxiii[+lii+]301:341[+xxii] pp., 4to, *contemp. tree calf, gilt, leather label, upper joint cracked* **£30.00**

359 **Pearson** (Anthony) The Great Case of Tithes Truly Stated, Clearly Open'd, And fully Resolv'd, with an Appendix. *Printed and sold by the Assigns of J. Sowle*, 1732, *ownership inscription on verso of title, fore margins trimmed with some loss*, viii+124[+viii—cat.] pp., sm. 8vo, *contemp. hf. calf, rubbed, upper joint cracked* (Kress 4030) **£18.00**

360 **Pepys** (Samuel) Memoirs of the Reigns of Charles II. and James II. Comprising his Diary from 1659 to 1669, deciphered by the Rev. John Smith, A.B. of St. John's College Library, Cambridge, from the Original Short-Hand MS. in the Pepysian Library, and a Selection from his Private Correspondence. Edited by Richard, Lord Braybrooke. 2 Vols. *Henry Colburn*, 1825, FIRST EDITION, *with 13 engravings (one folded), all foxed and off-set, 2 vignettes in text, hf. titles present, heavy foxing of first and last few gatherings in vol. i., short tears in lower margins of 2 ll., lacks the 2 pp. catalogue at end of vol. i*, [ii+]xlii+498[+ii+]xlix:[iv+]348+viii+311 pp., roy. 4to, *contemp. tan calf, gilt, edges rubbed, leather labels* **£250.00**

361 **Pole.** [BECCADELLI (Lodovico, *archbp. of Ragusa*)] Vita Reginaldi Poli, S.R.E. Cardinalis . . . Italice Conscripta, Latine Reddita . . . *Juxta Exemplar Venetiis excusum, An.* mdlxiii. *Londini, rec. imp. Jacobi Adamson*, 1690, *some staining, label on verso of title*, [viii+]108 pp. (Adams B434: Wing B1641):

[and]

[WYNGFELD (Robert, *diplomatist*)] Nobilissima Disceptatio super Dignitate et Magnitudine Regnorum Britannici & Gallici, habita ab utriusque Oratoribus & Legatis in Concilio Constantiensi. *Juxta Exemplar Lovaniis excusum, An. mdxvii. Londini, rec. imp. Jacobi Adamson*, 1690, *some staining, one lf. repaired, extensive contemp. notes on title and margins throughout, gatherings continuous with the above item, but separately paginated*, [xiv+]70[+xiv] pp. (Adams W209: Wing W3030):

Two works bound together, sm. 8vo, *new hf. tan calf, marb. bds. lettered, r.e.* **£45.00**

362 **Poll Tax.** AN ACT for Granting unto the Kings Majesty Twelve hundred and threescore thousand pounds, to be Assessed and Levied by an Assessment of Threescore and ten thousand pounds by the Moneth, for Eighteen Moneths. [*Printed by John Bill and Christopher Barker*, 1662], *drop title, lacks general title*, 96 pp., folio, *disbound* **£20.00**

363 **Popish Plot.** A NARRATIVE, being a true Relation of what Discourse passed between Dr. Hawkins and Edward Fitz-Harys, Esq., late Prisoner in the Tower; with the Manner of taking his Confession. *Printed for Samuel Carr*, 1681, [ii+]10 pp., folio, *unbound* **£35.00**

364 —— [NORTHLEACH (John)] The Parallel: or, the New Specious Association an Old Rebellious Covenant. Closing with a Disparity between a True Patriot, and a Factious Associator. *Printed for B. Tooke ,and T. Sawbridge*, 1682, [ii+]34 pp., folio, *disbound* (Wing N1301) **£30.00**

365 **Post Office.** AN ACT for Consolidating the Estates Tail and Reversion in Fee, which His Majesty hath in the Post-Office, and Twenty four thousand pounds per Annum of the Hereditary Excise. [*Printed by the Assigns of John Bill, deceas'd* . . . 1685], 4 pp., *drop title*, folio, *disbound* **£16.00**

366 **Postal Services.** DEBATES in both Houses of Parliament in the months of May and June 1808, relative to the Agreement made by Government with Mr. Palmer, for the Reform and Improvement of the Post-Office and its Revenue. With an Appendix containing several Documents therein referred to. *Printed by T. C. Hansard*, 1811, *some foxing, hf. title present*, [iii+]130+xlii pp., 8vo, *recent marb. bds., leather label* **£50.00**

367 —— [PALMER (John, *projector of the Mail Coaches*)] Papers relative to the Agreement made by Government with Mr. Palmer, for the Reform and Improvement of the Posts. *Printed for T. Cadell, jun. and W. Davies*, 1797, *upper margins cut close, with sl. loss of pagination*, vi+11+8+65 pp., 4to, *binder's cloth* **£65.00**

368 The **Present State of Europe,** or, the Historical and Political Monthly Mercury, giving an Account of all the Publick and Private Occurrances, Civil, Ecclesiastical and Military, that are most Considerable in every Court . . . with Political Reflexions upon every State. Vol. V. *Printed for Henry Rhodes and John Harris*, 1694, *divisional titles, lacking that for January, worming throughout, with some loss of letters*, pp. 3-425[+ix], sm. 4to, *new hf. tan calf, leather label, marb. bds.* **£75.00**

369 **Prideaux** (Mathias) An Easy and Compendious Introdvction for Reading all sorts of Histories: contrived in a more facile way then heretofore hath been published . . . Third Edition, in which is added a Synopsis of Councels by John Prideaux . . . *Oxford, Printed for Leonard Lichfield, and are to be sold by Tho. Robinson*, 1655, *sl. staining and browning*, [viii+]351[+xxxv+ii+]58[+iv] pp., sm. 4to, *new qtr. dark brown calf, leather label, grey paper bds.* (Wing P3442) **£30.00**

370 **Prince Regent.** PERCEVAL (Spencer) The Genuine Book. An Inquiry, or Delicate Investigation into the Conduct of Her Royal Highness the Princess of Wales; before Lords Erskine, Spencer, Grenville and Ellenborough, the Four Special Commissioners of Inquiry, appointed by His Majesty in the Year 1806. Reprinted from an Authentic Copy. *Printed by R. Edwards, and reprinted by George Wilson, Leeds for A. Cumming*, 1813, *engr. frontis.*, [ii+]360 pp., 12mo, *contemp. hf. calf, lettered, marb. bds.* **£25.00**

371 **Prussia.** FREDERICK III. TOWERS (Joseph) Memoirs of the Life and Reign of Frederick the Third, King of Prussia. 2 Vols. *Printed for Charles Dilly*, 1788, *vignette portrait on engr. title, general browning throughout*, [xvi+]392:[xii+]506[+ii] pp., 8vo, *contemp. marb. calf, newly rebacked, leather labels, y.e.* **£21.00**

372 **Public Prayers.** AN ACT for the Uniformity of Publique Prayers, and administration of Sacraments, and other Rites and Ceremonies; and for establishing the Form of Making, Ordaining, and Consecrating Bishops, Priests and Deacons, in the Church of England. *Printed by John Bill and Christopher Barker*, 1662, [ii+]29 pp., folio, *disbound* **£15.00**

373 **Railway Engineering.** BARLOW (Peter) Second Report addressed to the Directors and Proprietors of the London and Birmingham Railway Company, founded on an Inspection of, and Experiments made on the Liverpool and Manchester Railway. *B. Fellowes*, 1835, *with 3 full-page and other illusts. in text*, [ii+]116 pp., 8vo, *hf. calf, marb. bds., unlettered* **£75.00**

¶"Barlow was much occupied with experiments designed to afford practical data for steam locomotion. His two reports were regarded as of the highest authority both abroad and in this country". (D.N.B.)

374 **Raleigh.** THE ARRAIGNMENT and Conviction of Sr. Walter Rawleigh, at the Kings Bench-Barre at Winchester. on the 17. of November. 1603. before the right Honourable the Earle of Suffolke, Lord Chamberlaine, the Earle of Devonshire, Lord Henry Howard, Lord Cecill, Lord Wotton, Sir John Stanhope, Lord Chiefe Justice of the Common-Pleas, Popham and Andrewes [corrected to *Anderson* in early hand], Justice Gaudy, Justice Warberton, Sir William Wade, Commissioners, Coppied by Sir Tho. Overbvry. *Printed by William Wilson, for Abel Roper*, 1648, *sl. discolouration throughout, top edges only trimmed*, [ii+]38 pp., sm. 4to, *modern hf. brown calf, cloth matching sides, lettered* (Wing A3744) **£145.00**

375 **Reyd** (Everard van) Belgarvm Aliarvmqve Gentivm, Annales. Dionysio Vossio Interprete. *Lugduni Batavorum, ex off. Ioannis Maire*, 1633, *title in red and black*, [x+]561 (shd. read 563) pp., folio, *contemp. stamped vellum, ties present, upper joint split* **£60.00**

376 **Riots.** THE HUMBLE PETITION of the Lord Mayor . . . of London . . . as it was Presented to His Majesty in Council at Windsor, upon Monday the 18th of June 1683. Together with the Lord Keeper's Speech. *Printed by the Assigns of John Bill deceas'd: and by Henry Hills and Thomas Newcomb*, 1683, 10 pp., folio, *disbound* **£15.00**

377 **Robinson** (John) Archaeologia Graeca, or the Antiquities of Greece; being an Account of the Manners and Customs of the Greeks . . . chiefly designed to illustrate the Greek Classics . . . *Printed for Richard Phillips*, 1807, [lxiv+]618[xvi—cat.] pp., 8vo, *contemp. hf. calf, marb. bds., newly rebacked, leather label* **£25.00**

378 **Ross** (Alexander) *Πανδεβεια*: or, A View of all Religions in the World, with the several Church Governments, from the Creation to these times. Also, a Discovery of all known Heresies in all Ages and Places . . . Fourth Edition . . . to which are annexed, the Lives, Actions, and Ends of certain notorious Hereticks . . . *Printed for John Williams*, 1672, *portrait of the author and 17 copper engravings of 'heretics', some soiling throughout*, [xxix+]544[+viii]:[xx+blank+]78[+ii] pp., sm. 8vo, *contemp. calf, unlettered, corners wearing, backstrip defective* (Wing R1975) **£45.00**

379 **Rous** (Francis) Archaeologiae Atticae Libri Septem. Seven Books of the Attick Antiquities. Containing the description of the Citties glory, Government, division of the People, the Towns within the Athenisn Territories, their Religion, Superstition, Sacrifices, Account of the Year, a full relation of their Judicatories. Fifth Edition, corrected and enlarged. *Oxford, Printed by A. Lichfield and H. Hall, for John Adams and Edw. Forrest*, 1658, *embrowning throughout*, [viii+]374[+xii] pp., sm. 4to, *contemp. sprinkled sheep, unlettered, corners worn, backstrip sl. defective* (Wing R2035: Madan 2410) **£40.00**

380 **[Rowlands** (Richard)] The History of the Lives and Reigns of the Kings of Scotland from Fergus the First King, continued to the Commencement of the Union of the Two Kingdoms of Scotland and England . . . to which is added, An Account of the Rebellion in Scotland in the Year 1715 . . . *Dublin, Printed by John Harding for the Author*, 1722, *some embrowning, tears in two margins repaired, a few margins shaved close*, [xxiv+]188[+xxxvi] pp., sm. 4to, *19th cent. ecclesiastical calf, leather label, little rubbed, r.e.* **£35.00**

381 **Rowlands or V[erstegan]** (R[ichard]) A Restitvtion of Decayed Intelligence: in antiquities, concerning the most noble, and renowned English Nation. *Printed by Iohn Norton, for Ioyce Norton, and Richard Whitaker*, 1634, [xxiv+]338[+xii] pp., *title in red and black, and laid down, engravings in text, general browning throughout*, sm. 4to, *new qtr. sprinkled calf, leather label, marb. bds.* (STC 21363) **£30.00**

382 [——] A Restitution of Decayed Intelligence in Antiquities, concerning the most Noble and Renowned English Nation. *Printed for Samuel Mearne, John Martyn and Henry Herringman*, 1673, *engr. title, damaged and laid down, soiled, engravings in text*, [xxiv+]374[+xvi] pp., sm. 8vo, *contemp. sheep, rubbed and corners worn, newly rebacked, leather label* (Wing V271) **£25.00**

383 **Royal Progress.** AN ACT for the Providing necessary Carriages for His Majesty in His Royal Progress and Removals. *Printed by the Assigns of John Bill deceas'd* . . . 1685, [ii+]8 pp., folio, *disbound* **£12.00**

384 **Rushworth** (John) Historical Collections of Private Passages of State, Weighty Matters of Law, Remarkable Proceedings in . . . Parliaments, beginning the Sixteenth Year of King James, Anno 1618 . . . to the End of the Year, 1644. 3 Parts in 5 Vols. *Printed* . . . 1680/92, *folding map and engraved portraits*, folio, *18th cent. diced calf, backstrips tooled and lettered in gilt, vols. 1 & 2 misnumbered, small snag on one backstrip, otherwise in excellent condition* (Wing R2317/9) **£185.00**

¶Volume 1 is the second edition.

385 **Russell** (Lady Rachel) Letters; from the MS. in the Library at Wooburn Abbey to which are prefixed, an Introduction, vindicating the Character of Lord Russell against Sir John Dalrymple, &c. and the Trial of Lord William Russell for High Treason, extracted from the State Trials . . . Sixth Edition. *Printed for J. Mawman*, 1801, *with 3 engravings*, clxxi+351[+i] pp., 8vo, *marb. sheep, leather label, upper cover sl. damaged, joints beginning to crack* **£25.00**

386 **Russia.** RULHIERE (Claude-Carloman de) The History, or Anecdotes of the Revolution in Russia, in the year 1762. Translated from the French. *Printed for T. N. Longman*, 1797, *engr. port.*, xxiv+178[+ii] pp., 8vo, *orig. drab bds., recently rebacked, paper label, all edges untrimmed* **£21.00**

387 **Rye House Plot.** [SPRATT (Thomas)] A True Account and Declaration of the Horrid Conspiracy against the late King, his Present Majesty, and the Government . . . Second Edition. *Printed by Thomas Newcomb, and are to be sold by Sam Lowndes*, 1685, *Imprimatur lf. present*, [v+]167 pp. (Wing S5067):

[with]

Copies of the Informations and Original Papers relating to the Proof of the Horrid Conspiracy against the Late King, his Present Majesty and the Government. *Printed by Thomas Newcomb, and are to be sold by Sam. Lowndes*, 1685, *folding plate, lf. Dd² not present but stub after Ee²*, [ii+]141(shd. read 139) pp. (Wing S5029):

Two works bound together, folio, *contemp. calf, corners worn, rebacked, leather label* **£65.00**

88 **[Saint-Didier** (Alexander-Toussaint de Limojon, sieur de)] La Ville et la Republique de Venise. *Paris, chez Guillaume de Luyne*, 1680, *embrowning throughout*, [xxiv+]452 pp., 12mo, *contemp. calf, newly rebacked, leather label* (Brunet 5/37) **£30.00**

389 **[St. Germain** (Christopher)] The Dialoges in English, betwene a Doctor of Diuinity, and a Student in the lawes of England. Newly corrected and imprinted, with new additions. [*In Aedibus Richardi Tottelli*, 1580—colophon], **Black Letter,** *embrowning throughout, last lf. defective in two places with loss of letter-press, marginal notes and underlinings in contemp. hand*, 176[+iv] ff., sm. 8vo, *18th cent. hf. calf, leather label, marb. bds.* (STC 21574.5) **£55.00**

390 **St. Helena.** BROOKE (T. H.) History of the Island of St. Helena, from its Discovery by the Portuguese to the Year 1823. 2nd Edition. *Printed for Kingsbury, Parbury, and Allen*, 1824, *two plates, both foxed, outer margins on title fragile and sl. fragmented, title inscribed from 'Mr. H. Brooke to Mr. B. Brooke 1826, some marginalia pertaining to the Brookes, errata slip*, xvi+495 pp., 8vo, *green morocco, gilt, corners worn, rebacked, old backstrip mounted, g.e.* **£25.00**

391 **Schlegel** (Frederick von) The Philosophy of History; in a Course of Lectures delivered in Vienna. Translated from the German, with a Memoir of the Author by James Burton Robertson. 2 Vols. *Saunders and Otley*, 1835, FIRST ENGLISH EDITION, lxxxvi[+ii+]350:iv+336 pp., 8vo, *orig. drab bds., cloth backs, paper labels, somewhat soiled* **£45.00**

392 **Scotland.** AN ACCOUNT of the Proceedings of the Meeting of the Estates in Scotland, with the Letters of King William, and the late King James, to the said Estates. *Printed for Richard Chiswell*, 1689, *some soiling and few corners dog-eared*, [iv+]12 pp., folio, *disbound* **£20.00**

393 —— CHARLES II. His Majesties Gracious Letter to His Parliament of Scotland: with the Speech of His Royal Highness the Duke, His Majesties High Commissioner, at the Opening of the Parliament at Edinburgh, the 28th Day of July, 1681. Together with the Parliaments most Loyal and Dutiful Answer to His Majesties Letter. *In the Savoy, Printed by Thomas Newcomb*, 1681, 15 pp., folio, *disbound* (Wing C3025) **£15.00**

394 —— CRAIG (Sir Thomas) Scotland's Soveraignty Asserted. Being a Dispute concerning Homage, against those who maintain that Scotland is a Feu, or Fee-Liege of England, and that therefore the King of Scots owes Homage to the King of England. Wherein there are many Judicious Reflections upon most of the English Historians, who wrote before the Year 1600. And abundance of considerable Passages, which illustrate the History of both Kingdoms. Translated from the Latin MS. . . . by George Ridpath. *Printed for Andrew Bell and sold by Thomas Brown* . . . 1695, *stub of longitudinal title still attached to one outer margin, sl. worming in margin of last gathering, penetrating to lower cover*, [iv+]xliv+430 pp., 8vo, *contemp. sprinkled calf, lacks label* (Wing 6805: Aldis 3453) **£75.00**

395 —— DEMSTER (Thomas, *self-styled Baron of Muresk*) Scotorvm scriptorvm nomenclatvra Quartum Aucta . . . [with] Menologivm Scotorvm . . . [and] Apparatvs ad Historiam Scoticam lib. ii. . . . 4 Parts together. *Bononiae, Typis Nicolai Tebaldini*, 1622, *separate titles to each part, title and dedication ll. to bl. ii. of Apparatus are inserted, title of pt. i. defective in upper margin, with no loss of letters, some damp staining of first two parts*, [viii+]28:[xvi+]40:[xvi+]88[+iv+]89-152 pp., sm. 4to, *new qtr. brown calf, lettered, grey bds., new end papers, but one original preserved with brief list of contents on verso in early hand* (Graesse ii/361) **£55.00**

¶Demster spent most of his life on the continent, and has left a detailed (if sometimes incredible) account of his life in the form of an autobiography which is 'clearly marked', says the D.N.B., 'by the same habit of grotesquely extravagant falsehood which appears in some of his other writings . . .' In 1619, on his way to London, he passed through Bologna, and was appointed to the vacant professorship of humanities at the university there, where he stayed, apart from a brief pursuit of his errant wife as far as the Alps, until his death in 1625.

396 —— A LARGE DECLARATION concerning the late Tumults in Scotland, from their first originalls: together with a particular Deduction of the seditious Practices of the prime Leaders of the Covenanters: collected out of their owne foule Acts and Writings: by which it doth plainly appeare, that Religion was onely pretended by those Leaders, but nothing lesse intended by them. *Printed by Robert Young*, 1639, *title creased, staining throughout*, [i+]431[+i] pp., folio, *contemp. calf, corners worn, sometime rebacked with canvas, MS. label* (STC 21906 *marginal note in p*, 41) **£50.00**

¶This Declaration, attributed to A. Henderson, was answered in 1640 by W. Ker's *A True Representation*.

397 —— THE LAWS AND ACTS of Parliament made by King James the First, Second, Third, Fourth, Fifth, Queen Mary, King James the Sixth, King Charles the First, King Charles the Second who now presently Reigns, Kings and Queen of Scotland, collected and extracted, from the Publick Records of the said Kingdom, by Sir Thomas Murray. *Edinburgh, Printed by David Lindsay*,- 1681, *with engr. portraits of the monarchs but lacking those of Queen Mary and Charles i., three frayed in margins and misbound, genealogical table*, [vi+]521+19[+ii+]1-108[+iv+]109-198+6+19+11[iv+]45[+xxxvii] pp., lge. folio, *hf. calf, marb. bds., newly rebacked, leather label* (Wing S1265: Aldis 2243) **£50.00**

398 —— LOCKHART (George) The Lockhart Papers containing Memoirs and Commentaries upon the Affairs of Scotland from 1702 to 1715: His Secret Correspondence with the Son of King James the Second from 1718 to 1728: and his other Political Writings: also, Journals and Memoirs of the Young Pretender's Expedition in 1745, by Highland Officers of his Army, published from Original MSS. in the Possession of Anthony Aufrere [husband of Lockhart's great grand-daughter]. 2 Vols. *Printed by Richard and Arthur Taylor, for William Anderson*, 1817, *facsimiles and pedigree, plan of Cullenden inserted in Vol.* 2, xvi+616:xvi+586 pp., 4to, *hf. calf, marb. bds.* **£45.00**

399 —— [LOCKHART (George)] Memoirs concerning the Affairs of Scotland, from Queen Anne's Accession to the Throne, to the Commencement of the Union of the Two Kingdoms of Scotland and England, in May, 1707. With an Account of the Origine and Progress of the Design'd Invasion from France, in March 1708, and some Reflections on the Ancient State of Scotland. Third Edition. *Printed and sold by J. Baker*, 1714, xxx+420 pp., [with] A Key to the Memoirs of the Affairs of Scotland. *Printed for J. Moor*, 1714, 8vo, *contemp. panelled calf, unlettered, joints beginning to crack* **£21.00**

400 —— [RIDPATH (George)] An Historical Account of the Ancient Rights and Power of the Parliament of Scotland. Humbly offer'd to the Consideration of the Estates, when they come to settle Limitations for the next Successor. To which is prefix'd, A short Introduction upon Government in General [By Hume of Blackotter—MS. note]. *Printed in the Year* 1703, *some discolouration throughout, names on title*, xxxii+160 pp., 8vo, *contemp. sheep, worn, newly rebacked, leather label, incorrectly lettered* **£21.00**

401 —— SCOT (Sir John, *of Scotstarvet*) The Staggering State of the Scots Statesmen, for one hundred Years, from 1550 to 1650. Now first published from the original manuscript. *Edinburgh, Printed by Wal Ruddiman jun. and Company, and sold by R. Nimmo*, 1754, FIRST EDITION, *lacks final lf. (? blank)*, [ii+]xxxiv+190 pp., 12mo, *modern hf. calf, leather labels, marb. bds,, ex-libris labels and inscriptions* **£25.00**

402 —— SOME PAPERS of the Commissioners of Scotland, given in lately to the Houses of Parliament, concerning the Propositions of Peace. *Printed for Robert Bostock, April* 11., 1646, *one corner torn away with sl. loss*, [iv+]26 pp., sm. 4to, *new marb. bds.* **£25.00**

403 [**Scott** (Thomas)] Newes from Parnassvs. The Political Touchstone, taken from Mount Parnassus: whereon the Governments of the greatest Monarchies of the World are touched. *Printed at Helicon* (i.e. *Holland)*, 1622, *sl. enbrowning*, 92[+iii] pp., sm. 4to, *modern qtr. calf, marb. bds. lettered* (STC 22080) **£150.00**

¶Scott, sometime Chaplain to James I., wrote in his lifetime some 25 phamphlets, many against Spain, and the Roman Catholics. He was assassinated, while preacher to the English Garrison in Utrecht.

404 **A Seasonable Warning** to the Commoners of England; discovering to them their Present Danger, and the only means of Escaping it, to be by a Prudent Choice of old English Spirits, to serve their King and Countrey in the Approaching Parliament. [*London*, 1679], *drop title*, 4 pp., folio. *disbound* (Wing S2248) **£20.00**

405 **Secret Partition Treaties.** A STATE of the Proceedings in the House of Commons, with Relation to the Impeached Lords [Edward, Earl of Orford: John, Lord Somers: Charles, Lord Halifax]: and what happened thereupon between the Two Houses. *Printed for Edward Jones, and Timothy Goodwin*, 1701, *margins little frayed, lacks* A^1, 61 pp., folio, *disbound* **£25.00**

406 **Selden** (John) The Priviledges of the Baronage of England, when they sit in Parliament. Collected . . . out of the Parliament Rolles, and Journalls Patent, and close Rolls . . . *Printed by T. Badger for Matthew Wallbank*, 1642, *lacks* A^1 *(? blank), ink scoring in a few margins*, [vi+]167 pp., sm. 8vo, *contemp. calf, rubbed, joints beginning to crack, lacks label* (Wing S2434) **£45.00**

407 —— Titles of Honor. Second Edition. *Printed by William Stansby for Richard Whitakers*, 1631, *title in red and black, sl. soiled, some errors in pagination*, [xxxvi+]941[+i] pp., th. folio, *modern dark brown morocco, blind tooled, incorrectly titled* (STC 22178) **£65.00**

408 **Sheriffs.** AN ACT for preventing the unnecessary charge of Sheriffs, and for ease in passing their Accompts. *Printed by John Bill and Christopher Barker*, 1662, [ii+]11 pp., folio, *disbound* **£15.00**

409 **Ship Building.** AN ACT to Encourage the Building of Ships in England. [*Reprinted by Charles Bill* . . . 1691], *drop title*, 4 pp., folio, *disbound* **£15.00**

410 **Shropshire Militia.** AN ORDINANCE of the Lords and Commons assembled in Parliament, for raising of Monies for the Maintenance of such Forces as are and shall be raised in the County of Salop for the Service of the Parliament. *Printed for Christopher Meredith*, 1644, *small rubber stamp on title*, [ii+]6 pp., sm. 4to, *disbound* **£40.00**

411 **Sidney** (Algernon) Discourses concerning Government. Second Edition, carefully corrected, to which is Added, the Paper He deliver'd to the Sheriffs immediately before his Death, and an Alphabetical Table. *Printed by J. Darby*, 1714, *portrait*, [viii+]424[+xlviii] pp., folio, *contemp. panelled calf, corners worn, rebacked at sometime, but joints now cracking again, lacks label* **£65.00**

412 **Slatyer** (William) The History of Great Britanie from the first peopling of this Island to this present Raigne of o[u]r happy and peacefull Monarke K. James. *Printed by W. Stansby, for Rich. Meighen*, [1621], *lacks printed title and colophon lf. as usual, engraved title trimmed and inlaid, 'Declaration of the Frontispiece' trimmed close and laid down, last 3 lines defective, lower corner of* ¶^{8} *repaired, general staining and browning throughout*, [xxiv+]305[+xiv] pp., folio, 19*th cent. tan calf, corners bruised, newly rebacked, leather label* (STC 22634) **£65.00**

413 **Slavery.** DICKSON (William) Letters on Slavery . . . to which are added, Addresses to the Whites, and to the Free Negroes of Barbadoes; and Accounts of some Negroes eminent for their Virtues and Abilities. *Printed and sold by J. Phillips, and sold by J. Johnson, and Elliot and Kay*, 1789, *insertion in ink in one lower margin*, x+190[+i] pp., 8vo, *modern qtr. calf, cloth bds. unlettered* (Sabin 20094) scarce **£225.00**

414 —— [MACAULAY (Zachary)] The Slave Colonies of Great Britain; or a Picture of Negro Slavery drawn by the Colonists themselves; being an Abstract of the various Papers recently laid before Parliament on that Subject. *Printed by Ellerton and Henderson* . . . 1825, iv+164 pp., 8vo, *qtr. tan calf, mid brown cloth sides, lettered by hand*, scarce **£145.00**

415 —— TWO LETTERS on Slavery, by an Eminent and Learned Jurist. Originally published in the Charleston Courier. *Philadelphia*, 1841, *a little soiled*, 8 pp., 8vo, *sewed* **£35.00**

416 **Somers** (John, *Baron*) A Brief History of the Succession of the Crown of England, &c. collected out of the Records, and the most Authentick Historians. Written for the Satisfaction of the Nation. *Printed, and are to be sold by Richard Janeway*, 1688/9, *sl. soiling*, [ii+]18 pp., folio, *disbound* (Wing S4639) **£18.00**

417 **Spanish War.** ACT for the three Moneths Assessment in Ireland, for the Maintenance of the Spanish War, and other Services of the Commonwealth . . . [*Printed by Hen. Hills and John Field*, 1657—col.], *embrowned*, 3 pp., folio, *disbound* **£18.00**

418 **Sparrow** (Anthony, *bp.*) A Collection of Articles, Injunctions, Canons, Orders, Ordnances, and Constitutions Ecclesiastical, with other Publick Records of the Church of England, chiefly in the Times of King Edward vith. Q. Elizabeth. and K. James. Published to Vindicate the Church of England and to promote Uniformity and peace in the same. *Printed by R. Norton for Timothy Garthwait*, 1661, FIRST EDITION, *divisional titles, pagination irregular*, [xii+325] pp., sm. 4to, *contemp. panelled calf, rubbed and worn, sometime rebacked but joints now cracking again* (Wing S4823) **£25.00**

419 **Speed** (Iohn) The Historie of Great Britaine vnder the Conqvests of the Romans, Saxons, Danes and Normans. Their Originals, Manners, Habits, Warres, Coines, and Seales: with the Successions, Liues, Acts, and Issues of the English Monarchs, from Ivlivs Caesar, to our most gracious Soueraigne King Iames. Second Edition, reusied, and enlarged with sundry descents of the Saxons Kings, Their Marriages and Armes. *Printed by Iohn Beale, for George Hvmble*, 1623, *woodcuts of arms, banners, &c. one lf. repaired in lower corner with sl. loss, lacks* A^1. *(engr. title) and portrait of Speed*, pp. [xix+]1-308:363-430:391:1058:ff. 1059-1191(shd. read 1102): pp. 1107-1258[+lccciv], thick folio, 18*th cent. tan calf, gilt extra, some worm damage to surface of back cover* (STC 23246.3) **£80.00**

420 **Spelman** (Sir Henry) Villare Anglicum: or, a View of all the Cities, Towns and Villages in England: alphabetically composed . . . 2nd Edition, corr. and emend. *Printed by T.H. for Robert Pawlett, and are to be sold by Tho. Barrell*, 1678, *worming in a few fore-margins*, [vi+462] pp., 8vo, *hf. calf, corners worn, marb. bds., lettered* (Wing S4933) **£35.00**

421 **Sprigge** (Ioshua) Anglia Redivia; Englands Recovery: being the History of the Motions, Actions, and Successes of the Army under the Immediate Conduct of his Excellency Sr. Thomas Fairfax, Kt. Captain-General of all the Parliaments Forces in England. *Printed by R.W. for Iohn Partridge*, 1647. *folding equestrian portrait of Fairfax, with his armorial achievement facing (repaired and laid down), large folding map of Battle of Naseby, with a number of small defects, laid down on linen, folding table, additional portrait added to end free end-paper*, [xxii+]335[+iv] pp., folio, *hf. mottled calf, marb. bds., lettered* (Wing S5070) **£85.00**

422 **Stackhouse** (Thomas) A General View of Ancient History, Chronology, and Geography . . . *Printed for the Author* . . . 1770, *2 folding charts*, viii+76 pp., 4to, *new qtr. calf, marb. bds., unlettered* **£30.00**

423 [**Steele** (Richard)] The Spinster: in Defence of the Woollen Manufactures. To be continued Occasio-nally. Numb. 1. [all published]. *Printed for J. Roberts*, 1719, [ii+]16[+i] pp., 8vo, *sewed, enclosed in grey buckram fold-over case, leather label on front cover* (Kress 3119) **£70.00**

424 **Strada** (Famianvs) De Bello Belgico. The History of the Low-Countrey Warres. Written in Latine, in English by Sr. Rob. Stapylton Kt. *Printed for Humphrey Moseley*, 1650, *with 14 engraved portraits, one creased with small split in plate mark, title little soiled*, [viii+]143+83+58+24[+xliv] pp., folio, *contemp. mottled calf, rubbed, backstrip gilt, leather label, joints cracking* (Wing S5777) **£40.00**

425 **Talleyrand-Perigord** (Charles Maurice, *Prince*) Revelations of the Life of . . . edited from the papers of the late M. Colmache, private Secretary to the Prince. 2nd Edition. *Henry Colburn*, 1830, vii+375[+i] pp., *port.*, 8vo, *hf. morocco, edges little rubbed, t.e.g.* **£15.00**

426 **Tithes.** MOVNTAGV (Richard) Diatribae vpon the First Part of the late History of Tithes. [by John Selden] *Imprinted by Felix Kyngston, for Matthevv Lovvnes*, 1621, *damp staining throughout, many fore-margins rather fragile, small hole in title and last lf. (repaired), some worming in upper margin towards end, lacks* A^1, [x+]579[+i] pp., sm. 4to, *new qtr. sprinkled calf, leather label, marb. bds.* (STC 18037) **£75.00**

427 **Tooke.** REID (W. Hamilton) Memoirs of the Public Life of John Horne Tooke, Esq. containing a Particular Account of his Connections with the most eminent Characters of the Reign of George III. his Trials for Sedition, High Treason, &c. . . . *Printed for Sherwood, Neely & Jones*, 1812, xxviii+192 pp., 12mo, *contemp. hf. calf, leather label, marb. bds.* **£15.00**

428 **Trade.** AN ACT for Continuing and Establishing the Subsidie of Tunnage and Poundage, and for reviving an Act for the better Packing of Butter, and redress of abuses therein. *Printed by Henry Hills and John Field*, 1657, *embrowned*, [ii+]16 pp., folio, *grey bds.* (Wing E1016) **£20.00**

429 —— COLLINS (Sir Joseph) A New Discourse of Trade: wherein are recommended several weighty Points relating to Companies of Merchants, the Act of Navigation, Naturalization of Strangers, and our Woollen Manufacturers: the Balance of Trade, and the Nature of Plantations, with their Consequences in relation to the Kingdom, are seriously discussed . . . New Edition. *Printed for Richardson and Urquhart*, 1775, *lower blank margin of title and ff. lf. cut away*, [iv+]xxxix+224 pp., 12mo, *contemp. sprinkled tan calf, leather label, y.e.* scarce (Kress 7091: Goldsmith 11259) **£130.00**

430 —— GEE (Joshua) The Trade and Navigation of Great Britain considered: shewing . . . some account of the commodities each country we trade with takes from us, and what we take from them; with observations on the balance. Sixth Edition. *Glasgow, Printed by William Duncan junior*, 1755, [xvi+]166 pp., sm. 8vo, *contemp. grained calf, rebacked and orig. backstrip mounted, g.e.* (Kress 5441: Sabin 26827) **£45.00**

431 **Trogus Pompeius.** Givstino Historico belle Historie di Trogo Pompeo, tradotto per Thomaso Porcacchi. *Vinegia, appresso Gabriel Giolito de Ferrari*, 1561, *large engraving on title, book-plate of Lord Chesterfield on verso, device on verso of last lf., lower margin of which has been repaired, one other lf. repaired, many fine woodcut initials and decorations*, [xvi+]239[+i] pp., sq. 8vo, 19*th cent. cloth, faded and sometime rebacked, leather label* **£120.00**

¶The abridgement by Justine of the universal history by Trogus Pompeius containing 'a few striking passages, such as the description of the multitude of Athenians pouring out to see Alcibiades on his return from exile (bk. v.) and of Bennus and his army at Delphi (bk. xxiv).' (Harvey)

Once the property of W. M. Rossetti (brother of D.G.) with an inscription from his mother, 1876: also 'Mary E. Madox Rossetti from Papa's books, 1919'.

432 **Trombelli** (Giovanni Grisostomo) La Diplomatica o sia l'arte di conoscera l'eta', ed autentica de Codici latini, e italiani. *Napoli, Presso Giuseppi-Maria Porcelli*, 1780, *3 folding plates, some staining*, xiv+146 pp., sm. 8vo, *contemp. sprinkled calf, gilt, leather label* (Brunet 30206) **£35.00**

433 **Tudors.** [GODWIN (Francis, *bp. of Llandaff and Hereford*)] Rervm Anglicarvm Henrico viii., Edvvardo vi. et Maria regnantibus, Annales. *Apud Ioannem Billium*, 1628, *some outer margins sl. soiled*, [vii+]246[+i] pp., sm. 4to, *modern panelled sheep* (STC 11946) **£110.00**

434 **Turkey.** MIGNOT (Abbé) The History of the Turkish, or Ottoman Empire, from its Foundation in 1300, to the Peace of Belgrade in 1740. To which is prefixed an historical Discourse on Mahomet and his Successors. Translated from the French by A. Hawkins. 4 Vols. *Exeter, Printed and sold by R. Thorn*, 1787, 8vo, *contemp. tree calf, gilt, leather labels, short crack in two joints, y.e.* **£75.00**

435 **Valois.** MENESTRIER (Cl. Francois) Les Devoirs Funebres rendus a la Memoire de Madame Royale . . . et de Madame la Fuchesse Royale Francoise de Valois . . . [*s.a.l.n.* 1664], *drop title, embrowned throughout*, [iv+]31 pp., sm. 4to., *hf. brown roan, marb. bds., lettered* **£30.00**

436 —— MENESTRIER (Cl. Francois) Les Larmes de l'Amour et de la Maieste au duces de Madame la Duchesse Royale Francoise de Valois . . . dans l'année de son Mariage avec S.A.R. Charles Emmanuel II. [*s.a.l.n.* 1664], *drop title, some browning throughout*, 19 pp., sm. 4to, *hf. brown roan, marb. bds., lettered* **£35.00**

437 **A Vindication** of Addresses in general, and of the Middle Temple Address and Proceedings in particular. In Answer to the Impartial Account of Addresses, wherein the Popular pretences of some men are exposed. By a Barrester of the Middle Temple. [*Printed by N. Thompson*, 1681—col.], *two corners torn in upper margin*, 8 pp., folio, *disbound* (Wing V469) **£15.00**

438 **Voltaire** (Francois Marie Arouet de) Letters concerning the English Nation. [Trans. by John Lockman]. *Printed for C. Davis and A. Lyon*, 1733, FIRST EDITION, *portrait from another source tipped in, sl. soiling to verso of title*, [xiv+ii(adverts.)+]253[+xviii] pp., 8vo, *contemp. calf, corners sl. worn, newly rebacked, leather label* (Sabin 100751) **£120.00**
¶The first four letters are devoted to William Penn and to Quakers. Four other letters deal with Isaac Newton and his theories.

439 **Votes** of the House of Commons in the Parliament begun at Westminster the 4th day of November, in the Fourth Year of the Reign of King William and Queen Mary . . .[comprising 11 numbers]. *Printed by Thomas Braddyll and Robert Everingham*, 1692, *browning throughout*, 41 pp., folio, *disbound* (Wing *V2764) **£25.00**

440 **Wales.** AN ACT for taking away the Court holden before the President and Council of the Marches of Wales. *Printed by Charles Bill and Thomas Newcomb*, 1689, [ii+]2 pp., folio, *disbound* **£18.00**

441 —— WILLIAMS (W. R.) The Parliamentary History of the Principality of Wales, from the earliest Times to the present Day, 1541-1895 . . . together with Particulars of the various contested Elections, Double Returns and Petitions. *Brecknock, Privately Printed for the Author* . . . 1895, 300 *copies*, xiv+209[+xviii] pp., *some discolouration*, 4to, *orig. cloth* **£35.00**

442 **[Walpole** (Sir Robert)] A Letter from a Foreign Minister in England to Monsieur Pettecum, containing the True Reasons of the late Changes in the Ministry . . . transl. from the French Original. *Printed for J. Baker*, 1710, 15[+i] pp., sm. 8vo, *disbound*, scarce **£55.00**

443 **Walsingham** (Thomas) Historia Brevis, ab Edwardo primo, ad Henricum quintum. *Excusum apud Henricum Binnemann*, 1574, *title within woodcut border* [McK. 147], *woodcut portraits of the six monarchs on verso, large device on verso of last lf.*, *Bb²⁻⁶ slightly short in tail margins, some early marginal notes and underlinings*, folio, *English (London) blind-stamped calf over wooden bds.* [Oldham SWb5 with another unidentified roll], *sometime rebacked and lettered, lacks part of clasps* (STC 25004) **£750.00**

444 —— Ypodigma Nevstriae vel Normanniae: ab irruptione Normannorum vsq; ad annum 6. regni Henrici quinti. *In aedibus Iohannis Daii*, 1574, *title within woodcut border* [McK. 76—sl. modified], *woodcut portraits of the seven Norman dukes on verso, a few fox marks near end, otherwise a clean copy (? washed)*, [iv+]197[+v] pp., folio, *full crimson morocco, lettered, by Sangorski and Sutcliffe* (STC 25005) **£325.00**
¶The object of this work was to provide Henry v. with an instructive summary of the history of his predecessors, the dukes of Normandy; and to furnish an historical justification for his invasion of France.

445 **Warmstry** (Thomas) Ramus Olivae; or. an Humble Motion for Peace: Presented to His Sacred Majesty, and the Honourable Houses of Parliament: and commended to the consideration of the people, for the composing the miserable Distractions of this Kingdome, and for the prevention of a further shedding of Christian Bloud. *Oxford, Printed by H. Hall*, 1644, *sl. discolouration*, [ii+]54 pp., sm. 4to, *marb. wrappers* (Wing W889: Madan 1638) **£40.00**

446 **Weaving.** AN ACT for Regulating the Making of Stuffs in Norfolk and Norwich. *Printed by Edward Husband and John Field*, 1650, [ii+]9 pp., folio, *disbound* **£21.00**

447 **Webb** (Sidney) Labour in the Longest Reign, 1837-1897, issued under the Auspices of the Fabian Society. *Grant Richards*, 1897, *a few marginal pencil notes*, 62[+ii] pp., sm. 8vo, *orig. red cloth backstrip faded* **£30.00**

448 **Wellington.** ELLIOTT (George) The Life of the most noble Arthur duke of Wellington, from the period of his first Achievements down to the Battle of Waterloo, and his Invasion of France in 1815 . . . Second Edition, *Printed for Sherwood, Neely and Jones*, 1816, *portrait and 2 maps, one folding, some discolouration*, xiv+680[+xxii] pp., 8vo, *contemp. calf, elaborately gilt, lettered* **£38.00**

449 **[Wellwood** (James)] An Answer to the Late King James's Declaration to all his Pretended Subjects in the Kingdom of England, dated at Dublin Castle, May 8. 1689. Ordered . . . to be burnt by the Common-Hangman. *Printed for Dorman Newman*, 1689, *inner margin of title repaired, soiled and stained throughout*, [ii+]31[+i] pp., sm. 4to, *new blue wrappers* (Wing W1298) **£30.00**

450 **William III.** His Majesties Letter to the Lord Bishop of London, to be Communicated to the Two Provinces of Canterbury and York. *Printed by Charles Bill and Thomas Newcomb*, 1689/90, 4 pp., folio, *unbound* (Wing W2355) **£15.00**

451 —— Prince William of Orange his Declaration: shewing the Reasons why he Invades England. With a Short Preface and some modest Remarks on It. *Published by Randal Taylor*, 1688, *general soiling, some short tears in margins*, 32 pp., sm. 4to, *disbound* (Wing W2331) **£18.00**

452 **[Wolff** (Christian)] The Real Happiness of a People under a Philosophical King demonstrated, not only from the Nature of Things, but from the undoubted Experience of the Chinese under their first Founder Fohi, and his Illustrious Successors, Hoam Ti, and Xin Num. *Printed for M, Cooper*, 1750, FIRST EDITION IN ENGLISH, [viii+]viii+96 pp., 8vo, *contemp. mottled calf, corners worn, sides little rubbed, newly rebacked, unlettered, g.e.* **£50.00**

453 **Wolsey** (Cardinal) [CAVENDISH (George)] The Negotiations of Thomas Woolsey, the great Cardinall of England, containing his life and Death, viz. 1. The Originall of his promotion. 2. The Continuance of his Magnificence. 3. His Fall, Death, and Buriall . . . *Printed for William Sheares*, 1641, *engraved portrait, few marginal notes, discolouration throughout, sm. tear in upper margin of* H^3 *and* h^3, [xii+]118(shd. read 122) pp., sm. 4to, *early hf. calf, marb. bds., joints cracking, some rubbing* (Wing C1619) **£75.00**
¶Gathering h and i are additional and placed between G and H: while the text is conjugate, the pagination is erratic.

454 **Wood** (Anthony) Athenae Oxonienses. An Exact History of all the Writers and Bishops who have had their Education in the most Ancient and Famous University of Oxford, Oxford, from the fifteenth Year of King Henry the Seventh, A.D. 1500, to the Author's Death in November 1695 . . . to which are added, the Fasti, or Annals of the said University. 2 Vols. in 1, Second Edition. *Printed for R. Knaplock, D. Midwinter, and J. Tonson*, 1721, *titles in red and black, some discolouration throughout*, folio, *18th cent. hf. calf, leather label, marb. bds. rubbed* **£55.00**

455 **Wraxall** (N. William) Memoirs of the Courts of Berlin, Dresden, Warsaw, and Vienna, in the Years 1777, 1778, and 1779. 2 Vols. Third Edition. *Printed by Luke Hansard, for T. Cadell and W. Davies*, 1806, xii+418:xii+510 pp., 8vo, *contemp. tan calf, tooled in black and gilt, lettered, g.e., upper joint of vol. i cracked* **£20.00**

456 **Yarranton** (Andrew) England's Improvement by Sea and Land, to Out-do the Dutch without fighting, to pay Debts without Moneys . . . [Part I. only]. *Printed by R. Everingham*, 1677, *with 6 plates (ex8), three torn, but repaired, imprimatur lf. present*, [xxxix+]195 pp., sm. 4to, *contemp. mottled calf, corners worn, sl. rubbed, unlettered* (Wing Y13) **£50.00**

ADDENDA

457 **Ashton** (John, *Jacobite*). [FOWLER (Edward) *bp.*] An Answer to the Paper delivered by Mr. Ashton at his Execution to Sir Francis Child: Sheriff of London, &c. together with the paper it self. *Printed for Robert Clavell*, 1690, *lacks A1 (? blank), some browning*, 31[+i] pp., sm. 4to, *disbound* (Wing F.1695) **£45.00**
¶A Jacobite conspirator, John Ashton, who was a clerk of the closet to Mary of Modena, was hanged at Tyburn. His 'Paper' defending his principles was published in England, France and Holland, and greatly alarmed the authorities. Bp. Fowler's 'Answer' represented it as a manifesto of the Jacobite party, and tried to confute, in detail, his arguments against the lawfulness of William III's accession to the throne. (D.N.B.).

458 **CharlesI.** Julii 4. 1642. The Declaration . . . or, Five severall passages of State, viz. 1 His Maaiesties Commission of Array. 2. His Proclamation upon the same. 3. His Majestie Letter to the County of Leycester. 4. The Declaration of the Houses of Parliament concerning the said Commission of Array and His Majesties Proclamation. Lastly divers Acts and Statutes thereupon annexed. Whereby it appears that the said Commission is not warranted by any Act of Parliament . . . *Printed for Ioseph Hunscot and Iohn Wright*, 1642, *soiled throughout, small stamp on verso of last lf.*, 29 pp., sm. 4to, *disbound* (Wing E1446) **£35.00**

459 **Fens.** LABELYE (Charles) The Result of a View of the Great Level of the Fens, taken at the Desire of his Grace the Duke of Bedford, &c. Governor, and the Gentlemen of the Corporation of the Fens, in July 1745. *Printed by George Woodfall*, 1745, *errata lf. before text, rubber stamp on title, small hole in one margin*, viii+74 pp., sm. 4to, *new qtr. tan calf, leather label* **£100.00**
¶"These *Fenny* surrounded Grounds in former Times have been dry and profitable; and so may be hereafter, if due Provision be made." (Commissioner of Sewers, AD 1569).

460 **Godwin** (William) Enquiry concerning Political Justice, and its Influence on Morals and Happiness. Second Edition, corrected. 2 Vols. *Printed for G. G. and J. Robinson*, 1796, *hf. titles present*, xxiii+464: x+545 pp., 8vo, *an excellent copy in contemp. marb. calf, gilt, leather labels, y.e.* **£300.00**

461 **Kingston upon Hull.** The DECLARATION and Votes of both Houses of Parliament, concerning the Magazine at Hull, and Sir Iohn Hotham Governour thereof. *Printed by Robert Barker, and by the Assigns of John Bill*, 1642, *staining in inner margins, last lf. sl. damaged*, [ii+]6 pp., sm. 4to, *sewed, untrimmed* (Wing E1326) **£45.00**

462 **Letters** from the Living to the Living, relating to the Present Transactions both Public and Private, with their several Answers . . . written by Several Hands. *Printed in the Year* 1703, xv+215+22 pp., 8vo, *contemp. panelled calf, unlettered* **£20.00**

463 **[Love** (Christopher)] A Modest and Clear Vindication of the Serious Representation, and late Vindication of the Ministers of London, from the Scandalous Aspersions of John Price, in a Pamphlet of his, Entituled Clerico-Classicum or, the Clergies Alarum to a Third War. Wherein the King-killing Doctrine is confuted. The Authors by him alledged, as defending it, cleared. The Ministers of London vindicated. The follies and falsities of Iohn Price discovered. The Protestation, Vow and Covenant explained. *Printed for Stephen Bowtell*, 1649, iv+71 pp., sm. 4to, *sewed* (Wing L3168) **£40.00**

464 **Maunder** (Samuel) The Biographical Treasury; a Dictionary of Universal Biography reconstructed, thoroughly revised, and partly rewritten with above 1000 additional Memoirs and Notices, by William L. R. Cates . . . *Longmans, Green, & Co.*, 1876, *engr. frontis.*, [vi+]1313[+i] pp., th. sm. 8vo, *crimson calf, gilt, leather label, arms on side* **£45.00**

465 **Military.** To the Right Honorable the Lords and Commons assembles in High Covrt of Parliament. The humble Petition of the Lord Major . . . of the City of London, in Common Councell assembled. With the Answer of the Lords and Commons to the said Petition. *Printed by Richard Cotes*, 1646, 14[+i] pp., sm. 4to, *sewed, lower margins roughly trimmed* (Wing T1690) **£30.00**
¶The Petition calls for the disbanding of the Army assembled in London.

466 —— The Trve Coppy of a Letter sent by Mr. Speaker to the Sheriffes of severall Counties, namely: Worcester, Cambridge, Huntington, Leicester, Northampton, Warwick, and Rutland which have not as yet paid in the Poll-Money. With the Copy of an Order . . . for the speedy transportation of that Money to York for disbanding of his Majesties Army. *Printed in the Yeare*, 1641, *worming in upper qtr. with sl. loss of letters*, [ii+]5 pp., sm. 4to, *disbound* (Wing E2379) **£45.00**

467 **Peninsular War.** MOORE (James) A Narrative of the Campaign of the British Army in Spain, commanded by his Excellency Lieut. General Sir John Moore, authenticated by original Papers and original Letters. Second Edition, corrected. *Printed for Joseph Johnson*, 1809, *with portrait, a view of Corunna (lower margin trimmed) and 2 folding maps, inserted a broadside of 'Lines on the Burial of Sir John Moore, 1890', by Charles Woolfe, upper margin of which has been repaired, some foxing of plates and off-setting*, xii+88+238[+i] pp., 4to, *hf. calf, marb. bds., little rubbed* **£85.00**
¶The appendix, with the exception of the last lf., has been bound before the text.

468 **Raleigh** (Sir Walter) The Works, Political, Commercial, and Philosophical; together with his Letters and Poems. The Whole never before collected together, and some never yet printed. To which is prefix'd a new Account of his Life by Tho. Birch. 2 Vols. *Printed for J. Dodsley*, 1751, *portrait*, [ii+]cxx+280[+ii]: [ii+]400 pp., 8vo, *contemp. sprinkled calf, gilt, leather labels, edges and joints rubbed, lacks free and papers at rear of vol. ii* **£75.00**

469 **Scotland.** BROWNE (James) A History of the Highlands and of the Highland Clans; with an extensive Selection of the hitherto inedited Stuart Papers; a New Edition. 4 Vols. *A. Fullarton and Co.*, 1848, *with a folding map (splits in folds)*, 8 *portraits*, 26 *scenes*, 22 *Tartans (coloured)*, 9 *plates of arms, and numerous woodcuts in the text, some foxing to margins of plates*, 8vo, *hf. calf, sometime rebacked, orig. backstrips mounted* **£95.00**

470 **Scrinia Ceciliana:** Mysteries of State & Government: in Letters of the late Famous Lord Burghley, and other Grand Ministers of State: in The Reigns of Queen Elizabeth and King James. Being a further Additional Supplement to the Cabala. as also Many Remarkable Passages faithfully Revised, and no where else Published. With two exact Tables: the one of the Letters, the other of Things most Observable. *Printed for G. Bedel and T. Collins*, 1663, *title printed in red and black*, [xv+]224[+viii] pp., sm. 4to, *new qtr. tan calf, leather label* (Wing S2109) **£75.00**

471 **Shaftesbury** (Anthony Ashley Cooper, *earl of*) Characteristicks of Men, Manners, Opinions, Times. 3 Vols. Fifth Edition, corrected, with the Addition of a Letter concerning Design. [*Printed by John Darby*], 1732, *portrait, engr. titles, lacks final blank in vol. 3*, iv+364: 443: iv+410[+liv] pp., 8vo, *contemp. black calf, gilt, backstrips chipped, end papers soiled* **£85.00**

472 **[Sheridan** (Thomas)] A Discourse of the Rise & Power of Parliaments, of Law's, of Courts of Judicature, of Liberty, Property, and Religion, of the Interest of England in reference to the Designs of France; of Taxes and of Trade. In a Letter from a Gentleman of the Country to a Member in Parliament. *Printed in the Year*, 1677, *small flaw in inner margin of title and ff. lf., some soiling and general discolouration*, pp. [xxxiv+]7-245[+i], (has both errata), sm. 8vo, *contemp. calf, unlettered, split in upper joint* (Wing S3225: Kress 1453) **£160.00**
¶"When the Parliament have setled the Laws, I wish they woud think of som more fitting restraint of Offences, that what the penal Statutes direct almost for every crime, The *Loss of Life*." (The Author).

473 **Wiltshire Resolvtion,** presented with the Contributions of divers Gentlemen to His Majesties Commissioners at Oxford, also the Ingagement and Resolution of the Principall Gentlemen of the County of Salop, for the raising and maintaining of Forces at their owne charge, for the defence of His Majestie, their Country, and more particularly the Fortunes, Persons, and Estates of the Subscribers thereunto. *Oxford, Printed by L. Leichfield*, 1642, *all ll. becoming separated at fold*, 7 pp., sm. 4to, *unbound* (Wing W2961: Madan 1121) **£40.00**

474 **Witchcraft.** HUTCHINSON (Francis) An Historical Essay concerning Witchcraft, with Observations upon Matters of Fact; tending to clear the Texts of the Sacred Scriptures, and confute the vulgar Errors about that Point. and also Two Sermons: one in Proof of the Christian Religion; the other concerning Good and Evil Angels. Second Edition, with considerable Additions. *Printed for R. Knaplock, and D. Midwinter*, 1720, [xxxii+]336 pp., 8vo, *contemp. panelled calf, sometime rebacked and corners repaired, but now rubbed, unlettered* (Sabin 34063) **£90.00**

Catalogue A23

from

Blackwell's Rare Books

(1981)

ANTIQUARIAN HISTORY

HISTORY

PLEASE QUOTE CATALOGUE A23 WHEN ORDERING

Codeword: 'BUSBY'

Please address all orders from this catalogue to:–
BLACKWELL'S RARE BOOKS, FYFIELD MANOR, FYFIELD, NR. ABINGDON, OXON OX13 5LR
Please quote your Blackwell's account number when ordering. ***Telephone:*** **0865-390692**

1 **A'Beckett** (Gilbert Abbott) The Comic History of England. 2 Vols. *The Punch Office*, 1847/8, FIRST EDITION, *with 20 coloured steel engravings (one torn in margin) and 240 woodcuts, by John Leech, occasional slight foxing*, xii+320:xii+304., 8vo., *contemp. hf. calf, backstrips gilt, leather label, marbled bds. rubbed* **£45.00**

2 **Addington** (William) An Abridgement of Penal Statutes, which exhibit at one View, the Offence; the Punishment or Penalty annexed to that Offence; the Mode of Recovering and Application of the Penalty; the Number of Witnesses and Justices necessary to convict the Offender; with a Reference to the Chapter and Section of the enacting Statute. *W. Strahan and M. Woodfall, for P. Uriel, T. Cadell, E. & C. Dilly, and J. Robson*, 1775, viii+558[+xxxviii] pp., oblong 8vo, *contemp. hf. calf, leather label, new marbled paper to sides* **£35.00**

3 **America. Brissot de Warville** (Jacques Pierre) New Travels in the United States of America. Performed in 1788. Translated from the French [by Joel Barlow]. *Dublin, W. Corbet for P. Byrne, A. Grueber* ... 1792, *folding table, library stamp on title*, [iii+]483[+iii] pp., 8vo, *contemp. tree calf. leather label, y.e., head and tail of back-strip slightly worn* (Sabin 8026) **£95.00**

¶ 'The author came to the United States just before the French Revolution, for the purpose of selecting a suitable place for establishing a colony of respectable persons, who had determined to abandon the then despotic government of France, and seek an asylum under the mild and equal government of the United States.' (Sabin)

4 ——BROUGHAM (Henry Peter, *Baron Brougham and Vaux)* The Speech before the House of Commons, Friday, April 1, 1808, in Support of the Petitions from London, Liverpool and Manchester, against the Orders in Council ..*J. M'Creery, for J. Ridgway*, 1808, FIRST EDITION, *dust soiling of title, last page and some margins*, ix+84 pp., 8vo, *stab sewed as issued, edges untrimmed*, scarce **£85.00**

¶ Brougham's first speech in his battle to have the Orders in Council of Jan. and Nov. 1807 repealed. The ultimate repeal of these orders in 1812 came too late to avoid the war with America. (See Palgrave. Sabin 8415)

5 ——DUMMER, (Jeremiah) A Defence of the New-England Charters. *J. Almon*, [1765], 88 pp., 8vo, *new qtr. calf, lettered, marbled bds.* (Sabin 22197) **£120.00**

6 ——FORD (Timothy) Eulogy on John Adams, delivered, ... at the Request of the Honourable the Intendant and Wardens of the City of Charlston. *Charlston, Ellis & Neufville*, 1826, *embrowned, small hole in last lf. with part loss of two words*, 39 pp., 8vo, *blue bds., paper label* (Sabin 25071) **£16.00**

7 ——HAMILTON (Alexander, *Major-General*) Collection of the Facts and Documents, relative to the Death of Major-General Alexander Hamilton; with Comments: together with the various Orations, Sermons, and Eulogies, that have been published or written on his Life and Character. *New York, Printed by Hopkins and Seymour, for I. Riley and Co.*, 1804, *embrowned throughout, tears in a few margins*, [iii+]238 pp., 8vo, *contemp. sprinked calf, corners worn, newly rebacked, leather label* **£30.00**

8 ——JEWITT (John R.) The Adventures and Sufferings of John R. Jewitt, only Survivor of the Ship Boston, during a Captivity of nearly three Years among the Savages of Nootka Sound; with an Account of the Manners, Mode of living, and religious opinions of the Natives of Nootka Sound; with an Account [and Vocabulary] of the Manners, Mode of Living, and Religious Opinions of the Natives. *America Printed Edinburgh, Re-printed for Archd. Constable & Co., and Hurst, Robinson, & Co.* 1824, *embrowned throughout, library stamp on title*, iv+237 pp., 12mo, *contemp. calf, leather labels, tail of backstrip defective and joints cracking* (Sabin 36123) **£45.00**

9 ——[JOHNSTON (Elizabeth B.)] A Visit to the Cabinet of the United States Mint, at Philadelphia. *Press of J. B. Lippincott & Co.* 1876, *frontis. and 6 other wood engravings*, 92 pp., sm. 8vo, *tan cloth* **£35.00**

10 ——LAWRENCE (William Beach) The Origin and Nature of the Representative and Federative Institutions of the United States of America; an Anniversary Discourse, delivered before the New York Historical Society, on the 19th April, 1832. *New York, G. & C. & H. Carvill*, 1832, 44 pp., 8vo, *paper wrappers* **£18.00**

11 ——QUAKERS. RECKITT (William) and James GOUGH. Some Account of the Life and Gospel Labours of William Reckett [sic], also, Memoirs of the Life, Religious Experiences, and Gospel Labours of James Gough. *Philadelphia, Joseph Cruikshank*, 1783, [i+]164:xxiv+184 pp., 12mo, *contemp. sheep, sometime rebacked, leather label* (Sabin 68371) **£30.00**

12 ——STAMP ACT. A List of the Minority in the House of Commons, who voted against the Bill to Repeal the American Stamp Act. *Paris, chez J. W.*, 1766, 8pp., sm. 8vo, *recent tan calf over earlier marb. bds.* rare (Sabin 41453) **£75.00**

13 ——STAMP ACT. Protest against the Bill to repeal the American Stamp Act, Last Session. *Paris, chez J. W.*, 1766, *title sl. soiled*, 16 pp.:
[and]
Second Protest, with a list of Voters against the Bill to repeal the American Stamp Act, of Last Session. *Paris, chez J. W.*, 1766, 15 pp.:
Two items bound together, 8vo, *recent qtr. calf over earlier marb. bds.*, rare (Sabin 66103 – 2 pts.) **£100.00**

14 ——STAMP ACT. The Rights of Parliament Vindicated, on Occasion of the late Stamp-Act. In which is exposed the Conduct of the American Colonists. Addressed to all the People of Great Britain. *J. Almon*, 1766, *sl. discolouration of paper*, 44pp., sm. 8vo, *binders' cloth, old leather label mounted on upper cover* (Sabin 71374) **£70.00**

15 ——WEBSTER (Daniel) Discourse . . . in Commemoration of the First Settlement of New England. Second Edition. *Boston, Wells and Lilly*, 1821, *embrowned, some margins fragile, some corners dog-eared*, 55[+i] pp., 8vo, *sewed, lacks pale blue wrappers* (Sabin 102262) **£15.00**

16 ——Speech on the President's [Andrew Jackson] Protest: delivered in the Senate of the United States, May 7th 1834. *Washington, Gales and Seaton*, 1834, *dust soiled and little damp stained*, 31pp., 8vo, *sewed* (Sabin 102291) **£15.00**

17 ——WOOD (James G.) A Reply to the Speech of the Hon. C. Sumner on the "Alabama Claims." *Cambridge, Henry Wallis*, 1869, *discoloured, dust soiled*, 25 pp., 8vo, *sewed* **£15.00**

18 **Angliae Ducus & Tutamen:** or, the Glory and Safety of this Nation, under our Present King and Queen; plainly demonstrating, that it is not only the Duty, but the Interest of all Jacobites and Disaffected Persons to act for, and submit to, this Government. *Richard Baldwin*, 1691, *outer margins discoloured*, [ii+] 62 pp., sm. 4to, *disbound* (Wing A3181) **£85.00**

19 **Anne** [POVEY (Charles)] An Inquiry into the Miscarriages of the Last Four Years Reign . . . Presented to the Freeholders of Great Britain, against the next Election of a New Parliament. *Printed for the Author* . . . 1714, *small stamp on verso of title*, 32 pp., sm. 4to, *disbound* **£21.00**

20 ——SWIFT (Jonathan) The History of the Four Last Years of the Queen. Published from the last Manuscript copy, Corrected and Enlarged by the Author's own Hand. *A. Millar*, 1758, FIRST EDITION, *with Z3 so signed but 2A3 signed 2A4* [*see Rothchild 2187*], xiv+392 pp. 8vo, *contemp. sprinkled calf, unlettered, little rubbed, joints cracking* (Teerink 809) **£80.00**

¶With the book label of Tho. Drake Tyrwhitt on front paste-down.

21 [**Anon**] The Case of Dunkirk faithfully Stated, and Impartially Considered. *A. Moore*, 1730, *embrowned*, 32 pp.:
[?**Hoadley** (Benjamin)] Faults on both Sides: or, an Essay upon the Original Cause, Progress, and Mischievous Consequences of the Factions in this Nation . . . Second Edition, 1710, *embrowned*, 38 pp.:
[**Anon**]Two Letters. One from a Lady to a Friend who has married a Roman-Catholick Gentleman. The Other . . . to the said Gentleman, by which he was converted from the Popish Religion to the Protestant. *James and John Knapton*, 1727, *soiled*, 40 pp.:
[**Anon**] An Exact Alphabetical List of the Members of Parliament who Voted For and Against Bringing in the Tobacco or Excise Bill, March 16, 1722/3 . . . *W. Fowles*, 1733, *embrowned, all fore-edges trimmed with some loss*, 6 pp.:
[**Anon**] The Fundamental Laws of Physick. Or, the Nobility and Gentry cannot be Preserv'd by the Modern Practice in the Difficult and Dangerous Diseases, *J. Robinson, sold by A. Baldwin*, 1711, *embrowned and soiled*, 29 pp.:
[**Swift** (Johathan)] Schemes from Ireland, for the Benefit of the Body Natural, Ecclesiastical, and Politick . . . *Dublin Printed, London, Re-printed for J. Roberts*, 1732, 31[+i] pp., (see Teerink 958):
[**Anon**] A Short State of the War and the-Peace. *John Morphew*, 1715, *heavily foxed*, 24 pp.:
Seven pieces together, 8vo, *contemp. mottled calf, unlettered, corners slightly worn, upper joint cracking* **£100.00**

22 [**Anon**] The Thoughts of an Impartial Man upon the present Temper of the Nation; offer'd to the Consideration of the Freeholders of Great Britain. *J. Roberts*, 1733, *binder's blanks*, [i+] 29 pp., 8vo, *modern marbled bds., leather label* **£35.00**

23 **Anti-Papists.** An Act for Discovering, Convicting, and Repressing of Popish Recusants. *Henry Hills and John Field*, 1657, *embrowned*, [i+] 21 pp., folio, *grey bds.* (Wing E1030) **£18.00**

24 **Army Council.** A Particular Charge or Impeachment in the Name of his Excellency Sir Thomas Fairfax, and the Army under his Command, against Denzill Holles, Esquire, Sir Philip Stapleton . . . Members of the Honorable House of Commons. *George Whittington*, 1647, 28 [+i] pp., sm. 4to, *unstitched, edges untrimmed* (Wing E. 741) **£30.00**

25 [**Aulnoy** (Marie Catherine Jumelle de Berneville, *Comtesse d'*)] Memoirs of the Court of England: in the Reign of King Charles II. Containing the Amours of that Prince, the Duke of Monmouth, Earl of Argyle. —— of Buckingham, —— of A——n, Earl of Oxford —— Lord Grey, &c. —— St. Albans. Second Edition, Corrected. To which is added, The Lady's Packet of Letters . . . *J. Woodward; and J. Morphew*, 1708, *some browning throughout, paper fragile with some marginal tears and slight loss of a few letters, one lf, torn*, [viii+] 157+136+83 pp., 8vo, *modern brown morocco, leather label* **£45.00**

26 [**Ayscu** (Edward)] A Historie Contayning the VVarres, Treaties, Marriages, and other occurrents between England and Scotland, from King William the Conqueror, untill the happy Vnion of them both in our gratious King Iames. With a briefe declaration of the first Inhabitants of this Island: And what seuerall Nations haue sithence settles them – selues therin one after an other: *G. Eld.* 1607, *large woodcut on title, some marginal notes in early hand and long biographical sketch of Edgar Athelinge on free endpaper facing title, upper margin of title cut away with no loss, a few pp. slightly soiled, lacks A1 and A8 (both blanks)*, [xii+] 396 pp., sm. 4to, *contemp. tan calf, lined and decorated in gilt, paper label, lacking the ties* (STC 1014) **£300.00**

27 **Bacon** (Francis, *Lord Verulam*) and Francis **Godwyn,** *Bp. of Hereford*. The History of the Reigns of Henry the Seventh, Henry the Eighth, Edward the Sixth, and Queen Mary. . . . *W. G. for R. Scot, T. Basset, J. Wright, R. Chiswell, and J. Edwyn*, 1676, *engraved portrait of Bacon*, [xii+] 201 pp., folio, *contemp. dark brown calf, corners slightly worn, newly rebacked, leather label* (Wing B 300: Gibson 121) **£65.00**

28 [**Barnard** (Sir John, *Lord Mayor of London*) A Present for an Apprentice: or, a Sure Guide to gain both Esteem and an Estate. With Rules for his Conduct to his Master, and in the World. The Second Edition . . . *T. Cooper*, 1740, *tear across title, soiled, some browning*, [iv+] 76 pp., 8vo, *contemp. mottled sheep, unlettered, joints cracking* **£30.00**

29 **Bastille.** LINGUET (Simon Nicolas Henri) Memoirs of the Bastille. Containing a full Exposition of the Mysterious Policy and Despotic Oppression of the French Government, in the interior Administration of that State Prison. Interspersed with a Variety of curious Anecdotes. Translated from the French . . . *Dublin, J. A. Husband for Messrs. H. and W. Whitestone* . . . 1783, xii+ 114:162 pp., 12mo, *contemp. sheep, lettered, backstrip little defective* **£45.00**

30 ——RENNEVILLE (Constantin de) The French Inquisition: or, the History of the Bastille in Paris, the State-Prison of France: in which is an Account of the manner of the Apprehending of Persons sent thither; and of the barbarous Usage they meet with there . . . transl. from the Original . . . *A. Bell, T. Varnham, and J. Osbourne; W. Taylor and J. Baker*, 1715, *one fore margin defective with slight loss of letter press*, [iv+]322[+ii] pp., 8vo, *contemp. panelled calf, newly rebacked, leather label*, scarce **£42.00**

31 [**Beach** (Philip)] A Letter to Thomas Burnet, Esq; shewing that he hath used the same Fidelity in printing a Letter of Dr. Beach's in the Life of Bishop Burnet, as the Editors of Bishop Burnet's History of his own Times have exemplified in the Publication thereof: . . . *Richard Reily*, 1736, xii+64 pp., 8vo, *disbound* **£15.00**

32 [**Beaufort** (Louis de)] A Dissertation upon the Uncertainty of the Roman History during the First Five hundred Years. Translated from the French. *T. Waller*, 1740, *some staining, tear to* H5 *affecting running title and to lower margin of* [H10], [iv+]iv+334[+i – cat.] pp., 12mo, *contemp. calf, leather label, corners and edges worn, joints cracked but strong* **£45.00**
¶The first work to examine scientifically the histories of the early centuries of Roman History.

33 **Bégin** (E. A.) Histoire des Duches de Lorraine et de Bar, et des trois Évèchés (Meurthe, Meuse, Moselle, Vosges). 2 Vols. *Nancy, chez Vidart et Jullien*, 1833, *foxed*, [iii+]xx+380: [iii+] 404 pp., 8vo, *qtr. calf, lettered, marbled bds. rubbed* **£18.00**

34 **Bembo** (Pietro) Della Historia Vinitiana di M. Pietro Bembo Card. volgarmente scritta. Libri xii. *Vinegria*, [colophon:– *appresso Gualtero Scotto*], 1552, FIRST EDITION IN ITALIAN, *woodcut device on title and verso of last lf., historiated initials, slight marginal staining*, [xiv+]179[+i] ff., sm. 4to, *seventeenth century calf, corners worn, newly rebacked with orig. leather label* (Adams B599: Graesse i/p. 333) **£65.00**

35 **Bentivoglio** (Cardinal Guido) Della Gverra di Fiantra [1559–1607], 3 Parts in 1 Vol., *Venetia, appresso il Ciera*, 1702, *divisional titles*, [i+]256[+xii]:168[+viii]:236[+ xi] pp., sm. 4to, *contemp. sprinkled calf, leather label, backstrip gilt, joints cracked, corners little worn* **£65.00**

36 ——Lettres sur diverses matieres de Politique & autres importans sujets; écrites aux premiers Princes de l'Europe, & à plusieurs personnes considerables par leur scavoir & par leurs emplois. Traduites en Francois, avec l'Italien à côté; par le Sieur [J.] De Veneroni. *Bruxelles, chez les T' Serstevens*, 1713, *engraved title, printed title in red and black*, 399(shd. read 395) [+xi – cat.] pp., 12mo, *contemp. sprinkled sheep, leather label (partly defective), slight rubbing* **£45.00**
¶The work is dedicated by the translator to Bishop Bossuet, of Meaux.

37 **Bernardi** (John, *major*) A Short History of the Life of Major John Bernardi, written by himself in Newgate, where he has been for near 33 Years a Prisoner of State, without any Allowance from the Government, and could never be admitted to his Tryal. To which is added by Way of Appendix, a true copy of the Diploma, or Patent of Count of the Empire, granted to the Author's Grand-Father in the Year 1629, and a Translation of it into English, as also Copies of the Major's several Commissions, &c. *J. Newcomb, for the Benefit of the Author*, 1729, *engr. port. by Van der Gucht, errata lf. present, a skilfully washed copy*, [ii+]135+62[+i] pp., 8vo, *recased in contemp. mottled calf, and carefully rebacked, gilt, new marbled endpapers, armorial bookplate.* **£45.00**

38 **Blomfield** (Ezekiel) Lectures on the Philosophy of History, accompanied with Notes, and illustrative Engravings. *Black, Kingsbury, Parbury, and Allen. Bungay, Printed by Brightly and Childs*, 1819, *with* 12 *coloured maps*, xviii+ 161[+ix – list of subscribers] pp., 4to, *orig. drab bds., recently rebacked, paper label, edges untrimmed* **£85.00**

39 **Boufflers.** WEBSTER (Nesta H.) The Chevalier de Boufflers. A Romance of the French Revolution. *John Murray*, 1917, 9 *plates* (1 *folding*), xv+ 441 pp., 8vo, *hf. crimson calf, gilt, lettered, backstrip sunned, t.e.g., inscribed by Dennis Wheatley on front free endpaper* **£25.00**

40 **Bourne** (Thomas) A Concise History of the Moors in Spain, from their Invasion of that Kingdom to their final Expulsion from it. *F., C., and J. Rivington, and J. Hatchard*, 1811, *hf. title present, some discolouration*, xli+278 pp., 4to, *contemp. hf. calf, marbled bds. corners worn, newly rebacked, leather label* **£45.00**

41 [**Boyle** (Henry)] Honesty the best Policy: or, the History of Roger [i.e. Henry Boyle, 1st Earl of Shannon]. The Seventh Edition. Wherin the Characters and Passages, omitted by the Editor of the former Editions, are restored. To which is prefixed, a Letter from the Author to the Printer. *Dublin*, 1752, *ex libris rubber stamps*, 23 pp., 8vo, *disbound* **£25.00**

42 ——(John, *Earl of Corke and Orrery*) Letters from Italy, in the years 1754 and 1755. published from the Originals, with explanatory Notes by John Duncombe. Second Edition. *B. White*, 1774, *vignette on title, folding genealogical table, few ll. stained in margins*, [i+]lvi+268 pp., sm. 8vo, *contemp. tan calf, leather label, lower joint beginning to crack* **£40.00**

43 **Braithwait** (Richard) A Svrvey of History; or, a Nursery for Gentry. Contrived and Comprized in an Intermixt Discourse upon Historicall and Poeticall Relations . . . distinguished into several Heads for the Direction of the Reader, to all such Historical Mixtures, as be Comprehended in this Treatise . . . *I. Okes, for Iasper Emery*, 1638, *engraved title by William Marshall, slight embrowning throughout*, [xxvi+]415[+i] pp., sm. 4to, *early nineteenth-century tan calf, a little worn, newly rebacked, leather label, g.e.* (STC 3583a – variant imprint) **£85.00**

44 **Britain.** TALBOT (William) Narrative of the Whole of his Proceedings relative to Jonathan Britain [executed for forgery]. *Bristol, S. Farley* . . . [1772], *two small holes (? paper faults) with slight loss of letter-press*, 93[+i] pp., 8vo, *disbound* **£15.00**

45 **Brooke** (Henry Francis) Private Journal of Henry Francis Brooke, late Brigadier-General commanding 2nd Infantry Brigade Kandahar Field Force, Southern Afganistan, from April 22nd to August 16th, 1880. (Preface by Annie Brooke). *Dublin, William Curwen (for private circulation only)* 1881, *frontis. portrait*, viii+204 pp., 8vo, *orig. black morocco, unlettered, black edges* **£60.00**
¶This copy is inscribed by Annie Brooke for Sir Andrew and Lady Clarke. He served in India until 1880.

46 **Bruce** (Peter Henry) Memoirs of . . . a Military Officer, in the Services of Prussia, Russia, and Great Britain. Containing an Account of his Travels in Germany, Russia, Tartary, Turkey, the West Indies, &c. as also, several very interesting private Anecdotes of the Czar, Peter I. of Russia. *Dublin: J. and R. Byrn*, 1783, xv+527 pp., 8vo, *contemp. calf, leather label, y.e., two small blemishes on upper cover* **£100.00**

47 **Bryce** (James) The Holy Roman Empire. *Oxford, T. & G. Shrimpton*, 1864, FIRST EDITION, [i+] 176 pp., 8vo, *original brown cloth, recently rebacked, with old backstrip mounted, new end-papers* **£40.00**
¶The 'Arnold Prize Essay' for 1863.

48 **Buckingham.** M[ATTIEU] (P[ierre]) The Povverfvl Favorite, or the Life of Aelivs Seianvs. *Printed at Paris*, 1628, *early inscriptions in ink on title, and a small hole in title lf. (not touching letters), several contemp. small ink blots on K^3 and[K^4], corroded through with loss of a few letters, several page numerals shaved*, [ii+] 154 pp., sm. 4to, *qtr. tan morocco, linen sides, lettered* (STC 17664) **£140.00**

49 [**Budgell** (Eustace)] A Short History of Prime Ministers in Great Britain. *H. Haines*, 1733, 31 pp., 8vo, *disbound* **£10.00**
¶ Budgell, a cousin of Addison, was one of the Grub Street authors, contributor to the 'Craftsman' and originator of the 'Bee.'

50 **Burke** (Edmund) A Letter . . . to a Noble Lord [Grenville], on the Attacks made upon him and his Pension . . . by the Duke of Bedford and the Earl of Lauderdale . . . *J. Owen, and F. and C. Rivington*, 1796, FIRST EDITION, *lacking hf. title*, [ii+] 80 pp., 8vo, *disbound* (Todd 65) **£21.00**
¶ Owing to the absence of the hf. title, it is not possible to identify the impression, but certainly seventh or later.

51 ——Substance of the Speeches made in the House of Commons, on Wednesday, the 15th of December, 1779. on Mr. Burke's giving Notice of his Intention to bring in a Bill after the Christmas Recess, for the Retrenchment of Public Expences, and for the better securing the Independence of Parliament. *J. Almon*, 1779, FIRST EDITION, [ii+]17[+i] pp., 8vo, *sewed, unopened* (Todd 31) **£50.00**

52 ——Three Memorials on French Affairs. Written in the Years 1791, 1792 and 1793. *F. and C. Rivington*, 1797, FIRST EDITION, THIRD IMPRESSION, *lacks hf. title, embrowned, slight foxing at beginning and end*, [i+]xxxi+*4+ 199[+x] pp., 8vo, *contemp. hf. tan calf, leather label, crest in top compartment of backstrip, marbled bds., slightly rubbed, inscription on free endpaper by Dennis Wheatley, and with his bookplate* (Todd 69c) **£60.00**

53 ——Two Letters on the Conduct of our Domestick Parties, with regard to French Politicks; including "Observations on the Conduct of the Minority, in the Session of M.DCCXCIII." *F. and C. Rivington, also sold by J. Hatchard*, 1797, FIRST EDITION, THIRD IMPRESSION, *hf. title and advert-page little soiled*, lxxii+127[+ i]pp., 8vo, *sewed, unopened copy* (Todd 70c) **£30.00**

54 [**Burnet** (Gilbert, *Bp. of Sarum*)] An Enquiry into the Measures of Submission to the Supream Authority, and of the Grounds upon which it may be Lawful or necessary for Subjects, to defend their Religion, Lives and Liberties. [*London* 1688], *drop-title, margins cropped just touching letter press on one page, some soiling*, 8 pp., sm. 4to, *disbound* (Wing B 5808) **£20.00**

55 ——History of his Own Time, from the Restoration of K. Charles II. to the Conclusion of the Treaty of Peace at Utrecht, in the Reign of Queen Anne . . . together with the Author's Life, and some Explanatory Notes . . . 4 Vols., Third Edition. *T. Davies*, 1766, *portrait*, 8vo, *contemp. sprinkled calf, leather labels, one missing, backstrips gilt, small chip out of one, little rubbed, joints cracking* **£40.00**

56 ——The History of the Reformation of the Church of England. A New Edition. 3 Vols. in 6 (as issued). *Oxford, at the Clarendon Press*, 1816, ONE OF ABOUT 50 SETS PRINTED ON LARGE PAPER, *vignette on each title page, hf. titles to the first part of each vol., occasional slight foxing*, imp. 8vo, *contemp. hard-grained crimsom morocco, backstrips ornamentally gilded and with leather labels, sides with three line gilt fillets enclosing ornate gilt panels with floral corner-pieces, edges of covers and inner gilt borders, edges gilded over marbling, marbled end-papers* [*by Charles Lewis*] **£400.00**

57 **Burton** (John) Monasticon Eboracense: and the Ecclesiastical History of Yorkshire. Containing an Account of the first Introduction and Progress of Christianity in that Diocese, until the End of William the Conqueror's Reign. Also the Description of the Situation, Fabric, Times of Endowments of all Churches, Collegiate, Conventual, Parochial, or of peculiar Jurisdiction . . . *York, the Author, by N. Nickson*, 1758, *with 3 folding plates, snags in some folds, lacks last lf. of Index*, xii+448[+xxxii] pp., folio, *contemp. tan calf, tooled in blind and gilt* **£90.00**

59 **Byng** (John) The Torrington Diaries containing the Tours through England and Wales of the Hon. John Byng, between the years 1781 and 1794. Edited, with an Introduction, by C. Bruyn Andrews and with a general Introduction by John Beresford, [with the Supplementary volume] 5 Vols. together. *Eyre and Spottiswood*, 1934/8, *illustrations*, 8vo, *orig. cloth, a little soiled* **£85.00**

60 ['C'] A Friendly Conference concerning the New Oath of Allegiance to K. William, and Q. Mary, wherein the Objections against taking the Oaths are impartially examined, and the Reasons of Obedience Confirm'd . . . *Samuel Smith*, 1689, [ii+]35[+i] pp., sm. 4to, *grey wrappers* (Wing C1A) **£25.00**

61 **Caesar** (C. Julius) The Commentaries . . . of his Wars in Gallia; and the Civil Wars betwixt him and Pompey. Translated into English; with many Excellent and Judicious Observations thereupon. As also the Art of our Modern Training, or Tactick Practice. By Clement Edmonds. Whereunto is adjoyned the Eighth Commentary of the Wars in Gallia; with some short Observations upon it. Together with the Life of Caesar, and an Account of his Medals; revised, corrected, and enlarged. *In the Savoy, Tho. Newcomb, for Jonathan Edwin*, 1677, *frontis. portrait and 14 plates (of which 9 are folding), a few sl. frayed at fore-edge, divisional titles* [1+] 332 pp. folio, *contemp. mottled calf, corners little worn, sometime rebacked, gilt, leather label* (Wing C. 200) **£150.00**

62 **Camden** (William) Annales Regvm Anglicarvm, et Hibernicarvm, Regnante Elizabetha, ad annvm salvtis M.D.LXXXIX, [First Part]. *Guilielmi Stansbij, imp. Simonis Watersoni*, 1615, FIRST EDITION, *very slight wrinkling of ll. throughout*, [viii+]499[+xx] pp., folio, *contemp. dark brown calf, unlettered, slight rubbing at all edges, small piece missing from tail of backstrip, paste-downs lifted* (STC 4496) **£360.00**

63 **Camden** (William) Remaines concerning Britaine: their Languages. Names. Surnames. Allusions. Anagrammes. Armories. Monies . . . Epitaphes. The fift Impression, with many rare Antiquities never before imprinted. By the industry and care of Iohn Philipot. *Thomas Harper for John Waterson*, 1637, *engraved portrait and 26 armorial cuts in the text, lacks final blank, embrowned throughout, slight marginal worming*, [v+]420[+ii] pp., sm. 4to, *contemp. half calf, marbled bds., rubbed, sometime rebacked, leather label* (STC 4526) **£75.00**

64 ——BROOKE (Ralphe) A Discoverie of certaine Errovrs published in Print in the much commended Britannia, 1594. very prejudiciall to the Discentes and Successions of the auncient Nobilitie of this Realme. To which is added, the Learned Mr. Camden's Answer to this Book. *J. Bettenham, for James Woodman*, 1723, *title in red and black*, [vii+]77[+x]+32 pp., sm. 4to, *sprinkled sheep, lacks label, rubbed and corners worn, joints cracking* **£45.00**

65 [**Campbell** (Hugh Hume, *Earl of Marchmont*)] A State of the Rise and Progress of our Disputes with Spain, and of the Conduct of our Ministers relating thereto. *T. Cooper*, 1739, [ii+] 76 pp., 8vo, *grey bds, unlettered* **£21.00**

66 **Caroline** (*Princess of Wales*) The Book! or, Delicate Investigation; containing the whole Proceedings, Correspondence, Documents, Depositions, &c. upon the Subject of the Inquiry into the Conduct of H.R.H. the Princess of Wales, under a Commission, appointed by the King . . . to which is prefixed, a History of recent Events, with a full Statement of Facts, relative to the Child, now under the Protection of Her Royal Highness. *Edinburgh, James Sawers*, 1813, *light browning throughout*, xxiv+244 pp., 8vo, *modern dark brown calf, leather label* **£35.00**

67 **Cave** (William) Ecclesiastici: or, the History of the Lives, Acts, Death, & Writings, of the most Eminent Fathers of the Church, that Flourished in the Fourth Century. Wherein among other things an Account is given of the Rise, Growth, and Progress of Arianism, and all other Sects of that Age descending from it. Together with an Introduction, containing an Historical Account of the State of Paganism under the First Christian Emperours. *J. R. for Richard Chiswell*, 1683, *title in red and black, frontis., 5 cuts of coins and 9 portraits, 2pp. catalogue, some discolouration and marginal staining*, [lii+]lxxi+543[+i] pp., folio, *contemp. mottled calf, corners wearing, newly rebacked, leather label* (Wing C1596) **£75.00**

68 **Chaloner** (Thomas) De Rep. Anglorvm Instavranda libri decem, hvc accessit in Lavdem Henrici Octaui Regis quondam Angliae praestantis, carmen panegyricum. Item, de Illvstrivm qvorvndam Encomiis Miscellanea, cvm Epigrammatis, ac Epitaphiis nonnullis, eodem authore. *Thomas Vautrollerius*, 1579, *divisional titles, errata on verso of last lf. head of title neatly remargined, two small holes in one lf, a few marginal notes, stubs of two blanks before title still present*, sm. 4to, *contemp. limp vellum, gilt lines and ornaments, lacks ties, a very clean and large copy, at sometime carefully recased* (STC 4938) **£300.00**
¶ The title carries the signature of William Malim, a friend of the author and responsible for the commendatory verses. There is also another inscription at the foot on the title in a neat Chancery hand 'Malim mori; quam cedere amori . . . qth G. B.' The grandsons of Chaloner were among King Charles I's judges.

69 **Chamberlayne** (Edward) Angliae Notitia: or the Present State of England: the First [and Second] Part. Together with Divers Reflections upon the Antient State thereof. Nineth Edition, with several Additions. *In the Savoy. T. N. for J. Martin*, 1676, *title torn across and laid down, some general soiling*, [xxiii+]332:[xvii+] 287 pp., 12mo, *contemp. mottled calf, leather label, joints split at head and tail, backstrip sl. defective, arms in gilt of sides* (Wing C1827) **£50.00**

70 ——England's Wants: or, several Proposals very advantageous for England. Humbly offered to the Consideration of the Two Houses of Parliament, now Assembled at Westminster, under our most Gracious Lord and Lady, King William and Queen Mary. *R. Baldwin*, 1689, *outer margins stained*, 38 pp., sm. 4to, *disbound* (Wing C1842) **£50.00**

71 ——The Present VVarre parallel'd or a briefe Relation of the five yeares Civil Warres of Henry the Third . . . *Printed in the yeare*, 1647, *heavily embrowned, lower outer corner of A2 torn away with some loss, titled frayed at edges*, [i+] 33 pp., sm. 4to, *binder's cloth, faded* (Wing C1845) **£55.00**

72 **Charlemagne.** HEGEWISCH, (Dietrich Hermann) Histoire de l'Empereur Charlemagne, traduction libre d'Allemand. Avec un Avant-propos, quelques Notes et un Supplément du Traducteur [J. T. de Bourgoing]. *Paris, chez Henrichs*, 1805, xxiv+507[+ii – cat.] pp., 8vo, *contemp. calf, gilt, lettered, backstrip sunned* **£35.00**

72A ——UBALDINI (Petruccio) La Vita di Carlo Magno Imperadore, scritta in lingua Italiana da Petrvccio Ubaldino Cittadin Fiorentino. *Londra appresso Giouanni Wolfio Inghilese*, 1581, FIRST EDITION, *woodcut device on title* (McKerrow 216), *final lf.* [Q4] (*blank*) *present, slight dampstaining to gutters of first section*, 125 pp., sm. 4to, *eighteenth century mottled calf, gilt, leather label (chipped), joints beginning to crack, little rubbed, head and tail of backstrip little worn, silk place-marker, marbled endpapers, library label sometime removed with slight damage to endpaper* (STC 24486) **£225.00**
¶ The first book printed in Italian in London, and very scarce.

73 **Charles I.** Works: with a Collection of Declarations, Treaties, and other Papers concerning the Differences betwixt his said Majesty and his two Houses of Parliament, with the History of his Life; as also his Tryal and Martyrdome. Second Edition. *Ric. Chiswell*, 1687, *frontis., engraved title and 3 double page plates, divisional titles, damp staining throughout, heavy in places, small tear repaired*, [viii+]721[+iv] pp., folio, *contemp. sprinkled calf, rubbed and corners worn, newly rebacked, leather label* (Wing C2076) **£55.00**

74 ——Ειχωγ Βασιλιχη. The Povrtraictvre of His Sacred Maiestie in His Solitvdes and Svfferings. [*s.l., s.n.*] 1648, FIRST EDITION, THIRD ISSUE, *with A3 misnumbered A4, errata on r. [A4], misprint 180 for 108, and 'repaired' on p. 269, frontis.* [Madan 11.] *repaired, fore-edge dog-eared, no 'Explanation' lf. present, has the final blank some MS. corrections, embrowned throughout, a few small snags in some fore margins,* [viii+] 269 pp., 8vo, *contemp. calf, gilt, leather label, upper joint beginning to crack* (Madan 1) **£50.00**

75 ——By the King. A Proclamation for the prizing of Wines, [1st February], *Robert Barker and the Assigns of Iohn Bill*, 1635, **black letter,** 2 ll. printed on one side, *fold marks across centre*, 16×11½ ins. (STC 9054) **£80.00**

¶ The proclamation sets the wholesale and retail prices of imported wines, and indicated the additional charges to be made for carriage.

76 ——By the King. A Proclamation for restraining the use of Wine Casks, by Brewers and sellers of Beere and Ale, [19th November], *Robert Barker and the Assigns of John Bill*, 1637, **black letter,** 2 ll. printed on one side only, *fold marks across centre*, 15×11½ ins. (STC 9096) **£110.00**

¶ The illegal use of wine casks, etc. by the Brewers was bringing the Coopers into an inpoverished state, besides breaking existing statutes on the subject.

77 ——By the King. A Proclamation prohibiting the vse of the Net or Engine, called a Trawle, [2nd April]. *Robert Barker and the Assigns of Iohn Bill*, 1635, **black letter,** 2 ll. printed on one side, *fold marks across centre*, 15½×11 ins. (STC 9034) **£120.00**

¶ The proclamation points out that the trawl by its very action damages and destroys the spawn and fry, thereby causing an acute scarcity of fish. Previous legislation had, apparently, made little impression upon the fishermen.

78 ——By the King. A Proclamation touching common Maultsters, and Brewers [9th July], *Robert Barker and the Assigns of John Bill*, 1637, **black letter,** 3 ll. printed on one side only, *fold marks across centre*, 16×11½ ins. (STC 9089) **£100.00**

¶ Restricting the purchase of barley and other grain, for conversion to malt, to common Maltsters, and then not for the months of June to August. The proclamation also prohibited the brewing of ale by Inn-keepers, etc. unless no official brewer was operating in their locality.

79 ——HOLLINGWORTH (Richard, *the Younger*) A Defence of King Charles I. occasion'd by the Lyes and Scandals of many Bad Men of this Age. *Samuel Eddowes*, 1692, *some staining*, [ii+] 36 pp., sm. 4to, *disbound* (Wing H2502) **£45.00**

80 —— ——Defence of K. Charles the First's Holy and Divine Book, called Ειχων Βασιλιχη; against the Rude and Undutiful Assaults of the late Dr. Walker, of Essex. proving by Living and Unquestionable Evidences, the aforesaid Book to be that Royal Martyr's, and not Dr. Gauden's. *Samuel Eddowes*, 1692, iv+ 27 pp., sm. 4to, *disbound* (Wing H2503) **£45.00**

81 —— ——A Second Defence of King Charles I. by Way of Reply to an Infamous Libel, called, Ludlow's Letter to Dr. Hollingworth. *S. Eddowes . . . and Randal Taylor*, 1692, *slight staining on a few ll.*, [vii+]53[+ii] pp., sm. 4to, *disbound* (Wing H2504) **£45.00**

82 K[ILLIGREW] (H[enry]) A Sermon preached before the Kings most Excellent Majesty at Oxford [on Psalm 101. i.]. *Oxford, W. Web*, 1643, *woodcut portrait of K. Charles, paper fault to fore margin*, [iv+17] pp., (Wing K445: Madan 1272):
[and]
THREE Worthy Particulars. 1 A Letter or message sent by his Majestie to . . . Kingstone upon Hull. 2 A Catelogue of the names of all the Divines . . . 3 A true List of the Commanders . . . Also two Orders . . . from the House of Commons. *F. Cowles and T. Bates*, 1642, *arms on title, edges cropped with slight loss*, [ii+6] pp., [Wing T1125A) rare:
[and]
CHARLES I. His Majesties Declaration to all His loving Subjects, to His True Intentions in advancing lately to Brainceford [Brentford]. *Oxford, Leonard Lichfield*, 1642, [i+] 9 pp., (Wing C2246: Madan 1082):
[and]
——His Majesties Message to Both Houses of Parliament, April 28. 1642. Concerning his Refusall to passe the Bill for the Militia. *Robert Barker and the Assignes of John Bill*, 1642, *Royal Arms on verso of title*, [ii+] 5 pp., (Wing C4253):
[and]
AN ORDINANCE from His Majesty, and both Houses of Parliament. For the Ordering of the Militia of the Kingdome of England and Dominion of Wales. Also, for setting the same in a Posture of Warre. *R. O. and G. D. for F. Coules*, [1642], *Royal Arms on title and A⁴v., date cropped from title*, [i+] 5 pp., (Wing E1788)
Five Pieces bound together, sm. 4to, *hf. brown morocco, lettered, slightly rubbed* **£225.00**

¶ Of the two pieces noticed by Madan, there appear to be two contenders for the honour of authorship, in the first. Henry Killigrew was in Oxford at the time of the Sermon, but Henry King was not. A contemporary comment in *Mercurius Aulicus* is:– "They [the Parliament] have . . . printed a Sermon pretended to be Preached before His Majesty at *Oxford* by Doctor *H. K.* which is an errant forgery, the supposed author having not beene in *Oxford* . . . Neither is it usuall with His Majesty to cause those Sermons to be printed here, which are preached before His Majesty". "Presumably King was the 'supposed author' ". (Madan)

The second piece does not agree with Madan's collation in that p.9 begins 'desire Accommodation . . .'.

83 ——WALKER (Anthony) A True Account of the Author of a Book entituled Ειχωθ Βασιλιχη, or, the Portraiture of His Sacred Majesty in His Solitudes and Sufferings: Proved to be written by Dr. Gauden, Late Bishop of Worcester, with an Answer to all Objections made by Dr. Hollingworth and others. *Nathanael Ranew*, 1692, *discoloured throughout*, [ii+]37[+i] pp., sm. 4to, *disbound* (Wing W310) **£40.00**

84 ——WYNNE (Robert) Unity and Peace the Support of Church and State, a Sermon . . . the Anniversary of the Martyrdom of King Charles I. *T. W. for Thomas Bennet*, 1704, [ii+]22[+ii] pp., sm. 4to, *disbound* **£18.00**

85 **Charles Louis.** The Manifest of the Most Illustrious, and Soveraigne Prince, Charles Lodowick, Count Palatine of the Rhine . . . concerning the Right of His Succession both in the Princedome, Lands and Palatinate; as also in the Dignity, Voice, Session and Function of the Electorship-Palatine thereunto annexed. Translated . . . *A. G[riffin] for I. N[orton] and R. W[hitaker]*, 1637, FIRST EDITION IN ENGLISH, *lacks lf. before title (? blank), small piece torn from top outer corner of 2nd ff.*, [vii+77] ff., sm. 4to, *modern qtr. dark green crushed morocco, cloth sides, raised bands and lettered* (STC 5046) **£90.00**

86 [**Chesterfield** (Philip Stanhope Dormer, *Earl of*)] An Apology for a Late Resignation: in a Letter from an English Gentleman to his Friend in the Hague. *John Freeman*, [1748], *contemp. comment on title, last lf. soiled and creased*, 46 pp., 8vo, *disbound* **£25.00**

87 ——[and Edmund **Waller**] A Vindictation of a late Pamphlet, entitled The Case of the Hanover Troops considered: with some further Observations upon those Troops; being a Sequel to the said Pamphlet. By the same Author. *T. Cooper*, 1743, *some discolouration*, 47 pp., sm. 8vo, *disbound* (Gulick *306) **£30.00**

88 **Churchill** (Sir Winston) Divi Britannici: being a Remark upon the Lives of all the Kings of this Isle, from the Year of the World 2855. unto the Year of Grace 1660. *Tho. Roycroft, to be sold by Francis Eglesfield*, 1675, *title in red and black, engravings in text, divisional titles*, A[1] *frayed in margins, some discolouration*, [vi+]362[+ii] pp., folio, *contemp. calf, surface worn and rubbed, sometime rebacked, leather label* (Wing C4275) **£55.00**

89 **Civil War.** The Humble Petition of the Lord Major, Aldermen and Common of the City of London, in Common Councell assembled . . . with the Answer of the Lords to the said Petition. *Richard Cotes, August 8*, 1648, [ii+] 6 pp., sm. 4to, *folded but unstitched, top margin uncut* (Wing H3544) **£30.00**

90 **Cicero** (M. Tullius) Three Books touching the Nature of the Gods done into English; with notes and illustrations. Setting forth, (from all Antiquity,) What Perceptions, Men, by the Only Light of Reason, may Entertain, concerning a Deity! *Joseph Hindmarsh*, 1683, *a little embrowned throughout*, [iii+]cxl[+ii+] 252 pp., 12mo, *new mottled calf, leather label, gilt* (Wing C4323) **£45.00**

91 ——An Ordinance . . . to Appoint and Enable Committees in the severall Counties of Buckingham, Oxon, and Berks, to put in Execution this present Ordinance, and severall other Ordinances of both Houses of Parliament. *Edward Husbands*, June 27, 1644, 8 pp., sm. 4to, *folded but unstitched* (Wing E2090) **£40.00**

92 ——Two Ordinances . . . for the enabling of the Commissioners of the Great Seale, and other Committees in their severall Counties, to tender an Oath . . . For the discharging of the Members of both Houses from all places both Military and Civil. *Iohn Wright, April.* 7. 1645, *small hole in lower margin of last leaf*, [ii+] 6 pp., sm. 4to, *folded but unstitched* (Wing E2422) **£30.00**

93 ——WALKER (Clement) Animadversions upon the Armies Remonstrance, delivered to the House of Commons, Monday, 20. November, 1648. In vindication of the Parliaments Treaty with the King in the Isle of Wight. Printed in the year 1648, *browning throughhout*, [ii+]20[+ii] pp., sm. 4to, *disbound* (Wing W319) **£35.00**

94 [**Clarkson** (Daniel)] The Case of Protestants in England under a Popish Prince, if any should happen to Wear the Imperial Crown. *Richard Janeway*, 1681, *some discolouration*, 35 pp., sm. 4to, *disbound* (Wing C4569) **£40.00**

95 **Clèry** (Jean-Baptiste) A Journal of Occurrences at the Temple, during the Confinement of Louis xvi, King of France. Transl. from the original MS. by R. C. Dallas *Baylis*, 1798, *3 engraved plates, slight foxing*, [xviii+]255[+i] pp., 8vo, *qtr. morocco, leather label, marbled bds.* **£25.00**

96 The **Coalition:** or, an Historical Memorial of the Negotiations for Peace, between his High Mightiness of C——m——t [Claremont, Duke of Newcastle] and his Sublime Excellency of H—y—s [Hayes, i.e. William Pitt], with the Vouchers. Published by Authority of One of the Contracting Powers. *J. Hinxman*, 1762, *hf. title present*, 23 pp., 4to, *new marbled bds.* **£25.00**

97 **Cobbett** (William) Cobbet's Paper against Gold; containing the History and Mystery of the Bank of England, the Funds, the Debt, the Sinking Fund, the Bank stoppage, the lowering and raising of the value of Paper-Money; and shewing that Taxation, Pauperism, Poverty, Misery and Crimes have all increased, and ever must increase, with a Funding System. [in 15 parts, *W. Molineux*, 1817], *browning throughout*, viii+470 cols., 8vo, *contemp. hf. calf, corners worn, newly rebacked and lettered, marbled bds. and endpapers* (Pearl 81) **£50.00**

98 **Coke** (Roger) England's Improvements. In Two Parts. In the Former is Discoursed, how the Kingdom of England may be Improved, in Strength, Employment, Wealth, Trade. By the Encreasing the Value of Lands, the Revenues of the Crown and Church, Peace and Amity with Forein Nations, without any Charge to the Subject. In the Latter is Discoursed, how the Navigation of England may be Increased, and the Soveraignty of the British Seas more Secured to the Crown of England. Treatise III. [and IV.], *J. C. for Henry Brome*, 1675, *divisional title, some discolouration*, pp. [xx+]68:[xii+] 73–115, sm. 4to, *disbound* (Wing C4978: Kress 1380) **£150.00**

¶ Palgrave notes that Coke, accepting Fortrey's statistics as accurate and therefore believing the trade and commerce of England to be decaying, "made many sound suggestions for their improvement . . ." and sets down Coke's main proposals in some detail – a great many of which are taken from these treatises.

99 **Comines** (Philippe de) Memoires, contenans l'Histoire des Rois Louis xi. & Charles viii. depuis l'an 1464 jusques en 1498. Edition nouvelle, . . . augmentee de plusieurs Traittez, Contrats, Testamens & autres Pieces nouvelles. 5 Vols. *Brusselle, Francois Foppens*, 1723, *with engr. frontis., 11 portraits and 2 folding tables*, sm. 8vo, *contemp. sprinkled calf, gilt, edges rubbed, sprinkled edges, leather labels* **£185.00**

100 ——Memoirs. Containing the History of Lewis xi. & Charles viii. Kings of France, with the most Remarkable Occurrances in their particular Reigns from the Year 1464 to 1498. Revised and Corrected from divers MSS. and Antient Impressions by Denys Godefroy . . . Faithfully Translated into English. *John Starkey*, 1674, *engraved frontis., one lf. remargined, some soiling of prelims.*, [xxxviii+]611[+iv] pp., 8vo, *contemp. calf, corners little worn, newly rebacked, leather label* (Wing C5543) **£45.00**

101 **Commerce** CHILD (Sir Josiah) A New Discourse of Trade: wherin are recommended several weighty Points relating to Companies of Merchants, the Act of Navigation, Naturalization of Strangers, and our Woolen Manufacturers: the Balance of Trade, and the Nature of Plantations, with their Consequences in relation to the Kingdom, are seriously discussed . . . New Edition. *Richardson and Urquhart*, 1775, *lower blank margin of title and ff. lf. cut away*, [iv+]xxxix +224 pp., 12mo, *contemp. sprinkled tan calf, leather label, y.e.* scarce (Kress 7091: Goldsmith 11259) **£110.00**

102 ——GEE (Joshua) The Trade and Navigation of Great Britain considered: shewing . . . some account of the commodities each country we trade with takes from us, and what we take from them; with observations on the balance. Sixth Edition, *Glasgow, William Duncan junior*, 1755, [xvi+] 166 pp., sm. 8vo, *contemp. grained calf, rebacked and orig. backstrip mounted, g.e.*.(Kress 5441: Sabin 26827) **£45.00**

103 ——Grand Taris des réductions de la monnoie de France, courant la Brabant, et argent des Pays-Bas, et vice versâ; ainsi que des espèces d'or et d'argent contenues dans les Décrets de 1810, par Dulion, jaugeur. Suivi du tarif des espèces, fixée par Arrêté royal du 8 Décembre 1824 . . . Nouvelle édition . . . *Anvers, A. Grangé*, [1825?], 96[+i] pp., 8vo, *contemp. hf. vellum, unlettered, mottled bds. index with printed tabs on fore-edges* **£21.00**

104 ——Reasons for improving the Fisheries, and Linnen Manufacture of Scotland . . . Humbly submitted to the Consideration of . . . the Members of both Houses of Parliament. *J. Roberts*, 1727, [iv+]31[+iii] pp., 8vo, *disbound* **£45.00**

105 ——[SQUIRE (Samuel, *Bp. of St. David's*)] The Important Question discussed; or, a Serious and Impartial Enquiry into the True Interests of England, with Respect to the Continent. *Dublin, G. Faulkner*, 1746, *slight staining*, 50[+ii] pp., 8vo, *buff wrappers* **£15.00**

106 **Constitvtions** and Canons Ecclesiasticall, treated vpon by the Bishop of London . . . and agreed vpon by the Kings Maiesties Licence in their Synode begun at London Anno Dom. 1603 . . . *Robert Barker*, 1604, *prelims. soiled, some staining*, [xxiii+149+i] pp., sm. 4to, *new qtr. calf, lettered, marbled bds.* (STC 10070) **£55.00**

107 **Corn Laws.** WHITMORE (W. W.) A Letter to the Electors of Bridgnorth, upon the Corn Laws. *Edinburgh, William Blackwood: and T. Cadell*, 1826, *title soiled*, 84 pp., 8vo, *grey bds., paper label* **£16.00**

108 **Coronation.** WILLIAM iv. The Form and Order of the Service that is to be performed, and of the Ceremonies that are to be observed, in the Coronation of their Majesties King William IV. and Queen Adelaide, in the Abbey Church of S. Peter, Westminster, on Thursday, the 8th of September 1831. *George Eyre and Andrew Strahan*, 1831, iv+71 pp., sm. 4to, *orig. cloth, leather label on upper cover, recently rebacked* **£21.00**

109 [**Corry** (John)] The English Metropolis; or, London in the Year 1820. Containing Satirical Strictures on Public Manners, Morals, and Amusements; a Young Gentleman's Adventures; and characteristic Anecdotes of several eminent Individuals who now figure in this great Theatre of temporary Exhibition. *Barnard and Farley; sold by Sherwood, Neely, and Jones*, 1820, 320 pp., 8vo, *orig. bds., backstrip defective and paper label mostly torn away, upper joint split, all edges untrimmed*, scarce **£55.00**

110 **Craig** (Sir Thomas) The Right of Succession to the Kingdom of England, in Two Books; against the Sophisms of Parsons the Jesuite, who assum'd the Counterfeit Name of Dolman; by which he endeavours to overthrow not only the Rights of Succession in Kingdoms, but also the Sacred Authority of Kings themselves . . . now Faithfully Translated into English [by James Gatherer], *M. Bennet, for Dan. Brown* . . . 1703, *title creased*, pp. [xxxiv+]1–230:245–431[+xvi], folio, *contemp. sprinkled calf, corners worn, newly rebacked, leather label* **£65.00**

¶ Bears the signature in several places of Saltoun 1716 (i.e. Alexander Fraser, Master and 12th Baron Saltoun, 1684–1748)

111 **Cromwell** VAUGHAN (Robert, *ed.*) The Protectorate of Oliver Cromwell and the State of Europe during the early part of the Reign of Louis xiv. illustrated in a series of Letters . . . with an Introduction on the Character of Cromwell and of his Times. 2 Vols. *Henry Colburn*, 1838, 2 *portraits, slight foxing*, cxx+454:xi+518 pp., 8vo, *contemp. gray calf, gilt extra, leather labels, some discolouration through sunning* **£35.00**

112 **Crowne** (William) A Trve Relation of all the Remarkable Places and Passages observed in the Travels of the right honourable Thomas Lord Howard . . . Ambassadour Extraordinary to his sacred Majesty Ferdinando the second, Emperour of Germanie, Anno Domini 1636. *Henry Seile*, 1637, *title soiled, some discolouration, lacks final blank*, [iv+] 70 pp., sm. 4to, *nineteenth century calf, little scuffed, leather label* (STC 6097) **£220.00**

113 **Cumberland** (Richard) Memoirs . . . containing an Account of his Life and Writings, interspersed with Anecdotes and Characters of several of the most distinguished Persons of his Time . . . 2 Vols. *Lackington, Allen, & Co.* 1807, 4 *portraits, foxing*, [iii+]432:[iii+] 504 pp., 8vo, *contemp. marbled calf, backstrips gilt, and lettered, a little rubbed* **£21.00**

114 **Customs and Excise.** An Act for the Improvement of the Revenue of the Customs and Excize. *Hen: Hills and John Field*, 1657, [colophon], *drop title, embrowned*, 4 pp., folio, *grey bds.* (Wing E1113) **£21.00**

115 **Dawson** (Thomas) Memoirs of St. George the English Patron; and of the most Noble Order of the Garter. Being an Introduction to an intended History of the Antiquities of the Castle, Town and Borough of Windsor, and the Parts adjacent, in the County of Berks. *Henry Clements*, 1714, *title in red and black, frontis., and portrait of K. George I.*, [xix+] 336 pp., 8vo, *contemp. sprinkled calf, leather label, corners worn and joints cracking, but sound* **£40.00**

116 **Defoe** (Daniel) Defoe's Review, reproduced from the Original Editions, with an Introduction and Bibliographical Notes by Arthur Wellesley Secord. 9 Vols. in 22, *New York, For the Facsimile Text Society by Columbia University Press*, 1938, 8vo, *publishers' cloth, lettered in gilt, with the Graham Pollard/BHB label* **£110.00**

117 **Denmark.** The Present State of Denmark, in relation to its Government and Laws, its Trade and Manufacturers, its Revenues and Forces. Compiled from the Present Archives, and other authentic Materials. Being an exact Description of that Kingdom, as it now exists, and different from any Account hitherto published in the English Language. In a series of letters, mostly written by Monsieur Roger. *Tho. Osbourne*, 1762, xvi+338 pp., 8vo, *qtr. calf, grey bds., recently rebacked, leather label* **£50.00**

118 **De Ruiter.** BRANDT (Gerard) La Vie de Michel de Ruiter, Duc, Chevalier, LieutenantAmiral Général de Hollande & de Oüest-Frise. Où est comprise l'Histoire Maritime des Provinces Unies, depuis l'An 1652, jusques à 1676. Traduite du Hollandois [by N. Aubin] . . . *Amsterdam, P. & J. Blaeu, pour Waesberge, Boom, à Someren & Goethals*, 1698, *title in red and black, engraved title, portrait, 7 double-page and folding plates and 1 single plate, discoloured, some 14 ll. torn in lower quarter into letter press*, folio, *contemp. panelled calf, recently repaired and rebacked, leather label*, scarce **£250.00**

119 A **Dialogue** at Oxford between a Tutor and a Gentleman, formerly his Pupil, concerning Government. *Rich. Janaway*, 1681, *some discolouration*, [i+] 21 pp., sm. 4to, *grey wrappers* (Wing D1290) **£45.00**

120 [**Dicke** (James)] The History of the Last Parliament, begun at Westminster, the Tenth Day of February, in the Twelth Year of the Reign of King William, An. Dom. 1700. *Fra. Coggan, Robert Gibson, and Tho. Hodgson*, 1702, *sm. hole in 2 ll. of preface, staining of outer margins, extending to text in some ll.* [xxvii+] 211 pp., sm. 8vo, *modern qtr. morocco, leather label, drab bds., slightly rubbed* **£21.00**

121 **Disraeli.** MONYPENNY (W. F.) and G. E. BUCKLE. The Life of Benjamin Disraeli, Earl of Beaconsfield. 6 Vols. *John Murray*, 1910/20, *portraits and illustrations*, 8vo, *publishers' cloth, little faded* **£35.00**

122 **Dodington** (George Budd, *Baron of Melcombe Regis*) The Diary . . . with an Appendix, containing some curious and interesting Papers . . . *Dublin, William Porter, for Messrs. Price, Moncrieffe . . . and Marchbank*, 1784, xiv+346 pp., 12mo, *contemp. calf, leather label, two small areas of surface damage* **£25.00**

123 **Drinkwater** (John, *Captain*) A History of the late Siege of Gibraltar. With a Description and Account of that Garrison, from the earliest Periods. Second Edition, Corrected; *T. Spilsbury, sold by J. Johnson, T. and J. Egerton, and J. Edwards*, 1786, *with 2 charts (slight tears in folds), 2 plans and 6 views (all folding), additionally an albumen photograph of a drawn portrait of the author mounted and pasted to front fly, also the broadside description of the commemorative medal inserted, dated presentation inscription from the daughter of the author to her daughter on title, A2 misbound, some foxing throughout*, xxiv+356 pp., 4to, *contemp. marbled calf, rubbed, corners and edges worn, sometime rebacked, old backstrip mounted, new leather label* **£130.00**

124 **Dugdale** (Sir William) The Antient Usage in Bearing of such Ensigns of Honour as are commonly call'd Arms. With a Catalogue of the present Nobility and Baronets of England. To which is added, a Catalogue of the present Nobility of Scotland and Ireland, &c. Second Edition Corrected. *Oxford, at the Theater for Moses Pitt, and sold by Samuel Smith*, 1682, *woodcuts in text, folding chart, small tear in fold, small tear in one fore-margin neatly repaired, slight discolouration*, [iv+] 210 pp., sm. 8vo, *contemp. calf, recently repaired and rebacked, leather label* (Wing D2478) **£65.00**

125 **Duperrier Dumouriez** (Charles Francois, *General*) Memoirs, written by himself. Translated by John Fenwick. 2 Parts in 1 Vol. *Dublin, by Z. Jackson, [and] by William Porter for P. Wogan . . . and G. Folingby*, 1794, *rubber stamps*, xxviii+111:[iv+] 185 pp., 8vo, *contemp. diced calf, lacks label, slightly defective at base of backstrip and both joints* **£30.00**

126 **Echard.** CALAMY (Edmund) a Letter to Mr. Archdeacon Echard, upon Occasion of his History of England, wherein the true Principles of the Revolution are Defended . . . Second Edition, corrected. *John Clark*, 1718, *discoloured*, 100 pp., sm. 8vo, *disbound* **£18.00**

127 **East Indies.** [FEYNES (Henri de, *sieur de Monfart*) An Exact and Cvriovs Svrvey of all the East Indies, euen to Canton, the chiefe Cittie of China: All duly performed by land, by Monsieur de Monfart, the like whereof was neuver hetherto, brought to an end. VVherein also are described the hugh Dominions of the great Mogar, to whom that honourable Knight, Sir Thomas Roe, was lately sent Ambassador from the King. Newly translated out of the Trauailers Manuscript. *Thomas Dawson, for VVilliam Arondell*, 1615, FIRST EDITION, *woodcut initials, title margined and restored with pen-facsimile to a few letters, side notes on 4pp. just shaved*, [ix+] 40 pp., sm 4to, *19th cent. tan roan, gilt extra, lettered, by W. Pratt for John Bellingham Inglis* (STC 10840) **£500.00**

128 **Edward Prince of Wales.** LELAND (John) Genethliacon illustrissimi Eäduerdi Principis Cambriae, Ducis Coriniae, et Comitis Palatini: libellus ante aliquot annos inchaotus, nunc uero absolutus & editus . . . *Londini*: (*Colophon*:) *Renerum Vuolfium* . . . 1543, FIRST EDITION, *partly italic, woodcut of badge of Prince of Wales within the sun in its splendour on verso of title, one large historiated woodcut initial, printer's woodcut device* (McKerrow 96) *on verso of final lf., some staining or discolouration of first few ll.*, [30] ff., sm. 4to, *18th cent. marbled bds., rebacked modern brown morocco, unlettered, endpapers faintly stained, collation mark of Thomas Rawlines on front free endpaper, ownership stamp (initials) of Albert Ehrmann and Broxbourne Library bookplate* (STC 15443: Hazlitt iii/p.139) **£325.00**

129 **Elwes.** TOPHAM (Edward) The Life of the late John Elwes, Esquire; Member in Three successive Parliaments for Berkshire. First published in the Paper of The World . . . Ninth Edition. *John Jarvis, for James Ridgway*, 1791, *etched portrait by Wm. Austin, folded genealogical table creased, heavy stain in lower margins, some foxing*, viii+ 111 pp., 8vo, *binder's grey bds., printed lettering strip* **£21.00**

130 **Exports.** An Act for the Exportation of several Commodities of the Breed, Growth and Manufacture of this Commonvvealth. *Henry Hills and John Field*, 1657, *embrowned*, [i+] 10 pp., folio, *grey bds.* (Wing E1110) **£25.00**

131 **Eyre** (Edward *Ed.*) European Civilization, its Origin and Development, 7 vols., *Oxford University Press*, 1934, *maps and illustrations*, 8vo, *publishers' buckram, some backstrips faded, hinges of vol. i. becoming loose* **£65.00**

Contents:– Prehistoric Man and earliest known Societies: Rome and Christendom: The Middle Ages: The Reformation: Economic History of Europe since the Reformation: Political and cultural History of Europe since the Reformation: The Relations of Europe with Non-European Peoples.

132 ——(Sir Vincent) The Military Operations at Cabul, which ended in the Retreat and Destruction of the British Army, January 1842. with a Journal of Imprisonment in Afghanistan. Second Edition [ed. by Edward Eyre]. *John Murray*, 1843, *folding map*, xx+ 330 pp. + 4 pp. book list, 8vo, *orig. decorated green cloth, rather stained* **£25.00**

133 **Fabyan** (Robert) The New Chronicles of England and France . . . reprinted from Pynson's Edition of 1516. The first Part collated with the Editions of 1533, 1542, and 1559; and the second with a MS. of the Author's own time, as well as the subsequent Editions: including the different Continuations. To which are added a biographical and literary Preface, and an Index, by Henry Ellis. *F. C. and J. Rivington* . . . 1811, *slight foxing, small repair to one margin*, [i+]xxi[+i+]723[+lxxii] pp., imp. 4to, *hf. tan calf, leather label, cloth sides, shelf label at base of backstrip and ex-libris label on front pastedown* **£55.00**

134 **Fanshawe** (Anne, *Lady*) Memoirs, written by herself. To which are added Extracts from the Correspondence of Sir Richard Fanshaw. [Ed. by Sir N. Harris Nicolas]. *Henry Colburn*, 1829, *portrait, some foxing*, lxiii+395[+iv – cat.], 8vo, *orig. bds., a little worn, contemp. lending library label pasted to upper cover* **£20.00**

135 **Fens.** LABELYE (Charles) The Result of a View of the Great Level of the Fens, taken at the Desire of his Grace the Duke of Bedford, &c. Governor, and the Gentlemen of the Corporation of the Fens, in July 1745. *George Woodfall*, 1745, *errata lf. before title, small rubber stamp on title, small hole in one margin*, vi+ 74 pp., sm. 4to, *new qtr. calf, leather label, cloth sides* **£100.00**

¶ "These Fenny surrounded Grounds in former Times have been dry and profitable; and so may be hereafter, if due Provision be made." Commissioner of Sewers, A.D. 1596.

136 **Fiennes** (Nathaniel, *Lord*) A Speech in answere to the Third Speech of the Lord George Digby . . . in which is plainely cleared the severall objections, that are made against the Londoners Petition, and also the great and transcendent evills of Episcopal Government, are demonstrated and plainly laid open. *Printed in the yeare* 1641, *title and last page soiled*, [ii+] 28 pp., sm. 4to, *disbound* (Wing F880) **£25.00**

137 ——The Speech . . . made before His Highness and both Houses of Parliament, on Wednesday the 20th January, 1657 . . . *Henry Hills and John Field*, 1657[–8], *top margins of last 2 ll. cropped with slight loss, browned throughout*, sm. 4to, *disbound* (Wing F881) **£25.00**

138 ——The Speech . . . made before his Highnesse, and both Houses of Parliament: on Thursday the 27th of January, 1658, being the first day of their sitting. *Henry Twyford*. 1659, *a few upper margins shaved*, 30 pp., sm. 4to, *disbound* (Wing F882) **£25.00**

139 [**Fleetwood** (William, *Bp. of St. Asaph*)] Chronicon Preciosum: or, an Account of English Money, the Price of Corn, and other Commodities. In a Letter to a Student in the University of Oxford, *Charles Harper*, 1707, FIRST EDITION, *embrowned throughout*, [xvi+]181[+x] pp., 8vo, *new qtr. calf, lettered, marbled bds.* **£50.00**

140 **Fleury.** [Frey de] Neuville (Charles) The Funeral Oration upon Cardinal [Andre Hercule] de Fleury, Minister of State, &c. Translated into English. *M. Cooper*, 1743, *title and last page soiled*, [i+] 70 pp., 8vo, *edges untrimmed, disbound* **£15.00**

141 **Foote** ((Edward J.)) Captain Foote's Vindication of his Conduct, when Captain of His Majesty's Ship Sea-Horse, and Senior Officer in the Bay of Naples, in the Summer of 1799. Second Edition, with Observations on the Rev. J. S. Clarke's, and John McArthur's Life of Nelson; and a previous Correspondence on that Subject. *J. Hatchard*, 1810, [iii+] 198 pp., + 2 pp. adverts., 8vo, *orig. plain grey wrappers, backstrip slightly defective, untrimmed* **£30.00**

142 **Foss** (Edward) Biographia Juridica. A Biographical Dictionary of the Judges of England from the Conquest to the Present Time, 1066–1870. *John Murray*, 1870, xv+792 pp., thick 8vo, *orig. cloth, faded* **£18.00**

143 **Four Questions** Debated. Q.1. Whether the Exercise of the Government of England be totally Subverted? Affirm. Q.2. Admitting the Exercise of Government dissolved, whether the power of Settling is in the People? Affirm. . . . with an Answer to the Objection that the Convention will not have the Power of a Parliament. [*Edinburgh*], *Re-printed* 1689, *final blank present*, 30 pp., sm. 4to, *disbound* (Wing F1669) **£21.00**

144 **Fox.** TROTTER (John Bernard) Memoirs of the Latter Years of the Right Honourable Charles James Fox. *Richard Phillips, by George Sidney*, 1811, *some browning at beginning* xl+ 536 pp., 8vo, *contemp. mauve calf, gilt, lettered, backstrip little faded* **£25.00**

145 **France.** [——] An Impartial History of the late Revolution in France, from its Commencement to the Death of the Queen, and the Execution of the Deputies of the Gironde Party. 2 Vols. *G. G. and J. Robinson*, 1794, FIRST EDITION, *slightly foxed, one lower margin cut away, with no loss*, xi+518:vii+466 pp., 8vo, *contemp. hf. calf, leather labels, marbled bds.* **£80.00**

146 ——CODE NAPOLÉON. Edition originale et seule officielle. *Paris, Imprimerie Impériale*, 1811, [with] Table alphabétique des Matières: [and] Exposé des Motifs du Code Napoléon . . . pour faire Suite et server de Commentaire à l'Edition officielle du Code Napoléon. *Paris A. Galland*, 1810, *some discolouration throughout, small piece torn from one lower margin*, [i+]432:136[i+]522 pp., thick 8vo, *new qtr. calf, leather label, marbled bds.* **£40.00**

147 ——DAVILA (Henrico Caterino) The Historie of the Civill Warres of France, written in Italian. Translated out of the Original [by Charles Cotterell and William Aylesbury]. *R. Raworth . . . sold by W. Lee, D. Pakeman, and G. Bedell*, 1648, FIRST EDITION IN ENGLISH, *vignette of translators initials entwined, within a wreath, on title, Imprimatur and errata ll. present*, [ii+iii+]1478[+i] pp. folio, *contemp. sprinkled calf, corners worn, recently rebacked, leather label* (Wing D413) **£120.00**

148 ——The **Proceedings** of the parliament of Paris, upon the Pope's Bull, concerning the Franchises in the city of Rome, and the following Ordonance of the 26th of December. Translated into English by Order of his Excellency Monsieur Barillon . . . *R. Bentley, and Randal Taylor, – Colophon: Paris, Francis Muquets*, 1688 [ii+] 37 pp., sm. 4to, *sewed* (Wing F2053) **£45.00**

149 ——The QUEEN'S NECKLACE. [Balsamo (Joseph, *'Comte de Cagliostro'*)] Memorial, or Brief against the King's Attorney-General, Plaintiff: in the Cause of the Cardinal de Rohan, Comtesse de la Motte, and Others. From the French Original, published in Paris in February last; with an Introductory Preface by Parkyns MacMahon. *J. Debrett, J. Macklaw, J. de Boff*, 1786, *lacks* a1 (*? hf. title*), xvii+86 pp., 8vo, *disbound*, scarce **£55.00**

150 **French Revolution.** [SENAC DE MEILHAN (Gabriel)] Du Government, des Moeurs, et des Condition en France avant la Révolution, avec le Caractère des principaux Personnages du Règne de Louis xvi. *Londres, Benjamin et Jean White*, 1795, iv+334 pp.:
[with]
A TRANSLATION of a passage in a late Pamphlet by Monsieur Mallet du Pan, entitled, Correspondance Politique. Containing a Vindication of the late excellent King of France, Lewis the XVIth, from a false and wicked Charge brought against him by some of his Enemies. *Benjamin and John White*, 1796, [iii+]20 pp.:
[and]
QUESTIONS, sur lesquelles on souhaite de scavoir les Réponses de Monsieur Adhémar et de Monsieur De Lisle, et d'autres Habitants de la Province de Québec. *London, printed* 1784, 16 pp.:
[and]
MONTESQUIEU (Charles Louis de Secondat, *Baron de*) A View of the English Constitution, being a Translation of the Sixth Chapter of the Eleventh Book of his celebrated Treatise, intitled l'Esprit des Loix. *B. White and H., Payne*, 1781, [i+]74 pp.:
[and]
HALES (William) Observations on Tithes . . . to which is annexed, a Second Edition of The Moderate Reformer . . . [by Francis Maseres], *B. and J. White*, 1794, [i+]73 pp.
Five pieces bound together, 8vo, *contemp. tree calf, leather label, backstrip rubbed, upper joint beginning to crack* **£100.00**

151 A **Free Conference** concerning the Present Revolution of Affairs in England. *R. Baldwyn*, 1689, *tail margins fragile, one repaired*, [iv+] 36 pp., sm. 4to, *disbound* (Wing F2111) **£25.00**

152 **Froissart** (Sir John) The Antient Chronicles of England, France, Spain, Portugal, Scotland, Brittany, and Flanders, and the Adjoining Countries; translated from the original French, at the Command of King Henry the Eighth, by John Bouchier, Lord Berners. With the Names of Places and Persons carefully corrected, and the obsolete words modernised, with a copious Index. 4 Vols., *J. Davis*, 1814, 8vo, *contemp. hf. russia, lettered, upper qtr. of one backstrip missing, upper joint of vol. i. cracking* **£42.00**

153 ——Chronicles of England, France, Spain, and the adjoining Countries, from the latter Part of the Reign of Edward II. to the Coronation of Henry IV. Translated from the French Editions, with variations and additions from many celebrated MSS. by Thomas Johnes, to which are prefixed, a Life of the Author, an Essay on his Works, and a Criticism on his History. 2 Vols. *George Routledge and Sons*, 1868, *coloured titles, 70 coloured lithographs from MSS., and many wood engravings in the text*, xlvii+768:xiv+733 pp., 4to, *contemp. hf. crimson morocco, marbled bds., recently rebacked and orig. backstrips laid down, g.e.* **£95.00**

154 ——**Sleiden** (Jean) An Epitome of Frossard: or, a Summerie Collection of the most memorable Histories contained in his Chronicle, chiefly concerning the State of England and France. Wherein the famous Warres and Conquests of king Edward the third, with the honorable atchieuements of the Black Prince, and other his sonnes, both in Fraunce, Spaine, and Portugall, are compendiously described. Enter-mixed with other historicall occurrents of those times, very worthy, and profitable to be had in remembrance. Compiled in Latine by Iohn Sleydane, and translated into English, by P. Golding. *Tho: Purfoot, for Per: Golding*, 1608, FIRST EDITION, *small woodcut ornament of title, large woodcut initials, slight worming in fore margins*, [ii+] 215 pp., sm. 4to, *contemp. calf, rebacked at some time, lettered, head of backstrip bent and slight rubbing elsewhere, lacks pastedowns but modern free endpapers, book-plate* (STC 11399) **£300.00**

¶ The titlepage of this copy does not have the large head-piece composed from printer's flowers, or the full measure rule between lines two and three, but an additional rule has been inserted between lines twelve and thirteen.

155 **Froude** (James Anthony) History of England from the Fall of Wolsey to the Defeat of the Spanish Armada. 12 Vols., *Longmans, Green, and Co.*, 1870, cr.8vo, *publishers' cloth, becoming shabby* **£21.00**

156 **Gardiner.** DODDRIDGE (P.) Some Remarkable Passages in the Life of Col. James Gardiner, who was slain at the Battle of Prestonpans, September 21, 1745; with an Appendix, relating to the Antient Family of the Munro's of Fowlis. Fifth Edition. *J. Buckland, W. Strahan* . . . 1772, *portrait,* [xii+]272[+iv] pp., 12mo, *contemp. sprinkled calf, leather label, little worn, joints cracking* **£25.00**

157 ——(Samuel Rawson) History of the Commonwealth and Protectorate, 1649–1660. 3 Vols., *Longmans, Green, and Co.* 1894/1901, FIRST EDITIONS, 27 *maps,* xxiv+515:xxiv+503:xx+513 pp., 8vo, *orig. cloth, edges mostly uncut* **£25.00**

158 **The Gentleman's Magazine: or, Monthly Intelligencer.** 160 Consecutive Volumes + 4 Index Volumes. *E. Cave; Cave and Henry: John Nichols, etc.*, 1731–1836, *texts in excellent state, engraved plates, printed in double-column. 8vo., all but the final six volumes of the Magazine and the four Index volumes bound in a uniform style of half calf over marbled boards; joints generally weak and all volumes rubbed, two boards missing and twenty volumes have covers detached, the volumes dated in gilt; despite all – a remarkable survival with the early volumes being in generally better shape than the later ones* **£2,800.00**
All but the final six volumes bearing the *Huyshe* family provenance.
The Gentleman's Magazine, begun in 1731 by Edward Cave, survived until 1907. It is the most enduring periodical ever published. Our run as above covers the editorships of Cave (1731–1754); R. Cave and D. Henry (1754–1792) and from then until the middle of the nineteenth century it was in the hands of John Nichols and his successors.

159 **George I.** SOPHIA DOROTHEA (*Consort*) Memoirs . . . chiefly from the secret Archives of Hanover, Brunswick, Berlin and Vienna; including a Diary of the Conversations of illustrious Personages of those Courts, illustrative of her History, with Letters and other Documents. 2 Vols. Second Edition. *Henry Colburn,* 1845, *portraits, some foxing,* xxiv+452:vii+452 pp., catalogues, 8vo, *orig. cloth, faded and soiled* **£18.00**

160 **Gibbon** (Edward) The History of the Decline and Fall of the Roman Empire. 6 Vols. *W. Strahan, and T. Cadell,* 1776/89, *some discolouration, portrait and maps,* 4to, *nineteenth century hf. green morocco, lettered, a little scuffed, maroon cloth sides, r.e.* **£165.00**
¶ Vol. i. is Second Edition, vols. ii. and iii. are New Editions, vols. iv. v. and vi. are First Editions.

161 ——The History of the Decline and Fall of the Roman Empire. 12 Vols., with a Life of the Author: written for this Edition [unsigned]. *Edinburgh, Bell and Bradfute* . . . 1811, *portrait and 2 folding maps, occasional foxing,* 8vo, *excellent in modern hf. sprinkled tan calf, backstrips gilt, with leather labels, marbled bds., t.e.g.* (Norton 61) **£250.00**

162 **Godwin** (William) Enquiry concerning Political Justice, and its Influence on Morals and Happiness. Third Edition corrected. 2 Vols., *G. G. and J. Robinson,* 1798, *occasional foxing,* lvi+463:ix+554 pp., 8vo, *modern qtr. calf, lettered, marbled bds.* **£185.00**

163 **Goldsmith** (Oliver) The Grecian History, from the Earliest State to the Death of Alexander the Great. 2 Vols., *J. and F. Rivington* . . . 1774, FIRST EDITION, *lacks the preliminary blanks* [iii+]399; [i+]284[+lxiv] pp., 8vo., *newly bound in qtr. tan calf, marb. bds., leather labels* **£50.00**

164 **Gordon** (Charles George). COE (Charles C.) General Gordon in a new Light: the Cause of War, and the Advocate of Peace. *Bolton,* 1885, 60 pp., 8vo, *disbound disbound* **£10.00**

165 ——(Jacob) Opvs Chronologicorvm Annorvm Seriem, Regnorvm Mvtationes, & rerum toto orbe gestarum narrationem, à Mundi exordio ad annum vsq; Christi 1617 complectens. Curis secundis auctum & recognitum. *Auoustoriti Pictonum,* 1617, *discoloured throughout, pagination irregular, 2 ll. misbound,* [i+]287[+xix]:[iv+]630[+lxxxii] pp., folio, *early sprinkled sheep, leather label, worn and rubbed, joints beginning to crack* **£95.00**

166 **Grafton** (Richard) Chronicle; or, History of England. To which is added his Table of the Bailiffs, Sherriffs, and Mayors, of the City of London, from the Year 1189, to 1558, inclusive. 2 Vols., *J. Johnson, F. C. and J. Rivington* . . . 1809, xvi+677:[iii+]568[+lii] pp., imp. 4to, *hf. tan calf, leather labels, cloth sides, shelf label at base of backstrips and ex-libris labels on front pastedowns* **£110.00**

167 **Grammont.** HAMILTON (Antoine) Memoires du Comte de Grammont. Nouvelle edition, augmentée des notes & d'eclaircissemens necessaires par M. Horace Walpole. *Londres, chez J. Dodsley,* 1783, *light embrowning throughout,* xxiii+290[+iii] pp., sm. 4to, *hf. calf, marbled bds., rubbed* **£45.00**

168 **Greville** (Charles C. F.) The Greville Memoirs. A Journal of the Reigns of King George iv. and King William iv. ed. by Henry Reeve, 3 Vols., Second Edition. *Longmans, Green, and Co.*, 1874:
[with]
A Journal of the Reign of Queen Victoria from 1837 to 1852, 3 Vols., *Longmans, Green, and Co.* 1885:
[and]
A Journal of the Reign of Queen Victoria from 1852 to 1860, 3 Vols., *Longmans, Green, and Co.*, 1887:
Complete in the 8 Vols., 8vo, *dark green morocco, backstrips panelled and lettered in gilt, slightly sunned, green cloth sides, t.e.g., armorial book plate of* xix *Baron Willoughby de Broke* **£225.00**

169 **Guicciardi** (Diago, *Comte*) Relation Historique de la Révolution du Royaume d'Italie en 1814; traduit de l'Italien par M. Saint-Edme. *Paris, A. Corréard,* 1822, *slight foxing,* 204 pp., 8vo, *contemp. hf. calf, marbled bds.* **£15.00**

170 **Gunpowder Plot.** WILLIS (Richard) A Sermon preach'd . . . for the Happy Deliverance from the Gunpowder Treason Plot . . . *J. L. for Mat. Wotton,* 1705, 31[+i] pp., sm. 4to, *disbound* **£15.00**

171 **Hall** (Edward) Chronicle; containing the History of England, during the Reign of Henry the Fourth, and the succeeding Monarchs to the End of the Reign of Henry the Eighth in which are particularly described the Manners and Customs of those Periods. Carefully collated with the editions of 1548 and 1550. *J. Johnson, F. C. and J. Rivington* . . . 1809, viii+868[+xxxix] pp., 4to, *contemp. calf, sometime rebacked and repaired, lettered, with the Graham Pollard/BHB label* **£75.00**
¶ A. F. Pollard's copy, with innumerable marginal annotations in his neat holograph.

172 —— ——another copy *J. Johnson, F. C. and J. Rivington* . . . 1809, *occasional foxing,* viii+868[+xxxix] pp., imp. 4to, *hf. tan calf, leather label, cloth sides, shelf label at base of backstrip, ex-libris label on front-pastedown* **£50.00**

173 ——(Mrs. Matthew) The Queens before the Conquest. 2 Vols. *Henry Colburn,* 1854, 2 *portraits,* xvi+403[+i]:x+397[+iii] pp., 8vo, *publisher's red cloth, lettered* **£21.00**

174 **Hamilton and Castleherald.** BURNET (Gilbert, *Bp. of Sarum*) The Memoires of the Lives and Actions of James and William, Dukes of Hamilton and Castleherald, &c. in which an Account is given of the Rise and Progress of the Civil Wars of Scotland . . . together with many Letters, Instructions, and other Papers, written by King Charles the I. . . . In Seven Books. *J. Grover, for R. Royston,* 1677, *portrait of Charles I. and of James and William, Dukes of Hamilton, marginal notes by one Richard Martin, whose signature is on the title,* [xviii+]436[+xii] pp., folio, *contemp. mottled calf, corners worn, newly rebacked, leather label* (Wing B5832) **£95.00**

175 **Hardyng** (John) The chronicle, containing an Account of the Public Transactions from the earliest Period of English History to the Beginning of the Reign of Edward the Fourth. Together with the Continuation by Richard Grafton to the thirty fourth year of King Henry the Eighth. The former Part collated with two MSS. of the Author's own Time; the last, with Grafton's duplicate Edition. To which are added a biographical and literary Preface, and an Index, by Henry Ellis. *F. C. and J. Rivington,* . . . 1812, [iii+]xxi+607[+lxx] pp., imp. 4to, *hf. tan calf, leather label, cloth sides, shelf label at base of backstrip, ex-libris label on front pastedown* **£55.00**

176 **Hare** (Hugh) A Charge given at the General Quarter Sessions of the Peace for the County of Surrey, holden in Dorking on Tuesday the 5th day of April, 1692. and in the Fourth Year of their Majesties Reign. *John Newton,* 1692, *outer margins stained and very fragile,* [vii+] 32 pp., sm. 4to, *disbound* (Wing H760) **£55.00**

177 **Harris** (Stanley) The Coaching Age. *Richard Bentley,* 1885, *with 16 lithographs by John Sturgess,* viii+468 pp., 8vo, *full brown morocco, gilt, lettered and with equestrian symbols in backstrip compartments, which is lightly sunned, t.e.g., others untrimmed, by A. Taffin, inscribed by Dennis Wheatley on end-paper, and with his bookplate* **£100.00**

178 **Henry viii.** [RAYNAL (T.–G.–F. Abbé)] Histoire du Divorce de Henri viii. Roi d'Angleterre, et de Catherine d'Arragon. *Amsterdam,* 1763, 258 pp., sm. 8vo, *sewed, orig. upper wrapper intact but backstrip and lower wrapper replaced, edged untrimmed* **£25.00**

179 **Heraldry.** DUGDALE (Sir William) The Antient Usage in Bearing of such Ensigns of Honour as are commonly call's Arms . . . Second Edition Corrected. *Oxford, at the Theatre for Moses Pitt, and sold by Samuel Smith,* 1682, *with 13 woodcuts and a folding chart, rather soiled by use,* [viii+] 210 pp., sm. 8vo, *contemp. sheep, worn and rubbed* (Wing D2478) **£30.00**

180 ——[FISHER (Payne)] A Synopsis of Heraldry, or, the most plain, short, and easie way for a perfect attaining of that Art, containing all necessary Directions, in order thereunto . . . to which is added an Alphabetical Table, for the ready finding any Name whose Coat is herein Blazoned. *L. Curtis and T. Simmons,* 1682, engraved title (*sometime neatly coloured*) *and 33 engraved plates of arms and 4 of crests, one split in plate mark, divisional titles present,* [i+]xx[+ii+]114[+xx] pp., sm. 8vo, *modern hf. tan calf, lettered* (Wing F1039) **£84.00**

181 **Herne** (John) The Law of Charitable Uses. Wherein the Statute of 43. Eliz. Chap.4. is set forth and Explained; with Directions how to Sue out and prosecute Commissions grounded upon that Statute: also Presidents, Inquisitions, and Decrees, with divers Judgements, and Resolutions upon Exceptions and Appeals against Decrees; and other Proceedings upon the said Statute. *T. R. for Timothy Twyford,* 1660, [A1] blank *present,* [vi+]151[+v] pp., sm. 8vo, *contemp. sheep, leather label* (Wing H1568) **£75.00**

182 **Hervey** (John, *Lord*) Remarks on the Craftsman's Vindication of his two Hon[ble] Patrons, in his Paper of May 22. 1731. *J. Peele,* 1731, *hf.-title present,* 62 pp., 8vo, *disbound* **£15.00**

183 **Highwaymen.** An Act for the better Suppressing of Theft upon the Borders of England and Scotland, and for Discovery of High-way Men and other Felons. *Hen: Hills and John Field,* 1657, *embrowned,* [i+] 9pp., folio, *grey bds.* (Wing E1100) **£20.00**

184 **Holt** (J.) Characters of the Kings and Queens of England, selected from different Histories; with Observations and Reflections, chiefly adapted to common Life; and particularly intended for the Instruction of Youth. To which are added, Notes historical. *Dublin, by J. Moore,* 1789, *name on title,* xiv+409 pp., 8vo, *contemp. hf. tan calf, leather label, marbled bds., slightly scuffed* **£35.00**

185 **Hughes** (John) Letters by Several Eminent Persons deceased including the Correspondence of John Hughes and several of his Friends, published from the Originals: with notes explanatory and historical by John Duncombe. 3 Vols. Second Edition, with additions. *J. Johnson,* 1773, *engraved general title,* xxxvi+297:viii+272+lxxii:vi+184+c pp., 8vo, *contemp. sprinkled calf, backstrips gilt, lacks all labels, joints beginning to crack* **£40.00**

186 **Hume** (David) The History of England, from the Invasion of Julius Caesar to the Revolution of 1688. 8 Vols., to which is prefixed a Short Account of his Life, written by himself. *Edinburgh. Peter Hill and Silvester Doig* . . . 1810, *portrait foxed:*
[with]
Smollett (T.) A History of England, from the Revolution to the Death of George II . . . 5 Vols., to which is prefixed, the Life of the Author, with critical Observations on his Works by Robert Anderson. *Edinburgh, Peter Hill and Silvester Doig* . . . 1810, *portrait foxed:*
[and]
[**Campbell** (Thomas)] Annals of Great Britain from the Ascension of George III, to the Peace of Amiens. 3 Vols., *Edinburgh, Mendell, Doig, & Stevenson,* 1807:
The 16 Vols. together, 8vo, *uniformly bound in contemp. full calf, backstrips gilt and lettered, sides tooled in gilt and blind, some joints tender or beginning to crack, m.e.* **£110.00**

187 —— ——Continued to the Death of George the Second, by T. Smollett, with last corrections and improvements of the Authors, and a short Memoir of Hume, written by himself. *Henry G. Bohn,* 1868, *printed in double column, portraits,* xiv[+ix+]1352[+lxii][+i] pp. lge.8vo, *contemp. calf, leather label, little rubbed, m.e.* **£35.00**

188 The **Hungarian Rebellion:** or, an Historical Relation of the late wicked Practises of the three Counts, Nadasdi. Serini, and Frangepani; tending to subvert the Government of his present Imperial Majesty of Hungary, and introduce the Mahumetan. With their Arraignment, Condemnation, and manner of being Executed for the same. Translated into English by P[hilip] A[yres] Gent. *William Gilbert, and Tho. Sawbridge,* 1672, *discoloured throughout,* [xii+]115 pp., 12mo, *contemp. calf, unlettered, backstrip a little defective* (Wing – not recorded: Term Cat. i.110), scarce **£185.00**

189 **Hunt** (William) and Reginald L. **Poole**, *Eds.* The Political History of England. 12 Vols., *Longmans, Green, and Co.*, 1906, 8vo, *publishers' buckram, backstrips faded* **£25.00**

190 **Huntington** (Major Robert) Sundry Reasons inducing Major Robert Huntington to lay down his Commission. Humbly presented to the Honourable Houses of Parliament. *Printed in the Year.* 1648, [ii+] 14 pp., sm. 4to, *sewed, untrimmed* (Wing H3775) **£30.00**

191 **Hurault** (Jacques, *French Privy-Councellor*) Politicke, Moral, and Martial Discources, written in French . . . and translated into English by Arthur Golding. *Adam Islip.* 1595, FIRST EDITION IN ENGLISH, *large woodcut device on title, woodcut initials, some worming to lower fore-margins throughout, with no loss,* [xvi+]494 pp., sm. 4to in 8's, *contemp. limp vellum, lacking ties, sometime recased with antique rear free end-paper, orig. paste-downs worn, front hinge strained, lettered by hand* (STC 14000: Hazlitt ii.p. 297) **£450.00**
¶ The front free endpaper carries the signature of Sir Philip Mainwaring, sometime secretary for Ireland, and the purchase price of 3s.

192 **Hyde,** (Edward, *Earl of Clarendon*) The Life of . . . containing, I. An Account of the Chancellor's Life from his Birth to the Restoration in 1660. II. A Continuation of the same, and of his History of the Grand Rebellion, from the Restoration to his Banishment in 1667. Written by Himself. *Oxford, at the Clarendon Printing-House,* 1759, *portrait, offset onto title and foxed, many fine vignettes, slight discolouration,* folio, *contemp. qtr. tan calf, leather label, vellum corners, marbled bds. worn and torn, backstrip slightly defective, joints beginning to crack* **£50.00**

193 **Inclosures.** Observations on a Pamphlet entitled An Enquiry into the Advantages and Disadvantages resulting from Bills of Inclosure. To which are added, Outlines of a proposed Act of Parliament for a general Inclosure of Commons or Waste Lands; introduced by Reflections upon the Utility and Importance of such a Plan, also Calculations, shewing the Loss inevitably sustained by the Clergy or Laity, wherever Lands are given in lieu of Tithes. *Shrewsbury; P. Sandford, also J. Bew,* 1781, *lightly embrowned,* viii+103 pp., 8vo, *sewed, edges untrimmed* (Goldsmiths' 12137) **£50.00**

194 **Indemnity.** An Act for Indempnifying of such Persons as have Acted for the Service of the Publique. *Hen: Hills and John Field,* 1657, *embrowned,* [i+]5 pp., folio, *grey bds.* (Wing E1042) **£18.00**

195 The **Interest of England maintained:** the Honour of the Parliament vindicated: the Malignants Plott upon the Presbyters, to make them doe their worke discovered: the Designe to destroy Common Freedome, and all just Government, is under the specious pretence of rooting out Sectaries, and hereticks, evidenced: . . . *Printed* June the 8. 1646, 19 pp., sm. 4to, *disbound* (Wing 1266) **£30.00**

196 **Ireland.** An Act for the Assuring, Confirming and Setling of Lands and Estates in Ireland. *Henry Hills and John Field,* 1657, *embrowned,* [i+]21 pp., folio, *grey bds.* (Wing E1091) **£18.00**

197 ——[BORLASE (Edmund)] The Reduction of Ireland to the Crown of England. With the Governors since the Conquest by King Henry II. Anno mclxxii. With some Passages in their Government. A Brief Account of the Rebellion Anno Dom mdcxli. also, the Original of the Universitie of Dublin, and the Colledge of Physicians. *Andr. Clarke, for Robert Clavel,* 1675, *folding frontis. of Arms of Charles Stanley, Earl of Derby, to whom the work is dedicated, some staining and wrinkling by damp of early pp.,* 8vo, *contemp. mottled calf, gilt, leather label, joints starting to crack, Grosvenor book label on front paste-down,* (Wing B3771) scarce **£85.00**

198 ——BURKE (Edmund) Two Letters . . . to Gentlemen in the City of Bristol, on the Bills depending in Parliament relative to the Trade of Ireland. Second Edition. *J. Dodsley,* 1778, *hf.-title present,* [iv+] 32 pp., 8vo, *disbound* (Todd 29b) **£15.00**

199 ——CALDWELL (Sir James)] Debates relative to the Affairs of Ireland; in the Years 1763 and 1764. To which is added, an Enquiry how far the Restrictions laid upon the Trade of Ireland, by British Acts of Parliament, are a Benefit or Disadvantage to the British Dominions in general, and to England in particular, for whose separate Advantage they were intended . . . 2 Vols. *London,* 1766, x+853[+i(errata)+]iii pp., 8vo, *contemp. sprinkled tan calf, a little worn, joints beginning to crack* (Kress 6321: Goldsmiths 10149) scarce **£85.00**

200 ——[COOKE (Edward)] Arguements for and against an Union, between Great Britain and Ireland, considered. *Dublin printed: London reprinted, for J. Wright*, 1798, *hf.-title and advert.-lf. present*, [iv+]58[+ii] pp.:
[with]
Arguments . . . to which is prefixed, a Proposal on the same Subject by Josiah Tucker, a New Edition. *Reprinted for John Stockdale*, 1798, 31[+i] pp.:
The 2 Issues together, 8vo, *disbound* **£30.00**
¶ 'This pamphlet . . . is a temperate examination of the problem, resting the case for the union on grounds conciliatory to all classes of the Irish people.' (*D.N.B.*)

201 —— ——RUDD (Pemberton) An Answer to the Pamphlet, intituled, "Arguments for and against an Union," . . . New Edition. *Reprinted for John Stockdale*, 1798, 23[+i] pp., 8vo, *disbound* **£18.00**

202 ——CURRY (J.) An Historical and Critical Review of the Civil Wars in Ireland, from the Reign of Queen Elizabeth to the Settlement under King William. With the State of the Irish Catholics from that Settlement to the Relaxation of the Popery Laws, in the year 1778. A New and improved Edition. *Dublin, R. Conolly*, 1810, *occasional rubber stamps*, [xix+]xxvii+660[+xi] pp., 8vo, *original bds, rubbed, backstrip mostly defective, paper label, unpressed and untrimmed copy* **£65.00**

203 ——DOUGLAS (Sylvester) Speech . . . in the House of Commons, Tuesday, April the 23d, 1799, on seconding the Motion . . . for the House to agree with the Lords in an Address to his Majesty relative to a Union with Ireland. *J. Wright*, 1799, *hf.-title present* [iv+] 196 pp., 8vo, *disbound* **£21.00**

204 ——DUIGENAN (Patrick, *Irish politician*) The Speech . . . on the Subject of an Incorporating Union with Great Britain, earnestly recommended to the serious consideration of the Loyal Citizens of Dublin. *Dublin, REA*, 1800, *soiled and dog-eared*, [ii+] 24 pp., 8vo, *sewed, untrimmed* **£21.00**
¶ Duigenan was strongly in favour of the union, and was one of the leading speaker on the government side during the debates on this question. (D.N.B.)

205 ——FITZGIBBON (John, *Earl of Clare*) The Speech . . . in the House of Lords of Ireland, on a Motion made by him [. . .'it will be advisable to concur in such Measures as may best tend to unite the two Kingdoms . . .] on Monday, February 10, 1800. *Dublin, J. Milliken*, 1800, *hf. title present*, [iv+]101[+ii] pp., 8vo, *disbound* **£18.00**

206 ——FITZWILLIAM (William Wentworth, *Earl*) First Letter. A Letter . . . to the Earl of Carlisle, explaining the Cause of that Event [his dismissal from office of Lord Lieutenant]. *Dublin printed, London reprinted and sold by G. G. and J. Robinson*, 1795, 28 pp., 8vo, *hf. cloth, marbled bds.* **£15.00**

207 ——FOSTER (John Leslie) A Report of a Speech . . . on Mr. Grattan's Motion for a Committee on the State of the Penal Laws now in force against the Roman Catholics of Ireland. Friday, April 24, 1812. *J. Hatchard*, 1812, *top outer corner of first 2 ll. slightly defective*, [iv+] 36 pp., 8vo, *sewed, all edges untrimmed* **£18.00**

208 ——[JOHNSON (William)] Reasons for adopting an Union between Ireland, and Great Britain. *Dublin, J. Milliken*, 1799, [ii+] 61 pp., 8vo, *disbound* (Goldsmith 17531) **£25.00**

209 —— —— ——*J. Plymsell, at the Anti-Jacobin Press, and sold by C. Chappel*, [1799], [ii+] 62 pp., 8vo, *disbound* (Goldsmith 17532) **£20.00**

210 ——LUCAS (Charles) Seasonable Advice to the Electors of Members of Parliament at the ensuing General Election. Addressed to the Free and Independent Electors of the Kingdom of Ireland in general, to those of the City of Dublin in particular. *T. Davies, J. Coote, and T. Becket*, 1760, *hf.-title, with errata on verso, present*, [iv+] 72 pp., 8vo, *disbound* **£35.00**

211 ——M'KENNA (Theobald) Constitutional Objections to the Government of Ireland, by a separate Legislature, in a letter to John Hamilton . . . Third Edition *Dublin, N. Fitzpatrick*, 1799, 85 pp., 8vo, *disbound* **£18.00**

212 ——[SMITH (Sir William Cusac) Letters on the Subject of Union, in which Mr. Jebb's 'Reply' is considered, and the Competance of Parliament to bind Ireland to an Union is asserted. *Dublin printed, London reprinted for J. Wright*, 1799, *hf.-title present*, [iv+]115[+ii] pp., 8vo, *disbound* **£25.00**

213 ——STUART (James) Historical Memoirs of the City of Armagh, for a Period of 1373 Years, comprising a considerable Portion of the general History of Ireland; a Refutation of the Opinions of Dr. Ledwich, respecting the Non-Existence of St. Patrick; and an Appendix on the Learning, Antiquities, and Religion of the Irish Nation. *Newry, Alexander Wilkinson for Longman, Hurst, Rees* . . . 1819, *with 5 engravings, embrowned throughout, small tear in one lf.*, x+651[+x] pp., 8vo, *orig. bds., paper label, soiled, joints splitting* **£45.00**

214 **Isaacson** (Henry) Satvrni Ephemerides sive Tabvla Historico-Chronologica, containing A Chronilogical Series or Succession of the foure Monarchyes, with an Abridgment of the Annual Memorial Passages in them, as also a Succession of the Kings and Rulers ouer most Kingdomes and Estates of the World, with a Breife Chorographical Description of them, & theire Seueral Storyes Epitomized, with a Compend of the History of the Church of God from the Creation . . . lastly as Appendix of the Plantation and Encrease of Religion in this Monarchy of Britayne . . . *B. A[lsop] and T. F[awcet] for Henry Seile and Humphrey Robinson*, 1633, *engraved title by Will. Marshall, "The Frontispiece Explained" facing title, many outer corners worn and fragile, a few pp. torn with some damage of letter press*, [xix+]494[+xvi] pp., lge. folio, *contemp. calf, corners and edges worn, due to worming, backstrip defective, lacks label* (STC 14269) **£50.00**

215 **Jacob** (William) Tracts relating to the Corn Trade and Corn Laws: including the Second Report . . . *John Murray*, 1828, vii+293:58:41[+i] pp., 8vo, *orig. blue and drab paper bds., paper label, backstrip little torn*, scarce (Goldsmiths' 25512: Kress C2091) **£95.00**
¶ Comprises: Report . . . respecting the Agriculture and Trade in Corn, in some of the Continental States of Europe: Notices respecting the Commerce of the Black Sea and the Sea of Azoff . . .: Observations on the Benefits arising from the Cultivation of Poor Soils, by the application of Pauper Labour . . .

216 **James I.** His Maiesties Speach in the Starre-chamber. The xx. of Ivne. Anno 1616. *Robert Barker*, [1616], *soiled and embrowned throughout, lacks* A1 (*? blank*), bibliographical annotations on recto and verso of title by, and the armorial book label of Oliver Acton, a few running titles cropped, [i+] 57 pp., sm. 4to, *early marbled bds., word and joints cracked* (STC 14397)) **£45.00**

217 ——W[ELDEN (Sir A[ntony]) The Court and Character of King James . . . *R. J. and are to be sold by John Wright*, 1650, *Reprinted by G. Smeaton*, 1817, *portrait, foxing throughout*, iv+61[+iii] pp., sm. 4to, *contemp. hf. calf, rubbed, joints cracked, lacks label, marbled bds.* **£40.00**

218 **James II.** (King of England, &c) His last Expressions and Dying-words. *R. Rogers*, 1702, *portrait*, broadside, *folded and little creased in margins* **£45.00**

219 **James II.** [Ames (Richard)] The Character of a Bigotted Prince; and what England may Expect from the Return of such a One. *Richard Baldwin*, 1691, *outer margins slightly stained and becoming fragile*, [iv+]31[+i] pp., sm. 4to, *disbound* (New Wing A2975AB) **£75.00**

220 ——[WELLWOOD (James)] An Answer to the late King James's Declaration to all his pretended Subjects in the Kingdom of England, dated at Dublin Castle, May 8. 1689. *Dorman Newman*, 1689, *hf. title and final advert. page dust soiled*, [iii+]31[+i] pp., sm. 4to, *disbound* (Wing W1298) **£21.00**

221 **Jennings** (James) Description of Lord Exmouth's Attack upon Algiers, painted by Henry Aston Barker; now exhibited in his Panorama, Leicester Square. *Jas Adlard and Sons*, 1818, *large folding plate, foxed and worn at some folds* 12 pp., 8vo, *wrappers* **£16.00**

222 **Johnson** (Hewlett, *Dean of Canterbury*) Soviet Strength, its Source and Challenge. *Frederick Muller*, 1942, [vi+] 154 pp., sm. 8vo, *sewed* **£15.00**

223 **Justinus** (Marcus Junianus) The History of Ivstine, taken out of the four and forty Books of Trogus Pompeius: containing the Affairs of all Ages, and Countrys, both in Peace and War, from the beginning of the World untill the Time of the Roman Emperors. Together, with the Epitomie of the Lives and Manners of the Roman Emperors, from Octavius Augustus Caesar, to the Emperor Theodosius. Translated into English by Robert Codrington. *William Gilbertson*, 1654, *errata lf. present, some browning throughout*, [xii+]606[+xxxi] pp., sm. 8vo, *contemp. calf, corners repaired, sometime rebacked, leather label* (Wing J1271) scarce **£100.00**

224 **Karcher** (Théodore) Les Ecrivains militaires de la France. *Londres, Trübner*, 1866, *hf. title present, engravings in text*, [iv+]viii+348 pp., 8vo, *orig. cloth, partly faded and soiled* **£25.00**

225 **Kettell** (Thomas P.) History of the Great Rebellion, from its Commencement to its Close, giving an Account of its Origin, the Secession of the Southern States and of the Formation of the Confederate Government . . . *Hartford, Conn., L. Stebbins, F. A. Howe*, 1865, *portraits, maps, &c., overall faint browning*, thick 8vo, *contemp. sprinkled calf, newly rebacked, orig. labels retained* **£40.00**

226 The **Kingdomes Case:** or, the Question resolved, Whether the Kings Subjects of this Realm of England may or ought to ayd and assist each other, in repressing the persons now assembled together, under the name of the Kings Army . . . *Iohn Wright*, May 1, 1643, *embrowned throughout, small tear in head margin of last leaf with slight loss, upper margins cropped*, [ii+] 13 pp., sm. 4to, *wrappers* (Wing K583) **£25.00**

227 **Kinnaird** (Douglas) Remarks on the Volume of Hydrabad Papers, printed for the Use of the East India Proprietors. *J. M. Richardson, and James Ridgway*, 1825, [i+] 208 pp., 8vo, *grey bds., paper-label* **£18.00**

228 **Lacretelle** (Charles) Histoire de France pendent le Dix-huitième Siècle. Seconde Édition. 6 Vols. *Paris, F. Buisson*, 1810/12, *some staining*, 8vo, *qtr. purple sheep, lettered, marbled bds., a little rubbed* **£160.00**

229 **LaHarpe** (Jean-Francois) Du Fanatisme dans la Langue révolutionnaire, or de la Persecution suscitée par les Barbares du dix-huitième Siècle, contre la Religion Chrétienne et ses Ministres. Seconde Édition, revue et corrigée par l'Auteur. *Paris, chez Migneret*, 1797, [ii+]168[+i] pp., 8vo, *orig. bds., little worn* **£20.00**

230 **La Noue** (Francois de) The Politicke and Militarie Discovrses of the Lord de La Novve. Whereunto are adioyned certaine obseruations of the same Author, of things happened during the three late civill warres of France. With a true declaration of manie particulars touching the same. All faithfully translated out of the French by E. A[ggas]. *T. C[adman] and E. A[ggas] by Thomas Orwin*, 1587, *partly* **black letter,** *title within typographic border, large woodcut initials, tear in inner margin* [D[8]], *hole in* [M[8]] *with slight loss, paper faults in fore margins of* Y[2] *and* [Y[8]], *occasional rust marks, pagination erratic*, [xvi+] 460 pp., sm. 4to, *contemp. limp vellum, lettered by hand, upper inner hinge broken, lacks ties*, (STC 15215: Cockle 37) scarce **£950.00**

231 **La Tude** (Henry Masers de) Memoirs . . . containing an Account of his Confinement Thirty-five Years in the State Prisons of France; and of the Stratagems he adopted to escape, once from the Bastille, and twice from the Castle of Vincennes; with the Sequel to those Adventures. Translated from the French of the Amsterdam Edition. *J. Johnson*, 1787, *embrowned*, viii+63[+i] pp., 8vo, *contemp. qtr. calf, marbled bds.* **£65.00**

232 **Laud** (William, *Archbp. of Canterbury*) The History of the Troubles and Tryal . . . wrote by Himself, during his Imprisonment in the Tower. To which is prefixed the Diary of his own Life . . . and subjoined a Supplement to the Preceding History . . . *Ri. Chiswell*, 1695, *title in red and black, creased, lower margin repaired, divisional titles present, lacks portrait and final advert. lf., small snags in a few margins, some ll. damp stained*, [xx+]616 pp., folio, *contemp. panelled calf, rubbed, corners worn, recently rebacked, leather label* (Wing L586) **£45.00**

233 **Leases.** Tables for Renewing and Purchasing of the Leases of Cathedral Churches and Colleges, according to several Rates of Interest; with their Construction and Use explain'd . . . Second Edition . . . *J. Wyat*, 1722, xviii+29 pp.;
[and]
The Value of Church and College Leases consider'd: and the Advantage of the Lessees made very Apparent. Second Edition. *J. Wyat*, 1722, iv+26[+ii] pp.;
The 2 pieces together, 8vo, *disbound* **£25.00**

234 **Leather.** Observations on the Evidence relating to the Duties on Leather, taken before the Committee of the House of Commons: ordered to be printed, 5th April, 1813: shewing the chief Causes which have induced the Trade to petition Parliament for Relief. *Joseph Hartnell*, 1813, *2 folding tables, hf. title present*, [i+] 38 pp., 8vo, *sewed as issued, edges untrimmed* (Kress B6191) **£25.00**

235 **Lecky** (W. E. H.) A History of England in the Eighteenth Century, 7 Vols., *Longmans, Green, and Co.* 1919, cr. 8vo, *publishers' cloth, backstrips slightly faded* **£15.00**

236 **Legal** BIRD (James Barry) The Laws respecting Landlords, Tenants, and Lodgers, laid down in a plain, easy, and familiar Manner; together with Practical Directions . . . Ninth Edition. *W. Clarke and Sons*, 1811, [viii+]108[+iv] pp., 8vo, *disbound* **£12.00**

237 ——BIRD (James Barry) The Laws respecting Landlords, Tenants, and Lodgers . . . Ninth Edition. *W. Clarke and Sons*, 1809, [viii+]108[+viii] pp.:
[with]
The Laws respecting Parish Matters containing the several Offices and Duties of Churchwardens, Overseers of the Poor, Constables, Watchmen . . . Fifth Edition, *W. Clarke and Sons*, 1808, [viii+]135[+ix] pp.:
[and]
The Laws respecting Tithes, comprising all the Cases and Statutes on the subject of Tithes . . . Fourth Edition. *W. Clarke and Sons*, 1809, [vi+]98[+viii] pp.:
[and]
The Laws respecting Wills, Testements, and Codicils, and Executors, Administrators, & Guardians . . . Fifth Edition. *W. Clarke and Sons*, 1806, [x+]140[+iv] pp.:
Four piece bound together, 8vo, *contemp. tan calf, leather label, slight worming in head and tail of joints* **£45.00**

238 ——BURROW (Sir James) Reports of Cases adjudged in the Court of Kings Bench, since the Death of Lord Raymond . . . Part the Fourth, 2 Vols., Michaelmas Term 30 Geo. 2. 1756 to Trinity Term 1 Geo 3. 1761 (inclusive). *Dublin, R. Moncrieffe*, 1785, xviii+1–53 [54–607+lxx]: [xii+548+lxxii] pp., 8vo, *contemp. tan calf, leather labels* **£35.00**
¶ Vol. i. Fourth Edition: vol. ii. Third Edition.

239 ——CHRISTIE (James Traill) Concise Precedent of Wills; with an Introduction & Practical Notes. *A. Maxwell & Son*, 1849, *23pp. catalogue*, xv+267 pp., 8vo, *orig. bds., paper label, snags at extremities of backstrip* **£20.00**

240 ——CLARKE'S New Law List; being a List of the Judges and Officers of the different Courts of Justice: Councel, Certificated Special Pleaders, Conveyancers; and a complete and accurate List of certificated Attornies, Notaries, &c. in England and Wales . . . Sixteenth Edition *William Clarke and Sons, and R. Pheney*, 1812, 302 pp., sm. 8vo, *contemp. sheep, leather label, little worn* **£21.00**

241 ——The CLERK'S ENGLISH TUTOR. Shewing the Practice of the Courts of King's Bench and Common Pleas, as they are now settled, pursuant of the several late Acts of Parliament, and the respective Rules of both the Courts made consonant thereto . . . by an Attorney at Law. *E. and R. Nutt, and R. Gosling* . . . 1733, *light browning throughout*, vi+399 +xxiii :v+394 pp., 8vo, *contemp. sheep, leather labels, a little worn* **£35.00**

242 ——The Compleat Clark, containing the best Forms of all sorts of Presidents, for Conveyances and Assurances; and other Instruments now in Use and Practice: with the Forms of Bills, Pleadings, and Answers in Chancery; as they were penned and perfected by Eminent Lawyers, and Great Conveyancers, both Ancient and Modern . . . Third Edition, *T. R. for N. Brook*, 1671, *some soiling, a few margins slightly torn, a few ll. working loose*, [iv+]936[+lxxx] pp., sm. 4to (in 8s), *contemp. calf, rather worn at edges, split in backstrip, rear hinge loose, paste-downs lifted and defective* (Wing C5636) **£25.00**

243 ——CUMBERLAND (R.) De Legibus Naturae Disquisitio Philosophica . . . *Typis E. Flesher, prostat verò apud Nathanaelem Hooke*, 1672, FIRST EDITION, *title in red and black, imprimatur lf. present, marginal notes and markings in ink and pencil by various hands, signature of James H. Todd, Trin. Coll. Dublin at head of dedication page*, [lxv+]421[+i] pp., sm. 4to, *contemp. calf, blind tooled, rubbed and corners worn, sometime rebacked, old leather label retained* (Wing C. 7580) **£60.00**

244 ——[EGERTON (Sir Thomas, *Baron Ellesmere and Viscount Brackley*)] The Speech of the Lord Chancellor of England, in the Eschequer Chamber, touching the Post-nati. *Societie of Stationers*, 1609, FIRST EDITION, *A[1] & [Q[4]] both present, with double printed line borders*, [xii+]118[+ii] pp., sm. 4to, *qtr. crushed maroon morocco, lettered cloth sides*, (STC 7540) **£140.00**
¶ From the Phillipps collection.
The most important of Lord Ellesmere's judgements. The *Post-nati* were Scots born after the accession of James vi. of Scotland to the English throne. It was ruled that the *Post-nati* were natural-born subjects and therefore entitled to hold land in England.

245 ——HUTTON (Sir Richard) The Reports . . . containing many Choice Cases, Judgements, and Resolutions, in points of Law, in the several Raignes of King James and King Charles, being written in French by his owne hand and now faithfully translated into English according to Order. *T. R. for Henry Twyford and Thomas Dring*, 1656, *tear in title, title and dedication sometime crudely repaired in inner margins, paper discoloured throughout*, [xii+]136[+vii] pp., folio, *contemp. tan calf, corners worn, newly rebacked, leather label* (Wing H3843) **£40.00**

246 ——JACOB (Giles) A New Law Dictionary: containing the Interpretation and Definition of Words and Terms used in the Law; and also the Whole Law, and the Practice thereof, Under all the Heads and Titles of the same . . . Sixth Edition . . . *In the Savoy, Henry Lintot for R. Ware, J. and P. Knapton* [*et alia*], 1750, *slight worming in some lower gutters, and occasional staining*, [viii+398+iv] pp., folio, *contemp. rough calf, newly rebacked, leather label* **£50.00**

247 ——KING (P. J. Locke) Injustice of the Law of Succession to the Real Property of Intestates. Second Edition. *James Ridgway*, 1854, 78 pp., 8vo, *grey bds., paper label* **£16.00**

248 —— ——Speech on the Laws relating to the Property of Intestates, in the House of Commons, February 17, 1859. *James Ridgway*, 1859, 18[+i] pp., 8vo, *grey bds., paper label* **£15.00**

249 ——MITFORD (Eardley) The Law of Wills, Codicils and Revocations, with Plain and Familiar Instructions for Executors, Administrators, Devisees and Legatees. . . . Fifth Edition, *W. Flint*, 1812, iv+120[+iv] pp., 8vo, *disbound* **£12.00**

250 ——POLLOCK (Sir Frederick) and Frederic William MAITLAND. The History of English Law before the Time of Edward I. Second Edition, 2 Vols., *Cambridge University Press*, 1898, xxxviii+638: xv+691 pp., roy. 8vo, *orig. black buckram, lettered, faded* **£25.00**

251 ——SELDEN (Ionnes) De Iure Naturali & Gentium, iuxta Disciplinam Ebraeorum, libri septem. *Richardus Bishopius*, 1640, FIRST EDITION, *title in red and black, hf. title with imprimatur on verso present*, [xl+] 847 pp., folio, *contemp. rough calf, leather label, backstrip slightly defective at head and tail* (STC 22168) **£375.00**

252 ——STRANGE (John) Reports of Adjudged Cases in the Courts of Chancery, King's Bench, Common Pleas, and Exchequer, from Trinity Term in the second Year of King George I. to Trinity Term in the twenty-first Year of King George II. [1716–1747]. The Second Edition, Revised and Corrected . . . 2 Vols. *The King's Law-Printers* . . . 1782, iv+1272[+lxxxiv] pp., 8vo, *contemp. calf, leather labels* **£35.00**

253 **Leigh** (Edward) Select and Choyce Observations, containing all the Roman Emperours. The first eighteen by Edward Leigh, the others added by his Son Henry Leigh. Certain Choyce French Proverbs, alphabetically disposed and Englished . . . *Roger Daniel, for John Williams*, 1637, *lacks* A1/2, *a few headlines cut close, some staining*, [xi+] 277 pp., sm. 8vo, *modern panelled calf, leather label, marb. endpapers* (Wing L. 1003) **£75.00**

254 **L'Estrange** (Roger) A Memento: directed to all Those that Truly Reverence the Memory of King Charles the Martyr; and as Passionately with the Honour, Safety, and Happinesse of his Royall Successour, our most Gratious Sovereign Charles the II. The First Part. *Henry Brome*, 1662, *title soiled*, [viii+]251[+v] pp., sm. 4to, *disbound* (Wing L1270) **£30.00**

255 **Linen** [BINDON (David)] A Letter from a Merchant who has left the Trade to a Member of Parliament. In which the Case of British and Irish Manufacture of Linnen, Threads, and Tapes, is fairly stated, and all the Objections against the Encouragement proposed to be given to that Manufacture fully answered. *R. Willock*, 1738, 84 pp., 8vo, *new marbled bds., label on upper cover* (Kress 4373: Goldsmith's 7567) scarce **£95.00**

256 [**Lloyd** (David)] State Worthies, or, the States-men and Favourites of England since the Reformation their Prudence and Policies, Successes and Miscarriages, Advancements and Falls; during the Reigns of King Henry viii, King Edward vi, Queen Mary, Queen Elizabeth, King James, King Charles i. Second Edition, with Additions. *Thomas Milbourn for Samuel Speed*, 1670. *engr. frontis., title in red and black, one lf. torn, browning throughout*, [xvii+]680:721–1051[v] pp., sm. 8vo, *nineteenth century calf, gilt, leather label, m.e.* (Wing L2646) **£85.00**

257 **Lloyd** (Lodowick) The Marrow of History: or, the Pilgrimage of Kings and Princes. Truly representing the variety of Dangers inherent to their Crowns; and the lamentable Deaths which many of them, and some of the best of them, have undergone. Collected, not onely out of the best Modern Histories; but from all those which have been most famous in the Latine, Greek, or in the Hebrew Tongue . . . Corrected and Revived by R[obert] C[odrington]. *E. Alsop*, 1653, *has lf.* A[1], *embrowned throughout, with some other soiling*, [viii+] 311 pp., sm. 4to, *nineteenth century hf. calf, lettered, marbled bds, and end-papers* (Wing L2660) scarce **£120.00**

258 [——(William)] Pretences of the French Invasion Examined. for the Information of the People of England. *R. Clavel*, 1692, *sl. marginal staining*, [iv+] 16 pp., sm. 4to, *disbound* (Wing L2690) **£55.00**

259 **Locke** (John) Two Treatises of Government. [In the former the False Principles and Foundation of Sir Robert Filmer and his Followers are detected and overthrown. The latter is an Essay concerning the true original Extent and End of civil Government]. Reprinted, the Sixth Time by *A. Millar, H. Woodfall, I. Whiston and B. White* . . . 1764, [xii+] 416 pp., 8vo, *contemp. sprinkled calf, backstrip gilt, leather label, tail of backstrip chipped, joints becoming tender* **£75.00**

260 **London.** An Act for the preventing of the Multiplicity of Buildings in and about the Suburbs of London, and within Ten Miles therof. *Henry Hills and Iohn Field*, 1657, *embrowned*, [i+] 24 pp., folio, *grey bds.* (Wing E1119) **£25.00**

261 ——ARNOLD (Richard) The Customs of London, otherwise called Arnold's Chronicle; containing, among divers other Matters, the Original of the celebrated Poem of The Nut-Brown Maid. Reprinted from the first Edition, with the additions included in the second. *F. C. and J. Rivington* . . . 1811, liii+300 pp., imp. 4to, *hf. tan calf, leather label, cloth sides, upper joint cracking, shelf label at base of backstrip, ex-libris label on front pastedown* **£45.00**

262 ——To the Honovrable the House of Commons assembled in High Covrt of Parliament: the Humble Remonstrance and Petition of the Lord Major, Aldermen, and Commons of the city of London, in Common Councell Assembled [dealing in the main with the reform of Church and State] *Richard Cotes*, 1646, [ii+] 9 pp., sm. 4to, *sewed* (Wing T1447) **£30.00**

263 ——To the Right Honourable the Lords assembled in High Court of Parliament: the Humble Petition of the Lord Major, Aldermen, and Commons of the City of London, in Common Council Assembled, together with an humble Representation of the pressing grievances, and important desires of the well-affected Freemen, and Covenant-engaged Citizens of the City of London. *Richard Cotes*, 1646, *slight worming in fore-margins*, 8pp., sm. 4to, *disbound* (Wing T1664) **£35.00**

264 [**Long** (Thomas)] A Resolution of Certain Queries concerning Submissions to the Present Government . . . *R. Baldwin*, 1689, *title laid down, staining and browning throughout*, [viii+] 83 pp., sm. 4to, *disbound* (Wing L2980) **£20.00**

265 **Lope de Vega** HOLLAND (Henry Richard Lord) Some Account of the Life and Writings of Lope Felix de Vega Carpio. *Longman, Hurst, Rees, and Orme* . . . 1806, *portrait, offset onto title*, vii+294[+i – errata] pp., 8vo, *contemp. diced calf, lettered, marbled end-papers* **£30.00**

266 **Louis xii,** (King of France.) SAINT-GELAIS (Jean de) Histoire de Lovys xii. Roy de France, Pere dv Pevple, et de plvsievrs chose memorables aduenües en France, 9 en Italie, jusques en l'an 1510. Tirée de la Bibliotheque du Roy, & nouuelement mise en lumiere par Theodore Godefroy. *Paris, Abraham Pacard*, 1622, FIRST EDITION, *copper engraved vignette on title, title in red and black*, [viii+]315[+i] pp., 4to, *contemp. limp vellum, lettered by hand, pastedowns slightly torn* (Goldsmith S93) **£85.00**

267 **Louis xiv.** The Great Bastard, Protector of the Little One. Done out of French. And for which a Proclamation with a Reward of 5000 Lewes-dores, to Discover the Author, was Publish'd. *Printed at Cologne*, 1689, *outer margins browned*, [iv+] 32 pp., sm. 4to, *disbound* (Wing G1663) **£60.00**

268 **Louis xv.** MOUFFLE D'ANGERVILLE. The Private Life of Lewis xv. in which are contained the principal Events, remarkable Occurences, and Anecdotes of his Reign. Translated from the French by J. O. Justamond. 4 Vols. *Dublin, John Parker, for Messrs. Whitestone, Sleater, Williams* . . . 1781, 12mo, *contemp. sprinkled calf, leather labels, one side little damaged by insects* **£42.00**

269 **Louvet** (John-Baptist) Narrative of the Dangers to which I have been exposed since the 31st of May, 1793, with Historical Memorandums. *Dublin, P. Byrne*, 1795, *slight foxing, small tear in title and one margin*, vii+221 pp., 8vo, *disbound* **£18.00**

270 **Ludlow** (Edmund, *General and Regicide*) Memoirs. With a Collection of Original Papers, serving to confirm and illustrate many important Passages. 3 Vols. . . . *Switzerland, Printed at Vivay in the Canton of Bern*, 1698–99, *portrait, embrowned throughout*, viii+878:[vii]402[+lvi] pp., 8vo, *contemp. panelled calf, corners little worn, newly rebacked, leather labels* (Wing L3460–62) **£75.00**

271 —— ——to which is now added, the Case of King Charles the First. With a copious Index. *A. Millar; D. Brown; and J. Ward*, 1751, *title in red and black, portrait, occasional marginalia in ink*, [x+]502+[ii+]5–20[+xxviii] pp., folio, *contemp. sprinkled calf, leather label, surface damaged, joints cracking* **£55.00**

272 **Macaulay** (Thomas Babington) The History of England from the Accession of James II. [to the Death of William III.] 5 Vols., *Longman* . . . 1849/61, *a few gatherings working loose*, 8vo, *orig. brown cloth, lettered in gilt, blind tooled, backstrips faded* **£20.00**

¶ Vols. i. and ii. are the Second Edition; vol. v. is edited by Lady Trevelyan, sister of the author.

273 —— ——edited by Charles Harding Firth. 6 Vols. *Macmillan and Co.*, 1913, *plates in colour and in black and white*, roy. 8vo, *publishers' blue cloth, lettered in gilt, a little shabby* **£25.00**

274 **Maccartney** (George, *General*) A Letter to a Friend of His in London, dated at Ostend, Dec. 4–15. 1712. giving a Particular Account of what pass'd before and at the Unfortunate Duel between His Grace the D. of Hamilton and L. Mohun. *A. Baldwin*, 1713, *small stamp on verso of title, embrowned throughout*, 18[+ii] pp., sm. 4to, *disbound, untrimmed* **£21.00**

275 **MacKenzie.** LANG (Andrew) Sir George MacKenzie, King's Advocate, of Rosehaugh, his Life and Times 1636(?)–1691. *Longmans, Green and Co.*, 1909, *4 illusts.*, xii+347 pp., 8vo, *orig. red cloth, lettered, dulled by age* **£18.00**

276 **Maclaine** (James, *'gentleman-highwayman'*) ALLEN (Rev. Dr.) An Account of the Behaviour o Mr. James Maclaine, from the Time of his Condemnation to the Day of his Execution, October 3 1750. *J. Noon and A. Millar*, 1750, 32 pp., 8vo, *disbound* **£25.00**

277 [**Macpherson** (James)] A Short History of the Opposition during the last Session of Parliament. Sixth Edition. *T. Cadell*, 1779, *inner margin of hf. title repaired, some discolouration throughout*, vi+58 pp., 8vo, *new wrappers* **£16.00**

278 **Madox** (Thomas) The History and Antiquities of the Exchequer of the Kings of England, in Two Periods: to wit, from the Norman Conquest, to the End of the Reign of K. John; and from the End of the Reign of K. John, to the End of the Reign on K. Edward II: together with a Correct Copy of the Ancient Dialogue concerning the Exchequer, generally ascribed to Garvasius Tilburiensis; and a Dissertation concerning the most Ancient Great Roll of the Exchequer, commonly styled The Roll of Quinto Regis Stephani. *J. Matthews; and sold by Robert Knaplock*, 1711, *slight worming in few tail margins, early annotations on free endpapers*, folio, *contemp. sprinkled calf, corners little worn and sides rubbed, newly rebacked, leather label* **£100.00**

279 **Mahan** (A. T.) The Influence of Sea Power upon the French Revolution and Empire 1793–1812. 2 Vols., *Sampson Low*, 1892, 13 *maps and battleplans* (1 *folding*), *vol. i. inscribed by Dennis Wheatley*, xxi+380:xix+428 pp.:

[and]

Sea Power in its Relations to the War of 1812. 2 Vols., *Sampson Low*, 1905, 27 *plates and* 25 *maps and battle-plans* (4 *folding*), *vol. i. inscribed by Dennis Wheatley, vol. ii. has his marginal pencil marks, hf. titles*, xxiii+423:xix+456 pp.:

The 4 volumes together, 8vo, *uniformly bound in hf. crushed, peacock blue morocco, backstrips panelled, ornamented and lettered in gilt, slight scuffing to bands of one vol., pale blue cloth sides, g.e., marbled endpapers* **£200.00**

280 [**Mallet** (David)] A Congratulatory Letter to Selim, on the Three Letters to the Whigs. *M. Cooper*, 1748, *some soiling*, [iv+] 64 pp., 8vo, *disbound* **£15.00**

281 **Marines** A Letter to a Member of Parliament concerning the four Regiments commonly called Mariners. *A. Baldwin*, 1699, *final blank present*, 14 pp., (Wing L1670):

[and]

A Short Vindication of Marine Regiments, in Answer to a Pamphlet, Entituled, A Letter . . . concerning the Four Marine Regiments. *A. Baldwin*, 1699, *embrowned*, 11 oo., (Wing S3643): Two pieces together, sm. 4to, *disbound*, scarce **£185.00**

282 **Markham** (Francis) The Booke of Honovr. Or, Five Decads of Epistles of Honovr. *Augustine Matthews, and John Norton*, 1625, *some discolouration throughout*, [vi+] 200 pp., folio, *contemp. vellum gilt, sometime rebacked, new endpapers, ties still present* (STC 17331) **£175.00**

283 **Marlborough.** TRELAWNEY (Jonathan, *Bp. of Exeter*) A Sermon preached . . . for the Signal Successes Vouchsafed to Her Majesty's Forces by Sea and Land: Under the Command of the Earl of Marlborough in the Low Countries; . . . *Tho. Bennet*, 1702, [ii+]43[+i] pp., sm. 4to, *disbound* **£16.00**

284 **Mary Stuart.** CHALMERS (George) The Life of Mary, Queen of Scots, drawn from the State Papers, with subsidiary Memoirs. Second Edition, corrected and enlarged. 3 Vols., *John Murray*, 1822, *portraits and views, some foxing*, 4+xxiv+507:[iii+]584:[iii+] 652 pp., 8vo, *orig. drab bds., paper labels, rather shabby, edges untrimmed* **£25.00**

285 ——[KYFFIN (Maurice)] Apologie ov defense de l'honorable sentence & tres-juste execution de defuncte Marie Steuard derniere Royne d'Ecosse . . . Aprez la fin du liure sont adioustées les copies des lettres, actes & articles qui seruent à découuir & à bien verifier la trahison de ladite Royne d'Ecosse &c. à l'encontre de la Royne, de la Noblesse & de l'estat d'Angleterre. Le tout traduit d'Anglois en Francoise suiuant l'original imprimé à Londres, par Jean Ouinted, 1587. *Imprimé nouuellement* [*s.l.*] 1588, *small woodcut initials, occasional dampstaining, lacks* A^{m} (*blank*), [x+]287+4 pp., 12mo, *contemp. tan calf, backstrip gilt, leather label, upper joints cracked but strong, marbled endpapers* (Adams M825) **£85.00**

286 ——STEVENSON (Joseph) *Ed.* Selections from Unpublished Manuscripts in the College of Arms and the British Museum, illustrating the Reign of Mary Queen of Scotland mdxliii–mdlxviii. *Glasgow, The Maitland Club*, 1837, xxviii+329 pp., 4to, *hf. tan calf, marbled bds., lettered, backstrip slightly rubbed* **£20.00**

287 ——TYTLER (William) An Inquiry, historical and critical, into the Evidence against Mary Queen of Scots; and an Examination of the Histories of Dr. Robertson and Mr. Hume, with respect to that Evidence. The Fourth Edition, 2 Vols., *T. Cadell and W. Creech*, 1790, *errata lf. present, discoloured*, vi+381:viii+422[+i] pp., 8vo, *qtr. cloth, drab bds., paper labels, soiled* **£30.00**

288 **Matthew of Westminster.** Flores Historiarvm: praecipve de Rebvs Britannicis: ab exor dio mundi usque ad annum Domini mcccvii. et Chronicon ex chronicis ad initio mundi vsqve ad annum Domini mcxviii. deductum: auctore Frorentio Wigorniensi monacho. Cui accessit Continvatio vsqve ad annvm Christi mcxli. per quendam eiusdem coenobii eruditum. . . . *Francofvrti, Wechelianis apud Claudium Marnium & heredes Ioannis Aubrij*, 1601, *embrowning throughout, name rubbed from title leaving small hole*, [viii+]696[+xxiv] pp., folio, *nineteenth century brown sprinkled calf, leather label, 'greek-key' borders in gilt, m.e., sl. cracking of upper joint* **£135.00**

289 [**Maxwell** (John, *Archbp. of Tuam*)] Presbytery Displayed. For the Justification of Such as do not Like the Government. And for the Benefit of Those that do not Understand it. The Second Edition Corrected. *Henry Brome*, 1668, *slight discolouration*, [iv+] 52 pp., sm. 4to, *grey wrappers* (Wing M1382) **£40.00**

290 **Melvil** (Sir James, of Halhill) Memoirs, contining an Impartial Account of the most remarkable Affairs of State during the Sixteenth Century, not mentioned by other Historians . . . Published from the original MS. by George Scott. Third Edition corrected. *Glasgow, Robert Urie*, 1751, *a few marginalia, one outer margin repaired, title soiled*, large 12mo, *contemp. calf, backstrip worn, lacks label* **£21.00**

291 **Merlin.** [HEYWOOD (Thomas)] The Life of Merlin, Sirnamed Ambrosivs. His Prophesies, and Predictions Interpreted; and their truth made good by our English Annals. Being a Chronographicall History of all the Kings, and memorable passages of this Kingdome, from Brute to the Reigne of our Royall Soveraigne King Charles. A Subject never published in this kind before, and deserves to be knowne and observed by all men. *J. Okes, sold by Jasper Emery*, 1641, *engr. frontis. (attrib. to Hollar), lower sixth remargined, some foxing throughout*, [lxx+] 376 pp., sm. 4to, *nineteenth century tan calf, leather label, sprinkled edges* (Wing H1786) **£160.00**

292 **Military.** An Argument, proving, that a small Number of Regulated Forces Established during the Pleasure of Parliament, cannot damage our Present Happy Establishment. And that it is highly necessary in our present Circumstances to have the Matter fully determined. Being Considerations upon what has been objected against Standing Armies in General. *A. Baldwin,* 1698, *outer pp. soiled,* [iv+] 24 pp., sm. 4to, *disbound* (Wing A3634) **£35.00**

293 ——BARRET (Robert) The Theorike and Practike of Moderne Warre, discoursed in Dialogue vvise. Wherein is declared the Neglect of Martiall discipline: the inconuenience thereof: the imperfections of manie training Captaines: a redress by due regard had: the fittest weapons for our Moderne Warre: the use of the same: the parts of a perfect souldier in generall and in particular: the Officers in degrees, with their seuerall duties: the imbattailling of men in formes now most in vse with figures and Tables to the same: with sundrie other martiall points. Comprehended in sixe Bookes. *William Ponsonby,* 1598, *complete copy with folding sig. O, many other diagrams of military formations, arms of Henry Herbert, Earl of Pembroke, to whom the work is dedicated, on verso of title, arms of Barret on verso of last lf.,* [viii+]247[+vii] pp., folio, *contemp. limp vellum, soiled and wrinkled, front hinge breaking, lacks front free endpaper and most of ties* (STC 1500: Cockle 68) scarce **£1,350.00**

294 ——HISTOIRE DES ORDRES MILITAIRES ou des Chevaliers, des Milices Seculaires & Regulieres de l'un & de l'autre Sexe, qui ont été établies jusques à present. Contenant leur Origine, leurs Fondations, leurs Progrés, leur manier de Vie, leur Decadence, leurs Reformes, & les evenemens les plus considerables qui y sont arrivez. Nouvelle Edition, tirée de l'Abbé Giustiniani, du R. P. Bonanni . . . et un Traité Historique de Mr. Basnage sur les Duels. 4 Vols., *Amsterdam, chez Pierre Brunel,* 1721, *with 187 engraved plates, 23 of which are of regalia, lower margins of 2 plates sl. torn, a few water stains,* 8vo, *contemp. calf, gilt, leather labels, most covers sl. rubbed, joints of vol. i. tender* **£175.00**

295 ——Manual for the Royal Army Medical Corps. *War Office,* 1899, *numerous diagrams,* [vi+] 185 pp. *book lists on end-papers,* sm. 8vo, *orig. green cloth, lettered* **£18.00**

296 ——MARKHAM (Francis) Five Decades of Epistles of Warre. *Augustine Matthewes,* 1622, *lacks A1,* [x+] 200 pp., folio, *nineteenth century calf, leather label, blind 2 line fillets on both covers, arms of George Granville Leveson-Gower, K. G. (2nd Earl of Granville) on front cover* (STC 17332, Cockle 96) **£300.00**

297 ——[MORRIS (Corbyn)] A Letter from a By-stander to a Member of Parliament: wherein is Examined what Necessity there is for the Maintenance of a Large Regular Land-Force in this Island . . . Second Edition. *J. Roberts,* 1742, *discolouration throughout, lacking half title,* 110 (of 112) pp., 8vo, *disbound* **£20.00**

298 ——The News-Readers Pocket-Book: or, a Military Dictionary. Explaining the most difficult Terms made use of in Fortification, Gunnery, and the whole Compass of the Military Art. And a Naval Dictionary; explaining the Terms used in Navigation, Ship-Building, &c. . . . *J. Newbery,* 1759, FIRST EDITION, *folding map,* vi+216 pp., 12mo, *contemp. sheep, leather label, rubbed, corners worn, joints cracked* (Roscoe A385) **£30.00**

299 ——An Ordinance of the Lords and Commons assembled in Parliament, for Raising and Maintaining of Forces for the Defence of the Kingdom, under the Command of Sir John Fairfax knight, who is hereby Constituted and Ordained Commander in chief. *Edw. Husbands* Febr. 17. 1644, *dampstained,* 23 pp., sm. 4to, *sewed and untrimmed* (Wing E1906) **£30.00**

300 ——An Ordinance . . . for the speedy raising and levying of Money for the maintenance of the Army raised by the Parliament. And other great Affaires of the Common-wealth. By a Weekly Assessment . . . *Edw. Husbands,* 1643, [ii+] 29 pp., sm. 4to, *disbound* (Wing E2050) **£35.00**

301 ——PORTER (Whitworth), Colonel Sir Charles M. WATSON, and others. History of the Corps of Royal Engineers, 1066 to 1948, 9 Vols., 1951/58, *illusts. and maps,* 8vo, *publishers' cloth, lettered, dust jackets* **£45.00**

302 ——S[HEPPEN] (William), E. J[EFFRYS]. and Sir T[homas] H[ANMORE]. Three Speeches against continuing the Army, &c. . . . to which are added, the Reasons given by the Lords, who Protested against the Bill for Punishing Mutiny and Desertion. *John Morphew,* 1718, *lacks final blank,* 46 pp., sm. 8vo, *disbound* **£18.00**

303 ——A Trve Description of the Discipline of VVar both for Horse and Foot, used in His Maiesties Army, under their Excellencies, William Earle of New Castle, and Prince Robert. With the order and manner of their marching and excercising [sic] in the Field. N.P., N.D. [*London* 1642], *drop title, Royal Arms between ornate 'C' and 'R', catchword of sig.* A[1] *trimmed,* 7 pp., sm. 4to, *modern qtr. crimson morocco, cloth sides* (Wing T2677) rare **£250.00**

304 ——TURNER (Sir James) Pallas Armata. Military Essayes of the Ancient Grecian, Roman, and Modern Art of War. Written in the Years 1670 and 1671. *M. W. for Richard Chiswell,* 1683, *title in red and black, engraved portrait by R. White, small snag in lower margin of prelim. ll.,* [xviii+] 372 pp., folio, *contemp. mottled calf, backstrip gilt, leather label, corners worn* (Wing T3292) **£185.00**

305 ——The Vindication of the Parliament and their Proceedings or, their Military Designe proved Loyall and Legall. A Treatise, wherein these things are ingeniously and sincerely handled . . . *Printed in the yeare* 1642, *lower margins wormed,* 22 pp., (*mispaginated*), sm. 4to, *disbound* (Wing V521) **£25.00**

306 ——WARNERY (General C.E.) Remarks on Cavalry; by a Prussian Major General of Hussars. Translated from the Original [by Lt. Col. G. F. Koellier]. *T. Egerton,* 1805, *with 33 plates of military 'types' and 9 of diagrams of manoeuvres, some marginal staining,* xxii+125[+i] pp., 4to, *orig. grey bds., soiled, recently rebacked, paper label* **£130.00**

307 **Milton** (John) A Complete Collection of the Historical, Political, and Miscellaneous Works . . . Vol. 1 of 3 Vols. To which is Prefix'd The Life of the Author . . . *Amsterdam* [*London*], 1698, *portrait by William Faithorne, worming in lower margin of latter half of vol., with occasional partial loss of some letters, some staining throughout,* pp. 48+iv+1–568(shd. read 580)545–872(shd. read 868), folio, *modern qtr. calf, marbled bds. label supplied in MS.* **£35.00**

308 **Minehead Doctrine.** [BINSON (W.)] A Letter to Sir J[acob] B[ancks] . . . concerning the late Minehead Doctrine, which was establish'd by a certain Free Parliament of Sweden, to the utter Enslaving of that Kingdom. *A. Baldwin,* 1711, *light browning throughout,* [viii+] 40 pp., 8vo, *disbound* **£21.00**

309 A **Modest Attempt** for Healing the Present Animosities in England. Occasion'd by a late Book, Entituled, A Modest Enquiry, &c. in a Dialogue between Testimony, a Zealous Dissenter; and Hot-head, a Chollerick Bigot; Trimmer, Moderator. *R. Janeway,* 1690, *margins browned,* 28[+ii] pp., sm. 4to, *disbound* (Wing M2359) **£60.00**

310 A **Modest Enquiry** into the Causes of the Present Disasters in England. and who they are that brought the French Fleet into the English Channel, Described. *Richard Baldwin,* 1690, *outer margins stained and fragile,* ii+ 38 pp., sm. 4to, *disbound* (Wing M2367) scarce **£45.00**

311 A **Second Modest Enquiry** into the Causes of the Present Disasters in England. and who they are that brought the French Fleet into the English Channel, Described. Being a farther Discovery of the Jacobite Plot. Together with a List of those Noble-men, Gentlemen, and others now in Custody. *John Dunton and John Harris,* 1690, *outer margins stained,* 31 pp., sm. 4to, *disbound* (Wing S2292) scarce **£55.00**

312 **Monk.** SKINNER (Thomas) The Life of General Monk: Duke of Albermarle, Second Edition, corrected. *J. Graves, J. Isted and J. Hooke,* 1724, *lacks portrait, soiled and embrowned throughout, one lf. repaired,* [x+]xlvii+385[+vii] pp., 8vo, *contemp. panelled, calf, corners wearing, newly rebacked, leather label* **£25.00**

313 —— —— ——Second Edition corrected, *J. Graves, J. Isted and J. Hooke,* 1724, *portrait, laid down, soiled, embrowned throughout,* [x+]lxvii+385[+vii] pp., 8vo, *contemp. panelled calf, rubbed, corners worn, sometime rebacked, leather label* **£25.00**

314 **Monstrelet** (Enguerrand de) The Chronicles, containing an Account of the cruel Civil Warrs between the Houses of Orleans and Burgundy; of the Possession of Paris and Normandy by the English, – their Expulsion thence, – and of other memorable Events that happened in the Kingdom of France as well as in other Countries: a History of fair Example and of great Profit to the French, beginning in the year mccc. where that of Sir john Froissart finishes, and ending at the year mcccclxvii. and continued by others to the year mdxvi. Translated by Thomas Johnes. 5 Vols. *The Hafod Press, by James Henderson,* 1809, *vignette on titles,* 51 *plates uncoloured, slight foxing to some,* 4to, *hf. tan calf, leather labels, shelf mark labels at bottom of backstrips, ex-libris labels on front paste-downs* **£200.00**

315 **Montagu** (Charles, *Earl of Halifax*) The Works and Life of, including the History of his Lordship's Times. *E. Curll, J. Pemberton and J. Hooke,* 1715, *the 'Poem on the Marriage of Princess Anne' bound in the correct place, embrowning throughout, some marginal damp staining,* [v+]iii+92+264+viii pp., 8vo, *contemp. panelled calf, leather label, corners worn, upper cover almost detached* **£55.00**

316 [**Montesquieu** (Charles de Decondat, *Baron de*)] De l'Esprit des Loix ou du Rapport que les Loix doivent avoir avec la Constitution de chaque Gouvernement, les Moeurs, le Climat, la Religion, le Commerce, &c. à quoi l'Auteur a ajouté. Des recherches nouvelles sur les Loix Romaines touchant les Successions, sur les Loix Francoises, & sur les Loix féodales. 2 Vols. *Geneve, Barillot, & Fils,* [1748], FIRST EDITION, SECOND ISSUE, *errata lf. in vol. i., sig. K in vol. ii. misfolded,* [viii+]xxiv+552[+i]:[iii+]xvi+564 pp., 4to, *contemp. mottled 'French' calf, backstrips gilt, leather labels, m.e., corners slightly worn* (Tchemerzine viii:459/60) **£550.00**

317 ——The Spirit of Laws. Translated from the French by Thomas Nugent. Fifth Edition, carefully revised and improved with considerable Additions by the Author. *J. Nourse, and P. Vaillant,* 1773, xlvii+468:xvi+518[+xlvi] pp., 8vo, *contemp. tan calf, corners slightly worn and edges rubbed, newly rebacked, leather labels* **£50.00**

318 **More.** MORE (Thomas [Cresacre)] The Life of Sir Thomas More, Kt. Lord High Chancellor of England under K. Henry the Eighth, and his Majesty's Embassadour to the Courts of France and Germany, by his Great Grandson . . . *James Woodman and David Lyon,* 1726, *engr. portrait,* xxxi+336[+xii+iii(adverts.)] pp., 8vo, *contemp. panelled calf, gilt, leather label, joints cracking* **£40.00**

319 **Muratori** (Ludovico Antonio) A Relation of the Missions of Paraguay. Written Originally in Italian, and now done into English from the French Translation [of F. E. de Lourmel]. *J. Marmaduke,* 1759, *folding map, a few minor repairs, some pp. soiled,* 8vo, *new hf. mottled calf, marbled bds.* (Sabin 51422) **£75.00**

320 [**Nalson** (John)] Vox Populi, Fax Populi. or, a Discovery of an Impudent Cheat and Forgery . . . thereby Endeavouring to instill the Poysonous Principles of Rebellion into the Minds of His Majesties Subjects. Humbly Recommended to all Loyal Subjects and True Englishmen. *S. R. for Benj. Tooke,* 1681, *title little soiled,* [i+] 34 pp., sm. 4to, *disbound* (Wing N121) **£30.00**

321 **Napier** (Charles, *Admiral*)) An Account of the War in Portugal between Don Pedro and Don Miguel. 2 Vols. *T. and W. Boone,* 1836, *rubber stamp on title,* xvi+369[+i]:xi+336 pp., 8vo, *qtr. cloth, drab bds., very shabby, joints of vol. ii. split and backstrip defective, vol. i. sometime rebacked, orig. paper labels,* scarce **£25.00**

322 **Napoleon.** Copies of Original Letters from the Army of General Bonaparte in Egypt, intercepted by the Fleet under the Command of Admiral Lord Nelson. With an English Translation. 3 Parts in 1 Vol. [pt. iii. is the Second Edition], *J. Wright,* 1798/1800, 2 *folding maps, slight foxing,* [iii+]xxiii+248[+iv – cat.]:[iii+]xxxi+236:[iii+]xx+182 pp., 8vo, *hf. crimson morocco, lettered, t.e.g.* **£150.00**

323 —— ——Translated into English. *Dublin, J. Milliken,* 1799, *folding map, marginal discolouration,* xxx+184 pp., 8vo, *disbound, edges untrimmed,* scarce **£50.00**

¶ This is the first part of the above.

324 ——FAUVELET DE BOURRIENNE (Louis Antoine) Memoirs of Napoleon Bonaparte. To which are now first added, as Account of the Important Events of the Hundred Days, of Napoleon's Surrender to the English, and of his Residence and Death at St. Helena. With Anecdotes and Illustrative Notes from all the most authentic Sources, 4 Vols. *Richard Bentley,* 1836, *with 14 portraits, 12 views, a folding map and a facsimile,* 8vo, *hf. crimson morocco, lettered, gilt panels on backstrips with Napoleonic symbols, red cloth sides, edges gilt* **£110.00**

325 ——SÉGUR (Philippe-Paul, *General, Comte de*) Histoire de Napoleon et de la Grande-Armée pendant l'année 1812, et Examen Critique par le Général Gourgaud. 2 Vols. *Bruxelles, H. Tarlier,* 1825, *portrait, embrowned throughout,* [v+]x+323:[iii+]298[+i] pp., 8vo, *contemp. hf. blue calf, lettered, rubbed, marbled bds.* **£35.00**

326 ——WARDEN (William) Letters written on Board His Majesty's Ship the Northumberland, and at Saint Helena; in which the Conduct and Conversations of Napoleon Buonaparte, and his Suite, during the Voyage, and the first months of his Residence in that Island, are faithfully described and related. Sixth Edition. *For the Author by R. Ackerman,* 1817, *with Bertrand's sketch of the Battle of Arcola, but lacking the portrait of Napoleon and facsimile of the Medal, first three ll. extended and upper margin of title repaired,* [iii+] viii+215 pp., 8vo, *hf. crimson morocco, lettered, t.e.g.* **£45.00**

327 **Napoleon III.** JERROLD (Blanchard) The Life of Napoleon III. derived from State Records, from unpublished Family Correspondence, and from Personal Testimony. 4 Vols *Longmans, Green, and Co.,* 1874/82, *with 11 (ex 12) portraits and 16 facsimiles of letters and drawings of Napoleon I., Napoleon III. Queen Hortense, &c.,* 8vo, *contemp. tan calf, gilt extra, g.e., sometime rebacked matching morocco, leather labels, gilt compartments on backstrips with Napoleonic symbols, some corners slightly worn* **£65.00**

328 **Nassau.** BREVAL (John) The History of the Most Illustrious House of Nassau, continued from the Tenth Century (its earliest Known Origin) down to this present Time . . . there are likewise added, Original Letters of King William, while Prince of Orange. *Dublin, S. Powell for Abraham Bradley* . . . 1734, *2 folding genealogical tables, some browning,* [viii+]255[+xxii] pp., 12mo, *contemp. sprinkled, calf, leather label, upper joint cracked* **£35.00**

329 **Naudet** (J.) Histoire de l'Établissement, des Progrès, et de la Décadence de la Monarchie des Goths en Italie. Paris, Adrien Égron, 1811, *damp staining and some foxing,* [vi+] 328 pp., 8vo, *contemp. hf. straight grained crimson morocco, paper bds., damp staining on back cover, corners rubbed, carries library label of Prince Roland Bonaparte* **£25.00**

330 **Naunton** (Sir Robert) Fragmenta Regalia. Memoirs of Elizabeth, her Court and Favourites. A New Edition, with Notes, and a Memoir of the Author. *Charles Baldwyn,* 1824, 9 *portraits, some browning,* xxvi[+i+] 156 pp., 12mo, *calf, leather label, backstrip repaired* **£21.00**

331 **Naval.** COLLINGWOOD (Adam) Anecdotes of the late Lord Viscount Nelson; including copious Accounts of the Three Great Victories obtained over the combined Forces of France, Spain, &c. off The Nile, Copenhagen & Trafalgar . . . to which is added, the Ceremonial of his Funeral . . . *W. Stratford for J. Stratford,* 1806, *frontis., engr. title and plans in the text,* iv+148 pp., 12mo, *cloth, soiled* **£21.00**

332 ——JAMES (William) The Naval History of Great Britain, from the Declaration of War by France, in February 1793, to the Accession of George IV. in January 1820. A New Edition, with considerable additions and improvements. 6 Vols., *Harding, Lepard, and Co.,* 1826, *with 40 diagrams of actions and 28 folding 'Abstracts', 2 vols. rather foxed,* 8vo, *contemp. half calf, leather labels, marbled bds. little rubbed, m.e.* **£85.00**

333 **Necker** (Jacques) De l'Administration des Finances de la France. 3 Vols. [*Paris?*], 1785, *portrait and folding chart, holes in first four gatherings of vol. i. not seriously affecting letter press,* cvii+244: iv+376:vi+324 pp., 12mo, *orig. wrappers, unlettered, edges uncut, stitching weak in places* (Kress B916) **£40.00**

334 **Nethersole** (Sir Francis) 'Ο Αὐτοκατακριτος. The Self-condemned. Or, a Letter to Mr. Jo. Goodwin: shewing, that in his Essay to justifie the equity and regularnes of the late, and present proceedings of the Army by Principles of Reason, and Religion, he hath condemned himself of iniquity, and variablenesse in the highest degree, untill he shall explaine himself in publike. *Printed in the yeare* 1648, 8 pp., sm. 4to, *folded but unstitched* (Wing N495) **£30.00**

335 [**North** (Dudley, *4th Lord North*)] Observations and Advices Oeconomical. *T. R. for John Martyn,* 1669, *has first blank but lacks final one,* [xiii+]132[+ix] pp., sm. 8vo, *contemp. sprinkled calf, gilt, unlettered* (Wing N1286) **£75.00**

¶ The work terminates with *Morning and Evening Prayer for the Family.*

336 ——(Francis) NORTH (Roger) The Life of Francis North, Baron of Guilford, Lord Keeper of the Great Seal, under King Charles ii. and King James ii. Wherein are inserted the Characters of Sir Matthew Hale, Sir George Jeffries, Sir Leoline Jenkins, Sidney Godolphin, and others the most eminent Lawyers and Statesmen of that Time. *John Whiston,* 1742, *portrait, signatures of past owners on title,* [iv+]333[+x] pp., 4to, *contemp. hf. calf, leather labels, marbled bds., rubbed, joints cracking* **£45.00**

337 **Ockland** (Christopher) Anglorvm Praeiia ad anno Domini. 1327. anno nimirum primo inclytissimi Principis Eduardi eius nominis tertii vsque ad annu Domini.1558, Carmina summatim perstricta, item, de pacatissimo Anglicae statu, imperante Elizabetha compendiosa Narratio . . . *Radulphum Numerie, ex assign. Henrici Bynneman*, 1582, *divisional titles, lacks* A1 (*blank*) N1v. *last line commences 'Londini', some general soiling throughout, a few ll. slightly defective in margins*, [vi+119: ii+43+ii(blank)]:[xvi+]97[+vii] pp., *signatures continuous*, sm. 8vo, *contemp. panelled sheep, recently rebacked calf, leather label* (STC 18773) **£65.00**

338 [**Oldmixon** (John)] Clarendon and Whitlock Compar'd. To which is occasionally added, A Comparison between the History of the Rebellion, and other Histories of the Civill War . . . *J. Pemberton*, 1727, *slight discolouration, with the rare advert lf. before the title*, xxxiii+344[+xxiv] pp., 8vo, *contemp. calf, corners worn, newly rebacked, leather label* **£35.00**

339 [**Osbourne** (Sir Thomas)] Copies and Extracts of some Letters written to and from the Earl of Danby (now Duke of Leeds) in the Years, 1676, 1677, and 1673. with particular Remarks upon some of them. *John Nicholson*, 1710, xxvi+364[+iv] pp., 8vo, *contemp. panelled calf, lacks label, joints cracked* **£38.00**

340 **Owen** (N., *Ed.*) British Remains; or, a Collection of Antiquities relating to the Britons: . . . to which are also added, Memoirs of Edward Llwyd, Antiquary. Transcribed from a MS. in the Museum, Oxford. *Printed for J. Bew*, 1777, *some marginal notes and underlining, names on title, inner margins wormed*, viii+184 pp., 8vo, *new bds., unlettered, edges uncut* **£25.00**

341 **Oxford.** BARROW (John) The Case of Queen's College, Oxford; in a letter addresses to the Rt. Hon. W. E. Gladstone. *Oxford, John Henry Parker*, 1854, 59pp.:
[and]
THOMSON (William) An Open College best of All. A Reply. . . *Oxford, William Graham: James Ridgway*, 1854, [iii+] 49 pp.:
Two pieces together, 8vo, *grey bds., paper label* **£21.00**

342 ——BARRY (Henry Boothby) Remarks on the Three Proposals for reforming the Constitution of the University of Oxford. *Oxford, Joseph Vincent and James Ridgway*, 1854, 24 pp., 8vo, *grey bds., paper label* (Cordeaux and Merry 1731) **£15.00**

343 ——[NEWTON (Richard)] The Principles of the University of Oxford, as far as relates to Affection to the Government, stated. *R. Baldwin*, 1755, *title soiled*, iv+23 pp., sm. 8vo, *disbound* (Cordeaux and Merry 199) **£15.00**

344 ——[WILLOUGHBY (Sir Henry)] The Apology of an English Landowner, addressed to the Landed Proprietors of the County of Oxford. *Oxford, W. Baxter, for J. Parker; and J. Hatchard and Son*, 1827, [i+] 43 pp., 8vo, *grey bds., paper label* **£16.00**

345 **Paris** (Matthew) Angli, Historiae Maior, à Guilielmo Conquestore, ad vltimum annum Henrici tertii [edited by Archbishop Matthew Parker], cum Indice locupletissimo. *Londini*, 1571 [colophon – (latin motto) *Londini, Reginaldum Vuolsium* . . . 1570], FIRST EDITION, SECOND ISSUE, *title within woodcut border, soiled and extended, worming in 1st gathering, with no serious loss*, [ii+]1349[+xxxi] pp., folio, *new qtr. tan calf, leather label, grey bds.*, (STC 19209A) **£200.00**

346 [**Parker** (Samuel)] Reasons for Abrogating the Test, imposed upon All Members of Parliament Anno 1678. Octob. 30. *Henry Bonwicke*, 1688, *some staining with margins becoming fragile, worming throughout outer margins, heavy in places*, [iii+] 131 pp., sm. 4to, *nineteenth century calf* (Wing P467) **£35.00**

347 **Parliament.** A Declaration of the Parliament assembled at Westminster [setting forth the principles by which it intended to govern after the death of the Protector]. *John Streater and John Macock*, 1659, *discoloured*, 16 pp., sm. 4to, *sewed* (Wing E1491) **£40.00**

348 ——A Declaration of the Commons of England assembled in Parliament of their true Intentions concerning the Ancient and Fundamental Government of the Kingdom, The Government of the Church, the present Peace . . . *Edward Husbands*, 1646, *top inner margins damaged by damp*, 8pp., sm. 4to, *folded but unstitched* (Wing E2862) **£30.00**

349 ——A Declaration of the Parliament of England, in Vindication of their Proceedings, and Discovering the Dangerous Practices of several Interests, against the Present Government, and Peace of the Commonwealth, together with the Resolutions of Parliament thereupon. *John Field for Edward Husbands*, 1649, 32 pp., sm. 4to, *sewed, edges uncut* (Wing E1503) **£30.00**

350 ——An Exact Collection of the most Considerable Debates in the Honourable House of Commons, at the Parliament held at Westminster the One and twentieth of October, 1680. which was Prorogued the Tenth, and Dissolved the Eighteenth of January following. *R. Baldwin*, 1681, *slight foxing*, [viii+] 295 pp., sm. 8vo, *eighteenth century mottled calf, leather label, joints beginning to crack, y.e.* (Wing E2575) **£85.00**

351 ——THE HISTORY and Proceedings of the House of Commons from the Restoration to the Present Time. Containing the most remarkable Motions, Speeches, Resolves, Reports and Conferences to be met with in that Interval . . . together with a large Appendix containing exact Lists of every Parliament, the Names of the Speakers, their several Posts under the Government; and other valuable, Supplemental Pieces. 14 Vols. *Richard Chandler*, 1742/44, 8vo, *contemp. sprinkled calf, corners worn, newly rebacked, leather labels*, scarce **£220.00**

352 ——[LENTHAL (William)] Mr. Speakers Speech, with His Maiesties Speech to both Hovses of Parliament, at the passing of the Bill for Tonnage and Poundage *Printed in the yeare*, 1641, [ii+] 6 pp., sm. 4to, *disbound* (Wing L1089) **£30.00**

353 ——Modus Tenendi Parliamentum; an Ancient Treatise on the Mode of Holding the Parliament in England, ed. by Thomas Duffus Hardy. *George E. Eyre and William Spottiswood*, 1846, [iv+]xxxii+47 pp., 8vo, *contemp. tan calf, gilt, recently rebacked, original leather label, crest of Duke of Northumberland on both covers* **£35.00**

354 ——An Ordinance of the Lords and Commons assembled in Parliament. With the names of the Knights and Gentlemen entrusted in every County . . . also the Instructions agreed upon by both Houses, for the said Gentlemen appointed for this service. *Iohn Wright*, May 4. 1643, *some browning*, [ii+] 6 pp., sm. 4to, *disbound* (Wing E2112) **£35.00**

355 ——The Evidence given at the Bar of the House of Commons upon the Complaint of Sir John Pakington against William Lord Bishop of Worcester and Mr. Lloyd, his Son. Together with the Proceedings of the House of Commons thereupon. *Edward Jones, and Timothy Goodwin*, 1702, *embrowned*, 24pp., folio, *disbound, fold crease* **£21.00**

356 ——TODD (Alpheus) Parliamentary Government in England: its Origin, Development, and Practical Operation. New Edition, abridged and revised by Spencer Walpole. 2 Vols. *Sampson Low, Marston & Company*, 1892, xi+290:[iii+] 292 pp., 8vo, *full crimson morocco, lettered, g.e. by Roger de Coverly* **£30.00**

357 [**Pattenson** (Matthew)] Jerusalem and Babel: or the Image of both Churches. Being a Treatise historically discussing, whether Catholikes or Protestants be the better Subjects. by P. D. M. The Second Edition, Reviewed [sic] and Corrected. *Printed in the Year*, 1653, *three ll. torn, with no loss, slight worming at beginning only*, [xiii+]643[+i – errata] pp., 12mo, *early sheep, slightly worn, recently rebacked, unlettered* (Wing P868/9) scarce **£100.00**

¶Pattenson was physician-in-ordinary to Charles I. Reference is made to the 'Spanish Marriage' and also to the Colony of Virginia.
The work is dedicated to Prince Charles.

358 **Peake** (Thomas) Cases determined at Nisi Prius, in the Court of King's Bench, from the Sittings after Easter Term 30 George III. to the Sittings after Michaelmas Term 35 George III. both inclusive. *A. Strahan and W. Woodfall, for E. and R. Brooke*, 1795, *small tear in one outer margin*, xii+243[+xxiv] pp., 8vo, *orig. drab bds., paper label, soiled and worn, backstrip defective, joints cracked, all edges uncut* **£30.00**

359 **Peck** (Francis) Desiderata Curiosa: or, a Collection of divers Scarce and Curious Pieces relating chiefly to Matters of English History; consisting of Choice Tracts, Memoirs, Letters, Wills, Epitaphs, &c. . . . 2 Vols. in 1. *Thomas Evans*, 1779, *engravings*, pp. xvii[+vii+]1–238[+xxv+] 241–581[+ix], 4to, *contemp. tan calf, leather label, backstrip and sides chipped in places, corners worn* **£35.00**

360 **Pepys** (Samuel) Memoirs of the Reigns of Charles II. and James II. Comprising his Diary from 1659 to 1669, deciphered by the Rev. John Smith, A.B. of St. John's College Library, Cambridge, from the Original Short-Hand MS. in the Pepysian Library, and a Selection from his Private Correspondence. Edited by Richard, Lord Braybrooke. 2 Vols., *Henry Colburn*, 1825, FIRST EDITION, *with 13 engravings (one folded), all foxed and off-set, 2 vignettes in text, hf.-titles present, heavy foxing of first and last few gatherings in vol. i., short tears in lower margins of 2 ll., lacks the 2 pp. catalogue at end of vol. i.* [ii+]xlii+498[+ii+]xlix:[iv+]348+viii+311 pp., roy. 4to, *contemp. tan calf, gilt, leather labels, edges rubbed* **£250.00**

361 The **Phenix:** or, a Revival of Scarce and Valuable Pieces from the Remotest Antiquity down to the Present Times. Being a Collection of Manuscripts and Printed Tracts, no where to be found but in the Closets of the Curious [edited by John Dunton]. 2 Vols. *J. Morphew*, 1707/08, *some foxing throughout*, vi+570:xvi+552 pp., 8vo, *contemp. panelled calf, corners worn, sometime rebacked, leather labels, ex-library labels on end papers* **£95.00**

362 **Phillips** (Catherine) Considerations on the Causes of the High Price of Grain, and other Articles of Provision, for a number of Years back; and Propositions for reducing them: with occasional Remarks. *James Phillips*, 1792, FIRST EDITION, *hf. title present*, [iii+]v+90pp., 8vo, *sewn as issued,untrimmed* **£35.00**

363 **Pitt** (William, *1st Earl of Chatham*) CHAMPIGNY (Jean de, *Chevalier*) Suplément au Ministére de Mr. Pitt, avec une Récapitulation exacte de toutes les démarches de ce sage Politique depuis le 5 Septembre 1761, qu'il quitta le Ministére, jusqu'un 30 Juillet 1766, qu'il a été créé Comte de Chatham, et garde du sceau privé d'Angleterre, contenante un Espace de prés de cinq ans. *Cologne* . . . 1766, *portrait, errata lf. present*, viii+114[+i] pp., 8vo, *contemp. hf. sprinkled calf, leather label, marbled bds.* **£38.00**

364 ——GIBSON (Edward, *Lord Ashbourne*) Pitt: some Chapters of his Life and Times. *Longmans, Green, and Co.*, 1898, 11 *portraits, errata slip*, xiv+395 pp., 8vo, *hf. crimson calf, leather label, matching cloth sides, marbled endpapers, backstrip slightly sunned, inscribed by Dennis Wheatley on hf. title* **£20.00**

365 **Plain English:** in relation to the real and pretended Friends to the English Monarchy. Humbly offered to the Consideration of his Majesty, and his Great Council, the Lords and Commons in Parliament assembled. Second Edition, with a short Preface; and an Appendix, concerning the Coronation-Oath administered to King James the Second. *Printed for the Author*, 1690, *outer margins stained and fragile*, [ii+]viii+ 34 pp., sm. 4to, *disbound* (Wing P2359) **£45.00**

366 **Polybius.** The General History, in five books. Translated from the Greek by Mrs. Hampton. *J. Davis*, 1811, *some discolouration throughout*, 464 pp., 8vo, *hf. diced russia, marb. bds, y.e.* **£15.00**

367 **Pope Alexander vii.** [CAVALLI (Stephen)] A Short Account of the Life and Death of Pope Alexander the VII. with a Description of his Funeral Machin, and Elegies erected in St. Peter's Church in Rome. Together with an Exact Relation of the particular Ceremonies performed at the Creation and Coronation of this present Pope Clement the IX. with a Catalogue of all the Cardinals. Translated out of the Italian by P[hillip] A[yres]. *Moses Pitt*, 1667, *lacks portrait, embrowned, ex-libris stamps on verso of title and last lf.*, [iv+] 28 pp., sm. 4to, *early vellum, with paper backstrip, defective* (Wing C11579) **£25.00**

368 **Popish Plot.** A Brief Account of the several Plots, Conspiracies, and Hellish Attempts of the Bloody-minded Papists, against the Princes and Kingdoms of England, Scotland, and Ireland, from the Reformation to this present Year, 1678 . . . *J. R. and W. A.* 1679, *embrowned throughout, inner margin of title torn and slightly defective*, [i+] 46 pp., sm. 4to, *wrappers* (Wing B4520) scarce **£45.00**

369 **Popular Prejudices** against the Convention and Treaty with Spain, Examin'd and Answer'd. With Remarks on a Pamphlet, Entituled, Considerations upon the Present State of our Affairs at Home and Abroad. *T. Cooper*, 1739, *title dust soiled, final blank present*, 30 pp., 8vo, *new marbled bds., leather label on upper cover, edges untrimmed* (Goldsmith's Library 7680: Hanson 5316: Kress 4457) **£20.00**

370 **Porny** (M. A.) Modern Letters in French and English. Divided into two Parts . . . to which are annexed Accurate Directions with Regard to the Proper Form of writing to Superiors, Equals and Inferiors [French and English in parallel.] . . . *J. Nourse, and S. Hooper*, 1769, [viii+]307[+v] pp., 8vo, *contemp. sheep, little worn, unlettered* **£25.00**

371 **Porter** (Whitworth) A History of the Knights of Malta or the Order of the Hospital of St. John of Jerusalem. 2 Vols. *Longman, Brown* . . . 1858, *with 2 portraits, 2 other plates and a folding map, publishers' lists at end and on end-papers, one gathering becoming loose*, xvi+518:viii+ 522 pp., 8vo, *orig. brown cloth, gilt, backstrips faded* **£25.00**

372 **Portugal.** VERTOT (Rene Aubert de, Abbé) Révolutions de Portugal. Nouvelle Édition, revue & augmentée. *La Haye, Pierre Gosse Junior; et Daniel Pinet*, 1765, *some staining throughout*, xii+176 pp., 12mo, *contemp. sprinkled calf, backstrip gilt, leather label* **£35.00**

373 **Prescott** (William H.) History of the Conquest of Peru, with a Preliminary View of the Civilization of the Incas, 2 Vols. *Richard Bewntley*, 1847, FIRST EDITION, *with map, facsimile and 2 portraits, publisher's cat. at end of each vol.*, xxxvi+480:xx+490[+i] pp., 8vo, *publisher's cloth, faded* **£85.00**

374 The **Princess Cloria:** or, The Royal Romance. In Five Parts. Imbellished with divers Political Notions and singular Remarks of Modern Transactions. Containing the Story of most part of Europe, for many Years last past. Written by a Person of Honour. *Ralph Wood, and are to be sold by William Brooke*, 1661, FIRST EDITION, *frontis. defective in most margins and laid down, title extended, three ll. carefully repaired, generally embrowned, a few marginal snags, lacks final blank*, [ix+]614 pp., folio, *new qtr. calf, leather label, cloth sides* (Wing P2492) **£85.00**

375 **Prisons** GURNEY (Joseph John) Notes on a Visit made to some of the Prisons in Scotland and the North of England in Company with Elizabeth Fry . . . *Archibald Constable and Co.* 1819, *some foxing*, viii+170 pp., 8vo, *orig. bds., worn, backstrip defective* **£21.00**

376 **Purveyancy.** An Act for the taking away of Purveyance, and Compositions for Purveyance. *Hen: Hills and John Field*, 1657, *embrowned*, [i+]2 pp., folio, *grey bds.* (Wing E1131) **£20.00**

377 **Pütter** (John Stephen) An Historical Development of the present Political Constitution of the Germanic Empire. Translated from the German, with Notes, and a comparative View of the Revenues, Population, Forces, &c. of the respective Territories, from the Statistical Tables lately published in Berlin, by Josiah Dornford. 3 Vols. *T. Payne and Son; L. Davis;* . . . 1790, *occasional foxing*, pp. 321–384 *in vol. i. misbound following* p. 240, xxxix+512:xxxii+492: xxx+308+vi+71[+xlvi] pp., 8vo, *contemp. hf. calf, marbled bds., sometime rebacked, leather labels* **£45.00**

378 **Pym** (John) A Speech delivered at a Conference with the Lords, Ianuary 25. 1641. By occasion of the Petitions from the City of London, and the Counties of Middlesex, Essex, and Hertford. *John Wright*, 1641, *woodcut port. on title, title within typographic border, upper margins cut close, some staining*, sm. 4to, *hf. brown cloth, marbled bds.* (Wing P4280) **£45.00**

379 **Rapin-Thoyras** (Jean de) Histoire d'Angleterre, contenant ce qui s'est passé depuis l'Invasion de Jules César, jusqu'a . . . [l'Avenement de Guillaume III. et de Marie a la Couronne]. Seconde Édition. 10 Vols. *La Haye, Chrétien van Lom, Jean van Duren, Pierre de Hondt*, 1733, *titles in red and black, with frontis., 8 portraits, 5 maps and 11 genealogical tables*, 4to, *contemp. sprinkled calf, some joints cracking and lacking some labels* **£130.00**

380 **Rastell** (John) The Pastime of People, or, the Chronicles of divers Realms; and most especially of the Realm of England . . . now first reprinted, and systematically arranged, with fac-simile wood-cuts of the portraits of Popes, Emperors, &c. and the Kings of England, *F. C. and J. Rivington* . . . 1811, 13 *small woodcuts in the text and* 18 *full-page plates*, viii+299 pp., 4to, *hf. tan calf, cloth sides, leather label, shelf label at base of backstrip and ex-libris label on front paste-down* **£40.00**

381 **Robinson** (John, *of Leyden*) The Peoples Plea: fully vindicating the Povver and Proceedings of the Parliament. Occasioned by a defence of the Covenant . . . *Robert Bostock*, 1646, *discoloured*, [iv+]19 pp., sm. 4to, *disbound* (Wing R1697) **£35.00**

382 **Rocoles** (Jean Baptiste de) The History of [12] Infamous Impostors. Or, the Lives & Actions of Several Notorious Counterfeits, who from the most Abject, and Meanest of the People, have Usurped the Titles of Emperours, Kings, and Princes. And now Done into English. *William Cademan*, 1683, *lacking the frontispiece, embrowned throughout*, [xvi+]180[+iv – catalogue] pp., 8vo, *contemp. calf, worn, later drab end-papers, newly rebacked, unlettered* (Wing R1766) **£50.00**

383 **Roland** (Jeanne-Marie Phlipon – '*Madame*') The Works . . . containing her Philosophical and Literary Essays, written previous to her marriage; her Correspondence, and her Travels. To which are annexed the justificative Documents relative to her Imprisonment and Condemnation. The whole preceded by a preliminary Discourse, interspersed with Notes, illustrative and explanatory, by L. A. Champagneux. Translated from the French. *J. Johnson*, 1800, *portrait foxed*, lxiv+399 pp., 8vo, *contemp. hf. russia, lettered, marbled bds., corners slightly worn, joints cracking* **£75.00**

384 **Roll or List** of the Claims, entered in the Court of Session in Scotland, in pursuance of an Act of Parliament . . . entituled, Act for abolishing Heretable Jurisdictions, &c. distinguishing the Number of Claims, the Names of Claimers, the Jurisdictions, &c, specified in the Claims, and the Values demanded, in separate Columns. *M. Cooper*, 1748, *title soiled*, 28 pp., 4to, *disbound* (Hanson 6049, recording an issue of [1747]) **£18.00**

385 **Roscoe** (William) The Life and Pontificate of Leo the Tenth. The Second Edition, corrected, 6 Vols. *J. M'Creery for Cadell and Davies*, 1806, *engraved medallion portrain in vol. i., occasional spotting:*
[with]
The Life of Lorenzo de'Medici, called the Magnificent. The Fifth Edition, corrected, 3 Vols. *J. M'Creery for Cadell and Davies*, 1806, *engraved portrait in vol. i. and title-page vignettes, occasional spotting:*
[and]
Illustrations, historical and critical, of the Life of Lorenzo de 'Medici, called the Magnificent; with an Appendix of original and other Documents. (*J. M'Creery*) *for T. Cadell*, 1822, FIRST EDITION, *engraved bust-portrait and 3 plates* (1 *double-page*) 2 *of which are in sepia, all these slightly foxed:* 10 Vols. together, 8vo, *contemp. full green straight grain morocco, backstrips decorated and lettered in gilt, sides with wide borders in blind and large gilt corner pieces, all edges gilt, backstrips slightly faded and with occasional chafing* **£330.00**

386 **Rousset** (J.) Les Interêts Presens et les Prétensions des Puissances de l'Europe, fondez sur les Traitez depuis ceux d'Utrecht inclusivement, & sur les Preuves de leurs Droits particuliers. Seconde Edition. 2 Vols. [lacking the Supplement]. *La Haye, Adrien Moetjens*, 1736, *titles in red and black*, xxiv+1017:[i+]816[+xiv] pp., 4to, *contemp. sprinkled calf, newly rebacked, leather labels, new endpapers* **£45.00**

387 **Rudyerd** (Sir Benjamin) Two Speeches concerning the Palatinate. *Francis Constable*, 1641, [i+]5 pp., sm. 4to, *disbound* (Wing R2202) **£21.00**

388 **Russia.** MOTTLEY (John) The History of the Life of Peter I. Emperor of Russia. 3 Vols. *Dublin, by and for George Faulkner* . . . 1740, *titles in red and black, portraits, views and maps*, viii+336[+xl]:[viii+]348[+xxxix]:[viii+]434[+xxx] pp., sm. 8vo, *contemp. sprinkled calf, lacking one label* **£40.00**

389 [**Saumaise** (Claude de)] Defensio Regia, pro Carolo I. ad Serenissimum Magnae Britanniae Regem Carolum II. filium natu majorem, Haeredem & Successorem legitimum. [*s.l.n.*] 1649, 444 pp., 12mo, *contemp. calf, rubbed, corners worn, newly rebacked, leather label* (Wing S737) **£40.00**

390 [**Savile** (George) *Marquis of Halifax*)] Some Cautions offered to the Consideration of Those who are to chuse Members to serve in the Ensuing Parliament. *Printed in the Year* 1695, *some browning throughout*, 32 pp., sm. 4to, *buff bds*. (Wing H322) **£65.00**
¶ The issue with 'Cautions' 3½" and line 17 on p. 18 ending 'will be the Honester'.

391 **Scaffold Speeches.** HAMILTON (James, *Earl of Cambridge*) Henry, Earl of HOLLAND, and Arthur Lord CAPEL. The Several Speeches . . . upon the Scaffold immediately before their Execution, on Friday the 9. of March. Also the several Exhortations, and Conferences with them, upon the Scaffold, by Dr. Sibbald, Mr. Bolton, & Mr. Hodges. *Peter Cole, Francis Tyton, and John Playford*, 1649, *general discolouration*, 43 pp., sm. 4to, *disbound* (Wing H482) **£25.00**

392 **Schonberg.** DU CHASTELET DE LUZANCY, HIPPOLITE. A Panegyrick to the Memory of his Grace Frederick, late Duke of Schonberg . . . *R. Bentley*, 1690, *outer margins stained, with slight worming*, 40 pp., sm. 4to, *disbound* (Wing D2417A) **£55.00**
¶ After a long and distinguished military career which started at the age of 18, the Duke was killed at the Battle of the Boyne, at the age of 75.

393 **Scot** (Thomas) The High-Waies of God and the King. Wherein all men ovght to vvalke in holinesse here, to happinesse hereafter. Deliuered in tvvo Sermons preached at Thetford in Norfolke, Anno 1620. *Printed at London*. 1623, *some discolouration*, 88 pp., sm. 4to, *drab wrappers* (STC 22079) **£45.00**

394 **Scotland.** An Act for Raising of Fifteen Thousand pounds Sterling in Scotland, [towards the maintenance of the War against Spain]. *Hen: Hills and John Field*, 1657, *embrowned*, [i+]38 pp., folio, *grey bds*. (Wing E1054) **£20.00**

95 ——ALISON (William Pulteney) Observations on the Management of the Poor in Scotland, and its Effects on the Health of the Great Towns. *Edinburgh, William Blackwood & Sons, and Thomas Cadell*, 1840, xv+123 pp., 8vo, *hf. calf, marbled bds., rubbed, lacks label and rear free-endpaper* **£21.00**

96 ——CRAIG (Sir Thomas) Scotland's Soveraignty Asserted. Being a Dispute concerning Homage, against those who maintain that Scotland is a Feu, or Fee-Liege of England, and that therefore the King of Scots owes Homage to the King of England. Wherein there are many Judicious Reflections upon most of the English Historians, who wrote before the Year 1600. and abundance of considerable Passages, which illustrate the History of both Kingdoms. Translated from the Latin MS. . . . by George Ridpath. *Andrew Bell and sold by Thomas Brown* . . . 1695, *stub of longitudinal title still attached to one outer margin, sl. worming in margin of last gethering, penetrating to lower cover*, [iv+]xliv+430 pp., 8vo, *contemp. sprinkled calf, lacks label* (Wing 6805: Aldis 3453) **£75.00**

397 ——Customs. The Rates of His Majesties Customes, . . . According to the subjoined Alphabet of the said Rates, and Instructions for regulating the raising of the same. Together with the Act of Parliament concerning Custome and Excise, the Imposition on Tar and Iron; With the List of all Unexcisable Goods. And the Act Concerning Bullion. *Edinburgh, Andrew Anderson*, 1670, *piece cut from front free end-paper, some discolouration*, [vi+] 104 pp., sm. 8vo, *contemp. sprinkled sheep, unlettered* (Wing S1329: Aldis 1912) scarce **£100.00**
¶ In 1670 the *Customs* were placed in the hands of special commissioners and a new book of Rates became necessary. The Excise continued to be farmed until 1683.

398 ——A Declaration of the Lords and Commons assembled in Parliament, with the advice and concurrence of the Commissioners of Scotland, to publish their proceedings upon His Majesties Letter, touching a Treaty of Peace, and to declare their resolutions and endeavours, to put an end to the unhappy distempers of the Kingdome, by a safe and well grounded Peace. *Edward Husbands*, March 30. 1644, 40 pp., sm. 4to, *sewed* (Wing E1486) **£30.00**

399 ——The Declaration of the Rebels now in Arms in the West of Scotland. [*Edinburgh*, 1679 – *Aldis dates this title as* ?1681], *drop title, tail fore-corner of both ll. repaired*, 4pp., folio, *new qtr. calf, leather label, matching cloth sides* (Wing D761: Aldis 2265) scarce **£100.00**

400 ——DEMSTER (Thomas, *self-styled Baron of Muresk*) Scotorvm sciptorvm nomenclatvra Quartum Aucta . . . [with] Menologivm Scotorvm . . . [and] Apparatvs ad Historiam Scoticam lib. ii. . . . 4 Parts together. *Bononiae, Nicolai Tebaldini*, 1622, *separate titles to each part, title and dedication ll. to bk. ii. of Apparatus are inserted, title of pt. i. defective in upper margin, with no loss of letters, some damp staining of first two parts*, [viii+]28:[xvi+]40:[xvi+]88[+iv+]89–152 pp., sm. 4to, *new qtr. brown calf, lettered, grey bds. new end papers, but one original preserved with brief list of contents on verso in early hand* (Graesse ii/361) **£55.00**
Demster spent most of his life on the continent, and has left a detailed (if sometimes incredible) account of his life in the form of an autobiography which is 'clearly marked', says the D.N.B., 'by the same habit of grotesquely extravagant falsehood which appears in some of his other writings . . .' in 1619, on his way to London, he passed through Bologna, and was appointed to the vacant professorship of humanities at the university there, where he stayed, apart from a brief pursuit of his errant wife as far as the Alps, until his death in 1625.

401 ——GILLESPIE (George) Edinb. 28 April 1648. post meridiem. The Humble Representation of the Commissioners of the Generall Assembly, to the Honorable Estates of Parliament; upon their Declaration lately communicated to us. *John Dallom*, 1648, 24 pp., sm. 4to, *sewed, untrimmed* (Wing G751) **£25.00**

402 ——[HOLLES (Thomas Pelham, *Duke of Newcastle*)] Letter to . . . on certain Points of the last Importance to these Nations: being an Enquiry, I. Into the genuine Sources of Disaffection in both Parts of Great-Britain . . . and II. Into the most rational Measures for effectually extinguishing the Remains of the present detestable Rebellion . . . *H. Whitridge*, 1746, *contemp. comment on title, final blank present*, [i+]38 pp., 8vo, *disbound* **£21.00**

403 ——[——] Remarks upon a letter (just made Publick) on certain Points of the Last Importance to these Nations. Addressed to his Grace the Duke of Newcastle. In a Letter to the Author of that Pamphlet. *M. Cooper*, 1746, *contemp. comment on title*, 27 pp., 8vo, *disbound* **£20.00**

404 ——JACOBITE REBELLION. TAYLER (Henrietta, *Ed.*) The History of the Rebellion in the Years 1745 and 1746, from a Manuscript now in the Possession of Lord James Stewart-Murray. *Oxford, Printed for the Roxburghe Club by John Johnson*, 1945, 2 *Portraits and* 2 *other facsimiles*, xxi+427 pp., lge 4to, *qtr. roan, lettered, cloth sides, a little scuffed* **£200.00**
¶ The editor's own copy with her signature on front free end-paper. Tipped in are four letters relevant to the book, those by Lord Ilchester [President of the Club] and Sydney Cockerell in their holographs, the other typed and signed by [Sir] Owen Morshead and [Lord] Kennet.

405 —— —— ——A Jacobite Miscellany. Eight Original Papers on the Rising of 1745–1746, edited, with Introduction and Notes. *Oxford, Printed for the Roxburghe Club by Charles Batey*, 1948, *signed inscription on front free end-paper, 4 illustrations*, ix+196 pp., lge 4to, *qtr. roan, lettered, cloth sides* **£100.00**

406 ——JOHNSTONE (John) Sketch of Chap. xii. of the General Report of Scotland. On Embankments. Drawn up for the Board of Agriculture, *Edinburgh, Abernethy & Walker*, 1813, 5 *folding charts*, v+63 pp., 8vo, *disbound* **£16.00**

407——JOHNSTONE (John) Sketch of Chap. xii, sect. ii. of the General Report of Scotland. On Draining. Drawn up for the Board of Agriculture. *Edinburgh, Abernethy & Walker*, 1812, *with 17 plates, all foxed*, v+91 pp., 8vo, *disbound* **£16.00**

408——The Proceedings of the Parliament of Scotland: begun at Edinburgh, 6th May, 1703. with an Account of all the Material Debates which occur'd in that Session. To which are Subjoyn'd the several Acts passed in that Session . . . *Printed in the Year* 1704, *damp stained throughout, some edges fragile with slight loss, one lower margin trimmed with loss of last line*, [iv+]70[+xx] pp., sm. 4to, *drab wrappers* **£32.00**

409 **Scrinia Sacra;** Secrets of Empire, in Letters of illustrious Persons. A Supplement to the Cabala. In which Business of the same Quality and Grandeur is contained: with many famous Passages of the late Reigns of K. Henry 8. Q. Elizabeth, K. James, and K. Charls. *G. Bedel and T. Collins*, 1654, *title in red and black*, [xii+]355[+viii] pp., sm. 4to, *contemp. calf, worn, sometime carefully restored, initials 'H.L.' surmounted by viscount's coronet on both covers* (Wing S2110) **£65.00**

410 The **Scrupler's Case** considered: or the Unreasonableness of Refusing the Oaths of Allegiance to K. William and Q. Mary evinced. *J. H. for Henry Mortlock*, 1691, *small piece torn from one margin with slight loss to letterpress, some staining*, 40 pp., sm. 4to, *disbound* (Wing S2128) **£65.00**

411 [**Sedgewick** (William)] Animadversions upon a Letter and Paper, first sent to his Highness by certain Gentlemen and other in VVales: and since printed, and published to the world by some of the Subscribers. By One whose Desire and Endeavor is, to preserve Peace and Safety, by removing Offence and Enmity. *Printed in the year* 1656, *some embrowning, repair to last leaf* [vi+] 104 pp., sm. 4to, *disbound* (Wing S2383) **£25.00**

412 **Selden** (John) Table-Talk: being the Discourses of . . . or his Sense of various Matters of Weight and high Consequence; relating especially to Religion and State. Second Edition. *Jacob Tonson, and Awnsham and John Churchill*, 1696, *lightly browned throughout, small hole in outer margin of first three ll.*, [viii+]192 pp., 8vo, *contemp. mottled sheep, recently rebacked and repaired, leather label, new end papers, armorial book plate of* **Isambard Brunel** *facing title* (Wing S2438) **£75.00**

413 **Sévigné** (Marie de Rabutin-Chantai, *Marquise de*) Lettres de . . . de sa Famille et de ses Amis. 10 Vols. *Paris, J. J. Blaise*, 1818, *with portraits, views and facsimile, some discolouration*, 8vo, *contemp. qtr. calf, lettered, some backstrips a little defective* **£42.00**

414 ——The Letters. With an Introduction by A. Edward Newton, 7 Vols. *W. T. Morrell & Co.*, 1928, LIMITED EDITION, *portraits, views and facsimiles*, lge. 8vo, *orig. blue buckram, lettered, t.e.g., backstrips little faded* **£70.00**
¶ The Carnavalet Edition, newly re-edited, revised and enlarged, including over three hundred letters not previously translated into English.

415 **Sharp** (Granville) Memoirs, composed from his own Manuscripts, and other authentic Documents in the Possession of his Family and of the African Institution. By Prince Hoare. With Observations on Mr. Sharp's Biblical Criticisms, by the Right Rev. the Lord Bishop of St. David's. *Henry Colburn and Co.*, 1820, *portrait, hf. title, occasional foxing and discolouration*, xxxiv+524+xxxiii pp., 4to, *new qtr. calf, leather label* (Sabin 32288) **£45.00**

416 [**Sherlock** (William)] A Letter to a Friend, concerning a French Invasion, to restore the Late King James to his Throne. and what may be Expected from him, should he be Successful in it. *Randall Taylor*, 1692, FIRST EDITION, *some staining in outer margins*, [ii+] 30 pp., sm. 4to, *disbound* (Wing S3295) **£60.00**

417 [——] A Second Letter to a Friend, concerning the French Invasion. In which the Declaration lately dispersed under the Title of His Majesty's most Gracious Declaration . . . against the P. of Orange and his Adherants, is entirely and exactly Published . . . *Randal Taylor*, 1692, FIRST EDITION, [ii+] 32 pp., sm. 4to, *grey wrappers* (Wing S3339) **£70.00**

418 **Shipwreck.** [MACGREGOR (Lieut, General Sir Duncan)] A Narrative of the Loss of the Kent East Indiaman, by Fire, in the Bay of Biscay, on the 1st March 1825. in a Letter to a Friend, by a Passenger. Second Edition, with additions. *Edinburgh, Waugh and Innes*; . . . 1825, 96 pp., 12mo, *contemp. tan calf, leather label, tooled in blind and gilt, joints beginning to crack* **£30.00**

419 **Silhon** (Jean Sieur de) Le Ministre d'Estat, avec le veritable Usage de la Politique moderne. Seconde Edition. *Paris, Toussainct du Bray*, 1634, *title soiled and spotting elsewhere, not serious*, [xxiv+]499[+viii] pp., sm. 4to, *contemp. sprinkled calf, leather label, slight damage to head of backstrip, slight rubbing of edges of bds*. (Goldsmith – this edition not recorded) **£50.00**
¶ Several early signatures on front free endpaper, and that of Lord Widdrington on title.

420 **Sixtus V.** LETI (Gregorio) The Life of Pope Sixtus the Fifth . . . in which is included the State of England, France, Spain, Italy, the Swiss Cantons, Germany, Poland, Russia, Sweden, and the Low Countries, at that Time: with an Account of St. Peter's, the Conclave, and Manner of Chusing a Pope; the Vatican Library, the many Grand Obelisks, Aquaducts, Bridges, Hospitals, Palaces, Streets, Towns, and other Noble Edifices, Begun or Finish'd by Him . . . Translated from the Italian . . . by Ellis Farneworth. *W. Bowyer, and sold by C. Bathurst*, 1754, *slightly discoloured*, xvii[+i+]xxiv+484 pp., folio, *contemp. sprinkled calf, slightly rubbed, leather label, joints beginning to crack* **£65.00**

421 **Slatyer** (William) The History of Great Britanie from the first peopling of this Island to this present Raigne of o[u]r happy and peacefull Monarke K. James. *W. Stansby, for Rich. Meighen*, [1621], *lacks printed title and colophon lf. as usual, engraved title trimmed and inlaid, 'Declaration of the Frontispiece' trimmed close and laid down, last 3 lines defective, lower corner of* ¶3 *repaired, general staining and browning throughout*, [xxiv+]305[+xiv] pp., folio, *nineteenth century tan calf, corners bruised, newly rebacked, leather label* (STC 22634) **£65.00**

422 **Slavery.** STANSFORD (P. Thomas) The Tragedy of the Negro in America. A condensed History of the Enslavement, Sufferings, Emancipation, Present Condition and Progress of the Negro Race in the United States of America . . . *Boston, Mass. Author's Edition*, 1898, *with 20 plates*, xxii+230 pp., sm. 8vo, *blue cloth* **£35.00**

423 ——WIGHAM (Eliza) The Anti-Slavery Cause in America and its Martyrs. *A. W. Bennett*, 1863, vii+168 pp., sm. 8vo, *orig. red cloth, lettered in gilt on backstrip and upper cover, faded with stain on upper cover* **£35.00**

424 **Smith** (William) A Just Account of the Horrid Contrivance of John Cupper, and Judith Brown his Servant, in poysoning his Wife . . . together with their Dying Confessions. *Edward Robinson*, 1684, *outer margins stained and fragile, with single worm hole throughout*, 12 pp., sm. 4to, *disbound* (Wing S4261) **£75.00**

425 **Smyth** (Matthew) Remarks upon the D[uke] of S[hrewsbury]'s Letter to the House of Lords concerning Capt. Smyth. Being a Vindication of his Services from the Imputations therein laid upon them . . . *Printed and sold by the Booksellers of London and Westminster*, 1700, *corner of title paired*, xvi+31 pp., 8vo, *disbound* **£15.00**

426 **Spain.** An Account of Spain: being a New Description of that Country and People; and of the Sea Ports along the Mediterranean: of Centa, Tangier, &c . . . to which is added, a Large Preface concerning the Establishment of the Spanish Crown, on the Duke of Anjou. *Jonathan Wilde*, 1700, *soiling throughout*, [xxxii:]192 pp., 8vo, *contemp. calf, corners worn, sometime rebacked, unlettered* (Wing A226) scarce **£60.00**

427 ——ROCCA (Albert Jean Michel de) Memoirs of the War of the French in Spain. Translated from the second Paris Edition. *Philadelphia, Thomas Dobson and Son*, 1820, *some foxing*, vii+219 pp., 8vo, *contemp. tree calf, gilt, leather label, marbled endpapers, library label, y.e.* **£25.00**

¶ De Rocca was an Officer of Hussars and Knight of the Order of the Legion of Honour.

428 **Spelman** (Sir Henry) An Apology of the Treatise 'De non temerandis Ecclesiis'. against a Treatise by an unknowne Author, written against it in some particulars. Also his Epistle to Richard Carew Esquire, of Anthony in Cornwall concerning Tithes. *J. L. for Philemon Stephens*, 1646, [vi+]28+[ii+]27 pp., sm. 4to, *disbound* (Wing S4917) **£35.00**

429 **State Affairs.** A Choice Collection of Papers relating to State Affairs; during the Late Rebellion. Some whereof were never before Printed. Vol. I. [all published]. *In the Year* 1703, *embrowned throughout*, pp. [viii+]1–240:353–583, 8vo, *contemp. sprinkled calf, little rubbed, unlettered* **£45.00**

430 **Steinkopff** (Ch. Fr. A.) Letters relative to a Tour on the Continent, undertaken at the Request of the Committee of the British and Foreign Bible Society, in the Year 1812. *The Author, and sold by J. Hatchard and L. B. Seeley*, 1813, vii+106[+ii] pp., sm. 8vo, *grey bds., sometime rebacked, paper label, edges untrimmed, stitching starting to break* **£35.00**

431 **Strafford** (Sir Thomas Wentworth, *Earl of*) Letters and Dispatches, with an Essay towards his Life by Sir George Radcliffe . . . [edited by] William Knowler. 2 Vols. in 1. *William Bowyer*, 1739, 2 *portraits*, [x+]527[+iv]:[i+]439[+iv] pp. folio, *diced russia, rubbed, newly rebacked and repaired, leather label* **£95.00**

432 ——Two Speeches . . . the one concern – the Liberty of the Subject. The other the Priviledge of the Houses of Parliament. *John Ashton*, 1641, *lacks* [a1] (*?blank*), *contemp. writing on title, some staining*, [ii+] 7 pp., sm. 4to, *sewed, but untrimmed* (Wing S5802) **£30.00**

433 ——DIGBY (George, *Earl of Bristol*) His last Speech against the Earle of Strafford, occasioned upon the reading of the Bill of Attainder touching the point of Treason. *Printed*, 1641, *first and last blanks present*, [ii+] 14 pp., sm. 4to, *sewed, untrimmed* (Wing B4767) **£30.00**

434 **Stubbs** (William) Seventeen Lectures on the Study of Medieval and Modern History and Kindred Subjects. *Oxford, Clarendon Press*, 1886, vii+399 pp., 32 pp. catalogue, 8vo, *orig. qtr. roan, lettered, little rubbed* **£18.00**

435 **Sweden.** Harte (Walter) The History of the Life of Gustavus Adolphus, King of Sweden, surnamed, The Great. 2 Vols. *for the Author, and sold by G. Hawkins*, 1759, *portrait, 8 maps and charts* (5 *folding*) *and a large folding table of the 'Brigade of Pikemen'* (*this very defective and photo-facsimile supplied*), *some worming in lower margins of vol. i. a few catch words touched*, xxvii+40[+i+]452:[iv+]350[+xxxviii+]71[+xxix] pp. 4to, *contemp. sprinkled calf, backstrips gilt, leather labels, joints rubbed* **£45.00**

436 **Sully.** BETHUNE (Maximilian de, *Duke of Sully*) Memoirs, containing the History and Reign of that Monarch [Henry the Great], and his own Administration under Him. Translated from the French. [by Charlotte Lennox]. To which is added, the Tryal of Ravaillac for the Murder of Henry the Great. 3 Vols. *A. Millar, R. & J. Dodsley, and W. Shropshire*, 1756, FIRST EDITION, *some light foxing*, xxxii+540:viii+555:vii+407[+cxxii] pp., 4to, *contemp. sprinkled calf, leather labels, a little rubbed* **£75.00**

437 ————Memoirs . . . Translated from the French by Charlotte Lennox. A New Edition, revised and corrected: with additional Notes, some Letters of Henry the Great, and a brief historical Introduction. 5 Vols. *W. Miller*, 1810, *with portraits*, 8vo, *contemp. polished russia, lettered in gilt, backstrips panelled and with wide 'Greek Key' borders on sides within double fillets, m.e. backstrips lightly rubbed, one joint a little defective with loss of leather* **£85.00**

438 **Sweden.** VOLTAIRE (Francois Marie Arouet de) The History of Charles II. King of Sweden. Translated from the French. Fourth Edition. *C. Davis and A. Lyon*, 1732, *engraved portrait and folding map*, xii+371[+i] pp., 8vo, *contemp. panelled calf, unlettered, little rubbed, joints beginning to crack* **£25.00**

439 A **System** to secure and extend the Credit and Strength of the British Nation. *H. Kent, for E. Comyns*, 1747, 17[+i] pp., 4to, *disbound* (Goldsmith 8301: Hanson 6082) **£35.00**

¶ The endorsement agrees with that of the Goldsmiths' Library copy, and not with that described by Hanson.

440 **Tanner** (Thomas) Notitia Monastica: or, an Account of all the Abbies, Priories, and Houses of Friers, heretofore in England and Wales; and also of all the Colleges and Hospitals founded before A.D. MDXL. [edited by] John Tanner, *William Bowyer, sold by John Whiston, John Osborn, and Francis Changuion*, 1744, *portrait and 3 plates of arms, some light discolouration*, [iv+]xliv[+x+]722[+liv] pp., folio, *contemp. sprinkled calf, backstrip gilt, leather label, rubbed, corners worn, joints cracked* **£85.00**

441 The **Temple** of Mammon. Dublin, *P. Higly, for the United Company of Booksellers*, 1776, 32 pp., 12mo, *disbound* **£45.00**

¶ A satire against bankers, goldsmiths, merchants, Bank of England, etc.

442 [**Titus** (Silius)] Killing, No Murder: with some Additions briefly discourst in Three Questions, for Publick View; To deter and prevent Single Persons, and Councils, from Usurping Supream Povver. By William Allen [pseud.]. *London*, [i.e. *Holland*] *Printed* 1659, *soiled throughout, corner torn from final lf. with very slight loss*, 14[+ii] pp., sm. 4to, *grey wrappers* (Wing T1311) **£45.00**

443 **T[rapp]** (J[oseph]) The Royal Sin: or, Adultery Rebuk'd in a Great King . . . addressed to those whom it may concern. *J. Huggonson*, 1738, 29 pp., 8vo, *green cloth, unlettered* **£20.00**

444 **Truths Discovery of a black Cloud in the North:** shewing some Antiparliamentary, inhumane, cruell, and base proceedings of the Scotch Army against the well-affected in the North of England . . . [*London* 1646], *drop-title*, 12 pp., sm. 4to, *sewed* (Wing T3168) **£40.00**

445 **Tweddell** (John) Remains: being a selection of his Correspondence, a republication of his Prolusioned Juveniles, an Appendix containing some Account of the Author's Collections, MSS., Drawings, &c. and of their extraordinary Disappearance, preceded by a biographical Memoir of the Deceased by Robert Tweddell. Second Edition . . . *J. Mawson, by Joyce Gold*, 1816, *with 5 portraits, 4 views and 3 maps, with ll.* D^{*2} *added*, viii+591 (shd. read 595)+179[+xvii] pp., 4to, *contemp. hf. russia, marbled bds., recently rebacked calf, hand lettered paper label, ex-libris book plate on pastedown* **£45.00**

446 **Twi[y]sden** (Sir Roger) An Historical Vindication of the Church of England in point of Schism, as it stands Separated from the Roman, and was Reformed I. Elizabeth. *Robert Pawlet*, 1675, *Royal arms on title, title in red and black, worm hole in some outer margins, one torn*, [viii+]198[+ii] pp., sm. 4to, *new hf. tan calf, leather label, marbled bds.* (Wing T3554) **£45.00**

447 An **Universal,** Historical, Geographical, Chronological and Poetical Dictionary, exactly describing the Situation, Extant, Customs, Laws, Manners, Commodities, &c. of all Kingdoms, Common-wealths, Provinces, Islands and Cities, in the known World. . . . 2 Vols., *J. Hartley, W. Turner and J. Hodgson*, 1703, *discolouration*, [viii+749+i:i+558] pp., 8vo, *contemp. sprinkled calf, lettered, backstrips rubbed and joints starting to crack* (Cordell p. 167) **£45.00**

¶ An Abridgement of Moreri's, Baile's, Hoffman's and Danet's . . . Dictionaries, being a Curious Miscellany of Sacred and Profane History. (Drop title)

448 **Ursinus** (Fulvius) Familiae Romanae quae reperivntvr in Antiqvis Nvmismatibvs ab Vrbe Condita ad Tempora Divi Avgvsti . . . [colophon: *Romae, Francisci Tramezini, apud Iosephum de Angelis*, 1577], *engraved title, fore-edge just trimmed, and 218 engravings in the text, one with over-lay, some staining towards end, 2 pp. soiled and 4 ll. defective in inner margins with some loss, now repaired and text restored in MS., rubber stamp on title and elsewhere*, [viii+]403[+xi] pp., folio, *panelled calf, leather label, corners worn, sides heavily rubbed, sometime rejointed* (Adams U71), scarce **£180.00**

449 **Vagrancy.** An act against Vagrants, and Wandring, Idle, Dissolute Persons. *Henry Hills and John Field*, 1657 [colophon], *drop title, embrowned*, 3pp., folio, *grey bds.* (Wing E971) **£20.00**

450 **Varillas** (Antoine, Sieur de) Ανεκδοτα ετερουρɩαxα, or, the Secret History of the House of Medicis. Made English by Ferrand Spence. *R.E. for R. Bentley and S. Magnes*, 1686, *discoloured throughout*, [lxxvii+]470 pp., 8vo, *contemp. mottled calf, lettered, upper joint cracking* (Wing V112) **£95.00**

451 **Vertot** (René Aubert, *Abbé*) Histoire des Révolutions arrivées dans le Gouvernement de la République Romaine. Troisième Edition augmentée d'une Dissertation de l'Autheur, sur le Senat Romain, &c. 3 Vols. *La Haye, chez Henri Scheurleer*, 1724, *a little discoloured, vol. i. lacks final blank*, [vi+]xxii[+ii+]406:[i+]458:[i+]404[+li]42[+vi – cat.] pp., sm. 8vo, *contemp. sprinkled calf, leather labels, little rubbed, silk markers* **£75.00**

452 [**Walker** (Clement)] Relations and Observations, Historicall & Politick, upon the Parliament begun Anno Dom. 1640. Divided into II. Bookes: 1. The Mystery of the two Iunto's, Presbyterian and Independant. 2. The History of Independency, &c. Together with an Appendix, touching the proceedings of the Independent faction in Scotland. *Printed in the year*, 1650, *folding frontis., trimmed and laid down, stained and embrowned throughout, separate title to Appendix*, [vi+]266(shd. read 270)+264+71 pp., sm. 4to, *contemp. calf, corners worn, newly rebacked, leather label* **£45.00**

453 **Walpole** (Horace) The Yale Edition of Horace Walpole's Correspondence. Edited by W. S. Lewis. Volumes 1–34 in 33 Vols. *O.U.P. and Yale U.P.*, 1937–1965, roy. 8vo., *a fine set in orig. blue buckram, lettered in gilt* **£450.00**

454 [**Ward** (Nathaniel)] To the High and Honorable Parliament . . . the Humble Petitions, Serious Suggestions, and dutifull Expostulations of some of the moderate and loyall Gentlemen, Yeomen, and Freeholders of the Easterne Association . . . *Ralph Smith*, 1648, *upper and lower margins cropped with some loss, soiled throughout*, sm. 4to, *disbound* (Wing W791) **£25.00**

455 **Ward and Liveries.** An Act for the taking away the Court of Wards and Liveries. *Henry Hills and John Field*, 1657, *embrowned*, [i+] 2 pp., folio, *grey bds.* (Wing E1134) **£19.00**

456 [**Wase** (Christopher) Considerations concerning Free-Schools, as settled in England. *The Theater in Oxford and are to be sold there, and in London at Mr. Simon Millers* . . . 1678, *large vignette on title, slight browning at edges*, [viii+] 112 pp., 8vo, *modern maroon morocco, gilt backstrip lettered, sides panelled in gilt, armorial bookplate on front pastedown* (Wing W1015: Madan 3198) scarce **£300.00**

¶ 'There remains another advantage of publick Schools: the greatest benefit to Learners after the Master, is a good Library . . . And even in that affluence of Books, which this present Age daily furnishes, although a Parent can afford to provide his Son of such as are cheap and portable for his present use as he proceeds in Learning, yet there are voluminous Authors, Pillars of a Library, which would highly advance Study, yet are not the purchase of every one that is most studious: and therefore best able to use them. In which regard a Library would ever at present be reputed a necessary Member of a School-House.' (Author)

457 **Watermen and Lightermen.** The Constitutions of the Company of Watermen and Lightermen . . . to which is prefixed, a Table of Contents of those By-Laws: and thereunto annexed, an Abstract of the respective Duties of Rulers, &c. *Printed in the Year* 1730, *Reprinted in* 1790, *final blank present, some staining and soiling*, 8vo, *contemp. calf, rubbed, corners worn, newly rebacked, unlettered*, scarce **£100.00**

458 **Wellington.** Service and Anthems . . . Public Funeral of his Grace Field Marshall the Duke of Wellington, K.G. in the Cathedral Church of St. Paul, London. *George Edward Eyre and William Spottiswood*, 1852, 18 pp., 8vo, *sewed* **£15.00**

459 [**Whatley** (Stephen)] A Collection of White and Black Lists. Or, A View of those Gentlemen who have given their Votes in Parliament For and Against the Protestant Religion, and Succession, and the Trade and Liberties of this Country; ever since the Glorious Revolution to the Happy Accession of King George. Recommended for the Consideration of Electors . . . *S. Poppin* . . . 1715, *some foxing*, [ii+]39pp., 8vo, *nineteenth century hf. brown calf, lettered, marbled bds. slightly rubbed* **£45.00**

460 **Whitlocke** (Sir Bulstrode) Memorials of the English Affairs, from the Suppos'd Expedition of Brute to this Island, to the End of the Reign of King James the First . . . with some Account of his Life and Writings by William Penn, and a Preface by James Welwood. *E. Sanger, E. Curll, and J. Pemberton*, 1709, *some staining and embrowning*, [iv+]vii[+xxxii+]310 (shd. read 342) pp., folio, *contemp. panelled calf, corners and edges worn, recently rebacked, leather label* **£40.00**

461 **William I.** CLARKE (Samuel) the Life and Death of William, surnamed The Conqueror: King of England, and Duke of Normandy, who dyed Anno Christi, 1087. *Simon Miller*, 1671, *engr. portrait, foremargins frayed through damp, embrowned throughout*, [iv+] 40 pp., sm. 4to, *disbound* (Wing C4534) **£35.00**

462 **William III.** CHISHULL (Edmund) Gulielmo Tertio, Terra Marique Principi Invictissimo in Gallos pugna navali nuperrime de victos Carmen Heroicum. *Oxonii e Theatro Sheldoniano, prost. apud Joh. Crosley*, 1692, *outer margins stained*, [ii+] 21 pp., sm. 4to, *disbound* (Wing C3900) **£75.00**

463 ——Injunctions given by the Kings Majesty to the Archbishops of this Realm, to be Communicated by them to the Bishops and the rest of the Clergy. *Charles Bill and the Executrix of Thomas Newcomb deceas'd*, 1694, *head margins cropped with partial loss of pagination, soiled and stained throughout*, 11 pp., 8vo, *sewed* (Wing W2340) **£25.00**

464 **Willis** (Browne) Notitia Parliamentaria [Vol. III.], containing an Account of the First Returns and Incorporation of the Cities, Towns, and Boroughs, in England and Wales, that sent Members to Parliament . . . *for the Author*, 1750, xi+118+312[+lxxv] pp., sm. 8vo, *contemp. calf, sometime rebacked, worn and rubbed, lacks label* **£21.00**

465 **Wilmot** (John, *Earl of Rochester*). PARSONS (Robert) A Sermon preached at the Funeral of the Rt. Honourable John Earl of Rochester . . . *Oxford, at the Theater for Richard Davis and Tho: Bowman*, 1680, *soiled throughout*, [iv+] 48 pp., sm. 4to, *drab bds.* (Wing P570) **£21.00**

466 **Wiltshires Resolvtion,** presented with the Contributions of divers Gentlemen to His Majesties Commissioners at Oxford, also the Ingagement and Resolution of the Principall Gentlemen of the County of Salop, for the raising and maintaining of Forces at their owne charge, for the defence of His Majestie, their Country, and more particularly the Fortunes, Persons, and Estates of the Subscribers thereunto. *Oxford, L. Leichfield*, 1642, *all ll. becoming separated at fold*, 7 pp., sm. 4to, *unbound* (Wing W2961: Madan 1121) **£40.00**

467 **Windebanck.** The Articles or Charge exhibited in Parliament against Sir Francis Windebanck, Secretary of State to his Majesty whereunto is annexed the Letter that he sent to the Right Honourable the Lord Chamberlaine, from Callis, Ian:11. 1640. *Printed* 1641, [ii+] 6 pp., sm. 4to, *sewed and untrimmed* (Wing E1235) **£35.00**

468 **Wine.** An Act for Limiting and Setling the Prices of Wines. *Henry Hills and John Field*, 1657, *embrowned*, [i+] 2 pp., folio, *grey bds.* (Wing E1046) **£21.00**

469 **Witchcraft.** BOYS (J.) The Case of Witchcraft at Coggeshall, Essex, in the year, 1699 . . . printed from his MS. *A. Russell Smith*, 1901, *one of 50 copies*, 23pp., 8vo, *grey paper wrappers, edges untrimmed* **£25.00**

470 **Wolsey.** [CAVENDISH (George)] The Negotiations of Thomas Woolsey, the great Cardinall of England, containing his life and death, viz. 1. The Originall of his promotion. 2. The continuance of his Magnificence. 3. His Fall, Death, and Buriall. Composed by one of his owne Servants, being his Gentleman-Usher. With many Errours Corrected, and some Additions inlarged. Whereunto is added a Parallel between Thomas Lord Arch-Bishop of Yorke, and William Lord Arch-Bishop of Canterbury. *Printed for the good of the Commonwealth*, [1651], *some discolouration, some margins cut close*, [vi+]102[+ii] pp., sm. 4to, *nineteenth century hf. morocco, lettered, marbled bds.* (Wing C1619A) scarce **£100.00**

471 ——[GROVE (Joseph)] The History of the Life and Times of Cardinal Wolsey, Prime Minister to King Henry viii. . . . in which are interspersed the Lives and memorable Actions of the most eminent Persons: And the whole illustrated with Political and Moral Reflections. Collected from ancient Records, MSS., and Historians. 4 Vols., *J. Purser, for the Author* . . . 1742, *with 40 engraved plates of portraits and views*, 8vo, *contemp. sprinkled calf, leather labels, one missing, gilt lines, joints of vol. 1 cracking* **£140.00**

472 **Wool** SINCLAIR (Sir John) Address to the Society for the Improvement of British Wool; constituted at Edinburgh, on Monday, January 31, 1791. The Second Edition. *T. Cadell*, 1791, iv+46[+i] pp., 8vo, *disbound* **£45.00**
¶ Sinclair believed that the breeding and intensive farming of a strain of sheep which would produce better quality wool could halt the depopulation of the Highlands and greatly increase prosperity there. (See Mitchison's 'Agricultural Sir John)

473 **Wraxhall** (Nathaniel William) A Short Review of the Political State of Great Britain at the Commencement of the Year One Thousand Seven Hundred and Eighty-seven. Sixth Edition. *Debrett*, 1787, *inner margin of half title slightly defective*, iii+70[+ii] pp., 8vo, *disbound* **£16.00**

474 **Wyvill** (Christopher), *political reformer*). [Anon] A Letter to the Rev. Christopher Wyvill chairman of the late committee of Association of the County of York, On the Present State of this Country, by a Yorkshireman. *Printed for J. Johnson; W. Tesseyman, York; E. Hargrove, Harrogate; and other Booksellers*, 1793, [ii+] 14 pp., sm. 8vo, *sewed* **£30.00**
¶ The primary objects of the Yorkshire Association were to shorten the duration of parliaments and to equalise the representation.

ADDENDA

475 **Anne.** The History of the Reign of Queen Anne, digested into Annals. Year the Third. Containing the most Memorable Transactions, both at Home and Abroad: In which are Inserted several Valuable Pieces never before Printed. *A. Roper*, 1705, *folding plan of Battle of Blenheim, some marginal pencil marks and underlinings*, [viii+]264+76[+viii] pp., 8vo, *contemp. panelled calf, unlettered* **£35.00**

476 **Antoninus** (Marcus Aurelius) His Conversation with Himself. Together with the Preliminary Discourse of the Learned Gataker. As also, the Emperor's Life, Written by Monsieur D'acier, and Supported by the Authorities Collected by Dr. Stanhope. To which is added the Mythological Picture of Cebes the Theban, &c. Translated into English by Jeremy Collier. The Second Edition Corrected. *Richard Sare*, 1708, *with three portraits, one neatly repaired, a few ll. embrowned*, [x+]420 pp., 8vo, *contemp. panelled calf, small crack in upper joint, lacks label* **£45.00**

477 **Athenian Letters:** or, the Epistolary Correspondence of an Agent of the King of Persia, residing at Athens during the Peloponnesian War. A New Edition, to which is prefixed a Geographical Index. 2 Vols. *T. Cadell jun. and W. Davies*, 1798, *with portraits of Philip Earl of Hardwicke and the Hon. Charles Yorke, 12 engravings of classical personalities and a folding map of ancient Greece (slight tear in fold)*, lxiv+436:xv:466 pp., 4to, *contemp. diced russia, gilt, lettered, hinged in blue morocco, some corners beginning to wear, back-strips and inner margins of sides a little faded* **£160.00**

478 **Belsham** (W.) Memoirs of the Reign of George III. to the Session of Parliament ending A.D. 1793. 4 Vols., *G. G. and J. Robinson*, 1795, *occasional discolouration*, 8vo, *contemp. sprinkled calf, little rubbed, some joints tender, lacks all leather labels* **£35.00**

479 **Brady** (Robert) An Historical Treatise of Cities, and Burghs or Boroughs. Shewing, their Original, and Whence, and from Whom they Received their Liberties, Privileges and Immunities; What they were, and what Made and Constituted a Free Burgh, & Free Burgesses. As also, shewing when they first sent their Representatives to Parliament. With a Concurrent Discourse of most Matters, and Things incident, or Relating thereto. *Samual Lowndes*, 1690, *some staining with consequent brittleness of margins*, [i+]iv[+ii+]79+39+4 pp., folio, *contemp. sprinkled calf, backstrip defective, sides heavily worn* (Wing B4192) **£40.00**

480 **Caesar** (Sir Julius) LODGE (Edmund) Life of Sir Julius Caesar, Knt. Judge of the High Court of Admiralty, Master of the Rolls, Chancellor of the Exchequer, and a Privy Councellor to Kings James, and Charles, the First; with Memoirs of his Family and Descendants. To which is added, Numerus Infaustus, an historical Work, by Charles Caesar, Esq. Grandson to Sir Julius. *John Hatchard and Son* . . . 1827, *with 18 engraved portraits, 2 other plates and a folding pedigree, a few plates are slightly foxed and some ll. discoloured*, [i+]116 pp., 4to, *contemp. hf. roan, leather label, upper joints cracking, corners worn, marbled bds.* **£65.00**

481 **Campbell** (John) A Political Survey of Britain: being a Series of Reflections on the Situation, Lands, Inhabitants, Revenues, Colonies, and Commerce of this Island. Intended to shew that we have not yet approached near the Summit of Improvement, but that it will afford Employment to many Generations before they push to their utmost Extent the natural Advantages of Great Britain. 2 Vols. *for the Author; and sold by Richardson and Urquhart* . . . 1774, *a few ll. slightly discoloured*, [i+]vi[+i+]726[+xxiv]:[iii+]739[+xxxii] pp., lge. 4to, *contemp. mottled calf, leather labels, slightly rubbed* (Kress 6997) **£150.00**

482 **Caulfield** (James) Portraits, Memoirs, and Characters, of Remarkable Persons, from the Revolution in 1688 to the End of the Reign of George II. collected from the most authentic Accounts extant. 4 Vols., *H. R. Young and T. H. Whitely*, 1819/20., *with 155 engraved plates, tail pieces, most plates off-set on to letterpress, a few embrowned or foxed*, 8vo, *contemp. maroon morocco, lettered, heavily gilt, sides embossed in blind, g.e., in excellent condition* **£185.00**

483 **Charles II.** SAVILE (George, *Marquis of Halifax*) A Character of King Charles the Second: and Political, Moral and Miscellaneous Thoughts and Reflections. *for J. and R. Tonson*, 1750, *some discolouration*, [viii+]183 pp., 8vo, *contemp. calf, leather label, rubbed, joints beginning to crack* **£30.00**

484 **Cobbett** (William) A History of the Protestant 'Reformation,' in England and Ireland; showing how that event has impoverished and degraded the main body of the People in those Countries. In a Series of [16] Letters, addressed to all sensible and just Englishmen. *Charles Clement*, 1824, FIRST EDITION, *some discolouration*, [382 un-numbered] pp., 16mo, *hf. blue calf, lettered, marbled bds., a little rubbed* (Pearl 132) **£55.00**

485 **Colbert.** [COURTILZ DE SANDRAS (Gatien de)] The Life of the Famous John Baptist Colbert, late Minister and Secretary of State to Lewis xiv. the present French King. Done into English . . . *R. Bentley, J. Tonson, H. Bonwick, W. Freeman and S. Manship*, 1695, *frontis., slightly creased*, [xiv+]246[+viii] pp., 8vo, *contemp. sprinkled calf, unlettered, lacks free end-papers* (Wing C6599) **£35.00**

486 **Correspondence** in a Series of Letters between a Gentleman in Berlin and a Person of Distinction in London, from August 1803, to June 1804. *Dresden Printed: and sold by J. Budd, and Messrs. Richardsons*, [1805], *occasional light browning*, vii+190 pp., 8vo, *contemp. hf. russia, lettered, marbled bds., upper joint cracked* **£25.00**
"A very singular book – the work of a clever, but inexperienced man – who has thought, more than observed & who mistakes the facility of finding fault in these anxious times for a quickness of apprehension – but in no one instance offers a remedy for the evil he imagines he has discover'd." [Contemp. MS. note.]

487 **Hill** (Rowland) Journal through the North of England and Parts of Scotland . . . *T. Gillet* . . . 1799, xii+182 pp.:
[with]
A SERIES of Letters, occasioned by the late Pastoral Admonition of the Church of Scotland . . . *Edinburgh, J. Ritchie*, 1799, 45 pp.:
[and]
EWING (Greville) A Defence of Itinerant and Field Preaching: a Sermon . . . *Edinburgh, J. Ritchie* . . 1799, viii+58[+i] pp.:
Three pieces bound together, 8vo, *contemp. marbled sheep, leather label, upper joints cracked* **£28.00**

488 [**Howard** (Sir Robert)] Historical Observations upon the Reigns of Edward I. II. III. and Richard II. With Remarks upon their Faithful Counsellors and False Favourites. Written by a Person of Honour. *J. Partridge and M. Gillyflower*, 1789, *discolouration*, [ii+]192 pp., sm. 8vo, *contemp. sprinkled calf, joints cracked* (Wing H2997) **£45.00**

489 **Huntingdon.** [SEYMOUR (A.C.H.)] The Life and Times of Selina [Hastings, née Shirley] Countess of Huntingdon. By a Member of the Houses of Shirley and Hastings. Third Thousand. 2 Vols., *William Edward Painter*, 1840, *portrait*, [i+]xxviii+488:xxiv+544 pp., 8vo, *contemp. tan calf, gilt, leather labels, a little rubbed* **£45.00**

490 **Ireland.** DEWAR (Daniel) Observations on the Character, Customs, and Superstitions of the Irish; and on some of the Causes which have retarded the moral and political improvement of Ireland. *Gale and Curtis*, . . . 1812, *some discolouration*, [i+]vii+iv[+i+]164+158+331–353 pp., 8vo, *contemp. hf. mottled sheep, leather label, drab bds., joints cracking* **£40.00**

Catalogue A37

from

Blackwell's Rare Books

ANTIQUARIAN LAW & HISTORY (1982)

CATALOGUE A37

LAW & HISTORY

PLEASE QUOTE CATALOGUE A37 WHEN ORDERING

Codeword: "GORGON"

Please address all orders from this catalogue to:–
BLACKWELL'S RARE BOOKS, FYFIELD MANOR, FYFIELD, NR. ABINGDON, OXON OX13 5LR
Please quote your Blackwell's account number when ordering. Telephone: 0865-390692

LAW

1 **Aytta** (Vigleus Zichemus) Commentaria in decem titules Institutionum Iuris Ciuilis. Quibus omnia pene testamentorum Iura eleganter ac dilucide explicantur. Adsunt etiam praelectiones in titulum Pandectarum, De Rebus creditis, & ad titulum Codicii Iustinianaei, De Edicto Divi Hadriani Tollendo . . . *Lugduni, Petri Landry*, 1591, *staining and discolouration throughout*, 479 [+xxxii] pp., 8vo., *contemp. vellum, recently rebacked, red leather label, new endpapers* **£110.00**

2 **The Compleat Clark,** and Scriveners Guide. Containing Exact Draughts and Precedents of all manner of Assurances and Instruments now in use: as they are penned and perfected by divers Learned Judges, Eminent Lawyers, and Great Conveyancers, both Ancient and Modern. Whereunto is also added a Concordance of years, from the time of King Richard the third untill this present, very usefull for Conveyancers and others . . . *T.R. for H. Twyford* . . . 1655, *engr. title, general discolourations, single worm hole through lower gutter occasionally affecting a letter of text*, [vii+] 664 [+xvi] pp., sm.4to., *contemp. calf, rubbed, sometime rebacked, red leather label* (Wing C5633) scarce **£250.00**

3 **Disney** (John) An Essay upon the Execution of the Laws against Immorality and Prophaneness. With a Preface address'd to Her Majesty's Justices of the Peace. *Joseph Downing*, 1708, *with the Advertisement lf. and 4pp. Catalogue, some browning*, [i+] xxv+206 [+iv] pp., sm.8vo, *contemp. calf, unlettered, corners worn and joints cracking* **£60.00**

4 **Enchiridion** titulorum Iuris, quibus vniuersum pene ius summatim continetur de verborum Obligationibus, de verborum Significatione, de diuersis regulis iuris antiqui, Rubricae Iuris. Omnia secundum editionem Florentinam, & eum breuibus ac nouis annotatiunculis. *Lovanii, apud Petrum à Colonia Bibliop. Iurat*, 1554, *embrowned throughout*, 236 (shd. read 256) [+cxix] pp., sm.8vo, *contemp. sprinkled calf, backstrip gilt, brown leather label, (partly defective), rubbed and corners worn* **£90.00**
¶The work is followed by 30 pp. of legal notes in a 'secretary' hand.

5 **Fortescue** (Sir John) De Laudibus Legum Angliae, hereto are ioind the two Summes of Sir Ralph de Hengham, [edited by John Selden] Notes both on Fortescue and Hengham are added. *The Companie of Stationers*, 1616, *lacks first and final blanks, last leaf restored in lower half, some marginal notes in ink, embrowned*, [xvi+] pp. 132 ll. [vi+] 56 [+xii+] 159 (shd. read 161) pp., sm.8vo, *eighteenth century tan calf, sometime rebacked and repaired, lettered* (STC 11197) **£250.00**
¶The text is in parallel Latin and English.

6 **Hutton** (Sir Richard) The Reports, containing many Choice Cases, Judgments, and Resolutions, in points of Law, in the several Raignes of King James and King Charles, being written in French by his owne hand. And now faithfully Translated. *T.R. for Henry Twyford and Thomas Dring*, 1656, *tear in title, which with dedication leaf have sometime been crudely repaired in inner margins, embrowned throughout*, [xii+136] [+vii] pp., folio, *contemp. tan calf, corners badily worn, recently rebacked, red leather label* (Wing H 3843) **£40.00**

7 **Justinian.** Jurisprudentia Philologica., sive Elementa Juris Civilis, secundum Methodum et Seriem Institutionum Justiniani . . . per Roberto Eden. *Oxonii, e Theatro Sheldoniano*, 1744, *engr. portrait, a few fore-margins damp stained*, xx+307 pp., 4to, *tan calf leather label, upper joints cracked, r.e.* **£45.00**

8 **Leigh** (Edward) A Philologicall Commentary: or, an Illustration of the most Obvious and Useful words in the Law. With their Distinctions and divers Acceptations, as they are found as well in Reports, Antient and Modern, as well in Records, and Memorials never Printed: Usefull for all Young Students of the Law. Second Edition, Reviewed and Inlarged. *A.M. for Charles Adams*, 1658, *general discolouration, names of previous owners on end-papers, lacks first and last blanks*, [xiv+] 245 [xix] pp., sm.8vo, *contemp. sprinkled sheep, hand-lettered paper labels* (Wing L999) **£75.00**

9 **Leonard** (William) Reports and Cases of Lavv: argued and adjudged in the Courts of Law, at Westminster, in the time of the late Queen Elizabeth, from the 18th to the 33rd year of her Reign. With Alphabeticall Tables of the Names of the Cases, and of the Matters contained in the Book. *Tho. Roycroft, for Nath. Ekins*, 1658, *mostly* **Black letter,** *title and next leaf frayed and stained, general discolouration, some early marginalia*, [xii+] 336 [+vii]: [viii+] 226 [+iv] pp., folio, *modern qtr. tan sheep, black leather label, brown cloth sides* (Wing L1103) **£90.00**

10 **Littleton** (Sir Thomas) Les Tenures, ouesque certein cases added per auters de pursue temps queux cases troueres signes ouesque cest signe ✤ al cōmencement & al fin de chelcun deux au fine que ne poies eux misprender pour les cases de monsieur Littleton: pur quel inconuenience ils fuerent derniermént tolles de cest liuer, cy ūn fortzplus des gentil homes students en le ley dengleterre. 1572. [colophon: *Richard Tottyl*, 1574], **Black letter,** *extensive marginal glossing in various neat contemporary hands*. [i+] 170 [+i] ll., sm.8vo, *early tan calf, blind tooled, recently rebacked and repaired, red leather label* (STC 12742: Beale T27) **£45.00**

¶This is obviously a student's copy as the book, early in its career, was extended at both ends by some 60 ll, of blank paper, many of which have been used for annotations, etc.

11 —— —— *Companie of Stationers*, 1612, *mostly* **Black letter,** *title remargined, some lower margins cropped with slight loss of catchwords*, [i+] 170 [+xxiii] ll., 12mo, *modern tan sheep, red leather label* (STC 12756) **£325.00**

12 —— HARGRAVE (Francis) and Charles Butler. Notes on Lord Coke's First Institute, or Commentary upon Littleton. *E. and R. Brooke*, 1794, *light foxing throughout*, [xvi+474+xl] pp., 8vo, *contemp. half calf, marbled bds., rubbed, recently rebacked tan calf, black leather label, new end-papers* **£45.00**

13 [**Montesquieu** (Charles de Decondat, *Baron de*)] De l'Esprit des Loix ou du Rapport que les Loix doivent avoir avec la Constitution de chaque Gouvernement, les Moeurs, le Climat, la Religion, le Commerce, &c. à quoi l'Auteur a ajouté. Des recherches nouvelles sur les Loix Romaines touchant les Successions, sur les Loix Francoises, & sur les Loix féodales. 2 Vols. *Genève, Barillot, & Fils*, [1748], FIRST EDITION, SECOND ISSUE, *errata leaf, in vol. i., sig. K in vol. ii. misfolded*, [viii+] xxiv+552 [+i]: [iii+] xvi+564 pp., 4to, *contemp. mottled 'French' calf, backstrips gilt, leather labels, m.e., corners slightly worn* (Tchemerzine viii:459/60) **£550.00**

14 **Nelson** (W.) The Office and Authority of a Justice of Peace: collected out of all the Books, whether of Common or Statute Law, hitherto written on that Subject, The Eleventh Edition, 2 Vols. *E. and R. Nutt, and R. Gosling*. 1736, xlvii+572: [ii+]308 [+cclxiv] pp., 8vo, *contemp. calf, rubbed, backstrips worn and lacking labels* **£45.00**

15 **Peake** (Thomas) Cases determined at Nisi Prius, in the Court of King's Bench, from the Sittings after Easter Term 30 George III. to the Sittings after Michaelmas Term 35 George III. both inclusive. *A. Strahan and W. Woodfall, for E. and R. Brooke*, 1795, *small tear in one outer margin*, xii+243 [+xxiv] pp., 8vo, *orig. drab bds., paper label, soiled and worn, backstrip defective, joints cracked, all edges uncut* **£30.00**

16 **Perkins** ((John) A Profitable Booke, Treating of the Lawes of England. *Thomas Wight*, 1601, **Black letter,** *damp staining and slight worming in lower margins and gutters throughout*, [iv+] 168 [+xx] pp., 12mo, *modern half tan sheep, red leather label, red cloth sides, new end-papers* (STC 19641) **£220.00**

17 —— The Antient Right of the Commons of England Asserted; or, a Discourse proving by Records and the best Historians, that the Commons of England were ever an Essential part of Parliament. *F. Smith, T. Bassett, J. Wright, R. Chiswell, and S. Heyrick*, 1680, [18] *(blank) present, margins of title frayed, one lower margin repaired, general light browning throughout*, [ix+] 75+ 184 pp., 8vo., *contemp. tan sheep, corners worn, sometimes rebacked, blue leather label, new end-papers* (Wing P1945) **£65.00**

18 —— Miscellanea Parliamentaria: containing Presidents 1. Of Freedom from Arrests. 2. Of Censures. 1. Upon such as have wrote Books to the dishonour of the Lords or Commons. 2. Upon Members for Misdemeanours. 3. Upon persons not Members, for Contempts and Misdemeanours. 4. For Misdemeanours in Elections. Besides other Presidents and Orders of a various Nature, both of the House of Lords and Commons, *T. Basset and J. Wickins*, 1680, *some discolouration and staining*, [xix+] 220[+lxiv] pp., 8vo, *modern tan sheep, red leather label, new end-papers* (Wing P1948) **£140.00**

19 **Plowden** (Edmund) Les Commentaries, ou Reports . . . de diuers cases esteant matters en ley, & de les Argumentes sur yceux, en les temps des Raigns le roy Ed. le size, le Roign Mary, le Roy & Royne Ph. & Mary, & le Roign Elizabeth. Quesque un Table perfect des choses notable contenus en ycel, nouelment compose per VVilliam Fleetwood Recorder de Loundres, & iammais ey deuant imprimee. *Richardi Tottelli*, 1588, *mostly* **Black letter,** *title soiled*, [xviii+] 401 ff., folio, *contemp. tan calf, recently rebacked, red leather label, and corners repaired, new end-papers* (STC 20044: Beale R/489) **£120.00**

20 [**St. Germaine** (Christopher)] Doctor and Student: or Dialogues between a Doctor of Divinity, and a Student in the Laws of England, containing the Grounds of those Laws, together with Questions and Cases concerning the Equity and Conscience thereof; also comparing the Civil, Canon, Common and Statute Laws, and shewing wherein they vary from one another. *Eliz Nutt and R. Gosling (Assigns of Edward Sayer) for R. Gosling*, 1721, **Black letter,** *slight foxing*, [xii+] 366[+xxxviii] pp. 8vo, *contemp. tan calf, newly rebacked, brown leather label* **£85.00**

21 —— Two Dialogues in English, between a Doctour of Divinity, and a Student in the Laws of England, on the Grounds of the said Laws, and of Conscience. Newly Revised and Re-printed. *The Assigns of Richard Atkyns and Edward Atkyns*, 1673, **Black letter,** *name on title*, [i+] 366 [+viii] pp., sm.8vo, *contemp. tan calf, corners worn, sometimes rebacked, green leather label, new end-papers* (Wing S317 – variant imprint) **£95.00**

22 **Salkeld** (William) Report of Cases adjudged in the Court of King's Bench; with some Special Cases in the Courts of Chancery, Common Pleas and Exchequer, from the First Year of K. William and Q. Mary, to the Tenth Year of Queen Anne. 2 Vols. in 1. Second Edition carefully corrected. *In the Savoy, Printed by Eliz. Nutt, and R. Gosling, (Assigns of Edw. Sayer) for J. Walthoe and J. Walthoe, jun.*, 1721, *repair to upper margin of title*, [xiii+] 793 [+cviii] pp., folio, *contemp. tan calf, leather label, corners wearing, sides rubbed* **£45.00**

23 **Selden** (John) De Iure Naturali & Gentium, iusta Disciplinam Ebraeorum, libri septem. *Richardus Bishopius*, 1640, *title in red and black, half title with imprimatur on verso present*, [xl+] 847 pp., folio, *contemp. rough calf, red leather label, backstrip slightly defective at head and tail* (STC 22168) scarce **£375.00**

24 **Sheppard** (William) The Tovch-stone of Common Assurances. Or a Plain and Familiar Treatise, opening the learning of the Common Assurances or Conveyances of the Kingdome. *M.F. for W. Lee, M. Walbancke, D. Pakeman, and G. Bedell*, 1648, *discoloured throughout*, pp. [xii+] 1–348:353–529 [+vi] – complete, 4to, *modern half tan calf, leather label, linen sides* (Wing S3215: Kress 946) **£210.00**

25 —— —— Fourth Edition, revised and corrected, with Notes and additional References, by Edward Hilliard, to which is added, a Copious Index. *W. Strahan and M. Woodfall, for P. Uriel, E. Brooke, Whielden and Co. and R. Critchet*, 1780, *a few ll. stained*, [xxiii+] 504 [+xix] pp., folio, *contemp. tan calf, red leather label, corners little worn, upper joint cracked, but sound* **£45.00**

26 **Strange** (John) Reports of Adjudged Cases in the Courts of Chancery, King's Bench, Common Pleas, and Exchequer, from Trinity Term in the second Year of King George I. to Trinity Term in the twenty-first Year of King George II. [1716–1747]. The Second Edition, Revised and Corrected. 2 Vols. *The King's Law-Printers*, 1782, iv+1272 [+lxxxiv] pp., 8vo, *contemp, calf, leather labels* **£35.00**

27 **Wingate** (Edmund) An Exact Abridgment of all Statutes in Force and Use. From the beginning of Magna Charta untill 1641. With a Continuation, under their proper Titles, of all Acts in Force and Use, untill the Year, 1675. And Alphabetically digested under apt Titles. Whereto is annexed Four Tables, directing to the several Matters and Clauses throughout the said Statutes [Fifth Edition]. *John Streater, Eliz. Flesher . . . sold by George Sawbridge, John Bellinger . . . 1675, signature of early owner on title, which is dust soiled*, [v+] 756 (shd. read 752) [+cxxxv] pp. sm.8vo, *contemp. tan calf, corners worn, recently rebacked, red leather label, new end-papers* (Wing E908) **£75.00**

28 **The Young Clerk's Magazine:** or English Law-Repository: containing a Variety of the most useful Precedents of Articles of Agreement, Bonds, Bills, Recognizances, Releases . . . to which is added the Doctrine of Fines and Recoveries, and their Forms. Second Edition, Revised and Corrected. *E. and R. Nutt, and R. Gosling (Assigns of Edw. Sayer) for J. Hodges*, 1740, *2 plates embrowned*, [iv+] 192 [+viii] pp., 12mo, *contemp. sheep, corners worn, recently rebacked, red leather label* **£75.00**

HISTORY

29 **Aiken** (Lucy) Memoirs of the Court of Queen Elizabeth. 2 Vols. Third Edition. *Longman, Hurst, Rees, Orme, and Brown*, 1819, *portrait, slightly foxed and off-set*, xvi+488: [iv+] vii+522 pp., 8vo, *contemp. diced tan calf, gilt, lettered, small areas of insect damage to surface* **£45.00**

30 —— Memoirs of the Court of King James the First. 2 Vols. Third Edition. *Longman, Hurst, Rees, Orme, Brown, and Green*, 1823, *with 2 portraits, off-set on to titles*, xvi+444: x+413 pp., 8vo, *half tan calf, brown leather labels, marbles bds. and edges* **£45.00**

31 **Aitkin** (John) Annals of the Reign of King George the Third; from its Commencement in the year 1760, to the General Peace in the year 1815. 2 Vols. *Longman, Hurst, Rees, Orme, and Brown*, 1816, *occasional foxing*, xxiv+505: xix+480 pp. 8vo, *contemp. half tan calf, lettered, marble bds.* **£35.00**

32 **America.** AN ACT to prohibit all Trade and Intercourse with the Colonies of New Hampshire, Massachusett's Bay, Rhode Island, Connecticut, New York, New Jersey, Pennsylvania, the Three Lower Countries of Delaware, Maryland, Virginia, North Carolina, South Carolina, and Georgia, during the Continuance of the present Rebellion within the said Colonies respectively. *Charles Eyre and William Strahan*, 1776, [i+30] pp., folio, *disbound* **£30.00**

33 —— BRISTED (John) America and her Resources; or a View of the agricultural, commercial, manufacturing, financial, political, literary, moral and religious Capacity and Character of the American People. *Henry Colburn*, 1818, *library name on title*, xvi+504 pp., 8vo, *contemp. half calf, marbled bds., newly rebacked, brown leather label* (Sabin 8050) **£150.00**

34 —— TARIFFS. A Collection of 32 speeches, mostly made in the House of Representatives, on the subject of Tariffs. *Washington (mostly)*, 1820–1863, *some a little foxed*, 8vo, *sewed* **£85,00**

35 **Amhurst** (Nicholas) Terrae-Filius; or, the Secret History of the University of Oxford; in several Essays. To which are added, Remarks upon a late Book, entitled, University Education, by R. Newton, D.D. Principal of Hart Hall. Third Edition. *R. Francklin*, 1754, *title soiled, advert. leaf at end*, xxiii+370 pp., sm.8vo, *new half tan calf, brown leather label, marbled bds.* **£40.00**

36 **Andrews** (James Pettit) The History of Great Britain, connected with the Chronology of Europe: with Notes, &c. containing Anecdotes of the Times, Lives of the Learned, and Specimens of their Works. 2 Vols. in 1. *T. Cadell*, 1794, *with 4 folding genealogies*, [i+] vii+7+477 (shd. read 483): [i+] 366 [+ii] pp., 4to, *contemp. sprinkled calf, gilt, sometime rebacked and old backstrip laid down, leather labels* **£50.00**

37 [**Anquetil** (Louis Pierre)] L'Esprit de la Ligue, or Histoire Politique des Troubles de France pendant les xvi & xviie siecles. Seconde Edition, corr. and augm., 3 Vols. *Paris, Jean-Th. Herissant Fils*, 1771, lxxxvii+329: [iii+] 341: [iv+] 392 pp., 12mo, *contemp. mottled calf, backstrips gilt, red and green leather labels, one missing, little rubbed, m.e.* **£50.00**

38 **Austria.** GUILLIMANNUS (Franciscus) Habsbvrgiaca sive de Antiqva, et Vera origine Domvs Avstriae vita et rebvs gestis comitvm vindonissensium sive Altenburgiensium in primis Habsbvrgiorvm, libri septem. *Mediolani, ex officina Regia Pandulphi & M. Tullii Malatestae*, 1605, *large engraved coat of arms on title and a number of woodcut arms in the text, ruled throughout in red*, [xii+] 344 [+ii] pp., 4to, *contemp. brown calf, gilt backstrip, lettered, joints beginning to crack, a little rubbed, part of the front paste-down torn away* **£65.00**

39 **Aylmer** (John, *Bp. of London*) STRYPE (John) Historical Collections of the Life and Acts of . . . John Aylmer . . . wherein are explained many Transactions of the Church of England; and what Methods were then taken to preserve it, with respect both to the Papist and the Puritan. *Printed by W. Bowyer for Brabazon Aylmer*. 1701, *some discolouration*, [xxx+] 330 [+vi] pp., 8vo, *new qtr. calf, marbled boards, leather label* **£30.00**

40 **Ayloffe** (Sir Joseph) Calendars of the Ancient Charters, and the Welch and Scottish Rolls, now remaining in the Tower of London, to which are added Memoranda concerning the Affairs of Ireland, extracted from the Tower Records, to the Whole is prefixed an Introduction, giving some Account of the State of the Public Records from the Conquest to the present Time. *Benjamin White*, 1774, *with 4 copper plates showing the various hands used in writing the charters, to the reign of Elizabeth*, [lxx+] 462 [+xxxii] pp., 4to, *contemp. sprinkled calf, red leather label, joints cracked* **£65.00**

41 [**Bacon** (Sir James, *Barrister and Judge*)] The Life and Times of Francis the First, King of France. 2 Vols. *Edward Bull*, 1829, *portrait, some light foxing*, xv+492: xi+432 pp., 8vo, *contemp. half green calf, red leather labels, backstrips dulled, marbled sides a little rubbed* **£42.00**

42 **Baker** (Sir Richard) A Chronicle of the Kings of England from the Time of the Romans Goverment [sic] unto the Raigne of our Soveraigne Lord King Charles. Containing all Passages of State and Church, with all other Observations proper for a Chronicle. Faithfully Collected out of Authors, Ancient and Moderne; and digested into a new Method. *Daniel Frere*, 1643, FIRST EDITION, *engraved portrait of Prince Charles* [Charles II.] *by Dalen, and engraved title within an elaborate pictorial border by Wm. Marshall, these a little creased*. [ix+] 181+163+108+163 [+xxxv] pp., folio, *contemp. brown calf, red leather label, chipped, corners bruised, some rubbing, small splits in joints, upper hinge partly broken* (Wing B501) **£65.00**

43 **Balliols.** SCOTT (Benjamin J.) The Norman Balliols in England, compiled in part from Mr. Wentworth Huyshe's *Harold and the Balliols*, with illustrations and additional matter, including two introductory and two concluding chapters and a pedigree. 1914, *profusely illust.*, xx+467 pp., 8vo, *full green niger morocco, gilt panels and fillets, inner dentelle borders, lettered, by Rivière, backstrip v. sl. sunned, otherwise an excellent copy* **£85.00**

44 **Banking.** [TURNER (Thomas)] The Joyful News of Opening the Exchequer to the Gold-Smiths of Lombard-street, and their Creditors. As it was celebrated in a Letter to the same Friend in the Countrey, to whom the Bankers Case was formerly sent. *T.N. for William Place, and Thomas Basset*, 1677, *with the final blank leaf present, License dated April 7th. for May 7th., a few small stains*, 10pp., folio, *new wrappers, an excellent untrimmed copy* (Wing T3339: Goldsmiths' 2216) scarce **£115.00**

45 **Barlow** (Edward) Barlow's Journal of his Life at Sea in King's Ships, East & West Indiamen & other Merchantmen from 1659 to 1703. Transcribed from the original Manuscript by Basil Lubbock. 2 Vols. *Hurst and Blackett*, 1934, *with 8 coloured plates and 72coastline drawings reproduced in half-tone, foxing of fore-edges*, 575 pp., 8vo, *orig. blue cloth, lettered* **£45.00**

46 **Beckington** (Thomas) A Journal of one of the Suite of Thomas Beckington, afterwards Bishop of Bath and Wells, during an Embassy to negociate a Marriage between Henry vi. and a Daughter of the Count of Armagnac. A.D. MCCCCXLII. with Notes and Illustrations by Nicholas Harris Nicolas. *William Pickering*, 1828, *one of 250 copies*, 6 pp. *catalogue*, lxxvii [+i+] 130 pp., 8vo, *orig. brown cloth, paper label, faded and torn at head of backstrip* (Keynes p.52) **£25.00**

47 **Bede** (The Venerable) Historia Ecclesiastica Gentis Anglorum. Ad fidem Codicum Manuscriptorum recensuit Josephus Stevenson. 2 Vols. *English Historical Society*, 1838, MEMBER'S COPY, *2 coloured plates*, [v+] iv+xxxv+423: vi+v–xii+359 pp., roy. 8vo, *orig. cream paper bds., brown leather labels, all edges untrimmed, joints splitting* **£45.00**

48 —— ——, cum opusculis quibusdam et Epistola Bonifacii ad Cudbertum Archiepiscopum cura Roberti Hussey. *Oxonii, Typographeo Academico*, 1846, xiv+365 [+i] pp., 8vo, *contemp. prize calf, gilt, red leather label, college crest on sides, inscription on fly leaf* **£30.00**

49 **Belsham** (W.) Memoirs of the Kings of Great Britain of the House of Brunswick-Lunenburg [George I. and II.]. 2 Vols., Second Edition. *G.G. and J. Robinson*, 1796, *slight foxing*, [i+] 383: [i+] 384 [+xx] pp., 8vo, *contemp. half tan calf, gilt, lettered, marbled bds.* **£35.00**

50 —— Memoirs of the Reign of George III. [to the Commencement of the Year 1799]. 6 Vols., Second Edition. *G.G. and J. Robinson*, 1795/1801, *occasional foxing*, 8vo, *contemp. half brown calf, lettered, marbled bds.* **£45.00**

51 **Benger** (Elizabeth Ogilvy) Memoirs of the Life of Anne Boleyn, Queen of Henry VIII., Second Edition, 2 Vols. *Longman, Hurst, Rees, Orme, and Brown*, 1821, *portrait after Holbein*, viii+300: iv+305 [+i] pp., 8vo, *an elegant copy in contemp. marbled tan calf, backstrips lettered and decorated in gilt.* **£45.00**

52 —— Memoirs of the Life of Mary Queen of Scots. 2 Vols. *Longman, Hurst, Rees, Orme, and Brown*, 1823, *portrait, little foxed*, viii+382: viii+401 [+i] pp., 8vo, *contemp. half brown calf, lettered, marbled bds.* **£40.00**

53 **Bentham** (Jeremy) Defence of Usury; shewing the Impolicy of the present Legal Restraints on the Terms of Pecuniary Bargains. In a series of Letters to a Friend. To which is added, a Letter to Adam Smith, Esq; LL.D. on the Discouragements opposed by the above Restraints to the Progress of Inventive Industry. *Dublin, Messrs. D. Williams, Colles, White, Bryne, Lewis, Jones, and Moore*, 1788, *some paper faults, worm holes in inner margins throughout*, [viii+] 232 pp., 12mo, *orig. grey bds., soiled and a little worn, sometime crudely rebacked with canvas, edges uncut* (Kress B1368: Goldsmiths' 13615) **£200.00**

¶Closely followed the First London Edition and preceded the Second by some two years.

54 **Berkeley.** SMYTH (John) The Berkeley Manuscripts. The Lives of the Berkeleys Lords of the Honour, Castle and Manor of Berkeley in the County of Gloucester from 1066 to 1618, with a Description of the Hundred of Berkeley and of its Inhabitants. Edited by Sir John Maclean. 3 Vols. *Gloucester, John Bellows for the Subscribers*, 1883/5, [ix+] xii+397 [+v]: viii+476: iii+439 pp., lge 4to, *orig. quarter cloth, paper labels, grey bds., a little rubbed and corners worn* **£85.00**

¶Armorial book labels of Cecil H. S. Perceval, one of the subscribers, on inside paste-downs.

55 **Besdel** (P.F.) Abrégé des Causes célébres & intéressantes, avec les Jugemens qui les ont decidées. 3 Vols. *Londres, H. Hughs*, 1777/8, [iii+] viii+309 [+iii]: [iii+] 300 [+iii]: vii+240 [+iv] pp., 8vo, *modern half tan sheep, red leather labels, marbled bds., all edges untrimmed* **£110.00**

56 **Beugnot.** D'IDEVILLE (Count H.) Life and Adventures of Count [Jean Claude] Beugnot, Minister of State under Napoleon I. Edited [and translated] from the French by Charlotte M. Yonge. 2 Vols. *Hurst and Blackett*, 1871, FIRST EDITION, x+365: viii+343 pp., 8vo, *twentieth century half tan calf, lettered, marbled bds., corners bumped, backstrips faded and little rubbed* **£35.00**

57 **Bill** [with the Amendments] to Punish, by Imprisonment and Hard Labour, certain Offenders; and to establish proper Places for their Reception. 1778, *some few marginal notes, small hole in* 1st *leaf with no loss*, 40pp., folio, *disbound* **£25.00**

58 **B[lount]** (T[homas]) Glossographia: or a Dictionary interpreting all such Hard Words, whether Hebrew, Greek, Latin, as are now used in our refined English Tongue. Also the Terms of Divinity, Law Physick, Mathematick, Heraldry, Anatomy, War, Musick, Architecture; and of several other Arts and Sciences Explicated . . . *Tho. Newcomb, sold by Humphrey Moseley and George Sawbridge*, 1656, FIRST EDITION, *embrowned and stained by use throughout with margins becoming brittle*, [xvi+671] pp., 8vo, *modern quarter calf, red leather label, marbled bds.* (Wing B3334) **£95.00**

59 **Boccalini** (Trajano) Iragguagli di Parnasso: or, Advertisements from Parnassus: in Two Centuries. With the Politick Touchstone. Written Originally in Italian . . . and now put into English by the Right Honourable Henry Earl of Monmouth. Third Edition, Corrected. *Peter Parker*, 1674, *some staining at edges, last leaf laid down*, [xvi+] 291 pp., folio, *contemp. sprinkled calf, corners worn, recently rebacked, red leather label* (Wing B3384) **£35.00**

60 **Bohun** (Edmund) The Character of Queen Elizabeth, or a Full and Clear Account of Her Policies, and the Methods of Her Government both in Church and State. Her Virtues and Defects. Together with the Characters of Her Principal Ministers of State. And the greatest part of the Affairs and Events that Happened in Her Times. *Ric. Chiswell*, 1693, *portrait, torn and laid down, this and title soiled*, [xxx+] 376 pp., 8vo, *contemp. sheep, red leather label, sides worn* (Wing B3448) **£40.00**

61 **Bolingbroke.** COOKE (George Wingrove) Memoirs of [Henry St. John] Lord Bolingbroke. 2 Vols. *Richard Bentley*, 1835, *2 portraits, some dampstaining*, xx+416: viii+472 pp., 8vo., *half crimson roan, lettered, cloth sides faded* **£35.00**

62 **Bonamici** (Castrucci) Commentariorum de Bello Italico. 4 Parts in 2 Vols. *Lugduni Batavorum*, 1750/51, *some occasional soiling, lacks 2 half titles*, xviii+128: xx+122: xxii+130: 144 [+iii] pp., 8vo, *modern half calf, black leather labels, buckram sides* **£65.00**

63 [**Bonesana** (Caesar, *Marquis of Beccaria*)] An Essay on Crimes and Punishments, translated from the Italian; with a Commentary, attributed to Mons. De Voltaire, Translated from the French. Second Edition. *F. Newbery*, 1769, *some discolouration*, xii+179+lxxi pp., 8vo, *new quarter sheep, green leather label, cloth sides* **£75.00**

64 **Bossuet** (James-Benignus) A View of Universal History, from the Beginning of the World to the Empire of Charlemain. Transl. from the Louvre Original by James Elphinston. 2 Vols. *B. White; E. and C. Dilly* . . . 1778, vii+267: 287 pp., 12mo, *contemp. tree calf, red and green leather labels, upper joint of vol. i. cracked, y.e.* **£21.00**

65 [**Boyer** (Abel)] The History of King William the Third. 3 Vols. *A. Roper and F. Coggan, and Wm. Davis*, 1702, *frontis. to each vol., 5 portraits and a coat of arms, divisional titles*, [xvi+] 136+395 (shd. read 381): [viii+] 520 (shd. read 504) +51 [+vii]: [xvi+] 407+82 [+xii] pp., 8vo, *contemp. sprinkled calf, panelled in blind, sometime rebacked and lettered, backstrips gilt and blind, rubbed, one joint cracked* **£55.00**

66 [**Brady** (Robert)] A Great Point of Succession discussed. With a Full and Particular Answer to a late Pamphlet, Intituled, A Brief History of Succession, &c. *H. Rodes*, 1681, *margins discoloured, two small holes in final lf. with slight loss*, [i+] 38 pp., folio, *disbound* (Wing B4191) **£25.00**

67 **Brady** (Robert) An Historical Treatise of Cities, and Burghs or Boroughs. Shewing, their Original, and Whence, and from Whom they Received their Liberties, Privileges and Immunities; What they were, and what Made and Constituted a Free Burgh, & Free Burgesses. As also, shewing when they first sent their Representatives to Parliament. With a Concurrent Discourse of most Matters, and Things incident, or Relating thereto. *Samuel Lowndes*, 1690, *some staining with consequent brittleness of margins*, [i+] iv [+ii+] 79+39+4 pp., folio, *contemp. sprinkled calf, backstrip defective, sides heavily worn* (Wing B4192) **£40.00**

68 **Britton** (John) and E.W. **Brayley.** Memoirs of the Tower of London: comprising historical and descriptive Accounts of that national Fortress and Palace, *Hurst, Chance, and Co.*, 1830, *vignette on title and* 18 *engravings on wood by Branston and Wright, half title and advert. lf. present, some foxing*, xvi+374 pp., sm.8vo, *orig. quarter green cloth, drab bds., paper label chipped and soiled* **£40.00**

69 **Brooke** (Sir Robert) La Graund Abridgement, collect & escrie per le Iudge tresreuerend Syr Robert Brooke Chiualier . . . 2 parts in 1 Vol. *Ricardi Tottell*, 1576, *lacking title to part* 1., *this replaced by that of part* 2., *title within woodcut border* (McKerrow 196) *margins cropped, tear neatly repaired, signature of previous owner, dampstaining throughout, a few lower margins cut close with slight loss*, [iv+] 351: [blank+] 328 ff., sm.4to, *seventeenth century tan calf, little worn, recently rebacked, red leather label* (STC 3828: Beale 471/2) **£450.00**

70 [**Brown** (John)] An Estimate of the Manners and Principles of the Times. Third Edition. *L. Davis, and C. Reymers*, 1757, *title in red and black, 2 pp. catalogue at end*, 221 [+ii] pp., 8vo., *contemp. sprinkled calf, joints cracking, lacks label* **£40.00**

71 **Browne** (John, *Jesuit*) A Discovery of the Notorious Proceedings of William Laud, in bringing Innovations into the Church, and raising up troubles in the State . . . *Henry Walker*, 1641, *head margins cropped, soiled* [i+5] pp., sm.4to, *disbound* (Wing B5119) **£30.00**

72 **Buckingham** and **Chandos** (Duke of) Memoirs of the Courts and Cabinets of William iv. and Victoria, from original family Documents. 2 Vols., *Hurst and Blackett*, 1861, *2 portraits, slight foxing*, viii+401: viii+429 pp., 8vo., *contemp. half tan calf, backstrips gilt, black leather labels, little chipped, marbled bds. and end-papers* **£25.00**

73 **Burke** (Edmund) The Works, a New Edition, 16 Vols. *C. and J. Rivington*, 1826/7, 8vo, *contemp. tree calf, carefully rebacked and restored, having at some time been damaged in a fire, original backstrips laid down, red and green leather labels* **£200.00**

74 —— The Correspondence . . . edited by Thomas W. Copeland. 9 Vols. [lacking vol. x. – Index]. *Cambridge and Chicago, The University Presses*, 1958–70, *portraits*, 8vo, *blue cloth, lettered* **£190.00**

75 **Burton** (Henry) The Grand Impostor vnmasked; or a Detection of the notorious hypocrisie, and desperate Impiety of the late Archbishop (so called) of Canterbury, cunningly couched in that written Copy, which he read on the Scaffold at his execution, *Giles Calvert*, [1644/5], *embrowned, some running titles cropped, two corners torn with slight loss to text*, [iv+] 20 pp., sm.4to, *disbound* (Wing B6163) **£30.00**

76 —— (John) Monasticon Eboracense: and the Ecclesiastical History of Yorkshire. Containing an Account of the first Introduction and Progress of Christianity in that Diocese, until the End of William the Conqueror's Reign. Also the Description of the Situation, Fabric, Times of Endowments of all Churches, Collegiate, Conventual, Parochial, or of peculiar Jurisdiction, *York, the Author, by N. Nickson*, 1758, *with 3 folding plates, snags in some folds, lacks last lf. of Index*, xii+448 [+xxxii] pp., folio, *contemp. tan calf, lettered, tooled in blind and gilt* **£90.00**

77 —— (John Hill) Narratives from Criminal Trials in Scotland, 2 Vols. in 1. *Chapman and Hall*, 1852, [i+] iv+310: [i+] 319 pp., sm.8vo, *half tan calf, brown leather label, buff cloth sides* **£25.00**

78 —— (Thomas, *Cromwellian Member of Parliament*) Diary, now first published from the original autograph Manuscript, with an introduction containing an Account of the Parliament of 1654; from the Journal of Guibon Goddard and now first printed. Edited and illustrated with notes historical and biographical by John Towill Rutt. 4 Vols. *Henry Colburn*, 1828, *3 frontispieces, slight foxing*, 8vo, *nineteenth century green calf, slight rubbing, sometime neatly rebacked, faded, red leather labels* **£75.00**

79 **Calendar.** PHILIPP (Henry) Quaestiones Chronologicae de Annis Domini, Ivlianis et Nabonassari: et Aera Mvndi Ivdaica apte inter se componendis . . . [and] Quaestiones Chronologicae de Annis Nati et Passi Salvatoris . . . 2 Parts in 1 Vol. *Coloniae Agrippinensivm, Ioannem Kinckivm*, 1630, *folding tables, discoloured throughout*, [viii+] 154 (shd. read 146): [iv+] 107 [+i] pp., sm.4to, *new quarter calf, red leather label, drab bds.* **£75.00**

80 **Calmet** (Augustin) Suite des Portraits des Ducs et Duchesses de la Maison Royale de Lorraine dessinés et gravés d'apres les Medailles de St. Urbain par les plus habiles Maitres de Florence, avec la Dissertation historique et chronologique, 2 Parts in 2 Vols., *Florence, Francois Moucke*, 1762/3, *titles in red and black, with 65 portraits, 15 inscriptions, 5 vignettes, some light foxing, plates in vol. i. wrinkled*, v+lxxxxv: i+lxxxxiv pp., large folio, *contemp. half 'cats-paw' calf, leather labels, cloth sides a little worn, lettered on upper covers* **£160.00**

81 **Camden** (William) Annales Regvm Anglicarvm, et Hibernicarvm, Regnante Elizabetha, ad annvm salvtis M.D.LXXXIX, [First Part]. *Guilielmi Stansbij, imp. Simonis Watersoni*, 1615, FIRST EDITION, *very slight wrinkling of ll. throughout*, [viii+] 499 [+xx] pp., folio, *contemp. dark brown calf, unlettered, slight rubbing at all edges, small piece missing from tail of backstrip, paste-downs lifted*
(STC 4496) **£360.00**

82 —— The History of the most Renowned and Victorious Princess Elizabeth, late Queen of England; containing all the most Important and Remarkable Passages of State, both at Home and Abroad (so far as they were linked with English Affairs) during her Long and Prosperous Reign. The Third Edition, *E. Flesher, for Charles Harper, and John Amery*, 1675, *portrait by White, title in red and black, worming in a few early margins, some dampstaining with corners becoming fragile*, [xvii+] 661 (shd. read 671) [+xl] pp., folio, *contemp. dark brown calf, lacks label, slight cracks in joints, a little rubbed* (Wing C362) **£90.00**

83 —— Rerum Anglicarvm et Hibernicarvm Annales, Regnante Elisabetha, Ultima Editio. *Lvgd. Batavorvm, typis Elseviriorum*, 1639, *title in red and black, portrait of Queen Elizabeth, light discolouration throughout*, [xiv+] xiv+856 [+xxxviii] pp., 8vo, *contemp. vellum, MS. lettering faint, some edges worn and damaged, book-label cut from front paste-down* (Willems 475) **£55.00**

84 [**Campbell** (John)] The Present State of Europe; explaining the Interests, Connections, Political and Commercial Views of its Several Powers, comprehending also, a clear and Concise History of each Country, so far as to shew the Nature of their Present Constitutions. Fifth Edition, revised, corrected, and continued by the Author. *T. Longman, C. Hitch and L. Hawes* . . . 1757, *discoloured*, viii+517 [+iii] pp., 8vo, *contemp. tan calf, red leather label, head and tail of backstrip chipped, joints cracked* **£25.00**

85 **Canada. Newfoundland.** A REPORT from the Committee of Secrecy, appointed by Order of the House of Commons to examine several Books and Papers laid before the House, relating to the late Negotiations of Peace and Commerce, &c. Reported on the Ninth of June, 1715, by the Right Honourable Robert Walpole, Chairman of the said Committee. Together with an Appendix, containing Memorials, Letters, and other Papers referred to in the said Report. *Printed for Jacob Tonson, Timothy Goodwin, Bernard Lintot, and William Taylor*, 1715, *tear in last leaf repaired, staining to some lower margins*, [iv+] 94 pp., folio, *modern qtr. calf, marb. bds., unlettered* (Sabin 69729: Kress 2973) **£85.00**

¶Relates in part to the rights of fishing in Newfoundland, with an Appendix of letters etc. dealing with trade and commerce of Britain in various parts of the world.

86 **Cary** (Henry, *Editor*) Memorials of the Great Civil War in England from 1646 to 1652. Edited from Original Letters in the Bodleian Library of Charles the First, Charles the Second, Queen Henrietta, Prince Rupert, Oliver Cromwell, Sir Thomas Fairfax [&c. &c.]. 2 Vols. *Henry Colburn*, 1842, *some foxing, staining and discolouration*, xxxii+445: xii+464 pp., 8vo, *binder's red buckram, brown leather labels* **£35.00**

87 **Chalmers** (George) An Estimate of the Comparative Strength of Great Britain, during the present and four preceding reigns, and of the Losses of her Trade from every War since the Revolution. A New Edition, *John Stockdale*, 1794, [iii+] cxvi+ [v] -xi+254 [+xv] pp., 8vo, *late nineteenth century half tan calf, black leather label, marbled bds., end-papers and edges* (Sabin 11760: Kress B2666) **£45.00**

88 **Chamberlayne** (Edward) Angliae Notitia; or; the Present State of England, together with Divers Reflections upon the Antient State thereof. Third Edition, Corrected and much Augmented. *The Savoy, T.N. for John Martyn*, 1669, *discoloured, small hole in corner of penultimate leaf*, [xii+] 480 [+i] pp., 12mo, *contemp. black calf, recently rebacked, remains of orig. backstrip laid down, unlettered* (Wing C1821) **£35.00**

89 **Charles I.** *ΕΙΚΩΝ ΒΑΣΙΛΙΚΗ*. Vel Imago Regis Caroli, il illis suis Aerumnis & Solitudine. *Hagae-Comitis, Typis S.B. Impensis J. William*, 1649, *crowned sun and shield on verso of title, discoloured*, [xii+] 258 (shd. read 252) pp. (Madan 43, the rare variant title):
with
Rationes Serenissimi Caroli . . . Contra affectatam Curiae, quae dicebatur Justitiae, Jurisdictionem . . . ex Autographo fideliter Redditae. *Hagae-Comitis, typis S.B. Impensis Richardi Royston*, 1649, *lacks* [¶1] *and* [¶6], [ii+] 4 pp. (Madan 102):
Two pieces bound together, 12mo, *contemp. calf, rubbed, back strip defective* **£40.00**

90 —— The Kings Cabinet opened: or, Certain Packets of Secret Letters & Papers, written with the Kings own Hand, and taken in his Cabinet at Nasby-Field, June 14. 1645. by Victorious Sr. Thomas Fairfax; . . . *Robert Bostock*, 1645, *embrowned, some margins cut close*, [vi+] 56 pp. (Wing C2358 and K591: Madan 1790)
[and]
BRISTOL (George Digby, *Earl of*) The Lord George Digby's Cabinet and Dr. Goff's Negotiations; together with His Majesties, the Queen's and the Lord Jermin's, and other Letters: taken at the Battel at Sherborn in Yorkshire about the 15th of October last. Also Observations upon the said Letters. *Edward Husband*, 1646, *embrowned, title soiled*, 68 pp. (Wing B4763)
Two pieces bound together, sm.4to, *contemp. sheep, red leather label slightly rubbed* **£85.00**

91 —— HALFORD (Sir Henry) Essays and Orations, read and delivered at the Royal College of Physicians; to which is added an Account of the Opening of the Tomb of King Charles I. Second Edition. *John Murray*, 1833, *portrait and facsimile*, viii+173+lxx pp., 8vo, *contemp. half calf, brown leather label, marbled bds.* **£30.00**

92 —— SKELTON (Sir John) Charles I. *Goupil & Co.*, 1898, *with coloured portraits and 41 other portraits, views, etc.*, v+185 [+i] pp., lge. 4to, *green buckram, lettered, dulled by exposure* **£25.00**

93 **Charles II.** An Act for Regulating the Making of Stuffs in Norfolk and Norwich. *John Bill and Christopher Barker*, 1662, *embrowned*, pp. [i+] 97–113, folio, *disbound* **£20.00**

94 —— PRICE (John) The Mystery and Method of His Majesty's Happy Restauration, laid Open to Publick View. *James Vade*, 1680, *portrait of General Monck by R. White, the preliminaries have been misbound, some light browning*, [xvi+] 162 pp., 8vo, *contemp. sprinkled sheep, unlettered* (Wing P3335) **£75.00**
¶One of the most important sources for the events which culminated in the restoration of Charles ii.

95 —— [PRIMI-VISCONTI (J.B.) *Count de St. Maijole*] An Account of the Reasons which Induced Charles II. King of England to declare War against the States-General of the United Provinces in 1672. and of the Private League which He entered into at the same Time with the French King to carry it on. And to establish Popery in England, Scotland, & Ireland, *Richard Baldwin*, 1689, [iii+] 15 pp., *advert. pasted on verso of* [E2], folio, *disbound, edges untrimmed* (Wing M288) scarce **£40.00**

96 —— SAVILE (George, *marquis of Halifax*) A Character of King Charles the Second: and Political, Moral and Miscellaneous Thoughts and Reflections. *J. and R. Tonson*, 1750, *some discolouration*, [viii+] 183 pp., 8vo, *contemp. calf, red leather label, rubbed, joints beginning to crack* **£30.00**

97 The **Chronicles** of the White Rose of York. A Series of Historical Fragments, Proclamations, Letters, and other contemporary Documents relating to the Reign of King Edward the Fourth. *James Bohn*, 1845, *portrait and plan of Calais, foxed*, xc+310 [+ii] pp., 8vo, *quarter brown roan, lettered, brown paper bds., little scuffed* **£15.00**

98 **Church of England,** (temp. Edward vi.) INIUNCCIONS geuen by the most excellent prince Edwarde the sixt . . . To al and singular his louyng subiectes, aswel of the Clergie as of the Laietie. [colophon: *last daye of Iuly, by Rychard Grafton*, 1548], *title within woodcut border* (McK. and F. 63), [12 ff.], (STC 10091):
with
ARTICLES to be Inqvired of. 1548. (in visitacions to bee had, within the Diocess of Cantorbury – drop title), [colophon: *laste daie of August*, 1548, *by Richard Grafton*], *title within woodcut border*, [8 ff.], (STC 10148):
and
CERTAYNE SERMONS, or Homelies, appoynted by the kynges Maiestie, to be declared and redde, by all persones, Vicars, or Curates, euery Sondaye in their churches, where they haue Cure. 1548. [colophon: *the xxi daye of Iune, by Richard Grafton*, 1548], *title within woodcut border* (MCK. and F. 63), *large rebus of Grafton on verso of colophon leaf, very extensive marginal glosses in an early hand in the 'Homilie against Adultery' and in the final 3 pp.*, [93 ff.], (STC 13642):
Three pieces bound together, *some soiling by use, wormed throughout with some loss, mostly to single letters or parts of words*, sm.4to, *contemp. brown calf, panelled in blind, sometime rebacked and lettered and the sides extensively repaired* **£750.00**

99 **Churchill** (Winston S.) A History of the English-Speaking Peoples. 4 Vols. *Cassell and Company*, 1956/58, FIRST EDITIONS, *maps*, 8vo, *orig. red cloth, lettered, covers a little marked* **£15.00**

100 —— The World Crisis 1911–1918, 3 Vols. in 4, *Thornton Butterworth*, 1923–27, FIRST EDITIONS, *maps*, 8vo, *orig. blue cloth, lettered* **£20.00**

101 —— (*Editor*) The British Gazette. 8 issues [all published], *H.M.S.O.*, 5th–13th May 1926, *issues 1 and 2 printed on pp. 1 and 4 only (as usual), remainder printed on all 4 pp.*, 597×468 mm., *excellent set, each folded twice* (Woods p. 382) **£60.00**

102 **Civil War.** The GARRISON of Shropshire during the Civil War, 1642–48, *Shrewsbury, Leake and Evans*, 1867, *with 25 plates*, 87 [+ii] pp., 4to, *contemp. quarter calf, black leather label, plum paper sides, all rubbed* **£35.00**

103 **Clarendon** (Edward Hyde, *Earl of*) The History of the Rebellion and Civil Wars in England, begun in the Year 1641: with the precedent Passages and Actions, that contributed thereunto, and the happy end, and Conclusion thereof by the King's blessed Restoration, and Return upon the 29th of May, in the Year 1660. 3 Vols. in 6. *Oxford, at the Theatre*, 1705/20, *portrait, some discolouration*, 8vo, *contemp. tan calf, backstrips gilt, green leather labels, all vols. sometime neatly rebacked and orig. backstrips laid down and slightly restored* **£50.00**

104 —— The Life of . . . containing, I. An Account of the Chancellor's Life from his Birth to the Restoration in 1660. II. A Continuation of the same, and of his History of the Grand Rebellion, from the Restoration to his Banishment in 1667 . . . 3 Vols. *Oxford, The Clarendon Printing-House*, 1759, *some embrowning*, [iii+] vii+264 [+x]: [i+] 993 [+xxi] pp., 8vo, *contemp. sprinkled calf, red leather labels, some rubbing, joints cracked* **£45.00**

105 [**Clavell** (Robert)] His Majesties Propriety, and Dominion on the Brittish Seas Asserted: together with a true Account of the Neatherlanders Insupportable Insolencies, and Injuries, they have committed; and the Inestimable Benefits they have gained in their Fishing on the English Seas: as also their Prodigious and Horrid Cruelties in the East and West-Indies, and other Places, *T. Mabb, for Andrew Kembe, and Edward Thomas, and Robert Clavel*, 1665, *portrait, and folding map, this creased and slightly torn, soiling throughout*, [xvi+] 176 pp., 8vo, *contemp. sheep, unlettered, joints cracked* (Wing C4602) **£310.00**

106 [**Cobbett** (William)] Important Considerations for the People of this Kingdom. July, 1803, broadside, 20.25×15.3 ins., *folded* (Pearl 59) **£75.00**
¶"This violent denunciation of the French was written by Cobbett after the Peace of Amiens, which he opposed, had been shattered by Napoleon's renewal of the war. It was sent out, in this form, by the Government to the officiating minister of every English and Welsh parish for display and distribution in the churches." (Pearl)

107 **Commynes** (Philippe de) Mémoires. Nouvelle Edition, revue sur les Manuscrits de la Bibliothèque Royale, et publiée avec annotations et éclaircissements par Mlle. Dupont. 3 Vols. *Paris, Jules Renouard et Cie*, 1840, *some staining in vols. i and ii.*, cxlviii+413: [v+] 607: [v+] 579 pp., 8vo, *dark blue roan, red leather labels, rubbed, crack in joint of vol. i* **£35.00**

108 —— The History of . . . Third Edition, to which is now added out of the latest and best French copy. A Preface to the said History, the Life of Angelo Cattho, Arch-Bishop of Vienna, and two Epistles of John Sleiden relating to the said History never before published. *S.G. for Joshua Kirton*, 1665, *frontis., title within woodcut border*, [x+] 290 [+xii] pp., folio, *sprinkled calf, red leather label, joints cracked* (Wing C5541) **£75.00**

109 **Cooper** (C.P.) An Account of the most important Public Records in Great Britain, and their Publications of the Record Commissioners: together with other miscellaneous, historical, and antiquarian Information. Compiled from various printed Books and Manuscripts. 2 Vols. *Baldwin and Cradock*, 1832, xxiii+458: x+496 pp., 8vo, *orig. brown cloth, red leather labels, shelf marks on backstrips, ex-libris labels on front paste-downs* **£20.00**

110 [**Cosin** (Richard)] Regni Angliae sub Imperio Serenissimae Piae & Potentissimae Reginae Elizabethae Religio et Gubernatio Ecclesiastica. *T. Wood*, 1729, *with 16 tables (some folding) half title present, paste-downs lifted*, [iv+] vi+vi [+x+] 44 pp., 4to, *contemp. panelled calf, red leather label* **£75.00**
¶This edition was augmented by William Wekett. The 8 pp. list of subscribers contains numerous ecclesiastical and secular dignitaries of the time, including Sir Robart Walpole.

111 **Cotton** (Sir Robart) Cottoni Posthuma: Divers Choice Pieces . . . preserved from the Injury of Time, and exposed to publick light, for the benefit of Posterity. *M.C. for C. Harper, sold by W. Hensman and T. Fox*, 1679, light embrowning throughout, [viii+] 353 pp., 8vo, *contemp. sheep, rubbed, recently rebacked, red leather label* (Wing C6487) **£65.00**

112 [**Courtilz de Sandras** (Gatien de)] The Memoirs of the Count de Rochefort, containing an Account of what past most memorable, under the Ministry of Cardinal Richelieu and Cardinal Mazarin, with many particular passages of the Reign of Lewis the Great. Made English from the French. *F.L. for James Knapton, Richard Parker and Tho. Nott*, 1696, *some discolouration, two short tears with no loss of text, 1st blank present*, [xii+] 412 pp., 8vo, *contemp. sprinkled calf, recently rebacked, green leather label* (Wing C6600) **£95.00**

113 **Coxe** (William) Memoirs of the Kings of Spain of the House of Bourbon, from the Accession of Philip the Fifth to the Death of Charles the Third: 1700 to 1788. Drawn from original and unpublished Documents. 3 Vols. in 1. *Longman, Hurst, Rees, Orme, and Brown*, 1813, *some foxing*, xxii [+vii+] *19–*69 [+ii+] 434: [viii+] 465: [viii+] 540 [+xxxii+] 2 pp., 4to, *contemp. half tan calf, green leather label, marbled bds., rubbed* **£30.00**

114 **Craik** (George L.) The History of British Commerce, from the Earliest Times. Reprinted from the Pictorial History of England, with corrections, additions, and a continuation to the present day. 3 Vols. in 1. *Charles Knight*, 1844, *illustration of coins, divisional titles*, 272: 220: 284 pp., 12mo, *contemp. half brown calf, black leather label, brown cloth sides* (Kress 6267) **£30.00**

115 **Cromwell.** NOBLE (Mark) Memoirs of the Protectoral-House of Cromwell; deduced from an early Period, and continued down to the present Time . . . Second Edition, 2 Vols. *Birmingham, Pearson and Rollason* . . . 1787, *portraits and genealogies, some foxing*, xxxi+443: viii+464 pp., 8vo, *contemp. calf, newly rebacked, red leather labels* **£45.00**

116 —— SPITTLEHOUSE (John) The first Addresses to His Exellencie the Lord General, with the Assembly of Elders elected by him and his Council for the management of the affairs of this Commonwealth; as also to all the cordial Officers and Souldiers under his command. Containing Rules & Directions how to advance the Kingdom of Jesus Christ over the face of the whole earth. *J.C. for himself and Richard Moone*, 1653, *Moone's device on title, some discolouration, small repair to title, all inner margins guarded*, [iv+] 27 [+blanks] pp., sm.4to, *quarter buckram over earlier marbled bds., lettered* (Wing S5008) **£75.00**

117 **Dalrymple** (Sir John) Memoirs of Great Britain and Ireland, from the Dissolution of the last Parliament of Charles II. until the Sea-battle off La Hogue. Second Edition, [and from the Battle off La Hogue till the Capture of the French and Spanish Fleets at Vigo], 2 Vols. in 3. *W. Strahan and T. Cadell* . . . 1771/87, xv+509: xiv+325+342+246 [+i]: xiv+205 (shd. read 217) +84 (shd. read 82) pp., lge.4to, *binder's brown buckram, red leather labels* **£40.00**

118 **Dangerfield** (Thomas) Answer to a Certain Scandalous Lying Pamphlet, entituled Malice Defeated, or, The Deliverance of Elizabeth Cellier, *The Author, and are to be sold at Randal Taylor's*, 1680, 20 pp., folio, *disbound* (Wing D183) **£21.00**

119 **De Lolme** (J.L.) The Constitution of England, or an Account of the English Government; in which it is compared with the Republican Form of Government, and occasionally with the other Monarchies in Europe. *T. Spilsbury; and sold by G. Kearsley*, 1775, FIRST ENGLISH EDITION, vii+448 pp., 8vo, *contemp. sprinkled calf, covers little worn, newly rebacked, red leather label* **£35.00**

120 **de Moleville** (Ant. Fr. Bertrand) Private Memoirs relative to the last Year of the Reign of Lewis the Sixteenth, late King of France. 3 Vols. *A. Strahan; and T. Cadell jun. and W. Davies*, 1797, *with 5 portraits, some discolouration*, xii+418: x+418: viii: 446 pp., 8vo, *contemp. quarter tan calf, brown leather labels, lacking in vol. i., marbled bds., vellum corners, little rubbed* **£55.00**

121 **Dermoncourt** (Paul F.S., *General*) The Duchess of Berri in La Vendrée; comprising a Narrative of her Adventures, with her private Papers and secret Correspondence. *Philadelphia, Carey, Lea & Blanchard*, 1833, *foxing throughout, 32 pp. catalogue at end*, iv+188 pp., sm.8vo, *orig. red cloth, paper label, soiled and faded* **£21.00**

122 **De Ruiter.** BRANDT (Gerard) La Vie de Michel de Ruiter, Duc, Chevalier, Lieutenant-Amiral Général de Hollande & de Oüest-Frise. Où est comprise l'Histoire Maritime des Provinces Unies, depuis l'An 1652, jusques à 1676. Traduite du Hollandois [by N. Aubin], . . . *Amsterdam, P. & J. Blaeu, pour Waesberge, Boom, à Someren & Goethals*, 1698, *title in red and black, engraved title, portrait 7 double-page and folding plates and 1 single plate, discoloured, some 14 ll. torn in lower quarter into letter press*, folio, *contemp. panelled calf, recently repaired and rebacked, brown leather label*, scarce **£200.00**

123 **D'Israeli** (Isaac) Commentaries on the Life and Reign of Charles the First, King of England. 2 Vols. *Henry Colburn*, 1828, xxxi+355 [+i]: [i+] ii+246 pp., 8vo, *contemp. half tan calf, red and black leather labels, marbled bds., slight rubbing* **£35.00**

124 [**Dodd** (George)] Pictorial History of the Russian War, 1854–5–6, *Edinburgh, W. & R. Chambers*, 1856, *with coloured frontis., maps, plans and wood engravings*, x+584 pp., 4to, *orig. red cloth, lettered and decorated on backstrip and upper cover, short snag in upper joint* **£21.00**

125 **Dom Boc.** A Translation of the Record called Domesday, so far as relates to the Counties of Middlesex, Hertford, Buckingham, Oxford, and Gloucester. By the Rev. William Bawdwen. *Doncaster, W. Sheardown*, 1812, *divisional titles, lacking that of Bucks.*, [iv+] 26+76+3–82+62+72 [+ii+] 4+3+4+6 pp., 4to, *contemp. tan calf, lettered vol. ii., gilt and blind tooling* **£35.00**

126 **D'Orleans** (J.) The History of the Revolutions in England under the Family of the Stuarts from the Year 1603, to 1690 . . . to which is Prefix'd an Advertisment concerning this History. *E. Curll and R. Gosling*, 1711, *some staining at beginning*, [xxiv+] 328 [+xvi+] 44 pp., 8vo, *contemp. sprinkled calf, lacks label, joints cracking* **£30.00**

127 **Du Boys** (Albert) Catherine of Aragon and the Sources of the English Reformation. Edited from the French, with Notes by Charlotte M. Yonge. 2 Vols. *Hurst and Blackett*, 1881, xxiv+303: xii+322 pp., cr.8vo, *orig. purple cloth, lettered in gilt, backstrips faded* **£18.00**

128 **Duclos** (Charles) The History of Lewis xi. King of France. Translated from the French Original. 2 Vols. *C. Davis and P. Vaillant*, 1746, xxiv+304 [+xlvi]: [i+] 367 pp., 8vo, *contemp. sprinkled sheep, tan leather labels, incorrectly lettered, rubbed and joints cracked* **£30.00**

129 **Dumouriez** (Chas. Franc., *General*) Memoires . . . 2 parts, *Londres, P. Elmsley*, 1794, xvi+99: 164 pp.:
[with]
Coup-d'Oeil Politique sur l'Avenir de la France, *Hambourg*, 1795, [i+] 83 pp.:
[and]
Notice sur la Vie de Sieyes, membres de la Premiere Assemblée Nationale et de la Convention. *Suisse et à Londres*, 1795, 100 pp.:
4 pieces bound together, 8vo, *contemp. half tan calf, red leather label, marbled bds., y.e.* **£40.00**

130 **Echard** (Laurence) The History of England. From the First Entrance of Julius Caesar and the Romans, to the Conclusion of the Reign of King James the Second, and the Establishment of King William and Queen Mary upon the Throne, in the Year 1688. With a Compleat Index. The Third Edition, with Additions, 2 Vols. *Jacob Tonson*, 1720, *with 2 portraits, some staining at margins throughout*, [xvi+] 1150 [+xxxiii] pp., folio, *contemp. panelled calf, sometime rebacked and orig. backstrips laid down, joints now again cracked, leather labels, with the armorial bookplate of Chandos Leigh, First Baron Leigh of the second creation and a presentation inscription from the dowager Duchess of Chandos to Caroline Brydges* [*his Grandmother*] **£50.00**

131 **Ellis** (Henry, *Editor*) Original Letters illustrative of English History; including numerous Royal Letters from Autographs in the British Museum, and one or two other collections. with notes and illustrations, 3 series, 11 Vols., 1825–46, *frontispieces, slight foxing*, 8vo, *binder's buckram, red leather labels* **£130.00**
¶The first series is the second edition.

132 **Elwes.** TOPHAM (Edward) The Life of the late John Elwes, Esquire; Member in Three successive Parliaments for Berkshire. First published in the Paper of The World . . . Ninth Edition. *John Jarvis, for James Ridgway*, 1791, *etched portrait by Wm. Austin, folded genealogical table creased, heavy stain in lower margins, some foxing*, viii+111 pp., 8vo, *binder's grey bds., printed lettering strip* **£21.00**

133 **Estienne** (Charles) Dictionarium Historicum, Geographicum, Poeticum: Gentium Hominum, Deorum, Gentiliem, Regionum, Insularum . . . ad incudem vero revocatum, innumerisque pene locis auctum & emaculatum per Nicolaum Lloydium, editio novissima, *B. Tooke, T. Passenger, T. Sawbridge, A. Swalle & A. Churchill*, 1686, *lacks front free endpaper*, [v+190+i+161+vi] ff., folio, *contemp. mottled calf, unlettered, arms in compartments of backstrip* (Wing E3349 and L2664A) **£75.00**

134 **Eugene of Savoy** (Prince) Memoirs . . . written by himself. Translated from the Genuine French Edition, containing all those Passages which have since been suppressed by order of the French Government, by Frederic Shoberl. Second Edition. *Henry Colburn*, 1811, *portrait, some foxing throughout*, pp. xl+17–304, 8vo, *orig. drab bds., paper label, rubbed, edges untrimmed* **£21.00**

135 **Fell** (Sarah, *of Swarthmoor Hall*) The Household Account Book. Edited by Norman Penny. *Cambridge. The University Press*, 1920, xxxii+597 pp., 8vo, *orig. quarter linen, grey paper bds., paper label* **£21.00**

136 **Fenelon** (Fr. de Salignac de la Mothe de) Examen de Conscience pour un Roi. Ecrit pour l'usage de Mons. le Duc de Bourgogne, puis Dauphin de France, pére de Louis xv. avec la Vie de l'Auteur, une Liste compléte de ses Ouvrages, et des Memoires de sa Famille. *Londres, C. Davis, T. Osbourne, & L. Davis*, 1747, iv+232 pp., sm.8vo, *contemp. mottled calf, red leather label, backstrip gilt, very slightly rubbed* **£50.00**

137 —— Letters to the Duke of Normandy. *Dublin, W. Watson*, 1758, 27 [+i] pp., sm.4to, *contemp. marbled bds.* **£25.00**

138 **Forbes** (William) A Treatise of Church-lands & Tithes: in two Parts. Containing, an Historical Account of Ecclesiastical Revenues, Churches, Church-yards, Church-offices . . . and Actions about Ministers Stipends, Tithes, &c. falling under the Cognisance of the Lords of Session. *Edinburgh, Heirs and Successors of Andrew Anderson . . . sold at John Vallange's shop* . . . 1705, *slight embrowning, one outer margin trimmed with no loss*, [xvi+] 450 [+xxii] pp., sm.8vo, *new 'antique' calf, red leather label* **£85.00**

139 **France.** BAINES (Edward) History of the Wars of the French Revolution, from the Breaking out of the War in 1792, to the Restoration of a General Peace in 1815, comprehending the Civil History of Great Britain and France, during that Period. 2 Vols. *Printed for Longman*, 1817, *with portraits, maps, plans and charts*, [iv+] 539: [iv+] 595 pp., 4to, *contemp. calf, gilt extra, lettered, upper joint of vol. ii. cracked* **£55.00**

140 —— BARRUEL (Augustin de, Abbé) The History of the Clergy during the French Revolution. A Work dedicated to the English Nation. *J. P. Cochlan* . . . 1794, *light foxing throughout*, [i+] vii+vi+160+170+249 pp., 8vo, *contemp. black morocco, lettered, joints becoming tender* **£65.00**

141 —— LES CINQ CODES de l'Empire Francais. 1. Code Napoleon, 2. Code de Procédure civile, 3. Code de Commerce, 4. Code d'Instruction criminelle, 5. Code Pénal. Seconde edition. *Paris F. Guital [and] Ferra*, 1812, *portrait of Napoleon, some foxing*, [i+] 827 pp., 12mo, *half tan calf, gilt, brown leather label* **£65.00**

142 —— LES CODES FRANCAIS contenant: Le Code civil, le Code de procédure civile, le Code de commerce, le Code d'instruction criminelle, le Code pénal, le Code forestier, la Loi sur la police de la Chasse. Edition augmentée de la nouvelle Loi sur le recruitement de l'armée. *Paris, Bernardin Béchet*, 1879, *rubber stamp on title and half title, small hole in former, some foxing*, 720 pp., 8vo, *recent quarter tan sheep, red leather label, over original marbled bds.* **£45.00**

143 —— DUSAULX (Jean) De l'Insurrection Parisienne, et de la Prise de la Bastille; discours historique, prononcé par extrait dans l'assemblée nationale. *Paris, chez Debure*, 1790, xvi+269 [+iii] pp., 8vo, *contemp. tan morocco, green leather label, g.e., joints tender to cracking* **£55.00**

144 —— the GENUINE TRIAL of Marie Antoinette, late Queen of France, containing all the Charges brought against her by the Public Accuser . . . the whole containing a number of important Facts, and displaying a general View of the Causes of the late Revolution in France. Third Edition, Collated and revised with the last Paris edition. *J. S. Jordan, J. Mathews and T. Boosey*, [1793], *coloured portrait, slightly foxed*, 65 pp., 8vo, *full dark blue morocco, lettered, inner dentelle borders, g.e., by Rivière* **£65.00**

145 —— MEZERAY (Francois Eudes de) Abregé chronologique de l'Histoire de France. nouvelle edition, augmentee. 4 Vols. *Amsterdam, David Mortier*, 1755, 4to, *contemp. half tan calf, red and green leather labels, marbled bds., corners worn and bds. a little rubbed, all edges untrimmed* **£60.00**
¶The first edition of the corrected abridgement of Mezeray's great work on the *History of France* met with greater applause than the original work and was much sought after by foreigners as well as Frenchmen. (Chalmers' Biog. Dicty.)

146 —— MOTTEVILLE (Frances Bertaut de) Memoirs for the History of Anne of Austria, Wife of Lewis xiii. of France; and Regent of that Kingdom from his Death to the Accession of her Son Lewis xiv. containing all the remarkable Events during that King's Minority, and the Administration of her Favourite Cardinal Mazarin. Translated from the original French . . . 5 Vols. *J. Darby*, 1726, 12mo, *contemp. tan calf, gilt, red and brown leather labels, 1 missing, very slight rubbing* **£65.00**

147 —— PROVART (Lievain Bonaventura) Vie de la Reine de France, Marie Lecksinska, Princesse de Pologne, dédiée a Mesdames de France ses Filles, escrite sur les Mémoires de la Cour. *Bruxelles, Le Charlier*, 1794, *portrait, discolouration throughout*, [iv+] 397 [+i] pp., 12mo, *contemp. half sheep, red leather, drab bds., corners worn, upper joint cracking* **£45.00**

148 **Franklin** (Benjamin) Papers, 1734 to 1771. Edited by Leonard W. Labaree and others. Vols. 1–18 (of 21), *New Haven, Yale University Press*, 1960–74, *portraits*, 8vo, *orig. brown buckram, lettered* **£230.00**

149 **Fulke** (William) A briefe Confutation, of a Popish Discourse: lately set forth, and presumptuously dedicated to the Queens most excellent Maiestie: by Iohn Howlet, or some other Birde of the night, vnder that name. Contayning certain Reasons , why Papists refuse to come to Church, which Reasons are here inserted and set downe at large, with their several answeres. [*Thomas Dawson* – col.] *for George Byshop*, 1581, *title supplied in photo-facsimile, some margins trimmed close with slight loss of running titles and side notes*, [i+] 58 pp., sm.4to, *binders' black cloth, lettered* (STC 11421) **£85.00**

150 **Gardiner** (Samuel R.) History of England from the Accession of James I. to the Outbreak of the Civil War, 1603–1642. 10 Vols. *Longmans, Green and Co.* 1883, *maps*, cr.8vo, *orig. green cloth, paper labels, well used but sound* **£38.00**

151 —— History of the Great Civil War 1641–1649, New Edition, 4 Vols. *Longmans, Green, and Co.*, 1893/4, *maps, slight foxing*, 8vo, *orig. dark blue cloth, paper labels, label removed from one front cover* **£35.00**

152 **George II.** His Majesty's most gracious Speech to both Houses of Parliament, on Thursday the Seventeenth Day of January, 1750. *Thomas Baskett*, 1750, 4 pp., folio, *unstitched* **£25.00**

153 **Gibbon** (Edward) The History of the Decline and Fall of the Roman Empire. 6 Vols. *A. Strahan and T. Cadell*, 1789/8, *portrait and maps, some discolouration*, 4to, *nineteenth century diced russia, lettered, joints cracking* **£185.00**
¶Vols. i–iii are New Edition, vols. iv–vi are First Editions.

154 **Gingins la Sarra** (Frederik de) **Dépêches** des Ambassadeurs Milanais sur les Campagnes de Charles-le-Hardi duc de Bourgogne de 1474 a 1477; publiées d'après les pièces originales avec sommaires analytiques et notes historiques. 2 Vols. *Paris, Joel Cherbuliez*, 1858, *light foxing*, xix+391: [iii+] 406 pp., 8vo, *half calf, brown and black leather labels, marbled sides, slightly rubbed and faded* **£25.00**

155 **G[lanvill]** (J[oseph]) Some Philosophical Considerations touching the Being of Witches and Witchcraft. Written in a Letter to the much Honour'd Robert Hunt Esq. *E.C., for James Collins*, 1667, *date cut from title*, [i+] 62 [+i] pp., *binders' blanks*, sm.4to, *binders' buckram, lettered* (Wing G832) **£225.00**

156 **Goldsmith** (Oliver) The History of England, from the Earliest Times to the Death of George ii. 4 Vols. *T. Davies, Becket and De Hondt, and T. Cadell*, 1771, FIRST EDITION, FIRST ISSUE, *with the error in the headline on p. 149 in vol. ii., copper engraved portraits of the monarchs, lacking the half titles*, 8vo, *contemp. sprinkled tan calf, corners worn, recently rebacked, green leather labels* (Temple Scott p. 272/3) **£120.00**

157 —— The Roman History, from the Foundation of the City of Rome, to the Destruction of the Western Empire. Second Edition. 2 Vols. *S. Baker and G. Leigh, T. Davies and L. Davis*, 1770, *one leaf torn but no loss*, [ii+] x+487 [+xvi]: [ii+] vi+501 [+xi] pp., 8vo, *contemp. half tan calf, lettered, marbled bds.* **£30.00**

158 **Gordon** (Jacob) Opvs Chronologicorvm Annorvm Seriem, Regnorvm Mvtationes, & rerum toto orbe gestarum narrationem, à Mundi exordio ad annum vsq; Christi 1617 complectens. Curis secundis auctum & recognitum. *Auvustoriti Pictonum*, 1617, *discoloured throughout, pagination irregular, 2 ll. misbound*, [i+] 287 [+xix]: [iv+] 630 [+lxxxii] pp., folio, *early sprinkled sheep, leather label, worn and rubbed, joints beginning to crack* **£95.00**

159 **Gowrie.** SCOTT (James) A History of the Life and Death of John, Early of Gowrie, with Preliminary Dissertations. *Edinburgh, Balfour & Clarke, and sold by William Blackwood and David Morison, jun.*, 1818, *Ltd. to 150 copies, some dampstaining throughout*, [xi+] 342 pp., 8vo, *orig. drab bds., recently rebacked, paper label, edges untrimmed* **£35.00**

160 **Greville** Memoirs 1814–1860, edited by Lytton Strachey and Roger Fulford. 8 Vols. *Macmillan & Co.*, 1938, LTD. TO 630 SETS, *with 7 portraits*, 8vo, *orig. red buckram, lettered*, scarce **£350.00**

161 **Grey** (Richard) Memoria Technica: or, a New Method of Artificial Memory, applied to and exemplified in Chronology, History, Geography, Astronomy. Also Jewish, Grecian and Roman Coins, Weights, and Measures, &c. With Tables proper to the respective Sciences; and Memorial Lines adapted to each Table. Fourth Edition, Corrected and Improved. *D. Browne, J. Whiston* . . . 1756, *clean tear in one leaf*, xvi [+vii+] 159 [+xxviii] pp., sm.8vo, *contemp. tan calf, corners worn, newly rebacked, orig. label*, scarce **£75.00**

162 **Guicciardini** (Francesco) Della Istoria d'Italia. libri xx. 4 Vols. *Friburgo, Michele Kluch*, 1775/6, *portrait, some free end-papers missing*, 4to, *contemp. blind stamped vellum, lettered in gilt* **£45.00**

163 [**Halifax** (George Savile, *marquis of*)] The Anatomy of an Equivalent, [1688], *drop-title, some staining*, 16 pp., sm.4to, *disbound* (Wing H291) **£30.00**

164 [**Hall** (Edward)] The Vnion of the two noble and illustre famelies of Lancastre & Yorke, beeyjg long in continual discension for the croune of this noble realme, with all the actes done in bothe the tymes of the Princes, bothe of the one linage and of the other, beginnyng at the tyme of kyng Henry the fowerth, the first aucthor of this diuision, and so successiuely proceadyng to the reigne of the high and prudent prince kyng Henry the eight, the vndubitate flower and very heire of both the sayd linages. 1548, *title page trimmed and laid down, leaf 'Richard Grafton to the Reader' restored with no loss to text, several leaves remargined or repaired, several tears still extant, lacks 2 blanks, viz.* [Kk6] *and* [KKK8], *and last leaf with the colophon and device of Richard Grafton*, [iv+] 250 [+blank+] 59+61+263 ff., folio, *late nineteenth century calf, lettered, little rubbed, backstrip faded* (STC 12721: McKerrow and Ferguson 67) **£350.00**

165 **Hawarde** (John) Les Reportes del Cases in Camera Stellata 1593 to 1609, from the original MS., edited by William Paley Baildon. *Privately Printed*, 1894, *illusts.*, lxxv+502 pp., 4to, *orig. blue buckram*, scarce **£65.00**

166 [**Hazlitt** (William C. *Editor*)] Inedited Tracts: illustrating the Manners, Opinions and Occupations of Englishmen during the sixteenth and seventeenth Centuries: now first republished from the original Copies with a preface and notes. *The Roxburghe Library*, 1868, *slight foxing*, vii+218 pp., sm.4to, *quarter green roan, lettered, cloth sides* **£20.00**
¶Contains: The English Courtier . . . 1586: A Health to the Gentlemanly profession of Seruingmen . . . 1598: The Court and Country . . . by N.B., 1618.

167 **Henry VII.** BACON (Sir Francis) The Historie of the Raigne of King Henry the Seuenth. *W. Stansby for Matthew Lownes, and William Barret*, 1622, FIRST EDITION, *portrait trimmed to plate edge and laid down, title within woodcut border, marginal notes on 3 pp.*, [iv+] 248 pp. sm.folio, *contemp. mottled calf, a little pitted, recently rebacked, red leather labels, corners repaired* (STC 1160: Gibson 116B) **£95.00**
¶This is a mixed copy with some pp. in Gibson A. and some in Gibson B.

168 **Henry VIII.** NICOLAS (Nicolas Harris, *Ed.*) The Privy Purse Expences of King Henry the Eighth, from November MDXXIX, to December MDXXXII: with introductory Remarks and illustrative Notes. *William Pickering*, 1827, *title in red and black, occasional light foxing*, [v+] xlvi+372 pp., 8vo, *half black morocco, lettered, marbled bds., little rubbed* **£25.00**

169 **Heraldry.** ASHMOLE (Elias) The History of the most Noble Order of the Garter. Wherein is set forth an Account of the Town, Castle, Chappel, and College of Windsor, with their several Officers: The Foundation of the Order by King Edward III. With the Statutes, and Annals at large, as they have been altered and amended. An Account of the Habits, Ensigns, and Officers of the Order . . . To which is prefix'd, A Discourse of Knighthood in General, and the several Orders extant in Europe. *A. Bell, W. Taylor, J. Baker and A. Collins*, 1715, *portrait, 2 plates and a table*, [viii+] 565 (shd. read 561) [+iii] pp., 8vo, *contemp. tan calf, gilt extra, lettered, a little rubbed, head and tail of backstrip tender* **£65.00**

170 —— [BLOUNT (Thomas)] Glossographia Anglicana Nova: or, a Dictionary, interpreting such Hard Words of whatever Language, as are at present used in the English Tongue . . . also, the Terms of Divinity, Law, . . . History . . . Heraldry, Architecture . . . are here explain'd, from the best Modern Authors, as, Sir Isaac Newton, Dr. Harris, Dr. Gregory, Mr. Lock, Mr. Evelyn, Mr. Dryden, Mr. Blunt, &c., *Dan. Brown, Tim. Goodwin (and others)*, 1707, *with 63 cuts illustrative of heraldic terms*, [vi+ii+476] pp., 8vo, *modern half calf, leather label, marbled bds.* **£55.00**

171 —— [DOBSON (Mrs. Susannah)] Historical Anecdotes of Heraldry and Chivalry, tending to shew the Origin or many English and Foreign Coats of Arms, Circumstances and Customs. *Worcester, Holl and Brandish* . . . 1795, *with 5 engraved plates, light staining throughout*, [iii+] 3+316 pp., 4to, *contemp. half calf, marbled bds., corners worn, recently rebacked, red leather label* **£25.00**

172 —— DUGDALE (William) The Baronage of England, or an Historical Account of the Lives and most Memorable Actions of our English Nobility in the Saxon time, to the Norman Conquest; and from thence, of those who had their rise before the end of . . . [the Eleventh Year of King Richard the Second]. 2 Vols. in 1. *Tho. Newcomb, for Abel Roper, John Martin, and Henry Herringman*, 1675/6, *titles in red and black, some staining and a few marginal tears*, [xii+] 790 [+iii]: [viii+] 488 [+iii] pp., folio, *contemp. mottled calf, corners worn, sides rubbed, newly rebacked, red leather label, early arms on sides* (Wing D2460) **£65.00**

173 —— KENT (Samuel) The Grammar of Heraldry. Containing I. Rules of Blazoning . . . II. Practical Directions for Marshalling . . . III. A Large Collection of Arms . . . With Two Appendices, *J. Pemberton, sold by R. Tookey*, 1716, *illustrated by 6 cuts of achievements and 846 of coats of arms*, xliv [+176] pp., 8vo in 4s., *new quarter tan calf, red leather label, marbled bds.* **£45.00**

174 **Herzel** (Hans Caspar, *the Elder*) Le Socrate rustique, ou description de la conduite économique & morale d'un paysan philosophe [Klyiogg – a Swiss Farmer], trad. de l'allemand par un Officier Suisse au Service de France. Quatrième édition . . . 2 Vols. *Lausanne, Francois Grasset & Compag.*, 1777, *portrait, slight discolouration*, xlviii+394 [+ii]: [iii+] 400 pp., sm.8vo, *contemp. sheep, red leather labels, joint cracked in vol. ii.* **£35.00**

175 [**Hickeringill** (Edmund)] The Naked Truth. The Second Part. In Several Inquiries concerning the Canons and Ecclesiastical Jurisdiction, Canonical Obedience, Convocations, Procurations, Synodals and Visitations. Also of the Church of England, Church Wardens, and the Oath of Church-vvardens, and of Sacriledge. *Francis Smith*, 1681, *small stamp on last page*, [vi+] 59 [+iv] pp., folio, *disbound* (Wing H1822) **£25.00**

176 **Higgins** (Godfrey) The Celtic Druids; or an Attempt to shew, that the Druids were the Priests of Oriental Colonies who emigrated from India, and were the Introducers of the First or Cadmean System of Letters, and the Builders of Stonehenge, of Carnac, and of other Cyclopean Works in Asia and Europe. *Rowland Hunter, Hurst & Chance, and Ridgway and Sons*, 1829, *with lithograph title, 46 plates of plans, views and maps, 7 woodcut headpieces and 7 engraved tail pieces, woodcuts in the text*, [iv+] xcvi+324 pp., 4to, *green cloth, paper label, faded, head of upper joint split*, scarce **£200.00**

177 **Howard** (William, *Lord, of Escrick*) A Letter . . to a Friend. Together with his Protestation [against Edward FitzHarris's accusation of his authorship of 'The True Englishman . . .'], at his Receiving the Blessed Communion in the Tower, on July the Third, 1681, [colophon: *Robert Roberts*, 1681, *drop title, few worm holes in lower margins*, 4 pp., folio, *disbound* (Wing H3012) **£25.00**

178 **Huet** (Pierre Daniel, *Bp. of Avranches*) Opuscula duo quorum unum est De Optimo Genere Interpretandi et de Claris Interpretibus; alterum De Origine Fabularum. *Venetiis, Benedictum Milocco*, 1757, *title in red and black, portrait and vignettes, slight worming in few upper margins*, xvi+216 [+vi+] 130 pp., sm.8vo, *'cats-paw' sheep, leather label, slightly rubbed* **£35.00**

179 **Hume** (David, *of Godscroft*) The History of the House and Race of Douglas and Angus. 2 Vols. *Edingurgh, T.W. and T. Ruddiman, for L. Hunter*, 1743, *discolouration*, xxxii+388: iv+422 pp., 12mo, *half brown calf, black leather labels, marbled bds., rubbed and joints cracking* **£35.00**

180 —— (David) The History of England, from the Invasion of Julius Caesar, to the Revolution in 1688, a New Edition, 13 Vols. to which is prefixed a Short Account of his Life, written by Himself. *T. Cadell, sold by T.N. Longman*, 1793:
and
SMOLLETT (T.) The History of England from the Revolution to the Death of George the Second, a New Edition, 8 Vols. *T. Cadell, sold by T.N. Longman*, 1794:
Together 21 Vols., *illust. by portraits and scenes*, sm.8vo, *contemp. marbled calf, red and green leather labels, a little scuffed* **£75.00**

181 —— 10 Vols. *R. Scholey and B. Crosby and Co.* 1808: [with] Tobias Smollett's Revolution in 1688, to the Death of George ii. 6 Vols. *R. Scholey*, 1810, *with engravings on copper and wood from Thurston's designs, some foxing*, 8vo, *an excellent set of the* LARGE PAPER EDITION, *bound in tan russia, gilt and blind tooling, lettered, 3 vols. neatly rebacked and orig. backstrips laid down* **£300.00**

182 **Hutchinson** (Francis, *Bp. of Down and Connor*) A Defence of the Antient Historians: with a particular Application of it to the History of Ireland and Great-Britain, and other Northern Nations. In a Dialogue between a Protestant and a Papist, an Englishman and an Irishman. To which are added, Two Sermons, *Dublin, S. Powell, for John Smith and William Bruce*, 1734, *divisional titles*, xv+270 pp., 8vo, *contemp. sprinkled calf, gilt, leather label, corners little worn, joints cracked* **£65.00**

183 —— (Colonel John) Memoirs . . . with Original Anecdotes of many of the most distinguished of his Contemporaries, with a summary Review of Public Affairs: written by his widow Lucy . . . Second Edition, *Printed for Longman, Hurst, Rees and Orme*, 1808, *with 2 portraits, 3 other plates and a folding genealogical table, some off-setting*, vi+xiv+452 pp., 4to, *contemp. half calf, marbled bds., corners worn, newly rebacked, leather label* **£35.00**

184 **Imber** (Matthew) The Case, or, an Abstract of the Customs of the Mannor of Merdon, in the Parish of Hursely in the County of Southampton, which are to be Observed and Performed by the Lord and the Customary Tenants of the said Mannor, their Heirs and Successors for Ever. As they were taken out of a Decree Made and Inrolled in the Honourable Court of Chancery, for Ratifying and Confirming the said Customs, *Printed*, 1707, *embrowned throughout, lacks* [A1] *and* [F8] *blanks*, pp. 3–93, sm.8vo, *nineteenth century tan calf, lettered, backstrip little rubbed* **£75.00**

185 **Inquisition.** PUIGBLANCH (Antonio) The Inquisition Unmasked: being an historical and philosophical Account of that Tremendous Tribunal, founded on authentic Documents; and exhibiting the Necessity of its Suppression, as a Means to Reform and Regeneration. Translated by William Walton. 2 Vols. *Baldwin, Cradock, Joy, and J. Booth*, 1816, *with vignette and 11 engraved plates*, lxxxvi [+ii+] 362: iii+472 pp., 8vo, *contemp. diced calf, corners worn, newly rebacked, black leather labels* **£45.00**

186 **Insurance.** HAYES (Richard) A New Method for Valuing of Annuities upon Lives . . . with many useful Examples and Instructions for valuing of single Lives; two or more Lives; Lives taken in with other Lives; Reversion of Lives; Annuities in Expectation . . . Second Edition, Corrected, *W. Meadows*, 1746, *embrowned throughout*, [vii+] 128 pp., *advert. leaf before title*, 4to, *contemp. calf, gilt, unlettered, slightly rubbed* (Kress 4809: Goldsmiths' 8238) scarce **£100.00**

187 **An Intimation** of the Deputies of the States General, in a Late Discourse with Mr. Sidney, Extraordinary Envoy from His Majesty of Great Britain. [*London*, 1680], *drop titles few worm holes in lower margins*, 4 pp., folio, *disbound* (Wing E275) **£21.00**

188 **Ireland** An INQUIRY, but not a Parliamentary Inquiry into the Past and Present Abuses of the Irish Revenue, and into the Plunder of the Irish Patronage. *Dublin, the Author by P. Byrne*, 1824, [ii+] 94 pp., 8vo, *orig. blue wrappers, backstrip worn, recently restitched* **£35.00**

189 —— [JONES (John)] An Impartial Narrative of the most Important Engagements which took place between his Majesty's Forces and the Insurgents, during the Irish Rebellion, in 1798 . . . Second Edition, *South Newberlin, N.Y., Levi Harris*, 1834, *frontis., heavily embrowned throughout*, 227 pp., 8vo, *contemp. sheep, red leather label, heavily rubbed* **£35.00**

190 —— STUART (James) Historical Memoirs of the City of Armagh, for a Period of 1373 Years, comprising a considerable Portion of the general History of Ireland; a Refutation of the Opinions of Dr. Ledwich, respecting the Non-Existence of St. Patrick; and an Appendix on the Learning, Antiquities, and Religion of the Irish Nation. *Newry, Alexander Wilkinson for Longman, Hurst, Rees*, 1819, *with 5 engravings, embrowned throughout, small tear in one leaf*, x+651 [+x] pp., 8vo., *orig. boards, paper label, soiled, joints splitting* **£45.00**

191 **James II.** A Full Answer to the Depositions; and to all other the Pretences and Arguments whatsoever, concerning the Birth of the Prince of Wales. The Intreague thereof detected, the whole design being set forth, with the way and manner of doing it. Whereunto is annexed, a Map or Survey Engraven of St. James's Palace, and the Convent there: Describing the Place wherein it is supposed the true Mother was delivered: with the particular Doors and Passages through which the Child was convey'd to the Queens Bed Chamber. *Simon Burgis*, 1689, *folding plan*, [iv+] 21 pp., folio, *disbound* (Wing F2342) **£30.00**

192 **Jesse** (John Heneage) Memoirs of the Court of England during the Reigns of William and Mary, Queen Anne, and the First and Second Georges. 4 Vols., *Boston, L.C. Page & Company*, 1901, *frontis. portraits*, 8vo, *twentieth century half blue calf, tan leather labels, marbled bds., t.e.g.* **£50.00**

193 **Jourdan** (Jean-Baptiste, *Marshal of France*) Mémoires pour servir a l'histoire de la Campagne de 1796, contenant les opérations de l'Armée de Sambre et Meuse, sous les ordres du général en chef, Jourdan. *Paris, chez Magimel, Anselin, et Pochard*, 1818, *4 folding tables, with inscription of author to Mr. Tennyson [probably Charles, the politician]*, [iii+] 352 [+ii] pp., 8vo, *contemp. half calf, lettered, drab bds., worn but sound* **£50.00**

194 **Kennett** (Basil) Romae Antiquae Notitia: or, the Antiquities of Rome. In Two Parts . . . Twelfth Edition, Corrected and Improved. *W. Innys, J. and P. Knapton, S. Birt* . . . 1754, *title in red and black, portrait, 12 plates (some folding) and a folding map*, [xvi+] xxx+375 [+xxvi] pp., 8vo, *contemp. calf, rubbed, joints cracked, lacks label* **£21.00**

195 **Kinglake** (Alexander William) The Invasion of the Crimea: its Origin, and an Account of its Progress down to the Death of Lord Raglan. 8 Vols. *William Blackwood and Sons*, 1863, *maps*, 8vo, *orig. maroon cloth, lettered, faded and shabby* **£40.00**

196 **Land Tax.** An Act for granting an Aid to His Majesty by a Land Tax to be raised in Great Britain, for the Service of the Year 1744. *Thomas Baskett and Robert Baskett*, 1743, *title dust-soiled, last few leaves frayed in margin due to dampstaining which extends further into the work*, 95 pp., folio, *sewed* **£20.00**

197 —— for the Service of the Year 1750. *Thomas Baskett. and the Assigns of Robert Baskett*, 1749, *title and last leaf stained and creased*, pp. [i+] 15–111, folio, *stab-sewed, uncut* **£20.00**

198 —— for the Service of the Year One thousand seven hundred and seventy five. *Printed by Charles Eyre and William Strahan*, 1776, [ii+114] pp., folio, *half calf, marb. bds. little rubbed* **£15.00**
¶The text of the Oaths of Allegiance, Supremacy and Abjuration has been written out in a neat contemporary copper-plate hand on one of the free endpapers.

199 **La Primavdaye** (Pierre de) The French Academie, wherein is discoursed the institution of maners, and whatsoever els concerneth the good and happie life of all estates and callings, by precepts of doctrine, and example of the liues of ancient Sages and famous men. Newly translated into English by T. B[owes]. *Edmund Bollifant for G. Bishop and Ralph Newbery*, 1586, FIRST EDITION, *title trimmed to woodcut border and laid down, but slightly defective, lacks* [2K8] *and* [3F8] *(?final blank), small corner torn from* [3F7], *not affecting letter press*, [xxviii+] 812 [+x] pp., sm.4to, *contemp. calf, rubbed, sometime rebacked and repaired, red leather label* (STC 15233: Hazlitt Hdbk. 482) **£75.00**

200 **Laud** (William, *Archbp. of Canterbury*) A Speech delivered in the Starr-Chamber, on Wednesday, the XIVth of Iune, MDCXXXVII. at the Censvre, of Iohn Bastwick, Henry Burton, & William Prinn; concerning pretended Innovations in the Church. *Richard Badger*, 1637, [A1 *(blank)*] *present but soiled, some discolouration, worm hole through text but no serious loss, four outer margins also attacked*, [xiii+] 77 pp., sm.4to, *modern light brown morocco, sides panelled in gilt, lettered* (STC 15307 with rose, crown and thistle ornament on title) **£60.00**

201 —— CHARGE (The) of the Scottish Commissioners against Canterburie and the Lievertentant of Ireland. Together with their Demand concerning the Sixt Article of the Treaty. Whereunto is added the Parliaments Resolution about the Proportion of the Scottish charges and the Scottish Commissioners thankfull acceptance thereof. *Nath. Butter*, 1641, *title and verso of last leaf soiled embrowned*, [i+] 53 pp., sm.4to, *disbound* (Wing C4201k) **£30.00**

202 **Lecky** (William E.H.) Democracy and Liberty. 2 Vols. *Longmans, Green, and Co.* 1896, *Library Edition*, xvii+471: xvi+489 pp., 24 pp catalogue, 8vo, *orig. blue cloth, lettered, slightly faded* **£25.00**

203 —— A History of England in the Eighteenth Century. Fourth Edition Revised, 8 Vols. *Longmans, Green, and Co.*, 1888, LIBRARY EDITION, 8vo, *dull red cloth, lettered, backstrips faded* **£35.00**

204 **A Letter** from Flanders, giving an Account of the present State of the War in the Netherlands, the Weakness of the Allies and Strength of the French; with a View of the present Politics of Holland, of the Courts at War, and principal Neutral Powers of Europe. By an Old English Officer. *M. Cooper*, 1744, *slightly soiled*, 31 pp., 8vo, *disbound* **£25.00**

205 **Lilly** (William, *Astrologer*) History of his Life and Times, from the Year 1602, to 1681. Written by himself in the 66th Year of his Age to his worthy Friend Elias Ashmole, Esq. . . . Second Edition, *J. Roberts*, 1715, *some foxing throughout, many running-titles heavily cropped*, [iv+] 116 pp., 12mo, *tan sheep, recently rebacked, red leather label* **£35.00**

206 **Macaulay** (Thomas Babington, *Lord*) The History of England from the Accession of James the Second. Edited by Charles Harding Firth. *Macmillan and Co.*, 1913, *illusts., some in colour*, lge.8vo, *orig. blue cloth, lettered* **£35.00**

207 **MacCormick** (Charles, *Editor*) The Secret History of the Court and Reign of Charles the Second, by a Member of his Privy Council; to which are added Introductory Sketches of the preceding Period from the Accession of James I. with notes, and a supplement continuing the Narrative in a summary Manner to the Revolution; by the Editor. 2 Vols. *T. Gillet for J. Bew*, 1792, *corners of 2 leaves torn away*, 8vo, *contemp. half sheep, lettered, marbled bds., crack down spine of both vols.* **£25.00**

208 **Madox** (Thomas) The History and Antiquities of the Exchequer of the Kings of England, in Two Periods: to wit, from the Norman Conquest, to the End of the Reign of K. John; and from the End of the Reign of K. John, to the End of the Reign of K. Edward II: together with a Correct Copy of the Ancient Dialogue concerning the Exchequer, generally asctibed to Garvasius Tilburiensis; and a Dissertation concerning the most Ancient Great Roll of the Exchequer, commonly styled The Roll of Quinto Regis Stephani. *J. Matthews; and sold by Robert Knaplock*, 1711, *slight worming in few tail margins, early annotations on free endpapers*, folio, *contemp. sprinkled calf, corners little worn and sides rubbed, newly rebacked, green leather label* **£100.00**

209 **Malmesbury** (William of) The History of the Kings of England and the Modern History of . . . Translated from the latin by the Rev. John Sharpe. *W. Bulmer and Co.*, 1815, LARGE PAPER COPY ON THICK PAPER, *watermarked J. Whatman*, 1815, *a few marginal pencil notes*, xxiv+610 [+xiii] pp., lge.folio, *half mauve cloth over earlier marbled bds., unlettered* **£40.00**

210 **Marlborough.** COXE (William) Memoirs of John Duke of Marlborough, with his Original Correspondence: collected from the Family Records at Blenheim, and other authentic Sources illustrated with portraits, maps, and military plans. Second Edition. 6 Vols. *Longman, Hurst, Rees, Orme, and Brown*, 1820, 8vo, *contemp. half calf, gilt, red leather labels, marbled bds., sprinkled edges, upper joint of vol. vi. cracked* **£45.00**

211 **Margravine of Bareith.** Memoirs of Frederica Sophia Wilhelmina, Princess Royal of Prussia, Margravine of Bareith, Sister of Frederic the Great. Written by Herself. Translated from the original French. 2 Vols. *Henry Colburn, John Anderson and George Goldie, and John Cumming*, 1812, *slight discolouration*, [iv+] 374: [i+] 374 pp., 8vo, *contemp. tree calf, black leather labels, joints cracking, y.e.* **£40.00**

212 **Marie Antoinette.** CAMPAN (Jeanne-Louise-Henriette Genest, Madame) Memoirs of the Private Life of Marie Antoinette . . . to which are added, Recollections, Sketches, and Anecdotes, illustrative of the Reigns of Louis xiv. Louis xv. and Louis xvi. Third Edition, 2 Vols. *Henry Colburn*, 1824, *the 2 portraits foxed*, [viii+] xlvii+447 [+i]: [vii+] 462 pp., 8vo, *contemp. half grey calf, red leather labels, marbled bds.* **£50.00**

213 **Markham** (Francis) The Booke of Honovr. Or, Five Decads of Epistles of Honovr. *Augustine Matthews, and John Norton*, 1625, *some discolouration throughout*, [vi+] 200 pp., folio, *contemp. vellum gilt, sometime rebacked, new endpapers, ties still present* (STC 17331) **£175.00**

214 **Matthew of Westminster.** Flores Historiarvm: praecipve de Rebvs Britannicis: ab exor dio mundi usque ad annum Domini mcccvii. et Chronicon ex chronicis ad initio mundi vsqve ad annum Domini mcxvii. deductum: auctore Frorentio Wigorniensi monacho. Cui accessit Continvatio vsqve ad annvm Christi mcxli. per quendam eiusdem coenobii eruditum. *Francofvrti, Wechelianis apud Claudium Marnium & heredes Ioannis Aubrij*, 1601, *embrowning throughout, name rubbed from title leaving small hole*, [viii+] 696 [+xxiv] pp., folio, *nineteenth century brown sprinkled calf, leather label, "greek-key" borders in gilt, m.e., slight cracking of upper joint* **£135.00**

215 **May** (Thomas) The History of the Parliament of England: which began November the Third, M.DC.XI. with a short and necessary view of some precedent yeares. *Moses Bell, for George Thomason*, 1647, *title in red and black, lacks* [A1] *(license leaf)*, [xiv+] 119+128+115 pp., folio, *contemp. sprinkled tan calf, sometime rebacked, brown leather label, corners repaired, slightly rubbed, new endpapers* (Wing M1410) **£95.00**

216 **Military.** AN ACT for applying the Money granted in this Session of Parliament, for defraying the Charge of the Pay and Cloathing of the Militia . . . and for explaining, amending and rendering more effectual, several Acts of Parliament . . . relating to the raising and training of the Militia, *Mark Baskett, and the Assigns of Robert Baskett*, 1766, [i+18] pp., folio, *disbound* **£25.00**

217 —— AN ACT for defraying the Charge of the Pay and Cloathing of the Militia . . . for the more effectually punishing Serjeants, Drummers, and Fifers, for Misbehaviour and Desertion; for securing Deserters from the Militia Regiments, *Mark Baskett, and the Assigns of Robert Baskett*, 1767, [i+14] pp., folio, *disbound* **£30.00**

218 —— AN ACT for explaining, amending, and continuing, an Act . . . to reduce into One Act of Parliament, the several Laws now in being, relating to the Raising and Training of the Militia, *Mark Baskett, and the Assigns of Robert Baskett*, 1769, [i+29] pp., folio, *disbound* **£25.00**

219 —— AN ACT to explain and amend an Act . . . and reduce into One Act of Parliament, the several Laws now in being, relating to the raising and training the Militia, *Charles Eyre and William Strahan*, 1772, [i+8] pp., folio, *disbound* **£18.00**

220 —— BARRET (Robert) The Theorike and Practike of Moderne Warre, discoursed in Dialogue vvise. Wherein is declared the Neglect of Martiall discipline: the inconuenience thereof: the imperfections of manie training Captaines: a redress by due regard had: the fittest weapons for our Moderne Warre: the use of the same: the parts of a perfect souldier in generall and in particular: the Officers in degrees, with their seuerall duties: the imbattailling of men in formes now most in vse with figures and Tables to the same: with sundrie other maritall points. Comprehended in sixe Bookes. *William Ponsonby*, 1598, *complete copy with folding sig. O, many other diagrams of military formations, arms of Henry Herbert, Earl of Pembroke, to whom the work is dedicated, on verso of title, arms of Barret on verso of last leaf*, [viii+] 247 [+vii] pp., folio, *contemp. limp vellum, soiled and wrinkled, front hinge breaking, lacks front free endpaper and most of ties* (STC 1500: Cockle 68) scarce **£1,350.00**

221 —— BURN (Richard) A Digest of the Military Laws. *S. Richardson and C. Lintot*, 1760, viii+88 pp.
[preceded by]
MILITARY ACTS [5] for 1756–58, and index to the Acts. *Thomas Baskett and the Assigns of Robert Baskett*, 1759, *lacks* [A1.] pp. 3–175, 8vo, *half brown morocco, lettered, bookplate and initials of Henry Ellison* **£65.00**

222 —— COOP (J.O.) The Story of the 55th (West Lancashire) Division. *Liverpool, "Daily Post" Printers*, 1919, *portraits and maps*, 184 pp., cr.8vo, *orig. qtr. cloth, decorated boards stitching loose* **£21.00**

223 —— CUTHBERTSON (Bennett, *Capt. of 5th Foot* – [Northumberland Fusiliers]) A System for the compleat interior Management and Oeconomy of a Battalion of Infantry. *Dublin, Boulter Grierson*, 1768, *with 17 tables*, xl+239 pp., 8vo, *contemp. qtr. calf, leather label, marbled boards, corners beginning to wear*, scarce **£120.00**
¶The 16 pp. of Subscribers mainly comprise military men. Cuthbertson surveyed the currently available military manuals and observed "Scarcely one . . . has been wrote for the Instruction of the Subaltern Part of the Profession . . . when . . . by far the greatest number advance but very little beyond that Rank . . ."

224 —— A DESCRIPTION of all the Seats of the Present Wars of Europe, in the Netherlands, Germany, Hungary, Italy, Spain and Portugal, being a particular Survey of all these Countries; setting forth the Situation and Distances of their Provinces, Cities, Towns, Villages, &c. With Historical Remarks upon the Places of Note, especially such as are of Importance to the Contending Parties, *John Nicholson and Sam Ballard*, 1704, *with 7 folding maps*, [iv+] 244 [+xv] pp., sm.8vo, *contemp. panelled calf, brown leather label, backstrip torn at head, joints starting to crack, rubbed* **£70.00**

225 —— MARKHAM (Francis) Five Decades of Epistles of Warre. *Augustine Matthewes*, 1622, *lacks* [*A1*], [x+] 200 pp., folio, *nineteenth century calf, leather label, blind 2 line fillets on both covers, arms of George Granville Leveson-Gower, K.G. (2nd Earl of Granville) on front cover* (STC 17332, Cockle 96) **£300.00**

226 —— MINUTES OF EVIDENCE, taken before the Committee of the whole House, upon the Conduct of His Royal Highness the Commander in Chief. [*London*] 1809, [iii+] 480 pp., folio, *new quarter calf, red leather label, marbled bds., new end-papers* **£120.00**

¶The Committee was appointed to investigate the conduct of the Duke of York, the Commander in Chief, with regard to Promotions, Exchanges, and Appointments to Commissions in the Army, and Staff of the Army, and in raising Levies for the Army.

227 —— PENINSULAR WAR. MOORE (James) A Narrative of the Campaign of the British Army in Spain, commanded by his Excellency Lieut. General Sir John Moore, authenticated by original Papers and original Letters. Second Edition, corrected. *Printed for Joseph Johnson*, 1809, *with portrait, a view of Corunna (lower margin trimmed) and 2 folding maps, inserted a broadside of "Lines on the Burial of Sir John Moore, 1809", by Charles Woolfe, upper margin of which has been repaired, some foxing of plates and off-setting*, xii +88+238 [+i] pp., 4to, *half calf, marbled boards, little rubbed* **£85.00**

¶The appendix, with the exception of the last leaf, has been bound before the text.

228 —— SHROPSHIRE MILITIA. AN ORDINANCE of the Lords and Commons assembled in Parliament, for raising of Monies for the Maintenance of such Forces as are and shall be raised in the County of Salop for the Service of Parliament. *Printed for Christopher Meredith*, 1644, *small rubber stamp on title*, [ii+] 6 pp., sm.4to, *disbound* **£40.00**

229 —— TOWNSEND (Maj. Gen. Sir Charles V.F.) My Campaign in Mesopotamia. *Thornton Butterworth*, 1920, *portrait and 15 maps and plans*, 400 pp., 8vo, *orig. red cloth, backstrip faded* **£18.00**

230 —— A TRVE DESCRIPTION of the Discipline of VVar both for Horse and Foot, used in His Maiesties Army, under their Excellencies, William Earle of New Castle, and Prince Robert. With the order and manner of their marching and excercising [sic] in the Field. N.P., N.D., [*London* 1642], *drop title, Royal Arms between ornate* 'C' *and* 'R', *catchword of sig.* A[1] *trimmed*, 7 pp., sm.4to, *modern qtr. crimson morocco, cloth sides* (Wing T2677) rare **£250.00**

231 —— TURNER (Sir James) Pallas Armata. Military Essayes of the Ancient Grecian, Roman, and Modern Art of War. Written in the Years 1670 and 1671. *M.W. for Richard Chiswell*, 1683, *title in red and black, engraved portrait by R. White, small snag in lower margin of prelim. ll.*, [xviii+] 372 pp., folio, *contemp. mottled calf, backstrip gilt, brown leather label, corners worn* (Wing T3292) **£185.00**

232 —— WAVELL (A.P. *Colonel, later Field Marshal*) The Palestine Campaigns. Third Edition, *Campaigns and their Lessons, Constable and Co.*, 1935, *folding maps and plans, some marginal pencil notes*, xiv+252 pp., 8vo, *orig. red cloth, backstrip faded* **£21.00**

233 —— WARNERY (General C.E.) Remarks on Cavalry; by a Prussian Major General of Hussars. Translated from the Original [by Lt. Col. G.F. Koellier]. *T. Egerton*, 1805, *with 33 plates of military "types" and 9 of diagrams of manoeuvres, some marginal staining*, xxii+125 [+i] pp., 4to, *orig. grey bds., soiled, recently rebacked, paper label* **£130.00**

234 —— WITH A HIGHLAND REGIMENT in Mespotamia 1916–1917, by One of its Officers. *Bombay, The Times Press*, 1918, *maps and illusts.*, [xi+] 165 pp., cr.8vo, *orig. blue cloth, a little soiled* **£21.00**

235 The YEOMAN CAVALRY of Worcestershire, 1794–1922, 2 Vols., 1914/26, *maps and illusts.*, xii+238 [+i]: xi+251, 4to, *orig. buckram, not uniform in colour* **£35.00**

236 **Mills** (Charles) The History of the Crusades, for the Recovery and Possession of the Holy Land. 2 Vols. with a Memoir of the Author. Fourth Edition. *Longman, Rees, Orme, Brown, and Green*, 1828, *frontispieces and folding map, some foxing throughout*, x+cxxi+414: x+486 pp., 8vo, *modern half red calf, green leather labels, marbled bds. and endpapers, some fading and rubbing* **£30.00**

237 **Mitford** (William) The History of Greece. 10 Vols. *Luke Hansard & Sons, for T. Cadell and W. Davies*, 1820, *some foxing throughout*, 8vo, *contemp. half tan calf, green leather labels, marbled bds., slight rubbing* **£40.00**

238 [**Monson** (Sir John)] A Discourse concerning Supreme Power and Common Right. At first calculated for the Year 1641. and now thought fit to be published. By a Person of Quality. *R. Chiswell*, 1680, [vii+] 174 pp., 8vo, *contemp. sheep, leather label, corners and part of backstrip worn, joints cracking* (Wing M2462) scarce **£85.00**

¶An interesting association copy with the "Burton" armorial bookplate of Lord Monson and a MS note by [Wm. John, 6th Baron] Monson, dated 14 April 1851, which concludes "I found this copy after a long search in the library at Galton whither no doubt it was removed from Burton."

239 **Montagu** (William Drogo, *Duke of Manchester*) Court and Society from Elizabeth to Anne. Edited from the Papers at Kimbolton by the Duke of Manchester. 2 Vols. *Hurst and Blackett*, 1864, *portraits, some foxing, stitching becoming loose*, viii+405: vi+458 pp., publishers' catalogue, 8vo, *orig. blue cloth, gilt, arms of Manchester on upper covers, a little dust-soiled* **£25.00**

240 [**Montesquieu** (Charles Louis)] Considérations sur les Causes de la Grandeur des Romains, et de leur Décedence. Nouvelle Edition, *Amsterdam, Arkstée et Markus*, 1776, [i+] 440 pp., sm.8vo, *contemp. sprinkled calf, leather label, upper joint cracked* **£35.00**

241 **Monteth** (Robert, *of Salmonet*) The History of the Troubles of Great Britain: containing a particular Account of the most remarkable Passages in Scotland, from the Year 1633 to 1650, with an exact Relation of the Wars carried on, and the Battles fought by the Marquis of Montrose . . . Translated into English by Captain James Ogilvie, *Printed for G. Strahan and R. Williamson*, 1735, viii+557+xxii pp., folio, *contemp. sprinkled calf, rubbed, corners worn, covers almost detached* **£28.00**

242 **Napoleon.** O'MEARA (Barry E., *Surgeon to Napoleon*) Napoleon in Exile; or, A Voice from St. Helena. The Opinions and Reflections of Napoleon on the important Events of his Life and Government in his own Words. 2 Vols., Second Edition. *W. Simpkin and R. Marshall*, 1822, *with 3 portraits and a view*, xxviii+512: [i+] 542 pp., 8vo, *contemp. half brown calf, lettered, marbled bds.* **£45.00**

245 **Naunton** (Sir Robert) Fragmenta Regalia, or Observations on the late Queen Elizabeth, her Times and Favourites. *Printed* 1642, *embrowned throughout, one leaf fragile through damp, 2 letters of text affected, some flaws in margins*, 40 pp., sm.4to, *early half green roan, lettered, drab bds., slightly rubbed* (Wing N251) scarce **£75.00**

246 **The New Annual Register,** or General Repository of History, Politics, and Literature, for the Year 1786. To which is prefixed, the History of Knowledge, Learning, and Taste, in Great Britain, during the Reign of Henry the Seventh, from the Year 1485 to 1509. *G.G.J. and J. Robinson*, 1787, xxxi+175+187+299 pp., 8vo, *contemp. quarter sheep, grey bds., all edges untrimmed* **£25.00**

247 [**Nichols** (John)] Illustrations of the Manners and Expences of Antient Times in England, in the fifteenth, sixteenth, and seventeenth Centuries, deduced from the Accompts of Churchwardens, and other authentic Documents, collected from various Parts of the Kingdom, with explanatory notes. *John Nichols*, 1797, *light foxing*, x+320 (+38 inserted) +24+28+2+13+6+12 pp., 4to, *nineteenth century half tan calf, tan leather label, marbled bds. and endpapers* **£85.00**

248 [—— (*Editor*)] A Collection of all the Wills, now known to be extant, of the Kings and Queens of England, Princes and Princesses of Wales, and every branch of the Blood Royal, from the Reign of William the Conqueror, to that of Henry the Seventh exclusive. With Explanatory Notes, and a Glossary. *J. Nichols, sold by H. Payne, C. Dilly, J. Walter, N. Conant, and E. Brooke*, 1780, *sigs. Ff and Gg misbound*, x+434 pp., *C2–4 *additional*, 4to, *contemp. sheep, worn* **£40.00**

249 —— (*Editor*) The Progresses and Public Processions of Queen Elizabeth. Among which are interspersed other Solemnities, Public Expenditures, and Remarkable Events, during the Reign of that illustrious Princess. Collected from Original Manuscripts, Scarce Pamphlets, Corporation Records, Parochial Registers, &c. &c. illustrated with historical Notes. *John Nichols and Son*, 1823, *with portraits, views, facsimilies of signatures, etc.*, lvi+600: [iv+] 628 [+2]: [iv+] 682 pp., 4to, *tan polished calf, gilt extra, gilt backstrips and edges, brown and green leather labels, joints rubbed* **£140.00**

250 **Nicolas** (Sir Harris) History of the Battle of Agincourt, and of the Expedition of Henry the Fifth into France, in 1415; to which is added, the Roll of Men at Arms in the English Army. Third Edition. *Johnson & Co.*, 1833, *with portrait, coloured frontis. and 5 maps*, xvi+404+106 pp., 8vo, *orig. green cloth, newly recased, paper label* **£35.00**

251 —— (Nicholas Harris) Privy Purse Expenses of Elizabeth of York: Wardrobe Accounts of Edward the Fourth. With a Memoir of Elizabeth of York, and Notes. *William Pickering*, 1830, *title in red and black*, [vi+] civ+265 pp., 8vo, *original brown cloth, paper label, backstrip faded* (Keynes p. 82) **£30.00**

252 —— (*Editor*) Testamenta Vetusta: being Illustrations from Wills, of Manners, Customs, &c. as well as of the Descents and Possessions of many distinguished Families. From the Reign of Henry the Second to the Accession of Queen Elizabeth. 2 Vols. *Nichols and Son*, 1826, *some marginal browning*, pp. 16+lx+1–448: [iii+] 449–874, 8vo, *binder's green cloth, lettered, edges untrimmed* **£35.00**

253 **Nicolson** (William) The English Historical Library: or, a Short View and Character of most of the Writers now Extant, either in Print or Manuscript; which may be serviceable to the Undertakers of a General History of this Kingdom. [Part i.] *Abel Swail and D. Child*, 1696, *title and following leaf repaired in lower margin, discoloured*, [xxxiv+] 232 (shd. read 250) [+viii] pp., sm.8vo, *contemp. panelled calf, rubbed newly rebacked, red leather label* (Wing N1146) **£75.00**

254 **Nolan** (E.H.) The History of the British Empire in India and the East, 8 Vols., *James S. Virtue*, N.D., *portraits (mostly foxed or dampstained) and maps.*, roy.8vo, *orig. red cloth, lettered on backstrips and upper covers, rubbed, stain on back cover of vol. i.* **£25.00**

255 **North** (Roger) The Life of the Honourable Sir Dudley North, Knt. Commissioner of the Customs . . . and Dr. John North, Master of Trinity College in Cambridge, *John Whiston*, 1744, *portrait*, vi+288 [+vii] pp.:

[and]

The Life of the Right Honourable Francis North, Baron of Guildford, Lord Keeper of the Great Seal, *John Whiston*, 1742, *portrait*, [iv+] 333 [+x] pp.:

Two pieces bound together, 4to, *contemp. sprinkled calf, brown leather label, little rubbed* **£75.00**

256 **Orme** (Robert) A History of the Military Transactions of the British Nation in Indostan, from the Year mdccxlv. to which is prefixed a Dissertation on the Establishments made by Mahomedan Conquerors in Indostan. The Fourth Edition, revised by the Author, 2 Vols. in 3, *F. Wingrave*, 1803, *with 36 maps, plans and views (some folding), one misbound and one inserted upside down*, [i+] 436+xcvi: [i+] 365 [+xvi]: [i+] 367–739 [+xvi] pp., 4to, *contemp. sprinkled calf, slightly rubbed, sometime rebacked, black leather labels* **£145.00**

257 **Oxford.** AN ACCOUNT of the Visit of His Royal Highness the Prince Regent and Their Imperial and Royal Majesties the Emperor of Russia and the King of Prussia to the University of Oxford, in June 1814. *Oxford, at the Clarendon Press*, 1815, *with 2 engr. plates and a folded Broadsheet*, [ii+] 77 pp., 4to, *contemp. tan calf, gilt, leather label* **£45.00**

258 **Parliament.** HANSARD (T.C.) The Parliamentary Debates: forming a Continuation of the work entitled – "The Parliamentary History of England from the earliest period to the year 1803 [by William Cobbett]". Published under the superintendence of T.H. Hansard. New Series; commencing with the accession of George iv. [and terminating with the close of this reign]. 25 Vols. *Printed by T.C. Handard*, 1820–30, *printed in double column throughout*, 8vo, *uniformly bound in nineteenth century purple cloth, marbled bds., backstrips faded, library labels on front covers and pastedowns, in sound condition* **£200.00**

259 —— A SHORT HISTORY of all the Parliaments of England, in all Reigns, *A. Moore*, 1722, *title soiled and piece cut from top fore-corner*, [iv+] 76 pp., 8vo, *disbound* **£25.00**

260 **Paulden** (Capt. Thomas) An Account of the Taking and Surrendering of Pontefract Castle, and of the Surprisal of General Rainsborough in his Quarters at Doncaster, Anno 1648. Written upon the Occasion of Prince Eugene's surprising M. Villeroy at Cremona. *Oxford, The Theatre, sold by R. Clements and S. Parker, and by J. and J. Rivington*, 1747, *view, mounted, and double page plan of the castle, some soiling*, 26 pp., 8vo, *contemp. tan sheep, lettered, upper joint cracked* **£45.00**

261 **Pepys** (Samuel) Memoirs of the Reigns of Charles II. and James II. Comprising his Diary from 1659 to 1669, deciphered by the Rev. John Smith, A.B. of St. John's College Library, Cambridge, from the Original Short-Hand MS. in the Pepysian Library, and a Selection from his Private Correspondence. Edited by Richard, Lord Braybrooke. 2 Vols. *Henry Colburn*, 1825, FIRST EDITION, *with 13 engravings (one folded), all foxed and off-set, 2 vignettes in text, half titles present, heavy foxing of first and last few gatherings in vol. i., short tears in lower margins of 2 ll., lacks the 2 pp. catalogue at end of vol. i.* [ii+] xlii+498 [+ii+] xlix: [iv+] 348+viii+311 pp., roy.4to, *contemp. tan calf, gilt, leather labels, edges rubbed* **£250.00**

262 **Pitt** (William, *1st Earl of Chatham*) CHAMPIGNY (Jean de, *Chevalier*) Suplément au Ministére de Mr. Pitt, avec une Récapitulation exacte de toutes les démarches de ce sage Politique depuis le 5 Septembre 1761, qu'il quitta le Ministére, jusqu'un 30 Juillet 1766, qu'il a été,créé Comte de Chatham, et garde du sceau privé d'Angleterre, contenante un Espace de prés de cinq ans. *Cologne*, 1766, *portrait, errata leaf present*, viii+114 [+i] pp., 8vo, *contemp. half sprinkled calf, leather label, marbled bds.* **£38.00**

263 **Poland.** LA BIZADIERE (Michel David de) An Historical Account of the Divisions in Poland: from the Death of K. John Sobieski to the Settlement of the Present King on the Throne. Containing a Particular Relation of the late King's Death, and of all the Intrigues of the several Candidates, till the Coronation of the elector of Saxony. Translated from the French Original. *H. Rhodes, T. Bennet, A. Bell, and D. Midwinter and T. Leigh*, 1700, *some discolouration, pagination very erratic*, [viii+] 232 (shd. read 224) pp., 8vo, *contemp. sprinkled sheep, unlettered* (Wing L101) scarce **£95.00**

264 **Pole.** [BECCADELLI (Lodovico) *archbp. of Ragusa*] Vita Reginaldi Poli, S.R.E. Cardinalis . . . Italice Conscripta, Latine Reddita. *Juxta Exemplar Venetiis excusum, An.* mdlxiii. *Londini, rec. imp. Jacobi Adamson*, 1690, *some staining, label on verso of title*, [viii+] 108 pp.: (Adams B434: Wing B1641)

[and]

[WYNGFELD (Robert, *diplomatist*)] Nobilissima Disceptatio super Dignitate et Magnitudine Regnorum Britannici & Gallici, habita ab utriusque Oratoribus & Legatis in Concilio Constantiensi. *Juxta Exemplar Lovaniis excusum, An. mdxvii. Londini, rec. imp. Jacobi Adamson*, 1690, *some staining, one leaf repaired, extensive contemp. notes on title and margins throughout, gatherings continuous with the above item, but separately paginated*, [xiv+] 70 [+xiv] pp.: (Adams W209: Wing W3030)

Two works bound together, sm.8vo, *new half tan calf, marbled bds. lettered, r.e.* **£45.00**

265 —— NEVE (Timothy, *Rector of Middleton-Stoney, Oxfordshire*) Animadversions upon Mr. Phillips's History of the Life of Cardinal Pole. *Oxford, Clarendon Press [for] Dan. Price and J. Robson*, 1766, *some dampstaining*, [xvi+] 562 [+vi] pp., 8vo, *contemp. sprinkled calf, red leather label, rubbed, joints cracking* **£16.00**

266 **Popish Plot.** A BRIEF ACCOUNT of the several Plots, Conspiracies, and Hellish Attempts of the Bloody-minded Papists, against the Princes and Kingdoms of England, Scotland, and Ireland, from the Reformation to this present Year, 1678. *J.R. and W.A.*, 1679, *inner margin of title torn and slightly defective, embrowned throughout*, [ii+] 46 pp., sm.4to, *wrappers* (Wing B4520) scarce **£45.00**

267 —— THE HUMBLE PETITION of the Right Honourable the Lord Mayor, Aldermen, and Commons of the City of London, in Common-Council Assembled, on the thirteenth of January, 1680, *Samuel Roycroft*, 1680, *slight discolouration*, [ii+] 11 pp., folio, *disbound* (Wing H3577) **£21.00**

268 —— AN IMPARTIAL ACCOUNT of Divers Remarkable Proceedings the last Sessions of Parliament relating to the Horrid Popish Plot, &c., *Printed in the Year*, 1679, *some soiling, irregular leaf size, fold creases*, 16 pp., folio, *disbound* (Wing I61) **£30.00**

269 **Porter** (Whitworth) A History of the Knights of Malta or the Order of the Hospital of St. John of Jerusalem. 2 Vols. *Longman, Brown, Green, Longmans, & Roberts*, 1858, *frontispieces, folding map, a view and a woodcut, embossed stamp on titles*, xvi+518: viii+522 pp., 8vo, *half brown morocco, lettered, marbled bds. by de Coverly* **£30.00**

270 **Portugal.** VERTOT (Rene Aubert de, Abbé) Révoltuions de Portugal. Nouvelle Edition, revue & augmentée. *La Haye, Pierre Gosse Junior; et Daniel Pinet*, 1765, *some staining throughout*, xii+176 pp., 12mo, *contemp. sprinkled calf, backstrip gilt, leather label* **£35.00**

271 **Prescott** (William H.) History of the Reign of Ferdinand and Isabella, the Catholic, of Spain. Eleventh Edition, Revised, 2 Vols. *Richard Bentley*, 1858, *portraits, foxed, some foxing of fore-edges*, xxiv+568: xi+616 pp., 8vo, *original blue cloth, lettered* **£18.00**

272 **Prideaux** (Mathias) An Easy and Compendious Introdvction for Reading all sorts of Histories: contrived in a more facile way then heretofore hath been published . . . Third Edition, in which is added a Synopsis of Councels by John Prideaux, *Oxford. Printed for Leonard Lichfield, and are to be sold by Tho. Robinson*, 1655, *slight staining and browning*, [viii+] 351 [+xxxv+ii+] 58 [+iv] pp., sm.4to, *new qtr. dark brown calf, leather label, grey paper bds.* (Wing P3442) **£30.00**

273 **Prisons.** FIELD (John) The Life of John Howard [Prison Reformer]; with Comments on his Character and Philanthropic Labours. *Longman, Brown, Green, and Longmans*, 1850, *portrait and 2 charts*, xvi+495 pp., 8vo, *dark blue calf, gilt, red leather label* **£45.00**
¶The author was chaplain of Reading gaol and wrote a number of books on prison reform, etc.

274 —— A REPORT from the Committee appointed to Enquire into the State of the Gaols of this Kingdom: relating to the Fleet Prison. With the Resolutions and Orders of the House of Commons thereupon. *Robert Knaplock, Jacob Tonson, John Pemberton and Richard Williamson*, 1729, *title and last leaf soiled*, [ii+] 20 pp., folio, *disbound* **£20.00**

275 **Prynne** (William) A true and perfect Narrative of what was done, spoken by and between Mr. Prynne, the old and newly Forcibly late secluded Members, the Army Officers, and those now sitting both in the Commons Lobby, House, and elsewhere; on Saturday and Monday last (the 7. and 9. of this instant May;) with the Reasons, Ends including Mr. Prynne (a Member of the old Parliament thus ernestly to press for entry, to go and keep in the House as he did; And what proposals he intended there to make for publike peace, settlement, and preservation of the Parliaments privileges, *Printed in the Year*, 1659, *title within typographic border, one corner repaired, title and last page soiled*, [ii+] 99 (shd. read 109) pp., sm.4to, *nineteenth century tree calf, gilt, g.e., lettered, from the Sunderland/Evelyn Libraries, with their labels* (Wing P4113) **£85.00**

276 [**Pulteny** (William)] Plan of Re-Union between Great Britain and her Colonies, *John Murray*, 1778, *additional title tipped in at end*, xvi+211 pp., 8vo, *new quarter tan calf, brown leather label, marbled bds.* (Sabin 66645) **£35.00**

277 **Pymm** (John) The Speech of Declaration to the Lords of the upper House upon the delivery of the Articles of the Commons assembled in Parliament, against William Laud, Archbishop of Canterbury, in maintenance of their Accusation, whereby he stands charged of High Treason. Together with a true Copy of the said Articles. *Ralph Mabb*, 1641, *title soiled*, [i+] 34 pp., sm.4to, *disbound* (Wing P4295) **£35.00**

278 [**Rae** (Peter)] A Short History of the late Rebellion, and of the Conduct of Divine Providence; together with the Consequences if it had succeeded: in a Letter from Edinburgh to a Gentleman at Dumfries. *Edinburgh, Robert Brown*, [1716], *soiled and discoloured throughout, slight worming in few inner margins*, [i+] 46 pp., sm.4to, *disbound* **£35.00**

279 **Ralegh** (Sir Walter) The History of the World, in five books. Eleventh Edition. To which is prefix'd, the Life of the Author, newly compil'd, from Materials more ample and authentick than have yet been publish'd; by Mr. Oldys. Also his Trial, with some Additions: together with a new and more copious Index to the whole Work. 2 Vols. in 1. *G. Conyers, J.J. and P. Knapton*, 1736, *title in red and black, portrait and 8 folding maps, title and few other ll. stained, lacks 4d1/2 and A1 (sub-titles)*, [iv+] xxxii [+xxiv+] ccl [+viii+] 817 (shd. read 811) [+xlv] pp., folio, *early nineteenth century calf, lettered, heavily gilt on sides, gauffred edges* **£135.00**

280 —— Instrvctions to his Sonne: and to Posteritie. Third Edition, corrected and enlarged according to the Authors owne Coppy. *Beniamin Fisher*, 1633, *portrait, slightly trimmed*, [x+] 99 pp. [with] The dutifull Advice of a loving Sonne to his aged Father. *Benjamin Fisher*, 1632, [i+] 57 pp., sm.8vo, *brown morocco, backstrip gilt and lettered, g.e. by W. Pratt* (STC 20643 and 156.7) scarce **£350.00**
¶From the library of the late Dennis Wheatley, with his book plate and a signed memo on the fly leaf.

281 —— The Marrow of History or, an Epitome of all Historical Passages from the Creation, to the end of the last Macedonian War . . . now Abbreviated by A[lexander] R[oss], Second Edition. *John Place and William Place*, 1662, *lacks portrait, embrowned throughout, a few margins slightly frayed from use*, [xxiv+] 574 pp., 12mo, *contemp. calf, worn, sometime rebacked and lettered, now rubbed*, (Wing R173: Brushfield 228) **£35.00**

282 —— The Prerogative of Parlements in England. Proved in a Dialogue between a Counsellour of State and a Iustice of Peace. *William Shears Iunior*, 1657, *portrait by Robert Vaughan, browned throughout*, [x+] 122 pp., 12mo, *contemp. sheep, unlettered, little rubbed* (see Wing R180: Brushfield 219f) **£65.00**
¶Part 10 of "The Remains", issued with separate pagination, as Brushfield explains in his bibliography of Raleigh: the contemporary binding would confirm that these pieces were issued separately.

283 [**Rapin** (René)] The Modest Critick: or Remarks upon the most Eminent Historians, Antient and Modern. With Useful Cautions and Instructions, as well for Writing, as Reading History: wherein the Sense of the Greatest Men on this Subject is faithfully Abridged. *John Barnes*, 1689, *discoloured throughout, name cut from head of License leaf*, [xxii+] 151 pp., sm.8vo, *contemp. sprinkled sheep, corners worn, sometime rebacked, lettered* (Wing R264) scarce **£85.00**

284 **Rapin de Thoyras** (Paul) The History of England [from the Earliest Times to the Abdication of King James II.]. Translated into English with Additional Notes by N. Tindal. Second Edition. 2 Vols. *James, John and Paul Knapton*, 1732/3, *with 64 portraits and monumental effigies, 4 maps, 11 tables, 42 head and tail pieces and 63 cuts of coins, some dampstaining in inner margins*, [i+] x+849 [+i]: [i+] 807 [xix] pp., lge.folio, *contemp. panelled calf, backstrips gilt, leather labels, joints cracked but sound, carries the armorial book plate of Chandos Leigh, First Baron Leigh of the second creation* **£130.00**
¶A 2 pp. memorandum on the "Pretender" signed by Wm. Bentinck (2nd Earl of Portland) has been inserted.

285 **Ranken** (Alexander) The History of France, civil and military, ecclesiastical, political, literary, commercial, &c. &c. from the Time of its Conquest by Clovis, A.D. 486. 9 Vols. *A. Strahan for T. Cadell Jun. and W. Davies*, 1801, 8vo, *contemp. half roan, lettered, matching cloth sides little faded, rubbed at joints* **£25.00**

286 **Reyd** (Everard van) Belgarvm Aliarvmqve Gentivm, Annales. Dionysio Vossio Interprete. *Luvduni Batavorum, ex off. Ioannis Maire*, 1633, *title in red and black*, [x+] 561 (shd. read 563) pp., folio, *contemp. stamped vellum, ties present, upper joint split* **£60.00**

287 **Richard of Cirencester.** The Description of Britain, translated . . .: with the original Treatise De Situ Britanniae; and a Commentary on the Itinerary. *J. White and Co., by Richard Taylor and Co.*, 1809, *2 folding maps (slight tear in fold), and a facs. of the MS.*, xxiii [+i+] 166+127 [+i] pp., 8vo, *contemp. mottled calf, gilt, worn at corners, backstrip defective at head and tail* **£35.00**

288 **Ripperda** (Jan Willem,. *Duke de*) Memoirs: containing a Succinct Account of the most Remarkable Events which happen'd between 1715 and 1736 . . . The Second Edition Corrected, with Additions, *John Stagg and Daniel Browne*, 1740, xv [+i+] 390 [+ii (book list)] pp., 8vo, *contemp. tan calf, brown leather label, slightly chipped* **£30.00**

289 **Robertson** (William) The History of America: including the History of Virginia to the year 1688, and New England to the year 1652. A New Edition; to which is added, a Continuation, comprising the History of the Colonies from 1652 to the present Time . . . by David M'Intosh. *Richard Evans and John Bourne*, 1817, *with a portrait, 3 maps and 11 plates*, iv+588 pp., 4to, *contemp. tan calf, lettered, small blemish on upper cover*, scarce (Sabin 71977) **£140.00**

290 —— The History of Scotland during the Reigns of Queen Mary and King James VI. Eighteenth Edition, 3 Vols. *T. Cadell and W. Davies*, 1809: The History of the Reign of the Emperor Charles V. Thirteenth Edition, 4 Vols. *Cadell and Davies*, 1812: The History of America, Twelfth Edition . . . 4 Vols. *Cadell and Davies*, 1812: An Historical Disquisition concerning the Knowledge which the Ancients had of India; and the Progress of Trade with that Country prior to the Discovery of the Passage to it by the Cape of Good Hope. Fourth Edition. *A. Strahan for T. Cadell and W. Davies, and E. Balfour*, 1804: 12 Vols together, *engraved frontispieces foxed and off-set to titles*, 8vo, *contemp. tan russia, gilt, lettered, in excellent and sound condition* **£160.00**

291 **Robinson** (John, *of Leyden*) The Peoples Plea: fully vindicating the Povver and Proceedings of the Parliament. Occasioned by a defence of the Covenant, *Robert Bostock*, 1646, *discoloured*, [iv+] 19 pp., sm.4to, *disbound* (Wing R1697) **£35.00**

292 **Rocca** (Albert Jean Michel de) Memoirs of the War of the French in Spain. Translated from the second Paris Edition. *Philadelphia, Thomas Dobson and Son*, 1820, *some foxing*, vii+219 pp., 8vo, *contemp. tree calf, gilt, leather label, marbled endpapers, library label, y.e.* **£25.00**
¶De Rocca was an Officer of Hussars and Knight of the Order of the Legion of Honour.

293 **Rocoles** (Jean Baptiste de) The History of [12] Infamous Impostors. Or, the Lives & Actions of Several Notorious Counterfeits, who from the most Abject, and Meanest of the People, have Usurped the Titles of Emperours, Kings, and Princes. And now Done into English. *William Cademan*, 1683, *lacks frontispiece, embrowned throughout*, [xvi+] 180 [+iv – catalogue] pp., 8vo, *contemp. calf, worn, later drab end-papers, newly rebacked, unlettered* (Wing R1766) **£50.00**

294 **Rous** (Francis) Archaeologiae Atticae Libri Septem. Seven Books of the Attick Antiquities. Containing the description of the Citties glory, Government, division of the People, the Towns within the Athenian Territories, their Religion, Superstition, Sacrifices, Account of the Year, a full relation of their Judicatories. Fifth Edition, corrected and enlarged. *Oxford, Printed by A. Lichfield and H. Hall, for John Adams and Edw. Forrest*, 1658, *embrowning throughout*, [viii+] 374 [+xii] pp., sm.4to, *contemp. sprinkled sheep, unlettered, corners worn, backstrip slightly defective* (Wing R2035: Madan 2410) **£40.00**

295 [**Rowlands** or V[erstegan] (R[ichard)] A Restitution of Decayed Intelligence in Antiquities, concerning the most Noble and Renowned English Nation. *Printed for Samuel Mearne, John Martyn and Henry Herringman, 1673, engr. title, damaged and laid down, soiled, engravings in text*, [xxiv+] 374 [+xvi] pp. sm.8vo, *contemp. sheep, rubbed and corners worn, newly rebacked, green leather label* (Wing V271) **£25.00**

296 **Royal Memoirs** of the French Revolution: containing, I. A Narrative of the Journey of Louis xvi. and his Family to Varennes . . . II. A Narrative of a Journey to Bruxelles and Coblentz in 1791 . . . III. Private Memoirs of what passed in the Temple, *John Murray*, 1823, *map*, 302 pp., 8vo, *contemp. half green calf, corners rubbed, recently rebacked, red leather label* **£30.00**

297 **Rudyerd** (Sir Benjamin) Two Speeches concerning the Palatinate. *Francis Constable*, 1641, [i+] 5 pp., sm.4to, *disbound* (Wing R2202) **£21.00**

298 **Russell** (Lady Rachel) Letters; from the MS. in the Library at Wooburn Abbey to which are prefixed, an Introduction, vindicating the Character of Lord Russell against Sir John Dalrymple, &c. and the Trial of Lord William Russell for High Treason, extracted from the State Trials . . . Sixth Edition. *Printed for J. Mawman*, 1801, *with 3 engravings*, clxxi+351 [+i] pp., 8vo, *marbled sheep, leather label, upper cover slightly damaged, joints beginning to crack* **£25.00**

299 **Ruvigny and Raineval** (Marquis of) The Jacobite Peerage, Baronetage, Knightage and Grants of Honour, extracted, by permission, from the Stuart Papers now in the Possession of his Majesty the King at Windsor Castle, and supplemented by biographical and genealogical notes. *Edinburgh, T.C. and E.C. Jack*, 1904, xix+267 pp., folio, *orig. cream buckram, red leather labels, covers soiled by use* **£45.00**

300 **Rye House Plot.** [SPRAT (Thomas, *Bp. of Rochester*)] A True Acoount and Declaration of the Horrid Conspiracy against the Late King, His Present Majesty, and the Government: *Thomas Newcomb, and are to be sold by Sam. Lowndes*, 1685, [v+] 167 pp. (Wing S5066):
[with]
COPIES of the Informations and Original Papers relating to the Proof of the Horrid Conspiracy against the Late King, His Present Majesty, and the Government. *Thomas Newcomb*, 1685, [i+] 141 pp. (Wing S5029):
Two pieces bound together, folio, *contemp. mottled calf, newly rebacked, red leather label* **£100.00**

301 **Ryves** (Bruno) [*attrib. to* John Barwick]. Querela Cantabrigiensis: or, a Remonstrance by way of Apologie, for the banished Members of the late flourishing University of Cambridge. By some of the said Sufferers. *Oxoniae* 1646, *worming in lower eighth with slight loss*, [xii+] 28 [+viii], (Wing B1009: Madan 1889):
with
[——] Micro-Chronicon: or; A briefe Chronology of the Time and Place of the Battels, Sieges, Conflicts, and other most remarkable Passages . . . together, with a Catalogue of the Lords, Knights, Commanders, and persons of quality slain on either side therein, *Printed in the Year*, 1647, G1 *misbound*, [iv+106] pp., (Wing R2451)
Two pieces together, 12mo, *early calf, recently rebacked, red leather label* **£55.00**

302 [**Saint-Didier** (Alexandre-Toussaint de Limojon, sieur de)] La Ville et la Republique de Venise. *Paris, chez Guillaume de Luyne*, 1680, *embrowning throughout*, [xxiv+] 452 pp., 12mo, *contemp. calf, newly rebacked, leather label* (Brunet 5/37) **£30.00**

303 **St. John** (Henry, *Lord Viscount Bolingbroke*) A Letter to Sir William Windham. II. Some Reflections on the Present State of the Nation. III. A Letter to Mr. Pope. *Dublin, J. Smith*, 1753, *2 pp. catalogue at end*, iv+305 pp., 12mo, *contemp. tan calf, brown leather label* **£45.00**

304 **Scotland.** [GRIFFITHS (Ralph)] Ascanius; or, the Young Adventurer; containing an impartial History of the rebellion in Scotland in the years 1745, 1746, *Edinburgh, Ogle, Allardice & Thomson*, 1818, *portrait, 3 engravings and a folding chart*, 216 pp., 12mo, *contemp. half tan calf, red leather label, marbled bds.*, scarce **£30.00**

305 —— HOOCKE (Nathaniel, *Colonel*) Secret History of Colonel Hoocke's Négociations in Scotland in 1707. being the Original Letters and Papers which passed between the Scotch and Irish Lords and the Courts of Versailles and St. Germains. With a Translation of Letters, containing a Narrative of the Pretender's expedition into Scotland in 1708, and his return to Dunkirk, *Edinburgh, by the booksellers*, 1760, *embrowned throughout*, iv+210 pp., 8vo, *orig. drab bds., worn, paper label, edges untrimmed* **£35.00**

306 —— A LARGE DECLARATION concerning the late Tumults in Scotland, from their first originalls: together with a particular Deduction of the seditious Practices of the prime Leaders of the Covenanters: collected out of their owne foule Acts and Writings: by which it doth plainly appeare, that Religion was onely pretended by those Leaders, but nothing lesse intended by them. *Printed by Robert Young*, 1639, *title creased staining throughout*, [i+] 430 [+i] pp., folio, *contemp. calf, corners worn, sometime rebacked with canvas, ms. label*, (STC 21906 marginal note in p. 41) **£50.00**

307 —— THE PROCEEDINGS of the Parliament of Scotland: begun at Edinburgh, 6th May, 1703. with an Account of all the Material Debates which occur'd in that Session. To which are Subjoyn'd the several Acts passed in that Session, *Printed in the Year* 1704, *dampstained throughout, some edges fragile with slight loss, one lower margin trimmed with loss of last line*, [iv+] 70 [+xx] pp., sm.4to, *drab wrappers* **£32.00**

308 —— SOME PAPERS of the Commissioners of Scotland, given in lately to the Houses of Parliament, concerning the Propositions of Peace. *Printed for Robert Bostock, April 11*, 1646, *one corner torn away with slight loss*, [iv+] 26 pp., sm.4to, *new marbled boards* **£25.00**

309 —— STEVENSON (Joseph) *Ed.* Selections from Unpublished Manuscripts in the College of Arms and the British Museum, illustrating the Reign of Mary Queen of Scotland mdxliii–mdxlxviii. *Glasgow, The Maitland Club*, 1837, xxviii+329 pp., 4to, *half tan calf, marbled boards, lettered, backstrip slightly rubbed* **£20.00**

310 [**Scott** (Thomas)] Newes from Parnassvs. The Political Touchstone, taken from Mount Parnassus: whereon the Governments of the greatest Monarchies of the World are touched. *Printed at Helicon* (i.e. *Holland*), 1622, *slight embrowning*, 92 [+iii] pp., sm.4to, *modern qtr. calf, marbled boards lettered* (STC 22080) **£150.00**
¶Scott, sometime Chaplain to James I., wrote in his lifetime some 25 pamphlets, many against Spain, and the Roman Catholics. He was assassinated, while preacher to the English Garrison in Utrecht.

311 **Selden** (John) Titles of Honor. Second Edition. *William Stansby for Richard Whitakers*, 1631, *engravings, some foxing of early pp., lacks* 3Y 2/3, [xxxvi+] 941 (shd. read 921) [+i] pp., folio, *nineteenth century half tan calf, blue leather label, marbled bds., edges rubbed* (STC 22178) **£40.00**

312 —— Tracts. The first Entituled, Jani Anglorum Facies Altera, rendred into English, with large Notes thereupon, by Redman Westcot, Gent. The Second, England's Epinomis. The Third, Of the Original of Ecclesiastical Jurisdictions of Testaments. The Fourth, Of the Disposition or Administration of Intestates Goods. *Thomas Basset and Richard Chiswell, sold by Robert Clavell*, 1683, *portrait by White, divisional titles*, [xxxi+] 131 [+i]: [vii+] 39: [iv+] 24 pp., folio, *contemp. calf, joints cracking, paper label* (Wing S2441A) rare **£150.00**
¶With the signature Dan: Fleming on the fly-leaf – probably Sir Daniel Fleming the antiquary and lawyer.

313 **Serious Considerations** on the Present State of Affairs, both at Home and Abroad, and the Fatal Consequences reasonably to be expected from thence . . . as also that of the King of Prussia, upon his extraordinary Manifesto; and the Emperor's Commissorial Decree. The Whole in a Letter to the Lords B, [William Pulteney, Earl of Bath] and C. [John Carteret, Earl of Granville]. *C. Corbett*, 1744, *writing on title, some staining*, 76 pp., 8vo, *disbound* **£40.00**

314 [**Sherlock** (William)] A Second Letter to a Friend, concerning the French Invasion. In which the Declaration lately dispersed under the title of His Majesty's most Gracious Declaration . . . against the P. of Orange and his Adherants, is entirely and exactly Published, . . . *Randal Taylor*, 1692, FIRST EDITION, [ii+] 32 pp., sm.4to, *grey wrappers* (Wing S3339) **£70.00**

315 **Sidney** (Algernon) Discourses concerning Government. *Printed, and are to be sold by the Booksellers of London and Westminster*, 1698, FIRST EDITION, *small corner torn from title*, [i+] 462 [+v] pp., folio, *contemp. panelled calf, corners little worn, recently rebacked, tan label, new endpapers* (Wing S3761) **£375.00**

316 —— —— . . . to which is added, a Short Account of the Author's Life, and a copious Index. 2 Vols., *Edinburgh, G. Hamilton and J. Balfour*, 1750, *some foxing and browning throughout*, xxv+v+453: vi+390 [+xlvi] pp., 8vo, *contemp. "French" mottled calf, red leather labels, one missing, others chipped, rubbed, joints cracking, marbled endpapers and edges* **£50.00**

317 **Slatyer** (William) The History of Great Britanie from the first peopling of this Island to the present Raigne of o[u]r happy and peacefull Monarke K. James. *W. Stansby for Rich. Meighen* [1621], *lacks printed title and colophon leaf as usual, "Declaration of the Frontispiece" trimmed close and laid down, part of last 3 lines defective, engraved title trimmed and inlaid, lower corner of ¶3 repaired, general staining and browning throughout*, [xxiv+] 305 [+xiv] pp., folio, *nineteenth century tan calf, corners bruised, recently rebacked, black leather label* (STC 22634) **£65.00**

318 **Slavery.** BUXTON (Thomas Foxwell) The African Slave Trade and its Remedy. *John Murray*, 1840, *folding map, some foxing throughout*, viii+582 pp., 8vo., *orig. brown cloth, lettered, worn at edges and corners* (Sabin 9686) scarce **£65.00**

¶The work is preceded by a 14 pp prospectus for the short-lived "Society for the Extinction of the Slave Trade and the Civilisation of Africa."

319 —— [CLARKSON (Thomas)] An Essay on the Slavery and Commerce of the Human Species, particularly the African, translated from a Latin Dissertation, which was honoured with the First Prize in the University of Cambridge, for the year 1875, with Additions. *J. Phillips, and sold by T. Cadell and J. Phillips*, 1786, FIRST EDITION, *name cut from head margin of title, some slight foxing, gathering* b *misbound*, 256 pp., 8vo, *contemp. sprinkled calf, red leather label, a little rubbed* (Sabin 13485: Kress B1026) **£150.00**

320 —— WHITELEY (Henry) Verbatim Reprint of a Pamphlet . . . entitled Three Months in Jamaica, in 1832: comprising a Residence of Seven Weeks on a Sugar Plantation. *The Anti-Slavery Society*, [N.D., ?1833], *drop title*, 24 pp., sm.8vo, *grey wrappers* (Sabin 103670) **£25.00**

322 **Sleidan** (John) De Quatvorsvmmis Imperiis, libri tres, postrema editione hac accurate recogniti. *Amsteredami, Joannem Wolters*, 1705, *engraved title, light embrowning throughout*, 309 [+xix] pp., 16mo, *contemp. sprinkled calf, unlettered, joints rubbed* **£25.00**

323 **Smith** (Adam) Essai sur la première Formation des Langues, et sur la différence du gégie des langues originales et des langues composées; traduit de l'anglais Avec des notes suivi du premier livre des Recherches sur la langue et la philosophie des Indiens. Extrait et traduit de l'allemand de F. Schlegel, par J[aques Louis] Manget. *Genève, chez Manget et Cherbuliez*, 1809, *slight spotting and discolouration, 8 pp. catalogue and 2 pp. errata at end*, xix+229 [+x] pp., 12mo, *orig. pink marbled wrappers, surface rubbed, backstrip gone, an uncut copy* (Kress S5906) scarce **£100.00**

¶The text of this essay was first published in the 2nd ed. of "The Theory of Moral Sentiments" (1761).

324 —— An Inquiry into the Nature and Causes of the Wealth of Nations. 3 Vols. Sixth Edition. *A. Strahan and T. Cadell*, 1792, x+499: vi+518 [+v]: v+465 [+1] pp., 8vo, *contemp. tree calf, red and black leather labels, upper joint of vol. i. cracked* **£150.00**

325 —— —— With a Life of the Author. Also, a View of the Doctrine of Smith, compared with that of the French Economists; with a Method of facilitating the Study of his Works; from the French of M. Garnier. 3 Vols. *Edinburgh, Silvester Doig and Andrew Stirling*, 1811, *some foxing throughout*, lxiii+360: vi+514: v+448 [+1] pp., 8vo, *contemp. half calf, marbled bds., rubbed, sometime rebacked, red leather labels* **£95.00**

326 —— (William) The Particular Description of England. 1588. With Views of some of the chief Towns and armorial Bearings of Nobles and Bishops. Ed. . . . with an Introduction by Henry B. Wheatley and Edmund W. Ashbee. *Printed for Subscribers only*, 1879, *folding map, illuminated title, 17 plates of arms, and 11 plates of town plans and views, some dampstaining*, xix+75, 4to, *orig. "roxburghe" binding, rubbed at edges* **£35.00**

327 **Spain.** An EXACT RELATION of the Grand Ceremony of the Marriage of Charles the II. the Most Catholick King, with the most Illustrious Princess Madamoiselle Marie Louise d'Orleans . . . as it was performed at Fontainbleau . . . faithfully Translated. *Dorman Newman*, 1679, *discoloured, small stamps on verso of title*, [i+] 10 pp., folio, *disbound* (Wing E3690) **£30.00**

328 —— WATSON (Robert) The History of the Reign of Philip the Second, King of Spain, 2 Vols., *Dublin, Messrs. Price, W. Watson, Whitestone*, 1777, [and] The History of the Reign of Philip the Third, King of Spain. *Dublin, Messrs. Price, Whitestone, W. Watson*, 1783. 3 Vols. together, [iii+] 443: [i+] 437 [+xxi]: [xii+] 525 [+ix] pp., 8vo, *contemp. sprinkled calf, leather labels, vol. iii. rubbed and joints worn and cracked* **£65.00**

29 **Sparrow** (Anthony, *Bp*) A Collection of Articles, Injunctions, Canons, Orders, Ordnances, and Constitutions Ecclesiastical, with other Publick Records of the Church of England, chiefly in the Times of King Edward vith. Q. Elizabeth. and K. James. Published to Vindicate the Church of England and to promote Uniformity and peace in the same. *Printed by R. Norton for Timothy Garthwait*, 1661, FIRST EDITION, *divisional titles, pagination irregular*, [xii+325] pp., sm.4to, *contemp. panelled calf, rubbed and worn, sometime rebacked but joints now cracking again* (Wing S4823) **£25.00**

330 **Sprat** (Thomas, *F.R.S.*) Observations on Monsieur de Sorbier's Voyage into England. Written to Dr. Wren, Professor of Astronomy in Oxford. *John Martyn and James Allestry*, 1665, *some discolouration, lacks* [A1], [i+] 298 pp., sm.8vo, *contemp. calf, gilt, backstrip defective, joints cracked* (Wing S5035) scarce **£100.00**

331 **Sprott** (Thomas) Chronica. E Codice antiquo MS.[to] in Bibliotheca praenobilis Adolescentis Dni. Edvardi Dering, de Surrenden Dering in Agro Cantiano Baronetti, descripsit ediditque Tho. Hearnius, qui & alia quaedem Opuscula, è Codicibus MSStis. authenticis à seipso itidem descripta, subjecit. *Oxonii, Theatro Sheldoniano*, 1719, xxx+334 [+i] pp., 8vo, *binder's green cloth, red leather label, edges untrimmed* **£40.00**

332 **Statutes.** WASHINGTON (Jo.) An Exact Abridgment of the Statutes of King William and Queen Mary, and of King William III. in Force and Use. . . . Revised and Continued to the end of the last Session of Parliament, 27 Apr. 1696. with two new Tables. *The Assigns of the Kings Printers and of R. and E. Atkyns*, 1696, *both paste-downs lifted*, [xvi+] 331 [+v] pp., 8vo, *contemp. tan calf, green leather label, little rubbed* **£35.00**

333 [**Steele** (Richard)] The Spinster: in Defence of the Woollen Manufactures. To be continued Occasio-nally. Numb. 1. [all published], *Printed for J. Roberts*, 1719, [ii+] 16 [+i] pp., 8vo, *sewed, enclosed in grey buckram fold-over case, leather label on front cover* (Kress 3119) **£70.00**

334 **Strada** (Famian) Prolvsiones Academicae, sev Orationes Variae, ad Facvltatem Orationiam, Historicam, Poeticam spectantes. Editio Tertia. *Coloniae Agrippinae, Ioannem Kinckivm*, 1625, *embrowned throughout*, 481 [+xiv] pp., 8vo, *contemp. sprinkled calf, red leather label, backstrip gilt* (Ebert 12835 – vide) **£45.00**

335 **Strafford** (Sir Thomas Wentworth, *Earl of*) Letters and Despatches, with an Essay towards his Life by Sir George Radcliffe . . . [edited by] William Knowler, 2 Vols. in 1. *The Editor, by William Bowyer*, 1739, *2 portraits*, [x+] 527 [+iv]: [i+] 439 [+iv] pp., folio, *diced russia, corners repaired, rebacked, orig. backstrip laid down, black leather label, marbled end papers* **£90.00**

336 —— RUSHWORTH (John) The Tryal of Thomas Earl of Strafford . . . upon an Impeachment for High Treason by the Commons then Assembled in Parliament . . . to which is added a short Account of some other Matters of Fact transacted in both Houses of Parliament, precedent, concomitant and subsequent to the said Tryal: with some Special Arguments in Law relating to a Bill of Attainder. *John Wright and Richard Chiswell*, 1680, *engraved portrait by R. White*, [x+] 786 pp., folio, *contemp. calf, tan leather label, all surfaces rubbed, joints cracked, lacks free endpapers* (Wing W2333) **£75.00**

337 **Strickland** (Agnes) Lives of the Bachelor Kings of England. Fourth Thousand. *Simpkin, Marshall, and Co.*, 1861, *portraits, slightly foxed*, xi+433 pp., sm.8vo, *modern tan calf, gilt, green leather label, g.e.* **£30.00**

338 **Stuart** (Gilbert) A View of Society in Europe, in its Progress from Rudeness to Refinement: or, Inquiries concerning the History of Law, Government and Manners. *Edinburgh, John Bell and J. Murray*, 1778, *lacks half title, tear in one leaf*, xx+433 [+i] pp., 4to, *contemp. half calf, lettered, marbled boards, rubbed, joints cracking* **£90.00**

339 [—— (James Francis Edward, *the "Old Pretender"*)] Memoirs of the Chevalier de St. George: with some Private Passages of the Life of the late King James II. never before Publish'd. *Printed in the Year* 1712, *damp stained, lacks half title*, 8vo, *disbound* **£25.00**

340 **Sully.** BETHUNE (Maximilian de, *Duke of Sully*) Memoirs, containing the History and Reign of that Monarch [Henry the Great], and his own Administration under Him. Translated from the French. [by Charlotte Lennox]. To which is added, the Tryal of Ravaillac for the Murder of Henry the Great. 3 Vols. *A. Millar, R. & J. Dodsley, and W. Shropshire*, 1756, FIRST EDITION, *some light foxing*, xxxii+540: viii+555: vii+407 [+cxxii] pp., 4to, *contemp. sprinkled calf, leather labels, a little rubbed* **£75.00**

341 **Sussex.** LOWER (Mark Anthony) The Chronicle of Battel Abbey, from 1066 to 1176, now first translated, with notes, and an abstract of the subsequent history of the Establishment. *John Russell Smith*, 1851, *with 2 coloured plates*, xii+227 pp., 8vo, *orig. blue cloth, lettered* **£15.00**

342 **Sweden.** VOLTAIRE (Francois Marie Arouet de) The History of Charles II. King of Sweden. Translated from the French. Fourth Edition. *C. Davis and A. Lyon*, 1732, *engraved portrait and folding map*, xii+371 [+i] pp., 8vo, *contemp. panelled calf, unlettered, little rubbed, joints beginning to crack* **£25.00**

343 **Swift** (Jonathan) The History of the Four Last Years of the Queen. Published from the last Manuscript copy, Corrected and Enlarged by the Author's own Hand. *A. Millar*, 1758, FIRST EDITION, *with* Z3 *so signed but* 2A3 *signed* 2A4 [*see Rothchild 2187*], xiv+392 pp. 8vo, *contemp. sprinkled calf, unlettered, little rubbed, joints cracking* (Teerink 809) **£80.00**

344 **Switzerland.** [STANYAN (Abraham)] An Account of Switzerland. Written in the Year 1714. *Jacob Tonson*, 1714, [viii+] 247 pp., 8vo, *contemp. panelled calf, hand-written paper label, joints starting to crack otherwise an exceptionally clean and sound copy* **£80.00**

¶"Finding therefore, that there is no distinct Account of this Country, I thought it might be worth while, to publish the Observations I made upon it, while I lived there, both to make it better known to us, and to remove some Prejudices, which are taken upon trust from other Nations, and have no real Foundation." (Preface)

345 **Tangier.** CHARLES II. His Majesties Message to the Commons in Parliament, relating to Tangier. And the Humble Address of the Commons to His Majesty, in Answer to that Message. Presented upon Monday 29. Nov. 1680. *John Wright*, 1680, pp. [iii+] 71–85, folio, *disbound* (Wing – not recorded) **£35.00**

346 —— A PARTICULAR NARRATIVE of a Great Engagement between the Garison [sic] of Tangier, and the Moors, and of the Signal Victory which His Majesties Forces obtained against them on the 27th of October last. *In the Savoy, Thomas Newcombe*, 1680, *soiled throughout, piece torn from lower inner margins*, 8 pp., folio, *disbound* (Wing P593) **£40.00**

347 **Tasso.** BLACK (John) Life of Torquato Tasso; with an Historical and Critical Account of his Writings. 2 Vols. in 1. *Edinburgh, John Murray*, 1810, *with 2 frontispieces*, [i+] xxxiv+404 [+i]: vi+508 pp., 4to, *contemp. tan calf, backstrip gilt, red leather label, joints cracked, small piece missing from base of backstrip* **£55.00**

348 **Taxatio Ecclesiastica** Angliae et Halliae. Auctoritate P. Nicholae iv. circa A.D. 1291. *George Eyre and Andrew Strahan*, 1802, *facsimile*, [vii+] xvii+448 pp., folio, *contemp. half tan calf, marbled bds., rubbed, sometime rebacked buckram, red leather label, fresh endpapers* **£35.00**

349 **Temple** (Sir William) Miscellanea, The First [and Second] Part[s]. Containing I. A Survey of the Consitiutions and Interests of the Empire . . . II. An Essay upon the Original and Nature of Government. III. An Essay upon the Advancement of Trade in Ireland. IV. Upon the Conjuncture of Affairs in Octob. 1673. V. Upon the Excesses of Grief. VI. An Essay upon the Cure of the Gout by Moxa. The Third Edition. *Jacob Tonson, and Awnsham and John Churchill*, 1691, [iv+] 232 pp. [and] In Four Essays. I. Upon Ancient and Modern Learning. II. Upon the Gardens of Epicurus. III. Upon Heroick Vertue. IV. Upon Poetry. The Second Edition. *J.R. for Ri. and Ra. Simpson*, 1690, [i+] 341 pp.,
Two Parts bound together, 8vo, *contemp. mottled calf, corners little worn, newly rebacked, leather label, new endpapers* (Wing T648 and 653) **£75.00**

350 **Thiers** (Louis Adolphe, *President of France*) Histoire du Consulat et de l'Empire, faisant suite a l'Histoire de la Révolution Francaise. 20 Vols. *Paris, Paulin*, 1845/62, 8vo, *green cloth, lettered, backstrips just faded* **£45.00**

351 **The Thoughts** of an Impartial Man upon the present Temper of the Nation; offer'd to the Consideration of the Freeholders of Great Britain. *J. Roberts*, 1733, *binder's blanks*, [i+] 29 pp., 8vo, *modern marbled bds., leather label* **£35.00**

352 **Tobacco.** AN ACT for granting an additional Duty upon Tobacco and Snuff; and for repealing certain Duties payable upon the Importation of Brandy and Arrack, and for granting other Duties in lieu thereof. *Charles Eyre and William Strahan*, 1782, [i+vi] pp., folio, *disbound* **£20.00**

353 —— AN ACT to permit the Importation of British Plantation Tobacco from any Port or Place either in America, or the West Indies, or in Europe, during the present Hostilities. *Charles Eyre and William Strahan*, 1782, [ii+2] pp., folio, *disbound* **£20.00**

354 **Todd** (Alpheus) Parliamentary Government in England: its Origin, Development, and Practical Operation. New Edition, abridged and revised by Spencer Walpole. 2 Vols. *Sampson Low, Marston & Company*, 1892, xi+290: [iii+] 292 pp., 8vo, *full crimson morocco, lettered, g.e. by Roger de Coverly* **£30.00**

355 **Trevelyan** (Sir George Otto) The American Revolution, 3 Vols. in 4, [Vol. i. second edition]. *Longmans, Green, and Co.*, 1899–1907, *maps*, 8vo, *orig. red cloth, lettered, a little dulled* **£30.00**

356 **Trials.** COKE. The Tryal and Condemnation of Arundel Coke alias Cooks Esq. and of John Woodburne Labourer, for Felony, in Slitting the Nose of Edward Crispe Gent. *John Darby and Daniel Midwinter*, 1722, 37 [+i] pp., folio, *marbled wrappers* **£25.00**

357 —— GORDON (George) The Trial of, commonly called Lord George Gordon. for High Treason, at the Bar of the Court of King's Bench, on Monday, February 5th, 1781. Third Edition. Taken in short-hand by Joseph Gurney, 2 parts in 1 Vol. *G. Kearsly and M. Gurny*, 1781, *portrait*, [i+] 37+65 [+i] pp., folio, *contemp. tan calf, recently rebacked, red leather label, corners worn* **£80.00**

¶The last page carries an advertisment for Gurney's *Brachygraphy*.

358 —— HAMBDEN (John) The Tryal of; in the Great Case of Ship-Money, between his Majesty K. Charles I. and that Gentleman . . . to which is added, the Tryal of Thomas Harrison, Clerk, for Words spoken against Mr. Justice Hutton, *D. Browne, W. Mears, F. Clay, J. Sackfield, B. Creake, and J. Beal*, 1719, *worm hole through lower fore margins*, [vi+] 238 [+ additional Q & R (8 pp.)] pp., folio, *contemp. marbled bds., rubbed, recently rebacked quarter calf, red leather label* **£65.00**

359 —— LAYER (Christopher) A Report from the Committee appointed by Order of the House of Commons to examine Christopher Layer, and others; and to whom several Papers and Examinations laid before the House, relating to the Conspiracy mentioned in His Majesty's Speech, at the Opening of this Parliament, to be carried on against his Person and Government, are referred, *Jacob Tonson, Bernard Lintot, and William Taylor*, 1722/3, *4 ll slightly torn, several dust soiled*, folio, *contemp. half calf, marbled bds., recently rebacked, red leather label* **£85.00**

360 —— PARRY (William) A true and plain Declaration of the Horrible Treasons practised by William Parry, Dr. of the Civil Law, being a Papist, against Queen Elizabeth (of blessed memory,) because She was a Protestant; and of his Tryal, Conviction, and Execution for the same, *William Crook and Charles Harper*, 1679, *some soiling and discolouration*, [iv+] 36 pp., folio, *drab wrappers* (Wing T2572) **£40.00**

361 —— ROSEWELL (Thomas) The Arraignment and Tryal of, for High Treason; before the Lord Chief Justice Jefferies, at the Court of King's Bench, Westminster, in the Year 1684. And the Arguments offer'd in Arrest of Judgment by his Learned Council. To which is Prefix'd an Account of his Life and Death. Publish'd by Samuel Rosewell, A.M. *John Clark and Richard Ford*, 1718, *discolouration throughout*, vi+90 [+i]: 340 pp., 8vo, *contemp. panelled calf, newly rebacked, red leather label, corners repaired* **£55.00**

362 The **True State** of England. Containing the Particular Duty, Business and Salary of every Officer, Civil and Military in All the Publick Offices of Great Britain . . . Together with an Account of the Government of the Cities of London and Westminster: With the Names of the Magistrates, Principal Officers, &c. . . . *C. King, and J. Stagg, R. Francklin, and D. Browne*, 1734, [vi+] 128+5+82 pp., 8vo, *contemp. sprinkled sheep, brown leather label, part of surface damaged by insects* **£55.00**

363 **Tull** (Jethro) The Horse-Hoeing Husbandry: or, a Treatise on the Principles of Tillage and Vegetation, wherein is taught a Method of introducing a sort of Vineyard Culture into the Corn-Fields, in order to increase their Product and diminish the Common Expense. To which is prefixed, an Introduction, explanatory of some Circumstances connected with the History and Division of the Work; and containing an Account of certain Experiments of recent date, by William Cobbett. *William Cobbett*, 1829, *plate*, xxiv+466 (shd. read 468) pp., 8 pp. catalogue, 8vo, *new qtr. tan calf, red leather label, marbled bds.* **£85.00**

364 **Tullibardine** (Marchioness of, *Editor*) A Military History of Perthshire, 1660–1902. *Perth, R.A. & J. Hay*, 1908, *with portraits, illustrations and maps*, xxiii+634 pp., 4to, *orig. red buckram, lettered, backstrip faded* **£21.00**

365 **Turnpike Trusts.** COPIES of the Several Accounts transmitted to the Clerks of the Peace of the different Counties of England and Wales, from the Clerks of the Trustees of the several Turnpike Trusts in each County, *Ordered, by the House of Commons, to be Printed, 24 June*, 1824, 959 pp., folio, *contemp. half sheep, leather label, rubbed, joints cracking* **£65.00**

366 **Tursellinus Romanus** (Horatius) Historiarum, ab origine mundi, usque ad annum á Christo nato, mdxcvii. Epitomae, libri decem. Cum brevibus Notis, duplici item Accessione, usque ad annum mdcxlii. Ac duplici Indice. Editio ultima prioribus correctior. *Ultrajecti, Gulielmum vande Water*, 1710, *title in red and black, engraved title, some marginal notes*, [xiv+] 549 [+lxvii] pp., sm.8vo, *contemp. quarter leather, unlettered, marbled sides, rubbed, untrimmed edges* **£35.00**

367 **Tweddell** (John) Remains: being a selection of his Correspondence, a republication of his Prolusioned Juveniles, an Appendix containing some Account of the Author's Collections, MSS., Drawings, &c., and of their extraordinary Disappearance, preceded by a biographical Memoir of the Deceased by Robert Tweddell. Second Edition, *J. Mawson, by Joyce Gold*, 1816, *with 5 portraits, 4 views and 3 maps, with ll.* D*2 *added*, viii+591 (shd. read 595) +179 [+xvii] pp., 4to, *contemp. half russia, marbled bds., recently rebacked calf, hand lettered paper label, ex-libris book plate on pastedown* **£45.00**

368 **Ursinus** (Fulvius) Familiae Romanae quae reperivntvr in Antiqvis Nvmismatibvs ab Vrbe Condita ad Tempora Divi Avgvsti . . . [colophon: *Romae, Francisci Tramezini, apud Iosephum de Angelis*, 1577], *engraved title, fore-edge just trimmed, and 218 engravings in the text, one with over-lay, some staining towards end, 2 pp. soiled and 4 ll. defective in inner margins with some loss, now repaired and text restored in MS., rubber stamp on title and elsewhere*, [viii+] 403 [+xi] pp., folio, *panelled calf, leather label, corners worn, sides heavily rubbed, sometime rejointed* (Adams U71) scarce **£180.00**

369 **Varillas** (Antoine, Sieur de) *ANEKΔOTA ETEKOYIAKA*, or, the Secret History of the House of Medicis. Made English by Ferrand Spence. *R.E. for R. Bentley and S. Magnes*, 1686, *discoloured throughout*, [lxxvii+] 470 pp., 8vo, *contemp. mottled calf, lettered, upper joint cracking* (Wing V112) **£85.00**

370 **Vertot** (Rene D'Aubert de, *Abbé*) The History of the Knights of Malta, with lxxi. Heads of the Grand Masters, &c. engraved by the best Hands in France, from the Original Paintings, under the Inspection of Mons. Bologne, Director of the Royal Academy of Painting. With Maps by Mons. de Lille, and the Plans and Fortifications of Malta by the Chevalier de Tigné. And a compleat Index to the Whole. 2 Vols. *G. Strahan, F. Gyles*, 1728, *title in red and black, 71 portraits and 5 maps and plans*, [viii+] 487+155: [i+] 220+143+196 [+xxiv] pp., folio, *new qtr. tan calf, leather labels, matching cloth sides*, scarce **£400.00**

371 **Voltaire** (F.M. Aroute de) The Age of Lewis xiv. Translated from the French [by John Lockman], 2 Vols. *R. Dodsley*, 1752, *portrait and frontis., last leaf of vol. i. remargined and extended*, viii+436: [i+] 292 (shd. read 308) +90 [+xx] pp., 8vo, *contemp. sprinkled tan calf, backstrips gilt, red and green leather labels, marbled endpapers, joints tender* **£50.00**

¶". . . I dare affirm, that these two Volumes contain more interesting facts, and curious anecdotes than are in any of the immense collections which have hitherto been published upon the reign of Lewis XIV."

372 **W.** (T.) A Briefe Recitall of the unreasonable proceedings of Dr. Laud, against T.W. Minister of the Word of God: which he conveyed into his hands in a Letter very lately sent to him in the Tower. Together with his absurd answer to the same, *E.G. for H. Overton*, 1641, *discoloured*, [ii+] 5 pp., sm.4to, *disbound* (Wing W112) **£40.00**

373 **Walsingham** (Thomas) Historia Brevis, ab Edwardo primo, ad Henricum quintum. *Excusum apud Henricum Binnemann*, 1574, *title within woodcut border* [McK. 147], *woodcut portraits of the six monarchs on verso, large device on verso of last leaf, Bb*2-6 *slightly short in tail margins, some early marginal notes and underlinings*, folio, *English (London) blind-stamped calf over wooden bds.* [Oldham SWb5 with another unidentified roll], *sometime rebacked and lettered, lacks part of clasps* (STC 25004) **£750.00**

374 —— Ypodigma Nevstriae vel Normanniae: ab irruptione Normannorum vsq: ad annum 6. regni Henrici quinti. *In aedibus Iohannis Daii*, 1574, *title within woodcut border* [McK. 75 – sl. modified], *woodcut portraits of the seven Norman dukes on verso, a few fox marks near end, otherwise a clean copy* (?washed), [iv+] 197 [+v] pp., folio, *full crimson morocco, lettered, by Sangorski and Sutcliffe* (STC 25005) **£325.00**

¶The object of this work was to provide Henry v. with an instructive summary of the history of his predecessors, the dukes of Normandy; and to furnish an historical justification for his invasion of France.

375 **Walter de Hemingburgh.** Chronicon . . . de Gestis Regum Angliae. Ad fidem Codicum Manuscriptorum recensuit Hans Claude Hamilton. 2 Vols. *English Historical Society*, 1848, MEMBER'S COPY, xvi+356: viii+448 pp., roy.8vo, *orig. cream paper bds., red leather labels, joints cracked and backstrips chipped, all edges untrimmed* **£40.00**

376 **War with France.** Official Papers, presented by his Majesty's Command to both Houses of Parliament on Wednesday, the 18th of May, 1803, relative to the Negociation between Great Britain and the French Government. *Dublin, J. Shea*, 1803, *soiled and embrowned*, [i+] 88 pp., 8vo, *disbound* **£30.00**

377 **Warburton** (Eliot) Memoirs of Prince Rupert, and the Cavaliers. Including their Private Correspondence, now first published from the Original Manuscripts. 3 Vols. *Richard Bentley*, 1849, *with 9 portraits and a plan, foxing throughout*, x+539: vi+492: vi+596 pp., 8vo, *binder's buckram, black leather labels, backstrips faded* **£42.00**

378 **Waring** (Edward Scott) A History of the Mahrattas: to which is prefixed, an historical Sketch of the Decan: containing a short Account of the Rise and Fall of the Mooslim Sovereignties prior to the Aere of Mahratta Independence. *John Richardson*, 1810, *with 2 plates heavily foxed and off-set, otherwise slight discolouration throughout, rubber stamp on front paste-down and recto of frontis. plate*, xii+279 pp., 4to, *orig. drab bds., badly worn but intact, edges uncut*, rare **£265.00**

¶The list of Subscribers would indicate an edition of something over 125 copies.

379 **Warren Family.** WATSON (John) Memoirs of the Ancient Earls of Warren and Surrey, and their Descendants to the Present Time. 2 Vols. *Warrington, William Eyres*, 1782, *with 24 engraved plates, comprising portraits, views, armorial achievements, etc., 9 genealogical tables, 128 small coats of arms in the text, 51 head and tail pieces and 41 decorated initials*, vi+304 [+xvi]: [i+] 245 [+x] pp., lge 4to, *contemp. diced calf, lettered, by I. Bohn, joints rubbed, vol. i. sometime neatly rebacked, orig. backstrip laid down*, scarce **£230.00**

380 **Warwick** (Sir Philip) Memoirs of the Reign of King Charles the First. *Edinburgh, James Ballantyne and Co.*, 1813, *portraits, some discolouration throughout, heavy browning at beginning and end*, xii+473 pp., *advert. leaf*, 8vo, *nineteenth century half calf, black leather label, marbled bds.* **£21.00**

381 [**Wase** (Christopher)] Considerations concerning Free-Schools, as settled in England. *The Theater in Oxford and are to be sold there, and in London at Mr. Simon Millers* . . . 1678, *large vignette on title, slight browning at edges*, [viii+] 112 pp., 8vo, *modern maroon morocco, gilt backstrip lettered, sides panelled in gilt, armorial bookplate on front pastedown* (Wing W1015: Madan 3198) scarce **£300.00**

¶"There remains another advantage of publick Schools: the greatest benefit to Learners after the Master, is a good Library . . . And even in that affluence of Books, which this present Age daily furnishes, although a Parent can afford to provide his Son of such as are cheap and portable for his present use as he proceeds in Learning, yet there are voluminous Authors, Pillars of a Library, which would highly advance Study, yet are not the purchase of every one that is most studious: and therefore best able to use them. In which regard a Library would ever at present be reputed a necessary Member of a School-House." (Author)

382 **Webb** (Sidney and Beatrice) English Poor Law History: Part II: The Last Hundred Years. 2 Vols. *Private Subscription Edition*, 1929, ONE OF 400 SIGNED AND NUMBERED COPIES, *frontis. portraits*, pp. xvi+1–469: vii+469–1085, 8vo., *red and blue cloth as issued, lettered backstrips faded* **£40.00**

383 **W[eidner]** (J[oh.] L[udwig]) Jubileum, sive Speculum Jesuiticum, *s.l., s.n.*, 1643, [viii+] 240 [+xxviii] pp.:
with
BURGUS (Petrus Baptista) Mars Sveco-Germanicvs, sive Rerum à Gvstavo Adolpho Sueciae Rege gestarum libri tres, *Coloniae Agrippinae, Andreae Binghy*, 1641, *engraved title*, [xxii+] 334 pp.:
Two pieces bound together, 12mo, *contemp. vellum, brown leather labels* **£35.00**

384 **Wellington.** DE GREY (The Earl) Characteristics of the Duke of Wellington, apart from his Military Talents. *Thomas Bosworth*, 1853, [i+] 213 pp., 8vo, *orig. mauve cloth, backstrip faded* **£20.00**

385 **Wiesener** (Louis) The Youth of Queen Elizabeth 1533–1558. edited, from the French, by Charlotte M. Yonge. 2 Vols. *Hurst and Blackett*, 1879, xxv+302: viii+290 pp., cr.8vo, *orig. red cloth, decorated in black, lettered in gilt, backstrips faded* **£18.00**

386 **Wilson** (Arthur) The History of Great Britain, being the Life and Reign of King Iames the First, relating to what passed from his first Accesse to the Crown, till his Death. *Richard Lowndes*, 1653, FIRST EDITION, *large portrait, slight discolouration and staining, small piece torn from outer margin of C1, small paper fault in margin of S4, tear up gutter of G1*, [xii+] 292 (should read 300) [+vi] pp., folio, *nineteenth century half brown morocco, lettered, matching cloth sides* (Wing W2888) **£90.00**

¶"As an historian Wilson is very strongly prejudiced against the rule of the Stuarts, but his work is of value because it records contemporary impressions and reminiscences which are of considerable interest". (D.N.B.) There is a short description of New England on pp. 74–6.

387 [—— (John, *Recorder*)] A Discourse of Monarchy, more particularly, of the Imperial Crowns of England, Scotland, and Ireland, according to the Ancient, Common, and Statute-Laws of the same. With a Close from the whole, as it relates to the Succession of his Royal Highness, James Duke of York. *M.C. for Jes. Hindmarsh*, 1684, *lightly browned throughout*, [xiv+] 272 pp., sm.8vo, *contemp. morocco, gilt, g.e., unlettered, head of backstrip slightly defective, slight worming of covers only* (Wing W2921) **£50.00**

388 **Witchcraft.** GLANVIL (Joseph) Saducismus Triumphatus: or, Full and Plain Evidence concerning Witches and Apparitions. In Two Parts . . . Second Edition . . . With two Authentick, but wonderful Stories of certain Swedish Witches, done into English by Anth. Horneck. *Tho. Newcomb, for S. Lownds*, 1682, *engr. frontis. and cuts in the text, engr. title, general and divisional printed titles, one misbound, some ll. working loose, generally soiled by use*, [xx+] 52 [+x+] 162 [+vi+] 78 [+blank+ix+] 173+67+45 (shd. read 43) [+xvi+] 24 [+i] pp., 8vo, *contemp. calf, corners worn, rubbed, sometime rebacked, red leather label, but now rubbed and wearing* (Wing S823) **£120.00**

389 **Wolsey.** GALT (John) The Life and Administration of Cardinal Wolsey *T. Cadell and W. Davies*, 1812, *slight foxing, lacks the portrait*, xx+268+ccxxxiii pp., lge.4to, *contemp. russia gilt, sometime rebacked and orig. backstrip laid down, with the armorial bookplate of Chandos Leigh, First Baron Leigh of the second creation* **£35.00**

390 —— [GROVE (Joseph)] The History of the Life and Times of Cardinal Wolsey, Prime Minister to King Henry viii. . . . in which are interspersed the Lives and memorable Actions of the most eminent Persons: And the whole illustrated with Political and Moral Reflections. Collected from ancient Records, MSS., and Historians. 4 Vols., *J. Purser, for the Author* . . . 1742, *with 40 engraved plates of portraits and views*, 8vo, *contemp. sprinkled calf, leather labels, one missing, gilt lines, joints of vol. 1 cracking* **£140.00**

391 **Wool.** TUCKER (Josiah) Reflections on the Present Low Price of Course Wools, its immediate Causes, and its probable Remedies. *T. Cadell*, 1782, *fore-edges and corners dog-eared, a few marginal tears, name cut from head of title*, 46 [+i] pp., 8vo, *orig. wrappers, unlettered* **£46.00**

¶Tucker suggests national lotteries, etc., to fund the provision of allotments and housing to encourage the raising of a new generation who can be wrapped in wool from birth to death.

392 **Wraxall** (Sir N. William) Historical Memoirs of my own Time from 1772 to 1784. 2 Vols. *T. Cadell and W. Davies*, 1815, FIRST EDITION, *portrait, some browning*, iv+549: [iv+] 583 pp.:
[with]
Quarterly Review, 1815, pp. 193–215: British Critic, 1815, July, pp. 17–31: Edinburgh Review, 1815, June, pp. 168–220: Wraxall (Nath. W.) Answer to the Calumnious Misrepresentations . . . 1815, 62 pp. Edinburgh Review, 1815, pp. 527–541: Review and Reply to "An Answer . . .": Wraxall (Nath. W.) A Second Answer to the Calumnious Attacks . . . 1816, 27 pp.:
Bound into 2 Vols., 8vo, *contemp. sprinkled calf, backstrip gilt, black and green leather labels, corners worn, joints beginning to crack, lacks front free endpaper to vol. i.* **£65.00**

393 —— The History of France, under the Kings of the Race of Valois, from the Accession of Charles the Fifth, in 1364, to the Death of Charles the Ninth, in 1574. Second Edition, with very considerable Augmentations. 2 Vols. *C. Dilly*, 1785, [x+] 320: [vii+] 290 pp., 8vo, *contemp. grained calf, black leather labels slightly chipped, joints becoming tender* **£40.00**

394 —— —— to the Death of Louis the Fourteenth. Preceded by a View of the Civil, Military, and Political State of Europe, between the Middle, and the Close of the Sixteenth Century. 3 Vols. [all published], *A. Strahan and T. Cadell, sold by T. Cadell Junior and W. Davies*, 1795, *slight foxing*, xiv+588: viii+514: vii+462 pp., 4to., *contemp. tan calf, red leather labels, slight rubbing, two backstrips little defective, one joint cracked* **£55.00**

395 **Yarranton** (Andrew) England's Improvement by Sea and Land, to Out-do the Dutch without fighting, to pay Debts without Moneys . . . [Part I. only], *Printed by R. Everingham*, 1677, *with 6 plates (ex 8), three torn, bur repaired, imprimatur leaf present*, [xxxix+] 195 pp., sm.4to, *contemp. mottled calf, corners worn, slightly rubbed, unlettered* (Wing Y13) **£50.00**

RARE AND SCHOLARLY

BOOKS ON THE LAW
(1978)

JOHN SELDEN

"The giveing a booke seller his price for his bookes, has this advantage, he that will doe it shall be sure to have the refusall of what soever comes to his hands. and soe by that means gett many things which otherwise he never should have seen. So tis in giveing a Baud her price." Selden's Table Talk (see Items 373 and 374).

CATALOGUE ONE

MEYER BOSWELL BOOKS
SAN FRANCISCO

Illustrations by Cruikshank.
1. A'BECKETT, Gilbert Abbott. Comic Blackstone. A New Edition. London, Bradbury & Evans, 1856. **$65.00**
Attractively bound in ¾ blue calf and cloth, slightly rubbed, gilt-lined covers, elaborately gilt-decorated, lined and lettered spine, marbled end papers, and all edges gilt; endpapers lightly foxed. The classic spoof of Blackstone, patterned after the Commentaries' divisions of persons, property, private wrongs and public wrongs. With the copper-engraved frontispiece, pictorial title page and tail-piece by George Cruikshank, and a letter from the English bookseller Henry Sotheran laid in explaining the edition.

2. ACHESON, Patricia C. The Supreme Court. Dodd, Mead 1961. **$7.50**

3. AKITA, George. Foundations of Constitutional Government in Modern Japan, 1868 – 1900. Harvard, 1967. **$12.50**

4. ALEXANDROWICZ, Charles H. The Law-Making Functions of the Specialized Agencies of the United Nations. Angus & Robertson, 1973. **$10.00**

5. ALFANGE, Dean. The Supreme Court and the National Will. Kennikat, 1967. **$8.50**

6. ALLEN, Francis A. The Crimes of Politics. Harvard, 1974. **$10.00**
The 1973 Holmes Lectures.

7. AMERICANO, Jorge. The New Foundation of International Law. MacMillan, 1947. **$7.50**

8. ANDERSON, J.N.D. (ed.). Family Law in Asia and Africa. Praeger, 1967. **$10.00**

9. ANDRASSY, Juraj. International Law and the Resources of the Sea. Columbia, 1970. **$10.00**

10. ARNOLD, Thurman. The Symbols of Government. Yale, 1937. **$10.00**

11. (ARNOLD, Thurman). GENE M. GRESSLEY. Voltaire and the Cowboy, the Letters of Thurman Arnold. Colorado Associate University Press, 1979. New. **$15.00**

12. (ARNOLD, Thurman). EDWARD N. KEARNY. Thurman Arnold, Social Critic. New Mexico, 1970. **$8.50**

13. ARONSON, Moses J. Tendencies in American Jurisprudence. 19pp., wraps, slightly soiled. **$8.50**
Presentation Copy from Aronson; a reprint of his 1941 Toronto Law Journal article.

14. ASCH, Sidney H. The Supreme Court and Its Great Justices. Arco, 1972. **$7.00**

15. (ASSOCIATION OF THE BAR OF THE CITY OF NEW YORK). Lectures on Legal Topics, 1922-23. MacMillan, 1928. **$25.00**
Original maroon cloth, gilt lettering in a worn dust wrapper. Articles by **Roscoe Pound** and **Harlan F. Stone**, among others.

16. (ASSOCIATION OF THE BAR OF THE CITY OF NEW YORK). Report of the Special Committee on the Federal Loyalty-Security Program. Dodd, Mead, 1956. **$12.50**
Committee members included **Henry J. Friendly** and **Dudley Bonsal**; on the staff was **Elliott Cheatham**, among others.

17. AUERBACH, Jerold S. Unequal Justice. Oxford, 1976. **$12.50**

18. AUSTIN, John. Lectures on Jurisprudence. Abridged from the Larger Work for the Use of Students by Robert Campbell of Lincoln's Inn. Henry Holt, 1875. **$30.00**
Campbell edited the volume of Austin's Lectures published in 1869 and based in part on John Stuart Mill's lecture notes. This is the **first issuance** of the abridged edition, which was thereafter reprinted many times. An attractive copy, in the original cloth, gilt spine.

An Early Collected Edition.
19. BACON, Francis. The Works of Francis Bacon, Baron of Verulam, Viscount St. Alban, and Lord High Chancellor of England. Five volumes, quarto. London, 1778. **$225.00**
Full contemporary calf, elaborate gilt-decorated spines, contrasting red and black labels, but the binding quite worn, joints broken but reinforced. Internally, a wide-margined, clean copy. Volume II is devoted in substantial part to Bacon's legal works including his **Elements of the Common Laws of England** and his **Charge Touching Duels.** With a portrait of Bacon, 3 frontispieces and folding plan, and the **title pages in red and black.**

20. (BARRY, Sir John). Law and Crime: Essays in Honor of Sir John Barry. Edited by Norval Morris and Mark Perlman. Gordon and Breach, 1972. **$10.00**

21. BARNETT, Walter. Sexual Freedom and the Constitution. New Mexico, 1973. **$8.50**

22. BARROS, James. The Aland Islands Question. Yale, 1968. **$10.00**

23. BAUM, Daniel J. The Welfare Family and Mass Administration of Justice. Praeger, 1974. **$8.75**

24. BEATTIE, Ronald H. A System of Criminal Judicial Statistics for California. Berkeley, 1936. **$15.00**

25. BALLENTINE, James A. A Law Dictionary. Rochester, 1923. **$25.00**

Original limp green leather, gilt lettered, printed on "Bible" paper. A nice copy of an early issue.

26. BECCARIA, Caesar Bonesana, Marquis. An Essay on Crimes and Punishments. Academic Reprints, Stanford, 1954. **$12.50**
Reprinted from the Second American Edition of 1819.

27. BECK, James M. The Vanishing Rights of the States. Doran, 1926. **$12.50**
With Beck's complimentary card laid in.

29. BELLI, Melvin M. The Law Revolution. Sherbourne Press, 1968. First Printing. **$15.00**
Presentation copy from Belli to Jim Eason, a San Francisco media personality; with a publicity release laid in.

30. BENTHAM, Jeremy. Bentham's Theory of Legislation . . ., translated and edited from the French of Etienne Dumont by Charles Milner Atkinson. Two vols. O.U.P., 1914. **$30.00**
An important edition. This work first appeared in French in 1802, based on manuscripts Bentham made available to Dumont, but with additions of Dumont's own. The Bowring and Hildreth translations are of Dumont; this is the first translation based on an examination of Bentham's manuscripts.

31. (BENTHAM, Jeremy). CHARLES ATKINSON. Jeremy Bentham, His Life and Work. Greenwood Press, 1970. **$10.00**
Originally published in 1905.

32. BERGER, Raoul. Impeachment: The Constitutional Problems. Harvard, 1973. **$11.50**

33. BETH, Loren P. The American Theory of Church and State. University of Florida Press, 1958. **$7.50**

34. BICKEL, Alexander M. The Morality of Consent. Yale, 1975. **$10.00**
Includes a bibliography of Bickel's work.

35. BISHOP, Joseph W., Jr. Justice Under Fire, a Study of Military Law. Charterhouse, 1974. **$8.75**

36. BITTKER, Boris I. The Case for Black Reparations. Random House, 1973. **$8.50**

37. BLACK, Charles L., Jr. The Occasions of Justice. MacMillan, 1963. **$10.00**

38. BLACK, Donald. The Behavior of Law. Academic Press, 1976. **$10.00**

39. (BLACK, Hugo). HOWARD BALL. The Vision and the Dream of Justice Hugo L. Black. University of Alabama Press, 1975. **$8.50**

40. (BLACK, Hugo). HUGO BLACK, JR. My Father: A Remembrance. Random House, 1975. **$7.50**

41. (BLACK, Hugo.) IRVING DILLIARD (ed.). One Man's Stand for Freedom. Knopf, 1971. **$10.00**

42. (BLACK, Hugo). GERALD T. DUNNE. Hugo Black and the Judicial Revolution. Simon and Schuster, 1977. **$8.50**

43. (BLAKESLEE, George Hubbard). DWIGHT E. LEE & GEORGE E. McREYNOLDS (ed). Essays in History and International Relations in Honor of . . . Kennikat, 1969. **$8.50**

44. BLAUSTEIN, Albert P. and Charles O. Porter. The American Lawyer. Chicago, 1954. **$10.00**

45 B[LOUNT], T[homas]. Fragmenta Antiquitatis. Antient Tenures of Land, and Jocular Customs of Some Mannors. Made public for the diversion of some, and instruction of others. London, 1679. Wing B.3333. **$100.00**
First Edition. New half calf, marbled boards, spine gilt lettered and gilt & blind ruled, occasional very light foxing. An attractive copy of a work "for those weary with poring upon *Littletons Tenures* and his Learned Commentator" (presumably Coke), and termed by Holdsworth the "only really original book" produced on legal history in the latter part of the 17th century.

46. BODENHEIMER, Edgar. Treatise on Justice. Philosophical Library, 1967. **$8.50**

47. BOHANNAN, Paul (ed.) Law and Warfare, Studies in the Anthropology of Conflict. The Natural History Press, 1967. **$8.50**

48. BONNER, Robert J. Lawyers and Litigants in Ancient Athens. Barnes & Noble, 1969. **$10.00**
Originally published in 1927.

49. BORKIN, Joseph. The Corrupt Judge. Clarkson N. Potter, 1962. **$8.50**

50. BOTEIN, Bernard. Trial Judge. Simon & Schuster, 1952. **$8.50**

51. BOUDIN, Louis B. Government by Judiciary. William Godwin, 1932. Two vols. **$25.00**

52. BOYD, Julian P. Fundamental Laws and Constitutions of New Jersey. Van Nostrand, 1964. **$7.50**

53. BOZELL, L. Brent. The Warren Revolution. Arlington House, 1966. **$8.50**

"the crown and flower of English medieval jurisprudence" — Maitland
54. BRACTON, Henrici de. De Legibus & Consuetudinibus Angliae. London, Richard Tottel, 1569. 2 (blank), title, 15 leaves, folios 1-444, 2(blank). Beale T323, STC 3475, Printing and the Mind of Man 89. **$2,000.00**
First edition of one of the greatest works of English Law. Old calf, slightly worn, rebacked, gilt & blind tooled, gilt lettered spine, marbled endpapers; marginal annotations in Latin & French, & underlining throughout, title page slightly soiled, very occasional embrowning, but generally *a very clean, wide-margined and highly desirable copy.*

Professor Thorne's contributions to Bractonian scholarship lay the creation of this work not only to Bracton, but to others, and he places the writing of much of the treatise in the first third of the 13th century; yet his contributions to a near century of scholarly debate leave untouched Maitland's characterization (quoted above) of this work's place in English legal history.

With the **signature of Sir Francis Winnington**, created solicitor general in 1674, on the title page; likewise the signature (dated 1799) of **Arthur Browne,** Regius Professor of Civil and Canon Law at Trinity College, Dublin, and the author of "A Compendius View of the Civil Law"; and the bookplate of **S.M. Leake,** author of several highly regarded 19th century works on the law of property and contract.

A handsome copy of the first edition, in folio, termed by Plucknett "a stately volume, perhaps the best printed law book we have ever had."

55. (BRANDEIS, Louis D.). ALEXANDER M. BICKEL. The Unpublished Opinions of Mr. Justice Brandeis. Belknap, 1957. **$17.50**
With an introduction by **Paul A. Freund.**

56. (BRANDEIS, Louis D.). ALPHEUS THOMAS MASON. Brandeis, A Free Man's Life. The Viking Press, 1946. **$17.50**
Inscribed by **Mason.**

57. (BRENNAN, William J., Jr.). STEPHEN J. FRIEDMAN (ed.). An Affair with Freedom. Atheneum, 1967. **$10.00**
With a foreword by **Arthur J. Goldberg.**

58. BRIERLY, J. L. The Law of Nations. Fourth Edition. Clarendon Press, 1949. **$8.50**

59. BRYANT, Margaret M. English in the Law Courts. Ungar, 1962. **$8.50**

60. BRYSON, William Hamilton. Census of Law Books in Colonial Virginia. University Press of Virginia, 1978. New. **$12.00**

61. BRYSON, William Hamilton (ed.). The Virginia Law Reporters Before 1800. University Press of Virginia, 1977. New. **$9.75**

Articles on **Bushrod Washington, Thomas Jefferson** and **George Wythe,** among others

62. BURN, Richard. Ecclesiastical Law. Second Edition, London, 1767. Four volumes, 8 vo. (6) xxxi, 503; 488; 502; 380, (92) pp. **$125.00**
Arranged alphabetically, Burns' work first appeared four years previously in two volumes, expanded to four in this edition, with the bulk of Volume IV devoted to Wills; one of only two works on ecclesiastical law which, according to Blackstone, "can be relied on with any degree of certainty" (Commentaries *392, note). *Attractively and unusually bound* in contemporary crimson morocco, spines elaborately gilt-tooled; a very nice set, though (as the bookseller from whom we purchased the set — himself a binder — remarked) "it's clear the binder seldom got such ambitious commissions." Internally, apart from scattered and very lightish damp marking, an exceptionally clean set of the work Holdsworth called "the clearest and most successful of all the great treatises upon English ecclesiastical law."

63. BUTLER, William E. The Soviet Union and the Law of the Sea. Johns Hopkins, 1971. **$8.50**

64. CAHN, Edmond. Confronting Injustice. Gollancz, 1967. **$12.50**
With a foreward by **Hugo Black.**

A Unique Presentation Copy
65. CALHOUN, George M. The Growth of Criminal Law in Ancient Greece. Berkeley, 1927. **$35.00**
Presentation Copy from Professor Calhoun to **Orin K. McMurray,** whose manuscript suggestions Calhoun acknowledges in the Prefatory Note.

A Magnificent Set
66. CAMPBELL, John, Lord. The Lives of the Lord Chancellors and Keepers of the Great Seal of England, from the Earliest Times Till the Reign of King George IV. *Seven volumes.* London, 1846-47. **$250.00**
Uniformly and very handsomely bound in contemporary polished calf, spines richly gilt tooled, five raised bands, covers gilt & blind tooled, with some minor rubbing, marbled endpapers and all edges marbled.

With the bookplate & unobtrusive library stamp of Edward Bibby, and a few pencil notations, dated 1857, of J. Hartley, who (in the words of the bookseller from whom we purchased the set) "in the passage on the quarrel between Lord Eldon & Mr. Abercromby was outraged by the author's references to Abercromby's 'high sense of honour' and noted 'Abercromby acted towards me not only Dishonourably but as a *Scoundrel*. . . ' beyond which I can make very little of the note since the poor old boy obviously became quite incoherent with rage. For a more polished assassination of Abercromby see DNB: the final clause of the first sentence of the second paragraph is a nice example of how to put the knife in *quietly.* Of course a good many old scores were settled in DNB, and many an old man clung desperately to life in the hope of outliving rivals and having the chance to write their obituaries."

Beginning with the chancellors under the Anglo-Saxons, Campbell proceeds to **A Beckett, More, Bacon, Hardwicke** and **Camden**, among others, before finishing with **Eldon**.

67. CAPLOVITZ, David. The Poor Pay More. Free Press, 1963. **$8.50**

68. CARDOZO, Benjamin N. The Nature of the Judicial Process. Yale, 1925. **$17.50**
An uncut, early issue in the dustwrapper of Cardozo's 1921 **Storrs Lectures** at Yale.

69. CARLIN, Jerome E. Lawyers on their Own. Rutgers, 1962. **$10.00**

70. CARLSTON, Kenneth S. Law and Organization in World Society. Illinois, 1962. **$8.50**

71. CASPER, Jonathan D. Lawyers before the Warren Court: Civil Liberties and Civil Rights, 1957-66. Illinois, 1972. **$10.00**

72. CASTANEDA, Jorge. Legal Effects of United Nations Resolutions. Columbia, 1969. **$10.00**

73. CHAFEE, Zechariah, Jr. Free Speech in the United States. Harvard, 1942. **$25.00**

74. CHAFEE, Zechariah, Jr. State House versus Pent House, Legal Problems of the Rhode Island Race-Track Row. Providence, 1937. Illus., xxii, 165 pp., sewn wraps. **$20.00**
Dorr Pamphlet No. 1. The first issuance in a series devoted to Rhode Island affairs, edited by Chafee, a Rhode Island native.

75. CHALIDZE, Valery (trans. Guy Daniels). To Defend These Rights, Human Rights and the Soviet Union. Random House, 1974. **$8.50**

76. CHASE, Harold W. Federal Judges, The Appointment Process. Minnesota, 1972. **$8.75**

77. CHEATHAM, Elliot Evans. A Lawyer When Needed. Columbia, 1964. **$7.50**
The **1963 James S. Carpentier Lectures** at Columbia.

78. (CHOATE, Joseph H.). FREDERICK C. HICKS (ed.). Arguments and Addresses of Joseph H. Choate. West, 1926. **$22.50**
With a memorial by **Elihu Root**. Binding slightly worn.

79. CHOATE, Rufus. Addresses and Orations of . . . Little, Brown, 1879. Third Edition. **$35.00**
Original reddish-brown cloth; front cover very slightly spotted. Else a nice copy, with decorated & blind ruled covers & spine gilt-lettered, still bright.

80. CLARK, Grenville and Louis B. Sohn. World Peace Through World Law. Harvard, 1958. **$15.00**

81. CLAVIR, Judy and John Spitzer. The Conspiracy Trial. The extended edited transcript of the trial of the Chicago Eight. Complete with motions, rulings, contempt citations, sentences and photographs. Bobbs-Merrill, 1970. **$12.50**
With an introduction by **William Kunstler** and a foreword by **Leonard Weinglass.**

82. COHEN, Morris R. Law and the Social Order, Essays in Legal Philosophy. Harcourt, Brace, 1933. **$25.00**
Presentation Copy of the **First Edition**, in a worn dustwrapper.

83. (COKE, Sir Edward). W. O. HASSALL (ed.). A Catalogue of the Library of Sir Edward Coke. Yale, 1950. xxvii, 96 pp., sewn wraps. **$17.50**
Yale Law Library Publications, No. 12. With a Preface by **Samuel E. Thorne.**

84. COLLIER, Jane F. Law and Social Change in Zinacantan. Stanford, 1973. **$10.00**

85. (COLUMBIA LAW REVIEW). Essays on Jurisprudence from the Columbia Law Review. Columbia, 1963. **$25.00**
Foreward by **William O. Douglas;** articles by **Frankfurter, Friedmann, Hand, Llewellyn** and **Pound,** among others.

86. CONQUEST, Robert (ed.). Justice and the Legal System in the U.S.S.R. Praeger, 1969. **$7.50**

87. COOK, William W. American Institutions and Their Preservation. Two vols. Privately Printed, New York, 1929. Second Edition. **$20.00**
The author's largesse resulted in the Cook Law Quadrangle at Michigan.

88. COOPER, John Cobb. Explorations in Aerospace Law. McGill, 1968. **$15.00**

89. CORBETT, Percy E. The Growth of World Law. Princeton, 1971. **$8.50**

90. CORTNER, Richard C. The Apportionment Cases. Tennessee, 1970. **$10.00**

91. CORWIN, Edward S. The Twilight of the Supreme Court, A History of Our Constitutional Theory. Yale, 1935. **$15.00**
The **1934 Storrs Lectures;** with a foreward by *Charles E. Clark.*

92. COSTIGAN, George P. Handbook on American Mining Law. West, 1908. **$25.00**
First edition of this well-known work; original buckram, somewhat soiled, with contrasting red and black spine labels, gilt lettering, owner's name stamp liberally dotting front cover & edges, some pencil notations.

The early mining communities did not take kindly to lawyers; Costigan notes early regulations imposing "banishment for Asiatics, whipping and banishment for practising lawyers." (p.3).

93. COUDERT, Frederic R. A Half Century of International Problems. Columbia, 1956. **$7.50**

94. COX, Archibald. The Warren Court. Harvard, 1971. **$10.00**

95. (CRAVATH, Swaine & Moore). ROBERT T. SWAINE. The Cravath Firm and Its Predecessors, 1819-1947. Three Volumes. Privately Printed, New York, 1948. **$65.00**
Original red cloth, gilt-lettered spine; spines lightly and uniformly faded, bindings very lightly shaken, but sound.

96. CROSS, Rupert. Precedent in English Law. Oxford, 1961. **$12.50**
The fifth volume in the **Clarendon Law Series,** editied by *H.L.A. Hart.*

97. COOLEY, Thomas M. The General Principles of Constitutional Law in the United States of America. Second Edition. Little Brown, 1891. **$25.00**
Cooley intended this volume as a manual for law students, the first edition being published in 1880; this edition was edited by Alexis Angell of Detroit. A very nice copy in the original blue cloth, spine gilt-lettered and ruled.

98. DALTON, Michael. Officium Vicecomitum. The Office and Authority of Sheriffs: Gathered Out of the Statutes, and Books of the Common Laws of this Kingdom. London, 1682. Title page, (2), 1-500, (4), 501-564, (27). Wing D153. **$250.00**
A very nice copy, attractively bound in ¾ mottled calf, red label, gilt-lettered; occasional underscoring & marginal notations, some embrowning, insignificant worming to one leaf not affecting text. With the separate title page for the appendix.

A *handsome folio edition* of the work called by Holdsworth "a standard authority till the beginning of the eighteenth century."

99. DAUBE, David. Roman Law, Linguistic, Social and Philosophical Aspects. Edinburgh, 1969. **$10.00**
The **1966 Gray Lectures** at Cambridge.

100. DAVIS, Kenneth Culp. Discretionary Justice. Louisiana State, 1969. **$10.00**
The **1966 Edward Douglass White Lectures.**

101. DAWSON, Philip. Provincial Magistrates and Revolutionary Politics in France, 1789-1795. Harvard, 1972. **$11.50**

102. DEAN, Arthur H. William Nelson Cromwell 1854-1948. Privately printed, New York, 1957. **$17.50**
The Cromwell of Sullivan and Cromwell. With a foreword by John Foster Dulles, who notes his own 1911 starting salary of $50, an innovation gratefully received, young lawyers previously working for nothing "on the theory, no doubt correct, that what they learned was far more valuable than anything they contributed." (p.iii).

103. DE LOLME, J. L. The Constitution of England. A New Edition. London, 1821. **$50.00**
Bound in ¾ calf, the spine elaborately gilt and blind tooled, marbled endpapers. A nice copy of a classic work, by a man "whose genius and abilities were only obscured by his imprudent and extravagant habits" according to his biographer, **MacGregor.**

104. DEL VECCHIO, Giorgio (ed. RALPH A. NEWMAN; trans. A. H. CAMPBELL). Selected Essays. Notre Dame, 1969. **$20.00**
Presentation Copy from the editor to **Lewis M. Simes.**

105. DENG, Francis Mading. Tradition and Modernization, A Challenge for Law among the Dinka of the Sudan. Yale, 1971. **$12.50**
Foreward by **Harold D. Lasswell.**

106. DERRETT, J. Duncan M. Religion, Law and the State in India. Free Press, 1968. **$10.00**

107. DICEY, A.V. A Leap in the Dark or Our New Constitution. London, 1893. **$22.50**

108. DICKERSON, Reed. The Fundamentals of Legal Drafting. Little, Brown, 1965. **$10.00**

109. DIETZ, Arthur T. An Introduction to the Antitrust Laws. Bookman, 1951. **$10.00**

110. DIXON, Robert G., Jr. Democratic Representation, Reapportionment in Law and Politics. Oxford, 1968. **$10.00**

111. DONNER, André M. The Role of the Lawyer in the European Communities. Northwestern, 1968. **$10.00**
The **1966 Rosenthal Lectures** at Northwestern.

112. DONOVAN, James B. Challenges: Reflections of a Lawyer-at-Large. Atheneum, 1967. **$15.00**
Presentation Copy of the **First Edition**; with a foreward by **Erwin N. Griswold.**

113. DORSEN, Norman (ed.). The Rights of Americans. Pantheon, 1972. **$10.00**
Articles by **Anthony Amsterdam, Thomas Emerson** and **Michael Tigar,** among others.

114. DOUGLAS, William O. Go East, Young Man. Random House, 1974. **$35.00**
Presentation Copy of the **First Edition.**

115. (DUGUIT, Leon.). The Law and the State. Cambridge, 1917. **$20.00**
A special number (November, 1917) of the Harvard Law Review containing the first appearance of this essay; and devoted exclusively to it; with a note on Duguit by **Harold Laski,** who at the time was Book Review Editor of the Review; in the original wraps, with some chipping and embrowning and contemporary pencil annotations.

116. DUNKEL, Wilbur. William Lambarde, Elizabethan Jurist. Rutgers, 1965. **$10.00**

117. DWINELLE, John W. The Colonial History of San Francisco, Ross Valley, 1978. New **$10.00**
As attorney for San Francisco, Dwinelle submitted the major portion of this work as a brief, in effect a history of the city, designed to prove the existence of the Pueblo of San Francisco, and thus the city's entitlement to four leagues of land including the city site. The result was the city's vindication and one of the West's most important historical works. Reprinted from the 4th (and best) edition of 1867.

118. EDWARDS, J. LL. J. Mens Rea in Statutory Offences. MacMillan 1955. **$12.50**
The sixth volume of *English Studies in Criminal Science* edited by **Sir Leon Radzinowicz.**

119. ELZINGA, Kenneth G. and William Breit. The Antitrust Penalties: A Study in Law and Economics. Yale, 1976. **$8.50**

120. EMERSON, Thomas I. Toward A General Theory of the First Amendment. Random House, 1966. **$12.50**

121. ERNST, Morris. A Love Affair with the Law. MacMillan, 1968. **$7.50**

122. (EVIDENCE). The Law of Evidence, Some Proposals for Its Reform. Yale, 1927. **$25.00**
The results of the efforts of a committee of the *Commonwealth Fund,* formed in 1920 to encourage legal research; contributing committee members include **Edmund Morgan, Zachariah Chafee** and **John H. Wigmore,** among others. With a gilt lined & lettered front cover and spine, and a complimentary card of the Legal Research Committee of the Fund laid in.

123. FALK, Richard A. (ed.). The International Law of Civil War. Johns Hopkins, 1971. **$10.00**
Published under the auspices of the American Society of International Law.

124. FALLERS, Lloyd A. Law Without Precedent, Legal Ideas in Action in the Courts of Colonial Busoga. Chicago, 1969. **$10.00**

125. FAWCETT, J. E. S. The Law of Nations. Basic Books, 1968. **$7.50**

126. FEIFER, George. Justice in Moscow. Simon and Schuster, 1964. **$8.50**

127. FEINSTEIN, Isidor. The Court Disposes. Covici, Friede, 1937. **$8.50**

128. FENN, Percy Thomas. The Origin of the Right of Fishery in Territorial Waters. Crofton, 1974. **$10.00**
First published in 1926.

129. FERNALD, Charles. A County Judge in Arcady, Select Papers of Charles Fernald, Pioneer California Jurist. Arthur H. Clark, 1954. **$17.50**

130. FIELD, Stephen J. Personal Reminiscences of Early Days in California. DaCapo, 1968. **$15.00**
A reissue of the first edition of 1893; included is Gorham's account of Field's attempted assassination.

131. FLEMING, D. F. The United States and the League of Nations 1918-1920. Russell, 1968. **$12.50**

132. FLEMING, Donald and Bernard Bailyn (eds.). Law in American History. Little, Brown, 1971. **$17.50**
Essays by **James Willard Hurst** and **Morton J. Horwitz,** among others.

133. FLEMING, John G. An Introduction to the Law of Torts. Oxford, 1967. **$10.00**
The 10th volume in the *Clarendon Law Series* edited by **H. L. A. Hart.**

134. FLEMING, R. W. The Labor Arbitration Process. Illinois, 1965. **$8.50**

135. FLORIOT, Rene. When Justice Falters. Harrap, 1972. **$7.50**
Translated from the French by Rayner Heppenstall.

136. FORSYTH, William. History of Trial by Jury. Cockcroft, 1878. Second edition. **$35.00**
Original brown & decorated cloth, gilt spine; *a nice copy.*

137. FORTESCUE, Sir John. The Difference Between an Absolute and Limited Monarchy. London, 1714. Title page, (14), lxxxii, (4), 1-148, (4) pp. Octavo. First Edition. **$150.00**
A contemporary of Littleton, Fortescue initially sided with the Lancastrian cause during the War of the Roses; his subsequent reflections while in exile in the late 1400's led to this treatise (sometimes referred to as **The Governance of England**), his only work in English, in which he postulated the necessity for a limited or constitutional monarchy, whether Yorkist or Lancastrian.

A *handsome copy* – newly bound in dark, sprinkled calf, blind ruled, gilt-lettered spine – of the **First Edition** *of the seminal work on English constitutional history.*

139. FRANK, Jerome. Law and the Modern Mind. Coward-McCann, 1949. **$12.50**
The first issue with Frank's lengthy essay reconsidering this work, first published in 1930.

140. (FRANK, Jerome). J. MITCHELL ROSENBERG, Jerome Frank: Jurist and Philosopher. Philosophical Library, 1970. **$7.50**

140. FRANKEL, Marvin E. Criminal Sentences. Hill and Wang, 1973. **$7.50**

141. FRANKFURTER, Felix. Of Law and Life & Other Things That Matter. Belknap, 1965. **$10.00**
Frankfurter's papers and addresses between 1956 and 1963; edited by Philip B. Kurland.

142. (FRANKFURTER, Felix). HARLAN B. PHILLIPS. Felix Frankfurter Reminisces. Reynal, 1960. First Edition. **$10.00**

143. (FRANKFURTER, Felix). Roosevelt & Frankfurter, Their Correspondence 1928-1945. Bodley Head, 1968. **$12.50**

144. FREEDMAN, Max, William M. Beaney, and Eugene V. Rostow. Perspectives on the Court. Northwestern, 1967. **$10.00**
The **1966 Rosenthal Lectures** at Northwestern.

145. FRIEDMAN, Lawrence M. A History of American Law. Simon and Schuster, 1973. **$11.50**

146. FRIEDMAN, Leon (ed.). Argument: The Complete oral argument before the Supreme Court in Brown v. Board of Education of Topeka, 1952-55. Chelsea House, 1969. **$15.00**

147. FRIEDMANN, Wolfgang. Legal Theory. Fifth Edition. New. **$20.00**

148. FRIEDMANN, Wolfgang and J. F. Garner (eds.). Government Enterprise, A Comparative Study. Columbia, 1970. **$12.00**

149. FRIENDLY, Henry J. The Federal Administrative Agencies. Harvard, 1962. **$12.50**
The **1972 James S. Carpentier Lectures** at Columbia.

151. (FRY, Sir Edward). AGNES FRY. A Memoir of the Right Honorable Sir Edward Fry. Oxford, 1921. **$22.50**
Fry, Lord Justice of the Court of Appeal, authored the article on **Selden** for the D.N.B.

152. GAMBLE, John King (ed.). Law of the Sea: The Emerging Regime of the Oceans. Ballinger, 1973. **$10.00**

153. GANZGLASS, Martin R. The Penal Code of the Somali Democratic Republic. Rutgers, 1971. **$13.50**

154. GARVEY, Gerald. Constitutional Bricolage. Princeton, 1971. **$9.50**

155. GELLHORN, Walter. Security, Loyalty & Science. Cornell, 1950. **$12.50**

156. GIGEROFF, Alex. K. Sexual Deviations in the Criminal Law; Homosexual, Exhibitionistic, and Pedophilic Offences in Canada. Toronto, 1968. **$10.00**

157. GINGER, Ann Fagan. The Relevant Lawyers. Simon & Schuster, 1972. **$7.50**

158. GOLDBERG, Arthur J. The Defenses of Freedom. Harper & Row, 1966. **$10.00**

159. GOLDFARB, Ronald L. The Contempt Power. Columbia, 1963. **$12.00**

160. GOLDING, M. P. (ed.). The Nature of Law, Readings in Legal Philosophy. Random House, 1966. **$10.00**
Excerpts from the writings of **Maine, Hart, Holmes, Kelsen and Fuller,** among others.

161. GOULD, Wesley L. and Michael Barkun. International Law and the Social Sciences. Princeton, 1970. **$9.50**

162. GOULDEN, Joseph C. The Benchwarmers. Weybright and Talley, 1974. **$8.50**

163. GOULDEN, Joseph C. The Superlawyers. Weybright and Talley, 1972. **$8.50**

164. GREEN, Edward. Judicial Attitudes in Sentencing. MacMillan, 1961. **$9.00**
Volume XV in the **Cambridge Studies in Criminology** edited by *Sir Leon Radzinowicz.*

165. GREENBERG, Jack. Race Relations and American Law. Columbia, 1959. **$10.00**

166. (GROTIUS, Hugo). EDWARD DUMBAULD. The Life and Legal Writings of Hugo Grotius. Oklahoma, 1969. **$10.00**
The only work in English devoted exclusively to Grotius' legal works.

167. HADLEY, Eleanor M. Antitrust in Japan. Princeton, 1970. **$15.00**

168. HAIR, Paul (ed.). Before the Bawdy Court, Selections from Church court and other records relating to the correction of moral offences in England, Scotland and New England, 1300-1800. Elek, 1972. **$9.00**

169. HALE, Sir Matthew. Contemplations Moral and Divine. London, 1695. Wing H.230. **$90.00**
Hale is said to have set aside Sundays for his reflections, and as a matter of discipline to have recorded his thoughts for his own personal use; these thoughts, partly embodied in this volume, were published without his consent, the work in its original publication being in the press when he died in 1676.
A very nice copy in contemporary panelled and sprinkled calf, gilt, with George Baillie's bookplate.

The first general history of English Law
170. HALE, Sir Matthew. The History of the Common Law of England. Third Edition. London, 1739. (2), title page, (4), 1-261, (11).
bound with
HALE, Sir Matthew. The Analysis of the Law. Third Edition. London, 1739. (1), title page, (12), 1-148, (26). **$200.00**
Termed "one of the most remarkable characters of the seventeenth century" by Plucknett, Hale may have intended his Common Law for students. It was said by Holdsworth to be *"the ablest introductory sketch of a history of English law that appeared till the publication of Pollock and Maitland."*
Hale's Analysis may be viewed as complementary to his classic works on criminal law, treating as it does only civil matters; it was termed by Blackstone the "most natural, scientific . . . as well as the most comprehensive" of all attempts (prior to his own Analysis) to digest the Common Law.
Bounded in contemporary full calf, blind tooled covers, somewhat worn, five raised bands, new label; an exceptionally clean copy of two of the most important legal works of the 17th century.
With the bookplate of **Lord Beresford**, Archbishop of Dublin and Primate of Ireland in the early 1800's.

171. HALE, Sir Matthew. The History of the Common Law of England. Chicago, 1971. **$12.50**
Reprinted from the third edition (see above); with a lengthy introduction by Charles M. Gray.

172. (HALE, Sir Matthew). EDMUND HEWARD. Matthew Hale. Robert Hale, 1972. **$10.00**
The author is a member of the Council of the **Selden Society.**

173. HALL, Jerome. Comparative Law and Social Theory. Louisiana State, 1963. **$15.00**
The *1962 Edward Douglass White Lectures.*

174. HALLAM, Henry. The Constitutional History of England from the Accession of Henry VII to the Death of George II. *Second Edition.* Three volumes. London, 1829. **$85.00**
Handsomely bound in contemporary full calf, somewhat rubbed, gilt-lined covers and spine, gilt-lettered spine with contrasting red and black labels, marbled endpapers and all edges marbled. *An extremely attractive copy* of the second edition, published two years after the first, by a man who was ranked, by **Maitland, with Palgrave, Stubbs and Gneist.**

175. HALLECK, Seymour L. and Walter Bromberg (eds.). Psychiatric Aspects of Criminology. Thomas, 1968. **$8.50**
Included is a contribution by **Jerome Hall.**

176. (HAMILTON, Alexander). JULIUS GOEBEL, JR. (ed.). The Law Practice of Alexander Hamilton. Two volumes. Columbia, 1964. **$35.00**

177. (HAND, Learned). IRVING DILLARD (ed.). The Spirit of Liberty. Knopf, 1952. **$10.00**

Presentation Copy to Sir John Romilly
178. (HARDWICKE, Lord Chancellor). GEORGE HARRIS. The Life of Lord Chancellor Hardwicke. First Edition. Three Volumes. London, 1847. **$150.00**
Called by Holdsworth *the greatest lawyer of the 18th century after Mansfield,* Hardwicke was successively solicitor-general (at age 29), attorney-general and chief justice of the King's Bench before succeeding Talbot on the Woolsack in 1737. In his 20 years as Chancellor he then oversaw the attainment of the law of equity in its final form.
Very attractively bound in ¾ calf, slightly rubbed, gilt and blind tooled, gilt lettered spine with contrasting black and brown labels, marbled boards, and all edges marbled. Some foxing to the endpapers, else exceptionally clean; volume I contains an engraved frontispiece of Hardwicke, with some offsetting on title page.
With the presentation inscription, also on the title page, to **Sir John Romilly,** second son of Sir Samuel Romilly and the last Master of the Rolls who sat in the House of Commons.

179. (HARDY, Carlos S.). In the Matter of the Impeachment of Carlos S. Hardy. California State Printer, Sacramento, 1930. **$25.00**
Original buckram, very lightly soiled, contrasting red and black labels, gilt lettering still bright; a nice copy.

180. HART, H.L.A. The Concept of Law. Oxford, 1970. **$12.50**
The *first volume in the Clarendon Law Series,* which Hart edits.

181. HART, J. B. A Treatise on the Practice of the Courts of the State of California. New York, 1853. lxviii, 253 pp. **$125.00**
Full leather, worn and soiled, contrasting red and black spine labels, gilt lettered, front free endpaper dampstained, occasional foxing, but altogether *a clean, sound copy of the first treatise on California Law.*

182. HARTLAND, E. Sidney. Primitive Law. Kennikat, 1970. **$8.50**
Re-issue of the 1924 edition; *"streets ahead of the stuff from Kohler and Post"* – Laski to Holmes.

183. (HARVARD LAW SCHOOL). The Centennial History of the Harvard Law School 1817-1917. The Harvard Law School Ass'n., 1918. Fifty-five illustrations. **$30.00**
With a number of valuable appendices, including bibliographies of the Law School and the legal writings of its teachers.

184. HARVEY, William Burnett. Law and Social Change in Ghana. Princeton, 1966. **$8.50**

185. HAY, Peter. Federalism and Supranational Organizations. Illinois, 1966. **$8.50**

186. HAZARD, Leland. Attorney for the Situation. Carnegie-Mellon, 1975. **$8.50**

187. HEDGES, R. Yorke. International Organization. Pitman, 1935. **$12.50**

With Sir Henry Maine's bookplate
188. HEEREN, A.H.L. A Manual of the History of the Political System of Europe and Its Colonies. *Two volumes.* Oxford, 1834. **$50.00**
A nicely bound copy of the first appearance in English of this work; ¾ leather, scuffed, blind & gilt ruled, gilt lettered, marbled boards, five raised bands.
Maine's most recent biographer, George Feaver, notes the unusual nature of Maine's bookplate, and the dispersal of Maine's library, causing its scarcity (p.xix).

189. HERBERT, W. Antiquities of the Inns of Court and Chancery. London, 1804. **$125.00**
One of the few authoritative works on the *Inns of Court;* with 24 copper-engraved plates, slightly foxed. Bound in ¾ roan & marbled boards, quite rubbed yet still attractive; gilt-lined & lettered, raised bands, marbled endpapers. Some foxing and embrowning to preliminaries, else a very clean copy.

190. HERMAN, Lawrence. The Right to Counsel in Misdemeanor Court. Ohio State, 1973. **$7.50**

191. HEWART, Lord. The New Despotism. Cosmopolitan, 1929. **$17.50**

192. HILL, Martin. Immunities and Privileges of International Officials. Carnegie Endowment for International Peace, 1947. **$12.50**

193. HIRSCH, Andrew von. Doing Justice, The Choice of Punishments. Hill and Wang, 1976. **$10.00**
The Report of the Committee for the Study of Incarceration.

194. HOCKING, William Ernest. Freedom of the Press. Chicago, 1947. **$15.00**
A publication of the **Commission on Freedom of the Press,** luminaries of which included **Harold Lasswell and Zechariah Chafee,** among others.

195. HODGES, Edward P. The Anti trust Act and the Supreme Court. West, 1941. **$15.00**
With a foreword by **Thurman Arnold,** under whom Hodges served at the Antitrust Division.

196. HODGSON, D. H. Consequences of Utilitarianism. Oxford, 1967. **$10.00**

197. HOLBORN, Louise W., Gwendolen M. Carter, and John H. Herz (eds.). German Constitutional Documents Since 1871. Pall Mall, 1970. **$9.50**

198. HOLLAND, Thomas Erskine and Charles Lancelot Shadwell (eds.). Select Titles from the Digest of Justinian. Oxford, 1881. **$22.50**
Largely uncut.

199. HOLLANDER, Barnett. The English Bar: A Priesthood. Bowes, 1965. **$8.50**

200. HOLMES, Oliver Wendell. Collected Legal Papers. Harcourt, Brace 1920. **$25.00**
The *original edition* in the dustwrapper.

201. HOLMES, Oliver Wendell. The Common Law. Belknap, 1967. **$10.00**
Edited by **Mark DeWolfe Howe,** with a valuable introduction by him.

202. (HOLMES, Oliver Wendell). FRANCIS BIDDLE. Mr. Justice Holmes. Scribners, 1943. **$10.00**

203. (HOLMES, Oliver Wendell). FELIX FRANKFURTER. Mr. Justice Holmes and the Supreme Court. Second Edition. Belknap, 1961. **$15.00**
This edition adds Frankfurter's article on Holmes for the Dictionary of American Biography; with an introduction by **Paul A. Freund.**

Presentation Copy
204. (HOLMES, Oliver Wendell). MARK DeWOLFE HOWE (ed.). Holmes-Pollock Letters. Harvard, 1941. Two volumes. **$50.00**
Presentation Copy from Professor Howe, Holme's biographer, and the editor of the Holmes-Pollock and Holmes-Laski Letters, as well as Holmes' secretary in 1933-34.

205. (HOLMES, Oliver Wendell). ALFRED LIEF (ed.). Representative Opinions of Mr. Justice Holmes. Vanguard, 1931. **$15.00**

206. (HOLMES, Oliver Wendell). JAMES BISHOP PEABODY (ed.). The Holmes-Einstein Letters. MacMillan, 1964. **$12.50**

207. HONE, Nathaniel J. The Manor and Manorial Records. Kennikat, 1971. **$8.50**
First published in 1906.

208. HOOK, Sidney. Common Sense & the Fifth Amendment. Criterion, 1957. **$8.50**

209. HOWARD, J. Woodford. Mr. Justice Murphy. Princeton, 1968. **$12.50**

210. HSIUNG, James Chieh. Law & Policy in China's Foreign Relations. Columbia, 1972. **$10.50**

211. HUNTING, Roger Bryant and Gloria S. Neuwirth. Who Sues in New York City? Columbia, 1962. **$8.50**

212. HUTCHINSON, E. R. Tropic of Cancer on Trial. Grove Press, 1968. **$8.50**

213. HUTCHINSON, Thomas W. (ed.). Africa and Law. Wisconsin, 1968. **$8.50**

214. (INNS OF COURT). CECIL HEADLAM and GORDON HOME. The Inns of Court. London, 1909. **$35.00**
With 20 colored illustrations; *an attractive volume* in the original red cloth, unobtrusive stain on front cover, gilt lined and lettered front cover and spine, very slightly rubbed.

215. INTERNATIONAL COMMISSION OF JURISTS. Justice Enslaved, A Collection of Documents On the Abuse of Justice For Political Ends. The Hague, 1955. Sewn wraps, paper embrowned. **$15.00**

216. INTERNATIONAL COMMISSION OF JURISTS. Report of the International Congress of Jurists, Athens, Greece, June 13-20, 1955. The Hague, 1956. Sewn, wraps. Light embrowning. **$12.50**

217. JACKSON, Donald Dale. Judges. Atheneum, 1974. **$8.00**

218. JACKSON, R. M. The Machinery of Justice in England. Fifth Edition. Cambridge, 1967. **$10.00**

219. JACKSON, Robert H. Falstaff's Descendants in Pennsylvania Courts. Silvarado, 1955. 25 pp. **$37.50**
Privately printed by the "Silvarado Squatters", the camp of the Bohemian Club of which Jackson was a member; measuring 9" x 12", printed in red and black, red wraps, sewn, gold stamped. Unusual, and very nice.

220. (JACKSON, Robert H.). Mr. Justice Jackson: Four Lectures in His Honor. Columbia, 1969. **$8.50**
The Lecturers were **Judge Desmond, Professor Freund, Justice Stewart and Lord Shawcross.**

221. JAWORSKI, Leon. The Right and the Power. Reader's Digest Press, 1976. **$8.50**

222. JESSUP, Philip C. Elihu Root. Dodd, Mead, 1938. *Two volumes.* **$25.00**

223. JESSUP, Philip C. The Price of International Justice. Columbia. **$8.50**
The **1970 Jacob Blaustein Lectures.**

224. JESSUP, Philip C. and Francis Deak. Neutrality, Its History, Economics and Law. *Four volumes.* Octagon, 1976 **$48.00**
Reissue of the 1935 edition.

225. (JESSUP, Philip C.). WOLFGANG FRIEDMANN, LOUIS HENKIN AND OLIVER LISSITZYN (eds.). Transnational Law in a Changing Society, Essays in Honor of Philip C. Jessup. Columbia, 1972. **$10.50**

226. JOHNSTON, Douglas M. and Hungdah Chiu (eds.). Agreements of the People's Republic of China, 1949-1967, A Calendar. Harvard, 1968. **$12.00**
The third volume in **Harvard Studies in East Asian Law.**

227. JOINER, Charles W. Civil Justice and the Jury. Prentice Hall, 1962. **$9.00**
Forward by **Earl Warren.**

228. JONES, Eliot. The Trust Problem in the United States. MacMillan, 1929. **$12.50**

229. JONES, W. J. Politics and the Bench, The Judges and the Origins of the English Civil War. Allen and Unwin, 1971. **$8.50**

230. KAPLAN, John and Jon R. Waltz. The Trial of Jack Ruby. MacMillan, 1965. **$10.00**

231. KARLEN, Delmar. Appellate Courts in the United States and England. N.Y.U., 1963. **$10.00**
Forewords by **Lord Evershed and Justice Brennan.**

232. KAUPER, Paul G. Civil Liberties and the Constitution. Michigan, 1962. **$10.00**

233. KEETON, Robert E. Venturing to do Justice. Harvard, 1969. **$10.00**

234. KEIR, D. Lindsay. The Constitutional History of Modern Britain 1485-1937. Third Edition. Black, 1946. **$10.00**

235. KELSEN, Hans. General Theory of Law and State. Harvard, 1945. **$22.50**
The *first volume* in the **20th Century Legal Philosophy Series.**

236. KEMBLE, J. M. The Saxons in England. AMS Press, 1971. *Two volumes.* **$22.50**
A reissue of the New Edition revised by **Walter de Gray Birch** in 1876.

237. KENT, William. Memoirs and Letters of James Kent. Little, Brown, 1898. **$32.50**
Original maroon cloth, gilt lettering; spot on front cover, else fine.

238. KIRST, Michael W. Government Without Passing Laws. North Carolina, 1969. **$8.50**

239. KOESSLER, Maximilian (ed.). Masterpieces of Legal Fiction. Lawyers Publishing, 1964. **$17.50**

240. KONVITZ, Milton R. Fundamental Liberties of a Free People. Cornell, 1963. **$10.00**

241. KRONSTEIN, Heinrich. The Law of International Cartels. Cornell, 1973. **$10.00**

242. KUHN, Arthur K. Pathways in International Law. MacMillan, 1953. **$8.50**

243. LADAS, Stephen P. The International Protection of Trade Marks by the American Republics. Harvard, 1929. **$15.00**
Volume 1 of Harvard Studies in International Law, edited by Manley O. Hudson.

244. LaFAVE, Wayne R. (ed.). Law in the Soviet Society. Illinois, 1965. **$8.50**

245. LAMONT, Corliss. The Trial of Elizabeth Gurley Flynn by the American Civil Liberties Union. Horizon, 1968. **$7.00**

246. LANSING, John, Jr. The Delegate From New York. Kennikat, 1967. **$8.50**
Reissue of the 1939 edition.

247. LASSWELL, Harold D. World Politics Faces Economics. McGraw-Hill, 1945. **$10.00**

248. LEFCOURT, Robert (ed.). Law Against the People. Random House, 1972. **$7.50**
Essays by **Howard Moore, Jr., William M. Kunstler and Michael E. Tigar,** among others.

249. LEPAWSKY, Albert. The Judicial System of Metropolitan Chicago. Chicago, 1932. **$15.00**

250. LETWIN, William. Law and Economic Policy in America, The Evolution of the Sherman Antitrust Act. Random House, 1965. **$8.50**

251. LEVY, Leonard W. Judgments, Essays on American Constitutional History. Quadrangle, 1972. **$10.00**

252. LINDSEY, Edward. The International Court. Crowell, 1931. **$15.00**

253. LIPSON, Leon and Nicholas deB. Katzenbach. Report To The National Aeronautics And Space Administration On The Law of Outer Space. American Bar Foundation, 1961. **$15.00**

254. LOEBL, Eugene. Sentenced & Tried, The Stalinist Purges in Czechoslovakia. Elek, 1969. **$7.50**

255. (LONDON). HELENA M. CHEW AND WILLIAM KELLAWAY (eds.). London Assize of Nuisance 1301-1431. London Record Society, 1973. **$12.50**

256. McCLINTOCK, F. H. and Evelyn Gibson. Robbery in London. MacMillan, 1961. **$8.50**
Volume XIV in Cambridge Studies in Criminology, edited by Sir Leon Radzinowicz.

257. McCLOSKEY, Robert G. The American Supreme Court. Chicago, 1967. **$8.50**

258. McCONACHIE, Lauros G. Congressional Committees, A Study of the Origins and Development of Our National and Local Administrative Methods. Crowell, 1898. **$17.50**
Slightly rubbed.

259. MacDONAGH, Michael. The English King. Kennikat, 1971. **$8.50**
Reissue of the 1929 edition.

260. McGOWAN, Carl. The Organization of Judicial Power in the United States. **$8.50**
The **1967 Julius Rosenthal Lectures.**

261. McILWAIN, C. H. Constitutionalism & the Changing World. MacMillan, 1939. **$17.50**

262. MacKINNON, Sir Frank Douglas. On Circuit, 1924-1937. Cambridge, 1941. **$17.50**
Edges spotted, else quite nice.

263. McLAUGHLIN, Andrew Cunningham. The Confederation and the Constitution, 1783-1789. Harper & Row, 1968. **$8.75**
First issued in 1905.

The First Edition in Folio

264. MADOX, Thomas. The History and Antiquities of the Exchequer. London, 1711. (4), title page, (4), xviii, (2), 752; title page, iii-xii, 59; title page, 63-75, (5), (2). **$250.00**
Termed by Maitland a "beautiful" work, and *"one of the greatest historical works of the eighteenth century"*. Contemporary calf, rebacked, some wear and repairs to binding, six raised bands, blind decorated spine with a gilt label, occasional foxing and embrowning particularly to first and last leaves, but altogether *a tall, exceptionally clean, wide-margined and desirable copy*. Appended, with separate title pages, are the Dialogus de Scaccario and a Dissertation on the Great Roll of the Exchequer; the former, written in the late 1100's, provides an insight into the early administrative workings of the Exchequer — "an excellent and valuable little treatise" in Maitland's opinion.

265. MADOX, Thomas. The History and Antiquities of the Exchequer. *Two volumes*. Greenwood, 1969. **$50.00**
A reissue of the second edition of 1769, in facsimile.

266. MAINE, Sir Henry. Lectures on the Early History of Institutions. Kennikat, 1966. **$10.00**
Reissued from the Seventh Edition of 1914.

267. MAINE, Sir Henry. Village-Communities in the East and West. Henry Holt, 1876. **$22.50**
The first American edition, taken from the third and best English edition, which was expanded to include a number of Maine's other lectures, essays and addresses.
Original reddish-brown cloth, rubbed and worn.

268. MAITLAND, F. W. The Forms of Action at Common Law. Cambridge, 1965. **$15.00**

269. (MAITLAND, F. W.). H. E. BELL. Maitland, A Critical Examination and Assessment. Harvard, 1965. **$12.50**

270. (MAITLAND, F. W.). HELEN M. CAM. Selected Historical Essays of F. W. Maitland. Cambridge, 1957. **$17.50**

271. (MAITLAND, F.W.). C.H.S. FIFOOT (ed.). The Letters of Frederic William Maitland. Harvard, 1965. **$17.50**

272. MANNING, Bayless. Federal Conflict of Interest Law. Harvard, 1964. **$8.50**

273. MARSHALL, Burke. Federalism and Civil Rights. Columbia, 1964. **$7.50**
Based on the 1964 Gino Speranza Lectures.

274. MARSHALL, Geoffrey. Police and Government. Methuen, 1965. **$7.50**

275. MARSHALL, James. Intention in Law and Society. Funk & Wagnalls, 1968. **$7.50**
Forward by **William O. Douglas.**

276. MARSHALL, John. An Autobiographical Sketch. Michigan, 1937. **$17.50**
Written at **Story's** request, the Sketch was not printed until this edition, which is taken from the original manuscript at Michigan.

277. (MARSHALL, John). JOHN F. DILLON. John Marshall, Life, Character and Judicial Services. *Three Volumes*. Callaghan, 1903. **$35.00**
Original blue buckram, slightly rubbed, top edge gilt, gilt spine; a nice set.

278. (MARSHALL, John). STANLEY I. KUTLER (ed.). John Marshall. Prentice Hall, 1972. **$7.00**

279. (MARSHALL, John). IRWIN S. RHODES. The Papers of John Marshall, A Descriptive Calendar. Oklahoma, 1969. **$25.00**
Two volumes, boxed.

280. (MARSHALL, John). JAMES A. SERVIES. A Bibliography of John Marshall. Washington, 1956. **$17.50**
With a laid-in slip from the John Marshall Bicentennial Commission.

281. MARTIN, George. Causes and Conflicts, the Centennial History of the Association of the Bar of the City of New York 1870-1970. Houghton Mifflin, 1970. **$10.00**

282. MASON, Alpheus Thomas. The Supreme Court, Palladium of Freedom. Michigan, 1963. **$15.00**
The 1962 **Cooley Lectures** at Michigan.

283. (MASON, Jeremiah). G. J. CLARK. Memoirs of Jeremiah Mason 1768-1848. Boston Law Book Co., 1917. **$15.00**
Reissue of the privately printed edition of 1873; Webster termed Mason "eminently superior to any lawyer whom I ever met."

284. MAURER, Amira Karl von. Konrad von Maurer, Gedachtnisrede. Munchen 1903. 19 pp., sewn wraps, folded. **$17.50**

285. MAY, John G. The Lighter Side of the Law. Michie, 1956. **$12.50**

286. MAY, John Wilder. The Law of Crimes. Second Edition. Little, Brown, 1893. **$17.50**
An attractive little book, bound in full sheep, red label, gilt lettering, some wear to extremities; edited by **J. H. Beale** shortly after he began teaching at Harvard.

287. MAY, Thomas Erskine. The Constitutional History of England Since the Accession of George III 1760-1860. *Two volumes*. Widdleton, New York, 1865. **$75.00**
An extremely handsome set, bound in ¾ blue morocco, slightly rubbed, marbled boards and endpapers, top edge gilt, five raised bands with gilt designs, gilt decorated and lettered spines.

288. MAYER, Martin. The Lawyers. Harper & Row, 1967. **$8.50**

289. MEDINA, Harold R. The Anatomy of Freedom. Holt, 1959. First Edition; edited by C. Waller Barrett. **$12.50**
Presentation copy from the editor, C. Waller Barrett.

290. MELTSNER, Michael. Cruel and Unusual, the Supreme Court and Capital Punishment. Random House, 1973. **$8.50**

291. MEYER, Howard N. The Amendment that Refused to Die. Chilton, 1973. **$7.50**

292. (MIDDLE TEMPLE). Middle Temple Ordeal, Being an Account of what WORLD WAR II meant to the Inn. Privately printed, 1948. 55 pp., sewn wraps, illustrated. **$12.50**

293. MILLER, Arthur R. The Assault on Privacy. Michigan, 1971. **$10.00**

294. MINEAR, Richard H. Victors' Justice, The Tokyo War Crimes Trial. Princeton, 1972. **$9.50**

295. MOLLOY, Charles. De Jure Maritimo et Navali: or a Treatise of Affairs Maritime and of Commerce. Two volumes. Ninth Edition. London, 1769. **$100.00**
Bound in full calf, blind tooled covers, red labels gilt lettered and decorated. Bindings worn, front cover of volume II stained & joints cracked but firm; some foxing & embrowning.
Despite the foregoing litany, an attractive set of a work first appearing in the mid-1600's, and the first written by an English lawyer (Molloy was both a civilian and a member of two Inns of Court) on the evolving Law Merchant, influenced by England's expanding sea trade and by Continental law.

296. MOOTE, A. Lloyd. The Revolt of the Judges, the Parlement of Paris and the Fronde 1643-1652. Princeton, 1971. **$12.50**

297. MORGAN, Glenn G. Soviet Administrative Legality. Stanford, 1962. **$10.00**

298. MORRISON, Fred L. Courts and the Political Process in England. Sage, 1973. **$8.50**

299. MOWRER, Edgar Ansel and Lilian T. Mowrer. Umano and the Price of Lasting Peace. Philosophical Library, 1973. **$7.50**

300. MOYNIHAN, Cornelius J. Introduction to the Law of Real Property. West, 1962. **$10.00**

301. MURPHY, Paul L. The Meaning of Freedom of Speech. Greenwood, 1972. **$10.00**

302. MURPHY, Walter F. Elements of Judicial Strategy. Chicago, 1964 **$12.50**

303. MYERS, Gustavus. History of the Supreme Court of the United States. Kerr, 1912. **$15.00**

304. (NADER REPORT). MARK J. GREEN, et al. The Closed Enterprise System, Ralph Nader's Study Group Report on Antitrust Enforcement. Grossman, 1972. **$8.50**

305. NAGEL, Stuart S. (ed.). The Rights of the Accused. Sage, 1972. **$11.00**

306. NEALE, A. D. The Antitrust Laws of the U.S.A. Cambridge, 1962. **$12.50**
With a foreward by **Abe Fortas.**

307. NELSON, William. The Laws of England Concerning the Game. Third Edition. London, 1736. 12 mo; xvi, 248, 34. (index). **$55.00**
Newly and attractively rebound in ¾ leather, with marbled boards and endpapers, gilt decorated & lined boards and gilt lined & lettered spine, contrasting red & black labels; minor dampstaining to lower inner margins of some leaves, not affecting text, very minor & occasional foxing, but altogether *a very clean and desirable copy.*

308. NIMS, Harry D. Pre-Trial. Baker Voorhis, 1950. **$12.50**

309. NORTH, Roger. The Lives of the . . . North[s] A New Edition. *Three Volumes*. London, 1826. **$125.00**
Paired by Holdsworth with Fortescue and Samuel Romilly, North provides considerable and amusing detail of the daily life of the law in the latter half of the 17th century.
A particularly attractive set, bound in full calf, expertly rebacked, gilt decorated and ruled covers and spines very slightly darkened, contrasting red and black labels, gilt lettered, all edges gilt.
It is from this work that the Selden Society has taken from one of the two quotations found on the title pages of its Year Book series: "He [Sergeant Maynard] had such a relish of the old year books that he carried one in his coach to divert him in travel, and said he chose it before any comedy."

310. (NUREMBERG). Opening Speeches of the Chief Prosecutors. H.M.S.O., 1946. Sewn wraps, 173 pp. **$15.00**
The chief prosecutors: **Robert H. Jackson, Lord Shawcross, Francois de Menthon** and **R. A. Rudenko.** Some wear and embrowning.

311. NUSSBAUM, Arthur. Principles of Private International Law. Oxford, 1943. **$12.50**

312. OPPENHEIM, L. International Law. Seventh Edition. *Two volumes*. Longmans, Green, 1952. **$25.00**

Original maroon cloth, gilt lettering; slightly rubbed, but a nice set, edited by **Lauterpacht.**

313. OPPENHEIMER, In the Matter of J. Robert. Transcript of Hearing before Personnel Security Board and Text of Principal Documents and Letters. M.I.T. Press, 1971. **$12.50**
Reproduced from the original 1954 G.P.O. printings.

314. PACKER, Herbert L. The Limits of the Criminal Sanction. Stanford, 1973. **$12.50**

315. PARSONS, Theophilus. Commentaries on American Law. New York, 1836. **$45.00**
Full sheep, slightly rubbed, top of rear joint cracked, but holding, red label gilt lettered. An attractive copy.

316. PATTERSON, Edwin W. Law in a Scientific Age. Columbia, 1963. **$7.50**
The 1962 **James S. Carpentier Lectures.**

317. PFEFFER, Leo. Church, State and Freedom. Revised Edition. Beacon Press, 1967. **$10.00**

318. PFEFFER, Leo. This Honorable Court. Beacon Press, 1965. **$10.00**

319. PLUCKNETT, T. F. T. Edward I and Criminal Law. Cambridge, 1960. **$12.50**
The **Wiles Lectures** at Belfast, 1958.

320. POLLOCK, Sir Frederick. Jurisprudence and Legal Essays. MacMillan, 1961. **$12.50**
Selected and introduced by **A. L. Goodhart.**

First American publication of the Second Edition

321. POLLOCK, Sir Frederick and F. W. Maitland. The History of English Law Before the Time of Edward I. Second Edition. Two volumes. Little, Brown, 1899. **$65.00**
Issued only a few years after the first edition of 1895, this work – written primarily by Maitland – remains the classic modern work on medieval English law.

322. POLLOCK, Sir John. Time's Chariot. John Murray, 1950. **$8.50**
Slightly worn.

323. POUND, Roscoe. The Development of Constitutional Guarantees of Liberty. Yale, 1960. **$15.00**

324. POUND, Roscoe. The Formative Era of American Law. Peter Smith, 1960. **$12.50**
Originally published in 1938.

325. (POUND, Roscoe). Law in Action, an Anthology of the Law in Literature. Bonanza, 1947. **$12.50**
With an Introduction by Pound.

326. (POUND, Roscoe). PAUL SAYRE (ed.). Interpretations of Modern Legal Philosophies, Essays in Honor of Roscoe Pound. Oxford, 1947. **$22.50**
Essays by **A. L. Goodhart, Jerome Frank, Hans Kelsen, Albert Kocourek** and **Julius Stone,** among many others.

327. POWICKE, F. M. The Reformation in England. Oxford, 1949. **$8.50**
Slightly worn.

328. PRITCHETT, C. Herman. Civil Liberties and the Vinson Court. Chicago, 1954. **$10.00**

329. PRITCHETT, C. Herman. The Roosevelt Court. MacMillan, 1948. **$10.00**

330. PROTHERO, G. W. (ed.). Select Statutes and Other Constitutional Documents Illustrative of the Reigns of Elizabeth and James I. Fourth Edition. Oxford, 1965. **$15.00**

331. QUINNEY, Richard. The Social Reality of Crime. Little, Brown, 1970. **$8.50**

332. RADCLIFFE, Lord. The Law and Its Compass. Northwestern, 1960. **$8.50**
The 1960 **Julius Rosenthal Lectures** at Northwestern.

333. RADIN, Max. The Law and Mr. Smith. Bobbs-Merrill, 1938. **$10.00**
Slight wear.

334. RADZINOWICZ, Sir Leon. Ideology & Crime. Columbia, 1969. **$8.00**
The 1965 **James S. Carpentier Lectures.**

335. RADZINOWICZ, Sir Leon and Joan King. The Growth of Crime. Basic Books, 1977. **$8.50**

336. RADZINOWICZ, Sir Leon and Marvin E. Wolfgang (eds.). Crime and Justice. *Three Volumes*. Basic Books, 1971. **$25.00**
Boxed.

337. RAMASWAMY, M. The Creative Role of the Supreme Court of the United States. Stanford, 1956. **$7.50**

338. READ, John E. The Rule of Law on the International Plane. Clarke Irwin, 1961. **$7.50**

339. REEVE, Tapping. The Law of Baron and Femme. Source Book Press, 1970. **$17.50**
Reprinted from the Third Edition of 1862.

340. REITMAN, Alan (ed.). The Pulse of Freedom, American Liberties 1920-1970s. Norton, 1975. **$8.50**

341. REMBAR, Charles. The End of Obscenity, the Trials of Lady Chatterly, Tropic of Cancer and Fanny Hill. Random House, 1968. **$8.50**
Rembar was defense counsel in each of the cases.

342. (RHODE ISLAND). DOROTHY S. TOWLE. Records of the Vice-Admiralty Court of Rhode Island 1716-1752. American Historical Ass'n., 1936. **$25.00**
Volume 3 of **American Legal Records.**

343. RICHARDSON, H. G. A Norman Lawsuit. Cambridge, 1932. 11 pp., stapled wraps. **$5.00**
Offprinted from Speculum.

345. ROBERTS, Owen J. The Court and the Constitution. Harvard, 1951. **$10.00**
The 1951 **Holmes Lectures.**

346. ROBINSON, W. W. Lawyers of Los Angeles. Los Angeles Bar Association, 1959. **$25.00**
Handsomely printed at the **Ward Ritchie Press.**

347. ROBSON, William A. Civilisation and the Growth of Law. MacMillan, 1935. **$10.00**

348. RODELL, Fred. Nine Men. Random House, 1955. **$12.50**
Presentation copy.

349. ROSENBERG, Maurice. The Pretrial Conference and Effective Justice. Columbia, 1964. **$10.00**
Preface by **Justice Tom C. Clark.**

350. ROSENBLOOM, David H. Federal Service and the Constitution. Cornell, 1971. **$8.50**

351. ROSTOW, Eugene V. (ed.). Is Law Dead? Simon & Schuster, 1971. **$8.50**
Articles by **Charles L. Black, Jr., Edgar S. Cahn** and **Ronald Dworkin,** among others.

352. RUTHERFORD, M. Louise. The Influence of the American Bar Association on Public Opinion and Legislation. Foundation Press, 1937. **$12.50**

Printed in Black Letter

353. [St. GERMAIN, Christopher]. Doctor and Student: or Dialogues Between A Doctor of Divinity, and a Student in the Laws of England. London, 1721. 12 mo. Title page, (10), 365, (40) pp. **$60.00**
First appearing in the early 1500's, this work provided, according to Holdsworth, "the basis and starting point of the English system of equity," by borrowing from the canon law the principle of applying conscience to the law's generality – "circumstances alter cases."
This copy attractively bound in contemporary calf, slightly worn, blind tooled, five raised bands, brown label gilt lettered. With the bookplate, dated 1725, of Lord Charles Noel Somerset.

354. ST. JOHN-STEVAS, Norman. The Agonising Choice. Eyre & Spottiswoode, 1971. **$8.00**

355. SALMON, [Thomas]. A New Abridgement and Critical Review of the State Trials and Impeachments for High Treason. London, 1738. Title page, iii-iv, 922, (8) pp. **$150.00**
The State Trials have been published in various editions, reaching their apogee with Howells' 33 volume set in the early 1800's; this work, his last abridgement, is by Salmon, the original editor of the State Trials in their first appearance in 1719. A very handsome copy of the work which in its entirety has been called of "unique value for constitutional and legal historians" by Holdsworth.

356. SAMEK, Robert A. The Legal Point of View. Philosophical Library, 1974. **$10.00**

357. SANTVOORD, George van. Sketches of the Lives and Judicial Services of the Chief-Justices of the Supreme Court of the United States. Scribner, 1854, **$35.00**
Original cloth, slightly rubbed, light foxing to preliminaries, else a clean and attractive copy, gilt lettered spine.

358. SAYRE, Francis Bowes. A Selection of Cases on the Law of Admiralty. Lawyers Cooperative, 1929. **$15.00**
Some pencilling.

359. SAYRE, Paul. An Introduction To A Philosophy of Law. Iowa, 1951. **$12.50**
Presentation copy, with margin annotations.

360. SCANDINAVIAN Studies in Criminology. Volume 2. Oslo, 1968. **$8.50**

361. SCHRAG, Philip G. Counsel for the Deceived. Pantheon, 1972. **$8.50**

362. SCHUR, Edwin M. & Hugo Adam Bedau. Victimless Crimes. Prentice-Hall, 1974. **$7.50**

363. SCHWARTZ, Bernard. French Administrative Law and the Common-Law World. N.Y.U., 1954. **$15.00**
With an introduction by **Arthur T. Vanderbilt.**

364. SCHWARTZ, Helene E. Lawyering. Farrar, 1976. **$8.50**

365. SCHWARZENBERGER, Georg. International Law and Totalitarian Lawlessness. Jonathon Cape, 1943. **$8.50**
Wartime paper.

366. (SCHWARZENBERGER, Georg). Second Report on the Review of the Charter of the United Nations. Dubrovnik

Conference 1956. International Law Association, h.d. 122 pp., stapled. **$5.00**

367. SEAGLE, William. Law, The Science of Inefficiency. MacMillan, 1952. **$8.50**

368. SEEBOHM, Frederic. The English Village Community. Kennikat, 1971. **$8.75**
First published in 1883.

369. SEEBOHM, Frederic. Tribal Custom in AngloSaxon Law. Longmans, 1911. **$20.00**
Originally decorated cloth, soiled, boards slightly warped.

370. SEEBOHM, Frederic. The Tribal System in Wales. Longsmans, 1904. $20.00
Original decorated cloth, soiled, boards slightly warped.

371. SELDEN, John. De Dys Syris Syntagmata II. Small octavo. Leipzig, 1662. (1), title page,(36), 373, (51). **$120.00**
The first Leipzig edition (unrecorded by Fry in his D.N.B. article) of Selden's first work as an Orientalist, and *perhaps the first book written by him,* at age 21. Bound in black morocco, gilt ruled and lettered spine, slightly embrowned, but a nice copy, with the engraved frontispiece showing six scenes of adoration of various idols, including that of the Golden Calf.
It is this work of Selden's from which Milton drew many names and attributes of the heathen gods in Paradise Lost, and in the Areopagitica Milton calls Selden "the chief of learned men reputed in this land."

Suppressed by Public Authority
372. SELDEN, John. The History of Tithes. [London], 1618. (1), Title page, (4), xxii, (12), 491, (5), (2). Quarto. New S.T.C. 22172.7. **$225.00**
Said by Fry to be Selden's best known work other than his "Table Talk", the History of Tithes was immediately highly controversial, and shortly suppressed, being interpreted to deny divine right.
Old calf, slightly rubbed, gilt spine, red label gilt lettered, early manuscript annotations and underscoring, name erased on title page.
A nice copy of the work which Fletcher states "brought [Selden] at once to the forefront of the political stage"; with the title page in red and black.

373. SELDEN, John. Table Talk: Being the Discourses of John Selden, Esq. A New Edition, London, 1777. Small Octavo. Title page, (6), 181, (3) pp. **$75.00**
The work by which Selden is best known, and dedicated by its complier to Matthew Hale. "But the French (said I) have the art of accommodating literature."
Johnson: "Yes, sir: we have no such book as Moreri's Dictionary."
Boswell: "Their Ana are good."
Johnson: "A few of them are good: but we have one book of that kind better than any of them; Selden's Table Talk."
Old calf, considerably worn and crudely rebacked, black label gilt lettered; a pleasant copy, exceptionally clean.

374. SELDEN, John. Table Talk of John Selden. London, 1927. **$20.00**
Edited by Sir Frederick Pollock for the Selden Society from a Lincoln's Inn manuscript. Endpapers embrowned. With an introduction by Pollock and Fry's D.N.B. article appended.

375. SELDEN, John. Titles of Honor. **Second Edition.** London, 1631. Quarto. (4), title page, (34), 941 (not consecutive, but complete), (3) S.T.C. 22178. **$250.00**
Termed by Fletcher Selden's "first book of any importance", the Titles of Honor first appeared in 1614, and was much expanded in this edition.

376. (SELDEN Society). ELSIE SHANKS (ed.). Novae Narrationes. London, 1963. **$22.50**
Volume 80; completed and with a legal introduction by **S.F.C. Milsom.**

377. SELZNICK, Philip. Law, Society, and Industrial Justice. Sage, 1969. **$9.50**

378. (SERJEANTS' Inn). Old Serjeants' Inn Chancery Lane. Privately printed, 1912. **$17.50**
Top edge gilt, gilt-lettered covers, slightly crimped, five colored coats of arms & other illustrations; light foxing to preliminaries, but a nice copy.

379. (SHAKESPEARE). CUSHMAN K. DAVIS. The Law in Shakespeare. Washington Law Book Co., 1883. First Edition. **$25.00**
Original buckram, a bit dusty; gilt lettered cover and spine. "The most comprehensive contribution made in the nineteenth century to the explanation of legal terms in Shakespeare" (according to O. Hood Phillips) by Davis, who was to become Governor of Minnesota.

380. (SHAKESPEARE). GEORGE W. KEETON. Shakespeare's Legal & Political Background. Pitman, 1967. **$15.00**
"The most comprehensive survey made by a lawyer of the constitutional background to Shakespeare's plays" — Phillips.

381. SHAPIRO, Martin. Law and Politics in the Supreme Court. Free Press, 1964. **$10.00**

382. (SHEARMAN and Sterling). WALTER K. EARLE. Mr. Shearman and Mr. Sterling and How They Grew. Privately printed, 1963. **$25.00**
Original red cloth, gilt spine, slight wear. The firm traces its origins back to the mid-19th century, when Shearman was partner with **David Dudley Field.**

383. SHEPHERD, William G. The Treatment of Market Power, Antitrust, Regulation, and Public Enterprise. Columbia, 1975. **$10.00**

384. SHIENTAG, Bernard L. Moulders of Legal Thought. Kennikat, 1968. **$10.00**
Articles on **Cardozo, Lord Mansfield** and **Sir Frederick Pollock,** among others.

385. SHIRAS, Winfield (ed.). Justice George Shiras, Jr. of Pittsburgh. Pittsburgh, 1953. **$15.00**

386. SHORE, Thomas William. Origin of the Anglo Saxon Race. Kennikat, 1971. **$10.00**
Originally published in 1906.

387. SHUMAN, Samuel I. Legal Positivism. Wayne, 1963. **$10.00**

388. SHUMAN, Samuel I. (ed.). The Future of Federalism. Wayne, 1968. **$7.50**
Essays by **Paul Freund** and **Skelly Wright,** among others.

389. SIMON, James F. In His Own Image, The Supreme Court in Richard Nixon's America. McKay, 1973. **$7.50**

390. SIMON, James F. The Judge. McKay, 1976. **$7.50**

391. SLUSSER, Robert M. and Jan F. Triska. A Calendar of Soviet Treaties, 1917-1957. Stanford, 1959. **$15.00**

392. SMIGEL, Erwin O. The Wall Street Lawyer. Free Press, 1964. **$12.50**

393. (STANDARD OIL CASE). A collection of seven briefs filed in the U.S. Supreme Court and in the U.S. Circuit Court on behalf of Standard Oil and other defendants. **$40.00**
The first of modern antitrust actions, with a record over a score of volumes and five million words, leading to the Court's 1911 opinion that the Rule of Reason governs Sherman Act cases.
Original wraps, worn and soiled, one cover detached but present, all sound; an interesting collection – further details provided on request.

394. STANFORD, Leland G. Footprints of Justice . . . in San Diego. San Diego County Law Library, 1960. **$10.00**

395. STANFORD, Leland G. Tracks on the Trial Trail in San Diego. Law Library Justice Foundation, 1963. **$10.00**

396. STENTON, Doris, M. English Justice Between the Norman Conquest and the Great Charter, 1066-1215. American Philosophical Soc'y, 1964. **$10.00**
The 1963 Jayne Lectures.

397. STEPHEN, Sir James Fitzjames. A Digest of the Law of Evidence. Third Edition. MacMillan, 1877. **$25.00**
Full leather, some rubbing and scuffing, contrasting red and black labels, gilt lettered; an attractive copy.
First appearing the year before, and the first digest Stephen attempted, the work was warmly received and was followed shortly thereafter by Stephen's Digest of the Criminal Law.

First Edition
398. STEPHEN, Sir James Fitzjames. Liberty, Equality, Fraternity. London, 1873. **$60.00**
Original brown cloth, rubbed, spine darkened, gilt lettered, spot on front cover, occasional very light foxing, pencil notations; a sound copy.
Written in response to Mill's **On Liberty,** Stephen's work has been termed the "finest exposition of conservative thought in the latter half of the nineteenth century" (Sir Ernest Barker) and, by Sir Leon Radzinowicz in his Selden Society Lecture, "a contribution of lasting value to English political thought."

399. STEVENS, Robert. Law and Politics, The House of Lords as a Judicial Body, 1800-1976. North Carolina, 1978. New. **$30.00**
The latest publication of the American Society for Legal History.

400. STEWART, Robert B. Treaty Relations of the British Commonwealth of Nations. MacMillan, 1939. **$12.50**

401. STITES, Francis N. Private Interest and Public Gain: The Dartmouth College Case, 1819. Massachusetts, 1972. **$10.00**

402. (STONE, Harlan Fiske). ALFRED LIEF (ed.). Public Control of Business, Selected Opinions of . . . Howell, Soskin, 1940. **$12.50**

403. STONE, Julius. Law and the Social Sciences. Minnesota, 1966. **$10.00**
Based on Stone's Pattee Memorial Lectures.

404. (STORY, Joseph). WILLIAM W. STORY (ed.). The Miscellaneous Writings of Joseph Story. Boston, 1852. **$35.00**
Original olive cloth, quite worn and rubbed; occasional foxing, else sound.

405. STREET, A. L. H. American Cemetary Law. Park and Cemetary, n.d. **$7.50**
Somewhat soiled and damped, as might be expected.

406. STUART, Graham H. American Diplomatic and Consular Practice. Appleton, 1936. **$12.50**
Slight wear.

One of 250 hand-printed copies
407. STUBBS, William. Kettel Hall, Christmas 1873. Printed at the Golden Hind Press, 1950. **$25.00**
Copyrighted and with a note by Christopher Morley; very lightly soiled, but *an usual and very nice item.*

408. (STUBBS, William). CH. PETIT-DUTAILLIS AND GEORGES LEVEBRE. Studies and Notes Supplementary to Stubbs' Constitutional History. Manchester, 1968. **$15.00**
First published in separate parts in 1908, 1914 and 1929.

409. SUTHERLAND, Arthur E. Apology for Uncomfortable Change: 1865-1965. MacMillan, 1965. **$12.50**
The 1963 Holmes Lectures.

410. SUTHERLAND, Arthur L. (ed.). Government Under Law. Harvard, 1956. **$15.00**
Essays by **Felix Frankfurter, Erwin Griswold** and **Charles E. Wysanski, Jr.,** among others; very slight wear.

411. SWINDLER, William F. Court and Constitution in the 20th Century. Bobbs-Merrill, 1974. **$10.00**

412. SZASZ, Thomas S. Law, Liberty and Psychiatry. MacMillan, 1963. **$10.00**

413. TAFT, Henry W. Legal Miscellanies. MacMillan, 1941. **$10.00**

414. TAFT, William Howard. Liberty Under Law. New Haven, 1922. **$15.00**
The Cutler Lecture for 1921. Published for the University of Rochester by the Yale University Press; the first work published by the former university.

415. (TAFT, William Howard). ALPHEUS THOMAS MASON. William Howard Taft: Chief Justice. Oldbourne, 1965. **$10.00**

416. TASWELL-LANGMEAD, Thomas Pitt. English Constitutional History. Tenth Edition. Sweet 7 Maxwell, 1946. **$17.50**
Edited by **T.F.T. Plucknett.**

417. THACH, Charles C., Jr. The Creation of the Presidency 1775-1789, A Study in Constitutional History. Johns Hopkins, 1969. **$8.50**
Originally published in 1923.

418. THOMSON, George Malcolm. A Kind of Justice, Two Studies in Treason. Hutchinson, 1970. **$7.50**

A Superb Copy
419. (TOWER, Charlemagne). The Charlemagne Tower Collection of American Colonial Laws. Privately printed for the Historical Society of Pennsylvania, 1890. **$50.00**
Perhaps the most impressive collection of Colonial law ever amassed, and a valuable bibliographical work, Tower's Collection was formed in the last half of the 19th century, and presented by his widow to the Pennsylvania Historical Society in 1890.
Bound in black simulated leather, top edge gilt, gilt spine, very bright. Uncut and an exceptional copy.

420. TRISKA, Jan F. and Robert M. Slusser. The Theory, Law, and Policy of Soviet Treaties. Stanford, 1962. **$12.50**

421. TURNER, J. W. Cecil. Introduction to the Study of Roman Private Law. Bowes, 1953. **$10.00**

422. TURNER, Ralph V. The King and His Courts, The Role of John and Henry III in the Administration of Justice, 1199-1240. Cornell, 1968. **$10.00**

423. TUROW, Scott. One L, An inside account of life in the first year at Harvard Law School. Putnam, 1977. **$7.50**

424. ULC, Otto. The Judge in a Communist State. Ohio, 1972. **$10.00**

425. ULMER, S. Sidney. Military Justice & The Right to Counsel. Kentucky, 1970. **$7.50**

426. UNGAR, Sanford J. The Papers & The Papers, An Account of the Legal and Political Battle over The Pentagon Papers. Dutton, 1972. **$7.50**

427. (UNITED NATIONS). Charter of the United Nations and Statute of the International Court of Justice. Two volumes. California, 1945. **$45.00**
A handsome set, measuring 10 x 13 inches, with gilt lined and lettered covers. An exact facsimile of the volumes signed at San Francisco on June 26, 1945; in five languages (English, French, Spanish, Russian and Chinese), the edition was limited to 1000 copies. In a slightly worn slipcase.

First Printing of the
Civil Rights Act of 1866
428. (UNITED States). The Statutes at Large and Treaties of the United States of America. 39th Congress, First Session. Boston, Little Brown, 1866. **$35.00**
Original sewn wraps, lacking back cover, front cover badly chipped and stained. Internally clean.
The Civil Rights Act of 1866, the first federal statute to provide broad protection in the field of civil rights, carried into effect the 13th Amendment; vetoed by Johnson, & his veto overridden, it was eventually recast in part as the 14th amendment.

429. VANDERBILT, Arthur T. The Challenge of Law Reform. Princeton, 1955. **$10.00**
With a complimentary card of the author tipped in.

RARE AND SCHOLARLY
BOOKS ON THE LAW
(1979)

OLIVER WENDELL HOLMES, JR.

"These chance utterances of faith and doubt are printed for a few friends who will care to keep them." **(see Item 105).**

CATALOGUE TWO
MEYER BOSWELL BOOKS
SAN FRANCISCO

MEYER BOSWELL BOOKS

RARE AND SCHOLARLY BOOKS ON THE LAW
982 Hayes Street, San Francisco, California 94117
Telephone (415) 346-1839

With this catalogue, we continue our series of catalogues devoted exclusively to rare and scholarly law books; to the best of our knowledge, we remain the only bookshop in the world which is doing so, and which deals solely in this subject matter.

The response to our first catalogue, issued some few months ago, was *spectacular*, much better than we had anticipated or even hoped, and we are heartened. Which leads us to the following:

Have you been looking for a particular book, for years, without success? Are you interested in a subject matter which no "normal" person has ever even heard of? Are professors pestering you with requests for obscure titles no one seems to be able to find? Do you have a wants list moldering in your desk drawer? Do you just want to try us out? Well, just give us a call, or write, and at no obligation to you we will do our very best to find what you want.

For this catalogue, the following terms apply:

1. *Our Guarantee.* All items are guaranteed as described (if no express description is given, you may assume the item is in very good to mint condition), and may be returned for any reason within 30 days of receipt; please pack carefully and insure if received insured by you.
2. *Telephone Orders.* You may place your order by telephone 24 hours a day, seven days a week. Just call (415) 346-1839, and we will ship the next day.
3. *Domestic Shipments.* Handling, postage and insurance (which we obtain on all shipments over $25.00) are additional; on shipments under $25.00 we assume risk of loss or damage.
4. *Overseas Shipments.* Handling, postage, conversion charges, and insurance (where applicable) additional. Unless instructed otherwise, shipments under $100.00 are sent surface mail at your risk; shipments over $100.00 are insured and sent by air parcel post.
5. *Individual Billing.* If unknown to us, you may be billed pro-forma; we ship on receipt of payment. In all other instances, you will be billed upon shipment, and payment is due upon receipt of books, unless you wish to pay by either Visa (including BarclayCard) or Master Charge, in which case please provide us with your credit card number and its expiration date when you order; we will enclose your receipt with shipment.
6. *Library Billing.* Libraries will be billed to suit requirements.

1. ALEXANDROWICZ, C. H. An Introduction to the History of the Law of Nations in the East Indies. Oxford, 1967. **$15.00**
With the "ex libris" stamp of the O.U.P., Canadian Branch.

2. ALEXANDROWICZ, C. H. The Law of Global Communications. Columbia, 1971. **$12.50**

3. AMACHER, Ryan C. and Richard James Sweeney (ed.). The Law of the Sea: U.S. Interests and Alternatives. American Enterprise Institute, 1976. **$15.00**
Articles by *John Norton Moore* and *Myres S. McDougal*, among others.

4. ANDERSON, Robert Bowie (comp.). A Supplement to Beale's Bibliography of Early English Law Books. Harvard, 1943. **$25.00**
Issued 17 years after Beale's work, the foremost bibliography on early English law, which appeared in 1926. Spine slightly dulled.

5. (ARBITRATION). KATHARINE SEIDE (ed.). The Paul Felix Warburg Union Catalogue of Arbitration; A Selective Bibliography and Subject Index of Peaceful Dispute Settlement Procedures. Rowman & Littlefield. Three volumes. **$65.00**
Cross-indexed in six ways, the materials are taken from the holdings of 19 law libraries.

6. ARNOLD, Thurman. Democracy and Free Enterprise. Oklahoma, 1942. **$15.00**
The Baxter Memorial Lectures.

7. ARNOT, Hugo. A Collection and Abridgment of Celebrated Criminal Trials in Scotland from A.D. 1536 to 1784. Glasgow, 1812. **$100.00**
Irascible and eccentric, Arnot first published this work in 1785 at his own expense in defiance of the Edinburgh booksellers. It was immediately pirated in Ireland, and became his most popular work.
Arnot organizes the work by subject, from treason to murder to adultery and worse; attractively rebound in half calf over marbled boards, all edges marbled, red label gilt-lettered; some foxing to the title page and succeeding leaves, else very clean, and altogether a very attractive copy.

8. (ASSOCIATION of the Bar of the City of New York). Disorder in the Court. Pantheon, 1973. **$10.00**
The Report by the Association's Special Committee on Courtroom Conduct.

9. (ASSOCIATION of the Bar of the City of New York). Freedom of the Press and Fair Trial. Columbia, 1967. **$8.50**
Final Report by the Association's Special Committee on Radio, Television and the Administration of Justice, chaired by *Judge Harold Medina.*

10. BARD, Robert L. Food Aid and International Agricultural Trade, a Study in Legal and Administrative Control. Lexington, 1972. **$10.00**

11. BEANEY, William M. The Right to Counsel in American Courts. Michigan, 1955. **$15.00**

12. BENTHAM, Jeremy. The Church of England Catechism Examined. London, 1824. **$65.00**
Bentham's attack on the church catechism and the Church of England, first published in 1818; original boards, paper label, worn & soiled, occasional light spotting but quite a clean copy.
Bentham, in his manuscripts, referred to the Christian religion as the "Jug", short for "Juggernaut"; further evidence of his antipathy to the Church, if needed, is supplied by this little volume.

Bentham's Defense of Freedom of the Press.

13. BENTHAM, Jeremy. The Elements of the Art of Packing, As Applied to Special Juries, Particularly in Cases of Libel Law. London, 1821. First Edition. 12 leaves, 269 pp., 2 leaves. **$250.00**
3/4 calf over original marbled boards, worn, newly & attractively rebacked, black label,gilt-lettered; gilt-lined spine; foxing to preliminaries and title page, occasional light foxing elsewhere.
Bentham's "j'accuse" of the Crown's corruption in selecting obsequious special juries in libel cases, and selectively applying the law in deciding them, thus crushing the liberty of the press.
A clean and attractive copy of the first edition of one of Bentham's most important works, on the subject (fear of prosecution for libel) which delayed publication of many of his own books.

14. (BENTHAM,Jeremy). C.K. OGDEN. Jeremy Bentham 1832-2032. Kegan Paul, 1932. **$15.00**
Red cloth over boards, paper label. *An attractive little volume* issued on the centenary of Bentham's death.

15. (BENTHAM, Jeremy). TIMOTHY L.S. SPRIGGE (ed.). The Correspondence of Jeremy Bentham, 1752-1780. Two Volumes. Athlone Press, 1968. **$25.00**
The first two volumes of Bentham's correspondence, scrupulously edited and far surpassing earlier efforts.

16. BICKEL, Alexander M. Reform and Continuity: The Electoral College, The Convention, and The Party System. Harper & Row, 1971. **$12.50**

17. BISHOP, Joseph W., Jr. Obiter Dicta, Opinions, Judicious and Otherwise, on Lawyers and the Law. Atheneum, 1971. **$8.50**

18. BLACK, Charles L. Capital Punishment: The Inevitability of Caprice and Mistake. Norton, 1974. **$10.00**

19. BLACK, CYRIL E., et al. Neutralization and World Politics. Princeton, 1968. **$10.00**

20. (BLACK, Hugo). STEPHEN STRICKLAND (ed.). Hugo Black and the Supreme Court. Bobbs Merrill, 1967. **$15.00**
With a foreward by *Charles L. Black.*

21. (BLACK, Hugo). CHARLOTTE WILLIAMS. Hugo Black, A Study in the Judicial Process. Johns Hopkins, 1950. **$12.50**

E.D. Keyes Copy.

22. BLACKSTONE, Sir William. Commentaries on the Laws of England. Two Volumes. New York, 1836. Eller 97. **$125.00**
Often called *"Chitty's Blackstone"* because of the inclusion of Chitty's notes, this edition first appeared in New York in 1832, and was taken from the 18th English edition.
Original full calf, rubbed and worn but sound, contrasting red and black labels, gilt-lined and lettered ("Blackstone's Commentaries" "By Chitty"), occasional foxing and marginal dampstaining, but altogether a good set in the original binding.
With the signature in both volumes of E.D. Keyes, pioneer California lawyer and soldier, and author of "Fifty Years Observation of Men and Events."

23. BOZEMAN, Adda B. The Future of Law in a Multicultural World. Princeton, 1971. **$10.00**

24. (BRANDEIS, Louis D.). MELVIN UROFSKY and David W. Levy. Letters of Louis D. Brandeis. S.U.N.Y., 1971-73. Three volumes. **$50.00**
Superbly edited, these three volumes contain Brandeis' letters from 1915, immediately before he went on the Bench; a fourth volume has recently been printed (which we will be pleased to order for you), and a fifth is planned.

25. BRITTON, (John le, Bishop of Hereford). Britton on the Laws of England. Second Edition. London, 1640. Blank; title page; 15 leaves; 287 folios; 21 leaves. S.T.C. 3804. **$300.00**
Called *"the first great treatise upon the law written in the vernacular language [Law French] of the courts"*, Britton's work was written in the last years of the 1200's, most likely 1291-1292.
An attractive copy, old mottled boards, morocco-backed, a fair amount of age-browning to the text, some marginal annotations, black letter throughout.
The second edition of Britton, edited by Edmund Wingate, was published exactly 100 years after the issuance of the first edition in 1540, which itself was "exceeding full of manifest imperfections", including omission of an entire chapter; Wingate supplies this chapter and other emendations in an Appendix.
A desirable copy of the only reliable early rendition of Britton, and its last publication until Nichols' critical edition in 1865.

26. BRYSON, William Hamilton. (ed.). Dictionary of Sigla and Appreviations to and in Law Books before 1607. 1975. New. **$20.00**
Extremely valuable.

27. BURN, Richard. The Justice of the Peace and Parish Officer. Thirteenth Edition. Four Volumes. London, 1776. **$150.00**
Called the *"best of the books on the justices of the peace"* by Holdsworth, Burns' Justice ran through 15 editions in Burns' lifetime, and reached a 30th in 1869. This, the thirteenth, was published a mere 21 years after the first edition of 1755.
Attractively bound in the original calf, worn, joints unobtrusively cracked or cracking, elaborately gilt-decorated spines, contrasting red and black labels, gilt lettered, some occasional light spotting or foxing, but altogether *quite a nice set.*

28. CAM, Helen M. The Eyre of London, 14 Edward II, A.D. 1321. Two volumes. London, 1968-69. **$45.00**
Dr. Cam's last work, to which she was devoting herself at the time of her death. Selden Society volumes 85 & 86, and volume 26 of its Year Book Series.

29. (CAPITAL Punishment). Capital Punishment, Nineteenth Century Arguments. Arno, 1974. **$10.00**
Reprints of several extensive Massachusetts House reports originally published in 1836 and 1837.

30. (CARDOZO, Benjamin N.). Essays Dedicated to Mr. Justice Cardozo, N.P., 1939. **$25.00**
An unusual, perhaps unique, combined issue of the Columbia, Harvard and Yale law reviews and law journal, respectively, with essays by *Learned Hand, Felix Frankfurter and Harlan Stone*, among others; original sewn wraps, chipped and worn, cover marked, isolated underlining.

31. CARRINGTON, Frank G. Neither Cruel Nor Unusual, the Case for Capital Punishment. Arlington, 1978. **$8.50**

32. CAVERS, David F. The Choice-of-Law Process. Michigan, 1965. **$15.00**
Based on the *1964 Cooley Lectures at Michigan.*

33. CHAFEE, Zechariah, Jr. The Blessings of Liberty. Lippincott, 1956. **$15.00**

34. CHALIDZE, Valery. Criminal Russia, Crime in the Soviet Union. Random House, 1977. **$8.50**

35. CHEAPE, Douglas. An Introductory Lecture on the Civil Law. Edinburgh, 1827. **$45.00**
Well known for his "squibs", this is Cheape's only full-dress work, delivered upon his assuming the post of *Professor of Civil Law at Edinburgh* in 1827.
A clean copy, bound in modern gray wraps.

36. CHEVIGNY, Paul. Police Power, Police Abuses in New York City. Pantheon, 1969. **$10.00**

37. CHUTE, Marchette. The First Liberty, A History of the Right to Vote in America, 1619-1850. Dent, 1970. **$10.00**

38. (CLARK, Grenville), MARY CLARK DIMOND (comp.). Memoirs of a Man. Norton, 1975. **$15.00**
Reminiscences by *Henry Friendly, Charles Wyzanski and Jack Greenberg*, among many others.

39. (CLEMENTS Inn). SIR CECIL CARR (ed.). Pension Book of Clements Inn. London, 1960. **$22.50**
Printed from the only surviving Pension Book manuscript of this now defunct Inn of Chancery, the "Pension" being the Assembly of the Members of the Society, and related only indirectly to board, lodging, or retirement. Selden Society, Volume 78.

40. (COHEN, Morris R.). LEONORA COHEN ROSENFIELD. Portrait of a Philosopher: Morris R. Cohen in Life & Letters. Harcourt, 1962. **$15.00**
Includes the *Holmes-Cohen Correspondence.*

41. (COLUMBIA Law School). MONRAD G. PAULSON (ed.). Legal Institutions Today and Tomorrow. Columbia, 1959. **$20.00**
The centennial volume of the Columbia Law School.

42. COMMITTEE To Frame a World Constitution, The. Preliminary Draft of a World Constitution. Chicago, 1948. **$10.00**

Committee members included *Robert M. Hutchins, Mortimer J. Adler and C. H. McIlwain.*

43.(COMPUTERS and Civil Liberties). Records, Computers and the Rights of Citizens. G.P.O., 1973. Stiff wraps. **$15.00**
Report of the Secretary's [of H.E.W.] Advisory Committee on Automated Personal Data Systems; with the H.E.W. press release laid in.

44.(COPYRIGHT). THORVALD SOLBERG. Copyright in Congress, 1789-1904. G.P.O., 1905. **$45.00**
A bibliography, and a chronological record of all proceedings in copyright written by Solberg, the then Register of Copyrights. Original maroon cloth, slightly worn, foredge spotted, gilt-lettered spine; altogether quite nice.

45. CORWIN, Edward S. Constitutional Revolution, Ltd. Pomona, 1941. **$20.00**
Presentation copy from Corwin, signed by him on the title page; in a worn dust-wrapper.

46. (COWBOYS). HAROLD L. OPPENHEIMER and JAMES D. KEAST. Cowboy Litigation. Second Edition. Interstate, 1972. **$20.00**
The subtitle "Cattle and the Income Tax" fails to do this exceptional work justice.

A Wing Variant
47. Dalton, Michael. The Country Justice. London, 1643. Sixth Edition. 4 leaves; 496 pages; 4 leaves (table). Wing D143 (variant). **$225.00**
One of the very first books in a long line of works on the justices of the peace extending from the 17th to the 20th centuries, and perhaps the first book to adopt the alphabetical arrangement of subject matters concerning the justices' duties, so as to permit ease of reference.

Title within woodcut border, four woodcut rules and three initials; some pages a bit dusty, but in general a very good copy, handsomely rebound in full-dark calf, ruled in blind.

Bibliographically also of interest, in that Wing calls for a 12mo edition, while our copy is a quarto.

48. DANELSKI, David J. A Supreme Court Justice Is Appointed. Random House, 1964. **$10.00**

49. DAVENPORT, William H. (ed.). Voices in Court. MacMillan, 1958. **$15.00**
Essays by *Holmes, Wigmore, Learned Hand, Cardozo,* and many others.

50. DERRETT, J. Duncan M. (ed.). An Introduction to Legal Systems. Praeger, 1968. **$12.50**
Essays on Roman, Islamic, Chinese and African law, among others.

51. DICEY, A.V. Introduction to the Study of the Law of the Constitution. Ninth Edition, MacMillan, 1956. **$15.00**
Termed a "classic" by Holdsworth; this is the Ninth edition revised by E.C.S. Wade.

First Edition.
52. DICKENS, Charles. Bleak House. London, 1853. **$135.00**
One of Dickens' greatest novels, and certainly his most "legal", devoted to his castigation of the delay and expense in the Court of Chancery in the early 1800's.

An extremely handsome copy, in full green morocco, slightly rubbed, gilt-lined and lettered, matching labels, hand-tooled design on front cover, all edges gilt, the binding signed by A. Darling; with all plates present, some spotting to the edges only, some off-setting, lacking the half-title but altogether *a very attractive copy of what Holdsworth called "the greatest triumph of his [Dickens'] art,"* Holdsworth also quoting Gibbon on Roman Law at the time of Justinian as appropriately descriptive of Chancery: "a mysterious science and a profitable trade . . . the innate perplexity of the study [of which] was involved in tenfold darkness by the private industry of the practitioners."

53. DIGNAN, Rev. Patrick J. A History of the Legal Incorporation of Catholic Church Property in the United States (1784-1932). Kenedy, 1935. **$35.00**

54. DILLON, John F. The Laws and Jurisprudence of England and America. Little, Brown, 1894. **$35.00**
Called "interesting" and "suggestive" by *Augustus N. Hand* (while he was a student at Harvard Law, however), this work consists of Dillon's lectures at Yale given shortly before publication. Original brown cloth, gilt-lettered; occasional light foxing, but a nice copy.

55. DORSEN, Norman. Frontiers of Civil Liberties. Pantheon, 1968. **$10.00**

56. DOUGLAS, William O. Mr Lincoln and the Negroes. Atheneum, 1963. **$10.00**

57. DOUGLAS, William O. Towards a Global Federalism. N.Y.U., 1968. **$12.50**
The 1968 *James Stokes Lectureship.*

58. DRUG Addiction: Crime or Disease? Indiana, 1966. **$12.50**
The interim and final reports of the Joint Committee of the American Bar Association and the American Medical Association on Narcotic Drugs.

59. DUMBAULD, Edward. The Bill of Rights and What It Means Today. Oklahoma, 1957. **$10.00**

60. ELSYNGE, Henry. The Ancient Method and Manner of Holding Parliaments in England. Fourth Edition. London, 1679. Title page; 5 leaves (table); 371 pages. New Wing E646. **$110.00**
Termed the *"best book on Parliamentary procedure"* by Holdsworth, and "always . . . regarded as authoritative", the first edition of this work appeared some 19 years before, in 1660.

A nice copy, bound in early 19th century calf, marbled edges, elaborately gilt-decorated spine, somewhat worn; with the bookplate of Thomas Philip Earl de Grey, first Lord of the Admiralty 1834-35, and the first President of the Society of British Architects.

61. d'ENTREVES, A.P. Natural Law, an Introduction to Legal Philosophy. Hutchinson, 1970. **$12.50**
The Second Edition, with three additional essays.

62. FALK, Richard A. The Status of Law in International Society. Princeton, 1970. **$15.00**

63. FALK, Richard A. and Richard J. Barnet (eds.). Security in Disarmament Princeton, 1965. **$10.00**

64. FALK, Harry W. Timber and Forest Products Law. Howell-North, 1958. **$25.00**

65. (FEDERAL Trade Commission). Report of the Federal Trade Commission on Interlocking Directorates. G.P.O., 1951. **$17.50**
Original sewn wraps, slightly chipped and worn; with four folding tables, 510 pp.

66. FERRIS, David Frederic. Judge Marvin and the Founding of the California Public School System. California, 1962. **$10.00**
Sewn wraps.

A unique association and presentation copy.
67. (FIELD, Stephen J.). Some Account of the Work of Stephen J. Field. New York (?), 1895. **$225.00**
Originally issued in 1881, this work was re-published in 1895, considerably expanded by additions of George Gorham, Field's longtime friend and associate, the primary addition being an account of the famous Terry-Field episode, which Gorham denominates an assasination attempt.

Our copy contains *a presentation inscription from Justice Field;* and laid in are *a handwritten, signed letter from Gorham,* on the stationery of the Office of the Secretary of the U.S. Senate, and *a U.S. Post Office return receipt card, signed by Field.*

Bound in 3/4 leather over marbled boards, marbled endpapers; some rubbing to joints & extremities and short, unobtrusive cracks to the upper portions of the joints; gilt-lettered, and *a handsome copy.*

Interleaved Copy.
68. FITZHERBERT, Sir Anthony. La Nouvelle Natura Brevium. Title Page. 31 leaves (table); 271 folios; colophon. London, 1581. S.T.C. 10962. Beale T349. **$450.00**
One of the greatest law books of the 1500's, published through nine editions until 1794.

Called by Professor Boersma "the leading figure on the Bench in the reign of Henry VIII (1509-1547)", Fitzherbert intended this work to reveal the "divers Maximes and Fundamentals in

the knowledge of the Common Laws of the Land", this to be accomplished through the study of the entire writ system, with the writs set out, accompanied by Fitzherbert's commentary on them.

Contemporary calf, raised bands, covers ruled in blind with embossed device at center, remains of original cord ties, front joint skillfully renewed, one corner repaired; title within woodcut border, Gothic type, printed initials at outer margins, some contemporary marginalia, some minor dampstaining, spotting and embrowning, but in general *an exceptionally clean copy,* and interleaved throughout.

A highly desirable copy in the original binding of one of Fitzherbert's two great works, and *placed by Coke among the books which he considered "most necessary and of the greatest authority and excellency."*

69. FORTAS, Abe. Concerning Dissent and Civil Disobedience. Signet, 1968. Wraps, 64 pp. **$5.00**

70. FRANK, Jerome. Courts on Trial. Princeton, 1949. **$15.00**

71. FRANK, Jerome and Barbara Frank. Not Guilty. DaCapo, 1971. **$10.00**
With a foreward by *William O. Douglas.*

72. (FRANK, Jerome). BARBARA FRANK KRISTEIN. A Man's Reach, The Selected Writings of Judge Jerome Frank. MacMillan, 1965. **$15.00**

73. FRANK, John P. American Law, The Case for Radical Reform. MacMillan, 1969. **$12.50**
The Earl Warren Legal Center Dedication Lectures.

74. FRANK, John P. Justice Daniel Dissenting. A Biography of Peter V. Daniel, 1784-1860. Harvard, 1964. **$10.00**

75. FRANK, John P. Marble Palace, The Supreme Court in American Life. Knopf, 1968. **$10.00**

76. (FRANKFURTER, Felix). JOSEPH P. LASH. From the Diaries of Felix Frankfurter. Norton, 1975. **$10.00**

77. (FRANKFURTER, Felix). WALLACE MENDELSON (ed.). Felix Frankfurter, the Judge. Reynal, 1964. **$12.50**
Essays by *Henry J. Friendly, Louis Henkin and Louis Jaffe,* among others.

78. (FRANKFURTER, Felix). HELEN SHIRLEY THOMAS. Felix Frankfurter, Scholar on the Bench. Johns Hopkins, 1960. **$10.00**

79. FRANKLIN, Julian H. (ed.). Constitutionalism and Resistance in the Sixteenth Century, Three Treatises by Hotman, Beza, & Mornay. Pegasus, 1969. **$10.00**

80. FREEMAN, E.A. The History of the Norman Conquest of England. Five Volumes. Revised American Edition. Oxford, 1873, 1876. **$125.00**
A contemporary and close personal friend of Stubbs, Freeman devoted much of his life to this, his magnum opus, about which *Sir Frank Stenton* was later to say "as an introduction to the sources for the political history of the period the book is *of great and permanent value."*

Bound in the original lightish-red buckram, gilt-lined and lettered spines, slightly rubbed and chafed, but an attractive and sound set.

81. FRIEDMAN, Leon (ed.). Obscenity The Complete Oral Arguments Before the Supreme Court in the Major Obscenity Cases. Chelsea House, 1970. **$15.00**

82. FRIENDLY, Henry J. Federal Jurisdiction: A General View. Columbia, 1973. **$12.50**
Based on Friendly's *1972 James S. Carpentier Lectures* at Columbia.

83. FULLER, Lon. Legal Fictions. Stanford, 1967. **$15.00**

84. GAJENDRAGADKAR, P.B. Law, Liberty and Social Justice. Asia, 1965. **$10.00**
The author was *Chief Justice of India.*

85. GARVER, John A. John W. Sterling, A Biographical Sketch. Yale, 1929. **$35.00**
The Sterling of Shearman and Sterling, and one of Yale Law's most illustrious graduates; *a presentation copy from the author,* in the original blue cloth, gilt-lettered spine and cover; illustrated.

86. GATES, Paul W. Landlords and Tenants on the Prairie Frontier. Cornell, 1973. **$12.50**

87. GELDART, William. Elements of English Law. Fifth Edition. Oxford, 1957. **$10.00**
Revised by *Sir William Holdsworth* and *H.G. Hanbury.*

88. GLUECK, Sheldon and Eleanor. Criminal Careers in Retrospect. The Commonwealth Fund, 1943. **$17.50**
One of the *Harvard Law School Studies in Criminology.*

89. GOLDFARB, Ronald. Jails, the Ultimate Ghetto of the Criminal Justice System. Anchor Press, 1975. **$8.50**

90. GOLDFARB, Ronald. Ransom. Harper, 1965. **$10.00**

91. GOULDEN, Joseph C. The Million Dollar Lawyers. Putnam, 1978. **$10.00**

92. GRAGLIA, Lino A. Disaster by Decree, The Supreme Court Decisions on Race and the Schools. Cornell, 1976. **$10.00**

93. GREEN, Mark J. The Other Government, The Unseen Power of Washington Lawyers. Grossman, 1975. **$10.00**

94. GREENBERG, Douglas. Crime and Law Enforcement in the Colony of New York. Cornell, 1976. **$12.50**

95. GRIEVANCE Response Mechanisms in the Ghetto, a Symposium. DaCapo, 1971. **$8.50**
One of several symposia under the general editorship of *Leonard W. Levy.*

96. HALE, Sir Matthew. Contemplations Moral and Divine, in Two Parts. London, 1679. Wing H.223. **$125.00**
An early issue of one of Hale's most oft-reprinted works, in the press in 1676 when he died. Whether Hale intended these musings, principally theological and philosophical, to be printed remains debatable, their printing begun over his objection.

Contemporary panelled calf, worn, rebacked, red label gilt-lettered; *an attractive and clean copy, with the engraved frontispiece of Hale.*

97. HALLAM, Henry. View of the State of Europe During the Middle Three Volumes. 12th edition. London, 1868. **$85.00**
Hallam's first great work, appearing in 1818 after what is said to have been "ten years' assiduous labour."

Handsomely bound in full calf, blind and gilt decorated covers, richly gilt spine, contrasting red and black labels, all edges marbled and marbled endpapers, prize label in volume I, a bit of foxing to preliminaries, and a very little rubbing to the bindings, but altogether *an extremely attractive set.*

98. (HAMILTON, Alexander). JULIUS GOEBEL, JR. and Joseph H. Smith (eds.). The Law Practice of Alexander Hamilton. Columbia, 1964-79. Five volumes. **$250.00**
In preparation in excess of fifteen years, and co-edited by perhaps the greatest historian of American law in this century, Julius Goebels, the set includes in Volume V *Hamilton's manuscript Law Register* and his manuscript Cash Book. Individual volumes may also be purchased, at $50 each.

99. HART, H.L.A. Law, Liberty and Morality. Oxford, 1966. **$15.00**
The 1962 *Harry Camp Lectures* at Stanford.

100. HASKINS, George Lee. Law and Authority in Early Massachusetts. MacMillan, 1960. **$17.50**

101. HAZARD, John N. Soviet Housing Law. Yale, 1939. **$22.50**
Hazard's first work.

102. HOLLANDER, Barnett. Colonial Justice, The Unique Achievement of the Privy Council's Committee of Judges. Bowes, 1961. **$15.00**
Introduction by *Lord Shawcross.*

103. HOLLANDER, Barnett. The International Law of Art. Bowes, 1959. *Presentation copy.* **$25.00**

Presentation Copy of the First Edition.
104. HOLMES, Oliver Wendell, Jr. The Common Law. Boston, 1881. **$750.00**

Published when Holmes was 40, "The Common Law" may be the most famous of all American Law books. This copy of the first edition, *with an autographed, signed presentation slip tipped in*, dated November, 1896, *from Holmes to Sir Leslie Scott*, whom Mark de Wolfe Howe counts among Holmes "intimate" friends, and whose copious pencil annotations may be found throughout the text.

Scott, who was later to become Lord Justice of Appeal, wrote to thank Holmes in January, 1897, for the copy of the book; we have examined a copy of this letter, the original of which is at Harvard Law School, in which Scott (then 27) apologizes for his delay in replying noting that he was too tired at the end of the day to read Holmes' closely reasoned exegesis, thus having to save the work for Sundays; Scott further refers to his particular interest in torts and bailments, and it is indeed these chapters of the book which are most heavily annotated.

Handsomely rebound in full blue oasis leather, with hand-marbled endpapers and hand-tooled gilt lines, a tan label and matching brown slipcase. *A beautiful and unique copy of the first edition of Holmes' most important work.*

A Presentation Copy from Holmes in Mrs. Holmes' Hand.

105. HOLMES, Oliver Wendell, Jr. Speeches. First Edition. Boston, 1891. **$300.00**
The first edition of the first collection of Holmes' speeches, among which are several of his most famous, including "Memorial Day" and "The Law".

With an autograph, presentation inscription "To F.P. from O.W.H. Jr. December 1891" in the hand of Mrs. Holmes; the question "who is F.P.?" remains unanswered--the most tantalizing possibility is Sir Frederick Pollock, Holmes' long-time friend and correspondent whom Holmes addressed as "F.P.", but Pollock's thank-you letter to Holmes (in the Holmes-Pollock Letters) predates the inscription date; the most likely other possibility may be Francis Parkman, the renowned historian.

Bound in the original boards, slightly worn and rubbed, the top edge gilt, a *unique and extremely desirable copy of the first edition.*

106. (HOLMES, Oliver Wendell). SILAS BENT. Justice Oliver Wendell Holmes. Vanguard, 1932. **$15.00**
The Original Edition.

107. (HOLMES, Oliver Wendell). MARK DeWOLFE HOWE (ed.). Holmes-Pollock Letters. Second Edition. Harvard, 1961. **$17.50**

108. (HOLMES, Oliver Wendell, Jr.). MARK DE WOLFE HOWE. Justice Holmes: The Shaping Years 1841-1870. Harvard, 1957. **$15.00**
With a complimentary card of the Harvard University Press laid in.

109. (HOLMES, Oliver Wendell). ALFRED LIEF (ed.). The Dissenting Opinions of Mr. Justice Holmes. Vanguard, 1929. **$17.50**
Slightly worn.

110. HUNT, Aurora. Kirby Benedict, Federal Frontier Judge. Arthur H. Clarke, 1961. **$17.50**
Folding map; uncut.

111. HURST, Sir Gerald. Lincoln's Inn Essays. Constable, 1949. **$17.50**

112. INTERNATIONAL Commission of Jurists. African Conference on the Rule of Law. Geneva, 1961. **$15.00**

113. INTERNATIONAL Commission of Jurists. The Dynamic Aspects of the Rule of Law in the Modern Age. Geneva, 1965. Stiff wraps. **$15.00**

114.(ISAACS, Rufus). Rufus Isaacs, First Marquess of Reading. Putnam, 1940. **$17.50**
Written by Isaacs' son; Isaacs is said to have been the first advanced from commoner to Marquess since the Duke of Wellington, becoming Lord Chief Justice along the way; a nice copy.

115. JACKSON, Robert H. The Struggle for Judicial Supremacy. Knopf, 1949. **$17.50**

116. JACKSON, Robert H. The Supreme Court in the American System of Government. Harvard, 1955. **$25.00**
First printing of the *1955 Godkin lectures* at Harvard, on which Jackson was working the day before his death; *in the handsome red and black cloth binding.*

First Edition.

117. [Jacob, Giles]. Every Man His Own Lawyer, or A Summary of the Laws of England. First Edition. London, 1736. Blank; advertising leaf; title page; iii-vi; 454 pages; 7 leaves (table); blank. **$150.00**
The first edition of the first work by this name, written by one of the most prolific law writers of the 18th century; original calf, worn, *very nicely rebacked*, occasional very light spotting or embrowning; altogether *quite a desirable copy.*

118. JENKS, C. Wilfred. The Prospects of International Adjudication. Stevens, 1964. **$22.50**
With the corrigenda laid in.

119. JESSUP, Philip C. The Birth of Nations. Columbia, 1974. **$10.50**

120. JESSUP, Philip C. The Use of International Law. Michigan, 1959. **$20.00**
The *1958 Thomas M. Cooley Lectures* at Michigan.

121. [JOHNSON, John]. The Clergyman's Vade-Mecum. Fifth Edition. London, 1723. 12 leaves, 378 pp., 23 leaves. **$85.00**
Bound in contemporary panelled calf, *newly and well rebacked* lightish damping to portions of the index leaves.

An unusual volume, consisting of practical advice to young clergy, so as to avoid the expense of lawyers, and *a collection and commentary on codes governing the primitive church*, so as to justify the Anglican system of church government; *an attractive copy* of a work written by John Johnson, whom Holdsworth terms a "learned ecclesiastical historian" who "knew a good deal of law."

122. KATZ, Carol Hecht (ed.). The Law and the Low Income Consumer. N.Y.U., 1968. **$15.00**
Stiff wraps, slightly worn, the second of the Welfare Law Supplements published by the Project on Social Welfare Law at N.Y.U.

123. KEETON, Robert E. and Jeffrey O'Connell. After Cars Crash, The Need for Legal and Insurance Reform. Dow Jones-Irwin, 1967. **$15.00**

124. KELSEN, Hans. The Pure Theory of Law. California, 1967. **$20.00**

Fore-edge slightly spotted, small portion of first free endpaper cut away, else a fine copy in the dustwrapper.

125. KOEGEL, Otto E. Walter S. Carter, Collector of Young Masters, or the Progenitors of Many Law Firms. Round Table Press, 1953. **$35.00**
A superb work, and a presentation copy tracing Carter's influence in the Wisconsin, Chicago and Wall Street bars.

126. KRISLOV, Samuel. The Supreme Court and Political Freedom. Free Press, 1968. **$8.50**

127. KUH, Richard H. Foolish Figleaves? Pornography in-and out of-court. MacMillan, 1967. **$10.00**

128. LAFFAN, R.G.D. Select Historical Documents of European History, 800-1492. Henry Holt, 1929. **$12.50**

129. (LAMBARDE, William). CONYERS READ (ed.). William Lambarde & Local Government. Cornell, 1962. **$17.50**
Published for *The Folger Shakespeare Library.*

130. LATHAM, Frank B. The Great Dissenter, John Marshall Harlan, 1833-1911. Cowles, 1970. **$8.50**

131.(LAW-FRENCH). T.B.W. REID. Anglo-Norman Dictionary, Fascicle 1: A-Cyvere. London, 1977. Sewn wraps. **$60.00**
The first volume of the first major scholarly effort to include Law-French in an Anglo-Norman dictionary, and of great assistance in any study of early English law.

132. LEE, Guy Carleton. Historical Jurisprudence, An Introduction to the Systematic Study of the Development of the Law. MacMillan, 1911. **$25.00**
Dedicated to Pollock & Maitland; original green cloth, gilt-lettered, very slightly worn & a few pencil annotations.

133. LEWIS, Anthony. Gideon's Trumpet. Random House, 1964. **$10.00**

134. (LONDON Churches). The Acts of Parliament Relating to the Building Fifty New Churches in and about the Cities of London and Westminster. London, 1721. Blank; title page; 3-179 pages; 10 leaves (contents); blank. Octavo. **$100.00**
A massive undertaking, commenced in the early 1700's, costing hundreds of thousands of pounds, and financed initially by a tax upon coal, which apparently proved insufficient and was supplemented by lotteries. *A very nice copy* in the original, unlettered calf, gilt and blind decorated, five raised bands.

135. [MACONOCHIE, Allan (Lord Meadowbank)]. Considerations on the Introduction of Jury Trial in Civil Causes Into Scotland. First Edition. Edinburgh, 1814. **$65.00**
The issue whether the right to jury trial in civil causes should be recognized became a cause celebre in late 18th and early 19th century Scotland; this volume, published anonymously by Lord Meadowbank in 1814, praised (cautiously) the English system of trial by jury, and suggested its selective adoption by way of experiment, a suggestion adopted the succeeding year, eventually leading to the full-scale adoption of the jury trial in civil causes in 1830.

An attractive copy, newly rebound in half-calf over marbled boards, spine gilt-lined and lettered.

136. MACY, Jesse. The English Constitution, a Commentary on Its Nature and Growth. MacMillan, 1898. **$15.00**
Very slightly worn.

137. MAINE, Sir Henry. Ancient Law. Fourteenth Edition. London, 1891. **$20.00**
Maine's greatest work, his first, and the one which Holmes' said fed his *"philosophic passion"* and led to The Common Law. A nice copy in the original reddish-brown cloth, very slightly worn, gilt lettered.

138. MAINE, Sir Henry. International Law. London, 1890. **$45.00**
Maine's Whewell Lectures, his last work and published posthumously in 1888; this edition of bibliographical interest, not noted by Feaver, appearing after the first edition, but before the second edition of 1894. In the original reddish-brown cloth, very slightly rubbed, gilt-lettered and *quite nice.*

139. MAINE, Sir Henry. Lectures on the Early History of Institutions. Sixth Edition. London, 1893. **$25.00**
Maine's attempt, pursuing themes begun in his Ancient Law, to connect up *early Irish law with the law of India and Eastern Europe.* Original reddish-brown cloth, slightly worn and the front cover unobtrusively spotted, gilt-lettered spine altogether *an attractive copy.*

140. MAINE, Sir Henry. Popular Government. London, 1890. **$25.00**
A prolific writer, Maine revised four of his essays, *including one on the U.S. Constitution*, to express his reservations of democratic governments; *a nice copy*, in the original reddish-brown cloth, slightly rubbed, gilt-lettered spine.

141. MAINE, Sir Henry. Village Communities in the East and West. New Edition. London, 1890. **$25.00**
Maine's classic comparison of Indian practices and European property law, and his first book following Ancient Law. Original reddish-brown cloth, slightly worn, gilt-lettered; *nice.*

142. MAITLAND, F.W. The Constitutional History of England. Cambridge, 1911. **$22.50**
Slightly worn; with the bookplate of the Constitutional Club Library.

143. (MAITLAND). FREDEGOND. Fredegond and Gerald Shove. Cambridge, England, 1952. **$22.50**
Privately printed, in an edition of 250 copies, for Ermengard Maitland, one of Maitland's two daughters who contributes a preface to this work by her sister; original buckram-backed boards, a little rubbed and worn, with the Bodleian Library cancel stamps.

144. MALINOWSKI, Bronislaw. Crime and Custom in Savage Society. Harcourt Brace, 1926. **$35.00**
A very nice copy of the first American edition.

145. (MARSHALL, John). JOHN STOKES ADAMS (ed.). An Autobiographical Sketch by John Marshall. Written at the Request of Joseph Story, etc. Michigan, 1937. **$25.00**
Inscribed to Tappan Gregory, nature writer and lawyer at the Nuremburg trials.

146. (MARSHALL, John). ROBERT K. FAULKNER. The Jurisprudence of John Marshall. Princeton, 1968. **$15.00**

147. (MARSHALL, John). Final Report of the United States Commission for the Celebration of the Two Hundredth Anniversary of the Birth of John Marshall. Washington, 1955. **$17.50**

148. (MARSHALL, John). GERALD GUNTHER (ed.). John Marshall's Defense of *McCulloch v. Maryland.* Stanford, 1969. **$10.00**

149. (MARSHALL, John). MARY NEWTON STANARD. John Marshall and His Home. Richmond, 1938. 38 pp, stapled, wraps. **$17.50**
With six photographs and a brief genealogical chart of Marshall and his family.

150. MARTIN, Charles H. The Angelo Herndon Case and Southern Justice. Louisiana State, 1976. **$10.00**

151. MAYERS, Lewis. The American Legal System. Harper & Row, 1955. **$25.00**
Presentation copy.

152. MEGARRY, Sir Robert. Inns Ancient and Modern, A Topographical and and Historical Introduction to the Inns of Court, Inns of Chancery, and Serjeants' Inns. London, 1978. 57 pp. stiff wraps, stapled. **$7.50**
The reprint of Justice Megarry's 1971 Selden Society Lecture.

153. MENZIES, Walter. Some Early Law Books in Aberdeen University Library. Edinburgh, 1932. 16 pp plus ten facsimile plates. Sewn wraps, slightly worn & stained. **$20.00**
Based on Aberdeen's collection of early works on *Canon and Civil Law*, and designed in part to remedy the long neglect of early law as some of the best examples of topography.

154. MERITON, George. The Touchstone of Wills, Testaments, and Administrations. **First Edition.** London, 1668. **$125.00**
Newly rebound half leather over boards, gilt-lined and lettered spine, text generally embrowned, title page repaired, first leaf of index torn with loss of text.

Brother of the dramatist Thomas Meriton, the learned author is best known for his work "In Praise of Yorkshire Ale"; this, the first of three editions of his "Touchstone", is written upon a much drier subject.

155. MIDGLEY, E.B.F. The Natural Law Tradition and the Theory of International Relations. Barnes & Noble, 1975. **$17.50**

156. (MIGRATORY LABOR). Amending Migratory Labor Laws, Hearings before the Subcommittee on Migratory Labor of the Senate Committee on Labor and Public Welfare. 1st & 2d Sess., 89th Cong. G.P.O., 1966. **$15.00**

157. MILLER, Arthur Selwyn. The Supreme Court and American Capitalism. Free Press, 1968. **$10.00**

158. MITGANG, Herbert. The Man Who Rode the Tiger, the Life and Times of Judge Samuel Seabury. Lippincott, 1963. **$15.00**
One of the *Legal Studies of the William Nelson Cromwell Foundation.*

159. MOORE, John Bassett. Commencement Address . . . Together with a Bibliography of His Writings. Printed at the Yale University Press, 1944. **$35.00**
Valuable biographical detail in the address, and invaluable detail in the 25 page bibliography.

160. MORRIS, Norval. The Future of Imprisonment. Chicago, 1974. **$15.00**
Morris' *1974 Thomas M. Cooley Lectures* at Michigan, revised and expanded.

161. MORRIS, Richard B. Fair Trial. Knopf, 1952. **$12.50**

162. MOSCHZISKER, Robert von. Trial by Jury, a Brief Review of Its Origin, Development and Merits, etc. Bisel, 1922. **$25.00**
Slightly worn.

163. MURPHY, Earl Finbar. Man and His Environment: Law. Harper & Row, 1971. **$10.00**
Marston Bates' copy.

164. NADER, Laura (ed.). Law in Culture and Society. Aldine, 1969. **$17.50**

165. (NAPOLEON). ALEX de JONGE (trans.). Napoleon's Last Will and Testament. Paddington, 1977. **$15.00**
The original document reproduced in facsimile, with an English translation (the first) on the facing pages. *An unusual item.*

166. (NATIONAL Commission on the Causes and Prevention of Violence). Law and Order Reconsidered. Praeger, 1970. $15.00
One of several Task Force reports submitted to the Commission; this Praeger edition contains a number of supplemental materials.

167. (NATIONAL Commission on the Causes and Prevention of Violence). To Establish Justice, to Insure Domestic Tranquility. G.P.O., 1969. Sewn wraps, stapled. $17.50
The official issuance of *the Commission's Final Report.*

168. NIMMER, Raymond T. Diversion, The Search for Alternative Forms of Prosecution. American Bar Foundation, 1974. $10.00

169. NOONAN, John T., Jr. Persons & Masks of the Law. Farrar, Straus, 1976. $10.00
Based on Noonan's *1972 Holmes Lectures*, with superb essays on Holmes, Cardozo and Wythe, among others.

170. (NORTH Atlantic Treaty). KURT VOLK (typographer). The Signing of the North Atlantic Treaty. New York, 1949. $50.00
Limited to 1,000 copies and signed by Volk; a handsome issue, bound in leather over decorated boards, gilt-lettered spine slightly chafed and worn. With the Proceedings, the text of the Treaty itself, and facsimile signatures, red-lettered throughout, and strikingly designed, with a Christmas card from Volk laid in.

171. NORTON, Thomas James. Losing Liberty Judicially, Prohibitory and Kindred Laws Examined. MacMillan, 1931. $22.50

172. (NOVAE Narrationes). ELSIE SHANKS (ed.). Novae Narrationes. London, 1963. $22.50
The only modern and the only critical edition ever published of this famous collection of medieval "counts" or "narrations" by which lawyers, beginning in the late 1200's, "told the tales" of their clients, by formula, in court. *With a legal introduction by S.F.C. Milsom.* Selden Society Volume 80.

173. OAKS, Dallin H. & Warren Lehman. A Criminal Justice System and the Indigent, A Study of Chicago and Cook County. Chicago, 1968. $12.50

174. ORTON, William Aylott. The Liberal Tradition. Yale, 1945. $15.00

Inscribed by Pound
175. POUND, Roscoe. The Formative Era of American Law. Little, Brown, 1938. $27.50
Based on Pound's lectures, two years before at Tulane, on the centennial of Edward Livingston's death. In a worn dustwrapper.

176. POUND, Roscoe. An Introduction to the Philosophy of Law. Yale, 1922. $35.00
Pound's *Storr's Lectures*, given in 1921, immediately after Cardozo's the year before; *the original edition.*

177. POUND, Roscoe. Law and Morals. North Carolina, 1926. Second Edition. $25.00
Revised shortly after the issuance of the first edition in 1924, and based on Pound's *McNair Lectures* in 1923; with a valuable bibliography appended.

178. (POUND, Roscoe). MOSES J. ARONSON. Roscoe Pound and the Resurgence of Juristic Idealism. 36 pp., wraps, covers slightly embrowned. $12.50
A *presentation copy* of Aronson's article appearing in the October, 1960 issue of the Journal of Social Philosophy.

179. POWELL, James M. (trans.). The Liber Augustalis, or Constitutions of Melfi Promulgated by the Emperor Frederick II for the Kingdom of Sicily in 1231. Syracuse, 1971. $10.00

180. POWELL, Thomas Reed. Vagaries and Varieties in Constitutional Interpretation. Columbia, 1956. $15.00
The *1955 James S. Carpentier Lectures* at Columbia; with an introduction by *Paul Freund.*

181. (PUBLIC Television). Public Television Act of 1967, Hearings Before the Committee on Interstate and Foreign Commerce, House of Representatives. 1st. Sess., 90th Cong. G.P.O. 1967. $15.00
Occasional margin annotations.

182. QUINNEY, Richard. The Social Reality of Crime. Little, Brown, 1970. $8.50

183. RADIN, Max and A.M. Kidd (eds) Legal Essays in Tribute to Orrin Kip McMurray. California, 1935. $25.00
Essays by *Roscoe Pound, Karl Llewellyn* and *John H. Wigmore*, among others. Slightly worn.

184. RAMUNDO, Bernard A. Peaceful Coexistence. Johns Hopkins, 1967. $8.50

The first general history of English law.
185. REEVES, John. Reeves' History of the English Law (ed. W.F. Finlason). Three volumes. London, 1869. $125.00
First appearing in the late 1700's, Reeves' work remained the only history of English Law until Pollock and Maitland's appeared in 1895, and the only history treating matters after Edward I until the appearance of Holdsworth's great history in this century.
A very nice copy, bound in the original green cloth, gilt lined & lettered spines still bright, of the work Maitland termed "intelligent and trustworthy"; this edition edited by Finlason, *with a lengthy introductory essay on the influence of Roman Law in England.*

186. REICH, Charles A. Police Questioning of Law Abiding Citizens. June, 1966. $5.00
Reprinted from the Yale Law Journal.

187. RICHARDSON, H.G. The Coronation in Medieval England. Fordham, 1960. Sewn wraps. $10.00
Offprinted from Tradition; wraps sunned.

188. RICHARDSON, W.C. History of the Court of Augmentations 1536-1554. Louisiana State, 1961. $17.50

189. (ROMILLY, Sir Samuel). C.G. OAKES. Sir Samuel Romilly 1757-1818. London, 1935. $17.50
Top of spine lightly faded, edges spotted, else *quite nice.*

190. ROOT, Elihu. Addresses on Government and Citizenship. Harvard, 1916. $25.00
Subdivided into five portions, this volume includes Root's *1907 Dodge Lectures* at Yale, his *1913 Stafford Little Lectures* at Princeton, and his addresses on the 1894 and 1915 New York State Constitutional Conventions.

191. ROOT, Elihu. Addresses on International Subjects. Harvard, 1916. $35.00
Included are Root's addresses at the first eight annual meetings of the *American Society of International Law*, of which he was president; original green cloth, gilt lettering, top edge gilt; *a nice copy.*

192. ROOT, Elihu. Miscellaneous Addresses. Harvard, 1917. $22.50
Collected and edited by *Robert Bacon* and *James Brown Scott;* top edge gilt.

193. SAMEK, Robert A. The Legal Point of View. Philosophical Library, 1974. $10.00

194. SAVIGNY, Friedrich Carl von. Geschichte des Romischen Rechts im Mittelalter. Seven Volumes. Second Edition. Heidelberg, 1834-51. $200.00
Arguably Savigny's greatest work, and certainly *one of the foremost works on legal history ever written*, never translated in its totality in English.
Occasional spotting and minor dampstaining, later unlettered blue wrappers a trifle chipped, but in general *a very nice, clean and largely uncut copy* of the second (and last) edition of what Peter Stein has termed one of two "main works of reference . . . of the sources of Roman Law in the middle ages."

195. SAYLER, Richard, et. al. (eds.). The Warren Court, A Critical Analysis. Chelsea House, 1969. $12.50

196. SAYLES, G.O. The Medieval Foundations of England. Pennsylvania, 1950. $17.50

197. SCHAFER, Stephen. Restitution to Victims of Crime. Stevens & Son, 1960. $15.00

198. SCHAFER, Stephen. Theories in Criminology. Random House, 1969. $10.00

199. SCHIFFER, Walter. The Legal Community of Mankind. Columbia, 1954. $15.00

Oscar T. Schuck's personal copy, heavily annotated.
200. SCHUCK, Oscar T. Bench and Bar in California. San Francisco, 1889. $225.00
Schuck, perhaps the greatest early historian of California law, published this work (the first of its kind in California) in 1889. Some ten years later, M.M. Miller began a similar, but expanded, work which he abandoned in 1900 to resume the practice of law in Hawaii.
Schuck was then called upon to complete Miller's work, devoting virtually his entire energies during the ensuing 12 months to it; the new work was published in 1901 as the History of Bench & Bar of California.
Our copy is Schuck's personal copy of his 1889 work, which he incorporated in part, but with substantial revisions, into the 1901 work; *the revisions are in Schuck's own hand*, and their faithful introduction into the 1901 text may be followed.
Also included are numerous newspaper clippings and portraits, and other notes pinned in where applicable.
In the original reddish-brown, blind-decorated cloth, gilt-lettered, considerably worn (as might be expected) but clean and sound. *A one-of-a-kind copy of one of the premier works on California legal history.*

201. SCHUR, Edwin M. and Hugo Adam Bedau. Victimless Crimes. Prentice Hall, 1974. $7.50

202. SCHWARZENBERGER, Georg. A Manual of International Law. Two volumes. Fourth Edition. Stevens and Sons, 1960. $25.00
An exceptionally nice set, slightly chipped dustwrappers.

203. SCIGLIANO, Robert The Supreme Court and the Presidency. Free Press, 1971. $8.50

204. SCOTT, Arthur P. Criminal Law in Colonial Virginia. Chicago, 1930. $22.50

205. SELDEN, John. The History of Tithes. [London], 1618. Title page; (4); xxii, (12), 491, (5). Quarto. New S.T.C. 22172.7 $350.00
Termed by Holdsworth Selden's *"great work on ecclesiastical history"* and by Hazeltine "one of the greatest of all [his] works, and the one that has occasioned more controversy than any other", Selden's Tithes caused him to be summoned thrice before King James, and led to Selden's writing--at the King's orders--three additional works.
Perhaps the most attractive binding we have ever commissioned, in full dark brown calf, sewn in original fashion on four heavy cords, labelled in later 17th century style; with some aging and greying of the pages, occasional spotting, but altogether *a handsome, desirable copy*, with the title page in red and black.

206. SELDEN, John. Table Talk. Edinburgh, 1819. $75.00
An *exceptionally clean copy* in contemporary calf, newly rebacked, gilt-lined covers, somewhat worn and stained, gilt-lined and lettered spine, black label.
Selden's most popular work, compiled by Selden's secretary, Richard Milward, who dedicated the volume to *Sir Matthew Hale*, one of Selden's executors. This edition, the second of the 19th century, was part of the "British Prose Writers Series".

207 SHEPPARD, William. The Faithful Councellor: or the Marrow of the Law in English. London, 1651. First Edition. 2 leaves (lacking A1 blank? and A4 To the Reader?); 703 pages (irregular but complete); 6 leaves; blank. Wing S.3186 $185.00
One of the best known and most prolific legal writers of the 1600's, Sheppard wrote this volume, really two books in one on the procedures in the courts at common law and at equity.
Title page frayed in margin, marginal repairs to a few leaves, some dust marking and unobtrusive marginal dampstaining, contemporary blind-lined calf, nicely rebacked.
A desirable copy of the first edition of this work, written in the mid-1600's, the period during which treatises on specific legal subject matters first appeared, *certainly a scarce title, only one copy being recorded at auction in this century.*

208. SHKLAR, Judith N. Legalism. Harvard, 1971. $12.50

209. SHOGAN, Robert. A Question of Judgment, The Fortas Case and the Struggle for the Supreme Court. Bobbs-Merrill, 1972. $10.00

210. SIGLER, Jay A. Double Jeopardy The Development of a Legal and Social Policy. Cornell, 1969. $12.50
A volume in the *Cornell Studies in Civil Liberty.*

211. SIMES, Lewis M. The Improvement of Conveyancing by Legislation. Michigan, 1960. $15.00

212. SIMON, James F. In His Own Image, The Supreme Court in Richard Nixon's America. McKay, 1973. $7.50

213. SMITH, Franklin A. Judicial Review of Legislation in New York, 1906-1938. Columbia, 1952. $15.00
Issued in *Columbia's Studies in History, Economics and Public Law.*

214. (SPELMAN, Sir John). J. H. BAKER (ed.). The Reports of Sir John Spelman. Two Volumes. London, 1977-78. $45.00
The first volumes of Tudor law reports edited since the 18th century; *with Dr. Baker's superb introductory essay*, certain to become a classic on the law of the late 15th and early 16th centuries. Selden Society volumes 93 & 94.

215. STEINER, Peter O. Mergers. Michigan, 1975. $12.50

216. STEWART, Robert B. Treaty Relations of the British Commonwealth of Nations. MacMillan, 1939. $17.50

217. STORY, Joseph. Chief Justice Marshall, An Address. Lawyers Co-op, 1900. $20.00
60 pp., sewn wraps.
A re-issue of Story's address, given before the Suffolk Bar in 1835, shortly after Marshall's death, in commemoration of Marshall's accesion to the Bench in 1801; wraps soiled, worn and detached.

218. STUBBS, William. The Constitutional History of England. Three volumes. Oxford, 1875, 1878. $150.00
Maitland, terming it Stubbs' "great work", said he held an advantage over others, in that "I did not read it because I was set to read it, or because I was to be examined in it, or because I had to teach history or law. I found it in a London club, and read it because it was interesting."
Superbly bound in full tree calf, ornately gilt spine, six compartments and five raised bands, contrasting black and brown labels, and marbled edges and endpapers; very slight rubbing to the spines and joints, and some light foxing to the preliminary leaves, but altogether *an extremely handsome set of Stubbs' classic work*, with volumes II and III being the first editions, Volume I the second.

219. STUBBS, William. Lectures on European History. Longmans, 1904. $35.00
Bishop Stubbs' Lectures, delivered while Regius Professor of History at Oxford in the 1860's, devoted to the years from the reign of Charles V through the 30 Years War.

220. SULLIVAN, Francis S. Lectures on the Constitution and Laws of England: With a Commentary on Magna Charta, and Illustrations of Many of the English Statutes. Second Edition. London, 1776. Blank; title page; [v]-xvi; i-xxxii; 415 pages; blank. $125.00
First appearing in 1772 under the title *"An Historical Treatise on the Feudal Law, and the Constitution and Laws of England"*, the work was issued without supporting authorities, which were supplied by Gilbert Stuart, together with an introductory essay and a new title, in the second edition four years later. *An attractive copy*, bound in contemporary 3/4 leather over decorated boards, some rubbing to top and bottom of spine and joints, very occasional spotting and some manuscript marginalia, but altogether very clean, wide-margined and desirable.

221. SUMMERS, Robert S. (ed.). Essays in Legal Philosophy. California, 1972. $15.00
Essays by Ronald Dworkin, A.M. Honore, and Glanville Williams, among others; very lightly faded.

222. SWISHER, Carl Brent. The Growth of Constitutional Power in the United States. Chicago, 1946. $12.50
The *Walgreen Lectures* at Chicago, 1945.

223. SWISHER, Carl Brent. Roger B. Taney. MacMillan, 1935. $20.00

224. THOMAS, Ann Van Wynen & A. J. Thomas, Jr. Legal Limits on the Use of Chemical and Biological Weapons. S.M.U., 1970. $12.50

225. (THOMAS, Dylan). J. STEVENS COX (ed.). Under Milk Wood: Account of an action to recover the original manuscript. Toucan Press, Channel Islands, 1969. 17 pp., stapled wraps. $7.50

226. TOBIAS, J.J. Nineteenth-Century Crime: Prevention and Punishment. David & Charles, 1972. $10.00

Presentation Copy.
227. TOWER, Charlemagne. Essays Political and Historical. Lippincott, 1914. $35.00
The son of Charlemagne Tower, whose collection of early American law is one of the greatest ever amassed, Tower was a well-known lawyer and diplomat in his own right.
Presented by Tower to the Honorable Henry Galbraith Nord, and *signed by Tower, a nice copy* in the original blue cloth, gilt-lettered cover and spine.

228. TULLOCK, Gordon. The Logic of the Law. Basic Books, 1971. $8.50

229. (UNITED NATIONS). KURT VOLK (typographer). Charter of the United Nations. New York, 1948. $50.00
A beautifully designed and printed issue of the U.N. Charter, in green leather over decorated boards, top edge gilt, gilt spine, very slightly rubbed, *in a limited edition of 1,000*, with the text of the Charter and the facsimile signatures, and signed by Volk.

230. VANDERBILT, Arthur T. (ed.). Studying Law. N.Y.U., 1955. $17.50
Essays by *Roscoe Pound* and *John H. Wigmore*, among others.

231. (VIRGINIA Law School). JOHN RITCHIE. The First Hundred Years, A Short History of the School of Law of the University of Virginia for the Period 1826-1926. Virginia, 1978. New. $9.95

232. VIRTUE, Maxine Boord. Survey of Metropolitan Courts Detroit Area. Michigan, 1950. $15.00

233. DE VISSCHER, Charles. Theory and Reality in Public International Law. Princeton, 1969. $12.50
Translated by Percy Corbett from the third French edition.

234. WAKIN, Jeanette A. (ed.). The Function of Documents in Islamic Law. S.U.N.Y., 1972. $17.50

235. (WALES). IFAN AB OWEN EDWARDS (comp.). A Catalogue of Star Chamber Proceedings Relating to Wales. Cardiff, 1929. $20.00
The *first volume* in the *History and Law Series* published by the University of Wales.

236. (WALES). NATALIE FRYDE (ed.). List of Welsh Entries in the Memoranda Rolls 1282-1343. Cardiff, 1974. $10.00

237. WALKER, Thomas Alfred. The Science of International Law. Cambridge, 1893. $30.00
Original cloth, slightly spotted, endpapers lightly foxed; but a desirable copy, largely uncut, gilt-lettered spine bright.

238. WARE, Wallace L. The Unforgettables. Mimram, 1965. $7.50

239. WARREN, Charles. The Making of the Constitution. Little, Brown, 1937. $22.50

240. WARREN, Charles. The Supreme Court in United States History. Two volumes. Little, Brown, 1926. $35.00
A nice set, in the original blue cloth, spines gilt-lettered.

241. (WARREN, Earl). JOHN D. WEAVER. Warren: The Man, The Court, The Era. Little, Brown, 1967 $10.00

242. WASHINGTON, Joseph. An Exact Abridgment of All the Statutes of King William and Queen Mary, and of King William III and Queen Anne, in Force and Use. [Fifth Edition]. London, 1704. 3 blanks; title page; 40 leaves (titles of statutes); 661 pages; 43 leaves (table); 2 blanks. $85.00
First published in 1689, Washington's Abridgment continued that of Wingate, itself the foremost abridgment of the 1600's and first published, it is thought, in the 1640's.
Contemporary calf, worn, well rebacked, gilt-lettered, some upper margins cut close affecting headnotes on three leaves, very occasional embrowning.
Altogether, *quite a nice copy* of the Fifth Edition of 1704, one of several issued by Washington as he revised the text (but without additions) to take into account intervening statutory changes.

243. WATSON, Richard A. and Rondal G. Downing. The Politics of The Bench and The Bar. Wiley, 1969. $10.00

244. WEINSTEIN, Jack B. Reform of Court Rule-Making Procedures. Ohio State, 1977. $8.50

245. WEST, Ranyard. Conscience and Society, A Study of the Psychological Prerequisites of Law and Order. Methuen, 1950. $10.00

246. WEST, William. The First [and Second] Part[s] of Simboleography. London, 1610, 1611. Title page; 5 leaves; 326 folios; title page; 2 leaves; 304 folios; 7 leaves; blank. New S.T.C. 25272 and 25279.3. $425.00
Contemporary calf, worn, handsomely rebacked, occasional contemporary manuscript annotations, occasional very light spotting or dampstaining; title page dusty.
Perhaps the most important legal work of the late 1500's; first published in 1590, the first part of the Symbeology went considerably beyond earlier collections of precedents, which tended to be mere form books, by stating the underlying principles of the law.
With the issuance of the second edition in 1594, West divided the work into two parts, considerably enlarging the first, adding a second devoted largely to judicial precedents, and providing an account of equitable jurisdiction.
An attractive copy of an important work.

247. WHITE, G. Edward. The American Judicial Tradition. Oxford, 1976. $12.00

248. WHITING, William. The Government's War Powers Under The Constitution Of The United States. Rio Grande, 1971. $10.00
Printed from the Tenth Edition of 1864.

Signed by Wigmore
249. WIGMORE, John Henry. A Panorama of the World's Legal Systems. Three Volumes. West, 1928. $85.00
Limited to 1990 copies, and signed by Wigmore, this massive work considers those sixteen legal systems extant since recorded history began which Wigmore considered the most important--from the Egyptian to the English Common Law.
In the original blue cloth, slightly worn, gilt spines and covers; unobtrusive spotting to the front cover and top edge of Volume I.
A good copy of an exceptional work, termed by Plucknett "remarkable" and "fascinating".

David Louisell's copy
250. WIGMORE, John Henry. A Treatise on the Anglo-American System of Evidence, in Trials at Common Law. Second Edition. Five Volumes. Little, Brown, 1923. $85.00
The first revision by Wigmore of his classic treatise, termed by Beale upon its first publication in 1904 *"the most complete and exhaustive treatise on a single branch of our law that has ever been written."*
In the original buckram, gilt-lined and lettered and contrasting red and black spine labels, the binding somewhat worn and soiled, but sound.
Upon the appearance of this edition, Chafee wrote "No man since Jeremy Bentham has by his own unaided labor brought about such a marked improvement of our system of law as Wigmore."
Formerly the copy of *David Louisell*, late Professor of Law at Boalt Hall.

251. (WILDE, Oscar). H. MONTGOMERY HYDE. The Three Trials of Oscar Wilde. University Books, New York, 1956. $15.00
The verbatim transcripts of Wilde's three trials, and a lengthy introduction by Hyde.

252. WILKINSON, J. Harvie, III. Serving Justice, A Supreme Court Clerk's View. Charterhouse, 1974. $8.50

253. WILLIAMS, Glanville. The Sanctity of Life and the Criminal Law. Knopf, 1957. $10.00
Based on Williams' *1956 James S. Carpentier Lectures.*

254. WINDOLPH, F. Lyman. Reflections of the Law in Literature. Books for Libraries, 1970. $10.00
Three essays, on *Trollope, Shakespeare* and *Browning*, and the law, respectively.

255. WINES, E.C. The State of Prisons and of Child Saving Institutions in the Civilized World. Cambridge, 1880. $45.00
The John Howard of the late 19th century, Wines toured all of the prisons of the northern states of the U.S. in 1865. This work, his last, still partly in page proof at his death, surveys prison conditions throughout the world.
In the original green buckram, gilt lettered and lined spine, a small snag to the top of the spine, *else an exceedingly nice and largely uncut copy.*

256. WINSTON, Ambrose Pare. Judicial Economics, The Doctrine of Monopoly as Set Forth by Judges of the U.S. Federal Courts in Suits under the Anti-Trust Laws. Privately printed, 1957. $15.00

257. WITTENBERG, Philip. Dangerous Words, A Guide to the Law of Libel. Columbia, 1947. $7.50

258. WOLF-PHILLIPS, Leslie (ed.). Constitutions of Modern States, Selected Texts. Pall Mall, 1968. $10.00

259. WOLFF, Hans Julius. Roman Law, An Historical Introduction. Oklahoma, 1951. $15.00

Interleaved Throughout
260. WOOD, Thomas. An Institute of the Laws of England. Fifth Edition. London, 1734. Folio. (4), title page, xi, 663, (32), (4). $275.00
Bound in quarter sheep, worn, over boards; some staining to preliminary leaves, but in general *a very clean copy, and an impressive one*, enormous in size measuring 10 x 15½ inches. Called the "most important and most popular of his books" by Holdsworth, this work anticipated Blackstone's Commentaries. Blackstone himself spoke of it as "a valuable performance" in the Preface to his Analysis.

261. WRIGHT, E. Blackwood. The French Civil Code . . . Translated into English. Stevens, 1908. $17.50
Private library stamp on title page.

262. WYZANSKI, Charles E., Jr. Whereas--A Judge's Premises. Little, Brown, 1965. $12.50

263. (YALE Law School). DWIGHT C. KILBOURN. The Bench and Bar of Litchfield County, Connecticut 1709-1909. Privately printed, 1909. $45.00
One of 500 copies; original brown cloth slightly rubbed, gilt lettered spine.

264. YANKWICH, Leon R. An American Judge Looks at the Talmud. Western Jewish Institute, Los Angeles, 1936. $15.00
20 pp.; original wraps bound in.

265. ZEISEL, Hans, Harry Kalven, Jr. and Bernard Buchholz. Delay in the Court. Little, Brown, 1959. $15.00

MEYER BOSWELL BOOKS
RARE AND SCHOLARLY BOOKS ON THE LAW

CATALOGUE TWO

RARE AND SCHOLARLY
BOOKS ON THE LAW
(1980)

SIR WILLIAM BLACKSTONE
(1723-1780)

"Blackstone's Commentaries are the most correct and beautiful outline that ever was exhibited of any human science."—Sir William Jones

CATALOGUE THREE

MEYER BOSWELL BOOKS
SAN FRANCISCO

MEYER BOSWELL BOOKS

RARE AND SCHOLARLY BOOKS ON THE LAW

982 Hayes Street, San Francisco, California 94117
Telephone (415) 346-1839

This year marks the 200th anniversary of Blackstone's death, with a special exhibition in tribute at the Bodleian Library at Oxford, where Blackstone held the chair as the first Vinerian Professor of Law.

Though only a casual acquaintance of Dr. Johnson, Blackstone "made" Boswell's Life with the anecdote told Johnson by William Scott after Blackstone's death, that "Blackstone, a sober man, composed his 'Commentaries' with a bottle of port in front of him; and found his mind invigorated and supported in the fatigue of his great Work, by a temperate use of it."

When one thinks of Blackstone, of course, one does think of the "Commentaries," and we are pleased to offer as the "jewel" of this catalogue a first edition of this great work, which made its appearance in 1765 through 1769, as well as a facsimile issue of the first edition just published by the University of Chicago Press, in four volumes, both in hardcover and paperback, giving you a "feel" for the Commentaries' typography.

For this catalogue, the following terms apply:

1. ***Our Guarantee.*** **All items are guaranteed as described (if no express description is given, you may assume the item is in very good to mint condition), and may be returned for any reason within 30 days of receipt; please pack carefully and insure if received insured by you.**
2. ***Prices.*** **All prices are in U.S. dollars.**
3. ***Telephone Orders.*** **You may place your order by telephone 24 hours a day, seven days a week. Just call (415) 346-1839, and we will ship the next day.**
4. ***Domestic Shipments.*** **Handling, postage and insurance (which we obtain on all shipments over $25.00) are additional; on shipments under $25.00 we assume risk of loss or damage.**
5. ***Overseas Shipments.*** **Handling, postage, conversion charges and insurance (where applicable) additional. Unless instructed otherwise, shipments under $100.00 are sent surface mail at your risk; shipments over $100.00 are insured and sent by air parcel post.**
6. ***Individual Billing.*** **If unknown to us, you may be billed pro-forma; we ship on receipt of payment. In all other instances, you will be billed upon shipment, and payment is due upon receipt of books, unless you wish to pay by either Visa (including BarclayCard) or Master Charge, in which case please provide us with your credit card number and its expiration date when you order; we will enclose your receipt with shipment.**
7. ***Library Billing.*** **Libraries will be billed to suit requirements.**

★ ★ ★ ★

WE WILL BE DISPLAYING AT THE CONFERENCE OF THE AMERICAN ASSOCIATION OF LAW LIBRARIES IN ST. LOUIS THIS JUNE. WE HAVE BEEN SAVING UP SOME SPECIAL ITEMS FOR THE CONFERENCE, AND HOPE YOU WILL STOP BY TO SEE THEM AND MEET US.

1. **AMERY, L.S.** Thoughts on the Constitution. Second Edition. Oxford, 1953. **$25.00**
A presentation copy, originally based on Avery's *1946 Chichele Lectures.*

2. **ASSOCIATION of the Bar of the City of New York.** Bad Housekeeping, The Administration of the New York Courts. New York, no date [1955]. **$17.50**

3. **ASSOCIATION of the Bar of the City of New York, et al.** The Visual Artist and The Law. New York, 1971. **$15.00**

4. **AUSTIN, John.** The Province of Jurisprudence Determined. New York, 1954. **$15.00**
With an introduction by *H.L.A. Hart*; slightly worn.

5. **BAKER, J. H.** Manual of Law French. Avebury, 1979. New **$20.00**
The first glossary of law French produced since 1779, with an introduction by Dr. Baker; a valuable companion to the Anglo-Norman Dictionary now undergoing publication by the Modern Humanities Research Association.

6. **BARRINGTON, Daines.** Observationson the Statutes, Chiefly the More Ancient, from the Magna Carta [to 1623]. London, 1766. **$225.00**
Called to the bar and later a Bencher in the Inner Temple, Barrington (whose renaissance tastes are here reflected in his first work) won Bentham's approval for this work, which said Bentham, "is everything apropos of everything."
Nicely bound in contemporary calf, worn, the covers gilt-lined, rebacked, with a black morocco label, gilt lined and lettered, occasional very lightish spotting.
Altogether a handsome copy, with Barrington's observations, in addition to those upon the Magna Carta, on some of the most important statutes in English legal history, including the Statute of Merton, the Statutes of Westminster (including Quia Emptores), and the Charter of Forests.

The First Edition in English

7. **[BECCARIA, Cesare].** An Essay on Crimes and Punishment. London, 1767. Printing and the Mind of Man 209. **$350.00**
Eventually translated into twenty-two languages, *Beccaria's classic essay first appeared in English in this edition* three years after its initial publication in Italian.
Newly and attractively rebound in ¾ leather over decorated boards, red morocco label gilt lined and lettered. A very little lightish dampstaining, worsening in the last ten leaves, but *altogether a very nice copy of a work said by Holdsworth to anticipate Bentham and relied upon by Blackstone.*

8. **BELLOT, Hugh H. L.** The Inner and Middle Temple, Legal, Literary and Historic Associations. London, 1902. **$35.00**
Original blue cloth, gilt-decorated and lettered front cover and spine, *with ninety illustrations*; slightly worn.

9. **BICKEL, Alexander M.** The Least Dangerous Branch. Bobbs-Merrill, 1962. **$17.50**

10. **BICKEL, Alexander M.** The Morality of Consent. Yale, 1975. **$12.50**
Includes a bibliography of Bickel's work.

11. **BIDDLE, Francis.** Justice Holmes, Natural Law, and the Supreme Court. MacMillan, 1961. **$17.50**
The 1960 Oliver Wendell Holmes Devise Lectures.

12. **BLACK, Charles L.** The People and the Court, Judicial Review in a Democracy. MacMillan, 1960. **$15.00**

13. **BLACK, Charles L. and Bob Eckhardt.** The Tides of Power. Yale, 1976. **$8.50**

14. **(BLACK, Hugo L.).** JOHN P. FRANK. Mr. Justice Black, the Man and His Opinions, Knopf, 1949. **$15.00**
First edition; with the errata slip laid in.

The First Edition of the Most Renowned Work of English Law

15. **BLACKSTONE, Sir William.** Commentaries on the Laws of England. Four Volumes. Oxford, 1765-1769. Eller 1. **$5,500.00**
Arguably the greatest work on English law ever written, and certainly the most renowned, the first volume appearing in 1765, while Blackstone was Vinerian Professor of Law at Oxford, the first chair in English law ever established, and Blackstone its first occupant.
This set bound in full calf, somewhat worn and with some cracking to the joints, and chipping to the labels, the label of Volume II not uniform with the remaining three volumes, occasional spotting internally, more substantially to eight signatures of Volume II, but in general, *a fresh, large, wide-margined copy,* measuring 8½ by 10⅞ inches, *in a complete contemporary binding, of the foremost work of English legal history,* praised by Lord Mansfield, read three times by Gibbon, who is said to have made a full and careful abstract of the first volume, lauded by Bentham for its literary qualities, and said, by Sir James Fitzjames Stephen, to have "rescued the law of England from chaos."

First Edition in Facsimile

16. **BLACKSTONE, Sir William.** Commentaries on the Laws of England. Four volumes. Chicago, 1979. New. **$80.00**
The first edition of 1765-69, reproduced in facsimile, with separate introductions by Professors Katz, Simpson, Langbein and Green.

Blackstone in Paperback

17. **BLACKSTONE, Sir William.** Commentaries on the Laws of England. Four volumes. Chicago, 1979. New. **$35.80**
A facsimile of the first edition (see the above item), in paperback; individual volumes may be purchased at $8.85 per volume.

Association Copy

18. **(BLACKSTONE, Sir William).** A. EDWARD NEWTON. Newton on Blackstone. Pennsylvania, 1937. **$55.00**
Newton's well-known address, delivered at the University of Pennsylvania in 1935, having little to do with Blackstone, but with Newton, as raconteur, at his best. Limited to 2000 copies, of which this is1249, on all-rag paper, signed by Newton, and *with a lengthy and amusing presentation inscription by Newton's only son,* Swift.

19. **(BLACKSTONE, Sir William).** I. G. PHILIP. William Blackstone and the Reform of the Oxford University Press in the Eighteenth Century. Oxford, 1957. **$35.00**
Begun a decade before the publication of his Commentaries, and while he was appointed first Vinerian Professor of Law at Oxford, Blackstone's efforts inspired "*the most ruthless, single-handed reform in eighteenth-century Oxford.*"
Untrimmed, original green wraps, somewhat chipped and worn; with a full page portrait of Blackstone. Oxford Bibliographical Society Publications, New Series, Volume VII.

20. **(BLACKSTONE, Sir William).** I. G. PHILIP. William Blackstone and the Oxford University Press. Oxford, 1967. **$22.50**
The 1967 Christmas Keepsake of the Press, based on Philip's work immediately above; *a handsome little pamphlet, illustrated and printed in red and black.*

21. **(BLOUNT, Thomas).** THEO BONGAERTS. The Correspondence of Thomas Blount (1618-1679), A Recusant Antiquary. Amsterdam, 1978. New. Sewn wraps, illustrated. **$27.00**
A fine volume, with *the first reliable biography of Blount,* and an account of his writings.

22. **BONNER, Robert J.** Lawyers and Litigants in Ancient Athens. Chicago, 1927. **$35.00**
Sherman Moulton's copy, with his signature; very slightly worn.

23. **BOTEIN, Bernard and Murray A. Gordon.** The Trial of the Future. Simon and Schuster, 1963. **$10.00**
Based on Botein's *1960 Cardozo Lecture.*

24. **BRINTON, Jasper Yeates.** The Mixed Courts of Egypt. Revised Edition. Yale, 1968. **$17.50**

25. **BURN, Richard.** Ecclesiastical Law. Four Volumes. Volumes 1 and 4 the Fourth Edition, volumes 2 and 3 the Third Edition. London, 1775 and 1781. **$150.00**
An early set of the work which Holdsworth has called "the clearest and most successful of all the great treatises upon English ecclesiastical law." Uniformly bound in full contemporary calf, worn, gilt decorated covers and elaborately gilt spines, with contrasting red and black labels.
Altogether, a handsome and clean set, first published in 1763, and reaching a ninth edition by 1842.

Presentation Copies

26. **BURTON, Harold H.** Unsung Services of the Supreme Court of the United States. 1955 & 1956. **$65.00**
Three presentation copies, each inscribed, dated and signed by Justice Burton, to Chief Judge John Biggs, Jr.; two separate copies of Burton's article on the Supreme Court, and the third Burton's article on the Legal Tender Cases.
Specially bound in black buckram, gilt-lettered front cover and spine, with decorated endpapers; tears to the last three leaves, not affecting the text.

27. **BURTT, Harold Ernest.** Legal Psychology. Prentice-Hall, 1931. **$17.50**
Slightly worn.

28. **BUTLER, Charles Henry.** A Century at the Bar of the Supreme Court of the United States. Putnam, 1942. **$25.00**
Butler, who dedicated the work to Charles Evans Hughes, was reporter to the court from 1902 to 1916. Original blue cloth, gilt-lettered; very slightly worn, private library stamp.

First Edition

29. **BYNKERSHOEK, Cornelius van.** Opera Minora. Lugduni Batavorum, 1730. **$250.00**
The *first edition* of Bynkershoek's "minor works," including *two of his famed essays on international law,* since published by the Carnegie Endowment in their series of Classics of International Law: his Dissertatio de Domino Maris (his Dissertation on the Sovereignty of the Sea) and his De Foro Legatorum (On the Jurisdiction over Ambassadors).
Bound in contemporary vellum, a bit worn and soiled, with some spotting internally, but *in general an excellent copy, with the title page in red and black,* and with five additional essays, devoted to questions of Dutch and Roman law.

First Edition of Bynkershoek's Greatest Work

30. **BYNKERSHOEK, Cornelius van.** Quaestionum juris publici Libri Duo. Lugduni Batavorum, 1730. **$450.00**
The masterwork of Bynkershoek, President of the Supreme Court of Holland during the first part of the 1700's, praised by Lord Mansfield, the first book of which (De rebus bellicis) considers the most vital questions of international law and customs of war.

Bound in full, contemporary vellum, a bit worn and soiled, some spotting internally, with the title page in red and black; in general *an excellent copy of one of the foremost works on international law* by Grotius' countryman and a man who, according to Professor Hall, "was the earliest writer of real importance" on international law.

31. **CAHN, Edmond (ed.).** The Great Rights. MacMillan, 1963. **$15.00**
Based on the *James Madison Lectures at N.Y.U.,* with lectures by Justices Black and Douglas, among others.

32. **CALAMANDREI, Piero.** Eulogy of Judges. Princeton, 1942. **$35.00**
Translated from the Italian by John Clarke Adams and C. Abbott Phillips, Jr., and *handsomely printed* by Princeton, in the original cloth-backed decorated boards, paper label; an unusual work.

33. **CHAFEE, Zechariah, Jr.** Some Problems of Equity. Michigan, 1950. **$25.00**
Chafee's masterwork on his chosen field of the law, based primarily on his Cooley Lectures at Michigan; edges slightly spotted.

34. **CHAMBERLAIN, Joseph P., et al.** The Judicial Function in Federal Administrative Agencies. New York, 1942. **$22.50**
Under the auspices of the Legal Research Committee of the Commonwealth Fund, whose members included *Learned Hand, Austin Scott* and *Grenville Clark,* among others.

35. **CHRISTENSEN, Barlow, F.** Lawyers for People of Moderate Means. American Bar Foundation, 1970. **$12.50**

36. **CLANCHY, M. T.** From Memory to Written Record, England, 1066-1307. Harvard, 1979. New. **$18.50**
An exceptional work.

37. **(CLASSICS of English Legal History in the Modern Era).** 332 Volumes. Garland Publishing, New York, ongoing publication. **$50-$55 per volume**
Garland's ambitious program, edited by *Samuel E. Thorne* and *David S. Berkowitz,* and begun a few years ago, reprints legal classics from the "modern era," i.e., 1480 forward, with 80 new titles due to appear during this year.
Available singly at $50 or $55 (depending on the volume), the volumes may also be purchased in two series, at very substantial savings, and an especially attractive and additional discount for one of the series is available through June 30, 1980.
We will be pleased to provide further particulars of any or all of the volumes, and order them for you; *an unprecedented opportunity to acquire the great and near-great works of English legal history in the last 500 years.*

38. **COFFIN, William Sloane, Jr. and Morris I. Liebman.** Civil Disobedience: Aid or Hindrance to Justice? American Enterprise Institute, 1972. **$10.00**

Coke on Littleton

39. **COKE, Sir Edward.** The First Part of the Institutes of the Laws of England. Seventh Edition. Title page; 4 leaves; portrait; folios 1-206,222-395 (irregular but complete); 30 leaves. London, 1670. New Wing C4926. Folio. **$350.00**
The only part (the first of four) of Coke's Institutes published during his lifetime, commonly called "Coke on Littleton," and *one of the greatest classics of English law*
Bound in 3/4 19th century leather, rubbed, marbled endpapers, *with the fine engraved portrait of Littleton,* and the folding table; a bit of dustiness and staining to some pages, considerable contemporary annotations, but altogether a *very desirable copy of a work Holdsworth places among the five most pre-eminent law books in English history,* one of the remaining four being Littleton's Tenures, the subject of Coke's commentary in this volume.

40. **(COKE, Sir Edward).** EDMUND PLUNKETT BURKE(?). Sir Edward Coke. London, 1828. Title page; 32 pp.; advertising leaf. **$55.00**
Born in Lisbon of Irish parents, Burke first gained fame when, as an undergraduate, he wrote his "Essay on the Laws and Government of Rome." This effort, appearing when he was 26, was issued as part of the series published by the Society for the Diffusion of Useful Knowledge.
Bound in later ¾ cloth, a trifle rubbed, over decorated boards, the first and last leaves a bit embrowned and dusty.
With the unobtrusive release stamp of the Long Island Historical Society on the title page.

41. **COOKE, George Wingrove.** A Treatise on the Law and Practice of Agricultural Tenancies. First Edition. London, 1850. **$60.00**
One of the more prolific legal writers of the mid-19th century, and *unquestionably the leading legal writer on matters rural and agricultural,* Cooke worked for many years under the Enclosure Commission in London; this volume published in 1850, with a new edition issued in 1882, 17 years after his death.
Recently rebound in ½ leather over rather audacious decorated boards, paper label.

42. **CORWIN, Edward S.** John Marshall and the Constitution, A Chronicle of the Supreme Court, Yale, 1921. **$35.00**
A handsome issue, with elaborately decorated front cover and spine; extra-illustrated. Volume 16 in the Chronicles of America series.

Limited to 400 Copies

43. COSGRAVE, George. Early California Justice. The Grabhorn Press, San Francisco, 1948. **$75.00**
A choice example of fine printing from the Grabhorn Press, bound in red linen, very slightly rubbed, paper label, with the title page in red and black, decorative initials throughout the text, and seven facsimile documents laid in. *Very nice.*

An early law book, bridging to medieval times

44. (COURT Baron). Modus Tenendi Curiam Baronis. Title page; folios 2-31; colophon leaf. Thomas Berthelet, London, 1540. Beale T193, compare S.T.C. 7713 and 14876. **$850.00**
An intriguing volume, *printed in Black Letter throughout, in Latin, Law French, and English,* the languages alternating.

Several of Maitland's earliest works for the Selden Society, devoted to local courts in the 13th and 14th centuries, are echoed here, some 250 years later, the similarities between the courts' subject matters and procedures outweighing the differences, with glimpses of medieval life correspondingly apparent.

An exceptionally clean copy, newly and attractively bound in full tawny calf by Sangorski and Sutcliffe of London, the spine gilt-lettered; with considerable portions of the volume devoted to the Hundred Court and to the Court Leet, the latter concerning local criminal matters, as opposed to the civil matters normally the province of the Court Baron.

An unusual and rare volume, with volume one of the new S.T.C. (not yet issued) perhaps to posit this tract as one of several intended by the printer Berthelet to be issued as a series; Beale locating only the copies in the British Museum and Harvard Law School, *with no record of the work at auction in this century.*

45. COWAN, Robert G. Ranchos of California, a List of Spanish Concessions 1775-1822, and Mexican Grants 1822-1846. Los Angeles, 1977. New. **$9.00**

46. COX, Archibald. The Role of the Supreme Court in American Government. Oxford, 1976. **$12.50**
Based on Cox's *Chichele Lectures* at All Souls College, Oxford, 1974-75.

47. COY, Owen C. California County Boundaries. Sacramento, 1923. **$45.00**
The *first edition,* with Coy's essay "The Genesis of California Counties" included; *with a map, in color, for each county.* Original blue cloth, gilt-lettered, slightly worn.

48. CURRIE, Brainerd. Selected Essays on the Conflict of Laws. Duke, 1963. **$17.50**
Fore-and top-edge slightly spotted.

The First Edition of the First Work on Scottish Styles

49. DALLAS, George of Saint-Martins. System of Styles. Title page; leaf; 904 pp. (irregular but complete, with five additional dedication leaves); 6 leaves (index). Edinburgh, 1697. Folio. New Wing D137. **$350.00**
The first edition of the first work on Scottish "styles," or forms and precedents, styles being, according to Sir George Mackenzie, "to lawyers what the Chart is to Geographers, or the Compass to Seamen."

Bound in full contemporary calf, well worn, a small hole in the back cover, decorated spine, gilt-lettered label, the title page strengthened, leaf G2 repaired, some insignificant worming to a few leaves and minor dampstaining toward the end of the volume; but altogether quite clean and sound, and a desirable copy of what Lord Deas has termed *"the oldest and most authoritative formalist" of Scots' law.*

50. DAVIS, Winfield J. History of Political Conventions in California, 1849-1892. Sacramento, 1893. **$65.00**
The first volume in the series Publications of the California State Library; quite a nice copy, in the original brown cloth, gilt-lettered.

51. DE LOLME, J. L. The Constitution of England. New Edition. London, 1822. **$65.00**
Said to be *DeLolme's only work of permanent value,* first written in French, published in Holland, and translated into English some four years subsequently, in 1775 and prompting Bentham to remark (in contrast to Blackstone): "Our author has copied, but Mr. DeLolme has thought."

An attractive copy in full contemporary calf, rebacked, elaborate gilt dentilles on the covers, all edges marbled, marbled endpapers, a bit of spotting to the preliminary leaves only.

52. DERRETT, J. Duncan M. Henry Swinburne, Civil Lawyer of York. York, 1973. **$7.50**
The first critical monograph on Swinburne, perhaps *the most famous English canon lawyer;* 54 pages, stapled wraps.

53. DEVLIN, Patrick. The Criminal Prosecution in England. Yale, 1958. **$15.00**
Lord Devlin's *1956 Sherrill Lectures* at Yale Law School.

54. DEVLIN, Patrick. The Enforcement of Morals. Oxford, 1965. **$15.00**

55. (DICKENS, Charles). SIR WILLIAM HOLDSWORTH. Charles Dickens as a Legal Historian. Yale, 1928. **$35.00**
Holdsworth's highly enjoyable *Storrs Lectures at Yale in 1927,* with chapters on Bleak House and the Pickwick Papers; *a very nice copy,* buckram backed maroon cloth, gilt-lined and lettered leather label, with a complimentary card of Yale University Press laid in.

56. DICKINSON, John. Administrative Justice and the Supremacy of Law in the United States. Harvard, 1927. **$25.00**
Dedicated to Pound and Frankfurter, this volume is the second in the *Harvard Studies in Administrative Law;* original cloth, gilt-lettered, slightly worn.

57. DOUGLAS, William O. The Anatomy of Liberty, The Rights of Man Without Force. New York, 1963. **$12.50**

58. DOUGLAS, William O. Points of Rebellion. Random House, 1970. **$10.00**

59. (DOUGLAS, William O.). Tributes to Honorable William O. Douglas. Washington, 1976. **$25.00**
Occasioned by Douglas' retirement from the Court in November, 1975; original maroon cloth, gilt-lettered.

Justice Treby's Copy

60. DUGDALE, Sir William. A Perfect Copy of All Summons of the Nobility to the Great Councils and Parliaments of this Realm. Imprimatur leaf; Title Page; 5 leaves; 580 pp.; 12 leaves. London, 1685. New Wing D2491. **$275.00**
Dugdale's last work, published the year before his death in 1686; one of the great historians of the 17th century, and the friend of Sir Henry Spelman and Sir Christopher Hatton, Dugdale through them gained access to the records in the Tower, and to the Cottonian manuscript collection.

This work, extending from the reign of Henry III in the mid-1200's until Dugdale's day, sets forth the parliamentary summonses as issued; handsomely and recently bound in ½ leather over cockerel boards, the title page in a double woodcut border, with a piece torn away from the upper right hand margin, and a stain to it and the following leaf; some embrowning and occasional spotting, but altogether *an extremely nice copy.*

With the signature of George Treby, dated "Jul. 2. [16]98" on the title page, six years after Treby's appointment as Chief Justice of the Common Pleas.

61. EDWARDS, George. Pioneer-at-Law. Norton, 1974. **$10.00**
With a foreward by *Earl Warren.*

62. EGERTON, Robert. Legal Aid. Oxford, 1945. **$15.00**
With a preface by *A. L. Goodhart.*

63. EHRENZWEIG, Albert A. Psychoanalytic Jurisprudence. Leiden and Dobbs Ferry, 1971. **$22.50**
With an introduction by *Julius Stone.*

A Very Handsome Set

64. (ELDON, Lord). HORACE TWISS. The Public and Private Life of Lord Chancellor Eldon. *Three Volumes.* First Edition. London, 1844. **$175.00**
Called the most learned and capable lawyer of his day by Holdsworth, and compared by Lord Brougham to Coke, *Eldon was successively solicitor-general, Lord Chief-Justice of the Common Pleas, and Lord Chancellor,* succeeding to the woolsack in 1801 and serving as Lord Chancellor for a period of a quarter of a century.

An extremely handsome set of the first edition, bound in ¾ leather, very slightly rubbed, over marbled boards, all edges marbled and marbled endpapers, the spines uniformly and elaborately gilt and blind lined, with matching green and black labels, and with three engraved portraits of Lord Eldon, serving as frontispieces of the volumes.

65. ELIAS, T. O. (ed.). Nigerian Press Law. Lagos, 1969. **$15.00**
The first volume in the University of Lagos Law Series.

66. [ELLIS, William]. A Summary of the Roman Law. London, 1772. **$125.00**
The only edition summarizing John Taylor's "Elements of the Civil Law," which first appeared in 1755, and which had gone through four editions by 1828.

Handsomely bound in later, full crimson morocco, slightly worn, with the spine elaborately gilt, all edges gilt, and marbled endpapers.

The Subscribers' Edition

67. FARRAND, Max (ed.). The Records of the Federal Convention. First Edition. *Three Volumes.* Yale, 1911. **$250.00**
The first edition of Farrand's work, immediately recognized as a model of historical editing.

A magnificent set of the Subscribers' Edition, of which there were 250, this being set 241, *bound in ½ vellum over blue boards,* the edges untrimmed and largely uncut, with green morocco labels, gilt lined and lettered, some minor wear and soiling to the binding, and a bit of splitting where the vellum meets the boards.

68. (FIELD, David Dudley). Centenary Essays, Celebrating One Hundred Years of Legal Reform. N.Y.U., 1949. **$35.00**
Issued to commemorate the enactment of the New York Code of Procedure in 1848; with essays by *Roscoe Pound, Justice Jackson* and *Edmund Morgan,* among many others.

69. FINN, R. Welldon. The Making and Limitations of the Yorkshire Domesday. York, 1972. **$6.00**
31 pages, stapled wraps.

First Edition of the First Book in English About English Law

70. FORTESCUE, Sir John. The Difference Between an Absolute and Limited Monarchy. 2 blanks; Title Page; 7 leaves; lxxxii; 2 leaves; 148 pp.; 2 leaves; 2 blanks. London, 1714. **$350.00**
One of the two great legal figures (with Littleton) of the 1400's, Fortescue became serjeant in 1430 and Chief Justice of the King's Bench in 1442; this work, written towards the end of his life in the early 1470's, examines the comparative merits of despotic and constitutional government by contrasting comtemporary France and England.

This, *the first edition of 1714,* edited by one of Fortescue's descendants, *handsomely bound in 19th century full calf,* a bit worn, gilt and blind lined and decorated covers, elaborately gilt spine, inner gilt dentilles, all edges gilt, and decorated endpapers. Slight foxing and spotting, particularly to preliminaries, the title page in red and black, and with decorative woodcuts and woodcut initials throughout the text.

Altogether, an extremely handsome copy of the work said by Winfield to be the first book written in English about English law.

71. FRAENKEL, Osmond K. The Supreme Court and Civil Liberties. Oceana, 1960. **$10.00**

72. FRANKFURTER, Felix (ed.). Mr. Justice Brandeis. Yale, 1932. **$35.00**
Issued upon Brandeis' seventy-fifth birthday; with an Introduction by *Oliver Wendell Holmes,* and essays by *Frankfurter* and *Charles Evans Hughes,* among others.

Presentation Copy

73. FRANKFURTER, Felix. Mr. Justice Holmes and the Supreme Court. Harvard, 1938. **$125.00**
Dedicated to Justice Cardozo, these lectures were given by Frankfurter at Harvard in April, 1938.

With Frankfurter's presentation inscription to "Uncle Bill" Sheldon, whom Frankfurter thanks in his introduction to the volume for assistance in its preparation, and whom Frankfurter had asked to undertake certain affairs in case he should pre-decease his wife.

Sheldon's untimely death during the Second World War led to Frankfurter's tribute of him, recorded in the Roosevelt-Frankfurter correspondence.

The first edition, in the original cloth, gilt-lettered, the dustjacket considerably worn.

74. (FRANKFURTER, Felix). MOSES J. ARONSON. The Juristic Thought of Mr. Justice Frankfurter. 24 pp., stapled wraps. **$12.50**
Presentation copy from Aronson of his article published in the January, 1940 issue of the Journal of Social Philosophy.

75. (FRANKFURTER, Felix). LIVA BAKER. Felix Frankfurter, a Biography. Coward-McCann, 1962. **$15.00**

76. (FRANKFURTER, Felix). Proceedings of the Bar and Officers of the Supreme Court of the United States. Washington, 1965. **$25.00**
The proceedings held in memory of Justice Frankfurter, upon his death, with remarks by *Archibald Cox, Henry Friendly,* and *Archibald MacLeish,* among others. Original wraps, lightly soiled.

77. (FRY, Sir Edward). The Vanity Fair Cartoon, by Spy, showing Fry reflectively holding his pince-nez. May 30, 1891. **$35.00**
The caricature of Fry, Lord Justice of the Court of Appeal, and the author of the article on Seldon for the Dictionary of National Biography, measuring slightly in excess of 10x15 inches, with the second, equally-sized, "explanatory" sheet.

78. FULLER, Lon L. Anatomy of the Law. Praeger, 1968. **$15.00**

Selden and Coke

79. FULLER, Thomas. The Soveraigns Prerogative and the Subjects Priviledge. 2 blanks; Title Page; 9 leaves; 269 pp. (irregular but complete); leaf; 2 blanks. Second Edition. London, 1660. Wing F2469. **$225.00**
Prompted by the crisis secured by Charles' attempt to obtain £300,000 without parliamentary consent, leading to the Petition of Right and the Habeas Corpus Amendment Act.

With speeches and arguments made by and in response to the King, *on the most fundamental constitutional questions by the greatest men of the day,* including Selden and Coke.

Bound in contemporary blind-lined sheep, nicely rebacked, brown morocco label, gilt-lettered old style, some dustiness and embrowning, but *altogether a desirable copy;* with the title page in red and black.

80. GEIS, Gilbert (ed.). White-Collar Criminal. Atherton, 1968. **$15.00**
Articles by *Edwin Sutherland, David Caplovitz* and *Edmond Cahn,* among many others.

81. GILMORE, Grant. The Ages of American Law. Yale, 1977. **$12.50**
The *1974 Storrs Lectures* at Yale.

82. GLAD, Betty. Charles Evans Hughes and the Illusions of Innocence. Illinois, 1966. **$15.00**

83. [GLASSE, Samuel]. The Magistrate's Assistant. Second Edition. Glocester, 1788. **$85.00**
Designed by Glasse, an active county magistrate, to distill the "essentials" from Burn's classic, but by then massive Justice of the Peace; this work, Glasse's principal legal effort, first appeared in 1784, and went through four editions.

Bound in full contemporary calf, somewhat worn with the front joint unobtrusively cracked, red morocco label, occasional light spotting, but *altogether a nice copy.*

84. DE GRAZIA, Edward. Censorship Landmarks. Bowker, 1969. **$17.50**
An interesting collection of opinions from the 1600's to the present day.

85. GREEN, Mark J. et al. The Closed Enterprise System. Grossman, 1972. **$8.50**
Ralph Nader's Study Group Report on Anti-trust Enforcement.

86. GRINDEL, Carl W. (ed.). Concept of Freedom. Regnery, 1955. **$12.50**

87. GRISWOLD, Erwin N. Law and Lawyers in the United States. Harvard, 1965. **$15.00**
Dean Griswold's *1964 Hamlyn Lectures.*

88. GRISWOLD, Erwin N. Search and Seizure, A Dilemma of the Supreme Court. Nebraska, 1975. **$15.00**
Dean Griswold's *1974 Roscoe Pound Lectures* at Nebraska.

89. GROSS, Hyman. A Theory of Criminal Justice. Oxford, 1979. **$15.00**

Grotius' Greatest Work

90. GROTIUS, Hugo. De Jure Belli ac Pacis. Amsterdam, 1680. ter Meulen & Diermanse 582. **$250.00**
Grotius' most famous work, first appearing in Paris in 1625, and perhaps *the most famous of all works on international law.*

A handsome copy, bound in contemporary blind-stamped vellum, *with a superb extra-symbolic engraved title, and a fine engraved portrait of Grotius,* and the title page in red and black.

This edition of significance in the development of the later printings of Grotius, *containing for the first time the notes and commentary of the classicist Johann Friedrich Gronovius.*

A Family Copy of the First Edition

91. HALE, Sir Matthew. A Discourse of the Knowledge of God, and of Ourselves, London, 1688. 2 blanks; portrait title page; 17 leaves; 503 pages; blank. Wing H240. **$275.00**
Termed "one of the most interesting characters to be found in our legal history" by Holdsworth, and *one of the great polymaths of the 17th century,* Hale was respectively Justice of the Common Pleas, Lord Chief Baron of the Exchequer, and Lord Chief-Justice of Kings Bench, with works spanning legal, philosophical, religious and scientific topics.

This work, not discussed by Hale's most recent biographer, Lord Heward, was *published posthumously,* as many of Hale's were, and not intended by Hale for publication, though taken from a manuscript left in his hand.

Bound in contemporary calf, worn, *newly and attractively rebacked,* with the spine gilt-lined and lettered; some pages a little dusty, but altogether a very nice copy.

With the signature of R.H.B. Hale on the front paste-down, *and the bookplate of Hale of Alderly* on the second blank.

92. HALL, Jerome. Living Law of Democratic Society. Bobbs-Merrill, 1949. **$15.00**
Based on Hall's *1947 Isaac Hillman Lectures,* at Pacific University.

93. HALL, Jerome. Readings in Jurisprudence. Bobbs-Merrill, 1938. **$25.00**

94. HALLAM, Henry. View of the State of Europe During the Middle Ages. Three volumes. New York, 1880. **$125.00**
An extremely attractive set of Hallam's first major work, uniformly bound in ¾ black morocco over marbled boards, all edges marbled, and marbled endpapers, with the spines elaborately gilt, in six compartments.

"Do you know Hallam? Of course, I need not ask you if you have read his Middle Ages?"—Lord Byron.

95. HAMSON, C. J. Executive Discretion and Judicial Control, An Aspect of the French Conseil d'Etat. Stevens, 1954. **$17.50**
The *Hamlyn Lectures, Sixth Series,* given in 1954.

96. (HAND, Learned). KATHRYN GRIFFITH. Judge Learned Hand and the Role of the Federal Judiciary. Oklahoma, 1973. **$15.00**

A Superb Set

97. (HARDWICKE, Lord). GEORGE HARRIS. The Life of Lord Chancellor Hardwicke. *Three volumes.* London, 1847. **$175.00**
The *first edition* of Harris' work on Hardwicke, *called by Lord Chesterfield "perhaps the greatest magistrate that [England] ever had,"* and by Holdsworth "a great lawyer and a great Lord Chancellor."

An extremely handsome set, bound in full contemporary calf, the covers gilt-lined, and the spines elaborately gilt, with contrasting red and brown labels gilt-lettered, all edges marbled and marbled endpapers.

98. HARLAN, Justice John M. Typed letter signed, dated June 3, 1968, on Supreme Court letterhead, at the chambers of Justice Harlan. **$45.00**
Addressed to *Robert B. Williamson,* then Chief Justice of the Maine Supreme Court, *with Justice Harlan's signature in full.*

99. (HARVARD Law School). JOEL SELIGMAN. The High Citadel, the Influence of Harvard Law School. Houghton Mifflin, 1978. **$8.50**
With an introduction by *Ralph Nader*

100. HAVINGHURST, Harold C. The Nature of Private Contract. Northwestern, 1961. **$12.50**
The *1961 Rosenthal Lectures* at Northwestern.

101. HEYTING. W. J. The Constitutional Relationship Between Jersey and the United Kingdom. Stiff wraps. Jersey, 1977. New. **$12.50**

102. HILL, Constance. Good company in Old Westminster and the Temple. Bodley Head, 1925. **$28.50**
Original red cloth, decorated cover, slightly worn; *with 24 illustrations.*

Sir Sidney Colvin's Copy

103. HOLMES, Oliver Wendell. Speeches, Boston, 1896. **$150.00**
The second edition of Holmes' Speeches, issued five years after the first edition in 1891, and *including for the first time Holmes' famous speech 'The Soldier's Faith.'*

In the original printed boards, a bit worn and rubbed, but essentially quite nice, the edges untrimmed.

With the bookplate of Sir Sidney Colvin, the biographer and art critic, and fellow book-lover and acquaintance of Holmes.

104. (HOLMES, Oliver Wendell). MARK DE WOLFE HOWE (COMP.). The Occasional Speeches of Justice Oliver Wendell Holmes. Harvard, 1962. **$17.50**
In the original cloth-backed decorated boards, a trifle worn.

105. (HUNTINGTON Library). WILLARD O. WATERS. Check List of American Laws, Charters and Constitutions of the 17th and 18th Centuries in the Huntington Library. Sewn wraps. San Marino, 1936. **$35.00**

The *first volume of Huntington Library Lists;* slightly worn.

106. JACKSON, Robert H. Full Faith and Credit, the Lawyer's Clause of the Constitution. Columbia, 1945. **$17.50**
The *Fourth Annual Cardozo Lecture;* original maroon cloth, gilt lettered. *A nice copy,* though slightly worn, with unobtrusive spotting to the front cover.

107. (JACKSON, Robert H.). GLENDON SCHUBERT. Dispassionate Justice, A Synthesis of the Judicial Opinions of Robert H. Jackson. Bobbs-Merrill, 1960. **$15.00**

108. JACKSON, William A. Records of the Court of Stationers' Company, 1602-1640. London, 1957. **$45.00**
A work to which Professor Jackson devoted himself over a period of nearly twenty years, and published in 1957 by the Bibliographical Society on the fourth centenary of the grant of the Charter of Incorporation to the Company of Stationers; original canvas-backed boards, slightly worn.

109. JACOB, I. H. Later Legal Records and the Historian. 12 pages, stapled wraps. **$7.50**
Reprinted from the April, 1964 issue of Archives.

110. JESSUP, Philip C. Transnational Law. Yale, 1956. **$15.00**
The *1956 Storrs Lectures* at Yale.

111. JOHNSON, Herbert A. Imported Eighteenth-Century Law Treatises in American Libraries, 1700-1799. Tennessee, 1978. New **$16.50**

112. KAUFMAN, Irving R. The Message, the Medium, and the First Amendment. No date, no place. **$20.00**
Judge Kaufman's James Madison Lectures at N.Y.U. in 1970, with his *autograph, presentation inscription,* dated March 11, 1971; slightly worn.

113. KAUPER, Paul G. Frontiers of Constitutional Liberty. Michigan, 1956. **$17.50**

The *1956 Cooley Lectures* at Michigan; original blue cloth, slightly worn.

An Unrecorded Variant

114. KEBLE, Joseph. An Assistance to Justices of the Peace for the Easier Performance of Their Duty. 2 blanks; license leaf; title page, 2 leaves; 719 pp (irregular, but complete). Printed by W. Rawlins, S. Roycroft, and H. Sawbridge, Assigns of Richard & Edward Atkins Esq; for Samuel Keble at the Turks Head over against Fetter Lane End in Fleet-Street. MDCLXXIII [1683]. Compare Wing K113 and K113A. Folio. **$225.00**
Admitted to Gray's Inn in 1647, at age 15, Keble is best known for his reports, though perhaps infamously so, this work is seemingly more thorough.

This copy, bound in contemporary reverse calf, worn, rebacked, new label, an unrecorded variant, the volume being in any event uncommon, but three copies of Wing K113 and one of K113A recorded.

With the title page in double wood-cut borders, the two blanks somewhat loose, but *altogether a tall, impressive volume.*

115. KELSEN, Hans. What is Justice? Berkeley, 1960. **$20.00**
Professor Kelsen's collected essays.

116. KEMBLE, John Mitchell. The Saxons in England. Two Volumes. New Edition. London, 1876. **$125.00**
His reputation as an Anglo-Saxon scholar established in 1833 with the publication of his edition of the poems of Beowulf, Kemble began his work on The Saxons in England in the late 1840's, toward the end of the decade (from 1839 to 1848) which saw the publication of his massive Codex Diplomaticus aevi Saxonici in six volumes.

This the New Edition, revised by Walter de Gray Birch, *handsomely bound in full calf,* gilt-lined covers, elaborately gilt spines, a trifle rubbed, with matching red and black morocco labels, gilt-lined and lettered, all edges marbled, and marbled endpapers.

117. (KENT, James). A manuscript document, *signed by Kent,* one page, for the Supreme Court of Otsego County, New York, delivering William Garrett to bail, as taken and acknowledged before Kent. **$125.00**

Drawn for Kent, with his signature in full, and dated February 23, 1811; measuring 7¼ by 8 inches, a bit of age staining, *but the signature bold and easily recognizable.*

Kent had been appointed to the Supreme Court by Jay in 1798, and was to become Chancellor of the New York Court of Chancery in 1814.

118. KING, Donald B. and Charles W. Quick (eds.). Legal Aspects of the Civil Rights Movement. Wayne, 1965. **$15.00**

119. KISCH, Guido. Gestalten und Probleme aus Humanismus und Jurisprudenz. de Gruyter, 1969. **$25.00**
With a letter from Professor Kisch laid in.

120. LANDIS, James M. The Administrative Process. Yale, 1938. **$20.00**
The *1938 Storrs Lectures* at Yale; original blue cloth, gilt-lettered, slightly worn.

121. LANDON, Michael. The Triumph of the Lawyers, Their Role in English Politics, 1678-1689. Alabama, 1970. **$10.00**

122. (LAW SCHOOL EXAMINATIONS). EDWARD H. WARREN. Corporations. 4 pages, as issued. June, 1921. **$12.50**
Professor Warren's 1921 Corporations' Examination at Harvard Law School; considerable underlining, two folds, a bit worn.

123. LEAGE, R. W. Roman Private Law. MacMillan, 1909. **$22.50**
Original reddish-brown cloth, gilt-lettered, slightly worn.

124. LEE, R. W. The Elements of Roman Law. Fourth Edition, London, 1956. **$15.00**

125. LEVI, Edward H. An Introduction to Legal Reasoning. Chicago, 1961. **$10.00**

126. LEWIS, Edmund H. The Contribution of Judge Irving Lehman to the Development of the Law. New York, 1951. **$15.00**
The *tenth annual Cardozo Lecture* delivered before the Association of the Bar of the City of New York.

127. (LINCOLN'S Inn). Catalogue of Books of the Sixteenth to the Twentieth Centuries from the Lindoln's Inn Library. London, 1980. **$10.00**

The Sotheby Parke Bernet catalogue for its auction held in London on February 21, 1980, *with the estimate and prices realized lists laid in.*

128. LOPEZ-REY, Manuel. Crime, An Analytical Appraisal. Routledge, 1970. **$15.00**

129. LOTH, David. Chief Justice, John Marshall and the Growth of the Republic. Norton, 1949. **$15.00**

130. LYON, Leverett S. et al. Government and Economic Life. Two volumes. Washington, 1939. **$25.00**
Publication No. 79 of The Institute of Economics of the *Brookings Institution.*

131. McCLOSKEY, Robert G. (ed.). Essays in Constitutional Law. Knopf, 1957. **$15.00**
With essays by *James B. Thayer, Thomas Reed Powell,* and *Edward S. Corwin,* among others.

132. McCLOSKEY, Robert G. The Modern Supreme Court. Harvard, 1972. **$15.00**

133. McDOWELL, Banks, Jr. Foreign Personal Representatives. Michigan, 1957. **$17.50**
With a foreward by *Hessel Yntema;* original blue cloth, gilt-lettered, foredge spotted.

134. MacKINNON, F. B. Contingent Fees for Legal Services. American Bar Foundation, 1964. **$17.50**

135. MADOX, Thomas. Baronia Anglica. Blank; Title Page; 292 pp.; 14 leaves; blank. London, 1741. *Folio.* **$225.00**
Madox, one of England's greatest legal historians, and after whom Maitland considered naming the society bearing Selden's name.

This *Madox's only posthumous work,* first published in 1736, nine years after his death, examining the history of land-honors, baronies and tenure in capite.

Bound in old calf, the boards repaired and quite worn, *handsomely rebacked,* the spine elaborately gilt, occasional spotting, but in general an exceptionally clean, desirable and worthwhile copy, *with a handsome engraved vignette of Madox's principal works on the title page, and fine woodcut illustrations, designs and initials throughout the text.*

136. MAGUIRE, John MacArthur. The Lance of Justice, A Semi-Centennial History of the Legal Aid Society, 1876-1926. Harvard, 1928. **$17.50**

137. MAIDMENT, James. The Court of Session Garland. London, 1888. **$75.00**
A prolific author and collector, a renowned antiquary and friend of Tennyson, Maidment gained his legal reputation as a Scottish advocate engaged in genealogical and disputed cases.

This volume catches him in lighter humor, having first been published in 1839; *a very attractive copy* in blue cloth, very slightly rubbed, *with an exceptionally nice gilt-lettered and decorated spine.*

138. MAITLAND, F. W. (ed.). Select Pleas of the Crown. London, 1887. **$50.00**
One of Maitland's earliest works, the first volume which he edited for the Selden Society, and its first volume, comprised of Maitland's selections from among the earliest of plea rolls, from 1200 to 1225, during the reign of King John and the first part of the reign of King Henry III.

139. (MAITLAND, F. W.). H. E. BELL. Maitland, A Critical Examination and Assessment. Harvard, 1965. **$12.50**

The Only Edition in English

140. MARTENS, [Georg Friedrich]. Summary of the Law of Nations. Translated from the French by William Cobbett. Philadelphia, 1795. **$125.00**
One of Martens' three major works, written on the eve of the French Revolution while he was Professor at Gottingen, this its only translation into English.

The translator if William Cobbett, the great radical pamphleteer, residing at the time of publication as a political refugee in the United States. States.

Newly rebound in ½ leather, gilt-lined and lettered spine, some greying and spotting, particularly to preliminaries, but altogether a sound copy.

141. MASON, Alpheus Thomas. The Supreme Court from Taft to Warren. Lousiana State, 1958. **$12.50**

142. MASON, Alpheus Thomas. William Howard Taft, Chief Justice. Simon and Schuster, 1965. **$17.50**

143. MAY, Thomas Erskine. The Constitutional History of England. *Three Volumes.* Fifth Edition. London, 1875. **$85.00**

144. MIDWINTER, E. C. Law and Order in Early Victorian Lancashire. York, 1968. **$5.00**

42 pages stapled wraps.

145. MORGAN, Edmund Morris. Some Problems of Proof under the Anglo-American System of Litigation. Columbia, 1956. **$17.50**
The 13th *James S. Carpentier Lectures at Columbia.*

146. (MURPHY, Frank). RICHARD D. LUNT. The High Ministry of Government: The Political Career of Frank Murphy. Wayne, 1965. **$12.50**

147. NADER, Laura (ed.). The Ethnography of Law. Stiff wraps. Menasha, Wisconsin, 1965. **$12.50**
With articles by *Nader, Bohannan* and *Hoebel,* among others; a special publication of the American Anthropology Association, appearing in December, 1965.

148. NAGEL, Stuart S. (ed.). The Rights of the Accused. Sage, 1972. **$11.00**
The *first volume* in Sage's Criminal Justice System Annuals.

149. NELSON, Robert H. Zoning and Property Rights. M.I.T., 1977. **$12.50**

150. (NEW YORK). The Supreme Court of the State of New York, 1691-1941. Stamford, 1941. **$25.00**
Exercises upon the occasion of the 250th anniversary of the Court's founding, *with addresses by Irving Lehman, Arthur Goodhart* and *John W. Davis,* among others. *Handsomely printed* at the Overbrook Press, blue linen cloth, spine gilt-lettered.

151. OAKLEY, Thomas Pollock. English Penitential Discipline and Anglo-Saxon Law in Their Joint Influence. Columbia, 1923. **$25.00**
Issued in *Columbia's Studies in History, Economics and Public Law;* original sewn wraps, somewhat worn and embrowned.

In Six Volumes

152. OLDFIELD, T. H. B. The Representative History of Great Britain and Ireland. Six volumes. London, 1816. **$300.00**
This the final edition, revised and amplified, of Oldfield's two major works, first issued in the 1790's, namely his "Entire and Complete History . . . of the Boroughs of Great Britain" and his "History of the Original Constitutions of Parliaments."

A very attractive set, bound in full, contemporary leather, the covers blind decorated, and the spines elaborately gilt, with contrasting red and black labels, gilt-lined and lettered.

153. PALGRAVE, Sir Francis. The Rise and Progress of the English Commonwealth, Anglo-Saxon Period. *Two Volumes. London, 1832.* **$175.00**
The first edition of what is perhaps Palgrave's most famous work, *termed "ingenious and profound" by Kent* and "replete with omnifarious reading" by Hallam, published during the year in which Palgrave was knighted, and six years before he became Deputy-Keeper of the Public Records.
An attractive copy, bound in ¾, dark-brown morocco over marbled boards, slightly worn, all edges marbled, with marbled endpapers, and the spine gilt-lettered.

154. PARKER, John J. The American Constitution and World Order Based on Law. New York, 1953. **$15.00**
The *Twelfth Annual Cardozo Lecture.*

155. PATTERSON, Bennett B. The Forgotten Ninth Amendment. Bobbs-Merrill, 1955. **$20.00**
With an introduction by *Roscoe Pound;* foredge spotted.

156. PETERSON, Merrill D. (ed.). Democracy, Liberty and Property, the State Constitutional Conventions of the 1820's. Bobbs-Merrill, 1966. **$10.00**

157. PFENNIGSTORF, Werner. Legal Expense Insurance, The European Experience in Financing Legal Services. American Bar Foundation, 1975. Wraps. **$5.00**

158. PICTET, Jean. Le Droit humanitaire et la Protection des Victimes de la Guerre. Sijthoff, 1973. **$10.00**

159. PLUCKNETT, Theodore F. T. A Concise History of the Common Law. *First Edition.* Rochester, 1929. **$35.00**
The first edition of perhaps the best, and certainly the most highly enjoyable, introduction to the history of English law.

160. POLLOCK, Sir Frederick. Leading Cases Done Into English and Other Diversions. London, 1892. **$45.00**
Pollock's whimsical parodies of the law, in verse, dedicated to (and the dedication accepted by) *Algernon Swinburne; a highly unusual item,* in the original blue cloth, gilt-lettered, slightly worn.

161. POLLOCK, Sir Frederick and Frederic William Maitland. The History of English Law. Second Edition. *Two volumes.* Washington, 1959. **$55.00**
Unquestionably the classic modern work on medieval English law, written primarily by Maitland, and appearing first in 1895, with the second edition shortly thereafter in 1898; this issue *with an introduction by Roscoe Pound.* Original blue cloth, gilt-lettered, slightly worn.

162. POMEROY, Earl S. The Territories and the United States, 1861-1890, Studies in Colonial Administration. University of Washington, 1969. **$12.50**
A re-issue of the 1947 edition.

163. POUND, Roscoe. Criminal Justice in America. Harvard, 1945. **$17.50**
The second issue, with emendations, of *Pound's Colver Lectures,* delivered at Brown University in 1924.

164. POUND, Roscoe. New Paths of the Law. Nebraska, 1950. **$20.00**
The First Lectures in the Roscoe Pound Lectureship Series at Nebraska, Pound's alma mater, delivered, fittingly, by Pound.

165. POUND, Roscoe. The Spirit of the Common Law. Boston, 1931. **$17.50**
Pound's 1921 Dartmouth Alumni Lectures.

166. PRESTWICH, Michael. York Civic Ordinances, 1301. York, 1976. **$5.00**

28 pages, stapled wraps.

167. PULLING, Alexander. The Order of the Coif. Buffalo, 1975. New. **$20.00**
A reissue of Pulling's estimable work, first issued in 1884, on Serjeants-at-Law, the Order in decline as Pulling wrote, but among which were numbered almost all the great judges and lawyers of England through the 1800's.

168. (PULLING, Serjeant Alexander). Circuit Court Broadside. Cardiff, 1867. **$45.00**
An interesting, large broadside, measuring 13x26 inches, announcing that Pulling (who later wrote The Order of the Coif) and William Mills, will be holding court on circuit in County Glamorgan, with a listing of the locations at which the court is to be held, and the parishes, hamlets and places to attend, including Cardiff and its environs.

With five folds, and a bit of wear at the edges, but *generally very nice.*

169. PURVIS, J. S. Notarial Signs from the York archiepiscopal records. York, 1957. **$45.00**
One of the few modern works on the history of notaries public in England, *with 100 plates* of notarial signs, marks, signatures and seals from the 14th through the 18th centuries.

170. PURVIS, J. S. The Records of the Admiralty Court of York. York, 1962. **$5.00**

38 pages, stapled wraps.

171. PUSEY, Merlo J. Charles Evans Hughes. Two Volumes. New York, 1951. **$22.50**

172. RADIN, Max. Handbook of Anglo-American Legal History. West, 1936. **$35.00**
Dedicated to Justice Cardozo; in the original maroon buckram, a bit worn and faded.

173. RADIN, Max. Handbook of Roman Law. West, 1927. **$35.00**
Quite a nice copy, in the original maroon buckram, gilt-lettered.

First Edition of His First Work
174. REEVE, Tapping. The Law of Baron and Femme. **First Edition.** New Haven, 1816. **$150.00**
Founder of the Litchfield Law School (which may lay claim to being the first law school founded in this country) in 1784, Reeve published this volume, his first, at the age of 72, upon his retirement from the bench.
Bound in full contemporary calf, somewhat worn and rubbed, red morocco label, gilt-lined and lettered, occasional spotting, but essentially clean.
Altogether, an agreeable copy of a work which Hoffman proclaimed "if not read, an American lawyer can scarce be said thoroughly to understand the law of descents of this country."
With the signature (dated 1819) of Archibald Smith, who entered Litchfield in 1814, on the title page.

175. REGAN, Richard J. Private Conscience and Public Law, the American Experience. Fordham, 1972. **$12.50**

176. REISS, Albert J., Jr. The Police and the Public. Yale, 1971. **$10.00**
Professor Reiss' *Terry Lectures* at Yale.

177. REIWALD, Paul. Society and its Criminals. Heinemann, 1949. **$17.50**

Translated and edited by *T. R. James.*

178. RICE, William Gorham. A Tale of Two Courts, Judicial Settlement of Controversies between the States of the Swiss and American Federations. Wisconsin, 1967. **$12.50**

179. ROBINTON, Madeline Russell. An Introduction to the Papers of the New York Prize Court, 1861-1865. Columbia, 1945. **$25.00**
Published in *Columbia's Studies in History, Economics and Public Law*

180. ROBITSCHER, Jonas B. Pursuit of Agreement, Psychiatry & the Law. Lippincott, 1966. **$10.00**

181. (ROMILLY, Sir Samuel). PATRICK MEDD. Romilly, A Life of Sir Samuel Romilly, Lawyer and Reformer. London, 1968. **$17.50**

182. ROSENBLOOM, David H. Federal Service and the Constitution, the Development of the Public Employment Relationship. Cornell, 1971. **$12.50**

183. ROTTSCHAEFER, Henry. The Constitution and Socio-Economic Change. Michigan, 1948. **$35.00**
The first series of Cooley Lectures, delivered at Michigan Law School in 1947.

184. RUSSELL, Lord John. An Essay on the History of the English Government and Constitution. Second Edition. London, 1823. **$65.00**
One of the leaders in the Reform Movement which transformed England in the first half of the 19th century, Russell wrote this work, said to be his best, while still in his twenties, it first appearing in 1821, some few years after he had embarked on his parliamentary career.
Attractively bound in later ¾ morocco over marbled boards, the first leaf foxed, else exceptionally clean, save very occasional light spotting.

185. SCHICK, Marvin. Learned Hand's Court. Johns Hopkins, 1970. **$17.50**

186. SCHUBERT, Glendon. Human Jurisprudence. Hawaii, 1975. **$15.00**

187. SCHWARTZ, Bernard. The Law in America, A History. McGraw-Hill, 1974. **$15.00**

188. SCHWARTZ, Bernard. The Supreme Court, Constitutional Revolution in Retrospect. Ronald Press, 1957. **$15.00**

189. SCHWARZENBERGER, Georg. A Manual of International Law. Fourth Edition. **Two Volumes.** Stevens and Sons, 1960. **$25.00**

190. (DRED Scott). CHARLES MORROW WILSON. The Dred Scott Decision. Philadelphia, 1973. **$8.50**

191. SELDEN, John. Titles of Honor. Second Edition. Blank; title page; 14 leaves; 941 pp. (irregular, but complete); 2 blanks. London, 1631. New S.T.C. 22178. Folio. **$250.00**
Among Selden's most handsomely printed works, with many woodcut illustrations throughout, several nearly full page.
First published in 1614, when Selden was but 30, this work was reissued in 1631 much expanded, and was recently termed by Sir John Fletcher in his Selden Society lecture, Selden's "first book of any importance."
Bound in full leather, worn, the covers blind-ruled, *handsomely rebacked in mottled calf,* gilt-lettered, title page dusty, occasional spotting and embrowning, but in general, *a large, clean and desirable copy* of the work of which John Locke said "Selden's 'Titles of Honor' a gentleman should not be without."

Including Selden's First Published Work
192. SELDEN, John. Tracts. **First Edition.** Portrait; title pages; 15 leaves; 132 pp; title page; 3 leaves; 40 pp; title page; leaf; 24 pp. London, 1683. Wing S2441. **$425.00**
The first edition of Selden's Tracts, four in number, the first two of particular interest to the legal historian, being his first published work ("Janus") and his Epinomis, both published in 1610 when Selden was but 26 and comprising his first investigations of English law. Also of interest are the last two tracts, Selden's only published works concerning wills and estates.
Bound in full, contemporary panelled calf, *handsomely rebacked,* red morocco label, gilt-lettered.
With three separate title pages for each tract, saving the last two which are combined in one, and the separate title page for the entire volume, in red and black, all in double woodcut borders, and decorative woodcuts in the text.
Altogether a handsome copy, with wide margins, occasional black letter, and *a fine engraved portrait of Selden facing the first title page.*

193. SELZNICK, Philip. Law, Society and Industrial Justice. Sage, 1969. **$15.00**

194. SIGMUND, Paul E. Natural Law in Political Thought. Winthrop, 1971. **$10.00**

195. SIMPSON, A. W. B. (ed.). Oxford Essays in Jurisprudence. Oxford, 1973. **$17.50**
This the Second Series, with essays by *Honoré, Hart* and *Dworkin,* among others.

196. SMITH, Franklin. Judicial Review of Legislation in New York, 1906-1938. Columbia, 1952. **$15.00**

197. SQUIBB, G. D. The Law of Arms in England. London, 1979. 15 pp, stapled wraps. **$7.50**
An enjoyable essay by the author of *Doctors' Commons.*

198. STIMSON, Frederic Jesup. The American Constitution. Scribner's, 1914. **$35.00**
The *1907 Lowell Institute Lectures;* a very nice copy in the original blue cloth, gilt-lettered, uncut, and with a folding table.

199. STONE, Julius. Quest for Survival, The Role of Law and Foreign Policy. Harvard, 1961. **$15.00**
Dedicated to *Roscoe Pound* on his 90th birthday.

200. STONE, Victor J. (ed.). Civil Liberties and Civil Rights. Illinois, 1977. **$15.00**
The *David C. Baum Memorial Lectures,* with essays by *Francis Allen, Paul Freund* and *Charles Black,* among others.

201. STOUFFER, Samuel A. Communism, Conformity, and Civil Liberties. Doubleday, 1955. **$10.00**

202. STRUM, Philippa. The Supreme Court and "Political Questions," a Study in Judicial Evasion. Alabama, 1974. **$10.00**

203. SWISHER, Carl Brent. The Supreme Court in Modern Role. N.Y.U., 1958. **$15.00**
The *1957 James Stokes Lectures* at N.Y.U.

204. SZASZ, Thomas S. Psychiatric Justice. MacMillan, 1965. **$12.50**

205. TACHAU, Mary K. Bonsteel. Federal Courts in the Early Republic, Kentucky 1789-1816. Princeton. New. **$16.50**
An impressive work, pioneering the examination of the records of the early lower federal courts.

206. THIERRY, Augustin. History of the Conquest of England by the Normans. London, 1841. **Bound With. TOMLINS, T. E.** Chronicles of Jocelin of Brakelond. London, 1844. **$75.00**
Thierry, *one of the greatest French historians of the 19th century,* first published this work in 1825, its being called his great work ("grand ouvrage") and the first creation of his youth, and going through nine editions before his death.
Bound with T. E. Tomlins' translation from the Latin of the Chronicles of Jocelin, written at the close of the twelfth century, the basis for Carlyle's essay, written in 1843, on Abbott Samson.
Quite attractively bound in full contemporary calf, the spine elaborately gilt.

207. [THORPE, Benjamin]. Ancient Laws and Institutes of England. London, 1840. **Folio.** **$200.00**
First making his reputation, much as did Kemble, as an Anglo-Saxon scholar, Thorpe edited this work, published by the Records Commission in 1840, both in one single folio volume and in two octavo volumes, *our copy being the folio,* and comprised in the main of the old Anglo-Saxon laws from Aethelbert (c. 600 A.D.) to Canute (c. 1025 A.D.), *with the Anglo-Saxon and English texts, including manuscript variants, placed in double columns,* as appropriate.
Rather nicely rebound in later dark blue cloth, blue morocco label, gilt-lettered.

A Handsome Set
208. TOWNSEND, William C. Modern State Trials. Two volumes. London, 1850. **$125.00**
A valuable supplement to Howells' great State Trials, issued some thirty years' previously.
A very handsome set, bound in ¾ leather over marbled boards, elaborately gilt spines with matching red morocco labels, gilt-lined and lettered.

209. TRUSOV, Alexei. An Introduction to the Theory of Evidence. Moscow, no date [post 1960]. **$22.50**
Translated from the Russian, a rather startling exposure to Soviet evidence law.

210. (VICTIMLESS Crime). THE SAN FRANCISCO COMMITTEE ON CRIME. A Report on Non-Victim Crime in San Francisco. San Francisco, 1971. Wraps. **$10.00**

211. WADE, H. W. R. Administrative Law. Oxford, 1961. **$15.00**
The fifth volume in the *Clarendon Law Series,* edited by *H. L. A. Hart.*

212. (WALES). E. A. LEWIS. An Inventory of the Early Chancery Proceedings Concerning Wales. Cardiff, 1937. **$17.50**
The third volume in the *History and Law Series* published by the University of Wales.

213. (WALES). T. I. JEFFREYS JONES. Exchequer Proceedings Concerning Wales in Tempore James I. Cardiff, 1955. **$17.50**
The 15th volume in the *History and Law Series* of the University of Wales.

214. WARKOV, Seymour. Lawyers in the Making. Aldine, 1965. **$8.50**

215. WARREN, Earl. The Memoirs of Earl Warren. Doubleday, 1977. **$10.00**

216. (WARREN, Earl). LEO KATCHER. Earl Warren, a Political Biography. McGraw-Hill, 1967. **$12.50**

217. WARREN, Samuel. A Popular and Practical Introduction to Law Studies. London, 1835. **$75.00**
The first English edition of this well-received work, which went through several editions, in Warren's pointed and enjoyable style.
Newly and attractively rebound in canvas-backed boards, black leather label, gilt-lettered.

218. (WATER Law). CORWIN W. JOHNSON and Susan H. Lewis (eds.). Contemporary Developments in Water Law. Austin, 1970. **$15.00**

219. WECHSLER, Herbert. Principles, Politics, and Fundamental Law. Harvard, 1961. **$17.50**
Including Wechsler's famed *"Neutral Principles"* essay, given as the Holmes Lecture at Harvard.

220. WESTIN, Alan F. (ed.). An Autobiography of the Supreme Court, Off-the-Bench Commentary by the Justices. MacMillan, 1963. **$18.50**

221. WESTIN, Alan F. et al. Databanks in a Free Society, Computers, Record-Keeping and Privacy. Quadrangle, 1972. **$15.00**

222. WILLIAMS, Glanville L. Joint Torts and Contributory Negligence, A Study of Concurrent Fault in Great Britain, Ireland, and the Common-Law Dominions. Stevens, 1951. **$17.50**

Thomas Dorr's Copy with His Signature
223. WOOD, Tho[mas]. A New Institute of the Imperial or Civil Law. Second Edition. London, 1712. **$300.00**
Reaching a fourth edition by 1730, this work treats not only Roman law, but also canon law and the laws of several European countries.
A remarkable Rhode Island association, with the signature of T. W. Dorr (of the Dorr Rebellion) dated May 6, 1825, on the first blank (the blank somewhat torn, but not affecting the signature or date), and a letter tipped in, on the letter-head of the United States Courts, Providence, dated March 25, 1904, addressed to *S. S. Rider,* the noted Rhode Island lawyer and historian, informing him of the book.
Bound in later full sheep, a bit worn, leather label, gilt-lined and lettered, title within double woodcut border, lightly spotted, a few upper margins cut close, but altogether quite a desirable copy of one of Wood's best known works.

Thomas Dorr's Copy
224. [WOOD, Thomas]. A Treatise of the Principles of the Laws in General. First Edition. London, 1705. **$250.00**
First published in 1705, one year after Wood's Institutes, this volume was intended by Wood to be an introduction to the latter volume; translated from the French, it comprises a portion of Domat's great book "Les Lois Civiles dans leur Ordre Naturel."
Uniformly bound with the preceding item, in later sheep, somewhat worn and rubbed, but attractive; leather label, *with the signature of T. W. Dorr on the title page, dated 1825,* the title page in a double woodcut border with a portion of the upper right hand corner torn away, and woodcut initials throughout the text, somewhat embrowned and spotted.

225. WOODWARD, C. Vann (ed.). Responses of the Presidents to Charges of Misconduct. Delacorte Press, 1974. **$10.00**
Requested by *John Doar.*

The First Edition of the Most Famous Work on Court Hand
226. WRIGHT, Andrew. Court Hand Restored. London, 1776. **$175.00**
First published in 1776, Wright's work had, by 1912, appeared in ten editions, and was initially prompted by legislation enacted in the reign of George II requiring legal documents to be drawn in English, with an ensuing ignorance of Law French and Latin.
A very attractive copy, bound in 19th century ¾ calf, gilt-lined and lettered spine, five raised bands, and *twenty plates setting forth examples of court hand.*

227. WRIGHT, Benjamin F. The Growth of American Constitutional Law. Holt, 1946. **$15.00**

RARE AND SCHOLARLY

BOOKS ON THE LAW
(1980)

"Man must be noble, helpful and good."
— Johann Wolfgang von Goethe,
Das Göttliche (The Divine), 1785

CATALOGUE FOUR

MEYER BOSWELL BOOKS
SAN FRANCISCO

1. ABERNATHY, George L. The Idea of Equality, an Anthology. **$15.00**
With a *presentation inscription* by the author.

2. ABRAHAMS, Gerald. Morality and the Law. London, 1971. **$15.00**

3. ADLOW, Elijah. The Genius of Lemuel Shaw. Boston 1962. **$25.00**
With a presentation inscription from the author to *Arthur "Pops" Fielder.*

4. ARNOLD, Thurman. Fair Fights and Foul, A Dissenting Lawyer's Life. Harcourt, Brace, 1965. **$12.50**

5. ARNOLD, Thurman. The Folklore of Capitalism. Yale, 1938. **$15.00**

6. (ARNOLD, Thurman). EDWARD N. KEARNY. Thurman Arnold, Social Critic; the Satirical Challenge to Orthodoxy. New Mexico, 1970. **$12.50**

7. ASSOCIATION of the Bar of the City of New York. Jurisprudence in Action. New York, 1953. **$45.00**
With a foreward by *Robert H. Jackson*, and a selection of some of the greatest modern legal essays, including those of *Holmes (The Path of the Law), Cardozo, Maitland* and *Holdsworth*, among many others.

8. AVINS, Alfred (ed.). Open Occupancy vs Forced Housing Under the Fourteenth Amendment. New York, 1963. **$10.00**

Bacon's Proposed Restatement of English Law

9. BACON, Sir Francis. The Elements of the Common Lawes of England. London, 1639. Title Page: Title Page (Maxims); 7 leaves; 94 pp.; Title Page (Use); 3 leaves; 72 pp.; blank. S.T.C. 1136. Gibson 195. **$520.00**
Comprised of two works, Bacon's Maxims and his Use of the Law, neither published until after his death, but *of great importance*, the former having been dedicated to Queen Elizabeth and written in 1598, and *forming part of Bacon's scheme for a restatement of English law which was never to be realized.*
This, the third issue of 1639, nine years after the initial appearance in 1630; *a handsome copy bound in ¾ 19th century crimson morocco*, a bit rubbed, all edges gilt, and the spine gilt-lettered, with all three title pages as called for, a trifling bit of dampstaining to a few leaves, but altogether exceptionally clean and desirable, *with the Short Title Catalogue noting only the Huntington Library copy in this country.*

10. BACON, Gaspar G. The Constitution of the United States. Harvard, 1928. **$35.00**
The first Bacon lectures delivered at Boston University by Bacon, in the *Lectureship Series on the United States Constitution* which bears his name.

11. (BACON Lectures). The Bacon Lectures on the Constitution of the United States, 1940-1950. Boston University Press, 1953. **$35.00**
Given at Boston University, and including those by *Commager, Swisher, Fairman* and *Justice Owen J. Roberts.*

12. BARNETT, Walter. Sexual Freedom and the Constitution. New Mexico, 1973. **$12.50**

The First Edition of One of the Earliest Works on Husband and Wife

13. BARON and Feme. A Treatise of the Common Law Concerning Husbands and Wives. London, 1700. Leaf; Title Page; 14 leaves; 380 pp.; 18 leaves. New Wing B899. **$350.00**
This, the first edition, anonymously published in 1700, and perhaps written by the author of The Infants' Lawyer (see below), also published anonymously some three years previously, and, in any event, one of the earliest works on the subject, providing (according to Holdsworth) *"a clear summary of the main principles of the law as to marriage, separation and divorce, the status of married women, and the proprietary relations of husband and wife."*
Quite a nice copy, bound in full, 19th century calf, a trifle rubbed, the covers and spine blind-decorated with a red label, gilt-lined and lettered, and marbled endpapers.
Julius Rosenthal's copy, with his signature on the first free endpaper and also on the title page.

14. BARON and Feme. A Treatise of the Common Law Concerning Husbands and Wives. *Second Edition.* [London], 1719. 2 blanks; leaf; Title Page; 12 leaves; 422 pp.; 21 leaves; blank. **$225.00**
The second (of three) editions of this work, enlarged from the first, and published 19 years subsequently.
In a desirable full, contemporary calf binding, somewhat worn, the covers blind-decorated, the spine with a red label, gilt-lined and lettered, the base of the spine a trifle chipped, but in general *an exceptionally clean copy.* The copy of Julius Rosenthal.

15. BAUM, Daniel J. The Welfare Family and Mass Administrative Justice. Praeger, 1974. **$12.50**

16. BEANEY, William M. The Right to Counsel in American Courts. Michigan, 1955. **$15.00**

17. BEELEY, Arthur L. The Bail System in Chicago. Chicago, 1966. **$17.50**
A pioneering study, first published in 1927; with a new preface by the author.

18. BELKNAP, Michael R. Cold War Political Justice, The Smith Act, the Communist Party, and American Civil Liberties. Greenwood, 1977. **$12.50**

19. BELLAMY, John. The Tudor Law of Treason. London, 1979. **$15.00**

Bentham Proposes Universal Suffrage

20. BENTHAM, Jeremy. Plan of Parliamentary Reform. Second Edition. London, 1818. Title Page; leaf; 156 pp. **$250.00**
The work which signalled Bentham's conversion to the cause of radical reform, and written in 1809, but not published until 1817; this, the second edition, published a year later, with Bentham excluding only infants, idiots and people unable to read from the vote, parliaments to last but a year, the remedy of "democratical ascendancy" to erase the evils afflicting England.
A very attractive copy, newly bound in ½ calf over marbled boards, occasional very lightish and insignificant spotting, a tear in leaf G4 just affecting the text.

21. (BLACKSTONE, Sir William). Blackstone and Oxford, An Exhibition Held at the Bodleian Library, Oxford on the occasion of the bicentenary of Sir William Blackstone, 1723-1780. Bodleian Library, 1980. **$10.00**
Pictorial wraps; 43 pp. *With 156 items described; very enjoyable.*

The First Edition

22. B[LOUNT], T[homas]. Fragmenta Antiquatatis. Ancient Tenures of Land, and Jocular Customs of Some Mannors. Made public for the diversion of some, and instruction of others. London, 1679. License leaf; Title Page; 2 leaves; 175 pp.; 8 leaves; blank. New Wing B3333. **$180.00**
A very nice copy of Blount's most entertaining work, yet valuable, termed by Holdsworth *the "only really original book" produced on legal history in the latter part of the 17th century.*
Newly and attractively bound in ½ calf over marbled boards, the spine gilt-lined and lettered, a small tear in the third leaf expertly repaired.

23. BLUMBERG, Abraham S. Criminal Justice. Quadrangle, 1967. **$10.00**

24. BOGUSLAVSKY, Mark. The U.S.S.R. and International Copyright Protection. Moscow, 1979. **$17.50**

Coke and Ellesmere

25. BOHUN, William. Cursus Cancellariae; or, the Course of Proceedings in the High Court of Chancery. Second Edition. London, 1723. Leaf; Title Page; 2 leaves; 513 pages; 5 leaves; 8 advertising leaves. **$250.00**
Designed to provide a guide for the practitioner and student to the courts of Chancery, *this work may be even more valuable historically for its account of the result of the controversy between Coke and Ellesmere, omitted in the Reports in Chancery, over the respective provinces of the* Common Law and Equity, decided in Ellesmere's favor after reference to Bacon and others, and without which the court of Chancery may not have retained its independence.
The title page with the signature of Julius Rosenthal and in a double woodcut border, a small portion torn from the upper right hand corner slightly affecting the border, but not the text; a few marginal tears not affecting the text.
Altogether, an exceptionally clean copy, very attractively and newly bound in ¾ maroon calf over marbled boards, the spine gilt-lined, with a black label, gilt-lined and lettered.
Julius Rosenthal's copy.

Handsomely Printed

26. BOYD, Julian P. The Murder of George Wythe. Philadelphia, 1949. **$45.00**
An intriguing account of the murder of George Wythe, Jefferson's mentor, by the editor of the definitive edition of Jefferson's works. Privately printed for the Philobiblon Club, in very attractive cloth-backed marbled boards, the spine gilt-lettered.

27. BRYSON, William Hamilton. A Bibliography of Virginia Legal History Before 1900. Virginia, 1979. **New. $14.95**
Very useful.

28. (CASTBERG, Frede). Legal Essays, A Tribute to Frede Castberg on the Occasion of His 70th Birthday. [Oslo?], 1963. **$45.00**
In honor of Frede Castberg, perhaps the most eminent Norwegian legal scholar of this century; with essays by *Julius Stone, Max Sorenson and Gerhard Geibholz*, among many others. Bound in leather backed boards.

29. CEDERBLOM, J.B. and William L. Blizek (eds.). Justice and Punishment. Ballinger, 1977. **$12.50**

30. CHADBOURN, J.H. Lynching and the Law. North Carolina, 1933. **$25.00**
By the author of the current revision of Wigmore on Evidence.

31. CHEATHAM, Elliot Evans. A Lawyer When Needed. Columbia, 1964. **$12.50**
The 1963 James S. Carpentier Lectures at Columbia.

32. CHRISTENSEN, Barlow F. Lawyers for People of Moderate Means. American Bar Foundation, 1970. **$12.50**

33. CLARK, Leroy D. The Grand Jury, the Use and Abuse of Political Power. Quadrangle, 1972. **$12.50**

34. CLAUSEN, Henry C. Stanford's Judge Crothers. Privately Printed, San Francisco, 1967. **$17.50**
Illustrated; 157 pp., sewn printed wraps.

35. CLERKE, Francis. Praxis Supremae Curiae Admiralitatis. Fifth Edition. London, 1798. Half-title; Title Page; iv, 183 pp. **$150.00**
A very important book, first published in 1667, and one which Holdsworth called *"the leading book on the practice of the court [of Admiralty] right down . . . to 1859"*; with the Articles of Master Rowghton, containing the matters to be inquired of by maritime inquests, appended.
Full contemporary calf, worn, newly rebacked, red morocco label gilt-lined and lettered.
Julius Rosenthal's copy.

36. COFFIN, William Sloane, Jr. and Morris I. Liebman. Civil Disobediance: Aid or Hindrance to Justice? Washington, 1972. **$10.00**

Coke Upon Littleton With a Presentation Inscription

37. COKE, [Sir] Edw[ard]. The First Part of the Institutes of the Lawes of England. Or a Commentarie Upon Littleton. Second Edition. London, 1629. Blank; portrait; Title Page; 4 leaves; portrait; 395 folios; 35 leaves. S.T.C. 15785. **$1750.00**
One of the five greatest books in the history of English law, Coke's First Institute (or Coke on Littleton) is unquestionably the foremost work from Coke's pen, prolific as he was, and a work which, Holdsworth concludes, Coke "was engaged in writing all his life."
This, the second edition, of exceptional importance, the first edition having been published without Coke's authorization leading Coke within the year to bring out the second edition, with his corrections and emendations, this latter edition then used as the basis for printing of all subsequent editions until the critical edition of Hargraves and Butler close to 200 years later.
This copy, with a presentation inscription in a contemporary hand "ex dono Authoris . . . Coke", though not in Coke's hand.
Handsomely rebound in full tan sheep, the covers blind decorated, with a black morocco label, gilt-lined and lettered. First and last leaves somewhat dusty and soiled, with some marginal dampstaining, mainly lightish and not affecting the text, save for a few index leaves, very occasional lightish dampstaining elsewhere, marginal repairs to two leaves, copious annotations to the text, primarily in one early hand and to the first 250 folios; *in general, a very clean and extremely wide-margined copy, with two fine engraved portraits of Coke and Littleton respectively, and exceptional engraved title and index pages, with the Short Title Catalogue recording only the Huntington Library copy in this country.*

38. (COKE, Sir Edward). STEPHEN D. WHITE. Sir Edward Coke and "The Grievances of the Commonwealth," 1621-1628. North Carolina, 1979. **New $20.00**
The latest volume but two in the Studies in Legal History.

39. CONQUEST, Robert (ed.). Justice and the Legal System in the U.S.S.R. Praeger, 1969. **$12.50**

40. (CONSTITUTION, U.S.). The Constitution of the United States, An account of its travels since September 17, 1787. Washington, 1939. **$12.50**
An interesting pamphlet, issued by the Library of Congress; 6 plates, 12 pages, stapled wraps, a bit worn.

41. (CONSTITUTIONS). American Constitutions, Comprising an Astonishing Assemblage of Rare & Important Original Printings of "The Supreme Law of the Land". New York, 1964. **$45.00**
The famous catalogue issued by Edward Eberstadt & Sons, with valuable bibliographical notes, well-illustrated, and with the covers printed in red and blue; very attractive; 72 pages, sewn wraps, 210 items.

42. CORWIN, Edward S. Liberty Against Government. Louisiana State, 1948. **$22.50**
Based on Corwin's 1943 Edward Douglass White Lectures at Louisiana State; with a foreward by *Arthur T. Vanderbilt.*

43. CRELINSTEN, Ronald D. et al. Terrorism and Criminal Justice. Lexington, 1978. **$10.00**

44. CROSSKEY, William W. and William Jeffrey, Jr. Politics and the Constitution in the History of the United States. Three Volumes. Chicago, 1980. **New $100.00**
The first publication of all three volumes, the third volume left incomplete at Professor Crosskey's death and completed by Professor Jeffrey; perhaps the most controversial work on American Constitutional history published in this century. In a boxed collector's edition.
Volume III may be separately purchased at $27.

The First Edition of the First Work on the Law of Sheriffs

45. DALTON, Michael. Officium Vicecomitum: The Office and Authority of Sheriffs. London, 1623. 3 blanks; Title Page; 2 leaves; 192 folios; 4 leaves; 2 blanks. S.T.C. 6212. **$620.00**
The first edition of the first work ever published devoted exclusively to the law of the office of sheriff, and the work which, according to Holdsworth, "continued to be a standard authority till the beginning of the 18th century."
In full, contemporary calf, the corners and the head and tail of the spine expertly repaired, a bit of cracking to the lower portion of the front joint, but the cords very firm; an elaborate woodcut title page, the text exceptionally clean, with woodcut initials and decorations throughout, the last blank imperfect, but *altogether a very handsome volume, well-printed, and with considerable black letter throughout.*

46. DAUBE, David. Roman Law, Linguistic, Social and Philosophical Aspects. Edinburgh, 1969. **$15.00**
The 1966 Gray Lectures at Cambridge.

47. DAWSON, John P. Gifts and Promises, Continental and American Law Compared. Yale, 1980. **New $16.95**
The 1978 Storrs Lectures.

48. DENG, Francis Mading. Tradition and Modernization, A Challenge for Law Among the Dinka of the Sudan. Yale, 1971. **$15.00**
With a foreward by *Harold D. Lasswell.*

49. DEVOL, Kenneth S. (ed.). Mass Media and the Supreme Court. New York, 1971. **$12.50**

50. DOUGLAS, William O. An Almanac of Liberty. Doubleday, 1954. **$10.00**

51. DOUGLAS, William O. A Living Bill of Rights. Doubleday, 1961. **$10.00**

52. DUFFY, Herbert S. William Howard Taft. New York, 1930. **$22.50**
The first biography of Taft; *a nice copy.*

53. (DUGDALE, Sir William). FRANCIS MADDISON et al. Sir William Dugdale, 1605-1686, A List of His Printed Works and of His Portraits with Notes on His Life and the Manuscript Sources. Warwick, 1953. **$15.00**
The foremost bibliography, handsomely printed; 92 pages, printed wraps.

The First and Only Early Edition

54. DUKE, George. The Law of Charitable Uses. London, 1676. 2 blanks; leaf; Title Page; 2 leaves; 186 pp. (irregular but complete); 5 leaves; 2 blanks. Wing D2504 (not in New Wing). **$275.00**
Duke's volume, written upon The Statute of Charitable Uses (43 Eliz c.4), remains the sole work devoted to that statute, itself of seminal importance in the history of the English Poor Laws and the law of charity. *This is the first and only edition published until the early 1800's and including the reading upon the statute of Sir Francis Moore, said to be the statute's author.*
Bound in full, contemporary sheep, a bit worn, newly rebacked, red label gilt-lined and lettered, and the covers blind-lined. The title page in a double woodcut border, with woodcut initials and decorations in the text, occasional black letter, occasional light dampstaining to the lower margin, slightly affecting the text, and very occasional spotting, and with notes and lining in a contemporary hand on the blank leaves.
Altogether, a desirable copy of a work called by Bridgman "a standard authority upon this branch of the law."

The First Treatise on the Law of Women

55. [E., T.]. The Lawes Resolution of Womens Rights: or, The Lawes Provision for Women. London, 1632. Title Page; 6 leaves; 404 pp. (irregular but complete). S.T.C. 7437 **$750.00**
A work of the first importance in the history of the law, being the first work exclusively devoted to women's law, and the first treatise or textbook on a specific subject other than the land law.
Attributed by some to Thomas Edgar, and by others (with an inscription in a 19th century hand on the second front free end paper to the effect of the latter), to Sir James Dodderidge the work has been called by Lord Campbell "a learned work".
Bound in full, 19th century calf, a bit rubbed, the covers and spine blind-lined, red label gilt-lettered, the title page in a double woodcut border, with it and the succeeding two leaves dusty and repaired, slightly affecting the border but not the text, in black letter throughout, and with woodcut initials and decorations in the text.
A very good copy of a very important work with the Short Title Catalogue disclosing but one copy in this country, at the Huntington Library.
Julius Rosenthal's copy.

56. EHRENZWEIG, Albert A. Psychoanalytische Rechtswissenschaft. Duncker & Humblot, Berlin, 1973. Sewn wraps. **$22.50**
The first German translation.

57. EHRENZWEIG, Albert A. and Erik Jayme. Private Internatinal Law, A Comparative Treatise on American International Conflicts Laws, Including the Law of Admiralty. *Two volumes.* Sijthoff-Oceana, 1967 & 1973. **$35.00**

58. ELDRIDGE, William Butler. Narcotics and the Law. American Bar Foundation, 1962. **$15.00**

59. ESSER, Josef. Grundsatz und Norm in der richterlichen Fortbildung des Privatrechts. Mohr, Tubingen, 1956. **$17.50**

60. EULAU, Heinz and John D. Sprague. Lawyers in Politics, A Study in Professional Convergence. Bobbs-Merrill, 1964. **$10.00**

61. FALK, Richard A. The Role of Domestic Courts in the International Legal Order. Syracuse, 1964. **$15.00**

62. FODA, Ezzeldin. The Projected Arab Court of Justice. Nijhoff, 1957. **$17.50**
258 pp., sewn wraps.

Forsyth on Infants

63. FORSYTH, William. Law Relating to the Custody of Infants in cases of difference between parents or guardians. London, 1850. **$150.00**
A distinguished lawyer and man of letters, bencher and treasurer of the Inner Temple, and author of a Life of Cicero and the famed History of Trial by Jury, Forsyth wrote on a number of specific legal subjects, including this, his sole effort, on the law of infants, and this the only edition.

Newly and nicely rebound in ¾ calf over marbled boards, with the ownership stamp of Rosenthal, Hamill, Eldridge and King, the Rosenthal being Julius Rosenthal's son, Lessing Rosenthal.

64. FORTESCUE, Sir John. De Laudibus Legum Angliae. London, 1660. Title Page; 6 leaves; 132 folios; 3 leaves; 51 pages; Title Page; 5 leaves; 140 pages (irregular but complete). Wing F1612. **$350.00**
Said by Holdsworth to be "probably *the first legal book which was avowedly written to instruct a layman in the elements of the law",* this volume was designed by Fortescue for the instruction of the young Prince Edward.

Written circa 1470, the volume may also be viewed as *one of the earliest examples of comparative political method,* treating as it does of the differences between the English and French governments of the day, and *of value, in addition, for its description of the Inns of Court and the legal profession, and the first text to provide us with these insights.*

This edition *with the Latin text and English translation in double column,* the latter primarily black letter, and including two volumes (Summa Magna and Parva) dating from the 13th century on the procedures of the courts and written by Ralph Hengham, then Chief Justice of the King's Bench.

Bound in later ¾ vellum, a bit worn but sound, some spotting and embrowning, the title page a bit stained and some head and marginal notes shaved, but altogether *a desirable copy of a famous work, this the second issue to include the extensive notes and commentary of John Selden.*

65. (FORTESCUE, Sir John). Commendation of the Laws of England. London, 1917. **$27.50**
A re-issue of the translation by Francis Gregor of Fortescue's great De Laudibus Legum Angliae, *Gregor's translation having been first published in 1737.* Original cloth-backed printed boards, a bit of spotting to the endpapers and fore-edge.

Foster on Crown Law

66. FOSTER, Sir Michael. Report of Proceedings on the Commission of Oyer and Terminer and Goal Delivery for the Trial of the Rebels in 1746, in the County of Surrey, and of other Crown Cases, with discourses upon a few branches of the Crown Law. Second Edition. Dublin, 1791. **$175.00**
Termed "a very great master of crown law" by Blackstone, Foster was made a judge of the court of King's Bench, a post he held until his death in 1763, one year after the publication of the first edition of his Crown Law, in which he both collected apposite cases and added notes and discourse on them and the subject of crown law.

Attractively and newly bound in ¾ calf over marbled boards; Julius Rosenthal's copy.

67. FOX, Sanford J. Science and Justice, The Massachusetts Witchcraft Trials. Johns Hopkins, 1968. **$17.50**

68. FRANCK, Thomas M. The Structure of Impartiality, Examining the Riddle of One Law in a Fragmented World. MacMillan, 1968. **$15.00**

69. FRANK, Jerome. Fate and Freedom, A Philosophy for Free Americans. Simon and Schuster, 1945. **$15.00**

70. (FRANK, Jerome). BARBARA FRANK KRISTEIN. A Man's Reach, The Selected Writings of Judge Jerome Frank. MacMillan, 1965. **$17.50**
With a forward by *William O. Douglas.*

71. FRANKFURTER, Felix. Address to Harvard Law Society of Illinois, Annual Meeting, Chicago, Illinois, April 28, 1955. **$35.00**
16 pages, stapled wraps, a trifle embrowned; said to be "informal remarks spoken without notes and reproduced from a tape recording", and *highly enjoyable, with great spontaneity and wit.*

72. FRANKFURTER, Felix. Law and Politics, Occasional Papers of Felix Frankfurter 1913-1938. Harcourt-Brace, 1939. **$20.00**
Edited by Archibald MacLeish.

73. (FREEDOM of the Press). Association of the Bar of the City of New York. Freedom of the Press and Fair Trial. Columbia, 1967. **$15.00**
The Final Report with Recommendations.

74. FRIEDMAN, Lawrence M. A History of American Law. Simon & Schuster, 1973. **$15.00**

75. FRIENDLY, Henry J. The Federal Administrative Agencies, The Need for Better Definition of Standards. Harvard, 1962. **$17.50**
The 1962 Holmes Lectures at Harvard.

76. FRIENDLY, Henry J. Federal Jurisdiction: A General View, Columbia 1973. **$15.00**
Based on Judge Friendly's 1972 *James S. Carpentier Lectures at Columbia.*

The First Edition

77. FULBECKE, William. The Pandectes of the Law of Nations. London, 1602. Title Page; 3 leaves; 90 folios. S.T.C. 11414. **$400.00**
Preceding Grotius' great classic by a quarter-century, *Fulbecke's work was one of several by English civilians which, according to Nye, took a leading part in the development of the new international law.*

Handsomely and newly bound in full dark calf, tooled gilt and decorated spine; some embrowning, but an attractive work, with woodcut initials and decorations throughout the text.

Canon, civil and common law compared

78. FULBECKE, William. A Parallele or Conference of the Civil Law, the Canon Law, and the Common Law of this Realme of England. Second Edition. London, 1618. Title Page; 11 leaves; 104 folios; 8 leaves. S.T.C. 11416. **$350.00**
Termed "discursive and original" by Holdsworth, the work takes the form of 15 dialogues between a canonist, a civilian, and a barrister, much in the style of St. Germain, with the resemblances and differences between the three legal systems thereby appearing more readily.

Very attractively and uniformly bound with the copy of Fulbecke's Pandectes, immediately above, in full dark calf, tooled gilt and decorated spine; with some embrowning to the leaves, and woodcut initials and decorations throughout.

The First Edition

79. FULBECKE, William. The Second Part of the Parallele or Conference of the Civill Law, and the Canon Law, and the Common Law of this Realme of England. London, 1602. Title Page; 7 leaves; 74 folios; 8 leaves. S.T.C. 11415a. **$375.00**
Published just one year after the initial appearance of the first part of the Parallele (immediately above), this, *the second part, continues Fulbecke's series of dialogues with seven additional, the two parts being the complete work, and amounting to 22 dialogues total.*

Uniformly bound with the two preceding volumes, in full dark calf, tooled gilt and decorated spine; a little embrowning and spotting, and with woodcut initials and decorations throughout.

80. GERHART, Eugene C. Robert H. Jackson, Lawyer's Judge. Albany, 1961. **$15.00**

81. GIBSON, William Marion. Aliens and the Law. North Carolina, 1940. **$17.50**

82. GLASSEY, Lionel K.J. Politics and the Appointment of Justices of the Peace, 1675-1720. Oxford, 1979. **New. $29.00**
The latest volume in the series Oxford Historical Monographs.

83. GLICK, Henry Robert. Supreme Courts in State Politics. Basic Books, 1971. **$12.50**

84. GLUECK, Sheldon. Law and Psychiatry. London, 1963. **$22.50**
The 1962 Isaac Ray Award Lectures, dedicated to Justice Frankfurter; with a complimentary slip of the editor laid in.

85. GLUECK, Sheldon. Mental Disorder and the Criminal Law. Little, Brown, 1925. **$35.00**
The original edition of Glueck's first work; in a worn dustwrapper.

A Classic Work on the Law of Wills and Testaments

86. GODOLPHIN, John. The Orhan's Legacy: or, A Testamentary Abridgment. Fourth Edition. London, 1701. Title page; 3 leaves; 478 pp.; 10 leaves. **$225.00**
Despite its title, *Godolphin's work* covers more than orphans, treating of the law of wills and testaments comprehensively, and having been called by Holdsworth *one of "the two most famous books contributed by civilians"* upon this subject, the other being Swinburne's Briefe Treatise of Testaments and Last Willes.

Attractively and newly bound in ¾ dark green calf over marbled boards, the spine gilt-lined with a dark-red morocco label, gilt-lined, decorated and lettered; with lightish embrowning throughout, a few small holes on three leaves very slightly affecting the text, but not its legibility, and one leaf torn, perhaps very slightly affecting one marginal note. *A wide-margined, desirable copy.*

Julius Rosenthal's copy, with his signature laid in.

87. GOLD, Joseph. The Fund Agreement in the Courts. International Monetary Fund, 1962. **$15.00**

88. GOLDFARB, Ronald. Ransom, A Critique of the American Bail System. Harper & Row, 1965. **$10.00**
With a foreward by *Justice Arthur J. Goldberg.*

89. GOULDEN, Joseph C. The Superlawyers, The Small and Powerful World of the Great Washington Law Firms. Weybright, 1972. **$10.00**

90. GRAY, John Chipman. The Nature and Sources of Law. Second Edition. MacMillan, 1921. **$35.00**
A classic, praised by Pound, Holdsworth and Morris Raphael Cohen; this the original edition, a trifle rubbed, but very attractive, in the original maroon cloth, gilt still bright.

91. DE HAAS, Jacob. Louis D. Brandeis, A Biographical Sketch, With Special Reference to his Contributions to Jewish and Zionist History. New York, 1929. **$35.00**
Illustrated; *a very nice copy.*

5

6

"A Master of English Law"– Holdsworth

92. HALE, Sir Matthew. The Analysis of the Law. Third Edition. London, 1739. Leaf; Title Page; six leaves; 148 pp.; 13 leaves; blank. **$250.00**
One of the most important works in the history of the scientific arrangement of the law, setting forth an analytical scheme later adopted by Blackstone in his Commentaries, and in fact *termed by Blackstone "the most natural and scientifical . . . as well as the most comprehensive" scheme* for so doing.

An exceptionally fine copy, newly bound in full calf, the spine gilt-labelled.

Hale's Only Work Devoted Exclusively to the Law of Descents

93. HALE, Sir Matthew. De Successionibus apud Anglos: The Law of Hereditary Descents. London, 1700. Title Page; 3 leaves; folding table; 104 pp. **$250.00**
Written in English, and published after Hale's death, *this work treats of the transmission of land by hereditary descent, in which Hale investigates not only English, but also Jewish, Greek and Roman Law.*

A handsome volume, newly rebound in full dark calf, the spine gilt-lettered, lined and decorated; with some embrowning throughout, the folding table with one partial tear to one fold, but complete, and a bit of insignificant worming to the margins of a few pages. *An attractive, wide-margined copy.*

Julius Rosenthal's copy.

94. (HALE, Sir Matthew). EDMUND HEWARD. Matthew Hale. London, 1972. **$15.00**
The only 20th century biography of the great 17th century judge and polymath; illustrated.

95. (HAND, Learned). IRVING DILLIARD (ed.). The Spirit of Liberty, Papers and Addresses of Learned Hand. Knopf, 1952. **$12.50**

96. HARAGUCHI, Torao, et al. The Status System and Social Organization of Satsuma. Hawaii, 1975. **$15.00**
Satsuma Historical Documents Series No. 1.

97. HARDING, Alan. A Social History of English Law. Peter Smith, 1973. **$15.00**

Blackstone, Hale and the Rule in Shelley's Case

98. HARGRAVE, Francis. A Collection of Tracts Relative to the Law of England. Dublin, 1787. Title Page; leaf; li pp.; 578 pp. **$225.00**
This is the first, and only, volume published by Hargrave under this title, containing the first printings of hitherto unpublished manuscripts from his private collection, *including essays by Sir Matthew Hale and Sir William Blackstone, among others, the accomplishment of which Holdsworth termed Hargrave's "principal and greatest services to legal history."*

Newly and very nicely rebound in ¾ light calf over boards, the spine attractively gilt-lined and with a morocco label gilt lined, lettered and decorated; occasional spotting, primarily marginal, a very few leaves dampstained; generally a handsome copy, with the edges untrimmed.

With Julius Rosenthal's signature on the title page, and his pictorial bookplate on the front pastedown.

99. HARMER, Miss F.E. Anglo-Saxon Charters and the Historian. Manchester, 1938. **$17.50**
With a facsimile plate; 31 pp. sewn wraps, slightly worn; reprinted from the Bulletin of the John Rylands Library.

100. HARNO, Albert J. Legal Education in the United States. Bancroft-Whitney, 1953. **$25.00**

101. HARTLAND, E. Sidney. Primitive Law. Kennikat, 1970. **$12.50**
Originally published in 1924.

102. HAWKINS, William. A Treatise of the Pleas of the Crown. Second Edition. [London], 1724 & 1726. Blank; Title Page; 6 leaves; 266 pp.; 22 leaves; Title Page; 3 leaves; 464 pp.; 38 leaves; 2 blanks. **$300.00**
Of considerable importance in the history of the criminal law, this has been called by Holdsworth Hawkins' "great work" and by Winfield *"the starting-point of modern . . . treatises on the criminal law."*

Two volumes bound in one, in full contemporary calf, slightly worn, and newly rebacked, red label gilt-lined and lettered, the title pages in double woodcut borders, woodcut initials and decorations in the text; an exceptionally clean copy, save an occasional very lightish embrowning to some leaves of the second volume.

103. HEARN, William Edward. The Aryan Household, Its Structure and Its Development, An Introduction to Comparative Jurisprudence. London and Melbourne, 1891. **$45.00**
Recommended by Roscoe Pound for the study of legal institutions of Indo-European peoples; original blue-green cloth, slightly worn, inner hinges cracking, but a good copy with untrimmed edges, and largely uncut.

104. HILL, Frederick Trevor. Lincoln the Lawyer. New York, 1906. First Edition. **$25.00**
Pictorial cloth, gilt; *a very attractive copy,* though the slightest bit worn, of *the best legal biography of Lincoln.*

105. HILL, Helen. George Mason, Constitutionalist. Harvard, 1938. **$17.50**
Top edge spotted, else extremely nice.

106. HILL, Norman L. The Public International Conference, Its Function, Organization and Procedure. Stanford, 1929. **$15.00**
Slightly worn.

107. HINDUS, Michael Stephen. Prison and Plantation, Crime, Justice and Authority in Massachusetts and South Carolina, 1767-1878. North Carolina, 1980. **New. $20.00**
The latest volume in the Studies in Legal History.

Four Marvelous Holmes' Items All Presentation Copies

108. HOLMES, Oliver Wendell, Jr. (1) Speeches. Boston, 1913. (2) Speech of Mr. Justice Holmes at Commencement, Harvard University, June 28, 1911; (3) Speech of Mr. Justice Holmes at Commencement, Harvard University, June 28, 1911, a later issue; and (4) Speech of Mr. Justice Holmes at a Dinner of the Harvard Law School Ass'n of New York, February 15, 1913. Four items. **$1100.00**
All four items presentation copies from Justice Holmes, signed and in his hand, to Thomas Barbour and, in one instance, Barbour's daughter, Louise.

A highly interesting association, the Barbours being related to the Holmes, through the respective wives, who were cousins, and, as well, next door neighbors at Beverly Farms, Massachusetts, where the Holmes resided during the summer vacations of the Court.

Barbour is best known for reinvigorating and then presiding over the Agassiz Museum at Harvard; in his autobiography, published after Holmes' death, he devotes a chapter to his friendship with the Justice, whom he called *"a sincere, confirmed, and in some respects quite simple-minded atheist."*

Further details, including the text of the inscriptions, available upon request.

109. (HOLMES, Oliver Wendell, Jr.). MARK DeWOLFE HOWE (ed). Holmes-Laski Letters. Two Volumes. Harvard, 1953. **$27.50**
The most voluminous and wide-ranging of Holmes' correspondence. *With a foreward by Felix Frankfurter;* slightly worn.

110. HORWILL, Herbert W. The Usages of the American Constitution. Oxford, 1925. **$25.00**

111. HOULBROOKE, Ralph. Church Courts and the People during the English Reformation, 1520-1570. Oxford, 1979. **New $29.95**
The latest but one volume in the series of Oxford Historical Monographs.

112. (HUDSON, Manley O.). An extensive collection of essays written from 1913 to 1958 by this famous international law scholar, comprised of 44 pamphlets, typically stapled wraps, slightly worn. **$100.00**
A complete listing gladly supplied on request; individual titles available at $4.00 each.

113. HULL, William I. The Two Hague Conferences and Their Contributions to International Law. Boston, 1908. **$25.00**
A very nice copy.

The First Work on Infants' Law

114. THE INFANTS' LAWYER: or, The Law (Ancient and Modern) Relating to Infants. Second Edition. [London], 1712. Title Page; 11 leaves; 380 pp; 14 leaves. **$225.00**
The first book ever written on infants' law, first published in 1697, and reaching a third edition by 1726; this the much expanded second edition of 1712.

Rebound in an exceptionally handsome, antique panelled calf, red gilt label, sewn on five raised cords; a bit of spotting and embrowning, but altogether an extremely desirable copy of the work which Holdsworth said "was needed and . . . deals with the subject comprehensively."

The copy of Julius Rosenthal.

In Fourteen Volumes

115. (INTERNATIONAL Law). Procedural Aspects of International Law Institute. Fourteen Volumes. Syracuse and Virginia, various dates. **$115.00**
A complete run of the thirteen numbered titles (in fourteen volumes) of this valuable scholarly series, begun in the 1960's.

116. (JACKSON, Robert H.). Mr. Justice Jackson, Four Lectures in His Honor. Columbia, 1969. **$12.50**
With lectures by *Judge Desmond, Professor Freund, Justice Stewart* and *Lord Shawcross.*

117. JACOBS, Clyde E. Law Writers and the Courts, The Influence of Thomas M. Cooley, Christopher G. Tiedeman, and John F. Dillon Upon American Constitutional Law. California, 1954. **$17.50**

118. JESSUP, Philip C. The Birth of Nations. Columbia, 1974. **$15.00**
Based on Jessup's *1971 Barnette Miller Lectures at Wellesley.*

119. JESSUP, Philip C. The Price of International Justice. Columbia, 1971. **$12.50**
The 1970 Jacob Blaustein Lectures at Columbia.

120. (KELSEN, Hans). Essays in Honor of Hans Kelsen, Celebrating the 90th Anniversary of His Birth. Rothman, 1971. **$12.50**

With prefaces by Albert Ehrenzweig and Julius Stone, and a bibliography of Kelsen's works in the English language.

121. KLOOSTER, John W. The Granting of Inventive Rights. Minneapolis, 1965. **$15.00**

122. KONIG, David Thomas. Law and Society in Puritan Massachusetts, Essex County, 1629-1692. North Carolina, 1979. **New. $21.00**
The latest but one volume in the Studies in Legal History.

123. KRAINES, Oscar. The World and Ideas of Ernst Freund. Alabama, 1974. **$15.00**

124. KRIER, James E., and Edmund Ursin. Pollution & Policy, A Case Essay on California and Federal Experience with Motor Vehicle Air Pollution, 1940-1975. California, 1977. **$15.00**

125. KUTLER, Stanley, I. Judicial Power and Reconstruction Politics. Chicago, 1968. **$15.00**

126. (LAMBARDE, William). WILBUR DUNKEL. William Lambarde, Elizabethan Jurist, 1536-1601. Rutgers, 1965. **$15.00**

127. LATHAM, R.T.E. The Law and the Commonwealth. Oxford, 1949. **$15.00**

128. LEE, Dwight E., and George E. McReynolds (eds.). Essays in History and International Relations, in honor of George Hubbard Blakeslee. Kennikat, 1969 **$12.50**
Originally issued in 1949; with a bibliography of Blakeslee's works.

129. LETWIN, William. Law and Economic Policy in America, The Evolution of the Sherman Antitrust Act. Random House, 1965. **$15.00**

130. LEVY, Leonard W. Against the Law, The Nixon Court and Criminal Justice. Harper & Row, 1974. **$17.50**

The Tenures in English
131. [LITTLETON, Sir Thomas]. Littletons Tenures in English. London, 1604. Title Page; 142 folios; 2 leaves. New S.T.C. 15778. **$350.00**
One of the most famous works in all of English law, and the earliest treatise on the English law printed anywhere, Littleton's Tenures had gone through an amazing 70 editions by the time of the appearance of Coke's great commentary upon Littleton, in 1628.
This, the second issue to appear in the 1600's, in black letter throughout, bound in 18th century ½ calf over boards, morocco label, gilt-lined and lettered, the title page a bit dusty and chipped, with the contemporary signatures of William Boys and Sir Charles Peen, a very little bit of spotting and softening to the margins; *altogether a handy, desirable and uncommon copy of this great work*, the New Short Title Catalogue disclosing only three copies in this country, at the Folger Library, Harvard and Michigan.

132. LOKKEN, Roy N. David Lloyd, Colonial Lawmaker. U. of Washington Press, 1959. **$12.50**

133. (LONDON). PHILIP E. JONES (ed.). Calendar of Plea & Memoranda Rolls . . . of the City of London, 1437-1457. Cambridge, 1954. **$35.00**
With a presentation slip from The Corporation of London on the front pastedown.

134. (LONDON). PHILIP E. JONES (ed.). Calendar of Plea & Memoranda Rolls . . . of the City of London, 1458-1482. Cambridge, 1961. **$35.00**
With a presentation slip from The Corporation of London on the front pastedown.

135. LOWENSTEIN, Steven. Lawyers, Legal Education, and Development: An Examination of the Process of Reform in Chile. New York, 1970. **$15.00**
Printed wraps, 310 pp; with a complimentary slip from the publisher laid in.

136. MACAULAY, Stewart. Law and the Balance of Power, The Automobile Manufacturers and Their Dealers. Russell Sage, 1966. **$15.00**
With a forward by J. Willard Hurst.

137. McCLOSKEY, Robert G. The American Supreme Court. Chicago, 1971. **$12.50**

138. MacLACHLAN, Colin M. Criminal Justice in Eighteenth Century Mexico. California, 1974. **$15.00**

139. MADOX, Thomas. The History and Antiquities of the Exchequer of the Kings of England. Two Volumes. Greenwood, 1974. **$50.00**
A facsimile reissue of the second and best edition of 1769, a work termed by Maitland *"one of the greatest historical works of the eighteenth century."*

140. (MAGNA Carta). DORIS M. STENTON. After Runnymede, Magna Carta in the Middle Ages. Virginia, 1965. **$10.00**
Pictorial wraps, stapled, 54 pp., 4 plates; *Lady Stenton's essay on the 750th anniversary of the Magna Carta.*

141. (MAGNA Carta). THOMAS WOOD STEVENS. Magna Carta, a Pageant Drama. Chicago, 1930. **$45.00**
Limited to 1,000 copies, illustrated, with an introduction by Roscoe Pound, and a presentation inscription from the volume's editor, the pageant itself having been performed at the semicentennial of the American Bar Association in 1928.

142. MAINE, Sir Henry. Lectures on the Early History of Institutions. Kennikat, 1966. **$12.50**
Re-issued from the 7th edition of 1914.

143. MAITLAND, Frederic W. The Forms of Action at Common Law. Cambridge, 1936. **$25.00**
The first separate issue, the work formerly having been combined with Maitland's Equity.

144. (MAITLAND, Frederic W.). H.E. BELL. Maitland, A Critical Examination and Assessment. Harvard, 1965. **$15.00**
The best critical biography of Maitland.

145. (MAITLAND, Frederic W.). C.H.S. FIFOOT. Frederic William Maitland, A Life. Harvard, 1971. **New. $16.50**
The first volume in the Studies in Legal History, fittingly devoted to Maitland, primary founder and moving force of the Selden Society in its early years.

146. (MAITLAND, Frederic W.). H.A.L. FISHER (ed.). The Collected Papers of Frederic William Maitland. Three Volumes. Cambridge, 1911. **$250.00**
A handsome set, bound in ¾ green leather over linen boards, slightly rubbed, the front covers gilt-stamped, the spines gilt-lettered and with decorated endpapers, the prize copy awarded by Trinity College Cambridge for First Class in the Examination for the Law Tripos in June, 1921, with a presentation slip affixed to the front pastedown of the first volume to that effect.
A very attractive copy of this, the most difficult to find of Maitland's works, with his essays arranged chronologically from 1875 to 1906, the year of his death.

147. (MANSFIELD, Lord). EDMUND HEWARD. Lord Mansfield, A Biography of William Murray, 1st Earl of Mansfield 1705-1793, Lord Chief Justice for 32 Years. Barry Rose, 1979. **New. $35.00**
Highly praised by Lord Devlin.

148. (MARSHALL, John). GERALD GUNTHER (ed.). John Marshall's Defense of McCulloch v. Maryland. Stanford, 1969. **$15.00**
The remarkable series of contemporary essays prompted by Marshall's decision, edited by Professor Gunther.

149. MASTERSON, William E. Jurisdiction in Marginal Seas, with Special Reference to Smuggling. Kennikat, 1970. **$15.00**
A reissue of the 1929 edition

150. MAYER, Martin. Emory Buckner. Harper & Row, 1968. First Edition. **$12.50**
With an introduction by *Justice John M. Harlan.*

151. MEDINA, Harold R. The Anatomy of Freedom. Holt, 1959. **$10.00**

152. MENU, Bernadette. Le Regime Juridique des Terres et du Personnel Attache a la Terre dans le Papyrus Wilbour. Lille, 1970. **$25.00**
Cloth-backed printed wraps; 268 pp.; slightly worn.

153. MEURER, Christian. The Program of the Freedom of the Sea, a Political Study in International Law. Washington, 1919. **$25.00**
104 pp., sewn wraps, slightly worn and chipped; *George Grafton Wilson's copy, with his last name in his hand on the front cover.*

154. MEYERS, David W. The Human Body and the Law. Aldine, 1970. **$12.50**

155. MILLER, Arthur R. The Assault on Privacy, Computers, Data Banks, and Dossiers. Michigan, 1971. **$15.00**
With a foreward by *Sam Ervin.*

156. MILLER, George H. Railroads and the Granger Laws. Wisconsin, 1971. **$15.00**

157. MORRIS, Clarence. The Justification of the Law. Pennsylvania, 1971. **$15.00**

158. MUNZER, Stephen. Legal Validity. Nijhoff, 1972. **$15.00**
Sewn, printed wraps, 74 pp.

159. MURPHY, Jay, et al. Legal Profession in Korea: The Judicial Scrivener and Others. Oceana, 1967. **$17.50**
Korea Law Study Series Number 2.

160. NELSON, William. Lex Testamentaria: Or, A Compendious System of All the Laws of England . . . concerning Last Wills and Testaments. Second Edition. London, 1724. Title page; 6 leaves; 578 pages; 6 leaves. **$225.00**
Nelson, to whom the writing or editing of more than a dozen works, several multi-volume, have been credited, published this, his only work on the subject, in 1714, it reaching a third edition by 1728.
Newly and extremely handsomely bound in full dark calf, the covers blind-tooled and panelled, Oxford-style, and the spine gilt-lined and lettered; with a very little bit of spotting and embrowning. *Very Nice.*

Julius Rosenthal's copy.

The First Edition
161. NELSON, W[illiam]. The Rights of the Clergy of Great Britain; As Established by the Canons; the Common Law; and the Statutes of the Realm. London, 1709. Title Page; 7 leaves; 551 pp. (irregular but complete); blank. **$175.00**
Nelson, a Middle Temple barrister, and *one of the most prolific legal writers of the early 1700's*, and whose works were reprinted as late as 1872, arranged this volume, *his sole work devoted to the law of the clergy*, alphabetically, much in the manner of works on the Justices of the Peace and abridgments then popular.
This, the first edition of 1709 and Nelson's first treatise, nicely rebound in ½ dark calf over marbled boards, the spine gilt-lined with a red label gilt-lined and lettered; a bit of spotting to the title page, with two small holes expertly repaired, a bit of wear to the preliminary leaves, but altogether *a very attractive and clean copy.*

162. NODA, Yosiyuki. Introduction to Japanese Law. U of Tokyo Press, 1978. **$17.50**
With a complimentary slip of the editor and translator, Anthony H. Angelo, laid in.

163. O'BRIAN, John Lord. National Security and Individual Freedom. Harvard, 1955. **$17.50**
The 1955 Godkin Lectures at Harvard; with a complimentary card from the Fund for the Republic laid in.

164. (OBSCENITY). The Obscenity Report, Pornography and Obscenity in America. London, 1970. **$12.50**

165. (OXFORD Companion). DAVID M. WALKER. The Oxford Companion to Law. **New $49.95**
An absorbing volume, part dictionary, part encyclopedia, part biography, part bibliography; worth dipping into for a moment or an hour. *The perfect Christmas book for any lawyer — or even non-lawyer — in a bright, red dustwrapper.*

166. PATTERSON, Edwin W. Law in a Scientific Age. Columbia, 1963. **$12.50**
The 1963 James S. Carpentier Lectures at Columbia.

167. PAUL, John. Every Landlord or Tenant His Own Lawyer. Dublin, 1777. **$125.00**
The most popular of several treatises published on the law of landlord and tenant during this period, Paul's treatise reached an 11th edition in 1821.
Nicely bound in full contemporary calf, the spine gilt-lined, with a red label, gilt-lined and lettered, the very top of the back joint unobtrusively a bit cracked. *A handsome little volume.*

168. PFEFFER, Leo. Church, State and Freedom. Revised Edition. Beacon Press, 1967. **$15.00**

The First Work on Powers
169. POWELL, John Joseph. An Essay on the Learning respecting the Creation and Execution of Powers. Second Edition. Dublin, 1791. **$175.00**
Termed "a pioneer work" by Holdsworth, Powell's Powers first appeared in 1787, offering for the first time a systematic account of and comment on previously scattered authorities on the subject, and preceding Sudgen's great work by over 20 years.
A very nice copy in full contemporary calf, blind-lined covers and spine, with a red label, gilt-lined and lettered, the very top of the front joint just unobtrusively cracking; *altogether quite attractive.*

170. POWELL, Thomas. The Attourney's Academy. London, 1647. 2 blanks; Title Page; 4 leaves; 436 pp.; 8 leaves; blank. Wing P3068 **$350.00**
A much enlarged issue of Powell's work, first published in 1623, and *one of the oldest of a series of books of practice describing the procedure of all the different courts*, including (in addition to the Common Law Courts) the Courts of Chancery, The Court of Requests, the Star Chamber and the Court of Wards.
Bound in full, contemporary calf, unlettered, the covers blind ruled, the binding worn, but sound, with the head and tail of the spine expertly repaired, a great many notations and signatures in contemporary hands on the first blank, the first leaves a bit dusty, very small holes in two leaves, slightly affecting the text, and some very minor dampstaining to the upper margin, but *generally a very clean copy of this work, which Holdsworth stated "treated of procedure in general in a more modern style than any book that had yet appeared."*

171. (POWELL, Thomas Reed). A collection of essays written from 1917 to 1947 on a variety of subjects, comprised of nine pamphlets, typically stapled or sewn wraps, slightly worn. The Collection **$50.00**
A complete listing gladly supplied on request; individual titles separately available.

172. (PRISONS). American Prisons in Turmoil, Part 1. Hearings before the Select Committee on Crime, House of Representatives, 92nd Congress, First Sessions. G.P.O. 1972. **$10.00**
Prompted by Attica; slightly worn, a bit of underlining, 486 pp., sewn wraps.

173. QUINNEY, Richard. Critique of Legal Order, Crime Control in Capitalist Society. Little, Brown, 1974. **$12.50**

174. RADZINOWICZ, Sir Leon. Ideology and Crime. Columbia, 1969. **$15.00**
The 1965 James S. Carpentier Lectures at Columbia.

175. RADZINOWICZ, Sir Leon and Joan King. The Growth of Crime. Basic Books, 1977. **$10.00**

176. RAMUNDO, Bernard A. Peaceful Coexistence, International Law in the Building of Communism. Johns Hopkins, 1967. **$12.50**

177. REISS, Albert J. The Police and the Public. Yale, 1971. **$15.00**
Based on the author's *Terry's Lectures at Yale.*

178. REIWALD, Paul. Society and its Criminals. Heinemann, 1949. **$17.50**
Translated and edited by T.E. James.

179. REMBAR, Charles. The End of Obscenity. The trials of Lady Chatterly, Tropic of Cancer, and Fanny Hill. Random House, 1968. **$12.50**
Rembar served as defense counsel in these cases; *highly entertaining.*

A Very Early Law Book
180. RETURNA Brevium. London, [1538-40?]. Title Page; 11 folios, Beale T228; New S.T.C. 20900.5 **$850.00**
The Returna Brevium, or Return of Writs, has been said by Holdsworth to be "essential, because *the whole of the local government was carried on under judicial forms, and by means of writs original or judicial*", *the Returna Brevium providing the proper response, or "return"*, to the brevium, or writ, directed to the local forum.
This copy very attractively bound in new, tan calf by Sangorski and Sutcliffe, the title page in a fine, architectural woodcut border (McKerrow & Ferguson 30), a few contemporary annotations, the text exceptionally clean.
An extremely desirable copy of a rare, early law book, Beale disclosing but two copies, in the British Museum and Harvard, and the revised Short Title Catalogue three, at the Folger Library, Harvard and Minnesota, and with no copy of the work appearing at auction in this century; the precise date of the volume remaining uncertain, the title page showing 1534 in the woodcut border, the New S.T.C. estimating 1538-40, and Beale 1544.

181. RICE, Charles E. The Supreme Court and Public Prayer. Fordham, 1964. **$10.00**

182. RIDER, Sidney S. Historical Research and Educational Labor Illustrated in the Work of Elisha Reynolds Potter, Late Judge of the Supreme Court of Rhode Island. Providence, 1901. **$35.00**
Rider's address delivered before the Rhode Island Historical Society on July 11, 1882; 19 pp., stapled and printed wraps, somewhat worn.

183. ROBINSON, Edward S. Law and the Lawyers. MacMillan, 1935. **$17.50**

184. ROBINSON, W.W. Lawyers of Los Angeles, A History of the Los Angeles Bar Association and of the Bar of Los Angeles County. Los Angeles, 1959. **$45.00**
A scholarly and handsome volume, printed at the Ward Ritchie Press, *with the title page in red and black.*

185. RODELL, Fred. Nine Men, A Political History of the Supreme Court of the United States from 1790 to 1955. Random House, 1955. **$10.00**

With Sir Matthew Hale's Preface
186. ROLLE, Henry. Un Abridgment des plusieurs Cases et Resolutions del Common Ley. London, 1668. Portrait; Title Page; 6 leaves, 490 pp.; 836 pp.; 4 leaves. Wing R1872. **$275.00**
A gargantuan work, even for legal tomes, and *making an important new departure in the literature of abridgments through its summaries of Parliamentary records and statutes, as well as case law. Of value also for the preface by Sir Matthew Hale providing a summary of the common law's development to the time of the Restoration.*
Bound in full contemporary panelled calf, newly rebacked, the original label preserved, woodcut initials and decorations in the text, largely black letter, occasional spotting and embrowning, infrequent marginal annotations in a contemporary hand, and *with a fine engraved portrait of Rolle preceding the title page.*

187. (ROLT, Sir John). The Memoirs of the Right Honourable Sir John Rolt, Lord Justice of the Court of Appeal in Chancery, 1804-1871. London, 1939. **$17.50**
Privately printed by the Inner Temple, with nine plates, the fore-edge untrimmed; *a nice issue.*

188. ROSCOE, E.S. Lord Stowell, His Life and the Development of English Prize Law. Houghton Mifflin, 1916. **35.00**
Slightly worn; uncut.

189. ROSENBERG, Maurice. The Pretrial Conference and Effective Justice. Columbia, 1964. **$15.00**
With a preface by Justice *Tom C. Clark.*

190. ROSETT, Arthur and Donald R. Cressey. Justice by Consent: plea bargains in the American courthouse. Lippincott, 1976. **$15.00**

191. RUSCHE, Georg and Otto Kirchheimer. Punishment and Social Structure. Columbia, 1939. **$22.50**
With a forward by *Thorsten Sellin.*

192. SAWER, Geoffrey. Law in Society. Oxford, 1965. **$15.00**
The 8th volume in the *Clarendon Law Series.*

193. SAWYER, P.H. Anglo-Saxon Charters, an Annotated List and Bibliography. Royal Historical Society, London, 1968. **$35.00**

194. SCHRAG, Philip G. Counsel for the Deceived, Case Studies in Consumer Fraud. Pantheon, 1972. **$10.00**
With an introduction by *Ralph Nader.*

195. SCHWARTZ, Bernard (ed.). The Fourteenth Amendment, Centennial Volume. N.Y.U., 1970. **$17.50**
With essays by *Justice Brennan, Lord Denning, Dean Griswold,* and *Chief Justice Warren,* among many others.

196. SCHWARTZ, Helen E. Lawyering. Farrar, Straus 1976. **$10.00**

197. (SCOTT, Austin Wakeman). ROSCOE POUND, ERWIN N. GRISWOLD, and ARTHUR E. SUTHERLAND (eds.). Perspectives of Law, Essays for Austin Wakeman Scott. Little, Brown, 1964. **$35.00**
With essays by *Roscoe Pound, W. Barton Leach* and *Julius Stone,* among many others.

198. SCOTT, James Brown. Law, the State, and the International Community. Two Volumes. Greenwood, 1970. **$35.00**
Originally published in 1939.

199. SCURLOCK, John. Retroactive Legislation Affecting Interests in Land. Michigan, 1953. **$17.50**
With a foreword by *Lewis M. Simes;* slightly worn.

200. SEARLE, Eleanor (ed. & trans.). The Chronicle of Battle Abbey. Oxford, 1980. **New $55.00**
Written in the twelfth century, with considerable portions devoted to the law developing during the reigns of Henry I and II and of Stephen, the main chronicler the abbey's lawyer; *with the Latin text and English translation on facing pages.*

201. (SEDITION Act). The Kentucky-Virginia Resolutions and Mr. Madison's Report of 1799, an Historic Statement on State and Federal Relations. Richmond, 1960. **$10.00**
82 pages, sewn, printed wraps.

The First Edition Variant

202. SELDEN, John. The History of Tithes. [London], 1618. Title Page; 2 leaves; xxii pp.; 6 leaves; 491 pp.; 2 leaves. New S.T.C. 22172 (variant). **$260.00**
Undoubtedly Selden's most controversial work, called his *"great work on ecclesiastical history"* by Holdsworth, inferring that tithes were due, not by divine, but by merely human law, leading to many recriminations and replies, and to Selden's summons before the court of High Commission and before King James.

Controversial as it was, Selden's work apparently went through several issues in the first edition of 1618, this being the variant of the first issue noted at New S.T.C. 22172; *attractively, and newly, bound in ¾ leather over decorated boards,* four raised bands, red label, gilt-lined and lettered, the title page in red and black, embrowned and slightly chipped, occasional annotations in a contemporary hand, and occasional very lightish marginal dampstaining and spotting, with a very small hole in the last several leaves barely affecting the text.

203. SELZNICK, Philip. Law, Society, and Industrial Justice. Russell Sage, 1969. **$15.00**

**The First Edition of
Sheppard's Most Successful Work**

204. SHEPPARD, William. The President of Presidents. London, 1655. Title Page; 2 leaves; 361 pp. (irregular but complete); 6 leaves. **$350.00**
One of the most industrious writers of the 1600's, and the author of many law books, *Sheppard here provided a concise summary of the law of assurances, as well as the precedents, or forms, themselves; the work was extremely popular, and editions of it were published as late as the 1820's.* As with his Touchstone, however, Sheppard's authorship has been questioned, and the work attributed to Justice Dodderidge.

Newly and very attractively rebound in full, light calf, antique, with the label preserved, the title page in a double woodcut border, with slight loss to the outer lower portion of the border, cut close, and a very slight loss to two headnotes, not affecting legibility; some embrowning throughout, and very occasional marginal annotations in a contemporary hand.

With the signature of William Petyt, barrister of the Middle Temple and for many years Keeper of the Records in the Tower of London, we believe, on the title page, and the annotations by his hand.

Julius Rosenthal's copy.

**The First Edition of a
Classic in Real Property and
Conveyancing**

205. SHEPPARD, William. The Touchstone of Common Assurances. London, 1648. Title page; 5 leaves; 523 pp. (irregular but complete); 3 leaves. Wing S3214. **$500.00**
Termed by Holdsworth the earliest work exclusively devoted to the theory of conveyancing, Sheppard's Touchstone may in fact have been written by Sir John Dodderidge, whose manuscripts fell into Sheppard's hands.

A handsome volume, newly rebound in ¾ red morocco over marbled boards, the spine gilt-lined, with a black label gilt-lined and lettered; a few marginal tears and holes not affecting the text, save a small hole on Q8 affecting a few words; occasional lightish embrowning, a few leaves with lightish dampstaining in the margins and a bit of marginal worming in the first leaves, with a small portion torn from the upper right hand corner of the title page, all not affecting the text.

Altogether, a highly desirable copy of a famous work, the first book to go beyond mere collections of precedents, and to explain their use, in the law of conveyancing.

Julius Rosenthal's copy.

The First Latin Edition

206. SMITH, Sir Thomas. De Republica et Administratione Anglorum. London, [1610]. Blank; Title Page; 3-165 pp.; 2 blanks. New S.T.C. 22868. **$275.00**
Truly a Renaissance man, Smith was in turn an eminent public servant, a classical scholar, physician, mathematician, astronomer, architect and historian; but his place in English legal and constitutional history is due to his Republic, which Alston in his modern, critical edition of this work termed a *"pioneer treatise in comparative politics",* written while Smith was Ambassador to France.

This, the first Latin edition, of which there were four, bound in contemporary vellum, a bit worn, with an unobtrusive smallish stain to the lower right portion of the front cover, lightish dampstaining to the upper right hand corner of most leaves, some worming to the lower margins not affecting the text, and some embrowning, but altogether a good copy, with the binding well preserved, a red label gilt-lined and lettered, a trifle chipped.

**An Excellent Copy of
the Best Edition**

207. SPELMAN, Sir Henry. Glossarium archaiologicum. Third Edition. London, 1687. Blank; portrait; Title Page; 10 leaves; 576 pp.; blank. Wing S4926. Cowley 178 (variant). **$275.00**
Termed by Holdsworth a book "of first-rate importance in our legal history", Spelman's Glossarium was first published in 1626, in the first part only, at Spelman's own expense, after he had offered it to John Beale, the printer, for £5 or books of equal value, the offer being refused.

The remainder, left unfinished at Spelman's death in 1641, was completed by Dugdale, with the first complete edition appearing in 1664; this, the third and best edition with a memoir of Spelman, was the last edition, appearing in 1687.

Bound in full, contemporary calf, worn, early rebacked, with an elaborate gold spine, the bottom of the spine a bit chipped, but expertly repaired, six raised bands, red label, gilt-lined and lettered; with a handsome, full page portrait of Spelman, the title page in red and black, woodcut initials and decorations in the text, double-column.

Altogether quite an attractive copy, containing not only legal terms, but being a dictionary of Latin and other words to be found in the post-classical authors and documents, both English and foreign.

**The First Work Devoted Exclusively
to the Pleas of the Crown**

208. STANFORD, [William]. Les Plees del Corone. London, 1607. Blank; Title Page; 11 leaves; 198 folios. New S.T.C. 23224.

Bound With

STANFORD, William. An Exposition of the Kings Prerogative. London, 1607. Title Page; 4 leaves; 85 folios (irregular but complete). New S.T.C. 23218. **$600.00**
Made judge of the Common Pleas in 1554, Stanford founded his Pleas of the Crown primarily on Bracton and the Yearbooks, though he did not live to see its first publication in 1560, two years after his death, as the first work devoted exclusively to English criminal law.

This copy bound also with his Exposition of the Kings Prerogative, the preface (to Sir Nicholas Bacon) dated 1548, Stanford's summary of the King's feudal prerogatives, based on the Yearbooks and on the Prerogative Regis, the work also not appearing until after Stanford's death.

These, the last early printings of both works, in 1607, *attractively bound in full, contemporary calf, expertly rebacked,* red label, gilt-lined and lettered, the first title page within a double woodcut border, woodcut decorations and initials throughout the text, occasional black letter and annotations in a contemporary hand, some very lightish dampstaining to a few leaves only; *altogether a desirable copy.*

A Very Early Work on International Law

209. SUTCLIFFE, Matthew. The Practice, Proceedings, and Lawes of armes. London, 1593. 2 blanks; Title Page; 11 leaves; 342 pp. (irregular but complete); 3 blanks. **$700.00**
Termed an "original" work by Holdsworth, this is the sole legal effort of Sutcliffe, a clerical civilian, dealing at length with the justifiable causes of war.

This the first edition of 1593, bound in full 17th century calf, a few smallish holes to the leather only on the covers, the front joint cracked and the spine worn, lacking the label, but the cords sound and despite the foregoing *a pleasing copy, exceptionally clean,* save a bit of insignificant dustiness and lightish staining of the title page, *and well-printed with many woodcut initials and decorations throughout the text.*

The First and Only Edition

210. (WOMEN'S Law). Laws respecting Women, as they regard their natural rights or their connections and conduct, also the Obligations of Parent and Child and the Condition of Minors. London, 1777. **$275.00**
This, the chronological successor to Baron and Feme and the Treatise of Feme Coverts appearing earlier in the century, and said by Holdsworth to be *"large and better"* and *"to cover much ground [and be] clearly written."*

Very nicely and newly bound in ¾ calf over marbled boards, with contemporary marginal annotations; *Julius Rosenthal's copy,* with his signature on the title page.

RARE AND SCHOLARLY

BOOKS ON THE LAW

(1981)

"Britton composed a learned work . . . published . . . by the commandment of Edward I., our Justinian; the tenor whereof runneth in the King's name, as if it had been written by him, answerable to Justinian's Institutes, which Justinian assumeth to himself . . . This John Britton was . . . of great and profound judgment in the common laws." (Sir Edward Coke, Reports, Pt 10, Preface) (See items 27 and 45, and inside cover).

CATALOGUE FIVE

MEYER BOSWELL BOOKS

SAN FRANCISCO

1. ADAMS, George Burton. Council and Courts in Anglo-Norman England, Yale, 1926. **$35.00**
Yale Historical Publications, Studies, Volume V; *a very nice copy.*

2. ADAMS, Willi Paul. The First American Constitutions. North Carolina, 1980. **New $23.00**
Winner of the American Historical Association Bicentennial Prize.

3. ALLEN, David Grayson. In English Ways, The Movement of Societies and the Transferal of English Law and Custom to Massachusetts Bay in the Seventeenth Century. North Carolina, 1981. **New $27.00**
Winner of the Jamestown Prize for Early American History.

4. ARENS, Richard and Harold D. Lasswell. In Defense of Public Order, The Emerging Field of Sanction Law. Columbia, 1961. **$15.00**
With a foreword by David L. Bazelon.

5. (ASSOCIATION of the Bar of the City of New York). GEORGE MARTIN. Causes and Conflicts, the Centennial History of the Association of the Bar of the City of New York, 1870-1970. Houghton Mifflin, 1970. **$12.50**

6. (AUSTRALIA). J.M. BENNETT. Keystone of the Federal Arch, A Historical Memoir of the High Court of Australia to 1980. Canberra, 1980. **New $22.50**

7. BAKER, J.H. An Introduction to English Legal History. Second Edition. Butterworths, 1979. **New $39.25**
Likely to be the standard introduction for this generation; also available in paper at $23.60.

8. BALDWIN, Simeon. Modern Political Institutions. Little, Brown, 1898. **$45.00**
A nice copy in the original green cloth, gilt, with a presentation inscription from the author.

9. BARNES, James J. Authors, Publishers and Politicians, The Quest for an Anglo-American Copyright Agreement 1815-1854. London, 1974. **$20.00**

10. BELL, Walter George. London Rediscoveries. London, 1929. **$27.50**
With an essay on the Inns of Court libraries; a bit of spotting, but nice.

11. BENTHAM, Jeremy. The Principles of Morals and Legislation. New York, 1948. **$15.00**

12. BERGER, Raoul. Impeachment: The Constitutional Problems. Harvard, 1973. **$13.50**
The second volume in the Studies in Legal History.

13. (BERLIN). Violations of Human Rights, Illegal Acts and Incidents at the Sector Border in Berlin Since the Building of the Wall. Berlin, 1962. **$15.00**
27 pages, printed wraps; *illustrated,* with a fold-out map.

14. BEVERIDGE, Albert J. The Life of John Marshall. **Four Volumes.** Houghton Mifflin, 1919. **$50.00**
An attractive copy of the leading and standard biography; in the original maroon cloth, a bit rubbed, leather labels, gilt-lettered, with many illustrations.

15. (BIBLIOGRAPHY). J.H. BEALE. A Bibliography of Early English Law Books. Buffalo, 1966. **New $35.00**
A fine work, arguably the best bibliography of English law ever compiled, covering the period 1475-1600; this a reissue of both the 1926 original edition and the 1943 supplement.

16. (BIBLIOGRAPHY). JOHN WILLIAM WALLACE. The Reporters. Fourth Edition. Buffalo, 1959. **New $35.00**
By far the best work ever published on the English and American reporters, with emphasis on the former; an attractive reissue of the 4th edition of 1882.

17. BIEBERSTEIN, Wolfgang Frhr Marschall v. Reflexschaden und Regressrechte. Kohlhammer, 1967. **$50.00**
A presentation copy to Max Rheinstein, to whom the work is co-dedicated, the author a pupil of Rheinstein; a trifle worn.

18. BISHOP, Joseph W., Jr. Justice Under Fire, a Study of Military Law. Charterhouse, 1974. **$10.00**

19. BLACK, Charles L., Jr. The Occasions of Justice. MacMillan, 1963. **$15.00**

20. (BLACK, Hugo). HUGO BLACK, JR. My Father: A Remembrance. Random House, 1975. **$10.00**

21. (BLACK, Hugo). GERALD T. DUNNE. Hugo Black and the Judicial Revolution. Simon and Schuster, 1977. **$12.50**

22. (BLACK, Hugo). DANIEL J. MEADOR. Justice Black and His Books. Virginia, 1974. **$15.00**
With more than 150 pages devoted to Justice Black's library.

23. (BLACK, Hugo). Memorial Addresses and Other Tributes in the Congress of the United States on the Life and Contributions of Hugo LaFayette Black. Washington, 1972. **$35.00**
With the U.S. Supreme Court Proceedings included.

24. BLAUSTEIN, Albert and Charles O. Porter. The American Lawyer, A Summary of the Survey of the Legal Profession. Chicago, 1954. **$15.00**
With a foreward by Reginald Heber Smith.

25. (BODLEIAN Library). Manuscripts at Oxford: an Exhibition in memory of Richard William Hunt (1908-1979) Keeper of Western Manuscripts at the Bodleian Library Oxford, 1945-1975. Oxford, 1980. **New $35.00**
155 pages, printed wraps, very many illustrations, *with essays on the Holkham Library of Sir Edward Coke and the Coke family,* and the late fifteenth-century group of *Nova Statuta* manuscripts; *very nice.*

26. BOHANNAN, Paul (ed.). Law and Warfare, Studies in the Anthropology of Conflict. Natural History Press, 1967. **$12.50**

A Specially Important Copy of The First Edition of One of the Great English Law Books
27. BRITTON, John le. Britton [on the Laws of England]. London, [1540]. Title page; 5 leaves; 287 folios; leaf (irregular but complete). S.T.C. 3803, Beale T324. **$2750.00**
Most probably written in 1291-1292, during the 20th year of the reign of Edward I, *and the first great law book written in Law French,* the vernacular of the legal profession and the Courts, *Britton's treatise is unique, appearing as it does to be promulgated under Edward's royal authority.*
This the copy from the Broxbourne Library, formed by Albert Ehrman in this century, with an extraordinary range of 15th and 16th century works, with Ehrman's personal bookplate on the inside front board and his stamp and the Broxbourne bookplate on the inside rear board; *serving as end leaves, two leaves from a processional printed by Pynson in 1502 [S.T.C. 16232.8].*
A bit of lightish marginal dampstaining to the fore-margin, slightly affecting the last leaves, annotations in several early hands; *altogether, an exceptionally clean, wide-margined and exceedingly desirable copy, in a full contemporary English calf binding, the sides with roll-tooled panels* [Oldham HM.a(12)], some expert repairs to the spine, housed in a leather-backed, cloth folding box.

28. BUERGENTHAL, Thomas. Law-Making in the International Civil Aviation Organization. Syracuse, 1969. **$15.00**

29. (CARDOZO, Benjamin N.). IRVING LEHMAN. Benjamin Nathan Cardozo, A Memorial. Stamford, 1938. **$65.00**
One of 350 copies printed at the Overbook Press, on folded paper, the front cover and spine gilt-lettered; printed in red and black throughout, with Justice Cardozo's bookplate reproduced; a trifle worn.

A Very Early English Law Book
30. CARTA Foedi. Title Page; 38 folios; 2 leaves (irregular but complete). London, 1539. New S.T.C. 15584.5, Beale T171. **$950.00**
An important, though anonymous, work, termed by Holdsworth "the ancestor of the many collections of conveyancing and other forms and precedents which have appeared from that day [the late medieval period] to this", with the forms or precedents set forth, sometimes accompanied by short notes as to their proper use.
Nicely bound in recent full, tawny calf, the spine gilt-lettered, occasional spotting, but generally a very clean and desirable copy.
A rare work, Beale showing but two copies and the New S.T.C. six, with the work not appearing at auction in this century.

31. CATTAN, Henry. Palestine and International Law. Longman, 1974. **$15.00**

32. CECIL, Henry. The English Judge. London, 1970. **$20.00**
The 22nd Hamlyn Lectures.

33. (CENTER for the Study of Democratic Institutions). Natural Law and Modern Society. World, 1963. **$15.00**

34. CHAPIN, Bradley. The American Law of Treason, Revolutionary and Early National Origins. Seattle, 1964. **$15.00**

35. CHO, Sung Yoon. Japanese Writings on Communist Chinese Law, 1946-1974. Washington, 1977. **$15.00**

36. (COCKBURN, Lord). ALAN BELL (ed.). Lord Cockburn, A Bicentenary Commemoration, 1779-1979. Edinburgh, 1979. **New $15.00**

37. COHEN, Julius, et al. Parental Authority, The Community and the Law. Rutgers, 1958. **$15.00**

The Rarely Found First Edition
38. COKE, Sir Edward. La Size Part des Reports. Title page; 8 leaves; 80 folios; leaf; two blanks. London, 1607. S.T.C. 5509. **$300.00**
Coke's Reports, arguably the most famous law reports ever published, originally appearing in 13 parts, beginning with the first part in 1600, this the first edition of the sixth part, appearing in 1607.
An exceedingly clean, wide-margined copy, largely black-letter throughout, with attractive woodcut initials and decorations beginning each case, some annotations and underlining in an early hand, including notations on the title page and next to last blank, *nicely rebound in ¾ calf over linen boards, the spine with contrasting red and black morocco labels, gilt-lined and lettered.*
An attractive copy of a work whose influence in its totality Winfield termed "inestimable". *Coke in the preface defending the antiquity of the Common Law against foreign influence,* praising the Common Law's case approach, and defending his thesis, presented in an earlier preface, disposing of the Pope's supremacy in England.
With the Short Title Catalogue showing only one copy, at the Huntington Library.

With the Arguments of Francis Bacon, Dodderidge, Selden and Dugdale
39. COLLINS. Arthur. Proceedings, Precedents, and Arguments, on Claims and Controversies, concerning Baronies by Writ, and other Honours. London, 1734. Blank; Title Page; leaf; 415 pages; blank. **$300.00**
Best known for his mammoth work on the Peerage, which reached a sixth and final edition of nine volumes in 1812, *Collins here collects most of the cases respecting dignities from the late 1500's to 1740, preserving the arguments of Sir Francis Bacon, John Selden, Justice Dodderidge, and many others.*
Attractively bound in full, contemporary calf, worn, recently and nicely rebacked, dampstaining, mainly lightish, throughout; altogether a very tall wide-margined and desirable folio copy of the sole edition.

40. (COLUMBIA Law School). MONRAD G. PAULSON (ed.). Legal Institutions Today and Tomorrow. Columbia, 1959. **$20.00**
The centennial volume of the Columbia Law School.

41. CONLEY, Patrick T. The Constitutional Significance of *Trevett v. Weeden* (1786). Providence, 1976(?) **$5.00**
12 unnumbered pages; stapled wraps.

42. CONLEY, Patrick T. The Dorr Rebellion, Rhode Island's Crisis in Constitutional Government. Providence, 1976. **$5.00**
13 pages, pictorial printed wraps.

43. (CONSOLATO del Mare). STANLEY S. JADOS (ed.). Consulate of the Sea and Related Documents. Alabama, 1975. **$15.00**
One of the important collection of medieval maritime customs, in an English translation.

The First Edition
44. COOKE, William. A Compendious System of the Bankrupt Laws. London, 1785. **$175.00**
Termed "eminently lucid and a virtually exhaustive digest of the [bankrupt] .. law", this the first edition of Cooke's principal work, which went through eight editions by 1823.
A very nice copy in ¾ calf over marbled boards, the spine gilt-lined and decorated, with a crimson morocco label, gilt-lined and lettered.

The First Systematic Work on Law in Scotland—"Another Justinian"
45. CRAIG, Sir Thomas. Jus Feudale. Third Edition. Edinburgh, 1732. Portrait; Title page; iii-xxii, 524,52 pages. **$275.00**
Craig's great work, completed about 1603 but not published 'til 1655, this the third edition of 1732, said to be the first to present a reasonably correct text, *with the opening chapters tracing the history and development of the Civil, Canon and Feudal law, Burnet in his preface noting that "our Author rose, like another Justinian, and . . . embraced the whole body of our Scottish Jurisprudence . . ."*
A very nice, exceptionally clean copy, newly and handsomely bound in full, dark calf, a bit of worming to the lower margin, the covers and spine blind-lined, with the original crimson morocco label, gilt-lined and lettered, preserved.

46. CRESSEY, Donald R. (ed.). Crime and Criminal Justice. Quadrangle, 1971. **$10.00**

The Last Edition
47. CUNNINGHAM, T[imothy]. A New Treatise on the Laws Concerning Tithes. Fourth Edition. London, 1777. **$150.00**
One of the most prolific legal writers of the 1700's, with upwards of twenty separate works attributed to him, Cunningham saw this, his sole work on tithes, published in 1764, with this, the fourth edition, appearing in 1777.
Quite a nice copy, in full contemporary calf, a bit worn, the covers blind-lined and decorated, the spine unlettered.

48. CURRAN, Francis X. Catholics in Colonial Law. Loyola, 1963. **$15.00**

A Fine Edition
49. CUSHING, John D. (Comp.). The Laws and Liberties of Massachusetts, 1641-1691. **Three volumes.** Wilmington, 1976. **$125.00**
The best edition, in facsimile, containing also Council Orders and Executive Proclamations, *with a valuable introduction by Dr. Cushing, Librarian of the Massachusetts Historical Society.*

50. DAY, John and Clinton Walker Keyes (eds.). Tax Documents from Theadelphia, Papyri of the Second Century A.D. Columbia, 1956. **$45.00**
Columbia Papyri, Greek Series, Volume V.

51. (DENNING, Lord). Lord Denning's Report, Presented to Parliament by the Prime Minister by Command of Her Majesty, September, 1963. **$25.00**
The Profumo affair; 114 pages, sewn, printed wraps, a bit worn.

52. DIXON, Robert G., Jr. Democratic Representation, Reapportionment in Law and Politics. Oxford, 1968. **$15.00**

The First Edition
53. DODDERIDGE, [Sir] J[ohn]. The Compleat Parson. London, 1630. Leaf; Title Page; 2 leaves; 95 pages. S.T.C. 6980. **$325.00**
Dodderidge's readings delivered at New Inn in 1602 and 1603, readings still forming, according to Holdsworth, "an important part of the education of the law student", mainly upon statutes, Dodderidge's thus an exception.
Save a bit of embrowning, *a very clean and attractive copy, nicely rebound in ¾ calf over marbled boards,* a red morocco label, gilt-lined and lettered.

The First and Only Edition
54. DODDERIDGE, Sir John. The English Lawyer. London, 1631. Title page; 3 leaves; 271 pages. S.T.C. 6981. **$1000.00**
Dodderidge's most famous work, and one of the most renowned single volume treatises published in the early 1600's, termed by Holdsworth "the most notable . . . of books written about law to instruct students as to the kind of knowledge which they ought to acquire, and the best method of acquiring it".
An extremely nice copy in full, sprinkled calf, very neatly rebacked, the spine gilt-lined, with the label gilt-lined and lettered; a small repair to the corner of the title page, not affecting the text, *attractive woodcut decorations and initials throughout,* slightish dampstaining to the upper margin of a few leaves, with that margin cut just a bit close, perhaps barely affecting parentheses surrounding page numbers; and occasional underlining and marginal annotations in an early hand.
Altogether, a very desirable copy, with the Short Title Catalogue showing only the Huntington copy in this country.

The First Edition
55. DODDERIDGE, Sir John. The History of the ancient and moderne Estate of The Principality of Wales, Dutchy of Cornewall, and Earldome of Chester. London, 1630. Title Page; 7 leaves; 142 pages. S.T.C. 6982. **$350.00**
Published posthumously, though clearly written much earlier, possibly at the turn of the century at the accession of James I in 1603, and dedicated to him, *with Dodderidge becoming a serjeant-at-law within the year and, about the same time, being appointed the serjeant of Prince Henry of Wales.*
Quite a nice copy, with woodcut decorations and initials throughout, the title page just the slightest bit dusty. *Newly and handsomely bound in ¾ calf over marbled boards,* the covers gilt decorated and the spine gilt-lined, with a morocco label gilt-lettered and decorated.

56. DORSEN, Norman (ed.). The Rights of Americans, What They Are—What They Should Be. Pantheon, 1971. **$17.50**
Essays by Thomas I. Emerson, Harry Kalven and many others commemorating the 50th anniversary of the American Civil Liberties Union.

57. DORSEN, Norman and Leon Friedman. Disorder in the Court. Pantheon, 1973. **$15.00**
With a preface by Burke Marshall; the Report of the Association of the Bar of the City of New York, Special Committee on Courtroom Conduct.

58. DOUGLAS, William O. The Anatomy of Liberty. New York, 1963. **$15.00**

59. DOUGLAS, William O. Go East, Young Man; The Early Years, the Autobiography of William O. Douglas. Random House, 1974. **$15.00**

60. DRINKER, Henry S. Legal Ethics. Columbia, 1954. **$25.00**
One of the Legal Studies of the William Nelson Cromwell Foundation; a bit worn.

61. DUNHAM, William Huse. Lord Hastings' Indentured Retainers, 1461-1483, the Lawfulness of Livery and Retaining under the Yorkists and Tudors. Yale, 1955. **$22.50**
Transactions of the Connecticut Academy of Arts and Sciences, volume 39, pages 1-175; *separately issued, sewn and printed wraps, uncut.*

One of the Most Significant Cases in English Legal History
62. EGERTON, Sir Thomas. The Speech of the Lord Chancellor of England, in the Exchequer Chamber, touching the Post-nati. London, 1609. Title page; 4 leaves; 118 pages; leaf. S.T.C. 7540. **$275.00**
One of the great Lord Chancellors, during whose chancellorship the bounds of equity were finally established, Egerton (later Lord Ellesmere) was successively Solicitor General, Master of the Rolls, and Lord Chancellor.
This, the only edition of his only contemporaneously published work, containing Ellesmere's argument in the case of the post-nati, or those born in Scotland after the accession of James I; *termed by Coke "the weightiest [case] . . . for the present and for all posterity"* with the resolution that the post-nati were to be regarded, not as aliens, but as subjects, *with far-reaching results as the king's dominions increased in succeeding centuries.*
A bit of embrowning and dustiness throughout, especially to the title page and last leaf, the text in woodcut borders with attractive woodcut decorations and initials; *altogether, quite a clean and attractive copy, newly bound in ½ calf over linen boards, the spine gilt-lettered.*

A Very Early Issue of Statutes from the Reign of Henry VIII
63. ENGLAND, Statutes. Anno XXIII Henrici VIII. London, [1531]. Title Page; folios 2-24 (irregular but complete). S.T.C. 9374, Beale S141 (variant). **$1000.00**
The statutes of the 23rd year of the reign of Henry VIII, printed by Thomas Berthelet, in English, consisting of 18 acts.
The title page in an elaborate, woodcut border [McKerrow 18, state 1], annotations and underlining in an early hand, black letter throughout, with decorated woodcut initials; a bit of spotting to some leaves, *else a very tall, clean and desirable copy bound in 19th century ¾ light calf,* a bit rubbed, over linen boards, marbled endpapers, the spine gilt-lined and decorated and lettered, with a crimson morocco label, a bit chipped, gilt-lined and lettered.
A rare issue, the Short Title Catalogue showing only the British Library copy, Beale, in addition, the Harvard Law copy, and Bishop that of the Library of Congress, *with, possibly, one copy at auction in this century in 1920.*

64. FALK, Richard A. and Cyril E. Black (eds.). The Future of the International Order. **Four Volumes.** Princeton, 1969-1972. **$50.00**
The fourth volume in paper.

65. FALLERS, Lloyd A. Law Without Precedent, Legal Ideas in Action in the Courts of Colonial Busoga. Chicago, 1969. **$12.50**

66. FARRAND, Max (intro). The Laws and Liberties of Massachusetts, Reprinted from the Copy of the 1648 edition in the Henry E. Huntington Library. Harvard, 1929. **$65.00**
Termed "the great bibliographical prize among legal Americana" by Professor James, this reissue from the only known surviving copy (of 600) at the Huntington Library.

67. FELLMAN, David. The Defendant's Rights Under English Law. Wisconsin, 1966. **$12.50**

68. FIELD, Stephen J. California Alcalde. Oakland, 1950. **$75.00**
An attractive re-issue, limited to 600 copies, of Field's "Personal Reminiscences of early days in California", privately printed in 1880; *printed in red and black throughout, marbled edges, red-linen cloth, gilt.*

69. FINKELMAN, Paul. An Imperfect Union: Slavery, Federalism and Comity. North Carolina, 1981. **New $22.00**
The latest volume in Studies in Legal History.

70. FLEMING, R.W. The Labor Arbitration Process. Illinois, 1965. **$12.50**

The Earliest Work on the Inns of Court
71. FORTESCUE, Sir John. De Laudibus Legum Angliae. London, 1672. Title Page; 6 leaves; 132 folios; 3 leaves; 51 pages; Title Page; 5 leaves; 140 pages (irregular but complete). Wing F1613. **$350.00**
A very attractive copy of Fortescue's most famous work, written between 1468 and 1471, and, according to Professor Hazeltine, *providing "the earliest account of . . . the nature of the Inns of Court and of Chancery,* and their system of legal education".
A bit of marginal embrowning to the last leaves, a small hole in the last leaf not affecting the text, very occasional lightish marginal dampstaining and embrowning, but *altogether a very clean, desirable and wide margined copy, newly and attractively bound in ½ calf over marbled boards,* the spine gilt-lined and blind decorated, with a red morocco label, gilt-lined and lettered.

72. FRANK, Jerome. Law and the Modern Mind. Tudor, 1935. **$15.00**

73. FRANK, John P. Marble Palace, The Supreme Court in American Life. Knopf, 1968. **$12.50**

74. (FRANKFURTER, Felix). JOSEPH P. LASH. From the Diaries of Felix Frankfurter. Norton, 1975. **$12.50**

75. (FRANKFURTER, Felix). HARLAN B. PHILLIPS. Felix Frankfurter Reminisces. Reynal, 1960. **$12.50**

76. (FREEDOM of the Press). CANDOR, FATHER OF (pseud.). An Enquiry into the Doctrine Lately Propagated Concerning Libels, Warrants, and the Seizure of Papers. New York, 1970. **$15.00**
A facsimile reissue of the first edition of 1764.

77. FRIER, Bruce W. Landlords and Tenants in Imperial Rome. Princeton, 1980. **New $18.50**

One of 750 Copies
78. GALVIN, John (ed.). The Coming of Justice to California. San Francisco, 1963. **$75.00**
A very handsome volume, illustrated, printed in black, red and green throughout, largely uncut, with a folding map, red linen cloth, the spine gilt-lettered.

79. GELLHORN, Walter. Ombudsmen and Others, Citizens' Protectors in Nine Countries. Harvard, 1967. **$17.50**

80. GIGEROFF, Alex. K. Sexual Deviations in the Criminal Law, Homosexual, Exhibitionistic, and Pedophilic Offences in Canada. Toronto, 1968. **$15.00**

81. GOLDBERG, Arthur J. Equal Justice, The Warren Era of the Supreme Court. Northwestern, 1971. **$17.50**
The 1971 Rosenthal Lectures at Northwestern.

82. GOLDSTEIN, Abraham S. The Insanity Defense. Yale, 1967. **$16.50**

The First Edition in English of the Most Renowned Work of International Law

83. GROTIUS, Hugo. Of the Law of Warre and Peace. London, 1654. Portrait; Title Page; 38 leaves; 660 pages; 2 leaves; Title Page (biographical); 43 leaves. Wing G2119. **$1250.00**
Grotius' masterwork, a "tour de force [and] an extraordinary achievement", according to James Brown Scott, *the first systematic treatise on international law, appearing in Latin in 1625, this the first edition in English,* translated by Clement Barksdale, and published in London in 1654.

A bit of lightish embrowning and spotting, two margins torn without loss of text, the upper margin cut close, shaving a few headnotes, but not affecting legibility; *altogether, a very nice copy, well and newly rebound in full, light calf,* the covers blind-lined and the spine blind and gilt decorated, with matching dark-brown morocco labels, gilt-lined and lettered, *and with the fine engraved portrait of Grotius,* reinforced in the margin, facing the title page.

84. HAAR, Charles M. (ed.). The Golden Age of American Law [1820-1860]. New York, 1965. **$25.00**

The First and Only Edition

85. HALE, Sir Matthew. The Primitive Origin of Mankind. London, 1677, Portrait; Title Page; 4 leaves; 380 pages; 2 blanks. Wing H258. **$275.00**
Clearly a work of considerable importance to Hale, written during a period of seven years while he was on the bench, *and the chief subject to which he devoted himself during his retirement;* the only published part of a larger work left in manuscript at Hale's death, *in which Hale reviews religious and classical sources, both Greek and Roman, in treating of mankind's origin.*

Quite a nice copy, in full contemporary, double blind-lined calf, worn, newly rebacked, the spine gilt-lettered, occasional light spotting increasing on the first and last leaves, a few leaves a little dusty, but *altogether a very clean, tall and attractive folio, with a fine, full page engraved portrait of Hale by Van Houe.*

86. (HALE, Sir Matthew). GILBERT BURNET. The Life of Sir Matthew Hale. London, 1823. **$85.00**
The only contemporary biography of Hale, first appearing shortly after Hale's death.

Bound in contemporary tree calf, worn, adequately rebacked, with the Society for Christian Knowledge blind-embossed on the front cover, and John Fell's Life of Dr. Hammond bound in.

87. (HALE, Sir Matthew). D.E.C. YALE. Hale as a Legal Historian. London, 1976. **$10.00**
18 pages, sewn, printed wraps; *the 1976 Selden Society Lecture.*

88. HALL, Jerome. Living Law of Democratic Society. Bobbs-Merrill, 1949. **$22.50**

89. HALL, Kermit L. The Politics of Justice, Lower Federal Judicial Selection and the Second Party System, 1829-61. Nebraska, 1979. **New $19.50**

90. (HAND, Learned). KATHRYN GRIFFITH. Judge Learned Hand and the Role of the Federal Judiciary. Oklahoma, 1973. **$15.00**

91. (HAND, Learned). MARVIN SCHICK. Learned Hand's Court. Johns Hopkins, 1970. **$17.50**

92. (HAND, Learned). HERSHEL SHANKS (ed.). The Art and Craft of Judging, the Decisions of Judge Learned Hand. MacMillan, 1968. **$20.00**
Inscribed by the Editor.

93. HART, H.L.A. Punishment and Responsibility, Essays in the Philosophy of Law. Stanford, 1968. **$17.50**

94. HARTLAND, E. Sidney. Primitive Law. Methuen, 1924. **$35.00**
The original edition, in a worn dustwrapper.

95. (HARVARD Law School). The Centennial History of the Harvard Law School, 1817-1917. Harvard Law School Ass'n, 1918. **$45.00**
With a number of valuable appendices, and 55 illustrations; a nice copy in the original maroon cloth, the spine gilt-lined and lettered.

96. HAYNES, Evan. The Selection and Tenure of Judges. The National Conference of Judicial Councils, 1944. **$25.00**
With an introduction by Roscoe Pound; a bit worn.

97. HECTOR, L.C. The Handwriting of English Documents. Kohler & Coombes, 1980. **New $21.00**
A superb introduction to the study of paleography, first published in 1966. **We are the only source in North America for this valuable work.**

98. HESS, Albert G. and Shigeyo Murayama. Everyday law in Japanese folk art, Daily life in Meiji Japan as seen through petty law violations: woodcuts c. 1878. Scientia Verlag Aalen, 1980. **New $37.50**
With 70 plates reproduced.

99. HINDUS, Michael Stephen, et al. The Files of the Massachusetts Superior Court, 1859-1959. Hall, 1980. **New $50.00**
One result of the recent Massachusetts' inquiry into managing historical judicial records; *highly interesting.*

Successor to Coke

100. (HOBART, Sir Henry). The Reports of ... Sir Henry Hobart. Third Edition. London, 1671. Blank; Title Page; 7 leaves; 350 pages; blank. Wing H2208. **$225.00**
Successor to Coke as attorney general and Chief Justice of the Common Pleas, Hobart held the latter office until his death in 1625, his Reports appearing posthumously in 1641, this the third edition of 1671, *with a preface signed by "C.M.", thought by Heterick as, perhaps, Milton's brother, Christopher.*

Full, contemporary unlettered calf, a bit worn, the covers blind-lined, the joints and top and bottom of the spine very neatly repaired; *a very tall, clean and handsome folio,* a few marginal notations in an early hand, and largely in black le'ter throughout.

101. (HOLMES, Oliver W., Jr.). SILAS BENT. Justice Oliver Wendell Holmes. New York, 1932. **$17.50**

102. (HOLMES, Oliver W., Jr.). HARRY C. SHRIVER (ed.). The Judicial Opinions of Oliver Wendell Holmes. Buffalo, 1940. **$15.00**
Of value, selections from Holmes' opinions during his years on the Massachusetts' Supreme Judicial Court.

Justice Story's Copy

103. HORNE, Andrew. The Mirrour of Justices. London, 1768. Title Page; 15 leaves; 325 pages; 4 leaves. **$450.00**
Termed "the most fantastic work in our legal literature" by Plucknett, and written about 1290, during the reign of Edward I, this work Maitland attributed to Andrew Horne, fishmonger and later chamberlain of London during the reign of Edward II. Fortunately surviving in one medieval manuscript, and not printed until 1642, *this the sole complete edition of the 1700's, translated into English by William Hughes.*

Once the copy of Justice Joseph Story, *with his full signature on the title page,* together with a note by J. Elliot Cabot (Harvard 1840, Suffolk Bar 1847) that he purchased the volume "at Judge Story's sale: April 3, 1846."

A bit of spotting and marginal, lightish embrowning, else quite clean and attractive, *newly and handsomely bound in full blind-decorated sheep, the spine nicely gilt-decorated, with a red morocco label, gilt decorated and lettered.*

104. HOWELL, P.A. The Judicial Committee of the Privy Council 1833-1876, Its Origins, Structure and Development. **New $29.50**
The latest volume in *Cambridge Studies in English Legal History.*

105. HUNT, Alan. The Sociological Movement in Law. Temple, 1978. **$15.00**

106. HUTCHINSON, Thomas W., et al (eds.). Africa and Law Developing Legal Systems in African Commonwealth Nations. Wisconsin, 1968. **$15.00**

107. HYMAN, Allen and M. Bruce Johnson (eds.). Advertising and Free Speech. Lexington, 1977. **$12.50**

108. (INNS of Court). W[ILLIAM] HERBERT. Antiquities of the Inns of Court and Chancery. London, 1804. **$175.00**
One of a few early works on the Inns of Court; with 24 copper-engraved plates. Bound in full, diced calf, worn, nicely rebacked, the spine gilt-lined and lettered. A bit of foxing and embrowning to preliminaries, else *quite an attractive copy.*

A Very Early Law Book of Considerable Historical Value

109. INTRATIONUM liber omnibus legum Anglie. London, 1546. Title page; 23 leaves; 244 folios (irregular but comlete). S.T.C. 14117, Beale T284. **$1800.00**
Books of Entries (or Intrationum liber) so-called because taken from the entries of the clerks upon the plea rolls, and *essential to the proper pleading of a case; termed by Dr. Baker "replete with learning", and sources which "the legal historian ignores at his cost".*

This, the first and only appearance of this work, according to Winfield and Holdsworth, a reissue of the 1510 edition according to the S.T.C.

The title page well worn and soiled, repairs to it and to the next three leaves' margins and to the next to last leaf, some waterstaining, primarily marginal but extending into the text primarily on the preliminary and last leaves, with attendant softening of the margins throughout; despite the foregoing, *a desirable copy, handsomely printed in black letter throughout, and exceedingly well bound in 17th(?) century straight-grained morocco,* 19th century marbled endpapers, the edges gilt, and inner gilt dentelles, with the booksticker of Viscount Mersey, Bignor Park.

110. JACKSON, Robert H. The Struggle for Judicial Supremacy. Knopf, 1949. **$20.00**

A Handsome Copy

111. JACOB, Giles. The Statute-Law Common-plac'd. Fourth Edition. London, 1739. Blank; Title Page; five leaves; v, 409 pages; 3 leaves; 2 blanks. Cowley 233. **$175.00**
First appearing in 1719, and reaching a fifth edition by 1748, this the fourth edition of 1739, *Jacob's only work devoted to the abridgement of the statutes. A very nice copy,* very occasional marginal annotations, attractively rebound in full calf, the spine blind and gilt-lined and lettered.

112. JACOBSOHN, Gary L. Pragmatism, Statesmanship, and the Supreme Court. Cornell, 1977. **$12.50**

The Hanging Judge

113. (JEFFREYS, Lord). The Life and Character of the Late Lord Chancellor Jeffreys. London, 1725. [xiii], 47 pages. **$175.00**
The last near-contemporary account of Jeffreys, destined for ill-fame, but whose reputation has been partially redeemed in this century; *a nice copy, in full, blind-decorated later calf,* a bit worn, the spine with a black label gilt-lined and lettered, the half-title a bit dusty, else exceptionally clean.

114. JENKS, Edward. A Short History of English Law. Second Edition. London, 1920. **$25.00**
Dedicated to Maitland; a bit of spotting, else nice.

115. JOHNSTONE, Quintin and Dan Hopson, Jr. Lawyers and their Work, An Analysis of the Legal Profession in the United States and England. Bobbs-Merrill, 1967. **$22.50**

116. JOLOWICZ, J.A. The Judicial Protection of Fundamental Rights under English law. **And, JONES, G.** The Infiltration of Equity into English Commercial Law. Kluwer, 1980. **New $15.00**
The Cambridge-Tilburg Law Lectures, Second Series, 1979; sewn wraps.

117. (JURY). The American Jury System, Final Report. Cambridge, 1977. **$12.50**
107 pages, pictorial wraps; *sponsored by the Roscoe Pound-American Trial Lawyers Foundation.*

118. KARLEN, Delmar. Judicial Administration, The American Experience. Oceana, 1970. **$15.00**
Lectures given upon the founding of the *Institute of Judicial Administration* in England, in 1968.

119. (KELSEN, Hans). SALO ENGEL AND R.A. METALL (eds.). Law, State, and International Legal Order, Essays in Honor of Hans Kelsen. Tennessee, 1968. **$22.50**
With essays by *Roscoe Pound, Hans Morgenthau and Georg Schwarzenberger,* among many others.

120. (KELSEN, Hans). GEORGE A. LIPSKY (eds.). Law and Politics in the World Community, Essays on Hans Kelsen's Pure Theory and Related Problems in International Law. California, 1953. **$22.50**

121. KEYNES, Simon. The Diplomas of King Aethelred "The Unready" 978-1016, A Study of Their Use as Historical Evidence. Cambridge, 1980. **New $42.50**
Cambridge Studies in Medieval Life and Thought, Volume 13.

122. KORKOUNOV, N.M. Cours de Theorie Generale du Droit. Second Edition. Paris, 1914. **$45.00**
Termed a "through and original contribution to the study of jurisprudence", originally appearing in Russian in 1887, and discovered by Roscoe Pound while he was at Nebraska; rebound in an unprepossessing library buckram, gilt, a bit worn.

123. KROOSS, Herman E. (ed.). Documentary History of Banking and Currency in the United States. **Four Volumes.** Chelsea House, 1977. **$125.00**
With over 300 documents reprinted, grouped into ten historical periods, from 1637 to 1968; *with an introductory essay by Paul A. Samuelson.*

124. KURLAND, Philip B. Politics, the Constitution, and the Warren Court. Chicago, 1970. **$17.50**
The 1969 Cooley Lectures at Michigan.

125. KURLAND, Philip B. Religion and the Law of Church and State and the Supreme Court. Aldine, 1962. **$15.00**

126. LANG, Meredith. Defender of the Faith: The High Court of Mississippi, 1817-1875. Mississippi, 1977. **$15.00**

127. LASKI, Harold J. Law and Justice in Soviet Russia. Hogarth Press, 1935. **$25.00**
44 pages, sewn, printed wraps; a trifle worn; *one of the "Day to Day Pamphlets" published by Leonard and Virginia Woolf at the Hogarth Press.*

128. LASKI, Harold J. The State in Theory and Practice. New York, 1968. **$12.50**

129. LAUWAARS, R.H. Lawfulness and Legal Force of Community Decisions. Sijthoff, 1973. **$17.50**

130. (LEGAL Method). Science of Legal Method. Select Essays by Various Authors. MacMillan, 1921. **$35.00**
The Modern Legal Philosophy Series; with essays by *Geny,* **Pound** *and Freund,* among many others; slightly worn.

131. LEONI, Bruno. Freedom and the Law. van Nostrand, 1961. **$15.00**

132. LEVY, Leonard W. Judgments, Essays on American Constitutional History. Quadrangle, 1972. **$12.50**

133. LEVY, Leonard W. (ed.). The Supreme Court under Earl Warren. Quadrangle, 1972. **$15.00**
With articles by *Fred Rodell, Alexander Bickel, and Philip Kurland,* among many others.

134. LIEBHOLZ, Gerhard. Strukturprobleme der Modernen Demokratie, Karlsruhe, 1967. **$22.50**
Presentation copy.

135. LILLICH, Richard B. The Protection of Foreign Investment. Syracuse, 1965. **$15.00**

136. (LITCHFIELD Law School). Presentation of the Reeve Law School Building to the Litchfield Historical Society. Litchfield, 1911. **$45.00**
36 pages, sewn, printed wraps, many illustrations, a bit worn; *an unusual item.*

137. MAARSEVEEN, Henc van, and Ger van der Tang. Written Constitutions, A Computerized, Comparative Study, Oceana, 1978. **$15.00**

138. McCALL, Andrew. The Medieval Underworld, London, 1979. **New $23.00.**

A Beautiful Copy

139. (MAGNA Carta). Magna Charta, cum statutis, cum antiquis, tum recentibus, etc. Title Page; 6 leaves; blank; 247 folios; blank. [London], 1576. S.T.C. 9281, Beale S18. **$750.00**
An important edition of the Magna Carta, with the addition of many of the 16th century statutes, in Latin, Law French, and English, as appropriate, *primarily in English.*

Black letter throughout, a trifling bit of marginal worming and lightish dampstaining to a few leaves not affecting the text, and very occasional embrowning, but altogether *a very clean, crisp and wide-margined copy,* with woodcut initials throughout, some annotations in early hands, including some arithmetic notations on the title page.

Beautifully bound in a modern 17th century-style, full crimson morocco, the covers triple-gilt lined, gilt decorated edges, inner gilt dentelles, and the spine elaborately gilt-decorated, lined and lettered.

140. (MAGNA Carta). G.R.C. DAVIS. Magna Carta. British Museum, 1963. **$17.50**
31 pages, sewn, pictorial wraps, a bit worn; *with six plates and a map.*

141. (MAITLAND, Frederic W.). H.E. BELL. Maitland, A Critical Examination and Assessment. Harvard, 1965. **$15.00**
The best critical biography of Maitland.

142. MAKHNENKO, A. KH. The State Law of the Socialist Countries. Moscow, 1976. **$22.50**

143. MALLOY, William M., et al (comps.). Treaties, Conventions, International Acts, Protocols, and Agreements Between the United States of America and Other Powers, 1776-[1937]. **Four Volumes.** Greenwood, 1968. **$125.00**
First issued in 1910 and then supplemented in 1923 and 1937, covering the period 1776-1937, and *containing the English texts, with a number of valuable lists and cross-references in volume 4.*

144. MANCHESTER, A.H. A Modern Legal History of England and Wales 1750-1950. Butterworths, 1980. **New $51.95**
Also available in paper at $32.65.

The Douglas Case

145. (MANSFIELD, Lord). ANDREW STUART. Letters to the Right Honourable Lord Mansfield. Dublin, 1775. **$175.00**
Mansfield's most scandalous case, in which he argued Lady Douglas' cause in the House of Lords, she accused of the purchase of two children to become the heirs of the Douglas' fortune; these the letters of Andrew Stuart, sent to France by Lady Douglas' opponents, to obtain evidence of the purchase.

Bound in full, contemporary sheep, rubbed, a bit of cracking to the joints, but quite sound, with the spine gilt-lined, a red morocco label gilt-lined and lettered; *an exceedingly clean copy, and a pleasant one.*

An Inscribed Copy

146. (MARSHALL, John). FRANCES NORTON MASON. My Dearest Polly, Letters of Chief Justice John Marshall to His Wife, with Their Background, Political and Domestic, 1779-1831. Richmond, 1961. **$45.00**
With all of Marshall's letters to his wife; twelve illustrations.

147. MARTIN, Charles Trice. The Record Interpreter: A Collection of Abbreviations, Latin Words and Names used in English Historical Manuscripts and Records. Kohler & Coombes, 1976. **New $25.00**
A standard reference work, long out of print, this a reissue of the 1910 second edition. **We are the only source in Nor'h America for this valuable work.**

148. MARTIN, Donald L. and Warren F. Schwartz. Deregulating American Industry. Lexington, 1977. **$12.50**

149. MASON, Alpheus Thomas. Harlan Fiske Stone: Pillar of the Law. Viking, 1956. **$22.50**

150. (MASON, Alpheus T.). GOTTFRIED DIETZE (ed.). Essays on the American Constitution, A Commemorative Volume in Honor of Alpheus T. Mason, Prentice-Hall, 1964. **$17.50**

151. MELTSNER, Michael. Cruel and Unusual, the Supreme Court and Capital Punishment. Random House, 1973. **$12.50**

152. MILSOM, S.F.C. The Legal Framework of English Feudalism. Cambridge, 1976. **New $28.50**
Cambridge Studies in English Legal History.

Milton's Majestic Defense of Freedom of the Press
153. MILTON, John. Areopagitica. Cambridge, England, 1973. **$65.00**
Limited to 400 numbered copies on mould-made paper, with initials in a second color, typographically of unusual interest, with the print in two type faces and partially in double column, the main line of the argument in the larger, with new departures of thought indicated by a large initial.
An attractive issue, bound in black buckram, with morocco label, the top edge gilt and the remainder untrimmed.

154. MORGAN, Glenn G. Soviet Administrative Legality, the Role of the Attorney General's Office. Stanford, 1962. **$12.50**

155. MURPHY, James M. Laws, Courts, and Lawyers, Through the Years in Arizona. Arizona, 1970. **$15.00**

156. MURPHY, Walter F. Elements of Judicial Strategy. Chicago, 1969. **$15.00**

157. NAGEL, Stuart S., and Marian G. Neef. Legal Policy Analysis. Lexington, 1977. **$12.50**

158. NELSON, Robert H. Zoning and Property Rights. M.I.T., 1977. **$15.00**

159. NELSON, William E. Dispute and Conflict Resolution in Plymouth County, Massachusetts, 1725-1825. North Carolina, 1981. **New $19.50**
Studies in Legal History.

Limited to 2000 copies
160. NEWTON, A. Edward. Newton on Blackstone. Pennsylvania, 1937. **$45.00**
Newton's delightful address; printed on all-rag paper, this copy 749, *signed by Newton;* in a worn dust-wrapper.

The First Collected Edition
161. NICOLSON, W[illiam]. The English Historical Library . . . With an Account of our Records, Law-Books . . . and Other Matters. Second Edition. London, 1714. 3 blanks; Title Page; iii-xviii, 272 pages (irregular but complete); 2 blanks. **$300.00**
Called Nicolson's "great work", and initially issued in three parts, this the first collected edition of 1714, with the third part devoted chiefly to legal matters, including Parliamentary and judicial records, law-writers, year-books and reports, and (elsewhere) ecclesiastical courts and registers.
A handsome, folio edition, in full contemporary panelled calf, newly rebacked, occasional lightish spotting, ownership release stamp on front pastedown, the spine with six raised bands and elaborately gilt, a crimson label, double-gilt lined and lettered.

162. NOONAN, John T., Jr.. Persons and Masks of the Law, Cardozo, Holmes, Jefferson, and Wythe as Makers of the Masks. Farrar, 1976. **$12.50**

163. (NUREMBERG). WILBOURN E. BENTON AND GEORG GRIMM (eds.). Nuremberg, German Views of the War Trials. S.M.U., 1970. **$15.00**

164. OLLENNU, N.A. Principles of Customary Land Law in Ghana. Sweet & Maxwell, 1962. **$17.50**
Law in Africa, Volume 2.

165. OPPLER, Alfred. Legal Reform in Occupied Japan. Princeton, 1976. **$15.00**

166. OSBORN, Albert S. The Problem of Proof. Second Edition. Essex Press, 1926. **$35.00**
With an introduction by John Henry Wigmore, a bit worn, the top edge gilt.

167. OSBORNE, Thomas Mott. Society and Prisons. Yale, 1916. **$25.00**

168. PACKER, Herbert L. Ex-Communist Witnesses, Four Studies in Fact Finding. Stanford, 1962. **$15.00**

169. PACKER, Herbert L. The Limits of the Criminal Sanction. Stanford, 1968. **$15.00**

A Very Attractive Copy
170. PERKINS, John. A Profitable Book of Master John Perkins, fellow of the Inner Temple, Treating of the Lawes of England. London, [1593] (colophon). Title Page; 19 leaves; 168 pages. New S.T.C. 19639, Beale T425. **$600.00**
Termed "witty and learned" by Coke, and one of the most popular books of the 1500's, first appearing in 1528, and going through a 15th edition in 1827.
Occasional lightish dampstaining, primarily marginal or to preliminary leaves, occasional dustiness and a bit of staining to a few leaves, copious annotations in Law French, primarily in one early hand; *altogether quite a clean copy, with very ample fore and lower margins, and with substantial black letter throughout.*
A very attractive copy, newly and nicely bound in full, double blind-lined brown morocco, the spine blind-lined and gilt-lettered.

The First Edition
171. PETYT, William. Miscellania Parliamentaria. London, 1680. Blank; Title Page; 14 leaves; 220 pages; 32 leaves. Wing P1948. **$160.00**
For many years *Keeper of the Records in the Tower,* Petyt devoted this work, published in 1680, to Parliamentary privilege. *Altogether, a very nice, attractive and clean copy, newly bound in ¾ dark calf over marbled boards,* the covers blind decorated and the spine gilt-lined and lettered, a bit of marginal worming very occasionally just affecting the text, but not legibility.

172. PLUCKNETT, T.F.T. Early English Legal Literature. London, 1980. **$20.00**
A re-issue of Plucknett's absorbing Maitland Memorial Lectures, given to commemorate the 100th anniversary of Maitland's birth.

173. POLLOCK, Sir Frederick. A First Book of Jurisprudence. Sixth Edition. London, 1929. **$35.00**
Termed by Professor Goodhart *"probably the most original book published in England on this subject";* a very nice copy.

174. POLLOCK, Sir Frederick. The Land Laws. Second Edition. London, 1887. **$55.00**
A nice copy, bound in darkish blue ¾ calf over marbled boards, some marginal notes and underlining, of this "agreeable introduction to the technical treatises on the law of real property."

175. POULTER, Sebastian. Family Law and Litigation in Basotho Society. Oxford, 1976. **$15.00**

176. POUND, Roscoe. The Formative Era of American Law. Peter Smith, 1960. **$17.50**
Dean Pound's Lectures delivered at Tulane in 1936, in commemoration of the centennial of the death of Edward Livingston.

177. POUND, Roscoe. Organization of Courts. Little, Brown, 1940. **$35.00**

178. PREST, Wilfrid (ed.). Lawyers in Early Modern Europe and America. London, 1981. **New $30.00**
Highly interesting.

179. PRITCHETT, C. Herman. Congress versus the Supreme Court, 1957-1960. Minnesota, 1961. **$15.00**
Based on Pritchett's *1959 Guy Stanton Ford Lectures at Minnesota.*

180. (PROBATION). The Results of Probation. MacMillan, 1958. **$17.50**
English Studies in Criminal Science, volume 10, edited by *Sir Leon Radzinowicz.*

Charles Tennyson's Copy
181. PRYNNE, William. Brevia Parliamentaria Rediviva. London, 1662. 2 blanks; Title page; 11 leaves; 398 pages; leaf; 2 blanks. Wing P3902. **$200.00**
Appointed Keeper of the Records in the Tower shortly after the Restoration, *Prynne issued his work, termed valuable by Gross, in four separate volumes over a five year period,* this the third of four.
A desirable copy, in full contemporary speckled calf, early and very nicely rebacked preserving the old label; occasional very lightish spotting and embrowning, with woodcut decorations in the text.
The copy of Charles Tennyson, elder brother of Alfred Tennyson, with his bookplate on the front pastedown.

The First Separate Issue
182. PRYNNE, William. Historiarchos, or The Exact Recorder. London, 1659. Title Page; 4 leaves; 402 pages; leaf. Wing P3974. **$250.00**
An important part of Prynne's historical writings, first appearing in 1657, and then titled "A Seasonable Legall and Historicall Vindication and Chronologicall Collection of the good old fundamental Liberties of all English Freeman", *this portion devoted primarily to the period from 600 A.D. to the Norman Conquest.*
Altogether a handsome and attractive copy, newly bound in ½ sheep over maroon boards, occasional very lightish dampstaining, primarily to the upper margins, the spine gilt-lined with a red morocco label, double-gilt lined and lettered, *with Wing showing only the Harvard and Yale copies in this country.*

183. RAY, Isaac. A Treatise on the Medical Jurisprudence of Insanity. Harvard, 1962. **$22.50**
A fine, scholarly edition based on the text of the first edition of 1838.

184. SATOW, Sir Ernest. A Guide to Diplomatic Practice. Two volumes. Second and Revised Edition. London, 1922. **$45.00**
Issued in *Contributions to International Law and Diplomacy,* edited by Professor Oppenheim.

185. SCHLECHTRIEM, Peter H. Vertragsordnung und auservertragliche Haftung. Frankfurt, 1972. **$25.00**
A Presentation Copy to Max Rheinstein.

Charles I's Scottish Coronation
186. (SCOTLAND). The Acts Made in the First Parliament of Our Most High and Dread Soveraigne Charles. Edinburgh, 1633. Title Page; [3]-66 pages; 4 leaves; blank. New S.T.C. 21902. **$150.00**
The occasion of Charles' coronation in Scotland, his first visit in 30 years since his departure at age three, with the Parliament, controlled by Charles, putting its seal to 168 acts, *"a more*

industrious Parliament had never sat", with ominous consequences.
Quite a good copy, nicely rebound in ½ calf over marbled boards, woodcut decorations and initials throughout, the decorations on leaves A2 and I2 slightly shaved, a few marginal tears, and embrowning primarily marginal throughout; the spine gilt-lined and lettered.

187. SEEBOHM, Frederic. The English Village Community. Kennikat, 1971. **$12.50**
A re-issue of the first edition of 1883.

"A High Authority"—Holdsworth
188. SHEPPARD, William. The Touch-Stone of Common Assurances. Second Edition. London, 1651. Title Page; 5 leaves; 529 pages; 3 leaves (irregular, but complete). Wing S3215. **$400.00**
Termed by Holdsworth "the earliest work exclusively devoted to the theory of conveyancing". Sheppard's Touchstone first appeared in 1648, three years previously, reaching an 8th edition in 1826.
A desirable copy, newly and nicely bound in ½ calf over marbled boards, occasional underlining and marginal annotations in an early hand, some embrowning and chipping to the first and last leaves, occasional embrowning and spotting elsewhere, but altogether quite attractive, the spine gilt-lined and blind decorated, a red morocco label gilt-lined and lettered, and with woodcut decorations and initials in the text.

189. SHIENTAG, Bernard L. Moulders of Legal Thought. Viking, 1943. **$17.50**
A presentation copy, with essays on Cardozo, Lord Mansfield and Samuel Romilly, among others.

190. SHROPSHIRE, Denys W.T. The Bantu Woman Under the Natal Code of Native Law. Lovedale Press, 1941. **$12.50**
47 pp., stapled wraps, slightly worn.

191. SIGLER, Jay A. Double Jeopardy, The Development of a Legal and Social Policy, Cornell, 1969. **$12.50**

192. SINGH, Nagendra. Maritime Flag and International Law. Sitjhoff, 1978. **$15.00**

193. SMIGEL, Erwin O. The Wall Street Lawyer. Free Press, 1964. **$12.50**

194. SMITH, Reginald Heber. Justice and the Poor. New York, 1913. **$35.00**
A classic study, Bulletin number Thirteen of The Carnegie Foundation for the Advancement of Teaching. 271 pp., sewn wraps, somewhat worn, three folding tables; *with a foreward by Elihu Root.*

195. SORAUF, J. The Wall of Separation. The Constitutional Politics of Church and State. Princeton, 1976. **$15.00**

196. SPRENKEL, Sybille van der. Legal Institutions in Manchu China. Athlone Press, 1962. **$17.50**

197. STEIN, Peter. Legal Evolution, The Story of an Idea. Cambridge, 1980. **New $17.95**
The *R.M. Jones Lectures* in the Development of Ideas.

198. STENTON, Doris M. English Justice Between the Norman Conquest and the Great Charter, 1066-1215. American Philosophical Society, 1964.. **$15.00**
The 1963 Jayne Lectures.

199. STENTON, Doris Mary. The English Woman in History. Schocken, 1977. **$17.50**
Lady Stenton's work of love, written over the course of her lifetime; originally published in 1957.

200. STEPHENS, Otis H., Jr. The Supreme Court and Confessions of Guilt. Tennessee, 1973. **$12.50**

201. STONE, Bailey. The Parlement of Paris, 1774-1789. North Carolina, 1981. **New $19.00**

202. STONE, Julius. Human Law and Human Justice. Stanford, 1968. **$22.50**

203. STOPES, Marie. Contraception, Its Theory, History and Practice, A Manual for the Medical and Legal Professions. London, 1924. **$35.00**
A bit worn.

204. SUNDERLAND, Edson R. History of the American Bar Association and Its Work. Privately printed, 1953. **$17.50**
A bit worn.

A Handsome Copy of the First Edition
205. SWINBURNE, Henry. A Treatise of Spousals, or Matrimonial Contracts. London, 1686. First Edition. Title page; 7 leaves; 240 pages. Wing S6260. **$500.00**
Called by Professor Derrett "a true follower of Bartolus and Baldus, and a genuine colleague of the celebrated jurists of the European continent", Swinburne intended a full treatise on Marriage, living but to see this portion, on Spousals, completed, and it published posthumously.
Occasional spotting and lightish embrowning throughout, with the title page in a double woodcut border. *Very attractively and newly bound in full blind-lined and decorated calf,* the spine with a crimson morocco label, gilt-lined, decorated and lettered; *Julius Rosenthal's copy, with his signature on the title page.*

206. SWISHER, Carl Brent (ed.). Selected Papers of Homer Cummings, Attorney General of the United States, 1933-1939. Scribners, 1939. **$22.50**
A trifle worn.

207. SWINDLER, William F. A Bibliography of Law on Journalism. Columbia, 1947. **$20.00**

208. TAFT, Henry W. Legal Miscellanies. MacMillan, 1941. **$17.50**
With several essays on women and the bar; a bit worn.

209. TANSELLE, G. Thomas. Royall Tyler, Harvard, 1967. **$17.50**
The first book-length study of Tyler, Chief Justice of the Vermont Supreme Court and one of the most significant pre-Revolutionary literary figures.

210. TREBACH, Arnold S. The Rationing of Justice, Constitutional Rights and the Criminal Process. Rutgers, 1964. **$15.00**

211. TUGWELL, Rexford G. The Compromising of the Constitution (Early Departures). Notre Dame, 1976. **$12.50**

212. ULC, Otto. The Judge in a Communist State, A View From Within. Ohio, 1972. **$15.00**

213. VANDERBILT, Arthur T.II. Changing Law, A Biography of Arthur T. Vanderbilt. Rutgers, 1976. **$17.50**

214. VANDERBILT, Arthur T. Judges and Jurors: Their Functions, Qualifications and Selection. Boston, 1958. **$17.50**
The 1955 Bacon Lectures at Boston University.

The First Edition In English of One of the Classics of International Law
215. VATTEL, Emerich de. The Law of Nations. Two Volumes in One. London, 1760 & 1759. **$450.00**
A handsome copy of Vattel's foremost work, said by Professor Fenwick ultimately to have become better known than the work of Grotius himself, and of considerable value, according to Professor Grey, in shaping the constitutional ideas of the American colonists.
A handsome copy of the first edition in English, appearing shortly after the first edition in French; some damping to the title page, a few leaves dusty, holes in leaves 2G4 and 2H1 affecting the text, occasional spotting in volume 2, but in general a clean, wide-margined and highly desirable copy, *with two separate title pages, the first in red and black;* bound in full contemporary calf, worn, very attractively rebacked, with the original label preserved.

216. VLASIC, Ivan A. (ed.). Explorations in Aerospace Law, Selected essays by John Cobb Cooper. McGill, 1968. **$25.00**

217. WALKER, David M. The Oxford Companion to Law. Oxford, 1980. **New $49.95**
An outstanding reference work, clearly the best one volume resource for Western legal thought.

218. WARNER, Gerald. Being of Sound Mind, A Book of Eccentric Wills. London, 1980. **New $14.50**

219. WATKINS, Charles. An Essay Towards the Further Elucidation of the Law of Descents. Dublin, 1794. Title Page; viii, 130 pp.; folding table; 8 leaves. **$150.00**
Termed "excellent", "very valuable", and "masterly", Watkins' work first appeared in London in the previous year, and went through four editions (the last edited by Joshua Williams) by 1837.
This the first Irish edition, in full contemporary calf, worn, newly rebacked, red morocco label, gilt-lined and lettered.
Julius Rosenthal's copy.

A Handsome Copy of the First and Only Edition
220. WHITELOCK, Sir Bulstrode. Essays Ecclesiastical and Civil [with] a Treatise of the Work of Sessions of the Peace. London, 1706. Blank; Title Page; 3 leaves; 264 pages; blank. **$250.00**
Grouped by Hume with More, Bacon and Clarendon, and called "a man of great abilities and merit", Whitelock was Keeper of the Great Seal and a voluminous writer, *this one of his five legal works, with essays on high and petty treason, felonies and contempts, and several on ecclesiastical matters.*
An extremely nice copy, the title page within a double woodcut border, a few leaves a little dusty, some very lightish dampstaining to the last leaves, but altogether very clean, *in full contemporary sprinkled and panelled calf,* newly and exceptionally well rebacked, with a crimson spine label, triple gilt-lined and lettered.

221. WOODS, T.P.S. Prelude to Civil War 1642, Mr. Justice Malet and the Kentish Petitions. Michael Russell, 1980. **New $25.00**

The Origin of Feudal Tenures
222. WRIGHT, Martin. An Introduction to the Law of Tenures. Second Edition. London, 1734. Blank; Title Page; leaf; 222 pages; 3 blanks. **$225.00**
The work through which, according to Maitland, Englishmen "learned of feudal law as of a mediaeval jus gentium", and said by Holdsworth to "attain a high standard of learning".
A very clean and attractive copy, well printed, in full contemporary calf, a bit worn, blind-lined and decorated covers, the spine elaborately gilt-decorated, with the label gilt-lettered.

223. WYZANSKI, Charles E., Jr. Whereas—A Judge's Premises; Essays in Judgment, Ethics, and the Law. Little, Brown, 1965. **$15.00**

RARE AND SCHOLARLY

BOOKS ON THE LAW

Sir Edward Coke

1552 – 1634

"Coke . . . by his writings and his career . . . [made] medieval common law . . . fit to bear rule in a modern state. It is for this reason that, amongst all the many Makers of English Law, Coke is the most important." (Sir William Holdsworth, Some Makers of English Law, p. 113) (See items 39 – 44, 46, 77, 105 and inside front cover).

CATALOGUE SIX

MEYER BOSWELL BOOKS

SAN FRANCISCO

1. ALLEN, Eleanor Wyllys. The Position of Foreign States before National Courts Chiefly in Continental Europe. New York, 1933 **$22.50**

2. AMOS, Sheldon. The Science of Law. Fifth Edition. London, 1881. **$75.00**

One of three works for which Amos, Professor of Jurisprudence in University College, London, is best known, **with considerable reference to Maine, Austin and Bentham;** *a very handsome copy in a prize binding,* full, plum-colored calf, a bit rubbed, the covers double-gilt lined, the spine elaborately gilt, marbled edges and marbled endpapers.

3. ANSON, Sir William. The Law and Custom of the Constitution. Two Volumes. London, 1896 & 1897. **$150.00**

Termed "the most . . . comprehensive book . . . on the laws and framework of [the English] government" by President Lowell, and perhaps Anson's most famous work, with volume one devoted to Parliament, and volume two to the Crown. **A highly attractive set,** uniformly bound in ¾ brown morocco, gilt-lined covers, the spine gilt-lined, decorated and lettered, marbled endpapers, volume 1 the third edition of 1897, volume 2 the second of 1896.

4. ATIYAH, P.S. Promises, Morals, and Law. Oxford, 1981. **New $29.95**

Limited to 150 Copies

5. (AUSTRALIA). J.M. BENNETT. Portraits of the Chief Justices of New South Wales 1824 – 1977. Sydney, 1977. **$45.00**

A special edition, signed by the author, in ¾ red morocco, gilt, with full-page color portraits of each of the 14 Chief Justices; *very nice.*

6. BAADE, Hans W. (ed.). Jurimetrics. New York, 1963. **$15.00**

The First Edition of the First Significant Work on Arbitration

7. [BACON, Matthew]. The Compleat Arbitrator: or, the Law of Awards and Arbitraments. London, 1731. Title Page; iii-vi: 3 leaves; 308 pages. 8vo. **$275.00**

The first significant work on arbitration, (preceded by an anonymous work published in 1694 consisting of 93 pages) termed by Holdsworth "good, straightforward and . . . useful."

Quite a nice copy, exceptionally clean, bound in full contemporary calf, worn, the covers double blind-lined, *newly and very well rebacked,* the spine double blind and gilt-lined, blind decorated, and with a dark brown, morocco label, triple gilt-lined and lettered.

8. BAILEY, Cyril (ed.). The Legacy of Rome. Oxford, 1924. **$35.00**

With 75 photographs and an essay on the Science of Law, by Professor de Zulueta.

9. BERLANSTEIN, Lenard R. The Barristers of Toulouse in the Eighteenth Century (1740–1793). Johns Hopkins, 1975. **$17.50**

With Two Letters Tipped In

10. BEVERIDGE, Albert J. The Life of John Marshall. **Four Volumes.** Houghton, Mifflin, 1916–19. **$150.00**

Quite an attractive set of Beveridge's principal work, and the leading and standard biography of Marshall, specially bound in ¾ morocco over linen boards, a bit rubbed, the covers gilt-lined, the spines with gilt-panels, and gilt-lettered, marbled endpapers, the inner hinge to volume one cracked but firm.

With two typewritten, one page letters signed by Beveridge on his stationery, with their envelopes, tipped in, dated December 17, 1923 and January 4, 1926, to James H. Hustis, President of the Boston & Maine Railroad; attached to the former extracts of a speech used by Beveridge and provided by Hustis.

11. (BIBLIOGRAPHY). THEODORE BESTERMAN. Law & International Law. Rowman and Littlefield, 1971. **$25.00**

Very useful; extracted from Besterman's massive World Bibliography of Bibliographies.

12. (BIBLIOGRAPHY). FRAN GJUPANOVICH et al. Legal Sources and Bibliography of Yugoslavia. Praeger, 1964. **$25.00**

13. (BIBLIOGRAPHY) J.G. MARVIN. Legal Bibliography. Buffalo, 1953. **$35.00**

An attractive re-issue of the original 1847 edition, *Marvin's work the pre-eminent American legal bibliography of the 19th century, with valuable comment on earlier English, Scottish, Irish and American works.*

14. (BIBLIOGRAPHY). VIRGILIU STOICOIU. Legal Sources and Bibliography of Romania. Praeger, 1964. **$25.00**

15. (BLACK and Frankfurter). WALLACE MENDELSON. Justices Black and Frankfurter, Conflict in the Court. Chicago, 1961. **$17.50**

An Exceptional Set

16. BLACKSTONE, Sir William. Commentaries on the Laws of England, **Four Volumes.** Oxford, 1766–1769. 4to. **$3,000.00**

The most renowned of all English law books, Bentham praising it as one which "has taught Jurisprudence to speak the language of the scholar and the gentleman [and] put a polish upon that rugged science," this the first edition of volumes 2 through 4, and the second edition of volume 1, which appeared in 1766, one year after the first edition of 1765.

A highly attractive set, bound in full, contemporary mottled calf, the spines recently rebacked antique-style, elaborate gilt decorated and lined compartments, with crimson morocco labels, double-gilt lined and lettered. A bit of occasional spotting, particularly to the preliminary leaves, but altogether a tall, clean, wide-margined and desirable copy.

The First London and Last Quarto Edition

17. BLACKSTONE, Sir William. Commentaries on the Laws of England. Sixth Edition. **Four Volumes.** London, 1774. 4to. **$1500.00**

The first non-pirated edition printed in the United Kingdom other than at Oxford, and the only so published during Blackstone's lifetime, this the last quarto edition to be issued.

Quite a desirable set, *in full contemporary speckled calf, the spine with five raised bands and five gilt-decorated compartments with gilt rules and decoration;* a bit of chipping to the heads and tails of some spines and like cracking to to some joints, expertly repaired and very sound, contemporary marbled endpapers.

A bit of worming to the margins of volumes 2 and 3 not affecting the text, else *a very clean, wide-margined copy, and very attractive, with a fine engraved portrait of Blackstone in volume 1.*

A Re-issue of the First Edition with American Notes

18. (BLACKSTONE, Sir William). ST. GEORGE TUCKER. Blackstone's Commentaries. **Five Volumes.** Buffalo, 1965. **$130.00**

This a facsimile re-issue of the edition originally published in Philadelphia in 1803, and edited by St. George Tucker, professor of law at William and Mary and a judge of the General Court in Virginia, based on the London edition of 1783, with Tucker's American notes appended, expanding the set from four volumes to five; *rather nicely and uniformly bound in red buckram, gilt.*

We also have available the facsimile re-issue of the 1765-69 first edition, published by the University of Chicago Press, in 1980, in four volumes, at $90 (hardcover) and $48 (paper).

The First General History of English Boroughs

19. BRADY, [Robert]. An Historical Treatise of Cities and Burghs or Boroughs. London, 1777. Title Page; iv, 107, 55 pages; 4 leaves. 8vo. **$175.00**

Brady's treatise, said by Professor Gross to have had *"a greater influence than any other in mouldng public opinion", first appearing in 1690, Brady having been Keeper of Records in the Tower, and physician in ordinary to Charles II and James II.*

Quite a desirable copy, bound in full contemporary calf, a bit worn, the covers blind lined and decorated, *newly and very nicely rebacked, the spine double gilt-lined, and blind decorated, with a crimson morocco label double gilt-lined, decorated and lettered;* occasional underscoring and marginal annotations, very occasional spotting, but altogether a very clean and desirable copy, with the bookplate of Thomas Erskine.

20. (BRANDEIS and Frankfurter). NELSON L. DAWSON. Louis D. Brandeis, Felix Frankfurter, and the New Deal. Archon, 1980. **$19.50**

One of Two Great Sixteenth Century Abridgements, in Both Parts

21. BROOKE, Sir Robert. La Graunde Abridgement. Second Edition. London, 1576. Title Page; 3 leaves; 351 folios; blank; Title Page (2d part); folios 2-328. S.T.C. 3828; Beale T471 & 472; Cowley 70. **$950.00**

Perhaps the greatest, and certainly one of the two greatest, 16th century abridgements, the other being Fitzherbert's much earlier in the century, Brooke drawing (as Fitzherbert did not) upon the early treatises and particular statutes, as well as the Year Books.

An exceptionally clean and desirable copy, in black letter throughout, extensive printed sidenotes, a few notations in an early hand, occasional embrowning, bound in old, triple-blind-lined calf, recently and nicely rebacked, the spine unlettered and double blind-lined with five raised bands.

The copy complete with both the first and second parts of the work, the title pages in very attractive, elaborate woodcut borders [McKerrow 196], the fore and bottom edges just slightly shaved.

22. BROWNLIE, Ian. Basic Documents on Human Rights. Second Edition. Oxford, 1981. **New $65.00**

Also available in paper at $35.00

23. BRYSON, W.H. The Equity Side of the Exchequer. Cambridge, 1975. **$25.00**

Cambridge Studies in English Legal History.

A Handsome Copy of The First Statutes of California

24. (CALIFORNIA). The State of California, Passed at the First Session of the Legislature. San Jose [New York], 1850. **$350.00**

The 146 acts and 19 joint resolutions, with the state constitution and pertinent federal material prefixed, the San Jose imprint false, with the statutes printed in New York at half cost, and the State Printer charged with delaying their arrival, so as to sell at higher prices those copies he had received personally.

A handsome copy, newly bound in full sheep, the spine triple gilt-lined, with contrasting red and black morocco labels, gilt-lettered; a bit of dampstaining to the last leaves, primarily marginal, occasional pencil annotations, else a very clean and crisp copy.

Of Great Importance for Commercial and Maritime Law

25. [CALLIS, Robert]. The Reading . . . Upon . . . Sewers. Second Edition. London, 1685. Title Page; leaf; 291 pages; 36 leaves. New Wing C305. Quarto. **$250.00**

One of the most famous readings ever given at the Inns of Court, treating "sewers", not in the modern sense, but as freshwater trenches and small currents or little rivers, vital to those portions of England exposed to incursions of the sea and to flooding, *the Commissioners of Sewers being the most notable, oldest and permanent of English local authorities, dating to pre-Conquest times,* and Callis' reading treating of this history, with modern law based on a statute (23 Henry 8, c.5) enacted in 1531-32.

A very attractive copy, bound in full, contemporary calf, handsomely rebacked, a red morocco label, gilt-lined, decorated and lettered, a bit of spotting, but in general, a very clean, desirable and wide-margined copy.

A Magnificent Set in Eleven Volumes

26. CAMPBELL, Lord John. The Lives of the Chief Justices of England **uniformly bound with** The Lives of the Lord Chancellors of England. Eleven Volumes. London, 1846–69. **$500.00**

Perhaps the most famous of all works devoted to England's Chief Justices and Lord Chancellors, immensely readable and covering approximately eight centuries from the Conquest to the 1800's (with pre-Conquest treatment of the Chancellors as well), full of detail and anecdote difficult to locate in any other single source.

This an especially attractive set, uniformly bound in ¾ calf over linen boards, the spines richly gilt-decorated in triple gilt-lined compartments, contrasting crimson and brown morocco labels gilt-lettered, a bit of rubbing and chafing to the bindings, not detracting from overall exceptional appearance, the top edges gilt, and decorated endpapers.

This set with the sometimes elusive eighth and index volume to the Lord Chancellors.

27. CHAPLAIS, Pierre. Essays in Medieval Diplomacy and Administration. Hambledon Press, 1981. **New $72.00**

22 essays, nine of which are devoted to English diplomatic from 700 to 1300; 59 illustrations.

28. (CAESAR, Sir Julius). L.M. HILL (ed.). The Ancient State Authoritie and Proceedings of the Court of Requests. Cambridge, 1975. **$35.00**

Cambridge Studies in English Legal History.

29. CARDOZO, Benjamin N. The Growth of the Law. Yale, 1939. **$20.00**

Cardozo's lectures at Yale Law School in 1923, supplementing his Nature of the Judicial Process.

30. (CHATTERLY, Lady). C.H. ROLPH (ed.). The Trial of Lady Chatterly, Regina v. Penguin Books Ltd., The Transcript of the Trial. Privately printed, 1961. **$65.00**

A special issue, initialed by Allan Lane, who published the trade edition; *with illustrations by Paul Hogarth and a selection of cartoons.*

31. CHENEY, Mary G. Roger, Bishop of Worcester, 1164 – 1179. Oxford, 1981. **New $59.00**

With much on Becket and Henry II, and the "English" contribution to the new canon law; Oxford Historical Monographs.

32. (CHINA). GRANT F. RHODE and REID E. WHITLOCK. Treaties of the People's Republic of China, 1949 – 1978: An Annotated Compilation. Boulder, 1980. **$20.00**

33. CHINARD, G. (ed.). The Treaties of 1778. Johns Hopkins, 1928. **$45.00**

The treaties of alliance and amity and commerce between the Colonies and France; *an attractive issue in linen backed blue, printed boards,* slightly worn, with the bookplate of the Massachusetts Historical Society, and *a forward by James Brown Scott, the treaties' text in French and English, double column.*

34. CHROUST, Anton-Hermann. The Rise of the Legal Profession in America. Two volumes Oklahoma, 1965 **$37.50**

Quite valuable, covering the period to 1840; boxed.

35. CHO, Sung Yoon (comp.). Japanese Writings on Communist Chinese Law, 1946–1974. Washington, 1977. **$15.00**

36. CHOPER, Jesse H. Judicial Review and the National Political Process, A Functional Reconsideration of the Role of the Supreme Court. Chicago, 1980. **New $32.50**

37. COCKBURN, J.S. A History of English Assizes 1558–1714. Cambridge, 1972. **$45.00**

Cambridge Studies in English Legal History.

38. COHEN, Felix S. Ethical Systems and Legal Ideals. New York, 1933. **$45.00**

Slightly worn.

The Only Edition in English

39. (COKE, Sir Edward). THO[MAS] ASHE. Fasciculus Florum, or a Handfull of Flowers. London, 1618. Title Page; 6 leaves; 102 leaves; blank. S.T.C. 5529; 8vo. **$375.00**

A delightful little book, *extracting Coke's epigrams and sayings, primarily from his Reports, in Latin and English translation,* arranged alphabetically, with references to the folios of the reports from which they are taken, the compiler, Thomas Ashe, a contemporary of Coke's and author of several other legal works.

An extremely attractive volume, newly bound in full, 18th century style morocco, the covers gilt-lined, and the spine elaborately gilt-lined, decorated and lettered, the title page cut close and repaired with partial loss of imprint, some headnotes, catchwords and signatures cut close with loss of letters, but the text fully intact save for a few words on the penultimate leaf, the preliminary leaves a bit dusty, else quite a clean copy; *a choice little book, with the Short Title Catalogue showing but four copies, and only one in this country.*

With Two, Fine, Full-Page Portraits of Coke and Littleton

40. (COKE, Sir Edward). SIR HUMPHREY DAVENPORT. An Abridgement of the Lord Coke's Commentaries Upon Littleton. Blank; Littleton Portrait; Coke Portrait; Title Page; leaf; 459 pages (irregular but complete); 8 leaves; blank. New Wing C4906A; 8vo. **$450.00**

Of Coke on Littleton, Justice Story has reported his experience as a student: "It was a very large folio . . . and after trying it day after day with very little success, I sat myself down and wept bitterly", his case perhaps typical, leading to abridgements of this classic work, this example by Sir Humphrey Davenport, judge of the Court of Common Pleas and president of the court of exchequer in the 1630's.

A very handsome copy, arranged in accordance with the folios and sections of Coke on Littleton, *newly bound in full, dark sheep,* the covers and spine double blind-lined, the spine with a crimson morocco label, triple gilt-lined and lettered; a bit of dampstaining to the margins throughout, else a very clean and attractive copy.

A work not often found, New Wing showing but three copies in this country; with the signature of John Bond on the title page, perhaps the author of the Complete Guide for Justices of the Peace, published in its first edition in the same year, 1685.

Coke's Reports Indexed

41. (COKE, Sir Edward). Un General Table, A touts les several Livres de les Reports de le Tres-reverend Judge Sir Edward Coke. London, 1672. Blank; Title Page; 84 folios; blank. Folio. **$350.00**

The only folio index of Coke's Reports ever issued, and of considerable value, listing alphabetically all of the cases with reference to the part (of 13) of Coke's Reports in which the cases may be found, and, as valuably, *digesting the subject matter of the reports alphabetically, with similar references to the parts set forth.*

Quite a desirable copy, newly bound in half calf over marbled boards, the covers blind decorated and the spine with a crimson morocco label, double gilt-lined and lettered, the title page just a bit dusty, else an exceptionally clean, tall and wide-margined copy.

An Extremely Handsome Copy of Coke's Reports Abridged

42. (COKE, Sir Edward). SIR THOMAS IRELAND. An Exact Abridgment in English, Of the eleven Books of Reports of the Learned Sir Edward Coke. London, 1651. Blank; Title Page; 6 leaves; 428 pages; 20 leaves. New Wing 4920. 8vo. **Sold**

An exceptionally handsome copy of the most popular abridgement of Coke's Reports, treating of 11 of the 13 parts (the last two parts published only subsequently, and posthumously, in 1656 and 1659), this the only work of Ireland, a Reader in Gray's Inn.

Bound in full, 18th-century style mottled calf, the covers double blind-lined, the spine elaborately gilt-lined and decorated, with a black morocco label, gilt-lined, decorated and labelled; a bit of worming to the lower portion of many pages, affecting the text on occasion, some notations and underlining, most in an early hand, else quite a clean and desirable copy, and not often found, New Wing noting but four copies.

43. (COKE, Sir Edward). STEPHEN D. WHITE. Sir Edward Coke and "The Grievances of the Commonwealth," 1621–1628. North Carolina, 1979. **New $22.50**

Studies in Legal History.

Coke in Verse

44. (COKE, Sir Edward). JOHN WORRAL (comp.). The Reports of Sir Edward Coke, Kt., in Verse. London, 1742. 2 blanks; Title Page; 41 unpaged leaves; 2 blanks. 8vo in 4's. **$325.00**

The first edition of a highly entertaining work, attributed to John Worrall, the famed 18th century law-bookseller, *reducing the great majority of the cases in Coke's Reports to two-line verse,* Shelley's Case sufficing as an example:
"Shelley, Where ancestors a freehold take:
The words (his heirs) a limitation make."

Quite a desirable copy, bound in ¾ contemporary calf over marbled boards, worn, newly and very nicely rebacked, the spine double gilt-lined, with the original label preserved; a very little bit of spotting, tears to leaves B1 and B4, just affecting the text, this the American Antiquarian Society copy, with its circular stamp on the title page (released), and the bookplate of the Windham College Marvin Memorial Library on the front pastedown.

A Superb Copy

45. (COLONIAL Law). The Charlemagne Tower Collection of American Colonial Laws. Privately Printed for the Historical Society of Pennsylvania, 1890. **$75.00**

A valuable bibliographical work, with full collations and extensive title-page descriptions, Tower's perhaps the most impressive private collection of Colonial law ever amassed, this an exceptional copy, uncut and untrimmed, bound in black, simulated leather, top edge gilt, gilt spine, very bright.

The Dictionary That Enraged Sir Edward Coke

46. COWELL, John. The Interpreter: or Booke, Containing the Signification of Words. London, 1637. Title page; 3 leaves; 336 leaves. S.T.C. 5903; Cowley 128 and figure 34. 4to. **$600.00**

Originally appearing in 1607, *Cowell's work incensed Coke by its slighting references to Littleton, and its affirmation of the absolute sovereignty of the King led to its suppression in 1610,* not to be reissued until 1637, with the publication of this and one other issue, which were themselves used in the trial against William Laud.

An exceedingly attractive copy, bound in full, double blind-lined, contemporary sheep, well rebacked, the spine with a red morocco label, double gilt-lined, decorated and lettered; the lower margin of K3 torn not affecting the text, two small holes on R1 and 2B1 respectively, the former just affecting a few letters. *Altogether, a handsomely printed work, the title page in a double woodcut border, and the pages in double columns with woodcut borders, particularly fresh and crisp.*

The S.T.C. showing but one copy in this country, and Cowley two.

47. DAGGETT, Harriet Spiller. The Community Property System of Louisiana with Comparative Studies. Louisiana State, 1931. **$25.00**

237 pages, sewn, printed wraps, slightly worn.

48. (DARROW, Clarence). ABE C. RAVITZ. Clarence Darrow & The American Literary Tradition. Western Reserve, 1962. **$17.50**

49. DeLOLME J.L. The Consititution of England. New Edition. London, 1822. **$75.00**

Grouped by Gross with Blackstone's historical sketch as "the leading authorities on English constitutional history" of the late 1700's, DeLolme's work first appeared in English in 1771, shortly after the Commentaries; *this a very attractive copy,* in ¾ leather, the spine gilt-decorated and lined, the label gilt-lettered, all edges marbled and marbled endpapers.

50. DENNING, Lord. The Family Story. Butterworths, 1981. **New $35.00**

The family autobiography of England's "greatest as well as . . . most colorful judge."

51. DePAUW, Linda Grant. The Eleventh Pillar, New York State and the Federal Constitution. Cornell, 1966. **$17.50**

Winner of the 1964 Beveridge Award of the American Historical Association.

52. (DICTIONARY). LOUIS W. STONE et al. Anglo-Norman Dictionary. Fascicle 2. London, 1981. **$63.00**

A highly valuable work, **the first major scholarly effort to include Law French (to 1500) in an Anglo-Norman dictionary,** undertaken by the Modern Humanities Research Association in conjunction with The Anglo-Norman Text Society.

This volume two, comprising letters D-E volume one (letters A-C) still available at $60.00. We would be pleased to take standing orders for this first-rate work. 150 pages, double-column, sewn wraps.

53. (DUBLIN). A handsome, hand-colored, 19th century engraving of the Four Courts, Dublin, matted. 5 x 7 inches. **$50.00**

A Major Contribution to the Study of English Legal History

54. (ENGLISH Legal Manuscripts). J. H. BAKER (ed.). English Legal Manuscripts Project. Zug, Switzerland, 1975–79. Approximately **$10,000.00**

Perhaps the most significant contribution to the study of English legal history accomplished in this century, making available the great stores of manuscripts at the Harvard Law Library, Lincoln's Inn, the Bodleian Library, Gray's Inn, and the Yale Law Library, *with the microfiche reproduction of approximately 250 Year Books, 800 reports of cases, and 150 readings and moots in the Inns of Court.*

With two valuable bibliographies by Dr. Baker, in hardcover, describing the manuscripts in detail, and highly valuable in their own right, volume 1 (Harvard) available at $35.00, and volume 2 (the remaining libraries) at $50.00.

Also available, free of charge, are well-compiled, descriptive catalogues of the manuscripts; please write for your copies, and for further information about this exceptional project.

55. (EQUAL Rights Amendment). Hearings before the Subcommittee on Constitutional Amendments of the Committee on the Judiciary. Washington, 1970. **$25.00**

793 pages, sewn, printed wraps, slightly worn.

56. EUSDEN, John Dykstra. Puritans, Lawyers and Politics in Early Seventeenth-century England. Archon, 1968. **$17.50**

57. EWEN, C. L'Estrange (ed.). Witch Hunting and Witch Trials, The Indictments for Witchcraft from the Records of 1373 Assizes Held for the Home Court AD 1559-1736. London, 1971 **$25.00**

A re-issue of the original 1929 edition.

58. FINGARETTE, Herbert & Ann Fingarette Hasse. Mental Disabilities and Criminal Responsibility. California, 1979. **$15.00**

59. (FORENSIC Medicine). SUNG TZ'U. The Washing Away of Wrongs. Ann Arbor, 1981. **New $15.00**

The oldest extant work on forensic (or legal) medicine, this the first English translation, impressively done. 181 pages, sewn, pictorial and printed wraps.

60. FREEMAN, Edward A. The Growth of the English Constitution from the Earliest Times. Third Edition. London, 1876. **$65.00**

Freeman's sole work devoted to constitutional history, and termed a classic, Freeman himself placed by Maitland among the foremost of 19th century English historians.

A handsome copy, and a fine specimen of a full tree calf binding, the spine elaborately gilt, a bit of rubbing to the joints and just the slightest chipping to the head and tail of the spine, but still very attractive, with dentelles, all edges marbled and marbled endpapers.

61. FREEMAN, Edward A. Historical Essays. **Two Volumes.** London, 1871 & 1873. **$150.00**

A choice selection of Freeman's writings, volume one devoted to medieval history, the second to ancient or classical times, with essays on Edward III, the Holy Roman Empire, Charles the Bold, Athenian democracy, Mommsen's Rome, and many others.

A very handsome set, uniformly bound in ¾ dark brown morocco over linen boards, gilt-lined covers, the spines with five raised bands and gilt-lettered, all edges gilt, and decorated endpapers, a bit of occasional, very light spotting internally, else exceptionally fine.

62. GARGARIN, Michael. Drakon and Early Athenian Homicide Law. Yale, 1981. **New $25.00**

An Unrecorded Edition

63. (GAME Law). The Game Law: or, the Laws Relating to the Game. London, 1727. Title Page; 2 leaves; 86 pages; 5 leaves; Title Page (pt 2); 11 leaves; 180 pages. 8vo. **$300.00**

One of a number of works written on the game law in the early 1700's, *with much on the law pertaining to hunting, hawking, fowling and fishing, and to forests, chases, parks and warrens.*

This edition in two parts, both dated 1727, and *unrecorded in the Harvard Law catalogue, Sweet & Maxwell, the National Union Catalogue, and the British Museum Catalogue.*

A handsome copy, the title pages in double woodcut borders, some dampstaining to the upper margin, occasional embrowning, but altogether quite clean and crisp, and *very attractively and newly bound in full calf,* the covers and spine elaborately blind decorated, with a crimson morocco label, double gilt-lined, lettered and decorated.

64. GILBERT, Gustav. The Constitutional Antiquities of Sparta and Athens. London, 1895. **$125.00**

Termed "important [and] a recognized textbook" by Professor Sandys even while in the original German, *this the first English translation; a handsome copy,* in a prize binding, full, polished calf, a bit rubbed, all edges marbled, marbled endpapers, the spine elaborately gilt, with a black, morocco label, double gilt-lined and lettered.

65. GILBERT, Lord Chief Baron. Cases in Law and Equity. 2d. edition. Dublin, 1792. **$125.00**

Of value in containing, in addition to the reports, Gilbert's short treatises on debt and constitutional law, two of his 18 separate works, which Holdsworth called "some of the best text-books on legal topics published during this [18th] century".

A bit of spotting and embrowning throughout, particularly to preliminaries, else *quite a good copy, nicely rebound in ½ calf over marbled boards, marbled endpapers,* and the spine gilt lined and blind decorated, the label gilt lined, decorated and lettered.

66. GOLDZIHER, Ignaz. Introduction to Islamic Theology and Law. Princeton, 1981. **New $30.00**

A fine translation (& the first in English), with notes, of this classic work first appearing in German in 1910.

67. GRAGLIA, Lino A. Disaster by Decree, The Supreme Court Decisions on Race and the Schools. Cornell, 1977. **$15.00**

68. GREENWAY, George (ed.). English Historical Documents, 1042–1189. Second Edition. Oxford, 1981. **New $98.00**

The best single-volume reference source for documents of this period, from Edward the Confessor to Henry II; in English translation.

69. (GROTIUS, Hugo). EDWARD DUMBAULD. The Life and Legal Writings of Hugo Grotius. Oklahoma, 1969. **$15.00**

The only work in English devoted exclusively to Grotius' legal writings, very well done.

The Edition First Expressly Attributed to Hale

70. HALE, Sir Matthew. The History of the Common Law of England. Second Edition. London, 1716. Leaf; Title Page; 2 leaves; 261 pages; 5 leaves. 8vo. **$275.00**

First published anonymously in 1713, this the second edition of 1716, perhaps intended by Hale as a work for students, **Holdsworth terming it "the ablest introductory sketch of a history of English law that appeared till the publication of Pollock and Maitland."**

A handsome copy, newly bound in full, dark calf, the covers blind-lined and decorated, and the spine elaborately blind-decorated, a red leather label, double gilt lined and lettered; a bit of dampstaining to the first four leaves, some spotting and embrowning throughout, else quite clean and sound, the title page in a double woodcut border.

Limited to 1000 Copies

71. HAND, Learned. Liberty. Overbrook Press, 1941. **$65.00**

Hand's address delivered to the Elizabethan Club at New Haven, on May 10, 1941, *a handsomely printed, private edition in blue, decorated boards,* with a paper label on the front cover, printed in red and black; *very nice.*

The First and Only Edition

72. [HARBIN, George]. The Hereditary Right of the Crown of England Asserted. Title Page; 3 leaves; 274, lxiii pages; 2 leaves. London, 1713. Folio **$250.00**

An important part of the early 18th century literature debating the question of political and constitutional theory, whether allegiance was due a de facto sovereign, Harbin decidedly against, marshalling Fortescue, Coke, Grotius and Hale in his support, with a detailed examination of post-Conquest history and with a copy of Henry VIII's will included.

Quite an attractive copy, bound in full, panelled calf, very nicely and newly rebacked, the spine with a morocco label, double gilt lined and lettered; a very clean, tall & wide-margined copy, with woodcut decorations and initials throughout.

73. HASKINS, George Lee. Law and Authority in Early Massachusetts. MacMillan, 1960. **$25.00**

74. HASTINGS, Margaret. The Court of Common Pleas in Fifteenth Century England. Archon, 1971. **$17.50**

A re-issue of the 1947 edition.

75. HAZARD, John and Isaac Shapiro. The Soviet Legal System. Dobbs Ferry, 1962. **$25.00**

Parker School Studies in Foreign and Comparative Law.

76. HENDERSON, Dan F. Village "Contracts" in Tokugawa Japan, Fifty Specimens with English Translations and Comments. Washington, 1975. **$20.00**

Asian Law Series.

77. HOLDSWORTH, Sir William. Some Makers of English Law. Cambridge, 1938. **$45.00**

Holdsworth's 1937–38 Tagore Lectures, *with essays on Bracton, Littleton, Coke and Blackstone,* among many others; ownership sticker and date on title-page, else quite nice.

78. HONNOLD, John (ed.). The Life of the Law, Readings on the Growth of Legal Institutions. New York, 1964. **$45.00**

With much from **Maitland, Holmes, Pound, Cardozo** and **Holdsworth,** among many others.

An Unrecorded Edition

79. HUGHES, William. An Exact Abridgment of all the Statutes. London, 1663. Imprimatur; Title Page; 2 leaves; 246 pages; advertising leaf. See Wing H3320 and Cowley 151 & 153. 8vo. **$275.00**

One of several supplements to Wingate's statutory abridgment, arranged alphabetically, and covering five years in the reigns of Charles I and II.

This an unrecorded edition, the title page corresponding to item 153 of Cowley's Bibliography of Abridgments [Selden Society, 1932], but the contents a mix of Cowley 151 and 153, *with no copy shown in the Harvard Law Catalogue or Sweet and Maxwell, or* (for want of supplied collation) *the National Union Catalogue or the British Museum Catalogue;* further details of the collation and differences gladly supplied.

Quite a good copy, bound in full contemporary sheep, worn, rebacked, with a black morocco label, gilt-lined and lettered; a bit of insignificant marginal worming to the first and a few other leaves, just affecting the double woodcut border of the title page, but not the text, else exceptionally clean and sound.

80. HYAMS, Paul R. Kings, Lords, and Peasants in Medieval England, The Common Law of Villeinage in the Twelfth and Thirteenth Centuries. Oxford, 1981. **New $49.50**

Oxford Historical Monographs.

81. (INTERNATIONAL Commission of Jurists). The Decline of Democracy in the Philippines. Geneva, 1977. **$15.00**

97 pages, printed wraps.

82. (INTERNATIONAL Commission of Jurists). The Rule of Law in A Free Society. Geneva, 1959. **$25.00**
340 pages, sewn, printed wraps, a bit worn.

83. (IOWA). BENJ. F. SHAMBAUGH. The Constitutions of Iowa. Iowa City, 1938. **$55.00**
Handsome and valuable, in the original blue cloth, gilt, a bit worn.

With a Very Fine Woodcut Portrait of James VI

84. (JAMES VI). The XXIII Parliament . . . Halden at Edinburgh . . . 1621. Edinburgh, 1621. Title Page; leaf; 34 folios. New S.T.C. 21900. Folio. **Sold**
The last Scottish Parliament of James VI, King of Scotland, and afterwards James I of England; a very nice copy, newly bound in ½ calf over marbled boards, the spine gilt-lettered, with many striking woodcuts throughout, a bit of lightish embrowning to the margins, else quite a clean and crisp copy.

85. JESSUP, Philip C. Elihu Root. Two Volumes. New York, 1937. **$65.00**
A fine biography of Root, who was called "the foremost example of the lawyer in politics" at the turn of the century, *this is an especially interesting copy, with the presentation inscription from Charles K. Burdick to Robert E. Cushman, two of the leading constitutional scholars of that period,* on the half-title of volume one; slightly worn.
We also have an additional set, not inscribed, at $45.00; please inquire.

86. JESSUP, Philip C. The International Problem of Governing **Mankind.** Claremont, 1947. **$20.00**
Jessup's 1947 Claremont Lectures.

87. JESSUP, Philip C. et al. Neutrality, Its History, Economics, and Law. **Four Volumes.** New York, 1976. **$75.00**
Termed "a most important scientific work" and "a very creditable example of historical research" upon its publication, treating of neutrality from the 15th century through this century, with much on the Napoleanic period; *this the re-issue of the original 1935–36 edition.*

88. JOHNSON, Earl, Jr. Justice and Reform, The Formative Years of the OEO Legal Services Program. New York, 1974. **$17.50**
A review copy, with the publisher's slip laid in.

89. JONES, Gareth. History of the Law of Charity, 1532–1827. Cambridge, 1969. **$30.00**
Cambirdge Studies in English Legal History.

90. KAGAN, Richard L. Lawsuits and Litigants in Castile, 1500–1700. North Carolina, 1981. **New $23.00**
Studies in Legal History.

91. KAISER, Daniel H. The Growth of the Law in Medieval Russia. Princeton, 1980. **New $30.00**

92. KANTOROWICZ, Hermann. The Definition of Law. Cambridge, 1958. **$20.00**

93. KATZ, Jan and A.M. Capron. Catastrophic Diseases: Who Decides What? A Psychological and Legal Analysis of the Problems Posed by Hemodialysis and Organ Transplantation. Russell Sage, 1975. **$20.00**
With an unobtrusive stamp on the half-title.

94. KATZ, Milton. The Relevance of International Adjudication. Harvard, 1968. **$17.50**

95. KING, Willard L. Melville Weston Fuller, Chief Justice of the United States, 1888–1910. New York, 1950. **$17.50**

96. KORSTEN, F.J.M. Roger North (1651–1734), Virtuoso & Essayist. Amsterdam, 1981. **New $45.00**
The only modern biography of North, whose works provide unrivaled glimpses of 17th century law and legal training; 353 pages, sewn wraps.

97. KRAINES, Oscar. The World and Ideas of Ernst Freund: The Search for General Principals of Legislation and Administrative Law. Alabama, 1974. **$17.50**

98. LaFAVE, Wayne R. Arrest: The Decision to Take a Suspect into Custody. Little, Brown, 1965. **$25.00**
The Report of the American Bar Foundation's Survey of the Administration of Justice in the United States.

99. LAMBERT, Sheila. Bills & Acts, Legislative Procedure in Eighteenth-Century England. Cambridge, 1971. **$30.00**

100. LAMBTON, Ann K.S. State and Government in Medieval Islam, An Introduction to the Study of Islamic Political Theory: The Jurists. Oxford. 1981. **New $54.00**

101. LAUWAARS, R.H. Lawfulness and Legal Force of Community Decisions. Leiden, 1973. **$17.50**

The First and Only American Edition

102. LAWES, Edward. An Elementary Treatise on Pleading in Civil Actions. Portsmouth, 1808. **$125.00**
The first and only American edition of Lawes' first work, termed *"comprehensive and instructive"* upon its appearance; *quite a nice copy, in full, contemporary sheep,* a bit worn, the label gilt lined and lettered; occasional spotting throughout.

103. (LEGAL Philosophy). My Philosophy of Law, Credos of Sixteen American Scholars. Boston, 1941. **$45.00**
With essays by **Pound, Llewellyn, Fuller, Wigmore,** and many others.

104. LEPAWSKY, Albert. The Judicial System of Metropolitan Chicago. Chicago, 1932. **$25.00**

105. LITTLE, David. Religion, Order and Law, A Study in Pre-Revolutionary England. Harper & Row, 1969. **$15.00**
With much on John Calvin, the Puritans, and Sir Edward Coke.

106. LLEWELLYN, K.N. The Bramble Bush. Dobbs Ferry, 1978. **$15.00**

107. (LONDON). JOHN GREEN. The Priviledges of the Lord Mayor and the Aldermen of the City. London, 1722. Title Page; 6 leaves; 215 pages. 8vo. **$250.00**
This the re-issue of the first edition of 1707, *Green having been attorney in London's Mayor's-Court, with much on it and other local courts,* including the Court of Common Council, the Court of Aldermen, and the Court of Chancery, among many others. *An attractive copy, bound in full, contemporary, panelled calf,* worn, newly and quite nicely rebacked, the spine gilt-lined and lettered; the title page in a double woodcut border, a bit of lightish spotting and embrowning throughout, but generally a very clean and desirable copy.

108. LYTLE, Clifford M. The Warren Court and Its Critics. Arizona, 1968. **$17.50**
With a forward by John Frank.

109. MacDOWELL, Douglas M. The Law in Classical Athens, Cornell, 1978. **$22.50**

110. MacFARLANE, Alan. The Justice and The Mare's Ale, Law and Disorder in Seventeenth-Century England. Cambridge, 1981. **New $19.95**

111. McLEAISH, Donald C. The Laws of the State of Texas Affecting Church Property. Catholic University, 1960. **$25.00**
Canon Law Studies No. 405; 205 pages, sewn, printed wraps, a bit worn.

112. McCONNELL, W.H. Prairie Justice. Calgary, 1980. **New $30.00**
The first legal history of Saskatchewan.

113. (MADISON, James). ADRIENNE KOCH (ed.). Notes of Debates in the Federal Convention of 1787 Reported by James Madison. Ohio, 1976. **$17.50**
Valuable; the Hunt and Brown text of 1920, as read against Madison's manuscript in the Library of Congress.

An Early Issue of Magna Charta in Its Classic Form, with Both Parts

114. (MAGNA Carta). Magna Carta, cum statutis quae Antiqua vocantur. London, 1556. Title page; 7 leaves; 170 folios; 2 leaves; Title page (pt 2); folios 2–72. Beale S16 and S24b, S.T.C. 9278. 8vo. **$600.00**
Printed in 1556, with two other issues and *marking the last time Magna Carta was published as a text of the ancient statutes,* the issues thereafter including recent statutes as well, thereby approaching handbooks.
Bound in full, blind lined and decorated near-contemporary calf, rubbed, sometime rebacked, the spine gilt-lined and blind decorated, with a black label gilt-lined and lettered; some expert paper repairs to the first five and last two leaves, not affecting the text, save the last leaf, three words there just affected.
A very little bit of embrowning, particularly to the first leaves, throughout, but generally *quite a clean, attractive and desirable copy, with extensive annotations in a 16th century hand.*

115. MAITLAND, Frederic W. and Francis C. Montague. A Sketch of English Legal History. Putnam, 1915. **$35.00**
Primarily derived from the authors' contributions to Social England, with additions.

116. (MAITLAND, F.W.) HELEN M. CAM (ed.). Selected Historical Essays of F.W. Maitland. Cambridge, 1957. **$35.00**
The best of works selecting Maitland's writings, with Miss Cam's valuable introduction.

117. (MAITLAND, Frederic William). A. L. SMITH. Frederic William Maitland, Two Lectures and a Bibliography. Burt Franklin, 1971. **$15.00**
A re-issue of Smith's 1911 lectures; 71 pages, paper wraps.

118. (MAITLAND, F. W.) E. L. G. STONES (ed.). Letters to George Neilson. Glasgow, 1976. **$15.00**
A cache discovered too late to include in Fifoot's Maitland Letters; 76 pages, pictorial wraps, *scrupulously edited.*

119. MAKTARI, A.M.A. Water Rights and Irrigation Practices in Lahj, a Study of the Application of Customary and Shariah Law in South-West Arabia. Cambridge, 1971. **$25.00**

The First and Only Edition

120. MANBY, Thomas. An Exact Abridgement Of all the Statutes. London, 1674. Title Page; 19 leaves; 194 pages (irregular but complete); 12 leaves. New Wing E904; Cowley 166. 8vo. **$250.00**
A seldom-found work, covering the reigns of Charles I and II, from 1625 through 1673, and digesting the statutes alphabetically, in English, Cowley showing only the British Museum copy, and New Wing four copies with only the Library of Congress copy in this country.
Attractively and recently bound in ¾ calf over marbled boards, the spine gilt-lined and lettered; lightish staining to some leaves, a bit of embrowning, primarily to preliminaries, a very little bit of insignificant worming to the margins of a few leaves, not affecting the text, a small hole in b3 and a clean tear in B8 affecting a few letters of text, but not legibility.

121. MARSH, A.H. History of the Court of Chancery and of the Rise and Development of the Doctrines of Equity. Toronto, 1890. **$45.00**

122. MARSTON, Geoffrey. The Marginal Seabed in United Kingdom Legal Practice. Oxford, 1981. **New $55.00**
With Part 1 devoted to historical development.

123. MARTIN, Charles Trice. The Record Interpreter, A Collection of Abbreviations, Latin Words, and Names used in English Historical Manuscripts and Records. Dorking, 1976. **$25.00**
A standard reference work, long out of print, this a reissue of the 1910 second edition, with stock of the reissue itself (we are informed) running low. **Please do not miss the chance to obtain this valuable book.**

124. (MASSACHUSETTS). The Book of the General Lawes and Libertyes Concerning the Inhabitants of the Massachusetts. San Marino, 1975. **$15.00**
Reproduced in facsimile from the only surviving copy of the original 1648 edition at the Huntington Library, with a valuable introduction by Professor Barnes; 87 pages, printed wraps.

125. MILSOM, S.F.C. Historical Foundations of the Common Law. Second Edition. London, 1981. **New $63.25**
Perhaps the seminal work on English medieval legal history in this half-century, in a new edition; also available in paper at $24.00.

126. (MORE, Sir Thomas). J.A. GUY. The Public Career of Sir Thomas More. Yale, 1980. **New $22.50**
Highly praised as the most significant contribution to More's public (and legal) career yet published.

127. MORRIS, Thomas D. Free Men All, The Personal Liberty Laws of the North 1780–1861. Johns Hopkins, 1974. **$17.50**

128. (NEW York). HERBERT ALAN JOHNSON and RALPH K. ANDRIST. Historic Courthouses of New York State. Columbia, 1977. **$17.50**
With superb photographs by Milo V. Stewart.

The First Edition

129.(OATHS). RICHARD GARNET. The Book of Oaths, and the severall forms thereof, both Antient and Modern. London, 1649. Title Page; 5 leaves; 416 pages (irregular but complete). Wing G264. 12 mo. **$250.00**
A highly unusual collection, from the coronation oath to the oath for scavengers in London; a very clean copy, save staining to a few leaves, particularly the preliminary blanks, occasional black letter and woodcut decorations and initials, bound in contemporary double blind-ruled sheep, worn, newly and nicely rebacked, a red morocco label, gilt-lined and lettered.

130. O'BRIAN, John Lord. National Security and Individual Freedom. Harvard, 1955. **$20.00**
The 1955 Godkin Lectures at Harvard.

The First Edition

131. OLDFIELD, T.H.B. History of the Original Constitution of Parliaments. London, 1797. **$225.00**
Termed by Holdsworth a "keen advocate of Parliamentary reform", Oldfield did not live to see the great reforms of the 1830's, this one of his several works called, also by Holdsworth, the *"principal books written on Parliament"* of the preceding generation.
An extremely handsome copy, bound in full, contemporary calf, the covers elaborately gilt and blind-decorated, the spine gilt-lined, decorated and lettered, marbled edges and marbled endpapers.

132. OPPLER, Alfred C. Legal Reform in Occupied Japan. Princeton, 1976. **$15.00**

In Four Volumes

133. PARKER, Herbert. Courts and Lawyers of New England. American Historical Society, 1931. **$150.00**
A handsome set in the original light tan buckram, the spines with uniform red morocco labels, gilt-lined and lettered, a bit rubbed, *with a great many plates & photographs throughout.*

The First Edition in English

134. PERKINS, John. A Profitable Book . . . Treating of the Lawes of England. London, 1641. Title Page; 15 leaves; 388 pages (irregular but complete). Wing P1543. 8vo. **$375.00**
One of the most popular law books of the 1500's, running through 20 editions in Law French before this edition, the first in English and published in 1641; the only book that Holdsworth mentions with Littleton on the land law, conveyancing and other precedents.
A bit of lightish staining to a few leaves, else *an exceptionally clean and desirable copy, bound in a well-preserved, though unexciting, full, contemporary sheep,* a bit of rubbing to the joints, the covers and spine double blind-lined, with the spine unlettered and some expert repairs to its head.

135. PLESCIA, Joseph. The Oath and Perjury in Ancient Greece. Florida State, 1970. **$15.00**

136. (POLAND). W.J. WAGNER (ed.). Polish Law throughout the Ages, 1000 Years of Legal Thought in Poland. Hoover, 1976. **$35.00**

The First American Issue of the Second and Best Edition

137. POLLOCK, Sir Frederick and Frederic William Maitland. The History of English Law. Second Edition. **Two Volumes.** Boston, 1899. **$100.00**
The greatest modern work on English medieval legal history, primarily written by Maitland, still the source to which one must turn; this the second, and best, edition, issued four years after the first, in the original blue cloth, the spines gilt-lettered, a but rubbed, but still *quite imposing and desirable.*

138. POSNER, Richard A. The Economics of Justice. Harvard, 1981. **New $25.00**
Perhaps the most provocative and wide-ranging law book of this half century, auspiciously published on the centenery of Holmes' Common Law.

139. POUND, Roscoe. Contemporary Juristic Theory. Ward Ritchie, 1940. **$35.00**
Pound's lectures at Claremont in 1940.

140. PROVINE, Doris Marie. Case Selection in the United States Supreme Court. Chicago, 1980. **New $20.00**

141. QUINNEY, Richard. The Social Reality of Crime. Little, Brown, 1970. **$15.00**

142. RADIN, Max. The Lawful Pursuit of Gain. Riverside Press, 1931. **$45.00**
A presentation copy of Radin's Weinstock Lectures at the University of California in 1931; very nice.

The First American Edition of the First English Law Dictionary

143. RASTELL, John, Les Termes de la Ley. Portland, 1812. **$225.00**
First appearing in 1527, and actually preceding the appearance of the earliest English general dictionary,*Rastell's work had as long a life as any other English law book, passing through at least 29 editions* the last of which (excluding modern reprints) appeared in 1819, this the first American edition of 1812, in English, following the appearance of the first English edition by some 400 years.
An exceedingly attractive copy, bound in full, contemporary sheep, the spine with a red, morocco label, gilt-lined and lettered, and quite bright; a very little bit of spotting, but in general highly desirable.

144. REID, John Phillip. Law for the Elephant, Property and Social Behavior on the Overland Trail. Huntington Library, 1980. **New $18.50**

145. RICHARDSON, H.G. and G.O. Sayles. The English Parliament in the Middle Ages. Hambledon Press, 1981. **New $58.00**
The fruits of fifty years of collaboration between these great scholars; 26 essays with additional notes by Professor Sayles.

146. RIDER, Sidney S. Historical Research and Educational Labor Illustrated in the Work of Elisha Reynolds Potter, Late Judge of the Supreme Court of Rhode Island. Providence. 1901. **$35.00**
19 pages, stapled, printed wraps, a bit embrowned.

147. ROOT, Elihu. Experiments in Government and the Essentials of the Constitution. Princeton, 1913. **$35.00**
Root's 1913 Stafford Little Lectures; very nice in the original blue cloth, gilt.

148. ROSTOW, Eugene V. The Ideal in Law. Chicago, 1978. **$17.50**

An Early Edition of the Most Famous Work of English Equity

149. [St. GERMAIN, Christopher]. The dialoges in English, betwene a Doctour of divinitye, and a Student in the lawes of England. London, 1569. Title page; folios 2–177 (irregular but complete); 4 leaves. Beale T475, New S.T.C. 21572. 8vo. **$600.00**

The most enduring part of the literature occasioned by Sir Thomas More's promotion to the chancellorship in 1529, basing the chancellor's right to exercise jurisdiction (according to Professor Guy) on the application to English law of the Aristotelian principle of epikeia — **law leavened with conscience.**

A desirable copy bound in recent vellum, the title page in an elaborate decorated woodcut border [McKerrow 48], somewhat frayed and dusty, the inner margin strengthened, else quite clean and nicely margined, with many annotations in an early hand, printed in black letter throughout.

We also have in stock two later editions of Doctor and Student printed in the early 1600's, priced uniformly at $350, for which we invite your inquiries.

The First Edition

150. SELDEN, John. The Priviledges of the Baronage of England. Title Page; 2 leaves; 167 pages. London, 1642. Wing S2434. 8vo. **$250.00**

Written by Selden at the command of the House of Lords, and a valuable example of Selden's examination of Parliamentary and court records as bases for his writings.

An attractive copy, bound in full, speckled modern calf, the covers double blind-lined, a bit of unobtrusive rubbing and cracking to the joints, though very sound, the spine with a red morocco label, gilt-lined, decorated and lettered; the top margin cut a bit close, affecting some page numbers but not the text; in general, quite a clean, bright and desirable copy.

A Very Handsome Copy

151. SELDEN, John. Titles of Honor. Third Edition. London, 1672. Portrait; Title Page; 16 leaves; 756 pages. Wing S2440. Folio. **$250.00**

Termed Selden's "first work of any importance" by Sir Eric Fletcher, and praised by **Locke, Gibbon** and **Nicolson,** Selden's Titles was first published in 1614, this the third, and said to be the best, edition of 1672, *with Selden ranging far beyond England, to discuss titles in Rome, Greece, Eastern Europe, Russia, China and Islam.*

An extremely handsome copy, newly bound in ¾ speckled calf over marbled boards, the spine with a red morocco label, gilt-lined and lettered; exceedingly clean and crisp, with many attractive, woodcut figures throughout, *and the fine, full-page engraved portrait of Selden facing the title page.*

The Last 18th Century Edition

152. [SELDEN, John]. Seldeniana, or the Table-Talk of John Selden, Esq. London, [1797]. **$125.00**

The work for which Selden is best known, a remarkable collection, highly entertaining and instructive, culled by Selden's Boswell, Richard Milwood, over the last 20 years of Selden's life; *an attractive little copy, bound in full, contemporary tree calf,* the joints a bit rubbed, the spine elaborately gilt, with a black, morocco label, gilt-decorated and lettered, *and a very nice, full-page, frontspiece engraving of Selden.*

153. SHAPIRO, Martin. Courts, A Comparative and Political Analysis. Chicago, 1981. **New $20.00**

With chapters devoted to England, China, Islam and Western Europe.

154. SIEGAN, Bernard H. Economic Liberties and the Constitution. Chicago, 1980. **New $19.50**

155. SMITH, James Morton. Freedom's Fetters, the Alien and Sedition Laws and American Civil Liberties. Cornell, 1967. **$17.50**

The second printing , with a new preface.

A Pioneer Treatise in Comparative Law

156. SMITH, Sir Thomas. The Commonwealth of England. London, 1621. Title Page; 3 leaves; 134 pages. New S.T.C. 22864. 4to. **$250.00**

Written while Smith was Ambassador to France in the 1560's, and after he had been appointed first Regius Professor of Civil Law at Cambridge in 1540; first published in 1583, six years after Smith's death, of considerable interest, *Smith's disregard of notions of medieval law leading Professor Coquillette to term him the "English Humanist".*

Quite handsomely and newly bound in antique-style full mottled-calf, the covers double gilt-lined and decorated, the spine with a black, morocco label, gilt-decorated and lettered, a bit of insignificant worming to the upper margin, not affecting the text, the date of publication and part of the imprint shaved from the title page, a bit of lightish dampstaining, primarily marginal, throughout, else quite a clean and desirable copy, largely printed in black letter.

157. STAIR, James Viscount. The Institutions of the Law of Scotland. Yale, 1981. **New $74.50**

The first modern edition of the greatest work of Scots law, published on the tercentary of its first publication in 1681; edited by David M. Walker.

The First Edition of the Classic Tudor Work on The King's Prerogative

158. STANFORD, Sir William. An Exposicion of the Kinges Prerogative. First Edition. London, 1567. Title page; 4 leaves; 5–85 folios. Beale T491, New S.T.C. 23213. 8vo. **$750.00**

Termed by Professor Elton the "best opinion" whose "authority was still supreme . . . a half century later", Stanford's work first appeared in 1567, after Stanford's death, though written in 1548, *of considerable value in discounting notions of Tudor despotism, considering, as it does, the King's prerogative a part of the Common Law, and definable by statute.*

A very desirable copy, bound in full contemporary blind-lined calf, worn, expertly rebacked with much of the original spine laid down, the title page a bit dusty and with early ownership inscriptions, *this the Cashel Library copy, with its shelf markings in ink on the front pastedown.*

David Baker's Copy of the First Work on English Criminal Law

159. STANFORD, Sir William. London, 1567. Les Plees del coron. Title page; 13 leaves; 198 folios. Beale T488; New S.T.C. 23221. **$750.00**

The first work devoted exclusively to criminal law, or pleas of the crown, Stanford's arrangement of topics followed by later writers, among them Hale and Hawkins.

This the copy of David Baker, a Benedictine monk and member of Lincoln's Inn and the Middle Temple, remembered for his collections of ecclesiastical history, with his signature three times on the title page, and annotations in his and others' hands in the text.

A very attractive copy, bound in full, contemporary calf, the covers blind-lined and decorated, newly and well rebacked, the spine unlettered gilt and blind-lined and decorated, with five raised bands; bit of minor dampstaining, else a very clean, and desirable copy, the title page in an exquisite woodcut border [McKerrow 49].

160. STONE, Harlan F. Law and Its Administration. Columbia, 1924. **$35.00**

Stone's 1915 Hewitt Lectures at Columbia, while he was Dean; original maroon cloth, a bit chafed, gilt still bright.

161. (STONE, Harlan Fiske). ALFRED LIEF (ed.). Public Control of Business, Selected Opinions by Harlan Fiske Stone. New York, 1940. **$22.50**

Slightly worn.

The First Edition of Story's First Commentary

162. STORY, Joseph. Commentaries on the Law of Bailments. Cambridge, 1832. **$175.00**

Story's first Commentary, of which there were to be nine, and *the first fruits of Story's Dane professorship at Harvard, highly praised by Professor Dunne as "[s]uperbly organized, lucidly written, comprehensive in breadth, and accurate in research",* with much drawn from English common law, and with Story expressly attempting to compare civil law and the jurisprudence of the continent, including the works of Pothier and Domat.

Bound in full, contemporary sheep, well worn but sound, the spine with a red morocco label, double gilt lined and lettered, a bit of foxing, more pronounced to the preliminaries, else *very clean and desirable.*

163. (STORY, Joseph). JAMES McCLELLAN. Joseph Story and the American Constitution. Oklahoma, 1971. **$21.50**

164. STRYKER, Lloyd Paul. The Art of Advocacy. Zenger, 1979. **$19.50**

An attractive re-issue of the 1954 edition.

The First Book Ever Published on the Subject

165. SUGDEN, Edward. A Practical Treatise of the Law of Vendors & Purchasers of Estates. Fifth Edition. London, 1818. **$175.00**

The first significant work of Sugden, later Lord Chancellor, one which Sugden called "the foundation of my early success in life", Sugden himself called by Lord Cockburn *"the Nestor of the profession who has done more to teach the law and improve the law than any man of his age."*

An attractive copy, in full, contemporary calf, newly and well rebacked, the spine gilt-lined and decorated, with the original label, gilt-decorated and lettered, preserved.

166. (SUPREME Court). GEORGE L HASKINS and HERBERT A. JOHNSON. History of the Supreme Court of the United States. Volume II. MacMillan, 1981. **New $60.00**

The fourth volume of the Holmes Devise to appear, covering the first Marshall years, 1801–15; we would be pleased to take standing orders for this landmark set, and to order any of the three volumes already published, each at $60.00. Please write for details.

167. TAFT, Henry W. A Century and a Half at the New York Bar, being the Annals of a Law Firm and Sketches of Its Members. Privately printed, New York, 1938. **$35.00**

The firm of Cadwalader, Wickersham & Taft, *with the card of R. Keith Kane, a member of the firm at the book's writing, laid in,* slightly worn, in a worn box.

168. TAYLOR, Telford. Two Studies in Constitutional Interpretation; Search, Seizure and Surveillance, and Fair Trial and Free Press. Ohio State, 1969. **$15.00**

169. THOMAS, Seth. Some Speeches and a Thesis. Privately printed, 1955. **$25.00**

A presentation copy, the author a judge of the U.S. Court of Appeals for the Eighth Circuit.

170. THOMAS, Wayne H., Jr. Bail Reform in America. California, 1976. **$15.00**

171. TOURTOULON, Pierre de. Philosophy in the Development of Law. MacMillan, 1922. **$35.00**

With a preface by Morris R. Cohen. Modern Legal Philosophy Series. Vol XIII; somewhat worn.

172. TOUT, T.F. The Empire and the Papacy, 918–1273. London, 1909. **$20.00**

A bit worn.

173. (TROLLOPE, Anthony). CORAL LANSBURY. The Reasonable Man, Trollope's Legal Fiction. Princeton, 1981. **New $20.00**

174. (TROLLOPE, Anthony). WILLARD THORP. Trollope's America. and HENRY S. DRINKER. The Lawyers of Anthony Trollope. New York, 1950. **$45.00**

Two addresses delivered to the Grolier Club; *limited to 750 copies,* printed in the Netherlands, 47 pages, gray boards, with a paper label on the front cover; *quite nice.*

175. TUSHNET, Mark. The American Law of Slavery, 1810–1860. Princeton, 1981. **New $25.00**

176. (ULLMANN, Walter). BRIAN TIERNEY and PETER LINEHAN (EDS.). Authority and Power, Studies on Medieval Law and Government Presented to Walter Ullman on his Seventieth Birthday. Cambridge, 1981. **New $59.50**

177. VINOGRADOFF, Paul. The Growth of the Manor. Second, revised edition. London, 1911. **$35.00**

Slightly worn.

Dedicated to the Future King George II

178. (WALES). SIR JOHN DODDERIDGE. An Historical Account of the Ancient and Modern State of the Principality of Wales. Second Edition. London, 1714. Title page; 7 leaves; 147 pages. 8vo. **$225.00**

Dodderidge's account of Wales, which may have gained him the appointment as serjeant to Prince Henry in the early 1600's, this the second edition issued in 1714, coincident upon the reconcilliation of King George I and his son, the future King George II, upon the latter's creation as Prince of Wales.

An attractive copy, bound in recent, dark-brown, ¼ calf, the spine blind-decorated, and the label gilt-lined, decorated and lettered, a bit of light spotting and embrowning, but generally quite nice.

179. WARE, Gilbert (ed.). From the Black Bar, Voices for Equal Justice. Putnam, 1976. **$15.00**

180. WARE, Judge Wallace L. The Unforgettables. Hertford, 1964. **$12.50**

181. (WARREN, Earl). HENRY M. CHRISTIAN (ed.). The Public Papers of Chief Justice Earl Warren. Simon & Schuster, 1959. **$15.00**

182. WARSDOFF, Louis A. Equality and the Law. Liveright, 1938. **$20.00**

183. WASSERSTROM, Richard A. The Judicial Decision, Toward a Theory of Legal Justification. Stanford, 1961. **$15.00**

184. (WATERGATE). Submission of Recorded Presidential Conversations To the Committee on the Judiciary . . . by President Richard Nixon, April 30, 1974. Washington, 1974. **$25.00**

1308 pages, double-spaced typescript, printed wraps, slightly worn.

185. (WEBSTER, Daniel). MAURICE G. BAXTER. Daniel Webster & the Supreme Court. Massachusetts, 1966. **$17.50**

186. WESTIN, Alan F. Privacy and Freedom. Atheneum, 1967 **$15.00**

187. WESTIN, Alan F. et al. Databanks in a Free Society, Computers, Record-Keeping and Privacy. Quadrangle, 1972. **$15.00**

188. WESTON, Corinne Comstock and Janelle Renfrow Greenberg. Subjects and Sovereigns, The Grand Controversy over Legal Sovereignty in Stuart England. Cambridge, 1981. **New $39.50**

189. WESTPHAL, Albert C.F. The House Committee on Foreign Affairs. Columbia, 1942. **$35.00**

A presentation copy to Senator Tom Connolly of Texas; Columbia Studies in History, Economics and Public Law, Number 493.

190. WHEARE, K.C. The Statute of Westminster and Dominion Status. Third Edition. Oxford, 1947. **$20.00**

191. WHITEBREAD, Charles H. (ed.). Mass Production Justice and the Constitutional Ideal. Charlottesville, 1970. **$10.00**

Virginia Legal Studies.

192. WHITLOCK, F.A. Criminal Responsibility and Mental Illness. London, 1963. **$12.50**

RARE AND SCHOLARLY

BOOKS ON THE LAW
(1982)

William O. Douglas
1898 — 1980

"In these early years I met six seminal forces in the law who shaped my life . . . [one of whom was] Louis Brandeis . . ." (William O. Douglas. Go East, Young Man 179-80)(See items 27, 60-70, and 91, and inside front cover).

CATALOGUE SEVEN

MEYER BOSWELL BOOKS
SAN FRANCISCO

1. ARNOLD, Morris S., et al (eds.). On the Laws and Customs of England, Essays in Honor of Samuel E. Thorne. North Carolina, 1981. **$25.00**

Studies in Legal History.

2. (AUCTION Catalogue). Catalogue of Printed Books Including Law Books. London, 1974. **$15.00**

The sale at Sotheby's on December 12, 1974, *with 91 lots devoted to legal works;* prices realized provided.

3. (BACON, Francis). JOEL J. EPSTEIN. Francis Bacon, A Political Biography. Athens, Ohio, 1977. **$15.00**

With chapters on Bacon as Attorney General and Lord Chancellor.

Attributed to Selden

4. BACON, Nathaniel. An Historical and Political Discourse of the Laws & Government of England. London, 1689. 2 blanks; leaf; Title Page (1689); Title Page (1682); 7 leaves; 203 pages; Title Page (Part 2) (1682); leaf; 188 pages; 3 leaves; 2 blanks. Wing S2428; Folio in 4's. **$375.00**

The foremost work of Nathaniel Bacon, Francis Bacon's half-brother, called the work "to which he owes his reputation," *tracing the history of English political and legal institutions (both civil & ecclesiastical) from the earliest times through the reign of Queen Elizabeth,* hostile to Stuart claims of royal prerogative, the work first appearing in 1647, suppressed in 1665, its printer prosecuted in 1676, this a re-issue of the suppressed 1665 edition with new title pages, attributed (doubtfully) to manuscript notes of John Selden, based upon a statement said to have been made by Chief Justice Vaughan, one of Selden's executors, in the preface to this edition.

Quite an attractive copy; occasional spotting and embrowning, very minor dampstaining to the upper margin of some leaves, not affecting the text; bound in full, contemporary, speckled calf, worn, gilt designs on both covers, newly rebacked, the spine elaborately gilt-decorated, ruled and lettered, this the copy of a descendant of philanthropist August Heckscher, with his book sticker and the presentation plate to him on the front pastedown.

5. (BACON, Nicholas). ROBERT TITTLER. Nicholas Bacon, The Making of a Tudor Statesman. Athens, Ohio, 1976. **$15.00**

The first modern biography of Francis Bacon's father, with chapters on Bacon at Gray's Inn, as a young lawyer, and as attorney of the Court of Wards and Liveries.

Edward Boswell's Copy

6. [BECCARIA, Cesare]. An Essay on Crimes and Punishments. Edinburgh, 1788. **$150.00**

One of the most influential treatises on penal reform ever written, first appearing in Italian in 1764 and eventually translated into 22 languages, subsequently of importance in England through the efforts of Blackstone, John Howard, and others, this the fourth printing to appear in Scotland.

Minor tears to the margins of a few leaves, tears to two other leaves expertly repaired, *else an exceedingly clean and crisp copy, bound in full, contemporary calf, quite worn, very neatly rebacked,* the spine blind-ruled and the original label, gilt-decorated and lettered, a bit chipped, preserved. *An attractive copy.*

This once the copy of Edward Boswell, early 19th century solicitor & antiquary, with his bookplate.

7. (BENTHAM, Jeremy). CHARLES M. ATKINSON. Jeremy Bentham, His Life and Work. New York, 1969. **$17.50**

A reissue of the first edition of 1905.

8. (BENTHAM, Jeremy). L.J. HUME. Bentham and Bureaucracy. Cambridge, 1981. **$49.50**

With much on Bentham's *Comment* on Blackstone's Commentaries, his *Constitutional Code,* and other of his works on law and jurisprudence.

9. (BENTHAM, Jeremy). A.T. MILNE (ed.). The Correspondence of Jeremy Bentham, Volume 5, 1788-1797. London, 1981. **$84.00**

Superbly edited; the seventh volume in the Collected Works of Jeremy Bentham, begun in 1968; we would be pleased to provide further information. Orders for past & future volumes gladly taken.

10. BERNIER, Ivan. International Legal Aspects of Federalism. Archon, 1973. **$15.00**

11. (BIBLIOGRAPHY). THOMAS R. ADAMS. The American Controversy, A Bibliographical Study of the British Pamphlets About the American Disputes, 1764-1783. Two volumes. Providence, 1980. **$80.00**

A highly valuable work, in preparation for twenty years, with 1400 titles in about 2350 editions or issues, fully described, often annotated, and designed to include all pamphlets published in Great Britain bearing on the disputes in the British colonies in America, *including Canada and the West Indies.*

12. (BIBLIOGRAPHY). THOMAS R. ADAMS. American Independence, The Growth of an Idea, A Bibliographical Study of the American Political Pamphlets Printed Between 1764 and 1776 Dealing with the Dispute Between Great Britain and Her Colonies. Austin & New Haven, 1980. **$35.00**

A re-issue of the 1965 edition, a companion to the preceding item, *of considerable value,* encompassing works printed in this country.

Complete in Nine Volumes

13. (BIBLIOGRAPHY). JACQUES-CHARLES BRUNET. Manuel du Libraire et de l'Amateur de Livres. Nine Volumes. Copenhagan, 1966-68. **$300.00**

Perhaps the best-known and most comprehensive of all 19th century bibliographies, still widely cited, covering all subject matters and most of the western world, *with over 1,000 legal subject matter entries alone,* including significant sections on legal philosophy, international law, and Roman and canon law; this a reissue of the fifth (the last and best) edition, complete with the three supplementary volumes; in French.

14. (BIBLIOGRAPHY). PIERCE W. GAINES. William Cobbett and the United States, 1792-1835, A Bibliography with Notes and Extracts. Worcester, 1971. **$25.00**

15. (BIBLIOGRAPHY). WILLARD D. HUNSBERGER. Clarence Darrow: A Bibliography. Scarecrow, 1981 **$22.50**

16. (BIBLIOGRAPHY). Law Books, 1876-1981. Four Volumes. Bowker, 1981. **$375.00**

Of considerable value; over 5,000 pages, quadruple-columned, arranged by subject matter, cross-indexed by author and title, with some 130,000 entries.

17. (BIBLIOGRAPHY). THOMAS M. McDADE. The Annals of Murder, A Bibliography of Books and Pamphlets on American Murders from Colonial Times to 1900. Oklahoma, 1961. **$40.00**

1126 items, with full collations, extensive commentary, well-indexed; *highly desirable.*

18. (BIBLIOGRAPHY). ROBERT B. WINANS. A Descriptive Checklist of Book Catalogues Separately Printed in America, 1693-1800. Worcester, 1981. **$35.00**

A fine work, the first attempt to describe all separately printed book catalogues in this country to 1800, with almost 300 fully described, *including over 80 catalogues partly or entirely legal.*

An Unrecorded Variant of the First and Only Edition?

19. [BIRD, William]. A Treatise of the Nobilitie of the Realme, Collected out of the Body of Common Law. London, 1642. Title Page; leaf; 157 pages. New Wing B2956 (variant?); 8vo. **$200.00**

A short, elementary treatise on barons and baronies, their rights and privileges, with three chapters devoted to women, and consideration of the proper descent of the estates of Bergavenny in the 13th century; an apparent variant of New Wing B2956, the author's name not found on the title page and the imprint differing from that recorded.

A bit of very lightish dampstaining throughout, the title page a bit chipped and dusty, the last blank torn away, else *an exceedingly clean copy, bound in full, contemporary sheep,* quite worn, the covers and spine double blind-ruled, some repairs effected to the head and tail of the spine and to the joints.

20. BLACK, Charles L., Jr. Structure and Relationship in Constitutional Law. Baton Rouge, 1969. **$15.00**

The 1968 *Edward Douglass White Lectures* at Louisiana State.

The First University Law Lectures

21. BLACKSTONE, Sir William. An Analysis of the Laws of England. Fifth Edition. Oxford, 1762. Blank; Title Page; [iii]-lxxvii pages; Half-title; 2 leaves; 189 pages; 7 leaves. Eller 221; 8vo. **$350.00**

The syllabus for Blackstone's lectures at Oxford, *the first ever given on English law at a university, and ultimately the lectures given by Blackstone as the first Vinerian professor of law at Oxford,* which even Bentham conceded were popular, this the first and only edition to have the postscript concerning Blackstone's Vinerian professorship.

A highly desirable copy, a bit of occasional spotting, but in general quite clean, bound in full contemporary calf, a little worn, newly rebacked, the original spine, elaborately gilt, expertly laid down, the original crimson morocco label, double gilt-ruled and lettered, and the original marbled endpapers, preserved.

The Only Edition by John Taylor Coleridge

22. BLACKSTONE, Sir William. Commentaries on the Laws of England. Four Volumes. Sixteenth Edition. London, 1825. Eller 34; 8vo. **$375.00**

An attractive early 19th century edition of Blackstone, wherein, according to Lord Mansfield, one "may imbibe imperceptibly the first principles on which our excellent laws are founded."

This the only edition undertaken by John Taylor Coleridge, Middle Temple barrister, nephew of Samuel Taylor Coleridge, and later justice of the King's Bench.

A desirable set, in four volumes, a bit of spotting throughout, moreso to the frontispiece portrait in volume 1, with some attendant offsetting to the title page, and to the two folding tables, one neatly repaired with a bit of loss, else quite clean, newly and uniformly bound in ¼ calf over grey boards, the spines with contrasting crimson and black labels, double gilt-ruled and lettered.

The First Edition in Facsimile

23. BLACKSTONE, Sir William. Commentaries on the Laws of England. Four Volumes. Chicago 1979. **$100.00**

The most renowned of all works on English law, this the first edition of 1765-69 reproduced in facsimile, with separate, brief scholarly introductions to each volume; also available in paper at $48.00.

24. BLOOMFIELD, Maxwell. American Lawyers in a Changing Society, 1776-1876. Harvard, 1976. **$17.50**

Studies in Legal History.

25. (BOOKSELLERS). International Directory of Antiquarian Booksellers. Copenhagen, 1980. **$24.00**

Prepared by the International League of Antiquarian Booksellers; *the only handy, one volume work of its kind,* arranged geographically, cross-referenced alphabetically and by subject matter, with over 700 pages and 2,000 booksellers listed.

26. BOYLE, Leonard E. Pastoral Care, Clerical Education and Canon Law, 1200-1400. London, 1981. **$44.00**

To Mrs. Brandeis from Justice Roberts

27. (BRANDEIS, Louis D.). Autograph letter signed, Owen J. Roberts to Mrs. Louis D. Brandeis, [October 6, 1941(?)]. **$200.00**

On Supreme Court letterhead, two pages entirely in Justice Roberts' hand, with his full signature; to Mrs. Brandeis, a letter of condolence upon the death of Justice Brandeis, dated "Monday", presumably October 6, 1941, Brandeis having died on Sunday, October 5.

Justice Roberts paying tribute to Brandeis' "great and noble spirit" and expressing his gratitude for "what he generously gave me . . ." with notations suggesting a reply. *In very nice condition.*

28. (BRANDEIS and Frankfurter). BRUCE ALLEN MURPHY. The Brandeis/Frankfurter Connection, The Secret Political Activities of Two Supreme Court Justices. Oxford, 1982. **$18.95**

Justice Brandeis' Copy

29. (BRANDEIS, Louis D.) Proceedings at the Ceremonies in Commemoration of the One Hundred and Fiftieth Anniversary of the First Meeting of the Supreme Court of the United States. Washington, 1940. **$250.00**

64 pages, stapled self-wraps, one fold, a very little bit of wear, but in quite good condition.

Justice Brandeis's copy, with his bold, full signature, in ink, on the front wrap.

Justice Brandeis had retired from the Court the preceding year.

30. BRINKHORST, L.J. and J.D.B. Mitchell. European Law and Institutions. Edinburgh, [1968?]. **$10.00**

Sewn, printed wraps.

An Exceptionally Well-Preserved Copy of a Great English Law Book

31. [BRITTON, John le]. Britton [on the Laws of England]. Second Edition. London, 1640. 2 Blanks; Title Page; 15 leaves; 287 folios (irregular but complete); 21 leaves. S.T.C. 3804; 8vo. **$400.00**

One of the most famous of all English law books, most probably written in 1291-1292, and *unique among English legal treatises, appearing as it does to have been promulgated by the authority of the sovereign, then King Edward I.*

This the second edition of Britton, edited by Edmund Wingate, and published exactly 100 years after the first edition (in 1540), which itself was "exceeding full of manifest imperfections," including omission of an entire chapter, Wingate supplying this chapter and other emendations in an Appendix.

The foremargins of two leaves a bit trimmed, not affecting the text, *else an exceedingly clean and fresh copy, bound in full, contemporary calf,* a bit rubbed, the covers in a triple blind-ruled border, the spine unlettered and double blind-ruled, with four raised bands.

A particularly attractive example of a representative mid-17th century law binding.

32. BROWNING, Reed. Political and Constitutional Ideas of the Court Whigs. Lousiana State, 1982. **$32.50**

With a chapter devoted to Lord Hardwicke.

33. BUCKLAND, W.W. A Text-Book of Roman Law from Augustus to Justinian. Cambridge, 1975. **$59.50**

Perhaps the best introduction (together with item 101) *to the law of the Roman Empire.* This the last and best edition, revised by Peter Stein.

34. BUTLER, Benjamin F. Outline of the Constitutional History of New York. New York, 1848. **$48.00**

One of seven essays in the Collections of the New-York Historical Society, Second Series, Volume II, Part 1 *Butler Attorney General under Andrew Jackson, and U.S. Attorney for the Southern District of New York,* his essay the anniversary address before the Society, covering the years 1614 to 1846; in the original printed wraps, uncut, the covers somewhat dusty.

35. CAHN, Edmond. Confronting Injustice. London, 1967. **$25.00**

With a foreword by Justice Hugo L. Black.

36. CALABRESI, Guido. A Common Law for the Age of Statutes. Harvard, 1982. **$25.00**

The 1977 *Oliver Wendell Holmes Lectures* at Harvard.

37. (CANON Law). J.F. von SCHULTE. Die Geschichte der Quellen und Literatur des canonischen Rechts von Gratian bis auf die Gegenwart. Graz, Austria, 1956. **$125.00**

Still the most useful reference work on medieval canon law, with almost 2500 biographical sketches and at least 7500 bibliographical entries, ranging from the early 12th century to 1879. Three volumes bound in two; in German.

One of 20 Copies

38. (CARDOZO, Benjamin N.). A.L. SAINER (ed.). Law is Justice, Notable Opinions of Mr. Justice Cardozo. New York, 1938. **$225.00**

One of only twenty copies, of which this is number 8, a special deluxe issue by the publisher, *bound in full, dark ¾ blue morocco, a bit worn, over marbled boards, the spine gilt in compartments,* and gilt-lettered, the top edge gilt, marbled endpapers.

39. CAREY, John A. Judicial Reform in France before the Revolution of 1789. Harvard, 1981. **$22.50**

40. CHENEY, C.R. The Papacy and England, 12th-14th Centuries, Historical and Legal Studies. London, 1982. **$48.00**

41. (CHINA). CHING-HSI PERNG. Double Jeopardy: A Critique of Seven Yuan Courtroom Dramas. Ann Arbor, 1978. **$15.00**

Highly interesting, analysing all seven (of 161 surviving) plays centering on "judgment reversal" (the second trial's result reversing the first) from the Yuan Dynasty (1260-1368); printed wraps.

42. CHIU, Hungdah. The People's Republic of China and the Law of Treaties. Harvard, 1972. **$15.00**

Harvard Studies in East Asian Law, Volume 5.

The First Edition of Coke's Entries

43. [COKE, Sir Edward]. A Booke of Entries. First Edition. London, 1614. Title Page; 8 leaves; 713 folios (irregular but complete); blank; 9 leaves. New S.T.C. (draft) 5488; Folio. **$600.00**

The only work of Coke which Holdsworth groups in importance with Coke's Reports and Coke on Littleton (and which Holdsworth notes is one of 13 books recorded on Coke's tombstone, with the 11 books of his Reports and Coke on Littleton —"duodecim liberorum, tredecim librorum pater"), *a massive volume containing a vast number of precedents,* this the first edition of 1614, appearing eight years after Coke had become Chief Justice of the Common Pleas, thus embodying his experience both at the bar and on the bench.

The title page backed and repaired, two early ownership inscriptions crossed out, a bit of fraying and wear to the margins of the first and last leaves, some embrowning throughout, a bit of occasional lightish dampstaining essentially marginal, and a bit of insignificant worming to the foremargin of the latter part of the volume, *else quite a clean, tall and imposing folio, newly bound in full dark calf,* the covers blind-ruled and the spine unlettered, with five raised bands, ruled in blind.

Several Early Parts of Coke's Reports

44. COKE, Sir Edward. Le Quart [Quinta and Size] Part[s] des Reportes del Edwarde Coke. London, 1610, 1612 & 1607. Blank; Title Page (pt 4); 9 leaves; 128 folios; Title Page (pt 5); 41 folios; blank; Title Page (pt 5 #2); 6 leaves; 127 folios; leaf; blank; Title Page (pt 6); 8 leaves; 80 folios; leaf; 2 blanks. New S.T.C. (draft) 5503, 5507 & 5509; Folio. **$700.00**

The most famous of all law reports, referred to simply as "The Reports", published in 13 separate parts, the first 11 during Coke's lifetime, beginning during the first decade of the 1600's; their importance leading Winfield to say that "even at the present day where any point in the history of the law is involved . . . counsel . . . will almost invariably begin with Coke's Reports or his Institutes."

These the fourth, fifth and sixth parts, all early editions, including the first edition of part 6, both title pages of part 5, and the New S.T.C., in draft, showing but two copies of part 4, at Harvard and the Huntington Library.

The title page of part 4 and the next several leaves dampstained, occasional dampstaining, essentially marginal, elsewhere, a few marginal tears, just affecting the text (but not legibility) in two instances, some insignificant worming to part 6; *despite the foregoing, overall a very clean and crisp copy,* the three parts bound in one volume, in full contemporary calf, worn, the initials "W S" in gilt on both covers, newly rebacked, the spine with five raised bands, blind-ruled, and unlettered.

The First and Only Edition

45. COKE, Sir Edward. Three Law Tracts. London, 1764. Portrait; Title Page; [iii]-xii pages; Title Page (Copyholder); leaf; 364 pages; 2 leaves 8vo. **$375.00**

A valuable assemblage of three of Coke's minor works, including his reading on the Statute of levying fines, his treatise on bail and mainprize, and his Complete Copyholder.

The first of interest as the only reading of Coke's to have survived in print, the second termed by Holdsworth "useful," setting out the law "clearly and succinctly," and the third perhaps the most important, Plucknett crediting Coke with taking up "the cause of the copyholders, and finally extending to them the protection of the common law courts."

With the additional inclusion of the Old Tenures, written during the reign of Edward III, and William Hawkins' notes on Coke on Littleton.

A bit of occasional spotting, moreso to preliminaries, and a bit of chipping and fraying to the same leaves, but essentially *quite a clean copy, rather nicely rebound in ¾ calf over marbled boards*, the spine double gilt-ruled, with matching red leather labels, double gilt-ruled and lettered.

The First and Only 17th Century Abridgment of Coke on Littleton

46. (COKE, Sir Edward). SIR HUMPHREY DAVENPORT. Synopsis or, An Exact Abridgement of The Lord Cokes Commentaries upon Littleton. Portrait (Littleton); Portrait (Coke); Title Page; 2 leaves; 465 pages (irregular but complete); 15 leaves. New Wing C4958; 8vo. **$400.00**

Coke's greatest work, and, according to Holdsworth, one of the five great books on English law, Coke's Commentary on Littleton (the first part of his Institutes) was notoriously difficult, leading Daniel Webster to say "I read [it] through, without understanding a quarter part of it," perhaps indicating others' reaction, and the cause of this, its *first abridgment or synopsis.*

This the second edition of the *sole work of Sir Humphrey Davenport, judge of the Court of Common Pleas and president of the Court of Exchequer* in the 1630's, the first edition appearing the year before under a different title.

A bit of very lightish spotting and embrowning throughout, a number of annotations in an early hand, a few top margins cut close, just affecting some headnotes but not legibility, else *quite a clean copy, bound in full, contemporary, dark calf,* very worn, the covers double blind-ruled, sometime rebacked, the remains of the unlettered, original spine laid down, a very little bit of cracking to the front joint. *Altogether a sound, desirable copy, in a modest contemporary binding,* with two impressive, full page frontispiece portraits, one of Coke and the other of Littleton.

The First and Only Edition of the First Abridgment of Coke's Reports

47. (COKE, Sir Edward) EDWARD TROTMAN. Haec Epitome Undecim Librorum Relationum . . . Edwardi Coke. London 1640. Title Page; 4 leaves; 578 pages. S.T.C. 5527; 8vo. **$350.00**

Together with Coke's Institutes, called by Holdsworth *"[b]y far the most important of [Coke's] works,"* and by Plucknett as "the easiest way of finding medieaval authority," Coke's Reports eventually appeared in 13 parts, 11 of which were printed in his lifetime.

This the first of several "epitomes," or abridgments, of the enormous corpus of the Reports, Trotman's first work, in Law French, the cases arranged in the same order as they appeared in the Reports, with a valuable alphabetical table of cases added.

The title page a bit dusty, and some lightish embrowning throughout, else *quite a good copy, recently and pleasantly rebound in a ½ brown morocco,* the spine double gilt-ruled and lettered, with a black leather label, similarly gilt.

The Short Title Catalogue showing only the Huntington Library copy in this country.

Part of the Basic Documentation of American Architecture, With Approximately 8500 Visual Documents, on Microfiche

48. (COUNTY Courthouses). The County County Court Houses of America. Two Volumes. Princeton, 1982. **$550.00**

Published in Association with The Dunlap Society Visual Archive of American Art, and drawing on the historic picture files of the Library of Congress, among other sources, arranged alphabetically by state, with 179 fiche, and over 1800 courthouses. Each volume may be ordered separately, at $275.00; further information gladly provided.

49. COX, Archibald. The Role of the Supreme Court in American Government. Oxford, 1976. **$17.50**

Based on the *1974-75 Chichele Lectures* given at All Souls College, Oxford.

The Attempted Reformation of the Canon Law for the Church of England.

50. [CRANMER, Thomas]. Reformatio Legum Ecclesiasticarum. London, 1640. Title Page; 7 leaves; 303 pages; blank. S.T.C. 6007; 8vo. **$350.00**

Ultimately Archibishop of Canterbury, and confidant of Henry VII, Cranmer began this, termed *"his last great undertaking,"* during Henry's lifetime, but it remained incomplete at his death, and was never enacted, Cranmer seeking to reform the Canon law for the Church of England; first printed in 1571, sixteen years after his death; *this the second edition of 1640.*

An attractively printed work, the text surrounded by woodcut rules, with woodcut initials and decorations found throughout; some lightish dampstaining, primarily to the upper margin, occasional embrowning, the title page a bit dusty, but altogether *a desirable and well-preserved copy, nicely and newly bound in full, dark calf,* the covers double blind-ruled, the spine with a brown morocco label, double gilt-ruled and lettered.

With the signature of John Lightfoot, (Vice-Chancellor of Cambridge University and Biblical scholar), dated 1640, on the title page.

51. CUTTLER, S.H. The Law of Treason and Treason Trials in Later Medieval France. Cambridge, 1981. **$47.50**

52. DAINOW, Joseph (ed.). Essays on the Civil Law of Obligations. Baton Rouge, 1969. **$17.50**

The *1968 Bailey Lectures* at Louisiana State.

53. DAINOW, Joseph (ed.). The Role of Judicial Decisions and Doctrine in Civil Law and in Mixed Jurisdictions. Lousiana State, 1974. **$22.50**

to Congress which lead to changes in both the revised bankruptcy act and the Trust Indenture Act.

See also the inside front cover for further discussion of this item and Justices Douglas & Brandeis.

The Original Manuscript of Justice Douglas' Essay on Vietnam

63. DOUGLAS, WILLIAM O. Dark Days in Indo-China. [Washington], October 27, 1952. **$750.00**

The original manuscript *consisting of 16 pages, approximately 4,000 words, in double-spaced typescript, signed in full by Justice Douglas,* apparently used by the editors as copy, with changes throughout, accompanied by an unmarked carbon copy of the manuscript, also signed by Douglas and three letters, each on Justice Douglas' Court stationery, from his chambers, each one-page typewritten, concerning the manuscript and authorizing the changes, addressed to the editors, *and each signed by Douglas* (two in full and one by initials), dated October 27, October 28 and November 1, 1952, respectively.

Douglas' prescient analysis of Vietnam, based on his visit there the preceding summer, well over a decade before this country's full-scale involvement, subsequently appearing as one of five articles written by Douglas for Look Magazine in the fall of 1952, this essay appearing in the December 16 issue, under the title "Indo-China Near Disaster," condensed in the March, 1953 issue of Reader's Digest (as "Indo-China: A House Divided"), *and ultimately becoming a chapter in Douglas' book "North from Malaya, Adventures on Five Fronts," published by Doubleday in 1953, the succeeding year.*

Of considerable interest, Douglas most likely the most prolific writer to sit on the Supreme Court, with over 30 books to his credit, this the result of what one observer called Douglas' "travel books with a conscience," *through which Douglas "reached millions around the world and exposed them to his foreign policy ideas."*

Also of interest as Douglas' sole writing on Vietnam to have been preserved in book form, and, conceivably, of importance and bearing upon Douglas' political ambitions for the Presidency, the trip having been taken shortly before the Democratic Convention of 1952, ending in Korea, after the formation of the Independent Voters for Douglas committee.

64. DOUGLAS, WILLIAM O. Go East, Young Man, The Early Years, The Autobiography of William O. Douglas. New York, 1974. **$50.00**

A presentation copy of the first part of Justice Douglas' autobiography, with his full signature, and the presentation in his hand on the first free endpaper.

65. DOUGLAS, WILLIAM O. The Right of the People. New York, 1958. **$27.50**

In substantial part, Justice Douglas' 1957 North Lectures, delivered at Franklin and Marshall.

66. DOUGLAS, William. Strange Lands and Friendly People. New York, 1951. **$17.50**

First edition; covers somewhat marked.

67. DOUGLAS, William O. We the Judges, Studies in American and Indian Constitutional Law from Marshall to Mukherjea. Doubleday, 1956. **$45.00**

Justice Douglas' 1955 Tagore Lectures; a bit worn.

68. (DOUGLAS, William O.). VERN COUNTRYMAN (ed.). Douglas of the Supreme Court, A Selection of His Opinions. Doubleday, 1959. **$30.00**

With a biographical sketch by Professor Countryman.

69. (DOUGLAS, William O.). VERN COUNTRYMAN. The Judicial Record of Justice William O. Douglas. Harvard, 1975. **$15.00**

70. (DOUGLAS, William O.). Tributes to Honorable William O. Douglas. Washington, 1976. **$35.00**

Occasioned by Douglas' retirement from the Court in November 1975; original maroon cloth, gilt-lettered.

71. DUFF, E. Gordon. Early English Printing, A Series of Facsimiles of All the Types Used in England During the XVth Century. New York, 1976. **$25.00**

Re-issue of the 1896 edition, *with much on the early legal printers,* including Pynson and Lettou and Machlinia: with 40 plates reproduced, one from the 1482 edition of Littleton's Tenures, the first printed English law book.

72. DUGGAN, Charles. Canon Law in Medieval England; the Becket Dispute and Decretal Collections. London, 1982. **$48.00**

73. EMERSON, THOMAS I. Toward A General Theory of the First Amendment. New York, 1966. **$20.00**

74. FEENSTRA, R. and C.J.D. Wall. Seventeenth-Century Leyden Law Professors and Their Influence on the Development of the Civil Law, A Study of Bronchorst, Vinnius and Voet. Amsterdam, 1975. **$30.00**

124 pages, printed, sewn wraps.

Not in the Harvard Law Catalogue

54. DALRYMPLE, John. An Essay Towards a General History of Feudal Property in Great Britain. Second Edition. London, 1758. Title Page; [iii]-x pages; leaf; 276 pages. 8vo. **$175.00**

Written with a view to promoting the unification of English and Scots law, yet far more ambitious, *ultimately seeking, according to Professor Stein, "to trace the progress of the land laws of England and of Scotland, as far as they had a feudal origin,"* and "[t]he earliest published work to mention the four stages of society [hunting, herding, farming and commerce] based on modes of subsistence."

An immediately popular work, going through at least four editions within two years; an attractive copy, a bit of embrowning throughout, else quite clean, *newly bound in a ¼ vellum over marbled boards; quite nice.*

55. DAUBE, David. Civil Disobedience in Antiquity. Edinburgh, 1972. **$20.00**

A Highly Important Work, Just Completed

56. DAVIES, K.G. (ed.). Documents of the American Revolution, 1770-83. Twenty-one volumes. Dublin, 1972-81. **$1120.00**

Very highly praised, called "magnificent," "splendid," and "comprehensive," just completed in 21 volumes, providing a chronological calendaring and brief description of every letter surviving in the Colonial Record Office, amounting to some 28,000 documents, in volumes 1-7, with over 1800 printed in extenso in the remaining 14 volumes; with Professor Davies' valuable introductions to each volume. *Further details gladly provided.*

57. (DICEY, Albert V.). RICHARD A. COSGROVE. The Rule of Law, Albert Venn Dicey, Victorian Jurist. North Carolina, 1980. **$22.50**

Studies in Legal History.

The First Edition of the First Dictionary of Law French

58. (DICTIONARY). F.O. The Law-French Dictionary Alphabetically Digested . . . to which is added, the Law-Latin Dictionary. London, 1701. 2 blanks; Title Page; leaf; 150 unnumbered leaves; Title Page (Latin); leaf; 248 unnumbered leaves; 2 blanks. 8vo. **$500.00**

The first edition of the first Law-French dictionary, called by Dr. Baker a ***"pioneering effort"*** *and a* ***"valuable contribution,"*** with, I estimate, some 18,000 entries, arranged alphabetically, each page in double column; with an even more extensive Law-Latin dictionary appended; the works' author has never been identified.

Quite a desirable copy, bound in full and well-preserved contemporary calf, slightly worn, the covers double blind-ruled and decorated, the spine unlettered, with a bit of chipping to its base, a bit of very lightish dampstaining, the lower margin of the first title page cut close, affecting the outer border of the double woodcut rule, but not the text, *else exceptionally clean and fresh.*

The First Edition

59. DODDERIDGE, Sir John. The History of the ancient and moderne Estate of the Principality of Wales, Dutchy of Cornewall, and Earldome of Chester. London, 1630. Title Page; 7 leaves; 142 pages. S.T.C. 6982; 8vo. **$300.00**

Named Solicitor General in 1604, and succeeded by Francis Bacon, Dodderidge was created a justice of the King's Bench in 1612, joined by Coke a year later; *a man of wide accomplishments,* Dodderidge joined Henry Spelman, Robert Cotton and William Camden in establishing the Society of Antiquaries in 1585, *this the first edition of the only published result of his antiquarian interests.*

An acceptable copy, *nicely and recently rebound in ¾ calf over marbled boards,* the spine gilt-lettered; a bit of lightish dampstaining throughout, and occasional embrowning, the top margins of the title page and two other leaves repaired, not affecting the text, the foremargins cut a bit close, just affecting a few letters of some sidenotes, but not legibility, occasional worming, primarily marginal, affecting some letters on several pages, but not legibility.

60. DOUGLAS, William O. An Almanac of Liberty, Doubleday, 1954. **$20.00**

61. DOUGLAS, William O. America Challenged. Princeton, 1960. **$35.00**

Justice Douglas' 1960 Edge Lectures at Princeton.

Douglas to Brandeis

62. DOUGLAS, William O. Autograph note signed, William O. Douglas to Justice Brandeis, February 25, 1941. **$400.00**

On Supreme Court stationary, *entirely in Douglas' hand and signed by Douglas,* accompanying a copy of the slip opinion in *Wood v. City National Bank* [312 U.S. 262], decided by the Court that month, in a unanimous opinion written by Douglas.

A highly desirable item of many associations, Douglas having taken Brandeis' seat on the Court in 1939, with Douglas disclosing his conversations with Brandeis about the case, particularly its "problem of conflicts of interest which we discussed."

An excellent example of Brandeis' & Douglas' interest in protecting the "little guy," and a subject which attracted Douglas' interest throughout his his professional life, his years at Cravath substantially devoted to them, followed while at Yale by his 1934 Harvard Law Review article, and, as Director of the S.E.C. study, by his first significant efforts for the Roosevelt administration, resulting in the massive 8 volume study submitted

Aristotle, Grotius, Hobbes and Milton, and the Divine Right of Kings

75. FILMER, Sir Robert. The Freeholder's Grand Inquest [and five other tracts]. London, 1684. Wing F916; 8vo. **$350.00**

Six of Fuller's most important tracts in support of the theory of the divine right of kings, including his *Patriarcha,* called by Holdsworth the theory's "most popular exposition," his *Freeholder's Grand Inquest,* recently termed "the most formidable anticoordination tract of the century" (though Filmer's authorship has been challenged), and his *Reflections Concerning the Original of Government,* in which he considers the theories proposed by Aristotle, Grotius, Hobbes and Milton, together with his short tract on the difference between an English and a Hebrew witch.

Quite a good copy; a bit of spotting and embrowning throughout, very occasional lightish dampstaining, a bit of early underlining, two erasures on the first title page and another on the first contents' leaf, the lower margin of the title page of *Patriarcha* cut close, affecting one rule, but not the text; *altogether a desirable copy, handsomely rebound in full dark calf,* the covers double blind-ruled, the spine with a brown morocco label, double gilt-ruled and lettered.

"A forerunner of modern works on Jurisprudence" — Winfield

76. FINCH, Sir Hen[ry]. Law, Or a Discourse therof. London, 1678. 3 blanks; Title Page; 2 leaves; 506 pages (irregular but complete); 8 leaves; 2 blanks. Wing F932; 8vo. **$350.00**

Called a "considerable achievment" by Winfield, and "a pioneer book of the institutes of English law" by Holdsworth, Finch's work first appeared in 1627, this the fourth, and last, printing of the 17th century; *not in the Harvard Law Catalogue.*

A bit of lightish embrowning throughout, tears to the margins of two leaves, just affecting a few words in one case, else *quite a clean, desirable copy, bound in later full sheep, neatly rebacked,* the spine gilt-ruled and lettered, and elaborately blind decorated.

77. FLAHERTY, David H. (ed.). Essays in the History of Canadian Law. Toronto, 1981. **$35.00**

The first publication of the Osgoode Society, devoted to Canadian legal history.

78. (FRANKFURTER, Felix). PHILIP B. KURLAND. Mr. Justice Frankfurter and the Constitution. Chicago, 1971. **$15.00**

79. FRIEDMAN, Lawrence M. and Robert V. Percival. The Roots of Justice, Crime and Punishment in Alameda County, California, 1870-1910. North Carolina, 1981. **$27.50**

Studies in Legal History.

Coke and the Supremacy of the Common Law

80. [FULLER, Nicholas]. The Argument of Nicholas Fuller . . . in the Case of Tho. Lad, and Rich. Mansell. Second Edition. London, 1641. Title Page; leaf; 32 pages. Wing F2394; 4to. **$200.00**

An important part of Coke's first major conflict with James I, occuring in 1607, one year after Coke became Chief Justice of the Common Pleas, Coke maintaining the Court's power to issue prohibitions against the High Commission, thus seeking common law control over ecclesiastical judges and, indirectly, its independence of the Crown, here the argument of Fuller before the High Commission against its jurisdiction, leading to his being fined and imprisoned, and his seeking the review and protection of the Common Law courts.

This the second edition of 1641, most likely issued upon the abolition of the High Commission in that year; *quite a clean and desirable copy,* a very little bit of lightish embrowning, neatly bound in modern boards, with a paper label.

81. GALBRAITH, V. H. Kings and Chroniclers, Essays in English Medieval History. London, 1982. **$40.00**

Fifteen essays, including essays upon a draft of Magna Carta, and upon the *Modus Tenendi Parliamentum.*

82. (GÉNY François). JARO MAYDA. François Gény and Modern Jurisprudence. Baton Rouge, 1978. **$22.50**

The German War Trials, 1945-1966, A Massive Documentary, Just Completed in 23 Volumes

83. (GERMANY). C.F. RUTER, et al (eds.). Justiz und NS-Verbrechen, The German War Trials, 1945-1966, War Crimes and Crimes Against Humanity. 23 Volumes. Amsterdam, 1968-1981. About **$2200.00**

An extremely important work, containing full details of all of the judgments and penal sentences dealing with war crime capital offenses (numbering about 1,000) passed by German courts from the end of World War to 1965, "judgments" and "penal sentences" comprising much more than American usage imports, including witnesses' testimony, defense arguments (including motivations and justifications) and underlying local and historical circumstances; of further value, more than 95% of the judgments and penal sentences previously unpublished and of difficult access, scattered over 90 German archives.

Further information on this valuable work gladly supplied.

"[T]he first of our legal classics" —Maitland

84. [GLANVILLE, Ranulf de]. Tractatus de Legibus & Consuetudinibus regni

Angliae. [London], 1604. Title Page; 8 leaves; 116 folios; 17 leaves. S.T.C. 11906; 8vo.

bound with

ST. GERMAIN, Christopher. Dialogus de fundamentis Legum Angliae. [London], 1604. Title Page; 3 leaves; 73 folios; 2 leaves. New S.T.C. 21560; 8vo.. **$650.00**

One of the five great books of English law, and the earliest, written about 1187, traditionally attributed to Ranulf de Glanville, justiciar under Henry II, its significance uniformly acknowledged, Plucknett calling its author "the first exponent of the new common law which in the course of the centuries was to supersede the ancient legal institutions of the land;" this the second edition of 1604, published some 60 years after the first edition, and *the only issue of the early 1600's.*

Bound together with the second Latin edition of St. Germain's Doctor and Student, *"the basis and starting point of the English system of equity,"* according to Holdsworth.

The first and last leaves just a bit dusty, an early signature crossed out on the first title page, *else an exceptionally clean and wide-margined copy,* bound in full, contemporary calf, very worn, the covers double blind-ruled, recently and adequately rebacked, with a crimson morocco label, gilt-ruled and lettered.

85. GLASSEY, Lionel K.J. Politics and the Appointment of Justices of the Peace, 1675-1770. Oxford, 1979. **$29.00**

Oxford Historical Monographs.

86. HAAKONSSEN, Knud. The Science of a Legislator, The Natural Jurisprudence of David Hume and Adam Smith. Cambridge, 1981. **$34.50**

87. HALL, Jerome. Comparative Law and Social Theory. Baton Rouge, 1963. **$17.50**

The 1962 *Edward Douglass White Lectures* at Lousiana State.

88. (HAMILTON, Alexander). JULIUS GOEBEL, et al (eds.). The Law Practice of Alexander Hamilton: Documents and Commentary. Volume 5. New York, 1981. **$75.00**

The fifth, and final, volume of this superb work, whose first volume appeared in 1964, devoted primarily to Hamilton's law register and cashbook. Each prior volume is also available, at $60.00, as is the entire set at $315.00.

89. HARDING, Alan (ed.). Law-making and Law-makers in British History. Royal Historical Society. London, 1980. **$30.00**

Papers read to the biennial conference of legal historians, held at Edinburgh in 1977.

90. HOLDSWORTH, W.S. The Historians of Anglo-American Law. Archon, 1966. **$25.00**

The re-issue of *Holdsworth's 1927 Carpentier Lectures at Columbia,* with a chapter devoted to Maitland, and much on Coke, Selden, Hale, Blackstone, and many others.

Christmas Greetings from Holmes to Mrs. Brandeis

91. HOLMES, Oliver Wendell, Jr. Autograph letter signed, Justice Holmes to Mrs. Brandeis, December 22, 1932. **$400.00**

On Holmes' personal stationery, from Holmes' I Street residence, ***entirely in Holmes' hand,*** with his full signature, offering "reciprocal wishes for a Merry Christmas and a Happy New Year," one page, with the conjugate leaf, two folds, *in very nice condition.*

Holmes had retired from the Court in January of this year.

92. (HOLMES, Oliver Wendell). DAVID H. BURTON. Oliver Wendell Holmes, Jr. Boston, 1980. **$20.00**

The most recent Holmes' biography.

93. HONORE, Tony. Sex Law in England. Archon, 1978. **$15.00**

94. HUNT, Aurora. Kirby Benedict, Frontier Federal Judge. Glendale, 1961. **$50.00**

With a presentation slip from the author, and a prospectus, laid in, and a chapter on circuit riding with Abraham Lincoln in Illinois.

95. (ICELAND). ANDREW DENNIS et al (trans). Laws of Early Iceland, Volume 1. Winnipeg, 1980. **$35.00**

The first of three proposed volumes translating and discussing *Gragas, the earliest written Icelandic legal code,* reduced to writing in the early 1100's. Standing orders gladly taken.

Complete in Three Volumes

96. (INNS of Court). J. CONWAY DAVIES (ed.). Catalogue of Manuscripts in the Library of the Honourable Society of the Inner Temple. Three Volumes. Oxford, 1972. **$75.00**

Over 1500 pages, with an 80,000 word introduction, *each of the 772 volumes of manuscripts described in detail,* including works by Littleton, Coke, Francis Bacon, and innumerable others. *Highly desirable.*

97. IRONS, Peter H. The New Deal Lawyers. Princeton, 1982. **$27.50**

98. JACKSON, Robert H. Full Faith and Credit, the Lawyer's Clause of the Constitution. Columbia, 1945. **$17.50**

Justice Jackson's 1944 Cardozo Lecture.

99. (JACKSON, Robert H.). EUGENE C. GERHART. America's Advocate: Robert H. Jackson. New York, 1958. **$25.00**

100. JOHNSTON, Richard E. The Effect of Judicial Review on Federal-State Relations in Australia, Canada, and the United States. Louisiana State, 1969. **$15.00**

101. JOLOWICZ, H.F. Historical Introduction to the Study of Roman Law. Third Edition. Cambridge, 1972. **$79.00**

Perhaps the best introduction (together with item 33) *to Roman Law,* this the last and best edition.

102. (JUSTINIAN). TONY HONORÉ. Tribonian. London, 1978. **$56.00**

The first work written on Tribonian, Justinian's minister for legislation and propaganda, who composed about ¾ of Justinian's laws.

103. KEETON, Robert E. Venturing to Do Justice, Reforming Private Law. Harvard, 1969. **$15.00**

104. KETTERING, Sharon. Judicial Politics and Urban Revolt in Seventeenth-Century France. Princeton, 1978. **$17.50**

105. KIECKHEFER. Richard. European Witch Trials, Their Foundations in Popular and Learned Culture, 1300-1500. London, 1976. **$35.00**

106. KING, Jerome B. Law v. Order, Legal Process and Free Speech in Contemporary France. Archon, 1975. **$15.00**

107. (KIPLING, Rudyard). SHAMSUL ISLAM. Kipling's "Law," A Study of His Philosophy of Life. London, 1975. **$17.50**

108. KNAFLA, Louis A. Law and Politics in Jacobean England, the Tracts of Lord Chancellor Ellesmere. Cambridge, 1977. **$59.00**

Cambridge Studies in Legal History.

109. KNAFLA, Louis A. (ed.). Crime and Criminal Justice in Europe and Canada. Waterloo, Ontario, 1981. **$22.50**

Fifteen historical essays, ranging from the 16th to the 20th centuries.

110. KUTTNER, Stephan. The History of Ideas and Doctrines of Canon Law in the Middle Ages. London, 1980. **$11.00**

111. KUTTNER, Stephan. Medieval Councils, Decretals, and Collections of Canon Law, Selected Essays. London, 1980. **$44.00**

The Pre-eminent Work

112. LAMBARDE, William. Eirenarcha, or of the Office of the Justices of Peace. London, 1610. Title Page; 634 pages; 42 leaves. New S.T.C. 15172; 8vo.

bound with

LAMBARDE, William. The Duties of Constables. London, 1610. Title Page; pages 3-94. New S.T.C. 15158; 8vo. **$550.00**

Most likely the foremost work on Justices of the Peace ever written, placed by Holdsworth "at the head of that long list of books upon the justices of the peace which stretch in a continuous series from the seventeenth to the twentieth century," *essential to any study of English local government, and enormously successful,* the two books running through a combined 39 editions by 1640.

The first title page a bit dusty and a few upper margins cut close, just affect some headnotes, but not legibility, *else an exceedingly clean and fresh copy,* largely in black letter throughout, bound in an attractive, early ½ calf over decorated boards, a bit worn, a bit of chipping to the head of the spine; *altogether, quite a desirable copy.*

113. LAUTERPACHT, H[ans]. The Function of Law in the International Community. Archon, 1966. **$20.00**

A re-issue of the 1933 edition.

The Last Edition Prior to Coke on Littleton

114. [LITTLETON, Sir Thomas]. Littleton's Tenures in English. London, 1627. Title page; folios 2-142; 2 leaves. New S.T.C. 15783; 8vo. **$350.00**

Called one of the five most pre-eminent works of English law by Holdsworth, Winfield holding that "[b]etween Bracton and Blackstone there was not a treatise to be compared to it," *Littleton's Tenures was the most oft-printed law book of the sixteenth century; this edition of historical importance, the last to appear before Coke's famed gloss on Littleton,* first published in 1628, the next year.

A bit of lightish dampstaining to the last several leaves, the title page a bit dusty and a small paper repair to it and to the next leaf, just affecting three letters of the latter, the top margin cut a bit close, affecting a very few headnotes, but not legibility, *else an exceedingly clean and crisp copy,* bound in full contemporary calf, quite worn, the covers blind-decorated, sometime neatly rebacked, the spine double blind-ruled and gilt-lettered. *Altogether, a decent and quite fresh copy, black letter, in English.*

115. (LOMBARD Laws). KATHERINE FISCHER DREW. The Lombard Laws. Pennsylvania, 1973. **$22.50**

The first English translation, with an extensive foreword and introduction.

A Handsome Copy of the First Stuart Edition

116. (MAGNA Carta). Magna Carta, cum Statutis, tum antiquis, tum recentibus. London, 1608. Title Page; 5 leaves; 258 folios. S.T.C. 9284; 8vo. **$400.00**

The first edition of the Magna Carta printed during the reign of James I and the Stuart Period, the first to include statutes enacted under him, and the second to appear in the Seventeenth Century.

Quite an attractive copy, newly bound in full, dark calf, the covers double blind-ruled, the spine similarly blind-ruled, and unlettered, with four raised bands; a portion of the lower margin of 2D1 torn away, not affecting the text, a few annotations in an early hand, an early(?) library stamp on the title page, some embrowning, essentially marginal, throughout, else quite a clean, wide-margined copy.

The Short Title Catalogue showing but three copies, and only one in this country, at the Huntington Library.

117. MAGRATH, C. Peter. Yazoo, Law and Politics in the New Republic, The Case of *Fletcher v. Peck.* Providence, 1966. **$17.50**

118. (MAITLAND, Frederic W.). H.E. BELL. Maitland, A Critical Examination and Assessment. Harvard, 1965. **$15.00**

The best critical biography of Maitland.

119. (MAITLAND, Frederic W.). C.H.S. FIFOOT. Frederic William Maitland, A Life. Harvard, 1971. **$17.50**

The first volume in Studies in Legal History.

120. MARSHALL, John. The Life of George Washington. Five Volumes. New York, 1925. **$75.00**

Termed "the first serious memoir of Washington," and first appearing in 1804-1807, this the reissue in similar format, based on Marshall's revised edition of 1832, which Beveridge characterized as *"the fullest and most trustworthy treatment of that period* [post-independence], *from the conservative viewpoint."*

Quite nice, in the original tan buckram, contrasting red and black spine labels, gilt; with 40 illustrations.

The First Massachusetts' Laws Printed in England

121. (MASSACHUSETTS). Acts and Laws, passed by the Great and General Court or Assembly Of the Province of the Massachusetts-Bay in New-England, from 1692, to 1719. London 1724. Blank; Title Page; iii-xvi pages; Title Page (Charter); iii-xvi pages; 359 pages; blank. Benedict 121; Tower 214; Sabin 45567; Folio. **$850.00**

The acts and laws of the first 30 years under the Charter granted by William and Mary in 1691, the Charter itself prefixed to this edition, and *to remain as the governing document of the colony until shortly before the Revolutionary War,* its effect to extend even beyond, into the Massachusetts state constitution.

An exceptionally clean and crisp copy, handsomely printed, the separate title page of the Charter bearing the Royal arms, woodcut decorations and initials throughout, bound in full contemporary calf, somewhat worn, newly rebacked, the originally elaborately gilt spine well-imitated, a crimson morocco label double gilt-ruled and lettered.

122. MEEKINGS, C.A.F. Studies in 13th Century Justice and Administration. London, 1981. **$48.00**

Milton's Historic Defense of Freedom of the Press

123. MILTON, John. Areopagitica. Cambridge [England], 1973 **$65.00**

Limited to 400 numbered copies on mould-made paper, with initials in a second color; typographically of unusual interest, with the print in two type faces, partially in double column, the main line of argument in the larger, with the new departures of thought indicated by a larger initial.

An attractive, large issue, measuring about 10 x 13 inches, bound in black buckram, a morocco label gilt-ruled and lettered, the top edge gilt and the remainder untrimmed.

The First Work Written by an English Lawyer on the Law Merchant

124. MOLLOY, Charles. De Jure Maritimo et Navali: or, a Treatise of Affairs Maritime and of Commerce. Fourth Edition. London, 1688. Engraved frontispiece; Engraved Title Page; Title Page; 10 leaves; 433 pages; 7 leaves. Wing M2398; 8vo. **$350.00**

Termed "very successful" by Holdsworth and one of the "most popular books on the law of trade ever printed" by Professor Coquillette. Molloy's work went through a 10th edition by 1778, just over a century after the first edition of 1676, this the fourth edition of 1688.

Some embrowning and spotting throughout, occasional lightish dampstaining, primarily marginal, a few annotations in two hands, one early, one later, bound in full, contemporary calf, quite worn, sometime rebacked, the spine double blind-ruled, with the original red morocco label, gilt-ruled and decorated and lettered, preserved, the title page in a wood-ruled border, with the additional engraved title, and the engraved frontispiece, both full-page, preceding it.

His Most Famous Work

125. MOUNTAGU, Richard. Appello Caesarem, A Just Appeale from Two Unjust Informers. London, 1625. Title Page; 12 leaves; 322 pages. New S.T.C. 18030.5; 4to. **$250.00**

A variant of the first edition of Montagu's most famous work, *"certainly one of the most famous pamphlets in an age of controversial activity,"* offered in support of the Stuart theory of Kingship to the derogation of Parliament, *called by Coke "as dangerous a book as [he] ever saw,"* and suppressed by proclamation in 1629.

An attractive copy; the first and last leaves chipped and dusty, a bit of embrowning throughout, but essentially sound and clean, *quite pleasantly rebound in a ¾ calf over marbled boards,* the spine blind-decorated and gilt-ruled, with a brown morocco label, gilt-lettered.

126. MUNSCHE, P.B. Gentlemen and Poachers, The English Game Laws, 1671-1831. Cambridge, 1981. **$37.50**

127. (NEW York). The Burghers of New Amsterdam and the Freemen of New York, 1675-1866. New York, 1886. **$35.00**

With much on the "Burgher Recht" of the Dutch and the corresponding Freedom of the City under the English; Collections of the New York Historical Society for 1885. *Very nice,* in the original pebbled buckram gilt, uncut.

128. (NEW York). PAUL M. HAMLIN and CHARLES E. BAKER. Supreme Court of Judicature of the Province of New York, 1691-1704. Three Volumes. New York, 1959. **$75.00**

Highly desirable, volume 1 a valuable introduction to the Court, and volume 3 a biographical dictionary of the court's bench and bar, with additional extensive indexes. The New York Historical Society Collections for 1945, *in the original green cloth, gilt, very nice.*

129. (NEW York). Proceedings of the General Court of Assizes, Held in the City of New York, October 6, 1680 to October 6, 1682. New York, 1913. **$45.00**

Together with the minutes of the Supreme Court of Judicature, for 1693 to 1701, and *supplementing the Hamlin and Baker set described just above; very nice, in the original pebbled buckram gilt,* uncut; Collections of the New York Historical Society for 1912.

130. (PATENTS). W. M. HINDMARCH. A Treatise on the Law relating to Patent Privileges. Harrisburg, 1847. **$125.00**

Termed "the most complete work on the subject" by Holdsworth, and "very much more elaborate" than its predecessors, Hindmarch's Treatise first appeared in 1846, this the first American edition of the succeeding year, appearing as volume 8 in the Law Library series, with a second appendix devoted to American Law; bound in full, contemporary sheep, well rubbed but sound, contrasting red and black leather labels, double gilt-ruled and lettered, a bit of spotting throughout, moreso to preliminaries, but altogether quite a decent copy.

The Farnborough Abbey Copy

131. [PERKINS, John]. A Profitable Booke . . . Treating of the Lawes of England. London, 1609. Title Page; 23 leaves; 168 folios. New S.T.C. 19642; 12mo. **$450.00**

Termed by Dr. Baker one of the "two most successful law books of Henry VIII's reign," Perkins' Profitable Booke had appeared in 20 editions by 1640, being much devoted to the land law and conveyancing, with substantial chapters on testaments and devises; this the second 17th century edition, in Law French.

An exceptionally clean and very tall copy, from Farnborough Abbey; the title page a bit dusty, a small hole in the margin of leaf A4 not affecting the text, extensive marginal annotations in an early hand throughout, including (together with a 19th century hand) the preliminary blanks and title page.

Bound in full, 19th century mottled calf, a bit rubbed, sometime rebacked, the spine laid down, marbled endpapers, the covers gilt-decorated and the spine gilt-decorated and ruled, with a black leather label gilt-ruled, decorated and lettered.

The Only Work in English Devoted Exclusively to the Law of Piracy, Rarely Found

132. (PIRACY). A Discourse of the Laws Relating to Pirates and Piracies. London, 1726. Title page; [iii]-vi; leaf; 70 pages; 8vo. **$500.00**

Apparently the only work in English ever devoted exclusively to the law of piracy, appearing anonymously in this the first, and only, edition of 1726.

A work rarely found, not in the Harvard Law Catalogue, nor the massive 20 volume Harvard Catalog of International Law and Relations, nor in the Inns of Court libraries, the National Union Catalogue showing but one copy, at the Boston Public Library, and the recent Bibliography of Eighteenth-Century Legal Literature also but one, at the British Library.

Attractively printed, the title page in a double-ruled border and a bit dusty, else quite clean, *nicely rebound in a ¾ mottled calf over marbled boards,* a bit rubbed, the spine with a brown morocco label, double gilt-ruled and lettered.

Prynne's Important Contribution to the History of Parliamentary Sovereignty

133. PRYNNE, William. A Brief Register, Kalendar and Survey of the Several Kinds, Forms of all Parliamentary Writs. London, 1659-64. Four volumes in two. Wing P3956, P3902, P4071 and P3961; 8vo. **$650.00**

Perhaps Prynne's most important contribution to historical scholarship, based on his investigations as Keeper of Records in the Tower, disclosing the House of Commons to have originated much later — in the mid to late 13th century — than previously supposed, and correspondingly influencing notions of sovereignty and respective powers among the King and the two Houses of Parliament.

An extremely handsome set, bound in full 19th century diced calf, the covers elaborately gilt, sometime rebacked, the ornately gilt spines neatly laid down, all edges gilt, marbled endpapers, the top and bottom margins cut a bit close, occasionally affecting headnotes, woodrules and catchwords and the decorative woodcut borders of the title pages of parts 2 and 4, but never the text, a few leaves a bit dusty, but essentially a very clean, desirable copy.

Each volume containing the armorial bookplate of Charles W G Howard, *disclosing the set's presentation from Sir David Dundas,* Queen's Counsel and Solicitor General, respectively, in the 1840's.

134. RALEIGH, Sir Walter. Remains of Sir Walter Raleigh. London, 1661. Portrait; Title Page; 4 leaves; 264 pages. New Wing R181 (variant?); 12mo. **$250.00**

Seven of Raleigh's essays, *including those two essays which may in the broader sense be termed legal,* his "Maxims of State" and "The Prerogative of Parliaments," this the second edition of this collection, published four years after the first; this issue a possible unrecorded variant of New Wing R181, the imprint differing slightly.

The title page and a few other leaves a bit dusty, occasional spotting, but altogether a clean copy, *bound in an early panelled calf, quite worn, early marbled endpapers preserved,* the covers in double gilt-ruled borders, newly rebacked, the spine blind decorated and gilt-ruled, with a brown morocco label, gilt-lettered.

135. (RHODE Island). WILLIAM R. STAPLES. Rhode Island in the Continental Congress, with the Journal of the Convention that Adopted the Constitution, 1765-1790. Providence, 1870. **$75.00**

The first publication of the convention journal adopting the federal constitution, with much background material, Rhode Island being the last of the original 13 colonies to ratify; limited to 500 copies. *Extremely nice, in the original green, pebbled buckram, gilt.*

136. RIVERS, Theodore John. Laws of the Alamans and Bavarians. Pennsylvania, 1977. **$25.00**

The first English translation of these early Germanic legal codes, dating from the eighth century; with an extensive introduction.

137. (SCOTLAND). G.W.S. BARROW (ed.). The Acts of Malcolm IV, King of Scots 1153-1165. Edinburgh, 1971. **$40.00**

The first of a proposed eight volumes, *collecting all authenticated royal documents of Scotland, for the period 1153 to 1424.* Standing orders for this valuable series gladly taken.

138. SCHWOERER, Lois G. The Declaration of Rights, 1689. Johns Hopkins, 1981. **$26.50**

139. SMITH, Roger. Trial by Medicine, Insanity and Responsibility in Victorian Trials. Edinburgh, 1981. **$30.00**

140. SNOW, Vernon F. Parliament in Elizabethan England, John Hooker's *Order and Usage.* Yale, 1977. **$17.50**

141. STEIN, Peter. Regulae Iuris, from Juristic Rules to Legal Maxims. Edinburgh, 1966. **$20.00**

"[T]he first work . . . ever written on the principles of pleading"—Holdsworth

142. STEPHEN, Henry John. A Treatise on the Principles of Pleading in Civil Actions. Third American Edition. Philadelphia, 1837. **$150.00**

This the foremost work of Stephen on pleading, causing Holdsworth to state that he "did more than anyone else to demonstrate the logical and scientific character of its chief principles." *Nicely rebound in ¼ sheep and linen sides, the original label preserved,* a bit of lightish spotting and marginal dampstaining, but essentially very clean and desirable. *Not in the Harvard Law Catalogue.*

"[T]he masterpiece"
— Gerald T. Dunne

143. STORY, Joseph. Commentaries on Equity Jurisprudence. Fifth Edition. Two Volumes. Boston, 1849. **$150.00**

Said by Professor Dunne, Story's foremost biographer, *to crown the many efforts which Story had undertaken on equity's behalf,* and to go through fourteen American and three English editions; this the fifth (and only) edition, by Charles Sumner, *Story's pupil and friend at Harvard Law School, already famous as an orator, and to become one of the foremost anti-slavery spokesman of the 19th century.*

A very attractive set, quite clean, recently bound in ¼ leather, the covers and spines double gilt-ruled, with matching red morocco labels, gilt-ruled and lettered.

A Very Attractive Engraving

144. (SUPREME Court). WILLIAM JOHNSON. A shoulder-length, full-face engraved portrait, measuring about 5 x 6½ inches, matted. **$125.00**

A late 19th-century engraving of Johnson, quite attractive, done by Albert Rosenthal, (signed by him in pencil), son of Max Rosenthal, and well known for his portraits of historically important Americans.

Johnson the 14th justice appointed to the Court, by Jefferson in 1804, *serving 30 years during one of the Court's most important periods.*

The engraving mounted on archival-standard matting, measuring about 9 x 12 inches matted; *we will also be pleased to provide the matted engraving in a simple black frame,* at $150.

145. (SUPREME Court). CHARLES A. MILLER. The Supreme Court and the Uses of History. Harvard, 1969. **$17.50**

146. SUTHERLAND, Arthur E. (ed.). Government Under Law, A Conference Held at Harvard Law School on the Occasion of the Bicentennial of John Marshall. New York, 1968. **$17.50**

147. (TRIAL). (HENRY WARD BEECHER). The Beecher Trial: A Review of the Evidence. Fourth Edition. New York, 1875. **$75.00**

One of the most sensational trials of the 19th century, Henry Ward Beecher, the defendant, accused of adultery with one of his parishoners, resulting in a hung jury; this account reprinted from the New York Times of July 3, 1875, with revisions and additions.

Quite nice, in the original printed, gray wraps, a bit worn and spotted; 34 pages.

The First Collected Edition
of United States Laws

148. (UNITED States). The Laws of the United States of America. Three Volumes. Philadelphia, 1796. Evans 31356 and 32973; 8vo. **$500.00**

The first collected edition of United States' Laws, comprising the acts of the first four Congresses, the Constitution, and the treaties made with the Indians and with foreign nations, together with the subject index compiled by Zephaniah Swift.

A handsome set, some spotting and embrowning throughout, *newly and attractively bound in full, panelled calf,* the spines with uniform black morocco labels, gilt-ruled, decorated and labelled.

149. (VANITY Fair). ROY T. MATTHEWS and PETER MELLINI. In "Vanity Fair." Berkeley, 1982. **$45.00**

An exceedingly handsome volume, with a chapter devoted to the Bench and Bar, and with over 150 caricatures, many in color; $55.00 after January 1, 1983.

One of the Foremost Treatises
on International Law

150. VATTEL, [Emerich] de. The Law of Nations; or, Principles of the Law of Nature. London, 1793. 8vo. **$175.00**

Called a "work of the first magnitude," which "modernized the whole theory and business of International Law," Vattel's work first appeared in French in 1758, and was promptly translated into English and German, this one of several early English editions appearing soon thereafter.

A desirable copy, a bit of spotting, moreso to the preliminary and last leaves, else quite clean, bound in full contemporary tree calf, quite worn, neatly rebacked, the spine double-gilt ruled, with the original crimson morocco label, gilt lettered, preserved.

151. WALKER, David M. The Oxford Companion to Law. Oxford, 1980. **$49.95**

A unique compendium, with over 1300 double-column pages, treating virtually all of Western law.

152. (WEBSTER, Daniel). ALFRED S. KONEFSKY and ANDREW J. KING (eds.). The Papers of Daniel Webster, Legal Papers, Volume 1, the New Hampshire Practice. Hanover, 1982. **$35.00**

The first of three proposed volumes, superbly edited, devoted to Webster's New Hampshire practice, volumes 2 and 3 to treat of his Boston and federal practices, respectively; standing orders gladly taken.

Chancellor Kent's Copy

153. WEST, William. The First [and Second] Part[s] of Simboleography. Two Volumes. London, 1603 and 1601. Title Page; 3 leaves; 318 unnumbered folios; Title Page (pt 2); leaf; 308 folios; 7 leaves. New S.T.C. 25270 and 25278; 4to in 8's. **$600.00**

Recently termed "the first comprehensive collection of legal forms and precedents to be published in English" and the "standard precedent book used by English practitioners," West's Symboleography first appeared in 1590, with the second part first added in 1594; *this the first edition of the 1600's,* part 1 appearing in 1603 and part 2 in 1601, respectively.

Once the copy of Chancellor James Kent, with his full signature on the title page of part 1, which, together with the succeeding several leaves, is dusty, embrowned and somewhat chipped, diminishing to a lightish embrowning, essentially marginal, throughout, a bit of occasional lightish dampstaining, primarily to the lower margin, some ink smudges to 4 leaves, a small wormhole in the upper margin of part 2, not affecting the text, *else quite a clean copy, attractively and newly bound in a uniform ½ sheep over marbled boards,* the spines gilt-ruled, each with a red morocco label gilt-ruled and lettered.

An edition not commonly found, the New S.T.C. showing but four copies in this country, one of which is imperfect; this edition of part 1 not in the Harvard Law Catalogue.

Complete in Ten Volumes

154. WIGMORE, John Henry, et al (eds. and trans.). The Continental Legal History Series. Ten Volumes. New York, 1968. **$225.00**

Perhaps the single best introduction, in English, to continental law, this the reissue of the 1912 edition, with separate volumes on German, French and Italian law, respectively, a valuable introductory volume, and *a volume devoted to Great Jurists, including essays on Bartolus, Grotius, Pufendorf, Pothier and Savigny, among many others.*

Catalogue 24

LAW & RELATED SUBJECTS

(1978)

(Item #38 Roscoe)

OCTOBER BOOKS

Antiquarian & Scholarly Booksellers

A·B·A·C
A·L·A·C
111 Queen Street East. Suite 302
Toronto, Ontario, Canada M5C 1S2
(416) 863-9930
CABLE ADDRESS: OCTOBOOKS TORONTO

PART I: 1600-1850

1 ATKYNS, Robert. An Argument In The Great Case Concerning Election of Members, To Parliament: Between Sir Samuel Bernardiston, Bart. Plaintiff; and Sir William Soames, Sheriff of Suffolk, Defendant; In The Court of Kings-Bench, In An Action upon the Case; and Afterwards by Error; Sued in the Exchequer-Chamber. London: Printed for Tim. Goodwin, 1689. pp. 1 pl, 31-51. Folio. Disbound. 45.00

Atkyns held the appointments of Judge of the Court of Common Pleas and later was Chief Baron of the Exchequer. Bernardiston vs. Soames was one of Atkyns' most important civil cases as Judge of the Court of Common Pleas. Atkyns' legal judgement in this case led to the passing of a law forbidding sheriffs to make double returns in parliamentary elections. Atkyns' controversial judgement in this case and his dissident stand on other legal questions led to considerable pressure for his resignation as Judge of the Court of Common Pleas.

2 ----An Enquiry Into The Power of Dispensing With Penal Statutes Together With Some Animadversions Upon a Book writ by Sir Edw. Herbert, Lord Chief Justice of the Court of Common Pleas, Entituled, A Short Account of the Authorities in Law, upon which Judgment was given in Sir Edward Hales's Case. London: Printed for Timothy Goodwin, 1689. pp. 2 pl, 58. Folio. Disbound. 70.00

Wing A4138.
Atkyns wrote this tract in response to King James' plans to dispense with penal statutes. Atkyns' work gives a history of dispensation and also a forceful argument on the illegality of King James' actions.

3 ----The Power, Jurisdiction and Priviledge of Parliament; And The Antiquity Of The House of Commons Asserted. Occasion'd By an Information in the Kings Bench, by the Attorney General, against the Speaker of the House of Commons. As also a Discourse concerning the Ecclesiastical Jurisdiction In The Realm of England, Occasion'd by the Late Commission in Ecclesiastical Causes. London: Printed for Timothy Goodwin, 1689. pp. 1 pl, 74. Folio. Disbound. 50.00

Wing A4141.

4 AYLOFFE, Joseph. Calendars Of The Ancient Charters, And Of The Welch And Scottish Rolls, Now Remaining In The Tower of London: Also Calendars Of all the Treaties of Peace entered into by the Kings of England with those of Scotland; and of sundry Letters and public Instruments relating to that Kingdom, now in the Chapter-House at Westminster . Together with Catalogues of the Records Brought to Berwick from the Royal Treasury at Edinburgh; of such as were transmitted to the Exchequer at Westminster, and of those which were removed to different parts of Scotland by Order of King Edward I. The Proceedings relating the carrying back the records of Scotland into that Kingdom; and the Transaction of the Parliament there from the 15th of May 1639 to the 8th of March 1650. To Which Are Added Memoranda concerning the Affairs of Ireland, Extracted From The Tower Records. With Four Copper Plates, exhibiting all the various Hands in which the several Charters have been written, from the Reign of King William The Conqueror to that of Queen Elizabeth. To the Whole is prefixed an Introduction, giving some Account of the State of the Public Records from the Conquest to the present Time. London: Printed for Benjamin White, 1774. pp. 1 pl, lxx, 1 leaf, 462, [32] index & errata. 4 engraved plates, 2 text engravings. 4 to. contemporary calf, rebacked, morocco spine label, gilt. backstrip stamped in gilt & blind. calf worn, tape repairs to hinges, fr. bd. detached but present. I2 lacking outer corner, else, internally, a nice clean copy. With armorial bookplate of Charles Abbot & bookplate of the Constitutional Club acknowledging the gift of Lord Colchester, 1887. "Prefix to Mr. Abbot's copy" written in contemporary hand bound in at front. Second edition. 125.00

"In 1772 Ayloffe published the work by which he is still known to historical students...In a lengthy introduction the author impresses on historians the necessity of scholarly research among the state papers. The book was begun by the Rev. Philip Morant, who was at one time employed at the State Paper Office, and was published at first anonymously. But in 1774 a new issue gave Sir Joseph Ayloffe's name on the title-page." [DNB]

5 BRADY, Robert. An Introduction To The Old English History, Comprehended in Three Several Tracts. The First, An Answer to Mr. Petyt's Rights Of The Commons Asserted; and to a Book Intituled, Jani Anglorum facies Nova; the Second Edition very much Inlarged. The Second, An Answer to a Book Intituled, Argumentum Antinormanicum, much upon the Same Subject; Never Before Published. The Third, The Exact History of the Succession of the Crown of England: The Second Edition, also very much enlarged. Together With An Appendix Containing several Records, and a Series of Great Councils and Parliaments Before and After The Conquest, unto the End of the Reign of Henry the Third. And A Glossary Expounding many Words used frequently in our Ancient Records, Laws, and Historians. London: Printed by Thom. Newcomb, 1684. pp. 6 pl, 412, 60, 68, [15] index. Folio. Modern quarter morocco. Minor marginal worming to a few signatures affecting some letters of marginal notes of first few leaves only. First Edition. 325.00

Wing B4194.
Brady's work staunchly defended the royal prerogative. Entering into the controversy of royalist vs. parliamentary powers, Brady attacked William Petyt and William Atwood's views on parliamentary rights.

6 CAMPBELL, John, [first Baron] Campbell. The Lives Of The Chief Justices Of England. From The Norman Conquest Till The Death Of Lord Mansfield. In Two Volumes. London: John Murray, 1849. pp. xix, 588; xii, 584, +16 pp. of publisher's ads. 8 vo. Original blind and gilt stamped cloth. Backstrips faded and frayed. Bookplate of Baldwin of Spadina in The County of York Upper Canada. First Edition. 100.00

Campbell's work "contains a great deal of information about the history of law and lawyers which is not easily to be found elsewhere...Nor has time worn away the merit of his books; they still find many readers, and there is little probability that they will be displaced by anything more entertaining written on the subject." [DNB] Chapters on Edward Coke, Matthew Hale and Lord Mansfield.

7 COKE, Edward. The First Part Of The Institutes Of The Laws Of England. Or, A Commentary upon Littleton. Not the name of the Author, only, but of the Law itself. The Fourteenth Edition, Revised And Corrected. With The Addition Of Notes and References, From The Beginning To Folio 190 Inclusive, By Francis Hargrave, Esq. of Lincoln's-Inn. And From Folio 190 To The End, With the Preface and Index to the Notes, By Charles Butler, Esq. of Lincoln's-Inn. Including Also, The Notes Of Lord Chief Justice Hale, and Lord Chancellor Nottingham. And An Analysis of Littleton, Written by an Unknown Hand in 1658-9, but never before published. [Hargrave and Butler's Second Edition]. London: Printed for E. & R. Brooke, 1789. pp. 2 pl, [18], xx, 395 (numbered leaves), [59] index & tables. folding engraved plate. folio. contemporary

tree calf, morocco spine label, gilt back. calf rubbed, joints cracked, head of backstrip worn, internally a nice clean copy. 225.00

The First Part Of The Institutes is considered to be Coke's most "celebrated work on which his fame is permanently established". [Foss] "If Bracton first began the codification of the common law, it was Coke who completed it...It is a disorderly, pedantic work in which the common thread is a national dogmatism, tenacious of its continuous self-perpetuating life. With it the lawyers fought the battle of the constitution against the Stuarts; historical research was their defence for national liberties." [Printing And The Mind Of Man #259, of the 1st Ed.] Francis Hargrave and Charles Butler's critical notes on Coke in the 13th and 14th Editions provide added insight into Coke's work and distinguish these editions from previous ones.

8 COLLINS, Arthur. Proceedings, Precedents, And Arguments, On Claims and Controversies, Concerning Baronies by Writ, and other Honours. With The Arguments of Sir Francis Bacon, Sir Henry Montagu, the Lord Chief Justice Crew, the Lord Chief Justice Brampston, Judge Dodderidge, Judge Rolles, Mr. Selden, Sir Heneage Finch, Mr. Montagu, (afterwards Lord Chief Baron) Sir William Jones, Sir William Dugdale, Mr. Offley, Sir Edward Northey, Sir Thomas Powis, and others...With An Appendix containing several Papers copied from the Bodleian and Ashmolaean Libraries, at Oxford &c. London: Printed for Thomas Wotton, 1734. pp. 1 pl, 4 (Dedication and Preface), [2] errata leaf, 415, [12] index. Folio. Modern quarter antique morocco [by Seamus McClafferty], morocco spine label, gilt, gilt rules to spine, marbled bds. Armorial bookplate of Baron Maule laid in. 400.00

Collins spent his whole life researching the nobility. "Collin's indefatigable industry and general accuracy are worthy of all praise. In prosecuting his unrequited, or very tardily requited, labours, on which he expended not only a lifetime but all that he possessed, his only inducement to persevere was, as he himself has said ' an innate desire to preserve the memory of famous men'." [DNB]

9 [COOKE, Edward]. Letters Addressed To Lord Grenville And Lord Howick, Upon Their Removal From The Councils Of The King, In Consequence Of Their Attempting The Total Repeal Of The Test Laws Now in Force, with Respect to His Majesty's Army and Navy. By a Protestant [pseud.]. London: Printed for John Stockdale, 1807. pp. 37, [1] ad. 8 vo. disbound. light foxing to first two leaves, else VG. 50.00

Goldsmith 19523.

10 COWELL, John. A Law Dictionary: Or, The Interpretor Of Words and Terms, Used either in the Common or Statute Laws Of That Part Of Great Britain, Call'd England; And In Tenures and Jocular Customs: First Published by the Learned Dr. Cowel, and now very much Augmented and Improv'd, by the Addition of many Thousand Words, as are found in our Histories, Antiquities, Cartularies, Rolls, Registers, and other Manuscript Records, not hitherto Explain'd in any Dictionary, to the Year 1708. With An Appendix, Containing the Antient Names of Places in (that Part of Great-Britain call'd) England, very necessary for the use of all such, that Converse with Ancient Deeds, Charters &c. London: Printed for D. Browne...1708. No pagination[pp. 340]. Folio. Contemporary calf worn. Front board loose, back joint cracked, internally VG. First Edition of Enlarged Work. 275.00

Cowell's work was first published in 1607. Cowell "advanced the opinion that the English monarchy was an absolute monarchy, and that the king only consulted parliament by his 'goodness in waiving his absolute power to make laws without their consent'."[DNB] After charges that Cowell had insulted the King and the Commons civil law, the book was suppressed by royal proclamation in 1610. Cowell's work was enlarged and first re-issued in 1708.

11 CRAIG, Thomas. D. Thomae Cragii De Riccarton, Equitis, In Senatu Edinburgensi Patroni celeberrimi & jurisconsultissimi, Jus Feudale, Tribus Libris comprehensum: Quibus non solum consuetudines Feudales, & Praediorum jura, quae in Scotia, Anglia, & plerisque Galliae locis obtinent, contineutur; sed universum jus Scoticum, & omnes fere materiae juris clare & dilucide exponuntur; & ad fontes juris Feudalis & Civilis singula reducuntur. Editio Tertia, prioribus multo emendatior...Opera & Studio Jacobi Baillie Advocati. Edinburgi: Apud. Tho. & Walt Ruddimannos, 1732. pp. xxii, 524, [52] index. engraved frontis. portrait. Folio. contemporary sprinkled calf. backstrip bit worn, joints cracked, pen notes to front free-endpaper, else a nice copy. 225.00

The third edition, with biographical sketch of Craig by James Baillie & preface by Robert Burnet (Lord Crimond), a Scottish judge. "A very learned work, written with the avowed object of showing that the feudal law of Scotland and England had a common origin...No clearer statement of the feudal system in its legal relations exists, and it is still, although the law has been must altered, the standard authority in Scotland as to the original condition of its feudal landlaw, probably as complete as that of any European country."[DNB]

12 CRAUFURD, Q[uintin]. Researches Concerning The Laws, Theology, Learning, Commerce etc. Of Ancient and Modern India. In Two Volumes. [Bound in one]. London: T. Cadell & W. Davies, 1817. pp. vi, [2], 353; 2 pl, 378. 8 vo. half calf, morocco spine label, marbled bds. gilt rules & lettering to spine. binding rubbed, hint of foxing to index & outer blanks, else a very nice copy. First Edition. 125.00

An account of Hindu traditions, including chapters on religious and civil law.

13 DE LAPORTE, M.J.B. Le Nouveau Dunod, Ou Traite Des Prescriptions De Ce Celebre Auteur, Mis En Concordance Avec La Legislation Actuelle; Contenant tout ce qui peut etre encore utile de cet excellent Ouvrage, auquel on a ajoute toutes les Prescriptions introduites par les Codes Napoleon, de Procedure civile, de Commerce, d'Instruction criminelle, et par les Lois relatives aux Droits d'Enregistrement, de Timbre, de Greffe et d'Hypotheques, ainsi que par celles sur les Douanes, les Droits reunis, les Octrois municipaux, etc. Avec la Notice des Jugemens, et Arrets, tant anciens que modernes, sur les questions les plus importantes dans la matiere. Paris: Aux Archives Du Droit Francais..., 1810. pp. xii, 501. index. complete with half-title. 8 vo. contemporary quarter sheep, leather spine label, gilt back. preliminary leaves misbound but all present, v. slight pen scoring to first 6 chapters. binding worn, internally VG. 65.00

14 DE LOLME, J[ean] L[ouis]. The Constitution Of England, Or An Account Of The English Government; In Which it is compared with the Republican Form of Government, and the other Monarchies in Europe. The Fourth Edition, Corrected and Enlarged. London: Printed for G. Robinson & J. Murray, 1784. pp. 4 pl, xvi, 540, [20] index. engraved frontis. portrait. contemporary tree calf, morocco spine label, gilt back. small chip out of spine, upper corner of fr. bd. snubbed, extremities rubbed, internally a very nice clean copy. 50.00

De Lolme's work "appeared at a favourable moment, when the rise of modern radicalism made constitutional questions of engrossing interest; it flattered the national pride by representing England as the only country where the government was at once strong and free; it was written in an easy style; and until recently, it kept a secure place through the absence of any good systematic work on the English constitution." [DNB]

([DUNDAS, Henry, first] Viscount Melville). The Trial By Impeachment, Of Henry Lord Viscount Melville, For High Crimes and Misdemeanours, Before The House of Peers, In Westminster Hall, Between the 29th of April and the 17th of May 1806...The Impartial Edition. Edinburgh: Printed for and by J. Robertson, 1806. pp. 1 pl, 304, [9] appendix. engraved frontis. portrait. 8 vo. later cloth. corners frayed. 60.00

Lord Melville was charged with embezzlement of large sums of public money from the Treasury.

EAST, Edward Hyde. A Treatise Of The Pleas Of The Crown. 2 Volumes. Philadelphia: Printed for P. Byrne, 1806. pp. lxiii, 480; 2 pl, 481-1126, [2] ads. complete with half-title. 8 vo. contemporary sheep, gilt stamped leather labels. First American Edition. binding somewhat worn, some browning & foxing throughout, else VG. 200.00

This work was the result of 15 years of labour. The Treatise was conceived as a reference work for members of the legal profession. East classed offences under three categories: crimes against religion, crimes against property and crimes against persons, and summarized the legal judgements.

FEUERBACH, Anselm Ritter Von. Narratives Of Remarkable Criminal Trials. Translated from the German by Lady Duff Gordon. London: John Murray, 1846. pp. xi, 368 + 16 pp. of publisher's ads bound in at end. 8 vo. original blind & gilt stamped cloth, frayed. covers detached, some signatures roughly opened. 30.00

FORSYTH, William. Hortensius: Or, The Advocate. An Historical Essay. London: John Murray, 1849. pp. xix, 495. engraved frontis. & title vignette. 12 mo. contemporary cloth worn & crudely rebacked. Ex-lib. 20.00

A history of the advocates role and function in England, France, Rome and Greece, including accounts of important trials for witchcraft, trials by battle, &c.

GODWIN, William. An Enquiry Concerning Political Justice, And Its Influence on General Virtue and Happiness. In Two Volumes. Dublin: Printed for Luke White, 1793. pp. xiii, [21] contents, 411; 2 pl, [19] contents, 424. complete with half-titles. 8 vo. contemporary sheep, leather spine labels, gilt. bindings somewhat worn, joints cracking, some foxing throughout, sl. dampstain to lower edge of first few leaves of Vol. 1, small strip clipped from half-title of Vol. 1, else VG. First Irish Edition. 350.00

Kress B.2528. cf Goldsmith 15825 (1st English Edition).
Composed of carefully constructed arguments dealing with all aspects of legal rights and duties, this influential work established Godwin as the philosophical representative of English radicalism. The first Irish edition was published in the same year as the first English.

20 (GREAT BRITAIN). A Collection Of All The Wills, Now Known To Be Extant, Of The Kings and Queens of England, Princes and Princesses of Wales, And Every Branch Of The Blood Royal, From The Reign Of William The Conqueror, To That Of Henry The Seventh Exclusive. With Explanatory Notes, And A Glossary. London: Printed by J. Nichols..., 1780. pp. x, 429, [1] ad. index. 4 to. Trilingual work - English, French, Latin. Half morocco stamped in blind, morocco spine label, gilt, marbled endpapers, sprinkled edges. extremities very lightly rubbed, occasional bit of foxing, else a very nice copy. 65.00

21 (GREAT BRITAIN, LAWS, STATUTES).(An Act for the better preventing of Clandestine Marriages). Anno Regni Georgii II. Regis Magnae Brittanniae, Franciae, & Hiberniae, Vicesimo Sexto. At the Parliament begun and holden at Westminster, the Tenth Day of November, Anno Dom. 1747, in the Twenty First Year of the Reign of our Sovereign Lord George the Second, by the Grace of God, of Great Britain, France, and Ireland, King, Defender of the Faith, &c. And from thence continued by several Progrogations to the Eleventh Day of January, 1753, being the Sixth Session of this present Parliament. London: Printed by Mark Baskett..., 1761. pp. 1 pl, 471-478. 4 to. Disbound. 20.00

22 HALE, Matthew. A Discourse Of The Knowledge Of God, and of our Selves, 1. By the Light of Nature. II. By the Sacred Scriptures... To which are added a Brief Abstract of the Christian Religion, And Considerations seasonable at all Times, for the Cleansing of the Heart and Life. London: Printed by B.W. for William Shrowsbery, 1688. pp. 1 pl, [36], 503, [1] ad. engraved frontis. portrait. 8 vo. contemporary mottled calf. binding worn, upper backstrip chipped, internally a nice copy. First Edition. 150.00

Wing H240.
Religious treatise of Matthew Hale, Chief Justice, published posthumously.

23 ----The History of the Common Law. The Fourth Edition Corrected; With Notes, References, And Some Account of the Life of the Author, By Charles Runnington. [Also including "An Analysis of the Civil Part of the Law. The Fourth Edition"]. London: Printed by W. Strahan & M. Woodfall for T. Cadell, 1779. pp. 4 pl, xl, [305], [1] errata, 6 pl, 114, [8] index, [2] ads. engraved frontis. chart. 8 vo. modern quarter morocco, morocco spine label, gilt rules & lettering to spine. some browning throughout, dampstaining to lower edge of some leaves including prelims. & frontis. frontis. & title neatly mounted, but a good copy. 150.00

"In 1713 appeared his Analysis of the Law and History of the Common Law. Both were rough drafts, never intended for publication, but ran through several editions particulary the latter, which was indeed the first work of the sort ever written."(Grosse) The fourth edition published both works together, previous editions had issued the History and Analysis separately. This work is considered to be of considerable importance, providing an erudite interpretation of English civil law.

24 [HALHED, Nathaniel]. (Translator & Editor). A Code Of Gentoo Laws, Or, Ordinations Of The Pundits. From A Persian Translation, Made From the Original, Written In The Shanscrit Language. London:[Printed and Sold by Alexander Donaldson.], 1781. pp. cxx, 284, [4] ads, 8 engraved plates (some folding). contemporary calf. , morocco spine label, gilt. binding rubbed, fr. bd. detached, back joint cracking, internally a nice clean copy. Third Edition. 75.00

Warren Hastings, the Governor General of India, originally commissioned this work on the Hindu legal code in 1773; with chapters on the Indian judicial system prior to British administrative overhaul.

(HONE, William). The Three Trials Of William Hone, For Publishing Three Parodies; viz. The Late John Wilkes's Catechism, The Political Litany, And The Sinecurist's Creed; On Three Ex-Officio Informations, At Guildhall, London, During Three Successive Days, December 18, 19, & 20, 1817; Before Three Special Juries, And Mr. Justice Abbott, On The First Day, And Lord Chief Justice Ellenborough, On The Last Two Days. London: Printed By & For William Hone, 1818. pp. iv, 48, 45, [3] ads, 44. 8 vo. Disbound. (Prefatory address by William Hone, dated January 23, 1818. The first trial is of the 16th edition, the second of the fourteenth, the third of the twelfth). 85.00

cf Goldsmith 22265-66 (Variant editions).

([HOWARD], Thomas, [Earl of Surrey and Third] Duke of Norfolk). The Tryal, Of Thomas Duke of Norfolk By His Peers, For High Treasons Against The Queen; On Wednesday the 16th Day of January, in the Year of Our Lord, 1571 and in the XIVth Year of the Reign of Queen Elizabeth: For attempting to Marry Mary Queen of Scots without the Consent and Approbation of the said Queen Elizabeth. Together with the Learned Arguments of all the Judges and Queen's Council against the Duke, with his most excellent Defence and Noble Conduct of himself throughout the whole Tryal, from his Arraignment to his last Loyal Speech to the Lords after Sentence of Death had pass'd upon him, To which is added, An Historical Preface letting the Reader into the Nature of the Case, with an Epistle Dedicatory to his Grace the present Duke of Norfolk. London: Printed for J. Morphew, 1709. pp. 1 pl, [22], 150. 8 vo. Contemporary mottled calf, gilt stamped spine, with armorial bookplate of Rolle. extremities rubbed, else a very nice copy. 75.00

JUSTINIAN. D. Justiniani: Institutionum Libri Quatuor. The Four Books Of Justinian's Institutions, Translated into English, With Notes, By George Harris. London: Printed for C. Bathurst & E. Withers, 1756. pp. xv, 73, 121, 100, 92, 11, [4] index. contemporary calf, morocco spine label. gilt rules & lettering to spine. First edition of Harris' translation. binding rubbed. fr. joint cracked, except for very light foxing to several leaves, internally a very nice clean crisp copy. With armorial bookplate of Earl of Moray. 150.00

"Justinian I (483-565) was responsible for the code of Roman Law known as the Corpus juris civilis which is the basis of the form, as well as of much of the content, of modern law. It consisted of the Codex, the essence of the confused mass of statute law; the Pandects, a similar abridgement of juristic opinions; and the Novellae, new ordinances made since the Codex... The clarity which they achieved gave the Codex its permanent value."[Printing And The Mind Of Man #137 (of the 1st Ed.)].

The Lives Of All The Lords Chancellors, Lords Keepers, And Lords Commissioners, Of The Great Seal Of England; From William The Conqueror, to the Present Time: But more at large of those Two Great Opposites, Edward, Earl of Clarendon, and Bulestrode Lord Whitlock. With A Parallel of their Actions. To Which is added, An Appendix of many Rare and Valuable Speeches, Letters, &c., referring to the Said Lives. In Two Volumes. By an Impartial Hand. The Second Edition, with Additions. London: Printed and sold by R. Bonwicke, W. Freeman..., 1712. pp. 1 pl, [22], 216, [7] index, [1] ad.; 336; [1] ad., 1 pl, 520. 8 vo. contemporary panelled calf, morocco spine labels, gilt sprinkled edges. Vol. 1 rebacked, joints of Vol. II tender, bindings worn, some foxing thoughout, else VG. 175.00

Abbott 1251.

29 (LOUIS XVI and MARIE ANTOINETTE). The Accusation, Trial, Defence, Sentence, Execution, And Last Will, of Lewis XVI. Late King Of France and Navarre; Giving An Account of his magnaminous behaviour from the decree of the National Convention to bring him to Trial as a traitor, to his last affectionate interview with his unfortunate family, on the 21st day of January 1793, the day he was beheaded. Translated from the French. With a portrait of Lewis, and a View and Description of the Guillotine on Which He Suffered. Edinburgh: Printed for J.Elder, T.Brown...1793. pp. 1pl, 108. 2 engraved plates (incl. frontis. port.). 8vo.
Bound with
The Accusation, Trial, Defence, Sentence and Execution, of Marie Antoinette, Late Queen of France. Translated from the French. Edinburgh: Printed for J. Elder, T. Brown & Walter Berry, 1793. pp. 1 pl, 77. engraved frontis. portrait. 8 vo. contemporary half calf, marbled bds. joints cracked, backstrip worn, i2 misbound & torn (repaired at upper edge), else a nice copy. With the armorial bookplate of Robert Pitcairn, Writer to the Signet. 125.00

30 MARTENS, [George Friedrich von]. Summary Of The Law Of Nations, Founded On The Treaties And Customs Of The Modern Nations of Europe; With A List of The Principal Treaties, Concluded Since The Year 1748 Down To The Present Time, Indicating The Works In Which They Are To Be Found. TRANSLATED FROM THE FRENCH BY WILLIAM COBBETT. Philadelphia: Thomas Bradford, 1795. pp. xix, 379. incl. list of Subscribers. 8 vo. modern buckram. some foxing, mainly to outer leaves, else VG. First American Edition.

Sabin 44848. 150.00

31 MOILE, Nicholas Thirning. State Trials. Specimen Of A New Edition. London: Simpkin, Marshall & Co., 1838. pp. xxix, 402. complete with half-title. 8 vo. contemporary cloth rubbed & soiled. head & foot of backstrip worn, internally VG. (Including the trials of Anne Ayliffe for heresy, Sir William Stanley for high treason & Mary Queen of Scots; written in verse). 35.00

32 NELSON, William. Lex Manericorum: Or The Law And Customs Of England, Relating To Manors and Lords of Manors, their Stewards, Deputies, Tenants, and others viz. Of The Lords Right to Deodands, Felons, Goods, Waifs, Estrays, Wrecks, and Goods of Felo de fe. Of the Privileges of their Tenants in Ancient Demesne, and of Widow's Free Bench, &c.Of Copyhold Estates, Courts-Leer, Courts-Baron, and By-Laws there made, and of Amerciaments, Fines and Heriots, and how to be recovered. Of Surrenders and Admittances to Copyholds, and of Entailing them, and of Barring and Discontinuing such Entails by Fines and Recoveries in the Lord's Court, and by other Methods. Of Leases made by Copyholders with Licence, and without; Also of Forfeitures and other Determinations of their Estates. The whole being a methodical Collection of the Cases dispersed in the several volumes of the Law relating to Copyhold Estates, and to every thing depending on that Tenure. To which is added an Appendix of all the Modern Entries of Declaration, Pleas, Replications, Rejoinders, Demurrers, Issues, Special Verdicts, Writs of Recordari, Certiorari, &c. relating to the said Cases. With proper Tables to the Whole. In The Savoy: Printed by E. & R. Nutt, R. Godling...for John Hooke, 1726. pp. 5 pl, 198, 128, [8] appendix. Folio. Contemporary calf. crude tape mends to hinges & spine, some pen notes on fr. free-endpaper, binding worn. hint of foxing throughout, else a nice copy internally. First Edition. 200.00

33 [NICHOLSON], William, Bishop of Carlile. Leges Marchiarum, Or Border-Laws: Containing Several Original Articles and Treaties, Made and Agreed upon by the Commissioners of the Respective Kings of England and Scotland, for the better Preservation of Peace and Commerce upon the Marches of Both Kingdoms: From the Reign of Henry III. to the Union of the Two Crowns, in K. James I. With a Preface, and an Appendix of Charters and Records, relating to the said Treaties. London: Printed for Tim. Goodwin, 1705. pp. 4 pl, lvi, 388, [4]ads. 8 vo. complete with half-title. contemporary sprinkled panelled calf, sprinkled edges. binding rubbed, joints cracking, crude tape repairs to hinges & head & foot of backstrip, small acid-free tape mend to outer lower corner of title, else a nice copy. First Edition. 225.00

Goldsmith 4131.

34 NYE, Philip. The King's Authority in Dispensing with Ecclesiastical Laws Asserted and Vindicated. London: Printed for H.N. and Nathanael Ranew, 1687. pp. 3 pl, 64. 4 to. considerable browning to leaves.
Wing N1495.
Bound with
Free Thoughts of the Penal Laws,Tests and some Late Printed Papers Touching Both. In a letter from a Person of Quality. Np: 1688. pp. 8. 4 to.
Wing F2123.
Bound with
HERBERT, Sir Edw[ard]. A Short Account of the Authorities in Law, upon which Judgement was given in Sr. Edw. Hales His Case. London: Printed for M. Clark..., 1688. pp. 39. 4 to.
Wing H1496.
Leaves have been very closely trimmed and inlaid,with minimal effect to text of some leaves. (A collection of three tracts supporting dispensation). 90.00

35 PEARSON, Anthony. The Great Case of Tithes Truly Stated, Clearly Open'd, And Fully Resolv'd,...With an Appendix thereto. To which is added, A Defence of Some other Principles held by the People Call'd Quakers, in which they differ from other Religious Denominations. The Arguments of these are supported by Scripture, and the concurring Sentiments of Ancient and Modern Authors. By J[osiah] M[artin]. London: Printed and Sold by the Assigns of J. Sowle, 1730. pp. viii, 292. [8] ads. 8 vo. contemporary sprinkled panelled calf, paper spine labels. corners worn, else VG. 125.00

Kress 3884. Goldsmith 6788.

Pearson's work provides "...an Extract, or short History of Tithes, from the first Appointment of them under the Law, taken mostly from the History of Tithes by the Learned Antiquary J. Selden, he then considers the several claims made to them. As first, By Divine Right. Secondly, By the Gifts of Kings and Princes. Thirdly, By the Laws of Kings and Parliaments. Fourthly, By Particular Gifts, Appropriation, Consecration, and Donation of the Owners of the Land. Fifthly, By Prescription and Legal Possession. Sixthly, By Purchase. The Arguments advanced for each of these Claims, are particularly answered..." [pp.iv-v]

36 [PELHAM-HOLLES, Thomas] Duke of Newcastle. The Duke of Newcastle's Letter, By His Majesty's Order, To Monsieur Michell, the King of Prussia's Secretary of the Embassy, in Answer to the Memorial, and other Papers, deliver'd by Monsieur Michell to the Duke of Newcastle, on the 23rd of November, and 13th of December last. Published by Authority. London: Printed by Edward Owen, 1753. pp. 46, 2 fold-out lists.
Goldsmith 8803.
Bound with
A Short Epistle From A Country Gentleman To His Grace The Duke of Newcastle, On The Present Conjuncture Of Affairs; But Principally relative to the Subject of a Proper Constitutional Militia. London: Printed for Thomas Payne, 1756. pp. 1 pl, 13. 4 to. contemporary quarter leather, gilt spine lettering, marbled bds. front joint cracked, bds. sl.rubbed & & stained at edges, sl.dampstaining to lower edge of first few leaves, else VG. 150.00

After the War of the Austrian Succession, there were numerous unsettled claims for damages between England and Prussia. Newcastle's letter to the King of Prussia outlines the Principles of the Laws of Nations. Responding to Prussian violations of Maritime Law, Newcastle describes the legal jurisdiction for settling international disputes: "If a Subject of the King of Prussia is injured by, or has a Demand upon, any Person here, he ought to apply to your Majesty's Courts of Justice, which are equally open and indifferent to Foreigner or Native...Where the Judges are left free, and give Sentence according to their Conscience, though it should be erroneous, there would be no ground for Reprizals...and all a Friend can desire, is, that Justice should be as impartially administered to him, as it is to the Subjects of that Prince, in whose Courts the Matter is try'd." [pp. 16-17]

37 PUFENDORF, [Samuel]. On The Law Of Nature And Nations. Eight Books. Written in Latin...Translated into English from the Best Edition [By B. Kennett]. Oxford: Printed by A. Lichfield, 1703. pp. 1 pl, [4], 1 leaf, [17], 27, 400, 231, 143-262. main body of text printed in double columns. folio. contemporary panelled calf, morocco spine label, gilt. bds. detached, calf worn, internally VG. Folger Library duplicate, released. First English Edition First Issue. 450.00

Kress 2400.
"In the De jure naturae et gentium Pufendorf took up in great measure the theories of Grotius and sought to complete them by means of the doctrines of Hobbes and of his own ideas... He combatted Hobbe's conception of the state of nature and concluded that the state of nature is not one of war but of peace...As regards public law Pufendorf, while recognizing in the state a moral person, teaches that the will of the state is but the sum of the individual wills that constitute it, and that this association explains the state."[Encyc. Brit. 11th Ed.]

38 ROSCOE, Henry. Lives Of Eminent British Lawyers. (Lardner's Cabinet Cyclopaedia.Biography.). London: Longman, Rees, Orme, Brown, and Green, 1830. pp. [1] ad, 4 pl (incl. 2nd engraved title), 428. index. 12 mo. original cloth marked & faded. publisher's ad tipped-in to fr. free-endpaper.(Chapters on

11

Edward Coke, Matthew Hale, W. Blackstone &c.). 35.00

39 (SACHEVERELL, Henry). The Tryal Of Dr. Henry Sacheverell, Before the House of Peers, For High Crimes and Misdemeanors; Upon An Impeachment By The Knights, Citizens and Burgesses in Parliament Assembled, in the Name of themselves, and of all the Commons of Great Britain: Begun in Westminster-Hall the 27th Day of February 1709-1710, and from thence continued by several Adjournments until the 23rd day of March following. Published by Order of the House of Peers. London: Printed for Jacob Tonson, 1710. pp. 456.
With:
The Bishop of Salisbury's [Gilbert Burnet] And The Bishop of Oxford's Speeches [William Talbot] In The House of Lords, On The First Article of the Impeachment of Dr. Henry Sacheverell; Also the Bishop of Lincoln's [William Wake] and Bishop of Norwich's [Charles Trimnell] Speeches At The Opening of the Second Article of the said Impeachment. London: Printed and Sold by John Morphew, 1710. pp. 63. Contemporary calf, morocco spine label, gilt, sprinkled edges. binding rubbed, pen notes to endpapers. 150.00

Account of Sacheverell's trial for sedition and speeches supporting the legal validity of the four articles of impeachment.

40 [SAINT-GERMAIN, Christopher]. Doctor and Student: Or Dialogues Between A Doctor of Divinity, And A Student in the Laws of England, Containing the Grounds of those Laws, together with Questions and Cases concerning the Equity and Conscience thereof; also comparing the Civil, Canon, Common and Statute Laws, and shewing wherein they vary from one another. To which is now added an Account of the Author, and a General Table of the Principal Matters; never before printed. In The Savoy: Printed by Eliz. Nutt & R. Gosling...for R. Gosling, 1721. pp. 6 pl, 366, [39] index. [1] ad. 12 mo. Contemporary calf, gilt stamped leather label. binding bit rubbed else a very nice copy. Armorial bookplate of Lord Charles Noel Somerset. 225.00

Saint-Germain's popular work "Doctor and Student" was first published in 1523. Saint-Germain's work was "a handbook for legal students, which was not superseded until the appearance of Blackstone's 'Commentaries'." [DNB]

41 ([SANCROFT, William], Archbishop of Canterbury). The Proceedings and Tryal in the Case of the Most Reverend Father in God William Lord Archbishop of Canterbury...London: Printed for Thomas Basset and Thomas Fox, 1689. pp. 3 pl, 140. Engraved frontis. Folio. Contemporary pig skin. End papers wanting, some worming to margins, some staining to upper margin of most leaves, frontis loose, leather very worn. Book plate of Nicholas Buckeridge of Oxford. First Edition. 250.00

Wing S564.
An account of the proceedings of Sancroft's trial for seditious libel. Sancroft, as Archbishop of Canterbury, openly disputed the legislative powers of the King, James II, in ecclesiastical matters. Sancroft assisted in the publication of the first edition of his trial.

42 SAUNDERS, Sir Edmund. The Reports Of The Most Learned Sir Edmund Saunders, Knt. Late Lord Chief Justice of The King's Bench, Of Several Pleadings And Cases In The Court Of King's Bench, In The Time Of The Reign Of His Most Excellent Majesty

King Charles The Second. With Three Tables: The First, Of The Names of the Cases; the Second, of the Matters contained in the Pleadings; and the Third, of the Principal Matters contained in the Cases. The Third Edition. With Notes And References To The Pleadings And Cases, By John Williams. In 2 Volumes. London: Printed by A. Strahan for T. Cadell & W. Davies...1799-1802. pp. 4 pl, [364], [52]index; xii, 423, [82]index, [2]errata. 8 vo. Contemporary calf, rubbed. 125.00

Saunders was "abundantly versed in the mysteries and technicalities of law. His Reports, printed after his death, extend from 1666 to 1672, are esteemed for their simplicity and precision. They are composed in so dramatic a form that Lord Mansfield called him the Terence of reporters." [Foss]

43 SELDEN, John. The Historie of Tithes That is, The Practice of Payment of them. The Positive Laws made for them. The Opinions touching the Right of them. A Review of it Is also annext, which both Confirmes it and directs in the Use of it. [London]: 1618. pp. 1 pl, [4], xxii, [11], 491, [5]. small 4 to. title in red & black. old sprinkled calf, morocco spine label. gilt rules & lettering to spine. extremities rubbed, slight underscoring & notes in contemporary hand, name inked on title, else a very nice copy. 500.00

New STC 22172.7

In his historical analysis of the origin and development of tithes, Selden entered into the controversy between canon law and common law. Selden's denial of the clergy's "divine right" to tithes guaranteed the violent reaction of the Church. Selden was "summoned to answer for his opinions before some of the lords of the court of high commission and some of the privy council, and he acknowledged his error in a few lines of writing. The submission contained, as Selden contended, no confession of mistakes in the book, and expressed no change of opinion, but merely regret at the publication of the work... The book itself was suppressed by public authority, and by some command, probably of the king, he was forbidden to print any reply to his numerous antagonists." [DNB]

44 SPELMAN, Sir Henry. The English Works Of Sir Henry Spelman, Kt. Published in his Life-Time; Together with his Posthumous Works, Relating to the Laws and Antiquities of England; First Published by the Present Lord Bishop of Lincoln, in the Year 1695, Together with the Life of the Author, Now Revised by his Lordship. To which are added, Two more Treatises of Sir Henry Spelman, never before printed: One, of the Admiral-Jurisdiction, and the Officers thereof: The Other, Of Ancient Deeds and Charters. With A Compleat Index to the Whole. London: Printed for D. Browne..., 1723. pp. 1 pl, [26], xxvi, 38, 39-49(1 page), 1-lxv, blank, 67-194, [167]index; 1 pl, [14], 256, [23] index, [1] errata. complete with list of subscribers. engraved frontis. portrait. 2 folding genealogical tables & numerous engraved vignettes. folio. contemporary calf, morocco spine label, gilt. calf worn, fr. joint cracked, some foxing throughout, otherwise a very good copy. First Collected Edition. 300.00

"As an ecclestiastical lawyer he ranks among the best informed that this country has produced, and his 'Glossary' gives him a title to the name of the inaugurator of philological science in England." [DNB] Contains Spelman's chief works: De non Termerandis Ecclefius: Chuches Not to be violated, The Larger Treatise Concerning Tythes, De Sepultura.

45 SPELMAN, Sir Henry....The Second Edition. (Imprint & collation as 1st edn.,with the work on Spelman's life & contents of Part I bound in at beginning of Part II.). Half sheep, gilt stamped leather label. binding somewhat worn, some foxing throughout, a^4 loose, else VG. 200.00

46 [SPRAT, Bp. Thomas]. A True Account and Declaration of the Horrid Conspiracy against the Late King His Present Majesty And The Government: As It Was Order'd to be Published By His Late Majesty. The Second Edition. In The Savoy: Printed by Thomas Newcomb...Sold by Sam. Lowndes, 1685. pp. 3 pl, 167. folio. several engraved vignettes. upper corner of 1st prelim wanting.
Wing S5067.
Bound with
[SPRAT, Bp. Thomas]. Copies of the Informations and Original Papers Relating to the Proof of the Horrid Conspiracy against the Late King, His Present Majesty, And The Government: As they were Order'd to be Published By His Late Majesty. In The Savoy: Printed by Thomas Newcomb...sold by Sam. Lowndes, 1685. pp. 1 pl, 141. folding copper plate. Folio. Fore-edge of last leaf chipped, tear to plate. First Edition.
Wing S5029.
The two items bound in old calf. binding worn, fr. joint cracked. 250.00

After his new appointments as Bishop of Rochester and Dean of Westminster, Sprat published these works anonymously. "It purported to be an account of the Rye House plot, and he drew it up after much hesitation, as he subsequently pleaded, at the command of Charles II, who granted 'free liberty to consult the Paper-office and council books'." [DNB]

47 STARKIE, Thomas. Reports Of Cases, Determined At Nisi Prius, In The Courts Of King's Bench and Common Pleas, And On The Circuit, From The Sittings After Michaelmas Term, 55 Geo. III 1814 To The Sittings after Michaelmas Term, 57 Geo. III 1816. Inclusive. 2 Vols. [2nd Volume has variant title: ... Sittings after Michaelmas Term, 57 Geo. III 1816. To the Sittings after Michaelmas Term, 60 Geo. III 1819. Inclusive.]. London: Printed by A. Strahan..., 1817-1820. pp. xii, 564; xi, 623. index. 8 vo. Contemporary calf, bit worn. gilt lettering to spine. rebacked in morocco, joints rubbed, several pen notes in contemporary hand, else VG. 150.00

48 (STUART, James). The Trial Of James Stuart, Esq. Younger of Dunearn, Before The High Court Of Justiciary, At Edinburgh, On Monday, June 10, 1822. With An Appendix of Documents. Second Edition. Edinburgh: Archibald Constable & Co. & London: Hurst, Robinson..., 1822. pp. 2 pl, 186, 1 leaf, 16 (Appendix). 8 vo. Disbound. Small piece missing from fore-edge margin of contents leaf, not affecting text, last few leaves bit browned & sl.chipped at edges. 25.00

Goldsmith 23644.
Proceedings of famous Scottish murder trial. Stuart, a Whig politician, killed Sir Alexander Boswell in a duel. Stuart had taken offence to an article Boswell had written for a Tory newspaper.

49 (TRIALS). All The Proceedings In Relation to the Aylesbury-Men, Committed by the House of Commons; And The Report Of The Lords Journal, And Reports Of The Conferences, And Of The Free Conference. Together with what stands upon the Journal

of the House of Commons, in the Reign of King James I in the Case between Sir Francis Goodwin and Sir John Fortescue. London: Printed for Edward James & Timothy Goodwin, 1704. pp. 83. complete with half-title. Folio. Disbound. Some foxing thoughout. 55.00

50 (TRIALS). A Complete Collection of State-Trials, and Proceedings For High Treason, and other Crimes and Misdemeanours; The Fourth Edition; Commencing With the Eleventh Year of the Reign of King Richard II. And Ending With the Sixteenth Year of the Reign of King George III. With Two Alphabetical Tables To The Whole. To Which is Prefixed, A New Preface, By Francis Hargrave, Esquire. II Vols. in 6. London: Printed by T. Wright, And Sold by G. Kearsley, 1776-1781. (Title page varies slightly, text in double columns except for preface.). Contemporary calf, leather labels, gilt stamping, marbled endpapers. bindings worn, all but 2 covers loose, hint of foxing to outer leavers. Folio. 350.00

51 (TRIALS). The Humble Representation And Address, Of The Right Honourable the Lords Spiritual and Temporal In Parliament assembled, Presented To Her Majesty The Fourteenth Day of March, 1704. And Her Majesties Most Gracious Answer thereunto. With Their Lordships Thanks for the same. Together with the Papers Annexed to the said Address, and Laid before Her Majesty. London: Printed by the said Charles Bill...and the Executrix of Thomas Newcomb..., 1704. pp. 20. errata slip. Folio. Disbound. 40.00

52 (TRIALS). A Narrative Of The Apprehending, Commitment, Arraignment, Condemnation, And Execution of John James Who Suffered At Tiburne; Novemb. the 26th 1661. With several occasional Passages and Speeches, faithfully collected from such as were Eye and Ear Witnesses. Also, An Account of the Death of several Persons since the Execution of John James, known to be active and diligent in that matter. London: 1662. pp. 47. small 4 to. disbound. 65.00

Wing N175.

John James was indicted on 5 counts of high treason. As a preacher for the seventh-day baptists, James prophesized the millennial reign of Christ and hence the end of King Charles II's reign.

53 (TRIALS). The Proceedings Of The House Of Lords, Concerning The Scottish Conspiracy, And The Papers Laid Before that House, By Her Majesties Command, Relating thereunto. London: Printed by Charles Bill...& the Executrix of Thomas Newcomb..., 1704. pp. 67. Folio. Disbound. 50.00

Proceedings of two trials dealing with Parliament's legal jurisdiction in the prosecution of political offences.

54 (TRIALS)...A Report of the Trial On An Action For Damages, Brought By The Reverend Charles Massey Against The Most Noble The Marquis of Headfort, For Criminal Conversation With Plaintiff's Wife. Damages laid at 40,000[pounds] Taken in Short-Hand by an eminent Barrister. Dublin: M.N. Mahon, 1804. pp. viii, 95. complete with half-title. 8 vo. Disbound. Some staining to outer leaves, small piece missing from upper margin of D3 & D^4. Second Edition. 40.00

55 (TRIALS). The Speeches And Prayers Of Some of the late King's Judges, viz. Major Gen. Harrison, October. 13. Mr. John Carew, October. 15. Mr. Justice Cooke, Mr. Hugh Peters Octob. 16.

Mr. Tho. Scot, Mr. Gregory Clement, Col. Adrian Scroop, Col. John Jones, Oct. 17. Col. Dan Axtell, Col. Fran. Hacker, Octob. 19. 1660. The Times of their Death. Together with Several occasional Speeches and Passages in their Imprisonment, till they came to the place of Execution. Faithfully and Impartially Collected for further Satisfaction. [London]: 1660. pp. 2 pl, 96. 4 to. Disbound. Small hole in title page, some soiling to first few leaves. 60.00

Wing S4875. Abbott 1087.

56 (TRIALS). The Trials Of Patrick Maxwell Stewart Wallace, And Michael Shaw Stewart Wallace, For Willfully Destroying The Brig Dryad, Off Cuba, With Intent To Defraud The Marine Assurance Companies And Underwriters. London: Williams and Son, 1841. pp. 1 pl, viii, 294. 8 vo. Original blind stamped cloth, frayed and faded, backstrip off, internally VG. 60.00

57 TWISS, Horace. The Public And Private Life of Lord Chancellor Eldon, With Selections From His Correspondence. In Three Volumes. London: John Murray, 1844. pp. 514; xi, 614; viii, 518. 8 vo. 10 plates: 5 engravings, 5 lithographs,(4 plates of Vol. II bit damp stained at upper edge).Contemporary half calf, gilt stamped spine, morocco spine labels. extremities rubbed, one label off, light foxing to some plates, else VG. 100.00

58 WENTWORTH, Thomas. The Office and Duty of Executors: Or, A Treatise directing Testators to Form, and Executors to Perform their Wills and Testaments according to Law...And now enlarged with a Supplement containing Divers Matters and Things not comprised in former Impressions, relating to Wills, Executors, Administrators, Devises, Legacies, &c. Collected from the Common and Statute Laws, and methodically digested, rendring the whole compleat, and in all its Parts comformable to the present Time and Laws now in Force. With References to the several Acts of Parliament and authentick Books of Reports both Ancient and Modern authorizing and approving the same. By H. Curson. In the Savoy: Printed by Eliz. Nutt & R. Gosling, 1720. pp. 2 pl, vi, [10]contents, 468, [70]table, [2]ads. 8 vo. Contemporary calf, rubbed. Fr. bd. detached, back joint cracked, ink stain to fore edge. Library bookplate of J. Hall Pleasants, with number to lower spine, internally VG. 135.00

"The first two editions were anonymous, but the third, also appeared in 1641, bore the name of Thomas Wentworth. The work was, however, generally ascribed to the judge, Sir John Doddridge, and several indications in the book itself seem to support his claim." [DNB]

59 WIGHT, Alexander. A Treatise On The Laws Concerning The Election of the different Representatives sent from Scotland to the Parliament of Great Britain. With A Preliminary View of the Constitution of the Parliaments of England and Scotland, before the Union of the two Kingdoms. Edinburgh: Printed by Balfour & Smellie, 1773. pp. vii, 397, 16(index).8 vo. Contemporary calf, gilt lettered morocco spine label. Leather worn, fr. bd. detached, hint of foxing to 1st signature else a nice clean copy. Armorial bookplate of Sir James Stuart, Chief Justice of Lower Canada. 150.00

60 WILLIAMS, Edward. Precedents of Warrants, Convictions, And Other Proceedings, Before Justices Of The Peace,Chiefly Original; And Containing None That Are To Be Met With In Dr. Burn's Justice To Which This Publication Is Offered As A Supplement Of Practical Forms, Interspersed With Notes,

References to Cases, And Observations. London: Printed for R. Pheney, 1801. pp. vii, 667. index. 8 vo. contemporary calf, bit worn, gilt stamped morocco label. hint of foxing throughout,else a nice tight copy. 65.00

WILMOT, Sir John Eardley. Memoirs Of The Life Of The Right Honourable Sir John Eardley Wilmot, Knt. Late Lord Chief Justice Of The Court Of Common Pleas, And One Of His Majesty's Most Honourable Privy Council: With Some Original Letters. London: Printed by Luke Hansard & Sold by T. Cadell and W. Davies, 1802. pp. 2pl, 77. 2 engraved portraits (incl. frontis.). 4 to. original boards, worn and detached, some foxing, else a nice uncut copy. 60.00

WYNNE, William. The Life of Sir Leoline Jenkins, Judge of the High-Court of Admirality, and Prerogative Court of Canterbury, &c. Ambassador and Plenipotentiary For The General Peace At Cologn and Nimeguen, And Secretary of State to K. Charles II, And A Compleat Series of Letters, From The Beginning to the End of those Two Important Treaties, Wherein are related, The Most Remarkable Transactions of Those Times, both Foreign and Domestick. Together With Many valuable Papers and Original Letters, relating to the Rights and Privileges of the Universities, and other weighty Subjects. And the Resolution of many difficult and curious Points in the Common and Civil Law, Laws of Merchants and of Nations, that arose within the Time of his Ministry. Never Before Published. In Two Volumes. London: Printed for Joseph Dowing, William Taylor..., 1724. pp. xvii, [3]list of subscribers, civ, 552; iv, 792. engraved frontis portrait. numerous engraved vignettes. Folio. Contemporary calf, morocco spine labels, gilt backs. calf somewhat worn, head of spine of Vol. I repaired - new label, else a very nice clean copy. Folger Library duplicate, released. 350.00

Jenkins occupied posts in civil law, Pregrogative Court of Canterbury, and Maritime Law, Judge of High Court of Admirality. Jenkins' legal opinions on martime law are considered particulary valuable, as are his legal judgements on civil law.

BARGEN, Peter Frank. The Legal Status of the Canadian Public School Pupil. Toronto: Macmillan, 1961. pp. 172. biblio. 12.50

BARKER, Richard (Ed.). The Fatal Caress...and other accounts of English murders from 1551 to 1888. New York: Duell, Sloan, 1947. pp.210.biblio. 10.00

BARRY, Philip Beaufoy. Twenty Human Monsters In Purple And In Rags From Caligula To Landru A.D. 12-A.D. 1922. London: Jarrolds, [c1929]. pp. 286. illus. cloth slightly worn. 15.00

BARTH, Alan. The Price Of Liberty. New York: Viking, 1961. pp.212. index. 10.00

BARTON, George. Thrilling Triumphs Of Crime Detection. (Fwd. by J. Edgar Hoover). Philadelphia: David McKay, 1937. pp. 320. 10.00

BAR-YAACOV, Nissim. The Handling Of International Disputes By Means Of Inquiry. London: Published for The Royal Institute Of International Affairs by Oxford UP, 1974. pp. 370. biblio. index. 17.50

BELEBNOIT, Rene. Dry Guillotine: Fifteen Years Among The Living Dead. New York: Blue Ribbon, 1940. pp. 345. illus. 10.00

BELL, Charles W. Who Said Murder? Toronto: Macmillan, 1935. pp. 403. illus. index. 25.00

BELL, Clive. On British Freedom. New York: Harcourt, Brace, 1923. pp. 86. 12.50

BENSON, Allan L. The Usurped Power of the Courts. Chicago: Socialist Party, [c1911]. pp. 64. wrs. sl. chipped at edges. (Reprinted from Pearson's Magazine 1911). 15.00

BEZE, Theodore de. Du Droit Des Magistrats Sur Leurs Subiets.Avec une Introduction et des notes par M. Marabuto. Saint-Julian-L'Ars, France: Imprimerie Monastique, 1968. pp. 106. index. wrs. 10.00

BIERSTADT, Edward Hale. Curious Trials & Criminal Cases: From Socrates to Scopes. New York: Coward-McCann, 1928. pp. 366. illus. 12.50

BLACK, Ladbroke. Some Queer People. London: Sampson Row, Marston, nd. pp. 244. illus. front board slightly stained. 10.00

BOETTIGER, John. Jake Lingle or Chicago on the Spot. New York: E.P. Dutton, 1931. pp. 335. illus. 10.00

BOLITHO, William. Murder For Profit. New York: Garden City, 1926. pp. 332. 7.50

BOND, Raymond T. Handbook For Poisoners: A Collection Of Famous Poison Stories Selected, With An Introduction On Poisons. New York: Rinehart, 1951. pp. 311. 7.50

BORCHARD, Edwin M. Convicting the Innocent: Errors Of Criminal Justice. New Haven: Yale UP, 1932. pp. 421. cloth slightly soiled. 20.00

BORDWELL, Percy. The Law Of War Between Belligerents: A History And Commentary. Chicago: Callaghan, 1908. pp. 374. index. Publisher's letter tipped in to front pastedown presenting book to Col. Dudley. library stamp of Col. Dudley. 20.00

BORGEAUD, Charles. Adoption And Amendment Of Constitutions In Europe And America. New York: Macmillan, 1895. pp. xxi, 353. partially unopened. cloth worn, free endpapers soiled, damp stained. 15.00

BORNSTEIN, Joseph. The Politics of Murder. New York: William Sloane, 1950. pp. 295. illus. 10.00

BOWEN, Catherine Drinker. Yankee From Olympus: Justice Holmes and His Family. Boston: Little, Brown, 1944. pp. 475. illus. biblio.index. 7.50

BOYER, Raymond. Les Crimes Et Les Chatiments Au Canada Francais Du XVII Au XX Siecle: Le crime est un acte considere comme prejudiciable a la societe par un groupe d'hommes ayant le pouvoir de donner force de loi a ses considerations. Montreal: Le Cercle Du Livre De France,

ABRAHAMS, Gerald. According To The Evidence: An Essay on Legal Proof. London: Cassell, 1958. pp. 248. index. 12.50

ADAM, George. Treason And Tragedy: An Account Of French War Trials. London: Jonathan Cape, 1929. pp. 254. 10.00

ADAM, Hargrave Lee. Murder By Persons Unknown. London: W. Collins, 1931. pp. 286. 10.00

----Murder Most Mysterious. London: Sampson Low, Marston, [c1932]. pp. 270. back board stained. 10.00

AMNESTY INTERNATIONAL. Prison Conditions In East Germany: Conditions For Political Prisoners. A Factual Report Compiled By...London: 1966. pp. 56. wrs. 7.50

----Report On Torture. New York: Farrar, Straus & Giroux, 1975. pp. 285. biblio. 10.00

ANDREWS, Bert. Washington Witch Hunt. New York: Random House, 1948. pp. 218. front free endpaper wanting. dustjacket taped on. tape mend to title page. 10.00

ANGER, William H. & H.D. Anger. Summary of Canadian Commercial Law. 18th Ed. Revised by Frederick R. Hume. Toronto: Putnam & Sons, 1962. pp. 530. index. 12.50

ARMSTRONG, C.H.A. The Honourable Society Of Osgoode Hall with an appendix on The History and Architecture of the Fabric by E.R. Arthur. Toronto: Clarke, Irwin & Company, 1952. pp. 60. illus. biblio. 20.00

ARNOLD, Thurman W. The Symbols of Government. New Haven: Yale UP, 1935. pp. 278. index. 15.00

ARROW, Charles. Rogues And Others. London: Duckworth, 1926. pp. 224. illus. 12.50

ASHBURY, Herbert. The Barbary Coast: An Informal History Of The San Francisco Underworld. New York: Garden City, 1933. pp. 319, xi. biblio. index.illus. 12.50

----Gem Of The Prairie: An Informal History Of The Chicago Underworld. New York: Alfred A. Knopf, 1940. pp. 377, xix. illus. biblio. index.12.50

----The French Quarter: An Informal History Of The New Orleans Underworld. New York: Garden City, 1938. pp. 462, xvi. illus.biblio.index.12.50

----Sucker's Progress: An Informal History Of Gambling In America From The Colonies To Canfield. New York: Dodd, Mead, 1938. pp. 493. illus. biblio. index. 20.00

ASINOF, Eliot. People vs. Blutcher: Black Men And White Law In Bedford-Stuyvesant. New York: Viking, 1970. pp. 239. 7.50

ATLAY, J.B. Famous Trials Of The Century: Weare and Thurtell; The Burke and Hare Case; The Queen against Courvoisier; Barber's Case; The Queen against Madeleine Smith; The Road Mystery; The Queen against Pritchard; The Tichborne Case. London: Grant Richards, 1899. pp. 393. illus. back board slightly stained. 20.00

BALCHIN, Nigel. The Anatomy Of Villany. London: Collins, 1950. pp. 256. illus (Chapters on Francis Chateris, Marquis de Sade, Rasputin &c).12.50

BALLANTINE, Serjeant. Some Experiences Of A Barrister's Life. In Two Volumes. Third Edition. London: Richard Bentley, 1882. pp. xv, 321; xiv, 308, 48 [ads]. frontis. index. 30.00

BARBER, James David. The Lawmakers:Recruitment and Adaptation to Legislative Life. New Haven: Yale UP, 1965. pp. 314. index. 10.00

107 BOYD, Julian P. & W. Edwin Hemphill. The Murder of George Wythe: Two Essays. Williamsburg: Insitute of Early American History & Culture, 1955. pp. 64. frontis. wrs. 7.50

08 (BRANDEIS, Louis D.). The Curse Of Bigness: Miscellaneous Papers Of Louis D. Brandeis. Edited by Osmond D. Fraenkel As Projected By Clarence M. Lewis. New York: Viking Press, 1935. pp. 339. bds. faded.12.50

09 BROOKS, Collin (Ed.). The Royal Mail Case: Rex v. Lord Kylsant, and Another. Toronto: Canada Law Book, 1933. pp. 276. illus. fold out chart. some coloured pencil scoring. 10.00

10 BROWNE, Douglas G. & E.V. Tullett. Bernard Spilsbury: His Life and Cases. London: George Harrap, 1951. pp. 422. illus. index. 15.00

11 BRYAN, Geoffrey. Off With His Head! London: Hutchinson, 1954. pp. 288 + ads. illus. (History of Decapitation). 12.50

12 BRYSON, Thomas A. Walter George Smith. Washington: Catholic UP, 1977. pp. 225. biblio. index. 7.50

13 BURROWS, Roland. Phipson's Manual Of The Law Of Evidence For The Use Of Students. Sixth Edition. London: Sweet & Maxwell, 1943. pp. 341. index. 7.50

14 BUSCH, Francis X. Enemies Of The State: An Account of the Trials of The Mary Eugenia Surratt Case; The Teapot Dome Cases; The Alphonse Capone Case; The Rosenberg Case. Indianapolis: Bobbs-Merrill, 1954. pp. 299. First Edition. 15.00

15 ----Prisoners At The Bar: An Account of the Trials of The William Haywood Case; The Sacco-Vanzetti Case; The Loeb-Leopold Case; The Bruno Hauptmann Case. Indianapolis: Bobbs-Merrill, 1952. pp. 288. 15.00

16 ----They Escaped The Hangman: An Account of the Trials of The Caleb Powers Case; The Rice-Patrick Case; The Hall-Mills Case; The Hans Haupt Case. Indianapolis: Bobbs-Merrill, 1953. pp. 301. 15.00

17 [BYRNE, Julia Clara]. Curiosities Of The Search-Room: A Collection Of Serious, And Whimsical Wills. By The Author Of "Flemish Interiors", &c. London: Chapman & Hall, 1880. pp. 407. index. back board stained, joints cracked. 35.00

18 (CAMPBELL, John, [first Baron] Campbell. Life Of John, Lord Campbell, Lord High Chancellor of Great Britain: Consisting Of A Selection From His Autobiography, Diary, and Letters. Edited by His Daughter The Hon. Mrs. Hardcastle. In Two Volumes. London: John Murray, 1881. pp. 12, 528; 11, 410. 8 vo. engraved frontis. portrait. contemporary three quarter morocco, gilt stamping to spine, marbled endpapers. joints cracked, backstrips faded, extremities rubbed, internally a nice clean tight copy. 40.00

9 [CANADA]. Report to The Minister Of Justice of the Special Committee on Hate Propaganda In Canada. Ottawa: Queen's Printer, 1966. pp. 327. wrs. 12.50

0 CAREY, Arthur A. Memoirs Of A Murder Man. Garden City: Doubleday, Doran, 1930. pp. 326. illus. covers slightly soiled. 7.50

1 CARR, Robert K. Federal Protection of Civil Rights: Quest for a Sword. Ithaca: Cornell UP, 1947. pp. 284. index. 12.50

2 CECIL, Henry. Brief To Counsel. London: Michael Joseph, 1958. pp. 190. illus. index. 7.50

3 CECIL, William (Lord Burghley). Execution Of Justice In England (1583). New York: Scholars' Facsimiles & Reprints, 1938. pp. xiii, [80]. 12.50

4 CLARK, Sir George (Ed.). The Campden Wonder. London: Oxford UP, 1959. pp. 155. illus. index. 7.50

5 COCKBURN, Harry A. (Ed.). Some Letters Of Lord Cockburn With Pages Omitted From The Memorials Of His Time. Edinburgh: Grant & Murray, [illegible] 130. index. 12.50

COMMONWEALTH AND EMPIRE LAW CONFERENCE. Record Of The Commonwealth And Empire Law Conference. London, 20th-27th July, 1955. Published with the Authority of the Executive Committee of the Conference. London: Solicitors' Law Stationery Society, 1956. pp. 471.illus. (Articles on law reform, legal aid, including Canadian contributors).15.

COOPER, Courtney Ryley. Designs In Scarlet. Boston: Little, Brown, 1939. pp. 372. 10.0C

----Here's To Crime. Boston: Little, Brown, 1937. pp.454. 10.0C

COOPER, John Cobb. Explorations In Aerospace Law: Selected essays by John Cobb Cooper 1946-1966. Montreal: McGill UP, 1968. pp. 480.biblio. index. 10.00

COOPER, R. Weldon. Municipal Police Administration In Texas. Chicago: University of Chicago, 1938. pp. 320. index.wrs. [PHD Dissertation].10.0

CORRY, J.A. Law And Policy: The W.M. Martin Lectures, 1957. [Toronto]: Clarke, Irwin, 1959. pp. 78. 12.50

CORWIN, Edward S. The Constitution And What It Means Today. (Revised by Harold W. Chase & Craig R. Ducat). Princeton: Princeton UP, 1973. pp. 601. 15.00

COWAN, Samuel. The Lord Chancellors Of Scotland From The Institution Of The Office To The Treaty Of Union. 2 Vols. Edinburgh: W. & A.K. Johnston, 1911. pp. 307; 299. frontis. portraits. index. 45.00

COTLER, Irwin & Herbert Marx (Eds.). The Law and the Poor in Canada. Montreal: Black Rose, 1977. pp. 143. 7.5C

COX, Homersham. The British Commonwealth: or a Commentary on the Institutions and Principles of British Government. London: Longman, Brown, Green & Longmans, 1854. pp. 576. Rebound in buckram. 25.0C

CROUSE, Russel. Murder Won't Out. Garden City: Doubleday, Doran, 1932. pp. 261. illus. 10.0C

CRUMP, Paul. Grille, Assassin Grille! Paris: Presses De La Cite, 1963. pp. 345. 6.00

CULLEN, Tom. The Mild Murderer: The True Story of the Dr Crippen Case. Boston: Houghton Mifflin, 1977. pp. 211. illus. 6.00

CURRAN, John Philpot. Speeches Of John Philpot Curran, While At The Bar. Chicago: Callaghan & Co., 1877. pp. 618. frontis. portrait. cloth slightly stained. 15.0C

CURTIS, Benjamin Robbins. A Memoir Of Benjamin Robbins Curtis, LL.D. With Some Of His Professional And Miscellaneous Writings. 2 Vols. Boston: Little, Brown, 1879. pp. 490; 440. frontis. portraits. index. spines frayed. 35.00

DARK, Sidney. Twelve More Ladies: Good, Bad And Indifferent. [London]: Hodder & Stoughton, 1932. pp. 285. cloth stained, edges soiled. 10.00

DARROW, Clarence. Plea of Clarence Darrow August 22nd 23rd & 25th MCMXXIIII In Defense of Richard Loeb And Nathan Leopold Jr on Trial for Murder. Authorized and Revised Edition Together with a brief Summary of the Facts. Chicago: Ralph Fletcher Seymour, [c1924]. pp. 121. wrs. chipped & slightly soiled. 20.00

[DARROW, Clarence]. Darrow-Lewis Debate On The Theory Of Non-Resistance To Evil For: Clarence Darrow Against: Arthur Morrow Lewis. Kansas: Haldeman-Julius Publications, nd. pp. 24. wrs. 6.00

DAVENPORT, William H. Voices In Court: A Treasury of the Bench, the Bar, and the Courtroom. New York: Macmillan, 1958. pp. 588. index. l. pencil scoring. 10.00

DEMPERWOLFF, Richard. Famous Old New England Murders and Some That Are Infamous. Vermont: Stephen Daye Press, 1942. pp. 293. biblio. index. 10.00

DEMPSEY, Hugh A. (Ed.). William Parker: Mounted Policeman. Edmonton: Hurtig Publishers, 1973. pp. 163. illus. biblio. 7.50

DICEY, A.V. Lectures On The Relation Between Law & Public Opinion In England During The Nineteenth Century. London: Macmillan & Co., 1926. pp. 506. index. some pen scoring, cloth worn. 15.00

DILNOT, George. Celebrated Crimes. London: Stanley Paul, 1925. pp. 256. illus. 12.50

----Great Detectives And Their Methods. London: Geoffrey Bles, [c1930]. pp. 271. illus. index. 12.50

----Rogues' March. London: Geoffrey Bles, 1934. pp. 240. 12.50

----Triumps Of Detection: A Book About Detectives. London: Geoffrey Bles, [c1930]. pp. 273. illus. 12.50

DITTON, Jason. Part-Time Crime: An Ethnography of Fiddling and Pilferage. London: Macmillan, 1977. pp. 195. biblio. index. 20.00

DIXON, Hepworth. John Howard, And The Prison-World Of Europe. Slightly Abridged. Webster: Frederick Charlton, 1852. pp. 442. Original gilt and blind stamped cloth. spine slightly frayed, some foxing. 20.00

DOLCI, Danilo. Outlaws. New York: Orion, 1961. pp. 296. 10.00

DOUGHTY, Arthur G. & Norah Story. Documents Relatifs a l'Histoire Constitutionelle du Canada 1819-1828: Choisis et Edites Avec Notes Par... Ottawa: J.O. Patenaude, 1935. pp. xi,543. index. (Archives Publiques).40.0 wrs.

DOUTHWAITE, L.C. Mass Murder. London: John Long, 1928. pp. 288. illus. cloth slightly worn. 15.00

DUFF, John J. A. Lincoln: Prairie Lawyer. New York: Rinehart, 1960. 433. illus. biblio. index. first edition. 12.50

DUMAS, Alexander. Celebrated Crimes. 8 Volumes. New York: P F Collier, 1910. Gilt stamped cloth. (Deluxe Edition). Illus. 40.00

DUNCAN, Lewis & John D. Honsberger. Bankruptcy In Canada. Third Edition. Toronto: Canadian Legal Authors, 1961. pp. 1188. index. 20.00

DUNNE, Gerald T. Hugo Black And The Judicial Revolution. New York: Simon & Schuster, 1977. pp. 492. illus. biblio. index. 10.00

----Justice Joseph Story and the Rise of the Supreme Court. New York: Simon & Schuster, 1970. pp. 458. illus. biblio. index. 10.00

EATON, Harold. Famous Poison Trials. London: W. Collins, 1924. pp. 246. 7.50

EIDE, Asbjorn & August Schou (Eds.). International Protection of Human Rights: Proceedings of the Seventh Nobel Symposium Oslo, September 25-27, 1967. Stockholm: Almqvist & Wiksell, 1968. pp. 300. 20.00

ELIAS, T.O. (Ed.). Law and Social Change in Nigeria. Lagos: U of Lagos, 1972. pp. 292. index. 12.50

ELLIS, Havelock. The Criminal. London: Walter Scott, 1890. pp. 337. illus. index. cloth worn, back joint cracked. 15.0C

ELLIS, J.C. Black Fame: Stories of Crime and Criminals. London: Hutchinson, nd. pp. 320. 12.5

FAIRMAN, Charles. Mr. Justice Miller And The Supreme Court 1862-1890. Cambridge: Harvard UP, 1939. pp. 456. illus. index. 20.00

FEINSTEIN, Isidor. The Court Disposes. New York: Covici Friede, 1937. pp. 127. 10.00

FENTON, Frances. The Influence of Newspaper Presentations Upon the Growth of Crime and Other Anti-Social Activity. Chicago: U of Chicago Press, 1911. pp. 96. wrs. back wr. wanting. [PHD Dissertation]. 8.50

FERRI, Enrico. Criminal Sociology. New York: Appleton, 1898. pp. 284. half morocco, marbled boards. title leaf detached but present. 17.50

----The Positive School of Criminology. Chicago: Kerr, 1906. pp.125.12.50

FIELDING, Cecil. Justice Triumphant. London: Lang, 1958. pp. 167. index. 7.50

FLEMING, Amalia. A Piece of Truth. Boston: Houghton, Mifflin, 1973. pp. 257. 7.50

FLETCHER, Ronald. The Akenham Burial Case. London: Wildwood House, 1974. pp. 280. 12.50

FOUCHE, Joseph. Memoires De Joseph Fouche, Duc D'Obtrante, Ministre De La Police Generale. Reimpression de l'edition 1824. Osnabruck: Biblio-Verlag, 1966. In 2 Volumes. pp. 418; 384. gilt stamped cloth.15.00

FOWLER, Gene. The Great Mouthpiece: A Life Story of William J. Fallon. New York: Covici Friede, 1932. pp. 403. 7.5C

FRANK, Leonhard. The Cause Of The Crime. London: Peter Davies, 1928. pp. 188. 7.50

FRANKFURTER, Felix. The Public & Its Government. New Haven: Yale UP, 1930. pp. 169. 15.00

FRENCH, Joseph Lewis. The Book of The Rogue: Studies Of Famous Scoundrels. New York: Boni & Liveright, 1926. pp. 399. illus. 12.50

FRIDMAN, G.H.L. (Ed.). Studies In Canadian Business Law. Toronto: Butterworths, 1971. pp. 580. index. 20.00

FRIEDLAND, Martin L. Detention before Trial: A Study Of Criminal Cases Tried In The Toronto Magistrates' Courts. Toronto: U of Toronto Press, 1965. pp. 202. index. 15.00

GALTIER-BOISSIERE, Jean. Mysteries Of The French Secret Police. London: Stanley Paul, 1938. pp. 292. illus. index. 12.50

GAYLIN, Willard. In the Service of Their Country: War Resisters In Prison. New York: Viking, 1970. pp. 344. 7.50

GAZELL, James A. State Trial Courts As Bureaucracies: A Study In Judicial Management. np: Kennikat Press, 1975. pp.168. biblio. Lacking front free endpaper. 7.50

GIBSON, Dale & Lee. Substantial Justice: Law and Lawyers In Manitoba 1670-1970. Winnipeg: Peguis Publishers, 1972. pp. 357. illus.index.12.50

[GIFFARD, Hardinge Stanley], Earl Of Halsbury. The Laws Of England Being A Complete Statement Of The Whole Law Of England. 31 Vols. London: Butterworth & Co., 1907. quarter morocco, sl. worn. 150.00

GISNET, Morris. A Lawyer Tells The Truth. (Intro. Nroman Thomas). New York: Kahn, 1931. pp. 160. 12.50

GLUECK, Eleanor. Criminal Careers In Retrospect. New York: Commonwealth Fund, 1943. pp. 380. index. 15.00

GODWIN, William. Enquiry concerning Political Justice and its influence on Morals And Happiness. Photographic facsimile of the third edition corrected. Edited with variant readings of the first and second editions and with a critical introduction and notes by F.E.L. Priestley. 3 Vols. Toronto: U of Toronto Press, 1969. pp. 463; 554; 344. 35.00

-An Enquiry Concerning Political Justice And Its Influence On General Virtue And Happiness. Edited and Abridged by Raymond A. Preston. 2 Vols. New York: Alfred A. Knopf, 1923. pp. 255; 307. index. 15.00

----Enquiry Concerning Political Justice: With selections from Godwin's other writings. Abridged And Edited By K. Codell Carter. Oxford: At The Clarendon Press, 1971. pp. 347. index. 12.50

GOODWIN, John C. Crook Pie. London: Alston Rivers, 1927. pp. 319. 10.00

GOLDBERG, Louis P. & Eleanore Levinson. Lawless Judges. (Intro. Prof. Morris R. Cohen). New York: Rand School, 1935. pp. 303. index. 20.00

GOLLOMB, Joseph. Crimes Of The Year. New York: Horace Liveright, 1931. pp. 354. 10.00

----Master Highwaymen. New York: Macaulay, 1927. pp. 312. 10.00

----Master Man Hunters. New York: Macaulay, 1926. pp. 315. 10.00

----Spies. New York: Macmillan, 1928. pp. 389. 12.50

GOUDY, Henry. Trichotomy In Roman Law. Oxford: At The Clarendon Press, 1910. pp. 77. spine tips bit frayed, bds. bit sunned. 20.00

Goudy's work deals with the symbolic influence of the number 3 in Roman Law. "...many of the Roman lawyers were influenced by the symbolism of numbers, as regards both the external arrangement of their works and the classifications of the subject-matter contained in them..." [pp. 3].

GRAEME, Bruce. Passion, Murder and Mystery. London: Hutchinson, [c1930]. pp. 287. sl. stain to back bd. 15.00

GREENE, Ward (Ed.). Star Reporters and 34 of their stories. New York: Random House, 1948. pp. 402. 10.00

GRIFFITHS, Arthur. Mysteries Of Police And Crime. In Three Volumes. Special Edition. London: Cassell, [c1880]. pp. 464; 464; 464. profusely illustrated. index. joints weak, extremities sl. rubbed, else a very nice copy. (Chapters on police in France, England, Russia, India &c. Also chapters on every conceivable criminal activity and notorious criminal.) 100.00

GRISWOLD, H. Jack, Mike Misenheimer, Arts Powers, Ed Tromanhauser. An Eye For An Eye. New York: Holt, Rinehart, 1970. pp. 288. 7.50

GROSS, Fred L. What Is the Verdict? New York: Macmillan, 1944. pp. 311. 10.00

HADFIELD, R.L. Picturesque Rogues: A Chronicle Of The Lives And Adventures Of A Diversity Of Rogues In Which Will Be Found Something Of The Romantic, Something Of The Picturesque, And Occasionally Something Of The Saving Grace Of Humour. London: H.F. & G. Witherby, 1931. pp. 207. index. bk. bd. slightly stained. 12.50

HAINES, Charles Grove. The American Doctrine Of Judicial Supremacy. New York: Russell & Russell, 1959. pp. 705. index. 12.50

HALL, John. Four Famous Mysteries. London: Nisbet, 1922. 228.index.10.00

HALL, William Edward. A Treatise On International Law. Sixth Edition. Edited by J. B. Atlay. Oxford: At The Clarendon Press, 1909. pp. 768. index. some pencil notes. 15.00

HALLAM, Henry. The Constitutional History Of England From The Accession Of Henry VII To The Death Of George II. From the Fifth London Edition. New York: Harper, 1847. pp. xi, 737. Modern Buckram, marbled edges. slight foxing. 45.00

HAND, Learned. The Spirit Of Liberty: Papers And Addresses Of Learned Hand. Collected, And With An Introduction And Notes, By Irving Dilliard. Second Edition, Enlarged. New York: Alfred A. Knopf, 1953. pp. 285. 7.50

HARLAN, John M. The Evolution Of A Judicial Philosophy: Selected Opinions And Papers Of Justice John M. Harlan. Ed. by David L. Shapiro.

HARPER, Fowler V. Justice Rutledge And The Bright Constellation. Indianapolis: Bobbs-Merrill, 1965. pp. 406. illus. index. 10.00

HARPER, Lawrence A. The English Navigation Laws: A Seventeenth-Century Experiment In Social Engineering. New York: Columbia UP, 1939. pp. 502. biblio. index. 15.00

HARRIS, Sara. Hellhole: The Shocking Story of the Inmates and Life in the New York City House of Detention for Women. New York: E.P. Dutton, 1967. pp. 288. 7.50

HART, H.L.A. Punishment and Responsibility: Essays in the Philosophy of Law. New York: Oxford UP, 1968. pp. 271. index. 10.00

HARVEY, C.P. The Advocate's Devil. London: Stevens & Sons, 1958. pp. 177. 12.50

HASTINGS, Patrick. Cases In Court. London: William Heinemann, 1949. pp. 342. illus. index. 12.50

HAWORTH, Peter. Classic Crimes In History And Fiction. New York: D. Appleton, 1927. pp. 286. 10.00

HAYS, Arthur Garfield. Trial By Prejudice. New York: Covici Friede, 1933. pp. 369. illus. index. 15.00

HAWKES, C.P. Bench And Bar In The Saddle: The Pegasus Club During Three Reigns...London: Everleigh Nash & Grayson, 1928. pp. 243. illus. index. 20.00

HEAD, Richard & Francis Kirkman. The English Rogue Described In The Life Of Meriton Latroon A Witty Extravagant Being A Complete History of the Most Eminent Cheats of Both Sexes. New York: Dodd, Mead, 1928. pp. 660. 12 plates. large 8 vo. 35.00

HERLING, John. The Great Price Conspiracy: The Story of the Antitrust Violations in the Electrical Industry. Washington: Robert B. Luce, 1962. pp. 366. glossary index. 12.50

HJALMARSON, Glenn. Just Call Us Bandits. Toronto: Longmans, 1961. pp. 190. 7.50

HOLBROOK, Stewart H. Murder Out Yonder: An Informal Study of Certain Classic Crimes in Back-Country America. New York: Macmillan, 1941. pp. 255. index. 12.50

HOLLAND, Thomas Erskine. The Elements of Jurisprudence. Fourth Edition. Oxford: At The Clarendon Press, 1887. pp. 378. index. some pencil scoring, cloth slightly rubbed. 25.00

HOLLICK, Ann L. & Robert E. Osgood. New Eras Of Ocean Politics. (Studies in International Affairs Number 22). Baltimore: Johns Hopkins UP, 1974. pp. 131. 6.50

HOLMES, Grace W. & Mary I. Hiniker. The Liability Of Professionals: Malpractice. Ann Arbor: Institute of Continuing Legal Education, 1976. pp. 302. 12.50

(HOLMES, Oliver Wendell). Holmes-Pollock Letters: The Correspondence of Mr. Justice Holmes and Sir Frederick Pollock 1874-1932. Ed. by Mark DeWolfe Howe. (Intro. by John Gorham Palfrey). 2 Vols. Cambridge: Harvard UP, 1944. pp. 275, 359. illus. index. 40.00

HOOD, Roger. Borstal Re-Assessed. London: Heinemann, 1965. pp. 244. biblio. index. fr. endpaper clipped. 12.50

HOPKINS, Ernest Jerome. Our Lawless Police: A Study of the Unlawful Enforcement of the Law. New York: Viking, 1931. pp. 379. index. 12.50

HOSKINS, Percy. No Hiding Place! The full authentic story of Scotland Yard In Action. [London]: Daily Express, nd. pp. 192. illus. 10.00

KARPINSKY, V. The Social and State Structure of the U.S.S.R. Moscow: Foreign Languages Pub. House, 1952. pp. 240. illus. 7.50

KATKOV, George. The Trial of Bukharin. London: Batsford, 1969. pp. 255. illus. index. 10.00

KENNAN, George. Siberia and the Exile System. 2 Vols. New York: New Century, 1891. pp. xv, 409; x, 575. frontis & numerous illus. index. attractive blind & gilt stamped original publisher's cloth. 75.00

----Siberia and the Exile System. (Abridged from the 1st ed. of 1891). (Intro. George Frost Kennan). Chicago: Univ. of Chicago Press, 1958. pp. 244. illus. 12.50

KETCHUM, J. Davidson. Ruhleben: A Prison Camp Society. (Fwd. & Post-script Robert B. MacLeod). Toronto: University of Toronto Press, 1965. pp. 397. frontis. biblio. index. library stamps. 12.50

KING, Willard L. Melville Weston Fuller: Chief Justice Of The United States 1888-1910. New York: Macmillan, 1950. pp. 394. illus.index.12.50

KINGSTON, Charles. A Gallery of Rogues. London: Stanley Paul, 1924. pp. 243. illus. index. 10.00

----Law-Breakers. London: John Lane, 1930. pp. 280. index. 10.00

----Rogues And Adventuresses. London: John Lane, 1928. pp.238. illus. index. 10.00

KOBLER, John. Ardent Spirits: The Rise and Fall Of Prohibition. New York: Putnam, 1973. pp. 386. illus. biblio. index. 7.50

KRAVCHENKO, Victor. I Chose Freedom: The Personal and Political Life of a Soviet Official. New York: Scribners, 1946. pp. 496. index. 7.50

LAMBTON, Arthur. Echoes Of Causes Celebres. London: Hurst & Blackett, nd. pp. 277. illus. 10.00

----"Thou Shalt Do No Murder" London: Hurst & Blackett, nd. pp.282. illus. boards slightly stained. 10.00

LANDON, Michael. The Triumph Of The Lawyers: Their Role in English Politics, 1678-1689. Alabama: U of Alabama Press, 1970. pp.303. index. 12.50

LANE, Mark. Rush To Judgement: A Critique of the Warren Commission's Inquiry Into the Murders of President John F. Kennedy, Officer J.D. Tippit, and Lee Harvey Oswald. New York: Holt, Rinehart, 1966.pp. 478. index. 7.50

LANG, Andrew. James VI and the Gowrie Mystery. London: Longmans, Green, 1902. pp. 280 with 40 pp. literature catalogue bound in. frontis. 2 photogravure portraits & 11 other illus & 3 plans. index. spine dull and slightly frayed. gilt stamped cloth. 30.00

----The Valet's Tragedy And Other Studies. London: Longmans, Green, 1903. pp. 366. with 40 pp. of publisher's ads. illus. index.original gilt stamped cloth. rubbed.& stained. 25.00

LANG, O.E. (Ed.). Contemporary Problems Of Public Law In Canada: Essays in Honour of Dean F.C. Cronkite. Toronto: U of Toronto Press for College of Law U of Saskatchewan, 1968. pp. 171. frontis. 10.00

LASH, Joseph P. (Ed.). From The Diaries Of Felix Frankfurter. New York: W.W. Norton, 1975. pp. 366. index. 10.00

LAVINE, Emanuel H. The Third Degree: A Detailed and Appalling Expose of Police Brutality. New York: Vanguard, 1930. pp. 248. spine tips frayed, cloth spotted. 7.50

LAW SOCIETY OF UPPER CANADA. The Rules Of The Law Society Of Upper Canada Passed In Convocation, June 21st, 1928. Together With The Law Society Act; The Barristers Act And The Solicitors Act And An Index. Toronto: Printed For The Society By The Monetary Times, 1928. pp. 125. wrs. slightly stained. pen notes. 12.50

HOWE, Mark DeWolfe. Justice Oliver Wendell Holmes. 2 Vols. Includes The Shaping Years 1841-1870 & The Proving Years 1870-1882. Cambridge: Harvard UP, 1957. pp. 330; 295. illus. index. slight pencil scoring. 25.00

HUGHES, Graham (Ed.). Law, Reason and Justice: Essays in Legal Philosophy. New York: New York UP, 1969. pp. 269. 12.50

HUME-WILLIAMS, Ellis. The World, The House And The Bar. London: John Murray, 1930. pp. 272. illus. index. 15.00

HYND, Alan. Passport to Treason: The Inside Story Of Spies In America. New York: Robert M. McBride, 1943. pp. 306. 10.00

INGPEN, Arthur Robert (Ed.). Master Worsley's Book On The History And Constitution Of The Honourable Society Of The Middle Temple. London: Printed At The Chiswick Press & Published by Order Of The Masters Of The Bench, 1910. pp. 340. 14 plates & 4 plans. index. quarter morocco. uncut. slight staining to upper boards. 50.00

IREY, Elmer L. The Tax Dodgers: The Inside Story of the T-Men's War With America's Political and Underworld Hoodlums...As Told To William J. Slocum. New York: Greenberg, 1948. pp. 288. 7.50

IRVING, H.B. A Book Of Remarkable Criminals. London: Cassell, 1918. pp. 336. index. 2 small nicks to spine. 10.00

----Last Studies In Criminology. London: W. Collins, 1921. pp. 281.12.50

----Studies Of French Criminals Of The Nineteenth Century. London: William Heinemann, 1901. pp. 356. fr. free endpaper wanting, bit loose. 20.00

IWI, Edward F. Laws And Flaws: Lapses of the Legislators. London: Odhams, 1956. pp. 224. index. 15.00

JAFFARY, Stuart King. Sentencing of Adults in Canada. Toronto: U of Toronto Press, 1963. pp. 122. index. 7.50

JAMES, Marlise. The People's Lawyers. New York: Holt, Rinehart, 1973. pp. 368. 7.50

JELF, Ernest Arthur. Fifteen Decisive Battles Of The Law: Being A Study Of Some Leading Cases In The Law Of England. Second Edition. London: Sweet & Maxwell, 1921. pp. 124. coloured pencil scoring. 10.00

JENNINGS, W. Ivor. Cabinet Government. Cambridge: At The University Press, 1936. pp. 484. biblio. index. cloth slightly faded. 15.00

JOAD, C.E.M. Liberty To-Day. Revised Edition. London: Watts & Co., 1938. pp. 221. 7.50

JOHNSON, W. Branch. The Age Of Arsenic: Being an Account of the Life, Trial, and Execution of Catherine Montvoisin...together with a Relation of their various Transactions in Poison, Abortion, and Black or Satanic Masses...London: Chapman & Hall, [c1931]. pp. 260.illus.index. 10.00

JOHNSON, William R. Schooled Lawyers: A Study In The Clash Of Professional Cultures. New York: New York UP, 1978. pp. 215. illus. index. 12.50

JONAS, George & Barbara Amiel. By Persons Unknown: The Strange Death of Christine Demeter. Toronto: Macmillan, 1977. pp. 349. illus. 7.50

JONES, P. Asterley. Mozley And Whiteley's Law Dictionary. Sixth Edition. London: Butterworth, 1950. pp. 376. 10.00

JUSTINIAN. The Institutes Of Justinian; With English Introduction, Translation, And Notes By Thomas Collett Sandars. London: John W. Parker, 1853. pp. iv, 614[10]ads. modern buckram. 35.00

----Special Lectures Of The Law Society Of Upper Canada 1950: Company Law. Toronto: Richard De Boo, 1950. pp. 252. 15.00

----Special Lectures Of The Law Society Of Upper Canada 1968: Developments In Company Law. Toronto: Richard De Boo, 1968. pp. 396. index. front board spotted. 15.00

----Special Lectures Of The Law Society Of Upper Canada On Taxation 1944. Toronto: Richard De Boo, 1944. pp. 410. 15.00

LEAGE, R.W. Roman Private Law: Founded On The 'Institutes' Of Gaius And Justinian. London: Macmillan, 1906. pp. 429. index. cloth rubbed. a bit loose. 12.50

LEBOURDAIS, Isabel. The Trial Of Steven Truscott. Toronto: McClelland & Stewart, 1966. pp. 240. 10.00

LENOTRE, G. The Guillotine And Its Servants. London: Hutchinson, nd. pp. 282. illus. slight foxing to outer edges, cloth sl. stained. 20.00

----The September Massacres: Accounts Of Personal Experiences Written By Some Of The Few Survivors Of The Terrible Days Of September 2nd And 3rd, 1792, Together With A Series Of Hitherto Unpublished Police Reports. London: Hutchinson, nd. pp. 288. illus. some foxing. 20.00

LIEBER, Francis. On Civil Liberty And Self-Government. London: Richard Bentley, 1853. pp. xv, 552. index. Original blind stamped cloth. partially unopened. cloth faded, hinges cracked, spine chipped. First British Edition. 50.00

Sabin 40974.

LOADES, D.M. The Oxford Martyrs. London: B.T.Batsford, 1970. pp. 296. biblio. index. 12.50

LOBENTHAL, Joseph S. Power and Put-On The Law In America. New York: Outerbridge & Dienstfrey, 1970. pp. 187. 7.50

LOGAN, Guy. B.H. Dramas Of The Dock: True Stories of Crime. London: Stanley Paul, 1928. pp. 286. illus. 12.50

----Great Murder Mysteries. London: Stanley Paul, 1931. pp. 288.illus. 12.50

----Guilty Or Not Guilty? Stories Of Celebrated Crimes. London: Stanley Paul, nd. pp. 288. illus. 12.50

----Masters Of Crime: Studies Of Multiple Murders. London: Stanley Paul, 1928. pp. 288. illus. 15.00

----Rope, Knife And Chair: Studies Of English, French And American Crimes. London: Stanley Paul, nd. pp. 280. illus. 12.50

LORIMER, James. The Institutes Of The Law Of Nations: A Treatise Of The Jural Relations Of Separate Political Communities. In Two Volumes. Edinburgh: William Blackwood, 1883. pp. xviii, 449, 4[ads]; xx, 620. index. cloth rubbed, spines slightly frayed, joints weak. First Edition. 60.00

"Nine-tenths or more of this work is devoted to public international law, the remainder to a very rapid outline of private international law, on the basis of the classical work of Savigny, though modified and adapted to Lorimer's own system. His treatment of public international law differs from that of most other English writers in his endeavour to ascertain the principles on which it rests and to derive them, not from express or tacit convention, but, as Grotius did, from the law of nature." [DNB]

McCARDIE, [Henry]. Judicial Wisdom Of Mr. Justice McCardie or Famous Cases Of Mr. Justice McCardie: Domestic And Social Relations, Divorce Cases, Legal Cases Of General Interest. (Ed. by Albert Crew). London: Ivor Nicholson & Watson, 1932. pp. 298. index. 12.50

McCLUER STEVENS, C.L. From Clue To Dock. London: Stanley Paul, 1927. pp. 256. 10.00

MacCLURE, Victor. She Stands Accused: Being A Series Of Accounts of

McGOWAN, Carl. The Organization of Judicial Power in the United States. 1967 Rosenthal Lectures. Evanston: Northwestern University Press, 1969. pp. 131. 6.50

MacKENZIE, F.A. World-Famous Crimes. London: Geoffrey Bles, 1927. pp. 285. illus. 12.50

MacKINNON, Frank Douglas. On Circuit 1924-1937. Cambridge: At The University Press, 1940. pp. 311. index. 15.00

McRUER, James C. The Evolution Of The Judicial Process: The W.M. Martin Lectures, 1956. Toronto: Clarke, Irwin, 1957. pp. 115. biblio. 12.50

McWHINNEY, Edward (ed.). Law, Foreign Policy, and the East-West Detente Toronto: University of Toronto Press, 1964. pp. 123. biblio. 7.50

MACKEY, Philip English. Voices Against Death: American Opposition to Capital Punishment, 1787-1975. New York: Burt Franklin, 1976. pp. 362. index. biblio. 10.00

MAITLAND, F.W. The Constitutional History Of England: A Course Of Lectures Delivered By F.W. Maitland. Cambridge: At The University Press, 1911. pp. 547. index. cloth slightly rubbed. 25.00

MAJOR, Reginald. Justice In The Round: The Trial of Angela Davis. New York: Third Press, 1973. pp. 314. 7.50

MARJORIBANKS, Edward. The Life Of Sir Edward Marshall Hall. (Intro. by The Earl Of Birkenhead). London: Victor Gollancz, 1929. pp. 428. illus. index. 15.00

MARTIENSSEN, Anthony. Crime And The Police. London: Secker & Warburg, 1951. pp. 256. index. 10.00

MARTIN, John Bartlow. Break Down The Walls. London: Victor Gollancz, 1955. pp. 286. biblio. index. 10.00

MASON, Alpheus Thomas. Brandeis: A Free Man's Life. New York: Viking, 1956. pp. 713. frontis. biblio. index . 12.50

----Bureaucracy Convicts Itself: The Ballinger-Pinchot Controversy Of 1910. New York: Viking, 1941. pp. 224. illus. index. 12.50

----Harlan Fiske Stone: Pillar of the Law. New York: Viking, 1956. pp. 914. illus. biblio. index. 15.00

----The Supreme Court from Taft to Warren. Baton Rouge: Louisiana State UP, 1958. pp. 250. index. 7.50

MASON, Jeremiah. Memoir And Correspondence Of Jeremiah Mason. Cambridge: Riverside Press, 1873. (Privately Printed). pp. 467. frontis. index. Original gilt stamped cloth. spine faded & chipped. cloth rubbed. 35.00

MATTER, Joseph Allen. My Lords and Lady of Essex: Their State Trials. Chicago: Henry Regnery, 1969. pp. 374. illus. biblio. index. 12.50

MAY, Thomas Erskine. The Constitutional History Of England Since The Accession Of George Third 1760-1860. In Two Volumes. Boston: Crosby & Nichols, 1862. pp. 484; 596. spines slightly frayed. 50.00

MEGARRY, R.E. Miscellany-at-Law: A Diversion for Lawyers and Others. London: Stevens & Sons, 1955. pp. 415. index. 12.50

MELVILLE, Lewis & Reginald Hargreaves. Famous Duels And Assassinations. London: Jarrolds, 1929. pp. 288. illus. index. 12.50

MENCKEN, August. By the neck: A Book of Hangings. (Foreword by H.L.

Edition ornee de vignettes. Paris: Garnier Freres, nd. pp. 356. 6 engravings. gilt stamped calf gift binding, leather label, marbled edges & endpapers. shelf wear, upper spine frayed. front free endpaper loose. 35.00

542 PENNOCK, J. Roland & John W. Chapman (Eds.). Due Process. New York: New York UP, 1977. pp. 362. index. 12.50

543 PITT-LEWIS, G. Commissioner Kerr: An Individuality. London: T. Fisher Unwin, 1903. pp. 395. 2 portraits. index. Original gilt stamped cloth. spine faded & frayed, cloth rubbed, front free endpaper chipped. 20.00

44 POPPLE, A.E. Canadian Criminal Evidence: A Manual of instruction upon the admissibility and use of evidence in criminal cases with "Briefs" on evidence. Briefs On Evidence Canada Evidence Act. Second Edition. Toronto: Carswell, 1954. pp. 694. index. 15.00

45 POZEN, Robert C. Legal Choices for State Enterprises in the Third World. New York: New York UP, 1976. pp. 263. biblio. index. 10.00

46 PRINGLE, Henry F. The Life And Times Of William Howard Taft. 2 Vols. New York: Farrar & Rinehart, 1939. pp. 555; 556-1106. illus. biblio. index. 20.00

47 PROSSER, William L. Handbook Of The Law Of Torts. (Hornbrook Series). St. Paul: West, 1941. pp. 1309. index. 12.50

48 PUSEY, Merlo J. Charles Evans Hughes. 2 Vols. New York: Macmillan, 1951. pp. 409; 410-829. illus. index. 25.00

49 ROCHE, Philip Q. The Criminal Mind: A Study Of Communication Between The Criminal Law And Psychiatry. New York: Farrar, Strauss, 1958. pp. 299. index. First edition. 12.50

50 ROGERS, R. Vashon. The Law of the Road; Or, Wrongs and Rights of a Traveller. San Francisco: Sumner Whitney & Co., [1876]. pp. viii, 275. index. complete with half-title. 16 mo. original cloth, gilt. spotty & rubbed. Very scarce. 85.00

Not in Sabin or Gagnon.
A "brief summary of the rights and liabilities of carriers and passengers by land &by water" applicable in Britain, Canada and the US (Preface), written by a barrister at law of Osgoode Hall. This appears to be a first American edition of a work first published in Canada in 1875.

51 ROUGHEAD, William. Bad Companions. Edinburgh: W. Green, 1930. pp. 300. illus. 12.50

52 ----Classic Crimes: A Selection from the works of William Roughead. London: Cassell, 1951. pp. 449. 10.00

53 ----Glengarry's Way And Other Studies. Edinburgh: W. Green, 1922. pp. 307. illus. 12.50

4 ----In Queer Street. Edinburgh: W. Green, 1932. pp.259. illus. 12.50

5 ----Mainly Murder. London: Cassell, 1937. pp. 299. illus.index. 10.00

6 ----Neck Or Nothing. London: Cassell, 1939. pp. 277.frontis. 10.00

7 ----Rascals Revived. London: Cassell, 1940. pp. 332. illus. 10.00

8 ----The Rebel Earl And Other Studies. Edinburgh: W. Green, 1926. pp. 310. illus. 12.50

9 ----Reprobates Reviewed. London: Cassell, 1941. pp. 307. frontis.10.00

0 ----Rogues Walk Here. London: Cassell, 1934. pp. 301. illus. 10.00

1 ----The Seamy Side. London: Cassell, 1938. pp. 292.illus.index. 10.00

2 ----Trial of Jessie M'Lachlan. Toronto: Canada Law Book, [1925]. pp. 401. illus. 12.50

3 ----Twelve ScotsTrials. Edinburgh: W. Green, 1913. pp.302.illus. 12.50

MOOREHEAD, Alan. The Traitors: The Double Life of Fuchs, Pontecorvo, and Nunn May. London: Hamish Hamilton, 1952. pp.222. illus. 12.50

MORAIN, Alfred. The Underworld of Paris: Secrets of the Surete. New York: Blue Ribbon, 1931. pp. 320. illus. back board stained. 15.00

MORLAND, Nigel. An Outline Of Scientific Criminology. Second Completely Revised Edition. London: Cassell, 1950. pp. 242. biblio.index. 12.50

MORRIS, Richard B. Fair Trial: Fourteen Who Stood Accused from Anne Hutchinson to Alger Hiss. New York: Alfred A. Knopf, 1952. pp. 494.10.0

MORTON, J.B. The Bastille Falls And Other Studies of the French Revolution. London: Longmans, 1936. pp. 311. illus.slight foxing.15.00

MORTON, J.D. The Function of Criminal Law in 1962: Five Lectures for Radio in the Series CBC University of the Air. Toronto: Canadian Broadcasting Corporation, 1962. pp. 54. 7.50

MOULTON, Sherman Roberts. The Boorn Mystery: An Episode From The Judicial Annals Of Vermont. Montpelier: Vermont Historical Society, 1937. pp. 104. 10.00

NIZER, Louis. My Life In Court. New York: Doubleday, 1961. pp. 524. Square clipped from fr. free endpaper. 7.50

NUSSBAUM, Arthur. A Concise History Of The Law Of Nations. New York: Macmillan, 1950. pp. 361. index. 12.50

O'DONNELL, Bernard. The Old Bailey and Its Trials. London: Clerke & Cockeran, 1950. pp. 226. illus. index. 10.00

OHEARN, Peter J.T. Peace, Order and Good Government: A New Constitutior For Canada. Toronto: Macmillan, 1964. pp. 325. index. 10.00

ONTARIO. ROYAL COMMISSION INQUIRY INTO CIVIL RIGHTS. Report No. 1. 4 Vols. (James Chalmers McRuer, Commissioner). (Toronto): Frank Fogg, Queen's Printer, 1968. pp. 497; 499-956; 957-1331; 1332-1733. charts. wrs. 30.00

ORKIN, Mark M. Legal Ethics: A Study of Professional Conduct. Toronto: Cartwright, 1957. pp. 330. index. 12.50

PAGET, John. Paradoxes And Puzzles: Historical, Judicial, And Literary. Edinburgh: William Blackwood, 1874. pp. xii, 472. 35.00

PARKHILL, Forbes. The law goes West. Denver: Saga, 1956. pp.176. illus. index. 7.50

PAULSON, Monrad G. (Ed.). Legal Institutions Today and Tomorrow. (Centennial Conference Volume of The Columbia Law School). New York: Columbia UP, 1959. pp. 356. index. 12.50

PEARCE, Charles E. Unsolved Murder Mysteries. London: Stanley Paul, 1924, pp. 319. illus. 10.00

PEARSON, Edmund. More Studies In Murder. New York: Harrison Smith, 1936. pp. 317. 10.00

----Murder At Smutty Nose And Other Murders. New York: Doubleday, 1926. pp. 330. illus. back board cockled. 10.00

----Studies In Murder. New York: Macmillan, 1926. pp.295.illus. 10.00

PELLICO, Silvio. Mes Prisons Suivi Des Devoirs Des Hommes; Traduction Nouvelle Par Le Comte H. De Messey Revue Par Le Vicomte Alban de Villeneuve Avec une Notice biographique et litteraire sur Silvio Pellico et ses ouvrages par M.V. Philipon De La Madelaine. Nouvelle

SANSON, Henry (Ed.). Memoirs Of The Sansons from Private Notes and Documents. 1688-1847. London: Chatto & Windus, 1876. pp. 285;306. Original blind & gilt stamped cloth, rubbed. spine frayed. (A history of a family of French executioners.). 25.00

SCHLESINGER, Rudolf. Soviet Legal Theory: Its Social Background and Development. London: Kegan Paul, 1945. pp. 299. biblio. index. 12.50

SCHMIDT, Folke & Stig Stromholm. Legal Values In Modern Sweden. (Stockholm): Bedminster Press, 1964. pp. 87. 7.50

SCHWARTZ, Bernard. The Bill Of Rights: A Documentary History. 2 Vols. New York: Chelsea, 1971. pp. 623; 624-1234. index. 35.00

SELIGMAN, Joel. The High Citadel: The Influence of Harvard Law School. (Intro. by Ralph Nader). Boston: Houghton Mifflin, 1978. pp.262. index. 10.00

SERGEANT, Philip W. Liars And Fakers. London: Hutchinson, 1925. pp. 319. illus. index. 15.00

----Rogues and Scoundrels. New York: Brentano's, [1924]. pp.328. illus. index. 15.00

SHARSWOOD, George. Reports Of The American Bar Association Volume XXXII. An Essay On Professional Ethics. Fifth Edition. Philadelphia: T. & J.W. Johnson, 1907. pp. 196. frontis. 15.00

SIEGAN, Bernard H. The Interaction of Economics and the Law. Lexington: Lexington Books, 1977. pp. 171. 12.50

SLATTERY, T.P. "They Got To Find Mee Guilty Yet". Toronto: Doubleday, 1972. pp. 414. biblio. index. (On the trial of Whelan, Thomas D'Arcy McGee's assassin). 7.50

SMITH, Edward H. Mysteries Of The Missing. New York: Dial, 1927. pp. 317. illus. index. (Chapter on Ambrose Small). 12.50

(SMITH, F[rederick] E[dwin]). The Life of F.E. Smith First Earl of Birkenhead By His Son The Second Earl of Birkenhead. London: Eyre & Spottiswoode, 1960. pp. 572. biblio. index. 15.00

SMITH, Herbert A. The Law Of Associations Corporate And Unincorporate. Oxford: At The Clarendon Press, 1914. pp. 168. index. 15.00

SMITH, Sydney. Mostly Murder. Toronto: Clarke, Irwin, 1960. pp.318. illus. index. 12.50

SMITH-HUGHES, Jack. Unfair Comment Upon Some Victorian Murder Trials. London: Cassell, 1951. pp. 360. illus. 10.00

SOHM, Rudolph. The Institutes: A Textbook Of The History And System Of Roman Private Law. (Transl. James Crawford Leddie, Intro. by Erwin Grueber). Oxford: At The Clarendon Press, 1907. pp. 605. cloth worn, small nicks to front board. 15.00

SPENCE, Edward F. Bar and Buskin: Being Memories of Life, Law and the Theatre. London: Elkin Matthews, 1930. pp. 400. illus. index. pen scoring to front pastedown. 10.00

STALLYBRASS, W.T.S. Salmond's Law Of Torts: A Treatise On The English Law Of Liability For Civil Injuries. Tenth Edition. London: Sweet & Maxwell, 1945. pp. 678. index. 15.00

STILL, Charles E. Styles In Crime. Philadelphia: J.B. Lippincott, 1938. pp. 366. illus. 10.00

STOCKTON, Charles H. Outlines Of International Law. London: George Allen & Unwin, 1914. pp. 616. index. 15.00

STORY, Joseph. A Familiar Exposition Of The Constitution Of The United States: Containing A Brief Commentary On Every Clause, Explaining The True Nature, Reasons, And Objects Thereof...With An Appendix Containing Important Public Documents, Illustrative Of The Contribution. New York: Harper, 1847. pp. 372. index. Original blind stamped cloth, rubbed. spine chipped & frayed, some foxing.Fourth Edition.20.00

Sabin 93205.

SYMONS, Julian. A Reasonable Doubt: Some Criminal Cases Re-examined. London: Cresset, 1960. pp. 223. 10.00

TAFT, Henry W. Witnesses In Court With Some Criticisms of Court Procedure. New York: Macmillan, 1934. pp. 98. index. 15.00

Culver 5358.

THOMPSON, George. Prison Life And Reflections; Or, A Narrative Of The Arrest, Trial, Conviction, Imprisonment, Treatment, Observations, Reflections, And Deliverance of Work, Burr, and Thompson, Who Suffered An Unjust And Cruel Imprisonment In Missouri Penitentiary, For Attempting to Aid Some Slaves To Liberty. Three Parts In One Volume. Dayton: Published by Author, 1857. pp. xii, [13], 377. frontis. 12 mos. original blind stamped cloth, gilt spine lettering. extremities frayed, foxing to pastedowns and endpapers, else a nice copy. 35.00

THOMSON, George Malcolm. A Kind of Justice: Two Studies In Treason. London: Hutchinson, 1970. pp. 219. biblio. illus. 12.50

THOMSON, Richard. An Historical Essay On The Magna Charta Of King John: To Which Are Added, The Great Charter in Latin and English; The Charters of Liberties and Confirmations, Granted by Henry III, And Edward I; The Original Charter of the Forests; And Various Authentic Instruments Connected with Them: Explanatory Notes on their several Privileges; A Descriptive Account Of The Principal Originals and Editions Extant, Both In Print and Manuscript; And Other Illustrations, Derived From The Most Interesting And Authentic Sources. London: Printed for John Major & Robert Jennings, 1829. pp. engraved title, xxxii, 612. Each page illustrated with woodcut vignettes of the Charters of Liberties, Tombs, Monumental Effigies, Armorial Ensigns and Seals. index. 8 vo. hinges cracked, spine frayed, corners bumped, slight foxing to outer leaves, otherwise a nice copy. First Edition. 60.00

Goldsmith 26028.

TOBIAS, J.J. Crime and Industrial Society in the 19th Century. New York: Schocken, 1967. pp. 288. biblio. index. 12.50

TOPPING, C.W. Canadian Penal Institutions. Toronto: Ryerson, 1929. pp. 126. index. ex lib. sl. staining to front board. 30.00

TRAIN, Arthur. Mr. Tutt At His Best: A Collection Of His Most Famous Cases Selected, And With An Introduction, By Judge Harold R. Medina. New York: Charles Scribner's, 1961. pp. 357. 12.50

TRAVER, Robert. Trouble-Shooter: The Story Of A Northwoods Prosecutor. New York: Viking, 1943. pp. 294. 10.00

ALS

(BENNETT, D.M.). Trial Of D.M. Bennett, In The United States Circuit Cout, Judge Charles L. Benedict, Presiding, New York, March 18, 19, 20, and 21, 1879, Upon The Charge Of Depositing Prohibited Matter in the Mail. Reported by S.B. Hinsdale, Official Stenographer of the Court. New York: The Truth Seeker Office, (c1879). pp. viii, 189, [3]ads. original gilt & Blind stamped publisher's cloth, frayed & faded. staining to front free endpapers. 30.00

Bennett was the publisher of the radical paper The Truth Seeker. "Anthony Comstock, active agent for the Society for the Suppression of Vice, and informer, complainant, and prosecutor in this trial, sought in 1877 to find some pretext upon which to arrest the Defendant..." [Preface] Bennett was charged with distributing obscene matter through the mail. "The remarkable charge of the Judge as to the meaning of the term obscenity, and his test as to how it can be determined, will be noticed. Under his rigid ruling not a publisher of books or papers, not a bookseller in the country could escape imprisonment."[Preface]

Edward D. Ingraham. Philadelphia: T. & J.W. Johnson, 1854. pp. xlviii, 656. index. contemporary sheep, leather spine label, gilt. corners & head of spine a bit worn. 55.00

412 VYSHINSKY, Andrei. The Law Of The Soviet State. New York: Macmillan, 1948. pp. 749. index. 15.00

413 WALDMAN, Louis. Labor Lawyer. New York: E.P. Dutton, 1944. pp. 394. index. 15.00

414 WALKER-SMITH, Derek. Lord Reading And His Cases: the Study of a Great Career. New York: Macmillan, 1934. pp. 399. frontis.index. 12.50

415 WARDE, J.D. The Shareholders' and Directors' Manual A Practical Handbook of the Law Of The Dominion Of Canada And Of The Provinces Thereof, Relating To Joint Stock Companies Together With Information Respecting the Incorporation, Organization and Management of such Companies, And Forms and By-laws for the use Thereof. Seventh Edition. Toronto: Canada Railway News, 1907. pp. 619, xxix[ads]. 20.00

416 WEDGWOOD, C.V. The Trial Of Charles I. London: Collins, 1964. pp. 253. index. 10.00

417 WEINBERG, Arthur (Ed.). Attorney for the Damned. (Fwd. by Justice William O. Douglas.). New York: Simon & Schuster, 1957. pp. 552. index. biblio. (Clarence Darrow's legal pleas in Leopold & Loeb; Communist Trial, Chicago; Scopes Evolution Case; Sweet Case, &c.).20.00

418 WELLMAN, Francis L. Gentlemen Of The Jury: Reminiscences Of Thirty Years At The Bar. New York: Macmillan, 1926. pp. 298. illus. 12.50

419 WHEARE, K.C. Government By Committee: An Essay On The British Constitution. Oxford: At The Clarendon Press, 1955. pp. 264.index. 12.50

420 WHITELAW, David. Corpus Delicti: An Enquiry into the Various Methods by which Famous Murderers have Disposed of the Bodies of their Victims London: Geoffrey Bles, 1936. pp. 256. illus. 10.00

421 WHITTON, F.E. Service Trials & Tragedies. London: Hutchinson, (c1930). pp. 288. illus. 15.00

422 WILLISTON, Samuel & George J. Thompson. Selections From Williston's Treatise On The Law Of Contracts. Revised Edition. New York: Baker, Voorhis, 1938. pp. 1049. index. 12.50

423 WILSON, James. The Works Of James Wilson Associate Justice Of The Supreme Court Of The United States, and Professor Of Law In The College Of Philadelphia: Being His Public Discourses Upon Jurisprudence And The Political Science Including Lectures As Professor Of Law, 1790-2. (Ed. by James DeWitt Andrews). 2 Vols. Chicago: Callaghan, 1896. pp. 577; 623. index. small chip missing from front free endpaper. spine sl. frayed. 30.00

424 WOLFF, Robert Paul (Ed.). The Rule of Law. New York: Simon & Schuster, 1971. pp. 254. 7.50

425 WYLES, Lilian. A Woman At Scotland Yard. London: Faber & Faber, 1952. pp. 256. frontis. index. 15.00

426 WYNDHAM, Horace. Crime On The Continent. London: Thornton Butterworth, 1928. pp. 316. illus. index. 12.50

427 ----Crimes In High Life: Some Society Causes Celebres. New York: Dodd, Mead, 1927. pp. 323. 16 illus. index. corner clipped from last leaf of index. quarter cloth. corners rubbed. 12.50

428 ----Feminine Frailty. London: Ernest Benn, 1929. pp. 352. illus. index. 12.50

429 ZANE, John M. The Story Of Law. (Intro. James M. Beck). New York: Garden City, 1927. pp. 486. index. 10.00

430 ZIEGAL, Jacob S. Studies In Canadian Company Law. Toronto: Butterworths, 1967. pp. 717. index. (Articles in French and English). 20.00

MACKENZIE, F.A. (Ed.). The Trial Of Harry Thaw. London: Geoffrey Bles, nd. pp. 300. illus. 12.50

MANVELL, Roger. The Trial Of Annie Besant and Charles Bradlaugh. New York: Horizon, 1976. pp. 182. index. 7.50

(MORE, St Thomas). REYNOLDS, E.E. The Trial of St. Thomas More. Montreal Palm, 1964. pp. 169. illus. index. 7.50

(PALMER, William). Trial of William Palmer. (ed. by George H. Knott). Edinburgh: William Hodge, 1912. pp. 320, [5]. illus. 20.00

"Sir James Stephen, in his "History of the Criminal Law," observes that he was present at the trial of William Palmer, and that it made an impression on him which the subsequent experience of thirty-four years had only confirmed and strengthened. He considers that the trial, as a whole, was one of the greatest trials in the history of English law..." [Preface]

TENNYSON JESSE, F. (Ed.). Trials of Timothy John Evans And John Reginald Halliday Christie. London: William Hodge, 1957. pp. 379. 15.00

THOMAS, Donald (Ed.). State Trials. 2 Vols. London: Routledge, 1972. pp.236; 247. 20.00

U.S.S.R. Report Of Court Proceedings In The Case of The Anti-Soviet Trotskyite Centre Heard Before The Military Collegium Of The Supreme Court Of The U.S.S.R. Moscow, January 23-30, 1937 In Re: Y.L. Pyatakov, K.B. Radek, G.Y. Sokolnikov, L.P. Serebryakov, N.I. Muralov, Y.A. Livshitz...Accused of treason against the country, espionage, acts of diversion, wrecking activities and the preparation of terrorist acts, i.e., of crimes covered by Articles 58[1a], 58[8], 589, and 5811 of the Criminal Code of the R.S.F.S.R. Verbatim Report. Moscow: People's Commissariat Of Justice Of The U.S.S.R., 1937. pp. 580. bds. slightly discoloured & chipped. 35.00

----Report Of Court Proceedings In The Case Of The Anti-Soviet "Bloc Of Rights And Trotskyites" Heard Before The Military Collegium Of The Supreme Court Of The U.S.S.R. Moscow, March 2-13, 1938. In Re: N.I. Bukharin, A.I. Rykov, G.G. Yagoda, N.N. Krestinsky, K.G. Rakovsky A.P. Rosengoltz, V.I. Ivanov, M.A. Chernov, G.F. Grinko, I.A. Zelensky S.A. Bessonov...Verbatim Report. Moscow: People's Commissariat Of Justice Of The U.S.S.R., 1938. pp. 800. 35.00

----Wrecking Activities at Power Stations in the Soviet Union. The Case Of N.P. Vitvitsky, V.A. Gussev, A.W. Gregory, Y.I. Zivert, N. G. Zorin, M.D. Krasheninnikov...Heard Before The Special Session Of The Supreme Court Of The U.S.S.R. In Moscow, April 12-19, 1933. Translation of the Official Verbatim Report. pp. 798. wrs., stained and worn. 25.00

(WILDE, Oscar). The Trials Of Oscar Wilde. (ed. by H. Montgomery Hyde. fwd. by Sir Travers Humpreys). London: William Hodge, 1948. pp. 384. illus. 20.0

---oOo---

TUTT, Ephraim. Yankee Lawyer: The Autobiography of Ephraim Tutt. New York: Charles Scribner's, 1944. pp. 463. illus. index. 12.5

VAN VOLLENHOVEN, C. The Law Of Peace. (Trans. by W. Horsfall Carter, preface by Jonkheer W.J.M. Van Eysinga). London: Macmillan, 1936. pp. 261. 15.(

VATTEL, [Emmerich] de. The Law Of Nations; Or, Principles Of The Law Of Nature, Applied To The Conduct And Affairs Of Nations And Sovereigns. From The French Of Monsieur De Vattel. From The New Edition By Joseph Chitty, With Additional Notes And References By

ALLEN, John. Inquiry Into The Rise And Growth Of The Royal Prerogative In England. A New Edition. With The Author's Latest Corrections, Biographical Notices, &c. To Which Is Added An Inquiry Into The Life And Character Of King Eadwig. London: Longman, Brown, Green, & Longman, 1844. pp. xciv, 208. 8 vo. Original blind and gilt stamped cloth. Uncut. Spine chipped, corners slightly rubbed, some neat pencil scoring, else a nice copy. 60.00

Allen's work provides a historical analysis of the growth of monarchical power in English law. "The Inquiry opens with a striking and succint statement of the regal power, as described by the abstract theory of our constitution, which clothes the monarch with every degree of power, and every kind of perfection...The person invested with such mightly authority is, no doubt, merely ideal; he is a corporation, and a creature of legal theory; and in practice, his power is checked, and his defects supplied, in various ways; for he cannot act in anyway without some adviser, or some instrument answerable for what is done; so that the power which in the contemplation of law is supreme, in practice is exceedingly limited." [pp. xli]

BROUGHAM, Henry. Contributions To The Edinburgh Review. In Three Volumes. London: Richard Griffin, 1856. pp. 4 pl, 507; 3 pl, 544; 3 pl, 512. index. complete with half titles. 8 vo. Original blind and gilt stamped cloth. corners slightly rubbed. 60.00

CAMPBELL, John [first Baron] Campbell. The Lives Of The Chief Justices Of England. From The Norman Conquest Till The Death Of Lord Mansfield. In Three Volumes. Philadelphia: Blanchard & Lea, 1851, 1857. pp. 463; 442 [32]ads; 381, 16[ads]. 8 vo. Original blind and gilt stamped cloth. Spines slightly chipped and frayed else a very nice set. First American Edition. 100.00

DIX, D[orothea]L. Remarks On Prisons And Prison Discipline In The United States. Boston: Printed by Munroe & Francis, 1845. pp. 104. 8 vo. Disbound. First Edition. 100.00

Sabin 20336

Dix spent her life investigating conditions in mental asylums, poor houses and prisons. In this landmark work, Dix advocates a radical reform of the United States penal system.

[FITZGIBBON], John, Earl Of Clare. The Speech Of The Right Honourable John, Earl Of Clare, Lord High Chancellor Of Ireland, In The House Of Lords Of Ireland, On A Motion Made By The Earl Of Moria, Monday, February 19, 1798...By Authority. Dublin: Printed For John Milliken, 1798. pp. 2 pl, 87, ix. complete with half title. 8 vo. disbound. outer leaves slightly foxed, small tear in K1, not affecting text. 50.00

Goldsmith 17438.

Fitzgibbon was appointed Chancellor of Ireland in 1789. "In politics he maintained an uncompromising resistance to all popular movements, and especially to all atempts to improve the position of the Roman Catholics. A detailed record of his chancellorship would be a history of Ireland during the same period."[DNB] In this important speech, Fitzgibbon defended the government's harsh measures in crushing Catholic opposition. "Lord Moira attached the government for its coercive policy. Clare justified that policy in a long reply, containing an elaborate account of the progress of disaffection, and of the failure of conciliation during a period, as he considered it, of rapid advance."[DNB]

GIFFORD, John. The Complete English Lawyer; Or, Every Man his own Lawyer: Containing A Summary Of The Constitution Of England; Its Law and Statutes...Also, The Criminal Law of England, Comprising Every Species Of Public Offences With Their Punishments. To Which Is Added An Appendix, Containing the most approved Forms of Agreements, Leases, Wills and Testaments, Notices between Landlord and Tenant, Contracts, Articles of Copartnership, &c.&c. Also, A Supplement Containing The Excise Laws, The Customs' Laws, The Assessed Taxes, The Stamp Duties, &c. The whole carefully digested, and the Statutes and Term Reports brought down to the 4th Geo. Iv. The Eighth Edition. London: Printed by R. Macdonald...For A. Whellier, 1823. pp. 688, 2 pl, 17-148 [Supplement]. index. engraved frontis. portrait of Sir Charles Abbott, 5 engraved portraits of important legal figures, foxed. 8 vo. Contemporary calf, morocco spine label, gilt. calf worn, boards detached, free endpapers missing, library lettering to spine and library markings on front pastedown. 70.00

HIGHLY PRAISED BY WALPOLE

A Letter Concerning Libels, Warrants, The Seizure of Papers, And Sureties for the Peace of Behaviour; With A View to some late Proceedings, And The Defence of Them by the Majority. The Third Edition, Enlarged and Improved. London: Printed for J. Almon..., 1765. pp. 112. complete with half title. 8 vo. Disbound. 100.00

Goldsmith 10144. Higgs 3584.

This important work outlined the case for freedom of the press. "Some there may have been, but many agreed with Walpole that this pamphlet was 'the finest piece that I think has been written for liberty since Lord Somers.' It was, he added, 'the only tract that ever made me understand law.'"[Rea] Speculation as to the identity of the author continues: Halkett and Laing cite John Almon while Rea favours John Dunning.

PAGE, J. A Narrative Of Facts, Interesting, Mysterious, And Extra-Ordinary, As Connected With A Short History Of Two Servants, Named James Harper Peart, And Ann Thomas: Detailing The Particulars Of a Robbery in Great Bedford Street; Their Apprehension On Suspicion: Extraordinary Escapes of Peart; Together With Letters And Other Documents, Containing A Combination Of Diabolical Events, And A System Of Imposition, Fraud, And Cunning, To Which The Human Mind Can Scarcely Give Credit. Bath: Printed and Published By Mary Meyler, 1833. pp. 48. 8 vo. Disbound. 50.00

PRIESTLEY, Joseph. Remarks On Some Paragraphs In The Fourth Volume of Dr. Blackstone's Commentaries on the Laws Of England. Relating To The Dissenters. America: Printed For The Subscribers, By Robert Bell..., Philadelphia, 1773. pp. 1 pl, 119. [Including: Priestley's Remarks. Blackstone's Reply to Priestley's Remarks. Priestley's Answer To Blackstone's Reply. Blackstone's Case of the Middlesex Elections. Separate title-pages, but pagination is continuous.][Also Including: FURNEAUX, Philip. Letters To The Honourable Mr. Justice Blackstone, Concerning His Exposition of the Act of Toleration, And Some Positions relative to Religious Liberty, In His Celebrated Commentaries On The Laws Of England. The Second Edition With Additions. And An Appendix, containing Authentic Copies of the Argument of the late Honourable Mr. Justice Foster in the Court of Judges Delegates, and of the Speech of the Right Honourable Lord Mansfield in the House of Lords, in the Cause between the City of London and the Dissenters. America: Printed For The Subscribers, By Robert Bell..., Philadelphia, 1773. pp. xii, 155, [1]ad.]8 vo. Contemporary sheep, morocco label, gilt. Leather worn, head & foot of spine neatly reinforced, browned as usual. 400.00

See Sabin 65513.

Scarce American Edition of two important English works on the struggle for religious freedom. Priestley and Furneau wrote in opposition to Blackstone's classification of nonconformity as a civil offence. Both works provide a strong "...moral argument against enforcing religious truths by civil penalties."[DNB]

SELDEN, John. Titles of Honor. The Second Edition. London: Printed by William Stansby for Richard Whittakers...1631. pp. [36], 941, [1]errata. 6 engraved plates, numerous engraved vignettes. Folio. Old sprinkled calf, morocco spine label, gilt. Calf worn, joints tender, small tear in lower corner of $3A^2$ & $4D^1$, else a very nice copy. Armorial bookplate of Arthur Dalrymple. 2nd Edition. 400.00

STC 22178.

"In 1614 Selden published his 'Titles of Honour' dedicated to his friend and chamber-fellow, Edward Heyward. In the first part he deals with the titles and dignities of emperors, kings, and other rulers, beginning with the inquiry whether there were kings before the flood. In the second part he deals with inferior titles, commencing with those of heirs-apparent to thrones; and finally discusses feminine titles, honorary attributes such as 'clarissimus' and 'illustris' and the laws of precedence." [DNB]

SMITH, William. A Treatise On The Duties And Office Of A Receiver, Under The High Court Of Chancery In Ireland, Embracing The Present Practice Of The Court As Connected Therewith, From The Order Of Appointment To The Final Discharge And Vacating The Recognizance; As Also, A Summary View Of Certain Portions Of The Law Of Landlord And Tenant, Including Practical Directions For Making And Disposing Of A Distress For Non-Payment Of Rent; With An Appendix, Containing A Variety Of Useful Precedents. Dublin: Printed For Richard Milliken, 1827. pp. 1 pl, ii, 187, xliii. 8 vo. Half calf, marbled boards, morocco spine label, gilt. Armorial bookplate of Saunders. Boards slightly rubbed, else a nice copy. 85.00

SMITH, Thomas. The Commonwealth Of England, And The Maner Of Governement thereof. Compiled by the Honourable Sir Thomas Smith, Knight, Doctor of both Lawes, and one of the principall Secretaries unto two most worthy Princes, King Edward, and Queene Elizabeth. With new additions of the chiefe Courts in England, And The Offices thereof by the Said Author. Also a Table added thereto, of all the principall matters contained in this Treatise. New Corrected and Amended. London: Printed by William Stansby for John Smethwicke, 1621. pp. 4 pl, 134. small 4 to. several vignettes. modern half leather, marbled boards, gilt spine lettering, sprinkled edges. several brief marginal comments, else a very nice copy. 8th Edn. 300.00

STC 22864.

Written during his first embassy in France, "it is the most important description of the constitution and government of England written in the Tudor age." [DNB] It was originally published in 1583 under the title "De Republica Anglorum; the Maner or Governement or Policie of the Realm of England" and passed through 11 editions in English in little over a century.

STUART, Andrew. Letters to the Right Honourable Lord Mansfield, From Andrew Stuart, Esq; London: Printed in the Month of January 1773. pp. 2 pl, 39, 63, 47, 47. complete with half title. 4 to. contemporary tree calf, red morocco spine label, gilt. extremities rubbed, spine tips worn, joints cracked, else a very nice copy. Bookplate of the Right Honourable Earl of Moray. 100.00

An attack on Lord Mansfield for his conduct in the Douglas case; Mansfield favoured Douglas in his claims to the Douglas family estates, whereas Stuart conducted the case against the claimant. "In these epistles he assailed Mansfield for his 'want of impartiality with a force and eloquence that caused him at the time to be regarded as a worthy rival to Junius." [DNB]

ENDA TO PART II

BIRON, Chartres. Without Prejudice: Impressions of Life and Law. London: Faber & Faber, 1936. pp. 368. illus. index. 12.50

CLARK, Charles L. & Earle Edward Eubank. Lockstep and Corridor: Thirty-five Years of Prison Life. (Fwd. by Charles W. Hoffman). Cincinnati: University of Cincinnati Press, 1927. pp. 177. illus. biblio. 17.50

GERIN-LAJOIE, Paul. Constitutional Amendment In Canada. Toronto: University of Toronto Press, 1950. pp. 340. biblio. index. 20.00

HOSMER, William. The Higher Law, In Its Relations To Civil Government: With Particular Reference To Slavery And The Fugitive Slave Law. Auburn: Derby & Miller, 1852. pp. ix, 1 leaf, [13]-204. engraved frontis. portrait. 12 mo. Original blind and gilt stamped cloth. Last blank & endpaper chipped off at upper corner, inscriptions on endpapers and back of frontis, else a very good copy. Scarce. 85.00

Sabin 33113.

STEPHEN, James Fitzjames. Liberty, Equality, Fraternity. London: Smith, Elder & Co., 1873. pp. 350. 8 vo. Original cloth. Extremities beginning to fray, else VG. 60.00

Stephen developed this work while working on codification in India. Impressed by British legislative measures in India, Steven argued, in opposition to John Stuart Mill, that strong government would cure the British malaise.

9 The Texts Of The Trustee Act And Other Acts Relating To The Administration Of Estates In The Province Of Ontario. Toronto: National Trust Company, [c1955]. pp. 197.

OLD & RARE LAW BOOKS

CATALOGUE #33

(1979)

D & E Lake Ltd.
Old & Rare Books
(Formerly October Books)
111 Queen Street East Suite 302
Toronto, Canada M5C 1S2
Telephone: (416) 863-9930
Cable Address: Lakebooks, Toronto

OLD & RARE LAW BOOKS: 1550-1900

ANTHON, John [1784-1863]. The Law of Nisi Prius, Being Reports of Cases Determined at Nisi Prius, in the Supreme Court of the State of New-York, With Notes and Commentaries On Each Case. To Which Is Prefixed An Introductory Essay, On the Studies Preparatory to the Active Duties of the Bar. New-York: Gould & Banks & Albany: William Gould & Co., 1820. 8vo. pp. xxxi, [1], errata, 214. index. contemporary sheep. First Edition. 85.00

Marvin p. 64.

This work, compiled by the man who was largely responsible for the establishment of the Supreme Court of New York, contains the reports of 150 cases decided between the years 1808 and 1818. The whole is preceded by an introductory essay on the study of the law.

"PRIMOGENITURE DISPUTED"

[AP-ROBERT, J.]. The Younger Brother His Apologie, Or A Fathers Free Power disputed, for the disposition of his Lands, or other his Fortunes to his Sonne, Sonnes, or any one of them: as right Reason, the Lawes of God and Nature, the Civill, Canon, and Municipall Laws of this Kingdome doe command. Oxford: Printed by Iohn Lichfield for Edward Forrest, 1635 [colophon: 1634]. small 4to. pp. 1pl, [8], 56, [2]. several woodcut ornaments & initials. half pigskin [c1920's]. some dampstaining to lower outer corner of leaves, repair to fore-edge margin of title-leaf, else a very nice copy, with the bookplate of Sidney Fuller Smith, and, on title, the signature of James Chaloner (1603-1660), member of the Long Parliament and one of the judges who tried Charles I. 200.00

cfMadan I 174. cfSTC 715-717. cfGoldsmith 656. cfS.&M.I.478.36.

We can find no reference to this variant in the relevant bibliographies, the BM Catalogue or the National Union Catalogue. The first edition appeared in Douai in 1618 and 2 issues are recorded of the first edition printed in England in 1634, one giving incorrect date of 1624 on title, the other with the date corrected.

Madan incorrectly attributes the work to a John Allen and remarks: "This is a rare book, arguing against exclusive privileges of primogeniture, and for the right and in some cases duty of parents to disinherit the eldest son."

AYLIFFE, John [1676-1732]. A New Pandect of Roman Civil Law, As Anciently established in that Empire; and now received and practised in most European Nations: With Many useful Observations thereon; shewing, Wherein that Law differs from the Municipal Laws of Great-Britain, from the Canon Law in general, and from that Part of it now in Use here with us in England... London: Printed for Tho.Osborne, 1734. folio. pp. 4pl, xlviii, [8], 608[ie648]. several woodcut ornaments. contemporary calf, sometime rebacked. binding somewhat worn, joints cracked, paper repairs to lower margin of 2 preliminary leaves, else internally fine. First Edition. 400.00

S.&M.I.177.4. Marvin pp. 80-81.

Ayliffe's career and social position suffered much from his outspoken political views ("he was an ardent whig at a time when Oxford was the home of Jacobitism"), and his book on Oxford, in which he exposed the misappropriation of the funds of Clarendon Printing House led to his expulsion from

the unversity, stripped of all privileges and degrees. His most important undertakings, however, were his two treatises on canon and civil law. The 'Pandect' was not published until two years after his death, and "though it was never finished, it remains to our own day the most elaborate treatise on modern Roman law written in English." (DNB)

4 BACQUET, Jean [d1597]. Les Oeuvres de Iean Bacquet, Advocat en la Chambre du Thresor. Des Droicts du Domaine de la Couronne de France. Reveues, Corrigees, et Augmentees de plusieurs Arrests & Decisions notables; & du Traicte des Rentes du mesme Autheur. Derniere Edition, Enrichie D'Un Traicte de la Iurisdiction de la Chambre du Thresor, & conseruation du Domaine du Roy. Divisee En Cinq Tomes. A Paris: Chez Iean Gesselin, 1621. folio. pp. 6pl, 291, [12]index; 4pl, 240, [16]index; 2pl, 432, [16]index; 425-486, [4]index, [2]blank; 6pl, 170, [2]index. general title in red & black. title vignettes & several woodcut ornaments & initials. old calf, worn, joints cracked, dampstaining to some leaves, lacking middle index leaf of last vol. (other index leaves tatty), still, a good copy. From the library of T.C.Aylwin. (See note on provenance.) 400.00

Not in BM STC French Books (which lists only the editions of 1664 & 1688). The NUC locates only 1 copy, that in the New York Public Library.

The works of the French jurist, edited and augmented by his nephew, N. Belut, were first published in 1603. Included are chapters on the 'droit de francs-fiefs', 'droit d'amortissement', bastardy, disinheritance, &c.

Vols. II, III, & V have separate varying title leaf; despite irregular pagination & lack of title-leaf in Vol. IV, the signature collation is uninterrupted & the work appears to be complete.

5 BALLANTINE, William. Some Experiences of A Barrister's Life. In Two Volumes. Third Edition. London: Richard Bentley & Son, 1882. 8vo. pp. xv, 321; xiv, 308 + 48p. of ads. complete with half-titles. frontis. port. index. original cloth. 30.00

6 BALUZE, Etienne (Stephanus BALVZIVS) [1630-1718]. Capitularia Regum Francorum. Additae sunt Marculfi monachi & aliorum formulae veteres, & Notae doctissimorum virorum. 2 Volumes. Pariis: Excudebat Franciscus Muguet, 1677. folio. pp. 2pl, [66], 1448; 4pl, 1660. text printed in double columns. engraved title in Vol. I, engraved folding plate in Vol. II, several vignettes. indices. contemporary calf, rubbed, joints cracked, backstrips worn & dry, some inner marginal dampstaining in Vol. I, not affecting text, else very good. From the library of T.C.Aylwin. First Edition. 500.00

Graesse I p. 284. BM STC French Books B.171. Cioranescu, 17th Cent., I 9516.

A very important work on the earliest legal texts and statutes of the Merovingian and Carolingian Kings of France. Baluze was appointed professor of Canon law at the College de France in 1689, and subsequently became director of the institution. He unfortunately fell into disfavour and was exiled after the appearance of his works in support of the cardinal de Bouillon, who claimed to be a direct descendant of the old dukes of Guyenne. The 'Capitularia' is dedicated to Jean Baptiste Colbert, of whose library Baluze was curator for 33 years.

7 BARRINGTON, Daines [1728-1800]. Observations on the More Ancient Statutes, From Magna Charta to the Twenty-First of James I Cap. XXVII. With An Appendix, Being A Proposal For New Modelling the Statutes. The Third Edition, With Considerable Additions. London: Printed by W.Bowyer and J.Nichols: And Sold by S.Baker and G.Leigh, 1769. 4to. pp. xii, 516. index. contemporary sprinkled calf, sometime rebacked, endpapers renewed. extremities rubbed, author's name printed in white on lower spine, back paste-down snarled, internally very good. 250.00

See S.&M.I.546.3 & Marvin p. 96 (neither listing this edition).

"Mr Barrington, in his 'Observations', has contributed very much to the elucidation of the more ancient laws of England, by introducing historical illustrations of the times during which the statutes were enacted. The volume abounds in curious, learned, and valuable information." (Marvin) This is Barrington's first work.

BAYLEY, John [Whitcomb] [d1869]. The History and Antiquities Of the Tower of London, With Memoirs of Royal and Distinguished Persons, Deduced From Records, State-Papers, and Manuscripts, And From Other Original and Authentic Sources. 2 Volumes. London: Published by T.Cadell, 18[21]-25. 4to. pp. 3pl (incl. blank), [vii]-xiv, [2]list of plates & errata, 272, xxxiv; vi, [273]-671[ie679], [xxxv]-cxxviii, [17]index. [pp. 345-352 are numbered 345a & b, &c.]. extra-illustrated: 29 engraved plates [27 called for] plus 11 added illustrations, mostly inlaid, of portraits of distinguished prisoners of the Tower: Lady Jane Grey, Sir Thomas More, &c. contemporary half calf, gilt backs. front joint of Vol. I renewed, joints of Vol. II cracking, hint of foxing to some plates & adjoining leaves, else a very nice set. First Edition. 300.00

The greater portion of Bayley's work, which "ranks among the very best works of its kind for excellence of style, acuteness of judgment, and unfailing accuracy of statement" (DNB), is given over to an account of the Tower as a state prison, with biographical notices of the most distinguished personnages that have been confined there, and an appendix including a number of their letters.

"CORNERSTONE OF CRIMINAL JURISPRUDENCE"

[BECCARIA, Cesare Bonesana, Marchesi di] [1735-1793]. An Essay On Crimes and Punishments, Translated from the Italian; With A Commentary Attributed to Mons. De Voltaire, Translated from the French. The Second Edition. London: Printed for F. Newberry, 1769. 8vo. pp. xii, 179, lxxix. old quarter calf. binding rubbed, head & foot of backstrip wearing, internally very good. Second English Edition. 250.00

New CBEL II p. 1542. See S.&M.I.358.5 & Marvin p. 105 & PMM 352.

"Beccaria was the first writer to plead for humane views on the treatment of criminals. Opposing capital punishment, torture, and the use of force, he maintained that education and care of the criminal rather than revenge should be the aim of society in its treatment of the offender. The book had an immediate success, six editions being published, including a French one with an anonymous commentary by Voltaire. Its success led to the introduction of many reforms in the penal codes of the principal European nations." (PMM)

[BECCARIA, Cesare Bonesana, Marchesi di] Traite des delits et des peines, Traduit de L'Italien, D'apres la troisieme edition, revue, corrigee et augmentee par l'Auteur: Avec des Additions

de l'Auteur, qui n'on pas encore paru en Italien. A Lausanne: 1766. 12mo. pp. xxxi, 242. contemporary mottled sheep, gilt back. some spotting to leaves, but an excellent copy. First French Edition. 300.00

Brunet I, 729. Barbier IV, 776/77. Not in BM STC French Books. See S&M.I.358.5 & Marvin p. 105 & PMM 352.

Beccaria's celebrated treatise was first published in Milan in 1764. This French translation is by the radical-leaning abbe Andre Morellet.

11 BENTHAM, Jeremy [1748-1832]. The Works...Published Under the Superintendence of His Executor, John Bowring. 11 Volumes. Edinburgh: William Tait & London: Simpkin, Marshall, & Co., [1838]-1843. 8vo. numerous folding tables. text in double columns. contemporary half calf, gilt backs, marbled bds., edges & endpapers. extremities slightly rubbed, bookplates neatly removed from front paste-downs, else very good. A handsome set. First Edition of the Collected Works. 1,500.00

S.&M.II.27. Goldsmith 33105. Kress C.6008. New CBEL III p. 1717.

Many of Bentham's greatest contributions were made in the reform of English law and judicial procedure. According to Sir James Stephen, in his 'History of the Criminal Law of England', Bentham's legal writings "have had a degree of practical influence upon the legislation of his own and various other countries comparable only to that of Adam Smith and his successors upon commerce." Included in the 'Works' is a biography of Bentham by Bowring.

12 (BENTHAM, Jeremy).[WHIPPLE, John]. Jeremy Bentham and the Usury Law. [Signed: A Rhode-Islander], [New York?]: 1836. 8vo. pp. 20. stitched, as issued. hint of foxing, else fine. 60.00

Kress C.4283. Not in Goldsmith.

This criticism of Bentham's 'Defence of Usury' was also issued in the Banker's Magazine and Statistical Register, March, 1850 as "The Usury Laws" by the Hon. John Whipple. Bentham had argued that a contract for money, like all contracts, should be left open to the good sense of those bargaining.

"BEST GENERAL HISTORY OF ENGLISH LAW"

13 BLACKSTONE, Sir William [1723-1780]. Commentaries on the Laws of England, Book the First. [-------Book the Fourth]. 4 Volumes. Oxford: Printed at the Clarendon Press, 1766-69. 4to. pp. 2pl, iv, [3], 485; 4pl, 520, xix; 4pl, 455, xxvii; 4pl, 436, vii, [39]index. 2 engraved plates (1 folding) in Vol. II. contemporary calf. several joints cracked, but all quite firm, bindings bit rubbed, notes penned on final blank of Vol. I, else internally fine. A handsome set, with armorial bookplate of E.J.Curteis, Oxford, 1780, and his signature, as well as a presentation inscription to William H.White from Francis White, Boston, 1888. Second Editions of Vols. I & II; First Editions of Vols. III & IV. 2,000.00

S.&M.I.27.8. Rothschild 407. Winfield pp. 337-340. Higgs 4494. PMM 212. See Marvin pp. 122-126 & Grose p. 46.

Blackstone's 'Commentaries', based on his lectures given at Oxford beginning in 1753, constitute the first attempt since Bracton to provide a coherent account of English law as a whole. It is "the best general history of the English Law, needing comparatively little correction and told with admirable clearness and spirit." (DNB) Even one of his most furious critics, Jeremy Bentham, "allowed that it was he who first taught English law to speak the language of the scholar and the gentleman."

14 BLACKSTONE, Sir William. Commentaries on the Laws of England: Applicable to Real Property. Adapted to the Present State of the Law in Upper Canada By Alexander Leith, Of Osgoode Hall, Barrister-at-Law. Toronto: W.C.Chewett & Co., 1864. 8vo. pp. viii, 416. 3 tables (2 folding). index. modern half oasis morocco. With the signature and bookplate of Frederic William Cumberland (1821-1881), Canadian engineer & architect. 200.00

TPL 4284. Not in Lande or Gagnon. This edition not listed in S.&M. For an account of Cumberland, see the MacMillan Dictionary of Canadian Biography.

15 BOHIER, Nicolas de (Nicolaus BOERIUS) [1469-1539]. Decisiones Burdegalenses Summa Diligentia et Eruditione Collectae, Et Explicatae, Vna Cum Eiusdem Boerii Consiliis, Tractatibus De Statu et Vita Heremitarum de Seditiosis, de Custodia clauium portarum ciuitatis, & Additionibus in tractatum Ioan.Montani de Authoritate magni consilij. Collatis vetustissimis exemplaribus omnia recognita, a Guill.Nepote in Curia Lugdunensi Aduocato. Accesserunt huic editioni, nunc primum e Gallico in Gallico in Latinum conuersa, Decisiones insignes D.Aegidij Magistri, Equitis, & in Suprema Parisiensi Curia primi Prasidu. Cum rerum ac verborum locupletissimo Indice. np: Excudebat Philippus Albert, 1620. folio. pp. 6pl, 1020, [45]index. title in red & black. title vignette & several woodcut ornaments & initials. text in double columns. old calf, sometime rebacked. binding worn, front cover detached, title leaf detached but present, wanting front free-endpaper & front blank, some foxing, else internally very good. From the library of T.C.Aylwin & with the printed book label of the Court of Arches, London. 300.00

The NUC locates only 1 copy of this edition. See Adams B.2277 (1566, 1st edition).

This is the most esteemed of the works of the celebrated jurist Bohier. He became the third president of the parliament of Bordeaux in 1515.

16 BOUTMY, Emile [Gaston]. Studies in Constitutional Law: France, England, United States. Translated From the Second French Edition by E.M.Dicey. With an Introduction by A.V.Dicey. London & New York: Macmillan, 1891. 8vo. pp. xiv, [1], 183 + 55p. of ads. half-title. index. original cloth. S.&M.II.37. 30.00

17 BRADY, Rob[ert] [d1700]. An Historical Treatise of Cities and Burghs Or Boroughs. Shewing Their Original, and Whence, and From Whom They Received their Liberties, Privileges, and Immunities; What they were, and what Made and Constituted a Free Burgh, & Free Burgesses. As Also Shewing When they first sent their Representatives to Parliament. With a Concurrent Discourse of most Matters, and Things Incident, or Relating thereto. The Second Edition. London: Printed for A.L. and Sold by John Nutt, 1704. folio. pp. 1pl, iv, 88[ie90], 41 [ie43]. lacking A^4 [probably blank or fly-title]. several woodcut ornaments & initials. 19th century half hard-grained

leather. extremities rubbed, joints cracked, some light foxing, else internally very good. 150.00

S.&M.I.416.7.

Brady's work staunchly defended the royal prerogative. In the preface to this treatise, he claims that he is able to show that they "have nothing of the greatness and authority they boast of, but from the bounty of our ancient kings and their successors."

18 BROUGHAM, Henry [Peter, Baron Brougham and Vaux] [1778-1868]. Speeches of Henry Lord Brougham, Upon Questions Relating to Public Rights, Duties, and Interests; With Historical Introductions, And A Critical Dissertation Upon the Eloquence of the Ancients. In Four Volumes. Edinburgh: Adam and Charles Black..., 1838. 8vo. pp. 1pl, x, 676, [1]errata; 2pl, 632; iv, 626; iv, 571. index. full ribbed morocco, gilt lettering, edges & inside dentelles. extremities slightly rubbed, 2 nicks to front cover of Vol. II, pen notes to 2 leaves, else very good. A handsome set. First Edition. 120.00

Brougham made many important contributions to legal reform: his scheme of 1828 led to the vast improvement and simplification of the system of common law procedure; he was responsible for improvements in the court of chancery & the establishment of the judicial committee of the privy council and the central criminal court; although his Local Courts Bill of 1830 did not succeed, it laid the basis for the present system of County Courts. Included here is Brougham's famous speech in defence of J. & J.L.Hunt (1811), who were charged with libel for publishing an article in the 'Examiner' on military flogging.

19 BUGNYON, Philibert [d1590]. Legum Abrogatarum Et Inusitatarum In omnibus Curiis, Terris, Jurisdictionibus, & Dominiis Regni Franciae Tractatus. Edition Tertia, Mendis, quibus antea scatebat, repurgata...Accessere Additiones In Hac Editione Sesqui Altera Parte Adauctae: Quibus recentiores non modo Galliae, sed & universi Belgii, Hispaniae, Italiae, Germaniae, vicinorumque locorum Mores, & Leges tum Abrogatae, tum receptae demonstrantur... Bruxellis: Apud Petrum De Dobbeleer, 1702. folio. pp. 2pl, [21], 696, [86]index, [2]div.title, 81, [8] index. complete with half-title. woodcut ornaments. title in red & black. contemporary calf, gilt back. binding slightly rubbed, paper repair to title leaf, affecting several letters of imprint, else an excellent clean copy. From the library of T.C.Aylwin. 225.00

This edition not located in NUC. See BM STC French Books B.1847 (Paris: Buon, 1605).

Included is a commentary on the Moulin ordonnances proclaimed by Charles IX in February 1566, by which the judicial system of France was reorganized.

20 BURROW, Sir James [1701-1782]. A Series of the Decisions of the Court of King's Bench Upon Settlement-Cases; From the Death of Lord Raymond in March 1732: To Which Is Added A Complete Abridgment of the Substance of each Case, and Two Tables of the Names of them... 3 Volumes. [...Volume the Second: Containing near Fifteen Years, and including Lord Chief Justice Ryder's Time and the first Twelve Years of Lord Mansfield's. To this Volume is added an Index to both Volumes. And there are also Subjoined a few Thoughts upon Pointing and some other Helps towards Perspicuity of Expression; Vol. III: Continuation...By Four Additional Years, ending in July 1772 ...]. London: Printed by His Majesty's Law-Printers For J. Worrall and B.Tovey, 1768-72. 4to. pp. xv(incl. general title), 364; 2pl, 365-625, ix-xv, [36]index, [2]div.title, 631-652; 1pl, [6], 627-718, [4]index. contemporary calf. bindings bit rubbed, several joints cracked, clean tear to 1 leaf (no loss), erasures to lower margin of some leaves has caused paper to wear thin, some leaves misbound in Vol. III, but all are present except for final blank; otherwise a very good set. 300.00

S.&M.I.386.3. See Marvin p. 166(3rd edn.).

Burrow's great merits as a law reporter were his pains-taking accuracy and his belief in the "importance of sharp divisions between the facts, the arguments of counsel, and the judgment of the court." (See Winfield, p. 190) A further continuation [1772]-1776 was also published.

[BYRNE, Julia Clara (Busk)]. Curiosities of the Search-Room. A Collection of Serious and Whimsical Wills. By the Author of "Flemish Interiors", Etc. Etc. London: Chapman and Hall, 1880. 8vo. pp. ix, [1], 407 + 32p. of ads. complete with half-title & tipped-in errata slip. original cloth bit soiled, back cover stained, internally very good. First Edition. 35.00

CABASSUT, Jean (Joannis CABASSUTIUS) [1604-1685]. Notitia Ecclesiastica Historarum, Conciliorum, & Canonum invicem collatorum, veterumque juxta, ac recentiorum Ecclesiae Rituum, Ab ipsis Ecclesiae Christianae incunabulis ad nostra usque tempora, secundum cujusque saeculi seriem, accurate digesta. Editio Quarta, Ab Ipso Auctore Correcta, Plurimum Aucta, & quinque Indicibus locupletata... Lugduni (Lyon): Sumptibus Anisson & Posuel, 1725. folio. pp. 2pl, [20], 680, [76]index. complete with half-title. title in red & black. text in double columns. several ornaments. contemporary sprinkled calf, gilt back. some dampstaining to outer leaves & inner margins, binding bit rubbed, else very good. From the library of T.C.Aylwin. 225.00

No copy of this edition located in the NUC.

Cabassut was a French priest of the Oratory, eminent for his knowledge of the Canon law. "Ouvrage judicieux, utile, recommande par Mabillon dans ses Etudes monastiques". (Dict. de Theol. Cath. II/1297)

CAMERON, Geo., Alex.MacTavish, James Mackenzie. Report of the Sub-Committee of the Inverness Society For the Suppression of Begging. March 1828. Inverness: Printed at the Courier Office, 1828. 8vo. pp. 42, [2], xlv-lxxii(appendix). some foxing throughout, backstrip wanting, else a very nice uncut copy in original publisher's boards. signed presentation copy from Geo.Cameron. 75.00

Not in Kress, Goldsmith or the NUC.

CAMPBELL, John [first Baron] Campbell [1779-1861]. Life of John, Lord Campbell, Lord High Chancellor of Great Britain Consisting of a Selection From His Autobiography, Diary, and Letters. Edited by His Daughter The Hon. Mrs. Hardcastle. In Two Volumes. With Portrait. London: John Murray, 1881. 8vo. pp. 12, 528; 11, 410, [34]ads. engraved frontis. port. com-

plete with half-titles. full ribbed morocco, gilt lettering, edges & inside dentelles. Fine. First Edition. 100.00

25 CAMPBELL, John [first Baron] Campbell. The Lives of the Chief Justices of England. From the Norman Conquest Till the Death of Lord Mansfield. In Two Volumes. London: John Murray, 1849. 8vo. pp. xix, 588; xii, 584 + 16p. of publisher's ads. original blind & gilt stamped cloth. backstrips faded & frayed, internally very good. with the armorial bookplate of Baldwin of Spadina in The County of Upper Canada. First Edition. 100.00

S.&M.I.591.1.

Campbell's work "contains a great deal of information about the history of law and lawyers which is not easily to be found elsewhere...Nor has time worn away the merits of his books; they still find many readers, and there is little probability that they will be displaced by anything more entertaining written on the same subject. None the less are they among the most censurable publications in our literature." (DNB)

26 (CAMPBELL, John [first Baron] Campbell). HILDRETH, Richard (Ed.). Atrocious Judges. Lives of Judges Infamous As Tools of Tyrants and Instruments of Oppression. Compiled From the Judicial Biographies of John Lord Campbell, Lord Chief Justice of England. With an Appendix, Containing the Case of Passmore Williamson. Edited, With an Introduction and Notes, by... New York & Auburn: Miller, Orton & Mulligan, 1856. 12mo. pp. 432. original blind-blocked cloth, soiled & frayed. First American Edition, Second Issue. Sabin 31770. 45.00

"STANDARD AUTHORITY ON
MARITIME & COMMERCIAL LAW"

27 CASAREGI, Giuseppe Lorenzo Maria (Josephus Laurentius Maria de CASAREGIS) [1670-1737]. Discursus Legales De Commercio... Secunda Editione...4 Volumes in 3. [Vol. IV has variant title: Tomus Quartus Continens Elucubrationes Ac Resolutiones in aliquot, & ad integra Statuta De Decretis, Ac De Successionibus Ab Intestato...]. Venetiis: Ex Typographia Balleoniana, 1740. folio. pp. xxiv, 417, [1]; xii, 440, clvi; 223; xii, 268. indices. half-title in Vol. I. title of Vol. I in red & black. text in double columns. engraved portrait in Vol. I. numerous vignettes & ornamental initials. slight dampstaining to lower inner margin of Vol. I & outer margin of last few leaves in Vol. II, otherwise an excellent set in contemporary vellum. From the library of T.C.Aylwin. 1,000.00

S.&M.I.505.15. Goldsmith 7737. Marvin p. 178.

Casaregi, professor of law and for 20 years a judge at Florence, has long enjoyed the reputation of being a standard authority on commercial and maritime law and one of the best Italian writers on these subjects. "His commercial discourses are by far the most valuable of all his works to a modern lawyer. They embrace the whole circle of commercial law, including the law of prize. All that is most useful in the works of former jurists is collected and commented on with acuteness and accuracy, and for the most part the topics are examined until the whole subject matter is exhausted. Rarely have we looked into his works upon any contested question, without rising instructed and enlightened by the perusal. Higher praise cannot be bestowed upon him than the fact affords, that he is quoted by all subsequent writers on commercial law, as a leading and

safe authority, and Valin does not scruple to affirm, that he is beyond all contradiction the best of all the maritime authors." (Marvin) The third volume also includes the 'Il Cambista Istruito' and the 'Consolato del Mare', with a commentary.

Besides this edition (the best & most complete), S.&M. lists the following: Florence 1719 in 2 vols. & Florence 1729 in 3 vols. The NUC also locates 1 copy of an earlier 1707 edition.

28 CHASSENEUX, Barthelemy de. Consuetudines Ducatus Burgundiae, Fere'Que Totius Galliae...Commentariis amplissimis & doctissimis illustratae. Hac postrema editione infinitis erroribus omnia purgata genuinaequelectioni restituta opera & studio Iuliani Mallety. Accessit rerum, verborumque Index locupletissimus. Lugduni (Lyon): Apud Bartholomaeum Vincentium, 1582. folio. pp. 3pl, [112]index, [2], 1528. text in double columns. 7 engraved genealogical trees. title in red & black. woodcut ornaments & initials, title vignette. old sprinkled calf, sometime rebacked. binding worn, front cover detached, back joint cracked, front free-endpaper loose; except for some slight dampstaining to fore-edge margin of a few leaves, internally an excellent copy. From the library of T.C.Aylwin and the Court of Arches. 600.00

This edition not in BM STC French Books, Adams or Graesse. See Graesse II p. 289 (1534 edition).

This commentary on the customary law of Burgundy by the French judge and legal writer Chasseneux went through a number of editions; "c'est un des premiers ouvrages dans lesquels on ait essaye d'eclaircir le droit coutumier de France, en le conciliant avec le droit romain." (Michaud, Biographie Universelle)

29 CLARENDON, Edward [HYDE, first] Earl of [1609-1674]. A Collection of Several Tracts of the Right Honourable Edward, Earl of Clarendon, Author of the History of the Rebellion and Civil Wars in England. Published from his Lordship's Original Manuscripts. London: Printed for T.Woodward..., and J.Peele, 1727. folio. pp. 2pl, 348, [2]div.title, [369]-770. vignettes. contemporary calf. binding somewhat worn, else very good. with armorial bookplate of Sir Richard Bempde Johnstone, Bart. First Edition. 250.00

Included is Clarendon's 'Vindication' written in 1668 in answer to the articles of impeachment against him (his popularity had been on a quick and steady decline, largely due to his attempts to restrict the authority of the House of Commons).

30 COKE, Edward. The First Part of the Institutes of the Laws of England Or, A Commentary Upon Littleton. Not the Name of the Author, only, but of the Law Itself. The Thirteenth Edition [Hargrave and Butler's First Edition], Revised and Corrected. With the Addition of Notes and References, From the Beginning to Folio 195 Inclusive, By Francis Hargrave Esq...And From Folio 196 to the End, With the Preface and Index to the Notes, by Charles Butler...And An Analysis of Littleton, Written by an Unknown Hand in 1658-9, but never before published. London: Printed for E.Brooke..., 1788. folio. pp. 2pl, [18], xx, 395 (numbered leaves), [64]index & tables, [2]blank, [2]errata & directions to binder. 1 folding table. contemporary calf, sometime rebacked, endpapers renewed. binding rubbed, covers detached, small library stamp on front free-endpaper & label

on spine, internally very good. 225.00

S.&M.I.450.7. Winfield pp. 333-34. Marvin pp. 204-208. See PMM 259.

The First Part of the Institutes is considered to be Coke's most "celebrated work on which his fame is permanently established." (Foss) "If Bracton first began the codification of the common law, it was Coke who completed it. Ranging over the whole field of law, in comment, report, argument, and decision - it is a disorderly, pedantic, masterful work in which the common thread is a national dogmatism, tenacious of its continuous self-perpetuating life. With it the lawyers fought the battle of the constitution agains the Stuarts; historical research was their defence for national liberties. In the Institutes the basis of the constitution in the law of the land was firmly established." (PMM) Francis Hargrave and Charles Butler's critical notes on Coke in the 13th and 14th editions of the First Part of the Institutes provided added insight into Coke's work and distinguish these from previous editions.

31 COLLINS, Arthur [1682-1760]. Proceedings, Precedents, And Arguments, On Claims and Controversies, Concerning Baronies by Writ, and other Honours. With the Arguments of Sir Francis Bacon, Sir Henry Montagu, the Lord Chief Justice Crew, the Lord Chief Justice Heneage Finch, Mr. Montagu, (afterwards Lord Chief Baron) Sir William Jones, Sir William Dugdale, Mr. Offley, Sir Edward Northey, Sir Thomas Powis, and others... With an Appendix containing several Papers copied from the Bodleian and Ashmolaean Libraries, at Oxford &c. London: Printed for Thomas Wotton, 1734. folio. pp. 1pl, 4(dedication & preface), [2]errata leaf, 415, [12]index. An excellent copy in modern quarter antique oasis morocco, with armorial bookplate of Baron Maule laid in. First Edition. 400.00

S.&M.I.204.11. New CBEL II p. 1712.

Collins devoted his lifetime to researching the nobility and investigating disputed titles. Here recorded are the cases covering the period from the end of the reign of Queen Elizabeth to the year 1740.

32 COLQUOUN, P[atrick] [1745-1820]. A Treatise On Indigence; Exhibiting A General View of the National Resources For Productive Labour; With Propositions For Ameliorating the Condition of the Poor... London: Printed for J.Hatchard, 1806. 8vo. pp. 1pl, [iii]-xii, [2], [5]-302, [12]incl. index. & ads. tables (1 folding). lacking half-title. modern green buckram. Fine. First Edition. 300.00

Kress B.5028. Goldsmith 19292. McCulloch p. 286.

Colquoun's treatise contains considerable discussion of the poor laws (with a section on Blackstone's observations), the relation between poverty and crime, the police and law enforcement. To combat indigence and crime, he recommended "the establishment of a board of education, of a national savings bank with a state guarantee to the depositors, of a system of reproductive employment for those out of work, of a national poor-rate universally assessed, and the issue of a police gazette, containing instructive reading, with the statistics of crime and descriptions of the persons of offenders." (DNB)

33 COLQUOUN, P[atrick]. A Treatise on the Commerce and Police of the River Thames: Containing An Historical View of the Trade of the Port of London; And suggesting Means for preventing the Depredations thereon, by a Legislative System of River Police. With An Account of the Functions of the Various Magistates and Corporations Exercising Jurisdiction on the River; And A General View of the Penal and Remedial Statutes Connected With the Subject. London: Printed For Joseph Mawman, 1800. 8vo. pp. 2pl, xxxiv, 593, 609-676(appendix), [20]index. engraved folding map, 2 folding tables. contemporary quarter calf. bds. rubbed, internally fine. First Edition. 350.00

Kress B.4102. Goldsmith 18053. Marvin p. 215.

Colquoun was Lord Provost of Glasgow and police magistrate in London. Subsequent to the publishing of his chief work on the "Police of the Metropolis", East Indian merchants requested his assistance in preventing the stealing of goods from ships in the Thames. This work resulted in the establishment for the first time of an effective Thames police.

COMBERBACH, Roger. The Report of Several Cases Argued and adjudged in the Court of King's Bench at Westminster; From the First Year of King James the Second, to the Tenth Year of King William the Third. Collected By...late Recorder of Chester, and one of the Justices of North-Wales. Published by his son Roger Comberbach of the Inner-Temple, Esq. In the Savoy: Printed by E.andR.Nutt, and R.Gosling...for J.Walthoe, 1724. folio. pp. 2pl, [9]table, [1]errata, 484, [51]table. 19th century half calf. binding bit rubbed, cloth sides faded & spotty, some dampstaining & browning to outer leaves, numbers erased from lower margin of first two leaves, else very good. First Edition. 150.00

S.&M.I.298.33. See Marvin pp. 215-16.

COOTE, Richard Holmes. An Analysis, Arranged to Serve Also As A Compendious Digested Index of Mr. Fearne's Essay on Contingent Remainders and Executory Devises, And of Mr. Butler's Notes. London: Printed for W.Clarke & Sons, 1814. 8vo. pp. 2pl, [12], 198. contemporary calf. front joint tender. First Edition. 125.00

S.&M.II.77. Marvin p. 228.

A very useful and concise alphabetical index & analytical abridgement of Fearne's authoritative work on property law.

CROKE, George [1582-1641]. The Third Part (Though first publish't) of the Reports of Sr George Croke Kt, Late one of the Justices of Kings-Bench, And formerly one of the Justices of the Court of Common-Bench; Of Such Select Cases as ere Adjudged in the said Courts, during the first Sixteen Years Reign of King Charles the First. Collected and Written in French by Himself; Revised and Published in English by Sir Harbottle Grimston, Baronet, Master of the Rolls. The Third Impression, carefully Corrected, with the Addition of many Thousand of References never before Printed. London: Printed by W.Rawlins, S.Roycroft, and H.Sawbridge..., 1683. folio. pp. 1pl, [28], 610, [66]index. several woodcut ornaments & initials. old calf, quite worn. front free-endpaper loose, fore-edge of first few leaves bit tatty, few notes on back endpapers in old hand, else internally very good. From the library of T.C.Aylwin. The book also bears the signatures of the following previous owners: the Boston jurist John Leverett 1697, the Boston lawyer, theologian & Loyalist William Brattle 1734 & the Massachusetts lawyer & judge Jonathan Sewall.

Third Edition in English. 200.00

New Wing C.7020. S.&M.I.298.37. Marvin p. 240. Winfield p. 190.

"Croke's Reports form a continuation of Dyer's, and are among the most esteemed of the elder determinations, and are to this day familiarly referred to as authentic repositories of the Common Law." (Bridgman) "Precedents for almost any opinion may be found in Croke's Law Reports." (Judge Pendleton)

"INDEX TO THE WORKS OF THE GREATEST OF ALL CIVIL LAWYERS"

37 (CUJAS, Jacques [1522-1590]). ALBANESE, Domenico. Promptuarium Universorum Operum Jacobi Cujacii Variantibus inter se lectionibus, praesertim Titulorum, & Legum Florentinae, Vulgataeque editionis Pandectarum, sive Digestorum accomodatum Cura, Et Industria Dominici Albanensis In Supremis Regni Neapolitani Tribunalibus Causarum Patroni. 2 Volumes. Mutinae (Modena): Apud Societatem Typographicam, Superiorum Facultate, 1795. folio. pp. 1pl, [18], lxxii, 680; 146, 343. text in double columns. with divisional titles. title vignette. contemporary mottled calf, gilt backs. bindings bit rubbed, backstrips chipped, front cover of Vol. I detached, other joints cracked, otherwise a very good set. From the library of T.C.Aylwin & with the armorial bookplates & signatures of Alexander Buchanan. 400.00

Graesse II p. 306. The NUC locates only 3 copies of this edition.

A valuable index to the works of the eminent French jurist Cujas, who has been referred to as the greatest of all civil lawyers. "He is the outstanding representative of humanism in Roman law...The school of Cujas viewed the Roman texts as historical documents, interpreting them in the full setting of ancient history and literature. A consummate master of jurisprudence, philology and history, Cujas may claim to be the greatest legal scholar of all time...[this index] gives ready access to the eleven-volume Naples (1722-27) and Venice-Modena (1758-83) reprints of the Opera Omnia edited by C.A.Fabrot (10 vols., Paris 1658)." (Encycl. of Social Sciences)

38 DECISIONVM Novissimarum Diversorum Sacri Palatii Apostolici Auditorum...Opus Sane Perquam Utile, Et in Foro versantibus summe necessarium. His Accessit Practica Quaedam notabilium quorundam eiusdem Rotae perpetuo quidem memori & commendanda. Cum Summariis et Indice Locupletissimis. Omnia nunc recens in luce edita. 4 Volumes in 2. [Vol. IV with variant title:... Continens Cum Decisiones Varias, Tum Declarationes Consilii Tridenti: E Bibliotheca manuscripta. D.N.Prosperi Farinacii ...]. Lugduni (Lyon): Sumptibus Claudii Landry, 1618-19. folio. pp. 6pl, 519; 2pl, [517]-803, [79]index; 2pl, 491, [68] index; 118, [10]index. text in double columns. titles in red & black. title vignettes. old calf, sometime rebacked. binding worn, covers off, tears to 2 leaves (no loss), else internally very good. From the library of T.C.Aylwin and the Court of Arches. 400.00

Not in NUC.

The decisions of the papal courts are an "important source of our knowledge of the application and development of canon law by judicial practise." (Encycl. of Social Sciences)

) DE LOLME, J[ean] L[ouis] [1740?-1807]. The Constitution of England, Or An Account of the English Government; In Which It is compared with the Republican Form of Government, and the other Monarchies in Europe. The Fourth Edition, Corrected and Enlarged. [Edited by Charles Coote]. London: Printed for G. Robinson & J.Murray, 1784. 8vo. pp. 4pl, xvi, 540, [20]index. engraved frontis. port. contemporary calf. corners bumped, otherside a fine copy. 75.00

S.&M.I.100.27. New CBEL II p. 1734. Marvin p. 263.

De Lolme's work constitutes a good systematic treatment of the English constitution and is highly regarded. Four new chapters were added to the third edition as well as some corrections, and this fourth edition is further improved by Charles Coote.

DE LOLME, J[ean] L[ouis]. The Constitution of England...A New Edition. London: Sold by G.Kearsley and J.Ridley, 1777. 8vo. pp. 2pl, 404. contemporary calf. front cover & front free-endpaper detached, else a very nice clean copy with the armorial bookplate of the Hon. George Baillie, one of the Lords of the Treasury, with his signature on title. 75.00

[DESTUTT DE TRACY, Antoine Louis Claude, Comte] [1754-1836]. A Commentary and Review of Montesquieu's Spirit of the Laws. Prepared For Press From the Original Manuscript, in the Hands of the Publisher. To Which Are Annexed, Observations on the Thirty-First Book, By the Late M.Condorcet: And Two Letters of Helvetius, On the Merits of the Same Work. [Translated by Thomas Jefferson]. Philadelphia: Printed by William Duane, 1811. 8vo. pp. viii, 292. slight dampstain to inner margin of last few signatures, else very good. First American Edition, First Appearance in Print. Marvin p. 607.

Bound with:

[ANDREWS, William Eusebius]. An Historical Narrative of the Horrid Plot and Conspiracy of Titus Oates, Called the Popish Plot In Its Various Branches and Progress, Selected From the Most Authentic Protestant Historians, To Which Are Added Some Cursory Observations On the Test Act. London: Published by W. E.Andrews..., 1816. 8vo. pp. 2pl, vi, [7]-284. last leaf soiled, tear to upper margin of 2A2, resulting in loss of two words of text, else a nice copy.
The two works bound in contemporary half sheep. lacking free-endpapers & back blank. 250.00

Jefferson's English translation of Destutt de Tracy's commentary marks its first appearance in print. Although the manuscript in French dates from 1807, the first French edition was not published until 1819. The work presents a clear formulation of the author's political philosophy, in which he opposes the concept of absolute natural rights & compares the English constitution unfavourably to the American system.

(DOUGLAS, Archibald James Edward, first Baron Douglas of Douglas; formerly A.J.E.Stewart) [1748-1827]. Observations Servant de Reponse a Un Ecrit Anonime, Portant le titre de Memoire Abrege Pour M. De Douglas; Avec L'Articulation Des Faits De Supposition De Part, Et Les Quatre Lettres Du Pretendu Accoucheur Pier Lamarr. A Paris: 1763. 4to. pp. 1pl, 40, [24]. library buckram, several small library stamps, title browned, else very good. 50.00

The first brief here contained is signed A[ndrew] Stuart, who represented the Duke of Hamilton in the famous Douglas case. The Duke of Hamilton contested the will of Archibald Douglas (1761), which settled his estate upon his sister's surviving son, and claimed that, in fact, the young Douglas was a spurious child. The Scottish case lasted 5 years (1762-67); Douglas appealed the original decision against him and obtained a reversal in 1769.

43 [DUNNING, John, first Baron Ashburton] [1731-1783]. A Postscript to the Letter on Libels, Warrants, &c. In Answer to A Postscript in the Defence of the Majority, And Another Pamphlet, entitled, Considerations on the Legality of General Warrants. The Second Edition [actually the Third], Considerably Enlarged. London: Printed for J.Almon, 1765. 8vo. pp. 1pl, 5-25, [2]ads, [1], 16(additions to 2nd & 3rd editions). lacking the half-title. disbound. 75.00

Dunning's celebrated arguments against the legality of general warrants in the case of Leach vs Money established his great reputation.

44 DYER, [Sir James] [1511-1582]. Les Reports Des Divers Select Matters & Resolutions des Reverend Judges & Sages del Ley, Touchant & concernant mults principal Points occurrent estre debate per eux: En le several Reignes de les tres-hault & excellent Princes, Le Roys Hen. 8. & Edw. 6 & le Roignes Mar. & Eliz. Collect & Report per tres-Reverend Judge, Sr. Jacques Dyer Chivaler... London: Printed by W.Rawlins, S.Roycroft, and M.Flesher...for Samuel Keble..., 1688. folio. pp. 3pl, [10]table, 377 (numbered leaves), [2], [52]index. woodcut ornaments & vignettes. old calf, sometime rebacked. binding quite worn, covers detached, outer signatures loose, some dampstaining & marginal tearing to a few leaves (not affecting text), otherwise internally very good. Sixth Edition, in Law French. Edited by Chief Justice Treby. 275.00

S.&M.I.299.47. New Wing D.2927. Marvin p. 284. Winfield p. 187.

Dyer "reported the most remarkable cases that came before the Court of Common Pleas, together with those, which, on account of their difficulty, were adjourned into the Exchequeur Chamber before all the Judges. They are valuable records of the history of English jurisprudence and English manners." (S.&M.) "No Reports have been so frequently reprinted, and none have received higher homage..." (Marvin) Dyer's reports are also notable as being the first collection regularly called 'Reports' rather than 'Cases' or 'Commentaries'. This sixth Edition is the first to be altered; the notes and additions of Chief Justice Treby are held to be of equal authority to the Reports.

45 DYMOND, Jonathan [1796-1828]. Essays on the Principles of Morality and on the Private and Political Rights and Obligations of Mankind. Ninth Edition. Dublin: Easen and Son & London: Samuel Bagster and Sons, 1894. 8vo. pp. xiv, 294. text in double columns. index. original cloth spotty & soiled. 25.00

45 EAST, Edward Hyde [1764-1847]. A Treatise of the Pleas of the Crown. 2 Volumes. Philadelphia: Printed for P.Byrne, 1806. 8vo. pp. lxiii, 480; 2pl, 481-1126, [2]ads. complete with half-title. contemporary sheep. some browning & foxing to leaves. First American Edition. 200.00

S.&M.II.106 (not recording this edition). Marvin p. 284.

A clearly written thorough and standard account relating to criminal law at the end of the eighteenth century, this work was the result of 15 years of labour. East had access to private collections of cases during his research and his treatise is the sole source for many otherwise unreported decisions. Offences are classed under 3 categories: crimes against religion, crimes against property and crimes against persons.

47 ESPINASSE, Isaac. A Digest of the Law of Actions and Trials At Nisi Prius. The Second Edition, Corrected, With Considerable Additions From Printed and Manuscript Cases, And Three New Chapters On the Law of Corporations and Evidence. 2 Volumes in 1. Dublin: Printed for E.Lynch, 1794-93. 8vo. pp. x, [33], 426; 1pl, [427]-791, [66]index. contemporary calf. occasional light foxing else very good. 100.00

S.&M.I.335.6. See Marvin p. 298.

48 EXPILLY, Claude [1561-1636]. Plaidoyez de M^{re}..., Chevalier, Conseiller du Roy En Son Conseil D'Estat, & President au Parlement de Grenoble: Ensemble plusieurs Arrests & Reglemens notables dudit Parlement. Cinquiesme Edition. Reveue, augmentee, & corrigee d'un grand nombre de fautes, outre les precedentes impressions, & divisee en deux parties. Avec trois Tables... 2 Parts in 1. A Lyon: De l'Imprimerie de Simon Rigaud, 1631. 4to. pp. 2pl, [16], 291, [2]div.title, 295-450, [56]index.. title in red & black. title vignette & woodcut ornaments & initials. old sprinkled calf, sometime rebacked. binding rubbed, front cover detached, some age-browning to leaves, else internally very good. From the library of T.C. Aylwin and the Court of Arches. 200.00

This edition not listed in BM STC French Books or Cioranescu. See Cioranescu, 17th Cent., II 28629-30 (1608 & 1652 editions) & Andre, Sources, 6321. NUC locates 2 copies only.

Expilly, French lawyer, councillor of State and president of the Parlement de Grenoble, studied under Cujas. The sixth & seventh 'plaidoyes' deal with the commerce with Spain and Flanders.

49 FACHINEI, Andrea (Andreas FACHINAEUS). Controversiarum Opus: In Quatuor Tomos Sectum...Edition Postrema Cui primo accreuit Tomus quartus, deinde cuique Tomo argumenta praefixa, tertio superadditus est triplex Elenchus: vnus Capitum, alter Verb. Sentent. & Rerum: tertius V.I.locorum, vniuerso hoc opere cribratorum. Aureliae Allobrogum (Geneva): Excudebat Stephanus Gamonetus, 1609. 8vo. pp. 1pl, [15], 1859, [14], 1860-2415, [91]index. text in double columns. several woodcut ornaments & initials. title vignette. old sprinkled calf, gilt back. slight marginal dampstaining & some insignificant marginal worming to last few signatures, binding rubbed, head of spine worn, else very good. From the library of T.C.Aylwin. 275.00

NUC only locates a Lyon edition for 1609.

The Italian jurist frequently quotes Cujas & Bude, but is critical of Hotman for doubting the authenticity of a letter of Justinian inserted in the Code (de Summa Trinitate) asserting the pre-eminence of the Popes.

50 FAVRE, Antoine (Antonius FABER) [1557-1624]. Coniecturarum Iuris Civilis Libri viginti. In quibus difficiles perique Iuris Iustinianaei loci, nouis cum emendationibus, tum inter-

pretationibus explicantur, & vera rectaque Iuris principia stabiliuntur. Cume Indice Copiosissimo...Editio Postrema. Coloniae Allobrogum (Geneva): Apud Samuelem Crispinum, & Franciscum Fabrum, 1615. folio. pp. 1pl, [10], 798, [32]index. title vignette & several woodcut ornaments & initials. title in red & black. old mottled calf, gilt back. head of backstrip & spine label chipped, otherwise an excellent copy. From the library of T.C.Aylwin. 325.00

This edition not in Graesse or the NUC. For other editions, see Graesse II p. 540 (Lugduni, 1661) & BM STC French Books F.109 (Lugduni 1651).

The 'Coniecturarum' were first written when Favre was but 23 years of age; they reveal a profound knowledge of Roman laws and their interrelationships. Favre was deservedly hailed by Cujas, and became successively, 'juge-mage' of Bresse, Bugey, Valroney et Gex, senator of Chambery, president of the Council of Geneva, president at Annecy & Chambery, and finally governor of Savoy.

51 FAVRE, Antoine. Iurisprudentiae Papinianeae Scientia, Ad Ordinem Institutionum Imperialium efformata, In qua uniuersum Ius Civile, noua methodo, ad propria & indubitata sua Principia refertur, & ex iis clarissime ac certissime demonstratur. Editio Novissima, Et Emendata. Lugduni (Lyon): Sumptibus Philippi Borde, Laurentii Arnaud, & Claudii Rigaud, 1658. folio. pp. 3pl, 644, [15]index. text in double columns. title in red & black. title vignette. woodcut ornaments & initials. upper backstrip defective, else a fine copy in contemporary vellum. From the library of T.C.Aylwin. 275.00

Graesse II p. 540. BM STC French Books F.112.

"Ouvrage capital, qui avait pour but de reduire dans un ordre methodique et regulier toute la science du droit romain qui offre tant de confusion dans les cinquante livres des Pandectes. (Michaud, Biographie Universelle)

52 FOLEY, Robert. Laws Relating to the Poor, From the Forty-third of Queen Elizabeth to the Third of King George II. With Cases adjudged in the Court of King's Bench, upon the several Clauses of them. In a Method Entirely New. In the Savoy: Printed by E.and R.Nutt, and R.Gosling (Assigns of E.Sayer), Esq;) for T.Woodward..., 1739. 8vo. pp. 2pl, [28], 284, [19]index, [1]errata. crudely recased in old sheep binding from another source, taped label & hinges, title trimmed & mounted, lower margin of following leaf repaired, ad leaf chipped at fore-edge, otherwise a good sound copy. First Edition. 175.00

Kress 4435. S.&M.I.387.16. See Marvin p. 316.

53 FORSYTH, William. The History of Lawyers Ancient and Modern. With Illustrations. Boston: Estes & Lauriat, 1875. 8vo. pp. xvii, 404. 3 plates. original blind & gilt stamped cloth. First American Edition. 45.00

54 FURNEAUX, Philip [1726-1783]. Letters To the Honourable Mr. Justice Blackstone, Concerning His Exposition of the Act of Toleration, And Some Positions relative to Religious Liberty, In His Celebrated Commentaries on the Laws of England. London: Printed for T.Cadell, 1770. 8vo. pp. 1pl, xv, [1]errata, 166. disbound. First Edition. 150.00

S.&M.I.29.11 & Marvin p. 326 (not listing first edition).

An important work on the struggle for religious freedom, written in opposition to Blackstone's classification of nonconformity as a civil offence. "The moral argument against enforcing religious truths by civil penalties is presented with remarkable power." (DNB)

55 GODWIN, William. [1756-1836]. An Enquiry Concerning Political Justice, And Its Influence on General Virtue and Happiness. In Two Volumes. Dublin: Printed for Luke White, 1793. 8vo. pp. xiii, [21]contents, 411; 2pl, [19]contents, 424. complete with half-titles. contemporary sheep bit worn, joints cracking, slight dampstain to lower corner of first few leaves of Vol. I, small strip clipped from half-title of Vol. I, hint of foxing, else internally very good. First Irish Edition. 350.00

Kress B.2528. cfGoldsmith 15825 (1st English edition). S.&M. I.608.30. New CBEL II p. 1249. See PMM 384.

Composed of carefully constructed arguments dealing with all aspects of legal rights and duties, this influential work established Godwin as the philosophical representative of English radicalism. The first Irish edition was published in the same year as the first English.

56 GRIVEL, Jean (Ioannis Grivellus) [1560-1624]. Decisiones Celeberrimi Sequanorum Senatus Dolani. In quibus multa, tum ad theoriam iuris, tum ad praxim, & consuetudinem spectantia, dilucide explanantur: omnibus in foro versantibus admodum utilia & necessaria....Cum Indice rerum ac materiarum locupletissimo. Antverpiae: Apud Ioannem Keerbergium, 1618. folio. pp. 1pl, [25], 443, [41]index & errata. title vignette. woodcut ornaments & initials. text in double columns. old calf, sometime rebacked. binding worn, covers off, internally fine. From the library of T.C.Aylwin & the Court of Arches. 300.00

No copies located in NUC.

"Cet ouvrage est ecrit en bon latin avec beaucoup d'ordre, de nettete et d'erudition; de sorte qu'on peut le regarder comme un des meilleurs de ce genre." (Dunod de Charnage) The author, 'conseiller au parlement de Dole'. in 1608 became 'maitre de requetes' in the Privy Council of the Low Countries, and upon the death of Richardot, assumed control of the affairs of the province of Burgundy.

57 GROTIUS (or DE GROOT),Hugo [1583-1645]. De Veritate Religionis Christianae. Cum Notulis Joannis Clerici; Accesserunt Ejusdem De Eligenda Inter Christianos Dissentientes Sententia, & Contra Indifferentiam Religionum Libri Duo. Bostonii, Nov-Anglorum: Typis Thomas B.Wait Et Sociis, Sumptibus W.Wells, 1809. 12mo. pp. xvi, 388. bit of foxing, else a very nice uncut copy in modern buckram. 60.00

58 GUI-PAPE (Guidon de la Pape) [1400-1475]. Decisiones Parliamenti Delphinatus. Ex Prototypo, Matthaei Antonioni I.V. Cons. studio genuinae integritati restitutae, Anno 1561. Item Tractatus Imberti De Bovenco de Iuramento contractus seu actus invalidi confirmatorio, ex autentico, Sacramenta puberum. C. si adversus venditionem. Summis adhaec, notis & Indice illustrantur. Lugduni (Lyon): Apud haeredes Iacobi Iuntae, 1562. small 8vo. pp. 951, [84]index, [2]. lacking final blank. modern quarter oasis morocco, title & following leaf & corner of T^2 laminated, small wormhole to last 6 leaves of index (touching some

letters), some dampstaining to upper portion of leaves of last few signatures, else very good. original endpapers preserved. From the library of T.C.Aylwin and the Court of Arches. 350.00

Adams P.208. See Brunet II p. 1811. This edition not in BM STC French Books, Graesse or the NUC.

"Les decisions du Guy-Pape ont ete longtemps d'une grande authorite dans les pays de droit ecrit." (Brunet) "Dumoulin et Tiraqueau ont parle de lui avec de grands eloges. Taisand dit qu'il seta toujours recommendable et distingue parmi les jurisconsultes, parce qu'il a reuni la theorie a la pratique, chose si necessaire." (Michaud, Biographie Universelle)

59 HALE, Matthew. The History of the Common Law. The Fourth Edition Corrected; With Notes, References, And Some Account of the Life of the Author, By Charles Runnington. [With: "An Analysis of the Civil Part of the Law. The Fourth Edition"]. London: Printed by W.Strahan & M.Woodfall for T.Cadell, 1779. 8vo. pp. 4pl, xl, [305], [1]errata; 6pl, 114, [8]index, [2] ads. engraved frontis. chart. modern quarter morocco. some browning throughout, dampstaining to lower edge of some leaves, frontis. & title neatly mounted, else very good. With complimentary ticket of F.A.Alberger, Member of Assembly. 150.00

S.&M.I.239.18. See Marvin p. 359 & Winfield pp. 37-38 & 328.

The 'Analysis', treating of civil matters, was the first work of its kind ever written and had a considerable influence on Blackstone, who called it "the most rational, scientific...as well as the most comprehensive of all atempts [prior to his own analysis] to digest the common law." Of his 'History' Holdsworth has said that it is "the ablest introductory sketch of a history of English law that appeared till the publication of Pollock and Maitland." Both of the works were published posthumously from rough drafts never intended for publication, and this fourth edition marks their first appearance together.

60 HALES, William [1747-1831]. Observations On Tithes, Shewing the Inconveniences of all the Schemes that have been proposed for altering that antient Manner of providing for the Clergy of the Established Church of Ireland...To Which is annexed, A Second Edition of the Moderate Reformer, Or A Proposal for abolishing some of the most obvious and gross Abuses that have crept into the Church of England, and are the Occasion of frequent Complaints against it. By A Friend of the Church of England [Francis Maseres]. London: Sold by B.andJ.White, 1794. 8vo. pp. 1pl, 73. disbound. Goldsmith 16068. 35.00

61 HARDINGE, George. A Series of Letters to the Right Honourable Edmund Burke, Upon the Impeachment of Mr. Hastings. The Third Edition, With Many Corrections and Additions, A New Preface, and Appendix. London: Cadell..., 1791. 8vo. pp. 1pl, [v]-xii, 220, [12]appendix. contemporary half calf. binding rubbed, tear to title leaf (part of imprint torn away), else very good. 100.00

"DEFENCE OF ABSOLUTISM"

62 HOBBES, Thomas [1588-1679]. Leviathan, Or The Matter, Forme, & Power of a Common-Wealth Ecclesiasticall and Civill. London: Printed for Andrew Ckooke [sic], 1651. folio. pp. 1 248, 247-256, 261-[396]. engraved title leaf & folding broadside table. woodcut ornaments. contemporary calf, neatly rebacked. covers bit worn, inscription at top of engraved title, else an extremely nice copy. With armorial bookplate of John Lord Brownlowe, Baron Charleville, & Viscount Tyrconnel in the Kingdom of Ireland [John Cust]. Second Edition, First Pirate Edition. 1,500.00

Wing H.2247. Kress 831. MacDonald & Hargreaves 43. S.&M. I. 609.42. See PMM 272.

The second edition, first pirate edition, with the bear ornament on title-page & the long foliated ornament at head of introduction, with 2 winged figures holding a plaque with St. Christopher & initials C.C. in a central oval, was probably published in Amsterdam by Christoffel Cunradus, not long after 1651.

"Thomas Hobbes of Malmesbury is a unique figure in the history of English political thought. His defence of absolutism, unpopular from the day it was published to the present, is based on expediency. The individual (except to save his life) should always submit to the State, because any government is better than the anarchy of the natural state. Though his ideas have never appealed to proponents of the individual rights of man or to the modern totalitarians with their mystical visions of Volk, the fundamental nature of Hobbes's speculation has stimulated philosophers from Spinoza to John Stuart Mill." (PMM)

63 [HOME, Henry, Lord Kames] [1696-1782]. Remarkable Decisions of the Court of Session, From the year 1730 to the year 1752. Edinburgh: Printed for A.Kincaid and J.Bell, 1766. folio. pp. viii, 284, [9]index. contemporary sprinkled calf. joints & extremities rubbed, else a very good clean copy. First Edition. 150.00

S.&M.V.57. Marvin p. 394.

A further volume of 'Remarkable Decisions' by the Scottish judge & philosopher, covering the period 1716-1728, appeared in 1728.

64 HOPKINS, Tighe. The Dungeons of Old Paris: Being the Story and Romance of the most Celebrated Prisons of the Monarchy and the Revolution. New York and London: G.P.Putnam's Sons, 1897. 8vo. pp. v, 265, [2]ads. 12 illus. A fine uncut copy in original cloth, t.e.g. 35.00

"IDEAL OF PROTESTANT STATESMANSHIP"

65 HOTMAN (or HOTTOMAN), Francois [1524-1590]. Francogallia. [Geneva]: Ex officina Iacobi Stoerij, 1573. 8vo. pp. 8pl, 174, [9]index. title within fine arabesque border. ornamental initials. contemporary vellum bit soiled, some damp marks, upper corner of back cover & a few leaves chipped, hole in last leaf (not affecting text), else a very nice copy. With manuscript notes in contemporary hand on flyleaves. First Edition. 1,250.00

Adams H.1083. Graesse III p. 377. Cioranesco, 16th Cent., 11577. Hauser 2215. Tilley II, 231. Weill, Pouvoir Royal, 98.

The French publicist & jurist's most important work quickly established his reputation as a political theorist. Inspired by the St. Bartholomew massacre of the previous year, the 'Francogallia' "presented an ideal of Protestant statesmanship, pleading for a representative government and an elective monarchy." (Encyc. Brit., 11th ed.) Hotman advocates revolution

and tyrannicide when necessary. The treatise was much in advance of its age and its vogue is is comparable to that obtained later by Rousseau's 'Social Contract'.

The manuscript notes in contemporary hand are epigrams addressed to Francis Duke of Alencon, brother of Kings Francis II and Henry III. Many of the verses are dated 1583, after his defeat at Antwerp and before his death in 1584 , which revived the Catholic camp & gave a new turn to politics.

66 HOTMAN, Francois. Novus Commentarius De Verbis Iuris Franc-Hotomani...De Legibus. De Magistratibus populi R. De Senatu &c S.C., De Iuris consultis, eorumq formulis. Quibus propter argumenti affinitatem Typographus adiunxit Epitomen Gruchij De Comitijs. &c. Diuersas Rerumpub. formas, ex Polybio. Basileae: Per Nicolaum, 1563. folio. pp. 6pl (incl. blank), 519, [7]index. text in double columns. printer's device on title & last leaf. woodcut ornamental initials. modern quarter oasis morocco, gilt tooled ornaments from original backstrip laid down. thin, neat marginal repairs to first 3 leaves, otherwise an excellent, clean, crisp, wide-margined copy. From the library of T.C.Aylwin and the Court of Arches. First Edition. 700.00

Not in Adams. The NUC locates only two copies (entry indicates that at least one, if not both, are defective).

Possessed of a critical knowledge of Roman sources and a fine Latin style, Hotman made a significant contribution to sixteenth century jurisprudence. He followed in the tradition of the humanist school of Alciat & Cujas. The last 14 years of his life were spent in wandering exile in order to save his family from anti-Huguenot persecution.

67 (HOWARD, John). DIXON, Hepworth. John Howard, and the Prison-World of Europe. Slightly Abridged. Webster, Mass.: Frederick Charlton, 1852. 8vo. pp. xxxii, [33]-442. original blind & gilt stamped publisher's cloth. extremities frayed. 25.00

68 JAY, John. The Correspondence and Public Papers of...First Chief-Justice of the United States, Member and President of the Continental Congress...1763-1781. Edited by Henry P. Johnston. 4 Volumes. New York & London: G.P.Putnam's Sons, 1890-93. 8vo. pp. xxiii, 461; xiii, 452; xxvi, 489; xxii, 532. complete with half-titles. index. original quarter hard-grained leather, t.e.g. bindings rubbed, ex-lib. uncut. #191 of a letter-press edition of 750 copies. 50.00

69 JUSTINIAN I. Institutionum Libri Quatuor. The Four Books of Justinian's Institutions, Translated into English, With Notes, By George Harris. London: Printed for C.Bathurst & E.Withers, 1756. 4to. pp. xv, 73, 121, 100, 92, 11, [4]index. genealogical table. copper vignette. contemporary calf scuffed, front joint cracked, internally fine. Armorial bookplate of Earl of Moray. First Edition of Harris translation. 150.00

See S.&M.V.137 & Marvin pp. 432-33 (not listing this edition) & PMM 137 (1st edition).

"Justinian I (483-565) was responsible for the code of Roman Law known as the Corpus juris civilis which is the basis of the form as well as of much of the content, of modern law. It consisted of the Codex, the essence of the confused mass of statute law; the Pandects, a similar abridgement of juristic opinions; and the Novallae, new ordinances made since the

Codex...The clarity which they achieved gave the Codex its permanent value." (PMM) Mr. Harris's translation is accurate & well annotated.

70 KING, Edward [1735?-1807]. An Essay on the English Constitution and Government. London: Printed for Benjamin White..., 1767. 8vo. pp. viii, 184, [1]errata. contemporary calf, gilt back. extremities & joints slightly rubbed, else fine. The First Edition of King's First separate work. 135.00

S.&M.I.102.54. Marvin p. 441.

71 KNAPP, Andrew and William Baldwin. The Newgate Calendar; Comprising Interesting Memoirs of the Most Notorious Characters Who Have Been Convicted of Outrages On the Laws of England Since the Commencement of the Eighteenth Century; With Occasional Anecdotes and Observations, Speeches, Confessions, and Last Exclamations of Sufferers. 4 Volumes in 3. London: J. Robins and Co., 1824-28. 8vo. pp. iv, 514, [2]index; 1pl, 500, [2]index; 1pl, 499, [3]index; 1pl, 404, [2]index. text in double columns. numerous plates & cuts in the text. original blind & gilt stamped cloth. backstrips faded & frayed, hint of foxing, mostly to endpapers, else internally fine. 300.00

72 LAURENTIUS, Heironymus A. Decisiones Rotae, Sacri Palatii Apostolici Avenionis. Nunc Primum in Lucem Emissae, & cum suo debito splendore per earum auctorem traditae, & completae: multum utiles ad similes & quotidianos definiendos casus... Lugduni (Lyon): In Officina Iuntarum, Apud Horatium Cardon, 1600. folio. pp. 1pl, [10], 293, [19]index, 58, [4]index, [1]. title in red & black. title vignette, woodcut ornaments & initials. text in double columns.

Not in Adams or located in NUC.

Bound with:

GAMMA, Antonio de. Decisionum Supremi Senatus Regnilusitaniae ...Centuriae Quaturo, In quibus diuersi casus, tam Canonici, quam Civiles, Feudales, & Criminales...Francofurto: Cura et Studio Collegii Musarum Novenarum Paltheniani, 1599. folio. pp. 4pl, [13]index, [3], 356, [18]index. title in red & black. text in double columns. title vignette, woodcut ornaments & initials.

Adams G.202. The NUC locates 3 copies. Not in BM STC German.

The 2 items bound in old bds., reversed calf backstrip. binding rubbed, backstrip worn, front cover off, some age-browning, else internally very good. From the library of T.C. AYlwin and the Court of Arches. 600.00

73 LAW DISSERTATIONS. A Collection of 14 Law Dissertation (in Latin) published in Germany and Switzerland (various imprints) between 1719 and 1792. 4to. & 8vo. disbound. Detailed list available upon request. 600.00

73 LAWES, Edward. An Elementary Treatise on Pleading in Civil Actions. Portsmouth, N.H.: Thomas & Tappan, 1808. 8vo. pp. 3pl, 246. contemporary sheep. joints rubbed. First American Edition. 60.00

Marvin p. 452. S.&M.II.208 (1st edition, 1806).

"OLD DUTCH LAW"

74 LEEUWEN, Simon Van [1625-1682]. Censura Forensis Theoretico-Practica, Id Est, Totius Juris Civilis Romani, Usuque Recepti, & Practici Methodica Collatio. Qua non tantum ipsa Juris Romani fundamenta ad rationis, & veritatis censuram, methodice reducuntur; sed & ad usum practicum transferuntur...Editio quarta prioribus longe emendatior, & ex Auctoris Autographis locupletior. Gerardus De Haas, JC. recensuit & Observationes suas adjecit. 2 Parts in 1 Volume [Part I in 5 books; Part II in 2 books; with separate & cumulative indices]. Lugduni In Batavis (Leyden): Sumptibus Samuelis Luchtmans et Cornelii Haak, 1741. folio. pp. 1pl, [37], 623, [43]index; 1pl, [11], 248, [28]index. title of Vol. I in red & black. several woodcut ornaments & initials. text in double columns. 2 engraved plates in text (genealogical trees). contemporary calf. extremities bit rubbed, else fine. From the library of T.C.Aylwin. 450.00

Camus 518. Only 3 copies of this edition located in NUC.

An important manual on old Dutch law, written by the Dutch jurist Van Leeuwen, son of a member of the Dutch company of the East Indies.

75 LIEBER, Francis. On Civil Liberty and Self-Government. London: Richard Bentley, 1853. 8vo. pp. xv, 552. complete with half-title. index. original blind & gilt stamped cloth. cloth faded & frayed, upper backstrip chipped, internally very good - unopened. with the armorial bookplate & signature of James Whitall. First British Edition. Sabin 40974. 50.00

76 THE LIVES of All the Lords Chancellors, Lords Keepers, And Lords Commissioners, Of the Great Seal of England; From William the Conqueror, to the Present Time: But more at large of those Two Great Opposites, Edward, Earl of Clarendon, and Bulestrode Lord Whitlock. With A Parallel of their Actions. To Which is added, An Appendix of many Rare and Valuable Speeches, Letters, &c., referring to the Said Lives. In Two Volumes. By an Impartial Hand. The Second Edition, with Additions. London: Printed and sold by R.Bonwicke, W.Freeman..., 1712. 8vo. pp. 1pl, [22], 216, [7]index, [1]ad, 336; [1]ad, 1pl, 520. contemporary panelled calf. Vol. I rebacked, with new spine label, joints of Vol. II cracked, bindings rather worn, some foxing, else internally very good. 175.00

S.&M.I.591.8. Marvin p. 470. Abbot 125.

Although the greater portion of the work is devoted to the Earl of Clarendon & Bulestrode Lord Whitlock, the first section includes sketches of Sir Francis Bacon, Thomas Beckett, Sir John Fortescu, &c.

77 LORIMER, James. The Institutes of Law: A Treatise of the Principles of Jurisprudence As Determined By Nature. Second Edition, Revised and Enlarged. Edinburgh & London: William Blackwood and Sons, 1880. 8vo. pp. xx, 572. complete with half-title. index. original cloth. backstrip soiled & frayed, upper corner of 2 leaves of preface & contents wanting (no loss), else very good. 45.00

S.&M.II.219.

The Scottish jurist was the sole proponent in Great Britain at the time, of the concept of the law of nature. Opposed to democracy, he was a defender of natural inequalities.

MacLAURIN, [John, later Lord Dreghorn] [1734-1796]. Arguments and Decisions, in Remarkable Cases, Before the High Court of Justiciary, and other Supreme Courts, in Scotland. Collected by... Edinburgh: Printed for J.Bell and E.&C.Dilly, London, 1774. 4to. pp. xvi, [1]errata, [2]addenda [insert], [xvii]-xl, 776, [6]index, [2]ads. contemporary sprinkled calf. extremities worn, joints cracked, internally very good. With the armorial bookplate of Plummer of Middlestead. First Edition. 150.00

S.&M.V.76. Marvin p. 486.

A most interesting collection of cases of murder, madness, witchcraft, incest, and treason, with discussion of the effect of drunkenness on liability, the extent of Parliamentary privilege in regard to arrest & prosecution, &c. & an introductory essay on criminal cases.

"MOST IMPORTANT 18TH CENTURY SOCIALIST"

MABLY, Abbe [Gabriel Bonnot] de [1709-1785]. De La Legislation, Ou Principes Des Loix. 2 Parts in 1. A Amsterdam: 1776. 12mo. pp. viii, 264; iv, 264. vignettes. contemporary mottled calf, gilt back. several small perforated private library stamps, else a fine copy. First Edition. 375.00

Tchemerzine VII 267(b). Cioranescu, 18th Cent.,II 41180. Querard V 405.

"Physionomie originale, et apres Morelly et Rousseau, le plus important des socialistes moraux du siecle...C'est la propriete individuelle qui a donne possibilite a l'inegalite et a l'avarice de se developper...La societe s'est accomplir graduellement le changement...Il est peut-etre l'exemple le plus frappant de la forme sous laquelle se presente le plus souvent le socialisme au XIIIe siecle. C'est une doctrine morale, basee sur la philosophie du bonheur et la morale utilitaire." (Lichtenberger) This is Mably's main work in support of a system of community in goods, in which he recommends the restriction of inheritance laws as a means to bring about the more equitable distribution of property.

MAINE, Sir Henry Sumner. Ancient Law: Its Connection With the Early History of Society, And Its Relation to Modern Ideas. Seventh Edition. London: John Murray, 1878. 8vo. pp. 1pl, viii, [1], 415 + 20p. of publisher's ads. complete with half-title. index. modern buckram. some pencil markings, lower margin of last leaf of index clipped. 35.00

MAINE, Sir Henry Sumner. Lectures on the Early History of Institutes. New York: Henry Holt and Comapny, 1875. 8vo. pp. 1pl, viii, 412. complete with half-title. index. original cloth. First American Edition. 30.00

MAINE, Sir Henry Sumner. Village-Communities in the East and West: Six Lectures Delivered At Oxford To Which Are Added Other Lectures, Addresses and Essays. New York: Henry Holt and Company, 1876. 8vo. pp. xii, 413, [6]ads. complete with half-title. index. original cloth. First American Edition. 30.00

MARTINI, D.Nicolaus [1632-1713]. Praxis Criminalis Ad Theoricam accomodata In Qua Continentur Modus fabricandi Processus Criminales: Constitutiones Barbarina, & Cardinalis Sacchetti ...Commissiones admissionis ad novas: Feriae generales, &

particulares totius Status Ecclesiastici: Formula Actorum contumacialium...Eximio, ac Nobili Notariorum Tribunalis Illmi, &Rmi D.Auditoris Camerae Collegio Dicata Cura, Et Sumptibus D.Nicolai Martini... Romae: Typis Petri Ferri, 1728. 4to. pp. 1pl, [14], 224. contemporary mottled calf, gilt back. backstrip very slightly wormed, hint of foxing, else an excellent copy, with 2 cancels on imprimatur leaf. First Edition. 175.00

The NUC locates only the Library of Congress copy.

On Canon law criminal procedure & torture, with discussion of assassination, adultery, abortion, premeditation, &c.

"HIGHLY ESTEEMED BY LEIBNIZ"

4 MASCARDI, Giuseppe (JOSEPHUS MASCARDUS) [d1588]. Conclusiones Probationum omnium quibusvis in utroque Foro versantibus, Practicabiles, Utiles, Necessariae. In Quatuor Volumina Distinctae. Hisce Canonicae, Civiles, Feudales, Criminales, aliaeq; materiae, per Ampliationes, Limitationes, Intelligentiasque, ordine alphabetico distinctae, continentur. Iisdemque Additiones DD. Joann. Aloysii Ricii Canonici Neapolitani, & Bartholomaei Nigri ex arte Hannoni JCtorum hactenus in fine annexae, nunc pro majori legentis commoditate, suo quaevis loco insertae sunt. Accedit Repertorium Universale, Ex Summariis locupletissimis: magis receptis DD.opinionibus hoc *Asterisco notatis. Edition Ultima, Revisa et a Plurimis Mendis Repurgata. 4 Volumes. Francofurti ad Moenum: Impensis Johannis Davidis Zunneri, Typis Balthas/ Christophori Wustii, Sen., 1684. folio. pp. 2pl, [12], 500; 1pl, 510, [2]blank, [8]index; 1pl, [4], 513, [8]; 2pl, 267, [215]index. engraved title in Vol. I. half-title in Vol. IV. title vignettes, woodcut ornaments & initials. title of Vol. I in red & black. contemporary mottled calf, gilt backs. bindings rubbed, front joint of Vol. IV cracked, some insignificant marginal worming to first few leaves of Vol. I, else a very good set, internally clean & crisp. From the library of T.C.Aylwin. 800.00

The NUC locates only 1 copy of this edition. See Adams M.833 (2 Vols. Venice: 1584).

"Cette theorie de la preuve en matier civile, criminelle et canonique, rebute par l'immensite des details auxquels est descendu l'auteur; mais resserree dans ce qu'elle a d'important par une main exercee, elle serait un membre des traites les plus usites de la jurisprudence." (Michaud, Biographie Universelle)

Mascardi was successively Archbishop of Milan, Naples, Padua, and Plaisance. This, his magnum opus, was highly esteemed by Leibniz, who began but never completed an abridged translation of the work.

5 MAY, Thomas Erskine [Baron Farnborough] [1815-1886]. The Constitutional History of England Since the Accession of George Third 1760-1860. In Two Volumes. Boston: Crosby and Nichols, 1862. 8vo. pp. xiv, [15]-484; xvi, [17]-596. half-titles. indices. original cloth. First American Edition. S.&M.II.238 (not listing this edition). 50.00

6 MAY, Thomas Erskine [Baron Farnborough]. A Treatise on the Law, Privileges, Proceedings and Usage of Parliament. Sixth Edition, Revised and Enlarged. London: Butterworths, 1868. 8vo. pp. [1]ad, xxvi, 808 + [36]ads. index. original cloth, bit frayed. 50.00

S.&M.II.238.

"May was clerk of the House of Commons, 1871-86, and wrote the first clear and comprehensive description of parliamentary procedure as it then existed." (Grose, p. 38) Its authority was recognised by parliament.

MONTESQUIEU, [Charles Louis de Secondat, Baron De La Brede et de] [1689-1755]. Oeuvres de Monsieur Montesquieu, Nouvelle Edition, revue, corrigee, & considerablement augmentee par l'auteur. 3 Volumes. A Amsterdam & A Peipsick: Chez Arkstee & Merkus, 1758. 4to. pp. 2pl, lxxxvi, 527; 2pl, xvi, 634; 2pl, 638. complete with half-titles. 2 folding maps & copper vignette in Vol. I. contemporary mottled calf, rebacked, endpapers renewed. bindings bit rubbed, slight dampstain to fore-edge margin of first few leaves of Vol. II, else very good. Second Edition of the Collected Works, Edited by Richer. 750.00

Tchemerzine VIII, p. 463. Cioranescu, 18th Cent., II 46045.

The Works of the celebrated French political theorist include 'L'Esprit des Loix' with an appraisal by D'Alembert, 'Lysimaque', 'Les Lettres Persanes', 'Grandeur Des Romains et De Leur Decadence', 'Le Temple de Gnide', 'L'Essai Sur Le Gout'.

MONTESQUIEU, [Charles Louis] de Secondat, Baron [De La Brede et] de. The Spirit of Laws. Translated from the French of M. De Secondat, Baron De Montesquieu. By Thomas Nugent. 2 Volumes. The Fifth Edition. Carefully revised and improved with considerable Additions by the Author. London: Printed for J.Nourse, and P.Vaillant, 1773. 8vo. pp. 2pl, xlvii, 468; 2pl, xvi, 534, [46]index. complete with half-titles. some faint foxing to a few leaves, otherwise a fine set. 200.00

New CBEL II p. 1525. See PMM 342 (1st Edition; Geneva: 1748).

"Montesquieu is known for the destructive criticism of French legal and political institutions contained in the 'Lettres persanes' (1721) and for the constructive criticism of 'De l'esprit des lois', in which he compared the various kinds of constitution, with special reference to the defects of the French monarchical system. He put forward a liberal and benevolent form of monarchy subject to safeguards of individual liberty. His theories deeply influenced the political thinking which led to the French and the American Revolutions." (PMM)

MONTESQUIEU, [Charles Louis de Secondat, Baron De La Brede et] de]. A View of the English Constitution. By the late...Being A Translation [by Francis Maseres] of the Sixth Chapter of the Eleventh Book of his celebrated Treatise, intitled L'Esprit des Loix. London: Sold by B.White, and H.Payne, 1781. 8vo. pp. 1pl, 74. disbound. small piece wanting form inner edge of title (no loss), inner edges of outer leaves slightly soiled, else very good. 35.00

New CBEL II p. 1525. S,&M.I.104.69.

MOULTON, R.K. The Constitutional Guide; Comprising The Constitution of the United States; With Notes and Commentaries From the Writings of Judge Story, Chancellor Kent, James Madison, and Other Distinguished American Citizens. Compiled by... New-York: Sold by G.&C.Carvill & Co., 1834. 12mo. pp. v, 147, [1]errata. index misbound after title. WITH: MOULTON, R.K. Legislative and Documentary History of the Banks of the United

States, From the Time of Establishing the Bank of North America, 1781, to October, 1834: With Notes and Comments By... New-York: Sold by G.&C.Carvill & Co., 1834. 12mo. pp. v, 227, [1]errata. original cloth. extremities frayed, else very good. 145.00

See Kress C.3800 & Sabin 51134 (listing second work) & Sabin 51133 (listing both works together).

91 NISBET, John, [Lord Dirleton] [1609?-1687]. Some Doubts & Questions, In the Law; Especially of Scotland. As Also, Some Decisions of the Lords of Council and Session: Collected & Obser'd by...To which is Added, An Index, For finding the Principal Matters in the said Decisions. Edinburgh: Printed by George Mosman, 1698. folio. pp. 1pl, [10], 228, 226, [17] index. [Second part with separate title-page, variant title]. engraved frontis. portrait. contemporary calf, sometime rebacked. binding rubbed, covers off, internally very good. From the library of T.C.Aylwin and the Court of Arches. First Edition. 350.00

Wing N.1170. S.&M.V.31. Marvin p. 539. Aldis 3767.
Nisbet was lord advocate during the covenanting persecution; although a learned man, he was noted for his unscrupulous and expedient methods.

92 NOBLE, Mark [1754-1827]. The Lives of the English Regicides, and Other Commissioners of the Pretended High Court of Justice, Appointed to sit in Judgment upon their Sovereign, King Charles the First. In Two Volumes. London: Printed for John Stockdale, 1798. 8vo. pp. xlvi, [47]-383; iv, 340, [4]ads. contemporary half calf. bindings rubbed, joints cracked, occasional hint of foxing, else very good. First Edition. Abbot 1535. 100.00

93 O'FLANAGAN, J.Roderick. The Lives of the Lord Chancellors and Keepers of the Great Seal of Ireland, From the Earliest Times to the Reign of Queen Victoria. In Two Volumes. London: Longmans, Green, and Co., 1870. 8vo. pp. xxix, 555; xxii, 621. complete with half-titles. contemporary half calf. bindings rubbed, front joint of Vol. II & upper backstrip cracked, slight dampstaining to front endpapers & half-titles only, else internally very good. 60.00

94 D'OLIVE, Simon, Sieur du Mesnil [d1645]. Les Oeuvres de... Conseiller du Roy en la Cour de Parlement de Tolose: Divisee En Deux Volumes. Le Premier, Contenant les Questions Notables du Droict, decidees par divers Arrests de la Cour de Parlement de Tolose. Le Deuxiesme, Contenant les Actions Forenses, les Lettres & Notes sur les dictes Actions Forenses. [Vol. II has slight variation in title]. A Lyon: Chez Iacques Iustet..., 1649. 4to. pp. 1pl, [22], 494; 4pl, 396. ornaments. old calf. bindings rubbed, spinal extremities worn, occasional hint of foxing, else very good. With the armorial bookplate of Alexander Buchanan, & his signature on titles. From the library of T.C.Aylwin. 225.00

Only 1 copy located in NUC. Not in BM STC French Books.
The Works of the 17th century jurist include his commentaries on the law determined by cases heard before the Parlement of Toulouse, speeches, letters and analysis of legal actions.

PAGET, John. Paradoxes and Puzzles Historical, Judicial, and Literary. Edinburgh & London: William Blackwood and Sons, 1874. 8vo. pp. xii, [1], 472. complete with half-title. original cloth. First Edition. 35.00

(PALMER, William). Illustrated Life and Career of...of Rugeley: Containing Details of His Conduct As School-Boy, Medical-Student, Racing-Man and Poisoner; With Original Letters of William and Anne Palmer and Other Authentic Documents. Together With the Whole of His Private Diary Up to the Hour of His Arrest, and the Fullest Particulars Respecting His Execution At Stafford. Illustrated With Views, Portraits, and Representations of the Chief Incidents In His Career. London: Ward and Lock, 1856. 8vo. pp. 136. frontis. & text illus. original printed wrs. tatty & chipped. back wr.detached. 25.00

"UNRECORDED CANADIANA"

PELEUS, Julien [d.1625]. Les Questions Illustres de Me..., Advocat En Parlement. Disputees et Plaidees de Part et d'autre, & decidees par les Arrests du Parlement de Paris...Edition Seconde, Reveue et Augmentee Par l'Autheur. A Paris: Chez Nicolas Buon, 1608. 4to. pp. 1pl, [36], [1]blank leaf, 943, [59]index. title vignette. woodcut ornaments & intials. title in red & black. contemporary vellum, sometime rebacked in old sheep, gilt back. few marginal annotations in old hand, lacking front paste-down, binding rubbed, otherwise an excellent copy. 850.00

Cioranescu, 17th Cent., III 53942. Not in the BM STC French Books. The NUC locates 4 copies, none of them in Canadian libraries. Not in any of the relevant Canadian bibliographies.
One of the decisions (pp. 910-923) concerns violations of the terms of the trade monopoly of the Sieur de Monts trading company, committed by Corneille de Belloy and Henry Couillard. Pierre Du Gua De Monts (1558?-1628), governor of Acadia and founder of the first permanent settlement in Canada, was granted a trading monopoly in New France in 1603. The Dutchman, Cornelis de Bellois (or Corneille de Belloy), Rouen merchant, was his principal collaborator, but their association was severed when Bellois's nephew was caught trading illegally in 1606.
"Despite the tremendous contribution made by this far-seeing and broad-minded individual to the development of Canada, he has seldom been accorded his rightful place in accounts of its history. Here is the man who made possible so much of what Champlain accomplished. He it was who, inspired with the noble impulse of making a new France in America, founded the first permanent colony here...The energetic direction, support, and encouragement de Monts gave to exploration which was subsequently reported in the writings of such men as Champlain [his staunch ally] and Lescarbot represents a contribution of inestimable value." (Dict. of Canadian Biography, I, pp. 291-95)

PERKINS (or PARKINS), John [d.1545]. A Profitable Book...Treating of the Laws of England. Translated out of French into English for the benefit of young students and others. An.Dom. 1657. small 8vo. pp. 2pl, [27]index, 333. contemporary sheep. no endpapers. binding worn, head of backstrip gone, some insignificant marginal worming, corners of some leaves dog-eared otherwise very good. 450.00

Wing P.1544. S.&M.I.485.56. See Winfield p. 330 & Marvin p. 563.
Perkins' popular textbook for law students first appeared in law French in 1528 (Perutilis tractatus). An attempt to update Littleton's 'Tenures', it enjoyed an enormous success for nearly three centuries, and is still regarded as an authority.

99 PETIT, Samuel [1594-1643]. Leges Atticae Sam. Petitus Colligit, Digessit, Et Libro Commentario Illustravit. Opus Iuris, Literarum, Et Rei Antiquariae studiosis utilissimum, VIII. Libris distinctum, in quo varij Scriptorum veterum Graecorum et Latinorum loci explicantur et emendantur. Parisiis: Sumptibus Caroli Morelli, 1635. folio. pp. 5pl, [1]blank, 55, 557, [4]index. title vignette. woodcut ornaments & initials. title in red & black. contemporary panelled calf. binding worn, front cover detached, lacking front free-endpaper, marginal tear in last leaf of index (no loss), else very good. From the library of T.C.Aylwin. 300.00

Graesse V, p. 220. Not in BM STC French Books.
An important work on Greek law by the learned French orientalist & protestant minister, Petit, whose friendship was sought by such distinguished scholars as Selden, Gassendi and Vossius.

100 PITHOU, Francois [1543-1621]. Codex Canonum Vetus Ecclesiae Romanae A Francisco Pithoeo Ad Veteres Manuscriptos Codices Restitutus, Et Notis Illustratus. Accedunt Petri Pithoei Miscellanea Ecclesiastica; Abbonis Floriacensis Apologeticus Et Epistolae; Et Formulae Antiquae Alsaticae. Ex Bibliotheca Illustrissimi D.D.Claudii Le Peletier Regni Administri, Regni Administri, Regii Aerarii Praefecti, & Supremi Galliarum Senatus Praesidis Insulati. Parisiis: E Typographia Regia, Curante Sebastiano Mabre-Cramoisy, 1687. folio. pp. 7pl, 448, [1]. copper-engraved title vignette, head & tail pieces & initials. 19th century half-calf [John Lovell, Montreal, binder's ticket]. binding bit rubbed, 2 outer leaves slightly soiled & tatty at edges, otherwise an excellent uncut copy. From the library of T.C.Aylwin. First Edition. 275.00

Not in BM STC French Books. The NUC locates only 1 copy.
The two brothers, Francois and Pierre Pithou, both learned French jurists, collaborated on this edition of the 'Corpus Iuris Canonici', one of their most important works.

101 POLLET, Jacques. Arrests Du Parlement De Flandre Sur Diverses Questions De Droit, De Coutume, et De Pratique. Recueillis par ...Ouvrage utile pour l'intelligence des Coutumes & des Usages du Pais. 3 Parts in 1. A Lille: Chez Lievin Danel, 1716. 4to. pp. 1pl, [14], 118, [1]div.title, [11], 119-267, [1]div.title, [3], 268-376, [26]. woodcut ornaments & initials. contemporary sprinkled sheep. binding rubbed, joints cracking, internally fine. From the library of T.C.Aylwin. First Edition. 175.00

The NUC locates 3 copies.

102 POWELL, Edmund. A Treatise on the Law of Inland Carriers. Second Edition. London: Butterworths & Dublin: Hodges, Smith & Co., 1861. 8vo. pp. xv, 375 + [40]ads. original cloth. extremities frayed, paper spine label chipped, light marginal dampstain throughout, else very good. With the armorial bookplate of F[rederic] W[illiam] Cumberland, Pendarves. [Cumberland was archiect of St. James Cathedral, Osgood Hall & University College, Toronto.]. 50.00

S.&M.II.286.
The second edition is carefully revised and substantially re-written, with 2 new chapters on the Railway & Canal Traffic Act 1854.

PUFENDORF, Samuel [1632-1694]. The Divine Feudal Law: Or, Covenants With Mankind, Represented: Together With Means For the Uniting of Protestants. In which also The Principles of the Lutheran Churches are Stated and Defended. Translated from the Latin by Theophilus Dorrington. 8vo. pp. 2pl, [12], 365, [3]ads. complete with half-title. modern quarter oasis morocco. some foxing & age-browning, else very good. First English Edition. 150.00

PUFENDORF, Samuel. On the Law of Nature and Nations. Eight Books, Written in Latin...Translated into English from the Best Edition [By B.Kennett]. With A Short Introduction. Oxford: Printed by A.Lichfield, 1703. folio. pp. 1pl, [4], [2], 27, [17], 400, 231, 143-262. main body of text printed in double columns. old reversed calf. binding somewhat worn, joints cracked, some insignificant marginal worming to first few signatures (touching several letters on one page), else very good. First English Edition, First Issue. 500.00

S.&M.I.597.72. New CBEL II, p. 77. Kress 2400. See Marvin pp. 593-94.
"In the 'De jure naturae et gentium' Pufendorf took up in great measure the theories of Grotius and sought to complete them by means of the doctrines of Hobbes and of his own ideas...He combatted Hobbes's conception of the state of nature and concluded that the state of nature is not one of war but of peace...As regards public law Pufendorf, while recognizing in the state a moral person, teaches that the will of the state is but the sum of the individual wills that constitute it, and that this association explains the state." (Encyc. Brit., 11th Edn.)

PUTZLACHER, Thomas Antonius. Dissertation Juridica De Praescriptionibus...Addita Juris Bohemici Dispositione, Et Observationibus Practicis, Quam Sub Gloriosissimis Auspiciis Augustissimae Romanorum Imperatricis Mariae Theresiae Germaniae, Hungariae, Bohemiae, &c. Reginae... Praegae: Typis Catharinae Labaunin Viduae, per Factorem Michaelem Jans, 1754. 4to. pp. 8pl, 180, [3]. several woodcut ornaments. contemporary velvet binding, gilt edges. binding slightly soiled & faded, hint of foxing to last few leaves, else internally fine. 150.00

Only 1 copy located in NUC.

"FIRST ENGLISH LAW DICTIONARY"

[RASTELL, John] [d.1536]. [Translated by William Rastell]. Les Termes de La Ley Or, Certain difficult and obscure Words and Terms of the Common Laws and Statutes of this Realm now in use expounded and explained. Newly corrected and enlarged. With an Addition of above one hundred Words. London: Printed by John Streater, James Fletcher,..., 1671. small 8vo. pp. 2pl, [10]index, 613, [1]errata. modern quarter oasis morocco.

title leaf laminated, neat repairs to following 2 leaves & last leaf, some slight marginal dampstaining to a few leaves, several annotations in old hand, lacking first & last blanks, otherwise very good. 450.00

Wing R.291. S.&M.I.11.48. See Marvin p. 599 & Winfield p.17.

The first English law dictionary, by John Rastell, barrister of the Middle Temple & law printer, was also intended as a guide to law French. Originally composed in French, it was first published in 1527 with Latin title. The French and English texts are printed in parallel columns, and the editor's preface is signed T.B. [Thomas Blount]. Rastell's last years were unhappily spent in prison, in consequence of his criticism of the practice of paying tithes, and perhaps also, because of the suspicion attaching to him as the friend and brother-in-law of Sir Thomas More.

107 REBUFFI, Pierre (Petrus REBUFFUS) [1487-1557]. Commentaria In Constitutiones, Seu Ordinationes Regias. Non solum Iuris studiosis, verum etiam Pragmaticis utilissima, In quibus facilis ad praxim Curiarum Franciae via, & Iurium intellectus explicantur... 3 Volumes in 1. [Title varies]. Lugduni (Lyon): Apud Haeredes Gulielmi Rovillii, Sub Scuto Veneto, 1599. folio. pp. 952, [2]blank, [59]index. [continuous pagination]. title vignettes. woodcut ornaments & initials. title of Vol. I in red & black. old mottled sheep, gilt back. binding bit rubbed, lower backstrip worn, small hole in last 6 leaves of index, affecting some words, otherwise an excellent copy. From the library of T.C.Aylwin. 300.00

This edition not in Adams or BM STC French Books. See Adams R.244 (listing Lyon edition 1550-51). Only 1 copy located in NUC.

The distinguished French jurist Rebuffi was born near Montpellier in 1487. He lectured on law at Bourges and Paris, and published several works, mainly dealing with civil law and regal ordinances.

108 REBUFFI, Pierre. In Tit.Dig. De Verborum et Rerum Significatione Commentaria Amplissima. In quibus, praeter exactas verborum omnium, quae ad ius ciuile pertinent, significationes, Iurisconsultorum veterum phrases & locutiones,...Ex Tertia Editione... Lugduni (Lyon): Apud Haeredes Gulielmi Rouillij, 1614. folio. pp. 6pl, 701, [45]index. title in red & black. text in double columns. title vignette. woodcut ornaments & initials. old mottled calf, gilt back. binding bit rubbed, spinal extremities worn, upper outer corner of title leaf wanting (no loss), some inner marginal dampstaining, else very good. From the library of T.C.Aylwin. 250.00

BM STC French Books R.219. See Adams R.246 (1586 edition).

Included is a brief biography of the author.

109 REBUFFI, Pierre. Repetitiones Variae, Extrema Authoris manu recognitae, selectissimis Opusculis, Notis, & Summarijs hac postrema editione auctae & locupletae. Quarum Elenchum pagina quarta indicabit. Lugduni (Lyon): Apud Haeredes Guilielmi Rovillii, Sub Scuto Veneto, 1600. folio. pp. 4pl, 681, [34] index. title in red & black. text in double columns. title vignette. woodcut ornaments & initials. old sprinkled sheep, gilt back. binding bit rubbed, some wear to spinal extremities, otherwise an excellent copy. From the library of T.C. Aylwin. 250.00

Not in BM STC Fronch Books, Adams or NUC.

REBUFFI, Pierre. Tractatus Varii. Extrema Authoris manu recogniti, Selectissimis opusculis, Notis, & Summarijs hac postrema Editione aucti, & locupletati. Quorum Elenchum pagina quinta indicabit. Lugduni (Lyon): Apud Haeredes Gulielmi Rovillii, Sub Scuto Veneto, 1600. folio. pp. 4pl, 661, [1], [22]index, [1]blank, 51, [1], 70, [8]index, [1]blank. title in red & black. text in double columns. title vignette. woodcut ornaments & initials.

Not in BM STC French Books or Adams. NUC locates 3 copies.

Bound with:

REBUFFI, Pierre. Explicatio Ad Quatuor Primos Pandectarum Libros, Novaeque Eorundem et Subtiles Illustrationes...Adiecti sunt ad leg.Si debitori, de Iudiciis. 1. Imperatores, de priuil.cred.... Lugduni (Lyon): Apud Guilielmum Rouillium, sub scuto Veneto, 1589. folio. pp. 6pl, 507, [37]index. title in red & black. text in double columns. title vignette. woodcut ornaments & initials.

BM STC French Books p. 373. See Adams R.251 (1581 edition only). 3 copies located in NUC.

The two items bound in old sprinkled sheep, gilt back. binding bit rubbed, extremities of backstrip worn, some dampstaining to upper inner margin, title leaf of first item loose, otherwise very good. From the library of T.C.Aylwin. 550.00

ROSS, Walter. A Discourse Upon the Removing of Tenants, Published to Serve as a Specimen of the Lectures Intended to Be Delivered Upon the Practice of the Law of Scotland, By..., Writer to the Signet. [At bottom of title: The Class is to be opened upon the 18th of November next]. Edinburgh: Printed by Mandell and Wilson...and Sold by William Gibb, 1782. 8vo. pp. 170, [1]errata. upper outer corner of A^2 torn away (no loss), else a fine uncut copy in original publisher's boards (slightly soiled). First & only Edition. Rare. 150.00

S.&M.V.99. Marvin p. 620. Only 1 copy located in the NUC. Not in BM.

RUSSELL, Sir Charles, [first Baron Russell of Killowen] [1832-1900]. The Parnell Commission. The Opening Speech For the Defence. Delivered By...Carefully Revised by the Author. London & New York: Macmillan, 1889. 8vo. pp. xii, 615. complete with half-title. index. original cloth. perforated lib. stps. on title & several leaves, sticker removed from lower backstrip, else very good. With inscription on verso of front free-endpaper: "Presented to the Library of the Laval University of Quebec by the Author Lord Russell of Killowen, Lord Chief Justice of England". 50.00

"His famous speech for the defence occupied six days...and was undoubtedly his greatest forensic effort. The delivery was so slow and so deliberate as to divest the speech of all oratorical character. It began with an account of the land legislation in Ireland of much historical value." (DNB) In 1894 Lord Russell received an honorary LL.D. from Laval.

"DEFENCE OF REVOLUTION"

113 [RUTHERFORD, Samuel] [1600-1661]. Lex, Rex: The Law and the Prince. A Dispute for the just Prerogative of King and People. Containing the Reasons and Causes of the most necessary Defensive Wars of the Kingdom of Scotland, and of their Expedition for the ayd and help of their dear Brethren of England... London: Printed for Iohn Field, 1644. small 4to. pp. 2pl, [36], 467. later full red morocco, gilt back & edges. slight dampstaining to margins, some browning, edges of first 2 leaves bit tatty & soiled, else very good. with bookplate of ARchibald MacDiarmid Campbell. First Edition. 750.00

New CBEL I p. 2464. Wing R.2386. Marvin p. 624. cfS.&M.I. 117.52.

Rutherford, Scottish ecclesiastic and political theorist, vigourously defended presbytarianism and actively propagandized against the absolutist claims of the royalists. During the Commonwealth, he led the group of protesters who favoured Cromwell. 'Lex, Rex' was mainly written as a reply to John Maxwell's 'Sancto-sancto regum majestas'; in it he argues that the law is above the king, who is bound by oath to rule justly, and that sovereignty resides in the people, who have a natural right to depose an unjust ruler. In 1660, when Charles II was fully restored, the government took notice of the publication and ordered it to be publicly burned. Rutherford was summoned to appear for trial on a charge of high treason, but he died before the trial could be held.

114 [SADLER, John] [1615-1674]. Rights of the Kingdom: Or, Customs of our Ancestors. Touching The Duty, Power, Election, or Succession of our Kings and Parliaments, Our True Liberty, due Allegiance, three Estates, their Legislative Power, Original, Judicial, and Executive; With the Militia. Freely discussed through The British, Saxon, Norman Laws and Histories. With An occasional Discourse of Great Changes yet expected in the World. London: Printed for J.Kidgell, 1682. small 4to. pp. 4pl, 319[ie315]. several woodcut ornaments. contemporary calf newly rebacked. binding bit worn, no pastedowns, some browning to outer margins of leaves, front free-endpaper soiled & tatty, otherwise a very good copy. With armorial bookplate of Edward Whitaker Junior of the Middle Temple. Second Edition. 250.00

Wing S.279. Marvin p. 625 (incorrectly names 'Ralph' Sadler as the author). Grose p. 478. S.&M.I.106.99. Locke Library Bib. 2525.

Sadler, master-in-ordinary in the court of chancery, was highly esteemed by Oliver Cromwell, who offered him the office of chief justice of Munster in Ireland, a post which he declined.

This work, first published in 1649, is recommended by John Locke (Remains. 1720. p. 238) as containing the ancient Constitution of the Government of England.

115 SAINT-GERMAIN, Christopher [1460?-1540]. Doctor and Student: Or Dialogues Between A Doctor of Divinity, and A Student in the Laws of England, Containing the Grounds of those Laws, together with Questions and Cases concerning the Equity and Conscience thereof; also comparing the Civil, Canon, Common and Statute Laws, and shewing wherein they vary from one another. To which is now added an Account of the Author, and

a General Table of the Principal Matters; never before printed. In the Savoy: Printed by Eliz. Nutt and R.Gosling... for R.Gosling, 1721. 12mo. pp. 1pl, [10], 366, [40]index & ad. contemporary calf. A fine copy, with armorial bookplate of Lord Charles Noel Somerset. 225.00

S.&M.I.25.35. See Winfield pp. 321-234 & Marvin p. 626.

"The 'Doctor and Student' is one of the most esteemed of ancient law books, and has been an authority for about three centuries, having been constantly cited, from the time of Chief Justice Brooke to the present time." (Marvin) A handbook for legal students, it was first published in Latin in 1523, and was not superceded until the appearance of Blackstone's 'Commentaries'. Saint-Germain attempted to reconcile common law with the law of nature and the dictates of ethics, thus forming the "basis and starting point of the English system of equity". (Holdsworth)

[SARPI, Paolo] [1552-1623]. The Rights of Sovereigns and Subjects. By Father Paul the Venetian, Author of The History of the Council of Trent. Translated From the Italian and compared with the French. To which is prefix'd the Life of the Author, And An Account of His Writings [by Sir H.Wotton, Bp. Bedell, and Bp. Burnet]. London: Printed for J.Graves, C. King, W.Meadows, J.Hooke, 1720. 8vo. pp. 4pl, lxxxviii, viii, 392. engraved frontis. port. several woodcut ornaments. contemporary calf, slightly rubbed, front joint tender, else a nice crisp copy. First Edition in English. 250.00

A brilliant refutation of papal authority in secular matters, written in response to Pope Paul V's excommunication of the Venetians & his attempt to lay their dominions under an interdict, by the Venetian patriot, scholar & church reformer. "Never before in a religious controversy had the appeal been made so exclusively to reason and history; never before had an ecclesiastic of his eminence maintained the subjection of the clergy to the state, and disputed the pope's right to employ spiritual censures, except under restrictions which virtually abrogated it...The great victory, however, was not so much the defeat of papal pretensions, as the demonstration that interdicts and excommunications had lost their force." (Encyc. Brit., 11th Edn.)

SAUNDERS, Sir Edmund [d.1683]. The Reports of the Most Learned...Late Lord Chief Justice of the King's Bench, Of Several Pleadings and Cases In the Court of King's Bench, In the Time of the Reign of His Most Excellent Majesty King Charles The Second. With Three Tables...The Third Edition. With Notes and References To the Pleadings and Cases, By John Williams. In 2 Volumes. London: Printed by A.Strahan for T. Cadell & W.Davies..., 1799-1802. 8vo. pp. 4pl, [364], [52] index; xii, 423, [82]index, [2]errata. contemporary calf, rubbed, front cover of Vol. II detached, spinal extremities worn, otherwise very good. 150.00

S.&M.I.308.112. See Marvin pp. 629-630.

Saunders was "abundantly versed in the mysteries and technicalities of law. His Reports, printed after his death, extend from 1666 to 1672, and are esteemed for their simplicity and precision. They are composed in so dramatic a form that Lord Mansfield called him the Terence of Reporters." (Foss) According to Marvin, the Reports still remain the "Bible of the Law of Special Pleading."

SELDEN, John [1584-1654]. Table-Talk: Being the Discourses

of John Selden, Esq; Or His Sense of various Matters of Weight and high Consequence; Relating especially to Reason and State. Second Edition. London: Printed for Jacob Tonson ...and Awnsham and John Churchill..., 1696. 8vo. pp. 4pl, 192. contemporary panelled mottled calf. joints rubbed, else a fine copy. 350.00

Wing S.2438.

Perhaps Selden's most famous work, compiled by his secretary Richard Milward, it was not first printed until 1689, when the revolution had given freedom to the press. Although its authenticity was at one point disputed, "the work may safely be accepted as the most vivid picture extant of the habits of thought and the modes of expression of the great Erastian lawyer. The conversations cover a great range of subjects relative to human life and history..." (DNB)

119 SELDEN, John. Titles of Honor. The Second Edition. London: Printed by William Stansby for Richard Whittakers, 1631. folio. pp. 1pl, [34], 941, [1]errata. title in red & black. numerous engravings (6 of them 3/4 page in size) & woodcut ornaments. old sprinkled calf bit rubbed, head of backstrip loose, small pieces wanting from lower corner of $3A^2$ & $4D^1$ (no loss), else a fine copy. 400.00

STC 22178. S.&M.I.208.50. Winfield p. 320.

This is the second greatly enlarged edition of the first of Selden's great historical works treating of titles of nobility & knighthood, honorary attributes & the laws of precedence.

120 SHARP, Granville [1735-1813]. A Declaration of the People's Natural Right to Share in the Legislature; Which is the Fundamental Principle of the British Constitution of State. The Second Edition. London: Printed for B.White, 1775. 8vo. pp. 2pl, xl, 279, [4]ads. complete with half-title. index. uncut in original publisher's bds. bds. bit rubbed, backstrip wanting, stitching split, internally fine. 250.00

Sabin 79817. Howes S-331. Goldsmith 11368. Higgs 6484. S.&M.I.148.24.

Philanthropist and anti-slavery worker, Sharp's "sympathies were easily enlisted on behalf of the American colonies", and after the publication of the 'Declaration' he resigned his office in the ordnance department rather than assist in despatching war material to the colonies. Howes describes the work as having a "powerful influence in determining colonial resistance."

121 SHARP, Granville. A Tract on Duelling: Wherein The Opinions of some of the most celebrated Writers on Crown Law Are Examined and Corrected Either by the Authority of the same Writers, declared in contradictory Sentiments on the same Subject collated from other Parts of their Works, Or, by the solemn Decision of more ancient Writers of (at least) equal Authority; in order to ascertain the due Distinction between Manslaughter and Murder. Second Edition with Additions. London: Printed by B.White and Son and C.Dilly, 1790. 8vo. pp. xix, 75.

S.&M.I.45.15 (calling for pp. 102; the collation in NUC entry agrees with our copy). Marvin p. 639.

Bound with:

SHARP, Granville. A Declaration of the People's Natural Right to Share in the Legislature...Second Edition. London: Printed for B.White, 1775. 8vo. pp. 1pl, xl, 279, [4]. lacking the half-title. index.

Sabin 79817. Howes S-331. Goldsmith 11368. Higgs. 6484. S.&M.I.148.24.

The two items bound in full calf, rebacked, with original backstrip laid down. extremities rubbed, else fine. 400.00

In his interesting & learned tract on duelling, Sharp cites cases & decisions of Lord Bacon, Henry de Bracton, Sir William Blackstone, Sir Edward Coke, Sir Matthew Hale, John Selden, &c. See also note to item #120.

SIDNEY, Algernon [1621-1683]. Discourses Concerning Government...Publish'd from an Original Manuscript. The Second Edition carefully corrected. To which is Added, The Paper He deliver'd to the Sheriffs immediately before his Death. And an Alphabetical Table. London: Printed by J.Darby..., 1704. folio. pp. 3pl, 424, [47]index, [1]ads. engraved frontis. port. contemporary panelled calf. binding rubbed, part of backstrip wanting, joints cracked, some inner marginal dampstaining to latter portion of text, else very good. 200.00

S.&M.I.107.101.

Sidney served as ambassador to Sweden under Cromwell. This work, written, as was Locke's, in answer to Robert Filmer's 'Patriarcha'(1680), laid the theoretical foundation for English speaking republicanism.

SMITH, Horace & Thomas Spooner Soden. A Manual of the Law of Landlord and Tenant. Edited by Lewis W.Cave. London: Davis & Son, 1871. 8vo. pp. xxxvii, [1]addenda & errata, 386. complete with half-title. original cloth slightly spotty, extremities frayed, internally very good. First Edition. S.&M.II.329. 45.00

SMITH, Thomas [1513-1577]. The Commonwealth of England, And the Maner of Governement thereof. Compiled by the Honourable Sir Thomas Smith, Knight, Doctor of both Lawes, and one of the principall Secretaries unto two most worthy Princes, King Edward, and Queene Elizabeth. With new Additions of the chiefe Courts in England, And the Offices thereof by the Said Author. Also a Table added thereto, of all the principall matters contained in this Treatise. New Corrected and Amended. London: Printed by William Stansby for John Smethwicke, 1621. small 4to. pp. 4pl, 134. title vignette. several woodcut ornaments & initials. modern half hard-grained leather. several marginal annotations, else fine. 300.00

STC 22864. S.&M.I.107.105. New CBEL I, p. 2211.

Written during his first embassy in France, "it is the most important description of the constitution and government of England written in the Tudor age." (DNB) It was originally published in 1583 under the title "De Republica Anglorum; the Maner of Government or Policie of the Realm of England" and passed through 11 editions in English in little over a century.

SMITH, William . A Treatise On the Duties and Office of a Receiver, Under the High Court of Chancery in Ireland, Embra-

cing the Present Practice of the Court As Connected Therewith, From the Order of Appointment to the Final Discharge and Vacating the Recognizance... Dublin: Printed for Richard Milliken, 1827. 8vo. pp. 1pl, 187, xliii. index. contemporary half calf. binding slightly rubbed, else fine. Armorial bookplate of Saunders. First Edition. 85.00

S.&M.IV.86.

The first handbook to define & delineate the duties & responsibilities of the then relatively newly created Irish office of the receiver.

126 SOEFVE, Lucien. Nouveau Recueil de Plusieurs Questions Notables Tant De Droit Que De Coutumes, Jugees Par Arrests D'Audiances Du Parlement de Paris. Depuis 1640 jusques a present Divise Par Centuries. Par Maistre...ancien Avocat audit Parlement. 2 Volumes in 1. A Paris: Chez Charles De Sercy, 1682. folio. pp. 1pl, [54], 467, [49]index; 1pl, [50], 479, [42]index, [1]errata. several engraved vignettes (incl. titles). woodcut ornaments & initials. titles in red & black. contemporary calf, somewhat worn, backstrip cracked, internally fine. From the library of T.C.Aylwin. First Edition. 275.00

Not in BM STC French Books. NUC locates only 3 copies.

Sections on matters ecclesiastical, fiefs & seigneurial rights, legal obligations & contracts, testaments & succession, prescription, &c.

127 SORDI, Giovanni Pietro (Joannis Petrus SURDUS). Consiliorum Sive Responsorum Juris De grauissimis quaestionibus in vtroque foro quotidie occurrentibus & incidentibus Libri IV... Opus Nunc Denuo Ad Primam Editionem Venetam Diligenter recensitum & emendatum... 4 Volumes in 2. [Title varies]. Francofurti Ad Moenum: Typis Wechelianis, Sumptibus Clementis Schleichii & Petri de Zetter, 1629-30. folio. pp. 4pl, 509, [2]div.title, 513-978, [61]index; 618, 619-914, [53]index. title of Vol. I in red & black. text in double & index in triple columns. title vignettes. woodcut ornaments & initials. alum-tawed leather, emblem stamped in blind on centre covers. ties gone, backstrips worn & chipped, internally fine. From the library of T.C.Aylwin and the Court of Arches. 600.00

This edition not in NUC.

Treating of civil & criminal law, wills, hereditary rights, contracts, &c. A native of northern Italy, the author was one of the most celebrated jurists of his time.

128 SORDI, Giovanni Pietro. Decisiones Universae, Summo Labore et Studio Compilatae, Nec Hactenus sic editae: in quibus variae, & perplexae satis materiae, ultimas voluntates, contractus, judicia civilia, criminalia, fiscalia, feudalia, fideique materiam respicientes non minus docte, quam sententiose explicantur, & exactissime resolvuntur... 2 Books in 1 [No separate title-page for Book II]. Francofurti ad Moenum: Imprensis Joannis Baptistae Schonwetteri, Typis Matthaei Kempfferi, 1664. folio. pp. 4pl, 641, [77]index; 63, [7]index. title in red & black. text in double & index in triple columns.

Bound with:

HODIERNA, Giambattista. Novissimae Additiones, Et Observationes ad Decisiones Mantuani Senatus Io.Petri Surdi. Quibus hac quarta editione praeter antiquas nouae insigniores Quaestiones accesserunt, nouaeque Almi Consilii Neap. sententiae subnectuntur... Genevae: Sumptibus Ioannis Hermanni Widerhold, 1669. folio. pp. 3pl, 397, [54]index. complete with half-title. title in red & black. text in double columns. title vignette. several woodcut ornaments.

The NUC locates only 2 copies of the first work, and none of the second.

The two bound together in old calf, sometime rebacked. binding worn, front cover & prelims of first item detached, some foxing & age-browning, else very good. From the library of T.C.Aylwin and the Court of ARches. 450.00

SPICER, Henry. Judicial Dramas; Or the Romance of French Criminal Law. London: Tinsley Brothers, 1872. 8vo. pp. 4pl, 423. complete with half-title. original cloth. backstrips faded & chipped, hint of foxing to endpapers & 2 outer leaves, else very good. With armorial bookplate of F.W.Cumberland of Pendarves. [See note, item #102]. 45.00

SPOT[T]ISWOODE, Robert [1596-1646]. Practicks of the Laws of Scotland, Observed and Collected by...of Pendland, President of the College of Justice, and Secretary of State to K. Charles the I. As Also Abstracts Taken out of the Ancient Records...and Propositions and Questions in Law...With Memoir of His Life and Trial...1646. Publish'd by John Spotiswoode..., the Author's Grand-son. Edinburgh: Printed by James Watson..., 1706. small folio. pp. 2pl, xli, [3]index, 372. old calf, sometime rebacked. binding rubbed, front cover detached, some minor worming to lower portion of first few signatures, with minimal effect to text, otherwise very good. First Edition. From the library of T.C.Aylwin and the Court of Arches. 300.00

S.&M.V.108. Marvin p. 657.

Spotiswoode was the son of the Archbishop of St. Andrews; in 1622 he was promoted to the Scots bench & in 1633 he became president of the court of session. He was later tried & executed by the Presbyterian covenanters. This is his only work, published posthumously by his grandson.

STAIR, James [Dalrymple], Viscount of [1619-1695]. The Institutions of the Law of Scotland, Deduced from its Originals, and Collated with the Civil, Canon and Feudal Laws, and with the Customs of Neighbouring Nations. In IV. Books. ...The Second Edition, Revised, Corrected, and much Enlarged: With an Alphabetical Index to the whole work. Edinburgh: Printed by the Heir of Andrew Anderson..., 1693. folio. pp. 2pl, 2, 779, [1]errata, [39]index. engraved frontis. port. frontis. laminated, otherwise a fine copy.

Wing S.5178. Aldis 3296. S.&M.V.108. Marvin p. 657.

Bound in at end:

The Acts of Sederunt of the Lords of Session Beginning the 5th June 1661, and ending in February 1681. folio. pp. 45. AND Acts of Sederunt of the Lords of the Session Past since February 1681. Edinburgh: Printed by the Heir of Andrew Anderson..., 1691. folio. pp. 24, [3]index. corner of last leaf laminated, else fine.

Wing S.1171. Aldis 3130. New CBEL II, p. 2057.

Bound in modern quarter oasis morocco. 350.00

"The Institutes of Lord Stair are of the highest authority in Scotland, and are frequently cited by elementary legal writers of other countries, and in the Courts of both England and the United States. The author was the first writer who reduced to system, the Law of Scotland ...". (Marvin) This is the author's final text, no further edition appearing until 1825-32.

STEPHEN, James Fitzjames [1829-1894]. A General View of the Criminal Law of England. London & Cambridge: Macmillan & Co. 1863. 8vo. pp. xii, 499. complete with half-title. index. original cloth. First Edition. S.&M.II.339. 60.00

STEPHEN, James Fitzjames. A General View of the Criminal Law of England. Second Edition. London & New York: Macmillan & Co., 1890. 8vo. pp. 6pl, 399. index. original cloth. 40.00

STEPHEN, James Fitzjames. Liberty, Equality, Fraternity. London: Smith, Elder & Co., 1873. 8vo. pp. vi, [2], 350. complete with half-title. original cloth. extremities beginning to fray, else very good. First Edition. 60.00

Stephen developed this work while working on codification in India. Impressed by British legislative measures in India, Stephen argued, in opposition to John Stuart Mill (On Liberty), that strong government could cure the British malaise. Sir Ernest Barker has called it "the finest exposition of conservative thought in the latter half of the nineteenth century."

STERNE, Simon. On Representative Government and Personal Representation. Based In Part Upon Thomas Hare's Treatise, Entitled "The Election of Representatives, Parliamentary and Municipal". Philadelphia: J.B.Lippincott & Co., 1871. 12mo. pp. 237. complete with half-title. original cloth. small piece cut from backstrip, extremities frayed, else very good 30.00

STUART, Andrew [d.1801]. Letters to the Right Honourable Lord Mansfield, From Andrew Stuart, Esq; London: Printed in the Month of January 1773. 4to. pp. 2pl, 39, 63, 47, 47. complete with half-title. contemporary tree calf. spinal extremities worn, joints cracked, else very good. With the armorial bookplate of the Right Honourable Earl of Moray. 100.00

An attack on Lord Mansfield for his conduct in the Douglas case [see item #42]; Mansfield favoured Douglas in his claims to the Douglas family estates, whereas Stuart conducted the case against the claimant. "In these epistles he assailed Mansfield for his want of impartiality with a force and eloquence that caused him at the time to be regarded as a worthy rival to Junius." (DNB)

TALLACK, William. Penological and Preventive Principles, With Special Reference to Europe and America; And to the Diminution of Crime, Pauperism, and Intemperance; to Prisons, and Their Substitutes, Habitual Offenders, Sentences, Neglected Youth, Education, Police, Statistics, Etc. By..., Secretary of the Howard Association, London. London: Wertheimer, Lea & Co., 1889. 8vo. pp. [ii]-x, 414. index. lacking the half-title. modern buckram. Fine. First Edition. 60.00

"FRIEND OF RABELAIS"

TIRAQUEAU, Andre (Andreas TIRAQUELLUS) [c1480-1558]. Operum Omnium...7 Volumes in 2. [Title varies]. Francofurti; Curantibus Rulandii, Typis Ioannis Bringeri, 1616. folio. pp. 1pl, [10], 480, [18]index; 1pl, [10], 360, [22]index; 1pl, [6], 214, [16]index; 1pl, [37], 498, [23]index; 1pl, [9], 275, [9]index; 106, [6]index; 116, [5]index. text in double columns. index in triple columns. title vignettes. several woodcut ornaments. title of Vol. I in red & black. old blind-stamped calf. bindings rather worn, with some repairs, metal reinforcements to 2 corners, small hole in title leaf neatly mended (affecting numeral of date), some slight dampstaining near end of Vol. III, else very good. From the library of T.C.Aylwin and the Court of Arches. 700.00

Only 3 copies located in NUC. For earlier editions see BM STC German Books p. 863 (1597) & Adams T.726 (1574) & T.727 (1597).

Tiraqueau, French jurist, was one of the most important members of the 'Parlement de Paris' under Henri II. He was a man of integrity & celebrated ability, & was on close terms with all of the leading men of letters. While he held the office of judge, he released Rabelais, who had been imprisoned by the monks, & he is mentioned by Rabelais in his 'Pantagruel'. Included here are the author's writings on nobility & the law of primogeniture, hereditary rights ('Le Mort saisit le vif'), marriage laws, punishments, &c.

TOMKINS, Frederick J. & Henry D.Jencken. A Compendium of the Modern Roman Law, Founded Upon the Treatises of Puchta, Von Vangerow, Arndts, Franz Moehler, and the Corpus Juris Civilis. London: Butterworths, 1870. 8vo. pp. xix, 425, [35]ads. index. original blind & gilt stamped cloth. extremities frayed, else very good. First Edition. 20.00

(TRIALS). AMOS, Andrew. The Great Oyer of Poisoning: The Trial of the Earl of Somerset For the Poisoning of Sir Thomas Overbury, in the Tower of London, and Various Matters Connected Therewith, From the Contemporary Mss. London: Richard Bentley, 1846. 8vo. pp. 2pl, [555], [1]. 2 engraved portraits, with tissue guards. contemporary half calf. extremities rubbed, joints cracked, some dampstaining to upper & lower margins of some leaves, else very good. 75.00

An account of the poisoning of Sir Thomas Overbury by Robert Carr, Earl of Somerset, for opposing his projected marriage with the Countess of Essex, the case was important for its bearing on the constitutional aspects of state trials.

(TRIALS). BURKE, Peter. Celebrated Trials Connected With the Aristocracy in the Relations of Private Life. London: William Benning & Co., 1849. 8vo. pp. 1pl, v, 505. contemporary half sheep. binding rubbed, cloth sides faded & soiled, front co-

ver detached, else very good. 50.00

(TRIALS). (CARLILE, Richard). A Genuine Report of the Two Trials of Richard Carlile, For the Republication of Thomas Paine's Age of Reason and Palmer's Principles of Nature: In which are faithfully given the Whole of the Evidence, With Copies of the various Extracts read, &c. by the Defendant in His Defence, A List of the Jury, Speeches of the Attorney-General, The Judge's Remarks, Charge to the Jury &c.&c. Accurately Taken Expressly by an Eminent Short-Hand Writer. [At Head of Title: Correct Edition, Entered at the Stamp Office]. London: Duncombe, [1819]. 8vo. pp. 41, [1]. BOUND WITH: The Whole Proceedings in Passing Sentence on R.Carlile In the King's Bench, Westminster, On Tuesday, 16th November, 1819. [London]: J.Turner, [1819]. 8vo. pp. 4. modern bds., cloth backstrip. mild foxing to a few leaves, else fine. 75.00

Carlile was sentenced to 3 years imprisonment in Dorcester gaol & a 1500L fine. Despite his imprisonment, which lasted until 1825, & the subsequent imprisonment of his wife, sister & shopmen, his firm still managed to continue to publish & sell 'The Republican' and other radical works.

(TRIALS). (DUNDAS, Henry, first Viscount Melville). The Trial by Impeachment, of Henry Lord Viscount Melville, For High Crimes and Misdemeanours, Before the House of Peers, In Westminster Hall, Between the 29th of April and the 17th of May 1806...The Impartial Edition. Edinburgh: Printed for & by J.Robertson, 1806. 8vo. pp. 1pl, 304, [9]appendix. engraved frontis. port. later cloth. corners frayed, else very good. 60.00

Lord Melville, treasurer & later admiral of the Navy, was charged with the embezzlement of large sums of public money from the Treasury. He was acquitted by a narrow margin.

(TRIALS). (MOORE, John Hamilton). Trial of...for Pirating a Chart: Sittings after Ten March 1798, before Lord Kenyon and a special Jury of Merchants. Huildhall, London. Heather and Williams, v.John Hamilton Moore. [cLondon]: Plummer, Printer, [c1798]. 8vo. pp. 8. disbound. 25.00

(TRIALS). NIGHTINGALE, J[oseph] (Ed.). Report of the Proceedings Before the House of Lords, On A Bill of Pains and Penalties Against Her Majesty, Caroline Amelia Elizabeth, Queen of Great Britain and Consort of King George the Fourth. Collated With the Journals of the House of Lords. 3 Volumes. [Vol. I: ...The Charges; Vol. II: ...The Defence, Part I; Vol. III: ...The Defence Part II]. London: J.Robins & Co., 1821. 8vo. pp. 2pl, 611, [1]ads; 1pl, 604; 1pl, 758. 23 engraved plates (including 3 engraved titles & numerous portraits). disbound, first portrait mounted, occasional dammarks & brown stains, else very good. 100.00

A bill promoted in the House of Lords to deprive Queen Caroline of her rights & privileges as Queen Consort & to dissolve the marriage between herself & King George IV, was abandoned in view of popular opinion Brougham's defence of the Queen considerably enlarged his reputation.

(TRIALS). (PAGET, Arthur). Report of the Proceedings Under A Writ of Enquiry of Damages, In An Action in the Court of King's Bench, In Which the Right of Honourable Lord Boringdon was Plaintiff, and the Right Honourable Sir Arthur Paget, K. B. Defendant, Executed before the sheriff of Middlesex and a Special Jury, on Tuesday the 19th July, 1808. Taken in Short-Hand By M.Gurney. London: Printed for John Joseph Stockdaee [sic], 1808. 8vo. pp. 77, [3]ads.

Bound with:

(SMITH, Captain William). The Trial of...of the Hon. the East-India Company's Battalion of Artillery for Criminal Conversation With Mrs. Mary Bond, Wife of Lieutenant Charles John Bond, of the Same Corps; Before Sir Benjamin Sullivan, Knight, Recorder, And A Special Court, Assembled at Bombay, February 13, 1804. Damages 32,000 Rupees (4000L.Sterling). London: Printed for J.Ginger..., 1805. 8vo. pp. vii, 64.

Bound with:

(YELVERTON, William Charles). The Yelverton Marriage Case, Thewall v. Yelverton, Comprising An Authentic and Unabridged Account of the Most Extraordinary Trial of Modern Times, With All Its Revelations, Incidents, and Details Specially Reported. Illustrated With Portraits, Views ofLocalities, Leading Events, And Important Situations. [At Head of Title: Unabridged Copy Right Edition]. London: George Vickers, nd. 8vo. pp. [2]ads, viii, [9]-191, [1]. text illus. contemporary half roan. binding rubbed, some browning to outer leaves, else very good. 150.00

(TRIALS). (PATCH, Richard). The Trial of Richard Patch, For the Wilful Murder of Mr. Isaac Blight, on the 23rd of Sept. 1805, At Rotherhithe, in the County of Surry; Before the Right Hon. Sir A.MacDonald, Knt. Lord Chief Baron of His Majesty's Court of Exchequer; On Saturday, April 5, 1806. Taken in Short Hand by Blanchard and Ramsey. With Portraits of Richard Patch and Esther Kitchener, Taken in Court, expressly for the Publication, by an eminent Artist; Together with a View of the House, and a Ground Plan of the Premises, &c. &c. London: Printed by the Express Appointment of the Sheriff, For Edward Jeffery...Sold by John Walker, and H.D. Symonds..., 1806. 8vo. pp. xvi, 194, [2]. complete with half-title. 3 portraits, 1 folding plate & 1 facsimile. contemporary half calf. binding bit rubbed, part of backstrip wanting, hint of foxing to plates & neighbouring leaves, else very good. First Edition. 100.00

(TRIALS). (PERREAU, Robert & Daniel, & Margaret Carolina Rudd). The Whole Trials, At Large, of Robert Perreau, Daniel Perreau, and Margaret Carolina Rudd; For Divers Forgeries; With a full Account of the Execution of the tow Perreaus; Also, A true Copy of their Dying Declarations, delivered to the Ordinary of Newgate, and authenticated by themselves. Revised and Corrected by Serjeant Glynn, Recorder of London. [London]: Printed by T.Walker, 1776. 8vo. pp. 1pl, 102. disbound. 60.00

(TRIALS). (STRAFFORD, Thomas Wentworth, first Earl of). The Tryal of Thomas Earl of Strafford, Lord Lieutenant of Ireland, Upon an Impeachment of High Treason By The Commons Then Assembled in Parliament, In the Name of Themselves and of All the Commons in England: Begun in Westminster-Hall the 22th of March 1640. And Continued before Judgment was Given until 10th of May 1641. Shewing the Form of Parliamentary Proceedings In an Impeachment of Treason. To Which is Added A Short Account of Some other Matters of Fact Transacted in Both Houses of Parliament, Precedent, Concomitant and Subsequent to the said Tryal: With some Special Arguments in Law Relating to a Bill of Attainder. Faithfully Collected, and Impartially Published, Without Observation or Reflection, By John Rushworth... London: Printed for John Wright...and Richard Chiswell..., 1680. folio. pp. 1pl, [8], [76], 101-252, 401-786, [1]ad. contemporary calf, sometime rebacked. binding worn, front cover off, internally very good. (labelled Rushworth Historical Collection Vol. IV). From the library of T.C.Aylwin. 165.00

Wing T.2333. cfMarvin p. 623. See S.&M.I.106.96.

150 (TRIALS). (THISTLEWOOD, Arthur). The Trials of Arthur Thistlewood, At the Old Bailey Sessions-House, Commencing On Saturday, the 15th, and ending on Thursday, the 27th of April, 1820. Taken in Shorthand, According to the Method Invented By John Byrom, Esq. F.R.S. Illustrated by Back and Front Views of the Premises in Cato Street, Edgeware Road, London; and by Several Original Portraits of the Principal Conspirators and Witnesses connected with these Proceedings. With An Appendix, Containing Circumstantial Details of the Execution and Decapitation of Thistlewood, Tidd, Ings, Davidson, and Brunt. London: Printed For Sherwood, Neely, & James..., 1820. 8vo. pp. 2pl, 200. 9 plates (incl. 7 ports. & 2 views). 2 neat marginal paper mends, front cover detached, binding bit rubbed, else a nice uncut copy in original boards. 175.00

An account of the famous 'Cato Street Conspiracy' trial. Thistlewood and a number of his fellows had already been tried on similar charges and acquitted (in 1816 after their attempt to organise a large public meeting under the auspices of the Spencean & other revolutionary societies with the express purpose of fomenting a revolution). Thistlewood & 4 other conspirators were sentenced to death by hanging.

152 UBALDIS, Angelo degli (Angelus BALDUS DE UBALDIS or Angelo BALDESCHI) [c1328-c1407]. Consilia...Opus Sane Utilissimum, Tam In Scholis, quam foro versantibus, multarum grauium ac variarum Causarum & Quaestionum decisiones complectens. Iam de Novo In Gratiam Iurisprudentiae addictorum, multo vigilantius, accuratius, & tertius, infinitis mendis sublatis, pristiniq; nitoris habitaratione, recusa. Cum Indice Omnium Rerum Memorabilium locupletissimo, accuratissimeq; confecto. Francofurti: Typis Andreae Wecheli, sumptibus Sig.Feyrabend, 1575. folio. pp. 4pl (incl. blank), 294 (numbered leaves), [26]index. text in double columns. title vignette. woodcut initials. old calf, sometime rebacked. binding worn, covers off, last 2 signatures loose, else very good. From the library of T.C.Aylwin and the Court of Arches. 350.00

BM STC German Books p. 878. Only 1 copy located in NUC.

The author, born at Perugia, was an eminent Italian jurist & professor of law at Pisa, Bologna, Florence, and Padua.

VAN SANTVOORD, George. Sketches of the Lives and Judicial Services of the Chief-Justices of the Supreme Court of the United States. New-York: Charles Scribner, 1856. 8vo. pp. viii, 533. engraved frontis. port., with tissue guard. original blind & gilt stamped cloth. extremities slightly chipped, hint of foxing to frontis., lacking back free-endpaper, else very good. First Edition. 30.00

Sketches of the first 5 chief justices: John Jay, John Rutledge, Oliver Ellsworth, John Marshall, Roger B.Taney; according to the preface, the first substantial effort of its kind.

"LAW OF NATIONS"

VATTEL, [Emeric] de [1714-1767]. Le Droit des Gens, ou Principes de la Loi Naturelle, Appliques a la conduite & aux affaires des nations & des souverains. 3 Volumes. A Londres [Neuchatel]: 1758. 12mo. pp. lix, xlvi, [2]blank, 480; 1pl, 532; 510. contemporary sheep, gilt backs. binding rubbed, extremities worn, small paper labels on lower backstrips, else very good. From the library of D.Jose Maria de Mello. 450.00

See Graesse VI p. 265 & Cioranescu, 18th Cent., III 62938 (not listing this edition).
Published the same year as the first edition.

This classic in the literature of international law established the international reputation of the Swiss jurist & diplomat Vattel. He followed in the tradition of Leibniz & Wolff, but abandoned the mathematical method & Wolff's notion of the 'world state'. He claimed that one could discover the ultimate basis of all legal institutions, including the natural law of nations, in the concept of utility derived from the postulates of ideal reason. Vattel's theory, more in keeping with the practice of statesmen, was highly influential.

[WADE, John] [1788-1875]. The Cabinet Lawyer; Or, Popular Digest of the Laws of England...With the Criminal Law of England; Also, A Dictionary of Law Terms, Maxims, Acts of Parliament, and Judicial Antiquities; Correct Tables of Assessed Taxes...and Prison Regulations. Second Edition. London: Printed For W.Simpkin and R.Marshall, 1827. 12mo. pp. xxviii, 584. index. uncut in original boards. 85.00

See S.&M.II.368. This edition not in NUC.

WINCH, Humphrey [1555?-1625]. Reports of That Reverend and Learned Judge...; Sometimes one of the Judges of the Court of Common Pleas. Containing many Choice Cases, and excellent matters touching Declarations, Pleadings, Demurrers, Judgements, and Resolutionsin points of Law, In the foure last years of the Raign of King James, faithfully Translated out of an exact french Copie, with two Alphabetical, and necessary Tables, the one of the neames of the Cases, the others of the principal matters contained in this Book. London: Printed for W.Lee, D.Pakeman, and G.Bedell, 1657. small folio. pp. 4pl, 125, [7]index, [1]errata. several woodcut ornaments. modern buckram. few marginal annotations in old hand, else fine. First Edition. 300.00

S.&M.I.310.132. Wing W.2964. Marvin p. 741.

Winch was a judge of the Common Pleas, 1611-1625. His otherwise unblemished career is interrupted by his disgraceful condemnation & execu-

tion of nine women as witches on the scant testimony of a young boy who claimed to be charmed by them.

ADDENDA (Including a selection of 20th century publications)

157 AMERICAN HISTORICAL ASSOCIATION. Annual Report of the...For the Year 1896. Volume II. Proposed Amendments to the Constitution, 1789-1889. Washington: Government Printing Office, 1897. 8vo. pp. 442. index. original cloth spotty. 35.00

158 ANSON, William R. The Law and Custom of the Constitution. In [Three] Volumes. Vol. I: Parliament. [Vol. II: The Crown. Part I; Vol. III: The Crown. Part II]. Oxford: At the Clarendon Press..., 1911, 1907, 1908. 8vo. pp. [xxxiv], 404, 16 (ads); xxxii, 283, 16(ads); xxiv, 347, 16(ads). complete with half-titles & 2 tipped-in errata slips. indices. original cloth. Vol. II rubbed, else a very good set. Fourth Edition of Vol. I; Third Editions of Vols. II & III. 60.00

159 BAUER, Elizabeth Kelley. Commentaries on the Constitution 1790-1860. New York: Columbia University Press, 1952. 8vo. pp. 400. biblio. index. original cloth. 20.00

160 BEVERIDGE, Albert J. The Life of John Marshall...1755-1835. 4 Volumes. Boston & New York: Houghton Mifflin, 1919. 8vo. pp. xxvi, [2], 506; xviii, [2], 594; xxii, [2], 644; xviii, [2], 668. 40 plates (incl. 4 colour frontispieces, ports. & facsimiles). complete with half-titles. biblio. index. original cloth, t.e.g. 60.00

161 CALDWELL, James Stamford. A Treatise of the Law of Arbitration; With An Appendix of Precedents. The Second Edition. London: Joseph Butterworth and Son & Dublin: J.Cooke, 1825. 8vo. pp. xxiv, 310. complete with half-title. index. uncut. modern buckram. browning to lower portion of first 4 leaves, else very good. Marvin p. 170. 65.00

162 (CAPITAL PUNISHMENT). A Collection of 25 pamphlets, letters & reports issued by the League to Abolish Capital Punishment & the American League to Abolish Capital Punishment, dated 1923-1940. (Including 'Heywood Broun on Capital Punishment', 'The Story of Michigan: Abolition of the Death Penalty Has Saved Innocent Men' by George B.Catlin, 'Capital Punisment' by Clarence Darrow, 'Is It Possible to Execute Innocent Men?' by Michael Angelo Musmanno, &c.). Detailed list available upon request. 250.00

163 DARROW, Clarence & Wallace Rice. Infidels and Heretics: An Agnostic's Anthology. Boston: Stratford Company, 1929. 8vo. pp. 8pl, x, 293. half-title. index. original cloth. 25.00

164 [DUANE, William]. Experience The Test of Government: In Eighteen Essays. Written During the Years 1805 and 1806. To Aid the Investigation of Principles, and Operation of the Existing Constitution and Laws of Pennsylvania. Philadelphia Printed by William Duane, 1807. 8vo. pp. 60. uncut. disbound. Sabin 20986. 50.00

165 FAIRMAN, Charles. Mr. Justice Miller and the Supreme Court

1862-1890. Cambridge: Harvard Univ. Press, 1939. 8vo. pp. [xii], 456. 8 plates. half-title. index. original cloth. 20.00

GIESECKE, Albert Anthony. American Commercial Legislation Before 1789. New York: University of Pennsylvania, D.Appleton & Co., Agents, 1910. 8vo. pp. 4pl, 167. uncut. modern buckram. First Edition. 15.00

GROTIUS, Hugo [1583-1645]. Epistolas ad Gallos, nunc primum editae. Lugduni Batavorum (Leiden): Ex Officina Elzeviriorum, 1648. 12mo. pp. 12pl, 501, [1]blank. title in red & black. title vignette. several woodcut ornaments. First Edition, First Impression.

Willems 639.

The first edition, first impression, with the unsuppressed table & dedicatory epistle to Pierre & Jacques Du Puy. The letters of Grotius to his French friends consist of over 200 letters, 27 of which were written prior to his arrival in Paris in April 1621. Among his correspondents were the President De Thou, the brothers Du Puy, Pierre & Jacques, custodians of De Thou's celebrated library & the scholar Nicholas Claude de Fabre, sieur de Pieresc.

Bound with:

LANGUET, Hubert [1518-1581]. Viri Cl. Huberti Langueti Burgundi, Ad Ioachimum Camerarium Patrem, & Ioachimum Camerarium, Filium, Medicum, Scriptae Epistolae, Ob res politicas & historicas memorabiles lectu utilissimae, Nunc primum editae a Ludovico Ioach.F.Ioach.N.Camerario, Consiliario Regio Suecico & Explegato. Groningae: Typis Iohannis Nicolai, 1646. 12mo. pp. 1pl, [67]dedication, [3]blank, 284, [1]errata. First Edition.

Graesse IV p. 100. Not in the NUC.

The correspondence of the French Huguenot writer & diplomat Languet, best remembered for his famous political treatise 'Vindiciae Contra Tyrannos', is an important primary source for the history of the 16th century. This work consists of 108 letters to the German classical scholar Camerarius.

The two items bound in contemporary vellume. Excellent copies. 600.00

GROTIUS, Hugo. The Freedom of the Seas Or The Right Which Belongs to the Dutch to Take Part in the East Indian Trade. A Dissertation by...Translated With A Revision of the Latin Text of 1633 By Ralph Van Deman Magoffin...Edited With An Introductory Note by James Brown Scott. New York: Oxford University Press (for the Carnegie Endowment for International Peace, Division of International Law), 1916. 8vo. pp. xv[ie17], 83[ie162]. [English translation on recto; Latin text on verso]. index. original cloth. 40.00

"FOUNTAIN OF INTERNATIONAL LAW"

GROTIUS, Hugo. The Rights of War And Peace, In Three Books. Wherein are explained, The Law of Nature and Nations, And The Principal Points relating to Government. Written in Latin by the Learned..., And Translated into English. To which are added, All the large Notes of Mr. J.Barbeyrac, Professor of Law at Groningen, And Member of the Royal Academy of Sciences at Berlin. London: Printed for W.Innys and R.Manby, J. and P.Knapton, D.Brown, T.Osborn, and E.Wicksteed, 1738. folio. pp. 2pl, xxxvi, 817. complete with half-title. index. A fine copy in modern oasis morocco. 500.00

S.&M.I.595.52. Marvin pp. 352-53. See PMM 258 (1st Edition, Paris 1625).

"No legal work ever enjoyed a more extended reputation, and none ever exercised such a wonderful influence over the public morals of Europe... Grotius wrote in advance of his age, his book was forbidden to be read in Spain and Italy, and through the instrumentality of the clergy was placed in the Index Expurgatorius...The title does not convey an idea of the scope of the work, which is no less than an endeavor to digest a systematic Code, deeply imbued with morals and equity, for regulating the intercourse and reciprocal obligations of nations, in war and peace, and incidentally that of individuals." (Marvin)

170 (GROTIUS, Hugo). JAGER, Johann Wolfgang [1647-1720]. Hugonis Grotii Libri Tres De Jure Belli Et Pacis, Observationibus Theologicis, Moralibus & Politicis illustrati Auctore Joh. Wolfgango Jagero... Tubingae: Sumptibus Joh.Georgii Cottae, 1710. 8vo. pp. 2pl, [10], 738, [30]index. engraved frontis. portrait. A fine uncut, unopened copy in modern quarter oasis morocco. 200.00

Only 1 copy located in NUC, that in the Yale Law Library

Analysis of Grotius' magnum opus by the German Lutheran divine & theological writer Jager.

171 (GROTIUS, Hugo). KNIGHT, W.S.M. The Life and Works of Hugo Grotius. London: Sweet & Maxwell, Limited, 1925. 8vo. pp. 1pl, xiv, 304. half-title. biblio. index. original quarter cloth, bds. 30.00

172 (GROTIUS, Hugo). LYSEN, A. Hugo Grotius: Essays On His Life and Works Selected For the Occasion of the Tercentenary of His "De Iure Belli Ac Pacis" 1625-1925. With A Preface By Jacob Ter Meulen. Leyden: A.W.Sythoff's Publishing Co., 1925. 8vo. pp. 2pl, [x], 109. portrait. facsimile reproduction of title-page of 1st edition. original cloth. 35.00

Twelve essays by C.Van Vollenhoven, William Rattigan, John Edwin Sandys, &c., with a further article by Van Vollenhoven from the American Journal of International Law tipped in.

173 HAWKINS, William [1673-1746]. A Treatise of the Pleas of the Crown: Or A System of the Principal Matters relating to that subject, digested under their proper Heads. Book I. [Book II]. The Second Edition corrected, with the Addition of some References. 2 Books in 1. In the Savoy: Printed by E.andR.Nutt, and R.Gosling...for J.Walthoe..., 1724. folio. pp. 7pl, 266, [44]index; 4pl, 464, [74]index. old calf worn, joints cracked, some age-browning & marginal annotations, otherwise internally very good. 225.00

S.&M.I.362. See Marvin p. 375 & Winfield pp. 325-26.

"There are very few juridical writers, whose compilations are more full of useful knowledge, or more methodically digested, even down to the minute sub-divisions, than the Pleas of the Crown, by Mr. Serj. Hawkins. In this admired and authoritative work the studen will readily find information in almost every point of Law relating to Crime and Punishments."(Marvin)

KING, Willard L. Melville Weston Fuller Chief Justice of the United States 1888-1910. New York: Macmillan, 1950. 8vo. pp. [xiv], 394. 7 illus. cloth. publisher's blurb laid in. 12.50

KONEFSKY, Samuel J. The Legacy of Holmes and Brandeis: A Study in the Influence of Ideas. New York: Macmillan, 1956. 8vo. pp. [xii], 316. index. cloth. pencil notes on back paste-down. 15.00

KOS-RABCEWICZ-ZUBKOWSKI, L[udwik]. East European Rules on the Validity of International Commercial Arbitration Agreements. Manchester: Manchester Univ. Press, 1970. 8vo. pp. xii, 332. biblio. index. cloth. 15.00

MACKENZIE, Norman & Lionel H.Laing (Eds.). Canada and the Law of Nations: A Selection of Cases in International Law, Affecting Canada or Canadians, Decided by Canadian Courts, by Certain of the Higher Courts in the United States and Great Britain and by International Tribunals. (Fwd. Sir Robert Borden; Intro. James Brown Scott). Toronto: Ryerson Press, For the Carnegie Endowment For International Peace: Division of Economics & History, 1938. 8vo. pp. xxvi, [1], 567. index. cloth. covers bit warped & slightly soiled, else very good. 65.00

A Canadian case book of international law, with sections on territorial jurisdiction, fisheries & boundaries disputes, status of Indians, treaties, extradition, &c.

McMASTER, John Bach & Frederick D.Stone (Eds.). Pennsylvania and the Federal Constitution 1787-1788. Published for the Subscribers by the Historical Society of Pennsylvania, 1888. 8vo. pp. viii, 803. complete with half-title. 15 portraits, with tissue guards. index. original cloth, t.e.g. cloth slightly soiled, spinal extremities beginning to fray, else a very good uncut & unopened copy. First Edition. 50.00

MADDEN, Marie R. Political Theory and Law in Medieval Spain. (Fwd. Moorhouse I.X.Millar). New York: Fordham Univ. Press, 1930. 8vo. pp. xv, 198. 9 illus. biblio. index. quarter cloth, bds. binding bit faded, corners bumped, else very good. 20.00

(MASSACHUSETTS). The Laws and Liberties of Massachusetts. Reprinted From the Copy of the 1648 Edition In the Henry E. Huntington Library. With an Introduction by Max Farrand. Cambridge: Harvard Univ. Press, 1929. folio. pp. ix, [4], 59. 2 photo-facsimiles. cloth very slightly spotty, else fine, uncut & unopened. related blurb laid in. 65.00

"The Book of the General Lawes and Libertyes of 1648' is the next significant measure after the Body of Liberties in the legal development of Massachusetts. It is a more important work than its predecessor, standing as the basis of all Massachusetts legislation, and influencing as well the legislation of other colonies, notably Connecticut and New Haven. It is furthermore the first attempt at a comprehensive reduction into one form of a body of legislation of an English-speaking country. Because of its importance and because the copy in the Huntington Library is to the present time unique, it has seemed desirable to reprint it." (Max Farrand, Introduction)

181 MARSHALL, Geoffrey. Constitutional Theory. Oxford: At the Clarendon Press, 1971. 8vo. pp. ix, 238. biblio. index. cloth. (Clarendon Law Series). 15.00

182 NELSON, Benjamin N. The Idea of Usury: From Tribal Brotherhood to Universal Otherhood. Princeton Univ. Press, 1949. pp. xxi, 258. biblio. index. cloth. (The History of Ideas Series 3). 10.00

183 NORTH, Roger [1653-1734]. The Life of the Right Honourable Francis North, Baron of Guilford, Lord Keeper of the Great Seal, Under King Charles II. And King James II. Wherein Are Inserted The Characters of Sir Matthew Hale, Sir George Jeffries, Sir Leoline Jenkins, Sidney Godolphin, And Others The Most Eminent Lawyers and Statesmen of That Time. Second Edition. 2 Volumes. London: Printed for W.Clarke and Sons, 1808. 8vo. pp. xvi, 317, [3]ads; 1pl, 347, [21]index. 2 frontis. portraits. contemporary sprinkled calf, rubbed, front covers detached, back joints cracked, internally fine. 100.00

Roger North's classic biography of his illustrious brother forms the basis of all subsequent memoirs, & is an authoritative work on the period.

184 O'BRIEN, R.Barry. The Life of Lord Russell of Killowen. With A Portrait and Facsimiles. Second Impression. London: Smith, Elder & Co., 1901. 8vo. pp. 4pl, 405, [2]ads. frontis. port. 3 folding facsimile letters. index. original cloth slightly spotty, else very good. 20.00

185 PADELFORD, Norman J. International Law and Diplomacy in the Spanish Civil Strife. New York: Macmillan, 1939. 8vo. pp. xxvii, [2], 710. folding map. index. cloth. 45.00

186 PUFENDORF, Samuel [1632-1694]. Le Droit De La Nature Et Les Gens, Ou Systeme General Des Principes les plus importans De La Morale, De La Jurisprudence, Et De La Politique. Par le Baron De Pufendorf, Traduit Du Latin Par Jean Barbeyrac,... Avec des Notes de Traducteur; & une Preface qui sert d'Introduction a tout l'Ouvrage. Cinquieme Edition, revue de nouveau, & fort augmentee. 2 Volumes. A Amsterdam: Chez la Veuve de Pierre De Coup, 1734. 4to. pp. cxxi, [3], 716; 2pl, 613, [37]index, 52, [2]errata. engraved frontis. port. title in red & black. title vignettes. several ornaments. hint of foxing to outer leaves, else a fine set in modern quarter oasis morocco. 350.00

See Marvin p. 593 & our item #104 in this catalogue.

187 RICHARDSON, H.G. Bracton: The Problem of His Text. Being an expansion of a lecture delivered before the Selden Society in the Hall of Gray's Inn on March 28, 1961. London: Selden Society (Supplementary Series Vol. 2), 1965. 8vo. pp. xii, 165. 8 facsimile plates. biblio. index. cloth. 25.00

SAWYER, Geoffrey. Australian Federal Politics and Law 1929-1949. Melbourne: Melbourne Univ. Press, 1963. 8vo. pp. 4pl, 244. index. cloth. 15.00

(SELDEN, John, Translator). EADMER [d.1124?]. Eadmeri Monachi Cantuariensis Historiae Novorum Sive Sui Saeculi Libri VI. Res gestas (quibus ipse non modo spectator diligens sed comes etiam & actor plerunq interfuit) sub Guilielmis I & II & Henrico I Angliae Regibus, ab anno nempe Salutis MLXVI ad MCXXII potissimum complexi, In lucem ex Bibliotheca Cottoniana emisit Ioannes Seldenus, & Notae porro adjecit & Spicilegium. Londonini: Typis & Impensis Guilielmi Stanesbeij, ex officinis Richardi Meighen & Thomae Dew, 1623. folio. pp. 3pl, xvi, 218. title in red & black. 2 text illus. several ornamental headpieces & initials. modern buckram. First Edition. 250.00

STC 7438.

Selden edited Eadmer's main work from a manuscript in the Cotton Library, & in his preface he praises its merits. Sober & well-written, Eadmer's work is free of the trivial details & alleged miracles which mar the other monkish histories of the period.

STEWART-BROWN, Ronald. Isaac Greene: A Lancashire Lawyer of the 18th Century With The Diary of Ireland Greene (Mrs. Ireland Blackburne of Hale) 1748-9. With Three Portraits. Liverpool: 1921. 8vo. pp. vii, [92]. 3 ports. index. cloth. Edition limited to 250 copies. 25.00

STIMSON, F.J. Labor In Its Relations to Law: Four Lectures delivered at the Plymouth School of Ethics, July, 1895. New York: Charles Scribner's Sons, 1895. 12mo. pp. 3pl (incl. half-title), 145, [1]ad. original cloth. From the library of the Mechanic's Institute and Library Association, Goderich, Ontario. 20.00

STINSON, Alvah L. Woman Under the Law. Boston: Hudson Printing Company, 1914. 8vo. pp. 1pl, v, 406, viii(glossary). frontis. port. cloth. 20.00

STORY, Joseph. A Discourse Upon the Life, Character, And Services of The Honorable John Marshall, LL.D., Chief Justice of the United States of America, Pronounced on the Fifteenth Day of October, At the Request of the Suffolk Bar, By..., And Published at Their Request. Boston: James Munroe and Company, 1835. 8vo. pp. 74, [1]errata. improvised wrs. hint of foxing, several small library rubberstamps, else very good. Sabin 92302. 35.00

[TOWNSHEND, Charles] [1725-1764]. A Defence of the Minority in the House of Commons on the Question Relating to General Warrants. London: Printed for J.Almon, 1764. 8vo. pp. 2pl, 38. complete with half-title. disbound. 100.00

Sabin 96403.

This pamphlet was issued just a few weeks after his famous speech against the legality of general warrants & the outlawry of John Wilkes. Townshend upholds that a general warrant for apprehending and seizing the authors, printers & publishers of seditious libel, together with their papers, is not warranted by law.

Catalogue #39

ENGLISH LAW

1600-1850

(Item #83)

D & E Lake Ltd.
Old & Rare Books

111 Queen Street East Suite 302
Toronto, Canada M5C 1S2
Telephone: (416) 863-9930
Cable Address: Lakebooks, Toronto

AYLIFFE, John [1676-1732]. A New Pandect of Roman Civil Law, As Anciently established in that Empire; and now received and practised in most European Nations: With Many useful Observations thereon; shewing, Wherein that Law differs from the Municipal Laws of Great-Britain, from the Canon Law in general, and from that Part of it now in Use here with us in England...London: Printed for Tho. Osborne, 1734. folio. pp. 4pl, xlviii, [8], 608[ie648]. several woodcut ornaments. contemporary calf, sometime rebacked, binding somewhat worn, joints cracked, paper repairs to lower margin of 2 preliminary leaves, else internally fine. First Edition. 400.00

S.&M.I.177.4. Marvin pp.80-81.
Ayliffe's career and social position suffered much from his outspoken political views ("he was an ardent whig at a time when Oxford was the home of Jacobitism"), and his book on Oxford, in which he exposed the misappropriation of the funds of Clarendon Printing House led to his expulsion from the university, stripped of all privileges and degrees. His most important undertakings, however, were his two treatise on canon and civil law. The 'Pandect' was not published until two years after his death, and "though it was never finished, it remains to our own day the most elaborate treatise on modern Roman law written in English." (DNB)

BARRINGTON, Daines [1728-1800]. Observations on the More Ancient Statutes, From Magna Charta to the Twenty-First of James I Cap. XXVII. With An Appendix, Being A Proposal For New Modelling the Statutes. The Third Edition, With Considerable Additions. London: Printed by W. Bowyer and J. Nichols: And Sold by S. Baker and G. Leigh, 1769. 4to. pp. xii, 516. index. contemporary sprinkled calf, sometime rebacked, endpapers renewed. extremities rubbed, author's name printed in white on lower spine, back paste-down snarled, internally very good. 250.00

See S.&M.I.546.3 & Marvin p.96 (neither listing this edition).
"Mr. Barrington, in his 'Observations', has contributed very much to the elucidation of the more ancient laws of England, by introducing historical illustrations of the times during which the statutes were enacted. The volume abounds in curious, learned, and valuable information." (Marvin) This is Barrington's first work.

BAYLEY, John [Whitcomb] [d1869]. The History and Antiquities Of the Tower of London, With Memoirs of Royal and Distinguished Persons, Deduced From Records, State-Papers, and Manuscripts, And From Other Original and Authentic Sources. 2 Volumes. London: Published by T. Cadell, 18[21]-25. 4to. pp. 3pl (incl. blank), [vii]-xiv, [2]list of plates & errata, 272, xxxiv; vi, [273]-671[ie679], [xxxv]-cxxviii, [17]index. [pp. 345-352 are numbered 345 a & b, &c.]. extra-illustrated: 29 engraved plates [27 called for] plus 11 added illustrations, mostly inlaid, of portraits of distinguished prisoners of the Tower: Lady Jane Grey, Sir Thomas More, &c. contemporary half calf, gilt backs, front joint of Vol. I renewed, joints of Vol. II cracking, hint of foxing to some plates & adjoining leaves, else a very

nice set. First Edition. 300.00

The greater portion of Bayley's work, which "ranks among the very best works of its kind for excellence of style, acuteness of judgement, and unfailing accuracy of statement" (DNB), is given over to an account of the Tower as a state prison, with biographical notices of the most distinguished personnages that have been confined there, and an appendix including a number of their letters.

"BENTHAM'S CLASSIC DEFENCE OF FREEDOM OF THE PRESS"

4 BENTHAM, Jeremy [1748-1832]. The Elements Of The Art Of Packing, As Applied To Special Juries, Particularly In Cases Of Libel Law. London: Published by Effingham Wilson, Royal Exchange, 1821. 8vo. pp. 2pl, vii, 269, [2]Ads. Except for foxing to some leaves, a fine uncut copy in original cloth backed bds. First Trade Edition. 550.00

S.&M.II.27. Marke p.187. Goldmith 23350. McCoy B200.
Bentham's critique of English libel law was written in 1809 and printed in 1810. Bentham's work is a vivid expose of governmental corruption in the selection of juries, particularly the packing of juries to obtain favourable verdicts in criminal libel trials. In writing this work and pointing to the abuses of particular judges, Bentham exposed himself to prosecution under the very same law he condemned, the Libel Law. Thus, the original edition of 1810 was held back from publication, copies only being distributed to Bentham's friends. The work did not officially appear until 1821.

"BENTHAM'S MOST IMPORTANT WORK ON ENGLISH LAW"

5 BENTHAM, Jeremy. Rationale Of Judicial Evidence, Specially Applied To English Practice. From The Manuscripts Of...In Five Volumes. London: Published By Hunt And Clarke, York Street, Covent Gardens, 1827. 8vo. Index. Related book review mounted on fr.blanks. modern cloth. sl.tearing to lower corner of several gatherings of Vol. I, else a very nice set, complete with half-titles. First Edition. 650.00

S.&M.II.27. Marke p.524. Marvin p.113.
Bentham's 'Rationale' was edited by John Stuart Mill. Vol. I includes a Preface by Mill describing his editorial role. The epochal 'Rationale' is considered by many to be Bentham's most important work on English law. "The 'Rationale of Judicial Evidence' is one of the richest in matter of all Bentham's productions. The book contains, very fully developed, a great proportion of all his best thoughts; while among more special things it comprises the most elaborate exposure of the vices and defects of English law, as it then was, which is to be found in his works..."(John Stuart Mill. Autobiography)

"BEST GENERAL HISTORY OF ENGLISH LAW"

6 BLACKSTONE, Sir William [1723-1780]. Commentaries on the Laws of England, Book the First. [-------Book the Fourth]. 4 Volumes. Oxford: Printed at the Clarendon Press, 1766-69. 4to. pp. 2pl, iv, [3], 485; 4pl, 520, xix; 4pl, 455, xxvii; 4pl, 436, vii, [39]index. 2 engraved plates (1 folding) in Vol. II. contemporary calf. several joints cracked,

but all quite firm, bindings bit rubbed, notes penned on final blank of Vol. I, else internally fine. A handsome set, with armorial bookplate of E.J. Curteis, Oxford, 1780, and his signature, as well as a presentation inscription to William H. White from Francis White, Boston, 1888. Second Edition of Vols. I & II; First Editions of Vols. III & IV. 2,000.00

S.&M.I.27.8. Rothschild 407. Winfield pp.337-340. Higgs 4494. PMM 212. See Marvin pp. 122-126 & Grose p.46.
Blackstone's 'Commentaries', based on his lectures given at Oxford beginning in 1753, constitute the first attempt since Bracton to provide a coherent account of English law as a whole. It is "the best general history of the English Law, needing comparatively little correction and told with admirable clearness and spirit." (DNB) Even one of his most furious critics, Jeremy Bentham, "allowed that it was he who first taught English law to speak the language of the scholar and the gentleman."

BRADY, Rob[ert] [d1700]. An Historical Treatise of Cities and Burghs Or Boroughs. Shewing Their Original, and Whence, and From Who They Received their Liberties, Privileges, and Immunities; What they were, and what Made and Constituted a Free Burgh, & Free Burgesses. As Also Shewing When they first sent their Representatives to Parliament. With a Concurrent Discourse of most Matters, and Things Incident, or Relating thereto. The Second Edition. London: Printed for A.L. and Sold by John Nutt. 1704. folio. pp. 1pl, iv, ii[ie90], 41[ie43]. lacking A4 [probably blank or fly-title]. several woodcut ornaments & initials. 19th century half hard-grained leather. extremities rubbed, joints cracked, some light foxing, else internally very good. 150.00

S.&M.I.416.7
Brady's work staunchly defended the royal prerogative. In the preface to this treatise, he claims that he is able to show that they "have noting of the greatness and authority they boast of, but from the bounty of our ancient kings and their successors."

BROUGHAM, Henry [Peter, Baron Brougham and Vaux] [1778-1868]. Present State of the Law. The Speech of...In the House of Commons, On Thursday, February 7th, 1828, On His Motion, That An Humble Address Be Presented to His Majesty, Praying That He Will Graciously Be Pleased to Issue A Commission For Inquiring into the Measures Necessary for Removing the Same. Philadelphia: Carey, Lea & Carey, 1828. 8vo. pp. xii, 146, [1]postscript. index. complete with half-title. disbound. outer leaves slightly soiled, else very good. 45.00

S.&M.II.45.
The reform scheme proposed by Brougham in his famous six-hour speech led to the vast improvement and simplification of the system of common law procedure. This edition was revised by the author.

BROWNLOW, Richard [1553-1638]. Latine Redivivus: A Book Of Entries, Of Such Declarations, Informations, Pleas in Barr and Abatement, Replications, Rejoynders, Issues, Verdicts,

Bills of Exception to Verdicts, Judgements, Demurrers, and other Parts of Pleadings, (now in use) in Personal and Mixt Actions...London: Printed by the assigns of Richard and Edward Atkyns, Edquires; And are to be Sold by S. Heyrick in Holborn, T. and G. Sawbridge in Little-Britain, and M. Gilliflower in Westminster Hall, 1693. Folio. pp. 3pl, 506, [46]index. printed in black letter. modern quarter oasis morocco. first two leaves mounted (edges tatty), neat paper mend to third leaf, several ink marks on title, otherwise an excellent copy. First complete edition. 350.00

Wing B5197. S.&M.I.265.36. Marvin p.156.
Several surreptitious editions of Brownlow's 'Latine Redivivus' were published prior to the complete 1693 edition. Two English translations appeared in 1653 and 1654. The title-page of the 1693 edition reprobates the 1653 & 1654 editions as "unskilfully turned into English". The 1693 edition of Brownlow's work was issued in Latin, the original language, with additions in English.

10 BURROW, Sir James [1701-1782]. A Series of the Decisions of the Court of King's Bench Upon Settlement-Cases; From the Death of Lord Raymond in March 1732; To Which Is Added A Complete Abridgment of the Substance of each Case, and Two Tables of the Names of them...3 Volumes. [...Volume the Second: Containing near Fifteen Years, and including Lord Chief Justice Ryder's Time and the first Twelve Years of Lord Mansfield's. To this Volume is added an Index to both Volumes. And there are also Subjoined a few Thoughts upon Pointing and some other Helps towards Perspicuity of Expression; Vol.III: Continuation...By Four Additional Years, ending in July 1772...]. London: Printed by His Majesty's Law-Printers for J. Worrall and B. Tovey, 1768-72. 4to. pp. xv(incl. general title), 364;2pl, 365-625, ix-xv, [36]index, [2]div. title, 631-652; 1pl, [6], 627-718, [4]index. contemporary calf. bindings bit rubbed, several joints cracked, clean tear to 1 leaf (no loss), erasures to lower margin of some leaves has caused paper to wear thin, some leaves misbound in Vol.III, but all are present except for final blank; otherwise a very good set. 300.00

S.&M.I.386.3. See Marvin p.166(3rd edn.).
Burrow's great merits as a law reporter were his painstaking accuracy and his belief in the "importance of sharp divisions between the facts, the arguments of counssel, and the judgment of the court." (See Winfield, p.190) A further continuation [1772]-1776 was also published.

11 CAMPBELL, John, [first Baron]Campbell [1779-1861]. The Lives Of The Chief Justices Of England. From The Norman Conquest Till The Death Of Lord Mansfield. In Two Volumes. London: John Murray, 1849. 8vo. pp. xix, 588; xii, 584, 16 [Publisher's Ads]. Original blind and gilt stamped cloth. Backstrips faded and frayed. Bookplate of Baldwin of Spadina in The County of York Upper Canada. First Edition. SOLD

Campbell's work "contains a great deal of information about the history of law and lawyers which is not easily to be found elsewhere...Nor has time worn away the merit of his books; they still find many readers, and there is little probability that they will be displaced by anything more entertaining written on the subject."(DNB) Chapters on Edward Coke, Matthew Hale and Lord Mansfield.

CLARENDON, Edward [HYDE, first] Earl of [1609-1674]. A Collection of Several Tracts of the Right Honourable Edward, Earl of Clarendon, Author of the History of the Rebellion and Civil Wars in England. Published from his Lordship's Original Manuscripts. London: Printed for T. Woodward..., and J. Peele, 1727. folio. pp. 2pl, 348, [2]div. title, [369]-770. vignettes. contemporary calf. binding somewhat worn, else very good. with armorial bookplate of Sir Richard Bempde Johnstone, Bart. First Edition. 250.00

Included is Clarendon's 'Vindication' written in 1668 in answer to the articles of impeachment against him (his popularity had been on a quick and steady decline, largely due to his attempts to restrict the authority of the House of Commons).

COKE, Edward [1552-1634]. The First Part of the Institutes of the Laws of England Or, A Commentary Upon Littleton. Not the Name of the Author, only, but of the Law itself. The Thirteenth Edition [Hargrave and Butler's First Edition], Revised and Corrected. With the Addition of Notes and References, From the Beginning to Folio 195 Inclusive, By Francis Hargrave Esq...And From Folio 196 to the End, With the Preface and Index to the Notes, by Charles Butler ...And An Analysis of Littleton, Written by an Unknown Hand in 1658-9, but never before published. London: Printed for E. Brooke..., 1788. folio. pp. 2pl, [18], xx, 395(numbered leaves), [64]index & tables, [2]blank, [2]errata & directions to binder. 1 folding table. contemporary calf, sometime rebacked, endpapers renewed. binding rubbed, covers detached, small library stamp on front free-endpaper & label on spine, internally very good. 225.00

S.&M.I.450.7. Winfield pp.333-34. Marvin pp.204-208. See PMM 259.
The First Part of the Institutes is considered to be Coke's most "celebrated work on which his fame is permanently established."(Foss) "If Bracton first began the codification of the common law, it was Coke who completed it. Ranging over the whole field of law, in comment, report, argument, and decision - it is a disorderly, pedantic, masterful work in which the common thread is a national dogmatism, tenacious of its continuous self-perpetuating life. With it the lawyers fought the battle of the constitution against the Stuarts; historical research was their defence for national liberties. In the Institutes the basis of the constitution in the law of the land was firmly established." (PMM) Francis Hargrave and Charles Butler's critical notes on Coke in the 13th and 14th editions of the First Part of the Institutes provided added insight into Coke's work and distinguish these from previous editions.

COLLINS, Arthur [1682-1760]. Proceedings, Precedents, And Arguments, On Claims and Controversies, Concerning Baronies by Writ, and other Honours. With the Arguments of Sir Francis Bacon, Sir Henry Montagu, the Lord Chief Justice Crew, the Lord Chief Justice Heneage Finch, Mr. Montagu, (afterwards Lord Chief Baron) Sir William Jones, Sir Wil-

liam Dugdale, Mr. Offley, Sir Edward Northey, Sir Thomas Powis, and others...With an Appendix containing several Papers copied from the Bodleian and Ashmolaean Libraries, at Oxford &c. London: Printed for Thomas Wotton, 1734. folio. pp. 1pl, 4(dedication & preface), [2]errata leaf, 415, [12]index. An excellent copy in modern quarter antique oasis morocco,with armorial bookplate of Baron Maule laid in. First Edition. 400.00

S.&M.I.204.11. New CBEL II p.1712.
Collins devoted his lifetime to researching the nobility and investigating disputed titles. Here recorded are the cases covering the period from the end of the reign of Queen Elizabeth to the year 1740.

15 COLQUOUN, P[atrick] [1745-1820]. A Treatise On Indigence; Exhibiting A General View of the National Resources for Productive Labour; With Propositions For Ameliorating the Condition of the Poor... London: Printed for J. Hatchard, 1806. 8vo. pp. 1pl, [iii]-xii, [2], [5]-302, [12]incl. index & ads. tables(1 folding). lacking half-title. modern green buckram. Fine. First Edition. 300.00

Kress B.5028. Goldsmith 19292. McCulloch p.286.
Colquoun's treatise contains considerable discussion of the poor laws (with a section on Blackstone's obervations), the relations between poverty and crime, the police and law enforcement. To combat indigence and crime, he recommended "the establishment of a board of education, of a system of reproductive employment for those out of work, of a national poor-rate universally assessed, and the issue of a police gazette, containing instructive reading, with the statistics of crime and descriptions of the persons of offenders."(DNB)

16 COLQUOUN, P[atrick]. A Treatise on the Commerce and Police of the River Thames: Containing An Historical View of the Trade of the Port of London; And suggesting Means for preventing the Depredations thereon, by a Legislative System of River Police. With An Account of the Functions of the Various Magistrates and Corporations Exercising Jurisdiction on the River; And A General View of the Penal and Remedial Statutes Connected With the Subject. London: Printed for Joseph Mawman, 1800. 8vo. pp. 2pl, xxxiv, 593, 609-676(appendix), [20]index. engraved folding map, 2 folding tables. contemporary quarter calf. bds. rubbed, internally fine. 350.00

Kress B.4102. Goldsmith 18053. Marvin p.215. S&M.I.438.42.
Colquoun was Lord Provost of Glasgow and police magistrate in London. Subsequent to the publishing of his chief work on the "Police of the Metropolis", East Indian merchants requested his assistance in preventing the stealing of goods from ships in the Thames. This work resulted in the establishment for the first time of an effective Thames police.

17 COMBERBACH, Roger. The Report of Several Cases Argued and adjudged in the Court of King's Bench at Westminster; From the First Year of King James the Second, to the Tenth Year of King William the Third. Collected By...late Recorder of Chester, and one of the Justices of North-Wales. Published by his son Roger Comberbach of the Inner-Temple, Esq. In The Savoy: Printed by E. and R. Nutt, and R. Gosling...for J. Walthoe, 1724. folio. pp. 2pl, [9]table, [1]errata, 484, [51]table. 19th century half calf. binding bit rubbed,cloth sides faded & spotty, some dampstaining & browning to outer leaves, numbers erased from lower margin of first two leaves, else very good. First Edition. 150.00

S.&M.I.298.33. See Marvin pp.215-16.

[COOKE, Edward] [1755-1820]. Letters Addressed To Lord Grenville And Lord Howick, Upon Their Removal From The Councils Of The King, In Consequence Of Their Attempting The Total Repeal Of The Test Laws Now in Force, with Respect to His Majesty's Army and Navy. By a Protestant [pseud]. London: Printed for John Stockdale, 1807. pp. 37, [1]ad. 8vo. disbound. light foxing to first two leaves, else VG. 50.00

Goldsmith 19523.

COOTE, Richard Holmes. An Analysis. Arranged to Serve Also As A Compendious Digested Index of Mr. Fearne's Essay on Contingent Remainders and Executory Devises, And of Mr. Butler's Notes. London: Printed for W. Clarke & Sons, 1814. 8vo. pp. 2pl, [12], 198. Contemporary calf. front joint tender. First Edition. 125.00

S.&M.II.77. Marvin p.228.
A very useful and concise alphabetical index & analytical abridgement of Fearne's authoritative work on property law.

COWEL[L, John] [1554-1611]. A Law Dictionary: Or The Interpreter of Words and Terms, Used either in the Common or Statute Laws of Great Britain, And In Tenures and Jocular Customs...Augmented and Improved...With An Appendix, Containing Two Tables; one of the antient Names of Places in Great Britain, and the other of the antient Surnames; Both of them very necessary for the Use of all such, as converse with antient Deeds, Charters, &c. In the Savoy: Printed by E. and R. Nutt, and R. Gosling...for J. Walthoe..., 1727. folio. no pagination. [pp.340]. contemporary calf, bit worn, joints cracked, new spine label, pen notes to outer blanks, cancelled institutional bookplate on front paste-down, else internally a fine clean copy. Second Edition of the Enlarged Work. 275.00

S.&M.I.7.21. Marvin p.234. Winfield p.17.
First published in 1607 but suppressed by royal proclamation in 1610 as it contained passages offensive to the King and the Commons civil law. Cowell advanced the heretical notion that the English monarchy was absolute and the King was able to make laws without the consent of parliament. This considerably enlarged edition first appeared in 1708.
"Selden and other writers, of, and since his time, have freely used the work, and previous to Jacobs' it was the best existing Law Dictionary [it was based on Rastell's 'Les Termes de la Ley']. "With the exception of the prerogative doctrines in Cowell's Interpreter, it is a useful work, and is an excellent glossary to Coke Littleton and the old law books, and will be found of considerable utility to a modern student of English law and antiquities." (Marvin)

"FIRST SYSTEMATIC WRITER ON LAW IN SCOTLAND"

21 CRAIG, Sir Thomas [1538-1608]. Jus Feudale Tribus Libris Comprehensum. Quibus Non solum Consuetudines Feudales & Praeditorum Iura, quae in Scotia, Anglia, & plerisque Galliae locis obtinent,continentur; Sed Universum Ius Scoticum, Et omnes fere Materiae Iuris clare & dilucide exponuntur, Et ad fontes Iuris Feudalis & Civilis singula reducuntur. Edinburgi: 1655. small folio. pp. 6pl, 383. woodcut ornaments & initials. contemporary calf, rubbed, front cover detached, head & foot of backstrip chipped, some spotting & browning, title strengthened, but a very good copy internally. folio leaf tipped-in on back paste-down containing manuscript copy extract from Lord Jeffrays Essays, "The Scottish Dialect". First Edition, First Issue. 400.00

Wing C6801. S.&M.V.26. cfMarvin p.237 (later editions).
Although the Scottish lawyer's great work was apparently completed about 1603, it was not published until 1655. "A very learned work, written with the avowed object of showing that the feudal law of Scotland and England had a common origin...No clearer statement of the feudal system in its legal relations exists, and it is still, although the law has been much altered, the standard authority in Scotland as to the original condition of its feudal landlaw, probably as complete as that of any European country." (DNB) Its scholarship, organization & originality thoroughly distinguish it from previous compilations & textbooks & Craig is regarded as the first systematic writer on law in Scotland. A zealous promoter of the union of Scotland & England, Criag wrote with both public & patriotic ends in view, and has been compared to Bacon in this respect.

22 CROKE, George [1582-1641]. The Third Part (Though first publish't) of the Reports of Sr George Croke Kt, Late one of the Justices of Kings-Bench, And formerly one of the Justices of the Court of Common-Bench; Of Such Select Cases as ere Adjudged in the said Courts, during the first Sixteen Years Reign of King Charles the First. Collected and Written in French by Himself; Revised and Published in English by Sir Harbottle Grimston, Baronet, Master of the Rolls. The Third Impression, carefully Corrected, with the Addition of many Thousand of References never before Printed. London: Printed by W. Rawlins, S. Roycroft, and H. Sawbridge..., 1683. folio. pp. 1pl, [28], 610, [66]index. several woodcut ornaments & initials. old calf, quite worn. front free-endpaper loose, fore-edge of first few leaves bit tatty, few notes on back endpapers in old hand, else internally very good. From the library of T.C. Aylwin. The book also bears the signatures of the following previous owners: the Boston jurist John Leverett 1697, the Boston lawyer, theologian & Loyalist William Brattle 1734 & the Massachusetts lawyer & judge Jonathan Sewall. Third Edition in English. 200.00

New Wing C7020. S.&M.I.298.37. Marvin p.240. Winfield p. 190.
"Croke's Reports form a continuation of Dyer's, and are among the most esteemed of the elder determinations, and are to this day familiarly referred as to authentic repositories of the Common Law." (Bridgman) "Precedents for almost any opinion may be found in Croke's Law Reports."(Judge Pendleton)

DE LOLME, J[ean] L[ouis] [1740?-1807]. The Constitution of England, Or An Account Of The English Government; In which it is compared with the Republican Form of Government, and occasionally with the other Monarchies in Europe. London: Printed by T. Spilsbury...And Sold by G. Kearsley, 1775. 8vo. pp. vii, 448. Contemporary half calf, marbled bds. extremities rubbed, fr. joint cracked, else a very good copy. First English Edition. 200.00

S.&M.I.100.27. New CBEL II p.1734. Marvin p.263.
De Lolme's work, written in French, was first published in Amsterdam in 1771. "De Lolme was a native of Switzerland, and it is remarkable that a foreigner should have been the first to write a clear, concise, and accurate treatise upon the constitutional law of England."(Marvin). The work is still highly regarded today.

DE LOLME, J[ean] L[ouis]. The Constitution of England...The Fourth Edition, Corrected and Enlarged. [Edited by Charles Coote]. London: Printed for G. Robinson & J. Murray, 1784. 8vo. pp. 4pl, xvi, 540, [20]index. engraved frontis. port. contemporary calf. corners bumped, otherwise a fine copy. 125.00

S.&M.I.100.27. New CBEL II p.1734. Marvin p.263.

(DOUGLAS, Archibald James Edward, first Baron Douglas of Douglas; formerly A.J.E. Stewart) [1748-1827]. Observations Servant de Reponse a Un Ecrit Anonime, Portant le titre de Memoire Abrege Pour M. De Douglas; Avec L'Articulation Des Faits De Supposition De Part, Et Les Quatre Lettres Du Pretendu Accoucheur Pier Lamarr. A Paris: 1763. 4to. pp. 1pl, 40, [24]. library buckram, several small library stamps, title browned, else very good. 50.00

The first brief here contained is signed A[ndrew] Stuart, who represented the Duke of Hamilton in the famous Douglas case. The Duke of Hamilton contested the will of Archibald Douglas (1761), which settled his estate upon his sister's surviving son, and claimed that, in fact, the young Douglas was a spurious child. The Scottish case lasted 5 years (1762-67); Douglas appealed the original decision against him and obtained a reversal in 1769.

DYER, [Sir James] [1511-1582]. Les Reports Des Divers Select Matters & Resolutions des Reverend Judges & Sages del Ley, Touchant & concernant mults principal Points occurrent estre debate per eux: En le several Reignes de les tres-hault & excellent Princes, Le Roys Hen. 8 & Edw. 6 & le Roignes Mar. & Eliz. Collect & Report per tres-Reverend Judge, Sr. Jacques Dyer Chivaler...London: Printed by W. Rawlins, S. Roycroft, and M. Flesher...for Samuel Keble..., 1688. folio. pp. 3pl, [10]table, 377 (numbered leaves),[2] [52]index. woodcut ornaments & vignettes. old calf, sometime rebacked. binding quite worn, covers detached, outer signatures loose, some dampstaining & marginal tearing to a few leaves (not affecting text), otherwise internally very good. Sixth Edition, in Law French. Edited by Chief Justice Treby. 275.00

S.&M.I.299.47. New Wing D2927. Marvin p.284. Winfield p. 187.

Dyer "reported the most remarkable cases that came before the Court of Common Pleas, together with those, which, on account of their difficulty, were adjourned into the Exchequeur Chamber before all the Judges. They are valuable records of the history of English jurisprudence and English manners."(S.&M.) "No Reports have been so frequently reprinted, and none have received higher homage..."(Marvin) Dyer's reports are most notable as being the first collection regulary called 'Reports' rather than 'Cases' or 'Commentaries'. This sixth Edition is the first to be altered; the notes and additions of Chief Justice Treby are held to be of equal authority to the Reports.

27 EAST, Edward Hyde [1764-1847]. A Treatise of the Pleas of the Crown. 2 Volumes. Philadelphia: Printed for A. Bryne, 1806. 8vo. pp. lxiii, 480; 2pl, 481-1126, [2]ads. complete with half-title. contemporary sheep. some browning & foxing to leaves. First American Edition. 200.00

S.&M.II.106 (not recording this edition). Marvin p.284.
A clearly written thorough and standard account relating to criminal law at the end of the eighteenth century, this work was the result of 15 years of labour. East had access to private collections of cases during his research and his treatise is the sole source for many otherwise unreported decisions. Offences are classed under 3 categories: crimes against religion, crimes against property and crimes against persons.

28 ELLIS, Charles. The Law of Fire and Life Insurance and Annuities, With Practical Observations. Part I.-The Law of Fire Insurance. Part II.-The Law of Life Insurance. Part III.-The Law of Annuities. London: Saunders and Benning..., 1832. 8vo. pp. xv, 263, [1].index. contemporary half calf. First Edition. 85.00

S.&M.II.110. Kress C.3127. Marvin p.291. Not in Goldsmith.
Apparently the first work to be exclusively devoted to the subject.

29 ESPINASSE, Isaac. A Digest of the Law of Actions and Trials At Nisi Prius. The Second Edition, Corrected, With Considerable Additions From Printed and Manuscript Cases, And Three New Chapters On The Law of Corporations and Evidence. 2 Volumes in I. Dublin: Printed for E. Lynch, 1794-93. 8vo. pp. x, [33], 426; 1pl, [427]-791, [66]index. contemporary calf. occasional light foxing else very good. 100.00

S.&M.I.335.6. See Marvin p.298.

30 GODWIN, William [1756-1836]. An Enquiry Concerning Political Justice, And Its Influence on General Virtue and Happiness. In Two Volumes. Dublin: Printed for Luke White, 1793. 8vo. pp. xiii, [21]contents, 411; 2pl, [19]contents, 424. complete with half-titles. contemporary sheep bit worn, joints cracking, slight dampstain to lower corner of first few leaves of Vol. I, small strip clipped from half-title of Vol.I, hint of foxing, else internally very good. First Irish Edition. 350.00

Kress B.2528. cf Goldsmith 15825 (1st English edition). S.&M.I.608.30. New CBEL II p.1249. See PMM 384.

Composed of carefully constructed arguments dealing with all aspects of legal rights and duties, this influential work established Godwin as the philosophical representative of English radicalism. The first Irish edition was published in the same year as the first English.

(GORDON, Lord George [1751-1793]). The Trial of Lord George Gordon, For High Treason, At the Bar of the Court of King's Bench, On Monday, February 5th, 1781. Published under the Inspection of his Lordship's Friends. To which are subjoined, Several Original Papers Relating to the Subject. Edinburgh: Printed by J. Mennons, [1781]. 8vo. pp. viii, 200. disbound. some foxing & age-browning, small lib.stp. on title-withdrawn. SOLD

Account of the trial of Lord George Gordon for high treason for his role in instigating the famous Gordon riots of 1780. Gordon organized and headed the Protestant associations formed to secure the repeal of the Catholic Relief Act of 1778. Erskine's eloquent defence secured Gordon's acquittal. Of particular interest are the references to the Quebec Act of 1774, establishing the Roman Catholic religion in Canada, pointed up as one of the first instance of the alarming toleration of popery by the British government.

GRIFFITHS, Arthur. The Chronicles Of Newgate. New Edition. London: Chapman And Hall, 1884. 8vo. pp. xii, 596. frontis. 37 illus. (plates & text illus.). index. complete with half-title. original publisher's gilt stamped cloth. spine faded, head & foot of backstrip frayed, else internally fine. 50.00

Griffiths, an inspector of prisons, was an acknowledged authority on prison systems & London gaols. This work provides a comprehensive history of Newgate from 1218 to 1877, including vivid sketches of some of the prison's most notorious inmates.

HALE, Matthew [1609-1676]. A Discourse Of The Knowledge Of God, and of our Selves, I. By the Light of Nature. II. By the Sacred Scriptures...To which are added a Brief Abstract of the Christian Religion, And Considerations seasonable at all Times, for the Cleansing of the Heart and Life. London: Printed by B.W. for William Shrowsbery, 1688. 8vo. pp. 1pl, [36], 503, [1]ad. engraved frontis. portrait. contemporary mottled calf. binding worn, upper backstrip chipped, internally a nice copy. First Edition. 150.00

Wing H240.

HALE, Matthew. The History of the Common Law. The Fourth Edition Corrected; With Notes, References, And Some Account of the Life of the Author, By Charles Runnington. [With: "An Analysis of the Civil Part of the Law. The Fourth Edition"]. London: Printed by W. Strahan & M. Woodfall for T. Cadell, 1779. 8vo. pp. 4pl, xl, [305], [1]errata; 6pl, 114, [8]index, [2]ads. engraved frontis. chart. modern quarter morocco. some browning throughout, dampstaining to lower edge of some leaves, frontis. & title neatly mounted, else very good. With complimentary ticket of F.A. Alberger, Member of Assembly. 150.00

S.&M.I.239.18. See Marvin p.359 & Winfield pp.37-38 & 328.
The 'Analysis', treating of civil matters, was the first work of its kind ever written and had a considerable influence on Blackstone, who called it "the most rational, scientific...as well as the most comprehensive of all attempts [prior to his own analysis] to digest the common law." Of his 'History' Holdsworth has said that it is "the ablest introductory sketch of a history of English law that appeared till the publication of Pollock and Maitland." Both of the works were published posthumously from rought drafts never intended for publication, and this fourth edition marks their first appearance together.

35 HALE, Matthew. The Primitive Origination of Mankind, Considered And Examined According to The Light of Nature. London: Printed by William Godbid, for William Shrowsberry..., 1677. folio. pp. 5pl, 380. Engraved frontis. portrait of Hale by Van Houe. Contemporary calf, expertly & attractively rebacked. Covers rubbed, else an unusually fine & clean copy. First Edition. 500.00

Wing H258.
Hale devoted many of his leisure hours to scientific and philosophical concerns. The 'Origination' was written over a period of years when Hale was lord chief baron of the Exchequer, but the work was not published until 1677, a year after his death.
In the 'Origination' Hale defends the Mosaic account of creation & deals with objections to the Mosaic account in the light of the discovery of America. Hale conducts an interesting inquiry into the geography, wild life and native races of the Americas. In this work Hale reviews many of the ideas of the Greek philosophers, as well as the discoveries of Copernicus, Harvey &c.

36 HANWAY, Jonas [1712-1786]. The Defects of Police The Cause of Immorality, and the continual Robberies committed, particularly in and about the Metropolis: With Various Proposals For Preventing Hanging and Transportation: Likewise for the establishment of Several Plans of Police on a permanent basis, with respect to common beggars; the regulation of paupers; the peaceful security of subjects; and the moral and political conduct of the people: Observations on the Rev. Mr. Hetherington's Charity; and the most probable means of relieving the blind. In Twenty-nine Letters to a Member of Parliament. London: Printed for J. Dodsley..., 1775. 4to. pp. 1pl, xxxiv, 288. First Edition.

Kress 7093. Goldsmith 11353. Higgs 6458.

Bound with:

[HANWAY, Jonas]. **Common Sense: In Nine Conferences, Between A British Merchant And A Candid Merchant of America,** in their private capacities as friends; tracing the several causes of the present contests between the mother country and her American subjects; the fallacy of their prepossessions; and the ingratitude and danger of them; the reciprocal benefits of the national friendship; and the moral obligations of the individuals which enforce it:with various anecdotes, and reasons drawn from facts, tending to conciliate all differences, and establish a permanent union for the common happiness and glory of the British empire. **London: Sold by J. Dodsley..., 1775. 4to.pp. x, 117. First Edition.**

Howes C-646. Sabin 14998. Goldsmith 11221. Kress 7093. Higgs 6321.

The two works bound in contemporary sprinkled calf, bit rubbed, joints cracked, internally fine. 750.00

Hanway is one of the most notable of 18th century English philanthropists; his zealous efforts on behalf of social reform were many & varied: he was a chief promoter of the Marine Society, of the Magdalen Hospital, of plans for benefiting chimney-sweepers, for reforming the Foundling Hospital, for establishing Sunday schools & for lowering the infant mortality rate among the parish poor, &c. He is also remembered as the first man who made a practice of using an umbrella.
In the area of penal reform, Hanway argued for the abolition of imprisonment for fixed sentences & the institution of a system whereby offenders are released only upon proving penitence. He opposed the practice of transportation as too expensive & too difficult to enforce & advocated solitary confinement & labour for prisoners.
The second work, which is most certainly by Hanway, is listed as anonymous in all of the cited bibliographies.(See DNB entry). Among his relatively unconvincing arguments against American independence, he mentions Great Britain's generous & protective conduct towards Canada, citing his involvement in petitioning for the relief of the Canadians at Montreal, after the great fire of 1765. During the American war, Hanway helped to establish the Society for the Encouragement of British troops, an organization which provided clothing & prayer books for the troops.

HARGRAVE, Francis [1741?-1821]. Juridical Arguments and Collections. 2 Vols. London: Printed for G.G. and J. Robinson, 1797-99. 4to. pp. 3pl, xv, 570, [1]leaf, liii; 3pl, 391, xxiv. contemporary calf, rubbed, bds. off, lacking spine labels, slight staining to outer leaves of Vol. I, else internally fine & crisp. Armorial bookplate of Richard Spencer. First Edition. 135.00

S.&M.I.33.38. Marvin p.369.
Hargrave enjoyed considerable reputation as a learned & skilfull lawyer. With Charles Butler he produced an important critical edition of the First Part of Coke's Institute. The cases here include the equity suit against the Duke of Chandos about the Manor of Villiers in Ireland, the Thellusson will case (later separately reprinted), &c.

"COMMAND THEORY OF LAW"

HOBBES, Thomas [1588-1679]. The Art of Rhetòric, With A Discourse Of The Laws of England. London: Printed for William Crooke, 1681. 8vo. pp. 4pl (including engraved frontis portrait), 168, 208. K4 separate title: The Art of Rhetorick Plainly set forth; with Pertinent Examples For the more easie understanding and Practice of the same. London: Printed, for W. Crooke. 1681; last part with heading: A Dialogue Between A Philosopher and A Student, of the Common-Laws of England. old mottled calf, gilt back.

spinal extremities worn, front joint cracked, small hole in I4 of last part (defect in the paper, affecting several letters of text),else an excellent copy. Third Edition of the work on Rhetoric & First Edition of the Discourse of the Laws of England. 850.00

Wing H2212. Macdonald & Hargreaves 13. S.&M.I.240.23.
The abridgement of the useful part of Aristotle's Rhetoric was first published in 1637 & corresponds with a Latin version dictated to his young pupil William, the succeeding Earl of Devenshire. According to Macdonald & Hargreaves, quoting the Rev. Walter J. Ong, 'The Art of Rhetorick Plainly Set Forth' is not by Hobbes, although previously always attributed to him, but in fact is a reprint of an English adaptation of the Rhetorica of Ramus's collaborator Talon. (See M & H 12a)
'The Dialogue...of the Common-Laws of England', although written many years previously, was not first published until this point, after his death. It was John Aubrey, later his biographer, who encouraged Hobbes to write on the subject by sending him a copy of Bacon's 'Elements of the Laws of England'. It constituted "a trenchant criticism of the constitutional theory of English government as upheld by Coke" (Encyc. Brit., 11th Edn.). Hobbes unequivocally favouring the 'command theory of law'. The work anticipated the analytical school of jurisprudence of the nineteenth century. (See Encyc. of Philosophy)

39 [HOME, Henry, Lord Kames] [1696-1782]. Remarkable Decisions of the Court of Session, From the year 1730 to the year 1752. Edinburgh: Printed for A. Kincaid and J. Bell, 1766. folio. pp. viii, 284 [9]index. contemporary sprinkled calf. joints & extremities rubbed, else a very good clean copy. First Edition. 150.00

S.&M.V.57. Marvin p.394.
A further volume of 'Remarkable Decisions' by the Scottish judge & philosopher, covering the period 1716-1728, appeared in 1728.

40 (HONE, William) [1780-1842]. The Three Trials of William Hone, For Publishing Three Parodies; viz. The Late John Wilkes's Catechism, The Political Litany, And The Sinecurist's Creed; On Three Ex-Officio Informations, At Guildhall, London, During Three Successive Days, December 18, 19 & 20, 1817; Before Three Special Juries, And Mr. Justice, Abbott, On The First Day, And Lord Chief Justice Ellenborough, On The Last Two Days. London: Printed By & for William Hone, 1818. 8vo. pp. iv, 48, 45, [3]ads, 44. Disbound. Prefatory address by William Hone dated January 23, 1818. The first trial is of the 16th edition, the second of the fourteenth, the third of the twelfth. 85.00

cf Goldsmith 22265-66 (Variant editions).

"FIRST ENGLISH WORK OF POLITICAL THEORY"

41 HOOKER, Richard [1554?-1600]. Of The Lawes of Ecclesiastical Politie, Eight Bookes. London: Printed by Richard Bishop and are to be sold by George Lathum, [1638] [with separate titles & varying imprints]. folio. pp. 4pl, [50], 453, [verso blank], [1 leaf], 453-583[verso blank], [16]. index. engraved & printed titles, woodcut ornaments & initials. modern mottled calf. faint dampstaining to outer margin of leaves of last signature, lacking initial blank, else very good. Seventh Edition of Preface & Books I-IV, Sixth Edition of Book V, & Fourth Collected Edition (Second Issue) of 'Certain Divine Tractates'. 300.00

Hill 17 & 16(b). STC 13719-20. S.&M.I.170.69. NCBEL Ip.1949. PMM 233 (1st Edn).
In his great work, Hooker sought to defend, on philosophical & logical grounds, the Church of England as established in the reign of Elizabeth I. In his discussion of the authority & responsibility of the church in general, Hooker was led to consider the nature of human and divine laws; his treatise marks the first adequate presentation in the English language of the abstract theory of the law.(See S.&M.) "In it the theory of the 'original contract' as the basis of sovereignty, which originated in France, was first made known in England, where it became a major issue in the political struggles of the seventeenth century. The 'Ecclesiastical Politie' is in fact the first English work of political theory." (PMM)

HOWARD, [Gorges] E[dmond] [1715-1786]. A Treatise of the Exchequer and Revenue of Ireland. In Two Volumes. Dublin: Printed by J.A. Husband, For E. Lynch, 1776. 4to. 2 Vols. in 1. pp. 1pl, [4]list of subscribers, lxiii, 323; 2pl, 436, [1]errata. complete with half-titles.index. nineteenth century half calf. several private lib.stps., some dampstaining to outer margin of some leaves, occasional hint of foxing, but a very good large-paper copy. First Edition. 400.00

Kress 7217. Goldsmith 11472. Marvin p.400.
As a solicitor in the exchequer, Howard acquired a vast & detailed knowledge of legal procedure & the complicated systems of exchequer, revenue & forfeiture departments,& rendered many valuable services to the government. This is one of his most important professional works.

5 HUGHES, William. The Commentaries Upon Original Writs.Where most of the Cases in Bracton, Book of Entries, the Year of Term-Books, from King Edward the second to these Times.With the Plaints, Counts, Pleadings, Issues, Demurrers in matters of Law; the Debates, Opinions, Rules of Court, and Resolutions of the Judges therein: Are reduced to the Original Writs, under severall Head or Sections, for the better understanding of the Cases and Poynts of Law Collected, abridged, and taken out of the Books themselves. The First Part. [All Published]. London: Printed by Tho. Roycroft, for Henry Twyford, and John Place, 1655. 4to. pp. 8pl, (incl. blank), 272, 8index. woodcut headpiece & initial. contemporary calf, rebacked. armorial bookplate of Charles F. Crosbie Wood. binding rubbed, corners worn, some marginal dampstaining, mainly to last signatures, lacking paste-downs, else very good. First Edition. 250.00

S.&M.I.271.82. Marvin p.403. Wing H3322 (cites 6 copies - 1 in North America). The NUC locates 2 other copies in North America.
Basically a translation of the pleadings in Coke's Reports.

44 JUSTINIAN, D. Justiniani: Institutionum Libri Quatuor. The Four Books Of Justinian's Institutions, Translated into English, With Notes, By George Harris. London: Printed for C. Bathurst & E. Withers, 1756. 8vo. pp. xv, 73, 121, 100, 92, 11, [4]index. contemporary calf, morocco spine label, gilt rules & lettering to spine. binding rubbed, fr. joint cracked, except for very light foxing to several leaves, internally a very nice clean crisp copy. With armorial bookplate of Earl of Moray. First Edition of Harris' translation. SOLD

"Justinian I (483-565) was responsible for the code of Roman law known as the Corpus juris civilis which is the basis of the form, as well as of much of the content, of modern law. It consisted of the Codex, the essence of the confused mass of statute law; the Pandects, a similar abridgement of juristic opinions; and the Novallae, new ordinances made since the Codex...The clarity which they achieved gave the Codex its permanent value." (PMM 137[of the 1st Ed.])

45 KNAPP, Andrew and William Baldwin. The Newgate Calendar; Comprising Interesting Memoirs of the Most Notorious Characters Who Have Been Convicted of Outrages On the Laws of England Since the Commencement of the Eighteenth Century; With Occasional Anecdotes and Observations, Speeches, Confessions, and Last Exclamations of Sufferers. 4 Volumes in 3. London: J. Robins and Co., 1824-28. 8vo. pp. iv, 514, [2]index; 1pl, 500, [2]index; 1pl, 499, [3]index; 1pl, 404, [2]index. text in double columns. numerous plates & cuts in the text. original blind & gilt stamped cloth. backstrips faded & frayed, hint of foxing, mostly to endpapers, else internally fine. 300.00

46 KYD, Stewart [d1811]. A Treatise On The Law Of Awards. The Second Edition, Revised And Corrected; With very considerable Additions from Printed and Manuscript Cases: And An Appendix, Containing a Variety of useful Precedents. London: Printed for J. Johnson, G.G. & J. Robinson, & J. Butterworth; And B.C. Collins, 1799. 8vo. pp. 2pl, [vii]-xvii, 583, [1]errata. index. contemporary calf. lacking half title? bk. joint cracked, fr. joint starting to crack, bk.bd. sl. rubbed, faint dampstain visible at extreme outer edge of outer leaves, else a fine clean copy. Second and best edition. 150.00

S.&M.I.545.3. Marvin p.443.

Kyd's noted legal career included a high treason charge, along with Thomas Hardy & John Horne Tooke in 1794. After the acquittal of Hardy & Tooke, Kyd was discharged. Kyd also conducted a brilliant defence of Thomas Williams, a publisher of Paine's 'Age of Reason', on blasphemy charges.

47 LEICESTER [LEYCESTER], Peter [1614-78]. Two Books: The First being Styled A Reply to Sir Thomas Manwaring's Book Entituled An Answer to Sir Peter Leicester's Addenda. The Other Styled, Sir Thomas Manwaring's Law Cases Mistaken. [cLondon]. 1674. sm. 8vo. pp. 3pl, 96, 3pl, 31. modern morocco. title slightly soiled & chipped at corners, else very good. First Edition. 200.00

Oddly, not in Wing, although the BM has it. Also not in NUC. Lowndes V 1357 calls for 2p. dedication & 2p. of errata in second part, while our copy has a 3p. dedication (on 2 leaves) & no errata.

Leycester engaged in a fairly lengthy dispute with Sir Thomas Mainwaring over the question of whether a common ancestor Amicia, wife of Ralph Mainwaring, was the lawful daughter of Earl Hugh Cyrveliok. The judges itinerant & the College of Arms, under the lead of Sir William Dugdale, declared against Leycester & in favour of Amicia's legitimacy.

THE LIVES of All The Lords Chancellors, Lords Keepers, And Lords Commissioners, Of the Great Seal of England; From William the Conqueror, to the Present Time: But more at large of those Two Great Opposites, Edward, Earl of Clarendon, and Bulestrode Lord Whitlock. With A Parallel of their Actions. To Which is added, An Appendix of many Rare and Valuable Speeches, Letters, &c., referring to the Said Lives. In Two Volumes. By an Impartial Hand. The Second Edition, with Additions. London: Printed and sold By R. Bonwicke, W. Freeman..., 1712. 8vo. pp. 1pl, [22], 216, [7]index, [1]ad, 336; [1]ad, 1pl, 520. contemporary panelled calf. Vol. I rebacked, with new spine label, joints of Vol.II cracked, bindings rather worn, some foxing, else internally very good. 175.00

S.&M.I.591.8. Marvin p.470. Abbot 125.

Although the greater portion of the work is devoted to the Earl of Clarendon & Bulestrode Lord Whitlock, the first section includes sketches of Sir Francis Bacon, Thomas Beckett, Sir John Fortescu, &c.

LORIMER, James. The Institutes of Law: A Treatise of the Principles of Jurisprudence As Determined By Nature. Second Edition, Revised and Enlarged. Edinburgh & London: William Blackwood and Sons, 1880. 8vo. pp. xx, 572. complete with half-tile. index. original cloth. backstrip soiled & frayed, upper corner of 2 leaves of preface & contents wanting (no loss), else very good. SOLD

S.&M.II.219.

The Scottish jurist was the sole proponent in Great Britain at the time, of the concept of the law of nature. Opposed to democracy, he was a defender of natural inequalities.

MacLAURIN, [John, later Lord Dreghorn] [1734-1796]. Arguments and Decisions, in Remarkable Cases, Before the High Court of Justiciary, and other Supreme Courts, in Scotland. Collected by...Edinburgh: Printed for J. Bell and E. & C. Dilly, London, 1774. 4to. pp. xvi, [1]errata, [2]addenda [insert], [xvii]-xl, 776, [6]index, [2]ads. contemporary sprinkled calf. extremities worn, joints cracked, internally very good. With the armorial bookplate of Plummer of Middlestead. First Edition. 150.00

S.&M.V.76. Marvin p.486.

A most interesting collection of cases of murder, madness, witchcraft, incest, and treason, with discussion of the effect of drunkenness of liability, the extent of Parliamentary privilege in regard to arrest & prosecution, &c. & an introductory essay on criminal cases.

51 NISBET, John, [Lord Dirleton] [1609?-1687]. Some Doubts & Questions, In the Law; Especially of Scotland. As Also, Some Decisions of the Lords of Council and Session: Collected & Obser'd by...To which is Added, An Index, For finding the Principal Matters in the said Decisions. Edinburgh: Printed by George Mosman, 1698. folio. pp. 1pl, [10], 228, 226, [17]index. [Second part with separate title-page, variant title]. engraved frontis. portrait. contemporary calf, sometime rebacked. binding rubbed, covers off, internally very good. From the library of T.C. Aylwin and the Court of Arches. First Edition. 350.00

Wing N1170. S.&M.V.31. Marvin p.539. Aldis 3767.

Nisbet was lord advocate during the covenanting persecution; although a learned man, he was noted for his unscrupulous and expedient methods.

52 [OSBORNE, Thomas, first] Earl of Danby, [Marquis of Carmarthen], Duke of Leeds [1631-1712]. Copies & Extracts Of Some Letters Written to and from the Earl of Danby (now Duke of Leeds) In The Years 1676, 1677, and 1678. With particular Remarks Upon some of them. Published by his Grace's Direction. London: Printed for John Nicholson..., 1710. 8vo. pp. 1pl, v-xiii, [2], 364, [4]ads. lacking half-title or front blank. quarter calf. damp staining to outer leaves, else a very good copy. First Edition. 75.00

In 1678, Danby, the lord treasurer, was impeached on the charges of French intrigue and involvements in the Popish plot. In a final effort to clear himself, Danby published the incriminating letters in an altered form.

53 OVERALL, Bishop [John] [1560-1619]. Bishop Overall's Convocation Book, MDCVI. Concerning the Government of God's Catholick Church, And The Kingdoms of the Whole World. London: Printed for Walter Kettilby, 1690. 4to. pp. 4pl, 338. complete with license leaf & final blank. 2 engraved portraits. contemporary calf, bit rubbed, else fine. First Edition. 200.00

Wing O607. McAlpin IV, 393.

Bishop Overall was prolocutor of the lower house of the convocation of Canterbury which drew up these canons & constitutions relating to civil government at the request of James I during the years 1603-1610. The work, however, was denied royal assent on the basis of one passage, which affirmed that new forms of government originating in successful rebellion have divine authority. It remained in manuscript until it was published by William Sancroft, Archbishop of Canterbury, a few days before his suspension.

54 PAGE, J. A Narrative Of Facts, Interesting, Mysterious, And Extraordinary, As Connected With A Short History Of Two Servants, Named James Harper Peart, And Ann Thomas: Detailing The Particulars Of a Robbery in Great Bedford Street; Their Apprehension On Suspicion: Extraordinary Escapes of Peart; Together With Letters And Other Documents, Containing a Combination Of Diabolical Events, And A System Of Imposition, Fraud, And Cunning, To Which The Human Mind Can Scarcely Give Credit. Bath: Printed and Published By Mary Meyler, 1833. 8vo. pp. 48. Disbound. 50.00

"TRIAL FOR LIBEL AGAINST BRITISH CROWN"

(PAINE, Thomas [1737-1809]). The Whole Proceedings on the Trial of An Information Exhibited ex Officio by the King's Attorney-General against Thomas Paine For a Libel upon the Revolution and Settlement of the Crown and Regal Government as by Law established; and also upon the Bill of Rights, the Legislature, Government, Laws, and Parliament of this Kingdom, and upon the King. Tried by a Special Jury in the Court of King's Bench, Guildhall, on Tuesday, the 18th of December, 1792. Before the Right Honourable Lord Kenyon. Taken in Short-Hand By Joseph Gurney. Second Edition. London: Sold by Martha Gurney, 1793. 8vo. pp. 196. late 19th century cloth. title slightly soiled, else very good. 250.00

cf Goldsmith 15854 (1st Edn.). cf Sabin 96918 (1st Edn.).

Account of the famous trial of Thomas Paine for libels against the British crown contained in the second part of his 'Rights of Man'. Despite an able defence by Lord Erskine, Paine was found guilty & outlawed. Erskine, who had refused to heed friendly advice & attacks in the government newspapers by accepting the case, was subsequently dismissed from his office of attorney-general to the Prince of Wales.

PEARSON, Anthony [1628?-1670). The Great Case of Tithes Truly Stated, Clearly Open'd And Fully Resolv'd...With an Appendix thereto. To which is added, A Defence of Some Other Principles held by the People Call'd Quakers, in which they differ from other Religious Denominations. The Arguments of these are supported by Scripture, and the concurring Sentiments of Ancient and Modern Authors. By J[osiah] M[artin]. London: Printed and Sold by the Assigns of J. Sowle, 1730. 8vo. pp. viii, 292, [8]ads. contemporary sprinkled panelled calf. corners worn, else VG. 125.00

Kress 3884. Goldsmith 6788. S.&M.I.193.37. Marvin p.560.

[PECKWELL, Henry] [1747-1787]. The Account Of An Appeal From a summary Conviction on the Statute 22 Car. II. C.I. To the Hon. C--rt of K.B. Wherein the Effects of Persecution and Bigotry are disclosed, and the Privileges of Christian Worshippers made known. To Which Is Added An Appendix ...By A Friend to Civil and Religious Liberty. London: Printed and sold by the Booksellers in Town and Country, [1786]. 8vo. pp. 72, 34, [1]. Disbound. 35.00

[PELHAM-HOLLES, Thomas] Duke of Newcastle. The Duke of Newcastle's Letter, By His Majesty's Order, To Monsieur Michell, the King of Prussia's Secretary of the Embassy, in Answer to the Memorial, and other Papers, deliver'd by Monsieur Michell to the Duke of Newcastle, on the 23rd of November, and 13th of December last. Published by Authority. London: Printed by Edward Owen, 1753. 4to. pp. 46. 2 folding folio tables. First Edition.

Goldsmith 8803. Casey I 160. Higgs 484.

Bound With:

A SHORT EPISTLE From A Country Gentleman To His Grace The Duke of Newcastle, On The Present Conjuncture Of Affairs; But Principally relative to the Subject of a Proper Constitutional Militia. London: Printed for Thomas Payne, 1756. 4to. pp. 1pl, 13. First Edition. Not in Goldsmith.

The two items bound in contemporary quarter morocco, marbled bds. front joint cracked, bds. sl. rubbed & stained at edges, sl. dampstaining to lower edge of first few leaves, else very good. the second item untrimmed. 175.00

Pelham-Holles' letter to the King of Prussia outlines the modus operandi for the settlement of international disputes. After the war of the Austrian Succession, there were numerous unsettled claims for damages between England and Prussia. Continued post war Prussian violations of Maritime Law occasioned this letter outlining the principles of international law.

59 PERKINS (or PARKINS), John [d1545]. A Profitable Book... Treating of the Laws of England. Translated out of French into English for the benefit of young students and others. An.Dom. 1657. small 8vo. pp. 2pl, [27]index, 333. contemporary sheep. no endpapers. binding worn, head of backstrip wanting, some insignificant marginal worming, corners of some leaves curled, otherwise very good. 450.00

Wing P1544. S.&M.I.485.56. See Winfield p.330 & Marvin p.563.

Perkins' popular textbook for law students first appeared in law French in 1528 (Perutilis tractatus). An attempt to update Littleton's 'Tenures', it enjoyed an enormous success for nearly three centuries, and is still regarded as an authority.

60 PETYT, William [1641?-1707]. The Antient Right of the Commons of England Asserted; Or, A Discourse Proving by Records and the best Historians, that the Commons of England were ever an Essential part of Parliament. London: Printed for F. Smith, T. Bassett, J. Wright, R. Chiswell, and S. Heyrick, 1680. 8vo. pp. 5pl, 75, 184. contemporary calf. extremities bit rubbed, outer margin of title tatty & lower corner of d1 torn away (no loss of text), else very good. First Edition. 300.00

Wing P1945. S.&M.148.18.

Petyt's refutation of the notion that the Commons of England was established as an essential part of Parliament only in 1649 aroused considerable controversy & elicited a number of replies, incl. 'Jus Anglorum ab antiquo' by William Atwood & 'A Full and Clear Answer' by Robert Brady,&c.

"STRUGGLE FOR RELIGIOUS FREEDOM"

61 PRIESTLEY, Joseph et Al. An Interesting Appendix To Sir William Blackstone's Commentaries on the Laws of England. Containing, I. Priestley's Remarks on some Paragraphs in the Fourth Volume of Blackstone's Commentaries, relating to the Dissenters. II. Blackstone's Reply to Priestley's Remarks. III. Priestley's Answer to Blackstone's Reply. IV. The Case of the late Election of the County of Middlesex considered on the Principles of the constitution and the Authorities of Law. V. Furneaux's Letters to the Hon. Mr. Justice Blackstone concerning his Exposition of the Act of Toleration, and some Positions relative to Religious Liberty, in his celebrated Commentaries on the Laws of England. VI. Authentic Copies of the Argument of the late Hon. Mr. Justice Foster in the Court of Judges Delegates, and of the Speech of the Right Hon. Lord Mansfield in the House of Lords, in the Cause between the City of London and the Dissenters. [Separate Titles]. Philadelphia: Printed for the Subscribers, By Robert Bell, 1773. 8vo. pp. 2pl, iv, [5]-119, xii, 155, [1]ad. late 19th century half calf (labelled Vol. IV). occasional hint of browning. A remarkably fresh clean copy. 425.00

Short Title Evans 12684. cf Sabin 5697 (1772 edition). See Sabin 65513n. cf S.&M.I.29.11-13a. See Marvin p.326 & p.589. Marke pp.34-35.

Scarce American edition of two important English works on the struggle for religious freedom, written by Priestley & Furneaux in opposition to Blackstone's classification of nonconformity as a civil offence. In both works "The moral argument against enforcing religious truths by civil penalties is presented with remarkable power." (DNB)

"TREATISE ON CRIMINAL LAW"

PULTON, Ferdinando [1536-1618]. De Pace Regis Et Regni, viz. A Treatise declaring which be the great and generall Offences of the Realme, and the chiefe impediments of the peace of the King and the Kingdome, as Treasons, Homicides, and Felonies...Collected out of the Reports of the Common Lawes of this Realme, and of the Statutes in force, and out of the painfull workes of the Reverend Judges, Sir Anthonie Fitzharbert, Sir Robert Brooke, Sir William Stanford, Sir James Dyer, Sir Edward Coke, Knights, and other Learned Writers of our Lawes. London: Printed for the Companie of Stationers, An. Dom. 1610. folio. pp. 5pl, 243 [some leaves misnumbered], [33]index. Head & tail-pieces. ornamental initials. black letter. contemporary calf, sometime rebacked. extremities rubbed, internally very good. Second Edition. 500.00

S.&M.I.365.589. STC 204966. Davies & Keeler 1087. cf Marvin p. 595.

Pulton devoted his life to the study and compilation of statute law. "A more comprehensive and up-to-date book [than Staunford's Pleas of the Crown]...A comparison between ...[them] enables us to appreciate the effect of the additions to the criminal law made during the sixteenth century by the legislature, the common law courts, and the Star Chamber." (Holdsworth. Sources)

"FIRST ENGLISH LAW DICTIONARY"

[RASTELL, John] [d1536]. [Translated by William Rastell]. Les Termes de La Ley Or, Certain difficult and obscure Words and Terms of the Common Laws and Statutes of this Realm now in use expounded and explained. Newly corrected and enlarged. With an Addition of above one hundred Words. London: Printed by John Streater, James Fletcher..., 1671. small 8vo. pp. 2pl, [10]index, 613, [1]errata. modern quarter oasis morocco. title leaf laminated, neat repairs to following 2 leaves & last leaf, some slight marginal dampstaining to a few leaves, several annotations in old hand, lacking first & last blanks, otherwise very good. 450.00

Wing R291. S.&M.I.II.48. See Marvin p.599 &Winfield p.17.

The first English law dictionary, by John Rastell, barrister of the Middle Temple & law printer, was also intended as a guide to law French. Originally composed in French, it was first published in 1527 with Latin title. The French and English texts are printed in parallel columns, and the editor's preface is signed T.B. [Thomas Blount]. Rastell's last years were unhappily spent in prison, in consequence of his criticism of the practice of paying tithes, and perhaps also, because of the suspicion attaching to him as the friend and brother-in-law of Sir Thomas More.

64 ROSS, Walter. A Discourse Upon the Removing of Tenants, Published to Serve as a Specimen of the Lectures Intended to Be Delivered Upon the Practice of the Law of Scotland, By..., Writer to the Signet. [At bottom of title: The Class is to be opened upon the 18th of November next]. Edinburgh: Printed by Mandell and Wilson...and Sold by William Gibb, 1782. ivo. pp. 170, [1]errata. upper outer corner of A^2 torn away (no loss), else a fine uncut copy in original publisher's boards (slightly soiled). First & only Edition. Rare. 150.00

S.&M.V.99. Marvin p.620. Only 1 copy located in the NUC. Not in BM.

"DEFENCE OF REVOLUTION"

65 [RUTHERFORD, Samuel] [1600-1661]. Lex, Rex: The Law and the Prince. A Dispute for the just Prerogative of King and People. Containing the Reasons and Causes of the most necessary Defensive Wars of the Kingdom of Scotland, and of their Expedition for the ayd and help of their dear Brethren of England...London: Printed for Iohn Field, 1644. small 4to. pp. 2pl, [36], 467. later full red morocco, gilt back & edges. slight dampstaining to margins, some browning, edges of first 2 leaves bit tatty & soiled, else very good. with bookplate of Archibald MacDiarmid Campbell. First Edition. 750.00

New CBEL I p.2464. Wing R2386. Marvin p.624. cf S.&M.I. 117.52.

Rutherford, Scottish ecclesiastical and political theorist, vigourously defended presbyterianism and actively propagandized against the absolutist claims of the royalists. During the Commonwealth, he led the group of protesters who favoured Cromwell. 'Lex, Rex' was mainly written as a reply to John Maxwell's 'Sancto-sancto regum majestas'; in it he argues that the law is above the king, who is bound by oath to rule justly, and that sovereignty resides in the people, who have a natural right to depose an unjust ruler. In 1660, when Charles II was fully restored, the government took notice of the publication and ordered it to be publicly burned. Rutherford was summoned to appear for trial on a charge of high treason, but he died before the trial could be held.

66 SACHEVERELL, Henry [1674-1724]. The Communication of Sin: A Sermon Preach'd at the Assizes held at Derby, August 15th 1709. Publish'd at the Request of the Gentlemen of the Grand-Jury. London: Printed for Henry Clements..., 1709. First octavo edition. 8vo. pp. 16. disbound. 35.00

Rothschild 1778.

One of the controversial sermons which led to Sacheverell's 1709 impeachment for "high crimes & misdemeanours".

(SACHEVERELL, Henry). The Tryal Of Dr. Henry Sacheverell Before the House of Peers, For High Crimes and Misdemeanors; Upon An Impeachment By The Knights, Citizens and Burgesses in Parliament Assembled, in the Name of themselves, and of all the Commons of Great Britain: Begun in Westminster-Hall the 27th Day of February 1709-1710, and from thence continued by several adjournments until the 23rd day of March following. Published by Order of the House of Peers. London: Printed for Jacob Tonson, 1710. 8vo. pp. 456.

With:

The Bishop of Salisbury's [Gilbert Burnet] And The Bishop of Oxford's Speeches [William Talbot] In The House of Lords, On The First Article of the Impeachment of Dr. Henry Sacheverell; Also the Bishop of Lincoln's [William Wake] and Bishop of Norwich's [Charles Trimnell] Speeches At The Opening of the Second Article of the said Impeachment. London: Printed and Sold by John Morphew, 1710. 8vo. pp. 63.

Bound in contemporary calf. binding rubbed, pen notes to endpapers, internally very good. 150.00

Account of Sacheverell's trial for sedition and speeches supporting the legal validity of the four articles of impeachment.

[SADLER, John] [1615-1674]. Rights of the Kingdom: Or, Customs of our Ancestors. Touching The Duty, Power, Election, or Succession of our Kings and Parliaments, Our True Liberty, due Allegiance, three Estates, their Legislative Power, Original, Judicial, and Executive; With the Militia. Freely discussed through The British, Saxon, Norman Laws and Histories. With An occasional Discourse of Great Changes yet expected in the World. London: Printed for J. Kidgell, 1682. small 4to. pp. 4pl, 319[ie315]. several woodcut ornaments. contemporary calf newly rebacked. binding bit worn, no paste-downs, some browning to outer margins of leaves, front free-endpaper soiled & tatty, otherwise a very good copy. With armorial bookplate of Edward Whitaker Junior of the Middle Temple. Second Edition. 250.00

Wing S279. Marvin p.625 (incorrectly names 'Ralph' Sadler as the author). Grose p.478. S.&M.I.106.99. Locke Library Bib. 2525.

Sadler, master-in-ordinary in the courts of chancery, was highly esteemed by Oliver Cromwell, who offered him the office of chief justice of Munster in Ireland, a post which he declined.

This work, first published in 1649, is recommended by John Locke (Remains. 1720. p.238) as containing the ancient Constitution of the Government of England.

SAINT-GERMAIN, Christopher [1460?-1540]. Doctor and Student: Or Dialogues Between A Doctor of Divinity, and A Student in the Laws of England, Containing the Grounds of those Laws, together with Question and Cases concerning the Equity and Conscience thereof; also comparing the Civil, Canon, Common and Statute Laws, and shewing wherein they vary from one another. To which is now added an Account of the Author, and a General Table of the Principal Matters; never before printed. In the Savoy: Printed by Eliz. Nutt and R. Gosling...for R. Gosling, 1721. 12mo. pp. 1pl, [10], 366, [40]index & ad. contemporary calf. A fine copy, with armorial bookplate of Lord Charles Noel Somerset. 225.00

S.&M.I.25.35. See Winfield pp.321-234 & Marvin p.626.
"The 'Doctor and Student' is one of the most esteemed of ancient law books, and has been an authority for about three centuries, having been constantly cited, from the time of Chief Justice Brooke to the present time."(Marvin) A handbook for legal students, it was first published in Latin in 1523, and was not superceded until the appearance of Blackstone's 'Commentaries'. Saint-Germain attempted to reconcile common law with the law of nature and the dictates of ethics, thus forming the "basis and starting point of the English system of equity".(Holdsworth)

70 SAUNDERS, Sir Edmund [d1683]. The Reports of the Most Learned...Late Lord Chief Justice of the King's Bench, Of Several Pleadings and Cases In the Court of King's Bench, In the Time of the Reign of His Most Excellent Majesty King Charles The Second. With Three Tables...The Third Edition. With Notes and References To the Pleadings and Cases, By John Williams. In 2 Volumes. London: Printed by A. Strahan for T. Cadell & W. Davies..., 1799-1802. 8vo. pp. 4pl,[364], [52]index; xii, 423, [82]index, [2]errata. contemporary calf, rubbed, front cover of Vol. II detached, spinal extremities worn, otherwise very good. 150.00

S.&M.I.308.112. See Marvin pp.629-630.
Saunders was "abundantly versed in the mysteries and technicalities of law. His Reports, printed after his death, extend from 1666 to 1672, and are esteemed for their simplicity and precision. They are composed in so dramatic a form that Lord Mansfield called him the Terence of Reporters."(Foss) According to Marvin, the Reports still remain the "Bible of the Law of Special Pleading."

71 SELDEN, John [1584-1654]. Table Talk: Being the Discourses of John Selden, Esq; Or His Sense of various Matters of Weight and high Consequence; Relating especially to Reason and State. Second Edition. London: Printed for Jacob Tonson ...and Awnsham and John Churchill..., 1696. 8vo. pp. 4pl, 192. contemporary panelled mottled calf. joints rubbed, else a fine copy. 350.00

Wing S2438.
Perhaps Selden's most famous work, compiled by his secretary Richard Milward, it was not first printed until 1689, when the revolution had given freedom to the press. Although its authenticity was at one point disputed, "the work may safely be accepted as the most vivid picture extant of the habits of thought and the modes of expression of the great Erastian lawyer. The conversations cover a great range of subjects relative to human life and history..."(DNB)

72 SELDEN, John. Titles of Honor. The Second Edition. London: Printed by William Stansby for Richard Whittakers, 1631. folio. pp. 1pl, [34], 941, [1]errata. title in red & black. numerous engravings (6 of them 3/4 page in size) & woodcut ornaments. old sprinkled calf bit rubbed, head of backstrip loose, small pieces wanting from lower corner of $3A^2$ & $4D^1$ (no loss), else a fine copy. 400.00

STC 22178. S.&M.I.208.50. Winfield p.320.
This is the second greatly enlarged edition of the first of Selden's great historical works treating of titles of nobility & knighthood, honorary attributes & the laws of precedence.

SELDEN, John. Titles of Honor. The Third Edition carefully Corrected. With Additions and Amendments by the Author. London: Printed by E. Tyler, and R. Holt, for Thomas Bassett, 1672. folio. pp. 1pl, [32], 756. engraved frontis. port. several text engravings & numerous woodcut text illus. ornaments & initials. contemporary panelled calf, neatly rebacked with original gilt backstrip laid down. extremities bit rubbed, dampstain to inner margin of first few signatures, else a very good handsome copy. 400.00

Wing S2440. S.&M.I.208.50. Winfield p.320.
The third & best edition, corrected & enlarged, of the first of Selden's great historical works treating of titles of nobility & knighthood, honorary attributes & the laws of precedence. A long eulogy in verse by Ben Johnson prefaces the work.

"CONCISE ACCOUNT OF PREVAILING ENGLISH LAW"

(SELDEN, John). FLETA. Fleta Seu Commentarius Juris Anglicani sic nuncupatus, sub Edwardo Rege primo seu circa annos abhinc CCCXL. ab Anonymo conscriptus, atque e Codice veteri, autore ipso aliquantulum recentiori, nunc primum typis editus. Accedit Tractatulus vetus de Agendi Excipiendique Formulis Gallicanus, Fet Assavoir dictus. Subjungitur etiam Joannis Seldeni ad Fletam Dissertatio Historica. Londini: Typis M.F. Prostant apud Guilielum Lee, Mathaeum Walbancke, & Danielem Pakeman, 1647. 4to. pp. 4pl, 533, [3] errata. title in red & black. several woodcut ornaments. copper engraving in text. contemporary calf, sometime rebacked, some worming in lower margin touching text up to signature L; another in inner margin touches some text from 3M through $3P^4$, else a very good copy. The title leaf appears to be a cancel. 600.00

Wing F1290. Marvin p.314. Winfield pp.262-63. See Marke p.36 (listing a later edition). S.&M.I.53.20.
The 'Fleta',an ancient Latin text-book of English law based on Bracton, was evidently the work of a corrupt judge, written during his confinement in the Fleet Prison (whence its name) around the year 1290, during the reign of Edward I. The work is a concise account of prevailing English law: the practice of the Courts, the forms of writs, & the explanation of law terms. Although it is basically an updated abridgement of Bracton, it does contain some information not contained in Bracton, for example, an account of manorial organization. "It seems to have been a failure, though Coke enumerates it among his legal authorities and says that it was well written by a learned lawyer."(Winfield)
It was John Selden who brought the treatise to public attention & who was instrumental in procuring its publication. He edited it from the unique manuscript in the Cottonian

library & added a learned prefatory dissertation, dealing with the influence of Roman law on English jurisprudence, and discussing the place of civil law in the courts martial and the courts of the admiralty. "Such a work appears an ample justification of the founders (in 1887) of the Selden Society for the selection of Selden as their eponymous hero." (DNB)
Also included is another anonymous essay 'Fet Assavoir' written at about the same time as the 'Fleta', & dealing with the practice of the Courts.

75 SHARP, Granville [1735-1813]. A Declaration of the People's Natural Right to Share in the Legislature; Which is the Fundamental Principle of the British Constitution of State. The Second Edition. London: Printed for B. White, 1775. 8vo. pp. 2pl, xl, 279, [4]ads. complete with half-title. index. uncut in original publisher's bds. bds. bit rubbed, backstrip wanting, stitching split, internally fine. 250.00

Sabin 79817. Howes S-331. Goldsmith 11368. Higgs 6484. S.&M.I.148.24.
Philanthropist and anti-slavery worker, Sharp's "sympathies were easily enlisted on behalf of the American colonies", and after the publication of the 'Declaration' he resigned his office in the ordnance department rather than assist in despatching war material to the colonies. Howes describes the work as having a "powerful influence in determining colonial resistance."

76 SHARP, Granville. A Tract on Duelling: Wherein The Opinions of some of the most celebrated Writers on Crown Law Are Examined and Corrected Either by the Authority of the same Writers, declared in contradictory Sentiments on the same Subject collated from other Parts of their Works, Or, by the solemn Decision of more ancient Writers of (at least) equal Authority; in order to ascertain the due Distinction between Manslaughter and Murder. Second Edition with Additions. London: Printed by B. White and Son and C. Dilly, 1790. 8vo. pp. xix, 75.

S.&M.I.45.15 (calling for pp.102; the collation in NUC entry agrees with our copy). Marvin p.639.

Bound with:

SHARP, Granville. A Declaration of the People's Natural Right to Share in the Legislature...Second Edition. London: Printed for B. White, 1775. 8vo. pp. 1pl, xl, 279, [4].lacking the half-title. index.

Sabin 79817. Howes S-331. Goldsmith 11368. Higgs 6484. S.&M.I.148.24.

The two items bound in full calf, rebacked, with original backstrip laid down. extremities rubbed, else fine. 400.00

In his interesting and learned tract on duelling, Sharp cites cases & decisions of Lord Bacon, Henry de Bracton, Sir William Blackstone, Sir Edward Coke, Sir Matthew Hale, John Selden, &c.

77 SIDNEY, Algernon [1621-1683]. Discourses Concerning Government By Algernon Sydney With His Letters Trial Apology and Some Memoirs of His Life. London: Printed for A. Millar,

1763. 4to. pp. 2pl, [1], 46, [3leaves], [3]-497, 198. engraved frontis. port. modern half mottled calf. some offsetting to outer signatures, occasional hint of foxing, else very good. Fifth & Best Edition, First Thus. 200.00

S.&M.I.107.101.
Sidney's 'Discourses Concerning Government', written, as was Locke's treatise, in answer to Robert Filmer's 'Patriarcha' (1680), laid the theoretical foundation for English speaking republicanism. Immediately after the discovery of the Rye House Plot, Sidney was arrested & tried for conspiracy against the king, convicted & beheaded. One of the charges against him was that he had written a book (the 'Discourses', not first published until 1698) proving kingship unlawful. This fifth edition is substantially enlarged, including an account of the trial, correspondence, memoirs, &c.

SMITH, Thomas [1513-1577]. The Commonwealth of England, And the Maner of Governement thereof. Compiled by the Honourable Sir Thomas Smith, Knight, Doctor of both Lawes, and one of the principall Secretaries unto two most worthy Princes, King Edward, and Queene Elizabeth. With new Additions of the chiefe Courts in England, And the Offices thereof by the Said Author. Also a Table added thereto, of all the principall matters contained in this Treatise. New Corrected and Amended. London: Printed by William Stansby for John Smethwicke, 1621. small 4to. pp. 4pl, 134. title vignette. several woodcut ornaments & initials. modern half hard-grained leather. several marginal annotations, else fine. 300.00

STC 22864. S.&M.I.107.105. New CBEL I, p.2211.
Written during his first embassy in France, "it is the most important description of the constitution and government of England written in the Tudor Age."(DNB) It was originally published in 1583 under the title "De Republica Anglorum; the Maner of Government or Policie of the Realm of England" and passed through 11 editions in English in little over a century.

SMITH, William. A Treatise On The Duties And Office Of A Receiver, Under The High Court Of Chancery In Ireland, Embracing The Present Practice Of The Court As Connected Therewith, From The Order Of Appointment To The Final Discharge And Vacating The Recognizance; As Also, A Summary View Of Certain Portions Of The Law Of Landlord And Tenant, Including Practical Direction For Making And Disposing Of A Distress For Non-Payment Of Rent; With An Appendix, Containing A Variety Of Useful Precedents. Dublin: Printed For Richard Milliken, 1827. 8vo. pp. 1pl, ii, 187, xliii. contemporary half calf, marbled bds. bds. sl. rubbed, else a nice copy. 100.00

cf Marvin p.649 (listing later edition).

SPOONER, Lysander [1808-1887]. An Essay On The Trial By Jury. Boston: John P. Jewett And Company. Cleveland, Ohio: Jewett, Proctor & Worthington, 1852. 8vo. pp. 224. contemporary sheep. foxing to outer leaves, sl. dampstaining to margins of some leaves, joints cracked, extremities rubbed, paper browned, but a good sound copy. 75.00

Sabin 89608.

Spooner's legal career was characterized by repeated attempts to challenge the unconstitutionality of government action in certain spheres, such as mail service and slavery In this particular work Spooner turned his critical attention to English and American constitutional law pertaining to trial by jury. Spooner argued the selection of jurors was unconstitutional and in fact, a violation of English common law.

81 SPOT[T]ISWOODE, Robert [1596-1646]. Practicks of the Laws of Scotland, Observed and Collected by...of Pendland, President of the College of Justice, and Secretary of State to K. Charles the I. As Also Abstracts Taken out of the Ancient Records...and Propositions and Questions in Law... With Memoir of His Life and Trial...1646. Publish'd by John Spotiswoode..., the Author's Grand-son. Edinburgh: Printed by James Watson..., 1706. small folio. pp. 2pl, xli, [3] index, 372. old calf, sometime rebacked. binding rubbed, front cover detached, some minor worming to lower portion of first few signatures, with minimal effect to text, other wise very good. First Edition. From the library of T.C. Aylwin and the Court of Arches. 300.00

S.&M.V.108. Marvin p.657.

Spotiswoode was the son of the Archbishop of St. Andrews; in 1662 he was promoted to the Scots bench & in 1633 he became president of the court of session. He was later tried & executed by the Presbyterian covenanters. This is his only work, published posthumously by his grandson.

82 [SPRAT, Thomas] [1635-1713]. A True Account and Declaration of the Horrid Conspiracy against the Late King His Present Majesty And The Government: As It Was Order'd to be Published By His Late Majesty. The Second Edition. In The Savoy: Printed by Thomas Newcomb...Sold by Sam. Lowndes, 1685. folio. pp. 3pl, 167. several engraved vignettes. upper corner of 1st prelim wanting.

Wing S5067.

Bound with:

[SPRAT, Thomas]. Copies of the Informations and Original Papers Relating to the Proof of the Horrid Conspiracy against the Late King, His Present Majesty, And The Government: As they were Order'd to be Published By His Late Majesty. In The Savoy: Printed by Thomas Newcomb...sold by Sam Lowndes, 1685. folio. pp. 1pl, 141. folding copper-plate. Fore-edge of last leaf chipped, tear to plate. First Edition.

Wing S5029.

The two items bound in old calf. Binding worn, fr. joint cracked, else VG. 250.00

After much hesitation, Sprat published his account of the Rye House Plot. The work was undertaken as an expression of gratitude for his recent appointments as Bishop of Rochester and Dean of Westminster. Sprat's colleagues questioned his sources of information, Charles II's papers & council books.

"ENGLAND'S EARLIEST SCIENTIFIC CRIMINALIST"

STANFORD, Sir William [1509-88]. Les Plees del Coron, diuisees in plusors titles & comon lieux. Per queux home plus redemen & plenairement trouera quelque chose qu'il quira, touchaunt les dits Plees, composees par le tres reuerend Iude Monsieur Guilliaulme Staundforde Chiualer, derniement corrigee auecques vn table par faicte des choses notables contenues en ycelle, nouuelment reueu et corrigee. [London]: In aedibus Richardi Tottelli, 1574. 4to. ll. 2pl, [12]table, 193[ie 198]. woodcut title border & initials. Fourth Edition.

STC 23222. S.&M.I.365.68. Beale T.489. Winfield pp. 234-25. See Marke p.453 & Marvin pp. 662-63 (not listing this edition).

"Stanford's is the earliest professed Treatise upon the Criminal Law of England, and his mode of dividing and arranging the topics has been generally followed by succeeding writers in this department of the law. Lord Hale took 'Les Plees del Coron', as the foundation of his excellent works upon Criminal Law."(Marvin) The work was first published posthumously in 1557 and is divided into 3 books, dealing, respectively, with greater crimes; jurisdiction, appeals, &c.; & with different modes of trial, judgment and forfeiture. The work enjoyed a high reputation & has always been regarded as the ultimate authority for certain of the basic rules & aspects of the criminal law.

Bound with:

STANFORD, Sir William. An exposition of the Kinges Prerogatiue, collected out of the great abridgement of Iustice Fitzherbert, and other olde writers of the lawes of England, by the right worshipfull Sir William Staunford Knight, lately one of the Justices of the Queenes Maiesties Court of common pleas. Where vnto is annexed the Proces to the same Praerogatiue appertayning. London: Richard Tottel, 1577. 4to. ll. 1pl, 85. woodcut initials. Fourth Edition.

STC 23216. S.&M.I.119.79. Beale T.495. Winfield p.319. See Marvin p. 662 (not listing this edition).

This commentary on the statute 17 Edw. II was first published in 1567. An extremely erudite work, it is distinguished as being the earliest extant monograph on statutory interpretation.

The two works bound in old sprinkled panelled calf. binding bit rubbed, rebacked, else fine copies. Armorial bookplate of Algernon Capell, Second Earl of Essex, &c. on verso of title. manuscript notes of former owner (N.W. Mach) on front blank - with separate notes bound in, indicating that the volume also belonged to Henry Bickersteth, Baron Langdale & was sold at Sotheby's auction of 28 July 1851. 1,000.00

(STRAFFORD, Thomas Wentworth, first Earl of). KNOWLER, William [1699-1733]. The Earl of Strafforde's Letters And Dispatches, With An Essay towards his life By Sir George Radcliffe... 2 Vols. London: Printed for the Editor, by William Bowyer, 1739. First Edition. folio. pp. 5pl, 527, [4]index; 1pl, 439, [4]index. 2 engraved frontispieces. vignettes. contemporary calf. binding bit scuffed, neat repairs to spinal extremities of Vol. I, very faint damp-

stain to lower inner margin of some leaves of Vol. II, else internally fine. A very nice set. 250.00

Abbott 1340. Grose 83.

Main source of information on the statesman and reformer, the Earl of Strafford. Sacrificed to the intrigues of James I, Strafford was impeached and found guilty of high treason. The volumes contain his letters from 1611 to 1641, the year of his execution.

85 (STRAFFORD, Thomas Wentworth, first Earl of). The Tryal of Thomas Earl of Strafford, Lord Lieutenant of Ireland, Upon An Impeachment of High Treason By The Commons Then Assembled Parliament, In the Name of Themselves, and of All the Commons in England: Begun in Westminster-Hall the 22th of March 1640. And Continued before Judgment was Given until 10th of May 1641. Shewing the Form of Parliamentary Proceedings In an Impeachment of Treason. To Which is Added A Short Account of Some other Matters of Fact Transacted in Both Houses of Parliament, Precedent, Concomitant and Subsequent to the said Tryal: With some Special Arguments in Law Relating to a Bill of Attainder. Faithfully Collected, and Impartially Published, Without Observation or Reflection, By John Rushworth...London: Printed for John Wright... and Richard Chiswell..., 1680. folio. pp. 1pl, [8], [76], 101-252, 401-786, [1]ad. contemporary calf, sometime rebacked. binding worn, front cover off, internally very good. (labelled Rushworth Historical Collection Vol. IV). From the library of T.C. Aylwin. 165.00

Wing T2333. cf Marvin p.623. See S.&M.I.106.96.

86 STUART, Andrew [d1801]. Letters to the Right Honourable Lord Mansfield, From Andrew Stuart, Esq; London: Printed in the Month of January 1773. 4to. pp. 2pl, 39, 63, 47, 47. complete with half-title. contemporary tree calf. spinal extremities worn, joints cracked, else very good. With the armorial bookplate of the Right Honourable Earl of Moray. 100.00

An attack on Lord Mansfield for his conduct in the Douglas case [see item #25]; Mansfield favoured Douglas in his claims to the Douglas family estates, whereas Stuart conducted the case against the claimant. "In these epistles he assailed Mansfield for his want of impartiality with a force and eloquence that caused him at the time to be regarded as a worthy rival to Junius."(DNB)

"CORNERSTONE OF MEDICAL JURISPRUDENCE"

87 TAYLOR, Alfred S. [1806-1880]. Elements Of Medical Jurisprudence. Vol. I. [All Published]. London: Deacon, 1836. 8vo. pp. xix, 511. index. Original cloth backed bds. corners bumped, bds. spotted, faint staining to lower inner margins, else a very good uncut copy of the rare first edition. 300.00

S.&M.II.352. Garrison & Morton 1738.

Taylor was the first to lecture on medical jurisprudence in England. Within a short time, he became the acknowledged expert on the subject. The 'Elements', Taylor's first work formed the basis for the 'Manual' and 'Principles and Practice'. Taylor's 'Elements' is still "one of the best-

known English texts on the subject". (G&M)

[TOWNSHEND, Charles] [1725-1764]. A Defence of the Minority in the House of Commons on the Question Relating to General Warrants. London: Printed for J. Almon, 1764. 8vo. pp. 2pl, 38. complete with half-title. disbound. 100.00

Sabin 96403.

This pamphlet was issued just a few weeks after his famous speech against the legality of general warrants & the outlawry of John Wilkes. Townshend upholds that a general warrant for apprehending and seizing the authors, printers & publishers of seditious libel, together with their papers, is not warranted by law.

(TRIALS). ALL THE PROCEEDINGS In Relation to the Aylesbury-Men, Committed by the House of Commons; And The Report Of The Lords Journal, And Reports Of The Conferences, And Of The Free Conference. Together with what stands upon the Journal of the House of Commons, in the Reign of King James I in the Case between Sir Francis Goodwin and Sir John Fortescue. London: Printed for Edward Jones & Timothy Goodwin, 1704. folio. pp. 83. complete with half-title. disbound. some foxing throughout, else VG. 60.00

Grose 3033.

Controversial case of Ashby vs. White in which the House of Lords reversed the decision of the House of Commons & found the constables of Aylesbury guilty of election irregularities.

(TRIALS). (BYRON, William, fifth lord). The Trial Of William Lord Byron, Baron Byron of Rochdale, For The Murder of William Chaworth, Esq; Before the Right Honourable The House of Peers, In Westminster-Hall, in Full Parliament. On Tuesday the 16th, and Wednesday the 17th of April, 1765: On the last of which Days the said William Lord Byron was Acquitted of Murder, but found Guilty of Manslaughter. Published by Order of the House of Peers. London: Printed for Samuel Billingsley, in Chancery-Lane, 1765. Folio. pp. 2pl, 47. Disbound. hint of foxing, else VG. 50.00

Lord Byron, the poet's ancestor, was found guilty of the murder of his cousin Chaworth. No punishment was affixed, owing to Byron's privilege as a peer.

(TRIALS). (DUNDAS, Henry, first Viscount Melville). The Trial by Impeachment, of Henry Lord Viscount Melville, For High Crimes and Misdemeanours, Before the House of Peers, In Westminster Hall, Between the 29th of April and the 17 th of May 1806...The Impartial Edition. Edinburgh: Printed for & by J. Robertson, 1806. 8vo. pp. 1pl, 304, [9]appendix. engraved frontis. port. later cloth. corners frayed, else very good. 60.00

Lord Melville, treasurer & later admiral of the Navy, was charged with the embezzlement of large sums of public money from the Treasury. He was acquitted by a narrow margin.

(TRIALS) (FRASER, Simon, twelfth Baron Lovat). The Whole Proceedings In The House of Peers, Upon The Impeachment Exhibited By The Knights, Citizens, and Burgesses, in Parliament Assembled, in the Names of Themselves, and of all the Commons of Great Britain; **Against Simon Lord Lovat**, For High Treason: The Proceeding in Westminster-Hall being Begun on Monday the 9th day of March...On the last of which Days Judgment of High Treason was given against him. Published by Order of the House of Peers. London: Printed for Samuel Billingsley..., 1747. folio. pp. 2pl, 188. Disbound. some browning, else VG. First Edition. 100.00

Lovat's numerous intrigues included: involvement with the Scots plot of 1704, a full pardon in 1716, professed loyalty in 1745 while committing his son & clan to the Jacobite forces. In 1747 Lovat was charged of high treason. William Hogarth sketched Lovat before his trial. The subsequent engraving of Lovat proved immensely popular, reportedly the presses ran day & night. Lovat was found guilty & beheaded at the Tower.

93 (TRIALS) (KILMARNOCK, William Boyd, fourth Earl of). The Whole Proceedings In The House of Peers, Upon The Indictments Against William Earl of Kilmarnock, George Earl of Cromertie, and Arthur Lord Balmerino; For High Treason In Levying War against His Majesty: The Proceeding in Westminster Hall being begun on Monday the 28th day of July... 1746: On the last of which Days Judgment of High Treason was given against them. Published by Order of the House of Peers. London: Printed for Samuel Billingsley..., 1746. folio. pp. 2pl, 39. Disbound. hint of foxing, else a very good copy.First Edition. 100.00

Kilmarnock was involved in the 1745 Scottish rebellion. He was a general in the rebel army & fought at Falkirk & Culloden where he was taken prisoner. Kilmarnock's subsequent trial for high treason was characterized by a lack of judicial impartiality. He was found guilty & executed.

94 (TRIALS). NIGHTINGALE, J[oseph] (Ed.). Report of the Proceedings Before the House of Lords, On A Bill of Pains and Penalties Against Her Majesty, Caroline Amelia Elizabeth, Queen of Great Britain and Consort of King George the Fourth. Collated With the Journals of the House of Lords. 3 Volumes. [Vol.I: ...The Charges; Vol. II:...The Defence, Part I; Vol. III: ...The Defence Part II]. London: J. Robins & Co., 1821. 8vo. pp. 2pl, 611, [1]ads; 1pl, 604; 1pl, 758. 23 engraved plates (including 3 engraved titles & numerous portraits). disbound. first portrait mounted, occasional dampmarks & brown stains, else very good. 100.00

A bill promoted in the House of Lords to deprive Queen Caroline of her rights & privileges as Queen Consort & to dissolve the marriage between herself & King George IV, was abandoned in view of popular opinion. Brougham's defence of the Queen considerably enlarged his reputation.

95 (TRIALS). (PATCH, Richard). **The Trial of Richard Patch**, For the Wilful Murder of Mr. Isaac Blight, on the 23rd of Sept. 1805, At Rotherhithe, in the County of Surry; Before the Right Hon. Sir A. MacDonald, Knt. Lord Chief Baron of His Majesty's Court of Exchequer; On Saturday, April 5, 1806. Taken in Short Hand by Blanchard and Ramsey. With Portraits of Richard Patch and Esther Kitchener, Taken in Court, expressly for the Publication, by an eminent Artist; Together with a View of the House, and a Ground Plan of the Premises, &c. &c. London: Printed by the Express Appointment of the Sheriff, for Edward Jeffery...Sold by John Walker, and H.D. Symonds..., 1806. 8vo. pp. xvi, 194, [2]. complete with half-title. 3 portraits, 1 folding plate & 1 facsimile. contemporary half calf. binding bit rubbed, part of backstrip wanting, hint of foxing to plates & neighbouring leaves, else very good. First Edition. 100.00

(TRIALS). THE PROCEEDINGS OF The House Of Lords, Concerning The Scottish Conspiracy, And The Papers Laid Before that House, By Her Majesties Command, Relating thereunto. London: Printed by Charles Bill...& the Executrix of Thomas Newcomb..., 1704. folio. pp. 67. disbound. 50.00

Proceedings of two trials dealing with Parliament's legal jurisdiction in the prosecution of political offences.

(TRIALS). A REPORT OF THE TRIAL On An Action For Damages, Brought By The Reverend Charles Massey Against The Most Noble The Marquis of Headfort, For Criminal Conversation With Plaintiff's Wife. Damages laid at 40,000 [pounds]. Taken in Short-Hand by an eminent Barrister. Dublin: M.N. Mahon, 1804. 8vo. pp. viii, 95. complete with half-title. Stitched as issued. some staining to outer leaves, small piece missing from upper margin of D3 & D^4 (no loss of text). Second Edition. 40.00

(TRIALS). (STATE). A Complete Collection of State-Trials, and Proceedings For High Treason, and other Crimes and Misdemeanours; The Fourth Edition; Commencing With The Eleventh Year of the Reign of King Richard II. And Ending With the Sixteenth Year of the Reign of King George III. With Two Alphabetical Tables To The Whole. To Which is Prefixed, A New Preface, By Francis Hargrave, Esquire. 11 Vols. in 6. London: Printed for T. Wright, And Sold by G. Kearsley, 1776-1781. (Title page varies slightly, text in double columns except for preface). folio. contemporary calf, gilt stamping. bindings worn, all but 2 covers off, hint of foxing to outer leaves, else a very good set. 350.00

S.&M.I.369.8. Marvin p.660-661. Marke p.1030.

(TRIALS). (STUART, James). The Trial Of James Stuart, Esq. Younger of Dunearn, Before The High Court Of Justiciary, At Edinburgh, On Monday, June 10, 1822. With An Appendix Of Documents. Second Edition. Edinburgh: Archibald Constable & co. London: Hurst, Robinson..., 1822. 8vo. pp. 2pl, 186, 1 leaf, 16(Appendix). disbound. small piece missing from fore-edge margin of contents leaf, not affecting text, last few leaves bit browned & sl. chipped at edges. 25.00

Goldsmith 23644.

Proceedings of famous Scottish murder trial. Stuart, a Whig politician, killed Sir Alexander Boswell in a duel. Stuart had taken offence to an article Boswell had written for a Tory newspaper.

(TRIALS). THE TRIAL OF Lawrence Earl Ferrers, For The Murder of John Johnson, Before the Right Honourable The House of Peers, In Westminster-Hall, in Full Parliament, On Wednesday the 16th, Thursday the 17th, and Friday the 18th of April 1760: On the last of which Days, Judgment for Murder

was given against him. Published by Order of the House of Peers. London: Printed for Samuel Billingsley..., 1760. folio. pp. 2pl, 55. disbound. hint of foxing, some age browning, else VG. First Edition. 50.00

101 (TRIALS). (YORK, Frederick Augustus, Duke of). Stratford's Authentic Edition. Of the Investigation of the Charges Brought against His Royal Highness the Duke of York, By Gwyllym Lloyd Wardle, Edq. Member for Oakhampton. Containing the Whole of the Evidence. Printed from the Minutes of the House of Commons. With the Official Papers and The Debates At Large. 2 Vols. London: Printed for J. Stratford ..., 1809. 8vo. pp. 3pl, [5]-564; 1pl, 658. 16 engraved plates, incl. 2 frontis. portraits & 1 hand-coloured plate [12 plates after Rowlandson sketches]. contemporary calf. joints of Vol. I cracked, bds. of Vol.II detached, covers sl. rubbed, some plates sl. foxed, else a good set. 150.00

Account of the royal imbroglio in which Wardle exposed the Duke of York's indiscretion with the adventuress, Mary Anne Clarke. Trading on her relationship with the Duke of York, Mary Anne Clarke had promised officers' promotions after suitable payment for her recommendations. Although the Duke was acquitted of corrupt practices, the scandal forced him to resign his post as commander-in-chief of the army.

102 WALLACE, George [d1805?]. The Nature and Descent of Ancient Peerages, Connected With The State of Scotland, The Origin of Tenures, The Succession of Fiefs, And The Constitution of Parliament, in that Country: A Discourse Addressed to the Rt. Hon. William Earl of Mansfield, Lord Chief Justice of England. The Second Edition, With Additions and Corrections. Edinburgh: Printed for T. Cadell & C. Elliot, 1785. 8vo. pp. viii, [9]-520. index. contemporary calf bit rubbed, front joint cracking, internally fine & clean. 200.00

cfS.&M.I.459.113 (1st Edn.). Marvin p.716.

Principal work of the Scottish advocate & son of Robert Wallace, whose writings on the threatening prospects of over-population had considerable influence on Malthus. The work is chiefly concerned with the pivotal effects of 1587 on peerages & fiefs.

103 [WHELLIER, C.A.]. The Complete English Lawyer; Or, Every Man his own Lawyer: Containing A Summary Of The Constitution Of England: Its Law and Statutes...Also, The Criminal Law of England, Comprising Every Species Of Public Offences With Their Punishments. To Which Is Added An Appendix, Containing the most approved Forms of Agreements, Leases, Wills and Testaments...Also, A Supplement Containing The Excise Laws...The Eighth Edition. London: Printed by R. Macdonald...For A. Whellier, 1823. 8vo. pp. 688, 2pl, 17-148 [Supplement]. index. engraved frontis. portrait of Sir Charles Abbott, 5 engraved portraits of important legal figures. contemporary calf. bds. detached, calf worn, free endpapers missing, library lettering to spine & library markings on fr. pastedown, plates sl. foxed. 70.00

S.&M.II.377.

(THE WILKES CASE). A Collection of the Most Valuable Tracts Which Appeared During the Years 1763, 1764, and 1765, Upon the Subjects of General Warrants, Publication of Libels, Seizure of Papers, And Other Constitutional Points, Which arose out of the Case of Mr. Wilkes. [General Title, Vol.I]. London: Printed for J. Almon, 1766. 4 Volumes. 8vo. contemporary sprinkled calf. An excellent set. 1,000.00

One of the most important cases in the history of Anglo-American law, and particularly in the area of civil liberties, concerned with the legality of general warrants for apprehending & seizing the authors, printers & publishers of seditious libel together with their papers. This collection represents both sides of the controversy according to the preface by publisher Almon who was imprisoned & fined for supporting him. The 19 separate tracts included are:
1) [TOWNSHEND, Charles]. A Defence of the Minority in the House of Commons, On the Question Relating to General Warrants. The Fifth Edition. London: Printed for J. Almon, 1764. pp. 2pl, 38, [2]ads. complete with half-title.
2) [DUNNING, John, Lord Ashburton]. A Letter to the Public Advertiser. London: Printed for J. Almon, 1764. pp.51, [1]ad. [Also ascribed to Sir Francis].
3) [ALMON, John]. A Letter Concerning Libels, Warrants, The Seizure of Papers & Sureties for the Peace of Behaviour; With A View to some late Proceedings, And the Defence of Them by the Majority. With The Postscript and An Appendix. The Sixth Edition. London: Printed for J. Almon, 1766. pp. 1pl, [5]-132. lacking half-title?
4) SOMERS, John, Baron Somers. The Security of Englishmen's Lives: Or, The Trust, Power and Duty of Grand Juries of England Explained according to the Fundamentals of the English Government, and the Declaration of the same made in Parliament by many Statutes. First printed in the Year 1681. London: Printed for J. Almon, 1766. pp. 112.
5) THE TRIAL OF John Peter Zenger, of New-York, Printer: Who was charged with having printed and published a Libel against the Government; and acquitted. With a Narrative of His Case. To which is now added, being never printed before, The Trial of Mr. William Owen, Bookseller, near Temple-Bar, Who was also Charged with the Publication of a Libel against the Government; of which he was honourably acquitted by a Jury of Free-born Englishmen, Citizens of London. London: Printed for J. Almon, 1765. pp. 59,[1]ad.
6) [HARTLEY, David]. The Right of Appeal to Juries, in Causes of Excise, Asserted. The Second Edition. London: Printed for J. Almon, nd. pp. 28.
7) [ADAIR, James]. Thoughts On the Dismission of Officers, Civil or Military For Their Conduct in Parliament. London: Printed for J. Almon, 1765. pp. iv, [5]-39, 1ads.
8) [WALPOLE, Horatio, Earl of Orford]. A Counter-Address to the Public on the Late Dismission of a General Officer [General Conway]. The Fourth Edition. London: Printed for J. Almon, 1764. pp. 47, [1]ad.
9) A COLLECTION OF all the Remarkable and Personal Passages in the Briton, North Briton, and Auditor. Affecting the Dukes of Newcastle and Bedford, The Earls Temple, Powis, Bute, Halifax, Talbot and his Horse, The Lords Mansfield .....London: Printed in the Year 1766. pp. 1pl, 5-66. lacking half-title?

10) A PARALLEL: Drawn between the Administration In the Four last Years of Queen Anne, And the Four First of George the Third. By a Country Gentleman [pseud]. London: Printed for J. Almon, 1766. pp. 25, [2]ads. complete with half-title.
11) [GREVILLE, Richard, 1st Earl Temple]. The Principles of the Changes in 1765 Impartially Examined: And the Reasons of some Great Men for Refusing, and others Accepting, the Offers of the Court at that Time, Explained. In a Letter from a Son of Candor to the Public Advertiser [pseud]. The Fourth Edition, Corrected. London: Printed for J. Almon, 1766. pp. 1pl, [5]-89, [1]ad. lacking half-title?
12) [ALMON, John]. The History of the Minority; Dvring the Years 1762, 1763, and 1765. Exhibiting the Condvct, Principles, and Views, of That Party. The Fovrth Impression. London: Printed 1765 & Reprinted with some Additions 1766. pp. xii, [9]-332, [2]ads.
13) [LLOYD, Charles]. A True History of A Late Administration. London: Printed for J. Almon, 1766. pp. 22.
14) [COTES, Humphrey]. An Enqviry Into the Condvct of A Late Right Honovrable Commoner [William Pitt]. The Third Impression, Corrected. London: Printed for J. Almon, 1766. pp. 72. complete with half-title.
15) [LLOYD, Charles]. An Examination of the Principles and Boasted Disinterestedness of A Late Right Honourable Gentleman [William Pitt]. In a Letter from an Old Man of Business, to a Noble Lord. London: Printed for J. Almon, 1766. pp. 34, [2]ads.
16) SHORT CONSIDERATIONS Vpon Some Late Extraordinary Grants, And Other Particvlars of A Late Patriot's Condvct. London: Imprinted for J. Almon, 1766. pp. 1pl, 5-31, [3] ads. lacking half-title?
17) A FREE APPEAL To the People of Great Britain, On the Conduct of the Present Administration, Since the Thirtieth of July, 1766. Second Edition. London: Printed for J.Almon, 1767. pp. 45, [3]ads. complete with half-title.
18) [GRENVILLE, George]. A Speech, Against The Suspending and Dispensing Prerogative, &c. The Sixth Edition, with many Corrections and Additions. London: Printed for J.Almon, 1767. pp. 74.
19) [WILKES, John]. A Letter to His Grace the Dvke of Grafton, First Commissioner of His Majesty's Treasvry. The Seventh Edition. London: Printed for J. Almon, 1767. pp. 35, [2]ads. folding chart.

WINCH, Humphrey [1555?-1625]. Reports of That Reverend and Learned Judge...; Sometimes one of the Judges of the Court of Common Pleas. Containing many Choice Cases, and Excellent matters touching Declarations, Pleadings, Demurrers, Judgements, and Resolutions in points of Law, In the foure last years of the Raign of King James, faithfully Translated out of an exact french Copie, with two Alphabetical, and necessary Tables, the one of the names of the Cases, the others of the principal matters contained in this Book. London: Printed for W. Lee, D. Pakeman, and G. Bedell, 1657. small folio. pp. 4pl, 125, [7]index, [1]errata, several woodcut ornaments. modern buckram. few marginal annotations in old hand, else fine. First Edition. 300.00

S.&M.I.310.132. Wing W2964. Marvin p.741.
Winch was a judge of the Common Pleas, 1611-1625. His otherwise unblemished career is interrupted by his disgraceful condemnation & execution of nine women as witches on the scant testimony of a young boy who claimed to be charmed by them.

[WORMALL, J. and others]. The Prisoners' Defence Supported: Or An Answer To The Charges And Allegations Of George Markham, Vicar Of Carlton, In Yorkshire, Contained In His Book Entitled, "More Truth For The Seekers." By the Authors of the Defence. York: Printed for William Blancard..., [1797]. 8vo. pp. 1pl, 96. Disbound. age-browning, first two leaves detached. 75.00

Goldsmith 17079.
Testimony of members of the Society of Friends, imprisioned for their non-payment of Tithes.

"IMPORTANT SOURCE OF MEDIEVAL COMMON LAW"

[YEARBOOK] [LONGO QUINTO]. En cest Volume est conteinus Le Longe Report de Anno Quinto Edwardi Quarti, Ore Novelment imprimee & corrigee, Ovesque References al Abridgement de les Cases in Brooke addes in le Margent de chescun Case. London: Printed by the Assignes of John More Esquire, 1638. folio. pp. 5pl, 142 leaves. printed in black letter. modern quarter oasis morocco. title leaf mounted, edges of outer leaves tatty, perforated lib. stamp on title, age-browning to margins, else a very nice crisp copy. With the bookplate of the Biddle Law Library. 350.00

S.&M.I.312.15 & 318.16.
The Yearbooks are the most important source of medieval common law, providing first hand accounts of the legal doctrines established by the judges of the 14th and 15th centuries. The publication of Yearbooks flourished from 1481 to 1638 or 1640, after which publication ceased for 40 years.
The 'Longo Quinto' was published in 1552 and 1587, then re-published in 1638. This report of Edward IV's reign is considered to be one of the finest examples of law reporting contained in the various Yearbooks. "The Longo Quinto represents a more elaborate effort of reporting than had yet been seen. Often it seems to be more impersonal, and to give the gist of several reports rather than the actual account of the eye-witness. No doubt, too, the reporters became more skilful, more professional, as time went on; they allowed themselves fewer scattered notes, fewer personal details. The report of the case is the main thing, and the report grows fuller." (Holdsworth. A History II)

NDA

COTTON, Sir Robert Bruce [1571-1631]. Cottoni Posthuma: Divers Choice Pieces Of That Renowned Antiquary Sir Robert Cotton, Knight and Baronet, Preserved from the injury of Time, and Exposed to publick light, for the benefit of Posterity. By J.H. Esq. [James Howell]. London: Printed for Richard Lowndes..., 1672. 12mo. pp. 4pl, 351. Contemporary calf, rebacked. hinges cracked, calf rubbed, age-browning, else a very good copy. Second Edition. 300.00

Wing C6486. S.&M.I.129.22. cf Kress 820 (First Edition).

Catalogue #46.

Prior to the publication of 'Cottoni Posthuma', Cotton's works had been issued as separate parliamentary pamphlets during the English Civil War (only 2 works were printed during his lifetime). The work includes Cotton's most important tracts on English laws & essays by Sir Philip Sidney & Sir Francis Walsingham.

[PLOWDEN, Francis Peter] [1749-1829]. An Investigation Of The Native Rights Of British Subjects. London: Printed for the Author; And sold by R. Baldwin..., 1784. 8vo. pp. vii, [1]errata, 200. contemporary half calf, marbled bds. extremities rubbed, joints cracked, hint of foxing to outer leaves, else very good. 225.00

S.&M.I.155.14. Marvin p.576. Goldsmith 12788.
An important examination of English civil law attributed by Marvin and Goldsmith to Francis Plowden, the author of numerous works on English law. Halkett & Laing and Sweet & Maxwell attribute the work to John Davidson (Halkett & Laing give the date of the work as 1734).

[SANCROFT, William], Archbishop of Canterbury [1617-1693]. The Proceedings and Tryal in the Case of the Most Reverend Father in God William Lord Archbishop of Canterbury... London: Printed for Thomas Basset and Thomas Fox, 1689.pp. 3pl, 140. Engraved frontis. folio. contemporary pig skin. end papers wanting, some worming to margins, some staining to upper margin of most leaves,frontis loose, leather very worn. Book plate of Nicholas Buckeridge of Oxford. First Edition. 250.00

Wing S564.
An account of the proceedings of Sancroft's trial for seditious libel. Sancroft, as Archbishop of Canterbury, openly disputed the legislative powers of the King, James II, in ecclesiastical matters. Sancroft assisted in the publication of the first edition of his trial.

SEDGWICK, James [1775-1857]. Remarks, Critical And Miscellaneous, On The Commentaries Of Sir William Blackstone. London: Printed by M. Ritchie...For G.G. &J. Robinson..., 1800. 4to. pp. x, [2], 304. complete with half-title. uncut in original bds. extremities chipped, paper flaw in 2P4 causing small hole (no loss of text), some pencil annotations in margins, otherwise internally fine & crisp. A very attractive copy. First Edition. 300.00

S.&M.I.30.15. cf Marvin p.635 (2nd Edition).
Sedgwick's well-reasoned critique of Blackstone's 'Commentaries' is less well-known than those of his more famous contemporaries, Bentham & Priestley. Nevertheless Sedgwick's chapter by chapter critique of Vol. I of the 'Commentaries' is still remembered for its "spirit of great fairness & minute care".(DNB)

LAW &

CONSTITUTIONAL HISTORY

(1981)

D & E Lake Ltd.
Old & Rare Books

106 Berkeley Street
Toronto, Canada M5A 2W7
Telephone: (416) 863-9930
Cable Address: Lakebooks, Toronto

1 [ALMON, John] [1737-1805]. A Letter Concerning Libels, Warrants, The Seizure of Papers, And Sureties for the Peace or Behaviour; With A View to some late Proceedings, And The Defence of Them by the Majority. The Fourth Edition, Enlarged and Improved. London: Printed for J. Almon..., 1765. 8vo.pp. 112. complete with half-title. [WITH] [-----]. A Postcript To The Letter, On Libels, Warrants, &c. In Answer To A Postscript In The Defence of the Majority And Another Pamphlet, entitled, Considerations on the Legality of General Warrants. [cLondon]: Printed for J. Almon..., 1765. 12mo. pp. 7[ie9], [2]ads. First Edition. [WITH] [-----]. Additions To The Second Edition...& Additions To The Fourth Edition...8vo. pp. 16. disbound. except for some browning, a very good copy. $80

S.&M.I.245.3. cfGoldsmith 10144 & Higgs 3584 (112 pp.).

2 [ARNOLD, Richard] [d.1521?]. The Customs of London, Otherwise Called Arnold's Chronicle: Containing, Among Divers Other Matters, The Original Of The Celebrated Poem Of The Nut-Brown Maid. Reprinted From The First Edition, With The Additions Included In The Second. London: Printed For F.C. And J. Rivington..., 1811. 4to. pp. lii, 300. complete with half-title. later three-quarter polished sheep. a very fine copy. Third Edition. $200

cfS.&M.I.435.21.

Arnold's work, first published in 1502, is a medly of information on the history of London. Included is a list of mayors from 1189-1520, customs, charters, commercial regulations, & curiously, the 'Ballade of ye Nottebrowne Mayde'.

3 ATKYNS, Robert [1621-1709]. The Power, Jurisdiction and Priviledge of Parliament; And The Antiquity Of The House Of Commons Asserted. Occasion'd By an Information in the Kings Bench, by the Attorney General, against the Speaker of the House of Commons. As also a Discourse concerning the Ecclesiastical Jurisdiction In The Realm of England, Occasion'd by the Late Commission in Ecclesiastical Causes. London: Printed for Timothy Goodwin..., 1689. folio. pp. 1pl, 74. disbound. $80

Wing A4141.

Atkyns, Judge of the Court of Common Pleas and later Chief Baron of the Exchequer, was known for his dissident stands in a variety of legal judgments. "After Hale, there was no more learned lawyer of his time, and there was none more honest."(DNB)

4 AYLIFFE, John [1676-1732]. A New Pandect of Roman Civil Law, As Anciently established in that Empire; and now received and practised in most European Nations: With Many useful Observations thereon; shewing, Wherein that Law differs from the Municipal Laws of Great-Britain, from the Canon Law in general, and from that Part of it now in Use here with us in England...London: Printed for Tho. Osborne, 1734. folio. pp. 4pl, xlviii, [8], 608[ie648]. several woodcut ornaments. contemporary calf, sometime rebacked, binding somewhat worn, joints cracked, paper repairs to lower margin of 2 preliminary leaves, else internally fine. First Edition. $400

S.&M.I.177.4. Marvin 80-81.

Ayliffe's career and social position suffered much from his outspoken political views ("he was an ardent whig at a time when Oxford was the home of Jacobitism"), and his book on Oxford, in which he exposed the misappropriation of the funds of Clarendon Printing House led to his expulsion from the university, stripped of all privileges and degrees. His most important undertakings, however, were his two treatises on canon and civil law. The 'Pandect' was not published until two years after his death, and "though it was never finished, it remains to our own day the most elaborate treatise on modern Roman law written in English." (DNB)

BACQUET, Jean [d1597]. Les Oeuvres de Iean Bacquet, Advocat en la Chambre du Thresor. Des Droicts du Domaine de la Couronne de France. Reveues, Corrigees, et Augmentees de plusieurs Arrests & Decisions notables; & du Traicte des Rentes du mesme Autheur. Derniere Edition, Enrichie D'Un Traicte de la Iurisdiction de la Chambre du Thresor, & conseruation du Domaine du Roy. Divisee En Cinq Tomes. A Paris: Chez Iean Gesselin, 1621. folio. pp. 6pl, 291, [12]index; 4pl, 240, [16]index; 2pl, 432, [16]index; 425-486, [4]index, [2]blank; 6pl, 170, [2]index. general title in red & black. title vignettes & several woodcut ornaments & initials. old calf, worn, joints cracked, dampstaining to some leaves, lacking middle index leaf of last vol. (other index leaves tatty), still, a good copy. From the library of Thomas Cushing Aylwin (1806-71), lawyer, politician & high court justice of Lower Canada, with his signature on front free-endpaper.$400

Not in BM STC French Books (which lists only the editions of 1664 & 1688). The NUC locates only 1 copy, that in the New York Public Library.

The works of the French jurist, edited and augmented by his nephew, N. Belut, were first published in 1603. Included are chapters on the 'droit de francs-fiefs', 'droit d'amortissement', bastardy, disinheritance, &c. Vols. II, III, & V have separate varying title leaf; dispite irregular pagination & lack of title-leaf in Vol. IV, the signature collation is interrupted & the work appears to be complete.

BARRINGTON, Jonah [1760-1834]. Personal Sketches Of His Own Times. In Two Volumes. London: Henry Colburn..., 1827. 8vo. pp. xxvii, 476; xii, 480. engraved frontis. portrait. index. contemporary half calf, rebacked. corners rubbed, occasional foxing, otherwise a very nice set. First Edition. $175

Barrington, a judge in the Irish Court of Admiralty, provides a humorous look at the Irish legal profession in his 'Personal Sketches'. A third volume of this work was published in 1832.

CORNERSTONE OF CRIMINAL JURISPRUDENCE

[BECCARIA, Cesare Bonesana, Marchesi di] [1735-93]. An Essay On Crimes And Punishments, Translated from the Italian; With A Commentary, Attributed to Mons. De Voltaire, Translated from the French. London: Printed for J. Almon, 1767. 8vo. pp. xii, 179, lxxix. later marbled bds.,neatly rebacked. extremities very slightly rubbed, internally fine. First English Edition. $500

NCBEL II 1542. S.&M.I.358.5. Marvin 105. PMM 352 (1st Edn.).

"Beccaria was the first writer to plead for humane views on the treatment of criminals. Opposing capital punishment, torture, and the use of force, he maintained that education and care of the criminal rather than revenge should be the aim of society in its treatment of the offender. The book had an immediate success, six editions being published, including a French one with an anonymous commentary by Voltaire. Its

success led to the introduction of many reforms in the penal codes of the principal European nations." (PMM)

8 [BECCARIA, Cesare Bonesana, Marchesi di]. An Essay On Crimes And Punishments...The Fourth Edition. London: Printed for E. Newberry..., 1785. 8vo. pp. viii, [4]contents, 179,lxxix. contemporary calf. covers marked, spinal extremities chipped, otherwise a very good copy. $200

cfS.&M.I.358.15. Marvin 105. PMM 209.

9 [BECCARIA, Cesare Bonesana, Marchesi di]. Traite des delits et des peines, Traduit de l'Italien, D'apres la troisieme edition, revue, corrigee et augmentee par l'Auteur: Avec des Additions de l'Auteur, qui n'ont pas encore paru en Italien. A Lausanne: 1766. 12mo. pp. xxxi, 242. contemporary mottled sheep, gilt back. some spotting to leaves, but an excellent copy. First French Edition. $350

Brunet I, 729. Barbier IV, 776/77. Not in BM STC French Books. See S.&M.I.358.5 & Marvin 105 & PMM 352.

Beccaria's celebrated treatise was first published in Milan in 1764. This French translation is by the radical-leaning abbe Andre Morellet.

BENTHAM'S CLASSIC DEFENCE OF FREEDOM OF THE PRESS

10 BENTHAM, Jeremy [1748-1832]. The Elements Of The Art Of Packing, As Applied To Special Juries, Particularly In Cases Of Libel Law. London: Published by Effingham Wilson, 1821. 8vo. pp. 2pl, vii, 269, [2]ads. Apart from some foxing to a few leaves, a fine uncut copy in original cloth backed bds. First Trade Edition. $550

Goldsmith 253350. McCoy B200. S.&M.II.27. Marke 187.

Bentham's critique of English libel law was written in 1809 & printed in 1810. It is a vivid expose of governmental corruption in the selection of juries, particularly the packing of juries to obtain favourable verdicts in criminal libel trials. In writing this work & pointing to the abuses of particular judges, Bentham exposed himself to prosecution under the very same law he condemned. Consequently the original edition of 1810 was held back from publication, copies only being distributed to Bentham's friends, & the work did not officially appear until 1821.

BENTHAM'S MOST IMPORTANT WORK ON ENGLISH LAW

11 BENTHAM, Jeremy. Rationale Of Judicial Evidence, Specially Applied To English Practice. From The Manuscripts Of...In Five Volumes. London: Published By Hunt And Clarke, York Street..., 1827. 8vo. index. related book review glued on fr. blanks. modern cloth. sl. tearing to lower corner of several gatherings of Vol. I, else a very nice set complete with half-titles. First Edition. $650

S.&M.II.27. Marke 524. Marvin 113.

Bentham's 'Rationale' was edited by John Stuart Mill. Vol. I includes a Preface by Mill describing his editorial role.

The epochal 'Rationale' is considered by many to be Bentham's most important work on English law. "The Rationale Of Judicial Evidence' is one of the richest in matter of all Bentham's productions. The book contains, very fully developed, a great proportion of all his best thoughts; while among more special things it comprises the most elaborate exposure of the vices and defects of English law, as it then was, which is to be found in his works..."(John Stuart Mill.Autobiography).

BOHIER, Nicolas de (Nicolaus BOERIUS) [1469-1539]. Decisiones Burdegalenses Summa Diligentia et Eruditione Collectae, Et Explicatae, Vna Cum Eiusdem Boerii Consiliis, Tractatibus De Statu et Vita Heremitarum de Seditiosis, de Custodia clauium portarum ciuitatis, & Additionibus in tractatum Ioan. Montani de Authoritate magni consilij. Collatis vetustissimis exemplaribus omnia recognita, a Guill.Nepote in Curia Lugdunensi Aduocato. Accesserunt huic editioni, nunc primum e Gallico in Latinum conuersa, Decisiones insignes D. Aegidij Magistri, Equitis, & in Suprema Parisiensi Curia primi Prasidu. Cum rerum ac verborum locupletissimo Indice. np: Excudebat Philippus Albert, 1620. folio. pp. 6pl, 1020, [45]index. title in red & black. title vignette & several woodcut ornaments & initials. text in double columns. old calf, sometime rebacked. binding worn, front cover detached, title leaf detached but present, wanting front free-endpaper & front blank, some foxing, else internally very good. From the library of Thomas Cushing Aylwin (1806-71), lawyer, politician & high court justice of Lower Canada, with his signature on front free-endpaper & with the printed book label of the Court of Arches, London. $300

The NUC locates only 1 copy of this edition. See Adams B.2277 (1566, 1st edition).

This is the most esteemed of the works of the celebrated jurist Bohier. He became the third president of the parliament of Bordeaux in 1515.

BRADBY, James. A Treatise On The Law Of Distresses. First American Edition From The London Edition of 1808. New York: Printed and published by Isaac Riley, 1808. 8vo. pp. xx, 323. index. modern half calf. several repairs to outer margins, browned, else very good. $125

Marvin 141. Marke 790. S.&M.II.39.

BROUGHAM, Henry [1778-1865]. Contributions To The Edinburgh Review. In Three Volumes. London: Richard Griffen, 1856. 8vo. pp. 4pl, 507; 3pl, 544; 3pl, 512. index. complete with half-titles. original blind stamped cloth. corners bumped, else a very nice set with the bookplate of William Lynn Smart, judge of Hastings County, Canada West, 1850-65.First Edition. $80

Brougham wrote essays for the 'Edinburgh Review' on almost every conceivable subject. Included in this work are four of his legal essays: 'English Criminal Law', 'Bentham - Theory of Punishments', 'Law Of Libel - Liberty Of The Press', & 'English Orators - Lord Erskine' as well as 6 articles on constitutional questions.

BROUGHAM, Henry. The Life And Times Of Henry Lord Brougham Written By Himself. In Three Volumes. Second Edition. Edinburgh & London: William Blackwood And Sons, 1871. 8vo. pp. x, 552; xii, 516; xii, 524. engraved frontis. portrait. folding facsimile letter. contemporary half calf. corners sl. rubbed, else a very attractive set. $100

Marke 1062.

BROWNLOW, Richard [1533-1638]. Latine Redivivus: A Book Of Entries, Of Such Declarations, Informations, Pleas in Barr and Abatement, Replications, Rejoynders, Issues, Verdicts, Bills of Exception to Verdicts, Judgements, Demurrers, and other Parts of Pleadings, (now in use) in Personal and Mixt Actions...London: Printed by the assigns of Richard and Edward Atkyns, Esquires; And are to be Sold by S. Heyrick in Holborn..., 1693. folio. pp. 3pl, 506, [46]index.printed in black letter. modern quarter oasis morocco. first two leaves mounted (edges tatty), neat paper mend to third leaf, several ink marks on title, otherwise an excellent copy. First Complete Edition. $350

Wing B5197. S.&M.I.265.36. Marvin 156.
Several surreptitious editions of Brownlow's 'Latine Redivivus' were published prior to the complete 1693 edition. Two English translations appeared in 1653 and 1654. The title-page of the 1693 edition reprobates the 1653 & 1654 editions as "unskilfully turned into English". The 1693 edition of Brownlow's work was issued in Latin, the original language with additions in English.

17 BUGNYON, Philibert [d1590]. Legum Abrogatarum Et Inusitatarum In omnibus Curiis, Terris, Jurisdictionibus, & Dominiis Regni Franciae Tractatus. Edition Tertia, Mendis, quibus antea scatebat, repurgata...Accessere Additiones In Hac Editione Sesqui Altera Parte Adauctae: Quibus recentiores non modo Galliae, sed & universi Belgii, Hispaniae, Italiae, Germaniae, vicinorumque locorum Mores, & Leges tum Abrogatae, tum receptae demonstrantur... Bruxellis: Apud Petrum De Dobbeleer, 1702. folio. pp. 2pl, [21], 696, [86]index, [2]div.title, 81, [8]index. complete with half-title. woodcut ornaments. title in red & black. contemporary calf, gilt back. binding slightly rubbed, paper repair to title leaf, affecting several letters of imprint, else an excellent clean copy. From the library of Thomas Cushing Aylwin (1806-71), lawyer, politician & high court justice of Lower Canada, with his signature on front free-endpaper. $275

This edition not located in NUC. See BM STC French Books B.1847 (Paris: Buon, 1605). Brunet VI 2581.
Included is a commentary on the Moulin ordonnances proclaimed by Charles IX in February 1566, in which the judicial system of France was reorganized.

18 BURLAMAQUI, J[ean] J[acques] [1694-1748]. The Principles Of Natural and Politic Law, In Two Volumes...Translated into English by Mr. Nugent. The Second Edition, revised and corrected. London: Printed for J. Nourse..., 1763.8vo. pp. xvi, [24], 312; 4pl, 371, [1]ads. woodcut tailpieces & initials. contemporary tree calf, slightly scuffed. occasional marginal foxing, else very good. The best English edition according to Lowndes. $250

S.&M.I.592.8. cfMarvin 162 & cfMarke 933.
Combined edition of the two principal works of Swiss jurist Burlamaqui, foremost exponent of the law of nature school outside Germany: 'Principes du droit naturel' (Geneva 1747) & 'Principes du droit politique' (Geneva 1751). He "formulated the principles of popular sovereignty, of delegated power, of a constitution as a fundamental law, of a personal and functional separation of powers into three independent departments, of a system of checks and balances based upon coordinate departments and, finally, he provided for an institutional guardian of the fundamental law." (R.F. Harvey. 'Jean Jacques Burlamaqui; A Liberal Tradition in American Constitutionalism', pp. 178-79)

CABASSUT, Jean (Joannis CABASSUTIUS) [1604-1685]. Notitia Ecclesiastica Historarum, Conciliorum, & Canonum invicem collatorum, veterumque juxta, ac recentiorum Ecclesiae Rituum, Ab ipsis Ecclesiae Christianae incunabulis ad nostra usque tempora, secundum cujusque saeculi seriem, accurate digesta. Editio Quarta, Ab Ipso Auctore Correcta, Plurimum Aucta, & quinque Indicibus Iocupletata... Lugduni (Lyon): Sumptibus Anisson & Posuel, 1725. folio. pp. 2pl, [20], 680, [76]index. complete with half-title. title in red & black. text in double columns. several ornaments. contemporary sprinkled calf, gilt back. some dampstaining to outer leaves & inner margins, binding bit rubbed, else very good. From the library of Thomas Cushing Aylwin (1806-71), lawyer, politician & high court justice of Lower Canada, with his signature on front free-endpaper. $275

No copy of this edition located in the NUC.
Cabassut was a French priest of the Oratory, eminent for his knowledge of the Canon law. "Ouvrage judicieux, utile, recommande par Mabillon dans ses Etudes monastiques". (Dict. de Theol. Cath. II/1297)

STANDARD AUTHORITY ON
MARITIME & COMMERCIAL LAW

CASAREGI, Giuseppe Lorenzo Maria (Josephus Laurentius Maria de CASAREGIS) [1670-1737]. Discursus Legales De Commercio... Secunda Editione...4 Volumes in 3. [Vol. IV has variant title: Tomus Quartus Continens Elucubrationes Ac Resolutiones in aliquot, & ad integra Statuta De Decretis, Ac De Successionibus Ab Intestato...]. Venetiis: Ex Typographia Balleoniana, 1740. folio. pp. xxiv, 417, [1]; xii, 440, clvi; 223; xii, 268. indices. half-title in Vol. I. title of Vol. I in red & black. text in double columns. engraved portrait in Vol. I. numerous vignettes & ornamental initials. slight dampstaining to lower inner margin of Vol. I & outer margin of last few leaves in Vol. II, otherwise an excellent set in contemporary vellum. From the library of Thomas Cushing Aylwin (1806-71), lawyer, politician & high court justice of Lower Canada, with his signature on front free-endpaper. $1,000

S.&M.I.505.15. Goldsmith 7737. Marvin 178.
Casaregi, professor of law and for 20 years a judge at Florence, has long enjoyed the reputation of being a standard authority on commercial and maritime law and one of the best Italian writers on these subjects. "His commercial discourses are by far the most valuable of all his works to a modern lawyer. They embrace the whole circle of commercial law, including the law of prize. All that is most useful in the works of former jurists is collected and commented on with acuteness and accuracy, and for the most part the topics are examined until the whole subject matter is exhausted. Rarely have we looked into his works upon any contested question, without rising instructed and enlightened by the perusal. Higher praise cannot be bestowed upon him than the fact affords, that he is quoted by all subsequent writers on commercial law, as a leading and safe authority, and Valin does not scruple to affirm, that he is beyond all contradiction the best of all the maritime authors." (Marvin) The third volume also includes the 'Il Cambista Istruito' and the 'Consolato del Mare', with a commentary.

Besides this edition (the best & most complete), S.&M. lists the following: Florence 1719 in 2 vols. & Florence 1729 in 3 vols. The NUC also locates 1 copy of an earlier 1707 edition.

21 CASAREGI, Giuseppe [Lorenzo] Maria. Il Cambista Instruito Per ogni caso de'Fallimenti, O Sia Instruzione Per Le Piazze Mercantili Colla quale si puo giungere facilmente alla decisione di tutti i dubbj, che possono occorrere nelle Lettere di Cambio, loro Girate, e Accettazioni, per li Fallimenti tanto occulti, o prossimi, che attuali de'Mercanti. Opera Pratica, E Legale... In Firenze: 1723. 4to. pp. 12pl, 372. index. finely engraved full-page portrait of the author (name of engraver shaved off: Dom. Ferretti). woodcut ornaments & initials. A fine copy in contemporary vellum, with Landau bookplate. First Edition. $650

Kress 3501. Goldsmith 6198. NUC locates only 2 copies in North America.
This work, 'The Accomplished Money Changer', treats of commercial money transactions, such as letters of credit, &c. & especially cases of bankruptcy. It was incorporated into later editions of his 'Discursus Legales de Commercio'.

NEW CODE OF LAWS FOR THE RUSSIAN EMPIRE

22 CATHERINE II, EMPRESS OF RUSSIA. The Grand Instructions To The Commissioners Appointed to Frame A New Code of Laws For The Russian Empire: Composed by Her Imperial Majesty Catherine II. Empress of all the Russias. To which is prefixed, A Description of the Manner of opening the Commission, with the Order and Rules for electing the Commissioners. Translated from the Original, in the Russian Language, By Michael Tatischeff, a Russian Gentleman; And published by Permission. London: Printed for T. Jefferys, 1768. 4to. pp. xxiii, [1]errata, 3-258. contemporary sheep. binding worn, joints cracked, internally fine. First English Edition. $500

Crowther 790.
Shortly after her accession to the throne, Catherine II zealously embarked on her efforts to raise the intellectual & artistic levels of Russian society to those of Western Europe. It was during her reign that Russian established itself as one of the Great Powers. She was a great admirer of Voltaire & the Encyclopedistes & this work, based largely on the writings of Montesquieu & Beccaria, was an attempt to embody in a legislative form the principles of the enlightenment. The democratic principles unnerved many of Catherine's advisers & the Grand Commission, summoned to deliberate the proposals, was eventually dissolved.
According to the preface, this is the first English translation of a Russian book by a Russian.

23 CHASSENEUX, Barthelemy de. Consuetudines Ducatus Burgundiae, Fere'Que Totius Galliae...Commentariis amplissimis & doctissimis illustratae. Hac postrema editione infinitis erroribus omnia purgata genuinaequelectioni restituta opera & studio Iuliani Mallety. Accessit rerum, verborumque Index locupletissimus. Lugduni (Lyon): Apud Bartholomaeum Vincentium, 1582. folio. pp. 3pl, [112]index, [2], 1528. text in double columns. 7 engraved genealogical trees. title in red & black. woodcut ornaments & initials, title vignette. old sprinkled calf, sometime rebacked. binding worn, front cover detached, back joint cracked, front free-endpaper loose; except for some slight dampstaining to fore-edge margin of a few leaves, internally an excellent copy. From the library of Thomas Cushing Aylwin (1806-71), lawyer, politician & high court justice of Lower Canada, with his signature on front free-endpaper, & with book label of Court of Arches. $600

This edition not in BM STC French Books, Adams or Graesse. See Graesse II p. 289 (1534 edition). cf Brunet VI 2651.
This commentary on the customary law of Burgundy by the French judge and legal writer Chasseneux went through a number of editions; "C'est un des premiers ouvrages dans lesquels on ait essaye d'eclaircir le droit coutumier de France, en le conciliant avec le droit romain." (Michaud, Biographie Universelle)

COOTE, Richard Holmes. An Analysis, Arranged to Serve Also As A Compendious Digested Index of Mr. Fearne's Essay on Contingent Remainders and Executory Devises, And of Mr. Butler's Notes. London: Printed for W. Clarke & Sons, 1814. 8vo. pp. 2pl, [12], 198. contemporary calf. front joint tender. First Edition. $125

S.&M.II.77. Marvin 228.
A very useful and concise alphabetical index & analytical abridgement of Fearne's authoritative work on property law.

CRAIG, Sir Thomas [1538-1608]. Jus Feudale Tribus Libris Comprehensum. Quibus Non solum Consuetudines Feudales & Praeditorum Iura, quae in Scotia, Anglia, & plerisque Galliae locis obtinent, continentur; Sed Universum Ius Scoticum, Et omnes fere Materiae Iuris clare & dilucide exponuntur, Et ad fontes Iuris Feudalis & Civilis singula reducuntur. Edinburgi: 1655. small folio. pp. 6pl, 383. woodcut ornaments & initials. contemporary calf, rubbed, front cover detached, head & foot of backstrip chipped, some spotting & browning, title strengthened, but a very good copy internally. folio leaf tipped-in back paste-down containing manuscript copy extract from Lord Jeffrays Essays, "The Scottish Dialect". First Edition, First Issue. $400

Wing C6801. S.&M.V.26. cf Marvin 237 (later editions).
Although the Scottish lawyer's great work was apparently completed about 1603, it was not published until 1655. "A very learned work, written with the avowed object of showing that the feudal law of Scotland and England had a common origin...No clearer statement of the feudal system in its legal relations exists, and it is still, although the law has been much altered, the standard authority in Scotland as to the original condition of its feudal landlaw, probably as complete as that of any European country." (DNB) Its scholarship, organization & originality thoroughly distinguish it from previous compilations & textbooks & Craig is regarded as the first systematic writer on law in Scotland. A zealous promoter of the union of Scotland & England, Craig wrote with both public & patriotic end in view, and has been compared to Bacon in this respect.

INDEX TO THE WORKS OF THE
GREATEST OF ALL CIVIL LAWYERS

(CUJAS, Jacques [1522-1590]). ALBANESE, Domenico. Promptuarium Universorum Operum Jacobi Cujacii Variantibus inter se lectionibus, praesertim Titulorum, & Legum Florentinae, Vulgataeque editionis Pandectarum, sive Digestorum accomodatum Cura, Et Industria Dominici Albanensis In Supremis

Regni Neapolitani Tribunalibus Causarum Patroni. 2 Volumes. Mutinae (Modena): Apud Societatem Typographicam, Superiorum Facultate, 1795. folio. pp. 1pl, [18], lxxii, 680; 146, 343, text in double columns. with divisional titles. title vignette. contemporary mottled calf, gilt backs. bindings bit rubbed, backstrips chipped, front cover of Vol. I detached, other joints cracked, otherwise a very good set. From the library of Thomas Cushing Aylwin (1806-71), lawyer, politician & high court justice of Lower Canada, with his signature on front free-endpaper & with the armorial bookplates & signatures of Alexander Buchanan. $400

Graesse II p.306. The NUC locates only 3 copies of this edition.

A valuable index to the works of the eminent French jurist Cujas, who has been referred to as the greatest of all civil lawyers. "He is the outstanding representative of humanism in Roman law...The school of Cujas viewed the Roman texts as historical documents, interpreting them in the full setting of ancient history and literature. A consummate master of jurisprudence, philology and history, Cujas may claim to be the greatest legal scholar of all time..[this index] gives ready access to the eleven-volume Naples (1722-27) and Venice-Modena (1758-83) reprints of the Opera Omnia edited by C.A. Fabrot (10 vols., Paris 1658)." (Encycl. of Scoial Sciences)

27 DE LOLME, J[ean] L[ouis] [1740?-1807]. The Constitution Of England, Or An Account Of The English Government; In which it is compared with the Republican Form of Government, and occasionally with the other Monarchies in Europe. London: Printed by T. Spilsbury...And Sold by G. Kearsley, 1775. ivo. pp. vii, 448. contemporary half calf, marbled bds. extremities rubbed, fr. joint cracked, else a very good copy. First English Edition. $200

S.&M.I.100.27. NCBEL II 1734. Marvin 263.

De Lolme's work, written in French, was first published in Amsterdam in 1771. "De Lolme was a native of Switzerland, and it is remarkable that a foreigner should have been the first to write a clear, concise, and accurate treatise upon the constituional law of England." (Marvin) The work is still highly regarded today.

28 DE LOLME, J[ean] L[ouis]. The Constitution Of England... The Fourth Edition, Corrected and Enlarged. [Edited by Charles Coote]. London: Printed for G. Robinson & J.Murray, 1784. 8vo. pp. 4pl, xvi, 540, [20]index. engraved frontis. portrait. contemporary calf. corners bumped, otherwise a fine copy. $125

S.&M.I.100.27. NCBEL II 1734. Marvin 263.

Four new chapters were added to the third edition as well as some corrections,and this fourth edition is further improved by Charles Coote.

29 [DESTUTT DE TRACY, Antoine Louis Claude, Comte] [1754-1836]. A Commentary and Review of Montesquieu's Spirit of the Laws. Prepared For Press From the Original Manuscript, in the Hands of the Publisher. To Which Are Annexed, Observations on the Thirty-First Book, By the Late M. Condorcet:And Two Letters of Helvetius, On The Merits of the Same Work.[Translated by Thomas Jefferson]. Philadelphia: Printed by William Duane, 1811. 8vo. pp. viii, 292. slight dampstain to inner margin of last few signatures, else very good. First American Edition, First Appearance in Print. Marvin p.607.

Bound with:

[ANDREWS, William Eusebius]. An Historical Narrative of the Horrid Plot and Conspiracy of Titus Oates, Called the Popish Plot In Its Various Branches and Progress, Selected From the Most Authentic Protestant Historians, To Which Are Added Some Cursory Observations On the Test Act. London: Published by W.E. Andrews..., 1816. 8vo. pp. 2pl, vi, [7]-284. last leaf soiled, tear to upper margin of 2A2, resulting in loss of two words of text, else a nice copy. The two works bound in contemporary half sheep. lacking free- endpaper & back blank. $300

Jefferson's English translation of Destutt de Tracy's commentary marks its first appearance in print. Although the manuscript in French dates from 1807, the first French edition was not published until 1819. The work presents a clear formulation of the author's political philosophy, in which he opposes the concept of absolute natural rights & compares the English constitution unfavourably to the American system.

DIXON, Hepworth [1821-1879]. John Howard And The Prison-World Of Europe. From Original And Authentic Documents. Slightly Abridged. Webster: Published by Frederick Charlton, 1852. 8vo. pp. 442. original gilt & blind stamped cloth. backstrip sl. frayed, hint of foxing, else very good. $30

[DUANE, William] [1760-1835]. Experience The Test Of Government: In Eighteen Essays. Written During The Years 1805 And 1806. To Aid The Investigation Of Principles, And Operations Of The Existing Constitution And Laws Of Pennsylvania. Philadelphia: Printed by William Duane, 1807. 8vo. pp. 60. uncut. disbound. $50

Sabin 20986.

DYER, [Sir James] [1511-1582]. Les Reports Des Divers Select Matters & Resolutions des Reverend Judges & Sages del Ley, Touchant & concernant mults principal Points occurent estre debate per eux: En le several Reignes de les tres-hault & excellent Princes, Le Roys Hen. 8. & Edw. 6 & le Roignes Mar. & Eliz. Collect & Report per tres-Reverend Judge, Sr. Jacques Dyer Chivaler... London: Printed by W. Rawlins, S. Roycroft, and M. Flesher...for Samuel Keble..., 1688. folio. pp. 3pl, [10]table, 377(numbered leaves), [2], [52]index. woodcut ornaments & vignettes. old calf, sometime rebacked. binding quite worn, covers detached, outer signatures loose, some dampstaining & marginal tearing to a few leaves (not affecting text), otherwise internally very good. Sixth Edition, in Law French. Edited by Chief Justice Treby. $275

S.&M.I.299.47. New Wing D.2957. Marvin 284. Winfield 187.

Dyer "reported the most remarkable cases that came before the Court of Common Pleas, together with those, which, on account of their difficulty, were adjourned into the Exchequeur Chamber before all the Judges. They are valuable records of the history of English jurisprudence and English manners."(S.&M.) "No Reports have been so frequently reprinted, and none have received higher homage..."(Marvin) Dyer's reports are also notable as being the first collection regularly called

'Reports' rather than 'Cases' or 'Commentaries'. This sixth Edition is the first to be altered; the notes and additions of Chief Justice Treby are held to be of equal authority to the Reports.

33 ESCRICHE, D. Joaquin. Diccionario Razonado De Legislacion Y Jurisprudencia...[Revised And Enlarged]. 4 Vols. Madrid: Imprenta De Eduardo Cuesta, 1874. folio. pp. 2pl, [v]-viii [misbound], 955; 1167; 950 [1]; 1341 [1]errata. contemporary sheep. hinges cracked, extremities sl. rubbed, else a very good set. $150

Copy of James H. Blount [1837-1903], noted lawyer, congressman and diplomatic envoy. Each volume has Blount's signature and stamp noting his position of "Judge of First Instance, First Judicial District, Philippine Islands" with the date of July 3rd, 1901.

34 FACHINEI, Andrea (Andreas FACHINAEUS). Controversiarum Opus: In Quator Tomos Sectum...Edition Postrema Cui primo accreuit Tomus quartus, deinde cuique Tomo argumenta praefixa, tertio superadditus est triplex Elenchus: vnus Capitum, alter Verb. Sentent. & Rerum: tertius V.I. locorum, vniuerso hoc opere cribratorum. Aureliae Allobrogum (Geneva): Excudebat Stephanus Gamonetus, 1609. 8vo. pp. 1pl, [15], 1859, [14], 1860-2415, [91]index. text in double columns. several woodcut ornaments & initials. title vignette. old sprinkled calf, gilt back. slight marginal dampstaining & some insignificant marginal worming to last few signatures, binding rubbed, head of spine worn, else very good. From the library of Thomas Cushing Aylwin (1806-71), lawyer, politician & high court justice of Lower Canada, with his signature on front free-endpaper. $275

NUC only locates a Lyons edition for 1609.

The Italian jurist frequently quotes Cujas & Bude, but is critical of Hotman for doubting the authenticity of a letter of Justinian inserted in the Code (de Summa Trinitate) asserting the pre-eminence of the Popes.

35 FAVRE, Antoine (Antonius FABER) [1557-1624]. Coniecturarum Iuris Civilis Libri viginti. In quibus difficiles perique Iuris Iustinianaei loci, nouis cum emendationibus, tum interpretationibus explicantur, & vera rectaque Iuris principia stabiliuntur. Cume Indice Copiosissimo...Editio Postrema. Coloniae Allobrogum (Geneva): Apud Samuelem Crispinum, & Franciscum Fabrum, 1615. folio. pp. 1pl, [10], 798, [32]index. title vignette & several woodcut ornaments & initials. title in red & black. old mottled calf, gilt back. head of backstrip & spine label chipped, otherwise an excellent copy. From the library of Thomas Cushing Aylwin (1806-71), lawyer, politician & high court justice of Lower Canada, with his signature on front free-endpaper. $350

This edition not in Graesse or the NUC. For other editions, see Graesse II p.540 (Lugduni, 1661) & BM STC French Books F. 109 (Lugduni 1651).

The 'Coniecturarum' were first written when Favre was but 23 years of age; they reveal a profound knowledge of Roman laws and their interrelationships. Favre was deservedly hailed by Cujas, and became successively, 'juge-mage' of Bresse, Bugey, Valroney et Gex, senator of Chambery, president of the Council of Geneva, president of Annecy & Chambery, and finally governor of Savoy.

FAVRE, Antoine. Iurisprudentiae Papinianeae Scientia, Ad Ordinem Institutionum Imperialium efformata, In qua uniuersum Ius Civile, noua methodo, ad propria & indubitata sua Principia refertur, & ex iis clarissime ac certissime demonstratur. Editio Novissima, Et Emendata. Lugduni (Lyon): Sumptibus Philippi Borde, Laurentii Arnaud, & Claudii Rigaud, 1658. folio. pp. 3pl, 644, [15]index. text in double columns. title in red & black. title vignette. woodcut ornaments & initials. upper backstrip defective, else a fine copy in contemporary vellum. From the library of Thomas Cushing Aylwin (1806-71), lawyer, politician & high court justice of Lower Canada, with his signature on front free-endpaper. $325

Graesse II p.540. BM STC French Books F.112.

"Ouvrage capital, qui avait pour but de reduire dans un ordre methodique et regulier toute la science du droit romain, qui offre tant de confusion dans les cinquante livres des Pandectes." (Michaud, Biographie Universelle)

FERRIERE, Claude De. Corps Et Compilation De Tous Les Commentateurs Anciens Et Modernes Sur La Coutume De Paris... Seconde Edition, Revue, Corrigee Et Augmentee Par L'Auteur, Et par M. Claude Joseph De Ferriere, son Fils...Enrichie Des Scavantes Observations De Feu Monsieur [Nicolas] Le Camus, Lieutenant Civil de la Ville, Prevote & Vicomte de Paris. 4 Volumes. A Paris: Chez Henry Charpentier, 1714. folio. titles in red & black. engraved frontis. portrait of Le Camus by Tardieu after Rigaud & engraved dedication headpiece after Veritier. folding engraved map of Paris & environs by C. Inselin. several woodcut ornaments & initials. index. with half-title in Vol. II. printed in double columns. contemporary sprinkled calf. bindings quite worn, but apart from some age-browning & marginal dampstaining to some leaves, internally very good. $850

Brunet VI 2682.

A key work on the customary law of Paris, incorporating the interpretations & elucidations of its major commentators: Charles Du Moulin, Louis Charondas Le Caron, Gilles Fortin, Rene Chopin, Jean Troncon, Maitres Tournet, Labbe & July, Claude Guerin, Julien Brodeau, Jean Marie Ricard, Batthelemy Ausanet, Claude Duplessis, Jean Le Camus & Eusebe De Lauriere. Ferriere provides, in his preface, his own assessment of the writings of these various distinguished commentators, with a bibliographical listing of the texts.

FORD, Paul Leicester (Ed.). Essays On The Constitution Of The United States, Published During Its Discussion By The People 1787-1788. Brooklyn, N.Y.: Historical Printing Club, 1892. 8vo. pp. viii, 424. biblio. index. contemporary quarter morocco. First Edition. (Edition limited to 500 copies). $50

Marke 374.

The 17 essays were originally published in the press of the period, anonymously, as part of the debate on the U.S. Constitution. "Subsequently most of the writers were prominent in administering this Constitution or opposing its development, and were largely responsible for the resulting tendencies of our government."(Marke)

(FRANCE). Suite De La Marechaussee De France Ou Recueil

Des Ordonnances, Edits, Declarations, Lettres Patentes, Arrests, Reglemens & autres Pieces concernant la Creation, Establissement, Fonctions, Rang, Seances, Preeminences, Droits Prerogatives & Privileges de tous les Officiers & Archers des Marechaussees. Paris: Chez Joseph Saugrain..., 1717. Avec Privilege Du Roy. 4to. pp. 2pl, 240, [11]index. several woodcut ornaments & initials. contemporary calf. a very nice copy. $250

40 GRIVEL, Jean (Ioannis Grivellus) [1650-1624]. Decisiones Celeberrimi Sequanorum Senatus Dolani. In quibus multa, tum ad theoriam iuris, tum ad praxim, & consuetudinem spectantia, dilucide explanantur: omnibus in foro versantibus admodum utilia & necessaria...Cum Indice rerum ac materiarum locupletissimo. Antverpiae: Apud Ioannem Keerbergium,1618. folio. pp. 1pl, [25], 443, [41]index & errata. title vignette. woodcut ornaments & initials. text in double columns. old calf, sometime rebacked. binding worn, covers off, internally fine. From the library of Thomas Cushing Aylwin (1806-71), lawyer, politician & high court justice of Lower Canada, with his signature on front free-endpaper & with printed book label of the Court of Arches, London. $325

No copies located in NUC.

"Cet ouvrage est ecrit en bon latin avec beaucoup d'ordre, de nettete et d'erudition; de sorte qu'on peut le regarder comme un des meilleurs de ce genre." (Dunod de Charnage) The author, 'conceiller au parlement de Dole' in 1608 became 'maitre de requetes' in the Privy Council of the Low Countries, and upon the death of Richardot, assumed control of the affairs of the province of Burgundy.

PHILOSOPY OF INTERNATIONAL LAW

41 GROTIUS, Hugo [1583-1645]. Le Droit De La Guerre et De La Paix...Nouvelle Traduction, Par Jean Barbeyrac... Avec les Notes de l'Auteur meme, qui n'avoient point encore paru en Francois; & de nouvelles Notes Du Traducteur. Edition Nouvelle, faite d'apres un Exemplaire considerablement corrige, retouche, & augmente de la main de Mr. J. Barbeyrac. 2 Volumes. A Basle: Chez Emanuel Tourneisen, 1768. 4to. pp. 4pl, xxxii, 516; 2pl, 471, [33]index. engraved frontis. port. by Chovin, title vignettes, several woodcut ornaments, large engraved vignette & initial at head of dedication. contemporary calf, gilt backs. A handsome binding with elaborate oval stamp in blind within a double blind roll-stamp & triple gilt fillet border, a flower tool at the angles of inner border, on covers. corners bumped, occasional hint of foxing, slight dampstain to leaves of preface, else very good. In slip-off box. Eighth Edition in French. $500

Ter Meulen/Diermanse 658. Rogge 60. Marvin 352-53. cfS.&M. I.595.52. cfPMM 125.

Esteemed edition of the magnum opus of the celebrated Dutch jurist. Grotius' treatise, written against the stormy background of the Thirty Years' War, was the first attempt to establish a systematic code for regulating the intercourse and reciprocal obligations of nations in war & peace. This code is based on the theory of natural right & social contract; the principles are derived from reason rather than the divine order. "No legal work ever enjoyed a more extended reputation, and none ever exercised such a wonderful influence over the public morals of Europe." (Marvin)

HALE, Matthew [1609-1676]. The History of the Common Law. The Fourth Edition Corrected; With Notes, References, And Some Account of the Life of the Author, By Charles Runnington. [With: "An Analysis of the Civil Part of the Law. The Fourth Edition"]. London: Printed by W. Strahan & M. Woodfall for T. Cadell, 1779. 8vo. pp. 4pl, xl, [305], [1]errata; 6pl, 114, [8]index, [2]ads. engraved frontis. chart. modern quarter morocco. some browning throughout, dampstaining to lower edge of some leaves, frontis. & title neatly mounted, else very good. With complimentary ticket of F.A. Alberger, Member of Assembly. $175

S.&M.I.239.18. See Marvin 359 & Winfield pp. 37-38 & 328.

The 'Analysis', treating of civil matters, was the first work of its kind ever written and had a considerable influence on Blackstone, who called it "the most rational, scientific...as well as the most comprehensive of all attempts [prior to his own analysis] to digest the common law." Of his 'History' Holdsworth has said that it is "the ablest introductory sketch of a history of English law that appeared till the publication of Pollock and Maitland." Both of the works were published posthumously from rough drafts never intended for publication, and this fourth edition marks their first appearance together.

THE HARLEIAN MISCELLANY: Or A Collection Of Scarce, Curious, and Entertaining Pamphlets and Tracts, As well in Manuscript as in Print, Found in the late Earl of Oxford's Library. Interspersed With Historical, Political and Critical Notes. With A Table of the Contents, and an Alphabetical Index. [Introduction by Samuel Johnson]. 8 Vols. London: Printed for T. Osborne..., 1744-1776. 4to. contemporary panelled calf. binding rubbed, spinal extremities chipped, bds. of Vol. 1 & 5 detached, other volumes' joints tender, else very good set. Complete with List of Subscribers & 168 pp. Catalogue of Pamphlets in Harleian Library which is often missing. With the bookplate & rubber stamp of Thomas Fowell Buxton [1786-1845], noted author, philanthropist & legal reformer. First Edition. $500

S.&M.I.33.40. Kress 4707. Abbott 1365. NCBEL II 1143. cf Marvin 369.

"This invaluable, political, historical, and antiquarian record, an indispensable auxiliary in the illustration of British history, contains between 600 and 700 rare and curious tracts." (Lowndes)

HEARNE, Thomas [1678-1735]. A Collection Of Curious Discourses Written By Eminent Antiquaries Upon Several Heads In Our English Antiquities. Together with Mr. Thomas Hearne's Preface And Appendix To The Former Edition, To Which Are Added A Great Number Of Antiquary Discourses Written By The Same Authors. Most of Them Now First Published From The Original Manuscripts. In Two Volumes. London: Printed for Benjamin White..., 1775. 8vo. pp. 4pl, lxxi, 354; 3pl, 449, 14. index. 1 double-page engraving & 1 engraved plate of script. contemporary tree calf, armorial arms stamped in gilt on centre covers. hinges cracked, else a very good set. Second Edition. $125

S&M I.33.41. cfMarvin 379.

Includes numerous legal tracts: 'The Antiquity of the Laws of this Island', 'Of the Antiquity and Etymology of Terms and Times for Administration of Justice in England', 'Of the Antiquity of the Office of the Chancellor in England', 'Duello Foiled' &c.

45 HENRION DE PENSEY [PANSEY], [Pierre Paul Nicolas, baron] [1742-1829]. Traite Des Fiefs De Dumoulin, Analyse et Confere Avec les Autres Feudistes. A Paris: Chez Valade, 1773. 4to. pp. 2pl, iii, [1], 717, [2]. complete with half-title. several woodcut head & tailpieces. contemporary mottled calf, gilt back. joints cracking, head & foot of spine worn, occasional hint of foxing, small stamp on verso of title (Harvard Law Library Duplicate Sold), else a very good copy. First Edition. $350

Querard IV, 76.

An important treatise on feudal law based on the work of the celebrated Dumoulin, including a tribute to Dumoulin which appeared previously in 1769. According to Querard & Michaud, the chancellor Maupeou viewed the dedication to M. Mole de Champlatreux, son of the first president of Parliament, overthrown & exiled by Maupeou, as a fresh protestation against his regime. The Dedication was therefore suppressed & few copies include it; ours does not.

46 HOLST, H[ermann] E.Von. The Constitutional Law Of The United States Of America. Authorized Edition. Translated By Alfred Bishop Mason. Chicago: Callaghan & Company, 1887. pp. vi, [1 leaf], 369. index. original cloth. First American Edition. $45

Marke 398.

47 [HUMPHRYS-ALEXANDER, Alexander - self-styled Earl of Stirling] [1783-1859]. Narrative of the Oppressive Law Proceedings, And Other Measures, Resorted to By The British Government, And Numerous Private Individuals, To Overpower the Earl of Stirling, and Subvert His Lawful Rights. Written By Himself. Also A Genealogical Account of the Family of Alexander, Earls of Stirling, &c. Compiled From Mss. In the Possession of the Family: Followed By An Historical View of Their Hereditary Possessions in Nova Scotia, Canada, &c. By Ephraim Lockhart, Esq. With A Copious Appendix of Royal Charters and Other Documents. Edinburgh: [James Walker, Printer], 1836. 4to. pp. vi, [1 leaf], 176, 8, vi, 77. complete with tipped-in errata slip. 1 text illus., 2 facsimile letters & folding genealogical table. Original bds., rebacked in cloth with original spine mounted. except for little wear to bds., a fine uncut copy. $600

TPL 1974. Lande 461. Sabin 33826.

In 1621, the Scottish poet & statesman, Sir William Alexander of Menstrie (later Earl of Stirling & Viscount Canada) was granted virtually the whole of Nova Scotia, then known as 'New Scotland', by King James. The grant was further increased by King Charles to include the greater portion of what is now the north-eastern United States. The title lapsed in 1739 on the death of the fifth earl, who died without issue. In 1830, Alexander Humphrys-Alexander claimed the earldom through his mother, a daughter of the putative sixth earl. In this work, he sets forth his claim & reproduces the many charters relating to the Alexander lands in North America. Despite the fact that his claim was dismissed in 1833, he continued to offer land for sale in Nova Scotia until 1837, & in 1839, was tried and found guilty of forgery.

48 (HUMPHRYS-ALEXANDER, Alexander - self-styled Earl of Stirling). HAYES, John L[ord] [1812-1887]. Vindication Of The Rights And Titles, Political And Territorial, Of Alexander, Earl Of Stirling & Dovan, Hereditary Lieutenant General And Lord Proprietor Of Canada And Nova Scotia. Washington: Gideon & Co., Printers, 1853. 8vo. pp. 52. original printing wrs. slightly chipped, small rubberstamp on fr.wr., else a fine copy. First Edition. $100

Sabin 31025. Casey I 2375. Lande 415. Not in TPL or Gagnon.

Legal argument in support of Alexander Humphrys-Alexander's claim to the proprietorship of Nova Scotia & parts of Canada & Northeastern America, based on the charters issued by James I & Charles I to Sir William Alexander of Menstrie (later Earl of Stirling & Viscount Canada) & the judicial recognition of the lineal descent of the present Earl from the first.

[JACKSON, Helen Maria Fiske Hunt] [1830-1855]. A Century Of Dishonor A Sketch Of The United States Government's Dealings With Some Of The Indian Tribes. By H.H. New York: Harper & Brothers, 1881. 8vo. pp. x, 457, 6(ads). original cloth, institutional bookplate on fr. paste-down, tail of spine stained, else a fine copy. First Edition. $60

JOURGNIAC SAINT-MEARD, [Francois] [1745-1827]. Dernier Tableau De Paris. Pieces Justificatives. Prison De L'Abbaye. Mon Agonie de Trente-huit Heures; Ou Recit de ce qui m'est Arrive, de ce que j'ai vu & entendu pendant ma Dentention Dans La Prison De L'Abbaye St. Germain, Depuis le 22 Aout jusqu'au 4 Septembre; (Par Jourgniac Saint-Meard) Ci-devant Captaine-Commandant des Chaffeurs du Regiment d'Infanterie du Roi. [Paris]: [c1792]. 8vo. pp. lxxi. contemporary calf. backstrip bit chipped, else a very nice copy. $125

cfSaricks 3296(5th Edition).cfMartin & Wlater II 17543.

Royalist Jourgniac Saint-Meard's 'Mon Agonie' gives a day by day account of his imprisonment on a charge of high treason, as well as an account of his trial & acquittal. Also included is a letter from Alexandre De Tilly to M. De Condorcet (pp. lvii-lxxi).

[KELD, Christopher]. An Essay On The Polity Of England: With A View To Discover the True Principles of the Government, what Remedies might be likely to cure the Grievances complained of; And Why The several Provisions Made by the Legislature, and those recommended by Individuals, have failed. London: Printed For T. Cadell, In The Strand, 1785. 8vo. pp. 10pl (incl. 1p.errata), 518. contemporary calf, rubbed. front joint cracked, small piece torn from B4(affecting catchword & 2 letters of footnote), occasional foxing, else a pleasant copy. $300

Keld's work on English constitutional law demonstrates an extensive knowledge of the work of eminent legal writers, including references to Coke, De Lolme, Blackstone &c. The 'Essay' traces the origins of British constitutional law & concludes with a chapter on British policy errors in America and Ireland.

KELYNG, John [d.1671]. A Report Of Divers Cases In Pleas of the Crown, Adjudged and Determined; In the Reign of the late King Charles II. With Directions for Justices of the Peace and others...From the Original Manuscript, under his own Hand. To which is added, The Reports of Three Modern Cases, Viz. Armstrong and Lisle; The King and Plumer; The Queen and Mawgridge. London: Printed for Isaac Cleabe..., 1708. folio. pp. 3pl, 138, [14]index. black letter. later half calf. bds. detached, calf worn, browned but crisp. First Edition. $150

S.&M.I.303.75. cfMarvin 436 (later editions).

A valuable collection of cases on Crown law, including high treason & murder trials.

53 KYD, Stewart [d.1811]. A Treatise On The Law Of Awards. The Second Edition, Revised And Corrected; With very considerable Additions from Printed and Manuscript Cases: An Appendix, Containing a Variety of useful Precedents. London: Printed for J. Johnson, G.G. & J. Robinson, & J. Butterworth..., 1799. 8vo. pp. 2pl, [vii]-xvii, 583, [1]errata. index. contemporary calf. lacking half-title? bk. joint cracked, fr. joint starting to crack, bk.bd. sl. rubbed, faint dampstain visible at extreme outer edge of outer leaves, else a fine clean copy. Second and best edition. $150

S.&M.I.545.3. Marvin 443.

Kyd's noted legal career included a high treason charge, along with Thomas Hardy & John Horne Tooke, in 1794. After the acquittal of Hardy & Tooke, Kyd was discharged. Kyd also conducted a brilliant defence of Thomas Williams, a publisher of Paine's 'Age of Reason', on blasphemy charges.

54 LADD, William [1778-1841]. An Essay On A Congress Of Nations, For The Adjustment Of International Disputes Without Resort To Arms. Containing The Substance Of The Rejected Essays On That Subject. With Original Thoughts And A Copious Appendix. Boston: Whipple and Damrell, 1840. 8vo. pp. iv, [5]-192 [513-700: (double pagination)]. original cloth-backed bds. front joint tender, head & foot of backstrip frayed, lacking spine label, strip clipped from title (not affecting text), faint hint of foxing, else a very good copy. First Edition. $85

Sabin 38525. cfMarke 637.

The first original American proposal for international arbitration of disputes between nations.

55 LAMBARD[E], William [1536-1601]. Eirenarcha, Or Of The Office of the Justices of Peace, in foure Bookes, Reuised, corrected, and enlarged, in the eighth yeere of the peaceable Raigne of our most gracious King, James. London:Printed from the Companie of Stationers, 1614. 8vo. pp. 1pl, 634, [84]. black letter. title within ornamental woodcut border. numerous ornamental initials. small tear to Yy6 & Qq3 (no loss), else a fine copy.

STC 15172. S.&M.I.229.43. cfMarke 199. cfMarvin 444.

Bound with:

LAMBARD[E], William. The Dvties Of Constables, Borsholders, Tythingmen, and such other lowe and Lay Ministers, and Churchwardens, and Ouerseers for the Poore, Surueyours of the highwaies and Distributors of the prouision against noisome fowle and vermine. First collected by...And enlarged in the yeere. 1610. London: Printed for the Companie of Stationers, 1614. 8vo. pp. 94, black letter. ornamental initials a very good copy.

STC 15159. S.&M.I.234.9. cfMarvin 444.

Both works bound in old calf, gilt back (no paste-downs). corners worn. $500

Lambarde, antiquary, lawyer & justice, was the author of a number of works on legal subjects, the best known & most enduring being the 'Eirenarcha' (first published 1581), a treatise on the office of the justice of the peace. These justices had, by the end of the sixteenth century, become crucial to the working of local administration. Lambarde's treatment is thorough & his exposition remarkably lucid & coherent.

THE LAW OF EXECUTORS AND ADMINISTRATORS. Being a Common Law Treatise; Shewing, Directions for the managment of their Office and Duty, in the several Branches of it. Of Probate of Wills. and of Codicils. Of Executor de son Tort. Of Joynt Executors. Executor of Executor. Of Administration committed, how and by whom, and to whom. Of bona notabilia, and Pleadings. Several sorts of Actions, brought by and against Executors, with the Declarations and Pleadings thereon. Of the Plea Plene Administravit, n'unq, Executor. Of Notice, Retainer and Pleadings. Issue, Evidence, Costs, Judgment, Execution and Error... London: Printed by the Assigns of R. and Edw. Atkins, Esquires. For D. Waithoe..., 1702. 8vo. pp. [32], 493, [34]index. contemporary calf, rubbed (lacking leather label). staining to outer margins of first few gatherings, browned, otherwise good. First Edition. $150

S.&M.I.492.18. Marvin 301.

OLD DUTCH LAW

LEEUWEN, Simon Van [1625-1682]. Censura Forensis Theoretico- Practica, Id Est, Totius Juris Civilis Romani, Usuque Recepti, & Practici Methodica Collatio. Qua non tantum ipsa Juris Romani fundamenta ad rationis, & veritatis censuram, methodice reducuntur; sed & ad usum practicum transferuntur...Editio quarta prioribus long emendatior, & ex Auctoris Autographis locupletior. Geradus De Haas, JC. recensuit & Observationes suas adjecit. 2 Parts in 1 Volume [Part I in 5 books; Part II in 2 books; with separate & cumulative indices]. Lugduni In Batavis (Leyden):Sumptibus Samuelis Luchtmans et Cornelii Haak, 1741. folio. pp. 1pl, [37], 623, [43]index; 1pl, [11], 248, [28]index. title of Vol.I in red & black. several woodcut ornaments & initials. text in double columns. 2 engraved plates in text (genealogical trees). contemporary calf. extremities bit rubbed, else fine. From the library of Thomas Cushing Aylwin(1806-71), lawyer, politician & high court justice of Lower Canada, with his signature on front free-endpaper. $450

Camus 518. Only 3 copies of this edition located in NUC.

An important manual on old Dutch law, written by the Dutch jurist Van Leeuwen, son of a member of the Dutch company of the East Indies.

LIEBER, Francis [1800-1872]. On Civil Liberty and Self-Government. London: Richard Bentley, 1853. 8vo. pp. xv, 552. complete with half-title. index. original blind & gilt stamped cloth. cloth faded & frayed, upper backstrip chipped, internally very good - unopened. With the armorial bookplate & signature of James Whitall. First British Edition. $75

Sabin 40974.

FIRST TO DIVIDE 'TENURES' INTO SECTIONS

59 LITTLETON, [Thomas] [1422-1481]. Les Tenures du monsieur Littleton...[Edited by William West [fl.1568-1594]]. 1581. [Colophon on Y4v:] Imprinted at London in Fletestrete within Temple barre, at the Signe of the hande and Statte by Rychard Tottel, 1581. small 8vo. ff. 1pl, 170, 25[index]. black letter. contemporary calf, with oval ornament stamped in blind on covers (no paste-downs). some marginal notes in old hand. apart from some very insignificant worming to lower margin of some gatherings, a fine copy in a remarkably well-preserved binding. $800

STC 15745. S.&M.I.455.56. cf Marvin 467-69. cfPMM 23.

In his commentary Coke called Littleton's 'Tenures' "the ornament of the Common Law, and the most perfect and absolute work that ever was written in any human science". Littleton's work was the first systematization of the English law of property, complete with principles & precedents, & has become "the basis of the essential rights of property in all English-speaking countries." (PMM)

First published in 1481, there were numerous editions of the 'Tenures' in both Anglo-French & English. This 1581 edition in Anglo-French is edited by William West, author of 'Symboleography'. It is the first West edition & marks the initial appearance of the numbered sectional divisions (See W.S. Holdsworth, 'A History of English Law', 1914. Vol. II p.485).

THE FIRST ATTEMPT TO CREATE A WRITTEN CONSTITUTION

60 LOCKE, John [1632-1704]. A Collection of Several Pieces of Mr. John Locke, Never before printed, or not extant in his Works. Publish'd by the Author of the Life of the ever-memorable Mr. John Hales, &c. [P. Des Maizeaux under the direction of Mr. Anthony Collins]. London: Printed by J. Bettenham for R. Francklin, 1720. 8vo. pp. 1pl, [33]dedication, xxiv, [2], 362, [18]index, [1]errata, [3]ads. 1 engraved plate. engraved title vignette. woodcut ornaments & initials. contemporary panelled calf, newly rebacked. binding bit rubbed, text foxed throughout, otherwise very good. First Edition. $600

NCBEL II 1836. Sabin 41726. JCB 271. Streeter II 1119. Winsor V p.336.

This collection contains the 'Fundamental Constitutions of Carolina' (pp. 1-53),the distinguished beginnings of the Carolina constitution, "which may be considered the first instrument ever digested and written out, for the entire and perfect government of a political body." (Sabin) Lord Shaftesbury, who was one of the 'lords' proprietors of Carolina under a patent granted in 1663, laid out the constitution, but it was Locke who was entrusted with its final composition. The conception is in general aristocratic & provides for negro slavery; although may of the points & provisions were impracticable, "it undoubtedly suggested to the colonists many hints which were beneficial in their civil and political organization."

61 (MACKINTOSH, James) [1765-1832]. The Trial Of John Peltier, Esq. For A Libel Against Napoleon Buonaparte, First Consul, Of The French Republic, At the Court of King's-Bench, Middlesex, on Mondy the 21st of February, 1803. Taken in Short hand by Mr. Adams, and the Defence revised by Mr. Mackintosh. London: Printed by Cox, Son, and Baylis...For M. Peltier..., 1803. 8vo. pp. xxxii, 312, clii. 1 wood engraving. modern cloth. except for some browning, a very nice copy. First Edition. $125

Marke 1023.

Peltier's trial for libel was distinguished by his defence counsel's eloquent speech on constitutional law & history. Even though Peltier was convicted, Mackintosh's speech was duly praised by Perceval, Lord Ellenborough & Erskine for its "almost unparalled eloquence". (DNB)

MARTINI, D. Nicolaus [1632-1713]. Praxis Criminalis Ad Theoricam accomodata In Qua Continentur Modu fabricandi Processus Criminales: Constitutiones Barbarina, & Cardinalis Sacchetti...Commissiones admissionis ad novas: Feriae generales, & particulares totius Status Ecclesiastici: Formula Actorum contumacialium...Eximio, ac Nobili Notariorum Tribunalis Illmi, & Rmi D. Auditoris Camerae Collegio Dicata Cura, Et Sumptibus D. Nicolai Martini... Romae: Typis Petri Ferri, 1728. 4to. pp. 1pl, [14], 224. contemporary mottled calf, gilt back. backstrip very slightly wormed, hint of foxing, else an excellent copy, with 2 cancels on imprimatur leaf. First Edition. $175

The NUC locates only the Library of Congress Copy.

On Canon law criminal procedure & torture, with discussion of assassination, adultery, abortion, premedidation, &c.

HIGHLY ESTEEMED BY LEIBNIZ

MASCARDI, Giuseppe (JOSEPHUS MASCARDUS) [d.15-8]. Conclusiones Probationum omnium quibusvis in utroque Foro versantibus, Practicabiles, Utiles, Necessariae. In Quator Volumina Distinctae. Hisce Canonicae, Civiles, Feudales, Criminales, aliaeq; materiae, per Ampliationes, Limitationes, Intelligentiasque, ordine alphabetico distinctae, continentur. Iisdemque Additiones DD. Joann. Aloysii Ricii Canonici Neapolitani, & Bartholomaei Nigri ex arte Hannoni JCtorum hactenus in fine annexae, nunc pro majori legentis commoditate, suo quaevis loco insertae sunt. Accedit Repertorium Universale, Ex Summariis locupletissimis: magis receptis DD. opinionibus hoc *Asterisco notatis. Edition Ultima, Revisa et a Plurimis Mendis Repurgata. 4 Volumes. Francofurti ad Moenum: Impensis Johannis Davidis Zunneri, Typis Balthas/Christophori Wustii, Sen., 1684. folio. pp. 2pl, [12], 500; 1pl, 510, [2]blank, [8]index; 1pl, [4],513, [8]; 2pl, 267, [215]index. engraved title in Vol.I. half-title in Vol. IV. title vignettes, woodcut ornaments & initials. title of Vol. I in red & black. contemporary mottled calf, gilt backs. bindings rubbed, front joint of Vol. IV cracked, some insignificant marginal worming to first few leaves of Vol.I, else a very good set, internally clean &crisp. From the library of Thomas Cushing Aylwin (1806-71), lawyer, politician & high court justice of Lower Canada, with his signature on front free-endpaper. $800

The NUC locates only 1 copy of this edition. See Adams M.833 (2 Vols. Venice: 1584).

"Cette theorie de la preuve en matier civile, criminelle et canonique, rebute par l'immensite des details auxquels est descendu l'auteur; mais resserree dans ce qu'elle a d'important par une main exercee, elle serait un membre des traites les plus usites de la jurispurdence."(Michaud,

Biographie Universelle)
Mascardi was successively Archbishop of Milan, Naples, Padua, and Plaisance. This, his magnum opus, was highly esteemed by Leibniz, who began but never completed an abridged translation of the work.

64 (MASSACHUSETTS). The Laws and Liberties of Massachusetts. Reprinted From the Copy of the 1648 Edition In The Henry E. Huntington Library. With An Introduction by Max Farrand. Cambridge: Harvard University Press, 1929. folio. pp. ix, [4], 59. 2 photo-facsimiles. cloth very slightly spotty, else fine, uncut & unopened. related blurb laid in. $65

"'The Book of the General Lawes and Libertyes of 1648' is the next significant measure after the Body of Liberties in the legal development of Massachusetts. It is a more important work than its predecessor, standing as the basis of all Massachusetts legislation, and influencing as well the legislation of other colonies, notably Connecticut and New Haven. It is furthermore the first attempt at a comprehensive reduction into one form of a body of legislation of an English-speaking country. Because of its importance and because the copy in the Huntington Library is to the present time unique, it has seemed desirable to reprint it." (Max Farrand, Introduction)

65 MATHER, James. The Constitutions Of Great Britain, France, And The United States Of America. Consisting Of Magna Charta, Bill Of Rights, And Coronation Oath; French Declaration of Rights, Charter Of Louis XVIII, And Constitution Of 1830 ...From The Most Authentic Sources. London: Effingham Wilson, Edinburgh: William Tait..., 1834. 8vo. pp. 1pl, [v]-viii, 76. original cloth (bit stained), lacking front free-endpaper. $50

66 MAY, Thomas Erskine [Baron Farnborough] [1815-1886]. The Constitutional History of England Since the Accession of George Third 1760-1860. In Two Volumes. Boston: Crosby and Nichols, 1862. 8vo. pp. xiv, [15]-484; xvi, [17]-596. complete with half-titles. indices. original cloth. First American Edition. $50

cf S.&M.II.238.

67 MAY, Thomas Erskine [Baron Farnborough]. A Treatise On The Law, Privileges, Proceedings and Usage of Parliament. Sixth Edition, Revised andEnlarged. London: Butterworths,1868. 8vo. pp. [1]ad, xxvi, 808, [36]ads. index. original cloth, bit frayed. $50

S.&M.II.238.
"May was clerk of the House of Commons, 1871-86, and wrote the first clear and comprehensive description of parliamentary procedure as it then existed." (Grose, p.38)

68 MILLINGEN, J[ulius] G[ideon] [1782-1862]. The History Of Duelling: Including, Narratives Of The Most Remarkable Personal Encounters That Have Taken Place From The Earliest Period To The Present Time. In Two Volumes. London: Richard Bentley, 1841. 8vo. pp. xii, 399, [1]; xii, 428. original blind & gilt stamped cloth, rebacked, with original backstrips laid down. corners bumped. A very nice set. First Edition. $150

In addition to providing a lively national account of the rules & practice of duelling, Millingen also considers the evolution of its legal status. Several chapters are devoted to America & the West Indies.

THE SPIRIT OF LAW

[MONTESQUIEU, Charles Louis de Secondat, Baron De La Brede et de] [1689-1755]. De L'Esprit Des Loix Ou Du Rapport Que Les Loix Doivent Avoir Avec La Constitution De Chaque Gouvernement, Les Moeurs, Le Climat, La Religion, Le Commerce, &c. a quoi l'Auteur a ajoute Des recherches nouvelles sur les Loix Romaines touchant les Successions, sur les Loix Francoises, & sur les Loix Feodales. Tome Premier. [... Tome Second.]. 2 Volumes. A Geneve: Chez Barrillot & Fils, [1748]. 4to. pp. 2pl, xxiv[iexxxviii, with pagination beginning on p.[5]]. 522; 2pl, xvi, 564. complete with half-titles. With the 15 cancelled leaves, as listed by Tchemerzine at pp. 23/24, 27/28, 29/30, 37/38, 45/46, 47/48, 85/86, 87/88, 185/186, 227/228, & 261/262 in Vol. I & pp.267/268, 273/274, 425/426, 427/428 in Vol. II. title vignettes, woodcut head & tailpieces. contemporary mottled calf,gilt backs. Signature of former owner (B[eat] J[acob] Tscharner [1743-1816]) on half-title. bindings bit rubbed & scuffed, slight embrowning to some leaves, otherwise excellent crisp copies. First Edition. $5,000

Tchemerzine VIII 459. PMM 197. Cabeen 97. Dagneau 15. Le Petit 495-96. Kress 4920.
One of the most remarkable works of the eighteenth century, treating of the philosophical principles of law & government, & the determining influence of geographical & economic factors on social thought, customs, & legal & political institutions. Original & inspiring, the treatise is particularly distinguished by a singular absence of doctrinairism, egotism & oversystematization. Montesquieu was unanimously advised by his friends, including Helvetius & Fontenelle, not to publish, but he ignored them & despite Helvetius' criticism that the work was too moderate, it was placed on the Index & the Sorbonne planned a regular censure of it. During the printing, several passages were altered, either by threat or order of censure or through the desire of the author, resulting in 15 cancelled leaves.
Although largely misunderstood & ignored by his contemporaries, including the 'philosophes', "his theories underlay the thinking which led up to the American and French revolution, and the United States Constitution in particular is a lasting tribute to the principles he advocated." (PMM).

MONTESQUIEU, [Charles Louis] de Secondat, Baron [De La Brede et] de. The Spirit of Laws. Translated from the French of M. De Secondat, Baron De Montesquieu. By Thomas Nugent. 2 Volumes. The Fifth Edition. Carefully revised and improved with considerable Additions by the Author. London: Printed for J. Nourse, And P. Vaillant, 1773. 8vo. pp.2pl, xlvii, 468; 2pl, xvi, 534, [46]index. complete with half-titles. some faint foxing to a few leaves, otherwise a fine set. $200

NCBEL II 1525.

MONTESQUIEU, [Charles Louis de Secondate, Baron De La Brede et de]. A View Of The English Consitution. By the late... Being A Translation [by Francis Maseres] of the Sixth Chap-

ter of the Eleventh Book of his celebrated Treatise, intitled L'Espirit Des Loix. London: Sold by B. White and H. Payne, 1781. 8vo. pp. 1pl, 74. disbound. small piece wanting from inner edge of title (no loss), inner edges of outer leaves slightly soiled,else very good. $50

NCBEL II 1525. S.&M.I.104.69.

72 MORRIS, Alexander [1826-1889]. The Treaties Of Canada With The Indians Of Manitoba And The North-West Territories, Including The Negotiations On Which They Were Based, And Other Information Relating Thereto. Toronto: Belfords, Clarke & Co., Publishers, 1880. 8vo. pp. 375, [5]ads. original blind & gilt stamped cloth. occasional foxing, else a very nice copy. First Edition. $125

Peel 544.
"A valuable source book by one who played a leading role in settling the Indians' claims." (Peel)

73 NISBET, John, [Lord Dirleton] [1609?-1687]. Some Doubts & Questions, In The Law; Especially of Scotland. As Also, Some Decisions of the Lords of Council and Session: Collected & Obser'd by...To which is Added, An Index, For finding the Principal Matters in the said Decisions. Edinburgh: Printed by George Mosman, 1698. folio. pp. 1pl, [10], 228, 226, [17]index. [Second part with separate title-page, variant title]. engraved frontis. portrait. contemporary mottled calf, gilt backs. binding a bit rubbed, internally very crisp. contemporary manuscript notes of Ja. Wineam. First Edition. $400

Wing N1170. S.&M.V.31. Marvin 539. Aldis 3767.
Nisbet was lord advocate during the covenanting persecution; although a learned man, he was noted for his unscrupulous and expedient methods.

74 NOBLE, Mark [1754-1827]. The Lives of the English Regicides, and Other Commissioners of the Pretended High Court of Justice, Appointed to sit in Judgment upon their Sovereign, King Charles the First. In Two Volumes. London: Printed for John Stockdale, 1798. 8vo. pp. xlvi, [47]-383; iv, 340,[4] ads. contemporary half calf. bindings rubbed, joints cracked, occasional hint of foxing, else very good. First Edition. $125

Abbot 1535.

75 D'OLIVE, Simon, Sieur du Mesnil [d1645]. Les Oeuvres de... Conseiller du Roy en la Cour de Parlement de Tolose: Divisee En Deux Volumes. Le Premier, Contenant les Questions Notables du Droict, decidees par divers Arrests de la Cour de Parlement de Tolose. Le Deuxiesme, Contenant les Actions Forenses, les Lettres & Notes sur les dictes Actions Forenses. [Vol. II has slight variation in title]. A Lyon: Chez Iacques Iustet..., 1649. 4to. pp. 1pl, [22], 494; 4pl, 396. woodcut ornaments. old calf. bindings rubbed, spinal extremities worn, occasional hint of foxing, else very good. With the armorial bookplate of Alexander Buchanan, & his signature on titles. From the library of Thomas Cushing Aylwin (1806-71), lawyer, politician & high court justice of Lower Canada, with his signature on front free-endpaper. $250

Only 1 copy located in NUC. Not in BM STC French Books.
The Works of the 17th century jurist include his commentaries on the law determined by cases heard before the Parlement of Toulouse, speeches, letters and analysis of legal actions.

PERKINS (or PARKINS), John [d.1545]. A Profitable Book... Treating of the Laws of England. Translated out of French into English for the benefit of young students and others. An.Dom. 1657. small 8vo. pp. 2pl, [27]index, 333. contemporary sheep. no endpapers. binding worn, head of backstrip defective, some insignificant marginal worming, otherwise very good. $450

Wing P1544. S.&M.I.485.56. See Winfield 330 & Marvin 563.
Perkins' popular textbook for law students first appeared in law French in 1528 (Perutilis tractatus). An attempt to update Littleton's 'Tenures', it enjoyed an enormous success for nearly three centuries, and is still regarded as an authority.

PETIT, Samuel [1594-1643]. Leges Atticae Sam. Petitus Colligit, Digessit, Et Libro Commentario Illustravit. Opus Iuris, Literarum, Et Rei Antiquariae studiosis utilissimum, VIII. Libris distinctum, in quo varij Scriptorum veterum Graecorum et Latinorum loci explicantur et emandantur. Parisiis: Sumptibus Caroli Morelli, 1635. folio. pp. 5pl, [1] blank, 55, 557, [4]index. title vignette. woodcut ornaments & initials. title in red & black. contemporary panelled calf. binding worn, front cover detached, lacking front free-endpaper, marginal tear in last leaf of index (no loss) else very good. From the library of Thomas Cushing Aylwin (1806-71), lawyer, politician & high court justice of Lower Canada, with his signature on front free-endpaper. $325

Graesse V, p. 220. Not in BM STC French Books. cf Brunet VI 2448.
An important work on Greek law by the learned French orientalist & protestant minister, Petit, whose friendship was sought by such distinguished scholars as Selden, Gassendi and Vossius.

[PLOWDEN, Francis Peter] [1749-1829]. An Investigation Of The Native Rights Of British Subjects. London: Printed for the Author; And sold by R. Baldwin..., 1784. 8vo. pp. vii, [1]errata, 200. contemporary half calf, marbled bds. extremities rubbed, joints cracked, hint of foxing to outer leaves, else very good. $225

S.&M.I.155.14. Marvin 576. Goldsmith 12788.
An important examination of English civil law attributed by Marvin and Goldsmith to Francis Plowden, the author of numerous works on English law. Halkett & Laing and Sweet & Maxwell attribute the work to John Davidson (Halkett & Laing give the date of the work as 1734).

PLOWDEN, Francis. A Short History Of The British Empire During The Year 1794. London: Printed For G.G. And J. Robinson, Paternoster Row, 1795. 8vo. pp. x, 377. contemporary sheep. binding quite worn, fr. joint cracked, internally browned but crisp. With the bookplate of John Scott, Chester-Town, 1795. First Edition. $150

Plowden's 'Short History' contains a sweeping expose of the government's erosion of the principle of trial by jury in the 1794 State Trials of the English Jacobins.

80 POLLET, Jacques. Arrests Du Parlement De Flandre Sur Diverses Questions De Droit, De Coutume, et De Pratique. Recuellis par...Ouvrage utile pour l'intelligence des Coutumes & des Usages du Pais. 3 Parts in 1. A Lille: Chez Lievin Danel, 1716. 4to. pp. 1pl, [14], 118, [1]div.title, [11], 119-267, [1]div.title, [3], 268-376, [26]. woodcut ornaments & initials. contemporary sprinkled sheep. binding rubbed, joints cracking, internally fine. From the library of Thomas Cushing Aylwin (1806-71), lawyer, politician & high court justice of Lower Canada, with his signature on front free-endpaper. $225

The NUC locates 3 copies.

"THE GREATEST FRENCH JURIST
OF THE 18TH CENTURY"

81 POTHIER, [Robert Joseph] [1699-1722]. [Oeuvres Completes]. Traites Sur Differentes Matieres De Droit Civil, Appliquees A l'Usage Du Barreau; Et De Jurisprudence Francoise. Seconde Edition, Revue. 4 Volumes. Paris: Chez Debure l'Aine ...Orleans: Chez J.M. Rouzeau-Montaut..., 1781. 4to. engraved frontis. portrait. several woodcut headpieces & ornamental initials. index. complete with half-titles. [WITH] [-----]. Coutumes Des Duche, Bailliage Et Prevote D'Orleans, Et Ressort D'Iceux; Avec une Introduction generale auxdites Coutumes, & des Introductions particulieres a la texte de chaque Titre, corrigees & augmentees, dans lesquelles les principes des matieres contenues dans le Tire, sont exposes & developpes. La Texte Est Accompagne De Notes. Par M. Pothier...Nouvelle Edition. Paris: Chez Debure l'aine... Orleans: Chez la Veuve Rouzeau-Montaut, Imprimeur du Roi ..., 1780. 4to. several woodcut headpieces & ornamental initials. index. complete with half-title. [WITH] [-----]. Oeuvres Posthumes De M. Pothier Dediees A Monseigneur Le Garde Des Sceaux De France. 3 Volumes. Paris: Chez De Bure, fils aine, Libraire, Quai des augustins, 1777-78. 4to. engraved frontis. portrait. engraved title vignettes. several woodcut headpieces. index. complete with half-titles. All 8 volumes bound in modern half calf, binding not uniform. a few leaves washed, some staining to margins & foxing, else a good set. From the library of Jean Thomas Taschereau [1778-1832], judge of court of King's Bench at Quebec & later, his son Jean Thomas Taschereau [1814-1893], puisine judge of Supreme Court of Canada. Both signatures on titles & numerous markings throughout in their hand. $1,350

Benet IV 844-45. For English editions of specific works see Marvin 578-79. cf Marke 233 (later edition of collected works).

Pothier, a magistrate & professor of law, devoted his life to the study of French civil law. His complete works form virtually an encyclopaedia of French law. "Pothier [was] the greatest French jurist of the 18th century...The present French Civil Code contains more of the spirit of Pothier than of Rousseau - the works of Pothier are often almost textually embodied in the code: for instance book iii of the code of obligations is greatly indebted to Pothier's very famous treatise on the same subject."(Marke)

82 PUFENDORF, Samuel [1632-1694]. The Divine Feudal Law: Or, Covenants With Mankind, Represented: Together With Means for the Uniting of Protestants. In which also the Principles of the Lutheran Churches are Stated and Defended. Translated from the Latin by Theophilus Dorrington. London: Printed for John Wyat..., 1703. 8vo. pp. 2pl, [12], 365, [3]ads. complete with half-title. modern quarter oasis morocco. some foxing & age-browning, else very good. First English Edition. $150

83 PUFENDORF, Samuel. On the Law of Nature and Nations. Eight Books, Written in Latin...Translated into English from the Best Edition [By B. Kennett]. With A Short Introduction. Oxford: Printed by A. Lichfield, 1703. folio. pp. 1pl, [4], [2], 27, [17], 400, 231, 143-262. main body of text printed in double columns. old reversed calf. binding somewhat worn, joints cracked, some insignificant marginal worming to first few signatures (touching several letters on one page), else very good. First English Edition, First Issue. $500

S.&M.I.597.72. NCBEL II 77. Kress 2400. See Marvin 593-94.

"In the 'De jure naturae et gentium' Pufendorf took up in great measure the theories of Grotius and sought to complete them by means of the doctrines of Hobees and of his own ideas...He combatted Hobbes's conception of the state of nature and concluded that the state of nature is not one of war but of peace...As regards public law Pufendorf, while recognizing in the state a moral person, teaches that the will of the state is but the sum of the individual wills that constitute it, and that this association explains the state." (Encyc.Brit., 11th Edn.)

84 PUFENDORF, Samuel. Le Droit De La Nature Et Les Gens, Ou Systeme General Des Principes les plus importans De La Morale, De La Jurisprudence, Et De La Politique. Par le Baron De Pufendorf, Traduit Du Latin Par Jean Barbeyrac...Avec des Notes de Traducteur; & une Preface qui sert d'Introduction a tout l'Ouvrage. Cinquieme Edition, revue de nouveau, & fort augmentee. 2 Volumes. A Amsterdam: Chez la Veuve de Pierre De Coup, 1734. 4to. pp. cxxi, [3], 716;2pl, 613, [37]index, 52, [2]errata. engraved frontis. port. title in red & black. title vignettes. several ornaments. hint of foxing to outer leaves, else a fine set in modern quarter oasis morocco. $400

Brunet IV, 960. See Marvin 593 & S.&M.I.597.72.

TREATISE ON CRIMINAL LAW

85 PULTON, Ferdinando [1536-1618]. De Pace Regis Et Regni, viz. A Treatise declaring which be the great and generall Offences of the Realme, and the chiefe impediments of the peace of the King and the Kingdome, as Treasons, Homicides, and Felonies...Collected out of the Reports of the Common Lawes of this Realme, and of the Statutes in force, and out of the painfull workes of the Reverend Judges, Sir Anthonie Fitzharbert, Sir Robert Brooke, Sir William Stanford, Sir James Dyer, Sir Edward Coke, Knights, and other Learned Writers of our Lawes. London: Printed for the Companie of Stationers, An.Dom. 1610. folio. pp. 5pl, 243[some leaves misnumbered], [33]index. head & tail-pieces. ornamental initials. black letter. contemporary calf, sometime rebacked. extremities rubbed, internally very good. Second Edition. $500

S.&M.I.365.589. STC 204966. Davies & Keeler 1087.

Pulton devoted his life to the study and compilation of statute law. " A more comprehensive and up-to-date book [than Staunford's Pleas of the Crown]...A comparison between...[them] enables us to appreciate the effect of the additions to the criminal law made during the sixteenth century by the legislature, the common law courts, and the Star Chamber." (Holdsworth. Sources p.125)

86 PUTZLACHER, Thomas Antonius. Dissertation Juridica De Praescriptionibus...Addita Juris Bohemici Dispositione, Et Observationibus Practicis, Quam Sub Gloriosissimis Auspiciis Augustissimae Romanorum Imperatricis Mariae Theresiae Germaniae, Hungariae, Bohemiae, &c. Reginae... Praegae: Typis Catharinae Labaunin Viduae, per Factorem Michaelem Jans, 1754. 4to. pp. 8pl, 180, [3]. several woodcut ornaments. contemporary velvet binding, gilt edges. binding slightly soiled & faded, hint of foxing to last few leaves, else internally fine. $150

Only 1 copy located in NUC.

87 QUESTIONS Concernant Les Substitutions, Avec les Responses de Tous les Parlemens et Cours Souveraines Du Royaume, et Des Observations De M. Le Chancelier D'Aguesseau, sur lesdites Reponses. A Toulouse: Chez Joseph Dalles & Fris Vitrac, 1770. 4to. pp. xii, 567, 28. several woodcut ornaments. contemporary mottled calf, gilt back. extremities rubbed, narrow strip clipped from upper edge of title, else an excellent clean copy. First Edition. $250

NUC cites only the Library of Congress copy.

Questions composed by the Chancellor d'Aguesseau regarding the legal entailing of estates, with responses from the high judicial courts of Paris, Toulouse, Metz, Dijon, &c. & commentary by d'Aguesseau; also including the royal ordonnance issued August 1747.

88 [RASTELL, John] [d.1536]. Les Termes De La Ley: Or, Certain difficult and obscure Words and Terms of the Common and Statute Laws of this Realm, now in Use, expounded and explained. Corrected and Enlarged, with the Addition of many other Words; particularly of those that have been lately introduced into the Statute Law of Great Britain, never printed in any other Impression. In the Savoy: Printed by Eliz. Nutt and R. Gosling...for R. Gosling..., 1721. 8vo. pp. 2pl, 592. modern quarter oasis morocco. small tear to Pp8(affecting 1 letter of headline), occasional foxing, otherwise very good. $200

S.&M.I.11.48. Marvin 599. cfWinfield 17. cfMarke 1203.

"Rastell's Terms de la Ley is a book which, like St. Germain's Doctor and Student, reflects the common law at the close of the yearbook period with much fidelity."(Marke) The first English law dictionary, by John Rastell, barrister of the Middle Temple & law printer, was also intended as a guide to law French. Originally composed in French, it was first published in 1527 with a Latin title. The 1721 edition was considerably enlarged & has both French & English texts.

89 REBUFFI, Pierre (Petrus REBUFFUS) [1487-1557]. Commentaria In Constitutiones, Seu Ordinationes Regias. Non solum Iuris studiosis, verum etiam Pragmaticis utilissima, In quibus facilis ad praxim Curiarum Franciae via, & Iurium intellectus explicantur... 3 Volumes in 1. [Title varies]. Lugduni

(Lyon): Apud Haeredes Gulielmi Rovillii, Sub Scuto Veneto, 1599. folio. pp. 952, [2]blank, [59]index. [continuous pagination]. title vignettes. woodcut ornaments & initials. title of Vol. I in red & black. old mottled calf, gilt back. binding bit rubbed, lower backstrip worn, small hole in last 6 leaves of index, affecting some words, otherwise an excellent copy. From the library of Thomas Cushing Aylwin (1806-71), lawyer, politician & high court justice of Lower Canada, with his signature on front free-endpaper. $350

This edition not in Adams or BM STC French Books. See Adams R.244 (listing Lyon edition 1550-51). Only 1 copy located in NUC.

The distinguished French jurist Rebuffi was born near Montpellier in 1487. He lectured on law at Bourges and Paris, and published several works, mainly dealing with civil law and regal ordinances.

90 REBUFFI, Pierre. In Tit. Dig. De Verborum et Rerum Significatione Commentaria Amplissima. In quibus, praeter exactas verborum omnium, quae ad ius ciuile pertinent, significationes, Iurisconsultorum veterum phrases & locutiones ...Ex Tertia Editione... Lugduni (Lyon): Apud Haeredes Gulielmi Rouillij, 1614. folio. pp. 6pl, 701, [45]index. title in red & black. text in double columns. title vignette. woodcut ornaments & initials. old mottled calf, gilt back. binding bit rubbed, spinal extremities worn, upper outer corner of title leaf wanting (no loss), some inner marginal dampstaining, else very good. From the library of Thomas Cushing Aylwin (1806-71), lawyer, politician & high court justice of Lower Canada, with his signature on front free-endpaper. $275

BM STC French Books R.219. See Adams R.246 (1586 edition).

Included is a brief biography of the author.

91 REBUFFI, Pierre. Repetitiones Variae, Extrema Authoris manu recognitae, selectissimis Opusculis, Notis, & Summarijs hac postrema editione auctae & locupletae. Quarum Elenchum pagina quarta indicabit. Lugduni (Lyon): Apud Haeredes Guilielmi Rovillii, Sub Scuto Veneto, 1600. folio. pp. 4pl, 681, [34]index. title in red & black. text in double columns. title vignette. woodcut ornaments & initials. old sprinkled calf, gilt back. binding bit rubbed, some wear to spinal extremities, otherwise an excellent copy. From the library of Thomas Cushing Aylwin (1806-71), lawyer, politician & high court justice of Lower Canada, with his signature on front free-endpaper. $275

Not in BM STC French Books, Adams or NUC.

92 REBUFFI, Pierre. Tractatus Varii. Extrema Authoris manu recogniti, Selectissimis opusculis, Notis, & Summarijs hac postrema Editione aucti, & locupletati. Quorum Elenchum pagina quinta indicabit. Lugduni (Lyon): Apud Haeredes Gulielmi Rovillii, Sub Scuto Veneto, 1600. folio. pp. 4pl, 661, [1], [22]index, [1]blank, 51, [1], 70, [8]index, [1]blank. title in red & black. text in double columns. title vignette. woodcut ornaments & initials.

Not in BM STC French Books or Adams. NUC locates 3 copies.

Bound with:

REBUFFI, Pierre. Explicatio Ad Quator Primos Pandectarum Libros, Novaeque Eorundem et Subtiles Illustrationes... Adiecti sunt ad leg. Si debitori, de Iudiciis. 1. Imperat ores, de priuil. cred... Lugduni (Lyon): Apud Guilielmum Rouillium, sub scuto Veneto, 1589. folio. pp. 6pl, 507,[37] index. title in red & black. text in double columns. title vignette. woodcut ornaments & initials.

BM STC French Books p.373. See Adams R.251 (1581 edition only). 3 copies located in NUC.

The two items bound in old sprinkled calf, gilt back. binding bit rubbed, extremities of backstrip worn, some damp staining to upper inner margin, title leaf of first item loose, otherwise very good. From the library of Thomas Cushing Aylwin (1806-71), lawyer, politician & high court justice of Lower Canada, with his signature on front free-endpaper. $550

REYNOLDS, John [fl. 1620-1640]. The Triumphs Of Gods Revenge Against the Crying and Execrable Sin of Murther. Expressed in Thirty several Tragical Histories. The Sixth Edition, very carefully Corrected. To which is Added, Gods Revenge Against The Abominable Sin of Adultery, Containing Ten Several Histories, Never Printed before. Illustrated with New Sculptures. [6 books in 1, the first 5 with continuous pagination; Parts II-V dated 1678]. title in red & black. London: Printed by J. Bennet, for Thomas Lee..., 1679. folio. pp. 10pl, 481, [1 blank], [4], 182. engraved title by F.H. Van Houe. 40 engraved strip text illus. contemporary panelled calf, rebacked. some browning & occasional foxing, corners bumped, else a very nice copy. First Edition Thus. $500

Wing R1313. NCBEL I 2056.
Reynold's didactic work on divine law was first published in parts. The first collected eition of the parts on murder appeared in 1635. This sixth edition includes for the first time the hitherto unpublished work on adultery as well as 40 unusual engraved strip illustrations which outline the scenario of each chapter.

ROCCUS, [Francesco] [fl.1655]. A Manual Of Maritime Law. Consisting Of A Treatise On Ships And Freight And A Treatise On Insurance. Translated From The Latin Of Roccus.With Notes. By Joseph Reed Ingersoll. Philadelphia: Published By Hopkins And Earle, 1809. 8vo. pp. xvi, [17]-156, [8]index. contemporary quarter sheep, bds. fr. joint cracked, sheep rubbed, internally, except for some browning, a very good copy. First Edition in English. $125

Marke 269. cfMarvin 616 (Amsterdam edition).
First published in 1655 under the title of 'Notablia de Navibys et Naulo, item de Assecurationibus', Roccus' work went through several editions. The first English translation of this work was based on the 1708 Amsterdam edition. "This manual is very highly esteemed by commercial lawyers in all countries, for its compressed, methodical, and accurate learning, and is a book of high authority." (Marvin)

RYALLS, Charles Wager (Ed.). Transactions Of The National Association For The Promotion Of Social Science. Brighton Meeting, 1875. London: Longmans, Green, And Co., 1876. 8vo. pp. xxxix, 743. 1 photographic illus. folding chart. index. complete with half-title. original blind stamped cloth. spine tips frayed, institutional stamp on title, else very good. $50

Includes articles on international law, land law, law of evidence, the Prevention of Crime Act &c., as well as articles on public health & economics.

[SAINT-GERMAIN, Christopher] [1460-1540]. The Dialoges In Englishe, betweene a Doctor of Diuinitie, and a Student in the lawes of Englande, newly corrected and imprinted wyth new additions. [Colophon on Z_4]: Londini in aedibus Richardi Tottelli, Anno, 1575. small 8vo. ff. 177, [4]. black letter. title within ornamental woodcut border. several woodcut initials. margins of some leaves stained, else a very good copy.

S.&M.I.24.34. STC 21573. Winfield 321-324. For other editions see Marvin 626 & Marke 38.

Bound With:

MAGNA CHARTA, cum statutis, tum antiquis, tum recentibus, maximopere animo tenendis nunc demum ad vnum, tipis aedita, per Richardum Tottel. Anno domini. 1576. [Colophon on Hh_8]: Imprinted at London in Fleetestreete within Temple barre at the Signe of the Hand and Starre, by Richard Tottel, the 8. day of March, 1576. small 8vo. ff. [7], [1 blank], 3-247. several woodcut initials. lacking A_1 & A_2, P & Z gatherings. staining to outer margins of some gatherings.

STC 9281. S.&M.I.552.9.

Both works bound in late 18th century quarter roan (rubbed). $450

"It is impossible to read [Saint-Germain's 'Doctor and Student'] without being struck by the amount of fresh air which it pours upon the ill-ventilated technicalities of our medieval law. From beginning to end, legal rules are put in the witness-box and cross-examined to credit. Religious and ethical tests are applied to them, and Doctor and Student is surprisingly full of the speculative inquiries into the foundation of the Common Law which are almost entirely lacking in the earlier literature...Great men like Fitzherbert and Coke cited it freely, and there is reason to think that it partially filled a gap which only Blackstone's Commentaries were destined to close." (Winfield)

SEDGWICK, James [1775-1857]. Remarks, Critical And Miscellaneous, On The Commentaries Of Sir William Blackstone. London: Printed by M. Ritchie...For G.G. & J. Robinson...,1800. 4to. pp. x, [2], 304. complete with half-title. uncut in original bds. extremities chipped, paper flaw in 2P4 causing small hole (no loss of text), some pencil annotations in margins, otherwise internally fine & crisp copy. First Edition. $300

S.&M.I.30.15. cfMarvin 635 (2nd Edition).
Sedgewick's well-reasoned critique of Blackstone's 'Commentaries' is less well-known than those of his more famous contemporaries, Bentham & Priestley. Nevertheless Sedgewick's chapter by chapter critique of Vol. I of the 'Commentaries' is still remembered for its "spirit of great fairness & minute care." (DNB)

SMITH, Thomas [1513-1577]. The Commonwealth Of England: And

the manner and Governement thereof. Compiled By The Honourable Sir Thomas Smith, Knight, Doctor of both Lawes, and one of the principall Secretaries unto...King Edward, and Queene Elizabeth. With new Additions of the chiefe Courts in England, and the Offices thereof, by the said Author. London: Printed by R. Young for J. Smethwicke, and are to be sold at his shop in S. Dunstans Church-yard, 1640. 12mo. pp. 6pl. incl. engraved title, 272. contemporary calf, rebacked. covers lightly worn, else a very nice copy. $250

STC 22867. S.&M.I.107.105. NCBEL I 2211. cfMarke 368.
Written during his first embassy in France, "it is the most important description of the constitution and government of England written in the Tudor age."(DNB) It was originally published in 1583 under the title 'De Republica Anglorum; the Maner of Government or Policie of the Realm of England' and passed through 11 editions in English in little over a century.

SORDI, Giovanni Pietro (Joannis Petrus SURDUS). Consiliorum Sive Responsorum Juris De grauissimis quaestionibus in vtroque foro quotidie occurrentibus & incidentibus Libri IV... Opus Nunc Denuo Ad Primam Editionem Venetam Diligenter recensitum & emendatum... 4 Volumes in 2. [Title varies]. Francofurti Ad Moenum: Typis Wechelianis, Sumptibus Clementis Schleichii & Petri de Zetter, 1629-30. folio. pp. 4pl, 509, [2]div.title, 513-978, [61]index; 618, 619-914, [53] index. title of Vol. I in red & black. text in double & index in triple columns. title vignettes. woodcut ornaments & initials. contemporary alum-tawed pigskin over bds. oval ornament stamped in blind on centre covers. leather ties wanting, backstrips worn & chipped, internally fine. From the library of T.C. Aylwin, signed, & with printed book label of the Court of Arches, London. $600

This edition not in NUC.
Treating of civil & criminal law, wills, hereditary rights, contracts, &c. A native of northern Italy, the author was one of the most celebrated jurists of his time.

SORDI, Giovanni Pietro. Decisiones Universae, Summo Labore et Studio Compilatae, Nec Hactenus sic editae: in quibus variae, & perplexae satis materiae, ultimas voluntates, contractus, judicia civilia, criminalia, fiscalia, feudalia, fideique materiam respicientes non minus docte, quam sententiose explicantur, & exactissime resolvuntur... 2 Books in 1 [No separate title-page for Book II]. Francofurti ad Moenum: Imprensis Joannis Baptistae Schonwetteri, Typis Matthaei Kempfferi, 1664. folio. pp. 4pl, 641, [77]index; 63, [7]index. title in red & black. text in double & index in triple columns.

Bound with:

HODIERNA, Giambattista. Novissimae Additiones, Et Observationes ad Decisiones Mantuani Senatus Io. Petri Surdi.Quibus hac quarta editione praeter antiquas nouae insigniores Quaestiones accesserunt, nouaeque Almi Consilii Neap. sententiae subnectuntur... Genevae: Sumptibus Ioannis Hermanni Widerhold, 1669. folio. pp. 3pl, 397, [54]index. complete with half-title. title in red & black. text in double columns. title vignette. several woodcut ornaments.

The NUC locates only 2 copies of the first work, and none of the second.

The two bound together in old calf, sometime rebacked.binding worn, front cover & prelims of first item detached, some foxing & age-browning, else very good. From the library of T.C. Aylwin, signed, & with printed book labels of the Court of Arches, London. $500

"ENGLAND'S EARLIEST SCIENTIFIC CRIMINALIST"

STANFORD, Sir William [1509-88]. Les Plees del Coron, diuisees in plusors titles & comon lieux. Per queux home plus redemen & plenairement trouera quelque chose qu'il quira, touchant les dits Plees, composees par le tres reuerand Iudge Monsieur Guilliaulme Staundforde Chiualer, dernierment corrigee auecques vn table per faicte des choses notables contenues en ycelle, nouuelment reueu et corrigee. [London]: In aedibus Richardi Tottelli, 1574. 4to.ll. 2pl, [12]table, 193[ie198]. woodcut title border & initials. Fourth Edition.

STC 23222. S.&M.I.365.68. Beale T.489. Winfield 234-35. See Marke 453 & Marvin 662-63 (not listing this edition).
"Stanford's is the earliest professed Treatise upon the Criminal Law of England, and his mode of dividing and arranging the topics has been generally followed by succeeding writers in this department of the law. Lord Hale took 'Les Plees del Coron', as the foundation of his excellent works upon Criminal Law."(Marvin) The work was first published posthumously in 1557 and is divided into 3 books, dealing, respectively, with greater crimes; jurisdiction, appeals, &c; & with different modes of trial, judgment and forfeiture. The work enjoyed a high reputation & has always been regarded as the ultimate authority for certain of the basic rules & aspects of the criminal law.

Bound With:

STANFORD, Sir William. An exposition of the Kinges Prerogatiue, collected out of the great Abridgement of Iustice Fitzherbert, and other olde writers of the lawes of England, by the right worshipfull Sir William Staunford Knight, lately one of the Justices of the Queenes Maiesties Court of common pleas. Where vnto is annexed the Proces to the same Praerogatiue appertayning. London: Richard Tottel, 1577. 4to. ll. 1pl, 85. woodcut initials. Fourth Edition.

STC 23216. S.&M.I.119.79. Beale T.495. Winfield 319. See Marvin 662 (not listing this edition).
This commentary on the statute 17 Edw. II was first published in 1567. An extremely erudite work, it is distinguished as being the earliest extant monograph on statutory interpretation.

The two works bound in old sprinkled panelled calf. binding bit rubbed, else fine copies. Armorial bookplate of Algernon Capell, Second Earl of Essex, &c. on verso of title. manuscript notes of former owner (N.W. Mach) on front blank - with separate notes bound in, indicating that the volume also belonged to Henry Bickersteth, Baron Langdale & was sold at Sotheby's auction of 28 July 1851. $1,000

102 TALLACK, **William**. Penological and Preventive Principles, With Special Reference to Europe and America; And to the Diminution of Crime, Pauperism, and Intemperance; to Prisons, and Their Substitutes, Habitual Offenders, Sentences, Neglected Youth, Education, Police, Statistics, Etc. By ..., Secretary of the Howard Association, London. London: Wertheimer, Lea & Co., 1889. 8vo. pp. [ii]-x, 414. index. lacking the half-title. modern buckram. fine. First Edition. $60

103 TILLESLEY, Richard [1582-1621]. Animadversions upon M. Seldens History Of Tythes And His Review Thereof: Before which (in lieu of the two first Chapters purposely pretermitted) is premised a Catalogue of 72. Authors, before the year 1215. Maintaining the Jus diuinum of Tythes, or more, to by payd to the Priesthood under the Gospell. The second Edition newly corrected and much augmented, together with an Answer to an unprinted Pamphlet divulged against the former. London: Printed by N. Okes for Arthur Johnson,1621. small 4to. pp. 21pl, 263, [1 blank], 137[ie139], [1]errata. woodcut ornamental initials. 19th century half calf. light dampstaining to margins, lacking A1(blank?). An attractive copy with the printed label of the Court of Arches, London. $350

New STC 24074. S.&M.I.196.56.
A response to Selden's 'History', Tillesley's 'Animadversions' argues the divine origins of tithes & in the process gives a detailed history of tithes from the apostolic period. The second edition of this work contains an additional essay on some philogical passages of Selden's 'History'.

104 (TRIALS) (ANNESLEY, James) [1715-1760]. The Trial at Bar Between Campbell Craig, Lessee of James Annesley, Esq; Plaintiff, And the Right Honourable Richard Earl of Anglesey, Defendant. Before the Honourable the Barons of the Exchequer, At The King's Court, Dublin, in Trinity Term, In the 16th and 17th Years of the Reign of our Sovereign Lord George the Second, King of Great-Britain, &c. and in the Year of our Lord 1743. London: Printed by and for the Proprietor, R. Walker..., 1744. 8vo. pp. 448. engraved frontis. portrait. contemporary calf, rebacked. calf sl. scuffed, occasional foxing, else a very good copy. $150

Marke 962. cfSabin 1602 & Howes 283 (not listing this ed.).
Annesley's life reads like an 18th century novel: rejection by his father, kidnapped by his uncle, sold into slavery in America, rescued in Jamaica & returns to claim the title of Earl of Anglesey. It is no wonder that Smollett & Scott's imaginations were captured by Annesley's story: the former in 'Peregrine Pickle' and the latter in 'Guy Mannering'.
Annesley brought an action against his uncle, Richard Annesley, of trespass and ejectment for the recovery of the Irish estates. A record of this trial is included in this edition, as well as his trial for the murder of a poacher, Thomas Egglestone, in 1742.

105 (TRIALS). BURKE, Peter. Celebrated Trials Connected With The Aristocracy in the Relations of Private Life. London: William Benning & Co., 1840. 8vo. pp. 1pl, v, 505. contemporary half sheep. binding rubbed & faded, internally very good. $50

(TRIALS).(QUEEN CAROLINE) The Legislatorial Trial Of Her Majesty Caroline Amelia Elizabeth, Queen Of England, Consort Of George The Fourth, For The Alleged Crime of Adultery With Bartolomeo Bergami. By The Author Of "The Royal Wanderer". London: Printed And Published By H. Rowe..., 1820. 8vo. pp. viii, 763. folding frontispiece: 'A Sketch Of The Interior View Of The House Of Lords...' drawn by Cruikshank and etched by Roberts. 4 engraved portraits. contemporary half calf, gilt back. backstrip sl. rubbed, else a very nice copy. $125

(TRIALS).(QUEEN CAROLINE). NIGHTINGALE, J[oseph] (Ed.). Report of the Proceedings Before the House of Lords, On A Bill of Pains and Penalties Against Her Majesty, Caroline Amelia Elizabeth, Queen of Great Britain and Consort of King George the Fourth. Collated With the Journals of the House of Lords. 3 Volumes. [Vol. I: ...The Charges; Vol. II: ...The Defence, Part I; Vol.III: ...The Defence Part II]. London: J. Robins & Co., 1821. 8vo. pp. 2pl, 611,[1] ads; 1pl, 604; 1pl, 758. 23 engraved plates (including 3 engraved titles & numerous portraits). modern cloth.first portrait mounted, occasional damp marks & brown stains, else a very good uncut copy. $175

A bill promoted in the House of Lords to deprive Queen Caroline of her rights and privileges as Queen Consort & to dissolve the marriage between herself & King George IV, was abandoned in view of popular opinion. Brougham's defence of the Queen considerably enlarged his reputation.

(TRIALS). CUNNINGHAM, Francis. An Account Of The Death Of Philip Jolin, Who Was Executed For The Murder Of His Father, In The Island Of Jersey, October 3, 1829. London: J. Hatchard And Son, Piccadilly: Seeley And Sons..., 1830. 8vo. pp. 50. partially unopened. disbound. $25

(TRIALS). ELWALL, [Edward] [1676-1744]. The Triumph Of Truth Being an Account of the Trial of Mr. Elwall, Before Judge Denton, For publishing a Book in defence of The Unity of God. At The Stafford Assizes, In The Year 1726. Bilston: Printed And Sold By S. Bassford, 1808. 12mo. pp. 12. disbound. $20

(TRIALS). (DRED SCOTT CASE). Report Of The Decision Of The Supreme Court Of The United States, And The Opinions Of The Judges Thereof, In The Case Of Dred Scott Versus John F.A. Sandford. December Term, 1856. By Benjamin C. Howard, From The Nineteenth Volume Of Howard's Reports. Washington: Cornelius Wendell, Printer, 1857. 8vo. pp. 239. disbound, gatherings & leaves loose, outer leaves slightly tatty. First Separate Printing. $85

Howes S-218. Sabin 33240.
The momentous decision of the Supreme Court in the Dred Scott Case excited great interest throughout the country in view of its extreme pro-slavery position & probably did much to precipitate the Civil War. A negro slave, Scott sued for his freedom on the basis of having lived with his former master in the free state of Illinois for several years before resettling in the slave state of Missouri. The Supreme Court basically affirmed that blacks had never been intended to be considered as citizens by the designers of the Constitution & had no right

to sue in Federal courts, that the Missouri Compromise was unconstitutional & void & Scott was still a slave.

111 (TRIALS). (STATE). A Complete Collection Of State-Trials, And Proceedings For High-Treason, And Other Crimes and Misdemeanours; From The Reign of King Richard II. To The End Of the Reign of King George I. In Six Volumes [8 Vols. including 1735 supplemental volumes]. With two Alphabetical Tables to the Whole. The Second Edition, with great Additions. London: Printed for J. Walthoe Sen. R. Vincent..., 1730-1735. folio. woodcut vignettes & ornamental initials. titles in red & black. contemporary calf. bindings rubbed, joints cracked, covers of Vol. I detached, internally very good. $450

S.&M.I.369.8. For other editions see Marke 1030-31 & Marvin 660-61.

112 (TRIALS). (THISTLEWOOD, Arthur). The Trial Of Arthur Thistlewood, On a Charge Of High Treason. Tried at the Old Bailey, April 17th, 1820, Before The Lord Chief Justice Abbott. London: Printed and Published by Messrs. Clement and Benbow, No. 269, Strand, 1820. 8vo. pp. 95, [1]ad. engraved frontis. portrait. original bds. front covers detached, else a very good uncut copy. $75

An account of the famous 'Cato Street Conspiracy' trial. Thistlewood and a number of his fellows had already been tried on similar charges and acquitted (in 1816 after their attempt to organize a large public meeting under the auspices of the Spencean & other revolutionary societies with the express purpose of fomenting a revolution). Thistlewood & four other conspirators were sentenced to death by hanging.

113 (TRIALS). (YORK, Frederick Augustus, Duke of). Stratford's Authentic Edition. Of the Investigation of the Charges Brought against His Royal Highness the Duke of York, By Gwyllym Lloyd Wardle, Esq. Member for Oakhampton. Containing the Whole of the Evidence. Printed from the Minutes of the House of Commons. With the Official Papers and The Debates at Large. 2 Vols. London: Printed for J. Stratford ..., 1809. 8vo. pp. 3pl, [5]-564; 1pl, 658.16 engraved plates, incl. 2 frontis. portraits & 1 hand-coloured plate [12 plates after Rowlandson sketches]. contemporary calf. joints of Vol. I cracked, bds. of Vol. II detached, covers sl. rubbed, some plates sl. foxed, else a good set. $150

Account of the royal imbroglio in which Wardle exposed the Duke of York's indiscretion with the adventuress, Mary Anne Clarke. Trading on her relationship with the Duke of York, Mary Anne Clarke had promised officers' promotions after suitable payment for her recommendations. Although the Duke was acquitted of corrupt practices, the scandal forced him to resign his post as commander-in-chief of the army.

FRIEND OF RABELAIS

114 TIRAQUEAU, Andre (Andreas TIRAQUELLUS) [c1480-1558]. Operum Omnium... 7 Volumes in 2. [Title varies]. Francofurti; Curantibus Rulandii, Typis Ioannis Bringeri, 1616. folio. pp. 1pl, [10], 480, [18]index; 1pl, [10], 360, [22]index; 1pl, [6], 214, [16]index; 1pl, [37], 498, [23]index; 1pl, [9], 275, [9]index; 106, [6]index; 116, [5]index. text in double columns. index in triple columns. title vignettes. several woodcut ornaments. title of Vol. I in red & black. old roll-stamped calf. bindings rather worn, with some repairs, small hole in title leaf neatly mended (affecting numeral of date), some slight dampstaining near end of Vol. III, else very good. From the library of T.C. Aylwin, signed and the Court of Arches, London. $700

Only 3 copies located in NUC. For earlier editions see BM STC German Books p. 863 (1597) & Adams T.726 (1574) & T.727 (1597).
Tiraqueau, French jurist, was one of the most important members of the 'Parlement de Paris' under Henri II. He was a man of integrity & celebrated ability, & was on close terms with all of the leading men of letters. While he held the office of judge, he released Rabelais, who had been imprisoned by the monks, & he is mentioned by Rabelais in his 'Pantagruel'. Included here are the author's writings on nobility & the law of primogeniture, hereditary rights ('Le Mort saisit le vif'), marriage laws, punishments, &c.

FIRST COLLECTION OF
AMERICAN CONSTITUTIONS

[UNITED STATES OF AMERICA]. Recueil Des Loix Constitutives Des Colonies Angloises, Confederees Sous La Denomination D'Etats-Unis De L'Amerique-Septentrionale. Auquel on a joint les Actes d'Independance, de Confederation & autres Actes du Congres general, traduit de l'Anglois. Dedie a M. le Docteur Franklin. A Philadelphia [Printed Paris], Et se vend a Paris: Chez Cellot & Jombert...,1778. 12mo. pp. 6pl, 370. complete with half-title. occasional hint of foxing, backstrip chipped, otherwise a fine uncut copy in original wrs., preserved in folding morocco-backed box. First Collected Edition. $1,000

Howes R-111. Sabin 68448. JCB II 2507.
The first collective appearance of the constitutions of the original component states of the newly created United States of America. At this particular point, only 6 of the 13 states had drawn up, approved & published constitutions: Pennsylvania, New Jersey, Delaware, Maryland, Virginia, & Carolina. A complete collection was not published until 1781 in Philadelphia. Also included are the Declaration of Independence, the Articles of Confederation & the Laws of Navigation, &c. The work, compiled by Regnier, is,not unpredictably, dedicated to Benjamin Franklin, who no doubt had a hand in its appearance.

VAN SANTVOORD, George. Sketches Of The Lives And Judicial Services Of The Chief-Justices Of The Supreme Court Of The United States. New York: Charles Scribner, 1856. 8vo. pp. viii, 533. engraved frontis. portrait. original cloth, frayed. lacking back free endpaper, hint of foxing, else a very good copy. First Edition. $50

Marke 155.

JUDGE BRENTANO'S COPY
OF A CLASSIC OF INTERNATIONAL LAW

VATTEL, [Emeric] de [1714-67]. Le Droit Des Gens Ou Principes De La Loi Naturelle, Appliques a la Conduite & aux Affaires des Nations & des Souverains. Ouvrage qui conduit a developer les veritables Interets des Puissances.

2 Volumes in 1. A Leide: Aux Depens De La Compagnie, 1758. 4to. pp. 1pl, [34], 228; 1pl, [14], 162. title of Vol. I in red & black. title vignettes & woodcut ornaments. contemporary half calf somewhat worn, joints cracked, occasional hint of foxing, else internally very good. With engraved card & inscription of Theodore Brentano, American Chief Justice & diplomat. Published the same year as the first edition. $500

Camus 202. See Graesse VI p.265 & Cioranescu, 18th Cent., III 62938.

This classic in the literature of international law established the international reputation of the Swiss jurist & diplomat Vattel. He followed in the tradition of Leibniz & Wolff, but abandoned the mathematical method & Wolff's notion of the 'world state'. He claimed that one could discover the ultimate basis of all legal institutions, including the natural law of nations, in the concept of utility, derived from the postulates of ideal reason. Vattel's theory, more in keeping with the practice of statesmen, was highly influential.

118 VOLTAIRE, [Francois Marie Arouet] de [1694-1778]. A Treatise on Toleration; The Ignorant Philosopher; And A Commentary on the Marquis of Beccaria's Treatise on Crimes and Punishments. Translated From the Last Geneva Edition of M.R. De Voltaire, By the Rev. David Williams. London: Printed for Fielding and Walker, 1779. 3 Parts in 1, with separate titles. 8vo. pp. 2pl, iv, 224, [2], iii, 86, [2], ii, 50. A nice copy in original bds., sometime rebacked. $175

Voltaire's treatise on religious toleration was inspired by the celebrated judicial murder of Jean Calas, secured by popular Roman Catholic sentiment against Protestants. His 3 year effort in publicizing the case led to an anulment of the original verdict & the Calas family was declared innocent. The theme of intolerance & persecution is carried into the second work & that of judicial reform into the third. Voltaire was greatly influenced by Beccaria's systematic treatise & his commentary, which was later incorporated into editions of the latter, was the first work of Voltaire's to be published in America (1777). His reputation no doubt helped in popularizing & actualizing Beccaria's proposals.

119 [WADE, John] [1788-1875]. The Cabinet Lawyer; Or, Popular Digest of the Laws of England...With the Criminal Law of England; Also, A Dictionary of Law Terms, Maxims, Acts of Parliament, and Judicial Antiquities; Correct Tables of Assessed Taxes...And Prison Regulations. Second Edition. London: Printed For W. Simpkin and R. Marshall, 1827. 12mo. pp. xxviii, 584. index. uncut in original bds. $85

See S.&M.II.368. This edition not in NUC.

120 WRIGHT, William. Advice On The Study And Practice Of The Law: With Directions For The Choice Of Books. Addressed To Attorneys' Clerks. Third Edition, Enlarged. London: Printed For Charles Hunter, Law Bookseller..., 1824. pp. 1pl, x, [2], 248. original bds. except for occasional foxing & little rubbing to bds., a very nice uncut copy. $100

Marvin 750. Marke 232. S.&M.II.394.

121 (YEARBOOK) [EDWARD III]. Anni Decem Priores, Regis Edwardi Tertii, Mvlto Omnes, Qvam Ante, emendatius aediti, Signis istis ** in textu, principiis foliorum editionis prioris, praepositis: Numerisq; interlinearibus notatis in Margine, Iurisprudentissimorum vivorum Br. & Fitzh. Abbreuiamentorum foliis, quod in priore editione non obseruabatur, respondentibus. Londini: In Aedibus Ianae Yetsweirt relictae Caroli Yetsweirt Armigeri. Cvm Privilegio Regiae Maiestatis, 1596. folio. ff. 404. printed in black letter. title within elaborate woodcut border. numerous woodcut initials. modern quarter oasis morocco. few minor repairs to inner margins of some leaves, title & last leaf mounted, old manuscript notes on front free-endpaper. Biddle Law Library Duplicate. $450

S.&M.I.312.15 & 314.20. See Winfield 175. STC 9552.

The Yearbooks are the most important souce of medieval common law, providing first hand accounts of the legal doctrines established by the judges of the 14th and 15th centuries. The publication of Yearbooks flourished from 1481 to 1638 or 1640, after which publication ceased for 40 years.

(YEARBOOK) [LONGO QUINTO]. En cest Volume est conteinus Le Longe Report de Anno Quinto Edwardi Quarti, Ore Novelment imprimee & corrigee, Ovesque References al Abridgement de les Cases in Brooke addes in le Margent de chescun Case. London: Printed by the Assignes of John More Esquire, 1638. folio. pp. 5pl, 142 leaves. printed in black letter. modern quarter oasis morocco.title leaf mounted, edges of outer leaves tatty, perforated lib. stamp on title, age-browning to margins, else a very nice crisp copy. With the bookplate of the Biddle Law Library. $350

S.&M.I.312.15 & 318.16. See Winfield 176. STC 9804.

The 'Longo Quinto' was published in 1552 and 1587, then re-published in 1638. This report of Edward IV's reign is considered to be one of the finest examples of law reporting contained in the various Yearbooks. "The Longo Quinto represents a more elaborate effort of reporting than had yet been seen. Often it seems to be more impersonal, and to give the gist of several reports rather than the actual account of the eye-witness. No doubt, too, the reporters became more skilful, more professional, as time went on; they allowed themselves fewer scattered notes, fewer personal details. The report of the case is the main thing, and the report grows fuller."(Holdsworth. A History II p.456)

ENDA

BRIDGMAN, Orl[ando] [1606?-1674]. ...Conveyances: Being Select Precedents Of Deeds and Instruments Concerning the Most Considerable Estates in England...The Fourth Edition, With large Additions: And A New Table to the Whole. In the Savoy: Printed by John Nutt...for Susanna Battersby..., 1710. folio. pp. 3pl, 378, [25]index. old calf. former owner's signature (Macaulay) on front blank. old manuscript notes. binding worn, bds. detached, internally foxed but crisp. $200

S.&M.I.479.9. cfMarke779. cfMarvin 146-147.

"It is the first book of precedents of the modern type; and it is this book which has given to Bridgman the title of the father of modern conveyancers." (Marke)

ROBERT H. RUBIN BOOKS

Post Office Box 558 · Stoughton, Massachusetts 02072 USA
Cable Address: «RUBOOKS» Telephone: (617) 344-0740

CATALOG THREE 1979

ANTIQUARIAN AND OUT-OF-PRINT WORKS IN

LAW AND LEGAL HISTORY

(CHIEFLY ANGLO-AMERICAN)

PART I:	**Books published before 1900**	**items 1-114**
PART II:	**Books published 1900 and after**	**115-220**
	Addenda (continuation of Part I)	**221-225**

I take pleasure in sending to you my first law catalogue. Some of the highlights: **Gentili's Treatise on the Law of War; Livingston's Penal Code for the United States; an original unpublished manuscript treatise on American maritime insurance; the first English edition of Beccaria,** *and others. I hope all of it makes interesting reading, and I look forward to many more catalogues. Your offers of duplicates and specialized (though not exclusive) want lists will be most welcome.*

1. a BECKETT, THOMAS TURNER. Law reforming difficulties, exemplified in a letter to Lords Brougham and Vaux, accompanied by an analysis of a bill for the improvement of the law relating to the administration of deceased persons' estates, ... London, Butterworth, 1849. 79pp. Disbd. Presentation copy from the author. $ 25.00

2. ADAMS, JOHN. A Treatise on the principles and practice of the action of ejectment, and the resulting action for mesne profits. From the last London edition, to which have been carefully noted, the decisions of the Supreme Court of New-York, from January term, 1799 to October term, 1820. With references to decisions in the courts of Massachusetts and Pennsylvania, and the Supreme Court of the United States, by Philo Ruggles. N.Y., Gould, 1821. 421pp. Calf. Good copy. $ 42.50
*Marvin p. 31. Highly praised. First American Edition.

3. ANGELL, JOSEPH K. A treatise on the right of property in tide waters, and in the soil and shores thereof. 2nd edition, revised, corrected, and much enlarged. Boston, Little, 1847. 475pp. $ 45.00
*Marvin p. 62, "the only regular treatise on this branch of law" Best edition.

4. The attorney's companion, containing the rules of the Supreme Court, Court of Chancery, and the Court of Errors, of the State of New-York; notes of cases of practice at law; and practical forms. By a gentleman of the Bar. Poughkeepsie, Potter, 1818. 458pp. Cont. calf, spine a little worn, else a nice copy. $ 45.00
*Marvin p.78.

5. AUSTIN, HENRY. The liquor law in the New England States. Boston, (Berwick & Smith) 1890. 332pp. $ 12.50

6. (BACON, NATHANIEL). An historical discourse of the uniformity of the government of (Cont'd.)

6. (BACON, NATHANIEL). (Cont'd.) England. The first part ... till the reign of Edward III. (WITH:) The continuation of an historical discourse, of the government of England, until the end of the reigne of Queen Elizabeth, with a preface, being a vindication of the ancient way of Parliaments in England. London, Walbancke, 1647, 1651. Two parts bound together in one volume. Thick small 4to. Contemp. calf, expertly rebacked. Clean tear on p. 66 of part one; engraved illustration following title of part I. A very good copy. $ 110.00
*Wing B351,349. First editions of a classic attack on royal prerogative by way of a constitutional history of England; its libertarian spirit caused reprints of the work to be suppressed during the Restoration, and it re-appeared as late as 1760. Sweet and Maxwell, I, p. 99.

7. BAILEY, SAMUEL. The rationale of political representation. By the author of Essays on the Formation of Opinions. London, Hunter, 1835. $ 75.00
*Bailey was a follower of Bentham, and a highly original writer in both economic and political matters.

8. BALLANTINE, WILLIAM. A treatise on the statute of limitations. (21 Jac. I.c. 16). With references to American decisions. N.Y., Printed by C. Wiley, 1812. 251pp. Cont. 1/4 cf. Spine little rubbed, internally a fine copy. $ 37.50
*Marvin p. 90. First American edition.

9. BEAMES, JOHN. The elements of pleas-in-equity, with precedents of such pleas. First American edition, with notes and references to the subsequent decisions and American authorities, by William Halsted, Jun., Esq., solicitor and master in chancery. N.Y., Halsted, 1824. 362pp. Calf. Nice copy. $ 45.00
*Marvin p. 102. Highly praised.

10. BENNETT, M.L. The Vermont justice, being a treatise on the civil and criminal jurisdiction of justices of the peace, prepared primarily for the use of justices of (Cont'd.)

10. BENNETT, M.L. (Cont'd.) the peace, and the junior members of the bar in Vermont; ... Burlington, N.P. 1864. 802pp. Contemp full calf. Nice copy. First edition. $ 25.00

11. BENTHAM, JEREMY. An introduction to the principles of morals and legislation. Oxford. Clarendon, 1876. 336pp. Fine. $ 20.00
*Reprint of the author's edition of 1823.

12. BENTHAM, JEREMY. Theory of legislation; translated from the French of Etienne Dumont, by R(ichard) Hildreth. Boston, Weeks, Jordan, 1840. Two volumes. Orig. publ. cl. Fine. $ 75.00
*First appearance of the work in English. One of Bentham's major works, like so many others of his writings, appearing originally in Dumont's French translation from the author's ms.

13. BERNARD, MONTAGUE. A lecture on alleged violations of neutrality by England in the present war. London, Ridgway, 1863. 45pp. dsbd. $ 22.50
*Bernard was professor of international law at Oxford, greatly revered in England and America, and a signer of the subsequent Treaty of Washington.

14. BIGELOW, MELVILLE M. A treatise on the law of estoppel and its application in practice. Boston, Little, Brown, 1872. 656pp. Contemp. sheep, spine rubbed but a very good copy. First edition. $ 25.00

15. BISHOP, JOEL PRENTISS. Commentaries on the criminal law. Second edition, revised and enlarged. In two vols. Boston, Little, Brown, 1858. Contemp. sheep, little rubbed, but a very good set. $ 37.50

16. BLACK, CHARLES C. Proof and pleadings in accident cases. ... Jersey City, Linn, 1886. 301pp. Contemp. calf. Fine. First Edition. $ 15.00

17. BLACKSTONE, WILLIAM. Commentaries on the laws of England, in four books. From the last London edition. With the last corrections of the author; and with notes and additions by Edward Christian ... Portland, (Maine), Wait, 1807. 4 volumes. 8vo. Orig. full calf, lea. labels, minor rubbing, but an excellent set. $ 150.00
*With a specially executed portrait for this edition and the folding genealogical table in vol. 2. Marvin p. 123; Shaw-Shoemaker, 12159. The 5th American edition.

18. BROWNE, IRVING. Elements of the law of domestic relations and of employer and employed. Second edition, revised. Boston, Boston Book Co., 1890. 166pp. Calf, worn. $ 12.50

19. BUCHANAN, GEORGE. De jure regni adup Scotos. Or, a dialogue, concerning the due priviledge of government in the kingdom of Scotland. Betwixt George Buchanan and Thomas Maitland ... translated out of the original Latin into English by Philalethes. London, for Richard Baldwin, 1689. 3 p.l., 70pp. Sewn as issued. Quarto. Untrimmed. A nice copy. $ 75.00
*First published in 1579, this was a highly popular (and suppressed) tract defending the populace against absolute monarchy, advocating popular election of kings and upholding tyrannicide; he anticipated the great figures of the next century, Milton, Sydney, Locke, and according to Bishop Burnet, was Cromwell's guiding light.

20. BUMP, ORLANDO F., ed. U.S. stamp law: a compilation of all statutes now in force, relating to documentary and proprietary stamps; together with notes referring to all decisions and rulings, both the courts and the department. With a full index. N.Y., Baker, 1870. 60pp. $ 27.50
*An unusual and interesting treatise.

21. CAINES, GEORGE. Practical forms of the Supreme Court, taken (Cont'd.)

21. CAINES, GEORGE. (Cont'd.) from Tidd's appendix of the forms of the Court of King's Bench, in personal actions, and adapted to the Supreme Court of the State of New-York; with the forms in replevin and ejectment: preserving the references in I. Riley and Co.'s enlarged edition of Tidd's Practice. From the London copy of 1803. N.Y., Alsop, 1808. 526pp. Contemp. calf. Nice copy. $ 45.00
*Marvin p. 169.

22. CALIFORNIA. STATE. Compiled laws of the State of California: containing all the acts of the legislature of a public and general nature, now in force, passed at the sessions of 1850-51-52-53 ... By S. Garfielde and F.A. Snyder, compilers. By Authority. Benicia (Ca.), 1853. xix, 1071pp. 8vo. Modern buckram. $ 75.00
*The first compilation for the State of California.

23. CASPER, JOHANN LUDWIG. A handbook of the practice of forensic medicine, based upon personal experience ... translated from the third edition of the original by George William Balfour ... London, New Sydenham Society, 1861-1865. Four volumes. Orig. publ. cl. Nice set. $ 75.00
*First translation into English of a landmark in legal medicine; Casper assisted the translator in bringing this edition up to date with the simultaneously emerging fourth edition, the last in the author's lifetime. Scarce.

24. CHITTY, JOSEPH. A practical treatise on medical jurisprudence, ... and all the laws relating to medical practitioners; with explanatory plates ... second American edition with notes and additions adapted to American works and judicial decisions. Part I., (all published) Phila., Carey, Lea, 1836. xxxi, 509pp. 8vo. Old calf. $ 30.00
*Marvin p. 193.

25. CHITTY, JOSEPH. A practical treatise on pleading: and on (Cont'd.)

25. CHITTY, JOSEPH. (Cont'd.) parties to actions, and the forms of actions. With a second volume containing precedents of pleadings. N.Y., M'Dermut, 1809. 2 vols. large 8vo. Contemp. calf. $ 40.00
*Marvin p. 190f. "doubtless in more general use in the U.S. than England ... surpasses all others upon the law of pleading ... S&S, 17208. First American Edition.

26. CLARKE, EDWARD. A treatise upon the Law of Extradition. With the conventions upon the subject existing between England and foreign nations, and the cases decided thereon. 2nd. ed. London, Stevens, 1874. 194, clxxvipp. $ 17.50

27. COBBETT, PITT. Leading cases and opinions on international law, collected and digested from English and foreign reports, official documents, Parliamentary papers, and other sources, with notes and excursus, containing the views of the text writers on the topics referred to, together with supplementary cases, treaties, and statutes. London, Stevens and Haynes, 1885. 280pp. First Edition. $ 27.50
*Alfred Sutro's copy.

28. COKE, EDWARD. The complete copy-holder; being a learned discourse of the antiquity and nature of manors and copy-holds, with all things thereto incident. Whereto is added a supplement ... London, Streater, Flesher and Twyford, 1668. 4 pl., 173; 111(4)pp. Sm. 8vo. Contemp. calf, spine worn. $ 125.00
*S&M, I, 246: "marks the final triumph of the King's Court which virtually put an end to feudal jurisdiction in England. It is a book of first class importance." Jenks. Wing C4915.

29. COMBE, GEORGE. Remarks on the principles of criminal legislation, and the practice of prison discipline. London, Simpkin, Marshall, 1854. 105pp. Disbound. $ 35.00

(Cont'd.)

29. COMBE, GEORGE. (Cont'd.)
*In the great 19th century reform tradition, to which Combe, most famous as a phrenologist, brings the additional element of the physiology of the brain and nervous system as the fundamental concern on which penology must proceed.

30. (DE MOUNTENEY, THOMAS J. BARCLAY.) The case of a detenu. London, George Earle, 1838. 20pp. Wrps. $ 15.00
*The author sought indemnity from the British govt. for grievances suffered at the hands of the French during the Napoleonic Wars. Much discussion of points in international law.

31. (DUCPETIAUX, EDOUARD.) De la mission de la justice humaine et de l'injustice de la peine de mort. (AND) De le justice de repression, et particulierement de l'inutilite et des effets pernicieux de la peine de mort. Bruxelles, Cauterts, 1827. xiv, 16, 105pp. 8vo. Orig. prtd. wrps. removed from a bd. vol. but a very good copy. $ 45.00
*By a leading Belgian social reformer and writer. He was official inspector of prisons and charities, and best represents the movement in Belgium for prison reform, reflecting and referring to the work of Lucas, Mackintosh, Romilly and Ed. Livingston in France, England and America respectively.

32. The English pleader: being a select collection of various precedents of declarations on actions brought in the Courts of King's Bench and Common Pleas ... Dublin, Hoey, 1783. 347pp. Contemp. full calf. $ 45.00

33. EWING, JAMES. A treatise on the office and duty of a justice of the peace, sheriff, coroner, constable, and of executors, administrators, and guardians. ... Second edition, revised and corrected by a member of the bar. Trenton, Fenton, 1832. Contemp. calf, rubbed. Light damp stain. $ 30.00

34. FIELD, DAVID DUDLEY. Applicability of international law to Oriental nations. Paper presented to the Institute of International Law. N.Y., Polhemus, 1875. 12pp. Wrps. $ 17.50

35. FIELD, DAVID DUDLEY. Greater safety at sea, and international tribunals for questions of collision. Paper presented to the Assoc. for Reform & Codification of the Law of Nations. N.Y., Polhemus 1875. 7pp. Wrps. $ 12.50

36. FIELD, JOHN. Observations on the discipline and management of convicts, and on tickets of leave: with remarks ... on the more speedy trial and punishment of larceny in certain cases. London, Longman, 1855. 31pp. Dsbd. Author presentation copy. $ 50.00
*Author was Chaplain of Berkshire Gaol. Contains some observations on transportation, single cell confinement, and Pentonville. Field wrote prolifically and well on Penology. Ferguson 9597. NUC cites only one holding.

37. FILMER, ROBERT. Patriarcha: or the natural power of Kings. London, Davis, 1680. 7pl., 141pp. 8vo. Title within rules. 18th century calf, ruled in gilt, spine gilt. $ 200.00
*FIRST EDITION of a classic manifesto of absolutist doctrine which served as the target of Locke's attack in the first of the "Two Treatises on Government" of 1690. Filmer agreed with Hobbes' concept of total power but differed with his compact theory, while at the same time he took a less dismal view than did Hobbes, of man as a creature given to a natural state of war. The above work appeared posthumously. Wing F922.

38. FORSYTH, WILLIAM. History of trial by jury. London, Parker, 1852. 468pp. 1/2 mor. Nice copy. $ 50.00
*S&M III, p. 82. According to the author's preface, this is the first full-scale historical account of the rise and growth of the jury system in England.

39. FOX, CHARLES J. A guide to officers of towns; containing the statutes relating to their official duties, with forms, directions, and legal decisions: adapted to the revised statutes of New-Hampshire. A new edition, with some additions, including acts since passed. By Samuel D. Bell. Concord, Parker Lyon, 1847. 417pp. Contemp. fine calf. $ 15.00
*Marvin p. 322.

40. GELDART, T.C. Remarks on the Scotch judicature bill, with some account of the practice of the Court of Session. London, Butterworth, 1825. 61pp. Disbd. $ 25.00

THE FOUNDER OF THE SCIENCE OF INTERNATIONAL LAW

41. GENTILI, ALBERICO. De jure belli libri III. Hanau, William Antonius, 1598. Small 8vo. 4 p.l., 715pp. Bound in an early 19th century fine imitation binding of the early 17th century style. A fine, attractive copy. $ 350.00
*First complete edition of the first extensive treatise on the law of war, and the foundation for Grotius. Gentili, an Italian, became professor of law at Oxford in 1557, where he spent the rest of his life, after leaving his native country because of his Protestantism. "He has great claim to be considered the founder of the science of international law ... preceeding writers had dealt with various international questions ... singly and with servile submission to the church ... It was left to G. to group the whole relations of states ... to attempt solutions by principles entirely independent of Rome; he proclaims as his real guide Jus Naturae, the highest common sense of mankind ..." Encycl. Brittanica. Grotius, perhaps more well known, was indebted to his writings. This is the first complete edition, incorporating the three component parts (each published separately in 1588-89 in London) "with large additions and improvements." Encycl. Br. Adams G-424; NUC locates four copies in America.

42. GONZALES, THOMAS A. et al. Legal medicine and toxicology, with a foreword by Harrison S. Martland, M.D. N.Y., Appleton, (1937) 754pp. Illus. 244 plates. $ 22.50

43. GREAT BRITAIN. COURT OF EXCHEQUER. The Attorney General v. Sillem and others, claiming the Vessel "Alexandra" seized under the Foreign Enlistment Act. Report of the trial ... with an appendix. London, Eyre and Spottiswoode, 1863. 235, lxxxpp. 8vo. Orig. cl. $ 40.00
*The Alexandra was fitted out for Confederate use during the American Civil War. Contains incidentally a great deal of information on the involvement of certain English interests on behalf of the Confederacy.

44. GRIMKE, FREDERICK. Considerations upon the nature and tendency of free institutions. Cincinnati, Derby, 1848. viii, 544pp. 8vo. Orig. black publisher's cloth. Except for minimal wear to head of spine, a very nice copy. $ 125.00
*FIRST EDITION. Commenting on the absence of an early self-conscious literature by Americans on their government, John William Ward identifies a notable exception in Grimke: "If one of the tests of American scholarship is its responsibility to the sources of our common life, then Grimke's book deserves to be restored to its proper place. It is a penetrating analysis of the theory and institutions of American democracy. It fairly deserves comparison with Tocqueville ... and is in certain ways superior. It is in any event, the single best book written by an American in the 19th century on the meaning of our political life." From the preface to the John Harvard Library edition, Cambridge, 1968. The first edition is uncommon, especially in nice condition. $ 125.00

45. GRUBB, IGNATIUS. The Colonial and state judiciary of Delaware. Read before the Historical Soc. of Delaware, 1897. 70pp. Wrps. $ 10.00
*Papers of The Historical Soc. of Delaware, XVII.

46. GUY, WILLIAM A. Principles of medical jurisprudence, ... First American Edition edited by C.A. Lee, who has added 200 pages of original matter, adapting the work to the wants of the medical and legal profession in the United States. N.Y., Harper, 1845. 711pp. 8vo. Orig. publ. cl. fine copy. $ 50.00
*Marvin p. 355.

47. HAGUE, THOMAS. A Letter to William Garrow, Esq. in Which the Conduct of Counsel in the Cross-Examination of Witnesses, and Commenting on their Testimony, Is Fully Discussed, and the Licentiousness of the Bar Exposed. London [n.d.] 60pp. [and] [ANON.] A Letter to Mr. Thomas Hague, Containing Some Critical Remarks on His Letter to Wm. Garrow, Esq. London, 1808. 18pp. Removed. 2 items $ 30.00

48. HALE, MATTHEW. The jurisdiction of the Lords House, or Parliament, considered according to antient records. To which is prefixed, by the editor, Francis Hargrave, an introductory preface, including a narrative of the same jurisdiction from the accession of James the First. London, Cadell, 1796. 6 p.l., ccxxx, 208pp. 4to. New cloth. $ 65.00
*First edition. S&M, Rev. ed., I,144. Marvin, p. 358. Highly praised.

49. HALE, MATTHEW. The history of the Common Law of England ... second edition, corrected. London, Nutt for Browne et al., 1716. (BOUND WITH:) The analysis of the law: being a scheme or abstract, of the several titles and partitions of the law of England digested into method. Second edition corrected: with the addition of an alphabetical table. London, Nutt for Browne et al., 1716. 2 works bound in one volume, 8vo. 261 and 148pp. plus tables. Later 18th century calf, spine richly gilt, nice copy. $ 90.00
*Marvin P359f. S&M 1, rev. ed. p. 239, #18 and 16 respectively: "his concise but enlightening summary of the results of 600 years of growth can be accepted by students as the ripest product of his time ..."

50. HALL, ROBERT GREAM. An essay on the rights of the crown, and the privileges of the subject in the seashores of the realm: compiled from the text writers and decided cases. London, Walker, 1830. 297pp. Orig. boards, uncut, printed spine label. Tall 8vo. A very nice copy. $ 80.00
*An uncommon topic, with few predecessors. The author mentions Lord Hale's De Jure Maris published by Hargrave in a collection of law tracts, as the principal source for this treatise. Marvin p. 361.

51. HENING, WILLIAM WALLER. The New Virginia Justice, comprising the office and authority of a Justice of the Peace, in the Commonwealth of Virginia. Together with a variety of useful precedents adapted to the laws now in force ... Richmond, Nicholson, 1795. 8p.l., 456 (11), xxiv, 32, (19)pp. 8vo. Contemp. full calf, rubbed, lacking front free endpaper. First edition. $ 150.00
*A very important work, continuing an English tradition. Virginia was very early in creating original American manuals rather than issuing the popular British works (Webb's Justice ... of 1736 was the first full-scale original American work of its kind.) Hening's modernization remained popular throughout the early 19th century. This edition contains a list of works consulted and a long list of subscribers. Evans 28823. Shipton & Mooney notes that the amount of front and back matter differs among various copies. This copy seems to contain all the additional matter recorded.

52. HENING, WILLIAM WALLER. The Virginia justice, comprising the office and authority of a justice of the peace in the Commonwealth of Virginia. ... fourth edition, revised, corrected and enlarged, and adapted to the revised code of 1819, and the laws subsequently passed. Richmond, 1825. Printed for the author. 821 (1)p. 8vo. Contemp. calf. $ 50.00
*Marvin p. 381. Final edition of this prominent work.

53. HEPBURN, CHARLES M. The historical development of Code Pleading in America and England, with special reference to the codes of ... Cincinnati, Anderson, 1897. 318pp. $ 27.50
*Covers 27 of the United States including most states west of the Mississippi.

54. HIGHMORE, ANTHONY. A digest of the doctrine of bail; in civil and criminal cases. ... Dublin, More, 1791. 270pp. plus index. 8vo. Contemp. calf, front cover crudely rehinged, front free end-paper missing, internally a very good copy. $ 35.00
*S&M II, 76; Marvin 386.

55. HILLIARD, FRANCIS. The law of remedies for torts, or private wrongs. Boston, Little, Brown, 1867. 595pp. Contemp. sheep, spine rubed but a very good copy. First edition. $ 27.50

56. An historical essay on the jurisdiction of the Court of Chancery; and incidentally of the other courts. London, J. Shuckburgh, 1735. Quarto. 56pp. ornamental headpieces. Neatly disbound, a nice copy, untrimmed. (lacking the half-title.) $ 57.50
*S&M, I, 215. First and only edition.

AN UNPUBLISHED ORIGINAL AMERICAN WORK ON MARITIME INSURANCE

57. HOPKINS, (JAMES DEAN 1773-1840). A manual of insurance, containing the doctrine of Marine Insurance, Bottomry & Respondentia, Insurance on Lives, and insurance against fire; to which is added a chapter on agency. Comprising the latest authorities. By J.D. Hopkins, counsellor at law. (Portland, Maine, 1839) Small 4to. 3pl, 369, (46)pp. entirely in the author's manuscript. New 1/4 calf, antique style. $ 400.00
*The definitive, complete manuscript, prepared and intended for publication but never published, of a full scale American work begun around 1809, with special emphasis on marine law. Hopkins was a Maine lawyer of prominence (several published addresses are cited in NUC). In the work's preface, he recounts its origin and growth over a thirty year period, mentioning the encouragement received from Chief Justice Sewall of Massachusetts to provide a restatement of the law in light of the commercial revolutions of the time. Hopkins began to collect cases after reading Marshall's Insurance in 1805. He postponed publication in the 1820's because of the appearance of Willard Phillips' treatise, but the result was a work that went beyond Phillips both in the number of cases cited and in organizational concept (Hopkins' distinct idea was to bring together "all the law" on each subject through special organization and an elaborate index present here.)
This is a unique and invaluable source insofar as it displays the evolution of an important segment of the law over three formative decades: the text evinces these time layers through its numerous inserts and paste-downs.
A carefully wrought work of great scholarship and orderly detail and one of a very few contemporary American treatments of this subject.

58. HORNE, ANDREW. The mirrour of justices: ... to which is added, The Diversity of courts and their jurisdiction. Translated into English by William Hughes, of Gray's Inn, Esq. Manchester, England, Willis, 1840. 299 (5)pp. Frontispiece, 12mo. Orig. publ. cl., paper label. Fine. $ 27.50
*Of Anglo-Saxon origin, the Ms. first appeared in print in 1642 and remained a highly important influence upon conceptions of English law for the next two centuries. Winfield, Chief Sources of English Legal History, p. 268ff.

59. (JACOB, GILES). Every man his own lawyer: or a summary of the laws of England, in a new and instructive method, under the following heads, ... the seventh edition (But First American) corrected and improved, with many additions, ... New York, Hugh Gaine, 1768. iv, 289, 1 blank, 12 index. pp. 8vo. Orig. full calf, raised bands, lea. label, blind fillet borders; extremities a little rubbed, otherwise a very nice copy. $ 120.00
*First (and only 18th century) American edition of a classic. A very pleasant copy in thorough contemporary state. Evans 10935.

60. KILTY, JOHN. The landholder's assistant, and land office guide; being an exposition of original titles, as derived from the proprietary government, and more recently from the state of Maryland, ... the whole comprising, ... the history and practice of the land office. ... Baltimore, Dobbin and Murphy, 1808. 497, xliv, vi, (1)pp. 8vo. Contemp. calf, rubbed, lea. label. A very good copy. $ 50.00
*Strongly historical; author was registrar for the Western Shore of Maryland. Marvin p. 440.

61. LEAVITT, JONATHAN. A summary of the laws of Massachusetts relative to the settlement, support, employment and removal of paupers. Greenfield, Mass., Denio, 1810. 64pp. 8vo. Orig. marbled bds., calf spine, printed paper label on covers, a fine copy. $ 37.50
*The title conceals the fact that this, though a slim volume, is an able historical account of the laws of settlement, covering five periods from 1692 to 1810, and touching on slavery, apprenticeship-inheritance, debtors, etc. A valuable account. Marvin p. 456. S&S 20533.

62. LIEBER, FRANCIS. Legal and political hermeneutics, or principles of interpretation and construction in law and politics, with remarks on precedents and authorities. Enlarged ed. Boston, Little, 1839. 240pp. Orig. publ. cl. Very fine copy. $ 35.00

63. LIEBER, FRANCIS. On civil liberty and self-government. Enlarged Edition in one Vol. Philadelphia, Lippincott, 1859. 629pp. Orig. cl. Good copy. First of this copyrighted edition. $ 37.50

64. LOCCENIUS, JOANNES. De Jure Maritimo & Navali. Libri Tres. (Stockholm), ex officina Joannis Janssonii, 1650. 12mo. 288pp. Fine engraved title page with ship. Contemp. vellum. A very nice copy. $ 150.00
*First edition. The engraved title bears a date of 1651.

65. LONG, GEORGE. A treatise on the law relative to sales of personal property. First American, from the last London edition, improved by a digest of American decisions. Exeter, N.H., Lamson, 1823. 288pp. Calf. Nice copy. $ 40.00
*Marvin p. 474.

66. LORD, JOHN P. The Maine Townsman, or laws for the regulation of towns: with forms and judicial decisions. Adapted to the revised statutes of Maine. Third Ed. Portland, Sanborn, 1847. 395pp. Calf. $ 25.00
*A considerable revision of the first edition of 1844.

67. (LOUISIANA.) UPTON, WHEELOCK S. and NEEDLER R. JENNINGS, (compilers and annotators). Civil Code of the State of Louisiana. In two volumes, by authority. New Orleans, E. Johns, 1838. 2 vols. Roy. 8vo. Text in French and English on facing pages. 1/2 mor., spines little worn at extremities, neat blind stamp on title page, else a very good set. $ 125.00
*Marvin, p. 476. The first annotated edition of the civil code drawn up in 1824 by Edw. Livingston, et al.

68. McCLELLAND, MILO A., M.D. Civil malpractice: a treatise on surgical jurisprudence, with chapters on skill in diagnosis and treatment, prognosis in fractures, and on negligence. N.Y., Hurd & Houghton, 1877. 554pp. First Edition. $ 30.00

69. MARSHALL, (JOHN). Opinion of the Supreme Court of the United States, at January term, 1832, delivered by Mr. Chief Justice Marshall, together with the opinion of Mr. Justice McLean, in the case of Samuel A. Worcester, plaintiff in error, versus the State of Georgia. With a statement of the case, extracted from the records of the Supreme Court ... Washington, Gales & Seaton, 1832. 39pp. disbound. A good copy. $ 75.00
*A landmark case in which Andrew Jackson scorned Marshall's decision favoring the Federal status of the Cherokee Indians at the expense of the principle of States' Rights. Bruntjen, Am. Imprints 16104.

70. MARSHALL, JOHN AND EDWARD LIVINGSTON. Speech of the Hon. John Marshall, delivered in the House of Representatives, of the United States, on the resolutions of Hon. Edward Livingston, relative to Thomas Nash alias Jonathan Robbins. Philadelphia, printed at the office of the True American, 1800. 45pp. 12mo. Modern 1/4 calf. $ 75.00
*A very perceptive account by an unnamed third party of an important debate, narrating and commenting upon Marshall's brilliant defense of the President's action in surrendering to British authorities one Thomas Nash, a British national accused of committing murder on a British vessel and then seeking asylum in the U.S. At stake was the concept of separation of powers; Marshall compellingly demonstrates that the President, and not the Courts (or Congress) is "the sole organ of the nation in its external relations ..." Evans 37887.

71. MARSHALL, SAMUEL. A treatise on the law of insurance, in four books: ... First American, from the English Edition. Two vols. in one. Boston, Johnson, 1805. 8vo. 759pp. Contemp. calf., raised bands, nice copy. $ 57.50
*Emphasizes marine insurance. The standard work of its time, replacing Park. Marvin p. 500.

72. MARSHALL, SAMUEL. A treatise on the law of insurance, in four books; ... Second American from the second London edition, including the cases decided in the national and state
(Cont'd.)

72. MARSHALL, SAMUEL. (Cont'd.) courts of the United States, collected and arranged by J.W. Condy. In two volumes. Phila. Farrand, 1810. 2 vols. Lg. 8vo. Contemp. calf, lea. labels. Good set. $ 55.00
*Includes Marine insurance. Marvin p. 500.

73. MARTENS, GEORG FRIEDRICH. Summary of the law of nations, founded on the treaties and customs of the modern nations of Europe; with a list of the principal treaties concluded since the year 1748 ... translated from the French by William Cobbett. Phila., Bradford, 1795. xix, 378pp. 8vo., with a 7pp. list of American subscribers to this edition. New cloth. $ 45.00
*Evans 29025; Marvin p. 500.

74. (MILL, JAMES). On the Ballot; From the Westminster Review, for July, 1830. London 1830?. 3rd ed. with corrections and additions. 8vo. 28pp. Removed. $ 20.00
*Halkett and Laing Vol. 4. Argues for the secret ballot as a simple but revolutionizing political reform measure. First separate publication.

75. MINNESOTA. TERRITORY. The revised statutes of the Territory of Minnesota, passed at the second session of the Legislative Assembly commencing January 1, 1851. Printed and published persuant to law, under the supervision of M.S. Wilkinson. St. Paul, James M. Goodhue, 1851. xvi, 734, 45pp. Large 8vo. Contemp. calf, expertly rebacked. Light dampstaining to latter part of text; in all a very good copy. With the bookbinder's ticket of James Mackintosh, St. Paul. $ 175.00
*Minnesota Imprints #27. The first published code for Minnesota terr., replacing the Wisconsin code which had become increasingly unsuited to conditions in Minnesota.

76. MOHUN, BARRY. Mohun on Warehousemen: a compilation of Warehouse Laws and decisions, containing an annotated copy of the Uniform Warehouse Receipts Act, (Cont'd.)

76. MOHUN, BARRY. (Cont'd.) the statutes of each of the states and territorial possessions pertaining to Warehouse Men... 2nd. ed. Chicago, Nickerson, 1914. 1118pp. $ 15.00

77. MONTEFIORE, JOSHUA. A commercial dictionary: containing the present state of mercantile law, practice and custom. The first American edition: with very considerable additions relative to the laws, usages, and practice of the United States, in three volumes. Phila., printed and sold by James Humphreys. 1804. 562; 481; 479pp. 8vo., with the publisher's adds, and list of American subscribers. Later full mor., rubbed. A very good set. RARE. $ 250.00
*A very important economic and legal source, with much new American material added, including banking, insurance, the funding system, a section on Louisiana, etc. The author claims to have added over 200 new articles. He settled permanently in America after having left England and for a time experimented in an adventuring company in Africa. *Kress 4827; Marvin p. 525. S&S 6808.

78. O'DEDY, U. A vindication of the law of England: shewing that "Mesne Lords," derivative lessors, or middle-men, have no right, either at common law or under any statute to levy distress. London, Reed, 1812. 96pp. Wrps. $ 37.50
*A defense of the oppressed tenantry against the claims of middlemen. The author wrote also View of the Law of Landed Property in Ireland with a similar intent.

79. OLIVER, BENJAMIN L. Practical conveyancing; a selection of forms of general utility, with notes interspersed. Corrected and enlarged, by Peter Oliver. Hallowell, Masters, 1853. 622pp. Contemp. full calf. Fine. $ 25.00

80. PARK, JAMES ALLAN. System of the law of marine insurances, with three chapters on bottomry; (Cont'd.)

80. PARK, JAMES ALLAN. (Cont'd.) on insurances on lives; and on insurances against fire. Phila., Crukshank, 1789. 530pp. Contemp full calf, minor rubbing. $ 100.00
*Evans 22048. First American edition of a highly popular treatise.

81. PARKER, JOEL. Constitutional law and unconstitutional divinity. Letters to Rev. Henry M. Dexter, and to Rev. Leonard Bacon, D.D. Cambridge, Houghton, 1863. 63pp. Wrps. Fine. $ 15.00
*His most notable statement of conservative legal principles during the Civil War. He attacks those who urge abolition of slavery by executive action. Cited in DAB.

82. (PENOLOGY). On the abuse of the pardoning power. Phila., Clark, 1839. 13pp. Orig. plain wrps. chipped. $ 37.50
*An exchange of correspondence between Dr. P. Tidyman and Samuel Wood, warden of the Eastern State Penitentiary in Pa., where the concept of separate confinement began (it was to revolutionize penology in American and Europe). Both men discuss the nature and importance of the new system and its emulation elsewhere; at issue is the unjustified continuation of extensive pardoning at a time when intermingling and overcrowding were no longer prevalent.

83. PHILLIMORE, JOHN GEORGE. Letter to the Lord Chancellor on the reform of the law. Second edition with a preface. London, Ridgway, 1847. 87pp. Disbound. Presentation copy from the author. $ 30.00
*Largely a campaign against special pleading.

84. (POSTE, EDWARD, ed.) GAIUS. Gaii institutionum iuris civilis commentarii quattuor, or elements of Roman law, with a translation and commentary by Edward Poste. 2nd edition, revised and enlarged. Oxford, Clarendon Press, 1884. 680pp. o.p. $ 30.00

85. POTHIER, (ROBERT JOSEPH). A treatise on the law of obligations, or contracts. Translated from the French, with an introduction, appendix and notes, illustrative of the English law on the subject, by William David Evans. In two vols. Phila., Small, 1826. Contemp. calf. Very nice set. $ 55.00
*Marvin p. 578. First American edition.

86. POWELL, JOHN JOSEPH. Essay upon the law of contracts and agreements. Sixth American edition, revised and corrected. Two vols. in one. N.Y., Lamson, 1825. 271, 169; LXXXV. Contemp. calf, rubbed. $ 45.00
*Marvin p. 582.

87. The Principles of Law Reform. London 1835. 8vo. 53pp. Removed. $ 15.00
*Reprint from the London Review, no. 3. The article is signed P.Q. but is not in Halkett and Laing. A radical attack on the legal system; appended is a list of the publications of the radical Parliamentarian, J.A. Roebuck.

88. RAINY, ALEXANDER. A brief exposition of some existing abuses, regarding the transfer of real property by public auction and private contract; with the outline of a proposed remedy. (London,) (Brettell, 1838.) 15pp. Wrps. $ 17.50
*Kress C4712.

89. READ, COLLINSON. The American pleader's assistant, being a collection of approved declarations, writs, returns, and proceedings in the several actions now in use within the United States. N.Y., Riley, 1806. 450pp. Calf, rubbed. Occasional light dampstaining, but a good copy. FIRST EDITION. $ 45.00
*Marvin, p. 602.

90. (REDERN, SIGISMUND EHRENREICH, Graf von). De l'influence de le forme des gouvernemens sur las nations, ou fragment historique et politique. Bruxelles, Chez de (Cont'd.)

90. (REDERN, SIGISMUND EHRENREICH, Graf von). (Cont'd.) Mat, 1817. 119pp. Orig. wrps. uncut. $ 27.50

91. REESE, JOHN J. A manual of toxicology, including the consideration of the nature, properties, effects and means of detection of poisons, more expecially in their medico-legal relations. Philadelphia, Lippincott, 1874. 507pp. $ 27.50
*First edition.

92. ROMILLY, SAMUEL. Observations on the criminal law of England, as it relates to capital punishments, and on the mode in which it is administered. London, Cadell, 1810. 76pp. Disbound. $ 75.00
*FIRST EDITION. A landmark in English legal reform. Romilly was a leading force in the moderation of traditional punishment. A follower of Rousseau and Beccaria and an intimate of Bentham and Dumont, he succeeded at this time in removing the death penalty for numerous minor offences, in some cases substituting transportation.

93. (ROSEDALE, JOHN FREEMAN-MITFORD, baron). A treatise on the pleadings in suits in the Court of Chancery, by English Bill. Third ed. Phila. Byrne, 1812. 276pp. Calf. Nice copy. $ 47.50
*Marvin p. 517. First American edition. An important and classic treatise; highly influential in American law; Marvin notes that Story incorporated it into his Commentaries.

94. STARKIE, THOMAS. A treatise on the law of slander, libel, scandalum magnatum, and false rumours; including the rules which regulate intellectual communications, affecting the characters of individuals and the interests of the public. With a description of the practice and pleadings in personal actions, informations, indictments, attachments for contempts, & c. (Cont'd.)

94. STARKIE, THOMAS. (Cont'd.) connected with subject. First American edition, with notes and references to American and the English cases. By Edward D. Ingraham. N.Y., Lamson, 1826. 616pp. Calf. Nice copy. $ 50.00
*Marvin p. 659. "best work on this subject."

95. (SUGDEN, E.B. Ld. St. Leonards). A handy book on property law; in a series of letters, from the 5th London edition. N.Y., Appleton, 1858. 216pp. $ 20.00
*S&M, III, 221.

96. TATE, JOSEPH. A digest of the laws of Virginia, which are of a permanent character and general operation; illustrated by judicial decisions: to which is added, an index of the names of the cases in the Virginia Reporters. Richmond, 1823. viii, 562pp. 8vo. Contemp. calf, lea. label. Front free-endpaper missing, occasional foxing, otherwise a very good copy. $ 50.00
*Marvin p. 685.

97. TAYLOR, ALFRED SWAINE. A manual of medical jurisprudence. Revised and edited by Thomas Stevenson, M.D. ...eleventh American, edited with citations and additions from the twelfth English edition, by Clark Bell, Esq. Philadelphia, Lea Bros., 1892. 790pp. $ 20.00

98. TAYLOR, ALFRED SWAINE. A manual of medical jurisprudence. Revised and edited by Thomas Stevenson. 12th American, edited with citations and additions from the 12th English edition. By Clark Bell, Esq. ... N.Y., Lea, 1897. 832pp. $ 17.50

99. UPSHUR, ABEL P. A brief enquiry into the true nature and character of our Federal Government: being a review of Judge Story's commentaries on the constitution of the United States. Phila., Campbell, 1863. 131pp. (Cont'd.)

99. UPSHUR, ABEL P. (Cont'd.) 1/4 pol. calf. Extremely fine copy. $ 30.00
*One of the most important statements of southern political philosophy. Like Calhoun, Upshur attacked the idea of majority rule as a sufficient standard in deciding the fate of the South. This edition is a political reprint of the first edition of 1840.

100. VIRCHOW, RUDOLPH. Postmortem examinations with especial reference to medico-legal practice. Translated by T.P. Smith ... 3rd American edition from the 4th German edition with additional notes and plates. Phila., Blakiston, 1891. 143pp. Illus. 12mo. $ 17.50

101. VIRGINIA, COMMONWEALTH. The code of Virginia ... published pursuant to an act of the General Assembly ... August 1849. Richmond, Ritchie, 1849. xxxi, 898pp. 8vo. Contemp. calf, rubbed. $ 50.00
*The first revision since 1819, consolidating both the civil and criminal codes. The preface gives a long, excellent account of the history of all the revisions of Virginia law.

102. VIRGINIA, COMMONWEALTH. The revised code of the laws of Virginia: being a collection of all such acts of the General Assembly, of a public and permanent nature, as are now in force; with a general index. ... Richmond, Ritchie, 1819. Two volumes. 8vo. Contemp. calf rubbed (mixed bindings). $ 75.00
*Marvin p. 713. The supervisor of this important compilation was Benjamin Watkins Leigh (see DAB).

103. WALPOLE, CHARLES GEORGE. The Leeward Islands Magistrates Acts. With an appendix, containing a copious schedule of forms and other matters. London, Clowers, 1892. 314pp. $ 35.00
*First consolidation of these acts.

104. WARREN, SAMUEL. The moral, social, and professional duties of attorneys and solicitors. N.Y., Harper, 1861. 306pp. Orig. cl. Nice copy. $ 20.00

105. (WASHINGTON. STATE). SENATE JOURNAL of the extraordinary session, first Legislature of the State of Washington. Begun and held at Olympia, the State Capital, Sept. 3, 1890, adjourned, sine die, Sept. 11, 1890. Olympia, White, State Printer, 1891. 600, 325pp. $ 25.00

106. WATSON, WILLIAM. A treatise of the law of partnership. Albany, N.Y., Webster, 1795. 368pp. Contemp. calf, rubbed. $ 65.00
*First American edition. Evans 29139; Marvin p. 721, S&M, II, p. 171.

107. Westminster Hall: or professional relics and anecdotes of the Bar, Bench, and Woolsack. London, John Knight & Henry Lacey, 1825. 3 volumes. 12mo. Folding illustrations, numerous engraved portraits. Original publisher's cloth, paper labels, spines a little rubbed. Uncut. A very nice set. $ 65.00
*A skillfully assembled collection of dissertations, biographies, and anecdotes on English legal history, some original, others culled from a great variety of sources. Indexed. A very pleasant little anthology, nicely illustrated.

108. WHITAKER, RICHARD. A treatise of the law relative to the rights of lien, and stoppage in transitu. London, printed. N.Y., reprinted & publ. by I. Riley, 1816. 229pp. Contemp. 1/4 calf, nice copy. $ 37.50
*First American edition. Marvin p. 370; S&S 39805.

109. WHITCOMBE, RICHARD. An inquiry into some of the rules of evidence, relating to the incompetency of witnesses. London, Butterworth, 1824. 48pp. wrps. stitched. $ 27.50
*Marvin p. 730; S&M, III, p. 24.

110. WILLIAMS, JOSHUA. The seisin of the freehold, being twelve lectures delivered in Gray's Inn Hall, in the months of January and February, 1876. London, Sweet, 1878. 227pp. o.p. $ 25.00

111. WILLIAMS, THOMAS WALTER. Original precedents in conveyancing, ...interspersed with the observations and opinions of counsel upon various intricate cases. The whole selected from the draughts of actual practice ... in two volumes. Dublin, Watts et al., 1790. 2 vols 8vo. Contemp. full calf. Nice set. $ 37.50
*S&M II, 155. Marvin, p. 737. First Dublin edition.

112. WOOD, H.G. A treatise on the law of master and servant: covering the relation, duties and liabilities of employers and employees. Albany, N.Y., Parsons, 1877. 956pp. First edition. $ 20.00

113. WOODFALL, WILLIAM. The law of landlord and tenant; to which is added, an appendix of precedents. First American, from the fourth London edition, with considerable alterations and additions. N.Y., M'Dermut, 1816. 620pp. Contemp. calf, rubbed, else a good copy. $ 37.50
*S&S 39855. Marvin, p. 745: highly praised. First American edition.

114. (VINERIAN LECTURES). (WOODDESON, R.). Elements of Jurisprudence treated of in the preliminary part of a course of lectures on the laws of England. London, T. Payne, 1783. 4to. 4 p.l., 3-118pp. later wrps. $ 75.00
*Consists of the preliminary lectures intended to form, along with the three main divisions as outlined at the end, the course of law given at Oxford, known as the Vinerian Lectures. Marvin, p. 745. Of real value; complementary to Blackstone's Commentaries. S&M II, p. 33.

115. ADAMI, COLONNELLO VITTORIO. National frontiers in relation to International Law. Translated by T.T. Behrens, with an appendix on practical considerations when defining frontiers by watersheds. London, Oxford Univ. Press, 1927. 127pp. Illus. o.p. $ 17.50

116. ALLEN, ELEANOR WYLLYS. The position of foreign states before National Courts, chiefly in Continental Europe. N.Y., Macmillan, 1933. 354pp. o.p. $ 12.50

117. ANNUAL DIGEST OF PUBLIC INTERNATIONAL LAW CASES. Being a selection from the decisions of international and national tribunals. London, Longmans, 1929-1933. 4 vols., 8vo., each approx. 500 pp., fine copies. o.p. $ 75.00
*Complete coverage 1919-1928, in 4 vols. (1919/22; 1923/24; 1925/26 and 1927/28.) London School of Economics, Contributions to International Law and Diplomacy series.

118. BALCH, THOMAS WILLING. Legal and political questions between nations. Phila., Allen, 1924. 147pp. o.p. $ 15.00

119. BATY, THOMAS. International law in twilight. Tokyo, Maruzen, 1954. 327pp. Frontis. o.p. $ 17.50
*Author was distinguished writer and professor at Oxford, Trinity, and Cambridge. Consists of 17 essays.

120. BILLIAS, GEORGE ATHAN (ed.) Selected essays: law and authority in Colonial America. Barre, Barre Publishers, (1965). 208pp. o.p. $ 22.50
*10 original essays given at a conference sponsored by the American Antiquarian Society.

121. BODIN, JEAN. The six bookes of a Commonweale: a facsimile reprint of the English translation of 1606, corrected and supplemented in the light of a new comparison with the French and Latin texts. Edited with an intro- (Cont'd.)

121. BODIN, JEAN. (Cont'd.) duction by Kenneth Douglas McRae. Cambridge, Harvard Univ. Press, 1962. 214; 794pp. 4to. o.p. $ 37.50

122. BOS, MAARTEN, (ed.) The present state of International Law and other essays, written in honour of the Centenary Celebration of the Internat'l Law Assoc. 1873-1973. The Netherlands, Kluwer, 1973. 392pp. $ 12.50

123. BOSTON UNIVERSITY. The Bacon lectures on the Constitution of the United States, given at Boston University. 1928-1938. (Boston). 453pp. o.p. $ 15.00
*19 contribution including those of Chas. Warren and E.S. Corwin.

124. BUTLER, GEOFFREY, et al. The development of International Law. London, Longmans, 1928. 566pp. o.p. $ 22.50
*Series: Contributions to International Law and Diplomacy. A fine general history. (L.S.E.)

125. CALVERY, E. ROY. Capital punishment in the twentieth century: with an introduction by Lord Buckmaster. London, G.P. Putnam's. (1927). 204pp. d.j. $ 12.50

126. COOK, ARTHUR E., compiler, et al. Immigration Laws of the United States. Compiled and explained. Chicago, Callaghan, 1929. 499pp. $ 12.50

127. COOK, WILLIAM G.H. Insanity and mental deficiency in relation to legal responsibility: a study in psychological jurisprudence. London, Routledge, 1921. 192pp. o.p. $ 22.50

128. CRAIGMYLE, LORD. John Marshall in diplomacy and law. With an introduction by Nicholas Murray Butler. N.Y., Scribner, 1933. 145pp. cl. $ 10.00

129. CUTLER, JAMES ELBERT. Lynch-Law: an investigation into the history of lynching in the United States. N.Y., Longmans, 1905. 287pp. First edition. $ 12.50

130. DANGERFIELD, ROYDEN J. In defense of the Senate: a study in treaty making. Introduction by Quincy Wright. Norman, Univ. of Oklahoma Press, 1933. 357pp. 1st edition. Fine. $ 12.50

131. DE BEUS, J.G. The jurisprudence of the General Claims Commission United States and Mexico under the convention of Sept. 8, 1923. The Hague, Nijhoff, 1938. 342pp. $ 22.50

132. DELMAS, DELPHIN M. The scopes trial and the Constitution. (Los Angeles, 1926). 16pp. wrps. $ 12.50
*Published by the Unitarian Society in defense of free discussion. Not in McCoy.

133. DUMBAULD, E. Interim measures of protection in international controversies. The Hague, Nijhoff, 1932. 204pp. o.p. $17.50

134. DUNN, FREDERICK SHERWOOD. The diplomatic protection of Americans in Mexico. N.Y., Columbia Univ. Press, 1933. 439pp. $ 22.50
*Mexico in International Finance & Diplomacy, Columbia Univ. Vol. II.

135. EGERTON, HUGH EDWARD. Federations and unions within the British Empire. 2nd ed. Oxford, Clarendon, 1924. 306pp. o.p. $12.50

136. FINCH, GEORGE A. The sources of modern international law. Wash., D.C., Carnegie Endowment for Internat'l Peace, 1937. 124pp. $ 12.50
*Monograph Series of the Carnegie Endowment for International Peace, div. of Internat'l Law. No. I.

137. FISHER, HERBERT. The common weal. Oxford, Clarendon, 1924. 296pp. $ 10.00
*Series of lectures, including international law.

138. FLOURNOY, RICHARD W. (ed.) et al. A collection of nationality laws of various countries as contained in constitutions, statutes, and treaties. N.Y., Oxford Univ. Press, 1929. 776pp. o.p. $ 22.50

139. FOLLETT, M.P. The Speaker of the House of Representatives: with an introduction by Albert Bushnell Hart. N.Y., Longmans, Green. 1896. 378pp. $ 12.50

140. FORSYTH, WILLIAM. Hortensius: an historical essay on the office and duties of an advocate. Third edition. London, Murray, 1879. 412pp. Illus: 10 plates. o.p. $ 27.50

141. FREUND, ERNST. Standards of American legislation: an estimate of restrictive and constructive factors. Chicago, Univ. of Chicago Press, (1917). 321pp. $ 12.50

142. FROTHINGHAM, LOUIS ADAMS. A brief history of the Constitution and Government of Massachusetts, with a chapter on legislative procedure. Cambridge, Harvard Univ. Press, 1916. 140pp. o.p. $ 12.50

143. GARNER, JAMES WILFORD. Prize Law during the World War: a study of the jurisprudence of the Prize Courts, 1914-1924. N.Y., MacMillan, 1927. 712pp. o.p. $ 17.50

144. GARNER, JAMES WILFORD. Recent developments in international law. (Calcutta) Univ. of Calcutta, 1925. 840pp. o.p. $ 22.50
*Tagore Law Lectures, 1922.

145. GELLHORN, WALTER. Individual freedom and governmental restraints. Baton Rouge, Louisiana State Univ. Press, (1956). 251pp. $ 12.50

146. GETTYS, LUELLA. The law of citizenship in the United States. With a foreword by Quincy Wright. Chicago, Univ. of Chicago Press, (1934). 221pp. o.p. $ 12.50

147. HAAR, CHARLES M. (edited by.) Law and land: Anglo-American planning practice. Cambridge, Harvard Univ. Press. 1964. 290pp. o.p. $ 12.50

148. HABICHT, MAX. Post-war treaties for the pacific settlement of international disputes: a compilation and analysis of treaties of investigation, conciliation, arbitration, and compulsory adjudication, concluded during the first decade following the World War. Cambridge, Harvard Univ. Press, 1931. 1109pp. Fine copy. o.p. $ 37.50
*Concentrates on arrangements, other than those of Geneva and the Hague, which have not been hitherto frequently noticed.

149. HAMBRO, EDVARD. The case law of the International Court: a repertoire of the judgments, advisory opinions and orders of the permanent court of international justice and of the International Court of Justice. With a bibliography prepared by J. Douma, and an index prepared by Audrey Welsby. Leyden, Sijthoff, 1952. 699pp. o.p. $ 27.50

150. HARDY, E.G. (translator). Six Roman Laws. Translated with introduction and notes. Oxford, Clarendon, 1911. 176pp. o.p. $ 22.50

151. HARE, THOMAS. The election of representatives, parliamentary and municipal. A treatise. Third edition. Philadelphia, Lippincott, 1867. 350pp. o.p. $ 15.00

152. HARLEY, JOHN EUGENE. Documentary textbook on international relations: a text and reference study emphasizing official documents, and materials relating to world peace and international co-operation. Los Angeles, Suttonhouse, 1934. 848pp. (Incl. 27pp. bibliography). o.p. $ 22.50

153. HARLEY, JOHN EUGENE. World-wide influences of the cinema: a study of official censorship and the international cultural aspects of (Cont'd.)

153. HARLEY, JOHN EUGENE. (Cont'd.) motion pictures. Los-Angeles, Univ. of Southern Calif. Press, 1940. 320pp. $ 12.50
*Cinematography Series No. 2.

154. HARVARD TERCENTENARY PUBLICATIONS. The future of the common law. Cambridge, Harvard Univ. Press, 1937. 245pp. o.p. $ 15.00
*Incl. contributions by Roscoe Pound and H.F. Stone.

155. HEADLAM-MORLEY, JAMES. Studies in Diplomatic History. N.Y., King, (1930). 312pp. o.p. $ 15.00
*19th Century British relations with Mid-East and Cyprus the chief emphasis.

156. HEWART, (GORDON). The New Despotism. N.Y., Cosmopolitan Book Corp., 1929. 311pp. $ 15.00
*By the Chief Justice of England; attacks the growth of administrative law, among other examples of bureaucratic aggrandizement.

157. HIGGINS, A. PEARCE. Studies in international law and relations. Cambridge, Cambridge Univ. Press, 1928. 314pp. o.p. $ 15.00

158. HILL, MARTIN. Immunities and privileges of international officials; the experience of the League of Nations. Washington, D.C., Carnegie Endowment for International Peace, 1947. 281pp. $ 12.50
*Studies in Administration of International Law & Organization.

159. HOLLANDER, BARNETT. Confiscation, (Soviet) aggression, (German) and foreign-funds control in American law. N.Y., Baker, Voorhis, 1942. 265pp. $ 15.00

160. HOWARD-ELLIS, C. The origin, structure & working of the League of Nations. Boston, Houghton Mifflin, 1929. 528pp. o.p. $ 17.50

161. HUDSON, MANLEY O. The permanent court of international justice and the question of American participation, with a collec- (Cont'd.)

161. HUDSON, MANLEY O. (Cont'd.) tion of documents. Cambridge, Harvard Univ. Press. 1925. 387pp. $ 12.50

162. HURST, JAMES WILLARD. Law and economic growth: the legal history of the lumber industry in Wisconsin 1836-1915. Cambridge, Mass., Harvard University Press, 1964. 946pp. 8vo. d.j. o.p. $ 27.50

163. HUTZEL, ELEONORE L., et al. The policewoman's handbook: with an introduction by Leonard V. Harrison, Bureau of Social Hygiene, N.Y. N.Y., Columbia Univ. Press, 1933. 303pp. o.p. $ 17.50
*"The first effort to standardize the work of the policewoman ..." Preface.

164. KANN, JEROME H. California's code time table: containing an alphabetical arrangement of the various periods of time required by the code of civil procedure, the civil code, the penal code, and the rules of the Supreme Court, now in force, in all actions and proceedings in the courts of the State of California, with notes referring to the amendments of 1901. San Francisco, Dempster, 1902. 125pp. $ 12.50

165. KEITH, ARTHUR BERRIEDALE. The Constitution of England from Queen Victoria to George VI. London, Macmillan, 1940. 2vols. 485; 515pp. Orig. cl. Fine. o.p. $ 37.50

166. KELLOR, FRANCES, et al. The United States Senate and the International Court. N.Y., Seltzer, 1925. 353pp. o.p. $ 12.50

167. KERNER, ROBERT JOSEPH, et al. The Balkan conferences and the Balkan Entente 1930-1935: a study in the recent history of the Balkan and Near Eastern Peoples. Berkeley, Univ. of Calif. Press, 1936. 271pp. Illus. Maps. 1st ed. d.j. Fine. $ 12.50

168. JESSUP, PHILIP C. The law of territorial waters and maritime jurisdiction: the nature and extent of civil and criminal jurisdiction in marginal seas as evidenced by decisions of national and international Courts, statutes, treaties, state papers, text writers, and general principles of international law, with commentaries and a proposed code. N.Y., Jennings, 1927. 548pp. 1st ed. Fine. $ 22.50

169. KULSRUD, CARL J. Maritime neutrality to 1780: a history of the main principles governing neutrality and belligerency to 1780. Boston, Little, Brown, 1936. 351pp. o.p. $ 22.50

170. LARSON, LAURENCE M. (translator). The earliest Norwegian laws, being the Gulathing law and the Frostathing law. Translated from the old Norwegian. N.Y., Columbia Univ. Press, 1935. 451pp. $ 22.50

171. The League of Nations Starts: an outline by its organisers. London, Macmillan, 1920. 282pp. o.p. $ 12.50

172. LEONARD, L. LARRY. International regulation of fisheries. Issued in cooperation with the International Secretariat, Institute of Pacific Relations. Wash., D.C. Carnegie Endowment for Internat'l Peace, 1944. 201pp. $ 15.00
*Monograph Series of the Carnegie Endowment of Internat'l Peace, div. of Internat'l Law. No. 7.

173. LISSITZYN, OLIVER J. The International Court of Justice: its role in the maintenance of international peace and security. N.Y., Carnegie Endowment for Internat'l Peace, 1951. 118pp. $ 12.50
*United Nations Studies: No. 6.

174. LOEB, ISIDOR. The legal property relations of married parties: a study in comparative Legislation. N.Y., Columbia Univ. Press, 1900. 197pp. Wrps. $ 10.00
*Studies in History, (etc.) ... Vol. 13, #1.

175. MAGUIRE, JOHN MacARTHUR. The lance of justice: a semicentennial history of the Legal Aid Society, 1876-1926. Cambridge, Harvard Univ. Press, 1928. 305pp. o.p. $ 17.50

176. MULLER, W.H. Early history of the Federal Supreme Court. Boston, Chipman, 1922. 117pp. o.p. $ 12.50

177. MURPHY, PATRICK W. Florida real estate law. Miami, Royal Palm Press, 1925. 252pp. $ 15.00
*Written to fill the need for a comprehensive source in the midst of the Florida land-boom.

178. MARTIN, LAWRENCE, compiler. The Treaties of Peace 1919-1923. N.Y., Carnegie Endowment for Internat'l Peace, 1924. 2vols. Maps. 1098pp. Orig. cl. fine. o.p. $ 35.00
*Maps prepared especially for this edition, with a summary of the legal basis of the new boundaries.

179. MOLEY, RAYMOND. Politics and criminal prosecution. N.Y., Minton, 1929. 241pp. 1st ed. d.j. Fine. $ 12.50

180. MOYNIHAN, CORNELIUS J. A preliminary survey of the law of real property: an historical background of the common law of real property and its modern application. St. Paul, West, 1940. 154pp. $ 12.50

181. NEW YORK BAR ASSOCIATION. SPECIAL COMMITTEE ON RADIO AND TELEVISION. Radio, television, and the administration of justice: a documented survey of materials. N.Y. Columbia, 1965. 321pp. o.p. $ 15.00

182. NICHOLS, PHILIP. The Massachusetts law of planning and zoning. Massachusetts Federation of Planning Boards, 1943. 273pp. Illus. $ 17.50
*A first-rate account of the historical growth of the law by one who was active at the center of events as counsel for the city and later as chairman of the Mass. Fed. of Planning boards.

183. NORTH CAROLINA ADVISORY COMMITTEE. Equal protection of the laws in North Carolina. ...Report of the ... to the U.S. Commission on Civil Rights, 1959-1962. (Wash, GPO). Ca. 1962. 251pp. Wrps. $ 10.00

184. POUND, ROSCOE. An introduction to the philosophy of law. New Haven, Yale Univ. Press, 1922. 397pp. First edition. $ 10.00

185. PUENTE, JULIUS I. The Foreign Consul: his juridical status in the United States. Chicago, Smith, 1926. 157pp. o.p. $ 15.00

186. REMINGTON, ARTHUR. Notes on the Washington reports embracing vols. 1-3 Washington Territory and vols. 1-30 Washington State, showing the citations of Washington reports, fully digested, from all citing cases in the same court, in the United States Court and in all State Courts of last resort. With a complete table of cases of all Washington decisions, alphabetically arranged, with cross-references and reverse index, referring to all official and unofficial reports of the cases, and an index-digest of the notes. Tocoma, 1903. 572pp. $ 25.00

187. RIESENFELD, STEFAN A. Protection of coastal fisheries under International Law. Washington, D.C., Carnegie Endowment for International Peace, 1942. 296pp. $ 22.50
*Monograph Series of the Carnegie Endowment for International Peace, Div. of Internat'l Law No. 5.

188. ROBINSON, EDWARD STEVENS. Law and the lawyers. N.Y., Macmillan, 1935. 348pp. o.p. $ 10.00
*Stresses role of social and behavioral sciences in the "new law."

189. ROTTSCHAEFER, HENRY. The Constitution and socio-economic change: five lectures delivered at the University of Michigan, March ... 1947: with a foreword by E. Blythe Stason. Ann Arbor, Univ. of Michigan, 1948. 253pp. $ 15.00

190. ST. JOHN-STEVAS, NORMAN. Life, death and the law: law and Christian morals in England and the United States. Bloomington, Indiana Univ. Press. (1961). 375pp. o.p. $ 12.50

191. SALNY, SAMUEL M. Independent unions under the Wagner Act: a manual for attorneys, labor relations advisors and union officials acting for employers, employees or unions in relation to the National Labor Relations Act, with complete forms. Boston, Hildreth, 1944. 342pp. $ 12.50
*Much historical reference.

192. SAYRE, PAUL, ed. Interpretations of modern legal philosophies. Essays in honor of Roscoe Pound. Edited with an introduction. N.Y., Oxford Univ. Press, 1947. 807pp. Port. $ 22.50

193. SCHLESINGER, RUDOLF. Soviet legal theory: its social background and development. N.Y., Oxford Univ. Press. 1945. 297pp. o.p. $ 22.50

194. SCHROEDER, THEODORE. Constitutional free speech defined and defended in an unfinished argument in a case of blasphemy. N.Y., Free Speech League, 1919. 456pp. $ 17.50

195. SCHULYER, ROBERT LIVINGSTON. Parliament and the British Empire: some Constitutional controversies concerning Imperial Legislative jurisdiction. N.Y., Columbia Univ. Press, 1939. 279pp. 1st ed. d.j. Fine. $ 15.00

196. SHEALEY, R. PRESTON. The law of government contracts. N.Y., Ronald, 1919. 300pp. $ 12.50

197. SILVERS, E.B. Examination of Missouri titles: being designed to give immediate information as to what should appear from abstract of any transmission of title to real estate, at any date, in order that the abstract shall show a perfect record title. Kansas City, Pipes Reed, 1911. 650pp. $ 15.00

198. SILVERS, E.B. Missouri titles: being designed to give immediate information as to what should appear from the abstract of any transmission of title to real estate, at any date, in order that the abstract shall show a perfect record title. 2nd edition, revised and fully annotated. Kansas City, Vernon Law Book, 1923. 581pp. $ 15.00

199. SMITH, ELEAZER. Nine years among the convicts: or prison reminiscences. Boston, Magee, 1856. 287pp. o.p. $ 15.00
*Author was a prison chaplain.

200. STAHL, DAVID et al. (editors). The Community and racial crises. N.Y., Practising Law Institute, (1966). 364pp. $ 12.50

201. STEPHENS, HAROLD M. Administrative tribunals and the rules of evidence: a study in jurisprudence and administrative law. Cambridge, Harvard Univ. Press. 1933. 128pp. $ 12.50
*Harvard Studies in Administrative Law, Vol. 3.

202. SULLIVAN, HAROLD W. Trial by newspaper. Hyannis, Patriot Press. 1961. 250pp. o.p. $ 12.50

203. THAYER, JAMES BRADLEY. Legal essays. Boston, Boston Book Co. 1908. 402pp. Illus. Photogravure frontis. Fine copy. First edition. $ 20.00

204. THAYER, JAMES BRADLEY. Legal essays. Third impression. Boston, Chipman, 1923. 402pp. $ 12.50

205. THOINOT, L. Medicolegal aspects of moral offenses. Translated from the original French and enlarged by Arthur W. Weysse. Phila., Davis, 1911. 487pp. Illus. $ 22.50

206. THORNTON, JOHN WINGATE. The historical relation of New England to the English Commonwealth. (Boston, Alfred Mudge), 1874. 105pp. o.p. $ 17.50
*Privately printed and scarce.

207. UNITED NATIONS. Conference on the law of the sea. Geneva, 1958. 5to. wrps. Vol. I: Preparatory Documents; Vol. II: Plenary Meetings. $ 15.00
*In all there were 7 vols., the last 5 being the record of individual committees.

208. U.S. DEPT. OF LABOR. Growth of labor law in the United States. (Wash., GPO), 1967. 311pp. Wrps. $ 10.00

209. VAN VLECK, WILLIAM C. The administrative control of aliens: a study in administrative law and procedure. N.Y., The Commonwealth Fund, 1932. 260pp. $ 17.50

210. WAR OBVIATED, by an International Police: a series of essays, written in various countries. The Hague, Nijhoff, 1915. 223pp. o.p. $ 12.50

211. WASHINGTON (STATE) UNIVERSITY. BOARD OF REGENTS. Communism and academic freedom: The record of the tenure cases at the University of Washington including the findings of the committee on tenure and academic freedom and the president's recommendations. Seattle, Univ. of Washington Press, 1949. 125pp. wrps. $ 10.00

212. WEXLEY, JOHN. The judgment of Julius and Ethel Rosenberg. N.Y., Cameron & Kahn, 1955. 672pp. With the original dust-jacket by Rockwell Kent. Nice copy. $ 17.50

213. WHITE, EDW. J. Legal antiquities: a collection of essays upon ancient laws, and customs. St. Louis, F.H. Thomas, 1913. 349pp. o.p. $ 15.00

214. WIENER, LEO. Commentary to the Germanic laws and Mediaeval documents. Cambridge, Harvard (Cont'd.)

214. WIENER, LEO. (Cont'd.) Univ. Press, 1915. 224pp. Orig. cl., nice copy. o.p. $ 25.00

215. WILLIAMS, BRUCE. State security and the League of Nations. Baltimore, John Hopkins Press, 1927. 345pp. $ 12.50
*Albert Shaw Lectures on Diplomatic History, 1927.

216. WILLIAMS, JOHN FISCHER. Aspects of modern international law: an essay. London, Oxford Univ. Press, 1939. 117pp. o.p. $ 12.50

217. WILLIS, JOHN. The Parliamentary powers of English government departments. Cambridge, Harvard Univ. Press, 1933. 214pp. $ 12.50
*Harvard Studies in Administrative Law, Vol. 4.

218. WILSON, FRANCIS GRAHAM. Labor in the League system: a study of the International Labor Organization in relation to International Administration. Stanford, Calif. Stanford Univ. Press (1934). 384pp. o.p. $ 22.50

219. WITNEY, FRED. Indiana labor relations law. Indiana Univ., (1960). 123pp. o.p. $ 12.50
*Indiana business report no. 30.

220. ZURCHER, ARNOLD JOHN. The experiment with democracy in Central Europe: a comparative survey of the operation of Democratic Government in post-war Germany and in the Russian and Austro-Hungarian succession states. N.Y., Oxford Univ. Press, 1933. 328pp. Maps. o.p. $ 15.00

221. (BECCARIA, CESARE). An essay on crimes and punishments, Translated from the Italian; with a Commentary, Attributed to Mons. De Voltaire, translated from the French. London, J. Almon, 1767. 8vo. xii, 179 (1), lxxix, (1)pp. Contemp. calf, rubbed, spine gilt, label missing; hinges cracked but firm; internally very good. $ 225.00
*FIRST EDITION IN ENGLISH; Printing and the Mind of Man 209 (first edition of 1764). "The success of Beccaria's book was immediate, six editions being published within eighteen months, and it was eventually translated into twenty-two languages. Its principles have been incorporated into the criminal practice of all civilized countries ... (its) impact ... on the reform of criminal justice can hardly be exaggerated." (PMM)

222. (CIVIL WAR). PITMAN, BENN, Editor. The trials for treason at Indianapolis, disclosing the plans for establishing a North-western Confederacy ... to which is added the full report of Judge ... Holt on the Order of American Knights, alias the Sons of Liberty; a Western conspiracy in aid of the Southern rebellion. Cincinnati, Moore, Wilstach & Baldwin, 1865. 8vo. 340pp. Fine engraved frontis containing five portraits of the conspirators. Text in double column. Orig. publ. cl., trifle worn at head of spine, but a fine copy. $ 125.00

223. CUBIN, J. Sketch of a new national police bill: by which the progress of crime would be arrested, and the community protected: with suggestions for the more effectual detection of criminals: the speedy and cheap administration of justice, as submitted to ... the Duke of Wellington ... and Sir Robert Peel ... with emendations and additions. London, Smith, Elder, 1832. 31pp. Wraps. sewn as issued. $ 45.00
*Sane and interesting proposals, including the use of military transport ships for prisoners sent to Australia. Transportation and its reform is given substantial attention. Missed by Ferguson. Not in NUC, or BM cat. to 1965.

224. HAWAII. KINGDOM. MINISTERIAL REPORTS. Report of the Attorney General (John Ricord). By order of His Majesty King Kamehameha III. Read ... to the Hawaiian Legislature, on Wednesday, May 21st, 1845. Printed by Royal Authority, at the Polynesian Press, Honolulu, (1845). 31pp. 8vo. Stitched as issued; a very good copy. $ 250.00
*First edition. An interesting exposition of Anglo-American political spirit to the native Hawaiian legislature on the eve of the first complete codification of law for the new nation. The address emphasizes the main concepts of separation of powers, a bill of rights, and, above all, the idea of implied powers, the latter essential to fashion a workable system, not only for internal stability but also for gaining diplomatic recognition. Ricord was appointed Attorney General 10 days after his arrival in Hawaii on a visit in 1844 because he was the only lawyer in the island! NUC locates LC, BPL and AAS only.

225. LIVINGSTON, EDWARD. A system of penal law for the United States of America: consisting of a code of crimes and punishments; a code of procedure in criminal cases; a code of prison discipline; and a book of definitions. Proposed and presented to the House of Representatives ... by one of the Representatives from the State of Louisiana ... Wash., Gales & Seaton, 1828. Folio. x, 142, 187, 51, 45, 21pp. Contemp. polished tree claf, leather label, an exceptionally fine copy. FIRST EDITION. $ 350.00
*Sir Henry Maine described Livingston as "the first legal genius of modern times" (Cambridge Essays, 1856). Livingston's code marks an epoch in the broad international movement for prison reform. Profoundly influenced by Bentham, he stressed prevention over revenge in every facet of his work. Like its counterpart of a few years earlier designed for the state of Louisiana, this monumental, enlightened code failed to materialize into law; nonetheless it established its author in America and abroad as one of the great standards by which future efforts at reform would be judged. The work is now very rare in trade.

ROBERT H. RUBIN BOOKS

Post Office Box 558 · Stoughton, Massachusetts 02072 USA
Cable Address: «RUBOOKS» Telephone: (617) 344-0740

CATALOG FOUR FALL/WINTER: 1979

ANTIQUARIAN AND OUT-OF-PRINT WORKS IN

LAW AND LEGAL HISTORY

(CHIEFLY ANGLO-AMERICAN)

PART I:	**Books published before 1900**	**items 1-293**
PART II:	**Books published 1900 and after**	**294-409**
PART III:	**A special collection of monographs and serials on the beginnings of English legal history.**	**410-514**

•

A detailed index is enclosed

•

I take pleasure in sending you my fall-winter law catalogue. Some of the highlights: **John Dickinson's copy of Bradford's epoch-making tract on capital punishment; a fine manuscript account book of an important 18th century legal practice; the first edition of the Napoleonic Code; Mill on liberty, and Locke on civil government; major contributions to American political philosophy by John Taylor of Virginia and Zephaniah Swift; important editions of Blackstone and Kent; tracts on constitutional questions under Lincoln and on the penological controversy in America in the 19th century.** *Also of special interest is the greater than usual number of works on* **Southern law before the Civil War,** *and a very substantial collection of important scholarship on* **early English law** *which comprises Part III.*
I hope all of it makes interesting reading.

•

Offers of single items or entire collections from institutional duplicates and personal collections always welcome

1. (AIKENS, ASA). Practical forms; with notes and references explanatory of the law ... together with a lengthy note giving every legal requisite to the perfection of deeds and other conveyances of real estate ... Windsor, Vermont, printed and published by Simeon Ide, 1823. 409pp. 12mo. Contemp. 1/4 calf, First edition.
*Shaw-Shoemaker 11551 $ 27.50

2. (ALABAMA. LAWS, STATUTES.) AIKIN, JOHN G., Compiler. A digest of the laws of the state of Alabama: containing all the statutes ... in force ... in January 1833: to which are prefixed,... the act to enable the people of Alabama to form a constitution of the state of Alabama. With an appendix and a copious index, and also a supplement containing the public acts of the General Assembly ... Second edition. Tuscaloosa, Woodruff and Mobile, Smith, 1836. 8vo. xlvii, 664pp. Contemp. sheep, rubbed, but a very good, sound copy. $ 75.00
*The supplement continues to 1835. Marvin p. 50. Second digest of state law.

3. (ALABAMA. LAWS, STATUTES.) CLAY, C.C. A digest of the laws of the state of Alabama: containing all the statutes of a public and general nature, in force in Feb. 1843. To which are prefixed the ... act to enable the people of Alabama to form a constitution and state government, and the constitution of the state with an appendix, and a copious index. Tuskaloosa, Marmaduke L. Slade, 1843. 8vo. xliv, 766pp. Contemp. sheep. A very good copy. $ 75.00
*Marvin p. 199. This is the third digest of state law.

4. ALDRICH, P. EMORY. Equity pleadings and practice in the Courts of Massachusetts, with frequent references to the practice in other jurisdictions. With an appendix of forms. Boston, Little, Brown, 1885. 409pp. Full contemp. sheep. First edition. $ 25.00

5. AMERICAN LEGAL ASSOCIATION. Manual ... containing its plan, constitution and Secretary's Report together with a catalogue of its members, embracing the name and address of at least one efficient and trustworthy lawyer at almost every village and city in the Union. N.Y., 1851. 31pp. Wrps. $ 20.00

6. AMERICAN ARCHIVES. (Peter Force, Compiler). Wash., D.C., 1848. Fourth series: Vols. 1-6; Fifth series: Vols. 1-3. Two vols. rebound in 1/4 lea; the rest in original 1/4 calf, two covers detached. Institutional bookplates inside front covers. A sound, clean and reasonably attractive set, internally fine. Complete in nine vols. $ 350.00
*A complete set; the first three series were never published. The work was conceived in conjunction with the publication

(Cont'd.)

6. AMERICAN ARCHIVES. (Cont'd.)
of the American State Papers series and covers the period before Nationhood.

7. (AMERICAN PRECEDENTS OF DECLARATIONS.) (PERHAM, BENONI AND Joseph Story). American precedents of declarations. Collected chiefly from manuscripts of accomplished pleaders; digested and arranged under distinct titles and divisions; and adapted to the most modern practice. With a prefixed digest of rules and cases concerning declarations. Boston, printed by Manning and Loring, for Macanulty, Salem. 1802. xxiv, (9)-345, errata pp. 8vo. Contemp. calf. $ 100.00
*Tapley: Salem Imprints p. 193 states that Perham was the author, assisted by Joseph Story. The work was revised by Anthon a few years later. This first edition is quite uncommon and is of great importance in documenting the practical departure of American law from the rigid accrued forms of English common law; it is said to have been based in large part on the ms. notes of Theophilus Parsons. Shaw-Shoemaker 1766; The NUC cites 6 locations.

8. (AMERICAN PRECEDENTS OF DECLARATIONS.) ANTHON, JOHN. American precedents of declarations, collected chiefly from the manuscripts of Chief Justice Parsons ... and adapted to the most modern practice ... N.Y., Gould, 1810. xxxiv, (31)-370pp. 8vo. Contemp. calf, worn, internally a good copy. $ 45.00
*An enlarged and revised version of this important work which first appeared in 1801 under the editorship of B. Perham and Joseph Story. It is significant for its introduction into print of New England usages which differ in accordance with practical needs from English Common Law precedent. Marvin p. 65. (See the preceding item.)

9. AMES, JAMES BARR. A selection of cases on pleading at common law, with references and citations. Cambridge, Wilson, 1875. 299pp. contemp. sheep. Fine. Samuel Williston's copy with his notes. $ 20.00

10. ANCHER, PEDER. Dansk Lehns Ret. Kisbenhavn, Gyldendals, 1777. 12pl., 176pp. 8vo. Contemp. 1/4 calf. $ 30.00
*This work by this leading author on Danish law is not in the NUC.

11. ANTHON, JOHN. The law of Nisi Prius, being reports of cases determined at Nisi Prius, in the Supreme Court of the State of New-York, with notes and commentaries on each case. To which is prefixed an introductory essay, on the studies preparatory to the active duties of the bar. N.Y., Gould, 1820. 214pp. 1/4 calf, rubbed. $ 60.00
*An original and important work, indexed with table of cases, and a prefatory essay on legal education and bibliography. Marvin p. 64, DAB.

12. ARCHBOLD, JOHN FREDERICK. A summary of the law relative to pleading and evidence in criminal cases; with precedents of indictments, &c. and the evidence necessary to support them. First American from the first London edition, with considerable additions and corrections. N.Y., Gould, 1824. 429pp. 8vo. Contemp. calf, rubbed. $ 45.00

13. BACKUS, JOSEPH. The Justice of the Peace, being a general directory, and forms proper for the due execution of the office, according to the Common and Statute Laws now in force and use in the State of Connecticut. With many other forms not peculiarly appropriate to that office. Hartford, Russell, 1816. 264pp. Full contemp. sheep. $ 35.00

14. BACON, FRANCIS. The elements of the common lawes of England, branched into a double tract: the one containing a collection of some principal rules and maximes of the common law, ... the other the use of the common law, for preservation of our persons, goods, ... London, John Moore, 1639. 4to. 10pl., 94, (8),72pp. with separate title pages for the two parts. Ornamental headpieces. Contemp. calf; corner of title page cropped, no text affected. A very good copy. $ 225.00
*One of the earliest if not the first published collections of maxims of the English law. STC 1136; S&M, I, 237.. The third edition.

15. BANCROFT, GEORGE. History of the formation of the Constitution of the United States of America. N.Y., Appleton, 1882. In 2 vols. Approx. 1000pp. Orig. cl. Fine. o.p. $ 45.00

16. (BANKS & BROTHERS). A catalogue of law books, published or for sale by Banks & Bros., law publishers, booksellers, and importers. N.Y., Banks, 1872. 134pp. Covers stained. Includes British, Irish, Scottish, and Canadian works, and an o.p. service. With chronological lists of reports. $ 17.50

17. BAY, ELIHU HALL. Reports of cases argued and determined in the Superior Courts of Law, in the State of South Carolina, since the Revolution. Volume 2, only. N.Y., Riley, 1811. 591pp. Contemp. full sheep. $ 20.00
*Marvin p. 100. Published separately and complete in itself for 1796-1804.

18. BAYLEY, JOHN. Summary of the law of bills of exchange, cash bills, and promissory notes. From the fourth London edition, revised by the author. With notes and references to American decisions, by Willard Phillips and Samuel E. Sewall. Boston, Harrison Gray, 1826. 426pp. Full contemp. sheep. $ 45.00
*First American edition with a wealth of American material. Marvin p. 101, a very laudatory note.

19. BEADLE, DELOS W. The American lawyer and business man's form book; containing forms and instructions for (numerous categories) together with the laws of the various states on (numerous topics) and a map and seal for each state in the Union. N.Y. Phelps, Fanning, 1852. 359pp. Orig., prtd. bds. Illus. $ 27.50
*Contains recent states such as Texas and California, as well as the southern states.

20. BEALE, JOSEPH HENRY. A selection of cases and other authorities upon criminal law. Cambridge, Harvard Law Review Pub. Assoc., 1894. 983pp. cl. 1st ed. $ 17.50

21. BECK, THEODRIC ROMEYN, et al. Elements of medical jurisprudence. Sixth edition. In two vols. Phila., Cowperthwait, 1838. XXIII,670,743pp. $ 45.00
*The first American treatise on the subject; this edition considerably revised, extensive bibliography.

22. BENTHAM, JEREMY. Defence of usury: shewing the impolicy of the present legal restraints on the terms of pecuniary bargains. To which is added, a Letter to Adam Smith on the discouragement of inventive industry. Phila., printed for Mathew Carey, 1796. 149pp. plus 2pp. advts. Later half calf, joints worn but firm. Expert paper restoration to upper corner of title with several words supplied in neat facsimile, otherwise a very good copy. $ 100.00
*FIRST AMERICAN EDITION. A masterly treatment and "one of the first to be completely emancipated from the old prejudice against moneylending." Palgrave. Bentham's first appearance in America and curiously his last until the 1830's. Kress B3088. Vanderblue p. 51.

23. BENTHAM, JEREMY. Defence of usury; shewing the impolicy of the present legal restraints on the terms of pecuniary bargains; ... to which is added a letter to Adam Smith, ... on the discouragments opposed by the above restraints to the progress of inventive industry. The fourth edition. And to which is added, third edition, a protest against law-taxes. London, Payne and Foss, 1818. 206, 70pp. 12mo. Contemp. polished calf. Very fine copy. $ 80.00
*Kress C12; Vanderblue p. 51.

24. BIGELOW, LEWIS. A digest of Pickering's Reports, vols. II-VII, being a supplement to the digest of the previous volumes of the Massachusetts Reports. Boston, Milliard, 1830. 38,339pp. Full contemp. sheep. Fine. $ 22.50

25. BIGELOW, LEWIS. A Digest of the reported cases argued and determined in the Supreme Judicial Court of the Commonwealth of Massachusetts. Boston, Wells and Lilly, 1824. 856pp. Full contemp. sheep. $ 35.00
*Marvin p. 117.

26. BIGELOW, MELVILLE MADISON. Placita Anglo-Normannica: law cases from William I. to Richard I., preserved in historical records. London, Sampson, 1879. 328pp. cl. $ 30.00
*With good introduction. Bigelow was American and collected these sources while preparing his "Leading Cases on Torts."

<u>THE CONSTITUTIONAL QUESTION UNDER LINCOLN: BINNEY AND OTHERS</u>

27. (BINNEY, HORACE). The privilege of the Writ of Habeas Corpus under the Constitution. Phila., Sherman & Son, 1862. 58pp. Orig. prtd. wrps. $ 32.50
*Signed presentation copy from the author to S.A. Allibone. Defends presidential power. His three Habeas Corpus works taken together form an important treatise. (DAB.)

28. (BINNEY, HORACE). The privilege of the Writ of Habeas Corpus under the Constitution. Second ed. Phila., Sherman, 1862. 58pp. wrps. $ 22.50
*(Second printing of the preceding item.)

29. (BINNEY). BULLITT, J.C. A review of Mr. Binney's pamphlet on "The Privilege of the Writ of Habeas Corpus under the Constitution." Phila., J. Campbell, 1862. 56pp. wrps. $ 20.00

30. (BINNEY). JACKSON, TATLOW. Authorities cited antagonistic to Horace Binney's conclusions on the Writ of Habeas Corpus. Phila., J. Campbell, 1862. 8pp. wrps. $ 12.50

31. (BINNEY). MONTGOMERY, JNO. T. The Writ of Habeas Corpus and Mr. Binney. Second ed. Phila., J. Campbell Bookseller. 1862. 29pp. wrps. $ 17.50

32. (JOHNSTON, JAMES I.). The suspending power and the Writ of Habeas Corpus. Phila., J. Campbell, 1862. 48pp. wrps. $ 17.50

33. (KENNEDY, W. M.). The Privilege of the Writ of Habeas Corpus under the Constitution of the United States. In what it consists, how it is allowed, how it is suspended. It is the regulation of the law, not the authorization of an exercise of Legislative power. Phila., 1862. 17pp. wrps. $ 17.50
*Sabin 65729 (under title) and 37445 (under Kennedy).

34. BINNEY, HORACE. An eulogy on the life and character of John Marshall, Chief Justice of the Supreme Court of the United States. Delivered at the request of the Councils of Philadelphia, on the 24th Sept., 1835. Phila., printed by J. Crissy, 1835. 70pp. Illus., frontis. Orig. wrps. Signed by Binney. $ 20.00

35. BLACKSTONE, WILLIAM. Commentaries on the laws of England. Book of the First (Second-Third-Fourth). Oxford, Printed at the Clarendon Press, 1766-1769. Four volumes, 4to. Contemporary calf, raised bands, red leather labels, several joints cracked but all quite firm. Internally a very fine copy with generous margins and in all quite handsome and attractive. With the contemp. signature and bookplates of "G.J. Curteis, Oxford, 1780." $ 1250.00
*Volumes I and II are second editions; Volumes II and IV are first editions. Two engraved plates, one folding in Vol. II. The revised volume one contains corrections and slight amplification by the author. Sweet & Maxwell I, 27. Printing and the Mind of Man 212. Rothschild 407.

36. BLACKSTONE, WILLIAM. Commentaries on the laws of England. In four books. The twelfth edition. With the last corrections of the author; additions by Richard Burn, and continued to the present time by John Williams. Dublin, White, Jones and Rice. 1794. Four volumes, 12mo., folding tables in volume two. Contemp. polished calf, red and black leather labels. An exceptionally fine and attractive set. $ 225.00
*S&M, I, p. 28.

37. BLACKSTONE, WILLIAM. Commentaries on the laws of England: in four books, with an analysis of the work. In two vols. from the nineteenth London edition, with a life of the author, and notes: by Christian, Chitty, Lee, Hovenden, and Ryland: and also references to American cases, by a member of the New-York Bar. N.Y., Dean, 1849. Full contemp. sheep. Very good copy. $ 75.00
*Marvin p. 123. "This edition the most general in use in the U.S." It was first published in 1832. This is a stereotype reprint. There is a good deal of reference to differences between N.Y. State and British law; Blackstone had been an important influence upon the revision of N.Y. law.

38. BLACKSTONE, WILLIAM. Reports of cases determined in the several courts of Westminster-Hall from 1746-1779 taken and compiled by Sir William Blackstone ... published ... from his original manuscript, ... with a preface containing memoirs of his life. In two volumes. London, His Majesty's Law Printers for Strahan; Cadell ... 1781. Two vols. Folio. Title soiled. New cloth. A very good set. <u>FIRST EDITION.</u> $ 150.00
*S&M, I, 293.

39. BLACKSTONE, WILLIAM. Tracts, chiefly relating to the antiquities and laws of England. The third edition. Oxford, Clarendon Press, 1771. 4to. 353, lxxx, (19)pp. Contemp. mottled calf, rubbed, joints cracked though firm, internally fine. $ 175.00
*This is the first edition of the tracts to contain the <u>Analysis of the Laws of England</u>, which is here revised to conform with the recently published <u>Commentaries</u> of which it had originally been an outline. S&M, I, 30.

40. BLAGRAVE, J. (Notary Public). Laws for regulating bills of exchange, inland and foreign. The fourth edition, (i.e., First American edition). London, printed; and, New-York: re-printed by S&J Loudon, 1786. 36pp. sm. 8vo., sewn as issued, uncut, neat library blind stamp and release stamp, but a good copy. $ 55.00
*Not in Evans who lists only a 1787 edition. Bristol B6248 who notes two holdings.

41. BLAKE, D. T. An historical treatise on the practice of the Court of Chancery of the State of New-York; containing all the proceedings of a suit, as well in the Court of Chancery, as in the Court for the trial of impeachments and correction of errors. N.Y., printed by J. T. Murden, 1818. 483, 167pp. Full contemp. sheep. rubbed, some marginal dampstains. FIRST EDITION. $ 37.50
*Marvin p. 129. Shaw Shoemaker 43390.

42. BOLSTER, WM. W. Digest of the law of tax titles, and form book, embracing all practical tax forms in all departments of the law for the use of Town, County and State Officers, adapted to the New England States, also containing (with notes, directions and citations,) forms of proceedings, for Town Officers, School Committees, Trial Justices, Coroners, Sheriffs, Constables and County Commissioners, adapted to the revised statutes of Maine. Portland, Me., Dresser, 1871. 483pp. Full contemp., sheep. $ 25.00

43. (BOSTON. MUNICIPAL COURT). THACHER, PETER OXENBRIDGE. Reports of Criminal Cases, tried in The Municipal Court of the City of Boston before ... Edited by Horatio Woodman. Boston, Little & Brown, 1845. 733pp. Full contemp. sheep. Very good copy. $ 35.00
*Marvin p. 687. First edition.

44. BOUVIER, JOHN. A law dictionary, adapted to the constitution and laws of the United States of America, and of the several states ... with references to the civil and other systems of foreign law. Fifth edition, revised, improved, and greatly enlarged. Phila., 1855. 2 vols. 692; 745pp. Supreme 8vo. Contemp. sheep, near fine. $ 35.00

45. BRADFORD, WILLIAM. An inquiry how far the punishment of death is necessary in Pennsylvania. With notes and illustrations. To which is added, an account of the gaol and penitentiary house of Philadelphia, and of the interior management thereof. By Caleb Lownes, ... Phila., T. Dobson, 1793. 4,(3)-108pp. fold. table. 8vo. Original pale blue wrappers, stitched as issued, entirely uncut. A fine copy in original state, with the signature of John Dickinson. $ 350.00
*Evans 25225. A milestone in enlightened penal reform in America. Bradford, formerly Attorney General for Pa., "influenced (Cont'd.)

45. BRADFORD, WILLIAM. (Cont'd.) the revision of the criminal jurisprudence of Pennsylvania by his report of Dec. 3, 1792 which led to the statute of 1794 which substituted imprisonment at hard labor for the death penalty for all capital crimes except murder of the first degree." (DAB). This first published version contains material not in the original report, and was several times reprinted including a London edition. Pennsylvania led the way in this and in the matter of prison organization: Lownes, who contributed the appendix was at the center of the founding of the first penitentiary in 1790, the beginning of that system in America and the beginning of Pennsylvania's role as a crucible of penological reform for the countries of Europe as well as America. This is a very fine association copy, bearing the holograph signature of John Dickinson, member of the Continental Congress and author of <u>Letters from a Farmer in Pennsylvania.</u>

46. BROOM, HERBERT. The philosophy of law: being notes of lectures delivered during twenty-three years, in the Inner Temple Hall ... adapted for students and the Public. San Francisco, Sumner, Whitney; Boston, Houghton, Osgood, (1876?) xi, 271pp. cl. Nice copy. 1st American edition. $ 20.00

47. BROWN, SAMUEL GILMAN. The life of Rufus Choate. Fifth edition. Boston, Little, Brown, 1885. 498pp. cl. fine. $ 17.50

48. BROWN, WILLIAM H. An historical sketch of the early movement in Illinois for the legalization of slavery, read at the annual meeting of the Chicago Historical Society Dec. 5th, 1864. Chicago, Steam Press of Church, Goodman and Donnelley. 1865. 44pp. Orig. printed wrps. Blind stamp of the Ch. Hist. Soc. on the title page. A good copy. $ 45.00
*Howes B873. Ante-fire imprints 884. 1st edition.

49. BRYCE, JAMES. Legal studies in the University of Oxford: a valedictory lecture delivered before the University, June 10, 1893. London, Macmillan, 1893. 35pp. Orig. prtd. wrps, fine. Refers to American practice. $ 25.00

50. BULLER, FRANCIS. An introduction to the law relative to trials at Nisi Prius, containing additions to the present time, carefully corrected from the last London copy, by a gentleman of the Bar. N.Y., printed for J. Riley, 1806. 356pp. Full contemp. sheep. $ 35.00
*Marvin p. 158. First American Edition.

51. BURN, JOHN ILDERTON. A practical treatise or compendium of the law of marine insurances. London, printed, New York, reprinted, 1801. 235pp. 12mo. contemp. calf worn. $ 37.50
*Marvin p. 163. Same year as London edition, and the only editions to appear. Very uncommon.

52. CALLAN, JOHN F., compiler, and A.W. Russell. Laws of the United States relating to the Navy and Marine Corps, from the formation of the Government to 1859: to which are prefixed the Constitution of the United States, (with an index thereto), and a synopsis of the legislation of Congress, respecting Naval Affairs, during the Revolutionary Way. Baltimore, John Murphy, 1859. 464pp. Full contemp. calf. $ 45.00
*Arranged chronologically, with the decisions of the Supreme Court, and material on the slave trade, and the Neutrality Act. Includes defunct as well as active legislation, the two distinguished by typography. Well indexed. With a 4p. testimonial from Taney and other leading jurists, tipped in at the back. Scarce.

53. CARLE, GIUSSEPPE. La faillite dans le droit international prive ou du conflit des lois de differentes nations en matiere de faillite ... traduit et annote avec une analyse de la jurisprudence francaise et plusieurs autres additions par Ernest Dubois. Paris, Marescq, 1875. 163(1)pp. Wrps. $ 30.00

54. CHAMBERLAIN, DANIEL H. Oration on some of the relations and present duties of the legal profession to our public life and affairs, delivered by Hon. Daniel H. Chamberlain, Governor of South Carolina, before the Yale Law School, at its fifty-first anniversary, June 30th, 1875, at the Center Church in New Haven. New Haven, Yale College, 1875. 34pp. $ 15.00

55. CHAMBERLIN, FRANKLIN. American Commercial Law, relating to every kind of business: with full instructions and practical forms, adapted to all the States of the Union. Hartford, Conn, 1869. Full contemp. sheep. 991pp. Joints mended. $ 30.00
*First edition, with a very large chapter on insurance.

56. CHIPMAN, NATHANIEL. Principles of government: a treatise on free institutions, including the Constitution of the United States. Burlington, Edward Smith, 1833. 330pp. $ 47.50
*Chipman, like Zephanian Swift, was one of the most important judicial theorists whose legal thought extended to a comprehensive system of government. This is a much revised version of his "Sketches of the Principles of Government" which appeared in 1793.

57. CHOATE, RUFUS. The works of Rufus Choate with a memoir of his life by Samuel Gilman Brown. In two vols. Boston, Little Brown, 1862. 558, 523pp. Illus., frontis. Orig. cl., fine. 1st ed. $ 37.50

58. (CIVIL WAR. CONSTITUTIONAL PROBLEMS). Correspondence between S. Teackle Wallis, Esq. of Baltimore, and the Hon. John Sherman, of the U.S. Senate, concerning the arrest of the Maryland Legislature, and the Mayor and Police Commissioners of Baltimore in 1861. Baltimore, 1863. 30pp. wrps. $ 32.50
*A leader of the Maryland Bar for almost half a century, Wallis was imprisoned for four months in an attempt to stop the secessionist movement in Md. (DAB).

59. CLAVERING, HENRY. The new complete parish officer; or perfect guide to church-wardens, overseers, constables (etc.) ... explaining, ... the substance of all the Acts of Parliament, ... including a complete library of parish law down to Hilary Term, 1801. ... The third edition, considerably enlarged and improved. London, Stratford, (1801). 144pp. Disbound. $ 25.00
*S&M, III, 44.

60. (CLAYTON, JOHN). Topicks in the laws of England. Containing media, apt for argument and resolution of law cases; also an exposition of severall words, not touched by former glossaries. London, printed by R.L. for William Leake, 1646. 8vo. 5 pl, 138, 1 blank, 4 contents leaves, errata page. Contemp. calf, lea. label. A very good copy. FIRST EDITION. $ 225.00
*Dedicated to Oliver Cromwell. A book of rules or maxims, 167 in all, with side-note references to cases. Wing C4612; S&M I, 575.

61. The Clerk's Magazine: containing the most useful and necessary forms of writings, ... fourth edition. Albany, Websters and Skinners, 1812. 291, (18)pp. 12mo. New cl. $ 22.50
*The appendix contains certain key N.Y. laws, on debtors, money of account, the Constitution. Shaw Shoemaker 25097. First edition was 1803, published anonymously.

62. COKE, (EDWARD). An abridgement of the first part of my Ld. Coke's Institutes; with some additions explaining many of the difficult cases, and shewing in what points the law has been altered by late resolutions and acts of Parliament. London, Sayer, Walthoe, 1711. vi, (1 errata)495 (1 advt.)pp. Lg. 12mo. Contemp. calf, spine gilt, lea. label, joints cracked but firm. A very attractive copy. $ 150.00
*FIRST EDITION. The editor was William Hawkins. Marvin p. 376, much esteemed. This abridgement continued to be reprinted into the early 19th century. S&M, I, 452.

63. COKE, EDWARD. The first part of the Institutes of the Laws of England: or, a Commentary upon Littleton, ... also three learned tracts of the author ... the eleventh edition, carefully corrected ... to which is added, the Treatise of the Old Tenures of the Laws of England: with two new tables; and many references to the modern law cases, (Cont'd.)

63. COKE, EDWARD. (Cont'd.) never printed before, ... (London,) in the Savoy, Nutt and Gosaling, 1719. FOLIO. Contemp. calf, joints cracked, but cords firm. 10pl., 804pp. plus tables and large folding illustration. Internally a fine copy with an excellent engraved frontispiece portrait of Coke. $ 125.00
*S&M I, 450. Marvin 204ff. The most important of the Institutes, and one of the great summaries of learning and experience linking medieval and modern times; it remained a force in legal literature into the 19th century.

64. COKE, EDWARD, The reports ... in English, in thirteen parts complete; with references to all the ancient and modern books of the law, ... to which are now added, the respective pleadings in English. The whole newly revised, and carefully corrected and translated, with many additional notes and references. By George Wilson, ... Dublin, Moore, 1793. Complete in 7 vols. 8vo. contemp calf, lea. labels. An attractive set. $ 80.00
*This edition first appeared in 1776. S&M, I 296.

65. COLBY, H.G.O. The practice in Civil Actions and Proceedings at Law in Massachusetts. With copious references to decisions in New Hampshire, Maine, &c., with the rules of the State and United States Courts, and an appendix of forms. Boston, Little, Brown, 1848. 515pp. Full contemp. sheep. Very good copy. FIRST EDITION. $ 37.50

66. COLVIN, J.B. The magistrate's guide and citizen's counsellor; adapted to the state of Maryland and Washington County in the District of Columbia. Second edition, revised, added to, and improved. George Town, D.C., Elijah Weems, 1819. 8vo. 479pp. Contemp. calf, lea. label, minor rubbing but an excellent copy. $ 150.00
*Rare. Written in part to protect the public against the abuses of lawyers, according to the preface. Shaw-Shoemaker 476-79, 3 locations; Marvin p. 215. Not in Sabin.

67. COMYNS, JOHN. A digest of the laws of England ... the fifth edition, corrected, (with considerable additions to the text) and continued from the original edition to the present time; to which is added, A digest of the cases at nisi prius, by Anthony Hammond. The FIRST AMERICAN, from the fifth London edition. With the addition of the principle American decisions by Thomas Day. N.Y., Collins & Hanway, 1824-26. Eight volumes, 8vo. Complete. Approximately 7500pp. Contemp. calf, lea. labels. A very good set. $ 120.00
*Marvin p. 218. "... Comyn's Digest stands unrivalled in the annals of the law ... the American edition is ably edited ..." One of the best editions of one of the most important authorities.

68. CONKLING, ALFRED. The jurisdiction, law and practice of the Courts of the United States in admiralty and maritime causes including those of quasi admiralty jurisdiction arising under the Act of Feb 26, 1845, with an appendix containing the new rules of admiralty practice prescribed by the Supreme Court of the United States ... Albany, Little, 1848. 2 vols. 8vo. 950pp. with a 7pp. catalogue of law books published by Little in Albany. Contemp. calf, lea. labels. A very nice copy. $ 87.50
*See DAB for a long notice of Conkling. An interesting association copy belonging to George F. Shepley, with his signature (see DAB). He was District Attorney for Maine and was military governor of Louisiana. FIRST EDITION.

69. COOPER, GEORGE. A treatise of pleading on the equity side of the High Court of Chancery. N.Y., Riley, 1813. 385pp. Full contemp. sheep. First American edition. $ 37.50
*Marvin p. 288.

70. COOPER vs. GREELEY. Brief statement of the pleadings and argument in the case of J. Fenimore Cooper, versus Horace Greeley and Thomas McElrath, in an action for libel, tried at the Saratoga circuit ... 1842, together with running commentaries on the law of libel ... of the State of New York ... N.Y., Greeley, Tribune, 1843. 16pp. Orig. wrps. Nice copy. $ 50.00
*BAL II, 308. First edition. McCoy C543. Between 1837 and 1845 Cooper brought 16 libel suits against newspapermen and won most of the cases, but his victories resulted in a softening of the libel laws.

71. CROSS, TRUEMAN. Military laws of the United States; including those relating to the Marine Corps ... compiled by Colonel Trueman Cross, U.S. Army. Second edition. Washington City, George Templeman, 1838. xxvi, 288pp. 8vo. Contemp. calf. Nice copy. $ 75.00
*First ed. was 1824. This expanded version includes penal legislation as well as repealed laws and seeks to give a complete and connected view of the history and development of military law.

72. The Crown Circuit Companion. First American edition; into which has been incorporated the work formerly published under the name of the Crown Circuit Assistant. Both works have also been carefully revised, and such additions made thereto as modern statutes and decisions have rendered necessary. N.Y., M'Dermut, 1816. 540pp. 8vo. Contemp. calf, little rubbed. $ 40.00
*Marvin p. 242. S&M I, 360. First appeared 1738; last edition 1836.

73. CURTIS, GEORGE TICKNOR. History of the origin, formation, and adoption of the Constitution of the United States: with notices of its principle framers. In two volumes, N.Y., Harper, 1863. 581; 663pp. Original cloth, gilt. Roy. 8vo. A very fine copy. $ 45.00
*One of the major works on the Constitution in the 19th century. See DAB.

74. CURTIS, GEORGE TICKNOR. The strength of the Constitution: a discourse delivered at the Lowell Institute, in Boston, 7 Feb. 1850, as the conclusion of a course of twelve lectures on the history of the Constitution of the United States. Boston, Ticknor, 1850 39pp. Orig. prtd. wrps. Presentation copy from the author to Rufus Choate. $ 30.00
*Ticknor was a notable constitutional scholar and later formed these lectures into an influential text. (See preceding item.)

75. DANIEL, W.T.S. The history and origin of the law reports, together with a compilation of various documents shewing the progress and result of proceedings taken for their establishment, and the condition of the reports on the 31st December, 1883. London, Clowes, 1884. 359pp. New cloth. Illus., frontis., facsimile. Roy 8vo. Scarce. $ 45.00

76. DAVIS, JOHN C.B. The Massachusetts Justice: a treatise upon the powers and duties of the Justices of the Peace, with copious forms. Worcester, Lazell, 1847. 553pp. Full contemp. sheep. $ 35.00
*First edition of this new treatise. Surprisingly uncommon.

77. DEANE, JAMES PARKER. The law of blockade, as contained in the report of eight cases argued and determined in the High Court of Admiralty on the blockade of the coast of Courland, 1854. London, Butterworths, 1855. xvii, 193pp. with a 20pp. Butterworth law book catalogue. Orig. cl. $ 50.00
*Cases arose in the course of attempting to close off Russian ports by way of the Baltic during the Crimean War. Fine, detailed study. S&M, III, 62.

78. DE LOLME, J.L. The constitution of England or, an account of the English government: in which it is compared, both with the Republican form of government, and the other monarchies in Europe. A new edition enlarged. N.Y., Hodge & Campbell, 1792. xvi, (24)-376,(8)pp. 8vo. Contemp. calf. A good copy. $ 40.00
*Evans 24263. First and only American edition of this classic.

79. (DESTUTT DE TRACY, ANTOINE LOUIS CLAUDE, Comte). A commentary and review of Montesquieu's Spirit of Laws. Prepared for press from the original manuscript, ... to which are annexed, Observations on the thirty-first book, by ... Condorcet; and two letters of Helvetius, on the merits of the same work. Phila., Duane, 1811. vii, 292pp. Contemp. 1/4 calf. $ 75.00
*First publication of this work, in a translation by Thomas Jefferson who was a close friend of the author. The French ms. dates from 1807 and was not published until 1819.

80. DE WOLF, LYMAN E. The constable's guide, being a treatise on the duties of constables in the State of Pennsylvania ... Towanda, Pa., Published by the author. (Cont'd.)

80. DE WOLF, LYMAN E. (Cont'd.) 1845. 176pp. Contemp. calf. FIRST EDITION. $ 37.50
*Very uncommon and an unusual imprint, privately published by the author. Marvin p. 264f. A fine note, "an excellent guide."

81. DICKINSON, RODOLPHUS. A digest of the Common Law, the Statute Laws of Massachusetts, and of the United States, and the decisions of the Supreme Judicial Court of Massachusetts, relative to the powers and duties of Justices of the Peace, to which is subjoined an extensive appendix of forms. Deerfield, Wilson, 1818. 521pp. Full contemp. sheep. 1st ed. Good copy. *Marvin p. 266. $ 37.50

82. Digested index to the modern reports in Chancery: containing the points of equity determined in the High Court of Chancery, from the year 1689, to the year 1805. Second edition, corrected and enlarged. London, Butterworth, 1807. 625pp. Full contemp. sheep. $ 37.50
*S&M, I 286, best ed. (1st was 1802).

83. DILLON, JOHN F. Inns of Court and Westminster Hall: our law-its history, characteristics and influences. An address delivered before the Iowa State Bar Assoc., at Des Moines, May 14, 1878, Second edition. Des Moines, Mills, 1878. 31pp. See DAB for a fine account of the author whose career spanned N.Y. and Iowa. $ 17.50

84. DUER, JOHN. A discourse on the life, character, and public services of James Kent, late Chancellor of the State of New York; delivered by request, before the judiciary and bar of the City and State of New-York, April 12, 1848. N.Y., Appleton, 1848. 86pp. Illus., frontis. Dsbd. $ 22.50
*DAB gives an account of Duer.

85. EARDLEY-WILMOT, JOHN E. Lord Brougham's law reforms: comprising the acts and bills introduced or carried by him through the Legislature since 1811; with an analytical review of them. London, Longman, 1860. 251pp. $ 25.00
*By the President of the Society for the Amendment of the Law; much on criminal law reform. S&M, III, 69.

86. EDWARDS, CHARLES. The Juryman's Guide throughout the State of New-York, and containing general matter for the lawyer and law officer. N.Y., Halsted, 1831. 293pp. 1/4 leather. $ 55.00
*Marvin p. 289. An uncommon sort of work, as pointed out in the preface.

87. EDWARDS, CHARLES. Pleasantries about courts and lawyers of the State of New York. N.Y., Richardson, 1867. 528pp. Illus., frontis. o.p. $ 25.00
*Anecdotal accounts in great detail of lawyers, cases and practices in first half of 19th century by a member of the Bar.

88. ELMER, LUCIUS Q.C. Forms of proceedings under the laws of New Jersey. 2nd ed. revised and conformed to the (Cont'd.)

88. ELMER, LUCIUS Q.C. (Cont'd.) statutes as found in Nixon's Digest, by John T. Nixon. Trenton, Scott, 1858. 448pp. Buckram, fine. $ 37.50

89. (ENGRAVING). Edward Lord Coke. Fine engraved oval portrait hand colored. London, J. Wilkes, 1820. 8 1/2 x 11" including margins, unmatted and unframed. $ 40.00

90. (ENGRAVING). Sir William Blackstone. Fine engraved oval portrait hand colored. London, J. Wilkes, 1800. 8 1/2 x 11" including margins. Unmatted and unframed. $ 40.00

91. ERNST, GEORGE A.O. The law of married women in Massachusetts. 2nd ed. Boston, Little, Brown, 1897. 285pp. $ 15.00

92. EWALD, ALEX CHARLES. The life and times of the Hon. Algernon Sydney, 1622-1683. In two vols. London, Tinsley, 1873. 782pp. Illus., frontis. o.p. $ 25.00
*Author was of Her Majesty's Record Office and used State Papers in addition to secondary sources. One of the few main sources on this great Republican.

93. EWING, JAMES. A treatise on the office and duty of a Justice of the Peace, Sheriff, Coroner, Constable, Executors, Administrators, and Guardians; in which are particularly laid down, the rules for conducting an action in the Court for the trial of small causes. With new and approved forms. 4th ed. N.Y., Banks, 1848. 498pp. Legal buckram. $ 32.50
*Marvin p. 300. Entirely updated and revised in accordance with new statutes.

94. Examination of witnesses. Hints for conducting a trial. The examination-in-chief-duty of opposing counsel-cross examination. Des Moines: Mills, 1877. 46pp. $ 15.00

95. FARRAR, TIMOTHY. Report of the case of the Trustees of Dartmouth College against William H. Woodward. Argued and determined in the Superior Court of Judicature of the State of New Hampshire, Nov. 1817 and on error in the Supreme Court of the United States, Feb. 1819. Portsmouth, N.H., Foster, (1819). 2pl, 406pp. 8vo. Original boards, paper label. Minor wear to ends of spine, but a fine copy in original state. $ 75.00
*Marvin p. 303. A landmark case elucidating the contract clause of the Constitution and the rights of corporations.

96. FEARNE, CHARLES. An essay on the learning of contingent remainders and executory devises. Fifth edition, revised, corrected, and greatly enlarged by the author. Dublin, Watts, 1794-96. Cloth, a nice set. In two volumes. $ 45.00
*Final edition in the author's lifetime; (Cont'd.)

96. FEARNE, CHARLES. (Cont'd.) in fact the second volume was completed and published after the author's death by John Joseph Powell. Marvin p. 304f. "Still considered the best source of information upon these topics."

97. (FERRIERE, CLAUDE JOSEPH de.) The History of the Roman or Civil Law. Shewing its origin and progress; ... with some account of the principal writers and commentators thereupon: and of the method to be observed in studying the same. Written originally in French, by M. Claude Joseph de Ferriere. To which is added, Dr. Duck's Treatise of the Use and Authority of the Civil Law in England. Translated into English by J.B. 8vo. 8pl., 169, xxxviii pp. half-title present, title within rules. (BOUND WITH:) The history of the origine of the French laws. Translated from the French by J.B. With a preface and notes, shewing, the analogy of the laws of the antient Gauls and Britons. 8pl., 105, (8)pp. 8vo. Both published at London, printed for D. Browne, 1724. Contemp. polished panelled calf, stamped in blind, leather label, front joint cracked but firm, otherwise a very attractive copy. Two works...... $ 150.00
*S&M I, 612. Marvin 307. The second work, also by Ferriere, is rare; NUC cites one holding only.

98. FESSENDEN, THOMAS G. The American clerk's companion, and attorney's prompter: a collection of the most useful and approved forms ... with observations relative to the varieties of practice, introduced or sanctioned by the statutes and courts of the different states. Brattleborough, Vt., Holbrook, 1815. 377pp. 12mo. Calf, FIRST EDITION. $ 30.00
*Shaw Shoemaker 34697. Marvin p. 307.

99. (FIELD, DAVID DUDLEY). A letter to Gulian C. Verplanck, on the reform of the judicial system of this State, by a member of the New-York Bar, 1839. N.Y., University Press, 1840. 43pp. Orig. prtd. wrps., small piece torn from front wrapper, no text affected. $ 32.50
*An early work by this pioneer of legal codification and reform; here he recommends a constitutional amendment allowing the legislature to re-organize an outmoded court system.

100. FILANGIERI, GAETANO. La scienza della legislazione e gli opuscoli scelti. Livorno, 1827-27. Complete in 5 volumes, 8vo. Original wrps. entirely untrimmed, with engraved frontispiece portrait of the author. A very fine set. $ 125.00
*Filangieri was a major economic writer of the late 18th century; without knowing of Adam Smith's already well established work, he nonetheless arrived at similar strong convictions in behalf of freedom of economic activity. However, he rejected universal abstraction in economics and stressed the importance of individual national circumstance in determining policy, thus anticipating the historical school of the 19th century. This edition contains the biography by Tommasi (Cont'd.)

100. FILANGIERI, GAETANO. (Cont'd.) and the collected miscellaneous minor works. All editions are scarce in U.S. holdings.

101. FINCH, THOMAS. Precedents in chancery: being a collection of cases argued and adjudged in the High Court of Chancery ... 1689-1722. The second edition, revised and corrected, with notes and references to theformer and latter reports ... Dublin, Moore, 1792. xiv, approx. 500pp. plus table. 8vo. New cloth. *S&M I, 348. $ 37.50

102. FORTESCUE, JOHN. De Laudibus Legum Angliae: a treatise in commendation of the laws of England, with translation by Francis Gregor, notes by Andrew Amos, and a Life of the Author by Thomas (Fortescue) Lord Clermont. Cincinnati, Clarke, 1872. lxiv, 302pp. $ 17.50

103. FOWLER, WILLIAM CHAUNCEY. Local law in Massachusetts and Connecticut, historically considered: and the historical status of the Negro, in Connecticut; also a speech delivered in the Senate of Connecticut June 22, 1864. Albany, Munsell, 1872. 171pp. Orig. cl. $ 22.50

THE NAPOLEONIC CODE

104. (FRANCE. CODE CIVIL.) Code civil des Francais. Edition originale et seule officielle. Paris, De l'imprimerie de la Republique. An XII, 1804. 4to. Ornamental vignette on title page. 479pp. Contemp. marbled bds., rebacked, spine rubbed, joints cracked but firm, internally an excellent copy. (BOUND IN at the end:) Table alphabetique des matieres du code civil des Francais, redigee sur l'edition originale ... Paris, Rondonneau, 1804, uniform with the above, 111pp. $ 500.00
*First official edition, in the finest format (an octavo was issued at the same time), of one of the landmarks of modern European history. Combining the legacy of the past with the innovations of the French Revolution this great code endured at home and spread its influence abroad; through its clearness of provisions and its spirit of equity and equality it became the model for modernization and reform of law in the Netherlands, Italy, Portugal, Spain and the Central and South American Republics, and served as the code for Belgium and the Rhine Provinces. (Encyl. Britannica, 11th ed.) The NUC cites three holdings of this edition.

105. (FRANCE. LAWS, STATUTES. Code civil). The Code Napoleon; or, The French Civil Code. Literally translated from the original and official edition, 1804. By a Barrister of the Inner Temple. London, Hunter, 1824. xix, 627pp. 8vo. new cloth. A very good copy. $ 40.00
(Cont'd.)

105. (FRANCE. LAWS, STATUTES. Code civil). (Cont'd.)
*First of this translation of one of the landmark codes in modern history.

106. FREEDLEY, EDWIN T. The legal adviser; or how to diminish losses, avoid lawsuits, and save time, trouble, and money, by conducting business according to law, as expounded by the best and latest authorities. Phila., Lippincott, 1859. 397pp. Orig. cl. $ 22.50

107. GARDINER, SAMUEL RAWSON, ed. The Constitutional documents of the Puritan Revolution 1628-1660. Oxford, Claredon Press, 1889. 376pp. 1st ed. Orig. cl. Fine. $ 10.00

108. GLOAG, W.M., et al. Law of rights in security heritable and moveable including cautionary obligations. Edinburg, Green, 1897. 1023pp. Full calf. $ 40.00
*A massive treatise on a hitherto undeveloped topic in Scottish law. S&M, V, 36, (1937 ed.).

109. GOODWIN, ISAAC. New England Sheriff: or digest of the duties of civil officers; being a compendium of the Laws of Massachusetts, with reference to those of the neighboring states, upon those subjects, with copious forms. Worcester, Dorr, 1830. 312pp. Full contemp. sheep. $ 25.00
*Marvin 342. "Useful compilation." 1st ed.

110. GOULD, JAMES. A treatise on the principles of pleading in civil actions. Boston, Lilly, 1832. 536pp. New cloth. FIRST EDITION. $ 45.00
*Marvin p. 342: "A legal classic of the highest order, it has placed its author among the very best legal writers of the age."

111. GOULD, JAMES. A treatise on the principles of pleading, in civil actions. Second edition, revised and corrected by the author. N.Y., Collins, 1836. 536pp. Full contemp. sheep. $ 35.00
*Marvin p. 342. "A classic of the highest order."

112. GRANT-DUFF, M.E. Sir Henry Maine, a brief memoir of his life, with some of his Indian speeches and minutes, selected and edited by Whitley Stokes, with portrait. N.Y., Holt, 1892. 451pp. First American edition. Orig. cl. Fine. o.p. $ 37.50
*Reflects Maine's brilliant legal contributions while serving in India for 7 years.

113. GRAYDON, WILLIAM (compiler). An abridgment of the laws of the United States. or: a complete digest of all such acts of Congress as concern the United States at large, to which is added, an appendix, containing, all existing treaties, the Declaration of Independence, the Articles of Confederation, the rules and articles (Cont'd.)

113. GRAYDON, WILLIAM (compiler). (Cont'd.) for the government of the Army, and the Ordinance for the government of the Territory NorthWest of the Ohio. Harrisburgh, John Wyeth, 1803. 476, 169pp. Full contemp. sheep.
*Shaw-Shoemaker 5194 under U.S. $ 55.00

114. GREAT BRITAIN. COURTS OF KINGS-BENCH. An abridgement of the three volumes of reports of the learned Sr. George Croke of such select cases as were adjudged in the Courts of Kings-Bench and Common Bench, during the reigns of Queen Elizabeth, King James, and King Charles the First. By William Hughes. London, Starkey, Bassett, and Speed, 1665. 25pl., 884,(16)pp. including table of cases, index and license leaf. 8vo., unbound, in a contemporary leather jacket. $ 75.00
*Marvin p. 403. S&M I, 298. Wing C7009.

115. GREENLEAF, SIMON. A discourse pronounced at the inauguration of the author as Royal Professor of Law, in Harvard University, August, 27, 1834. Cambridge, Munroe, 1834. 28pp. Original prtd. wrps., inscribed to Rufus Choate by a third person. Nice copy. $ 27.50
*"To the efforts of Story and Greenleaf is to be ascribed the rise of the Harvard Law School to its eminent position." DAB.

116. GRINNELL, CHARLES E. The Law of deceits and incidents in its practice, illustrated by an analysis of Massachusetts cases, and by references to some other authorities. Boston, Little, Brown, 1886. 169pp. Orig. cl. Good copy. $ 22.50

117. GUTHRIE, WILLIAM D. Lectures on the Fourteenth Article of Amendment to the Constitution of the United States delivered before the Dwight Alumni Association, New York, April-May, 1898. Boston, Little, Brown, 1898. 265pp. cl. Fine. $ 22.50

118. HALL, EVERARD. A digested index to the Virginia reports, containing all the points argued and determined in the Court of Appeals of Virginia, from Washington to Second Randolph inclusive: with a table of the names of the cases reported, to which are added, rules of the Court of Appeals, General Court, and Courts of Chancery for the Richmond and Lynchburg Districts, with instructions for Commissioners in Chancery. Richmond, Cottom, 1825. 654pp. Full contemp. calf. First edition. Marvin 361. $ 65.00

119. HAMILTON, ALEXANDER. The works of Alexander Hamilton: comprising his most important official reports; an improved edition of the Federalist, ... in three volumes. N.Y., Williams and Whiting, 1810. Three engraved frontispieces of Hamilton, Madison and Jay respectively. Contemp. tree calf; front joint of volume 1 strengthened. A very nice set. $ 125.00
*First collected edition of Hamilton's (Cont'd.)

119. HAMILTON, ALEXANDER. (Cont'd.) writings. Ford, Bibliotheca Hamiltoniana p. 87. "edited by John Wells, who gives the authorship of the different numbers of the Federalist from a private memorandum in [Hamilton's] own handwriting." The first appearance thus in print. Also contained here is the Report on Manufactures.

120. HARRIS, RICHARD. Mr. Bumpkin's lawsuit: or how to win your opponent's case. London, Stevens, 1883. xvii, 385 pp. cl. fine. $ 20.00
*Plea for law reform, particularly slowness and expense of suits. Fictional treatment. Author was barrister of Middle Temple and wrote "Hints on Advocacy."

121. HARRISON, JOSEPH. The accomplished practiser in the High Court of Chancery, shewing the whole method of proceedings, according to the present practice, from the bill to the appeal: containing the original, power and jurisdiction of the Chancery, both as a court of law and equity ... also the best forms and precedents ... together with a list of the officers and their fees ... The Second edition, with all the practice enlarged ... and an addition of precedents of all kinds; also the proceedings upon a Commission of Lunacy. In two volumes. (London), Lintot, 1745. 2vols. 8vo. Contemp. calf, a very good set. $ 150.00
*An extremely informative and rather uncommonwork; this enlarged edition is of particular merit because of the inclusion of the material on mentally abnormal persons, an early chapter in the jurisprudence of insanity. S&M I, 339. Marvin 371.

122. HEARD, FRANKLIN FISKE. Curiosities of the law reporters. Boston, Lee, 1871. 212pp. $ 17.50

123. HENRY, MORTON P. The jurisdiction and procedure of the Admiralty Courts of the United States in civil causes. (On the instance side.) Phila., Kay, 1885. 496pp. Full contemp. sheep. Good copy. 1st ed. $ 35.00

124. HERBERT, W. Antiquities of the Inns of Court and Chancery; containing historical and descriptive sketches ... with a concise history of the English law. London, Vendor and Hood, 1804. 8vo. xii, 377,(8)pp. Illustrated. Contemp. tree calf, spine and labels worn, joints cracked but holding. Internally near fine, some very light occasional foxing, but the plates mostly in very clean state. $ 55.00
*One of the best authorities on the Inns of Court, with twenty-four fine steel-engraved views.

125. HILL, JOHN W. A manual of the Law of Fixtures. N.Y., Voorhis, 1867. 64pp. 1/2 calf. 1st ed. $ 25.00

126. a) HILLHOUSE, (JAMES). Propositions for amending the Constitution of the United States; submitted by ... to the Senate ... with his explanatory remarks. New Haven, Oliver Steele, 1808. 31pp. Sewn as issued. Fine. (second ed., revised.) $ 27.50

(Cont'd.)

126. a) HILLHOUSE, (JAMES). (Cont'd.)
*Though a Federalist, Hillhouse had proposed a series of checks to the centralization of power. See DAB.
b) SAME: Speech of the Hon. James Hillhouse ... to which is added the amendments referred to. Troy, N.Y. Wright, Goodenow and Stockwell, 1808. 39pp. Dsbd. $ 22.50
*Another printing of the above text.

127. HOAR, GEORGE F. The function of the American lawyer in the founding of States: an address delivered before the graduating classes at the fifty-seventh anniversary of the Yale Law School on June 28th, 1881. New Haven, Tuttle, 1881. 22pp. wrps. Fine. $ 10.00

128. HOFFMAN, MURRAY. The office and duties of masters in chancery and practice in the master's office. With an appendix of precedents. N.Y., Gould and Banks, 1824. 437,(2)pp. new cloth. FIRST EDITION. $ 37.50
*Marvin p. 390. Hoffman was one of the masters in the N.Y. court.

129. HOLMES, OLIVER WENDELL. Address delivered at the dedication of the new hall of the Boston University School of Law, January 8, 1897. Boston, (1897). 29pp. Orig. prtd. wrps. Nice copy. Scarce. $ 25.00

130. JACOBS, VICTOR. Etude sur les assurances maritimes et les avaries faite en vue du Congres de Droit commercial d'Anvers. Bruxelles, 1885. 83pp. wrps. $ 27.50

131. JARMAN, THOMAS. Treatise on wills. First American ed., with notes and references to American decisions, by J.C. Perkins. 2 vols. Boston, Little & Brown, 1845. Full contemp. sheep. Very fine copy. $ 60.00
*Marvin p. 420: "This is by far the most voluminous and complete treatise on the subject of wills extant."

132. JENKINS, JOHN S. The new Clerk's Assistant, or Book of Practical Forms; containing numerous precedents and forms for ordinary business transactions, with references to the various statutes, and latest judicial decisions: ... to which is added an appendix, containing The New Constitution of the State of New York. Auburn, Derby, 1854. 644pp. Full contemp. sheep. $ 27.50

133. JOHNSON, WILLIAM. A digest of the cases decided and reported in the Supreme Court of Judicature, the Court of Chancery, and the Court for the Correction of Errors, of the State of New York; from 1799 to 1823; with tables of the names of the cases and of titles and references. In two vols. Albany, Backus, 1825. 654, 660pp. Full contemp. sheep. Good copy. $ 40.00
*Marvin p. 426. A third volume appeared later. This is complete as originally issued.

134. JONES, WILLIAM. An essay on the Law of Bailments, from the last London edition, with introductory remarks, and notes, comprising the most modern authorities, by John Balmanno. Albany, Backus, 1806. 132, 21pp. Full contemp. sheep. $ 25.00
*Marvin p. 428f.

135. JOY, EDMUND STEELE. The right of the Territories to become States of the Union. Newark, Advertiser Printing House, 1892. 43pp. wrps. o.p. $ 12.50

136. (KENDALL, AMOS). Mandamus Case. Letter of the Postmaster General and opinion of the Attorney General in reference to the power of the circuit court for the District of Columbia to control executive officers of the United States in the performance of their official duties: also an exposition of the reasons of the postmaster general for refusing to execute a part of the award of the solicitor in favor of messrs. Stockton, Stokes, and others. Wash., Blair & Rives, 1837. 76pp. Stitched as issued. $ 40.00
*Amos Kendall as Postmaster refused to obey a court order to make an award on the grounds of separation of powers; he was supported by Benj. F. Butler as Attorney General.

137. KENT, JAMES. Commentaries on American Law. In four volumes. Second edition. New York, O. Halsted, 1832. Four vols., 8vo. Original sheep, red leather labels, a little rubbed and dry; internally a fine set. $ 250.00
*Probably the most important single interpretation of American law, in effect "the American Blackstone." This edition contains substantial additions and revisions as outlined in Kent's new preface in which he refers to changes occuring since the first edition of 1826. Of particular importance is the adoption of the Revised Statutes of New York and a number of Supreme Court decisions.

138. KILTY, WILLIAM. A report of all such English statutes as existed at the time of the first emigration of the people of Maryland, and which by experience have been found applicable to their local and other circumstances; and of such others as have since ... been introduced ... by the courts of law or equity ... and also all such ... as may be proper to be introduced and incorporated into the statute law. Made according to the directions of the Legislature, by ... Chancellor of Maryland. To which are prefixed, an introduction and lists of the statutes which had not been found applicable ... with full and complete indexes ... Annapolis, Jehu Chandler, 1811. 4to. 289, (1 errata)pp. Contemp. calf, front joint cracked, some foxing but a very good copy. $ 150.00
*Kilty produced the 1799 laws of the state, an important treatise on land law, and this uncommon piece of legal research commissioned by the legislature towards a further revision of the law. Marvin p. 440. Sabin 45320. Shaw-Shoemaker 23158.

139. KINNE, ASA. The most important parts of Blackstone's Commentaries, reduced to questions and answers. 2nd ed. N.Y., Dean, 1839. 266pp. Full contemp. sheep, very fine copy. $ 30.00
*Marvin p. 441. Updated and expanded beyond the 1835 edition.

140. KINNE, ASA. The most important parts of Kent's Commentaries, reduced to questions and answers. 2nd edition. N.Y. Dean, 1840. 249pp. Full contemp. sheep. Very good copy. $ 30.00
*Marvin p. 441. A greatly expanded edition.

141. KINNE, ASA. Questions and answers on law. Alphabetically arranged with references to the most approved authorities. 4th ed. N.Y., 1844-5. 5 vols. Contemp. sheep, very good copies. $ 40.00
*Marvin 441. A quasi serial publication which extended to another few volumes. It was begun in 1842 and the run offered here contains those early volumes in later editions.

142. (LADD, WILLIAM, editor). Prize essays on a Congress of Nations, for the adjustment of international disputes, and for the promotion of universal peace without resort to arms. Together with a sixth essay, comprising the substance of the rejected essays. Boston, Whipple and Damrell, 1840. 700pp. 8vo. Orig. cl. Nice copy. $ 45.00
*The work of the American Peace Society. The judges appointed to select these essays were Joseph Story, Wm. Wirt, John M'Lean, John Quincy Adams, James Kent, and Daniel Webster. A copy of the volume was to go to all heads of states, colleges, etc. A nice association copy, presented to a New England library by Robert Rantoul 2 months before the declaration of War with Mexico.

143. LAWES, EDWARD. An elementary treatise on pleading in civil actions. First American from first London ed. Portsmouth, N.H., Thomas, 1808. 246pp. Cont. calf, rubbed. $ 45.00
*Marvin p. 452.

144. (LEGAL DIRECTORY). J.A. GRAFT & Co's Legal Directory, 1889. For lawyers, merchants and all business men, containing a synopsis of the collection laws of each State, Territory and Canada, also forms adapted to the laws of each State, the address of one of the leading and most reliable attorneys in over five thousand cities and towns in the United States, Canada and Europe. ... N.Y., Graft, 1889. 462pp. plus 9pp. lawyer's advertisements. $ 25.00

145. LEONARD, JOHN EDWARDS. A digest of the decisions of the Supreme Court of the United States, in Louisiana cases, with an appendix, containing a short treatise on the jurisdiction and practice of the Federal Courts. New Orleans, Johnson Armstrong, 1875. 377pp. Lib. stamp. $ 25.00

146. LIEBER, FRANCIS. Guerrilla parties, considered with reference to the laws and usages of war. Written at the request of Major-General Henry W. Halleck. N.Y., Van Nostrand, 1862. 22pp. Orig. printed wrps., fine. $ 45.00

147. LIVERMORE, SAMUEL. A treatise on the law relative to principals, agents, factors, auctioneers, and brokers. Boston, Wait, 1811. xii, 250pp. 8vo. Orig. bds. Fine copy. FIRST EDITION. $ 47.50
*Marvin p. 470. The first work of its kind from an American writer. See also Warren, History of the American Bar, 1911, p. 337. Livermore was interesting as one of the early historically minded writers who gave his impressive library to Harvard Law School.

148. LIVINGSTON, JOHN. Livingston's Law Register; containing the name, post office county and state of every lawyer in the United States; also ... legal rates of interest ... forms for deeds in every state, N.Y., 1851. 227p. 12mo. cl. $ 22.50
*Early issue of the first comprehensive census of American lawyers.

149. (LOCKE, JOHN). Du gouvernement civil, ou l'on traitte de l'origine, des fondemens, de la nature, du pouvoir, & des fins des societez politiques. Traduit de l'Anglois. Amsterdam, chez Abraham Wolfgang ... 1691. 6pl., 321pp. 12mo. Woodcut vignette on title page, ornamental head and tailpieces. Contemporary calf, leather label. Old institutional stamp on verso of title page, otherwise a fine copy. $ 500.00
*The very rare first French edition of Locke's second treatise on government (first edition L. 1690). No copy in the BM Catalogue; the NUC cites only the University of Michigan copy. Printing and the Mind of Man, no. 163, (the first edition.)

150. LUFF, ARTHUR P. Text-book of forensic medicine and toxicology. In two vols. London, Longmans, 1895. 416, 360pp. Illus., frontis, plates. 1st ed. $ 32.50

151. McCALL, H.S. The Constable's Guide; being a concise treatise on the powers and duties of Constables in the State of New York; to which is added an appendix, containing most of the practical forms. Albany, Gould, 1862. 234pp. Full contemp. sheep. 1st ed. $ 20.00

152. McCLELLAND, MILO A. M.D. Civil malpractice: a treatise on surgical jurisprudence, with chapters on skill in diagnosis and treatment, prognosis in fractures, and on negligence. N.Y., Hurd & Houghton, 1877. 554pp. FIRST EDITION. $ 35.00

153. McKELVEY, JOHN JAY. Principles of common-law pleading: a brief explanation of the different forms of common-law actions, and a summary of the most important principles of pleading therein, with illustrations taken from the cases. N.Y., Baker, 1894. 193pp. $ 15.00

CRIME IN THE STREETS

154. (MADAN, MARTIN). Thoughts on executive justice, with respect to our criminal laws, particularly on the Circuits. Dedicated to the judges of Assize; and recommended to the perusal of all magistrates; and to all persons who are liable to serve on Crown juries. By a sincere well wisher to thepublic. London, Dodsley, 1785. (BOUND WITH:) Appendix to the Thoughts on Executive Justice ... London, Dodsley, 1785. Two items, 170,(1);77pp. Sm. 8vo. Contemp. polished calf, lea. label, spine gilt, a fine attractive copy. FIRST EDITIONS. $ 150.00
*Madan was a prolific and often controversial author; he wrote theological and musical works and produced a notorious defense of polygamy. Here he defends severe penal legislation and laments the leniency of judges and juries, attributing the epidemic of crime to slow and uncertain punishment--a familiar charge. This brought forth a response from Samuel Romilly, later responsible for liberalization of English penal law, and from Benjamin Franklin. There is no copy of the first edition in the BM cat. or the NUC. S&M, I, 364.

155. MAINE, HENRY SUMNER. Popular Government, four essays. London, Murray, 1885. 261pp. Original cloth. spine a little darkened, but a very nice copy. FIRST EDITION. $ 25.00

156. MAINE, HENRY SUMNER. Village-Communities in the East and West. Six lectures delivered at Oxford. Third edition, to which are added other lectures addresses, and essays. London, Murray, 1876. 413pp. Orig. cl. $ 25.00

157. MAITLAND, F.W. Justice and police. London, MacMillan, 1885. 176pp. Cloth. 1st ed. Fine. $ 15.00

158. MANNING, EDWARD WINDHAM. The law of bills of exchange, promissory notes, bank-notes, bankers notes, drafts and checks, containing all the statutes cases, ... and decisions to Trinity Term 1801, including the arguments in the case of Lawson v. Weston ... when some essential information occurred respecting country banks, and their very extraordinary multiplication ... London, Stratford, 1801. 92(4)pp. Neatly disbound. $ 27.50
*First edition. Occasioned by the increase in paper currency and the virtual disappearance of specie in commercial transactions. Marvin p. 496. S&M, III, 146.

159. MANNING, JAMES. A digest of the Nisi Prius Reports, with notes and references, and some original cases, chiefly collected on the Western Circuit. First American, from the last London edition. Exeter, Lamson, 1823. 465, 124pp. Full contemp. sheep.
*Marvin p. 495. S&M, I, 287. $ 37.50

160. MARCH, JOHN. Amicus Reipublicae. The Commonwealths Friend. Or an exact and speedie course to justice and right, and for preventing and determining of tedious law suits. With many other things considerable for the good of the public. All which are fully controverted and debated in law. London, Will. Bentley for Francis Eaglesfield, 1651. 8vo. 8pl., 160pp. complete with the terminal blanks. Contemp ruled calf, and printed spine label. An excellent copy. $ 250.00
*A strong and forthright attack on the sacrosanct authority attached to custom: " ... a common error cannot make a law ... there is no building of a law where reason is not the foundation," the author's preface "remarkable for the enlightenment with which he discusses a series of eighteen questions." DNB. S&M, *, 250. Wing M57. S&M, I. First and only edition.

161. MARRIOT, WILLIAM. The country gentleman's lawyer; and the farmer's complete law library. Containing all the laws now in force ... the third edition ... London, Stratford, 1801. 128pp. disbound. $ 27.50
*This edition adds acts from 1797 to 1801 and relates the law concerning horses, coaches, gaming, bridges, enclosures, woods, etc., etc. Marvin p. 499. S&M, I, 160.

162. MARTINDALE, JAMES B. Martindale's United States Law Directory for 1875-6: containing the names of one or more of the most reliable firms, banks, and real estate agents in each of the principal cities and towns of the United States and Canada; an extensive digest of the commercial laws of each of the states and territories, and the bankrupt law in full, with forms and rules of court. N.Y., Martindale Law and Collection Assoc., (1875). 812pp. Full contemp. sheep. Good copy. $ 27.50

163. (MASSACHUSETTS COLONY. LAWS). The charters and general laws of the colony and province of Massachusetts Bay. Carefully collected from the publick records and ancient printed books. To which is added an appendix, tending to explain the spirit, progress and history of the jurisprudence of the state; especially in a moral and political view. Published by order of the General Court. Boston, Wait, 1814. vii, 830,(30)pp. incl. index. 8vo. Contemp. tooled calf, fine. $ 65.00
*The Committee appointed to make this collection consisted of Nathan Dane, William Prescott and Joseph Story; they were to report also on those laws still in effect which ought to be repealed.

164. MENANT, JOACHIM. Organisation de la famille d'apres les lois de Manou. Paris, Derache, 1846. 44pp. wrps. $ 27.50
*Study of family law in India, under the generic series title of "Recherches sur l'Organisation des familles."

165. MERCHANTS' UNION LAW COMPANY. N.Y. Second monthly report of the correspondents and members ... comprising the name and residence of an efficient and relia-
(Cont'd.)

165. MERCHANTS' UNION LAW COMPANY. N.Y. (Cont'd.) ble practising lawyer for every county of the U.S. ... N.Y., 1866. 79pp. wrps. $ 17.50
*Covers all states and territories, east and west. Rare.

166. MILL, JOHN STUART. On liberty. London, John W. Parker, 1859. 207pp., wanting the advertisements. Small 8vo. Later three-quarter morocco gilt. A very good copy. $ 250.00
*FIRST EDITION. Printing and the Mind of Man 345: " 'Mill on Liberty' remains his most widely read book (Mill himself considered it his most important and most likely to endure work). It represents the final stage in the growth of utilitarian doctrine, and its central point is one which had escaped both Mill's father and Bentham. Mill realized that the 'greatest good' of the community is inseparable from the liberty of the individual ... (he) extended tyranny to include a custom ridden majority ... Many of Mill's ideas are now the commonplace of democracy. His arguments for freedom of every kind of thought or speech have never been improved upon."

167. MITFORD, EARDLEY. The law of wills, codicils, and revocations. With ... a clear and distinct account of the law's disposal of the estates of those who die intestate ... the second edition with additions. London, Stratford, 1801. 110pp. Disbound. (Index incomplete.) $ 17.50

168. MONTEFIORE, JOSHUA. Commercial and notarial precedents: consisting of the most approved forms, ... each set of precedents preceded by a summary of the law on the subject. Particularly on bills of exchange, insurance, salvage, &c. Second American, from the last London edition with an introduction, and considerable alterations and additions by Clement C. Biddle, ... Phila., Carey & Lea, 1822. xx, 480pp. 8vo. Contemp. calf., little rubbed. $ 75.00
*The author was of Spanish-Jewish descent and came to America after 1812 from England and enjoyed a great success in the practice and writing of law. This is the final edition of a scarce title (all of his works are rather uncommon), in which he calls attention to the special role of the notary in civil law, mentioning specifically Louisiana. Not in Marvin.

169. MORIARTY, GERALD P., translator. The Paris Law Courts: sketches of men and manners. Translated from the French by Gerald P. Moriarty. N.Y., Scribner, 1894. 293pp. Illus., plates. o.p. $ 30.00
*Taken from "Palais de justice ..." written by French journalists to acquaint the public with the spirit of French justice; translator was of Balliol College.

170. MORISON, JOHN H. Life of the Hon. Jeremiah Smith, LL.D. Boston,
(Cont'd.)

170. MORISON, JOHN H. (Cont'd.) Little, Brown, 1845. 516pp. Illus., frontis. $ 27.50
*Smith was Chief Justice of N.H. and one of the counsels for the Trustees of Dartmouth College. See DAB.

171. MOYLAN, D. CREAGH. The right of search, as between France, America, and Great Britain. Second edition. London, Butterworth, 1843. 48pp. wrps. $ 22.50
*Presentation to "W.C. Rives, U.S. Senate."

172. MURRAY, J.B.C. The history of usury from the earliest period to the present time together with a brief statement ... concerning the conflict of laws ... and an examination into ... their effect upon commerce. Phila., Lippincott, 1866. 158pp. Orig. cl., fine. First edition. $ 55.00
*State by state coverage as well as numerous citations. 4pp. list of subscribers.

173. MUSGRAVE, W.A.B. A dissertation on the common law of waters and its application to natural circumstances other than those of England. London, Stevens & Son, 1890. 47pp. Dsbd. $ 35.00
*Written in response to the movement in Australia towards public ownership; much reference to American practice. S&M, III, 1159. Not in Ferguson.

174. NEW MEXICO. TERRITORY. Actas de la asamblea legislativa ... sesion trigesima primera. Santa Fe, 1895. 145pp. orig. prtd. wrps. $ 25.00

175. NORTH CAROLINA. LAWS, STATUTES. Revised code of North Carolina, ... 1854; together with other acts ... passed at the same session ... prepared by Bartholomew F. Moore and Asa Biggs ... Boston, Little, Brown, 1855. 728pp. Roy. 8vo. Contemp. calf, rubbed. A good copy. $ 45.00
*First revised code for the state.

176. NORTH CAROLINA. SUPREME COURT. REPORTS. Cases at Law. IREDELL. Vol. I. June 1840-June 1841. Raleigh, 1841. IREDELL. Vol. III. Dec. 1842-June 1843. Raleigh, 1843. IREDELL. VOL. V. Dec. 1844-June 1845. Raleigh, 1845. JONES. Vol. IV. Dec. 1856-Aug. 1857. Salisbury, 1857. SAME: Cases in Equity. IREDELL. Vol. II Dec. 1841-June 1843. Raleigh, 1843. All contemp sheep, 8vo. very good condition. Per Volume, $ 20.00

177. O'CONOR, CHARLES. Commemoration of the one hundredth anniversary of the adoption of the Constitution of the State of New York. Address by Charles O'Conor delivered before the New York Historical Society at the Academy of Music, May 8th, 1877. N.Y., Randolph, 1877. 40pp. Neatly removed. $ 15.00

178. OLIVER, BENJAMIN LYNDE. Practical conveyancing, a selection of forms of general utility with notes interspersed. Second ed. corrected and enlarged.
(Cont'd.)

178. OLIVER, BENJAMIN LYNDE. (Cont'd.) Hallowell, Maine, Glazier, 1827. 581pp. Full contemp. sheep. $ 37.50
*Marvin p. 547. " ... the best American manual on conveyancing."

179. OLIVER BENJAMIN, L. Practical conveyancing; a selection of forms of general utility, with notes interspersed, Fourth ed., corrected and enlarged, by Peter Oliver. Hallowell, Glazier, 1845. 622pp. Full contemp sheep. Very fine copy. $ 35.00
*Marvin p. 547. "best American manual on conveyancing in use."

180. PARKER, EDWARD G. Reminiscences of Rufus Choate, the great American advocate. N.Y., Mason- 1860. 522pp. Illus., frontis. Orig. embossed cl. fine. o.p. $ 27.50

A MANUAL FOR THE WHISKEY REBELLION

181. PARKER, JAMES. The conductor generalis: or, tha office, duty and authority of justices of the peace, ... compiled chiefly from Burn's Justice ... by James Parker, late one of the Justices of the Peace for Middlesex County, in New Jersey; and now revised and adapted to the United States of America. By a Gentleman of the Law ... to which are added, the excise and militia laws of the U.S.; and the Acts called the Ten Pound Act of the States of Pennsylvania and New York. Phila., Campbell, 1792. xv, 464pp. 8vo. Contemp. calf, rubbed. A good copy. $ 150.00
*Evans 24661. The second appearance of this calssic work in its adaptation to the new union. An extremely interesting edition containing the revenue laws and the means of their enforcement which led soon to the Whiskey Rebellion extending from western Pennsylvania to Georgia. Later editions of course omitted this material.

182. (PARKER, JAMES.) The conductor generalis: or, the office, duty and authority of justices of the peace, ... compiled chiefly from Burn's Justice ... by James Parker, late one of the Justices of the Peace for Middlesex County, in New Jersey; and now revised and adapted to the United States of America, by A Gentleman of the Law. ... Albany, Webster, 1794 ... 8vo. 467pp. Contemp. calf, lea. label. An excellent copy, especially considering the use to which such a volume was subjected. $ 100.00
*Fourth appearance (1st was 1788) of this U.S. adaptation of the standard English work which first appeared, unaltered, in N.Y. and Pennsylvania editions early in the century. This national adaptation emphasizes N.Y., N.J., and Pennsylvania law.

183. PARKER, JOEL. The Law School of Harvard College. N.Y., Hurd, 1871. 56pp. Wrps. Fine. $ 20.00
*Parker was Royall professor for 20 years and defends and elucidates the educational philosophy of the school against a slanderous article.

184. PARKER, THEODORE. The trial of Theodore Parker, for the "misdemeanor" of a speech in Faneuil Hall against kidnapping, before the Circuit Court of the United States, at Boston, April 3, 1855, with the defence. Boston, Published for the author, 1855. 221pp. Orig. cl. Fine copy. $ 30.00
*Concerned with the fight over the fugitive slave act and a vehement attack on George Ticknor Curtis who delivered the charge to the grand jury.

185. PARSONS, THEOPHILUS. The laws of business for business men, in all the States of the Union, with forms for mercantile instruments, deeds, leases, wills, &c. Boston, Little, Brown, 1857. 504pp. cl. First edition of this enduring work. Good copy. $ 27.50

186. PARSONS, THEOPHILUS. Laws of business for all the States of the Union, and the Dominion of Canada. With forms and directions for all transactions. Revised and enlarged ed. Hartford, Scranton, 1877. 693pp. $ 37.50
*This appears to be the first edition to include Canada.

187. PARSONS, THEOPHILUS. Laws of business for all the States and Territories of the Union, and the Dominion of Canada ... New revised edition. Hartford, Scranton, 1889. 864pp. Full contemp. sheep. $ 20.00

188. PARSONS, THEOPHILUS. Memoir of Theophilus Parsons, Chief Justice of the Supreme Judicial Court of Massachusetts, with notices of some of his contemporaries, by his son. Boston, Ticknor, 1859. 476pp. Frontis. Cl. Fine $ 27.50
*"Probably no man except Story did more to carry on the common law and restate it in intellible form to suit American needs." DAB.

189. PASSY, FREDERIC, et al. De la Propriete intellectuelle: etudes par Mm. Passy, Victor Modeste et P. Paillottet, avec une preface par M. Jules Simon. Paris, Dentu, 1859. xxiv, 347pp. 8vo. Orig. prtd. wrpas. Partly unopened. $ 30.00
*Reform-oriented studies on patent and property law.

190. PATERSON, JAMES. The liberty of the press, speech, and public worship. Being commentaries on the liberty of the subject and the laws of England. London, Macmillan, 1880. xxi, 568pp. 8vo. cl. Fine First edition. o.p. $ 45.00

191. (PATERSON, SAMUEL). Joinerianas or the book of scraps. London, Johnson, 1772. Two volumes in one. New cl. $ 45.00
*Maxims, including large chapters on booksellers and lawyers.

192. PEAKE, THOMAS. A compendium of the law of evidence. From the last London edition with additions and the American cases in notes, by Josiah Randall. Phila., Printed for F. Byrne, Law Bookseller, 1812. xlix,470,(60)pp. Full contemp. calf., (Cont'd.)

192. PEAKE, THOMAS. (Cont'd.) lea. label, little rubbed but a very good copy. FIRST AMERICAN EDITION. $ 45.00
*Marvin p. 559. With very substantial American case notes.

193. (PENNSYLVANIA. COURT OF COMMON PLEAS). The opinion of the Court of Common Pleas of Lancaster County, in the case of Robert W. Houston against Gen. John Dicks, and others, on the question respecting the authority under which courts-martial should be constituted, for the trial of militiamen charged with delinquency, in disobeying the President's call into the service of the U.S. as delivered, on the 10th of February, 1817. Lancaster, Pennsylvania, William Dickson, 1817. 21pp. removed. $ 55.00
*A rare little work on federal-state relationship; a state-ordered court martial was invalidated on the grounds that the U.S. only possessed the power to call a court martial. Shaw Shoemaker 41756, locating only the AAS copy.

THE "PENNSYLVANIA SYSTEM" AND 19th CENTURY AMERICAN PENOLOGY

194. BOSTON PRISON DISCIPLINE SOCIETY. Annual Reports. 1st - 8th, 12th, 17th, 19th, 21/22nd, 23rd, 26th (1826-1851). Many in original wrappers; each approx. 100-200pp. each $ 10.00
*The Boston Society's annual reports were the only documents of the period in which the progress, method and statistics of American prisons were compiled. Largely through its secretary, Louis Dwight, the Society led the attack on the Pennsylvania System, effectively limiting its spread in the U.S. Its reports were intensively distributed and "it is probably not too much to say that (Dwight) in large measure conditioned the form of prison structure and method adopted in many a state." Teeters, They were in prison: a history of the Pennsylvania Prison Society. 1937. p. 237f.

195. FOULKE, WILLIAM PARKER. Remarks on cellular separation. Read by appointment of the American Association for the Improvement of Penal Institutions, at the annual meeting in N.Y. ... 1860. Phila., 1861. 112pp. Orig. prtd. wrps. $ 50.00
*Foulke was for sixteen years a leading participant in the Pennsylvania Prison Society. "In 1860 he presented what may be considered one of the best and most logical defenses of the separate system ever penned. It was read by appointment before the American Association (etc.) ..." Teeters, They were in prison: a history of the Pennsylvania Prison Society 1937, p. 286.

196. HOWE, (SAMUEL GRIDLEY). An essay on separate and congregate systems of prison discipline; being a report made to the Boston Prison Discipline Society. Boston, Ticknor, 1846. xi, 90pp. Orig. prtd. wrps. Nice copy. $ 75.00
*Presentation copy inscribed by Howe to Rufus Choate. A remarkable defense of

196. HOWE, (SAMUEL GRIDLEY). (Cont'd.) the Pennsylvania system of separate confinement based upon his own investigation of the facts and aimed at the intensely biased and hostile Boston Society, of which Howe had previously been an adherent. Howe failed to have the Society print this "minority report" which was the work also of Horace Mann and Charles Sumner, and finally, after a battle to secure the manuscript from the Society, published it himself. A fine association copy of a scarce and important document in the most critical controversy in 19th century American penology.

197. LIEBER, FRANCIS. A popular essay on subjects of penal law, and on uninterrupted solitary confinement at labor, as contradistinguished to solitary confinement at night and joint labor by day, in a letter to John Bacon ... Phila., Society for Alleviating the miseries of Public Prisons, 1838. 94pp. errata slip. Disbound, marginal dampstaining. $ 47.50
*Lieber, in addition to translating the favorable report of Beaumont and Tocqueville produced this ardent defense of the new Pennsylvania system; he is credited with inventing the term "penology."

198. LINDSLEY, J. BERRIEN. On prison discipline and penal legislation; with reference to the State of Tennessee ... Nashville, 1874. 64pp. Orig. prtd. wrps. $ 45.00
*Lindsley was an M.D. and ardent reformer in the areas of public health and prisons in his capacity as leader of the Robertson Association (see DAB). This is very knowledgably written and informative plea for modernization of conditions in Tennessee, with statistics and a fine general chronology intended to give readers some perspective Scarce.

199. (TIDYMAN, PHILIP). Letters on the Pennsylvania System of solitary imprisonment. Charleston, S.C., 1835. 16pp. Orig. prtd. wrps. stitched as issued. $ 45.00
*Tidyman was an ardent proselytizer for the new system developed at the Eastern Penitentiary; he carried on a substantial correspondence with Samuel Wood, first warden, and used it as the basis of this and other pamphlets. The humane and progressive views of Wood's replies are also printed here. A very uncommon pamphlet.

END OF PENOLOGY SECTION

200. PHELPS, OLIVER, JR. (Attorney at Law, and Agent for Claims). A set of forms and instructions for bounty land claimants: under the Act of Sept. 28, 1850. To which is appended a synopsis of the most important bounty land and pension laws. Wash., D.C., C. Alexander, printer, 1851. 8pp. wrps. $ 35.00
*Scarce. The author practiced in D.C. and surrounding Maryland and Virginia counties.

201. PHILLIMORE, ROBERT. Commentaries upon international law. Phila., Johnson, 1854-57. Three volumes bound in two. (Cont'd.)

201. PHILLIMORE, ROBERT. (Cont'd.) Cloth. $ 32.50
*One of the most important treatises of the period. A final volume was issued in 1861. This first American edition appeared simultaneously with the British. According to the preface, volume three was originally intended to "complete the system of international law." Phillimore pays special recognition to the works of Story and Wheaton in shaping his own work.

202. PHILLIPPS, W(ILLIAM). The principles of the law reduced to practice. London, Twyford, Dring and Place, 1661. (36),167pp. Contemp. calf, rubbed, recased. 12mo. $ 140.00
*An early attempt to present a methodical digest of cases in the form of rules and maxims. Wing P2059; S&M, I, 28; Marvin p. 567. Second edition.

203. PHILLIPS, RICHARD. On the powers and duties of Juries, and on the criminal laws of England. London, Sherwood, 1811. 379pp. Contemp. calf, covered with cloth. $ 30.00
*Marvin 571. First edition.

204. PIKE, LUKE OWEN. A history of crime in England, illustrating the changes of the laws in the progress of civilisation. In two vols. Vol. I, from the Roman invasion to the accession of Henry VII. Vol. 2, from the accession of Henry VII to the present time. London, Smith, 1876. Illus. frontis. 1258pp. First edition, full embossed cloth, fine. $ 30.00

205. PIRTLE, HENRY. A digest of the decisions of the Court of Appeals of Kentucky. In two volumes. Louisville, Penn., 1832. 2 vols. 8vo. New cloth. First edition. $ 75.00

SAME. Volume II, only. (Jail to Writ). Contemp. calf, very good copy. $ 25.00

206. POMEROY, JOHN NORTON. An introduction to the Constitutional Law of the United States. Especially designed for students, general and professional. N.Y., Hurd, 1868. 549pp. FIRST EDITION. $ 45.00
*"His popular treatises really marked a break with the teaching of Blackstone, Bentham and Austin and exercised very considerable influence on American law." DAB.

207. PORTER, WILLIAM A. An essay on the life, character and writings of John B. Gibson. Phila., Johnson, 1855. 140pp. Neatly removed. $ 25.00
*Gibson was Chief Justice of Pennsylvania 1827-1851 and had a profound effect on the development of its law, especially on constitutional issues. See DAB.

208. POTHIER, ROBERT JOSEPH. A treatise on maritime contracts of letting to hire, translated from the French, with notes and a life of the author, by Caleb (Cont'd.)

208. POTHIER, ROBERT JOSEPH. (Cont'd.) Cushing. Boston, Cummings, 1821. 170pp. Original boards, printed paper label on spine, uncut. LC release stamp, otherwise a very nice copy. $ 65.00
*First American edition, and one of Cushing's earliest publications. The latter reviews the great American admiration for this work and its author; he dedicates this first translation to Joseph Story, and his original notes contain a wealth of bibliographic reference and some mention of American decisions. Uncommon.

209. POTHIER, (ROBERT JOSEPH). A treatise on obligations, considered in a moral and legal view. Translated from the French of Pothier. In two volumes. Newbern, N.C., Martin & Ogden, 1802. 364; 315pp. 8vo. 2 vols. bound in one, modern blue 1/4 mor., a very good copy. $ 125.00
*Shaw Shoemaker 2917, Marvin p. 578. First American edition and first translation into English, by Francois Xavier Martin, later to become the first Attorney General and first Chief Justice for the state of Louisiana. DAB.

210. POTTER, HENRY. The office and duty of a Justice of the Peace, and a guide to Sheriffs, Coroners, Clerks, Constables, and other Civil Officers, according to the Laws of North Carolina. With an appendix, containing theDeclaration of Rights and Constitution of this State, the Constitution of the United States, with the amendments thereto: and a collection of the most approved forms. Raleigh, Gales, 1816. 418pp. First edition. $ 65.00

211. POWELL, JOHN JOSEPH. Essay upon the law of contracts and agreements. In two vols. Walpole, N.H., Thomas, 1802. Full contemp. sheep, lea. label. 2 vols. in 1. A good copy. First American edition. $ 47.50
*Shaw Shoemaker 2923. Marvin p. 382.

212. POWELL, JOHN JOSEPH. An essay upon the learning of devises from their inception by writing, to their consummation by the death of the devisor. First American edition. Hartford, Riley, 1806. xii, (364),(28)pp. 8vo. Contemp. calf, with the gilt stamp of the Charleston Library Society. $ 47.50
*Marvin p. 582. S&M, I, 493.

213. POWELL, JOHN JOSEPH. A treatise on the law of mortgages. First American, from the fourth London Edition, revised, corrected and greatly enlarged, together with an appendix of precedents. Hartford, Sidney's Press, 1807. Approx. 600pp. Contemp. full sheep. $ 35.00
*Marvin 581.

214. PRATT, A.S. Pratts' Digest, comprising the laws relating to national banks, with annotations, references to decisions of the courts, and tables of cases cited, also information in regard to the organization and conduct of national banks ... edition of 1896. Wash., D.C., Pratt, (1896). xvii, 319pp. cl. 8vo. [illegible]

214. PRATT, A.S. (Cont'd.)
*Pratt & Sons was a National Bank Agent; this edition incorporates changes arising from the new banking acts.

215. QUEBEC. LAWS, STATUTES. Collection de plusiers des actes et ordonnances les plus utiles en force dans le Bas Canada concernant la loi criminelle et les devoirs des magistrats. Publiee par Autoritee. Quebec, Derbishire & Desbarats, 1854. New cl. $ 65.00
*These laws were selected for use by justices of the peace especially in rural areas.

216. (QUEBEC. PROVINCE. LAWS, STATUTES). Code civil du Bas Canada ... Civil Code of Lower Canada from the ammended roll deposited in the office of the Clerk of the Legislative Council 1865. Ottawa, Malcolm Cameron, 1866. 747pp. 1/4 sheep. indexed. 8vo. Bilingual. $ 50.00
*TPL 4472. First edition of this code.

217. (QUEEN V. CHADWICK). FOSTER, T. CAMPBELL. A review of the law relating to marriages within the prohibited degrees of affinity; and of the canons and social considerations by which the law is supposed to be justified. London, Benning, 1847. Disbound. $ 35.00
*The author had been counsel to prosecution in Queen v. Chadwick, but came to see the need for reform of the law against marriage to a sister of a deceased wife. S&M, III, 82.

218. (QUEEN V. CHADWICK). Report of the Commissioners appointed "to enquire into the state and operation of the law of marriage, as related to the pronibited degrees of affinity, and to marriages solemnized abroad or in the British colonies," together with brief extracts from the evidence given before the Commission. London, Benning, 1849. 71pp. Dsbd. $ 35.00
*Recommends change in the law and refers to American practice.

219. RALEIGH, WALTER. The perogative [sic] of Parliaments in England. Proved in a dialogue betweene a counsellor of state, and a justice of peace. Written by ... Dedicated to the Kings Majesty, and to the House of Parliament now assembled. Preserved to be now happily (in these distracted times) published, and printed 1640. 4to. 4pl., 65(1)pp. Later 1/4 mor., rubbed. $ 160.00
*A classic defense of Parliamentary institutions in response to the proceedings of the Star Chamber. New STC 20650. S&M, I, 137. Third edition.

220. REEVES, JOHN. History of the English law from the time of the Saxons, to the end of the reign of Philip and Mary. The second edition. In four volumes. London, Brooke, 1787. 4 vols. 8vo. Contemp. calf, leather labels. A very nice set. $ 100.00
*S&M, I, 21. "A remarkable book, before its time."

221. (REFORMATORY CONVENTION OF 1859). Proceedings of the second convention of managers and superintendents of houses of refuge, schools of reform, and institutions for the prevention and correction of juvenile destitution, delinquency and crime, in the United States ... N.Y., 1860. 175pp. 8vo. Orig. prtd. wrps, fine. $ 30.00
*Contains also 8 papers delivered at the Convention. Affords a good view of the thought of the time.

222. RICHECOURT, A. De. Essai sur l'histoire et la legislation des formes requises pour la validite du mariage. Paris, Douniol, 1856. 135(5)pp. Orig. wrps. $ 27.50
*No copy found in the NUC.

223. (ROBERTSON, JAMES). An account of the trial of Thomas Muir, ... before the High Court of Justiciary at Edinburgh ... for sedition. N.Y., Samuel Campbell, 1794. 4,vii, 148,viipp. with frontis portrait. (name excised from frontis without affecting image.) New wrappers. $ 50.00
*Classic account of the notorious sedition trial in which Muir and others were sentenced to transportation; Muir became the chief symbol of the "Scottish martyrs." In fact Muir's case excited sympathy in the United States and he was rescued from Sydney by an American ship sent out from New York. This edition combines the main pagination of the first with the prefatory and appendix material of the second American edition (Evans 27633-34). Ferguson 158f., not recording the American editions.

224. (ROBERTSON, JAMES). An account of the trial of Thomas Muir, ... before the High Court of Justiciary at Edinburgh ... for sedition. N.Y., Campbell, 1794. vii, 110pp. Orig. wrappers, sewn as issued. $ 35.00
*"Third American Edition," variant of Evans 27635, with prefatory material not noted by Evans for this edition.

225. (ROBINSON, ROBERT). The law of inheritances in fee, laid down in a new method, with a KALENDAR of the persons inheritable, curiously engraved: to which is added, a supplement, containing a review of the said discourse. By a barrister of Lincoln's-Inn. The second edition. London, Ward and Chandler. (1724). xiv, 104pp., fldg. plate. sm. 8vo. new cloth. *S&M, I, 476. $ 55.00

226. (RUPP, DANIEL?) The new American Clerk's Magazine, and complete conveyancer ... adapted to the use of the citizens of the United States, and more particularly to those of the State of Maryland; with necessary instructions and forms of precedents for the use of justices of the peace, sheriffs (ec. ...) by a Gentleman of the Bar. Hagers-Town, (Md.) Dietrick, John F. Thomson, printer, Frederick-Town, 1806. 526pp. With 28pp. index and a 40pp. list of subscribers from Maryland, D.C., Virginia, Pennsylvania, N.J., Tennessee and Kentucky. Large thick 12mo. (Cont'd.)

226. (RUPP, DANIEL?) (Con'd.) Contemp. tree calf, lea. label, in very nice condition and most attractive. $ 135.00
*FIRST EDITION, Not in Sabin or Marvin. Listed in the NUC under title. Shaw-Shoemaker 10952.

227. RYAN, EDWARD G. An address delivered before the law class of the University of Wisconsin, June 16, 1873, by Hon. Edward G. Ryan. Madison, Published under the auspices of the Law Class, 1873. 26pp. $ 22.50
*"His address is a legal and literary classic and is probably more often referred to and quoted than any other production." DAB. As justice of the Supreme Court of Wisconsin he made notable decisions on state regulation of corporations. (Neatly disbound, a good copy.)

228. (SAINT GERMAIN, CHRISTOPHER). Doctor and student: or dialogues between a doctor of divinity and a student in the laws of England, containing the grounds of those laws ...; also comparing the civil, canon, common and statute laws ... To which is now added an account of the author, and a general table of the principle matters; never before printed. (London), Nutt and Gossing, 1721. 6pl., 366,(20)pp. 12mo. Contemp. blind calf, leather label, near fine and very attractive copy. $ 125.00
*An enduring classic, "of considerable importance in the history of equity." Holdsworth, Sources and literature, 185088. This is a nice association copy, with the signature of Richard Saltonstall, (Sibley, VII, 117ff.) Harvard class of 1722, Chief Justice of the Massachusetts Superior Court and member of the legislature.

229. (SAINT-ROMAN, ALEXIS-JACQUES de serre, comte de). Refutation de la doctrine de Montesquieu, sur la balance des pouvoirs, et apercus divers sur plusiers questions de droit public; faisant suite a la Proposition de M. le Cte. de Saint-Roman, dans la seance de la Chambre de Paris, ... Paris, Chez Mme. Ve. Perronneau, Imprimeur-Libraire, 1816. 229(1)pp. 1/4 calf, spine rubbed. $ 60.00
*No copy in the BM cat. NUC cites 4 holdings.

230. SAMPSON, WILLIAM. An anniversary discourse delivered before the Historical Society of New-York, on Saturday, December 6, 1823, showing the origin, progress, antiquities- curiosities, and nature of the Common Law. N.Y., Bliss, 1824. 68pp. Neatly disbound. Foxed. $ 22.50

231. SANFORD, H.S. The different systems of penal codes in Europe: also a report on the administrative changes in France, since the Revolution of 1848. Wash., Beverly Tucker, Senate Printer, 1854. 404pp. Orig. cl. $ 30.00
*Also issued as U.S. 33C 1st session. S. Ex. Doc68.

232. SAYER, JOSEPH. The law of damages. Dublin, Moore, 1792. 248pp. 12mo. calf, repaired. $ 30.00
*1st ed. was L. 1770. S&M, I, 241.

233. SCHIEFER, JOHN FREDERIC. An explanation of the practice of law: containing the elements of special pleading, ... also elements of a plan for a reform: showing that the plaintiffs costs ... need not exceed 10 pounds, and those of the defendant ... 6 pounds. Dublin, Stockdale, 1793. xxxi, 340pp. Calf, joints cracked but firm. Good copy. $ 45.00
*S&M, I, 278. Marvin p. 632. This and the London edition of the preceeding year are the only ones of this work.

234. SCHLEGEL, J.F.W. Neutral rights; or an impartial examination of the right of search of neutral vessels under convoy, and of a judgment pronounced by the English Court of Admiralty, the 11th June, 1799, in the case of the Swedish convoy; with some additions and corrections. Translated from the French. Philadelphia, Aurora Office, 1801. 162pp. 8vo. Neatly removed. $ 35.00
*Schlegel was professor of law at the University of Copenhagen. In this work he brings his knowledge of international law to bear against England's interference with the neutral commerce of his own country. In America it became a forceful argument for the anti-British forces. Sabin 77646. Shaw-Shoemaker 1299.

235. SCOTT, ROBERT N. An analytical digest of the military laws of the United States: a compilation of the constitutional and statutory provisions concerning the military establishment, in all its branches and relations, accompanied by judicial and executive decisions explanatory of the text. Phila., Lippincott, 1873. 510pp. $ 30.00
*pp. 337-350 cover Indian affairs.

236. SEEBOHM, FREDERIC. The English Village Community. Examined in its relations to the manorial and tribal systems, and to the common or open field system of husbandry: an essay in economic history. London, Longmans, 1890. 464pp. Illus., frontis map, also 13 maps and plates. Fourth ed. cl. $ 15.00

237. SERGEANT, THOMAS. View of the land laws of Pennsylvania, with notices of its early history and legislation. Phila., Kay, 1838. 303pp. 8vo. New cloth; marginal dampstains, nonetheless a very good copy. $ 75.00
*Rare. An important book by one of the most distinguished persons in Pennsylvania law in this period. Marvin p. 638. See DAB for account of the author.

238. THOMAS SEYMOUR and THOMAS SEYMOUR, JR. Manuscript account book for their legal practice, 1762-1775. Narrow folio, approx. 280 pages, contemp. calf, excellent condition. $ 375.00
*A fine record of a significant 18th century law practice in the Hartford, Connect-

238. THOMAS SEYMOUR and THOMAS SEYMOUR, JR. (Cont'd.). icut area. Seymour (1705-1767) was born at Hartford, attended Yale 1724, "became a lawyer of reputation in Hartford and represented the town in five sessions of the General Assembly ... In 1764 he received the appointment of agent and Atty. General for the Governor and Company of the Colony to appear in their behalf ..." Yale Biographies, 1st Series, 307f. Thomas Seymour Jr. 1734/35-1829, Yale 1755, "studied law and early gained a prominent position at the Hartford County Bar ... in 1767 he succeeded his father as King's Attorney" ... served in the Revolution, was the first mayor of Hartford and represented it in the General Assembly. Yale Biographies, 2nd series, p. 370f. The ledger contains accounts for about 200 clients including Silas Deane who was practising law at Wethersfield. The accounts were tidied-up by T.S., Jr., who upon succeeding his father also began a series of separate accounts, some continuing to 1774 at the back of the ledger.

239. SHAW, LEMUEL. A charge delivered to the grand jury for the County of Essex, at the Supreme Judicial Court held at Ipswich, May term, 1831. Published at their request. Boston, Steam Power Press, 1832. 16pp. Neatly removed, a good copy. $ 30.00
*Bruntjen, American Imprints, 14682. Scarce, citing 5 holdings. Reviews the nature and duties of the grand jury system.

240. SHOWER, BARTHOLOMEW. Reports of cases adjudged in the Court of King's Bench, during the reigns of Charles the Second; James the Second; and William the Third. In two volumes. The second edition, corrected, with notes and marginal references by Thomas Leach ... London, Clarke, 1794. 540; 410pp. plus indices. 8vo. Contemp. calf. Nice copy. $ 45.00
*S&M, I, 309.

241. SIDNEY, ALGERNON. Discourse concerning government, published from an original manuscript of the author. London, printed and are to be sold by the booksellers of London and Westminster. 1698. Folio. 1pl.,462,(5)pp. Contemp. panelled calf. Joints cracked but firm; spine in compartments, with ornaments and leather labels; internally a fresh, bright copy. FIRST EDITION. $ 300.00
*Wing S-3761. Written in answer to Robert Filmer's Patriarcha, 1680, probably at that time, and first published posthumously, the Discourse ranks with the works of Bodin, Milton and Locke in the forefront of modern libertarian political philosophy and is the great foundation of the Republican idea.

242. SOUTH CAROLINA. COURT OF APPEALS. Reports of equity cases determined in the Court of Appeals of the State of South Carolina. By the State Reporter. Columbia, S.C., Black and Sweeney, 1825. 301 pp. plus index. 8vo. Contemp. calf, minor staining. A very good copy. $ 45.00
*Marvin p. 370. Covers Mar.-Dec. 1824.

243. SOUTH CAROLINA. CONSTITUTIONAL COURT. Reports of judicial decisions in the Constitutional Court of South Carolina, held in Charleston and Columbia in 1817, 1818. A new edition. Two volumes in one. Charleston, Riley, 1837. 8vo. 486pp. incl. index. Contemp. sheep, very good copy. $ 45.00
*Marvin p. 513. Judges included J.F. Grimke, Abraham Nott and Langdon Cheeves.

244. (SPAIN). The political Constitution of the Spanish Monarchy promulgated at an assembly of the general and extraordinary Cortes, held at Cadix, March 19, 1812. Translated ... by Daniel Robinson ... London, Stockdale, 1813. 93pp. uncut, stitched as issued. Fine. $ 30.00
*One of two editions in English, the first and only contemporary ones to appear, for this important constitution. Not in Sabin, though of American interest.

245. SPOTISWOODE, ROBERT. Practicks of the laws of Scotland, observed and collected by Sir Robert Spotiswoode of Pentland, President of the College of Justice ... as also Abstracts taken out of the ancient record of this kingdom, whereby is declared the manner and questions in law made by the same author, with memoirs of his life and trial ... published by John Spotiswoode ..., advocate, the author's grand-son. Edinburgh, James Watson, 1706. Folio. 2pl, xli,(3),372pp. Title within rules. Contemp. Calf, rubbed, a very good copy. FIRST EDITION. $ 150.00
*S&M, V, 108. See DNB for an account of Spotiswoode.

246. STEPHEN, JAMES FITZJAMES. A history of the criminal law of England. In three volumes. London, Macmillan, 1883. Original publisher's brick-red cloth, spines lettered in gilt. FIRST EDITION, an exceptionally fine set. $ 60.00

A COMMENTARY ON THE COMMENTARIES

247. STORY, JOSEPH. Commentaire sur la constitution federale des etats-unis ...traduit du Commentaire abrege de J. Story ... et augmente des observations de Jefferson, Rawle, Tocqueville,...et de notes sur la jurisprudence et l'organisation judiciaire, par Paul Odent ... Paris, Joubert, 1843. 2 vols. 8vo. Cont. 1/4 calf, gilt. Fine. $ 150.00
*First French edition with a great wealth of material taken from Tocqueville, Chevalier and others. The editor proposes to present to Europeans the American system as seen by an American, around which the observations of foreign writers can then be organized. His own notes are very extensive, and he acknowledges the special assistance of Paul Quemper, "avocat a la Nouvelle Orleans" The first edition is rare: the NUC cites only the University of Michigan copy. No copy of any edition in the BM Catalogue.

248. STORY, JOSEPH. A discourse pronounced upon the inauguration of the author, as Dane Professor of Law, in Harvard University, on 25th of Aug., 1829. Boston Hilliard, 1829. 60pp. Neatly removed. (Cont'd.)

248. STORY, JOSEPH. (Cont'd.) $ 27.50
*On common law and role of the lawyer.

249. STORY, JOSEPH. A discourse upon the life, character and services of the Hon. John Marshall, Chief Justice of the United States of America, pronounced on the 15th of October at the request of the Suffolk Bar. Boston, Munroe, 1835. 74pp. Neatly removed. $ 27.50

250. STORY, JOSEPH. A familiar exposition of the Constitution of the United States: containing a brief commentary ... with an appendix ... N.Y., (1840). 372 pp. Original publisher's cloth. $ 40.00
*First edition (paralleled by a Boston printing) of a classic which continued to be published for the next 50 years.

251. STORY, JOSEPH. The miscellaneous writings of Joseph Story, ... edited by ... William W. Story. Boston, Little, Brown, 1852. 8vo. x,828pp. New cl. $ 27.50
*First of this edition which contains additional papers not included in the 1835 edition published by Story himself.

252. STORY, WILLIAM W. A treatise on the law of sales of personal property, with illustrations from the foreign law. Boston, Little, Brown, 1847. 488pp. Full contemp. sheep. Very fine copy. $ 50.00
*First edition. According to its preface, the first American work on the subject outside of the outline in Kent's Commentaries. He considers the law in England and America with reference also to French and Scotts law.

253. SUTTON, ROBERT. A complete guide to landlords, tenants, and lodgers; being a methodical arrangement of the whole law ... with clear and practical directions for making a distress for rent, &c. with all new and adjudged cases & acts of Parliament down to 1801. The third edition. London, Stratford, 1801. 104pp. Disbound. S&M, III, 223. $ 25.00

254. SWIFT, ZEPHANIAH. A digest of the law of evidence, in civil and criminal cases, and a treatise on bills of exchange, and promissory notes. Hartford, Cooke, 1810. 361pp. Full contemp. calf. Front joint neatly mended. FIRST EDITION. *Marvin p. 671. $ 50.00

"THE FIRST AMERICAN LAW TEXT"

255. SWIFT, ZEPHANIAH. A system of the laws of the State of Connecticut. In six books. Windham, John Byrne, for the author, 1795-96. In two volumes. 8vo. 452;479(12)pp. incl. list of subscribers. Folding table of descents in vol. I. New 1/4 morocco, raised bands, a very nice copy. FIRST EDITION. $ 150.00
*"The first American law text; it displayed a thoughtful philosophy of government as well as a thorough presentation of the constitutional and working govern-
(Cont'd.)

255. SWIFT, ZEPHANIAH. (Cont'd.) ment of the State." DAB. It also defined the role of the common law in American society in a pragmatic and flexible way, reconciling tradition with the necessary innovation of a new nation in a new time. See Horwitz, Transformation of American Law, 1780-1860, p. 25-26. Evans 29600 & 31260. Marvin p. 651.

256. TAYLOR, ALFRED S. Medical jurisprudence. Second American, from the third London edition, with notes and additions by R. Eglesfeld Griffith, M.D. Phila., Lea, 1850. 670pp. Full contemp. sheep. rubbed, but sound. $ 35.00

257. TAYLOR, HANNIS. The origin and growth of the English Constitution: an historical treatise, in which is drawn out, by the light of the most recent researches, the gradual development of the English Constitutional System, and the growth out of that system of the Federal Republic of the United States. Fourth edition, in two parts. Part I, The Making of the Constitution. Part II, The After-Growth of the Constitution. Boston, Houghton, Mifflin, 1898. 616pp,645pp. 2vols., orig. cl. o.p. $ 37.50

258. TAYLOR, JOHN. An inquiry into the principles and policy of the government of the United States. ... By John Taylor, of Caroline County, Virginia. Fredericksburg, Green and Cady, 1814. 8vo. vii,656, (1)pp. Contemp. tree calf, lea. label, hinges cracked but firm, light wear to extremities of binding; a very good copy. FIRST EDITION. $ 250.00
*"First conceived in 1794 as an answer to John Adams' Defense of the Constitution ... 'it deserves to rank among the two or three really historic contributions to political science which have been produced in the United States.' (Beard) ... one of America's greatest disciples and philosophers of agrarian liberalism ... local democracy ... and states' rights." Dictionary of American Biography.

259. TAYLOR, JOHN N. A treatise on the law of landlord and tenant, in a series of letters addressed to a citizen of New-York. N.Y., Wells, 1840. 164pp. Original embossed cloth. A very good copy. FIRST EDITION. $ 40.00
*Marvin p. 686. Written at the time of the rent wars, its chief aim is to supply a neutral account of existing law; however in the preface the author defends the right of the landlord to a lien on the goods of the tenant, and opposes current plans for substitutes in distress.

260. (TENNESSEE. LAWS, STATUTES). CARUTHERS, R.L., et al. A compilation of the Statutes of Tennessee, general and permanent nature, from the commencement of the Government to the present time. With reference to judicial decisions, in notes, to which is appended a new collection of forms. Nashville, James Smith, 1836. 808,108pp. Lib. buckram. Inst. stamp on title. $ 35.00
*Marvin p. 177. Commended for its organization.

261. THOMAS, BENJAMIN F. Goodwin's Town Officer. Fourth ed., adapted to the revised statutes. Worcester, Dorr, 1837. 365pp. Full contemp sheep. Scarce ed. $ 22.50

262. TUCKER, GEORGE. The life of Thomas Jefferson, ... with parts of his correspondence never before published, and notices of his opinions on questions of civil government, national policy and constitutional law. In two volumes. Phila., Carey, Lea & Blanchard, 1837. Two volumes, 8vo. Frontis portrait. Orig. publisher's cloth. printed paper labels, spines a bit faded, but an excellent set. FIRST EDITION. $ 75.00

263. TUCKER, JOHN RANDOLPH. The history of the Federal Convention of 1787 and of its work. An address delivered before the graduating class at the sixty-third anniversary of the Yale Law School, on June 28th, 1887, by Hon. John Randolph Tucker. New Haven, Yale, 1887. 54pp. Orig. rptd. wrps. fine. $ 15.00

264. TYLER, SAMUEL. Memoir of Roger Brooke Taney, Chief Justice of the Supreme Court of the United States. Second revised and enlarged edition. Baltimore, Murphy, 1876. 672pp. Illus. frontis. Orig. sandstone cl., gilt. $ 30.00
*This revised edition not reprinted.

265. ULMAN, CHARLES H. Lawyers' record and official register of the United States: containing federal officers ... state, county, and city officials; judiciary, with jurisdiction and time of holding courts; ... and a record of practising lawyers throughout the U.S. Together with a convenient and comprehensive digest of the laws of several states ... N.Y., Barnes, 1872. 1143pp. Full contemp. sheep. Very good copy. $ 45.00
*First of this series, it includes all western states and territories.

266. UPHAM, THOMAS C. The manual of peace, embracing I, Evils and remedies of war, II, Suggestions on the law of nations, III, Considerations of a Congress of Nations. N.Y., Leavitt, Lord; Brunswick, Griffin, 1836. 408pp. 8vo. Orig. publisher's emb. cloth, lea. label, near fine. First edition. $ 50.00
*"One of the earliest American advocates of international peace." DAB.

267. U.S. COMMISSION OF CLAIMS. Report of the decisions of the Commission of Claims under the Convention of February 8, 1853, between the United States and Great Britain, transmitted to the Senate by the President ... August 11, 1856. Wash, Nicholson, 1856. vii, 478pp. Orig. embossed cl., spine lettered in gilt, Fine. Single page map, index of cases and claims. $ 45.00
*This copy belonged to the Chief U.S. Commissioner, Nathaniel G. Upham, with his signature. All outstanding issues were negotiated including Florida, Texas bonds, and especially Canadian affairs. Nice association copy.

268. U.S. COMMISSIONER OF PENSIONS. A Treatise on the practice of the Pension Bureau, governing the adjudication of Army and Navy Pensions. Wash., GPO, 1898. 140pp. $ 15.00

269. (UNITED STATES. LAWS. FIRST CONGRESS 1789-1791). Acts passed at a Congress of the United States of America, begun and held at the city of New York ... 1789 ... Being the acts passed at the first (-Third) sessions of the First Congress ... Hartford reprinted and sold by Hudson and Goodwin, 1791. 5pl.,(3)-327pp. 8vo. Cont. calf. rubbed; marginal staining, missing front free end paper. $ 75.00
*Evans 46319; Bristol B 7862. Evans lists this also as #23843 with erroneous pagination. This is one of the first printed compilations of the laws of the first Congress in all its sessions; New York and Philadelphia editions appeared also in 1791, presumably preceeding this issue. Those editions bore the title: "Laws of the U.S. Vol. I."

270. U.S. PUBLIC LAND COMMISSION. Laws of the United States of a local or temporary character and exhibiting the entire legislation of Congress upon which the public land titles in each state and territory have depended. Dec. 1, 1880 ... also a digest of all Indian treaties ... and a table of judicial and executive decisions. Wash., GPO, 1884. 1371pp., in 2 vols. cl. fine. $ 37.50

271. U.S. SUPREME COURT. Decisions of the U.S. Supreme Court in relation to treaties, contracts, courts of claims, etc. Exhibit to report of Cherokee Delegation. 1898. $ 10.00

272. UPHAM, N.G. Opinion in the case of the Barque Jones. London, Whittingham, 1854. 40pp. Printed. wrps. $ 17.50
*American ship siezed by British along African Coast in 1840 in attempt to suppress the slave trade. Upham was U.S. Commissioner in claims settlement convention.

273. UPHAM, N.G. Opinion in the case of the Enterprise, pending before the Mixed Commission ... London, Taylor, 1854. 24pp. $ 15.00
*British interference with American carrying trade involving freeing of 73 slaves in Bermuda. Upham was U.S. Commissioner in the 1853 settlement convention between Britain and the U.S.

274. UPHAM, N.G. Opinion in the case of the Schooner Washington, pending before the mixed commission ... London, Taylor, 1854. 16pp. map of Gulf of St. Lawrence. $ 17.50
*Vessel siezed by British while fishing in Bay of Fundy; question of meaning of Treaty of 1818 relative to fishing on coasts of North America. Upham was U.S. Commissioner in claims settlement convention.

275. UPSHUR, ABEL P. Address to the Literary Societies of William and Mary College, Va. delivered by Judge Upshur, July 2d, 1841. at the request of the
(Cont'd.)

275. UPSHUR, ABEL P. (Cont'd.) Lyciveronian Society of that college. Phila., Waldie, printer, 1841. 29pp. $ 35.00
*One of the most important southern conservative ideologists. Along with Calhoun he opposed "democracy" or rule by numerical majority and "rejected almost in toto the natural rights philosophy" DAB - referring to the work offered here.

276. VAN SANTVOORD, GEORGE. Sketches of the lives and judicial services of the Chief-Justices of the Supreme Court of the United States. N.Y., Scribner, 1854. 533pp. Illus., Frontis. Orig. embossed publ. cl. First edition. Nice copy. o.p. $ 27.50
*According to the preface, the first substantial memoirs of the first five chief justices, concentrating on judicial and professional aspects in a connected scheme.

277. VATTEL, (EMMERICH de.). The law of nations: or principles of the law of nature applied to the conduct and affairs of nations and sovereigns ... First American Edition, corrected and revised from the latest London edition. Translated from the French. N.Y., Samuel Campbell, 1796. 563pp. 8vo. Contemp. calf, rebacked. $ 50.00
*Evans 31483. Actually the second American edition.

278. VERPLANCK, GULIAN. A letter to Col. William Drayton, of South Carolina, in assertion of the Constitutional power of Congress to impose protecting duties. N.Y., printed for E. Bliss, 1831. 31pp. $ 17.50
*Kress C2990. Argued from British and Colonial precedent.

279. VIRGINIA. COMMONWEALTH. GENERAL COURT. A collection of cases decided by the General Court ... chiefly relating to the penal laws ... commencing in the year 1789, and ending in 1814. Copied from the records of said court, with explanatory notes, by Judges Brockenbrough and Holmes. Philadelphia, Webster, 1815. viii, 326pp. with an 8 page catalogue of law books for sale by the publisher. Contemp. sheep, lea. label, front joint tender. A very good copy. 8vo. FIRST EDITION. $ 75.00
*Marvin p. 150 under William Brockenbrough. Shaw Shoemaker 36447. A second volume continuing coverage from 1815-1826 was later issued.

280. (VIRGINIA. LAWS, STATUTES.) THE CODE OF VIRGINIA. Including legislation to the year 1860. 2nd ed. Richmond, Ritchie, 1860. 1022pp. Full contemp. calf. $ 30.00

281. The Virginia scrivener, being a collection of forms of bond, contracts, conveyancing, and other instruments ... adapted to the use of the people of Virginia. Prepared by a Gentleman of the Bar of Staunton. To which are prefixed ... the new Constitution of Virginia. Staunton, Va.,
(Cont'd.)

281. The Virginia scrivener (Cont'd.) Kenton Harper, 1833. 8vo. 181pp. Contemp. calf, moderate foxing but a very good copy. First edition. $ 100.00
*Swem 6142 and 10689; Sabin 100565. Not in Marvin. An attractive and scarce little book. We have seen but one other copy in six years.

282. VON HOLST, H. The Constitutional Law of the United States of America. Authorized edition translated by Alfred Bishop Mason. Chicago, Callaghan, 1887. 369pp. o.p. $ 27.50

283. WASHBURN, ISRAEL. The North-Eastern Boundary. Read before the Maine Historical Society, at Portland, May 15, 1879. 106pp. Orig. wrps., bound in. Presentation copy signed by the author. $ 17.50

284. WATERMAN, THOMAS G. The justice's manual; or, a summary of the powers and duties of justices of the peace in the State of New York, comprising a variety of practical forms adapted to cases civil and criminal. Binghamton, N.Y., Morgan & Canoll, 1825. 222pp. 8vo. Contemp. calf, minor staining. $ 32.50
*Marvin p. 720. 1st ed.

285. WATERMAN, THOMAS G. The Justice's Manual: or a summary of the powers and duties of Justices of the Peace, in the State of New York; containing a variety of practical forms, adapted to cases civil and criminal. Second edition. Albany, Printed by Webster & Skinners, 1829. 294pp Full contemp. sheep. $ 30.00

286. WATSON, WARREN, preparer. A manual for Commissioners of the Circuit Courts of the United States. Second ed. Chicago, Callaghan, (1881). 152pp. $ 15.00

287. WHITING, SAMUEL. The Connecticut town officer; in three parts. ...Danbury, Skinner, 1814. 287(1)pp. 12mo. calf. First edition. $ 27.50
*Shaw Shoemaker 33668.

288. WILSON, WOODROW. Congressional Government: a study in American politics. Second ed. Boston, Houghton, Mifflin, 1885. 333pp. Orig. cl. fine. $ 15.00
*Exact reprint of 1st ed. of same year. A very important work reflecting the ascendancy of Congress over the President from the Civil War to the New Deal.

289. WOOLRYCH, HUMPHREY W. The life of Judge Jeffreys, Chief Justice of the King's Bench under Charles II., and Lord High Chancellor of England during the Reing of James II. Phila., Lindsay, 1852. 316pp. Orig. emb. cl., very fine. $ 25.00

290. WRIGHT, DAVID. Executor's, administrator's and guardian's guide: containing a summary of the laws of New York ... forms ... and also, a copy of "An Act respecting the fees of surrogates," ... Auburn, N.Y., Derby, 1845. 304pp. calf. $ 22.50

EARLY AMERICAN LEGAL EDUCATION

291. (WRIGHT, WILLIAM). Advice on the study of the law, with directions for the choice of books, addressed to attornies' clerks, with additional notes for the American student. Baltimore, Edward J. Coale, 1811. 167pp. 8vo. Contemp. boards, leather spine and label, minor wear but very good. $ 75.00
*A very uncommon example of early legal educational guides in America; although of British origin, this appears to be the true first edition, with the American insertions either by an unnamed editor or quite possibly by the author himself; it is the only American edition. Two later London editions appeared; however none appears to have been published earlier than or contemporary with this (Sweet and Maxwell and the Br. Museum Cat.) RARE. Shaw-Shoemaker locates only the Harvard Law school copy.

* * * * * * * * * PART II: WORKS PUBLISH.

294. ADAMS, HENRY, et al. Essays in Anglo-Saxon law. Boston, Little, Brown, 1905. 392pp. cl. Fine copy. $ 20.00

295. ALEXANDER, G.G., et al. Cambridge legal essays, written in honour of and presented to Doctor Bond, Professor Buckland and Professor Kenny. Cambridge, Heffer, 1926. 331pp. Illus., frontis. cl. o.p. $ 22.50

296. ARIAS, HARMODIO. The Panama Canal: a study in International Law and Diplomacy. London: P.S. King, 1911. 192pp. $ 10.00
*Studies in Economics and Political Science, #25, London School of Ecs.

297. ASSOCIATION OF AMERICAN LAW SCHOOLS. Anatomy of legal education: an inquiry into the adequacy and mobilization of certain resources in American Law Schools, by Special Committee on Law School Administration and University Relations ... St. Paul, West Publishing, 1961. 515pp. $ 15.00

298. ASSOCIATION OF THE BAR OF THE CITY OF NEW YORK. Mental illness, due process and criminal defendant: a second report and additional recommendations by the Special Committee on the Study of Commitment Procedures and the Law Relating to Incompetents of the ... in cooperation with Fordham Univ. School of Law. N.Y., Fordham Univ. Press, 1968. 261pp. $ 12.50

299. AYRINHAC, H.A. Marriage legislation in the new code of canon law. Revised and enlarged by Rev. P.J. Lydon. New revised edition. N.Y., Benziger, 1935. 398pp. $ 15.00

300. BAILEY, S.J. Sir Percy Henry Winfield 1878-1953. London, Oxford Univ. Press. Offprint. Proceedings of the British Academy, Vol. 41. pp. 329-337. Plate. $ 3.50

292. WYCHE, WILLIAM. A treatise on the Practice of the Supreme Court of Judicature of the State of New-York in civil actions. 2nd ed. N.Y., Swords, 1794. xvi, 355pp. Contemp. calf. $ 75.00
*Wyche was a recent emigrant from England and brings an immediate sense of the contrast between English and American practice to this work. Marvin 751. Evans 28140.

293. YATES, JOHN V.N. A collection of pleadings and practical precedents, with notes thereon, and approved forms of bills of costs: containing, also references, &c. to Graham's Practice. 2nd. edition. Albany, Gould, 1837. 866pp. Contemp. sheep. 1st ed $ 35.00
*Marvin p. 752.

301. BALDWIN, ROGER N., et al. Civil liberties and industrial conflict. Cambridge, Harvard Univ. Press, 1938. 137pp. o.p. $ 12.50

302. BALDWIN SIMEON E. The American Judiciary. N.Y., Century, 1905. 403pp. *The American State Series. o.p. $ 15.00

303. BERMAN, WILLIAM H., et al. Federal and State responsibilities for radiation protection: the need for Federal Legislation. Ann Arbor, Michigan Law School, 1959. 120pp. Wrps. o.p. $ 12.50

304. BERRY, C.P. A treatise on the law relating to automobiles. Chicago, Callaghan, 1909. 305pp. A very early treatise on this topic. $ 15.00

305. BILLIAS, GEORGE ATHAN (ED.) Selected essays: law and authority in Colonial America. Barre, Barre Publishers, (1965). 208pp. o.p. $ 22.50
*10 original essays given at a conference sponsored by the American Antiquar.an Society.

306. BLAKEY, ROY G., et al. The Federal income tax. 1st ed. London, Longmans, 1940. 640pp. o.p. $ 22.50
*Major scholarly history.

307. BOCZEK, BOLESLAW ADAM. Flags of convenience: an International legal study. (Forword by Myres S. McDougal). Cambridge, Harvard Univ. Press, 1962. 323pp. o.p. $ 22.50

308. BURDICK, CHARLES K. The law of the American Constitution, its origin and development. With two introductory chapters by Francis M. Burdick. N.Y., Putnam's Sons, 1922. 687pp. o.p. $ 17.50

309. CARNEGIE ENDOWMENT FOR INTERNATIONAL PEACE. Carnegie Endowment Conference on the Newly Independent States and International Law. (Geneva, Oct. 9 to 13, 1963). Some reflections and a selected bibliography. (Geneva, 1964). 46pp. Wrps. $ 7.50

310. CARNEGIE ENDOWMENT FOR INTERNATIONAL PEACE. Carnegie Endowment Conference on the Process of Change in International Law. (Menton, Jan. 3 to 8, 1965). Report. 34pp. Wrps. $ 7.50

311. CHANDOS, JOHN, ed. To deprave and corrupt: original studies in the nature and definition of obscenity. (London, Souvenir Press, (1962). 207pp. o.p. $ 17.50

312. (CHINA). The code of criminal procedure of the Republic of China and the Court agreement relating to the Chinese Courts in the International Settlement of Shanghai, China. Translated by the Legal Department of the Shanghai Municipal Council. Shanghai, Commercial Press, 1936. 378pp. Text in English and Chinese. $ 25.00

313. CLEVENGER, WILLIAM M. The courts of New Jersey: their origin composition and jurisdiction. Also some account of their origin and jurisdiction by Edward Q. Keasbey. Plainfield, N.J., New Jersey Law Journal, 1903. 143pp. Full contemp. sheep, rubbed. $ 22.50

314. DAGGETT, HARRIET SPILLER. The Community Property System of Louisiana, with comparative studies, with foreword by Robert Lee Tullis. Baton Rouge, Louisiana State Univ. Press, 1931. 237pp. Wrps. o.p. $ 15.00
*Louisiana State Univ. Studies No. I.

315. DAWSON, JOHN P. Unjust enrichment, a comparative analysis: a series of lectures delivered under the auspices of the Julius Rosenthal Foundation at Northwestern University School of Law, in April 1950. Boston, Little, Brown, 1951. 201pp. o.p. $ 17.50

316. DE BECKER, J.E., (solicitor and legal translator). De Becker's Japanese law of trading partnerships and companies. First ed. Yokohama, Kelly, 1906. 133pp. cl. $ 30.00

317. DE QUIROS, C. BERNALDO. Modern theories of criminality. Translated from the Spanish by Alfonso De Salvio, with an introduction by Wm. W. Smithers. Boston, Little, Brown, 1912. 249pp. $ 12.50

318. DE VISSCHER, CHARLES. Theory and reality in public international law. Translated from the French by P.E. Cobbett. Princeton, Princeton Univ. Press, 1957. 381pp. $ 15.00

319. DOWDELL, E.G. A hundred years of quarter sessions: the government of Middlesex from 1660-1760, with an introduction by Sir William Holdsworth. Cambridge, Univ. Press, 1932. 75, 215pp. 1st ed. d.j. (Cont'd.)

319. DOWDELL, E.G. (Cont'd.) fine copy. o.p. $ 25.00
*. Cambridge Studies in English Legal History.

320. DRAHMS, AUGUST. The Criminal, his personnel and environment. A scientific study, with an introduction by Cesare Lombroso. N.Y., Macmillan, 1900. 402pp. $ 12.50
*1st ed. Author was chaplain at San Quentin and a follower of Lombroso.

321. DRAPER, FRANK WINTHROP. A textbook of legal medicine, fully illustrated. Phila., Saunders, 1905. 573pp. $ 22.50

322. DUNKEL, WILBUR. William Lambarde, Elizabethan Jurist, 1536-1601. New Brunswick, Rutgers Univ. Press, (1965). 210pp. Orig. cl. D.j. o.p. $ 15.00

323. EMERSON, R.L. Legal medicine and toxicology. N.Y., Appleton, 1909. 593pp. Illus. First edition. $ 25.00
*Covers each state individually.

324. FOLSOM, CHARLES FOLLEN. Studies of criminal responsibility and limited responsibility. Privately printed, 1909. 153pp. o.p. $ 22.50
*Six important case studies. Author was professor of mental diseases at Harvard.

325. FRANK, ELI. Title to real and leasehold estates and liens. Baltimore, Baltimore City Printing, 1912. 348pp. $ 22.50
*Study of Maryland law.

326. GATES, PAUL W. History of public land law development. Written for the Public Land Law Review Commission, with a chapter by Robert W. Swenson. Wash., D.C. (GPO), 1968. 828pp. Lg. 8vo., illus. cl. $ 25.00

327. GIERKE, OTTO. Political theories of the Middle Ages. Translated with an introduction by Frederic William Maitland. Cambridge, University Press, 1900. lxxx, 197pp. o.p. $ 25.00

328. GLUECK, SHELDON. Crime and correction: selected papers. Cambridge, Addison, 1952. 273pp. $ 15.00

329. GODWIN, GEORGE. Crime and social action. London, Watts, (1956). 277pp. o.p. $ 15.00
*Historical overview of various penal ideologies; lengthy treatment of the M'Naghten trial.

330. GOEBEL, JULIUS, ed. Cases and materials on the development of legal institutions. N.Y., Ad Press, 1937. 784pp. Cloth. 4to. o.p. $ 25.00

331. GOODNOW, FRANK J. Social reform and the Constitution. N.Y., Macmillan. 1911. 365pp. $ 15.00

332. GROTIUS, HUGO. The freedom of the seas, or the right which belongs to the (Cont'd.)

332. GROTIUS, HUGO. (Cont'd.) Dutch to take part in the East Indian Trade. Translated with a revision of the Latin text of 1633, by Ralph Van Deman Magoffin, edited with an introductory note by James Brown Scott. N.Y., Oxford Univ. Press, 1916. 83pp. $ 12.50

333. HAINES, CHARLES GROVE. The American doctrine of judicial supremacy. N.Y., Macmillan, 1914. 365pp. First edition, fine. A classic work. $ 15.00

334. HAMILTON, ALLAN McLane, et al. A system of legal medicine. Illustrated. In two vols. Second edition. N.Y., Treat, 1900. 657, 738pp. cl. $ 37.50

335. HARNO, ALBERT J. Legal education in the United States. A report prepared for the survey of the legal profession. San Francisco, Bancroft, 1953. 211pp. $ 17.50
*Historical and contemporary.

336. HART, H.L.A. The morality of the criminal law. Two lectures. Jerusalem, Magnes Press, 1965. 54pp. cl. o.p. $ 12.50
*Hebrew Univ. of Jerusalem, Lionel Cohen Lectures, tenth series.

337. HOANG, PIERRE. Le mariage Chinois au point de vue legal ... deuxieme ed. revue et corrigee par l'auteur avec deux appendixes sur le mariage en Chine d'apres le nouveau code par Jerome Tobar. Chang-Hai, Imprimerie de la Mission Catholique, 1916. 259, 86pp. tables, some folding. Fine copy. $ 27.50
*Author was a member of the clergy of Nan King. Text in French with original Chinese codes. Varietes Sinologiques #14.

338. HOANG, PIERRE. Notions techniques sur la propriete en Chine, avec un choix d'actes et de documents officiels (deuxieme ed.) Chang-hai, Imprimerie de l'Orphelinat de T-ou-se-we Zi-ka-wei., 1920. 200p. Includes some text and documents in original Chinese. $ 20.00
*Varietes Sinologiques #11.

339. HUGHES, CHARLES EVANS. The Supreme Court of the United States, its foundation, methods and achievements, an interpretation. Garden City, Garden City Publishing, (1936). 269pp. Orig. cl. fine. $ 10.00

340. HYDEMAN, LEE M., et al. International control of Nuclear Maritime activities. Ann Arbor, 1960. 384pp. wrps. o.p. $ 17.50

341. INTERNATIONAL ATOMIC ENERGY AGENCY. Agreements registered with the International Atomic Energy Agency. Second edition, (up to 31 December 1966) Vienna, Internat'l Atomic Energy Agency, 1968. 68pp. $ 10.00
*Legal series No. 3.

342. INTERNATIONAL ATOMIC ENERGY AGENCY. Civil liability for nuclear damage: official records of the International Conference on (Cont'd.)

342. INTERNATIONAL ATOMIC ENERGY AGENCY. (Cont'd.) Civil Liability for Nuclear Damage held by the International Atomic Energy Agency, in Vienna, 29 April-19 May 1963. Vienna, International Atomic Energy Agency, 1964. 522pp. $ 15.00
*Legal Series No. 2.

343. INTERNATIONAL ATOMIC ENERGY AGENCY. International Conventions on civil liability for nuclear damage. International Atomic Energy Agency, Vienna, 1966. 250pp. Wrps.
*Legal Series No. 4. $ 12.50

344. INTERNATIONAL ATOMIC ENERGY AGENCY. Liability of operators of Nuclear Ships: report of a panel of legal experts convened by the Director General ... Vienna, International Atomic Energy Agency, 1960. 42pp. Wrps. $ 10.00

345. JAMIESON, G. Chinese family and commercial law. Shanghai, Kelly, 1921. 188pp. $ 22.50

346. JENKS, EDWARD. A short history of English law, from the earliest times to the end of the year 1919. Second ed, revised. Boston, Little, Brown, 1922. 390pp. o.p. $ 20.00

347. John Marshall bicentennial celebration 1955. Final report of the United States Commission for the celebration of the two hundredth anniversary of the birth of John Marshall. Wash., D.C. (1955). 94pp. Illus., frontis. $ 12.50
*Good account of publications, projects, seminars.

348. KEITT, LAWRENCE. An annotated bibliography of bibliographies of statutory materials of the United States. Cambridge, Harvard Univ. Press, 1934. 191pp. $ 6.50

349. KELLOR, FRANCES, et al. Protocol for the Pacific settlement of International disputes in relation to the sanction of war. 1925. 183pp. Wrps. $ 10.00

350. THE LAW ASSOCIATION OF PHILADELPHIA. Addresses delivered March 13, 1902, and papers prepared or republished to commemorate the Centennial Celebration of the Law Association of Philadelphia, Pennsylvania, 1802-1902. Phila. (1906). 462pp. illus., plates. $ 20.00
*Extensive treatments of Binney, Rawle, Sergeant, Tilghman and others.

351. LEE, GUY CARLETON. Historical Jurisprudence: an introduction to the systematic study of the development of law. N.Y., Macmillan, 1900. 517pp. o.p. $ 22.50
*One of the earliest American works on comparative historical jurisprudence; author was professor at Johns Hopkins.

352. LEE, JOHN. Religious liberty in South America, with special reference to recent legislation in Peru, Ecuador, and Bolivia. With an introduction by Bishop John H. Vincent. Cincinnati, Jennings, (1907). 266pp. o.p. $ 22.50

353. LERNER, DANIEL, ed. Evidence and inference. The Hayden Colloquium on Scientific Concept and Method. Glencoe, Free Press, (1959). 164pp. o.p. $ 12.50

354. LEVY, ROBERT J. Selected materials on family law, custody, the unwed mother, adoption, parental neglect. Chicago, Nat'l Council on Legal Clinics, 1964. 235pp. 4to. $ 12.50

355. LEWIS, JOHN FREDERICK. Thomas Spry, lawyer and physician. The first attorney admitted to practise under English law in the Delaware River settlements now included in the States of Pennsylvania, New Jersey and Delaware. Phila., (Patterson), 1932. 126pp. Illus, Frontis., plts. $ 15.00

356. LIBRARY OF CONGRESS. PALMER, THOMAS W. Guide to the law and legal literature of Spain. Wash., GPO, 1915. 174pp. 4to. cl. fine. o.p. $ 15.00

357. LINCOLN, CHARLES Z. The constitutional history of New York, from the beginning of the Colonial period to the year 1905, showing the origin, development, and judicial construction of the Constitution. In 5 vols. Rochester, Lawyers Co-op. Publishing Co., 1906. o.p. $ 75.00
*Approx. 2600pp. Index, table of cases and statutes; Author was member of Const. Convention of 1894 and Chairman of Statutory Revision Committee as well as legal advisor to three governors of N.Y. incl. Roosevelt (Theodore).

358. LOWENSTEIN, STEVEN. Lawyers, legal education, and development: an examination of the process of reform in Chile. N.Y., Internat'l Legal Center, (1970). 310pp. $ 12.50

359. MACHEN, ARTHUR W., JR. A treatise on the modern law of corporations with reference to formation and operation, under general laws. In two vols. Boston, Little, Brown, 1908. 1797pp. First edition. $ 30.00

360. MAGILL, ROSWELL. Taxable income. N.Y., Ronald Press, (1936). 437pp. o.p. $ 17.50
*Classic delineation of administrative and judicial definition of the tax base since the income tax act of 1913. Intro. by Robert Murray Haig.

361. MAITLAND, ERMENGARD. F.W. Maitland, a child's-eye view. Selden Society. London, Quaritch, 1957. 16pp. Illus., Frontis., plates. Wrps. $ 7.50

362. MEGARRY, ROBERT. Inns ancient and modern: a topographical and historical introduction to the Inns of Court, Inns of Chancery, and Serjeants' Inns. London, Selden Society, 1972. 61pp. Illus. frontis., plates. Wrps. $ 7.50

363. MIKELL, WILLIAM E. Dental jurisprudence, the law relating to dentists and the practice of dentistry. Phila., Lea, 1912. 570pp. cl. fine. $ 25.00
*Covers U.S., G.B. and colonies. 1st systematic treatise on the subject.

364. MILLER, PEYTON F. A group of great lawyers of Columbia County, New York. With portraits. Privately printed, 1904. 264pp. o.p. $ 17.50
*Includes Edward and Robert Livingston, Van Buren, others of distinction and a chapter on the anti-rent war.

365. MORRIS, WILLIAM ALFRED. The Frankpledge system. N.Y., Longmans, 1910. 194pp. o.p. $ 22.50
*Harvard Historical Studies, vol. XIV.

366. MOYNIHAN, CORNELIUS J. A preliminary survey of the law of real property: an historical background of the common law of real property and its modern application. St. Paul, West, 1940. 154pp. $ 12.50

367. MUELLER, GERHARD O.W. Crime, law and scholars: a history of scholarship in American criminal law. Seattle, Univ. of Washington Press, (1969). 302pp. o.p. $ 17.50

368. NATIONAL MUNICIPAL LEAGUE. CONFERENCE FOR GOOD CITY GOVERNMENT. Proceedings of the annual meetings. 1894-1909. (1st through 16th national conferences, held at various places. 1895 is called the 1st annual meeting so that 1909 is the 15th annual meeting). $ 200.00
*Each volume is a substantial collection of articles, papers etc. by numerous important participants; this publication is essential as a source for the broad urban reform movement of this period, in all of its important aspects including politics, administration, health, education, finance and social control.

369. NEWHALL, GUY. The settlement of estates of deceased persons and others in Massachusetts. Boston, Jackson, 1915. 339pp. $ 15.00

370. NEW YORK TEMPORARY COMMISSION OF INVESTIGATION. Syndicated gambling in New York State, a report of the New York State Commission of Investigation Feb., 1961. 136pp. Wrps. $ 10.00

371. NOYES, C. REINOLD. The institution of property: a study of the development, substance and arrangement of the system of property in modern Anglo-American Law. N.Y., Longmans, 1936. 645pp. First edition. o.p. $ 37.50

372. O'MALLEY, AUSTIN. The ethics of medical homicide and mutilation. N.Y., Devin-Adair, (1919). 273pp. Illus. o.p. $ 22.50

373. PARKER, HERBERT. Courts and lawyers of New England. N.Y., American Historical Society, 1931. 4vols. 4to. 1015pp. Illus., portraits. Cl. covers of one vol. stained, contents fine. $ 45.00
*Finely illustrated study of 18th and 19th century pillars of the legal profession.

374. POLLOCK, FREDERICK. The genius of the common law. N.Y., Columbia Univ. Press, 1912. 141pp. 1st ed. Fine. $ 12.50

375. POUND, ROSCOE. Law and morals: the McNair Lectures, 1923, delivered at the Univ. of North Carolina. Chapel Hill, Univ. of No. Carolina Press, 1924. 156pp. First edition, signed by the author. $ 17.50

376. POUND, ROSCOE, ed., and compiler, et al. Readings on the history and system of the Common Law. Third ed. completely revised. Rochester, Lawyers Co-operative Pub. Co., 1927. 731pp. $ 22.50

377. REED, H. CLAY, ed., et al. The Burlington Court Book: a record of Quaker Jurisprudence in West New Jersey, 1680-1709. Wash., D.C., American Historical Assoc. 1944. 372pp. 4to. o.p. $ 35.00
*American Legal Records, vol. 5.

378. RIASANOVSKY, V.A. Customary law of the Mongol tribes (Mongols, Buriats, Kalmucks). Parts I-III complete. Harbin, China, 1929. 306pp. 4to. Original wrps. Very good copy. o.p. $ 37.50

379. RITCHIE, DAVID G. Natural rights: a criticism of some political and ethical conceptions. 2nd. ed. London, Swan, 1903. 304pp. o.p. $ 17.50

380. ROBERTS, OWEN J. The Court and the Constitution: the Oliver Wendell Holmes lectures, 1951. Cambridge, Harvard Univ. Press, 1951. 102pp. o.p. $ 10.00

381. RUNES, DAGOBERT D. The disinherited and the law. N.Y., Philosophical Lib., (1964). 79pp. o.p. $ 12.50

382. SELECT ESSAYS IN ANGLO-AMERICAN LEGAL HISTORY, by various authors. Compiled and edited by a Committee of the Assoc. of American Law Schools. In 3 vol. Boston, Little, Brown, 1907. cl. fine set. Approx. 2500pp. $ 45.00

383. SIEBERT, FREDRICK SEATON. The rights and privileges of the press. N.Y., Appleton-Century, (1934). 429pp. $ 17.50
*McCoy S391.

384. SIMPSON, ALEX, JR. A Treatise on Federal Impeachments: with an appendix containing, inter alia, an abstract of the Articles of Impeachment in all the Federal Impeachments in this Country and in England. Phila., The Law Assoc. of Phila., 1916. 230pp. o.p. $ 17.50

385. SINGER, B. Trade mark laws of the world and unfair trade. Chicago, 1913. 685pp. Cloth. First edition of a massive and thorough treatise. $ 27.50

386. SINGER, H. DOUGLAS, et al. Insanity and law: a treatise on forensic psychiatry. Phila, Blakiston, (1924). 428pp. o.p. $ 27.50

387. SMITH, F.E., et al. International law as interpreted during the Russo-Japanese War. Boston, Boston Book, 1905. 494pp. cl. Roy. 8vo. Fine copy. o.p. $ 25.00

388. SMITH, W. RAMSAY. Medical jurisprudence from the judicial standpoint. London, Stevens, 1913. 331pp. $ 22.50

389. (THE STAIR SOCIETY). Miscellany One by various authors, with a preface by Rt. Hon. Lord Clyde. Edinburgh, Stair Society, 1971. 284pp. Illus., frontis., plates. $ 20.00
*8 essays on Scottish law.

390. STRAIT, GEORGE A. A bibliography of the writings of Roscoe Pound 1940-1960. Cambridge, Harvard Law School Library, 1960. 52pp. Illus., frontis. Wrps. o.p. $ 10.00

391. STROMHOLM, STIG. Right of privacy and rights of the personality: a comparative survey. Working paper prepared for ... International Commission of Jurists ... Stockholm, Norstedt, 1967. 250pp. wrps. Entirely in English. $ 12.50
*Acta, Upsala Institute for Comparative Jurisprudence, VIII.

392. SULLIVAN, HAROLD. Contempt by Publication: the Law of Trial by Newspaper. (Privately printed under the direction of the Yale Univ. Press), 1940. 208pp. $ 17.50
*Historical with reference to numerous cases and a comparison between England and America.

393. SUNDERLAND, EDSON R. History of the American Bar Association and its work, with a concluding chapter on the Committee on Scope and Correlation of Work and its program by William J. Jameson. 1953. 251pp. $ 12.50

394. SUPREME COURT REPORTER. (West edition). Vol. 1-92A Bound in 105 physical volumes. Good condition. $ 750.00

395. The Supreme Judicial Court of Massachusetts, 1692-1942. Boston, Massachusetts Bar Assoc., (1942). 72,61pp. Illus., frontis., numerous portraits. $ 12.50

396. THOMAS, DONALD. A long time burning: the history of literary censorship in England. New York: Praeger, (1969). 546. Illus. Numerous plates. o.p. $ 22.50
*Fine, detailed comprehensive study.

397. U.S. DEPARTMENT OF THE INTERIOR. Laws, decisions, and regulations affecting the work of the Commissioners to the Five Civilized Tribes, 1893-1906, together with maps showing classification of lands in the Chickasaw, Chocktaw, Cherokee, Creek, and Seminole Nations, and recording districts, railroads, and principal towns of the Indian territory. Wash., GPO, 1906. 8vo. 250pp. With five very large folding colored maps, each approx. 36 x 32" full of remarkable detail. Some minor tears at folds, but a very good copy. A scarce and extremely useful source compiled by the Commissioner. $ 60.00

398. U.S. SUPERINTENDENT OF DOCUMENTS. Catalogue of Public Documents. Vol. 1-25 (Cont'd.)

398. U.S. SUPERINTENDENT OF DOCUMENTS. (Cont'd.) (53rd-76th Congress, 1895-1940) Bound. Original edition. Excellent condition. $ 500.00

399. U.S. TREATIES. Treaties, conventions, international acts, and agreements between the United States of America and other powers 1923-1937. Wash., GPO, 1938. Large 8vo. $ 35.00
*Volume 4 (and final vol. with index to vols. 1-4) of this series.

SAME. Vols. I and II (1789-1909). each $ 25.00

400. VANDERBILT, ARTHUR T. Judges and Jurors: their functions, qualifications and selection. Boston, Boston Univ. Press, 1956. 76pp. $ 12.50
*The Bacon Lectures. Author was Chief Justice of N.J.

401. WARREN, CHARLES. Congress, the Constitution and the Supreme Court. Boston, Little, Brown, 1925. 308pp. First ed. Fine. $ 15.00

402. WARREN, CHARLES. The making of the Constitution. Boston, Little, Brown, 1929. 824pp. o.p. $ 15.00

404. WEI-TUNG, PAN. The Chinese Constitution: a study of forty years of constitution-making in China. Wash, D.C.: Institute of Chinese Culture, 1945. 327pp. o.p. $ 22.50

405. WEITZEL, FRED W. The law of deposits. Wash, D.C., Economy Publishing, (1910). 127pp. cl. $ 12.50

406. WEST, RANYARD. Conscience and society: a study of the psychological prerequisites of law and order. N.Y., Emerson Books, Inc., 1945. 261pp. d.j. fine copy. $ 12.50

407. WILLOUGHBY, W.F. Principles of judicial administration. Wash., D.C., Brookings Inst., 1929. 662pp. o.p. $ 17.50
*Institute for Government Research.

408. WOETZEL, ROBERT K. The Nuremberg Trials in international law. London, Stevens, 1960. 287pp. o.p. $ 15.00

409. WRIGHT, BENJAMIN FLETCHER. Consensus and continuity, 1776-1787. Boston, Boston Univ. Press, 1958. 60pp. cl. hardcover o.p. $ 12.50
*Boston Univ. The Gasper G. Bacon Lectures on the Constitution of the United States.

403. WARREN, CHARLES. The Supreme Court and sovereign States. Princeton, Princeton Univ. Press, 1924. 157pp. Orig. c., d.j., fine, first ed. $ 15.00

* * * * PART III: A COLLECTION OF WORKS ON

a.) MONOGRAPHS

410. BALLARD, ADOLPHUS. The Domesday Inquest. With 27 Illus. London, Methuen, (1906). Illus. plates. o.p. $ 20.00
*Classic analysis of the descriptive and statistical content of the Domesday Book. W.J. Ashley's copy.

411. BALLARD, ADOPHUS. The English Borough in the twelfth century: being two lectures delivered in the Examination Schools Oxford on 22 and 29 October 1913. Cambridge, University Press, 1914. 87pp. Blind stamp on title. o.p. $ 15.00

412. BARRACLOUGH, GEOFFREY, ed. Facsimiles of early Cheshire Charters. Oxford, Blackwell, 1957. cl. 4to. xiv, 54pp. plus 21 plates. o.p. $ 20.00

413. BELL, H.E. An introduction to the history and records of the Court of Wards & Liveries. Cambridge, University Press, 1953. 215pp. 1st ed. d.j., fine. o.p. $ 22.50
*Cambridge Studies in English Legal History.

414. BISHOP, T.A.M., (editor)., et al. Facsimiles of English Royal Writs to a.d. 1100, presented to Vivian Hunter Galbraith. Oxford, Clarendon Press, 1957. 4to. Profusely illsutrated with facsimiles, d.j., fine. o.p. $ 30.00

415. CAM, HELEN. The Hundred and the Hundred Rolls: an outline of local government in medieval England with illustrations and two maps. N.Y., Burt Franklin, reprint of 1930 edition. 296pp. cl. $ 15.00

416. CAM, HELEN. Law-finders and law-makers in Medieval England: collected studies in legal and constitutional history. London, Merlin Press, (1962). 240pp. d.j., fine. $ 10.00

417. CAMERON, JAMES R. Frederick William Maitland and the history of English law. Norman, Univ. of Oklahoma Press, (1961). 214pp. Illus., frontis, plates, d.j., fine. First edition. $ 15.00

418. CHADWICK HEALEY, CHARLES E.H., ed. Somersetshire Pleas (civil and criminal). from the rolls of the Itinerant Justices, (close of 12 century-41 Henry III). (London, Harrison, Printer,) 1897. 520pp. cl. o.p. $ 35.00
*Somerset Record Society, vol. XI.

419. CHEW, HELENA M., et al., eds. London assize of nuisance 1301-1431. A Calendar. London Record Society, 1973. cl. Fine. $ 12.50
*Vol. 10 of the Publications.

420. CHEW, HELENA M., et al., eds. The London eyre of 1244. London Record Society, 1970. cl. Fine. $ 12.50
*Vol. 6 of the Publications.

421. DE HAAS, ELSA. Antiquities of bail: origin and historical development in criminal cases to the year 1275. N.Y., Columbia Univ. Press, 1940. 174pp. Orig cl., fine. First edition. $ 15.00

422. Dialogus de Scaccario (The Course of the Exchequer by Richard, Son of Nigel, Treasurer of England and Bishop of London) AND Constitutio Domus Regis (The King's Household) translated ... with notes by Charles Johnson. London, Nelson, (1950). 66, 270pp. and index. Illus., frontis. D.j., fine. 1st ed. o.p. $ 17.50
*Medieval Classics Series.

423. DOVE, P. EDWARD, ed. Domesday Commemoration, 1086 A.D.-1886 A.D. Domesday studies: being the papers read at the meetings of the Domesday Commemoration, 1886, with a bibliography of Domesday Book and accounts of the MSS and printed books exhibited at the Public Record Office and at the British Museum. In two vols. London, Longmans, 1888. 710pp. Illus., frontis. map. Cloth. 4to. 1st ed. fine. *S&M, I, p. 91. $ 40.00

424. DUNHAM, WILLIAM HUSE, ed. Radulphi De Hengham Summae. Cambridge, Univ. Press, 1932. lxxxiv, 94pp. cl. o.p. $ 25.00
*Cambridge Studies in English Legal History.

425. EARLE, JOHN. A hand-book to the Land-Charters, and other Saxonic Documents. Oxford, Clarendon Press, 1888. 519pp.
*By a leading Anglo-Saxon scholar. o.p. $ 27.50

426. ELLIS, HENRY. A general introduction to Domesday Book; accompanied by indexes of the tenants in chief, and under tenants, ... the holders of land, ... an abstract of the population of England, ... numerous notes and comments. In two vols. London, 1921. Reprint of the 1883 edition. $ 25.00

427. FIFOOT, CECIL H.S. Pollock and Maitland: being the thirty-first lecture on the David Murray Foundation in the Univ. of Glasgow delivered on 28th Oct., 1970. Glasgow, Univ. of Glasgow, 1971. 30pp. Wrps. $ 7.50

428. FINN, R. WELLDON. The Domesday Inquest and the making of Domesday Book. (London). Longmans, (1961). 201pp. d.j., fine. First edition. $ 15.00

429. FINN, R. WELLDON. An introduction to Domesday Book. (London), Longmans, (1963). 306pp. cl. o.p. $ 17.50

430. GALBRAITH, V.H. The making of Domesday Book. Oxford, Clarendon Press, 1961. 242pp. cl. Illus., d.j., fine. o.p. $ 17.50

431. GEOFFREY OF MONMOUTH. The Historia Regum Britanniae ... with contributions to the study of its place in early (Cont'd.)

431. GEOFFREY OF MONMOUTH. (Cont'd.) British history by Andrew Griscom together with a literal translation of the Welsh manuscript ... by Robert Ellis Jones. With 17 photographs of manuscripts. London, Longmans, 1929. 672pp. cl. fine copy, first edition. o.p. $ 27.50

432. GREAT BRITAIN. DEPUTY KEEPER OF THE RECORDS. Liber feodorum. The book of fees commonly called Testa de Nevill. Reformed from the earliest mss. Part II. A.D. 1242-1293 and appendix. London, HMSO, 1923. pp. 637-1483. Roy. 8vo. Orig. cl. Fine. $ 20.00

433. HALL, G.D.G., ed. The treatise on the laws and customs of the realm of England commonly called Glanvill, with introduction, notes and translation by ... (London), Nelson, (1965). 213pp. cl. o.p. $ 22.50

434. HARMER, F.E. Anglo-Saxon writs. Manchester, Manchester Univ. Press, (1952). 604pp. o.p. $ 22.50

435. HATTON, CHRISTOPHER. Sir Christopher Hatton's book of seals, to which is appended a select list of the works of Frank Merry Stenton. Edited by the late Lewis C. Loyd and Doris Mary Stenton. Oxford, Claredon Press, 1950. 452pp. Illus., frontis., numerous fine plates. 4to. o.p. $ 30.00
*Shows 529 seals and charters of the 12-13th centuries.

436. HEMMEON, MORLEY DE WOLF. Burgage tenure in Mediaeval England. Cambridge, Harvard Univ., Press, 1914. 235pp. o.p. $ 27.50
*Harvard Historical Studies, vol, 20. 1st ed. fine.

437. HUNNISETT, R.F. The medieval coroner. Cambridge, The University Press, 1961. 217pp. 1st ed., d.j., fine. $ 17.50
*Cambridge Studies in English Legal History.

438. JOHN, ERIC. Land tenure in early England: a discussion of some problems. (Welwy Garden City), Leicester Univ., Press, 1960. 184pp. d.j., fine. $ 12.50
*Studies in Early English History.

439. JOSSIFFE, J.E.A. The constitutional history of medieval England, from the English Settlement to 1485. Second edition. London, Adam & Charles Black, 1948. 524pp. cl. hardcover o.p. $ 15.00

440. KANTORWICZ, H. Bractonian problems: being the ninth lecture on the David Murray Foundation in the Univ. of Glasgow prepared, but not delivered, with a short memoir of the author by Doris M. Stenton. Glasgow, Jackson, 1941. 133pp. wrps. $ 10.00
*Glasgow Univ. Publications LVI.

441. KEETON, GEORGE W. The Norman Conquest and the Common Law. London, Benn, (1966). 238pp. d.j., fine. o.p. $ 17.50

442. KELHAM, ROBERT. Domesday Book illustrated: containing an account of that antient record; as also of the tenants ... a translation of the difficult passages with occasional notes; an explanation of the terms ... an alphabetical table of the tenants ... London, Nichols for Brooke, 1788. 8vo. Original boards, uncut, rebacked somewhat later in paper, half-title present, a very nice copy.
*S&M, I, 92. First edition. $ 75.00

443. MACRAY, WILLIAM DUNN, ed. Chronicon Abbatae De Evesham, ad annum 1418. London, Longman, 1863. 394pp. Folding frontis. o.p. $ 25.00
*Chronicles and Memorials of G.B. and Ireland Series.

444. MAITLAND, F.W. (Editor). Bracton's Note Book. A collection of cases decided in the King's courts during the reign of Henry the Third, annotated by a lawyer of that time, seemingly by Henry of Bratton. London, C.J. Clay, 1887. 3 volumes, complete. 337; 720; 723pp. 8vo. Orig. cl., minor wear but a very good set. First edition. o.p. $ 75.00

445. MAITLAND, FREDERIC WILLIAM, ed., et al. The charters of the Borough of Cambridge. Edited for the Council of Borough of Cambridge and Cambridge and Cambridge Antiquarian Society. Cambridge, University Press, 1901. 209pp. Illus., frontis. cl. o.p. $ 25.00

446. MAITLAND, FREDERIC WILLIAM. The collected papers of Frederic William Maitland, edited by H.A.L. Fisher. In 3 vols. Cambridge, University Press, 1911. 497, 496, 566pp. cl. o.p. $ 50.00

447. MAITLAND, F.W. Equity, also the forms of action at common law; two courses of lectures, edited by A.H. Chaytor, and W.J. Whittaker. Cambridge, University Press, 1916. 411pp. o.p. $ 25.00

448. MAITLAND, F.W., ed. Pleas of the Crown for the County of Gloucester before the Abbot of Reading and his fellows justices itinerant, in the fifth year of the reign of King Henry the third, and the year of grace 1221. London, MacMillan, 1884. lvi, 155pp. cl. o.p. $ 27.50

449. MAITLAND, FREDERIC WILLIAM, ed. Records of the Parliament holden at Westminster, on the twenty-eighth day of February, in the thirty-third year of the reign of King Edward the First, (A.D., 1305). London, H.M.S.O., 1893. 373pp. o.p. $ 30.00

450. MAITLAND, F.W. Selected historical essays of ..., chosen and introduced by Helen M. Cam. Cambridge, University Press, 1957. 278pp. d.j., fine. First edition. $ 22.50

451. MARTIN, CHARLES TRICE, compiler. The record interpreter; a collection of abbreviations, Latin words and names used in English historical manuscripts and records. Second edition. London, Stevens, 1910. 464pp. cl. $ 15.00

452. PLUCKNETT, T.F.T. Early English legal literature. Cambridge, Univ. Press, 1958. 120pp. o.p. $ 22.50
*Cambridge Studies in English Legal History. Fine, with d.j., First edition, with TLS from the author.

453. PLUCKNETT, T.F.T. Legislation of Edward I: the Ford Lectures delivered in the Univ. of Oxford in Hilary term 1947. Oxford, Clarendon, 1949. 168pp. 1st ed. d.j., fine. o.p. $ 22.50

454. PLUCKNETT, THEODORE F.T. Statutes and their interpretation in the first half of the fourteenth century. Cambridge Univ. Press, 1922. 200pp. Orig. cl., cl., fine. 1st ed. o.p. $ 25.00
*Cambridge Studies in English Legal History.

455. POLLOCK, FREDERICK W. AND F.W. MAITLAND. The history of English law before the time of Edward I. Second edition in two volumes. Cambridge, University Press, 1899. cl. Good set. $ 25.00

456. PUTNAM, BERTHA HAVEN, ed. Proceedings before the justices of the peace in the fourteenth and fifteenth centuries, Edward III to Richard III, with commentary by Theodore F.T. Plucknett. London, Spottiswoode, 1938. 590pp. 4to. o.p. $ 30.00
*Ames Foundation Publications.

457. The Records of the Honourable Society of Lincoln's Inn. The Black Books. Volume I. From A.D. 1422 to A.D. 1586. Lincoln's Inn, 1897. xl, 521pp. Roy. 8vo. cl. fine. $ 30.00
*Documentary archives of Lincoln's Inn, showing the entire range of life and activities there.

458. RILEY, HENRY THOMAS, ed. Munimenta Gildhallae Londoniensis; Liber Albus, Liber Custumarum, et Liber Horn. In 4 vols. London, Longman, 1859-1862. Illus. Roy. 8vo. 1/4 mor. rubbed, approx. 2000pp. $ 75.00
*Chronicles and Memorials of Great Britain series.

459. RYLANDS, J. PAUL, ed. The exchequer lay subsidy roll of Robert De Shireburn and John De Radcliffe, taxers and collectors in the County of Lancaster, A.D. 1332. London, Wyman, 1896. 148pp. o.p. $ 12.50

460. SAWYER, P.H. Anglo-Saxon charters: an annotated list and bibliography. London, Royal Historical Society, Univ. College. 1968. 538pp. cl. $ 15.00
*Royal Historical Society Guides and Handbooks No. 8.

461. SCRUTTON, THOMAS EDWARD. Commons and common fields, or the history and policy of the laws relating to commons and enclosures in England. Being the Yorke Prize Essay of the Univ. of Cambridge for the year 1886. Cambridge, Univ., Press, 1887. 179pp. 1st ed. $ 15.00

462. SEEBOHM, FREDERIC. Tribal custom in Anglo-Saxon law: being an essay supplemental to (1) "The English Village Community," (2) "The Tribal System in Wales." London, Longmans, 1911. 538pp. cl. $ 20.00

463. SELDEN, JOHN. Ad fletam dissertatio. Reprinted from the edition of 1647 with parallel translation, introduction and notes by David Ogg. Cambridge, Univ. Press, 1925. 66, 197pp. d.j., fine copy. 1st ed. o.p. $ 25.00
*Cambridge Studies in English Legal History.

464. SELDEN, JOHN. Table talk ... newly edited for the Selden Society by Frederick Pollock ... together with an account of Selden and his work by the late Sir Edward Fry ... London, Quaritch, 1927. xxiv, 200pp. 8vo. 1/4 cl. Illustrated, portrait, facsimiles. Stamp on title page, else a good copy. $ 25.00
*This ed not reprinted.

465. SHILLIBEER, H.B. The ancient customs of the manor of Taunton Deane; ... to which are prefixed, some introductory observations on copyholds in general, and remarks on those of this manor in particular, with the origin, history, and nature of Courts Leet, and Courts Baron. (Taunton), for the Author, 1821. 132, xixpp. New cl. $ 35.00

466. STENTON, F.M., ed. Documents illustrative of the social and economic history of the Danelaw from various collections. London, Humphrey Milford. Oxford Univ. Press, 1920. 554pp. cl. o.p. $ 30.00
*Records of the Social and Economic History of England & Wales, vol. 5.

467. STENTON, F.M. The first century of English feudalism 1066-1166, being the Ford Lectures delivered in the Univ. of Oxford in Hilary Term 1929. Oxford, Clarendon Press, 1954 reprint of 1932 ed., d.j., fine. o.p. $ 20.00

468. STENTON, F.M. The Latin charters of the Anglo-Saxon period. Oxford, Clarendon Press, 1955. 103pp. cl. o.p. $ 12.50

469. THORNE, SAMUEL E., ed. A discourse upon the exposicion & understandinge of statutes, with Sir Thomas Egerton's additions. Edited from manuscripts in the Huntington Library. San Marino, Calif., Huntington Library, 1942. 194pp. d.j., Fine. o.p. $ 30.00
*"Earliest treatise brought to light on the interpretation of statutes in England."

470. THORPE, BENJAMIN, ed. The Anglo-Saxon Chronicle, according to the several original authorities. Edited with a translation by ... In 2 vols. Vol. 1, contains original texts, vol. 2, contains translation. London, Longman, 1861. 415,319pp. Illus. Fold. facsimiles. o.p. $ 50.00
*Chronicles and Memorials of G.B. and Ireland Series.

471. THORPE, BENJAMIN. Diplomatarium Anglicum Aevi Saxonici: a collection of English charters, from the reign of King Aethelberht of Kent, A.D. D.C.V. to that of William the Conqueror. Containing, I. miscellaneous charters, II wills, III. guilds, IV. manumissions and acquittances, with translation of the Anglo-Saxon. London, MacMillan, 1865. 683pp. cl. o.p. $ 40.00

472. TOUT, T.F. Chapters in the administrative history of Mediaeval England; the wardrobe, the chamber, and the small seals. Manchester, Manchester Univ. Press, 1937. 325, 367pp. cl. In two vols. $ 20.00
*Univ. of Manchester Historical Series, No. XXXV. First printed 1920, reprinted with minor additions and corrections 1937.

473. TWISS, SIR TRAVERS, ed. Monumenta Juridica. The Black Book of the Admiralty, with an appendix. In 4 vols. London, Longman, 1871-1876. Illus. Roy. 8vo. 1/4 morocco. approx. 2000pp. Spines rubbed. o.p. $ 100.00
*Chronicles and memorials of Great Britain and Ireland Series.

474. VINOGRADOFF, PAUL. English society in the eleventh century: essays in English mediaeval history. Oxford, Clarendon Press, 1968. 599pp. d.j., fine. Reissue of the 1908 ed. $ 22.50

475. VINOGRADOFF, PAUL. The growth of the manor. London, Allen, 1951. 384pp. d.j., fine. Reprint of 1911 ed. $ 15.00

476. WHITELOCK, DOROTHY, ed. Anglo-Saxon wills, edited with translation and notes by ... Cambridge, University Press, 1930. 244pp. 1st ed. fine. $ 15.00
*Cambridge Studies in English Legal History.

477. WILLIAMS, GWYN A. Medieval London from commune to capital. London, Univ. of London, 1963. 377pp., d.j., fine. $ 17.50
*U. of London Historical Studies XI. Hardcover o.p.

b.) RECORD SOCIETY PUBLICATIONS

PIPE ROLL SOCIETY. The following:

478. The Great Roll of the Pipe for the fifth year of the reign of King Henry the Second, A.D. 1158-1159. London, 1884, reprinted 1910. 80pp. cl. $ 15.00
*Pipe Roll Society Publications vol. I.

479. ROUND, JOHN HORACE, ed. Ancient Charters royal and private, prior to A.D. 1200. Part I. Printed from the originals. London, 1888. 133pp. cl. (Facsimile Reprint). $ 15.00
*Pipe Roll Society Publication, Vol. X.

480. Feet of Fines of the ninth year of the reign of King Richard I. A.D. 1197 A.D. 1198. London, reprinted from the 1898 ed. in 1929. 178pp. cl. $ 15.00
*Pipe Roll Society Publication, vol. XXIII.

481. Feet of Fines of the tenth year of the reign of King Richard I, A.D. 1198 to A.D. 1199, excepting those for the counties of Bedford, Berkshire, Buckingham, Cambridge, Devon, and Dorset. Also a Roll of the Kings Court in the reign of King Richard I. London, 1900, reprinted 1929. 267pp. cl. $ 17.50
*Pipe Roll Society Publications, vol. XXIV.

482. The Great Roll of the Pipe for the twenty-second year of the reign of King Henry the Second, A.D. 1175-1176. London, 1904. 268pp. cl. $ 20.00
*Pipe Roll Society Publications, vol. XXV.

483. BARNES, PATRICIA M., editor, et al. A Medieval Miscellany for Doris Mary Stenton. London, 1962. 345pp. Illus. frontis., including 22 plates. cl. $ 17.50
*Pipe Roll Society Publications, vol. LXXIV (New Series vol. XXXVI).

484. BROWN, R.A., ed. Pipe Roll 17 John, and Praestita Roll 14-18 John, Roll of Summonses 1214, Scutage Roll 16 John, edited by J.C. Holt. London, 1964. 161pp. cl. $ 17.50
*Pipe Roll Society Publications vol. LXXV. (New Series vol. XXXVII).

485. EBDEN, E. PAULINE, ed. The Great Roll of the Pipe for the second year of the reign of King Henry III, Michaelmas 1218, (Pipe Roll 62). Now first printed from the original in the Public Record Office. London, 1972. 145pp. cl. $ 15.00
*Pipe Roll Society Publications vol. LXXVII (New Series vol. XXXIX).

486. DODWELL, BARBARA, ed. The Charters of Norwich Cathedral Priory, part one. London, 1974. 279pp. Illus., frontis, plates. cl. $ 17.50
*Pipe Roll Society Publications vol. LXXVIII. (New Series Vol. XL).

487. The Great Roll of the Pipe for the third year of the reign of King Henry III. Michaelmas 1219 (Pipe Roll 63). Now first printed from the original in the Public Record Office, with an introduction by B.E. Harris. London, 1976. 314pp. cl. $ 17.50
*Pipe Roll Society Publications, vol. LXX. (New Series vol. XLII).

488. The Great Rolls of the Pipe for the second, third and fourth years of the reign of King Henry the Second, A.D. 1155, 1156, 1157, 1158. London, 1844. 186pp. cl. Reprinted 1930. Not in series. $ 17.50

* * * * * * * * * * * * * * * *

489. SELDEN SOCIETY. Publications. London. (1887-1972). Volumes 1-4; 7-8; 11; 13; 15; 17-22; 24; 26-27; 50; 53; 55-63; 65-70; 72-79; 82-89. Original cloth, all in very good to fine condition.
per volume: $ 20.00

* * * * * * * * * * * * * * * *

SELDEN SOCIETY. Supplementary Series.

490. FIFOOT, C.H.S., ed. The letters of Frederic William Maitland. London, Selden Society, 1965. 397pp. Illus., Frontis. $ 17.50
*Selden Society Supplementary Series vol. I.

491. BLAND, D.S., compiler. A bibliography of the Inns of Court and Chancery. London, Selden Society, 1965. 75pp. cloth. $ 15.00
*Selden Society Supplementary Series, vol. 3.

492. KAYE, J.M., ed. Placita Corone or La Corone Pledee devant Justices, edited with introduction, notes and translation by ... London, Selden Society, 1966. xxxix, 42pp. cl. $ 15.00
*Selden Society Supplementary Series, vol. 4.

SELDEN SOCIETY. Lecture Series.

493. RADZINOWICZ, LEON. Sir James Fitzjames Stephen 1829-1894, and his contribution to the development of criminal law. Selden Society Lecture. 30th July, 1957, London, Quaritch, 1957. 79pp. frontis. Large bibliography. $ 7.50

494. SAYLES, GEORGE O. The Court of King's Bench in law and history. Selden Society Lecture. London, Quartitch. 1959. 21pp. wrps. $ 15.00

495. FLETCHER, SIR ERIC. John Selden 1584-1654. Selden Society Lecture, July 9th, 1969. London, Quaritch, 1969. 16pp. Illus, frontis. wrps. $ 5.00

496. WIENER, FREDERICK BERNAYS. Uses and abuses of legal history: a practitioner's view. Selden Society Lecture ... 1962. London, Quaritch, 1962. 32pp. wrps. $ 7.50

497. FIFOOT, C.H.S. Law and history in the nineteenth century. Selden Society Lecture, 13th March, 1956. London, Quaritch, 1956. 23pp. Wrps. $ 5.00

498. THORNE, SAMUEL E. Sir Edward Coke 1552-1952. Selden Society Lecture 17th March, 1952. London, Quaritch, 1957. 18pp. Wrps. $ 6.00

499. CAM, HELEN M. Magna Carta--event or document? Selden Society Lecture, July 7th, 1965. London, Quaritch, 1965. 26pp. Wrps. $ 6.00

500. WILLIAMS, N.J., ed. Collectanea, with a foreword by T.F.T. Plucknett. Devizes, 1956. 207pp. cl. $ 17.50
*Wiltshire Record Society, vol. XII.

501. FARR, M.W., ed. Accounts and surveys of the Wiltshire Lands of Adam De Stratton. Devizes, 1959. 266pp. cl. $ 17.50
*Wilshire Record Society, vol. XIV.

502. MEEKINGS, C.A.F., ed. Crown pleas of the Wiltshire Eyre, 1249. Devizes, 1961. 334pp. cl. $ 20.00
*Wiltshire Record Society, vol. XVI.

503. CLANCHY, M.T., ed. Civil pleas of the Wiltshire Eyre, 1249. Devizes, 1971. 214pp. cl. $ 17.50
*Wiltshire Record Society, vol. XXVI.

c.) YEARBOOKS. Various series.

504. YEAR BOOKS. EDW. I. Years 20-22, 30-35 (1292-1307), in five volumes, complete, all published in this series. Edited by Alfred Horwood. London, Longmans, 1866-1879. $ 150.00
*Chronicles and Memorials of G.B. Series. Sweet & Maxwell I, 313-314.

505. YEAR BOOKS. EDW. III. Years 11-20 part I. (1337-1346), in 14 volumes. Except for a final volume (Year 20 pt. II) a complete run of all published in this series. Edited by Luke Owen Pike. London, HMSO, 1883-1908. Large 8vo.s 1/4 cloth, very good to fine. $ 400.00
*Chronicles and Memorials of G.B. series. Sweet & Maxwell I, 313-314.

506. (YEAR BOOKS. RICHARD II). Year Books of Richard II: 11 Richard II 1387-1388. Edited for the Ames Foundation by Isobel D. Thornley ... with a commentary upon the cases by Theodore F.T. Plucknett. London, Spottiswoode, 1937. lxii, 576, (60)pp. Orig. cl. fine. 4to. o.p. $ 35.00
*Ames Foundation Publications.

507. (YEAR BOOKS. RICHARD II). 13 Richard II, 1389-1390. Edited ... by Theodore F.T. Plucknett. London, Spottiswoode, 1929. xlix, 370,20pp. 4to. Orig. cl. Fine. o.p. $ 30.00
*Ames Foundation Publications.

YEAR BOOKS. Maynard's edition - 11 parts with notes to Brooke and Fitzherbert. London, 1678-79. folios. each with tables, black letter. each $ 50.00
*S&M, I, 312. The following volumes: (1, 2, 3, 4, 6, 8, 9, and 11).

508. Les Reports des cases ... in le temps del' Roy Edward Le Second ... solonq les ancient manuscripts de Sir Jehan Maynard ... London, Sawbridge, et al., 1679. 685pp. plus index. FOLIO. New cl.
*Edw. II, 1-19. $ 50.00

509. Le premier part de les reports des cases en ley ... en le temps de ... Roy Edward le tierce ... nouvelment imprimes, corriges et amendes avec les notations et references a ... Brook et Fitzherbert. London, Sawbridge, 1679. Approx. 450pp. FOLIO. new cloth. $ 50.00
*Edw. III, 1-10.

510. Le second part de les reports des cases en ley en le temps de ... Edward le tierce ... nouvelment imprimes, corriges et amends avec les notations et references a ... Brook et Fitzherbert. In 2 volumes (volume II lacks title pate). London, Sawbridge, 1679. 2vols. FOLIO. new cloth. two volumes $ 100.00
*Edw. III, 17, 18, 21-30, 38, 39, 40-50.

511. Les reports des cases en ley. . . en le temps de ... les roys Henry le IV et Henry le V ... nouvelment imprime, corriges et amendes ... a Brook, Fitzherbert et Statham. London, Sawbridge, 1679. Thick FOLIO. New cloth. $ 50.00
*Henry IV, 1-14; Henry V, 1,2,5, 7-9.

512. Les reports des cases contenus en les ans (21 and after) en temps du Roy Henry le VI (Henry VI part II). ... London, Sawbridge, 1679. Thick FOLIO. New cloth (last leaf of table lacking). $ 50.00
*Henry VI, 21, 22, 27, 28, 30-39.

513. Les reports des cases en ley ... en le temps du Roy Edward le Quart ... avec les notations de ... Brook et Fitzherbert ... London, Sawbridge, 1680. Large thick FOLIO. New cloth. tables.
*Edw. IV, 1-22. $ 50.00

514. Les reports des cases en les ans des roys Edward V, Richard III, Henri VII, et Henri VIII... nouvelment imprime, corrige et revue ... London, Sawbridge, 1679. Thick FOLIO. New cloth. $ 50.00
*Edw. V; Rich. III; Henry VII, 1-16, 20, 21; Henry VIII, 12-14, 18, 19, 26, 27.

ROBERT H. RUBIN BOOKS

Post Office Box 558 · Stoughton, Massachusetts 02072 USA
Cable Address: «RUBOOKS» Telephone: (617) 344-0740

CATALOG SEVEN 1980

ANTIQUARIAN AND OUT-OF-PRINT WORKS IN

LAW AND LEGAL HISTORY

(CHIEFLY ANGLO-AMERICAN)

A detailed index is enclosed

We take pleasure in sending you our spring catalogue of law and legal history, chiefly Anglo-American, but with a few Continental works as well. The emphasis is on a variety of topics including **constitutional law, freedom of speech, international law, medical jurisprudence, penology, political theory and women's rights.** *There are also a number of works pertaining to the law of specific states, and we have added a brief addendum of serials. We invite you to consult the enclosed index for greater detail.*
We hope you find it interesting and useful reading.

Offers of single items or entire collections from institutional duplicates and personal collections always welcome

1. (ARCHBOLD, JOHN) ARCHBOLD'S SUMMARY of the law relative to pleading and evidence in criminal cases; with precedents of indictments, &c. and the evidence necessary to support them. Third American from the fifth and last London Edition, enlarged, with an appendix of statutes, and the decisions to the present time, by John Jervis. N. Y., Gould, 1835. xxiv, 524, clxxvii, pp. New cloth. $ 37.50
* Marvin p. 67: "standard work of great practical utility in England and America."

2. The attorney's compleat pocket-book. Containing ... precedents in law, equity and conveyancing ... fourth edition, corrected, with large editions. (London, Lintot, 1756.) 2 volumes, 12mo. Contemporary polished calf, raised bands, leather labels. A very nice set. $ 87.50
* S &M I, 478. A popular work which went through numerous editions throughout the 18th century.

3. BAKER, H. K. The Maine Justice; or powers and duties of Justices of the Peace, with the necessary forms, adapted to the revised statutes of this state. Hallowell, Glazier, 1842. 424pp. Full contemporary sheep. $ 45.00
* Major revision of the last Perley edition of 1835. Actually quite uncommon.

4. BEAUSSIRE, EMILE. La liberte dans l'ordre intellectuel et moral: etudes de droit naturel. Paris, Durand et Pedone-Lauriel, 1866. xxiv, 500pp. 8vo. Original Printed wrappers. Fine. First edition. $ 45.00
* Includes discussion on the family and marriage, freedom of the press, intellectual property, etc.

5. (BECCARIA, CESARE.) An essay on crimes and punishments, translated from the Italian; with a commentary, attributed to Mons. De Voltaire, translated from the French. London, J. Almon, 1767. 8vo. xii, 179, xxix, pp. Later marbled boards, expertly rebacked. Internally a fine copy. $250.00
* FIRST EDITION IN ENGLISH. Printing and the Mind of Man 209. (first edition of 1764.) "The success of Beccaria's book was immediate, six editions being published within eighteen months, and it was eventually translated into twenty-two languages. Its principles have been incorporated into the criminal practice of all civilized countries ... (its) impact ... on the reform of criminal justice can hardly be exaggerated."

6. (BENSON, WILLIAM.) A letter to Sir J___B___, by birth a Swede, but naturalized and a M___r of the present P___t: concerning the late Minehead Doctrine which was established by a certain free Parliament of Sweden, to the utter enslaving of that Kingdom. London, Baldwin, 1711. First edition. 8 vo.

6. (Continued)
40pp. Very good copy. Half-title present. $ 45.00
* A sharp attack on Royal Absolutism in the form of the assertion that the king is accountable only to God, as put forth by Sir John Bankes, MP for Minehead. Rothschild 361.

7. BERNARD, MONTAGUE. A lecture on alleged violations of neutrality by England in the present war. London, Ridgway, 1863. 45pp. Disbound. $ 22.50
* Bernard was professor of international law at Oxford, greatly revered in England and America, and a signer of the subsequent Treaty of Washington.

8. BIGELOW, MELVILLE MADISON. Placita Anglo-Normannica: law cases from William I to Richard I, preserved in historical records. London, Sampson, 1879. 328pp. cloth. $ 25.00
* With good introduction. Bigelow was American and collected these sources while preparing his "Leading Cases on Torts."

9. BIRRELL, AUGUSTINE. Seven lectures on the law and history of copyright in books. London, Cassell, 1899. 228pp. Original cloth. First edition. $ 17.50

10. BLACKSTONE, WILLIAM. Commentaries on the laws of England. In four books. The twelfth edition. With the last corrections of the author; additions by Richard Burn, and continued to the present time by John Williams. Dublin, White, Jones and Rice. Contemporary polished calf, red and black leather labels. An exceptionally fine and attractive set. 4 vols 12mo. fold tables. 1974 $225.00
* S & M I., p. 28.

11. BLACKSTONE, WILLIAM. Commentaries on the laws of England, in four books. From the last London edition, with the last corrections of the author, and with the notes and additions by Edward Christian ... Portland Maine., Wait, 1807. 4 volumes, 8vo. Engraved frontispiece portrait of the author in volume one. Folding table of descents in volume two. Contemporary calf, leather labels, rubbed. A good set. $125.00
* S & M I, 29; Marvin p. 123. This is the fifth edition to appear in America.

12. BLACKSTONE, WILLIAM. Commentaries on the laws of England ... with notes selected from the editions of Archbold, (et al.), Barron Field's analysis, and additional notes, and a life of the author, by George Sharswood. Phila., Lippincott, 1875. 2 vols. roy. 8vo., frontis portrait, folding table. Original sheep, leather labels. A very nice set. $ 55.00

13. (BRADLEY, CHARLES S. Comp.) The methods of changing the constitutions of the states, especially that of Rhode Island. 118pp. (BOUND WITH:) THAYER, J. B. Memorandum on the legal effect of opinions given by judges to the executive and the legislature under certain American constitutions. Boston, Mudge, 1885. 118pp. Cloth. Two items. $ 22.50

14. CAINES, GEORGE. Practical forms of the Supreme Court, taken from Tidd's appendix of the forms of the Court of King's Bench, in personal actions, and adapted to the Supreme Court of the State of New York; with the forms in replevin and ejectment: preserving the references in I. Riley and Co's enlarged edition of Tidd's Practice. From the London copy of 1803. N. Y., Alsop, 1808. 526pp. Contemporary calf. Rubbed. $ 45.00
* Marvin p. 169.

15. (CAXTON.) The statutes of Henry VII. In exact facsimile from the very rare original, printed by Caxton in 1489. Edited, with notes and introduction, by John Rae. London, John Camden Hotten, 1869. xxxi, 32, (40 leaves of facsimile)pp. 4to. Later cloth. Bound in is the publishers prospectus and subscription leaflet for the work. $ 75.00
* The earliest printed book of English laws, and the first laws to be made in the ordinary language of their period. Probably Caxton's last effort. The facsimile is done by hand lithography on Holland paper.

16. CHALMERS, GEORGE. Opinions of eminent lawyers on various points of English jurisprudence, chiefly concerning the Colonies, fisheries and Commerce of Great Britain: collected and digested, from the originals in the Board of Trade, and other depositories. (First American Edition) Burlington, Goodrich, 1858. 787pp. New cloth. Uncut, a fine copy. $ 80.00
* Intended by the editor to supply a need created by the rarity of the first and only edition of 1814; he dedicates this edition to both Canadians and United States citizens to whose ongoing disputes the work is relevant. Both editions are extremely scarce. Chalmers was one of the great compilers of this kind of record.

17. CHALMERS, M. D. A digest of the law of bills of exchange, promissory notes and checks, rewritten and adapted to the law as it exists in the United States, by W. E. Benjamin. Chicago, Callaghan. 1881. 328pp. Full contemporary sheep. First edition. $ 25.00

18. CHIPMAN, DANIEL. The life of Hon. Nathaniel Chipman, LL. D., formerly member of United States Senate, and Chief Justice of the State of Vermont, with selections from his miscellaneous papers. Boston, Little Brown, 1846. 402pp. original cloth. $ 47.50

* Included are his addresses and writings; Chipman was one of the most important early expositors of a flexible point of view reconciling common law tradition with the competing realities and needs of a new time and place.

19. CHITTY, JOSEPH. A practical treatise on bills of exchange, checks on bankers, promissory notes, bankers' cash notes and bank notes. The sixth American, from the sixth London edition, with notes of all the recent decisions and statutes, an appendix of precedents, to which are added the cases decided in the Courts of the United States, by a Gentleman of the Philadelphia Bar. Philadelphia, printed for H. C. Carey & L. Lea. 1826. xxxiii, xlvii, 799pp. new cloth. $ 37.50

* Marvin p. 191: "Standard and most complete treatise on the subject in England and America."

20. (CIVIL WAR) GREAT BRITAIN. COURT OF EXCHEQUER. The Attorney General vs. Sillem and others, claiming the Vessel "Alexandra" seized under the Foreign Enlistment Act. Report of the trial ... with an appendix. London, Eyre and Spottiswoode, 1863. 235, lxxxpp. 8vo. Original cloth. $ 40.00

* The Alexandra was fitted out for Confederate use during the American Civil War. Contains incidentally a great deal of information on the involvement of English interests on behalf of the Confederacy.

21. COKE, EDWARD. The first part of the Institutes of the Laws of England: or, a Commentary upon Littleton, ... also three learned tracts of the author ... the eleventh edition, carefully corrected ... to which is added, the Treatise of the Old Tenures of the Laws of England: with two new tables; and many references to the modern law cases, never printed before, ... (London), in the Savoy, Nutt and Gossling, 1719. FOLIO. Contemp. calf, joints cracked, but cords firm. 10pl. 804pp. plus tables and a large folding illustration. Internally a fine copy with an excellent engraved frontispiece portrait of Coke. $125.00

* S & M I, 450. Marvin 204ff. The most important of the Institutes, and one of the great summaries of learning and experience linking medieval and modern times; it remained a force in legal literature into the 19th century.

22. COLLYER, JOHN. Practical treatise on the law of partnership, with notes of American cases; by Willard Phillips and Edward Pickering. Springfield, Merriam, 1834. 728pp. Full contemp. sheep. $ 40.00

* FIRST AMERICAN EDITION. Marvin p. 215; "best English treatise on the law of partnership.

23. COLQHOUN, PATRICK. A treatise on the police of the metropolis; containing a detail of the various crimes and misdemeanors ... and suggesting remedies for their prevention. The sixth edition corrected and considerably enlarged. London, Baldwin for Mawman, 1800. 8vo. 8pl, xvi, 655pp. Contemporary tree calf, spine ornately gilt with leather label. An exceedingly fine and attractive copy. With folding tables. $150.00

* A substantially expanded edition of this very informative classic. It affords an excellent view of society during the upheavals of the early industrial revolution, with sections on the state of the poor, prostitution, transportation to New South Wales, etc. including an up-to-date summary of the statistics of transported felons, and an account of the penal systems being proposed by Jeremy Bentham. Ferguson 305.

24. COODE, GEORGE. On legislative expression; or the language of the written law. Second edition. London, Turpin, 1852. 69pp. wrappers. $ 20.00

25. COOLEY, THOMAS M. A treatise on the law of torts on the wrongs which arise independent of contract. Chicago, Callahan, 1880. cl, 755pp. Full contemp. sheep. Apparently first edition. $ 30.00

26. COOPER, THOMAS. Tracts on medical jurisprudence. Including Farr's Elements ..., Dease's Remarks ..., Male's Epitome ..., and Haslam's Treatise on Insanity. With a preface, notes and digest of the law relating to the insanity and nuisance. To which is added an appendix, containing ... an abstract of a report of the trial of Abraham Kessler, indicted for poisoning his wife ... and a memoir on the chromat of Pot-ash, as a test for detecting arsenic ... Phila., James Webster, Thomas Town, Printer, 1819. 8pl., 456,(1)pp. Contemp. calf, leather label, spine a little rubbed, but an excellent copy. FIRST EDITION. $250.00

* The first book on this subject to be published in America. While the body consists of four standard British treatises, Cooper has added a wealth of American notes, a digest of American law, a report of a critical N. Y. case and his own experiments in arsenic detection. Throughout he stresses the importance of applying modern science in the courtroom. A rare book in commerce.

27. (DAGGE, HENRY.) Considerations on criminal law. London, T. Cadell, 1772. xxxii, 434, errata slip. 8vo. New cloth. Very good copy, with the half title and errata slip. $100.00

* First edition (there was a Dublin reprint and a later London edition.) The author's analysis proceeds along historical and indeed sociological lines. He concludes by opposing sanguinary and excessive punishment and even advances the idea that the criminal ought to make retribution to his victim, a practice which formerly existed and whose loss he considers responsible for the growth of penal barbarism in modern society. The work thus shares in two main currents of the time: enlightened feeling toward humanity, and the beginning of historical and comparative sociology. S & M, I., 361. Marvin p. 249.

28. (DALRYMPLE, DAVID, LORD HAILES.) The additional case of Elisabeth, claiming title and dignity of Countess of Sutherland, by her guardians, wherein the facts and arguments in support of her claim are more fully stated, and the errors in the additional cases exhibited for the other claimants are detected. n.p., ca. 1770. 21, 70, 177pp. large fold. table. 4to. Contemp. 1/4 calf, spine little worn but a very nice copy. $150.00

* An unusual and important written pleading relating to woman's rights in matter of inheritance, obviously printed in a very small edition for the occasion before the bar of the House of Lords. "There is no better specimen of (written) pleadings than the case for the Countess ... which was drawn by Hailes as her guardian after he became judge. It won the cause and is still appealed to by peerage lawyers for the demonstration of descent of the older Scottish titles to and through females. DNB.

29. DANIEL, W. T. S. The history and origin of the law reports, together with a compilation of various documents shewing the progress and result of proceedings taken for their establishment, and the condition of the reports on the 31st December, 1883. London, Clowes, 1884. 359pp. New cloth. Illus., frontis., facsimile. Roy 8 vo. Scarce. $ 45.00

30. DE LOLME, J. L. The constitution of England or, an account of the English government: in which it is compared, both with the Republican form of government, and the other monarchies in Europe. A new edition enlarged. N. Y., Hodge & Campbell, 1792. xvi, (25)-376,(8)pp. 8vo. Contemp. calf. a good copy. $ 40.00

* Evans 24263. First and only American edition of this classic.

31. DRAKE, CHARLES D. A treatise on the law of suits by attachment in the United States. Fourth edition, revised, corrected and enlarged: with an appendix, containing the leading statutory provisions of the several states and territories of the United States in relation to suits by attachment. Boston, Little, Brown, 1873. lix, 699pp. Full contemp. sheep. $ 30.00

32. DUNLAP, JAMES D. A book of forms: containing 600 of the most approved precedents for conveyancing, and for practice in the Courts of the Commonwealth: also, for use in public offices and for men of business generally, adapted to the present Acts and Assembly, with explanatory notes and references, and a glossary of technical law terms. Philadelphia, Biddle, 1845. 360pp. Full contemp. sheep. $ 35.00

* First edition. Entirely on Pennsylvania law.

33. (EDEN, WILLIAM. First Baron Auckland.) Principles of penal law. London, Printed for B. White and T. Cadell, 1771. iv, 300pp. plus errata leaf. Large 8vo. Contemp. 1/4 calf, a fine copy. FIRST EDITION. $250.00

* An enlightened analysis and a plea for reform and restraint. Eden's first book, written upon completion of law studies. His interest in penal reform continued as his career changed towards that of political activist: in 1788 he delivered a notable speech in Parliament advocating hard labor in place of transportation to America. Marvin p. 288: "This justly admired work, from its philosophical character and enlightened humanity, ranks the author with Montesquieu, Beccaria and other advocates of a mild and improved system of legislation. Hoffman, Leg. St."

34. EMERIGON, BALTHAZARD-MARIE. Traite des assurances et des contrats a la grosse. Marseille, Jean Mossy, 1788. Two volumes, 4to. xvi, 686; 680,(4)pp. 19th century half-calf. preliminary and final leaves stained, otherwise a good copy. $150.00

* One of the great and influential classics on insurance law. "Of all the French writers upon commercial law, E. holds the first rank. His writings and his reputation are not confined to France alone, for the jurists of England and the United States have equally derived assistance from his labors ... Chancellor Kent ... remarks that his Treatise 'very far surpasses all preceeding works ...' " Marvin p. 293.

35. FARRAR, TIMOTHY. Report of the case of the Trustees of Dartmouth College against William H. Woodward. Argued and determined in the Superior Court of Judicature of the State of New Hampshire, Nov. 1817 and on error in the Supreme Court of the United States, Feb. 1819.

35. (Continued) Portsmouth, N. H. Foster, (1819). 2pl, 406pp. 8vo. Original boards, paper label. Minor wear to ends of spine, but a fine copy in original state. $ 75.00

* Marvin p. 303. A landmark case elucidating the contract clause of the Constitution and the rights of corporations.

36. FORSYTH, WILLIAM. History of Trial by Jury. New edition, prepared by James Appleton Morgan. N. Y., Cockcroft, 1875. cl. $ 45.00

* First published in England in 1852, this is the first full scale account of the rise and development of the jury system; the American edition adds a few notes and makes a few corrections to American references. Fine copy.

37. FOULKE, WILLIAM PARKER. Remarks on cellular separation. Read by appointment of the American Association for the Improvement of Penal Institutions, at the annual meeting in N. Y. ... 1860. Phila., 1861. 112pp. Orig. prtd. wrps. $ 50.00

* Foulke was for sixteen years a leading participant in the Pennsylvania Prison Society. "In 1860 he presented what may be considered one of the best and most logical defenses of the separate system ever penned. It was read by appointment before the American Association (etc) ..." Teeters, They were in prison: a history of the Pennsylvania Prison Society, 1937. p. 286.

38. FREEMAN, SAMUEL. The probate directory; or, an assistant to probate courts, executors, administrators, and guardians, being the laws of ... Massachusetts ... to which are added a variety of forms ... third edition, enlarged and improved. Boston, Thomas and Andrews, 1812. 264pp. (BOUND WITH:) An appendix to the third and last edition of the Probate Directory ... Boston, 1818. 65,(3)pp. Contemp. calf. 12mo. $ 37.50

* Marvin, p324. (2nd edition) Shaw-Shoemaker 25457 & 44079 (for the appendix). Best and final edition. Two separately published works.

39. FREEMAN, SAMUEL. The town officer: or the power and duty of selectment ... and other town officers as contained in the laws of the Commonwealth of Massachusetts, with a variety of forms ... the third edition, corrected, improved and greatly enlarged. Boston, I. Thomas and E. T. Andrews, 1794. 240pp. 12 mo. Cont. calf. $ 37.50

* The new statutes include those relating to small pox, the poor, the militia, and appointment of grand jurors. Evans 27016.

40. GARDNER, DANIEL. A treatise on representative government, and its probable durability: prepared by appointment and read before the Phi Beta Kappa Society of New York, at Union College, in January, 1837. Troy, Gates, 1837. 23pp. wrps. $ 15.00

* Cf. Sabin 26640f for others of his works on international and constitutional law. This title not in Sabin.

41. GAZZAM, AUDLEY W. Gazzam's treatise on the Bankrupt Law for business men, containing all the recent ammendments to the Bankrupt Act, and copious notes covering the latest English and American decisions. N. Y., Deller, 1870. 328pp. cloth. $ 22.50

42. (GILBERT, GEOFFREY). The law of evidence. The second edition, corrected; and many new references added, with a complete table to the whole. In the Savoy, Printed by Catherine Lintot, 1760. 289, 74pp. Full contemp. calf. A very nice copy. $ 85.00

* S & M I, 379. A popular work which continued to be republished throughout the rest of the century.

43. GOULD, JAMES. A treatise on the principles of pleading, in civil actions. Second edition, revised and corrected by the author. N. Y., Collins, 1836. 536pp. Full contemp. sheep. $ 35.00

* Marvin p. 342. "a classic of the highest order."

44. GREENLEAF, SIMON. Three ALS's to Thomas J. Wharton of Philadelphia, Nov. 2, June 14, and Dec. 8, 1842, all 4to. each 1 page. All three deal with Greenleaf's recommendation of English treatises worthy of American republication in a series undertaken by Wharton and known as the Law Library. Greenleaf especially recommends treatises by H. H. Joy, William Wills, and James Wigram. He reminds Wharton of his belief that the great subscription project should be "a repository of the lesser (not the greater) treatises in the law." Greenleaf was, with Story, the great architect of legal education as developed at the Harvard Law School. Wharton occupied a most prominent position in Pennsylvania legal profession and was, of course, one of the editors of the ambitious "Law Library"; see Marvin, p. 449 for comment on this series. $125.00

45. GUTHRIE, WILLIAM D. Lectures on the Fourteenth Article of Amendment to the Constitution of the United States delivered before the Dwight Alumni Association, New York, April-May, 1898. Boston, Little, Brown, 1898. 265pp. Cloth. Fine. $ 22.50

46. HEARD, FRANKLIN FISKE. A concise treatise on the principles of equity pleading, with precedents. Boston, Soule, 1882. 217pp Full Contemp. sheep. FIRST EDITION. $ 30.00

47. HICKMAN, WILLIAM. A treatise on the law and practice of Naval Courts-Martial. London, Murray, 1851. 319pp. cloth. $ 37.50

* S & M, III, 105.

48. HILLIARD, FRANCIS. The law of taxation. Boston, Little, Brown, 1875. 636pp. Full contemp. sheep. FIRST EDITION. $ 35.00

49. HOFFMAN, MURRAY. The office and duties of masters in chancery and practice in the master's office. With an appendix of precedents. N. Y., Gould and Banks, 1824. 437,(2)pp. new cloth. FIRST EDITION. $ 37.50

* Marvin p. 390. Hoffman was one of the masters in the N. Y. court.

50. HONE, WILLIAM. The first (second-third) trial of William Hone ... for publishing a parody on the late John Wilke's Catechism of a ministerial member, (The Political Litany, and the Sinecurist's Creed, respectively). London, by and for Hone, 1818. 14th, 13th, and 10th editions, respectively. $ 27.50

* McCoy H. 336 etc.

51. HOWLAND, J. D., et. al. A manual for executors, administrators, and guardians; with forms, adapted to the Statutes of Indiana. Indianapolis, Merrill, 1862. 278pp. Full Contemp sheep. Nice copy. First Edition. Very uncommon. $ 45.00

52. HUGHES, DAVID. A treatise on the law relating to insurance; in threeparts, viz. 1-of Marine Insurance, 11- of Insurance on Lives, 111- of Insurance Against Fire. First American edition, with notes and references to American Decisions. N Y., Halsted, 1833. xxxii, 471pp. Full contemp. sheep. $ 47.50

* Marvin p. 403; London edition was 1828.

53. HURLBUT, E. P. Essays on human rights and their political guarantees. With notes by George Combe. N. Y., 1852. Fowler and Wells, Publishers. 249pp. Orig. cl. Fine. $ 30.00

* A rather reform -minded work, with a large chapter on woman, defending their campaigns for change, on debtors, on copyright law., etc. Actually an uncommon work, though first published in 1845. (Horace Greeley was the original publisher.)

54. HUTH, ALFRED HENRY. The marriage of near kin: considered with respect to the laws of Nations, the results of experience, and teachings of biology. London, Churchill, 1875. 359pp. $ 27.50

55. INDERWICK, F. A. The King's Peace: a historical sketch of the English Law Courts, with 15 illustrations and one map. London, Swan Sonnenschein, 1895. 254pp. orig. cl. $ 15.00

56. (IOWA) General laws of the state of Iowa relating to the duties of the board of supervisors and township officers, including civil and criminal procedure in justices' courts. Printed by authority of the Eighth General Assembly ... Des Moines, John Teesdale, 1860. viii, 456pp. 8vo. Orig. 1/4 calf., spine a little frayed, otherwise an excellent copy. First edition. $ 90.00

* Copy belonging to the township assessor, Boone Township. Issued on the occasion of a major transformation in the assignment of jurisdiction.

57. (IOWA) BRADFORD, JOHN M. The Iowa form book, or book of practical forms, containing precedents and forms for ordinary business dealings and transactions, with statements of the law; adapted and designed for the use of merchants, mechanics, farmers, business men, and especially Justices of the Peace. Davenport, House of Luse, Lane Co. 1857. 335pp. Orig. prtd. brds. A very nice copy. $100.00

* NUC records two copies only, both in Iowa. Rare. Moffit #266.

58. ITO, COUNT HIROBUMI Commentaries on the Constitution of the Empire of Japan. Translated by Miyoji Ito. Tokyo, Igirisu-Horitsu Gakko, 1889. xiii, 259pp. Orig. cl. Fine. Published by the English Law College in Japan. $ 37.50

59. JACOB, GILES The complete court-keeper: or, land-steward's assistant: containing the nature of courts leet and courts baron (etc.) ... seventh edition, with large additions and ammendments to the present time. London, for Rivington, etc., 1781. 8 vo. 4 pl.; 538pp. plus index. New cloth. $ 50.00

59. (Continued)
* S & M I, 400, There were 8 editions from 1713-1819 of this most standard work for rural administration of justice.

60. JACOBS, VICTOR. Etude sur les assurances maritimes et les avaries faite en vue du Congres de Droit commercial d'Anvers. Bruxelles, 1885, 83pp. Wrps. $ 27.50

61. JONES, WILLIAM. An essay on the law of bailments. From the Press of Samuel Etheridge, for John West, Boston, 1796. 178,(1)pp. 12mo. Cont. calf. $ 50.00

* First American Edition. Evans 30646.

62. (KENT, JAMES) A lecture introductory to a course of law lectures in Columbia College, delivered Feb. 2, 1824. Published at the request of the trustees of the college. N. Y., Clayton, 1824. 23pp. new cl. $ 45.00

* Not in Marvin. The NUC locates 8 copies.

63. LEWIS, FRANCIS A. Law relating to stocks, bonds, and other securities, in the United States. Philadelphia, Rees, 1881. 196pp. orig. cl. $ 27.50

* According to the author's preface the first systemmatic treatise on the stock exchange in America. First trade edition (privately printed with fewer chapters the previous year.

64. LINDLEY, SIR NATHANIEL, et. al. A treatise on the Law of Partnership. Fifth edition with a supplement consisting of the Partnership Act, 1890, with notes, and an introduction and notes on the Law of Scotland by J. Campbell Lorimer. London, Sweet, 1891. 844, 155pp. cl. $ 25.00

* S & M, III, 136.

65. McDONALD, W. J. (Compiler) Constitution of the United States of America, ... to which are added the rules of the Senate, the joint rules of the two houses ... Printed for the use of the Senate. Wash., GPO, 1868. 356pp. Contemp. full red mor. Fine Copy. $ 40.00

* Contains the newly adopted rules for proceedings in impeachment.

66. MACLAREN, J. J. Bills, notes and chequees. The bills of exchange act, 1890, Canada, and amending acts, with notes and illustrations from Canadian, English and American decisions, and references to ancient and modern French Law. Second edition. Toronto, Carswell, 1896. 546pp. 1/2 calf, fine copy. $ 30.00

67. McCLELLAND, MILO A., M.D. Civil malpractice: a treatise on surgical jurisprudence, with chapters on skill in diagnosis and treatment, prognosis in fractures, and on

67. (Continued)
neglegence. N. Y., Hurd & Houghton, 1877. 554pp. First Edition. $ 35.00

68. McKELVEY, JOHN JAY. Principles of common-law pleading: a brief explanation of the different forms of common-law actions, and a summary of the most important principles of pleading therein, with illustrations taken from the cases. N. Y., Baker, 1894. 193pp. $ 15.00

69. McKENZIE, GEORGE. Pleadings, in some remarkable cases, before the Supreme Courts of Scotland, since the year, 1661. To which the decisions are subjoined. Edinburgh, Printed by George Swinton, James Glen, and Thomas Brown: 1672. 4to. 4 pl., 232,(4)pp with the preliminary and final blanks. Contemp. blind calf, extremities moderately worn, lower edge trimmed a bit close, just touching two digits of the imprint date; no other text affected. A very good copy in contemporary binding. $250.00

* A very interesting collection of cases including the determination of sanity, inheritance, treason, witchcraft, wife-beating, liabilities of minors, prize law, right to trade with foreigners, as well as an essay on proper eloquence before the bar and a translation of an essay on pleading out of the French. MacKenzie's career (see DNB for a lengthy account) combined cultivation of the law and its restraints (he opposed torture of witches) with often brutal excess as King's advocate against the covenanters. Wing M191. First edition.

70. (MAINE) The powers and duties of the Town Officer, as contained in the Statutes of Maine, with forms adapted thereto, including also the powers and duties of Plantation & Parish Officers, and other useful matter. Third edition, improved. Hallowell, Glazier, 1833. 357pp. Full contemp. calf. Fine. $ 30.00

* Bruntjen 19872.

71. (MAINE) SMITH, FRANCIS O. J. Reports of decisions in the Circuit Courts Martial, of questions arising on trials in said courts. ... to which is added an appendix of practical forms of proceedings ... Portland, Todd and Holden, 1831. 113pp. 8vo. Orig. 1/4 calf. $ 45.00

* According to the author's preface, this is the "first of the kind ever published under any government ..." Marvin p. 651. American Imprints 5105, 9207.

72. MAINE, HENRY SUMNER. Popular Government, four essays, London, Murray, 1885. 261pp. Original cloth. spine a little darkened, but a very nice copy. FIRST EDITION. $ 25.00

73. MAINE, HENRY SUMNER. Village-Communities in the East and West. Six lectures delivered at Oxford. Third edition, to which are added other lectures addresses, and essays. London, Murray, 1876. 413pp. Orig. cl. $ 25.00

* Best edition.

74. MANSFIELD, EDWARD D. The legal rights, liabilities and duties of women; with an introductory history of their legal condition in the Hebrew, Roman and Feudal Civil Systems, including the law of marriage and divorce, the social relations of husband and wife, parent and child, of guardian and ward, and of employer and employed. First Edition. Salem, Jewett, 1845. 369pp. orig. cl. $ 37.50

* One of the earliest popular expositions of woman's legal status in America.

75. MARSHALL, (JOHN). Opinion of the Supreme Court of the United States, at January term, 1832, delivered by Mr. Chief Justice Marshall, together with the opinion of Mr. Justice McLean, in the case of Samuel A.Worcester, plaintiff in error, versus the State of Georgia. With a statement of the case extracted from the records of the Supreme Court ... Washington, Gales & Seaton, 1832. 39pp. Disbound. A good copy. $ 75.00

* A landmark case in which Andrew Jackson scorned Marshall's decision favoring the Federal status of the Cherokee Indians at the expense of the principle of States' Rights. Bruntjen, Am. Imprints 16104.

76. MARSHALL, THOMAS F. Speeches and writings of Hon. Thomas F. Marshall, edited by W. L. Barre. Cincinnati, Applegate, 1858. 462pp. Illus., frontis. New cloth. $ 25.00

* Kentucky lawyer and legislator, and nephew of John Marshall.

77. (MASSACHUSETTS, COLONY. LAWS.) The charters and general laws of the colony and province of Massachusetts Bay. Carefully collected from the publick records and ancient printed books. To which is added an appendix, tending to explain the spirit, progress and history of the jurisprudence of the state; especially in a moral and political view. Published by order of the General Court. Boston, Wait, 1814. vii, 830,(30)pp. incl. index. 8vo. Contemp. tooled calf, fine. $ 65.00

* The Committee appointed to make this collection consisted of Nathan Dane, William Prescott and Joseph Story; they were to report also on those laws still in effect which ought to be repealed.

78. MERCHANTS' UNION LAW COMPANY. N. Y. Second monthly report of the correspondents and members ... comprising the name and residence of an efficient and reliable practising lawyer for every county of the U.S. ... N. Y., 1866. 79pp. wrps. $ 17.50
* Covers all states and territories, east and west. Rare.

79. MITFORD, EARDLEY. The law of wills, codicils, and revocations. With ... a clear and distinct account of the law's disposal of the estates of those who die intestate ... the second edition with additions. London, Stratford, 1801. 110pp. Disbound. (Index incomplete.) $ 17.50

80. MOLLOY, CHARLES. De jure maritimo et navali: or, a treatise of affairs maritime and of commerce. In three books. The fourth edition. London, Bellinger and Walthoe, 1688. 12pl,433,(13)pp. 8vo. with fine double engraved frontispiece. Contemp. panelled calf, very expertly rebacked. A very nice copy. With the inscription "H. Walrond 1692" on the front end-paper, quite likely Henry Walrond, governor of Barbados (see DAB under Humphrey Walrond.) $200.00
* An early and attractive edition of a classic not superceded until the 19th century. With sections on slavery, insurance, Jews, planters. With a very attractive double-page frontis of maritime commerce. Sabin 49924; Wing 2398.

81. MURRAY, J. B. C. The history of usury from the earliest period to the present time together with a brief statement ... concerning the conflict of laws ... and an examination into ... their effect upon commerce. Phila., Lippincott, 1866. 158pp. Orig. cl., fine. First edition. $ 55.00
* State by state coverage as well as numerous citations. 4pp. list of subscribers.

82. NELSON, HORACE. Selected cases, statutes and orders illustrative of the principles of private international law as administered in England, with a commentary by ... London, Stevens, 1889. 483pp. Contemp. 1/2 mor. fine. First edition. $ 37.50

83. NEW MEXICO. TERRITORY. Actas de la asamblea legislativa ... sesion trigesima primera. Santa Fe, 1895. 145pp. orig. prtd. wrps. $ 25.00

84. (NEW YORK. PROVINCE.) Laws of New York from the Year 1691, to 1773 inclusive. Published according to an Act of the General Assembly. New York, Printed by Hugh Gaine ... 1774. Folio. Two volumes in one. iv, 835pp. Each volume with separate title page, ornamental em-

84. (Continued)
blems on titles. Contemporary calf, leather label; front cover detached. Internally about fine. $250.00
* Gaine was the largest and most successful publisher-printer in colonial New York. This is a meticulous and historically important compilation deliberately including both private and repealed acts in order to show the development of the colony and the foundation of its courts of jurisdiction, and is supplied at the conclusion with an elaborate subject index. Evans 13467.

85. O'CONOR, CHARLES. Commemoration of the one hundredth anniversary of the adoption of the Constitution of the State of New York. Address by Charles O'Conor delivered before the New York Historical Society at the Academy of Music, May 8th, 1877. N. Y. Randolph, 1877. 40pp. Neatly removed. $15.00

86. OLIVER, BENJAMIN, L. Practical conveyancing; a selection of forms of general utility, with notes interspersed, fourth ed. corrected and enlarged, by Peter Oliver. Hallowell, Glazier, 1845. 622pp. Full contemp. sheep. Very fine copy. $ 35.00
* Marvin p. 547. "best American manual on conveyancing in use."

87. PAGANO, FRANCESCO MARIA Principi del codice penale e considerazioni sul processo criminale. Lugano, Ruggia, 1832. 252pp. Orig. front wrp. only. uncut. First edition. $ 25.00
* Third appearance of this posthumous work. Pagano was an Italian jurist devoted to the principles of enlightened reform.

88. PARKER, EDWARD G. Reminiscences of Rufus Choate, the great American advocate. N. Y., Mason, 1860. 522pp. Illus., frontis, orig. embossed cl. fine. $ 27.50

89. A MANUAL FOR THE WHISKEY REBELLION
PARKER, JAMES. The conductor generalis: or, the office, duty and authority of justices of the peace, ... compiled chiefly from Burn's justice ... by James Parker, late one of the Justices of the Peace for Middlesex County, in New Jersey; and now revised and adapted to the United States of America. By a Gentleman of the Law ... to which are added, the excise and militia laws of the U.S.; and the Acts called the Ten Pound Act of the States of Pennsylvania and New York. Phila., Campbell, 1792. xv,464pp. 8vo. Contemp. calf, rubbed. A good copy. $150.00
* Evans 24661. The second appearance of this classic work in its adaptation to the new union. An extremely interesting edition con-

89. (Continued)
taining the revenue laws and the means of their enforcement which led soon to the Whiskey Rebellion extending from western Pennsylvania to Georgia. Later editions of course ommitted this material.

90. PARSONS, THEOPHILUS. Laws of business for all the States of the Union, and the Dominion of Canada. With forms and directions for all transactions. Revised and enlarged. Hartford, Scranton, 1877. 693pp. $ 37.50
* This appears to be the first edition to include Canada.

91. PARSONS, THEOPHILUS. Laws of business for all the States and Territories of the Union, and the Dominion of Canada... New revised edition. Hartford, Scranton, 1889. 864pp. Full contemp. sheep. $ 25.00

92. PARSONS, THEOPHILUS. Memoir of Theophilus Parsons, Chief Justice of the Supreme Judical Court of Massachusetts, with notices of some of his contemporaries, by his son. Boston, Ticknor, 1859. 476pp. Frontis. Cl. Fine. $ 27.50
* "Probably no man except Story did more to carry on the common law and restate it in intelligible form to suit American needs." DAB

93. PASSY, FREDERIC et al. De la Propriete intellectuelle: etudes par Mm. Passy, Victor Modeste et P. Paillottet, avec une preface par M. Jules Simon. Paris, Dentu, 1859. xxiv, 347pp. 8vo. Orig. prtd. wrps. Partly unopened. $ 30.00
* Reform-oriented studies on patent and property law.

94. (PHILADELPHIA. FARMERS' AND MECHANICS' BANK.) The charter and by-laws of the ... to which are added the several acts of Assembly relative to banks ... Phila., Lippincott, 1849. 187pp. calf, covers worn, contents very good. $ 25.00

95. POWELL, JOHN JOSEPH. Essay upon the law of contracts and agreements. Dublin, Byrne, 1796. 2 vols, in 1. Thick 8vo. Orig. calf, front cover detached, contents very good. $ 45.00
* Marvin p. 582. First edition was 1790.

96. POWELL, JOHN JOSEPH. An essay upon the learning of devises, from their inception by writing, to their consummation by the death of the devisor. Third American from the last London edition, improved by a digested index of American decisions from reports of the several states. Exeter, N. H., Lamson, 1822. 523,xxvi pp. Full contemp. sheep. $ 37.50
* Marvin p. 582, a laudatory note.

97. PRIESTLEY, JOSEPH. An Essay on the First Principles of Government and on the Nature of Political and Civil Liberty. London, 1835. 8vo. 27pp. New wrappers. $ 15.00
* Published as part of the reform effort by the Society for the Diffusion of Moral and Political Knowledge amongst the People.

98. QUEBEC. LAWS, STATUTES. Collection de plusiers des actes et ordonnances les plus utiles en force dans le Bas Canada concernant la loi criminelle et les devoirs des magistrats. Publie par Autoritee. Quebec, Derbishire & Desbarats, 1854. New cl. $ 65.00
* These laws were selected for use by justices of the peace especially in rural areas.

99. (QUEBEC. PROVINCE. LAWS, STATUTES.) Code civil du Bas Canada ... Civil Code of Lower Canada from the ammended roll deposited in the office of the Clerk of the Legislative Council 1865. Ottawa, Malcolm Cameron, 1866. 747pp. 1/4 sheep. indexed. 8vo. Bilingual. $ 50.00
* TPL 4472. First edition of this code.

100. RAM, JAMES. A treatise on facts as subjects of inquiry by a jury. Second American edition by John Townsend with an appendix, containing David Paul Brown's golden rules for the examination of a witness; Cox's advice ... N. Y., Baker, 1870. 407pp. Full contemp. sheep. $ 25.00

101. RAWLE, WILLIAM HENRY. Some contrasts in the growth of Pennsylvania and English law. A lecture delivered before the students of the law department of the University of Pennsylvania, October 3, 1881, by ... Philadelphia, Republican State Committee. 32pp. Wrps. $ 17.50

102. REEVES, JOHN. History of the English law from the time of the Saxons, to the end of the reign of Philip and Mary. The second edition. In four volumes. London, Brooke, 1787. 4 vols. 8vo. Contemp. calf, leather labels. A very nice set. $100.00
* S & M, I, 21. "A remarkable book, before its time."

REFORM TRACTS. Four caustic attacks published by "The Royal Watchman" under two series titles: Peep into the Focus of Corruption and Peep into Westminster Hall, advertised for sale at "The Watchman's Legal Libel Warehouse, 51 Swallow St." Concerned with judicial corruption, iniquities of the legal system, political censorship, inequality of wealth and legislation against the interests of the poor.
* Rare. Not in McCoy, Goldsmiths' or Kress Catalogues. Not in Halkett and Laing, or the NUC. Harvard Law School records among its holdings a single number not present here and attributes it to a Samuel Keen (e.). No trace of these found in the BM catalogue.

103a. The prescription; or, a radical cure for rascality without hanging, in a letter addressed to the Prince Regent, being the first number of an original work, entitled, A Peep into the Focus of Corruption; or, the battle between the Genuine and Spurious Law of Libels. London, J. MacDonald for the author,(1812). $ 35.00

103b. The third number of an original work, entitled, a peep into the focus of corruption: containing the second letter to the Prince Regent; showing the ways and means of protecting the honest man, ... London, G. Hayden, 1812. 40pp. Neatly dsbd. $ 35.00
* Argues for the right of tenant s to pay rent in bank notes.

103c. The second number of the Peep into Westminster Hall; being the Barons allarmed, or the position proved, that libel is lawful when it is for the public good; being a motion in the Court of Exchequer Jan. 25, 1812, to set aside a nonsuit which was founded on a mistake. To which is added some rook-tricks to ruin honest men... By the Royal Watchman, London, (1812) 48pp. Neatly dsbd. $ 35.00

103d. The fifth number of the Peep into Westminster Hall; or the tricks, quibbles, & juggles of law and the lawyers detected & exposed. Addressed to the Court of Common Pleas, being a Branch of the Check Knave System, or Poor Man's Parliament. By the Royal Watchman. London, (1812). 64pp. Neatly dsbd. $ 35.00

104. RICHECOUR, A. De. Essai sur l' histoire et la legislation des formes requises pour la validite du mariage. Paris, Dounoil 1856. 135(5)pp. Orig. wrps. $ 27.50
* No copy found in the NUC.

105. RICHMOND, WELLINGTON H. Richmond's book of legal forms and law manual, for the legal transaction of business ... second edition, revised and enlarged. Toronto, Lovell and Gibson for Richmond, 1854. xvi, 600pp. 8vo. Contemp. Sheet, near fine. $ 75.00
* The author did the first form book for this province, presumably the first edition of the work offered here (1850). This edition is, according to the author's preface, three times the size and scope of the first, and is in any case the best "early" work of its kind we have come across in commerce. NUC locates only three American holdings. TPL 3471.

106. (ROBERTSON, JAMES) An account of the trial of Thomas Muir, ... before the High Court of Justiciary at Edinburgh ... for sedition. N. Y., Samuel Campbell, 1794. 4, viii, 148, viiipp. with frontis portrait (name excised from frontis without affecting image.) New wrappers. $ 50.00
* Classic account of the notorious sedition trial in which Muir and others were sentenced to transportation; Muir became the chief symbol of the "Scottish martyrs". In fact Muir's case excited sympathy in the United States and he was rescued from Sydney by an American ship sent out from New York. This edition combines the main pagination of the first with the prefatory and appendix material of the second American edition (Evans 27633-34). Ferguson 190.

107. SAMPSON, WILLIAM. An anniversary discourse delivered before the Historical Society of New-York, on Saturday, December 6, 1823, showing the origin, progress, antiquities, curiosities, and nature of the Common Law. N. Y., Bliss, 1824. 68pp. Neatly disbound. Foxed. $ 22.50

108. (SEDITION TRIALS) (Robertson, James) Account of the trial of Thomas Muir ... before the High Court of Justiciary at Edinburgh ... Aug. 1793. for sedition. N. Y., Sam. Campbell, 1794. 4, viii, 148pp. engr. frontis. port. (WITH) RAMSEY, MR. The trial of Joseph Gerrald ... at Edinburgh ... March 1794. for Sedition. N. Y., Sam. Campbell, 1794. 207pp. Engr. frontis. port. (WITH) RAMSEY, MR. The Trial of Maurice Margarot ... at Edinburgh ... January 1794 on an indictment for seditious practices. London, printed, -New York: re-printed, by James Carey (1794). 166pp. Engr. frontis port. (WITH) Report of the Trial of Archibald Hamilton Rowan ... for the distribution of a libel ... N. Y., re-printed by Tiebout & O'Brien 1794. 152, 1pp. Engr. frontis port. 4 works bound together in contemp. calf. $125.00
* First American editions (except no. 3) of these sedition trials all involving the movement for parliamentary reform and universal suffrage. Muir, Gerrald and Margarot were

108. (Continued)
transported to Australia and became the symbolic "Scottish martyrs;" Rowan, a leader of the United Irishmen, escaped to America where for a time he set up in Delaware as a calico printer. There was a good deal of American interest and sympathy for these men; it was a New York vessel which set out and rescued Muir from Sydney. Evans 27633; 27591; 27594; 27643. Ferguson 190; 179; 188.

109. SEEBOHM, FREDERIC. The English Village Community. Examined in its relations to the manorial and tribal systems, and to the common or open field system of husbandry; an essay in economic history. London, Longmans, 1890. 464pp. Illus., frontis map, also 13 maps and plates. Fourth ed. cl. $ 15.00

110. SERGEANT, THOMAS. A treatise upon the law of Pennsylvania relative to the proceeding by foreign attachment, with the acts of assembly now in force in Pennsylvania on the subject of Foreign and Domestic Attachments. Phila., Farrand, 1811. 331pp. Full contemp. sheep. First edition. $ 50.00
* Marvin p. 638.

111. SHAW, JOSEPH. The practical justice of the peace and parish and ward-officer ... the sixth edition, corrected and very much enlarged ... (London) Lintot, 1756. Two volumes, large thick 8vo. Contemp. blind calf, leather labels, very nice set. $100.00
* This edition brought up to the statutes of the most recent session of Parliament, with a table added for the first time. This is the final edition of the work (1st was 1728). S & M, I, 231.

112. SHEPPARD, WILLIAM. The president of presidents. Or, One general president for common assurances by deeds: wherein there is contained an extract or abridgement of all the readings and presidents thereof extant. Of singular use and profit to all men. London, Henry Hills for Humphrey Tuckey, 1655. 4to. 3 pl., 361, (12)pp. Contemp. blind calf, spine quite worn; internally light browning, but a decent copy. $150.00
* First edition of a treatise which endured through various editions into the 1820's. Marvin p. 642. S & M, I, 486. Wing S3209.

113. SMITH, ELEAZER. Nine years among the convicts: or prison reminiscences. Boston, Magee, 1856. 287pp. $ 15.00
* Author was a prison chaplain.

114. SMITH, JOHN WILLIAM. A selection of leading cases, on various branches of the law; with notes, by ... Front the third English edition, by Henry Singer Keating and James Shaw Willes. Fourth American edition, with additional notes, and references to American decisions by J. L. Clark Hare, and H. B. Wallace. In two vols. Phila., Johnson, 1852. 840, 627pp. Full Contemp. sheep. $ 40.00

115. SOMERS, (LORD JOHN). The judgement of whole kingdoms and nations, concerning the rights, power and prerogatives of kings, and the rights, powers and prerogatives of the people: shewing the nature of government in general ... an account of the British government; and the rights and privileges of the people in the time of the Saxons ... London, reprinted and sold by J. Williams, ... 1771. 168pp. neatly disbound, very good copy. $ 40.00
* A highly popular 18th century catechism of limited monarchy, right of resistance to tyranny, etc. The work was reprinted in the American colonies on the eve of the Revolution. S & M, I, 108.

116. STEPHEN, JAMES FITZJAMES. A history of the criminal law of England. In three volumes. London, Macmillan, 1883. Original publisher's brick-red cloth, spines lettered in gilt. FIRST EDITION, an exceptionally fine set. $ 60.00

117. STORY, JOSEPH. Commentaries on the law of bailments, with illustrations from the civil and the foreign law. Fifth edition, revised, corrected and enlarged. Boston, Little, Brown, 1851. xlvi, 667pp. Full contemp. sheep. $ 45.00
* Includes additions to the law occuring since the appearance of the 4th edition (1846); this edition was prepared apparently by William W. Story and contains a prefatory remark by Charles Sumner.

118. STORY, JOSEPH. A discourse pronounced before the Phi Beta Kappa Society, at the anniversary celebration, on the thirty-first day of August, 1826. Boston, Hilliard, 1826. 58pp. Orig. prtd. wrps. uncut, fine. Deals with humanistic learning in general and its current status in America. $ 20.00

119. SWAN, JOSEPH R. A manual for executors and administrators, in the settlement of the estates of deceased persons, with practical forms, etc. Columbus, Ohio, Whiting, 1843. 332pp. Full contemp. sheep. Very good copy. $ 50.00
* First edition. Marvin 1.680.

121. SWAN, JOSEPH R. A treatise on the law relating to the powers and duties of Justices of the Peace, and Constables, in the State of Ohio: with practical forms, &c. Third edition, revised and corrected. Columbus, Whiting, 1841. 602pp. Full contemp. sheep. Very good copy. Roy. 8vo. $ 55.00
* Revised to include the statutes of the most recent session of the legislature. Tipped in the front is a 5pp. publisher's advertisement for Swan's other works. Marvin p. 679.

"THE FIRST AMERICAN LAW TEXT"

122. SWIFT, ZEPHANIAH. A system of the laws of the State of Connecticut. In six books. Windham, John Byrne, for the author, 1795-96. In two volumes. 8vo. 452;479(12)pp, incl. list of subscribers. Folding table of descents in vol. I. A very good set in mixed contemporary binding. FIRST EDITION. $150.00
* "The first American law text; it displayed a thoughtful philosophy of government as well as a thorough presentation of the constitutional and working government of the State." DAB. It also defined the role of the common law in American society in a pragmatic and flexible way, reconciling tradition with the necessary innovation of a new nation in a new time. See Horwitz, Transformation of American Law, 1780-1860, p. 25-26. Evans 29600 & 31260. Marvin p. 651.

123. TABARAUD, (MATHIEU) Principes sur la distinction du contrat et du sacrament de mariage, sur le pouvoir d'etablir des empechements dirimants et d'en dispenser ... Paris, Librarie de Fortic, 1825. xv, 506pp. Orig. prtd. wrps. fine. $ 45.00
* NUC records only the Harvard Law School copy in America.

124. TAYLOR, JOHN. An inquiry into the principles and policy of the government of the United States. ... By John Taylor, of Caroline County, Virginia. Fredericksburg, Green and Cady, 1814. 8vo. viii, 656, (1)pp. Contemp. tree calf, leather label, hinges cracked but firm, light wear to extremities of binding; a very good copy. FIRST EDITION $250.00
* "First conceived in 1794 as an answer to John Adams' Defense of the Constitution ... 'It deserves to rank among the two or three really historic contributions to political science which have been produced in the United States.' (Beard) ... one of America's greatest disciples and philosophers of agrarian liberalism ... local democracy ... and states rights." Dictionary of American Biography.

125. TIFFANY, ALEXANDER R. A treatise on the powers and duties of Justices of the Peace in the State of Michigan, under chapter ninety-three of the revised statutes: with practical forms. Adrian, Ingals, 1850. 341pp. Full contemp. sheep. A very nice copy. $100.00
* The rare first edition of the standard guide for Michigan which reached a tenth edition in 1905. NUC records only the Library of Congress copy of the edition offered here. A very uncommon inprint as well.

126. TUCKER, GEORGE. The life of Thomas Jefferson, ... with parts of his correspondence never before published, and notices of his opinions on questions of civil government, national policy and constitutional law. In two volumes. Phila., Carey, Lea & Blanchard, 1837. Two volumes, 8vo. Frontis portrait. Orig. publisher's cloth, printed paper labels, spines a bit faded, but an excellent set. FIRST EDITION. $ 75.00
* A very important account, "supplementing extensive research ... by many conferences with Madison." DAB. Tucker was the first professor of political economy at the Univ. of Virginia, and nominally a faithful agrarian democrat, but as Dorfman notes, he was really a Federalist in disguise: "in his urbane manner he took J. to task for his criticism of cities, debt, tariff ... and especially national bank." II, 881.

127. TYLER, SAMUEL. A commentary on the law of partnership, with an appendix of forms. Wash., D. C., Morrison, 1877. 159pp. Full contemp. sheep. Covers detached. $ 17.50

128. ULMAN, CHARLES H. Lawyers' record and official register of the United States: containing federal officers ... state, county, and city officials; judiciary, with jurisdiction and time of holding courts; ... and a record of practising lawyers throughout the U. S. Together with a convenient and comprehensive digest of the laws of several states ... N. Y., Barnes, 1872 1143pp. Full contemp. sheep. Very good copy. $ 45.00
* First of this series, it includes all western states and territories.

129. (UNITED STATES. LAWS. FIRST CONGRESS 1789-1791). Acts passed at a Congress of the United States of America, begun and held at the city of New York ... 1789 ... Being the acts passed at the first (- Third) sessions of the First Congress ... Hartford, reprinted and sold by Hudson and Goodwin, 1791. 5pl., (3)-327pp. 8vo. Cont. calf, rubbed; marginal staining, missing front free end paper. $ 75.00
* Evans 46319; Bristol B 7862. Evans lists this also as #23843 with erroneous pagination. This is one of the first printed compilations of the laws of the first Congress in all its sessions; New York and Philadelphia editions appeared also in 1791, presumably preceeding this issue. Those editions bore the title: "Laws of the U. S. Vol. I."

130. (UNITED STATES OF AMERICA). The Constitutions of the several independent states of America; the Declaration of Independence; the Articles of Confederation ... The second edition. Boston, Printed by Norman and Bowen, 1785. 8vo. in fours. 180, (1), 29pp. Slight tear to lower corner of of page 85 touching a few words; contemp. calf, a very good copy. $165.00

130. (Continued)
* The first edition of 1781 was printed in only 200 copies for official use. The edition offered here is the first to contain the Constitution of Georgia. Howes C716; Sabin 16092 (date misprinted); Evans 19306.

A LANDMARK IN THE AMERICAN DOCTRINE OF JUDICIAL SUPREMACY

131. VARNUM, James M. The case, Trevett against Weeden: on information and complaint, for refusing paper bills in payment for butcher's meat, in market, at par with specie. Tried before the honourable Superior Court, in the County of Newport, September Term, 1786. Also, the case of the judges of said court, before the honourable General Assembly, at Providence ... wherein the rights of the people to trial by jury, &c. are stated and maintained, and the legislative, judiciary and executive powers of government examined and defined. Providence, printed by John Carter, 1787. iv, 60pp. Contemp. plain blue wrappers, stitched as issued. A fine copy. FIRST EDITION. $350.00
* A major landmark in the establishment of the doctrine of judicial review. We cannot imagine a clearer and more prohetic argument, not only for the right of the judiciary to reject legislation which violates the Constitution, but also for the primacy of the judiciary in the scheme of political authority. Varnum's bold defense echoed 17 years later in the statement of John Marshall in "Marbury v. Madison" that "it is emphatically the province and duty of the judicial department to say what the law is." Of the five or so colonial cases involving judicial review (see Beveridge, Life of Marshall, III, p. 610f and Charles Warren, Congress, the Court and the Const. p. 43ff) this is the most important because it was separately published and heavily advertised in the Philadelphia papers at the time of the Convention. Madison took special note of it in the Debates and Warren maintains that the founding fathers agreed that the Supreme Court would, like its colonial and state counterparts, be the ultimate judge of a law's validity.
Varnum also gives a good account of the social and financial background to the affair and reproduces the currency act and obnoxious forcing acts which denied right of trial by jury and appeal. He later became justice for the new Northwest Territory and helped frame its laws. Evans 20825; Sabin 98638; JCB 1772-1800, p. 267. Kress B1355. Rare in fine condition.

132. VATTEL, EMMERICH DE The law of nations; or, principles of the law of nature: applied to the conduct and affairs of nations and sovereigns ... a new edition corrected. Translated from the French. London, Robinson, 1793. lvi, 444pp. large 8vo. Contemporary tree calf, spine and borders

132. (Continued)
gilt, with floral devices in compartments, leather label. A very fine and attractive large paper copy. $125.00

133. VERPLANCK, GULIAN. A letter to Col. William Drayton, of South Carolina, in assertion of the Constitutional power of Congress to impose protecting duties. N.Y. printed for E. Bliss, 1831. 31pp. $ 17.50
* Kress C2990. Argued from British and Colonial precedent.

134. (VIRGINIA. LAWS, STATUTES.) THE CODE OF VIRGINIA. Including legislation to the year 1860. 2nd ed. Richmond, Ritchie, 1860. 1022pp. Full contemp. calf. $ 30.00

135. The Virginia scrivener, being a collection of forms of bonds, contracts, conveyancing, and other instruments ... adapted to the use of the people of Virginia. Prepared by a Gentleman of the Bar of Staunton. To which are prefixed ... the new Constitution of Virginia. Staunton, VA., Kenton Harper, 1833. 8vo. 181pp. Contemp. calf, moderate foxing but a very good copy. First edition. $100.00
* Swem 6142 and 10689; Sabin 100565. Not in Marvin. An attractive and scarce little book. We have seen but one other copy in six years.

136. (WASHINGTON. STATE. LAWS, STATUTES, Etc.) NICHOLS, SAM H., compiler. Session laws of the State of Washington. Eleventh session, conve ned Jan. 11, adjourned March 11, 1909, compiled in chapters, with marginal notes by ... Olympia, Wash., Published by Authority, Boardman, Public Printer, 1909. 1172pp. Full contemp. sheep. $ 20.00

137. WATERMAN, THOMAS G. The justice's manual; or, a summary of the powers and duties of justices of the peace in the State of New York, comprising a variety of practical forms adapted to cases civil and criminal. Binghamton, N. Y., Morgan & Canoll, 1825. 222pp. 8vo. Contemp. calf., minor staining. $ 32.50
* Marvin p. 720. First edition.

138. WATKINS, CHARLES. An essay towards the further elucidation of the Law of Decents. The second edition, corrected and enlarged; with an appendix on the distribution of the personal effects of intestates. London, printed for R. Pheney, 1801. 311pp. Full contemp. sheep. With large folding tables, joints mended. $ 45.00
* S & M, I, 478.

139. (WILLARD PEELE et al. versus THE MERCHANTS' INSURANCE COMPANY). Argument of plaintiffs' counsel in the case of ... before the Supreme Court of the United States, February Term 1826, upon the question of admiralty jurisdiction, in cases of policies of insurance. With extracts from various learned treatises upon this subject. Boston, Howe and Norton, 1826. 35, 132pp. 8vo. Cont. plain wrps. Fine. $ 45.00
* An uncommon work; remarkably well documented and well argued case for admiralty jurisdiction in contract cases, publishing (in some cases probably the first American appearances) extracts from historical treatises, and citing American precedent. Shaw-Shoemaker 25593 listing the work (the argument only) under Benj. Ropes Nichols.

140. (WISCONSIN. LEGISLATURE). The trial in the Supreme Court, of the information in the nature of a Quo Warranto, filed by the Attorney General, on the relation of Coles Bashford vs.Wm. A. Barstow, contesting the right to the Office of Governor of Wisconsin. Madison, Calking, 1856. 368pp. Prtd. wrps. $ 50.00

140. (CONTINUED)
* Concerns a contested election; Bashford was a Republican challenger to Barstow, then Governor. Published by order of the legislature with thorough revision by A. D. Smith, Judge of the Supreme Court.

141. (YORKE, CHARLES). Some considerations on the law of forfeiture, for high treason. Occasioned by a clause in the late Act ... with an appendix concerning Estates-Tail in Scotland. Third edition, further corrected and enlarged. London, Rivington, 1748. 8vo. 190pp. Neatly disbound. Very good copy. $ 65.00
* An essay with far reaching implications about the limits of power. "This work richly deserves its popularity with the profession ... Hoffman, Legal Studies ..." Marvin p.758. Yorke defends this harsh, seemingly unjust measure, as necessary to protect the state and constitution and denies it to be an instrument for arrogating undue power to the government. S & M, I, 368.

142. ABBOTT, FREDERICK. The administration of Indian affairs in Canada. Report of an investigation made in 1914 under the direction of the Board of Indian Commissioners. Wash., D.C., 1915. 148pp. Illus. frontis, numerous plates, tables. Orig. cl. Fine. $ 55.00
* This is not a government publication, or at least not a government document. The report was, however, intended for the consideration of the U.S. Secretary of the Interior, to be used in the improvement of Indian administration in the United States. Duncan Campbell Scott was the Canadian superintendent, Abbott was Secretary of the American board. Much on western Canada.

143. BLAKEY, LEONARD STOTT. The sale of liquor in the South: the history of the development of a normal social restraint in Southern Commonwealths. N. Y., Columbia Univ., 1912. 52pp. wrps. 4to. Plates. $ 15.00

144. (BRITTON). Britton, an English translation and notes. By Francis Morgan Nichols ... with an introduction by Simeon E. Baldwin ... Wash., Byrne, 1901. 649pp. cl. Fine. $ 25.00
* Legal Classic. Series.

145. BROWN, ESTHER LUCILE. Lawyers and the promotion of justice. N. Y., Russell Sage Foundation, 1938. 302pp. $ 22.50

146. BURDICK, CHARLES K. The law of the American Constitution, its origin and development. With two introductory chapters by Francis M. Burdick. N. Y., Putnam's Sons, 1922. 687pp. $ 17.50

147. CAHN, EDMOND N. The sense of Injustice: an anthropocentric view of law. N. Y., New York Univ., Press, 1949. 186pp. orig. cl. $ 10.00

148. CALVERT, E. ROY. Capital punishment in the twentieth century; with an introduction by Lord Buckmaster. London, G. P. Putnam's. (1927) 204pp. $ 12.50

149. CAMERON, JAMES R. Frederick William Maitland and the history of English law. Norman, Univ. of Oklahoma Press, (1961). 214pp. Illus., frontis, plates. d.j., fine. First edition. $ 15.00

150. CHESHIRE, GEOFFREY CHEVALIER International contracts: being the fifteenth Lecture on the David Murray Foundation in the University of Glasgow, delivered on March 4th, 1948. Glasgow, Jackson, 1948. 90pp. Wrps. $ 12.50
* Glasgow Univ. Publications LXXVI.

151. CLARKE, MARY PATTERSON. Parliamentary privilege in the American Colonies. New Haven, Yale Univ. Press, 1943. 303pp. orig. cl. d.j. Fine copy. First Edition. $ 22.50
* Yale Historical Publications, XLIV.

152. DENNING, SIR ALFRED. Freedom under the law. London, Stevens, 1949. 126pp orig. cl. $ 12.50
* Hamlyn Lectures, first series.

153. DUNN, FREDERICK SHERWOOD. The diplomatic protection of Americans in Mexico. N. Y., Columbia Univ. press, 1933. 439pp. $ 22.50
* Mexico in International Finance & Diplomacy, Columbia Univ. Vol. II.

154. EAGLETON, CLYDE. The responsibility of States in International Law. N. Y., New York Univ. Press, 1928. 291pp. orig. cl. d.j. Fine. First edition. $ 17.50

155. EDSALL, PRESTON W., ed. Journal of the Courts of Common Right and Chancery of East New Jersey, 1683-1702, with an introduction by ... Phila., American Legal History Society, 1937. 356pp. cl. 4to. $ 32.50
* Publications of the American Legal History Society, series one.

156. EGERTON, HUGH EDWARD. Federations and unions within the British Empire. Second edition. Oxford, Clarendon, 1924. 306pp. $ 12.50

157. ELIOT, THOMAS D. The juvenile court and the community. N. Y., MacMillan, 1914. 234pp. orig. cl. $ 12.50

158. FIFOOT, C.H.S. Judge and jurist in the reign of Victoria. London, Stevens, 1959. 140pp. orig. cl. $ 7.50
* Hamlyn Lectures, eleventh series.

159. FIFOOT, C. H. S., ed. The letters of Frederick William Maitland. London, Selden Society, 1965. 397pp. Illus., Frontis. $ 17.50
* Selden Society Supplementary Series Vol. I.

160. FLOURNOY, RICHARD W. ed., et al. A collection of nationality laws of various countries as contained in constitutions, statutes, and treaties. N. Y., Oxford Univ. Press, 1929. 776pp. $ 22.50

161. FOLLETT, M. P. The Speaker of the House of Representatives: with an introduction by Albert Bushnell Hart. N. Y., Longmans, Green. 1896. 378pp. $ 12.50

162. FRANK, ELI. Title to real and leasehold estates and liens. Baltimore, Baltimore City Printing, 1912. 348pp. $ 22.50
* Study of Maryland law.

163. FRANKFURTER, FELIX. Mr. Justice Holmes and the Supreme Court. Cambridge, Harvard Univ. Press, 1938. 139pp. Frontis. orig. cl. Fine. $ 12.50

164. GATES, PAUL W. History of public land law development. Written for the Public Land Law Review Commission, with a chapter by Robert W. Swenson. Wash., D. C. (GPO) 1968. 828pp. Lg. 8vo., illus. cl. $ 25.00

165. (GLANVILLE). A translation of Glanville by John Beames to which are added notes With an introduction by Joseph Henry Beale. Wash., Byrne, 1900. 306pp. cl. Fine. $ 25.00
* Legal Classic Series.

166. GOODHART, A.L. English Law and the moral law. London, Stevens, 1953. 151pp. orig. cl. $ 12.50
* Hamlyn Lectures, fourth series.

167. GOODHART, ARTHUR L. Five Jewish lawyers of the common law. London, Oxford Univ. Press, 1949. 74pp. orig. cl. $ 10.00

168. GOODNOW, FRANK J. Municipal home rule: a study in administration. N. Y. Columbia Univ. Press, 1916. 283pp. orig. cl. $ 15.00
* Chiefly a legal, constitutional study.

169. GRAY, JOHN CHIPMAN. The nature and sources of the law. N. Y., Columbia Univ. Press, 1916. 332pp. cl. First Edition. $ 10.00
* Columbia Univ. Lectures, the Carpentier lectures, 1908-1909.

170. GREAT BRITAIN. DEPUTY KEEPER OF THE RECORDS. Liber feodorum. The book of fees commonly called Testa de Nevill. Reformed from the earliest mss. Part II. A. D. 1242-1293 and appendix. London, HMSO, 1923. pp.637-1483. Roy 8vo. Orig. cl. Fine. $ 20.00

171. GREENMAN, FREDERICK F. Wire-tapping: its relation to civil liberties, to which are appended the leading opinions on this subject. Stamford, Connecticut, Overbrook Press, 1938. 228pp. orig. cl. $ 35.00
* A fine production of the Overbrook Press. Very scarce.

172. GROTIUS, HUGO. The freedom of the seas, or the right which belongs to the Dutch to take part in the East Indian Trade. Translated with a revision of the Latin text of 1633, by Ralph Van Deman Magoffin, edited with an introductory note by James Brown Scott. N. Y., Oxford Univ. Press, 1916. 83pp. $ 12.50

173. HALLER, WILLIAM, ed. Tracts on liberty in the Puritan Revolution, 1638-1647, with a commentary by ... In three vols. N. Y. Columbia Univ. Press, 1934. 197, 339, 405pp. Illus., frontis., plates. orig. cl. d.j.'s. Very fine set. First edition. $ 65.00
* Vol. I is commentary, Vols II & III consist of facsimile reprints of a number of major tracts.

174. HAMILTON, OTTO TEMPLAR. The courts and the curriculum. N.Y., Teachers College, Columbia Univ., 1927. 168pp. orig. cl. $ 12.50

175. HAMSON, C. J. Executive discretion and judicial control: an aspect of the French Counseil d'Etat. London, Stevens, 1954. 222pp. orig. cl. $ 12.50
* Hamlyn Lectures, sixth series.

176. HARMER, F. E. Anglo-Saxon writs. (Manchester, University of Manchester Press, 1952). 604pp. Frontis. orig. cl. Folding plate. Fine copy. $ 22.50

177. HOANG, PIERRE. Notions techniques sur la propriete en Chine, avec un choix d' actes et de documents officiels (deuxieme ed.) Chang-hai, Imprimerie de l'Orphelinat de T-ou-se-we Zi-ka-wei., 1920. 200p. Includes some text and documents in original Chinese. $ 20.00
* Varietes Sinologiques #11.

178. HORNE, ANDREW. The mirrour of justices ... to which is added The Diversity of Courts and their Jurisdiction, translated into English by W. H. of Gray's Inn. With an introduction by William C. Robinson. Wash., Byrne, 1903. 337p. Cl. Fine. $ 15.00
* Legal Classic Series

179. HUGHES, CHARLES EVANS. The Supreme Court of the United States, its foundation, methods and achievements, an interpretation. Garden City, Garden City Publishing, (1936). 269pp. $ 10.00
* Orig. cl. fine.

180. KAYE, J. M., ed. Placita Corone or La Corone Pledee devant Justices, edited with introduction, notes and translation by ... London, Selden Society, 1966. xxxix, 42pp. cl. $ 15.00
* Selden Society Supplementary Series, vol.4.

181. LEWIS, O. F. The development of American prisons and prison customs, 1776-1845, with special reference to early institutions in the State of New York. (Albany), Prison Assoc. of N. Y., (1922). 350pp. cl. $ 15.00

182. LOWENSTEIN, STEVEN. Lawyers, legal education, and development: an examination of the process of reform in Chile. N.Y. International Legal Center, (1970). 310pp. $ 12.50

183. MACRAY, WILLIAM DUNN, ed. Chronicon Abbatae De Evesham, ad annum 1418. London, Longman, 1863. 394pp. Folding frontis. $ 25.00
* Chronicles and Memorials of G. B. and Ireland Series.

184. MacDERMOTT, LORD. Protection from power under English Law. London, Stevens, 1957. 196pp. orig. cl. $ 12.50
* Hamlyn Lectures, ninth series.

185. MAITLAND, F. W. Equity, also the forms of action at common law; two courses of lectures, edited by A. H. Chaytor, and W. J. Whittaker. Cambridge, University Press, 1916. 411pp. $ 25.00

186. MEGARRY, ROBERT. Inns ancient and modern: a topographical and historical introduction to the Inns of Court, Inns of Chancery, and Serjeants' Inns. London, Seldon Society, 1972. 61pp. Illus. frontis. plates, wrps. $ 7.50

187. MERIAM, LEWIS, et al. The problem of Indian administration: report of a survey made at the request of Hon. Hubert Work, Secretary of the Interior, and submitted to him, Feb. 21, 1928. Baltimore, Johns Hopkins Press, 1928. 872pp. orig. cl. Nice copy. $ 35.00

188. MICHIGAN. HOUSE OF REPRESENTATIVES. LEGISLATIVE COMMITTEE. Michigan tax study: staff papers. Lansing, (1958). 573pp. orig. cl. $ 17.50

189. NATIONAL INDUSTRIAL CONFERENCE BOARD. Mergers and the law. N. Y., N.I.C.B., 1929. 153pp. cl. $ 15.00

190. NATIONAL INDUSTRIAL CONFERENCE BOARD. Public regulation of competitive practices. N. Y., N.I.C.B., 1929, 320pp. cl. Best ed., Revised $ 15.00

191. NATIONAL MUNICIPAL LEAGUE. CONFERENCE FOR GOOD CITY GOVERNMENT. Proceedings of the annual meetings. 1894-1909. (1st through 16th national conferences, held at various places. 1895 is called the 1st annual meeting so that 1909 is the 15th annual meeting) $200.00
* Each volume is a substantial collection of articles, papers etc. by numerous important participants; this publication is essential as a source for the broad urban reform movement of this period, in all of its important aspects including politics administration, health, education, finance and social control.
** Please inquire about shorter runs.

192. NORTON, ROBERT F., et al. A treatise on deeds. Founded upon, and in lieu of a second edition of, rules for the Interpretation of Deeds, by H. W. Elphinstone, the author, and James William Clark. London, Sweet, 1906. lxx, 694pp. cl. Roy. 8vo. $ 22.50
* S & M, III, 71.

193. OSBORN, ALBERT S. The mind of the Juror as judge of the facts or the Layman's view of the law: a study of the contentious trial. Introduction by John H. Wigmore. Albany, Boyd Printing, 1937. Second Printing. 239pp. cl. $ 25.00

194. OSBORN, ALBERT S. The problem of proof especially as exemplified in disputed document trials: a discussion of the proof of the facts in Courts of Law, with some general comments on the conduct of trials. Introduction by John Henry Wigmore. Second edition. Newark, Essex Press, 1926. 539pp. Illus., frontis. cl. Author presentation copy. Fine. $ 25.00

195. O'SULLIVAN, RICHARD. The inheritance of the common law. London, Stevens, 1950. 118pp. orig. cl. $ 12.50
* Hamlyn Lectures, second series.

196. PARRY, SIR DAVID HUGHES. The sanctity of contracts in English Law. London, Stevens, 1959. 77pp. orig. cl. $ 12.50
* Hamlyn Lectures, tenth series.

THE PIPE ROLL SOCIETY
The following:

197. ROUND, JOHN HORACE, ed. Ancient Charters royal and private, prior to A.D. 1200. Part I. Printed from the originals. London, 188. 133pp. cl. (facsimile reprint). $ 15.00
* Pipe Roll Society Publication, Vol. X.

198. Feet of Fines of the ninth year of the reign of King Richard I. A.D. 1197-1198. London, reprinted from the 1898 ed. in 1929. 178pp. cl. $ 15.00
* Pipe Roll Society Publication, vol. XXIII.

199. Feet of Fines of the tenth year of the reign of King Richard I. A.D. 1198 to A.D. 1199, excepting those for the counties of Bedford, Berkshire, Buckingham, Cambridge, Devon, and Dorset. Also A Roll of the Kings Court in the reign of King Richard I. London, 1900, reprinted 1929. 267pp. cl. $ 17.50
* Pipe Roll Society Publication, vol. XXIV.

200. The Great Roll of the Pipe for the twenty-second year of the reign of King Henry the Second, A.D. 1175-1176. London, 1904. 268pp. cl. $ 20.00
* Pipe Roll Society Publications, vol. xxv.

201. BROWN, R.A., ed. Pipe Roll 17 John, and Praestita Roll 14-18 John, Roll of Summonses 1214, Scutage Roll 16 John, edited by J. C. Holt. London, 1964. 161pp. cl. $ 17.50
* Pipe Roll Society Publications vol. lxxv. (New Series vol. XXXVIL.)

202. EBDEN, E. Pauline, ed. The Great Roll of the Pipe for the second year of the reign of King Henry III, Michaelmas 1218, (Pipe Roll 62). Now first printed from the original in the Public Record Office. London, 1972. 145pp. cl. $ 15.00
* Pipe Roll Society Publications vol. LXXVII. (New Series vol. XXXIX.)

203. DODWELL, BARBARA, ed. The Charters of Norwich Cathedral Priory, part one. London, 1974. 279pp. Illus., frontis, plates. cl. $ 17.50
* Pipe Roll Society Publications vol. LXXVIII (New Series vol. XL.)

204. The Great Roll of the Pipe for the third year of the reign of King Henry III. Michaelmas 1219 (Pipe Roll 63). Now first printed from the original in the Public Record Office, with an introduction by B. E. Harris. London, 1976. 314pp. cl. $ 17.50
* Pipe Roll Society Publications, vol. LXXX. (New Series vol. XLII.)

205. The Great Rolls of the Pipe for the second, third and fourth years of the reign of King Henry the Second, A.D. 1155, 1156, 1157, 1158. London, 1844. 186pp. cl. $ 17.50
* Reprinted 1930. Not in Series.

END OF PIPE ROLL SERIES

206. POUND, ROSCOE. Criminal justice in America. N.Y., Holt, (1930). 226pp. $ 15.00

207. POUND, ROSCOE. The formative era of American law. Boston, Little, Brown, 1938. 188pp. orig. cl. Signed by Pound on the title. D.J., fine copy. First edition. $ 15.00

208. POUND, ROSCOE. Law and morals: the McNair Lectures, 1923, delivered at the Univ. of North Carolina. Chapel Hill, Univ. of No. Carolina Press, 1924. 156pp. First edition, signed by the author. $ 17.50

209. POUND, ROSCOE. New paths of the law. First lectures in the Roscoe Pound Lectureship Series. University of Nebraska Press, 1950. 69pp. orig. cl. $ 15.00

210. POUND, ROSCOE. Outlines of lectures on jurisprudence. Fourth ed. Cambridge, (Printed at the Harvard Univ. Press), 1928. 158pp. wrps. $ 10.00

211. PRUYN, JOHN V.L. Catalogue of books relating to the literature of the law, collected by the late ... Albany, Riggs, 1901. 300pp. frontis. orig. cl. $ 45.00
* 1/120 copies printed. Pruyn was Chancellor of the State Univ. at Albany.

212. RALSTON, JACKSON H. International arbitration from Athens to Locarno. Stanford, Calif., Stanford Univ. Press, 1929. 417pp. orig. cl. $ 22.50

213. REED, H. CLAY, ed., et al. The Burlington Court Book: a record of Quaker Jurisprudence in West New Jersey, 1680-1709. Wash., D. C., American Historical Assoc. 1944. 372pp. 4to. $ 35.00
* American Legal Records, vol. 5.

214. RIDDELL, WILLIAM RENWICK. The Constitution of Canada in its history and practical working. New Haven, Yale Univ. Press, 1917. 170pp. cl. $ 12.50

215. ROTTSCHAEFER, HENRY. The Constitution and socio-economic change: five lectures delivered at the University of Michigan, March 1947: with a foreword by E. Blythe Stason. Ann Arbor, Univ. of Michigan, 1948. 253pp. $ 15.00

216. RUNES, DAGOBERT D. The disinherited and the law. N.Y., Philosophical Lib., (1964). 79pp $ 12.50

217. RUSHMORE, ELSIE MITCHELL. The Indian policy during Grant's administrations. Jamaica Queensborough N.Y., Marion Press, 1914. 81pp. wrps. $ 17.50

218. RUSSELL, ELMER BEECHER. The review of American Colonial Legislation by the King in Council. N. Y., Columbia Univ. 1915. 227pp. orig. cl. $ 12.50
* Columbia Studies No. 155.

219. SCHROEDER, THEODORE. Free Speech for radicals. Enlarged edition. Riverside, Hillacre Bookhouse, 1916. 206pp. orig. cl. $ 17.50

****

220. SELDEN SOCIETY. Publications. London. (1887-1972)
Volumes: 1 - 4, 7 - 8, 11, 13, 15, 17 - 22, 24, 26 - 27, 50, 53, 55 - 63, 65 - 70, 72 - 79, 82 - 89.
Original cloth, all in very good to fine condition. Per volume $ 15.00

****

221. SHERRILL, GEORGE RAYMOND. Criminal procedure in North Carolina, as shown by criminal appeals since 1890. Chapel Hill, Univ. of No. Carolina Press, 1930. 173pp. orig. cl. $ 15.00

222. STAHL, DAVID et al., (editors) The Community and racial crises. N.Y., Practising Law Institute, (1966). 364pp. $ 12.50

223. STATHAM, (NICHOLAS) Statham's Abridgement of the Law. Translated by Margaret Center Klingelsmith ... Boston, Boston Book Company, 1915. 2vols. large thick 4tos. xxxiv, 684;(685)-1308pp. Cl. Fine set. Autograph presentation copy from the translator. $125.00
* Cf. Marvin p.661. Considered to be the earliest work of its kind. This is the only translation.

224. STINSON, ALVAH L. Woman under the Law. Boston, Hudson, 1914. 406pp. Illus., frontis. cl. $ 25.00

225. SULLIVAN, HAROLD W. Trial by Newspaper. Hyannis, Patriot Press. 1961. 250pp. $ 12.50

226. SUNDERLAND, EDSON R. History of the American Bar Association and its work, with a concluding chapter on the Committee on Scope and Correlation of Work and Its program by William J. Jameson. 1953. 251pp. $ 12.50

227. SUTHERLAND, J. G. A treatise on the law of damages embracing an elementary exposition of the law, and also its application to particular subjects of contract and tort. Third edition by John R. Berryman. Four vols. Chicago, Callaghan, 1903. 4221pp. Full contemp. calf. $ 45.00

228. TRULL, EDNA. The administration of regulatory inspectional services in American Cities. N.Y., Municipal Adm. Service, 1932. 184pp. orig. cl. $ 12.50
* Publication No. 27.

229. U.S. TREATIES. Treaties, conventions, international acts, and agreements between the United States of America and other powers 1923-1937. Wash., G.P.O., 1938. Large 8vo.
* Volume 4 (and final vol. with index to vols. 1-4) of this series. $ 35.00
** SAME: Vols. I and II (1789-1909) each $ 25.00

230. WALKER, HARVEY. The Legislative process: lawmaking in the United States. N.Y., Ronald Press, (1948). 482pp. cl. $ 15.00

231. WARREN, CHARLES. A history of the American Bar. Boston, Little Brown, 1911. 586pp. orig. cl. $ 17.50

232. WILLIAMS, BRUCE. State security and the League of Nations. Baltimore, John Hopkins Press, 1927. 345pp. $ 12.50
* Albert Shaw Lectures on Diplomatic History, 1927.

233. WILLISTON, SAMUEL. Life and law: an autobiography, with illustrations. Boston, Little, Brown, 1941. 347pp. orig. cl. $ 15.00

234. WRIGHT, BENJAMIN FLETCHER. Consensus and continuity, 1776-1787. Boston, Boston Univ. Press, 1958. 60pp. cl. $ 12.50
* Boston Univ. The Gasper G. Bacon Lectures on the Constitution of the United States.

235. YEAR BOOKS. EDW. I. Years 20-22, 30 - 35 (1292 - 1307). in five volumes, complete, all published in this series. Edited by Alfred Horwood. London, Longmans, 1866-1879. Large 8vo. $125.00
* Chronicles and Memorials of G.B. Series. Sweet & Maxwell I, 313-314.

236. YEAR BOOKS. EDW. III. Years 11-20 Part I. (1337-1346), in 14 volumes. Except for a final volume (Year 20 pt. II) a complete run of all published in this series. Edited by Luke Owen Pike. London, HMSO, 1883-1908. Large 8vo. & 1/4 cloth, very good to fine. $350.00
* Chronicles and Memorials of G. B. series. Sweet & Maxwell I, 313-314.

237. (YEAR BOOKS. RICHARD II) Year books of Richard II: 11 Richard II 1387-1388. Edited for the Ames Foundation by Isobel D. Thornley ... with a commentary upon the cases by Theodore F. T. Plucknett. London, Spottiswoode, 1937. lxii, 578,(60)pp. Orig. cl. fine. 4to. $ 25.00
* Ames Foundation Publications.

238. (YEAR BOOKS. RICHARD II) Year Books of Richard II: 13 Richard II 1389-1390. Edited ... by Theodore F.T. Plucknett. London, Spottiswoode, 1929. xlix, 370, 20pp. 4to. Orig. cl. Fine. $ 25.00
* Ames Foundation Publications.

239. ZURCHER, ARNOLD JOHN. The experiment with democracy in Central Europe: a comparative survey of the operation of Democratic Government in post-war Germany and in the Russian and Austro-Hungarian succession states. N.Y., Oxford Univ. Press, 1933. 328pp. Maps. $ 15.00

240. ANDERSON, ROBERT BOWIE, comp. A supplement to "Beale's bibliography of early English law books." Cambridge, Harvard Univ. Press, 1943. xii, 50p. 4to. Cl. $ 20.00

241. ANGELL, JOSEPH K. A treatise on the law of fire and life insurance, with an appendix, containing forms, tables &c. 2nd ed., enlarged. Boston, Little, 1855. 644p. Sheep. $ 37.50
* Autographed presentation copy from the author.

242. ANGELL, JOSEPH K., et al. A treatise on the law of highways. Third edition, with notes and references to the later cases by George F. Choate. Boston, Little, Brown, 1886. 625pp. full contemp. sheep. $ 30.00

243. BARLOW, E.R., et al. Foreign investment and taxation. (West Hanover) Halliday Lithograph Corp., 1955. 481pp. $ 15.00
* Harvard Law School, International Program in Taxation.

244. BENTHAM, JEREMY The rationale of reward. London, Published for John and H.L. Hunt, 1825. viii, errata, 325pp. Entirely uncut and mostly unopened. Quarter calf, marbled bds., antique style. A fine copy. $300.00
* First separate English edition. The material had first appeared in Dumont's publication from two manuscripts given him by Bentham, one in English, the other in French. This is the first appearance based on a "confrontation" with the original English ms. The editor notes that it differs from a literal translation of Dumont, and prints Bentham's remarks apropos this edition.

245. BOURINOT, SIR J.G. A manual of the Constitutional History of Canada, from the earliest period to 1901, including the British North America Act of 1867, a digest of judicial decisions on important questions of legislative jurisdiction and observations on the working of Parliamentary Government. New edition, revised and enlarged. Toronto, Copp, 1901. 246pp cl. $ 35.00
* Contains a section on Indian titles, the Rebellion of 1837-1838, Roman Catholics, Railroads, etc. Very well annotated with lists of references and authorities. First published in 1888, this is a major revision.

246. BOUTWELL, GEORGE S. A manual of the direct and excise tax system of the United States: ... Boston, Little, Brown, 1863. 500pp. Full contemp. sheep. Fine copy. $ 27.50
* First edition. The first manual to appear in connection with the new Civil-War tax laws.

247. CHAMBERLIN, FRANKLIN. American Commercial law, relating to every kind of business: .... adapted to all the states of the Union. Hartford, 1870. 991pp. sheep. very good copy. $ 25.00

248. CHANDLER, PELEG W. The bankrupt law of the United States, with an outline of the system; together with the rules and forms in Massachusetts, and references to recent decisions. Boston, Weeks, 1842. vi, 102pp. (pp. 1 and 2 in facsimile). Contemp. 1/4 calf. $ 45.00
* An interesting copy, edited and supplied with continuation sheets, partly manuscript and partly printed rules and regulations pertaining to cases and ruling for New Hampshire in matters of bankruptcy. It has the appearance of an adaptation to N.H. law intended for publication as such, and bears the signature of A. R. Hatch. The manuscript portions are in his hand.

249. CURTIS, GEORGE T. The American Conveyancer; containing a large variety of legal forms and instruments, ... together with forms and directions for applicants under the Patent Laws of the United States, and the Insolvent Act of Massachusetts, revised according to the Act of 1844. Boston, Little, Brown, 1844. 269pp. Full contemp. sheep. Good copy. $ 27.50

250. DALTON, MICHAEL. Officium Vicecomitum. The office and authoritie of sherifs. Written for the better incouragement of the gentrie (upon whom the burthen of this office lyeth) to keepe their office, and undersherife, in their houses; that so by their continuall care of the businesse, and eye over their officers, they may the better discharge their dutie to God, their prince, and countrey, in the execution of this their office. Gathered out of the statutes, and bookes of the common lawes of this Kingdome. London, printed for the Companie of Stationers, 1623. 2 leaves (conjugate blanks), 3 leaves (title and dedication), 194 leaves numbered (text), 5 leaves (index), 2 leaves (conjugate blanks). Elaborate woodcut bordered title; ornamental headpieces. Folio. Original limp vellum A very fine copy. FIRST EDITION. $400.00
*STC 6212. A classic work which remained in use throughout the 17th century and passed through a number of reprints and revisions. The first edition is quite uncommon and this copy is especially desireable. At the end of the text and again at the end of the index is the contemporary manuscript inscription "Liber Thome Thornton ex dono Michaelis Dalton" probably in the author's hand. A very attractive copy in original state.

251. DENISART, JEAN B. Collection de decisions nouvelles et de notions relatives a la jurisprudence actuelle. A Paris, per l'auteur, chez Savoye, etc., 1763-64, 1768.
251. (Continued)
Large, thick 4 to. Contemp. calf, rubbed; spines worn. In 4 volumes. $150.00
* Actually the third edition of this work; the 4th volume being a supplement of materials subsequent to the completion of the third and last volume of the main collection (Denisart died in 1765). The content is predominantly related to internal affairs, but there are occasional references to America under Colonies, Negroes, etc. Denisart pioneered in publishing this collection.

252. DUNOD, (de CHARNAGE, FRANCOIS IGNACE). Traites de La Mainmorte, et des Retraits. Dijon, chez de Fay, 1733. 234, (18); 67, (1), (8)p. Illus: woodcut device on title page. 4to. Cont. calf, rubbed; spine gilt. Title-page neatly restored at top-margin, no text affected. A very good copy. $ 85.00
* FIRST EDITION. NUC locates only one copy and that one with a different place of publication. The work was important enough to go through several later revisions.

253. FOURNEL, (JEAN FRANCOIS). Traite du voisinage. Considere dans ses rapports avec L'Ordre, Judiciare. Paris, Rondonneau, (1800)., xlvii, 454;456p. Half-titles present. 8vo. Original boards, leather labels. Complete in 2 volumes. $ 75.00
* The author begins this work with the statement that he seeks to re-introduce order and tradition into the field of jurisprudence left ravaged in the past decade and chooses this subject because of the universality of these problems to all classes of society.

254. FREEMAN, SAMUEL. The Probate Directory: or an assistant ... being the Laws of the Commonwealth of Massachusetts, respecting the estates of testators, intestates, and wards, to which are added, a variety of forms, ... Second edition, greatly enlarged and improved. Boston, Thomas, 1803. 228pp. Full contemp. sheep. Nice copy. $ 27.50

255. GALE, GEORGE. Forms, with notes and references, adapted to the statutes of Wisconsin; being a convenient manual for men of business, attorneys, sheriffs, constables, town officers, and justices of the peace. Second ed. rev. and enlgd. Milwaukee, Hale & Chapman, 1848. 368pp. calf, A very good copy. $ 55.00
* A vastly augmented edition (the first was published 2 years earlier in a small prtng. of 500 copies). Scarce. The NUC reports only LC and Harvard Law copies.

256. The Gentleman's Law Magazine: containing a variety of the most useful practical forms of writings, which occur in the course of business: ... By a Gentleman of the Bar. Middlebury, Vt., Printed by Huntington and Fitch, 1804. 348pp. Full contemp. sheep. Nice copy. FIRST EDITION. $ 32.50

THE FIRST SYSTEMATIC WORK IN ENGLISH ON THE LAWS AND CUSTOMS OF INDIA

257. (HALHED, NATHANIEL BRASSEY). A Code of Gentoo Laws, or ordinations of the pundits, from a Persian translation, made from the original in the sanskrit language. London, printed in the year 1776. 4to. lxxiv, 322pp. Illustrated with 8 finely engraved sanskrit plates. Large 4to. Contemporary calf, expertly rebacked. A very good copy. FIRST EDITION. $275.00
* The first complete presentation of the laws and customs of India for the English speaking world. The project was sponsored by Warren Hastings on behalf of the East India Company and was dedicated by him to them. "The importance of the commerce of India, and the advantage of a territorial establishment in Bengal, have at length awakened the attention of the British legislature to every circumstance that may conciliate the affections of the natives ... nothing can so favorably conduce to this as ... an adoption of such original institutes of the country, as do not clash immediately with the laws or interests of the conquerors." From the translator's preface. The translator was apparently of a very young age. All the more striking is his performance: the long introductory section is an extremely able and valuable sociological commentary, raising this work from a mere compilation of laws to a much more significant whole view of a society. The First edition is uncommon.

258. HALLECK, H. W. International Law: or, rules regulating the intercourse of states in peace and war. N. Y., Van Nostrand, 1861. 907pp. Full contemp. sheep. $ 45.00
* FIRST EDITION. Conceived originally while the author was serving in the Mexican War as commander of the Pacific Squadron and as Secretary of State of California. The preface is dated San Francisco, May, 1861.

259. HILL, JAMES. A practical treatise on the law relating to trustees, their powers, duties, privileges, and liabilities. Second American edition, containing the notes to the former edition, by Francis J. Troubat, with full notes and references to English and American decisions, by Henry Wharton. Phila., Johnson, 1854. Old sheep. $ 47.50

260. HILLHOUSE, (JAMES). Speech of ... in the Senate of the U.S. ... explanatory of his proposed ammendments to the Constitution of the United States, to which is added the ammendments referred to. Troy, N.Y., Wright Goddenow, and Stockwell, 1808. 39pp. removed. $ 27.50
* Though a Federalist, Hillhouse proposed a series of checks to the threat of overly centralized power. DAB gives an account.

261. KINGSBURY, BENJAMIN, Jr. The justice of the peace: designed to be guide to justices of the peace, for the state of Maine. Portland, Sanborn & Carter, 1854. vii, 407pp. Old sheep. $ 27.50

262. (LOCKE, JOHN). Du gouvernement civil, ou l'on traitte de l'origine, des fondemens, de la nature, du pouvoir, & des fins des societez politiques. Traduit de l'Anglois. Amsterdam, chez Abraham Wolfgang ... 1691. 6 pl, 321pp. 12mo. Woodcut vignette on title page, ornamental head and tailpieces. Contemporary calf, leather label. Old institutional stamp on verso of title page, otherwise a fine copy. $500.00
*THE VERY RARE FIRST FRENCH EDITION of Locke's second treatise on government (first edition L. 1690). No copy in the BM Catalogue; the NUC cites only the University of Michigan copy. Printing and the Mind of Man, no. 163, (the first edition).

263. MUSGRAVE, PEGGY B. United States taxation of foreign investment income: issues and arguments. Cambridge, Mass., 1969. 162pp. wrps. $ 12.50
* Harvard Law School. International tax program.

264. (NEW-HAMPSHIRE). STRAFFORD COUNTY. Probate forms, for the use of executors, administrators, &c., in the County of Strafford, together with the probate laws of the state. Dover, printed by John Mann, 1832. 129pp. Small 8vo. Contemp. calf, leather label. Fine. $ 30.00
* Not found in Bruntjen-Am. Imprints 1832.

265. (OKLAHOMA. LAWS, STATUTES). General Statutes of Oklahoma, 1908. A compilation of all the laws of a general nature including the session laws of 1907. Examined and approved by Wm. L. Curtis. Published by authority. Kansas City, Pipes-Reed, 1908. 1774p. 4to. Cl. Leather labels. $ 50.00
* Annotated to vol. 18 Oklahoma reports, 96 Pacific Reporter, 76 Kansas reports and 150 California reports. This is the first published compilation of territorial and state law from 1870 to 1907/1908. There had been several territorial compilations before 1907 when Oklahoma became a state.

266. (PERION, JOACHIM) 1499?-1559. De Romanorum et Graecorum Magistratibus. Libri Tres. Ad Odonem Collignium Castilionaeum Cardinalem Ampliss. Paris, In officina Caroli Perier ... 1560. 4to. 4pl., 51 leaves, 3 leaves index and errata. Woodcut device on title page, ornamental initials, partly printed in Greek. Very minor staining along lower inner margin, otherwise a very nice copy with generous margins bearing occasional annotations in a very early hand. Bound in later full vellum. $125.00
* The NUC reports only the Library of Congress copy in America. This is the only edition.

267. REPPY, ALISON. Historical and statutory background of the law of wills: descent and distribution, probate and administration. Chicago, Callaghan, 1928. 427p. Cl. Fine. $ 22.50

268. ROUSSET, GUSTAVE. Nouveau code annote de la presse pour la France, l'Algerie et les colonies, ou concordance synoptique et annotee de toutes les lois sur l'imprimerie, la librairie, ... les theatres, et tous autres moyens de publication, depuis 1789 jusqu'a 1856, suivie 1. des circulaires ministerielles importantes sur la matiere; 2. du Catalogue des ouvrages condamnes depuis 1814 jusqu'a 1850; 3. d'une table analytique alphabetique des crimes, delits et contraventions de la parole, de l'ecriture, de la presse, etc., y compris les delits d'audience; ... Paris, Imprimerie et Librairie Generale de Jurisprudence, 1856. (xxi), 296, errata pages. Illus: numerous tables. Half-title present. Folio. Contemp. leather, spine gilt decorated, raised bands. $125.00

A LANDMARK IN THE PHILOSOPHY OF REPUBLICAN GOVERNMENT

269. SIDNEY, ALGERNON. Discourse concerning government, published from an original manuscript of the author. London, Printed and are to be sold by the booksellers of London and Westminster. 1698. Folio. 1pl, 462, (5)pp. Contemp. panelled calf. Joints cracked but firm; spine in compartments, with ornaments and leather labels; internally a fresh, bright copy. FIRST EDITION. $300.00
* Wing S-3761. Written in answer to Robert Filmer's Patriarcha, 1680, probably at that time, and first published posthumously, the Discourse ranks with the works of Bodin, Milton and Locke in the forefront of modern libertarian political philosophy and is the great foundation of the Republican idea.

270. STANFORD (or STAUNFORD), WILLIAM. An exposition of the Kings prerogatiue, collected out of the great abridgement of Justice Fitzherbert, and other old writers of the laws of England by the right worshipfull ... Whereunto is annexed the process to the same prerogatiue appertaining. London, printed for the Company of Stationers, 1607. 86 leaves, 4to. Partly in black letter; ornaments, initials, head and tail pieces. Later boards, in a cloth slip case. An attractive copy. $250.00
* STC 23224. Marvin p 662. Winfield p. 319. This is the final edition of this very popular and influential work which first appeared in 1567.

270a. SWAN, JOSEPH R. A treatise on the law relating to the powers and duties of Justices of the Peace, and Constables, in the State of Ohio: with practical forms &c. &c. Columbus, Whiting, 1837. 582pp. Full contemp sheep. Good copy. $ 85.00
*Marvin p. 679 First Edition of the Standard major guide which reached a tenth edition in 1875.

271. TAYLOR, JOHN N. A treatise on the American law of landlord and tenant; embracing the statutory provisions and judicial decisions of the several united states in reference thereto; with a selection of precedents. Fifth edition, revised and enlarged. Boston, Little, Brown, 1869. lxii, 736pp. sheep. $ 37.50

272. TEXAS. LAWS, STATUTES. A digest of the general statute laws of the state of Texas: to which are subjoined the repealed laws of the republic and state of Texas, ... also, the colonization laws of Mexico, and Coahuila, and Texas which were in force before the declaration of independence by Texas. Prepared by Williamson S. Oldham and George W. White. Published by authority of the legislature. Austin, 1859. iv, 836, (3)p. 4to. Cont. calf, rubbed but a very good copy. $125.00
* Winkler 1229.

273. WHITING, WILLIAM. War powers under the Constitution of the United States. Military arrests, Reconstruction, and Military Government, also, now first published, war claims of aliens, with notes on the acts of the Executive and Legislative Departments during our Civil War, and a collection of cases decided in the National Courts. Forty-third edition. Boston, Lee, 1871. 695pp. cl. $ 30.00
* An interesting and important treatise first published in 1862. It defends the acts of the President and later, of Congress against Southern objections. This edition adds significant developments in the issue of war powers to previous editions and the author urges that this rather new branch of law continue to be developed.

WORLD TAX SERIES. Sponsored by the Harvard Law School International Program in Taxation.

The following: (all are out-of-print, and are the latest or only edition published)

274. Taxation in Australia. Boston, Little, Brown, 1958. 326pp. cl. $ 17.50

275. Taxation in Brazil. Boston, Little, Brown, 1957. 373pp. cl. $ 17.50

276. Taxation in Colombia. Chicago, Commerce Clearing House, 1964. 586pp. cl. $ 20.00

277. Taxation in India. Boston, Little, Brown, 1960. 552, 22pp. cl. $ 22.50

278. Taxation in Sweden. Boston, Little Brown, 1959. 723pp. cl. $ 20.00

ADDENDA II:

Serials

279. ACADEMY OF POLITICAL SCIENCE. PROCEEDINGS. V. 1 - 30, 1910-1970/72. Partly reprint. $625.00

280. AMERICAN ACADEMY OF POLITICAL AND SOCIAL SCIENCES. ANNALS. V 1-396, 1890 - 1971 with all supplements. Partly reprint, a few issues in photocopy. $2995.00

SAME. V 25-396, 1905 - 1971, lacks 2 issues and several supplements. $2195.00

281. AMERICAN BAR ASSOCIATION. Annual report ... incl. proceedings. Chicago. Bd. V. 63 - 64, 67 - 81. Each. $ 8.00

282. AMERICAN LAW REGISTER (Current Title: Univ. of Pennsylvania Law Review). Phila., V. 9, 12 - 19, 21 - 22, 25, 27, 28, 31. (1861 - 1883). Contemp. sheep. per vol. $ 12.50

283. AMERICAN POLITICAL SCIENCE REVIEW. V. 43 - 66, 1949 - 1972. $325.00

284. ANNALS OF CONGRESS. V. 1 - 42, March 4, 1789 - May 27, 1824.
* Comprising the first to eighteenth Congresses (Congressional classification nos. X 1-X 42). Complete set.

Together with
REGISTER OF DEBATES. V. 1 - 14, Dec. 6, 1824 - Oct. 16, 1837.
* Comprising 2nd session of the Eighteenth Congress to First session of the Twenty-Fifth Congress (Congressional Classification nos. X 43 - X 71). Complete Set. In all, 71 volumes in contemp. full calf binding. $1750.00

285. Annual Survey of Massachusetts Law. A Comprehensive analysis of the significant developments in the law ... Boston, Little, Brown, ... 8vo. Cl. d. j. s. Vols. 1 - 9 (1954 - 1962). $125.00

286. CALIFORNIA LAW REVIEW. V. 1 - 32, 1912 - 1944. Bd. $ 750.00

287. HARVARD LAW REVIEW. V. 1 - 90, 1887 - 1977 (V. 1 - 81 bd., indices 1/50, 50/75). $1325.00

SAME. Reprint $2250.00

288. IOWA LAW REVIEW. V. 1 - 36, 1915 - 1950/51. Mostly bound, partly reprint. $625.00

289. JOURNAL OF LEGAL EDUCATION. V. 10 - 21, 1957 - 1968. $150.00

290. MINNESOTA LAW REVIEW. V. 1 - 23, 27, 1917/18 - 1942/43, index and digest V. 1/11. Bd. $350.00

291. MONTHLY LAW REPORTER (Formerly: Law Reporter). Boston.
Old Series: V. 5 - 8, 1842/43 - 1845/46.
New Series: V. 1, 2, 5 - 10, 23, 24, 1848/49 1861/62.
Full sheep. per vol. $ 15.00

292. NATIONAL MUNICIPAL LEAGUE. CONFERENCE FOR GOOD CITY GOVERNMENT. Proceedings of the annual meetings. 1894 - 1909. (1st through 16th national conferences, held at various places. 1895 is called the 1st annual meeting so that 1909 is the 15th annual meeting). $200.00
* Each volume is a substantial collection of articles, papers etc. by numerous important participants; this publication is essential as a source for the broad urban reform movement of this period, in all of its important aspects including politics, administration, health, education, finance and social control.

293. SPECULUM. V. 1 - 50, 1926 - 1975. $900.00

294. U.S. DEPARTMENT OF STATE. Papers relating to the foreign relations of the U. S. Partly original, partly reprint, a few volumes needing rebinding. V. 1 - 205, 1861 - 1942. w/ general indeces 1861 - 99, 1900 - 1918. $6750.00

SAME: 1907; 1914; 1917suppl. 1, pt. 1; 1919 pts. 1, 2; 1931 pt. 3; 1932 pt. 2; 1939 pt. 3; 1940 pts. 1, 2, 3; 1941 pts. 1, 6, 7; 1942 pts. 2, 3, 5, 6.
per vol./part $ 30.00

295. YALE LAW JOURNAL V. 36 - 80. Bd. except 2 vols. $750.00

RUBIN 1980 — APPELLANT BRIEFS COLLECTION — RUBIN 1980

A collection of 250 appellant briefs, arguments, etc. published primarily between 1875 and 1900, with a minority between 1900 and 1920. A very good sampling with respect to both region and content. Many points of law as well as interesting fact are included in these discussions. Topics include: jurisdiction and states rights, immunity of witnesses, voting rights, contested elections, trade marks, and patents, wills, railroads, public utility regulation, maritime jurisdiction, etc.

The following states are represented:

Alabama (1)
California (2)
Connecticut (4)
Delaware (2)
Florida (1)
Georgia (3)
Illinois (19)
Indiana (7)
Iowa (2)
Kansas (2)
Kentucky (2)
Louisiana (4)
Maine (8)
Massachusetts (84)
Michigan (3)
Minnesota (4)
Mississippi (1)
Missouri (3)
Nebraska (1)
New Hampshire (4)
New Jersey (5)
New York (22)
Pennsylvania (6)
Ohio (6)
Rhode Island (3)
South Carolina (5)
Tennessee (4)
Vermont (4)
Virginia (4)
Washington, D.C.
U.S. Supreme Court (40)

While we are primarily interested in selling this material as an entire lot, uncatalogued, we will consider requests for single state groups provided that the lot remains unsold. We can list the shorter groups if necessary, and send the larger groups, such as Mass. on approval. Prices for smaller groups or possibly single items will have to be higher, of course, but will range between $ 5.00 and 15.00 per item. Prices for whole intermediate size groups such as Mass. or N. Y. would be less.

Price for the entire lot: (250 items).
$ 350.00

ROBERT H. RUBIN BOOKS

Post Office Box 558 · Stoughton, Massachusetts 02072 USA
Cable Address: «RUBOOKS» Telephone: (617) 344-0740

CATALOG NINE AUTUMN/WINTER 1980

ANTIQUARIAN AND OUT-OF-PRINT WORKS IN

LAW AND LEGAL HISTORY

(CHIEFLY ANGLO-AMERICAN)

PART I:	Books published before 1900	items 1-300
PART II:	Books published 1900 and after	301-504
PART III:	Addenda to both periods	505-525

Please see page i for detailed index and collection advertisement

Please see page ii for notes on condition, binding, and cited references

We are pleased to send you our fall/winter catalogue. We have been actively purchasing what we hope you will regard as interesting works in a variety of fields. A few well represented special topics are: **criminology, domestic relations, international law, medical jurisprudence,** *and* **political and constitutional theory.** *Included are important editions of works by* **Bentham, Blackstone, Hamilton, Locke,** *and* **Story,** *among others, as well as fine copies in original state of* **Parks' Laws of Maryland, 1729** *and the* **Code Napoleon,** *and a healthy selection of* **early American legal works** *of both regional and general interest. We hope you find it interesting and useful reading.*

Offers of single items or entire collections, institutional or private, are always welcome.

TELEPHONE ORDERS

Please feel free to phone at any time. In the unlikely event that you fail to reach us in the afternoon, please try again before noon, E.S.T.

CABLE ORDERS

It is essential that cable messages be confirmed immediately by letter.

1. ABBOTT, CHARLES. A treatise on the law relative to merchant ships and seamen ... With the copious annotations of Joseph Story... Third American edition, improved by a digest of American decisions subsequent to Judge Story's notes. Exeter, N. H., Lamson, 1822. 668, xxviiipp. Cloth. $ 50.00
* Marvin p. 47. " a legal classic of high character ... Kent made it the basis of the forty-seventh lecture of his Commentaries..."

2. ADAMS, JOHN. A treatise on the principles and practice of the action of ejectment, and the resulting action for mesne profits. From the last London edition to which have been carefully noted, the decisions of the Supreme Court of New York, from January Term, 1799, to October Term, 1820. With references to decisions in the Courts of Massachusetts and Pennsylvania, and the Supreme Court of the United States, by Philo Ruggles. N. Y., Gould, 1821. 421pp. Full contemp. sheep, good copy. First American edition. $ 45.00
* Marvin p. 51. A laudatory note but he fails to note this first American appearance.

3. (AIKENS, ASA). Practical forms; with notes and references... together with a lengthy note, giving every legal requisite to the perfection of deeds and other conveyances of real estate, in most of the States of the Union... being a convenient manual, for men to business, conveyances, judges of probate, executors and administrators, sheriffs, town officers, and justices of the peace. Windsor, Vt., Simeon Ide, 1823. 409pp. Full contemp. calf. 12mo. Nice copy. First edition. Shoemaker 11511. $ 27.50

4. ANCHER, PEDER. Dansk Lehns Ret. Kisbenhavn, Gyldendals, 1777. 12pl., 176pp. 8vo. Contemp. 1/4 calf. $ 30.00
* This work by this leading author on Danish law is not in the NUC.

5. Ancient laws and institutes of Wales; comprising laws supposed to be enacted by Howel the Good, modified by subsequent regulations under the native Prices prior to the conquest by Edward the First, and anomalous laws, consisting principally of institutions which by the statute of Ruddlan were admitted to continue in force. With an English translation of the Welsh text, to which are added a few Latin transcripts, containing digests of the Welsh laws, principally of the Dimetian Code, with indexes and glossary. In two vols. Printed by command of his late Majesty King William IV, under the direction of the Commissioners on the Public Records of the Kingdom, 1841. 904;1, 128pp. Orig. cl. Roy. 8vo. Nice set. $125.00

6. ANGELL, JOSEPH K. An inquiry into the rule of law which creates a right to an incorporeal hereditament by an adverse enjoyment of twenty years. With remarks on the application of the rule to light, and in certain cases to a water privilege. Boston, Hilliard, 1827. 117pp. Full contemp. sheep,

6. (Continued). leather label, fine copy. $ 75.00
* First and only edition, and quite uncommon in trade. Marvin p. 62. Shoemaker 27875.

7. ANGELL, JOSEPH K. and SAMUEL AMES Treatise on the law of private corporations aggregate. Fifth edition, revised, corrected and enlarged. Boston, Little, Brown, 1855. 939pp. New cloth. $ 35.00

8. ANGELL, JOSEPH K. A treatise on the right of property in tide waters, and in the soil and shores thereof. 2nd edition, revised, corrected, and much enlarged. Boston, Little, 1847. 475pp. Fine copy. $ 75.00
* Marvin p. 62, "the only regular treatise on this branch of law" Best edition.

9. ANSON, SIR WILLIAM R. Principles of the English law of contract and of agency in its relation to contract. Eighth edition, first American copyright edition, edited with American notes by Ernest W. Huffcut... N. Y., Banks, 1895. 456pp. Cloth. $ 25.00

10. ARCHBOLD, JOHN FREDERICK. The law and practice in bankruptcy, as founded on the recent statute; with forms. London, Sweet, 1825. 170pp. Full contemp. sheep. 12mo. $ 45.00
* First edition of a very popular work which appeared regularly with revisions to 1856. S & M, III, p. 6.

11. (AUCTION CATALOGUE. LAWYER'S LIBRARY.) Catalogue of the valuable and extensive library of Thomas Thomson, Esq., Advocate; consisting of a rare assemblage of works on history, antiquities, general literature, and law. To be sold by auction by Mess. C. B. Tait and Co., No. 11, Hanover St., Edinburgh, on Monday, June 28, 1841, and twelve following days. (Edinburgh, Printed by Ballantyne.) 110pp. Frontis. 1/4 mor. Not priced. $ 50.00
* See DNB for an account of Thomson (1768-1852), an important legal scholar and antiquarian as well as jurist.

THE FIRST FULL-SCALE AMERICAN WORK ON INTERNATIONAL LAW ?

12. BARTON, WILLIAM. A dissertation on the freedom of navigation and maritime commerce and such rights of states, relative thereto, as are founded on the law of nations; adapted more particularly to the United states ... Phila., Conrad, 1802. 340, xlv, (3)pp. Contemp. 1/4 calf. First and only edition. $150.00
* One of the earliest, and quite possibly the first (we invite comment), works of real substance on international law published in America by an American; certainly it is the first on the topic of neutral rights. This is a very able defense of American commercial rights against the claims and reprisals of Great Britain during

12. (Continued). the Napoleonic Wars. It combines a sophisticated knowledge of the classics with a wealth of commentary on recent events to support the dictum that "free ships make free goods," a doctrine which lay at the basis of the "Armed Neutrality" of 1780. Barton was a prominent Philadelphia lawyer and member of the Am. Phil. Society. He dedicated this work to Jefferson. Sabin 3853. Not in Marvin!

13. BEADLE, DELOS W. The American lawyer and business man's form book; containing forms and instructions for (numerous categories) together with the laws of the various states on (numerous topics) and a map and seal for each state in the union. N. Y., Phelps, Fanning, 1852. 359pp. Orig. prtd. bds. Illus. $ 27.50
* Contains recent states such as Texas and California, as well as the southern states.

14. BECCARIA, (CESARE). An essay on crimes and punishments ... with a commentary by M. de Voltaire. A new edition corrected. Edinburgh, Donaldson, 1788. 238pp. 12mo. Contemp. calf, rubbed. $ 65.00

15. BELL, SAMUEL D. Justice and sheriff. Practical forms, for the use of justices of the peace, sher iffs, coroners and constables: containing forms of proceedings and the revised statutes of New-Hampshire... Second edition, including acts since passed, and additional forms. Concord, Lyon, 1850. 495pp. Full contemp. sheep. Nice copy. $ 25.00
* Marvin p. 107 (1st ed. of 1843).

16. (BENSON, WILLIAM). A letter to Sir J____ B____, by birth a Swede, but naturalized and a M____r of the present P____t concerning the late Minehead Doctrine which was established by a certain free Parliament of Sweden, to the utter enslaving of that Kingdom. London, Baldwin, 1711. First edition. 8vo. 40pp. Very good copy. Half-title present. $ 45.00
* A sharp attack on Royal Absolutism in the form of the assertion that the King is accountable only to God, as put forth by Sir Jacob Bankes, MP for Minehead. Rothschild 361.

17. BEMIS, GEORGE. Precedents of American neutrality, in reply to the speech of Sir Roundell Palmer, Attorney-General of England, in the British House of Commons, May 13, 1864. Boston, Little, Brown, 1864. 83pp. Wrps. Fine copy. $ 30.00
* The first of 4 important pamphlets by Bemis on international law questions during the Civil War. "...these pamphlets were distinguished for their uniformly high level of thought ... which stamped their author as a publicist of outstanding merit." --DAB. He played an important role also in the Alabama Claims. A professorship in international law at Harvard was established in his name.

18. BENTHAM, JEREMY. Benthamiana: or select extracts, from the works of ..., with an outline of his opinions on the principal subjects discussed in his works. Edited by John Hill Burton. Phila., Lea., 1844. 446pp. Orig. cl. $ 37.50
* First American edition a year after the Edinburgh edition. Bentham was not published in America between 1796 and 1830 so that this was an appropriate overview for the general public of that time.

19. BENTHAM, JEREMY. The book of fallacies: from unfinished papers of Jeremy Bentham. By a friend. London, John & H. L. Hunt, 1824. xi, 411pp. 8vo. Contemp. 1/4 calf, spine with ornamental tooling, very lightly rubbed, otherwise a fine copy. $250.00
* FIRST EDITION in English, and first appearance of a significant portion of this treatise on the art of government through the process of Parliamentary debate. The editor notes that Dumont had published this work earlier in French, omitting "with a view to Continental circulation ... many applications of the writer's principles to British Institutions and British interests ..." The works on fallacies and tactics constitute together "the first and only purely theoretical and scientific treatise on Parliamentary procedure that has ever been written." Holdsworth, XIII, p. 94.

20. BENTHAM, JEREMY. The elements of the art of packing, as applied to special juries, particularly in cases of libel law. London, Effingham Wilson, 1821. vii, 269pp. plus the final leaf of ads. Original boards and cloth spine with publisher's label, entirely uncut, a bit of foxing to first and last leaves, but a fine copy, in completely original state. $350.00
* FIRST EDITION. A classic in the struggle for freedom of speech. "...some of Bentham's attacks upon the legal and political abuses of his time were so outspoken that Romilly advised him not to publish them. He feared, not without reason, that, if he were prosecuted for libel, a special jury ... would be very likely to convict. This state of the law inspired (this work)." Holdsworth, XIII, p. 99. McCoy B200.

21. BENTHAM, JEREMY. A fragment on government. With an introduction by F. C. Montague. Oxford, Claredon Press, 1891. 241 pp. $ 30.00
* Bentham's first work and a major criticism of Blackstone. This is an important edition with long critical introduction. There is no edition currently in print.

22. BENTHAM, JEREMY. Plan of Parliamentary reform in the form of a catechism, with the reasons for each article, with an introduction shewing the necessity of radical, and the inadequacy of moderate reform. London, Printed for R. Hunter, 1817. 8vo. iv, cccxxxvii, 52, 16, (1)pp. including final leaf of publisher's ads. Early 19th

22. (Continued). century straight grained binder's cloth and leather label. A very nice copy. $750.00
* FIRST EDITION. "Bentham signalized his conversion to the crred of the radical reformers by writing in 1809 a book called 'Plan of Parliamentary Reforms ...' ... Bentham maintained the thesis that the only remedy for the evils that were afflicting the country was a reform of Parliament which would ensure 'democratical ascendancy.' He maintained that the experience of the United States, the constitution of which he considered to be almost perfect, showed that an entirely democraticconsitution was by far the best ... 'Talk of balance,' he said, 'never will it do: leave that to Mother Goose and Mother Blackstone.'" -- Holdsworth, His. of English Law, XIII, 104. Cobett refused to publish the original "Catechism" of 1809 in his Political Register, so it first appeared here with an introduction six times its length. This 1817 edition is apparently quite uncommon, the second edition of 1818 being the one usually found.

23. BENTHAM, JEREMY. Tactique des assemblees legislatives, suivie d'un Traite des Sophismes Politiques; ouvrage extrait des manuscrits de M. Jeremie Bentham ... par Et. Dumont ... Geneve, Paschoud; Paris, 1816 In 2 volumes. 8vo. 361;396pp. Later full morroco, richly gilt with raised bands, spines, covers and inner dentelles gilt with coat of arms on all covers, a.e.g. A fine and very attractive copy; with the half-titles to both volumes. $400.00
* FIRST EDITION in French of the "Tactics" and FIRST EDITION of the "Sophisms", both works concerned with the art of governing by parliamentary bodies. Bentham published in 1791 a fragment of the "Tactics" (see Amano, Bibliography of the Classical Economics, V. 4, pt. 5, p. 490, Tokyo, 1964); Dumont has presented here a much more complete version of that work based on Bentham's unpublished manuscripts. The "Sophisms" was first sketched in outline by Bentham in 1806 - this is its first appearance in print; in 1824 its English version was published. "It was the first and only purely theoretical and scientific treatise on Parliamentary procedure that has ever been written." Holdsworth, XIII, p. 94.

24. BENTHAM, JEREMY. A treatise on judicial evidence, extracted from the manuscripts of Jeremy Bentham by M. Dumont... translated into English. London, From the Law Journal - published by J. W. Paget, 1825. xvi, 366pp. 4to. Modern quarter calf. Half-title present. A very good copy. $325.00
* FIRST EDITION in English. The original edition appeared in 1823, in French. "(The) works on evidence and procedure are the most finished of Bentham's works, and the most fruitful in their suggestions of practical reform." Holdsworth, XIII, p. 83f. John Stuart Mill, who shortly after the appearance of this trans-
24. (Continued). lation edited a five volume work from the same aggregate of manuscripts on evidence, wrote: "He found the philosophy of ... evidence, in a more wretched state than even any other part of the philosophy of law; he carried it at once almost to perfection." In our experience this edition is quite scarce.

25. BEXON, SCIPION. Parallele du code penal d'Angleterre avec les lois penales francaises, et considerations sur les moyens de rendre celles-ci plus utiles. Paris, Fauvelle et Sagnier, an VIII (1800). 8vo. iv, 430pp. Contemp. 1/4 calf, leather label. $125.00
* Uncommon. NUC cites three locations.

26. BIGELOW, ABIJAH. The voters' guide: or, the power, duty & privileges of the constitutional voters in the Commonwealth of Massachusetts ... Leominster, Mass., Wilder, 1807. 156pp. 12mo. Orig. boards, calf spine, very nice copy. $ 50.00
* The earliest such work we have come across; it covers voter and office-holder qualifications from town officials to the Presidency. Shaw-Shoemaker 12144 locates only 4 copies.

27. BINNS, JOHN. Binns's Justice, or Magistrate's Daily Companion: a treatise on the office and duties of aldermen and justices of the peace, in the Commonwealth of Pennsylvania ... Eighth edition, revised, corrected and greatly enlarged by Frederick C. Brightly. Phila., Kay, 1870. 870pp. Full contemp. sheep. $ 22.50

28. BLACKSTONE, WILLIAM. Commentaries on the laws of England ... the first Worcester edition, carefully reprinted from the last London edition, containing the last corrections of the author, the additions by Richard Burn, and continued to the present time by John Williams. Printed at Worcester, Mass., by Isaiah Thomas, 1790. Four volumes, 12mo. Engraved frontis. portrait in volume one, folding table. Bound in the original edition binding of plain sheep, blind cover borders and red leather labels gilt. An extraordinarily fine set in a remarkable state of preservation, virtually free of imperfection or wear. $ 1000.00
* This is the second appearance of Blackstone in America and the first to be published by Isaiah Thomas. It is in fact much less common in holdings than the Phila., 1772 edition. Today both editions have become extremely scarce in trade, and the appearance of a copy such as this is indeed a pleasant surprise. Since it was intended to be a popular, affordable edition in an unsophisticated and relatively fragile binding, it can be expected to turn up, if at all, with substantial wear or defects, which is exactly the case with the single copy we have handled in the past ten years and the very few others we have seen. This copy is about as ideal a set of any work from this period in America that one can hope for. A perfect collector's copy. Printing and the Mind of Man, 212 (1st English edition). Evans 22360.

29. BLACKSTONE, WILLIAM. Commentaries on the laws of England, in four books ... the 14th edition with the last corrections of the author and with notes and additions by Edward Christian ... London, Strahan, 1803. 4 vols. 8vo. Contemporary calf, all spines rebacked in cloth, bindings unattractive but sound; contents good throughout. Engraved frontis-portrait in first vol. Folding table of descents in second vol. $ 85.00

30. BLACKSTONE, WILLIAM. Commentaries on the laws of England, in four books ... the fifteenth edition, with the last corrections of the author and with notes and additions by Edward Christian ... London, Strahan for Cadell & Davies, 1809. In 4 volumes. Engraved frontis-portrait, fold. table. Full contemporary calf, stamped in blind and gilt, spines lettered in gilt. A fine, handsome set. $250.00

31. BLACKSTONE, WILLIAM. Commentaries on the laws of England ... from the eighteenth London edition, with a life of the author and notes by Christian, Chitty, Lee, Hovenden and Ryland: and also references to American cases by a Member of the New York Bar. N. Y., Collins, 1832. In 2 volumes bound as 4. Contemporary sheep and leather labels, a little rubbed but an excellent set. $150.00
* First edition of this Americanized text which according to Marvin p. 123, writing in 1847, was then the most generally used in the United States. This copy is of special interest in that it is interleaved throughout and is annotated, sporadically but in several places substantially, by its original owner, J. S. Carleton, a New Haven lawyer, with comments on American practice and development. The set was purchased by him in 1834 and has both the original bookseller's ticket and the original bill of sale tipped in.

32. BLACKSTONE, WILLIAM. Commentaries on the laws of England: in four books, with an analysis of the work. In two vols. From the nineteenth London edition, with a life of the author, and notes: by Christian, Chitty, Lee, Hovenden, and Ryland: and also references to American cases, by a member of the New-York Bar. N. Y., Dean, 1859. Full contemp. sheep. Very good copy. $ 75.00
* Marvin p. 123. "This edition the most general in use in the U.S." It was first published in 1832. This is a stereotype reprint. There is a good deal of reference to differences between N. Y. State and British law; Blackstone had been an important influence upon the revision of N. Y. law.

33. (BLACKSTONE, WILLIAM). A letter to the author of the Question Stated, by another member of Parliament. London, Printed for Charles Bathurst ... 1769. 24pp. Disbound. A very good copy. $275.00
* FIRST EDITION of a rare Blackstone item concerned with his defense of the House of

33. (Continued). Commons in its expulsion of John Wilkes; Blackstone declared that Wilkes was disqualified by common law from sitting in the House, to which Grenville replied by quoting from the Commentaries the causes for disqualification, none of which applied to Wilkes. Blackstone was too fatigued to say something in his own defense but later stated his case (here) and ammended later editions of the Commentaries to account for his position. This work is part of a pamphlet war which swirled about Wilkes and involved Sir W. Meredith (to whom Blackstone here responds), Junius, Samuel Johnson, and Wilkes himself. (DNB) The NUC locates 4 holdings. There is no copy in Rothschild. Eller #241.

AN EARLY LEGAL-AID SOCIETY

34. (BOUCHER d'ARGIS, Andre-Jean-Baptiste, and others). Recueil de pieces concernant l'Association de Bienfaisance Judiciaire fondee en 1787. Paris, Clousier. Imprime aux frais de M. le Duc De Charost, Pair de France, 1788. 12mo. 222pp. Original marbled wraps, uncut. SOLD
* A remarkable document concerning the founding of a legal society whose purpose is to defend the poor gratis and effect compensation for innocent victims of the law. Boucher's address, contained here with other items including articles of association and a long membership list concluding with Lafayette, is an unsparing attack on class opporession, harsh penal laws and administrative abuse. cf. I.N.E.D. #689 which cites the main address but not this more complete work. The NUC cites only a single location. A rare work marking the earliest such endeavor we have come across.

35. (BOURGUIGNON DUMOLARD, CLAUDE SEBASTIEN). Manuel du juri, ou commentaire sur la legislation relative a l'organisation du juri, ... precede de la theorie du juri ... Paris, Moreau, 1827. 8vo. 548pp. 1/4 calf. $ 55.00
* A substantial work. The NUC cites only the LC copy.

36. BRICE, JOHN. A supplement to the selection of all the laws of the United States, now in force, relative to commercial subjects, with marginal notes & references to the same, classed under separate heads; including in continuation, all the laws passed during the third session of the thirteenth, and the first session of the fourteenth Congress of the United States. Baltimore, published by the editor, 1816. 80pp. Orig. prtd. wrps., uncut. $ 27.50
* Shaw-Shoemaker 37082. Scarce.

37. BROWN, DAVID PAUL. Review of the speech of Henry Brougham upon the state of the law. Phila., Dobson, 1828. 64pp. dsbd. A very good copy. $ 35.00
* Brown was a very eminent Philadelphia jurist. He began as a student of William Rawle to whom this very early work is dedicated. In it he considers Brougham's epochal call for reform of
37. (Continued). the common law in its relation to America whose legal system he considers to have anticipated and vindicated Brougham's ideas. (See DAB).

38. (BROWN, WILLIAM). A compendious and accurate treatise of recoveries upon writs of entries in the post and fines upon writs of covenant with ample and copious instruction ... London, Sawbridge ... 1678. 23pl, 303pp. including privilege leaf and tables. Contemp. calf, extremities of spine little worn, front joint rather crudely repaired, internally a fine copy. $225.00
* FIRST EDITION. Wing B5081. Marvin p. 152. There were 6 further editions to 1725.

39. BROWNE, IRVING. Elements of the law of domestic relations, and of employer and employed. Second edition, revised. Boston, Boston Book Co., 1890. 166pp. Orig. cl. $ 22.50

40. BROWNSON, (ORESTES A.). The American Republic: its constitution, tendencies, and destiny. N. Y., P. O'Shea, 1866. xvi, 439pp. Orig. cl. A fine copy. $ 55.00
* First edition. An important work on constitutional theory with application to Reconstruction Brownson was closer to Sumner than Calhoun, whom he once supported for President. He writes here as a converted Catholic, and has much to say about church-state relationship. Published by a Catholic house.

41. BRYCE, JAMES. The American Commonwealth. In two vols. ... London, MacMillan, 1889. 750;743pp. Orig. cl. Fine. $ 30.00
* Original edition, in 2 volume format, rather than 3, preserving textual material later edited out.

42. BURN, RICHARD. The Justice of the Peace, and Parish Officer ... continued to the present time by John Burn ... The seventeenth edition; including the statutes of the last session of Parliament (32 Geo. III.) to which is added an appendix, containing the Act Respecting Aliens, and such others as have passed in the present session. In four volumes. London, Printed by A. Strahan, 1793. 4 vols. 8vo., contemp. calf, one joint repaired but a very good set. $150.00
* Marvin p. 163. "The most useful book ever published on the law relating to justices of the peace ..." It continued to be published until the mid-19th century. The edition offered here is of particular interest for its appendix on aliens and treason, reflecting English (and American) reaction to the French Revolution. Burn's work was adapted to American law as early as 1773.

ORIGIN OF THE "THREE MILE LIMIT"

43. BYNKERSHOEK, CORNELIUS VAN (1673 - 1743). A treatise on the law of war. Translated from the original Latin of ... being the first book of his Quaestiones Juris Publici. With notes by Peter Stephen Du Ponceau. Phila., Farrand & Nicholas ... 1810. 8vo. xxxiv, 218pp Contemp. polished calf. Very fine. $135.00
* First American edition and the first systematic translation into the English language. It ranks as one of the classics of international law, and was accepted widely as an authority. -- Marvin p. 168. Du Ponceau came to America during the Revolution. His background in European law and languages resulted in his attaining a foremost position in American legal practice for the litigation of international disputes associated with the Napoleonic Wars. This work reflects his intimate practical experience as well as his considerable scholarship. An extremely attractive copy.

A MAJOR SOUTHERN INTERPRETATION OF THE CONSTITUTION

44. CALHOUN, JOHN C. A disquisition on government and a discourse on the Constitution and Government of the United States. Edited by Richard K. Cralle. Published under the direction of the General Assembly of the State of South Caroline. Charleston, Steam Power Press of Walker & James, 1851. 406pp. New cl. $ 87.50
* First edition, appearing posthumously and with the blessing of the State of South Carolina, of a very important Southern contribution to American political theory. As John Taylor earlier gave perfect expression to "states' rights" theory, Calhoun further developed the rationale for Southern rights through the distinction of "constitutional" or "concurrent" as opposed to "numerical" majorities. His view of the origin and nature of the Constitution was carried on by Upshur, in sharp opposition to Story. Surprisingly uncommon book in trade!

45. CAMPBELL, JOHN W. Biographical sketches with other literary remains ... Columbus,Ohio, Scott & Gallagher, 1838. 279pp. Engr. portraits, original linen, good copy. $ 45.00
* Campbell was an Ohio lawyer, politician and briefly U. S. District Judge. Includes his legal and political writings along with other miscellania and several good biographical sketches. See DAB for an account.

46. CAMPBELL, JOHN D. and STEPHEN CAMBRELENG. The American chancery digest; being a digest index of all the reported decisions in equity, in the United States courts, and in the courts of the several states. N. Y., Gould, 1828. 584pp. Full contemp. sheep. $ 45.00
* Marvin p. 172. First edition.

47. (CANADA). LORTIE, EDMOND. Le guide des coroners ... Quebec, "Le Soleil", 1902. 138pp. 12mo. cl. $ 12.50

Please consult index for other items relating to Canada

48. CARE, HENRY. English liberties, or the free-born subject's inheritance. Containing Magna Charta ... Habeas Corpus Act (etc.) ... also a declaration of the liberties of the subject ... petition of right ... of trials by juries ... lastly of justices of the peace, and coroners: With many law cases throughout the whole. Compiled first by Henry Care, and continued with large additions, by William Nelson ... the sixth edition, corrected and improved. Providence, Rhode Island, John Carter, 1774. viii, 350, (6)pp, including list of subscribers. Square 8vo. Contemp. plain calf, border stamped in blind. A very nice copy in the original American binding. $125.00
* A timely reappearance of this libertarian classic, actually its second publication in America, the first being 1721. Evans 13185. Marvin p. 173.

49. CHAMBERLIN, FRANKLIN. American commercial law, relating to every kind of business: ....adapted to all the states of the Union. Hartford, 1870. 991pp. Sheep, v. good copy. $ 25.00

50. CHITTY, JOSEPH. A practical treatise on the criminal law; comprising the practice, pleadings, and evidence, which occur in the course of criminal prosecutions ... with additional notes of decisions in the courts of the United States, and of many of the State courts, by Richard Peters Jr. ... Two vols. in three. Phila., Riley, 1819. 823, 1027pp. Full contemp. sheep. Nice set. $ 75.00
* First American edition, from the first London of 1816. Marvin p. 192: "This is one of the author's best productions. It has had an extended circulation throughout the United States, and has hitherto been more generally used than any other book upon criminal law."

51. CHRISTISON, ROBERT. A treatise on poisons, in relation to medical jurisprudence, physiology, and the practice of physic. First American, from the fourth Edinburgh edition. Phila., Barrington, 1845. 743pp. Full contemp. sheep. $ 50.00
* Marvin p. 196. "It exhausts the subject, and is of the highest authority."

52. (CHURCH-STATE RELATIONSHIP). Address to the American people by the Provisional National Association for the Complete Secularization of the State ... Chicago, Religio-Philosophical Journal, 1881. 23pp. Orig. prtd. wrps. $ 12.50

53. (CHURCH-STATE RELATIONSHIP). GLADSTONE, RIGHT HON. W. E. The Vatican Decrees in their bearing on civil allegiance: a political expostulation. With the replies of Archbishop Manning, Lord Acton, and the Right Rev. Monsignor Capel. N. Y., Appleton, 1874. 96pp. Orig. prtd. wrps. Fine. $ 17.50

54. (CHURCH-STATE RELATIONSHIP). (MORMONS). Marriage: monogamy and polygamy on the basis of divine law, of natural law, and of constitutional law. An open letter to the Massachusetts Members of Congress, by one of their constituents, with observations on the opinion of the Supreme Court in Reynolds vs. United States, 98 U. S. Supreme Court Reports, by a citizen of Massachusetts. Boston, Campbell, 1882. 76pp. Wrps. $ 50.00
* An unusual pro-Mormon defense based upon principles of religious toleration.

55. (CHURCH-STATE RELATIONSHIP). NATIONAL CONVENTION TO SECURE THE RELIGIOUS AMENDMENT OF THE CONSTITUTION OF THE UNITED STATES. Proceedings ... with an account of the origin and progress of the movement. Phila., Rodgers, 1872. xvi, 72pp. wrps. $ 17.50
* Attempt to rejoin church and state. Cincinnati Conv.

56. (CHURCH-STATE RELATIONSHIP). NATIONAL CONVENTION TO SECURE THE RELIGIOUS AMENDMENT OF THE CONSTITUTION OF THE UNITED STATES. Proceedings ... with an account of the origin and progress of the movement. N. Y., Polhemus, 1873. xvi, 78pp. Orig. prtd. wrps. $ 17.50
* Attempt to rejoin church and state. N. Y. Convention.

57. (CIVIL WAR). PITMAN, BENN, Editor. The trials for treason at Indianapolis, disclosing the plans for establishing a Northwestern Confederacy ... to which is added the full report of Judge ... Holt on the Order of American Knights, alias the Sons of Liberty; a Western conspiracy in aid of the Southern rebellion. Cincinnati, Moore, Wilstach & Baldwin, 1865. 8vo. 340pp. Fine engraved frontis containing five portraits of the conspirators. Text in double column. Orig. publ. cl., trifle worn at head of spine, but a fine copy. $ 85.00

58. CLARK, E.C. Early Roman law: the regal period. London, MacMillan, 1872. 151pp. Orig. cl. $ 20.00

59. COKE, EDWARD. The first part of the Institutes of the Laws of England: or, a commentary upon Littleton ... also three learned tracts ... the twelfth edition, carefully corrected ... to which is added, the Treatise of the Old Tenures of the Laws of England ... (London) Nutt & Gosling, 1738. Folio, 1pl., 804pp. plus tables and large fold. illustration. Contemp. calf, rebacked. Lacks the frontis-portrait; contents fine. A good copy. $125.00
(Continued on next page)

59. (Continued).
* S & M, I, 450. Marvin 204ff. The most important of the Institutes and one of the great summaries of learning and experience bridging the medieval and modern periods; it remained a force in legal literature into the 19th century.

60. COLEMAN, MRS. CHAPMAN., ed. The life of John J. Crittenden, with selections from his correspondence and speeches. Edited by his daughter ... In 2 vols. Phila., Lippincott, 1871. 389, 391pp. Frontis. Orig. cl. $ 45.00
* "A valuable source" DAB. Crittenden was an important Kentucky lawyer and national statesman, especially prominent in the McLeod incident and, later, in the rupture of the Union.

61. COLQHOUN, PATRICK. A treatise on the police of the metropolis; containing a detail of the various crimes and misdemeanors ... and suggesting remedies for their prevention. The sixth edition corrected and considerably enlarged. London, Baldwin for Mawman, 1800. 8vo. 8pl, xvi, 655pp. Contemporary tree calf, spine ornately gilt with leather label. An exceedingly fine and attractive copy. With folding tables. $150.00
* A substantially expanded edition of this very informative classic. It affords an excellent view of society during the upheavals of the early industrial revolution, with sections on the state of the poor, prostitution, transportation to New South Wales, etc. including an up-to-date summary of the statistics of transported felons, and an account of the penal systems being proposed by Jeremy Bentham. Ferguson 305.

Pamphlets relating to the constitutional crisis under Lincoln.

Horace Binney, 1780-1875, a prominent Philadelphia lawyer, wrote a series of three pamphlets defending Lincoln's action in suspending the writ; they begot considerable critical replies.

62. (BROWN, D.B.) Reply to Horace Binney on the privilege of the writ of habeas corpus under the Constitution. By a member of the Philadelphia Bar. Phila., Challen, 1862. 31pp. Orig. wrp. $ 20.00

63. BULLITT, J.C. A review of Mr. Binney's pamphlet on "The Privilege of the Writ of Habeas Corpus under the Constitution." Phila., J. Campbell, 1862. 56pp. Wrps. $ 20.00

64. (GROSS, CHARLES H.) A reply to Horace Binney's pamphlet on habeas corpus. Phila., 1862. 40pp. Orig. wrp. $ 20.00

65. (MONTGOMERY, JOHN T.) The writ of habeas corpus and Mr. Binney. (Phila., 1862). 35pp. disbound. First edition. $ 20.00

66. (WHARTON, GEORGE M.) Remarks on Mr. Binney's treatise on the writ of habeas corpus. By a member of the Philadelphia Bar. Phila., 1862. 29pp. Orig. wrp. $ 20.00

67. CURTIS, BENJAMIN R. Executive power. Boston, Little, Brown, 1862. 29p. Wrps. $ 25.00
* Attacks Lincoln's "usurpation" of power in connection with the Emancipation Proclamation.

68. KIRKLAND, CHARLES P. A letter to the Hon. Benjamin R. Curtis late Judge of the Supreme Court of the United States in review of his recently published pamphlet on the "Emancipation Proclamation ..." second edition. N. Y., Randolph, 1863. 20p. Wrps., fine.
* Defends Lincoln's action. $ 22.50

End of Section

69. (CONSTITUTIONS AND ARTICLES OF CONFEDERATION). The Constitutions of the several independent states of America; the Declaration of Independence; and the Articles of Confederation. To which are now added, the Declaration of Rights; the Non-Importation Agreement; and the Petition of Congress to the King ... with an appendix, containing the treaties between His Majesty and the United States; the Provisional Treaty with America; and (never before published) an authentic copy of the Treaty between ... the States-General, and the United States ... the whole arranged, with a preface and dedication by William Jackson. London, Stockdale, 1783. 8vo. 19pl., 472, 4pp. publ. ads. With an engraved frontis portrait of Washington. Contemporary calf, gilt, little rubbed but a very good copy. $225.00
* Second and best London edition, with added material present here for the first time in any edition. Howes C 716. Sabin 16088.

70. COWDERY, JABEZ F. The Pacific Law Encyclopedia, a complete handbook of all matters ordinarily coming before judges, attorneys, justices of the peace, (etc.) ... with forms in conformity with the statutes of, and designed for use in, the States and Territories of the Pacific Coast. Third ed. San Francisco, Bancroft, 1872. 814pp. Full contemp. sheep. Very good copy. Rare. $ 65.00

71. COWEN, ESEK. A treatise on the civil jurisdiction of a justice of the peace in the State of New York. Albany, Gould, 1821. 748pp. Full contemp. calf. Good copy. $ 55.00
* First edition. Marvin p. 234: "No law book, local in its character, enjoys a better or more widely extended reputation ... from its excellent method, completeness and accuracy, it is found to be very well adapted to the wants of justices in several of the new states ..."

72. (COXE, TENCH). An examination of the conduct of Great Britain respecting neutrals, since the year 1791. Second ed. with corrections and ammendments. Boston, Oliver, 1808. 72pp. dsbd. $ 35.00
* Strong attack on British policy in 15 letters signed "Juriscola". Gaines 8-23. Kress B5329. Sabin 17297.

73. CRUISE, WILLIAM Essay on the nature and operation of fines and recoveries. Second edition, revised, corrected, and enlarged. 2 vols, in one. London, Brooke, 1786. 342;304;56pp. Full contemp. calf, front joint mended. A good copy. $ 65.00
* Marvin 243. First edition was 1783, third and last 1794.

74. CURTIS, GEORGE TICKNOR. The American conveyancer; containing a large variety of legal forms and instruments ... together with forms ... under the patent laws ... new edition. Boston, Little and Brown, 1847. 283pp. Calf. $ 37.50
* Marvin p. 247f.

75. CUSHING, ABEL. Historical letters on the first charter of Massachusetts government. Boston, Bang, 1839. 204pp. 1/4 cl. 12mo. Author presentation copy. $ 22.50

76. CUSHING, LUTHER STEARNS. Lex Parliamentaria Americana. Elements of the law and practice of legislative assemblies in the United States of America. Boston, Little, Brown, 1856. 1063pp. Original cloth. Imperial 8vo. A fine copy. $ 85.00
* FIRST EDITION on the first and greatest work by an American on this subject. It was recognized immediately as a classic, authoritative performance.

77. DANIEL, JOHN W. A treatise on the law of negotiable instruments, including bills of exchange, promissory notes; negotiable bonds and coupons, checks; bank notes; certificates of deposit, certificates of stock; bills of credit; bills of lading; guaranties; letter of credit; and circular notes. In two vols. N. Y., Baker, 1876. 707, 798pp. Full contemp. calf. First edition. $ 45.00

78. DAVIS, CHARLES G. Report of the trial of Samuel M. Andrews, indicted for the murder of Cornelius Holmes, before the Supreme Judicial Court of Massachusetts, Dec. 11, 1868. Including the rulings of the court upon many questions of law, and a full statement of authorities upon the subject of transitory insanity. N. Y., Hurd, 1869. 287pp. Orig. prtd. wrps, soiled. $ 27.50
* A trial which attracted much attention. Contains ample matter relating to the plea of insanity, which however failed to absolve the defendant.

79. DE LOLME, J.L. The constitution of England or, an account of the English government: in which it is compared, both with the Republican form of government, and the other monarchies in Europe. A new edition enlarged. N. Y., Hodge & Campbell, 1792. xvi, (25)-376, (8)pp. 8vo. Contemp. calf. A good copy. $ 50.00
* Evans 24263. First and only American edition of this classic. "...it is remarkable that a

79. (Continued). foreigner should have been the first to write a clear, concise, and accurate treatise upon the constitutional law of England ... Judge Story remarks that the author 'has presented a view of English equity jurisprudence far more exact and comprehensive than many of the English text writers on the same subject.'" Marvin p. 263.

80. DICKINSON, RODOLPHUS. A digest of the common law, the statute laws of Massachusetts and of the United States, and the decisions of the Supreme Judicial Court of Massachusetts, relative to the powers and duties of justices of the peace, to which is subjoined an extensive appendix of forms. Deerfield, Wilson, 1818. 521pp. Full contemp. sheep. First edition. A fine copy.
* Marvin p. 266. $ 45.00

81. DICKINSON, RODOLPHUS. A digest of the powers and duties of sheriffs, coroners, constables and collectors of taxes. Springfield, Massachusetts, Dickman, 1810. 232p. Orig. calf., nice copy. First edition. $ 45.00
* Marvin p. 266. Shaw-Shoemaker 19964.

82. DIGBY, KENELM EDWARD, et al. An introduction to the history of the law of real property, with original authorities. Fifth edition. Oxford, Clarendon Press, 1897. 448pp. Orig. cl. $ 22.50

83. (DOMAT, JEAN). Les loix civiles dans leur ordre naturel, suivie du Droit Public &c. Nouvelle ed., rev. et corrigee de nouveau. Luxembourg, Chevalier, 1702. Folio. 2 volumes in one. Contemp. calf, raised bands. A very good copy. $175.00
* Domat's work was the "first successful attempt to reduce to order the civil law of France" (Marvin p. 171 citing Story and Hoffman). "It was the first step in that movement to cut through traditional categories which culminated in the French Revolution and the civil code ... (it had) a vogue that spread beyond France (and) was frequently cited in England ... Domat was in a sense the founder of the science of public law in France, since his little treatise Le Droit Public... was the first French work on this subject." Encyclopaedia of the Social Sciences.

84. DRAKE, CHARLES D. A treatise on the law of suits by attachment in the United States. Fourth edition, revised, corrected and enlarged: with an appendix, containing the leading statutory provisions of the several states and territories of the United States in relation to suits by attachment. Boston, Little, Brown, 1873. lix, 699pp. Full contemp. sheep. $ 30.00

85. (HIGGINS, JESSE) Sampson against the Philistines, or the reformation of lawsuits; and justice made cheap, speedy... agreeably to the principles of the ancient trial by jury, before the same was innovated by judges and lawyers. Compiled for the use of the honest citizens of the United States, to whom it is dedicated. Second ed. Phila., Prtd. by B. Graves, for W. Duane, 1805. 98pp. disbound. $ 35.00
* Marvin p. 627.

86. DUMERIL, HENRI Lord Erskine: etude sur le barreau anglais a la fin du xviii siecle. Paris, Thorin, 1883. 375pp. 1/4 cl. Fine. $ 20.00
* Good study of this critical figure in political and free speech trials. Not in McCoy.

87. EATON, DORMAN B. Civil Service in Great Britain: a history of abuses and reforms and their bearing upon American politics. N. Y., Harper, 1880. 469pp. Orig. cl. o.p. $ 17.50
* Author was Chairman of U.S. Civil Service Commission.

88. EMERIGON, BALTHAZARD-MARIE. Traite des assurances et des contrats a la grosse. Marseille, Jean Mossy, 1788. Two volumes, 4to. xvi, 686;680(4)pp 19th century half-calf, preliminary and final leaves stained, otherwise a good copy. $150.00
* One of the great and influential classics on insurance law. "Of all the French writers upon commercial law, E. holds the first rank, His writings and his reputation are not confined to France alone, for the jurists of England and the United States have equally derived assistance from his labors ... Chancellor Kent ... remarks that his Treatise 'very far surpasses all preceeding works ...'." Marvin p. 293.

89. ERNST, GEORGE A.O. The legal status of married women in Massachusetts. Boston, Mass. Woman Suffrage Assoc., 1895. 81pp. Orig. cl. Autograph presentation by author. $ 22.50

90. FARRAR, TIMOTHY. Report of the case of the Trustees of Dartmouth College against William H. Woodward. Argued and determined in the Superior Court of ... the State of New Hampshire ... and on error in the Supreme Court of the United States ... Portsmouth, Foster, (1819). 2pl., 406pp. Contemp. calf, rubbed, some pencil marginalia but a good copy. $ 50.00
* Marvin p. 303. A landmark case elucidating the contract clause of the constitution and the rights of corporations.

91. FELL, WALTER WILLIAM. A treatise on the law of mercantile guarantees, and of principal and surety in general. First American edition, from the second and last English edition, with notes and references to American decisions by Charles Walker. N. Y., Lamson, 1825. 435pp. Full contemp. calf. Fine. Very Scarce. $ 75.00
* A good example of an English work which was taken over by the American profession. The last English edition appeared in 1820, but the work continued to be published with revisions in America to 1872. This first edition is quite uncommon in trade. Marvin p. 305. S & M, III p. 77.

92. FIELD, RICHARD S. The Provincial Courts of New Jersey, with sketches of the bench and bar: a discourse read before the New Jersey Historical Society. N. Y., Bartlett, 1849. 311pp. Orig. pict. cl. Fine copy. Author presentation copy. $ 55.00
* Collections of the New Jersey Historical Society, Vol. III.

93. FIELD, STEPHEN J. Personal reminiscence of early days in California with other sketches. To which is added the story of his attempted assassination by a former associate on the supreme bench of the state, by Hon. George C. Gorham. Printed for a few friends. Not Published. (1893). vi, 406pp. Original cloth, a fine copy. Inscribed "With the compliments of Stephen J. Field." $125.00
* The judicial reminiscences of this Supreme Court and California State justice. They were dictated in 1877 and published in an edition of 50 copies in 1880. To the original reminiscences are added here for the first time "Annoyances of my Judicial Life" and the account of the attempted assassination, about two-thirds of the book.

95. FILMER, ROBERT. Patriarcha: or the natural power of kings. London, Davis, 1680. 8pl., 141pp. Engraved frontis portrait, title within rules. New full blind-stamped calf, leather label, in attractive period style. $300.00
* FIRST EDITION of a classic manifesto in defense of absolute government, and the target of John Locke's counterattack in the first of the "Two Treatises on Government" of 1690. Filmer differed with Hobbes' compact theory as well as with his dismal view of human nature, but he arrived at about the same destination, defending the absolute sovereignty of the monarch. The work appeared posthumously; in this same year Algernon Sydney, another libertarian, wrote (though did not publish) his great defense of republican government directly in response to Filmer. Wing F922. Other copies we have seen or handled usually lack the frontispiece present here.

96. FISHER, R. A. A digest of reported cases determined in the House of Lords & Privy Council, and in the Courts of Common Law, Divorce, Probate, Admiralty & Bancrupty, from Michaelmas term, 1756, to Hilary term, 1870: with references to the statutes and rules of court. Founded on the Analytical Digest by Harrison, and adapted to the present practice of the law. In five vols... London, Sweet, 1870. 10053pp. Roy. 8vos. Contemp. 3/4 mor. $ 75.00
* The work was continued annually but this is the complete basic set as first published. S & M, III, 79.

97. FLANDERS, HENRY. A treatise on the law of shipping. Phila., Johnson, 1853. 580pp. Full contemp. sheep. First edition., $ 45.00

98. FOLLEVILLE, DANIEL De. Etude sur les associations commerciales en participation: leurs caracteres distinctifs. Paris, Durand 1865. 94pp. Stiff prtd. wrps. Fine. $ 30.00
* Original, and perhaps unique detailed study of a special type of corporate commercial entity in the French legal system.

99. FOSS, EDWARD. Biographia Juridica: a biographical dictionary of the judges of England, from the conquest to the present time, 1066-1870. London, Murray, 1870. 792pp. Orig. cl. Double col. text. $ 45.00

100. (FRANCE. CIVIL CODE) JOUSSE, (DANIEL). Nouveau commentaire sur l'ordonnance civile du mois d'Avril 1667. Nouvelle edition, augmentee de l'idee de la justice civile. Paris, Debure, 1767. 2 vols. 850pp. Contemp. mottled calf. $ 75.00
* Final edition of this very prominent commentary. The NUC cites 3 holdings.

THE NAPOLEONIC CODE

101. (FRANCE. LAWS). Code civil des Francais. Edition originale et seule officielle. Paris, De l'Imprimerie de la Republique. An XII - 1804. Large quarto, ornamental vignette on title page, with half-title. 579pp. A magnificent copy in completely original and perfect condition, in pink publisher's wraps, printed paper spine label, entirely uncut. $500.00
* FIRST EDITION, IN THE FINEST FORMAT (An octavo was issued at the same time.) of one of the landmarks of modern European history. Combining the legacy of the past, from Justinian to Domat and Pothier, with the innovations of the French Revolution, this was the first modern code of private substantive law. It is divided into three books, treating of persons, property and the acquisition of ownership, heavily though not entirely influenced in form and substance by Roman law - it made the first provisions in modern western law for legislation on divorce and adoption. Napoleon conceived of the code as the unifying element in his vision of a European empire; in fact it achieved something of this nature by becoming the model, and in some cases by being itself adopted, wherever the law was in need of restatement, both in Europe and Latin America. "The Code Civil, being the pioneer, was eagerly accepted as the model and became 'to a great extent the code of all the Latin races.' From its promulgation to the end of the century no civil code was framed anywhere which it did not profoundly influence, and many of the later codes do little more than reproduce it." Encyclopaedia of the Social Sciences, v II, p. 604ff. See also the article in the Encyclopaedia Britannica 11th ed. A highly desireable copy of this "deluxe" edition of this singular document. The NUC cites only three holdings of this format in America. It is especially rare in pristine original state.

102. (FRANCE. LAWS). Code civil des Francais. Edition originale et seule officielle. Paris, De l'Imprimerie de la Republique. An XII -1804. 8vo. 436pp., with half title. Ornamental vignette on title page. Entirely uncut, in contemporary boards, a fine copy. $100.00
* FIRST EDITION, in octavo format, of the Civil Code, known as the Napoleonic Code, the first modern code of its kind, intended by Napoleon to serve as the basis of a united European empire, and in fact a profound influence throughout the rest of the century on European and Latin American law.

103. (FRANCE. LAWS). Code civil des Francais. Edition originale et seule officielle. ISSUED WITH: Table alphabetique des matieres du code civil ... Paris, De l'Imprimerie de la Republique, (and) Paris, chez Rondonneau, (respectively) An XII-1804. 436;240pp. 8vo. Original wraps worn, contents fine. $150.00
* FIRST EDITION, in octavo format and with the supplementary tables separately published, of the Civil Code, known as the Napoleonic Code.

104. (FRANCE. LAWS). Code de procedure civile. Edition originale et seule officielle. Paris, De l'Imprimerie Imperiale, 1806. 4to. 358pp. Entirely uncut, in the original pink wrappers and printed spine label, paper backstrip worn partially through age, nevertheless a fine copy internally in completely original state. $150.00
* FIRST EDITION, in finest format, large quarto, of the code of civil procedure, the second of the great reforms of French law to come out of the Napoleonic era, and the practical handmaiden of the monumental Code Civile of 1804. A very desireable copy of this important work.

105. (FRANCE. LAWS, STATUTES). Les huit codes en miniature avec indication de leurs articles correlatifs suivis du tarif des frais et depens en matiere civile et criminelle, d'un appendice progressif contenant les lois et ordonnances principales rendues jusqu'a ce jour, et d'un table analytique des matieres. Paris, Roret, 1833. 16mo. 828pp. 1/4 calf., fine. $ 75.00
* A pocket size library of French law from the Napoleonic era with all of its major reforms; included are the code politique, civil, du procedure civil, commerce, penal, etc... along with legal fees and additional statutes.

106. (FRANCE. CONSTITUTIONS). Examen impartial de l'Acte Additionnel du 22 avril 1815, aux constitutions de l'Empire. Paris, Alexis Eymery, 1815. 4to. 16pp. Text in double column. Original plain wrps., uncut. Fine. $ 25.00

107. (FRANCE. MINING LEGISLATION). Recueil des lois, arretes et instructions sur les mines, minieres, carrieres et usines. Contenant toute la legislation en cette matiere, depuis ... 1791, jusqu'a ce jour; divers extraits des Chartes du Hainaut; les decisions ministerielles ... Mons, Monjot, 1824. 255pp. Orig. bds. $ 60.00
* Not in Kress Catalogue. Deals in part with safety, public health and regulation of workers. Not found in the NUC which records similar works of this period in France.

108. FREEMAN, SAMUEL. The town officer; or the power and duty of (various officers) as contained in the laws of the Commonwealth of Massachusetts ... Portland, Benjamin Titcomb, 1790. Small 4to. Contemp. calf. 178(?)pp. Very good copy. $ 75.00
* FIRST EDITION. Evans 23389. Marvin p. 323. This edition is rare. Interesting material on poor-laws, regulation of foodstuffs, tobacco, etc.

109. GALLAUDET, EDWARD M. A manual of international law. Fourth edition, with an introductory note relating to recent American diplomacy. N. Y., Holt, 1892. 338pp. Orig. cl. $ 27.50
* Gallaudet is best known as pioneer educator of the deaf and dumb; this text is based on a treatise by Charles Calvo published in Paris 1870 - 72, with original material added. The whole was intended to provide a usable, intelligent source for American general education.

110. GALLY, HENRY. Some considerations upon clandestine marriages. Second edition, with additions. London, Printed by J. Hughs, 1750. 164pp. Full contemp. calf, joints cracked. $ 85.00
* The author places the matter of the family and its well-being squarely within the control of government and urges strict enforcement of the laws against clandestine marriages. The work was noticed in the contemporary Parliamentary debates on the Marriage Laws (DNB). S & M, I, 499.

111. (GAME LAWS). A view of the principal parts of the most important statutes relating to game; with explanatory cases and observations. By an attorney. Ashburton, (Devonshire), printed and sold for the compiler by J. Ellis: sold in London by Lackington, Allen & Co., 1801. Original boards, spine and edges worn, covers a little soiled, but a very good, uncut copy. $100.00
* A very appealing and able work on game laws and apparently a very rare provincial imprint. We are unable to trace this work in Halkett & Laing, the NUC or BM catalogue, or Sweet & Maxwell; the imprint is not mentioned in Powers' Typographical Gazetteer, 1870, which was an attempt at a complete listing of provincial printing in Great Britain.

112. GARDNER, DANIEL. A treatise on international law, and a short explanation of the jurisdiction and duty of the government of the United States. T N. Y., Tuttle, 1844. 315p. Cl. $ 25.00

113. GNEIST, DR. RUDOLF. The English Parliament in its transformations through a thousand years. Translated by R. Jenery Shee. Boston, Little, Brown, 1886. 380pp. Orig. cl. o.p. $ 20.00

114. GODOLPHIN, JOHN. The orphans legacy: or a testamentary abridgement. In three parts... wherein the most material points of law ... are succintly treated, as well according to the common and temporal, as ecclesiastical and civil laws ... with a great variety of select cases ... the second edition much augmented and enlarged. London, Wilkinson, 1677. 4to. 4pl., 478pp. Plus index matter. New cloth. $150.00
* S & M, I, 492. Wing G974. Marvin p. 340.

115. GODOLPHIN, JOHN. The orphans legacy: or, a testamentary abridgement. In three parts... wherein the most material points of law relating to that subject are succinctly treated, as well according to the common and temporal, as ecclesiastical and civil laws ... illustrated with a great variety of select cases ... the third edition much augmented and enlarged. London, Atkins for Wilkinson ... 1685. 4to. 4pl,478pp. Plus index matter. New cloth. $150.00
* S & M, 1, 492. Wing G948. Marvin p. 340.

116. GOODRICH, JOHN. The civil and executive officers' assistant, containing the forms of bonds, bills, deeds, (etc.) ... with the power and duty of justices of the peace as contained in the laws of the State of Connecticut and exhibiting the duty and province of select-men, constables, grand-jurors, ... New Haven, Abel Morse, 1793. xii,(9)-305pp. 8vo. Contemp. calf., leather label. A very good copy. FIRST EDITION. $125.00
* Apparently the first such work for the state of Connecticut. Evans 25556.

117. GRAHAM, DAVID. An essay on new trails. N. Y., Halsted, 1834. 636pp. Full contemp. sheep. Very nice copy. $ 75.00
* FIRST EDITION. Marvin p. 344. Essentially the first serious attempt by an American writer to treat this topic; Graham notes in his introduction the only other works at his disposal being Grant's "Summary" and Morgan's "Essay" - both British texts. This treatise was conceived with special reference to N. Y. State but is intended to have general utility. Graham soon became the first Professor of Pleading and Practice at the newly founded law School of New York University. A scarce book.

118. GRANT-DUFF, M.E. Sir Henry Maine, a brief memoir of his life, with some of his Indian speeches and minutes, selected and edited by Whitley Stokes, with portrait. N. Y., Holt, 1892. 451pp. First American edition. Orig. cl. Fine. o.p. $ 37.50
* Reflects Maine's brilliant legal contributions while serving in India for seven years.

119. GREENLEAF, SIMON. A discourse pronounced at the inauguration of the author as Royal Professor of Law, in Harvard University, August, 26, 1834. Cambridge, Munroe, 1834. 28pp. Disbound. A very good copy. $ 20.00
* "To the efforts of Story and Greenleaf is to be ascribed the rise of the Harvard Law School to its eminent position." DAB.

120. GROSS, CHARLES. The gild merchant: a contribution to British municipal history. In two vols. Oxford, Clarendon Press, 1890. 332,447pp. o.p. $ 65.00
* S & M, I, 531.

121. HALE, SIR MATTHEW. The history of the pleas of the Crown... First American edition, with notes and references to later cases by W. A. Stokes and E. Ingersoll.... In two vols. Phila., Small, 1847. 752, lxiv, 644pp. Full contemp. sheep. Good set. $ 45.00

122. HALL, JOHN E. The practice and jurisdiction of the court of admiralty; in three parts. 1. An historical examination of the civil jurisdiction ... 2. A translation of Clerke's Praxis, with notes on the jurisdiction and practice of the district courts. 3. A collection of precedents. Baltimore, Dobbin & Murphy, 1809. xxviii, iv, 211, (5)pp. Original paper boards, spine worn; internally fine, largely unopened and entirely uncut. In all a very nice copy. $125.00
* First edition of the author's first book, one of the earliest, if not the first, original American treatises on admiralty law. In the previous year Hall began the first American legal periodical, The American Law Journal. Both it and this treatise reflect the growing involvement of the legal profession in commercial law and particularly in mercantile insurance causes. See Horwitz, Transformation of American Law, 1977, p. 141. Marvin p. 362. DAB.

123. HALLECK, H. W. International law: or, rules regulating the intercourse of states in peace and war. N. Y., Van Nostrand, 1861. 907pp. Full contemp. sheep. $ 45.00
* FIRST EDITION. Conceived originally while the author was serving in the Mexican War as commander of the Pacific Squadron and as Secretary of State of California. The preface is dated San Francisco, May 1861.

FINAL EDITION IN THE AUTHOR'S LIFETIME WITH HIS REVISIONS

124. (HAMILTON, ALEXANDER and others). The Federalist on the new Constitution. By Publius. Written in 1788, to which is added, Pacificus on the Proclamation of Neutrality, written in 1793. Likewise the Federal Constitution with all the ammendments. Revised and Corrected. In two volumes. N. Y., George F. Hopkins, 1802. 2vols., new 1/4 calf, a very good set. $150.00
* "This edition was probably edited by William Coleman, and was the last issued during Hamilton's lifetime ... the text is much altered ..." Sabin 23981. Ford, Bibliotheca Hamiltoniana., #21, notes that the editor was John Wells who proceeded under the direct supervision of Hamilton himself. Howes H 114. A rather scarce and textually significant set.

125. HAMMOND, ANTHONY. A treatise on the law of Nisi Prius: combining theory with practice, and including the pleadings in the several actions. First American, from the last London edition. Exeter, N. H., Lamson, 1823. 498pp. Full contemp. sheep, v. good copy. $ 65.00
* Marvin p. 364 "written in quite a different style from Buller ... more elaborate and systematic ..."

126. HARRINGTON, JAMES. The Oceana and other works ... with an account of his life by John Toland. London, Becket and Cadell, 1771. xi, 598pp. plus index and leaf of publisher's ads. 4to. Contemp. calf, joints worn but firm. Engraved portrait and two other plates, including one which depicts the ballot. $165.00
* A desireable edition of the work in that it includes a number of tracts omitted from the earlier edition of Toland. The Oceana was described by Hume as "the only valuable model of a commonwealth extant." DNB. "It was in America that Harrington's influence was strongest. The written constitution, the unlimited use of elective principle and the separation of powers are all points which may hve been derived directly from the Oceana, while all the minor points ... seem to have been first formulated by (him) ... His influence is best seen in the early constitutions of the proprietary colonies, Carolina, New Jersey, Pennsylvania." Encyclopaedia of the Social Sciences.

127. HARRIS, RICHARD. Hints on advocacy, intended for practitioners in civil and criminal courts, with suggestions as to opening a case, examination-in-chief, cross-examination, re-examination, reply, conduct of a prosecution and of a defense, etc; and illustrative cases. Second American from the fourth English edition, revised and enlarged, by William L. Murfree. St. Louis, Stevenson, 1881. 200pp. Orig. cl. $ 22.50

128. HAUTEFEUILLE, L.B. Quelques questions de droit international maritime a propos de la Guerre d'Amerique. Leipzig, Paris, 1861. 74pp. wrps. $ 30.00

129. HAWKINS, WILLIAM. A treatise of the pleas of the Crown; or a system of the principal matters relating to that subject, digested under proper hands. The seventh edition: in which the text is carefully collated with the original work; the marginal references corrected; new references from the modern reporters added; a variety of manuscripts cases inserted; and the whole enlarged by an incorporation of the several statutes upon subjects of criminal law, to the thirty-fifth year of George the Third. To which an explanatory preface is prefixed, and new and copious indexes are subjoined. By Thomas Leach. In four vols. London, Prtd. for Robinson, 1795. Contemp., calf, wanting the labels, a very good set. 4 vols. 659; 562;376;511pp., each volume with extensive tables. The first ed. was 1716. This is the penultimate edition and the last in the 18th century. $100.00
* Marvin p. 375, a laudatory note. S & M, I, 362-63.

130. HENNEN, WILLIAM D. A digest of the reported decisions of the Superior Court of the late Territory of Orleans; the late Court of Errors and Appeals, and the Supreme Court of the State of Louisiana. Contained in the sixty-five volumes of reports, from First Martin to Fifteenth Louisiana Annual. In two vols. New edition. Cambridge, Mass., Houghton, 1861. 174pp. Full contemp. calf. $ 75.00

131. (HENSHAW, DAVID). Remarks upon the rights and powers of Corporations, and of the rights, powers, and duties of the legislature toward them, embracing a review of the opinion of the Supreme Court of the United States, in the case of Dartmouth College, in New Hampshire, given in 1819. By a Citizen of Boston. Boston, Beals and Greene, 1837. 31pp. wrps. $ 22.50

132. HEROLD, JUSTIN. A manual of legal medicine, for the use of practitioners and students of medicine and law. Phila., Lippincott, 1898. 678pp. Orig. cl. $ 32.50
* First edition, written by a leading N. Y. medico-legal official. Uncommon.

133. HEYWOOD, SAMUEL. A dissertation upon the distinctions in society, and ranks of the people, under the Anglo-Saxon governments. London, printed for W. Clarke, 1818. 435pp. Contemp. diced calf, expertly rebacked, with the gilt seal of the Signet Society on the front cover. $125.00
* First and only edition. Of interest as both legal history and early sociological investigation along empirical lines as recently established by the Scottish school; Ferguson, Millar and Stuart. This is the first work we know of to concentrate on the legal evidence. S & M, I, p. 46. Marvin, p. 385.

134. HOBBES, THOMAS. Elementa philosophica de cive. Amsterodami, apud Ludovicum Elzevirium, 1647. 12mo. Engraved title page and portrait, contemporary vellum. A very good copy. $225.00
* Second Elzevir edition and the first to have the portrait; it is a reissue of the sheets of the first Elzevir of the same year. The work appeared originally in 1642; that edition is exceedingly rare. This work is the predecessor of and foundation for Leviathan. Both were intended to elucidate the nature of man as a social being and constituted one of the legs of Hobbes' tripod, the others being the study of man physically, and psychologically. MacDonald & Hargreaves 26.

135. (HOGDON, MOSES). The complete justice of the peace, containing extracts from Burn's Justice, and other justiciary productions. The whole altered and made conformable to the laws and manners of administering justice, particularly in the State of New Hampshire, and generally in the other of the United States ... by a Gentleman of the Profession. Dover, N.H ., printed for Charles Peirce, 1806. 431pp. Full contemp. sheep. Nice copy. $ 45.00
* Shaw-Shoemaker 10569. First edition.

136. HUMPHREYS, JAMES. Observations on the actual state of the English laws of real property; with the outline of a code. London, Murray, 1826. xi, 442pp. Large fldg. diagrams. 8vo. Contemp. calf. $ 90.00
* First edition. "Mr. Humphreys' writings are distinguished by bold and original thought ... the present work is remarkable for profound knowledge, and a liberal and philosophical spirit ... As a compendium, concise yet clear, it is unrivalled." Marvin p. 405. This copy bears a presentation from the author to Herman Merivale, statesman and political economist - see DNB.

137. (HUNT, GALLIARD). The American passport, its history and a digest of laws, rulings, and regulations governing its issuance by the Department of State. Wash., GPO, 1898. 233pp. Cl. $ 20.00

138. HUNTER, WILLIAM A. A systematic and historical exposition of Roman Law in the order of a code. Embodying the Institutes of Gaius and the Institutes of Justinian, translated into English by J. Ashton Cross ... London, Maxwell, 1876. 927pp. Full contemp. calf. First edition. $ 35.00

139. (ILLINOIS). HEGELER, EDW. C. A protest against the Supreme Court of Illinois and also against its legal and moral doctrine ... in the case of Hegeler vs. First National Bank of Peru ... Chicago, Open Court Publishing Co., 1890. 51p. Wrps. Concerns claims of a creditor and reputation. $ 15.00

140. ILLINOIS. LAWS, STATUTES. The revised code of laws of Illinois, containing those of a general and permanent nature passed by the sixth general assembly, at their session held at Vandalia ... commencing December 1828; and those enacted previous thereto and ordered ... to be republished. Published in pursuance of law. Shawneetown, Ill., published by Alexander F. Grant & Co.; Lodge, L'Hommedieu & Hammond - printers, Cincinnati, 1829. 278pp., 8vo. Contemp. 1/4 calf. Very nice copy. $125.00
* The second published code for the State, the first having appeared in 1827, Vandalia. NUC locates 8 copies.

141. ILLINOIS. LAWS, STATUTES. Revised statutes of the State of Illinois adopted ... 1844-5 together with an appendix ... revised and prepared for publication, with notes, index &c. by M. Brayman. Published by Authority. Springfield, Walters & Weber, 1845. xvi, 749pp. Calf. $ 75.00

142. IMPEY, JOHN. The office of sheriff shewing its history and antiquity ... together with their respective powers and duties ... with many useful precedents ... Dublin, Hoey, 1788. 522pp. plus index. 12mo. Contemp. calf, front joint cracked but firm, some moderate dampstains, but a good sound copy. $ 85.00
* Marvin p. 408, citing its importance as one of the first works to embody the general principles of the topic. First edition was 1786. S & M, I, 222 does not show this edition.

143. (INTERSTATE COMMERCE). Argument of Franklin B. Gowen before the Committee on Interstate Commerce ... March 24, 1888, on ammendments suggested by him to the I. C. C. act giving exemplary damages ... and authorizing ... writs of mandamus against common carriers. Phila., Allen, Lane, 1888. 46p. wrps., fine. $ 22.50
* Aimed at discriminatory rates in oil and other shipments and tendencies towards monopoly.

144. (INTERSTATE COMMERCE. STANDARD OIL). Argument of Franklin B. Gowen ... before the I.C.C. Jan. 17th, 1888 in the cases of George Rice vs. the Railroad Companies: known as the Standard Oil Monopoly Cases ... Phila., Allen, Lane, 1888. 40p. wrps., fine. Charges Standard Oil and the railroads with unjust rate discrimination fostering monopoly. Seeks redress and damages for Rice, a victimized competitor, under the new I. C. C. Law. Vital. $ 35.00

145. (IOWA). Citizens of Council Bluffs, Iowa, vs. Union Pacific Railway Co. Filed April 30th 1886. Investigation made by order of the Governor. Report of the Railroad Commissioner. Omaha Republican Print Co. 1886. 37p. wrps., fine. Charges mismanagement and discrimination in favor of Omaha. $ 35.00

146. (IOWA). General laws of the state of Iowa relating to the duties of the board of supervisors and township officers, including civil and criminal procedure in justices' courts. Printed by authority of the Eighth General Assembly ... Des Moines, John Teesdale, 1860. viii, 456pp. 8vo. Orig. 1/4 cl., spine a little frayed, otherwise an excellent copy. First edition. $ 90.00
* Copy belonging to the township assessor, Boone Township. Issued on the occasion of a major transformation in the assignment of jurisdiction.

147. JACOB, GILES, compiler. The law-dictionary: explaining the rise, progress, and present state of the English Law; defining and interpreting the terms or words of art; and comprising copious information on the subjects of law, trade, and government. Originally compiled by ... Corrected and greatly enlarged, by T. E. Tomlins. In six vols. Phila., Byrne, 1811. 531, 543, 618, 472, 553, 472pp. Full contemp. sheep. Good set. $ 75.00
* First American, from Tomlins' second edition.

148. JACQUET, (P.), Avocat au Parlement. Traite des justices de Seigneur, et des droits en dependants, conforme'ment a la jurisprudence actuelle des differents tribunaux du royaume, suivi des pieces justificatives qui ont trait a la matiere. Lyon, Reguilliat; Paris, Cellot, 1764. 4to. xvi, 448, lxviii, xxxii pp. Contemporary mottled calf, minor wear to corners, else a fine copy. $125.00
* I.N.E.D. 2336. A study of municipal law from its feudal origins to the present, reprinting many contemporary arrets. The author recommends a national unification of rules under a "Code general de Louis XV." Only edition. The NUC cites LC and Harvard only.

149. JOHNSTON, WILLIAM. Arguments to courts and juries, 1864 - 1874. Cincinnati, Clarke, 1887. 543pp. Orig. cl. $ 15.00
* Arguments in various cases by Ohio Superior Court Judge.

150. (JUDICIARY ACT OF 1801). Debates in the Congress of the United States, on the Bill for repealing the Law, "for the more convenient organization of the Courts of the United States:" during the first session of the seventh Congress, and a list of the yeas and nays on that interesting subject. Albany, Whiting, printer, 1802. 796pp. Full contemp. calf, front joint mended. $125.00
* "The repeal debate thoroughly canvassed the issue of judicial review, set forth the Jeffersonian theory of legislative supremacy and furnished the political setting for Marbury v. Madison." Adams, J. T. Dictionary of Am. History V. 3, p. 189.

151. (KANSAS). Crawford, S. J. Attorney for the State. Before the Jon. H. M. Teller, secy. of the Interior, in the matter relating to the excess of lands certified to the Atchison, Topeka and Santa Fe RR Co. within the State of Kansas. Wash., D.
151. (Continued). C., Moore, 1883. 23p., wrps., fine. Plea for the state against the railroad. Important on points of law, fed-state relations, Fed. land policy; a harsh attack on the railroads. $ 25.00

152. KING, JOHN. A commentary on the law and true construction of the Federal Constitution. Cincinnati, Clarke, 1871. 496pp. cl. $ 22.50

153. KINNE, ASA. The most important parts of Kent's Commentaries, reduced to questions and answers. Third edition. N. Y., Gould, 1843. 246pp. Full contemp. sheep. $ 30.00

154. LATHAM, FRANCIS LAW. A treatise on the law of window lights. London, Butterworths, 1867. 253pp. Orig. cl., paper spine label. A fine copy. $ 45.00
* First edition of a rather unusual work reflecting the problems or urban growth, specifically obstruction of light and air by tall buildings.

155. (LAW LIBRARY CATALOGUE). ESSEX COUNTY LAW LIBRARY ASSOCIATION. Catalogue of the library ... compiled by Frank V. Wright. Salem, Mass., Webb, 1897. 424pp. 1/2 calf. $ 27.50

156. LEAKE, STEPHEN MARTIN. A digest of the law of uses and profits of land. London, Stevens, 1888. 603pp. Orig. cl., moderate wear, internally very good. $ 37.50

157. LEAVITT, JOSHUA. The Monroe Doctrine. N. Y., Sinclair Tousey, 1863. 50p. Prtd. wrps. fine. Concerns events in Mexico. $ 17.50

158. LEE, EDWARD. The statute law of Ireland common-placed. Or, a general table to all the publick printed English and Irish Acts of Parliament now in force and use in Ireland ... digested under proper titles ... with proper marginal notes and references ... Dublin, Grierson, 1734. 4to. viii(4), 351,(19)pp., including tables. Contemp. calf, edges and joints worn, rubbed but sound, contents good. $135.00
* First and only edition, and quite uncommon. The NUC locates but two holdings. S & M, IV, p. 36. Marvin 456.

159. LEE, RICHARD. A treatise of captures in war. London W. Sandey, 1759. viii, 264pp. 8vo. New cl. First edition. $ 75.00
* A timely appearance, in the midst of the Seven Years War, of this treatise based partly on Bynkershoek, but containing as well contemporary material especially on Dutch contraband trade and mentioning specifically the American colonies. A second edition appeared in 1803 when the Napoleonic Wars renewed interest in the neutrality question. Marvin p. 457. S & M, I, 352.

160. LIEBER, FRANCIS. Essays on property and labour, as connected with natural law and the constitution of society. N. Y., Harper, 1841. 225pp. Orig. cl. 12mo. $ 37.50
* First edition! Usually this popular work turns up in reprint editions. It was issued in the Harper Family Library Series and became a respected and influential conservative defense of peoperty rights. Kress C5544.

161. LOCKE, JOHN. An essay concerning the true original extent and end of civil government. Boston, Re-printed and sold by Edes and Gill, 1773. 8vo. in fours. 129pp. Later portrait inserted. Later 3/4 morocco. A very good copy. $225.00
* FIRST AMERICAN EDITION. The greatest statement in the English language of libertarian political theory and a profound influence on the course of events in the American colonies. This is, to be sure, a late-coming edition, but it must have signified the fruition of Lockeian ideas as they appeared during the century in such popular writers as Trenchard and Gordon and in numerous other journalists and pamphleteers throughout the colonies. Evans 12834. Printing and the Mind of Man, 163. Rather scarce. (The NUC cites 6 holdings.)

THE FOUNDATION OF POLITICAL LIBERALISM

162. (LOCKE, JOHN). Two treatises of government: in the former the false principles and foundation of Sir Robert Filmer, and his followers, are detected and overthrown. The latter is an essay concerning the true original, extent, and end of civil government. London, Awnsham & Churchill, 1698. 8vo. 3pl., 358pp. Title within rules. Some foxing, light browning. New full blind, panelled calf in attractive period style. In all a very good copy. $300.00
* Third edition, and final one in the author's lifetime, of the singlemost influential statement in the English language of the contract theory and the rights of the individual. All three contemporary editions are, in our experience, quite uncommon in trade. Printing and the Mind of Man, 163. Pforzheimer 613, citing the third edition only. Wing L2768.

163. LORD, JOHN P. The Maine Townsman, or laws for the regulation of towns; with forms and judicial decisions, adapted to the revised statutes of Maine. Boston, White, 1844. 300pp. Full contemp. sheep. 12mo. First edition. Not common. $ 30.00

164. (LOUISIANA). Circuit Court of the U. S. Eastern District ... Myra Clark Gaines vs. The City of New Orleans. Opinion of Judge Edw. C. Billings. N. p., 1883. Landmark heirship case. $ 25.00

165. LOUQUE, CHARLES. A digest of decisions of the Supreme Court of Louisiana, from the 15th to the 30th Annual, p. 800, inclusive; also: of the Circuit Court of the Fifth Circuit, sitting in Louisiana, and the Louisiana cases decided in the Supreme Court of the United States. New Orleans, Clark, 1878. 836pp. Full contemp. calf. First edition. $ 50.00

166. LUCE, ENOS T. Hand book of practice in the probate courts of the State of Maine ... revised by John A. Waterman... Third edition, with an appendix containing references to the revised statutes of 1883, by a member of the Cumberland Bar. Portland, Me., Hoyt, 1884. 284pp. Full contemp. sheep. $ 30.00

167. McDONALD, W. J. (Compiler). Constitution of the United States of America, ... to which are added the rules of the Senate, the Joint rules of the two houses ... Printed for the use of the Senate. Wash., GPO, 1868. 356pp. Contemp. full red mor. Fine copy. $ 40.00
* Contains the newly adopted rules for proceedings in impeachment.

168. (McDOUGALL, MRS. FRANCIS HARRIET GREENE). Might and right; By a Rhode Islander. Providence, A. H. Stilwell, 1844. Port. 345pp. cl. $ 27.50
* A vigorous defense of the Dorr Rebellion.

169. MABLY, (GABRIEL BONNOT, Abbe de). Le droit public de l'Europe, fonde sur les traites. Nouvelle edition, corrigee & augmentee. A Geneve, Par la Compagnie des Libraires, 1748. 1748. 2 volumes, 12mo. Contemporary calf, spines gilt in compartments, leather labels, very light wear to joints but a fine, attractive set. $350.00
* Second edition of the second of Mably's works and his first of major importance. "After the appearance of his 'Droit ...' which was based upon a digest of available international treaties from 1648 to 1748 and which became a standard work throughout Europe he was ranked with Grotius and Pufendorf as an authority in international relations." E. A. Whitefield in Encycl. of the Social Sciences. Tchemerzine VII, 263.

170. (MAINE). Proceedings of the Bench and Bar of the Circuit Court of the United States, District of Maine, Sept. 28, 1878, upon the decease of Hon. George Foster Shepley. Portland, Berry, 1878. 45pp. Orig. wrps. Shepley was Circuit Judge. $ 7.50

171. MAINE, SIR HENRY SUMNER. Lectures on the early history of institutions. (A sequel to "Ancient Law.") N. Y., Holt, 1884. 412pp. Orig. cl. Fine. $ 22.50

172. MARRIAGE LAW DEFENCE UNION. (London). Publications ... 1882-83. $ 50.00
* A bound volume of its Tracts # 1 - 47 complete, originally published separately and here bound up with general title page and index. This organization opposed legislation then pending to allow marriage to the sister of a deceased wife; this liberalization of the law had begun in the British colonies and was now being taken up at home where it caused intense controversy. A very desireable and scarce collection of documents.

173. (MARRIAGE LAW). Specimens of the correspondence of a single year, showing the bad effects of the law prohibiting marriage with a deceased wife's sister. Marriage Law Reform Assoc., Parliament St., 1886. 47pp. Orig. prtd. wrps. $ 25.00

174. MARSHALL, (JOHN). Opinion of the Supreme Court of the United States, at January term, 1832, delivered by Mr. Chief Justice Marshall, together with the opinion of Mr. Justice McLean, in the case of Samuel A. Worcester, plaintiff in error, versus the State of Georgia. With a statement of the case, extracted from the records of the Supreme Court ... Washington, Gales & Seaton, 1832. 39pp., disbound. A good copy. $ 75.00
* A landmark case in which Andrew Jackson scorned Marshall's decision favoring the Federal status of the Cherokee Indians at the expense of the principle of States' Rights. Bruntjen, Am. Imprints 16104.

175. MARSHALL, JOHN. Reports of cases decided by the Hon. John Marshall, late Chief Justice of the United States, in the Circuit Court of the United States, for the District of Virginia and North Carolina, from 1802 to 1833 inclusive. Edited by John W. Brockenbrough. In two vols. Phila., Kay, 1837. 596, 580pp. Full contemp. calf, leather labels, fine set. $150.00
* Marvin p. 150 (under Brockenbrough.) Servies, A bibliography of John Marshall, 1656, #1178: "The source of eighty-eight Circuit opinions. B's note is of interest: 'It was, indeed the practice of the late Chief Justice, to commit his opinions to writing, only in cases of real difficulty: and the fact that all the opinions contained in these volumes were written by Marshall with his own hand and were carefully preserved by him furnishes ample guarantee of their intrinsic value and importance.' " The work is prefaced by Joseph Hopkinson's memoir of John Marshall. A fine copy of a scarce and desireable set.

176. MARSHALL, SAMUEL. A treatise on the law of insurance, in four books: ... First American, from the English Edition. Two vols. in one. Boston, Johnson, 1805. 8vo. 759pp. Contemp. calf, raised bands, nice copy. $ 65.00
* Emphasises marine insurance. The standard work of its time, replacing Park. Marvin P. 500.

177. MARSHALL, SAMUEL. A treatise on the law of insurance, in four books; ... Second American from the second London edition, including the cases decided in the national and state courts of the United States, collected and arranged by J. W. Condy. In two volumes. Phila., Farrand, 1810. 2vols. Lg. 8vo. Contemp. calf, lea. labels. Good set. $ 75.00
* Includes marine insurance. Marvin p. 500: "It was for some time the best treatise in use...' Marshall and Park were the standard insurance texts in America prior to the appearance of a native literature. This is the first of the editions to contain American notes.

178. MARTIN, CHARLES TRICE, compiler. The record interpreter: a collection of abbreviations, Latin words and names, used in English historical manuscripts and records. London, Reeves, 1892. 341pp. Orig. cl. First edition. Fine. $ 20.00

179. (MASSACHUSETTS). Reasons for repealing the laws of Massachusetts, which render the members of manufacturing companies personally liable for their debts. Boston, Dutton, 1830. 12pp. wrps. $ 20.00

180. (MASSACHUSETTS. COMMONWEALTH. LAWS, STATUTES). The perpetual laws of the Commonwealth of Massachusetts, from the commencement of the Constitution in October 1780, to May 1789 ... Published by order of the General Court. Boston, Adams and Nourse, 1789. Folio. 3 pl., 3-495, vipp. including index. Contemp. calf, raised bands, extremities little worn, somewhat rubbed, otherwise a very nice copy. $150.00
* First edition of the first official compilation of state law. Evans 21948.

181. MASS. GENERAL COURT. L. S. Cushing et al. State papers on nullification including the public acts of ... South Carolina ... the Proclamation of the President ... and the proceedings of the several state legislature ... Boston, Dutton, 1834. 381pp. Orig. sheep, fine. Major source for the great constitutional crisis. $27.50

182. (MASSACHUSETTS. LAWS). The Colonial Laws of Massachusetts. Reprinted from the edition of 1660, with the supplements to 1672, containing also the Body of Liberties of 1641 ... With a complete index. Boston, Publ. by order of the City Council of Boston, 1889. 332pp. 4to. 1/4 mor. $ 27.50
* A facsimile reprint of the original with ample scholarly notes.

183. (MASSACHUSETTS. SUPERIOR COURT). Rules of the Superior Court of Massachusetts, 1886. n.p., 1886. 83p. Cloth. $ 7.50

184. (MEDICAL JURISPRUDENCE). ROGERS, STEPHEN. Can chloroform be used to facilitate robbery. (Reprinted from the Journal of Psychological Medicine, Oct. 1871). N. Y., Appleton, 1871. 21pp. Orig. prtd. wrps. $ 10.00

185. METCALF, THERON. Digest of the cases decided in the Supreme Judicial Court of the Commonwealth of Massachusetts, from March, 1816 to October, 1823, inclusive, as contained in the five last volumes of Tyng's, and the first of Pickering's reports, with the names of the cases, and a table of the titles and references, to which is added, a digested index of the names of the cases in the eighteen volumes of Massachusetts Reports. Boston, Richardson, 1825. 513pp. Full contemp. calf. Fine. Marvin p. 511 $ 35.00

186. (MICHIGAN). State Supreme Court. Oct. Term 1878. E. H. Van Deusen vs. Nancy J. Newcomer. Argument for plantiff in error ... Kalamazoo, 1878. 35pp. wrps., fine. Concerns false imprisonment for insanity and view of insanity as disease vs. crime. $ 15.00

187. (MIRANDA EXPEDITION). LLOYD, THOMAS, Stenographer. The trials of William Smith and Samuel G. Ogden for misdemeanours had in the Circuit Court of the United States for the N. Y. District, in July 1806. N. Y., 1807. xxxiii, 287pp. Contemp. calf, nice copy. $ 75.00
* "Smith, the son-in-law of John Adams ... was tried on the charge of initiating the Miranda expedition (Latin American Filibustering) ... counsel for the defense attempted to show that Smith & Ogden, though they had taken part in the affair, had not actually begun it, that members of the government, including even Jefferson, were cognizant of Miranda's plans, and that moreover Spain and the U.S. were at the time practically in a state of war." Sabin 84904.

188. (MISSISSIPPI STATE, LAWS, STATUTES). Laws of the State of Mississippi; embracing all acts of a public nature from January session, 1824, to January session 1838, inclusive. Published by authority. Jackson, Miss., printed for the State of Miss. (J. Toy, prtr.) 1838. 932pp. Contemp. sheep. $ 75.00

189. (MISSISSIPPI STATE. LAWS, STATUTES). The revised code of the statute laws of the State of Mississippi. Published by authority of the Legislature. Jackson, Miss., Barksdale, 1857. 943pp. Full contemp. sheep. $ 75.00

190. (MISSISSIPPI STATE. LAWS, STATUTES). The statutes of the State of Mississippi, of a public and general nature ... and a manual for clerks, sheriffs and justices of the peace, compiled by V. E. Howard and A. Hutchinson, by authority. New Orleans, Jones, 1840. 885pp. Full contemp. sheep. $ 85.00
* Marvin p. 400.

191. MONNER, BASILIUS (d. 1566). Tractatus duo. Prior De matrimonio: posterior De clandestinis coniugiis ... secunda editione. Jena, Steinmann, 1603. 8pl., 348pp. $150.00
BOUND WITH: DAMHOUDER, JOOST, 1507-1581 Sententiae selectae pertinentes ad materiam praxis rerum criminalium ... Antwerp, Ioan. Belleri, 1601. 6pl., 192pp. Two works bound in one vol., 4to. Contemp. vellum. Nice copy.
* Three 16th century treatises, on marital and criminal law, in early 17th century editions. The NUC locates only the Harvard copy of the Monner treatises, and no copy at all of the "Sententiae ..." Bound at the end is an additional item: Regimen Academicum illustri Hessorum Giessena. 1609. Giessae Hessorum, N. Hampelius, 1610. 4pl., 168pp.

192. MONTEFIORE, JOSHUA. Commercial and notarial precedents: consisting of all the most approved forms, common and special, which are required in transactions of business: with an appendix containing principles of law relative to bills of exchange, insurance, and shipping. Philadelphia, Humphreys, 1803. xvi, 350pp. Contemp. calf, red leather label. A near fine copy. $125.00
* First American edition, following the London edition of 1802. Montefiore was an English Jew who finally settled in America. This work is quite important as an early attempt to define the legal status of commercial forms and particularly the work of the notary. It was later reprinted in America, and this first American edition does include American forms not present in the English edition. It is quite uncommon in our experience. Missed by Marvin. Not in Rosenbach. Shaw-Shoemaker 4761.

193. MONTESQUIEU, (CHARLES DE SECONDAT, baron de) The Spirit of the laws. First American from the fifth London edition. In two volumes. Worcester, Isaiah Thomas, sold by him and Matthew Carey ... 1802. 2 vols. 8vo. 19th c. 1/4 calf rubbed, internally very good. $125.00
* FIRST AMERICAN EDITION.

194. MOREHEAD, C.S. and MASON BROWN. A digest of the statute laws of Kentucky, of a public and permanent nature, from the commencement of the Government to the session of the Legislature ending on the 24th Feb., 1834. With references to judicial decisions. In two vols. Frankfort, Ky., Prt. by Hodges, 1834. 1648pp. Full contemp. sheep. 2 vols. $125.00
* Marvin p. 528. First edition. Includes Virginia acts and English statutes incorporated into Ky. law.

195. MORGAN, HENRY J., ed. The Canadian Legal Directory: a guide to the bench and bar of the Dominion of Canada. Toronto, Carswell, 1878. 279pp. Orig. cl. First edition. $ 50.00
* Includes 26? law publisher's catalogue and 26p. lawyers ads. A very detailed directory.

196. MORRIS, EDWARD S. Maine Civil Officer: a complete guide for justices of the peace, sheriffs, deputy sheriffs, coroners, and constables: containing forms of proceedings, and the law relating to their duties ... revised and corrected by Hon. Ether Shepley ... Portland, Bailey, 1861. 408pp. Full contemp. sheep. Scarce edition. $ 30.00

197. MORRISON, CHARLES R. The New-Hampshire Probate Directory: containing the general statutes and acts since passed, with full notes of decisions and forms of wills, petitions, citations, orders and decrees, and all other matters relating to probate courts and proceedings therein. Concord, Sanborn, 1870. 205pp. Full contemp. sheep, lea. label. Fine. $ 17.50

198. MOSES, MYER. The commercial directory and a digest of the laws of the United States relating to commerce; including a tariff, or rates of duties; and tables of calculation, applicable to all manufactures of wool or cotton imported into the United States. N. Y., Printed by Ludwig & Tolefree, 1830. 280pp. Full contemp sheep. $ 75.00
* First edition and scarce. Marvin p. 531. Shoemaker 2645. Not in Rosenbach.

199. MURRAY, J.B.C. The history of usury from the earliest period to the present time together with a brief statement ... concerning the conflict of laws ... and an examination into ... their effect upon commerce. Phila., Lippincott 1866. 158pp. Orig. cl. First edition. $ 55.00
* State by state coverage as well as numerous citations. 4pp. list of subscribers.

200. NATIONAL PRISON ASSOCIATION OF THE UNITED STATES OF AMERICA. Proceedings of the National Prison Congress held at Atlanta, Georgia, 1886. Chicago, Donnelley, 1888. 333pp. Orig. prtd. wrps. Fine. Includes Canadian material. $ 27.50

201. (NEUTRAL RIGHTS CONTROVERSY). A collection of publick acts and papers relating to the principles of Armed Neutrality brought forward in the years 1780 and 1781. London, Strahan, 1801. 278pp. 8vo. Old 1/4 calf, spine worn. $ 50.00
* Intended to support Britain's right to search neutral ships, it includes documents among the European powers and the U. S. up to 1801. Presentation copy from Rufus King, then Minister in London, to Joseph Hall of Boston, with Edward Everett's notation and signature on fly-leaf. Marvin p. 213.

202. (NEW JERSEY). The Law Instructor, or farmer's and mechanic's guide: containing a commentary on the act entitled "An act constituting courts for the trial of small causes," with its supplements, together with concise and correct precedents ... in various actions ... By a Gentleman of the Bar. Bridgeton, N. J., 1824. 100pp. 12mo. Contemp. 1/4 calf. A good copy of a very scarce book and unusual imprint. The act in question relates to New Jersey procedure and was passed in 1818. Shoemaker 16869 locates only one copy. $ 50.00

203. (NEW YORK). A New Conductor Generalis: being a summary of the law relative to the duty and office of justice of the peace ... With many new and improved subjects, alphabetically arranged; comprising a variety of practical forms, all which have been carefully collated with the new revised laws of the State of New York ... by Gentlemen of the Bar. Albany, Backus. 1819. 482pp. 1/2 calf, very good copy. First edition. $ 45.00
* Shaw-Shoemaker 48832.

204. N. Y. STATE. The amended Constitution of the State of New York adopted by the Convention of 1867-'8 together with the manner and form of submission and an address to the people ... Albany, Weed, Parsons, 1868. 83pp. Wrps. With extensive index. $ 17.50

205. N. Y. STATE. CHAMBER OF COMMERCE. Report of the special committee on railroad transportation ... on the subject of the regulation of commerce by railroads and the Reagan and Henderson Bills now pending in Congress. N. Y., 1881. 19p. Wrps. $ 27.50
* Marks the genesis of the Interstate Commerce Act and Commission. Both Federal bills are printed here.

206. (N. Y. STATE. LAWS, STATUTES). The code of procedure of the State of New York as amended April 16, 1852, with copious notes and references, and an appendix containing the recent rules of the Court of Appeals, Supreme Court, etc. Voorhies' second edition. N. Y., Voorhies, 1852. Full contemp. sheep. $ 30.00

207. (N. Y. STATE. LEGISLATURE). General index of the documents and laws of the State of New-York. Prepared and published under a joint resolution of the Senate and Assembly of the 26th March 1841, by the clerks of the two Houses. Albany, Weed, printer, 1842. 565pp. Full contemp. sheep. Fine. $ 47.50
* An extremely useful reference; both documents and laws are separately organized by subject classification which includes canals, railroads, banking, Indians, prisons, aliens, land, N. Y. city, and a wealth of other classes of information.

208. (NEW YORK UNIVERSITY. SCHOOL OF LAW). Inaugural addresses delivered by the Professors of Law in the University of the City of New York at the opening of the Law School of that Institution. N. Y., Clayton, 1838. 68pp. Disbound, small marginal stain but a very good copy. $ 45.00
* The faculty consisted of Benjamin F. Butler, Principal of the Faculty (his address on "The usefulness of the legal profession and the necessity and importance of providing additional means for instruction in legal science,") William Kent ("The rise and progress of commercial law in English Jurisprudence"), and David Graham ("The practice of the law as illustrated in the study of pleading ...").

209. NOY, WILLIAM. The principal grounds and maxims, with an analysis of the laws of England. Third American, from the ninth London edition, with references to modern authorities, both British and American, by William Waller Hening. Burlington, Vt., Goodrich, 1845. 219pp. 1/4 calf, fine. $ 37.50
* Marvin p. 542f.

210. (O'BRIEN, JOHN MAURICE). The powers and duties of the town officer, as contained in the statutes of Maine, with forms adapted thereto; including also the powers and duties of plantation and parish officers, and other useful matter. Brunswick, Griffin, 1822. 324pp. Full contemp. calf. 12mo. Fine copy. First edition. Shoemaker 9748. $ 35.00

211. (O'BRIEN, JOHN MAURICE). The powers and duties of the town officer, as contained in the statutes of Maine; with forms adapted thereto, including also the powers and duties of plantation and parish officers, and other useful matter. Second edition, improved. Hallowell, Spaulding, 1824. 324pp. Full contemp. calf. 12mo. Shoemaker 17482, one location only. $ 35.00

212. Officina brevium. Select and approved forms of judicial writs and other process: with their retorns and entries in the Court of Common Pleas at Westminster as also special pleadings to writs of scire facias. London, Sawbridge (et al.) for Thomas Bassett, 1679. Folio. 4pl., 414,(29)pp. including imprimatur leaf and publisher's ads. Contemp. panelled calf, front cover detached. Contents good. $150.00
* Wing O-152. Marvin p. 545. First and only edition (There was a variant issue the same year).

213. (OHIO). Court in Bank, Dec. Term, 1848. John P. Vieder & Co. ats. Mansfield and Sandusky Railroad Co. 6pp. sewn as issued. Fine. Concerns a railroad construction contract dispute. $ 20.00

214. (OHIO). The Ohio Officer's Guide, and Clerk's Companion, containing a summary view of the principal provisions of the statutes, as revised in 1830-31, and the statutes since passed, relating to the duties of justices of the peace, township trustees, constables, and other township officers ... and a concise treatise on the law of partnership ... Third edition. Steubenville, Turnbull, 1835. 404pp. Contemp. calf, rebacked. 12mo. $ 65.00
* Third and final edition, (others 1832, 1833). The NUC locates only 2 holdings, 3 each of the earlier editions. Missed by Marvin.

215. OLIVER, BENJAMIN LYNDE. Practical conveyancing, a selection of forms of general utility, with notes interspersed. Boston, Cummings, 1816. 486pp. Contemp. sheep, very good copy. $ 75.00
* Marvin p. 547. "The best American manual upon conveyancing ... in use." This is the first edition and is very uncommon. It continued through 1884. Shaw-Shoemaker 38519. The NUC locates only 4 holdings.

216. PARKER, EDWARD G. Reminiscences of Rufus Choate, the great American advocate. N. Y., Mason, 1860. 522pp. Illus., frontis. $ 27.50

217. PARSONS, THEOPHILUS. Laws of business for all the States of the Union. With forms and directions for all transactions. Hartford, Scranton, 1870. 685pp. $ 30.00
* First published in 1869, this became the enduring and leading text of its kind.

218. PARSONS, THEOPHILUS. Laws of business for all the States of the Union, and the Dominion of Canada, with forms and directions for all transactions, and abstrcact of the laws of all the States on various topics. Greatly enlarged and improved. Hartford, Scranton, 1880. 848pp. cl. $ 30.00

219. PARTRIDGE, J.A. From feudal to federal; or free church, free school, the complete bases of equality; with some of its results in State, Constitution, and Empire. London, Trubner, 1872. 591pp. Orig. pict. cl. $ 27.50

220. PAYNE, ABRAHAM. Reminiscences of the Rhode Island Bar. Providence, Tibbitts, 1885. 277pp. Orig. cl. Fine. $ 25.00

221. PEAKE, THOMAS. A compendium of the law of evidence. From the third London edition with additions: and an appendix containing a digest of the American cases ... by Samuel Bayard, presiding judge of the Court of Common Pleas of the County of Somerset in New Jersey. Phila., Nicklin, 1818. 460, (99), 134pp. plus index. Contemp. calf. $ 45.00
* Marvin p. 559. A good edition with the Bayard digest of 1810.

222. PENNSYLVANIA. City of Phila., Court of Common Pleas, No. 3 Dec. term 1877. In the matter of Henry T. Helmbold, an alleged lunatic. Paper book of (same) sur his petition to supercede commission of lunacy. Reply to respondents analysis. n.p., 1877. 24pp. wrps. Fine. Concerns alleged misuse of insanity ruling to defraud. $ 12.50

223. (PENNSYLVANIA). (INGERSOLL, CHARLES). Some objections to a joint resolution, passed at the last session of the Legislature and about to be submitted at the approaching session recommending to the people of Pennsylvania an elective judiciary. No place or publ., December 1849. 61pp. dsbd. $ 27.50

224. (PENNSYLVANIA ATTORNEY'S RECEIPT AND MEMORANDA BOOKS) SMITH, FREDERICK. Three manuscript volumes, oblong 12mo, total 446 pages of entries, kept between 1806 - 1824, being a record of his financial transactions in hundred of cases with clients, sher ifs, notaries, etc., as well as with his partner William Witman. The cases range from assault and battery to bankrupcy, the latter especially prominent in the years of the 1819 Depression when Smith was apparently attorney for the Farmer's Bank of Reading. $150.00
* Smith was a prominent attorney and local politician from Reading and was admitted, one of the first to be so, to the Berks County bar in 1795; he was active in county Democratic politics and served as Prosecuting Attorney from 1818-1820 and 1824-47. (Amos K. Strunck, Officers of Berks County, 1859) Record books of great detail such as these are especially valuable for providing insight into the financial and organizational aspects of early American law practice.

225. (PENNSYLVANIA. PETROLEUM). Argument of Mr. Franklin B. Gowen before the Comm. on RR of the House of Rep. of Pa., upon the bill presented by Mr. Hulings, of Venango Cty, to prevent unjust discrimination by RR companies ... Phila., Allen, Lane, 1883. 32pp. wrps., fine. Defends rate discrimination. Much on Standard Oil and other oil companies. $ 20.00

226. PHILLIPS, WILLARD. The inventor's guide, comprising the rules, forms, and proceedings, for securing patent rights. Boston, Colman, 1837. 385pp. Full contemp. calf. Fine copy. $ 37.50.
* First edition. Marvin p. 570. A practical abridgement of the author's treatise on patent law, the best work of its period in America.

227. POWELL, JOHN JOSEPH. Essay upon the law of contracts and agreements. Sixth American ed., revised and corrected. Two vols. in one. N. Y., Lamson, 1825. 271, 169; LXXXVpp. Cont. calf, very good copy. $ 45.00
* Marvin p. 582. Final American edition.

228. PRICE, RICHARD. Additional observations on the nature and value of civil liberty, and the war with America: also observations on ... public loans ... national debt ... and a brief account of the debts and resources of France. London, Cadell, 1777. xvi, 176pp. 1/4 calf, nice copy. First edition. $100.00
* A classic censure of Britain's attempt to coerce the American colonies into submission; contains a wealth of observation on finance (including paper money and coinage) and Britain's foreign trade. Kress B71. Sabin 65444.

PRISON REFORM

The following all relate to the internationally important controversy over prison discipline which arose in America in the 1830's and centered around the innovative Eastern State Penitentiary of Pennsylvania.

229. BEAUMONT, GUSTAVE DE & ALEXIS DE TOCQUEVILLE. Systeme penitentiaire aux Etats-Unis et de son application en France; suivie d'un appendice sur les colonies penales et de notes statistiques ... troisieme edition, augmentee ... Paris, Gosselin, 1845. 446pp. Contemp. 1/4 mor. Nice copy. $ 85.00
* The most famous European account of American prison experiments especially the "Pennsylvania system" of separate confinement; Francis Lieber, one of the systems ardent proponents, actually translated the work for the American public in 1833! The system in some form was adopted throughout Europe in the next decade. This edition is particularly desireable because it contains for the first time the newly adopted French prison code of 1844 along with Tocqueville's advisory report to the Chamber of Deputies. Monaghan 165.

230. BOSTON PRISON DISCIPLINE SOCIETY. Annual Reports. 1st - 6th, 21/22nd, (1826-1847). Many in original wrappers; each approx. 100-200pp. each $ 10.00
* The Boston Society's annual reports were the only documents of the period in which the progress, method and statistics of American prisons were compiled. Largely through its secretary, Louis Dwight, the Society led the attack on the Pennsylvania System, effectively limiting its spread in the U.S. Its reports were intensively distributed and "it is probably not too much to say that (Dwight) in large measure conditioned the form of prison structure and method adopted in many a state." Teeters, They were in prison: a history of the Pennsylvania Prison Society. 1937. p. 237f.

231. DYER, DAVID. History of the Albany Penitentiary. Albany, Joel Munsell, 1867. 237pp. Orig. cl. $ 27.50
* An important prison in 19th century penology. It was an internationally recognized application of the "silent system", the chief alternative to the "separate system" in Pennsylvania.

232. EASTERN STATE PENITENTIARY. First and second annual reports of the inspectors of the ... of Pennsylvania ... Phila., Kite, 1831. 23pp. dsbd. $ 17.50
* Earliest reports of the most important prison experiment of its time, instituting the widely imitated system of separate confinement.

233. FOULKE, WILLIAM PARKER. Remarks on cellular separation. Read by appointment of the American Association for the Improvement of Penal Institutions, at the annual meeting in N. Y. ... 1860. Phila., 1861. 112pp. Orig. prtd. wrps. $ 50.00
* Foulke was for sixteen years a leading participant in the Pennsylvania Prison Society. "In 1860 he presented what may be considered one of the best and most logical defenses of the separate system ever penned. It was read by appointment before the American Association (etc.) ..." Teeters, They were in prison: a history of the Pennsylvania Prison Society, 1937. p. 286.

234. (GREAT BRITAIN. PARLIAMENT). First (- Second) report from the Select Committee of the House of Lords appointed to inquire into the present state of the several gaols and houses of correction in England and Wales; with the minutes of evidence and appendix. (London), 1835. Folio. 400, 274pp. 5 fold. plates. 1/4 leather, a very nice copy. $200.00
* The first two reports (two others were subsequently issued) of one of the major inquiries leading directly to the creation and extension of the model prison at Pentonville, based on the American system of "separate confinement". The latter issue dominates these hearings along with the treadmill (which is illustrated), treatment and employment of female prisoners, and other topics of prisoner welfare and reform. Witnesses include William Crawford, Whitworth Russell and Elizabeth Fry. The committee concluded that a national system based on some form of separation was essential, and it was precisely this that was accomplished in the following decade.

235. HOWE, (SAMUEL GRIDLEY). An essay on separate and congregate systems of prison discipline; being a report made to the Boston Prison Discipline Society. Boston, Ticknor, 1846. xi, 90pp. Later boards. $ 45.00
* A remarkable defense by this important reformer, of the Pennsylvania system of "separate discipline", based on his own investigation of the facts and aimed directly at the intensely biased and hostile Boston Society to which Howe had previously been an adherent. This was conceived originally as a minority report and was written with the help of Horace Mann and Charles Sumner; theSociety refused to publish it and finally, after a struggle to secure the manuscript, Howe published it himself.

THE HUMANITARIAN RECONSTRUCTION OF ENGLISH PRISONS

236. (JEBB, SIR JOSHUA, Surveyor-General of Prisons and Commissioner of Pentonville). Report of the Surveyor General of Prisons on the construction, ventilation, and details of Pentonville Prison, 1844. London, Clowes, 1844. 62pp. plus 22 large folding lith. plates. TOGETHER WITH: Second report of the Surveyor-General of Prisons. London, Clowes, 1847. 220pp. 22 large folding plates. 2 volumes. Original cloth, spines faded, otherwise fine. 8vo. First book editions of the Parliamentary papers. $400.00
* The two land mark reports which document in great detail respectively the final creation and the extension of Pentonville, the model prison based on the American system of separate confinement. In fact this was the logical culmination of reform begun in England 70 years earlier by Howard and brilliantly advocated more recently by William Crawford who worked closely with Jebb in the final planning stages. Jebb was remarkably able to wed his technical training as an engineer in the Military (he served in Canada) to a very sympathetic understanding of the "separate system." As the second report shows, he vigorously promoted its application to other prison sites, work which he continued later as a national administrator. The choice of the "separate" over the so-called "silent" system meant, among other things, the virtual elimination of corporal punishment. Whatever the relative merits of the competing systems, and they were endlessly disputed, the idea of moral improvement through meticulous and humane attention to mental and physical well-being permeates every facet of these reports.
The plates include detailed and overall plans, elevations, and several views, one of which (plt. 21, 1844 report) is an idyllic visiting day promenade down the central hall. See DNB for an account of Jebb.

237. LIEBER, FRANCIS. Remarks on the relation between education and crime ... to which are added some observations by H. N. Julius, M. D. of Hamburg ... Phila., Philadelphia Society for Alleviating the Miseries of Public Prisons, 1835. 24pp. Orig. prtd. wrps. Fine. $ 45.00
* A scarce Lieber item, connected with the major reforms at the new Eastern Penitentiary. Julius was the leading German reform counterpart of Beaumont and Crawford and was visiting Philadelphia at this time.

238. (PACKARD, FRED A.). Memorandum of a late visit to the Auburn Penitentiary; prepared for the Phila., Society for the Alleviation of the Miseries of Public Prisons. Phila., Harding, 1842. 8pp. dsbd. $ 17.50
* Describes changes and improvements, use of cold head bath punishment, defends Pennsylvania system above Auburn system.

239. VAUX, ROBERTS. Notices of the original and successive efforts to improve the discipline of the prison at Philadelphia and to reform the criminal code of Pennsylvania: with a few observations on the penitentiary system. Phila., Kimber & Sharpless, 1826. 76pp., new boards. Inscribed presentation copy from the author. $ 75.00
* Vaux was one of the founders of the Pennsylvania system of separate confinement. His arguments in its favor were ideal and persuasive; he was a member of the planning commission for the Eastern Penitentiary and drafted the legislation for its administration. See DAB. Also, Teeters, N. K. The Prison at Philadelphia, 1957, p. 28f. This is his most important work in defense of penal reform.

END OF PENOLOGY SECTION

240. PULLING, ALEXANDER. The order of the Coif. London, Clowes, 1897. 297pp. Illus., eight plates. Orig. cl. Small blind stamp. $ 25.00
* History of the earliest form of the Bench and Bar.

241. RAWLE, WILLIAM. A view of the Constitution of the United States of America. Second edition. Phila., Nicklin, 1829. 349pp. cl. $ 47.50
* One of the earliest such works, first published in 1825. Marvin p. 599 "This is a very good elementary book ..."

242. REED, JOHN C. Conduct of lawsuits out of and in court: practically teaching and copiously illustrating the preparation and forensic management of litigated cases of all kinds. Being a new edition of "Practical Suggestions." Revised and rewritten. Boston, Little, Brown, 1885. 434pp. Full contemp. sheep, v. good. $ 20.00

243. REEVE, TAPPING. The law of baron and femme; of parent and child; of guardian and ward; of master and servant; and of the powers of Courts of Chancery, with an essay on the terms, heir, heirs, and heirs of the body. New Haven, Printed by Oliver Steele, 1816. 494pp. Full contemp. calf, a very good copy. $125.00
* FIRST EDITION of Reeves first book, published upon his retirement from the bench at age 72! Intended to exhibit the common law of England and such statutes as were adopted in America, it is the first extensive work of its kind in this country and was highly regarded by Kent and Hoffman. Marvin p. 603.

244. (RICHARDSON, WILLIAM). The New-Hampshire just'ce of the peace. Concord, printed by I. Hill, 1824. 320pp. Full contemp. sheep. 12mo. Nice copy. $ 27.50
* Shoemaker 17823. Marvin p. 609.

245. RICHARDSON, WILLIAM M. The New-Hampshire justice of the peace. Second edition, improved. Concord, Hill, 1831. 29pp. Full contemp. sheep. $ 25.00
* Marvin p. 609.

246. (ROCCO, FRANCESCO). A manual of maritine law. Consisting of a treatise on ships and freight and a treatise on insurance. Translated from the Latin of Roccus. With notes by Joseph Reed Ingersoll. Phila., Hopkins and Earle, 1809. xvi, 156, (8)pp. New cloth. $ 55.00
* Marvin p. 616: "This manual is very highly esteemed by commercial lawyers in all countries for its compressed, methodical and accurate learning, and is a book of high authority." This is not only the first American edition, but the first edition in English of this 17th century classic.

247. RYAN, MICHAEL. A manual of medical jurisprudence ... being an analysis of a course of lectures on forensic medicine annually delivered in London. First American edition, with notes and additions by R. Eglesfeld Griffith, M. D. Phila., Carey and Lea, 1832. viii, 327pp. 8vo. Original boards, entirely uncut. $100.00
* This appears to be the first single, systematic work on the subject to be adapted for American use, if one excludes Thomas Cooper's publication of four briefer English works without alterations but with his own digests of American laws in 1819. It falls between Beck's landmark work of 1823, the first original American work on the subject, and Taylor's book, first edited for Americans by Griffith in 1845. Griffith has added to Ryan's treatise by expanding the chapters on medical evidence and laws relating to the profession, etc. and in doing so has improved as well upon Beck. Marvin p. 625.

248. SAMS, C. WHITTLE. A brief comparison of the most important statutes of the Codes of Virginia of 1873 and 1887: being especially those referred to in "Minor's Institutes of Common and Statute Law." Richmond, Va., West, Johnson, 1888. 160pp. Cloth. $ 25.00

249. SAYER, JOSEPH. Law of costs. Second edition, corrected and much enlarged. London, Prtd. by W. Strahan for T. Cadell. 1777. 336pp. Full contemp. sheep. $ 65.00
* Marvin p. 631. S & M, I, 284.

250. (SCULLY, DENYS). A statement of the Penal Laws which aggrieve the Catholics of Ireland: with commentaries. In two parts. Second edition, enlarged. Dublin, Fitzpatrick, 1812. 370pp. Contemp. boards, rebacked in cloth. $ 75.00
* Scully was one of the leading Catholic agitators. He "prepared a famous 'Statement of the Penal laws' which appeared in 1812 and resulted in the prosecution of the printer, Fitzpatrick, who was fined 200 pounds and imprisoned for 18 months ... " DNB.

251. SEDGWICK, THEODORE. A treatise on the measure of damages, or, an inquiry into the principles which govern the amount of pecuniary compensation awarded by courts of justice. Third revised edition. N. Y., Voorhies, 1858. 689pp. Full contemp. sheep. $ 30.00

252. SELDEN, JOHN. Titles of honor. The third edition carefully corrected. With additions and ammendments by the author. London, Tyler and Holt, for Bassett ... 1672. Folio. 17pl., 756pp. Contemp. panelled calf, extremeties and joints worn but holding. Internally a very good copy, lacking the frontis-portrait. $100.00
* Final and textually the best edition. S & M, I, 208. Wing S 2440.

253. SHARP, GRANVILLE. Remarks on the opinions of some of the most celebrated writers on Crown Law, respecting the due distinction between manslaughter and murder, being an attempt to show that the plea of sudden anger cannot remove the imputation and guilt of murder ... that indulgence allowed by the courts to voluntary manslaughter ... is indiscriminate ... London, B. White, 1773. xvii, 76pp., half title present. Contemp. boards, front cover detached, internally very good. $ 85.00
* First edition of this great and effective philanthropist's attack on duelling by way of a reconsideration of criminal law. Marvin p. 639, citing a later edition. S & M, I, 365 and 45. Reprinted also in Phila., 1778.

254. SHEPPARD, WILLIAM. The touch-stone of common assurances: or a plain and familiar treatise opening the learning of the common assurances or conveyances of the Kingdom. The sixth edition. Revised and corrected, with notes and additional references by Edward Hilliard, to which is added a copious index. Dublin, printed by John Exshaw, 1785. 504pp. Full contemp. sheep. $ 75.00
* A true classic first published in 1641, last in 1826! Marvin p. 643. S & M, I, 487.

255. (SOUTH CAROLINA). Circuit Ct. of the U. S. for S. C. U. S. vs. Bates, et al. Arguments on motion of the government to stand aside jurors. Charleston, Perry, 1882. 22p. wrps. Fine. Jury selection. $ 12.50

256. (SPENCER, THOMAS). The new vade mecum; or, young clerk's magazine; digested and improved to correspond with the laws of the state of New York in particular and the United States in general ... The first edition ... Lansingburgh, Tiffany for Spencer, 1794. 12mo. 346pp. Contemp. calf, edges worn but a very good copy. $ 57.50
* First American edition of a standard English work, with original American material inserted in place of irrelevant English material. Evans 27728.

257. STEVENS, JAMES G. Stevens on indictable offences and summary convictions, founded on Dominion Statutes 32 - 33 Vic, Caps 29, 30 and 31. Toronto, Carswell, 1880. 256pp. 1/4 sheep. First edition. $ 40.00
* Author was a New Brunswick judge.

258. STOKES, ANTHONY. A view of the constitutions of the British Colonies in North America and the West Indies at the time the civil war broke out ... in which notice is taken of such alterations as have happened ... down to the present period. With a variety of colony precedents, which are chiefly adapted to the British West India Islands; and may be useful to those who have any intercourse with the colonies. London, Printed for the author ... 1783. 8vo. xvi-555pp. Half-title present. Contemporary calf, rubbed, small corner of upper spine chipped but not affecting label, internally a very nice copy. $325.00
* First and only edition. A marvelous source, first-hand, for the legal as well as constitutional practice of the colonies and Caribbean islands. Stokes was Chief Justice of Georgia and a practicing attorney in the Islands who chose loyalty and fled when the Revolution occurred. He speaks of his failure in 1762 to find any good sources of colonial precedent; this work is intended to fill the need, and indeed it describes in great detail the constitutions, powers of office, court structure, behavior of judges, counsel and attornies, vice admiralty in all the British possessions, and covers a great variety or normal precedents and forms, including the manumission and conveyancing of Negro slaves. Of great West Indian interest. Ragatz p. 379. Marvin p. 668. Sabin 91994. Uncommon.

259. (STORY). HORNE, ANDREW. The mirrour of justices: written originally in the old French ... to which is added, The diversity of courts ... translated into English by W. H. London, Worral & Tovery, 1768. 16pl., 325,(9)pp. 8vo. Old. calf very worn, spine split, cover detached, contents very good. $125.00
* Joseph Story's copy with his signature on the title page and several paragraphs of notes to a case (Woods vs. Sprague) pencilled on the rear free end-paper. A further note on the title page by one J. Elliot Cabot indicates that this copy was "bought at Judge Story's sale, April 3, 1846." Marvin p. 396f., citing this edition of Horne's classic.

260. STORY, JOSEPH. Commentaries on the law of agency as a branch of commercial and maritime jurisprudence, with occasional illustrations from the civil and foreign law ... Eighth edition, revised, with additions, by N. St. John Green. Boston, Little, Brown, 1874. 706pp. Full contemp. sheep. Nice copy. $ 30.00

261. STORY, JOSEPH. A discourse delivered before the Society of the Alumni of Harvard University, at their first anniversary, Aug. 23, 1842 ... Boston, Little, Brown, 1842. 40pp. Orig. prtd. wrps. Concerns national literary culture and standards. $ 12.50

262. STORY, JOSEPH. A familiar exposition of the Constitution of the United States; containing a brief commentary ... with an appendix ... N. Y., 1884, Harper Bros. 372pp. Fine. $ 27.50
* This is an exact re-issue of the first edition of 1840.

263. STORY, JOSEPH. A selection of pleadings in civil actions, subsequent to the declaration, with occasional annotations on the law of pleading. Salem, Macanulty, 1805. 697pp. Full contemporary sheep, label. A very good copy. $250.00
* FIRST EDITION OF THE AUTHOR'S FIRST BOOK, and intrinsically a fine achievement in a field then new to American legal literature. See the long praiseworthy note in Marvin p. 668. Shaw-Shoemaker 9435. We have not before handled or seen offered a copy of this work.

264. SWAN, JOSEPH R. A treatise on the law relating to the powers and duties of justices of the peace, and constables, in the State of Ohio; with practical forms, &c. &c. Columbus, Whiting, 1837. 582pp. Full contemp. sheep. Good copy. $ 85.00
* Marvin p. 679. FIRST EDITION of the standard major guide which reached a tenth edition in 1875.

265. TAYLOR, ALFRED S. Medical jurisprudence. Edited with notes and additions by R. Egglesfield Griffith, M. D. Phila., Lea, 1845. 539pp. Full contemp. sheep. $ 65.00
* First American edition, from the first English edition of 1843. The material added by the American editor reflects differences between the two countries. The preface to this edition states that a work such as this was necessary as a practical alternative to Beck's more specialized work. Taylor's treatise achieved this purpose, becoming perhaps the leading fundamental text in America and reaching a 12th edition by 1897. The first edition is scarce.

266. TAYLOR, CHARLES W. Biographical sketches and review of the bench and bar of Indiana, containing biographies and sketches of eminent judges and lawyers of Indiana, together with a history of the judiciary of the State and review of the bar from the earliest times to the present, with anecdotes reminiscences, etc. Illustrated. Indianapolis, Bench and Bar Publ. Co., 1895. 848pp. Cl. $ 45.00

267. TAYLOR, JOHN. Tyranny unmasked. Washington City, Davis & Force, 1822. 349pp. with errata paste-down. Title within rule. Contemporary calf, light wear to joints. $185.00
* First edition. A very nice copy which is unusual for this and other of Taylor's books. Charles Beard and others have recognized Taylor as one of the most important political theorists of the early national period. He is without doubt the greatest spokesman for the states' rights school. This work elaborates further his theory of the Constitution and deals with banking, tariffs, and taxation. Howes T-65. DAB.

268. (THOMAS, B. F). Thomas' Town Officer: a digest of the laws of Massachusetts in relation to the powers, duties and liabilities of towns, and of town officers; with the necessary forms. New edition, revised corrected and brought down to the present time, by Dwight Foster and James E. Estabrook. Worcester, Dorr., 1856. 486pp. Full contemp. sheep. $ 25.00
* Marvin p. 44.

269. TIDY, CHARLES MAYMOTT. Legal medicine. In two vols. N. Y., Wood, 1882. 314, 298pp. Orig. cl. $ 37.50
* First American edition from London edition of same year.

270. TRUMBULL, BENJAMIN. An appeal to the public relative to the unlawfulness of marrying a wife's siter. From the Press of E. Hudson, 1810. 18p. Orig. wrps. uncut. Presentation copy from the author. $ 27.50
* Shaw-Shoemaker 21562.

271. TYLER, SAMUEL. (ed.) Memoir of Roger Brooke Taney, LL.D. Chief Justice of the Supreme Court of the United States. Baltimore, Murphy, 1872. 659pp. Frontis. Orig. cl. Nice copy. First edition. $ 35.00

272. U.S. CONGRESS. HOUSE OF REPRESENTATIVES. Constitution ... to which are added Jefferson's manual ... and standing rules and orders for conducting business in the House ... and Senate ... Printed for the use of the House ... Washington, Steedman, 1859. 254pp., interleaved. Calf, with name plate of Hon. W. Saulsbury. $ 20.00

273. UPDIKE, WILKINS. Memoirs of the Rhode-Island Bar. Boston, Webb, 1842. 309pp. Orig. cl. Nice copy. $ 45.00
* 15 lawyers of the 18th century, including a large section on James Varnum. Marvin p. 703.

274. (U.S.) COMMISSIONER OF LABOR. Carroll D. Wright. Labor laws of the United States. Prepared for the Committee on Interstate and Foreign Commerce of the House of Representatives, to accompany a report submitted by Hon. John J. O'Neill of that Committee, July 20, 1892. Second special report of the ... Second Edition, revised... Wash., GPO, 1896. 1383pp. $ 22.50

275. (U.S.) COMMISSIONER OF LABOR. Carroll D. Wright. Labor Laws of the United States, with decisions of courts relating thereto. Tenth special report of the ... Wash., GPO, 1904. 1413pp. $ 25.00

276. (U.S.) COMMISSIONER OF LABOR. Carroll D. Wright. Regulation and restriction of output. Eleventh special report of the ... Wash., GPO, 1904. 932pp. $ 22.50

277. (U.S. COMMISSIONER OF LABOR). Carroll D. Wright. A report on marriage and divorce in the United States 1867 to 1886; including an appendix relating to marriage and divorce in certain countries in Europe. Wash., GPO, 1889. 1074pp. $ 35.00

278. (UTAH). In the Supreme Court ... Mary Ann Pratt et al. vs. Alexander Ramsay. Brief for respondents. n.p. 1883. 31pp. Orig., prtd. wrps., fine. Concerns voting rights and jurisdiction of Congress over territories. Plaintiffs were denied right to vote on account of polygamy issue, with special disabilities against women. $ 35.00

279. VANDEWEYER, SYLVAIN. Dissertation sur la realite, la connaissance et la pratique du devoir comme naturelles. Louvain, Cuelens, 1823. 52pp. Orig. marbled wrps., uncut. Fine. $ 37.50
* A discussion of the philosophy of natural rights and obligations in opposition to the ethics of utilitarianism. The author defends the former, and a substantial portion of the work is a commentary on Bentham. No copy in the NUC.

280. VAN VLEET, A. The Ohio Justice and Township Officers' Assistant, ... Also matters relative to the duties of executors and administrators, &c. To which is added an appendix; containing a variety of practical forms in conveyancing. Lebanon, (O.) Printed and published by the author, 1821. 222, 70pp. Full contemp. calf. $125.00
* First and only edition, and as far as we can tell the earliest Ohio justice. Shoemaker 7503.

A LANDMARK IN THE GENIUS OF THE AMERICAN POLITICAL SYSTEM

281. VARNUM, JAMES M. The case, Trevett against Weeden: on information and complaint, for refusing paper bills in payment for butcher's meat, in market, at par with specie. Tried before the honourable Superior Court, in the county of Newport, September term, 1786. ... wherein the rights of the people to trial by jury, &c. are stated and maintained, and the legislative, judiciary and executive powers of government examined and defined. Providence, printed by John Carter, 1787. iv, 60pp. 4to. Bound in late 19th century black morocco gilt, front joint worn, the work itself in fine condition. $300.00
* FIRST AND ONLY EDITION. A major landmark in the establishment of the doctrine of judicial review, one of the unique features of the American political system. Varnum's defense of the right of the judiciary to reject legislation which violates the Constitution and of the independence and primacy of the judiciary was the most extensive and forceful to appear in this formative period. Of the five or so colonial cases involving judicial review (see Beveridge, Life of Marshall, III, p. 610f. and Charles Warren, Congress, the Court and the Constitution, p. 430) this is the most important because Varnum's views were made available to his contemporaries in this separately published pamphlet which was heavily advertised in the Philadelphia papers at the time of the Constitutional Convention. Madison took special note of it in the debates and Warren maintains that the founding fathers agreed that the Supreme Court would, like its colonial counterparts, be the ultimate judge of the validity of a law. Varnum's bold words echoed 17 years later in the statement of John Marshall in Marbury v. Madison that "it is emphatically the province and duty of the judicial department to say what the law is." Varnum also gives a good account of the social and financial background to the affair and reproduces the currency and obnoxious forcing acts which denied trial by jury and appeal. He later became justice for the new Northwest Territory and helped frame its law. Evans 20825. Sabin 98638. JCB 1772-1800, p. 267. A very nice copy of an important work.

282. VATTEL, EMMERICH DE. Le droit des gens, ou, Principes de la loi naturelle, appliques a la conduits & aux affaires des nations & des souverains. A Leide, aux Depens de la Compagnie 1758. 4to. Two volumes in one. Engraved vignette on title page; title page in red and black. Contemporary calf, raised bands, sides a little rubbed, otherwise a very nice copy. $300.00
* Along with the "Londres" edition of this same year this is the first appearance of this great work - "a classic in the literature of international law, for decades (exercising) a decisive influence upon statesmen." Encycl. of the Social Sciences. Notable is its restriction of the role of warfare. "He has done for the morality of nations what Paley did for the morality of individuals ... he is more generally read than any other writer upon the law of nations, and in no country more than ours..." Marvin p. 706. This last comment is borne out by the profusion of English language edition throughout the 19th century, outlasting the French.

283. VATTEL, M. D. The law of nations; or principles of the law of nature, applied to the conduct and affairs of nations and sovereigns: a work tending to display the true interest of power ... Translated from the French. Northhampton, Mass., Butler, 1820. 560pp. Full contemp. sheep, rubbed. Second American edition. $ 45.00
* Marvin p. 706. "He is more generally read than any other writer upon the law of nations, and in no country more than ours."

284. (VIRGINIA. LAWS, STATUTES). A collection of all such acts of the General Assembly of Virginia of a public and permanent nature as are now in force ... Richmond, Pleasants, 1803. (WITH:) A collection of all such acts ... as have been passed since the session of 1801 ... with a complete index to the whole. Richmond, Pleasants, 1808. 2 vols. Small 4to's Contemp. calf, nice copies. $100.00
* The third code of the state, revising the 1794 revised code and bringing it up to 1808. Volume 2 has interesting appendices on special acts regarding lands, internal improvements, etc. Marvin p. 713.

285. WARDENS' ASSOC. OF THE UNITED STATES AND CANADA. Statistics of Prisoners, 1890. ... with an introduction by Roland P. Falkner. (Chicago) published by the Association, 1892. 56pp. Orig. prtd. brds. Includes Canadian material. $ 27.50

286. WASHBURN, EMORY. A treatise on the American law of easements and servitudes. Third edition. Boston, Little, Brown, 1873. 776pp. New cloth. $ 37.50
* Much on water rights.

287. (WATTERSTON, GEORGE). Letters from Washington, on the Constitution and laws; with sketches of some of the prominent public characters of the United States, written during the winter of 1817-18. By a foreigner. Washington, Gideon, 1818. 139pp. Original printed boards, rebacked in matching paper, uncut. Some very minor staining and covers a bit darkened, but a very good copy in original state. Contemporary annotations with an account of news of the taking of Florida written on the end-papers. $ 87.50
* Sabin 102164. Written by the first librarian of Congress.

288. WEBSTER, DANIEL. A defense of the Christian Religion, and of the religious instruction of the young. Delivered in the Supreme Court of the United States, Feb. 10, 1844 in the case of Stephen Girard's will, by ... N. Y., Newman, 1844. 76pp. Orig. prtd. wrps. On cover: "This edition has been submitted to the revisal of Mr. Webster ..." $ 25.00

289. WENDELL, JOHN L. A digest of cases decided and reported in the Supreme Court of Judicature, and in the Court for the Correction of Errors, of the State of New York from May 1828 to May 1835; with tables of the names of the cases reported and of cases determined in the Court ... from the commencement of the reports in the State of New York until Jan., 1835. Albany, Hoffman, 1836. 684pp. Full contemp. calf. $ 35.00
* Marvin p. 724.

290. WHEATON, HENRY. American legal scholar, first Ambassador to the Court of Berlin, and author of the first great American work on international law. Fine ALS, 3 pages 4to. entirely in his hand, dated Berlin 17 Nov. 1842, written to Thomas Caute Reynolds, later to become Governor of Missouri during the Civil War and at this time a student at Heidelberg, having just finished his dissertation (cf. Marvin p. 607), a copy of which is being sent to Wheaton who advises him on the present prospect of his obtaining a post in the diplomatic corps in Berlin and assures him of his support. $ 45.00

291. WHEATON, HENRY. Elements of international law. Eight edition, edited with notes by Richard Henry Dana, Jr. Boston, Little, Brown 1866. 749pp. Orig. sheep. Very good copy. $ 60.00
* First of this famous edition. William Beach Lawrence had edited two editions of Wheaton, the second in 1863. That edition was considered disloyal to the union cause and Wheaton's widow engaged Dana. The result led to a copyright suit by Lawrence. In any event, Dana's edition quickly attained the stature of an authority. See DAB.

292. (WILLARD PEELE et al. versus the MERCHANTS' INSURANCE COMPANY). Argument of plaintiffs' counsel in the case of ... before the Supreme Court of the United States, February Term 1826, upon the question of admiralty jurisdiction, in cases of policies of insurance. With extracts from various learned treatises upon this subject. Boston, Howe and Norton, 1826. 35,132pp. 8vo. Cont. plain wrps. Fine. $ 45.00
* An uncommon work; remarkably well documented and well argued case for admiralty jurisdiction in contract cases, publishing (in some cases probably the first American appearances) extracts from historical treatises, and citing American precedent. Shaw-Shoemaker 25593 listing the work (the argument only) under Benj. Ropes Nichols.

293. WINGATE, EDMUND. Maximes of reason: or, the reason of the common law of England. London, R. & W. L. for W. Lee ... 1658. Folio. 8pl., 772,(12)pp. Light browning around edges. Contemporary plain calf, rebacked, In all a good copy. $275.00
* First and only edition. Wing W-3021. Marvin p. 741.

294. WINSLOW, FORBES. On insanity. London, John Churchill, 1854. 8vo. (8), 160pp. and 32pp. advertisements. Original publisher's red blind cloth. A very nice copy. $250.00
* FIRST EDITION of Winslow's Lettsomian Lectures to the Medical Society of London. Founder of the first British psychiatric journal, Winslow devoted his career to the study and treatment of insanity and to its relationship with the law. He founded asylums where he employed humane treatment, then still controversial, and he pioneered in the development of the medical jurisprudence of insanity: "The frequent establishment of the plea of insanity in criminal cases was largely due to his influence, and he was called as a witness in many celebrated trials." DNB. The third and longest of these lectures is devoted to the latter topic, and the second to the matter of treatment.

THE PRECURSOR OF BLACKSTONE

295. (WOOD, THOMAS). Some thoughts concerning the study of the laws of England in the two Universities, in a letter to the Reverend ... Head of ... College in Oxford. London, Morphew, 1708. 26pp. 4to. Disbound. Lower edge closely trimmed, touching imprint date, small stain to lower corner of title, otherwise a good sound copy. $200.00
* FIRST EDITION. an Important landmark in the development of modern legal education. Wood argues here for the necessity of incorporating English Common Law in the university curriculum, and urges the production of a systematic treatise. Wood answered this need in 1720 with his Institute of the Laws of England, which remained the leading work on law until superceded by Blackstone, who perfected the project of which Wood can be considered the first great proponent. The work offered here was reissued in 1727 and later incorporated in editions of the Institute. Marvin p. 743. S & M I, 38. Holdsworth XII, p. 418f. The NUC cites 3 locations. This edition not in the BM catalogue.

296. WOOLSEY, THEODORE D. Divorce and divorce legislation especially in the United States. Second edition revised. N. Y., Scribner's Sons, 1882. 328pp. cl. o.p. $ 35.00

297. WRIGHT, MARTIN. An introduction to the law of tenures. The third edition. Dublin, printed for Mary Owen, in Skinner Row, 1750. 222pp. New cl. $ 75.00
* Marvin p. 750, noting at the end of his very laudatory note that Blackstone incorporated in the second volume of the Commentaries the substance of this treatise. S & M, I, 460.

298. WYTHE, GEORGE. Decisions of cases in Virginia by the High Court of Chancery, with remarks upon decrees by the Court of Appeals reversing some of those decisions ... second and only complete edition, with a memoir of the author, analyses of the cases, and an index, by B. B. Minor ... with an appendix, ... by William Green. Richmond, Randolph, 1852. xliii,471(3)pp. 8vo. Contemp. calf, leather label. A fine copy. $ 75.00
* A desireable edition of this Virginia classic first published in 1795. Marvin p. 752 (1st edition).

299. YEAR BOOKS. EDW. I. Years 20 - 22. 30 - 35 (1292 - 1307). In five volumes, complete all published in this series. Edited by Alfred Horwood. London, Longman, 1866 - 1879. Large 8 vo. $150.00
* Chronicles and Memorials of G. B. Series. Sweet & Maxwell I, 313-315.

300. YEAR BOOKS. EDW. III. Years 11 - 20 part I. (1337 - 1346), in 14 volumes. Except for a final volume (Year 20 pt II) a complete run of all published in this series. Edited by Luke Owne Pike. London, HMSO, 1883, 1908. Large 8vo. 1/4 cloth, very good to fine. $350.00
* Chronicles and Memorials of G. B. series. Sweet & Maxwell I, 313-314.

301. ABRAMS, CHARLES. Forbidden neighbors: a study of prejudice in housing. N. Y., Harper, (1955). 404pp. o.p. $ 12.50

302. AL-GHUNAIMI, MOHAMMAD TALAAT. The Muslim conception of international law and the western approach. The Hague, Martinus Nihjoff, 1968. 228pp. Orig. prtd. wrps. o.p. $ 17.50

303. AMADEO, SANTOS P. Argentine constitutional law: the judicial function in the maintenance of the federal system and the preservation of individual rights. With a foreword by L. S. Rowe. N. Y., Columbia Univ. Press, 1943. 243pp. Orig. cl. o.p. $ 22.50
* Columbia Legal Studies, No. IV.

304. AMERICAN ARBITRATION ASSOCIATION. Suggestions for the practice of commercial arbitration in the United States. N. Y., Oxford Univ. Press, 1928. 247pp. Orig. cl. $ 22.50

305. ASSOCIATION OF THE BAR OF THE CITY OF N.Y. Jurisprudence in action: a pleaders anthology ... legal essays selected by ... with a foreword by Robert H. Jackson. N. Y., Baker, 1953. 494pp. o.p. $ 17.50

306. AUSTIN, JOHN. The provine of jurisprudence determined; and the uses of the study of jurisprudence, with an introduction by H.L. A. Hart. London, Weidenfeld, (1954). 396pp. cl. 12mo. o.p. $ 20.00

307. BAILEY, W. F. A treatise on the law of habeas corpus, and special remedies, including mandamus, certiorari, quo warranto and prohibition, and also the subject of contempts. In two vols. Chicago, Flood, 1913. 1,592pp. Orig. cl. Firsted. $ 35.00

308. BATES, LINDELL THEODORE. The divorce and separation of aliens in France. 308. (Continued). N. Y., Columbia Univ. Press, 1929. 334pp. Orig. cl. o.p. $ 17.50

309. BAYLES, GEORGE JAMES. Woman and the law. With an introduction by Prof. L. F. Russell. N. Y., Century Co., 1901. 274pp. Orig. cl. o.p. $ 17.50
* A review of legal condition of women.

310. BELL, ALBERT H. Memoirs of the Bench and Bar of Westmoreland County, Pennsylvania. n.p. (1924). 300pp., frontis, Orig. cl. $ 22.50

311. BENNETT, MARION T. American immigration policies: a history. Wash., Public Affairs Press, (1963). 362pp. Orig. cl., d.j. Fine. o.p. $ 22.50
* Heavily legal.

312. BENTHAM, JEREMY. A fragment on government, and an Introduction to the principles of morals and legislation. Edited with an introduction by, Wilfrid Harrison. Oxford, Basil Blackwell, 1948. 435pp. Orig. cl., d.j. o.p. $ 22.50
* Text and this edition with 66 page scholarly intro. are out-of-print. The Fragment was B's first work and was a criticism of Blackstone.

314. BERNARD, WILLIAM S., ed. et al. American immigration policy - a reappraisal. N. Y., Harper (1950). First ed. 341pp. Cl. $ 10.00

315. BERNS, WALTER. Freedom, virtu e & the First Amendment. Baton Rouge, Louisiana State Univ. Press, (1957). 264pp. cl. $ 12.50

316. BEUTEL, FREDERICK K. Some potentialities of experimental jurisprudence as a new branch of social science. Lincoln, Univ. of Nebraska Press, (1957). 440pp. Orig. cl. o.p. $ 22.50

317. BILLIG, THOMAS CLIFFORD. Equity receiverships in the Common Pleas Court of Franklin County, Ohio. In the years 1927 and 1928. Baltimore, John Hopkins Press, 1932. 159pp. Orig. cl. o.p. $ 12.50
* Study of Judicial Administration in Ohio, Inst. of Law, JH Univ.

318. BLAUSTEIN, ALBERT P., et al. Desegregation and the law: the meaning and effect of the school segregation cases. New Brunswick, Rutgers Univ. Press, 1957. 333pp. Orig. cl. o.p. $ 22.50

319. BLUME, WILLIAM WIRT, ed. Unreported opinions of the Supreme Court of Michigan 1836-1843. Foreword by Walter H. North. Historical introduction by Clark F. Norton. Ann Arbor, Univ. of Michigan Press, 1945. 217pp. Cl. o.p. $ 17.50
* Michigan Legal Studies.

320. BOASSON, CHARLES. Sociological aspects of law and international adjustment ... Amsterdam, North Holland, 1950. 118pp. Wrps. $ 12.50

321. BODIN, JEAN. The six bookes of a Commonweale: a facsimile reprint of the English translation of 1606, corrected and supplemented in the light of a new comparison with the French and Latin texts. Edited with an introduction by Kenneth Douglas McRae. Cambridge, Harvard Univ. Press, 1962. 214; 794pp. 4to. d.j., fine. o.p. $ 45.00
* Best scholarly edition of Knolles' 1606 translation of Bodin's great work, considered the first to present the contract theory of government.

322. BOND, CARROLL T. The Court of Appeals of Maryland: a history. Baltimore, Barton - Gillett, 1928. 213pp. Illus., frontis, many plates. Orig. cl. o.p. $ 25.00
* Mainly from 1694 to 1867, written by Chief Justice of the Court.

323. BRANDEIS, LOUIS D. The curse of bigness: miscellaneous papers of Louis D. Brandeis, edited by Osmond K. Frankel. N. Y., Viking Press, 1934. 339pp. Orig. cl. o.p. $ 17.50

324. BROTHERS, ELMER D. Medical jurisprudence: a statement of the law of forensic medicine. St. Louis, Mosby, 1914. 301pp. Cl. First edition. $ 25.00

325. BROWN, ESTHER LUCILE. Lawyers and the promotion of justice. N. Y., Russell Sage Foundation, 1938. 302pp. First edition. $ 22.50

326. BROWN, ESTHER LUCILE. Lawyers, law schools and public service. N. Y., Russell Sage Foundation, 1948. 258pp. Orig. cl., d.j. First edition. $ 22.50

327. BURDICK, CHARLES K. The law of the American Constitution, its origin and development. With two introductory chapters by Francis M. Burdick. N. Y., Putnam's Sons, 1922. 687pp. o.p. $ 17.50

328. CALVERT, THOMAS H. Regulation of commerce under the Federal Constitution. Long Island, N. Y., Thompson, 1907. 380pp. Orig. cl. o.p. $ 22.50

329. CARDOZO, BENJAMIN N. The nature of the judicial process. New Haven, Yale Univ. Press, (1946). 180pp. Orig. cl. $ 12.50

330. CARLSTON, KENNETH S. Law and structures of social action. London, Stevens, 1956. 288pp. Orig. cl., d.j. o.p. $ 15.00

331. CARRIO, GENARO R. Legal principles and legal positivism. Buenos Aires, 1971. 29pp. Orig. prtd. wrps. $ 5.00

332. CASNER, A. JAMES. Trusts under which beneficiaries are to be determined, with an introduction by Abraham. S. Guterman. The first Mortimer N. Hess Memorial Lecture, delivered before the Assoc. of the Bar of the City of N. Y., on Nov. 5, 1969. N. Y., 26pp. Orig. cl. $ 7.50

333. CENTRE NATIONAL DE RECHERCHES DE LOGIQUE. Le fait et le droit: etudes de logique juridique. Bruxelles, Bruylant, 1961. 278pp, wrps., fine. $ 12.50

334. CHANG, YI-TING. The interpretation of treaties by judicial tribunals. N. Y., (Columbia Univ. Press) 1933. 197pp. Orig. wrps. $ 12.50
* Col. Studies 389.

335. COOK, ARTHUR E. and JOHN J. HAGERTY. Immigration laws of the United States, compiled and explained. Chicago, Callaghan, 1929. 499pp. Cl. Author presentation copy. $ 15.00

336. COWLES, WILLARD BUNCE. Treaties and constitutional law, property interferences and due process of law ... Wash., D. C., American Council on Public Affairs (1941). 315pp. Orig. prtd. wrps. $ 15.00

337. COX, ARCHIBALD. Law and the national labor policy. Los Angeles, Univ. of Calif. (1960). 111pp. Orig. prtd. wrps. $ 12.50
* Institute of Industrial Relations, Univ. of Calif. Monograph Series: 5.

338. CUSHMAN, ROBERT EUGENE. Excess condemnation. N. Y., Appleton, 1917. 323pp Orig. prtd. wrps. o.p. $ 17.50
* Study of a variety of eminent domain of European origin recently adapted to American cities. Scarce.

339. CUSHMAN, ROBERT E. The Independent Regulatory Commissions. N. Y., Oxford Univ. Press, 1941. 780pp. Orig. cl., d.j. Fine. $ 22.50
* Larson 4430. Traces historical development and present functions of every major agency. A standard study of its period.

340. DAVIS, KENNETH CULP. Discretionary justice, a preliminary inquiry. Baton Rouge, Louisiana State Univ. Press, (1969). 233pp. Orig. cl., d.j. o.p. $ 12.50

341. DAWSON, JOHN P. A history of lay judges. Cambridge, Harvard Univ. Press, 1960. 310pp. Orig. cl. o.p. $ 17.50

342. DE BECKER, J.E. (solicitor and legal translator). De Becker's Japanese law of trading partnerships and companies. First ed. Yokohama, Kelly, 1906. 133pp. Cl. $ 30.00

343. DEL VECCHIO, GIORGIO. General principles of law. Translated by Felix Forte. Boston, Boston Univ. Press, 1956. 111pp. Orig. cl. o.p. $ 12.50

344. DEL VECCHIO, GIORGIO. Humanite et unite du droit: essais de philosophie juridique. Paris, Pichon, 1963. 310pp., wrps, fine. $ 12.50

345. DE QUIROS, BERNALDO. Modern theories of criminality. Translated from the Spanish by Alfonso De Salvio, with an introduction by Wm. W. Smithers. Boston, Little, Brown, 1912. 249pp. $ 12.50

346. DEVINE, ROBERT A. American immigration policy, 1924-1952. New Haven, Yale Univ. Press, 1957. 220pp. cl., d.j. Fine. $ 17.50
* Yale Historical Pub., miscellany 66. Largely a legislative study.

347. DOUGHERTY, J. HAMPDEN. Constitutional history of the State of New York. Second edition, revised and enlarged by the author. N. Y., Neale Publ. Co., 1915. 408pp. Orig. cl. o.p. $ 22.50

348. DUCKWORTH, LAWRENCE. An encyclopaedia of marine law. Second edition. London, Pitman (1908). 336pp. Orig. cl. Appendices contain full text of all latest acts: exhaustively indexed, with table of cases. $ 17.50

349. EASTMAN, FRANK M. Courts and lawyers of Pennsylvania: a history, 1623-1923. In 4 vols. Illustrated. N. Y., American Historical Society, 1922. 1345pp. 4to. 4vols. 1/4 leather. Numerous engraved plates of portraits. $ 75.00
* A good coverage of all the important legal developments of the colony and state, as well as a detailed biographical encyclopaedia.

350. EDWARDS, NEWTON. The courts and the public schools: the legal basis of school organization and administration. Chicago, Univ. of Chicago Press (1940). 591pp. Orig. cl. $ 12.50

351. EISENSTEIN, LOUIS. The ideologies of taxation. N. Y., Ronald Press, (1961). 263pp. Orig. cl., d.j. o.p. $ 15.00
* By a foremost tax-lawyer.

352. EVANS, WILLIAM FRANKLIN. Federal contracts with land titles: a treatise on administering Federal statutes in relation to the real estate laws of the States. Charlottesville, Va., Michie Co., 1944. 256pp. $ 17.50

353. EWING, CORTEZ A.M. The judges of the Supreme Court, 1789-1937: a study of their qualifications. Minneapolis, Univ. of Minnesota Press (1938). 124pp. Orig. cl. o.p. $ 15.00

354. (EX PARTE MILLIGAN). KLAUS, SAMUEL ed. The Milligan Case. N. Y., Knopf, 1929. 476pp. Cl. Reproduction of entire trial with lengthy introduction concerning this landmark Civil War case. Fine copy, original edition. $ 22.50

354a. FIFOOT, C.H.S., ed. The letters of Frederic William Maitland. London, Selden Society, 1965. 397pp. Illus., frontis. $ 17.50
* Selden Society Supplementary Series Vol. I.

355. (CATALOGUE U.S. DEPT. OF JUSTICE) FINCH, JAMES A. Catalogue of the Library of the Department of Justice to September 1, 1904. Wash., GPO, 1904. 1135pp. Orig. cl. $ 25.00

356. FOX, DIXON RYAN, ed. The minutes of the Court of Sessions, (1657-1696) Westchester County, New York, with an essay by G. B. Harrington. White Plains, N. Y., Westchester County Historical Society, 1924. 138pp. Orig. cl. $ 15.00
* Publications of the Westchester County Historical Society, (founded 1874) vol. II, Source Series, Vol. I.

357. FRANCK, THOMAS M. Comparative constitutional process: cases and materials, fundamental rights in the common law Nations. N. Y., Praeger, (1968). 595pp. Cl. o.p. $ 17.50

358. FRANK, ELI. Title to real and leasehold estates and liens. Baltimore, Baltimore City Printing, 1912. 348pp. $ 22.50
* Study of Maryland law.

359. (FRANKFURTER, FELIX). Felix Frankfurter reminisces, recorded in talks with Dr. Harlan B. Phillips. N. Y., Reynal (1960). 310pp. 1/4 cl., d.j. First edition. $ 12.50

Holmes and the Supreme Court. Cambridge, Harvard Univ. Press, 1938. 139pp. Frontis. Orig. cl. Fine. o.p. $ 12.50

361. FREUND, ERNST. Administrative powers over persons and property, a comparative survey. Chicago, Univ. of Chicago Press, (1928). 620pp. Orig. cl. $ 15.00

362. FREUND, PAUL A. On understanding the Supreme Court: a series of lectures delivered under the auspices of the Julius Rosenthal Foundation at Northwestern Univ. School of Law, in April 1949. Boston, Little, Brown, 1950. 128pp. Cl., d.j. $ 12.50

363. FRIEDMANN, W. Law and social change in contemporary Britain. With a foreword by the Right Hon. Sir Alfred Denning. London, Stevens, 1951. 322pp. Orig. cl. o.p. $ 17.50

364. FRIEDRICH, CARL J. ed. Liberty. N. Y., Atherton, 1962. 333pp. $ 12.50
* NOMOS IV. Year book of the American Society for Political and Legal Philosophy.

365. GALL, MORRIS. Judicial decision and practical judgment. Morningside Heights, N. Y. King's Crown Press, 1946. 95pp. Orig. prtd. wrps. o.p. $ 12.50

366. GELLHORN, WALTER, ed. The States and subversion. Ithaca, N. Y., Cornell Univ. Press, 1952. 454pp. Orig. cl. $ 15.00
* Cornell Studies in Civil Liberty.

367. GROSS, BERTRAM M. The legislative struggle: a study in social combat. N. Y., McGraw-Hill, 1953. 472pp. Cl. $ 15.00

368. HAIG, ROBERT MURRAY. A history of the general property tax in Illinois. Champaign, Ill., 1914. 229pp. Orig. wrps. $ 10.00

369. HAINES, CHARLES GROAL. The American doctrine of judicial supremacy. N. Y., Russell, 1959. 705pp. Orig. cl. Second edition with revisions. $ 15.00

370. HALE, ROBERT L. Freedom through law; public control of private governing power. N. Y., Columbia Univ. Press, 1952. 591pp. Orig. cl., d.j. o.p. $ 17.50

371. HARARI, ABRAHAM. The place of negligence in the law of torts. Sydney, Australia, The Law Book Co., 1962. 194pp. Orig. cl., d.j. o.p. $ 15.00

372. HARRIMAN, EDWARD A. The Constitution at the cross roads: a study of the legal aspects of the League of Nations, the Permanent Organization of Labor, and the Permanent Court of International Justice. N. Y., Doran (1925). 274pp. Orig. cl. o.p. $ 12.50

373. HARRIS, ROBERT JENNINGS. The judicial power of the United States. Louisiana, Louisiana State Univ. Press, 1940. 238pp. Orig. cl. o.p. $ 15.00
* Louisiana State Univ. Studies No. 40.

374. HARRIS, SILAS A. Appellate courts and appellate procedure in Ohio. Baltimore, Johns Hopkins Press, 1933. 181pp. Orig. prtd wrps. o.p. $ 12.50
* Study of Judicial Admin. in Ohio, Inst. of Law, JH Univ.

375. HAWES, FRANCES. Henry Brougham, N. Y., St. Martin's Press (1956). 325pp. Illus., frontis., plates. Orig. cl., d.j. Biography of this important legal reformer. o.p. $ 17.50

376. HEATH, HERBERT M. A manual of Maine corporation law: containing the statutes regulating business corporations, a digest of these statutes, and the principal corporation forms used in Maine. N. Y., Ronald Press, 1907. 300pp. Orig. cl., lea. labels. $ 22.50

377. HENDERSON, GERARD CARL. The position of foreign corporations in American constitutional law: a contribution to the history and theory of juristic persons in Anglo-American law. Cambridge, Harvard Univ. Press, 1918. 199pp. Orig. cl. o.p. $ 22.50
* Harvard Studies in jurisprudence vol. II.

378. HESSELTINE, NORMAN F. A digest of the law of trade-marks, and unfair trade. Boston, Little, Brown, 1906. 390pp. Orig. cl. $ 22.50

379. HEXNER, ERWIN. Studies in legal terminology. Chapel Hill, Univ. of North Carolina Press, 1941. 150pp. Orig. cl. o.p. $ 15.00

380. HOLCOMBE, ARTHUR N. Human rights in the modern world. N. Y., N. Y. Univ. Press, 1948. 162pp. Orig. cl. o.p. $ 12.50

381. HOLLAND, THOMAS ERSKINE. The elements of jurisprudence. Twelfth edition. N. Y., Oxford Univ. Press, 1917. 454pp. cl. $ 30.00
* In this edition Holland has "aimed at producing a text which may be regarded as final ... the task ... has required an expenditure of time and labour exceeding that demanded by any preceeding new edition." Preface. Holland was the direct intellectual heir of John Austin and the venture towards scientific jurisprudence.

382. HOLLAND, THOMAS ERSKINE. Lectures on international law. Edited by Thomas Alfred Walker and Wyndham Legh Walter. London, Sweet, 1933. 576pp. Orig. cl. Roy 8vo. Fine. $ 50.00
* First edition, posthumously published from

382. (Continued). the lectures and other notes of this great scholar. See DNB for an account. Not in print or reprinted.

383. HUFFCUT, ERNEST W., ed. The law of negotiable instruments, statutes, cases and authorities. Second edition, revised and enlarged by Frederick D. Colson. N. Y. Baker, 1920. 885pp. Orig. cl. $ 15.00

384. HUFSTEDLER, SHIRLEY M. The directions and misdirections of a constitutional right of privacy. With an introduction by Mendes Hershman. Twenty-eighth annual Benjamin N. Cardoza Lecture, delivered before the Assoc. of the Bar of the City of N. Y., May 11, 1971. N. Y., 1971. 31pp. Orig. cl. $ 7.50

385. HUGHES, CHARLES EVANS. The Supreme Court of the United States, its foundation, methods and achievements, an interpretation. Garden City, Garden City Publishing, (1936). 269pp. Orig. cl., Fine. $ 10.00

386. INSTITUTE OF LAW AND OHIO INSTITUTE. Ohio criminal statistics 1931: an experiment in methods and techniques of reporting. Baltimore, Hopkins, 1932. 189p. wrps. $ 12.50

387. JENKS, EDWARD. Law and politics in the Middle Ages, with a synoptic table of sources. N. Y., Holt, 1[illegible]. 352pp. Orig. cl. $ 15.00

388. JENSEN, O. C. The nature of legal argument. Oxford, Basil Blackwell, 1957. 166pp. Orig. cl. o.p. $ 15.00

389. JONES, J. MERVYN. British nationality: law and practice. With a foreword by W. E. Beckett. Oxford, Clarendon Press, 1947. 452pp. Cl., d.j. o.p. $ 15.00

390. KARRAKER, CYRUS HARRELD. The seventeenth-century sheriff; a comparative study of the sheriff in England and the Chesapeake Colonies, 1607 - 1689. Chapel Hill, Univ. of No. Carolina Press, 1930. 217pp. Orig. cl. o.p. $ 22.50

391. KEENEY, BARNABY C. Judgment by peers. Cambridge, Harvard Univ. Press, 1949. 191pp. Orig. cl., d.j. o.p. $ 12.50
* Harvard Historical Monographs, XX.

392. KEITH, ARTHUR BERRIEDALE. Responsible government in the Dominions. In three vols. Oxford, Clarendon Press, 1912. 1,670pp. Orig. cl. o.p. $ 60.00
* Monumental treatment of history and working of parliamentary government throughout the British Commonwealth: includes chapters on Chinese immigration and native policy.

393. KELLOR, FRANCES. Arbitration and the legal profession: a report prepared for the survey of the legal profession. N. Y., Am. Arbitration Assoc., (1951). 64pp. Orig. prtd wrps. $ 7.50

394. KENDALL, WILLMOORE. John Locke and the doctrine of majority-rule. Urbana, Univ. of Illinois Press, 1941. 141pp. Orig. cl. $ 4.50
* Illinois Studies in the Social Sciences, vol. XXVI, No. 2.

395. KILBOURN, DWIGHT C. The Bench and Bar of Litchfield County, Connecticut, 1709-1909: biographical sketches of members, history and catalogue of the Litchfield Law School, historical notes. Litchfield, Published by the Author, 1909. (Edition limited to 500). 344pp Illus., frontis., numerous plates. Orig. cl. Fine. Scarce. $ 50.00
* Chronicles the development of one of the greatest legal traditions of the country, particularly the first professional law school, and such leaders as Tapping Reeve and James Gould

396. KING, DONALD B. 100 injustices to the child. St. Louis, St. Louis Univ., National Juvenile Law Center, 1970-1971. 120pp. Orig. prtd. wrps. $ 12.50

397. KNOCKER, DOUGLAS, ed. Accidents in their medico-legal aspect, by leading medical and surgical authorities. London, Bailliere, 1912. 1235pp. Illus., frontis, plates. Orig. cl. $ 25.00

398. KONESFSKY, SAMUEL J. Chief Justice Stone, and the Supreme Court. With a prefatory note by Charles A. Beard. N. Y., MacMillan, 1945. 290pp. Orig. cl. $ 15.00

399. KONEFSKY, SAMUEL J. The legacy of Holmes and Brandeis: a study in the influence of ideas. N. Y., MacMillan, 1956. 316pp. Orig. cl., d.j. Author presentation copy. Fine. $ 15.00

400. KONVITZ, MILTON R., ed., et al. Aspects of liberty. Essays presented to Robert E. Cushman. Ithaca, N. Y., Cornell Univ. Press (1958). 355pp. Frontis. Cl. $ 15.00
* Cornell Studies in Civil Liberty.

401. KONVITZ, MILTON R. A century of civil rights, with a study of state law against discrimination by Thoedore Leskes. N. Y., Columbia, 1961. 293p. d.j., fine. o.p. $ 22.50

402. KONVITZ, MILTON R., ed. Law and social action: selected essays of Alexander H. Pekelis. Ithaca, Cornell Univ. Press, 1950. 272pp. Orig. cl. $ 15.00

403. KULSRUD, CARL J. Maritime neutrality to 1780: a history of the main principles governing neutrality and belligerency to 1780. Boston, Little, Brown, 1936. 351pp. Orig. cl. o.p. $ 22.50

404. LEE, MAURICE W. Tax structure of the State of Washington. Pullman, Washington, State College of Wash. Press, (1950). 134pp. o.p. $ 15.00

405. LEHMAN, IRVING. The influence of Judge Cardozo on the common law. Garden City, N. Y., Doubleday, 1942. 33pp. Orig. cl. 12mo. $ 7.50

406. LEPAWSKY, ALBERT. The judicial system of Metropolitan Chicago. Chicago, Univ. of Chicago Press, (1932). 265pp. Orig. cl., d.j. o.p. $ 17.50

407. LEWIS, WM. DRAPER. Cases on specific performance. Phila., Univ. of Pennsylvania, 1903. 143pp. Cl. $ 12.50

408. LOEB, ISIDOR. The legal property relations of married parties: a study in comparative legislation. N. Y., Columbia Univ. Press 1900. 197pp. Orig. prtd. wrps. $ 12.50
* Studies in History, Economics and Public Law, Vol. XIII, No. I.

409. LONG, JOSEPH R. A treatise on the law of domestic relations. St. Paul, Keefe-Davidson, 1905. 455pp. Orig. cl. $ 25.00

410. McBAIN, HOWARD LEE. American city progress and the law. N. Y., Columbia Univ. Press, 1918. 269pp. Orig. cl. o.p. $ 17.50

411. McGEHEE, LUCIUS POLK. Due process of law under the Federal Constitution. Long Island, N. Y., Thompson, 1906. 451pp. Orig. cl. o.p. $ 17.50
* Studies in Constitutional Law, series.

412. MACMAHON, ARTHUR W. The statutory sources of New York City government. N. Y., (Columbia Univ.) 1923. 169pp. Orig. wrps. o.p. $ 12.50

413. McNAIR, ARNOLD DUNCAN. The law of treaties; British practice and opinions. N. Y., Columbia Univ. Press, 1938. 578pp. Orig. cl. o.p. $ 22.50

414. MAC VEAGH, ROGERS. The Transportation Act, 1920, its sources, history and text, together with its amendments to the Interstate Commerce Act: explained, analyzed, and compared; comprising extracts from reports and debates in Congress, rulings, interpretations, and decisions of the Interstate Commerce Commission, opinions of the United States Supreme Court, prescribed forms, and complete texts of related acts, including the Federal Control Act, Merchant Marine Act, 1920 and Interstate

414. (Continued) Commerce Act, all as amended to and including August 18, 1922. N. Y., Holt, 1923. 968pp. Cl. o.p. $ 22.50

415. MATTERN, JOHANNES. Principles of the constitutional jurisprudence of the German National Republic. Baltimore, Johns Hopkins Press, 1928. 682pp. Orig. cl. o.p. $ 27.50

416. MAUNG, MAUNG. Law and custom in Burma and the Burmese family. The Hague, Martinus, 1963. 155pp. Orig. cl., d.j. o.p. $ 17.50

417. MILLER, DAVID HUNTER. The Geneva Protocol. N. Y., MacMillan, 1925. 279pp. Orig. cl. o.p. $ 17.50
* A legal study of the document.

418. MILLER, HAROLD ACTON et al. A digest of New Jersey negligence cases ... April, 1790 to July, 1906. Neward, Soney & Sage, 1906. Cl. $ 15.00

419. MILLER, PERRY, et al. Religion and freedom of thought. Foreword by Henry P. Van Dusen. Garden City, N. Y., Doubleday, 1954. 64pp. Wrps. $ 6.50

420. MOORE, JOHN BASSETT. International law and some current illusions and other essays. N. Y., MacMillan, 1924. 381pp. Orig. cl. Fine. o.p. $ 22.50

421. MORRIS, CLARENCE. How lawyers think. Cambridge, Harvard Univ. Press, 1937. 144pp. Orig. cl. o.p. $ 15.00

422. Natural law and world law: essays to commemorate the sixtieth birthday of Kotaro Tanaka, Chief Justice of the Supreme Court of Japan. Yuhikaku, 1954. 241, 200pp. Cloth. $ 15.00
* Most in English, including ones by Kelsen, Yntema.

423. NICHOLSON, LOWELL S. The law schools of the United States: A statistical and analytical report. Prepared for the Survey of the Legal Profession by ... Baltimore, Lord Baltimore Press, 1958. 245pp. Orig. cl. o.p. $ 15.00

424. NIPPOLD, OTFRIED. The development of international law after the world war. Translated from the German by Amos S. Hershey. Oxford, Clarendon Press, 1923. 241pp. Orig. cl. o.p. $ 22.50

425. NORGREN, PAUL H., et al. Toward fair employment. N. Y., Columbia Univ. Press, 1964. 296pp. $ 12.50
* Account of FEP Committee, its activity and conditions surrounding its development.

426. OAKES, C. G. Sir Samuel Romilly, 1757-1818. "The friend of the oppressed," his life and times ... London, Allen, 1934. 440pp. Illus., frontis., plates Orig. cl. o.p. $ 15.00

427. OAKES, EUGENE E. Studies in Massachusetts town finance. Cambridge, Harvard Univ., Press, 1937. 237pp. o.p. $ 15.00
* Harvard Economic Studies vol. 57.

428. OSBORN, ALBERT S. Questioned document problems: the discovery and proof of the facts. Revised and edited by Albert D. Osborn. Introduction by Dean Roscoe Pound Albany, Boyd Printing, 1944. 486pp. Illus., frontis, plates. Orig. cl. $ 20.00

429. OUTLER, ALBERT C., et al. Natural law and natural rights. Edited with an introduction by Arthur L. Harding. Dallas, So. Methodist Univ. Press, 1955. 99pp. Cl., d.j. o.p. $ 12.50
* Studies in jurisprudence: II.

430. PECK, EPAPHRODITUS. The property rights of husband and wife under the law of Connecticut. Hartford, Dissell, 1904. 277pp Full contemp. sheep. $ 25.00

431. PENNOCK, J. ROLAND, ed., et al. Political and legal obligation. N. Y., Atherton Press, 1970. 455pp. Orig. cl. $ 12.50
* Yearbook, Am. Soc. for Political & Legal Philosophy, No. XII. (NOMOS)

432. PENNOCK, J. R. ed. Representation. N. Y., Atherton, 1968. 317pp. $ 12.50
* NOMOS X, Yearbook of the Am. Soc. for Political and Legal Philosophy.

433. PIERSON, WILLIAM WHATLEY, JR. Texas versus White: a study in legal history. Durham, N. C., Seeman Printery, 1916. 103pp. Orig. prtd. wraps. o.p. $ 15.00

434. PIGGOTT, SIR FRANCIS. Exterritoriality: The law relating to consular jurisdiction and to residence in Oriental countries. New edition, revised and enlarged. Hongkong, Kelly, 1907. 325pp. Orig. cl. $ 40.00
* Fine historical treatment of treaties, acts, theory and practice throughout the Pacific, India, Africa, Australasia in the 19th century. Final edition. S & M I, 179.

435. PLUCKNETT, T. F. T. Legislation of Edward I: the Ford Lectures delivered in the Univ. of Oxford in Hilary term 1947. Oxford, Clarendon, 1949. 168pp. 1st ed. d.j. Fine. o.p. $ 22.50

436. POUND, ROSCOE. Appellate procedure in civil cases. Boston, Little, Brown, 1941. 431pp. Orig. cl. d.j. First edition. Fine. o.p. $ 22.50

437. POUND, ROSCOE. An introduction to the philosophy of law. New Haven, Yale Univ. Press. 1922. 397pp. First edition. $ 12.50

438. POUND, ROSCOE, et al. Jubilee law lectures 1889-1939, School of Law and the Catholic University of America. Wash. The Catholic Univ. of Am. Press, 1939. 182pp. Cl. First edition. Fine. $ 15.00
* Autograph presentation copy from Pound.

439. POUND, ROSCOE. The lawyer from antiquity to modern times, with particular reference to the development of Bar Associations in the United States. St. Paul, Minn., West Publ. Co., 1953. 404pp. Frontis. $ 15.00

440. POUND, ROSCOE. Legal immunities of labor unions. Wash., D. C., Am. Enterprise Assoc., 1957. 58pp. Prtd. wrps. $ 6.50

441. Proceedings of International Conference, under the auspices of American Society for Judicial Settlement of International Disputes, December, 15-17, 1910. Washington, D. C. Baltimore, Waverly Press, 1910. 400pp. Orig. cl. $ 15.00

442. RADIN, MAX, ed. et al. Legal essays in tribute to Orrin Kip McMurray. Berkeley, Univ. of Calif. Press,, 1935 691pp. Frontis., orig. cl. o.p. $ 20.00
* Contributions by Pound, Wigmore, Manley Hudson and others.

443. RAPKIN, CHESTER et al. The demand for housing in racially mixed areas: a study of the nature of neighborhood change. Berkeley, Univ. of Calif. Press, 1960. 177pp. o.p. $ 12.50

444. READ, HORACE EMERSON. Recognition and enforcement of foreign judgments in the common law units of the British Commonwealth. Cambridge, Harvard Univ. Press, 1938. 371pp. Orig. cl., d.j. Author presentation copy. o.p. $ 27.50
* Harvard Studies in the Conflict of Laws, Vol. II.

445. RICHES, CROMWELL, A. The unanimity rule and the League of Nations. Baltimore, Johns Hopkins Press, 1933. 224pp. $ 12.50
* Johns Hopkins Univ. Studies, New Series, No. 20.

446. RIGNANO, EUGENIO. The social significance of the inheritance tax. Translated and adapted by William J. Shultz, with an introduction by Edwin R. A. Seligman. N. Y., Knopf, 1924. 128pp. Cl. o.p. $ 15.00

447. ROALFE, WILLIAM R. The libraries of the legal profession: A study prepared for the Survey of the Legal Profession, under the auspices of American Bar Association. St. Paul, Minn., West Publ. co., 1953. 471pp. $ 15.00

448. ROBINTON, MADELINE RUSSELL. An introduction to the papers of the New York Prize Court, 1861-1865. N. Y., Columbia Univ. Press, 1945. 203pp. Orig. cl., d.j. First edition. Fine. $ 12.50
* Studies in History, Economics and Public Law, Columbia Univ. Number 515.

449. RODICK, BURLEIGH CUSHING. The doctrine of necessity in international law. N. Y., Columbia Univ. Press, 1928. 195pp. Orig. wrps. o.p. $ 15.00

450. ROSS, ALF. Constitution of the United Nations: analysis of structure and function. N. Y., Rinehart, 1950. 226pp. Orig. cl. o.p. $ 15.00

451. ROSS, ALF. Towards a realistic jurisprudence: a criticism of dualism in law. (Translated from the Danish by Annie I. Fausboll, M.A.). Copenhagen, Munksgaard, 1946. 304pp. Orig. cl. Very scarce. o.p. $ 27.50

452. ROUBIER, PAUL. Theorie generale du droit. Histoire des doctrines juridiques et philosophie des valeurs sociales. Second ed. rev. et augm. Paris, Sirey, 1951. 334p. Wrps. $ 12.50

453. RUNES, DAGOBERT D. The disinherited and the law. N. Y., Philosophical Lib., (1964). 79pp. o.p. $ 12.50

454. ST. JOHN-STEVAS, NORMAN. Obscenity and the law. With an introduction by Sir Alan P. Herbert. London, Secker, 1956. 289pp. Orig. cl. $ 12.50

455. SAMUEL, HORACE B. Shareholders' money: an analysis of certain defects in company legislation with proposals for their reform. London, Pitman, 1933. 392pp. Cl., Fine. $ 25.00

456. SATOW, RT. HON. SIR ERNEST. A guide to diplomatic practice. In two vols. London, Longmans, 1917. 407,405pp. Orig. cl. o.p. $ 40.00
* Actually a full-scale treatise and not merely a "handbook". The author notes this to be the first such work published in England (compared with other well-known Continental predecessors). Issued under the auspices of the series "Contributions to International Law and Diplomacy."

457. SAVILL, STANLEY. The police service of England & Wales: its organization, disposition, finance, powers and duties, pay, pension, conditions of service, &c. With notes on other British and Colonial Forces. London, Kempster, (ca. 1900). 289pp. Orig. cl. Fine. Extremely detailed, with statistics. $ 25.00

458. SCECHTER, FRANK I. The historical foundations of the law relating to trade-marks. With foreword by Munroe Smith. N. Y., Columbia Univ. Press, 1925. 211pp. Orig. cl. Illustrated. o.p. $ 22.50

459. SCHMIDT, FOLKE AND STIG STROMHOLM. Legal values in modern Sweden. Svenska Bokforlaget, Norstedts (1964). 86pp. Orig. cl. $ 7.50

460. SCHOFIELD, HENRY. Essays on constitutional law and equity, and other subjects. Edited by the Faculty of Law, Northwestern University. In two vols. Boston, Chipman, 1921. 1006pp. Frontis., orig. cl. First edition. Fine. $ 45.00

461. SCHRAMM, GUSTAV L. Piedpoudre Courts: a study of the small claim litigant in the Pittsburgh District. Pittsburgh, The Legal Aid Society, 1928. 219pp. Orig. wrps. Many fold. tables. o.p. $ 12.50

462. SCOTT, JAMES BROWN ed. Resolutions of the Institute of International Law dealing with the law of nations, with an historical introduction and explanatory notes. N. Y., Oxford, 1916. Carnegie Endowment Series. o.p. $ 17.50

463. SEAVEY, WARREN A. Studies in agency. St. Paul, Minn., West Publ. Co., 1949. 451pp. cl. $ 17.50

464. SELDEN SOCIETY. Publications. London (1887 - 1972). Volumes 79, 83, 84, 87 - 89. Original cloth, all in very good to fine condition. per vol. $ 15.00

465. SERTORIO, LUIGI. La prigionia di guerra e il diritti di postliminio. Milan, Bocca, 1916. 198pp. Orig. wrps., Fine. $ 15.00

466. SHARTEL, BURKE. Our legal system and how it operates: Five lectures delivered at the Univ. of Michigan, Feb. 23, 24, 25, 26, and 27, 1948. on the Thomas M. Cooley Lectureship, enlarged and revised. Ann Arbor, Univ. Mich. Law School, 1951. 629pp. Cl. Fine. $ 22.50

467. SHIENTAG, BERNARD L. The personality of the judge. N. Y., Assoc. of the Bar, N. Y. City, 1944. 97pp. Orig. cl. 12mo. o.p. $ 8.50

468. SHIENTAG, BERNARD L. Summary judgment. N. Y., The Viking Press, 1941. 130pp. Orig. cl. o.p. $ 15.00
* N. Y. State Supreme Court Justice.

469. SHILTON, DOROTHY O., et al. High Court of Admiralty examinations (Ms volume 53) 1637 - 1638. With an introduction by Eric G. M. Fletcher. (N. Y.,) 1932. 330pp. o.p. $ 27.50
* Anglo-American Records Foundation, Vol. II. The first publication of Admiralty case records of the 17th century; considerable reference to colonial expansion in North America.

470. SIEVEKING, ALFRED. Das deutsche Seerecht (mit Ausschluss des Seeversicherungsrechtes). Ein praktische Lehrbuch. Hamburg, Meissners, 1907. Cl., orig. wrps. bound in. 471pp. $ 22.50

471. SIMKINS, W. S. Title by limitation in Texas. Kansas City, Mo., Vernon Law Book Co., 1924. 232pp. Cl. $ 25.00

472. SIMMS, HENRY H. Life of John Taylor: the story of a brilliant leader in the early Virginia state rights school. Richmond, Va., Byrd, 1932. 234pp. Frontis., Orig. cl. o.p. $ 22.50
* Taylor produced one of the most important statements of political theory in the early Republic (his "Inquiry into the principles and policy of the government of the U.S." 1814). Charles Beard considered him one of the greatest American political theorists. See DAB.

473. SIMONTON, THOMAS C. Simonton on the law of checks, notes and banks, including the right of parties in dealing with banks. N. Y., Van Horen, (1906). 176pp. Orig. cl., lea. labels. $ 12.50

474. SMITH, DAVID WRIGHT. The law relating to the rule of the road at sea, with diagrams and an appendix; containing extracts from the Merchant Shipping Act, 1894; The Admiralty Court Act, 1861, etc. Glasgow, J. Brown, 1910. 333pp. Orig. cl. $ 22.50

475. SMITH, FRANKLIN A. Judicial review of legislation in New York, 1906 - 1938. N. Y. (Columbia Univ. Press) 1952. 250pp. Orig. prtd. wrps. $ 12.50

476. SPALDING, HUGH M. Encyclopaedia of business law and forms ... for all the States and Canada. With notes and authorities. Revised edition. Phila., Ziegler, 1903. 702pp. Full contemp. sheep. $ 20.00

477. STAHL, DAVID et al. (editors). The community and racial crises. N. Y., Practising Law Institute, (1966). 364pp. $ 12.50

478. STEWART, GEORGE R., et al. The year of the oath: the fight for academic freedom at the University of California. Garden City, N. Y., Doubleday, 1950. 156pp. Orig. cl., d.j. $ 12.50

479. STONE, JULIUS. Legal education and public responsibility: report and analysis of the Conference on the Education of Lawyers for Their Public Responsibilities, 1956. The Univ. of Colorado, Boulder ... 1959. 430pp. Orig. cl. Fine. $ 15.00

480. STORY, JOSEPH. Commentaries on equity jurisprudence, as administered in England and America. Fourteenth edition by W. H. Lyon. In three vols. Boston, Little, Brown, 1918. cxcii, 2053pp. Orig. cl. Fine. $ 55.00

481. Studies in Polish and comparative law: a symposium of twelve articles, with a foreword by Professor H. C. Gutteridge. London, Stevens, 1945. 274pp. Orig. cl. $ 17.50

482. SUTHERLAND, GEORGE. Constitutional power and world affairs. N. Y., Columbia Univ. Press, 1919. 202pp. Orig. cl. $ 12.50

483. (TANSILL, CHARLES S. Compiler) Documents illustrative of the formation of the union of the American states. Wash., GPO, 1927. FOLIO. 1115pp. Cl. Fine. A few facsimile illustrations. $ 25.00

484. TARTER, HARRY. Legal resolvents. N. Y., Merlin Press, (1951). 114pp. Orig. prtd. wrps. o.p. $ 12.50

485. TAYLOR, JOHN. An inquiry into the principles and policy of the government of the United States. London, Routledge, (1950). 562pp. Orig. cl. o.p. $ 25.00
* Reprint of 1814 original ed. Intro. by Roy F. Nichols. One of the great landmarks of American political theory.

486. TITE, COLIN G.C. Impeachment and parliamentary judicature in early Stuart England. London, Univ. of London, 1974. 249pp. Cl., d.j. $ 15.00
* Univ. of London Historical Studies XXXVII.

487. TUMIN, MELVIN M. et al. Desegregation: resistance and readiness. Princeton, N. Y., Princeton Univ. Press, 1958. 270pp. $ 10.00

****

488. U. S. INTERSTATE COMMERCE COMMISSION. Annual report. 29-30, 36-53, 55-61 (1915 - 1947). per year $ 12.50

489. U.S. TREATIES. Treaties, conventions, international acts, and agreements between the United States of America and other powers 1923-1937. Wash., GPO., 1938. Large 8vo. $ 35.00
* Volume 4 (and final vol. with index to vols. 1-4) of this series.

SAME: Vols. I and II (1789-1909) each: $ 25.00

490. VAN DYNE, FREDERICK. Citizenship of the United States. Rochester, N. Y., Lawyers' Co-op. Publ. Co., 1904. 385pp. Full contemp. sheep. First edition. $ 17.50

491. VAN VLECK, WILLIAM C. The administrative control of aliens: a study in administrative law and procedure. N. Y., The Commonwealth Fund, 1932. 260pp. $ 17.50

492. VREELAND, HAMILTON JR. Hugo Grotius, the father of the modern science of international law. N. Y., Oxford Univ. Press, 1917. 258pp. Frontis., orig. cl. o.p. $ 17.50

493. WARREN, CHARLES. Bankruptcy in United States history. Cambridge, Harvard Univ. Press, 1935. 195pp. Orig. cl., d.j. Fine. First edition. $ 17.50

494. WARREN, CHARLES. Congress, the Constitution and the Supreme Court. New revised and enlarged edition. Boston, Little, Brown, 1935. 346pp. Orig. cl., d.j., fine. o.p. $ 17.50
* This revised edition not reprinted.

495. WARREN, EARL. "All men are created equal." With an introduction by Mendes Hershman. Twenty-seventh annual Benjamin N. Cardozo Lecture delivered before the Assoc. of the Bar of the City of New York, 1970. N. Y., 1970. 22pp. Orig. cl. $ 6.00

497. WESTRUP, C.W. Family property and patria potestas. Copenhagen, Levin, 1936. 72pp. Orig. prtd. wrps. 4to. Fine. $ 12.50

498. WHITE, EDW. J. Legal antiquities: a collection of essays upon ancient laws and customs. St. Louis, F. H. Thomas, 1913. 349pp. o.p. $ 22.50

499. WIDDIFIELD, CHARLES HOWARD. The law and practice relating to the passing of executors' accounts. Toronto, Carswell, 1916. 302pp. Cl. $ 27.50

500. WIGMORE, JOHN HENRY. A panorama of the world's legal systems. In three vols., with five hundred illustrations. St. Paul, West Publ. Co., (1928). 1,206pp. Orig. cl. o.p. $ 30.00

501. WILCOX, ARTHUR RUSSELL. The Bar of Rye Township, Westchester County, New York. An historical and biographical record, 1660-1918. (N. Y., Knickerbocker Press, 1918). 347pp. Illus., frontis., including numerous plates. Orig. cl. One of 250 copies printed. Roy 8vo. Fine. $ 47.50

502. WILKIN, ROBERT N., et al. Origins of the natural law tradition. Edited with an introduction by Arthur L. Harding. Dallas, So. Methodist Univ. Press, 1954. 96pp. Cl., d.j. o.p. $ 12.50
* Studies in Jurisprudence: I.

503. WILSON, GEORGE GRAFTON. The Hague arbitration cases: compromise and awards with maps in cases decided under the provisions of the Hague Conventions of 1899 and 1907 for the Pacific Settlement of International Disputes and texts of the conventions. Boston, Ginn, 1915. 525pp. Orig. cl. $ 25.00

504. WITTMANN, ERNO. The inalienable rights of aliens. With an introduction by Roger N. Baldwin. Wash., Hobard Publ. Co., (1946). 46pp. Orig. prtd wrps. $ 5.00

ADDENDA TO PARTS I and II

505. AIKIN, JOHN. A view of the life, travels and philanthropic labors of the late John Howard ... Phila., Ormrod, 1794. 12mo. 196pp. and 5pp. publ. ads; with list of American subscribers. Fine engraved frontis portrait. Orig. calf. Fine copy. $ 47.50
* First American edition and a most pleasant copy of the life of this great prison reformer.

506. AMES, JAMES BARR. Lectures on legal history and miscellaneous legal essays. With a memoir. Cambridge, Harvard Univ. Press, 1913. Frontis. 553pp. Orig. cl. $ 27.50

507. BANCROFT, GEORGE. History of the formation of the Constitution of the United States of America. N. Y., Appleton, 1889. In 2 vols. Approx. 1000pp. Orig. cl. Fine. o.p. $ 45.00

508. BARKER, LUCIUS J. and TWILEY W. BARKER, JR. Freedoms, courts, politics: studies in civil liberties. Englewood Cliffs, N. J., Prentice-Hall, (1965). 324pp. Cl., d.j. o.p. $ 22.50

509. BEBR, GERHARD. Judicial control of the European Communities. N. Y., Praeger, (1962). 268pp. Cl., d.j. o.p. $ 15.00

510. CAIRNS, HUNTINGTON. Legal philosophy from Plato to Hegel. Baltimore, Johns Hopkins Press, 1949. 583pp. o.p. $ 27.50

511. CHAPMAN, HENRY C. A manual of medical jurisprudence and toxicology. With thirty-six illustrations, some of which are in colors. Phila., Saunders, 1892. 237pp. Orig. cl. $ 17.50

512. GINSBERG, MORRIS. (ed.) Law and opinion in England in the 20th century. Berkeley, Univ. of Calif., Press, 1959. 407pp. Cl., d.j. First edition. Fine. $ 20.00

514. HALL, WILLIAM EDWARD. A treatise on international law. Third edition. Oxford, Clarendon Press, 1890. 788pp. Orig. cl. $ 27.50

515. (JACOB, GILES). Every man his own lawyer: or a summary of the laws of England in a new and instructive method, under the following heads ... the seventh edition (but first American) corrected and improved, with many additions ... N. Y., Hugh Gaine, 1768. iv, 289, 12pp. 8vo. Contemp. blind calf, moderately rubbed; some light staining towards rear. In all a very good copy. $120.00
* First and only 18th century American edition of a classic; a good copy of a book meant for heavy use. Evans 10935.

516. JENKINS, JOHN S. The new clerk's assistant, or book of practical forms... and adapted to the New England, Northern and Western States, and California. N. Y., Miller, 1857. Fourth edition. 620pp. Full contemp. sheep. $ 27.50

517. (MABLY, GABRIEL BONNOT, Abbe de) Le droit public de l'Europe, fonde' sur les traitez conclus jusqu'en l'annee 1740. A la Haye, Van Duren, 1746. Two volumes, 12mo. Half-titles present. Contemporary calf gilt, leather labels, fine set. $350.00
* FIRST EDITION. The second of Mably's works and the first of real importance. "After the appearance of his 'Droit ...' which was based upon a digest of available international treaties ... and which became a standard work throughout Europe he was ranked with Grotius and Pufendorf as an authority in international relations." E. A. Whitefield in Encyclopaedia of the Social Sciences. Tchemerzine VII, 263.

518. MILLER, ARTHUR S. Racial discrimination and private education: a legal analysis. Chapel Hill, Univ. of No. Carolina Press, (1957). Cl., d.j. o.p. $ 15.00

519. MINNESOTA. TERRIRTORY. The revised statutes of the Territory of Minnesota, passed at the second session of the Legislative Assembly commencing January 1, 1851. Printed and published pursuant to law, under the supervision of M.S. Wilkinson. St. Paul, James M. Goodhue, 1851. xvi, 734, 45pp. Large 8vo. Original full calf, front cover detached but present. With orig. binder's ticket of James Mackintosh, Saint Paul. Internally a fine copy. $150.00
* Minnesota Imprints #27. The first published code for Minnesota terr., replacing the Wisconsin code which had become increasingly unsuited to conditions in Minnesota.

520. PARSONS, THEOPHILUS. Laws of business for all the States of the Union. With forms and directions for all transactions. Hartford, Scranton, 1874. 679pp. Full contemp. calf. $ 25.00

521. POORE, GEORGE VIVIAN. A treatise on medical jurisprudence, based on lectures delivered at University College, London. With illustrations. Second edition. London, Murray, 1902. 536pp. Orig. cl. $ 27.50

522. REPPY, ALISON. Civil rights in the United States. N. Y., Central Book Co., 1951. 297pp. Cl., d.j. o.p. $ 15.00

PARKS' LAWS OF MARYLAND IN THE ORIGINAL BINDING WITH THE ERRATA SLIP

525. MARYLAND, COLONY. LAWS. A compleat collection of the laws of Maryland. With an index and marginal notes, directing to the several laws and the chief matters contained in them. Collected and printed by authority. Annapolis: printed by William Parks, 1727. Folio. (3), 300, (6)pp. In the original full calf binding, raised bands, panels consisting of blind ornamental rows within rules, ruled border, corner fleurons. Minor wear, confined mainly to rear panel and lower front joint; small old institutional stamp on title page. In all a fine and most desireable copy, with the original publisher's errata slip pasted down inside rear cover. $1250.00
* A legal and typographical landmark. "Until the appearance of Bacon's great work in 1765 it remained as the most ambitious production of the Maryland press." -- Wroth p. 63. Parks was one of the great pioneer printers in Colonial America. This compilation was the product of his first year as public printer to the colony (see DAB, Wroth and Oswald for accounts of his varied and ubiquitous career.) It is the only attainable edition for the "old body of law" of Maryland: its several predecessors of 1700, 1707, and 1718 are known in one or two copies only. It is the most complete collection of law prior to Bacon. The copy offered here is well preserved in its original binding which is almost certainly the work of Parks himself who quickly gained a reputation for his excellent and innovative binding -- See Lehmann-Haupt, et al. Bookbinding in America, p. 37. Copies are rare in trade: none has appeared at auction in the last 40 years. Evans 2897. Sabin 45111. Wroth 38. Wroth-Parks 12

ROBERT H. RUBIN BOOKS

Post Office Box 558 · Stoughton, Massachusetts 02072 USA
Cable Address: «RUBOOKS» Telephone: (617) 344-0740

CATALOG FOURTEEN 1981

ANTIQUARIAN AND OUT-OF-PRINT WORKS IN

LAW AND LEGAL HISTORY

(CHIEFLY ANGLO-AMERICAN)

Please see page i for detailed index

Please see page ii for notes on condition, binding, and cited references

We are pleased to send you our spring/summer catalogue. In the first part we continue to emphasize early American legal literature of both regional and general interest. Throughout the catalogue some well represented topics are **constitutional and international law, criminology, domestic relations, law reform, legal education, military and maritime law,** *and* **political theory.** *Included are important editions of works by* **Bentham, Blackstone,** *and* **Story,** *among others. We hope you find it interesting and useful reading.*

Offers of single items or entire collections, institutional or private, are always welcome.

1. AMERICAN BAR ASSOCIATION. Relief of U. S. Supreme Court. Report of a majority of the Select Committee... n.p., c.1881. 19pp. Orig. wrap. Recommends establishment of intermediate Appellate Courts in the Circuits. $ 15.00

2. (AMERICAN PRECEDENTS OF DECLARATIONS) (PERHAM, BENONI and JOSEPH STORY). American precedents of declarations Collected chiefly from manuscripts of accomplished pleaders; digested and arranged under distinct titles and divisions; and adapted to the most modern practice. With a prefixed digest of rules and cases concerning declarations. Boston, printed by Manning and Loring, for Macanulty, Salem. 1802. xxiv, (9)-345, errata pp. Sheep, rubbed but sound. $100.00
* Tapley: Salem Imprints p. 193 states that Perham was the author, assisted by Joseph Story. The work was revised by Anthon a few years later. This first edition is quite uncommon and is great importance in documenting the practical departure of American law from the rigid accrued forms of English common law; it is said to have been based in large part on the ms. notes of Theophilus Parsons. Shaw-Shoemaker 1766; The NUC cites 6 locations.

3. ANGELL, JOSEPH K. and THOMAS DURFEE. A treatise on the law of highways. Third edition, with notes and references to the later cases, by George F. Choate. Boston, Little, Brown, 1886. 625pp. New cl. $ 45.00

4. Attorneys General - Construction of Public Laws. Message from the President (Martin Van Buren) of the United States, transmitting copies of opinions given by Attorneys General, &c. which give construction to the public laws not of a temporary character, March 3, 1841... Wash., GPO, 1841. 182pp. Bound in contemp. calf. A very good copy. $ 47.50
* U.S. 26th Congress, 2d S. Doc. 123. An exhaustive one-time compilation from the beginning of the government to March 1, 1841.

5. AUSTIN, HENRY. The law concerning farms, farmers and farm laborers, together with the game laws of all the states. Boston, Soule, 1886. 256pp. $ 25.00

6. BACKUS, JOSEPH. Digest of laws relating to the offices and duties of sheriff, coroner and constable. In two vols. N. Y., printed for the author, 1812. 489, 477pp. New cl.
* Marvin p. 83. $ 55.00

7. BEADLE, DELOS W. The American lawyer and business man's form book; containing forms and instructions for (numerous categories) together with the laws of the various states on (numerous topics) and a map and seal for each state in the union. N. Y., Phelps, Fanning, 1852. 359pp. New cloth. $ 37.50
* Contains recent states such as Texas and California, as well as the southern states.

8. BEAUMONT, GUSTAVE DE & ALEXIS DE TOCQUEVILLE. Systeme penitentiaire aux Etats-Unis et de son application en France; suivie d'un appendice sur les colonies penales et de notes statistiques ... troisieme edition, augmentee ... Paris, Gosselin, 1845. 446pp. Contemp. 1/4 mor. Nice copy. $ 85.00
* The most famous European account of American prison experiments especially the "Pennsylvania System" of separate confinement; Francis Lieber, one of the systems ardent proponents, actually translated the work for the American public in 1833! The system in some form was adopted throughout Europe in the next decade. This edition is particularly desireable because it contains for the first time the newly adopted French prison code of 1844 along with Tocqueville's advisory report to the Chamber of Deputies. Monaghan 165.

9. BECCARIA, (CESARE). An essay on crimes and punishments: with a commentary by Voltaire, a new edition corrected. Phila., Young, 1793. 12mo. Contemp. calf, front hinge repaired. $ 75.00
* A significant American edition, appearing at the time and place of the beginning of major agitation for reform of prisons and penal law. Through the efforts of men like William Bradford, Benj. Rush and Roberts Vaux, Pennsylvania's reforms achieved international influence.

10. BENET, CAPT. S. V. A treatise on military law and the practice of courts-martial. Third edition, with additions. N. Y., Van Nostrand, 1863. 370pp. Full contemp. calf. A very nice copy. $ 75.00
* A scarce work. This copy is of special interest, having been used during the Civil War and Reconstruction in Arkansas, with manuscript ownership inscriptions dated 1864 and 1867 at Pine Bluffs. First edition was 1862.

11. BENTHAM, JEREMY. The book of fallacies: from unfinished papers of Jeremy Bentham. By a friend. London, John & H. L. Hunt, 1824. xi, 411pp. 8vo. Contemp. 1/4 calf, spine with ornamental tooling, very lightly rubbed, otherwise a fine copy. $250.00
* FIRST EDITION in English, and first appearance of a significant portion of this treatise on the art of government through Parliamentary debate. The editor notes that Dumont had published this work earlier in French, omitting "with a view to Continental circulation ... many applications of the writer's principles to British institutions and British interests ..." The works on fallacies and tactics constitute together "the first and only purely theoretical and scientific treatise on Parliamentary procedure that has ever been written." Holdsworth, XIII, p. 94.

12. BENTHAM, JEREMY. Defense of usury; shewing the impolicy of the present legal restraints on the terms of pecuniary bargains. To which is added a Letter to Adam Smith on the discouragement of inventive industry. Phila., Matthew Carey, 1796. 149, (2-ads)pp. 12mo. Contemporary

(Continued)

12. (Continued) boards, expertly rebacked recently in calf and leather label, in period style. Old ink name on top corner of title page. A very nice copy. $165.00
* FIRST AMERICAN EDITION. Evans 30057. Kress B3088. Vanderblue p. 51.

13. BENTHAM, JEREMY. The elements of the art of packing, as applied to special juries, particularly in cases of libel law. London, Effingham Wilson, 1821. vii, 269pp. plus the final leaf of ads. Original boards and cloth spine with publisher's label, entirely uncut, a bit of foxing to first and last leaves, but a fine copy, in completely original state. $350.00
* FIRST EDITION. A classic in the struggle for freedom of speech. "... some of Bentham's attacks upon the legal and political abuses of his time were so outspoken that Romilly advised him not to publish them. He feared, not without reason, that, if he were prosecuted for libel, a special jury ... would be very likely to convict. This state of the law inspired (this work)." Holdsworth, XIII, p. 99. McCoy B200.

14. BENTHAM, JEREMY. A fragment on government; or, A comment on the Commentaries: being an examination of what is delivered on the subject of government in general, in the introduction to Sir William Blackstone's Commentaries; with a preface, in which is given a critique on the work at large. Second edition, enlarged. London, E. Wilson, 1823. 8vo. xii, lii, 143pp. In the original publisher's boards and cloth spine with printed paper label, very slight wear along head of spine. Entirely uncut and a fine copy. $400.00
* Bentham's first book, published originally in 1776, that edition quite scarce, and a significant criticism of Blackstone. "(It) represented and expressed the ideas of those who were conscious that radical reforms in the law were becoming necessary ... It was as Bentham truly said, 'the very first publication by which men at large were invited to break loose from the trammels of authority and ancestor wisdom in the field of law.' " -- Holdsworth, XII, 731.

15. BENTHAM, JEREMY. Plan of Parliamentary reform in the form of a catechism, with the reason for each article, with an introduction showing the necessity of radical, and the inadequacy of moderate reform. London, R. Hunter, 1817. iv, cccxxxvii, 52, 16, (1)pp. incl. final leaf of ads. Later half-calf, antique. Upper corner margin of last few leaves browned, otherwise a very good copy. $650.00
* FIRST EDITION. "Bentham signalized his conversion to the creed of the radical reformers by writing in 1809 a book called 'Plan of Parliamentary Reforms ...' ... Bentham maintained the thesis that the only remedy for the evils that were afflicting the country was a reform of Parliament which would ensure 'democratical ascendancy.' He maintained that the experience of the United States, the constitution of which he considered to be almost perfect, showed that an entirely democratic constitution was by far the best ... 'Talk of balance,' he said,

15. (Continued) 'never will it do: leave that to Mother Goose and Mother Blackstone.' " Hist of English Law, XIII, 104. Cobbett refused to publish the original "Catechism" of 1809 in his Political Register, so it first appeared here with an introduction six times its length. This 1817 edition is apparently quite uncommon, the second edition of 1818 being the one usually found.

16. BENTHAM, JEREMY, Tactique des assemblees legislatives, suivie d'un Traite des Sophismes Politiques; ouvrage extrait des manuscrits de M. Jeremie Bentham... par Et. Dumont ... Geneve, Pascoud; Paris, 1816. In 2 volumes. 8vo. 361; 396pp. Later full morroco, richly gilt with raised bands, spines, covers and inner dentelles gilt with coat of arms on all covers, a.e.g. A fine and very attractive copy; with the half-titles to both volumes. $400.00
* FIRST EDITION in French of the "Tactics" and FIRST EDITION of the "Sophisms", both works concerned with the art of governing by parliamentary bodies. Bentham published in 1791 a fragment of the "Tactics" (see Amano, Bibliography of the Classical Economics, v. 4, pt. 5, p. 490, Tokyo, 1964); Dumont has presented here a much more complete version of that work based on Bentham's unpublished manuscripts. The "Sophisms" was first sketched in outline by Bentham in 1806 - this is its first appearance in print; in 1824 its English version was published. "It was the first and only purely theoretical and scientific treatise on Parliamentary procedure that has ever been written." Holdsworth, XIII, p. 94.

17. (BERNARD, RICHARD) The isle of man: or the legal proceeding in Man-shire against sinne. Wherein, by way of a continued allegory, the chief malefactors disturbing both church and Commonwealth are detected ... with their arraignment and judicial trial according to the laws of England ... sixteenth edition. London, Printed by T.M., 1683 12mo. 11pl, 218pp. Later mor. $75.00
* A famous 17th century religious allegory heavily steeped in the legal practice of the time. Bernard also wrote a guide to juries in witchcraft trials (1627) and in the introduction here discusses injustices connected with those trials and in fact with whole penological system. The NUC cites only one holding for this edition in America. Wing 1683.

18. BINNEY, HORACE. A pamphlet volume containing:

a. The Privilege of the writ of habeas corpus under the Constitution. All three parts, each separtely published, 1862-1865, forming together a significant constitutional treatise and defending Lincoln's actions during the Civil War. The complete work is rarely found thus.

b. The Alienigenae of the United States under present naturalization laws. Second edition. Phila., Sherman, 1853. Written to correct a defect in the law which rendered alien the children of natural-born citizens, if the former were born outside the U.S. A rare pamphlet.

c. Address to the Centennial Meeting of the Phila. Contributorship for the Insurance of Houses ... Phila., Sherman, 1852.

d. Two pamphlets by William Strong and Edmund Quincy, respectively, each eulogies of Binney. (Continued)

18. (Continued) with an envelope laid-in, full of contemporary obituaries clipped from newspapers. All bound in contemp. 3/4 mor. Fine. $75.00

19. (BINNEY, HORACE) The privilege of the writ of habeas corpus under the Constitution. Second Part. Philadelphia, Campbell, 1862. 50pp. Disbound. Good copy. $22.50
* Separately published and continuing the argument of the first part published the same year. Binney defended Lincoln's suspension of the writ. "The three (parts) together compose a very valuable constitutional treatise." --DAB.

20. (BINNEY, HORACE) The privilege of the writ of habeas corpus under the Constitution. Third part. Phila., Sherman, 1865. 74pp. errata slip. Disbound. Good copy. $25.00
* Separately published three years after the first two parts, and defending Lincoln's actions. "The three (parts) together compose a very valuable constitutional treatise." --DAB.

21. (BINNEY) JACKSON, TATLOW. Authorities cited antagonistic to Horace Binney's conclusions on the Writ of Habeas Corpus. Phila., J. Campbell, 1862. 8pp. wrps. $12.50

22. (BIRD, JAMES BARRY) The law respecting commons and commoners; comprising the law relative to the rights and privileges of both Lords and commoners and in which the law relative to the inclosing of commons is particularly attended to ... third edition, corrected. London, Clarke, 1817. 108, (4)pp. Neatly removed. $37.50
* Final edition. S&M, II, p. 31. NUC locates only the copy at Kress (B6870).

23. (BIRD, JAMES BARRY) The laws respecting tithes: comprising all the cases and statutes ... and of leases and agreements concerning tithes ... fifth edition, improved and enlarged. London, Clarke, 1818. 102, (4)pp. Very neatly removed. Fine. $27.50
* S&M, II, p. 32. NUC shows no copy of this final or penultimate edition.

24. BISHOP, JOEL PRENTISS. New commentaries on marriage, divorce, and separation as to the law, evidence, pleading, practice, forms and the evidence of marriage in all issues on a new system of legal exposition. In two vols. Chicago, Flood, 1891. 759, 831pp. Orig. cl. $50.00

25. BLACKSTONE, WILLIAM. Commentaries on the laws of England in four books ... the first Worcester edition, carefully reprinted from the last London edition, containing the last corrections of the author, the additions by Richard Burn, and continued to the present time by John Williams. Printed at Worcester, Mass., by Isaiah Thomas, 1790. Four volumes, 12mo. Engraved frontis. Portrait in volume one, folding table. Bound in the original edition binding of plain sheep, blind cover borders and red leather labels gilt. An extraordinarily fine set in a remarkable state of preservation, virtually free of imperfection or wear. $1000.00

25. (Continued)
* This is the second appearance of Blackstone in America and the first to be published by Isaiah Thomas. It is in fact much less common in holdings than the Phila., 1772 edition. Today both editions have become extremely scarce in trade, and the appearance of a copy such as this in splendid original state is indeed a pleasant surprise. Since it was intended to be a popular, affordable edition in an unsophisticated and relatively fragile binding, it can be expected to turn up, if at all, with substantial wear or defects, which is exactly the case with the single copy we have handled in the past ten years and the very few others we have seen. This copy is about as ideal a set of any work from this period in America that one can hope for. A perfect collector's copy. Printing and the Mind of Man, 212 (1st English edition). Evans 22360.

26. BLACKSTONE, WILLIAM. Commentaries on the laws of England, in four books ... the fifteenth edition, with the last corrections of the author and with notes and additions by Edward Christian... London, Strahan for Cadell & Davies, 1809. In 4 volumes. Engraved frontis-portrait, fold. table. Full contemporary calf, stamped in blind and gilt, oines lettered in gilt. A fine, handsome set. $250.00

27. BLACKSTONE, SIR WILLIAM. Commentaries on the Laws of England: in four books; with an analysis of the work. In two volumes. From the nineteenth London edition, with a life of the author and notes: by Christain, Chitty, Lee, Hovenden, and Ryland: and also references to American cases, by a member of the New York Bar. N. Y., Dean, 1844. 404, 468, 369, 402pp. Full contemp. sheep, rubbed. $75.00
* Marvin p. 123; "in the most general use in the United States." This is a stereotype reprint of the first edition of 1832, and was commonly referred to as Chitty's Blackstone. There is a good deal of material on differences between N. Y. State and British law; Blackstone had in fact been an important influence on the revision of N. Y. law.

8. (BLACKSTONE). An interesting appendix to ir William Blackstone's Commentaries on the Laws f England ... Phila., Printed for the Subscribers y Robert Bell, 1773. Small 4to. New cloth. $125.00
Second American edition. Contains exchanges etween Blackstone and Joseph Priestley (Crook S/315), as well as Furneau and Foster on the issue f Dissenters raised in Book Four of the Commenaries, together with Blackstone's defense of his osition in the Wilkes affair in Parliament. Evans 2328.

29. BODIN, (JEAN) Les six livres de la republique. Paris, chez Jacques du Puys, 1583. Thick small 8vo. 1060pp. plus tables and preliminaries. Bound in modern full calf, spine lettered in gilt. Repairs to title page and first few leaves, text not affected; some worming mostly marginal but occasionally affecting text, though not legibility, and some light staining. Basically a good working copy and priced accordingly. $75.00
* Printing and the Mind of Man, 94 (1st ed. 1576). Considered to be the first systemmatic modern treatise on politics and the source of the contract theory of government.

30. BOISOT, LOUIS, JR. A treatise on mechanics' liens. St. Paul, West Publ., 1897. 969pp. Full contemp. sheep. $27.50

31. (BOOKSELLER'S CATALOGUE. LAW) A catalogue of law books published or for sale by John Campbell & Son, law publishers, booksellers and importers. Second ed. Phila., Campbell, 1872. 188pp. 12mo. Orig. cl. Fine. Includes antiquarian and current works. Very detailed. SOLD

32. BOREGEAUD, CHARLES. Adoption and amendment of constitutions in Europe and America. Translated by Charles D. Hazen. With an introduction by John M. Vincent. N. Y., MacMillan, 1895. 353pp. Orig. cl. Library stamp on title-page. $22.50

33. BOSTON PRISON DISCIPLINE SOCIETY. Annual Reports. 1st - 6th, 21/22nd, (1826-1847). Many in original wrappers; each approx. 100-200pp. each, $10.00
* The Boston Society's annual reports were the only documents of the period in which the progress, method and statistics of American prisons were compiled. Largely through its secretary, Louis Dwight, the Society led the attack on the Pennsylvania System, effectively limiting its spread in the U.S. Its reports were intensively distributed and "it is probably not too much to say that (Dwight) in large measure conditioned the form of prison structure and method adopted in many a state." Teeters, They were in prison: a history of the Pennsylvania Prison Society. 1937. p. 237f.

34. (BRADLEY RALPH). Practical points, or, maxims in conveyancing, drawn from the daily experience of a very extensive practice ... to which are added critical observations on the various and essential parts of a deed. Second edition, corrected. London, Clarke, 1820. 147pp. Very neatly removed. Fine. $40.00
* The added material on deeds is by Joseph Ritson. Marvin p. 611. NUC cites 2 copies.

35. BRICE, SEWARD. A treatise on the doctrine of Ultra Vires: being an investigation of the principles which limit the capacities, powers, and liabilities of corporations, and more especially of Joint Stock Companies. London, Stevens, 1874. 599pp. Orig. cl. $55.00

36. BROWN, DAVID PAUL. The Forum; or, forty years full practice at the Philadelphia Bar. Phila., Robert Small, 1856. 2 volumes. Stout 8vo's. 588;521pp. Orig. publ. cl. A very good set. $50.00
* Chief source for the professional life and surroundings of this very prominent lawyer; he was a student of William Rawle, associate of the leaders of the Phila. Bar, and practitioner in both U.S. and State courts. Appended to the first volume are 8 pages of facsimile autographs of Phila. lawyers and judges. See DAB for a lengthy account.

37. BULLER, FRANCIS. An introduction to the law relative to trials at Nisi Prius, containing additions to the present time, carefully corrected from the last London copy, by a gentleman of the Bar. N. Y., printed for J. Riley, 1806. 356pp. Full contemp. sheep. $65.00
* Marvin p. 158. First American Edition. The Standard work of its period, originating in 1760 as the work of Henry Bathurst, and subsequently edited and taken over in name by his nephew Buller. "It is a good deal more than a book of practice." ---Holdsworth, XII, 354.

38. BURN, JOHN ILDERTON. A practical treatise or compendium of the law of marine insurances. London, printed, New York, reprinted, 1801. 235pp. 12mo. Contemp. calf, worn. $65.00
* Marvin p. 163. Same year as London edition, the only editions to appear. Very uncommon.

39. CALLAN, JOHN F. The military laws of the United States, relating to the army, volunteers, militia, and to bounty lands and pensions, from the foundation of the government to the year 1863 ... Phila., Child, 1863. 607pp. New cl. $35.00

40. (CANADA, NEW BRUNSWICK. LAWS, STATUTES). The consolidated statutes of New Brunswick. Fredericton, Fenety, 1877. 1187pp. Contemp. 1/2 calf. V. Good. $55.00

41. (CARE, HENRY). English liberties, or the free-born subjects inheritance, containing I. Magna Charta, the Petition of Right, The Habeas Corpus Act, and diverse other most useful statutes, with large comments ... II. The proceeding in appeals of Murther (etc. ...) London, G. Larkin, for How, (1680). 12mo., 5pl., 228pp. Disbound, but a very good copy. $ 85.00
* First edition of what became virtually a revolutionary tract, oft reprinted in the 17th and 18th centuries, including American editions in 1721 and 1774. Wing C 516.

42. Catalogue of the Instructors in the Law Schools of the United States in 1891 ... Hartford, Case, 1893. 41pp. Orig. prtd., wrps. 12mo. $ 12.50

43. CHANDLER, PELEG W. The bankrupt law of the United States with an outline of the system: together with the rules and forms in Massachusetts and references to recent decisions. Boston, Weeks, 1842. 102pp. Orig. cl. Old library stamp on title page, else a good copy. $ 27.50

44. CHIPMAN, DANIEL. An essay on the law of contracts for the payment of specific articles. Middlebury, published by the author, 1822. xvi, 222pp. Contemp. sheep, red leather label, little rubbed and a few scuffs, but a very good copy. $ 75.00
* FIRST EDITION. Along with the work of Verplanck, a classic in the early American contract literature. Marvin p. 189. See also DAB, and Horwitz, Transformation of American Law, p. 181.

45. CHITTY, JOSEPH. A practical treatise on bills of exchange, checks on bankers, promissory notes, bankers' cash notes, and bank notes. A new edition, from the fifth London edition, recomposed, enlarged, and improved, with notes of the leading cases, an index to their names, and an appendix of precedents; to which is added the most important cases decided in the Courts of the United States, and of the several states. Phila., Carey, 1821. Full contemp. sheep. $ 45.00
* Marvin p. 191, a long note of praise describing the importance and popularity of this work in both England and America.

46. CHITTY, JOSEPH. A treatise on the game laws and on fisheries; with an appendix containing all the statutes and a copious collection of precedents... the second edition, greatly improved, with all the new enactments and decisions. London, Samuel Brooke, 1826. Roy 8vo, xx 878pp. Contemp. polished calf, spine gilt with ornaments, borders gilt, front joint worn, a very nice copy. $125.00
* Final and best edition. Marvin p. 193. S & M, II. Holdsworth, Vol. XIII, p. 489. A comprehensive and desireable work. Scarce.

47. (CIVIL WAR). Observations respecting the test oath, imposed upon attorneys by Congress. Caption title, as issued; original plain wrps. 46pp. ca. 1865. (N.Y?). $ 27.50
* Protests the oath of allegiance passed by Congress, 24 January 1865, seeking to bar from practice in Federal courts lawyers involved with the Confederacy. Rare.

48. (CIVIL WAR) READ, JOHN M. Opinion of ... of the Supreme Court of Pennsylvania, in favor of the constitutionality of the Act of Congress of March 3, 1863. "For enrolling and calling out the National Forces and for other purposes." Delivered at Pittsburg, on Monday, Nov. 9, 1863. Phila., Sherman, 1863. 20pp. Orig. prtd wrps. Concerns Civil War draft. $ 25.00

49. CLARKE, EDWARD. A treatise upon the Law of Extradition. With the conventions upon the subject existing between England and foreign nations, and the cases decided thereon. 2nd ed. London, Stevens, 1874. 194, clxxvipp. Orig. cl. Fine. With 48pp. Stevens, Haynes Law Publisher's catalogue. $ 35.00

50. COKE, EDWARD. The first part of the Institutes of the Laws of England: or, a commentary upon Littleton ... also three learned tracts ... the twelfth edition, carefully corrected ... to which is added, the Treatise of the Old Tenures of the Laws of England ... (London) Nutt & Gosling, 1738. Folio, 7pl., 804pp. plus tables and large fold. illustration. Contemp. calf, rebacked. Lacks the frontis-portrait; contents fine. A good copy. $125.00
* S & M, I, 450. Marvin 204ff. The most important of the Institutes and one of the great summaries of learning and experience bridging the medieval and modern periods; it remained a force in legal literature into the 19th century.

51. COOKE, WILLIAM. A compendious system of the bankrupt laws. Dublin, Davis, 1786. 372, (8), 233, (16), (4), (6)pp. Bound with: Addenda to the compendious system of bankrupt laws. Dublin, Lynch ..., 1790. 150pp. Contemp. calf, some marginal damp-stains, but a good sound copy. $ 45.00
* Dublin issue from the first edition, London 1785, with supplement. It went through 8 editions by 1823 S & M, I, 541. Marvin p. 226.

52. COX, JACOB D. The republicanism of the English Government. An address before the Association of Alumni, of the Cincinnati Law School ... May 14, 1879. Cincinnati, Pugh, 1879. 20pp. Orig. prtd. wrps. $ 12.50

53. CRUISE, WILLIAM. A digest of the laws of England respecting real property. First American edition, carefully corrected from the London copy. N. Y., Gould, 1808. In 5 volumes, complete with index. Contemp. calf, some joints crudely repaired a few leaves dampstained, still a good sound set. $100.00
* First American edition. Marvin p. 243f, notes that it served as the basic American text until Kent and Hilliard.

54. CUNNINGHAM, T. The law of bills of exchange, promissory notes, bank-notes, and insurances: containing all the statutes, cases at large, arguments, resolutions, judgments, decrees, and customs of merchants concerning them methodically digested ... The sixth edition corrected, with additions of the late Acts of Parliament ... London, His Majesty's Law Printers, 1778. 539pp. Later 1/4 cloth, ex-library. Marvin p. 245. $ 55.00

55. CURTIS, GEORGE TICKNOR. History of the origin, formation, and adoption of the Constitution of the United States; with notices of its principle framers. In two volumes. N. Y., Harper, 1854. 2 vols. Roy. 8vo. Orig. cl., gilt, extremities of spine worn, otherwise a good copy, "From the author" inscribed on front free end-paper of vol. 1. $ 50.00
* First edition of one of the major works on the Constitution in the 19th century. See DAB.

56. CUSHING, CALEB. The Treaty of Washington: its negotiation, execution, and the discussions relating thereto. N. Y., Harper, 1873. 280pp. Orig. cl. Fine. 1st ed. $ 20.00

57. CUSHING, LUTHER S. Rules of proceeding and debate in deliberative assemblies. Second edition. Boston, Reynolds, 1845. 173pp. Full contemp. calf. 12mo. $ 27.50
* Marvin p. 248. The classic manual of parliamentary law in 19th century America. 1st ed. was 1844.

58. DANIEL, JOHN W. A treatise on the law of negotiable instruments ... In two vols. Second edition. N. Y., Baker, 1879. 771, 841pp. Full contemp. sheep. $ 55.00
* A very much expanded edition

59. DAVIS, CHARLES G. Report of the trial of Samuel M. Andrews, indicted for the murder of Cornelius Holmes, before the Supreme Judicial Court of Massachusetts, Dec. 11, 1868. Including the rulings of the court upon many questions of law, and a full statement of authorities upon the subject of transitory insanity. N. Y., Hurd, 1869. 287pp. Orig. prtd wrps., soiled. $ 27.50
* A trial which attracted much attention. Contains ample matter relating to the plea of insanity, which however failed to absolve the defendant.

60. DE HART, WILLIAM C. Observations on military law, and the constitution and practice of courts martial, with a summary of the law of evidence, as applicable to military trials; adapted to the laws, regulations and customs of the army and navy of the United States. N. Y., Appleton, 1862. 433pp. New cl. $ 45.00

61. DE LOLME, J. L. The Constitution of England or an account of the English government; in which it is compared with the republican form of government, and occasionally with the other monarchies in Europe. London, Spilsbury for Kearsley, 1775. 448pp. 8vo. Contemp. calf, good copy. $125.00
* FIRST EDITION IN ENGLISH. One of the best 18th century books on comparative constitutional law. It was very successful, deservedly so in the opinion of Holdsworth, "because it did call attention to some of the most salient features of the British constitution." (Hist. of English Law, V. XII, 344.) "It is remarkable that a foreigner should have been the first to write a clear, concise and accurate treatise upon the constitutional law of England ... Judge Story remarks that the author 'has presented a view of English equity jurisprudence far more exact and comprehensive than many of the English text writers on the same subject.' " -- Marvin, p. 263.

62. DE LOLME, J. L. The Constitution of England; or an account of the English government; in which it is compared both with the republican form of government, and the other monarchies in Europe. A new edition; with supplemental notes, and a preface biographical and critical. London, Wilkie, 1807. 535pp. Contemp. calf, gilt. $ 65.00
* Good edition of this highly regarded work on both comparative constitutional law and English equity jurisprudence. See Holdsworth XII, 344, and Marvin p. 263 who quotes the lavish praise of Story.

63. DICKINSON, RODOLPHUS. A digest of the common law, the statute laws of Massachusetts and of the United States, and the decisions of the Supreme Judicial Court of Massachusetts, relative to the powers and duties of justices of the peace, to which is subjoined an extensive appendix of forms. Deerfield, Wilson, 1818. 521pp. Full contemp. sheep. 1st ed. $ 45.00
* Marvin p. 266.

64. DIGBY, KENELM EDWARD. An introduction to the history of the law of real property, with original authorities. Oxford, Clarendon Press, 1875. 359pp. Orig. cl. 1st ed. $ 25.00

65. DOMAT, (JEAN). The civil law in its natural order: together with the public law ... translated by William Strahan ... with additional remarks on some material differences between the civil law and the law of England. London, Bell ..., 1722. 2 vols. FOLIOS. Contemp. reverse calf, minor binding wear, still a very good set. $200.00
* FIRST EDITION IN ENGLISH. Domat's work was the "First successful attempt to reduce to order the civil law of France" -- Marvin p. 171. "It was the first step in that movement to cut through traditional categories which culminated in the French Revolution and the civil code ... (it had) a vogue that spread beyond France (and) was frequently cited in England ..." -- Encyl. of the Social Sciences.

66. DUANE, WILLIAM JOHN. The Law of Nations, investigated in a popular manner. Addressed to the farmers of the United States ... Phila., Duane, 1809. 103pp. Neatly removed. $ 45.00
* In fact a learned exposition and defense of the rights of neutrals in wartime. This is among the very first original American works of substance on international law, all of which were occasioned by the Napoleonic Wars and the friction with Great Britain.

67. DWIGHT, THEODORE W. Education in law schools in the City of New York compared with that obtained in law offices. A lecture delivered to the students of Columbia College Law School ... February 7, 1875. N. Y., Trow, 1876. Wanting wraps. $ 30.00
* A strong defense of the school against its critics, especially the N.Y. Bar Association. Scarce.

68. EASTERN STATE PENITENTIARY. First and second annual reports of the inspectors of the ... of Pennsylvania ... Phila., Kite, 1831. 23pp. dsbd. $ 17.50
* Earliest reports of the most important prison experiment of its time, instituting the widely imitated system of separate confinement.

69. EDMONDS, JOHN WORTH. An address on the Constitution and Code of Procedure and the modifications of the law effected thereby, delivered ... before the class of Attorneys ... N. Y., Code Reporter Office, 1848. vii, 47pp. Neatly removed. Good copy. $ 45.00
* An exposition, by the Judge of the N. Y. Supreme Court to the newly qualified practicing attorneys, of the landmark Revised Code of N. Y.

70. ENDLICH, G. A. A commentary on the interpretation of statutes. Founded on the treatise of Sir Peter Benson Maxwell. Jersey City, Linn, 1888. 871pp. Sheep, rebacked. $ 50.00
* First edition. An American adaptation of an earlier British work. Uncommon.

71. FESSENDEN, THOMAS G. An essay on the law of patents for new inventions. With an appendix containing the French patent law, forms & c. Boston, Mallory, 1810. 229pp. Two inner leaves soiled. New cloth. $ 75.00
* First edition of the first American work on the subject. Marvin p. 307.

A CLASSIC DEFENSE OF ABSOLUTE POWER

72. FILMER, ROBERT. Patriarcha: or the natural power of kings. London, Davis, 1680. 8pl., 141pp. Engraved frontis portrait, title within rules. New full blind-stamped calf, leather label, in attractive period style. $300.00
* FIRST EDITION of a classic manifesto in defense of absolute government, and the target of John Locke's counterattack in the first of the "Two Treatises on Government" of 1690. Filmer differed with Hobbes' compact theory as well as with his dismal view of human nature, but he arrived at about the same destination, defending the absolute sovereignty of the monarch. The work appeared posthumously; in this same year, Algernon Sydney wrote (though did not publish) his great defense of republican government directly in response to Filmer. Wing F922. Other copies we have seen or handled usually lack the frontispiece present here.

73. FLANDERS, HENRY. The lives and times of the Chief Justices of the Supreme Court of the United States. Second series; William Cushing-Oliver Ellsworth-John Marshall. Phila., Lippincott, 1858. 560pp. Orig. cl. Roy. 8vo. Fine. First edition. $ 30.00

74. FLETA. Fleta, seu commentarius juris anglicani ... editio secunda, multis erroribus purgata. London, Twyford, 1685. 4to. Title within rules, woodcut at p. 462. Contemporary panelled calf rubbed, later rebacked with red label, raised bands. A good copy. $150.00
* Second edition (1st was 1647). Wing F 1291. One of the chief sources for the legal history of the period of Edward I, and the object of Selden's editorial care in his own edition of this work. "The two important books of Ed. I's reign are Britton and Fleta. They are mainly epitomes of Bracton's Treatise brought up to date." -- Holdsworth, Sources and Lit. of English Law, p. 32. "Fleta, when written, was a concise account of the whole English law as it then prevailed ..." --Marvin p. 314. This is the final edition.

75. FOX, CHARLES J. Guide to officers of towns; containing the statutes relating to their official duties, with forms, directions and legal decisions, adapted to the revised statutes of New-Hampshire. Concord, Lyon, 1843. 343pp. Full contemp. sheep. $ 27.50
* Marvin p. 322.

76. (FRANCE. CIVIL CODE) JOUSSE, (DANIEL). Nouveau commentaire sur l'ordonnance civile du mois d'Avril 1667. Nouvelle edition, augmentee de l'idee de la justice civile. Paris, Debure, 1767. 2 vols. 850pp. Contemp. mottled calf. $ 75.00
* Final edition of this very prominent commentary; the NUC cites 3 holdings.

77. (FRANCE. CONSTITUTIONS) Examen impartial de l'Acte Additionnel du 22 avril 1815, aux constitutions de l'Empire. Paris, Alexis Eymery, 1815. 4to. 16pp. Text in double column. Original plain wrps., uncut. Fine. $ 25.00

78. (FRANCE. LAWS). Code civil des Francais. Edition originale et seule officielle. ISSUED WITH: Table alphabetique des matieres du code civil ... Paris, De l'Imprimerie de la Republique, (and) Paris, chez Rondonneau, (respectively). An XII, 1804. 436;240pp. 8vo. Original wrps. worn, contents fine. $150.00
* FIRST EDITION, in octavo format and with the supplementary tables separately published, of the Civil Code, known as the Napoleonic code.

79. (FRANCE. LAWS, STATUTES). Les huit codes en miniature avec indication de leurs articles correlatifs suivis du tarif des frais et depens en matiere civile et criminelle, d'un appendice progressif contenant les lois et ordonnances principales rendues jusqu'a ce jour, et d'un table analytique des matieres. Paris, Roret, 1833. 16mo. 828pp. 1/4 calf, fine. $ 75.00
* A pocket size library of French law from the Napoleonic era with all of its major reforms; included are the code politique, civil, du procedure civil, commerce, penal, etc... along with legal fees and additional statutes.

80. FREEMAN, SAMUEL. The town officer; or the power and duty of (various officers) as contained in the laws of the Commonwealth of Massachusetts ... Portland, Benjamin Titcomb, 1791. Small 4to. Contemp. calf. 178(2)pp. Very good copy. $ 75.00
* FIRST EDITION. Evans 23389. Marvin p. 323. This edition is rare. Interesting material on poor-laws, regulation of foodstuffs, tobacco, etc. The standard work for this region for the next two decades.

81. FREEMAN, SAMUEL. Valuable Assistant for Every Man, or, The American Clerk's Magazine, containing the most useful and necessary forms of writings ... and other instruments ... conformable to law. Boston, I. Thomas, 1794. 12mo. 223pp. New cloth. $ 60.00
* First edition. One of the first works in America of its kind to go beyond a mere reprint of a British source. Evans 27017. Popular and reprinted for the next decade or so.

82. GALE, LEVIN of Elkton, Maryland. A list of English statutes supposed to be applicable to the several States of the Union (Caption title, no date or place of publication). 40pp. Neatly disbound. $ 45.00
* A questionnaire with provisions for reply, intended for distribution to the various states. Rare: not (Continued)

82. (Continued) in American Imprints Inv., NUC, or Sabin. Marvin p. 367 does note it! We would guess the date of publication to be between 1810-1825.

83. GASTON, H. A. The little lawyer: or the farmers, mechanics, miners, laborers, and business men's adviser and legal help ... New Constitution of the State of California. Sixth edition, revised. San Francisco, Bancroft, 1881 328pp. Strong on mining and land law in California and Nevada. $ 45.00

84. GRANT-DUFF, M.E. Sir Henry Maine, a brief memoir of his life, with some of his Indian speeches and minutes, selected and edited by Whitley Stokes, with portrait. N. Y., Holt, 1892. 451pp. First American edition. Orig. cl. Fine. o.p. $ 37.50
* Reflects Maine's brilliant legal contributions while serving in India for 7 years.

85. GRAY, JOHN CHIPMAN. Restraints on the alienation of property. Second edition. Boston, Boston Book, 1895. 309pp. Orig. cl. $ 65.00
* A fervent attack on the doctrine of "spendthrift trusts" arising from the case Nichols v. Eaton, whereby estates were protected against creditors. First edition was 1883. This is the final and best edition, with additions. "The most considerable contribution to this branch of the law is to be found in the works of ... Gray ... recognized at once as books of authority both in England and America." Holdsworth, Historians... p. 107.

86. (GREAT BRITAIN. PARLIAMENT). First (- Second) report from the Select Committee of the House of Lords appointed to inquire into the present state of the several gaols and houses of correction in England and Wales; with the minutes of evidence and appendix. (London), 1835 Folio. 400,274pp. 5 fold. plates. 1/2 leather, a very nice copy. $200.00
* The first two reports (two others were subsequently issued) of one of the major inquiries leading directly to the creation and extension of the model prison at Pentonville, based on the American system of "separate confinement." The latter issue dominates these hearings along with the treadmill (which is illustrated), treatment and employment of female prisoners, and other topics of prisoner welfare and reform. Witnesses include William Crawford, Whitworth Russell and Elizabeth Fry. The committee concluded that a national system based on some form of separation was essential, and it was precisely this that was accomplished in the following decade.

87. GREEN, JAMES. An historical essay on different governments. Edinburgh, Printed for the author, 1793. 317pp. and errata leaf. New cloth. $ 80.00
* First and only edition of a scarce work combining an inquiry into the nature of governments and political constitutions with a defense of democratic Parliamentary reform. He favors a mixed form of government, with emphasis on the democratic, and shows the vicissitudes of English gov-

87. (Continued) ernment from its Anglo-Saxon origins as it gains or loses its balance vis a vis the power of the Crown. The NUC locates only Yale and U. Chicago copies.

88. GREINER, M. Code of Practice of the State of Louisiana, containing the rules of procedure in civil actions; with an abstract of the decisions of the Supreme Court ... laws creating the city court, and the laws relative to justices of the peace. New Orleans, Printed by M. Greiner, 1839. 10pl., 281pp. Orig. sheep, leather label, a very good copy. $165.00
* A rare work. It is dedicated to F.X. Martin, and was privately printed by the author. The NUC notes only the LC and University of Texas copies.

89. GRIFFITHS, ARTHUR. Secrets of the prison-house or gaol studies and sketches. Illustrations by George D. Rowlandson. In two volumes. London, Chapman and Hall, 1894. 2 vols. Roy. 8vo. Orig. cl., gilt. Illustrations in text. A very nice set. First edition. o.p. $ 75.00
* A very good, first-hand view of international penal systems, with emphasis in the second volume on England. Author was one of H.M. Inspectors of Prisons.

90. (GRIMKE, JOHN FAUCHERAUD) The duty of executors and administrators: with full and clear directions to a man's relations how his estate will be distributed among them according to the laws of South Carolina ... the statutes and acts relative to these subjects, Mr. Blackstone's rules ... and a table of inheritance (etc.) ... N. Y., Swords, 1797. 8vo. xvii, 343,(2)pp. 2 tables, 1 folding. Original boards, front cover detached but present, internally fine and entirely uncut. $135.00
* First edition of one of the earliest and possibly first original American works on the subject. It is entirely concerned with South Carolina law and was copyrighted in S. C., though published in New York. Grimke was a member of the Constitutional Convention, a legal scholar and jurist, and author of the major compilation of 1790 for S. C. This work is rarely seen in trade. Evans 32214.

91. GRIMKE, FREDERICK. Considerations upon the nature and tendency of free institutions. Cincinnati, Derby, 1848. viii,544pp. 8vo. Orig. publ. cl., spine lettered in gilt. A fine bright copy. $150.00
* FIRST EDITION. A very important work analyzing the legal, political and constitutional nature of American society within the framework of the idea of progress and the deep conviction that the American political "genius" represents a major advance whose lessons should not be lost on emerging European republics. Commenting on the absence of an early self-conscious literature by Americans on their own government, John William Ward cites in Grimke a notable exception: "If one of the tests of American scholarship is its responsibility to the sources of our common life, then Grimke's book deserves to be restored to its proper place. It is a penetrating analysis of the theory and institutions of American democracy. It fairly deserves comparison with Tocqueville ... and is in certain ways superior. It is in any event the single best book

91. (Continued) written by an American in the 19th century on the meaning of our political life." --Preface to the Harvard, 1968 reprint. The first edition is uncommon, and especially so in such nice fresh condition.

92. GROSS, CHARLES. The gild merchant: a contribution to British municipal history. In two vols. Oxford, Clarendon Press, 1890. 332,447pp. o.p. $ 65.00
* S &M, I, 531. Holdsworth, Historians of Anglo-American Law, p. 111.

93. (GUILD REGULATIONS). Statutes, privileges, ordonnances, et reglemens de la Communaute des Maitres Menuisiers & Ebenistes de la Ville, Fauxbourgs, & Banlieue de Paris. Paris, J. Chardon, 1751. 12mo. 521pp. Contemporary mottled calf, spine gilt, a very pretty copy. $185.00
* An uncommon and interesting set of regulations for the gild of carpenters and cabinet-makers of Paris. Although dated 1751, this copy includes the new laws of 1768 as well and is not recorded in the NUC which cites 1751 and 1769 editions with lesser paginations, only, each in one or two holdings. Kress 5164.

94. (HANDS, W.) The modern practice of levying fines and suffering recoveries in the Court of Common Pleas, at Westminster. With an appendix of select precedents. London, Butterworth, 1800. 155pp. Full Contemp. calf. $ 65.00
* First edition. Marvin p. 365. S &M, II, p. 489. Holdsworth XIII, p. 470: "gives a clear account of the many formalities ... and of fees."

95. HANSON, (CHARLES W.). Opinion on the law of warranty by Judge Hanson of Baltimore. Baltimore, Lucas, 1831. 32pp. Sewn as issued. Author presentation copy. $ 27.50

96. HARGRAVE, FRANCIS and CHARLES BUTLER. Notes on Lord Coke's First Institute, or Commentary upon Littleton. London, Brooke, 1794. Large 8vo. binding worn. $ 25.00
* Comprises vol. 3 of the 15th ed. of Coke's First Institute. S &M, I, 451.

97. HARRINGTON, JAMES. The Oceana and other works ... with an account of his life by John Toland. London, Becket and Cadell, 1771. xl,598pp. plus index and leaf of publisher's ads. 4 to. Contemp. calf, joints worn but firm. Engraved portrait and two other plates, including one which depicts the ballot. $165.00

(Continued)

* A desireable edition of the work in that it includes a number of tracts omitted from the earlier edition of Toland. The Oceana was described by Hume as "the only valuable model of a commonwealth extant." DNB. "It was in America that Harrington's influence was strongest. The written constitution, the unlimited use of elective principle and the separation of powers are all points which may have been derived directly from the Oceana, while all the minor points ... seem to have been first formulated by (him) ... His influence is best seen in the early constitutions

97. (Continued) of the proprietary colonies, Carolina, New Jersey, Pennsylvania." Encyclopaedia of the Social Sciences.

98. (HAUTERIVE, ALEXANDRE MAURICE BLANC de LANAUTTE, comte d') Memoire sur les principes et les lois de la neutralite maritime, accompagne de pieces officielles justificatives. Paris, chez les Marchands de Nouveautes, 1812. 160pp. Neatly removed. Good copy. $ 37.50

99. HENING, WILLIAM WALLER. The Virginia justice ... the fourth edition, revised, corrected, greatly enlarged and adapted to the revised Code of 1819 and the laws subsequently passed. Richmond, Printed for the Author, 1825. 821, (1)pp. Orig. calf. A very nice copy. $ 85.00
* Final edition of this classic justice of the peace manual. Hening was one of the most highly regarded and authoritative legal writers of his time and region. See DAB.

100. (HIGGINS, JESSE) Sampson against the Philistines, or the reformation of lawsuits; and justice made cheap, speedy ... agreeably to the principles of the ancient trial by jury, before the same was innovated by judges and lawyers. Compiled for the use of the honest citizens of the United States, to whom it is dedicated. Second ed. Phila., Prtd. by B. Graves, for W. Duane, 1805. 96pp. Disbound. $ 35.00
* Marvin p. 627.

101. HOBBES, THOMAS. Elementa philosophica de cive. Amsterodami, apud Ludovicum Elzevirium, 1647. 12mo. Engraved title page and portrait, contemporary vellum. A very good copy. $225.00
* Second Elzevir edition and the first to have the portrait; it is a reissue of the sheets of the first Elzevir of the same year. The work appeared originally in 1642; that edition is exceedingly rare. This is the predecessor of and foundation for Leviathan. Both were intended to elucidate the nature of man as a social being and constituted one of the legs of Hobbes' tripod, the others being the study of man physically, and psychologically. MacDonald & Hargreaves 26.

102. HOCHHEIMER, LEWIS. A manual of criminal law as established in the State of Maryland. Baltimore, Scrimger, 1889. 200pp. Orig. cl. $ 30.00

103. (HOGDON, MOSES). The complete justice of the peace, containing extracts from Burn's Justice, and other justiciary productions. The whole altered and made conformable to the laws and manners of administering justice, particularly in the State of New Hampshire, and generally in the other of the United States ... by a Gentleman of the Profession. Dover, N. H., printed for Charles Peirce, 1806. 431pp. Calf, rubbed. Occasional pencilling. $ 45.00
* Shaw-Shoemaker 10569. First edition.

104. HOUARD, (DAVID) Dictionnaire analytique, historique, etymologique, critique et interpretatif de la coutume de Normandie, Ou l'on trouve la resolution des questions ... de droit civil & ecclesiastique de cette Province, conformement a la jurisprudence des arrets. A Rouen, chez Le Boucher le jeune, 1780. Four volumes, large thick 4 to's. Approx. 3000pp. Supplement and general index, fold. table. All half-titles present. Contemp. mottled calf, spines gilt, raised bands, minor wear to extremities. A very nice set. $250.00

105. HOWE, (SAMUEL GRIDLEY) An essay on separate and congregate systems of prison discipline; being a report made to the Boston Prison Discipline Society. Boston, Ticknor, 1846. xi, 90pp. Later boards. $ 45.00
* A remarkable defense by this important reformer, of the Pennsylvania system of "separate discipline", based on his own investigation of the facts and aimed directly at the intensely biased and hostile Boston Society to which Howe had previously been an adherent. This was conceived originally as a minority report and was written with the help of Horace Mann and Charles Sumner; the Society refused to publish it and finally, after a struggle to secure the manuscript, Howe published it himself.

106. HUBBELL, J.H., ed, and compiler. Hubbell's Legal Directory for lawyers and business men, containing the names of one or more of the leading and most reliable attorneys in nearly three thousand cities and towns in the United States: also a synopsis of the collection laws of each state... and times for holding courts throughout the United States and Territories for the year 1871. 280pp. Orig. cl. $ 32.50

107. HUBBELL, J.H., ed., compiler. Hubbell's Legal Directory for lawyers and business men, containing the names of one or more of the leading and most reliable attorneys in nearly three thousand cities and towns in the United States and Canada. Also a synopsis of the collection laws of each state, and Canada, ... also, times for holding courts throughout the United States and territories, for the year ending May 1, 1874. N. Y., Hubbell, 1374. $ 32.50
* Fourth annual volume. Covers territories. Includes many lawyers' ads.

108. HUNT, THOMAS. A defence of the charter and municipal rights of the City of London and the rights of other municipal cities and towns of England. Directed to the citizens of London. London, Richard Baldwin, 1683. 4to. 46pp. uncut and stitched as issued. A bit dusty but a very good copy. $125.00
* Sweet & Maxwell, I, noting that the work was answered by L'Estrange in Lawyer Outlawed. It is also an attack on John Dryden. MacDonald 221.

109. HUTCHINSON, JOHN A. A treatise on the laws of West Virginia pertaining to the powers and duties of justices, clerks of courts, prosecuting attorneys, sheriffs, constables, notaries, etc... also rules of evidence, definitions, notes of

109. (Continued) decisions, etc., etc. With references to the law and practice in Virginia. Second edition, revised by ... Cincinnati, Clarke 1889. 1177pp. Cloth. $ 45.00

110. INDERWICK, F. A. The King's peace: a historical sketch of the English law courts. With 15 illustrations and 1 map. London, Swan, 1895. 254pp. 1st ed. Fine. $ 15.00

111. (IOWA. LAWS, STATUTES) Revised statutes of the Territory of Iowa, revised and compiled by a Joint Committee of the Legislature - session 1842-43, and arranged by the Secretary of the Territory. Published by authority. Iowa City, Hughes & Williams, 1843. viii, 904pp. Orig. 1/4 calf, rubbed, still quite a good copy. $250.00
* THE FIRST AND ONLY COMPILED LAWS OF THE TERRITORY OF IOWA. An important source and an early Iowa imprint.

112. (IOWA) BRADFORD, JOHN M. The Iowa form book, or book of practical forms, containing precedents and forms for ordinary business dealings and transactions, with statements of the law; adapted and designed for the use of merchants, mechanics, farmers, business men, and especially Justices of the Peace. Davenport, House of Luse, Lane Co., 1857. 335pp. New cloth. $100.00
* NUC records two copies only, both in Iowa. Rare. Moffit # 266.

113. IRVINE, ALEXANDER FORBES. A treatise on the game laws of Scotland with an appendix containing the principal statutes and forms. Edinburgh, Clark, 1850. xxiv, 155pp. Orig. boards and cloth spine. A very good copy. Uncut. $ 60.00
* First edition. In part strongly historical.

114. JACOB, GILES. The modern justice: containing the business of a justice of peace in all its parts ... London, Sayer for Lintott, 1716. 8vo. 409pp., plus tables. Top inch of title page cropped affecting first word, "The", of title, else a very good copy. Contemp. calf, ruled in blind, small repair to head of spine. $ 75.00
* First edition. Scarce. NUC cites 3 locations. Marvin p. 416. S & M, I, p. 228.

THE HUMANITARIAN RECONSTRUCTION OF ENGLISH PRISONS

115. (JEBB, SIR JOSHUA, Surveyor-General of Prisons and Commissioner of Pentonville.) Report of the Surveyor General of Prisons on the construction, ventilation, and details of Pentonville Prison, 1844. London. Clowes, 1844. 62pp. plus 22 large folding lith. plates. TOGETHER WITH: Second report of the Surveyor-General of Prisons. London, Clowes, 1847. 220pp. 22 large folding plates. 2 volumes. Original cloth, spines faded, otherwise fine. 8vo. First book editions of the Parliamentary papers. $400.00
* The two land-mark reports which document in great detail respectively the final creation and the extension of Pentonville, the model prison based on the American system of separate confinement. In fact this was the logical culmination of reform begun (Continued)

115. (Continued) in England 70 years earlier by Howard and brilliantly advocated more recently by William Crawford who worked closely with Jebb in the final planning stages. Jebb was remarkably able to wed his technical training as an engineer in the Military (he served in Canada) to a very sympathetic understanding of the "seperate system". As the second report shows, he vigorously promoted its application to other prison sites, work which he continued later as a national administrator. The choice of the "separate " over the so-called "silent" system meant, among other things, the virtual elimination of corporal punishment. Whatever the relative merits of the competing systems, and they were endlessly disputed, the idea of moral improvement through meticulous and humane attention to mental and physical well-being permeates every facet of these reports.
The plates include detailed and overall plans, elevations, and several views, one of which (plt. 21, 1844 report) is an idyllic visiting day promenade down the central hall. See DNB for an account of Jebb.

116. (JUDICIARY ACT OF 1801) The speeches of Mr. Giles and Mr. Bayard in the House of Representatives ... on the bill received from the Senate entitled "An act to repeal certain acts respecting the organization of the courts of the United States." Boston, Munroe & Francis, 1802. 56pp. Sewn as issued. $ 35.00
* The two most representative arguments, pro and con respectively on the attack on an independent judiciary, an episode which led directly to Marbury v. Madison. Shaw-Shoemaker 2324.

117. KELLY, JAMES BIRCH. A summary of the history and law of usury, with an examination of the policy of the existing system, and suggestions for its amendment, together with an analysis of the parliamentary proceedings relative to the subject, up to the present time and a collection of statutes ... London; Kennett, 1835. 275pp. Orig. boards, spine worn and repaired, internally fine and uncut. $ 75.00
* S & M, II, p. 196. Marvin p. 435. Uncommon.

118. KERR, WILLIAM WILLIAMSON. A treatise on the law and practice as to receivers appointed by the Court of Chancery. With notes and references to American authorities by Geo. Tucker Bispham. Phila., Kay, 1872. 288pp. 1st Am. ed. $ 37.50

119. KINGSBURY, BENJAMIN. The Maine Townsman, or the laws for the regulation of towns with forms and judicial decisions adapted to the revised statutes of Maine. Eighth edition. Portland, Sanborn, 1860. 396pp. New cloth. $ 25.00

120. KINGSBURY, BENJAMIN, JR. The Maine townsman, or laws for the regulation of towns, with forms and judicial decision, adapted to the revised statutes of Maine. Fourteenth edition. Portland, Bailey, 1872. 480pp. Full contemp. sheep. $ 25.00

121. LADD, WILLIAM. A congress of nations: an essay by ... founder of the American Peace Society. Boston, Am. Peace Society., 1869. 124pp. Orig. cl. 12mo. $ 25.00
* An American classic first published in 1840. This edition adds a new supplementary chapter covering the post-Civil War period.

FIRST VERNACULAR EDITION OF A CRUCIAL EARLY WORK ON POLITICAL LIBERTY

122. (LANGUET, HUBERT) De la puissance legitime du Prince sur le peuple et du peuple sur le Prince. Traite tres-utile & digne de lecture en ce temps, escrit en Latin par Estienne Junius Brutus, & nouvellement traduit en Francois. N.p. 1581. 8 vo. 264pp. Some moderate staining confined to upper corner margin of first portion. Old expert and inconspicuous repair to minor worming in lower outer margin of middle portion, and very slight inconspicuous worming at lower inner margin towards middle just touching text in a few places. Despite these minor faults a very well preserved copy. Bound in 18th century polished calf, spine with floral gilt, borders gilt with corner fleurons. Slight wear at top of spine. In all a very pleasant, attractive copy. With a 16 line poem in contemporary hand on verso of A2 by L. Scribonius. $2750.00
* THE VERY RARE FIRST EDITION IN FRENCH of one of the most important early manifestos of basic political freedom. Attributed sometimes to Du Plessis Mornay as well as to Languet, it grew out of the French Protestant conflict. Published in Latin in 1579 as Vindiciae Contra Tyrannos, "it is an eloquent vindication of the people's right to resist tyranny, while affirming that resistance must be based on properly constituted authority. It is in fact the practical demonstration of Bodin's theory, and some measure of its impact and continuing relevance may be estimated from a study of the places and dates at which it has been translated and reprinted - London 1648, London 1689, Paris 1789, Berlin 1848. Like Rights of Man it is one of the perennial documents of anti-tyranny." Printing and the Mind of Man, 94. This "edition originale" is rare, in fact far more so than the earlier Latin edition, and is of special importance because it marks the first appearance of this revolutionary tract in the vernacular. Carteret Vol. I, p. 558: "plus recherchee que l'original Latin." Rothschild IV, 3126, p. 508. Adams, Cat. of Books printed on the Continent, 1500-1600, L-151.

123. The law of arrests in both civil and criminal cases: showing for what causes, by what authority, by whom, and how arrests are to be made ... necessary for sheriffs (etc. ...) in two parts. By an Attorney at Law. The second edition. (London) Henry Lintot, 1753. 12mo. vi, 264pp., plus tables and preliminary leaf of publisher's ads for law books. Contemporary calf, leather label, a very nice copy. $150.00
* An uncommon and attractive anonymous work. There were no further editions, and the first of 1742 has the same pagination. S & M, I, p. 260. NUC cites 4 copies.

124. (LAW SCHOOL CATALOGUE). University of Albany. ... Department of Law. c. 1855-56. 15pp. Neatly disbound. One of the earliest circulars, of a prospectus character, for this newly organized school. $ 20.00

125. (LAWYER'S DIRECTORY) Gould's lawyers' diary for the year 1868. N. Y., Gould, (1868). 137, 29printed pages plus diary; cloth, fine. $ 35.00
* A nice surviving example partly filled-in in the diary portion, belonging to Walston H. Brown. The printed sections contain a long list of N. Y. lawyers, plus commissioners for all states and territories, Gould's law blanks, and statistics and schedules for all local courts.

126. LEAVITT, JONATHAN. A summary of the laws of Massachusetts relative to the settlement, support, employment and removal of paupers. Greenfield, Mass., Denio, 1810. 64pp. 8vo. Orig. marbled bds., calf spine, printed paper label on covers. $ 65.00
* The title conceals the fact that this, though a slim volume, is an able historical account of the laws of settlement, covering five periods from 1692 to 1810, and touching on slavery, apprenticeship, inheritance, debtors, etc. A valuable account. Marvin p. 456. S & S 20533.

127. LEWIS, GEORGE CORNEWALL. An essay on the influence of authority in matters of opinion. London, Parker, 1849. xi, 424pp. Orig. bds., cl. spine, rubbed, edges worn, uncut. $ 45.00
* First edition. Part of the author's attempt to create a science of politics, using scientific method to organize social experience. He was student, friend, and follower of John Austin, and was greatly influenced by the latter's attempt to construct a scientific jurisprudence.

THE SCIENTIFIC STUDY OF POLITICS

128. LEWIS, GEORGE CORNEWALL. A treatise on the methods of observation and reasoning in politics. In two volumes. London, John W. Parker, 1852. 2 vols. 8vo. Contemp. 1/2 calf, a nice set. $125.00
* First and only edition of the author's most important work. In this well developed treatise he sought to do for government and the political process what his close personal friend and teacher, John Austin had done for jurisprudence, namely to determine the "province" of politics and apply scientific method to its analysis - to establish an orderly system of universally recognized truths comparable to the physical sciences. See DNB and the article in Encyclopaedia of the Social Sciences.

129. (LIBEL LAW) The speech of George Ponsonby in the House of Commons of Ireland ... upon the subject of fiats, to which are subjoined the several affidavits on which said fiats were granted against John Magee. Dublin, W. Gilbert, 1790. 55pp. Neatly removed. Fine copy. $ 37.50
* Concerns the setting of high bail on the accused in libel cases based upon vague charges. Very

129. (Continued) detailed on points of law. Magee was the most outstanding figure of this time in Ireland in connection with challenges to free speech McCoy 146 & 147 cites 2 items with long annotations concerning Magee, but this relevant tract on procedure goes unnoticed.

130. LILLY, JOHN. A collection of modern entries or select pleadings in the Courts of King's Bench, Common Pleas, and Exchequer ... to which is added, a collection of writs ... with two tables... The Fourth edition, carefully translated into English with many additional references. London, Strahan and Woodfall, for Worrall (et al.) 1771 Folio. 676pp. plus tables. Contemp. calf. rubbed, joints worn but holding. A good copy. $160.00
* One of the standard works on pleading, first published in 1723. This is a re-issue of the 1741 edition, the first to be rendered in English. S & M, I, 273. Holdsworth, Hist. of English Law, XII, p. 358.

131. LIVINGSTON, EDWARD. Introductory report to the code of prison discipline: explanatory of the principles on which the code is founded. Being part of the system of penal law prepared for the State of Louisiana. London, John Miller, 1827. 78pp. Neatly removed. A very good copy. $150.00
* An interesting example of American influence on prison reform abroad. This work was printed this same year in Philadelphia; the London issue consists of the same sheets with new title. Philadelphia was the center of American penological controversy; within a few years the "separate system" of confinement was instituted and was soon widely adopted elsewhere, especially in England. Livingston was the foremost American advocate of humanitarian reform-he drafted codes for Louisiana and the U.S., neither of which were adopted, but his international influence was enormous. All of his published works of the 1820's are quite scarce.

132. (LOGAN, JAMES) The charge delivered from the Bench to the Grand Jury at the Court of Quarter Sessions held for the County of Philadelphia, the second day of September 1723. Published at the desire of the said Grand Jury. Together with their address. Philadelphia, printed and sold by Andrew Bradford ... 1723. 4to. 16pp. Title within double rules. Sewn as issued and entirely uncut and unopened. A very fine copy. Contained in a folding cloth. box. $550.00
* The earliest of Logan's writings in connection with the beginning of his judicial career. He was leader of the aristocratic faction in Pennsylvania and formed one of the great early American libraries. This work deals with the broad issues of political and juridical philosophy and with the duties of man in society, "a subject upon which he began a treatise which was apparently never completed." --DAB, referring to his 1736 "Charge ..." which is erroneously suggested as being his first work in this genre. He concludes by defining a long list of crimes and the court's jurisdiction, and the names of the 17 jurors are given. Sabin 41793. Evans 2441.

133. LOWDEN, FRANK O. The lawyer's allegiance to the law. An address delivered ... before the

133. (Continued) graduating class of the law department of the State University of Iowa ... Iowa City, 1894. 19pp. Wrps. Fine. Laid in is a 4 page leaflet on the curriculum and faculty of the law school for 1894-5. Very nice. $ 15.00

134. McARTHUR, JOHN. Principles and practice of naval and military Courts Martial, with an appendix illustrative of the subject ... The fourth edition, on the entire new plan, with considerable additions and improvements. In two vols. London, Strahan, 1813. 463, 464pp. Full contemp. calf. Top margin of title page cropped just touching a few letters, still a very good set. $ 65.00
* This copy was bound in Philadelphia and bears the contemporary inscription: "U.S. Ship Natchez, J.T. Newton."

135. M'KINNEY, MORDECAI. The Pennsylvania justice of the peace: containing the law, practice and process, in proceedings before justices of the peace and aldermen, in criminal cases, with numerous precedents therein: also, the laws, adjudications, (with notes) forms of docket entries, process and practice, relative to their jurisdiction, and its exercise, in civil cases. Two vols. in one ... Harrisburg, prtd. by Guyer, 1839. 294, 353pp. Full contemp. calf, contrasting leather labels. A very good copy. $ 75.00
* A very uncommon and substantial Pennsylvania justice. Part of its scarcity may be explained by the fact that it was printed for and published by the author himself. Marvin p. 490.

137. (MADAN, MARTIN) Thelyphthora; or a treatise on female ruin ... under the following heads, viz. marriage, whoredom, fornication, adultery, polygamy, divorce ... particularly including an examination of the principles and tendency of Stat. 26 Geo. II, c. 33, commonly called the Marriage Act. The second edition enlarged. London, Dodsley, 1781. 2vols. 8vo. 404;382plus indeces. Later half-leather. Some heavy browning, mostly confined along outer margin. $ 75.00
* Madan's most important and notorious work, "in which he advocated polygamy, taking his stand on the Mosaic law, and elaborately arguing that it is in accordance with Christianity, properly understood .... when it was actually published it raised a storm of indignation, criticism, and opposition." --DNB. Madan will be remembered also as the author of "Thoughts on executive justice" which occasioned a reply by the young Romilly.

138. (MALLORY, JOHN) Modern entries in English: being a select collection of pleadings in the Courts of King's Bench, Common Pleas and Exchequer ... also...writs ... translated from the most authentic books ... with readings and observations on the several cases in the Reports ... references to all the other entries ... three distinct tables ... By a Gentleman of the Inner Temple. (London) Nutt & Gosling, 1734-1735. Two volumes, Folio. Contemp. leather, worn,

138. (Continued) covers loose or detached. Contents very good. $160.00
* First and only edition. S & M, I, 273. Holdsworth, History of English Law, V. XII, p.358. Not to be confused with the work of similar title by John Lilly.

139. MANSFIELD, EDWARD D. The political grammar of the United States; or, a complete view of the theory and practice of the general and state governments, with the relations between them. Dedicated and adapted to the young men of the United States. N. Y., Harper, 1834. 275pp. Orig. cl. 12mo. $ 27.50
* First edition. A popularization of American constitutional law and practice, avowedly modelled after Kent and Story. Mansfield was a lawyer.

140. (MARRIAGE LAW) KEEBLE, REV. JOHN. Sequel of the argument against immediately repealing the laws which treat the nuptial bond as indissoluble. Oxford, Parker, 1857. 220pp. Disbound. $ 27.50

141. MARSHALL, (JOHN). Opinion of the Supreme Court of the United States, at January term, 1832, delivered by Mr. Chief Justice Marshall, together with the opinion of Mr. Justice McLean, in the case of Samuel A. Worcester, plaintiff in error, versus the State of Georgia. With a statement of the case, extracted from the records of the Supreme Court ... Washington, Gales & Seaton, 1832. 39pp., disbound. A good copy. $ 75.00
* A landmark case in which Andrew Jackson scorned Marshall's decision favoring the Federal status of the Cherokee Indians at the expense of the principle of States' Rights. Bruntjen, Am. Imprints 16104.

142. MARTENS, (GEORG FRIEDRICH von, 1756-1821). Summary of the law of nations, founded on the treaties and customs of the modern nations of Europe ... translated from the French by William Cobbett. Phila., published by Thomas Bradford, 1795. xix, 379pp. incl. list of subscribers. Contemporary tree calf, leather label, a very nice copy. $150.00
* First American, and First English Language Edition, translated by William Cobbett and dedicated to George Washington. "Martens was one of the cofounders of postivism in international law, which began with Bynkershoek ... he was the first to banish the law of nature from international law ..." This is his chief work and was first published in Gottingen in 1785. -- See Encyclopaedia of the Social Sciences. Evans 29025. Gaines 8c.

143. (MARYLAND) Rules for the transaction of business in the Circuit Court for Frederick County, Maryland, as a court of law and as a court of equity. Frederick, Baughman, 1868. 51pp. with some interleaved mss. additions. Contemp. calf. Rare. $ 32.50

144. MASSACHUSETTS, LAWS, STATUTES. The laws of the Commonwealth of Massachusetts passed from the year 1780 to the end of 1800 ... in two volumes. Boston, Manning and Loring, 1801. 1073pp. plus indexes. Orig. calf, very good copies. $ 60.00
* The official committee consisted of Nathan Dane, George Richards Minot and John Davis. First edition of this major new compilation.

145. MASSACHUSETTS. LAWS, STATUTES. The laws of the Commonwealth of Massachusetts from (February 1801) to February 28, 1807 ... Boston, Thomas & Andrews ... 1807. 403pp. plus index. Calf, fine. $ 35.00
* This is denoted as "Volume three" and is in fact a continuation of the compilation published in 2 volumes in 1801. For this volume the Committee appointed on behalf of the Commonwealth consisted of Joseph Story and John Davis.

146. MAY, HENRY. Speech of ... late member of the Bar of the Circuit Court, on reform in the judiciary of the District of Columbia. Wash., Gideon, 1850. 15pp. Disbound. $ 25.00

147. (M., J). A guide to English juries: setting forth their antiquity, power, and duty from the common law and statutes, with a table. By a person of quality. Also a letter to the author upon the same subject. London, Thomas Cockerill, 1682. 12mo. 6pl., 176pp. plus 4pp. publisher's ads. Dsbd. but a very good copy. $100.00
* First and only edition. Wing MJ 37.

148. (MONTANA) Constitution of the State of Montana as adopted by the Constitutional Convention held at Helena, July 4, 1889 ... and also an address to the people. Helena, Published by Authority by the Independent Publ. Co., (1889). 76pp. Orig. pink wrps., fine. $ 50.00
* Official publication of the Montana State Constitution under which Montana was admitted to the Union. Kuhlman, p. 43.

149. MONTESQUIEU, (CHARLES DE SECONDAT) The spirit of the laws, translated from the French ... by Thomas Nugent. The fifth edition carefully revised and improved with considerable additions by the author. London, Nourse and Vaillant, 1773. 2 vols., 8vo. Contemp. calf, gilt, leather labels, a bit rubbed, but a very good set. $ 75.00

150. MORINEAU, AUGUSTE DE Essai statistique et politique sur les Etats-Unis d'Amerique ... comprenant 27 tableaux synoptiques et analytiques de la constitution federale et de celles des etats particuliers ... Paris, G. Thorel, 1848. Folio v, (5)-39, 27 full double page synoptic tables, full-length lithographed portrait of George Washington. Contemp. 1/4 calf, front joint repaired, internally fine. $165.00
* First edition. An unusual travel account of America. The author says that he has spent the best years of his life travelling in the New World and is fully committed to American democracy. This work presents American political and con-

150. (Continued) stitutional practice, with each state described in tabular detail, to Frenchmen in the midst of their own revolution; it has been expedited into print because of events, and is in fact part of a larger work not yet ready for press (actually never published). Howes M180. Sabin 50706. Monaghan 1115. Uncommon.

151. MORRISON, CHARLES R. The New-Hampshire Probate Directory: containing the general statutes and acts since passed, with full notes of decisions and forms of wills, petitions, citations, orders and decrees, and all other matters relating to probate courts and proceedings therein. Concord, Sanborn, 1870. 205pp. Full contemp. sheep, lea. label. Fine. $ 17.50

152. MORRISON, CHARLES ROBERT. New Hampshire Town Officer: containing the general laws of 1878, (other than school laws) and acts since passed relating to towns and cities, with decisions, directions, and forms. Concord, Sanborn, 1886. 498pp. Full sheep. 1st ed. $ 22.50

153. NATIONAL PRISON ASSOCIATION OF THE UNITED STATES OF AMERICA. Proceedings of the National Prison Congress held at Atlanta, Georgia, 1886. Chicago, Donnelley, 1888. 333pp. Orig. prtd. wrps. Fine. Includes Canadian material. $ 27.50

154. NESS, JOHN WILLIAM. A treatise on the game laws of Scotland with an appendix containing the principal statutes and leading cases on the subject. Edinburgh, Michael Anderson ..., 1818. x, 240pp. Half-title present. Original two-toned boards, printed paper label, a fine and attractive copy. $100.00

155. A new and useful table of costs as between attorney and agent, showing ... the whole of the charges as allowed for writs & c. and the costs for plaintiff and defendant. London, Clarke, 1819. 9pp. Neatly removed. $ 25.00
* A useful and elusive little source. Not in NUC, BM catalogue, or S & M.

156. O'BRIEN, JOHN. A treatise on American military laws, and the practice of courts martial; with suggestions for their improvement. Phila., Lea, 1846. 570pp. Orig. cl. $ 65.00
* Marvin p. 543: "...it is the most instructive treatise on the subject which has appeared in the United States; and for practical purposes it cannot fail to be more useful in our country than any of the English works ..." Surprisingly uncommon. FIRST EDITION.

157. OKE, GEORGE C. The synopsis of summary convictions; showing, at one view, the penalties, &c. for 1300 offences, when proceedings must be commenced ..., with an introduction, practical observations, forms and notes, embodying the entire law and practice relating thereto;... and an abstract of the juvenile offenders act ... London, Butterworth, 1848. 397pp. Orig. cl., fine. $ 50.00
* An unusual tabular presentation in ten catagories, showing in great detail the state of enforcement practice.

158. (PACKARD, FRED A.) Memorandum of a late visit to the Auburn Penitentiary; prepared for the Phila., Society for the Alleviation of the Miseries of Public Prisons. Phila., Harding, 1842. 8pp. dsbd. $ 17.50
* Describes changes and improvements, use of cold head bath punishment, defends Pennsylvania system above Auburn system.

A MANUAL FOR THE WHISKEY REBELLION

159. PARKER, JAMES. The conductor generalis: or, the office, duty and authority of justices of the peace, ... compiled chiefly from Burn's Justice .... by James Parker, late one of the Justices of the Peace for Middlesex County, in New Jersey; and now revised and adapted to the United States of America. By a Gentleman of the Law ... to which are added, the excise and militia laws of the U.S.; and the Acts called the Ten Pound Act of the States of Pennsylvania and New York. Phila., Campbell, 1792. xv, 464pp. 8vo. New cloth. A good copy. $100.00
* Evans 24661. The second appearance of this classic work in its adaptation to the new union. An extremely interesting edition containing the revenue laws and the means of their enforcement which led soon to the Whiskey Rebellion extending from western Pennsylvania to Georgia. Later editions of course om itted this material.

160. PARSONS, THEOPHILUS. The laws of business for business men, in all the States of the Union, with forms for mercantile instruments, deeds, leases, wills, &c. Boston, Little, Brown, 1857. 504pp. First edition of this enduring work Orig. cl., very fine. $ 37.50

161. PARSONS, THEOPHILUS. Laws of business for all the States of the Union. With forms and directions for all transactions. Hartford, Scranton, 1870. 685pp. $ 30.00
* First published in 1869, this became the enduring and leading text of its kind.

162. PARSONS, THEOPHILUS. Laws of business for all the States of the Union. With forms and directions for all transactions. Hartford, Scranton, 1874. 679pp. Full contemp. calf. $ 30.00

163. PARSONS, THEOPHILUS. Laws of business for all the States of the Union, with forms and directions for all transactions. Hartford, Scranton, 1875. 679pp. Full contemp. sheep. $ 30.00
* Early edition (1st was 1869) of the standard work of its time. Much on land law.

164. PARSONS, THEOPHILUS. Laws of business for all the States and Territories of the Union and the Dominion of Canada ... New enlarged edition, revised to date, with valuable fresh chapters on recent business legislation. Hartford, Scranton, 1908. 903pp. Contemp. cloth. $ 30.00

165. PAYNE, ABRAHAM. Reminiscences of the Rhode Island Bar. Providence, Tibbitts, 1885. 277pp. Orig. cl. Fine. $ 25.00

166. PHILLIPS, WILLARD. A treatise on the law of insurance. Boston, Wells and Lilly, 1823. 550pp. New cloth. A very good copy. $ 85.00
* First edition of the first original American work on the topic. Scarce. Marvin p. 569.

167. (PLATT, JONAS) Report of the evidence and reasons of the award between Johannis Orlandos & Andreas Luriottis, Greek Deputies of the one part, and Le Roy, Bayard & Co., and G. G. & S. Howland, of the other part. By the Arbitrators. N. Y., W. E. Dean, 1826. 72pp. Disbound. $ 25.00
* Involves contract suit in connection with American outfitting of ships for Greek War of Independence. Shoemaker 25789.

168. (PLATT) CONTOSTAVLOS, ALEXANDER. A narrative of the material facts in relation to the building of the two Greek frigates. N. Y., 1826. 88pp. Disbound. $ 25.00

169. POLLOCK, FREDERICK W. and F. W. MAITLAND. The history of English law before the time of Edward I. Second edition in two volumes. Cambridge, University Press, 1899. cl. Good set. $ 30.00

170. POPHAM, JOHN. Reports and cases collected by the learned ... late Lord Chief Justice of England written in his own hand in French and now translated into English, to which are added some remarkable cases ... with an alphabetical table ... London, Roycroft for Twyford and Place, 1656. Small folio, Contemp. calf, worn, internal moderate browning, still a reasonable copy. $ 75.00
* Marvin p. 577. See Holdsworth, V, pp. 360-61. Wing P-2942. FIRST EDITION.

171. POWNALL, THOMAS. The administration of the colonies. The third edition, revised, corrected and enlarged. To which is added, an Appendix, No. III, containing, Considerations on the points lately brought into question as to the Parliament's right of taxing the colonies, and of the measures necessary to be taken at this crisis. London, Dodsley, 1766. 8vo., 14pl., 202, 60, 52pp. Half-title present. 19th century 1/4 calf. A very nice copy, entirely uncut. $250.00
* Pownall's most important political work presenting his view that all British possessions in North America should be united into one commercial empire. He deals at length with the issue of colonial legislative rights, with Indian affairs, and with the currency question; he prints Tench Francis' tract on paper money (See Dorfman I, 174, 189) along with his own strong views - in fact he and Franklin togetherproposed a scheme for providing a currency for the colonies. Appendices I and II deal entirely with Canada and propose a defensive union with the Indians. Appendix III appears here for the first time. Sabin 64816; Howes 539. TPL 424.

172. Proposals humbly offer'd to the Parliament for remedying the great charge and delay of suits at law and in equity. The fourth edition, with additions. By an Attorney. London, N. Mist, 1724. v,48pp. later wrps. $ 55.00
* The NUC locates only 2 copies of a fifth edition and 4 of a sixth edition.

173. PUTNAM, SAMUEL jurist. ALS, 8pp. 4to., signed and dated Mar. 6, 1849. $ 75.00
* Putnam, 1768-1853 was born in Danvers, Mass., graduated Harvard, practiced law in Salem from 1790-1814, attained a high rank in the Essex County Bar, represented that county in the legislature and from 1814 to 1842 was judge of the Supreme Court of Mass. (see Appleton's Am. Biography.) This is an autobiographical letter written to classmate Abiel Abbott, intended to fill in the gap which had occurred in their earlier intercourse. Putnam describes his law career and personal life in detail.

174. PUTTER, JOHN STEPHEN. An historical development of the present political constitution of the Germanic Empire ... translated from the German with notes and a comparative view of the revenues, population, ... of the respective territories ... in three volumes ... London, Payne, 1790. 3 vols. Red buckram. $125.00
* First and only edition in English. Quite valuable as comparative legal and constitutional history, as well as a contemporary social survey.

175. RAFF, GEORGE W. A guide to executors and administrators in the settlement of the estates of deceased persons within the State of Ohio, to which is prefixed a brief comment upon the statute of wills. Third edition, revised and enlarged. Cincinnati, Clarke, 1864. 317pp. Full contemp. sheep, rubbed. $ 37.50

176. RAFF, GEORGE W. A guide to executors and administrators in the settlement of the estates of deceased persons within the State of Ohio, to which is prefixed a brief comment upon the statute of wills. Fourth edition, revised and enlarged. Cincinnati, Clarke, 1871. 327pp. Full sheep. $ 35.00

177. RAFF, GEORGE W. The law relating to roads and highways in the State of Ohio ... also, a brief consideration of ways existing by grant, dedication, and prescription. Second edition, greatly enlarged. Cincinnati, Clarke, 1871. 334pp. Full sheep. Expanded 2nd edition. $ 32.50

178 READ, COLLINSON. Precedents in the office of a Justice of Peace. To which is added a short system of conveyancing in a method entirely new with an appendix containing a variety of the most useful forms. Second edition with considerable additions. Harrisburgh, John Wyeth, for the author, 1801. (4)63,36,(1)pp. Square 8vo. Contemporary 1/4 calf, marbled boards. A very good copy. $100.00

179. READING, DANIEL. The English clerk's instructor in the practice of the Court of King's Bench and Common Pleas ... and several other matters necessary for the practice of an attorney, to which are added, several choice precedents of declarations never before printed. (London), Nutt and Gossling, for Bettesworth (et al.), 1733. 2 volumes, 8vo. 2pl,420,(16)pp; 1pl, 372,(14)pp. Contemp. calf, red leather labels, raised bands, very light rubbing, otherwise a fine unsophisticated copy. $225.00
* An uncommon work, not found in the BM catalogue or Marvin. The NUC records only the copy in the William Andrews Clark Library at UCLA. S & M, I, 277. Not in Marvin. A very pleasing copy.

180. REEVES, JOHN. Considerations on the Coronation oath to maintain the Protestant Reformed Religion and the settlement of the Church of England ... second ed. with additions. London, Wright, 1801. 69pp, with half-title. Removed. $ 30.00
* A defense of religious discrimination by this high Tory historian of English law.

181. RICHARDSON, WILLIAM M. The New-Hampshire justice of the peace. Second edition, improved. Concord, Hill, 1831. 299pp. Full contemp. sheep. $ 25.00
* Marvin p. 609.

182. ROBINSON, JAMES HARVEY. The German Bundesrath: a study in comparative constitutional law. Phila., Univ. of Pennsylvania, 1891. 68pp. Orig. prtd. wrps. $ 15.00

183. ROGERS, STEPHEN. The true object of medical legislation. Albany, Argus, 1873. 15pp. Orig. prtd. wrps. Fine. $ 15.00

184. ROPER, R. S. DONNISON. A treatise on the revocation and republication of wills and testaments; together with the tracts upon the law concerning baron and feme ... Phila., Byrne, 1803. 239,(1)pp. Corner of title page cropped, no text affected. Contemporary calf, label. A very good copy. $ 60.00
* First American edition, from the London edition of 1800. Marvin p. 619, not noticing the American editions. Uncommon.

185. ROWE, WILLIAM HENRY. Practical observations on certain points of frequent occurrence in conveyancing arising from an ommission to express the fact of signature ... on the late decision respecting some of those points and on the insufficiency of the late act (a copy of which is subjoined) together with a full answer to ... a recent letter to Sir Samuel Romilly ... London, Butterworth, 1815. 60pp. Neatly removed from a bound vol. Fine. $ 35.00
* First edition. S & M, II, p. 309. Marvin p. 622.

186. (RUGGLES, THOMAS) The barrister: or, strictures on the education proper for the bar. London, printed for J. Deighton, 1792. Two volumes, contemporary tree calf, spines gilt, leather labels. Small 8vo's. Inscribed: "From the author" on the title-pages, with contemporary bookplates (Freeland). Half-titles in both volumes. A very pretty copy. $250.00
* An uncommon and interesting work, treating the topic of legal education both very broadly and in technical detail. The work was later reprinted and there is a Dublin issue of the same year. This is the first time we have seen this book in any form; works of this sort and of this period seem to be particularly scarce in any case. The NUC lists only the Dublin reprint (one volume). cf. Marvin p. 622f. First edition.

187. SAMS, C. WHITTLE. A brief comparison of the most important statutes of the Codes of Virginia of 1873 and 1887: being especially those referred to in "Minor's Institutes of Common and Statute Law." Richmond, Va., West, Johnson, 1888. 160pp. Cloth. $ 25.00

188. SCROGGS, SIR WILLIAM. The practice of courts-leet and courts-baron: containing full and exact directions for holding the said courts ... etc.) To this fourth edition are added very large additions ... (London,) Nutt & Gosling, 1728. 8vo. 510(13)pp. Later 1/4 calf, rubbed, contents very good. $125.00
* S & M, I, p. 405. See Holdsworth VI, p. 504-7.

189. SEDGWICK, THEODORE. A treatise on the rules which govern the interpretation and construction of statutory and constitutional law. Second edition, with numerous additional notes by John Norton Pomeroy. N. Y., Baker, 1874. 692pp. Full contemp. sheep. $ 37.50

190. SELDEN, JOHN. Titles of honor. London, William Stansby for John Helme, 1614. Small 4to. Contemporary calf, raised bands, moderately rubbed, otherwise a very good copy. $250.00
* FIRST EDITION. STC 22177.

191. SELDEN, JOHN. Titles of honor. The third edition carefully corrected. With additions and ammendments by the author. London, Tyler and Holt, for Bassett ... 1672. Folio. 17pl., 756pp. Contemp. panelled calf, extremities and joints worn but holding. Internally a very good copy, lacking the frontis-portrait. $100.00
* Final and textually the best edition. S & M, I, 208. Wing S2440.

192. SERGEANT, THOMAS. A treatise upon the law of Pennsylvania relative to the proceeding by foreign attachment, with the acts of assembly now in force in Pennsylvania on the subject of Foreign and Domestic Attachments. Phila., Farrand, 1811. 331pp. New cloth. $ 50.00
* Marvin p. 638.

193. SHARP, GRANVILLE. Remarks on the opinions of some of the most celebrated writers on Crown Law, respecting the due distinction between manslaughter and murder, being an attempt to show that the plea of sudden anger cannot remove the imputation and guilt of murder ... that indulgence allowed by the courts to voluntary manslaughter ... is indiscriminate ... London, B. White, 1773. xvii, 76pp., half-title present. Contemp. boards, front cover detached, internally very good. $ 85.00
* First edition of this great and effective philanthropist's attack on duelling by way of a reconsideration of criminal law. Marvin p. 639, citing a later edition. S & M, I, 365 and 45. Reprinted also in Phila., 1778.

194. A short history of all the Parliaments of England in all reigns, showing the use they have made of their Parliamentary power ... and particularly the extraordinary laws they have enacted for government of the Kingdom ... London, Peele, 1722. 2pl., 76pp. Ornamental vignette headpiece. Nice copy. $ 75.00
* A knowledgeable overview of the past, by way of an attack on the present Parliament. Signed in print at the conclusion of the dedication, "G.J."

195. SITES, CLEMENT MOORE LACEY. Centralized administration of liquor laws in the American Commonwealths. N.Y., (Columbia Univ.), 1899. 164pp. Orig. prtd. wrps. $ 12.50

196. SMITH, E. FITCH. Commentaries on statute and constitutional law and on statutory and constitutional construction containing an examination of adjudged cases on constitutional law ... of the United States and ... of the respective states concerning legislative power and also the consideration of the rules of law in the construction of statutes and constitutional provisions. Albany, Gould, Banks, 1848. xv, 976pp. New cloth. $ 75.00
* First edition of a very uncommon treatise.

197. SMITH, JOHN WILLIAM. The law of contracts. Sixth American from the sixth London edition, by Vincent T. Thompson, with notes and references to both English and American decisions by William Henry Rawle, and with additional notes and references to recent American cases by George Sharswood. Phila., Johnson, 1878. 543pp. Full contemp. sheep. Very good. $ 27.50

198. SNYDER, WILLIAM L. The geography of marriage or legal perplexities of wedlock in the United States. N. Y., Putnam, 1889. 334pp. Orig. cl. $ 35.00

199. SPENCE, JAMES CARMICHAEL. The conscience of the King. London, Swan Sonnenschein, 1899. 280pp. Orig. cl. o.p. $ 22.50
* A philosophical work, with contemporary focus, on the perennial problems of law-making. Scarce.

200. SPOTISWOODE, ROBERT. Practicks of the laws of Scotland, observed and collected by Sir Robert Spotiswoode of Pentland, President of the College of Justice ... as also Abstracts taken out of the ancient record of this kingdom, whereby is declared the manner of administering justice in civil causes ... and propositions and questions in law made by the same author, with memoirs of his life and trial ... published by John Spotiswoode ..., advocate, the author's grandson. Edinburgh, James Watson, 1706. Folio. 2 pl., xli,(3), 372pp. Title within rules. Contemp. calf, little rubbed, but a very good copy. FIRST EDITION. $150.00
* S & M, V, 108. See DNB for an account of Spotiswoode.

201. STEARNS, ASAHEL. A summary of the law and practice of real actions; with an appendix of practical forms. Boston, Cummings, 1824. 528pp. Orig. bds., rebacked. $ 45.00
* First American edition. Marvin p. 663, citing laudatory notice in Hoffman's Legal Studies.

202. STOKES, ANTHONY. A view of the constitutions of the British Colonies in North America and the West Indies at the time the civil war broke out ... in which notice is taken of such alterations as have happened ... down to the present period. With a variety of colony precedents, which are chiefly adapted to the British West India Islands; and may be useful to those who have any intercourse with the colonies. London, Printed for the author ... 1783. 8vo. xvi, 555pp. Half-title present. Contemporary calf, rubbed, small corner of upper spine chipped but not affecting label, internally a very nice copy. $325.00
* First and only edition. A marvelous first-hand source for the legal as well as constitutional practice of the colonies and Caribbean Islands. Stokes was Chief Justice of Georgia and a practicing attorney in the Islands who returned to England when the Revolution occurred. He speaks of his failure in 1762 to find any good sources of colonial precedent; this work is intended to fill the need, and indeed it describes in great detail the constitutions, powers of office, court structure, behavior of judges, counsel and attornies, and vice-admiralty in all the British possessions, and covers a great variety of normal precedents and forms, including the manumission and conveyancing of Negro slaves. Of great West Indian interest. Ragatz p. 379. Marvin p. 668. Sabin 91994. Uncommon.

203. STORY, JOSEPH. Commentaries on the conflict of laws, foreign and domestic in regard to contracts, rights and remedies, and especially in regard to marriages, divorces, wills, successions, and judgements. Boston, Hilliard, Gray, 1834. xxv, 557pp. Contemp. sheep, little rubbed, still a very good copy. $150.00
* FIRST EDITION. Marvin p. 670f in an extensive laudatory note identifies this as the first work on this "most difficult chapter of public law" in America or England, and cites instances of its enthusiastic reception abroad.

204. STORY, JOSEPH. Commentaries on the Constitution of the United States; with a preliminary review of the constitutional history of the colonies and states before the adoption of the Constitution Abridged by the author for the use of colleges and high schools. Boston, Hilliard & Gray, 1833. xliii, 736pp. Contemp. sheep, rubbed and worn, but sound, leather label, internally light to moderate foxing but a good copy. $ 80.00
* First edition thus, of one of the greatest works on the U.S. Constitution, published in 3 volumes in the same year, and the format by which the work became known for many, including foreigners; for example the French translation was made from this abridgement. Marvin p. 670.

205. STORY, JOSEPH. Commentaries on the Constitution of the United States: with a preliminary review of the constitutional history of the colonies and states, before the adoption of the constitution. Third edition. In two vols. Boston, Little, Brown, 1858. 735, 702pp. Sheep, rebacked in cloth. $ 90.00
* Contains substantial revision and updating by the editors, kept distinct from the original text. One of the great classics of American legal and political thought.

206. STORY, JOSEPH. Commentaries on the law of bailments, with illustrations from the civil and the foreign law. Cambridge, Hilliard and Brown, 1832. xxxiv, 411pp. Contemp. sheep, rubbed, front cover bit scuffed, but sound, internally very good. $150.00
* FIRST EDITION. Marvin p. 668f, a long praiseworthy note: "The only complete and satisfactory treatise upon the law of bailments ... Had he written no other work than this his reputation as a learned jurist ... would have been secure..."

207. STORY, JOSEPH. Commentaries on the law of partnership as a branch of commercial and maritime jurisprudence, with occasional illustrations from the civil and foreign law. Boston, Little & Brown; London, Maxwell, 1841. xxi, 690pp. Roy 8vo. Contemp. sheep. leather label, binding worn, covers loose but holding, contents very good. $ 85.00
* FIRST EDITION. Marvin p. 672. Story's success was great not only in America, but overseas as well, as the dual publisher's imprint suggests.

208. STORY, JOSEPH. Commentaries on the law of partnership, as a branch of commercial and maritime jurisprudence, with occasional illustrations from the civil and foreign law. Fifth ed. Boston, Little, Brown, 1859. 754pp. Sheep. rubbed. $ 45.00

209. (STORY, JOSEPH, et al.) Report of the Commissioners appointed to consider and report upon the practicability and expediency of reducing to a written and systematic code the common law of Massachusetts, or any part thereof ... Boston, Dutton, 1837. 46pp. Neatly disbound. $ 35.00

210. SUGDEN, EDWARD BURTENSHAW. A practical treatise of powers. London, Reed, 1808. 604pp. Full calf, little rubbed, still a very good copy. $125.00
* FIRST EDITION. "A masterly elucidation... held in the highest esteem..." Marvin p. 676f. "The subject embraced a large part of the law of real property ... It is the best authority both for the present law and for its history." Holdsworth, XIII, p. 477.

211. SULLIVAN, JAMES. The history of land titles in Massachusetts. Boston, I. Thomas and E. T. Andrews, 1801. 392pp. Tables of descents in text. New cloth. $ 75.00
* First edition. Intended to "reduce the principles which govern real estates in this Commonwealth to an easy and concise system."--Preface. A work of considerable historical scholarship as well as a contribution to the American conception of the common law. The work concludes with a general philosophical defense of the common law tradition in the commercial jurisprudence of the new Republic. See Horwitz, Transformation of American Law 1780-1860, pp. 21-22, and 144. A significant work.

212. TAIT, GEORGE. A summary of the powers and duties of a justice of the peace in Scotland ... with forms of proceedings &c. comprising a short view of the criminal duty, and of the greater part of the civil duty, of sheriffs and magistrates of Burghs. Third edition. Edinburgh, Anderson, 1821. 470,38pp. Full polished calf. Marvin p. 684. $ 75.00

213. TAYLOR, JOHN (of Caroline County, Virginia) Construction construed, and Constitutions vindicated. Richmond, Shepherd & Pollard, 1820. iv,344pp. Original tree calf, spine gilt with contrasting leather label; some minor rubbing and wear to extremities but still an attractive binding. Moderate foxing throughout which is apparently inevitable with this book. A very good copy. $225.00
* First edition. An important book, Taylor was the greatest spokesman for the states-rights view of the Constitution. Charles Beard considered him one of the few really major original political theorists (see DAB). All of his works elaborate the same theme - this one is particularly interesting, coming in the wake of the Missouri Compromise and important tariff and banking legislation. This is also a very desireable copy in the original trade binding with the binder's ticket of Frederick A. Mayo ... Richmond, Va. Mayo was one of the best binders working in this region. Howes T60.

214. (TEXAS) County Commissioners' Legal Guide (for the State of Texas). Defining the powers, duties, immunities and privileges of a county commissioner. This compilation embraces the acts of the twenty-third legislature, which adjourned May 9, 1893. St. Louis, Barnard, (1894). 340pp. Full contemp. sheep. $ 47.50

215. THAYER, JAMES BRADLEY. A preliminary treatise on evidence at the common law. Boston, Little, Brown, 1898. 636pp. Orig. cl. 1st ed. V. good copy. $ 45.00

215. (Continued) * "Thayer's great book ... was the first to treat the development of this branch of the law historically ... (it) gave us at length an entirely adequate history of the jury, and of those older modes of trial." Holdsworth, Historians of Anglo-American Law, p. 104.

216. (TRIAL) Report of the case of Charles Stearns against J. W. Ripley in the Circuit Court ... at Boston, Nov. term, 1850, for malicious prosecution ... Judge Sprague presiding. Springfield, Wilson, 1851. 76,14pp., fold map. Neatly removed. $ 35.00
* Concerns abuse of military power and prosecution without probable cause in connection with land-title dispute between Stearns and the Springfield Armory. Judge and jury were in conflict, the latter finding for the plaintiff.

217. TUCKER, GEORGE F. Monroe Doctrine: a concise history of its origin and growth. Boston, Reed, 1885. 138pp. Orig. cl. o.p. $ 17.50

218. TUCKER, JOHN RANDOLPH. The Constitution of the United States: a critical discussion of its genesis, development, and interpretation. Edited by Henry St. George Tucker. In two vols. Chicago, Callaghan, 1899. 1015pp. Orig. cl. Boxed. Fine. o.p. $ 45.00

219. TWISS, TRAVERS. The law of nations considered as independent political communities: on the rights and duties of nations in time of war. Oxford, Clarendon, 1863. 506pp. Orig. cl. First edition. $ 50.00

220. (UNITED STATES CONSTITUTIONS). The Constitutions of the United States according to the latest ammendments ... Phila., John Conrad, 1804. 12mo. xxiv,391pp. Contemporary calf, leather label, slight wear to upper hinge but a very good copy. $150.00
* A very desireable edition with current material of great interest including "all the Federal Acts concerning the government of the new states down to March 1804," as well as the Constitution of the State of Ohio (Nov. 1802), Acts to incorporate the District of Columbia (1802-04), the 12th ammendment then being considered by the states, and especially, the Act for the creation and governance of the new Territory of Louisiana, 26 March 1804, quite possibly in its first book appearance. Sabin 16101.

221. (U.S. SUPREME COURT). Rules of practice for the Courts of Equity of the United States promulgated by the... January Term, 1842. Wash., Langtree, 1842. 56pp. Neatly removed. Rare. Not a government document. $ 27.50

222. UPDIKE, WILKINS. Memoirs of the Rhode-Island Bar. Boston, Webb, 1842. 309pp. Orig. cl. Nice copy. $ 45.00
* 15 lawyers of the 18th century, including a large section on James Varnum. Marvin p. 703.

223. VALLANDIGHAM, JAMES L. A life of Clement L. Vallandigham, by his brother ... Baltimore, Turnbull, 1872. 573pp. Frontis., Orig. cl. o.p. $ 35.00
* Of great interest in connection with the Constitutional crisis during the Civil War.

224. VANDEWEYER, SYLVAIN. Dissertation sur la realite, la connaissance et la pratique du devoir comme naturelles. Louvain, Cuelens, 1823. 52pp. Orig. marbled wrps., uncut. Fine. $ 37.50
* A discussion of the philosophy of natural rights and obligations in opposition to the ethics of utilitarianism. The author defends the former, and a substantial portion of the work is a commentary on Bentham. No copy in the NUC.

A LANDMARK IN THE GENIUS OF THE AMERICAN POLITICAL SYSTEM

225. VARNUM, JAMES M. The case, Trevett against Weeden: on information and complaint, for refusing paper bills in payment for butcher's meat, in market, at par with specie. Tried before the honourable Superior Court, in the county of Newport, September term, 1786. ... wherein the rights of the people to trial by jury, &c. are stated and maintained, and the legislative, judiciary and executive powers of government examined and defined. Providence, printed by John Carter, 1787. iv,60pp. 4to. Bound in later cloth, in fine condition. $300.00
* FIRST AND ONLY EDITION. A major landmark in the establishment of the doctrine of judicial review, one of the unique features of the American political system. Varnum's defense of the right of the judiciary to reject legislation which violates the Constitution and of the independence and primacy of the judiciary was the most extensive and forceful to appear in this formative period. Of the five or so colonial cases involving judicial review (see Beveridge, Life of Marshall, III, p. 610f and Charles Warren, Congress, the Court and the Constitution, p. 43f) this is the most important because Varnum's views were made available to his contemporaries in this separately published pamphlet which was heavily advertised in the Philadelphia papers at the time of the Constitutional Convention. Madison took special note of it in the debates and Warren maintains that the founding fathers agreed that the Supreme Court would, like its colonial counterparts, be the ultimate judge of the validity of a law. Varnum's bold words echoed 17 years later in the statement of John Marshall in Marbury v. Madison that "it is emphatically the province and duty of the judicial department to say what the law is." Varnum also gives a good account of the social and financial background to the affair and reproduces the currency and obnoxious forcing acts which denied trial by jury and appeal. He later became justice for the new Northwest Territory and helped frame its laws. Evans 20825. Sabin 98638. JCB 1772-1800, p. 267. A very nice copy of an important work.

226. VATTEL, EMMERICH DE Le droit des gens, ou, Principes de la loi naturelle, appliques a la conduite & aux affaires des nations & des souverains. A Leide, aux Depens de la Compagnie, 1758. 4to. Two volumes in one. Engraved vignette on title page; title page in red and black. Contemporary calf, raised bands, sides a little rubbed, otherwise a very nice copy. $300.00

226. (Continued) * Along with the "Londres" edition of this same year this is the first appearance of this great work - "a classic in the literature of international law, for decades (exercising) a decisive influence upon statesmen." Encycl. of the Social Sciences. Notable is its restriction of the role of warfare. "He has done for the morality of nations what Paley did for the morality of individuals ... he is more generally read than any other writer upon the law of nations, and in no country more than ours ..." Marvin p. 706. This last comment is borne out by the profusion of English language editions throughout the 19th century, outlasting the French.

227. VAUCHER, J. A guide to marine insurances; containing the policies of the principal commercial towns in the world ... also remarks on the mutual relation between insured and insurers: and comparative tables ... London, Baily, 1834. iv,xii,205pp., 3 fold. tables. A very nice copy, bound in original publisher's linen, with the full title page printed on both covers. A very nice example of this early cloth binding practice, little darkened. Internally fine, uncut and unopened. $100.00
* A scarce book in any condition. This is an especially nice copy. Contains American ports - Boston, Phila., Baltimore, N. Y. and New Orleans. Not in Kress or Goldsmiths'. Marvin p. 707. The NUC cites 2 copies.

228. (VENICE. LAWS STATUTES) NOVELLUS, J. Volumen statutorum, legum, ac iurium d. Venetorum cum amplissimo indice ... additis correctionibus ... cum sua pratica iudiciali ... Venice, (Apud Cominum de Tridino Montisferrati), 1564. 4to. 32pl., 211,(1),69,(3) leaves. A perfect copy, with woodcut plates, ornamental initials. Some staining, not serious, towards rear and minor worming at lower corner blank margin at end, otherwise a good copy, in later vellum. $ 350.00
* First edition of this important compilation, including much on family law and women. The second part consists of a supplement of recent laws. Adams, Continental Books ..., #359. The NUC cites four copies (the copy used for its entry omits the supplement present here).

229. (VERMONT. LAWS, STATUTES) Laws of the State of Vermont; revised and passed by the legislature ... 1797 ... with an appendix... and the titles of all the acts which have not been repealed, or become obsolete. Rutland, Josiah Fay, 1798. 8vo. 621,205,(2)pp. Contemp. calf rubbed, leather label, a very good copy. $ 75.00
* Evans 34925. McCorison 507.

230. VIRGINIA. LAWS, STATUTES, etc. A collection of all such acts of the General Assembly of Virginia as have passed since the session of 1801, to which are added appendices ... Richmond, Samuel Pleasants, 1808. Roy 8vo. vi,322pp. Contemp. calf, a good copy. $ 45.00
* This is actually the second volume of this revision, of which volume one was published in 1803. The volume offered here is, of course, complete by itself and contains the laws from 1802 through 1808. The appendices and index relate to the entire work.

231. VIRGINIA. LAWS, STATUTES. A collection of all such acts of the General Assembly of Virginia of a public & permanent nature as are now in force comprising the first volume of the revised code. The second edition, with copious notes .. and a new and much enlarged index ... Richmond, Pleasants, 1814. 762pp., errata. Contemp. sheep, quite worn, covers loose, internally a very good copy. $ 45.00
* This is the first volume of the 1814 revision of the revised code of 1803 - 1808; it is complete by itself and contains the laws from 1782 through 1801.

232. VON SAVIGNY, FRIEDRICH CARL. A treatise on the Conflict of Laws, and the limits of their operation in respect of place and time. Translated, with notes by William Guthrie, Advocate. With an appendix containing the treatises of Bartolus, Molinaeus, Paul Voet, and Huber. Second edition, revised. Edinburgh, Clark, 1880. 567pp. Orig. cl. $ 50.00

233. WALLIS, S. TEACKLE. Address ... at the unveiling of the statue of Chief Justice Taney ... Baltimore, Murphy, 1879. 18pp. Orig. prtd. wrps. Fine. $ 12.50

234. WARDENS' ASSOC. OF THE UNITED STATES AND CANADA. Statistics of prisoners, 1890 ... with an introduction by Roland P. Falkner. (Chicago) published by the Association, 1892. 56pp. Orig. prtd. brds. Includes Canadian material. $ 27.50

235. WASHINGTON, BUSHROD (Reporter) Reports of cases argued and determined in the Court of Appeals of Virginia. Richmond, Thomas Nicolson, 1798-99. Complete in two volumes. 8vo's. Contemporary calf, little scuffed and rubbed, with the original red leather labels. Light to moderate foxing. Old faint institutional stamp on each title page. A very good set with the original oval nameplates of William Owsley, Kentucky jurist and governor. $250.00
* FIRST EDITION of the first Virginia reports, which include numerous cases argued by JOHN MARSHALL between 1790 and 1796. Washington himself served in the U.S. Supreme Court with Marshall, whom he supported. This is a very nice association copy, having been part of the library of the Governor of Kentucky and Chief Justice of the Kentucky Court of Appeals, William Owsley, 1782-1862.--See DAB. Servies, Bibliography of John Marshall, #1791. Marvin p. 719. Sabin 100038. Swem 7696 and 7806. Evans 34958 and 36670.

236. WHEATON, HENRY. American legal scholar, first Ambassador to the Court of Berlin, and author of the first great American work on international law. Fine ALS, 3 pages 4to. entirely in his hand, dated Berlin 17 Nov. 1842, written to Thomas Caute Reynolds, later to become Governor of Missouri during the Civil War and at this time a student at Heidelberg having just finished his dissertation (cf. Marvin p. 607), a copy of which is being sent to Wheaton who advises him on the present prospect of his obtaining a post in the diplomatic corps in Berlin and assures him of his support. $ 50.00

237. WHEATON, HENRY. Elements of international law: with a sketch of the history of the science. Philadelphia, Carey, Lea & Blanchard 1836. xiv,375pp. and publ. ads. Orig. publisher's linen, printed paper label, little rubbed, light foxing, still a very good copy. $100.00
* FIRST EDITION. A classic in its field. Marvin p. 728.

238. (WHEATON vs. PETERS) Argument for the defendants, on an appeal from the Circuit Court of Pennsylvania. Wheaton and Donaldson versus Peters and Grigg. Phila., Kay, 1834. 31pp. Removed from a bound volume. Foredge worn, else a good copy. $ 35.00
* Landmark case in which Henry Wheaton sued Richard Peters for exclusive rights when the latter became involved in publishing the reports of the Supreme Court. It was decided that there could be no exclusive rights for that material.

239. WHITE, DANIEL APPLETON. A view of the jurisdiction and proceedings of the courts of probate of Massachusetts with particular reference to the County of Essex. Salem, Cushing and Appleton, 1822. 158pp. Very neatly removed from a bound volume. Very good. $ 80.00
* An excellent and very uncommon work. White was probate judge of Essex County for 38 years. He wrote this lengthy tract primarily to clarify and justify the reforms he was attempting to make in his new position; additionally the work reaches back and contains deliberately a good deal of history.

240. WHITING, SAMUEL. The Connecticut town officer; in three parts. ... Danbury, Skinner, 1814. 287(1)pp. 12mo. calf. First edition. $ 37.50
* Shaw Shoemaker 33668. Fine copy.

241. WHITMAN JOHN W., (reporter) Report of a trial in the Supreme Judicial Court, holden at Boston, Dec. 16th and 17th, 1828, of Theodore Lyman, Jr., for an alleged libel on Daniel Webster ... Boston, Putnam, 1828. 76pp. Neatly removed. $ 45.00
* "The style of the indictment is of special interest based upon the law of scandalum magnatum, or slander of great men ... the offense originated with the English Star Chamber but was never recognized in the common law of the United States." --McCoy L388. Shoemaker 35002.

242. WHITMAN, JOHN W., (reporter) Trial of the case of the Commonwealth versus David Lee Child, for publishing in the Massachusetts Journal a libel on the Honorable John Keyes, before the Supreme Judicial Court, holden at Cambridge, in the County of Middlesex, October Term, 1828. Boston, Dutton, 1829. 119pp. Neatly removed. Shaw-Shoemaker 40671. McCoy C318. $ 25.00

243. WHITMORE, WILLIAM H. A bibliographical sketch of the laws of the Massachusetts Colony from 1630 to 1686, in which are included the Body of Liberties of 1641, and the records of the Court of Assistants, 1641-1644, Arranged to accompany (Continued)

243. (Continued) the reprints of the laws of 1660 and of 1672. Boston, Rockwell, 1890. xliii, 150pp. Half-morocco. Scarce. $ 30.00

244. WILD, E. N. Municipal law of Indiana, containing the statutes to cities and incorporated towns, with notes of legislation and judicial decisions. Cincinnati, Clarke, 1870. 200pp. Full contemp sheep. $ 45.00

245. WINSLOW, FORBES. On insanity. London, John Churchill, 1854. 8vo. (8), 160pp. and 32pp. advertisements. Original publisher's red blind cloth. A very nice copy. $250.00
* FIRST EDITION. of Winslow's Lettsomian Lectures to the Medical Society of London. Founder of the first British psychiatric journal, Winslow devoted his career to the study and treatment of insanity and to its relationship

245. (Continued) with the law. He founded two asylums where he employed humane treatment, then still controversial, and he pioneered in the development of the medical jurisprudence of insanity: "The frequent establishment of the plea of insanity in criminal cases was largely due to his influence, and he was called as a witness in many celebrated trials.." DNB. The third and longest of these lectures is devoted to the latter topic, and the second to the matter of treatment.

246. WYTHE, GEORGE. Decisions of cases in Virginia by the High Court of Chancery, with remarks upon decrees by the Court of Appeals reversing some of those decisions ... second and only complete edition, with a memoir of the author, analyses of the cases, and an index, by B. B. Minor ... with an appendix ... by William Green. Richmond, Randolph, 1852. xliii, 471(8)pp. 8vo. Contemp. calf, leather label. A fine copy. $ 75.00
* A desireable edition of this Virginia classic first published in 1795. Marvin p. 752 (1st ed.).

247. ABEL-SMITH, BRIAN et al. Lawyers and the courts: a sociological study of the English Legal System, 1750-1965. Cambridge, Harvard, 1967. 504pp. o. p. $ 22.50

248. AMES, JAMES BARR. Lectures on legal history and miscellaneous legal essays. With a memoir. Cambridge, Harvard Univ Press, 1913. Frontis. 553pp. Orig. cl. $ 27.50

249. ASSOCIATION OF THE BAR OF THE CITY OF N.Y. Jurisprudence in action: a pleaders anthology ... legal essays selected by... with a foreword by Robert H. Jackson. N. Y., Baker, 1953. 494pp. o. p. $ 17.50

250. BAKER, ELIZABETH FAULKNER. Protective labor legislation with special reference to women in the State of New York. N. Y., Columbia, 1925. 467pp. Wrps. Fine. $ 17.50
* Studies in History, Economics and Public Law, #259.

251. BARKER, LUCIUS J. and TWILEY W. BARKER, JR. Freedoms, courts, politics: studies in civil liberties. Englewood Cliffs, N. J., Prentice-Hall, (1965). 324pp. cl., d. j. o. p. $ 22.50

252. BENTHAM, JEREMY. The theory of legislation. Edited with an introduction and notes by C. K. Ogden. London, Routledge, 1931. 555pp., frontis., orig. cl. $ 22.50
* Best scholarly edition with ample introductions, based on Hildreth's translation, with corrections.

253. BILLIAS, GEORGE ATHAN (ed.) Selected essays: law and authority in Colonial America Barre, Barre Publishers, (1965). 208pp. o. p. $ 22.50
* 10 original essays given at a conference sponsored by the American Antiquarian Society.

254. BILLIG, THOMAS CLIFFORD. Equity receiverships in the Common Pleas Court of Franklin County, Ohio. In the years 1927 and 1928. Baltimore, John Hopkins Press, 1932. 159pp. Orig. cl. o. p. $ 12.50
* Study of Judicial Administration in Ohio, Inst. of Law, JH Univ.

255. BODENHEIMER, EDGAR. Jurisprudence. First edition. N. Y., McGraw-Hill, 1940. 357pp. o. p. $ 20.00

256. BODIN, JEAN. Six books of the Commonwealth. Abridged and translated by M. J. Tooley. Oxford, Blackwell, n. d. (1956?). 211pp. Only modern English translation since Knolles' of 1606. This edition o. p. $ 22.50

257. BOGSCH, ARPAD. Universal Copyright Convention: an analysis and commentary. N.Y., Bowker, 1958. 279pp. o. p. $ 20.00

258. BOND, CARROLL T. The Court of Appeals of Maryland: a history. Baltimore, Barton-Gillett, 1928. 213pp. Illus., frontis., many plates. Orig. cl. o. p. $ 25.00
* Mainly from 1694 to 1867, written by Chief Justice of the Court.

259. BOORSTIN, DANIEL J. The mysterious science of the law: an essay on Blackstone's Commentaries, showing how Blackstone, employing eighteenth-century ideas of science, religion, history, asthetics, and philosophy, made of the law at once a conservative and a mysterious science. Cambridge, Harvard, 1941. 257pp. Frontis. 1st ed. $ 15.00

260. BORCHARD, EDWIN. Declaratory judgments. Cleveland, Banks-Baldwin, 1934. 669pp. Roy 8vo. First edition, fine. o. p. $ 30.00

261. BRAXTON, A.CAPERTON. The Fifteenth Amendment, an account of its enactment. Address delivered before Virginia State Bar Association for the year 1903. Lynchburg, Bell, (c. 1903). 78pp. Frontis. d. j. $ 15.00

262. BROWN, ESTHER LUCILE. Laywers, law schools and public service. N. Y., Russell Sage Foundation, 1948. 258pp. Orig. cl., d. j. First ed. $ 22.50

263. BRYSON, WILLIAM HAMILTON. A bibliography of Virginia legal history before 1900. Charlottesville, Univ. of Virginia, 1979. 133pp. New. $ 12.50

264. BURGESS, JOHN W. Recent changes in American constitutional theory. N. Y., Columbia, 1923. 115pp. First ed. $ 10.00

265. BUTLER, CHARLES HENRY. A century at the Bar of the Supreme Court of the United States. Illustrated. N. Y., Putnam's Sons, (1942). 222pp. Author was S. C. Reporter. o. p. $ 15.00

266. BUTZNER, JANE, compiler. Constitutional chaff- rejected suggestions of the Constitutional Convention of 1787, with explanatory argument. From the notes of James Madison of Virginia, Major William Pierce of Georgia, Dr. James McHenry of Maryland, Rufus King of Massachusetts, and the Hon. Robert Yates of New York. N. Y., Columbia, 1941. 197pp. o. p. $ 22.50

267. CAIRNS, HUNTINGTON. Law and the social sciences. Foreword by Roscoe Pound. N. Y., Harcourt, 1935. 279pp. D. j. First edition. Fine. With inscribed presentation from author. $ 15.00

268. CAIRNS, HUNTINGTON. Legal philosophy from Plato to Hegel. Baltimore, Johns Hopkins Press, 1949. 583pp. o. p. $ 27.50

269. GALLAHER, RUTH A. Legal and political status of women in Iowa: an historical account of the rights of women in Iowa from 1838 to 1918. Iowa City, State Historical Society, 1918. 300pp. Cl. Fine. $ 20.00

270. (CANADA). ROYAL COMMISSION ON PATENTS, COPYRIGHT, TRADE MARKS AND INDUSTRIAL DESIGNS. Report on copyright. Ottawa, Cloutier, 1957. 151pp. Orig. prtd. wrps. $ 12.50

271. CARDOZO, BENJAMIN N. Law and literature, and other essays and addresses. N. Y., Harcourt, (1931). 190pp. First ed. Fine. o. p. $ 17.50

272. CARR, SIR CECIL THOMAS. Concerning English administrative law. N. Y., Columbia, 1941. 189pp. $ 15.00

273. CARTER, KEITH. The Texas Court of Criminal Appeals. Austin, n. p., 1932. 104pp. Orig. prtd. wrps. o. p. $ 15.00
* Partly historical.

274. CHAFEE, ZECHARIAH, JR. State House versus Pent House: legal problems of the Rhode Island race-track row. Providence, The Book Shop, (1937). 165pp. wrps. $ 12.50

275. CHAFEE, ZECHARIAH, JR. Three human rights in the Constitution of 1787. Lawrence, Univ. of Kansas Press, 1956. 245pp. Illus., plates. d. j. Auto-presentation from author to M. D. Howe. o. p. $ 22.50

276. CHAMBERLAIN, JOSEPH P., et al. The judicial function in federal administrative agencies. N. Y., The Commonwealth Fund, 1942. 258pp. $ 15.00

277. CHARLES, JOHN FREDERICK. Statutes of limitations at Athens ... Chicago, Univ. of Chicago, 1938. 74pp. Orig. prtd. wrps. $ 12.50

278. CHASE, FREDERIC HATHAWAY. Lemuel Shaw, chief justice of the Supreme Judicial Court of Massachusetts, 1830-1860. Boston, Houghton Mifflin, 1918. 330pp. Frontis. o. p. $ 17.50

279. CLARK, AUBERT J. The movement for international copyright in nineteenth century America ... Wash., D. C., Catholic Univ. of Am. Press, 1960. 215pp. Orig. prtd. wrps. $ 10.00

280. CLARK, TOM C. et al. Prejudice and property: an historic brief against racial covenants. Submitted to the Supreme Court by ... Wash., D. C., Public Affairs Press, (1948). 104pp. $ 12.50

281. COLIN, DAVID H. The law of unemployment insurance in New York. N. Y., New York Univ., 1950. 412pp. 4to. o. p. $ 22.50

282. CORWIN, EDWARD S. Liberty against government: the rise, flowering and decline of a famous juridical concept. Baton Rouge, Louisiana State Univ. Press, 1948. 210pp. First ed. $ 17.50

283. COWLES, WILLARD BUNCE. Treaties and constitutional law, property interferences and due process of law... Wash., D. C., American Council on Public Affairs, (1941). 315pp. Orig. prtd. wrps. $ 15.00

284. CRAWFORD, CLARENCE C. A guide to the study of the history of English law and procedure. With an introduction by John H. Wigmore. Toronto, Carswell, 1923. 83pp. Orig. cl. o. p. $ 22.50

285. DEENER, DAVID R. The United States Attorneys General and international law. The Hague, Hijhoff, 1957. 416pp. o. p. $ 22.50

286. DENMAN, D. R. Origins of ownership: a brief history of land ownership and tenure from earliest times to the modern era. London, Allen, (1959). 190pp. D. j. Fine. o. p. $ 22.50

287. DE QUIROS, C. BERNALDO. Modern theories of criminality. Translated from the Spanish by Alfonso De Salvio, with an introduction by Wm. W. Smithers. Boston, Little, Brown, 1912. 249pp. $ 12.50

288. DEVLIN, PATRICK. The criminal prosecution in England. New Haven. Yale, 1958. 150pp. $ 12.50
* Sherrill Lectures. Author was Justice of the High Court in England.

289. DILLON, JOHN F. A commemorative address on Chief Justice Marshall ... N. Y., 1901. 58pp. Orig. prtd. wrps. Author presentation copy. $ 12.50
* Servies # 1285.

290. DOUGHERTY, J. HAMPDEN. Power of Federal Judiciary over legislation: its origin; the power to set aside laws; boundaries of the power; judicial independence; existing evils and remedies. N. Y., Putnam, 1912. 125pp. o. p. $ 15.00

291. EAGLETON, CLYDE. The responsibility of States in International Law. N. Y., New York Univ. Press, 1928. 291pp. Orig. cl. d. j. Fine. First ed. $ 17.50

292. EDWARDS, GEORGE. Public domain, or government law. San Francisco, (1934). 369pp. o. p. $ 22.50

293. EMERY, LUCILIUS. A. Concerning justice. New Haven, Yale Univ. Press, 1914. 170pp. 12mo. Yale Storrs Lectures. $ 12.50

294. ESS, HENRY N. A treatise on the power of special taxation: a critical analysis of special taxes for local and public improvements, considered with reference to the Constitution, State and Federal, and restrictions therein contained. Kansas City, Pipers-Reed Book Co., 1907. 389pp. $ 27.50

295. EVAN, WILLIAM M., ed. Law and sociology, exploratory essays. With a foreword by Lehan K. Tunks. (N. Y.) Free Press of Glencoe, (1962). 235pp. D. j. First ed. $ 17.50
* Includes essays by Riesman and Parsons.

296. FAIRMAN, CHARLES. Mr. Justice Miller and the Suprme Court, 1862-1890. Cambridge, Harvard, 1939. 456pp. Illus., frontis., plates. $ 15.00

297. FAULKNER, ROBERT KENNETH. The jurisprudence of John Marshall. Princeton, Princeton Univ. Press, 1968. 307pp. d. j. Fine. $ 22.50

298. FIELD, OLIVER P. The effect of an unconstitutional statute. Minneapolis, Univ. of Minnesota, 1935. 355pp. $ 22.50

299. FISHER, H.A.L. Frederick William Maitland ... a biographical sketch. Cambridge, University Press, 1910. 179pp. Frontis. Orig. cl., slight wear to spine. o. p. $ 25.00

300. FOLSOM, CHARLES FOLLEN. Studies of criminal responsibility and limited responsibility. Privately printed, 1909. 153pp. o. p. $ 22.50
* Six important case studies. Author was professor of mental diseases at Harvard.

301. FRANKFURTER, FELIX and JAMES M. LANDIS. The business of the Supreme Court: a study in the Federal Judicial System. N. Y., MacMillan, 1928. 349pp. First ed. $ 22.50

302. FRANKFURTER, FELIX and NATHAN GREENE. The labor injuction. N. Y., MacMillan, 1930. 343pp. First ed. $ 12.50

303. FREUND, ERNST. Administrative powers over persons and property, a comparative survey. Chicago, Univ. of Chicago Press, (1928). 620pp. Orig. cl. $ 15.00

304. FREUND, ERNEST. Legislative regulation a study of the ways and means of written law. N. Y., The Commonwealth Fund, 1932. 458pp. o.p. $ 22.50

305. FRIEDMAN, LAWRENCE M. Contract law in America: a social and economic case study. Madison, Univ. of Wisconsin, 1965. 280pp. $ 12.50

306. FRIEND, WILLIAM L. Anglo-American legal bibliographies: an annotated guide. Wash., GPO, 1944. 166pp. 4to. Cloth. $ 10.00

307. GELLHORN, WALTER, ed. The States and subversion. Ithaca, N. Y., Cornell Univ. Press, 1952. 454pp. Orig. cl. $ 15.00
* Cornell Studies in Civil Liberty.

308. (GEORGIA. SUPREME COURT) A history of the Supreme Court of Georgia. A centennial vol. With an introduction by Alexander A Lawrence. (Macon) Georgia Bar Assoc., 1948. 292pp. Illus., frontis., plates. $ 25.00

309. GLANVILL. De Legibus et Consuetudinibus Regni Angliae. Edited by George E. Woodbine. New Haven, Yale University Press, and London ... 1932. ix, 306pp. Original half cloth; paper label. A very fine copy. First Edition. $ 50.00
* A fine scholarly edition based on first hand study of numerous manuscripts, with an appendix of contemporary cases, and index. Holdsworth, writing in 1928 anticipated with great enthusiasm this edition by Woodbine whom he considered foremost among American scholars in this field. See Historians of Anglo-American Law, p. 113.

310. GOLDFARB, RONALD L. The contempt power. N. Y., Columbia, 1963. 349pp. Fine. $ 15.00

311. GRABER, DORIS APPEL. The development of the law of belligerent occupation, 1863-1914. A historical survey. N. Y., (Columbia Univ.) 1949. 343pp. Orig. prtd. wrps. Fine. *Columbia Studies, whole #543. $ 17.50

312. GRAY, JOHN CHIPMAN. The nature and sources of the law. N. Y., Columbia, 1909. 332pp. Orig. cl. good copy. First ed. $ 25.00
* "Gray was a great lawyer, a great teacher, and, as his book on the Nature ... shows, a great legal philosopher." Holdsworth, Historians ... p. 107f.

313. GRAY, JOHN CHIPMAN. The rule against perpetuities. Third edition. Boston, Little, Brown. 1915. 714pp. cloth. $ 50.00
* Final and best edition in the author's lifetime, with his last substantial revisions. "... the most considerable American contribution to this branch of law ... recognized at once as (being) of authority in England and America ... cited in reported cases over the English speaking world from Manitoba to ... New Zealand." Holdsworth, Historians ... p. 107.

314. GROTIUS, HUGO. The freedom of the seas, or the right which belongs to the Dutch to take part in the East Indian Trade. Translated with a revision of the Latin text of 1633, by Ralph Van Deman Magoffin, Edited with an introductory note by James Brown Scott. N. Y., Oxford Univ. Press, 1916. $ 17.50

315. GUEST, C. W. GRAHAM. The law of valuation in Scotland. Edinburgh, Hodge, 1930. 300pp. Roy. 8vo. Fine. $ 25.00

316. HAINES, CHARLES GROVE, et al. The role of the Supreme Court in American government and politics 1835-1864. Berkeley, Univ. of Calif., (1957). 533pp. First ed. Fine. $ 25.00

317. HART, JAMES. Tenure of office under the constitution: a study in law and public policy. Baltimore, Johns Hopkins, 1930. 384pp. Author presentation to Edw. Corwin. $ 22.50
* Johns Hopkins Studies, extra vols. New Series, No. 9.

318. HENDERSON, GERARD CARL. The position of foreign corporations in American constitutional law: a contribution to the history and theory of juristic persons in Anglo-American Law. Cambridge, Harvard Univ. Press, 1918. 199pp. Orig. cl. o.p. $ 22.50
* Harvard Studies in Jurisprudence Vol. II.

319. HILL, HELEN. George Mason, constitutionalist. Cambridge, Harvard, 1938. 300pp. Illus., frontis., plates. First ed. o.p. $ 27.50

320. HIMES, CHARLES F. Life and times of Judge Thomas Cooper, jurist, scientist, educator, author, publicist. Lectures before the Dickinson School of Law, Carlisle, Pa. Carlisle, Dickinson School of Law, 1918. 70pp. Illus., frontis. cloth. Fine copy. $ 17.50

321. A history of the School of Law, Columbia University, by the Staff of the Foundation for Research in Legal History under the direction of Julius Goebel, Jr. N. Y., Columbia, 1955. 542pp. Illus., frontis., plates. D. j. Fine copy. First edition. o.p. $ 30.00

322. HOGG, FREDERICK DRUMMOND. Parliamentary divorce practice in Canada. Toronto, Canada Law Book, 1925. 135pp. Perf. stamp on title page. $ 22.50

323. HOLLAND, THOMAS ERSKINE. The elements of jurisprudence. Twelfth edition. N. Y., Oxford Univ. Press, 1917. 454pp. $ 25.00
* Holland was the intellectual heir of John Austin.

324. HOROWITZ, JACOB I. Manual of divorce and other matrimonial actions: explaining and illustrating the procedure for the prosecution of matrimonial actions in New York State. N. Y., Central Book Co., 1938. 450pp. $ 15.00

325. HORWILL, HERBERT W. The usages of the American Constitution. Humphrey, Oxford Univ., 1925. 251pp. First ed. $ 15.00

326. HUFFCUT, ERNEST W. The law of agency, including the law of principal and agent and the law of master and servant. Second edition, revised and enlarged. Boston, Little, Brown, 1901. 406pp. $ 22.50

327. HUGHES, WILLIAM T. Datum posts of jurisprudence. Chicago, Usonia, 1907. 250pp. Orig. cl. Unusual compendium of leading cases, cross-referenced. $ 25.00

328. HUSTON, CHARLES ANDREWS. The enforcement of decrees in equity. Cambridge, Harvard, 1915. 189pp. o.p. $ 22.50
* Harvard Studies in Jurisprudence Vol. I.

329. INSTITUTE OF LAW AND OHIO INSTITUTE. Ohio criminal statistics 1931: an experiment in methods and techniques of reporting. Baltimore, Hopkins, 1932. 189pp, wrps. $ 12.50

330. INTERNATIONAL BAR ASSOCIATION. Eleventh Conference ... Lausanne, Switzerland, July 11-15, 1966. Summary of proceedings, official papers and reports ... The Hague, Nijhoff, 1966. 308pp. $ 15.00

331. IRELAND, GORDON, et al. Divorce in the Americas. Buffalo, Dennis, (1947). 306pp. $ 22.50

332. JAMES I. The political works of James I. Reprinted from the edition of 1616, with an introduction by Charles Howard McIlwain. Cambridge, Harvard, 1918. 354pp. 4to. $ 25.00
* Harvard Political Classics, Vol. I. First edition. Fine.

333. JENKS, EDWARD. The book of English law. Boston, Houghton Mifflin, 1929. 460pp. o.p. $ 17.50

334. JUDSON, FREDERICK N. The judiciary and the people. New Haven, Yale Univ. Press, 1913. 270pp. 12mo. Yale Storrs Lectures. $ 15.00

335. KALES, ALBERT M. Unpopular government in the United States. Chicago, Univ. of Chicago, (1914). 263pp. $ 12.50
* Author was Law Professor at Northwestern.

336. KEETON, GEORGE W. The elementary principles of jurisprudence. London, Black, 1930. 324pp. o.p. $ 27.50
* In the acknowledged tradition of Austin & Holland.

337. KEITH, ARTHUR BERRIEDALE. Dominion autonomy in practice. London, Oxford Univ., 1929. 92pp. 12mo. o.p. $ 12.50

338. KELSEN, HANS. Law and peace in international relations: the Oliver Wendell Holmes Lectures, 1940-41. Cambridge, Harvard, 1942. 181pp. Fine. o.p. $ 15.00

339. KENNEDY, W. P. M. Some aspects of the theories and workings of constitutional law. The Fred Morgan Kirby Lectures delivered at Lafayette College, 1931. N. Y., MacMillan, 1932. 142pp. o.p. $ 17.50

340. KILLINGSWORTH, CHARLES C. State labor relations acts: a study of public policy. Chicago, Univ. of Chicago, (1948). 327pp. D. j. o.p. $ 22.50

341. KING, DONALD B. 100 injustices to the child. St. Louis, St. Louis Univ., National Juvenile Law Center, 1970-1971. 120pp. Orig. prtd. wrps. $ 12.50

342. KONKLE, BURTON ALVA. The life of Chief Justice Ellis Lewis 1798-1871, of the First Elective Supreme Court of Pennsylvania. Phila., Campion, 1907. 285pp. Illus., frontis., plates. $ 25.00

343. KONVITZ, MILTON R. The alien and the Asiatic in American law. Ithaca, Cornell, 1946. 299pp. $ 17.50

344. KONVITZ, MILTON R. Civil rights in immigration. Ithaca, Cornell, 1953. 216pp. $ 15.00

345. LADD, WILLIAM. An essay on a Congress of Nations for the adjustment of international disputes without resort to arms. Reprinted from the original edition of 1840 with an introduction by James Brown Scott. N. Y., Oxford, Univ. Press, 1916. (50), 162pp. $ 22.50

346. LAKE, ISAAC BEVERLY. Discrimination by railroads and other public utilities. Raleigh, Edwards, 1947. 346pp. o.p. $ 22.50

347. LEONARD, L. LARRY. International regulation of fisheries. Wash., 1944. 201pp. Orig. prtd. wrps. Fine. $ 17.50

348. LIEF, ALFRED. Brandeis: the personal history of an American ideal. N. Y., Stackpole, 1936. 508pp. Illus., frontis., plates. $ 15.00

349. LINDESMITH, ALFRED R. The addict and the law. Bloomington, Indiana Univ. Press, (1965). 337pp. $ 10.00

350. LINDEY, ALEXANDER. Plagiarism and originality. N. Y., Harper, (1952). First edition. 366pp. $ 12.50

351. LOEB, ISIDOR. The legal property relations of married parties: a study in comparative Legislation. N. Y., Columbia Univ. Press, 1900. 197pp. Wrps. $ 10.00
* Studies in History, (etc.)... Vol. 13, #1.

352. LONG, JOSEPH R. A treatise on the law of domestic relations. St. Paul, Keefe-Davidson, 1905. 455pp. Orig. cl. $ 25.00

353. LONGENECKER, ROLLA R. Some hints on the trial of a lawsuit. Foreword by John Henry Wigmore. Rochester, Lawyers Co-op. Publ. Co., 1927. 314pp. $ 17.50

354. LOUISELL, DAVID W. Modern California discovery: a text on discovery in civil and criminal cases. San Francisco, Berkley Press, 1963. 426pp. o.p. $ 17.50

355. LUCE, ROBERT. Legislative procedure: Parliamentary practices and the course of business in the framing of statutes. Boston, Houghton Mifflin, 1922. 628pp. $ 27.50

356. (McILWAIN, CHARLES HOWARD). Essays in history and political theory in honor of Charles Howard McIlwain. Cambridge, Harvard, 1936. 371pp. Frontis. Fine. First edition. $ 15.00
* English and American constitutional history.

357. McINTYRE, STUART HULL. Legal effect of World War II on treaties of the United States. The Hague, Nijhoff, 1958. 392pp. o.p. $ 22.50

358. MCKEAG, EDWIN C. Mistake in contract: a study in comparative jurisprudence. N. Y., Columbia Univ., 1905. 132pp. Orig. prtd. wrps. $ 15.00

359. (MADISON, JAMES) SCOTT, JAMES BROWN (ed). James Madison's notes of debates in the Federal Convention of 1787 and their relation to a more perfect society of nations. 149pp Illus., frontis. N. Y., Oxford, 1918. $ 17.50

360. MAGUIRE, JOHN MacARTHUR. The lance of justice: a semi-centennial history of the Legal Aid Society, 1876-1926. Cambridge, Harvard, 1928. 305pp. Frontis. 3/4 mor., spine little worn. Signed by the author. o.p. $ 15.00

361. MAINE, SIR HENRY SUMNER. Ancient law: its connection with the early history of society and its relation to modern ideas. With introduction and notes by the Right Hon. Sir Frederick Pollock. New edition. London, Murray, (1930). 440pp. With a new introduction and a few alterations by Pollock. $ 22.50

362. MAITLAND, F. W. The constitutional history of England: a course of lectures delivered by ... Cambridge, University Press, 1919. 548pp. Some occasional light pencilling, still a reasonable copy. $ 22.50

363. MAITLAND, FREDERIC W. and FRANCIS C. MONTAGUE. A sketch of English legal history. Edited with notes and appendices by James F. Colby. N. Y., Putnam's (1915). 229pp. First edition. $ 17.50

364. MARSH, HAROLD, JR. Marital property in conflict of laws. Seattle, Univ. of Washington, (1952). 263pp. $ 10.00

365. MARSHALL, BURKE. Federalism and civil rights. Foreword by Robert F. Kennedy. N. Y., Columbia, 1964. 85pp. Cloth. o.p. $ 12.50

366. MASTERSON, WILLIAM E. Jurisdiction in marginal seas, with special reference to smuggling. N. Y., MacMillan, 1929. 423pp. $ 17.50

367. MATTERN, JOHANNES. Principles of the constitutional jurisprudence of the German National Republic. Baltimore, Johns Hopkins Press, 1928. 682pp. Orig. cl. o.p. $ 27.50

368. MAY, GEOFFREY. Marriage laws and decisions in the United States. A manual. N. Y., Russell Sage, 1929. 477pp. o.p. $ 22.50

369. MAYER, JOSEPH. The regulation of commercialized vice: an analysis of the transition from segregation to repression in the United States. N. Y., Klebold Press, 1922. 55pp. Orig. prtd. wrps. With bibliography. o.p. $ 15.00

370. MAYO, LAWRENCE SHAW. The St. Mary's River, a boundary. (Cambridge) privately printed, 1914. 24pp. Orig. brds. $ 17.50
* Reprints, with comment a 1763 document concerning establishment of the boundary between East Florida and Georgia.

371. MOTT, RODNEY L. Due process of law: a historical and analytical treatise of the principles and methods followed by the courts in the application of the concept of the "Law of the Land." Indianapolis, Bobbs-Merrill, (1926). 702pp. $ 27.50

372. NADELMANN, KURT H., ed., et al. XXth century comparative and conflicts law: legal essays in honor of Hessel E. Yntema. Leyden, Sythoff, 1961. 544pp. Frontis. Fine copy. o.p. $ 27.50
* A fine Festschrift with contributions by Pound, Schlesinger, von Mehren, et al.

373. NEKAM, ALEXANDER. The personality conception of the legal entity. Cambridge, Harvard, 1938. 131pp. $ 17.50
* Harvard Studies, vol. III. First ed. Fine.

374. NEW YORK CITY BAR ASSOC. Impartial medical testimony: a report by a special committee of the ... on the medical expert testimony project. N. Y., MacMillan, 1956. 188pp. D.j. o.p. $ 15.00

375. N.Y. CITY. BAR ASSOCIATION. THE SPECIAL COMMITTE TO STUDY COMMITMENT PROCEDURES. Mental illness and due process: report and recommendations on admission to Mental Hospitals under New York law. Ithaca, Cornell, 1962. 303pp. $ 17.50

376. NEW YORK UNIVERSITY. HENRY SELLIN, ed. Proceedings of the New York University Conference on practice and procedure under the Immigration and Nationality Act, (McCarran-Walter Act) ... N. Y., N. Y. U. Press, (1954). 145pp. o.p. $ 15.00

377. NORTHROP, F.S.C. The complexity of legal and ethical experience: studies in the method of normative subjects. Boston, Little, Brown, (1959). 331pp. 1st ed. $ 17.50

378. ORFIELD, LESTER BERNHARDT. The amending of the Federal Constitution. Foreword by Henry M. Bates. Ann Arbor, Univ. of Michigan Press, 1942. 242pp. $ 15.00

379. OSWALD, JAMES FRANCIS. Oswald's Contemp. of Court: committal, attachment, and arrest upon civil process. With an appendix of forms ... Third edition, English and American edition by George Stuart Robertson... Canadian edition by A. C. Forster Boulton ... London, Butterworth, 1911. 295pp. $ 27.50
* Canadian notes, statutes and cases.

380. PENNOCK, J. ROLAND, ed., et al. Political and legal obligation. N. Y., Atherton Press 1970. 455pp. Orig. cl. $ 12.50
* Yearbook, Am. Soc. for Poltical & Legal Philosophy, No. XII. (Nomos).

381. PENNOCK, J. R. ed. Representation. N. Y., Atherton, 1968. 317pp. $ 12.50
* NOMOS X, Yearbook of the Am. Soc. for Political and Legal Philosophy.

382. PERGLER, CHARLES. Judicial interpretation of international law in the United States. N. Y., MacMillan, 1928. 222pp. o.p. $ 22.50

383. PIERSON, WILLIAM WHATLEY, JR. Texas versus White: a study in legal history. Durham, N. C., Seeman Printery, 1916. 103pp. Orig. prtd. wrps. o.p. $ 15.00

384. POLLOCK, SIR FREDERICK. A first book of jurisprudence for students of the common law. Third edition. London, MacMillan 1911. 369pp. Orig. cl. Fine. $ 17.50

385. POLLOCK, SIR FREDERICK. Jurisprudence and legal essays. Selected and introduced by A. L. Goodhart. London, MacMillan, 1961. 243pp. D.j. Fine. First ed. $ 22.50

386. POUND, ROSCOE. Justice according to law. New Haven, Yale, 1951. 98pp. D.j. Fine. First ed. o.p. $ 12.50

387. POUND, ROSCOE. The spirit of the common law. Francestown, Marshall Jones, (1947). 224pp. $ 12.50

389. RAIT, ROBERT S., ed. Memorials of Albert Venn Dicey: being chiefly letters and diaries. London, MacMillan, 1925. 304pp. Illus., frontis. o.p. $ 20.00

390. RANSONE, COLEMAN B., JR. The office of Governor in the United States. University, Alabama, Univ. of Alabama, 1956. 417pp. o.p. $ 17.50

391. READ, CONYERS, ed. The Constitution reconsidered. Edited for the American Historical Association. Morningside Heights, Columbia, 1938. 424pp. o.p. $ 27.50
* Original papers by Beard, Thorne, McIlwain, et al.

392. READ, HORACE EMERSON. Recognition and enforcement of foreign judgments in the common law units of the British Commonwealth. Cambridge, Harvard, 1938. 371pp. o.p. $ 22.50
* Harvard Studies in the Conflict of Laws, Vol.II.

393. REED, ALFRED ZANTZINGER. Training for the public profession of the law: historical development and principal contemporary problems of legal education in the United States with some account of conditions in England and Canada. N. Y., Carnegie Foundation, 1921. 498pp. Orig. prtd. wrps. $ 22.50

394. REPPY, ALISON. Civil rights in the United States. N. Y., Central Book Co., 1951. 297pp. Cl., d.j. o.p. $ 15.00

395. RICH, BENNETT MILTON. The Presidents and civil disorder. Wash., Brookings Inst., 1941. 235pp. D.j. $ 15.00

396. ROALFE, WILLIAM R. The libraries of the legal profession: A study prepared for the Survey of the Legal Profession, under the auspices of American Bar Association. St. Paul., Minn. West Publ. Co., 1953. 471pp. $ 20.00

397. ROBINTON, MADELINE RUSSELL. An introduction to the papers of the New York Prize Court, 1861-1865. N. Y., Columbia Univ Press 1945. 203pp. Orig. cl., d.j. First ed. Fine. $ 15.00
* Studies in History, Economics and Public Law, Columbia Univ. Number 515.

398. ROBSON, WILLIAM A. Civilisation and the growth of law: a study of the relations between men's ideas about the Universe and the institutions of law and government. N. Y., MacMillan, 1935. 354pp. First ed. $ 17.50

399. ROGERS, JOSEPH W. U. S. national bibliography and the copyright law: an historical study. Foreword by Verner W. Clapp. N. Y., Bowker, 1960. 115pp. o.p. $ 15.00

400. ROSCOE, EDWARD STANLEY. The growth of English law: being studies in the evolution of law and procedure in England. London, Stevens, 1911. 260pp. First ed. v.g. $ 25.00

401. ROSS, ALF. On law and justice. Berkeley, Univ. of Calif. Press., 1959. 383pp. d.j. $ 17.50
* Author was Professor of Law at the University of Copenhagen.

402. ROTHENBERG, STANLEY. Copyright and public performance of music. The Hague, Nijhoff, 1954. 188pp. d.j. o.p. $ 20.00

403. RUNES, DAGOBERT D. The disinherited and the law. N. Y., Philosophical Lib., (1964). 79pp. o.p. $ 12.50

404. RYAN, FRANKLIN W. Usury and usury laws: a juristic-economic study of the effects of state statutory maximums of loan charges upon lending operations in the United States. Boston, Houghton Mifflin, (1924). 249pp. $ 22.50

405. SAYRE, PAUL ed. Interpretations of modern legal philosophies. Essays in honor of Roscoe Pound. Edited with an introduction. N.Y., Oxford Univ. Press, 1947. 807pp. Port. o.p. $ 27.50

406. SCHMIDT, FOLKE. The law of labour relations in Sweden. Cambridge, Harvard, 1962. 343pp. o.p. $ 22.50

407. SCHMIDT, FOLKE and STIG STROMHOLM. Legal values in modern Sweden. Svenska Bokforlaget, Norstedts, (1964). 88pp. Orig. cl. $ 7.50

408. SCOTT, JAMES BROWN. Sovereign States and suits before arbitral tribunals and courts of justice. N. Y., New York Univ. Press, 1925. 360pp. o.p. $ 25.00

409. SCOTT, JAMES BROWN. The status of the International Court of Justice. With an appendix of addresses and official documents. N. Y., Oxford Univ. Press, 1916. 93pp. cloth. o.p. $ 15.00

410. SELDEN SOCIETY. Publications. London. (1887-1972).
Volumes 79, 83, 84, 87-89
Original cloth, all in very good to fine condition. per vol. $ 15.00

411. SHAIN, MARK. Res ipsa loquitur: presumptions and burden of proof. With a foreword by the Hon. Jesse W. Carter, and an introduction by Albert Levitt. Second edition. (Los Angeles, Parker) 1947. 486pp. 4to. Cloth Fine. $ 25.00

412. SHARTEL, BURKE. Our legal system and how it operates: Five lectures delivered at the Univ. of Michigan, Feb. 23, 24, 25, 26, and 27, 1948 on the Thomas M. Cooley Lectureship, enlarged and revised. Ann Arbor, Univ. Mich. Law School, 1951. 629pp. cl. Fine. $ 22.50

413. SIEVEKING, ALFRED. Das deutsche Seerecht (mit Ausschluss des Seeversicherungsrechtes). Ein praktische Lehrbuch. Hamburg, Meissners, 1907. Cl., orig. wrps. bound in 471pp. $ 22.50

414. SIMMS, HENRY H. Life of John Taylor: the story of a brilliant leader in the early Virginia state rights school. Richmond, Va., Byrd, 1932. 234pp. Frontis., orig. cl. o.p. $ 22.50
* Taylor produced one of the most important statements of political theory in the early Republic (his "Inquiry into the principles and policy of the government of the U.S." 1814). Charles Beard considered him one of the greatest American political theorists. See DAB.

415. SIMONTON, THOMAS C. Simonton on the law of checks, notes and banks, including the right of parties in dealing with banks. N. Y., Van Horen, (1906). 176pp. Orig. cl., lea. labels. $ 12.50

416. SMITH, BRUCE. Rural crime control. N. Y., Columbia, 1933. 306pp. D.j. $ 15.00

417. SMITH, FRANKLIN A. Judicial review of legislation in New York, 1906-1938. N. Y. (Columbia Univ. Press) 1952. 250pp. Orig. prtd. wrps. $ 12.50

418. SMITH, JOSEPH HENRY. Appeals to the Privy Council from the American plantations. With an introductory essay by Julius Goebel, Jr. N. Y., Columbia, 1950. 770pp. 1st ed. $ 27.50

419. SPELLING, THOMAS C. and JAMES HAMILTON LEWIS. A treatise on the law governing injunctions. St. Louis, Thomas Law Book Co., 1926. 851pp. cloth. $ 30.00

420. SPRING, SAMUEL. Risks & rights in publishing, television, radio, motion pictures, advertising and the theater. N. Y., Norton (1952). First edition. 385pp. o.p. $ 12.50

421. STEVENS, E. A. Liens and priority and foreclosure of liens. Austin, Von Boeckmann-Jones, 1922. 175pp. $ 37.50
* Wholly on Texas Law

422. STINSON, ALVAH L. Woman under the law. Boston, Hudson, 1914. 406pp. Illus., frontis. cl. Author's inscribed presentation. $ 25.00

423. STONE, JULIUS. Legal system and lawyer's reasonings. Stanford, Stanford Univ., 1964. 454pp. D.j. First ed. Fine. $ 15.00

424. STOREY, MOORFIELD, The reform of legal procedure. New Haven, Yale Univ. Press, 1911. 263pp. 12mo. $ 15.00

425. (TANSILL, CHARLES S. Compiler) Documents illustrative of the formation of the union of the American states. Wash., GPO, 1927. Folio. 1115pp. cl. Fine. A few facsimile illustrations. $ 25.00

426. THOMAS, J. H. Town Government in the sixteenth century, based chiefly on the records of the following provincial towns ... Illustrated. London, Allen (1933). 188pp. D.j. Fine. First edition. $ 12.50

427. THORPE, FRANCIS NEWTON. The Federal and State Constitutions, colonial charters and other organic laws of the states, territories, and colonies ... compiled and edited under the Act of Congress of June 30, 1906. Wash., GPO, 1909. 7 vols., cloth. Complete (Reprinted at 250.00) $100.00

428. TURNER, DONALD F. The scope of "attempt to monopolize." The first Milton Handler Lecture delivered before the Assoc. of the Bar of the City of New York May 15, 1975. With an introduction by Milton Handler. N. Y., 1975. 28pp. Cloth. $ 8.50

429. TURNER, R. W. The equity of redemption: its nature, history and connection with equitable estates generally. Cambridge, University Press, 1931. 198pp. Fine copy. o.p. $ 27.50
* Cambridge Studies in English Legal History

430. (U.S. COPYRIGHT OFFICE). Letter to the Librarian of Congress, concerning certain aspects of the Copyright Act of March 4, 1909, in their relation to the public interest and existing problems of Copyright Office Administration, with proposed amendments. Wash., GPO, 1938. 72pp. Orig. prtd. wrps. 4to. $ 12.50

431. (U. S. COPYRIGHT OFFICE). SOLBERG, THORVALD. Copyright in Congress, 1799-1904: a bibliography, and chronological record of all proceedings in Congress in relation to copyright from April 15, 1789 to April 28, 1904... Wash., GPO, 1905. 468pp. 4to. $ 22.50
* Copyright Office Bulletin No. 8.

432. U. S. INTERSTATE COMMERCE COMMISSION. Annual report 29-30, 36-53, 55-61 (1915 - 1947). per year $ 12.50

****

433. (U.S.) NATIONAL LABOR RELATIONS BOARD. Legislative history of the National Labor Relations Act. 1935. Wash., GPO, 1949. Two vols. clxxxi, 3305pp. Buckram. Definitive and scarce. $ 75.00

434. VANDERBILT, ARTHUR T., ed. Minimum standards of judicial administration: a survey of the extent to which the standards of the American Bar Association for improving the administration of justice have been accepted throughout the country N. Y., New York Univ., 1949. 752pp. o.p. $ 25.00

435. VAN DYNE, FREDERICK. Citizenship of the United States. Rochester, N. Y., Lawyers' co-op. Publ. Co., 1904. 385pp. Full contemp. sheep. First ed. $ 17.50

436. VAN VLECK, WILLIAM C. The administrative control of aliens: a study in administrative law and procedure. N. Y., The Commonwealth Fund, 1932. 260pp. $ 17.50

437. VAN WAGENEN, THEO. F. International mining law. First edition. N. Y., Mc-Graw, Hill, 1918. 342pp. $ 22.50

438. VINOGRADOFF, PAUL. Common-sense in law. N. Y., Holt, n.d. 256pp. 12mo. $ 12.50

439. VOORHEES, HARVEY CORLANDT. The law of arrest in civil and criminal actions. Boston, Boston Book Co., 1904. 198pp. $ 25.00

440. WARREN, CHARLES. History of the Harvard Law School, and of early legal conditions in America. In three vols. Illustrated. N. Y., Lewis, 1908. 543, 560, 397pp. 1/2 mor. Fine. First edition. $ 55.00

441. WEEDEN, WILLIAM B. War government. federal and state in Massachusetts, New York, Pennsylvania and Indiana, 1861-1865. Boston, Houghton, Mifflin, 1906. 389pp. Fine. $ 22.50

442. WENDELL, MITCHELL. Relations between the Federal and State Courts. N. Y., (Columbia Univ), 1949. Orig. prtd. wrps. Fine. $ 17.50
* Columbia Studies, whole #555.

443. WERLINE, ALBERT WARWICK. Problems of church and state in Maryland, during the seventeenth and eighteenth centuries. South Lancaster, College Press, (1948). 236pp. o.p. $ 17.50

444. WEXLEY, JOHN. The judgment of Julius and Ethel Rosenberg. N.Y., Cameron & Kahn, 1955. 672pp. Orig. cl. $ 22.50

445. WHEATON, HENRY. Elements of international law: a literal reproduction of the 1866 edition of Richard Henry Dana, Jr., edited by George Grafton Wilson, with a chronological list of editions and translations of Wheaton's Elements of International Law, a table of cases, and indexes; to which are prefixed a note on Henry Wheaton and International Law, and a sketch of the life of Richard Henry Dana, Jr., by George Grafton Wilson. Oxford, Clarendon Press, 1936. 642pp. Frontis. 4to. $ 35.00
* The Classics of International Law, edited by James Brown Scott. This valuable scholarly edition out-of-print.

446. WHITE, EDW. J. Legal antiquities: a collection of essays upon ancient laws and customs. St. Louis, F. H. Thomas, 1913. 349pp. o.p. $ 30.00

447. WOODBINE, GEORGE E. Four thirteenth century law tracts. New Haven, Yale, 1910. 181pp. Orig. cl. Fine copy. $ 27.50
* First edition. "Pre-eminent among the American lawyers who have elucidated the sources of our law is Professor Woodbine. His little book ... has cleared up the position in our legal literature of certain short tracts of the last years of the 13th century." Holdsworth, Historians of Anglo-American Law, p. 113.

448. WRIGHT, BENJAMIN F. The growth of American constitutional law. N. Y., Reynal, (1942). 276pp. D.j. Hardcover. o.p. $ 15.00

449. WU, C. H. Fountain of justice: a study in the natural law. N. Y., Sheed, 1955. 287pp. $ 12.50

450. ZIEGLER, BENJAMIN MUNN. The international law of John Marshall: a study of first principles. Chapel Hill, Univ. No. Carolina, 1939. 386pp. D. j. Fine. o.p. $ 27.50

ROBERT H. RUBIN BOOKS

Post Office Box 558 · Stoughton, Massachusetts 02072 USA
Cable Address: «RUBOOKS» Telephone: (617) 344-0740

CATALOG FIFTEEN 1981/1982

ANTIQUARIAN AND OUT-OF-PRINT WORKS IN

LAW AND LEGAL HISTORY

(CHIEFLY ANGLO-AMERICAN)

PART I: **Books published before 1900** **items 1-377**
PART II: **Books published 1900 and after** **378-477**

Please see page i for detailed index

Please see page ii for notes on condition, binding, and cited references

We are pleased to issue our fall/winter catalogue of law books. In the first part we continue to emphasize early American legal literature of both general and regional interest, including a number of books which are the first works in their respective fields to appear in America. Throughout the catalogue some well represented subjects are **constitutional law, criminal law** *and* **penology, domestic relations, international law, legal education** *and* **legal reform,** *and* **justice of the peace manuals;** *there is also a good run of first or early editions of works by* **Joseph Story.** *We hope you find it interesting and useful.*

Offers of single items or entire collections, institutional or private, are always welcome.

TELEPHONE ORDERS

Please feel free to phone at any time. If the *unlikely* event that you fail to reach us in the afternoon, please try again before noon, E.S.T.

CABLE ORDERS

It is essential that cable messages be confirmed immediately by letter.

1. ADAMS, THATCHER M. A letter addressed to A. H. Brown, Esq. M.P., on the settlement of land and system of land transfer in the United States. London, Lane, 1872. 51pp. Orig. prtd wrps. $ 45.00

2. ALABAMA. CONSTITUTIONAL CONVENTION, 1875. Journal of the Constitutional Convention of the State of Alabama, assembled in the City of Montgomery, September 6th, 1875. Montgomery, Screws, State Prtr., 1875. 231pp. Orig. 1/4 lea., v. g. $ 50.00

3. The American jurist and law magazine. Volumes 1, 2 and 5. Jan. - Dec. 1829 and Jan. - June 1831. Boston, Freeman (et al.), 1829-31. 8vo's Contemp. 1/4 calf. Full of very interesting material, reviews, essays, bibliographic content, etc. One of the most influential of the early American legal journals. It was published until 1841. $ 45.00

4. AMES, FISHER. The works of ... compiled by a numer of his friends. To which are prefixed notices of his life and character. Boston, Wait, 1809. 519pp. Contemp. 1/4 calf., gilt. A very attractive copy. With portrait. $ 45.00
* First edition of the writings of this arch-conservative.

5. AMOS, SHELDON. The science of law. N. Y., Appleton, 1874. 417pp. Orig. pict. cl. $ 45.00
* "Amos carried on the Bentham-Austin tradition in jurisprudence ... yet Amos outsteps his master by recognizing the existence of international law, to which Austin had denied the title of law 'properly so called' ..." --Encyclopaedia of the Social Sciences. First American edition, same year as the London.

6. ANDERSON, W. C. The substance of four discourses on the Bible in common schools, delivered in the First Presbyterian Church, San Francisco ... San Francisco, Towne & Bacon, 1859. 31p. Orig. prtd. wrps. Opposes separation of church and state, urges restoration of Bible in California schools. Cowan, p. 15. $ 35.00

7. ANGELL, JOSEPH K. A treatise on the common law in relation to watercourses ... second edition with an appendix, containing forms of declarations. Boston, Hilliard, Gray, 1833. xxi, 221, 12, xi pp. Contemp. sheep, wanting label, few light marginal stains, still a good copy. $ 75.00
* Second edition of a classic treatise, first published in 1824, and here revised to take account of the rapid changes in the concept of property rights which were arising from the industrial revolution. See Horwitz, Transformation of American Law, 1977, pp. 38-40. Marvin p. 62, note.

8. ANGELL, JOSEPH K. A treatise on the law of carriers of goods and passengers, by land and by water. Second edition, revised and enlarged. Boston, Little, Brown, 1851. 802pp. Full contemp. sheep, rubbed. $ 50.00

9. ANGELL, JOSEPH K. A treatise on the right of property in tide waters, and in the soil and shores thereof, to which is added an appendix, containing the principal adjudged cases. Boston, Gray, 1826. 246pp. Full contemp. sheep, rubbed, wants label. FIRST EDITION. $ 125.00
* "The only regular treatise upon this branch of law, beside the one under consideration, is Lord Hale's ... Mr. Angell has furnished the profession ... with a work that was much needed. He has collected materials for his book with great industry ... a valuable contribution to our jurisprudence." --Marvin p. 62.

10. ANTHON, JOHN. The law of nisi prius, being cases determined at nisi prius in the Supreme Court of the State of New York, with notes and commentaries on each case, to which is prefixed an introductory essay on the studies preparatory to the active duties of the bar. N. Y., Gould and Banks, 1820. xxxi, 214pp. Contemp. sheep, leather label, top of spine chipped, front joint neatly repaired, a good copy. $ 65.00

11. ARCHBOLD, JOHN FREDERICK. The practice of the Court of King's Bench in personal actions, and ejectment. First American, from the first London edition, with considerable additions and corrections. In two vols. N. Y., Gould, 1823. 344, 319pp. Full contemp. sheep. Lea. labels. $ 65.00
* This work shared with Tidd the leading position in the field of procedure. Holdsworth XIII, 454. Marvin p. 66. First London edition was 1819.

12. ARGOU, (GABRIEL). Institution au droit Francais. Dixieme edition, revue, corrigee & augmentee conformement aux nouvelles ordonnances, par A. G. Boucher d'Argis ... Paris, Desaint, 1771. 2 vols. 12mo. Fold table. Contemp. mottled calf rubbed. $ 85.00
* Henry Wheaton's copy with his signature in both volumes and with a nice early Philadelphia bookseller's ticket (Lewis D. Belair at his European Bookstore, S. W. corner of Sixth and Chestnut streets ...)

13. ASHE, THOMAS. Un perfect table a touts les severall livers del Reportes de Sir Edward Coke ... ouesque un catalogue de touts les cases in larguments de les principall cases la remembre & in le temps le raigne le dit Roigne Elizabeth, & in auter temps ... et ... un brief & alphabeticall collection de touts les ornatiue & memorable texts de Latine, comprise in les dits seuerall liuers ... London, For the Company of Stationers, 1606. 16;148 leaves. Small 8vo. Contemporary unlettered blind calf. An excellent copy. $ 275.00
(Continued)

13. (Continued)
* First edition of Ashe's first abridgment of Coke, with a dedicatory espistle to the latter. A fairly scarce book missed by DNB; Holdsworth cites only a later edition. It consists of a digest with index to cases and subject matter. Ashe specialized in this kind of work and performed similar services for Dyer, Plowden, etc. STC 5525. S&M i, 297. Marvin p. 72. Winfield 180f. Holdsworth V, 374f. The NUC cites four holdings.

14. AUSTIN, BENJAMIN Jr. Constitutional Republicanism in opposition to fallacious Federalism; as published occasionally in the Independent Chronicle... to which is prefixed a prefatory address ... never before published. Boston, Adams & Rhoades, 1803. 327pp. Uncut. Later 1/4 cl. Foxed. Ex-library. $ 75.00
* A work of more than passing interest. It summed up the tone of New England supporters of Jefferson and especially the caustic, almost fanatical quality of Austin's opposition. His verbal attacks on the Federalist lawyer T. O. Selfridge resulted in Austin's son Charles being murdered by Selfridge, and in a subsequent court trial which added to party conflict. Austin also wrote a piece on legal reform in 1786 urging abolition of lawyers and the common law. See DAB.

****

15. BACON, FRANCIS. The works of Francis Bacon ... Lord High Chancellor of England. In three volumes. To which is prefixed, A life of the author by Mr. Mallet. London, A. Millar, 1753. 3 vols. Large thick folios. Engraved frontis. in each vol., titles in red and black. Contemp. panelled calf rubbed but quite sound and still somewhat attractive. Internally quite good. $250.00
* Volume two contains Bacon's Law Tracts including Elements of the Common Laws of England.

16. BADEN-POWELL, B.H. Forest law: a course of lectures on the principles of civil and criminal law and on the law of the forest. (Chiefly based on the laws in force in British India.) Addressed to the forest students at the Royal College of Engineering, Coopers' Hill. London, Bradbury, 1893. 495pp. Orig. cl. $ 37.50

17. BANCROFT, GEORGE. History of the formation of the Constitution of the United States of America. N. Y., Appleton, 1885. In 2 vols. Approx. 1000pp. Orig. cl. $ 45.00

18. BARTON, CHARLES. An historical treatise of a suit in equity: in which is attempted a scientific deduction of the proceedings used on the equity sides of the Courts of Chancery and Exchequer ... and an introductory discourse on the rise and progress of the equitable jurisdiction of those courts. London, W. Clarke, 1796. 22pl. 227, (14)pp. incl. publ. ads. and index. Contemp. calf neatly rebacked. A very good copy of an uncommon title. $135.00
* Marvin p. 97f. Praiseworthy note. Holdsworth XII, 181f. Barton was the author of several later works on conveyancing.

22. BATCHELDER, SAMUEL Jr., A manual of the laws of Massachusetts, in relation to manufacturing corporations. Together with a summary of the laws affecting corporations generally in this Commonwealth, especially those organized for business purposes. Boston, Little, Brown, 1868. 268pp. Orig. cl. $ 27.50

23. BATEMAN, J. The General Highway Act, 5 & 6 W. IV. c. 50, with notes and an index, also practical forms ... London, Maxwell (and) Sweet, 1835. Frontis and 1 plate. 132pp. 1/2 calf, rubbed. 12mo. $ 45.00
* First edition of this critical consolidation and revision of legislation, reflecting improved systems of road making. The introduction contains a brief history of English road legislation from Edw. III to the present. Marvin p. 99. S & M II, 22.

24. BAYLEY, JOHN. Summary of the law of bills of exchange, cash bills, and promissory notes. From the fourth London edition, revised by the author. With notes and references to American decisions, by Willard Phillips and Samuel Seqall. Boston, Harrison Gray, 1826. 426pp. Full contemp. sheep. $ 65.00
* First American edition with a wealth of American material. Marvin p. 101, a very laudatory note. "The best book upon bills of exchange." -- Holdsworth XII, 389f.

25. BAYLEY, SIR JOHN. Summary of the law of bills of exchange, cash bills, and promissory notes. Second American from the fifth London edition, edited by Francis Bayley, ... with notes and references to American and recent English decisions, by Willard Phillips and Samuel E. Sewall. Boston, Hilliard, 1836. 651pp. Full contemp. sheep. Nice copy. $ 45.00
* Marvin p. 101, a long, laudatory note. Cited as the best work on this topic by Holdsworth, XII, 389f.

26. BEACH, CHARLES FISK. Company law: commentaries on the law of private corporations whether with or without capital stock, also of joint-stock companies and of all the various voluntary unincorporated associations organized for pecuniary profit or mutual benefit. In two vols. Chicago, Flood, 1891. 1487pp. Orig. cl. First edition. $ 50.00

27. BEACH, CHARLES FISK, Jr. The modern law of railways, as determined by the courts and statutes of England and the United States. In two vols. San Francisco, Bancroft-Whitney, 1890. 1544pp. Orig. cl. 12mo. First edition. $ 40.00

28. BEADLE, DELOS W. The American lawyer and business man's form book; containing forms and instructions for (numerous categories) together with the laws of the various states on (numerous topics) and a map and seal for each state in the
28. (Continued) union. N. Y., Phelps, Fanning, 1852. 359pp. New cl. $ 37.50
* Contains recent states such as Texas and California, as well as the southern states.

29. BEALE, JOSEPH HENRY Jr., A treatise on criminal pleading and practice. Boston, Little, Brown, 1899. 400pp. Contemp. sheep, rubbed but sound. First edition. $ 35.00

30. BEAUMONT, (GUSTAVE) DE and (ALEXIS) DE TOQUEVILLE (sic). On the penitentiary system in the United States, and its application in France; with an appendix on penal colonies ... translated from the French, with an introduction, notes and additions by Francis Lieber. Phila., Carey, Lea & Blanchard, 1833. xlvii, 301, (2-ads) pp. Original publ. boards, cl. spine, printed paper label, extremities lightly worn, label rubbed. Light foxing. Entirely uncut and a very good copy in original condition. $200.00
* First edition in English from the French of the same year. Probably the singlemost influential work in the spread of American prison reforms to Europe. Central to this effort was the Pennsylvania system of "separate confinement" of which Lieber was a principle advocate. By the 1840's it had become a major factor in England and Europe. Lieber's speedy translation was no mere exercise, for the system had its opponents in the United States, and this work by two French visitors was ideal domestic propaganda. A good copy of an American penological classic. Monaghan 166.

31. BEMIS, GEORGE. American neutrality: its honorable past, its expedient future. A protest against the proposed repeal of the neutrality laws, and a plea for their improvement and consolidation. Boston, Little Brown, 1866. vi, 211pp. Orig. prtd. wrps. $100.00
* A choice association copy inscribed: "Hon. Schuyler Colfax (-) Speaker with the regards of George Bemis." Colfax was at this time Speaker of the U.S. House and later became Vice President. Bemis's writings on international law "were distinguished for their uniformly high level of thought." --DAB. Of particular interest in this work is a long section devoted to the Fenian movement against Canada. There is also much on the Monroe Doctrine and filibustering in Latin America. A nice copy.

32. BENNETT, EDMUND H. Farm law: a treatise on the legal rights and liabilities of farmers ... adapted to the statutes of all the states. Portland, (Maine) Hoyt, (1880). 120pp. Orig. cl. 12mo. $ 22.50

33. BENTHAM, JEREMY. Benthamania: or, select extracts from the works of Jeremy Bentham with an outline of his opinions on the principle subjects discussed in his works. Edited by John Hill Burton. Phila., Lea & Blanchard, 1844. Later cloth. Old stain to lower margin of preliminary leaves, else a good copy. First American edition. $ 45.00

34. BENTHAM, JEREMY. Plan of Parliamentary reform in the form of a catechism, with the reasons for each article, with an introduction shewing the necessity of radical, and the inadequacy of moderate reform. London, Printed for R. Hunter, 1817. 8vo. iv, cccxxxvii, 52, 16, (1)pp including final leaf of publisher's ads. Early 19th century straight-grained binder's cloth and leather label. A very nice copy. $750.00
* FIRST EDITION. "Bentham signalized his conversion to the creed of the radical reformers by writing in 1809 a book called Plan of Parliamentary Reforms ... Bentham maintained the thesis that the only remedy for the evils that were afflicting the country was a reform of Parliament which would ensure 'democratical ascendancy.' He maintained that the experience of the United States, the constitution of which he considered to be almost perfect, showed that an entirely democratic constitution was by far the best ... 'Talk of balance,' he said, 'never will it do: leave that to Mother Goose and Mother Blackstone.' " -- Holdsworth, Hist. of English Law, XIII, 104. Cobbett refused to publish the original Catechism of 1809 in his Political Register, so it first appeared here with an introduction six times its length! This 1817 edition is apparently quite uncommon, the second edition of 1818 being the one usually found.

35. BENTHAM, JEREMY. Principles of legislation: from the Ms. of Jeremy Bentham ... by M. Dumont ... translated ... with notes and a biographical notice of Jeremy Bentham and of M. Dumont. By John Neal. Boston, Wells and Lilly, 1830. 310pp. Large 8vo. Engraved frontis portrait ofBentham, with original brown publisher's cloth, red leather label. Quite a good copy. $200.00
* An attractive Bentham piece on several counts. This is the first publication in English of the work, which appeared in French editions in 1802 and 1820. Moreover it marks only the second publication in America of a work by Bentham (the first being his Defense of Usury, Phila., 1796) and the first of a work about him. Neal's biographical and critical chapters occupy more than half the book and were written from sheer enthusiasm for Bentham, with whom Neal resided for a time, and a strong committment to utilitarianism. The portrait was done from life, under Neal's supervision, by Robert M. Sully of Virginia, nephew of Thomas Sully. A nicely preserved copy of this book which turns up infrequently and usually in shabby condition.

36. BENTHAM, JEREMY. The rationale of reward. London, John and H. L. Hunt, 1825. viii, errata, 353pp. Original publisher's boards, cloth spine and printed paper label, light wear along edges, old paper shelf-label at foot of spine, old institutional stamp on title and following leaf, light marginal foxing. In all a good copy, uncut in the original binding. $250.00

36. (Continued)
* First published in French as the second volume of Bentham's Theorie des peines et des recompenses edited by Dumont. This first separate English edition makes use of the latter, but in addition uses the original mss., both in French and English, from which Dumont worked. There is a prefatory note by Bentham himself in this edition.

37. BEVER, THOMAS. A discourse on the study of jurisprudence and the civil law; being an introduction to a course of lectures. By ... Fellow of All Souls College; and an advocate of the Court of Arches. Oxford, Clarendon Press, 1766. 2pl., 43pp. Neatly removed. Large 4to. A fine copy. $150.00
* One of a handful of original English works on Roman law in this period. The lectures, to which this discourse served as introduction, were given at Oxford by Bever, acting as regius professor, in 1762. Holdsworth XII, 644f. Marvin p. 116. S&M i, 611.

38. BIERLY, WILLIS R. The rights and duties of county and township officers. Williamsport, Pa., 1879. 298pp. Full contemp. sheep. Very uncommon. $ 45.00

39. BIGELOW, MELVILLE M. A treatise on the law of estoppel and its application in practice. Second edition. Boston, Little, Brown, 1876. 603pp. New cloth. $ 37.50

40. BISHOP, JOEL PRENTISS. Commentaries on the non-contract law, and especially as to common affairs not of contract, or the every-day rights and torts. Chicago, Flood, 1889. 818pp. Orig. cl. First edition. $ 30.00

41. BISHOP, JOEL PRENTISS. The first book of the law; explaining the nature, sources, books, and practical applications of legal science, and methods of study and practice. Boston, Little, Brown, 1868. 608pp. Orig. cl. Slt. wear to crown of spine. $ 65.00
* Contains a wealth of bibliographical information; a work of high quality by the author of greatly esteemed treatises on criminal law and marriage and divorce. William L. Friend, Anglo-American Legal Bibliographies, 1944, p. 23 and #29: "Chapters 12 to 16 are devoted to ... reports, treatises or commentaries, digests, abridgements, selections of cases and other works not included in the above ..." First edition. A very good copy.

42. BISSET, ANDREW. A practical treatise on the law of partnership, including the law relating to joint-stock companies: with an appendix of precedents, forms and statutes. With notes of American cases. Harrisburg, M'Kinley, 1847. 460pp. New cl. $ 45.00
* First American, same year as the first London edition.

43. (BLACK, CHAUNCY F. ed.) Some account of the work of Stephen J. Field as a legislator, state judge, and judge of the Supreme Court of the United States. With an introductory sketch by John Norton Pomeroy ... 1881. 63;464pp. Orig. publ. cl. faded. $200.00
* A choice presentation copy from Field: "Chester Averill Esq. with regards from his uncle Stephen J. Field, Washington D. C. March 8-1895." First edition of an uncommon book celebrating Field's career and made up of contributions by "political and personal friends of Judge Field ... and by members of the California Bar" -- editor's preface. It was apparently privately published and intended in part to influence opinion favorable to Field in California, where his decisions on the Chinese question caused him difficulties, and elsewhere during a time when his name was mentioned for the Democratic presidential nomination. The work is copyrighted 1882 and was probably printed in N. Y. Howes B-485. Cowan p. 209. A good copy of a scarce book and a nice association.

44. (BLACK, CHAUNCY F. ed.) Some account of the work of Stephen J. Field as a legislator, state judge, and judge of the Supreme Court of the United States. With an introductory sketch by John Norton Pomeroy ... 1881. 63;464pp. Orig. publ. cl. faded. Preliminary blank excised. A very good copy. $125.00
* Please refer to the previous note.

45. BLACK, JEREMIAH S. Essays and speeches ... with a biographical sketch by Chauncey F. Black. N. Y., Appleton, 1885. Illus., frontis. 621pp. Orig. cl. $ 30.00
* Best single source on the man who was Buchanan's Attorney General and played a central role in the dispute over California land titles and later in the Habeas Corpus cases of the Civil War. -- See DAB.

46. BLACKSTONE, WILLIAM. Commentaries on the laws of England, In four books. The sixth edition. Printed page for page with the last Oxford edition. Dublin, John Colles, 1775. 4 vols. 12mo. Contemp. polished calf, spines gilt, raised bands, leather labels, joints a little rubbed and upper joints on two volumes with old slight splits; labels a bit rubbed. Overall a well preserved and attractive set in unrestored contemporary state. With the folding tables in volume two. S & M., I, 27. $350.00

47. BLACKSTONE, WILLIAM. Commentaries on the laws of England ... together with copious ... notes by Thomas M. Cooley. Fourth edition by James Dewitt Andrews. Chicago, Callaghan, 1899. 2 vols. New cl. $ 47.50

48. BLACKWELL, ROBERT S. A practical treatise on the power to sell land for the non-payment of taxes, embracing the decisions of the Federal Courts, and of the Supreme Judicial Tribunals of the several states and territories. Fourth edition, revised and enlarged. Boston, Little, Brown, 1875. 761pp. Full contemp. sheep. Wanting label. $ 45.00

49. BOISOT, LOUIS Jr. The law of by-laws of private corporations. Chicago, U. S. Corporation Bureau, 1892. 129pp. Full contemp. sheep. Fine. $ 27.50

50. BOISOT, LOUIS Jr. A treatise on mechanics' liens. St. Paul, West Publ., 1897. 969pp. Full contemp. sheep. $ 27.50

51. BOLSTER, W. W. A practical treatise upon the authority and duty of towns and town officers in town business, ... adapted to the statutes and laws of Maine. Portland, Dresser, 1880. 444pp. Full contemp. sheep. First edition. $ 22.50

52. BORGEAUD, CHARLES. Adoption and amendment of constitutions in Europe and America. Translated by Charles D. Hazen. With an introduction by John M. Vincent. N. Y., MacMillan, 1895. 353pp. Orig. cl. Lib. stamp. $ 25.00

53. BOUCHAUD, (MATHIEU ANTOINE) Theorie des traites de commerce entre les nations. Paris, La Veuve Duchesne, 1777. 12mo. 8pl., 538, (1)pp. Half-title present. Contemp. mottled calf gilt, slight rubbing. A very good copy. $200.00
* First edition. Kress B 13. I.N.E.D. 686. Not in Sabin though there is brief mentionof the slave trade. Deals mainly with maritime commerce.

54. BOUTMY, EMILE. The English Constitution. Translated by Isabel M. Eaden, with an introduction by Sir Frederick Pollock, Bart. London, MacMillan, 1891. 212, 55pp. Orig. cl. $ 27.50

55. BOUTMY, EMILE. Studies in Constitutional law: France-England-United States. Translated from the second French edition by E. M. Dicey, with an introduction by A. V. Dicey. London, MacMillan, 1891. 175, 55pp. Origl. cl. Neat pencil underlining. $ 27.50

56. (BOWDITCH, NATHANIEL INGERSOLL) Wharf property or the law of flats; being remarks before the judiciary committee of the Senate of Massachusetts, April 14, 1852. Boston, Wilson, 1852. 40p. Orig. prtd. wrps. Diagrams. $ 35.00
* A very learned discussion in opposition to redistribution of tidal property through a series of legal adjudications. (p. 6).

57. BRADBY, JAMES. A treatise on the law of distresses. First American edition, from the London edition of 1808. N. Y., Riley, 1808. 323pp. New cl. $ 55.00
* A scarce work. There is no copy of the London edition of the same year in the NUC.

58. BROWN, DAVID PAUL. The Forum; or, forty years full practice at the Philadelphia Bar. Phila., Robert Small, 1856. 2 volumes. Stout 8vo's. 588;521pp. Orig. publ. cl. A very good set. $ 50.00
* Chief source forthe professional life and surroundings of this very prominent lawyer; he was a student of William Rawle, associate of the leaders of the Phila. Bar, and practitioner in both U. S. and State courts. Appended to the first volume are 8 pages of facsimile aut ographs of Phila. lawyers and judges. See DAB for a lengthy account.

59. BROWN, JAMES BALDWIN. An historical account of the laws enacted against the Catholics both in England and Ireland ... to which is added a short account of the laws for the punishment of heresy in general; a brief review of the merits of the Catholic Question ... London, Underwood, & Blacks, 1813. xv, 366, 180pp. 8vo. Contemp. 1/4 mor. A good copy. $100.00
* A sympathetic and extremely well-documented account. Brown practised law and held a judgeship. His son was an important non-conformist writer. See DNB for both.

60. BRYCE, JAMES. The American Commonwealth. Second edition, revised. In two vols. London, MacMillan, 1891. 724, 764pp. Orig. cl. $ 25.00

61. BULLER, FRANCIS. An introduction to the law relative to trials at Nisi Prius, containing additions to the present time, carefully corrected from the last London copy, by a Gentleman of the Bar. N. Y., J. Riley, 1806. 336pp. plus index. Contemp. sheep. $ 65.00
* First American edition. A standard book, originating in 1760 as the work of Henry Bathurst, subsequently edited and taken over in name by his nephew, Buller. "It is a good deal more than a book of practice."--Holdsworth XII, 354. Marvin p. 158.

62. BUMP, ORLANDO F. Law and practice in bankruptcy. The practice in bankruptcy, with the bankrupt law of the United States as amended, ... Fifth edition. N. Y., Baker, 1872. xxii, 740pp. New cloth. $ 37.50

****

63. CAIN, JOHN. The officer's guide and farmer's manual containing a comprehensive collection of judicial and business forms adapted to the jurisprudence of Indiana ... Indianapolis, Douglass & Maguire, 1832. 347pp. Contemp. polished calf, leather label. Some light wear and foxing, still a very good copy. $125.00
* First edition of a very scarce Indiana manual. Not in Marvin. American Imprints, 1832, #11613 locates 5 copies of which 3 are in Indiana. A still attractive copy of a perishable book

64. (CANADA. NEW BRUNSWICK. LAWS, STATUTES.) The consolidated statutes of New Brunswick. Fredericton, Fenety, 1877. 1187pp. Contemp. 1/2 calf. Very good. $ 55.00

65. CARTER, A.G.W. (JUDGE). The old court house: reminiscences and anecdotes of the courts and bar of Cincinnati. Cincinnati, Thompson, 1880. Illus., frontis., plates. 466pp. Orig. pict. cl. $ 27.50

66. CHASE, HORACE. The New-Hampshire Probate Directory: ... adapted to the revised statutes and acts since passed, including June session, 1854. ... Second edition. Concord, Lyon, 1854. 342pp. Full contemp. sheep, rubbed. $ 27.50
* Marvin p. 188.

67. CHEEVER, GEORGE B. The Republic or the Oligarchy? Which? An appeal against the proposed transfer of the right to vote from the people to the State. N. Y., Am. News Co., 1866. 36pp. Orig. prtd. wrps. $ 30.00
* A strong attack on section 2 of the 14thammendment to the Constitution.

68. CHITTY, J. Supplement to a treatise on pleading, containing a copious collection of practical precedents of pleadings and proceedings in personal, real, and mixed actions. With American precedents. Phila., Riley, 1818. xxiv, 728pp. New cloth. $ 45.00
* Shaw-Shoemaker 43608. First American edition.

69. CHITTY, JOSEPH. A treatise on the game laws and on fisheries; with an appendix containing all the statutes and a copious collection of precedents ... the second edition, greatly improved, with all the new enactments and decisions. London, Samuel Brooke, 1826. Roy. 8vo. xx, 878pp. Contemp. polished calf, spine gilt with ornaments, borders gilt, front joint worn, a very nice copy. $125.00
* Final and best edition. Marvin p. 193. S & M, II. Holdsworth, Vol. XIII, p. 489. A comprehensive and desireable work. Scarce.

70. CLARKE, FRANCIS G. The American ship-master's guide and commercial assistant, being an enlargement of the Seaman's Manual; containing a variety of matter useful to all those who are engaged in commerce ... together with an analysis of the law of ships and shipping, and of the law of marine insurance ... second edition. Boston, Allen & Co., 1838. Large 8vo. 376pp. Fold. plate and separate title page illustrated with woodcut vignette. Contemp. tree calf, leather label; a well-preserved and attractive copy. $125.00
* An interesting book from the point of view of marine law. In addition to the usual technical material it contains an original digest, actually
(Continued)
a small treatise, on marine law and insurance, occupying a third of the book, prepared by James Dean Hopkins, a Portland lawyer. We handled some time ago a fine full-scale manuscript treatise on this subject written between 1809 and 1839 by Hopkins, complete with revisions - it was never published. It would have made a fine sequel to Willard Phillips' treatise of 1823, the first major American work on the subject. This appears to be the only printed version of Hopkins' careful scholarship and is fully recognized in Clarke's preface and in the testimonial of Simon Greenleaf. The book is copyrighted 1837.

71. The clerk's instructor in the ecclesiastical courts: consisting of a variety of the best precedents in English, now made use of in the practice of the civil law ... By a Gentleman of Doctors Commons. Dublin, Sarah Cotter, 1766. 343, (14)pp. 12mo. Contemp. calf rubbed, front joint cracked. $ 90.00
* This appears to be the only edition beyond the first of 1740, of which the NUC cites only the Library of Congress; it cites no holding of this edition. Holdsworth XII, 618. S & M I, 84.

72. COCKER, EDWARD. The young clerk's tutor enlarged: being a most useful collection of the best presidents ... the fourteenth edition. London, Battersby ... 1700. 8pl., 208, (8)pp. Sm. 8vo. Contemp. plain calf. Fore-edge of text on two leaves just touched in trimming without affecting intelligibility. Actually a nicely preserved copy of a perishable little book. Half-title present, with the final 4 leaves of court-hand facsimiles. $125.00
* Described by Holdsworth as a "very successful book, devoted to the conveyancing rather than to the pleading side of the clerk's work." --VI, 602f. First edition was 1660. Wing C-4862c. S & M I, 480.

73. COKE, (EDWARD). Le reading del mon Seignior Coke sur lestatute de 27 E. I. appelle Lestatute de Finibus Levitas. London, T. R. for G. Lee (etc) 1662. Small 4to. (4), 46pp. plus final original blank. Later wraps. A very good copy. $250.00
* A scarce Coke piece. The NUC cites only the LC and Harvard copies. Wing C-4943. S & M I, 489. First edition.

74. COOKE, WILLIAM. The bankrupt laws ... The seventh edition, with alterations and additions, including the Author's more recent notes, and the cases down to the present period. By George Roots. In two vols. London, printed for William Reed, 1817. 649, 300pp. New cl. $ 50.00
* Marvin p. 226: "The most complete of the early works on bankrupt law."

75. COOPER, THOMAS. A treatise on the law of libel and the liberty of the press; showing the origin, use, and abuse of the law of libel: with copious notes and references to authorities in Great Britain and the United States ... N. Y.,
75. (Continued) G. F. Hopkins, 1830. 184pp. Contemp. 1/4 calf, marbled boards. Old bookplate inside front cover. An excellent copy. $200.00
* FIRST EDITION. One of the outstanding early American works on free speech. "His legal researches led him to protest against the common law doctrine of libel..."—McCoy C558. It is interesting to note that Cooper was himself a victim of the Alien and Sedition Law in 1800. An uncommon book, especially welcome in nice condition. Missed by Marvin and strangely absent from the long account on Cooper in the DAB.

76. COTTU, (CHARLES). De l'administration de la justice criminelle en Angleterre et de l'esprit du gouvernement anglais. Paris, Nicolle, 1820. xii, 317, (2)pp. Calf rebacked in cloth. $ 50.00
First edition of an influential work. There were two further editions in French, as well as English and Spanish translations. The NUC citesonly the Harvard copy of this edition. The author visited England and upon his return to France founded the Societe de l'amelioration des prisons. (Nouv. Biogr. Gen.).

77. COWEN, ESEK. Reports of cases argued and determined in the Supreme Court, and in the Court for the Trial of Impeachments and the Correction of Errors, of the State of New-York. Albany, Gould, 1824, 1825. Approx. 3244pp. Full contemp. sheep. $ 40.00
First four of nine volumes. These cover May 1823 - July 1825. Wallace p. 580.

78. COWEN, ESEK. A treatise on the civil jurisdiction of justices of the peace in the State of New-York. Second edition revised by Sidney J. Cowen. In two vols. Albany, Gould, 1841. Portrait. 1251pp. Contemp. sheep, rubbed. 2 volumes. $ 65.00
* "No law book, local in its character, enjoys a better or more widely extended reputation ... Since its first publication it has been a favorite work ... it is found to be very well adapted to the wants of justices in several of the new states... --Marvin p. 234f. With a nice engraved frontis portrait.

79. COX, JOSEPH MASON. Practical observations on insanity: in which some suggestions are offered towards an improved mode of treating diseases of the mind, and some rules proposed which it is hoped may lead to amore humane and successful method of cure. To which are subjoined Remarks on medical jurisprudence as connected with diseased intellect. From the second corrected and enlarged London edition. Phila., Dobson, 1811. 238pp. Contemp. tree sheep, leather label, front cover detached but present, aside from this a very good copy. In an attractive cloth folding box. $250.00
* First American edition. This is the second psychiatric treatise published in the United States and, as far as we can determine, it is the first American publication to feature the subject of
79. (Continued) medical jurisprudence of insanity - that topic is dealt with in an appendix divided into sections on certification and jurisprudence proper; in fact, the first London edition of 1804 was the first treatise on insanity which carried this topic on the title page. Cox was the first writer on insanity who studied medicine in order to specialize in mental disease. Tuke called this "the best medical treatise of the day on insanity." (Chapters on the history of the insane ... 1882.) Hunter & MacAlpine, 594ff. Austin 551. Shaw-Shoemaker 22633.

80. CROSS, JOHN. A treatise on the law of lien, and stoppage in transitu. Phila., 1841. (WITH:) EDEN, ROBERT HENLEY. A practical treatise on the bankrupt law as amended by the new act of the 6 Geo. IV c. 16 with an appendix of precedents. From the last London edition. 269pp. Phila., Littell, 1841. New cl. $ 45.00
* First American editions of both works. (London eds. 1840 and 1825 respectively.)

81. CROSWELL, SIMON G. A treatise on the law relating to electricity. Boston, Little, Brown, 1895. 765pp. Full contemp. sheep. $ 45.00
* First edition and according to the author, the first really comprehensive treatment of the subject.

82. CRUISE, WILLIAM. An essay on uses. Dublin, prtd. for Exshaw, Byrne ..., 1796. 208pp. Contemp. sheep. A very good copy. $ 65.00
* An historical work on the early origins of conveyancing. Its substance found its way into his later digest on real property. London edition was 1795. Marvin p. 244f.

83. CUNNINGHAM, FRANCIS. Notes recueillies en visitant les prisons de la Suisse et remarques sur les moyens de les ameliorer, avec quelques details sur les prisons de Chambery et de Turin ... suivies de la description des prisons ameliorees de Gand, Philadelphie, Bury, Ilchester et Millbank, et d'un rapport sur le Comite des Dames a New Gate par T. F. Buxton. Geneve et Paris, Paschoud, 1820. lxviii, 87pp. Orig. pale blue wrappers. Uncut. A fine copy. $100.00
* First and only edition. Not a translation. The proceeds from its sale were to benefit the Women's Committee of Newgate. The author was Vicar of Lowestoft. An excellent copy of an uncommon early piece on prison reform. The NUC cites 3 holdings.

84. CURTIS, BENJAMIN ROBBINS. Jurisdiction, practice andpeculiar jurisprudence of the Courts of the United States. Edited, with notes, by George Ticknor Curtis and Benjamin R. Curtis. Boston, Little, Brown, 1880. 298pp. Orig. cl. $ 30.00
* First and posthumous edition of lectures delivered by the elder Curtis at Harvard 1872-73.

85. CURTIS, GEORGE T. The American conveyancer: containing a large variety of legal forms and instruments in use throughout the United States. Together with forms and directions for applicants under the patent laws of the United States. Second edition, revised, corrected, and enlarged, with an appendix of useful tables. Boston, Little, Brown, 1871. 351pp. Full contemp. sheep. $ 35.00

86. CURTIS, GEORGE TICKNOR. The inventor's manual of legal principles, and guide to the patent office. Boston, Phillips, 1851. 328pp. Original cl., little chipped. $ 37.50
* First edition, abridged from the author's Treatise on the Law of Patents, 1849.

87. CURTIS, GEORGE TICKNOR. A treatise on the rights and duties of merchant seamen, according to the general maritime law, and the statutes of the United States. Boston, Little, 1841. 456pp. New cl. $ 75.00
* First edition. Apparently thefirst original American work on the subject, hitherto served in America by Abbott's English treatise. "This work was highly esteemed by ... Story, and has the reputation of a carefully written and well digested volume .... It forms a suitable and necessary accompaniment to Abbott ..."--Marvin p. 248.

88. CUSHING, LUTHER STEARNS. Lex Parliamentaria Americana. Elements of the law and practice of legislative assemblies in the United States of America. Ninth edition. Boston, Little, Brown, 1874. 1063pp. Orig. sheep, leather labels. Good copy. $ 35.00

89. CUSHING, L.S. A practical treatise on the trustee process, or foreign attachment, of the laws of Massachusetts and Maine; with an appendix containing the statutes of Massachusetts, Connecticut, Rhode Island, New Hampshire, Vermont, and Maine, on that subject. Cambridge, Brown, 1833. 211pp. New cl. $ 65.00
* Marvin p. 248, a praiseful note. This is Cushing's first book, so it would appear from scanning the NUC, and is quite uncommon. He is, of course, best known for his classic works on legislative procedure.

****

90. DAKOTA (TERRITORY). LAWS, STATUTES. The revised codes of the Territory of Dakota ... By authority of the Legislative Assembly. Yankton, Bowen & Kingsbury, 1880. xliii, 946pp. Roy. 8vo. Contemp. sheep, labels, joints cracked, edges worn. Internally very good, with the embossed stamp of the District Court of Griggs County, Dakota Territory and the ownership inscription of E. K. Smart, justice of the peace for the county with a few annotations in his hand. $150.00
* Includes the political, civil, probate, justice's and penal codes, and codes of civil and criminal
(Continued)

90. (Continued) procedure, with a brief history of each in the preface, indicating borrowings from New York law as well as borrowings by California. Second edition, first published in 1877.

91. (DALHOUSIE UNIVERSITY LAW SCHOOL) ARCHIBALD, A. G. and WELDON, R. C. The inaugural addresses, & c. delivered at the opening of the law school in connection with Dalhousie University ... 1883. Halifax, Nova Scotia Printing Company, 1884. 62pp. Libr. stamp on title page. Wanting front wrapper. A good copy. Contains also a description of the library and a pitch for support. $ 27.50

92. DANIEL, JOHN W. A treatise on the law of negotiable instruments ... In two vols. Second edition. N. Y., Baker, 1879. 771, 841pp. Full contemp. sheep. SOLD
* A very much expanded edition.

93. DAVIS, DANIEL. A practical treatise upon the authority and duty of justices of the peace in criminal prosecutions. Third edition, revised and greatly enlarged by F. F. Heard. Boston, Little, Brown, 1853. 753pp. Full contemp. sheep. Very substantially altered beyond the first two editions, according to the preface. $ 45.00

94. DELAWARE. LAWS, STATUTES. Laws of the State of Delaware, to the year of our Lord one thousand eight hundred and twenty nine inclusive: to which are prefixed the Declaration of Independence and Constitution of the United States. Revised edition. Arranged and published under the authority of General Assembly. Wilmington, Prtd. by Porter, 1829. 760pp. Contemp. sheep, good copy. $ 85.00
* A landmark consolidation and revision of Delaware law, performed between 1824 and 1829 by Willard Hall, judge of U.S. District Court of Delaware 1823-1871. See DAB.

95. (DELAWARE. LAWS, STATUTES). Revised statutes of the State of Delaware, to the year of our Lord one thousand eight hundred and fifty-two inclusive; to which are added, the Constitution of the United States and of this State: the Declaration of Independence: and an appendix; &c. &c. Published by Authority of the General Assembly. Dover, Kimmey, Prtr., 1852. 574pp. Full contemp. sheep, rubbed. $ 60.00

96. DEVEREUX, JOHN C. The most material parts of Blackstone's Commentaries, reduced to questions and answers, upon the plan and in place of Kinne's Blackstone. New edition. N. Y., Baker, 1868. 392pp. Full contemp. sheep. $ 35.00

97. DEVEREUX, JOHN C. The most material parts of Kent's Commentaries reduced to questions and answers. New edition. N. Y., Baker, Voorhis, 1873. viii, 418pp. New cl. $ 35.00

98. DICKINSON, RODOLPHUS. A digest of the powers and duties of sheriffs, coroners, constables and collectors of taxes. Springfield, Massachusetts, Dickman, 1810. 232pp. Fold. table. Contemp. sheep rubbed. A very good copy. First edition. $ 45.00
* Marvin p. 266.

99. DOGHERTY, THOMAS. The Crown circuit assistant: being a collection of precedents ... in criminal and penal proceedings. Together with an alphabetical table to the statutes relating to felony, brought down to the twenty-fifth year of His present Majesty King George the Third. London, Uriel, 1787. 551pp. Full contemp. calf, rubbed, wanting label. $ 75.00
* Marvin p. 270. S & M. I, 361. Only edition except for a Dublin reprint.

100. DOGHERTY, THOMAS. The Crown circuit assistant: being a collection of precedents of indictments, informations, convictions by justices, inquisitions, pleas, and other entries in criminal and penal proceedings, together with an alphabetical table to the statutes relating to felony, brought down to the twenty-sixth year of His present Majesty King George the Third. Dublin, Prtd. by P. Byrne, 1788. 373pp. Contemp. sheep. $ 50.00
* Only edition beyond the first London of 1787. S & M I, 361.

101. DOLE, EDMUND P. Talks about law: a popular statement ofwhat our law is and how it is administered. Boston, Houghton, Mifflin, 1887. 557pp. Orig. cl. Fine. A notable attempt at legal education for the layman. $ 20.00

102. DRAKE, CHARLES D. A treatise on the law of suits by attachment in the United States. Fifth edition, revised, corrected and enlarged with an appendix containing the leading statutory provisions of the several states and territories of the United States in relation to suits by attachment. Boston, Little, Brown, 1878. 770pp. Full contemp. sheep. Wanting label. $ 45.00

103. (DREGHORN, JOHN MACLAURIN) Observations on some points of law. With a system of the judicial law of Moses. Edinburgh, Sands (et al.), 1759. viii, 203, 64pp. 12mo. Contemp. calf ruled in gilt, leather label. A fine copy. $250.00
* An uncommon and unusual book. It consists of 42 headings relating to Scottish law, 17 to Jewish law, with the "system" occupying the final 64pp. The NUC cites 4 holdings. An attractive copy.

104. DUANE, WILLIAM. A view of the relation of landlord and tenant in Pennsylvania, as affected by acts of assembly and judicial decisions. Phila., Kay, 1844. 136pp. 12mo. Full contemp. sheep. $ 45.00
* First edition. Marvin p. 276.

105. DUNCOMBE, GILES. Trials per pais, or the law of England concerning juries by nisi prius, &c. With a compleat treatise of the law of evidence ... The fifth edition with large additions, to which are now added such resolutions and acts of Parliament as have made any alteration in the laws relating to trials by juries ... (London,) Nutt & Gosling, 1718. 486pp. Contemp. calf, worn but sound. $ 75.00
* S & M I, 375. Marvin p. 280. First edition was 1665, the last 1793.

106. DUTCHER, SALEM. Minority or proportional representation, its nature, aims, history, processes, and practical operation. N. Y., United States Publ. Co., 1872. 165pp. Orig. cl. $ 22.50

****

107. EDWARDS, GEORGE C. A treatise on the powers and duties of justices of the peace and town officers in the State of New York, under the revised statutes: with practical forms. Second edition, revised and improved. Ithaca, Mack, 1834. 408pp. Full contemp. sheep. Marvin p. 289. $ 45.00

108. ELMER, LUCIUS Q. C. Practical forms of proceedings under the laws of New Jersey. Bridgeton, James M. Newell, 1839. 479pp. Contemp. sheep., front joint mended. $ 55.00
* A scarce book missed by Marvin.

109. ENDLICH, G. A. A commentary on the interpretation of statutes. Founded on the treatise of Sir Peter Benson Maxwell. Jersey City, Linn, 1888. 871pp. Sheep, rebacked. $ 45.00
* First edition. An American adaption of an earlier British work. Uncommon

110. 'ESPINASSE, ISAAC. Cases argued and ruled at Nisi Prius, in the Court of King's Bench, and Common Pleas, from Easter Term 33 George III to Hilary Term 34 George III with some additional cases of an earlier period. First American edition with additional references. London, printed, Baltimore: Re-printed by Clayland, Dobbin & Co. for Keatinge's Book Store. 1795. viii, 127, (1 blank), xiipp. Contemp. sheep rubbed. A very good copy. $ 75.00
* First American edition. Evans 28636. Uncommon.

111. 'ESPINASSE, ISAAC. A digest of the law of actions and trials at Nisi Prius. The second edition, corrected, with considerable additions from printed and manuscript cases, and three new chapters on the law of corporations and

111. (Continued) evidence. Dublin, Prtd. for E. Lynch, 1794. 791pp. Full contemp. calf, rubbed, wanting label. $ 50.00
* Marvin p. 298. S & M I, 335.

112. 'ESPINASSE, ISAAC. Practical treatise on the settling of evidence for trials at Nisi Prius: and on the preparing and arranging the necessary proofs. Phila., Carey, 1822. 302pp. New cl. $ 45.00
* First American, from the first London edition of 1819. Marvin p. 298.

113. An essay on naturalization & allegiance. Washington City, Daniel Rapine, 1816. 127, xv, (1)pp. Neatly removed. Foxed. A good copy. $ 55.00
* An anonymous little treatise on a special topic in international law, with repeated attacks on the doctrine of unalienable allegiance and a marked hostility towards England. The author cites an American treatise on expatriation by George Hay published in 1814. One of several very early American works on international law growing out of the Napoleonic Wars and marking the beginning of a distinctive literature. Shaw-Shoemaker 37526. Not in Marvin.

****

114. FARRAR, TIMOTHY. Report of the case of the Trustees of Dartmouth College against William H. Woodward. Argued and determined in the Superior Court of Judicature of the State of New Hampshire ... and on error in the Supreme Court of the United States. Portsmouth, Foster, (1819). 2pl., 406pp. 8vo. Contemp. sheep. Very good. $ 75.00
* First edition. A landmark case elucidating the contract clause of the Constitution and the rights of corporations. Marvin p. 303.

115. FESSENDEN, THOMAS G. An essay on the law of patents for new inventions. With an appendix containing the French patent law, forms & c. Boston, Mallory, 1810. 229pp. Contemp. sheep, rubbed. Internally very good. $ 75.00
* First edition of the first American work on the subject. Marvin p. 307.

116. FILMER, ROBERT. The free-holders grand inquest, touching our Sovereign Lord the King and his Parliament. To which are added Observations upon forms of government. Together with directions for obedience to governours in dangerous and doubtful times. London, 1679. Engraved portrait. 18th c. mor. gilt, joints worn. $225.00
* A posthumous reissue of virtually all of Filmer's political writings (except Patriarcha which was published for the first time from ms. in 1680). It consists of: the Free-holders grand inquest; Observations upon Aristotle's politics...; Observations concerning the original of government (against Hobbes, Milton and Grotius); The anarchy of a mixed or limited monarchy; An advertisement ... touching witches. His works (Continued)

116. (Continued) expound the virtues of absolutism based on his patriarchal theory and are important for provoking both Locke and Algernon Sydney.. First edition of this collected version. A very good copy. Wing F-913.

117. FINLASON, W. A selection of leading cases on pleading and parties to actions, with practical notes ... From the London edition. Harrisburg, M'Kinley, 1847. 218pp. New cl. $ 45.00
* First American, from the first London edition of the same year.

118. (FISHER, SIDNEY GEORGE) The law of the territories. Phila., C. Sherman, 1859. 127pp. Orig. cl. $ 35.00
* A conservative's attack on popular sovereignty and the Kansas-Nebraska Bill. Sabin 39336.

119. The form book: containing ... the most approved precedents for conveyancing (etc.) ... by a Member of the Philadelphia Bar. Phila., Towar and Hogan, ... 1830. 12mo. 288pp. New cl. $ 45.00
* American Imprints, 1830, #1411.

120. FOSTER, SIR MICHAEL. A report of some proceedings on the Commission for the Trial of the Rebels in the year 1746, in the County of Surry; and of other Crown cases: to which are added discourses upon a few branches of the Crown law. The second edition, corrected, with additional notes and references by his nephew, Michael Dodson, Esq. of the Middle Temple. Dublin, Moore, 1791. 412pp. Full contemp. sheep. $ 75.00
* One of the most highly esteemed works on Crown Law in the 18th century. See Holdsworth XII, 135ff, who notes also that "his book is an anticipation of the plan of collecting a book of leading cases with notes appended, which John William Smith, at the suggestion of Samuel Warren, carried out in 1837-1840." Marvin p. 321. Winfield p. 328.

121. FOX, CHARLES J. A guide to officers of towns; containing the statutes relating to their official duties, with forms, directions, and legal decisions: adapted to the revised statutes of New-Hampshire. A new edition, with some additions, including acts since passed. By Samuel D. Bell. Concord, Parker Lyon, 1847. 416pp. Sheep rubbed. $ 25.00
* Marvin p. 322.

122. (FRANCE. CIVIL CODE) JOUSSE, (DANIEL). Nouveau commentaire sur l'ordonnance civile du mois d'Avril 1667. Nouvelle edition, augmentee de l'idee de la justice civile. Paris, Debure, 1767. 2 vols. 850pp. Contemp. mottled calf. $ 75.00
* Final edition of this very prominent commentary. The NUC cites 3 holdings.

123. (FRANCE. LAWS, STATUTES) Les huit codes en miniature avec indication de leurs artic les correlatifs suivis du tarif des frais et depens en matiere civile et criminelle, d'un appendice progressif contenant les lois et ordonnances principales rendues jusqu'a ce jour, et d'un table analytique des matieres. Paris, Roret, 1833. 16mo. 828pp. 1/4 calf, fine. $ 75.00
* A pocket size library of French law from the Napoleonic era with all of its major reforms; included are the code politique, civil, du procedure civil, commerce, penal, etc... along with legal fees and additional statutes.

124. FREEMAN, SAMUEL. The probate auxiliary; or, a director and assistant to probate courts, executors, administrators and guardians, being the laws of Massachusetts ... to which are added a variety of forms ... Portland, Massachusetts (i.e. Maine), Benjamin Titcomb, 1793. xi, (1)156, (3)pp. 12mo. Contemp. sheep, rubbed. A good copy. $ 75.00
* First edition. Like Freeman's other guides and manuals, this remained a standard, often re-issued work for the next 25 years. Evans 25511. An early piece of Maine printing.

125. FREEMAN, SAMUEL. The Probate Directory: or an assistant ... being the Laws of the Commonwealth of Massachusetts, respecting the estates of testators, intestates, and wards, to which are added, a variety of forms, ... Second edition, greatly enlarged and improved. Boston, Thomas, 1803. 228pp. New cloth. $ 37.50

126. FREEMAN, SAMUEL. The town officer, or the power and duty of (various officers) as contained in the laws of the Commonwealth of Massachusetts ... Portland, Benjamin Titcomb, 1791. Sm. 8vo. Contemp. calf. 178, (2)pp. Good copy. $ 75.00
* First edition, and rare thus, containing interesting material on poor-laws, regulation of foodstuffs, tobacco, etc. A standard regional work for the next two decades. Evans 23389. Marvin p. 323.

127. FREEMAN, SAMUEL. The town officer: or the power and duty of selectmen ... and other town officers as contained in the laws of the Commonwealth of Massachusetts, with a variety of forms ... the third edition, corrected, improved and greatly enlarged. Boston, I. Thomas and E. T. Andrews, 1794. 240pp. 12mo. Cont. calf. $ 45.00
* The new statutes include those relatingto small pox, the poor, the militia, and appointment of grand jurors. Evans 27016. First published in Portland in 1791 and reissued over the next two decades. A standard work.

128. FRIEZE, JACOB. Concise history of the efforts to obtain an extension of suffrage in Rhode Island: from the year 1811 to 1842. Second edition. Providence, Moore, prtr., 1842. 179pp. Orig. boards, nice copy. $ 30.00
* An important account of one of the great constitutional crises in American history, critical of the Dorr faction.

129. GAROFOLO, ANTONIO MARIA. Vero metodo, ed ordine da tenersi da nodari nella formazione di qualunque processo criminale, ed ancora in via mista fino alla loro ultimazione con cio, che s'appartiene in qualche parte anco alli procuratori, con altre osservabili, e non piu usate particolarita esenzialissime pratica criminale ... Verona, Dionisio Ramanzini, 1751. 4pl., 102pp. Fine engr. headpiece. Contemporary vellum lightly worn. 4to. $ 50.00
* Not found in either the NUC or theBLC.

130. GEORGE, STAUGHTON et al., (compiler). Charter to William Penn, and laws of the Province of Pennsylvania, passed between the years 1682 and 1700, preceded by Duke of York's laws in force from the year 1676 to the year 1682, with an appendix containing laws relating to the organization of the Provincial Courts and historical matter ... Harrisburg, Hart, 1879. Illus., frontis., 3 large folding facsimile charters in pockets. 614pp. Orig. cl. $ 55.00

131. GILBERT (GEOFFREY). The law of devises, revocations and last wills. To which is added, Choice precedents of wills. London, Lintot, 1756. 10pl., 254(38)pp. Contemp. calf wanting label, front joint little worn, still a very good copy. $125.00
* First edition. A valuable work on land law, dealing as much with rules of law as with equity, and among the earliest modern texts on the principles of equity. See Holdsworth XII, 187f. Marvin p. 333. S & M I, 491.

132. GILBERT, (GEOFFREY). The law of executions. To which are added the history and practice of the Court of King's Bench ; and some cases touching wills of lands and goods. The second edition, carefully corrected from the many errors in the London impression. Dublin, Prtd. for Eliz. Watts, 1763. 427pp. Contemp. calf, rubbed & worn but sound. $ 75.00
* "(Gibert's) works are some of the best text books on legal topics published during this century."--Holdsworth, XII, 140, also p. 355. Marvin p. 332. London edition was same year.

133. (GILBERT, GEOFFREY). A treatise on the Court of Exchequer: in which the revenues of the Crown; the manner of receiving and accounting for the several branches of them; the duty of the several officers employed in the collection and receipt; the nature of the processes for the recovery of debts due to the Crown are clearly explained: as also occasionally, the nature of the feudal and antient tenures; the origin of Parliaments, Convocations, and several Courts of Justice; and many other curious and useful particulars are shewn. By a late Lord Chief Baron of that Court .... (London,) Lintot, 1758. 343pp. Contemp. calf, worn & rubbed but sound. $ 75.00
* First edition. "One of the best (on this branch of law). It is an able and clearly written book by one who was a master both of the present

133. (Continued) practice... and of the older authorities."--Holdsworth XII, 411. Marvin p. 334.

134. GLUCK, JAMES FRASER, et al. The law of receivers of corporations including National Banks, illustrated by abstracts of the facts of and excerpts from the opinions in leading cases. N.Y., Banks, 1891. 580pp. New cl. $ 27.50

135. GRANT-DUFF, M.E. Sir Henry Maine, a brief memoir of his life, with some of his Indian speeches and minutes, selected andedited by Whitley Stokes, with portrait. N. Y., Holt, 1892. 451pp. Orig. cl. Fine. $ 37.50
* Reflects Maine's brilliant legal contributions while serving in India for 7 years. First American edition.

136. GREENLEAF, SIMON. A collection of cases overruled, denied, doubted, or limited in their application, taken from American and English reports. Third edition revised and enlarged. N. Y., Halsted, 1840. 467pp. Full contemp. sheep. $ 45.00
* Marvin p. 348, a long laudatory note on the usefulness and publishing history of this work.

137. GLANVILLE. A translation of Glanville, by John Beames... to which are added notes. London, A. J. Valpy for W. Reed, 1812. xl, 362pp. plus index and ads. Some neat pencil marginalia and underlining. Modern (1937) ink ownership inscription on title page. Contemp. calf neatly rebacked. $ 75.00
* "The only English translation is by John Beames, which is accurate, and his notes learned and valuable."--Marvin p. 338.

138. GRIFFITHS, ARTHUR. Secrets of the prison-house or gaol studies and sketches. Illustrations by George D. Rowlandson. In two volumes. London, Chapman and Hall, 1894. 2 vols. Roy. 8vo. Orig. cl., gilt. Illustrations in text. A very nice set. First edition. $ 75.00
* A very good, first-hand view of international penal systems, with emphasis in the second volume on England. Author was one of H.M. Inspectors of Prisons.

139. GROSS, CHARLES. The gild merchant: a contribution to British municipal history. In two vols. Oxford, Clarendon Press, 1890. 332, 447pp. $ 65.00
* S & M, I, 531. Holdsworth, Historians of Anglo-American Law, p. 111.

140. GROTIUS, HUGO. De jure belli ac pacis libri tres ... accesserunt ejusdem Dissertatio de mari libero ... editio novissima ... Amsterdam Apud Janssonio-Waesbergios, 1712. Large thick 8vo. With fine engraved portrait of Grotius and engraved separate title-page. Includes ample notes of J. F. Gronovius. Appended at the end is Grotius's "Libellus singularis de aequitate, indulgentia, & facilitate." Old boards. A good copy. $ 85.00

141. HALSTED, WILLIAM. A digested index to the decisions of the Superior Courts of the State of New Jersey. Trenton, printed by Joseph Justice, 1830. 392pp. Contemp. sheep, leather label, bit rubbed but a very good copy. First edition.
* Marvin p. 363. $ 55.00

142. HAMMOND, ANTHONY. A digest of reports in equity ... containing the digest and names of cases. First American edition. Brookfield, Hammond, 1822. 860pp. Full contemp. sheep, rubbed, wanting label. $ 50.00
* Marvin p. 364.

143. HARRISON, R. TARRANT. Harrison's analytical digest of all the reported cases determined in the House of Lords, the several Courts of Common Law ... (etc.) 1756 ... 1843, including also ... a full selection of equity decisions, with manuscript cases ... not elsewhere reported. Second American edition from the third London ... to which is added a supplement ... carefully arranged by a member of the Philadelphia Bar. Phila., Small, 1846-1853. Complete in 7 volumes Buckram. Approx. 12,000pp. $125.00
* The supplementary volumes bring the coverage up to 1852. "...the whole execution is perhaps as perfect and accurate as could well be made from the magnitude and nature of the undertaking." --Marvin p. 372f.

144. (HARVARD LAW SCHOOL). A catalogue of the law school of the University at Cambridge for the academical year 1854-55. First term. Cambridge, Metcalf, 1854. 28pp. Orig. prtd. wrps. $ 17.50

145. (HARVARD LAW SCHOOL) A catalogue of the law school of the University at Cambridge for the academical year 1857-58. First term. Cambridge, Bartlett, 1857. 28pp. Orig. prtd. wrps. $ 17.50

146. (HAUTERIVE, ALEXANDRE MAURICE BLANC de LANAUTTE, comte d'). Memoire sur les principes et les lois de la neutralite maritime, accompagne de pieces officielles justificatives. Paris, chez les Marchands de Nouveautes, 1812. 160pp. Neatly removed. Good copy. $ 37.50

147. HAWLEY JOHN G., et al. The criminal law. Second edition. Detroit, Collector Publ., 1897. 316pp. Full contemp. sheep. $ 22.50

148. HAYWARD, JOHN. The New-England and New-York Law-Register for the year 1835: containing an almanac, descriptions of the courts, and the times of their sessions, the names of the judges, counsellors and attorneys at law, sheriffs and other law officers ... Boston, Hayward, (1835). 262pp. Contemp. 1/4 leather. 12mo. $ 45.00
* First and only issue. Sabin 31076.

149. HEARN, WILLIAM EDWARD. The Aryan household, its structure and its development. An introduction to comparative jurisprudence. London, Longmans, 1891. 494pp. Orig. cl. $ 35.00
* Second edition (1st was 1878) of a very highly regarded work in comparative jurisprudence, one of the best works in the social sciences to come out of Australia in the 19th century. Lib. stamp but a very good copy.

150. (HIGGINS, JESSE). Sampson against the Philistines, or the reformation of law-suits; and justice made cheap, speedy ... agreeable to the principles of the ancient trial by jury, before the same was innovated by judges and lawyers. Compiled for the use of the honest citizens of the United States, to whom it is dedicated. Second ed. Phila., Prtd. by B. Graves, for W. Duane, 1805. 96pp. disbound. $ 35.00
* Marvin p. 627.

151. HINKLEY, EDWARD OTIS. The testamentary law and the law of inheritance and apprentices in Maryland. Baltimore, Murphy, 1878. 784pp. New cl. $ 37.50

152. HISTORICAL SOCIETY OF PENNSYLVANIA. The Charlemagne Tower Collection of American Colonial Laws. Privately prtd. for the Historical Soc. of Pa., 1890. Engr. portrait. Fine copy, uncut. 298pp. Orig. cl. 4to. Detailed bibliographical descriptions and collations. $ 50.00

153. (HOGDON, MOSES). The complete justice of the peace, containing extracts from Burn's Justice, and other justiciary productions. The whole altered and made conformable to the laws and manners of administering justice, particularly in the State of New Hampshire, and generally in the other of the United States ... by a Gentleman of the Profession. Dover, N. H., printed for Charles Peirce, 1806. 431pp. Calf, rubbed. $ 45.00
* Shaw-Shoemaker 10569. First edition.

154. HOLLAND, THOMAS ERSKINE. The elements of jurisprudence. Second edition enlarged. Oxford, Clarendon Press, 1882. Original cloth. A fine copy. $ 60.00
* Holland was the most important direct successor to Austin in the development of a literature on scientific jurisprudence. This edition is substantially altered beyond the first of 1880. The work continued to be revised and reissued well into the 20th century. The very early editions are scarce.

155. HONDURAS. Estado de Honduras. Codigo de comercio, (1898). Tegucigalpa, 1898. 234pp. 4to. Sheep, orig. wrps. bound in. $ 45.00

156. HOPKINSON, JOSEPH. An address delivered before the Law Academy of Philadelphia at the opening of the session of 1826-7. Phila., The Law Academy, 1826. 21pp. Removed. General, on duties of the profession. $ 15.00

157. HOUCK, LOUIS. A treatise on the law of navigable rivers. Boston, Little, Brown, 1868. 235pp. New cl. $ 45.00

158. HOUCK, LOUIS. A treatise on the mechanics' lien law in the United States. Chicago, Callaghan, 1867. 256pp. Full contemp. sheep, rubbed. $ 45.00
* Ante-Fire Imprints 1213.

159. HOWE, SAMUEL. The practice in civil actions and proceedings at law in Massachusetts. Edited by Richard S. Fay and Jonathan Chapman. Boston, Hillard, 1834. 599pp. New cl. $ 80.00
* First edition. Of particular interest for early legal education in the United States. Howe formed a law school at Northampton, Mass. modelled after Litchfield, his own alma mater, in 1823. This work is a posthumous publication of his lectures, organized by his colleagues. The school "acquired areputation not inferior to that of the older institution ... Howe possessed a zeal ... which made him an excellent teacher and attracted many students."--DAB. In 1881 Howe's text was made the basis for a similarly titled work by Joseph W. Spaulding, who described it as "for many years ... so useful and valuable to the profession in this (Maine) and other States."

160. HULLOCK, JOHN. The law of costs. London, prtd. for C. Nicol, 1792. 626pp. Contemp. sheep, worn but sound. First edition. Marvin p. 404 $ 47.50

161. HUNT, THOMAS. A defence of the charter and municipal rights of the City of London and the rights of other municipal cities and towns of England. Directed to the citizens of London. London, Richard Baldwin, 1683. 4to. 46pp. uncut and stitched as issued. A bit dusty but a very good copy. $125.00
* Sweet & Maxwell, I, noting that the work was answered by L'Estrange in Lawyer Outlawed. It is also an attack on John Dryden. MacDonald 221.

162. HURD, JOHN CODMAN. The theory of our national existence, as shown by the action of the government of the United States since 1861. Boston, Little, Brown, 1881. xl, 550pp. Orig. cl. Fine. With ALS tipped in from the author to John Codman Ropes presenting the book, and with the author's photo tipped in. $ 85.00
* A desireable and sophisticated work on the Constitution and the theory of political sovereignty, centering around Reconstruction. "He believed that the nature of the Union was determined by social and political forces, not by provisions of the Federal Constitution ... these ideas he expounded with many nice distinctions in (this work) ..."--DAB. Hurd was also author of Law of Freedom and Bondage. "This work established his reputation as one of the most learned legal writers in the country."--DAB.

163. HUTCHINSON, JOHN A. A treatise on the laws of West Virginia pertaining to the powers and duties of justices, clerks of courts, prosecuting attorneys, sheriffs, constables, notaries, etc... also rules of evidence, definitions, notes of decisions, etc., etc. With references to the law and practice in Virginia. Second edition, revised by... Cincinnati, Clarke, 1899. 1177pp. cloth. $ 45.00

****

164. (IOWA) BRADFORD, JOHN M. The Iowa form book, or book of practical forms, containing precedents and forms for ordinary business dealings and transactions, with statements of the law; adapted and designed for the use of merchants, mechanics, farmers, business men, and especially Justices of the Peace. Davenport, House of Luse, Lane Co., 1857. 335pp. New cloth. $100.00
* NUC records two copies only, both in Iowa. Rare. Moffit #266.

165. IRVINE, ALEXANDER FORBES. A treatise on the game laws of Scotland with an appendix containing the principal statutes and forms. Edinburgh, Clark, 1850. xxiv, 155pp. Orig. boards and cloth spine. A very good copy. Uncut. $ 60.00
* First edition. In part historical.

166. JACKSON, CHARLES. A treatise on the pleadings and practice in real actions: with precedents of pleadings. Boston, Wells, 1828. xx, 396pp. Full contemp. sheep. Lacking label. $ 75.00
* First edition. "A very learned work... 'in addition to its value as a book of practical forms, it must rank very high as a clear and profound exposition of the ancient law of real actions, and such as few men in England or the United States could have produced...' "--Marvin p. 415. Jackson graduated from Harvard College, read law with Theophilus Parson who recognized in him great promise, served on the Mass. Supreme Court and sat in court in London.--DAB. A fairly scarce book.

167. JACOB, GILES. A new law dictionary... the seventh edition. The law proceedings being done into English, with great additions and improvements ... In the Savoy, Lintot ..., 1756. Large thick folio, unpaginated. Contemp. calf expertly rebacked, later end-papers. A very good copy. $150.00
* The most popular work of its kind in the 18th and early 19th centuries. "... a fine piece of work ... a new departure because it attempted, with a considerable measure of success, to combine in one work a dictionary and an abridgement ..."--Holdsworth, XII, 176ff.

168. JAMES, EDWIN. The Bankrupt Law of the United States, 1867. With notes, and a collection of American and English decisions upon the principles and practice of the law of bankruptcy. Adapted to the use of the lawyer and merchant. N. Y., Harper, 1867. 325pp. Full contemp. sheep. First edition. $ 35.00

169. JENKINS, JOHN S. The new clerk's assistant, or book of practical forms ... adapted to the New England, Northern and Western States, and California. New York, Saxton, 1858. 620pp. Full contemp. sheep. $ 37.50

170. JOHNSON, CUTHBERT WILLIAM. The life of Sir Edward Coke ... with memoirs of his contemporaries. In two volumes. London, Colburn, 1837. 2 vols. 8vo. Frontis. portrait. Contemp. half calf gilt. A fine set. $ 75.00
* First edition. Marvin p. 425.

171. JOHNSON, WILLIAM. Reports of cases adjudged in the Supreme Court of Judicature of the State of New York from January term 1799 to January term 1803, both inclusive; together with cases determined in the Court for the Correction of Errors during that period. In 3 vols. N. Y., Riley, 1808, 1810, 1812. 544, 520, 437pp. Full contemp. calf. Good sound set. 3 vols. $ 50.00
* First edition, complete. Marvin p. 426. Wallace 579.

172. JONES, SAMUEL. A treatise on the right of suffrage, with an appendix. Boston, Otis, 1842. 274pp. Orig. cl., a little worn, foxing. First edition. Preface dated: Stockbridge Mass., August 30, 1841. $ 37.50

173. JONES, WILLIAM. An essay on the law of bailments, from the last London edition, with introductory remarks and notes comprising the most modern authorities, by John Balmanno. Albany, Backus, 1806. 132, 21pp. New cloth. $ 45.00

174. JONES, WILLIAM. An essay on the law of bailments. From the last London edition with introductory remarks and notes ... by John Balmanno. Brattleborough, Vt., William Fessenden, 1813. 6pl., 144, xxipp. Contemp. sheep little rubbed. 12mo. A good copy. $ 45.00
* Marvin p. 428f. A classic and long-enduring treatise.

175. JONES, SIR WILLIAM. An essay on the law of bailments. From the last London edition, with notes and an appendix. Phila., Hogan, 1836. Full contemp. sheep, nice copy. $ 65.00
* An extremely interesting edition illustrating the reciprocal influence of American upon English jurisprudence. The editor notes that the latest London edition from which this edition is printed incorporates many notes as illustrations from Joseph Story's Commentaries on Bailments, a work whose great appreciation abroad had occasioned this new edition of Jones. A lengthy

175. (Continued) appendix consists of Nichols' noteon the Law of Carriers, with American authorities, parts of which are of maritime interest. This is the final edition. Marvin p. 428.

176. JONES, WILLIAM (translator) Institutes of Hindu law; or, the ordinances of Menu ... comprising the Indian system of duties, religious and civil. Verbally translated from the original sanscrit with a preface by Sir William Jones. Calcutta: printed ... London: reprinted for J. Sewell andJ. Debrett, 1796. 8vo. xvi, 366, (1)pp. Later half black mor. Few damp stains on title page and last few leaves, internally very good. $125.00
* Jones was appointed judge of the high court at Calcutta in 1783, and during his ten years of service there he undertook a complete codification of Indian law with the help of living native authorities. Helived just long enough to complete the first stages as embodied in this work, which is of interest both as "a masterly rendering" (DNB) of thelaw, andas a linguistical product, for Jones was the father of modern Indo-European philology.

177. JONES, SIR WILLIAM. The speeches of Isaeus in causes concerning the law of succession to property at Athens, with a prefatory discourse, notes ... and a commentary. London, J. Nichols, 1779. vii, xxxix, 204, (1-errata). Plates. 4to. Contemp. calf gilt, joints lightly rubbed. With the gilt oval stamp of University College, Oxford, Jones' own college. A very good copy. $175.00
* Jones was both a great linguist and orientalist and a distinguished legal scholar. This uncommonand interesting book on comparative law with digressions on the law of England combines both roles. He is best known for his Law of Bailments and Institutes of Hindu Law.

178. (JUDICIARY ACT OF 1801). The speeches of Mr. Bacon and Mr. Nicholson in the National House of Representatives in defence of the bill received from the Senate entitled "An act to repeal certain acts respecting the organization of the courts of the United States" February 1802. Boston, Munroe, 1802. 44pp. Uncut. Sewn as issued. $ 27.50
* Clear statements of the Jeffersonian theory of legislative supremacy in this early battle over the national court system. Shaw-Shoemaker 1794.

179. JUSTINIAN. The Institutes of Justinian: with English introduction, translation, and notes by Thomas Collett Sandars ... First American, from the fifth London edition, with an introduction by Wm. G. Hammond. Chicago, Callaghan, 1876. 693pp. New cloth. $ 45.00

180. KANT, IMMANUEL. Metaphysische Anfangsgrunde der Rechtslehre. Konigsberg, bey Friedrich Nicolovius, 1797. xii, 235, (1)pp. Contemp. stiff marbled wraps. Entirely uncut and a fine copy. In a 1/4 mor. slip case. $550.00
* First edition, first issue. Subsequent issues carry an added title: "Metaphysik der Sitten", of which this became part one, part two being Metaphysische Anfangsgrunde der Tugendlehre, separately published later in the same year. "Kant holds that legal obligations are a subspecies of moral obligation; thus the rational will, and neither force nor the commands of God, is the basis of law. His standpoint in Philosophy of law is thus broadly liberal, though his attitude on many particular legal issues is far from liberal as the term is now understood."--Edwards, Encycl. of Phil. Warda 171 (a.).

181. KENT, JAMES. Commentaries on American law. Third edition N. Y., Printed for the author, 1836. Four vols. Thick 8vo's. Contemp. sheep wanting labels, rubbed and dry but sound. Internally good. $150.00
* A substantially altered edition, taking into account the many changes which had occured since the second edition of 1832.--Kent's preface to this edition. Marvin p. 437ff.

182. KERR, WILLIAM WILLIAMSON. A treatise on the law and practice as to receivers appointed by the Court of Chancery. With notes and references to American authorities by Geo. Tucker Bispham. Phila., Kay, 1872. 288pp. First American edition. $ 37.50

183. KINGSBURY, BENJAMIN Jr. The Maine townsman, or, laws for the regulation of towns, with forms and judicial decisions, adapted to the revised statutes of Maine. Revised and enlarged by ... Sixth edition. Boston, Sanborn, 1857. 432pp. Full contemp. sheep, rubbed. $ 25.00

184. KINGSBURY, BENJAMIN, Jr. The Maine townsman, or laws for the regulation of towns, with forms and judicial decisions, adapted to the revised statutes of Maine. Fourteenth edition. Portland, Bailey, 1872. 480pp. Full contemp. sheep. $ 25.00

185. KINNE, ASA. The most important parts of Blackstone's Commentaries, reduced to questions and answers. N. Y., Dean, 1838. 180pp. Full contemp. sheep. $ 45.00

186. KYD, STEWART. A treatise on the law of awards. Dublin, prtd. by J. Stockdale, 1791. 251pp. Full contemp. calf. Faint stains to preliminary leaves. $ 50.00
* First Dublin from the first London edition of the same year. Marvin p. 443 notes a first American edition in 1808. It reflects the growing practice of arbitration, especially among merchants. "The best book on this subject ... describes historically the growth of the rules ... and discusses intelligently the modern cases ..." --Holdsworth XII, 392f and 429.

187. (LADD, WILLIAM editor) Prize essays on a Congress of Nations, for the adjustment of international disputes, and for the promotion of universal peace without resort to arms. Together with a sixth essay, comprising the substance of the rejected essays. Boston, Whipple and Damrell, 1840. 700pp. 8vo. Orig. cl. little spotted else a nice copy. $ 45.00
* The work of the American Peace Society. The judges appointed to select these essays were Joseph Story, Wm. Wirt, John M'Lean, John Quincy Adams, James Kent, and Daniel Webster. A copy of the volume was to go to all heads of state, colleges, etc.

188. The lady's law: or, a treatise of feme coverts: containing all the laws and statutes relating to women, under several heads... the second edition. To which is added, Judge Hide's very remarkable argument ... in the case of Manby and Scot, whether, and in what cases the husband is bound by the contract of his wife... In the Savoy, Nutt and Gosling, 1737. viii, 264, (16)pp. wanting half title. Title within rules. New cloth. A very good copy. $185.00
* A re-issue of the first edition of 1732 (same pagination) which appeared under the title: "A treatise of feme coverts ..." One of a small but important group of 18th century works on the legal status of women. The NUC cites only a copy at Yale, on microfilm. S & M I, 500.

189. (LAW LIBRARY CATALOGUE) A catalogue of the Social Law Library in Boston. Second edition. Boston, Printed for the proprietors, 1849. 197pp. Contemp. 1/4 leather. $ 50.00

190. LAWES, EDWARD. An elementary treatise on pleading in civil actions. First American from first London ed. Portsmouth, N. H., Thomas, 1808. 246pp. Contemp. sheep, rubbed. Light marginal stains. $ 45.00
* Marvin p. 452.

191. LAWES, EDWARD. A practical treatise on pleading in assumpsit. With the addition of the decisions of the American Courts, by Joseph Story. Boston, Burditt, 1811. 621pp. Contemp. sheep rubbed, wants label. $ 55.00
* First American, from the first London edition of 1810. Marvin p. 452.

192. LAWRENCE, WILLIAM BEACH. Disabilities of American Women married abroad: foreign treaties of the United States in conflict with state laws relative to the transmission of real estate to aliens. Appendix: conventions of naturalization and for the abolition of the Droit D'Aubaine-marriage laws of various countries, as affecting the property of married women. N. Y., Baker, 1871. 144pp. Orig. cl. $ 27.50

193. (LIBEL LAW). The speech of George Ponsonby in the House of Commons of Ireland ... upon the subject of fiats, to which are subjoined the several affidavits on which said fiats were granted against John Magee. Dublin, W. Gilbert, 1790. 55pp. Neatly removed. Fine copy. $ 37.50
* Concerns the setting of high bail on the accused in libel cases based upon vague charges. Very detailed on points of law. Magee was the most outstanding figure of this time in Ireland in connection with challenges to free speech. McCoy 146 & 147 cites 2 items with long annotations concerning Magee, but this relevant tract on procedure goes unnoticed.

194. LIEBER, FRANCIS. Manual of political ethics, designed chiefly for the use of colleges and students at law. In two vols. Second edition, revised. Edited by Theodore D. Woolsey Phila., Lippincott, 1893. 472, 459pp. Orig. cl. $ 45.00

195. LILLY, JOHN. A collection of modern entries or select pleadings in the Courts of King's Bench, Common Pleas, and Exchequer ... to which is added, a collection of writs ... with two tables ... The Fourth edition, carefully translated into English with many additional references. London. Strahan and Woodfall, for Worrall (et al.) 1771. Folio. 676pp. plus tables. New cloth. $150.00
* One of the standard works on pleading, first published in 1723. This is a re-issue of the 1741 edition, the first to be rendered in English. S & M, I, 273. Holdsworth, Hist. of English Law, XII, p. 358.

196. LILLY, JOHN. A collection of modern entries: or select pleadings in the Courts of King's Bench, Common Pleas, and Exchequer ... to which is added a collection of writs in most cases now in practice. With two tables, one of the names of the cases, and theother of the pleadings and writs. The fifth edition. In two vols. London, Prtd. by A. Strahan, 1791. Roy 8vo's. Contemp. calf, rubbed, wants labels. Approx. 1200pp. 2 volumes. $ 75.00
* "Lilly's is the only book of Entries and Writs that goes through the whole alphabet, published since the law proceedings have been in English. Clarke."--Marvin p. 465. S & M I, 273. The last edition of the work appeared in a Dublin reprint a year later.

197. LINN, WILLIAM. The legal and commercial lawyer: a common-place book for farmers, merchants, and mechanics, containing the decisions of the Supreme Court of the United States, and of the respective State Courts, on bills of exchange, checks, promissory notes, &c. ... Utica, Brooks, 1859. 294pp. Contemp. sheep, joints cracked but sound. $ 35.00

198. LIVINGSTON, EDWARD. The complete works of Edward Livingston on criminal jurisprudence: consisting of systems of penal law for the State of Louisiana and for the United States of America; with the introductory reports to the same, to which is prefixed an introduction by Salmon P. Chase. In two vols. N. Y., Nat'l. Prison Assoc., 1873. 589pp. Orig. cl. $ 35.00

199. LIVINGSTON, EDWARD. A system of penal law for the state of Louisiana: consisting of a code of crimes and punishments ... procedure... evidence... reform and prison discipline, a book of definitions... to which are prefixed a preliminary report on the plan of a penal code, and introductory reports to the several codes embraced in the system of penal law. Phila., Kay, (1833). v, 745pp. Contemp. sheep, leather label, rubbed but a very good copy. $150.00
* First complete edition of this landmark penal code which, though never adopted, remained influential here and abroad. There is an earlier Louisiana printing in 1824, but that version omits the reports, and is in any case almost impossible to find.

200. LONG, GEORGE. A treatise on the law relative to sales of personal property. First American from the last London edition, improved bya digest of American decisions. Exeter, N. H., Lamson, 1823. 288pp. plus index. Contemp. sheep. Very good copy. $ 55.00
* First American edition. Marvin p. 474.

201. LORD, JOHN P. The Maine townsman, or laws for the regulation of towns; with forms and judicial decisions, adapted to the revised statutes of Maine. Second edition. Portland, Sanborn, 1846. 372pp. Full contemp. sheep. 12mo. $ 27.50

202. LOUISIANA. LAWS, STATUTES. Civil code of the State of Louisiana. By authority. New Orleans, Printed by J. C. De St. Romes., 1825. Thick small 4to. xxxi, 1348pp. Text in English and French on opposite pages. The usual foxing, occasionally heavy in those portions where paper of variant quality was used. Overall a sound copy. New cloth. $250.00
* First edition of the landmark civil code, the first for the State of Louisiana, prepared by Edward Livingston, Pierre Derbigney and Moreau-Lislet. "... by the act of promulgation the legislature declared that ... the Spanish, Roman, and French laws in force at the time of cession ... should be repealed in reference to every case in which the code contains special provisions." --Marvin p. 476. Sabin 42204. Foote p. 166.

203. LOUISIANA. LAWS, STATUTES. Civil code of the State of Louisiana; with annotations by Wheelock S. Upton and Needler R. Jennings. By authority. New Orleans, E. Johns & Co., 1838. Large 8vo. Contemp. calf, moderate wear, light staining to first few leaves, still a good sound copy. $100.00
(Continued)

* First edition of this newly annotated version of the great Civil Code of 1825 prepared by Edward Livingston, Pierre Derbigny and Moreau-Lislet. Marvin p. 476.

204. LUBE, D. G. An analysis of the principles of equity pleading; containing a compendium of the practice of the High Court of Chancery and the foundation of its rules, together with an illustration of the analogy between pleadings at common law and in equity. Second American from the last London edition, with notes and references to American cases by J. D. Wheeler. N. Y., Banks, 1846. 415pp. Full contemp. sheep, rubbed. $ 45.00
* Marvin p. 478.

****

205. M'DONALD, DAVID. A treatise on the law relative to the powers and duties of justices of the peace and constables in the State of Indiana: with practical forms, and essays on various titles of the common law. Revised to conform to the statutes in force January 1, 1863, by Edwin A. Davis. Cincinnati, Clarke, 1867. 755pp. Full Contemp. sheep, rubbed. $ 55.00

206. (McDOUGALL, MRS. FRANCIS HARRIET GREENE). Might and right: By a Rhode Islander. Providence, A. H. Stilwell. 1844. Port. 345pp. Orig. cl. Fine. $ 27.50
* A vigorous defense of the Dorr Rebellion.

207. McKELVEY, JOHN JAY. Principles of common-law pleading: a brief explanation of the different forms of common-law actions, and a summary of the most important principles of pleading therein, with illustrations taken from the cases. N. Y., Baker, 1894. 193pp. $ 17.50

208. M'KINNEY, MORDECAI. The Pennsylvania justice of the peace: containing the law, practice and process, in proceedings before justices of the peace and aldermen in criminal cases, with numerous precedents therein: also, the laws, adjudications, (with notes), forms of docket entries, process and practice, relative to their jurisdiction, and its exercise, in civil cases. Two volumes, in one ... Harrisburg, prtd. for the author, by E. Guyer, 1839. 294, 353pp. Contemp. sheep rubbed. First edition. $ 75.00
* A very uncommon and substantial Pennsylvania justice. Part of its scarcity may be explained by the fact that it was printed for and published by the author himself. Marvin p. 490.

209. McMASTER, JOHN BACH (ed.), et al. Pennsylvania and the Federal Constitution, 1787-1788. (Lancaster) Historical Society of Penn., 1888. Illustrated with 15 engraved portraits. 803pp. Roy. 8vo. Orig. cl. Reprints many primary sources. $ 50.00

210. (MADAN, MARTIN) Thoughts on executive justice, with respect to our criminal laws, particularly on the circuits. Dedicated to the judges of assize; and recommended to the perusal of all magistrates; and to all persons who are liable to serve on Crown Juries. With an appendix ... by A Well-wisher to the Public. The second edition. London, Dodsley, 1785. iv, 256pp. Sm. 8vo. Contemp. bookplate of Charles Sturt, 1787. Contemp. polished calf, spine richly gilt, leather label. A very nice copy. $150.00
* Madan was a versatile and controversial writer best known for his notorious defense of polygamy. In this work he calls for severity in the treatment of criminals, lamenting upon lenient judges and juries and attributing the epidemic of crime to slow or uncertain punishment - a familiar charge. The work is especially interesting because it brought forth a sharp response from the young Romilly, his first effort in behalf of liberal penal reform (1786). At about the same time Benjamin Franklin wrote a piece in response to Madan. This is an entirely new setting of the book whose first edition appeared also in 1785. DNB. S& M. I, 364.

211. MAINE, SIR HENRY SUMNER. Dissertations on early law and custom chiefly selected from lectures delivered at Oxford ... N. Y., Holt, 1883. 402pp. Orig. cl. $ 20.00

212. MANSFIELD, EDWARD D. Thepolitical grammar of the United States; or, a complete view of the theory and practice of the general and state governments, with the relations between them. Dedicated and adapted to the young men of the United States. N. Y., Harper, 1834. 275pp. Orig. cl. 12mo. $ 27.50
* First edition. A popularization of American constitutional law and practice, avowedly modelled after Kent and Story. Mansfield was a lawyer.

213. (MARRIAGE LAW) KEBLE, REV. JOHN. Sequel of the argument against immediately repealing the laws which treat the nuptial bond as indissoluble. Oxford, Parker, 1857. 220pp. Disbound. $ 27.50

214. MARSHALL, SAMUEL. A treatise on the law of insurance, in four books ... First American, from the English edition. Two volumes in one. Boston, Johnson, 1805. 759pp. Contemp. calf, raised bands, rubbed. $ 75.00
* First American appearance of the standard work on marine insurance of this period, replacing Park. Marvin p. 500. Holdsworth XIII, 484.

215. (MARTIN, FRANCOIS-XAVIER translator and publisher) GREAT BRITAIN. COURT OF KING'S BENCH. Cases determined in the ... during theI, II, & III years of Charles I. Collected by John Latch ... first published in Norman French (1661) ... translated into the English languageby Francois-Xavier Martin. Newbern, N. C., from the Translator's Press, 1793.

215. (Continued) 8vo. Unpaginated (approx. 250pp) with final leaf of errata and ads. Contemp. sheep rubbed. A very good copy. $150.00
* First edition in English, and especially noteworthy as one of Martin's earliest productions. Martin started his career as a North Carolina printer and legal writer, contributing several important compilations, translations and practice books; in 1813 he became the first attorney general of Louisiana, and later chief justice. See DAB. Evans 25451 or (25702 under Latch). Wallace p. 262-65, describing this edition then (1882) as scarce. Copy belonging to Daniel Moreau Barringer, North Carolinian lawyer, congressman, diplomat, minister to Spain.

216. (MARYLAND) The Constitution of the State of Maryland: formed and adopted by the Convention which assembled at ... Annapolis, May 8, 1867 ... with marginal notes and references ... and an appendix and index by Edward Otis Hinkley ... Baltimore, Murphy, 1867. 156pp. Contemp. sheep. $ 27.50

217. (MARYLAND). General rules for the regulation of the pleading and practice of the Courts of Equity in this State, devised and promulgated by the judges of the Court of Appeals, in pursuance of section 18 of Article 4 of the Constitution of this State. Baltimore, Prtd. by King Bros., (1883). 27pp. Orig. cl. $ 15.00

218. (MARYLAND) Speech of Judge Chambers on the judicial tenure in the Maryland Convention, April 1851. Baltimore, Murphy, 1851. 41pp. Disbound. Defends an independent judiciary. $ 15.00

219. MARYLAND COLONY. LAWS, STATUTES, etc. Laws of Maryland made since M, DCC, LXIII, consisting of Acts of Assembly under the Proprietary Government, Resolves of Convention, Declaration of Rights, the Constitution and Form of Government, the Articles of Confederation, and, Acts of Assembly since the Revolution. Annapolis; Printed by Frederick Green, 1787. Folio. (4), (438), (12), (1)pp. Some foxing and browning. Handsomely bound in recent 1/4 calf, marbled sides, leather label with raised bands gilt. A good copy. $250.00
* A scarce compilation coming between the great work of Bacon in 1765 and William Kilty's laws of 1799-1800. Edited by A. C. Hanson. Sabin #45189 notes: "One hundred copies printed."

220. MASSACHUSETTS. LAWS (NATHAN DANE, WILLIAM PRESCOTT, and JOSEPH STORY). The charters and general laws of the colony and province of Massachusetts Bay, carefully collected from the publick records and ancient printed books, to which is added an appendix, tending to explain the spirit, progress, and history of the jurisprudence of the state ... published by Order of the General Court. Boston, Wait, 1814. Med. 8vo. vii, 830pp. plus index. 19th century 1/4 calf, front joint a little weak. $ 80.00
(Continued)

220. (Continued)
* First edition of the first modern compilation intended to serve as a reliable source of precedent in contemporary jurisprudence; many of these laws were still in force; others, though repealed, remained relevant to the construction of new statutes. The committee appointed to perform this compilation consisted of Story, Dane and Prescott, who were instructed also to report those laws still in effect which in their opinion ought to be repealed. This was JaredSpark's copy with his name on the title-page.

221. MASSACHUSETTS. LAWS, STATUTES. The laws of the Commonwealth of Massachusetts passed from the year 1780 to the end of 1800 ... in two volumes. Boston, Manning and Loring, 1801. 1073pp. plus indexes. Orig. calf, very good copies. $ 60.00
* The committee consisted of Nathan Dane, George Richards Minot and John Davis. First edition of this major new compilation.

222. MASSACHUSETTS. LAWS, STATUTES. The laws of the Commonwealth of Massachusetts from (February 1801) to February 28, 1807 ... Boston, Thomas & Andrews ... 1807. 403pp. plus index. Calf, fine. $ 35.00
* This is denoted as "Volume Three" and is in fact a continuation of the compilation published in 2 volumes in 1801. For this volume the committee appointed on behalf of the Commonwealth consisted of Joseph Story and John Davis.

223. (MASSACHUSETTS. REVISED CONSTITUTION). Discussions on the Constitution proposed to the people of Massachusetts, by the Convention of 1853. Boston, Little, Brown, 1854. 306pp. Orig. cl. $ 35.00
* Anthology of six discussions of the new proposed Constitution, all of which had been previously published separately. Includes The letters of Phocion, by G. T. Curtis; also works by G. S. Hillard, Samuel Hoar, Marcus Morton, C. F. Adams, and J. G. Palfrey.

224. MAY, HENRY. Speech of ... late member of the Bar of the Circuit Court, on reform in the judiciary of the District of Columbia. Wash., Gideon, 1850. 15pp. Disbound. $ 25.00

225. MAY, JOHN WILDER. The law of crimes. Boston, Little, Brown, 1881. 239pp. Full contemp. sheep, rubbed, wants label. $ 25.00

226. MAYO, JOSEPH. A guide to magistrates: with practical forms for the discharge of their duties out of court. To which are added precedents for the use of prosecutors, sheriffs, coroners, constables, escheators, clerks, &c. Second edition, in which the laws are brought down to the present time, with notes. Richmond, prtd. by Wynne, 1860. 726pp. Full contemp. calf rubbed but a good sound copy. $ 45.00

227. METCALF, THERON. Principles of the law of contracts as applied by courts of law. Second edition by Franklin Fiske Heard. Boston, Boston Book, 1893. 433pp. Full contemp. sheep. rubbed. $ 30.00

228. MILTON, JOHN. A defence of the people of England ... in answer to Salmasius's Defence of the King. Printed in the year 1692. 4pl., xxii, 1 blank leaf, 246, (1)pp. 8vo. Contemp. blind ruled calf, spine gilt, light wear along joints and head of spine, inner hinges later reinforced. A good copy with the original front blank, and with the final leaf of publisher's ads for books sympathetic to Charles I. $250.00
* First edition in English. Wing M-2104.

229. MINOT, GEORGE, ed. Digest of the decisions of the Supreme Judicial Court of Massachusetts, reported in the seventeen volumes of Massachusetts reports, the twenty-four volumes of Pickering's reports, and the first four volumes of Metcalf's reports. Boston, Little, Brown, 1844. xciii, 804pp. Full contemp. sheep, rubbed. $ 45.00

230. MISSISSIPPI TERRITORY. LAWS, STATUTES, etc. Statutes of the Mississippi Territory, The Constitution ... The Articles of Agreement and Cession between the United States and the State of Georgia; and such acts of Congress as relate to the Mississippi Territory. Digested by the authority of the General Assembly. Natchez, Peter Isler, Printer to the Territory, 1816. 495, (1), (28)pp. Contemp. sheep, leather label, light wear along joints and a little rubbed but quite a good copy in fresh contemporary state. $375.00
* Digested by Edward Turner and known as "Turner's Code..." Contains the laws from 1798 through the session of 1816. McMurtrie 96. Shaw-Shoemaker 38269. A choice copy of these early laws of the new south.

231. (MISSOURI. SUPREME COURT). A digest of the decisions of the ... on all subjects from 1820 to 1845; also the Constitution of the United States, to which is attached the construction given to the same. Compiled by Evans Casselberry. St. Louis, S. W. Meech, 1845. 482, (3)pp. New cl. $ 75.00
* American Imprints Inv. Missouri, 434. Not in Sabin.

232. (MONTANA). Constitution of the State of Montana as adopted by the Constitutional Convention held at Helena, July 4, 1889 ... and also an address to the people. Helena, Published by Authority by the Independent Publ. Co., (1889). 76pp. Orig. pink wrps., fine. $ 50.00
* Official publication of the Montana State Constitution under which Montana was admitted to the Union. Kuhlman, p. 43.

233. MOORE, JOHN BAYLY. A digested index to the term reports, analytically arranged containing all the points of law argued and determined in the Court of King's Bench from Michaelmas Term 1785, to Michaelmas Term 1819; in the Court of Common Pleas from Easter Term 1788, to Trinity Term 1819; and in the Court of Exchequer from Easter Term 1792, to Hilary Term 1818; with notes, references, tables to titles and statutes, and names of cases. In two vols. Second edition, with considerable additions and improvements. London, printed for J. Butterworth, 1821. 945,325pp. New cl. $ 50.00
* Last edition (but there were supplements 1822-25). Marvin p. 528. S & M II, 287.

234. MORAWETZ, VICTOR. A treatise on the law of private corporations. Second edition. In two volumes. Boston, Little, Brown, 1886. 2 vols. New cloth. $ 45.00

235. MOREHEAD, JAMES T. The practice in civil actions and proceedings at law in Kentucky; together with various precedents of declarations, with practical notes. Cincinnati, Derby, 1846. 783pp. Old sheep, rebacked. $ 50.00

MORMON SUFFRAGETTES

236. "Mormon" women's protest. An appeal for freedom, justice and equal rights ... against the tyranny and indecency of Federal Officials in Utah, and against their own disfranchisement without cause Full account of the Proceedings at the Great Mass Meeting held in the Theater ... Salt Lake City, Deseret News, 1886. 91pp. Orig. prtd. wrps. Fine. Laid in is a hand list of Mormon publications available at the store of Cannon & Sons, Ogden, Utah. $125.00
* In 1870 the territorial legislature had enfranchised women, according to the petitioners, in the misguided hope that they would vote down Mormon institutions. Now that first grant of woman suffrage was under attack by the Federal government. Also present is a petition against the cruelties of the Edmunds Act which prohibited future plural marriages. A choice pamphlet. Flake 5533.

237. MORRISON, CHARLES R. The New-Hampshire Probate Directory: containing the general statutes and acts since passed, with full notes of decisions and forms of wills, petitions, citations, orders and decrees, and all other matters relating to probate courts and proceedings therein. Concord, Sanborn, 1870. 205pp. Full contemp. sheep., lea. label. Fine. $ 17.50

238. MORRISON, CHARLES ROBERT. New Hampshire Town Officer: containing the general laws of 1878 (other than school laws) and acts since passed relating to towns and cities, with decisions, directions, and forms. Concord, Sanborn, 1886. 498pp. Full sheep. First edition. $ 22.50

239. MORSE, JOHN T., Jr. The law of arbitration and award. Boston, Little, Brown, 1872. 670pp. New cloth. First edition. $ 45.00

****

240. NATIONAL ASSOCIATION FOR THE PROMOTION OF SOCIAL SCIENCE. Transactions of the ... Norwich meeting, 1873. Edited by C. W. Ryalls. London. Longmans, 1874. 687pp. Orig. cl. $ 45.00
* Part I, pp. 137-307, is devoted to jurisprudence; participants include T. Erskine Holland, David Dudley Field, et al.

241. NATIONAL ASSOCIATION FOR THE PROMOTION OF SOCIAL SCIENCE. Transactions of the ... Glasgow meeting 1874. Edited by Charles Wagner Ryalls. London, Longmans, 1875. 976pp. Orig. cl. $ 37.50
* Part I, pp. 149-358 is devoted to jurisprudence and criminology.

242. NECKER, (JACQUES). An essay on the true principles of executive power in great states. Translated from the French ... London, Robinson, 1792. Two volumes, 8vo. Contemporary polished calf, red leather labels. A very good set. $250.00
* FIRST EDITION IN ENGLISH. A significant part of the second volume is a commentary on the American political system and constitution. An early and notable work on comparative constitutional systems which also discusses the question of social equality and criticizes the new revolutionary order. INED 3369. Not in the BM or Goldsmith's catalogues. Not in Sabin, or New Sabin, despite significant American interest.

243. NEILSON, JOSEPH. Memories of Rufus Choate, with some consideration of his studies, methods, and opinions, and of his style as a speaker and writer. Boston, Houghton, Mifflin, 1884. Frontis. 460pp. Orig. cl. $ 25.00

244. NESS, JOHN WILLIAM. A treatise on the game laws of Scotland with an appendix containing the principal statutes and leading cases on the subject. Edinburgh, Michael Anderson ..., 1818. x,240pp. Half-title present. Original two-toned boards, printed paper label, a fine and attractive copy. $100.00

245. (NEW HAMPSHIRE) The probate directory: or a complete system of forms for the use of probate courts ... according to the existing laws of New-Hampshire: and containing also, the substance of the probate laws of Massachusetts and Vermont and adapted to the practice in those states. By a Counsellor at Law. Concord, Hough, 1829. 504pp. Full contemp. sheep. $ 35.00
* First edition. Shoemaker 40157. Scarce.

246. NEW HAMPSHIRE. LAWS, STATUTES. The laws of the State of New-Hampshire, the Constitution of the State of New-Hampshire, and the Constitution of the United States, with its proposed amendments. Printed by order of the Honorable the General-Court. Portsmouth, Melcher, 1797. 492pp. Full contemp. sheep. Evans 32536. $ 75.00

247. NEW HAMPSHIRE. LAWS, STATUTES. Constitution and laws of the State of New-Hampshire; together with the Constitution of the United States. Published by Authority. Dover, Bragg, 1805. 531pp. Full contemp. sheep. $ 55.00

248. NEW-HAMPSHIRE. LAWS, STATUTES. The Public laws of New-Hampshire, enacted since the passage of the compiled statutes; June Session, 1853, to June Session, 1859, inclusive; with a copious index. Concord, Lyon, 1860. Full contemp. sheep. $ 37.50

249. NEW YORK STATE. SUPREME COURT. Reports of cases of practice, determined in the Supreme Court of Judicature of the State of New-York; from April term, 1794, to November term, 1805, both inclusive, to which is prefixed all the rules and orders of the court to the present time. N. Y., Riley, 1808. 530pp. Full contemp. sheep. $ 35.00
* Sometimes listed under William Coleman and George Caines. Coleman's Cases were the first published N. Y. reports. This is a reprint of that 1801 volume to which are added cases of practice selected from Caines' reports. Marvin p. 213. Wallace p. 579.

250. NEW ZEALAND. The New Zealand Constitution Act; together with correspondence between the Secretary of State for the Colonies and the Governor-in-Chief of New Zealand in explanation thereof. Wellington, R. Stokes, 1853. 127pp. Contemp. 1/4 morocco, spine lettered in gilt. A very nice copy. $250.00
* First edition of the first New Zealand constitution establishing representative self-government for the colony. There had been an attempt at a similar constitution in 1846 but it failed because of pressure from the governor. This act still remains New Zealand's basic constitutional document, though much altered by the very parliament it created. McLintock, Encyclopaedia of N. Z. 1966, II, p67ff. Hocken p. 172.

****

251. OKE, GEORGE C. A handy book of the game and fishery laws ... throughout the United Kingdom, and private and salmon fisheries in England; systematically arranged, with the acts, decisions, notes, forms, suggestions, etc. ... Second edition. London, Butterworths, 1863. 374pp. Orig. cl., gilt. $ 65.00

252. OLIVER, BENJAMIN L. Forms of practice; or American precedents in personal and real actions, interspersed with annotations. Fourth edition, revised and enlarged by a Member of the Cumberland Bar ... embracing also rules, forms at law and precedents, according to the practice acts of Massachusetts, supervised by a Member of the Suffolk Bar. Portland, Dresser, 1874. xxxvi,869pp. Full contemp. sheep $ 45.00
* A heavily augmented edition, especially with respect to the new Massachusetts codes.

253. OLIVER, PETER. Practical conveyancing; a selection of forms of general utility, with notes interspersed. Fourth edition, corrected and enlarged. Hallowell, Glazier, 1845. 622pp. cl. $ 30.00
* Marvin p. 547, highly praised.

254. OLMSTEAD, DWIGHT H. Land transfer reform. An address delivered before the New York State Bar Association ... with an appendix containing a synopsis of the New Zealand Land Transfer Act. Albany, Argus, 1883. 19pp. Orig. prtd. wrps. Urges a registry to facilitate land transfer. $ 27.50

255. OLMSTEAD, DWIGHT H. Transfer of title to real estate: a lecture delivered before the (West Side) Association ... with a synopsis of the New Zealand Land Transfer Act. N. Y., Evening Post, 1881. 28pp. Orig. prtd. wrps. Urges strong reform, including a registry system for facilitating transfer of real property. $ 27.50

256. ONSLOW, ARTHUR. An institute of the law relative to trials at Nisi Prius, originally published in the year 1760. A new edition, with alterations and additions. London, Prtd. for T. Wheildon, 1789. 284pp. Contemp. calf, joints worn but sound. $ 50.00
* Another edition of Buller, adding, however, some modern cases. See Holdsworth XII, 354n. Marvin p. 412 and 158.

257. Ordonnances, statuts, et reglements du Comte Venaissin. Avignon, Jean Piot, 1638. Sm. 8vo. 3pl.,67pp. Woodcut device on title. Contemp. vellum. Stained. $ 50.00
* Consists entirely of a reformed set of fees and regulations governing all legal and court officers from clerks to judges.

258. ORTOLAN, (JOSEPH LOUIS ELZEAR). Explication historique des Instituts de l'Empereur Justinien, avec le texte, la traduction ... les explications sous chaque paragraphe, et une table ... precedee d'une generalisation du droit Romain ... deuxieme ed. rev. et considerablement augmentee. Paris, Joubert, 1840-1843. 2 volumes. 8vo. Contemp. calf, ruled in blind, contrasting labels, little rubbed. Contemp. bookplate of William Ramsay, University of Glasgow, and binder's ticket of Carss & Co., Glasgow. $ 75.00

259. PANCOUCKE, (CHARLES LOUIS FLEURY). De l'exposition, de la prison et de la peine de mort. Essai. (With:) Lettre de M. Francois (de Neufchateau), a M. Pancoucke ... au sujet de son essai ... Paris, Agasse, 1807. 41,15pp. Half title present. 19th century boards. Fine. $125.00
* Inscribed presentation: "offert par l'auteur au Major Poussin ... a Paris." The NUC cites only the NYPL copy.

260. PARKER, EDWARD G. Reminiscences of Rufus Choate, the great American advocate. N. Y., Mason, 1860. 522pp. Illus. Cl. $ 27.50

261. PARKER, JAMES. The conductor generalis: or the office, duty and authority of justices of the peace ... compiled chiefly from Burn's Justice ... by James Parker, late one of the justices ... in New Jersey; and now revised and adapted to the United States of America, By a Gentleman of the Law ... to which are added ... the Ten Pound Act, and the Militia Law of the State of New York. N. Y., Hugh Gaine, 1788. xv,461pp. 8vo. Contemp. sheep worn. A sound copy of a perishable book. $100.00
* First edition to be adapted to the U.S. A basic English work, it passed through 10 American editions between 1711 and 1794, the first ones unaltered beyond their model, the later ones, including this, full of reference to American practice. Evans 21358.

A MANUAL FOR THE
WHISKEY REBELLION

262. PARKER, JAMES. The conductor generalis: or, the office, duty and authority of justices of the peace ... compiled chiefly from Burn's Justice ... by James Parker, late one of the Justices of the Peace for Middlesex County, in New Jersey, and now revised and adapted to the United States of America. By a Gentleman of the Law ... to which are added, the excise and militia laws of the U.S.; and the Acts called the Ten Pound Act of the States of Pennsylvania and New York. Phila., Campbell, 1792. xv,464pp. 8vo. New cloth. A good copy. $100.00
* Evans 24661. The third appearance of this classic work in its adaptation to the new union. An extremely interesting edition containing the revenue laws and the means of their enforcement which led soon to the Whiskey Rebellion extending from western Pennsylvania to Georgia. Later editions of course omitted this material.

263. (PARKER, JAMES). The conductor generalis: or, the office, duty and authority of justices of the peace, ... compiled chiefly from Burn's Justice ... by James Parker, late one of the Justices of the Peace for Middlesex County, in New Jersey; and now revised and adapted to the United States of America, by A Gentleman of the Law. ... Albany, Webster, 1794. 8vo. 467pp. Contemp. calf, lea. label. A very good copy, especially considering the use to which
263. (Continued) such a volume was subjected. $100.00
* Fourth appearance (1st was 1788) of this U. S. adaptation of the standard English work which first appeared, unaltered, in N. Y. and Pennsylvania editions early in the century. This national adaptation emphasizes N. Y., N. J., and Pennsylvania law. Evans 27472.

264. PARSONS, THEOPHILUS. The law of contracts. Sixth edition. In three vols. Boston, Little, Brown, 1873. 609,801,746pp. New cloth. $ 75.00

265. PARSONS, THEOPHILUS. Laws of business for all the States of the Union, with forms and directions for all transactions. Hartford, Scranton, 1869. 685pp. 1/4 sheep. $ 30.00
* Second edition (first was 1857), much altered, of what became the most enduring text in its field.

266. PARSONS, THEOPHILUS. Laws of business for all the States of the Union, and the Dominion of Canada. With forms and directions for all transactions. Revised and enlarged ed. Hartford, Scranton, 1877. 693pp. Very good copy. $ 37.50
* This appears to be the earliest edition to include Canada.

267. PARSONS, THEOPHILUS. Laws of business for all the States of the Union, and the Dominion of Canada. With forms and directions for all transactions. Revised and enlarged edition. Hartford, Scranton, 1878. 693pp. Full contemp. sheep. $ 30.00
* An early Canadian issue.

268. PARSONS, THEOPHILUS. Laws of business for all the States of the Union, and the Dominion of Canada, with forms and directions for all transactions, and abstracts of the laws of all the States on various topics. Greatly enlarged and improved. Hartford, Scranton, 1882. 848pp. cl. $ 30.00

269. (PENNSYLVANIA. CONSTITUTION). CREIGH, ALFRED. The Constitution of the Commonwealth of Pennsylvania. Adopted January 1, 1874. With an analytical index ... Washington, Pa., Reporter Steam Job Office Print, 1874. 66pp. Orig. limp lea. $ 17.50

270. PENNSYLVANIA STATE LIBRARY. Catalogue of the law books of the Pennsylvania State Library. Prepared by William Wallace Chisolm, official cataloguer. n.p., Ray, State prtr., 1899. 963pp. Frontis. Library stamp on title page. Large thick 4 to. A massive catalogue of a major collection. $ 50.00

271. PENNYPACKER, SAMUEL W. Pennsylvania Colonial cases: the administration of law in Pennsylvania prior to A. D. 1700 as shown in the cases decided and in the court proceedings. Phila., Bisel, 1892. 185pp. Orig. cl. lea. labels. $ 25.00

272. PERLEY, JEREMIAH. The Maine Justice; containing the laws relative to the powers and duties of justices of the peace, with the necessary forms. Hallowell, Goodale, Glazier & Co., 1823. vii, 304pp. 8vo. Contemp. sheep little rubbed but a very good copy. $ 75.00
* First edition of the first justice of the peace for the new State of Maine. A well preserved copy of a book which is uncommon today.

273. PERRY, R. ROSS. Common-law pleading; its history and principles, including Dicey's rules concerning parties to actions and Stephen's rules of pleading. Boston, Little, Brown, 1897. Cl. First edition. $ 40.00

274. PHILLIPPS, S. M. A treatise on the law of evidence. First American, from the second London edition; with notes and references to American authorities by John A. Dunlap. To which is added the theory of presumptive proof, &c. N. Y., Gould, 1816. Two vols. in one. xliii, 520, 106pp. Full contemp. sheep. $ 75.00
* First American edition. Nice copy of a scarce edition. This work passed through numerous further American edition. "Phillipps' Evidence has been one of the most successful of modern textbooks ... from sometimes discordant matter (it) evolves a principle. ... This text book ... has been frequently referred to by eminent judges with approbation, and has always been treated by the Bench with respect."--Marvin p. 569.

275. PHILLIPS, WILLARD. A treatise on the law of insurance. Boston, Wells and Lilly, 1823. 550pp. Contemp. sheep, leather label. Rubbed with some minor wear along lower spine, but sound and internally a very good copy. $100.00
* FIRST EDITION of the first original American work on the subject. Marvin p. 569. DAB.

276. The pocket conveyancer: or attorney's useful companion: containing variety of the most approved precedents, both special and common ... second edition with the addition of many excellent original precedents. In two volumes. London, Strahan and Woodfall, 1773. 2 vols. 12mo. Contemp. calf rubbed, front covers detached but present, contents good. $ 50.00
* The only other edition beyond the first of 1760. The NUC cites a single holding.

277. POLLOCK, FREDERICK. A first book of jurisprudence for students of the common law. London, MacMillan, 1896. 348pp. Orig. cl. First edition. Nice copy. $ 30.00

278. POMEROY, JOHN NORTON. An introduction to municipal law. Designed for general readers, and for students in colleges and higher schools. N. Y., Appleton, 1864. xxxviii, 544pp. Orig. cl. Fine. $ 75.00
* The author's first book and a very important one. "The book, which purportedto be an ele-

278. (Continued) mentary text for law students, really marked a departure from the conventional treatises based upon Blackstone. It disclosed Pomeroy's acquaintance with Roman and other legal systems, as well as with the ideas which Bentham and Austin were then spreading in England."--DAB. The work displays a high degree of scholarship and scientific method.

279. POWELL, JOHN JOSEPH An essay on devises. Third edition with copious notes and an appendix of precedents; also a treatise on the construction of devises by Thomas Jarman. In two volumes. London, Sweet, 1827. New cl. 751; 800pp. $ 45.00
* S & M I, 493. Marvin p. 582. This is the final edition.

280. POWELL, JOHN JOSEPH. An essay on the learning respecting the creation and execution of powers; and also respecting the nature and effect of leasing powers, in which the doctrine of the judgment delivered by the Court of King's Bench, in the case of Pugh and the Duke of Leeds, and the principal authorities for and against it, are considered. Second edition. Dublin, prtd. for E. Lynch, 1791. 582pp. Contemp. calf worn but sound. $ 65.00
* "To Mr. Powell belongs the merit of first collecting and systematizing the decisions upon the subtle doctrine of powers."--Marvin p. 581. "A pioneer work on the powers of appointment ..." --Holdsworth XII, 382. First edition was 1787.

281. The present state of the practice and practicers of the law, wherein is shewn the obscurity, uncertainty and expensiveness thereof with some methods humbly propos'd for remedying the same; in a familiar dialogue between Philalethes and Philonomous. By an impartial hand. London, Printed for the author and sold by T. Cooper, c. 1730. 8, 64pp. Stiched as issued and uncut. A fine copy in original state. $225.00
* An attractive piece of 18th century legal reform, highly specific and detailed and obviously by an able practitioner. Very uncommon. The NUC cites 3 locations of a second edition only. Not found in the BLC. S & M I, 214, suggesting ca. 1730.

282. RAFF, GEORGE W. A guide to executors and administrators in the settlement of the estates of deceased persons within the State of Ohio, to which is prefixed a brief comment upon the statute of wills. Third edition, revised and enlarged. Cincinnati, Clarke, 1864. 317pp. Full contemp. sheep, rubbed. $ 37.50

283. RAFF, GEORGE W. A guide to executors and administrators in the settlement of the estates of deceased persons within the State of Ohio, to which is prefixed a brief comment upon the statute of wills. Fourth edition, revised and enlarged. Cincinnati, Clarke, 1871. 327pp. Full sheep. $ 35.00

284. RAFF, GEORGE W. The law relating to roads and highways in the State of Ohio ... also, a brief consideration of ways existing by grant, dedication, and prescription. Second edition, greatly enlarged. Cincinnati, Clarke, 1871. 334pp. Full sheep. $ 32.50

285. (RAITHBY, JOHN). The study and practice of the law, considered in their various relations to society, in a series of letters by a Member of Lincoln's Inn. First American edition. Portland, Wait, 1806. 364pp. plus 3pp. ads. New cloth. $ 75.00
* First American edition from the London edition of 1798. Sometimes attributed mistakenly to James Mackintosh. Halkett & Laing. Marvin p. 596f. A good copy with the 3 pages of Thomas Wait's ads announcing American editions of Sullivan's Lectures and a deluxe Blackstone.

286. RAM, JAMES. A treatise on facts as subjects of inquiry by a jury. Third American edition by John Townsend, with an appendix containing David Paul Brown's golden rules for the examination of a witness; Cox's advice for conducting the examination of a witnesses and opening a case to the jury; Whewell on theory and fact; Hoffman's fifty resolutions in regard to professional deportment; cases of mistaken identity, and of erroneous conviction. N. Y., Baker, 1873. 486pp. Full contemp. sheep, rubbed. $ 35.00

287. RAWLE, WILLIAM HENRY. Equity in Pennsylvania. A lecture delivered before the Law Academy of Philadelphia ... with an appendix, being the Registrar's Book of Governor Keith's Court of Chancery. Phila., Kay, 1868. 93, 46pp. New cl. $ 35.00

288. READ, COLLINSON. Precedents in the office of a justice of the peace. To which is added a short system of conveyancing in a method entirely new, with an appendix containing a variety of the most useful forms. Second edition with considerable additions. Harrisburgh, John Wyeth for the author, 1801. (4), 63, 36, (1)pp. Square 8vo. Contemporary 1/4 calf, marbled boards, a very good copy. $100.00

289. READ, JOHN M. Opinion of ... of the Supreme Court of Pennsylvania, in favor of the constitutionality of the Act of Congress of March 3, 1863." For enrolling and calling out the National Forces and for other purposes." Delivered at Pittsburgh, on Monday, Nov., 9, 1863. Phila., Sherman, 1863. 20pp. Orig. prtd. wrps. Concerns Civil War draft. $ 25.00

290. REEVES, JOHN. Considerations on the Coronation Oath to maintain the Protestant reformed religion and the settlement of the Church of England ... second edition with additions. London, Wright, 1801. 69pp. with half-titles. Disbound. $ 30.00
* A defense of religious discrimination by this high Tory historian of English law.

291. (RHODE ISLAND). A collection of forms adapted to the use of justices of the peace, public notaries, sheriffs and constables (etc) together with miscellaneous forms; making every man his own conveyancer: conformable to the laws and usages of the State of Rhode Island ... Providen John Miller, (1824). 352pp. sheep rubbed. $ 45.00
* First edition. Uncommon. Shoemaker 15811

292. (RHODE ISLAND). The Rhode Island clerk's magazine, or civil officer's assistant: containing forms of writing ... of conveyancers, justices of the peace (etc. ...) particularly adapted to ... Rhode Island ... Providence, Heaton for Cushing, 1803. 351pp. New cloth. $ 45.00

293. RICARDO, JOHN LEWIS. The anatomy of the navigation laws. London, Gilpin, 1847. 336pp. Orig. publ. cl., spine chipped and repaired, otherwise a very good copy. First edition. $ 75.00
* An influential analysis and criticism of Britain's regulations of her colonial commerce in Asia, Africa and America, with an accountof their past and present effects on British shipping and on competition with other countries. The author, a nephew of David Ricardo, was a free-trader and an effective opponent of the Navigation Laws in Parliament. See DNB.

294. RICHARDSON, WILLIAM M. The New-Hampshire justice of the peace. Second edition, improved. Concord, Hill, 1831. 299pp. Full contemp. sheep, worn. $ 20.00
* Marvin p. 609

295. RICHARDSON, WILLIAM M. The New-Hampshire town officer. Concord, Moore, 1829. 299pp. Full contemp. sheep. 12mo. A very good copy. First edition. $ 27.50

296. ROBERTS, WILLIAM. A treatise on the statute of frauds ... to which is prefixed a systematic dissertation upon the admissibility of parol and extrinsic evidence, to explain and controul written instruments. Second American, from the last London edition, with references to, and a digest of the American decisions ... by a Member of the Bar. Hartford, Cooke, 1823. 537pp. Full contemp. sheep. Marvin p. 612. $ 45.00

297. ROSCOE, HENRY. A digest of the law of evidence in criminal cases. With considerable additions by T. C. Granger. Third American, from the third London edition, with notes and references to American decisions and to the English common law and ecclesiastical reports, by George Sharswood. Phila., Johnson, 1846. xxxix, 990pp. New cloth. $ 45.00

298. ROSS, GEORGE. A treatise on the law of purchasers and vendors of personal property considered chiefly with a view to mercantile transactions. Second edition with considerable

298. (Continued) additions ... by S. B. Harrison. From the London edition.211pp. (WITH:) ROBERTSON, DAVID. A treatise on the rules of the law of personal succession ... and on the cases regarding foreign and international succession which have been decided in the British Courts. 296pp. Phila., Littell, 1836. New cl. (Law Library, Vol. XII) $ 45.00
* Both first American editions (London 1836 and 1811 respectively). Of theRoss-"a pioneer treatise."--Holdsworth XIII, 486. Marvin p. 621. and 613 respectively.

****

299. SAINT GERMAIN, CHRISTOPHER. Dialogus de fundamentis legum Angliae et de conscientia ... In aedibus Thomae Wight. 1604. Small 8vo. Neatly removed, 80 leaves including original final blank. Good margins. Very faint marginal stain. A very good copy. $100.00
* A classic work of authority which appeared in numerous editions for three centuries, Winfield, Chief Sources of English Legal History, 321 - 324, citing this edition which contains a biography of the author, a list of his works, and his will. First Latin edition since 1528. S & M I, 24. STC 21560.

300. SCHOULER, JAMES. A treatise on the law of bailments including carriers, innkeepers and pledge. Third edition. Boston, Little, Brown, 1897. 782pp. New cloth. $ 35.00

301. SCHOULER, JAMES. A treatise on the law of the domestic relations: embracing husband and wife, parent and child, guardian and ward, infancy, and master and servant. Fourth edition. Boston, Little Brown, 1889. 773pp. Full contemp. sheep. $ 35.00

302. SCHOULER, JAMES. A treatise on the law of wills. Boston, Boston Book Co., 1889. lv, 689pp. Full contemp. sheep, rubbed. $ 32.50

303. SELDEN, JOHN. Titles of honor. London, William Stansby for John Helme, 1614. Small 4to. Contemporary calf, raised bands, moderately rubbed, otherwise a very good copy.
* FIRST EDITION. STC 22177 $250.00

304. SERGEANT, HENRY J. Treatise on the lien of mechanics and material men in Pennsylvania: with the acts of assembly relating thereto: and various forms of claims. Phila., Kay, 1839. 132pp. New cl. $ 37.50
* First edition. Marvin p. 637.

305. SERGEANT, THOMAS. A treatise upon the law of Pennsylvania relative to the proceeding by foreign attachment, with the acts of assembly now in force ... on the subject ... Phila., Farrand, 1811. 331pp. Contemp. sheep, little rubbed but a very good copy. $ 65.00
* Marvin p. 368. First edition of the author's first important book. See DAB.

306. SHARSWOOD, GEORGE. The common law of Pennsylvania. A lecture read before the Law Academy of Philadelphia at the opening of the session 1855-6. Phila., L. R. Bailey, 1855. 30pp. Orig. prtd. wrps. Sharswood was provost of the Academy. $ 27.50

307. SHELFORD, LEONARD. A practical treatise of the law of marriage and divorce; containing also the mode of proceeding on divorces in the Ecclesiastical Courts and in Parliament; the right of the custody of children; voluntary separation between husband and wife; the husband's liability to wife's debts; and the conflict between the laws ofEngland and Scotland respecting divorce and legitimacy. Phila., Littell, 1841. 519pp. New cl. $ 55.00
* First American, same year as first London ed. Marvin p. 641.

308. SHEPPARD, WILLIAM. The touchstone of common assurances: or a plain and familiar treatise opening the learning of the common assurances ... First American, from Hilliard's last London edition. (WITH:) An appendix to the touchstone ... containing the laws of the several states of the Union ... by John Anthon. N. Y., I. Riley, 1808-1810. 3 vols. bound in 2. New cloth. Foxed. $ 65.00
* First American edition of this hardy classic. Marvin p. 643. Included is the separately published supplement for the American states by John Anthon.

309. SHIPPEN, EDWARD. et al., defendants. Report of the trial and acquittal of Edward Shippen, and Jasper Yeates and Thomas Smith... of the Supreme Court of Pennsylvania on an impeachment before the Senate of the Commonwealth January 1805. By William Hamilton, editor of the Lancaster Journal. Lancaster, Pa. Printed by the reporter, (1805). 491,96pp. Calf, rubbed. $ 60.00
* A notable trial involving the abuse of contempt of court proceedings in the case of Thomas Passmore. Shaw-Shoemaker 9353. Marvin p. 363. DAB on Shippen.

310. SHIRAS, OLIVER P. Equity practice in the United States Circuit Courts: a compilation of the provisions governing the same as found in the statutes of the United States, rules in equity and decisions of the Supreme Court. Chicago, Callaghan, 1889. 149pp. cl. $ 27.50

311. SMITH, SIR THOMAS. The Common-Wealth of England, and manner of government thereof ... with new additions of the chiefe courts in England, & the offices thereof, by the said author ... London, James Roberts for Gregorie Seton, 1601. Woodcut vignette on title, 4pl., 148pp. Small 4to. Recent full speckled calf ruled in blind, raised bands gilt, leather label. Light marginal stain to last few leaves. A very good copy in an attractive period style binding. $350.00
* The most important description of the actual working of the English constitution in the Tudor age, including the administration of justice

311. (Continued) through the medieval court system and the common law, a feature which Smith considers to be the chief difference between the English and continental systems of government. In addition it stands as "a pioneer treatise in comparative politics."--Holdsworth IV, p. 210f. See also DNB. It was first published in 1583 and passed through numerous editions and translations throughout the next century. STC 22861.

312. SPAULDING, JOSEPH WHITMAN. The practice in civil actions and proceedings at law in the courts where the common law practice is in vogue; with the amendments thereto necessary to incorporate the provisions of the statutes of Maine. Portland, Dresser, 1881. xxxvii, 739pp. Full contemp. sheep. $ 55.00
* First edition. Based largely on Samuel Howe's text of similar title, 1834 with extensive alterations necessitated by time - this is apparently the first such revision since the older works of Howe and Colby, so cited in the preface. See item # 159.

313. SPENCER, HERBERT. Justice: being Part IV of the Principles of Ethics. London, Williams & Norgate, 1891. vi, 291pp. plus ads. Orig. publisher's embossed cloth, slight wear to crown of spine, a near fine copy. $ 80.00
* First edition. Actually the second part to be published in his projected work on ethics, the first being The Data of Ethics, in 1879. "This work covers a field which, to a considerable extent, coincides with that covered by Social Statics (his first book, 1851) ... though the two differ, alike in extent, form, and partially in their ideas."-- author's preface. Topics include the concept of justice, free speech, property rights, and the nature and limits of the state.

314. STEARNS, ASAHEL. A summary of the law and practice of real actions; with an appendix of practical forms. Boston, Cummings, 1824. 528pp. Orig. bds., rebacked. $ 75.00
* First edition. Stearns was one of the first appointees to the newly founded Harvard Law School in 1817. This work contains the substance of his lectures delivered there. "(It) proved to be one of the notable early American law books and was welcomed by a bar in need of accurate available information on technical procedure."--DAB. Marvin p. 663, citing the laudatory notice in Hoffman's Legal Studies.

315. STEARNS, ASAHEL. A summary of the law and practice of real actions; with an appendix of practical forms. The second edition with additions. Hollowell, Glazier, 1831. xxxiv, 495pp. New cloth. $ 45.00
* The preface is dated Harvard University 1824. Marvin p. 663, this edition.

316. STEPHEN, HENRY JOHN. A treatise on the principles of pleading in civil actions: comprising a summary view of the whole proceedings in a suit at law. Corrected in conformity with the rules of H. T. 1834, and otherwise improved. Fifth American edition, with notes; and additions from the first London edition, by Francis J.
(Continued)

316. (Continued) Troubat. Phila., Small, 1845. 453, clxxxpp. Full contemp. sheep. Nice copy. $ 50.00
* Marvin p. 664: "a masterpiece of exhaustive and elegant legal writing." "Of the later works which make any claim to a scientific treatment ... the best is ... Stephen's"--Winfield, p. 308. Holdsworth XIII, 458; Holdsworth, Sources and Literature ... p. 119.

317. STEPHEN, SIR JAMES FITZJAMES, et al. A digest of the law of criminal procedure in indictable offences. London, MacMillan, 1883. 230pp. Orig. cl. V. Good. $ 65.00

318. STEPHEN, JAMES FITZJAMES. Liberty, equality, fraternity. N. Y., Holt, 1873. 350pp. Orig. cl. Fine. $ 37.50
* First American, same year as the first London edition. The author's chief work, aside from his writings on the criminal law, expressing a conservative political philosophy.

319. STERNE, SIMON. On representative government and personal representation: based in part upon Thomas Hare's treatise, entitled, "The Election of Representatives, Parliamentary and Municipal." ... Phila., Lippincott, 1871. 237pp. Orig. cl. Fine copy. 1st ed. Scarce. $ 27.50

320. STORY, JOSEPH. Commentaries on equity jurisprudence, as administered in England and America. In two vols. Boston, Hilliard, 1836. 689, 769pp. New cl. Very good set. $150.00
* FIRST EDITION. Marvin p. 671, extensively praising this essential work and noting its esteemed position in England.

321. STORY, JOSEPH. Commentaries on equity pleadings, and the incidents thereto, according to the practice of the Courts of Equity of England and America. Boston, Little, Brown, 1838. 734pp. New cl. A very good copy. $100.00
* FIRST EDITION. Marvin p672, quoting Greenleaf's lavish praise of this work.

322. STORY, JOSEPH. Commentaries on equity pleadings, and the incidents thereof, according to the practice of the courts of equity of England and America. Ninth edition, revised, corrected, and enlarged, by John M. Gould. Boston, Little, Brown, 1879. 762pp. Full contemp. sheep. $ 40.00

323. STORY, JOSEPH. Commentaries on the conflict of laws, foreign and domestic in regard to contracts, rights and remedies, and especially in regard to marriages, divorces, wills, successions, and judgements. Boston, Hilliard, Gray, 1834. xxv, 557pp. Contemp. sheep, little rubbed, still a very good copy. $150.00
* FIRST EDITION. Marvin p.670f in an extensive laudatory note identifies this as the first work on this "most difficult chapter of public law" in America or England, and cites instances of its enthusiastic reception abroad.

324. STORY, JOSEPH. Commentaries on the conflict of laws, foreign and domestic, in regard to contracts, rights and remedies, and especially in regard to marriages, divorces, wills, successions, and judgements. Third edition, revised, corrected, and greatly enlarged. Boston, Little, Brown, 1846. 1068pp. Full contemp. sheep, rubbed $ 65.00
* Contains the final revisions of the author. Marvin p.670f.

325. STORY, JOSEPH. Commentaries on the law of agency as a branch of commercial and maritime jurisprudence. With occasional illustrations from the civil and foreign law. Third edition, revised, corrected, and enlarged. Boston, Little, 1846. 677pp. New cl. $ 50.00
* A reprint of the second edition, the final one from Story's hand.

326. STORY, JOSEPH. Commentaries on the law of parternship, as a branch of commercial and maritime jurisprudence, with occasional illustrations from the civil and foreign law. Second edition. Boston, Little, 1846. $ 55.00
* A posthumously published enlargement of the first edition of 1841, based upon Story's own manuscript.

327. STORY, JOSEPH. Commentaries on the law of partnership, as a branch of commercial and maritime jurisprudence, with occasional illustrations from the civil and foreign law. Fifth ed. Boston, Little, Brown, 1859. 754pp. Sheep, rubbed. $ 45.00

328. STORY, JOSEPH. Selection of pleadings in civil actions, with occasional annotations. A second edition, with additions by Benjamin Oliver. Boston, Carter, 1829. 709pp. New cloth. $ 55.00
* Second edition of Story's first formal law work originally published in 1805. See Marvin 668, noting it as a welcome achievement in a field then new to American legal literature.

329. STOW, MRS. J.W. Probate confiscation and the unjust laws which govern women. (San Francisco, the author, 1876). 258pp. Frontis Orig. embossed cl., gilt. $ 50.00
* Attacks California probate law from personal experience. Cowan p. 620.

330. SUGDEN, EDWARD B. A practical treatise of powers. London, Reed, 1808. 604pp. Full calf, little rubbed, still a very good copy. $125.00
* First edition. "A masterly elucidation ... held in the highest esteem ..."--Marvin p. 676f. "The subject embraced a large part of the law of real property ... It is the best authority both for the present law and for its history."--Holdsworth XIII, p. 477.

331. SUGDEN, EDWARD. A practical treatise of powers. Second American from the seventh

331. (Continued) London edition, with additional references to American cases. Phila., Johnson, 1847. 2 vols. in 1. 403, 406pp. New cl. $ 40.00
* "It is the best authority both for the present law and for its history."--Holdsworth XIII, p. 477.

332. SULLIVAN, FRANCIS STOUGHTON. Lectures on the constitution and laws of England: with a commentary on Magna Charta, and illustrations of many of the English statutes. The second edition, to which authorities are added, and a discourse is prefixed, concerning the laws and government of England, by Gilbert Stuart. Dublin, prtd. for Wm. Jones, 1790. 570pp. Full contemp. calf, worn but sound. Light stains in text. $ 75.00
* Sullivan attempted at his post in the University of Dublin lectures like those of Blackstone, designed, however, for less advanced students. "A good introduction to the study both of the law of real property and of constitutional law."--Holdsworth XII, 342f. Marvin p. 678f, giving an appreciative notice. This is the best edition with the supporting notes by Gilbert Stuart.

333. SULLIVAN, JAMES. Observations upon the government of the United States of America. Boston, Samuel Hall, 1791. 55pp. Half-title present. Small marginal stain. Recent 1/4 calf, gray boards. A very good copy. $250.00
* First and only edition of a very scarce and significant work. "A treatise on the suability of states ... credited with having been influential in securing the adoption of the Eleventh Ammendment..."--DAB. At issue was the case of Jacob and Nicholas Van Staphorst vs. Maryland, involving the apparent willingness of the State of Maryland to recognize a suit against it in a Federal court. Sullivan was at this time Attorney General of Massachusetts, later to become governor. He was "one of the most prominent lawyers in Massachusetts ... perhaps the richest, ablest and most powerful of the Democrats ... his writings ... carried great weight."--DAB. Evans 23812.

****

334. THAYER, JAMES BRADLEY. A preliminary treatise on evidence at the common law. Boston, Little, Brown, 1898. 636pp. Orig. cl. First edition. Very good copy. $ 45.00
* "Thayer's great book ... was the first to treat the development of this branch of the law historically ... (it) gave us at length an entirely adequate history of the jury, and of those older modes of trial." Holdsworth, Historians of Anglo-American Law, p. 104.

335. THOMPSON, ISAAC GRANT. The supervisor's manual: containing the laws relating to the powers and duties of supervisors, both in their individual and collective capacities. With an appendix of forms. Second edition. Albany, Parsons, Jr., 1869. 292pp. Full contem. sheep. rubbed. $ 27.50

336. THOMPSON, SEYMOUR D., et al. A treatise on the organization, custody and conduct of juries, including grand juries. St. Louis, Stevenson, 1882. 782pp. Full contemp. sheep, rear joint repaired. A scarce treatise. First edition. $ 55.00

337. TIDD, WILLIAM. The practice of the Courts of King's Bench and Common Pleas in personal actions and ejectment: to which are added the law and practice of extents; and the rules of court, and modern decisions, in the Exchequer of Pleas. In two vols. Third American, from the ninth London editions. With notes of recent English statutes and decisions, by Francis J. Troubat. Phila., Small, 1840. 1549pp. 2 vols. Buckram. $ 45.00
* "No practical treatise in modern times approaches nearer to judicial authority than this ... in more general use than any English reprint of this description."--Marvin p. 691.

338. TIDD, WILLIAM. The practice of the Courts of King's Bench, and Common Pleas, in personal actions, and ejectment, to which are added, the law and practice of extents, and the rules of court, and modern decisions, in the Exchequer of Pleas. In two vols. Third American, from the ninth London edition, with notes of recent English statutes and decisions, by Francis J. Troubat. Fourth American edition, with additional notes, by Asa I. Fish. Phila., Small, 1856. 1550pp. Later buckram. Ex-library. $ 45.00
* First published 1790-1798. "The success of this work was instantaneous, and for nearly fifty years it was almost the sole authority for common law practice."--Holdsworth XIII, p. 450ff. In America it shared with Archbold's treatise the leading position in this field; in fact, as Holdsworth notes, its usefulness persisted longer in this country, the last English edition appearing in 1828. This is the final edition. Marvin p. 691.

339. TIEDEMAN, CHRISTOPHER G. A treatise on the limitations of police power in the United States, considered from both a civil and criminal standpoint. St. Louis, Thomas Law Book, 1886. 662pp. New cl. $ 37.50

340. TOWNSEND, CALVIN. A compendium of commercial law, analytically and topically arranged with copious citations of legal authorities ... N. Y., Ivison, 1872. 587pp. Full contemp. sheep, rubbed. $ 27.50

341. (TURNBULL, ROBERT JAMES) The crisis: or, essays on the usurpations of the Federal Government. By Brutus. Charleston, A. E. Miller, 1827. 166pp. Tall 8vo. Uncut and stitched as issued. First few leaves foxed. A very good copy, in a cloth folding box. $175.00
* A very important document propounding the states rights theory of the constitution and the theory of nullification. "...his most important
(Continued)

341. (Continued) work ... It is doubtful if the thinking of the people of any other state has ever been so impressed and influenced by a single publication as was that of South Carolina by this work ...' it was the first bugle call to the South to rally' and it prepared the ground admirably for the seed others were to sow ... the essays are effectively written, well-reasoned, and admitting their premises, unanswerable ... The legislature in 1828 passed a series of resolutions written by him affirming the compact theory.. --DAB. Howes T -420. Sabin 8776.

****

342. U.S. PUBLIC LAND COMMISSION. COMMITTEE OF CODIFICATION. The Public Domain: its history, with statistics, with references to the National Domain, colonization, acquirement of territory, the survey, administration and several methods of sale and disposition of the Public Domain of the United States, with sketch of legislative history of the land states and territories, and references to the land system of the colonies, and also that of several foreign governments ... Revised July 16, 1881. Addenda to June 30 and Dec. 1, 1883, - pages 517-1302. All forms and regulations to Dec. 1, 1883. Revision and addenda to June 30 and Dec 1, 1883, prepared in pursuance of a joint resolution of Congress, approved Aug. 7, 1882, by Thomas Donaldson. Wash., GPO, 1884. Folding maps and diagrams. 1343pp. Orig. cl. $ 75.00

343. UPDIKE, WILKINS. Memoirs of the Rhode-Island Bar. Boston, Webb, 1842. 309pp. Orig. cl. Nice copy. $ 45.00
* 15 lawyers of the 18th century, including a large section on James Varnum. Marvin p. 703.

****

344. VANFLEET, JOHN M. The law of collateral attack on judicial proceedings. Chicago, Callaghan, 1892. xciv, 1016pp. Contemp. sheep rubbed. First edition. $ 40.00

345. VAN HEYTHUSEN, F. M. The equity draftsman, being a selection of forms of pleadings in suits in equity, originally compiled by ... revised and enlarged ... by Edward Hughes, ... Fourth American (edition) with copious notes and references to American cases, By a Member of the Phila. Bar. Phila., Small, 1861. 926pp. New cl. $ 37.50
* Marvin p. 705. (The third Am. ed. of 1842).

A LANDMARK IN THE GENIUS OF THE AMERICAN POLITICAL SYSTEM

346. VARNUM, JAMES M. The case, Trevett against Weeden: on information and complaint, for refusing paper bills in payment for butcher's meat, in market, at par with specie. Tried before the honourable Superior Court, in the county of Newport, September term, 1786. ...wherein the rights of the people to trial by jury, &c. are

346. (Continued) stated and maintained, and the legislative, judiciary and executive powers of government examined and defined. Providence, printed by John Carter, 1787. iv, 60pp. 4to. Bound in later 3/4 red morocco. A very nice copy. $325.00
* FIRST AND ONLY EDITION. A major landmark in the establishment of the doctrine of judicial review, one of the unique features of the American political system. Varnum's defense of the right of the judiciary to reject legislation which violates the Constitution and of the independence and primacy of the judiciary was the most extensive and forceful to appear in this formative period. Of the five or so colonial cases involving judicial review (see Beveridge, Life of Marshall, III, p. 610f and Charles Warren Congress, the Court and the Constitution p. 43f) this is the most important because Varnum's views were made available to his contemporaries in this separately published pamphlet which was heavily advertised in the Philadelphia papers at the time of the Constitutional Convention. Madison took special note of it in the debates and Warren maintains that the founding fathers agreed that the Supreme Court would, like its colonial counterparts, be the ultimate judge ofthe validity of a law. Varnum's bold words echoed 17 years later in the statement of John Marshall in Marbury v. Madison that "it is emphatically the province and duty of the judicial department to say what the law is."
Varnum also gives a good account of the social and financial background to the affair and reproduces the currency and obnoxious forcing acts which denied trial by jury and appeal. He later became justice for the new Northwest Territory and helped frame its laws. Evans 20825. Sabin 98638. JCB 1772-1800, p. 267. A very nice copy of an important work.

347. VATTEL, EMMERICH DE Le droit des gens, ou, Principes de la loi naturelle, appliques a la conduite & Aux affaires des nations & des souverains. A Leide, aux Depens de la Compagnie, 1758. 4to. Two volumes in one. Engraved vignette on title page; title page in red and black. Contemporary calf, raised bands, sides a little rubbed, otherwise a very nice copy. $300.00
* Along with the "Londres" edition of this same year this is the first appearance of this great work - "a classic in the literature of international law, for decades (exercising) a decisive influence upon statesmen." Encycl. of the Social Sciences. Notable is its restriction of the role of warfare. "He has done for the morality of nations, what Paley did for the morality of individuals ... he is more generally read than any other writer upon the law of nations, and in no country more than ours ..." — Marvin p. 706. This last comment isborne out by the profusion of English language editions throughout the 19th century, outlasting the French.

348. VATTEL, (EMERICH DE) The law of nations, or, principles of the law of nature, applied to the conduct and affairs of Nations and Sover-

348. (Continued) -eigns From the French of Monsieur De Vattel. A new edition, revised, corrected, and enlarged with many valuable notes never before translated into English. London, prtd. for Robinson, 1797. 500pp. Full contemp. calf, worn but sound, some light stains. $ 45.00

349. VATTEL, EMERICH DE. The law of nations ... From the new edition by Joseph Chitty. With additional notes and references by Edward D. Ingraham. Phila., Johnson, 1856. 656pp. Full contemp. sheep, wants label, rubbed but sound. $35.00

350. (VIRGINIA, COLONY. LAWS, STATUTES). MERCER, JOHN. An exact abridgement of all the public acts of assembly of Virginia in force and use, January 1, 1758. Together with a proper table. Glasgow, Bryce and Paterson, 1759. xxii, 482pp. Title-page in excellent facsimile on early paper. Recent 1/4 mor. A very good copy. $ 85.00
* A completely updated version of Mercer's abridgement first published at Williamsburg in 1737. (Evans 4204) Marvin 509. This version was not published in America at any time.

351. VON HOLST, H. The Constitutional law of the United States of America. Authorized edition. Translated by Alfred Bishop Mason. Chicago, Callaghan, 1887. 369pp. $ 27.50

****

352. (WARREN, SAMUEL). The experiences of a barrister. By Warren Warner, Esq. of the Inner Temple. N. Y., Cornish, Lamport, 1852. 240pp. Orig. embossed publ. cl. faded, light wear to extremities of spine. Endpapers printed with publ. ads. A good copy. $ 35.00
* First edition in book form; it precedes the London edition by 4 years (Sadleir 3504.) Some copies have a frontis which was clearly never issued here.

353. WARREN, SAMUEL. A popular and practical introduction to law studies. N. Y., The Law Press, 1837. 425pp. Full contemp. calf. Some very light occasional marginal staining, but still an attractive copy. $ 75.00
* Second American edition of this classic. "It stands at the head of all the works of its class..." --Marvin p. 719

354. (WARREN, SAMUEL). Ten thousand a-year. Philadelphia, Carey and Hart, 1840-1841. Six volumes. Original publisher's boards, linen spines, paper labels. Some even wear and rubbing, light occasional foxing, some light marginal staining in volumes 1, 4, 5, and 6. With the original ownership inscription of Robt. Robertson, Norfolk, Va. 1841. $300.00
* First edition, first issue, of one of the most popular novels of the 19th century, and one of the most famous with a legal setting. "The first chapter ... appeared in Blackwood's (Magazine) for October 1839, and at once excited a powerful interest ... When the novel was completed and

354. (Continued) appeared in three dense volumes in 1841 (sic), it had an enormous sale, was translated into French, Russian and other languages, and was applauded ... in the English reviews. The well-constructed plot turns upon the validity of certain title deeds, and a number of legal points are involved. Warren's handling of these was criticised by experts, and was justified by the author in elaborate notes in subsequent editions. His legal portraits were declared to be caricatures, but the cleverness of the farcical portraits ... established the book as one of the most popular novels of the century." --DNB. Its first book form appearance is this American printing, prior to the English (Edinburgh) printing of 1841. Sadleir 3304.

355. WARREN, SAMUEL. Ten thousand a-year A new edition, carefully revised by the author. 2 vols. in one. Paris, Baudry's European Library, 1842. 1/4 calf, little rubbed. $ 35.00
* One of the most popular novels of the century, based on 19th century legal life and practices.

356. WASHBURN, EMORY. A treatise on the American law of real property. In two volumes. Boston, Little, Brown, 1860-1862. 688,771pp. New cloth. First edition. $ 75.00

357. WATSON, WILLIAM. A treatise of the law of partnership. Albany, N. Y., Webster, 1795. 368pp. New cloth. $ 65.00
* First American edition. Evans 29139. Marvin p. 721.

358. WEDGWOOD, WILLIAM B. The government and laws of the United States, comprising a complete and comprehensive view of the rise, progress, and present organization of the state and national governments. N. Y., Schermerhorn, 1867. 477pp. Orig. cl. $ 27.50
* Important for its attempt to present thecommon law to the general public. Despite the title, only a minority of thework is concerned with state and national government, the rest being devoted to common law.

359. WELFORD, RICHARD GRIFFITHS. A practical treatise on equity pleadings, with observations on the new orders of 1841, and an appendix containing those orders. From the London edition. Harrisburg, M'Kinley, 1846. 271pp. New cl. First American edition (from the London of 1842). $ 45.00

360. WENTWORTH, THOMAS. The office and duty of executors, from the 14th London edition ... by Henry Jeremy ... with references to ... American decisions by E. D. Ingraham. Phila., Nicklin, 1832. 547pp. New cl. $ 45.00
* First American edition (first London was 1641).

361. WHARTON, FRANCIS. A treatise on the law of homicide in the United States: to which is

361. (Continued) appended a series of leading cases on homicide, now out of print or existing only in manuscript. Phila., Kay, 1855. 537pp. New cl. First edition. $ 65.00

362. WHEATON, HENRY. American legal scholar, first Ambassador to the Court of Berlin, and author of the first great American work on international law. Fine ALS, 3 pages 4to entirely in his hand, dated Berlin 17 Nov. 1842, written to Thomas Caute Reynolds, later to become Governor of Missouri during the Civil War and at this time a student at Heidelberg having just finished his dissertation (cf. Marvin p. 607), a copy of which is being sent to Wheaton who advises him on the present prospect of his obtaining a post in the diplomatic corps in Berlin and assures him of his support. $ 50.00

363. WHEATON, HENRY. Enquiry into the validity of the British claim to a right of visitation & search of American vessels suspected to be engaged in the African slave trade. London, John Miller, 1842. 175pp with errata slip. Original cloth. A very good copy. $150.00
* Written in defence of the American position, by the author of the first great American works on international law. Wheaton was highly respected in Europe, having been the first American ambassador to the Court of Berlin since 1797, and having already published in England and France his two major treatises on international law which gained immediate recognition. This is the first London edition, appearing simultaneously with a Philadelphia printing, intended no doubt to influence British readers on this highly vexatious issue.

364. WHITE, DANIEL APPLETON. A view of the jurisdiction and proceedings of the courts of probate of Massachusetts with particular reference to the County of Essex. Salem, Cushing and Appleton, 1822. 158pp. Very neatly removed from a bound volume. Very good. $ 80.00
* An excellent and very uncommon work. White was probate judge of Essex County for 38 years. He wrote this lengthy tract primarily to clarify and justify the reforms he was attempting to make in his new position; the work is partly historical.

365. WHITING, SAMUEL. The Connecticut town officer; in three parts ... Danbury, Skinner, 1814. 287,(1)pp. 12mo. Calf. Fine. $ 37.50
* First edition. Shaw-Shoemaker 33668.

366. WHITMAN, JOHN W., (reporter) Report of a trial in the Supreme Judicial Court, holden at Boston, Dec. 16th and 17th, 1828, of Theodore Lyman, Jr., for an alleged libel on Daniel Webster ... Boston, Putnam, 1828. 76pp. Neatly removed. $ 45.00
* "The style of the indictment is of special interest based upon the law of scandalum magnatum, or slander of great men ... the offense originated

366. (Continued) with the English Star Chamber but was never recognized in the common law of the United States." --McCoy L388. Shoemaker 35002.

367. WILLARD, JOSEPH A. Half a century with judges and lawyers. Boston, Houghton, Mifflin, 1895. Frontis. 371pp. Orig. cl. Author was clerk of the Mass. Superior Court. $ 22.50

368. (WILLARD PEELE et al versus THE MERCHANTS' INSURANCE COMPANY.) Argument of plaintiffs' counsel in the case of ... before the Supreme Court of the United States, February Term 1826, upon the question of admiralty jurisdiction, in cases of policies of insurance. With extracts from various learned treatises upon this subject. Boston, Howe and Norton, 1826. 35, 132pp. 8vo. Cont. plain wrps. Fine. $ 45.00
* An uncommon work; remarkably well documented and well argued case for admiralty jurisdiction in contract cases, publishing (in some cases probably the first American appearances) extracts from historical treatises, and citing American precedent. Shaw-Shoemaker 25593 listing the work (the argument only) under Benj. Ropes Nichols.

369. WILLIAMS, JOSHUA. Principles of the law of personal property, intended for the use of students in conveyancing. American editors, Benjamin Gerhard and Samuel Wetherill. Third American from the fifth London edition, with notes and references by Samuel Wetherill. Phila., Johnson, 1866, 570pp. Full contemp. sheep. $ 30.00

370. WILSON, JAMES. The works of the Honourable James Wilson, L.L.D., lateone of the Associate Justices of the Supreme Court of the United States, and professor of law in the College of Philadelphia. Published under the direction of Bird Wilson. Phila., at the Lorenzo Press, for Bronson and Chauncey, 1804. 3 vols. 8vo. Portrait in volume one. Contemp. sheep, leather labels, slight wear but still a rather attractive set. $150.00
* First edition of the works of this great jurist. In fact the great majority of the work consists of his law lectures delivered at the college in 1790-91, making this an important early first-hand source for American legal education. Marvin p. 740.

371. WILSON, W. D. Attainder of treason and confiscation of the property of rebels. A letter to the Hon. Samuel A. Foot, L.L.D. on the Constitutional restrictions upon attainder and forfeiture for treason against the United States ... with Judge Foot's answer ... Albany, Weed, Parsons, 1863. 30pp. Orig. prtd. wrps. $ 30.00
* "An open letter ... both writers striving to prove that there were no constitutional restrictions on confiscation in such cases." --DAB for William Dexter Wilson.

372. WOOD, THOMAS. Some thoughts concerning the study of the laws of England. Particularly in the two universities. In a letter to the Reverend ______ Head of ______ College in Oxford. The second edition. London, J. Stagg ..., 1728. 1pl., 62pp. Nice ornamental woodcut headpiece. Neatly disbound. A very good copy. $125.00
* A landmark in the development of legal education and the precursor, in many respects, of Blackstone. In this tract, first published in 1708, Wood argued for the incorporation of English Common Law into the university curriculum and called for the production of a systematic treatise, a need answered in part by the publication in 1720 of Wood's own Institute of the Laws of England, but more fully realized by Blackstone, who nonetheless recognized the merit of Wood's pioneering efforts. Holdsworth XII, 418f. Marvin p. 743. S & M, I, 38.

373. WRIGHT, R. W. A practical digest of the election laws of Pennsylvania, together with all the forms required by the election officers in the discharge of their duties. Allentown, Blumer, 1840. 168pp. Full contemp. sheep 12mo. Marvin p. 749. Uncommon. $ 45.00

374. WYCHE, WILLIAM. A treatise on the practice of theSupreme Court of Judicature of the State of New York in civil actions. Second edition. N. Y., Swords, 1794. xvi, 355, (4)pp. Contemp sheep wanting label, rubbed, joint repaired, still a sound copy, internally very good. $ 90.00
* Wyche was a recent emigrant from England and writes with an immediate sense of contrast between English and American practice. Marvin p. 751; Evans 28140. This copy contains two leaves of ads for other works by this author.

375. WYTHE, GEORGE. Decisions of cases in Virginia by the High Court of Chancery, with remarks upon decrees by the Court of Appeals reversing some of those decisions ... second and only complete edition, with a memoir of the author, analyses of the cases, and an index, by D. B. Minor ... with an appendix . . . by William Green. Richmond, Randolph, 1852. xliii, 471(8)pp. 8vo. Contemp. calf, leather label. A fine copy. $ 75.00
* A desireable edition of this Virginia classic first published in 1795. Marvin p. 752. (1st edition).

376. The young clerk's magazine; or, English law repository: containinga variety of the most useful precedents ... the seventh edition, revised and corrected. Philadelphia, Crukshank, 1792. 12mo. 2pl., 299, (6)pp. Contemp. sheep, leather label, rubbed but a good copy. Wanting the terminal blanks. $ 50.00
* A standard English work which appeared regularly in the American colonies since 1708. Evans2162:

377. The young clerk's magazine: or, English law-repository: containing a variety of the most useful precedents ... eighth edition, revised and corrected. Phila., Crukshank, 1795. 2pl., 299, (6-ads)pp. 12mo. Contemp. sheep rubbed, leather label. A good copy. $ 50.00
* Evans 29944. A standard English work which appeared regularly in the colonies since 1708. This appears to be essentially the same as the 1792 edition. Although the pagination is the same, the text has been reset with a few minor changes.

378. ANDERSON, WILLIAM. in collaboration with ALBERT J. LOBB. A history of the Constitution of Minnesota, with the first verified text. Minneapolis, Univ. of Minnesota, 1921. 323pp. Orig. prtd. wrps. $ 30.00

379. ANGLE, PAUL M. One hundred years of law: an account of the law office which John T. Stuart founded in Springfield, Illinois, a century ago. Springfield, Brown, 1928. Illus., frontis. plates. 53pp. Orig. cl. $ 20.00

380. ARISTOTLE. The politics of ... Translated with an introduction, notes, and appendixes by Ernest Barker. Oxford, Clarendon Press, (1948). 411pp. D.j. $ 17.50

****

381. THE BAR ASSOCIATION OF ST. LOUIS. Walter Henry Sanborn. A testimonial volume. Compiled and published by ... St. Louis, 1927, Illus., frontis., plate. 180pp. Cl. $ 15.00

382. BEALE, JOSEPH HENRY, compiler. A bibliography of early English law books. London, H. Milford, Oxford Univ., Press, 1926. 304pp. Perforated stamp on title page. $ 10.00

383. BRYCE, JAMES. Studies in history and jurisprudence. In two vols. Oxford, Clarendon Press, 1901. 553, 543pp. First edition. $ 45.00

384. CAIRNS, HUNTINGTON. Legal philosophy from Plato to Hegel. Baltimore, Johns Hopkins Press, 1949. 583pp. $ 27.50

385. CALLCOTT, MARY STEVENSON. Child labor legislation in New York: the historical development and the administrative practices of child labor laws in the State of New York, 1905-1930. N. Y., MacMillan, 1931. 267pp. Orig. prtd. wrps. $ 17.50

386. CALLENDER, CLARENCE N. American courts, their organization and procedure. First edition. N. Y., McGraw-Hill, 1927. 284pp. $ 17.50

387. CHASE, FREDERIC HATHAWAY. Lemuel Shaw, chief justice of the Supreme Judicial Court of Massachusetts, 1830-1860. Boston, Houghton Mifflin, 1918. 330pp. Frontis. $ 17.50

388. CHERMAK, LAWRENCE E. The law of revenue bonds. Wash., Nat'l. Inst. of Municipal Law Officers, 1954. 236pp. Orig. cl., d.j. $ 17.50

389. CLARK, JANE PERRY. Deportation of aliens from the United States to Europe. N. Y., Columbia, 1931. 524pp. $ 15.00

****

390. DANIEL, JOHN W. A treatise on the law of negotiable instruments, ... In two vols. Fifth edition, re-edited and enlarged with notes and references to American and English cases, by John W. Daniel and Charles A. Douglass. N. Y., Baker, 1903. 936, 1004pp. Orig. cl. $ 40.00

391. DICEY, A. V. Lectures on the relation between law & public opinion in England during the nineteenth century. London, MacMillan, 1914. 506pp. Best edition. $ 22.50

392. DILLON, JOHN F. A commemorative address on Chief Justice Marshall ... N. Y., 1901. 58pp. Orig. wrps. Fine. $ 22.50
* Inscribed presentation copy from the author to his daughter. See DAB for an account of Dillon. Servies #1285.

393. (DIRECTORY) Sharp & Alleman Co.'s lawyers' and bankers' directory for 1909, July edition, containing the names of over seven thousand capable and trustworthy attorneys in all the cities and larger towns in the United States and Canada; also the names of one or more banks or bankers in every banking town in the United States, including the county, capital, etc. ... Phila., Sharp & Alleman, 1909. 1464pp. Cloth. Fine. Scarce. $ 30.00

****

394. ENCYCLOPAEDIA OF THE SOCIAL SCIENCES. Edited by E. R. A. Seligman et al. 15 vols. bound in 8, as issued. N. Y., (ca 1937). Large thick 8vo's. Orig. cl. Very good set. $200.00
* Still an important reference, holding a position comparable to the 11th Britannica.

****

395. FAGAN, JOHN T. The Maine townsman: containing the statutory laws of Maine respecting the duties of town officers, powers and obligations of towns, cities and plantations, and laws affect-
395. (Continued) ing general business. Revised to January 1, 1911. Portland, Loring, 1910. 930pp. Full contemp. sheep. Lacking label. $ 22.50

396. FARSON, CHARLES T. A commentary on the mechanics' lien law of Illinois. Chicago, Callaghan, 1902. 377pp. New cl. $ 27.50

397. FELL, EDGAR TREMLETT. Recent problems in admiralty jurisdiction. Baltimore, (John Hopkins Press) 1922. 136pp. Orig. prtd. wrps. $ 15.00

398. FINEBERG. S. ANDHIL. The Rosenberg case, fact and fiction. (N.Y., Oceana, 1953.) 159pp. Orig. cl. $ 17.50

399. FRANKFURTER, FELIX, ed. Mr. Justice Brandeis: essays by Charles E. Hughes, Max Lerner, Felix Frankfurter, Donald R. Richberg, Henry Wolf Bikle, Walton H. Hamilton. Introduction by Oliver Wendell Holmes. New Haven, Yale, 1932. 232pp. Frontis. First edition. $ 27.50

400. GALLAHER, RUTH A. Legal and political status of women in Iowa: an historical account of the rights of women in Iowa from 1838 to 1918. Iowa City, State Historical Society, 1918. 300pp. Cl. Fine. $ 20.00

401. GATES, PAUL W. History of public land law development. Written for the Public Land Law Review Commission, with a chapter by Robert W. Swenson. Wash., D. C. (GPO), 1968. 828pp. Lg. 8vo., illus. cl. $ 25.00

402. GOLDFARB, RONALD L. The contempt power. N. Y., Columbia, 1963. 349pp. $ 15.00

403. GOULD, JOHN M. and ARTHUR W. BLAKEMORE. The Bankruptcy Act of 1898, annotated and explained, with the amendments thereto, all the important and latest Federal and State decisions thereon, and the general orders and forms established by the U.S. Supreme Court. Boston, Little, Brown, 1904. 263pp. Full contemp. sheep. Fine. $ 25.00

404. HAINES, CHARLES GROVE, et al. The role of the Supreme Court in American government and politics 1835-1864. Berkeley, Univ. of Calif., (1957). 533pp. Occasional neat pencil underlining. $ 25.00

405. HAMMURABI. Theoldest code of laws in the world: the code of laws promulgated by Hammurabi, King of Babylon, B. C. 2285-2242. Translated by C. H. W. Johns. Edinburgh, Clark, 1903. 88pp. Orig. cl. 12mo. $ 12.50

406. HARRIS, SILAS A. Appellate courts and appellate procedure in Ohio. Baltimore, Jonns Hopkins Press, 1933. 181pp. Orig. prtd. wrps. $ 15.00

407. HARRISON, EDWARD R. A digest and index of the official reports of tax cases ... being a judicial dictionary of tax law. Prepared for the Board of Inland Revenue by ... Fourth edition, revised, re-arranged and considerably enlarged. London, His Majesty's Stationery Office, 1929. 903pp. $ 20.00

408. HAWKINS, CHARLES A., (compiler). Legal counselor and form book: a hand book of business law and legal forms for all the States and the Provinces of Canada ... Written, arranged and compiled by ..., assisted by Members of the Bar in all the States and Canadian Provinces. Revised edition. N. Y., Leslie-Judge, (1910). 620pp. $ 27.50

409. HIGH, JAMES L. A treatise on the law of receivers. Fourth edition, by Shirley T. High. Chicago, Callaghan, 1910. 1102pp. Orig. cl. $ 30.00

410. (HOLMES, OLIVER WENDELL). Justice Oliver Wendell Holmes, his book notices and uncollected letters and papers. Edited and annotated by Harry C. Shriver. Introduction by Harlan Fiske Stone. (First edition). N. Y., Central Book, 1936. 280pp. d.j. $ 22.50

411. HUFFCUT, ERNEST W. The law of agency including the law of principal and agent and the law of master and servant. Second edition, revised and enlarged. Boston, Little, Brown, 1902. 406pp. Cloth, fine. Author was professor at Cornell. This rev. edition covers the whole field of agency. $ 25.00

412. HUTCHINSON, JOHN. A catalogue of notable Middle Templars, with brief biographical notices. (London), Prtd. for Society of the Middle Temple, 1902. 284pp. Orig. cl., gilt. Roy 8vo. Very fine copy. $ 50.00
* A careful collection of about 1000 sketches from 1501 to 1901.

****

413. INSTITUTE OF LAW AND OHIO INSTITUTE. Ohio criminal statistics 1931: an experiment in methods and techniques of reporting. Baltimore, Hopkins, 1932. 189pp. wrps. $ 12.50

414. INTERNATIONAL BAR ASSOCIATION. Eleventh Conference ... Lausanne, Switzerland, July 11-15, 1966. Summary of proceedings, official papers and reports ... The Hague, Nijhoff, 1966. 308pp. $ 15.00

****

415. JAMES, HERMAN G. The introductory articles of the Constitution of Illinois. Lancaster, Wickersham, 1911. 105pp. Orig. prt. wrps. $ 20.00

416. JAMIESON, G. Chinese family and commercial law. Shanghai, Kelly, 1921. 188pp. $ 35.00

417. JOHNSON, ARLIEN. Public policy and private charities: a study of legislation in the United States and of administration in Illinois ... Chicago, Univ. of Chicago, 1931. 230pp. Orig. prtd. wrps. $ 22.50

418. KOUSHNAREFF, SERGE GEORGE. Liability of carriers of good by sea. N. Y., Delphic Press, 1943. 167pp. Orig. prtd. wrps. $ 17.50

419. LASKI, HAROLD J. A grammar of politics. New Haven, Yale Univ., (1931). 672pp. $ 15.00

420. LASKI, HAROLD J. The state in theory and practice. London, Allen, (1935). 336pp. D.j. $ 22.50

421. THE LAW ASSOCIATION OF PHILADELPHIA Addresses delivered March 13, 1902, and papers prepared or republished to commemorate the centennial celebration of the Law Association of Philadelphia, Pennsylvania, 1802-1902. (Phila., 1906, reprint edition 1954) Illus., plates. 462pp. $ 20.00

422. LEWIS, JOHN FREDERICK. Thomas Spry, lawyer and physician: the first attorney admitted to practice under English law in the Delaware River Settlements ... Phila., (Patterson, prtr.) 1932. Illus., frontis., plates 125pp. $ 20.00

423. LINDESMITH, ALFRED R. The addict and the law. Bloomington, Indiana Univ. Press, (1965). 337pp. $ 10.00

424. LONG, JOSEPH R. A treatise on the law of domestic relations. St. Paul, Keefe-Davidson, 1905. 455pp. Orig. cl. $ 25.00

425. LOVELAND, FRANK O. A treatise on the law and proceedings in bankruptcy. Second edition. Cincinnati, 1904. 1422pp. Full contemp. sheep. $ 30.00

426. LUCAS, A. Forensic chemistry and scientific criminal investigation. Second edition. London, Arnold, 1931. 324pp. Fine. $ 15.00

427. LUCE, ROBERT. Legislative procedure: Parliamentary practices and the course of business in the framing of statutes. Boston, Houghton Mifflin, 1922. 628pp. $ 27.50

428. MacELREE, WILMER W. Side lights on the bench and bar of Chester County. West Chester, Penn., 1918. Illus., frontis., many plates. 435pp. Orig. cl., fine. Covers 18th-19th centuries in Pennsylvania. $ 37.50

429. MASON, JEREMIAH. Memoirs of ... reproduction of privately printed edition of 1873, illustrated and annotated, with enlarged index by G. J. Clark ... Boston, Boston Law Book (1917). Illus., frontis., plates. 491pp. N. H. lawyer and Senator, considered by Choate, Story et al. as one of the great lawyers of his time--DAB $ 22.50

430. MASTERSON, WILLIAM E. Jurisdiction in marginal seas, with special reference to smuggling. N. Y., MacMillan, 1929. 423pp. $ 17.50

431. MAY, GEOFFREY. Marriage laws and decisions in the United States. A manual. N. Y., Russell Sage, 1929. 477pp. $ 22.50

432. MERSHON, STEPHEN L. The power of the Crown in the valley of the Hudson. Montclair, Mershon, 1925. 209pp. Illus., plates. $ 25.00

433. MISSALL, J. ELLSWERTH. The Moreland Act; executive inquiry in the State of New York. N. Y., King's Crown Press, 1946. 145pp. Orig. prtd. wrps. $ 17.50

434. MOORE, IRA M. A treatise on contracts, torts, damages, evidence, and practice and procedure in civil cases in justice and other courts, and on the powers and duties of justices of the peace and constables in the State of Illinois. Fourth edition, revised. 2 vols. Chicago, Callaghan, 1900. 1810pp. New cl. $ 45.00

435. MYERBERG, HERBERT. The practical aspects of divorce practice. (Baltimore) Daily Record Co., 1951. 104pp. Cloth. $ 12.50

****

436. NELSON, MARGARET VIRGINIA. A study of judicial review in Virginia, 1789-1928. N. Y., (Columbia), 1947. 249pp. Orig. prtd. wrps. $ 20.00

437. NEW YORK UNIVERSITY. HENRY SELLIN, ed. Proceedings of the New York University Conference on practice and procedure under the Immigration and Nationality Act (McCarran-Walter Act) ... N. Y., N.Y.U. Press, (1954). 145pp. $ 15.00

438. NUSSBAUM, ARTHUR. Money in the law, national and international: a comparative study in the borderline of law and economics. A complete revised edition of "Money in the Law." Brooklyn, Foundation Press, 1950. 618 pp. $ 27.50

439. OAKLEY, THOMAS POLLOCK. English penitential discipline and Anglo-Saxon Law in their joint influence. N. Y., Columbia, 1923. 227pp. Orig. prtd. wrps. $ 17.50

****

440. PARKER, HERBERT. Courts and lawyers of New England. N. Y., American Historical Society, 1931. 4 vols. 4to. 1015pp. Illus., portraits. Cl. Little soiled, contents fine. $ 50.00
* Finely illustrated study of 18th and 19th century pillars of the legal profession.

441. PHILLIPSON, COLEMAN. The effect of war on contracts, and on trading associations in territories of belligerents. London, Stevens, 1909. 114pp. $ 17.50

442. PHILLIPSON, COLEMAN. Three criminal law reformers: Beccaria, Bentham, Romilly. London, Dent, 1923. 344pp. $ 15.00

443. POMEROY, JOHN NORTON. A treatise on equity jurisprudence as administered in the United States of America ... 4th edition (WITH:) A treatise on equitable remedies, 2nd edition. Rochester, Lawyers' Coop., 1918-1919. 6 vols. complete, including combined table and index. 6317pp. Cloth. Fine. $ 75.00

444. PUFENDORF, SAMUEL VON. De officio hominis et civis juxta legem naturalem libri duo. Vol. I. A photographic reproduction of the edition of 1682, with an introduction by Walter Schucking and a list of errata. Vol. II. A translation of the text, by Frank Gardner Moore, with a translation (by Herbert F. Wright) of the introduction by Walter Schucking, and an index by Herbert F. Wright. In two vols. N. Y., Oxford Univ., 1927. 167, 152pp. 4to. Perf. stamp. $ 45.00
* Series: Classics of International Law, edited by James Brown Scott.

****

445. RANSONE, COLEMAN B., Jr. The office of Governor in the United States. University, Alabama, Univ. of Alabama, 1956. 417pp. $ 17.50

446. READ, CONYERS, ed. The Constitution reconsidered. Edited for the American Historical Association. N. Y., Columbia, 1938. 424pp. $ 27.50
* Original papers by Beard, Thorne, McIlwain, et al.

447. READ, HORACE EMERSON. Recognition and enforcement of foreign judgments in the common law units of the British Commonwealth. Cambridge, Harvard, 1938. 371pp. $ 22.50
* Harvard Studies in the Conflict of Laws, Vol. II.

448. REPPY, ALISON. Civil rights in the United States. N. Y., Central Book Co., 1951. 297pp. cl., d.j. $ 17.50

449. REYNOLDS, WILLIAM. The theory of the law of evidence as established in the United States, and of the conduct of the examination of witnesses. Fourth edition. Chicago, Callaghan, 1905. 268pp. $ 22.50

450. RIENOW, ROBERT. The test of the nationality of a merchant vessel. N. Y., Columbia, 1937 247pp. Orig. prtd. wrps. $ 22.50

451. ROBSON, WILLIAM A. Civilisation and the growth of law: a study of the relations between men's ideas about the universe and the institutions of law and government. N. Y., MacMillan, 1935. 354pp. First edition. $ 17.50

452. ROOT, WILLIAM T., Jr. A psychological and educational survey of 1916 prisoners in the Western Penitentiary of Pennsylvania ... a report on the Italian Convict by Giovanni Giardini ... 246pp. Orig. prtd. wrps. n.p., ca. 1926. $ 15.00

453. ROSENBERG, JULIUS, petitioner. Transcript of record: Supreme Court of the U.S., Oct. term, 1951. No. 111, Rosenberg vs. U. S. No. 112, Morton Sobell vs U. S. Petitions for writs of certiorari and exhibit thereto ... N. Y., National Committee to Secure Justice in Rosenberg Case, (1952). vi, 1715pp. Complete in 8 parts. Boxed. $ 27.50

454. RUNES, DAGOBERT D. The disinherited and the law. N. Y., Philosophical Lib., (1964). 79pp. $ 12.50

****

455. SAYRE, PAUL. The life of Roscoe Pound. Iowa City, State Univ. of Iowa, (1948). Illus., frontis., plates. 412pp. $ 22.50

456. SCHROEDER, THEODORE. Constitutional free speech defined and defended in an unfinished argument in a case of blasphemy. N. Y., Free Speech League, 1919. 456pp. Orig. prtd. wrps. $ 22.50

457. SCOTT, JAMES A. The law of interstate rendition, erroneously referred to as interstate extradition: a treatise on the arrest and surrender of fugitives from the justice of one state to another; the removal of Federal prisoners from one district to another; and the exemption of persons from service of civil process; with an appendix of the statutes of the States and Territories on fugitives from justice. Chicago, Hight, 1917. 534pp. $ 30.00

458. SHARTEL, BURKE. Our legal system and how it operates: Five lectures delivered at the Univ. of Michigan, Feb. 23, 24, 25, 26, and 27, 1948, on the Thomas M. Cooley Lectureship, enlarged and revised. Ann Arbor, Univ. of Mich. Law School, 1951. 629pp. Cl. Fine. $ 22.50

459. SHAW, HENRY, M. D. The settlement laws of Massachusetts: in their application to poor relief outside institutions. With citations of some of the leading judicial decisions in the last thirty years, and practical suggestions to visitors among the poor. Boston, Ellis, 1900. 205, 84pp. Orig. cl. $ 22.50
* Bound with 1909 supplement of 84pp.

460. SIMPSON, FRANK LESLIE. Cases on torts. To accompany "The Law of Torts" by Melville M. Bigelow. Boston, Little, Brown, 1908. 709pp. Cloth. Author was professor at Boston University. $ 22.50

461. SPITZ, EDWARD F. An elementary treatise on conditional and future interests in property. N. Y., Baker, 1928. 298pp. $ 20.00

462. SPRING, SAMUEL. Risks & rights in publishing, television, radio, motion pictures, advertising and the theater. N. Y., Norton, (1952). First edition. 385pp. $ 12.50

463. STEPHENSON, GEORGE M. The political history of the public lands, from 1840 to 1862, from pre-emption to homestead. Boston, Badger, (1917). 296pp. First ed. Fine. $ 12.50

464. STOREY, MOORFIELD. The reform of legal procedure. New Haven, Yale University Press, 1911. 263pp. 12mo. $ 17.50

465. STULL, HARRY N. A case in the United States Court of Claims: a treatise on the rules of practice and procedure in the United States... and the jurisdiction of the court, with the citation of leading cases. Wash. D. C., Byrne, 1924. 150pp. $ 22.50

466. SUNDERLAND, EDSON R. History of the American Bar Association and its work ... n.p., 1953. 251pp. Cl. Fine. $ 15.00

****

467. TAPPAN, PAUL WILBUR. Delinquent girls in court: a study of the Wayward Minor Court of New York. N. Y., Columbia, 1947. 265pp. Orig. prtd. wrps. $ 10.00

468. TARTER, HARRY. Legal resolvents. N. Y., Merlin Press, (1951). 114pp. Orig. prtd. wrps. $ 12.50

469. TIFFANY, HERBERT THORNDIKE. The law of real property and other interests in land. Enlarged edition. Chicago, Callaghan, 1920. Three vols. complete. Cloth. Fine. $ 45.00

470. TOBEY, JAMES A. Public health law. Third edition. N. Y., Commonwealth Fund, 1947. 419pp. Orig. cl., d.j. $ 17.50

471. TRACHTENBERG, ALEXANDER. The history of legislation for the protection of coal miners in Pennsylvania, 1824-1915. Introduction by Henry W. Farnam. N. Y., International Pub., (1942). 239pp. D.j., fine. $ 17.50

****

472. (U.S. COPYRIGHT OFFICE). SOLBERG, THORVALD. Copyright in Congress, 1799-1904: a bibliography, and chronological record of all proceedings in Congress in relation to copyright from April 15, 1789, to April 28, 1904 ... Wash., GPO, 1905. 468pp. 4to. $ 22.50
* Copyright Office Bulletin No. 8

****

473. U.S. INTERSTATE COMMERCE COMMISSION. Annual report. 29-30, 36-53, 55-61. (1915 - 1947). per year $ 12.50

****

474. (U.S. LIBRARY OF CONGRESS) BORCHARD EDWIN M. Guide to the law and legal literature of Germany. Wash., GPO, 1912. 226pp. $ 22.50

475. UNIVERSAL CONGRESS OF LAWYERS AND JURISTS. Official report of the ... held at St. Louis Missouri, U.S.A., September 28, 29, and 30, 1904. ... St. Louis, Publ., by the Executive Committee, 1905. 423pp. $ 27.50
* Organized by the U.S. for the Louisiana Purchase Centennial. Much on international law and a proposed international bar association.

****

476. VERLIE, EMIL JOSEPH, ed. Illinois Constitutions. Springfield, Illinois State Historical Library, 1919. 231pp. $ 22.50
* Vol. XIII, Ill. State Hist. Library, Constitutional series, Vol. I.

****

477. WEXLEY, JOHN. The judgement of Julius and Ethel Rosenberg. N. Y., Cameron & Kahn, 1955. 672pp. Original cloth, with the Rockwell Kent dust jacket, little frayed around edges. $ 22.50

ROBERT H. RUBIN BOOKS

Post Office Box 558 · Stoughton, Massachusetts 02072 USA
Cable Address: «RUBOOKS» Telephone: (617) 344-0740

CATALOG EIGHTEEN 1982/1983

ANTIQUARIAN AND OUT-OF-PRINT WORKS IN

LAW AND LEGAL HISTORY

(CHIEFLY ANGLO-AMERICAN)

Please see page i for detailed index

We are pleased to send you our new catalogue. It emphasises both **early American legal literature** *and* **English law of the 17th-19th centuries,** *and includes a good many* **treatises,** *both American and English, as well as other types of works on a wide variety of topics, including* **constitutional law and history, criminal law and reform, international law, medical jurisprudence,** *and* **political theory.** *We hope you find it interesting.*

Offers of single items or entire collections, institutional or private, are always welcome.

TELEPHONE ORDERS

Please feel free to phone at any time. In the *unlikely* event that you fail to reach us in the afternoon, please try again before noon, E.S.T.

CABLE ORDERS

It is essential that cable messages be confirmed immediately by letter.

1. ADAMS, JOHN (and DANIEL LEONARD). Novanglus, and Massachusettensis; or political essays, published in the years 1774 and 1775, on the principle points of controversy between Great Britain and her colonies ... to which are added ... letters, lately written by President Adams to ... William Tudor ... Boston, Hews & Goss, 1819. 312pp. 8 vo. Orig. boards, front cover detached but present; internally fine, uncut. $ 55.00
* First edition in book form of these classic essays originally published in newspaper form, in response to the Loyalist articles by Daniel Leonard (at this time incorrectly attributed by Adams himself to Jonathan Sewall) which are also printed here. Howes A-63. DAB for Leonard.

2. (ADMIRALTY LAW) Admiralty proceedings in the cases of the British vessels Contest and Achsah, before the Hon. John K. Kane, Judge of the U.S. District Court of Eastern Pennsylvania. (Caption title.) (1850.) n.p. 24pp. Plain wrps. $ 30.00
* This appears to be a British publication, protesting the attempts by the U. S. Admiralty Court to exercise jurisdiction over foreign ships. Includes the British protests.

3. AMOS, SHELDON. The science of Law. N. Y., Appleton, 1876. 417pp. Orig. pict. cl. $ 45.00
* "Amos carried on the Bentham-Austin tradition in jurisprudence ... yet Amos outsteps his master by recognizing the existence of international law, to which Austin had denied the title of law 'properly so called' ..." Encyclopaedia of the Social Sciences. First London (and American) edition was 1874.

4. ANDREWS, ISRAEL WARD. Manual of the Constitution of the United States, designed for the instruction of American youth in the duties, obligations, and rights of citizenship. Cincinnati, Wilson, (1874). 370,xxxviiipp. $ 22.50

5. ATKYNS, ROBERT An enquiry into the power of dispensing with penal statutes. Together with some animadversions upon a book writ by Sir Edw. Herbert ... London, Timothy Goodwin, 1689, Folio. 2 p.l., 58pp. Neatly disbound. Preliminary advt. leaf present. Light marginal stains. A good copy. $ 50.00
* "Sums up the whole history of dispensations and denies their antiquity; a reply to ... Herbert's review of the authorities in Hale's case, which raised the question of the dispensing power ... After Hale there was no more learned lawyer of his time ..." -- DNB. Wing A 4138. S&M I, 358. First edition.

6. ATKYNS, SIR ROBERT. The power, jurisdiction and priviledge of Parliament; and the antiquity of the House of Commons asserted. Occasion'd by an information in the King's Bench, by the Attorney General, against the Speaker of the House of Commons. (Continued)

6. (Continued) As also a discourse concerning the ecclesiastical jurisdiction in the realm of England ... London, Timothy Goodwin, 1689. Folio. 1 p.l., 74pp. Early ¼ calf neatly rebacked. With the bookplate of Chandos Leigh. $125.00
* An interesting tract on separation of powers, growing out of Atkyn's defense of the speaker of the House, who had been indicted for publishing, by order of the House, Dangerfield's narrative of the Popish Plot. Atkyns zealously asserted the rights of Parliament, maintaining that "the courts have no jurisdiction to inquire into their limitations." -- Holdsworth. Atkyns held several judicial positions ... "he was a very learned lawyer, and a man of well-balanced mind." -- Holdsworth VI, 515f. DNB. S&M I, 127. Wing A 4141. First edition.

SCIENTIFIC JURISPRUDENCE

7. AUSTIN, JOHN. The province of jurisprudence determined. Second edition. Being the first part of a series of lectures on jurisprudence, or, the philosophy of positive law. London, John Murray 1861. WITH: Lectures on jurisprudence, being the sequel to "The province of jurisprudence determined." To which are added notes and fragments. Now first published from the original manuscripts. London, John Murray, 1863. Designated Volume II and Volume III. Together three volumes, complete. 8vo. Original uniform publisher's cloth, bit faded, unobtrusive repair to joints of volume three, but essentially a fine set, uncut and unopened. $500.00
* First complete edition of a classic of modern jurisprudence. Austin published The Province of Jurisprudence originally in 1832. That edition apparently became quite scarce - it is now exceedingly difficult to find - and Austin was occasionally asked to reissue the work (though generally it was a book ahead of its time. He could never bring himself to the task, which was left to his wife Sarah Austin. Two years after Austin's death, she produced the reissue of the Province, inserting Austin's manuscript alterations and additions, and published for the first time the remainder of his lectures (the majority of his work) and other writings, to which she added a long and moving biographical account including information directly connected with the progress and fortunes of the present work. Austin established jurisprudence, for the English speaking world, as a scientific, "analytical" discipline and became the major point of reference for important ideological opponents such as Henry Maine. See DNB for both Austins. S&M II, 15. Though well represented in institutional holdings copies in trade are notably uncommon.

8. (BACON, NATHANIEL) An historical and political discourse of the laws & government of England ... with a vindication of (Continued)

8. (Continued) the ancient way of parliaments in England, Collected from some manuscript notes of John Selden ... London, John Starkey, 1689. Folio. Two parts in one. 10 p.l.,203; 2 p.l.,189(5)pp. incl. preliminary advertisement leaf. Contemp. speckled calf, spine ornately gilt, very slight slight wear to lower joints. A fine fresh copy. With a handsome contemporary bookplate (Hon. James Bertie). $250.00
* An important 17th century constitutional history "pervaded by a strong spirit of hostility to the claims of the royal pre rogative and to hierarchical pretensions."-- DAB. It was first published in 1647; several subsequent editions met with severe government repression on account of its liberal leanings. This edition, appearing immediately after the Glorious Revolution, is interesting particularly for the publisher's account of the difficulties encountered by the book, in which he cites the offending passages; also, for the first time, Selden's name appears on the title page - that association is almost certainly apocryphal. A nice copy of a key book. Winfield, Chief Sources of English Legal History, p. 320f. DNB. S&M I, 99. Wing S 2428, under Selden.

9. BAILY, LAURENCE R. Perils of the sea and their effects on policies of insurance, pratically considered. London, Effingham Wilson, 1860. vii,lix,(1),227pp. Top margin of title page cropped, no text affected. Orig. publ. cl. bit faded. A good sound copy. $ 50.00
* First and only edition of a very uncommon treatise on a special topic in the law of marine insurance. S&M II, 17.

10. BANCROFT, GEORGE. History of the formation of theConstitution of the United States of America. In two volumes. N. Y., Appleton, 1882. 520;501pp. Orig. publ. cl. gilt. An exceptionally fine set. First edition, first printing. BAL680. $ 75.00

11. (BARTLETT, JAMES) Probate forms, for the use of executors, administrators, &c. in the County of Strafford, together with the probate laws of the State. Dover, (N.H.) John Mann, 1832. 129pp. Publ. linen. Fine. $ 30.00
* Am. Imprints 11223, three locations. Very uncommon.

12. BEADLE, DELOS W. The American lawyer and business man's form book; containing forms and instructions for (numerous categories) together with the laws of the various states on (numerous topics) and a map and seal for each state in the union. N. Y., Phelps, Fanning, 1852. 359pp. $ 35.00
* Contains recent states such as Texas and California, as well as the southern states.

13. BEALE, JOSEPH HENRY JR. A treatise on criminal pleading and practice. Boston, Little, Brown, 1899. 400pp. Contemp. sheep, rubbed but sound. First edition. $ 35.00

14. (BECCARIA, CESARE) An essay on crimes and punishments; translated from the Italian of Marquis Beccaria; with the commentary by Voltaire ... the fifth edition, revised and corrected. London, H. D. Symonds, 1804. 8vo. Contemp. polished calf, spine gilt with leather label. A very fine copy. With bookplate and contemporary signature of R. B. AE. Macleod. $125.00

15. (BECCARIA, CESARE) Traite des delits et des peines, traduit de l'italien d'apres la sixieme edition ... Auquel on a joint plusieurs pieces tres interessantes pour l'intelligence du texte ... Paris, Pichard, 1784. 12mo. iv,xxviii,424,iv, 93,iiipp. Contemp. mottled calf, spine gilt panelled. A fine copy. $135.00
* A new translation by E. Chaillou de Lisy which is considered to be superior to the original French version of Morellet. Included is the commentary by Voltaire. Barbier IV, 777. This edition is not in the NUC, which does listan earlier printing with the same pagination.

16. BELL, CHARLES H. The bench and bar of New Hampshire, including biographical notices of deceased judges of the highest court and lawyers of the province and state and a list of names of those now living. Boston, Houghton, Mifflin, 1894. Orig. cl. 795pp. Roy 8vo. $ 35.00

17. BEMIS, GEORGE. Precedents of American neutrality, in reply to the speech of Sir Roundell Palmer, Attorney-General of England, in the British House of Commons, May 13, 1864. Boston, Little, Brown, 1864. 83pp. Wrps. Fine copy. $ 35.00
* The first of 4 important pamphlets by Bemis on international law questions during the Civil War. "...these pamphlets were distinguished for their uniformly high level of thought ... which stamped their author as a publicist of outstanding merit." --DAB. He played an important role also in the Alabama Claims. A professorship in international law at Harvard was established in his name.

18. BENNETT, EDMUND H. Farm law: a treatise on the legal rights and liabilities of farmers ... adapted to the statutes of all the states. Portland (Maine), Hoyt, (1880). 120pp. Orig. cl. 12mo. $ 22.50
* Includes a chapter on water rights.

19. BENTHAM, JEREMY A defense of usury; showing the impolicy of the present legal restraints on the terms of pecuniary bargains, to which is added, A letter to Adam Smith on the discouragement of inventive industry. Phila., Manly and Orr, 1841. 124pp. 12mo. Orig. cl. Fine. $ 37.50
* First of this edition, with a preface by the editor. Not in Kress. No copy in the NUC which does list a later printing

20. BENTHAM JEREMY A fragment on government; or, a comment on the Commentaries: being an examination of what is delivered on the subject of government in general, in the introduction to Sir William Blackstone's Commentaries: with a preface, in which is given a critique on the work at large. Second edition, enlarged. London, W. Pickering and E. Wilson, 1823. 8vo, xii,lii, 143pp. Original publisher's cloth, printed paper spine label (little chipped along edges) spine skillfully and unobtrus ively laid down(entirely preserved). Some very light occasional foxing; on the whole quite a nice copy. $375.00
* Benthams first book, and a major criticism of Blackstone. It was first published in 1776 - that edition is exceedingly scarce. "(It) represented and expressed the ideas of those who were conscious that radical reforms in the law were becoming necessary ... it was, as Bentham truly said, 'the very first publication by which men at large were invited to break loose from the trammels of authority and ancestor wisdom in the field of law.' "-- Holdsworth XII, 731.

21. BIGELOW, MELVILLE M. Leading cases on the law of torts, determined by the Courts of America and England. With notes. Boston, Little, Brown, 1875. xli,754pp. Cl. First edition. $ 45.00
* In actuality a careful, scholarly historical work, so admitted in the author's preface. Bigelow was greatly respected as an historian, "perhaps the earliest of your (i.e. American) historical pioneers" -- Holdsworth, Historians of Anglo-American Law, pp. 101-103.

22. BIGELOW, MELVILLE M. (comp.) Reports of all the published life and accident insurance cases ... with notes ... N. Y., Hurd, Houghton, 1872-1875. 4 vols. $ 50.00
* Includes cases in American, English, Irish, Scottish, and Canadian courts prior to 1871 and thereafter to 1875. There was a fifth and final volume for 1876, not present here.

23. BILLINGHURST, GEORGE Arcana clericalia, or, the mysteries of clarkship: being a sure way of settling estates by deeds, fines, and recoveries. With the forms of all manner of charter parties in maritime cities, towns and corporations. With a table ... London, Henry Twyford, 1674. 8vo. Engraved title-frontispiece. (16), 240, (2), 179-351,(1), 67,(1), (2), 57, (1), (16)pp. Contemporary plain calf, wanting the label, light wear along joints, but quite sound, and in all a very good, well preserved copy. $300.00
* First edition of an attractive and elaborate manual on clerkship, consisting of several parts, including one on merchants and traders. Pagination is irregular but complete (copies seem to vary in the arrangement of sections.) It was reissued in 1705. A nice copy. S&M I, 489. Wing B 2905.

24. BISHOP, JOEL PRENTISS. The first book of the law; explaining the nature, sources, books, and practical applications of legal science, and methods of study and practice. Boston, Little, Brown, 1868. 608pp. Orig. cl. Slt. wear to crown of spine. $ 65.00
* Contains a wealth of bibliographical information; a work of high quality by the author of greatly esteemed treatises on criminal law and marriage and divorce. William L. Friend, Anglo-American Legal Bibliographies, 1944, p. 23 and #29: "Chapters 12 to 16 are devoted to ... reports, treatises or commentaries, digests, abridgements, selections of cases and other works not included in the above ..." First edition. A very good copy.

25. BISHOP, JOEL PRENTISS. Thoughts for the times. Boston, Little, Brown, 1863. 36pp. Orig. prtd. wrps. Fine. $ 25.00
* Defends the war and the emancipation of slaves, with reference to the Constitution. Bishop was a foremost and prolific legal writer and scholar. This represents one of his "lay" efforts. DAB.

26. BLACKSTONE, (WILLIAM) Commentaire sur le code criminel d'Angleterre, traduit de l'anglais ... par M. L'Abbe Coyer ... Paris, Chez Knapen, 1776. 8vo. Two volumes in one. Contemporary ½ calf, red leather label, light wear to corners otherwise a fine copy. $250.00
* First and only edition of a very early French translation of Book Four of the Commentaries, which concerns criminal law, all that appeared in this particular translation This and an entirely different French translation of the whole of the Commentaries published in Bruxelles 1774-1776 appear, based on the NUC, to be the first and only contemporary French versions of Blackstone; in fact, the general absence of early European translated editions is striking. Blackstone and Oxford, an Exhibition, 1980, #121. The NUC lists four holdings.

27. BLACKSTONE, WILLIAM Commentaries on the laws of England, in four books. From the last London edition. With the last corrections of the author; and with notes and additions by Edward Christian ... Portland (Maine), Wait, 1807. Four volumes, 8vo's. Contemp. sheep rubbed, labels. With the portrait in volume one. Neat ink institutional stamp on each title page and on fore-edges, otherwise a clean sound set. Fold. table in volume two. $135.00
* Fifth American edition, intended by the publisher as a more lavish alternative to its immediate predecessors, the 12mo Thomas-Worcester editions. S & S 12159. Marvin p. 123.

28. (BLOUNT, THOMAS) Fragmenta antiquitatis. Antient tenures of land, and jocular customs of some mannors. Made public for the diversion of some, and instructions of others. ByT. B. of the Inner

(Continued)

28. (Continued) Temple ... London, Atkins, 1679. 8vo. 4 p.l., 175, (15)pp. including privilege and errata leaves. Contemp sheep, worn. Some light marginal stains, but sound. $135.00
* First edition of an important book, intended both to amuse and to instruct, and characterized by Holdsworth as a singularly original and valuable piece of legal history. "It is a painstaking piece of work taken from the original authorities which preserved the memory of many old customs which were rapidly decaying..." -- Holdsworth VI, 611. Wing B 3333. S&M I, 398.

29. BOHUN, WILLIAM Cursus Cancellariae: or the course of proceedings in the High Court of Chancery, wherein the authority, jurisdiction, and modern practice of that court are methodically and distinctly treated ... with a variety of useful precedents ... In the Savoy, J. Nutt ..., 1715. 4 p.l., 510,(10)pp. 8vo. Title within rules. Contemp. unlettered plain calf, raised bands. Some foxing to preliminary leaves, otherwise a very good copy. $200.00
* First edition of an important work on practice which possesses added historical interest in the form of an account of "the result of the controversy between Coke and Ellamere (concerning the relationship between law and equity) which was inserted to supply the omission of this information in the account given in the Reports of Chancery." --Holdsworth, XII, 180. Marvin p. 131. S & M I, 5.

30. BOOTE, R. An historical treatise of an action or suit at law, and of the proceedings used in the King's Bench and Common Pleas ... The second edition with additions. London, W. Owen, 1781. xxxi, (1),268,(4)pp. Contemp. calf, a little rubbed, otherwise a very good copy. $100.00
* An important book which passed through numerous editions well into the 19th century. "The history of procedure is represented by (this work). It is an able summary ... one of the objects ... was to lay a foundation for some very necessary reforms in this branch of the law, the need for which was clearly explained by the author." -- Holdsworth XII, p. 411. Marvin p. 134. S&M I, 258.

31. BROWNLOW, RICHARD Brownlow Latine redivivus: a book of entries, of such declarations, informations, pleas ... (etc.) contained in the first and second parts of the declarations and pleadings of Richard Brownlow, late chief prothonotary of the Court of Common Pleas ... now published in Latin, their original language, with additions of authentick modern precedents ... and a copious table ... London, Richard and Edward Atkyns ... 1693. Folio. 3p.l.,506,(46)pp. incl. privilege leaf. Recent ¼ calf antique, leather label. Some browning but a good copy. $250.00
31. Continued
* First complete and reliable edition. The title page faults the two "surreptitious" editions of 1653 and 1654 as being "unskillfully turned into English". The present edition is complete, in the original Latin, with additions in English. Wing B 5197. S&M I, 265. Marvin p. 156.

32. BRYCE, JAMES. The American Commonwealth. Second edition, revised. In two vols. London, MacMillan, 1891. 724, 764pp. Orig. cl. $ 25.00

33. BULLER, FRANCIS An introduction to the law relative to trials at nisi prius. The fifth (i.e. first American) edition, with additions and corrections. London, printed: New-York: re-printed by Hugh Gaine, 1788. v,(1),336,(30)pp. Contemp. sheep worn but sound. Internally good, some light foxing. $100.00
* First American edition of a work which remained in standard use for a number of years. A later American edition, published in 1806, turns up with some frequency, but this one is quite uncommon. Evans 20987. Marvin p. 158.

34. BURN, RICHARD Ecclesiastical law. The second edition. In four volumes. London, H. Woodfall & W. Strahan, for A. Millar, 1767. Four vols., 8vo. Contemp. calf, leather labels, light rubbing but an excellent set. $150.00
* Second edition of perhaps the best work of its kind in this period. By 1842 it had reached a ninth edition. "Burn's learning in all these sources of the law, and his gift of clear exposition enabled him to write the clearest and most successful of all the great treatises upon English ecclesiastical law." -- Holdsworth, XII, p. 613. "Blackstone ... mentions it as one of the very few publications on the subject ... on which the reader can rely with certainty." -- Marvin p. 163. This edition appears to be an unaltered republication of the first edition of 1763 (2 vols. 4to).

35. BUTLER, BENJAMIN F. A brief of the authorities upon the law of impeachable crimes and misdemeanors, prepared by Hon. Wm. Lawrence, M.C. of Ohio; revised and presented by B.F. Butler ... as a part of his opening argument on the impeachment of the President. Wash., GPO, 1868. 27pp. Orig. wrps. Issued as a trade publication though printed by the GPO. Fine. $ 27.50

36. BUTLER, CHARLES Horae juridicae subsecivae: a connected series of notes, respecting the geography, chronology and literary history of the principle codes and original documents of the Grecian, Roman, feudal and canon law. With additional notes and illustrations by an eminent American civilian. Phila., Farrand, 1808. xv,136pp. Orig. ¼ leather, front cover

(Continued)

36. (Continued) detached but present, internally good. $ 75.00
* First American edition with interesting and substantial notes by an American editor. The book is full of bibliographic information on areas of law as yet little written about in America; on that account, as well as for its being among the very earliest works on Roman or Civil law to appear in America (Cooper's Justinian appeared in 1812), it is of more than passing interest. In one lengthy note the American editor notices the attempt of Edward Livingston to produce a translation of the whole body of civil law (p. 72a). Marvin p. 167. Missed in Friend, Anglo-American Legal Bibliographies.

ORIGIN OF THE "THREE MILE LIMIT"

37. BYNKERSHOEK, CORNELIUS VAN (1673-1743). A treatise on the law of war. Translated from the original Latin of ... being the first book of his Quaestiones Juris Publici. With notes by Peter Stephen Du Ponceau. Phila., Farrand & Nicholas ... 1810. 8vo. xxxiv,218pp. Contemp. polished calf. Fine copy. $150.00
* First American edition and the first systemmatic translation into the English language. It ranks as one of the classics of international law, and was accepted widely as an authority. -- Marvin p. 168. Du Ponceau came to America during the Revolution. His background in European law and languages resulted in his attaining a foremost position in American legal practice for the litigation of international disputes associated with the Napoleonic Wars. This work reflects his intimate practical experience as well as his considerable scholarship.

38. (CANADA) FAREWELL, A. and G.P. URE. The Maine Law illustrated: being the result of an investigation made in the Maine Law States by ... president and secretary of the Canadian Prohibitory Liquor Law League ... February 1855. Toronto, The ... League, (1855). 94pp. Orig. front prtd. wrps. TPL 3543. $ 45.00

39. CARPENTER, MARY Reformatory prison discipline as developed by the Rt. Hon. Sir Walter Crofton, in the Irish Convict Prisons. London, Longman, 1872. 143pp. Cl. 12mo. $ 30.00

40. CARTER, A.G.W. (JUDGE) The old court house: reminiscences and anecdotes of the courts and bar of Cincinnati. Cincinnati, Thompson, 1880. Illus., frontis, plates. 466pp. Orig. pict. cl. $ 27.50

41. CHASE, HORACE. The New-Hampshire Probate Directory: ... adapted to the revised statutes and acts since passed, including June session, 1854, ... Second edition, Concord, Lyon, 1854. 342pp. Full contemp. sheep, rubbed. $ 27.50
* Marvin p. 188.

42. CHRISTIAN, EDWARD Practical instructions for suing out and prosecuting a commission of bankrupt; with the best modern precedents, and a digest of supplemental cases. London, W. Clarke & Sons, 1816. xxvi,468pp. Contemp. calf (little rubbed). A very good copy. $ 65.00
* First edition of a timely and useful work on the subject of bankrupt law, which the author notes "now includes the whole mercantile law of England." Christian was the first Downing Professor at Cambridge, and the younger brother of Fletcher Christian, of Bounty fame. He also edited a standard version of Blackstone. DNB. Holdsworth XIII, 480f. Marvin p. 196. S&M II, 65.

43. CHRISTIE, JAMES TRAILL Concise precedents of wills; with an introduction & practical notes. London, A. Maxwell, & Son, 1849. xv,267pp. plus 4pp. ads, plus 23pp. publisher's catalogue devoted entirely to English (and some American) law books. Orig. boards, printed spine label. A fine copy. First edition. $ 65.00

44. (CHURCH STATE. N.Y. STATE) Argument of Henry A. Cram, against the so-called "Freedom of Worship Bill" before the Committee of Cities of the Assembly ... 1885. (Cover title.) n.p., 1885. 27pp. Orig. prtd. wrps. Fine. Attacks efforts to introduce religious rites and education into non-sectarian institutions. $ 27.50

45. CLARENDON, EDWARD (HYDE, First) Earl of. A brief view and survey of the dangerous and pernicious errors to church and state, in Mr. Hobbes's book entitled Leviathan. (Oxford.) Printed at the Theater, 1676. 4to. 5p.l.,322pp. plus final blank. Engraved frontis, and engraved title vignette, headpieces, and initials. Contemp. blind tooled panelled calf, old rebacking, most of original spine preserved. Internally fresh and clean with good margins (first few leaves with some marginal browning). In all a very good copy. $350.00
* First edition of the foremost contemporary critique of Hobbes's Leviathan. For the illustrious career of the author, see DNB and Holdsworth V & VI. Wing C-4420. Madan 3110.

46. COKE, EDWARD (and others) The compleat copy-holder, wherein is contained a learned discourse of the antiquity and nature of mannors and copy-holds ... whereunto is newly added, The relation between the Lord of a mannor and the copy-holder his tenant ... together with The Forme of keeping a copy-hold court and court baron: also two tables newly added. London, W. Lee and D. Pakeman, 1650. 4to. 4p.l.,179;76,(4);51pp. One inner leaf of text in excellent facsimile on acid-free paper. Contemp. plain calf. A very nice copy. $150.00
* An early edition of a major book. Coke's

(Continued)

46. (Continued) Copy-holder "marks the final triumph of the King's Court which virtually put an end to feudal jurisdiction in England. It is a book of first class importance." --Jenks in S & M I, 246. The second and third works, each with seperate pagination and title page, are by Charles Calthrop (2nd ed., S&M I, 398) and John Kitchin, respectively. Wing C-4914, for the entire volume.

47. COKE, EDWARD The first part of the Institutes of the laws of England; or, a commentary upon Littleton ... the fifteenth edition; revised and corrected with further additions ... by Francis Hargrave and Charles Butler ... including also the notes of ...Hale and... Nottingham and an analysis of Littleton, written by an unknown hand in 1658-9. London, Brooke, 1794. Three volumes, Stout 8vo's. Contemporary calf, later rebacked with new red leather labels. A very good set. With a fine 18th century American bookplate in each volume. $200.00
* A major edition of Coke's First Institute, one which became the standard text in use in England and American during the early 19th century. Marvin in fact notes that American editions were "a pretty accurate reprint of the 15th English edition (i.e. this one.)" The Hargrave-Butler version first appeared in 1788: here their notes constitute the entire third volume. This is a desireable copy, with three fine 18th century bookplates engraved by James Akin, from the library of Peter A. Browne, a Philadelphia lawyer and reporter. Allen, American Bookplates, p. 117f., describes this bookplate (in a variant form) and only one other by Akin. Signed 18th century bookplates are uncommon Marvin p. 204f. A nice association copy and an important text, of American interest in both respects. S&M I, 451.

48. The conductor generalis: or, the office, duty and authority of justices of the peace, ... compiled chiefly from Burn's Justice ... by James Parker, late one of the Justices of the Peace for Middlesex County, in New Jersey; and now revised and adapted to the United States of America, by A Gentleman of the Law. ... Albany, Webster, 1794 ... 8vo. 467pp. Contemp. calf, lea. label. A very good copy, especially considering the use to which such a volume was subjected. $100.00
* Fourth appearance (1st was 1788) of this U.S. adaptation of the standard English work work which first appeared, unaltered, in N.Y. and Pennsylvania editions early in the century. This national adaptation emphasizes N.Y., N. J., and Pennsylvania law. Evans 27472.

49. The conductor generalis: or, the office, duty and authority of justices of the peace... compiled chiefly from Burn's Justice ... and lately revised and adapted to the United States of America... Phila., Matthew Carey, 1801. xv,480,(3)pp. 8vo. Contemp. sheep, leather label. A very good copy. $ 75.00
* This standard work first appeared in the Colonies in 1749, adapted from the English original by James Parker, a New Jersey magistrate. There were four editions between 1788 and 1794, all modified for the new union and emphasizing New York, New Jersey, and Pennsylvania law. This is the fifth national edition, and the first to be published by Carey, with a new list of subscribers. Shaw-Shoemaker 338.

50. COOPER, THOMAS A treatise on the law of libel and the liberty of the press; showing the origin, use, and abuse of the law of libel: with copious notes and references to authorities in Great Britain and the United States ... N. Y., G. F. Hopkins, 1830. 184pp. Contemp, ¼ calf, marbled boards. Old bookplate inside front cover. An excellent copy. $200.00
* FIRST EDITION. One of the outstanding early American works on free speech. "His legal researches led him to protest against the common law doctrine of libel..."--McCoy C558. It is interesting to note that Cooper was himself a victim of the Alien and Sedition Law in 1800. An uncommon book, especially welcome in nice condition. Missed by Marvin and strangely absent from the long account on Cooper in the DAB.

51. (CORNWALLIS, CATHERINE FRANCES) On the principles of criminal law. London, William Pickering, 1846. 148pp. Orig. publ. cl. Light wear to spine extremities. $ 75.00
* First edition. A good general review of existing conditions, with the recommendation of compassionate reforms, especially in the treatment of juveniles and women. There is ample reference to Australia and to the desirability of transportation to Canada. The authoress conceived and was the major contributor to the series "Small Books on Great Subjects" to which the present work belongs. "These volumes ... were widely read both in England and America."--DNB. Not in Ferguson despite appropriate content

52. (COWELL), MANLEY, THOMAS ΝΟΜΟΘΕΤΗΕ: The interpreter, containing the genuine signification of such obscure words and terms used either in the common or statute lawes of this realm, first compiled by the learned Dr. Cowel, and now enlarged... with an addition of many words...also tenures whether jocular, or others... (and) an appendix containing the ancient names of places... London, J. Streater for H. Twyford ... 1672. Folio. 4p.l.,(292)pp. Half-title present. Title within rules, Ornamental head and tail pieces. Bound in contemporary calf, blind tooled border, raised bands (wanting label). A fine fresh copy. $350.00
* First edition of this important revision of Cowell. This copy is from the Evelyn family library and is in fine contemporary state. Cowell's dictionary was the first large scale work of its type for the common

52. (Continued) law; first published at the beginning of the 17th century, it remained the standard authority, in new editions and in revisions such as this one, for well over a century. DNB for Manley. cf. Holdsworth V, 21f. Wing C-6645, under Cowell. S&MI, 7.

53. COWEN, ESEK. A treatise on the civil jurisdiction of justices of the peace in the State of New-York. Second edition revised by Sidney J. Cowen. In two vols. Albany, Gould, 1841. Portrait. 1251pp. Contemp. sheep, rubbed. 2 volumes $ 65.00
* "No law book, local in its character, enjoys a better or more widely extended reputation ... Since its first publication it has been a favorite work ... it is found to be very well adapted to the wants of justices in several of the new states..."--Marvin p. 234f. With a nice engraved frontis portrait.

54. CROKE, ALEXANDER A report of the case of Horner against Liddiard, upon the question of what consent is necessary to the marriage of illegitimate minors; determined on the 24th of May 1799, in the Consistorial Court of London by ... Sir William Scott ... with an introductory essay upon the theory and the history of laws relating to illegitimate children, and to the encouragement of marriage in general. London, Strahan for Butterworth, 1800. viii,189,(1)pp. Contemp. calf, spine very slightly rubbed, otherwise a fine copy. $125.00
* A very uncommon book on an interesting topic. The introductory essay takes up the major part of the book. Croke, a member of the College of Advocates, was commissioned by the presiding judge to report this case; as a result he came to the attention of the government and eventually was awarded an admiralty judgeship in Halifax, Nova Scotia. DNB. Marvin p. 241. S&M I, 498. Only edition.

55. CROSWELL, SIMON G. A treatise on the law relating to electricity. Boston, Little, Brown, 1895. 765pp. Full contemp. sheep. $ 45.00
* First edition and according to the author, the first really comprehensive treatment of the subject.

56. CURTIS, GEORGE TICKNOR The American conveyancer; containing a large variety of legal forms and instruments, adapted to popular wants and professional use throughout the United States ... Boston, Little, Brown, 1844. 269pp. 12mo. Sheep. Good copy. $ 37.50
* First published in 1839, and here revised to take into account the 1844 Massachusetts Insolvent Act, this became a standard manual, passing through numerous editions during the next thirty or so years. Highly commended by Marvin, p. 247f. DAB.

57. CURTIS, GEORGE TICKNOR The case of the Virginius, considered with reference to the law of self-defence. N.Y., Baker, Voorhis, 1874. 40pp. Orig. prtd. stiff wrps. Fine $ 37.50
* An interesting tract on international law. At issue was the seizure by Spain of an American vessel being used by Cuban insurgents and the murder by Spanish authorities of a large number of persons on board. Curtis, in opposition to the doctrines enunciated by the U.S. President, defends the seizure of the vessel but not the treatment of the prisoners. Rare.

58. CUSHING, LUTHER STEARNS. Lex Parliamentaria Americana. Elements of the law and practice of legislative assemblies in the United States of America. Ninth edition, Boston, Little, Brown, 1874. 1063pp. Orig. sheep, leather labels. Good copy. $ 35.00

59. CUSTANCE, GEORGE. A concise view of the Constitution of England. Second edition, corrected and enlarged. London, Longman ... ca. 1809. 4p.l.,(5)-491,(1)pp. Contemp. ¼ calf. $ 75.00
* An uncommon and thoroughgoing account which acknowledges debts to Blackstone, De Lolme, Burke, Hume and others; it is dedicated to Wilberforce. S&M II, 89. Uncommon.

FROM THE LIBRARY OF JOSEPH STORY

60. DARD, H.J.B. Code Civil, avec des notes indicatives des lois romaines, coutumes, ordonnances, edits et declarations, qui ont rapport a chaque article; ou Conference du Code Civil avec les lois anciennes Troisieme edition revue et augmentee ... Paris, Waree, 1827 xxii,653pp. 8vo. Contemp. half calf slightly rubbed, otherwise a fine copy. $150.00
* Joseph Story's copy with his signature in its customary position at the top right margin of the title page (no annotations in the text). The NUC lists only this edition (2 copies).

61. (DARTMOUTH COLLEGE CASE) NEW HAMPSHIRE, SUPERIOR COURT. Opinion of theSuperior Court of the State of New Hampshire in the case of the Trustees of Dartmouth College versus William H. Woodward ... Concord, Isaac Hill, 1818. 27pp. Neatly disbound. $ 45.00
* A rare printing of a decision of major constitutional importance. The state court upheld the challenge of the legislature to the charter of the college; its opinion was overturned by the Supreme Court in a decision which marked a milestone in the development of the doctrine of corporate rights and laissez faire. Shaw-Shoemaker 44995, locating only two copies.

62. (DARTMOUTH COLLEGE CASE.) FARRAR, TIMOTHY Report of the case of the Trustees of Dartmouth College against William H. (Continued)

62. (Continued) Woodward. Argued and determined in the Superior Court of Judicature of the State of New Hampshire ... and on error in the Supreme Court of the United States ... Portsmouth, Foster, (1819). 2p.l.,406pp. 8vo. Contemp. sheep. Very good. $ 75.00
* First edition. A landmark case elucidating the contract clause of the Constitution and the rights of corporations. Marvin p. 303.

64. (DEDHAM COURT HOUSE) Souvenir of the dedicatory exercises at the new Norfolk County Court House at Dedham, Mass., June 20, 1895 together with an historical and descriptive sketch of the several court houses and biographical sketches of the leading participants. Boston, Heintzmann, 1896. Oblong 4to. 60pp. plus photogravure plates of interior and exterior views. $ 25.00
* Of interest historically and architecturally; also the scene of part of the Sacco-Vanzetti trial.

65. DELAFONS, JOHN A treatise on naval courts martial. London, P. Steel, 1805. xii,(6),385pp. Contemp. polished calf, some old scuffing to covers, otherwise a very nice copy. $ 90.00
* First and only edition of an uncommon book, with a six page list of subscribers. The author, who served in the navy as a deputy judge advocate, states that the work goes beyond a review of forms and precedents and attempts to uncover the principles which underly the naval code and trace institutions to their causes. Marvin p. 262. S&M II, 97. NUC lists 6 holdings. Seldom seen in trade.

66. DESTUTT DE TRACY, (ANTOINE LOUIS CLAUDE, comte) Commentaire sur L'Esprit des Lois de Montesquieu...suivi d'observations inedites de Condorcet... et d'un memoire sur cette question... Paris, Th. Desoer, 1822. xv,437pp, half-title present. Early cloth, leather label. A good copy. $ 75.00
* An early French edition of a work on political philosophy which contains a defense of the republican constitution of America against claims made for the superiority of the British system. It was written during the author's stay in America and first appeared in 1811 in an English translation by Thomas Jefferson. A French edition did not [illegible] until 1817. The work is omitted from the Kress catalogue, but in fact it contains [illegible]ntial discu[illegible]nomic policy.

68. DILLON, JOHN F. Commentaries on the law of municipal corporations. Fourth edition, thoroughly revised and enlarged. In two vols. Boston, Little, Brown, 1890. In two vols., clxxiv,1516pp. Full contemp. sheep. Fine. $ 45.00
* Penultimate edition, significantly revised by the author beyond the previous edition of 1881. "...(a) monumental treatise ... which created municipal corporations as a separate field of the law."--DAB.

69. DILLON, JOHN F. Removal of causes from state courts to federal courts, with forms, adapted to the several Acts of Congress on the subject. Fifth edition, revised and enlarged, and adapted to the Act of Congress of March 3, 1887, by Henry Campbell Black. St. Louis, Central Law Journal Co., 1889. 238pp. Cl. $ 25.00

70. DIX, WILLIAM GILES A national constitution the only road to national peace. A letter to the President of the United States. Boston, Estes & Lauriat, 1875. 23pp. Orig. prtd. wrps. Fine. $ 27.50
* A radical call for a new constitution embodying in explicit form the national idea vindicated by the outcome of the Civil War. Uncommon.

71. DOGHERTY, THOMAS The Crown circuit assistant: being a collection of precedents ... in criminal and penal proceedings. Together with an alphabetical table to the statutes relating to felony, brought down to the twenty-fifth year of His present Majesty King George the Third. London, Uriel, 1787. 551pp. Full contemp. calf, rubbed, wanting label. $ 75.00
* Marvin p. 270. S&M I, 361. Only [illegible]tion except for a Dublin reprint.

72. DOUGLAS, SYLVESTER, Lord Glenbervie. The history of the cases of controverted elections which were tried and determined during the first and second sessions of the fourteenth Parliament of Great Britain, 15 & 16 Geo. III. In four volumes. Second edition, with corrections and additions. London, Brooke...1802. Four vols. 8vo. Contemp. calf, very minor rubbing but an excellent set. $125.00
* "A collection of excellent reports on the law of parliamentary election...with an instructive historical preface and very judicious annotations...the only work of its kind except one lately published from Mr. Glanvill's manuscript...they are both particularly valuable..."--Marvin p. 273, quoting Hargrave. Holdsworth XII, 109 and

73. (Continued) tains some excellent hints upon the best method of reporting... Douglas' reports are noted for accuracy, care, and method ... and are of the highest authority."--Marvin p. 274. Wallace p. 529.

74. DRAKE, CHARLES D. A treatise on the law of suits by attachment in the United States. Fifth edition, revised corrected and enlarged with an appendix containing the leading statutory provisions of the several states and territories of the United States in relation to suits by attachment. Boston, Little, Brown, 1878. 770pp. Full contemp. sheep. Wanting label. $ 45.00

75. DU CANE, SIR EDMUND F. The punishment and prevention of crime. London, MacMillan, 1885. 235pp. Orig. cl. Fine. $ 50.00
* First edition of the only published book by this leading prison reformer. Du Cane was active in both Australia and England in the improvement of prisons. This historical sketch of British prisons and treatment of crime up to this time includes a long chapter on transportation. DNB 1901-1911. Ferguson 9252.

76. DUFF, SIR M.E. GRANT. Sir Henry Maine: a brief memoir of his life, with some of his Indian speeches and minutes selected and edited by Whitley Stokes. London, Murray, 1892. Portrait. 451pp. Cl. Fine. First edition. $ 37.50
* Reflects Maine's brilliant legal contributions while serving in India.

77. DUKE, GEORGE The law of charitable uses, revised and much enlarged with many cases in law both ancient and modern, whereunto is now added, the learned reading of Sir Francis Moor...methodically digested by... London, Henry Twyford, 1676. Folio. 4p.l.,186,(10)pp. Pagination irregular but complete. Imprimatur leaf and original terminal blanks present. Title within rules. Contemp. panelled calf gilt, neatly rebacked. Fine royal arms gilt on both covers. Bookplate of Edw. Sach. Sitwell. Cover edges a little rubbed otherwise a fine copy. $250.00
* First and only early edition of a principal authority on this topic. The work did not reappear until the beginning of the 19th century. It is devoted to an exposition of the Statute of 43 Eliz. concerning charitable uses, of considerable importance in the development of the poor-law. Marvin p. 279: "A standard authority on this branch of the law." Old Wing D-2504. S&M, I, 496.

78. (DUMONT, ETIENNE et al.) Recueil de documens relatifs a la prison penitentiaire de Geneve. Geneve, J. Barbezat, Paris, 1830. xvi,180pp. 3 double-page tables, 2 engraved plates. Contemp. half calf. Signet arms on covers. A nice copy. $150.00

78. (Continued)
* A collection of proposals for the reform of prison discipline and construction, in which the efforts of Dumont, the great Bentham disciple, figure heavily. A note on the verso of the half title indicates that this book was to be sold at the prison, and that the proceeds were to be given to prisoners who, by good conduct, obtained early release. Rare: not in the BLC; the NUC records Harvard only. Not seen in trade.

79. DU PONCEAU, PETER S. A dissertation on the nature and extent of the jurisdiction of the courts of the United States, being a valedictory address to the students of the Law Academy of Philadelphia...to which are added, A brief sketch of the national judiciary powers exercised in the United States prior to the adoption of the present Federal Constitution, by Thomas Sergeant...and the author's Discourse on legal education...with an appendix and notes. Phila., Abraham Small, 1824. xxxii,(2), 254,(1)pp. Old L.C. stamp on title page, internally good. New cloth. $ 65.00
* A collection of three interesting pieces. The last address, on legal education, is by Du Ponceau

80. The duty and power of jurymen; addressed to the freeholders of Great Britain. Manchester, J. Pratt, 1817. 16pp. 12mo Orig. plain wrps. Fine. $ 55.00
* An exposition and defense of the institution of trial by jury. Rare: not traced in the NUC, BLC or in Sweet & Maxwell.

81. EATON, (DORMAN BRIDGMAN) Should judges by elected? or the experiment of an elective judiciary in New York. N. Y., Amerman, (1873). 92pp. Sewn as issued. $ 35.00
* A substantial work by a pioneer crusader for civil service and municipal law reform. Eaton began his career as editor of Kent's Commentaries. DAB gives a good account. A scarce work, missed by DAB.

A SEMINAL BOOK IN ENGLISH PENAL REFORM

82. (EDEN, WILLIAM, First Baron Auckland.) Principles of penal law. London, B. White and T. Cadell, 1771. iv,300pp., errata leaf, final blank. Large 8vo. Contemporary speckled calf. A fine copy, printed on thick paper. $450.00
* First edition of a seminal work in the reform of English criminal law. It is the first book in English to consider reform in a systematic and philosophical manner. "Eden's book is a pioneer treatise. It discussed topics which, under the influence of Bentham and Romilly, aroused much attention in the last years of the eighteenth and the first years of the nineteenth century; and it discussed them effectively... not as abstract propositions, 'but rather as argumentative inferences...from observations on the penal systems of different governments.'... The book is a remarkable precursor of that new era of agitation for the reform of the law which, under Bentham's

82. (Continued) leadership, was soon to begin."--Holdsworth, XII, 364f. A choice copy, on thick paper, probably one of a number of copies printed for presentation. With contemp. bookplate of Earl Spencer (over Althorp label).

83. EDMONDS, JOHN WORTH An address on the Constitution and Code of Procedure and the modifications of the law effected thereby, delivered ... before the class of attorneys... N. Y., Code Reporter Office, 1848. vii,47pp. Original prtd. wrps. A fine copy. $ 45.00
* An exposition, given by the judge of the N.Y. Supreme Court to newly qualified practicing lawyers, of the landmark procedural reforms contained in the landmark Revised Code for the State of New York, which had just taken effect. A most interesting copy, bearing an inscribed presentation from Edmonds, with a few textual corrections in his hand, and with editorial markings by the unnamed recipient or later owner suggesting its use in a further publication.

84. 'ESPINASSE, ISAAC Cases argued and ruled at Nisi Prius, in the Court of King's Bench, and Common Pleas, from Easter Term 33 George III to Hilary Term 34 George III with some additional cases of an earlier period. First American edition with additional references. London, printed, Baltimore: Re-printed by Clayland, Dobbin & Co. for Keatinge's Book Store 1795. viii,127, (1 blank),xiipp. Contemp. sheep rubbed. A very good copy. $ 75.00
* First American edition. Evans 28636. Uncommon.

A REPLY TO BLACKSTONE

85. A fair trial of the important question, or the rights of election asserted; against the doctrine of incapacity by expulsion or by resolution: upon true constitutional principles, the real law of Parliament, the common right of the subject... in which two pamphlets... The Case of the ate Middlesex Election considered... and Serious Considerations upon a late Important Determination, are very fully examined ... London, J. Almon, 1769. 1p.l.,248pp. plus 8 pages of ads for Almon's publications. Contemp. sheep, rubbed but sound. Some foxing but a very good copy. $125.00
* Part of the intense pamphlet war that swirled around John Wilkes on the occasion of his ejectment from Parliament. Contributors to the melee included Blackstone, Samuel Johnson, William Meredith. Junius, and here Almon Wilkes's champion and publisher. Blackstone had defended the action of Parliament; the present work is, in part a reply to a pamphlet, The Case of the Late Middlesex Elections, which is attributed to Blackstone (see DNB, II, 602), and is included in the tracts published as an appendix to the Commentaries.

86. FESSENDEN, THOMAS G. An essay on the law of patents for new inventions. With an appendix containing the French patent law, forms &c. Boston, Mallory, 1810. 229pp. Contemp. sheep, rubbed. Internally very good. $ 75.00
* First edition of the first American work on the subject. Marvin p. 307.

FIELDING DEFENDS CAPITAL PUNISHMENT

87. FIELDING, HENRY A true state of the case of Bosavern Penlez, who suffered on account of the late riot in the Strand, in which the law regarding these offences, and the statute of George the First, commonly called the Riot Act, are fully considered. London, A. Millar, 1749. 1p.l., 54pp. Old ink inst. stamp on title and last leaf. Terminal leaves a bit dusty, internally fine. New marbled wrappers. $125.00
* Fielding's defense of his conduct in sentencing to death Penlez, a participant in a recent serious riot in the Strand involving housebreaking, looting, and arson; the sentence was carried out against the protest of the jury who convicted Penlez. This appears to be Fielding's earliest work on criminal law to be published in connection with his career as magistrate. Rothschild 852. Only edition.

88. FINLASON, W. A selection of leading cases on pleading and parties to actions, with practical notes ... From the London edition. Harrisburg, M'Kinley, 1847. 218pp. New cl. $ 45.00
* First American, from the first London edition of the same year.

89. (FISHER, SAMUEL) Lectures on the law-merchant, etc. (Running title.) (Boston ? 1824.) 16pp. Sewn as issued. Uncut. $ 45.00
* A rare prospectus and synopsis for a series of lectures on commercial law about to be given in Boston. Not recorded in Shaw-Shoemaker, American Imprints. Not found in the NUC.

90. FITZHERBERT, ANTHONY The new natura brevium... the ninth edition carefully revised... the writs accurately translated into English... to which is added, a commentary ... by the late Lord Chief Justice Hale... Dublin, Printed by H. Watts, Law Bookseller, 1793. Thick 8vo. Contemp. calf, leather label. $ 75.00
* One of the outstanding early works on procedure, first published in 1534. This is the penultimate edition, followed by a 1794 London edition. Winfield p. 302f. S&M I, 269. Marvin p. 311f.

91. (FOSTER, SIR MICHAEL) An examination of the scheme of church power laid down in the Codex Juris Ecclesiastici Anglicani, &c. Dublin, R. Reilly, 1735. 102pp. Neatly disbound. $ 65.00
* A refutation of some of the high ecclesiastical claims made by Edmund Gibson in

(Continued)

91. (Continued) his great work on ecclesiastical law published in 1713. Foster is best known for his treatise on criminal law. Holdsworth XII, 136, and 607ff, for Gibson. Marvin p. 321. DNB. S&M I, 168. First Dublin edition, the same year as the London. Both are sparsely represented in the NUC.

92. FOSTER, ROGER. A treatise on federal practice in civil causes, with special reference to patent cases and the foreclosure of railway mortgages. In two volumes. Boston, Boston Book, 1892. cxviii,1482pp. In two vols. $ 25.00

93. FREEMAN, SAMUEL The Massachusetts Justice: being a collection of the laws... relative to the power and duty of justices of the peace... forms... appendix... third edition, much improved. Boston, Thomas & Andrews, 1810. 8vo. 296pp. Contemp. sheep, lea. label. A very good copy. $ 37.50
* Rearranged and brought up to date beyond the previous edition of 1802. Marvin p. 324, earlier edition only. Shaw-Shoemaker 20148.

94. FREEMAN, SAMUEL The probate auxiliary; or, a director and assistant to probate courts, executors, administrators and guardians, being the laws of Masschusetts ... to which are added a variety of forms ... Portland, Massachusetts (i.e., Maine), Benjamin Titcomb, 1793. xi,(1),156,(3)pp. 12mo. Contemp. sheep, worn. A good copy. $ 80.00
* First edition. Like Freeman's other guides and manuals, this remained a standard, often re-issued work for the next 25 years. Evans 25511. An early piece of Maine printing. Laid into this copy is a partly printed form of recognizance filled in and signed by Samuel Freeman, acting as Justice of the Peace in an action for debt, in Cumberland County, Maine.

95. FREEMAN, SAMUEL The probate Directory: or an assistant... being the Laws of the Commonwealth of Massachusetts, respecting the estates of testators, intestates, and wards, to which are added, a variety of forms,... Second edition, greatly enlarged and improved. Boston, Thomas, 1803. 228pp. New cloth. $ 37.50

96. FULLWOOD, FRAN. Leges Angliae. The lawfulness of ecclesiastical jurisdiction in the Church of England, asserted and vindicated in answer to Mr. Hickeringill's late pamphlet stiled Naked Truth... London, R. Royston, 1681. Sm. 8vo. (24),78,(2)pp. Incl. engraved frontis. and final leaf of publ. advts. Contemp. plain calf, light wear to edges, otherwise an excellent copy. $ 75.00
* Only edition of an uncommon tract. S&M, I, 179. Wing F-2509. Marvin p. 326. The NUC lists four holdings.

97. (GARDNER, ROBERT ?) The compleat constable. Directing constables, head-

97. (Continued) boroughs (etc.) ... in the duty of their several offices...continued to...1700. Also directions for the London constables. To which is added, a treatise of warrants and commitments... the 2nd edition with additions. London, T. Beaver, 1700. 12mo. 6p.l.,190pp. Contemp. plain calf, some wear to spine, otherwise an excellent copy of a perishable book. $150.00
* Second edition of a popular manual whose early editions appear to be rare. This is the earliest edition listed in the NUC (two holdings only). Wing G-53 attributes the work to Gardner. S&M I, 233 and the NUC list it under title.

98. GILBERT, (GEOFFREY) The law of devises, last wills, and revocations. To which is added, a select number of wills, drawn by men eminent in the profession. The third edition, revised, corrected, and improved. London, Strahan & Woodfall for T. Waller, 1773. (xiv),255,(8),(2)pp. Orig. boards, paper spine, covers rather dust-soiled, internally fine. $100.00
* A valuable work on land law, dealing as much with rules of law as with equity, and among the earliest modern texts on the principles of equity. Holdsworth described Gilbert's works as "some of the best text books on legal topics published during this century." Holdsworth XII, 140 and 187f. Marvin p. 333 (this edition). S&M I, 491.

99. GILBERT, (GEOFFREY) The law of executions. To which are added, The history and practice of the Court of King's Bench; and some cases touching wills of lands and goods. London, W. Owen, 1763. 6p.l.,427, (5)pp. Contemp. calf, wanting label, otherwise a very good copy (very minor worming to lower blank margin, quite away from any text), internally clean and fresh. $150.00
* First edition. "(Gilbert's) works are some of the best text books on legal topics published during this century."--Holdsworth III, 140 and 355. Marvin p. 332. S&M I, 270. The only other edition of this work is a Dublin reprint of the same year.

100. GLANVILL, RANULPH DE Tractatus de legibus et consuetudinibus regni Angliae, tempore Regis Henrici secundi compositus... qui nunc imprimatur post 50. annos a priori & prima impressione... In aedibus Thomae Wight. 1604. Sm. 8vo. 9p.l.,116 numbered leaves,(33)pp. Original front signed blank present. A very good copy with good margins. Laid in to a contemporary vellum binding (bearing the appropriate lettering but possibly belonging originally to another copy). $200.00
* Third edition of a seminal work, the earliest treatise on the beginnings of the system of common law, first published in 1554, and again in 1557. S&M I, 54. STC 11906.

101. GOODWIN, ISAAC Town officer: or, laws of Massachusetts relative to the duties (Continued)

101. (Continued) of municipal officers; together with a digest of the decisions of the Supreme Judicial Court ... Worcester, Dorr & Howland, 1825. xii,336pp. 12mo. Orig. sheep, lea. label. Very good copy. $ 45.00
* First edition. "Mr. Goodwin has adopted the plan of Dickinson ...(etc)... and has done his work more thoroughly than any of his predecessors."--Marvin p. 341. Shoemaker 20722.

102. GREENHOOD, ELISHA The doctrine of public policy in the law of contracts. Reduced to rules. Chicago, Callaghan, 1886. xcv,860pp. Cl. First edition. $ 27.50

103. GREENLEAF, SIMON A discourse pronounced at the inauguration of the author as Royall Professor of Law in Harvard University, August 26, 1834. Cambridge, Munroe, 1834. 28pp. Orig. prtd. wrps. Fine. $ 35.00
* A choice copy of this pamphlet which usually turns up disbound. "To the efforts of Story and Greenleaf is to be ascribed the rise of the Harvard Law School to its eminent position."--DAB.

104. GRIFFITH, (WILLIAM) A treatise on the jurisdiction and proceedings of justices of the peace in civil suits; with an appendix containing advice to executors, administrators, guardians, also an epitome of the law of landlord and tenant... the second edition, with improvements, and a new chapter on conveyancing. Newark, New Jersey, John Woods, for the author, 1797. 12mo. xii,320,(22)pp. New cloth. $ 75.00
* A valuable early work on New Jersey law, with material on conveyancing. The DAB describes the author as "the state's ablest lawyer on N.J. land titles." Evans 32211. Marvin p. 351, listing the third edition (1813). The first edition appeared in 1796.

105. GUY, WILLIAM A. Principles of forensic medicine. First American edition, with notes and additions by Charles A. Lee. N. Y., Harper, 1845. xvi,711pp. 8vo. Contemp. sheep, very good copy. $125.00
* First American appearance, simultaneous with the London edition. A major comprehensive work including the jurisprudence of insanity. The American editor has made very substantial additions of American material, including the personal advice and opinions of Chancellor Kent, which he acknowledges in the preface. Guy acknowledges the influence of the American pioneers, Beck and Ray. An interesting example of interaction between English and American jurisprudence in an area still relatively new. Some copies of this American edition were issued with a variant title page: "Principles of medical jurisprudence..." They are otherwise identical with the present issue. S&M II, 149.

106. HAINES, ELIJAH M. Laws of Wisconsin concerning the organization and government of towns and the powers and duties of town officers and boards of supervisors, with numerous practical forms. Chicago, Wm. B. Keen...1858. 189,(1)pp. Orig. prtd. wrps. Slight chipping at edges, else fine. $125.00
* A well preserved copy of a work with official standing, made to conform to the new revised statutes. The Chicago publisher's ads for law books, etc. appear on the rear cover. A scarce book, particularly in the original wrappers. Ante-Fire Imprints #353. The NUC locates five copies.

107. HALL, JOHN E. The practice and jurisdiction of the court of admiralty; in three parts. 1. An historical examination of the civil jurisdiction... 2. A translation of Clerke's Praxis, with notes on the jurisdiction and practice of the district courts. 3. A collection of precedents. Baltimore, Dobbin & Murphy, 1809. xxviii,iv,211,(5)pp. Original boards, front cover detached but present. Some foxing, otherwise a good uncut copy. $125.00
* First edition of the author's first book, one of the earliest, if not the first, original American treatises on admiralty law. In the previous year Hall began the first American legal periodical, The American Law Journal. Both it and this treatise reflect the growing involvement of the legal profession in commercial law and particularly in mercantile insurance case. See Horwitz. Transformation of American Law, 1977, p. 141. Marvin p. 362. DAB.

108. (HAMILTON, ALEXANDER et al.) The Federalist: a commentary on the Constitution of the United States...reprinted from the original text... edited by Henry Cabot Lodge. N. Y., Putnam, 1888. 586pp. Cl. First of this edition, which contains a long introduction by Lodge. $ 25.00

109. HAMILTON, ALEXANDER The works of Alexander Hamilton: comprising his most important official reports; an improved edition of the Federalist... and Pacificus... In three volumes. N. Y., Williams and Whiting, 1810. 12mo. Three volumes. Three engraved frontis. portraits, of Hamilton, Madison, and Jay. Contemporary tree calf, contrasting leather labels. A fine set. $250.00
* The first collected edition of Hamilton's writings, "edited by John Wells, who gives the authorship of the different numbers of the Federalist from a private memorandum in (Hamilton's) own handwriting."--Ford, p. 87. Also present is the Report on Manufacturers. An attractive, well preserved copy of a scarce set.

110. HAMMOND, ANTHONY A digest of reports in equity ... containing the digest and names of cases. First American edition. Brookfield, Hammond, 1822. 860pp. Full Contemp. sheep, rubbed, wanting label. *Marvin p. 364. $ 50.00

"INSANE CRIMINALS SHOULD BE PUNISHED"

111. HAMMOND, WILLIAM A. Insanity in its relations to crime. A text and a commentary N. Y., Appleton, 1873. 77pp. plus ads. Original limp publisher's cloth gilt. A fine copy. $135.00
* First edition of a scarce work by an important American neurologist. Hammond produced the first text-book on nervous diseases in the English language and contributed several works devoted entirely to the jurisprudence of insanity, as well as founded and edited the Quarterly Journal of Psychiatric Medicine and Medical Jurisprudence. The lengthy article in the DAB fails to note the present work, which contains an important normative statement to the effect that the deterrent effect of punishment is not lost upon insane persons, and that, except in cases of extreme delusion or imbecility, they ought to be considered legally responsible and subject to penalties based on circumstantial degree like those applied to the normal population.

112. (HARGRAVE, FRANCIS, compiler) Collectanea Juridica. Consisting of tracts relative to the law and consitution of England, Volume the first (-second). London, E. and R. Brooke, 1791, (-1792). Two volumes, 8vo. Contemporary boards, paper spines, covers rather soiled. Internally fine uncut copies. $200.00
* First editions, all published, and one of Hargrave's major contributions to legal history. It contains forty tracts concerning English legal history taken from Hargrave's extraordinary manuscript collections; most were previously unpublished or poorly represented in earlier printed sources. Holdsworth singles out this work as one of Hargrave's two principal historical contributions. The work is also of considerable bibliographical interest in that each volume concludes with a register of recently published law books described in great detail. A very well preserved copy in original boards. Holdsworth XII, p. 410f. Marvin p. 369. S&M I, 32.

113. (HAUTERIVE, ALEXANDRE MAURICE BLANC de LANAUTTE, comte d') Memoire sur les principes et les lois de la neutralite maritime, accompagne de pieces officielles justificatives. Paris, chez les Marchands de Nouveautes, 1812. 160pp. Neatly removed. Good copy. $ 37.50

114. (HAWLES, JOHN) The Englishman's right; a dialogue in relation to trial by jury. Reprinted from the edition of 1772. Boston, 1883. 56pp. Orig. cl. $ 20.00

115. HENING, WILLIAM W. The American pleader and lawyer's guide, in commencing, prosecuting and defending actions at common law, and suits in equity, with full and correct precedents ... adapted to the practiceof the United States...Vol. I.... N. Y., Riley, 1811. xlvii,509pp. Contemp. sheep worn but sound. $ 35.00
(Continued)
* The first half, complete in itself, covering the headings "account" to "covenant", of a scarce two-volume work by a distinguished Virginia legal writer. The concluding volume appeared separately, in 1826 at Richmond. Not surprisingly the two rarely appear together, and, in fact, singly they are uncommon.

GEORGE FITZHUGH'S COPY

116. HENING, WILLIAM WALLER The Virginia justice... the fourth edition, revised, corrected, greatly enlarged and adapted to the revised Code of 1819 and the laws subsequently passed. Richmond, printed for the author, 1825. 821,(1)pp. Contemp. calf. Very good copy. $ 85.00
* Final edition of this classic Virginia manual. A nice association copy, bearing the signature of George Fitzhugh of Virginia, author of "Sociology for the South" and "Cannibals all", foremost defender of slavery and Southern society. He practiced law in his early years. See DAB for both Hening and Fitzhugh.

117. HEYL, LEWIS, compiler. Statutes of the United States relating to revenue, commerce, navigation, and currency... Boston, Little, Brown, 1868. 960pp. Full contemp. sheep. Roy 8vo. First such compilation since 1843. Painstakingly comprehensive. $ 50.00

118. HILLIARD, FRANCIS. The law of remedies for torts, or private wrongs. Boston, Little, Brown, 1867. xlvii, 595pp. Full contemp. sheep. First edition. $ 35.00

119. (HISTORICAL CHART) A correct account of the names of the most eminent professional men, who have presided in the several courts of judicature (with the official dates of their appointments), from the earliest periods of their institution to the present time. (London), Cunningham & Salmon, printers, ca. 1836. Large broadside, sectioned and mounted on linen as issued, measuring 31.5 x 24.5 inches, folded to 8.5 x 5.5 inches in ¼ leader folder, printed label (spine little worn). Fine copy of a very detailed and useful chart. $ 37.50

120. HOAR, E.R. Charge to the Grand Jury at the July Term of the Municipal Court in Boston, 1854. By ... one of the Justices of the Court of Common Pleas... Boston, Little, Brown, 1854. 22pp. Orig. prtd. wrps. Fine. Concerns suppression of riots connected with the Fugitive Slave Law. $ 25.00

121. HOBBES, THOMAS Leviathan, or, the matter, form, and power of a common-wealth ecclesiastical and civil. London, Andrew Crooke, 1651 (i.e. ca. 1680). Folio. Separate frontispiece title, fold. table. Contemp. plain calf, neatly rebacked, new endpapers. Some browning, mostly confined (Continued)

121. (Continued) to margins. A good copy. $350.00
* Third edition, with the ornamental device on the title page. It is identical in appearance with the first edition of 1651 and even bears that date in its imprint, but it was probably published in 1680. In any case it indicates the strong continued popular interest in Hobbes's challenging classic. MacDonald and Hargreaves, #44 and p. 27ff. PMM 138 (first edition).

122. (HOGDON, MOSES) The complete justice of the peace, containing extracts from Burn's Justice, and other justiciary productions. The whole altered and made conformable to the laws and manner of administering justice, particularly in the State of New Hampshire, and generally in the other of the United States... by a Gentleman of the Profession. Dover, N. H., printed for Charles Peirce, 1806. 431pp. Calf, rubbed. $ 45.00
* Shaw-Shoemaker 10569. First edition.

123. HOLMES, OLIVER WENDELL Address delivered at the dedication of the new hall of the Boston University School of Law, January 8, 1897. Boston, (1897). 29pp. Orig. prtd. wrps. Fine. $ 27.50
* First edition. Actually a substantial statement of his legal philosophy. Scarce.

124. HOUCK, LOUIS A treatise on the mechanics lien law in the United States. Chicago, Callaghan, 1867. 256pp. Full contemp. sheep, rubbed. $ 45.00
* Ante-Fire Imprints 1213.

125. HOWARD, JOHN The state of the prisons in England and Wales, with preliminary observations, and an account of some foreign prisons and hospitals. The fourth edition. London, Johnson...1792. Large thick 4to. 3p.l.,540pp. Twenty-two fine engraved plates, most folding, including many architectural plans and views. Contemporary tree calf neatly rebacked. A very good copy. $225.00
* Howard's book is the first major practical work on prison reform, and his efforts mark the beginning of enlightened reform in England. This posthumous edition is complete with the important supplements of 1780 and 1784. Printing and the Mind of Man, 224 (first edition of 1777).

126. HUNT, WILLIAM A collection of cases on the Annuity Act, with an epitome of the practice relative to the enrolement of memorials... the second edition, considerably enlarged and improved, with many manuscripts, and all the printed cases to hilary term, 36 Geo. 3. inclusive. London, W. Clarke, 1796. x,387pp. Original boards, paper spine. Entirely uncut and partly unopened. Printed on blue rag paper. Contemp. annotations on title page $ 75.00
* Final edition, much enlarged beyond the first of 1794. S&M I, 532. Marvin p. 406. A well preserved copy in original state.

127. HUTCHINSON, JOHN A. A treatise on the laws of West Virginia pertaining to the powers and duties of justices, clerks of courts, prosecuting attorneys, sheriffs, constables, notaries, etc... also rules of evidence, definitions, notes of decisions, etc., etc. With references to the law and practice in Virginia. Second edition, revised by ... Cincinnati, Clarke, 1899. 1177pp. Cloth. $ 45.00

128. IOWA HISTORICAL LECTURES. Delivered before the State Historical Society... 1892. Iowa City, 1893. 92pp. Orig. prtd. wrps. Fine. $ 25.00
* Includes: The introduction of the common law into Iowa, by Chancellor Emlin McClain.

129. JAMES, EDWIN The Bankrupt Law of the United States, 1867. With notes, and a collection of American and English decisions upon the principles and practice of the law of bankruptcy. Adapted to the use of the lawyer and merchant. N. Y., Harper, 1867. 325pp. Full contemp. sheep. First edition. $ 35.00

130. JAMESON, JOHN ALEXANDER A treatise on constitutional conventions; their history, powers, and modes of proceeding. Fourth edition, revised, corrected and enlarged. Chicago, Callaghan, 1887. 684pp. Later cl. Fine. $ 55.00
* Final and best edition of this unique and highly respected study. It was first published in 1867; the author was professor of law at the University of Chicago and Superior Court Judge. See Larned #2758.

THE HUMANITARIAN RECONSTRUCTION OF ENGLISH PRISONS

131. (JEBB, SIR JOSHUA, Surveyor-General of Prisons and Commissioner of Pentonville.) Report of the Surveyor General of Prisons on the construction, ventilation, and details of Pentonville Prison, 1844. London, William Clowes, 1844. 62pp. errata slip, with 22 large folding lithographed plates. Lge. 8vo. Orig. cloth little faded. $200.00

* First commercial edition of the landmark Parliamentary report on the American system of separate confinement. In fact it was the logical culmination of reforms begun 70 years earlier by Howard and continued more recently by William Crawford, who worked closely with Jebb in the final planning. Jebb, trained as a military engineer (he served in Canada), was able to fuse his technical proficiences with a very sympathetic understanding of the humane possibilities of the "separate system." The spread of this sytem throughout England was due to his subsequent efforts. The plates, of considerable architectural interest, include plans, sections, elevations, and a large overall view depicting an idyllic visiting-day promenade down the central hall. DNB gives a good account of Jebb.

132. JENKINS, HOWARD M. The republican form: a constitutional inquiry. Wilmington, Del., Jenkins & Atkinson, 1867. 12pp. Orig. prtd. wrps. Fine. Presentation copy from the author. $ 27.50
* A protest against inequality of representation in Delaware state government, and exclusion of Negro voters. The author calls for a Congressional law to alter such violations in this and other states, maintaining that Congress is obliged by the Constitution to guarantee the states a republican form of government. Scarce.

133. (JOHNSON, SAMUEL, 1649-1703) A history and defence of Magna Charta, containing a copy of the original charter at large with an English translation...with an introductory discourse containing a short account of the rise ... of freedom ... also the liberties which are confirmed by the Bill of Rights, &c. to which is added, an essay on parliaments describing their origin in England ... London, J. Bell, 1769. lxii,284pp. Contemp. polished calf, joint cracked but firm. A nice copy. $100.00
* First publication of a work written in the 17th century. S&M I, 550.

134. JONES, WILLIAM An essay on the law of bailments. The second edition, with introductory remarks and notes ... by John Balmanno. London, Strahan for Dilly 1798. 8p.l.,(246),xxviii,(2)pp. Contemp. calf, spine little rubbed, else a nice copy. $ 75.00
* The first appearance of Balmanno's edition, which served as the basis for a number of early American editions. Jones' treatise was an important contribution to this branch of law and remained preeminent until the appearance of Story's work. Marvin p. 428f. S&M I, 240.

135. JONES, WILLIAM (translator) Institutesof Hindu law: or, the ordinances of Menu ... comprising the Indian system of duties, religious and civil. Verbally translated from the original sanscrit with a preface by Sir William Jones. Calcutta: printed ... London: reprinted for J. Sewell and J. Debrett, 1796. 8vo. xvi, 366,(1)pp. Later half black mor. Few damp stains on title page and last few leaves, internally very good. $125.00

* Jones was appointed judge of the high court at Calcutta in 1783, and during his ten years of service there he undertook a complete codification of Indian law with the help of living native authorities. He lived just long enough to complete the first stages as embodied in this work, which is of interest both as "a masterly rendering" (DNB) of the law, and as a linguistical product, for Jones was the father of modern Indo-European philology.

136. KEITH, GEORGE SKENE A prize dissertation on the excellence of the British Constitution. Aberdeen, J. Chalmers for F.

136. (Continued) and C. Rivington... 1800. 2p.l.,(3)-58pp. Original pale blue wrps. sewn as issued, uncut. A fine copy $125.00
* In part a comparative study, with mention of the American Constitution, which the author finds too liberal. Scarce. The NUC lists LC only. Not in Sweet & Maxwell.

LEGAL EDUCATION FOR AMERICANS

137. KENT, JAMES An introductory lecture to a course of law lectures delivered November 17, 1794, by James Kent, Esquire, Professor of Law in Columbia College. Published at the request of the trustees. New York, Francis Childs, 1794. 23pp. Neatly disbound. A very good copy. $425.00
* The author's first published work, and one of the earliest works on American legal education. Kent had just been appointed to the first professorship of law at Columbia, where, in 1794, he delivered a course of 26 lectures. This broad introductory statement is especially interesting for its exposition and support of the doctrine of judicial review, as Kent attempts to show the special importance to Americans of the study of constitutional law. Rare in commerce. Evans 27183. DAB.

138. KERR, WILLIAM WILLIAMSON A treatise on the law and practice as to receivers appointed by the Court of Chancery. With notes and references to American authorities by Geo. Tucker Bispham. Phila., Kay, 1872. 288pp. First American edition. $ 37.50

139. KERR, WILLIAM WILLIAMSON. A treatise on the law of fraud and mistake. With notes to American cases, by Orlando F. Bump. N. Y., Baker, 1872. 505pp. Full contemp. sheep. First American edition. $ 25.00

140. KILTY, WILLIAM A report of all such English statutes as existed at the time of the first emigration of the people of Maryland, and which by experience have been found applicable to their local and other circumstances; and of such others as have been ... introduced, used and practiced by the courts of law or equity; and also all such ... as may be proper to be introduced and incorporated into the body of the statute law of the state. Made according to the directions of the Legislature... To which are prefixed, an introduction and lists of the statutes which had not been found applicable... with full indexes... Annapolis, Jehu Chandler, 1811. 4to. 289,(1)pp. Terminal leaves stained, some wear confined to margins. New cloth. $100.00
* Kilty, chancellor of Maryland, produced the 1799 laws of the State as well as this uncommon piece of legal research commissioned by the Legislature in connection with further revision of the law. Marvin p. 440. Sabin 45320. Shaw-Shoemaker 23158.

141. KINGSBURY, BENJAMIN Jr. The Maine townsman, or, laws for the regulation of towns, with forms and judicial decisions, adapted to the revised statutes of Maine. Revised and enlarged by ... Sixth edition. Boston, Sanborn, 1857. 432pp. Full contemp. sheep, rubbed, $ 25.00

142. (KITTRIDGE, E.W. ?) An examination of the recent cases of conflicting jurisdiction between the Federal and State Courts. Cincinnati, Truman & Spofford, 1857. 41pp. Orig. prtd. wrps. Fine. With rear wrap inscribed to Robert Rantoul. $ 55.00
* Deals with the Fugitive Slave Law, particularly with the cases ex parte Jenkins, and Ohio v. Marshals, the first concerning a Pennsylvania jurisdiction. Rare. NUC, three copies, listed under title. We make the author attribution on the basis of a pencil presentation present in this copy.

143. KYD, STEWART A treatise on the law of bills of exchange and promissory notes. The first American edition, from the third London edition, with considerable additions. Boston, Manning and Loring for Hall, 1798. xii,288pp. 12mo. Some stains to lower margin. New cloth. $ 35.00
* First American edition (the additions are to the London edition). Holdsworth XII, 390: "a good clear statement of the law." Marvin p. 443. Evans 33971.

144. (LAW REFORM) The law and lawyers laid open, in twelve visions. To which is added, Plain truth, in three dialogues, between Truman, Skinall, Dryboots, three attorneys, and Season, a bencher. London T. Woodman, 1737. xlviii,269,(1)pp. 12mo. Later calf in the style of the period, some wear to label. With the ownership signature of Gilbert Burnett, second son of Bishop Burnett. $150.00
* A broad-ranging satire on the common law as an overgrown, chaotic system full of uncertainty, danger and excessive expense, and on lawyers as predators and knaves, all by way of demonstrating the need for codification. Most of the work is cast in the form of allegorical fiction framed by a long introductory manifesto and a concluding dialogue. A nice, substantial piece of early legal reform. Halkett & Laing attributes the work to J. A. Purves. The NUC and BLC list it under title. S&M I, 215. Scarce.

145. LAWES, EDWARD A practical treatise on pleading in assumpsit. With the addition of the decisions of the American Courts, by Joseph Story. Boston, Burditt, 1811. 621pp. Contemp. sheep rubbed, wants label. $ 55.00
* First American, from the first London edition of 1810. Marvin p. 452.

146. (LAWYERS DIRECTORY) MERCHANTS' UNION LAW COMPNAY. Second monthly report of

146. (Continued) the correspondents and members of the ... giving its organization, officers, members: comprising the name and residence of an efficient and reliable practising lawyer for every county in the United States... N. Y., December 1866. 79pp. Orig. prtd. wrps. Fine. Second issue of an early directory which includes all Western territories as well as the States. $ 25.00

147. (LEGAL SATIRE) Law and laziness, or students at law of leisure. New York, printed for the author at the Golden Rule Office, 1846. 48pp. BOUND WITH: A BECKETT, GILBERT ABBOTT. The comic Blackstone Part I (-part IV). Philadelphia, Carey and Hart, 1844 (-1846). Four parts complete. Engraved frontis. and engraved title page for part I. Contemp ¼ calf. a nice copy. $100.00
* A biting satirical attack on the fraternity of professional lawyers, with the moral that law practice should be thrown open to all - a recurrent theme in American radical legal reform. Scarce. Wright, American Fiction, Vol. I, 1606 locates 3 copies. Bound with the first American edition of the Comic Blackstone.

THE SCIENTIFIC STUDY OF POLITICS

148. LEWIS, GEORGE CORNEWALL A treatise on the methods of observation and reasoning in politics. In two volumes. London, John W. Parker, 1852. 2 vols. 8vo. Contemp ¼ calf, a nice set. $125.00
* First and only edition of the author's most important work. In this well developed treatise he sought to do for government and the political process what his close personal friend and teacher, John Austin had done for jurisprudence, namely to determine the province of politics and apply scientific method to its analysis - to establish an orderly sytem of universally recognized truths comparable to the physical sciences. See DNB and the article in Encyclopaedia of the Social Sciences.

149. LINDSLEY, J. BERRIEN On prison discipline and penal legislation; with reference to the State of Tennessee... Nashville, 1874. 64pp. Orig. prtd. wrps. $ 45.00
* Lindsley was a medical doctor and an ardent reformer in the areas of public health and prisons; he was a leading figure in the Robertson Association, a philanthropic group which sponsored this work. It is a knowledgeable and informative plea for modernization, with statistics and a good chronology of penal reform. Scarce.

150. LINN, WILLIAM The legal and commercial lawyer; a common-place book for farmers, merchants, and mechanics, containing the decisions of the Supreme Court of the United States, and of the respective State Courts, on bills of exchange, checks, promissory notes, &c ... Utica, Brooks, 1859. 294pp. Contemp. sheep, joints cracked but sound. $ 35.00

151. LIVINGSTON, JOHN H. A dissertation on the marriage of a man with his sister in law. New Brunswick, (N.J.), Deare & Myer, 1816. 169pp. Contemp. sheep, front cover detached but present. $ 45.00
* A severe blast at what the author calls "gross incest of the highest order", based on the doctrine of the Reformed Dutch Church, of which Livingston was a leading representative in America. The issue continued to be a vexing one in the English speaking world for the rest of the century. This copy belonged to Nathan Allen, physician and writer on population and marriage, who wrote a book on intermarriage among descendants. See DAB for both Livingston and Allen S&S 38084.

152. LOCKE, JOHN Two treatises of government ... London printed MDCLXXXVIII Reprinted the sixth time, by A. Millar, H. Woodfall, (et al.) 1763. 8vo. Contemporary speckled calf, spine ornately gilt with raised bands, red leather label. A quite attractive copy (very slight wear to spine extremities). $225.00
* An edition of some textual interest bearing the following advertisement: "The present edition of this book has not only been collated with the first three editions, which were published during the author's life, but also has the advantage of his last corrections and improvements, from a copy delivered by him to Mr. Peter Coste, communicated to the editor, and now lodged in Christ College, Cambridge."

154. LONG, GEORGE A treatise on the law relative to sales of personal property. First American, from the last London edition, improved by a digest of American decisions. Exeter, N. H., Lamson, 1823. 288pp. plus index. Contemp. sheep. Very good copy. $ 55.00
* First American edition. Marvin p. 474.

155. LORD, JOHN P. The Maine townsman, or laws for the regulation of towns; with forms and judicial decisions, adapted to the revised statutes of Maine. Second edition. Portland, Sanborn, 1847. 327pp. Full contemp. sheep. 12mo. $ 27.50

156. LOWELL, ABBOTT LAWRENCE and LOWELL, FRANCIS C. The transfer of stock in private corporations. Boston, Little, Brown, 1884. xx,297pp. Contemp. sheep. Fine copy. $ 37.50
* First edition.

157. LUBE, D. G. An analysis of the principles of equity pleading; containing a compendium of the practice of the High Court of Chancery and the foundation of its rules, together with an illustration of the analogy between pleadings at common law and in equity. Second American from the last London edition, with notes and references to American cases by J.D. Wheeler. N. Y., Banks, 1846. 415pp. Full contemp. sheep, rubbed. $ 45.00
* Marvin p. 478.

158. McCLELLAN, ROBERT H. The executor's guide: a complete manual for executors, administrators and guardians, with a full exposition of their rights...and of the rights of widows...with forms. Albany, Gould, 1862. 204pp. Sheep, very rubbed but sound. $ 27.50

159. McLAREN, JOHN The law of Scotland in relation to wills and succession; including the subjects of intestate succession, and the construction of wills, entails, and trust-settlements. In two vols. Edinburgh, Bell, 1868. lxi,728,781pp. Contemp. half morocco. Roy. 8vo's $ 80.00
* First edition of a very substantial treatise, and apparently the author's own copy, with several small corrections and additions towards a future edition.

160. (MAINE.CONSTITUTION) PERLEY, JEREMIAH The debates, resolutions and other proceedings of the Convention of Delegates assembled at Portland...October, 1819, for the purpose of forming a constitution for the State of Maine. To which is prefixed the Constitution taken in Convention. Portland, A. Shirley, 1820. 300pp. 12mo. Contemp. sheep, rubbed, A very good copy. $125.00
* First edition and the first publication of the proceedings which gave Maine separate statehood. Perley was a Maine lawyer and was the author of the first justice's manual for the state. Shoemaker 2073. Sabin 43920.

161. MAINE, HENRY SUMNER Dissertations on early law and custom chiefly selected from lectures delivered at Oxford. London, John Murray, 1883. 402pp. plus publ. ads. Original publ. cl., spine faded, otherwise a fine copy. First edition. $ 50.00

162. MAINE, SIR HENRY SUMNER Dissertations on early law and custom chiefly selected from lectures delivered at Oxford ... N. Y., Holt, 1883. 402pp. Orig. cl. $ 25.00

163. MARSHALL, (JOHN) The opinion of Chief Justice Marshall in the case of Garnett, Ex'r of Brooke v. Macon et al. Published by Joseph Tat e Counsellor at law. Richmond, Shepherd and Pollard, 1825. 60pp. 8vo. Contemp. ¼ calf. Light wear to joints but sound. Internally fine. $125.00
* A very extensive opinion by Marshall in a complex case involving breach of contract in the sale of land subsequently discovered to be encumbered with debt. Tate abstracts no less than twenty points, prior to giving the full account, dealing with contract, conveyancing, and liability of estates for debt. Servies 771. Marvin p. 499. Shaw-Shoemaker 21334.

MARSHALL ON SEPARATION OF POWERS AND FOREIGN AFFAIRS

164. MARSHALL, JOHN and EDWARD LIVINGSTON. Speech of the Hon. John Marshall, delivered in the House of Representatives, of the United States, on the resolutions of Hon. Edward Livingston, relative to Thomas Nash alias Johnathan Robbins. Phila., printed at the office of the True American,,1800. 45pp. 12mo. Orig. wrps. Sewn as issued. A fine copy. $150.00
* First edition of a landmark speech in which Marshall compellingly vindicated the conduct of the Administration and stated the dictum, based upon the separation of powers, that the President, and not the Courts, or Congress, is "the sole organ of the nation in its external relations..." Henry Adams called this "a speech that still stands without a parallel in our Congressional debates." Evans 37887. Servies #232: "Very widely reprinted and anthologized."

165. MARTINDALE, W.B., A treatise on the examination of titles to real estate and the preparation of abstracts, with an appendix of forms, Second edition, revised and enlarged by Lyne S. Metcalfe, Jr. St Louis, Central Law Journal, 1890. 208pp. Cl. (First edition was 1885.) $ 20.00

166. (MARYLAND) The Constitution of the State of Maryland: formed and adopted by the Convention which assembled at ... Annapolis, May 8, 1867... with marginal notes and references ... and an appendix and index by Edward Otis Hinkley ... Baltimore, Murphy, 1867. 156pp. Contemp. sheep. $ 27.50

FIRST EDITION OF ONE OF THE MOST ENDURING STATE CONSTITUTIONS

167. MASSACHUSETTS. A constitution or frame of government agreed upon by the delegates of the people of the State of Massachusetts-Bay, in Convention... Boston, Benjamin Edes, 1780. 8vo. 53pp. including the half-title. Bound in later ¼ morocco, covers detached but present, the pamphlet itself in exceptionally fine condition, entirely untrimmed; a fresh clean copy. $250.00
* First edition of the state constitution adopted after an abortive attempt in 1778 at a more radical document. It has remained in effect in its essentials, making it one of the longest enduring of state constitutions. Evans 16844. Kuhlman p. 34. A choice copy in perfectly preserved original state.

168. MASSACHUSETTS. LAWS. (NATHAN DANE, WILLIAM PRESCOTT, and JOSEPH STORY) The charters and general laws of the colony and province of Massachusetts Bay, carefully collected from the publick records and ancient printed books, to which is added an appendix, tending to explain the spirit, progress, and history of the jurisprudence of the state... published by
168. (Continued) Order of the General Court. Boston, Wait, 1814. Med. 8vo. vii,830pp. plus index. Contemp. calf. $ 75.00
* First edition of the first modern compilation intended to serve as a reliable source of precedent in contemporary jurisprudence; many of these laws were still in force; others, though repealed, remained relevant to the construction of new statutes The committee appointed to perform this compilation consisted of Story, Dane and Prescott, who were instructed also to report those laws still in effect which in their opinion ought to be repealed. This was Jared Spark's copy with his name on the title-page.

169. (MASSACHUSETTS. REVISED CONSTITUTION) Discussions on the Constitution proposed to the people of Massachusetts, by the Convention of 1853. Boston, Little, Brown, 1854. 306pp. Orig. cl. $ 35.00
* Anthology of six discussions of the new proposed Constitution, all of which had been previously published separately. Includes The letters of Phocion, by G. T. Curtis; also works by G. S. Hillard, Samuel Hoar, Marcus Morton, C. F. Adams, and J. G. Palfrey.

170. MAUDSLEY, HENRY Responsibility in mental disease. N. Y., Appleton, 1898. $ 27.50
* A standard work first published in 1874 in London. It contains a good section on jurisprudence, with some reference to American decisions.

171. MAYO, JOSEPH A guide to magistrates: with practical forms for the discharge of their duties out of court ... precedents for the use of prosecutors, sheriffs ... adapted to the new code of Virginia. Richmond: Colin, Baptist and Nowlan, 1850. 702pp. Large 8vo. Contemp. calf. A good copy. $ 50.00
* First edition, variant printing following an issue of the previous year by a different publisher. Necessitated by the appearance of the new Revised Code of 1849.

172. MAYO, JOSEPH A guide to magistrates; with practical forms for the discharge of their duties out of court. To which are added precedents for the use of prosecutors, sheriffs, coroners, constables, escheators, clerks, &c. Second edition, in which the laws are brought down to the present time, with notes. Richmond (Virginia), prtd. by Wynne, 1860. 726pp. Full contemp. calf. rubbed but a good sound copy. $ 50.00

173. (MICHIGAN) State Supreme Court. Oct. Term 1878. E. H. Van Deusen vs. Nancy J. Newcomer. Argument for plaintiff in error ... Kalamazoo, 1878. 35pp. wrps, fine. Concerns false imprisonment for insanity and view of insanity as disease vs. crime. $ 15.00

174. MILTON, JOHN A defence of the people of England ... in answer to Salmasius's Defence of the King. Printed in the year 1692. 4p.l.,xxii,1blank leaf,246,(1)pp. 8vo. Contemp. blind ruled calf, spine gilt, light wear along joints and head of spine, inner hinges later reinforced. A good copy with the original front blank, and with the final leaf of publisher's ads for books sympathetic to Charles I. $250.00
* First edition in English. Wing M-2104.

175. MISSISSIPPI. TERRITORY. LAWS, STATUTES, etc. Statutes of the Mississippi Territory, the Constitution ... The Articles of Agreement and Cession between the United States and the State of Georgia; and such acts of Congress as relate to the Mississippi Territory. Digested by the authority of the General Assembly. Natchez, Peter Isler, Printer to the Territory, 1816. 495,(1),(28)pp. Contemp. sheep, leather label, light wear along joints and a little rubbed but quite a good copy in fresh contemporary state. $350.00
* Digested by Edward Turner and known as "Turner's Code..." Contains the laws from 1798 through the session of 1816. McMurtrie 96. Shaw-Shoemaker 38269. A choice copy of these early laws of the new south.

176. (MISSOURI. SUPREME COURT) A digest of the decisions of the ... on all subjects from 1820 to 1845; also the Constitution of the United States, to which is attached the construction given to the same. Compiled by Evans Casselberry. St Louis, S. W. Meech, 1845. 482,(3)pp. New cl. $ 75.00
* American Imprints Inv. Missouri, 434. Not in Sabin.

177. (MOCKET, RICHARD) God and the King: or, a dialogue shewing that our Soveraign Lord the King of England, being immediately under God ... doth rightly claim whatsoever is required by the Oath of Allegiance. Formerly compiled and printed by the especial command of King James ... and now commanded to be reprinted ... London, by His Majesties special Priviledge and Command, 1663. Sm. 4to. 2p.l.,40pp. Disbound. $ 50.00
* A characteristic tract propounding the theory of divine right, first published in 1615. Wing M-2302. S&M I, 117.

A PROFOUND INFLUENCE ON AMERICAN CONSTITUTIONAL THOUGHT

178. (MONTESQUIEU, CHARLES LOUIS SECONDAT, Baron de) De l'esprit des loix ou du rapport que les loix doivent avoir avec la constitution de chacque gouvernement, les moeurs, le climat, la religion, le commerce, &c... A Geneve, chez Barillot, & Fils., (1748). Two volumes 4to. 4p.l.,xxiv, 552,(1); 2p.l.,xvi,564pp. Complete with both half-titles, and with the errata leaf at the end of the first volume. Title vignettes, woodcut head and tailpieces.

178. (Continued) A handsome copy bound in contemporary mottled calf, raised bands, leather labels, spine with rich ornamental gilt. Slight partial rubbing along joints, very minor wear to spine ends. A fine, fresh copy throughout, in an attractive and well preserved binding. $1850.00

* First edition, second issue. This is the earliest version of this issue, with the errata leaf at the conclusion of the first volume. "One of the greatest masterpieces of the political theory and a pioneering work in sociology. The work enjoyed considerable immediate success- at least twenty-four editions in the first eighteen months - and its reputation continued to grow throughout the century. In its stress on the historical role of the nobility as a check to royal power, it provided a theoretical justification for the resurgence of artistocratic power, which was so important in the origins of the French Revolution. Furthermore, its emphasis on the separation of powers of government and on a system of checks and balances ...profoundly influenced constitutional thought in both America and France. Indeed, during the early and later stages of the French Revolution, Montesquieu's theories were much more important than those of Rousseau." -- France in the Age of Revolution: an Exhibition, by Charles B. McNamara, Cornell Univ., 1981. p. 11. PMM 197. Tchemerzine viii, 459/460. Cabeen 97. Kress 4920 (this issue).

179. MORIARTY, GERLAD P,, translator. The Paris law courts: sketches of men and manners. Translated from the French by Gerald P. Moriarty. N. Y., Scribner, 1894. 293pp. Illus. Orig. pict. cl. Fine. $ 35.00
* Based on the "Palais de Justice de Paris" written by French legal journalists in order to acquaint the general public with the workings of French justice. The translator, of Balliol College, has added his own introduction comparing English and French law. Reviewer's copy, with 1894 review for The Nation laid in.

180. MORISON, JOHN H. Life of the Hon. Jeremiah Smith. Member of Congress during Washington's administration, Judge of the United States Circuit Court, Chief Justice of New Hampshire, etc. Boston, Little, Brown, 1845. Frontis. 516pp. Buckram. $ 20.00

181. MORRISON, CHARLES R. New Hampshire probate law and directory containing the general laws of 1878, and acts since passed ... Concord, Sanborn, 1884. 321pp. Full contemp. sheep. Very good. $ 22.50

182. MORSE, JOHN T., Jr. The law of arbitration and award. Boston, Little, Brown, 1872. lxxi,670pp. Contemp. sheep. Fine copy. $ 50.00
* First edition, and according to the author's preface, the first American treatise on this subject.

183. NELSON, WILLIAM The rights of the clergy of ... England; as established by the canons, the common law, and the statutes of the realm, being a methodical collection under alphabetical heads ... of such things ... in cases concerning the rights, duties, power, and privileges of the clergy. The third edition, corrected with large additions. In the Savoy, E. and R. Nutt...1732. xii,628pp. Contemp. calf rubbed. $ 75.00
* Final edition of a compendious work first published in 1709. S&M I, 173. Holdsworth XII, 623. Marvin p. 534. NUC holdings of all editions are sparse.

184. The new commercial law: a practical text book with an appendix containing chapters on courts, pleadings and practice, and forms of ordinary legal and business documents ... (Rochester, N.Y., Andrews, printer), 1894. 262pp. Orig. pict. cl. $ 17.50

185. (NEW HAMPSHIRE) (SANBORN, CHARLES P.) Justice and sheriff, and attorney's assistant, for the use of attorneys, justices, sheriffs, coroners, and constables; with practical forms and notes of decisions and authorities. Revised edition. Concord, Sanborn, 1888. 557pp. Contemp. sheep. $ 17.50

186. (NEW YORK STATE) The clerk's magazine: containing the most useful and necessary forms of writings ... calculated for the use of the citizens of the United States ... the fourth edition. Albany, Websters and Skinners, 1812. 291,(17)pp. 12mo in sixes. Contemp. sheep. Nice copy. $ 35.00
* A standard work first published in 1803. This edition is substantially updated, with appendixes on money, debtor laws, State and Federal Constitutions, and recent census figures. Shaw-Shoemaker 25907.

187. NOYE, WILLIAM A treatise of the rights of theCrown declaring how the King of England may support and increase his annual revenues. Collected out of the records ... 1634. By William Noy, the attorney General. Now first publish'd from the original ms. with some account of the author London, B. Lintott, 1715. 12mo. xii, 113,(6)pp. Contemp. sheep. A very good copy. $150.00
* Noy was respected as one of the most learned lawyers and most reliable reporters of his time; like Hargrave, he amassed a major collection of manuscripts from which his works issued. See the account in Wallace, Reporters, p. 154ff. DNB. Marvin p. 542. S&M I, 330. First and only edition.

188. (O'BRIEN, JOHN MAURICE) The powers and duties of the town officer as contained in the statutes of Maine, with forms ... Second edition improved. Hallowell, Spaulding, 1824. 324pp. 12mo. Contemp. sheep. Shoemaker 17462, 1 location. $ 37.50

189. OLIVER, BENJAMIN L. Forms of practice; or American precedents in personal and real actions, interspersed with annotations. Fourth edition, revised and enlarged by a Member of the Cumberland Bar ... embracing also rules, forms at law and precedents, according to the practice acts of Massachusetts, supervised by a Member of the Suffolk Bar. Portland, Dresser, 1874. xxxvi,869pp. Full contemp. sheep. $ 45.00
* A heavily augmented edition, especially with respect to the new Massachusetts codes.

190. OLIVER, BENJAMIN LYNDE Practical conveyancing, a selection of forms of general utility, with notes interspersed. Boston, Cummings, 1816. 486pp. Contemp. sheep. A very good copy. $ 75.00
* First edition of a classic. It remained in use throughout the 19th century, passing through many editions, the last being 1884. The first edition is very uncommon. "The best American manual upon conveyancing ... in use."--Marvin p. 547. Shaw-Shoemaker 38519. The NUC cites only 4 holdings.

191. OLLYFFE, GEORGE An essay humbly offer'd for an act of Parliament to prevent capital crimes and the loss of many lives; and to promote a desireable improvement and blessing in the nation. London, J. Downing, 1731. 25pp. plus leaf of adds. Neatly removed. A fine copy. $125.00
* An atavistic pamphlet giving detailed proposals for a number of gruesome executions, the regular kind having apparently too little deterrent effect, also proposing a system of indelible marking of criminals, and transportation to the plantations to be sold into slavery as a means of dealing with vagrants. Like most such arguments, this one believes that crime itself will be eliminated by terror. The author was a cleric, and the son of John Ollyffe (DNB). S&M I, 364. The NUC lists two holdings.

192. ORTOLAN, (JOSEPH LOUIS ELZEAR) Explication historique des Instituts de l'Empereur Justinien, avec le texte, la traduction... les explications sous chaque paragraphe, et une table ... precedee d'une generalisation du droit Romain... deuxieme ed. rev. et considerablement augmentee. Paris, Joubert, 1840-1843. 2 volumes. 8vo. Contemp. calf ruled in blind, contrasting labels, little rubbed. Contemp. bookplate of William Ramsay, University of Glasgow, and binder's ticket of Carss & Co., Glasgow $ 75.00

193. (PALFREY, JOHN GORHAM) Remarks on the proposed state constitution. By a free-soiler from the start. Twelfth thousand. Boston, Crosby, Nichols, 1853. 53pp. Sewn as issued. $ 15.00
* A detailed criticism of the new Massachusetts Constitution. Sabin 58324. DAB.

194. PARKER, EDWARD G. Reminiscences of Rufus Choate, the great American advocate. N. Y., Mason, 1860. 522pp. Illus. cl. $ 27.50

195. PARSONS, THEOPHILUS The law of contracts. Sixth edition. In three vols. Boston, Little, Brown, 1873. 609,801pp. New cloth. $ 75.00

196. PARSONS, THEOPHILUS The law of contracts. Eighth edition, edited by Samuel Williston. Three vols. Boston, Little, Brown, 1893. In three vols., cclxiii,609,929,718pp. Cloth. $ 50.00

197. PARSONS, THEOPHIUS The laws of business for businessmen, in all the States of the Union, with forms for mercantile instruments, deeds, leases, wills &c. Boston, Little, Brown, 1857. 504pp. cl. First edition of this enduring work. $ 37.50

198. PARSONS, THEOPHILUS Laws of business for all the States of the Union, with forms and directions for all transactions. Hartford, Scranton, 1869. 685pp. ¼sheep. $ 30.00
* Second edition (first was 1857), much altered, of what became the most enduring text in its field.

199. PARSONS, THEOPHILUS Laws of business for all the states and territories of the Union, and the Dominion of Canada ... New revised edition. Hartford, Scranton, 1890. 864pp. Contemp. sheep. $ 30.00

200. PARSONS, THEOPHILUS Laws of business for all the States and Territories of the Union and the Dominion of Canada... New revised edition. Syracuse, Watson Gill, 1899. 864pp. Cl. $ 27.50

201. PEAKE, THOMAS A compendium of the law of evidence. Walpole, N. H., Thomas & Thomas, 1804. xvi,199pp. Contemp. sheep $ 45.00
* An early American edition of a work which "for many years, was in general use in the United States..." --Marvin. It first appeared in this country in 1802, just shortly after the London edition, and there were several later editions which included American notes. Shaw-Shoemaker 6996. Marvin p. 559.

202. PEARCE, ROBERT R. A guide to the Inns of Court and Chancery; with notices of their ancient discipline, rules,orders ... including an account of the eminent men of the honourable societies ... with the regulations of the four Inns of Court ... London, Butterworths, 1855. 440pp. New cloth. $ 45.00

203. (PENNSYLVANIA.) The form book; containing nearly three hundred of the most approved precedents for conveyancing...etc. By a member of the Philadelphia Bar. Phila., Tower, 1829. 278pp. Full contemp. sheep. 12mo. $ 37.50
* First edition. Shoemaker 38608.

204. PERLEY, JEREMIAH The Maine Justice; containing the laws relative to the powers and duties of justices of the peace, with the necessary forms. Hallowell, Goodale, Glazier & Co., 1823. vii,304pp. 8vo. Contemp. sheep little rubbed but a very good copy. $ 75.00
* First edition of the first justice of the peace for the new State of Maine. A well preserved copy of a book which is uncommon today.

205. (PHILA. DISTRICT COURT) The District Court of the City and County of Philadelphia. An address delivered at the final adjournment of the Court ... by Hon. James T. Mitchell... Phila., Wallace, (1875). 34pp. wrps. unopened, fine. Good history of the court. $ 17.50

206. POLLOCK, FREDERICK and FREDERIC WILLIAM MAITLAND The history of English law before the time of Edward I. Cambridge, University Press, 1895. Two volumes. Roy 8vo. Orig. publ. cl. Very slight rubbing and fraying to spine extremities, otherwise an excellent set. First edition. $ 75.00

207. POWELL, THOMAS The attornies almanacke. Provided & desired for the generall ease and daily use of all such as shall have occasion to remove any person, cause or record, from an inferiour court to any the higher courts at Westminster... London, Printed by B.A. and T. F. for Ben: Fisher...1627. Sm. 4to. 4p.l., 72pp. First signed blank present, good margins with fore-edge untrimmed. Recent half-morocco. A fine copy. $450.00
* First and only edition of a scarce piece of early legal ephemera, giving jurisdictions and modes of address for some 340 localities, procedural information necessary in the removal of cases or records to the Westminster Courts. Powell is best known as the author of The Attorney's Academy, 1623, one of the most distinguished early practice books, to which the present work and one other published in 1622 relating to the search of records are complementary. "Both the above (i.e. the Almanacke and the Academy) are of interest to the Shakesperian student. See Sydney Lee's Catalogue of Shakesperiana."--S&MI, 275. New STC 20165. Holdsworth V, 381f. Marvin p. 580. DNB.

BROADENING THE LEGAL DEFINITION OF INSANITY

208. PRICHARD, JAMES COWLES On the different forms of insanity in relation to jurisprudence, designed for the use of persons concerned in legal questions regarding unsoundness of mind. London, Bailliere, 1842. xi,243pp. plus ads. Orig. pub. cl. 12mo. A very good copy. $250.00
* First edition of an early and very significant work on the jurisprudence of insanity. Besides being one of a hand-full of first books devoted to this topic, and

208. (Continued) probably the first to be concerned with untechnical presentation for practical use, it is especially important on account of its recognition, for legal purposes, of "moral insanity", a category first recognized by Prichard and described in his long-influential Treatise on Insanity ... 1853. " 'I am fully persuaded that the time is not far distant when the existence of mental disorder unaccompanied by illusion or any lesion whatever of intellect, will be generally recognized.' ... Today when the whole question of criminal responsibility is under review, Prichard's work has gained renewed importance, for instance in such concepts as diminished responsibility and irresistable impulse. On this aspect he himself enlarged in a separate book... On the different forms of insanity (i.e. the present work)..."--Hunter and Macalpine p. 838 and 836ff. Garrison and Morton 4928 for the Treatise. DNB. Marvin p. 588.

209. PUTERBAUGH, SABIN D. Puterbaugh's chancery pleading and practice: a practical treatise on the forms of chancery suits, pleading and practice now in use in the State of Illinois, and wherever the same system prevails... and practice in the Supreme and Appellate Courts. Revised by Leslie D. Puterbaugh. Fourth edition. Chicago, Callaghan, 1896. 1075pp. Full contemp. sheep. (covers detached). $ 25.00

210. QUINCY, JOSIAH An address delivered at the dedication of Dane Law College in Harvard University, October 23, 1832. Cambridge, Metcalf, 1832. 27pp. Orig. prtd. wrps. Extols Nathan Dane and the virtues of university legal education, frequently citing Blackstone. $ 27.50

212. RAWLE, WILLIAM HENRY Equity in Pennsylvania. A lecture delivered before the Law Academy of Philadelphia ... with an appendix, being the Registrar's Book of Governor Keith's Court of Chancery. Phila., Kay, 1868. 93,46pp. New cl. $ 35.00

213. RAY, (ISAAC) A treatise on the medical jurisprudence of insanity. Second edition with additions. Boston, Ticknor, 1844. xv,490pp. Orig. publ. cl. Shelf numeral at foot of spine. A clean, sound, copy. $100.00
* First published in 1838, this is the first American book on the subject, and is described by Garrison and Morton (#1739) as "The first modern treatise on the medicolegal aspects of insanity." A landmark, it retained a good deal of authority throughout the century. (DAB) Both editions are scarce. One Hundred Years of American Psychiatry, 1944, pp. 547-556. Hunter & McAlpine, p. 974. DAB.

214. READ, COLLINSON Precedents in the office of a justice of the peace. To which is added a short system of conveyancing in a method entirely new, with an appendix·
214. (Continued) containing a variety of the most useful forms. Second edition with considerable additions. Harrisburgh, John Wyeth for the author, 1801. (4),63, 36,(1)pp. Square 8vo. Contemporary ¼ calf, marbled boards, a very good copy. $100.00

215. (REEVE, TAPPING) The sixth of August or the Litchfield festival. An address to the people of Connecticut. (caption title). n.p., (printed by Hudson and Goodwin), 1806. 16pp. Self-wrps Sewn as issued, untrimmed. $ 45.00
* The work of Tapping Reeve, judge, founder of the Litchfield Law School, and legal writer. An attack upon the Connecticut Jeffersonians who would revolutionize the government and constitution of the State. The title refers specifically to a celebration held by the democrats in support of Selleck Osborn, imprisoned for libel against the Federalist "Crowbar Justice" (Julius) Deming. Reeve was himself indicted by a U.S. grand jury in April of the same year for a libel on Jefferson. See DAB for Reeve and Osborn, Gaines, Political works of concealed authorship, 3rd, ed., 06-35. Shaw-Shoemaker 11366. Sabin 81493, (the latter two without attribution). Uncommon.

216. (RHODE ISLAND) A collection of forms adapted to the use of justices of the peace, public notaries, sheriffs and constables (etc.) together with miscellaneous forms; making every man his own conveyancer; conformable to the laws and usages of the State of Rhode Island... Providence, John Miller (1824). 352pp. Sheep rubbed. $ 45.00
* First edition. Uncommon. Shoemaker 15811.

217. RICHARDSON, WILLIAM M. The New-Hampshire justice of the peace. Second edition, improved. Concord, Hill, 1831. 299pp. Full contemp. sheep, worn. $ 20.00
* Marvin p. 609.

218. ROBERTS, DANIEL. A digest of all the reported decisions of the Supreme Court of the State of Vermont: contained in the reports of N. Chipman, Tyler, Brayton, D. Chipman, Aikens, and in forty eight volumes of Vermont reports; also, of all the decisions of the Courts of the United States for the District of Vermont, which are found in the Vermont reports. Burlington, n.p.,1878. 865pp. Contemp. sheep. Super Roy 8vo. $ 40.00

219. ROBERTSON, DAVID A treatise on the rules of the law of personal succession, in the different parts of the realm, and on the cases, regarding foreign and international succession, which have been decided in the British Courts. Phila., Littell, 1836. 296pp. Disbound (Law Library Vol. XII). $ 15.00

220. ROPER, R.S. DONNISON A treatise on the revocation and republication of wills and testaments: together with tracts upon the law concerning baron and femme... London, Butterworth, 1800. 233pp. Orig. boards, paper spine (slight wear). Internally fine and uncut; in all an excellent copy. $ 85.00
* First edition. This was the only London edition of the work, but there were at least two succeeding American editions. S&M I, 494, Marvin p. 619.

221. ROSCOE, HENRY A digest of the law of evidence in criminal cases. With considerable additions by T. C. Granger. Third American, from the third London edition, with notes and references to American decisions and to the English common law and ecclesiastical reports, by George Sharswood. Phila., Johnson, 1846. xxxix, 990pp. New cloth. $ 45.00

222. ROSS, WALTER A discourse upon the removing of tenants, published to serve as a specimen of the lectures intended to be delivered upon the practice of the law of Scotland. By Walter Ross, Writer to the Signet. The class is to be opened upon the 18th of November next. Edinburgh, Mundell & Wilson, 1782. 170,(1)pp. A fine copy, entirely uncut, in the original publisher's boards. $165.00
* A nice example of 18th century legal education, combining the features of a regular treatise with the promotion of law lectures. A choice copy. Rare. The NUC cites one holding. There is no copy in the BLC to 1975. S & M V, 99. Marvin p. 620.

223. RUNNINGTON, CHARLES The history, principles and practice (ancient and modern) of the legal remedy by ejectment; and the resulting action for mesne profits ... London, Robinson, 1795. 9p.l.,537pp. plus index. Contemp. calf, lightly rubbed, an excellent copy. $ 85.00
* First edition of an important standard treatise. This was the only London edition, but there were a number of succeeding editions in America. Marvin p. 623: "An excellent work." S&M I, 448.

224. (SADLER, JOHN) Rights of the Kingdom: or, customs of our ancestors. Touching the duty, power, election, or succession of our Kings and Parliaments, our true liberty, due allegiance, three estates, their legislative power, original, judicial and executive ... freely discussed through the British, Saxon, Norman laws ... with an occasional discourse of great changes yet expected in the world. London, J. Kidgell, 1682. 4to. 4p.l.,319pp. Title within rules. Modern ink signature along inner margin of title, slight marginal embrowning. Recent ¼ calf gilt, leather label. A very good copy. $125.00
* "Recommended by Mr. Locke as containing the ancient constitution of the government of England. An answer to it was written by (Continued)

224. (Continued) Sir Roger L'Estrange. --Marvin p. 625. S&M I, 106. Wing S-279. There was a 1649 edition.

225. (SAINT GERMAIN, CHRISTOPHER) Two dialogues in English, between a doctor of divinity, and a student in the laws of England, of the grounds of the said laws.. newly revised and re-printed. London, John Streater ... 1668. Sm 8vo. 1p.l., 366,(8)pp. Later full speckled panelled calf nicely tooled in blind in the style of the period. Tiny bit of worming to first few leaves $150.00
* "This book, right down to the middle of the eighteenth century, remained a lead ing text-book; and it is of considerable important in the history of equity."--Holdsworth, Sources and Literature, 185ff. An interesting association copy bearing the ownership signature of Thomas Astle, 18th century antiquary and palaeographer. In a later but very attractive binding, preserving contemporary blanks. Wing S-316. S&M I, 25.

226. (SAINT GERMAIN, CHRISTOPHER) Doctor and student: or, dialogues between a doctor of divinity and a student in the laws of England, containing the grounds of those laws...also comparing the civil, canon, common and statute laws...to which is added an account of the author and a general table... In the Savoy: printed by Eliz. Nutt...1721. 6p.l.,366,(40)pp. Contemp. calf, spine rubbed, otherwise a very good copy. Eighteenth century bookplate of John Mills (the actor?) $100.00
* An enduring classic "of considerable importance in the history of equity"--Holdsworth, Sources and literature... p. 185 -188.

227. SAYER, JOSEPH The law of costs. London, Woodfall & Strahan, 1768. xvi, 280pp. Contemp. calf, joints cracked but firm. Light foxing. A good copy. $ 90.00
* First edition. Holdsworth XII, p. 356. citing it as a comprehensive work. Marvin p. 631. There were several later 18th century editions. S&M I, 284.

228. SCHOMBERG, ALEXANDER C. An historical and chronological view of Roman Law, with notes and illustrations. Oxford, D. Prince and J. Cooke, 1785. 4p.l. 204,(4)pp. A fine copy in original boards, uncut. $100.00
* One of a relatively small number of original 18th century English works on the civil law; it was translated into French and appeared in English again in the mid-nineteenth century. First edition. Marvin p. 632.

229. SELDEN, JOHN Titles of honor. London, William Stansby for John Helme, 1614. Small 4to. Contemporary calf, raised bands, moderately rubbed, otherwise a very good copy. $250.00
* FIRST EDITION. STC 22177.

230. (SELDEN) FLETA. Fleta, seu commentarius juris anglicani... subjungitur etiam Joan. Seldini ad Fletam dissertatio historica. Editio secunda, multis erroribus purgata. London, Twyford, 1685. 4to. 4p.l.,553pp, final blank; woodcut at p. 462. Light browning. Recent ¼ calf antique, unlettered spine, attractively done. $225.00
* Second edition of one of the chief sources for the legal history of the period of Edward I, and the object of Selden's inquiry, here appended. "The two important books of Edw. I's reign are Britton and Fleta. They are mainly epitomes of Bracton's treatise brought up to date."--Holdsworth, Sources, p. 32. "Fleta, when written, was a concise account of the whole English law as it then prevailed..."--Marvin p. 314. S&M I, 53. Holdsworth, HIST. II, 321f. Winfield, Chief Sources, 262f. Wing F-1291.

231. SHARP, GRANVILLE Remarks on the opinions of some of the most celebrated writers on Crown Law, respecting the due distinction between manslaughter and murder: being an attempt to show that the plea of sudden anger cannot remove the imputation and guilt of murder... that the indulgence allowed by the courts to voluntary manslaughter in rencounters, and in sudden affrays and duels, is indiscriminate and without foundation in law... London, B. White, 1773. xvii,76pp., half-title present. A very good uncut copy (first few leaves lightly browned). Contemp. boards. $ 85.00
* First edition of this great and effective philanthropist's reconsideration of criminal law and attack on duelling. Marvin p. 639, citing a later edition. S&M I, 365 and 45. The work was reprinted in Philadelphia in 1778.

232. SHAW, LEMUEL An address delivered at the opening of the new Court House in Worcester, September 30, 1845. Worcester, Henry J. Howland, 1845. 14pp. Orig. prtd. wrps. On the administration of justice, with a passing reference to mob rule, meaning abolitionism. $ 25.00

233. SHEARMAN, THOMAS G., et al. A treatise on the law of negligence. Fifth edition, substantially rewritten. In two vols. N. Y., Baker, 1898. In two vols, clxxxiv,1427pp. Contemp. sheep. $ 40.00

234. SHEPPARD, WILLIAM The touchstone of common assurances: or, a plain and familiar treatise opening the learning of the common assurances or conveyances of the Kingdom. The fourth edition, revised and corrected, with notes and additional references, by Edward Hilliard ... London, Strahan and Woodfall, 1780. Folio. Contemp. calf, slight wear to front joint, otherwise a fine copy. $175.00
*An important and esteemed edition, in its first appearance, of this classic - "not only the earliest work exclusively devoted to the theory of conveyancing, but also a

234. (Continued) work which is still regarded as a high authority..."--Holdsworth Sources and Lit., p. 124. Hilliard revived this work, which "for a long time... lay on the stalls of the second-hand booksellers in Moorsfield unnoticed, and of no repute."--preface. His became the standard edition for future generations. Marvin p. 643. A rather handsome folio volume.

235. SHEPPARD, WILLIAM The touchstone of common assurances: or a plain and familiar treatise open ing the learning of the common assurances ... First American, from Hilliard's last London edition (WITH): An appendix to the touchstone ... containing the laws of the several states of the Union ... by John Anthon. N. Y., I. Riley, 1808-1810. 3 vols. bound in 2. New cloth,foxed. $ 65.00
* First American edition of this hardy classic. Marvin p. 643. Included is the separately published supplement for the American states by John Anthon.

236. (SHORE RIGHTS) The speech of Mr. Serjeant Merewether, in the Court of Chancery...December 8, 1849, upon the claim of The Commissioners of Woods and Forests to the sea shore and the soil and bed of tidal harbours and navigable rivers; the nature and extent of the claim and its effect upon such property. London, Butterworth, 1850. 48pp. Orig. prtd. wrps. A detailed, scholarly discussion of points of law. $ 35.00

237. SKENE, JOHN De verborum significatione. The exposition of the termes and difficill wordes, conteined in the four buiks of Regiam Maiestatem, and uthers...of this realme, and with divers rules, and common places, or principles of the lawes. London, E.G., 1641. Sm. 4to. 2p.l.,172pp. Contemp. plain calf, expertly rebacked. $225.00
* Skene was a pioneer scholar in Scottish law; his principal work, which appeared in 1609, was an edition of the Regiam Majestatem, an ancient source of Scots law which, as the DNB notes, is in reality based on the legal system of England. The present related work was first published in Edinburgh in 1597; this is its second appearance. Wing 7681. Marvin p. 647. DNB. S&M V, 105.

238. SMART, T.B. The Republican's manual, for the use of a free people. Liberty, equality, security, sovereignty. Phila., Printed for the author, by R. Cochran, 1806. Sm. 8vo. 30pp. Neatly removed. A fine copy. $125.00
* An uncompromisingly radical little tract in the form of a master-pupil dialogue, promoting the ideas of political equality and popular sovereignty along the lines of Rousseau's Social Compact (sic), a recent translation of which the author laments having encountered obstacles to (Continued)

238. (Continued) publication in America. He proposes law making by initiative and referendum, opposes executive veto power, judicial review, patronage, and presidential electors, and repeatedly urges that the constitution and law codes be widely taught. A nice copy of a scarce catechism. Only edition. The NUC shows but one holding; S&S adds four others.

239. SMITH, WILLIAM (LOUGHTON) A comparative view of the constitutions of the several states with each other, and with that of the United States: exhibiting in tables the prominent features of each constitution, and classing together their most important provisions under the several heads of administration; with notes and observations. Dedicated to the people of the United States. Phila., John Thompson, 1796. 4to. (6), (1)-4, 9-34pp. 6 fold. tables. Recently bound in fine ¼ calf. Some light uniform embrowning, nonetheless an excellent copy. SOLD
* The first comparative analysis of American state constitutions, intended to familiarize Americans with the constitutions of their neighbors and to broaden the understanding of future delegates charged with constitutional revision. This marks the beginning of a conscious attempt to make the study of constitutional law a popular affair. DAB notes that the work "was much admired and is said to have been used as a text at Princeton." Smith was a South Carolina congressman, diplomat, devout Federalist, and a vigorous pamphleteer. The work is notable scarce in trade. Evans 31209. Sabin 84820. DAB.

241. SPAULDING, JOSEPH WHITMAN. The practice in civil actions and proceedings at law in the courts where the common law practice is in vogue; with the amendments thereto necessary to incorporate the provisions of the statutes of Maine. Portland, Dresser, 1881, xxxvii,739pp. Full contemp. sheep. $ 55.00
* First edition. Based largely on Samuel Howe's text of similar title, 1834 with extensive alterations necessitated by time - this is apparently the first such revision since the older works of Howe and Colby, so cited in the preface.

242. SPOTTISWOOD, JOHN An introduction to the knowledge of the stile of writs, simple and compound, made use of in Scotland... written for the use of the students in Spottiswood's College of Law... the third edition with additions. Edinburgh, Brown, 1727. 12mo. Contemp. calf worn. Embrowing but sound copy. $ 65.00
* Spottiswood founded his own college of law in 1703 to redress the omission of a legal curriculum at the University of Edinburgh. This work was composed for his students. DNB. Marvin p. 657. S&M V, 108.

243. SQUIRE, SAMUEL An enquiry into the foundation of the English Constitution; or, an historical essay upon the Anglo-Saxon (Continued)

243. (Continued) government both in Germany and England. London, W. Bowyer for C. Bathurst, 1745. vi,291,(1)pp. Contemp. panelled calf gilt, spine and label rubbed, but a good copy. $ 100.00
* First edition of a fairly uncommon title. This copy belonged to Maurice Johnson, the antiquary (DNB). S&MI, 108. Marvin p. 657.

244. STEARNS, ASAHEL A summary of the law and practice of real actions; with an appendix of practical forms. The second edition with additions. Hallowell, Glazier 1831. xxxiv,495pp. New cloth. $ 45.00
* The preface is dated Harvard University 1824. Marvin p. 663, this edition.

245. STEPHEN, HENRY JOHN A treatise on the principles of pleading in civil actions: comprising a summary view of the whole proceedings in a suit at law. Corrected in conformity with the rules of H.T. 1834, and otherwise improved. Fifth American edition, with notes; and additions from the first London edition, by Francis J. Troubat. Phila., Small, 1845. 453, clxxxpp. Full contemp. sheep. Nice copy. $ 50.00
* Marvin p. 664: "a masterpiece of exhaustive and elegant legal writing." "Of the later works which make any claim to a scientific treatment... the best is ... Stephen's"--Winfield, p. 308. Holdsworth XIII,458; Holdsworth, Sources and literature ... p. 119.

246. STOCKTON, ALFRED A. Reports of cases decided in the Vice-Admiralty Court of New Brunswick, from 1879 to 1891. With an introduction on admiralty jurisdiction; tables of the cases reported and cited: the Imperial and Canadian statutes relating to admiralty jurisdiction and practice; the new rules of 1893, and a full digest of all Canadian Vice-Admiralty cases. St. John, N. B., McMillan, 1894. 702pp. Orig. ½ calf. $ 45.00
* A substantial, scholarly account of cases during the tenure of Justice Watters, with a long historical introduction, several useful digests and tabulations, and several accounts from an earlier period including the Chesapeake Affair, and the White Fawn (Canadian-American fishing dispute). The compiler was Registrar of the court.

247. STORY, JOSEPH Commentaries on the Constitution of the United States; with a preliminary review of the constitutional history of the colonies and states before the adoption of the Constitution. Abridged by the author for the use of colleges and high schools. Boston, Hilliard & Gray, 1833. xliii, 736pp. Contemp. sheep rubbed, but a very good, sound copy, internally fine. $125.00
* First edition of this abridgement published in the same year as the three volume work; it was this format by which the work became known to many, especially foreigners

247. (Continued) - the French translation, for example, was made from the abridgement. Marvin p. 670.

248. STORY, JOSEPH Commentaries on the conflict of laws, foreign and domestic, in regard to contracts, rights, and remedies, and especially in regard to marriages, divorces, wills, successions, and judgments. Seventh edition by Edmund H. Bennett. Boston, Little, Brown, 1872. lvi, 823pp. Contemp. sheep. $ 37.50

249. STORY, JOSEPH Commentaries on the law of agency as a branch of commercial and maritime jurisprudence, with occasional illustrations from the civil and foreign law. Boston, Little, Brown, 1839. xxiii, 544pp. Contemp. sheep, rubbed, red leather label. Some light foxing, but an excellent copy. $100.00
* First edition. One of a series of stunning works on special topics (some nine commentaries appeared within the space of twelve years), which earned Story an international reputation.

250. STORY, JOSEPH Commentaries on the law of agency as a branch of commercial and maritime jurisprudence. With occasional illustrations from the civil and foreign law. Third edition, revised, corrected, and enlarged. Boston, Little, 1846. 677pp. New cl. $ 50.00
* A reprint of the second edition, the final one from Story's hand.

251. STORY, JOSEPH A discourse pronounced before the Phi Beta Kappa Society at the anniversary celebration ... August 1826. Boston, Hilliard, Gray... 1826. 58pp. Neatly disbound. A good copy. $ 45.00
* Presentation copy inscribed on the title page: "His Excellency Levi Lincoln with the respects of the author." In Story's hand, with one small ms. correction also in Story's hand. Deals with the state of humanistic learning in America, and supports equal education and intellectual emancipation for women. Lincoln was at this time governor of Massachusetts.

252. STORY, JOSEPH A discourse upon the life, character, and services of the Honorable John Marshall... pronounced on the the fifteenth day of October at the request of the Suffolk Bar. Boston, Munroe, 1835. 74,(1)pp. Disbound. $ 37.50
* First edition. "Biographically, the most important and influential of all the eulogies. Written by M's friend and colleague for almost twenty five years, it remains the major biographical account..." --Servies 1713.

JOSEPH STORY'S COPY OF A SEMINAL BOOK ON CONSTITUTIONAL THOUGHT

253. (STORY, JOSEPH and SIMON GREENLEAF) HOOKER, RICHARD Of the lawes of ecclesiastical politie, eight (i.e. five) bookes. London, Printed by William Stansbye, (1622).

253. (Continued) Folio. 29p.l., 453, 1 leaf, 453-583, (15)pp. Engraved title page and six sectional engraved title pages, ornamental head and tail pieces, and initials. Contemporary calf ruled in blind, rubbed, joints worn and cracked but holding; internally good with some light marginal browning. $500.00
* A remarkable association copy of this classic work, bearing the ownership signatures of both Joseph Story and Simon Greenleaf, the latter inscribed just beneath the former along the upper margin of the title. The two share a preëminent position in the development of early American legal education - in a real sense they can be regarded as the founding fathers of the Harvard Law School - and in the creation of an American legal literature of international distinction. Hooker's treatise on the nature of law and government is an extremely fitting book to have come from the library of Joseph Story, whose own Commentaries on the Constitution of the United States is a landmark in American political science: "(It) is the earliest statement of the 'original contract' as the basis of government ... Hooker's theory formed the basis of Locke's Treatise of Civil Government, and can thus be considered the first statement of the principles behind the Constitution of England."--Printing and the Mind of Man, 104 (the first edition of 1593-1597). This is an early edition of the work, the sixth according to the preface. STC 13717. See Pforzheimer 500, note. Marvin p. 395. Sabine, George A History of Political Theory, 1950, p. 437ff. The copy contains no marginalia.

254. SULLIVAN, RICHARD JOSEPH Thoughts on martial law, with a mode recommended for conducting the proceedings of general courts martial, inscribed to the gentlemen of the army. Second edition enlarged. London, T. Becket, 1784. 104pp. Neatly removed. $ 75.00
* Best edition of a small but systematic treatise intended for the use of officers and as a supplement to Ayde. The author served in India. See DNB. Holdsworth XII, 630. S&M I, 602. The NUC lists four copies.

255. SWAN, JOSEPH R. A treatise on the law relating to the powers and duties of justices of the peace and constables, in the State of Ohio: with practical forms, etc. etc. Sixth edition; revised, corrected and enlarged. Cincinnati, Derby, 1857. 772pp. Full contemp. sheep. $ 55.00

256. SWIFT, ZEPHANIAH A digest of the law of evidence, in civil and criminal cases, and a treatise on bills of exchange and promissory notes. Hartford, Cooke, 1810. 361pp. New cloth. A very good copy. $ 75.00
* First edition of an important work. Swift describes this as the first Ameri-

256 (Continued) can digest on evidence and extols the common law tradition while stressing the need for flexibility and modification in keeping with American conditions. Works such as this and his System of the Laws of the State of Connecticut mark an important stage in the evolution of the common law in American legal literature. Marvin p. 671. Horwitz, The Transformation of American law 1780-1860, 1977, p. 25f.

257. TAYLOR, JOHN N. A treatise on the American law of landlord and tenant. Eighth edition, edited by Henry F. Buswell. In two vols. Boston, Little, Brown, 1887. In two vols., cv,509, 573pp. Full contemp. sheep. Fine. $ 37.50

258. TAYLOR, JOHN N. A treatise on the American law of landlord and tenant ... Sixth edition, revised and enlarged by John N. Taylor. Boston, Little, Brown, 1873. lxiii,769pp. Full contemp. sheep. $ 27.50

259. THATCHER, ERASTUS A digest of statutes, equity rules, and decisions, upon the jurisdiction, pleadings, and practice of the Circuit Courts of the United States; including decisions relating to pleadings and practice at common law, in equity, appeals in admiralty, and in criminal cases. Boston, Little, Brown, 1883. xiv,976pp. Full contemp. sheep. First edition. $ 45.00

260. THOMPSON, ISAAC GRANT The supervisor's manual: containing the laws relating to the powers and duties of supervisors, both in their individual and collective capacities. With an appendix of forms. Second edition. Albany, Parsons, Jr., 1869. 292pp. Full contemp. sheep. $ 27.50

261. TIDY, CHARLES MEYMOTT Legal medicine. In three volumes. N. Y., Wood, 1882- 1884. 314;298;321pp. Orig. emb. publ. cl. Large 8vo's, a fine set. $ 85.00
* First American edition published about simultaneously with the London edition. Perhaps the leading text of its kind in the latter part of the 19th century.

262. TOCQUEVILLE, ALEXIS DE Democracy in America. Translated by Henry Reeve, with an original preface and notes by John C. Spencer. Fourth edition, revised and corrected from the eighth Paris edition. In two volumes. N. Y., Henry G. Langley, 1845. 2 vols., 8vo. Original publisher's embossed cloth, spines gilt with eagle ornament. A fine bright set. $125.00

FRANCIS SCOTT KEY FOR THE PROSECUTION

263. The trial of Reuben Crandall, M. D. charged with publishing and circulating sedi-

263. Continued) ous and incendiary papers &c. in the District of Columbia, with the intent of exciting servile insurrection, carefully reported. .. By a Member of the Bar. Washington, City, printed for the proprietors, 1836. Large 8vo. 48pp. Original printed blue front wrapper, bound in later ¼ calf, spine rubbed. Some foxing, still a well preserved copy of a rare pamphlet. $225.00
* First edition of a rare and significant trial for abolitionist activities. The prosecutor was Francis Scott Key (his remarks on the case were also separately published) and the charge concerned the possession and 'distribution' of anti-slavery propaganda by Crandall, who had recently come from N.Y. and had opened an office in Georgetown where he practiced botany. He was tried under the common law of libels - such were the contortions in the plea that the threat to the integrity of the law itself outweighed local distaste for abolitionism and Crandall was acquitted. The preface states that "the trial...presents the first case of a man charged with endeavoring to excite insurrection among slaves and free colored population that was ever brought before a judicial tribunal." McCoy C627. Sabin 96855. cf. BAL, vol. 5, P. 250. There was a N. Y. reprint.

264. TWISS, TRAVERS Belligerent right on the high seas since the Declaration of Paris (1856). London, Butterworth, 1884. Orig. prtd. wrps. Fine. Critical of U.S.rulings. $ 27.50

265. (U.S. CONSTITUTION) MASSACHUSETTS. CONSTITUTIONAL CONVENTION, 1788. Debates, resolutions and other proceedings of the Convention of the Commonwealth of Massachusetts, convened at Boston on the 9th of January, 1788... for the purpose of assenting to and ratifying the Constitution recommended by the Grand Federal Convention ... to which the Federal Constitution is prefixed. Boston, Adams and Nourse, 1788. 8vo. 219pp. Contemp. speckled sheep, rubbed but quite sound, internally very good with light foxing. $150.00
* First edition. Evans 21242. Sabin 45702.

266. UPDIKE, WILKINS Memoirs of the Rhode-Island Bar. Boston, Webb, 1842. 309pp. Orig. cl. Nice copy. $ 45.00
* 15 lawyers of the 18th century, including a large section on James Varnum. Marvin p. 703.

267. (VALLANDIGHAM TRIAL) The trial of Hon. Clement L. Vallandigham, by a military commission: and the proceedings under his application for a writ of habeas corpus in the Circuit Court of the United States for the southern district of Ohio. Cincinnati, Rickey and Carroll, 1863. 272pp. Contemp. sheep. $ 65.00
* First edition of a full account of one of the major episodes in the Constitutional crisis under Lincoln.

268. VIDAURRE (Y ENCALADA, MANUEL LORENZO DE) 1773-1841. Proyecto de un codigo penal; contiene una explicacion prolija de la entidad de los delitos en general, y de la particular naturaleza de los mas conocidos, Se senalan las penas que paracen proporcionadas ... Boston, Hiram Tupper, 1828. 230,(2)pp. Full contemp. calf extra gilt, chain borders, ornamental lettered spine. A fine copy in an attractive, well-preserved binding, intended, no doubt, for presentation. $275.00
* First and only edition of the new penal code for Peru, written by this Peruvian statesman and champion of liberal reform, exiled in 1822 to the U.S. because of his views. In 1823 he published several works in Philadelphia. Upon his return to Peru in the following year he was appointed chief justice and foreign minister by Bolivar. He continued to visit the U.S., publishing 3 works in Boston during 1828, including this one with its preface dated Sept. 1828, Boston. The code is a humanitarian one, fully in keeping with the Enlightenment. A superior copy of a desireable work. Sabin 99493. Shoemaker 37019 (4 copies only).

269. (VIRGINIA. CIVIL WAR DEBT.) Virginia State Debt. Report of Mr. John Collinson and Mr. E. R. Leland to the Council of Foreign Bondholders and the Funding Association of the U.S.A. on the Funding Act, 1879; with appendix of documents. (London, 1879.) 29pp. Wrps. Urging creditors to accept the terms of the plan, printed here, in order to avoid repudiation. $ 25.00

270. (VIRGINIA. LAWS, STATUTES.) Supplement to the Revised Code of the laws of Virginia: being a collection of all the acts of the General Assembly...passed since the year 1819, with a general index. To which are prefixed the acts organizing a convention, the Declaration of Rights, and the amended Constitution of Virginia. Richmond, Samuel Sheperd, 1833. viii, 584pp. Contemp. sheep, leather label. A very good copy. $ 75.00
* A substantial work, complete in itself, presenting a needed compilation of Virginia law as it developed since the landmark code of 1819; it stands at midpoint between that and the code of 1849 and, except for a digest by Tate, appears to be the only work of this character for the period. Uncommon. This is the first copy we have seen on the market. Missed by Marvin.

271. VON HOLST, H. The Constitutional Law of the United States of America. Authorized edition translated by Alfred Bishop Mason. Chicago, Callaghan, 1887. 369pp. cl. Fine. $ 27.50

272. WARREN, SAMUEL The experiences of a barrister, and confessions of an attorney. Boston, Estes and Lauriat, 1880. 376pp. Orig. decorated cl. $ 20.00
* A popular collection of fictional pieces about English legal life, by the

272. (Continued) author of Ten Thousand a Year. The original American edition of 1852 actually preceded the London edition by four years. See Sadleir 3504.

273. WARREN, SAMUEL A popular and practical introduction to law studies. N. Y., The Law Press, 1837. 425pp. Full contemp. calf. Some very light occasional marginal staining, but still an attractive copy. $ 75.00
* Second American edition of this classic. "It stands at the head of all the works of its class..." --Marvin p. 719.

274. WATKINS, CHARLES An essay towards the further elucidation of the law of descents. London, Strahan...1793. vii, 192pp. plus index. Contemp. calf, rubbed but a very good copy. $100.00
* First edition of an important work which passed through numerous subsequent editions. S&M L, 478. Marvin p. 721: "A very valuable treatise."

275. WATT, FRANCIS. The law's lumber room. First and second series. In two vols. London, Lane, 1895, 1898. 139,202pp. Orig. cl. Entertaining accounts of early English legal customs, First edition. $ 25.00

276. WEBB, EDMUND F. The railroad laws of Maine, containing all public and private acts and resolves, relating to railroads in said state, with references to decisions of Supreme Judicial Court, also a digest of the decisions of the courts ... and copies of all mortages, deedsof trust, leases and contracts, made by said railroads. Portland, Dresser, 1875. 720pp. Full contemp. sheep. Fine. $ 50.00
* A one-time compilation of the entire body of railroad law of the State from 1831 to 1875, including repealed acts. Organized by individual line. Very useful.

277. WELFORD, RICHARD GRIFFITHS A practical treatise on equity pleadings, with observations on the new orders of 1841, and an appendix containing those orders. From the London edition. Harrisburg, M'Kinley, 1846. 271pp. New cl. First American edition (from the London of 1842.) $ 45.00

278. WHATELY, RICHARD Thoughts on secondary punishments, in a letter to Earl Grey. To which are appended two articles on transportation to New South Wales, and on secondary punishments; and some observations on colonization. London, B. Fellowes, 1832. 204pp. WITH: Remarks on transportation, and on a recent defence of the system; in a second letter to Earl Grey. By Richard Whately. London, B. Fellowes, 1834. 172pp., errata slip. 8vo. Contemporary half-calf gilt, raised bands. Fine. $550.00
* First editions of Whately's two chief

278. (Continued) works advocating enlightened penal form. "In the spirit of a philosopher he studied our penal system, which he proposed to reform by the abolition of all punishments but such as were strictly and merely deterrent ... his public utterances in regard to transportation did much to awaken the public mind to a sense of its futility and mischievous results..."--DNB. Fine copies of two important penological works with considerable Australian interest. Ferguson 1616 and 1870, quoting under the former, from Whately's biography: "One of Dr. Whately's singular and favourite pastimes was the use of this curious implement (the Australian boomerang) which he would throw with the utmost dexterity, at the same time holding forth on the mathematical principles which its flight illustrated."

AN AMERICAN MASTERPIECE ON INTERNATIONAL LAW

279. WHEATON, HENRY Elements of international law: with a sketch of the history of the science. In two volumes. London, B. Fellowes 1836. Two vols. 8vo. Original cloth backed boards with printed paper labels. A nice copy. $150.00
* First (London) edition of Wheaton's masterful work, for which he is best known today, the first such major work by an American and one which quickly established his reputation both in America and abroad. It appeared in a one volume Philadelphia edition, also in 1836. Wheaton was then assigned to the diplomatic service in Berlin, whence the preface is dated; it is conceivable that the London edition precedes the American, which is rather more common. DAB.

280. WHITE, DANIEL APPLETON A view of the jurisdiction and proceedings of the courts of probate of Massachusetts with particular reference to the County of Essex. Salem, Cushing and Appleton, 1822. 158pp. Very neatly removed from a bound volume. Very good $ 60.00
* An excellent and very uncommon work. White was probate judge of Essex County for 38 years. He wrote this lengthy tract primarily to clarify and justify the reforms he was attempting to make in his new position; the work is partly historical.

281. WHITMAN, JOHN W., (reporter.) Trial of the case of the Commonwealth versus David Lee Child, for publishing in the Massachusetts Journal a libel on the Honorable John Keyes, before the Supreme Judicial Court, holden at Cambridge in the County of Middlesex, October Term, 1828. Boston, Dutton, 1829. 119pp. Neatly removed. Shaw-Shoemaker 40671. McCoy C318 $ 25.00

282. WILLIAMS, SIR EDWARD VAUGHAN A treatise on the law of executors and administrators. Seventh ed. ... sixth Ameri-

282. (Continued) can edition in which the subject of wills is...enlarged upon. By J.D. Perkins. Phila., Kay & Brother, 1877. Three vols. 2560,(1)pp. $ 45.00

283. WOERNER, J.G. A treatise on the American law of administration. Second edition. In two vols. Boston, Little, Brown, 1899. In two vols., clxxii,1501pp. Full contemp. sheep. Fine. $ 40.00
* Heavily revised beyond the first edition of 1889.

AN IMPORTANT CONSERVATIVE ATTACK ON HARRINGTON

284. WREN, (MATTHEW) Monarchy asserted or the state of monarchicall & popular government in vindication of the considerations upon Mr. Harrington's Oceana. Oxford, W. Hall for F. Bowman, 1659. Sm. 8vo. 8p.l.,189pp. Contemp. calf, little rubbed, joints worn but entirely sound, internally a fresh clean copy (very minor worming to outer blank corner margin.) In all a very good copy. $200.00
* One of the principal critiques of Harrington defense of republican government. "The most capable of his (i.e. Harrington's) opponents was Matthew Wren... (he) directed a searching criticism against the agarian law, and warned that sovereignty divided between senate and assembly would cause quarrels which might destroy the state. He could see no reason why the members of a popular assembly should discern their true interest, and affirmed that there will always be men irrational enough to think it to their advantage to subvert the supreme power..." Zagorin, History of political thought in the English Revolution, (1966). p. 143. Wing W-3677. Madan 2463. S&H I, 611. First edition.

285. WRIGHT, R.W. A practical digest of the election laws of Pennsylvania, together with all the forms required by the election officers in the discharge of their duties. Allentown, Blumer, 1840. 168pp. Full contemp. sheep. 12mo. Marvin p. 749. Uncommon $ 45.00

286. WYNNE, RICHARD Eunomos: or dialogues concerning the law and constitution of England. With an essay on dialogue. The third edition. Dublin, James Moore, 1791. xli,444,(8)pp. Contemp. calf. $ 75.00
* A classic introduction to the study of English law. "He uses the machinery of a dialogue, as Fortescue...and as Saint Germain used it... to explain and justify in clear and untechnical language some of the most salient characteristics of English law."-- Holdsworth XII, 422. Marvin p. 751, highly praised.

A SEMINAL WORK ON MEDICAL JURISPRUDENCE

287. (ZACCHIA, PAOLO 1584-1659) Pauli Zacchiae...quaestiones medico-legales. Accedunt interpolationes, & auctaria ex novis inventis, & observationibus recentiourum auctorum cura Joannis Danielis Horstii... edition quarta Veneta... Venetiis, apud Simonem Occhi, 1789. Folio Three volumes in one, containing all nine books plus supplementary material, each volume with separate title page with woodcut vignettes, ornamental headpieces. Contemporary ¼ vellum, leather labels. A very good copy. $225.00

287. (Continued)
* An attractive edition of an early classic in medical jurisprudence. "Zacchias, a Papal physician, was one of the founders of medical jurisprudence. His treatise includes... (a) section on the medico-legal aspects of insanity."-- Garrison-Morton 1720. It was first published in 1621-1666. This edition, not listed in the NUC, appears to be one of the last; other listed editions are sparsely held.

288. ANNUAL DIGEST OF PUBLIC INTERNATIONAL LAW CASES: Being a selection from the decisions of international and national courts and tribunals given during the years ... London, various dates. Each vol. about 500pp. Cl. each $ 17.50
* London School of Economics, Dept. of International Studies, Contributions to International Law and Diplomacy series.

The following volumes:
a. 1919-1922
b. 1923-1924
c. 1925-1926
d. 1927-1928

289. ARISTOTLE. The politics of... Translated with an introduction, notes and appendixes by Ernest Barker. Oxford, Clarendon Press, (1948). 411pp. D.j. $ 17.50

290. BAILEY, HOLLIS R. Attorneys and their admission to the bar in Massachusetts. Boston, Nagel, 1907. 167pp. Detailed historical study from Colonial days to present. $ 22.50

291. BAYLES, GEORGE JAMES Women and the law. With an introduction by Prof. L. F. Russell. N. Y., Century Co., 1901. 274pp Orig. cl. Review of existing legal conditions. $ 27.50

292. BISHOP, JOEL PRENTISS. Bishop on criminal law. Ninth edition, edited by John M. Zane and Carl Zollmann. In two volumes. Chicago, Flood, 1923. ccxcii, 918,1148pp. In two vols. $ 32.50

293. BLAUSTEIN, ALBERT P. Manual on foreign legal periodicals and their index. N. Y., Columbia, 1962. 137pp. $ 12.50

294. BRADLEY, JOSEPH P. Miscellaneous writings of...Associate Justice of the Supreme Court of the United States...with a sketch of his life...review of his judicial record...account of his "dissenting opinions"... edited by...Charles Bradley. Newark, Hardham, 1902. 435pp. $ 32.50
* Appointed to the S.C. 1870. "Many notable opinions"--DAB.

295. BRYCE, JAMES Studies in history and jurisprudence. N. Y., Oxford Univ. Press, (1901). 926pp. Cl. First American edition. $ 22.50

296. CAIRNS, HUNTINGTON Legal philosophy from Plato to Hegel. Baltimore, Johns Hopkins Press, 1949. 583pp. $ 27.50

297. CALLENDER, CLARENCE N. American courts, their organization and procedure. First edition. N. Y., McGraw-Hill, 1927. 284pp. $ 17.50

298. CARR, SIR CECIL THOMAS Concerning English administrative law. N. Y., Columbia, 1941. 189pp. Author pres. copy. $ 17.50

299. COOK, WILLIAM W. A treatise on the law of corporations having a capital stock. Sixth edition. Chicago, Callaghan, 1908. 4 vols. 4309pp. A very important revision, with a new, long preface. $ 60.00

300. COOK, WILLIAM W. A treatise on the law of corporations having a capital stock. Seventh edition. In five volumes. Boston, Little Brown, 1913. 5 vols. Heavily revised by the author. 4984pp. $ 75.00

301. COOK, WILLIAM W. A treatise on the law of coporations having a capital stock. Eight edition in six volumes. N. Y., Baker, Voorhis, 1923. 5936pp. Cl. $ 60.00

302. COOLEY, THOMAS M. A treatise on the law of torts, or the wrongs which arise independently of contract. Students' edition by John Lewis. Chicago, Callaghan, 1907. 820pp. $ 20.00

303. CORNELL, JULIEN. The conscientious objector and the law. Foreword by Harry Emerson Fosdick. N. Y., Day, (1943). 158pp. Cl., d.j. $ 10.00

304. CORWIN, EDWARD S. A constitution of powers in a secular state. Three lectures on the William H. White foundation at the University of Virginia, April 1950, and an additional chapter. With a foreword by F.D.G. Ribble. Charlottesville, Michie, 1951. 126pp. $ 22.50

305. CRAWFORD, JOHN J. The Negotiable Instruments Law from the draft prepared for the Commissioners on Uniformity of Laws... the full text of the law as enacted with copious annotations. Third edition. N. Y., Baker, 1908. 212pp. $ 22.50
* Crawford was the author of the draft itself, which was enacted in 35 states.

306. DANIEL, JOHN W. A treatise on the law of negotiable instruments,... In two vols. Fifth edition, re-edited and enlarged with notes and references to American and English cases, by John W. Daniel and Charles A. Douglass. N. Y., Baker, 1903. 936,1004pp. Orig. cl. $ 40.00

307. ELLIOTT, BYRON K. and ELLIOTT, WILLIAM F. A treatise on the law of roads and streets. Second edition. Indianapolis, Bowen-Merrill, 1900. cxxxiv,1185pp. Full contemp. sheep. $ 25.00
* Revised by the authors (1st ed. 1890).

308. ELLIOT, CHARLES. A treatise on the law of private corporations. Third revised edition. Indianpolis, Bowen-Merrill, 1900. 748pp. Cl. $ 22.50

309. FAIRMAN, CHARLES Mr. Justice Miller and the Supreme Court, 1862-1890. Cambridge, Harvard, 1939. 456pp. Illus., frontis., plates. First edition. Nice copy. $ 15.00

310. FARNHAM, HENRY PHILIP The law of waters and water rights: international, national, state, municipal, and individual ... irrigation, drainage, and municipal water supply. In three vols. Rochester, Lawyers' Co-op. Publ. Co., 1904. In three vols., clxxx,2956pp. Contemp. sheep. Fine set. $ 90.00
* First edition of an exhaustive treatment of this important topic.

311. FARSON, CHARLES T. A commentary on the mechanics' lien law of Illinois. Chicago, Callaghan, 1902. 377pp. New. cl. First edition. $ 27.50

312. FIGGIS, JOHN NEVILLE. Studies of political thought from Gerson to Grotius, 1414-1625. The Birbeck lectures delivered in Trinity College, Cambridge, 1900. Second edition. Cambridge, University Press, 1931. 224pp. 12mo. Cl. Fine. $ 22.50

313. FLETCHER, WILLIAM MEADE A treatise on equity pleading and practice with illustrative forms and precedents. St. Paul, Keefe Davidson, 1902. 1368pp. Contemp. sheep. $ 25.00
* First edition.

314. FOSTER, ROGER A treatise on Federal practice, civil and criminal, including... equity pleading and practice... in the State courts. Fourth edition, revised and enlarged, in three volumes. Chicago, Callaghan, 1909. 3 vols. $ 35.00
* Heavily revised and supplemented. First edition was 1890.

315. FRIEDLANDER, BERNARD, et al. Rent control. Federal, State and Muncipal, with an appendix containing statutes, regulations, local laws, interpretations, and forms. Edited by Arthur I. Winard. N. Y., Central Book, 1948. 493;352;lviipp. $ 25.00

316. GALLAHER, RUTH A. Legal and political status of women in Iowa: an historical account of the rights of women in Iowa from 1838 to 1918. Iowa City, State Historical Society, 1918. 300pp. Cl. Fine. $ 20.00

317. GATES, PAUL W. History of public land law development. Written for the Public Land Law Review Commission, with a chapter by Robert W. Swenson. Wash, D.C., (GPO), 1968. 828pp. Lg. 8vo., illus. cl. $ 25.00

318. GATHINGS, JAMES A. International law and American treatment of alien enemy property. Introduction by Edwin Borchard. Wash., Am. Council on Public Affairs, (1940). 143pp. o.p. $ 17.50

319. GOLDFARB, RONALD L. The contempt power. N. Y., Columbia, 1963. 349pp. $ 15.00

320. GRAY, JAMES M. Limitations of the taxing power including limitations upon public indebtedness: a treatise upon the Constitutional Law governing taxation and the incurrence of public debt in the United States, in the several States, and in the Territories. San Francisco, Bancroft-Whitney, 1906. lx,131pp. Contemp. sheep. Fine. First edition. $ 35.00

321. GRAY, JOHN CHIPMAN. The nature and sources of the law. Second edition, from the author's notes, by Roland Gray. N. Y., MacMillan, 1921. 348pp. Perf. stamp on t.p. else fine. $ 17.50
* "Gray was a great lawyer, a great teacher, and, as his book... shows, a great legal philosopher."-- Holdsworth, Historians, p. 107. Best edition.

322. HACKWORTH, G.H. Digest of International Law. Wash., GPO, 1942- volumes 3,4,5,7,8 per volume $ 15.00

323. HARRIS, ROBERT JENNINGS. The judicial power of the United States. Louisiana, Louisiana State Univ. Press, 1940. 238pp. orig. cl. o.p. $ 22.50
* Louisiana State Univ. Studies No. 40.

324. HART, HEBER The law relating to auctioneers, house agents, and valuers, and to commission. Second edition. London, Stevens, 1903. xxxix,552pp. Cl. Very substantially revised and enlarged by the author. $ 27.50

325. (HARVARD LAW REVIEW.) Selected essays on the law of torts. Cambridge, Harvard Law Review Assoc., 1924. 770pp. Cloth. Roy. 8vo. $ 25.00

326. HENDERSON, JOHN G. Chancery practice with especial reference to the office and duties of masters in chancery... etc. Chicago, Flood, 1904. 1087pp. $ 22.50

327. (HOLMES, OLIVER WENDELL) Justice Oliver Wendell Holmes, his book notices and uncollected letters and papers. Edited and annotated by Harry C. Shriver. Introduction by Harry C. Shriver. Introduction by Harlan Fiske Stone. (First edition) N. Y., Central Book, 1936. 280pp. d.j. $ 22.50

328. HUBERICH, CHARLES HENRY. The law relating to trading with the enemy, together with a consideration of the civil rights and disabilities of alien enemies, and of the effect of war on contracts with alien enemies. N. Y., Baker, 1918. 485pp. $ 25.00

329. HUFFCUT, ERNEST W. The law of agency including the law of principal and agent and the law of master and servant. Second edition. Revised and enlarged. Boston, Little, Brown, 1902. 406pp. Cloth, fine. Author was professor at Cornell. This rev. edition covers the whole field of agency. $ 25.00

330. HUGHES, T.W. An illustrated treatise on the law of evidence. Chicago, Callaghan, 1907. lvi,676pp. Cl. (First edition, third impression.) $ 22.50

331. ILBERT, SIR COURTENAY Legislative methods and forms. Oxford, Clarendon Press, 1901. 372pp. $ 45.00
* An important, authoritative study of the nature and development of statute law, with special emphasis on India and other Commonwealth countries. The author had a distinguished career as legal draftsman and codifier while serving as Parliamentary draftsman and counsel and as member of the Council of the Governor General of India. DNB 1922-1930. First edition. Fine copy.

332. (ILLINOIS STATE TAX COMMISSION.) WILKEN, RALPH H., compiler. Compilation of tax and judicial decisions of the State of Illinois. (Springfield, Illinois State Journal Co., 1925.) 379pp. $ 17.50

333. JONES, LEONARD A. The law of bonds and bond securities. Fourth edition, rewritten and enlarged. In three volumes Indianapolis, Bobbs, Merrill, (1935). 3 volumes, with 1950 supplement. $ 37.50

334. JONES, WILLIAM C. et al. A practical treatise upon the jurisdiction of and practice in the county and probate courts of Illinois. Fourth edition by Mason H. Newell, in two volumes. Chicago, T. H. Flood, 1918. 2 vols. 1485pp. $ 30.00

335. JOYCE, JOSEPH A. et al. A treatise on the law of defenses in actions on commercial paper including the Uniform Negotiable Instruments Law, with full annotations. Second edition, rev. and enlarged by D. W. Crockett. Indianapolis, Bobbs-Merrill, (1924). 2158pp. In two volumes. $ 30.00

336. JUDGES, A.V., compiler. The Elizabethan underworld: a collection of Tudor and early Stuart tracts and ballads telling of the lives and misdoings of vagabonds, thieves, rogues and cozeners, and giving some account of the operation of the criminal law... London, Routledge, 1930. 4to. lxiv,543pp. Illustrated. Orig. cl., spine gilt. A fine copy of a handsome book. $ 65.00
* First edition. Of considerable interest as both social history and criminology, with a long historical introduction, and with twenty illustrations including some fine facsimiles of early printed works. Scarce and valuable.

337. JUDSON, FREDERICK N. The law of interstate commerce and its federal regulation. Second edition. Chicago, Flood, 1912. 805pp. Heavily revised by the author since the first edition of 1905.

338. KEEDY, CHARLES C. Delaware corporation law and equity practice... N.Y., Corporation trust Co., 1931. 317pp. $ 20.00

339. LABATT, C.B. Commentaries on the law of master and servant, including the modern laws on workmen's compensation, arbitration, employer's liability, etc. In eight volumes. Rochester, Lawyers Co-op., 1913. 8 vols. 10,190pp. cl. $125.00
* First edition of thecomplete work; a massive and important treatise.

340. THE LAW ASSOCIATION OF PHILADELPHIA. Addresses delivered March 13, 1902, and papers prepared or republished to commemorate the centennial celebration of the Law Association of Philadelphia, Pennsylvania, 1802-1902. (Phila., 1906, reprint edition 1954.) Illus., plates. 462pp. $ 20.00

341. LAWSON, JOHN D. The principles of the American law of contracts at law and in equity. Second edition. St. Louis, Law Book Co., 1905. 688pp. $ 27.50

342. LEWIS, WILLIAM DRAPER Great American Lawyers: the lives and influence of judges and lawyers who have acquired permanent national reputation and have developed the jurisprudence of the United States: a history of the legal profession in America. In eight vols. Phila., Winston, 1907-1909. Illus., frontis., many plates. Approx. 4300pp. Orig. cl. Fine. $150.00
* An impressive collection of 96 biographies of major figures from the 18th to early 20th century; the writing is of high quality throughout and is the work of numerous distinguished scholars and practitioners including Ames, Beale, J.C. Gray, J. B. Scott, Williston. Limited to 1000 sets.

343. LONG, JOSEPH R. A treatise on the law of domestic relations. St. Paul, Keefe-Davidson, 1905. 455pp. Orig. cl. $ 25.00

344. LOVELAND, FRANK O. A treatise on the law and proceedings in bankruptcy. Second edition. Cincinnati, 1904. 1422pp. Full contemp. sheep. $ 30.00

345. LUCAS, A. Forensic chemistry and scientific criminal investigation. Second edition. London, Arnold, 1931. 324pp. Fine. $ 15.00

346. LUCE, ROBERT Legislative procedure: Parliamentary practices and the course of business in the framing of statutes. Boston, Houghton, Mifflin, 1922. 628pp. $ 27.50

347. McCARTHY, CHARLES H. Lincoln's plan of Reconstruction. N. Y., McClure, 1901. 532pp. Orig. cl. Fine. First edition. $ 45.00
* One of the most thorough and expansive studies of the subject.

348. MACHEN, ARTHUR W., Jr. A treatise on the modern law of corporations with

348. (Continued) reference to formation and operation under general laws. In two vols. Boston, Little, Brown, 1908. 2 vols. ccxxv,1797pp. Full sheep. Fine set. First edition. $ 45.00

349. MAGUIRE, JOHN MacARTHUR The lance of justice: a semi-centennial history of the Legal Aid Society, 1876-1926. Cambridge, Harvard, 1928. 305pp. Frontis. $ 22.50

350. MARSHALL, JOHN The Constitutional decisions of John Marshall. Edited with an introductory essay by Joseph P. Cotton. In two volumes. N. Y., Putnam, 1905. Frontis. One of 600 copies especially bound for subscribers. 462,464pp. ¼ leather. $ 45.00
* A useful compilation with introduction and prefatory note to each of the forty-four cases presented. Servies #1.

351. (MARSHALL, JOHN) John Marshall: the tribute of Massachusetts, being the addresses delivered at Boston and Cambridge, February 4, 1901. 120pp. Frontis, and portraits of contributors. Cl. Fine. $ 25.00
* Addresses by J. B. Thayer, Henry St. George Tucker, Richard Olney; remarks by Oliver Wendell Holmes. Servies # 1284.

352. MASON, JEREMIAH Memoirs of... reproduction of privately printed edition of 1873, illustrated and annotated, with enlarged index by G.J. Clark... Boston, Boston Law Book, (1917). Illus., frontis, plates. 491pp. N.H. lawyer and Senator, considered by Choate, Story et al. as one of the great lawyers of his time.--DAB. $ 22.50

353. MASTERSON, WILLIAM E. Jurisdiction in marginal seas, with special reference to smuggling. N. Y., MacMillan, 1929. 423pp. $ 17.50

354. MAY, GEOFFREY Marriage laws and decisions in the United States. A manual. N. Y., Russell Sage, 1929. 477pp. $ 22.50

355. MOORE, IRA M. A treatise on contracts, torts, damages, evidence, and practice and procedure in civil cases in justice and other courts, and on the powers and duties of justices of the peace and constables in the State of Illinois. Fourth edition, revised. 2 vols. Chicago, Callaghan, 1900. 1810pp. New cl. $ 45.00

356. MORGAN, EDMUND M., et al. The law of evidence: some proposals for its reform. New Haven, Yale University, 1927. 98pp. $ 17.50
* Includes Chafee and Wigmore.

357. MOSES, WALTER H. Stockbrokerage law for stockbrokers and their employees.

357. (Continued) Chicago, Lincoln Prt. Co., 1937. 310pp. First edition. $ 22.50

358. NEWPORT, CECIL A. Income tax law and practice. Second edition. London, Sweet, 1928. 304pp. $ 22.50

359. NEW YORK UNIVERSITY. HENRY SELLIN, ed. Proceedings of the New York University Conference on practice and procedure under the Immigration and Nationality Act (McCarran-Walter Act)... N. Y., N. Y. U. Press, (1954). 145pp. $ 15.00

360. OAKLEY, THOMAS POLLOCK English penitential discipline and Anglo-Saxon Law in their joint influence. N. Y., Columbia, 1923. 227pp. Orig. prtd. wrps. $ 17.50

361. OGDEN, JAMES MATLOCK The law of negotiable instruments including promissory notes, bills of exchange, bank checks and other commercial paper with the negotiable instruments law annotated and forms of pleading, trial evidence and comparative tables arranged alphabetically by states. Chicago, Callaghan, 1909. lxix,550pp. Cl. First edition. $ 25.00

362. PAGE, WM. HERBERT A treatise on the law of taxation by local and special assessments... In two volumes. Cincinnati, Anderson, 1909. 2 vols. 2497pp. First edition. $ 35.00

363. PARSONS, THEOPHILUS Laws of business for all the states and territories of the Union, and the Dominion of Canada ... New enlarged edition, revised to date, with valuable fresh chapters on recent business legislation. Hartford, Scranton, 1911. 903pp. Cloth. $ 27.50

364. PERRY, JAIRUS WARE A treatise on the law of trusts and trustees. Seventh edition, revised and enlarged by Raymond C. Baldes. In two volumes. Boston, Little, Brown, 1929. clxxxi,1729pp. Orig. cl. In two vols. $ 27.50

365. POLLOCK, SIR FREDERICK Principles of contract at law and in equity: a treatise on the general principles concerning the validity of agreements in the law of England and America. Third American from the seventh English edition with annotations and additions by Gustavus H. Wald and Samuel Williston. N. Y., Baker, 1906. cliv, 985pp. $ 27.50

366. POMEROY, JOHN NORTON A treatise on equity jurisprudence, as administered in the United States of America; adapted for all the states, and to the union of legal and equitable remedies under the reformed procedure. Fourth edition by John Norton Pomeroy, Jr. In four volumes. San Francisco, 1918, 1919, Bancroft-Whitney Co. 1878pp. Cl. In four vols. $ 60.00

367. POMEROY, JOHN NORTON A treatise on the specific performance of contracts as it is enforced by courts of equitable jurisdiction in the United States of America. Third edition by John Norton Pomeroy, Jr., et al. Albany, Banks, 1926 xl,1045pp. $ 25.00
* Heavily revised beyond the previous edition of 1897. The final edition from Pomeroy (jr's) hand.

368. POND, OSCAR L. A treatise on the law of public utilities operating in cities and towns. Indianapolis, Bobb-Merrill, (1913). liv,954pp. Cloth. Fine. First edition. $ 25.00

369. POUND, ROSCOE An introduction to the philosophy of law. New Haven, Yale 1924. 307pp. $ 27.50

370. PUTERBAUGH, SABIN D. Puterbaugh's common law pleading and practice: a practical treatise on the forms of common law actions, pleading and practice now in use in the State of Illinois, and wherever the same system prevails. Revised by Basil Jones. Tenth edition. Chicago, Callaghan, 1926. 1491pp. Cl. $ 25.00

371. READ, CONYERS, ed. The Constitution reconsidered. Edited for the American Historical Association. N.Y., Columbia, 1938. 424pp. $ 27.50
*Original papers by Beard, THorne, McIlwain, et al.

372. READ, HORACE EMERSON Recognition and enforcement of foreign judgments in the common law units of the British Commonwealth. Cambridge, Harvard, 1938. 371pp. $ 22.50
* Harvard Studies in the Conflict of Laws, Vol. II.

373. REED, ALFRED ZANTZINGER Present-day law schools in the United States and Canada. N.Y.,(Carnegie Foundation), 1928 598pp. $ 15.00

374. REMSEN, DANIEL S. The preparation and contest of wills with plans of and extracts from important wills. N.Y., Baker, 1907. 839pp. CL. First edition. $ 27.50

375. REPPY, ALISON Civil rights in the United States. N.Y., Central Book Co., 1951. 297pp. cl., d.j. $ 17.50

376. REYNOLDS, WILLIAM The theory of the law of evidence as established in the United States, and of the conduct of the examination of witnesses. Fourth edition. Chicago, Callaghan, 1905. 268pp. $ 22.50

377. (RICHARDS, GEORGE.) Richards on the law of insurance in all its branches, especially fire, life, accident, and marine, with an appendix of statutes affec- (continued)

377. (continued) ting the insurance contract and a collection of forms. Fourth edition, by Rowland, H. Long. N.Y., Baker, 1932. 1346pp. Heavily revised since the previous ed. of 1909, to take into account new forms of insurance.

378. ROBERTS, GEORGE LITCH Patentability of inventions and the interpretation of patents: criteria for the determination of questions relating to patentability and patent- interpretation, derived from analysis of judgments of the Supreme Court of the United States. In two vols. Boston, Little, Brown, 1927. 1183pp. Cl. Fine. First edition $ 45.00

379. ROBERTS, M.G. Federal liabilities of carriers; a treatise upon the duties and liabilities of common carriers by railroads under all federal laws, with an appendix containing a copy of the federal statutes affecting railroads, and the general orders of the Director General of railroads under the Federal Control Act of 1918. In two vols. Chicago, Callaghan, 1918. lv,2029pp. First edition. $ 30.00

380. ROBERTSON, C. GRANT, ed. Select statutes, cases, and documents to illustrate English Constitutional history, 1660 - 1832. With a supplement from 1832-1894. London, Methuen, (1904). 447pp. $ 22.50

381. ROBERTSON, REYNOLDS Appellate practice and procedure in the Supreme Court of the United States... N.Y., Prentice-Hall, 1928. 360pp. $17.50

382. ROBSON, WILLIAM A. Civilisation and the growth of law: a study of the relations between men's ideas about the universe and the institutions of law and government. N.Y., MacMillan, 1935. 354pp. First edition. $ 17.50

383. ROOD, JOHN R. A treatise on the law of wills, including also gifts causa mortis and a summary of the law of descent, distribution and administration. Chicago, Callaghan, 1904. lxvi,635pp. First edition. $ 22.50

384. ROTHENBERG, L. HERBERT Rothenberg on labor relations. Buffalo, Dennis, 1949. lxiii,824pp. First edition. $ 20.00.

385. RUSH, GEORGE FREDERICK The essentials of equity pleading and practice, state and federal: with illustrative forms and analytical tables, and including forms and procedure in the master's office, also the reforms and changes effected by the United States Equity Rules, in force February 1, 1913. Chicago, Callaghan, 1913. 265pp. First. ed. $ 20.00

386. SCHROEDER, THEODORE Constitutional free speech defined and defended in an unfinished argument in a case of blasphemy.
386. (Continued) N.Y., Free Speech League, 1919. 456pp. Orig. prtd. wrps. $ 22.50

387. SCHOULER, JAMES Law of wills and administration. Boston, Boston Book Co., 1910. xcvii,647pp. Cloth. $ 27.50
* First edition thus; supercedes jointly his treatises on "Wills" and "Executors and Administrators." The author's own revision.

388. SCHOULER, JAMES Law of wills, executors and administrators. Fifth edition In two volumes. Albany, Bender , 1915. lxxxiii,xci,1734pp. In two vols. $ 30.00
* In 1910 Schouler had combined his "Law of Wills" and "Law of Executors..." Here he re-edits the original works in an entirely new edition.

389. SCOTT, JAMES A. The law of interstate rendition, erroneously referred to as interstate extradition: a treatise on the arrest and surrender of fugitives from the justice of one state to another; the removal of Federal prisoners from one district to another; and the exemption of persons from service of civil process; with an appendix of the statutes of the States and Territories on fugitives from justice. Chicago, Hight, 1917. 534pp. $ 30.00

390. SCOTT, JAMES BROWN, (compiler) Judicial settlement of the controversies between States of the American Union; cases decided in the Supreme Court of the United States. In two vols. N.Y., Oxford Univ. Press, 1918. 1775pp. 4to. $ 45.00
* Publications of the Carnegie Endowment for International Peace.

391. SEARS, JOHN H. Minimizing taxes: part I, selection of business methods, places of incorporation, personal domicile, investments, etc. Part II: synopses of the tax systems of each of the states and of the United States. Kansas City, Vernon Law Book, 1922. 706pp. Cl. $ 22.50

392. SEARS, JOHN H. Trust estates as business companies. Second edition. Kansas City, Vernon Law Book, 1921. 782pp. $ 25.00
* Heavily revised by the author, beyond the first edition of 1912.

393. SELDEN SOCIETY. Publications London. (1887-1972)
Volumes: 15, 83, 87, 89
Original cloth, all in very good to fine condition.
per vol. $ 15.00

394. SERVIES, JAMES A., compiler. A bibliography of John Marshall. Wash.,

395. SHAW, HENRY, M.D. The settlement laws of Massachusetts; in their application to poor relief outside institutions. With citations of some of the leading judicial decisions in the last thirty years, and practical suggestions to visitors among the poor. Boston, Ellis, 1900. 205,84pp. Orig. cl. $22.50
* Bound with 1909 supplement of 84pp.

396. STATE LAW INDEX: An index and digest to the legislation of the states of the United States enacted during the biennium... Wash, G.P.O., v.d.
Vols. 1 (1925-26); 6, (1935-36); 7, (1937-38); 8, (1939-40); 9, (1941-42) 11, (1945-46); 12, (1947-48)
each $ 12.50

397. STIMPSON, FREDERICK JESUP. The American Constitution: the national powers, the rights of the states, the liberties of the people. Lowell Institute Lectures, delivered at Boston, Oct. - Nov., 1907. N.Y., Scribner, 1908. 272pp. $ 22.50

398. STULL, HARRY N. A case in the United States Court of Claims: a treatise on the rules of practice and procedure in the United States... and the jurisdiction of the court, with the citation of leading cases. Wash. D.C., Byrne, 1924. 150pp. $ 22.50

399. The Supreme Judicial Court of Massachusetts, 1692 - 1942. Boston, Massachusetts Bar Assoc., (1942). Illus., frontis., many portraits. Approx. 125pp. Good history; contains many portraits of judges. $ 17.50

400. SUTHERLAND, ARTHUR, E., ed. Government under law: a conference held at Harvard Law School on the occasion of the bicentennial of John Marshall, Chief Justice of the United States, 1801-1835. Cambridge, Harvard, 1956. Orig. cl., dust jacket. Illus., frontis., plates 587pp. $22.50

401. TAFT, WILLIAM HOWARD. The Anti-trust Act and the Supreme Court. N.Y., Harper, 1914. 133pp. Scarce. $22.50

402. TAPPAN, PAUL WILBUR. Delinquent girls in court: a study of the Wayward Minor Court of New York, N.Y., Columbia, 1947. 265pp. Orig. prtd. wrps. $ 10.00

403. TAYLOR, HANNIS Due process of law and the equal protection of the laws: a treatise based, in the main, on the cases in which the Supreme Court of the United states has granted or denied
403. (Continued) relief upon the one ground or the other. Chicago, Callaghan, 1917. 988pp. First edition. By one of the leading writers of the time on the Constitution.

404. THAYER, JAMES BRADLEY John Marshall. Boston, Houghton, Mifflin, 1901. 157pp. 12mo. cl. fine. $ 15.00
* Servies 1740. "an excellent short biography" First edition.

405. THRING, (HENRY) Practical legislation: the composition and language of acts of Parliament and business documents. Toronto, Morang; Boston, Little, Brown, 1902. 140pp. Orig. cl. Fine. $ 45.00
* An important treatise on the making of statute law, by an outstanding Parliamentary draftsman. Thring designed numerous major 19th century British acts, of which some account is given in the new autobiographical introduction appended to this reissue (with slight revisions) of his chief work first published in 1877. See DNB 1901-1911. First Canadian/American edition.

****

406. U.S. INTERSTATE COMMERCE COMMISSION. Annual report. 29-30, 36-53, 55-61 (1915-1947).
per year $ 12.50

****

407. WARREN, CHARLES Bankruptcy in United States history. Cambridge, Harvard Univ. Press, 1935. 195pp. Orig. cl. $ 15.00

408. WARREN, GEORGE Traffic Courts. Boston, Little, Brown, 1942. 280pp. National Conf. of Judicial Councils, Judicial Admin. Series. $ 15.00

409. WATT, FRANCIS Terrors of the law: being the portraits of three lawyers "Bloody Jeffreys," "The Bluidy Advocate Mackenzie," The Original Weir of Hermiston. London, John Lane, 1922. Portraits 129pp. Cl. 12mo. $ 15.00

410. WEBSTER, DANIEL The writings and speeches... in 18 volumes. Illustrated with portraits and plates. Boston, Little Brown, 1903. Original cloth, a very nice set. $275.00
* The National Edition, limited to 1050 copies.

411. WHITEHOUSE, ROBERT TREAT., et al. Directions and forms for criminal procedure for the State of Maine. Portland, Loring, 1912. 223pp. $ 17.50

412. WIGMORE, JOHN HENRY A treatise on the system of evidence in trials at common law, including the statutes and judicial decisions of all jurisdictions of the U.S. In four volumes. Boston, Little, Brown, 1904-1905. WITH: A supplement... containing the statutes and judicial decisions 1904-1914. Boston, Little, Brown, 1915. Together 5 volumes, roy. 8vo's. Contemp. sheep. leather labels, A fine set. $125.00
* First edition of this classic (the supplementary 5th volume is a second edition). "His great treatise... not only gives a complete account of the existing law...it is also a most skillful and interesting history of the whole of this branch of the law."-- Holdsworth, Historians of Anglo-American Law, p. 105. Uniformly bound and in choice condition.

413. WILLISTON, SAMUEL The law governing sales of goods at common law and under the Uniform Sales Act. N.Y., Baker, Voorhis, 1909. cix,1304pp. Orig. cl. Fine copy. First edition. $ 50.00

414. WILLISTON, SAMUEL Life and law: an autobiography, with illustrations. Boston, Little, Brown, 1941. 347pp. Orig. cl. o.p. $ 15.00

415. YALE LAW SCHOOL Two centuries' growth of American law, 1701 - 1901. By members of the faculty of the Yale Law School. N. Y., Scribners, 1901. 538pp. Orig. cl. Fine. o.p. $ 30.00
* Eighteen articles on a variety of subjects, by eleven authors.

416. ZOLINE, ELIJAH N. Zoline on federal appellate jurisdiction and procedure, with forms. Revised by Stephen A. Day. N. Y., Boardman, 1917. 480pp. $ 17.50

ADDENDA

417. (AUCTION CATALOGUE) Law library to be sold by auction Thursday, November 5th, 1874... Leonard & Co. No. 50 Bromfield St., Boston. 8pp. listing 246 lots, unpriced. Fine. McKay #1893. $ 25.00

418. BACON, MATTHEW A treatise on leases and terms for years. London, Strahan for Cadell...1798. Roy 8vo. 2p.l.,352pp. Orig. boards, Internally fine and uncut. $ 75.00
* First edition in separate book form of this treatise thought to be based on a manuscript by Geoffrey Gilbert. It first appeared in Bacon's Abridgement. The proporietors of that work supervised this edition, to which they added at the end an original and quite substantial collection of precedents of leases. Marvin p. 84. S&M I, 479.

419. BALCH, THOMAS International courts of arbitration. Cambridge (Massachusetts), 1874. 27pp. Orig. wrps. Fine. Inscribed presentation copy from the author's son, Thos. Willing Balch. $ 27.50
* First edition. Balch claimed that he was the architect of the Alabama Claims arbitration. Balch's son later republished the work in a much expanded version.

420. BUCK, EDWARD Massachusetts Ecclesiastical Law. Boston, Gould, 1866. 310pp. Cl. Fine. First edition. Scarce. $ 27.50

421. BOND, (JOHN) A complete guide for justices of peace, according to the best approved authors. In two parts. The first containing the common and statute laws... the second consisting of the most authentick and useful precedents... London, W. Freeman, 1687; T. B. for Hannah Sawbridge, 1685 (part II). 6p.l.,252,(4)pp; 150,(10)pp. Two parts in one volume. Contemporary plain calf. Contemp. owner's name, and a few neat contemp. marginal notes. A very good copy. $225.00
* First edition (mixed issue, second of part one, first of part two). A successful work which went through several editions. Wing B 3567A, 3567. S&M I, 225. Marvin p. 133, later ed. NUC holdings of all editions are sparse.

422. COOLEY, THOMAS M. A treatise on the law of taxation, including the law of local assessments. Second edition greatly enlarged. Chicago, Callaghan, 1886. lxxxviii,991pp. Contemp. sheep. $ 35.00
* Heavily revised by the author, beyond the first edition of 1876.

423. DRAPER, FRANK WINTHROP A text-book of legal medicine, fully illustrated. Phila., Saunders, 1905. 573pp. $ 25.00
* First edition.

424. HAMILTON, ALLAN MCLANE A manual of medical jurisprudence, with special reference to diseases and injuries of the nervous sytem, with illustrations. N. Y., Bermingham, 1883. 380pp. Orig. cl. Fine. First edition. $ 45.00
* Hamilton was one of the leading writers in this field; he also played an active role in numerous court cases including the trial of Guiteau. See DAB for an account.

425. JACOB, GILES The complete court-keeper; or, land-steward's assistant... the sixth edition, with large additions and amendments...to the present time. London, J. Worrall...,1764. 8vo. viii, 534,(25)pp. Contemp. calf. A very good copy. $100.00
* A standard and comprehensive 18th century practical work on landlord and tenant. It was first published in 1713 and by 1819 had reached an eighth edition. Holdsworth XII, 380f, speaking well of it. Marvin p. 416. S&MI, 400, recording a new edition as late as 1819.

PROFESSIONAL BOOKS

CATALOGUE of SECONDHAND LAW BOOKS

(1982)

PROFESSIONAL BOOKS LTD
46 MILTON TRADING ESTATE
ABINGDON
OXFORDSHIRE OX14 4 SY
ENGLAND

PB

Major Works
Texts and Treatises, including Rare Books

English—Scottish—Irish—International

ENGLAND

MAJOR WORKS

*M1 **All England Law Reports: 1936-1980:** 128 volumes and index: Indiv. volumes also available:

M2 **All England Law Reports Reprint: 1558-1935:** 37 volumes and index: Indiv. volumes also available.

M3 **Annotated Tax Cases: 1922-1975:** Volumes 1-54:

M4 **Annual Register: 1758-1898:** Volumes 1-140:

*M5 **Annual Statutes (Chitty's): 1864-1948:** Volumes 1-42:

M6 **Aspinall's Maritime Cases: 1870-1940:** 22 volumes:
These reports contain "all the decisions of the courts of law and equity in the United Kingdom, and selections from the more important decisions in the Colonies and the United States," and contain reports of many important decisions not to be found elsewhere.

M7 **Atkin's Encyclopaedia of Court Forms:** 2nd Ed. (Current): Volumes 1-41:

*M8 **British and Foreign State Papers: 1812-1968:** Volumes 1-168: (from 1925 it incorporates Hertslets Commercial Treaties):

M9 **British Maritime Cases: 1776-1871:** Volumes 1-36: Indiv. volumes also available:

*M10 **British Tax Review: 1956-1981 and index:**

*M11 **Butterworth's Annotated Legislation Service: 1939-1981:** Volumes 1-280 and index:

M12 **Butterworth's Workmen's Compensation Cases:**1909-1950: Volumes 1-41 and supplements:

*M13 **Butterworth's Emergency Legislation Service:** Volumes 1-158:

M14 **Butterworth's Rating Appeals: 1913-1931:** 4 volumes:

*M15 **Cambridge Law Journal: 1920-1981:** Volumes 1-40:

*M16 **Commercial Cases (Reports of): 1895-1941:** Volumes 1-46: Contains full Reports of the most important cases heard in the Commercial List of the King's Bench Division. The set contains many important decisions not reported in any other series: (Also available in reprint):

*M17 **Commons Journal:** Volumes 136-226 plus index:

*M18 **Conveyancer: 1915-1939:** Volumes 1-22:

*M19 **The Conveyancer and Property Lawyer: 1936-1980:** Volumes 1-44 and index:

'M20 **Conveyancer's Yearbooks:** 1940-1951: Vols 1-12:

M22 **Cox's Criminal Cases: 1843-1941:** Volumes 1-31: This world-famous series may well be described as the most comprehensive record of English criminal law cases. The cases reported are those heard in the Courts of Criminal Appeal, the Superior Courts, the Central Criminal Court, at the Assizes and in Ireland:

M23 **Criminal Appeal Reports: 1908-1980:** Volumes 1-72 and index: The series now covers the House of Lords, Court of Criminal Appeal, Privy Council, Divisional Court and, in matters involving important points of law, Assize Courts:

M24 **Criminal Law Review: 1954-1980:**

*M25 **Current Law Statutes Annotated: 1947-1980:**
An annotated edition of the statutes usually available within six weeks of the text first becoming available and consolidated into annual volumes:

*M26 **Current Law Yearbook: 1947-1980:**
Indiv. volumes also available:

Encyclopaedia of Forms and Precedents:
M27 ________ 2nd Ed. Volumes 1-20:
M28 ________ 3rd Ed. Volumes 1-20:
M29 ________ 4th Ed. (current): Volumes 1-24 and index, service tables and noters up:

Encyclopaedia of the Laws of England:
M30 ________ 1st Ed. Volumes 1-13 (1897-1903):
M31 ________ 2nd Ed. Volumes 1-18 (1906-1918):

English and Empire Digest or The Digest:
M32 ________ 1st Ed. volumes 1-49 and supplements (1919-1932):
M33 ________ 2nd Ed. Volumes to 1980 and continuation volumes and green band reissue volumes to date:
The Digest contains a summary of every English Case that will ever be mentioned in a brief, together with a considerable body of cases from the Courts of Scotland, Ireland, Canada, Australia, New Zealand, India and other countries of the British Commonwealth, and South Africa:

M34 **English Reports: 1220-1865:** Volumes 1-178 :
This set reprints practically all reports of value for the years covered, as contained in some 274 different report series. About one hundred thousand cases are reprinted verbatim with parallel citations to reports of the cases in other series.. Some editorial notes are provided . . . Price and Bitner — Effective Legal Research:
Indiv. volumes also available: (Also available in reprint):

*M35 **Estates Gazette Digest of Cases: 1902-1980:**

*M36 **Estates Gazette Journal: 1858-1980:**

Halsbury's Laws of England:
M37 ________ 1st Ed. Volumes 1-31 (1907-1917): Plus annual supplements to 1939:
M38 ________ 2nd Ed. Volumes 1-37 (1931-1942) and supplements:
M39 ________3rd Ed. Volumes 1-43 (1952-1964), services and supplements:
M40 ________ 4th Ed. (All vols. so far published):
Indiv. volumes of all editions also available:

Halsbury's Statutes of England:
M41 ________ 2nd Ed. Volumes 1-52, services and supplements: 1948-1972:
M42 ________ 3rd Ed. Volumes 1-50, services and supplements 1968-1981:
Indiv. volumes also available:

ENGLAND
Major Works

M1	£1,100.00
M2	£295.00
M3	£950.00
M4	£1,450.00
M5	£150.00
M6	£575.00
M7	£550.00
M8	£4,750.00
M9	£675.00
M10	£425.00
M11	£840.00
M12	£780.00
M13	£300.00
M14	£60.00
M15	£1,250.00
M16	£775.00
M17	Price on App
M18	£190.00
M19	£600.00
M20	£350.00
M21	SOLD
M22	£490.00
M23	£750.00
M24	£495.00
M25	£280.00
M26	£190.00
M27	£85.00
M28	£150.00
M29	£425.00
M30	£120.00
M31	£150.00
M32	£80.00
M33	£300.00
M34	£4,750.00
M35	£2,800.00
M36	£5,500.00
M37	£140.00
M38	£90.00
M39	£495.00
M40	£975.00
M41	£160.00
M42	£780.00

M43 **Halsbury's Statutory Instruments:** Volumes 1-24 and services (fully up to date): Indiv. volumes also available:

M44 **Hertslet's Commercial Treaties: 1827-1926:** Volumes 1-31: (From 1925 see British & Foreign State Papers):

M45 **Howell's State Trials: 1163-1820:** 34 volumes:

M46 **Industrial Cases Reports: 1972-1981:**

M47 **Industrial Tribunal Reports: 1966-1978:** Volumes 1-13:

*M48 **Journal of Planning and Environmental Law: 1948-1981:**
Volumes 1-7 called The Journal of Planning Law; Volume 8-25 called The Journal of Planning and Property Law; Volume 26-34 called Journal of Planning and Environmental Law.
Indiv. volumes also available:

*M49 **Journal of Society of Public Teachers of Law:** 1947-1981: 22 vols: (New reprint may be available shortly):

*M50 **Jurist:** 1834-1866: 30 volumes:
Old Series 1843-1854: Volumes 1-18:
New Series 1855-1866: Volumes 1-12:
Indiv. volumes also available:

*M51 **Justice of the Peace:** 1837-1981:
Review and Reports (1837-1981), from 1932 Reports bound separately.
Indiv. volumes also available: Digests are available for all or most years:

*M52 **Knights Local Government Reports: 1903-1980:**
Part 1 Reports 1903-1980:
Part 2 Orders 1903-1980:
Part 3 Statutes 1903-1980:
Indiv. volumes also available:

M53 **Law Commission Reports: (1-95):** 10 vols: (Reprint also available):

M54 **Law Commission Working Papers (1-74):** 9 vols: (Reprint also available):

M55 **Law Journal County Court Reports: 1934-1947:** 14 volumes:

*M56 **Law Journal Reports:**
Old Series 1822-1831: Volumes 1-9:
New Series 1832-1949: Volumes 1-118:
At first these reports were prepared for general practitioners. In 1830, the New Series started to compete with the regular reports, which lacked unity of system, and paid too little attention to the requirements of the profession or public. The superiority of the Law Journal Reports was evident by their wide acceptance and long-lasting success: Indiv. volumes also available: Digests are available for all or most years:

*M57 **Law List: 1938-1969:**

*M58 **Law Magazine: 1828-1835:** Volumes 1-13:

*M59 **Law Notes: 1882-1980:** Volumes 1-99:
Indiv. volumes also available:

*M60 **Law Quarterly Review: 1885-1980:** Volumes 1-97 plus index:
Indiv. volumes also available:

*M61 **Law Reports (The): 1865-1980:** Incorporates all courts (KB, QB, Chancery, Appeals, Probate — now Family):
1st series 1865-1875:
2nd series 1876-1890:
3rd series 1890-1980:
Indiv. volumes also available:

*M62 **Law Reports Digest: 1865-1950:** (originally bound in 12 vols): Provides an accurate guide to all cases reported in the Law Reports and most of the other major series. Invaluable to any persons using the Law Reports Reprint which omits the table of cases: (Also available in reprint form):

*M63 **Law Reports Statutes: 1866-1970:**
Indiv. volumes also available:

*M64 **Law Society's Gazette: 1903-1980:** Volumes 1-77:
Indiv. volumes also available:

*M65 **Law Times Reports: 1859-1947:** Volumes 1-177:

*M66 **Law Times Journal: 1843-1965:** Volumes 1-236:
Indiv. volumes also available: Digest are available for all or most years:

*M67 **Lloyds Law Reports: 1919-1980:** 91 volumes:
1 vol per annum 1919-1950:
2 vols per annum 1951-1980:
This series of law reports is the only current publication specialising in maritime, insurance and commercial cases heard in the English Courts and includes important decisions given by the Scottish, Commonwealth and United States Courts. Only one-fifth of the cases reported will be found in any other series: Indiv. volumes also available:

M68 **Lloyds Law Reports Digest:** Volumes 1-15:

*M69 **Local Government Law and Administration (Macmillan's): 1934-1970:** Volumes 1-51: (including emergency legislation):

M70 **Local Government Forms and Precedents: 1953-1956:** Volumes 1-5 and index:

M71 **Local Government Review: 1909-1914:** Volumes 1-7:

M72 **The Magistrate: 1921-1975:** Volumes 1-31:

*M73 **Mew's Annual Digest of English Case Law: 1881-1969:** (last published)

M74 **Modern Law Review: 1937-1980:** Volumes 1-43:

*M75 **Nominate Reports:** We have most series, send for detailed list. The Nominate Reports are a collected series of reports by various editors, most of which are incorporated in the English Reports and/or the Revised Reports (see M34 and M83):

*M76 **Northern Ireland Law Reports: 1925-1980:** Volumes 1-56:

M77 **O'Malley and Hardcastle's Election Cases: 1869-1929:** Volumes 1-7:

*M78 **Patent Cases (Reports of): 1884-1980:** Volumes 1-96:

M80 **Planning and Compensation Reports: 1950-1980:** Volumes 1-41: This series of Reports covers fully all the important planning and compensation cases which come before the House of Lords and Court of appeal:

*M81 **Public General Statutes: 1831-1979:**
Indiv. volumes also available:

M82 **Railway and Canal Traffic Cases:** 1835-1950:
1835-1854: Volumes 1-7:
1855-1950: Volumes 1-29:

M83 **Revised Reports: 1785-1866:** Volumes 1-149 and index and table of cases: The matter which it incorporates is frequently more enlightening to the historical student than the original reports. Head notes are collected and references are added to later decisions . . . Winfield:

M84 **Ryde's Rating Cases: 1956-1976:** Volumes 1-20:

M85 **Solicitor's Journal: 1855-1981:** Volumes 1-125:
Recognised as the leading periodical expressing the practitioner's view of the contemporary legal scene:
Indiv. volumes also available: (Also in Microfiche form):

M86 **State Trials: (New Series) 1820-1858:** 8 volumes:

M87 **Statutes revised (3rd Ed.): 1235-1948:** Volumes 1-32:

M88 **Statutes at Large: Magna Charta — 1869:** Various editions, Ruffhead, Runnington, Tomlins etc.

M90 **Statutory Instruments (HMSO Ed.): 1935-1980:** Incorporates Statutory Rules and Orders:

M91 **Tax Cases: 1875-1980:** Volumes 1-52 and index:

M93 **Times Law Reports: 1884-1952:** Volumes 1-68:
It is possible by combining the contents of the four sets Times Law Reports, Law Journal Reports, Law Times Reports and the Law Reports to find a report of nearly every case decided in a Superior Court . . . Hicks:
Indiv. volumes also available: Digests are availabe for all or most years:

*M94 **Weekly Notes: 1866-1952:** Volumes 1-87:
Most of these cases were later fully reported in the "Law Reports" themselves, but many others were not, so that the periodical reported more cases than the main "Law Reports" series . . . Price and Bitner — Effective Legal Research:

*M95 **Weekly Law Reports: 1953-1982:** 90 volumes
Probably the most complete of all current series in its coverage of general reports is this one, which superseded the Weekly Notes. It is said to cover every decision likely to appear in any general series of reports. . . . Price and Bitner — Effective Legal Research: Indiv. volumes also available:

*M96 **Weekly Reporter: 1853-1906:** Volumes 1-54: Incorporated into Solicitors' Journal from 1906:
Indiv. volumes also available:

M43	£245.00	M52	£2,750.00
M44	£450.00	M53	£200.00
M45	£1,350.00	M54	£125.00
M46	£190.00	M55	£275.00
M47	£550.00	M56	£5,310.00
M48	£390.00	M57	From £8.00 per vol
M49	£375.00	M58	£350.00
M50	£850.00	M59	£1,150.00
M51	£5,900.00	M60	£1,150.00
M61	£5,900.00	M71	£95.00
M62	£300.00	M72	£400.00
M63	£870.00	M73	£575.00
M64	£1,600.00	M74	£495.00
M65	£5,600.00	M75	Price on App
M66	£4,700.00	M76	£780.00
M67	£3,700.00	M77	£110.00
M68	£400.00	M78	£3,900.00
M69	£250.00	M79	SOLD
M70	£60.00	M80	£580.00

M81	£1,250.00
M82	£675.00
M83	£2,600.00
M84	£480.00
M85	£5,500.00
M86	£200.00
M87	£250.00
M88	£1,550.00
M89	SOLD
M90	£850.00
M91	£775.00
M92	SOLD
M93	£3,450.00
M94	£1,700.00
M95	£2,350.00
M96	£275.00

1 **Acts and Statutes made in a Parliament began at Dublin 1769:** 1770: Contains two chapters, chapter 1 an act for granting His Majesty Additional duty on beer, ale etc. chapter 2 Duties and Taxes on payment of sums.

2 **An Act for the Amendment of the Law and the better advancement of Justice, Anno quarto and quinto. Annae Reginae:** 1706:

3 **Adams (J): Principles and Practice of Action of Ejectment:** 2nd Ed. 1818: The Author corrected most errors and defects which appeared in the 1st Ed. S & M v2 p2.

4 **Addington (Sir Wm): Abridgment of Penal Statutes:** 3rd Ed. 1786: S & M v2 p3.

5 **Adlington (J. H): Cyclopaedia of Law: or, Correct British Lawyer:** 1820: S & M v2 p3.

6 **Ainsworth: Latin Dictionary:** 2nd Ed. by J. Carey: 1823: First improved and enlarged by Dr. Thomas Morell, then by J. Carey, this is J. Carey's 2nd Ed.

7 **Aleyn (J): Select cases in B. R. 22, 23, and 24 CAR I regis:** 1st Ed. 1681: Years covered 1646-48:
8 ________ 2nd Ed. 1688:

9 **Ambler (C): Reports Court of Chancery [1737-83]:** 1st Ed. 1790: Printed in London: S & M v1 p344.
10 ________ Minature Ed.

11 **Anderson (E): Les Reports des mults principals cases, cibien en le Common Bank. [1534-1604]:** 2 parts in 1 vol. 1664: S & M v1 p292.

12 **Anno Regni George III Regis Magnae Britanniae, Franciae and Hiberniae, Nono at the parliament begun and holden at Westminster 10th May 1768:** 1769:

13 **Antiet Tenures of land:** 1679:

14 **Antonio (D): Forms and Procedure in the Bill Chamber:** 1905:

15 **Apologie Royale pour Charles I:** 1650:

16 **Archbold (J F): Practice of the Court of Queens Benc. Common Pleas & Exchequer:** 7th Ed. 2 vols: 1840: Contains th. latest Statutes on the subjects and latest Law Court dicisions: S & M v2 p9.

17 **Atkyns (J. T): Reports, Court of Chancery, temp Lord Hardwicke:** 3rd Ed. by F. W. Sanders: S & M v1 p344.

18 **Atterbury (F): Rights, Powers and Privileges of an English Convocation, stated and vindicated in Answer to a late book of Dr. Wake's entitled "The Authority of christian Princes over their Ecclesiastical Synods asserted etc." and several other pieces:** 2nd Ed. 1701: S & M v1 p164.

19 **Attorney's compleat Pocket Book; by an Attorney at Law:** 3rd Ed. Part 1 only: 1751: Published in 2 parts. S & M v1 p263.

20 **Bacon (J): Liber Regis: vel. Thesaurus Rerum Ecclesiasticarum with appendix [of] directions and precedents relating to Presentations etc:** 1786: S & M v1 p164.

21 **Bacon (M): New Abridgment of the Law:** 1st Ed. 5 vols: 1736-1766: The transition to the new type of abridgment is complete in Bacon's Abridgment . . . It is not surprising to find that Bacon's Abridgment had a much larger popularity and a longer life than Viner's. Between 1736 and 1832 it had run through seven editions, it had expanded from three to eight volumes and Maine called it 'Our classical English Digest' . . . Holdsworth — History of English Law. S & M v1 p16.
22 ________ 6th Ed. with additions by Sir H. Gwillim: 7 vols: 1807:
23 ________ 7th Ed. with additions by Sir H. Gwillim & C. Dodd: 8 vols: 1832:

Treatises

1	£85.00
2	£45.00
3	£25.00
4	£50.00
5	£40.00
6	£30.00
7	£70.00
8	£40.00
9	£60.00
10	£50.00
11	£60.00
12	£150.00
13	£175.00
14	£35.00
15	£75.00
16	£35.00
17	£60.00
18	£25.00
19	£30.00
20	£125.00
21	£275.00
22	£200.00
23	£240.00

24 **Baker (Sir R): A chronicle of the Kings of England from the time of the Roman Government, unto the death of King James, added Charles I and the first 13 years of Charles II:** 6th Impression 1674:

25 **Baker (Sir R): A chronicle of the Kings of England from the time of the Roman Government to the death of James I. Continued to the death of George I:** 1730 by E. Phillips:

26 **Barlow (T): Justice of the Peace; The power and duty of that Magistrate; with precedents, [also] appendix being a summary of the Acts of Parliament whereby Justices are authorized to Act:** 1745: S & M v1 p224.

27 **Barnardiston (T): Reports, Court of Chancery [1740-41]:** 1742: This book had many critics saying it would mislead students, but according to Lord Mansfield it was a marvellous book well worth having: S & M v1 p345.

28 **Barnes (H): Notes of cases in points of practice, taken in the Court of Common Pleas at Westminster 1732-39 by a Gentleman of the Middle Temple:** 1st Ed. 1740:S & M v1 p292.

29 ________ 2nd Ed. 1772-57:

30 **Barnes (W): A Summary of the Law of Exchange Cash Bills and Promissory notes:** 3rd Ed. by J. Baylay: 1813: Contains new section omitted from previous editions — Proof of Bills and notes under a commission of Bankruptcy:

31 **Barnham (J. C): A series of questions on the most important points connected with a legal education:** 2nd Ed. 1837: Designed for students preparing for entrance examinations. The Author was prompted to write the book when Westminster first introduced exams for Attorneys:

32 **Barron (A) & Austin (A): Reports of Cases of Controverted Elections 1842:** 1844: S & M v2 p21.

33 **Barton (C): Modern Precedents in Conveyancing:** 3rd Ed. 7 vols: 1821: S & M v2 p22.

34 **Bawdwen (The Rev. William): A Translation of record called Domesday, so far as it relates to the county of York:** 1809: The book contains many Laws and punishments imposed by the Normans. Also tries to explain how the original was undertaken:

35 **Beawes (W): Lex Mercatoria Redivius:** 2nd Ed. 1761:

36 **Bell (T): Crown Cases Reserved 1858-60:** 1861: S & M v2 p25.

37 **Benloe (W): Les Reports divers Pleadings et cases Court del Comon-Bank, en le Roignes de Henry VII, VIII, Edw. VI et Mary et Elizabeth [1532-79]:** 1689: Known as "Old Benloe" Though published with Dalison's Reports there is no connection between them except that they were both edited by Mr. Rowe and have a common preface: S & M v1 p292.

38 **Benloe (W): Les Reports des divers Resolutions et Judgments par les Judges en le temps del raigne de Hen. VIII, Edw. VI, Phil et Mar. et Elizab. avecque autres select cases en le temps de regne de Jacques et Charles les Premier [Kings Bench, 1530-1627]:** 1661: Known as "New Benloe". S & M v1 p293.

39 **Bentham (Jeremy): Treatise on Judicial Evidence:** 1825 with notes By M. Dumont: (reprint shortly available): S & M v2 p27.

40 **Bentham (J): Rationale of Judicial Evidence, specially applied to English Practice:** 5 vols: 1827 by J. S. Mill: (reprint shortly available): S & M v2 p27.

41 **Bentham (Jeremy): Theory of Legislation. Translated by R. Hildreth:** 1st Ed. 1864: S & M v2 p27. (reprint shortly available):

42 **Bentham (Jeremy): Introduction to the Principles of Morals and Legislation:** 1879:(reprint shortly available): S & M v2 p28.

43 **Bigelow (M M): History of Procedure in England from the Norman Conquest:** 1880: S & M v1 p51.

44 **Birkenhead (Lord): Famous Trials of History:** 2nd Ed. 1926: S & M v2 p32.

45 **Blackerby (S): Justice of the Peace, his Companion, or, Summary of the Acts of Parliament, to June 12, 1711:** 3rd Ed. 1715: S & M v1 p225.

46 **Blackstone (H): Reports, Courts of Common Pleas and Exchequer Chamber, 1788-96:** 1st Ed. 2 vols: 1791/1796: S & M v1 p293.

47 ________ 2nd Ed. 2 vols: 1793/1796:

48 **Blackstone (Sir W): Reports, Courts of Westminster-Hall 1746-79, with preface containing Memoirs of his life:** 2nd Ed. By C. H. Elsley: 2 vols: 1828: S & M v1 p27.

49 **Blackstone (Sir W): Commentaries of the Laws of England:** 2nd Ed. 4 vols: 1766. S & M v1 p27-28.

50 ________ 5th Ed. 4 vols: 1773:

51 ________ 8th Ed. 4 vols: 1774:

52 ________ 13th Ed. 4 vols: 1800:

53 ________ 14th Ed. by Edward Christian: 4 vols: 1803:

54 ________ 15th Ed. by Edward Christian: 4 vols: 1809: Portrait in first Volume: (Reprint also available):

55 ________ New Edition by J. F. Archbold: 4 vols: 1811:

56 ________ 16th Ed. by Coleridge: 4 vols: 1825:

57 ________ 18th Ed. by T. Lee, J. E. Hovenden and A. RyLand: 4 vols: 1829: Portrait in First Volume:

58 ________ 3rd Ed. by R. M. Kerr: 4 vols: 1862: This book is the 3rd Edition of F. M. Kerr's New Edition: The Commentaries were the most complete book on English Law which had yet appeared in the whole course of its long history. Blackstone is a classic of literature as well as of law. Other editions also in stock — details on request:

59 **Blackstone (Sir W): Analysis of the Laws of England. [with] introductory discourse on the study of the Law:** 3rd Ed. 1757: This edition contains a folding table of descents: S & M v1 p27.

60 **Blount (T): A Law Dictionary. Interpreting difficult and obscure words and terms in Common or Statute, Ancient or Modern Lawes:** 1st Ed. 1670: Contains references to several Statutes, Records, registers Law Books Charters, Ancient Deeds and Manuscripts: S & M v1 p6.

61 **Bohun (W): Privilegia Londini: or, Laws, Customs, and Priviledges of London:** 3rd Ed. 1723: Contains charters granted to the city 1066- date, The Magistrate and officers Authorities, Law and Customs of persons related to freemens wills etc. Proceedings of several courts, and several statutes: S & M v1 p436.

62 **Bond (J): Complete guide for Justices of the Peace, containing the Common & Statute Laws, and most authentic Precedents which concern the same:** 1687: S & M v1 p225.

63 **Bone (S. V) and Western (T. G): Precedents in conveyancing:** 1838: 4 vols: S & M v1 p36.

64 **Bosanquet (J) and Puller (C): Reports of Cases in the Courts of Common Pleas, Exchequer Chamber and in H of Lords, from 1796-1804:** 1st Ed. 3 vols: 1800-04: S & M v1 p293.

65 **Bosanquet (J) and Puller (C): New Reports, Courts of Common Pleas and other Courts 1804-07:** 2nd Ed. 2 vols: 1826: These reporters first prepared 3 volumes of reports, which were published in folio from 1800-04 In 1804 they commenced reporting the decisions of the Court of Common pleas, and styled them New Reports, to distinguish them from the preceding volumes: S & M v1 p293.

66 **Boyer (A): The History of Queen Anne where in all the Civil and Military Transactions of that Memorable reign are faithfully compiled from the Best Authorities, and impartially related:** 1735: Contains several remarkable papers, all important debates, a list of all eminent persons who died during the Reign and a number of illustrations.

67 **Bracton (H. De): De Legibus et consuetudinibus Angliae Libri quinq:** 1st Ed. 1569: "It gave the most extensive exposition of the English Law that the Middle Ages have to show — Brunner: S & M v1 p51.

68 **Brady (R): Historical Treatise of Cities, and Burghs or Boroughs, showing the original, and whence and from whom they received their liberties, privileges, and immunities, what they were, and what made and constituted a free burgh and free burgesses, as also when they first sent their representatives to Parliament:** New Ed. 1777: S & M v1 p416.

69 **Braithwaite (T): Oaths in Chancery; Manual for Commissioners:** 1st Ed. 1854: S & M v2 p40.

70 **Bramwell (G): Analytical table of the Private Statutes, 1727-1812 arranged chronologically, alphabetically and according to subject matter:** 1st Ed. 1813: S & M v1 p548.

71 **Bridgman (Sir O): Conveyances;Precedents of Deeds and Instruments concerning the most considerable Estate in England:** 2nd Ed. 2 vols: 1689: S & M v1 p480.

72 ________ 5th Ed. 2 volumes contained in 1 Book: 1725: This contains portrait:

73 **Bridgman (Sir O): Special Cases argued and resolved:** 1688: Written in the 18-19 years of King Charles II in the time when Sir O. Bridgman sat Chief Justice, by S. Carter: S & M v1 p293.

74 **Bridgman (Sir J): Reports [Court of Common Pleas, 1613-21]:** 2nd Ed. 1659: S & M v1 p293.

75 **Bridgman (R W): Thesaurus Juridicus; the Decisions of the Several Courts of Equity, and of the High court of Parliament, from the revolution to end of Easter Term 1798 Digested [Abatement — Demise le roi]:** 2 vols: 1798: S & M v1 p286.

76 **Bridgman (R W): Analytical Digest of Cases in the Courts of Equity, etc:** 2 vols & supplement: 1805-1807: The supplement also contains decisions of Lord Chancellor Redesdale in Ireland: S & M v1 p286.

77 ________ 2nd Ed. 3 vols: 1813:

78 **Briefe Treatise of the Testaments and last Wills, very profitable to be understoode of all the subjects of this Realme of England:** 1611.

79 **British Acts, from 6 Anne to 11-12 Geo. III:** 30 vols: 1718-1772: this is the official Scot's edition of the Sessional Acts with special title pages for the volumes. "British Acts" is only a binder's title: S & M v1 p563.

80 **Brook (Sir R): Le Livre des Assises et pleas del' corone, moves and Dependants devant les Justices sibien en lour circuits come aylours, en temps de Roy Edward le Tiers:** 1679: A book of assises and pleas of the crown also includes a table of the principle matters of the pleas of the crown:

81 **Brooke (Sir R): La Graunde Abridgment:** 2 vols: 1576: It is based on Fitzherbert's Abridgment, but contains much new matter. In particular it abridges fully the Year Books of Henry VII's and Henry VIII's reigns: S & M v1 p17.

No.	Price
24	£45.00
25	£25.00
26	£70.00
27	£50.00
28	£30.00
29	£30.00
30	£25.00
31	£30.00
32	£30.00
33	£75.00
34	£30.00
35	£120.00
36	£60.00
37	£70.00
38	£90.00
39	£45.00
40	£45.00
41	£85.00
42	£55.00
43	£45.00
44	£25.00
45	£36.00
46	£45.00
47	£40.00
48	£85.00
49	£350.00
50	£220.00
51	£200.00
52	£120.00
53	£130.00
54	£200.00
55	£100.00
56	£120.00
57	£120.00
58	£100.00
59	£90.00
60	£150.00
61	£45.00
62	£70.00
63	£60.00
64	£75.00
65	£60.00
66	£30.00
67	£1,800.00
68	£25.00
69	£20.00
70	£20.00
71	£70.00
72	£55.00
73	£75.00
74	£85.00
75	£70.00
76	£65.00
77	£50.00
78	£120.00
79	£600.00
80	£260.00
81	£350.00
82	£160.00
83	£110.00
84	£30.00
85	£25.00

82 **Brown (J): Reports, Court of Parliament from 1701 to 1779:** 1st Ed. 7 vols: 1779-83: In the first edition the cases are arranged chronologically while in the second edition they are arranged alphabetically under subjects: S & M v1 p146.

83 ________ 7 vols: Dublin Ed. 1784-89:

84 **Brown (T): Practical Treatise on Borough Courts of Records:** 1836: S & M v2 p45.

85 **Browne (J): General Law Lists 1787, being an alphabetical register of the Names and Residence of all the Judges etc:** 8th Ed. 1787: Also contains a list of common and civil Law-Offices, a list of Mail and Stage Coaches and has written notes by former owner:

86 **Brown (W): Reports, Court of Chancery [1788-94]:** 1st Ed. 4 vols: 1785-1794: S & M v1 p345.

87 ________ 2nd Ed. 4 vols: 1794:

88 **Brown or Browne (W): Formulae bene placitandi; a Book of Entries, containing Precedents:** 1st Ed. Vol 1 (of 2): 1671: Collected from manuscripts of some of the late and learned prothonetaries of the court of Common Pleas and eminent practicers of the Kings Bench. Published in 2 volumes: S & M v1 p264.

89 ________ 2nd Ed. 2 parts in 1 volume: 1675:

90 **Brown or Browne (W): Methodus Novissima Intrandi Placita. Generalia; or a new complete and exact method of drawing and entering declarations, pleas issues, continuances etc:** 1699: The method described used the new rules of court that had just been introduced at that time:

91 **Brown or Browne (W): Modus Intrandi Placita Generalia; the Entring Clerk's Introduction. Precedents of Declarations and other pleadings:** Part 2 only: 1703: Published in 2 parts in formation collected from the presidents of a late practitioner of the Court of Common Pleas: S & M v1 p265.

92 **Brown or Browne (W): Modus transferendi Status per Recorda; a collection of Precedents for Fines upon Writs of Covenant and Common Recoveries upon writs of Entry in the Post, in cases, whereby lands may be settled:** 1st Ed. 1698: Written mainly for country practitioners who could not get to Westminster-Hall Records: S & M v1 p489.

93 **Brown or Browne (W): Praxis Almae Curiae Cancellariae, with an Introduction [prefixed to the second part] shewing the original and antiquity of that court etc.** 4th Ed. 2 vols: 1725: Volume 1 is to acquaint the clerks of common law with the proper and authentic methods in use: S & M v1 p337.

94 **Brown or Browne (W): Entring Clerk's Vade Mecuni; Precedents for Declarations and Pleadings in most actions:** 1st Ed. 1678: S & M v1 p265.

95 **Brown or Browne (W): Clerk's Tutor in Chancery; giving the directions by authentick Precedents, how to draw affidavits, petitions, etc:** 3rd Ed. 1705: S & M v1 p337.

96 **Brownlow (R) & Goldesborough (J): Reports of divers choice Cases in Law, Common Pleas, [1569-1624]:** 1st Ed. Part 1 1651: S & M v1 p294.

97 **Brownlow (R): Latine redivivus; a book of entries of such declarations, informations, pleas in bar of abatement, replications, rejoinders, issues, verdicts, & c., contained in the first and second parts of his declarations:** 1693: The first complete edition of Brownlow's Forms: S & M v1 p265.

98 **Bullingbrooke (E) & Belcher (J): An Abridgment of the Statutes of Ireland from 3 Edw. II to 25 Geo. II and all the English and British Statutes which extend to and bind Ireland:** 1st Ed. 1754: Published in 1 volume but supplemented every other year:

99 **Bulstrode (E): Reports in Kings Bench, 1609-26:** 1st impression: Part 3 only: 1659: Published in 3 parts: S & M v1 p294.

100 **Bulstrode (E): Of Divers resolutions and judgements given by The learned Judges and Sages of the Law. Reasons and causes given in the court of Kings Bench James 1st — Charles 1st:** 2nd Ed. 3 parts in 1 volume: 1688:

101 **Bunbury (W): Reports, Court of Exchequer [1713-1741]:** 1st Ed. 1755: Published by his son-in-law George Wilson (Serjeant at Law) using his manuscripts: S & M v1 p322

102 **Burn (R): Justice of the Peace and Parish Officer:** 12th Ed. 4 vols:1772: S & M v1 p226

103 ________ 19th Ed. by John Burn Jnr. 4 vols: 1800:

104 ________ 20th Ed. by William Woodfall: 4 vols: 1805:

105 ________ 22nd Ed. by John King: 5 vols: 1814:

106 ________ 23rd Ed. By Chetwyned: 5 vols: 1820:

107 **Burn (R): Ecclesiastical Law:** 2nd Ed. 4 vols: 1767:

108 ________ 3rd Ed. 3 vols: 1775:

109 ________ 5th Ed.4 vols: 1788:

110 **An Abridgment of Burn's Justice of the Peace and Parish officer to which is added an appendix containing some general rules and directions necessary for all J/P:** American Ed. 1773: Printed in Boston for J. Greenleaf. It omits all acts which do not affect America:

111 **Burnett: Life and Death of Sir Mathew Hale:** 1682:

112 **Burrow (Sir J): Reports Kings Bench 1756-72:** 1st Ed. 5 vols: 1766-1780: Adjudged in the Court of Kings Bench since the death of Lord Raymond: S & M v1 p294.

113 ________ 2nd Ed. 5 vols: 1771 & 1779:

114 ________ 3rd Ed. 5 vols: 1777:

115 **Burrow (Sir J): Decision, Kings Bench, upon Settlement Cases, from 1732-76:** 3 vols in 1 volume: 1768/1772/1776: Includes both continuation volumes: S & M v1 p286.

116 **Caldecott (T): Reports of cases [of settlement] relative to a Justice of the Peace, 1776-85:** 1st Ed. 1786: this is a continuation of the "Decisions upon orders of Justice" series: S & M v1 p286.

117 **Campbell (Lord): Lives of the Lord Chief Justices:** 2nd Ed. 3 Vols: 1849-57: S & M v2 p54.

118 **Campbell (Lord): Lives of the Lord Chancellors:** 2nd Ed. 8 vols: 1846: More notorious than famous at the time of ublication these 'Lives' were the source of great controversy amongst the lawyers. They have become accordingly a recognized 'tool of the trade' of legal historians: 8 vols: 1846: S & M v2 p54.

119 **Carter (S): Reports of sevral special cases, Court of Common Pleas. (1664-75):** 1688: Cases argued in the 16th — 19th years of Charles II: S & M v1 p294.

120 **Carthew (J): Reports Kings Bench, [1687-1700]:** 1st Ed. 1728: Published by his son Thomas Carthew Jnr. with 2 tables: S & M v1 p294.

121 ________ 2nd Ed. 1748: Published with 3 tables:

122 **Cary (Sir G): Report or Causes in Chancery [1557-1604] out of the labours of William Lambert/Lambard:** 2nd Ed. 1665: In Cary are numerous and sometimes interesting decisions of Lord Ellesmere: S & M v1 p245.

123 **Case of James Blackman:** 2nd Ed. 1779:

124 **Cases Adjudged in the court of Kings Bench from 2 William III to the end of his reign:** 1738 with additions by a late Barrister of the Middle Temple:

125 **Cases argued and Decreed in the High Court of Chancery:** 1st Ed. Part 1: 1697: S & M v1 p345.

126 ________ 2nd Ed. Part 1: 1707:

127 ________ 4th Ed. 3 parts in 1 volume: 1735:

128 **Cases in Equity, during the time of Chancellor Talbot, [1730-37], from notes of Alexander Forrester:** 1st Ed. 1741: S & M v1 p345.

129 **Cases temp. Hardwicke: Cases argued in Court of King's Bench, 7-10 K. George II in the time of Lord Hardwicke, and Lord Lee, also two in Equity, determined by Lord Chancellor Hardwicke:** 1769: Printed in Dublin. Supposed to have been edited by Baron Annaly, and sometimes cited in his name: S & M v1 p295.

130 ________ 1770: Printed in London:

131 **Cay (J): Abridgment of the Public Statutes in force from Magna Charta, in ninth year of Henry III to eleventh year of George II inclusive, continued to first year of George III, inclusive:** 2nd Ed. with additions by H. B. Cay: 2 vols: 1762: Cay's Abridgment used to be continued by the Abstract of Acts to 35 George III, after which period they were not printed . . Clarke: S & M v1 p567.

132 **Chitty (J): A supplement to the first, second and third parts of Mr. Chitty's treatise on the general practice of the Law:** 1st Ed. 1835: For use with 1st edition but sometimes useful for 2nd Edition:

133 **Chitty (J): Law of the Bills of Exchange:** 3rd Ed. 1809: S & M v2 p63.

134 ________ 5th Ed. 1818: Includes many new laws, some chapters considerably enlarged and index much improved:

135 **Chitty (J): Practice of Law in All its Departments:** 1st Ed. Vol 1 (part 1) Vol 2 (parts 1 and 2) Vol 3 (parts 1 and 2): 1833: Published in 7 parts in 3 vols: S & M v2 p63.

136 ________ 3rd Ed. Vol 4 (part VII) only: 1838:

137 **Chitty (J): A practical treatise on the criminal Law containing precedents of Indictments:** 1st Ed. 4 vols: 1816:

138 **Chitty (H): Law of Descents:** 1825: When the author was researching the Law of Real Property he noticed that there was no comprehensive work on the above subject, so he set about the task and this is the result: S & M v1 p63.

139 **Chitty (J): Treatise on Pleading and Parties to actions with precedents:** 7th Ed. 3 vols:1844: S & M v2 p64.

140 **Christian (E): Dissertation shewing that the House of Lords in Cases of Judicature are bound by the same Rules of Evidence as are observed by all other Courts:** 1st Ed. 1792:S & M v1 p378.

141 **Chronica Juridicialis: or, A General Calendar of Years, from the First Year of William the Conqueror, to this First Year of James II. Together with a chronological table of the Names of all the Lord Chancellors, Lord Keepers of the Great Seal of England, Justices of the King's Bench and Common Pleas, Barons of the Exchequer, and Sergeants at Law:** 2nd Ed. 1736: S & M v1 p21.

142 **Circuit regulation commission: Reports of the commissioners with appendices:** 1845: Presented to both houses of Parliament by command of her Majesty:

143 **Clarendon (E. Earl of): A collection of such of the Orders heretofore used in Chancery with such alterations and additions thereunto as the right Honorable Edward Earl of Clarendon and Sir Harbottle Grimston saw fit to ordaine:** 1st Ed. 1661:

144 **Clarendon (E Earl of): The History of the rebellion and civil wars in England:** New Ed. 3 vols in 6 Books: 1807:

145 **Clerk's English Tutor; showing the practice of the courts of K. B. and C. P., with precedents, writs etc. with additions by an Attorney-at-Law:** Volume 2 only: 1733: Published in 2 volumes: S & M v1 p265.

146 **Clift (H): New Book of Declaration, Pleadings, Verdicts, Judgments , and Judicial Writs, with the entries thereupon;** digested by Sir C. Ingleby: 1st Ed. 1703: S & M v1 p266.

147 ________ 2nd Ed. 1719:

148 **Code Napoleon: or the French Civil Code by a Barrister of the Inner Temple:** 1825: Translated from the original and official edition published in Paris 1804:

149 **Coke (Sir Edward): First Part of the Institutes of the Lawes of England: or, commentarie upon Littleton:** 1st Ed. 1628: "Coke on Littleton has exercised a most wonderful and abiding influence upon the Common Law. The annotating of Littleton was a favorite pursuit of Lord Coke's and in his commentary he has gathered most that was valuable from all the books that existed pertinent to the subject when he wrote, adding his own reflections, which have commanded equal respect and consideration, and possess the same authority as the text which he elucidates. The highest encomiums have been bestowed upon the wonderful industry and learning of the commentator." — Holdsworth, History of English Law: S & M v1 p449.

150 ________ 2nd Ed. 1629: Carefully revised and corrected by the Author:

151 ________ 4th Ed. 1639:

152 ________ 8th Ed. 1670:

153 ________ 9th Ed. 1684: Added to this Edition are two Tracks, Statute of Levying Fines, and Bail and Main-prize:

154 ________ 10th Ed. 1703: Added to this edition are two tracts: Statute of Levying Fines, Bail and Mainprize, also his Complete Copy-holder, with references by an eminent Lawyer:

155 ________ 16th Ed. with additions by F. Hargrave & C. Butler: 3 vols: 1809: Also includes the notes of Chief Justice Hale and Chancellor Nottingham, and an Analysis of Littleton:

156 ________ 18th Ed. with additions by F. Hargrave & C. Butler:2 Vols:1823: Also includes the notes of Chief Justice Hale and Chancellor Nottingham, and an Analysis of Littleton:

157 **Coke (Sir Edward): Second Part of the Institutes of the Lawes of England; containing the exposition of many ancient and other Statutes:** 1st Ed. 1642: The Second, Third & Fourth Institutes were published after Cokes death by order of the House of Commons, dated 12th May 1641: Some 39 statutes were commented on, of which 36 belong to the mediaeval period. In the case of certain 16th century statutes Coke's comments are historically very valuable as they give us the reasons for passing them, and first hand information as to the etfects of their working . . . Holdsworth: S & M v1 p546.

158 ________ 3rd Ed. 1669:

159 ________ 4th Ed. 1671:

160 ________ 6th Ed. 1809:

161 **Coke (Sir Edward): Third part of the Institutes of the Laws of England; Concerning High Treason and other pleas of the Crown, and Criminal causes:** 6th Ed. 1680: The third institute was devoted to Criminal Law . . . His (Coke's) concern as a law officer and a judge enabled him to give a good deal of new itormation on the important new developments of the law . . . His work is more elaborate than that of his predecessors . . .Coke's writings were accepted and make the basis of our constitutional law and our common law . . . Holdsworth: S & M v1 p360.

162 **Coke (Sir Edward): 2nd, 3th & 4th Institutes of the Laws of England:** 4 vols: 1779:

163 **Coke (Sir Edward): A Systematic Arrangement of Lord Cokes First Institute on the plan of Sir Mathew Hale's Analysis:** 3 vols with additions by J. H. Thomas: 1818: S & M v2 P356.

164 **Coke (Sir Edward): Reports in English, with pleadings in English:** Part 9 only: 1738: S & M v1 p296.

165 **Coke (Sir Edward) Reports in English:** 7 Vols (parts 1-13) with additions by G. Wilson: 1776/1777: S & M v1 p296.

166 **Coke (Sir Edward): Reports, in French [K. B., C. P., Exch., etc.]:** Ed.1st Ed. Part 12 only: 1656: S & M v1 p296.

167 ________ 12nd Ed. Part 12 only: 1677:

86	£80.00	124	£20.00
87	£60.00	125	£40.00
88	£95.00	126	£25.00
89	£65.00	127	£25.00
90	£90.00	128	£30.00
91	£25.00	129	£85.00
92	£85.00	130	£65.00
93	£85.00	131	£90.00
94	£95.00	132	£50.00
95	£35.00	133	£45.00
96	£50.00	134	£25.00
97	£85.00	135	£40.00
98	£60.00	136	£20.00
99	£25.00	137	£50.00
100	£75.00	138	£30.00
101	£65.00	139	£45.00
102	£90.00	140	£40.00
103	£95.00	141	£35.00
104	£90.00	142	£25.00
105	£100.00	143	£85.00
106	£120.00	144	£60.00
107	£150.00	145	£25.00
108	£100.00	146	£45.00
109	£130.00	147	£30.00
110	£50.00	148	£45.00
111	£15.00	149	£450.00
112	£300.00	150	£375.00
113	£180.00	151	£300.00
114	£150.00	152	£180.00
115	£120.00	153	£225.00
116	£55.00	154	£180.00
117	£80.00	155	£200.00
118	£200.00	156	£200.00
119	£180.00	157	£395.00
120	£55.00	158	£280.00
121	£40.00	159	£240.00
122	£60.00	160	£130.00
123	£25.00	161	£250.00
		162	SOLD
		163	£175.00
		164	£45.00
		165	£140.00
		166	£40.00
		167	£45.00

168 ________ Parts 4-9 in 2 volumes: 1697:

169 **Coke (Sir Edward): Compleate copy Holder; where in is contained a learned Discourse of the antiquity and Nature of Manors and Copy-Holds, with the forme of keeping a Copy-Hold Court and Court Baron:** 1673: The publication of this book marks the final triumph of the King's Courts over the feudal courts which virtually put an end to feudal jurisdiction in England. It is a 'book of first-class importance' . . . Jenks H. E. L. 73, 82: S & M v1 p399.

170 **Coke (Sir Edward): Three Law Tracts: Compleat Copyholder Reading on 27 Edward the first, Treatise of Bail and Mainprize. [with] Old Tenures; also Notes and Additions to [his] Commentary upon Littleton:** 1764 with additions with William Hawkins: (Reprint also available): S & M v1 p575.

171 **Collection of Cases of Privilege of Parliament, from the earliest record to 1628 [by John Hatsell]:** 1776: This formed Vol 1 of Hatsell's parliamentary precedents:

172 **Collection of debates in the House of commons, in the year 1680 relating to the bill of exclusion of the then Duke of York:** 1775.

173 **Collection of Treaties between Great Britain and other Powers 1688-1771:** 2 vols: 1772: S & M v1 p603.

174 **Collins (A): Peerage of England:** 5 vols: 1756:

175 **Comberbach (R): Reports of several cases, King's Bench at Westminster (1685-98):** 1724: Published by his son Roger Comberbach: S & M v1 p298.

176 **Complete Collection of Protests from 1641 to 1737:** 1737: S & M v1 p145.

177 **Complete Collection of State-Trials, and Proceedings for High Treason, and other crimes and misdemeanours. Richard II — George I [1407-1709]:** 2nd Ed: 8 vols: 1730-35: Volumes 5-8 are supplemental volumes: S & M v1 p369.

178 **Compleat Constable; directing all Constables, Head-boroughs, Tithing-men, Church-wardens, Over-seers of the Poor, surveyors of the Highway, Scavengers in the duty of their several offices; according to the power allowed them by the Laws and Statutes:** 2nd Ed. 1700:

179 **The Complete English Lawyer, or every man his own Lawyer, containing a summary of the Laws of England and the Constitution of England:** 3rd Ed. by a student of the Inner Temple: 1810: The Book uses the writings of Blackstone, Bracton, Burn, Coke, Foster, Lyttleton, Raymond and Viner with other authors:

180 ________ 5th Ed. by John Gifford: 1820:

181 **Complete Juryman: or a Compendium of the Laws Relating to Jurors:** 1752: S & M v1 p375.

182 **Comyns (Sir J): Digest of the Laws of England:** 2nd Ed. 5 vols: 1780: "His Opinion alone is of great authority and he was considered by his contempories as the most able Lawyer in Westminster Hall" — 3 D & E., 64: S & M v1 p17.

183 ________ 5th Ed. with additions by A. Hammond: 8 vols: 1822:

184 **Comyns (Sir J): Reports, Kings Bench, Common Pleas, and Exchequer, [with] special cases in chancery and before the Delegates [1695-1741]:** 1st Ed. 1744: S & M v1 p298.

185 **Comyn (S): Law of Contracts and Argreements not under Seal:** 1st Ed. 2 vols: 1807: S & M v1 p74.

186 **Cooke (Sir G): Rules, orders and Notices in the Court of Kings Bench from the Second of James I to Michaelmas Term in the 15th George II, 1741:** 1st Ed: 1742.

187 **Corbett (U) and Daniell (E. R): Cases of Controverted Elections in the Sixth Parliament:** 1821: S & M v2 p78.

188 **County Courts Chronicle and Gazette of Bankruptcy:** New Series: Volume 12: 1891:

189 **Cowell (J): Interpreter; or, Booke containing the Signification of Words. Wherein is set forth the meaning of words and termes mentioned in the Lawe Writers or Statutes:** 2nd Ed. 1637:

190 **Cowper (H): Reports, Kings Bench 1774-78:** 1783: Papers given to the author by Sir James Burrow formed the basis of this book: S & M v1 p298.

191 **Croke (Sir G): Reports of Cases in King's Bench and Common Bench [1582-1641]. Written in French; revised and published in English by Sir H. Grimston:** 3 vols: 1669: S & M v1 p298.

192 ________ 4th Ed. with additions by Thomas Leach: 4 vols: 1790-92:

193 **Criminal Recorder:** 4 vols: 1804-09: S & M v2 p85.

194 **Crompton (G): Practice Common-placed; or, Rules and Cases of Practice in the Courts of King's Bench and Common Pleas:** 1st Ed. 2 vols: 1780: S & M v1 p267.

195 ________ 2nd Ed. 2 vols: 1783:

196 **Crown Circuit Companion:** 9th Ed. by J. Minchin & A. Herbert: 1820: Minchin was prevented from finishing this Edition by an appointment overseas at which point Herbert took over: S & M v2 p86.

197 **Cross (P. B): Interesting and impartial view of the practical benefits and advantages of the Laws and Constitution of England:** 1797:

198 **Cruise (W): Digest of the Laws of England, respecting Real Property:** 1st Ed. 7 vols: 1804-07: S & M v2 p87.

199 ________ 2nd Ed. 7 vols: 1818:

200 **Cruise (W): Essay on Nature and Operation of Fines:** 3rd Ed. 2 vols: 1794: S & M v1 p489.

201 **Cunningham (T): New and Complete Law Dictionary; or General Abridgment of the Law:** 1st Ed. 2 vols: 1764/1765: S & M v1 p8.

202 **Cunningham (T): New Treatise on the Laws concerning Tithes: By a Gentleman of the Middle Temple:** 3rd Ed 1748: S & M v1 p191.

203 **Cunningham (T): Law of Bills of Exchange, Promissory Notes, Bank-Notes, and Insurances:** 6th Ed. 1778: Also contains acts of Parliament to the present (1778) session that refer to the relevant subjects and several cases determined by the Earls of Hardwick and Mansfield: S & M v1 p521.

204 **Dalton (M): Countrey Justice, the Practice of the justices of the peace out of their sessions:** 1626: (Reprints also available): S & M v1 p227.

205 **Dalton (M): Office and Authoritie of Sherifes Abridged:** 1st Ed. 1628: S & M v1 p222.

206 **Dalton (M): Officum Vicecomitum; the Office and Authoritie of Sherifs:** 5th Ed. 1700: "It continued to be a standard authority until the beginning of the eighteenth century." — Holdsworth History of English Law: S & M v1 p222.

207 **Daniell (E. R): Practice in the High Court of Chancery:** 8th Ed. With notes by Williams: 2 vols: 1914: (Reprint may also be shortly available):

208 **D'Anvers (Knightley): General Abridgment of the Common Law:** 1st Ed. Vol 1 & 2 (of 3): 1713: Translation of Rolle to the title "Extinguishment": S & M v1 p17.

209 ________ 2nd Ed. 3 vols: 1725/1737:

211 **Davies or Davys (Sir John): Le Primer Report des Cases et matters en Ley resolutions et adjudges, en les Courts del Roy en Ireland [1604-12]:** 1674: S & M v1 p299.

212 **Dax (T): Practice on the Plea Side of the Exchequer:** 1st Ed. 1831: Includes an appendix of forms in general use and a table of costs as at present (1831) allowed on taxation: S & M v2 p94.

213 **Dearsly (H. R) and Bell (T): Crown Cases Reserved. In continuation of Dearsly's, 1856-58:** 1858: S & M v2 p96.

214 **Decisions of the English Judges during the Usurption:**

215 **De Lolme (J. L): Constitution of England. In which it is compared with the republican form of Government and the other monarchies in Europe:** 2nd Ed. 1775: S & M v1 p100.

216 **De Moleyns: Land Owners Guide:** 8th Ed. 1899:

217 **Denning (A): Freedom under the Law:** 1949: S & M v2 p98.

218 **De Secondant (M): The spirit of Laws:** 5th Ed. Volume 1 only: 1767: Translated into English by Thomas Nugent:

219 **D'eses: Journals of all the Parliament's Queen Bench:** 1693:

220 **Dictionarii Calepini, Octo-Lingvis, et novissime recogniti, Plyrimisave dictionbus: L-Z only:**

221 **Digest of Adjudged Cases in the Court of Kings Bench, from the Revolution to present Period By a Gentleman of Lincoln's Inn [1698-1773]:** 1st Ed. 1773: "Originally published in periodical parts, probably in 1773" — Cowley Bib: S & M v1 p287.

222 **Digested Index of the Chancery Reports, Containing the points of Equity, determined in the High Court of Chancery: 1689-1806:** 2nd Ed. 1807:

223 **Douglas (S. Baron Glenbervie): History of Cases of Controveted Elections during first and second sessions of fourteenth Parliament of Great Britain: (1774-76):** 1st Ed. 4 vols: 1775-77: S & M v1 p150:

224 **Douglas (S) (Baron Glenbervie): Reports, Kings Bench [1778-81]:** 1st Ed. 1783: S & M v1 p299.

225 ________ 2nd Ed. 2 parts in 1 volume: 1786:

226 ________ 2nd Ed. 1789: Printed in Dublin:

227 ________ 3rd Ed. 1970:

No.	Price
168	£40.00
169	£225.00
170	£250.00
171	£40.00
172	£25.00
173	£75.00
174	£85.00
175	£25.00
176	£45.00
177	£475.00
178	£130.00
179	£40.00
180	£35.00
181	£30.00
182	£250.00
183	£180.00
184	£70.00
185	£50.00
186	£35.00
187	£30.00
188	£25.00
189	£250.00
190	£40.00
191	£120.00
192	£100.00
193	£100.00
194	£45.00
195	£30.00
196	£55.00
197	£25.00
198	£225.00
199	£120.00
200	SOLD
201	£150.00
202	£25.00
203	£25.00
204	£240.00
205	£240.00
206	£90.00
207	£80.00
208	£60.00
209	£85.00
210	SOLD
211	£130.00
212	£20.00
213	£35.00
214	£120.00
215	£40.00
216	£25.00
217	£20.00
218	£25.00
219	£125.00
220	£30.00
221	£45.00
222	£25.00
223	£150.00
224	£50.00
225	£40.00
226	£50.00
227	£40.00

228 **Du Cange (Ch. Dufresne, Seigneur): Glossarium ad Sciptores Mediae et Infirmae Latinitatis:** 6 vols: 1733-36: This learned work comprehends the terms used by Bracton, Glanvil, and our older law writers, and explains words omitted by Spelman, and in our English dictionaries: S & M v1 p8.

229 **Dugdale (Sir W): Monasticon Anglicanum:** 8 Vols and volume 1 of J. Steven's additional volumes: 1723: John Stevens produced 2 additional volumes to the Monasticon: S & M v1 p197.

230 **Dugdale (Sir W): The History of St. Pauls Cathedral in London from its foundation:** 1818 with additions by H. Ellis: Also including the re-publication of Sir William Dugdale's Life:

231 **Dugdale (Sir W): Origines Juridiciales; or historical memorials of the English Laws, courts of justice, forms of trials, punishment in cases criminal, law writers, law books, grants and settlements, of estate, degrees of serjeats etc.** 1st Ed. 1666: "I cannot give the reader a better view of this most elaborate treatise than by telling the reader that it fully answers it's title page" — Nic Eng. Hist Lib:

232 **Dugdale (Sir W): Baronage of England: or an historical account of the lives and actions of the English nobility in the Saxons' time to the Norman Conquest, and from thence, of those who had their rise before the end of King Henry III reign:** 1675: Cowley p171.

233 **Duncombe (G): Trials per Pais: or Law concerning Juries by Nisi Prius:** 8th Ed. 2 vols: 1766: S & M v1 p375.

234 **Durnford (C): Reports of adjudged cases in the court of common Pleas during the time of Lord Chief Justice Willes:** 1799: Published using the Manuscripts of Willes:

235 **Durnford (C) and East (Sir E. H): King's Bench Reports [1785-1800]:** 7 vols: 1786-1798: These Reports were published at the end of each term, and are cited as "Term Reports":

236 **Dyer (Sir J): Ascun Novel Cases. Les Reports des divers select matters et Resolutions [K. B., C. P., Exch., Ch., 1513-82]:** 5th Ed. 1672: He reported the most remarkable cases that came before the Court of Common Pleas, together with those which, on account of their difficulty, were adjourned into the Exchequer Chamber before all the Judges. They are a valuable record of the History of English jurisprudence and English manners — Wallace Rep.

237 ________ 6th Ed. 1688: Contains many new cases and references, edited by Chief Justice Treby:

238 **East (Sir E H): Pleas of the Crown; or Principles and Practice of Criminal Law:** 2 vols: 1803: (Reprint also available): S & M v2 p106.

239 **Eden (R. H): Reports of Cases argued and determined in the High Court of Chancery, from 1757 to 1776 from the MSS of Lord Chancellor Northington:** 1st Ed. 2 vols: 1818: S & M v1 p346.

240 **Edwards (Thomas): Admiralty Reports, 1808-12:** 1812: S & M v2 p108

241 **Elmes (J): Treatise on Ecclesiastical and Civil Dilapidations, with Appendix of Cases:** 3rd Ed. 1829:

242 **Election Acts:** 1602:

243 **English Pleader; being a select collection of various Precedents of Declarations on actions brought in the Courts of King's Bench and Common Pleas at Westminster by a Gentleman of Lincoln's Inn:** 1734: S & M v1 p268.

244 **Espinasse (I): Reports of cases in Nisi Prius, King's Bench and Common Pleas 1793-1807:** 4 vols: 1797-1804: S & M v1 p335

245 **Evans (Sir W. D): Essays: on the Action for Money had and received, on the Law of Insurances, and on the Law of Bills of Exchange and Promissory notes:** 1802: S & M v1 p111

246 **Falconer (T) and Fitzherbert (E. H): Cases of Controverted Elections 1835-39:** 1839: S & M v2 p117

247 **Farresley (T): Modern cases argued and adjudged in the Court of King's Bench 1702-03:** 1st Ed. 1716: Incorporated in the Modern Reports (pt 7): S & M v1 p300 & 305

248 **Fearne (C): Essay on the Learning of Contingent Re-mainders and Executory Devises:** 4th Ed. edited by J. J. Powell 2 vols: 1795: S & M v1 p491

249 ________ 6th Ed. with additions by C. Butler: 1809:

250 **Finch (Sir H): Law: or, Discourse thereof. Written in French done into English by the author:** 1759: Finch's Law, till the publication of Blackstone's Commentaries, was regarded as the best elementary book to be placed in the hands of the Law Students. It is one of the few attempts that have been made to reduce the Common Law into System: S & M v1 p23

251 **Finch (Heneage): Reports, Court of Chancery [1673-81] during the time Finch was Lord Chancellor; collected by a gentleman who attended said court [William Nelson]:** 1725 S & M v1 p34

252 **Fiore: Derecho International Publico:** 3 vols: 1894:

253 **Fisher (R. B): Practical Treatise on Copyhold Tenures; with the method of Holding Courts Leet, Courts Baron, and other Courts; and an appendix containing Forms of Entries on Court Rolls and Minute Books, Surveys, Steward's fees, and a variety of Precedents on the Mode of Conveying Copyhold Estates:** 2nd Ed. 1803: S & M v1 p3

254 **Fitz-Gibbons (J): Reports, King's Bench at Westminster, with Special Cases, Courts of Chancery, Common Pleas and Exchequer [1727-32]:** 1732: S & M v1 p3

255 **Fitzherbert (Sir Anthony): La Graunde Abridgment:** 157 "Was first printed in 1514. It is remarkable not only for its accuracy but also for its research. It contains extracts from many still unprinted Year Books and also from Bracton's Note Book. It was a model to all future writers of Abridgments" — Holdsworth History of Enlish Law: (reprint shortly available) S & M v1 p

256 **Fitzherbert (Sir Anthony): New Natura Brevium; with a table of the most material things contained therein, composed by William Rastal, [also] the Authorities in Law Newly translated [by William Hughes]:** 1st Ed. 1652: Rastell's edition of the Register printed in 1531 was made the basis of Fitzherbert's Commentary. Its accuracy and completeness obtained for it high reputation, and Lord Coke terms it "an exact work exquisitely penned". S & M v1 p2

257 ________ 5th Ed. 1687:

258 ________ 6th Ed. 1718:

259 ________ 8th Ed. 1755: The Writs translated into English by an able hand [Serjeant Wilson] with a commentary By Lord Chief Justice Hale:

260 **Flather (J): Index — Digest to the Reports of Cases in Chancery and other Courts of Equity in England and Ireland from 1808-22; with a Digest of Reported Cases upon Equity Practice from the Earliest Printed Reports:** 1823: This is a supplementary volume to the 2nd Edition of Bridgman's index S & M v2 p1

261 **Florum Historae ecclesiasticae gentis anglorum:** 1654:

262 **Fonblanque (J): Treatise of Equity:** 5th Ed. 2 vols: 1820: S & M v2 p1

263 **Fortescue (Sir J): De Laudibus Legum Angliae. Latin and English. [With] the Two Summes of Sir Ralph de Hengham, commonly call'd Hengham Magna and Hengham Parva [with notes by John Selden]:** 1660: This a reprint of the 1616 Edition: S & M v1 p22.

264 ________ 3rd Ed. 1672:

265 **Fortescue First Baron (Sir John Fortescue Aland): Reports of select cases in all the Courts of Westminster-Hall, [1695-1738]; also the Opinion of all the Judges of England relating to the grandest Prerogative of the Royal Family, and some observations relating to the Prerogative of a Queen Consort:** 1748:

266 **Foss (E): Judges of England, 1066-1864:** 9 vols: 1848-64: (also available in reprint): S & M v2 p127.

267 **Foster (Sir Michael): Crown Laws:** 1st Ed. 1762: "His Discourses are much admired for their sound and accurate learning": (also available in reprint): S & M v1 p367.

268 **Fox: Acts and Monuments of Martyrs':** 3 vols: 1684.

269 **Fry (Sir E): Specific Performance of contracts; including those of Public companies:** 5th Ed. 1911: (Reprint may also be shortly available): S & M v2 p131.

270 **Gabbett (J): Abridgment of Statute Law:** 4 vols: 1812/1818: The main work covers the years upto 1811, the supplement continued this to the year 1817. The supplement is sometimes called the fourth volume: S & M v2 p132.

272 **Gardiner (S R): Constitutional Documents of the Puritan Revolution, 1625-1660:** 3rd Ed. 1906: S & M v1 p110.

273 **Gardiner (R): Doctrine of Demurrers by R. G.** 1706: For later edition see his Instructor Clericalis, Pt 6 (Vol 7): S & M v1 p269.

274 **General Abridgment of Cases in Equity argued and adjudged in the High Court of Chancery, etc., with several cases never before published, alphabetically digested under proper titles:** 1st Ed. 2 vols: 1732/1766: "The above mentioned volumes enjoy an unequal reputation. The first is reputed work of Mr. Pooley, a lawyer of great eminence in his time, and the volume has commanded a tolerable share of judical commendation". — Martin: The compiler of the second volume is unknown. Volume 2 is a supplementary volume: S & M v1 p286.

275 ________ 2nd Ed. 2 vols: 1734/1769:

276 ________ 3rd Ed. 2 vols: 1739.

277 ________ 4th Ed. 2 vols: 1756.

278 **General system of the Laws concerning Bankrupts; containing every case that may happen either to a bankrupt, creditor or assignee; with full instructions from the taking out a commission to the making a final dividend; together with** approved precedents, etc. 2 vols: 1761: S & M v1 p547.

279 **General Treatise of Naval Trade and Commerce as founded on the Laws and Statutes of this realm:** 2 vols: 1740: S & M v1 p508.

280 **Gibson (E): Codex Juris Ecclesiastici Anglicani: or Statutes, Constitutions, Canons, Rubricks, and Articles of the Church of England digested with a commentary historical and judicial, an introductory discourse, and appendix of instruments:** 2nd Ed. 2 vols: 1761: S & M v1 p168.

281 **Gilbert (Sir G): Law of tenures, including the theory and practice of copyhold:** 3rd Ed. 1757: "Gilbert's treatise contains explanations on many points of the feudal Law which are not as fully displayed by any other writer. The author uniformly traces principles to their origin." — Marvin, Leg. Bib: S & M v1 p453.

282 **Gilbert (Sir G): History and practice of the High Court of Chancery [Forum Romanum and Lex Pretoria]:** 1758: Printed in England: S & M v1 p338.

283 **Gilbert (G): Reports of Cases in Equity, Courts of Chancery and Exchequer [1705-26; with] Cases in Equity, Court of Exchequer, Ireland:** 1st Ed. 1734: S & M v1 p346.

284 ________ 2nd Ed. 1742:

285 **Gilbert (G): Law of Distresses and Replevins [with] appendix of English precedents in Replevins:** 3rd Ed. with additions by William Hunt: 1794: S & M v1 p460.

286 **Glanville (R): Tractatvs de legibus et consuetudinibvs regni Angliae tempore Regis Henrici secundi compositus, Iustice gubernacula tenente. Et illas solu leges continet et consuetudines secundum quas placitatur in Curia Regis ad scaccarium et coram Iusticiis vbicunque fuerint:** 1932 Edited by G. E. Woodbine: This book was written 1187-9 "It is the first of our classical textbooks. It gives us an accurate picture of the working of the royal court — The Law contained in it is mostly Land Law: as yet it is with Land that the royal court is chiefly concerned . . . The book marks an important stage in the development of common Law —" Maitland Const. Hist., 14: It is the earliest treatise on the common Law. It is doubtful whether it was written by Glanville himself, probably the author was Hurbert Walter. A full description is given in Holdsworth History of English Law: S & M v1 p54.

287 **Glyn (T. C) and Jameson (R. S): Reports in Bankruptcy, 1821-28:** 2 vols: 1824/28: S & M v2 p140.

288 **Godolphin (J): Orphans Legacy; or Testamenary Abridgment. In three parts; 1, Last Wills and Testaments, 2, Executors and Administrators, 3, Legacies and Devises:** 4th Ed. 1701: S & M v1 p492.

289 **Gothofredi (D): Corpus Juris Civilis Pandectis Ad Florestinum archetypum expreffis, institutionibus, Codice et Novellis:** 1663:

290 **Greenwood (W): Authority, Jurisdiction and Method of Keeping County-Courts, Courts-Leet, and Courts-Baron. Explaining the Judicial and Ministerial Authority of Sheriffs. Also the Office and Duty of a Coroner:** 9th Ed. 1730: Contains an act 27 Eliz. for the government of the City of Westminster. This act was not printed in any edition of the Statutes at large, because it was classed as a private act: S & M v1 p391.

291 **Grey (R): A system of English Ecclesiastical Law extracted from the Codex Juris Ecclesiastici Anglicani of the Reverend the Lord Bishop of London Edmund Gibson:** 2nd Ed. 1732: Designed for the use of students:

294 **Gurney (W): The trials of Jeremiah Brandreth, William Turner, Isaac Ludlam, George Weight-man and others for High Treason:** 2 vols: 1817:

295 **Gwillim (Sir H): Collection of Acts and Records of Parliament, with Reports of Cases in Courts of Law and Equity [1224-1800] respecting Tithes:** 1st Ed. 4 vols: 1801: S & M v1 p192.

296 **Hale (Sir M): Historia Placitorum Coronae: The History of the Pleas of the Crown, with notes by Sollom Emlyn:** 1st Ed. 2 vols: 1736: Hale gives us a complete statement of the principles and evolution of the law. It was at once accepted, and has ever since been regarded as a legal classic . . . Holdsworth: S & M v1 p362.

297 ________ New Edition By George Wilson: 2 vols: 1778: (Reprint also available):

298 **Hale (Sir M): Summary of the Pleas of the Crown; or a Brief but full account of whatsoever can be found relating to that subject:** 1716: (also available in reprint): S & M v1 p362.

No.	Price	No.	Price
228	£395.00	275	£60.00
229	£600.00	276	£65.00
230	£40.00	277	£75.00
231	£900.00	278	£25.00
232	£120.00	279	£45.00
233	£35.00	280	£120.00
234	£25.00	281	£60.00
235	£90.00	282	£45.00
236	£95.00	283	£55.00
237	£80.00	284	£40.00
238	£120.00	285	£40.00
239	£40.00	286	£35.00
240	£45.00	287	£50.00
241	£20.00	288	£30.00
242	£55.00	289	£150.00
243	£35.00	290	£45.00
244	£75.00	291	£30.00
245	£25.00	292	SOLD
246	£25.00	293	SOLD
247	£30.00	294	£75.00
248	£75.00	295	£75.00
249	£60.00	296	£180.00
250	£95.00	297	£100.00
251	£70.00	298	£85.00
252	£60.00		
253	£35.00		
254	£45.00		
255	£475.00		
256	£195.00		
257	£120.00		
258	£130.00		
259	£150.00		
260	£45.00		
261	£65.00		
262	£50.00		
263	£225.00		
264	£140.00		
265	£70.00		
266	£375.00		
267	£130.00		
268	£180.00		
269	£25.00		
270	£75.00		
271	SOLD		
272	£25.00		
273	£30.00		
274	£90.00		

299 **Hallam (H): Constitutional History of England: (1485-1760):** 7th Ed. 1850: S & M v1 p101.

300 **Hammond (A): Digested Index to the Term Reports and others during the Reigns of Geo. III and IV:** 2nd Ed. 2 vols: 1827: S & M v2 p153.

301 **Hands (W): Treatise on Fines and Recoveries:** 3rd Ed. 1817: S & M v2 p154.

302 **Hardres (Sir J): Reports, Court of Exchequer, 1655-69:** 1st Ed. 1693: There is a chasm in all copies of the first Edition (pp 233-300):

303 **Hardy (T D): Rotuli Litterarum Clausarum in turri Londinensi 1204-27:** 2 vols: 1833/1844: The Rotuli Litterarum Clausarum or close rolls are a series of parchment rolls commencing 1204 on which are recorded or enrolled all man-dates, letters and writs of a private nature. They are denomonated closed, in contradiction to another series of Rolls called patent. The entries registered on the closed rolls are letters addressed in the King's name to individuals, for special and particular purpose, and were folded, or closed up, and sealed on the outside with the great seal. The letters "Patent" were addressed to all the King's subjects and not folded up, but had the great seal on the bottom. These are enrolled on the patent rolls. The work was done by Command of King William IV in 1833 but was suspended until 1844.

304 **Hardy (T D): Rotuli Litterarum patentium in turri Londinensi asservati 1201-1216:** Volume 1 part 1: 1835: These are the Patent Rolls mentioned in prior entry:

305 **Hargrave (F): Juridical Arguments and Collections:** 2 vols: 1797-99: S & M v1 p33

306 **Hargrave (F): Collection of tracts relative to the Law of England, from manuscripts never before Published:** 1787: (also available in reprint): S & M v1 p32.

307 **Harington (J): Art of Law-Giving. In III books: First, Foundations and Superstructures of all the kinds of Government: Second, Frames of the Commonwealths of Israel and of the Jewes: Third Model fitted unto the present State of this Nation. [With] appendix concerning an House of Peers:** 1659: S & M v1 p608.

308 **Harrison (J): Accomplish'd Practiser in the High Court of Chancery, [with] forms and precedents:** 3rd Ed. 2 vols: 1750: S & M v1 339.

309 ———— 7th Ed. 2 vols: 1790: Different arrangment of subjects to former editions:

310 **Harrison (S B): Analytical Digest of all the reported Cases from 1756:** 3 vols: 1837: S & M v2 p158.

311 ———— 3rd Ed. 4 vols: 1844:

312 **Hawke (M): The Grounds of the Lawes of England, extracted from the Fountaines of all other learning; and digested methodically into cases for the use and benefit of all Practicers and Students. With a Commixtion of divers scattered grounds concerning the reasonable construction of the Law By M. H.** 1657: S & M v1 p243.

313 **Hawkins (W): Pleas of the Crown:** 2nd Ed. S & M v1 p362.
314 ———— 3rd Ed. 1724:
315 ———— 4th Ed. 1739:
316 ———— 5th Ed. 1771:
317 ———— 7th Ed. with additions by Thomas Leach: 4 vols: 1795:
318 ———— 8th Ed. with additions by John Curwood: 2 vols: 1824: (also available in reprint):

319 **Heartfree: Murder of Anne Bell:** 1760: (also available in repri

320 **Herberts (E. Lord): Life of Henry VIII:** 1683:

321 **Hetley (Sir T): Reports and Cases 3-7 Charles I, as they wer argued by most of the King's Serjeants at the Common Plea Barre:** 1657:

322 **History of the damnable popish plot in its various branche and progress:** 1680:

323 **Hobart (Sir H): Reports in the reign of James I with some fe cases in the reign of Queen Elizabeth [King's Bench. 160 25]:** 1st Ed. 1641: S & M v1 p30

324 ———— 2nd Ed. 1650:
325 ———— 2nd Ed. 1658:
326 ———— 5th Ed. with additions by Edward Chilton: 1724:

327 **Hobart (Sir H): Reports in the court of Common Pleas:** 3rd Ed 1671:

328 **Hodges (W): Law Relating to Railways and Railway Com panies:** 7th Ed. with additions by J. M. Lely: 2 vol 1888-89: S & M v2 p18

329 **Holt (Sir J): Modern Cases argued and adjudged in the cou of Queens Bench at Westminster (1703-05):** 2nd Ed. 1719: Th is also known as part 6 of the Modern Reports: S & M v1 30

330 **Holt (Sir J): Reports of Cases determined by Holt, [King Bench], 1688-1710; cases from an original manuscript Thomas Farresley also Cases in Chancery and Excheque Chamber:** 1738: Said to have been edited by Giles Jacob: S & M v1 p30

331 **Hooker (R): Of the Lawes of Ecclesiasticall Politic:** 168 "Remarkable as the first adequate presentation in the Englis Language of the abstract theory of law" — Salmond Jurisprudence: S & M v1 p1

332 **Horne (A): Book called the Mirrour of Justices; with the boo [by Sir Anthony Fitzherbert], called the Diversity of Cour and their jurisdictions. Translated out of the Old French b William Hughes:** 1646: Nobody can say for sure when this boo was first written. But according to Holdsworth's History English Law the evidence suggests it was written or compile before 1290: S & M v1 p

333 **Horsman (G): Precedents in Conveyancing:** 3rd Ed. 2 vol 1768: S & M v1 p4

334 ———— 4th Ed. 3 vols: 1785.

335 **Hovenden (J. E): Principles and Practice by which Courts Equity are guided as to the Prevention or Remedial Co rection of Fraud:** 2 vols: 1825: S & M v2 p17

336 **Hughes (W): Grand Abridgment of the Law continued, a collection of the Principal Cases and Points of the Commo Law of England in the Reports, from the first of Elizabet with appendix:** 3 vols: 1660-63: S & M v1 p

337 **Hughes: Nomotomia: 2 parts:** 1657: S& M v1 p

338 **Hunt (W): Cases on the Annuity Act ; with an epitome of th practice relative to the Enrolment of Memorials:** 1st Ed. 179 S & M v1 p5

339 **Hutcheson (G): Justice of the Peace:** 1st Ed. 1806:

340 **Hutton (Sir R) & Croke (Sir G): Arguments with the certifica of Sir John Denham upon a Scire Facias in the court Exchequer against John Hampden:** 1641: S & M v1 p3

341 **Hutton (Sir R): Reports containing many choice cases, jud ments and resolutions on points of law in the Court Common Pleas, [1617-38]; Written in French, now translated:** 1st Ed. 1656: S & M v1 p301.

342 ———— 2nd Ed. 1682:

343 **Impartial Lawyer. (i) Setting forth such special adjudged Cases as immediately concern such persons as are exercis'd in the Laws of England; (ii) with references to all sorts of precedents and pleadings:** 2nd Ed. 1731: S & M v1 p271.

344 **Impey (J): Office of Sheriff; shewing its history and antiquity, [with] the mode of electing Coroners and returning Members of Parliament:** 1786: S & M v1 p222.

345 **Impey (J): New Instructor Clericalis; stating the Authority, Jurisdiction, and Modern Practice of the Court of Common Pleas:** 3rd Ed. 1790: S & M v1 p271.

346 **Inglis (A. P): Consular Formulary. Forms and Precedents for Consular Officers:** 2nd Ed. 1898: S & M v2 p181.

347 **Isaacs (S. C): Law Relating to Theatres, Music Halls and other Public Entertainments:** 1927: S & M v2 p182.

348 **Jacob (G): Compleat Court Keeper; or, Land-Steward's Assistant, containing the nature of Courts Leet and Courts Baron:** 3rd Ed. 1724: S & M v1 p400.

349 **Jacob (G): Law Dictionary; explaining the Rise, Progress and Present State of the English Law etc.** 10th Ed. with additions by J. Morgan: 1782: S & M v1 p9.

350 ———— 2nd Ed. by T. E. Tomlins: 2 vols: 1809: This is Tomlin's 2nd Ed. (his first being 1797) but the 13th Edition of the dictionary altogether:

351 **Jacob (G): Compleat Chancery-Practiser; or, Whole Proceedings and Practice of the High Court of Chancery:** 2 vols: 1730: S & M v1 p339.

352 **Jenkins (D): Eight Centuries of Reports; or, Eight hundred cases, Exchequer-Chamber or upon Writs of Error [1220-1623]. Published originally in French and Latin (fol. 1661) now translated:** 2nd Ed. by a gentleman of the Middle-Temple: 1734: "Consists in the main of abstracts from the old abridgments, the Year Books, Keilway, Benloe, Dalison, Dyer, Plowden, Coke, and some other persons. It is a work of admitted accuracy and posseses very considerable authority" — Wallace Rep: S & M v1 p322.

353 ———— 3rd Ed. translated by Theodore Barlow: 1771:

354 **Jones (E): Index to the Records called the Originalia and Memoranda on the Remembrancer's side of the Exchequer:** 2 vols: 1793-95: S & M v2 p86.

355 **Jones (Sir T): Les Reports de divers Special Cases en le Common Bank et en le Court del Bank le Roy, [1667-84]:** 1st Ed. 1695: S & M v1 p301.

356 ———— 2nd Ed. in French and English: 1729:

357 **Jones (Sir W): Les Reports de divers Special Cases cy bien in le Court de Bank le Roy, come le Common-Bank, Angleterre [1620-40]:** 1675: Pages 266-98 contain, "Notes taken at a justice seat for the forest of Windsor". S & M v1 p302.

358 **Justin: Institutes:** 1622:

359 **Kames (Lord H. H): Historical Law tracts:** 1st Ed. 2 vols:1758: "Conducted upon a very judicious system of investigating the natural principles of some of the most important objects of judicial science, and tracing the application of them in the Laws of Rome, of Scotland and England" — I Evans: Pothier, Intro: S & M v1 p34.

360 **Keble (J): Reports, King's Bench, at Westminster [1661-79]:** Pts 1-3: 1665: All Parts contain Table of Matters: S & M v1 p302.

299	£25.00	331	£150.00
300	£25.00	332	£100.00
301	£25.00	333	£60.00
302	£65.00	334	£60.00
303	£180.00	335	£35.00
304	£75.00	336	£180.00
305	£150.00	337	£195.00
306	£95.00	338	£25.00
307	£300.00	339	£80.00
308	£40.00	340	£75.00
309	£45.00	341	£100.00
310	£50.00	342	£70.00
311	£60.00	343	£25.00
312	£95.00	344	£55.00
313	£85.00	345	£50.00
314	£60.00	346	£25.00
315	£50.00	347	£25.00
316	£55.00	348	£75.00
317	£80.00	349	£70.00
318	£70.00	350	£80.00
319	£30.00	351	£75.00
320	£70.00	352	SOLD
321	£40.00	353	£120.00
322	£80.00	354	£95.00
323	£120.00	355	£60.00
324	£75.00	356	£80.00
325	£80.00	357	£65.00
326	£65.00	358	£60.00
327	£70.00	359	£175.00
328	£45.00	360	£180.00
329	£45.00	361	£75.00
330	£50.00	362	£90.00
		363	£110.00

Lambarde (W.)
Archaionomia sive de priscis Anglorum legibus libri . . .
(Ref. No. 369)

362 **Keilway (R): Relationes quorundam Casuum Selectorum ex libris Roberti Keilway; [King's Bench, Common Pleas, 1496-1531 By J. Croke]:** 2nd Ed. 1633: Also contains Dalison and Benloe's cases, and a table not in the first: S & M v1 p302.

363 **Keilway (R): Reports d'Ascuns Cases (qui ont evenus aux temps du Roy Henry le Septieme et du Roy Henry le Huitiesme, et ne sont comprises deins les livres des Terms et Ans demesmes les Roys) [1496-1531]; Seliges hors des papiers de Keilway, par Jean Croke. 3rd ed., ovesque les Reports d'Ascuns cases prises per Guilleaume Dallison, [1553-65], et per Guilleaum Bendloe [1514-78]:** 1688: Includes the Year Books of the missing Years of HenryVII and of some years of Henry VIII: S & M v1 p302.

364 **Kelham: Britton, continuing Ancient Pleas of the Crown:** 1762:

365 **Kelyng (Sir J): Reports of divers Cases in Pleas of the Crown [1662-69], with directions for Justice of the Peace; [with] the reports of three modern cases, viz., Armstrong and Lisle, the King and Plumer, the Queen and Mawgridge:** 1st Ed. 1708: S & M v1 p302.

366 **Kilburne (R): Choice Presidents upon Acts of Parliament relating to the Office and Duty of a Justice of the Peace, with notes and cases: made publick by G. F:** 7th Ed. 1703: S & M v1 p229.

367 **Kingsley (M): The Crown and the Establishment:**

368 **Knapp (J. W) and Ombler (E): Cases of Controverted Elections in the Twelfth Parliament of the United Kingdom:** 1837: S & M v1 p199.

369 **Lambarde (W): Archaionomia sive de priscis Anglorum legibus libri, sermone Anglico, vetustate antiquissimo, aliquot abhinc seculis conscripti, nunc demum e tenebris in lucem vocati Anglo-Saxon and Latin:** 1568: S & M v1 p47.

370 **Lambard (W): Eirenarcha: or of the Office of the Justice of Peace:** 1st Ed. 1581: "It is far more complete than any preceding work on the subject, and is written in a style "which few writers upon the law had condescended to imitate since the time of Bracton, Fleta and Britton" " — Marvin's Leg Bib: (also available in reprint): S & M v1 p229.

371 **Lane (R): Reports in the Court of Exchequer, beginning in the third and ending in the ninth year of the Reign of the Late King James, containing several cases of information upon intrusion, touching the King's Perogative, Revenue, and Government. [1605-11]:** 1657:

372 **Laws of Commons and Commoners; or A Treatise shewing the Original and Nature of Common, and several kinds thereof, or, Commons in Gross and Sans Number; with the Pleadings in reference to every of them. Also the Powers and Privileges of Commoners; and of the Remedies and Actions they may have; together with the Learning of Prescription in General; the forms and manner of Pleadings Prescription in Reference to Common in several Rules; of Prescription and Pleading by a Copyholder in reference to Common; of Evidence to prove Prescriptions for Common; the several Customs of Commoners, and of Enclosures; With several forms of Presidents adapted to every sort of Common:** 1698: S & M v1 p402.

373 **Laws, Customs, Rights, Liberties and Privileges of the City of London, containing the several Charters etc.** 1st Ed. 1765: S & M v1 p440.

374 **Law Government of England:** 2nd Ed. 1906:

375 **Grant (F): Law, Religion, and Education considered; in three essays. [with a letter from a T . . . ry Lawyer to the publisher]:** 1715: Contains essays 1 and 2 only, the compiler having died before printing of the third essay:

376 **Lawyer's Magazine or Attorney's or Solicitor's universal library:** 2nd Ed. 2 vols: 1761-62: First published in parts: S & M v1 p573.

377 **Leach (T): Cases in Crown Law, determined by the Twelve Judges, by Kings Bench and by commissioners of Oyer and Terminer and General Gaol Delivery [1730-89]:** 3rd Ed. 2 vols: 1800: Continued to 1800: S & M v1 p303.

378 **Lord Archbishop of Carlisle: Leges Marchiarium (Border Laws);** 1705:

379 **Leigh (E. C) and Cave (L. W): Crown Cases Reserved 1860-65:** 1866: S & M v2 p213.

380 **Leonard (W): Reports and Cases of Law in the Courts at Westminster [1540-1615]:** 1st Ed. 1688: S & M v1 p303.

381 ________ 2nd Ed. Parts 1-4 in 1 volume: 1687:

382 **Levinz (Sir C): Reports of Cases in the Court of King's Bench and Common Pleas, during the time of Sir R. Foster, Sir R. Hyde, and Sir J. Kelying were Chief Justice: also in other Courts during that time [1660-96]:** 1st Ed. Parts 1-3 in 2 vols: This Edition is in French: S & M v1 p303.

383 **Lex Parliamentaria: or, Treatise of the Law and Custom of the Parliament of England. By George Petyt. With appendix of a case in Parliament between Sir F. Goodwyn and Sir J. Fortescue for the Knight's place for the County of Bucks from an original French manuscript, translated into English:** 2nd Ed. S & M v1 p132.

384 **Ley (Sir J): Reports of Resolutions in Law arising upon cases in the Court of Wards and other courts at Westminster, [1608-29 with a treatise concerning Wards and liveries]:** 1659: S & M v1 p357.

385 **Liber Placitandi; a Book of Special Pleadings containing Precedents of pleas in Abatement, Declaration, Barrs, etc., in the now most common and ordinary actions, also the Forms of Entries in Writs of Error etc:** 2nd Ed. 1674: Cited as Thompson's Entries: S & M v1 p273.

386 **Lilly (J): Collection of Modern Entries; or Select Pleadings in the Courts of King's Bench, Common Pleas, and Exchequer:** 3rd Ed. 1758: Lilly's was the first book of Entries to go through the whole alphabet: S & M v1 p271.

387 **Lilly (J): Practical Register; or, General Abridgment of the Law, as practiced in the Courts of Chancery, King's Bench, Common Pleas and Exchequer, with rules of Court:** 2nd Ed. 2 vols: 1745: Also contains supplement continuing rules of the respective courts to Mich. 1744: S & M v1 p271.

388 **Lilly (J): Practical Conveyancer, in 2 parts: I. Rules and Instructions for drawing Conveyances of Estates and Interests, also rules for the exposition of Deeds, wills etc. II. The first part reduced into Practice, in a collection of precedents [with] cases in Chancery:** 2nd Ed. Parts I and II in 1 volume: 1732: S & M v1 p483.

389 **Lilly (J): Reports and Pleadings of case in Assize, for Offices, Nusances, Lands, and Tenements [England, 1688-93, with Writs of Assize, etc; [with] a prefatory discourse shewing the nature of this action and reasons for putting it in practice [by W. Nelson]:** 1719: S & M v1 p335.

390 **Littleton (Sir E): Les Reports en le Courts del Common Bank et Exchequer (1626-32):** 1683: S & M v1 p303.

391 **Littleton (Sir T): Tenures:** 2 vols: 1612: "Littleton's book is the first great book upon English law not written in Latin and wholly uninfluenced by Roman Law — Holdsworth History of English Law: S & M v1 p454.

393 **Lofft (C.): Reports, King's Bench, with select cases, Court of Chancery and of Common Pleas [1771-74] with the cases of General Warrants and a collection of Maxims [in Latin]** 1776. S & M v1 p034.

394 **Lovelass (P): Law's Disposal of a Person's Estate who dies without Will or Testament. The Disposal of estates by Will Form of Wills. Directions for Executors etc:** 10th Ed. 1809: S & M v1 p482.

395 **Lucas (R): Cases in Law and Equity, chiefly temp Maccleafield (1709-25):** 2nd Ed. 17?1: This is part 10 of the Modern Reports: S & M v1 p304.

396 **Luder (A): Reports of Proceedings in Committees, House of Commons [1785-87]:** 3 vols: 1789/1790: S & M v1 p151.

397 **Lutwyche (Sir E): Un Livre des Entries; contenant auxi un Report des Resolutions del Court sur diverse Exceptions prises as Pleadings et sur auters matters en ley surdant (Pur la plupart) en le Court de Common Bank [1683-1704]:** 1st Ed. Translated By William Nelson: 2 vols: 1704: S & M v1 p304.

398 **Macassey (L): Private Bill Legislation and Provisional Orders:** 1887: S & M v2 p223.

399 **Mackintosh: Defence of the French Revolution:** 1791:

400 **Maddock (H): Principles and Practice of the High Court of Chancery:** 2nd Ed. 2 vols: 1820: S & M v2 p299.

403 **Maine (Sir H. S): Ancient Law:** 10th Ed. 1885: Compares English and Roman Law etc: S & M v1 p612.

404 **Maine (Sir H. S): Lectures on Early History of Institutions:** 7th Ed. 3rd impression: 1905: S & M v1 p597.

405 **Maine (Sir H. S): An Introduction & Notes to Sir Henry Maine's Ancient Law:** 1925 By H. Pollock:

406 **Maitland (F. W): Collected Papers of. Edited by H. A. L. Fisher:** 3 vols: 1911: S & M v2 p230.

407 **Mallory (J): Modern Entries in English; being a select collection of Pleadings in the Courts of King's Bench, Common Pleas and Exchequer; and also all kinds of Writs, with readings and observations on the cases in the Reports. By a Gentleman of the Inner Temple** 1st Ed. 2 vols: 1734: S & M v1 p273.

408 **Mallory (J): Quare Impedit:** 1737: This is Volume 3 of Mallory's Modern Entries: S & M v1 p273.

409 **Manby (R): Law and Practice of Fines and Recoveries:** 1738: S & M v1 p489.

410 **Manby (T): Collection of the Statutes made in the reigns of Charles the I and Charles the II [to 19 Ch. II], with the abridgment of such as stand repealed or expired; continued after the method of Pulton:** 1st Ed. 166?: S & M v1 p556.

411 **Manning (J): Digested Index to the Nisi Prius Reports and some original cases:** 1st Ed. 1813: Founded on the reports of Peake, Esspinasse, and Campbell, under-taken on the original plan of Comyn's Digest, which it was originally designed to supplement: S & M v2 p231.

412 **Modern Cases in Law and Equity in 2 parts. I, Cases in the King's Bench (1721-26). II, Cases in Chancery (1721-24):** 1st Ed. 2 parts in 1 volume: 1730: This makes up parts 8 and 9 of the Modern Reports: S & M v1 p305.

413 **Maxims of Equity and the arguments of the Lord Chancellor Macclesfield, the master of the rolls, Mr. Baron Price and Mr. Baron Gilbert in the case of the Earl of Coventry concerning the defective execution of Powers:** No date:

414 **McKechnie (W. S): Magna Carta; a Commentary on the Great Charter of King John, with historical introduction:** 1st Ed. 1905: Printed in Glasgow: S & M v1 p551.

415 **Middle Temple Records [1501-1703] By C. Hopwood:** 1903-5: S & M v1 p214.

416 **Modern Cases Temp Holt: 1703-04:** 1st Ed. 1713: This makes up part 6 of the Modern Reports: S & M v1 p305.

417 **Molloy (C): De Jure Maritimo et Navali; or Treatise of Affaires Maritime and of Commerce:** 9th Ed. 2 vols: 1769: S & M v1 p511.

418 **Montagu (B): Summary of the Law of Composition with Creditors:** 1823: S & M v2 p246.

419 **Moore (J. B): Index to the Term Reports:** 2nd Ed. 2 vols: plus supp: 1821/1822: S & M v2 p247.

420 **Moore (Sir F): Cases collect et report per Sir Fra. Moore; imprime et publie per l'original Jadis remainent en les mains de Sir Gefrey Palmer:** 1st Ed. 1663: His reports have always enjoyed a reputation for accuracy: S & M v1 p305.

421 ________ 2nd Ed. 1675:

422 **Nelson (W): Office and Authority of a Justice of Peace, also the Duty of other Parish Officers [with] presidents of indictments and warrents, and judgments and resolutions; by W. N.** 2nd Ed. 1707: S & M v1 p230.

423 ________ 11th Ed. 1736:

434 **Nelson (W): Lex Maneriorum; or, Law and Customs of England relating to Manors and Lords of Manors, their Stewards, Deputies, Tenants, and others, [with] appendix of all the Modern entries:** 1st Ed. 1726: S & M v1 p403.

425 **Nelson (W): Law of Evidence; wherein all the cases that have yet been printed in any of our Law Books or tryals, and that in any wise to relate to points of Evidence are collected:** 3rd Ed. 1739: S & M v1 p379.

426 **Newnam (W) and Others: Complete Conveyancer; or, Theory and Practice of Conveyancing in all its branches:** 1st Ed. 3 vols 1781: S & M v2 p484.

427 **New Precedents in Conveyancing, containing great variety of curious draughts, many of them on special occasions, drawn or settled by Mr. Piggot, Northey Webb and other eminent hands:** 1742:

428 **Noy (W): Treatise of the Principal Grounds and Maximes of the Lawes of this Kingdome by W. N. [with] a Dialogue and Treatise of the Laws of England and on Tenures, Estates, Hereditaments and Chattels [6th Ed] In which is included a Treatise of Estates ascribed to Sir John Doderidge, and Observations on a Deed of Feoffment [by T. H]. With a sketch of the authors Life:** 9th Ed. By W. N. Bythewood: 1821: S & M v1 p242.

429 **Noy (W): Reports of Cases, in the time of Queen Elizabeth and King Charles [1559-1649]; containing most excellent matters of exceptions to all manner of Declarations, Pleadings and demurrers:** 1st Ed. 1656: S & M v1 p306

430 **Observer, being a collection of Maral Literary and familiar Essays:** 2nd Ed. 4 vols: 1788:

431 **Odgers (W. B): Principles of Pleading in Civil Actions in the High Court of Justice:** 3rd Ed. 1897: S & M v2 p260.

432 **Officium Clerici Pacis; a book of Indictment, Informations, Appeals, and Inquisitions; also the Manner of holding the Sessions Peace By J. W.** 1st Ed. 1675: S & M v1 p232.

433 **Old Bailey: Session Papers, Justice Hall:**

434 **Order of the High Court of Chancery, made By Lord Hardwicke, Ld. Chan, by and with the Advice and Assistance of Wm. Fortesque Esq. M. R., relating to the fees of officers of the said Court, and other regulations for the benefit of the**

364	. £90.00
365	£175.00
366	. £35.00
367	. £30.00
368	. £25.00
369	£450.00
370	£450.00
371	. £75.00
372	. £60.00
373	. £80.00
374	. £25.00
375	. £35.00
376	. £40.00
377	. £65.00
378	. £80.00
379	. . £25.00
380	. . £90.00
381	. £65.00
382	. £80.00
383	. £40.00
384	. £85.00
385	. £95.00
386	. £45.00
387	. . £60.00
388	. . £30.00
389	. . £55.00
390	£120.00
391	£275.00
392	. . SOLD
393	. £45.00
394	. £35.00
395	. £25.00
396	. £85.00
397	£110.00
398	. £25.00
399	. £25.00
400	£25.00
401	. . SOLD
402	. . SOLD
403	. . £30.00
404	. . £20.00
405	. £25.00
406	. £45.00
407	£120.00
408	£130.00
409	. £30.00
410	. £75.00
411	. £50.00
412	£60.00
413	£70.00
414	. . SOLD
415	£45.00
416	£25.00
417	£180.00
418	£30.00
419	£45.00
420	£70.00
421	£55.00
422	£60.00
423	£45.00
424	£75.00
425	£45.00
426	£65.00
427	£40.00
428	£85.00
429	. £70.00
430	. £50.00
431	. £25.00
432	. £50.00
433	. £30.00
434	. £25.00

suitors thereof; to which are added, three other subsequent General orders of the said court: 1744: S & M v1 p343.

435 **Ordinances and Orders of the Lords and Commons concerning Sequesting:** 1646:

436 **Orme (R): Practical Digest of the Election Laws:** 1st Ed. 1796: S & M v1 p152.

437 **Oughton (T): Ordo Judiciorum; sive Methodus Procedendi in negotiis et Litibus in Foro Ecclesiastico Civili Britanico et Hibernico:** 1st Ed. 1728: S & M v1 p187.

438 **Owen (T): Reports in the King's Bench and Common Pleas [1556-1615]:** 1656: There is a gap in the paging from 77-80 inclusive: S & M v1 p306.

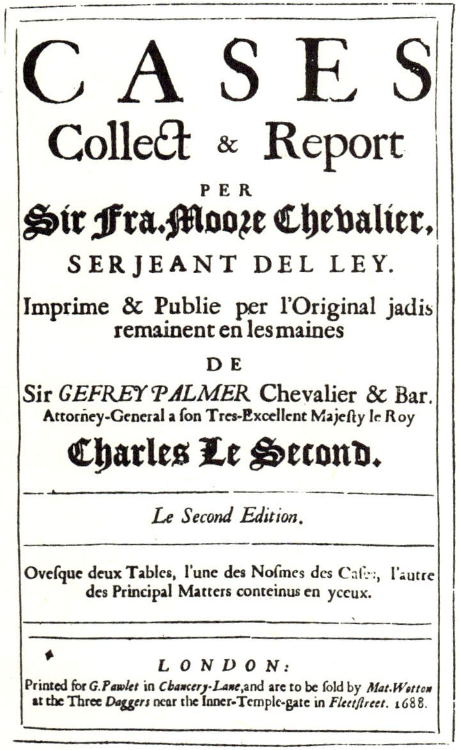
CASES
Collect & Report
PER
Sir Fra. Moore Chevalier,
SERJEANT DEL LEY.
Imprime & Publie per l'Original jadis remainent en les maines
DE
Sir GEFREY PALMER Chevalier & Bar. Attorney-General a son Tres-Excellent Majesty le Roy
Charles Le Second.
Le Second Edition.
Ovesque deux Tables, l'une des Nosmes des Cases, l'autre des Principal Matters conteinus en yceux.
LONDON:
Printed for G. Pawlet in Chancery-Lane, and are to be sold by Mat. Wotton at the Three Daggers near the Inner-Temple-gate in Fleetstreet. 1688.

439 **Palgrave (Sir F): Parliamentary writs and writs of Military Summons, together with the Records and Muniments relating to the suit and service due and performed to the King's High Court of Parliament and the Counsels; of the Realm or affording evidence of attendance given at Parliaments and Councils; with alphabetical Digest and Index:** 4 books in 2 volumes: 1827-34: This collection includes all the records which show the constituent parts of the ancient legislative and remedial assemblies of England, beginning with the reign of Edward I, the period when they first assumed a definite organisation: S & M v1 p135

440 **Palmer (F. B): Company Law:** 3 vols: 1976: S & M v2 p284

441 **Palmer (F. B): Company Precedents:** 2st Ed: 1968 & 1972 supplement: S & M v2 p284

442 **Palmer (Sir G): Les Reports [King's Bench 1619-29]:** 1st Ed. 1688: S & M v1 p306

443 **Park (J. J): Law of Dower:** 1819: S & M v1 p265

444 **Parker (Sir T): Reports of Cases concerning the Revenue, Court of Exchequer 1743-67, with appendix [of] cases, [1678-1717]:** 1st Ed. 1776: S & M v1 p321

435	£55.00
436	£50.00
437	£45.00
438	£50.00
439	£75.00
440	£20.00
441	£25.00
442	£120.00
443	£30.00
444	£60.00
445	£45.00
446	£50.00
447	£150.00
448	£80.00
449	£50.00
450	£50.00
451	£50.00
452	£60.00
453	£75.00
454	£25.00
455	£25.00
456	£25.00
457	£80.00
458	£55.00
459	£60.00
460	£130.00
461	£45.00
462	£35.00
463	£50.00
464	£175.00

465	£45.00
466	£200.00
467	£150.00
468	£75.00
469	£125.00
470	£175.00
471	£120.00
472	£85.00
473	£150.00
474	£60.00
475	£25.00
476	£95.00
477	£35.00
478	£42.00
479	£25.00
480	£60.00
481	£25.00
482	£35.00
483	£35.00
484	£25.00
485	£40.00
486	£30.00

Palmer
Les Reports (King's
(Ref. N

445 **Parliamentary History of England:** 6, 7, and 8 only: 1751:

446 **Parliamentary Reports: Copy of the first report made by his Majesty by the commissioners appointed to inquire into the Law of England respecting real property:** 1829:

447 **Parliamentary Reports: Copy of the 1st-4th reports made by his Majesty by the commissioners appointed to inquire into the practice and proceedings of the superior courts of common law:** 4 reports in 3 volumes:

448 **Parliamentary Reports: Reports from the select committee appointed to inquire into the state of the public records of the Kingdom:** 2 reports in 1 volume: 1800:

449 **Parliamentary Reports: Report from the commissioners appointed by his Majesty to execute the measures recommended by the report on Public Records of the Kingdom 1800-1812:** 1812:

450 **Parliamentary Reports: Report from the commissioners appointed by his Majesty to execute the measures recommended by a select committee of the House of Commons respecting Public Records: 1800-1819:** 1819:

451 **Parliamentary Reports: The seventh Report of the deputy keeper of the public records:** 1846:

452 **Parliamentary Reports: General report to the King in Council from the honourable board of commissioners on the public records:** 1837:

453 **Parliamentary Reports: Indexes to the subject matters of the subject of the reports of the House of Commons 1801-1834:** 1834:

454 **Parry (Sir E): Concerning Many Thing:** 1888:

455 **Paterson (J): Compendium of English and Scotch Law:** 2nd Ed.1865: S & M v2 p274.

456 **Peake: Compendium of the Law of Evidence:** 1st Ed. 1801:

457 **Peere Williams (W): Reports of Cases, Court of Chancery, and of some special cases, King's Bench [1695-1735]; with notes by his son, William Peere Williams:** 1st Ed. 3 vols: 1740-49: S & M v1 p247.

458 ——— 2nd Ed. 3 vols: 1746-49:

459 ——— 3rd Ed. 3 vols: 1768:

460 **Perkins (J): A Profitable booke treating of the lawes of Englande:** 9th Ed. 1604: S & M v1 p485.

461 **Perkins (J): Profitable Book, treating of the Laws of England principally as they relate to conveyancing:** 15th Ed. Translated and revised by R. Greening: 1827: Contains notes for the use of students: S & M v1 p485.

462 **Perry (H. J) and Knapp (J. W): Cases of controverted Elections in the Eleventh Parliament:** 1833: S & M v2 p277.

463 **Petersdorff (C): Index to the Precedents in Civil and Criminal Pleadings:** 1822: S & M v2 p277.

464 **Petersdorff (C): Abridgment of Cases in the Court of King's Bench, Common Pleas, Exchequer, and at Nisi Prius, and of the rules of Court 1660-1823:** 15 vols: 1825-30: This is primarily a case finder, suited to the modern analytical method and resembles current digests . . . Price and Bitner — Guide to Legal Research. That it never gained great favour is surprising, since it comprised of all the features of Comyn's and most of the later digests . . . Hicks: S & M v2 p277.

465 **Petersdorff (C): Practical Precedents in Pleading:** 1835: S & M v2 p278.

466 **Petersdorff (C): Abridgment of common and Statute Law:** 1st Ed. 5 vols: 1841-44:

467 ——— 2nd Ed. 6 vols: 1861-64:

468 **Pigott (N): Common Recoveries, their nature and use, [with] the case of Page and Hayward, a case between the Earl of Derby and the co-heirs of his elder brother, [and] precedents:** 1st Ed. 1739: S & M v1 p490.

469 **Placita de quo warranto temporibus Edward I, II and III in curia receptae Scaccarii Westm, asservata:** 1818: Edited by W. Illingworth: S & M v1 p87.

470 **Plowden (E): Commentaries or Reports: Divers cases upon matters of Law, [1550-80]; written in French, now translated, [with his] Queries rendered into English:** 1st Ed. 2 parts in 1 volume: 1761/1761: "In every sort of professional excellence Plowden's Reports rank among the best reports of any age" — Wallace Rep. S & M v1 p306.

471 ——— 2nd Ed. 2 parts in 1 volume: 1778/1761:

472 ——— 5th Ed. 2 parts in 1 volume: 1792:

473 **Plowden (E): Les Commentaries, ou les Reportes, de dyvers cases esteantes matters en ley, en les temps des raygnes le Rove Edwarde le sixe, le Roigne Mary, le Roy and Roigne Phillipp and Mary and le Roigne Elizabeth [1550-71]:** 1684: S & M v1 p306.

474 **Pollexfen (Sir H): Arguments and Reports in some special Cases, [England 1669-85], with Decrees in Court of Chancery upon Limitations of Trusts of Terms of Years:** 1702:

475 **Pollock (Sir F): The Law of Torts:** 3rd Ed. 1892: S & M v1 p284.

476 **Popham (Sir J): Reports and Cases [King's Bench, Common Pleas, Chancery, 1592-97], written in French; and now translated [with] some remarkable cases reported by other learned pens [1618-27]:** 2nd Ed. 1682: S & M v1 p307.

477 **Powell (J. J): Law of Morgages:** 4th Ed. 2 vols: 1799: S & M v1 p257.

478 **Power (D), Rodwell (H) and Dew (E. L): Reports of the Decisions on Controverted Elections, 1847-56:** 2 vols: 1857: S & M v2 p287.

479 **Practising Attorney, or New King's Bench Guide; being a Compendious Introduction to the Knowledge of the Practise of that Court: also Proceedings on a writ of Error and Variety of Useful Precedents:** 1779: S & M v1 p276.

480 **Precedents in Chancery; Cases, Court of Chancery 1689-1722:** 1st Ed. 1733: S & M v1 p348.

481 **Precedents of proceedings in the House of Commons under seperate titles, with observations:** 1781:

482 **Present Practice of the High Court of Chancery; in which are contained the nature and course of proceedings, from the bill filed to the decree inrolled, By a Gentleman of the Six Clerks Office:** 2 vols: 1741: S & M v1 p341.

483 **Preston (R): Treatise on Conveyancing:** 1st Ed. 1806: S & M v2 p289.

484 ——— 2nd Ed. 3 vols: 1815/1816:

485 **Preston (R): Essay on Abstract of Title:** 1st Ed. 3 vols: 1818-19: S & M v2 p289.

486 **Prothero (G. W): Select Statutes and other Constitutional Documents illustrative of the reigns of Elizabeth and James I:** 2nd Ed. 1989: S & M v1 p111.

487 **Pufendorf (S): De Jure Naturae et Gentium:** 1st Ed. 1672: S & M v1 p593.

488 **Pufendorf (S): Law of Nature and Nations:** 1st English Ed. Translated By B. Kennett: 8 books in 1 volume: 1703: S & M v1 p597.

489 ________ 2nd Ed. abridged by J. Sparen: 1716:

490 **Pufendorf (S): Le droit de La Nature et des Gens:** 2 vols: Translated from Latin to French By Jean Barheyrac: 1734:

491 ________ 1750:

492 **Pufendorf (S): Introduction:** 2 vols: 1748:

493 **Pulton (F): Collection of sundrie Statutes frequent in use, with notes and references:** 1640: S & M v1 p555.

494 **Rashadall: Universities of Europe in the Middle Ages:** 2 vols: 1895:

495 **Raymond (R. First Baron): Reports, King's Bench and Common Pleas [1694-1732]:** 1st Ed. 1743: S & M v1 p307.

496 ________ 2nd Ed. 1765:

497 **Raymond (Sir T): Reports, King's Bench, Common Pleas, and Exchequer, [1660-83]:** 1st Ed. 1696: S & M v1 p308.

498 ________ 2nd Ed. 1743:

499 **Rayner (J): Cases at Large concerning Tithes [1575-1782]:** 3 vols: 1783: S & M v1 p194.

500 **Reeves (J): History of the English Law from the Saxons to the end of the reign of Hen VII [1509] continued to the end of the reign of Phillip and Mary:** 2nd Ed. 4 vols: 1787: "A remarkable book, before its time" — Ames: The books are divided into reigns, in each reign there is a history of changes made in Law by the Courts of Legislature, some with examples of actual incidents: S & M v1 p16.

501 **Registrum omniu brevium tam originaliu qs iudicialium:** 4th Ed. 1687: "The invention of writs was really the making of the English Common Law" — Jenks HEL: S & M v1 p277.

502 **Reports of Cases argued and decreed in the High Court of Chancery:** 1st Ed. 3 vols: 1701-1702:

503 **Reports of Cases taken and adjudged in the High Court of Chancery in the reign of King Charles I, Charles II, James II and Queen Anne:** 3rd Ed. 3 parts in 1 volume: 1836:

504 **Reports in Chancery. Reports of cases in Chancery in the reign of Cha. I and II and James II being special cases all of them referring to the register books, & c., to which are added, learned arguments relating to the antiquity of the said court, its dignity, power, and jurisidiction, & c.** 3rd Ed. 3 volumes in 1 book: 1736: S & M v1 p348.

505 **Return of Owners Land:** 1873:

506 **Ritson (J): Jurisdiction of the Court Leet, exemplified in the Articles which the Jury or Inquest for the King, in that Court, is charged and sworn, and by Law enjoined, to inquire of and present, with Precedents, and an introduction containing an account of the origin, nature and present State of this insitution:** 2nd Ed. 1809: S & M v1 p404.

507 **Robinson (T): Common Law of Kent; or, Customs of Gavelkind with appendix concerning Borough English:** 2nd Ed. 1788: S & M v1 p477.

508 **Robinson (W): The Landlord's pocket Lawyer; or, the complete Landlord and Tenant:** No date on title page. Probably done between 1790-1810:

509 **The roll for Election of M. P. for Newcastle-upon-Tyne:** 1741:

510 **Rolle (Sir H): Les Reports de divers Cases, Banke Le Roy, [1614-16] et un continuation [1618-25]:** 2 vols: 1675/1676: S & M v1 p308

511 **Rolle (Sir H): Reports of common Law P-Z:** No date or edition:

512 **Rolle (Sir H): Abridgment des plusieurs Cases et Resolutions del Common Ley [with preface by Sir Mathew Hale]:** 2 vols: 1688: It abridges many of the Parliamentary Rolls and other authentic Records, and contains many cases that came under the author's own observation, when he was Chief Justice of the King's Bench (during the usuration) which are not otherwise reported. Mr. Hargrave mentions this work as "excellent in its kind" — Bridgman Leg Bib: S & M v1 p19.

513 **Roscoe (E. S): Jurisdiction and Practice of the Court of Admiralty:** 2nd Ed. 1882: S & M v2 p306.

514 ________ 5th Ed. 1931:

515 **Roscoe (E. S): History of English Prize Court: 1932:**

516 **Rose (G): Cases in Bankruptcy:** 2nd Ed. 2 vols: 1821: S & M v1 p307.

517 **Ross (G): Law of Vendors and Purchasers of Personal Property:** 1st Ed. 1811: S & M v2 p307.

518 **Rotuli Parliamentorum: ut et Petitiones et Placita in Parliamento [ab anno 1278 ad annum 1503]:** 6 vols: 1767: The rolls of parliament: S & M v1 p137.

519 **Rules, Orders and Notices, in the Court of King's Bench from 2 James I to 25 George II [1605-1747]:** 2nd Ed. 1747:

520 **Russell (W. O): On Crimes and Misdemeanors:** 1st Ed. 2 vols: 1819: S & M v2 p312.

521 **Rymer (T) and Sanderson (R): Foedera, Conventiones, Literae et Cujuscunque Generis Acta Publica inter Reges Angliae et alios quosvis Imperatores, Reges, Pontifices, Principes, vel Communitates ab 1066 ad nostra usque tempora:** 2nd Ed. 20 vols: 1727: Mr. Rymer was the historgrapher Royal and was warranted to search all public offices for this undertaking (August 26th 1693). Mr. Sanderson joined the undertaking in 1707 (May 3rd) and a similar warrant was granted to him: S & M v1 p604.

522 **Salkeld (W): Reports of cases in the Court of Kings Bench, with some special cases in the courts of Chancery, Common Pleas and Exchequer, alphabetically digested under proper heads for the 1st of William and Mary to the 10th of Anne [1689-1712]:** 1st Ed. 3 vols: 1717-18/1724: S & M v1 p308.

523 ________ 2nd Ed. 2 vols: 1721-22:

524 ________ 3rd Ed. 2 vols in 1 book: 1731-32:

525 ________ 4th with additions by K. D'Anvers: 2 vols: 1742:

526 ________ 5th Ed. with additions by Serjeant Wilson: 1773:

527 **Sanders: Essay on Uses and Trusts:** 4th Ed. 2 vols: 1824: S & M v2 p314.

528 **Sandrars: Institutes of Justinian:** 2nd Ed. 1926:

529 **Saunder (Sir E): Les Reports des Divers Pleadings et Cases en le Court del Bank le Toy en le temp del Reign de le Roy Charles II:** 1st Ed. 2 vols: in 1 book: 1686: In the case of Bullythorpe v's Turner, Lord Chief Justice Willes having cited the authority of Saunders, observed that he was so very learned a man, and so skilled in pleading that no authority needed to be mentioned after him: S & M v1 p308.

530 ________ 2nd Ed. with addition of reports translated into English: 2 vols: 1722:

531 **Savile (Sir J): Les Reports de divers special cases cybien en le Court de Common Bank come L'Exchequer [1580-94]:** 1st Ed. 1675: S & M v1 p308.

532 **Sayer (J): Reports, King's Bench [1751-56]:** 1st Ed. 1775: S & M v1 p309.

533 **Scarlatini (R): Homo et ejus partes figuatus & symbolicus:** 1695:

534 **Scroggs (Sir W): Practise of Courts Leet and Courts Baron:** 4th Ed. 1728: S & M v1 p405.

535 **Secondant Spirit of Laws:** 5th Ed. 3 vols: 1770:

536 **Selden (J): Opera Omnia, tam edita quam inedita collegit ac recensuit, vitam auctoris [&] praefationes adjecit D. Ilkims:** 6 vols: 1726: S & M v1 p36.

537 **Selden (J): Fleta: seu commentarius Juris Anglicani Accedit Tractatulus vetus de agendi excipiendique formulis Gallicanus, Fet assavoir dictus; subjungitur etiam Joannis Seldeni ad Fletam Dissertatio Historica:** 2nd Ed. 1685: S & M v1 p53.

538 **Selden (J): Fleta: Ad Fletam Dissertatio (Appendix to Fleta 1647):** 1st Ed. 1647: S & M v1 p53.

539 **Select Cases, Court of Chancery, 1724-33, before Lord Commissioners of the Great Seal and Lord Chancellor King: By a gentleman of the Middle Temple:** 1st Ed. 1740:

540 **Selwyn (W): Abridgment of the Law of Nisi Prius:** 4th Ed. 2 vols: 1817: S & M v2 p321.

541 **Service (J): Pocket Conveyancer:** 1845:

542 **Seton (H. W): Forms of Decrees, Judgments and Orders in Equity:** 7th Ed. 3 vols: 1912: (Reprint may be shortly available): S & M v2 p32.

543 **Shaw (J): Practical Justice of the Peace; or, Treatise shewing the power and authority of that office:** 2nd Ed. 1733: S & M v2 p231.

544 **Sheppard (W): Touch-stone of Common Assurances; or, Treatise opening the Learning of Common Assurances or Conveyances of the kingdome:** 2nd Ed. 1648: There is some evidence to suggest that Sheppard was not the author, but that John Dodderidge actually wrote the book. According to Holdsworth ,History of English Law, there is good secondhand evidence that Sheppard, having purchased Dodderidge's library he also aquired the M. S. of the treatise and published it as his own. The style in which it is written also points to Dodderidge. It was one of the earliest works exclusively devoted to conveyancing and has a good reputation as a high authority on the subject: S & M v1 p487.

545 ________ 3rd Ed. 1651:

546 ________ 4th Ed. with additions By E. Hillard: 1780:

547 ________ 5th Ed. with additions By E. Hillard: 1784:

548 ________ 7th Ed. with additions by R. Preston: 1821:

549 ________ 8th Ed. with additions by P. G. Atherley: 2 vols 1826:

550 **Sheppard (W): Faithful Councellor; or, Marrow of the Law in English:** 2nd Ed. 1653: The first part showing how actions may be laid for the relief in most cases of wrongs done; the second part in what cases relief is to be had in Chancery, a good deal of of law is grouped round the forms of action, especially the actions for the case . . Holdsworth: S & M v1 p278.

551 **Sheppard (W): Practical Councellor in Law; touching Fines, common Recoveries, Judgments, and the Execution thereof, Statutes, Recognizances and Bargain and sale:** 1671: S & M v1 p490:

552 **Sheppard (W): England's Balme; or, Proposals by way of Grievance and Remedy, presented to his Highness and the Parliament towards the Regulation of the Law and better Administration of Justice:** 1657: S & M v1 p251.

553 **Sheppard (W): Grand Abridgment of the Common and Statute Law of England:** 3 vols: 1675: S & M v1 p19.

554 **Shower (Sir B): Cases in Parliament resolved and adjudged upon Petition and Writs of Error (1694-99):** 1699: S & M v1 p146.

555 ________ 3rd Ed. 1740:

556 **Shower (Sir B): Reports, King's Bench [1678-94]:** 1st Ed. 2 parts: 1708/1720: S & M v1 p309.

557 **Siderfin (Sir T): Les Reports des divers Special Cases, Bank le Roy, Co, Ba, & L'Exchequer [1657-71]:** 1st Ed. Parts 1 and 2: in 1 volume: 1683/1684: S & M v1 p308.

558 ________ 2nd Ed. with notes by E. Chilton & R. Skinner: 1714:

559 **Skinner (R): Reports of Cases adjudged in the King's Bench [1681-97]: with some arguments in special cases. Published by his son M. Skinner:** 1728: S & M v1 p309.

560 **Skirrow (G): Complete Practical Undersheriff:** 1811: S & M v1 p327.

562 **Smith (J. W): Leading Cases in various branches of the Law:** 13th Ed. 2 vols: 1929: S & M v2 p331.

487	£750.00	525	£50.00
488	£275.00	526	£65.00
489	£180.00	527	£25.00
490	£120.00	528	£20.00
491	£100.00	529	£95.00
492	£95.00	530	£65.00
493	£250.00	531	£75.00
494	£25.00	532	£25.00
495	£120.00	533	£45.00
496	£85.00	534	£40.00
497	£95.00	535	£135.00
498	£60.00	536	£150.00
499	£90.00	537	£250.00
500	£120.00	538	£275.00
501	£85.00	539	£50.00
502	£75.00	540	£35.00
503	£25.00	541	£25.00
504	£30.00	542	£60.00
505	£25.00	543	£25.00
506	£25.00	544	£250.00
507	£30.00	545	£200.00
508	£30.00	546	£90.00
509	£20.00	547	£90.00
510	£150.00	548	£100.00
511	£120.00	549	£120.00
512	£450.00	550	£175.00
513	£45.00	551	£130.00
514	£30.00	552	£150.00
515	£50.00	553	£180.00
516	£45.00	554	£95.00
517	£25.00	555	£75.00
518	£420.00	556	£130.00
519	£25.00	557	£70.00
520	£75.00	558	£45.00
521	£180.00	559	£60.00
522	£90.00	560	£25.00
523	£60.00	561	SOLD
524	£60.00	562	£35.00

563 **Snell (E. H. T): Principles of Equity:** 1st Ed. 1868: S & M v1 p332.

564 **Speeches made in Parliament on several important occasions. Recommended to the Electors of Great Britain as a seasonable preparative for the ensuing Elections:** 1733:

565 **Spelman (Sir H): Spelmanni Reliquiae the Posthumous works of Sir Hen. Spelman, relating to the laws and antiquity of England; containing, I The original growth, propagation and condition of feuds and tenures by knight-service in England. II. Of the ancient government of England. 3. Of Parliaments. 4. Of the Original of the four terms of the year (Published from the original M. S. in the Bodleian Library) 5. Of the original of testaments and wills, and of their probats, and to whom it anciently belonged; with several other tracts, Chiefly relating to the history and antiquities of England:** 1st Ed. 1698: S & M v1 p37.

566 **Spelman (Sir H): Work of Sir H. Spelman published in his life time, together with his posthumous works:** 2nd Ed. collected by Edmund, Bishop of London: 1727: S & M v1 p37.

567 **State papers, published under the authority of his Majesty's commission King Henry VIII:** Parts 1-4 in 5 vols: 1831-36:

568 **Stanfield: Trial of James Evans:** 1826:

569 **Stephen (Sir J. F): History of the Criminal Law of England:** vols: 1883: (also available in reprint): S & M v2 p339.

570 **Stephen (Sir J. R.): General View of the Criminal Law of England:** 2nd Ed: 1890:

571 **Stephen (H. J): Commentaries on the Laws of England:** 21st Ed. 4 vols: 1950: S & M v2 p339.

572 **Stephen (H. J): On Pleading:** 5th Ed. 1843: S & M v2 p339.

573 **Stephen (H. J): Commentaries on the Laws of England:** 2nd Ed. 4 vols: 1848: S & M v2 p339.

574 **Strange (Sir J): Reports of Cases [1716-1749] in the courts of Chancery, King's Bench, Common Pleas and Exchequer:** 1st Ed. 2 vols: 1755: S & M v1 p309.

575 **Street (H. A): Ultra vires: Being and Investigation of the Principles which limit the Powers and Liabilites of Corporations, Quasi-Corporate Bodies and Non-Sovereign Legislature (Based on the work by S. Brice K. C):** 1930: S & M v2 p344.

576 **Stroud (D. A): Mens Rea, or imputability under the law of England:** 1914: (Reprint may be shortly available): S & M v2 p345.

577 **Stryne (J): Memorials of the most reverend father in God, Thomas Cranmer, sometime Lord Archbishop of Canterbury:** 3 books in 1 volume: 1694:

578 **Stubbs (W) and Talmash (G): Crown circuit companion; containing the practice of the Assizes on the Crown Side And of the Courts of General and General Quarter Sessions of the Peace (with) the Clerk of Assise's Circuit Companion:** 5th Ed. 1783: S & M v1 p360.

579 **Style (W): Regestrum Practicale, or the Practical Register; or Accomplish'd Attorney consisting of Rules, Orders, and Observations concerning the practice of the Common-Law in [the] Courts at Westminster, particulary the King's Bench:** 1st Ed. 1657: S & M v1 p279.

580 **Style (W): Narrationes Modernae, or, Modern Reports, Upper Bench Court at Westminster [1646-55], as well on the criminal as on the pleas side:** 1658: S & M v1 p310.

581 **Sullivan (F. S): Historical Treatise on the Feudal Law and the Constitution and Laws of England, with a commentary on Magna Charta and illustrations of many English Statutes: Lectures in the University of Dublin:** 2nd Ed. 1772: S & M v1 p18.

582 **Swinburne (H): Briefe Treatise of Testements and Last Willes, [with] divers Statutes: besides notes, and Quotations,** 4th Ed. 1677: "A very useful summary" — Holdsworth, History of English Law: S & M v1 p494.

583 ______ 5th Ed. 1728:

584 ______ 7th Ed. with additions by J. J. Powell: 3 vols: 1803:

585 **Taxatio Ecclesiastica Angliae et Walliae. Auctoritate P. Nicholai IV circa 1291:** 1802: The Taxation of Pope Nicholas is a most important record, because all the taxes, as well to our Kings as the Popes, were regulated by it, until the survey made in 26 Henry VIII: S & M v1 p88.

586 **Testa de Nevill, sive Liber Feodorum in Curia Scaccarii temp Hen. III and Edw. I [1216-1307]:** 1807: An account of Knights fees, Serjeanties, Widows and Heiresses of Tenants in Capite, Escheats, Scutages and Aids: S & M v1 p88.

587 **Tables of all the cases printed in the books of Reports, digested under proper heads; to which is added the names of all the cases in alphabetical order:** 1719:

588 **Table of Fees of the Courts at Westminster, as they were delivered in Parliament, with the Fees of the Clerk of Assize of the Peace of Middlesex, Surry, Clerk of Assize of the home circuit, and of the cursitor's office. Also the fees settled by Act of Parliament for the relief of insolvent debtors, with respect to the imprisonment of their persons, fees taken by wardens of the Fleet, and other gaolers. Likewise the fees of several Courts of request in the counties throughout England:** 1760: S & M v1 p284.

589 **Thesaurus Linguae Romanae Britannicae:** 1578:

590 **Thomas (R): Historical Essay on the Magna Charta of King John [with] the Great Charter in Latin and English, the Charters of Liberties and Confirmations granted by Henry II and Edward I, the original Charter of the Forests, and instruments connected with them, notes and other illustrations:** 1829: S & M v1 p551.

591 **Tidd (W): Forms of Practical proceedings in the Courts of King's Bench:** 6th Ed. 1824: S & M v2 p357.

592 **Tidd(W): The Practice of the Court of King's Bench and Common Pleas, in personal actions and ejectments:** 6th Ed. 2 vols: 1824:

593 ______ 9th Ed. 2 vols: 1828:

594 **Tithe Communication Returns:** 1853: Ordered to be printed by the House of Commons 1848:

595 **Toller(Sir S): Law of Tithes:** 1st Ed. 1808: S & M v2 p358.

596 ______ 3rd Ed. 1822:

597 **Toller (Sir S): Law of Executors and Administrators:** 6th Ed. 1827: S & M V1 p358.

598 **Tomlin (Sir T. E): Law Dictionary, explaining the Rise, Progress, and Present State of the British Law:** 3rd Ed 2 vols: 1820: S & M v2 p259.

599 **Tomlin (Sir T. E): Index to the Term Reports:** 1806: S & M v2 p359.

600 **Touching Ships Money:** 1641:

601 **Traill (J C): New Parishes Acts 1843, 1844, and 1856:** 1857: S & M v2 p360.

602 **Treatise of Sanguinary Law against Papists:** 1664:

603 **Tremaine (Sir J): Placita Coronae; or Pleas of the Crown in matters Criminal and Civil. Containing a collection of modern Precedents Digested by John Rice:** 1723: S & M v1 p366.

604 **Tryal of John Aycliffe:** 1759:

605 **Trial Between Craig and Armesly:** 1744:

606 **Trial Between Sir W. Pritchard and Thomas Papillan before Judge Jeffreys:** 1689:

607 **Trial of Colonel Montague Burgoyne:** 1800:

608 **Trial of the Earl of Macclesfield:** 1725:

609 **The Tryal of Dr. H. Sacheverall:** 1710:

610 **The Times Reports of the Trial of William Palmer:** 1856:

611 **Trial of Miss Madeline H. Smith:** 1857

612 **Trial of the Regicides:** 1660:

613 **Tryals 1678-1680:** 1689:

614 **Turner (S): Present Practice and Costs in the High Court of Chancery, with directions [and] appendix of precedents:** 4th Ed. with additions by R. Venables: 2 vols: 1810: S & M v1 p342.

615 **Tyler (J E): Oaths:** 1st Ed. 1834: S & M v2 p363.

616 **Uniformity of the Government of England:** 1647:

617 **Valor Ecclesiasticus temp. Hen VIII auctoritate regia institutuo A. D. 1535. Edited by J. Caley and J. Hunter:** Parts 1-4 in 6 volumes: 1810-34: This is a kind of Domesday of Church property, taken for the purposes of ascertaining the whole and true value of all possessions, as well spiritual as temporal, belonging to any manor of dignity, monastery, priory etc., in England, Wales, Calais and the Marches: S & M v1 p89.

618 **Vaughan (Sir J): Reports and Arguments in the Common Pleas, being all of them Special Cases and many wherein he pronounced the resolution of the whole Court of Common Pleas at the time he was Chief Justice there; to which is added a tract concerning the Process out of the Courts of Westminster into Wales; Published by his son Edward Vaughan [1665-74]:** 1st Ed. 1677: S & M v1 p310.

619 ______ 2nd Ed. 1706:

620 **Ventris (Sir P): Reports in two parts. Part I containing cases of the King's Bench [1668-84] with three learned arguments, one in the K. B. by Sir F. North, and two in the Exchequer by Sir M. Hale. Part II containing cases in the Common Pleas [1669-91] with Special Pleadings in the same; together with many remarkable and curious cases in the Court of Chancery:** 1701: 2 parts: 1701: S & M v1 p310.

621 ______ 3rd Ed. 2 parts: 1716:

622 **Vernon (T): Cases argued and adjudged in the High Court of Chancery [1681-1720]:** 1st Ed. 2 vols: 1726-1728: S & M v1 p349.

623 **Vesey (F. Snr): Reports of Cases in Chancery 1746-55 in the time of L. C. Hardwicke:** 1st Ed. 2 vols: 1771: S & M v1 p349.

624 ______ 2nd Ed. 2 vols: 1773:

625 **Viner (C): General Abridgment of Law and Equity; Alphabetically digested under Proper Titles, with Notes and References:** 1st Ed. 24 vols: 1741-58: S & M v1 p20.

626 **Voet (J): Commentanus ad pandectas:** 2 vols: 1707:

627 **Wake (W): The state of the Church and Clergy of England. Historically deduced from the conversation of the Saxons to the Present time:** 1703, occasioned by Dr. Atterbut:

628 **Watkins (C): Treatise on Copyholds:** 1st Ed. 1797: S & M v1 p406.

629 ______ 2nd Ed. 1804:

630 ______ 4th Ed. with additions by T. Coventry: 2 vols: 1825:

631 **Watson (S): Law of Partnership:** 2nd Ed. 1807: S & M v2 p372.

632 **Watson (W H): Law relating to the office and Duty of Sheriff:** 1st Ed. 1827: Written to guide Undersheriffs: S & M v2 p372.

633 **Watson: The Office of Sheriff:** 2nd Ed. 1848:

634 **Webb, Piggot and Northey: New Precedents in Conveyancing containing great variety of curious draughts, many of them on special occassion:** 1742:

635 **Wentworth (J): Complete system of Pleading; comprehending precedents and Forms of Practice, with an index to the principal work; incorporating and making it a continuation of Townshends and Cornwall's Tables:** 10 vols: 1797-99: S & M v1 p280.

636 **Wentworth (T): Office and Duty of Executors; or treatise of Wills and Executors directed to Testators in the choice of their Executors and contrivance of their Wills with the supplement By H. Curson** 1774: with additions by G. Wilson: The first two editions were ananymous. It has been ascribed to Judge Dodderidge: S & M v1 p494.

637 **Whishaw (J): New Law Dictonary:** 1829:

638 **White (F. T) and Tudor (O. D): Leading Cases in Equity:** 8th Ed. 2 vols: S & M v2 p377.

639 **Wilkins (D): Leges Anglo-Saxonicae Ecclesiasticae & Civiles, accedunt Leges Edvardi Latinae, Guilielmi Conquestoris Gallo-Normannicae, et Henrici I, Latinae; Subjungitur Henr. Spelmanni Codex Legum Veterum Statutorum Regni Angliae, quae ab ingressu Dissertatio Epistolaris admodum Guilielmi Nicolsoni de Jure Feudali Veterum Saxonum:** 1721:

640 **Williams (G. L): Liability for Animals:** 1939: S & M v1 p43.

641 **Williams: Proof of Guilt:** 2nd Ed. 1958:

642 **Williams (T. W): Abstract of Public Acts:** 1816-18: S & M v2 p284.

643 **Williams (W): Jus Appellandi ad Regum ipsum a Can-cellaria; or Manifestation of the King's Part and Power to relieve his Subjects against erroneous and unjust Decrees in Chancery:** 1783: S & M v1 p342.

644 **Williams (T. W): Compendious Digest of the Statute Law; an abridgment of all Public Acts of Parliament from Magna Charta:** 1st Ed. 1787: S & M v1 p567

645 ______ 3rd Ed. 2 vols: 1790:

646 **Willis (B): Notitia Parliamentaria; or History of Counties, Cities and Boroughs in England and Wales:** 1st Ed. 2 vols: 1716: S & M v1 p418.

647 **Eardley-Wilmot (Sir J. E): Notes of Opinions and Judgments delivered in different Courts:** 1802: S & M v2 p106.

648 **Wilmot: Memoirs of Sir John Eardley-Wilmot:** 1811:

649 **Wilson (G): Reports, King's Court at Westminster; King's Bench [1742-53], Common Pleas [1753]-74:** 1st Ed. Parts 1-3 in 2 vols: 1770-1775: S & M v1 p310.

650 ______ 2nd Ed. Parts 1-3 in 2 vols: 1779-84:

563	£55.00		
564	£25.00		
565	£180.00	624	£40.00
566	£85.00	625	£475.00
567	£50.00	626	£200.00
568	£30.00	627	£25.00
569	£100.00	628	£80.00
570	£50.00	629	£25.00
571	£45.00	630	£35.00
572	£25.00	631	£45.00
573	£90.00	632	£40.00
574	£75.00	633	£30.00
575	£30.00	634	£55.00
576	£30.00	635	£100.00
577	£50.00	636	£50.00
578	£85.00	637	£25.00
579	£75.00	638	£45.00
580	£80.00	639	£45.00
581	£35.00	640	£25.00
582	£110.00	641	£20.00
583	£70.00	642	£30.00
584	£85.00	643	£40.00
585	£140.00	644	£35.00
586	£75.00	645	£30.00
587	£25.00	646	£100.00
588	£30.00	647	£25.00
589	£120.00	648	£25.00
590	£35.00	649	£90.00
591	£45.00	650	£60.00
592	£85.00		
593	£70.00		
594	£25.00		
595	£50.00		
596	£30.00		
597	£30.00		
598	£90.00		
599	£25.00		
600	£140.00		
601	£20.00		
602	£85.00		
603	£150.00		
604	£70.00		
605	£125.00		
606	£180.00		
607	£60.00		
608	£95.00		
609	£75.00		
610	£40.00		
611	£25.00		
612	£160.00		
613	£350.00		
614	£25.00		
615	£30.00		
616	£60.00		
617	£550.00		
618	£95.00		
619	£45.00		
620	£65.00		
621	£40.00		
622	£85.00		
623	£55.00		

652 **Company Law: Principal distinctions between the Laws of England and Scotland:** 1912: S & M v2 p388.

653 **Winch (Sir H): Le Beau-Pledeur; a Book of Entries, containing, Declarations, Informations, and other Pleadings, with Special Verdicts and Demurrers in most actions Real, Personal and Mixt, argued and adjudged in the Court of Westminster:** 1680: S & M v1 p280.

654 **Winch (Sir H): Reports containing many choice cases [in Court of Common Pleas] and excellent matters touching declarations, pleadings, demurrers, judgments, and Resolutions in points of Law 1621-25:** 1657: S & M v1 p310.

655 **Wood(E): Complete Body of Conveyancing in theory and practice:** 1st Ed. Parts 1 and 2 in 3 vols: 1749: S & M v1 p488.

656 **Wood (H): A collection of decrees by the Court of Exchequer [1650-1798] in Tithe Causes:** 4 vols: 1798-99: S & M v1 p197.

657 **Wood (T): An institute of the Laws of England; or, Laws of England in their natural order according to common use:** 2nd Ed. 4 books in 1 vol: 1722: S & M v1 p38.

658 ——— 3rd Ed. 4 books in 1 vol: 1724:

659 ——— 7th Ed. 4 books in 1 vol: 1745:

660 ——— 9th Ed. 4 books in 1 vol: 1763:

661 ——— 10th Ed. 4 books in 1 vol: 1772:

662 **Wooddeson (R): Systematical View of the Laws of England as treated of in a course of Vinerian Lectures at Oxford, commencing in 1777:** 3 vols: 1792-93: S & M v1 p38.

663 **Wordsworth (C F): Law and Practice of Elections:** 2nd Ed. 1835: S & M v2 p392.

664 **Wright (A): Court Hand restored ; or, Student's Assistant in reading Old Deeds, Charters etc. with appendix containing the ancient names of Places in Great Britain and Ireland; also table of ancient surnames:** 7th Ed. 1834: S & M v1 p14.

665 **Wright (Sir M): Introduction to the Law of Tenures:** 3rd Ed. 1750: Dublin Edition: A work well recieved by the profession: S & M v1 p460.

666 ——— 3rd Ed. 1768:

652	£25.00	662	£50.00
653	£75.00	663	£25.00
654	£85.00	664	£25.00
655	£150.00	665	£85.00
656	£75.00	666	£60.00
657	£180.00	667-676	Orig. Eds. — Full
658	£140.00		details on application.
659	£90.00		Also available in reprint
660	£85.00		see Classical English Law
661	£90.00		Texts series.

PRINTING AND BINDING FACILITIES

We have a modern workshop on the premises in which we print and bind a wide range of our own publications from vast series such as the **English Reports** to monographs. Our binding is mainly by hand, using traditional methods to give a long lasting and handsome finish to our products and we are able to offer this service to institutions or individuals who wish to rebind some or all of their libraries

667 **Year Book:** Edward III: 1-10: 1679: S & M v1 p312/313

668 ——— Edward III: 1-10: with notes by Brooke and Fitzherbert 1596:

669 ——— Edward III: 1-39: 1619:

670 ——— Edward III: 17-39: 1619: Printed for the company of Stationers:

671 ——— Edward III: 40-50: 1679:

672 ——— Henry IV: 1-14 and Henry V 1, 2, 5, 7, 8, 9 with notes by Tottell:

673 ——— Henry VI: 1-20: 1609: Printed for the company of Stationers:

674 ——— Henry VI: 21-39: notes by Wight 1601:

675 ——— Edward IV: 1-22: notes by Wight and Norton: 1599:

676 ——— Edward IV: 1-22: 1640:

677 **Yelverton (Sir H): Les Reports de divers special cases en le Court del Bank le Roy [1602-13]:** 1st Ed. 1661: Published from a Manuscript owned by Thomas Twisden and published by W. Wyled: S & M v1 p310.

678 ——— 2nd Ed. 1674:

679 **Yelverton (Sir H): Reports of divers special cases, King's Bench, [1602-13] originally Published in French, now Translated into English:** 3rd Ed. 1735: S & M v1 p311.

680 **Young Clerk's Magazine; or English Repository. Containing a variety of the most useful Precedents of Articles of Agreements, Bonds, Bills, Recognizances, Releases, and other instruments, with directions for making Distresses for Rent etc., the doctrine of Fines and Recoveries, and their forms, together with those of Common Writs, Affidavits, Memorials for registering Deeds, etc., in Middlesex, also Declarations in the King's Bench and Common Pleas:** 2nd Ed. By the author of the Students Law Dictonary: 1740: S & M v1 p280.

681 **Zouchei (R): Quaestionum Juris Civilis centuria im Decem classes distributae:** 2nd Ed. 1682:

677	£60.00
678	£40.00
679	£55.00
680	£30.00
681	£70.00

...s Lane, Chichester, Sussex.
...ID (tel. 0243 784531).

Short-run reprint service

PROFESSIONAL BOOKS, based at 46 Milton Trading Estate, Abingdon, Oxon OX14 4SY (tel. 0235 834821), offers a short-run reprint service to publishers of professional books for the reprinting of textbooks and journals which have gone out of print but which are still of importance in certain jurisdictions.

The facility is restricted to runs of at least 100, but the company is prepared to consider lower figures.

As well as being a publisher and bookseller, Professional Books also has its own bindery on the premises and can offer facilities for handbinding books, journals and reports with a wide range of binding materials available.

SCOTLAND

MAJOR WORKS

M97 **Brown's Synopsis of Decisions in the Court of Session: 1540-1827:** Volumes 1-4:

M98 **Encyclopedia of Laws of Scotland: 1926-1935:** Volumes 1-16:

M99 **Faculty Digest of all reported Decisions in the Court of Session: 1868-1922:** 6 volumes with supplementary volumes to 1960(last published):

M100 **Faculty Decisions of the Court of Session(Original Ed.): 1752-1841:**

Old Series 1752-1808:(14 volumes)
New Series 1808-1825:(7 volumes)
Third Series 1825-1841:(16 volumes)

M101 **Green's Encyclopedia of Scots Law: 1896-1904:** 14 vols:

M102 **House of Lords: Reports of Scotch Appeals: 1707-1873:**

Robertson 1 vols: 1707-1727:
Paton 6 vols: 1726-1831:
Shaw 2 vols: 1821-1824:
Wilson & Shaw 7 vols: 1825-1834:
Shaw & Maclean 3 vols: 1835-1838:
Maclean & Robinson 1 vol: 1839:
Robinson 2 vols: 1840-1841:
Bell 7 vols: 1842-1850:
Macqueen 4 vols: 1851-1865:
Paterson 2 vols: 1851-1873:

M103 **Juridical Review: 1889-1980:** Volumes 1-92:
Indiv. volumes also available:

M104 **Morison's Dictionary of Decisions: 1540-1808:** 24 volumes:

M105 **Public General Statutes affecting Scotland(Blackwood Ed.):** 3 volumes,1707-1847 and annual volumes 1848-1947,103 volumes:

M106 **Scots Current Law Statutes 1949-1980:** volumes 1-32:

M107 **Scottish Current Law Yearbook: 1948-1980:** Volumes 1-33:
Indiv. volumes also available:

*M108 **Scots Digest of appeals in House of Lords from 1707 and of Cases in Supreme Court of Scotland: 1800-1944:** 11 volumes:
Indiv. volumes available:

M109 **Scottish Jurist: 1829-1873:** Volumes 1-45:
Indiv volumes also available:

*M110 **Scots Law Times: 1893-1980:**

M111 **Scottish Land Court Reports: 1913-1954:** Volumes 1-42 (Continuing):

M112 **Scottish Law Reporter and Digest: 1865-1924:**
Reports: Volumes 1-61:
Digest: Volumes 1-32:
Indiv volumes also available:

M113 **Scottish Law Review and Sheriff Court Reports: 1885-1963**
Volumes 1-79:
Indiv. volumes also available:

*M114 **Scots Revised Reports:** 45 vols: These are a reissue of many Scots decisions prior to 1873: They were published between 1898-1908:

M115 **Scots Statutes Revised: 1424-1900:** 10 volumes:

M116 **Scots Statutes Revised: 1901-1948:** 12 volumes:Continues previous entry:

*M117 **Session Cases:**
1st series 1-16: 1824-1838: (Shaw & Dunlop):
2nd series 1-24: 1838-1862: (Dunlop):
3rd series 1-11: 1862-1873: (Macpherson):
4th series 1-25: 1873-1898: (Rettie):
5th series: 1898-1906: (Fraser):
New series: 1907-1972:(Continuing):

M118 **Sheriff's Court Digest: 1893-1943:**

M119 **The Stair Society:24 volumes:(Continuing):**

SCOTLAND
Major Works

M97	£160.00	M98	£120.00	M106	£650.00	M115	£180.00
		M99	£300.00	M107	£300.00	M116	£300.00
		M100	£900.00	M108	£120.00	M117	£7,500.00
		M101	£75.00	M109	£850.00	M118	£20.00
		M102	£950.00	M110	£3,000.00	M119	£180.00
		M103	£1,500.00	M111	£480.00		
		M104	£650.00	M112	£800.00		
		M105	£540.00	M113	£750.00		
				M114	£900.00		

682 **The Acts Made in the first Parliament of our most high and dread soveraign Charles the first:** 1683: S & M Scot p113

683 **Acts of Parliament James VII:** 1731: S & M Scot. p117.

684 **Act of Sederunt of the Lords of Council and Session; from the Institution of the College of Justice, in May 1532 to January, 1553. Taken from Records of the Court of His Majesty General Register House. To which are added some of the Acts made at after periods, the records of which are lost. Taken from old manuscripts By Ilay Campbell.** 1811: S & M Scot p3.

685 **Acts of Sederunt from January 15, 1553 to July 11, 1790. Collected by W. Tait:** 1790: S & M Scot p3.

686 **Acts of Sederunt of the Court of Session (1628-1740):** 2 vols: 1740: S & M Scot p2.

687 **Acts of Sederunt from 1810-21:** 1821: S & M Scot p3.

688 **Alexander (W): Abridgment of the Acts of Sederunt from 1532 to 1838:** 1838: S & M Scot p4.

689 **Alexander (W): Digest of the Bankruptcy (Scotland) Act 1856:** S & M Scot p5.

Teatises

682	£130.00
683	£120.00
684	£60.00
685	£120.00
686	£60.00
687	£45.00
688	£60.00
689	£20.00

690 **An Analytical Digest of cases decided in the Supreme Courts of Scotland and on appeal by the House of Lords:** 1867-1895: 3 vols: S & M Scot p8.

691 **Anderson (W): The Speeches and Judgments of the Right Honourable The Lords of Council and Session in Scotland, George-James Duke of Hamilton against Archibald Douglas:** 1768:

692 **Anderson (A. M): Criminal Law:** 2nd Ed. 1904: S & M Scot p6.

693 **Arnot (H): Celebrated Criminal Trials in Scotland 1536-1784:** 1st Ed. 1784: S & M Scot p6.

694 **Balfour (Sir J): Practicks of the Law of Scotland:** 1754: A collection from the books of law, Acts of Parliament and decrees of the session, compiled in sixteenth century and traditionally ascribed to Balfour: S & M Scot p8.

695 **Barclay (H): Digest of the Law of Scotland for Justices of the Peace:** 2nd Ed. 1855: S & M Scot p9.
696 _______ 3rd Ed. 1865:

697 **Bayne (A): Notes for Students of Municipal Law:** 1s Ed. 1731: S & M Scot p10.

698 **Begg (J. H): Law of Scotland relating to Law Agents:** 2nd Ed. 1883: S & M Scot p10.

699 **Bell (A. M): Lectures on Conveyancing:** 2nd Ed. 2 vols: 1876: S & M Scot p10.
700 _______ 3rd Ed. 2 vols: 1882:

701 **Bell (G. J): Commentaries on the Laws of Scotland in relation to Mercantile and Maritime Laws, Moveable and Heritable Rights and Bankeruptcy:** 2 vols: 3rd Ed. 1819: Having no detailed and authoritative precedent on which to rely Bell . . . practically created the Law Merchant for Scotland . . . Stair Society Pub: S & M Scot p10.
702 _______ 4th Ed. 2 vols: 1821:
703 _______ 7th Ed. 2 vols: 1870:

704 **Bell (G. J): Principles of the Law of Scotland:** 3rd Ed. 4 vols: Intended originally for use of students and for "sudden ccasions of practice," it gradually expanded until it attained the status of an institute in all but form . . . Stair Society Pub: 1833: S & M Scot p11.
705 _______ 6th Ed. with notes By W. Guthrie: 1872:
706 _______ 7th Ed. with notes By W. Guthrie: 1876:
707 _______ 8th Ed. with notes By W. Guthrie: 2 vols: 1885:
708 _______ 10th Ed. with notes By W. Guthrie: 1899:

709 **Bell (G. J): Illustrations from Adjudged Cases of the Principles of the Law of Scotland:** 3 vols:1836-38: S & M Scot p10.

710 **Bell (J. M): Law of Arbitration in Scotland:** 2nd Ed. 1877: S & M Scot p11.

711 **Bell (R): Cases decided in the Court of Session from 1790-92:** 1794: S & M Scot p11.

712 **Bell (R): Cases decided in the Court of Session 1793-95:** 1796: S & M Scot p11.

713 **Bell (R): System of the Forms of Deeds:** 1st Ed. 7 vols: 1801: S & M Scot p11.
714 _______ 2nd Ed. 7 vols:
715 _______ 3rd Ed. 7 vols: 1817:

716 **Bell (W): Dictionary and Digest of the Laws of Scotland, with short explanations of the most ordinary English Law Terms:** 4th Ed. with notes By G. Watson: 1890: S & M Scot p12.

717 **Birnie (J. B. L): Married Women's Property (Scotland) Act 1881 with Notes:** 1883: S & M Scot p13.

718 **Birnie (J. B. L): Notes on Issues in Jury Trials:** 1881: S & M Scot p13.

719 **Burn-Murdoch (H): Interdict in the Law of Scotland with a Chapter on Specific Performance:** 1933: S & M Scot p18.

720 **Burnet (J): Criminal Law of Scotland:** 1811: S & M Scot p18.

721 **Cockburn (Lord): Journal of Henry Cockburn being a continuation of the memorials of his time 1831-1834:** 2nd Ed. 2 vols: 1874: S & M Scot p22.

722 **Cockburn (Lord): Examination of the Trials for sedition:** 1888: S & M Scot p22.

723 **Clark (A. J): Destinations and Vesting according to the Law of Scotland:** 1927: S & M Scot p22.

724 **Connolly (R. J): Handbook on Workmen's compensation Acts, 1906-23:** 1925: S & M Scot p24.

725 **Connell (I): Agricultural Holdings (Scotland) Acts, the Ground Game Act, and other Acts:** 1923: S & M Scot p23.

726 **Craig (Sir T): Jus Feudale, etc. Ed. 3a, accessit rerum et verborum index una cum regularum seu axiomatum ac vocabulorum, forensium interpretatione. Opera Jacobi aille:** 1732: "One of the greatest Lawyers this Country has produced". S & M Scot p26.

727 **Craigie (J): Conveyancing Statutes 1214-1894:** 1895: S & M Scot p27.

728 **Craigie (J): Digest of the Scottish Law of Conveyancing. Heritable Rights:** 1st Ed. 1887: S & M Scot p27.
729 _______ 2nd Ed. 1891:
730 _______ 3rd Ed. 1890:
731 _______ 4th Ed. 1909:

732 **Craigie (J): Digest of the Scottish Law of Conveyancing Moveable Rights:** 2nd Ed. 1894: S & M Scot p27.

733 **Crichton (D): Analysis of the Ballot Act:** 1873: S & M Scot p27.

734 **Currie (J. G): Confirmation of Executors in Scotland:** 5th Ed. 1945: S & M Scot p27.

735 **Dallas (G): Systems of Stiles:** 1st Ed. 1697: S & M Scot p28.

736 **Dalrymple (Sir H): Decisions, Court of Session (1697-1718)** 1792: S & M Scot p29.

737 **Dalrymple (Sir D): Decisions of the Court of Session 1766-1791:** 2 vols: Edited by M. P. Brown: 1826: S & M Scot p28.

738 **Dirleton (Lord): (Sir J. Nisbet): Doubts and Questions in the Law as also some Decisions 1665-77:** 1st Ed. 1698: S & M Scot p31.

739 **Douglas (R): Peerage of Scotland:** 2 vols: 1764:
740 _______ with notes by J. P. Wood: 1813:

741 **Edgar (J): Decisions, Court of session, 1724-25:** 1st Ed. 1742: S & M Scot p38

742 **Ellis (C C): Local Government act, 1894, etc.** 1912: S & M Scot p29

743 **Erskine (John): Institute of the Law of Scotland:** 1st Ed. 1773: 2 vols: S & M Scot p40.
744 _______ New Ed. with notes by J. Ivory: 1828: 2 vols:
745 _______ New Ed. With notes by A. Macallen: 1838:
746 _______ 4th Ed. 2 vols: 1805:

747 **Erskine (J): Principles of the Law of Scotland:** 1st Ed. 2 vols: 1754: S & M Scot p40.

748 **Esslemont (W. D): Handbook of the Commercial Law of Scotland:** 3rd Ed. 1929: S & M Scot p40.

749 **Fraser (P): Husband and Wife, according to the Law of Scotland:** 2nd Ed. 2 vols: 1876/1878: S & M Scot p44.

750 **Ferguson (J): Reports of some recent decisions, by the Constitutional court of Scotland in Actions of Divorce, 1811-17:** 1st Ed. 1817: S & M Scot p42.

751 **Fyfe (T. A): Law and Practice of the Sheriff Courts:** 1913: S & M Scot p45.

752 **General Report of the Commissioiners appointed to inquire into the State of municipal corporations in Scotland:** 1835:

753 **Gibson (Sir A): Decisions of the Lords of Council and Session, 1621-42:** 1690: S & M Scot p46.

754 **Glegg (A. T): Law of Reparation:** 1st Ed. 1892: S & M Scot p46.

755 **Gloag (W. M) and Hederson (R. C): Introduction to the Law of Scotland:** 6th Ed. 1956: S & M Scot p47.

756 **Gloag (W. M) and Irvine (J. M): Law of Rights in Security, Heritable and Moveable:** 1897: S & M Scot p47.

757 **Guthrie (G): Digest of Cases in Sheriff Court prior to December, 1894, as reported in the S. L. Review and Guthries Select Cases:** 1895: S & M Scot p48.

690 .... £60.00
691 .... £45.00
692 .... £25.00
693 .... £70.00
694 .... £95.00
695 .... £25.00
696 .... £20.00
697 .... £25.00
698 .... £25.00
699 .... £35.00
700 .... £35.00
701 .... £95.00
702 .... £80.00
703 .... £120.00
704 .... £40.00
705 .... £40.00
706 .... £40.00
707 .... £45.00
708 .... £45.00
709 .... £35.00
710 .... £25.00
711 .... £30.00
712 .... £30.00
713 .... £120.00
714 .... £65.00
715 .... £80.00
716 .... £55.00
717 .... £25.00
718 .... £30.00
719 .... £28.00
720 .... £75.00
721 .... £150.00
722 .... £60.00
723 .... £30.00
724 .... £20.00
725 .... £20.00
726 .... £95.00
727 .... £25.00
728 .... £45.00
729 .... £25.00
730 .... £25.00
731 .... £30.00
732 .... £35.00
733 .... £25.00
734 .... £20.00
735 .... £85.00
736 .... £150.00
737 .... £90.00
738 .... £175.00
739 .... £40.00
740 .... £30.00
741 .... £55.00
742 .... £25.00
743 .... £200.00
744 .... £140.00
745 .... £85.00
746 .... £95.00
747 .... £160.00
748 .... £30.00
749 .... £45.00
750 .... £60.00
751 .... £25.00
752 .... £25.00
753 .... £120.00
754 .... £40.00
755 .... £20.00
756 .... £30.00
757 .... £35.00

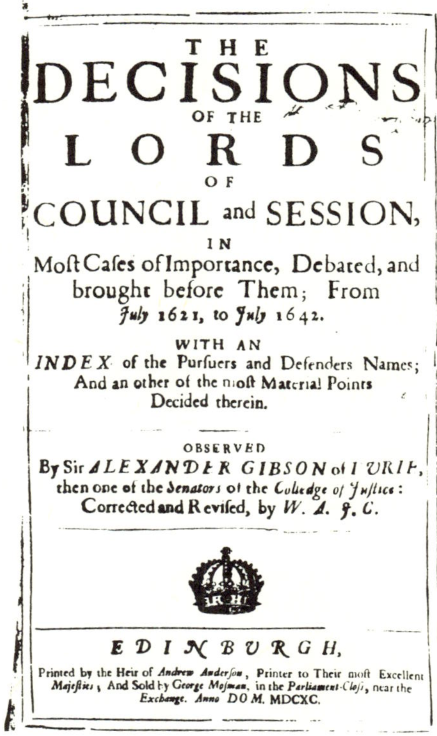
THE
DECISIONS
OF THE
LORDS
OF
COUNCIL and SESSION,
IN
Most Cases of Importance, Debated, and brought before Them; From *July* 1621, to *July* 1642.
WITH AN
INDEX of the Pursuers and Defenders Names; And an other of the most Material Points Decided therein.
OBSERVED
By Sir *ALEXANDER GIBSON* of *DURIE*, then one of the *Senators* of the *Colledge of Justice*: Corrected and Revised, by *W. A. J. C.*
EDINBURGH,
Printed by the Heir of *Andrew Anderson*, Printer to Their most Excellent *Majesties*, And Sold by *George Mosman*, in the *Parliament-Closs*, near the *Exchange*. *Anno* DOM. MDCXC.

758 **Grierson (P. J. H): Law of Stamp Duties on Written Instruments:** S & M Scot p48.

759 **Goudy (H): Law of Bankruptcy:** 2nd Ed. 1895: S & M Scot p47.

760 ———— 3rd Ed. 1903:

761 **Halkerston (P): Compendium, or Index of the Decisions reported by the Faculty of Advocates from 1752-1817:** 1819: S & M Scot p49.

762 **Herbert (D): Fish and Fisheries, a selection of prize essays of the International Fisheries Exhibition:** 1883: S & M Scot p51.

763 **Henderson (R. C): Principles of Vesting in the Law of Succession:** 2nd Ed. 1938: S & M Scot p30.

764 **Hog (Sir R. of Harcarse): Decisions of the Court of Session from 1681-91:** 1st Ed. 1757: S & M Scot p51.

764 **Hume (D): Decisions of the court of Session, 1781-1822, in the form of a Dictionary:** 1839: S & M Scot p52.

766 **Hume (D): Commentaries on the Law of Scotland respecting Trial for Crimes:** 1800: S & M Scot p52.

767 **Inquisitionum ad Capellam Domini Regis retornatum, quae in publicis archivis Scotiae adhuc servantur, Abbrevato [circa 1546-1700]:** 3 vols: 1811-16 Edited by T. Thompson: S & M Scot p54.

768 **Juridical Styles a complete system of conveyancing adapted to the present practice of Scotland and the recent Statutes:** 3 vols (1 & 2 are 5th Ed., 3 is 3rd Ed.): 1881-88:
Vol 1 = Heritable rights:
Vol 2 = Movable Rights:
Vol 3 = Forms of Process:

769 **Johnston (C. N): Agricultural Holdings Acts:** 6th Ed. 2 vols: 1909: S & M Scot p55.

770 **Kames (Lord): Remarkable Decisions in the Court of Session 1716-52:** 2nd Ed. 2 vols: 1799: S & M Scot p57.

771 **Kames (Lord) (H. Home): Statute Law of Scotland abridged with Historical Notes:** 1st Ed. 1757: S & M Scot p57.

772 **Kames (Lord) (H. Home): Elucidations respecting the common and Statute Law of Scotland:** New Ed. 1800: S & M Scot p56.

773 **MacBrair (D. J): Digest of Decisions in the Supreme Court of Scotland and House of Lords from 1840-55:** 2 vols: 1852-56: S & M Scot p72.

774 **MacKay (A. E. J. G.): Manual of Practice in the Court of Session:** 1893: S & M Scot p73.

775 **Mackenzie (Sir G): Laws and Customs of Scotland in matters Criminal. Wherein is to be seen how the Civil Law and Laws and Customs of other nations do not agree with and supply ours:** 1678: S & M Scot p74.

776 **MacKenzie (Lord): Studies in Roman Law with Comparative views in the Laws of France, England and Scotland:** 2nd Ed. 1865:

777 **M'Laren (Lord J): Law of Wills and Succession:** 1st Ed. 2 vols: 1868: S & M Scot p75.

778 ———— 3rd Ed. 2 vols: 1894:

779 **MacKenzie (Sir G): Institutes of the Laws of Scotland:** 8th Ed. 1758: S & M Scot p73.

780 **Miller (W. G): Law of Nature and Nations in Scotland:** 1896: S & M Scot p80.

781 **Menzies (A. J. P): Lectures on Conveyancing according to the Law of Scotland:** 1856: S & M Scot 79.

782 **Menzies (A. J. P): Law of Scotland affecting Trustees:** 2nd Ed. 1913: S & M Scot p79.

783 **Mure (W. J): A handbook to the Local Government (Scotland) act:** 1889:

784 **Proceedings of the commissioners for the arrangments and preservation of the public records of the Kingdom:** 1808:

785 **Renton(R. W) and Brown (H. H): Criminal Procedure according to the Law of Scotland:** 1909: S & M Scot p96.

786 **Registrum Magni Sigilli Regum Scotorum in Archivis publicis asservatum Register of the Great Seal, 1306-1668:** 1814: S & M Scot p96.

787 **Ross (G): Leading Cases in the Commercial Law of England and Scotland:** 3 vols: 1853-57: S & M Scot p99.

788 **Ross (G): Leading Cases in the Law of Scotland [Land Rights, 1638-1849], prepared from the Original Pleadings arranged in systematic order, and elucidated by opinions of the Court. Never before Published:** 3 vols: 1849-51: S & M Scot p99.

789 **Rotuli Scotiae in Turri Londinensis et in Domo Capitularii Westm asservati temp 19 Edw. 1 — Hen. VIII [1290-1547] Edited by D Macpherson and others:** 2 vols: 1814-1818:

790 **Seton (G): Practical Analysis of the Act 17 & 18 Vict. c. 80 . . for the better Registration of Births, Deaths and Marriages in Scotland:** 4th Ed. 1861: S & M Scot p103.

791 **Shaw (P): Digest of Cases in the Supreme Courts of Scotland 1800-1863, House of Lords from 1726-1821:** 4 vols: 1843-1864: S & M Scot p104.

792 **Shaw (P): Digest of Cases decided in the Supreme Courts of Scotland from 1800-1867, and on Appeal by the House of Lords from 1726-1867. Being a new edition of the Digest from 1800-1852 by P. Shaw:** New Ed. by A. Bell and W. Lamond: 1867: S & M Scot p104.

793 ———— New Ed. continued to 1868 By A. Beatson & W. Lamond: 3 vols: 1869:

794 **Shaw (P) and Ballantine (J): Digest of Cases in the Court of Session 1821-24:** 2 vols: 1822/1824:

795 **Skene (Sir J) (Lord Curriehill): Lawes and Acts of Priliament maid be King James the First and his successours Kinges of Scotland [1424-1597]. Visied, collected and extracted furth of Register:** 1597:

796 **Skene (Sir J): Regiam Majestatem; Scotiae, Veteres Leges et Constitutiones, ex archivis publicis et antiquis libris manuscriptis collectae, recognite, et notis Juris Civilis, canonice, Nortmannici auctoritate confirmatis. Annotantur in margine concordantiae Juris Divini, Legum Angliae, et juris novissimi Scotiae quod Acta Parliamenti Vulgo Vocant etc.** 1st Ed. 1609 S & M Scot p106.

797 ———— 2nd Ed. 1774:

798 **Stair (Sir James Dalrymple) (First Viscount): An institute of the Laws of Scotland in Civil rights with observations upon the agreement or diversity between them and the laws of England:** 4 books in 3 vols: 1751-53 with notes By A. McDougall:

799 **Stair (Sir James Dalrymple) (First Viscount): Institutions of the Law of Scotland; deduced from its originals and collated with the civil, canon, and feudal Laws and with the customs of neighbouring nations:** 3rd Ed. 1759: S & M Scot p108.

800 ———— New Edition: 2 vols: 1832:

801 **Stephen (Sir J. F): General View of the criminal law of Scotland:** 1st Ed. 1863:

802 **Stuart (Sir J): Answers to Dirleton's Doubts in the Laws of Scotland:** 1st Ed. 1715: S & M Scot p117.

803 **Stuart (R), Milne (J) and Peddie (W): Reports of cases decided in the Court of Session, Teind Court. Court of Exchequer Court of Justiciary, and the House of Lords:** 2 vols: 1882:

804 **Swinton (A): Digest of Decisions by the Registration Appeal Court at Glasgow in the Year 1835-40:** 1840: S & M Scot p119

805 **Swinton (J): Abridgment of the Public Statutes (Scot):** 2 vols: 1788:

806 **Tod (T. H): Scots Black Kalendar:** 1938: S & M Scot p122.

IRELAND

Irish Jurist: 1935-1980:
*M120 Old Series: 1935-1965: Vols 1-31:
*M121 New Series: 1966-1980: Vols 32-46:

*M122 **Irish Law Times: 1867-1980:** Volumes 1-114:
Indiv. volumes also available:

Irish Reports: 1838-1974: Reports all the important cases heard in Ireland. Important to libraries which need a good comparative law collection:
*M123 Series I-IV: 1838-1894:
*M124 Series V: 1894-1925 (64 vols):
*M125 Series VI: 1926-1980 (55 vols):
Indiv. volumes also available. (Also available in reprint):

807 **Walder (N. M. L): Digest of Sheriff Court Practice:** 1932: S & M Scot p123.

808 **Walker (N. M. L): Digest of Sheriff Court Cases 1893-1943:** 1944: S & M Scot p123.

809 **Walker (J): Justice of the Peace (Scotland):** 1931: S & M Scot p123.

810 **Walton (F. P): Law of Husband and Wife in Scotland:** 2nd Ed. 1922: S & M Scot p124.

811 **Wight (A): Inquiry into the Rise and Progress of Parliament, chiefly in Scotland; and a complete System of the Law concerning the Elections of Representatives from Scotland to the Parliament of the United Kingdom:** 2 vols: 1806: S & M Scot p126.

812 **Wilton (G. W): Company Law and Practice in Scotland:** 1912: S & M Scot p127.

813 **Yorke (C): Considerations of Forfeiture for High Treason; with an Appendix concerning Estates Tail in Scotland:** 1775: S & M Scot p128

MAJOR WORKS

Irish Reports Digest: 1867-1970): Provides a brief summary of all the cases reported in the Irish Reports, Irish Law Times Reports and some cases reported in other series:
*M126 Stubbs: 1867-1893:
*M127 Maxwell: 1894-1918:
*M128 Rylands: 1919-1938 (2 volumes):
*M129 Harrison: 1939-1958 (2 volumes):
*M130 Ryan: 1959-1970:
(Also available in reprint):

*M131 **Irish Statutes (Acts of the Oireachtas): 1922-1980** Covers all acts passed in Ireland after 1922: English translation only except where the act was passed in Gaelic in which case the Gaelic version is also printed:
(also available in reprint: 1922-1976)

TEXTS AND TREATISES (including RARE BOOKS)

814 **Cherry (R. R) and Wakely (J): Irish Land Law and Land Purchase Acts:** 1st Ed. 1888: S & M Irish p15

815 ———— 2nd Ed. 1893:

816 ———— 1906 Supplement by J H Maxwell:

817 **Dixon (G. Y) and Gilleland (W. L): Law Relating to Sheriffs in Ireland:** 1888: S & M Irish p25

818 **Humphreys (H): Justice of the Peace for Ireland:** 8th Ed. notes by J. B. Sandford: 1897: S & M Irish P42

819 **Hunt (E): Abridgment of all the Statutes in Ireland, in the Reigns of Queen Anne and King George [1702-1718] in force and use:** 1718: S & M Irish p42

820 **Molloy (C): Justice of the Peace for Ireland:** 1st Ed. 1890: S & M Irish p59

821 **O'Connor (J): Irish Justice of the Peace:** 1st Ed. 1911: S & M Irish p64

822 **Oulton (A. N): Index to Statutes in force affecting Ireland 1310-1838:** 2nd Ed. 1839: S & M Irish p67

823 **Rules of the Supreme Court (Ireland) 1905:** S & M Irish p82. 1905:

824 **Robbins (N): Exact Abridgment of all the Irish Statutes from the first session of Parliament in the 3rd Year of Edward II to the end of the 8th Year of George II. Together with an abridgment of all the English Statutes in force in Ireland:** 1736: S & M Irish p80

825 **Treaties on Tenures (Dublin):** 1754:

M120 .... £750.00
M121 .... £280.00
M122 .... £3,500.00
M123 Available in Micro form only — Price on Application.
M124 .... £1,100.00
M125 .... £1,150.00
M126 .... £45.00
M127 .... £42.00
M128 .... (2 vols) £40.00
M129 .... (2 vols) £43.00
M130 .... £20.00
M131 .... £950.00

Texts and Treatises

814 .... £60.00
815 .... £30.00
816 .... £15.00
817 .... £25.00
818 .... £45.00
819 .... £75.00
820 .... £60.00
821 .... £50.00
822 .... £45.00
823 .... £25.00
824 .... £90.00
825 .... £30.00

758 .. £20.00
759 .. £30.00
760 .. £20.00
761 .. £70.00
762 .. £20.00
763 .. £20.00
764 . £90.00
765 . £130.00
766 . £35.00
767 . £120.00
768 . £45.00
769 . £25.00
770 . £200.00
771 . £180.00
772 £225.00
773 . £50.00
774 . £20.00
775 £275.00
776 . £85.00
777 . £60.00
778 . £35.00
779 £180.00
780 . £30.00
781 . £40.00
782 . £20.00
783 . £25.00
784 . £45.00
785 . £20.00
786 . £75.00
787 £120.00
788 £120.00
789 . £60.00
790 . £25.00
791 £100.00
792 £140.00
793 £120.00
794 . £30.00
795 £350.00
796 £240.00
797 £130.00
798 £280.00
799 . £75.00
800 £120.00
801 . £75.00
802 £220.00
803 . £35.00
804 . £25.00
805 . £45.00
806 . £25.00
807 . £20.00
808 . £20.00
809 . £20.00
810 . £30.00
811 . £90.00
812 , £20.00
813 . £60.00

Commonwealth and International

REPORTS, STATUTES ETC.

M132-M189 Sets and parts available. Condition varies. Details on application.

M132 **Acts of Parliament (Australia): 1901-1978:**

M133 **Aden: Knox-Mawer: Law of workmens compensation in the Colony of Aden (as on March 31st 1957):** 1957: S & M v7 p189.

M134 **American Journal of International Law: 1907-1980:** Volumes 1-74:

M135 **American Journal of Legal Education: 1948-1980:** Volumes 1-32:

M136 **American Law Reports Annotated:** Indiv. volumes also available:

M137 **Antigua: New edition of the Statutes of the Presidency of Antigua:** 1921: S & M v7 p314.

M138 **Ashanti, British Togoland and Northen Territories: Smith (E. G): Laws in force on the 1st day of January 1928:** London 1928: S & M v7 p171.

M139 **Atlantic Reports:** Indiv. volumes also available

M140 **Australian Law Journal:** Volumes 1-54:

M141 **Bechuanaland: Protectorate and BSA Companies Territory. High Commissioners Notices and Proclamations (1888-1895):** 1895: S & M v7 p136.

M142 **Bechuanaland: Laws of Bechuanaland Protectorate:** 3 vols: 1948:

M143 **Bechuanaland: Laws of Bechuanaland:** 4 vols: 1959:

M144 **Basutoland: Laws of Basutoland, Rev. Ed:** 3 vols: 1949:

M145 **Basutoland: Laws of Basutoland:** 5 vols: 1960:

M146 **Bahamas: Statute Law of the Bahamas comprising all Acts in force on January 1st 1929:** 2 vols: 1929: S & M v7 p280.

M147 **Barbados: Laws of Barbados, Revised and Consolidated by C. V. M. Archer and W.I.K. Fergusson:** 5 vols: 1946: S & M v7 p296.

M148 **Barbados: Proclamations, Orders and Regulations (1916-1946):**

M149 **Bermuda: Private Acts 1709-1953:** 2 vols: 1954: S & M v7 p287.

M150 **Bermuda: Private Acts 1956-1965:**

M151 **Bermuda: Public Acts 1956-1964:**

M152 **Bermuda: Statute Law of Bermuda 1620-1952:** 5 vols: 1960: S & M v7 p287.

M153 **British Honduras: New Edition of the "Consolidated Laws" containing the orders in force on July 21 1924:** 2 vols: 1924: S & M v7 p365.

M154 **British Guiana: Laws of British Guiana: Rev. Ed. to July 1st 1953 by Sir D. Kingdon:** 11 vols: 1954: S & M v7 p38.

M155 **California Law Review: 1912-1980:** Volumes 1-68:

M156 **Columbia Law Review: 1901-1980:** Volumes 1-80:

M157 **Commonwealth Law Reports: 1903-1980:** Volumes 1-143:

M158 **Cornell Law Review: 1915-1980:** Volumes 1-65 and index:

M159 **Corpus Juris Secundum:** 148 volumes plus 5 volumes index:

M160 **Fiji: Laws of Fiji enacted on or before 16 April 1955:** 7 vols (vols 1-4 ordinances, vol 5 & 6 Sub. legislation, vol 7 index): 1956: S & M v7 p397.

M161 **Fiji: Laws of Fiji:** 1958-1966:

M162 **Gambia: Laws of Gambia in force on 1st January 1955:** 6 vols:1955: S & M v7 p155.

M163 **Gibraltar: Revised edition of Laws of Gibraltar:** 4 vols: 1950: S & M v7 p379.

M164 **Harvard Law Review: 1887-1980:** Volumes 1-93:

M165 **Hong Kong: Laws of Hong Kong containg the Ordinances enacted until the 1st Sept. 1950 and Subsidiary Legislation:** 11 vols: 1953: S & M v7 p238.

M166 **Illinois/North Western University Law Review: 1906-1980:** Volumes 1-74:

M167 **International and Comparative Law Quarterly: 1952-1980:** Volumes 1-29: I. C. L. Q. was formed when the International Law Quarterly and Journal of Comparative Legislation combined:

M168 **International Law Association Conference: 1873-1972:** and index:

M169 **International Law Reports:** Volumes 1-61:

M170 **Jamaica: Statutes and Laws of Jamaica. 1681-1888:** 12 vols 1890: S & M v7 p302.

M171 **Kenya: Laws of Kenya containing Laws in force on Sept. 21, 1948:** 8 vols: 1951: S & M v7 p74.

M172 **Leeward Islands: Federal Acts of the Leeward Islands, containing the Acts of the General Legislative council in force on Dec 31, 1927:** 3 vols: 1927: S & M v7 p311.

M173 **Malta: Revised Edition of Malta Laws to end of 1942:** 6 vols: 1943: S & M v7 p390.

M174 **Mauritius: Laws of Mauritius in force on July 31, 1945 (by Sir C. Lane):** Rev. Ed. 5 vols: 1946: S & M v7 p96.

M175 **Michigan Law Review: 1902-1980:** Volumes 1-78:

M176 **Nyasaland: Laws of Nyasaland in force on Jan 1, 1957:** 6 vols: 1959: S & M v7 p66.

M177 **Palestine: Laws of Palestine in force on 31 December 1933:** 3 vols: 1934: S & M v7 p196.

M178 **Rhodesia: Laws of Northern Rhodesia containing the Laws in force on Dec 31, 1947:** 8 vols: 1948: S & M v7 p55.

M179 **Rhodesia: Statute Law of North-Eastern Rhodesia, 1908-11, North-Western Rhodesia, 1910-11, Northern Rhodesia, 1911-16:** 1 vol: 1917: S & M v7 p58.

M180 **Sarawak: Laws of Sarawak:** Rev. Ed. 9 vols: 1958: S & M v7 p211.

M181 **South Africa Statutes:** Volumes 1-26.

M182 **Stanford Law Review: 1948-1980:** Volumes 1-32:

M183 **Swaziland: Laws of Swaziland in force 1st July 1959:** 4 vols:

M184 **Trinidad & Tobago: Laws of Trinidad & Tobago (1832-1904):** 6 vols: 1905: S & M v7 p329

M185 **Uganda: Laws of Uganda Protectorate in for 1st Jan 1951:** 9 vols: 1951: S & M v7 p78.

M186 **University of Chicago Law Review: 1933-1980:** Volumes 1-47:

M187 **University of Detroit Journal of Urban Law: 1931-1980:** Volumes 1-57:

M188 **Western Australian Law Reports: 1898-1959:** Volumes 1-30:

M189 **Yale Law Journal: 1891-1980:** Volumes 1-89: Some spare volumes available between 1903 and 1973:

TEXTS AND TREATISES (including RARE BOOKS)

Texts and Treatises

826-850 Details on application.

826 **Amerasinghe (C. F): Defamation and other aspects of the actio iniuriarum in Roman-Dutch Law (in Ceylon and South Africa).**

827 **Arbitration between government of Saudi Arabia and Arabian American Oil Company:-**
Award
Saudi Arabia's Memorials.
Aramco's first memorial.
Aramco's second and final mermorials.
Sessions of the tribunal verbatim transcript.

828 **Bosman (D. B): Tweetalige Woordeboek, Africaans-Engels.** 1936.

829 **British and Colonial Prize cases heard and decided in the prize court during the great war:** 3 vols: By Samuel Evans 1914-1922:

830 **Burnett (G): The Life and Death of Sir Mathew Hale:** 1862: 1972 reprint by Rothman:

831 **Carnegie Endowment for International peace recommendation on international Law and official commentary thereon of the second Par-Amercian Scientific Congress, held in Washington, Dec 27, 1915 — Jan 8, 1916: Edited by James Brown Scott: 1916:**

832 **Colombos (C. J): A treatise on the Law of Prize:** 1926: 2nd Ed. 1940:

833 **Conferance de la Haye de Droit Internatiol prive. Actes de la cinquieme session:** 1925:

834 **Conferance de la Haye de Droit International prive. Actes de la sixieme session:** 1928: Volume I acts: Volume II documents:

835 **Correspondence respecting the second peace conference held at the Hague in 1907:**

836 **Correspondence respecting the peace conferences held at the Hague 1899-1908:**

837 **Grotius (H): The freedom of the seas, or the right which belongs to the Dutch to take part in the East Indian Trade:** A dissertation by Hugo Grotius: Translated with a revision of the Latin text of 1633 by Ralph Van Deman Magoffin: Edited with an introductory note by James Brown Scott: 1916:

838 **Grotii (H): Ivre Belli Ac Pacis Libritres:** Nova: 1646:

839 **Grotius (H): The Jurisprudence of Holland:** 2 vols: 1953:

840 **Hertz (W. A): Burma gazetteer: Myitkyina District:** Volume A: 1912:

841 **Hurst (C. J. B): Russian and Japanese Prize cases, being a collection of translations and summaries of the principle cases decided by the Russian and Japaneses prize courts arising out of the Russo-Japanese war:** 1904-1905:
Volume I Russian Cases: 1912:
Volume II Japanese Cases: 1913:
By F. E. Bray:

842 **International Court of Justice Yearbook:** 1946-1947:

843 **Jorba (J. P): new vocabulary containing all usual words and their rigured pronunciation:** English-Spanish: 1908:

844 **Ladas (S. P): The international protection of trade marics by the american republics:** 1929:

845 **Library of the palace of peace. Concise alphabetical subject index:** To the catalogue (1916) and to the supplements: (1922 and 1929): 1933:

846 **MacKeurtan (H. G): The Sale of goods in South Africa being a handbook of the Law relating to the purchase and sale of corporal moveables in South Africa:** 1935: By T. B. Horwood:

847 **Miller (D. H): The drafting of the covenant:** With an introduction by Nicholas Murray Butler: 2 vols: 1928:

848 **Penn (W): The peace of Europe, the fruits of solitude and other writings by William Penn:**

849 **Prize Cases decided in the United States supreme court, 1789-1918 including also cases on the instances side in which questions of prize Law were involved:** 3 vols: 1923:
Pufendorf(S) — see ref nos 487-492

850 **Union Interparliementarie, resolutions des conferences et decision principles du conseil:** Volume II only: 1935:

Addenda

A1 **Acts of 1688 William & Mary etc.**

A2 **Acts of 1702 Queen Anne etc.**

A3 **A'Beckett: The Comic Blackstone:** 3rd Ed. 1887:S & M v2 p1.

A4 **Bentham: Complete Works:** 11 vols: 1843: Edited by Dr. Bowring: (reprint shortly available):

A5 **Birkenhead (Lord): More Famous Trials:** 1928: (See Ref. 44): S & M v2 p32.

A6 **Blount (T): Law Dictionary:** 1st Ed. 1670: S & M v1 p6.
A7 ________ 2nd Ed. 1691:

A8 **Borrow (G): Celebrated Trials and Remarkable Cases of Criminal Jurisprudence, from the earliest records to the year 1825:** 6 vols: 1825: S & M v2 p36.

A9 **Davies (Sir J): Le Primer Report des Cases et matters en ley resolues et adiudges, en les Courts del Roy a Ireland: (1604-12):** 2nd Ed. 1674: S & M Irish p23
A10 **Davies (Sir J): Historical Tracts:** 1786: S & M Irish p25

A11 **Edwards (T): Admiralty Reports 1808-1812:** 1812: (see British Maritime Cases ref. M9):

A12 **Gibson (Sir A) (Lord Durie): Decisions of the Lords of Council and Session, 1621-42:** 1660: S & M Scot p46

A13 **Goodhart (A. L): Essays in Jurisprudence and the Common Law:** 1931: S & M v2 p142.

A14 **Goodhart (A. L): English Contributions to the Philosophy of Law:** 1949: S & M v2 p142.

A15 **Goodhart (A. L): English Law and the Moral Law (The Hamlyn Lectures):** 1953: S & M v2 p142.
A16 **Hale (Sir M): History of the Common Law of England:** 5th Ed. with additions by C. Runnington: 2 vols: "His History of the Common Law and its analytical arrangment lie at the basis of all subsequent works . . . His concise, but enlightening, summary of the results of 600 years of growth, can be producte of his time — 4 AM. Law School: S & M v1 p239

A17 **Havelock Ellis: The Criminal:** 4th Ed. (Revised & Illustrated): 1910:

A18 **Holdsworth (Sir W. S): Sources and Literature of English Law:** 1925: S & M v2 p170.

A19 **Holdsworth (Sir W. S): Some Lessons from our legal History:** 1928: S & M v1 p169

A20 **Holdsworth (Sir W. S): History of English Law to 1700:** 12 volumes: 1932: (also available in reprint): S & M v2 p169.

A21 **Holt (Sir J): Modern Cases temp Holt:** 1712: Makes up part 6 of the modern Reports:

A22 **Kames (Lord H. H): Historical Law Tracts:** 1st Ed. 2 vols: 1758: (see Ref. 360):

A23 **Kerr (W. W): Law and Practice on Injunctions:** 6th Ed. 1927: (also available in reprint): S & M v2 p198.

A24 **Laws and Acts of Parliament made by King James 1st (1424-1597):** 1597: S & M Scot p116

A25 **Laws & Acts of Parliament made by James I — Charles II (1424-1681):** 1681: S & M Scot p116

A26 **Laws & Acts of Parliament: James VII — Anne (1685-1707):** (Anderson Edition): 1731: S & M Scot p117
A27 **Mackenzie (Sir G): Institutions of the Laws of Scotland:** 5th Ed. 1723: S & M Scot p73
A28 ________ 8th Ed. 1754:

A29 **Mallory (J): Modern Entries in English; Being a select collection of pleadings in the Courts of King's Bench, Common Pleas and Exchequer, and also all kinds of Writs, with readings and observations on the cases in the Reports; By a Gentlemen of the Inner Temple:** 1734: S & M v1 p273
A30 **McKenchnie (W. S): Commentary on Great Charter of King John:** 1913: S & M v1 p55

A31 **McNair (A. D): Law of the Air:** 3rd Ed. 1953: S & M v2 p228

A32 **Notable British Trials (incorporating Notable Scottish Trials):** Guy Fawkes: S & M v2 p259.
A33 ________ Lord Lovat:
A34 ________ James Stewart:
A35 ________ Deacon Brodie:
A36 ________ Madelane Smith:
A37 ________ The Baccarat Case:
A38 ________ Sir Roger Casement:

A39 **Selden (J): History of Tythes:** 1618: S & M v1 p194

A40 **Selden (J): Titles of Honour:** 3rd Ed. 1672: S & M v1 p208

A41 **Skene (Sir J): Scotch Acts 1536-1784:** 1785:

A42 **Stair (Sir James Dalrymple): Institutions of the Law of Scotland; deduced from its originals and collated with the customs of neigbouring nations:** 2nd Ed. 2 vols: 1693: With hand written additions and corrections of 1st Ed. by the author: S & M Scot p108

A43 **State Trials for High Treason: (containing Trial of Thomas Hardy):** 1794:

A44 **Stephen (Sir J. F): General View of the Criminal Law of England:** 1st Ed. 1863: S & M v2 p339

A45 **Tidd (W): Practice of the Court of King's Bench in Personal Actions:** 7th Ed. 2 vols: 1821: S & M v1 p279

A46 **Trial of Henry — Viscount Melville:** 1806:

A47 **Trial of the Regicides: (Exact & impartial account of 29 Regicides for the murder of late Sacred Majesty):** 1660:

A48 **Trial of William McGavin:** 1821:

A49 **Year Book Edward III 1-10 with notes to Brooke and Fitzherberts Abridgment:** 1678: S & M v1 p312

A50 **Acts of the Parliament of Scotland: (Thomson and Innes):** 11 vols in 12 with General Index: 1124-1707: Large folio: 1875: Rare newly bound: This is the authoritative edition. Thomas Thomson laboured nearly fifty years on this great work, the **record** edition of the Acts of the Parliament of Scotland, which is associated with his name. His work was completed by Cosmo Innes, who described him as "The foremost of record scholars" . . . Stair Soc. Publ.

ADDENDA

A1 .... **£125.00**
A2 .... **£85.00**
A3 .... **£35.00**
A4 .... **£240.00**
A5 .... **£40.00**
A6 .... **£150.00**
A7 .... **£95.00**
A8 .... **£350.00**
A9 .... **£130.00**
A10 .... **£90.00**
A11 .... **£45.00**
A12 .... **£180.00**
A13 .... **£50.00**
A14 .... **£35.00**
A15 .... **£30.00**
A16 .... **£120.00**

A17 .... **£25.00**
A18 .... **£45.00**
A19 .... **£40.00**
A20 .... **£240.00**
A21 .... **£60.00**
A22 .... **£180.00**
A23 .... **£45.00**
A24 .... **£250.00**
A25 .... **£200.00**
A26 .... **£180.00**
A27 .... **£110.00**
A28 .... **£90.00**
A29 .... **£120.00**
A30 .... **£45.00**
A31 .... **£20.00**
A32 .... **£18.00**
A33 .... **£18.00**
A34 .... **£18.00**
A35 .... **£18.00**
A36 .... **£18.00**
A37 .... **£18.00**
A38 .... **£18.00**
A39 .... **£180.00**
A40 .... **£150.00**
A41 .... **£225.00**
A42 .... **£350.00**
A43 .... **£75.00**
A44 .... **£50.00**
A45 .... **£65.00**
A46 .... **£45.00**
A47 .... **£160.00**
A48 .... **£20.00**
A49 .... **£375.00**
(see also **667-676**)
A50 .... **£1,200.00**

Additional Items

Dalloz: Jurisprudence Generale 1865-1933 plus Tables **£2,400.00**

Selden (J): Mare Clausum 1663 .... **£220.00**

Malynes: Lex Mercatoria 16 .... **£250.00** (see also Classical English Law Texts series)

Stair (Sir J): Institutions of the Law of Scotland 1st. Ed. 1681: **£300.00**

Humanities List 15

Social.Sciences (1976)

Law

Richard Adamiak
1545 East 60th St.
Chicago, Illinois 60637
312-955-4571

Terms of Sale: Prices Net, Postage Extra; 30 days.

1) ADAMS, Henry, History of the United States During the Administrations of Jefferson and Madison. NY, 1889-91, 8vo, nine volumes, original cloth, excellent, first edition, $275.00

2) ADDINGTON, William, An Abridgment of the Penal Statutes... L, 1795, 4to, 861p plus 90pp. table; bound with this: An Appendix to Addington's Abridgment.. to the Present Year 1802. bound in later 3/4 buckram, margins of title and following leaf slightly worn, else excellent, $100.00

3)AMOS, S., Fifty Years of the English Constitution, 1830-80. B, 1880, 8vo, $15.

4) Archiv für Geschichte der Philosophie, ed. by Ludwig Stein, et al, Berlin, 1888-1909. vols. 1-20 plus 2vol. index, Reprint, de Gruyter, 1970, roy8vo, buckram, new set, $450.00

5)BACON, Francis, Opera Omnia quae Extant. Frankfurt/M, 1665, folio, 324pp., contemp. calf, slight sporadic foxing & browning,bit worn, $125.00

6) BARTHELEMY, J. J., Oeuvres Diverses. Paris, An 6me, 8vo, 2vols., bound in ear 19th century 1/2 morocco and marbled boards, bit rubbed, $47.50

7) BAYLE, Peter, The Dictionary Historical & Critical, second edition, carefull collated with the several editions of the original in which many passages are restored and the whole greatly augmented. L, 1734-38, folio, 5vols., contemp. tree calf, expertly rebacked, $475.00

8) BECCARIA, Cesare, An Essay on Crimes & Punishments, translated from the Itali with a Commentary, Attributed to Mons. de Voltaire, translated from the French. L, 1770, third ed., 8vo, vii,iv,179pp, lxxixxpp., later morocco, corners of title neatlyrestored, nice copy, $125.00

9) BENTHAM, Jeremy, A Treatise on Judicial Evidence Extracted from the Manuscri of Jeremy Bentham by M. Dumont, translated into English. L, 1825, 8vo, xvi 366pp., original boards, rebacked, first English edition, $185.00

10)BENTHAM, Jeremy, Plan of Parliamentary Reform, inthe Form of a Catechism, Shewing the Necessity of Radical and the Inadaquacy of Moderate Reform. L, 1817, 8vo, iv,cccxxxviipp., later calf, fine copy, $250.00

11) BLACKSTONE, Sir William, Commentaries on the Laws of England. Oxford, 1765-69 4to, 4vols., later 1/2 calf and modern baards, fine set, first edition wit the supplement bound in vol. 2; $2500.00

12) BLACKSTONE, Sir William, Commentaries on the Laws of England. Oxford, 1775, 8 4vols., later 1/2 calf, fine set, $200.00

13) BLACKSTONE, Sir William, Commentaries on the Laws of England. Philadelphia, 1771-1772, roy8vo, 4vols.; with the Appendix volume together 5vols., all bound in contemp. roan, hinges tender, crowns sl. worn, subscribed editior with list of subscribers, first American edition, $1250.00

14) (Blackstone), REED, John, The Pennsylvania Blackstone, Being a Modification the Commentaries of Sir Wm. Blackstone, with Numerous Alterations and Add

--2--

tions Designed to Present an Elementary Exposition of the Entire Laws of Pennsylvania. Carlisle, 1831, roy8vo, 3vols., bound in contemp. roan, fine set, rare, $175.00

15) BLISS, Wm., New Encyclopedia of Social Reform. NY, 1908, 4to, 1321pp., $27.5

16) BOUFLERS, Duc C. Stanislas, Oeuvres de. Paris, An XI, 8vo, 352pp., bound in early 19th centmry 1/2 morocco and marbled boards, bit rubbed, $37.50

17) BOURRIENNE, Memoires de M. Bourrienne. 3rd ed, Paris, 1830, 8vo, 10vols., bound in contemp. 1/2 calf and marbled boards, all hinges tender, all vols .a bit rubbed. $150.00

18) BRANTOME, Oeuvres de Seigneur Brantome. Nouvelle Edition. P, 1787, 8vo, 8vols., mid 19th century marbled boards, rebacked in linen, $87.50

19) BREMNER, Robert, Excursions in the Interior of Russia, Including Sketches of the Character & Policy of the Emperor Nicholas. L, 1839, 8vo, 2vols., contemp. marbled bds,rebacked in linen, $87.50

20) BUCHANAN, George, Rerum Scotiarum Historia...Accesit De Jure Regni apud Scot Utrecht, 1668, 8vo, 787pp., contemp. calf, joints cracked but firm, cover worn, rare, $175.00

21) BUCKLE, Henry Thomas, History of Civilization in England. L, 1857-61, 8vo, 2vols., later 1/2 morocco, fine set, first edition, $325.00

22) BUTLER, Chs., Reminiscences of Lincoln's Inn.... B, 1827, small8vo, 284pp., orig. bds, reblcked, excellent, $25.00

23) CABET, Etienne, Le Vrai Christianisme Suivant Jesus-Christ. Paris, April, 1846, 12mo, xii, 636pp., later 19th century calf, fine copy, first editio first issue, of extreme rarity, $375.00

24) (CANTERBURY, Archbishop of), The Proceedings and Tryal in the Case of the Mo Rev. Father in God William Lord, Archbishopfof Canterbury....L, 1716, 8vo 377pp., contemp. calf, reblacked in calf, frontis, $47.50

25) CARLYLE, Thomas, Past & Present. L, 1843, 8vo, vi,399pp.,later 1/2 calf & marbled bds, excellent, first edition, $175.00

26) CARLYLE, Th., History of Frederick II of Prussia, Called Frederick the Great L, 1858-65, 8vo, 6vols., orig. cl., extremeties a bit worn and crown of II a bit chipped, else a very nice set, first edition, $175.00

27) CARRINGTON, S., History ofthe Life & Death of His Most Serene Highness Olive Late Lord Protector..... L, 1659, 8vo, 272pp., 18th century calf, engrave fold-out frontis, front hinge skillfully mended, nice copy, $125.00

28) CHAMBERLIN, Franklin, American Commercial Law Relatingto Every Kind of Busin Hartford, 1869, roy8vo, xxxi,991pp., contemp. roan, rubbed, $22.50

29) CIESZKOWSKI, Count August, Notre Pere, traduit par M. V. Gasztowtt et par le Fils de l'Auteur. P, 1906-29, roy8vo, 4vols., later linem, $125.00

30) COLQUHOUN, P., A Treatise on Indigence.....L, 1806, 8vo, xii,302pp., plus ad & index, bound in contemp. marbled bds, rebacked in calf, first ed, $250.

31) Commercial Code of France,with the Motives or Discourses of the Counsellors State, Delivered Before the Legislative Body, Illustrative of the Princip and Provisions of the Code, trans. w/explanatory Notes by John Rodman, NY, 1814, 8vo, xiv,383pp.,ex lib, later buckram, $37.50

32) (CONSTITUTIONAL CONVENTION OF 1787), Journal, Acts & Proceedings of the Convention Assembled at Philadelphia, Monday, May 14, and Dissolved, Monday, September 17, 1787, which formed the Constitution of the United States. Published under Direction of the President of the United States, Conforma to a Resolution of Congress, March 27, 1818. Boston, Thomas B. Wait, 1819 8vo, 510pp., contemp. roan, rebacked, light sporadic foxing, a clean, cri copy in exceptionally good condition for a publication of this period; wi the bookplate and signature of Henry Augustus Muhlenberg (1823-54),

--3--

Pennsylvania lawyer & politician and member of a family which played a prominent role in early state & national affairs; copies of the Journal have become quite rare and records indicate that only two have been available in this century, first edition, $2250.00

33) (CONSTITUTIONAL CONVENTION OF 1787) MADISON, James, ThePapers of James Madiso ....Now Published from the Original Manuscripts, under the Superintendence of Henry D. Gilpin. DC, 1840, roy8vo, 3vols., later 1/2 morocco, fine set, first edition, $350.00

34) DOMAT, Jean, Corpus Juris Civilis, Legum ex Libris Digestorum & Codicis Opera Joannis Domat, editio secunda, Amsterdam, 1703, folio, contemp. calf, $13

35) CRABB, Geo., A History of EnglishLaw.... L, 1829, 8vo, 579pp., later linen, title trifle soiled, some marginal dampstain, $37.50

36)CURREY, W. S., Manufacturing and Wholesale Industries of Chicago. C, 1918, 4to, 4vols., later linem, fine, $87.50

37) DE LOLME, M., Constitution de l'Angleterre.... new ed., rev. & corr. Geneve, 1788, 8vo, 2vols., (bound as one), early 19th century marbled boards, rebacked in linen, frontis, $47.50

38) STAEL DE HOLSTEIN, Baronness, A Treatise on Ancient & Modern Literature.... L, 1803, roy8vo, 2vols., orignal bds, hinges cracked & tender, bit worn, with the bookplates of Richard Brinsley Sheridan, forst English ed, $175.(

39) DE WITT, David M., The Judicial Murder of Mary E. Surratt. Balto, 1895, 8vo, 259pp., orig. cl., first ed., Howes D306, $57.50

40) DUMONT, Etienne, Recollections of Mirabeau and of the First Two Legislative Assemblies of France. L, 1832, 8vo, xxxv,404pp., contemp. 1/2 morocco & marbled bds, hinges tender, bit rubbed, $25.00

41) DU PONCEAU, Peter, A Dissertation on the Nature & Extent of the Jurisdiction the Courts of the U.S. P, 1824, 8vo, contemp. roan, $67.50

42) ELLIOT, Edw., The Colleges & the Courts.B, 1936, roy8vo, $10.00

43) ELSTER, Ludwig, et al., Handwörterbuch der Staatswissenschaften. 4th ed., Jer 1923-28, 4to, 9vols., orig. 1/2 buckram, clean & tight, $275.00

44)ENGELS, Friedrich, Anti-Duehring. trans. & ed. by Austin Lewis, C, 1907, 8vo, 266pp., orig. cl., fine copy, first English edition, $125.00

45) FAQUET, Emile, Politiques et Moralistes du Dix-Neuvieme Siecle. P, 1901, 8vo, 3vols., 1/2 morocco & bds, $37.50

46) FENELON, Les Adventures de Telemaque, Fils D'Ulysse. P, An IV (1796), roy8vo, 2vols., orig. cloth covered bds, rebacked in morocco, with 25 engravings, handsomeset, $135.00

47) FERGUSON, Adam, An Essay on the History of Civil Society. Dublin, 1767, 8vo, viii,416pp., contemp. calf, light sporadic foxing, front free end sheet missing, first Dublin edition, rare, $275.00

48) FREUD, Sigmund, Neue Folge der Vorlesungen zur Einfuhrung in die Psychoanalys Wien, 1933, 8vo, 254pp., orig. cl., covers a bit faded and light traces of wear in a few spots, first edition, first issue, $125.00

49) FRIEDBERG, Emile, Das Recht der Eheschliessung....Leipzig, 1865, roy8vo, 827p later buck., bit soiled, an exceptionally comprehensive treatment of the history of the law of marriage in all times & places, $37.50

50)GARNER, Jas. W., Studies in Government & International Law. Urbana, 1943, roy8vo, 574pp., $13.50

51) GODWIN, William, Mandeville. Edinburgh, 1817, 8vo, 3vols., contemp. marbled bds, rebacked in calf, first edition, $225.00

52) GODWIN, William, Fleetwood. L, 1805, 8vo, 3vols., contemp. marbled boards, rebacked in morocco, first ed., $225.00

--4--

53) GODWIN, William, The Enquirer. London, 1797, 8vo, xii,481pp., original bds, rebacked, fine, first edition, $285.00

54) GODWIN, William, History of the Commonwealth of England. L, 1824-28, 8vo, 4vols., later 1/2 morocco, fine, first edition, $250.00

55) GODWIN, William, Thoughts on Man. London, 1831, 8vo, vi,471pp., contemp. ca & marbled bds, joints cracked & crown a bit chipped, first edition, $225.

56)GODWIN, William, Lives of the Necromancers. L, 1834, 8vo, xiii,465pp., orig. bds rebacked & corners restored, excellent copy, first edition, $265.00

57) GUIZOT, F., History of the Origin of Republican Government in Europe. L, 186 8vo, $22.50

58) HARRIS, Ethel, Lamartine et le Peuple. P, 1932, roy8vo, 547pp., $15.00

59) The Hibbert Journal: A Quarterly Review of Religion, Theology & Philosophy. Vols. I-XIV, (1902-1916), Reprint: Amsterdam, orig. wrps, new $375.00

60) HOLBACH, Baron, Systeme Social. Londres, 1773, 8vo, 3vols., (bound as one), contemp. 1/2 calf & paper covered bds, first edition, $185.00

61) HOLDSWORTH, Wm., Sources & Literature of English Law. Ox, 1952, 8vo, 247pp,$

62) HUEBNER, Rudolf, History of Germanic Private Law. B, 1918, roy8vo, 785pp, $1

63) HULL, Brigadier General W., Defense of....Delivered before the General Court Martial.... B, 1814, small8vo, xviii,215pp., orig. bds, rebacked, $37.50

64) HUME, David, The History of England. London, 1754-62, 4to, 6vls., bound in contemp. calf, skillfully rebacked, foredge of T2 in vol. 5 neatly restor and part of the same leaf somewhat discolored bu haat, first editions of the volumes, scarce complete, $475.00

65) HUME, David, Essays & Treatises on Several Subjects. New Ed., London1772, 8vo, 2vols., contemp. polished calf, beautiful set, $225.00

66) HUME, David, The Historyof England.... NY, 1879, 8vo, 6vols, later linen, frontis, nice set, $87.50

67) JACOB, Giles, The New Law Dictionary....first American fromthe 2nd London ed P, 1811, roy8vo, 6vols., contem. roan, bit rubbed & scuffed, $150.00

68) JANIN, Jules, Paris et Versailles. P, 1874, roy8vo, 406pp., contemp. 1/2 morocco, $25.00

69) JEVONS, W. Stanley, The Theory of Political Economy. L/NY, 1871, 8vo, xvi, 267pp., orig. cl., crown neatlyrestored, first edition, $225.00

70) KANT, Immanuel, Sämmtliche Werke. Leipzig, 1838-42, roy8vo, 12 Parts bound 10 vols., orig. paper covered boards & paper labels, sl. worn, first collected edition, $450.00

71) KAUFMAN, Felix, Logik und Rechtswissenschaft. Tub, 1922, roy8vo, 134pp, $22.

72) KEYNES, John Maynard, Economic Consequences of the Peace. L, 1919, 8vo, vii, 279pp., orig. cl., trifle worn & lettering faded, first edition, $75.00

73) LAUTERDALE, Earl of, An Inquiry into the Nature & Origin of Public Wealth... Edinburgh, 1804, 8vo, 482pp., bound in later 1/2 morocco & linen, slight marginal chipping of first & last few leaves, last leaf of text laid in, first edition, $175.00

74)LAVELEYE, Emile, Socialisme Contemporain. P, 1894, 12mo, 413pp., $17.50

75) LEAKE, Stephen, An Historical Account of English Money.... 2nd ed., with gre Additions & Improvements, Tables of Gold & Silver Money & Six New Cuts. L 1745, 8vo, viii,428pp., plus plates & index, later 1/2 calf & linen, $87.

76) LENORMANT, Francois, La Monnaie dans l'Antiquite. P, 1897, 8vo, 3vols., $57.

77) LOCKE, John, The Reasonableness of Christianity. L, 1695, 8vo, 304pp., conte calf newly rebacked, minor flaw in B4 skillfully restored, first ed, $375

--5--

78) LOCKE, John, Second Vindication of the Reasonableness of Christianity. L, 1697, 8vo, A-a4,480pp., later calf, first edition, $350.00

79) MACHIAVELLI, Opere. Firenze, 1782-83, 4to, 6vols.,contemp. tree calf rebacke title of 5 in fine facsimile on period paper, $275.00

80) MALTHUS, T. R., Principles of Political Economy. L, 1820, 8vo, vi,601pp., co 1/2 calf & marbled boards, fine copy, first edition, $475.00

81) MALVEZZI, Virgilio, Discourses upon Cornelius Tacitus. L, 1642, 4to, 504pp., contemp. calf, front hinge tender, nice copy, WingM359, $225.00

82) MARTIN, R. M., The British Colonies. L/NY, (1885), 4to, 3vols.,$145.00

83) MARX, Karl, Das Kapital......Erster Band. Buch I: Der Produktionsprocess des Kapitals. 2nd ed., rev., Hamburg, 1872, 8vo, 830pp., bound in contemp. 1 morocco & linen, clean, tight copy, $350.00

84) M'CULLOCH, J. R., Principles of Political Economy. Edinburgh/London, 1825, 8 x,423pp., later 1/2 morocco & marbled bds, first edition, $225.00

85) MC LAUGHLIN, Andrew & HART, Alb. (eds.), Cyclopedia of Ameircan Government. 1914, 4to, 3vols., $75.00

86) MC NALLY, Leonard, The Rules of Evidence on the Pleas of the Crown. L, 1802, 8vo, 2vols., contemp. calf, worn, $37.50

87) MEINECKE, Friedrich, Die Idee der Staatsräson in der Neuren Geschichte. M/B, 1924, roy8vo, 545pp., orig. cl., first edition, $47.50

88) MENGER, Anton, Neue Staatslehre. 2nd ed.,Jena, 1904, 8vo, 263pp., $17.50

89) MIGNET, F. A., De la Feodalite. P, 1822, 8vo, 253pp., later linen, $37.50

90) MIGNET, F. A., Histoire de la Revolution Francaise. Brux, 1839, roy8vo, 452p contemp. marbled bds rebacked in linen, ill., $25.00

91) MILLAR, John, An Historical View of the English Government. L, 1803, 8vo, 4v contemp. calf, nice set with bookplates of Richard Brinsley Sheridan, $87

92) MOLIERE, Oeuvres de. P, 1876-1907, roy8vo, 13vols., bound in contemp. 1/2 ca and marbled bds, sl. sporadic dampstain, clean & tight, $275.00

93) The Monist. Chicago, Open Court, 1890-1910, vols. 1-20, roy8vo, $775.00

94) MORE, Sir Thomas,Utopia. NY, Scott-Thaw, 1903, folio, 265pp., bound in the c two-tone linen, #143 of 210 copies printed by the Chiswick Press, $47.50

95) MOREHEAD, Jas., The Practice in Civil Actions & Proceedings at Law in Kentuc Louisville, 1846, roy8vo, 783pp., later linen, $35.00

96) NOTOVICH, Nicholas, L'Empereur Alexandre III et Son Entourage. P, 1893, roy8 284pp., contemp. 1/2 calf & marbled bds, $22.50

97) OFFICE OF THE UNITED STATES CHIEF COUNSEL FOR THE PROSECUTION OF AXIS CRIMI ITY. Nazi Conspiracy & Aggression. DC, GPO, 1946-48, roy8vo, 11vols, $25

98) OPPENHEIMER, Franz, System der Soziologie. 2nd ed, Stut, 1964, 4to, 9vols.,$

99) OWEN, Robert, Debate on the Evidences of Christianity.....2nd ed., Cincinnat 1829, 8vo, two vols bound as one, later linen, $115.00

100) OWEN,,Robert, A New View of Society....London, 1813, 8vo, 24pp., later 1/2 morocco, of great rarity, first edition, Printing & the Mind of Man. $32

101) PARETO, Vilfredo, The Mind & Society. NY, 1935, roy8vo, 4vols., $87.50

102) PEAKE, Th., A Compendium of the Law of Evidence. P, 1802, 8vo, contemp.calf,

103) PETTY, Sir William, Political Arithmetic.... Glasgow, 1751, 12mo, x,97,44pp., later linen, $87.50

104) PISTOR, G. H., Memoires sur la Revolution de la Pologne. P, 1806, 8vo, civ,2 later buck, two fold out maps, $77.60

--6--

105) PLACE, Francis, Illustrations & Proofs of the Principles of Population. L, 182 8vo, xv,280pp., later 1/2 morocco, first edition, $235.00

106) PLECHANOW, Georg, Beiträge zur Geschichte des Materialismus. Stut, 1896, 8vo, vii,254pp., orig. cl., first edition, $67.50

107) QUETELET, A. D., Physique Sociale. Brux, 1869, roy8vo, 2vols., with a new pref by the author to this secnnd ed., later linen, ex lib, $125.00

108) RAUMER, Friedrich von, Uber die Geschichtliche Entwicklung der Begriffe von Recht, Staat u. Politik. 3rded., enl., L, 1861, 8vo, 308pp, rebacked, $27.5

109) RAYNOUARD, M., Histoire du Droit Municipal en France. P, 1829, 8vo, 2vols., orig. ptd. wrps, sl. soiled & sl. worn, $37.50

110) RICARDO, David, On the Principles of Political Economy & Taxation. 2nd ed., L, 1819, 8vo, vii,550pp., contemp. calf, $125.00

111) ROBERTS, Wm., A Treatise on the Statute of Frauds. 2nd American from the last Londoned., Hartford, 1823, 8vo, contemp. calf, $35.00

112) RODRIGUES, Eugene, Lettres sur la Religion et la Politique....P, 1831, 8vo, xvi, 180pp., later linen with orig. wrps bound in, first edition, $150.00

113) (ROMAN LAW), Institutionum Iuris Civilis Libri III.....per D. Jacobum Curtium. Venice, 1588, 12mo, 535p., contemp. vellum, bit worn, $125.00

114) ROPER, R. S., A Treatise on the Revocation & Republication of Wills & Testaments. P, 1803, 8vo, cantemp. roan, but worn, $37.50

115) ROSCHER, Wilhelm, Politik. 2nd ed., Stut, 1893, roy8vo, 722pp., rebacked,$22.5

116) SANDERSON, Edgar, The British Empire at Home & Abroad. L, 1901, 6large 8vo, vols bound as 3, 1/2 morocco & buckram, $125.00

117) SAINT-SIMON ET ENFANTIN, Oeuvres. P, 1865-78 (Reprint: 1964), 8vo, 47vols., (bound as 24), like new, $425.00

118) SAVIGNY, F. M. C., Traite de Droit Romain. traduit par M, Ch. Guenoux, Paris, 1840-1851, 8vo, 8vols., contemp. bds, rebacked, $150.00

119) SAY, J. B., Traite d'Economic Politique. 4th ed., corr. & aug., P, 1819, 8vo, 2vols., contemp. polished calf, fine set, $75.00

120) SEYBERT, Adam, Annales Stastiques des Etats-Unis. P, 1820, 8vo, 455pp., later linen, $57.50

121) SHAKESPEARE, Wm., Oeuvres Completes....translated by Francois-Victor Hugo. 2nd ed., P, 1866-73, 8vo, 18vols., bound in contemp. 1/2 morocco & marbled boards. superb set, $275.00

122) SIDNEY, Algernon, Discourses Concerning Government. 2nd ed., to Which is Added the Paper....L, 1704, folio, 424pp., engr. frontis, contemp. calf, rebacked $135.00

123) SISMONDI, Simonde de, Histoire des Republiques Italliennes du Moyen Age. 5th e Brux, 1838, 8vo, 8vols., contemp. 1/2 calf, bit worn, $175.00

124) SISMONDI, Revue des Progres des Opinions Religieuses. P, n.d. (1826), 8vo, 51p orig. ptd. wrps., first published ed., $47.50

125) SISMONDI, Etudes sur l'Economie Politique. Brix, 1837-8, 8vo, later 1/2 morocco, fine set, first edition, $250.00

126) SMITH, Adam, An Inquiry into the Nature & Causes of the Wealth of Nations. P, 1789, 8vo, 3vols., contemp. calf, first American edition, $1000.00

127) SMITH, Adam, Essays on Philosophical Subjects....L, 1795, 4to, xcv,244pp., orig. bds, rebacked, fine copy, first edition, $425.00

128) SMITH Adam, Untersuchungen uber das Wesen und die Ursachen des Nationalreichtums. Deutsch mit Anmerkungen von MAX STIRNER. Leipzig, Wigand, 1846-47, 8vo, 4vols., bound as one, later line, rare, $185.00

--7--

129) SOUTHEY, Rob., Sir Thomas More. L, 1829, 8vo, 2vols., contemp. 1/2 morocc & marbled bds, sl. worn, first edition, $125.00

130) SPELMAN, Sir Hwnry, Glossarium Archiologicum....L, 1664, folio, 576pp., bound in later 1/2 morocco & linen, first edition, $250.00

131) SPELMAN, Sir Henry, History & Fate of Sacrilege. 2nd ed., w/Adds., L, 1853, 8vo, xxix,371pp., orig. cl., sl. worn, $37.50

132) SPINOZA, Benedict, Opera. ed. Carl Gebhart, Heidelberg, n.d. (1925), 4to, 4vols., orig. buckram, $125.00

133) SPENGLER, Oswald, Jahre der Entscheidung: Erster Teil. M, 1933, 8vo, 165pp first edition, $37.50

134) SQUIRE, Samuel, An Enquiry into the Foundation of the English Constitution new ed., w/Adds. L, 1753, 8vo, 427pp., later linen, $100.00

135) STEPHEN, Henry, New Commentaries on the Laws of England. L, 1858, roy8vo, 4vols., orig. cl., $75.00

136) STORY, Jos., A Familiar Exposition of the Constitution of the US.... NY, 1 12mo, 372pp., orig. cl., rebacked, $37.50

137) STORY, Jos., A Discourse Pronounced upon the Inauguration of the Author as Dane Professor of Law in Harvard University. 1829, 8vo, orig wrps, $37.

138) STORCH, Henri, Cours d'Economic Politique....avec des Notes Explicatives e Critiques par J. B. SAY. P, 1823, 8vo, 4vols., later 1/2 morocco, $235.

139) STRAUSS, David Friedrich, Das Leben Jesu Kritisch Bearbeitet. 4th ed, Tub., 1840, 8vo, 2vols., wontemp. 1/2 calf, bit rubbed, $125.00

140) STRAUSS, David Friedrich, Die Christliche Glaubenslehre.... Tub, 1840-41, 8vo, 2vols., later 1/2 morocco, first edition, $250.00

141) THOMAS, William I., & ZNANIECKI, Florian, The Polish Peasant in Europe & America. Boston, n.d. (1920), roy8vo, 5vols., orig. cl., first complete edition, $175.00

142) TONNIES, Ferdinand, Gemeinschaft und Gesellschaft. L, 1887, 8vo, xxx,294pp contemp. 1/2 calf & marbled bds, first edition, $125.00

143) TORRENS, Robert, An Essay on the Production of Wealth. L, 1821, 8vo, xvi, 430pp., later linen, first edition, $145.00

144) U.S. Commission on Industrial Relations: Industrial Relations: Final Repor & Testimony Submitted to Congress. DC, 1916, 8vo, 11vols., $175.00

145) (VANDAM, Albert D.), An Englishman in Paris. L, 1892, 8vo, 700pp., 2nd ed. contemp. 1/2 calf & linen, fine, $37.50

146) VATTEL, M. de., The Law of Nations. NY, 1796, 8vo, xlviii,563pp., contemp. roan, rebacked, bit worn, first American edition, $125.00

147) VEBLEN, Thorstein, Theory of Business Enterprise. NY, 1904, 8vo, vii,400pp orig. cl., few margins bit jagged from hasty cutting, else fine, first edition, $75.00

148) VILLENEUVE-BARGEMONT, Alban de, Histoire de l'Economie Politique. P, 1841, 8vo, 2vols., later 19th cent. buck, rare, $150.00

149) VOLTAIRE, The Philosophy of History. L, 1766, 8vo, viii,316pp., later 1/2 morocco & linen, first English edition, $100.00

150) VOLTAIRE, Oeuvres Completes. P, 1818-25. 8vo, 66vols., (bound as 33), cont 1/2 morocco, bit rubbed & scuffed, $675.00

151) VOLTAIRE, M., La Philosophie de l'Histoire. Amsterdam, 1765, 8vo, viii,268 contemp. calf, bit worn, same year as first edition, $125.00

--8--

152) VON HOLST, Hermann, Constitutional & Political History of the US. C, 1889, roy8vo, 8vols., $110.00

153) WATSON, Wm., A Treatise on the Law of Partnesship. L, 1794, 8vo, contemp. calf, $47.50

154) WEBER, Adolf, Sozialpolitik. M, 1931, roy8vo, 235pp., $22.50

155) WEBER, MAX, Wirtschaft und Gesellechaft. 2nd ed., enl., Tub, 1925, 4to, 2vo orig. cl., $87.50

156) WHITNEY, Henry, Life on the Circuit with Lincoln. B, 1892, 4to, 601pp., ori cl., ill. w/67 plates, first edition, $30.00

157) WIGMORE, John Hanry, Chairman, Committee of American Law Schools, Select-Essays in Anglo-American Legal History. B, 1907-19, roy8vo, 3vols, $75.

158) WILDE, Oscar, Trials of. L, 1952. 8vo, 384pp., $15.00

159) WILSON, Joshua, Biographical Index to the Present House of Commons.... L, 1807, 8vo, 596pp., later buckram, $47.50

160) YEARBOOK. De Termino Michaelis Anno iiii Regni Regis Henrici vi. (1422-61) L, Tottel, 1556, 4to, xxxii leaves, later bds, $125.00

161) YEARBOOK. De Termono Trinitatis An xii, Hen VIII. (1509-47), L, 1548, 4to, bds, $125.00

162) YEARBOOK. Pascal Term of the 27th Year of Henry VIII. L, 1556, 4to, 30leav modern boards, sporadic underlining & marginal annotations in an antique hand, black letter, $125.00

List 16

Law (1977)

Richard Adamiak
1545 East 60th St.
Chicago, Illinois 60637
312-955-4571

1) ADAMS, John, A Treatise on the Principles and Practice of the Action of Ejectment, and the Resulting Action for Meane Profit. from the 3rd.... with Notes of the Decisions Made by the Supreme Court and Circuit Court of the United States, & by the Courts of the Several States where Decisions have been Reported, by John L. Tillinghast. New York, 1840, roy8vo, xii, 544pp., contemp. roan, rebacked, $25.00

2) Archiv für Urkundenforschung (Journal of Document Research), edited by Karl Brandi, Harry Bresslau, Michael Tangl. Leipzig. Volumes I through XIV, 1908 to 1938, bound in 7 stout volumes of about 1000pp/ each, later buckram, $175.00

3) ATHERLEY-JONES, L.A. & BELLOT, Hugh H.L., Commerce in War. London, 1907, roy8vo, 654pp., orig. cl., ex lib, $15.00

4) BARUCH, Bernard M., & HANCOCK, John M., Report on War and Post-War Adjustment Policies. n.p., Feb 15, 1944, 8vo, 108pp., orig.ptd.wrps., $12.50

5) BANKS, John, A Short Critical Review of the Political Life of Oliver Cromwell.... 4th edition, London,1760. sm8vo, 330pp.,contemp.calf, crown a trifle worn, else excellent, $37.50

6) BEVERIDGE, Albert J., The State of the Nation. Ind., 1924, 8vo, 277pp., $12.50

7) BIENER,Fried.August, Das Englische Geschworengericht (The English Jury), Leipzig, 1852-55, 8vo, 3vols bound as 2, about 1000pp., later linen, extremeties a bit worn, blind stamp on title, $37.50

8) BLAND, A.E., BROWN, M.A., & TAWNEY, R.H., (eds), English Economic History Select Documents. London, 1914, 8vo, xx, 730pp., $12.50

9) BLUNTSCHLI, J. K., The Theory of the State. translated from the 6th German edition, Oxford, 1892, 8vo, xxv, 550pp., $12.50

10) BONNIER, Edouard, Traité Theoretique et Practique des Preuves en Droit Civil et en Droit Criminel. 5th edition, rev. & updated, Paris, 1888, 8vo, 788pp.,later linen, $22.50

11) BOUTWELL, George S., A Manual of the Direct and Excise Tax System of the United States: Including the Forms and Regulations Established by the Commissioner of Internal Revenue, the Decisions and Rulings of the Commissioner....4th edition, Boston, 1864, roy8vo, 333pp.,orig. cloth, covers & title a bit soiled, else excellent, $15.00

12) BROWN, John, Thoughts on Civil Liberty, on Licentiousness, and Faction. Newcastle Upon Tyne, 1765, 8vo, 167pp., later linen, small stamp on verso, excellent, $67.50

13) BRUNNER, Heinrich, Abhandlungen zur Rechtsgeschichte: Gesammelte Aufsätze ed. by Karl Rauch, Weimar, 1931, roy8vo, 2vols., 1400pp., orig. cl.,vg, $37.50

14) BULLER, Francis, An Introduction to the Law Relative to Trials at Nisi Prius, Containing Additions to the Present Time, Carefulle Corrected from the Last London Copy, by a Gentleman of the Bar. New York, 1806, 8vo, 336pp. plus index, contemp. roan, $37.50

15) BURGE, William, Commentaries on the Law of Suretyship and the Rights and Obligations of Parties Thereto.....and of Obligations in Solido, under the Laws of England, Scotland and the Other States of Europe, the British Colonies and the United States, and on the Conflict of Laws. 1st American, from the London edition. Boston, 1847, roy8vo, 500pp., contemp. roan, rebacked, $30.00

16) BURN, Richard, The Justice of the Peace and Parish Officer. 11th edition London, 1769, 8vo, 4vols., 2000pp., later linen, $125.00

17) BURN, Richard, Ecclesiastical Law. 2nd edition, London, 1767, 8vo, 4vol 2000pp., contemp. polished calf, joints a bit cracked and some minor wear of extremeties, else excellent, $125.00

18) CARNEGIE ENDOWMENT OF INTERNATIONAL PEACE: DIVISION OF INTERNATIONAL LAW Reports to the Hague Conference of 1899 and 1907....edited, with an introduction by James Brown Scott. Oxford, 1917, 4to, 940pp., orig. cl., stamp on title, $27.50

19) CARNEGIE ENDOWMENT OF INTERNATIONAL PEACE: DIVISION OF INTERNATIONAL LAW: The Hague Court Reports (Second Series), edited with an Introduction by James Brown Scott, Oxford, 1932, 8vo, xlvii, 234pp., orig. cl., trace of wear at crown, $15.00

20) CHITTENDEN, L.E., A Report of the Debates and Proceedings in the Secret Sessions of the Conference Convention, for Proposing Amendments to the Constitution of the United States, Held at Washington, D.C., in February, A.D. 1861, by L.E. Chittenden, One of the Delegates. New York, 18 roy8vo, 626pp., orig. cloth, some light sporadic foxing and watermark, else vg, $37.50

21) CLAUSEWITZ, General von, Vom Kriege, mit einer Einführung von Graf von Schliessen. 10th edition, Berlin & Leipzig, 1915, roy8vo, xxxvi, 827pp orig. 1/2 linen and bds, inner hinges skillfully mended, $25.00

22) DOMAT, Jeanne, (ed.), Legum Delectus ex Libris Digestorum & Codicis, ad Usum Scholae & Fori. Accedunt Singulis Legibus quae summae earum brevi complexae. Editio Secunda, a Mednis Purgata. Amsterdam, 1703, 4to, 629pp., contemp. calf, rubbed in spots, else vg, "Domat was in a sense the founder of the science of public law in France," Max Radin, "Jean Domat," Encyclopedia of the Social Sciences, V, 194, $135.00

23) HARDCASTLE, THE hon. Mrs. (ed.), The Life of John, Lord Campbell, Lord High Chancellor of Great Britain, Consisting of a Selection from His Autobiography, Diary and Letters. 2nd ed., London, 1881, 8vo, 2vols., 950pp., 3/4 morocco & marbled boards, joints slightly cracked, else vg, $37.50

24) COMYNS, Sir John, A Digest of the Laws of England. 4th Edition, Correcte and Continued to the Present Time by Samuel Rose. London, 1800, roy8vo 6vols., later buckram, $140.00

25) COOLEY, Thomas M., A Treatise on the Law of Torts, or the Wrongs which Arise Independently of Contracts. Student's Edition by John Lewis, Chicago, 1907, 4to, cxcvii, 820pp., orig. cl., $17.50

26) CORPUS JURIS CIVILIS, edited by Mommsen, Krueger & Schoell, Berlin, 1896 4to, 3 vols., later linen, $75.00 (still the definitive edition)

27) CROMPTON, Geo., The Practice of the Court of Kings Bench & Common Pleas, Corr., Rev. & Newly Arranged by John S. Baker, 1st American from the last London edition, with the Addition of New Cases as Found in the English Reports to the Present Day. New York, 1813, 8vo, 2vols., 1100pp., later cloth, blindstamped, $47.50

28) CUSHING, Lther, Elements of the Law and Practice of Legislative Assemblie in the United States. 2nd ed., Boston, 1866, roy8vo, xxvii, 1061pp., contemp. roan, trace of wear at crown, else vg, $25.00

29) DAVID, Rene, & HAZARD, John, Le Droit Sovietque. Paris, 1954, roy8vo, 2vols., 750pp. org. ptd.wrps., $25.00

30) DEBATES IN THE CONGRESS OF THE United States on the Bill for Repealing the Law "for the More Convenient Organization of the Courts of the United States" During the First Session of the Seventh Congress, and a List of Yeas and Nays on that Interesting Subject/Albany,1802, 8vo, 796pp., contemp. roan, hinge a bit worn, front free end paper lacking, edges of title a trifle worn, else vg, $37.50

31) DILLON, E.J., The Peace Conference. London, n.d. (c. 1920), 8vo, 439pp., extremities a bit worn, else vg, $15.00

32) DIXON, William H., Her Majesty's Tower. 7th edition, London, 1885, roy8vo, 4vols., ill., extrmeties a trifle worn, else vg, $37.50

33) DUGDALE, William, Origines Juridicales: or Historical Memorials of the English Laws, Courts of Justice,Forms of Tryal, Punishment in Cases Criminal, Law-Writers, Law Books, Grants and Settlements of Estates, Degree of Serjeant, Innes of Court & Chancery; Also a Chronologie of the Lord of Chancellors & Keepers of the Great Seal, Lord Treasures, Justices Itinerant Justices of the Kings Bench & Common Pleas, Barons of the Exchequer, Masters of the Rolls, Kings Attorneys and Solicitors & Serjeants at Law; Second Edition, with Additions. In the Savoy, 1671, folio, 336, 117pp., with six full page engraved portraits (Coke, Clarendon etc.), and several full pages of engravings of arms, later half-calf and linen, $225.00

34) ENDEMAN, W., Die Beweislehre des Civilprocess. Heidelberg, 1860, 8vo, xv, 668pp., contemp/bds, $22.50

35) ERBE, Walter, Die Fiduzia im Römischen Recht. Weimar, 1940, 8vo, 212pp., orig. ptd. wrps, $12.50

36) FINN, R. Welldon, The Domesday Inquest and the Making of Domesday Book. London, 1961, 8vo, 201pp., $10.00

37) FLETCHER, C. R. L., An Introductory History of England. New York, 1907-09, 8vo, 3vols., 1200., extremeties a bit worn, else vg, the author was Late Fellow of Magdalen College, Oxford, $30.00

38) FOSTER, John W., American Diplomany in the Orient. Noston, 1903, 8vo, 498pp., $15.00

39) FOSS, Edward, A Biographical Dictionary of the Judges of England from the Conquest to the Present Time. London, 1870, roy8vo, 791pp.,orig. cl., redbacked, $37.50

40) GARDINER, Samuel R., A Student's History of England. New Edition. London, 1902, 8vo. 3 vols., 996pp., some ligth sporadic pencil underlining, else vg, $22.50

41) GILBERT, Lord Chief Baron, The Law of Evidence. 5th edition, Corrected wit Many Additions, Lonon/&Philadephia, 1788, 8vo, 286pp., later linen, title a trifle soiled, else vg, $37.50

42) GNEIST, Rudolf, Englische Verfassungsgeschichte. (English Constitutional History), Berlin, 1882, roy8vo, 731pp., later linen, $27.50

43) GUIZOT, M., History of the Origin of Representative Government in Europe. trans.by Andrew Scoble. London, 1852, 8vo, 538pp., crown trifle worn, else vg, $22.50

44) HAMMOND, Elisha, A Treatise on the Law of Fire Insurance and Insurance on Inland Waters....with an Appendix of Forms. New York, 1840,8vo, xi, 182pp., contemp/3/4 roan and marbled boards, $27.50

45) HAWKINS, Sir Henry, The Reminiscences of Sir Henry Hawkins, Baron Brampto edited by Richard Harris, New York, 1904, 8vo, 2vols., $27.50

46) HEADLAM-MORLEY, Agnes, The New Democratic Constitutions of Europe: A Comparative Study of Post-War Constitutions with Special Reference to Germany, Czechoslovakia, Poland, Finland, the Kingdom of the Serbs, Croats and Slovenes and the Baltic States. Oxford, 1929, 8vo, 298pp., $15.00

47) HEINECCIUS, Johann G., A Methodological System of Universal Law: or: the Laws of Nature & Nations Deduced from Certain Principles & Applied to Proper Cases. Written in Latin by the Celebrated Jo. Got.Heineccius, Counsellor of State to the King of Prussia & Professor of Philosophy at Hall. Translated and Illustrated with Notes & Supplements by Geo. Turnbull, LL.D., to which is Added a Discourse Upon the Nature & Origin of Moral & Civil Laws in Which They are Deduced by an Analysis of the Human Mind in the Experimental Way from our Internal Principles & Dispositions. London, 1741, 8vo, 2vols., contemp. calf, rebacked, nice set, "one of the most important and influential jurists of the 18th century," Encyclopedia of the Social Sciences, VII, 316, $185.00

48) HENRIOT, Eug., Moeurs Juridiques et Judiciaires de l'Ancienne Rome. Paris, 1865, 8vo, 3vols., 1500pp., contemp. 1/2 linen and bds, crowns a bit worn, else vg, (reprinted at $115.00), $65.00

49) HEYTHUYSEN, F.M. van, The Equity Draftsman, Being a Selection of Forms of Pleadings in Suits in Equity....Revised & Enlarged with Numerous Additional Forms and Practical Notes by Edw. Hughes. 3rd American from the last London edition. New York, 1843, roy8vo, xxxvii, 919pp., contemp. roan, some marginal watermark, $27.50

50) HOME, Henry (ed.), Historical Law Tracts. 2nd edition, Edinburgh, 1761, 8vo, xv, 463pp., later linen, $87.50

51) INTERNATIONAL COURT OF JUSTICE, Pleadings and Oral Arguments, Document: International Status of South-West Africa; Advisory Opinion of July 11, 1950, roy8vo, 371pp., $15.00

52) KENDALL, E.A., An Argument for Construing Largely the Right of an Appelle of Murder to Insist on Trial by Battle; and Also for Abolishing Appeals with an Appendix Containing a Report of a Debate in the House of Commons on Abolishing Appeal of Murder in the British North American Colonies. 3rd edition, Including Remarks on the ....Appellee, Ashford V. Thornton in the King's Bench, Jan 24, 1818. London, 1818, 8vo, 304pp., later linen with orig. wrps bound in, ex lib, $37.50

53) LABAND, Paul, Die Vermögensrechtlichen Klagen nach den Sächsischen Rechtsquellen des Mittelalters. Berlin, 1869, roy8vo, ix, 406pp., 1/2 linen & bds, $25.00

54) LEAGUE OF NATIONS: Committee of Experts for the Progressive Codification o International Law; Report to the Council of the League of Nations on th Questions which Appear Ripe for International Regulation. Geneva, 1927, folio, orig. ptd. wrps, 282pp; League of Nations: Conference for the Codification of International Law; Basis of Discussion Drawn up for the Conference by the Preparatory Committee: Vol. I: Nationality, Geneva,

-5-

1929, folio, orig. ptd. wrps; Vol. II: Territorial Waters, Geneva, 1 folio, orig. ptd. wrps; Vol. III: Responsibility of States for Dama Caused in Their Territory to the Person or Property of Foreigners, Geneva, 1929, folio, orig. ptd. wrps, the four volume set, about 1000pp. $87.50

55) LEWIS, Abram H., Sunday Legislation: Its History to the Present Time and Its Results. New ed., rev. & enl., New York, 1902, 8vo, xiv, 297pp., bit soiled, else vg, $12.50

56) LIEBER, Francis, Legal & Political Hermeneutics, or Principles of Inte pretation & Construction in Law & Politics with Remarks on Precedent and Authorities. Enlarged Edition. Boston, 1839, 8vo, xii, 240pp., orig. cl., excellent, first published edition, $65.00

57) LORD SHAW OF DUNFERMLINE, The Law of the Kinsmen, with a Forward by William Howard Taft, Chief Justice of the United States. New York, 1923, roy8vo, 178pp., orig. cl., nice copy, $22.50

58) MARSHALL, John, The Life of George Washington....to which is Prefixed Introduction Containing a Compendious View of the Colonies Planted the English on the Continent of North America, from their Settlement to the Commencement of that War which Terminated in their Independe Philadelphia, 1804-1807, 8vo, 5vols., bit rubbed and scuffed in spo trace of external wear, else a beautiful set, $185.00, first editio

59) MATTINGLY, Garrett, Renaissance Diplomacy. London, 1962, 8vo, 323pp., $10.00

60) MOMMSEN, THEODOR, Römisches Staatsrecht, 8vo, 5vols.,reprint of the 3 edition, excellent, $125.00, still the leading work on the subject.

61) NOVICON, J., La Federation de l'Europe. Paris, Alcan, 1901. 8vo. 807p contemp. 1/2 linen & marbled bds, 1/2 title mended, bit soiled & sh else vg, $15.00

62) Official Report of the Universal Congress of Lawyers and Jurists, Hel at St. Louis, 1904, Under the Auspices of the Universal Exposition the American Bar Assn., St. Lous, 1905, roy8vo, 423pp.,orig. cl.,$2

63) OLIPHANT, T.L. Kingston, The Old and Middle English. London, 1878, 8v 668pp., "especially valuable on account of the collateral illustrat it affords of the political & social events of the time," Gardiner Mullinger, Introduction to the Study of English History, 208, $17.5

64) PAL, Justice R.B., International Military Tribunal for the Far East: Dissentient Judgment of Justice R. B. Pal. Calcutta, 1953, roy8vo, xvii, 701pp., $22.50

65) PECK, Francis, Desiderata Curiosa: Or, A Collection of Diverse, Scarc Curious Pieces Relating Chiefly to Matters of English History, Consisting of Choice Tracts,Memoirs, Letters, Wills.... A New Edition, Greatly Corrected. London, 1779, 4to, 2 vols. bound as one, 581pp., contemp. pol. calf, rebacked, $47.50

66) PLANCK, J.W., Das Deutsche Gerichtsverfahren im Mittelalter, Nach dem Sachsenspiegel und den verwandten Rechtsquellen. Braunschweig, 1879 roy8vo, 2vols., 1300pp., later linen, covers bit soiled, else vg, $

67) POWELL, John Jos., A Treatise on the Law of Mortgages, 1st American f the 4th London edition, Rev. Corr. & Greatly Enl., with an Appendix Precedents. two vols in one, Hartford, 1811, roy8vo, viii, 1199pp., temp roan, a few minor cover flaws & some very slight sporadic wate mark, nice copy, $47.50

68) PRICE, M.P. (ed.), The Diplomatic History of the War... New York, n.d (1914), roy8vo, 344,102pp ,orig. cl., spine faded, $17.50

69) PRZEDZIECKI, M.P. (ed.), The Diplomatic History of the War....New York n.d. (1914), roy8vo, 344, 102pp., orig. cl., spine faded, $17.50

69) QUINCY, Edmund, The Life of Josiah Quincy...by His Son. Boston, 1867, 560pp., orig. cl., bit shaken & inner hinges mended, $15.00

70) RAY, I., A Treatise on the Medical Jurisprudence of Insanity. 3rd ed., w/ Additions, Boston, 1853, roy8vo, 521pp., later buck, margine of title skillfully restored, $25.00

71) RICHARDSON, Rob., The Attorney's Practice in the Court of Common Pleas 7th ed., with large Additions. Dublin, 1792, 8vo, 2vols. as one (as issued), 650pp., later linen, $37.50

72) ROOT, Elihu, Experiments in Government & the Essentials of the Constit Princeton, 1913, 8vo, iv, 83pp., orig. cl., $12.50

73) Уложение о Наказанияхъ: Уголовныхъ и Исправительныхъ (Uloshenie o Nakazaniiax: Ugolevnyx i Ispravitelnyx)-Kodex Kar Gełownych i Poprawczych- The (Russian) The (Russian) Criminal Code (for the realm of Poland). Warsaw, 1847, 946pp., contemp. 1/2 calf and marbled boards, joints a bit cracked a some minor wear of extremeties, else vg, text in Russian with facing Polish translation, $135.00

74) SAVIGNY, Friedrich Carl von, Das Obligationsrecht als Theil des Heutig Römischen Rechts. Berlin, 1851, 8vo, 2vols., later 19th century line bds, some slight external wear, else excellent, first edition, $75.0

75) SAVIGNY, Friedrich Carl von, System des Heutigen Römischen Rechts. Ber 1840-1849, 8vo, 8vols., I-V in contemp. bds, VI-VIII later linen, $1

76) SAVIGNEY, Friedrich Carl von, Vermischte Schriften, Berlin, 1850, 8vo, 5vols.,orig., bds. uncut, extremeties a bit worn, else excellent, fi edition, $175.00

77) SAVIGNY, Friedrich Karl von, Geschichte des Römischen Rechts im Mittel alter. 8vo, 7vols., 2nd ed., rev., later linen, 1834-1851, $185.00

78) S.N.D., William Howard, Viscount Stafford, 1612-80. London, 1929, 8vo, 252pp., $12.50

79) STAMMLER, Rudolf, SOHM, Rudolf & GAREIS, Karl, Systematische Rechtswis schaft. 2nd ed., imp., Leipzig-Berlin, 1913, 4to, xiii, 583pp.,orig. 3/4 linen & bds, $37.50

80) STAMMLER, Rudolf, Praktische Pandectenübungen für Anfänger. Leipzig, 1896, 8vo, 536pp., orig. cl., stamp on title, $15.00

81) STATE PAPERS ON NULLIFICATION: Including the Public Acts of the Conve of the People of South Carolina, Assembled at Columbia, November 19, and March 11, 1833; the Proclamation of the President of the United States and the Proceedings of the Several State Legislatures which Acted on the Subject; Collected and Published by Order of the Gener Court of Massachusetts. Boston, 1834, 8vo, vii, 381pp., title neatl mended, lacks blank leaves, later linen, $37.50

82) STEPHEN, Henry John, A Treatise on the Principles of Pleading in Civi Actions: Comprising a Summary View of the Whole Proceedings in a Su of Law. 6th American edition, with Notes & Additions, from the firs London edition, by Francis J. Troubat. Phil., 1851, 8vo, xvi, 443pp contemp. roan, $27.50

83) STORY, Joseph, The Life and Letters of Joseph Story, Edited by His So William W. Story. Boston, 1851, roy8vo, 2vols., frontis, orig. cl., rebacked, first ed. $87.50

84) STORY, Jos. (ed.), The Public & General Statutes Passed by the Congre

-7-

the United States of America from 1789 to 1827 Inclusive, Whether Expired, Repealed or in Force; Arranged in Chronological Order, with Marginal References and a Copious Index, to which is Added the Constitution of the United States and an Appendix. Published under the Inspection of Joseph Story. Boston, 1827, roy8vo, 3vols., contemp. roan, bit rubbed and scuffed in spots, nice set, $225.00

85) SWINBURNE, Henry, A Treatise on Testaments and Last Wills, Compiled out of the Laws Civil, Ecclestiastical & Canon, as Also out of the Common Laws, Customs and Statutes of this Realm. 5th Edition, Corr. & very much Enl., London, 1728, folio, 540pp., plus index, later linen, $75.00

86) THIERRY, Augustin, Histoire de la Conquete de l'Angleterre par les Normands, de ses Causes et de ses Suites Jusqu'à nos Jours. Nouvelle Editio suive de la Liste des Conquerants et de la Discription de la Tapisserie de Bayeaux. Paris, 1870, 8vo, 816pp., 1/2 morocco and bds, nice copy, $27.50, superseded by Freeman's Norman Conquest but still useful for the history of that event and necessary for the study of its historiography.

87) TRANSCRIPT OF THE PROCEEDINGS OF THE EMERGENCY BOARD (Appointed by the President of the United States). Chicago, 1948. Wage-Rules Case. Brotherhood of Locomotive Engineers....vs. Designated Railroads. 4to, 2vols., 2670pp., bit soiled, else vg, $37.50

88) VANGEROW, Karl Adolf von, Lehrbuch der Pandecten. Munich & Leipzig, 1863-69, 7th ed., rev. & enl., 3vols., 8vo, 2300pp., orig. bds, rebacked, $75.00(reprinted for $175.00) "not an exact treatise but a skeleton outline accompanied by dissertations arbitrarily selected (which) nevertheless furnish models of juridical discussion upon those questions." Girard, Short History of Roman Law, 195.

89) WEISKE, Julius (ed.), Rechtslexikon für Juristen aller teutschen Staaten, enthaltend die Gesammte Rechtswissenschaft. Leipzig, 1839-1862, roy8vo, 16vols., 500 to 900pp. in each, extremeties a trifle worn, else excellent, quite scarce, $275.00

90) WILCOX, Francis P., The Ratification of International Conventions. London, 1935, 8vo, 349pp., $15.00

91) WILSON, Joshua, A Biographical Index to the Present House of Commons, Corrected to April, 1807. London, 1807, 12mo, xvi, 596pp., later buckram ex lib, $25.00

92) (WONTER, Th.,) Old Bailey Experience: Criminal Jurisprudence and the Actual Working of Our Penal Code of Law; Also an Essay on Prison Discipline, to Which is Added a History of Crimes Committed by Offenders in the Present Day. London, 1833, 8vo, 447pp., orig. bds, rebacked, $37.50

93) WUNDERLICH, Frieda, German Labor Courts,with a Chapter on the Labor Courts in the German Judicial System by Ernst Fraenkel. Chapel Hill, Univ. of North Carolina Press, 1946, 8vo, 252pp., $15.00

94) ZEITSCHRIFT FÜR RECHTSGESCHICHTE, edited by Rudorff, Bruns, Roth, Merkel & Böhlau, Weimar, complete run of volumes I through XIII, 1861-1878, roy8vo, 13vols. bound in later linen, excellent; the continuation of the Zeitschrift für geschichtliche Rechtswissenschaft founded by Savigny in 1815, $275.00

95) ZUMPF, A. W., Das Criminal Recht der Römischen Republik. Belin, 1865-68, 8vo, 4vols bound as two, 1800pp., contemp. linen,rebacked, $75.00 (reprinted at $165.00)

96) Public & General Statutes of the United States, a continuation of #84 above to the year 1837, edited by Geo. Sharswood, Philadephia, 1837, 8vo, later buckram, $37.50

End of Law List 16

Addenda of Books in Various Field - Including Law

97) RIBIER, Guillaume, Lettres et Memories d'Estat, Des Roys, Princes, Ambassadeurs, et Autres Ministres, sous les Regnes de Francois Premier, Henry II, & Francois II; Continens les Intelligences de ces Roys avec les Princes de l'Europe, contre les Menees de Charles-Quint, principa ment a Constantinople aupres du Grand-Seigneur; en Angleterre avec He VIII, en Allemagne avec les Princes de l'Empire; en Italia avec le Pa & les Venitiens....Ouvrage Compose de Pieces Originales, la Plupart Chiffres, Negotiations & Instructions a nos Ambassadeuts....rangees l'order des temps, & formans comme un copps d'Histoire, par Messire Guillaume Ribier, Conseiller d'Estat. Paris, 1666, folio, 2vols., ab 1400pp., contemp. calf, 2 engraved frontises, title in red & black, forecorners a bit worn, else a very good set, a collection of the Fre diplomatic papers during one of the most turbulent periods of Europe history, $275.00

98) MASEREEL, Frans, Geschichte ohne Worte: 60 Holtzschnitte von Frans Mase Einleitung von Max Brod. München, 1927, 12mo, 72pp,, org. bds. extrem ties just a bit worn, else excellent, first edition, first issue, $4

99) BUCHEZ, P.J.P., Essai d'un Traite Complet de Philosophie du Point de Vu du Catholicisme et du Progres. Paris, 1838-1840, 8vo, 3vols., later h calf and marbled boards, some light watermark of extreme lower forecorner of first few leaves of volume one, else excellent, first editio of one of the most significant and rare socialist works of the 19th century; National Union Catalogue of pre-1956 Imprints notes only th copies in the United States, $350.00

100) EISNER, Kurt, Die Neue Zeit von Kurt Eisner, Ministerpräsident des Volk staates Bayern. München, Müller, 1919, sm8vo, 124pp., orig. ptd. wrp edges a bit browned, else excellent, of extreme rarity, not even one copy in the United States according to the National Union Catalogue Pre-1956 Imprints, $225.00

101) COKE, Sir Edward, The First Part of the Institutes of the Laws of Engla or, A Commentary Upon Littleton, Not in the Name of the Author, but the Law Itself.15th Edition, rev. & corr., with the addition of note references and proper tables by Francis Hargrave and Charles Butler.. including also the notes of Lord Justice Hale & Lord Chancellor Nott ham, with an analysis of Littleton written by an unkown hand in 1658- London, 1794, 8vo, 3vols., later linen, $135.00

102) COKE, Sir Edward, The Second Part of the Institutes of the Laws of Eng Containing the Exposition of Many Ancient and Other Statutes. London, 1817, 8vo, 2vols., later linen, $87.50

103) COKE, Sir Edward, The Third Part of the Institutes of the Laws of Engla Concerning High Treason and Other Pleas of the Crown & Criminal Caus 6th edition, London, 1680, 4to, 243pp., later half-linen and marbled boards, $145.00

104) COKE, Sir Edward, The Fourth Part of the Institutes of the Laws of England; Concerning the Jurisdiction of Courts. 6th Edition, London, 1681, 4yo, 364pp., later hanf-linen and marbled boards, $145.00

105) COKE, Sir Edward, The Fourth Part of the Institutes of the Laws of Eng Concerning the Jurisdiction of Courts. London, 1817, 8vo, 364pp., la linen, $47.50

106) BLACKSTONE, Sir William, Commentaries on the Laws of England. Oxford, 1775 Seventh Edition, 8vo, 4vols., contemp. calf, rebacked, nice set, $225.00

107) PETITUS, Samuel, Leges Atticae.... Paris, 1635, small folio, iii,55,5 contemp. calf, nicely rebacked in calf (17th century), minor externa wear, $175.00

1978

List 17

Law

With an Addenda of Interesting Titles in Various Fields and A Bronze Relief of Theodore (#160) Roosevelt by James Earle Fraser

Richard Adamiak
1545 East 60th St.
Chicago, Illinois 60637
312-955-4571
By Phone: 0700-1300

1) ANTHON, John, American Precedents of Declarations, Collected Chiefly from the Manuscripts of Chief Justice Parsons and Other Accomplished Pleaders in the State of Massachusetts....Adapted to Modern Practice with a Prefixed Digest of Rules & Cases Concerning Declarations. 3rd Edition, Corrected, Brookfield, 1821, roy8vo, xxxii, 516pp., later 1/2 linen and marbled boards, $35.00

2) ATKYNS, Sir Robert, The Power, Jurisdiction & Priviledge of Parliament, & the Antiquity of the House of Commons Asserted....as also a Discourse Concerning the Ecclesiastical Jurisdiction of the Realm of England. London, 1689, folio, 74pp., later1/2 linen and marbled bds. $85.00.

3) BACON, Chs. W., & MORSE, Franklyn S., The Reasonableness of the Law: The Adaptability of Legal Sanctions to the Needs of Society. NY, 1924. roy8vo, 400pp., $15.00.

4) BACON, Sir Francis, Recuscitatio; Or, Bringing into Publick Light Several Pieces of the Works, Civil, Historical, Philosophical & Theological, Hitherto Sleeping, of the Right Honorable Francis Bacon. 3rd ed., Corrected According to the Best Copies, Together with His Lordships Life by William Rawley. London, 1671, folio, 675pp, contemp. pannelled calf, skillfully rebacked, raised bands, engraved frontis. portrait misbound, handsome copy, $125.00

5) BARBEYRAC, Jean, Traite de la Morale des Peres de l'Eglise; ou en Defenent un Article de la Preface sur Puffendorf contre l'Apologie de la Morale des Peres du P. Ceillier. Amsterdam, 1728, 4to, xlii, 334pp., later 1/2 linen and marbled boards, $125.00

6) BENET, Capt. S. V., A Treatise on Military Law and the Practice of Courts-Martial. NY, 1862, 8vo, 377pp., later 1/2 linen, slight marginal dampstain of first few leaves, else excellent. $37.50.

7) BIOGRAPHICAL DIRECTORY OF THE AMERICAN CONGRESS, 1774-1927 Inclusive. DC, GPO, 1928, smfolio, 1740 (2col)pp., $65.00

8) BLACKSTONE, Sir William, Commentaries on the Laws of England, Together with a Copious Analysis of the Contents; and Notes, with References to English & American Decisions & Statutes to Date which Change the Law of the Text....& Some Considerations Regarding the Study of the Law by Thomas M. Cooley. Chicago, 1884, roy8vo, 2vols., later 1/2 linen.$75.00

9) BODENHEIMER, Edgar, Treatise on Justice. NY, 1967, 8vo, 314pp. fine, $6.50

10) BONGER, W. A., Criminalité et Conditions Economique. Amsterdam, 1905, roy8vo, 750pp., light soil, inner hinges reinforced, $30.00

11) BONNEY, Ch. C., Rules of Law for the Carriage and Delivery of Persons & Property by Railway. Chicago, 1864, 8vo, 267pp., marginal watermark of lower forecorners of first & last few leaves, later1/2 linen, $37.50

12) BRASOL, Boris, The Elements of Crime (Psycho-Social Interpretation), with Introductions by John Henry Wigmore & William A. White. Oxford Univ. Press, 1927, 8vo, 433pp., $12.50

--2--

13) BROUGHAM, Henry Lord, Historical Sketches of Statesmen Who Flourished in the Time of George III; to which is Added Remarks on Party, & an Appendix. Ist, 2nd, & 3rd Series. London, 1839-43, 3vols., roy8vo, numerous engraved plates of prominent legal & political figures, bit of light marginal sporadic watermark in II, else vg, later linen, $37.50

14) BROWN, Jas. D., The Collection Laws of the Several States and the District of Columbia, Comprising in a Condensed Form the Laws Relating to Imprisonment for Debt, Attachment, Judgement & Execution, Jurisdiction of the Justices of the Peace, Exemption, the Statute of Limitations, Rights of Married Women, Interest & Usury. Phil., 1885, 8vo, 282pp., contemp. roan, extremeties a bit worn, else vg, $27.50

15) BUCHANAN, George, Opera Omnia: Historica, Chronologica, Juridica, Politica, Satyrica & Poetica....edited by Thomas Ruddiman, Preface by Peter Berman Amsterdam, Lugduni Batavorum, 1725, 4to, 2vols., contemp. vellum, title in red & black, vol II lacks sciver, else excellent, $225.00

16) BULLER, Francis, An Introduction tb the Law Relative to Trials at Nisi Prius, 5th ed., with Adds, & Corrs. NY, 1788, 8vo, 336,29pp., contemp. roan, bit rubbed & scuffed, else vg, $37.50 SOLD

17) BURLAMAQUI, J.J., The Principles of Natural & Politic Law, translated into English by Mr. Nugent. 5th ed., Corr. Cambridge, 1807, 8vl, 2vols., contemp. calf, extremeties a bit worn, else vg, $47.50

18) CAPGRAVE, Johannis, Liber de Illustribus Henricis. edited by Francis Ch. Hingeston. London, 1858, r8vo, lvii, 319pp., (in the series: Chronicles & Monuments of Great Britain & Ireland During the Middle Ages, published under direction of the Master of the Rolls), later 1/2 linen * bds.$27.50

19) CARDOZO, Benjamin, The Growth of the Law. New Haven, 1924, 8vo, 145pp., orig. linen, first edition, $37.50

20) CHITTY, Joseph, A Practical Treatise on-Medical Jurisprudence, first American Edition, with Notes and Additions Adapted to American Works & Judicial Decisions. Part I (all published) Phil., 1835, roy8vo, xxxi, 509pp., later linen, $37.50

21) CLANCY, Jas, A Treatise of the Rights, Duties and Liabilities of Husband & Wife at Law & in Equity. first American from the 3rd London edition, with great additions, NY, 1828, roy8vo, 684pp., contemp. roan, $37.50

22) THE CLERK'S MAGAZINE, Containing the Most Useful Forms which Occur in Business Between Man & Man... Made Conformable to Law by a Member of the Massachusetts Bar. 2nd ed., rev. & enl., Boston, 1833, 8vo, 333pp., contemp roan, bit worn, wlse vg, $25.00

23) THE CODE OF 1650; Being a Compilation of the Earliest Laws and Orders of the General Court of Connecticut: Also the Constitution or Civil Compact Entered into & Adopted by the Towns of Windsor, Hartford and Wethersfield in 1638-39; to Which is Added Some Extracts from the Laws & Judicial Proceedings of the New Haven Colony, Commonly Called Blue Laws. Hartford n.d. (1882), sm8vo, 119pp., orig. cl., crown trifle worn, else vg, $30.00

24) COKE, Sir Edward, The First Part of the Institutes of the Laws of England; A Commentary Upon Littleton. First American from the 16th European Edition, rev. & corr., with the addition of Notes, References & Proper Tables by Francis Hargrave & Charles Butler, Including Also the Notes of Lord Chief Justice Hale & Lord Chancellor Nottingham....to which are now added considerable improvements by Thomas Day. Phil., 1812, roy8vo, 3 parts bound as one volume, about 600pp., later1/2 linen & bds, $75.00

25) COLEGROVE, Kenneth, The American Senate & World Peace. NY, 1944, 8vo, 209pp., $12.50

--3--

THE COMMENTARIES OF GAIUS AND THE RULES OF ULPIAN, translated with notes by J. T. Abdy & B. Walker, new ed., Cambridge, 1874, 8vo, xxvii, 479pp., crown trifle worn, else vg, $22.50

CONSTITUTIONS DES TREIZE ETATS-UNIS DE L'AMERIQUE. A Philadelphie, et se trouve a Paris; chez Ph. -D. Pierres; Pissot, pere et Fils, 1783, 8vo, 540pp., contemp. mottled calf, skillfully rebacked, raised bands, excellent copy, $750.00

First French Edition; these Constitutions were brought to France by Benjamin Franklin and at his suggestion they were translated into French by Duc de la Rochefoucault; Franklin added over fifty footnotes of his own and published the work in an edition of 600. Its publication engendered intense debate in Europe among those who were closely following the American constitutional & political experiment; three leading critics of the Constitutions were Turgot, Priestly and following author:

MABLY, L'Abby de, Observations sur le Gouvernement et les Loix des Etats-Unis d'Amerique. A Amsterdam, Rosart, 1784, sm8vo, 213pp., contemp. bds., skillfully rebacked, escellent copy, first edition, $225.00

This work, along with those of Turgot & Priestly, provoked John Adams; brilliant Defence of the Constitutions of Government of the United States; in it all three are refuted but Mably was singled out for special attention in a letter to him appended to the first volume of the first edition.

COVODE INVESTIGATION (of Naval Contracts and Public Printing), House of Representatives, 36th Congress, 1st Session, Report #648. June 16, 1860. roy8vo, 838pp., extremeties a bit worn, else vg, $30.00

CROMPTON, Geo., The Practice of the Court of King's Bench and Common Pleas. rev. corr. & newly arr. by Baker J. Sellon, first American from the last London edition, with the Addition of the New Cases, as Found in the English Reports, Down to the Present Day, by a Gentleman of the New York Bar. NY, 1813, roy8vo, 1100pp., later 1/2 linen & bds. $47.50

DARROW, Clarence, Farmington, NY, 1925, 8vo, 255pp., orig. cl., $12.50

DEAN, Amos, Principles of Medical Jurisprudence, Designed for the Professions of Law and Medicine. Albany & NY, 1850, roy8vo, 664pp., later1/2 linen and bds, $37.50

DE CHAMBRUN, Adolphe, The Executive Power in the United States: A Study of Constitutional Law. tr. by Dalghren. Lancaster, 1874, 8vo, xvii, 288pp., orig. cl., $25.00

De LOLME, M. de, Constitution de l'Angleterre; or, Etat du Gouvernement Anglais, compare avec la Form Republicaine & avec les autres Monarchies de l'Europe. new ed., rev. & corr. Geneva, 1788, 8vo, 2vols bound as one, xxi, 247, 286pp., contemp. bds, rebacked in linen, excellent, $47.50

DEL VECCHIO, Giorgio, Justice, edited with Additional Notes by A.H. Campbell. NY, 1955, 8vo, 236pp., $15.00

DIGEST OF OPINIONS OF THE JUDGE ADVOCATE GENERAL OF THE ARMY, 1912-1940. DC, GPO, 1942, 8vo, 1148pp., $22.50

DOBYNS, Fletcher, The Amazing Story of Repeal: An Expose of the Power of Propaganda. Chicago, 1940, roy8vo 457pp., $17.50

DOVE, P. Edward (ed), Domesday Studies: London, 1888, roy8vo,. xvi, 399pp., extremeties a bit worn, else vg, volume I only (of 2), $12.50

ELLIOT, William Yandell, The Need for Constitutional Reform. NY, 1935, roy8vo, 286pp., $15.00

--4--

ELWELL,John, J., A Medico-Legal Treatise on Malpractice and Medical Evidence, Comprising the Elements of Jurisprudence. NY, 1860, roy8vo, 588pp., later1/2 linen & bds. $37.50

EVERYMAN'S OWN LAWYER: A Handy Book of the Principles of Law & Equity, by a Barrister. 61st edition, rev., to Which is Added a Concise Dictionary of Legal Terms. London, 1931, 8vo, 839pp., $17.50

FERGUSON, Adam, An Essay on the History of Civil Society. Edinburg, 1768, 4to, contemp. tree calf, skillfully rebacked, raised bands, two tiny & hardly visible rents in title page, fine copy, first edition; General Nathanael Greene's copy with his signature on the title page; after Washington, Greene was the most brilliant military strategist of the American Revolution; he presided at the court-martial of Major John Andre. $650.00

FREEMAN, Edward A., William the Conqueror. London, 1907, 8vo, 200pp., $12.50

FREEMAN, Samuel A., A Valuable Assistant to Everyman; or, The American Clerk's Magazine....Made Conformable to Law. 7th ed., rev. & enl., Boston, 1814, 12mo, 324pp., contemp. roan, crown trifle worn, tiny piece missing from last leaf (index) with slight loss of text, $22.50

GARDINER,Samuel Rawson, A School Atlas of English History. London, 1905, 8vo, 88pp., $15.00

GIERKE,Otto von, Das Deutsche Genossenschaftsrecht. Berlin, 1868-1913. 4vols., roy8vo, 3500pp., later linen, excellent; the author was described by Maitland as "the greatest legal historian of the century in any tongue"; this is his master work. $250.00

GILLET, Ransom H., Democracy in the United States; What it Has Done, What it is Doing, What it Will Do. NY, 1868, 8vo,xiv, 414pp., $22.50

GILBERT, Geoffrey Lord, Law and Practice of Distressed and Replevin. ed. by William Hunt, 3rd ed., London, 1794, 8vo, xii, 339pp., contemp. calf $40.00

GIRARD, Paul F., Textes de Droit Romain. 5th ed., rev. & enl., Paris, 1923, 8vo, 926pp., 1/2 morocco & bds, $35.00

GROTIUS, Hugo. The Rights of War & Peace, Including the Law of Nature & Nations. trans. with Notes from Political & Legal Writers by A. C. Campbell. DC & London, 1901, roy8vo, 423pp., $17.50

HALE, William, A Series of Precedents and Proceedings in Criminal Causes, Extending from the Year 1475 to 1640, Extracted from the Act-Books of Ecclesiastical Courts in the Diocese of London....to Which is Prefixed an Introductory Essay. London, 1874, roy8vo, lxiii, 280pp., extremeties a bit worn, else vg, $35.00

HART,Albert Bushnell, Salmon Portland Chase. Boston, 1899, 8vo, 465pp., $12.50

HAWES, Frances, Henry Brougham. NY, n.d. (1956), 8vo, 325pp., $12.50

HEINECCUIS, Io. Gottlieb. Antiquitatum Romanarum Iurisprudentiam Illustrantium Syntagma, Secundum Ordinem Institutionum Iustiniani Digestum. ed. Got. Haubold. Frankfurt/M, 1822, 8vo, xxvi, 960pp., contemp. bit rubbed, else vg, $47.50

HEINEMANN, Franz, Die Richter u. die Rechtspflege in der deutschen Vergangenheit, mit 159 abbildungen u. Beilagen nach den Originalen aus dem funfzehnten bis achzehnten Jahrhundert. n.e., n.p. (Leipzig, 1900), 4to, 144pp., orig. 1/2 linen and bds, profus. illustrated (vol IV in the series Monographien zur deutschen Kulturgeschichte, ed. by Georg Steinhausen. Issued in a livited edition of only 100 copies, scarce, $35.00

--5--

56) HENRIOT, Eug., Moeurs Juridiques et Judiciares de l'Ancienne Rome. Paris, 1865, 8vo, 3vols, 1500pp., later 1/2 linen, $65.00

57) HEPBURN, Ch. M., The Historical Development of Code Pleading in America & England. Cincinnati, 1897, roy8vo, 318pp., $25.00

58) HERAUX, Aug. A., Code de Procedure Civile, avec les Derniers Modifications. Port-au-Prince, 1928, 8vo, 263pp., 1/2 calf and linen, $22.50

59) HEYL, Lewis (ed), US Duties on Imports. DC, 1872, 8vo, 280pp., $17.50

60) HICKEY, W., The Constitution of the United States, with an Alphabetical Analysis; with an Account of the State Papers, Published Documents and Other Sources of Political and Statistical Information at the Seat of Government. 2nd ed., Phil., 1847, 8vo, 497pp., later linen, lacks frontis., $27.50

61) HIGH, Jas., A Treatise on the Law of Injunctions as Administered in the Courts of the United States and England. Chicago, 1873, 4to, 642pp., contemp. roan, bit worn, $25.00

62) HOLCOMBE, Arthur N., The Foundations of the Modern Commonwealth. NY, 1923 roy8vo, 491pp., some pencil underlining, $17.50

63) HOOVER, Herbert, American Individualism. NY, 1923, 8vo, 72pp., $10.00

64) HUGHES, Ch., The Federal Constitution of Switzerland. NY, 1954, 8vo, 223pp., $7.50

65) JENKS, J. J., The Trust Problem. rev. ed. NY, 1905, 8vo, 361pp., $15.00

66) JENKS, Edward, The Government of the British Empire. Boston, 1918, 8vo 369pp., $17.50

67) JOHNSON, Samuel, A History & Defence of Magna Carta, Shewing the Manner of Its Being Obtained from King John, with Its Preservation and Final Establishment in the Succeeding Reigns, with an Introductory Discourse... also the Liberties which are Confirmed by the Bill of Rights.... to Which is Added an Essay on Parliaments Describing their Origin in England. 2nd ed. London, 1772, 8vo, lxiv, 284pp., contemp. calf, rebacked, bit rubbed, $125.00

68) JONES, William, An Essay on the Law of Bailments. Boston, 1796, 8vo, 174pp., contemp. roan, bit rubbed, $37.50

69) (JUSTICE, Alexander,) A General Treatise of the Dominion of the Sea: and a Compleat Body of Sea Laws, Containing what is Most Valuable on that Subject in Antient and Modern Authors.... with Curious Notes & Observations As also that Excellent Body of Sea Laws Lately Published in France, with A Collection of Marine Treaties Concluded During the Last Century, together with Several Discourses about the Jurisdiction and Manner of Proceeding in the Admiralty of England, both in Civil & Criminal Matters, and Adjudged Cases in Several Courts Concerning Trade and Navigation...2nd Edition, with Large Additions and Improvements and a New Appendix Containing Several Eminent Lawyer's Opions in Important Marine Cases...an Abstract of All the Acts of Parliament Relating to the Marine....London (1709?), stout and marbled boards, nice copy, $225.00

70) JUSTINIAN, The Digest of, trans. by Ch. H. Monro, Cambridge, 1909, 4to, 2vols., $47.50

71) KELSEN, Hans, Society and Nature: A Sociological Inquiry. Chicago, Univ of Chicago Press, 1943, roy8vo, 391pp., $15.00

72) KENT, James, Commentaries on American Law New York, 1826-1830, roy8vo, 4vols., contemp. roan, skillfully rebacked, first edition, $850.00

--6--

73) (KENT, James,) Rules and Orders of the Court of Chancery in the State of New York, Revised and Digested by the Present Chancellor. New York, 1815 first edition; bound with this: Rules & Orders of the Mayor's Court of the City of New York, July 1, 1815; bound in the original 1/2 roan and boards; Kent's Chancery Rules are of great importance and extreme rarity; he "became practically the creator of equity jurisdiction in the United States". DAB. $225.00

74) (KENT,James,) Rules of the Supreme Court of the State of New York, with Short Notes of Cases in Relation to the Rules. 3rd ed., rev., original boards, rebacked, 8vo, 92pp.; as Kent wrote most of the decisions of this court, although they were reported as per curiam, we may assume that if he did not draft them himself he did make the major contribution. $ 85.00

75) (KENT, James) BLAKE, D. T., An Historical Treatise on the Practice of the Court of Chancery in the State of New York. New York, 1818, roy8vo, 483pp contemp. roan, bit rubbed and scuffed, else vg, $65.00

76) (KENT, James,) HOFFMAN, Murray, The Office and Duties of Masters in Chancery. New York, 1824, roy8vo, 437pp., contemp. roan, bit worn and hinges tender, else vg, $45.00

77) LABAND, Paul, Die Vermögensrechtlichen Klagen nach dem Sadsischen Rechtsquellen des Mittelalters. Berlin, 1869, roy8vo, ix, 406pp., $25.00

78) LANDON, Judson, S., The Constitutional History and Government of the United States. Boston, 1889, roy8vo, 389pp., $17.50

79) LAWS AND LIBERTIES OF MASSACHUSETTS, Reprinted from the Copy of the 1648 Edition in the Harry E. Huntington Library, Introduction by Max Farrand. Harvard University Press, 1929, folio, ix, 59pp., $22.50

80) LAWS OF THE UNITED STATES OF AMERICA. PUBLISHED BY AUTHORITY. Philadelphia, 1796-99, 8vo, 4vols., contemp. roan, skillfully rebacked, excellent first collected edition, $375.00

81) LECKY, William Edw., Hartpole, A History of England in the 18th Century. London, 1903, 8vo, 7vols, nice set, $75.00

82) LEONARD, William, Reports and Cases of Law Argued and Adjudged in the Courts at Westminster in the Reigns of the Late Queen Elizabeth and King James.in Four Parts, 2nd ed., corr., with the Addition of Many Thousand References Never Before Printed. London, 1687, folio, 336,226, 279, 252pp., black letter, later 1/2 linen and bds, $165.00

83) LLOYD, Lord of Hampstead, Introduction to Jurisprudence. 3rd ed., Ny, 1972 4to, 873pp., $22.50

84) LEWIS, Geo. G., & MEWHA, John, History of Prisoner of War Utilization by The United States Army, 1776-1945, Dept. of the Army, 1955, 8vo,278pp $17.50

85) LIVINGSTON, Edward, The Complete Works of Edward Livingston on Criminal Juridprudence, with an Introduction by Salmon P. Chase. NY, 1873, roy8vo, 2vols., orig. cl., reb.; "When we begin presently to think in terms of a creative period, of a period of legal growth, I cannot doubt that Livingston will be held the great jurist of nineteenth century America, and one to rank with Bentham among English speaking jurists" Pound, Formative Era of American Law, 167, first collected edition, $125.00

86) MACAULAY, Lord, The History of England from the Accession of James II London, 1896, roy8vo, 5vols., nice set, $47.50

87) MAITLAND, Frederic W., Domesday Book and Beyond. Cambridge, 1897, roy8vo, 527pp., later linen, $35.00

--7--

MAITLAND, Frederic W., Township and Borough. Cambridge, 1898, roy8vo, 220pp., crown & base a trifle worn, inner hinges reinforced, $25.00

MAITLAND, Frederic W., Collected Papers, ed. H.A.L. Fisher. Cambridge, 1911, 8vo, 3vols., $75.00

MATHERS, Jas., From Gun to Gavel; The Courtroom Recollections of James Mathers of Oklahoma. NY, 1954, 8vo, 246pp., $12.50

MC ILWAIN, Chs. Howard, The High Court of Parliament and Its Supremacy. New Haven, 1910, 8vo, xviii, 409pp., first edition, presentation copy, signed by the author with a one page ALS from him, $37.50

MC LENNAN, John Ferguson, The Patriarchal Theory. London, 1885, 8vo, 355pp., crown trifle worn, $22.50

MONSTRELET, Enguerrand, The Chronicles of, Containing an Account of the Civil Wars between the Houses of Orleans and Burgundy, and the Possession of Paris and Normandy by the English. London, 1810, 8vo, 12vols.(of13) text complete, plate vol. lacking, later 1/2 linen and bds, $150.00

MONTAGUE, Basil, A Summary of the Law of Set-Off. NY, 1806, 8vo, 122pp., contemp. roan, rebacked, $30.00

MONTESQUIEU, Charles L., Baron de. Oevres. Amsterdam & Leipzig, 1758, 4to, 3vols., contemp. mottled calf, skillfully rebacked, raised bands, gilt, first complete collected edition, corrected and considerably augmented by the author, $650.00

The NEW AMERICAN LAWYER IN THE UNITED STATES. An Indispensable Form Book & Assistant for Everyone....as well as for Notaries, Lawyers, Constables, and County & Town Officers. in English and German. 2nd ed., NY, 1855, 8vl, xxii, 448pp., later 1/2 linen, $25.00

NOLAN, Michael, A Treatise on the Laws for the Relief and Settlement of the Poor. London, 1805, 8vo, 2vols., 390,384,170pp., later 1/2 linen,$85.00

OPIE, R., The Search for Peace Settlements. DC (Brookings), 1951, roy8vo, 366pp., $17.50

(PARLIAMENT) An Act to Enable the Adventurers, Owners and Proprietors of Taxable Lands, of Deeping Fens...to Raise a Complete Sum of Money for the Effectual Draining of the Fens. (Eigth Year of George II), London, 1738, folio, 20pp., unbound as issued, mostly black letter, $25.00

)PASCHAL, Geo. W., The Constitution of the United States Defined and Carefully Annotated. DC, 1868, 8vo, xxviii, 407pp., orig. cl., inscribed by the author, a Texan and a member of the bar of the US Supreme Court, a very interesting work, $37.50

)PHILLIPS, P., The Statutory Jurisdiction and Practice of the Supreme Court of the United States, Together with Forms of Process and Rules established for the Supreme Court, the Court of Claims, the Courts of Equity, the Courts of Admiralty and the Courts in Bankruptcy. DC, 1876, 8vo, 548pp., $30.00

PIGOTT, N., A Treatise of Common Recoveries. London, 1739, 8vo, contemp. calf, 248pp., $57.50

)POSTAL LAWS AND REGULATIONS OF THE UNITED STATES. DC, GPO, 1949, 8vo, 973pp. $17.50

)POUND, Roscoe, Interpretations of Legal History. NY, 1923, 8vo, xvii, 171pp. orig. cl., first edition, with the extensive marginal annotations of Prof. Frank Knight of the University of Chicago, $27.50

)POUND, Roscoe, The Formative Era of American Law. Boston, 1938, 8vo, x, 188pp., first edition, signed by the author, $25.00

)POWELL, John Jos., An Essay Upon the Learning of Devises from their Inception by Writing to their Consummation by the Death of the Devisor. 1st American edition, NY, 1807, 8vo, about 450pp., contemp. roan, bit worn, $37.50

)PRINGLE, Patrick, Hue and Cry: The Story of Henry and John Fielding and Their Bow Street Runners. London, n.d. (c. 1955, 8vo, 230pp., $12.50

)PROCEEDINGS OF THE 45TH ANNUAL CONFERENCE ON TAXATION. Sacramento, 1953, roy8vo, 733pp., $15.00

)RALSTON, Jackson H., International Arbitration from Athens to Locarno. Stanford, 1929, roy8vo, 417pp., $17.50

)RAM, Jas., A Practical Treatise of Assets, Debts and Incumbrances. from the London edition. Phil., 1835, roy8vo, xvi, 430pp., later 1/2 linen$37.

)RAM, Jas, A Treatise on the Exposition of Wills of Landed Property. from the London ed. Phil., 1835, roy8vo, 164pp., later 1/2 linen. $37.50

)RAMSAY, Sir Jas. H., The Angevin Empire; or the Reigns of HenryII, Richard I and John (1155-1216), Cambridge, 1900, roy8vo, 556pp., $22.50

)RANNIE, David W., Historical Outline of the English Constitution for Beginners. NY, 1882, 12mo, 180pp., $12.50

)RAPIN, Thoyras, Dissertation sur les Whigs et les Torys. A la Haye, 1717, 12mo, 162pp., contemp. calf, $85.00

)RAUMER, Fried, von, The Political History of England During the 16th, 17th, and 18th Centuries. London, 1837, roy8vo, 2vols, (I & II of 3), $37.50

)REEVE, Tapping, A Treatise on the Law of Descents in the Several United States. NY, 1825, 8vo, lxxxvii, 515pp., contemp. roan, bit worn, $37.50

)REIWALD, Paul, Society and Its Criminals. Trans. by T.W. James. London 1949,8vo, xix, 315pp., $15.00

)RICHTER, M. Francis, Causes Celebres et Interessantes, avec les Jugemens qui les ont Decidees. Redigees de nouveau par M. Richer, ancien Advocat au Parlement. A Amsterdam, 1772ff., 8vo, 18vols., contemp. calf, a few spines neatly restored and several hinges cracked but most firm, quite rare, $225.00

)ROGERS, Ammi, Memoirs of....Falsely Accused and Imprisoned in Norwich Jail, for two Years on the Charge of Crimes Said to Have been Committed in the Town of Griswold, when he was not within about 100 miles of the Place, and of which He was as Absolutely Innocent as the Judge who Pronounced the Sentence. 11th edition, with Additions, Omissions and Alterations. Watertown, 1846,12mo, 264pp., later 1/2 linen, $35.00

ROMMEN, Heinrich, The Natural Law : A Study in Legal and Social History. tr. by Hanley. St. Louis, 1947, roy8vo, 290pp., light v ery sporadic underlining, $17.50

ROSENBERG, J. Mitchell, Jerome Frank: Jurist and Philosopher. NY, 1970, 8vo, 274pp., fine, $6.50

SCHERGER, Geo. L., The Evolution of Modern Liberty. NY, 1904, 8vo 284pp., $17.50

SCHICK, Marvin, Learned Hand's Court. Balto, 1970, roy8vo, 371pp., $17.50

SCHLEGEL,J.F.W., Neutral Rights; or, An Impartial Examination of the Right of Search of Neutral Vessels under Convoy, and of a Judgment Pronounced by the English Court of Admiralty on the 11th June, 1799, in the Case of the Swedish Convoy, with Some Additions and Corrections. Phil., 1801, 8vo, 162pp., orig. ptd. wrps, boxed, $85.00

SHAFTSBURY, Anthony Earl of, Characteristicks of Men, Manners, Opinions Times. 6th edition, with the Addition of a Letter Concerning Design. London, 1737, 8vo, 3vols., contemp. calf, raised bands, spine gilt, extremeties a bit rubbed, joints a bit cracked but firm, $125.00

SPANISH TREATY CLAIMS COMMISSION. Collection of Documents and Opinions of the Commission. DC, GPO, 1902-3, 8vo, 478pp., complete as issued, $30.00

SPELMAN, Sir, Henry, Concilia, Decreta, Leges, Constitutiones in Re Ecclesiarum orbis Britannici....ab Initio Christianae ibidem Religionis ad Nostram usque Aetatem; Uti reperiuntur in eorundum Actis, Canonibus, Ecclesiasticis, Regnorum Constitutionibus, Senatus Consultis, Principium Rescriptis....usque ad Introitum Normannorum.London, 1639, large folio, 637pp., old calf, skillfully rebacked; a handsome copy, first ed, $225.00

STARKIE, Thomas, A Treatise on the Law of Slander and Libel, and Incidentally of Malicious Prosecutions, from the 2nd English ed., with Notes and References to American Cases & English Decisions Since 1830 by John L. Wendell, Hartford, 1858, roy8vo, 2vols, later 1/2 linen, $47.50

STEPHENS, W.R.W., & HUNT,Wm. (eds.), A History of the English Church. London, 1907ff. 8vo, 9vols., few crowns a bit worn, ex lib, $125.00

STEVENS,C. Ellis, Sources of the Constitution of the United States Considered in Relation to Colonial & English History. NY, 1894, 8vo, 277pp., $15.00

STORY, Joseph, Commentaries on the Law of Bailments. 2nd ed., rev. & enl. Boston, 1840, roy8vo, 409pp., later 1/2 linen, $37.50

STORY, Joseph, Commentaries on the Law of Agency as a Branch of Commercial and Maritime Jurisprudence, with Occasional Illustrations from the Civil and Foreign Law. 2nd ed., rev. corr. & enl., Boston & London, 1844, roy8vo, xxviii, 669pp., later 1/2 linen, $40.00

STRAUS, Oscar, The Origin of Republican Form of Government in the United States. 2nd ed. rev. NY, 1901, 8vo, xli, 151pp., $15.00

TAFT, Mrs. William Howard, Recollections of Full Years. NY, 1914, roy8vo, 395pp., $22.50

TAFT, Henry W., Occasional Papers and Addresses of An American Lawyer. NY, 1920, 8vo, 331pp., $15.00

TAYLOR, Alfred Swaine, M.D., Medical Jurisprudence. 5th American from the 7th London edition, with additions by Edw. Hartshorne. Phil., 1861, roy8vo, 714pp., rebacked, $37.50

TAYLOR, Hannis, The Science of Jurisprudence. NY, 1908, roy8vo, 676pp.$20.00

TAYLOR, Hannis, The Origin and Growth of the English Constitution: An Historical Treatise in Which is Drawn Out the Gradual Development of the English Constitutional System and the Growth out of that System of the Federal Republic of the United States. Boston, 1889-1898, roy8vo 2 vols., 1250pp., orig. cl, $45.00

THAYER, Jas./Bradley, Legal Essays. Boston 1908, 8vo, 402pp., $12.50

TODD, Alpheus, Parliamentary Government in England: Its Origin, Development and Practical Operation. New Ed., Abr. & Rev. by Spencer Walpole, London, 1892, 8vo, 2vols., $35.00

TRIAL OF JOHN H. SURRATT, in the Criminal Court for the District of Colombia DC, GPO, 1867, roy8vo, 2vols, later 1/2 linen, $75.00,Lincoln Assasination.

UNITED STATES LAW JOURNAL, Volume II, No. 5, January, 1862, 8vo, 165pp., hinges weak, $27.50

--10--

USSR Academy of Sciences: Institute of State and Law: Literature on Soviet Law; Index and Bibliography. Moscow, 1960, 8vo, 279pp., text in Russian and English, $17.50

VATTEL, M. de., The Law of Nations; or, Principles of the Law of Nature Applied to the Conduct and Affairs of Nations and Sovereigns. First American Edition, Corr. & Rev. from the Last London Ed., NY, 1796, 8vo xlviii, 536pp., contemp. roan, small rent in title neatly restored, light external weat, nice copy, $85.00

VIRGILIUS, Polydorus, Anglicae Historiae Libri Vigintisex, Ab ipso Autore Postremum iam Recogniti adque amusim, salva tamen historiae veritate expoliti. Access Anglorum Regum Chronices Epitome per Georgium Lilium Britannum. Gandavi Cornelius Manilius. n. d. (1603?), 12mo, 1742pp., later 1/2 linen and bds, $87.50: For the value of this work see the 11th Britannica, XXVIII, 116

WARDEN, Alex J. (ed.), Burgh Laws of Dundee, with the History, Statutes and Proceedings of the Guild of Merchants and Fraternities of Craftsmen. London, 1872, 8vo, 625pp., extremeties a bit worn, else vg, $30.00

WESSER, Rob. F., Charles Evans Hughes: Politics and Reform in New York: 1905-1910. Ithaca, 1967, roy8vo, 366pp., fine, $12.50

WEST, Julius, A History of the Chartist Movement. Boston, 1920, 8vo, 316pp., $7.50

WHARTON, Francis, A Digest of the International Law of the United States. DC, 1886, roy8vo, 3vols, 2500pp., orig. roan, trifle worn, tight, $75.00

WHEATON, Henry, Elements of International Law, with a Sketch of the History of the Science. Philadelphia, 1836, roy8vo, 375pp., orig. cl., rebacked, first edition, $125.00

WIGMORE, John Henry, Chairman, Committee of the Association of American Law Schools. Select Essays in Anglo-American Legal History. Boston, 1907, roy8vo, 3vols, 2500pp., later linen, $75.00

WILLIAM OF MALMESBURY'S Chronicle of the Kings of England from the Earliest Period to the Reign of Stephen. ed. by J.A. Giles, London, 1847, 8vo, 574pp., $22.50

WILLIAMS, Benjamin H., American Diplomacy: Policies and Practice. NY, 1936, roy8vo, 517pp., $17.50

WOODFALL, William, The Law of Landlord and Tenant. 2nd ed., with three new chapters. London, 1804, 8vo, 475pp., contemp. roan, bit rubbed,$40.00

WORMSER, Rene A., Foundations: Their Power and Influence. NY, 1958, 8vo, 412pp., $15.00

(XYZ AFFAIR), Instructions to the Envoys Extraordinary and Ministers Plenopotentiary from the United States of America to the French Republic, Their Letters of Credence and Full Powers and the Dispatches Received from Them Relative to Their Mission, Published by the Secretary of State in Conformity with the Resolution of Congress of the 22nd June, 1798, Phil., 8vo, 131pp., orig. ptd. wps under later wrps, $95.00 In 1797 envoys John Marshall, Charles C. Pinckney and Elbridge Gerry were sent to France; their experiences, recorded in this collection, precipitated the passage of the Alien and Sedition Acts in 1798.

FLOWERDEW, D. C., An Exposition of the Three Orders in Council of the 11th of November, 1807, on the Trade Restricted, Permitted and Regulated in the New System of Blockade, and also of Other Orders. 8vo, 89pp., later 1/2 linen and bds, $65.00

BARING, Alexander, M.P., An Inquiry into the Cause and Consequences of the Orders in Council and an Examination of the Conduct of Great Britain towards the Neutral Commerce of America. London, 1808, 8vo, 179pp., $75.00

List 17 (SUPPLEMENT)

March, 1978

With the Editio Princeps of The Mirror of Justices (#26)

Richard Adamiak
1545 East 60th St.
Chicago, Illinois 60637
312-955-4571
By Phone: 0700-1300

ABBOTT, Austin, A Brief on the Modes of Proving the Facts Most Frequently in Issue or Collaterally in Question in the Trial of Civil or Criminal Cases. 3rd ed. Rochester, 1912, 8vo, 1007pp., later linen, $17.50

ADAMI, Colonello Vittorio, National Frontiers in Relation to International Law. trans. by T.T. Behrens, Oxford Univ. Pr., 1927, roy8vo, 138pp., crown trifle worn, else vg, $15.00

ADDINGTON, William, An Abridgement of the Penal Statutes....3rd ed., with Large Additions & Annotations, to Which are Subjoined, Extracted from Reporters of the Best Authority....a Great Variety of Adjudged Cases. London, 1786, 4to, 694pp., contemp calf, rebacked, $125.00

Archiv fur Luftrecht (Journal of Aviation Law), Berlin, 1931-1937, Vols. I-VII, roy8vo, 7vols., orig. cl., scarce, $125.00

BUTLER, Chs., Reminiscences of Ch. Butler of Lincoln's Inn, with a Letter to a Lady on Ancient & Modern Music. NY, 1825, 2nd American ed., 8vo, 350pp., contemp. bds, rebacked, $27.50

Centennial History of the Harvard Law School 1918, roy8vo, 412pp., $22.50

The Charters and General Laws of the Colony and Province of Massachusetts Bay, Carefully Collected from the Public Records and Ancient Printed Books, to Which is Added an Appendix Tending to Explain the Spirit, Progress and History of the Jurisprudence of the State, Especially in a Moral and Political View, Boston, 1814, roy8vo, 868pp., contemp. roan, rebacked, $87.50

CLARK, Grenville, & Sohn, Louis (eds.) World Peace Through World Law. Cambridge, Harvard Univ. Press, 1960, 4to, 387pp., $17.50

CLARK, Grenville, (ed.) The Future of the Common Law. Cambridge, 1937. 8vo, 247pp., $15.00

COCHRAN, William C., Law Lexicon, Pronouncing Edition: A Dictionary of Legal Words and Phrases,Including Latin & French Maximx Translated, and Abbreviations Found in Law Books & Reports. rev. & enl. by Howard L. Lewis. Cincinnati, 1924, sm8vo, 362pp., $15.00

The Colonial Laws of Massachusetts, Reprinted from the Edition of 1672, with Supplements through 1686, Published....under the Supervision of William H. Whitmore, Boston, 1887, 4to, ix, 395pp., orig 1/2 morocco, $85.00

CRAIK, Sir Henry, The Life of Edward Earl of Clarendon, Lord High Chancellor of England. London, 1911, 8vo, 2vols., $30.00

CREASY, E.S., The Rise and Progress of the English Constitution. 3rd ed., rev. with adds., NY, 1855, 8vo, 359pp., $17.50

CROOK, J.A., Law & the Life of Rome. London, 1967, 8vo, 349pp., 17.50

DAVIDSON, William, Political Thought in England: The Utilitarians from Bentham to J.S. Mill., NY, 1910, 12mo, 256pp., $12.50

DEBATES AND PROCEEDINGS IN THE CONVENTION IN MASSACHUSETTS IN 1788 which Ratified the Constitution of the United States. Boston, 1856, 8vo, 442pp. a reprint of an earlier edition of the Debates, but also containing the first printing of the Journal of the Convention, and the first printing of the Notes of the debates of Chief Justice Parsons of Mass., printed from his original MS., contemp. roan, bit worn, $47.50

--2--

DICKINSON, John, Administrative Justice and the Supremacy of Cambridge, 1927, roy8vo, 403pp., $17.50

FRIEDRICH, Carl Joachim, Constitutional Government and Politics 1937, roy8vo, 591pp., $14.00

GERHART, Eugene, America's Advocate: Robert H. Jackson. NY, 1950, roy8vo, 545pp., $17.50

GREEN, Andrew Wilson, Political Integration by Jurisprudence. Leyden, 1969, 4to, 846pp., $22.50

GREENLEAF, Simon, Discourse Commemorative of the Life and Character of the Honorable Joseph Story. Boston, 1845, 8vo, 48pp., orig. ptd. wrps, bit soiled, else vg, $37.50

HAWARDE, John, Les Reportes del Cases in Camera Stellata, 1593-1609 the Original Ms. of John Hawarde of the Inner Temple, ed. by William Paley Baildon of Lincoln's Inn, one of 250 copies privately printed for Alfred Morrison, 1894, 4to, lxxv, 502pp., orig.cl., rare, $125.00

HILDRETH, Richard (ed.) Atrocious Judges: Lives of Judges Infamous as Tools of Tyrants and Instruments of Oppression. NY, 1856, 8vo, later linen, $37.50

HINE, Reginald L., Confessions of An Uncommon Attorney. NY, 1947, 8vo, 268pp., $12.50

HOCKETT, Homer C., The Constitutional History of the United States, 1776-1879. NY, 1939, roy8vo, 2vols., $27.50

EDITIO PRINCEPS OF A CLASSIC

HORN, Andrew, La Somme Appelle Mirroir des Justices vel Speculum Iustidiariorum, factum per Andream Horne. London, Printed by E. G. for Matthew Walbanke & Richard Best. 1642, 8vo, 311 (i.e. 291)pp. bound in 18th century calf, skillfully rebacked, black letter, beautiful copy, the editio princeps; for the character and significance of this classic see Maitland's Introduction to the Selden Society edition, rare,$1250.00

JOHNSON,Alvin, W., The Legal Status of Church-State Relationships in the US, with Special Reference to the Public Schools. Minneapolis, Univ. of Minnesota Press, 1934, roy8vo, 332pp., $15.00

Journal of the Convention for Framing a Constitution of Government for the State of Massachusetts Bay, from the Commencement of their First Session September 1, 1779, to the Close of their Last Session, June 16, 1780. Published by Order of the Legislature. Boston 1832, 8vo, 264pp., contemp. roan, front hinge a bit cracked near crown, else excellent, nice copy, first edition; John Adams played a leading role regarding the ideas embodied in this constitution and it was a prototype of the Federal Constitution of 1787, $65.00

The Journals of Each Provincial Congress of Massachusetts in 1774 & 1775, and of the Committee of Safety, with an Appendix Containing the Proceedings of the County Conventions....published under the supervision of William Lincoln. Boston, 1838, roy8bo, lix, 778pp., contemp roan, rebacked, $87.50

KELLOR, Frances, & HATVANY, Antonia, The United States Senate and the International Court. NY, 1925, 8vo, 353pp., lacks free end sheet, $15.00

LATHAM, Earl, The Communist Controversy in Washington from the New Deal McCarthy. Harvard University Press, 1966, roy8vo, 446pp., $15.00

LAURENCE, John, A History of Capital Punishment, with a Comment on Capital Punishment by Clarence Darrow. NY, 1960, 8vo, 230pp., ill., $15.00

LIEBER, Francis, On Civil Liberty and Self-Government. Phil., 1881, roy8vo, 662pp., $25.00

Life and Corresponcence of John Duke Lord Coleridge, Lord Chief Justice of England, written and ed. by E. H. Coleridge. London, 1904, roy8vo, 2vols. half-calf and linen, $37.50

LUCE, Robert, Legislative Principles: The History and Theory of Lawmaking by Representative Government. B & NY, 1930, 8vo, 665pp., $15.00

MARNELL, William H., The First Amendment: The History of Religious Freedom in America. NY, 1964, 8vo, 247pp., $15.00

MASON, Alpheus Thomas, Harlan Fiske Stone. NY, 1956, roy8vo, 914pp., $22.50

MAYER, Martin, The Lawyers, NY, 1967, 8vo, 586pp., $15.00

MAYERS, Lewis, The American Legal System. NY, 1955, roy8vo, 589pp., $17.50

O'BRIEN, R.B., The Life of Lord Russell of Killowen. London, 1901, roy8vo 405pp., $15.00

PARKER, Joel, Daniel Webster as a Jurist: An Address to the Students in the Law School of the University at Cambridge. 2nd ed., Cambridge, 1853, 8vo, 71pp., later 1/2 linen, $35.00

The Public and Private Life of Lord Chancellor Eldon, with Selections from His Correspondence, ed. H. Twiss. London, 1844, roy8vo, 2vols. (I&II of 3), 1/2 calf, rubbed and hinges tender, $22.50

REID, Helen D., International Servitudes in Law and Practice. Univ of Chicago Pr., 1932, 8vo, 254pp., $15.00

Report of the Special Committee of the Federal Loyalty-Security Program of the Association of the Bar of the City of NY. NY, 1956, 8vo, 301pp., $15.00

Reports of Controverted Elections in the House of Representatives of the Commonwealth of Massachusetts from 1780 to 1852 Inclusive; the Cases from 1780 to 1834 Compiled by Luther S. Cushing, and the Cases from 1835-1852 by Luther S. Cushing, Ch. W. Storey & Lewis Josselyn, Boston, 1853, roy8vo, xx, 757pp., later 1/2 linen, $45.00

ROSCOE, E. S., Lord Stowell: His Life and the Development of English Prize Law. London, 1916, 8vo, x, 116pp., $15.00

RUSSELL, Ruth B., A History of the United Nations Charter: The Role of the United States, 1940-45. DC, Brookings, 1958, roy8vo, 1140pp., $25.00

SMITH, Herbert A., Federalism in North America: A Comparative Study of Institutions in the US & Canada. NY, 1923, 8vo, 328pp., $17.50

SPEAR, Charles, Essays on the Punishment of Death. 2nd ed., Boston & London, 1844, 8vo, 237pp., orig. linen, extremeties worn, $35.00

STORY, Joseph, et al., Report of the Commissioners Appointed to Consider and Report Upon the Practicability & Expediency of Reducing to a Written and Systematic Code the Common Law of Massachusetts, or Any Part Thereof. Boston, 1837, 8vo, 46pp., orig. ptd. wrps, $37.50

STUART, Graham, American Diplomatic and Consular Practice. 2nd ed., NY, 1952, roy8vo, 477pp., $15.00

SWISHER, Carl Brent, The Growth of Constitutional Power in the United States. Univ of Chicago Pr., 1947, 8vo, 261pp., $12.50

--4--

WALKER-SMITH, Derek, Lord Reading and His Cases. NY, 1934, roy8vo, 394pp., $17.50

WHEELER, Jacob D., Reports of Criminal Law Cases Decided at the City Hall of the City of New York; titles of volumes II & III: Reports of Criminal Law Cases, with Notes and References Containing also a View of the Criminal Laws of the United States; 8vo, 3vols., 1930;;., a very comprehensive work; rom the preface of volume III, the work is to contain "all the criminal cases tried in the courts of the United States and of several states since the period of the revolution...it is intended to embrace the whole range of criminal jurisprudence." later 1/2 linen, $125.00

WORMSER, Rene, The Law: The Story of Lawmakers and the Law We Have Lived by from the Earliest Times to the Present Day. NY, 1949, roy8vo, 608pp., $15.00

WRIGHT, Benjamin F., The Growth of American Constitutional Law. Boston, 1942, 8vo, 275pp., $12.50

Addenda

MACK, William & NASH, Howard, Cyclopedia of Law and Procedure. Chicago, 1901-1912, 4to, 40vols., orig. buckram, $675.00

ENCYCLOPEDIA OF THE SOCIAL SCIENCES. Ed. Edwin R. A. Seligman & Alvin Johnson, NY, 1937, 4to, 15vols, bound as 8, ex lib., clean, tight set, $175.00

List 19

Summer 1978

Law

With an Addenda of Interesting Titles in Various Fields

Richard Adamiak
1545 East 60th St.
Chicago, Illinois 60637
312-955-4571
By Phone 8AM-Noon

1) ADAMS, John, A Treatise on the Principles and Practice of the Action of Ejectment....from the Last London edition, to which have been added the Decisions of the Supreme Court of New York....References to Decisions in the Courts of Mass., Penn. and the Supreme Court of the United States, by Philo Ruggles. NY, 1821, roy8vo, 421pp., contemp roan, rebacked, $38.50

2) ALEXANDER, Gilchrist, After Court Hours. L, 1950, 8vo. 278pp., $13.50

3) AMES, Jas. Barr, Lectures on Legal History. Cambridge, 1913, 4to, 553pp., light wear of extremeties, else vg, $30.00

4) BARROWS, Samuel, Children's Courts in the United States: Their Origin, Development & Results: Reports Prepared for the Int'l Prison Comission. DC, GPO, 1904, 8vo, 203pp., $13.50

5) BEAWES, Wyndham, Lex Mercatoria Rediviva; Or, The Merchants Directory, Being a Complete Guide to All Men in Business, Traders, Remitters, Owners, Captains, Insurers, Brokers, Factors, Agents, Containing an Account of Our Trading Companies and Colonies...and an Abstract of their Charters; the Duty of Consuls and the Laws Subsisting about Aliens, Naturalization & Denization,....the Whole Calculated for theUse & Service of the Merchant, Lawyer, Senator & Gentleman. 3rd edition, with large additions. London, 1771, large folio, 898pp., plus index, bound in later 1/2 linen and boards, large folding table of currence conversions neatly mended and one small portion supplied in excellent facsimile on period paper (the table is usually missing altogether); in addition to containing, as one might expect from the title, a great mass of information on the law merchant, much of its content is directly related to international law and admiralty law; $235.00

6) BECK, Jas, M., May It Please the Court. Atlanta, 1930, roy8vo, 511pp., $12.50

7) BIGELOW, L.J., Bench & Bar: A Complete Digest of the Wit, Humor, Asperities & Amenities of the Law. NY, 1868, roy8vo, 364pp., $15.00

8) BINNEY, Ch.C., Life of Horace Binney. Phil, 1903, roy8vo, 460pp., $17.50

9) BONGER, W.A., Criminalité et Conditions Économique. Amsterdam, 1905, roy8vo 750pp., light sporadic soil, else vg, a classic work, $22.50

10) BOONE, CH.T., Pleading Under the Codes, Adapted to the Use in Several States & Territories which have Adopted the System of Reformed Procedure, and in All the Courts where that System Prevails. San Francisco, 1885, 12mo, 581pp., $25.00

11) BOOS, William, M.D., The Poison Trail. B, 1939, 8vo, 380pp.; the author was a leading toxicologist and expert witness in many famous cases.$15.00

12) BORGEAUD, Ch., Adoption & Amendment of Constitutions in Europe & America. by Ch. Hazen. NY, 1895, 8vo, 353pp., tiny rent in cover, $17.50

13) (Boyden, Albert) Ropes-Gray, 1865-1940. Boston, Privately Printed, 1942, 8vo, 215pp., ltd. ed., history of a leading law firm, $15.00

14) BRADBY, Jas., A Treatise on the Law of Distresses. 1st American ed.NY,1808, roy8vo, xx, 325pp., contemp. roan, rebacked, $42.00

15) BROUGHAM, Henry Lord, Historical Sketches of Statesmen who Flourished in the Time of Geo.III.London, 1839-43, roy8vo, 3vols. with numerous engravings of political and legal luminaries. $35.00

BROWN, Basil, Law Sports at Gray's Inn (1594), Including Shakespeare's Connection with the Inns of Court, the Origin of the Capias Utlegatum re Coke & Bacon, Francis Bacon's Connection with Warwickshire, Together with a Reprint of the Gesta Grayorum. NY, Privately Printed, 1921, 8vo, xciv, 187, 88pp., orig. 1/2 linen & bds, light pencil annotations, $22.50

BROWN, David Paul, The Forum; or, Forty Years Full Practice at the Philadelphia Bar. Phil., 1856, roy8vo, 2vols., 1100pp., orig. cl., $45.00

BROWN, Marshall, Wit & Humor of Bench & Bar. Chi, 1899, 8vo, 578pp., $12.50

BROWNE, D., Sir Travers Humphries: A Biography, London, 1960. 8vo, 384pp., $17.50

BROWNE, Irving, Short Studies of Great Lawyers. Albany, 1878,8vo,322pp,$22.50

BRUNDAGE, Albert, M.D., A Manual of Toxicology. NY, 1929,8vo,444pp.,$12.50

BUCHANAN, George, Opera Omnia: Historica, Chronologica, Juridica, Politica Satyrica et Poetica. Amsterdam 1725, 4to, 2vols., ed. by Thomas Ruddiman Pref. by Peter Burman. contemp. vellum.II lacks label, $150.00

BURN, Richard, The Justice of the Peace and Parrish Officer. 11th ed. London, 1769,8vo,4vols., contemp roan, rebacked, extreme lower portions of titles in fine facsimile on period paper, clean tight set, $125.00

BUSH, Francis, In and Out of Court. Forward by Russell Whitman of the Chicago Bar. Chicago, De Paul Univ. Press, 1942, 8vo, 303pp., $13.50

CARR, Sir Cecil (ed.) The Pension Book of Clements Inn. London, 1960, 4to, 347pp., (Selden Society #78), $13.00

CARR, Rob. K., The Supreme Court & Judicial Review. NY, 1942,8vo,304pp.$8.50

CARSON, Hampton, A Sketch of Horace Binney. n.p., 1907, 4to, 94pp., 3/4 morocco and bds, bit rubbed. $15.00

CHISHOLM, John, Sir Walter Scott as a Judge: His Decisions in the Sheriff Court of Selkirk, Edinburgh, 1918, roy8vo, 221pp., $15.00

CHITTY, J., The Practice of Law in All Its Departments, with a View of Rights Injuries and Remedies...and Showing the Practice in Arbitrations before Justices, in Courts of Common Law, Equity, Ecclesiastical and Spiritual, Admiralty & Courts of Appeal. Phil., 1836, roy8vo, 3vols., 2800pp., contemp. roan, rebacked, $105.00

THE CLERMONT ASSIZES OF 1665: A Merry Account of a Grim Court, by W.W. Comfort, forward by Hon. W.B. Lonn. Phil., University of Penn. Press, 1937, 8vo, 291pp., $16.50

COLES, Edw., History of the Ordinance of 1787.....read before the Historical Society of Pennsylvania, June 1856, Published by the Press of the Society roy8vo, 33pp., author was governor of Illinois, $10.00

DANIEL, Hawthorne, Judge Medina: A Biography. NY, 1952, 8vo, 373pp., $12.50

DARLING, Hon. Mr. Justice., On the Oxford Circuit and Other Verses. London, 1909, 12mo, 79pp., ill., $10.00

DEAN, Arthur H., William Nelson Cromwell: 1854-1948: An American Pioneer in Corporation, Comparative and International Law. NY, Privately Published, 1957, roy8vo, viii, 237pp., (history of the Sullivan & Cromwell firm)$20.00

(CROMWELL), Addresses on the Occasion of a Meeting in Memory of William Nelson Cromwell. Ass. of the Bar of the City of New York and New York County's Lawyer Assn, 1949, 8vo, 27pp., $7.50

--3--

DERENUSSON, Philippes, Traite de la Communaute de Biens entre l'Homme et la Femme, Conjoints par la Mariage, et de la Continuation de communaute.... new ed., corr. & aug., Paris, 1723, 4to, 784pp., later 1/2linen, $125.00

DESTY, Rob.,A Manual of Praotice in the Courts of the United States,., with Notes & Decisions. 7th ed. San Francisco, 1889, 12mo,1010pp,roan, $22.50

DESTY, Rob., The Constitution of the United States, with notes. 2nd ed., San Francisco, 1887, 12mo, 504pp., roan, rebacked, $22.50

Digest of Opinions of the Judge Advocate of the Army, 1912-1940, DC, 1942 roy8vo, 1148pp., $10.00

DOVE, P. Edw., (ed.) Domesday Studies. London, 1888, 4to, 399pp., vol I only (of 2) $12.50

DRIVER, Cecil, Tory Radical: The Life of Richard Oastler. NY, Oxford Univ.Pr. 1946, roy8vo, 597pp., $15.00

DUGGAN, Sephan, (ed.) The League of Nations: The Principle and the Practice Boston, 1919, 8vo, 357pp., $15.00

DUNKEL, Wilbur, William Lambarde: Elizabethan Jurist, 1536-1601. New Jersey Rutgers Univ Press, 1965, roy8vo, 210pp., $15.00

EARLE, Walter, Mr. Shearman and Mr. Sterling and How they Grew, Being Annals of Their Law Firm, with Biographical & Historical Highlights. Privately Published, printed by Yale Univ. Press, 1963, roy8vo, 443pp., $20.00

THE CLERK'S MAGAZINE...by a Member of the Mass, Bar, Boston, 1833, 8vo, 333pp. contemp. roan, front hinge a bit worn, tight, $22.50

Everyman's Own Lawyer: A Handbook of the Principles of Law & Equity, by a Barrister. 61st ed. rev, to which is added a concise dictionary of legal terms. London, 1931, 8vo, 839pp., $12.50

FAY, E.S., Life of Mr. Justice Swift. London, 1939, roy8vo, 287pp., $15.00

FELL, Walker W., A Treatise on the Law of Mercantile Guarantees and of Principal & Surity. 1st American from the2nd & last London ed., with Notes & References to American Decisions by Charles Walker of the New York Bar. NY, 1825, roy8vo, 435pp., roan, rebacked, $42.50

FELSTEAD, Sidney T., (& edited by Lady Muir), Sir Richard Muir: A Memoir of a Public Prosecutor. London, 1927, roy8vo, 382pp., $16.50

FISKE, John, Civil Government in the US Considered with Some Reference to Its Origins. B, 1890, 8vo, 360pp., $12.50

FOOTE, Caleb, (ed.), Studies on Bail. Phil, Univ of Penn. Inst. of Legal Res. 1966, roy8vo, 288pp., $15.00

FOSTER, John W., Arbitration and the Hague Court. B & NY, 1904, 8vo, 148pp., $12.50

FREUND, Ernest, Legislative Regulation: A Study of the Ways and Means of Written Law. NY, 1932, roy8vo, 458pp., $17.50

GARFIELD, President,"My Experiences as a Lawyer", (autobiographical notes), furnished to Edmund Kirke: in North American Review, June, 1887, $7.50

GETZ, Geo, A General Collection of Precedents in Conveyancing. 3rd ed., rev. enl. & imp. Phil., 1845, roy8vo, 270pp., roan, rebacked, $32.50

GILLETT, Ransom, Democracy in the US: What it Has Done, What it is Doing & What it Will Do. NY, 1868, 8vo, 414pp., $12.50

GODDARD, Henry, Memoirs of a Bow Street Runner. NY, n.d. (1950) 8vo, 253pp., $12.50

--4--

GOLDSMITH, J., A Brief Grammar of the Laws and Constitution of England, Intended for the Use of Schools and the Junior Students of the Law. London, 1809, 12mo, 150pp., with 2 fold out engravings, later1/2 linen, $30.00

John Chipman Gray. Boston, Privately Ptd., 1917, roy8vo, 143pp., (of the firm Ropes and Gray), $12.50

GUILHERMET, E, The Judicial Errors. Chicago, n.d. (1920), 8vo, 208pp., (the author was professor of juridical psychology in the Univ. of Paris) $ 12.50

HALL, Edgar Vine, The Romance of Wills and Testaments. London, 1912, 256pp., $12.50

HAMMOND, Harold, A Commoner's Judge: The Life and Times of Charles P. Daly. Boston, 1954, 8vo, 456pp., $15.00

HARMON, Nolan, The Famous Case of Myra Clark Gaines. Baton Rouge. Louisiana State Univ. Press, 1946, roy8vo, 481pp., $15.00

HARRIS, Richard, Illustrations in Advocacy: Examples of Conducting the Prosecution & Defense of Civil and Criminal Cases, Including Methods of Cross-Examination, Cicero's Defense of Roscius for Murder, and the Story of the Trial Re-Told. 1st American from the 1st London ed., Adapted to the American Practice by an American Lawyer. St. Louis, 1885, sm8vo, 256pp., $22.50

M'HENRY, John & HARRIS, The Maryland Reports: Being a Series of the Most Important Law Cases Argued and Determined in the Provincial Court and Court of Appeals of the then Province of Maryland, from the Year 1700 down to the American Revolution, Selected from the Records of the State and from the Notes of Some of the Most Eminent Counsel who Practiced Law within that Period. NY, 1809, roy8vo, 609pp., roan, rebacked, $45.00

HAYS, Arthur Garfield, City Lawyer: The Autobiography of a Law Practice. NY, 1942, 8vo, 482pp., $15.00

HEYL, Lewis (ed), US Duties on Imports: 1872, DC, 1872, 280pp., $7.50

HINDMARCH, A Treatise on the Law Relative to Patent Privileges for the Sole Use of Inventions. Harrisburg, 1847, roy8vo, xxi,512pp.,roan,$45.00

HIGH, as., A Treatise on the Law of Injunctions. Chi,1873,4to,642pp.$12.50

HOAG, Clarence & HALLETT, Geo., Proportional Representation. NY, 1926, 8vo 546pp., $15.00

HOLCOMBE, Arthur, The Foundations of the Modern Commonwealth. NY, 1923, 8vo, 491pp., $12.50

HOLMES, Oliver Wendell, The Speeches of. Boston 1896, 8vo, 69pp., orig.ptd. bds, extremeties a bit worn, $15.00

HOOVER, J. Edgar, Persons in Hiding. Boston 1938, 8vo, 325pp., $15.00

HORN, Andrew, La Somme Appelle Mirroir des Justices vel Speculum Iusticiarioum, factum per Andream Horne. London, Printed by E.G. for Matthew Walbanke and Richard Best, and to be Sold at Their Shops at Grayes Inne Gate. 1642, 8vo, 311 (i.e.291pp.,) erratic pagination, bound in 18th century calf, skillfully rebacked, black letter, the editio princeps of this classic work; for the details of its character and significance, see Maitland's introduction to the Selden Society edition; $1250.00

HUDSON, Manley O., The World Court 1922-29, new edition, rev.Boston, 1929, 8vo, 199pp., $12.50

HUMPHRIES, Travers, Criminal Days: Recollections & Reflections. London 1946, 8vo, 227pp., $13.50

--5--

HYDE, H. Montgomery, Lord Justice: The Life and Times of Lord Birkett of Ulverston. NY, 1965, roy8vo, 638pp., $15.00

JACKSON, Fred. H., Simeon Eben Baldwin: Lawyer, Social Scientist, Statesman, NY, Columbia Univ. Press, 1955, roy8vo, 291pp., $13.00

JACKSON, S., The Life and Cases of Mr. Justice Humphries. NY,1952,239p.$13.00

JEREMY, Henry, The Law of Carriers, Inn-Keepers, Warehousemen and Other Depositories of Goods for Hire. NY, 1816, 8vo, 163pp., bds,rebacked.$35.00

JONES, William, An Essay on the Law of Bailments. Boston 1796, 8vo, 174pp., later1/2 linen, $37.50

KENEALEY, Arabella, Memoirs of Edward Vaughn Kenealy, LL.D., London, 1908, roy8vo, 303pp., extremeties a bit worn, else vg, $12.50

KNUDSON, John, A History of the League of Nations. Atlanta, 1938, 8vo, 445pp light sporadic pencil underscoring, $15.00

KUHNE, Fred, The Fingerprint Instructor. 2nd ed, NY, 1935, 8vo, 184pp., $13.50

KYD, Stewart, A Treatise on the Law of Bills of Exchange and Promissory Notes. 2nd American from the 3rd London ed., with Adds., Albany 1800. 12mo, 288pp., contemp roan, rebacked, $40.00

KYD, Stewart, A Treatise on the Law of Awards. Dublin, 1791, 8vo, 251pp., contemp. calf, rebacked, $46.50

(LANGDELL), Harvard Law School Association, Report of the9th Annual Meeting, June 25th, 1895, in Esoecial Honor of Christopher Columbus Langdell. Boston, Publ. by the Assn., 1895, roy8vo, 90pp., orig. ptd. wrps., contains an oration by Pollock and addresses by, among others, Holmes & Langdell, $22.50

The Law of Uses and Trusts: Collected and Digested in a Proper Order from Reports of Adjudged Cases, in the Courts of Law & Equity, and Other Books of Authority; Together with a Treatise of Dower. Savoy, 1734, 8vo, 437pp., contemp. calf, hinges a bit cracked, lacks label, $67.50

LEIGH, P. Brady, Abridgement of the Law of Nisi Prius, with Notes and References to the Latest American Cases by Geo. Sharswood. Phil, 1838, roy8vo, 2vols., contemp. roan, rebacked, $67.50

LOVEDAY, A., Reflections on International Administration. Oxford Univ.Press, 1956, 8vo, 334pp., $15.00

MACKINNON, Sir Frank Douglas, On Circuit, 1924-1937. Cambridge Univ. Press, 1940, roy8vo, 311pp., $17.50

MAJORIBANKS, Edw., Carson the Advocate. NY, 1932, roy8vo, 455pp., $15.00

MAJORIBANKS, Edw., For the Defence: The Life of Sir Edward Marshall Hall. NY, 1930, roy8vo, 471pp., $15.00

MARKS, A.H., Historical Notes on Lincoln's Inn Fields. London, 1922, 12mo, 103pp., $10.00

MAYER, Martin, Emory Buckner, intro. by Justice John M. Harlan. NY, 1968, 8vo, 304pp., $15.00

MAYER, Martin, The Lawyers. NY, 1967, 8vo, 586pp., $12.50

MC ELWEE, Will., The Murder of Sir Thomas Overbury. Oxford Univ. Press, 1952, roy8vo, 280pp., $15.00

MC LENNAN, The Patriarchal Theory. London, 1885, 8vo, 355pp., $12.50

MONTESQUIEU, Charles L., Baron de. Oevres. Amsterdam and Leipzig, 1758, 4to, 3vols, contemp. mattled calf, skillfully rebacked, first complete collected edition, corrected and considerably augmented by the author, nice set, $ 550.00

)MUSMANNO, Michael, Verdict! The Adventures of the Young Lawyer in the Brown Suit. NY, 1958, 8vo, 384pp., $15.00

)ODGERS, W. Blake, Six Lectures on the Inns of Court and Chancery. London, 1912, 12mo, 271pp., $12.50

)OPIE, Reduen, The Search for Peace Settlements.DC (Brookings), 1951, 8vo, 366pp., $15.00

)The Paris Law Courts: Sketches of Men and Manners. London, 1894, roy8vo, 293pp., $20.00

)PARRY, Sir Edward, The Bloody Assize. London, 1929, roy8vo, 310pp., $15.00

)PARRY, Edward, The Overbury Mystery: A Chronicle of Fact and Drama of the Law. NY, n.d. (c.1950), roy8vo, 328pp., $15.00

)PEAKE, Thomas, A Compendium of the Law of Evidence, from the last London edition, with additions, and American Cases and Notes by Josiah Randall. Phil., 1812, roy8vo, 470pp., contemp. roan, rebacked, $42.00

)The Pleader's Assistant, Containing a Select Collection of Precedents of Modern Pleadings, in the Courts of King's Bench and Common Pleas, Interspersed with Cursory Observations & Instructions, the Whole Drawn and Settled by the Most Eminent Counsel of Their Time. Dublin, 1795, 8vo, 520pp contemp. calf, rebacked, nice copy, $45.00

)POTTER, Paraclete, Every Man His Own Lawyer; or, the Clerk and Magistrates Assistant.....greatly enlarged by a Gentleman of the Bar. Poughkeepsie, 1834, sm8vo, 383pp., later 1/2 linen, $30.00

)POWELL, John, Jos., Essay Upon the Law of Contracts and Agreements. Dublin 1796, 8vo, 2vols., bound as one, 288pp., plus index, contemp.calf, rebacked, $47.50

)PUENTE, Julius. The Foreign Consul: His Juridical Status in the United States Chicago, 1926, roy8vo, 157pp., inscribed by the author, who was a member of the Chicago Bar, trace of wear at crown, $15.00

)RADCLIFFE, Viscount, Not in Feather Beds: Some Collected Paperc. London, 1968, 8vo, 277pp., $12.50

)RALSTON, Jackson H., International Arbitration from Athens to Locarno. Stanford Univ. Press, 1929, roy8vo, 417pp., $17.50

)RAM, Jas., The Science of Legal Judgement. fron the London edition, bound with many blank leaves for notes. Phil., 1835, roy8vo, 140pp., contemp. roan, rebacked, $42.50

)RAM, Jas., A Practical Treatise of Assets, Debts and Incumbrances. Phil., 1835, roy8vo, 430pp., later 1/2 linen & bds., $37.50

)RAMSAY, Sir Jas. H., The Angevin Empire, or the Reigns of HenryII, Richard I and John (1154-1216). Oxford Univ. Press, 1900, roy8vo, 556pp., $22.50 reprinted at $42.50

)REINWALD, Paul, Society and Its Criminals. London, 1949, 8vo, 315pp., $12.50

)Reports of Controverted Elections in the House of Representatives of the Commonwealth of Massachusetts from 1780- 1834..... and from 1835 to1852. Boston, 1853, roy8vo, 757pp., later 1/2 linen, $35.00

)REPPY, Alison, Civil Rights in the United States. NY, 1951, 8vo, 298pp., $13.50

--7--

)RICH, Bennett, The Presidents and Civil Disorder. DC (Brookings), 1941, 8vo, 235pp., $13.50

)RINGROSE, HAYACINTHE, The Inns of Court. London, 1909, 12mo, 147pp., $12.50

)ROBERTS, Owen, TheCourt and the Constitution. Cambridge, Harvard Univ.Press, 1951, 8vo, 102pp., first edition, $25.00

)Rogers, Ammi, Memoirs of....Falsely Accused and Imprisoned in Norwich Jail, for two years, on the Charge of Crimes...of which he Was as Absolutely Innocent as the Judge Who Pronounced the Sentence. 11th ed., Watertown, 1846 12mo, 264pp., later 1/2 linen and bds, $22.50

)ROLT, Sir John, Memoirs of....Lord Justice of the Court of Appeal in Chancery 1804-1871. Printed by the Society of the Inner Temple. 1939, roy8vo, 273pp., $15.00

)ROSENFARB, Jos., Freedom and the Administrative State. NY, 1948, roy8vo, 273pp., $13.50

)SCHLESINGER, Rudolf, Soviet Legal Theory. Oxford Univ. Pr., 1945, roy8vo, 299pp., $15.00

)SCHUBERT, Glendon (ed.), Judicial Behavior: A Reader in Theory and Research. Chicago, 1964, roy8vo, 603pp., $15.00

)SEAGLE, Will., The Quest for Law. NY, 1941, roy8vo, 439pp., $16.50

)SELDEN, John, Table-Talk: Being the Discourses of John Selden Esq., Or His Sence of Various Matters of Weight & Consequence Relating Especially to Religion and State. London, 1689, 8vo, bound in later 1/2 calf and marbled boards, lower portion of two margins trimmed a bit close, nice copy, first edition, scarce, $325.00

)Selected Essays in the Law of Torts. Cambridge, 1924, 4to, 770pp., intro by Roscoe Pound, $25.00

)SHEIL, Richard, Sketches of the Irish Bar, with Memoir & Notes by R. Shelton Mackenzie. NY, 1854, 8vo, 2vols., about 800pp., orig cl. $42.50

)SHEW, E.Spencer, A Companion to Murder...with a Note on the British Judicial System. NY, 1961, roy8vo, 303pp., contains biographical sketches of many judges. $13.50

)SINGER, Berthold, International Law. Chicago, 1918, 8vo, 335pp., $15.00

)SMITH-HUGHES, Jack, Unfair Comment Upon Some Victorian Murder Trials. London, 1951, 8vo, 360pp., $16.50

)SPELMAN, Sir Henry, Concilia, Decreta, Leges, Constitutiones in Re Ecclesiarum urbis Britannici....ab Initio Christianae ibidem Religionis ad nostram usque aetatem....Part I....usque ad Introitum Normannorum. London 1639, large folio, 637pp., bound in old calf, skillfully rebacked in calf a second part was published in 1664; this work the first collection of its kind, contains a vast store of information on early legal and constitutional history; there was no sharp distinction between church and state in either spiritual or temporal affairs before the Norman Conquest; moreover, clerks filled the majority of state positions, first edition, $225.00

)STERN, Rob., & GRESSMAN, E., Supreme Court Practice. DC, 1950, roy8vo, 523pp., $17.50

)THE STATUTES OF HENRY VII, in Exact Facsimile, from the Very Rare Original Printed by Caxton in 1489, edited with Notes and Introduction by John Rae. London, 1869, folio, xxi, 80, 32pp., bound in full contemp.morocco, printed on exceptionally high quality paper, a very beautiful book, $75.00

)STRAUS, Oscar, The Origin of Republican Form of Government in the United States. 2nd ed., rev., NY, 1901, 8vo, xli, 151pp., $12.50

)STRYKER, Lloyd Paul, Courts and Doctors. NY, 1932, 8vo, 236pp., $8.50

)Studies in Wills. Balto, 1926, 8vo, 25pp., ill., $6.50

)SWAINE, Robert T., The Cravath Firm & Its Predecessors 1819-1947: Vol.I: The Predecessor Firms 1819- 1906. NY, Privately Printed, 1946, roy8vo, 782pp., $27.50

)SWISHER, Carl Brent, American Constitutional Development. Boston, 1943, roy-8vo, 1079pp., light sporadic underlining, $15.00

)TAFT, Henry W., A Century and a Half at the New York Bar, Being the Annals of a Law Firm and Sketches of Its Members. NY, Privately Printed, 1938, roy8vo, xv, 305pp., $22.50

TAYLOR, Alfred S., Medical Jurisprudence. 4th American edition...with Adds. by Edw. Hartshorne. Phil., 1856, roy8vo, 697pp., roan, rebacked, $35.00

TAYLOR, Telford, Grand Inquest: The Story of Congressional Investigations NY, 1955, 8vo, 358pp., $12.50

TODD, Alpheus, Parliamentary Government in England: Its Origin, Development & Practical Operation. new ed., abr. & rev. by Spencer Walpole. London, 1892, 8vo, 2vols., $27.50

UNITED STATES LAW JOURNAL, Vol. II, 1826, 165pp., $22.50

WALKER-SMITH, Derek, The Life of Lord Darling. London, 1938, roy8vo, 316pp., $15.00

)WALPOSE, Spencer, The Life of Lord John Russell. London, 1889, roy8vo, 2vols. $30.00

)WARDEN, Rob., A Familiar Forensic View of Man and Law. Columbus, 1840 roy8vo, 550pp., rebacked, light watermark of last and first tew leaves $35.00

)WARREN, Samuel, Experiences of a Barrister & Confessions of an Attorney. Boston, 1857, 8vo, 376pp., later linen, $30.00

)WATSON, Will., A Treatise of the Law of Partenership. first American from the 2nd English ed., with many new References to American Decisions. Phil., 1807, roy8vo, 400pp., contemp. roan, rebacked, $42.50

)WHEATON, Henry, Elements of International Law, with a Sketch of the History of the Science. Phil., 1836, roy8vo, 375pp., orig. linen, crown just a trifle worn, new label, an excellent copy, uncut, first edition, $125.00

)WHITAKER, Richard, A Treatise of the Law Relative to Rights of Lien and Stoppage in Transit. London, & NY, 1816, 8vo, 228pp., contemp. bds, rebacked $40.00

WHITE, Leonard D., The Federalists: A Study in Administrative History. NY, 1959, roy8vo, 538pp., $12.50

WHITE, Leonard D., The Jeffersonians: A Study in Administrative History, 1829-1861, NY, 1956, roy8vo, 593pp., $12.50

WHITING, Will., War Powers Under the Constitution. (Boston, 1864,) Reprint: 1971, roy8vo, 342pp., $17.50 (list $35.00)

)WHITMORE, Will., A Bibliographical Sketch of the Laws of the Massachusetts Colony from 1630-1686, in Which are Included the Body of Liberties of 1641, and the Records of the Court of Assistants, 1641-44. Boston, 1890, 4to, xliii, 149pp., contemp. 1/2 morocco and linen, front hinge tender.$30.00

)WILD, Roland & CURTIS, B., King's Counsel: The Life of Sir Henry Curtis-Bennett. NY, 1938, 8vo, 282pp., $12.50 (crown trifle worn)

)WILLIAMS, Montague, Leaves of a Life. London, 1890, 8vo, 2vols., $25.00

)WILLIAMS, Montague, Later Leaves. B&NY, 1891, roy8vo, 423pp., $15.00

--9--

)WILLIAMS, Montague, Round London. London, 1892, 8vo, 244pp., $12.50

)WILLIAMS, J. Bruce, The Middle Temple Bench Book; Being a Register of the Benchers of the Middle Temple from the Earliest Records to the Present Time with an Historical Introduction. London, 1937, 4to, 368pp., with Numerous engravings, 1/2 morocco & linen, $35.00

)WOODRUFF, Douglas, The Tichborne Claimant: A Victorian Mystery. NY, 1957, 479pp., 8vo, $15.00

WORMSER, Rene, The Law: The Story of Lawmakers and the Law We Have Lived by from the Earliest Times to the Present Day. NY, 1949, roy8vo, 608pp.$17.50

YOUNG, Andrew, First Lessons in Civil Government, Including a Comprehensive View of the Government of the State of Ohio, and an Abstract of the Laws, Showing the Rights, Duties and Responsibilities of Citizens in the Civil & Domestic Relations, with an Outline of the Government of the United States, Adapted to the Capacities of Children & Youth. Cleveland, 1846, 12mo, 224pp roan, rebacked, $30.00

ZANE,John M., The Story of Law. NY, 1927, 8vo, 486pp., $15.00

ADDENDA

United States Commission on Industrial Relations: Industrial Relations; Final Report and Testimony Submitted to Congress. DC, GPO, 1916, roy8vo, 11vols., 11,000pp., orig. cl., $165.00

STAEL de HOLSTEIN, Baroness, A Treatise on Ancient & Modern Literature Illustrated by Striking Reference to the Principal Events and Characters that Have Distinguished the French Revolution. From the French of Baroness Stael de Holstein. London, 1803, roy8vo, 2vols., bound in the original boards, rebacked, from the library of Richard Brinsley Sheridan with his bookplate, first English edition, $125.00

GODWIN, William, Fleetwood: Or; The New Man of Feeling. London 1805, sm8vo, 3vols., contemp. marbled boards, newly rebacked in morocco, forecorners a bit worn, else excellent, first edition, $225.00

EISLER, Robert, Weltmantel und Himmelzelt: Religionsgeschichtliche Untersuchungen zur Urgeschichte des Antiken Weltbildes. Munchen, 1910, roy8vo, 2vols., $35.00

ENCYCLOPEDIA OF THE SOCIAL SCIENCES. NY, 1937, 15vols., bound as 8, orig. buckram, excellent, $175.00

WEBSTER'S INTERNATIONAL UNABRIDGED DICTIONARY: SECOND EDITION. Sp., 1946, orig. buckram, excellent, $125.00

MACHIAVELLI, Niccolo, Opere. Ferenze, 1782-3. 4to, 6vols., bound in later 1/2 linen and marbled boards, title of vol. V in fine facsimile on period paper, nice set, $175.00

SPENSER, Edmund, The Works of, edited by J. Payne Collier. London, Bell & Daldy, 1862, tall 8vo, 5vols., bound in later 1/2 linen and marbled boards, titles in red & black, beautifully printed on high quality paper, with woodcuts and ornamental letters at chapters, heavily annotated with very scholarly notes, nice set, $125.00

BAYLE, Pierre, Dictionnaire Historique et Critique. 5th edition, rev. & corr., & augmented. Amsterdam, 1740, folio, 4vols., bound in contemp calf, skillfully rebacked in calf, raised bands, spine gilt, light sporadic foxing and browning, $375.00

STERNE, Laurence, The Works of, NY, Taylor, 1904, roy8vo, 12vols., bound in 3/4 red morocco and marbled boards, marbled end papers, raised bands, spines gilt, ill., titles in red & black, uncut, York edition, #140 of an issue limited to 250, t/e/g, beautiful set in fine condition, $250.00

--10--

)DE FOE, Daniel, The Works of. NY, Jenson, 1905, tall 8vo, 16vols., bound in contemp. linen with paper labels, ill., uncut, #514 of an edition ltd. to 1000 sets, t/e/g, labels a bit faded, else excellent, $150.00

)ELIOT, George, Scenes of Clerical Life. London, Blackwood, 1858, 8vo, 2vols., bound in contemp. 3/4 calf and marbled boards, raised bands, spines gilded, forecorners a bit rubbled, half-titles lacking, first edition, author's first novel, $185.00

DICKENS, Charles, Master Humphrey's Clock. with Illustrations by Geo. Cattermole & Hablot Browne. London, Chapman, 1840, roy8vo, 3vols., bound in contemp. 3/4 calf and marbled boards, forecorners a bit rubbed and scuffed, spines gilded & tooled, nice set, first edition, $95.00

ADAMS, John, The Works of...Second President of the United States, with a Life of the Author, Notes and Illustrations. Boston, 1856, roy8vo, 10vols. orig. cl., small blind stamps on title pages, clean tight set, $225.00

SWIFT, Johnathan, The Works of, Arranged by Thomas Sheridan, with Notes, Historical and Critical. A New Edition, Corr. & Rev. by John Nichols, NYm 1812, sm8vo, 24vols., bound as 12 (as issued), contemp. roan, rebacked, excellent set, $225.00

BUCHEZ, P.J.B., Essai d'un Traite Complet de Philosophie, du Point de Vue du Catholicisme et du Progres. Paris, 1838-1840. 8vo, 3vols., bound in later 1/2 calf and marbled boards, one of the most important socialist works of the 19th century; Buchez was a Saint-Simonian who broke with the school to found his own movement; applying his radical interpretation of Christianity to society, he advocated the formation of a universal system of craft guilds with shared capital; under his influence many of these were established, some of them very successful; the newspaper l'Atelier, for which he provided the initial inspiration and ideas, was the only radical paper of the period written, published and printed by workingmen; this work is of extreme rarity, first (and only) edition, $275.00

CLEMENT, Pierre, Histoire de la Vie et de l'Administration de Colbert. Paris, 1846, 8vo, 520pp., later wraps, $27.00

SMITH, Adam, An Inquiry into the Nature & Causes of the Wealth of Nations. with a Life of the Author, an Introductory Discourse, Notes, and Supplemental Dissertations by J. R. M'Culloch. New Edition, Revised, Corrected and Improved. Edinburgh, 1863, roy8vo, lvi, 669pp., orig. cl., new end sheets, spine a bit rubbed, clean, tight copy, $37.50

SINCLAIR, Upton, The Jungle. NY, Doubleday, Page and Company, 1906. 8vo, original decorated cloth, an exceptionally clean, tight, bright copy, first edition, first issue, rare in this condition, $85.00

List 19
Summer 1978
SUPPLEMENT

Law

With an Addenda of Interesting Titles in Various Fields

Richard Adamiak
1545 East 60th St.
Chicago, Illinois 60637
312-955-4571
By Phone 8AM-Noon

1) AMERICAN BAR ASSOCIATION: Special Committee on Supplementing Canons of Professional Ethics, Compiled by the Chairman for theUse of the Committee. January, 1926, 8vo, 280pp., $17.50

2) BECKNER, Earl, History of Labor Legislation in Illinois. Chicago, University of Chicago Press, 1929, 8vo, 539pp., $17.50

3) BILLING, Sidney, A Practical Treatise on the Law of Awards and Arbitrations with Forms of Pleadings, Submissions and Awards. London, 1854, 8vo, xvi, 300, 72pp., bds, rebacked, $38.50

4) BLANSHARD, Paul, The Right to Read: The Battle Against Censorship. Boston, 1955, 8vo, 339pp., $13.50

5) BRYCE, James, International Relations. NY, 1922, 8vo, 275pp., $12.50

6) BUTLER, Charles Henry, A Century at the Bar of the Supreme Court of the United States. NY, 1942, 8vo, xxii, 222pp., $15.00

7) CURTIS, Charles, P., Jr., Lions Under the Throne: A Study of the Supreme Court of the United States......Boston, 1947, 8vo, 368pp., $12.50

8) DE BUSTAMENTE, Antonio Sanchez, The World Court, trans. by Eliz. Read. NY, 1925, roy8vo, xxv, 379pp., $17.50

9) EASTERBY, William, The History of the Law of Tithes in England. Cambridge University Press, 1888, 8vo, 110pp., $13.50

10) FRANKFURTER, Felix, The Case of Sacco and Vanzetti. Boston, 1927 sm8vo, 118pp., first edition, $27.50

11) GURNEY-CHAMPION, F.C.G., Justice and the Poor in England. London, 1926, 8vo, 245pp., $15.00

12) HAYNES, E.S.P., The Lawyer: A Conversation Piece...with an Autobiographical Intro. & Memoir by R. Haynes. London, 1951, xliii, 355pp., $17.50

13) HOLDSWORTH, William, Charles Dickens as a Legal Historian. New Haven, Yale Univ. Press, 1928, 8vo, 151pp., first edition, $25.00

14) HOLLAND, Sir Thomas Erskine, The Elements of Jurisprudence. 13th ed. Oxford Univ. Press, 1924, roy8vo, xxvi, 458pp., $22.50

15) HOPKINS, Albert, Autobiography of a Lawyer. Chicago, Privately ptd., 1966, 8vo, 236pp., inscribed by the author, $15.00

16) LAWSON, John, D., A Concordance of Words and Phrases Construed in the Judicial Reports and of Legal Definitions Contained Therein. San Francisco, 1887, roy8vo, 783pp., later linen, light sporadic marginal dampstain, $30.00

17) THE LAWS OF ENGLAND, Being a Complete Statement of the Whole Law of England by the Late Earl of Halsbury...and Other Lawyers. 3rd ed. under the editorship of Lord Simonds. London, 1952, roy8vo, 49vols. ie., 39vols., plus 1 vol. Table of Cases, 2vol. Index; 1vol. table of Statutes; and 6vols Supplements (1971,1972,1973), fine, $750.00

--2--

LEE, Howard B., The Story of the Constitution, Forward by John W. Davis, Charlottesville, 1932, roy8vo, xxii, 292pp., $13.50

MACY, Jesse, The English Constitution: A Commentary on Its Nature & Growth. NY, 1897, 8vo, 534pp., $15.00

MASTERMAN, J. Howard, A History of the British Constitution. London, 1912, 8vo, 291pp., $13.50

MC CARTER, Robert H., Memoirs of a Half Century at the New Jersey Bar. New Jersey State Bar Assn., 1937, 8vo, 178pp., $15.00

MC LAUGHLIN, Andrew C., The Courts, the Constitution and Parties: Studies in Constitutional History and Politics. Chicago. Univ. of Chicago Press, 1912, 8vo, 299pp., $15.00

MITCHELL, Edwin V., The Doctor in Court. NY, 1913, 8vo, 152pp., $10.00

MORSE, Charles, Apices Juris and Other Legal Essays in Prose & Verse. Toronto, Canada Law Book Co., 1906, 8vo, 356pp., $17.50

OSBORN, Albert S., Questioned Documents. Intro. by John Henry Wigmore. Rochester, 1910, roy8vo, xxiv, 501pp., $37.50

POLLOCK, Sir Friedrich, Leading Cases Done into English and Other Diversions. London, 1892, 8vo, x, 92pp., $17.50

ROBERT, Henry M., Parliamentary Law. NY, 1923, roy8vo, 588pp., trifle worn, $17.50

SEAGLE, Will., Men of Law from Hammurabi to Holmes. NY, 1948, 8vo, 391pp., $10.00

TAFT, William Howard, Popular Government: Its Essence, Its Permanence and Its Perils. New Haven, Yale Univ. Press, 1913, 8vo, 283pp., faint sporadic damp stain along lower margin, first edition, $22.50

TAFT, William Howard, Our Chief Magistrate and His Powers. NY, Columbia Univ. Press, 1916, 8vo, 165pp., first edition, $37.50

WARREN, Samuel, A Popular and Practical Introduction to Law Studies. ed. with Alterations & Adds. by Isaac G. Thompson. Albany, 1870, 8vo, 406pp., contemp. roan, bit scuffed and shaken, $27.50

WEAVER, Samuel, Autobiography of a Pennsylvania Dutchman. NY, 1951, 8vo, 228pp., $12.50

VIOLATIONS OF FREE SPEECH AND RIGHTS OF LABOR: Hearings before a Subcommittee of the Committee on Education and Labor: United States Senate, 74th Congress, 2nd Session, Pursuant to Senate Resolution 266, a Resolution to Investigate Violations of the Right of Free Speech and Assembly and Interference with the Right of Labor to Organize and Bargain Collectively.DC, GPO, 1936-43. Contains the following: Hearings, Senate, Parts 1-75 inc. (lacking22-23); House Hearings, Parts 1-9; Senate Reports for 1937, 1939, 1941, 1942, 1943, Proposed Amendments to the National Labor Relations Act, 1-4; bound in 29 volumes in 1/2 morocco, excellent condition, $375.00

INVESTIGATION OF CONCENTRATION OF ECONOMIC POWER: Hearings Before the Temporary National Economic Committee, Congress of the US, 75th Cong. 3rd Sess., Pursuant to Public Resolution No. 113. DC, GPO, 1938-41. Contains the following: Hearings, Parts 1-31A (inc.); Monographs, 1-43; Final Report of the Executive Secretary; Final Report and Recommendations; bound in 35vols., in 1/2 morocco, excellent, $375.00

CATALOGUE 22
LAW AND LEGAL HISTORY

With the unrecorded Dublin edition of Bentham's critique of Blackstone; and Austin's Jurisprudence.

Richard Adamiak
1545 East 60th St.
Chicago, Illinois 60637
312-955-4571

Jan, 1979

ABEL-SMITH, Brian, & STEVENS, R., In Search of Justice: Society & the Legal System. L, 1968, 8vo, 384p., $15.00

ABRAHAMS, Gerals, According to the Evidence: An Essay on Legal Proof. L, 1958, 8vo, 248p., $15.00

ADAMS, John, The Doctrine of Equity....2nd American ed. with Notes and References to the Latest American Chancery Decisions by Jas. Ludlow & John Collins. Phil., 1852, roy8vo, 760p., contemp. roan, rebacked, sl. marg. dampstain first & last few leaves, $47.50

ADAMS, John, Treatise on the Principles & Practice of the Action of Ejectment....from the Last London ed, to which have been carefully noted the Decisions from the Supreme Court of New York from Jan Term 1799 to Oct Term 1820, with References to the Decisions in the Courts of Mass. & Pa., & the Supreme Court of the U.S., by Philo Ruggles. NY, 1821, roy8vo, 421p., roan, rebacked, $35.00

ALBOIZE, M., & MAQUET, A., Les Prisons de l'Europe. P, 1845, roy8vo, 8vols. bound as 4, contemp/ 1/2 calf & bds, extremities bit worn, else vg, $85.00

ALEXANDER, Franz, & STAUB, H., The Criminal, the Judge & the Public: A Psychoanalysis, trans Zilboorg. NY, 1931, 8vo, 348p., $15.00

ALLMAN, NOrwood, Shanghai Lawyer. NY, 1943, 8vo, 283p., $13.50

ALTGELD, John, Live Questions: Including Our Penal Machinery & Its Victims. C, 1890, 8vo, 320pp., later linen, inscribed by the author, $27.50

ALVERSTON, Rt. Hon., Recollections of Bench and Bar. L, 1914, roy8vo, 331p., $20.00

) ANGELL, J.K., Treatise on the Limitations of Actions at Law & Suits in Equity & Admiralty, with an Appendix Containing the American and English Statues of Limitations. 2nd ed., rev., corr. & much enl., B, 1846, roy8vo xxiv, 707p., later 1/2 linen & marbled boards, $45.00

) ASSOCIATION OF AMERICAN LAW SCHOOLS, COMMITTEE (ed.), Selected Readings on the Law of Contracts from American and English Legal Periodicals. Intro. by Benjamin Cardozo. NY, 1931, 4to, 1320p., tiny nick in spine, $35.00

) AUSTIN, John, The Province of Jurisprudence Determined. L, 1832, 8vo, xx, 391, lxxvipp., bound in contemp. 1/2 calf and marbled boards, trace of wear at crown, bit rubbed, handsome copy, the first edition, $1000.00
Of great rarity, no copy recorded as available in this century: "the founder of the English 'analytical' or imperative school of jurisprudence. Despite some distinguished dissenters, it is still dominant in England, Canada, Australia and New Zealand." Patterson, Jurisprudence,84.

) BACON, Francis, Works of. New Edition. L, 1826, 8v9, 10vols., later 1/2 linen and marbled boards, excellent, $250.00

) BACON, Francis, Works of. L, 1871, sm4to, xvols., lxx, 797, 832pp., bound in contemp/ 1/2 calf and linen, bit rubbed, else excellent, $87.50

) BALDWIN, Simeon E., The American Judiciary. NY, 1905, 8vo, 403p., $16.50

) BALDWIN, Simeon, The Young Man & the Law. NY, 1920, 8vo, 160p., $14.50

17) BANCROFT, Geo., History of the Formation of the Constitution of the United States. NY, 1882, roy8vo, 2vols., $40.00

ER, Chs., Henry George. Oxford Univ. Pr., 1955, roy8vo, 696p., $17.50

ER, Lucius & BARKER, T., Freedoms, Courts, Politics: Studies in Civil erties. NJ, 1955, roy8vo, 324p., $15.00

S, Ernest, Story of the Supreme Court. Ind., 1936, 8vo, 377p. $15.00

EY, Sir John, Summary of the Law of Bills of Exchange, Cash Bills & missory Notes, from the 4th London ed., rev. by the author; with Notes eferences to American Decisions by Willard Philipps & Samuel E. Sewall. 1826, 8vo, 426p., contemp. roan, rebacked, marginal dampstain of first ast few leaves, $38.50

UT, John, An Ancient Partnership: Local Government, Magna Carta and the ional Interest. Univ. Press of Virginia, 1966, 8vo, 93p., orig. wrps,$10.

ANTINE, Henry, Problems in Law for Law School & Bar Examination Review. Paul, 1927, 4to, 1110p., $15.00

ENTINE, Jas., The College Law Dictionary, Foreword by Roscoe Pound. hester, 1931, 4to, 998p., $18.50

for International Settlements: Documents. C, 1930, 8vo, 172p., $13.50

RD, Jas., A Brief Exposition of the Constitution of the United States. , 1840, 12mo, 178p., later linen, 2nd ed., some dampstain of first last few leaves, $27.50

, Jas., The Constitution of the United States. Foreword by Calvin lidge. NY, 1924, roy8vo, 362p., $15.00

ER, Carl Lotus, New Liberties for Old. Yale Univ. Pr. 1941, 8vo, p., $14.50

U, Hugo, The Death Penalty in America: An Anthology. C, 1964, 8vo, p., $15.00

I, Melvin, Blood Money: Ready for the Plaintiff. NY, 1956, 8vo, 338p. $15

IETT, H.A., The Constitution in School and College. NY, 1935, roy8vo, p., $17.50

SON, Allan, Our Dishonest Constitution. NY, 1914, 8vo, 182p., $13.50

THAM, Jeremy, A Fragment on Government; Being an Examination of What Delivered on the Subject of Government in General, in the Introtion to Sir William Blackstone's Commentaries: With a Preface in ich Is Given a Critique of the Work at Large. Dublin, 1776, 8vo, xli, p., light sporadic foxing, some dampstain pp. xxxii-8, bound in later ? morocco and marbled boards, first Dublin edition; an unrecorded ition, not in Kress, not in National Union Catalogue, not in British seum Catalogue; $650.00

EZNIAK, Leon, The Theatrical Counselor. C, 1923, 8vo, 223p., $15.00

MAN, Harold, The Nature & Functions of Law. NY, 1958, roy8vo, 662p. $17.50

NAL, J.D., World Without War. L, 1958, 8vo, 308p., $13.50

ERIDGE, Albert, Life of John Marshall. B/NY, 1929, roy8vo, 4vols. bound 2, spine lettering faded, $45.00

LING, Sidney, Practical Treatise on the Law of Awards and Arbitrations. 1845, 8vo, 300p., bds, rebacked, $37.50

D, Otto, The Idea of Justice. NY, 1967, 8vo, 192p., $14.50

HOP, Jim, Murder Trial of Judge Peel. NY, 1962, 8vo, 210p., $12.50

-3-

41) BLACKHAM, Rob., Wig & Gown: The Story of the Temple, Gray's & Lincoln's Inn. L, (1925), roy8vo, 240p., ill., $22.50

BLACKSTONE, The Most Material Parts of Blackstone's Commentaries Reduced to Questions & Answers by John Devereux, Upon the Plan and in Place of Kinne's Blackstone. new ed., NY, 1870, 8vo, xxi,392p., later buck, $35.00

BLACKSTONE, Sir William, Commentaries on the Laws of England, from the 19th London Edition, with a Life of the Author & Notes by Christian, Chitty, Lee, Hovenden, & Ryland, and Also References to American Cases by a Member of the New York Bar. Phil., 1879, roy8vo, 4vols. bound as two, later 1/2 linen and marbled boards, $87.50

BLACKSTONE, Sir William, Commentaries on the Laws of England. 5th ed., Oxford, 1773, 8vo, 4vols., bound in contemp. calf, skillfully rebacked in calf, raised bands, spines gilt, slight marginal worming in volume two and in index of volume four, nice set, $275.00

A'BECKETT, Gilbert Abbott, The Comic Blackstone, revised and extended by Arthur A'Beckett of Gray's Inn, with ten full page coloured illustrations and others by Harry Furniss. L, 1887, 8vo, 324p., $35.00

BLANSHARD, Paul, God and Man in Washington. B, 1960, 8vo, 251p. (church-state relations), $13.50

BLAUSTEIN, Albert, & FERGUSON, C., Desegregation and the Law. NJ, Rutgers Univ. Pr., 1957, 8vo, 333p., $15.00

BLAUVELT, Mary, The Development of Cabinet Government in England. NY, 1902, 8vo, 300p., $14.50

BLISS, Edw., Defense Investigation. Springfield, 1956, roy8vo, 304p., $14.50

BLOOM, Murray, The Trouble with Lawyers. NY, 1968, 8vo, 351p., $13.50

BLOOM, Sol., Story of the Constitution. DC, 1937, 8vo, 192p., $12.50

BOARMAN, Patrick, Union Monopolies and Antitrust Restraints. DC, 1963, 8vo, 203p., $13.50

BONTECOU, Eleanor, The Federal Loyalty-Security Program. Cornell Univ. Pr., 1953, roy8vo, 377p., $16.50

BOQUET, Henry, An Examen of Witches Drawn from Various Trials of Many of This Sect....Including the Procedure Necessary to Judge in Trials for Witchcraft. trans by E. Allen Ashwin, ed. Rev. M. Summers. L, Priv. Pub., 1929, 8vo, 328p., spine bit faded, scarce, $27.50

BORCHARD, Edwin, Convicting the Innocent. NY, 1932, roy8vo, 383p., bit rubbed, $13.50

BORCHARD, Edwin, & Lage, W., Neutrality for the United States. Yale Univ. Pr., 1937, roy8vo, 380p., $16.50

BORCHARD, Edwin, Guide to the Law and Legal Literature of Germany. DC, Library of Congress, 1912, 4to, 226p., $22.50

BORKIN, Jos., The Corrupt Judge: An Inquiry into Bribery and Other High Crimes and Misdemeanors in the Federal Courts. NY, 1962, 8vo, 310p., $14.50

BORGESE, G.A., Foundations of the World Republic. Univ. of Chicago Pr., 1953, 4to, 328p., $16.50

BORTHWICK, Will., Remarks on British Antiquities: The Origin and Ceremony of Judicial Combats; the Solemnities of Ancient Writs;.... Edinburgh, 1776, 8vo, 144p., contemp. bds, rebacked, $67.50

BOURINOT, John, Manual of the Constitutional History of Canada Montreal, 1888, 12mo, 238p., ex lib, $13.50

BOUVIER'S Law Dictionary and Concise Encyclopedia. 3rd ed., rev., KC/St. P., 1914, 4to, 3vols., $47.50

NELSON, M., Judicial Review in Virginia. NY, 1947, 8vo, 249pp., wrps, $5.00

-4-

63) BOWEN, Cath., Yankee from Olympus: Justice Holmes and His Family. B, 1945, 8vo, 465p., $12.50

BOWKER, A.E., Behind the Bar. NY/L, 1949, 8vo, 323p., (clerk to Sir Edw. Marshall Hall & Lord Birkett), $15.00

BOX, Muriel, Birth Control & Libel: Trial of Marie Stopes. NY, 1967, roy8vo 392p., $16.50

BOZELL, L.B., The Warren Revolution. NY, 1966, roy8vo, 366p., $15.00

BRADBY, Jas., Treatise on the Law of Distresses. 1st American from the London ed. of 1808, NY, 1808, roy8vo, 325p., roan, rebacked, $35.00

BRADLEY, Hon Jos. P., Miscellaneous Writing....and a Review of His Judicial Record by Will. D. Lewis, and an Account of His "Dissenting Opinions" by A.Q. Keasby, ed. & compiled by his Son, Chs. Bradley. Newark, 1902, roy8vo, 435p., ex lib, bit soiled, $22.50

BRANT, Irving, The Bill of Rights. NY, 1965, roy8vo, 565p., $17.50

BRENNAN, Ellen, Plural Office-Holding in Mass., 1760-1780: Its Relation to the "Separation"of Departments of Government. Univ. of N. Carolina Pr., 1945, 8vo, 227p., $13.50

BRENTON, Myron, The Privacy Invaders. NY, 1964, 8vo, 240p., $13.50

BRITTON, An English Translation & Notes by Francis M. Nichols, Intro. by Simeon Baldwin, DC, 1901, roy8vo, 649p., later linen, $35.00

BRODRICK, Geo., English Land and English Landlords: An Inquiry into the Origin and Character of the English Land System with Proposals for Its Reform. L, 1881, roy8vo, 515p., $25.00

BROMHEAD, P.A., The House of Lords in Contemporary Politics, 1911-57. L, 1958, roy8vo, 283p., $16.50

BROWNE, G.L., Narratives of State Trials in the Nineteenth Century. B, 1882, 8vo, 2vols., rebacked, $27.50

BRYCE, Jas., Hindrances to Good Citizenship. Yale Univ. Pr., 1910, 8vo, 138p., $12.50

BUCKLAND, W.W., Elementary Principles of Roman Private Law. Cambridge Univ. Press, 1912, 8vo, 419p., $22.50

BUCKLAND, W.W., Main Institutions of Roman Private Law. Cambridge Univ. Press, 1931, 8vo, 410p., $25.00

BUSCH, Francis, Casebook of the Curious & True. NY, 1957, 8vo, 228p., $13.50

BUSCH, Francis, They Escaped the Hangman. Ind. 1953, 8vo, 301p., $14.50

BUTLER, Sir Geoffrey, & MACCOBY, Simon, The Development of International Law. L, 1928, roy8vo, xxxv, 566p., $22.50

CAENEGEM, R.C. van, Royal Writs in England from the Conquest to Glanville. L, 1959, 4to, 556p., (Selden Soc, vol. 77), $18.50

CAHN, Edmund, The Moral Decision: Right and Wrong in the Light of American Law. Indiana Univ. Pr., 1956, roy8vo, 453p., $17.50

CAMPBELL, Mildred, The English Yeoman under Elizabeth and the Early Stuarts. Yale Univ. Press, 1942, roy8vo, 453p., $17.50

CAMPION, G.F., An Introduction to the Procedure of the House of Commons. L, 1929, roy8vo, 308p., $16.50

CARMEN, Ira, Movies, Censorship and the Law. Univ. of Michigan Pr., 1966, 8vo, 339p., $7.50

DUFF, John, A.Lincoln:Prairie Lawyer. NY, 1960, roy8vo, 433p., ill., $22.50

GOODMAN, Gilbert, Government Policy Toward Commercial Aviation: Competition & the Regulation of Rates. NY, 1944, 8vo, 122p., wrps, $12.50

RADCLIFFE, G. & CROSS, G., English Legal System. L, 1937, 428pp., $16.50

ROCCA, Fer., Canonical Procedure. Mil., 1961, 8vo, 384pp., $16.50

-5-

87) CARNEGIE ENDOWMENT FOR INTERNATIONAL PEACE: Report of the International Commission to Inquire into the Causes and Conduct of the Balkan Wars. DC, 1914, 4to, 413p., $18.50

CARNEGIE ENDOWMENT FOR INTERNATIONAL PEACE: Yearbook for 1940. $14.50

Same for 1943, $14.50

Same for 1938, $14.50

CARR, Edward, Conditions of Peace. NY, 1943, 8vo, 282p., $12.50

CARR, Robert, The House Committee on Un-American Activities, 1945-50. Cornell Univ. Press, 1952, roy8vo, 489p., $17.50

CARRALBO, Claire, & SPARKES, B., Crime in Ink. NY, 1929, 8vo, 296p., $14.50

Catalogue of the Library of the Chicago Law Institute. C, 1887, 8vo, 371p., $22.50

CATLIN, Geo., Story of the Political Philosophers. NY, 1939, roy8vo, 802p., $16.50

CERNY, Joe, Courtroom Knowhow: Observations by a Court Reporter. Intro. by Hon. Earl Welch. Cincinnati, 1958, roy8vo, 326p., $16.50

CHADBOURN, Jas., Lynching and the Law. Univ. of N. Carolina Press, 1933, 8vo, 221p., $7.50

CHANLER, John A., Four Years Behind the Bars of "Bloomingdale" or; the Bankruptcy of Law in New York. Roanoke Rapids, N.C., 1906, roy8vo, 322p. (member of the NY bar), $17.50

CHAPMAN, Guy, The Dreyfus Case. NY, 1955, 8vo, 400p. $15.00

CHOATE, Jos. H., Arguments and Addresses., ed. Hicks, with Memorial by Elihu Root. St. Paul, 1926, 4to, 1189p., $25.00

CHUTE, Marchette, The First Liberty: History of the Right to Vote in America, 1619-1850. NY, 1969, roy8vo, 371p., $13.50

CLAPP, Edwin, Economic Aspects of the War: Neutral Rights, Belligerent Claims and American Commerce in the Years 1914-1915. Yale Univ. Pr., 1915, 8vo, 340p., $16.50

CLARK, Grenville, & SOHN, L., World Peace Through World Law. Harvard Univ. Press, 1958, roy8vo, 540p., $17.50

CLARKE, Catherine, The Loyolas and the Cabots: The Story of the Boston Heresy Case. B, 1950, 8vo, 301p., $14.50

CLARKE, Will., The Soul of the Law. Intro. by John H. Wigmore. B, 1942, roy8vo, 582p., few pp. underlined, $17.50

COBBAN, Alfred, The Debate on the French Revolution, 1789-1800. L, 1950, 8vo, 496p., (includes sections on Natural Rights & Sovereignty, Fox's Libel Act, The Treason Trials, Suspension of Habeus Corpus), $16.50

COHN, Alfred, & CHISHOLM, J. Take the Witness! NY, 1934, 8vo, 315p., (life of celebrated criminal lawyer Earl Rogers), $15.00

COLBERT, Evelyn, Retaliation in International Law. NY, 1948,8vo,220p,$13.50

COLEMAN, N., The Constitution & Its Framers. C, 1910, 8vo, 642p., $16.50

COMMAGER, Henry S. et al., Civil Liberties Under Attack. Univ. of Penn Press, 1951, roy8vo, 155p., $13.50

CONRAD, Earl, Mr. Seward for the Defense. NY, 1956, 8vo, 336p., $15.00

CORBETT, P.E., Law and Society in the Relations of States. NY, 1951, 8vo, 337p., $16.50

COX, Jos., The Recluse of Herald Square: The Mystery of Ida Wood. NY, 1964, 8vo, 246p., $13.50

SAMUEL, Maurice, Blood Accusation. NY, 1966, 8vo, 286pp., $12.50

-6-

114) The Counter Case of Great Britain as Laid Before the Tribunal of Arbitration Convened at Geneva under the Provisions of the Treaty between the United States and Her Majesty, the Queen of Great Britain, Concluded at Washington, May 8, 1871, Together with Volumes V, VI and VII of the Appendix to the British Case. DC, GPO, 1872, roy8vo, 1105p., light wear of extremities,$35.00

Corpus Juris Civilis. Recognoverunt Adnotationibusque Criticis Instructum Eididerunt D. Albertus, D.M.F. Kriegelii, D.A. Hermann, D.E. Osenbrueggen. Impressio Septima, Novis Curis Emendiator. Leipzig, 1856, 4to, 3vols., 3000pp. bound in 1/2 contemp. morocco and paper covered boards, paper worn a bit here and there, otherwise excellent, beautifully printed on very high quality paper, raised bands, spines nicely gilded, a scarce and very scholarly early modern edition, $145.00

CRANDALL, Samuel, Treaties: Their Making and Enforcement. NY, 1904, 8vo, 251p., orig. ptd. wrps, $8.50

CROSSKEY, Will. W., Politics and the Constitution in the History of the United States. Univ. of Chicago Press, 1953, 4to, 2vols., $30.00

CUQ, Eduard, Manuel des Institutions Juridiques des Romains. 2nd ed. rev., P, 1928, roy8vo, 953p., later linen, $37.50

CURRAN, Henry, Pillar to Post. NY, 1941, roy8vo, 387p., (Chief Magistrate of New York City), $14.50

CURTIS, George Ticknor, Constitutional History of the United States. NY, 1899-1902, roy8vo, 2vols., author argued the Dred Scott Case, $47.50

DARROW, Clarence, Verdicts Out of Court. ed. Weinberg. C, 1963, roy8vo, 448p., $17.50

DAVIS, Geo. B., Elements of International Law with an Account of Its Origin, Sources & Historical Development. 3rd rev ed. NY, 1908, 8vo, 673p., $17.50

DAVITT, Thomas, The Elements of Law. B, 1959, roy8vo, 370p., $14.50

DE HUZAR, Geo. (ed.), New Perspectives on Peace. Univ. of Chicago Press, 1944, 8vo, 261p., $12.50

Delon, Floyd (ed.), Yearbook of School Law 1974. Topeka. 8vo, 264p., $14.50

DESTY, Rob., The Constitution of the United States, 2nd ed., with a Supp. Table of Cases by A. Brunner, SF, 1887, 8vo, 504p., roan, rebacked, $22.50

DILLON, John F., The Laws and Jurisprudence of England and America. B, 1895, roy8vo, 431p., $25.00

DILNOT, Geo., The Bank of England Forgery. NY, 1929, roy8vo, 274p., $15.00

DOWNIE, Leonard, Justice Denied: The Case for Reform of the Courts. NY, 1971, 8vo, 221p., $13.50

DUBLIN, Lewis, & LOTKA, A., The Money Value of a Man. NY, 1930, 8vo, 264p. $17.50

DUFFY, Herbert, William Howard Taft. NY, 1930, roy8vo, 345p., $17.50

DURANT, W.C. (ed.), Law Observance: Shall the People of the United States Uphold the Constitution. NY, 1929, roy8vo, 573p.(pieces submitted in the contest "for the best and most practicable plan to make the 18th Amendment effective," $16.50

EAGLETON, Clyde, The Responsibility of States in International Law. NY, New York Univ. Press, 1928, roy8vo, 291p., $15.00

EHRLICH, J.W. A Reasonable Doubt. Clev. 1964, 8vo, 297p., $13.50

EKIRCH, Arthur, The Civilian and the Military. Oxford Univ. Press, 1956, roy8vo, 340p., $15.00

STORY, Jos., Equity Jurisprudence. 6th ed., B, 1853, roy8vo, 2vols, $85.00

135b) ELTON, G.R., Reform and Reformation in England, 1509-1558. Harvard Univ. Press, 1977, roy8vo, 423p., $12.50

Special Committee of the Association of the Bar of the City of New York and the National Legal Aid & Defender Assn., Equal Justice for the Accused. NY, 1959, 8vo, 144p., $13.50

ERNST, Morris, & SCHWARTZ, A., Privacy: The Right to Be Let Alone. NY, 1962, 8vo, 238p., $13.50

ERNST, Morris, A Love Affair with the Law. NY, 1968, 8vo, 181p. $12.50

ERNST, Morris, & LINDLEY, Alex, Hold Your Tongue! The Layman's Guide to Libel and Slander. rev. ed. NY, 1950, 8vo, 304p., $13.50

EVANS, E.P., The Criminal Prosecution and Capital Punishment of Animals. NY, 1906, 8vo, 384p., $17.50

FARMER, Robert, Rights of the Mentally Ill. NY, 1967, 8vo, 140p., $13.50

The Federalist.....Also the Continentalist and Other Papers by Alexander Hamilton. ed. John C. Hamilton, P, 1904, roy8vo, 658p., $17.50

FELL, Walter W., Treatise on the Law of Mercantile Guarantees, 1st American from the 2nd & last London ed., with Notes and References to American Decisions by Chs. Walker of the New York Bar. NY, 1826, roy8vo, 435p., contemp. roan, rebacked, $45.00

FELLMAN, David, The Constitutional Right of Association. Univ. of Chicago Press, 1963, 8vo, 110p., $5.00

FELSCHER, Howard, & ROSEN, M., The Press in the Jury Box. NY, 1966,239p.$13

FERBER, Nat, A New American: From the Life Story of Salvatore A. Cotillo, Supreme Court Justice, State of New York. NY, 1938, 8vo, 321p., $14.50

FISCHER, Edw., People's Court. Evanston, 1947, roy8vo, 164p., $12.50

FLEMING, Denna, The United States and World Organization, 1920-1933. NY, Columbia Univ. Press, 1938, 4to, 569p., light sporadic underlining, $12.50

FOLEY, Hamilton (ed.), Woodrow Wilson's Case for the League of Nations: Compiled with His Approval. Princeton Univ. Press, 1923, 8vo, 288p., $7.50

FOORD, A.S., His Majesty's Opposition: 1715-1830. Oxford Univ. Press, 1964, roy8vo, 494p., $15.00

FOREVILLE, R., L'Eglise et la Royaute en Angleterre sous Henri II Plantagenet (1154-1189). P, 1943, roy8vo, 611p., orig. ptd. wrps, $22.50

FORTESCUE, Sir John, De Laudibus Regum Angliae: A Treatise in Commendation of the Laws of England. trans by A. Gregor, Notes by A. Ames. Cininnati, 1874, roy8vo, 302p., $30.00

FOX, A.W., The Earl of Halsbury: Lord High Chancellor, 1823-1821. L, 1929, roy8vo, 358p., ex lib, $16.50

FOX, Harold, Monopolies and Patents: A Study of the History and Future of the Patent Monopoly. Univ. of Toronto Press, 1947, roy8vo, 388p, $14.50

FRANK, Jerome, Fate and Freedom: A Philosophy for Free Americans. NY, 1945, 8vo, 373p., $15.00

FRANK, John, Mr. Justice Black: The Man and His Opinions. NY, 1949, roy8vo, 357p., $14.50

GALSWORTHY, John, Justice: A Tragedy in Four Acts. NY, 1910,8vo,109p,$12.50

GARBETT, Cyril, Church & State in England. L, 1950, roy8vo, 320p., $16.50

GERHART, Eugene (ed.), The Lawyer's Treasury. Ind, 1956, roy8vo, 520p., $16.50

) HARRISS, Clement, Gift Taxation in the US. DC, 1940, 8vo,175p.wrps,$12.5C

183) HARRIS, Richard, Hints on Advocacy. 3rd American from the English Ed., rev. & enl. by Will. Murfree. St. Louis, 1884, 8vo, 208p., crown & base bit worn, $22.50

HARRISON, Joseph, The Practice of the Court of Chancery, enlarged by John G. Williams, 8th edition with considerable additions by Wilmot Parker. L, 1796, roy8vo, later 1/2 linen and marbled boards, last leaf or two of index lacking, $85.00

HASKINS, Chs. Homer, The Normans in European History. L, 1916 8vo, 258p;$12.

HASTINGS, Sir Patrick, Autobiography. NY, 1954, roy8vo, 302p., $15.00

HAYES, John E.R. (Of the Boston Bar), Invention: Its Attributes and Definition. Cambridge, Priv. Pub., 1942, 8vo, 133p., $16.50

HAYNES, Geo., The Election of Senators. NY, 1906, 8vo, 295p., $14.50

HERSHEY, Amos, The Essentials of International Public Law and Organization. rev. ed., NY, 1927, roy8vo, 784p., $17.50

HERSHEY, Amos, Essentials of International Public Law. NY, 1912, roy8vo, 558p., rebacked, $13.50

HILL, Frederick, Decisive Battles of the Law: Narrative Studies of Eight Legal Contests Affecting the History of the United States Between the Years 1800 and 1886. NY, 1907, 8vo, 267p., $16.50

HILL, Frederick, Lincoln the Lawyer. NY, 1906, roy8vo, 332p., $18.50

HILL, Norman, The Public International Conference: Its Functions, Organization and Procedure. Stanford Univ. Press, 1929, 8vo, 267p., $14.50

HOBSON, John A., Towards International Government. NY, 1915, 8vo, 216p., $14.50 (Reprinted at $33.00)

HODGKIN, R.H., History of the Anglo-Saxons. 3rd ed. Oxford Univ. Pr., 1959, roy8vo, 2vols., $35.00

HODGSON, D.H., Consequences of Utilitarianism: A Study in Normative Ethics and Legal Theory. Oxford Univ. Pr., 1967, 8vo, 187p., few pp. underlined, $13.50

HOFFMAN, Stanley (ed.), Conditions of World Order. B, 1968, roy8vo, 379p., (Daedalus #10), $15.00

HOLMES, G.A., The Estates of the Higher Nobility in XIV Century England. Cambridge Univ. Pr., 1957, 8vo, 180p., $13.50

HOOK, Sidney, The Paradoxes of Freedom. Univ. of California Press, 1962, 8vo, 152p., $6.50

HOOKER, Richard, The Works of, with Life by Isaac Walton, edited and arr. by John Keble. Oxford Univ. Press, 1836, roy8vo, 3vols. bound as 4, original binders boards, excellent, $85.00

HOOVER, Herbert, & GIBSON, H., Problems of a Lasting Peace. NY, 1943, 8vo, 303p., $8.50

HOWARD, Pendleton, Criminal Justice in England. NY, 1931, 8vo, 436p., $16.5C

HOWE, M.A. De Wolfe, Portrait of an Independent: Moorfield Story, 1845-1929. B, 1932, 8vo, 384p., $12.50

HUDSON, Sanford, Law for the Clergy. C, 1877, 12mo, 192p., $13.50

HUGHES, Charles Evans, Our Relations to the Nations of the Western Hemisphere. Princeton Univ. Pr., 1928, 8vo, 123p., faint blind stamp on title, first edition, $35.00

HURST, Jas., The Growth of American Law: The Law Makers. B, 1950, 8vo, 502p., paste-ins removed from end sheets, $12.00

CARY, Rich., Le Necessarie Use & Fruit de les Pleadings...L, 1601, 12mo, 98pp., some marginalia, title sl. chipped, later 1/2 morocco, $175.00

160) GERTZ, Elmer, A Handful of Clients. C, 1965, roy8vo, 379p.,$15.00

GIRARD, Paul F., Manuel Elementaire de Droit Romain. 6th ed., rev. & enl. P, 1924, roy8vo, 1158p., later linen, $45.00

GLAISTER, John, Medical Jurisprudence & Toxicology. Edinburgh, 1945 roy8vo, 687p., $22.50

GNEIST, Rudolf, The English Parliament in Its Transformation Through 1000 Years. trans. Shee. B, 1886, roy8vo, 380p., $22.50

GOLDSTEIN, Irving, Trial Technique. C, 1935, 4to, 790p., $17.50

GODWIN, Geo., The Middle Temple. L, 1954, 8vo, 174p., $15.00

GOEBEL, Julius (ed.), The Law Practice of Alexander Hamilton. NY, Columbia Univ. Press, 1964, roy8vo, 2vols., 1800pp., $45.00

GOODRICH, Leland, & SIMONS, A., The UN and the Maintenance of International Peace and Security. DC, Brookings, 1955, roy8vo, 709p., $17.50

GRAY, Rob., Some Legal and Constitutional Aspects of Deductions from Gross Income. Louisville, 1942, roy8vo, 175;., $13.50

GREEN, Harold, & ROSENTHAL, A., Government of the Atom: The Integration of Powers. NY, 1963, roy8vo, 281p., $15.00

GREEN, Sanford, A Treatise on Townships and the Powers and Duties of Township Officers. Detroit, 1879, roy8vo, 533p., $27.50

GRISWOLD, Erwin, Law and Lawyers in the United States: The Common Law Under Stress. Harvard Univ. Press, 1964, 8vo, 152p., $13.50

GROSS, Bertram, The Legislative Struggle. NY, 1953, 8vo, 472p., $16.50

GROSS, Hans, Empire & Sovereignty: A History of the Public Law Literature in the Holy Roman Empire, 1599-1804. Univ. of Chicago Pr., 1973, 8vo, 541p., orig. ptd. wrps, $12.50

GUTHRIE, William, The League of Nations and Miscellaneous Addresses. NY, Columbia Univ. Press, 1923, roy8vo, 383p., $16.50

GUY, William A., Principles of Medical Jurisprudence......First American Edition, edited by C.A. Lee, who has added 200 pages of original matter adapting the work to the wants of the medical and legal professions in the United States. NY, 1845, roy8vo, xvi, 711pp., later 1/2 linen and marbled boards; from the title page: "The Editor has enjoyed the advantages of freely consulting Chancellor Kent on many of the legal questions which come under discussion; and the opinions of this eminent jurist on several important points will be found embodied in the text, from his own notes kindly furnished, and which he has permitted the editor to publish."$87.50

HADFIELD, Stephen, Law and Ethics for Doctors. L, 1958, 8vo, 399p., $14.50

HALL, Jas. Parker, Cases on Constitutional Law, with Supplements Selected from Decisions of State & Federal Courts. St. Paul, 1926, 4to, 1867p., sporadic pencil underlining and marginal notes, $27.50

HALLOCK, Will., & WADE, Herb., Outlines of the Evolution of Weights and Measures and the Metric System. NY, 1906, 8vo, 304p., $15.00

HANKIN, Greg., & HANKIN, C., The US Supreme Court,1928-1929. DC, 1929, 8vo, 321p., $14.50

HANNAH, Harold, Law on the Farm: A Discussion of Legal Problems Which Arise in the Business of Farming. NY, 1950, 8vo, 399p., $13.50

HARMON, Nolan, The Famous Case of Myra Clark Gaines. Baton Rouge, Louisiana State Univ. Press, 1946, roy8vo, 481p., $15.00

HARRIS, Arthur, Letters to Young Lawyers. St. Paul, 1912, 8vo, 191p., orig. ptd. wrps., $13.50

TOBIN, H., Termination of Multipartite Treaties. NY, 1933, 8vo,wrps,$7.50

207) International Conciliation: 16 Issues, as follows: No. 223 (10/19); No. 224 (11/26); No. 230 (5/27); No. 231 (6/27); No. 232 (9/27); No. 234 (11/27); No. 235 (12/27); No. 236 (1/28); No. 238 (3/28); No. 243 (10/28); No. 244 (11/28); No. 247 (2/29); No. 248 (3/29); No. 249 (4/29); Docs for 1926; Docs for 1927; all in the orig. ptd. wrps, $75.00

JACKSON, E. Hilton, Law Latin: A Treatise in Latin with Legal Maxims and Phrases as a Basis of Instruction. DC, 1910, 8vo, 236p., $15.00

JACKSON, Robert H., Report of....US Representative to the International Conference on Military Trials, London, 1945: A Documentary Record of Negotiations.....Culminating in the Agreement and Charter of the International Military Tribunal. DC, Dept of State. 1949, 8vo, 440p., $18.50

JOHNS, Claude, Babylonian and Assyrian Laws, Contracts and Letters. NY, 1904, roy8vo, 424p., $22.50

JOHNSON, Allen (ed.), Readings in American Constitutional History. NY, 1912, 8vo, 584p., $12.50

JOHNSTON, Henry, What Rights are Left. NY, 1930, 8vo, 177p., $13.50

JONES, Harry (ed.), Law and the Social Role of Science. Rockefeller Univ. Press, 1966, roy8vo, 243p., $7.50

JONES, J.W., Law and Legal Theory of the Greeks. Oxford Univ. Press, 1956, roy8vo, 327p., $22.50

KAPLAN, Morton, & KATZENBACH, N. Political Foundations of International Law. NY, 1961, roy8vo, 372p., $16.50

KAUPER, Paul, Civil Liberties and the Constitution. University of Michigan Press, 1962, 8vo, 237pp., $13.50

KEETON, Geo., Trial for Treason. L, 1959, 8vo, 256p., $13.50

KENNEDY, Ludovic, Trial of Stephen Ward. NY, 1965, 8vo, 256p., $13.50

KENT, William (ed.), Memoirs and Letters of James Kent. B, 1898, 8vo, 341p., new front end sheet, $15.00 (Reprinted for $32.50)

KILPATRICK, Jas.,The Sovereign States: Notes of a Citizen of Virginia. C, 1957, 8vo, 347p., $15.00

KING, Willard, & PILLINGER, D., A Study of the Law of Opinion Evidence in Illinois. C, 1942, roy8vo, 389p., $15.00

KNOX, John, A Judge Comes of Age. NY, 1940, roy8vo, 353p., $15.00

KNOX, John, Order in the Court. NY, 1943, 8vo, 341p., $15.00

KOEGEL, otto E., Walter S. Carter: Collector of Many Masters or the Progenitor of Many Law Firms. NY, Priv. Pub., 1953, roy8vo, 491p., $22.50

KOESSLER, Max., (ed.), Masterpieces of Legal Fiction. Rochester, 1964, 4to, 862p., $25.00

KOHLMEIER, Louis, God Save This Honorable Court! NY, 1922,roy8vo,309p.,$15.

LAKE, Lewis, How to Win Lawsuits Before Juries. NJ, 1954, 8vo, 303p.,$15.50

LAMBERT, Richard, The Innocence of Edmund Galley. L, 1935, 8vo, 209p.,$12.50

LAURENCE, John, History of Capital Punishment. L, 1930, 8vo, 242p., $13.50

LEAMING, Thomas, Philadelphia Lawyer in the London Courts. NY, 1911, roy8vo, xiii, 199p., $16.50

LEBUFFE, F., & HAYS, Jas., The American Philosophy of Law with Cases to Illustrate Principles. 4th ed., NY, 1947, 8vo, 418p., $16.50

LEE, Richard Henry, An Additional Number of Letters from the Farmer to the Republican Leading to a Fair Examination of the System of Government Proposed by the Late Convention (1788). C, 1962, 8vo, 181p., $14.50

-11-

233) LEOPOLD, Nathan, Life Plus 99 Years. NY, 1958, roy8vo, 381p.,$14.50

LEVY, Beryl, Our Constitution: Tool or Testament. NY, 1941, 8vo, 315p.,$13.50

LEWIS, John, Thomas Spry: Lawyer and Physician. Phil., Priv. Ptd, 1932, 8vo, 126p., $14.50 (Reprinted at $25.00)

LIEF, Alfred, Brandeis. NY, 1936, roy8vo, 508p., $16.50

LILLY, John, A Collection of Modern Entries; or, Select Pleadings in the Court of King's Bench, Common Pleas and Exchequer, as also Special Assignments of Errors, Writs and Proceedings Thereupon, both in the Said Courts & in Parliament, with the Method of Suing to and Reversing Outlawries by Writ of Error and Otherwise, to Which Is Added a Collection of Writs in Most Cases Now in Practice. 4th ed., carefully translated into English, with Many Additional References. L, 1771, folio, 676p., contemp. calf., skillfully rebacked in calf, handsome copy, $225.00

LINDER, Gen. Usher, Reminiscences of the Early Bench and Bar of Illinois. with Intro. & Appendix by Hon. Jos. Gillespie. C, 1879, 8vo, 406p., orig. cl., rebacked, $30.00

LISSITZYN, Oliver, International Air Transport and National Policy. NY, 1942, roy8vo, 478p., $17.50

LITTLETON, Tenures, ed. Eugene Wambaugh. DC, 1903, roy8vo, 340p., $30.00

LODGE, Henry Cabot, The Senate and the League of Nations. NY, 1925, 8vo, 424p., $15.00

LOKOS, Lionel, The New Racism: Reverse Discrimination in America. NY, 1971, 8vo, 470p., $15.00

LONGENECKER, Rolla, Proving and Defending a Lawsuit. C, 1932, 8vo, 437p.,$15.

LOWENBERG, Henry, Until Proven Guilty: Forty Years as a Criminal Defense Counsel. B, 1971, 8vo, 236p., writing on end sheets, $12.50

LUARD, Evan, First Steps to Disarmament. NY, 1965, 8vo, 279p., $13.50

LUSTGARTEN, Edgar, The Murder & the Trial. NY, 1958, 8vo, 340p., $14.50

LYON, Hastings, & BLOCK, H., Edward Coke: Oracle of the Law. B/NY, 1929, 8vo, 385p., $20.00

MAC DOWELL, D.M., Athenian Homicide Law in the Age of the Orators. Manchester Univ. Pr., 1963, 8vo, 161p., $13.50

MACKENZIE, Jeanne, & Norman, The Murder of Maria Marten....to Which Is Added the Trial of Will. Corder, compiled by J. Curtis, 1828. NY, 1948, 8vo, 256p., $13.50

MACKINNON, Sir Frank, ON Circuit. Cambridge Univ. Pr., 1940, roy8vo, 311p., $17.50

MAINE, Sir Henry Sumner, Ancient Law, Introduction and Notes by Sir Friedrich Pollock, L, 1909, 8vo, xxiv, 426p., $22.50

MAINE, Sir Henry Sumner, Lectures on the Early History of Institutions. NY, 1888, roy8vo, 412p., $15.00

MAINE, Sir Henry Sumner, Ancient Law., Intro. by Theodore Dwight. 3rd American ed., NY, 1888, roy8vo, 400p., $22.50

MAINE, Sir Henry Sumner, Dissertations on Early Law and Custom. NY, 1886, roy8vo, 402p., $17.50

MARQUARDT, Joachim, Das Privatleben der Römer. 2nd ed., Leipzig, 1886, roy8vo, 885p., rebacked, $30.00

MARRIOT, Sir John, The Mechanism of the Modern State. Oxford Univ. Pr., 1927, roy8vo, 2vols., crown of II trifle worn, $30.00

HOSONO, Gunjii, International Disarmament. NY, 1926,8vo,315p,wrps,$13.50

-12-

257) MARSHALL, John, Complete Constitutional Decisions, edited with Annotations Historical, Critical and Legal, by John M. Dillon. C, 1903, roy8vo, 799p., rebacked, $35.00

John Marshall: The Tribute of Massachusetts, Being the Addresses Delivered at Boston & Cambridge, Feb 4, 1901, ed. Marquis Dickinson. (Addresses by Knowlton, Homes, Walcott, Thayer, Gray), Boston, 1901, roy8vo, 120p., ill., ltd. ed., inscribed by Knowlton, $25.00

John Marshall Day: Centennial Proceedings of the Chicago Bar, Feb 4, 1901, Including Proceedings Before the Supreme Court of Illinois. C, 1901, 4to, 193p., later linen, $22.50

MARSHALL, John, The Life of George Washington. Phil., 1804-1807, roy8vo, 5vols., contemp. calf, skillfully rebacked in calf, 1st edition, $275.00

MARTIN, Chs., The Politics of Peace. Stanford Univ. Press, 1929, roy8vo, 458p., $16.50

MARTIN, Chs., The Policy of the United States as Regards Intervention. NY, Columbia Univ. Pr., 1921, 8vo, 173p., wrps, $6.50

MASON, Alpheus T., Harlan Fiske Stone. NY, 1956, roy8vo, 914p., $22.50

MASON, Alpheus T., Brandeis. NY, 1956, roy8vo, 713p., $18.50

MASON, Alpheus, & Beaney, W., The Supreme Court in a Free Society. NJ, 1959, 8vo, 343p., $14.50

MAYERS, Lewis, The Federal Service. NY, 1922, roy8vo, 607p., $15.00

MAYO, Robert, & MOULTON, Ferdinand, Army and Navy Pension Laws and Bounty Land Laws of the United States, Including Sundry Resolutions of Congress from 1776-1852; Executed at the Department of the Interior with an Appendix Containing the Opinions of the Attorneys General of the United States, with the Decisions, Rules and Regulations, Adopted by Different Secretaries Relative to the Execution of Those Laws, DC, 1852, roy8vo, iii, 754p., contemp/roan, rebacked, $45.00

MC BAIN, Howard, The Living Constitution: A Consideration of the Realities and Legends of Our Fundamental Law. NY, 1934, 8vo, 284p., $13.50

MC CLURE, Wallace, World Legal Order: Possible Contributions by the People of the United States. Univ. of N. Carolina Pr., 1960, 8vo, 366p., $15.00

MC COOK, Philip, The Days of My Age. Conn. Priv. Ptd. 1964, 4to, 581p., ltd. ed., (for 25 years a justice of the NY Supreme Court, state referee & federal master), $22.50

MC DONALD, Forest, We the People: The Economic Origins of the Constitution. Univ. of Chicago Pr., 1958, roy8vo, 436p., $16.50

MC KAY, Rob., Reapportionment: The Law & Politics of Equal Representation. NY, 1965, 4to, 498p., $17.50

MC KEAN, Dayton, The Integrated Bar. B, 1963, 8vo, 151p., $13.50

MC LAUGHLIN, Andrew, Constitutional History of the United States. NY, 1935, 8vo, 833p., $15.00

MEDLEY, Dudley, A Student's Manual of English Constitutional History. 4th ed., Oxford Univ. Pr., 1907, 8vo, 650p., $25.00

MERCIER, Chs., Criminal Responsibility. NY, 1929, roy8vo, 256p., $13.50

MEYER, Ernest, Nominating Systems: Direct Primaries Versus Conventions in the United States. Madison, 1902, roy8vo, 501p., $17.50

MICHAEL, Will., & PULSIFER, P., Tariff Acts Passed by the Congress of the US, 1789-1895, Including All Acts, Resolutions and Proclamations Modifying or Changing Those Acts. DC, GPO, 1896, 4to, 588p., $35.00

LEONARD, L., International Regulation of Fisheries. DC,1944,201p,wrps,$12.50

-13-

279) MONTGOMERY, Rob., Sacco-Vanzetti: The Murder and the Myth. NY, 1960, 8vo, 370p., $16.50

MOORE, Blaine, The Supreme Court and Unconstitutional Legislation. NY, Columbia Univ. Pr., 1913, 8vo, 158p., wrps, $7.50 (bit worn)

MOORE, John Bassett, Report on Extradition with Returns of All Cases from August 9, 1842 to Jan 1, 1890. DC, GPO, 1890, 4to, 239p., $25.00

MOORE, Judge Chs., One Thing and Another: A Book of Essays. NY, 1924, roy8vo, 260p., ltd ed., $16.50

MORRIS, M.F., An Introduction to the History of the Development of Law. DC, 1909, roy8vo, 315p., (Assoc. Justice, Court of Appeals, Dist. of Columbia), $16.50

MORRIS, Richard, Fair Trial. NY, 1952, roy8vo, 494p., $16.50

MORRISON, Herbert, Government & Parliament. Oxford Univ. Pr., 1954, 8vo, 363p., $13.50

MORSE, John, Famous Trials: The Tichbourn Claimant; Troppmann; Prince Pierre Bonaparte; Mrs. Wharton; The Meteor; Mrs. Fair. B, 1874, 8vo, 342p., rebacked, $17.50

MORTON, Geo., & MALLOCH, D., Law & Laughter, Ill. with Portraits of Eminent Members of Bench & Bar. B/L, 1900, 8vo, 259p., $17.50

MOSCHZISKER, Rob. von, Stare Decisis, Res Judicata & Other Selected Essays. Phil., 1929, 8vo, 375p., $17.50

MUDDIMAN, J.G., Trial of King Charles the First. Edin., 1928, 8vo, 282p.,$15

NATIONAL INDUSTRIAL CONFERENCE BOARD, Mergers and the Law. NY, 1929, roy8vo, 153p., $13.50

NEALE, J.E., Elizabeth I and Her Parliaments, 1559-1581. NY, 1958, 8vo, 435p., $14.50

NEVILLE, Henry, Plato Ridivivus: Or, A Dialogue Concerning Government, Wherein by Observations Drawn from Other Kingdoms and States, Both Ancient and Modern, an Endeavor Is Used to Discover the Present & Politick Distemper of Our Own, with the Causes and Remedies. London, 1681, 8vo, 271p., later calf, first edition, some lower marginal worming and dampstain, occasional loss of a letter, $225.00

NILES, John, The Conn. Civil Officer. Hartford. 1854, 8vo, 367p., later linen, $27.50

NIZER, Louis, Between You and Me. rev. ed. NY, 1963, 8vo, 290p., $14.50

NIZER, Louis, Thinking on Your Feet. NY, 1940, 8vo, 312p., $6.50

NORTON, Th., The Constitution of the US. B, 1922, 8vo, 295p., $13.50

Notable Lawyers of the West. C, 1902, 4to, 186p., ill., $22.50

NOY, Wil., The Grounds and Maxims, & Also an Analysis of the English Laws, to Which Is Annexed a Treatise on Estates by Sir John Doderidge; Observations on a Deed of Feoffment by T.H. Gent; with Notes and Additions by Chs. Barton, from the 7th London ed., Middletown, 1808, 12mo, 160p., rebacked, $37.50

NUSSBAUM, Arthur, Concise History of the Law of Nations. NY, 1947, 8vo, 361p., $14.50

O'BRIEN, Will. (ed.), The New Nations in International Law and Diplomacy. (Yearbook of World Polity III), DC/NY, 1965, 8vo, 323p., $13.50

O'CONNOR, Richard, Courtroom Warrior: The Combative Career of William Travers Jerome. B, 1963, 8vo, 342p., $13.50

O'DONNELL, Bernard, Cavalcade of Justice. L, 1951, 8vo, 264p., "the history of our courts of law throughout the ages." $15.00

-14-

303) O'DONNELL, Bernard, Old Bailey & Its Trials. NY, 1951, 8vo, 226p., $12.50 (Reprinted for $20.00)

OGILVIE, Paul, International Waterways; Evolution of the Principle of International Waterways; Reference Manual to the Treaties, Conventions, Laws....Governing the International Use of Inland Waterways. NY, 1920, roy8vo, 424p., $20.00

ORFIELD, Lester, Criminal Procedure from Arrest to Appeal. NYU Pr/Oxford Univ. Pr., 1947, roy8vo, 614pp., $17.50

OSBORN, Albert, Questioned Documents. Intro. by John H. Wigmore. Rochester, 1910, 4to, 510p., $22.50

OSBORNE, Th., Society & Prisons. Yale Univ. Pr, 1916, 8vo, 246p., $10.00

OUTRAM, Geo., Legal and Other Lyrics. L, 1916, 8vo, 201p., $14.50

PACKE, Michael, Life of John Stuart Mill. NY, 1954, roy8vo, 567p., $17.50

PAINTER, Sidney, Studies in the History of the English Feudal Barony. Johns Hopkins Univ. Pr., 1943, roy8vo, 211p., wrps, $13.50

PARMELEE, Maurice, Principles of Anthropology & Sociology in Their Relations to Criminal Procedure. NY, 1911, 8vo, 410p., $14.50

PARRY, Edw., Drama of the Law. L, 1914, roy8vo, 310p., rebacked, $16.50

PARRY, Eds. The Persecution of Mary Stewart: The Queen's Case: A Study in Criminology. NY, 1931, roy8vo, 363p., $15.00

PARTRIDGE, Bellamy, Country Lawyer. NY, 1939, roy8vo, 317p., $13.50

PATTERSON, Edwin, Jurisprudence: Men and Ideas of the Law. NY, 1953, roy8vo, 649p., $22.50

Peace & War: US Foreign Policy, 1931-1941. DC, GPO, 1943, roy8vo, 874p., $15.

PEAKE, Th., Compendium of the Law of Evidence; from the Last London ed. with adds; and American Cases & Notes by Josiah Randall. Ph, 1812, roy8vo, 470p., roan, rebacked, $37.50

PEARSON, Lester, Diplomacy in a Nuclear Age. Toronto, 1959, 8vo, 114p.,$6.50

PEPPER, Geo., Philadelphia Lawyer. Ph, 1944, roy8vo, 407p., $15.00

PEPYS, Samuel, Diary of, ed. Whatley. NY, Heritage Pr, 1942, 2vols., $25.00

PIRSIG, Maynard, Cases and Materials on Legal Ethics. St. Paul, 1949, 4to, 208p., light sporadic underlining, $13.50

PLUNKET, Wm., Lord High Chancellor of Ireland, Speeches of, at the Bar and in the Senate, with Memoir and Historical Notices by John HOey.

POLESWORTH, John, Uncle Sam and His Lawsuits. NY, Priv. Ptd., 1944, 8vo, 91p., $12.50

POUND, Roscoe, Organization of Courts. B, 1940, roy8vo, 322p., $25.00

POUND, Roscoe, The Lawyer from Antiquity to Modern Times. St. Paul, 1953, 4to, 404p., $22.50

POWERS, Edwin, Crime and Punishment in Early Massachusetts, 1620-1692. B, 1966, roy8vo, 647p., $17.50

PRESTON, Richard, An Elementary Treatise on Estates. L, 1820-1827, 4to, 2vols. bound as one, xxxi, 511, 554p., later 1/ linen and bds, $85.00

PRICE, Don, The Secretary of State. NJ, 1960, 8vo, 200p., $12.50

PRITCHETT, C. Herman, American Constitutional Issues. NY, 1962, roy8vo, 473p., wrps, $13.50

LUST, Herbert (ed.), Commodities & Localities in the Decisions of the Interstate Commerce Commission, 1887-1933. C, 1933, 4to, 499p., $22.50

-15-

330) Proceedings in the Senate of the United States in the Matter of the Impeachment of Chs. Swayne, Judge of the District Court of the US in and for the Northern District of Florida. DC, GPO, 1905, roy8vo, 734p., $30.00

PROTHERO, G.W. (ed.), Select Statutes and Other Constitutional Documents Illustrative of the Reigns of Elizabeth and James I. 2nd ed., Oxford Univ. Pr., 1898, 8vo, 478p., $22.50

Ralli, Paul, Nevada Lawyer. Calif., 1949, 2nd ed., rev. & enl., 8v9, 320p., inscribed by the author, $15.00

RAM, Jas., Practical Treatise of Assets, Debts and Incumbrances. from the London ed., Phil., 1835, 8vo, 430p., later 1/2 linen $35.00

RAMSEY, Paul, The Just War: Force and Political Responsibility. NY, 1968, roy8vo, 554p., $17.50

RANSMEIER, Jos., The Tennessee Valley Authority. Vanderbilt Univ. Press, 1942, roy8vo, 486p., $15.00

RANSOM, Will., Majority Rule and the Judiciary. NY, 1912, 8vo, 183p., $12.50

REDDEN, Kenneth, So You Want To Be a Lawyer: A Vocational Guidance Manual. Ind., 1951, 8vo, 125p., $13.50

REED, Alfred, The Territorial Basis of Government under the State Constitutions: Local Divisions and Rules for Legislative Apportionment. NY, Columbia Univ. Pr., 1911, 8vo, 250p., wrps, bit worn, $9.00

REEL, A.FA., The Case of General Yamashita. Univ. of Chicago Pr., 1949, 8vo, 324p., later linen, $9.50

Regulations Prescribed for the Use of the Consular Service of the US. DC, GPO, 1888, 8vo, 715p., bit rubbed, $22.50

REIFFENSTUEL, R.P.F. Anacleto, Jus Canonicum Universum, Clara Methodo Juxta Titulos Quinque Librorum Decretalium....Editio Novissima, cui, Accessit Tractatus de Regulis Juris. Antwerp, 1755, folio, 2 vols. bound as one, 499, 530pp., bound in 19th century 1/2 calf and marbled boards, bit rubbed; deals not only with canon law but also with civil law, natural law and international law, $175.00

REVES, Emery, The Anatomy of Peace. NY, 1945, 8vo, 275p., $12.50

REUSCHLEIN, Harold, Jurisprudence: Its American Prophets. Ind., 1951 roy8vo, 527p., $17.50

RICHARDS, John, Abraham Lincoln: The Lawyer Statesman. B, 1916, roy8vo, 260p., bit rubbed, $16.50

RICHARDSON, H.G., & SAYLES, G., The Governance of Medieval England from the Conquest to Magna Carta. Edinburgh Univ. Pr., 1963, 5to, 514p., $17.50

RICHARDSON, W.C., Tudor Chamber Administration, 1485-1547. Louisiana State Univ. Pr., 1952, roy8vo, 541p., $16.50

RISEN, Maurice, Legal Aspects of Separation of Races in the Public Schools. Phil., 1935, 8vo, 142p., later linen, $16.50

ROBERTSON, A.H., Characterization in the Conflict of Laws. Harvard Univ. Press, 1940, roy8vo, 310p., sporadic pencil underlining, $15.00

ROBERTSON, C.G., Select Statutes Cases and Documents to Illustrate English Constitutional History, 1660-1832. L, 1919, roy8vo, 591p., $17.50

ROBERTSON, Edgar et al., Powers of the President in Foreign Affairs. San Francisco, 1966, roy8vo, 279p., $16.50

ROBINSON, Edw., Law and the Lawyers. NY, 1935, 8vo, 348p., $16.50

COUDERT, Frederic, Marriage & Divorce Laws in Europe. NY, 1893, 8vo, 108p., wrps, bit worn, $12.50

-16-

352) ROBINSON, Wm., Notes on Elementary Law. New Haven, 1875, roy8vo, 152p., $22.50

ROGGE, O.J., Our Vanishing Civil Liberties. NY, 1949, 8vo, 287p., $12.50

ROGGE, O.J., The First and the Fifth with Some Excursions into Others. NY, 1960, roy8vo, 358p., $14.50

ROSSITER, Clinton, Seedtime of the Republic: The Origin of the American Tradition of Political Liberty. NY, 1955, roy8vo, 553p., $16.50

ROTHWELL, Andrew, Laws of the Corporation of the City of Washington, to the End of the 13th Council, June, 1833; with a Digested Index; also an Abstract of Appropriations, to Which Is Added an Appendix, Containing Laws of the United States Relating to the City. Washington, 1833, roy8vo, vii, 508p., with a large fold-out map of the city; contemp. roan, bit rubbed and scuffed, nice copy, $75.00

RUSSELL, John Earl, An Essay on the History of the English Government and Constitution. (1865) Reprint, 1971, 8vo, 300p., $12.50

ST. GEORGE, Max, & DENNIS, Laurence, A Trial on Trial: The Great Sedition Trial of 1944. DC, 1946, roy8vo, 503p., $16.50

SANDERSON, Edgar, Judicial Crimes: A Record of Some Famous Trials in English History in Which Bigotry, Popular Panic and Political Rancor Played a Leading Part. L, 1902, 8vo, 263p., some pencil underlining,$14.50

SCHMALZGRUEBER, R.P. Francisco, Jus Ecclesiasticum Universum Brevi Methodo ad Discentium Utlitatem Explicatum Seu Lucubrationes Canonicae in Quinque Libros Decretalium Gregorii ix Pontificis Maximi. Rome, 1845, 4to, 2vols., contemp. 1/2 calf and bds, bit rubbed and scuffed, $75.00

SCHMIDT, Richard, & GRABOWSKY, Adolf, Disarmament and Equal Rights: Facts and Problems Dealt with in the Negotiations on Disarmament and Equal Rights 1933/34. Berlin, 1934, roy8vo, 284p., $18.50

SCHULZ, Fritz, Classical Roman Law. Oxford Univ. Pr., 1969, roy8vo, 650p., $30.00

SCHULZ, Fritz, Principles of Roman Law. Oxford Univ. Pr., 1936, 8vo, 268p., $16.50

SCOTT, James Brown, Cases on International Law Principally Selected from Decisions of English and American Courts. St. Paul, 1922, 4to, 1196p.$27.50

SCOTT, Jas. Brown, Final Act and Interpretive Commentary on the Second Pan-American Scientific Congress. DC, 1916, 4to, 516p., $22.50

SCOTT, Jas. Brown, Proceedings of the Second Pan-American Scientific Congress: Section VI: International Law, Public Law and Jurisprudence. Vol. VII. DC, GPO, 1917, roy8vo, 867p., $17.50

SEEBOHM, Frederic, The English Village Community Examined in Its Relation to the Manoral & Tribal Systems and to the Common or Open Field System of Husbandry. L, 1905, 8vo, 464p., $16.50

SELDEN, John, Table Talk....with a Biographical Preface & Notes by S.W. Singer. 3rd ed., L, 1860, 12mo, 270p., $22.50

SELDEN, John, An Historical and Political Discourse of the Laws and Government of England from the First Times to the End of the Reign of Queen Elizabeth; with a Vindication of the Ancient Way of Parliaments in England; collected from the Manuscript Notes of John Selden Esq by Nathaniel Bacon of Gray's Inn; 4th edition, corr. & imp. by a Gentleman of the Middle Temple. L, 1739, folio, xix, 202, xii, 178pp., contemp. calf, rebacked, handsome copy, $265.00

SHIRAS, Geo III, Justice George Shiras of Pittsburg, Assoc. Justice of the United States Supreme Court, 1892-1903. Univ. of Pittsburg Pr., 1953, roy8vo, 256p., $16.50

-17-

371) SHOTWELL, James T., War as an Instrument of National Policy and Its Renunciation in the Pact of Paris. NY, 1929, roy8vo, 310p., signed by Geo. W. Blakeslee, $16.50

SIBLEY, Mulford, & JACOB, P., Conscription of Conscience: The American State and the Conscientious Objector 1940-1947. Cornell Univ. Pr., 1952, roy8vo, 580p., $15.00

SIEBERT, Frederick, The Rights and Privileges of the Press. NY, 1934, 8vo, 429p., $12.50

SIMONDS, Frank, How Europe Made Peace Without America. NY, 1927, roy8vo, 407p., $16.50

SPAIGHT, J.M., Air Power and War Rights. 3rd ed., L, 1947, roy8vo, 523p., $17.50

STASON, E.B., & ESTEP, S., Atoms and the Law. Univ. of Michigan Law School, 1959, 4to, 1512p., $25.00

STEAMER, Rob., The Supreme Court in Crisis: A History of Conflict. Univ. of Mass. Press, 1971, roy8vo, 333p., $8.50

STEWART, Irvin, Consular Privileges and Immunities. NY, Columbia Univ. Press, 1926, 8vo, 216p., $15.00

STIMSON, Frederic, The American Constitution as It Protects Private Rights. NY, 1923, 8vo, 239p., $12.50

STOREY, Moorfield, & EMERSON, Edw., Ebenezer Rockwood Hoar: A Memoir. B, 1911, 8vo, 355p., $15.00

STREET, C.J., Lord Reading. L, 1928, 8vo, 286p., $15.00

STRONG, C.F., Modern Political Constitutions. L, 1952, 8vo, 383p., $11.50

STUBBS, William, The Constitutional History of England. Oxford, 1874, 8vo, 3vols., light wear of vol. I, $47.50

SUGDEN, Sir Edw., A Practical Treatise of Powers, from the 7th London ed., with Additional References to American Cases. Phil., 1847, roy8vo, 2vols., slight dampstain of first few leaves, $77.50

SWISHER, Carl Brent, The Growth of Constitutional Power in the United States. Univ. of Chicago Pr., 1946, 8vo, 261p., $13.50

SWISHER, Carl Brent, American Constitutional Development. 2nd ed., B. 1954, roy8vo, 1145p., $25.00

SYDNEY, Algernon, Discourses Concerning Government, with His Letters, Trial Apology and Some Memoirs of His Life. L, 1763, 4to, 497, 198pp., bound in later 1/2 morocco and marbled boards, light sporadic foxing, slight transfer from frontis. to title, $150.00

SZTUCKI, Jerzy, Jus Cogens and the Vienna Convention on the Law of Treaties. Wien/NY, 1974, 8vo, 204p., wrps (Osterreichische Zeitschrift für öffentliches Recht; Supp. #3), $17.50

TAFT, William Howard, The Anti-Trust Act and the Supreme Court. NY, 1914, 8vo, 133p., first edition, $37.50

TANNER, J.R., English Constitutional Conflicts of the 17th Century. Camb. Univ. Pr., 1966, 8vo, 315p., $15.00

TANNER, J.R.,Constitutional Documents of the Reign of James I, 1603-25, with an Historical Commentary. Camb. Univ. Pr., 1930, roy8vo, 389p.,$17.50

TAYLER, Wm., Federal States and Labor Treaties. NY, Columbia Univ. Pr., 1935, 8vo, 171p., wrps, $12.50

TAYLOR, Albion, Labor Problems and Labor Law. NY, 1944, roy8vo, 663p.,$16.00

COOPER, M.C.P., Lettres sur la Cour de la Chancellerie d'Angleterre. P, 1830, 8vo, xcviii, 402pp., contemp. 1/2 calf & bds, $47.50

-18-

394) TEAD, O., & METCALF, H., Labor Relations under the Recovery Act. NY, 1933, 8vo, 259p., $13.50

TAYLOR, Hannis, The Origin and Growth of the American Constitution. B, 1911, roy8vo, 676p., $25.00

THAYER, Jas. Bradley, Legal Essays. B, 1908, 8vo, 402p., $13.50

THAYER, Jas. Bradley, Cases on Constitutional Law, with Notes. Cambridge, 1895, 4to, 2vols., 2434p., some underlining and annotations, $65.00

THOMAS, Helen, Felix Frankfurter. Balto, 1960, 8vo, 381p., $16.50

THOMAS, Sam., & WILLIAMS, E., Our Weakened Constitution. NY, 1932, roy8vo, 321p., $14.50

THORNTON, Samuel, The Book of Yearly Recollections (M.P. for Surry) np. n.d. (c.1895), priv. pub., 8vo, 240p., $15.00

THORPE, Francis N., Constitutional History of the United States. NY, 1901, 8vo, 3vols., $75.00

HAZEN, Chs., & THAYER, Wm. Roscoe, Three Peace Congresses of the 19th Century Harvard Univ. Press, 1917, 8vo, 93p., $10.00

Treaty of Versailles and After: Annotations of the Text of the Treaty. DC, GPO, 1947, roy8vo, 1018p., wrps, $20.00

BERBER, Fritz (ed.), Das Diktat von Versailles: Entstehung, Inhalt, Zerfall....Intro. by Ribbentrop. Essen, 1939, roy8vo, 2vols., xliv, 1672p., scarce, $65.00

TRUMBULL, J.H., Public Records of the Colony of Connecticut Prior to the Union with New Haven Colony, May, 1665. Hartford, 1850, roy8vo, 604p., later linen, sporadic pencil underlining, $67.50

TRUMBULL, Wm., Materials on the Lawyer's Professional Responsibility. B, 1957, 8vo, 409p., $17.50

TUNKIN, Gregory (ed.), Contemporary International Law. Moscow, 1969, 8vo, 291p., $13.50

TURNER, Ralph, The King and His Courts: The Role of John and Henry III in the Administration of Justice, 1199-1240. Cornell Univ. Pr., 1968, 8vo, 310p., $12.50

TWYSDEN, Sir Roger, Certaine Considerations Upon the Government of England. from the unpublished Ms by John Kemble. L, Camden Soc, 1849, 8vo, $16.50

TYLER, Samuel, Memoir of Roger Brooke Taney. Balto, 1872, roy8vo, 659p., rebacked, $25.00

ULMAN, Jos. A Judge Takes the Stand. NY, 1933, 8vo, 289p., $15.00

UN Conference on International Organization: San Francisco, April 25-June 26, 1945: Select Documents. DC, GPO, 1946, roy8vo, 991p., $25.00

VANDERBILDT, Arthur, Studying Law: Selections from the Writings of Beveridge, Zane, Smith, Pound, Goodhart, Wambaugh, Wigmore and Stephens. NY, 1945, roy8vo, 753p., $18.50

VASQUEZ, Modesto, Cosmic International Law. trans. Malley. Wayne State Univ. Press, 1965, roy8vo, 293p., $16.50

VATTEL, M. de, The Law of Nations. Dublin, 1792, 8vo, 728p., later 1/2 linen and marbled boards, $75.00

VON GIERKE, Otto, Labands Staatsrecht und die deutsche Rechtswissenschaft. Reprint, 1961, 8vo, 99p., $13.50

VON IHERING, Rudolf, The Struggle for Law. trans. from the 5th German ed. by John Lalor. C, 1879, 8vo, xxiii,130p., extremities a bit worn, clippings concerning Ihering pasted in blank leaves, $16.50

MARTENS, Geo., Precis du Droit des Gens,2nd ed.,rev. Gott, 1801,8vo,502p. contemp. bds, $47.50

-19-

419) WARREN, Earl, Public Papers. NY, 1959, 8vo, 237p., $13.50

WATT, Francis, The Law's Lumber Room. L, 1895, 8vo, 139p., $13.50

WELLINGTON, Barrett, History of Elizabeth Canning. Intro. by John H. Wigmore. NY, 1940, 8vo, 209p., $15.00

WELLS, David, Theory & Practice of Taxation. NY, 1900, 8vo, 648p., $15.00

WHITE, Albert, Making of the English Constitution. 2nd ed. rev. NY, 1925 8vo, 461p., $15.00

WHITE, Leonard, Introduction to the Study of Public Administration. NY, 1926, 8vo, 495p., $16.50

WIGMORE, John H., Chairman, Committee of the Assn. of American Law Schools. Select Essays in Anglo-American Legal History. B, 1907, roy8vo, 3vols., 2500p., later linen, $75.00

WILCOX, Henry, Frailties of the Jury. C, 1907, 8vo, 141p., $13.50

WILKIN, Rob., Eternal Lawyer: A Legal Biography of Cicero. NY, 1947, 8vo, 264p., $14.50

WILLIAMS, Brad, Due Process: The Fabulous Story of Criminal Lawyer Geo. T. Davis. NY, 1960, 8vo, 336p., $15.00

WILLOUGHBY, Westel, American Constitutional System. NY, 1904, 323p., $13.50

WIPRUD, Arne, Justice in Transportation: An Expose of Monopoly Control. C, 1945, 8vo, 196p., $13.50

WISE, John, Treatise on American Citizenship. NY, 1906,8vo, 340p., $16.50

WISE, Maurice, Requisition in France & Italy: The Treatment of National Private Property. NY, Columbia Univ. Pr., 1944, 207p., wrps, $12.50

WOOLSEY, Theodore Dwight, Introduction to the Study of International Law. 6th ed. rev. & enl. by Theodore S. Woolsey. NY, 1899, 8vo, 527p., $16.50

WRIGHT, Benjamin F., Growth of American Constitutional Law. NY, 1946, 8vo, 276p., $13.50

WRISTON, Henry, Diplomacy in a Democracy. NY, 1956, 8vo, 115p, $10.00

WU, John, Fountain of Justice: Study in Natural Law. NY, 1955, 287p., $13.50

YOUNG, Edw., Constitutional Powers and Limitations. Dept. of Law, U.S. Military Academy, West Point, 1941, 8vo, 215p., wrps, $14.50

ZANE, John, The Story of Law. NY, 1927, 8vo, 486p., $13.50

ZOELLER, Max, Römische Staats--und Rechtsaltertümer. Breslau, 1895, 8vo, 520p., $17.50

ADDENDA INCLUDING LAW

AXTELL, Silas, Merchant Seamen's Law. NY, 1943, 8vo, 156p., bit worn, $12.50

BAKUNIN, Michael, God and the State, with a Preface by Carlo Cafiero & Elisee Reclus. First American Edition. NY, Mother Earth Publishing Assn., n.d. (1911), 8vo, 86p., later linen, $125.00

The Book of a Thousand Nights and a Night. A Plain and Literal Translation of the Arabian Nights Entertainments Made and Annotated by Richard F. Burton, Decorated with Illustrations by Valenti Angelo. NY, Heritage Pr., 1962, 8vo, 3vols., orig. 1/2 linen and marbled boards, boxed, fine, $45.00

BUCKLE, Henry Thomas, History of Civilization in England. L, 1857-61, 8vo, 2vols., later 1/2 morocco and linen, first edition, $250.00

CHAUFFEPIE, Jacques, Nouveau Dictionnaire Historique et Critique pour Servir de Supplement ou de Continuation au Dictionnaire Historique et Critique de Pierre Bayle. Amsterdam, 1750-56, folio, 4vols., later 1/2 morocco & linen, very scarce, $550.00

-20-

445) ENGELMAN, W., Die Wiedergeburt der Rechtskultur in Italien durch die Wissenschaftslehre. Leipzig, 1938, 8vo, 585p., $25.00

ENSIGN, Forest, Compulsory School Attendance & Child Labor Law. NY, 1921, 8vo, 263p., wrps, bit soiled, $6.50

DE GOBINEAU, Comte, Nouvelles Asiatiques. Paris, 1876, 8vo, 436p., contemp. 1/2 morocco and marbled boards, first edition, $125.00

ENCYCLOPEDIA OF THE SOCIAL SCIENCES. NY, 1937, 4to, 15vols., bound (as issued) as 8, original buckram, excellent, $175.00

GIBBON, Edward, The Decline and Fall of the Roman Empire. edited by J.B. Bury, Illustrated from the Etchings by Piranesi. NY, Heritage Press, 1946, roy8vo, 3vols., orig. 1/2 linen and pictorial boards, boxed, $45.00

GOEBEL, Julius, The Recognition Policy of the United States. NY, 1915, 8vo, 225p., wrps, $7.50

GERMANN, Geo., National Legislation Concerning Education: Its Influence & Effect in the Public Land States East of the Mississippi River Admitted Prior to 1820. NY, 1899, 8vo, 148p., wrps, $13.50

GROAT, Geo., Trade Unions and the Law in New York. NY, 1905, 8vo, 133p., wrps, $6.50

HARPER, Heber, What European and American Students Think on International Problems: A Comparative Study of the World-Mindedness of University Students. NY, 1931, 8vo, 255p., wrps, $12.50

HATCH, Leonard, Government Industrial Arbitration. NY, 1905, 8vo, 300p., later linen, $13.50

HONE, William, The First Trial of....for Publishing a Parody on the Late John Wilke's Catechism of a Ministerial Member. 18th ed., L, 1818, 8vo, 48p., later linen, $22.50

HONE, William, The Second Trial of....for Publishing a Parody with an Alleged Intent to Ridicule the LItany and LIbel the Prince Regent, the House of Lords and the House of Commons. 16th ed. L, 1818, 8vo, 45p., later linen, $22.50

HONE, William, The Third Trial of....for Publishing a Parody on the Athanasian Creed, entitled the 'Sinecurists Creed' 15th ed., L, 1818, 8vo, 44p., later linen, $22.50

JONES, Marvin, Should Uncle Sam Pay---When & Why: Selected Opinions of Marvin Jones, Chief Judge, US Court of Claims. rev. ed., 1963, 8vo, 159p., $13.50

LOEWENSTEIN, Karl, Beiträge zur Staatssoziologie. Tübingen, 1961, roy8vo, 485p., $22.50

MALTHUS, Rev. T.R., Principles of Political Economy Considered with a View to Their Practical Application. 2nd ed., with Considerable Additions from the Author's Own Manuscript and an Orginal Memoir. L, 1836, 8vo, liv, 446p.,bound in the original boards, expertly rebacked in calf, $275.00

MCGOLDRICK, Jos., Law & Practice of Municipal Home Rule, 1916-1930. NY, 1923, 8vo, 431p., wrps, bit soiled, $7.50

MIRABEAU, De la Monarchie Prussienne sous Frederic le Grand. L, 1788, 4to, 3vols., contemp. mottled calf, bit rubbed, first edition, $275.00

MIRABEAU, Correspondence entre Comte de Mirabeau et le Comte de la Marck. Pendent les Anees 1789,1790 & 1791. ed. by Bacourt. P, 1851, 8vo, 3vols., later linen, $67.50

PARK, Jas., The English Reform Bill of 1867. NY, 1920, 8vo,283p.,wrps, $6.50

MULLER, Wilhelm, Politische Geschichte der Gegenwart. Berlin, 1868-1899, 8vo, 33vols. bound in 31, contemp. 1/2 morocco, bit rubbed, $275.00

List 23

Philosophy 1979

Law Political Economy

Richard Adamiak
1545 East 60th St.
Chicago, Illinois 60637
312-955-4571
(By Phone: 8AM-Noon; 4-5

1) ALDEN, Jos., The Science of Government in Connection with American Institutions. NY, 1867, 8vo, 248p., trifle worn, $22.50

2) ALLEN Stephen, The Evolution of Governments & Laws. Princeton Univ.Pr., 1916, roy8vo, 1221., scarce, $30.00.

3) ANDREWS, John, An Inquiry Into the Manners, Taste and Amusements of the Last Two Centuries in England. L, 1782, 12mo, 147., later 1/2 linen, $35.00.

4) AUSTIN, John, The Province of Jurisprudence Determined. L, 1832, 8vo, xx, 391, lxxvipp., contemp. 1/2 calf and marbled boards, trace of wear at crown, trifle rubbed, the first edition, of extreme rarity, no copy recorded as available in this century, $1000.00.

5) BACON, Francis, Works of, with Intro., L, 1871, sm4to, 2vols., lxx, 797 832p. contemp. 1/2 calf & linen, bit rubbed, clean & tight, $87.50.

6) BARRIE, J.M., The Works of, NY, Scribners, 1929ff/, in the orig. 1/2 li & bds, roy8vo, 14vols., #79 of a limited edition of 1030; signed by Barrie, excellent, $250.00.

7) BASTIAT, Fred., Cobden et la Ligue ou l'Agitation Anglaise pour la Liberté du Commerce. P, 1845, 8vo, xcvi, 426pp., contemp. linen, excellent copy, first edition, $125.00.

8) BAYLE, Pierre, Dictionaire Historique et Critique. 5th ed., rev. corr., enl., avec la vie de l'Auteur par M. Des Maizeau. Amsterdam, 1740, large folio, 4vols., contemp. calf, expertly rebacked in calf, raise bands, light sporadic foxing & browning, nice set, $750.00.

9) BENDER, Johann H., Der Verkehr mit Staatpapieren im In- und Ausland. 2r ed., rev., Göttingen, 1830, 8vo, 685pp., contemp. bds, $75.00.

10) BENTHAM, Jeremy, The Works of, Published under the Superintendence of his Executor, John Bowring. Edinburgh, Tait, 1843, roy8vo, 11vols., contemp. 1/2 calf & marbled bds, raised bands, spines heavily gilded, trifle rubbed in a few spots, superb set, first collected edition, $850.00.

11) BERGMANN, Eugen von, Die Wirtschaftkreisen: Geschichte der National-ökonomischen Kreisentheorie. Stut., 1895, roy8vo, 440p., $47.50.

12) BEVERIDGE, Albert, Life of John Marshall, B/NY, 1929, 4vols, bound (as issued) as two, lettering bit faded, $50.00.

13) BLACKSTONE, Sir William, Commentaries on the Laws of England, from the 19th London ed., with Life of the Author and Notes by Christian, Chitty, Lee, Hovenden & Ryland, and References to American Case by Member of the NY Bar. Phil., 1887, roy8vo, 4vols. bound (as issued) as 2, later 1/2 linen and marbled bds, nice set, $87.50.

14) BLACKSTONE, Sir William, Commentaries on the Laws of England. Oxford, 1765-69, 4to, 4vols., contemp. calf, skillfully rebacked in calf, first edition, $2750.00.

15) BLACKSTONE, SIR William, Commentaries on the Laws of England, edited w Notes by Geo. Sharswood, Phil., 1860, roy8vo, 4vols. bound (as iss as 2, later 1/2 linen & marbled bds, excellent, $85.00.

-2-

16) BONNO, G., La Constitution Britannique devant l'Opinion Francaise de Montesquieu a Bonaparte. P, 1832, 8vo, 317p., later linen, $27.50.

17) BRENTANO, Lujo, Zur Kritik der Englischen Gewerkvereine. Leipzig, 1872, 8vo, xiv, 369pp., contemp. 1/2 linen & marbled bds, trace of marginal embrowning, nice copy, first edition, $145.00.

18) BUNGE, N.Ch., Esquisse de Litterature Politico-Economique. traduit de Russe. Geneva/P. 1898, roy8vo, xliii, 455pp., contempt/ 1/2 linen & marbled bds, few tiny marginal tears in first few leaves, else excellent, scarce & important work by an important Russian economist and Minister of Finance, $75.00.

19) BURNHAM, Jas. Congress & the American Tradition. C, 1959, roy7vo, 363p, $16.50.

20) BUXTON, The. F., Der Afrikanische Sklavenhandel und seine Abhülfe, aus dem Englischen übersetzt von G. Julius. Mit Einer Vorrede: Die Nigerexpedition und ihre Bestimmung von Karl Ritter. Leipzig, 1841, 8vo, lxx, 453pp., contemp. 1/2 calf and marbled bds, $85.00.

21) CARPENTER, Wm., Foundations of Modern Jurisprudence. NY, 1958, 8vo, 230p., light underlining, $13.50.

22) CLAUS, Ru., Das Russische Bankwesen. L, 1908, 8vo, 162p., wrps, $17.50.

23) CLINTON, Henry Lauren, Extraordinary Cases. NY, 1896, 8vo, 403p., $18.50.

24) COKE, Sir Edward, The First Part of the Institutes of the Laws of England, or, a Commentary Upon Littleton. 14th Edition, Rev. & Corr. with the Addition of Notes & References by Francis Hargrave & Chs. Bulter, Including also the Notes of Lord Chief Justice Hale and Lord Chancellor Nottingham, & an Analysis of Littleton written by an Unknown Hand in 1658-59 but Never Before Published. Dublin, 1791, very large folio, xx, 790, 57pp., bound in later 1/2 linen and bds, $145.00.

25) CONTZEN, Heinrich, Geschichte der Volkswirtschaftlichen Literature im Mittelalter . 2nd ed., enl., B, 1872, 8vo, 246p., $35.00.

26) COQUELIN, Ch., Du Credit et des Banques, P, 1848, 8vo., 424pp., contemp. linen, first edition, $135.00.

27) CORBERT, Thomas, An Inquiry into the Causes & Modes of the Wealth of Individuals; or the Principles of Trade and Speculation Explained. L, 1841, sm8vo, 256p., contemp., 1/2 calf, bit rubbed & scuffed, $45.00.

28) DAVIS, Daniel, A Practical Treatise Upon the Authority and Duty of Justices of the Peace in Criminal Prosecutions. B, 1824, roy8vo, 687pp.; orig. bds, rebacked, uncut, $47.50.

29) de COBINEAU, Comte, Nouvelles Asiatiques. P, 1876, 8vo, 436pp., contemp. 1/2 morocco and marbled bds,first edition, $125.00.

30) DE SMITH, S.A., Judicial Review of Administrative Action. L, 1968, roy8vo, 628pp., $17.50.

31) DE TOQUEVILLE, Alexis, Democracy in America. translated by Henry Reeve. London, 1838, 3rd ed. 8vo, 2vols., later 1/2 linen & marbled bds. $65.00

32) DOUBLEDAY, Th., A Financial, Monetary & Statistical History of England from the Revolution of 1688 to the Present Time. L, 1847, 8vo, 444pp. later linen, $45.00.

33) DROZ, Joseph, Economie Politique ou Principes de la Science des Richesses. Bruxelles, 1829, 12mo, 365p., contemp. 1/2 linen and marbled bds, $75.00

34) DUNNE, Gerald, Hugo Black & the Judicial Revolution. NY, 1977, 8vo, 492pp. $7.50.

35) DYKES, D. Oswald. Source Book of Constitutional History from 1660. L, 1930, roy8vo, 505pp., $17.50.

-3-

36) ENGELMAN, Woldemar, Die Wiedergeburt der Rechtskultur in Italien durch die Wissenschaftslehre. Leipzig, 1938, roy8vo, 585pp. $30.00.

37) EVARTS, William Maxwell. Arguments & Speeches of, ed. by His Son. NY, 1919, roy8vo, 3vols., $47.40.

38) Examination of the Charges of the Board of Trade Against the Phoenix Bank, Prepared by the Counsel of the Bank. NY, 1838, 8vo, 28pp., linen, $27.50.

39) FAUCHER, Leon, Études sur l'Angelterre. P, 1845, 8vo, 2vols., 900pp., contemp. linen, fine, first edition, $105.00.

40) FEHRENBACHER, Don, The Dred Scott Case: Its Significance in American Law & Politics. Oxford, UP, 1978, roy8vo, 741pp., $17.50.

41) FENWICK, Chas., Wardship in International Law. DC, GPO, 1919 (Confidential) 8vo, 39pp., linen, $13.50.

42) FERGUSON, Adam, An Essay on the History of Civil Society. 7th ed. Edinburgh, 1814, 8vo, 468pp., contemp. marbled bds, rebacked, $65.00.

43) FOOT, Samuel, An Argument in Favor of the Constitutionality of the General Banking Law of this State, Delivered before the Supreme Court at the July Term, 1839. Geneva, NY, 1839, 8vo, 101pp., linen, $35.00.

44) FORDHAM, Edw., Notable Cross-Examinations. L, 1951, 8vo, 202p., $13.50.

45) FRANKFURTER, Felix, & GREENE, Nathan, The Labor Injunction. NY, 1930, roy8vo, 343pp., orig. cl., first edition, $37.50.

46) FREEMAN, Edward, The Growth of the English Constitution from the Earliest Times. L, 1894, 8vo, 234pp., $22.50.

47) Gegenwartigen Zustand derer Finantzen von Frankreich, Worinnen die bisherigen Unternehmungen des Herrn Law, Insbesonderheit aber, die Historie der Königlichen Banco der Indianischen nach Mississippi handelnden Compagnie, und die in dem Münzwesen gemachte Veränderungen aus denen Hiervon eingelauffenen Nachtrichten mit allerhand Reflexions über dieses neue Systema angufführt und erläutert werden; Als ein ander Teil der Beschreibung des Mississippischen Handels und Supplement zu der Europäischen Fama. Leipzig, 1720, sm8vo, 252pp., engraved frontis. (of Law) later 1/2 morocco and marbled bds, Kress 3214, $175.00.

48) GRAHAM, David, A Treatise on the Practice of the Supreme Court of the State of New York. NY, 1832, roy8vo, 848pp., later linen, two tiny holes in title with loss of last number of imprint date, $37.50.

49) GRANT, M., The Bench and the Bar. L, 1837, 8vo, 2vols., contemp. marbled boards, rebacked, $47.50.

50) GRAY, Louis, Spitzbergen & Bear Island. DC, GPO, 1919, 8vo, 129pp., later linen, (Confidential), $14.50.

51) GRENADE, Pierre, Essai sur les Origines du Principat: Investure et Renouvellement des Pouvoirs Imperiaux. P, 1961, roy8vo, 494pp., later linen, $23.00.

52) GRIFFIN, Appleton, List of Discussions of the 14th and 15th Amendments with Special Reference to Negro Suffrage. DC, GPO, 1906, roy8vo, 18pp., orig. ptd. wrps, spine taped, $13.50.

53) GROTE, George, The Minor Works of, with Critical Remarks on His Intellectual Character, Writings & Speeches by Alexander Bain, L. 1873, 8vo, 364pp., orig. linen, rebacked, nice copy, $30.00.

54) GROTIUS, Hugo, The Rights of War and Peace in Three Books....translated into English, to which are Added all the Large Notes of J. Barbeyrac. L, 1738, large folio, xxxvi, 817pp., later 1/2 calf & marbled bds, $250.00.

-4-

55) GUTERBOCK, Carl, Bracton and His Relation to the Roman Law: A Contribution to the History of the Roman Law in the Middle Ages. trans. by Brinton Coxe. Phil., 1866, roy8vo, x, 182pp., orig. cl. $35.00.

56) GUY, William, Principles of Forensic Medicine, first American ed. with Notes and Adds. by Chs. Lee. NY , 1845, roy8vo, 711p., later 1/2 linen and marbled bds, $57.50.

57) GUYAU, M., Esquisse d'Une Morale sans Obligation ni Sanction. 5th ed., P, Alcan, 1900, roy8vo, 254pp., contemp. 1/2 morocco, $35.00.

58) GUYAU, M., L'Irreligion del'Avenir: Etude Sociologique. 7th ed. P, Alcan, 1900, roy8vo, 479pp., contemp. 1/2 morocco, $45.00.

59) HARRIS, Richard, Before & After Trial: What Should be Done by Counsel Solicitor & Client. Northport, NY, 1890, 8vo, 399pp., $25.00.

60) HASSELS, Georg, Statistischer Abriss der Russischen Kaisertums nach seinen neuesten politischen Beziehungen. Nurn/Leip, 1807, 8vo, 300pp., contemp. bds, $75.00.

61) HAYNES, Evan, The Selection and Tenure of Judges. National Conference of Judicial Councils, 1944, roy8vo, 308pp., $22.50.

62) HAZLITT, W.C., The Venetian Republic: Its Rise, Growth & Fall: 421-1797. L, 1900, roy8vo, 2vols., 1600pp., $45.00.

63) HERODOTUS, Herodoti Historiarum Libri IX Musarum Nominibus Inscripti Gr. & Lat. cum Interpretatione Laurentii Vallae. Ex MS, membrana Medicae Aldi Manutii, Joach. Camerii, Henk. Stephani, Goth, Junvermanii, Th. Gale....industria Jacovi Gronovii cujus accedunt Notae. Ejusdem Narratio de Vita Homeri Gr. Lat. interprete Conr. Heresbachio. Accedunt Excerpta ex Xenophonte, Strabone, Dinone, Hericlide Cymaeo, Clearcho,...Plutarcho Nymplodro, de Perciis, Aegyptis, & Indicis. Amsterdam, 1715, smfolio, 1000pp., plus index, contemp. calf, bit rubbed and scuffed, title in red & black, beautiful engraved frontis., and one fold-out engraving in the text, ornamental letters and several woodcuts, $225.00.

64) HUBNER, Otto, Die Banken. Leipzig, 1854, roy8vo, 476pp., contemp. bds, trace of wear at extremeties, else excellent, $65.00.

65) HUSKISSON, Wm., Substance of Two Speeches Delivered in the House of Commons....Respecting the Colonial Policy and Foreign Commerce of the Country, Balto, 1826, 8vo, 88pp., later linen, $35.00.

66) HYDE, Chs. C., Certain Effects of Change of Sovereignty. DC, GPO, 1918, (Confidential), 8vo, 31pp., later linen, $13.50

67) HYDE, Chs. C., National Character in Relation to Property in Time of War. DC, GPO, 1918, (Confidential), 8vo, 42pp., later linen, $13.50.

68) HYDE, Chs., C., Blockade, D.C, DC, GPO, 1918 (Confidential) 8vo, 43p, linen $13.50.

69) Inaugural Addresses Delivered by the Professors of Law in the University of the City of New York, at the Opening of the Law School of that Institution. NY, 1838, 8vo, 68pp., later linen, $35.00.

70) JACKSON, Robert H., The Supreme Court in the American System of Government. Harvard UP, 1955, 8vo, 92pp., 1st edition, $27.50.

71) JESSUP, Ph., American Neutrality & Int'l Police. B, 1928, 8vo, 1701, $14.50

72) JEVONS, W. Stanley, The State in Relation to Labour. L, 1882, 8vo, vii, 166pp., orig. dec. cl., slight cover soil, else excellent, first edition, $145.00.

73) JOHNSTON, Wm., England as It is, Political, Social and Industrial, in the Middle of the 19th Century. P, 1851, 8vo, 266 (2col.)pp., linen, $45.00.

74) (Justinian) Imperatoris Iustiniani Institutionem Libri Quattuor with Intro. Commentary & Excursus by J. B. Moyle. 2nd ed., Oxford UP, 1890, roy8vo, 683pp., rebacked, $27.50.

75) KEYNES, John Maynard, A Revision of the Treaty; Being a Sequel to the Economic Consequences of the Peace. L, 1922, 8vo, 223pp., orig. cl; first edition, $125.00.

76) KINNE, Asa, The Laws of the Different States and Territories of the US on Imprisonment for Debt. NY, 1842, 8vo, 56pp., linen, $25.00.

The First Work of the Historical School
of Political Economy.

77) KNIES, Karl, Die Politische Oekonomie vom Standpunkt der Geschichtlichen Methode. Braunschweig, 1853, 8vo, xii, 355pp., contemp. 1/2 linen and grain cloth, first edition, excellent copy, rare, $750.00.

78) LABAND, Paul, Die Vermögensrechtlichen Klagen nach den Sächsischen Rechtsquellen des Mittelalters. B, 1869, roy8vo, 406pp., $27.50.

79) LALANDE, Andre, La Dissolution Opposeee a l'Evolution dans les Sciences Physiques et Morales. P, Alcan, 1899, roy8vo, 492p., contem. 1/2 morocco, $40.00.

80) Livy, The Romane Historie, written by T. Livius of Padua. Also, the Breviaries of L. Florus, with a Chronologie to the Whole Historie and the Topography of Rome in Old Time. Translated Out of the Latin into English by Philemon Holland. London, 1600, folio, 1403pp., contemp. calf, front hinge expertly reinforced, arms embossed on covers, first English edition, $650.00.

81) LOCKE, John, The Works of. 12th edition, L, 1824, 8vo, 9vols., full contemp calf, red and black labels, spines heavily gilded, few hinges a bit tender, handsome set, $325.00.

82) LOVELL, Colin, English Constitutional & Legal History. Oxford UP, 1962, roy8vo, 589pp., some sporadic underlining, $17.50.

83) LUSTGARTEN, Edgar, Verdict in Dispute. NY, 1950, 8vo, 253pp., one page underlined in red, $12.50.

84) MAC-CULLOCH, J. R., Grundsätze der Politischen Oekonomie....As dem Englischen übersetz und mit einer Vorrede versehen von Georg Michael von Weber. Stut., 1831, 8vo, xxxvi, 399pp., contemp. paper covered bds, covers rubbed, not in Kress $110.00.

85) MACKIE, J.D., The University of Glasgow 1451-1951. Glasgow, 1954, 8vo. 341pp., $15.00.

86) MAITLAND, Fred., Constitutional History of England. Cambridge UP, 1920, roy8vo, 548pp., $25.00.

87) MAITLAND, Fred. & MONTAGUE, Francis, A Sketch of English Legal History. NY, 1915, 8vo, 229pp., $22.50.

88) MARQUARDT, Joachim, Das Privatleben der Römer. 2nd ed. Leipzig, 1886, roy8vo, 2vols. bound as one, 885pp., $30.00.

89) MARSHALL, John, The Life of George Washington. Virginia, 1926, roy8vo, 5vols., orig. cl., ill., fine set, $87.50.

90) MARSHALL, John, The Life of George Washington. Phil., 1804-07, 8vo, 5vols. contemp. tooled calf, skillfully rebacked in calf, first edition, $375.00

91) MARSHALL, John, Complete Constitutional Decisions, ed. with Annotations by John Dillon, C, 1903, roy8vo, 799pp., bit rubbed, $35.00.

-6-

92) MARTENS, G. F., Precis du Droit des Gens Moderne de l'Europe, new ed. with Notes by P. Ferreica. Paris, 1831, 8vo, 2vols., contemp. marbled bds, rebacked, $75.00.

93) MAYERS, Lewis, The American Legal System, 2md ed., rev., NY, 1964, roy8vo, 594pp., $18.50.

94) MC CALL, H.S., Precedents or Practical Forms in Actions at Law in the Supreme Court of the State of New York. Albany, 1852, roy8vo, 340pp. later linen, $30.00.

95) Memoir of Theophilus Parsons, Chief Judge of the Supreme Judicial Court of Massachusetts, with Notices of Some of His Contemporaries, by His Son. B, 1861, 8vo, 476pp., orig. linen, trifle worn, $30.00.

96) MILLER, David; Secret Statutes of the United States. DC, GPO; 1918 (Confidential), 8vo, 44pp., linen, $13.50.

97) MIRABEAU, Correspondence entre Comte de Mirabeau e le Comte de la Marck pendent les Anees 1789, 1790 & 1791. ed. by Bacourt. Paris, 1851, 8vo, 3vols., contemp. marbled bds, rebacked, $75.00.

98) MISES, Ludwig, Die Gemeinwirtschaft: Untersuchungen über den Sozialismus. Jena, 1922, roy8vo, 503pp., orig. cl., first edition, $75.00.

99) MITFORD, John, A Treatise on the Pleadings in Suits in the Court of Chancery by English Bill. Dublin, 1795, 8vo, 263p., later linen, $57.50

100) MONTESQUIEU, Baron de, Oeuvres. Nouvelle Edition, revue, corrige et considerablement augmentee par l'auteur. Amsterdam/Leipsick, 1758, 4to, 3vols., contemp. mottled calf, skillfully rebacked in calf, beautiful set, $550.00.

101) MORTENSON, Ernest, You be the Judge, Intro. by John H. Wigmore, DC, 1943, 439pp., ill. by Alain, $22.50.

102) NEBENIUS, Fried., Bemerkungen über den Zustand Grossbritanniens in Staatswirtschaftlicher Hinsicht, nebst einem Worte über Deutschlands auswärtige Handelsverhältnisse....mit einer Uebersetzung der französischen Schrift: über England und die Engländer, von J. B. Say. Karlsruhe/Baden, 1818, 8vo, xii, 59, 158pp., orig. bds. not in Kress, $115.00.

103) NEVILLE, Sir Henry, Plato Ridivivus: Or a Dialogue Concerning Government Wherein, by Observations drawn from Other Kingdoms and States, both Ancient & Modern, an Endeavor is Used to Discover the Present Politick Distemper of Our Own, with the Causes and Remedies. L, 1681, 8vo, 271pp., later calf, sporadic lower marginal worming and slight discoloration, occasional loss of a letter, first edition, $250.00.

104) NIETZSCHE Friedrich, Gesammelte Werke. München, 1922-29, roy8vo, 23vols. original 1/2 calf and buff boards, spines gilded, Musarion Edition, 240 of a limited edition of 1500 sets, a large paper edition, beautifully printed on rag paper, trifle rubbed here and there, excellent, scarce, $750.00.

105) OWEN, Robert, & CAMPBELL, Alexander, Debate on the Evidence of Christianity, Containing an Examination of the "Social System"....with an Appendix written by the Parties. Bthany, Va., 1829, 8vo, 2vols. bound (as issued) as one, 51, 301pp., light sporadic foxing & browning, later 1/2 morocco and marbled bds, $145.00.

106) PALGRAVE, Francis, The Rise and Progress of the English Commonwealth. Anglo-Saxon Period, Containing the Anglo-Saxon Policy and Institutions Arising Out of Laws and Usages which Prevailed before the Conquest.

107) PARMENTIER, Ch., Essais Economiques. P, 1904, 8vo, 485pp., full calf, one of 40 copies, $45.00.

108) PAYNE, Abraham, Reminisciences of the Rhode Island Bar. Providence, 1885, 8vo, 277pp., later linen, $30.00

109) PEREIRE, Isaac, La Banque de France et l'Organisation de Credit en France. 2nd ed., P, 1864, 8vo, 216p., later linen, $57.50.

110) Plain Advice to All Persons Going to Law; with Suggestions Addressed to the Common Sense and the Pockets of All Suitors in Courts of Justice. L, 1838, 12mo, 70pp., later linen, $27.50.

111) Plenge, Johann, Grûndung u. Geschichte des Credit Mobilier. Tübingen, 1903, roy8vo, 156pp., contemp. linen, $25.00.

112) POLLOCK, Sir Fried., & MAITLAND, F.W., History of English Law Before the Time of Edward the First. 2nd ed., DC, 1959, roy8vo, 2vols, $45.00

113) Prize Cases Decided in the United States Supreme Court, 1789-1918.... Prepared under the Supervision of James Brown Scott, Oxford UP, 1923, 4to 3vols., 2182pp., fine set, $110.00 (Carnegie Endowment)

114) RAND, Benajim, Selections Illustrating Economic History Since the Seven Years War. 2nd ed., rev. & enl., Cambridge UP, 1892, roy8vo, 567p, $22.50.

115) RICHARSON, Hamilton, The Journal of the Federal Convention Analyzed.... San Francisco, 1899, roy8vo, 244pp., orig. buck, $25.00.

116) ROPER, R. S. Donnison, Treatise on the Rvocation & Republication of Wills and Testaments, together with Tracts Upon the Law Concerning Baron & Feme. Phil. 1820, 8vo, 239pp., later linen, $37.50.

117) The "Rose" Book of Chile: Communications Exchanged Between Chile & Peru Regards the Question of Tacna & Arica (1905-08). D.C. GPO, 1918, (Confidential), 8vo, 88pp., linen, $15.00.

118) ROUSSEAU, J.J., Oeuvres Completes.P, 1793, 12mo, 37vols., contemp. full Levant morocco, spines & Covers gilt, a.e.g., beautiful set, $450.00.

119) SAINT-GERMAN, Christopher, Two Dialogues in English between a Doctor of Divinity and a Student of the Laws of England.newly revised & reprinted. L, 1687, 12mo, 366pp., mainly black letter, bound in 19th century morocco, nice copy, $185.00.

120) SCHAFFLE, Alb., Aus Meinem Leben. B, 1905, roy8vo, 2vols., contemp. 1/2 calf and linen, first edition, fine set, $75.00.

121) SCHAFFELE, Alb., Das Gesellschaftliche System der Menschlichen Wirtschaft. 3rd ed., rev., Tübingen, 1873, 8vo, 2vols., contemp. 1/2 linen & marbled bds, clean tight set, $95.00.

122) HONITZ, Hans, Der Kleingewerbliche Kredit in Deutschland. Karlsruhe, 1912, roy8vo, 542pp., orig. ptd. wrps, $27.50.

123) SCHOPENHAUER, Arthur, Parerga und Paralipomena: Kleine Philosophische Schriften. 2nd ed., rev. & enl., ed. by J. Frauenstadt. B, 1862, roy8vo, 2vols., 1250pp., contemp. 1/2 morocco & linen, light sporadic pencil underlining, nice set, $75.00.

124) Secret Proceedings and Debates of the Convention Assembled at Philadelphia in the Year 1787, for the Purpose of Forming the Constistution of the United States of America, from the Notes Taken by the Late Robert Yates, Chief Justice of New York, Copies by John Lansing, Jun., Late Chancellor of that State, Members of that Convention,....also Other Historical Documents Relative to the Federal .Compact of the North American Union. Albany, 1821, 8vo, 308pp., orig. bds. uncut, rebacked in the style of the original, first edit. $245.00

125) SCOTT, Jas. Brown, (ed.), American Addresses at the Second Hague Peace Conference. B, 1910, 4to, 217pp., $20.00.

126) SCOTT, Jas. Brown, The Status of the International Court of Justice. Oxford UP, 1916, 4to, 93pp., $17150.

127) SEUBERT, Rudolf, Aus der Praxis des Taylor-Systems mit eingehender Beschreibung seiner Anwendung bei der Tabor Manufacturing Co. in Philadelphia. B, 1914, roy8vo, 156pp., linen, $22.50.

128) SOMBART, Werner, Die Juden und das Wirtschaftsleben. Leipzig, 1911, roy8vo, vii, 476pp., orig. 1/2 vellum & bds, first edition, $75.00.

129) SOMBART, W., Luxus u. Kapitalismus. M/L, 1913, 8vo, 220pp., $22.50.

130) SPENGLER, Oswald, Der Untergang des Abendlandes. M, Beck, 1930, roy8vo, 2vols., orig. linen, handsome set, $65,00.

131) STEPHEN, Sir Geo., Adventures of an Attorney in Search of Practice. B, 1874, 8vo, 422pp., $30.00.

132) STODDART, Sir John, An Address Delivered on the 13th of Jan, 1831, by the Hon. Chief Justice of Malta, Sir John Stoddart, on the Opening of the Commission for that Year, Issued under the Law for Establishing at Malta a Modified Trial by Jury in Certain Criminal Cases, L, 1831, 8vo, 40pp., later linen, $30.00.

133) STONE, Narlan, F., Law and Its Administration. Columbia UP, 1915, 8vo, 232pp.., vl., first edition, $40.00.

134) STORY, Joseph, A Familiar Exposition of the Constitution of the United States: Containing a Brief Commentary....NY, 1874, 8vo, 373pp., later linen, $35.00.

135) STORY, Jos., Life and Letters, edited by His Son William Story, B, 1851, roy8vo, 2 vols., orig. cl., rebacked, first edition, $87.50.

136) STORY, Jos., Miscellaneous Writings, ed. by His Son Wm. Story, B, 1852, roy8vo, 828pp., later linen, contains almost twice as much material as the 1835 edition, $75.00.

137) STUBBS, William, The Constitutional History of England in Its Origin & Development. Oxford, UP, 1875, 8vo, 3vols., later linen, $75.00.

138) SUAREZ, Francisco, Opera Omnia. Paris, 1856-78. thick4to, 28 vols., contemp. 1/2 calf and marbled bds, blind stamps on titles, several volumes rebacked in the style and color of the others, an excellent set, the best edition of Suarex and rare complete; "At the time of his death, Suarez' reputation as a philosopher and theologian was extraordinary and his metaphysics deomnated thought at Catholic and many Protestant universities for the next two centuries. After Aquinas, to whom he owed much, Suarez is generally recognized as the greatest of the Scholastics...He was a highly original and influential thinker in the philosophy of law. He effected the transition from the medieval to the modern conception of natural law and his influence is particularly noticeable in the work of Hugo Grotius." Dictionary of Philosophy, VIII, 31-2. $875.00.

139) SUESS, Eduard, Die Zukunft des Goldes. Wien, 1877, 8vo, 8vo, 389pp. later linen, $27.50.

140) TELLKAMPF, J. L., Die Principien des Geld- und Bankwesens. B, 1867, 8vo 221pp., contemp. 1/2 cal and bds, bit rubbed, $37.50

141) THOL, Heinrich, Der Verkehr mit Staatspapieren. Göttingen, 1835, 8vo 272pp., orig. paper covered bds, trace of wear, $57.50.

142) THORNTON, Henry, An Inquiry into the Nature and Effects of Paper Credit

in Great Britain. Phil., 1807, roy8vo, 272pp., contemp. buff marbled boards, rebacked in 19th century linen, light sporadic foxing and browning, uncut, new label, first American edition, $65.00.

143) A Plain and Literal Translation of the Arabian Nights Entitled the Book of the Thousand Nights and a Night, with Introduction and Explanatory Notes by Richard F. Burton. Printed by the Burton Club for Private Subscribers Only, n.d. (1939), roy8vo, 17vols,, orig. cl., ill., #421 of ar edition of 1000, paper lables trifle worn, clean & tight, $175.00.

144) TIDD, Wm., Practical Forms: Being Chiefly Designed as an Appendix to the Practice of the Court of Kings Bench. London/Albany, 1803, 8vo, 371pp., contemp. roan, bit rubbed, $37.50.

145) TOUT, T. F., Edward the First. L, 1896, 8vo, 238pp., $13.50

146) TOWLE, Nathaniel, History and Analysis of the Constitution of the United States. 3rd ed. rev. & enl., B, 1871, 8vo, 449p., reb., $37.50

147) TRACY, John,Hints on Entering the Practice of Law. Ann Arbor, 1933, roy8vo, 255pp., $16.50.

148) (STRUBE, Julius M.), Untersuchung der Frage: ob das Silbergeld zu erhoben sei? Worin die sogenannte Vernünftige Verteidigung, des Schreibens: die Teutsche und Andere Volker Munz Verfassung betreffend, beantwortet wird. Hannover, 1752, sm4to, 132pp., 19th century bds, Kress5235, $135.00.

149) VANDERBILDT, Arthur (ed.) Minimum Standards of Judicial Administration. NY, 1949, roy8vo, 753pp., $27.50.

150) BERBER, Fritz (ed.), Das Diktat von Versailles: Entstehung, Inhalt, Zerfal Intro by Ribbentrop. Essen, 1939, roy8vo, 2vols., $75.00.

151) VIALLATE, Achielle, Essais d'Histoire Diplomatique Americaine. P, 1905, 8vo, 303pp., rebacked, $25.00.

152) VILLON, Francois, Oeuvres. P, 1934, sm4to, 151pp., orig., ptd. wrps, with 67 color illustrations by Dubout, #2809 of 3000, $37.50.

153) VIOLETTE, Eugen, English Constitutional Documents Since 1832. NY, 1936, 8vo, 225pp., $12.50.

154) VON HARTMANN, Eduard, Die Sozialen Kernfragen. Leipzig, 1894, 8vo, 571pp., contemp. 1/2 morocco, $37.50

155) von REIBNITZ, Kurt, Die New Yorker Fondsbörse (Stock Exchange): Ihre Geschichte, Verfassung..Jena, 1912, roy8vo, 126pp., wrps, $17.50.

156) von STEIN, Lorenz, Die Volkswirtschaftslehre. 2nd ed., rev., Wien, 1878, 8vo, xv, 578pp., orig. wrps over bds, $87.50.

157) WAGNER, Adolf, Die Geld-und Credittheorie der Peel'schen Bankacte. Wien, 1862, 8vo, 320pp., later linen, first edition, $125.00.

158) WAKEMAN, Henry, & Hassall, A. (ed.), Essays Introductory to the Study of English Constitutional History by Resident Members of the University of Oxford. L, 1896, 8vo, 349pp., $16.50.

159) WARDEN, Louis, The Life of Blackstone. Charlottesville, Va., 1938, roy8vo 325p., $17.50.

160) WARNER, Warren, The Experiences of a Barrister. NY, 1852, 8vo, 240p. $30.(

161) WEBSTER, Hutton, Rest Days: A Study in Early Law and Morality. NY, 1916

162) WHITE, G.E., The American Judicial Tradition. Oxford UP, 1976, roy8vo, 441pp., $12.50.

163) WIGMORE, John H., The Australian Ballot System. B, 1889, roy9vo, 205pp., $25.00.

164) WILLIAMS, Edw., A Treatise on the Law of Executors and Administrators

with Notes and References to American Decision by Francis Troubat. 2r American from the 2nd London e., Phil., 1841, roy8vo, 2vols. 1616pp., 1/2 linen and marbled bds, light sporadic fixing, $95.00.

165) WILLIAMS, Glanville, The Sanctity of Life and the Criminal Law. NY,195? 8vo, 350pp., $15.00.

166) WILLOUGHBY, W.W., & FENWICK, C.G., Types of Restricted Sovereignty and Colonial Autonomy. DC, GPO, 1919 (Confidential), 215pp., linen, $17.

167) WILSON, Woodrow, Constitutional Government in the United States. NY, Co bia University Press, 1908, 8vo, 236pp., first edition, $35.00

168) ZIELENZIGER, Kurt, Die Alten Deutschen Kameralisten: Ein Beitrag zur Ge schichte der Nationalökonomie and zum Problem des Merkantilismus. Jer 1914, roy8vo, 468pp., contemp. 1/2 linen and marbled bds, $45.00.

ADDENDA

169) SELIGMAN, Edwin (ed.), Encyclopedia of the Social Sciences. NY, 1937, 15vols. bound (as issued) as 8, orig. buck, clean, tight set $175.00.

170) Webster's International Unabridged Dictionary; Second Edition. India Pa bound in the original leather, minor tears in a few leaves neatly me nice copy, $140.00

171) Another copy, India Paper, bound in the original buckram,$140.00.

172) Another copy, Regular Paper, $130.00 (original backram)

173) SOMBART, Werner, Die Deutsche Volkswirtschaft im Neunzehnten Jahrhunde B, 1903, roy8vo, 647pp., contemp. 1/2 morocco, bit rubbed, $27.50.

174) Shakespeare, Comodies, Tragedies, Histories. NY, Heritage Press, roy8v 3vols., boxed, excellent, $57.50.

175) JELLINEK, Geo., Allgemeine Staatslehre. 3rd ed., B, 1914, roy8vo, 831p contemp. 1/2 morocco, $30.00

176) CONRAD, J. et al. (eds.), Handwörterbuch der Staatswissenschaften. 3rd rev., Jena, 1909, 4to, 8vols., orig. 1/2 morocco, $275.00.

177) NIZER, Louis, The Jury Returns. NY, 1966, 8vo, 467pp., NY, 1966, 8vo, $13.50.

178) BANKER'S SERVICE CO., Bank and Corporation Attorneys. B, 1927, 8vo, 943pp., $22.50.

179) Considerations Upon the Expediency of Abolishing Damages on Protested of Exchange, and the Effect of Establishing a Reciprocal Exchange wi Europe, and an Examination into the Nature and Operation of Bills of change. NY, 1829, 8vo, 67pp., linen, $30.00.

180) MORLEY, Henry (ed.(, Collection of Works on English Law and Politics; follows: Filmer, Patriarcha; Locke, Two Treatises of Civil Governmen Ellwood, Life of Thomas Ellwood;De Foe, Journal on the Plague Year. 900pp., orig. linen, handy collection, $27.50.

181) MORLEY, Henry (ed.), Collection of Works on English Law & Politics; as follows: Hobbes, Leviathan; Harrington, Oceana; Milton, Areopagitia; De Foe, The Shortest Way with Dissenters; Steele, The Crisis; Whatle Historical Doubts Respecting Napoleon. 8vo, 900pp., orig. linen, $27

182) SINCLAIR, Upton, The Jungle. NY, Doubdleday, 1906, 8vo, 413pp., orig. cloth, first edition, first issue, excellent, $125.00.

183) CAMPBELL, Wm., Lecture on the Life and Nilitary Services of General Ja Clinton. NY, 1839, 8vo, 23pp., linen, $25.00

If you do not wish to order from this list but would like to remain on our mailing list, please notify us; this does not appl old customers.

List 27

Law

JAN, 1980

Richard Adamiak
1545 East 60th St.
Chicago, Illinois 60637
312-955-4571
(By Phone: 7-11 AM & by Chance)

Prices net; postage extra; remittance must accompany order; usual institutional terms

ACOMB, Evelyn, The French Laic Laws, 1879-89. (1941), Reprint: 1967, roy9vc, 280pp., $12.50

American Bar Association Visit to England, Scotland & Ireland, 1924: Memorial Volume. NY, 1926, 4to, 500pp., $27.50

AMES, Jas. Barr, Lectures on Legal History & Miscellaneous Legal Papers. Harvard, 1913, 4to, 552pp., trifle rubbed, $35.00

APPLEMAN, JOHN (ed.), Successful Jury Trials: A Symposium. Indianapolis,1952, 4to, 586pp., $22.50

AUSTIN, John, The Province of Jurisprudence Determined. London, 1832, roy8vc, xx, 391, lxxvipp., contemp. 1/2 calf & marbled boards, trifle worn at crown, bit rubbed, first edition, of extreme rarity, no available copy reported in this century, $1250.00
The founder of the Analytic School of Jurispurdence: "The first English attempt to deal systematically with the fundamental ideas & forms involved in any developed legal system....Just as Machiavelli separated the science of politics from that of ethics, and Grotius made the theory of law independent of theology, Austin made jurisprudence a distinct science by sharply distinguishing between the legal and the normal." Morris R. Cohen, "John Austin," Encyclopedia of the Social Sciences.

BACON, Francis, Legum Leges: Sivi Francisci Baconi in Tractatus de Fontibus Universi Juris: Per Aphorismos Extractum ex Ejusdem Auctoris Opere, Adnctationis Quasdam Subjecit A.M.J.J. Dupin. Paris, 1822, 12mo, 147pp., later 1/2 linen & marbled bds, $27.50

BACON, Francis, The Works of. London, 1826, 8vo, 10vols., contemp. marbled boards, skillfully rebacked in linen, excellent set, $265.00

BARUCH, Bernard, The Making of the Reparation & Economic Sections of the Treaty. NY, 1920, 8vo, 352pp., $17.50

BELLI, Melvin & JONES, Dan, Belli Looks at Life & Law in Russia. Ind, 1963, roy8vo, 381pp., $15.00

BEMAN, Lamar, Selected Articles on Censorship of the Theater & Moving Pictures. NY, 1931, 8vo, 385pp., $16.50

BENT, Silas, Justice Oliver Wendell Holmes. NY, 1932, roy8vo, 386pp., $18.50

BEVERIDGE, Albert, The Life of John Marshall. B/NY, 1919, roy8vo, 4vols., orig. cloth with leather labels, #387 of an edition limited to 500, signed by the author, $87.50

BIGELOW, L.J., Bench & Bar: A complete Digest of the Wit, Humor....of the Bar. new ed., greatly enl., NY, 1871, 8vo, 532pp., bit rubbed, $27.00

BIRD, Fred., & RYAN, Fr., The Recall of Public Officers. NY, 1930, 8vo, 403pp., $16.50

BIRKENHEAD, Rt. Hoon. Earl of, Famous Trials of History. L, 1926, 8vo, 316p., $16.50

BLACHLY, Fred., & OATMAN, M., Administrative Legislation & Adjudication. DC, 1934, 8vo, 296pp., $15.00

BLACKBURN, Colin, A Treatise on the Effect of a Contract of Sale on the Legal Rights of Property & Possession. P, 1847, roy8vo, 172pp., lat.lin., $37.50

BLACKSTONE, Sir William, An Analytical Abridgement of the Commentaries of Sir Wm. Blackstone on the Laws of England, Together with an Analytical Synopsis of Each, by John Anthon. NY, 1809, 8vo, xx,279pp., later 1/2 linen & marbled bds, sl. sporadic dampstain, $47.50

BLACKSTONE, A Beckett, Gilbert Abbot, The Comic Blackstone, Ill. by Geo. Cruickshank, C, 1869, roy8vo, 376pp., orig. cl., rebacked & spine remounted, nice copy, $37.50

BLACKSTONE, Sir William, Commentaries on the Laws of England, the 20th Edition, Incorporating the Alterations to the Present Time, by James Stewart. London, 1841, roy8vo, 4vols., bound in full contemp. polished calf, raised bands, spines gilt, contrasting labels, edges and end sheets marbled, front hinges expertly reinforced, handsome set of a rare edition, only four copies reparted in No. America; Stewart's Notes appear in part in almost all American editions but are complete only in this edition, $265.00

BLACKSTONE, Sir William, Commentaries on the Laws of England. A New Edition with the Last Corrections of the Author....with Notes by John Frerderick Archbold. London, 1811, roy8vo, 4vols., in the original boards, uncut, repacked in the style & color of the original, large paper edition, the editor's notes are excerpted in almost all subsequent editions but are complete only in this edition, $325.00

SPRAGUE, Wm., An Abridgment of Blackstone's Commentaries. Detroit, 1893, 8vo, 533pp., later linen, $37.50

BLOM-COOPER, Louis, The Literature of the Law: An Anthology of Great Writing in and About the Law. NY, 1965, 8vo, 448pp., $14.50

BOUSH, G. M., Rulings by the Civil Courts Governing Religious Societies. Cleveland, 1915, roy8vo, 215pp., $15.00

BRANCH, Thomas, Principia Legis Aequitatis....first American edition, with Additions & Corrections by Wm. Hening. Richmand, 1824, 8vo, 168pp., later linen, $37.50

Broadcasting Bill of Rights. Statements Presented by Representatives of the Broadcasting Industry During Hearings on the White Bill to Amend the Communications Act of 1934. np., n.d., 8vo, 322pp., $14.50

BROWN, Louis, Freedom of the Seas. NY, 1919, 8vo, 262pp., $15.00

BRUNS, Karl (ed.), Fontes Juris Romani Antiqui. 7th ed., Tbg, 1909, 8vo, 2vols., $27.50

BRUCE, Alexander, Principia Juris Feudalis......Edinburgh, 1713, 8vo, 352pp., contemp. calf, nice copy, $235.00

BURKE, Edmund, The Works of, with Biographical & Critical Introduction by Henry Rogers. L, 1854, small4to, 2vols., comtemp. polished calf, raised bands, spines & covers gilt, spine gilt a bit faded, nice set, $87.50

BUSCH, Francis X., Enemies of the State. Ind, 1954, 8vo, 299pp., $15.00

CALLENDER, Clarence, American Courts: Their Organization & Procedure. NY, 1927, roy8vo, 284pp., $17.50

CAMPBELL, John Lord, Shakespeare's Legal Achievements Considered. NY, 1859, 8vo, 146pp., orig. cl., $30.00

CARDOZO, Benjamin, The Growth of the Law. Yale UP, 1924, 12mo, 145pp., orig. cloth, first ed., $45.00

CORDOZO, Benjamin, Law is Justice: Notable Opinions. ed. by S. Sainer, NY, 1938, roy8vo, 441pp., $17.50

CARLE, Guiseppi, Le Origini del Diritto Romano. Torino, 1888, roy8vo, 638pp., contemp. 1/2 calf & marbled bds, $30.00

CHENERY, Wm., Freedom of the Press. NY, 1955, 8vo, 256pp., $13.50

CHILD, Gilbert, Church & State under the Tudors. L, 1890, roy8vo, 429pp, $17.50

CHITTY, Jos., A Treatise on Pleadings and Parties to Actions. 9th American from the 6th London ed., w/New Matter from the 7th London ed., & w/Notes & Adds. by Dunlap & Ingraham & Add. Notes & References by J. C. Perkins. Springfield, 1844, roy8vo, 3vols., later 1/2 linen & marbled bds, excellent, $115.00

CLARK, G.J., Great Savings by Great Lawyers. KC, 1926, 4to, 801pp., $22.50

CLARKE, M. V., Medieval Representation & Consent: A Study of Early Parliaments of England & Ireland. (1936), NY, 1964, roy8vo, 408pp., $17.50

CLINTON, Henry, Extraordinary Cases. NY, 1896, 8vo, 403pp., $20.00

COHEN, Morris, Reason in Law. Glencoe, 1950, 8vo, 211pp., $14.50

COKE, Sir Edward, The First Part of the Institutes of the Laws of England: or, a Commentary Upon Littleton. 14th edition, rev. & Corr, with the Addition of Notes & References by Francis Hargrave & Chs. Butler; also the Notes of Lord Chief Justice Hale & Lord Chancellor Nottingham, and an Analysis of Littleton written by an Unknown Hand in 1658-59, but Never before Published. Dublin, 1791, large folio, xx,790, 57pp., bound in later 1/2 simulated leather & marbled bds, large paper copy, excellent, $145.00

COLLINET, Paul, Histoire de l'Ecole de Droit de Beyrouth. Paris, 1925, roy8vo, 333pp., later burkram, $27.50

COMER, John, Legislative Functions of National Administrative Authorities. Columbia UP, 1927, roy8vo, 274pp., ex lib, $15.00

The Constitution of the United States of America (Annotated). DC, GPO, 1938, 4to, 1246pp., $27.50

House of Representatives, 83rd Congress, 2nd Ses., Tax-Exempt Foundations. Report of the Special Committee (#2681), DC, 1955, 8vo, 432pp., $16.50

Corpus Juris Civilis: Cum Lectionum Florentiarum varietatibus, diligentius quam antea in margine appositis. Post sane Acurii Commentarios, Contii Scolia, Cuiacii paratitla, Duarani, aliorum clarissimorum i.c. additiones, nunc recene Iacobi Anelli de Bottis ac Augustini Caravitae....adnotationibus illustratus. Venice, 1606, 4to, 4vols., (I-IV of 5), about 2700pp. in each, contemp. vellum, sl. marginal dampstain in I, clean, tight set, $425.00

Corpus Juris Civilis Romani, in Quo Institutiones, Digesta ad Codicem Florentium emendata, codex item et Novellae, nec non Justiniani Edicta, Leonis et Aliorum Imperatorum Novellae, Conones Apostolorum, Feudorum Libri, Leges XII Tabb., et alis ad Jurisprudentiam Ante-Justinianiam Pertinentia Scripta, Dyonysii Gottofredi, Quibus Accesserunt Francisci Modii...Editic Nova, corr. Coloniae, 1756, large folio, 2vols., later 1/2 linen & marbled bds, $275.00

CORWIN, Edw., Total War & the Constitution. NY, 1947, 8vo, 182pp., $14.50

CORWIN, Edw., The President: Office & Powers. NYU Pr., 1948, 3rd ed., rev. roy8vo, 552pp., $16.50

COUPER, Chs., Report of the Trial....Against the Directors & Manager of the City of Glasgow Bank....with Lithographs of the Scroll Abstracts of Accounts & the Report of the Investigators. Edinburgh, 1879. 4to, 476pp., $22.50

COWEN, Esek, A Treatise on the Civil Jurisdiction of a Justice of the Peace in the State of New York. Albany, 1821, 8vo, 750pp., contemp. roan, bit rubbed & scuffed, $65.00

COX, Samuel, Three Decades of Federal Legislation, 1855-85. Providence, 1885, 4to, 726pp., later linen, $25.00

CRAVEN, Wesley, The Legend of the Founding Fathers. New York Univ. Press, 1956, 8vo, 191pp., $13.50

CROSS, Harold, The People's Right to Know: Legal Access to Public Records& Proceedings. Columbia Univ. Press, 1953, roy8vo, 405pp., $16.50

CUMMINGS, Homer, & McFarland, Carl, Federal Justice: Chapters in the History of Justice & the Federal Executive. NY, 1937, roy8vo, 576pp., $22.50

CURRAN, Barbara, Trends in Consumer Credit Legislation. Univ. of Chicago Press, 1965, 4to, 394pp., $17.50

CURTIS, Chs., The Oppenheimer Case: The Trial of a Security System. NY, 1955, 8vo, 281pp., $14.50

DABIN, Jean, La Philosophie de l'Ordre Juridique Positif, Specialment dans les Rapports de Droit Prive. Paris, 1929, roy8vo, 789pp., $25.00

DARROW, Clarence, Attorney for the Damned. ed. by A. Weinberg, forward by Wm. O. Douglas, NY, 1957, roy8vo, 552pp., $17.50

DAVIDSON, Eugene, The Trial of the Germans. NY, 1966, roy8vo, 636pp., $16.00

DAVIS, Daniel, A Practical Treatise Upon the Authority & Duty of Justices of the Peace in Criminal Prosecutions. Boston, 1824, roy8vo, 687pp., orig. boards, uncut, rebacked in the style of the original, $47.50

DERRETT, J., An Introduction to Legal Systems. NY, 1968, 8vo, 203pp., $13.50

DE SCHUTTER, et al, (eds.), Bibliography on International Criminal Law. Leiden, 1972, roy8vo, 423pp., $17.50

DE SMITH, S. A., Judicial Review of Administrative Action. London, 1968, roy8vo, 629pp., $17.50

DICEY, A. V., Introduction to the Study of the Law of the Constitution. London, 1927, roy8vo, 577pp., stamp on verso, $16.50

DICKINSON, Edwin, Law & Peace. Univ. of Pa. Press, 1951, 8vo, 147pp., $12.50

DONALD, David, Lincoln's Herndon. NY, 1948, 8vo, 378pp., (biography of Lincoln's law partner, circuit companion & biographer), $14.50

DUCHESNE, L., The Beginnings of the Temporal Sovereignty of the Popes, 754-1073. NY, 1908, 8vo, 312pp., $16.50

DUNHAM, Allison, & KURLAND, Ph.,Mr. Justice. Chicago, 1956, 8vo, 241pp., $14.50

DUNHAM, Wm. (ed.), Radolphi di Hengham Summae. Cambridge Univ. Press, 1932, roy8vo, lxxxiv, 94pp., $27.50

DU PASQUIER, L., Introduction a la Theorie Generale et a la Philosophie du Droit. Neuchatel/Paris, 1942, 8vo, 402pp., wrps, $16.50

EDWARDS, Chs., Pleasantries About Courts & Lawyers of the State of New York. NY, 1867, 8vo, 528pp., trifle worn, $30.00

ENSOR, R. C., Courts & Judges in France, Germany & England. Oxford Univ. Press, 1933, 8vo, 141pp., $14.50

ERNST, Morris, & SCHWARTZ, A., Censorship: The Search for the Obscene. NY, 1964, 8vo, 288pp., $14.50

--5--

ERNST, Morris, The Ultimate Power. NY, 1937, roy8vo, 344pp., $16.50

ERNST, M., The First Freedom. NY, 1946, 8vo, 316pp., $14.50

EVARTS, Wm. Maxwell, Arguments & Speeches of. ed. by His Son, NY, 1919, roy8vo, 3vols., $47.50

FARRAR, Timothy, Report of the Case of the Trustees of Dartmouth College Against William H. Woodward, Argued and Determined in the Superior Court of Judicature of the State of New Hampshire....and on Error in the Supreme Court of the United States. Portsmouth, 1819, roy8vo, 406pp., light sporadic foxing, in the original boards, uncut, light wear of extremeties; contains all the materials related to the case, including the arguments of Webster, Holms, Wirt & Hopkinson, and the opinions of Marshall, Washington and Story, in slipcase, first edition, $145.00

FAURE, Antonio, Codex Fabrianus Definitionum Forensium et Rerum in Sacro Sabaudiae Senatu Tractatarum, ex Ordine Titulorum Codicis Iustinianei, quantum fieri potuit, accommodate ad usum Forensem. 3rd ed., rev. & enl. London, 1610, folio, 2vols. bound as one, 458(58)632pp., bound in later full calf, light sporadic foxing, this edition is not in the National Union Catalogue and is ten years earlier than the earliest listed there, which is the Frankfurt edition of 1620; the author was president of the Senate of Savoy, a leading jurist of the period and a noted authority on Roman Law, $225.00

FENWICK, Chs., Wardship in International Law. (Confidential), D.C. GPO, 1919, 8vo, 39pp., later linen, $13.50

FINDLAY, Bruce & ESLER, J., Your Rugged Constitution. Stanford Univ. Pr., 1956, 8vo, 282pp., $13.50

FORDHAM, Edw., Notable Cross-Examinations. London, 1951, 8vo, 202pp., $13.50

FORTESCUE, Sir John, De Laudibus Legum Angliae....Hereto are Added the Sums of Sir Ralph de Hengham, Chief Justice to King Edward the First, Commonly Called Hengham Magna & Hengham Parva. With Notes of Both Fortescue and Hengham by that Famous and Learned Antiquary John Selden. London, 1672, 8vo, 134,51,140pp., text of Fortescue is two column, Latin with English translation facing, the latter in black letter, bound in later calf, beautiful copy, $335.00

FOSDICK, Raymond et al., Criminal Justice in Cleveland: Reports of the Cleveland Foundation Survey of the Admin. of Criminal Justice in Cleveland. Cl, 1922, roy8vo, 729pp., (Directed & Edited by Roscoe Pound and Felix Frankfurter), $30.00

FOSTER, Sir Michael, An Examination of the Scheme of Church Power, Laid Down in the Codex Juris Ecclesiastici Anglicani. London, 1735, 8vo, 168pp., later full calf, $87.50

FRANK, Jerome, Law & the Modern Mind. NY, 1938, roy8vo, 368pp., $17.50

FRANKFURTER, Felix (ed.), Mr. Justice Brandeis, Intro. by Oliver Wendell Holmes. Yale Univ. Press, 1932, roy8vo, 232pp., first edition, $37.50

FRANKFURTER, Felix, Mr. Justice Holmes and the Supreme Court. Harvard Univ. Press, 1938, 8vo, 139pp., small verso stamp, first edition, $37.50

FRANKFURTER, Felix, & LANDIS, Jas., The Business of the Supreme Court. NY, 1928, roy8vo, 349pp., first edition, $37.50

FRANKFURTER, Felix, & GREENE, Nathan, The Labor Injunction. NY, 1930, roy8vo, 343pp., first edition, $37.50

FREEMAN, Edw. A., The Growth of the English Constitution. L, 1894, 8vo, 234pp., $17.50

FREUND, Ernst, Standards of American Legislation. Univ. of Chicago Pr., 1917, roy8vo, 327pp., small verso stamp, $18.50

FREUND, E., Administrative Powers Over Persons & Property.C,1928,620pp.,$18.50

--6--

FULBECKE, William, A Parallele or Conference of the Civil Law, the Canon Law, and the Common Law of This Realm of England. Wherein the Agreement & Disagreement of These Three Laws and the Causes & Reasons of the Said Agreement and Disagreement are Opened and Discussed; bound with this is his: The Pandectes of the Law of Nations: Contayning Severall Discourses of the Questions, Points and Matters of Law, wherein the Nations of the World doe Consent & Accord. London 1618, sm4to, about 350pp., title a bit soiled and minor marginal chipping of the first few leaves with the loss of a few letters from two marginal notes, bound in later 1/2 blue calf and marbled boards, $365.00

FULLER, Chs., Law Manual: A Compend & Digest of Illinois Law, Designed as a General Manual of Reference for Illinois Lawyers, Justices and Business Men, and Embracing a Treatise on the Powers and Duties of Justices of the Peace in Civil & Criminal Cases. Chicago, 1878, roy8vo, 720pp., $35.00

GABEL, Richard, Public Funds for Church & Private Schools. D.C., Catholic Univ. Press, 1937, roy8vo, 858pp., ex lib, $22.50

GAIUS, Gaii Institutionum Iuris Civilis Commentarii Quattuor; or, Elements of Roman Law by Gaius, with a translation & commentary by Edw. Poste, 3rd ed., rev. & enl., Oxford Univ. Press, 1980, roy8vo, 685pp., $30.00

GAMELLI, Agostino, Cesare Lombroso, i Funerali di un Uomo e di una Dottrina. 3rd ed., rev. & enl., Firenze, 1911, 8vo, 189pp., $15.00

GARLAN, Edwin, Legal Realism & Justice. NY, 1941, 8vo, 161pp., $14.50

GARRATY, John (ed.), Quarrels that Have Shaped the Constitution. NY, 1964, 8vo, 276pp., $13.50

GASPAROLO, Francisco, Ius Civille Romanum. Senis, 1899-1903, 5vols.. bound as 2, thick roy8vo, contemp. 1/2 calf, bit rubbed, nice set, 47.50

GENTILE, Alberici, De Iuris Interpretibus: Dialog Sex. Text of the 1582 ed. introduction by G. Astoti and prepface by Salvatore Riccobono. Torino, 1937, roy8vo, 49,230pp., later linen, $27.50

GERANDO, M. Le Baron de, Institutes du Droit Administratif Francais. 2nd ed. rev. & enl., contemmp. 1/2 linen and marbled bds, 8vo, 5vols., $115.00

GIERKE, Otto, Political Theories of the Middle Age. trans. with intro. by F. W. Maitland. Cambridge Univ. Press, 1900, roy8vo, lxxx, 197pp, reb,$15.00

GLUECK, Sheldon, The Nuremberg Trial & Aggressive War. NY, 1946, 8vo, 121pp., $12.50

GNEIST, Rudolf von, History of the EnglishParliament....800-1887. 3rd ed. rev. NY, 1892, 8vo, 462pp., sporooadic neat underlining, rebacked, $22.50

GOODNOW, Frank, Comparative Administrative Law. NY, 1902, roy8vo, 700pp., $22.50

(GOODNOW) HAINES, CHS. G, & DIMOCK, M., Essays on the Law & Practice of Governmental Administration: A Volume in Honor of Frank Goodnow. Balto, Johns Hopkins Univ. Press, 1935, 8vo, 319pp., $17.50

GOGLIOLO, Pietro, Manuale delle Fonti del Diritto Romano Secondo i Risultati della piu Recente Critica Filologica e Giuridica. 2nd ed., Torino, 1911, roy8vo, 855pp., later linen, $30.00

GRAHAM, David, A Treatise on the Practice of the Suppreme Court of the State of New York. NY, 1832, roy8vo, 848pp., later linen, two tiny rents in title page, $37.50

GRANERIS, G., Contributi Tomistici alla Filosofia del Diritto. Torino, 1949, 8vo, 235pp., $13.50

GREENIDGE, A.H., Handbook of Greek Constitutional History. London, 1920, 8vo, 276pp., ex lib, $17.50

GRISWOLD, Erwin, The Fifth Amendment Today. Harvard UP, 1955,8vo,82pp.,$11.50

--7--

GROSS, Fred., What is the Verdict?, NY, 1944, 8vo, 311pp, $12.50

GROTIUS, Hugo, The Rights of War and Peace, trans. with Notes & Illustrations by A.C. Campbell, NY, 1901, roy8vo, 423pp, $20.00

GROTIUS, Hugo, The Rights of War and Peace in Three Books, Wherein are Explained the Law of Nature and Nations and the Principal Pionts Relating to Government..... translated into English, to which are added all the Large Notes of J. Barbeyrac. London, 1738, very largefolio, xxxvi, 817pp. bound in later 3/4 calf and marble boards, raised bands, spines gilt, beautiful copy, $300.00

GUTERBOCK, Carl, Bracton and His Relation to the Roman Law. trans. by Coxe, Philadephia, 1866, roy8vo, 182pp., orig. cl., $30.00

GUY, Wm., Principles of Forensic Medicine, first American edition with Notes & Adds. by Chs. Lee, NY, 1845, roy8vo, 711pp., later 1/2 linen $65.00

HADLEY, Jas., Introduction to Roman Law. NY, 1873, 8vo, 332pp, $22.50

HAINES, Chs. G., Revival of Natural Law Concepts. Harvard, 1930, roy8vo, 388pp., $17.50

HAINES, Chs. G., The American Doctrine of Judicial Supremacy. 2nd ed. rev. and enl., Univ. of CalifornisPress, 1932, roy8vo, 705pp., $27.50

HALLER, Wm. (ed.), Tracts on Liberty in the Puritan Revolution, 1638-47. Columbia Univ. Press, 1934, roy8vo, 3vols., $45.00

HARRIS, Richard, Before & after Trial: What Should be Done by Counsel, Solicitor & Client. 1st American ed., Northport, 1890, 8vo, 399pp, $22.50

HARRIS, Virgil, Ancieent, Curious & Famous Wills, B, 1911, roy8vo,472p, $16.50

HARRIS, Whitney, Tyranny on Trial: The Evidence at Nuremberg. Intro. by (American Prosecutor) Robert H. Jackson. Dallas, Southern Methodist University Press, 1954, roy8vo, 608pp., $22.50

HARTLAND, E.S., Primitive Law. London, 1924, 8vo, 216pp., $14.50

HAYEK, F., The Constitution of Liberty. Chicago, 1960, roy8vo, 569pp, $16.50

HENNESSEY, L. et al (ed.) , Bench and Bar of Illinois. Chicago, 1920, 4to, 443p., profus. ill., $30.00

HERSHEY, Amos, Essentials of Int'l Public Law. NY, 1918, 8vo, 558p. $16.50

HILLING, Nicholas, Procedure at the Roman Curia. NY, 1907, 8vo, 355p., $15.00

HOLAIND, Rene, Natural Law & Legal Practices. NY, 1899, 8vo 344p, $17.50

HOLLAND, Thomas E., Elements of Jurisprudence. 11th edition, Oxford Univ. Press, 1910, roy8vo, 415pp., $17.50

HOLLAND, Th. E., The Institutes of Justinian edited as a Recension of the Institutes of Gaius. Oxford Univ. Press, 1881, 12 mo, 243pp., ex lib, $14.50

HOLMES, Oliver Wendell, Collected Legal Papers. NY, 1921, roy8vo, 316p, $17.50

HOMEBURG, R., The Legal Rights of Performing Artists. trans. with Adds. by Maurice Speiser. NY, 1934, roy8vo, 184pp., $16.50

HONE, William, The First, Second & Third Trials of (for Publishing Parodies of Wilke's Catechism, the Litany & Athanasian Creed), London, 1818, 8vo, 137pp., later linen, $27.50

HOPKINS, John, The American Citizen: His Rights and Duties According to the Spirit of the Constitution of the US. NY, 1857, 8vo, 459pp, $30.00

HORNWILL, Herbert, The Ussages of the American Constitution. Oxford Univ. Press, 1925, roy8vo, 251pp., $17.50

HUDSON, Manley, International Tribunals. DC, 1944, 8vo, 287pp., $15.00

HUDSON, M. The World Court: 1921-34. Boston, 1934, 8vo, 289pp., $14.50

--8--

HUSCHKE, Edw., Imp. Iustiani Institutionum Libri Quarttuor. Leipzig, 1899, 8vo, xix, 643pp., 1/2 vellum, $22.50

HUSCHKE, Edw., Iurisprudentiae Anteiustinianae. 3rd ed. rev. Leipzig, 1874, 12mo, 820pp., 1/2 morocco, $27.50

HYAMSON, M., Mosaicarum et Romanarum Legum Collatio, with Intro. Facsimili & Transcription of the Berlin Codex, translation & notes. Oxford Univ. Press, 1913, roy8vo, 293pp., $22.50

HYDE, Chs., Certain Effects of Change of Sovereignty. DC, Gpo, 31p, $12.50

HYDE, Chs., National Character in Religion to Property in Time of War. DC, GPO, 1918 (Confidential), 8vo, 214pp., $13.50

HYDE, Chs., Blockade. DC, GPO (Confidential), 1918, 8vo, 43p, linen, $12.50

ICKES, Harold, America's House of Lords: An Inquiry Into the Freedom of the Press. NY, 1939, 8vo, 214pp., $13.50

Inaugural Addresses Delivered by the Professors of Law in the University of the City of New York at the Opening of the Law School of that Institution. NY, 1838, 8vo, 68pp., later linen, $27.50

INDERWICK, F.A., The King's Peace: A Historical Sketch of the English Law Courts. London, 1895, 8vo, 254pp., $17.50

JACOBS, Giles, A New Law Dictionary: Containing the Interpretation and Definition of Words and Terms Used in the Law; as also the Law & Practice Under the Proper Heads & Titles, Together with Such Learning as Explains the History & Antiquity of the Law; Our Manners, Customs and Original Government. 9th edition, with great additions and improvements, newly corrected and greatly enlarged by Owen Ruffhead & J. Morgan. London, 1772, very large folio, 974pp., contemp. calf, expertly rebacked in calf, raised bands, spine tooled, beautiful copy, $245.00

JONES, Jas., A Compendium of Forms with the Mode of Procedure in the Various Courts of the State of Illinois, which with Little Variation will Apply to Those of the Neighboring States and Territories. 3rd ed., enl. & imp. Chicago, 1872, roy8vo, 782pp., later linen, $35.00

JOLOWICZ, Herbert, Historical Introduction to the Study of Roman Law. 2nd ed., Cambridge Univ. Press, 1954, roy8vo, 596pp, $18.50

KANTOROWICZ, Ernst, The King's Two Bodies: A Study in Medieval Political Theology. Princeton Univ. Press, 1957, roy8vo, 567pp, $17.50

KAVANAUGH, Marcus, You Be the Judge: Dramatic Narratives of Some High-Light Cases Decided During 33 Years. NY, 1929, 8vo, 316pp., $15.00

KARPMAN, Benj., The Sexual Offender. NY, 1957, roy8vo, 744pp., $16.50

KELSEN, Hans, General Therory of Law and State. trans. by Wedberg. NY, 1961, roy8vo, 516pp., $16.50

(KENT) The Most Material Parts of Kent's Commentaries Reduced to Questions NY, 1860, roy8vo, 418pp., later 1/2 linen, $45.00

KENT, James, Commentaries on American Law. 4th Edition. New York, Printed for the Author, 1840, roy8vo,4vols., bound in later 1/2 calf and marble boards, excellent; an important association copy which belonged to Charles Sumner: each volume is signed by him and volume one has the following inscription: "This copy of Kent's Commentaries, a present to me from the author, is offered with pleasure to the library of Olivet College, Michigan, (signed) Chs. Sumner, Boaston, Dec 26, 1847". light sporadic foxing, $275.00

KERN, Fritz, Kingship & Law In the Middle Ages. Oxford, 1939, 8vo,214p, $12.50

KLUGER, Rich., Simple Justice: A History of Brown vs the Board of Education. NY, 1975, 8vo, 2vols., 1071pp., $$25.00

KOENIG, Louis, The Chief Executive. NY, 1964, roy8vo, 435pp., $15.50

KOMARNICKI, Titus, Rebirth of the Polish Republic: A Study of the Diplomatic History of Europe: 1914-20. L, 1957, roy8vo, 776pp., $27.50

--9--

KRISLOV, Samuel, The Supreme Court and Political Freedom. NY, 1968, 8vo, 239pp., $13.50

KRUEGER, Paul, (ed.), Ulpiani Liber Singularis Regularum; Pauli (in the Series Collectio Librorum Iuris Anteiustiniani ed. by Kruegr & Mommsen), $22.50

LABAND, Paul, Die Vermogensrechtlichen Klagen nach den Sachsischen Rechtsquellen des Mittelalters. B, 1869, roy8vo, 406pp., bds, $22.50

LADAS, Stephen, International Protection of Literary and Artistic Property. Vol. I: International Copyright and Inter-American Copyright. NY, 1938, 8vo, 679pp., later linen, $17.50

LASOK, D. (ed.), Polish Civil Law. Leiden, 1973, roy8vo, 277pp., (Series : Law in Eastern Europe, No. 18 (I),). $17.50

LAWERENCE, T.J., Les Principes de Droit International, traduit par Dumas et Lapradelle, pref by Jas. Brown Scott. (Carnegie Foundation), Oxford Univ. Press, 1920, 4to, xxxiv, 775pp., $30.00

LEAGE, R.W., Roman Private Law Founded on the Institutes of Gaius and Justinian. 2nd ed., by Ziegler. London, 1951 roy8vo, 458pp., $22.50

LEARNED, Henry, The President's Cabinet: Studies in the Orgin, Formation and Structure of an American Institution. Yale UP, 1912, roy8vo, 417p, $20.00

LE BUFFE, Francis, & HAYS, Jas., Jurisprudence: with Casess to Illustrate Principles. Fordham UP, 1938, 8vo, 285pp., 3rd ed. enl, $14.50

LEGAL DEPT., NAT'L CATHOLIC WELFARE CONFERENCE, School Bus Transportaion Laws in the U.S., D.C., 1946, roy8vo, 257pp., $14.50

LE VAYER DE BOUTIGNY (also ascribed to P. de Renusson), A Dissertation Shewing the Invalidity of All Proff by Similitude of Hands in Criminal Cases... translated from the Works of an Eminent Frenech Proper to be Read by a Free People if All Times, but Particularly the Pressent, when a New Species of Treason, and that by Way of Correspondence, Has been Lately Created.... London, 1744, 8vo, xxvi, 82pp., later calf, $125.00

LEVY, Beryl, Cardozo and the Frontiers of Legal Thinking, with Selected Opinions. Oxford Univ. Pr., 1938, roy8vo, $16.50

LEWIS, Walker, Without Fear or Favor: A Biography of Chief Justice Roger Brooke Taney. Boston, 1965, 8vo, 556pp., $16.50

LEWIS, Wm. D. Interpreting the Constitution. Va, 2937, 8vo, 117p, $12.50

Lieber, Francis, Manual of Political Ethics Designed Chiefly for the Use of Colleges and Students at Law. 2nd ed., rev., edited by Theodore Woosley, Phil., 1892, roy8vo, 2vols., nice set, $35.00

LOCKWOOD, Henry, Constitutional History of France. NY, 1890, roy8vo, 424p, $17.50

LORD RUSSELL OF LIVERPOOL, Trial of Eichman. L, 1962, 8vo, 324pp, $14.50

LOWTHER, Jas. Viscount Ullswater, A Speaker's Commentaries. L. 1925, roy8vo, 2vols., with ALS, $35.00

LUNC, L.A., Miedzynarodowe Prawo Prywante. (Int'l Private Law), Warsaw, 1951, 8vo, 434pp., $17.50

LUSTGARTEN, Edgar, Verdict in Dispute, NY, 1950, 8vo, 253pp, underlined, $12.50

MACMAHON, Arthur, (ed.), Federalism: Mature & Emergent. NY, 1955, roy8vo, 557pp., $17.50

MAINE, Sir Henry, Ancient Law. Second Edition. London, 1863, 8vo, 415pp., later linen, stamp on verso, trimmed, $65.00

MAINE, Sir Henry Sumner, Popular Government. NY, 1886, roy8vo, 261pp., nice copy, $22.50

--10--

MAINE, Sir Henry Sumner, Ancient Law: Its Connection with the Early History of Society and Its Relation to Modern Ideas. Introduction by Theodore Dwight, NY, 1871, 8vo, lxix, 400pp., original linen, rebacked and original spine expertly remounted, excellent copy, first American edition, $125.00

MAITLAND, F.W., Constitutional History of England. Cambridge University Press, 1920, roy8vo, 548pp., $22.50

MANDEVILLE, Bernard, The Fable of the Bees: Or, Private Vices, Publick Benefits. with a Commentary, Critical, Historical and Explanatory, by orig. cl., titles in red & black, rag paper, one of 875 copies, $95.00

John Marshall: The Tribute to Massachusetts. Boston/Cambridge, 1901, roy8vo 120pp., (addresses by Knowlton, Walcott, Holmes, Thayer, Gray), #690 of a limited edition of 750, inscribed by Thayer, $27.50

MARSHALL, John, The Life of George Washington. Virginia, 1926, roy8vo, 5vols., ill., orig. linen with labels, fine set, $87.50

MARSHALL, John, The Life of George Washington. Philadelphia, 1804-1807, 8vo, 5vols., bound in contemp. calf, skillfully rebacked in calf, raised bands, spines gilt, first edition, beautiful set, $425.00

MARSHALL, P., Impeachment of Warren Hastings. Oxford, 1965, 8vo, 217p, $13.50

MARTENS, G.F., Precis du Droit des Gens Moderne de l'Europe. Paris, 1831, 8vo, 2vols., contemp. bds, rebacked, $75.00

MARTIN, Edward, The Role of the Bar in Electing the Bench in Chicago. Univ. of Chicago Press, 1936, roy8vo, 385pp., $17.50

MASON, Alpheus T., Harlan Fiske Stone. NY, 1956, roy8vo, 914pp, $22.50

MASON, Alpheus, Brandeis & the Modern State. DC, 1936, 12mo, 263pp, $13.50

MASON, Alpheus, Brandeis: A Free Man's Life. NY, 1946, roy8vo, 713pp., $17.50

MC GRATH, John, Church & State in American Law: Cases & Materials. Milwaukee, 1962, roy8vo, 413pp., $14.50

MC LAUGHLIN, Raymond, A History of State Legislation Affecting Private Elementary & Secondary Schools in the US, 1870-1945. DC, 1946, roy8vo, 348pp., ex lib, $14.50

MERRIAM, Chs. History of American Political Theories. NY, 1918, 8vo, 364p, $13.50

MILLIOT, Louis, Introduction a l'Etude du Droit Musulman. Paris, 1953, roy 8vo, 822pp., orig. ptd. wrps, $25.00

MITFORD, John, A Treatise on the Pleadings in Suits in the Court of Chancery by English Bill. Dublin, 1795, 8vo, 263,pp., later 1/2 linen & bds, $65.00

MONTGOMERY, John, Cases in Vietnamese Administration. Saigon, 1959, roy8vo, xix, 481pp., with facing English translation, $22.50

MOORE, John Bassett, A Digest of International Law, as Embodied in Diplomatic Discussions, Treaties and Other Int'l Agreements, Int'l Awards, the Decisions of Municipal Courts, and the Writings of Jurists.... & the Decisions of Courts, Federal & State. DC, GPO, 1906ff. roy8vo, 8vols., 7000pp., bound in contemp. roan with red & black labels, excellent, $175.00

MOORE, John B., The Principles of American Diplomacy. NY, 1918, 8vo, 477pp., minor pencil underscoring, $16.50

MORTENSON, Ernest, You Be the Judge., Intro. by John H. Wigmore. DC, 1943, roy8vo, 439pp., ill. by Alain, $22.50

MORRIS, M.F., An Introduction to the History of the Development of Law. DC, 1928, roy8vo, 315p., $16.50

PARRY, LEONARD, Some Famous Medical Trials. L, 1927, 8vo, 326., $16.50

--11--

MORRIS, Gouverneur, The Life of, with Selections from His Correspondence & Miscellaneous Papers. ed. by Jared Sparks. B, 1832, roy8vo, 3vols., orrig. bds, rebacked in linen, first edition, important member of the Constitutional Convention, $75.00

MOYLE, J.B., Imperatoris Iustiniani Institutionem Libri Quattour, with Intro, Excursus & Translation. Oxford UP, 1883, roy8vo, 2vols., bit worn, $30.00

MUHLENBRUCH, C.F., Doctrina Pandectarum. rev. ed. Bruxelles, 1838, roy8vo, 724pp., contemp. 1/2 vellum & bds, nice copy, $37.50

NEALE, A.D., The Antitrust Laws of the US. Cambridge UP, 1970, roy8vo, 520pp., new linen, $18.50

INTERNATIONAL MILITARY TRIBUNAL: Trial of the Major War Criminals Before the International Military Tribunal: Official Text (English Edition), Nuremberg, 1947-49, roy8vo, 42vols., orig. cloth, some internal dampstain in the latter portion of vol. 5, nice set, $675.00

Trials of War Criminals Before the Nurenberg Military Tribunals Under Control Council Law No. 10, October, 1946-April, 1949. DC, GPO, 1953, roy8vo, 13 volumes (of 15, lacking 1 & 2), $350.00

OFFICE OF UNITED STATES CHIEF COUNSEL FOR PROSECUTION OF AXIS CRIMINALITY. Nazi Conspiracy and Aggression. DC, GPO, 1946-48, roy8vo, 9vols., without Supplements A & B, spines bit faded, $175.00

OBERHOLTZER, Ellis, The Referendum in America, Together with Some Chapters on the Initiative & Recall. new ed., NY, 1912, 8vo, 533pp., $17.50

Official Report of the Universal Congress of Lawyers & Jurists Held at St. Louis, 1904, roy8vo, 423pp., $17.50

O'NEILL, J., Religion & Education Under the Constitution. NY, 1949, 8vo, 338p, $14.50

On Trial: The Soviet State versus "Abram Tertz" & "Nikolai Arzhak," trans. & ed. by Max Hayward. rev. & enl. ed., NY, 1967, 8vo, 310pp., $14.50

ORTOLAN, Signor, Storia della Legislazione Romana dalla Sua Origine Fimo alla Legislazione Moderna; 2nd Italian ed., Napoli, 1857, 168 (2 col.)pp: bound with this companion work by the same author: Spiegazione Storica delle Instituzioni dell' Imperatore Giustiniano. Napoli, 1856, 486, 451 (2col.)pp., the three bound in one thick roy8vo, volume, contemp. 1/2 calf and boards, $65.00

The Paris Law Courts: Sketches of Men & Manners. London 1894, roy8vo, 293pp., rebacked & original spine remounted, $22.50

PALEOTTI, Gabriele, Tractatus Singularis de Nothis Spuriisque Fillis Omnibus Juris Studiosis....in quo omnia....Accessit Tractatus Utilissimus de Liber Hominis Nativitate seu de Liberis Naturalibus (by) Ponto Heutero Delfio. The Hague, 1655, 12mo, 341, 87pp., both works: $175.00

Memoir of Theophilus Parsons, Chief Judge of the Supreme Judicial Court of Massachsetts, ed. by His Son. B, 1861, 8vo, 476pp., $27.50

PATTERSON, Caleb, The Adminstration of Justice in Great Britain. Austin, Univ. of Texas Press, 1936, roy8vo, 326pp., $17.50

PAULSEN, Monrad (ed.), Legal Institutions Today & Tomorrow: Centennial Volume of the Columbia Law School. Columbia UP, 1959, roy8vo, 346pp., $20.00

PAYNE, Abraham, Reminiscences of the Rhode Island Bar. Providence, 1885, 277pp., $30.00 (later linen)

Trial of John Peltier for Libel Against Napoleon Buonaparte. L, 1803, 8vo, xxvii, 312, cxxxviipp., later linen, minor internal soil, $57.50

PHILBRICK, Fred, Language & the Law: The Semantics of Forensic English. NY, 1949, 8vo, 253pp., $15.50

--12--

PHILLIMORE, Robert, The Law of Domicil. Phil., 1847, roy8vo, 153pp., later 1/2 linen & marbled bds, $37.50

PITMAN, BENN (ed.), The Assassination of Lincoln and the Trial of the Conspirators, Containing the Orders Convening the Commission, Rules for Its Guidance; Pleas of the Accused & the Jurisdiction of the Commission & for Severance of Trial, Testimony in Full Concerning the Assassination and Attending Circumstances....Findings & Sentences of the Accused. Cincinnati/ NY, 1865, roy8vo, 421(2col.)pp., later 1/2 linen & marbled bds, $75.00

PITMAN, Benn (ed.), The Trials for Treason at Indianapolis, Disclosing the Plans for Establishing a North-Western Confederacy, Being the Official Record of the Trials before the Military Commission Convened by Special Orders No. 129, Hq. Dist. of Indiana. Cincinnati, 1865, roy8vo, 339 (2col.)p. later linen, $47.50

POLLOCK, Sir Federick, & MAITLAND, Frederic, The History of English Law Before the Time of Edward I. DC, 1959, roy8vo, 2vols., $40.00

POLLOCK, Sir Fred., An Introduction to the History of the Science of Politics. L, 1890, 8vo, 126pp., $12.50

POST, Chs. Supreme Court & Political Questions. Balto, Johns Hopkins Univ. Press, 1936, roy8vo, 145pp., $14.50

POUND, Roscoe, Masonic Addresses & Writings. NY, 1953, 8vo, 348pp., $17.50

POUND, Roscoe, Contemporary Juristic Theory. Cal, 1940, 8vo, 83pp., $17.50

POUND, Roscoe, The Formative Era of American Law. Boston, 1938, 8vo, 188pp., first edition, signed by Pound, $35.00

POUND, Roscoe, (et al), Jubilee Law Lectures: 1889-1939, Catholic University of America, School of Law. DC, 1939, 8vo, 181pp., $14.50

POWELL, John Jos., A treatise Upon the Law of Mortgages. 3rd ed. rev. & corr. Dublin, 1791, 8vo, xvi, 558pp, contemp. calf, rebacked in calf with old label preserved, $65.00

POWELL, Theo, The School Bus Law. Wesleyan Up, 1960, roy8vo, 334pp, $15.00

Prize Cases Decided in the United States Supreme Court, 1789-1918, ed. by James Brown Scott, Oxford, UP, 1923, 4to, 3vols., 2183pp., $95.00

Proceedings of the Electoral Commission of the Two Houses of Congress in Joint Meeting Relative to the Count of Electoral Votes Cast Dec 6, 1876. DC, GPO, 1877, roy8vo, 1087pp., $30.00

PROSTE, Francis, Canonical Procedurein Disciplinary & Criminal Cases of Clerics. NY, 1887, 8vo, 268pp., $14.50

PULLING, Alex, A Practical Compendium of the Law & Usage of Mercantile Accounts. Phil., 1847 roy8vo, 117pp., later 1/2 linen & bds, $35.00

PUTNEY, Albert (of the Chicago Bar), United States Constitutional History & Law. Chicago, 1908, roy8vo, 599pp., $17.50

RAITHBY, John, The Study and Practice of Law, Considered in their Various Relations to Society. 1st American ed., Portland, 1806, 8vo, 364pp. later 1/2 linen & marbled bds, $75.00

RANDALL, Jas. G., Constitutional Problems Under Lincoln. Urbana, Univ. of Illinois Press, 1964, 8vo, 596pp., wraps over boards, ex lib, $17.50

Records of the Federal Convention of 1787, edited by Max Farrand. New Haven, Yale University Press, 1911, tall thick 4to, bound in the original 1/22 vellum & buff boards, #9 of an edition limited to 250, large paper edition on rag paper, uncut, fine set, sscarce, $250.00

REED, Alfred, Carnegie Endowment for the Advancement of Teaching: Training for the Public Profession of Law. (Bull. #15), NY, 1921, roy8vo, 498pp., $22.50

REPPY, Alison (ed.), David Dudley Field Centenary Esssays. New York Univ. School of Law, 1949, 4to, 400pp., $20.00

--13--

REYNOLDS, Wm., The Theory of the Law of Evidence in the United States. 3rd ed. C, 1897, 8vo, 206pp., $17.50

RICE, Chs., The Supreme Court & Public Prayer. Fordham UP, 1964, 8vo, 202p, $12.00

RICE, Clinton, Manual of the U.S. Bankruptcy Act, 1867, with the Rules, Orders & Forms....Approved by the Justices of the Supreme Court. DC, 1867, roy8vo, 442pp., later linen, $30.00

RICHARDS, John, Abraham Lincoln: The Lawyer Statesman. Boston, 1916, roy8vo, 260pp., fine, $20.00

RIVALTA, Valentino, Diritto Naturale e Positivo. Bologna, 1898, roy8vo, 467pp., later 1/2 linen, $22.50

ROBBINS, Alexander, A Treatise on American Advocacy. St. Louis, 1904, roy8vo, 295pp., inscribed by the author, $22.50

ROBSON, Wm., Jsutice and Administrative Law: A study of the British Constitution. London, 1928, 8vo, 346pp., $17.50

RODELL, Fred, Woe Unto You Lawyers!, NY, 1939, 8vo, 274pp., $14.50

ROMMEN, Heinrich, The Natural Law: A Study in Legal and Social History Philosophy. St. Louis, 1947, roy8vo, 290pp., $16.50

ROSCOE, Henry, The Lives of Eminent British Lawyers. London, 1830, sm8vo, 428pp., contemp. linen, rebacked, $45.00

ROOT, Elihu, Addresses on International Subjects. ed. by R. Bacon & Jas. Brown Scott, Harvard University Press, 1916, roy8vo, 463pp., $22.50

ROOT, Elihu, Men & Policies: Addresses. Harvard, 1926, roy8vo, 509pp, $25.00

ROPER, R.S. Donnison, A Treatise on the Revocation and Republication of Wills Together with Tracts upon the Law Concerning Baron & Feme. Phil, 1820, 8vo, 239pp., later buckram, foxed, $35.00

RUTHEFORD, M.L., The Influence of the American Bar Association on Public Opinion & Legislation. Phil., 1937, roy8vo, 393pp., $18.50

SABINE, GEO., A History of Political Theory. NY, 1961,3rd ed.,8vo,948p, $17.50

SACHER, Hermann (ed.), Staatslexikon, 5th ed., rev., Freiburg, 1926-32, 4to, 5vols., about 1800 (2col)pp. in each, a wealth of information on law, politics and economics, 1/2 morocco & linnen, bit rubbed, $125.00

The Tryal of Dr. Henry Sacheverell Beforre the House of Peers for High Crimes and Misdemeanors Upon an Impeachment by the Knights, Citizens and Burgesses in Parliment Assembled....London, 1710, folio, 335pp; bound with this and individually paginated: The Bishop of Salisbury & Bishop of Oxford's Speechs in the House of Lords....and also the Bishop of Lincoln's & Bishop of Norwich' Speeches; the Bishop of Lincoln's and Bishop of Norwiche's Speeches at the Opening of the Second Article of Impeachment; An Impartial Review of What Passed Most Remarkable in the Last Session of Parliment; the Names of Some of the Peers who Protested Against Some of the Proceedings ....with Reasons for their Protestations; An Exact List of Members of the House of Commons Who Voted for and Against Him; this is a very complete edition, bound in later calf, $135.00

SAINT-GERMAN, Christopher, Two Dialogues in English between a Doctor of Divinity and a Student of the Laws of England. Newly Revised & Repr'td. London, 1681, 12mo, 366pp., mainly black letter, 19th century morocco, $225.00

SCHACHT, Hjalmar, The End of Reparations. tr. by Gannett. NY, 1931, 8vo, 248p, scarce, author was tried and acquitted at Nurnberg, $22.50

SCHMIDHAUSER, John (ed.), Constitutional Law in the Political Process. Chicago, 1963, roy8vo, 544pp., $17.50

SCHUBERT, GLENDON, Constitutional Politics: The Political Behavior of Supreme Court Justices. NY, 1960, 4to, 735pp., $17.50

--14--

SCHNORR VON CAROLSFELD, Ludwig, Geschichte der Juristischen Person: Vol. I: Universities, Corpus, Collegium im Klassischen Römischen Recht. M, 1933, roy8vo, 431pp., later linen, $27.50

SCOTT, Chs. Photographic Evidence: Preparation and Presentation. Kansas City, 1942, 4to, 922pp., ill. with photos, $30.00

SHARSWOOD, Hon. Geo., An Essay on Professional Ethics. 5th ed., Phil., 1896, 8vo, 214pp., $22.50

SHEIL, Richard, Sketches of the Irish Bar, with Memoir & Notes by R. S. Mackenzie. NY, 1854, 8vo, 2vols., $57.50

SIDLO, Th., Chairman, Standing Committee on Public Relations of the ABA, Public Relations for Bar Associations. n.p., n.d. (1952), 4to, 227p, $17.50

SMIEGL, Erwin, The Wall Street Lawyer: Professional Orgañization Man? Glencoe, 1964, roy8vo, 369pp., $16.50

SMITH, J.M. Powis, The Origin and History of Hebrew Law. University of Chicago Press, 1931, 8vo, 285pp., $15.00

SMITH, S.B., Elements of Ecclesiastical Law. 9th ed. rev. NY, 1893, roy8vo, 3vols., $47.50

SPAULDING, Hugh, An Encyclopedia of Law and Forms for All the States & Canada. Phil., 1880, roy8vo, 702pp., bit worn, $27.50

STEPHEN, Sir Geo. (or Sir Jas. Stephen, or Samuel Warren), Adventures of an Attorney in Search of Practice. London, 1839, 8vo, 407pp., bound in full later calf, raised bands, spine gilt, fine copy, $37.50

STIMSON, Fred., Popular Law Making: A Study of the Origin, History & Present Tendencies of Law-Making by Statute. NY, 1910, roy8vo, 390pp., $17.50

STOKES, Anson, & Pfeffer, Leo, Church and State in the United States. rev. one volume ed., NY, 1964, roy8vo, 660pp., $17.50

STONE, Harlan, Law and Its Adminstration. NY, Columbia Univ. Press, 1915, 8vo, 232pp., orig. cl., first edition, $45.00

STOREY, Moorfield, The Reform of Legal Procedure. Yale Univ. Press, 1911, 8vo, 262p, $14.50

STORY, Joseph, A Familiar Exposition of the Constitution of the United States Containing a Brief Commentary. NY, 1874, 8vo, 372pp., later linen, $35.00

STORY, Joseph., Commentaries on the Constitution of the United States. Boston, 1833, roy8vo, 3vols., contemp. 1/2 calf and marbled boards, bit rubbed, light sporadic foxing, very attractive set, first edition, rare, after the Federalist this remains the single most important work on the Constitution, $1500.00

STORY, Jos., Miscellaneous Writings, ed. by His Son. Boston, 1852, roy8vo, 828pp., contemp. 1/2 calf and linen, rubbed, $75.00

STRONG, Theron, Landmarks of a Lawyer's Lifetime. NY, 1914, roy8vo, 552pp., slight shelf wear, signed by the author, highly informative, $27.50

STUBBS, William, The Constitutional History of England in Its Origin and Development. Oxford Univ. Pr, 1875, 8vo, 3vols., slight external wear & light sporadic underling (neat), $47.50

Studi Dedicati alla Memoria de Pier Paolo Zanzucci dalla Faculta di Giurisprudeza. milano, 1927, roy8vo, 520pp., later buckram, $27.50

SUAREZ, Francisco, Opera Omnia. Paris, 1856-78, 4to, 30vols, contemp. 1/2 calf and marbled bds, several volumes rebacked in the color and style of the others, excellent set, $675.00

SUGDEN, Wm., A handy Book on Property Law. from the 5th London ed., NY, 1858, 8vo, 216pp., $30.00

SWISHER, Carl B, Supreme Court in Modern Role. NYU Pr., 1958, 8vo,214p, $14.50

--15--

THURSTON, John. Government Proprietary Corporations in the English-Speaking Countries. Harvard UP, 1937, roy8vo, 294p, $27.50

TODD, A. L., Justice on Trial: The Case of Lewis D. Brandeis. NY, 1964, 8vo, 275pp., $14.50

Told Out of Court: Personal Experiences by Members of the Chicago Bench & Bar. C, 1909. 12mo, 256pp., $22.50

TOLLER, Samuel, The Law of Executors and Administrators. 3rd ed. corr. with adds., NY, 1815, 8vo, 522pp., later 1/2 linen, $45.00

TOWLE, Nathaniel, A History and Analysis of the Constitution of the United States. 3rd ed. rev. & enl., Boston, 1871, 8vo, 449pp., rebacked, $35.00

The Treaties of Peace, 1919-1923....with Maps Compiled Especially for this Edition and a Summary of the Legal Basis of the New Boundaries by L. Martin. NY, Carnegie Endowment, 1924, 8vo, 2vols. as one, lxxvii, 1098pp., $25.00

TYRRELL, James, Bibliotheca Politica; or, An Enquiry into the Antient Constitution of the English Government, with Respect to the Just Extent of the Regal Power and the Rights and Liberties of the Subject, wherein all the Chief Arguments Both for and Against the Late Revolution are Impartially Considered. London, 1718, folio, xv, 739pp., contemp. calf, skillfully rebacked in calf, light sporadic foxing, nice copy, $245.00

ULRICH, Bartow, Abraham Lincoln and Constitutional Government. London, 1916, roy8vo, 406pp., scarce, $27.50

UMBREIT, Ken., Our Eleven Chief Justices: A History of the Supreme Court in Terms of their Personalities. NY, 1938, roy8vo, 539pp., $17.50

VAN BYNKERSHOEK, Cornelius, De Foro Legatorum: A Monograph on the Jurisdiction Over Ambassadors in Both Civil & Criminal Cases. Photo Repro. of the 1744 ed. with English Translation (Classics of Int'l Law), Oxford Univ. Press, 1946, 4to, xxv, 134, 140pp., lightly soiled, $30.00

VATTEL, Monsieur de, The Law of Nations; or Principles of the Law of Nature Applied to the Conduct & Affairs of Nations & Soverigns. from the New Edition by Jos. Chitty, with Additional Notes & References by Edw. Ingraham. Phil, 1872, roy8vo, lxvi, 500pp, later 1/2 linen and marbled boards; this is the best critical edition of Vattel, $75.00

VIGNALI, Giovanni, Corpo del Diritto Corre dato delle Note di Dionisio Gotofredo, e di C.E. Freisleben, Altrimenti Ferromontano, con le Varianti delle Leggi e la Conciliazione delle Stresse Fra Loro, Preceduto della Leggi de Roma....coll' Aggiuzione delle Instituzioni de Cajo, dei Frammenti de tutt le Leggi Relative al Diritto Romano, sia che Sieno Mentovate nel Corpo del Diritto sia chi Siano Raccolte in altre Opere, dei Frammenti di Ulpiano, di Paulo e de' Frammenti cosi detti Vaticani. Napoli, 1856, 4to, 10 vols., contemp. 1/2 calf and bds, bit rubbed, beautiful set, only 3 copies of this learned and comprehensive work in the U.S., $345.00

VOET, Johannis, Commentariorum ad Pandectas Libri Quinquaginta, Inquibus, Praeter Romani Juris Principia ac Controversias Illustriores, Jus etiam hodiernum & praecipuae Fori Quaestiones Excutiuntur. 5th edition, revised. nunc primum accedunt Alii duo Tractatus de Familia Erciscunda et de Juri Militari. Venice, 1827-28, sm4to, 7vols., contemp. 1/2 vellum and marbled bds, nice set; according to NUC, no copy of any edition of this work in the U.S., $225.00

VON HALLER, Sigmund (ed.), Encyclopädie der Bayerischen Gesetzgebung. Fürth, 1853-55, roy8vo, 6vols. bound as 3, 2000pp., 1/2 calf, $85.00

VON HOLST, Herman, The Constitutional and Political History of the United States. Chicago, 1889, roy8vo, 8 vols., fine set, $125.00

WEDGWOOD, WM. & HOMANS, I., A Law Manual for Notaries Public & Bankers. NY, 1867, roy8vo, 779pp., later linen, $27.50

--16--

WARREN, Charles, The Supreme Court in United States History. rev. ed. B, 1926, roy8vo, 2vols, 1600pp., $45.00

WENGER, Leopold, Institutes of the Roman Law of Civil Procedure. trans. Fisk, Intro. by Pound, NY, 1940, roy8vo, xxix, 440pp, $25.00

WESTERMARCK, Edw., History of Human Marriage. 5th ed., rev., NY, 1922, roy8vo, 3vols., $65.00

WHITAKER, Rich, Treatise of the Law Relative to Rights of Lien & Stoppage in Transitu. L/NY, 1816, 8 vo, 228pp., bds, rebacked, $35.00

WIENER, Leo, Commentary to the Germanic Laws and Medieval Documents. Harvard Univ. Press, 1915, roy8vo, 224pp., $17.50

WILL, Arthur (of the Chicago Bar), A Treatise on the Law of Circumstantial Evidence. P, 1896, roy8vo, 555pp., roan, $25.00

WILLIAMS, Edw., A Treatise on the Law of Executors and Administrators, with Notes & References to the Decisions of the Courts of this Country, by Francis Troubat, Phil., 1841, roy8vo, 2vols., 1616pp, 1/2 linen, $85.00

WILLOUGHBY. W. Westel, Principles of the Constitutional Law of the United States. NY, 1930, roy8vo, 883pp., $25.00

WILLOUGHBY, W. F., Principles of Judicial Administration. DC, 1929, roy8vo, 622pp., $17.50

THE WILKES CASE: A Collection of the Most Valuable Tracts which Appeared During the Years 1763, 1764, and 1765, Upon the Subjects of General Warrants, Publication of Libels, Seizure of Papers, and Other Constitutional Points, which Arose out of the Case of Mr. Wilkes. London, Printed for J. Almon, 1766, 8vo, 4vols., contemp. calf, bit rubbed, excellent.

One of the most important cases in the history of Anglo-American law, and particularly in the area of civil liberties. Publisher Almon, an associate of Wilkes, was imprisoned & fined for supporting him. This collection, according to Almon's preface, representing both sides of the controversy, contains the following pieces, each with its own title page and individual pagination: (Townshend, Chs.), A Defense of the Minority in the House of Commons on the Question Relating to General Warrants: A Letter to the Public Advertiser; (Almon, J.), A Letter Concerning Libels, Warrants, & Seisure of Papers & Sureties for the Peace or Behaviour; (Somers, John), The Security of Englishmen's Lives; or, the Trust, Power & Duty of Grand Juries of England....; The Trial of John Peter Zenger, of New York, Printer....with a Narrative Of His Case, to Which is Now Added....the Trial of Mr. William Owen, Bookseller; (Hartley, David), The Right of Appeal to Juries in Causes of Excise Asseeted; (Adair, Jas.), Thoughts on the Dismission of Officers, Civil & Military, for Their Conduct in Parliament; A Counter-Address to the Public on the Late Dismission of a General Officer; A Collection of All the Remarkable & Personal Passages in the Briton, North Briton, and Auditor; A Parallel Drawn Between the Administration in the Four Last Years of Queen Anne, & the Four First of George the Third; The Principles of the Changes in 1765 Impartially Examined; (Almon, J.), The History of the Minority During the Years 1762, 1763, 1764 & 1765, Exhibiting the Conduct, Principles & Views of that Party; A True History of a Late Short Administration; An Enquiry into the Conduct of a Late Right Honourable Commoner; An Examination of the Principles....of a Late Right Honourable Gentleman; Short Considerations Upon Some Late Extraordinary Grants; An Appeal to the People of Great Britain on th Conduct of the Present Administration; (Grenville, Geo.), A Speech against the Suspending & Dispensing Prerogative; A Letter to His Grace, the Duke of Grafton, First Commissioner of His Majesty's Treasury. the four volume collection: $850.00

WINKELMAN, Barnie, John G. Johnson: Lawyer & Art Collector, 1841-1917. Univ. of Va. Press, 1942, roy8vo, 327pp., $16.50

WOLDMAN, Albert, Lawyer Lincoln. B/NY, 1936, roy8vo, 347pp., bit faded, $22.50

--17--

WOODBINE, Geo. (ed.), Four Thirteenth Century Law Tracts. Yale Univ. Press, 1910, 8vo, 181pp., $15.00

WRIGHT, Sir Almoth, The Unexpurgated Case Against Woman's Suffrage. NY, 1913, sm8vo, 188pp., $17.50

WRIGHT, David, The Executor's, Administrator's & Guardian Guide. 3rd ed., rev. & enl., Alburn, 1852, 8vo, 408pp., later linen, $35.00

WU, John C., The Fountain of Justice: A study in the Natural Law. NY, 1955, 8vo, 287pp., $16.50

WITTINGHAM, Richard, Martial Justice: The Mass Execution in the U.S. Chicago, 1971, 8vo, 281pp., $14.50

ZEUMER, Carl, Leges Visigothorum Antiquiores. Han/Leip, 1894, roy8vo, 395pp., $25.00

ADDENDA VARIA (INCLUDING LAW)

(French Revolution), Accusator Public, edited by Richer-Serizy,a complete run of 34 numbers (#13 never published), (Paris), 1796-1797, 8vo, 2vols., 572, 576pp., contemp. 1/2 calf and marbled boards, a rare complete run of a very influential periodical, $145.00

BAUHI , Kaspar, Pinax: Theatri Botanici suive index in Theophrasti Dioscoridis Plinii et Botasnicorum quo a seculo scripserunt Opera: Plantarum Circiter Sex Millium ab Ipsis Exhibitarum Nomina cum earundem Synonymijs & Differentijs methodice secundum genera & species proponens, Basil, 1671, 12, 518pp; bound with this is his: Prodpomos Theatri Botanici in quo Plantae Supro Sexcentae ab ipso primum Descriptae cum Plurimus figuris proponuntur. 2nd ed. corr. Basil, 1671, 160pp., with numerous woodcuts in the text; both works bound in one 4to volume in full contemp. vellum, beautiful copy, the major works of a leading botanist of the period, $245.00

BUSINESS HISTORIES AND BIOGRAPHIES, Collection of 100, all different, all bound in cloth, all in very good condition; the lot: $1000.00

Cobbett's Complete Collection of State Trials & Proceeding for High Treason & Other Crimes and Misdemeanors from the Ancient Period to the Present Time. London, 1809, roy8vo, 34vols., contemp. 1/2 calf and marbled bds, light external wear, clean, tight set, $750.00

CONRAD, Joseph, Works, NY, 1926, 8vo, 26 volumes, original linen, rebacked in linen with labels, excellent set, $225.00

Correspondance Originale des Emigres, ou, les Emigres Peint par Eux-Memes. Paris, 1793, roy8vo, 290, 208pp., early 19th century vellum and marbled boards, excellent, with one preliminary leaf, Certificat du Comite de Surete, attesting the authenticity of documents, signed (printed) by Anacharsis Cloots, et al; engraved frontis., $145.00

CRIME, Collection of 100 Titles, all different, all non-fiction, all cloth bound and in very good condition, $850.00

DE FLOTTE, Paul, Souverainete du Peuple: Essais sur l'Espirit de la Revolution. Paris. 1851, roy8vo, 468pp., bds, rebacked, $75.00

DE WITT, David Miller, The Judicial Murder of Mary E. Surratt. Baltimore, Murphy, 1895, 8vo, 259pp., orig. cl., $47.50

DICKSON, Adam, A Treatise on Agriculture. 2nd ed., with large adds. Edinburgh, 1765, 8vo, 2vols., contemp. polished calf, nice set, $150.00

Encyclopedia Britannica, 11th Edition, 1910, 8vo, 29vols. Handy Volume Issue, India Paper, bound in the original full brown morocco, a few very tiny tears very neatly mended, handsome set, $350.00

Encyclopedia Britannic, 11th Edition, 1910, 8vo, 29vols. Handy Volume Issue, India Paper, bound in the original 3/4 Levant morocco, light external wear, nice set. $300.00

--18--

FENELON, Oeuvres de, preceds d'Etudes sur sa Vie par M. Aime-Martin. Paris, 1835, sm4to, 3vols., about 700 (2col.)pp. in each, engraved frontis., contemp. 1/2 calf and marbled boards, raised bands, spines gilt, extremities a trifle worn, $225.00

GOUGENOT-DESMOUSSEAUX, R., Des Proletaires, Necessite et Moyens d'Ameliorer leur Sort. Paris, 1846, 8vo, 568pp., contemp. marbled bds, rebacked, scarce, $150.00

HUGHES, Charles Evans, State of New York: Public Papers of Governor Charles E. Hughes, 1907-1910. Albany, 1908-10, roy8vo, 4vols., $47.50

HUME, David, Four Dissertations. London, 1757, 12mo, (3), 240pp., contemp. calf, new label, half-title present but without the dedication to Hume which was deleted from the first 800 copies printed; thus: first edition and one of the first 800 copies; Rothschild, 1176; Jessop, p.33; $525.00

HUNT, Leigh, Autobiography. London, 1850, 8vo, 3vols., orig. cloth, rebacked and original spines remounted, nice set, first edition, $145.00

JAMES, Henry, Transatlantic Sketches. Boston, Osgood, 1875, 8vo, vi, 401pp., in the original rust-brown cloth, extremities very slightly rubbed, an excellent copy, first edition, Edel & Laurence, A2, $225.00

JENKS, Edw, A Short History of English Law. London 1912, roy8vo, xxxv, 396p, $25.00

JEVONS, W. Stanley, Methods of Social Reform and Other Papers. London, 1883, roy8vo, viii, 383pp., orig. cloth excellent copy, first edition, $150.00

KIPLING, Rudyard, Writings in Prose & Verse. NY, Scribners, 1925ff. roy8vo, 36 volumes, original gilt cloth, fine set, scarce complete, $375.00

LAVISSE, Ernest, Histoire de la France. Paris, 1903, 4to, 9vols., later linen, $175.00

LOCKE, John, Works. Third Ed. London, 1727, tall folio, contemp. calf, skillfully rebacked in calf, raised bands, spines gilt, fine set, engraved frontis, $525.00

LYON, H., & BLOCK, H., Edward Coke: Oracle of the Law. Boston, 1929, roy8vo, 329pp., $20.00

MACDONALD, Geo, How Successful Lawyers were Educated. NY,1896,8vo,127p, $15.00

NATTA, Marco Antonio, Consiliorum sive Responsorum Tomi Quatuor, Opus Optimas Quasque et Quam Maxime Quotidianas Materias Complectens: Ideoque tam in Scholis quam inforo Versantibus, cum Peritis tum Studiosis Iuris eijusque Praxis apprime Necessarium. Frankfurt/M, 1588, tall folio, 4vols. bound as one, 388, 346, 386, 107pp., with very lengthy indexes, contemp. calf, minor external wear, rear hinge a bit cracked but firm, the author was a leading jurist of the period and member of the Pavian school; rare, only one copy recorded in the U.S., $325.00

NECKER, (J.), De l'Administration des Finances de la France. (Paris), 1784, 8vo, 3vols, contemp. calf, all half-titles present, minor cover wear & worming, clean, tight set, first edition, $575.00

PLUTARCH, The Lives and Writings of, edited by Clough & Goodwin, translations revised by Prof. Goodwin, Intro. by Ralph Waldo Emerson. B/NY, 1909, roy8vo, 12vols., orig. cloth with paper labels, #317 of an edition limited to 1000; extra illustrated, uncut & unopened, fine set, $175.00

(SHAKERS), A Summary View of the Millennial Church, or United Society of Believers, (Commonly Called Shakers), Comprising the Rise, Progress and Practical Order of the Society, together with the General Principles of their Faith and Testimony. Albany, 1823, xvi, 320pp., contemp. roan, bit rubbed, else excellent, $125.00

--19--

WALLON, H., Histoire de l'Esclavage dans l'Antiquite. 2nd ed., P, 1879, 8vo, 3vols., some dampstain lower portion of 3, later linen, $75.00

STEPHAN, Henry, Treatise on the Principles of Pleading in Civil Actions. P, 1837, 8vo, 3rd American ed., 8vo, 453pp., later 1/2 linen, $45.00

BORCHARD, Edwin, Convicting the Innocent. NY, 1932, 8vo, 385pp., $15.00

CARB, Alfred, & EDELMAN, R., Bar, Bench & Table: An Arbitral Drama. NY, 1957, roy8vo, 42pp., $14.50

CLARK, Chs., & SHULMAN, A Study of Law Admistration in Connecticut. Yale UP, 1937, roy8vo, 237pp., $16.50

MC LEOD, Grover, Sketches from the Bar. Birmingham, 1967, 8vo, 139pp, $13.50

VON HOLST, Herman, The Constitutional Law of the United States. trans. Mason, C, 1887, roy8vo, 369pp., $17.50

WARNER, Sam, & CABOT, H., Judges & Law Reform. Harvard, 1936, 242pp, $16.50

WILLOUGHBY, Westel, Ethical Basis of Political Authority. NY, 1930,460p,$17.50

WILLOUGHBY, W.F., Principles of Public Adminsitration. JH UP,1927,720pp,$17.50

WILSON, Woodrow, Constitutional Government in the United States. NY, 1908, 8vo, 236pp., orig. cl., first edition, $35.00

WRIGHT, Benjamin, Growth of American Constitutional Law. NY, 1946,8vo, $13.50

WILLIAMS, Glanville, The Sanctity of Life and the Criminal Law. NY, 1958, 8vo, 350pp., $15.00

WATSON, Ruth, & DOWNING, R., Politics of Bench & Bar. NY,1969,8vo,393p,$16.50

WARTON, Michael (ed.), The Nation's Security: The Case of Dt. J. Robert Oppenheimer. L, 1955, 8vo, 398pp., $14.50

VON SHUSCHNIGG, Kurt, International Law. Mil, 1959, roy8vo, 510pp., $15.00

TOUT, T.F., Edward the First. L, 1896, 8vo, 238pp., $13.50

SUTLIFFE, Rob., Impressions of an Average Juryman. NY, 1931,8vo,114pp.,$12.50

NEAVE, F., & TURNER, G., Mozley & Whiteley's Law Dictionary. 5th ed., L, 1930,8vo, 360pp., $15.00

NICHOLS, Egbert (ed.), Congress or the Supreme Court. NY, 1935,8vo,476p,$16.50

NILES, John, Connecticut Civil Officer. H, 1854, 8vo,367pp, later linen,$27.50

NELSON, Marg, Study of Judicial Review in Virginia. NY, 1947, 249pp, $5.00

ROCCA, Fernando, Canonical Procedure. Mil, 1961, 8vo, 384pp., $16.50

SAMUEL, Maurice, Blood Accusation. NY, 1966, 8vo, 286pp., $12.50

STORY, Jos., Commentaries on Equity Jurisprudence. 6th ed., rev. cor. & enl., B, 1853, roy8vo, 2vols., later linen, $85.00

TOBIN, Harold, Termination of Multipartite Treaties. NY, 1933, 8vo,wrps, $7.50

WASHBURN, Emory, Treatise on the American Law of Real Property. B, 1860, roy8vo, vol. I only of 2, later linen, $16.50

RECORDS OF THE FEDERAL CONVENTION OF 1787. ed. Max Farrand, Yale, 1911, 4to, 3vols., later linen, $75.00

TAFT, Geo., Compilation of Senate Election Cases, 1789-1885. (49th Con, 1st Ses, Misc. Docs. 47), DC, 1885, roy8vo, 654pp., $22.50

TAYLOR, John, Memoir of His Honor Samual Phillips, LL.D. B, 1856, roy8vo, 391pp., orig. cl., reb & spine remounted, $35.00

Treaties Between the United States of America and the Several Indian Tribes. DC, 1837, roy8vo, lxxxiii, 699pp., contemp. 1/2 calf & marbled bds, $145.00

WARDEN, Lewis, Life of Blackstone. Charlottesville, 1938, roy8vo,451pp, $27.50

--20--

ALVERSTONE, Rt. Hon, Recollections of Bar & Bench. NY/L, 1915, 331pp, $25.00

AMES, Jas. Barr, A Selection of Cases on Pleading at Common Law....Cambridge, 1875, roy8vo, 299pp., contemp. cl, fine, first edition, scarce, $75.00

BATES, Er., Story of the Supreme Court. NY, 1936, 8vo, 377pp, $16.50

BLACK, Hugo, One Man's Stand for Freedom. ed. Dillard, NY, 1963, 504pp, $17.50

BLANSHARD, Paul, The Right to Read. B, 1955, 8vo, 339pp., $14.50

BLAUSTEIN, Alb, The American Lawyer. Univ. Chicago, 1954, 8vo, 360pp, $17.50

BOWKER, A.E., Behind the Bar. 2nd ed., NY, 1951, 8vo, 323pp., $16.50

BRANDT, Irv., James Madison: 1787-1800. Ind, 1950, roy8vo, 520pp., $22.50

BRUMBAUGH, Jesse, Legal Reasoning & Briefing. Indi, 1917,roy8vo,775pp., $25.00

BUSCH, Francis, Prisoners at the Bar. Ind, 1952, 8vo, 288pp;, $15.50

CAMPBELL, Lord, Lives of the Lord Chancellors & Keepers of the Great Seal of England. 7th ed., NY, 1878, 8vo, 10vols., $115.00

CANFIELD, Geo & DALZELL, The Law of the Sea. NY, 1921, 8vo, 315pp., $16.50

CERNY, Joe, Courtroom Know-How. Cincinnati, 1958, roy8vo, 326pp., $17.50

CONNELL, John, A Treatise on the Law of Scotland Respecting the Erection, Union....of Parishes. Edin, 1818, 8vo, 547, 75pp, contemp. calf, bit scuffed & hinges tender, $37.50

CONRAD, Earl, Mr. Seward for the Defense. NY, 1956, 8vo, 306pp., $15.00

EDWARDS, Gus., Legal Laughs. Ga, 1915, roy8vo, 416pp., $15.00

GOODEN, Francis, Laughter is Legal. Ny, 1951, 8vo, 280pp., $13.50

GOODNOW, Frank, Social Reform & the Constitution. NY, 1911, 8vo, 365pp, $15.00

HOFFMAN, Paul, What the Hell is Justice. C, 1974, 8vo, 247pp., $12.50

HONNOLD, John (ed.), The Life of the Law. Glencoe, 1964, roy8vo,581pp., $22.50

HOWARD, Pendleton, Criminal Justice in England. NY, 1931, 8vo, 436pp., $16.50

HUIE, Wm., The Execution of Private Slovik. NY, 1954, 8vo,247pp,scarce, $16.50

HYDE, H.M., Lord Justice. NY, 1965, roy8vo, 638pp., $16.50

JACKSON, Percival, Justice & the Law. Va., 1960, roy8vo, 620pp., $17.50

KINGSTON, Chs., The Bench & the Dock. NY, 1925, 8vo, 290pp., $17.50

KOESSLER, Arthur, Masterpieces of Legal Fiction. Ro, 1964, roy8vo,862pp,$26.50

KUHN, Arthur, Comparative Commentaries on Private International Law or Conflict of Laws. NY, 1937, roy8vo, 381pp., $17.50

LEOPOLD, Nathan, Life Plus 99 Years. NY, 1958, roy8vo, 381pp., $17.50

LYON, Hastings, The Constitution & Men who Made It. B, 1936, 314pp., $17.50

MARTIN, Sanford, Life of Joseph Hodges Choate. L, 1920, roy8vo, 2vols., $27.50

MAYERS. Lewis, American Legal System. rev. ed., NY, 1964, roy8vo,594pp, $22.50

NEALE, J.E. Elizabeth the First & Her Parliments, 1559-1581. NY, 1958, 8vo, 452pp., $16.50

NEALE, J.E., Elizabeth I & Her Parliments, 1584-1601. NY,1958,8vo,452pp,$16.50

NIZER, Louis, My Life in Court. NY, 1961, roy8vo, 524pp., $16.50

O'DONNELL, Bern, Old Bailey & Its Trials. L, 1950, 8vo, 305pp., $14.50

PECK, David, The Greer Case. NY, 1955, 8vo, 209pp., $12.50

PLAYFAIR, G. & SINGLETON, The Offenders. NY, 1957, 8vo, 305pp., $14.50

RADIN, Max, The Law & Mr. Smith. Ind, 1938, roy8vo, 333pp., $17.50

CATALOGUE 29

LAW January, 1981

WITH AN ADDENDA OF VARIA

Including: Webster's Dictionary (1828); Wallace's Population (1753); the first American Das Kapital; the first Collected Freud; Fine Bindings; Cuvier's Theory of the Earth (1813).

RICHARD ADAMIAK
1545 EAST 60th St.
CHICAGO, ILL. 6063
312-955-4571
(By phone: 8-11AM
& by chance

S OF SALE: Prices are net, postage extra; all books returnable upon receipt for any reason. Deferred remittance for institutions; Past private purchasers are expected to remit without undue delay. New private purchasers may be asked to remit upon receipt of a pro-forma invoice.

: We buy single volumes and collections in all fields, including law, for cash or credit; we also buy institutional duplicates. We will pay the indicated prices for the first good copies offered of the following odd volumes: Blackstone, Commentaries, P, 1772, vol 3, $500.00; Kent, Commentaries on American Law, 1830, vol 4; Story, Commentaries on the Constitution, 1833, vol 2, $300.00 each. We do appraisals.

Abridgment of the Debates of Congress from 1789 to 1856, by the Author of the Thirty Years View. (Th. Benton), NY/L, 1857, 4to, 16vols., contemp. 1/2 morocco, bit rubbed, sound set, $550.00

ADAMS, John, The Doctrine of Equity...2nd American ed. w/Notes & References to the Latest American Chancery Decisions by Jas. Ludlow & John Collins. P, 1852, roy8vo, 760pp., contemp. roan, bit rubbed, $47.50

ADDISON, Alexander, Reports of Cases in the County Courts of the Fifth Circuit & in the High Court of Errors & Appeals, of the State of Pennsylvania: and Charges to Grand Juries of those County Courts, by Alexander Addison, President of the Court of Common Pleas. DC, 1800, 8vo, 396,318pp.,contemp. roan, bit scuffed, tight, beautiful copy, scarce, $325.00
Before the Republicans began their attack on the national level against the Federalist judiciary,which culminated in the impeachment of Chase, they took action in Pennsylvania. Addison's aggressive Federalist views, contained in the Charges, infuriated the Republicans who impeached and removed him in the celebrated action. The Charges in fact have little to do with matters at hand but taken together thry constitute a disquisition on government from the Federalist standpoint, written with, clarity, cogency & erudition. The Charge "had not the least reference to any business before the court and were no more appropriate than sermons. They were, however, written with uncommon ability. It is doubtful whether any arguments more weighty have sincebeen produced against what Geo. Cabot called 'excessive democracy.'" Beveridge, Life of John Marshall, III, 46; Addison sent one of the Charges, entitled "A Defence of the Alien Act," to Geo. Washington and the latter, in a letter printed on the verso of the title, responded with approbation.

ALEXANDER, Jas., A Brief Narrative of the Case & Trial of John Peter Zenger. Harvard, 1963, 8vo, 238pp., $17.50

ALLEN, Sir C. K., Law & Orders. L, 1965, 8vo, 412pp., $20.00

ALSOP, Jos. & STEW, We Accuse! NY, 1954, 8vo, 88pp., orig. wrps, $16.50

ALTON, Edmond, Among the Law Makers. NY, 1905, 8vo, 308pp., $16.50

AMERICAN PEACE SOCIETY, Prize Essays on a Congress of Nations. B,1840,8vo,706pp. $37.50

AMES, Jas. Barr, Lectures on Legal History.. Harvard, 1913, 4to, 552pp, $37.50

--2--

AMES, Jas. Barr, A Selection of Cases in Equity Jurisdiction.. Vol. I, Pts, 1-6, Harvard Law Rev., 1904, 8vo, 665pp., sporad. pencil underlineing, $17.50

ANDREWS, F. E., Legal Instruments of Foundations. NY, 1958, 8vo, 318pp, $17.50

ANTIEAU, Chs., Freedom from Federal Establishment.Mil, 1964,8vo, 272pp, $17.50

APPLEMAN, John, Cross-Examination. Va, 1963, 8vo, 226pp., $17.50

ASSN OF THE BAR OF THE CITY OF NY, Conflict of Interest & Federal Service. Harvard, 1960, roy8vo, 336pp., $18.50

AUERBACH, Jos., The Bar of Other Days. NY, 1940, roy8vo, 364pp., $25.00

AUERBACH, Jos., De Lancy Nicol. NY, 1931, 8vo, 125pp., $14.50

AUSTIN, John, Province of Jurisprudence Determined. intro. H.L.A. Hart, NY, 1954, 8vo, 396pp., $20.00

AUSTIN, John, Lectures on Jurisprudence. 4th ed, rev, L, 1873, 8vo,2vols.$75.00

BACON, Francis, Works of, P, 1859, small 4to, 3vols., sl. wear, nice set,$135.00

An Account of the Life & Times of Francis Bacon Extracted from the Edition of His Occasional Writings by Jas. Spedding. B, 1878, 8vo, 2vols., $57.50

BAILEY, Step., Congress Makes a Law. Columbia, 1950, 8vo, 282pp., $17.50

BAKAL, Carl, The Right to Bear Arms. NY, 1966, 8vo, 392pp., $17.50

BAKER, Eliz, Henry Wheaton. Unv Penn Pr, 1937, roy8vo, 425pp., $27.50

BALLARD, Emerson (ed.), The Cream of the Law. Crawfordsville, Indiana, Vol. I, No. 1 (Jan, 1905) to Vol. II, No. 4 (Oct, 1906), 2vols., $65.00

BANCROFT, Geo., Historyof the Formation of the Constitution of the United States. NY, 1896, 8vo, 495pp., $25.00

BANCROFT-WHITNEY CO., "Exposition Catalogue of Law Books" 1912, w/Supp, 1916, 8vo, 63,231pp., later linen with orig. wrps bound in, $27.50

BARBOSA, Augustinus, Lusitani, (Portugese, 1590-1649), Tractatus Varii: I; De Axiomatibus; II; De Appelativa; IIIDe Locis; IV; De Causulis; V; De Dictionibus. Lugduni, 1644, folio, 818pp., engraved title & dedication leaf, later 1/2 calf & bds, $300.00

BARRY, Rich, Mr. Rutledge of South Carolina. NY, 1942, 8vo, 430pp., $17.50

BARTLEY, Ernest, Tidelands Oil Controversy. Univ. of Texas,1953, 8vo,312p,$17.50

BARTON, Chs., An Historical Treatise of a Suit in Equity.... Dublin, 1796, 8vo, 44,227pp., contemp.roan, bit scuffed, $75.00

BARTON, D. P. et al, Story of the Inns of Court. B/NY, 1928, 8vo, 320pp, $25.00

BEARD, Chs. & Mary, American Citizenship. NY, 1918, 8vo, 330pp., $13.50

BECK, Jas, Evidence in the Case (War Guilt)rev. ed, NY, 1915, 8vo, 275pp,$22.50

BEDFORD, Sybille, Trial of Dr. Adams. NY, 1959, 8vo, 245pp., $14.50

BELLI, Melvin, Ready for the Plaintiff. NY, 1956, 8vo, 338pp., $17.50

BELLI, Melvin, The Law Revolution, I. LA, 1961, roy8vo, 288pp., $17.50

BEMIS, Samuel, American Secretaries of State. NY, 1929, 8vo, 9vols., $75.00

BENNETT, Edmund, Farm Law. Portland, 1880, 8vo, 120pp., $12.50

BENNETT, Edmund, Four Gospels from a Lawyer's Standpoint. B, 1899, 12mo,$12.50

BENT, Silas, Justice Oliver Wendell Holmes. NY, 1932, roy8vo, 386pp., $17.50

BENTON, Wilbourn, Nuremberg: German Views. Dallas, 1955, 8vo, 232pp., $17.50

BENTHAM, Jeremy, The Rationale of Punishment. L, 1830, 8vo, xv,441pp., bound in contemp. 1/2 calf & linen, first edition in English, $275.00

BERGER, Raoul, Impeachment. Harvard, 1973, 8vo, 345pp., $12.50

--3--

BERKMAN, Ted., The Lady & the Law. B, 1976, 8vo, 403pp., $17.50

BERLE, Adolf, Three Faces of Power. NY, 1967, 8vo, 83pp., $14.50

BERNSTEIN, Vic., Final Judgment: Story of Nuremberg. NY, 1947, 8vo, 289p, $20.00

BEVERIDGE, Albert, Life of John Marshall. B, 1916, 8vo, 4vols as 2, $57.50

BICKEL, Alex, Politics & the Warren Court. NY, 1965, 8vo, 299pp., $15.50

BICKNELL, Geo., Practice of the Superior Courts of Indiana in Criminal Cases. Cincinnati, 1866, roy8vo, 517pp., later 1/2 linen, $45.00

BIDDLE, Francis, Mr. Justice Holmes. NY, 1942, 8vo, 214pp., $13.50

BIGELOW, Melville, Law of Bills, Notes & Cheques. 2nd ed,,B, 1900, 349pp,$27.50

BIGELOW, M, Treatise on the Law of Fraud. B, 1888, roy8vo, 714pp., $30.00

BIGELOW, M., Treatise on the Law of Estoppel. 6th ed., rev, B, 1913, 4to, $27.50

BILLIAS, Geo. (ed), Law & Authority in Colonial America. Barre,1965,208p, $16.50

BLACKSTONE, Sir William, Commentaries on the Laws of England...with Notes & Add by Edw. Christian. Portland, 1807, 8vo, 4vols., contemp. roan, rebacked in calf, sporadic foxing, handsome set, $275.00

BLACKSTONE, Sir William, Commentaries on the Laws of England....by Thomas M. Cooley, 3rd ed., rev., C, 1884, roy8vo, 4vols., bound (as issued), as 2, later 1/2 linen, $125.00

BLACKSTONE, Sir William, Commentaries on the Laws of England....with Notes by John Frederick Archbold, L, 1811, roy8vo, 4vols., original binders boards, extertly rebacked inclaf, uncut, largevpaper capy, rare edition, $375.00

BLAND, A., et al (eds.), English Economic History: Select Documents. 2nd ed., L, 1915, 8vo, 730pp., $22.50

BLANSHARD, Paul, Religion in the Schools. B, 1963, 8vo, 265pp., $16.50

BLAUSTEIN, Alb. (ed.), Fiction Goes to Court. NY, 1954 ,8vo, 303pp., $17.50

BLESSIN, Geo., et al, Bundesentschädigunggesetze. 2nd ed, reb., M/B, 1957, roy8vo, 1321pp., $30.00

BLOOMSTEIN, Morris, Verdict: The Jury System. NY, 1968, 8vo, 176pp., $16.50

BONNER, Rob., Lawyers & Litigants in Ancient Athens. NY, 1927, 8vo, 276p, $14.50

BORCHARD, Edwin, Diplomatic Protection of Citizens Abroad. NY, 1916, 988p,$35.00

BORCHARD, Edwin, Guide to the Law & Legal Literature of Germany.DC, 1912,4to, 226pp., $27.50

BOUTMY, Emile, The English Constitution. Intro. by Pollock, L, 1891,8vo, $22.50

BRADLEY, Hon. Jos. Miscellaneous Writings. Newark, 1902, roy8vo, 435pp, $30.00

BOWLER, E. C., An Album of the Attornies of Rhode Island.... Bethel, 1904, roy8vo, 208pp., later linen, $27.50

BRANDT, Irving, The Bill of Rights. NY,1965,roy8vo, 565pp., $25.00

BOVEE, Marvin, Reasons for Abolishing Capital Punishment. C, 1878, 8vo, 328pp., sl. worn, $27.50

BRANDT, Irving, Story over the Constitution. Ind, 1936, 8vo, 294pp, $17.50

BRANTLEY, Wm., Chief Justice Stone of Alabama. Blim, 1943, roy8vo, 286pp,$22.50

BRIGGS, Herbert, The Law of Nations: Cases.. NY, 1938, roy8vo, 984pp., $25.00

BRISSAUD, Jan, History of French Public Law. B, 1915, roy8vo, 649pp., $30.00

BRITTON, An English Translation & Notes by Francis Nichols. Dc, 1901, roy8vo, 649pp., $45.00

BROUGHAM, Henry Lord, The British Constitution. L, 1844, 132pp, rebacked, $45.0

--4--

BROOM, Herbert, Commentaries on the Common Law. P, 1856, roy8vo, 674pp., later 1/2 linen, scarce, $75.00

BROWN, Alexander (ed.), Genesis of the United States. B, 1890, roy8vo, 2vols., few maps mended, $75.00

BROWN, Basil, Law Sports at Gray's Inn. NY, Priv. Pub., 1921, 8vo, xciv,188,88p, orig. 1/2 linen & bds, sl.wear & sl. soil, $30.00

BROWN, Esther, Lawyers & the Promotion of Justice. NY, 1938, 8vo, 292pp, $17.50

BROWN, Jethro, Underlying Principles of Modern Legislation. L, 1917, 8vo, $17.50

BROWN, Wm., Life of Oliver Ellsworth. NY, 1905, roy8vo, 369pp., $27.50

BROWNE, J. H. B., Medical Jurisprudence of Insanity. 2nd ed, SF, 1875,713p,$37.5

BROWNELL, Emery, Legal Aid in the US. Ro, 1951, 8vo, 333pp., $22.50

BRUNNER, Emil, Justice & the Social Order. NY, 1945, 8vo, 304pp., $14.50

BRYCE, Jas., American Commonwealth. 3rd ed., rev. & enl., NY, 1908, 8vo, 2vols., fine, $30.00

BRYCE, Jas., Impressions of South Africa. 3rd ed, rev, L, 1899, 8vo, 499p,$27.50

BRYCE, Jas., Treatment of Armenians in the Ottoman Empire. L, 1916, 8vo, $27.50

HORTON, R. G., Life & Public Services of James Buchanan. NY, 1856, 8vo, 428pp., $27.50

BUCHLER, Sam, "Cohen Comes First" & Other Cases. NY, 1933, 8vo, 256pp., worn dust jacket pasted to covers, sl.worn, $22.50

BUCKLAND, W., Some Reflections on Jurisprudence. Camb, 1945, 8vo, 118pp., $14.50

BUCKLAND, W. & MC NAIR, Roman Law & Common Law. 2nd ed., rev. by Lawson, Camb, 1965, 8vo, 439pp., $27.50

BUCKLAND, W., Main Institutions of Roman Private Law. Camb, 1931, 8vo,410p, $27.

BULLER, Francis, Introduction to the Law Relative to Trials at Nisi Prius.5th ed., L, 1788, 8vo, 336pp., contemp. calf, expertly rehinged, $65.00

BURGESS, John, Recent Changes in American Const. Theory. NY, 1923, 8vo,115p,$13.

BURKE, Edmund, Works. London, 1886, 8vo, 8vols., later linen, $95.00

BURRILL, Alexander, A Law Dictionary & Glossary... 2nd ed., NY, 1859-60, 4to, 2vols., later buck, splendid work, scarce, $85.00

BURROW, Sir Jas., Reports of Cases Argued & Adjudged in the Court of King's Bench... Dublin, 1794, 8vo, 5vols., contemp.roan, sl. worn, nice set, $250.00

BURTT, Harold, Legal Psychology. NY, 1931, roy8vo, 467pp., $17.50

BUTLER, Chs., Century at the Bar of the Supreme Court. NY, 1942, 8vo, 222p, $17.

BUTLER, Geoffrey, Handbook of the League of Nations. L, 1919, 8vo, 90pp, $12.50

BUTT, Ronald, The Power of Parliament. NY, 1967, 8vo, 468pp., $20.00

BUTTS, I.R. The Seaman's Assistant... B, 1849, 12mo, 108pp, lat. lin, $27.50

BUTTS, I. R., Improved Edition of the Landlord & Tenant's Asst.. B, 1848, 12mo, 108pp., later linen, $27.50

BUTTS, I.R.,Business Man's Asst...B, 1849, 12mo, 108pp., later linen, $27.50

BUTTS, I. R., Creditor's & Debtor's Asst.... B, 1849, 12mo, 108pp., $27.50

BUTTS, I. R., Shipper & Carrier's Asst.... B, 1849,12mo, 108pp.,lat. lin, $27.50

CAHN, Edmund, The Sense of Injustice. NYU, 1949, 8vo, 186pp., $15.50

CAIN, N. R., War Contracts. NY, 1945, roy8vo, 809pp., sl. soil, $22.50

CALCOTT, Mary, Russian Justice. NY, 1935, 8vo, 265pp., $17.50

CALVOCORESSI, Peter, Nuremberg. NY, 1948, 8vo, 176pp., $17.50

--5--

The Life of John Lord Campbell, edited by His Daughter, Mrs. Hardcastle. Jersey City, 1881, roy8vo, 2vols., $57.50

CAMPBELL, W. E. (ed.), Last Letters of Blessed Thomas More. L,1924, 123p,$15.50

CANNING, Geo., Select Speeches..P, 1835, 8vo, 583pp, roan, rubbed, $37.50

CANTOR, Nathan, Criminals & Criminal Justice. NY, 1932, 8vo, 470pp., $17.50

CARDOZO, Nathan, Selected Writings. NY, 1947, 8vo, 456pp., $22.50

CARPZOV, Benedict, Practicae Novae Imperalis Saxonicae Rerum Criminalum.... Leipzig/Frankfurt, 1695, folio, three vols bound (as issued) as 1; 334, 345, 406pp., separate titles, engraved frontis, text in Latin & German, the latter in black letter, light sporadic foxing & trace of browning, bound in later 1/2 calf & marbled bds, major work of one of the most distinguished jurists of the period, $335.00

CARROLL, Donald, Handbook for Judges. C, 1961, 8vo, 195pp., $17.50

CARSON, Hampton, The Supreme Court of the US; Its History & Centennial Celebration. P, 1891, small folio, 744pp., with 54 etchings of all the justices to that date, original buckram, $125.00

CARSON, Hampton, History of the Supreme Court of the United States... P, 1902, 4to 2vols., contemp. 1/2 morocco & linen, ill. with steel engravings,$125.0

CARTER, Orrin, Ethics of the Legal Profession. C, 1915, 8vo, 116pp., $22.50

Celebrated Speeches of Chatam, Burke & Erskine....P, 1835, 8vo, 540pp., later linen, $35.00

CHAFFEE, Zechariah, Three Human Rights in the Constitution of 1787. Univ. of Kansas, 1956, 8vo, 245pp., $14.50

CHAFFEE, Zech., Some Problems of Equity. Ann Arbor, 1950, 8vo, 441pp., $17.50

CHAFFEE, Zech., The Blessings of Liberty. P, 1956, 8vo, 350pp., $19.50

The Challenge of Crime in a Free Society. DC, GPO, 1967, 4to, 340pp., $17.50

Charges against the Doorkeeper of the House (John W. Polk) 45th Con, 2nd Ses, HR#422, 399pp; bound with: Report, Senate, 42nd Con, 3rd Ses, Rep#519 (Credit Mobilier), 161pp; and with: House of Reps: Inquiry into Impeachment in Credit Mobilier Testimony. 42nd Con, 3rd Ses, Rep#481; all in one 8vo, volume, contemp. 1/2 morocco, scuffed but tight, $35.00

Charters & General Laws of the Colony & Province of Massachusettes Bay.... Boston, 1814, roy8vo, 868pp., contemp. roan, rehinged, bit scuffed, $125.00

CHEATHAM, Elliot, Cases & Materials on the Legal Profession. C, 1938, 4to, 558pp., penciled, $22.50

CHESHIRE, G.C., Modern Law of Real Property. 10th ed, L, 1967, roy8vo,901p $22.

CHICAGO LAW INSTITUTE: Index Catalogue of the Library to Dec 31st, 1901. C, 1902, roy8vo, 699pp., later linen, $75.00

__________, Subject Index, 1902-1927. roy8vo, 264pp., $37.50

CHOATE, Rufus, Works of. B, 1862, roy8vo, 2vols., $47.50

PARKER, Edw., Reminiscences of Rufus Choate. NY, 1860, 8vo, 522pp, shaken,$30.0

NEILSON, Jos., Memories of Rufus Choate.B, 1884, roy8vo, 400pp., $25.00

CHUTE, Chs, Crime, Courts & Probation. NY, 1956, 8vo, 268pp., $17.50

CICERO, Works. London, 1812-29. various translators; as follows: Last Two Pleadings against Verres; Letters to Severalof His Friends; (2vols.) On Oratory & Orators (2vols); Old Age & Friendship; Orations (2vols); Letters to Atticus (2vols); Tusculan Disputations; De Finibus; The Nature of the Gods; The Officiis; Life of Cicero by Middleton. together 17vols. uniformly bpund in contemp. 1/2 calf & marbled bds, raised bands, spines gilt, contrasting labels, beautiful set, $375.00

--o--

The Civil Rights Act of 1964; Text. DC, 1964, roy8vo, 424pp., $22.50

CLARKE, Wm., The Soul of the Law. B, 1942, 8vo, 582pp., $18.50

COCKBURN, J.S., History of the English Assizes, 1558-1714. Cambridge UP, 1972, 8vo, 372pp., $25.00

COHEN, Louis, Murder, Madness & the Law. Cl, 1952, 8vo, 173pp., $16.50

COLERIDGE, S. T., On the Constitution of the Church & State.... Lay Sermons. L, 1839, 12mo, xxix,430pp., orig. cl., label worn, $37.50

COLLIE, Sir John, Fraud inMedico-Legal Practice. L, 1932, 8vo, 276p, $17.50

COMFORT, W.W., The Clermont Assizes of 1665. Pa, 1937, 8vo, 291pp., $17.50

COMMAGER, Henry, Freedom & Order. NY, 1966, 320pp., $17.50

A Complete Collection of State Trials & Proceedings for High Treason....4th ed. with New Prefaceby Francis Hargrave. L, 1776, folio, 11vols., contemp. marbled bds, rebacked in linen, $475.00

CONE, Al.,& LAWLER, Art of Persuasion in Litigation. Da, 1966, 366pp, $18.50

57th Con, 2nd Ses, HR Doc 431, State Papers & Correspondence Bearing upon the Purchase of the Territory of Louisiana. DC, GPO, 1903, roy8vo, 299p, $27.50

COOK, Wm., American Institutions & Their Preservation. 2nd ed., NY, 1929, roy8vo, 2vols., $30.00

COOLEY, Thomas, Treatise on the Constitutional Limitations....8th ed., B, 1927, 4to, 2vols., $47.50

COOLEY, Th. M., Treatise on the Law of Torts. StuEd, C, 1907, 8vo, 820p, $17.50

COOLEY, Th. M., The Law of Taxation. 4th ed., C, 1924, 4to, 4vols., $100.00

COOPER, Kent, The Right to Know. NY, 1956, 8vo, 335pp., $17.50

COUDERT, Frederic, Certainty & Justice. NY, 1914, 8vo, 319pp., $17.50

COUNTRYMAN, Edwin, The Supreme Court of the United States.... Albany, 1913, 8vo, 282pp., inscribed, $18.50

COHEN, Zelman & CARTER, Essays on the Law of Evidence. Oxford,1956, 8vo, $22.50

COWLES, Willard, Treaties & Constitutional Law. DC, 1941, roy8vo, 315pp,$17.50

COWPER, Henry, Reports of Cases Adjudged in the Court of King's Bench.... Dublin, 1788, roy8vo, 846pp., contemp. calf, rebacked, $96.00

CRABB, Geo., A History of English Law. L, 1829, 8vo, 579pp, later calf, $95.00

CRANE, Wm., & MOSES, Politics. NY, 1884, 8vo, 305pp., $17.50

CRAWFORD, Earl, The Construction of Statutes. StL, 1940, 4to, 1008pp, $25.00

CRESEE, F. A., Practical Pointers for Patenters. NY, 1902, 12mo, 144pp, $14.50

CURRAN, John A., Reminiscences of... L, 1915, roy8vo, 300pp., $25.00

CURRAN, Rt. Hon. John P., Speeches of... Dublin, 1811, 8vo, 486p, buck, $35.00

CURTIS, Geo. T., Constitutional History of the US. NY, 1895-6, roy8vo, 2v, $57.

CUSHING, Caleb, Treaty of Washington. NY, 1873, 8vo, 280p, ex lib, $20.00

CUSHING, Harry, Voting Trusts. rev. ed., NY, 1927, 8vo, 257pp., $17.50

CUSHMAN, Rob., Civil Liberties in the US. Ithaca, 1956, 8vo, 248pp., $12.50

CZERNIN, Ferd, Versailles, 1919. NY, 1964, 8vo, 437pp., $18.50

DARROW, Clarence, Verdicts Out of Court. C, 1963, roy8vo, 448pp., $18.50

DARROW, Clarence, Story of My Life. NY, 1932, roy8vo, 465pp., orig. cl., spine lettering faded, signed by Darrow, first edition, $47.50

DARROW, Clarence, Farmington. C, 1904, 8vo, 277pp., orig. pict. cl., first edition, excellent, $75.00

--7--

DARROW, Clarence, Attorney for the Damned. NY, 1957, roy8vo, 552pp, $18.50

DAVIDSON, Eugene, Trial of the Germans. NY, 1966, roy8vo, 636pp., $22.50

DAVIS, Geo. B., Elements of International Law. 4thed, NY, 1916, 8vo,668p,$22.50

DAVIS, Geo., Treatise on the Military Laws of the United States. NY, 1898, roy8vo, 754pp., $25.00

DEAN, Amos, A Manual of Law for the Use of Businessmen. Albany, 1838, 12mo, 242pp., later linen, $35.00

DEAN, Jos., Hatred, Ridicule or Contempt. NY, 1954, 8vo, 271pp., $15.00

DECLAREUIL, J., Rome the Law Giver. NY, 1926, roy8vo, 400pp., $22.50

Dedicatory Exercises of the Law Quadrangle, University of Michigan Law School 1934, 4to, 106pp., $27.50

DE MADRIAGA, Salvadore, Disarmament. NY, 1929, roy8vo, 378pp., $17.50

DE TOCQUEVILLE, Alexis, Democracy in America, trans. Henry Reeve, with an Original Preface & Notes by John C. Spencer. 2nd American ed., NY, 1838, roy8vo, xxvii,464pp., later 1/2 linen, important edition, $75.00

DE TOCQUEVILLE, Alexis, De la Democratie en Amerique. Vol.I: Paris Gosselin, 1836 (4th ed.); Vol.II: Paris, Gosselin, 1840, first edition; the four volumes bound (as issued) as two, both in contemp. matched marbled bds, rebacked in calf; early and first editions of the French edition are quite scarce, $285.00

DEUTSCH, Sam, & BALICER, How to Prove a Prima Facie Case.NY, 1928, 616p, $25.00

DE VISSCHER, Ch., Belgium's Case. L, 1916, 8vo, 164pp., $17.50

DEVLIN, Pat, The Criminal Prosecutor in England. Yale, 1958, 8vo, 150p., $15.50

DEWITT, David, Impeachment & Trial of Andrew Johnson. NY, 1903, 8vo,646p, $22.5

DICEY, A. V., Lectures on the Relation between Law & Public Opinion in England During the 19th Century. L, 1905, roy8vo, 503pp., $22.50

DICKERSON, Reed, Legislative Drafting. B, 1954, 8vo, 149pp., $17.50

DIEBOLD, Wm., The Schuman Plan. NY, 1959, 8vo, 750pp., $22.50

DIGBY, K. E., Introduction to the History of the Law of Real Property. 5th ed., Oxford, 1897, $22.50

DILNOT, Geo., Trial of the Detectives. NY, 1928, roy8vo, 301pp., $16.50

DIXON, Hepworth, John Howard & the Prison World of Europe....sl. abridged. Webster, Mass, 1852, 8vo, 441pp., orig. cl., rebacked, $37.50

DODD, Walter, Administration of Workman's Compensation. NY, 1936, 845pp,$25.00

DONALDSON, Sam, The Roentgenologist in Court. Ill, 1954, 8vo, 348pp, $17.50

DONALDSON, Th., The Public Domain. (1884), Rep: 1970, roy8vo, 1343pp, $27.50

DONOVAN, J. W., Tact in Court. L, 1915, 8vo, 182pp., $17.50

DONOVAN, J. W., Art of Advocates & Public Speaking. Ro, 1905, 8vo, 145p, $16.50

DORMAN, Michael, King of the Courtroom. NY, 1969, 8vo, 327pp., $16.50

DORSEN, Norman, Disorder in the Court...NY, 1973, roy8vo, 432pp., $17.50

DOUGLAS, Wm. O., We the Judges. NY, 1956, 8vo, 480pp., first edition, $27.50

DOUGLAS, Wm. O., Of Men and Mountains. NY, 1950, 8vo, 338pp., $17.50

DREYFUS, Alfred, The Dreyfus Case. Yale, 1937, roy8vo, 303pp., $18.50

DRUMMOND, Isabel, The Sex Paradox. NY, 1953, 8vo, 369pp., $17.50

DUNCAN, John, The Strangest Cases on Record. C, 1940, roy8vo, 272pp., $17.50

DUNNE, Gerald, Justice Joseph Story. NY, 1970, 8vo, 458pp., $16.50

DWARRIS, Fortunatus, A General Treatise on Statutes & Their Rules of Construction. P, 1835, 8vo, 100pp., later linen, $45.00

DYKSTRA, Gerald, The Business Law of Aviation. NY, 1946, 8vo, 523pp., $22.50

EARLE, Walter, Mr Sherman & Mr. Sterling & How They Grew. NY, 1963, 443p.$20.0

EDWARDS, Kathleen, English Secular Cathedrals in the Middle Ages: A Constitutional Study. Manchester UP, 1949, 8vo, 413pp., $22.50

EHRLICH, J. W., A Life in My Hands. NY, 1965, roy8vo, 379pp., $17.50

EHRLICH, J. W., Ehrlich's Blackstone, San Carlos, 1959, roy8vo, 987pp., $27.50

EHRLICH, Walter, Fundamental Principles of the Sociology of Law. trans. Moll, Intro. by Pound, Harvard, 1936, 8vo, 541pp., $25.00

EHRMANN, Herb., The Case that Will Not Die. B, 1969, roy8vo, 518pp., $22.50

ELLIOT, Byron, & ELLIOT, The Work of the Advocate. Ind, 1911, 8vo,605p, $27.50

ELLIS, Wm., Jonathan Blair. Cl/NY, 1954, roy8vo, 464pp., $17.50

ELTON, G. R., Star Chamber Stories. L, 1974, 8vo, 244pp., $15,50

ELY, Richard, Property & Contract. NY, 1914, 8vo, 2vols., $20.00

The Enduring Federalist, edited by Chs. A Beard. NY, 1948, 8vo, 391pp, $17.50

(ERASMUS), The Complaint of Peace...B, 1813, 8vo, 160pp., roan, $37.50

ERBSTEIN, Chs., The Show-Up. C, 1926, 8vo, 243pp., $16.50

ERNST, Morris, & SCHWARTZ, A., Censorship. NY, 1964, 8vo, 243pp., $16.50

ESMEIN, A/, History of Continental Criminal Procedure. B, 1913, 640pp, $30.00

Essays on Jurisprudence from the Columbia Law Review. 1963, 4to, 413p, $22.50

FEAVER, Geo., From Status to Contract. L, 1969, 8vo, 366pp., $25.00

The Federalist, ed. w/Notes by Cooke. Wesleyan UP, 1961, roy8vo, 672pp, $25.00

The Federalist...A New Edition with the Names & Portraits of the Several Writers. P, 1818, 8vo, 504pp., later 1/2 calf & bds, $95.00

The Federalist, on the New Constitution....A New Edition, the Numbers Written By Mr. Madison Corrected by Himself. Washington, 1818, 8vo, 671pp., contemp. tree calf, extremeties slightly worn but a very sound copy, $750.00

The Federalist....P, 1866, roy8vo, clxv,659pp., $75.00

FELIX, David, Protest: Sacco-Vanzetti...Indiana, 1965, 8vo, 274pp., $16.50

FERGUSON, Adam, An Essay on the History of Civil Society. 8th ed., P, 1819, 8vo, later 1/2 linen & marbled bds, $65.00

FERRERO, Guglielmo, Problems of Peace. NY, 1919, 8vo, 219pp., $17.50

FIELD, Henry, Life of David Dudley Field. NY, 1898, 8vo, 361pp., $22.50

FIFOOT, C. H., Frederic William Maitland. Harvard, 1971, 8vo, 313pp., $17.50

FINS, Harry, Illinois Motion & Petition Practice. C, 1939, 4to,1322pp, $27.50

FISHER, Harold & SMART, Canadian Patent Law. Toronto, 1914, roy8vo, 478pp, $25.

FONBLANQUE, John, A Treatise of Equity. Dublin, 1793, 8vo, 2vols., contemp. roan, beautiful set, $145.00

FORSYTH, Wm., Hortensius. 3rd ed., L, 1879, roy8vo, 412pp., $75.00

FOSS, Edw., The Judges of England, L, 1848-64, roy8vo, 9vols., orig. cl, $200.0

FOWLER, William, The Sectional Controversy. NY, 1863, 8vo, 269p, linen $47.50

FRANK, Jerome, Law & the Modern Mind. NY, 1936, roy8vo, 368pp., $17.50

FRANKFURTER, Felix (ed.), Mr. Justice Holmes. NY, 1931, 8vo, 241pp., $22.50

____, Mr. Justice Holmes & the Supreme Court. Camb,1938, 8vo,139p, 1st ed,$37.5

--9--

FRANKFURTER, Felix (ed.), Mr. Justice Brandeis. Intro. by Oliver Wendell Holmes. Yale, 1932, 8vo, 232pp., first edition, $37.50

FRANKFURTER, Felix, & GREENE, N., The Labor Injunction. NY, 1930, roy8vo, 343pp., first edition, $37.50

FRANKFURTER, Felix, Reminiscences. NY, 1960, 8vo, 310pp., $22.50

FREEMAN, Max (ed), Roosevelt & Frankfurter: Correspondence, 1928-1945. B, 1967 roy8vo, 772pp., $25.00

FREEMAN, Kathleen, The Murder of Herodes...L, 1955, 8vo, 239pp., $17.50

FREUND, Ernst, Administrative Powers over Persons & Property. C, 1928, roy8vo, 620pp., $22.50

FREUND, Ernst, The Police Power. C, 1904, 4to, 819pp., $37.50

FREUND, Paul, On Law & Justice. Harvard, 1968, 8vo, 259pp., $15.50

FRIEDMAN, Leon (ed.), Southern Justice. NY, 1965, 8vo, 259pp., $14.50

FUESS, Claude, Daniel Webster. B, 1930,roy8vo, 2vols., $37.50

GALL, F. J., & SPURZHEIM, G., Des Dispositions Innees de l'Ame et de l'Esprit. P, 1811, 8vo, 397pp., later 1/2 calf, first edition thus, $95.00

GARBET, Cyrl, Church & State in England. L, 1950, 8vo, 320pp., $17.50

GENTILI, Alberica, De Jure Belli Libri Tres. (Classics of Int'l Law), Oxford UP, 1933, 4to, 2vols., $75.00

GERBER, Albert, Sex, Pornography & Justice. NY, 1965, 8vo, 349pp., $16.50

GERHART, Eugene (ed.), The Lawyer's Treasury. Ind, 1956, roy8vo, 520pp, $18.50

GERHART, Eugene, America's Advocate. Ind, 1958,roy8vo, 545pp., $22.50

GETTY, Luella, Law of Citizenship in the US. C, 1934, 8vo, 221pp., $16.50

GOERKE, Otto, Natural Law & the Theory of Society, 1500-1800. Trans. Barker, B, 1957, 8vo, 423pp., linen, $22.50

GIESLER, Jerry, The Gerry Giesler Story. NY, 1960, 8vo, 341pp., $17.50

GILBERT, Gustav, Constitutional Antiquities of Sparta & Athens. (1895), Rep: 1968, roy8vo, 463pp., $18.50

GILLETTE, Wm., The Right to Vote. Balto, 1965, 8vo, 181pp., $15.50

GILMORE, Myron, Humanists & Jurists. Harvard, 1963, 8vo, 184pp., $16.50

GIRAUD, Ch., Essai sur l'Histoire du Droit Francais au Moyen Age. P, 1846, 8vo, 2vols., contemp. 1/2 morocco, 900pp., $125.00

GISNET, Morris, A Lawyer Tells the Truth. NY, 1931, 8vo, 160pp., $14.50

GLEN, W. C., Acts Regulating the Duties of the Justices of the Peace.... L, 1861, 12mo, 222pp., later linen, $37.50

GLUECK, Sheldon & Eleanor, After-Conduct of Discharged Offenders. foreword by Felix Frankfurter, L, 1945, 8vo, 114pp., $17.50

GLUECK, Sheldon, Nuremberg Trial & Aggressive War. NY, 1946, 8vo, 121p, $15.50

GNEIST, Rudolf, History of the English Constitution.L, 1891, 8vo, 790p, $25.00

GNEIST, R., Institutionum et Regularum.. L, 1858, 8vo, 356pp., $37.50

GOLDFARB, Ronald, The Contempt Power. NY, 1963, roy8vo, 361pp., $17.50

GOODHART, A. L., Precedent in English Continental Law. L, 1934, 8vo,55p,$15.50

GOODHART, Arth, Essays in Jurisprudence... Camb, 1931, roy8vo, 295pp, $25.00

GOODNOW, Frank, Principles of Constitutional Govt. NY, 1916, 8vo, 396pp, $20.0

GORDON, Thomas, Digest of the Laws of the US.. P, 1827, 8vo,884p, linen, $65.0

GRABER, Doris, Development of the Law of Belligerent Occupation. NY, 1948,$17.

--10--

GRAHAM, Harry, The Mother of Parliaments. B, 1911, roy8vo, 314pp, sl. soil, $20.00

280) GRAHAM, Willard & Kate, Accounting in Law Practice. 2nd ed, C, 1938,553p,$27.50

281) John Chipman Gray: An Appreciation. B, 1917, roy8vo, 141pp., $22.50

282) GRAY, John Chipman, Rule against Perpetuities. 2nd ed, B, 1906, 4to, 664p,$25.0

283) The Great Libel Case: Geo. Opdyke against Thurlow Weed....NY, 1865, 8vo, 156pp., later linen, $47.50

284) GREEN, Leon, Rationale of Proximate Cause. KC, 1927, roy8vo, 216pp., $22.50

285) The Green Bag: A Useless but Entertaining Magazine for Lawyers. Vol. I, No. 1 (Jan, 1889) to Vol. X, No. 12, (Dec, 1898), 4to, 10vols., contemp. 1/2 morocco, scuffed but sound, $375.00

286) GRISWOLD, Irwin, Law & Lawyers in the US. Harvard, 1964, 8vo, 152pp., $14.50

287) GROSSMAN, Joel, & NELLS, Constitutional Law & Judicial Policy Making. NY, 1972, 4to, 869pp., $17.50

288) GROTIUS, Hugo, The Rights of War & Peace...trans. with Notes by A. C. Campbell Pontefract, 1814, 8vo, 3vols., later 1/2 linen & marbled bds, scarce,$165.00

289) GROTIUS, Hugo, De Jure Praedae Commentarius. Oxford UP, 1950, 2vol., 4to & folio, (Classics of Int'l Law), $95.00

290) GROTIUS, Hugo, Freedom of the Seas. Oxford UP, 1916, roy8vo, 83pp., $17.50

291) GUTTMACHER, M., & WEIHOFFEN, Psychiatry & the Law. NY, 1952, 8vo, 476pp,$22.50

292) HAINES, Chs. G., Role of the Supreme Court in American Govt. & Politics..... m (1944), 1960, roy8vo, 679pp., $25.00

293) HAIR, Paul (ed.), Before the Baudy Court, NY, 1972, roy8vo, 271pp., $20.00

294) HALLAM, Henry, Constitutional History of England. NY, 1876, 8vo, 731pp, $37.50

295) HAMBLIN, P. R., United States Criminal History... Fayetteville, 1836, roy8vo, 550pp., contemp. roan, bit rubbed & scuffed, sl. sporad, foxing & sl. worming of front cover, $75.00

296) HAMILTON, Rob., & MORT, Law & Public Education. C, 1941, 4to, 579pp., $22.50

297) HAMLIN, Paul, Legal Education in Colonial NY. NY, 1939, roy8vo, 262pp., $17.50

298) HAMPE, Theo., Crime & Punishment in Germany. L, 1929, 8vo, 175pp., $22.50

299) HARBAUGH, Wm., Lawyer's Lawyer. Oxford, 1973, roy8vo, 648pp., $22.50

300) HARON, Albert, Legal Education in the US.SF, 1952, 8vo, 211pp., $17.50

310) HARRISON, A. R., The Law of Athens. Oxford, 1968, 8vo, 346pp., $22.50

302) HARVARD LAW REV. ASSN, Selected Essays on the Law of Torts. 1924, 4to,770p, sl. soil, preface by Pound, wrps, $27.50

303) HASKINS, Chs. H. & LORD, Some Problems of the Peace Conference. Cam,1920, 8vo, 307pp., $20.00

304) HASTINGS, Margaret, The Court of Common Pleas in 15th Century England. Cornell UP, 1947, roy8vo, 302pp., $22.50

305) HAUSNER, Gideon, Justice in Jerusalem. NY, 1966, roy8vo, 528pp., $18.50

306) HAWKINS, Sir John, Life of Samuel Johnson. ed. Davis, NY, 1961, 8vo,441p, $17.5

307) HAWLEY, Lowell, & POTTS, Counsel for the Damned. P, 1953, 8vo, 320pp., $17.50

308) HAYES, H. G., Complete History of the Life & Trial of Chs. Julius Guiteau... St.L, 1882, 8vo, 528pp., later line, title soiled, $25.00

309) HAYNES, Geo., The Senate of the US. B, 1938, 8vo, 2vols., $45.00

310) HEARD, Frank, Oddities of the Law. B, 1881, 8vO, 192pp., $22.50

311) HEATLEY, D. P., Diplomacy & the Study of Int'l Relations. 1919, 292pp., $17.50

--11--

HEDGES, R.Y., & WINTERBOTTOM, Legal History of Trade Unionism.L, 1931, $15.50

HELLMAN, Geo., Benjamin Cardozo. NY, 1940, roy8vo, 339pp., $17.50

HENSON, Allen, Confessions of a Criminal Lawyer. NY, 1959, 8vo, 236pp, $15.50

HERMAN, Louis, & GOLDBERG, You May Cross-Examine. NY, 1937, 8vo, 194p, $14.50

HEROLD, Justin, Manual of Legal Medicine. P, 1899, roy8vo, 768pp., $25.00

HERTZ, Emanual (ed.), The Hidden Lincoln. NY, 1938, 8vo, 461pp., $17.50

HESSE, Konrad (ed.), Grundzuge des Verfassungsrechts der Bundesrepublik. Karlsruhe, 1967, 8vo, 283pp., orig. ptd. wrps, $17.50

HEXNER, Erwin, Studies in Legal Terminology. UNo.C, 1941, 8vo, 150p., $16.50

HEYDECKER, Joe, & LEEB, The Nuremberg Trial. Cl, 1962, 8vo, 398pp., $17.50

HIGDON, Hal, The Crime of the Century. NY, 1975, roy8vo, 380pp., $17.50

HILL, Geo., Treasure Trove in Law & Practice. Ox, 1936, roy8vo, 311p, $22.50

HILLIARD, Francis, Elements of Law... B, 1835, roy8vo, 335p, lat. lin, $47.50

HIRSCHL, Andrew, Trial Tactics. C, 1906, roy8vo, 264pp., sl. worn, $16.50

Histoire Complet du Proces de...M. de Fualdes. P, 1818, 8vo, 390p, linen,$45.00

HOAG, Ernest, & WILLIAMS, Crime, Abnormal Minds & the Law. 1923, 8vo, 405pp,$17

HOBART, Henry, Reports of....3rd ed., L, 1671, folio, 350pp., lt. sporad. foxing tiny holes in last few leaves, engraved frontis with one corner neatly mended, black letter, later 1/2 calf, $150.00

HOEBEL, E. A., The Law of Primitive Man. Harvard, 1964, 8vo, 357pp., $16.50

HOFFMAN, Malcolm, Government Lawyer. NY, 1956, 8vo, 242pp., $16.50

HOGUE, Arthur, Origins of the Common Law. Ind, 1966, 8vo, 276pp., $15.50

HOLBOURN, Louis, German Constitutional Docs. L, 1970, roy8vo, 243pp., $17.50

HOLDSWORTH, Wm., Sources & Literature of English Law. Ox, 1952, 8vo,247p,$27.50

HOLDSWORTH, Wm., Some Makers of English Law. Cam, 1966, 8vo, 308pp., $27.50

HOLDSWORTH, Wm., Charles Dickens as a Legal Historian. Yale,1928, 8vo, $27.50

HOLMES, Oliver Wendell, Representative Opinions. NY, 1931, roy8vo,319p, $22.50

HOLMES, Oliver W., Dissenting Opinions. NY, 1929, roy8vo, 314pp., $22.50

HOLMES, Oliver W., Constitutional Opinions...Buf, 1940, 8vo, 360p, $22.50

HOLTZENDORF, Franzvon & KOHLER, Josef (eds.) Encyclopädie der Rechtswissenschaften. 7th ed. of the 2nd ed., M/L/B, 1915, 4to, 5vols., contemp. 1/2 calf & linen, sl. scuffed & sl. worn, an outstanding work; editor Kohler who also contributed the monograph "Legal Philosophy & Universal Legal History," was the leader of the neo-Hegelian school of jurisprudence; the book-length contribution of Bruns "History & Sources of Roman Law," is regarded as a classic, $150.00

HOMO,Leon, Roman Political Institutions. NY, 1930, roy8vo, z402pp., $20.00

HOOK, Sidney, Heresy Yes, Conspiracy No. NY, 1953, 8vo, 283pp., $14.50

HORNE, Andrew, The Mirror of Justices. DC, 1903, 8vo, 337pp., $37.50

HOOKER, Richard, The Works of....London, 1705, tall folio, 553pp., superb engraved frontis & half-title, contemp. calf, expertly rebacked in calf, beautiful copy, $265.00

HOROWITZ, Harold, & KARST, K, Law, Lawyers & Social Change. In,1969,531p,$25.00

HOUSER, M.L., Lincoln's Education. NY, 1957, 8vo, 356pp., $17.50

HOWARD, J. W., Mr. Justice Murphy. Princeton, 1968, roy8vo, 578pp., $22.50

HOWE, Mark (ed.), Holmes-Pollock Letters. Harvard, 1941, roy8vo, 2vols,$37.50

--12--

HOWE, Wm. W., Studies in the Civil Law. 2nd ed., B, 1905, roy8vo,391p,$35.00

Howl of the Censor, ed. J.W. Ehrlich. Ca, 1961, 8vo, 144pp, $14.50

HOXIE, R. G. (ed.), Presidency in the 70's. NY, 1972, 8vo, 196pp., $16.50

Plan for the Admin. of Justice US Zone, 1945, 8vo, 19pp, wrps, $17.50

HUBBELL"S Legal Directory...NY, 1871, 8vo, 289pp., new linen, $37.50

HUGHES, Chs. Evans, Pathway of Peace. NY, 1925, roy8vo, 329pp., $22.50

HUGHES, Chs. Evans, Supreme Court of the US. NY, 1928, 8vo, first edd., $37.50

HUMPHREYS, Travers, A Book of Trials. L, 1953, roy8vo, 243pp., $17.50

Jus Georgicum Regni Hungaricae... ed. Carolus Pfahler, Keszthely, 1820, roy8vo cxxxv,352,175p; later linen, stamp on verso, $75.00

HUNT, Aurora, Kirby Benedict. Ca, 1961,roy8vo, 268pp., $22.50

HYDE, H. M., Cases that Changed the Law. NY, 1951, 8vo, 203pp., $17.50

HYDE, H. (ed.), Trials of Oscar Wilde. L, 1952, 8vo, 384pp., $22.50

HYMAN, Harold, To Try Men's Souls. Ca, 1959, roy8vo, 414pp., $22.50

ICKES, Harold, Freedom of the Press Today. NY, 1941, 8vo, 308pp., $16.50

INGERSOLL, Edw., An Abridgment of the Acts of Congress Now in Force...., P, 1825, roy8vo, 784pp., contemp. roan, bit scuffed, $65.00

INTERNOCSIA, Jerome, New Code of Int'l Law, NY, 1910, smfolio,1002p, $37.50

JACKSON, Percival, Wisdom of the Supreme Court. Nor, 1962, roy8vo, 524pp, $20.0

JACKSON, Percival, Look at the Law. NY, 1940, 8vo, 377pp., $17.50

GUIDE TO THE ECONOMIC LAWS OF JAPAN. T, 1950, 8vo, 876pp., $25.00

JEFFREY, Life of Lord Jeffrey, ed. Lord Cockburn, P, 1856, 8vo, 2vols, $47.50

JENKS, Edw., The New Jurisprudence. L, 1933, 8vo, 290pp., $25.00

JENNINGS, Geo., An Anecdotal History of the British Parliament.3rd ed., w/Adds. L, 1892, roy8vo, 718pp., sl.wear, $27.50

JENNINGS, W. I., Law of the Constitution. 5th ed, L, 1959, 8vo, 354pp, $17.50

JENNINGS, W. I., British Constitution. 3rd ed., Cam, 1950, 8vo, 220pp, $15.50

JENNINGS, W.I., Modern Theories of Law. Rep: 1963, 8vo, 229pp., $22.50

Trial of Andrew Johnson.... DC, 1868, roy8vo, 3vols., orig. cl., $75.00

JOHNSON, Jas., Draftsman's Handbook.. B, 1961, roy8vo, 694pp., $30.00

JONES, Alonzo, Due Process of Law & the Divine Right of Dissent (NY, 1892); with this: RINGGOLD, Jas, Church & State (60pp); and JONES, A., The National Sunday Law (1888,191pp.); and RINGGOLD, Jas, Sunday Laws in the US. (1892), 126pp., later linen, $37.50

JONES, Ben, Sam Jones: Lawyer. Norman, 1947, 8vo, 218pp., $15.00

JONES, J. W., Historical Introduction to the Theory of Law. Oxford, 1956, $14.5

JONES, Leonard, Memoirs of the Judiciary & Bar of New England. B, 1909, folio, 5vols., ill., later linen, $185.00

JORDAN, E., The Theory of Legislation. Ind, 1930, roy8vo, 486pp., $22.50

JONES, Alfred, Life, Liberty & Property. P, 1941, roy8vo, 397pp., $17.50

JONES, Marvin, Should Uncle Sam Pay. n.p, 1963, 8vo, 159pp., $16.50

KAHN, Alfred, A Court for Children. NY, 1953, roy8vo, 359pp., $17.50

KAISER, John, Law, Legislative & Municipal Reference Libraries. B, 1914, 8vo, 466pp., scarce, $37.50

KALVEN, Harry, & ZEISEL, The American Jury. B, 1966, 8vo, 559pp, $22.50

--13--

KAPLAN, A, et al, The Rosso Case. NY, 1934, 8vo, 346pp., $16.50

KELLEN, Wm., Henry Wheaton. B, 1902, 8vo, 52pp., $17.50

KELLER, Wm., The Nation's Advocate. Pit, 1956, roy8vo, 451p., sl. soil,$22.50

KELLOGG, Louise, American Colonial Charters. Balto, 1903, 8vo, 150p, $17.50

KELLOR, Francis & HATVANY, The US Senate & the Int'l Court. NY, 1925,353p,$18.5

KELSEN, Hans, Society & Nature. Univ. of Chicago, 1943, roy8vo, 391p, $17.50

KENT, James, Commentaries on American Law, 12th ed. by Oliver Wendell Holmes & 13th ed. by Chs. Barnes, B, 1884, roy8vo, 4vols., best edition, $250.00

(KENT), JOHNSON, Wm., Reports of Cases Argued & Determined in the Supreme Court of Judicature,...in the State of New York. NY, 1807-08, Vols. I & II, roy8vo, 2vols., contemp. calf, Kent was chief justice & many of the opinions were written by him, $145.00

KISSINGER, Henry, Nuclear Weapons & Foreign Policy. NY, 1957, 8vo,463p, $17.50

KLAUS, Sam (ed.), The Molineux Case. NY, 1929, roy8vo, 409pp., $22.50

KLEIN, Fannie, Judicial Administration & the Legal Profession: A Bibliography. NY, 1963, roy8vo, 650pp., $30.00

KLING, Sam, Sexual Behavior & the Law. NY, 1965, roy8vo, 301pp., $15.00

KNAPPEN, M. T., Constitutional & Legal History of England. (1942), Rep:1964 roy8vo, 607pp., $20.00

KOCOUREK, Albert, Jural Relations. Ind, 1928, roy8vo, 484pp., $27.50

KOCOUREK, Alb, & WIGMORE, John, (eds.), Sources of Ancient & Primitive Law. B, 1915, roy8vo, 702pp., later linen, ex lib, few leaves mended, $27.50

KOESSLER, Max, Masterpieces of Legal Fiction. Ro, 1964, roy8vo, 862pp, $27.50

KONKLE, Burton, Life of Chief Justice Ellis Lewis. P, 1907, 8vo, 285pp, $22.50

KONKLE, Burton, Geo. Bryan & the Constitution of Penn. P, 1922, 381pp., $22.50

KOTHE, Chs. (ed.), A Tale of 22 Cities. NY, 1965, 8vo, 168pp., $16.50

KRONHAUSEN, E. & P., Pornography & the Law. NY, 1959, 8vo, 317pp., $15.50

KROHSTEIN, Heinrich, The Law of International Cartels. Cornell, 1973,489p,$25.0

KROUT, John, The Originsx of Prohibition. NY, 1925, 8vo, 328pp., $17.50

KUENZLI, F. A., Right & Duty. NY, 1916, 8vo, 225pp., $17.50

KUKIEL, M., Czartoryski & European Unity. Princeton, 1955, 8vo, 354pp, $22.50

KUNKEL, Wolfgang, Introduction to Roman Legal & Constitutional History. Oxford, 1966, 8vo, 217pp., $14.50

KURLAND, Philip, Religion & the Law. C, 1962, roy8vo, 127pp., $14.50

KYD, Stewart, Treatise on Bills of Exchange & Promissory Notes. D, 1791, 8vo, 160pp., contemp. calf, rebacked in calf, $75.00

LA BRIE, Francis, The Meaning of Income in the Law of Income Tax. Univ. of Toronto, 1953, roy8vo, 380pp., $17.50

LAKE, Lewis, How to Win Lawsuits before Juries. NY, 1955, 8vo, 303pp., $17.50

LAKE, L., How to Cross-Examine Witnesses. NY, 1957, roy8vo, 342pp., $20.00

LANGDELL, C. C., A Summary of Equity Pleading. Camb, 1883, 8vo, 282pp, $22.50

LANDGELL, C. C., Brief Survey of Equity Jurisdiction. 2nd ed., enl., Camb., 1908, 4to, 434pp., $25.00

LANGER, Rob., Seizure of Territory. Princeton, 1947, 8vo, 313pp., $17.50

LASKI, Harold, Studies in the problem of Sovereignty. Yale, 1917, 297pp, $17.50

LASKI, H., The American Presidency. NY, 1940, 8vo, 278pp., $16.50

--14--

LAWSON, F. H., A Common Lawyer Looks at the Civil Law. AA, 1953, 8vo, $17.50

LAWSON, F. H., Negligence in the Civil Law. Ox, 1955, 8vo, 341pp., $25.00

Lawyer to Lawyer Consultation Panel. Solon, 1974, 2nd ed, 312pp, wrps, $14.50

LEDER, Lawrence, The Genesis of American Freedom. Brandeis,1961, 4to, 26 facs & 31pp. text, 1/2 linen & bds, boxed, $22.50

LEE, Guy, Historical Jurisprudence. NY, 1927, roy8vo, 517pp., $25.00

LEE, Richard Henry, An Additional Number of Letters from a Federal Farmer.... (1788), NY, 1962, 8vo, 181pp., $16.50

LEE, R. W., Introduction to Roman Dutch Law. 2nd ed, Ox, 1925, 8vo,442, $27.50

LEE, R. W., Elements of Roman Law. 4th ed., L, 1956, 8vo, 499pp., $25.00

L'Intrigue de Rodez....P, 1818, 8vo, 249pp., later linen, $37.50

Les Six Codes.... P, 1828, 32mo, 878,107pp., contemp. roan, rubbed, $45.00

LEVIN, A.L., & WOOLEY, E., Dispatch & Delay. Pa, 1961, roy8vo, 426pp, wrp,$14.

LEVY, Leonard, Origins of the Fifth Amendment. Ox, 1968, roy8vo, 561pp, $22.50

LEWIN, Julius, Politics & Law in So. Africa. L,1963, 8vo, 115pp., $14.50

LEWIS, Anthony, Portrait of a Decade. NY, 1964, roy8vo, 322pp., $17.50

LEWIS, John, & BOMBOUGH, C., Stratagems & Conspiracies to Defraud Life Insur-insurance Companies. 2nd ed., rev/enl., Balto, 1896, 8vo, 682pp, $27.50

LEWIS, Walker, Without Fear or Favor. B, 1965, 8vo, 556pp., $17.50

LEWIS, Wm. Draper, Great American Lawyers. P, 1907-09, roy8vo, 8vols., orig. buck w/leather labels, ill. Special University Edition, #582 of 1000, uncut, excellent, $210.00

LIEBER, Francis, On Civil Liberty & Self-Government. Enl. ed, P, 1859, roy8vo, 629pp. orig. cl., sl. worn, $37.50

LIEF, Alfred, Brandeis. NY,1936, 8vo, 508pp., $17.50

LINDMAN, Frank, & MC INTYRE, The Mentally Disabled & the Law. Unv of Chiaago, 1961, 4to, $25.00

LIPPMANN, Walter, Liberty & the News. NY, 1920, 8vo, 104pp., $14.50

LISSITZYN, Oliver, International Air Transport & National Policy. NY, 1942, 8vo, 478pp., $25.00

LITTLETON, Tenures. DC, 1903, 8vo, 340pp., $44.00

LIVINGSTON, Edward, Complete Works on Criminal Jurisprudence.... to which is prefixed an Intro. by Salmon P. Chase. NY, 1873, roy8vo, 2vols., orig. cl., reblcked, first 3dition thus, $125.00

LOGAN, Andy, Against the Evidence.NY, 1970, roy8vo, 376pp., $16.50

LONDON, Ephraim, The World of Law. NY,1960, roy8vo, 2vols., $35.00

LOOMIS, Dwight & CALHOUN J., The Judicial & Civil History of Connecticut. B, 1895, 4to, 639pp., numerous steel engravings, later linen, $75.00

LUMMUS, Henry, Trial Judge. C, 1937, 8vo, 148pp., $16.50

LUNDSTEDT, A. V., Superstition or Rationality in Action for Peace. L, 1925, roy8vo, 239pp., $17.50

MAC DONAGH, Michael, The English King.... (1929) 1971, 8vo, 318pp., $13.50

LUSTGARTEN, Edgar, Defender's Triumph. L, 1951,12mo, 238pp., $12.50

MAC DONALD, John, No Deadly Drug. NY, 1968, 8vo, 656pp., $16.50

MAC DONNELL, John, Historical Trials. Oxford, 1927, roy8vo, 324pp., $17.50

MAC KENZIE, Jeanne, The Murder of Maria Martin...NY, 1948, 8vo, 256pp, $14.50

--15--

MACKINTOSH, Rt. Hon. Sir. Jas., Miscellaneous Works. B, 1856, roy8vo, 3vols. as one, later linen, $37.50

MAC NALLY, Leonard, The Rules of Evidence on Pleas of the Crown. P, 1804, 8vo, 2vols., hinges expertly reinforced, President James Buchanan's copy with his signature on both title pages, $150.00

MAGNUS, Julius, Die Rechtsanwaltschaft. L, 1929, 8vo, 536pp., $27.50

MAINE, Nenry S., International Law. NY, 1888, roy8vo, 234pp, sl. wear, $30.00

MAINE, Hnery S., Ancient Law, Intro. & Notes by Pollock. L, 1930, 8vo, 440pp., new linem, $25.00

MAINE, Henry S., Lectures on the Early History of Institutions. L, 1875, roy8vo, viii,412pp., orig. cl., rebacked & spine remounted, first edition, $125.00

MAITLAND, Frederic, Township & Borough. Camb, 1964, roy8vo, 220pp, $25.00

MAITLAND, F. W., Constitutional History of England. Camb,1920, 8vo,548p,$22.50

MANTOUX, Etienne, The Carthaginian Peace. Ox, 1946, 8vo, 210pp., $17.50

MARSHALL, Jas., Intention in Law & Society. NY, 1968, 8vo, 237pp., $16.50

MARSHALL, John, Life of George Washington. P, 1804-07, 8vo, 5vols., bound in contemp. calf, skillfully rebacked in calf, beautiful set,first ed, $475.00

MARSHALL, John, Life of George Washington. 2nd ed., rev. & corr., P, 1848, roy8vo, 2vols., later 1/2 linen, $75.00

MARSHALL, John, Autobiographical Sketch...AA, 1937, 4to, 48pp., $14.50

MARSZALEK, John, Court Martial. NY, 1972, roy8vo, 320pp., $17.50

MARTIN, CHs., Introduction to the Study of the American Constitution. Ox, 1928, roy8vo, 440pp., sl. spotted & rubbed, $22.50

MASON, Alpheus, & BEANY, American Constitutional Law. NJ, 1958, 8vo,669p,$22.5

MASON, Alpheus, & BEANY, Supreme Court in a Free Society. NJ, 1959, 8vo, 346pp., $16.50

MASON, Alpheus, Harlan Fiske Stone. NY, 1956, roy8vo, 914pp., $25.00

MASON, Alpheus, William Howard Taft. NY, 1965, 8vo, 354pp., $16.50

MASON, Alpheus, The Brandeis Way. Princeton, 1938, roy8vo, 336pp., $17.50

MASON, Alpheus, Brandeis. NY, 1946, roy8vo, 713pp., $22.50

MASON, Chs., Elementary Treatise on the Structure & Operations of the National & State Govts. in the US. B, 1843, 8vo, 233pp., $22.50

MASON, Jeremiah, Memoirs. Autobiography..B, 1917, roy8vo, 491pp., $25.00

MASSEL, Mark, Competition & Monopoly. DC, 1962, roy8vo, 477pp., $20.00

MATHEWS, John, Principles of American State Admin. NY, 1922, 8vo,513p, $17.50

MAY, Thomas E., Treatise on the Law, Privileges, Proceedings & Usages of Parliament. L, 1844, 8vo, 496pp., orig. cl., rebacked, $47.50

MEYER, Milton, Tradition of Freedom. NY, 1957, 8vo, 766pp., $17.50

MAYES, Edw., Lucius Q. C. Lamar. 2nd ed., Nashville, 1896, 4to, 820pp., ill., orig. cl., rebacked & spine remounted, scarce, $45.00

MAYNE, John, Treatise on Hindu Law & Usage. Madras, 1878, 8vo, 607pp, $27.50

MC CALL, Henry, The Clerk's Assistant... 2nded, Albany, 1866, 616pp., contemp. roan,bit scuffed, $37.50

MC CARTY, Dwight, Law Office Man-gement. NY, 1926, roy8vo, 386pp., $22.50

MC CLOSKEY, Rob., Essays in Constitutional Law. NY, 1962, 8vo, 429pp., $17.50

MC CLURE, S.S., Obstacles to Peace. B/NY, 1917, 8vo, 487pp., $17,50

MC GEHEE, Lucius, Due Process of Law...Northport, 1906, roy8vo, 451pp.,$22.50

--16--

MC ILWAIN, Chs. H., Constitutionalism Ancient & Modern. Cornell, 1947, 8vo, 180pp., ex lib, $16.50

MC ILWAIN, Chs. H., Growth of Political Thought in the West. NY, 1932, 8vo, 417pp., $1850

MC KAY, Robert, Reapportionment. NY, 1965, roy8vo, 498pp., $17.50

MC KECHNIE, W. S., Magna Carta. 2nd ed. rev.(1914), reprint, roy8vo,530p,$22.

MC NAIR, Lord, The Law of Treaties. Oxford, 1961, roy8vo, 789pp., $35.00

MEDLEY, Dudley, Student's Manual of English Constitutional History. L, 1894, 8vo, 583pp., $22.50

Mendelson, Wallace (ed.), Felix Frankfurter. NY, 1964, 8vo, 285pp., $15.00

MENDELSON, Wallace, (ed.), The Supreme Court. Ind, 1967, 8vo, 509pp, $16.50

METTERNICH, Prince, Memoirs of. trans Napier. NY, 1880, roy8vo, 2vols, $47.50

MILLER, Chs., Supreme Court & Use of History. Harvard, 1969, 8vo,334p, $13.50

MILSOM, S. F., Historical Foundations of the Common Law. L, 1969, 466p, $25.00

MIRABEAU, Count de, Enquiries Concerning Lettres de Cachet... Dublin, 1787, 8vo, 2vols. bound (as issued) as 1, 503pp., later 1/2 calf, scarce,$150.00

MITCHELL, C. A. The Expert Witness. Camb, 1923, 8vo, 188pp., $17.50

MITFORD, John, Treatise on the Pleadings in Suite in the Court of Chancery... 3rd ed,(American), NY, 1833, 8vo, 401pp., later 1/2 linen, $47.50

MITGANG, Herbert, Man Who Rode the Tiger. P, 1963, 8vo, 380pp., $17.50

MONTGOMERY, Rob., Sacco-Vanzetti. NY, 1960, 8vo, 370pp., $17.50

MOORE, John B., Digest of International Law. DC, GPO, 1906ff., 8vols., 7000pp. contemp. roan, bit rubbed, $175.00

MOORE, John B., Collected Papers. Yale, 1944, roy8vo, 7vols., $175.00

MORAWETZ, Victor, Essay on the Elements of a Contract.NY, 1926, 8vo,167p,$16.5

MOREY, Wm., Outlines of Roman Law...NY/L, 1900, 12mo, 433pp., $22.50

MORGAN, Donald, Justice William Johnson. So.Car, 1954, roy8vo, 326pp, $14.50

MORRIS, Geo. F., Reminiscences of a Yankee Jurist. N.H., 1953, 8vo,351p,$25.00

MORRIS, Richard, The Peacemakers. NY, 1965, roy8vo, 572pp., $22.50

MORRISON, Herbert, Government & Parliament. 2nd ed, Ox, 1959, 8vo,386p,$22.50

MOWER, Edmund, International Government. B, 1931, 8vo, 736pp., $22.50

MUIRHEAD, Jas., Historical Introduction to the Private Law of Rome. 2nded., rev/enl., L, 1899, roy8vo, 457pp., later linen, $25.00

MULLINS, Claude, In Quest of Justice. L, 1931, 8vo, 448pp., $27.50

MUNRO, Wm., Government of American Cities. 3rd ed, NY, 1920, roy8vo,456p,$17.5

MURPHY, W., Triumph of Nationalism. C, 1967, roy8vo, 434pp., $18.50

My Philosophy of Law: Credos of Sixteen American Scholars. B, 1941, sm4to, 321pp., scarce, $47.50

OFFICE OF THE U.S. CHIEF COUNSEL FOR THE PROSECUTION OF AXIS CRIMINALITY, Nazi Conspiracy & Aggression. DC, 1946-8, roy8vo, 11vols., $325.00

NELSON, Jack, & ROBERTS, The Censors & the Schools. B, 1963, 8vo,208p, $14.50

Report & Proceedings of the Senate Committee Appointed to Investigate the Police Dept. of the City of New York. Albany, 1895, 8vo, 5vols., $125.00

NIMS, Harry, Pre-Trial. NY, 1950, roy8vo, 334pp., $20.00

NIZER, Louis, The Jury Returns. NY, 1966, roy8vo, 438pp., $17.50

NIZER, Louis, What to Do with Germany. C/NY, 1944, 8vo, 213pp., $16.50

--17--

NOBLE, John & AUERBACH, Never Plead Guilty. NY, 1955, 8vo, 306pp., $16.50

NOTH, Martin, Laws in the Pentateuch. L, 1966, 8vo, 289pp., $17.50

"O", Forensic Fables. L, 1961, 8vo, 456pp., $17.50

OGG, Frederick, & RAY, Introduction to American Govt. 9th ed., rev., NY, 1948, roy8vo, 1135pp., $25.00

O'GORMAN, Hubert, Lawyers & Matrimonial Cases. Glencoe, 1963, 8vo,206p, $14.50

OMMESLAGHE, Pierre, Le Regime des Societes., Brux, 1960, 8vo, 595pp, $22.50

O'NEILL, Chs., The American Electoral System. NY, 1895, 8vo, 284pp., $16.50

OSBORN, Albert, The Mind of the Juror. Albany, 1937, roy8vo, 239pp., $27.50

OWEN, Wilbur, Questions & Answers on 25 of the Most Important Legal Subjects. St.P., 1900, roy8vo, 613pp., $22.50

PADILLA Y MENESES, Antonio, In Quaedam Imperatorum Rescripta et Nonulla Iuriu-consultorum Responsa... Venice, 1580, folio, 1131l., double column, wood-cut title & ornamental woodcut letters, contemp. calf, front hinge expertly restored, sl. worn, rare, only one copy reported in No. America, $325.00

PALMER, Ben, Courtroom Strategies. NY, 1959, roy8vo, 393pp., $17.50

Papers Relating to the Treaty of Washington. DC, GPO, 1872, 8vo,5vols, $125.00

PARKER, Jas., The Conductor Generalis. NY, Hugh Gain, 1788, 8vo, xv,461pp., contemp. calf, tiny piece missing from base of spine, extremeties slightly worn, front hinge expertly reinforced, nice cooy, $225.00

PARRY, Albett, Persecution of Mary Stewart.NY, 1931, roy8vo, 363pp., $22.50

PATMEN, Wright, The Robinson-Patman Actt NY, 1938, 8vo, 408pp., $17.50

PATTERSON, L., & CHEATHEM, Profession of Law. NY, 1971, 4to, 489pp., $25.00

PAYNE, Stanley, The Art of Asking Questions. Princeton, 1951, 8vo, 249p,$15.50

PEABODY, Jas (ed.), Holmes-Einstein Letters. NY, 1964, 8vo, 377pp., $22.50

PEKELIS, Alex, Law & Social Action. Cornell, 1950, roy8vo, 272pp., $17.50

PELTASON, J. W., Fifty-Eight Lonley Men. NY, 1961, 8vo, 270pp., $16.50

PERKINS, Dexter, Charles Evans Hughes...B, 1956, 8vo, 200pp., $16.50

PERRY, R. R., Common Law Pleading. B, 1897, roy8vo, 494pp., $27.50

PERRY, Richard,(ed.), Sources of Our Liberties. C, 1959, 4to, 456pp., $20.00

PETERSON, Leroy, & ROSSMILLER, Law & Public School Operation. NY, 1969, $22.50

PHILLIPS, Orie & MC COY, Conduct of Judges & Lawyers. LA, 1952, 8vo,247p,$17.5

PHILLIPS, Hubert, Development of a Residential Qualification for Representa-tives in Colonial Legislatures. Cincy, 1921, roy8vo, 251pp., $17.50

PIKE, Luke O., A History of Crime in England. L, 1873, 8vo, 2vols, $75.00

Pioneers of Religious Liberty in America... B, 1903, 8vo, 396pp., $22.50

PLUCKNETT, T. F., Legislation of Edward I. Ox, 1979, 8vo, 168pp., $18.50

POLE, J. R., Political Representation in England & the Origins of the American Republic. NY, 1966,roy8vo, 606pp., $22.50

POLLARD, A. F., Evolution of Parliament. 2nd ed, rev, 1926,8vo,459pp, $20.00

POLLITT, Basi, A Lawyer's Stpry. Miami, 1958, roy8vo, 170pp., $16.50

POLLOCK, Frederick, & MAITLAND, The History of English Law before the Time of Edward I. 2nd ed., DC, 1959, roy8vo, 2vol ., $57.50

POLLOCK, Sir F., Expansion of the Common Law. L, 1904, 8vo, 164pp., $15.50

POLLOCK, Sir F., The League of Nations. L, 1920, 8vo, 251pp., $27.50

--18--

POLLOCK, Frederick & WRIGHT, Rob. , An Essay on Possession in the Common Law. Oxford, 1888, 8vo, 244pp., $30.00

POLSON, Archer, Law & Lawyers. L, 1858, 12mo, 199pp, bds, rebacked, $47.50

POPE, Benjamin, Legal Definitions. C, 1919, 4to, 2vols., $57.50

POTTER, Pitman, Manual Digest of Common Int'l Law. NY, 1932, 8vo,284p, $18.50

POUND, Roscoe, Criminal Justice in America. NY, 1930, 8vo, 226pp., $17.50

POUND, Roscoe, Labor Unions & the Concept of Public Service. DC, 1959,63p,$15.

POUND, Roscoe, Law & Morals. No.Ca., 1926, 8vo, 144pp, inscribed, $22.50

POUND, Roscoe, Justice According to Law. Yale, 1951, 8vo, 98pp., $15.50

PRETTYMAN, Barnett, Death & the Supreme Court. NY, 1961, 8vo, 311pp., $13.50

PREUSS, Hugo, Recht, Staat und Freiheit. Tub, 1926, roy8vo, 588pp., $27.50

PRINGLE, Henry, Life & Times of Wm. Howard Taft. NY, 1939, roy8vo,2vols,$37.50

PRITCHETT, C. Herman, The Roosevelt Court. NY, 1948, 8vo, 314pp., $17.50

Proceedings of the Int'l Conference under the Auspices of the American Society for the Judicial Settlement of Int'l Disputes. DC, 1910, 4to, 400p, $25.00

PROTHERO, G. W. (ed.), Select Statutes....of the Reigns of Elizabeth & James I. 4th ed., Ox, 1913, 8vo, 490pp., $25.00

PUFENDORF, Samual, De Jure Naturae et Gentium. Oxford, 1934, 4to, 2vols,$125.00

PUFENDORF, Samuel, Elementorum Jurisprudentiae. Ox, 1931, 4to, 2vols., $95.00

PUSEY, Merlo, Charles Evans Hughes. NY, 1952, roy8vo, 2vols., $37.50

QUINBY, G. W., The Gallows, the Prison & the Poor House. Cincy, 1860, 8v0, 326pp., nice copy, scarce, $37.50

Quinquennial Catalogue of the Law School of Harvard University. Camb, 1895, roy8vo, 373pp., few leaves bit chipped, $27.50

RADIN, Max, Handbook of Anglo-American Legal History. St.P, 1936, 8vo,612p,$35.

RADIN, Max, Manners & Morals of Business. Ind, 1939, 4to, 270pp., $17.50

RAM, Jas., Science of Legal Judgment. P, 1835, 8vo, 146pp., linen, $57.50

RAM, Jas., Expositionof Wills of Landed Property. P, 1835, 8vo,164pp, lin,$47.5

RAM, Jas., Practical Treatise of Assets.... P, 1835, 8vo, 430p, lat.lin, $47.50

RAMSAY, Jas., The Angevin Empire.Ox,1900, 8vo,556pp., $30.00

RAY, I., M.D., Medical Jurisprudence of Insanity. 3rd ed., w/Adds, B, 1853, 8vo, 521pp., contemp. roan, worn but tight, $45.00

REDDEN, Kenneth, Introductory Survey of the Place of Law in our Civilization. Chatlottesville, 1946, roy8vo, 272pp., $18.50

REDDIE, John, Historical Notices of the Roman Law & of the Recent Progress of Its Study in Germany. Edinburgh, 1826, 8vo, 136pp., later linen, rare,$57.50

REES, J. R. (ed.), Case of Rudolf Hess. NY, 1948, 8vo, 224pp., $16.50

REIK, Theodore, The Compulsion to Confess. NY, 1959, 8vo, 493pp., $16.50

REMBAR, Chs, The End of Obsenity. NY, 1968, 8vo, 528pp., $16.50

Report of the Court Proceedings in the Case of the Anti-Soviet Bloc of Rights & Trotskyites....Moscow, 1939, 8vo, 799pp., $25.00

Report of Robert H. Jackson to the Int'l Conference on Military Trials. L, 1945, roy8vo, 445pp., $22.50

REYNOLDS, Quentin, Courtroom. NY, 1951, roy8vo, 419pp., $16.50

REYNOLDS, W., Theory of the Law of Evidence, Established in the United States. 4th ed., C, 1905, 8vo, 268pp., $22.50

--19--

RICE, Cy, Defender of the Damned. NY, 1964, 8vo, 258pp., $16.50

ROALFE, Wm., Libraries of the Legal Profession. St.P, 1953, 8vo, 471p, $30.00

ROBBINS, Caroline (ed.), Two English Republican Tracts. Cambridge UP, 1969, 8vo, 275pp., $22.50

ROBERTS, Owen, The Court & the Constitution. Harvard, 1951, 8vo,102p, $22.50

ROBINSON, Edw., Law & the Lawyers. NY, 1937, roy8vo, 349pp., $18.50

ROBINSON, Wm., Elements of American Jurisprudence.B, 1900, 8vo, 401p, $27.50

ROBY, Henry, Introduction to the Study of Justinian's Digest...., Camb, 1886, 8vo, 279pp., $30.00

RODENBECK, Adolf, Anatomy of the Law. B, 1925, 8vo, 292pp, inscribed, $17.50

ROOSEVELT, Theodore, National Strength & Int'l Duty. P, 1917, 8vo,103p, $22.50

Argument of the Hon. Elihu Root on Behalf of the US before the North Atlantic Fisheries Arbitration Tribunal...B, 1912, roy8vo, 523pp., $27.50

ROOT, Elihu, Addresses on Government & Citizenship. Har, 1916, 8vo,552p, $25.0

ROSE, Rob., Advocates & Adversaries. C, 1977, 8vo, 328pp., $22.50

ROSTOW, Eugene, The Sovereign Prerogative. Yale, 1962, 8vo, 318pp., $16.50

ROTTSCHAEFFER, H., Handbook of American Constitutional Law. St.P, 1939, $25.0

ROXBURGH, Ronald, Origins of Lincoln's Inn.Cam, 1963, 8vo, 90pp., $17.50

ROY, Jules, Trial of Marshall Petain. NY, 1966, 8vo, 262pp;, $16.50

SAINT-GERMAIN, Chr., The Doctor & Student...Cincy, 1886, roy8vo,401pp, $45.00

SAIT, Edw., American Parties & Elections. NY, 1927, 8vo, 608pp., $17.50

SANGER, Margaret, My Fight for Birth Control. NY, 1931, 8vo, 360p., $20.00

SARTORI, Mario, The War Gasses. NY, 1939, 8vo, 360pp., $17.50

SAUCERMAN, Sophia, Int'l Transfers of Territory in Europe. DC, GPO, 1937, 4to, 344pp., color maps, $22.50

SAYER, Paul, Life of Roscoe Pound. IC, 1948,roy8vo, 412pp;, $27.50

SCHLEGEL, J. W. F., Neutral Rights.... P, 1801, 8vo, 163pp., later linen,$105.

SCHLOSSER, Alexander, Lawyers Must Eat. NY,. 1933, 8vo, 248pp.,, $15.40

SCHOULER, Jas., Law of Domestic Relations. B, 1870, 4to, 670p, rebacked,$27.5

SCHRIFTGEISSER, K., The Lobbyists. B, 1951, 8vo, 297pp., $17.50

SCHROEDER, Theodore, "Obscene"Literature & Constitutional Law. NY, 1911, roy8vo, 439pp., new label $25.00

SCHUBERT, Glendon, The Presidency in the Courts. Univ. of Minnesota, 1957, 8vo, 391pp.., $22.50

SCHUCKING, Walther, International Union of the Hague Conferences. Oxford, 1918, roy8vo, 341pp., $27.50

SCHULZ, Fritz, History of Roman Legal Science, w/New Addenda. Oxford, 1967, 8vo, 358pp., $17.50

GREEN, A. W., Political Integration by Jurisprudence. Leyden, 1969, roy8vo, 847pp., $37.50

PINNER, H. L. (ed.), World Unfair Competition Laws. Leyden, 1965, 4to, 2vols., $50.00

ATLAY, J. B., The Victorian Chancellors. L, 1908, 8vo,2vols, $47.50

FELSTEAD, Sidney T., Famous Criminals and Their Trials. NY, 1926, roy8vo, il., $25.00

--20--

SCHWARTZ, Bernard, The American Heritage History of the Law in America NY, 1974, 4to, 2vols., ill., boxed, $47.50

SCOTT, E. H., The Federalist & Other Constitutional Papers. C, 1894, 4to, 2vols., $37.50

SCOTT, Jas. Brown, The Controversy Over Neutral Rights Between the United States & France, 1797-1800. Oxford, 1917, 4to, 510pp., $30.00

SCOTT, Jas. Brown, Cases in International Law. B, 1902, 4to, 961pp, $27.50

SCOTT, Jas. Brown, Law, the State & the Int'l Community. 1968, 8vo, 2vols,$37

SCTUTTON, Thomas E., The Land in Fetters. Camb, 1886, 8vo, 162pp., $22.50

SEAWELL, Jos., Law Tales for Laymen. Raleigh, 1925, 8vo, 314pp, inscr,$17.50

SECKEL, E., Heumanns Handlexikon zu den Quellen des Römischen Rechts. 9th ed, rev., Jena, 1907, roy8vo, 643pp., $35.00

SEDGWICK, Theodore, A Treatise on the Rules which Govern the Interpretation and Application of Statutory & Constitutional Law. NY, 1857, roy8vo, 712pp., later 1/2 linen, $65.00 (scarce)

SEEBOHM, Frederic, The English Village Community. L, 1905, 8vo, 464pp.,$27.50

Selected Essays on the Law of Evidence Reprinted from the Harvard Law Review. Camb, 1936, roy8vo, 300pp., wrps, $22.50

SHAY, Frank, Judge Lynch. NY, 1938, 8vo, 288pp; $16.50

SHIENTAG, Bernard, Mouldersof Legal Thought. NY, 1943, 8vo, 253pp., $12.50

SCHILLER, A. A., Military Law & Defense Legislation. St. Paul, 1941, 4to, 647pp., $35.00

SCHWARTZ, Bernard, The Supreme Court. NY, 1957, roy8vo, 429pp., $17.50

SHINDELL, Sidney, The Law in Medical Practice. Pa, 1966, 8vo, 297pp, $16.50

SHKLAR, Judith, Legalism. Harvard, 1964, 8vo, 246pp., $16.50

SHOTWELL, Jas. , At the Paris Peace Conference. NY, 1937, 8vo, 444pp., $22.50

SIDNEY, Algernon, Discourses on Governement.... NY, 1805, 8vo, 3vols., contemp. marbled bds, rebacked in calf, contains the full trial text, $175.00

SINGER, B., Patent & Trademark Laws of the World.C, 1911, 8vo, 539pp., $20.00

SIKES, Earl, State & Federal Corrupt Practices Legislation. Duke UP, 1928, 8vo, 321pp., $17.50

SMIGEL, Irwin, The Wall Street Lawyer. Glencoe, 1964, 8vo, 369pp., $17.50

SMITH, Chs., Roger B. Taney. No.Car., 1936, 8vo, 239pp., $17.50

SMITH, John W., A Compendium of Mercantile Law. P, 1837, 8vo, 320pp., later linen, $37.50

SMITH, John Allen, The Growth & Decadence of Constitutional Government. NY, 1930, 8vo, 300pp., $17.50

SMITH, Talbot, Lawyer. NY, 1961, 8vo, 201pp., $16.50

SMITH, Toulmin (ed.), English Guilds. L, 1870, 8vo, 483pp., $45.00

SOWLE, Claude (ed.), Police Power & Individual Freedom. C, 1962, 8vo, 287pp., $17.50

SPEAR, Chs. Essays on the Punishment of Death. B/L, 1845, 12mo, 237pp., sl.worn, $37.50

Radio, TV & the Administration of Justice...Columbia Univ Pr., 1965, 8vo, 321pp., $17.50

STAFF OF THE PUBLIC SERVICE COMMISSION OF WISCONSIN, Depreciation: A Review of Legal & Accounting Problems. NY, 1933, 8vo, 196pp, $15.50

STATE OF NEW YORK, First Report of the Commissioners on the Practice & Pleadings. Code of Procedure. Albany, 1848, 8vo, 275,31,20pp., later linen, $27.50

STEGEMANN, Hermann, The Mirage of Versailles. NY, 1928, 8vo, 360pp, $17.50

STEPHEN, Henry John, Treatise on the Principles of Pleading in Civil Actions. C, 1894, roy8vo, 554pp., $27.50

STEPHEN, Sir Jas., Digest of the Law of Evidence. 2nd American ed., NY, 1898, 8vo, 469pp., $22.50

STEPHENS, W. R., & HUNT, History of the English Church. L, 1907-12, 8vo, 9vols., $125.00

Stephen's Commentaries on the Laws of England. 21st ed. by Warmington, L, 1950, 8vo, 4vols., $75.00

STEUER, Aaron, Max D. Steuer. NY, 1950, 8vo, 301pp., $14.50

ST.JOHN-STEVAS, Norman, Life, Death & the Law. Ind, 1961, 8vo, 375pp, $17.50

STONE, Harlan F., Law & Its Administration. Colmmbia, 1915, 8vo, 232pp., orig. cl., first edition, $37.50

STONE, Irving, Clarence Darrow. NY, 1941, 8vo, 510pp., $17.50

STORY, Jos., Commentaries on the Law of Agency....9th ed., B, 1882, roy8vo, 674pp., later buckram, $75.00

STORY, Jos., Commentaries on the Law of Bailments.... 4th ed., B/L, 1846, roy8vo, 648pp., later 1/2 linen, $75.00

STORY, Jos., Commentaries on the Law of Bills of Exchange... B/L, 1843, roy8vo 608pp., later 1/2 linen, $125.00

STORY, Jos., Commentaries on the Law of Partnership.... 5th ed., B, 1859, roy8vo, 754pp., later 1/2 linen, $125.00

STORY, Jos., Commentaries on the Conflict of Laws.... B, 1834, roy8vo, 557pp., contemp. roan, bit rubbed & scuffed, $75.00

STORY, Jos., Commentaries on Equity Jurisprudence... 5th ed., rev/cor/enl., B/L, 1849, roy8vo, 2vols., later 1/2 linen, $150.00

STORY, Jos., Commentaries on the Law of Promissory Notes... 5th ed., B, 1859, roy8vo, 703pp., later 1/2 linen, $125.00

STORY, Jos., An Address by Mr. Justice Story on Chief Justice Marshall... Rochester, 1900, 8vo, 60pp., orig. wrps, $5.00

STRANGE, John, Reportsof Adjudged Cases in the Courtsof Chancery, King's Bench, Common Pleas & Exchequer...L, 1795, thick roy8vo, 2vols., contemp. calf, beautiful set, $145.00

STRAUSS, Pat., Cripps: NY, 1942, roy8vo, 423pp., $17.50

STREET, H., Freedom, the Individual & the Law. rev. ed., London, 1967 8vo, 302pp., $16.50

STUART, Graham, American Diplomatic & Consular Practice. 2nd ed., NY 1952 roy8vo, 477pp., $17.50

STUBBS, William, Constitutional History of England in Its Origin & Development. 4th ed., Oxford, 1883, 8vo, 3vols., rebacked, $75.00

STUBBS, Wm., Select Charters & Other Illustrations of English Constitutional History. 5th ed., Oxford, 1884, 8vo, 552pp., last edition to contain the full text of the Dialogus de Saccario, $27.50

STUBBS, W., & TALMASH, G., The Crown Circuit Companion...6th ed., with Several Additions, Improvements & Modern References by Thomas Dougherty. Dublin, 1791, 8vo, 442pp., contemp. calf, front hinge expertly reinforced, light sporadic foxing, nice copy, $125.00

STUMBERG, Geo., Principles ofthe Conflict of Laws. NY, 1951, 8vo, 475pp., $20.00

SUGDEN, Sir Edward, A Practical Treatise of Powers. from the 6th London ed., P, 1837, 8vo, 2vols., later 1/2 linen, $95.00

SUGDEN, Edw., A Series of Letters to a Man of Property on Sales, Purchases.. P, 1834, 8vo, 54pp., later linen, $37.50

SUGDEN, Sir William, A Practical Treatise of the Law of Vendors & Purchasers of Estates. 7th American from the 11th London edition, with Notes & References to the American Law....by J. C. Perkins. Springfield, Mass, 1851, roy8vo, 2vols., later linen, $115.00

SUMNER, Chs., Works. B, 1870-77, 8vo, 12vols., later linen, stamps on titles, nice set, $175.00

SUMNER, Chs., Memoir & Letters.. B, 1877, roy8vo, 4vols., later buckram, stamps on titles, $50.00

SUMNER, Chs., Life & Services of. ed. G. E. Lester, NY, 1874, roy8vo, 596pp., $27.50

SUNDERLAND, Edw., History of the American Bar Association. 1953, roy8vo, 251pp., $17.50

SUNDSTROM, G. O., Three Discussions on the Conflict of Laws... Stockholm, 1970, 8vo, 149pp., wrps., $17.50

SUTHERLAND, J.G., Treatise on the Law of Damages. 4th ed., C, 1916, 4to, 5vols., $125.00

SWAINE, Rob. T., The Cravath Firm & Its Predecessors. NY, 1946-48, roy8vo, 2vols., $75.00

SWINBURNE, Henry, A Treatise of Testaments and Last Wills....7th ed., Corr. & much Enlarged, Dublin, 1793, roy8vo, 2vols., contemp.roan, bit scuffed nice set of a classic work, $150.00

SWINFORD, Mac, Kentucky Lawyer. Cinncinnati, 1963, 8vo, 121pp., $14.50

SWISHER, Carl B., The Growth of Constitutional Power in the United States. C, 1946, 8vo, 261pp., $14.50

SWISHER, Carl B., Roger B. Taney. NY, 1935, roy8vo, 608pp., $27.50

SWISHER, Carl B., Stephen J. Field, DC, 1930, roy8vo, 473pp., $17.50

A Synoptical Index to theLaws and Treatiesof the United States from March 4 1789 to March 3, 1851....B, 1852, 4to, 747pp., contemp. roan,bit rubbed and scuffed, $45.00

TACITUS, Cornelius, Works of. w/an Essay on His Life & Genius by Arthur Murphy. new ed., corr, NY, 1859, 8vo, 742pp., contemp/ 1/2 calf, $47.50

TAFT, William Howard, The Anti-Trust Act and the Supreme Court. NY/L, 1914 8vo, 133pp., first edition, $37.50

TAFT, William Howard, Four Aspects of Civic Duty. NY, 1906, 8vo, 111pp., ex lib, first edition, $22.50

TAFT, William Howard, Liberty under Law. Yale, 1922, 8vo, 51pp., orig. cloth, sl. marginal discoloration of frontis, first edition, $35.00

TANNER, J. R., English Constitutional Conflicts of the 17th Century. Camb, 1962, 8vo, 315pp., $17.50

TAYLER, Thomas, The Law Glossary.... 7th ed., rev, corr, & enl., NY, 1864, roy8vo, 580pp., later linen, $47.50

TAYLOR, Hannis, Origin & Growth of the American Constitution. B, 1911, roy8vo, 676pp., $27.50

TAYLOR, Hannis, Due Process of Law & the Equal Protection of the Laws. C, 1917, 4to, 988pp., buckram, bit soiled, $35.00

TAYLOR, John L., A Memoir of His Honor Samuel Phillips, LL.D., B, 1856, roy8vo, orig. cl., rebacked & spine remounted, $36.50

TAYLOR, John, Treatise on the American Law of Landlord & Tenant. 7th ed., B, 1879, roy8vo, 824pp., roan, bit scuffed, $27.50

THAYER, Jas. B., A Selection of Cases on Evidence at the Common Law. 2nd ed., Camb, 1900, 4to, 1263pp., lt sporad underlining, $30.00

THAYER, Jas. B., Cases on Constitutional Law with Notes. Camb, 1895 4to, 2vols., rebacked, $75.00

THOMAS, Helen, Felix Frankfurter. Balto, 1960, roy8vo, 381pp., $22.50

THOMPSON, Jas. W. & PADOVER, S., Secret Diplomacy. NY, 1963, 8vo, 303pp, $14.[illegible]

THORNTON, Alfred, On Patents. L, n.d.1910, 4to, 556pp., $25.00

THORPE, Francis N., Constitutional Historyof the American People. NY, 1898, 8vo, 2vols., 1000pp., $37.50

Three Tracts Published at Amsterdam in the Years 1691 & 1692 under the Name of Letters of General Ludlow....L, 1812, 4to, 150pp., later linen, $85.00

TIEMANN, Wm., The Right to Silence. Richmond, 1964, 8vo, 160pp., $14.50

TIFFANY, Herbert, The Law of Real Property & Other Interests in Land. enl. ed., C, 1920, 4to, 3vol., $75.00

TILLOTSON, Lee, Articles of War Annotated. Pa, 1942, roy8vo, 266pp, $22.50

TOBEY, Jas., Public Health Law. NY, 1939, roy8vo, 404pp., $17.50

TORREY, Geo., A Lawyer's Recollections. B, 1910, 8vo, 227pp., $17.50

TRACY,John, The Successful Practice of Law. NY, 1947, 8vo, 470pp., $22.50

TRAIN, Arthur (ed.), Confessions of Artemas Quibble. NY, 1926, 8vo,227p,$16.50

TRAIN, Arthur, From the District attorney's Office. $16.50

TRAIN, Arthur, The Prisoner at the Bar. 2nd ed., rev/enl,NY, 1908,386p,$17.50

IRVING, H., Trial of Franz Muller. P, 1911, 8vo, 194pp., $16.50

Translation of the Civil Code in Force in Cuba, Puerto Rico & the Philippines. DC, 1899, 322pp; bound with this: Translation of the Code of Commerce in Force in Cuba, Puerto Rico & the Philippines. DC, 1899, 291pp., contemp. 1/2 morocco, scuffed but tight, $30.00

Trial of Jeanne D'Arc, translated into English from the Original Latin & French Documents by W. D. Barrett...NY, 1932, roy8vo, 544pp., ex lib, new linen, $30.00

MAC KAY, David (ed.), Trial of Simon, Lord Lovat. P, 1911, 8vo, 314pp, $16.50

KNOTT, Geo. (ed.), Trial of Sir Roger Casement. L, 1926, 8vo, 304pp., $17.50

MOULTON, F. (ed.), Trial of Steinie Morrison. Toronto, 1922, 8vo,280pp., sl. worn, $16.50

TRUMBULL, J. H., The True Blue Laws of Connecticut & New Haven and the False Blue Laws Forged by Peters. Hartford, 1876, 8vo, 360pp., $27.50

TUCKER, Robert, The Just War. Johns Hopkins, 1960, 8vo, 207pp., $16.50

--24--

TWISS, Horace, The Public & Private Life of Lord Chancellor Eldon with Selections from His Correspondence. 2nd ed., L, 1844, roy8vo, 3vols., orig. cl., sl. worn, $95.00

TYLER, Samuel, Memoir of Roger Brooke Taney....Balto, 1872, roy8vo, 659pp., sl. marg. dpst of frontis., later linen, $27.50

UN SECRETARIAT, A Survey of Treaty Provisions for the Pacific Settlement of International Disputes, 1949-62. NY, 1966, 4to, 901pp., $27.50

USHER, Roland, Institutional History of the House of Commons, 1924, roy8vo, 70pp., orig. ptd. wrps., $17.50

VAN BYNKERSHOEK, Cornelius, Quaestionum Juris Publici Libri Duo. Oxford, 1930, 4to, 2vol., text & translation, $75.00

VAN WINKEL, Marshall (ed.), Sixty Famous Cases. NY, 1956, 8vo, 10vols., excellent, $125.00

VEEDER, Van Vechten, Legal Masterpieces. C, 1912, roy8vo, 2vols., 1324pp., sl wear, $37.50

VEENHOVEN, Willem (ed.), Case Studies on Human Rights & Fundamental Freedoms Hague, 1975-6, roy8vo, 5vols., $175.00 (List Proce: $295.00)

VON HOLST, Hermann, The Constitutional Law of the United States. C, 1897, 8vo, 369pp., rebacked, $22.50

VON RAUMER, Frederick, America and the American People. NY, 1946, roy8vo, 512pp., later linen, $47.50

VORHEES, Harvey, The Law of the Public School System. B, 1916, roy8vo, 429pp., $22.50

VREELAND, Hamilton, Hugo Grotius. Columbia, 1917, 8vo, 246pp., $25.00

VREELAND, Ham., Twilight of Individual Liberty. NY, 1944, 8vo, 171pp., $14.50

WAITE, John, Prevention of Repeated Crime. AA, 1943, 8vo, 221pp., $17.50

WALKER-SMITH, Derek, & CLAUDE, Life and Famous Cases of Sir Edward Clarke. L, 1942, 8vo, 351pp., $18.50

WALLER, Geo., Kidnap: Story of the Lindberg Case. NY, 1961, 8vo,595p, $18.50

WALSH, Robert, An Appeal from the Judgments of Great Britain Respecting the United States. 2nd ed., P, 1819, 8vo, liii,512pp., contemp. 1/2 calf and bds, few leaves browned & a few marginally dampstained, bit rubbed and scuffed, hinges tender, $65.00

WAMBAUGH, Eugene, The Study of Cases. 2nd ed., B, 1894, 8vo, 333pp., $27.50

WARDEN, Robert, An Account of the Private Life and Public Services of Salmon Portland Chase. Cincinnati, 1874, roy8vo, 838pp, later linen,$35.00

WARREN, Chs., The Supreme Court in US History. 2nd ed., rev., B, 1926, 8vo, 2vols., $47.50

WARREN, Geo., Traffic Courts. B, 1942, roy8vo, 280pp., $17.50

WAREVILLE, Geo., Essays in Legal Ethics. C, 1902, 8vo, 234pp., $22.50

WATSON, Alan, The Law of Obligations in the Later Roman Republic. Oxford, 1965, 8vo, 295pp., $25.00

WATSON, Alan, The Law of Persons in the Later Roman Republic. Oxford, 1967 8vo, 269pp., $25.00

WATSON, David, The Constitution of the United States.C, 1910, 4to, 2vols. $57.50

WATSON, Wm., A Practical Treatise on the Law Relating to the Office and Duty of Sheriff....P, 1834, 8vo, later linen, 370pp., sl. dpst, $47.50

WATSON, Wm., Treatise on the Law of Arbitration & Awards... P, 1836, 8vo, 260pp., later linen, $47.50

WELLMAN, Francis, Day in Court. NY, 1937, roy8vo, 257pp., $20.00

WELLMAN, Francis, Gentlemen of the Jury. NY, 1944, 8vo, 244pp., $22.50

WESTIN, Alan, Privacy & Freedom. NY, 1967, roy8vo, 487pp., $17.50

WESTLAKE, John, A Treatise on Private International Law. P, 1859, 8vo, 251pp., edges of title sl. chipped, later linen, scarce, $47.50

WEYL, Nathaniel, Treason. Story of Disloyalty & Betrayal in American History DC, 1950, 8vo, 491pp., $17.50

WHARTON, Francis, A Treatise on Mental Unsoundness... 4th ed., P, 1882, 4to, 781pp., Vol I (all published), $37.50

WHITE, Leonard, Introduction to the Study of Public Administration. rev ed. NY, 1939, roy8vo, 611pp., $22.50

WHITE, Wm., Insanity & the Criminal Law. NY, 1923, 8vo, 281pp., $17.50

WHITLOCK, Brand, On the Enforcement of Law in Cities. Ind, 1913, 8vo, 281pp., $13.50

WHITMAN, Bernard, Two Letters to theReverend Moses Stuart on the Subject of Religious Liberty. B, 1830, 8vo, 165pp., later linen, $37.50

WHITMORE, Wm., Bibliographical Sketch of the Laws of Massachusetts Colony from 1630 to 1686.... B, 1890, 4to, 150pp., later linen, $45.00

WHITNEY, Henry, Marriage & Divorce. P/NY, 1894, 8vo, 377pp, sl. soil, $17.50

WIGMORE, John Henry, Code of the Rules of Evidence in Trials at Law. 2nd ed. B, 1935, 8vo, 621pp., $25.00

WIGMORE, John H., Panorama of the World's Legal Systems. St.P, 1928, sm4to, 3vols., w/500 ills., $75.00

WIGMORE, John H., (Chairman, Committee of the Association of American Law Schools), Select-Essays in Anglo-American Legal History. B, 1807-08, roy8vo, 3vols., nice set, $115.00

WIGMORE, John & KOCOUREK, (eds.), Rational Basis of Legal Institutions. Intro. by Holmes, NY, 1927, 8vo, 603pp., ex lib, new linen, $30.00

WILL, Britton, Liberty Under Law.... 2nded., rev/enl, St.L, 1880, 8vo, 385pp., inscribed, $27.50

WILLARD, Jos., Half-Century with Judges & Lawyers. B,1895, 8vo, 371p, $27.50

WILLIAMS, Glanville, Learning the Law. 6th ed.,L, 1957, 8vo,220pp, $17.50

WILLIAMS, Glanville, Liability for Animals. Camb, 1939, 4to, 409p, $27.50

WILLIAMS, Joshua, Principles of the Law of Personal Property.... 11th ed., L, 1881, 8vo, 556pp., $22.50

WILLIAMS, W. E., Lectures on the Constitution and Supreme Court of the US. Dallas, 1924, roy8vo, 97pp., $17.50

WILLIAMS, Roger, Free & Unequal: Biological Basis of Individual Liberty. Austin, 1953, roy8vo, 177pp., $16.50

WILLISTONM Samuel, Law Governing the Sale of Goods at Common Law. 2nd ed., NY, 1924, 4to, 2vols., $47.50

WILLISTON, Samuel, The Law of Contracts. NY, 1927, 4to, 5vols, $125.00

WILLISTON, Samuel, A Selection of Cases on the Law of Sales at Common Law. 2nd ed., Camb, 1905, 4to, 1086pp., underlined, $27.50

WILLMORE, J. S., The Great Crime & Its Moral. NY, 1917, 8vo, 323pp, $17.50

WILSON, Fred, Our Constitution & Its Makers. NY, 1937,8vo, 585pp., $17.50

WILSON, Louis, & TAUBER, The University Library.C, 1945, 8vo, 570pp, $27.50

WINES, Frederick, Punishment & Reformation. NY, 1910, 8vo, 387pp., $17.50

--20--

WINFIELD, Percy, The Present Law of Abuse of Legal Procedure. Camb, 1921, roy8vo, 256pp., $22.50

WISE, Raymond, Legal Ethics. NY, 1966, 8vo, 290pp., $17.50

WITTENBERG, Ph, Law of Literary Property. Cl, 1956 8vo, 284pp, $15.50

WITTKE, Carl (ed.), Essays in History & Political Theory in Honor of Charles Howard Mc Ilwain. Harvard, 1936, 8vo, 371pp., $17.50

WODDESSON, Richard, Lectures on the Law of England, w/Notes & Adds by W. R. Williams. P, 1842, 8vo, 3vols, later 1/2 linen, $150.00

WOERNER, J. G., Treatise on the American Law of Administration. 3rd ed., rev B, 1923, 8vo, 3vols., $75.00

WOOD, Earl, Fee Contracts for Lawyers. NY, 1936 ,4to, 432pp., $25.00

WRIGHT, Benjamin, Growth of American Constitutional Law.NY, 1946, 8vo, 276pp., $14.50

WRIGHT, Edw., Ladies & Gentlemen of the Jury. NY, 1962, 8vo, 166pp, $14.50

ZACCHIAS, Paolo, Totius Status Ecclesiastici. Quaestiones Medico-Legales. 2nd ed., Venice, 1751, folio, 3vols., bound as one, 347,328,296pp., contemp. vellum, bit worn, sporadic marginal worming with the occasional loss of a letter, "one of the founders of medical jurisprudence." Garrison-Morton. #720, $335.00

ADDENDA

COWEN, Esek, A Treatise on the Civil Jurisdiction of a Justice of the Peace in the State of New York. Albany, 1821, 8vo, 750pp., contemp. roan, bit worn but a nice copy, $75.00

MORRIS, Gouvenor,. Life of, with Selections from his Correspondence & Miscellaneous Papers. ed. Jared Sparks. B, 1852, 8vo, 3vds. later linen, $75.00

CATALOGUE 33
LAW AND LEGAL HISTORY

January, 1982

With first editions of: Bentham, Blackstone, Clarendon, Dane, Hegel, Leibnitz, Livingston, Marshall, Montesquieu & Story; an outstanding trial collection; numerous early treatises and scholarly works, and a collection of Law Prints.

WITH AN ADDENDA OF VARIA

INCLUDING SCIENCE POLITICAL ECONOMY LITERATURE REFERENCE

RICHARD ADAMIAK
1545 EAST 60th St.
CHICAGO, ILL.60637
312-955-4571 (from 7AM to 3PM)

TERMS OF SALE: All titles are offered on a subject-to-prior-sale basis. Prices are net in US dollars; shipping charges extra. Deferred remittance for institutions. Past private clients are expected to remit upon receipt; new private clients may be asked to remit upon receipt of a pro-forma invoice. We will ship in the manner most appropriate to the order & destination. Air-freight (via KLM Royal Dutch Airlines) available on request. All books, unless otherwise noted, are in very good condition; all significant defects are noted. Any book is returnable within five days of receipt only if deemed not as described. All cable and phone reserves must be confirmed in writing within seven days.

REFERENCES: Marvin, Legal Bibliography, 1847; Encyclopedia Britannica, Eleventh Edition (EB11); Encyclopedia of the Social Sciences, 1937 (ESS); where no reference is given the material is usually drawn from one or more of the following: Allgemeine Deutsche Biographie (1875); Grand Dictionnaire Universel (1875); Jöchers Allgemeines Gelehrten Lexikon (1750).

"The Law Library" This catalogue contains an unusually large number of early 19th century English treatises published in America in the Law Library series, Philadelphia, Littel, 1834ff. It was begun because of the inconvenience of procuring these works in America and their prohibitive cost. It consists of the most notable works of the period, many of them classics. The American editions in this series are complete texts but appear to be shorter versions because of the printing format: 11 point type and about 50 lines per page. For example, the Dublin edition of Joy's Confessions is 248pp; the same text in the Law Library format is 112pp. This format enabled the publisher to offer for $10.00 works which would otherwise cost $60.00. The series was very well received: James Kent wrote, "The Law Library is a work most advantageous to the profession and I hope and trust that you will find encouragement to persevere in it." It was a subscribed series and thus limited. When Marvin wrote in 1847 the early volumes were already out-of-print. Most of the titles are scarce and many rare. While the individual works are of intrinsic merit, the series as a whole is an important chapter in the history of American law. For further details, see Marvin under the series title. Works in the series in this catalogue are indicated by "LL."

---

1)ABBIATECI, A., & BILLACOIS, F. et al, Crimes et Criminalite en France sous l'Ancien Regime 17e--18e Siecles. F, Colin, 1971, roy8vo, 268pp., linen, $22.50.

2) ABBOT, Everett, Justice & the Modern Law. B, 1913, 8vo, 299pp., $18.50

3) ABBOTT, Nathan (ed.), Brief Making and the Use of Law Books, by Wm. Lile, Redfield, Wambaugh, Mason & Jas. Wheeler. St. P, 1906, roy8vo, 472pp., $27.50

4) ABBOTT, Wilbur, Bibliography of Oliver Cromwell. Harvard, 1929, roy8vo, 540pp., $27.50

5) A BECKETT, Gilbert, The Comic Blackstone, with Ills by Cruikshank. Detroit, 1897, 8vo, 160pp., $35.00

6) ACTON, Lord, Essays on Church & State, ed. Douglas Woodruff. NY, 1953, roy8vo, 518pp., $25.00

7) ADAMIAK, Richard, Justice & History in the Old Testament: The Evolution of Divine Retribution, with a Foreword by David Noel Freedman. C, forthcoming, 8vo, about 115pp; the author is a doctoral candidate in the University of Chicago; David Freedman is Director of the Program on Studies in Religion in the University of Michigan, Director of Publications of the American Schools of Oriental Research and editor of the Anchor Bible Series. $12.50

8) ADAMS, Geo. B., The Origin of the English Constitution. Yale, 1912, roy8vo, 378pp., $25.00

9) ADAMS, Geo. B., Council & Courts in Anglo-Norman England. Yale, 1926, roy8vo, 403pp., $25.00

10)ADAMS, John, The Legal Papers of, ed. by Wroth & Zobel, Harvard, 1965, roy8vo, 3vols., $65.00

11)AIKENS, Asa, Practical Forms with Notes & References....Concerning the Cases to which they are Applicable. 2nd ed., rev, corr & enl., Windsor, Vt., 1836, 12mo, 447pp., later linen, $37.50

12)ALEXANDER, G. G., The Administration of Justice in Criminal Matters (in England & Wales). Cambridge, 1915, roy8vo, 235pp., $22.50

13)ALLEN, J.W., History of Political Thought in the 16th Century. L, 1928 (1960), 8vo, 527pp., $22.50

14)ALLEN, Stephen, Evolution of Government & Laws. rev ed. Princeton, 1922, roy8vo, 2vols, 1300pp. $45.00

15)ALLNATT, Chs., A Practical Treatise on the Law of Partition with an Appendix Containing the Statutes & a Selection of Precedents. P, 1834, 8vo, 104pp., LL, later linen, $37.50

16)A MACHICADO AC ROSSILLO, Emanuele, & DE VALLARNA, Francisco, Additiones Legales Hispanicae ad Bibliothecam R. P. Fr. Lucii Ferraris, per Alphabeticum Auctoris Ordinem Distributae, Hodiernis, Antiquisque Ordinationibus, tam Castellae, quam Indarum, Accommodata,....Opus....Utilissimum, et Necessarium Omnibus R. R. Archiepiscopis,...Abbatibus, Judicibus, Advocatis, atque utriusque juris Professoribus. Madrid, 1782, 4to, 2vols., contemp. vellum, $175.00

17)AMERICAN CORRESPONDENCE SCHOOL OF LAW, Chicago (c. 1925), series of 19 lectures on law each by a different author; all in the orig. ptd. wrps., boxed, scarce and important, $75.00

18)AMERICAN LAW REGISTER, New Series, Vol. I (Old Series, Vol. 10), edited by Redfield, Dwight, Dean & Wharton. P, 1862, roy8vo, 188pp., later linen, $35.00

19)AMES, Fisher, The Works of, Compiled by His Friends, to which are Prefixed Notices of His Life & Character. B, 1809, 8vo, 519pp., scarce, important American statesman, orator & polical writer, $75.00

20)AMOS, Sheldon, Political & Legal Remedies for War. NY, 1880, 8vo, 254pp., $22.50

Ancient Laws and Institutes of Wales: Comprising the Laws Supposed to be Enacted by Howel Good....& Anomalous Laws....with an English Translation of the Welsh Text, to which are Added a Few Latin Transcripts Containing Digests of the Welsh Laws. L, 1841, 4to, 2vols., 904, 1128pp., later linen, $125.00

ANGELL, Jos., A Treatise on the Law of Carriers of Goods & Passengers by Land & Water. 2nd ed. rev & enl., B, 1851, roy8vo, 802pp., later linen, $45.00

ANGLE, Paul, One Hundred Years of Law: An Account of the Law Office which John T. Stuart Founded in Springfield a Century Ago. Springfield, 1928, 8vo, 53pp., $25.00

Annals of the American Academy of Political & Social Science. various volumes, all in the original ptd. wrps., vol. numbers & dates as indicated; $15.00 each: 24-1)The Administration of Justice (167, May, 1933)256pp; 24-2)Economics of World Peace (150, July, 1930), 324pp; 24-3)Prohibition: A National Experiment (163, Sept, 1932), 269pp; 24-4)Ownership & Regulation of Public Utilities (201, Jan, 1939), 295pp.; 24-5) Our Foreign Commerce in Peace & War (211, Sept, 1940), 225pp; 24-6) When War Ends: Consideration of the Conditions Necessary to Bring About a Lasting Peace (210, July, 1940), 195pp; 24-7) Labor Relations & the War (224, Nov, 1942), 244pp; 24-8) Power & the Public (159 Pt. 1, Jan, 1932), 190pp; 24-9)Organized Commodity Markets; and: Zoning in the US (May, 1931), 500pp; 24-10) Prisons of Tomorrow (157, Sept, 1941), 262pp; 24-11) The Constitution in the 20th Century (185, May, 1936), 280pp; 24-12) The State Constitution of the Future (181, Sept, 1935), 233pp; 24-13) The Attainment & Maintainence of World Peace (186, July, 1936), 251pp; 24-14) Government Finance in the Modern Economy (183, Jan, 1936), 313pp; 24-15) Banking & Transportation Problems (171; Jan, 1934), 313pp; 24-16) Increasing Government Control in Economic Life (178; March, 1935), 248pp; 24-17) American Policy in the Pacific (168; July, 1933), 274pp; 24-18) The International Labor Organization (166; March, 1933), 239pp; 24-19) China (152; Nov, 1930), 431pp; 24-20) Our State Legislators (195; Jan, 1938), 250pp;and Constitutional Rights, ed. by Herbert Goodrich, 123pp; 24-21) Crime in the United States (217; Sept, 1941), 237pp; 24-22) Administrative Regulation of Private Enterprise (221; May, 1942), 256pp; 24-23) Anti-Trust Laws of the United States (147; Jan, 1930), 236pp; 24-24) Police & the Crime Problem (146; Nov, 1929), 293pp; 24-25) America & Japan: A Survey (215; May, 1941), 247pp; 24-26) Frontiers of Legal Aid Work (205; Sept, 1939), 225pp; 24-27) Government Expansion in the Economic Sphere (206; Nov, 1939), 229pp; 24-28) Intergovernmental Relations in the US (207; Jan, 1940), 276pp; 24-29) Freedom of Inquiry & Expression (200; Nov, 1938), 365pp; 24-30) Refugees (203; May, 1939), 271pp.

La Salle Extension University: Department of Law; Annual Catalogue, 1912-13. 4to, 103pp., ill., orig. ptd. wrps, sl. lower foredge dampstain throughout; with 4pp. brochure describing books used, $35.00

ANSON, Sir Wm. et al, Rights of Citizenship: Survey of Safeguards for the People. L, 1912, 242p. $18.50

ANTHONY, Elliot, A Treatise on the Law of Consolidation of Railroad Companies, Being an Argument in the Case of Julius Wadsworth....vs Chicago & Northwestern Railway Co. Chicago, Beach & Barnard,1865, roy8vo, xvi, 288pp., contemp. bds., rebacked, $125.00

Archives de Philosophie du Droit, No. 14; Le Droit et la Crise Universitaire; Recents Apports Sociologiques a la Philosophie du Droit. P, 1969, roy8vo, 404pp., orig. ptd. wrps., $22.50

ARGUILLIERE, H. X., Saint Gregoire VII: Essai sur sa Conception du Pouvoir Pontifical.P, 1934, 599pp., orig. ptd. wrps., $27.50

Argument in Defense of the Rev. Eliphalet Nott, Pres. of Union College, in Answer to the Charges Made Against Him....Presented before the Committee of the Senate Appointed to Investigate Certain Pecuniary Affairs of the College, by John Spencer. Albany, 1853, 8vo, 113,111pp., later linen, $35.00

Arguments of the Defendant's Counsel (Horace Binney) and Judgment of the Supreme Court (Jos. Story) in the Case of Vidal & Another, versus the Mayor of Phila delphia....to which is Added the Will of Stephen Girard. Phil., 1854, roy8vo, 348pp., orig. cl., crown sl. worn, $37.50

ARNAUD, A-J., Les Origines Doctrinales du Code Civil Francais. P, 1969, roy8vo, 326pp., wrps, $22.50

ARNOLD, G.F., Psychology Applied to Legal Evidence. 2nd ed., Calcutta, 1913, roy8vo, 607pp., $25.00

ASHTON, Arthur, As I Went on My Way. L, 1924, 8vo, 267pp, bit rubbed, (Bencher of Inner Temple) $20.00

ATHERLEY, Edmund, A Practical Treatise of the Law of Marriage & Other Family Settlements. P, 1840,8vo, xxii,226pp., later linen, LL "an able & excellent treatise," Jas. Kent in Marvin, 74, $57.50

ATKINSON, S., An Essay on Marketable or Doubtful Titles to Real Estate. P, 1838, 8vo, 334pp.LL, $47.50

ATOMIC ENERGY COMMISSION: LOS ALAMOS SCIENTIFIC LABORAROTY, Effects of Atomic Weapons. DC, 1950, roy8vo, 456pp., $25.00

ATTON, Henry, & HOLLAND, Henry, The King's Customs: An Account of Maritime Revenue & Contraband Traffic ....from the Earliest Times. L, 1908, 8vo, 489pp., $25.00

A Volume Relating to the Early History of Boston, Containing the Aspinwall Notarial Records, 1644-51. B, 1903, roy8vo, 455pp., $35.00

AYLIFFE, John, A New Pandect of Roman Civil Law, As Anciently Established in that Empire; & Now Received & Practiced in Most European Nations; with Many Useful Observations Thereon, Shewing Wherein that Law Differs from the Municipal Laws of Great Britain, from the Canon Law in General and from that Part of It Now in Use Here with Us in England; Whereunto is Prefixed by Way of Introduction A Preliminary Discourse, Touching upon the Rise & Progress of the Civil Law, from the Most Early Times of the Roman Empire; Wherein is also Comprised a Particular Account of the Books Themselves Containing this Law, the Names of the Authors & Compilers of them, the Several Editions, and the Best Commentators Thereon. L, 1734, folio, xlviii, 608pp., later 1/2 calf & boards, $350.00

BABCOCK, Fred., The Appraisal of Real Estate. NY, 1927, 8vo, 380pp., $22.50

BABINGTON, Richard, A Treatise on the Law of Auctions. P, 1838, 8vo, 124pp., later linen, LL, $37.50

BABINGTON, R., Treatise on the Law of Set-Off & Mutual Credit.P, 1834, 8vo, 85pp, later lin, LL,$37.50

The Babylonian Laws, trans with Commentary by G. Driver & J. Mills, Oxford, 1952, roy8vo, 2vols,$75.00

BACON, Francis, Opera Omnia, Quatuor Voluminibus Comprehensa: Hactenus Edita, ad Autographorum maxime fidem, emendantur; Nonnulla etiam, ex MSS Codicibus deprompta, nunc primum prodeunt. (text in Latin & English) London, 1730, very tall folio, 4vols., one of 24 subscribed large paper copy sets, engraved frontis in each volume, bound in later 1/2 calf and marbled boards, beautiful, $475.00

BACON, Francis, The Works of....a New Edition with a Life of the Author by Basil Montague, P, 1841, small 4to, 3vols.,(reprints of his works available at $495.00 & $1050.00), $150.00

BACON, Francis, The Works of Lord Bacon, with An Introductory Essay & Portrait. L, 1871, small4to, 2vols., contemp. 1/2 calf & linen, bit rubbed, $125.00

(BACON) DIXON, William, The Personal History of Lord Bacon from Unpublished Papers. B, 1861, 8vo, 424pp., orig. cl., sl. trace of wear, nice copy, $35.00

49) BACON, Matthew, A New Abridgment of the Law, with Considerable Additions by Henry Gwillim, first American from the 6th London edition, with the Addition of the Later English & American Decisions by Bird Wilson. P, 1813, roy8vo, 7vols., bound in full contemp. calf, bit rubbed and scuffed & a trifle worn in spots; a very attractive set, $750.00

"Bacon's Abridgment, so well known to the profession, was first published in 1736 & has passed through six large editions. The contents of the work owe very little to the nominal author, and were chiefly extracted from the manuscript collections of Lord Chief Baron Gilbert....It consists of a series of tracts, or dissertations, upon various topics of the law, generally illustrated by adjudications, and, though incomplete, exhibiting a rare union of sagacity and industry. As a text-book for students it has long maintained an unrivalled reputation, and, as the expositions of a very able and learned judge upon a large survey of the law, dealing with its history and its reasons, it must forever hold a high rank among the treasures of the profession. Mr. Gwillim's edition is by far the best, and this edition has been republished in America under the superintendence of Bird Wilson, who has enriched it with many valuable additions." Joseph Story, Miscellaneous Writings, 1835, 327.

BAER, Jules, & BALICER, S., Cross-Examination & Summation. NY, 1933, roy8vo, 622pp., $27.50

BAGEHOT, Walter, The English Constitution. London, 1867, 8vo, viii,348pp., orig. cloth, new end sheets, first edition, $275.00

"This classic account of that most elusive and least codified of entities, the Constitution of England, has never lost its popularity, and shows signs of being elevated from the rank of a first-class handbook to a place with de Tocqueville as one of the most important texts in political literature. It showed how the close cooperation between executive government and legislature established by the cabinet system is the effective part of the English Constitution & the real centre of power. Some measure of the importance of what might seem at first sight an insular topic--the practical working of one nation's constitution-- can be gained from the number of times it has been translated. Bagehot's work is of more than English importance: it is the great defence of empirical as against theoretical politics." Printing and the Mind of Man, 358.

BAGEHOT, Walter, The English Constitution & Other Political Essays. rev ed. NY, 1878, 8vo, 468p. $35.00

BAGLEY, Wm., The Practice at the Chambers of the Judges of the Courts of Common Law, in Civil Actions. P, 1837, 8vo, 200pp., later linen, LL, $57.50

"As good as a work can be on the subject--he has attempted with as much success as was possible to do that which is next to impossible, namely, to separate the practice at Chambers from the practice of the Courts generally." Marvin, 88.

BALDWIN, Simeon, The Young Man and the Law. NY, 1924, 8vo, 116pp., $17.50

BALLARD, Adolphus, The Domesday Inquest. L, 1906, roy8vo, 283pp., $25.00

BANCROFT, Hubert, Popular Tribunals. SF, 1887, roy8vo, 2vols., 1600pp., $57.50

BARKER, Dudley, Lord Darling's Famous Cases. L, 1936, 8vo, 256pp., $22.50

BARKER, John, Missouri Lawyer. P, 1949, 8vo, 391pp., spine faded, $17.50

BARNES, Alb., The Throne of Iniquity: Or, Sustaining Evil by Law: A Discussion on Behalf of a Law Prohibiting the Traffic in Intoxicating Drinks.P, (1852), 8vo, 31p., orig. ptd. wrps, $27.50

BARNESBY , Norman, Medical Chaos & Crime. L/NY, 1910, 8vo, 384pp., $25.00

BARRINGTON, Daines, Observations upon the Statutes, Chiefly the More Ancient,from Magna Carta, to the 21st of Jas 1st....with an Appendix for New Moddeling the Statutes. 2nd ed., with corrs. & adds. Dublin, 1767, 8vo, 428pp., later 1/2 calf, $150.00

"Contributed very much to the elucidation of the more ancient laws of England by introducing historical illustrations of the times during which the statutes were enacted....abounds in curious, learned and valuable information." Marvin, 96.

BARROW, G.W., Feudal Britain: Completion of the Medieval Kingdoms. L, 1956, 8vo, 452pp., $22.50

BARTON, Tilney, Life of a Country Lawyer in Peace & Wartime. Oxford, Shakespeare Head Press, (1937) crown sl. worn, (solicitor in the S.C. of Judicature & Official Receiver in Bankruptcy), $18.50

BATEMAN, Thomas, A Treatise on Agistment Tithe, in which the Nature, Right, Objects, Mode of Payment & Method of Ascertaining the Value of Each Species of It are Fully Stated & Explained. 2nd ed., with large adds, (1778); bound with this his Appendix (1779); 8vo, 102,133pp., contemp. 1/2 calf and marbled boards, scarce, $145.00

BATY, T., & MORGAN, J., War: Its Conduct & Legal Results. L, 1915, 8vo, 578pp., $30.00

BAXTER, Ian, Essays on Private Law, Foreign Law & Foreign Judgments. Toronto, 1966, 8vo, 210pp, $17.50

BEALE, Joseph Henry, Cases on Taxation. Harvard, 1922, 4to, 511pp., $27.50

BEAMES, John, A Summary of the Doctrine of Courts of Equity, with Respect to Costs, Deduced from Leading Cases. P, 1838, 8vo, 152pp., later linen, LL, $47.50

"All of this author's writings denote a mind thoroughly imbued with, & capable of grasping, his subjects....his comments upon other writers are models of judicious legal criticism." Marvin, 102.

BECK, Theodoric & John, Elements of Medical Jurisprudence. 12th edition, rev. by E. C. Gilman, P, 1863, roy8vo, 2vols., 1900pp., contemp. roan, bit rubbed & scuffed but sound, scarce, $125.00

BECKNER, Earl, History of Labor Legislation in Illinois. Univ. of Chicago, 1929, 8vo, 539pp., $25.00

BECKWITH, Edmund, Lawful Action of State Military Forces. NY, 1944, 8vo, 210pp., $22.50

BELL, H.E., An Introduction to the History & Records of the Court of Wards & Liveries. Cambridge, 1953, 8vo, 215pp., $25.00

BEMIS, Geo., Report of the Case of John W. Webster....Indicted for the Murder of Geo. Parkman, Before the Supreme Judicial Court of Mass....& An Appendix Containing Several Interesting Matters Never before Published. B, 1850, roy8vo, 628pp., later linen, $47.50

BENNETT, W. H., A Short Dissertation on the Nature of the Various Proceedings in the Master's Office in the Court of Chancery. P, 1842, 8vo, 222pp., later linen, LL, $57.50

BENTHAM, Jeremy, The Works of Jeremy Bentham, Published under the Superintendence of His Executor, John Bowring. Edinburgh, 1843, roy8vo, 11vols., bound in later 1/2 oasis morocco & boards, raised bands, very elegant set, first collected edition, $1250.00

BENTHAM, Jeremy, The Correspondence of, ed. T. Sprigge. Vols. I & II, 1752-1780; Univ. of London, 1968, roy8vo, 2vols., 425,560pp., (List price: $120.00), $70.00

BENTHAM, Jeremy, Oeuvres, en 4 Tomes, traduits par P.E. Dumont et B. Laroche (1829), Reprint, 1969, 4to, 4vols., $125.00

BERGMAN, Carl, History of the Reparations. B, 1927, 4to, 333pp., $27.50

A) BROWN, Esther, Lawyers & the Promotion of Justice. NY, 1938, 8vo, 302pp., $20.00

79) BEVERIDGE, Albert, The Life of John Marshall. B, 1929, roy8vo, 4vols, nice set, $75.00

80) BEVERIDGE, Alb., The Vitality of the American Constitution: An Address. Pittsburgh, 1898, 8vo, 22pp., linen, scarce, $27.50

81) BEVILL, Rob., A Treatise on the Law of Homicide & Of Larceny at Common Law. L, 1799, 8vo, 287pp., later 1/2 sheep & bds, $75.00

BIDDLE, Geo. & MC MURTRIE, Rich., A General Index to the English Common Law Reports, Vols. I to LXXXIII Inclusive. 2nd ed. P, 1857, roy8vo, 2vols., later linen, $65.00

BIGELOW, L. J., Bench & Bar: A Complete Digest of the Wit, Humor, Asperities & Amenities of the Law. NY, 1867, 8vo, 364pp., $35.00

(BIGELOW, Melville,) Centralization & the Law: Scientific Legal Education. B, 1906, 8vo,296p. $17.50

BILLSON, Wm., Equity in Its Relation to Common Law: A Study in Legal Development. B, 1917, roy8vo, 234pp., $25.00

BINGHAM, Peregrine, The Law & Practice of Judgments & Executions, Including Extents at the Suit of the Crown. P, 1836, 8vo, 238pp., later 1/2 linen & bds, LL, $57.50

BINKLEY, W. E., The Powers of the President. NY, 1937, 8vo, 332pp., $20.00

BINMORE, Henry, Probate Practice in the State of Illinois. C, 1896, roy8vo, 788p. roan, rubbed,$35.00

Biographical Directory of the American Congress, 1774-1927. DC, 1928, folio, 1740pp., $47.50

BIRCH, Walter, The Royal Charters of the City of Lincoln, Henry II to William III, transcribed & translated with an Introduction. Cambridge, 1911, roy8vo, xlix,308pp., $30.00

BIRKENHEAD, Rt. Hon. Earl of, Law, Life & Letters. NY, 1927, roy8vo, 2vols., $45.00

BIRKENHEAD, Rt. Hon., Points of View. L, 1922, 8vo, 2vols., learned essays on law, $55.00

BIRKS, Michael, Gentlemen of the Law. L, 1960, roy8vo, 304pp., ill. quite interesting, $30.00

BIRRELL, Augustine, Res Judicatae: Papers & Essays. L, 1892, 12mo, 277pp., $25.00

BISHOP, Joel, Commentaries on the Criminal Law. 3rd ed. B, 1865, roy8vo, 2vols., later linen, $115.00

BISHOP, Prentiss, The First Book of the Law: Explaining the Nature, Sources, Books & Practical Applications of Legal Science & Methods of Study & Practice. B, 1868, roy8vo, 466p, later linen, $57.50

BISSETT, Andrew, A Practical Treatise on the Law of Estates for Life. P, 1843, 8vo, 206pp., later linen, LL, $57.50

"contains all that is essential & displays equal learning & judgment," Marvin, 121.

BLACKMER, R. C., Student's Manual of Medical Jurisprudence. St. L, 1890, 8vo, $17.50

BLACKSTONE, Sir Wm., An Analysis of the Laws of England. Second Edition. Oxford, 1757, 8vo, 180pp., later 1/2 calf & boards, $250.00

)BLACKSTONE, Sir Wm., A Treatise on the Law of Descents in Fee-Simple. Oxford, 1759, 8vo, 87pp., contemp. calf, skillfully rebacked, first edition, $650.00

)BLACKSTONE, Sir Wm., Commentaries on the Laws of England, the 13th Edition with the Last Corrections of the Author, and with Notes & Additions by Edward Christian. London, 1800, 8vo, 4vols., later 1/2 calf & boards, an extra illustrated edition with engravings of Fortescue, Somers, Blackstone, Raymond, Foster, Hale, Hardwicke, Comyns, Gilbert, Mansfield, Holt & Coke. handsome set, $450.00

)BLACKSTONE, Sir Wm., Commentaries on the Laws of England, with a Life of the Author & Notes by Christian, Chitty, Lee, Hovenden & Ryland, and also References to American Cases by a Member of the New York Bar. P, 1844-1857, roy8vo, 4vols. bound (as issued) as 2, later linen, $150.00

)BLACKSTONE, Sir Wm., Commentaries on the Laws of England, with a Life of the Author & Notes by Christian, Chitty.... P, 1874, roy8vo, 2vols., later linen, few leaves skillfully mended, $125.00

)BLACKSTONE, Wm., An Analytical Abridgment of the Commentaries of Sir Wm. Blackstone together with an Analytical Synopsis of Each, by John Anthon. NY, 1809, 8vo, 279pp., with 4 fold out tables, later 1/2 linen, slight sporadic dampstain, $75.00

)(BLACKSTONE) CHRISTIAN, Edw., Notes to Blackstone's Commentaries which are Calculated to Answer all the Editions. B, 1801, 12mo, 280pp., later linen, Christian's complete notes which are only excerpted in the other editions. $47.50

)BLAKEY, Roy & Gladys, The Federal Income Tax. NY, 1940, roy8vo, 640pp., $27.50

)BLEDSOE, S. T., Indian Land Laws: Being a Treatise on Indian Land Titles in Oklahoma....Also a Compilation of Treaties, Agreements, Statutes....KC, 1913, 4to, 967pp., 2nd ed., $47.50

)BLOCH, Marc, Feudal Society. trans. L. Manyon. Univ. of Chicago, 1962, roy8vo, 498pp., $25.00

)BLOCH, Louis, Labor Agreements in Coal Mines. NY, 1931, 8vo, 513pp., $22.50

)BLUNTSCHLI, J.K. Theory of the State, trans. from the 6th German ed. Oxford,1885, roy8vo,518p, $25.00

)BÖHMER, Iusti Henningus, Consultationum et Decisionum Iuris: Tomus I; in Duas Partes Divisus: Quarum Prior, Iuris Ecclesiastici; Posterior Iuris Publici et Feudalis; Selectiora Argumenta Adiectis Observationibus Necessariis exhibit, ex Schedis Paternis Collegit, Convenient Ordine Digessit..... Filius Carolus Augustus Böhmer. Halle/Magdeburg, 1733, tall folio, 2vols. bound as one, 608,596pp. contemp. vellum, nice copy, $275.00

Complete in itself with two additional collections published subsequently; Böhmer, (1674-1749) was professor of law in Halle, a celebrated jurist & legal historian, especially of Roman and Canon Law.

BOLINGBROKE, Works of, ed. Mallet.(1754), Reprint: 1968, roy8vo, 5vols., $150.00

BOORSTIN, Daniel, The Mysterious Science of Law. Harvard, 1941, 8vo, 251pp.,$25.00

BORDWELL, Percy, The Law of War between Belligerents: History & Commentary. C, 1908, roy8vo,374p$27.50

BORGHERS, A.R., Precis de l'Histoire de la Constitution d'Angleterre....d'Apres Hallam. Paris/Leipsick, 1828, 8vo, xii, 396pp., later linen, uncut, $57.50

Boston Slave Riot: Trial of Anthony Burns, Containing the Report of the Faneuil Hall Meeting; the Murder of Batchelder; Parker's Lesson for the Day, Speeches of Counsel on Both Sides, and a Verbatim Report of Judge Lorings Decision. B, 1854, 8vo, 86pp., later linen, Burns was captured in Mass. and extradited under the Fugitive Slave Law. $57.50

(Burns Trial) PARKER, Theodore, A New Crime Against Humanity: A Sermon Preached at the Music Hall. B, 1854, 8vo, 76pp., later linen, (denunciation of the trial), $30.00

BOTEIN, Bernard & GORDON, M., The Trial of the Future. NY, 1963, 8vo, 185pp., $20.00

A) BROWN, Esther, Lawyers & the Promotion of Justice. NY, 1938, 8vo, 302pp.,

119) BOUTMY, Emile, The English Constitution. trans. I. Eaden, Intro. by Sir. Fred. Pollock, L, 1891, 8vo, xvii, 212pp., tiny spine tear, $22.50

120) BOUTMY, Emile, Essai d'une Psychologie politique du Peuple anglais au xix Siecle. P, 1901, 8vo, 453pp., $22.50

121) BOWEN, Catherine, The Lion & the Throne: The Life & Times of Sir Edward Coke. B, 1957, roy8vo, 652pp., $22.50

BOWEN-ROWLANDS, Ernest, Seventy-Two Years at the Bar. L, 1924, 8vo, 410pp., sl. worn, $22.50

BRADSHAW, Henry (ed.), Statutes of the Lincoln Cathedral, with Illustrative Documents, ed. by Ch. Wordsworth; Pt. I, containing the complete Text of the 'Liber Niger.' Cambridge, 1892, roy8vo, 468pp., sl. worn, $27.50

BRANDEIS, Louis, The Curse of Bigness: Miscellaneous Papers, NY, 1934, roy8vo, 339pp., $35.00

BRANDT, Irving, James Madison: Father of the Constitution. NY, 1950, roy8vo, 520pp., $25.00

BRENTANO, Lujo, Relation of Labor to the Law of Today. trans. Sherman. NY, 1891, 12mo, 305p, $25.00

BRINDZE, Ruth, All About Courts & the Law, foreword by Erwin Griswold. NY, 1964, roy8vo, 138pp., children's book & directly related to the sociology of law, $15.00

BRISSON, Barnabe, De Verborum quae ad Ius Civile Pertinent Significatione: Opus Praestantissimum in Meliorem Commodiorumque Ordinem Redactum Innumeris Meddis Emaculatum et Post Aliorum Curas Plurimis Accessionibus Observationibusque, Philologicis, Criticis, Iuridicis Locuplatum. Produit Opera Studioque Io. Gottliebii Heinecci,...Praemissa Praefatione Nova, De Interpretationibus Gramaticae in Iure Civili Fatis et Vario Usu Nec non Huis Novae Editionis Praerogativis Iusti Henningii Böhmeri. Halle, 1743, folio, 1436pp., contemp. vellum, slight trace of wear at crown; also contains Francois Hotman's De Verbis Feudalibus Commentarius, nice copy, $350.00
Three legal luminaries are connected with this work; Brisson (1531-1591), a major jurist & legal historian; Böhmer; and Heineccius, "one of the most important and influential jurists of the 18th century." ESS, VII, 316.

BRODERICK, Hon. Geo., English Land and Landlords: An Inquiry into the Origin & Character of the English Land System, with Proposals for Its Reform. L, 1881, roy8vo, 515pp., $35.00

BROOM, Herbert, A Selection of Legal Maxims, Classified & Illustrated, ed. by W. Byrne, 9th ed. L, 1924, 4to, 668pp., handsome book, "best book of the kind extant," Marvin, 152, $37.50

BROOM, Herbert, The Philosophy of Law, Being Notes of Lectures Delivered During Twenty-Three Years (1852-75) in the Inner Temple Hall. NY, 1876, 8vo, 307pp., title reinforced, scarce, $57.50

BROSSARD, Jac., La Cour Supreme et la Constitution: La Forum Constitutionnol au Canada. Montreal, 1968, 8vo, 427pp., orig. ptd. wrps, $20.00

BROWN, GG., Law Administration & Negro-White Relations in Philadelphia. P, 1947, roy8vo,183p, $17.50

BROWN, Irving, Law & Lawyers in Literature. B, 1883, 8vo, 413pp., $22.50

BRUCE, Andrew, The American Judge. NY, 1924, 8vo, 218pp., $20.00

BRYCE, Jas., Studies in History & Jurisprudence. Oxford, 1901, 8vo, 2vols., 926pp., $57.50

BRYCE, Jas., Modern Democracies. NY, 1921, roy8vo, 2vols., $37.50

BRYCE, Jas., The Holy Roman Empire. Rev. ed., NY, 1921, 8vo, 515pp., $22.50

(Bryce), FISHER, H.A., James Bryce. NY, 1927, roy8vo, 2vols., $35.00

BURGESS, W. R. Reserve Banks and the Money Market. NY, 1927, 8vo, 328pp., $20.00

BURKE, Edmund, The Works of, with Biographical and Critical Introduction by Henry Rogers. L, 1837, small4to, 2vols., later linen, $75.00

BURKE, Edmund P., An Historical Essay on the Laws and Government of Rome, Designed as an Introduction to the Study of the Civil Law. Cambridge, 1827, 8vo, 298pp., later 1/2 sheep & bds, bit scuffed but sound; $95.00
"the best historical view of the Roman Constitution that has yet appeared from the hands of any English civilian or historian and exceeded by few if any of the continental essays." Marvin, 161.

BURKE, Peter, Celebrated Trials Connected with the Aristocracy. L, 1849, roy8vo, 505p. linen, $37.50

BURKE, Peter, Recollections of the Court Room, or, Narratives, Scenes & Anecdotes from the Courts of Justice. NY, 1859, 8vo, 305pp., later linen, $47.50

BURN, Richard, The Justice of the Peace and Parish Officer. 13th edition, rev., L, 1776, 8vo, 4vols. bound in full contemp. calf, beautiful set, $225.00
"most useful book ever published on the law relating to the Justice of the Peace," Marvin, 163.

(BURR) ROBERTSON, David, Reports of the Trials of Colonel Aaron Burr (Late Vice President of the United States) for Treason, and for a Misdemeanor, in Preparing the Means of a Military Expedition against Mexico....in the Circuit Court of the U.S. held in the City of Richmond....to which is Added an Appendix Containing the Arguments & Evidence....to Commit A. Burr, H. Blannerhasset & I. Smith, to be Sent for Trial to the State of Kentucky for Treason or Misdemeanor Alleged to be Committed There. P, 1808, 8vo, 2vols., mid 19th century 1/2 morocco, trifle rubbed, $250.00
One of the most famous trials in American history; John Marshall & Cyrus Griffin presided; Geo. Hay, William Wirt & Alex MacRae prosecuted; Burr was defended by himself, an accomplished lawyer, John Wickham, the ablest lawyer of the Richmond bar, and Luther Martin, former member of the Constitutional Convention of 1787 and defender of Chase at his celebrated trial a few years before.

(Burr) BEIRNE, Francis, Shout Treason: The Trial of Aaron Burr. NY, 1959, 8vo, 298pp., $22.50

(Burr) PARTON, J., Life & Times of Aaron Burr. NY, 1858, 8vo, 696pp., $30.00

(Burr) WANDELL, Sam, & MINNIGERODE, M., Aaron Burr: A Biography Written in Large Part from Original & Hitherto Unused Material. NY, 1927, roy8vo, 2vols., $37.50

BURR, Geo. (ed.), Narratives of the Witchcraft Cases, 1648-1706. NY, 1914, 8vo, 467pp, $25.00

BURROW, Sir Jas., Reports of Cases Adjudged in the Court of King's Bench During the Time of Lord Mansfield's Presiding in that Court, from 1756 to 1772. 5th ed., corr., with the Addition of Marginal Notes & References to the Reports of the Same Cases. Dublin, 1794, 8vo, 5vols., bound in contemp. roan, bit rubbed & scuffed & three hinges expertly reinforced, $225.00
"These volumes are the faithful repositories of Lord Mansfield's decisions. Burrow is an indefatigable, accurate & painstaking reporter. From his constant attendance in the Court, as well as the access afforded him by his office, he was able to give a complete history of each case." Marvin.

BURTON, Walter, An Elementary Compendium of the Law of Real Property. P, 1839, 8vo, 277pp. later lin. LL, $57.50 "a most valuable publication....learned, precise & accurate." Marvin, 166.

BUTLER, Chs., Horae Juridicae Subsecivae: A Connected Series of Notes Respecting the Geography, Chronology, & Literary History of the Principal Codes & Original Documents of the Grecian, Roman, Feudal & Canon Law, with Additional Notes & Illustrations by an Eminent American Civilian. P, 1808, 8vo, 136pp.linen, $75.00

BUTLER, Wm., Lawyer & Client: Their Relation, Rights & Duties. NY, 1871, 12mo, 76p, reb, $25.00

BYLES, John, A Practical Treaties on the Law of Bills of Exchange, Promissory Notes, Bank Notes, Bankers' Cash Notes. P, 1837, 8vo, 180p., later linen, $45.00 (LL)

CAIRNS, Huntington, Legal Philosophy from Plato to Hegel. Johns Hopkins, 1949, roy8vo,583p. $30.00

CAIRNS, J.S. Loom of the Law: Experiences of a Metropolitan Magistrate.L, 1925, 8vo, 320pp, $25.00

CALCOTT, Mary, Principles of Social Legislation. NY, 1932, 8vo, 416pp., $22.50

CALHOUN, Geo., Growth of Criminal Law in Ancient Greece. Univ. of Cal, 1927, 8vo, 149pp, $22.50

CALVERT, Frederic, Treatise upon the Law Respecting Parties to Suits in Equity. P, 1837, 8vo, xxx,228pp., LL, $47.50

CALVERT, Rob., Patent Practice & Management. NY, 1950, roy8vo, 371pp., $22.50

KAHL (alias Calvinus), Johannis, Magnum Lexicon Juridicum: Juris Nimirum Caesarei simul, & Canonici Feudalis item Civilis, Criminalis, Theoretici ac Practici: & in Schola, & in Foro usitatarum, ac tum ex ipso Juris Utriusque Corpore, tum ex Doctoribus & Glossis, tam veteribus, quam recentionibus collectarum vocum Penus: Simul & Locorum communium, & Dictionarii vi cem sustinens. Feudale Lexicon Leges ac Magistratus Romanos, & Caetera huic Operi adjecta vide in complemento, post finem operis ipsius. Collectum vero est Hoc Opus ex Collatis inter Sese Juridicis, quotquot hactenus fere prodierunt, & antiquioribus & recentioribus Lexicis. Auctum deinde, Expolitum et Emendatum ex Hacteuns editis accuratissimis lucubrationibus D. D. Jac. Cujacii, Barn. Brissoni, Hug. Donelli, Dion. Gothofredi,....cum Prefationibus Clar. & Emin. Jurisconsultorum Dion. Gothofredi,...Editio Postrema, Auctior, & ab Innumeris Mendis Expurgata, cui de novo accesit Jus Publicum, in quo Praecipilae Voces Doctrinae Juris Publici Romano-Germanici, breviter enuncleantur & asterisco* distinguuntur. Coloniae Allobrogum, 1734, large folio, 2vols., 910, 787pp., bound in contemp. vellum, excellent, scarce, only 4 copies in No. America, $350.00
Kahl (15'5-1614) was professor of law in Heidelberg, author of several notable works of which this is the best known; it appeared in several editions, this being the last; Denis Godefroy (1549-1622) was professor of Roman Law in Strassburg & later in Heidelberg. His edition of the Corpus Juris Civilis was the first to present Justinian's law as a complete typographical entity in the modern form; it went through some 20 editions and remained the standard text for about two centuries. EB11, XIII, 171; ESS, VI, 684; a most learned & comprehensive work.

Cambridge Legal Essays Written in Honour of & Presented to Dr. Bond, Prof. Buckland & Prof. Kenny. Cambridge, 1926, 8vo, 331pp., (contributors include Duff, Jenks, Jolowicz, Pound), $30.00

CARDAHII, Choucri, La Vente en Droit Compare Occidental et Oriental. P, 1968, roy8vo, 456p, $25.00

CARDOZO, Benj., The Nature of the Judicial Process. Yale, 1921, 8vo, 180p., $17.50

CARDOZO, Benj., The Paradoxes of Legal Science. NY, 1928, 8vo, 142pp., first edition, $47.50

CARDOZO, Benj., Selected Writings. ed. Hall. NY, 1947, roy8vo, 456pp., $25.00

CARLTON, Frank, History and Problems of Organized Labor. B, 1911, 8vo, 483pp., $20.00

CARLYLE, Sir R. W. & CARLYLE, A. J., A History of Medieval Political Theory in the West. NY, 1955, 8vo, 6vols., names on titles inked out, (Reprint: $175.00), $95.00

CARLYLE, A. J., The Christian Church & Liberty. L, 1924, 8vo, 159pp., $20.00

CARPENTER, S. C., Select American Speeches, Forensic & Parliamentary, with Prefatory Remarks.P, 1815, 8vo, 2vols., 1000pp., later linen, sl. dampstain few leaves of I; important speeches by Edmund Randolph, Patrick Henry, Madison, Jas. Wilson, Hamilton, Wirt, Governeur Morris), $75.00

CARTER, Judge A. G., The Old Court House: Reminiscences & Anecdotes of the Courts & Bar of Cincinnati. Cincinnati, 1880, 8vo, 466pp., later linen, $30.00

CARY, Henry, A Practical Treatise on the Law of Partnership.P, 1834, 8vo, 162pp. LL, $37.50

CASE, Nelson, European Constitutional History. NY, 1902, 8vo, 421pp., $22.50

The Case of the Private Armed Brig of War General Armstrong, Before the U.S. Court of Claims at Washington, with the Decision of the Court, reported by Sam Reid. NY, 1857, 8vo, 240pp., margins of title and last leaf slightly chipped, later linen, $47.50

The Case of the General Assembly of the Presbyterian Church in the U.S. before the Supreme Court of Pennsylvania, by Rev. D.W. Lathrop. P, 1839, 8vo, 628pp., sl. dampstain, later linen, $45.00

The Case of John Doggett vs Wm. Emerson & Others, in Equity, in the Circuit Court of the U. S. for the first Circuit, Dist. of Maine. B, 1844, roy8vo, 212pp., later linen, $37.50

LAW BOOK PUBLISHER CATALOGUES

Carswell Company, Catalogue of Modern Law Books. Toronto, 1931, 8vo, 168pp., linen, $30.00

Callaghan & Co., General Law Text Books, Chicago, 1940, 8vo, 69pp., linen, $27.50

Carswell Co., Catalogue of Modern Law Books, 1934-35. 8vo, 183pp., linen, $35.00

West Publishing Co., Catalogue of Law Books. St. Paul, 1941, 12mo, 210pp., linen, $35.00

Burdette Smith Co., Catalogue of Law Books. C, 1934, 12mo, 183pp., linen, $35.00

W. H. Anderson, Catalogue of Law Books. Cincinnati, 1929, 12mo, 182pp., linen, $35.00

Lawyer's Co-Operative Publishing Co., Catalogue of Works. Rochester, 1934, 12mo, 183pp, linen,$30.00

Baker, Voorhis & Co., Catalogue of Law Books. NY, 1932, 8vo, 177pp., linen, $30.00

Canon Law Studies, Catholic University of America: volume numbers as indicated; bound in linen or laminated boards unless otherwise indicated; $17.50 each

CHATHAM, Josiah, Force or Fear as Invalidating Marriage. #310, 1950, 187pp.

CLUNE, Robert, Judicial Interrogation of the Parties. #269, 1948, 142pp.

FINDLAY, Stephen, Canonical Norms Governing the Depositinn & Degradation of Clerics. #130, 1941,279p.

EIDENSCHINK, John, Election of Bishops in the Letters of Gregory the Great. #215, 1945, 200pp.

DOWNS, John, The Concept of Clerical Immunity. #126, 1941, 163pp., wrps.

SWEENEY, Francis, The Reduction of Clerics to the Lay State. #223, 1945, 199pp.

PICKARD, Wm., Judicial Experts, #389, 1958, 226pp.

193) MARX, Adolph, Declaration of Nullity of Marriages Contracted Outside the Church. #182, 1943, 151pp., wrps.

194) HESTON, Edw., Alienation of Church Property in the US. #132, 1941, 222pp.

195) RISTUCCIA, Bernard, Quasi-Religious Societies. #261, 1949, 318pp.

DUBE, Arthur, General Principles for Reckoning Time in Canon Law. #144, 1941, 299pp.

HUSER, John, The Crime of Abortion in Canon Law. #162, 1942, 187pp.

DUERR, Chs., The Judicial Notary. #312, 1951, 112pp.

PARO, Gino, The Right of Papal Legation. #211, 1947, 221pp.

KREMER, Michael, Church Support in the United States. #61, 1930, 130pp.

O'DONNELL, Cletus, The Marriage of Minors. #221, 1945, 268pp.

CIESLOK, Jos., National Parishes in the United States. #190, 1944, 178pp.

CROWE, Martin, The Moral Obligation of Paying Just Taxes. #84, 1944, 175pp.

CHRIST, Jos., Dispensation from Vindictive Penalties. #174, 1943, 285pp.

GOODWINE, John, Right of the Church to Acquire Temporal Goods. #131, 1941, 119pp.

BEGIN, Raymond, Natural Law & Positive Law. #393, 1959, 177pp.

MC DEVITT, Gilbert, Legitimacy and Legitimation. #138, 1941, 247pp.

HOGAN, Jas., Judicial Advocates & Procurators. #133, 1941, 200pp., wrps.

MC GRATH, Jas., The Privilege of the Canon. #242, 1946, 156pp.----end of CUA series.

Centennial History of the Harvard Law School, 1817-1917. Harvard, 1918, roy8vo, 412pp., $25.00

CHANDOS, Sir Edw., Bar, Bat & Bit: Recollections. ed. F. Bush. L, 1913, roy8vo, 232pp., $22.50

CHANNING, Edward, HART, Albert Büshnell, &,TURNER, Frederick Jackson, Guide to the Study & Reading of American History. rev. & augmented ed. B, 1912, 8vo, 650pp., a fine book, $30.00

CHANNING, Wm. Ellery, A Lecture on War. B, 1839, 8vo, 50pp., orig. ptd. wrps. $27.50

CHANNING, Walter, Thoughts on Peace & War: Address to the American Peace Society. B, 1844, 8vo, 38pp., orig. ptd. wrps, $27.50

CHAPMAN, Cecil, The Poor Man's Court of Justice: Twenty Five Years as a Metropolitan Magistrate. L, (1925), 8vo, 320pp., later linen, $22.50

Charity Still a Christian Virtue: or, An Impartial Account of the Trial and Conviction of the Rev. Mr. Hendley for Preaching a Charity Sermon at Chisselhurst, and of Mr. Chapman & Mr. Pratt, for Collecting at the Same Time the Alms of the Congregation. L, 1719, 8vo, 72pp; with two other pieces related to the matter, 27, 30pp., later linen, $65.00

The Charters & General Laws of the Colony & Province of Massachusetts Bay, Carefully Collected from the Publick Records & Ancient Printed Books, to which is Added an Appendix, Tending to Explain the Spirit, Progress & History of the Jurisprudence of the State. B, 1814, small4to, 868pp., contemp. roan, front hinge restored, sl. wear; by Nathan DANE, JOSEPH STORY & William PRESCOTT, $150.00

(CHASE) Report of the Trial of the Hon. Samuel Chase, One of the Associate Justices of the Supreme Court of the United States, Before the High Court of Impeachment, Composed of the Senate of the Senate of the United States, for Charges Exhibited Against Him by the House of Representatives.... for High Crimes & Misdemeanors, Supposed to have been by Him Committed, with the Necessary Documents & Official Papers, from His Impeachment to Final Acquittal, taken in Short Hand by Charles Evans, and the Arguments of Counsel Revised by Them from His Manuscript. Baltimore, 1805, 8vo, 268pp; bound with this: Impeachment of Samuel Chase, Esq....with the Articles Exhibited Against Him by the House of Representatives,...with His Answer & Pleas, likewise the Replication of the House of Representatives. Baltimore, 1805, 68pp., both works bound together in later 1/2 calf and marbled boards, $375.00

CHASE, Salmon P., Diary & Correspondence. DC, GPO, 1903, roy8vo, 527pp., $35.00

CHEEVER, Geo., A Defence in Abatement of Judgment for an Alleged Libel in the Story Entitled "Inquire at Amos Giles' Distillery," Addressed to Chief Justice Shaw. Salem, 1836, 12mo, 28pp., wrps, $30.00

CHEHATA, Chafik, Etudes de Droit Musulman. P, 1971, 8vo, 256pp., wrps, $20.00

CHESTER, Samuel, Anomalies of the English Law. L, 1920, 8vo, 287pp., later linen, $27.50

CHICAGO, T. H. Flood & Co., Publishers, Salesman's Sample Book of the Firm's Legal Publications, with excerpts from various works published by the firm and sample skivers (c. 1900) roy8vo, about 300 pp., inner hinges reinforced. $30.00

Chicago Conference on Trusts: Speeches, Debates, Resolutions. C, 1900, 8vo, 626pp., later linen,$35.00

Chicago Law Institute, Index Catalogue of the Library to December 31, 1901. C, 1902, roy8vo,700p,$75.00

the same continued: Subject Index from 1902 to 1932. C, 1932, 8vo, 332pp., later linen, $37.50

Chicago Voting Machine Investigation: Report of the Legislative Committee Appointed under House Joint Res. No. 23 of the 48th Illinois Gen. Ass. 1915, 4to, 776pp., $45.00

Chicago Municipal Court, Annual Reports, 3rd, 4th, 5th, 6th, 8th & 9th, 1908-1915. bound in 5 vols. orig. ptd. wrps, $75.00

(Chicago) Sullivan's Chicago Law Directory: 1921-1922: An Official List of Members of the Bar, with full Information abouts the Courts, Officials & Rules of Practice. (45th Annual ed.)8vo, 290pp. orig. ptd. cloth. with numerous ads, $30.00

(Chicago) Gunthorp's Legal Directory of Chicago, 1928, Containing Rules of Practice and a Complete Catalogue of the Chicago Bar Assn. Library (25th Annual Ed.) 8vo, 408pp., orig. cl., with numerous ads, $30.00

(Chicago) Sullivan's Chicago Law Directory, 1932-33 (56th Annual Ed.) 8vo, 470pp., w/ ads, $27.50

CHITTY, Jos. & Hulme, John, A Practical Treatise on Bills of Exchange, Checks on Bankers, Promissory Notes, Banker's Cash Notes & Bank Notes, with References to the Law of Scotland, France & America. 12th American from the 9th London ed, rev. & enl. by J.C. Perkins. Springfield, 1854, 4to, cvi, 1007pp. later linen, $57.50
"The most complete treatise on the subject in England & America, not equalled in the variety & extent of its learning by any similar production in our own or in any other language." Marvin,192.

CHITTY, Thomson, & TEMPLE, Leofric, A Practical Treatise on the Law of Carriers of Goods and Passengers by Land, Inland Navigation, & in Ships, with Notes & References to American Decisions by David Sellers. P, 1857, roy8vo, 642pp., later linen, $47.50

CHITTY, Jos. A Practical Treatise on the Law of Nations, Relative to the Legal Effect of War on the Commerce of Belligerents & Neutrals & On Orders in Council & Licenses to Which are Added extracts from Grotius, Bynkershoek & Vattel; also the Letter of Sir William Scott, & of the Duke of Newcastle, Containing Matters Applicable to the Law of Prize. B, 1812, 8vo, xii,340pp., contemp. roan, bit scuffed but tight; sporadic foxing & browning; nice copy of a scarce book; according to the preface to this American edition, the letters of Newcastle & Scott were prepared at the insistance of John Jay. $165.00

CHRISTY, David, Pulpit Politics; or, Ecclesiastical Legislation on Slavery in Its Disturbing Influences on the American Union. Cincy, 1862, 8vo, 624pp., sl. wear of extremeties, sound, scarce, $57.50

CHUTE, Marchette, The First Liberty: History of the Right to Vote in America, 1619- 1850. NY, 1969, roy8vo, 371pp., $22.50

CICERO, Opera Omnia, ex Recensione O. Augusti Ernesti, cum Eiusdem Notis et Clave Cicerniana. Halis Saxonum, 1774-1777. 8vo, 5vols. bound as 8; later buckram; sporadic foxing, title of vol 4 lacking, minor internal dampstain in vol. 5; sound set of a good edition, $175.00

(CICERO) FORSYTH, Wm., The Life of Marcus Tullius Cicero. NY, 1865, 8vo, 2vols., $45.00

CIVIL WAR PAMPHLET COLLECTION, 1852-1865; about 140 titles, none military but rather dealing with the political & constitutional aspects of the conflict, and especially with: Kansas-Nebraska, Dred Scott, Lecompton Constitution, presidential elections of 1860 and 1864; slavery & abolition; Lincoln's political & constitutional actions; most are scarce, many rare; details on request.

CLARENDON, Edward Earl of, A Brief View & Survey of the Dangerous & Pernicious Errors to Church & State in Mr. Hobbes's Book, Entitled Leviathan. London, 1676, small4to, 8,322pp., contemp. calf, hinges very slightly cracked but quite firm, new title skiver on spine, an exceptionally clean, crisp copy, first edition, $575.00

CLARENDON, Edward Earl of, The History of the Rebellion and Civil Wars in England, Begun in the Year 1641, with the Precedent Passages & Actions that Contributed Thereunto, and the Happy End..... Written by the Rt. Hon. Edward Earl of Clarendon, Late Lord High Chancellor of England. Oxford, 1702, tall folio, 3vols., contemp. calf, sometime expertly rebacked, beautiful set, first edition, Grolier Club List of 100 Books Famous in English Literature, $675.00

CLARKE, R.F., The Science of Law & Lawmaking, Being an Introduction to Law, a General View of Its Forms & Substance, & a Discussion of the Question of Codification. NY, 1898, roy8vo, 473p., $35.00

CLEPHANE, Jas., Official Report of the Trial of Mary Harris, Indited for the Murder of Adoniram J. Burroughs, before the Supreme Court of the District of Columbia (Sitting as a Criminal Court). DC, 1865, 8vo, 18?pp., later linen, $45.00

CLIFFORD, G.A., A Guide for Administrators, Executors & Guardians....2nd ed., rev. & enl. with the Rules of Court & Instructions promulgated by Judge Bradwell of the Cook County Court, ed. by Jas. Bassett. Chicago, Myers, 1870, 8vo, viii,308pp., later linen, $75.00

COCKBURN, Henry T., Circuit Journeys. Edinburgh, 1889, 8vo, 420pp., $25.00

COCKBURN, Wm., The Clerk's Assistant in the Practice of the Ecclesiastical Courts....Interspersed with Some Observations in Matters of Law. 4th ed. Dublin, 1792, 8vo, 221,92pp. later 1/2 calf, $75.00

Code Napoleon; or, The French Civil Code, Literally Translated from the Original & Official Edition Published at Paris in 1804, by a Barrister of the Inner Temple. NY, 1841, roy8vo, 627p. buck, $75.00

The Code of 1650, Being a Compilation of the Earliest Laws & Orders of the General Court of Connecticut also the Constitution or Civil Compact entered into & Adopted by the Towns of Windsor, Hartford & Wethersfield, in 1638-39, to which is Added some Extracts from the Laws & Judicial Proceedings of New Haven Colony, Commonly Called the Blue Laws. Hartford, 1842, 12mo, 119pp., later linen, $37.50

COGLEY, John, & HUTCHINS, Rob. Natural Law & Modern Society. Clev., 1961, 8vo, 285pp., $20.00

COGLIOLO, Pietro, Manuale delle Fonti del Diritto Romano. 2nd ed., Torino, 1911, roy8vo, bit of very sporadic underlining & marginalia, later linen, $35.00

COHEN, Herman, History of the English Bar & Attornatus to 1450. L, 1929, 8vo, 622pp., $37.50

COHEN, Jerome, Criminal Process in the People's Republic of China. Harvard, 1968, 4to, 706pp, $25.00

COHEN, Morris & Felix, Readings in Jurisprudence & Legal Philosophy. NY, 1951, 4to, 944pp., $35.00

COHEN, Morris, Reason in Law: Studies in Juristic Philosophy. Glencoe, 1950, 8vo, 211pp., $22.50

COKE, Sir Edward, The First Part of the Institutes of the Laws of England, Or, A Commentary Upon Littleton, Not in the Name of the Author, but of the Law Itself. 13th edition, rev. & corr, with the Addition of Notes & References by Francis Hargrave & Chs. Butler, and an Analysis of Littleton, written by an Unknown Hand, in 1658-59, but never before Published. London, 1788, tall folio, xx, about 800pp., bound in later 1/2 calf, beautiful copy, $250.00

COLE, Arthur (ed.), The Constitutional Debates of 1847. Springfield, 1919 (Collections of the Illinois State Historical Library, XIV; Constitutional Ser II,) roy8vo, 1018pp., sl. embrowning, $37.50

COLEMAN, Chris, The Treatise of Lorenzo Valla on the Donation of Constantine: Text & Translation. Yale, 1922, roy8vo, 183pp., ex lib, $25.00

COLERIDGE, Ernest, Life and Correspondence of John Duke Lord Coleridge, Lord Chief Justice of England. NY, 1904, roy8vo, 2vols., $47.50

AMICUS CURIAE (Collier, John Payne), Criticisms on the Bar: Including Strictures on the Principal Counsel Practising in the Courts of King's Bench, Common Pleas, Chancery & Exchequer. L, 1819, 12mo, 308pp., later linen, $75.00

COMMONS, John & ANDREWS, John, Principles of Labor Legislation. 4th ed, rev. NY, 1936, 606pp. $22.50

A Complete Collection of All the Protests Made in the House of Lords, from 1641 to....1747, Wherein is Contained the Sentiments of the Independent Gentlemen of that House, in Many Important Matters, of the Utmost Consequence to the Constitution & Liberties of Great Britain. L, 1747, 12mo, 487pp., contemp. calf, rear hinge cracked but firm, front hinge reinforced, nice copy, $75.00

COMYN, Rob., Treatise on the Law of Usury. P, 1834, 8vo, 121pp., later linen, LL, $57.50

COMYN, Rob., Treatise on the Law of Landlord & Tenant, 2nd ed., enl & corr. by Geo. Chilton. P, 1834, xxvii, 391pp., later linen, LL, $47.50

CONRAD, J. et al., Handwörterbuch der Staatswissenschaften. 2nd ed., rev. Jena, 1909, 4to, 8vols., contemp. 1/2 morocco, $300.00

Constitution of the U.S., with the Amendments thereto, to Which are Added Jefferson's Manual of Parliamentary Practice, & the Standing Rules & Orders for Conducting Business in the House of Representatives & Senate. DC, 1859, 8vo, 254pp., full contemp. calf, $37.50

266) The Constitution Reconsidered, ed. for the American Historical Assn. by Conyers Read. Columbia, 1938, roy8vo, 424pp., a fine collection of essays including contributions by McIlwain, Thorne, Beard, Elliot, Commager, Holborn & Becker), $27.50

267) The Constitutions of the Several States of the Union & the United States....NY, 1853, roy8vo, 555pp., $35.00

CONSTITUTIONAL CONVENTION OF 1787

MADISON, James, The Papers of James Madison, Purchased by Order of Congress, Being His Correspondence & Reports of Debates During the Congress of the Confederation & His Reports of Debates in the Federal Convention. Now Published from the Original Manuscripts, Deposited in the Dept. of State, Under the Superintendence of Henry Gilpin. Washington, 1840, roy8vo, 3vols., bound in contemp. 1/2 morocco & marbled boards, sl. rubbed & faint trace of sporadic dampstain on lower margin of vol. I; handsome set, first edition, $375.00

Secret Proceedings and Debates of the Convention Assembled at Philadelphia, in the Year 1787, for the Purpose of Forming the Constitution of the United States of America, from the Notes taken by the Late Robert Yates, Chief Justice of New York, and Copied by John Lansing Jr., Late Chancellor of that State, Members of that Convention; Including the "Genuine Information" Laid before the Legislature of Maryland, by Luther Martin, then Attorney General of that State, & a Member of the Same Convention. Albany, 1821, 8vo, 308pp., contemp. roan, hinges expertly reinforced, clean, crisp copy, first edition, $250.00

When the delegates to the Constitutional Convention convened in Philadelphia on May 15, 1787, all were sworn to secrecy, and that seal of secrecy endured until 1819 when Pres. Monroe ordered to be published the Journal of the Convention, a badly kept record of votes only. The secrecy breached, Yates notes were published which "threw a great deal of light upon what had taken place & in particular upon the attitude of individuals in the debates." The notes of Madison, "Father of the Constitution," are the most extensive & detailed record. He took full and careful notes of the proceedings and because he was regarded by his fellow-delegates as a semi-official reporter, several took pains to see that he was supplied with copies of their speeches & motions. Only 36 at the time, he was well aware of the momentous nature of the proceeding and was determined to leave a faithful account of it to posterity. Very much under the influence of the Classical Republicans (Harrington, Sydney, Neville & Moyle) and the accounts of the Legislators of Antiquity, he believed that the American Constitution, if properly drafted, would endure, as the Venetian Constitution, "for a thousand years." At the time, he was a firm proponent of national supremacy & foe of state soveréignty. He repeatedly declined to publish his notes despite frequent urgings. By 1821 he had become a champion of states' rights and his notes of 1787 would have compromised him politically.

MADISON) ADAMS, John Quincy, An Eulogy on the Life & Character of James Madison. B, 1836, 8vo, 87pp., later linen, $35.00

CONYNGTON, Th., KNAPP, H., Wills, Estates & Trusts. NY, 1924, roy8vo, 825pp., $27.50

COOLEY, Judge T. M.,et al, The Constitutional History of the United States as Seen in the Development of American Law. NY, 1889, 8vo, 296pp., later linen, $27.50

COOLEY, Th. M., A Treatise on the Constitutional Limitations which Rest Upon the Legislative Power of the States. 8th ed., enl. by W. Carrington. B, 1927, 4to, 2vols., $57.50

COOLEY, Th. M., The Law of Taxation. 4th ed., by Clarke Nichols, C, 1924,4to, 4vols., $125.00

COOTE, Richard, A Treatise on the Law of Mortgage. P, 1837, 8vo, 320pp., later 1/2 linen and bds, LL "most succinct & accurate," James Kent in Marvin, 228, $47.50

COREY, Henry, Law Without Lawyers: A Compendium of Business & Domestic Law for Popular Use. NY, 1886, 12mo, 396pp., sl. cov. soil, $27.50

CORNISH, Wm., An Essay on Uses. P, 1834, 8vo, 95pp., later linen, LL, $37.50

CORVINUS, Joh. A., Enchiridium seu Institutiones Imperiales, Insertis Latioribus Materys Theorice ac Practice Digeste et Explicate per Erotemata. Amsterdam, Elzevir, 1644, 12mo, 714pp., later 1/2 oasis morocco & linen, engraved title; professor of law in Mainz and author of numerous law text books of which this is one; this work is rare, NUC listing only one copy in No. America, $250.00

CORWIN, Edw., The Commerce Power versus States Rights. Princeton, 1936, 8vo, 273pp., $20.00

COULTON, G.G., The Medieval Village. Cambridge, 1926, roy8vo, 603pp., sl.worn, $22.50

COVENTRY, Th., On Conveyancers Evidence. P, 1839, 8vo, 158pp., later linen, LL, $45.00

COWELL, John, A Law Dictionary: Or the Interpreter of Words and Terms Used in Either the Common or Statute Laws of Great Britain and in Tenures & Jocular Customs....and in this Edition very much Augmented & Improved, by the Addition of Many Thousand Words, Found in Our Histories, Antiquities, Cartularies, Rolls, Registers & Other Ms Records, with an Appendix Containing Two Tables....Both of Them very Necessary for the Use of All Such, as Converse with Antient Deeds, Charters, etc. L, 1727, very tall quarto, 675pp., bound in later 1/2 calf & boards, minor title tear neatly mended; a very crisp copy of a beautifully printed book, $275.00

Some of Cowell's enemies, among them Coke, discovered that the Interpreter contained dangerous doctrines under the titles Subsidy, Parliament, King etc. Through Coke's influence Cowell was imprisoned and the book publicly burned. Selden and other writers of and since his time have freely used the work and previous to Jacobs it was the best existing law dictionary. It is an excellent glossary to Coke Littleton and the old law books. Marvin, 234.

CROSS, John, Treatise on the Law of Lien & Stoppage in Transitu. P, 1841, 8vo, 286pp, LL, $45.00

CRANSTON, Leslie, Early Criminal Codes of Illinois & Their Relation to the Common Law of England. DuQuin, Ill., 1930, roy8vo, 491pp., one leaf mended, scarce, $35.00

CREASY, Sir Edw., First Platform of International Law. L, 1876, roy8vo, 710pp, $37.50

CREASY, Sir Edw., The Rise & Progress of the English Constitution. L, 1853, 8vo, 340pp., $37.50

CROSS, Harold, The People's Right to Know: Legal Access to Public Records & Proceedings. Columbia, 1953, roy8vo, 405pp., $22.50

CROSSKEY, Wm., Politics & the Constitution in the History of the US. Univ. of Chicago, 1953, 4to, 2vols., ex lib, $47.50

CULVER, Dorothy, (ed.), Bibliography of Crime & Criminal Justice, 1927-1931. Univ. of California, 1934, 4to, 413pp., $25.00

CULVER, Dorothy, (ed.), Bibliography of Crime & Criminal Justice, 1932-1937. Univ. of Cal., 1939, roy8vo, 391pp., $22.50

CUMBERLAND, Richard, Les Loix de la Nature Expliquees....ou L'on Recherche et L'on Etablit, par la Nature des Choses, la Forme de ces Loix ....on y refute aussi les Elemens de la Morale et de la Politique de Thomas Hobbes; traduits du Latin par Mon. Barbeyrac, avec des Notes du Traducteur Leiden, 1757, 4to, xxviii,425pp., contemp. calf, sl. worn, lacks frontis, nice copy, $175.00

CUMMINGS, Homer, Liberty Under Law & Administration. NY, 1934, 12mo, 136pp, $18.50

CURRIE, Brainerd, Selected Essays on the Conflict of Laws. Duke UP, 1963, roy8vo, 761pp., $30.00

CURTIS, Benjamin R., A Memoir of....LL.D., with some of His Professional & Miscellaneous Writings, ed. by His Son, B, 1879, roy8vo, 2vols., sl. worn, faint trace dampstain in I, scarce, $45.00

CURTIS, George Ticknor, History of the Origin, Formation & Adoption of the Constitution of the United States, with Notices of Its Principal Framers.NY, 1854-58, roy8vo, 2vols., orig. cloth, rebacked & spines remounted, first edition, first issue, with the tipped-in publisher notice concerning Curtis' letter regarding his discovery of the conclusive proof of Nathan Dane's authorship of the Northwest Ordinance, a fact which had been disputed by some, $115,00.

Curtis was a major legal thinker and constitutional authority & historian of the period. He also appeared before the Supreme Court in many important cases, including the Dred Scott Case, in which he argued the constitutional question for Scott, and the "Legal Tender Cases." His constitutional historiography is by no means obsolete, & manifests itself in his biographies also.

CURTIS, Geo. T., History of the Origin, Formation & Adoption of the Constitution of the United States, NY, 1854-59, roy8vo, 2vols., later 1/2 linen, $85.00

CURTIS, Geo. Ticknor, Commentaries on the Jurisdiction, Practice & Peculiar Jurisprudence of the Courts of the United States: Vol. I, Containing a View of the Judicial Power, and the Jurisdiction & Practice of the Supreme Court of the United States. P, 1854, roy8vo, xxiv, 635pp., later 1/2 linen, (all published), an important and very rare work, $150.00

CURTIS, Geo. T., The Constitutional History of the United States from the Declaration of Independence to the Close of the Civil War. NY, 1895, roy8vo, 2vols., 1500pp., rebacked, $75.00

CURTIS, Geo. T., The Life of Daniel Webster. 2nd ed., NY, 1870, roy8vo, 2vols., contemp. 1/2 morocco, sl. dampstain f a few leaves, $65.00

CURTIS, Geo. T., The Life of James Buchanan. NY, 1883, roy8vo,2vols., 1300pp., orig. cl, $65.00

CURTIS, Geo. T., A Discourse on the Nature of the American Union, as the Principal Controversy Involved in the Late Civil War. NY, 1875, 8vo, 35pp., later linen, $35.00

CUSHING, Luther, An Introduction to the Study of Roman Law. B, 1844, 8vo, 243p., contemp. roan, $57.50

CUSHING, Luther, Elements of the Law of Procedure of Legislative Assemblies in the United States. 9th ed., B, 1874, roy8vo, 1063pp., later linen, $45.00

) CUTLER, Jas., Lynch-Law: An Investigation into the History of Lynching in the United States. NY, 1905, 8vo, 287pp., $20.00

5) DANE, Nathan, A General Abridgment and Digest of American Law, with Occasional Notes and Comments. Boston, 1823-1829. roy8vo, 9vols., vols. 1-8 bound in contemp. roan, a bit rubbed with a very slight trace of wear of extremeties; vol. IX rebound in later roan, an almost exact reproduction of the first eight volumes; rare and in this condition virtually unobtainable, $2500.00

The work is unique and of fundamental importance. The following excerpts from Dane's Introduction provide some idea of its nature and scope:

"At the close of the American revolutionary war, when the United States being an independent nation, it was very material to inquire & to know what was law in them, collectively & individually....The author turned his attention to these subjects (and he) found there was nothing like one collected body of American Law, ...all was found in scattered fragments. Scarcely any native American Law was in print, but the colony statutes, charters & some of the constitutions. No judicial decisions, made in America, of any importance, had been published, No one had attempted to embody our laws, dispersed in numerous local charters, constitutions, statutes....and also English books, even to the ancient Germans, in several cases, and in some to the Hebrews.In this state of things, a very important object naturally presented itself to one, who, for several years, had been in a situation highly to appreciate American principles, especailly those of the American revolution, which was, a collected body of American Law, formed with a constant reference to those principles, & to our character & situation. Formerly, the word Digest, in law books, meant much more than an alphabetical arrangement of marginal notes, or of several indexes. But as this seems to be nearly its modern meaning, it applies but to an inconsiderable part of this work, the principal parts of which are described by the other words in the title...Abridgment, Notes & Comments. The first object has been to abridge & compress cases within narrow limits, but not so as to loose or obscure the law, decided or settled in them. Next, on proper occasions, by remarks, notes & comments, to examine & explain a few obscure points of law, and sometimes to show the law is not, as it has been in some decisions stated to be.

The evil to be feared in our country is, that so many sovereign legislatures, & so many Supreme courts, will produce too much law, & in too great a variety; so much & so various, that any general revision will become impracticable. It may be observed that a complete system of law & equity, best calculated to preserve the power of the magistrate & the rights of the people, is the last thing men attain to in society. The reason is seen in the almost infinite variety, extent, & combination of ideas, founded in nature, ex perience, & cultivated morality, so essential in forming & completing such a system. It is very clear that a great republic, in which there is room for talents; in which thoughts & actions are not restrained by religious or political despotism; in which education is encouraged, and moral character is esteemed; in which the law rules & not the sword, in which each one asserts his rights by law, & not by force; & in which there is representation, jury-trial, and a free press, it is the natural field of law & equity.; but to produce these in perfection, there must be a national character. The rules of law & equity, in important matters, must be uniform, & pervade the whole nation; for if there be a code for each inconsiderable part, laws, & so law books, must necessarily be so extremely multiplied in the numerous parts, making & executing laws independently of each other, that soon, but few, even of the lawyers, can know what the law is, except in his own limited part, & not even there, if judges allow an innundation of law books, of every kind to be used in hearing and deciding cases. A serious evil we are fast running into, in most of our states....Our true course is plain, that is, by degrees, to make our laws more uniform & national, especially where there is nothing to make them otherwise, but local feelings & prejudices. We have in the common & federal law, the materials of national uniformity in numerous cases, We have a national judiciary promoting this uniformity; & we have lawyers, learned, industrious, & able to second this judiciary. We only want a general efficient plan, supported with zeal, energy, & national feeling....History & experience prove, that good laws, and an accurate legal style once established in a nation, preserve their character long after every thing else corrupts & decays.

As to the inquiry sometimes made, why the publication of this work has been delayed to so late a period in the author's life; it may perhaps be sufficient to observe, that a very large part of our law has in rapid increase, revisions, & alterations, come into existence of late years.....On a fair examination it will be found , that no law work in the English language has ever required so much labour, research & revision, as this has; especially in deciding what law, in a monarchy once feudal, is in force in free republic; what State law, in so many States, is annulled or altered by national law; & which of the authorities on a subject, of late so vastly multiplied, are most to be relied on; or what is the legal result of all, especially when often diverse, & sometimes contradictory....He now submits his labours to a learned & liberal profession, sincerely wishing this first essay to form a general....system of American law, on a large & national plan....may in time, lead to one more perfect."

Following the example of Viner, Dane established the Dane Professorship in Harvard, endowing it with the proceeds from the sale of the Digest, and he first consulted with Story, persuading him to accept the first Dane professorship. (For the full details of Dane's endowment, see: Story's Life & Letters, II, 3-6.) Story, who had written a lengthy review of the work (Misc. Writ., 1835, 321ff.)said in his Inaugural Discourse as Dane Professor: "Dane was almost immediately engaged in the duties of legislation in this, his native state, and to him we are chiefly indebted for the first general revisal of our Provincial Statutes, as well as for other improvements in our code of positive law....and to him in a great measure, we owe the valuable collection of our Colonial & Provincial Statutes which now adorns our libraries To him belongs the glory of the formation of the celebrated Ordinance of 1787, which constitutes the fundamental law of the states northwest of the Ohio. It is a monument of political wisdom, and sententious skillfulness of expression. It was adopted unanimously by Congress, according to his original draft, with scarcely the alteration of a single word. In the midst of an extensive practice he found time to compile his Digest & Abridgment of American Law which comprehends a general survey of all our jurisprudence, & attests the depth of his learning, his unwearied industry, and his independent but cautious judgment. Mr. Dane has nobly dedicated the whole proceeds of his great work to the establishment of this professorship; and thus has become, to our parent university, in the highest sense, the American Viner." Jos. Story, Inaugural Discourse as Dane Professor of Law in Harvard.

306) DANIELL, Edmund R., Pleading & Practice of the High Court of Chancery, 3rd English ed., rev. & enl. by Headlam, 3rd American ed., to which are added several New Chapters....Adapting the Work to American Practice in Chancery, by J. C. Perkins. B, 1865, 4to, 3vols., later linen, $135.00
"unequalled in the extent of its learning, the comprehensiveness of its plan & the general accuracy of its execution....of great general value to the American lawyer." Marvin, 253.

307) DANTAS DE BRITO, A. H., La Philosophie du Droit des Gens. DC, 1944, 8vo, 254pp., wrps, $17.50

308) DARROW, Clarence, Story of My Life. NY, 1932, roy8vo, 465pp., later linen, $27.50

309) DARROW, Clarence, Story of My Life. NY, 1932, roy8vo, 465pp., first ed., $37.50

310) DARROW, Clarence, Story of My Life. NY, 1932, roy8vo, 465pp., original cloth in dust jacket, signed by Darrow on the 1/2 title, exceptionally nice copy, $125.00

311) DARROW, Clarence, Farmington. NY, 1932, 8vo, 255pp., $22.50

312),DARROW, Clarence, Attorney for the Damned. ed. A. Weinberg, foreword by Wm. O. Douglas. NY, 1957, roy8vo, 552pp., $27.50

313) DAVIS, C.K., The Law in Shakespeare. DC, 1883, 8vo, 303pp., $25.00

314) DAVIS, Daniel, Precedents of Indictments, to Which is Prefixed a Concise Treatise Upon the Office & Duty of Grand Jurors. B, 1831, 8vo, 319pp., contemp. roan, bit worn, "authoritative," Marvin, $45.00

315) DAVIS, Jos., Essays in the Earlier History of American Corporations. Harvard, 1917, roy8vo, 975pp.$57.5

316) DAWES, Rufus, The Dawes Plan in the Making. Ind, 1925, 8vo, 525pp., $25.00

317) Debates in the British Parliament 1911-1912, on the Declaration of London & the Naval Prize Bill. DC, GPO, 1919, roy8vo, 716pp., $22.50

318) A Debate on Slavery, Held in October, 1845 in Cincinnati, Between Rev. J. Blanchard & N.L. Rice,D.D., Cincinnati, 1857, 8vo, 482pp., $45.00

319) de BECKER, J.E., Annotated Civil Code of Japan, Intro. by Count Hayashi. L/Yokohama, 1919-10. 4to, 4vols., $125.00

320) DE HAAS, Elsa, Antiquities of Bail: Origin & Historical Development in Criminal Cases to 1275. Columbia, 1940, 8vo, 174pp., wrps, $22.50

321) DE LAVELEYE, Emile, Primitive Property, trans. F. Marriot. L, 1878, 8v , 356pp., $25.00

322) DE LOLME, J.L., The Constitution of England, or An Account of the English Government, in which it is Compared, both ith the Republican Form of Government, and the Other Monarchies of Europe. 4th ed., corr. & enl., L, 1784, 8vo, 540pp., later 1/2 calf, $125.00
A classic....has been held in high estimation from its first publication and still holds a distinguished place....a bold, ingenious outline, written in a clear & vigorous style." Marvin, 263.

323) DEL VECCHIO, Giorgio, The Formal Basis of Law. trans. J. Lisle, NY, 1921, roy8vo, 412pp, $27.50

324) DEL VECCHIO, G., Philosophy of Law. trans. T. Martin. DC, 1953, roy8vo, 474pp., $30.00

325) DEL VECCHIO, G., Justice: An Historical & Philosophical Essay. Edinburgh, 1956, 8vo, 236pp., $27.50

326) DE PEYSTER, J.W., Secession in Switzerland & in the U.S. Compared. Catskill, 1863, 8vo, 72p. $30.00

327) DE SCHUTTER, Bart, Bibliography of International Criminal Law. Leiden, 1972, roy8vo, 423pp, $27.50

328) DESTY, Rob., The Removal of Causes from State to Federal Courts. SF, 1882, 12mo, 283pp., $27.50

329) DESTUTT DE TRACY, Antoine, A Commentary and Review of Montesquieu's Spirit of Laws. Prepared for Press from the Original Manuscript in the Hands of the Publisher. To Which are Annexed Observations on the 31st Book, by the Late M. Condorcet, and Two Letters of Helvetius on the Merits of the Same Work. P, 1811, 8vo, 292pp., bound in the original 1/2 paper & boards, sl. dampstain of front cover and first & last few leaves & trace of lower marginal sporadic dampstain, a very attractive copy in the original binding, first edition, translated by Thomas Jefferson, the first French edition did not appear until 1819; $275.00

330) DE TOCQUEVILLE, Alexis, Democracy in America, translated by Henry Reeve, with an Original Preface & Notes by John C. Spencer, Counsellor at Law. 4th edition, corr. & rev. from the 8th Paris edition, NY, 1841, 8vo, 2vols., bound in the original cloth, rebacked & spines remounted, the first complete uniform American edition, $250.00

331) DEWING, Arthur, The Financial Policy of Corporations. 4th ed., NY, 1941, roy8vo, 2vols., $47.50

332) DIDIER, Eugene, Report of the Trial of Dr. Wm. Stokes & Mary Blenkensup of Mount Hope Institution before the Circuit Court for Baltimore County, Held at Towsontown. Balto, 1866, 8vo, 202pp, $45.00

333) DILLON, John, The Laws & Jurisprudence of England & America. B, 1894, roy8vo, 431pp., $27.50

334) DIMSDALE, Th., The Vigilantes of Montana; or, Popular Justice in the Rocky Mountains. 4th ed., Helena, n.d. (1910), 8vo, 350pp., ex lib., $25.00

335) DI TULLIO, Benigno, Principi de Criminologia Clinica e Psichiatria Forense. 2nd ed., rev. & enl. R, 1960, roy8vo, 510pp., orig. ptd. wrps, $22.50

336) (DOANE), Record of Proceedings of the Court of Bishops....for the Trial of Rt. Rev. Geo. Wash. Doane Bishop of New Jersey, NY, 1853, 8vo, 44pp.; with this: DOANE, Geo. W., Protest & Appeal of,& His Reply to the False....P, 1852, 8vo, 52pp.; and: An Historical Review of the Proceedings in the Case of Bishop Doane. NY, 1853, 8vo, 30pp., the three in later linen, $47.50

336-A) MC CARTY, Dwight, Psychology & the Law. NJ, 1960, roy8vo, 463pp., $25.00

337) DOMAT, Jean, The Civil Law in Its Natural Order; trans. by Wm. Strahan, ed. from the 2nd London ed. by Luther Cushing. B, 1850, roy8vo, 2vols., 1700pp., later 1/2 linen and bds, $150.00
"a truly wonderful performance....his works were the first successful attempt to reduce to order the Civil Law of France and their authority is still invoked throughout the civilized world." Jos. Story quoted by Marvin, 271.

338) DONALD, David, Lincoln's Herndon. NY, 1948, 8vo, 378pp, (Lincoln's law partner), $20.00

339) DOUGLAS, Wm. O., Democracy & Finance: The Addresses and Public Statements as a Member & Chairman of the Securities & Exchange Commission. ed. Jas. Allen. Yale, 1940, 8vo, 301pp., $25.00

340) DOUGLAS, Wm. O., Russian Journey. NY, 1956, 8vo, 255pp., stamp on verso,sl. cov. soil, $17.50

341) DOUGLAS, Wm. O., West of the Indus. NY, 1958, 8vo, 513pp., $22.50

342) DOUGLAS, Wm. O., The Bible & the Schools. B, 1966, 8vo, 65pp., $22.50

343) DOUGLAS, Wm. O., My Wilderness. NY, 1961, roy8vo, 290pp., $22.50

344) DREWRY, Chs. Treatise on the Law & Practice of Injunctions. P, 1842, 8vo, 306pp., later lin,LL, $47.50

345) DUCOUDRAY, Gustave, Les Origines du Parlement de Paris et la Justice aux XIII et XIV Siecles (1902) Reprint: 1970, roy8vo, 2vols., excellent work, $65.00

346) DUGUIT, Leon, Law in the Modern State. trans. H. Laski, NY, 1919, 8vo, 245pp.,$25.00

347) DUNCAN, G.I., The High Court of Delegates. Cambridge, 1971, 8vo, 318pp. ($47.00), $27.50

348) DUNIWAY, Clyde, Development of Freedom of the Press in Massachusetts. Harvard, 1906, 202p.,$22.50

349) DUNNE, Gerald, Monetary Decisions of the Supreme Court. Rutgers UP, 1960, 8vo, 112pp., $15.00

350) DUPIN, Andre, Profession d'Advocat: Recueil de Pieces Concernant l'Exercise de Cette Profession. P, 1832, 8vo, 2vols., 740,877pp., bound in later 1/2 calf, $250.00
A scarce and very valuable work containing among numerous important pieces Boucher d'Agis' Histoire Abrégée de l'Ordre des Advocats and the Dialogue des Advocats by Loysel; vol. II (Bibliotheque Choisie des Livres de Droit, 5th ed., rev. & aug. by Camus) is a spectacular bibliography of law and legal history for all the European nations and the Americas, with some notice of the Asian countries & Mohamedan law.

351) DURRAN, Wm., The Lawyer: Our Old Man of the Sea. L, 1913, roy8vo, 551pp., $27.50

352) DYMOND, Jonathan, Essays on the Principles of Morality and on the Private & Political Rights and Obligations of Mankind. NY, 1834, roy8vo, 434pp., orig. cl., sl. wear, scarce, $47.50

353) EAST, Edward Hyde, A Treatise of the Pleas of the Crown. P, 1806, 8vo, 2vols., later 1/2 calf & boards, nice set, $175.00
"Because he had access to private collections of cases, his treatise is the result of a most thorough examination & sifting of all the English Common Law writers....though somewhat antiquated it is still a standard work upon criminal law." Marvin, 286.

354) EDEN, Hon. Rob., A Practical Treatise on the Bankrupt Law. P, 1841, 8vo, 2vols. later 1/2 linen, LL, $95.00

355) EDWARDS, Chs., Pleasantries about Courts & Lawyers in the State of New York. NY/L, 1867, 8vo, 528pp., $37.50

356) EHRENZWEIG, Albert, Psychoanalytic Jurisprudence. Leiden, 1971, roy8vo, 395pp., $25.00

357) EINAUDI, Mario, The Physiocratic Doctrine of Judicial Control. Harvard, 1938, 8vo, 96pp., $17.50

358) Election of William Lorimer: Hearings before a Committee of the Senate of the United States....to Investigate Whether Corrupt Methods & Practices were Used or Employed in the Election of Wm. Lorimer as a Senator from the State of Illinois. DC, GPO, 1912, 62nd Cong., 2nd Ses., Doc. # 484; roy8vo, 9vols., $225.00

359) ELLIOT, Jonathan, The Debates in the Several State Conventions on the Adoption of the Federal Constitution, as Recommended by the General Convention at Philadelphia in 1787, together with the Journal of the Federal Convention..... DC, 1836-45, roy8vo, 5vols., bound in later 1/2 linen and boards, beautiful set, $265.00

360) ELLIOT, Mabel, Conflicting Penal Theories in Statutory Criminal Law. Univ. of Chi,1931, 274pp, $25.00

361) ELLIS, Chs., The Law of Fire & Life Insurance. P, 1834, 8vo, 158pp., later linen, LL, $37.50

362) ELLIS, Sir Henry, A General Introduction to Domesday Book, Accompanied by Indexes of the Tenants in Chief & Under Tenants....with an Abstract of the Population of England at the Close of the Reign of William the Conqueror, Illustrated by Numerous Notes & Comments. L, 1833, 8vo, 2vols., 1100pp., later 1/2 linen and boards, $125.00

363) ELLUL, Jacques, The Theological Foundation of Law: A Radical Critique of Natural Law. NY, 1960, 8vo, 160pp., $17.50

364) EMDEN, Cecil., The People & the Constitution. 2nd ed., Oxford, 1956, 8vo, 339pp.,$25.00

365) EMERSON, Th., The System of Freedom of Expression. NY, 1970, roy8vo, 754pp., $27.50

366) ENGELMAN, Woldemar, Die Wiedergeburt der Rechtskultur in Italien durch die wissenschaftliche Lehre. Leipzig, 1938, roy8vo, 585pp., $36.00

367) ENSLIN, T. C., & ENGELMAN, W., et al., Bibliotheca Juridica: Handbuch der Gesamten Juristischen und Staatswissenschaftlichen Literatur,..,von 1750 -- 1876. (1840-1877) Reprint: 1968, 8vo, 4vols., $100.00 one of the most important law bibliographies.

368) EPPSTEIN, John, The Catholic Tradition of the Law of Nations. DC, 1935, roy8vo, 525pp., $30.00

369) ERNST, Morris, & SCHWARTZ, A., Censorship: Search for the Obscene. NY, 1964, 8vo, 287pp., $16.50

370) ERNST, Morris Too Big. B, 1940, 8vo, 314pp., $25.00

371) ESMEIN, A., Cours Elementaire d'Histoire du Droit Francais. P, 1892, roy8vo, 765pp., $37.50

372) ESMEIN, A., Melanges d'Histoire du Droit et de Critique: Droit Romain (1886), Rep.1970, 8vo, 420pp., $35.00

373) ESPINASSE, Isaac, A Digest of the Law of Actions & Trials at Nisi Prius, 3rd American ed. from the 3rd London ed. Walpole, N.H., 1808, 8vo, 2vols. contemp. roan, bit scuffed, nice copy, $75.00

374) Extraodinary Trial of the Rev. John Seys....for an Alleged Assault & Battery on Mrs. Eliz. Cram. NY, 1847, 8vo, 12pp., orig. wrps, $27.50

375) FALK, Richard, Status of Law in International Society. Princeton, 1970, roy8vo, 678pp., $27.50

375-A) MASTERS, Ruth, International Law in National Courts. Columbia, 1932, roy8vo, 245pp, $20.00

376) FARRAND, Max (ed.), Records of the Federal Convention of 1787.rev ed., Yale, 1966, 8vo, 4vols., $95.00

377) FARRAR, Timothy, Report of the Case of the Trustees of Dartmouth College Against Wm. Woodward, Argued & Determined in the Superior Court of Judicature of the State of New Hampshire, and on Error, in the Supreme Court of the U.S. Portsmouth, 1819, roy8vo, 406pp., later linen, lt. sporadic foxing, uncut, first edition; still the major source for this fundamentally important case, $125.00

FAY, Sidney, The Origins of the World War. NY, 1928, roy8vo, 2vols., $37.50

FELLMAN, David, Constitutional Right of Association. Univ. of Chicago, 1963, 8vo, 110pp., $10.00

FENWICK, The Proceedings Against Sir John Fenwick, Bar., Upon a Bill of Attainder for High Treason ....Printed in the Year 1702. 8vo, 348pp., contemp. calf, front hinge cracked but firm, $75.00

FERGUSON, Jan, Manual of International Law for the Use of Navies, Colonies & Consulates. Hague/London/Hong Kong, 1884, 8vo, 2vols., contemp. 1/2 calf, scuffed but sound, scarce, $47.50

FIELD, David Dudley, Draft Outlines of an International Code. NY, 1872, 8vo, 463pp., scarce, $37.50

FIELD, Oliver, Civil Service Law. Univ. of Minnesota. 1939, roy8vo, 286pp., $25.00

FIFOOT, C.H., Frederic Wm. Maitland. Harvard, 1971, 8vo, 313pp., $16.50

FIFOOT, Ch., Lord Mansfield. Oxford, 1936, roy8vo, 262pp., $27.50

FINNEY, H.A., & OLDBERG, R., Lawyer's Guide to Accounting. NJ, 1955, 4to, 291pp., $25.00

FISHER, H.A.L., Frederic Wm. Maitland. Cambridge, 1910, 8vo, 179pp., $22.50

FISHER, Irving, League or War. NY, 1923, 8vo, 268pp., $22.50

FISHER, Sydney, The Evolution of the Constitution of the United States, Showing that It is a Development of Progressive History, and Not an Isolated Document Struck off at a Given Time or an Imitation of English or Dutch Forms of Government. P, 1897, 8vo, 389pp., $30.00

FITZPATRICK, Wm., Ireland before the Union, with Revelations from the Unpublished Diary of John Scott, Chief Justice of the King's Bench in Ireland. 2nd ed., rev. & enl. D, 1867, 12mo, 268pp. lin, $37.50

FLETA, Seu Commentarius Juris Angli'ani, Sic Nuncupatus sub Edwardo Rege Primo, Seu Circa Annos Abhinc CCCXL ab Anonymo Conscriptus, atque e Codice Veteri, Auctore Ipso Aliquantilum Recentiori Nunc Primum Typis Editus. Accedit Tractatus Vetus de Agendi Excipiendi Formulis Gallicanus Fet Assavoir Dictus. Subjungitur etiam Joan. Seldini ad Fletam Dissertatio Historica. Editio Secunda, Multis Erroribus Purgata. L, 1685, small4to, 553pp., later 1/2 calf, lt. sporadic foxing and sl. trace of embrowning, $275.00
"The author of this Treatise is unknown. He is supposed to have been one of the judges who was imprisoned during the reign of Edw. I. Fleta, when written, was a concise account of the whole English law as it then prevailed....Mr. Selden first called the public attention to this ancient treatise & was instrumental in pro uring its publication to which he prefixed a dissertation abounding in varied antiquarian learning." Marvin, 314.

FLETCHER, Chs., An Essay on the Estates of Trustees. P, 1835, 8vo, 46pp.,later linen, LL, $35.00

FLORY, Wm., Prisoners of War: A Study in the Development of International Law. DC, 1942, roy8vo, 179pp.,$25.00

FLOYER, Philip, The Proctor's Practice in the Eccelsiastical Courts as It is Regulated by the Rules of Practice Now in Force. L, 1744, 8vo, 176pp., later 1/2 roan, $85.00

FLUEGEL, Maurice, The Spirit of Biblical Legislation in Parallel with Talmud, Moralists, Casuists, New Testament, Ancient & Modern Law. Balto, 1893, 8vo, 248pp., $22.50

FONBLANQUE, John, A Treatise of Equity....3rd American edition with References to American Chancery Decisions & Additional Notes by Anthony Laussat. P, 1831, roy8vo, 2vols. bound as one, contemp. calf, sl. rubbed, handsome copy; "until the appearance of Maddok & Story "Fonblanque was the best equity elementary treatise in existence." Marvin, 317. $115.00

FORNEY, John, Address on Religious Intolerance & Political Proscriptions. DC, 1855, 51pp, lin, $35.00

FORSTER, John, LL.D., The Debates on the Grand Remonstrance, Nov-Dec, 1641, with an Introductory Essay on English Freedom under Palntagenet & Tudor Sovereigns. L, 1860, 8vo, 500p., $57.50

FORTESCUE, Sir John, De Laudibus Legum Angliae, translation into English published in 1775, and Original Latin Text with Notes, by A. Amos. Cambridge, 1825, 8vo, xvi,280pp., later 1/2 calf, $85.00

FOSTER, Geo., Lawyer's Legal Research: Rules & Problems of Search Illustrated by Diagrams or Geometric Charts. Rochester, 1920, 8vo, 104pp., $18.50

FOSTER, Jeremiah, An Authentic Report of the Testimony in a Cause at Issue in the Court of Chancery in the State of New Jersey, between Thomas Shotwell, Complainant, & Jos. Hendrickson & Stacy Decow, Defendants. P, 1831,roy8vo, 2vols., orig. bds, $75.00

FOSTER, Roger, Commentaries on the Constitution of the U.S., Historical & Judicial, with Observations Upon the Ordinary Provisions of State Constitutions, and a Comparison with the Constitutions of Other Countries. B, 1895, Vol. I (all publ.) roy8vo, 713pp., scarce & important, $45.00

FOWLER, John, American Investment Trusts. NY, 1928, 8vo, 415pp., $20.00

FRAENKEL, Osmond, The Sacco-Vanzetti Case. NY, 1931, roy8vo, 550pp., $27.50

FRANK, John, Justice Daniel Dissenting: A Biography of Peter V. Daniel, 1784-1860. Harvard, 1964,$20.00

FRANKFURTER, Felix, The Case of Sacco & Vanzetti. B, 1927, 8vo, 118pp., 1st ed, sl. soil, $35.00

FRANKFURTER, Felix, Mr. Justice Holmes & the Supreme Court. Harvard, 1938, 8vo, 139pp., spine sl. faded, first edition, $37.50

FRANKFURTER, Felix, & GREENE, Nathan, The Labor Injunction. NY, 1930, roy8vo, 343pp, 1st ed. $45.00

FRANKLIN, Julian, Constitutionalism & Resistance in the 16th Century. NY, 1969, 8vo, 207pp., $17.50

FRASCA, Chs., Stock Swindlers & Their Methods. NY, 1931, 8vo, 209pp., $17.50

FRAZER, Sir JamesG. Folk-Lore in the Old Testament: Studies in Comparative Religion, Legend & Law. Abr. ed., NY, 1927, roy8vo, 476pp., $27.50

FREEDMAN, Max (ed.), Roosevelt & Frankfurter: Their Correspondence, 1928-1945. B, 1967, 772pp, $27.50

FREEMAN, Edw. A., The Growth of the English Constitution. L, 1894, 8vo, 234pp., 27.50

FRESKA, Frederick (ed.), A Peace Congress of Intrigue (Vienna, 1815). NY, 1919, 8vo, 448pp, $22.50

FRIEDMAN, Wolfgang, Legal Theory. L, 1944, roy8vo, 448pp., $25.00

FRIEDRICH, Carl, Philosophy of Law in Historical Perspective. Univ. of Chicago, 1958, 252pp, $22.50

FRIEDRICH, Carl (ed.), Nomos: Yearbook of the American Society for Political & Legal Philosophy. Vol. IV, Liberty. NY, 1962, 8vo, 333pp., $22.50

Nomos, Vol. VI; Justice. NY, 1963, 8vo, 325pp., $22.50

Nomos, Vol. VII; Rational Decision. NY, 1964, 8vo, 228pp., $20.00

FROUDE, Jas. Anthony, The History of England from the Fall of Wolsey to the Death of Elizabeth. 3rd ed. rev., L, 1862, roy8vo, 12vols., bound in later 1/2 morocco & linen (by Zaehnsdorf) raised bands, spines gilt, covers gilt, t.e.g., marbled end sheets, fine set, $335.00

FUCHS, Jos., Natural Law: A Theological Investigation. NY, 1965, 8vo, 193pp., $22.50

FUGATE, Wilbur, Foreign Commerce & Anti-Trust Laws. B, 1958, roy8vo, 384pp., $25.00

FULLER, Thomas, The Holy State & the Profane State (1642), ed. with Intro, Notes & Appendix by Max Graff-Walken. Columbia, 1938, roy8vo, 2vols., $47.50

GAIUS, Gai Institutiones, or Institutes of Roman Law by Gaius, with a translation & commentary by Edw. Poste, 4th ed, rev. & enl. by E. A. Whittuck, with an historical introduction by A. H. Greenidge. Oxford, 1925, roy8vo, lv, 668pp., bound with Supplements to the Institutes of Gaius, by F. de Zulueta (1935), 12pp., $50.00

GARDINER, W., A Survey of the Roman or Civil Law: An Extract from Gibbon's Decline & Fall, with Notes by Prof. Hugo of Goettingen, trans. fromthe German. Edinburgh, 1823, 12mo, 232pp., later linen,$47.50

GARDNER , Daniel, Institutes of International Law Public & Private, as Settled by the Supreme Court of the U.S. and by Our Republic. NY, 1860, roy8vo, 719pp., later linen, scarce, $65.00

GARDNER, Percy, A Lawyer's Philosophy of Life. B, 1935, 8vo, 45pp., $15.00

GARIS, Roy, Immigration Restriction: A Study of the Oppositinn to & Regulation of Immigration into the U.S. NY, 1927, roy8vo, 376pp., $27.50

GARNER, Jas. Wilford, International Law & the World War. L, 1920, roy8vo, 2vols.,$47.50

GARNER, Jas. W., Recent Developments in International Law. Calcutta, 1925, roy8vo, 840pp., $35.00

GARNER, Jas. W., Government in the U.S.: National & State. NY, 1911, 8vo, 410pp., $17.50

GARRETT, Paul, & MAC CORMICK,A., Handbook of American Prisons & Reformatories. NY, 1929, 1035p, $30.00

GAUPP, Ernst, Recht u. Verfassung der Alten Sachsen in Verbindung mit einer kritischen Ausgabe der Lex Saxonum. (1837), Rep: 1968, 8vo, 228pp., $22.50

GAYLEY, Chs., Shakespeare & the Founders of Liberty in America. NY, 1917, 8vo, 270pp., $25.00

_____? A Generation of Judges by Their Reporter. L, 1886, 8vo, 217pp., later linen, $25.00

A GENTLEMAN OF DOCTOR'S COMMONS, The Clerk's Instructor in the Ecclesiastical Courts....Also a Treatise Concerning Pluralities. L, 1740, 8vo, 528pp., later 1/2 calf, rare, one copy in No. America.$150.00

GENTRY, Curt, Frame-Up. NY, 1967, roy8vo, 495pp. (the 1916 San Francisco labor bomb case), $25.00

GEORGE, Jas., Constitutional Limitations on Evidence in Criminal Cases. NY, 1969, roy8vo, 413pp,$22.50

GEST, John, The Lawyer in Literature. B, 1913, 8vo, 249pp., $22.50

GIACON, Carlo, La Seconda Scholastica: I Problemi Giuridico-Politici Suarez, Bellarmino, Mariana. Milan, 1950, roy8vo, 296pp., wrps, $20.00

GIANNINI, Amedeo, La Convenzione di Diritto Internazionale Privato. Milan, 1928, 8vo, 196p, $17.50

GIBBONS, David, A Manual of the Law of Fixtures. P , 1836, 8vo, 24pp., later linen, LL, $30.00

GILBERT, Lord Chief Baron, The Law of Evidence, Considerably Enlarged....to Which is Prefixed Some Account of the Author, & His Argument in a Case of Homicide in Ireland. Dublin, 1795-97. roy8vo, 3vols. bound (as issued) as 2; bit rubbed & scuffed tut a nice set, $150.00
"For many years a standard practical book. When Blackstone wrote his Commentaries, he apologizes for not treating the subject of evidence more at length 'because of the fullness & excellence of Lord Chief Baron's Treatise;" Marvin, 334.

GILBERT, Lord, A Treatise on Rents. P, 1838, 8vo, 65pp., later 1/2 line , $47.50 (LL)

GILBERT, Lord, The History and Practice of the High Court of Chancery, first American ed. by Samuel Tyler. DC, 1874, roy8vo, 380pp., later linen, $65.00
"It has traced out the reasons for many parts of our modern practice from the feudal institutions and the primitive construction of our Courts in a most clear & ingenious manner," Blackstone quoted by Marvin, 334.

GILBERT, Lord, The Law of Devises, Last Wills & Revocations to Which is Added a Select Number of Wills Drawn by Men Eminent in the Profession. 4th ed., rev. Dublin, 1792, 8vo, 255p, contemp. roan, $95.00

GILBERT, Frank, Railway Law in Illinois with an Appendix Showing the Condition of all the Railways in the State & the Tariff Schedule. C, 1873, roy8vo, 337pp. later linen. $37.50

GLAISTER, John, Medical Jurisprudence & Toxicology. 8th ed. Edinburgh, 1945, roy8vo, 691pp, $25.00

GLANVILLE, A Translation by John Beames, to Which are Added Notes & Intro.by Geo. Beale. DC, 1900, (Legal Classics Series), 8vo, xxxiv, 306pp., $47.50

GLUECK, Sheldon, Crime & Justice. B, 349pp., tear in title neatly mended, $22.50

GLUECK, Sheldon, Law & Psychiatry. L, 1963, 8vo, 181pp., $18.50

GLUECK, Sheldon, War Criminals: Their Prosecution & Punishment. NY, 1944, 8vo, 249pp, sl. soil, $25.00

GLUECK, Sheldon, & Eleanor, Preventing Crime: A Symposium. NY, 1936, 8vo, 509pp., $27.50

GLUECK, Sheldon & Eleanor, Unraveling Juvenile Delinquency. Harvard, 1957, 4to, 399pp, $25.00

GLUECK, Sheldon (ed.), Probation & Criminal Justice: Essays in Honor of Herbert Parsons. NY, 1933, roy8vo, 344pp., $25.00

GNEIST, Rudolf, The History of the English Constitution, trans. by P. Ashworth. NY, 1886, roy8vo, 2vols., sl. wear, sound set, $47.50

GNEIST, Rudolf, Die Bildung der Geschworenengericht in Deutschland. (1849) (Evolution of the Jury in Germany), Rep: 1967, 8vo, 248pp, $22.50

GNEIST, Rudolf, Institutionum et Regularum Iuris Romani Syntagma. L, 1858, 8vo, 356pp, $35.00

GOLDEN, Harry, A Little Girl is Dead. Cl, 1965, 8vo, 363pp., (lynching of Leo FRank), $18.50

GOLDSMITH, G., The Doctrine & Practice of Equity....P, 1843, 8vo, 112pp., later linen, LL, $45.00. "As an Outline of Equity Law & Practice it is entitled to all praise." Marvin, 341.

GOMME, Geo., Primitive Folk Moots.(1880), Det, 1968, 8vo, 316pp.,$25.00

462) GOODHART, A.L., English Law & the Moral Law.L, 1953, 8vo, 151pp., $22.50

463) GOODRICH, Leland & HAMBRO, Edw., Charter of the UN: Commentary & Documents. B, 1946, 8vo, 413pp., $22.50

464) GORECKI, Jan (ed.), Sociology & Jurisprudence of Leon Petrazycki. Univ. of Illinois, 1975, 8vo, 144pp., $10.00

465) GOULD, Wesley & BARKUN, M., International Law & the Social Sciences. Princeton, 1970, 338p, $25.00

466) GRAHAM, David, Treatise on the Organization & Jurisdiction of the Courts of Law & Equity in the State of New York. NY, 1839, 8vo, 659pp., contemp. roan, sl. marg. dpst. & sl. wear, $45.00

467) GRANGE, Wm., & STAUB, W., Wills, Executors & Trustees. NY, 1933, roy8vo, 844pp., $25.00

468) (GRANT, Jas.), Random Recollections of the House of Lords, from 1830-1836, Including Personal Sketches of the Leading Members. L, 1836, 8vo, 408pp., contemp. 1/2 calf, sl. scuffed, $45.00

469) GRATIAN, Decretum Emendatum et Notationibus Illustratum, Una cum Glosis, Gregorii XIII Pont. Max iussu editum, Ad Exemplar Romanum diligenter Recognitum, Editio Ultima. Paris, 1612, large folio, 1273pp., bound in contemp. vellum, expertly rebacked, a beautiful copy, with a superb engraved title and numerous ornamental woodcut letters throughout the text; paper in an excellent state. $450.00

The fundamental work of Canon Law & thus one of the cornerstones of the Middle Ages: "In the Decretum Gratian (12th century) assembled close to 3500 texts, canons of the councils, decretals, Roman laws, extracts from the church fathers and the like--bringing togher the materials from the existing collections which circulated in the west after the Gregorian reform. Upon every point Gratian grouped the divergences of authorities and in his dicta, or comments, attempted to reconcile them by virtue of a method which was historical as well as logical. Since the 12th century it has formed the basis of instruction in canon law. It is the sum of the ancient canon law as well as one of the principal sources of the living law. Gratian had the great merit to apply a juridical method to the texts, and he thus contributed to the creation of an autonomous science of canon law, which in the future was taught in accordance with the Decretum, side by side with theology. As a result, the Decretum has had a great influence upon political & social doctrine....and many of its views of the state, the relation between church & state, the theory of war, rights of property & contract, and the law of civil & criminal procedure, were based in large part on the texts of the Decretum. ESS, VII, 156.

470) GRAVESON, R. H., Law: An Outline for Intending Students. L, 1967, 8vo, 207pp., $18.50

471) GRAY, John, The Country Attorney's Practice in Conducting Actions in the Superior Courts of Law at with....Bills of Cost. 5th ed., L, 1841, 8vo, 412pp., orig. cl., sl. soiled & sl. worn, $57.50

472) GREELEY, Horace, & CLEVELAND, John, Political Text-Book for 1860: Comprising a Brief View of the Presidential Nominations & Elections....also a History of the Struggle Respecting Slavery in the Territories, & the Action of Congress as to the Freedom of Public Lands. NY, 1860, roy8vo, 248 (2col.)pp., later linen, $45.00

473) The Green Bag: A Useless but Entertaining Magazine for Lawyers. Vol. I, No. 1 (Jan, 1889) to Vol. VII (1895), 4to, bound in 7vols., rebacked, $275.00

474) GROTIUS, Hugo, The Jurisprudence of Holland, Text & Translation with Brief Notes & Commentary by R. W. Lee. I: Text, Translation & Notes, Oxford, 1926, roy8vo, xxv, 531pp., $65.00

475) GROTIUS, Hugo, The Rights of War & Peace in Three Books, Wherein are Explained the Law of Nature & Nations, and the Principal Points Relating to Government, translated into English, to Which are Added All the Large Notes of Mr. J. Barbeyrac. L, 1738, folio, xxxvi, 817pp., bound in later 1/2 calf & marbled boards, raised bands, a very crisp, attractive copy, $475.00

476) GURVITCH, Geo., Le Temps Present et l'Idee du Droit Social. P, 1931, roy8vo, 336pp, $22.50

477) GUTHRIE, John, Elementary Principles of the Laws of England Traced Down to the Present Time. L, 1843, 8vo, 363pp., contemp. calf, sometime rebacked in roan, sl. scuffed, $65.00

478) GUY, Wm., Principles of Forensic Medicine, first American edition with Notes & Additions by Chs. Lee. NY, 1845, roy8vo, 711pp., contemp. roan, sl. internal dampstain, nice copy, $85.00

479) GWATHMEY, John, Legends of Virginia Courthouses. Richmond, 1934, roy8vo, 141pp., ill., $22.50

480) GYSIN, Arnold, Rechtsphilosophie und Grundlagen des Privatrechts: Begegnung mit grossen Juristen. F/m, 1969, 8vo, 358pp., $22.50

481) HAINES, Elijah, A Practical Treatise on the Powers & Duties of Justices of the Peace & Constables in the State of Illinois. 4th ed., rev. & enl., C, Meyers, 1868, roy8vo, 804pp., later lin, $87.50

482) HAINES, Chs. G., Role of the Supreme Court in American Government & Politics, 1789-1835. NY, 1960, roy8vo, 679pp., $27.50

483) HALE, Sir Matthew, A History of the Common Law of England and an Analysis of the Civil Part of the Law. 6th edition, with Additional Notes & References, and some Account of the Life of the Author by Chs. Runnington. L, 1820, roy8vo, li,368,104pp., contemp. calf, sometime rebacked, $150.00

484) HALE, Sir Matthew, Contemplations Moral and Divine, by a Person of Great Learning & Judgment. L, 1676, 8vo, 528pp., later 1/2 calf & bds, first edition. $285.00

485) HALE, Wm., The Law of the Press. St. P., 1923, roy8vo, 503pp., $25.00

486) HALEVY, Elie, History of the English People in the 19th Century. L, 1949, 2nd ed, rev, 4vols. $65.00

487) HALL, Sir Edw, Selections from the Charges & Other Papers of Baron Alderson, with an Introductory Notice of His Life by Chs. Anderson. L, 1858, 8vo, 311pp., later linen, $37.50

488) HALL, Wm., A Treatise on International Law. 7th ed., Oxford, 1917, roy8vo, 864pp., $30.00

489) HALLAM, Henry, The Constitutional History of England from the Accession of Henry VII to the Death of Geo. III. B, 1829, 8vo, 3vols., later linen, $65.00

490) HAMILTON, E. R., The Art of Interrogation. L, 1929, roy8vo, 173pp., $20.00

491) HANDS, Wm., The Solicitor's Practice on the Crown Side of the Court of King's Bench with an Appendix of Forms. L, 1803, 8vo, 524pp., contemp. calf, bit rubbed, nice copy, $85.00

492) HARDING, Arthur (ed.), Origins of the Natural Law Tradition. Dallas, 1954, 8vo, 96pp., $17.50

493) HARDING, W.P.G., Formative Period of the Federal Reserve System. NY, 1925, 8vo, 320pp., $17.50

494) HARGRAVE, Francis, Collectanea Juridica, Consisting of Tracts Relative to the Law & Constitution of England. L, 1791-92. 8vo, 2vols., 1000pp., later 1/2 linen & bds, $185.00

495) HARRIMAN, Edw., The Constitution at the Crossroads: A Study of the Legal Aspects of the League of Nations, Permanent Organization of Labor, & the Permanent Court of International Justice. NY, 1925, 8vo, 274pp., $25.00

495-A) MARNELL, Wm., The Right to Know: Media & the Common Good. NY, 1973, 8vo, 221pp., $17.50

496) The Harleian Miscellany; or, A Collection of Scarce, Curious & Entertaining Pamphlets & Tracts, as Well in Manuscript as in Print, found in the Late Earl of Oxford's Library, Interspersed with Historical, Political & Critical Notes. L, 1808, 8vo, 12vols. contemp. 1/2 morocco & marbled boards, raised bands, beautiful set, $450.00

497) HARRIS, Rob., The Judicial Power of the US. Louisiana St. UP, 1940, 8vo, 238pp., $22.50

498) HARVARD University: Conference on the Future of the Common Law. Harvard, 1937, 8vo, 246pp. $22.50

499) HARVEY, Peter, Reminiscences & Anecdotes of Daniel Webster. B, 1901, 8vo, 480pp., $22/50

500) HASKINS, Chs. H., Norman Institutions. NY, 1960, roy8vo, 377pp., $25.00

501) HASSARD, Alb. Famous Canadian Trials. Toronto, 1924, roy8vo, 246pp., $25.00

502) HASTIE, W., Outlines of the Science of Jurisprudence: An Intro. to the Systematic Study of Law; trans. & ed. from the Juristic Encyclopedias of Puchta....Ahrens. Edinburgh, 1887, 8vo, 325p, $30.00

503) HAWKINS, Wm., A Treatise of Pleas of the Crown. 8th ed. by John Curwood. L, 1824, thick roy8vo, 2vols., later 1/2 calf, $250.00

"There are very few juridical writers whose compilations are more full of more useful knowledge, or more methodically digested, even down to the minute subdivisions, than the Pleas of the Crown. In this authoritative work, the student will readily find information in almost every point of law relating to Crimes & Punishments." Marvin, 375.

504) HAYES, John, The Trial of Lord Stirling; Being Part II of the Vindication of the Rights & Titles, Political & Territorial, of Alexander, Earl of Stirling & Donovan, Hereditary Lieutenant General & Lord Proprietor of Canada & Nova Scotia. DC, 1853, roy8vo, 71pp., later linen, $45.00

505) HAYES, Wm., Principles for Expounding Dispositions of Real Estate to Ancestor & Heirs in Tail, Parent & Issue, with an Elementary Essay & Dissertations on Several of Mr. Fearne's Doctrines. P, 1835, 8vo, xxvii, 109pp., later linen, LL, $37.50

506) HAYNES, Evan, The Selection & Tenure of Judges. Nat'l Council, 1944, roy8vo, 308pp., $25.00

507) HEGEL, Georg Wilhelm Friedrich, Grundlinien der Philosophie des Rechts, (Naturrecht und Staatswissenschaft in Umrisse). Berlin, 1821, 8vo, xxvi, 355pp., bound in contemp. 1/2 calf and marbled boards, rubbed but a very sound and attractive copy, new title skiver, first edition, $1250.00

The cornerstone of Hegel's political & legal philosophy "in which his final system of a sciology of the perfectly organized state, such as an ideal Prussia might be, was laid down. The Grundlinien is a complete system, in which the concept of a sociology dominated by the idea of the state is laid down. It turns away from the apparent chaos of the democratic advocates of individual right in favor of an overwhelming sense that liberty cannot exist apart from order, and that the vital connection of all parts of the body politic is the source of all good. Taken apart from the rest of his system, Hegel's political philosophy has been much misrepresented by totalitarian propagandists. He was, however, one of the most profound & influential thinkers of the 19th century." Printing and the Mind of Man, 283.

This is the first work of the Philosophical School of Jurisprudence, and also had a major influence on the Historical School since many of its members were Hegelians. It is the subject of one of Marx's earliest works (1842), his Critique of Hegel's Philosophy of Law.

508) HENING, Wm. The Virginia Justice: Comprising the Office & Authority of the Justice of the Peace in the State of Virginia. 4th ed., rev. corr. & enl. Richmond, 1825, 8vo, 821pp., later linen, $75.00

509) HENNELL, Chs., Forms of Declarations, etc., Prepared in Conformity with the New General Rules of all the Courts, Intended Principally for the Use of Attorneys in Drawing Affadavits to Hold to Bail, Declarations, Particulars of Demand...P, 1834, 8vo, xvi,99pp., later linen, LL, $45.00

510) HENRY, Rob., Contracts in the Local Courts of Medieval England. L, 1926, roy8vo, 250pp., $25.00

511) HERBERT, A. P., Misleading Cases in the Common Law. NY, 1930, 8vo, 236p., $22.50

512) HIBBERT, W. N., Jurisprudence. L, 1932, roy8vo, 332pp., $30.00

513) HICKS, Fred, Men & Books Famous in the Law. Rochester, 1921, 8vo, 259pp., $25.00

514) HICKS, Fred (ed.) Famous American Jury Speeches. St. P., 1925, roy8vo, 1181pp., $35.00

515) HIGGINS, A.P., War & the Private Citizen: Studies in International Law. L, 1912, 8vo, 200p, $22.50

516) HIGH, Jas (ed.), Speeches of Lord Erskine while at the Bar. C, 1876, roy8vo, 2vols., new linen, $57.50

517) HILDRETH, Richard, Atrocious Judges: Lives of Judges Infamous as Tools of Tyrants & Instruments of Oppression, Compiled from the Judicial Biographies of John Lord Campbell, with an Appendix Containing the Case of Passmore Williamson. NY, 1856, 8vo, 432pp., contemp. 1/2 morocco, sl. wear, $45.00

518) HILL, Sir Francis, Medieval Lincoln. Cambridge, 1965, roy8vo, 487pp., ex lib, $35.00

519) HILL, Frederick, Decisive Battles of the Law. NY, 1907, 8vo, 267pp., sl. dpst., $17.50

520) HILLIARD, Edw., Sheppard's Touchstone of Common Assurances; Or, A Plain & Familiar Treatise, Opening the Learning of the Common Assurances, or Conveyances of the Kingdom....from the last London ed., with the Addition of Various Criticisms & Distinctions by the Late Richard Preston. P, 1840, 8vo, LL 2vols., later 1/2 linen. $125.00

"One of the most esteemed of the old treatises, a copious fountain of the law; the most esteemed editions are Hilliard's and subsequent ones." Marvin, 643.

521) The History and Antiquities of the Four Inns of Court....and of the Nine Inns of Chancery, Containing Every Particular Circumstance Relative to Each of Them, Comprised in the Well Known and Justly Celebrated Work, Written by Sir. Wm. Dugdale and Published in Folio in 1666,...under the title of Origines Juridicales, to Which is Subjoined an Appendix, Containing Several Modern Orders Made Up by the Society of Lincoln's Inn,...also a list of the Benchers of the Four Inns of Court, The Whole is Published by the Desire of Some Members of Parl. in Order to Point Out the Abuses in the Government of the Four Inns of Court & Chancery, and to Propose such Expedients for Remedying Them, and Regulating the Study & Practice of the Law, by Act of Parliament, as Shall be Judged Necessary. L, 1780, 8vo, xx, 251pp., contemp. calf, sometime rebacked, nice copy, $175.00

522) The History & Proceedings of the House of Commons from the Restoration, in the Year 1660, ...to the Death of Queen Anne, Containing the Most Remarkable Motions, Speeches, Resolves, REports & Conferences,...as also Exact Estimates of the Charge of Government; State of the Public Revenue, the Rise & Growth of the National Debt, Expense of War, Proceedings on Ways and Means, Speeches, Messages from the Throne, Addresses & Remonstrances, and also the Numbers Pro & Con Upon Every Division, Many of Which Particulars were Never before Printed, Collected from the Best Authorities,...and Illustrated with a Great Varietyof Historical & Explanatory Notes,...with All the Continuations to 1773. L, 1742-74. 8vo, 23vols., bound in later linen, scarce complete, $475.00

523) HOAR, Roger, Constitutional Conventions: Their Nature, Powers & Limitations. B, 1917, 8vo, 240p, $22.50

523-A) Manuel du Conseil de l'Europe: Structure, Fonctionnement. P, 1970, roy8vo, 406pp, $20.00

524) The History and Proceddings of the House of Lords from the Restoration in 1660 to the Present Time, Containing the Most Remarkable Motions, Speeches, Debates, Orders & Resolutions, Together with All the Protests of That Period, and the Numbers Pro & Con upon Each Division....Connected with the Transactions of the Commons and History of the Times & Illustrated with Historical Notes and Observations. L, 1742, 8vo, 8vols.,linen,$250.00

History of the Ordinance of 1787 & the Old Northwest Territory. Marietta, 1937, 8vo, 95p. wrps, $17.50

HOAR, Roger, Patent Tactics & Law. NY, 1950, 3rd ed., roy8vo, 352pp., $20.00

HOBSON, John, Toward International Government. L, 1916, 8vo, 216pp., $17.50

HOLAIND, Rene, Natural Law & Legal Practice. NY, 1899, 8vo, 344pp., $25.00

HOLLAMS, Sir John, Jottings of an Old Solicitor. NY, 1906, 8vo, 247pp., $20.00

HOLLAND, Thomas, The Elements of Jurisprudence. 13th ed., Oxford, 1917, roy8vo, 454pp., $30.00

HOLLAND, T. E., & SHADWELL, Chs., Select Titles from the Digest of Justinian. Oxford, 1881, roy8vo, 466pp., sl. wear, $37.50

HOLLAND, T. E., The Laws of War on Land (Written & Unwritten). Oxford, 1908, 8vo, 149p., $22.50

HOLMES, John, The Statesman: Or, Principles of Legislation & Law. Augusta, Me., 1840, 8vo, 510pp., contemp. roan, sl. worn, scarce, $65.00

HOLMES-POLLOCK, The Correspondence of Mr. Justice Holmes & Sir Frederick Pollock, 1874-1932. ed. Mark de Wolfe. Harvard, 1941, roy8vo, 2vols., sl. spine fade, $45.00

HOLMES, Oliver Wendell, Collected Legal Papers. sl. rubbed, $20.00

HOLMES, Oliver Wendell, His Book Notices & Uncollected Letters & Papers. ed. H. Shriver, Intro. by Harlan Fiske Stone. NY, 1936, 8vo, 280pp., sl. faded, $27.50

HOLZMAN, Rob., Federal Taxation of Capital Assets. NY, 1969, roy8vo, 349pp., $25.00

HOME, Henry (Lord Kames), Historical Law Tracts. 4th ed., with Adds. & Corrs. Edinburgh, 1792, 8vo, 487pp., later 1/2 sheep and boards, $125.00

HORSKY, Chs., The Washington Lawyer. B, 1952, 8vo, 179pp., $20.00

HOUSE, Edw. & SEYMOUR, Chs., What Really Happened at Paris: The Story of the Peace Conference by American Delegates. NY, 1921, roy8vo, 528pp., $25.00

HOUSE, Edw., The Intimate Papers of, arr. by Chs. Seymour. B, 1926, roy8vo, 2vols., $45.00

HOWE, Mark., Justice Oliver Wendell Holmes. Harvard, 1957-1963, roy8vo, 2vols., sl. rubbed, $35.00

HUGHES, Charles Evans, The Pathway of Peace: Representative Addresses Delivered During His Term as Secretary of State. NY, 1925, 8vo, 329pp., (several deal with law, including international) first edition, one of 200 copies signed by Hughes, $37.50

HUGHES, Chris, The British Statute Book. L, 1957, 12mo, 168pp., $22.50

HUGHES, Paul, & FRIES, Rob. (eds.), Crown & Parliament in Tudor-Stuart England: A Documentary Constitutional History, 1485-1714. NY, 1959, 4to, 359pp., $22.50

HUGHES, Paul & LARKIN, Jas. (eds.), Tudor Royal Proclamations. Yale UP, 1964, roy8vo, 3vols, $85.00

HUIE, Wm., The Execution of Private Slovik. NY, 1954, 8vo, 247pp., $17.50

HURLSTONE, Edwin, A Practical Treatise on the Law of Bonds. P, 1835, 8vo, 130pp, LL, later lin, $45.00

HUTCHINS, B. L., & HARRISON, A., History of Factory Legislation. 3rd ed. L, 1926, 8vo, 298pp. $22.50

HYDE, Charles, Maritime War (Confidential) DC, Gpo, 1918, 210pp.; bound with this: Declarations of War: Severances of Diplomatic Relations, 1914-18 (Confidential), DC, GPO, 1919, 99pp; and with: WRIGHT, Herb. (ed.), Constitutions of the States at War. DC, GPO, 1919, 679pp., roy8vo, $37.50

HYDE, H. M. (ed.), The Trials of Oscar Wilde. L, 1952, 8vo, 384pp., $22.50

ILBERT, Courtenay, The Mechanics of Law Making. Columbia, 1914, 8vo, 209pp., $22.50

Illinois: Journal of the Constitutional Convention of the State of Illinois, Convened at Springfield, 1869. Springfield, 1870, roy8vo, 1022pp., later linen, $75.00

Institutes of Hindu Law; Or, The Ordinances of Menu, According to the Gloss of Calcutta....Verbally Translated from the Original, with a Preface by Sir. Wm. Jones, a New Edition, Collated with the Sanskrit Text, by G. C. Haughton. L, 1825, 4ro, 450pp., later linen, $85.00

Information for Alexander Donaldson & John Wood, Booksellers in Edinburgh, against John Hinton, Bookseller in London. (Lord Coalston, Reporter) n.p. n.d. (1773), 4to, 82pp., later linen, $45.00

INTERNATIONAL LAW ASSOCIATION, Report of the 34th Conference, Vienna, 1926, 8vo, 742pp., $30.00

the same, Report of the 35th Conference, Warsaw, 1928, 8vo, 487pp., $30.00

the same, Report of the 38th Conference, Budapest, 1934, 8vo, 356pp., $30.00

In the Court for the Trial of Impeachments and the Correction of Errors: Henry Jackson & Maria, His Wife, vs. Benjamin Edwards & Others. NY, 1839, 8vo, 84pp., later linen, $35.00

Investigation of the Wonderful Charge Made Against Daniel Burtnett (The Wealthy Butcher) of Incest on His Daughters. NY, 1846, 8vo, 23pp., wrps, $35.00

Irish State Trials (NY, 1844), 8vo, 229pp., later linen, title on text, $45.00

IRVING, David, An Introduction to the Study of the Civil Law. 4th ed. L, 1837, 8vo, 284pp., later linen, "No other work in our language contains so much useful information in a small compass. The bibliographical criticism with which it abounds gives it a peculiar value." Marvin, 415.$65.00

JACKSON,R. M., The Machinery of Justice in England. Cambridge, 1940, 8vo, 348pp., $25.00

JACOBINI, H. B., International Law: A Text. Illinois, 1962, roy8vo, 324pp., $22.50

JACOBS, Clyde, Law Writers & the Courts: The Influence of Cooley, Tiedeman & Dillon Upon American Constitutional Law. Univ. of California, 1954, 8vo, 223pp., $22.50

JAY, Cyrus, The Law: What I have Seen, What I Have Heard, & What I have Known. L, 1868, 8vo, 351pp; later linen, $37.50

JEAFFRESON, John, A Book About Lawyers. NY, 1867, 8vo, 432pp., later linen, $45.00

JENKS, Edw., A Short History of English Law. 4th ed., L, 1928, 8vo, 420pp., $22.50

JENKS, Edw., The State & the Nation. NY, 1919, 8vo, 312pp., $22.50

JESSUP, Philip, Elihu Root. NY, 1938, roy8vo, 2vols., 1150pp., $37.50

JESTAZ, Phil., L'Urgence et les Principes Classiques du Droit Civil. P, 1968, roy8vo, 327p, wrps,$22.50

JOHNSON, Wm., Memoirs of John Selden & Notices of the Political Contests During His Time. L, 1835, 8vo, 374pp., later linen, $65.00

JOHNSON, Harold, Self-Determination within the Community of Nations. Leyden, 1967, roy8vo, 232pp., $22.50

JOHNSON, Walter, Maxims of the Civil Law: Essays in the Evolution of Law. Montreal, 1929, 8vo, 252pp., $30.00

JOHNSTON, Frank, Modern Conception of Law. C, 1925, roy8vo, 352pp., $25.00

JOHNSTON, Henry (ed.), The Correspondence & Public Papers of John Jay, 1763-1826. Reprint: 1971 (Orig. ed. 1890-93), 4to, 4vols. bound as one, ($150.00), $85.00

JONES, Chester, Statute Law Making in the United States. B, 1912, 8vo, 325pp., $22.50

JONES, J.W., The Position & Rights of a Bona Fide Purchaser for Value of Goods Improperly Obtained. Cambridge, 1921, 8vo, 128pp., $22.50

JONES, Sir William, An Essay on the Law of Bailments. 4th ed., with Notes by Wm. Theobald.L, 1833, 8vo, 123, lxiipp., bds, rebacked, $45.00

JOUFFROY, Th., Cours de Droit Naturel. 2nd ed., P, 1843, 8vo, 2vols., later linen, $75.00

JOY, Henry, On the Admissibility of Confessions & Challenge of Jurors in Criminal Cases in England and Ireland. P, 1843, 8vo, 112pp., later linen, $47.50 LL

Journal of the Commissioners for Trade & Plantations....from 1704 to 1734. (1920), Reprint: 1969, 4to, 6vols., $150.00

JUDSON, Frederick, The Judiciary & the People. Yale, 1913, 12mo, 270pp., $20.00

Jus Civile Antejustinianeum Codicum et Optimarum Editionum. Ope a Societate Jurisconsultorum Curatum Praefatus est et Indicem Editionum Adjecit Gustavus Hugo. Berlin, 1815, 8vo, 2vols., 1609pp., contemp. 1/2 calf, bit rubbed, $95.00

KEETON, Geo., The Elementary Principles of Jurisprudence. L, 1930, roy8vo, 324pp., $27.50

KENNEDY, John, Memoirs of the Life of William Wirt, Attorney-General of the U.S., new ed., rev. P, 1860, 8vo, 2vols. bound as one, 750pp., sl. wear, $45.00

KENNEDY, W.P., Some Aspects of the Theories & Workings of Constitutional Law. NY, 1932, 8vo,142p, $16.5

KENT, Jas., An Anniversary Discourse Delivered before the New York Historical Society. NY, 1829, 8vo, 40pp., later linen with orig. wrps. bound in, first edition, $85.00

KILGORE, Carrol, Judicial Tyranny. Nashville/NY, 1977, roy8vo, 370pp., $17.50

KIRBY, Jas., Selected Articles on Criminal Justice. NY, 1926, 8vo, 314pp, $22.50

KISCH, Guido, Die Anfänge der Juristischen Facultät der Universität Basel, 1459-1529. Basil, 1962, roy8vo, 397pp., orig. ptd. wrps, $35.00

KISCH, Guido, The Jews in Medieval Germany: Their Legal & Social Status. Univ.of Chicago, 1949, roy8vo, 655pp., a scarce and excellent book, $37.50

KLAUS, Samuel, (ed.), The Milligan Case. NY, 1929, roy8vo, 476pp., $22.50

(Klu Klux Klan) Report of the Joint Select Committee to Inquire Into the Condition of Affairs in the Late Insurrectionary States. DC, GPO, 1872, roy8vo, 632pp., $47.50

KNITTEL, Eberhard, Das Englische Schwurgericht, Bonn, 1968, 8vo, 124pp., wrps, $15.00

KOCOUREK, Albert, An Introduction to the Science of Law. B, 1930, 8vo, 343pp., $27.50

KOEGEL, Otto, Walter S. Carter: Collector of Young Masters, or, Progenitor of Many Law Firms. NY, 1953, roy8vo, 491pp., $25.00

KOHLER, Max, Immigration & Aliens in the U.S; Studies of American Immigration Law and the Legal Status of Aliens in the U.S. NY, 1936, roy8vo, 459pp., $30.00

KONVITZ,Milton, Fundamental Liberties of a Free People. Cornell, 1957, roy8vo, 420pp., $22.50

KONVITZ, M., Expanding Liberties: Freedom's Gains in Postwar America. NY, 1966, 8vo, 429pp., $18.50

KONVITZ, M., A Century of Civil Rights; with a Study of State Law Against Discrimination, by Theodore Leskes. Columbia, 1961, roy8vo, 293pp. ex lib, $18.50

KOVALEVSKY, Maxim, Modern Customs & Ancient Laws of Russia. L, 1891, roy8vo, 260p. sl. rubbed, $30.00

KREILKAMP, Karl, The Metaphysical Foundations of Thomistic Jurisprudence. DC, 1939, 8vo,183p, $17.50

KULSRUD, Carl, Maritime Neutrality to 1780. B, 1936, 8vo, 351pp., $25.00

KURTSCHEID, Bert., History of the Seal of Confession. St.L., 1927, 8vo, 342pp., $22.50

KUTNER, Luis, World Habeas Corpus; foreword by Pound. NY, 1962, 8vo, 295pp., $22.50

KYD, Stewart, A Treatise on the Law of Awards. 2nd ed., rev. L, 1799, 8vo, 583pp., contemp. calf,$95.00

KYD, Stewart, Treatise on the Law of Bills of Exchange & Promissory Notes. Dublin, 1791, 8vo, 160p. contemp. calf, rebacked, $57.50

LAMB, Frederick, Forty Years in the Old Bailey, with a Summary of the Leading Cases & Points of Law & Practice. L, 1913, 8vo, 356pp., $25.00

LANG, Andrew, Social Origins, and ATKINSON, J.J., Primal Law. L, 1903, roy8vo, 311pp. $22.50

LASPEGRES, Ernest, Uber die Entstehung und alteste Bearbeitung der Libri Feudorum. (1830), Rep: 1969, 8vo, 468pp., $25.00

LATOUR, Jos., La Mer Territoriale. P, 1889, 8vo, 380pp., contemp. 1/2 morocco, scarce, $45.00

The Law & Woman's Work, A Contribution to the Study & Status of Women. Geneva, 1939, roy8vo, 590pp. spine faded, sl. mag. embrowning, (Int'l Labor Off., Stud. & Rep., Ser I, No. 4), $27.50

LAWES, Edw., APractical Treatise on Pleading in Assumpsit, with the Addition of the Decisions of American Courts, by Joseph Story. B, 1811, roy8vo, 621pp., contemp. calf, rebacked, $75.00

LAWRENCE, Jos., Wall Street & Washington. Princeton, 1929, roy8vo, 468pp., $25.00

LAWRENCE, T. J., The Principles of International Law. 5th ed. B, 1910, 8vo, 745pp.,$27.50

Law & Justice: Proceedings of the American Academy of Political Science. NY, Columbia, Vol. X, NO. 3 July, 1923, 229pp., wrps, $15.00

The Laws of England, Being a Complete Statement of the Whole Law of England by the Late Earl of Halsbury...& Other Lawyers. 3rd ed.under the editorship of Lord Simonds. L, 1952ff. roy8vo, 39vols. plus Table of Cases (1 vol); Index (2vols); Table of Statutes (1 vol) and 6 vols of Supps (to 1972) together 49vols., in excellent condition. $675.00

619) Law Quibbles; Or, A Treatise of the Evasions, Tricks, Turns & Quibbles Commonly Used in the Profession of the Law, to the Prejudice of Clients & Others, Necessary to be Perused by All Attornies, & Those who May be Concerned in Law Suits, Trials, & etc. to Avoid the Many Abuses, Delays & E penses Introduced into Practice, with Abstracts of All the late Statutes for Amending the Law Relating to Attornies ....and an Essay on the Amendment & Reduction of the Laws of England, & a New Proposed Act of Parliament for a Thorough Regulation of the Practice of the Law. 4th edition, corrected & much enlarged, to Which is now Added a Second Part, Containing very Curious Precedents of Conveyances in Extraordinary Cases.... L, 1736, 8vo, 132, 135, 72pp., later 1/2 calf & bds, title margins expertly reinforced. $275.00

The Laws of Neutrality as Existing on Aug 1, 1914. DC, GPO, 1918; roy8vo, 578pp; bound with: WARRIN, Frank, The Neutrality of Belgium. GPO, 1918, 110pp; and with: Neutrality Proclamations, 1914-18. GPO, 1919, 64pp; and with: HYDE, Chs., Neutral Persons & Property within Belligerent Territory. GPO (Confidential), 1919, 24pp., $47.50

The Laws of the Northwest Territory, 1788-1800, ed. with Intro. by Calvin Pease. Springfield, 1925, roy8vo, 591pp., Collections of the Ill. State Hist. Lib, Vol. XVII; Law Ser, Vol. I), $37.50

LAZAREFF, Serge, Status of Military Forces Under Current Int'l Law. Leiden, 1971, roy8vo, 458p, $27.50

LEA, Henry C., Studies in Church History: The Rise of the Temporal Power, Benefit of Clergy, Excommunication. P, 1869, 8vo, 515pp., rebacked, $30.00

LEA, Henry C., Superstition & Force: Essays on the Wager of Law, the Wager of Battle, the Ordeal, Torture. 2nd ed., rev., P, 1870, 8vo, 480pp., $35.00

LECLERCQ, Jac., Du Droit Naturel a la Sociologie. P, 1960, 12mo, 159pp., $15.00

LEFEBURE, Victor, The Riddle of the Rhine: Chemical Strategy in Peace & War. NY, 1923, 282pp, $22.50

Legislative History of the Labor-Management Reporting & Disclosure Act of 1959. DC, GPO, 1959, 4to, 2vols., $50.00

LEONARD, John (ed.), Who's Who in Jurisprudence: A Biographical Dictionary of Contemporary Lawyers & Jurists. NY, 1925, roy8vo, 1618pp., $37.50

LEGRAND, Andre, L'Ombudsman Scandinave: Etudes Compare sur le Controle de l'Administration. P, 1970, roy8vo, 549pp., orig. ptd. wrps., $22.50

A Landmark of International Law

LEIBNITZ, Gottfried Wilhelm, Codex Juris Gentium Diplomaticus, in Quo Tabulae Authenticae Actorum Publicorum, Tractatuum, Aliarumque Rerum Majoris Momenti per Europam Gestarum....A Fine Seculi Undecimi ad Nostra usque Tempora....Hannover, 1693-1700, small folio, (16),479,180,380pp; Part II (Mantissa Codicis Juris Gentium) has separate title; bound in contemp. vellum; very light sporadic foxing and the very faintest trace of dampstain at the upper margin of a very few leaves, a superb copy, first edition, $2500.00
The only systematic work on the subject by the celebrated philosopher and polymath, an adherent of Grotius and masterful critic of Pufendorf.

LEIGH, J. & DALZELL, R., A Treatise on the Equitable Doctrine of the Conversion of Property. P, 1834, 8vo, 112pp., later linen, LL, $45.00

Les Reportes del Cases in Camera Stellata, 1593-1609, from the Original Ms of John Hawarde, ed. by Wm. P. Baildon. L, Privately Printed, 1894, 4to, lxxv, 502pp., $125.00

LEVIN, Laurence, The Political Doctrine of Montesquieu's Esprit des Lois in Its Classical Background. Columbia, 1936, roy8vo, 359pp., $25.00

LEVY, Beryl, Our Constitution: Tool or Testament? Introduction by Robert H. Jackson. NY, (1941) 1965, 8vo, 315pp., $22.50

LEVY, Ernst, West Roman Vulgar Law: The Law of Property. P, 1951, roy8vo, xix,305pp., $35.00

LEVY, Isaac, & SMOLENS, B. (eds.), Court is in Session, foreword by Owen J. Roberts. NY, 1950, 8vo, 241pp., $18.50

LEVY, Leonard, Origins of the Fifth Amendment: The Right Against Self-Incrimination. Oxford, 1968, roy8vo, 561pp., $27.50

LEVY, Leonard, Judgments: Essays on American Constitutional History. C, 1972, roy8vo, 341pp, $25.00

LEWIN, Th., A Practical Treatise on the Law of Trusts & Trustees. P, 1839, 8vo, liv, 410pp., later 1/2 linen, LL "few text books merit higher praise than this." Marvin, 461. $57.50

LEWIS, Walker, Without Fear or Favor: Biography of Chief Justice Roger B. Taney. B, 1965, roy8vo, 556pp., $25.00

LIEBER, Francis, A Lecture on the History & Uses of Athenaeums. Columbia, S.C., 1846, 8vo, 32pp., later linen, rare, leading American jurist and political philosopher, $47.50

LILLY, John, A Collection of Modern Entries, or Select Pleadings in the Courts of King's Bench, Common Pleas & Exchequer....to Which is Added a Collection of Writs in Most Cases Now in Practice. 5th ed. L, 1791, sm4to, 2vols., later 1/2 sheep & bds, $175.00
"The only book of Entries & Writs that goes through the whole alphabet since the law proceedings have been in English." Marvin, 465.

(LINCOLN) The Trial of John H. Surratt in the Criminal Court for the District of Columbia. DC/P, 1867, roy8vo, 2vols., 1383pp., later linen, $150.00

LINDLEY, Nathaniel, An Introduction to the Study of Jurisprudence, Being a Translation of the General Part of Thibaut's System des Pandekten Rechts, with Notes. P, 1855, roy8vo, 311pp., later lin, $45.00

LIPPMANN, Walter, Public Opinion. NY, 1934, 8vo, 427pp., $22.50

LIVERMORE, Sam., A Treatise on the Law Relative to Principals & Agents, Factors, Auctioneers & Brokers. B, 1811, 8vo, 260pp., contemp. roan, sl. foxing, "Learned & perspicuous, drawing illustrations from the Civil as well as the Common Law." Marvin, 470. $57.50

LIVERMORE, Shaw, Early American Land Companies: Their Influence on Corporate Development. NY, 1939, roy8vo, 327pp., $27.50

LIVINGSTON, Edward, A System of Penal Law for the United States of America: Consisting of a Code of Crimes & Punishments; A Code of Procedure in Criminal Cases; A Code of Prison Discipline and a Book of Definitions. Prepared & Presented to the House of Representatives of the United States, by Edward Livingston, one of the Representatives from the State of Louisiana. Printed by Order of the House of Representatives. Washington, Gales & Seaton, 1828, folio, x,142,187,51,45pp., bound in contemp. tree roan, rear hinge expertly reinforced, slight trace of wear at crown and front hinge very slightly cracked, a very sound, crisp, beautiful copy, first edition, $1250.00

Livingston (1764-1836) was admitted to the bar in 1785 and began law practice in New York City, rapidly rising to distinction. As a representative in Congress he led the opposition to Jay's Treaty and also opposed the Alien & Sedition Laws. In the debate on the extradition of Jonathan Robbins, who had claimed American citizenship when accused of murder on an English frigate, he was opposed by John Marshall. In 1804 he moved to Louisiana where he prepared a provisional code of judicial procedure. As Secretary of State under Jackson, he prepared a number of state papers, the most important being the famous anti-nullification proclamation of 1832.

His System of Penal Law for the United States, which was never adopted, in content & organization, with the necessary modifications required by its larger scope, follows the code of criminal law & procedure which he had prepared for Louisiana in 1824, but which was not published in full until 1833. His ultimate object in that endeavor was to adapt it for the use of the entire country. That code, known as the "Livingston Code," "foreshadowed nearly every reform in penology in the last half century." ESS, IX, 552; it attracted wide praise in America & Europe by its remarkable simplicity and vigor, and especially by reason of its philanthropic provisions in the code of reform & prison discipline, which notably influenced the penal legislation of various countries. Kent, Story, Marshall, Madison & Jefferson expressed their admiration & enthusiasm for his work. Kent wrote: "You have done more in giving precision, specification, accuracy & moderation to the system of crimes & punishments than any other legislator of the age., and your name will go down to posterity with distinguished honor." It was reprinted in England, translated into French, and German reviewers reproduced it almost in full in their notices. Bentham proposed that the whole work be printed for the use of the English nation and Sir Henry Maine called Livingston "the first legal genius of modern times." EB11, XVI, 811; Hunt, Life of Livingston, 281. (The article on Livingston in the 11th edition of the Britannica is the length of a full double-column quarto page; in the latest edition he merits only 30 lines.)

649) HUNT, Chs. The Life of Edward Livingston. NY, 1864, roy8vo, 448pp., later linen, $35.00

650) LLOYD, T. & CAINES, Geo., Reporters, The Trial of Thomas Selfridge, Counsellor at Law...for Killing Chs. Austin on the Public Exchange in Boston. 2nd ed., np.n.d. (NY, 1806), 8vo, 168pp., $47.50

651) LLOYD, Th., The Trials of William Smith & Samuel Ogden, for Misdemeanors, Held in the Circuit Court of the U.S. for the N. Y. District. NY, 1807, 8vo, 287pp., later lin, sl. soiled, $37.50

652) LOBINGIER, Chs., The People's Law, or Popular Participation in Law Making from Ancient Folk Moot to Modern Referendum. NY, 1909, 8vo, 429pp, $25.00

653) LOCKE, John The Works of, a New Edition, Corrected. L, 1823, 8vo, 10vols., later linen with leather labels, nice set, $350.00

654) LOKKEN, Roy, David Lloyd: Colonial Lawmaker. Univ. of Washington, 1959, 8vo, 305pp., $22.50

655) The London Missionary Society's Report of the Proceedings against the Late Rev. J. Smith of Demerara who was Tried under Martial Law & Condemned to Death on a Charge of Aiding & Assisting in a Rebellion....Including Documentary Evidence Omitted in the Parliamentary Copy. L, 1824, 8vo, 204p, $47.50

656) LONG, Robert The Mythology of Reparations. L, 1928, 8vo, 199pp., sl. worn, $22.50

657) LONGENECKER, Rolla, Hints on the Trial of a Lawsuit; foreword by Wigmore. R, 1927, 8vo, 314p, $25.00

658) LORD CRAIGMYLE, John Marshall in Diplomacy & Law. NY, 1933, 8vo, 145pp, signed, $25.00

659) LORD LLOYD OF HAMPSTEAD, Introduction to Jurisprudence. 3rd ed., NY, 1972, roy8vo, 873pp., $30.00

660) LORD RUSSELL OF LIVERPOOL, The Royal Conscience. L, 1961, 8vo, 253pp., (historical study of the office of Lord Chancellor and of the major chancellors.), $25.00

661) LORING, Jas., The Hundred Boston Orators, Appointed by the Municipal Authorities and Other Public Bodies from 1770 to 1852, Comprising Historical Gleanings Illustrating the Principles & Progress of Our Republican Institutions. B, 1852, roy8vo, 694pp., sl. wear, scarce, $35.00

662) LOVELASS, Peter, The Law's Disposal of a Person's Estate who Dies without Will or Testament, to Which is Added the Disposal of a Person's Estate by Will & Testament, with an Explanation of the Mortmain Act, from the 12th London ed. enl. P, 1839, 8vo, xxiv, 322pp., later 1/2 linen, LL, $57.50

663) LUCAS, Arthur, Legal Minimum Age in Massachusetts. (Supp. to the AAAPSS, vol. 130) 1927, 84p, wrps, $12.5

664) LUEHR, Elmer, The New German Republic: The Reich in Transition. NY, 1929, roy8vo, 442pp., covers sl. spotted, $27.50

665) LUNING, Johann, Corpus Iuris Militaris. Reprint of the 1723 ed., folio, 2vols., $125.00

666) LYON, Hastings, & BLOCH, H., Edward Coke: Oracle of the Law. B, 1929, roy8vo, 385p, sl. faded, $35.00

667) LYON, J. N. & ATKEY, R. (ed.), Canadian Constitutional Law in Modern Perspective. Univ. of Toronto, 1970, roy8vo, 351pp., $20.00

668) MABLY, Abbe, Remarks Concerning the Government & Laws of the United States of America, in Four Letters Addressed to Mr. Adams, Minister Plenipotentiary from the U.S.....from the French of Abbe de Mably, with Notes by the Translator. Dublin, 1785, 8vo, 280pp., contemp. calf, front hinge sl. cracked but firm; (occasioned Adams' masterful Defense of the Constitutions of Government of the United States.), $175.00

669) MAC COMBAICH DE COLQUHOUN, Patrick, A Summary of the Roman Civil Law, Illustrated by Commentaries on and Parallels from the Mosaic, Canon, Mohammedan, English & Foreign Law. L, 1849, roy8vo, 4vols. 2200pp., orig. cl., newly recased, $175.00

670) MACKELDY, Ferdinand, Compendium of Modern Civil Law, edited by Ph. Kaufmann, 2nd American from the 12th German ed, with Numerous Adds. NY, 1849, roy8vo, xxxv,400pp., later linen, $57.50

671) MAITLAND, F. W., Historical Essays. ed. Cam, Cambridge, 1951, 8vo, 277pp., $22.50

672) Maitland, F. W., Constitutional History of England, 1920, 8vo, 540pp., ($49.00), $32.50

673) MAKOWER, Felix, Constitutional History of the Church of England (1895), 1972, roy8vo, 545pp, $25.00

674) MAC KINNON, Sir Frank, On Circuit. Cambridge, 1940, 4to, 311pp., sl. wear, $25.00

675) MAC KINNON, F. B., Contingent Fees for Legal Services. C, 1964, roy8vo, 246pp., $22.50

676) MACKINTOSH, Jas., The Roman Law of Sale, with Modern Illustrations, Digest XVIII, 1; and XIX, 1; trans. with Notes & References to Cases and the Sale of Goods Act. 2nd ed., enl., Edinburgh, 1929, roy8vo, 299pp., $27.50

677) MACMILLAN, Hugh P. (Lord Macmillan), Law & Other Things. Cambridge, 1938, 8vo, 283pp., $22.50

678) MAC NEIL, John, & FIDGELY, O., An Index to Form Precedents in the Reports of the Supreme & Appellate Courts of Illinois. C, 1899, roy8vo, 211pp., later linen, $27.50

679) MACPHERSON, Wm., A Treatise on the Law Relating to Infants. P, 1843, 8vo, 430pp., linen, LL, $47.50

680) MAGNUS, Julius, Die Rechtsanwaltschaft. L, 1929, 8vo, 536pp; $25.00

681) MALONE, Dumas, Story of the Declaration of Independence. Oxford, 1954, 4to, 282pp, $25.00

682) MADDEN, R. R., The Connection between the Kingdom of Ireland & the Crown of England, with an Appeddix, of the Privy Council Correspondence During the Great Part of the Years 1811, 1812, 1816, 1817. Dublin, 1845, 8vo, 340pp., sl. wear & soil, $37.50

683) MAGUIRE, John, Lance of Justice: A Semi-Centennial History of the Legal Aid Society, 1876-1926. Harvard, 1928, 8vo, 305pp., $22.50

MAINE, Henry Sumner, Ancient Law: Its Connection with the Early History of Society, and Its Relation to Modern Ideas, with an Intro. by Theodore Dwight. First American from the Second London Edition. NY, 1864, roy8vo, LXIX, 400pp., orig. cloth, rebacked; the work is "almost the only one in the English language in which general jurisprudence is regarded from the historical point of view." Dwight. $125.00

Another copy of the First American Edition, original cloth, rebacked and the original spine remounted; with an ALS from Maine, to his American publisher, Henry Holt, August 16, 1874, discussing the sale of previous works and impending publication of works in progress, and mentions the revisions in Ancient Law necessitated by the criticisms of Edward Freeman, James Bryce and others. $250.00

MAINE, Sir Henry, Dissertations on Early Law & Custom. L, 1901, roy8vo, 402pp., $25.00

MAINE, Sir Henry, Lectures on the Early History of Institutions. L, 1875, roy8vo, viii, 412pp., orig. cloth, rebacked & spine expertly remounted, first edition, $125.00

MAINE, Sir Henry, Ancient Law, with Intro. & Notes by Pollock. NY, 1906, 8vo, xxiii, 462pp., later linen, $25.00

MAITLAND, F. W., & MONTAGUE, T., A Sketch of English Legal History. NY, 1915, 8vo, 229pp., $25.00

MANSEL, Geo., A Treatise on the Law & Practice of Demurrer to Pleadings & Evidence....in Personal Actions, with an Introduction to the Nature & Forms of Pleadings. P, 1839, 8vo, 298pp., later 1/2 linen, LL, $47.50

MARCHANT, Ronald, The Puritans & the Church Courts in the Diocese of York, 1560-1642. L, 1960, 8vo, 330pp., $27.50

MARIANO, John, A Psychoanalytic Lawyer Looks at Marriage & Divorse. NY, 1952, 8vo, 276pp., $17.50

MARSHALL, John, The Life of George Washington. Va, 1926, 8vo, 5vols. ($247.50), $125.00

MARSHALL, John, The Life of George Washington. P, 1804-07, 8vo, 5vols., contemp. calf, expertly re-backed in calf, beautiful set, first edition, $475.00

(MARSHALL), DICKINSON, Marquis (ed.), John Marshall: The Tribute of Massachusetts; Addresses Delivered in Commemoration of the 100th Anniversary of His Elevation to the Bench as Chief Justice. B, 1901, roy8vo, 120pp., (addresses by Holmes, Thayer, Gray, Olney & Others.) #484 of 750 copies, uncut & unopened, sl. trace of wear at crown, $37.50

John Marshall Bicentennial Celebration, 1955: Final Report of the U.S. Commission. DC, 1955, roy8vo, 94pp., $25.00

MARTIN, Edw., The Life of Joseph Hodges Choate, as Gathered Chiefly from His Letters. (leading lawyer, public figure & ambassador), NY, 1920, roy8vo, 2vols., $35.00

MARTIN, G. H. & MC INTYRE, S. (eds.), A Bibliography of British & Irish Municipal History, Vol. I: General Works. NY, 1972, roy8vo, 806pp, $27.50

MARTIN, P-M., Le Conflit Israelo-Arabe: Recherches sur l'Emploi de la Force en Droit International Public Positif. P, 1973, roy8vo, 345pp., wrps, $25.00

MASNATA-RUBATTEL, Claire, L'Amerique Blanche et les Droits des Noirs. P, 1969, 8vo, 295pp., $20.00

MASON, Alpheus T., Harlan Fiske Stone: Pillar of the Law. NY,1956, roy8vo, 914pp., ex lib, $25.00

MASON, Alpheus & BEANEY, W., American Constitutional Law: Introductory Essays & Selected Cases. NJ, 1958, roy8vo, 669pp;, $22.50

MASON, Alpheus, Brandeis: A Free Man's Life. NY, 1946, roy8vo, 713pp., $25.00

MATTERN, Johannes, Principles of the Constitutional Jurisprudence of the German National Republic. Johns Hopkins, 1928, roy8vo, 682pp., $35.00

MATTHEWS, Richard, A Practical Guide to Executors & Administrators, intended also for the Use of Attornies & Solicitors. P, 1835, 8vo, 171pp., later linen, LL, $45.00

MAY, Arthur, The Valuation of Residential Real Estate. NY, 1942, roy8vo, 309pp, sp. faded, $25.00

MAY, Gaston, Elements de Droit Romain. 3rd ed., P, 1894, roy8vo, 684pp., $45.00

MAY, Sir Thomas Erskine, A Treatise on the Law, Privileges & Proceedings of Parliament. 13th ed., by S. T. Webster, L, 1904, 4to, 914pp., sl. wear, sound copy, $37.50

MAYERS, Lewis, The American Legal System. rev. ed., NY, 1964, roy8vo, 594pp., $27.50

MAYHEW, Henry & BINNY, J., The Criminal Prisons of London & Scenes of Prison Life, with Numerous Illustrations. L (1862), roy8vo, 632pp., orig. cl., rebacked, $37.50

MAYHEW, Leon, Law & Equal Opportunity: A Study of the Massachusetts Commission against Discrimination. Harvard, 1968, 8vo, 313pp., $25.00

MC DOUGAL, Myres, LASSWELL, Harold, & VLASIC, I., Law & Public Order in Space. Yale, 1963, 4to, 1147pp., $35.00

MC MICHAEL, Stanley, Appraising Manual. 3rd ed., NY, 1944, 8vo, 715pp., $30.00

MC NUTT, John, Catalogue of the Indiana State Law Library. Ind, 1898, roy8vo, 725pp., $75.00

MEDER, Walter, Das Sowjetrecht: Grundzüge der Entwicklung, 1917-1970. F/m, 1971, 8vo, 588pp, $30.00

MERIAM, Lewis (et al), The Problem of Indian Administration. Johns Hopkins, 1928, roy8vo,872p,$35.00

MERRIAM, Chs E., The Written Constitution and the Unwritten Attitude. NY, 1931, 12mo, 89p, $22.50

MERSHON, S.L., English Crown Grants NY, 1918, 8vo, 266pp., $22.50

MICHAEL, Jerome & ADLER, Mortimer, Crime, Law & Social Science. NY, 1933, 8vo, 440pp., $25.00

MILLER, Clarence, Legislative Evolution of the Interstate Commerce Act. DC, 1930,roy8vo, 519p, $30.00

MILLER, Hunter (ed.), Treaties & Other International Acts of the U.S. DC, GPO, 1931-42, Vols. I-VII, thick 4to, ex lib, $175.00

MILLER, John, An Inquiry into the Present State of the Civil Law of England. L, 1825, 8vo, 533pp;, contemp. calf, sometime rebacked, $65.00

MILLER, Wm. G., Lectures on the Philosophy of Law, Designed Mainly as an Introduction to the Study of International Law. L, 1884, 8vo, 432pp., $30.00

MILNE, A. H., Freedom & Rights. L, 1968, 8vo, 376pp., $20.00

MIRABEAU, Oeuvres de, Precedes d'une Notice sur sa Vie et ses Ouvrages, par M. Merilhou, --22-- P, 1834-35, 8vo, 8vols., later linen, $250.00

MIRAGLIA, Luigi, Comparative Legal Philosophy Applied to Legal Institutions. B, 1912, 8vo, 793pp., (Mod. Leg. Phil. Ser., III), $30.00

MITGANG, Herb., The Man Who Rode the Tiger: Life & Times of judge Samuel Seabury. P, 1963, roy8vo, 380pp., $18.50

MOLLOY, Charles, De Jure Maritimo et Navali; Or a Treatise of Affairs Maritime and of Commerce. Third Editinn, Enlarged. L, 1682, 8vo, 432pp., bound in later 1/2 sheep and marbled boards, extremeties of upper fore-corners slightly chipped nn first few leaves, name sometime erased from title; sound, attractive copy, $325.00

MONAGHAN, Frank, John Jay: Defender of Liberty. NY, 1935, roy8vo, 497pp., $30.00

MONELL, Claudius, A Treatise on the Practice of the Courts in the State of New York,....and the Rules of the Supreme Court, to which is Added the Practice in Courts of Justices of the Peace. Albany, 1849, roy8vo, 575pp., later linen, $37.50

MONTESQUIEU, Oeuvres Completes de, avec des Notes de Dupin, Crevier, Voltaire, Mably, Servan, La Harpe. P, 1846, 4to, 770pp., contemp. 1/2 calf & bds, bit rubbed and scuffed but a sound copy of an excellent edition, $125.00

MONTESQUIEU, The Spirit of Laws, translated from the French of M. de Secondat Baron de Montesquieu, with Corrections and Additions Communicated by the Author. L, 1750, 8vo, 2vols., bound in later 1/2 calf and boards, raised bands, spines gilt, excellent set, first English edition, Printing and the Mind of Man, 197, $950.00

Monumenta Historica Britannica; or, Materials for the History of Britain from the Earliest Period to the End of the Reign of King Henry VII. Vol. I (all published) Extending to the Norman Conquest, prepared and illustrated with Notes by the Late Henry Petrie, asstd. by Rev. John Sharpe. 1848, very large folio, 1035pp., a mine of primary source material, illustrated with ms facsimiles; the "Descriptive Catalogue of British Coins" contains 17 full page plates, bound in later buck,$150.0

MONEYPENNY, Wm., & BUCKLE, Geo., Life of Benjamin Disraeli, NY, 1914, roy8vo, 6vols., $115.00

MONTAGUE, Basil, A Summary of the Law of Lien....Improved by a Digest of the American Decisions. Exeter, 1822, 8vo, 236pp., contemp. calf, hinges cracked but firm, $45.00

MONTAGUE, Francis, The Limits of Individual Liberty, L, 1885, 8vo, 242pp., sl. wear, $22.50

MONTGOMERY, Rob., Excess Profits Tax Procedure. NY, 1921, 8vo, 594pp., $22.50

MORGAN, John, The Attorney's Vade Mecum and Client's Instructor Treating of Actions, of Prosecuting & Defending Them: Of the Pleadings of Law, also of Hue & Cry,...with an Appendix, Containing a Few Precedents. Dublin, 1787, 8vo, 3vols. bound as 2, contemp. calf, beautiful set, $150.00

MORGAN, Lewis Henry, Ancient Society. NY, 1907, 8vo, 560pp., sl. wear, $30.00

MORSE, Wayne, A Survey of the Grand Jury System (reprinted from the Oregon Law Rev, 1931) roy8vo, 140pp., $20.00

MOSCHZISKER, Rob., Trial by Jury: A Brief Review of Its Origins & Developments and Practical Discussion of Actual Conduct of Jury Trials, Toghether with a Consideration of Constitutional Provisions & Other Cognate Subjects of Importance. 2nd ed., rev, & enl. P, 1930, roy8vo, 489pp;, $27.50

MOULTON, Harold, The Reparation Plan: An Interpretation of the Reports of the Expert Committees Appointed by the Reparation Commission. NY, 1924, 8vo, 325pp., $25.00

MOULTON, Harold, & MC GUIRE.C., Germany's Capacity to Pay: A Study of the Reparation Problem. NY, 1923, 8vo, 384pp., $25.00

MOYLE, Walter, The Works of,...None of Which Were Ever Before Published. L, 1726, 8vo, 2vols., contemp. calf, expertly rebacked, fine set, first edition. $500.00

Contains the first publication of his "Essay Upon the Roman Government," a classic of Republican political thought "which deserves now the closest scrutiny by students of 18th century political theory....Analogy between their contemporary world and that of the ancients was no novelty, but no one before Moyle examined in such detail the causes of the rise & fall of republican Rome and related these pronouncements so precisely to current political controversy. He was followed....by a whole series & essays by Englishmen and quite probably stimulated the greatest of 18th century analysts (Montesquieu) to write the Grandeur et Decadence in 1734" Robbins, Two English Republican Tracts, 37.

MUNRO, Wm., The Makers of the Unwritten Constitution. NY, 1930, 12mo, 136pp.,$20,00

MYERS, Wm., Woman & the Law. Albany, 1918, 8vo, 544pp.,$25.00

NASH, S. G. Attorney, His Manuscript Account Book; Nash was an attorney in Boston;from 1848 to 1864. a very detailed record of all expenses beginning with his freshman year at Dartmouth and continuing through his 19th year of law practice, in a neat hand, bound, 180pp, highly informative,$175.

NASSE, E., On the Agricultural Community of the Middle Ages & Inclosures of the 16th Century in England. trans. by H. A. Ouvry. L, 1871, 8vo, 100pp., later linen, $27.50

Natural Law and the Legal Profession: Lectures Delivered Under the Auspices of the Catholic Lawyer's Guild of Chicago. 1949, 8vo, 89pp., wrps, $18.50

NEILSON, Jos. Memories of Rufus Choate, with Some Consideration of His Studies, Methods, Opinions, and of His Style as a Speaker & Writer. B, 1884, 8vo, 460pp., fine copy, $30.00

NEWLAND, John, A Treatise on Contracts within the Jurisdiction of the Court of Equity. P, 1808, 8vo, xxxi, 543pp., sl. sporadic foxing, contemp. calf; "Its decisions at Common Law are often contrasted with those of Equity & the subject of every species of Contract cognizable in that Court is treated with singular ability and perspicuity." Marvin, 536. $85.00

The New Laws of the Indies for the Good Treatment & Preservation of the Indians, Promulgated by the Emperor Charles V, 1542-1543; A Facsimile Reprint of the Original Spanish Edition together with a Literal Translation into English, to which is Prefixed an Historical Introduction by the Late Henry Stevens & Fred. Lucas. L, Priv. Ptd. at the Chiswick Press, 1903, folio, xciv,26,xxxpp., original 1/2 linen & pictorial boards, sl. cover soil & trace of wear at extremeties, #37 of 88 copies, $85.00

NICHOLSON, Harold, The Congress of Vienna: A Study in Allied Unity. NY, 1946, 8vo, 312pp., $18.50

NIZER, Louis, My Life in Court. NY, 1961, roy8vo, 524pp., $17.50

NIZER, Louis, Thinking on Your Feet: Adventures in Speaking, NY, 1940, roy8vo, 312pp., $22.50

Notable Lawyers of the West. Chicago, 1902, 4to, 186pp., ill., $37.50

NOVICOV, J., L'Affranchisemment de la Femme. P, Alcan, 1903, 8vo, 267pp., $22.50

NOYES, C.R., The Institution of Property: A Study of the Development, Substance and Arrangement of the System of Property in Modern Anglo-American Law. Univ. of Toronto, 1936, roy8vo, 645pp, $35.00

NUMELIN, Ragnar, The Beginnings of Diplomacy: A Sociological Study of Intertribal & International Relations. Oxford, 1950, sm4to, 372pp., $27.50

OFFICE OF THE UNITED STATES CHIEF COUNSEL FOR THE PROSECUTION OF NAZI CRIMINALITY: Nazi Conspiracy and Aggression. (Nurenberg Trials), DC, GPO, 1946-48, thickroy8vo, 11vols., sl. faded, $350.00

762) OLIVER, Benjamin, Practical Conveyancing, with a Selection of Forms, 2nd ed, corr & enl. Me, 1827, roy8vo, 581pp., later linen, "highly esteemed," Marvin, $47.50

763) O'MALLEY, Austin, The Ethics of Medical Homicide & Mutilation. NY, 1922, roy8vo, 285pp., $22.50

764) ORFIELD, Lester, The Growth of Scandinavian Law. Univ. of Penn, 1953, roy8vo,363p.$22.50

OSBORN, Albert, The Problem of Proof, Especially as Exemplified in Disputed Document Trials; Discussion of the Proof of Facts in Courts of Law, with Comments on the Conduct of Trials. Intro. by John Henry Wigmore. 2nd ed., Newark, 1926, roy8vo, 539pp., $45.00

PAGET, John, Judicial Puzzles Gathered from the State Trials (Legal Recreations III). SF, 1876, 12mo, 155pp., later linen, $22.50

PAINE, Thomas, Life & Works. NY, 1925, roy8vo, 10vols., excellent, $150.00

Original Papers; with an Authentic State of the Proofs & Proceedings before the Coroner's Inquest Assembled at Madras in May, 1777, upon the Death of Lord Pigot, Likewise the Subsequent Proofs and Proceedings before the Justices at Madras, with the Opinions of the Judges of the Supreme Court of Judicature in Bengal; to the Whole Subjoined the Defence of Mr. Stratton, and the Other Members of Council, Accused by the Verdict of the Coroner's Inquest. L, 1778, 4to, 254pp., later linen, title bit soiled, $75.00

PALEY, Wm., A Treatise on the Law of Principal & Agent, Chiefly with Reference to Mercantile Transactions. 2nd Am. ed. P, 1840, 8vo, 202pp., later linen, LL, $45.00

PARK, John, A Treatise on the Law of Dower, Particularly with a View to the Modern Practice of Conveyancing. P, 1836, 8vo, 187pp., "much esteemed for its sound & copious learning," Marvin, $47.50

PARK, John Jas., A Contre-Projet to the Humphreysian Code; and to the Projects of Redaction of Messrs Hammond, Uniacke & Twiss. L, 1828, 8vo, 260pp., later linen, $125.00
"The object of this volume is to show that a complex system of laws belongs to a highly civilized state of society, and that the evil would not be removed by recasting them or adapting themto any of the plans of redaction. The author was a self-educated man and his writings are remarkable for their bold & independent thoughts....in the best sense of the word, a free thinker."Marvin, 554.

PARKER, James, The Conductor Generalis; or, the Office, Duty and Authority of Justices of the Peace, High Sheriffs, under Sheriffs, Coroners, Constables, Gaolers, Jury-men and Overseersof the Poor; Compiled Chiefly from Burn's Justice, and the Several Other Books on those Subjects by Jas. Parker, one of the Justices of the Peace for Middlesex County in New Jersey....and Now Adapted to the United States of America by a Gentleman of the Law. NY, 1788, 8vo, 461pp; contemp. calf, front hinge expertly restored, sl. wear at base of spine, nice copy, $150.00

PARKER, Jas., The Conductor Generalis....P, 1801, 8vo, 480pp., later linen, $75.00

PARKER, Joel, The Law School of Harvard College. NY, 1871, 8vo, 65pp., linen, $35.00

PARKES, Jos., A History of the Court of Chancery, with Practical Remarks on the Recent Commission Report & Evidence, & on the Means of Improving the Administration of Justice in the English Courts of Equity. L, 1828, 8vo, 616pp., later 1/2 linen, $75.00

The Parliamentary or Constitutional History of England from the Earliest Times to the Restoration of King Charles II, Collected from the Records & the Rolls of Parliament, the Journals of Both Houses, the Public Libraries, Original Manuscripts, Scarce Speeches & Tracts, All Compared withthe Several Contemporary Writers, and Connected Throughout with the History of the Times, by Several Hands. 2nd ed., L, 1762, 8vo, 24vols., later linen, $650.00

PARRY, Hon. Edw., The Drama of the Law. L, 1924, 8vo, 319pp., later linen, $22.50

PARRY, Sir Edw., The Bloody Assize. NY, 1929, roy8vo, 301pp., slightly faded, $22.50

PARRY, Leonard, Some Famous Medical Trials. NY, 1928, roy8vo, 326pp., $22.50

PARSONS, Theophilus, The Law of Contracts. 6th ed., B, 1873, 4to, 3vols., later linen, $75.00

PAYLER, Frederick, Law Courts, Lawyers & Litigants. L, 1926, 8vo, 241pp., $22.50

PEARCE, Robert, A Guide to the Inns of Court & Chancery, with Notices of their Ancient Discipline, Rules, Orders & Customs, Readings, Moots, Masques, Revels & Entertainments, together with the Regulations in the Four Inns of Court as to the Admission of Students, Keeping Terms, Lectures, Examinations, Call to the Bar. L, 1855, 8vo, 440pp., later linen, $125.00

PECK, David, Decision at Law. NY, 1961, 8vo, 303pp., $17.50

PERKINS, Dexter, The Monroe Doctrine, 1823-1826. Harvard, 1932, roy8vo, 280pp., $22.50

PERKINS, John, A Profitable Book of Mr. John Perkins, Sometimes Fellow of the Inner Temple, Treating of the Laws of England, translated out of the French into English, for the Benefit of Young Students and Others. L, 1658, 12mo, 333pp., black letter, later calf, $285.00
First published in 1528, "formerly much esteemed, and still regarded as an authority, though not equal to Littleton." Marvin, 563.

PERPIGNA, A., The French Law & Practice of Patents for Inventions, Improvements & Importations. P, 1834, 8vo, 54pp., later linen, LL, "very useful & practical." Marvin, 564, $45.00

PETERSDORFF, Chs., A Practical Treatise on the Law of Bail in Civil & Criminal Proceedings. P, 1835, 8vo, xxviii,327pp., later 1/2 linen, LL, $57.50

PETYT, William, The Antient Right of the Commons of England Asserted; Or, A Discourse Proving by Records & the Best Historians, that the Commons of England were Ever an Essential Part of Parliament. L, 1680, 8vo, 184pp., contemp. calf, sometime rebacked, new skiver, $225.00

PHELPS, Richard, Newgate of Connecticut: Its Origin & Early History, Being a Full Description of the Famous & Wonderful Simsbury Mines & Caverns & the Prison Built Over Them. Hartford, 1876, 8vo, 111pp., sl. wear, $30.00

PHILLIPS, S. N., Famous Cases of Circumstantial Evidence with an Introduction on the Theory of Presumptive Proof. B, 1873, roy8vo, xxix,153pp., $27.50

PHILLIPSON, Coleman, Termination of War & Treaties of Peace. L, 1916, 4to, 486pp; $30.00

No Copy in North America

PITHOU, Pierre & Francois, Corpus Juris Canonici Gregorii XIII, Pont. Max. Jussu Editum a Petro Pithoeo, et Francisco Fratre, Jurisconsultis, ad Veteres Codices Manuscriptas Restitutum, et Notis Illustratum. Ex Bibliotheca Illustrissimi D. D. Claudii Le Peletier, Regni Administri et Regnii Franciae Aerarii Praefecti. Paris, 1695, large folio, 2 vols. bound as one, 492, 488,140pp., contemp. vellum, top of front hinge very slightly cracked, a very sound copy; rare; not in NUC. $375.00
The authors, both eminent jurists & legal scholars, were students of the celebrated Cujas whose surpassing merit as a jurisconsult "consisted in the fact that he turned from the ignorant commentators on Roman Law to the Roman Law itself."EB11; Cujas held the brothers in high regard, calling them Pithoei fratres, clarissima lumina; following his example, in addition to authoring treatises, they established reliable editions of significant older works, of which this is one example. Although both were distinguished legal scholars, Pierre is better known due to his involvement in the public affairs of that turbulent time.

PITMAN, Edw., A Treatise on the Law of Principal & Surity. P, 1843, 8vo, 171pp., LL, $45.00

A Plain Statement about the Rights Claimed by Our Colonists, Under the Charters Granted to them by Our Sovereigns; and the Light in Which these Rights have been Viewed by the Parent State, in Various Statutes, Especially in Those of the 18th Geo III, Chapts. 11,12,13. L, 1833, 8vo, 118pp., contemp. bds., rebacked, $47.50

PLATT, Th., A Practical Treatise on the Law of Covenants. P, 1834, 8vo, 303pp., later 1/2 lin,LL,$45.00

PLAYFAIR, Giles, & SINGLETON, A., The Offenders: Society & the Atrocious Crime. L, 1957, 8vo, 278pp. (American subtitle: The Case Against Legal Vengeance), $18.50

PLUCKNETT, Theo., A Concise History of the Common Law. 5th ed., B, 1956, roy8vo, 746pp., $25.00

PLUCKNETT, Th. Early English Legal Literature. Cambridge, 1958, 8vo, 120pp., $22.50

POLLOCK, Sir Frederick, Leading Cases Done into English & Other Diversions. L, 1892, 8vo, 98p, $30.00

POLLOCK,Sir Fred., Personal Remembrances. L, 1887, 8vo, 2vols., $65.00

POLLOCK, Sir Fred., A Treatise on the Law of Torts, from the 3rd London ed., with Notes & References to American Cases by Jas. Webb. St. L., 1894, roy8vo, 803pp., later linen, $47.50

POLLOCK, Sir Fred., A Digest of the Law of Partnership. St. L., 1878, 12mo, 169pp., sl. wear, $37.50

POLLOCK, Sir John, The Popish Plot. Cambridge, 1914, 8vo, 379pp., $22.50

PONTICH, Henri, Administration de la Ville de Paris et du Departement de la Seine. P, 1884, 8vo, 1032pp., contemp. 1/2 morocco, bit rubbed & scuffed but sound, $37.50

POOLE, Austin, Obligations of Society in the XII & XIII Centuries. Oxford, 1946, 8vo, 115pp, $22.50

PORTER, Wm., A Paper on the Qualifications of the Advisor & the Advocate, Read before the Law Academy of Philadelphia. P, 1878, 8vo, 27pp., later linen, $27.50

POTHIER, M., A Treatise on the Law of Obligations, translated from the French, with an Introduction, Appendix & Notes Illustrative of the English Law on the Subject, by Wm. Evans. P, 1826, 8vo, 2vols. 516, 631pp., contemp. roan, sl. rubbed, beautiful set, $150.00
"I seize with pleasure an opportunity of recommending Pothier's admirable treatise to the English lawyer; exhorting him to read it again & again; for if his great master Littleton has given him a taste for luminous method, opposite examples, & a clear & manly style, in which nothing is redundant nothing deficient, he will surely delight in works in which all these advantages are combined, & the greatest portion of which is law at Westminster as well as at Orleans....not only a good book of law but an excellent book of morals, a work of all nations, a book to which antiquity can present no rival but the Offices of Cicero." Marvin, 578.

POTHIER, M., A Treatise on the Contract of Partnership: with the Civil Code & Code of Commerce Relating to that Subject, trans. from the French, with Notes Referring to the Decisions of English Courts, by O. D. Tudor. P, 1854, roy8vo, 113pp., contemp. roan, bit rubbed, $57.50

POUND, Roscoe, The Lawyer from Antiquity to Modern Times. St.P., 1953, roy8vo, 404pp., $35.00

POUND, Roscoe, Social Control Through Law. Yale, 1942, 8vo, 138pp., $20.00

POUND, Roscoe, The Formative Era of American Law. B, 1938, 8vo, 188pp., sl. faded, first edition, signed by Pound, $35.00

POUND, Roscoe, Development of Constitutional Guarantees of Liberty. Yale, 1957, 8vo, 207p., $17.50

POUND, Roscoe, Lectures on the Philosophy of Freemasonry. Ia., 1915, 8vo, 96pp., $22.50

POUND, Roscoe, The Spirit of the Common Law. B, 1925, 8vo, 224pp., $20.00

POWELL, Edw., Nullification & Secession in the United States: A History of the Six Attempts During the First Century of the Republic. NY, 1897, 8vo, 461pp., $25.00

POWELL, J. J., A Treatise on the Law of Mortgages, Reprinted from the 6th London Edition, Much Enl. & Improved, with Copious Notes by Th. Coventry, & Notes & References to American Cases by Benj. Rand. B, 1828, roy8vo, 3vols., contemp. roan, slight trace of wear at extremeties, handsome, $175.00
"The author selected with commendable industry the cases pertaining to this important subject, and wrought up his materials with skill, learning and sound judgment." In the opinion of James Kent, Rand did a splendid job on the American cases and "the immense body of English learning with which Mr. Coventry has enriched every part of the work is not only uncommon but extraordinary."Marvin,581.

POWELL, J. J., An Essay on the Learning Respecting the Creation & Execution of Powers, and also Respecting the Nature & Effect of Leasing Powers. 2nd ed., Dublin, 1791, 8vo, 582pp., contemp. calf, bit rubbed & minor cover worming in one spot, nice copy, $95.00
"To Mr. Powell belongs the merit of first collecting & systematizing the decisions upon the subtle doctrines of Powers." Marvin, 581.

POWELL, J. J., An Essay on Devises, with Copious Notes, An Appendix of Precedents; Also: A Treatise on the Construction of Devises, by Thomas Jarman. P, 1838, 8vo, 2vols., later 1/2 linen, LL, $115.00

POYNTER, Th., A Concise View of the Doctrine & Practice of the Ecclesiastical Courts in Doctor's Commons, on Various Points Relative to the Subject of Marriage & Divorce. 2nd ed., rev. & enl. P, 1836, 8vo, 123pp., later linen, LL, $45.00

PRESTON, Richard, An Essay on the Quantity & Quality of Estates, with More Immediate Reference to the Law of Merger. P, 1843, 8vo, 244pp., later linen, LL, a highly regarded author, $47.50

Preliminary Draft of the Rules of Civil Procedure for the District Courts of the United States & the Supreme Court of the District of Columbia; Prepared by the Advisory Committee on Rules for Civil Procedure, Appointed by the Supreme Court ofthe U.S. May, 1936, 8vo, 182pp., wrps, rare, $30.00

PRINGLE, Pat., Hue & Cry: The Story of Henry & John Fielding & their Bow St. Runners. L,1950, $17.50

PRINGLE, P., Stand & Deliver: Story of the Highwaymen. NY, 1955, 8vo, 287pp., ill., $17.50

LAW PRINTS---All Very Attractively Framed

"Alexander, Lord Loughborough, Lord High Chancellor of Great Britain," steel engraving by F. Bartolozzi, 1800 after Northcote), 14X19; framed: 23X28, $175.00

"An Amiable Judge," Original Color Lithograph by "Spy." 1898, 8X13; 16X22; $175.00 (Leslie Ward)

"The Barrister," by S. Van Abbe, original artist's proof dry point etching, #3 of 60 numbered & signed by the artist; 7X12; fromed: 14X19, $250.00

"Briefing Counsel," by S. Van Abbe, original artist's proof dry point etching, #5 of 60 numbered & signed by the artist; 12X8; framed: 19X15; $250.00

"Counsel's Opinion," by S. Van Abbe, original artist's proof dry point etching, #22 of 60; numbered & signed by the artist; 10X11; fromed: 16X20, $250.00

"Cross Examination," by S. Van Abbe, original artist's proof dry point etching, #55 of 60 numbered & signed by the artist; 10X11; framed: 16X20, $250.00

"Evidence," by S. Van Abbe, original artist's proof dry point etching, #11 of 60, numbered & signed by the artist; 11X11; framed: 17X20, $250.00

"A Flaw in the Title," by Dendy Sadler, original etching in color, signed by Sadler; 13X18; framed: 19X25, $175.00

"The Gatehouse, Lincoln Inn," by Sydney R. Jones, original artist's proof etching, signed by the artist; 9X12 ; framed: 14X19, $175.00

"The House of Commons" by Thomas Rowlandson & Pugin; aquatint in color, 1807; 10X9; framed 16X15; $150.00

"The House of Lords," by Rowlandson & Pugin, aquatint in color, 1807; 10X9; framed: 16X15, $150.00

"Inner Temple Lane, Fleet Street," by Sydney R. Jones, original artist's proof etching, signed by the artist; 5X13; framed: 14X19; $175.00

"John Randolph of Roanoke." Etching, artist not identified, 6X7; framed: 12X15; $65.00

"Judicial Light Weight," by "Spy," Original color lithograph, 8X14; framed: 16X21; $175.00

"The Lawyer," by Dendy Sadler, etching in color; 9X14; framed: 15X21; $150;00

"Lincoln's Inn" by Nathaniel Sparks, original artist's proof etching, signed by the artist; 9X12; framed: 14X19; $175.00

"Lloyd, Lord Kenyon, Lord Chief Justice of England," steel engraving by Wm. Holl, 1804, 13X20; framed: 21X29; $175.00

"Lord Rutherford," etching, artist not identified, 10X13; framed: 20X26; $125.00

"Old Baily Session House," by T. Hosmer Shepherd, original water color drawing; 1811; 7X5; framed: 14X12; $125.00

"Oxford Circuit," by "Spy," original color lithograph, 1896, 8X13; framed: 16X21; $175.00

"A Point of Law," by S. Van Abbe, original artist's proof dry point etching; #50 of 60; numbered and signed by the artist; 11X11; framed: 17X20, $250.00

"Prosecuting Counsel," by S. Van Abbe, original artist's proof dry point etching; #2 of 60; numbered and signed by the artist; 7X12; framed: 14X19; $250.00

"Rufus," by "Spy," original color lithograph, 1904, 8X13; framed: 14X19; $175.00

"Rufus Choate," etching, artist unidentified, 6X8; framed: 13X16; $75.00

"Sergeant's Inn, Chancery Lane," by T. Hosmer Shepherd, 1810; original water color drawing; 10X8; 14X14; $150.00

"Sergeant's Inn, Fleet Street," by Sydney R. Jones, original artist's proof etching, signed by the artist; 7X11; framed: 14X19; $175.00

"Sir Lloyd Kenyon, Bart., Late Master of the Rolls & Now Chief Justice of the Court of King's Bench," by T. Fittler, steel engraving, 1783, 14X19; framed: 22X28; $175.00

"Slim," by "Spy," original color lithograph, 1904, 8X13; framed: 16X21; $175.00

"Slow and Steady," by "Spy," original color lithograph, 1900; 8X13; framed: 16X21; $175.00

"Staple Inn, Holborn," by Sydney R. Jones, original artist's proof etching; signed by the artist; 5X13; framed: 14X19; $175.00

"Summing Up," by S. Van Abbe, original artist's proof dry point etching, #32 of 60; numbered & signed by the artist; 10X11; framed: 16X20; $250.00

"Ulsterman, K. C." by "Spy," original color lithograph, 1903, 8X13; framed: 16X21; $175.00

"William Murray, Earl of Mansfield, Lord Chief Justice of the Court ofKing's Bench," steel engraving; drawn by John Jackson (after Reynolds); engraved by H. Meyer, 1812; 9X12; 17X21; $175.00

Proceedings by the Bar of the United States Courts for the Second Circuit on the Retirement of Mr. Justice Nelson from the Supreme Court of the United States. NY, 1873, 8vo, 30pp., $35.00

Proceedings in the Klu Klux Trials at Columbia, S.C., in the U.S. Circuit Court, Nov. Term, 1871. Columbia, 1872, 8vo, 835pp., later linen, stamp on title, $57.50

Proceedings in the Trial of Andrew Johnson, President of the United States, on Articles of Impeachment, Exhibited bythe House of Representatives. DC, 1868, roy8vo, 1090,50pp., later linen, $95.00

Proceedings of the Bar & Offices of the Supreme Court of the United States in Memory of William Howard Taft. DC, 1931, 4to, 123pp., orig. ptd. wrps, rare, $47.50

Proceedings of the Bar & Offices of the Supreme Court of the United States in Memory of Edward Douglas White. DC, 1921, 4to, 103pp., orig. ptd. wrps, rare, $37.50

Proceedings of the Bar & Offices of the Supreme Court of the United States in Memory of Pierce Butler. DC, 1940, 4to, 58pp., orig. ptd. wrps, $37.50

Proceedings of the Bar & Offices of the Supreme Court of the United States in Memory of Edward Terry Sanford. DC, 1931, 4to, 47pp., orig. ptd. wrps, $35.00

Proceedings of the Court Convened Under the Third Canon of 1844....for the Trial of the Rt. Rev. Benjamin Onderdonk, Bishop of New York, on a Presentment Made by the Bishops of Virginia, Tennessee & Georgia. NY/P, 1845, 8vo, 333pp., later linen, $45.00

PROCTOR, Rob., Tarrif Acts Passed by the Congress of the U.S. from 1789 to 1897. DC, 1898, 4to, 689pp., $45.00

PROEHL, Paul (ed.), Legal Problems of International Trade. Univ. of Ill., 1959, 4to, 453pp., $25.00

PUFENDORF, Le Baron de, Les Devoirs de L'Homme et du Citoyen, tels qu'ils lui sont prescrits par la Loi Naturelle. Traduit du Latin par Jean Barbeyrac, 3rd ed., carefully revised and augmented with a great number of notes by the translator. Amsterdam, 1715, 8vo, lii,424pp., contemp. calf, rebacked; Pufendorf's abridgment of his De Jure Naturae et Gentium, with voluminous notes by the learned Barbeyrac. $225.00

PULSZKY, Augustus, The Theory of Law & Civil Society. L, 1888, roy8vo, 443pp., new linen, $35.00

PARKER, Edw., Reminiscences of Rufus Choate, the Great American Lawyer. NY, 1860, 8vo, 522pp., nice copy, $35.00

PUSEY, Merlo, Charles Evans Hughes. NY, 1952, roy8vo, 2vols., $37.50

PUSEY, Merlo, The Supreme Court Crisis. NY, 1937, 8vo, 108pp., $17.50

PUTERBAUGH, Sabin, Illinois Pleading & Practice, 2nd ed., rev. & enl., C, 1867, roy8vo, 899p, $75.00

QUELLER, Don., The Office of Ambassador in the Middle Ages. Princeton, 1967, 8vo,251pp., $17.50

Quinquennial Catalogue of the Law School of Harvard University, 1817-1909. 1910, roy8vo, 625p, $25.00

(RADDE, Wm,) Internal Relations of the Cities, Towns, Villages, Counties & States of the Union; or, the Municipalist. 2nd ed., NY, 1859, 8vo, 302pp., sl. wear, scarce, $45.00

RADIN, Max, Handbook of Roman Law. St. P., 1927, roy8vo, 576pp., $37.50

RAMSAY, Sir Jas. Bamff Charters, A.D. 1232-1703, with Introduction, Biographical Summary & Notes. Oxford, 1915, 4to, 392pp., sl. wear, $37.50

RAPER, Arthur, The Tragedy of Lynching. Univ. of No. Carolina, 1938, roy8vo, 499pp., $25.00

RASTELL, John, Les Terms de la Ley; or; Certain Difficult & Obscure Words & Terms of the Common Laws and Statutes of the Realm Now in Use, Expounded and Explained, Newly Imprinted and Much Enlarged and Augmented, with a New Addition of Above Two Hundred and Fifty Words. L, 1659, 12mo, 271leaves, later 1/2 calf and boards, trimmed close; title a bit soiled with former owner names and a few ink markings; a few missing words from one leaf expertly restored; sound copy; $225.00
First published in 1527, it was a standard work for centuries, passing through almost 30 editions.

Records, Computers and the Rights of Citizens: Report of the Secretary's Advisory Committee on Automated Personal Data Systems. DC, 1973, 8vo, 344pp., $22.50

REGAN, Louis, Medical Malpractice. St. L., 1943, roy8vo, 256pp., $20;00.

REEVE, Tapping, The Law of Baron & Femme, of Parent & Child, Guardian & Ward, Master & Servant; and of the Powers of the Courts of Chancery, with an Essay on the Terms Heir, Heirs...2nd ed, with Notes to English & American cases by L. Chittenden. Burlington, 1846, roy8vo, 493pp., later 1/2 linen; $57.50 "That excellent lawyer & venerable man has discussed every branch of the subject in a copious manner." James Kent in Marvin, 603.

REEVES, John, A History of the Law of Shipping & Navigation. Dublin, 1792, 8vo, 435pp., later 1/2 sheep & bds; bit rubbed, $125.00 "written with admirable clearness, method & accuracy,"Kent, ibid.

REIBSTEIN, Ernst, Völkerrecht: Eine Geschichte seiner Ideen in Lehre u. Praxis; II: Die Letzten Zweijahrhundert. (Int'l Law: A History of Its Ideas in Theory & Practice ;II: the Last Two Centuries) M, 1963, roy8vo, 784pp., few lines underlined, with a very extensive bibliography. $35.00

REID, John, Chief Justice: the Judicial World of Chs. Doe. Harvard, 1967,roy8vo, 489pp., $22.50

Repeal of the Union: Report of the Debate in the House of Commons on Mr. O'Connell's Motion, and the Proceedings in the House of Lords on Earl Gray's Motion. L, 1834, 8vo, 200p. sl. discoloration $35.00

Report of the Case of the Canadian Prisoners with an Introduction on the Writ of Habeas Corpus by Alfred Fry, one of the Counsel in the Case. L, 1839, roy8vo, 106pp., later linen, $45.00

A Report of the Case of the Rt. Rev. R. D. Hampden, Lord Bishop Elect of Hereford, in Hereford Cathedral, the Ecclesiastical Courts, and the Queen's Bench, by R. Jebb. L, 1849, roy8vo,518p,$45.00

Report of the Court Proceedings in the Case of the Anti-Soviet "Bloc of Rights and Trotskyites,"Heard Before the Military Collegium of the Sup. Crt. of the USSR. M, 1938, roy8vo, 799pp. sl. wear,$25.00

Report of the Court Proceedings in the Case of the Anti-Soviet Trotskyite Center, Heard before the Military Collegium of the Sup. Court of the USSR. M, 1937, roy8vo, 580pp., $25.00

Report of the Forrest Divorce Case.....NY, 1852, roy8vo, 185pp., later linen, $37.50

Report of the Proceedings of the 1st & 2nd Trials of the Cause of Fisher against Ward, Master of the Ship Fishburn, Detained in Russia During the Late Embargo...L, 1803, 8vo, 152pp., lat. lin, $47.50

Report of the Proceedings in the Nature of a Quo-Warranto at the Suit of the King against Waller O'Grady, Respecting the Right of Appointment to the Office of the Clerk of the Pleas in His Majesty's Court of Exchequer in Ireland. D/L, 1816, 8vo, 191pp., later linen, $45.00

Report of the Trial of the Dynamitards....before the Court of Justiciary at Edinburgh, by Chs. Couper. Edinburgh, 1884, 8vo, 254pp., later linen, $45.00

Report of the Trial on an Action for Damages, brought by Rev. Chs. Massy, against the Most Noble Marquis of Headfort, for Criminal Conversation with the Plaintiff's Wife. NY, 1804, 94pp, $45.00

Reports of the Proceedings of the American Branch of the International Law Assn: Annual Meetings: 11th thru 16th, 1932-1937, 8vo, 5vols in the orig. wrps, $45.00

Report on the Constitutionality of the National Labor Relations Act by the National Lawyer's Committee of the American Liberty League. Pit., 1935, 8vo, 132pp., wrps, $22.50

Research in International Law: Harvard Law School; I. Diplomatic Privileges & Immunities; II. Legal Position & Function of Consuls; III. Competence of Courts in Regard to Foreign States; IV. Piracy; V. Piracy Laws of Various Countries; Drafts of the Conventions Prepared for the Codification of International Law. Cambridge, Harvard Law School, 1932, 4to, 1013pp., $57.50

RICHARDS, John, Abraham Lincoln: The Lawyer Statesman. B, 1916, roy8vo, 260pp., $25.00

RICHARDSON, A. D., A Full & Authentic Report of the Testimony on the Trial of Matthew F. Ward. NY, 1854, roy8vo, 176pp., later linen, $35.00

RICHES, Cromwell, Majority Rule in International Organizations. Johns Hopkins, 1940, 8vo,322p, $22.50

RICHMOND, A.B., Leaves from the Diary of an Old Lawyer: Intemperance the Great Source of Crime/ NY, 1880, 8vo, 387pp., later linen, $27.50

RIVALTA, Valentino, Diritto Naturale e Positivo. Bologna, 1898, roy8vo, 467pp., $25.00

ROBERTSON, David, Treatise on the Rules of Law of Personal Succession in the Different Parts of the Realm; & on Cases, Regarding Foreign & International Succession, which have been Decided in the British Courts. P, 1836, 8vo, 296pp., later 1/2 linen, LL,$65.00

ROBINSON, Jacob, And the Crooked Shall Be Made Straight: New Look at the Eichman Trial.NY, 1965,$22.50

ROMMEN, Heinrich, The Natural Law: A Study in Legal & Social History & Philosophy. trans. T. Hanley. St. L., 1947, roy8vo, 290pp., $25.00

ROOT, Elihu, Addresses on International Subjects, ed. R. Bacon & Jas. Brown Scott. Harvard, 1916, roy8vo, 463pp., (most are on law, particularly international), $25.00

908) ROOT, Elihu, Addresses on Government & Citizenship, ed. R. Bacon & Jas. Brown Scott. Harvard, 1916, roy8vo, 552pp, (law, lawyers & constitutionalism), $25.00

909) ROOT, Elihu, The United States & the War, Mission to Russia, Political Addresses. ed. R. Bacon & Jas. Brown Scott. Harvard, 1918, roy8vo, 362pp; $25.00

ROPER, R. S., A Treatise of the Law of Property Arising from the Relation between Husband & Wife. LL new ed. with Notes by Jacob. P, 1841, 8vo, 2vols.,(as one), 630pp., later 1/2 linen, $75.00

ROSCOE, Henry, Treatise on the Law of Actions Relating to Real Property. P, 1840, 8vo, 2vols., 600p. later 1/2 linen, LL, "only work of merit on these ancient remedies." Marvin, 620, $95.00

ROSS, Geo., Treatise on the Law of Purchasers & Vendors of Personal Property, Considered Chiefly with a View to Mercantile Transactions. 2nd ed., enl. P, 1836, 8vo, 211pp., later linen, LL, $47.50

ROUSSE, Edmund, Advocats et Magistrats. P, 1903, roy8vo, 333pp., $37.50

ROYSE, M. A., Aerial Bombardment & the Int'l Regulation of Warfare. NY, 1928, roy8vo, 256pp, $25.00

RUNNINGTON, Chs., History, Principles & Practice (Ancient & Modern) of the Legal Remedy by Ejectment; & the Resulting Action for Mesne Profits; the Evidence Necessary to Sustain & Defend Them. NY, 1806, 8vo, 537pp., contemp. roan, sl. wear, "an excellent book," Marvin, 623. $75.00

RUSKOWSKI, Casimir, The Constitutional Governor. B, 1943, 4to, 61pp., $17.50

RUSSELL, F. A., Essays & Excursions in Law. L, 1929, 8vo, 144pp.,$22.50

RUSSELL, Frank, The Saar: Battleground & Pawn. Stanford UP, 1951, roy8vo, 204pp., $22.50

RUTLAND, Rob., Birth of the Bill of Rights: 1776-91. U of No. Carolina, 1955, 8vo, 243pp, $20.00

RYAN, John, & MILLAR, M., The State & the Church. NY, 1922, 8vo, 331pp;.

RZADZIEWICZ, Arnold, The Philosophical Basis of Human Liberty According to St. Thomas Aquinas. DC, Catholic Univ., 1949, 8vo, 185pp., $17.50

SABINE, Geo., History of Political Theory.3rd ed., NY, 1961, 8vo, 948pp., $25.00

SACHER, Hermann (ed.), Staatslexikon. Freiburg, 1926, 4to, 5vols., contemp. 1/2 morocco, $225.00

SADLER, Th. (ed.), Reminiscences & Correspondence of Henry Crabb Robinson, Barrister at Law. B, 1870, 8vo, 2vol., crowns sl. worn, $45.00

SALKOWSKI, Carl, Institutes & History of Roman Private Law, with a Catena of Texts, translated in full & edited by E. Whitfield, L, 1886, roy8vo, 1048pp., rebacked, $75.00

SANDARS, Th., The Institutes of Justinian, with an English Intro., Translation & Notes, rev. & corr. L, 1900, 8vo, 608pp., rebacked, some underlining & marginalia, $25.00

SANDERS, Francis, An Essay on Uses & Trusts & on the Nature & Operation of Conveyances at Common Law, & of Those which Derive their Effect from the Statute of Uses. 4th ed., rev. corr. & enl. L, 1824, roy8vo, 2vols., later 1/2 linen, "possesses more than ordinary merits," Marvin, 628. $85.00

SAVIGNY, Carl von, The History of the Roman Law During the Middle Ages. Edinburgh, 1829, 8vo, 459pp. Vol. I (all published), contemp. calf, bit rubbed & scuffed, $57.50

SAYAG, Alain, Essai sur le Besoin Creatur de Droit. P, 1969, roy8vo, 320pp., wrps, $17.50

SCHAACK, Michael, Anarchy & Anarchists: A History of the Red Terror & the Social Revolution in America & Europe, Communism, Socialism & Nihilism in Doctrine & Deed. The Chicago Haymarket Conspiracy and the Detection & Trial of the Conspirators, by Michael Schaack, Captain of Police, with Numerous Illustrations. C, 1889, roy8vo, 698pp., later linen, $75.00

SCHERER, Jas., The Lion of the Vigilantes: William T. Coleman & the Life of Old San Francisco. Ind., 1939, roy8vo, 335pp., $25.00

SCHIFFER, Walter, The Legal Community of Mankind: A Critical Analysis of the Modern Concept of World Organization. Columbia, 1954, roy8vo, 367pp., $22.50

SCHLATTER, Richard, Private Property: History of an Idea. Rutgers UP, 1951, 8vo, 283pp., $22.50

SCHOULER, James, Constitutional Studies: State & Federal. NY, 1897, 8vo, 332pp., $22.50

SCHULTES, Henry, An Essay on Aquatic Rights. P, 1839, 8vo, 56pp., later linen, LL, $37.50

SCORRAILLE, Raoul, Francisco Suarez. P, 1912, 8vo, 2vols., wrps, $37.50

SCOTT, Sir Walter, A Collection of Scarce & Valuable Tracts, on the Most Interesting & Entertaining Subjects, but Chiefly Such as Relate to the History and Constitution of These Kingdoms, Selected from an Infinite Number in Print & Manuscript, in the Royal, Cotton, Sion, & Other Public as well as Private Libraries, Particularly that of the Late Lord Somers, 2nd ed., rev. augmented & arr. by Walter Scott. L, 1809-1815, 4to, 13vols., bound in later 1/2 sheep and marbled boards, bit rubbed and scuffed but a sound, attractive set of a very valuable work; Somers (1651-1716) was Lord Chancellor. $950.00

SELLON, Baker, The Practice of the Court of King's Bench & Common Pleas. D, 1793, 8vo, 591pp., contemp. calf, minor dampstain first & last few leaves, $87.50

SHELFORD, Leonard, A Practical Treatise of the Law of Marriage & Divorce; Containing also the Mode of Proceeding on Divorces in the Ecclesiastical Courts & in Parliament; the Right to the Custody of Children; Voluntary Separation; the Husband's Liability to the Wife's Debt, andthe Conflict Between the Laws of England & Scotland Respecting Divorce & Legitimacy. P, 1841, 8vo, 519pp, LL, $65.00

SHULTZ, W., American Public Finance & Taxation. rev. ed. NY, 1936, roy8vo, 635pp., $27.50

SCHWARZENBERGER, Georg., A Manual of International Law. 2nd ed., L, 1950, 8vo, 428pp., $22.50

SCOTT, Jas. Brown, Peace Through Justice: Three Papers. Oxford, 1917, 4to, 102pp., $22.50

SCOTT, Jas. Brown, The Spanish Origins of International Law: Francisco de Vitoria & His Law of Nations. Oxford, 1934, 4to, 460pp., (with a trans. of selections from Vitori's works.) scarce, $50.00

SCOTT, Jas. Brown, Law, the State & the International Community.(1939), 1968, roy8vo, 2vols.,$45.00

SCOTT, Wm., Economic Problems of Peace after War. Cambridge, 1918, 8vo, 2vols.,ex lib, $30.00

SEATON, Henry, Forms of Decrees in Equity & of Orders Connected with Them. NY, 1831, 8vo, 321pp., contemp. roan, sl. rubbed, not in Marvin, $47.50

SEITZ, Don (ed.), The Tryal of Capt. William Kidd for Murder & Piracy....with a biography & bibliography. NY, 1936, roy8vo, 254pp, $22.50

Selected Essays in Constitutional Law Reprinted from the Harvard Law Review. Cambridge, 1952, roy8vo, 460pp., wrps, $27.50

SEYFARTH, Shaw, et al., Labor Relations & the Law in West Germany & the United States. Univ. of Michigan, 1969, roy8vo, 606pp., $22.50

SHARP, Gustavus, Confessions of An Attorney, to Which are Added Several Papers on English Law & Lawyers by Charles Dickens. NY, 1853, 8vo, 228pp., later lin, $57.50

LORD SHAW OF DUNFERMLINE, (Th. Craigmyle), The Law of the Kinsmen. NY, 1923, 8vo, 178pp, $22.50

SHELFORD, Leonard, A Practical Treatise of the Law of Mortmain, & Charitable Uses & Trusts. P, 1842, 8vo, 509pp., later 1/2 linen, LL, $65.00

SHELTON, Thomas, Spirit of the Courts. Balto, 1918, 8vo, 264pp., sl. wear, $20.00

SMITH, F. E. & SIBLEY, N., International Law as Interpreted During the Russo-Japanese War. B, 1905, 4to, 494pp., sl. cov. soil, scarce, $37.50

SMITH, Herbert, Federalism in North America. B, 1923, 8vo, 328pp., $22.50

SMITH, J. M., Origin & History of Hebrew Law. Univ. of Chicago, 1931, 8vo, 285pp., $22.50

SMITH, John W., A Selection of Leading Cases on Various Branches of the Law, with Notes. P, 1838-40. 8vo, 3vols., later linen, LL, $145.00
"One of the three Reports which every lawyer ought to possess....all the Cases are noted foundations of important prevailing legal doctrines....His method is to trace legal principles chronologically, pointing out their modifications & divergences, and furnishing rules for reconciling apparent antagonistic Cases. His Notes are not surpassed for extent of learning, depth of thought and have been frequently cited, with approbation, by the Bench." Marvin, 651.

SMITH, Sherman, Relation of the State to Religious Education im Massachusetts. Syr, 1926,350pp, $22.50

SOHM, Rudolf, Die Frankische Reichs- und Gerichtsverfassung. (1871), 1971, 8vo, 588pp., $30.00

SOHM, R., Wesen u. Voraussetzungen der Widerspruchsklage. (1908), 1970, 8vo, 172pp., $22.50

SOVERN, Michael, Legal Restraints on Racial Discrimination in Employment. NY, 1966, roy8vo,270p,$25.00

SPELMAN, Sir Henry, The History & Fate of Sacrilege, Discovered by Examples of Scripture, of Heathens and of Christians, from the Beginning of the World Continually to this Day....Wrote in the Year 1632....A Treatise Omitted in the Late Edition of His Posthumous Works, and Now Published for the Terror of Evil Doers....L, 1698, 8vo, 292,40pp., contemp. calf, skillfully rebacked, 1st ed, $275.00
His celebrated argument against the appropriation of ecclesiastical property; publication was begun in 1663 but it was suppressed by the government & beneficiaries of the appropriations. It was supposed to have perished in the Great Fire, but the ms was discovered in the Bodleian.

The Contrary Argument

BURGES, Cornelius, No Sacrilege or Sinne to Aliene or Purchase the Lands of Bishops or Others Whose Offices are Abolished. 2nd ed., rev. & enl. L, 1659, 12mo, 188pp., bound in early 19th century roan, scuffed but tight, $175.00
The author, who had invested heavily in church property, draws his argument from civil, common & canon law.

SPENCE, Geo., The Equitable Jurisdiction of the Court of Chancery, Comprising Its Rise, Progress & Final Establishment to which is Prefixed a Concise Account of the Course of Procedure in the Courts of Common Law in Regard to Civil Rights, with an Attempt to Trace them to Their Sources. P, 1846, roy8vo, 2vols., contemp. roan, sl. rubbed, nice set of a classic work, $125.00

SPOONER, Lysander, An Essay on the Trial by Jury. B, 1852, 8vo, 224pp., later linen,$65.00

STAMMLER, Rudolf, Lehrbuch der Rechtsphilosophie.(1928), 1970, roy8vo, 396pp., $25.00

STANSBURY, Arthur, Report of the Trial of James H. Peck, Judge of the U.S. District Court for the District of Missouri, before the Senate of the United States....for High Misdemeanors in Office. B, 1833, roy8vo, 592pp., later linen, $85.00

STARKIE, Th., A Practical Treatise on the Law of Evidence & Digest of Proofs in Civil & Criminal Proceedings, with Ref. to American decisions by T. Metcalf, 2nd American ed., with Add. Notes by Edw. Ingraham. B, 1828, roy8vo, ccxcvii, 1772pp., later 1/2 linen, $175.00
"More comprehensive & minute than any similar work in the language." Marvin, 660.

STATHAM, Nicholas, Abridgment of the Law, translated of the 15th century texf by Margaret Klingelsmith. B, 1915, thick 4to, 2vols, uncut, $115.00
The first work of its kind and not superseded until Fitzherbert. "Abridges some decisions not found elsewhere....the cases are distributed chronologically, without much regard for the connection of the matter and, though a rude performance, it has the merit of originality and served as a model for similar productions." Marvin, 661.

STEIN, Peter, Regulae Juris: From Juristic Rules to Legal Maxims. Edin., 1966, 8vo, 206p., $22.50

STEPHEN, Sir Geo. (also attributed to Sir Jas. Stephen & Samuel Warren), Adventures of an Attorney in Search of Practice; A Deliniation of Professional Life. L, 1840, 8vo, 450pp., linen, $45.00

STEPHEN, Henry, A Summary of the Criminal Law. P, 1840, 8vo, 207pp., later linen, LL, $57.50

STEPHENSON, Andrew, A History of Roman Law, with a Commentary on the Institutes of Gaius. B, 1912, roy8vo, 513pp., $35.00

STEPHENSON, Carl, Medieval Institutions: Selected Essays. ed. B. Lyon. Cornell, 1954, roy8vo, $22.50

STEVENS, Chs., Anthony Burns: A History (slave case), B, 1856, 8vo, 295pp, linen, $45.00

ST. GERMAIN, Christopher, The Dialogue in English between a Doctor of Divinity and a Student in the Laws of England. Newly Corrected & Imprinted with Additions. L, 1638, 8vo, 176leaves, contemp. calf, sometime rebacked, black letter, beautiful copy, $250.00
First published in 1518 it is "one of the most esteemed of the ancient law books and an authority for about three centuries....the author noted the demise of the ecclesiastical courts which would be out of favor in Protestant England. These courts had brought warmth & understanding in their handling of judicial matters which was not possible in the writ-bound common pleas courts where rigidity held full sway...St. Germain laid the groundwork for what we now call equity." CLJ, 9, 1947.

STIMSON, Fred., Popular Law Making: A Study of the Origin, History & Present Tendencies of Lawmaking by Statute. L, 1911, roy8vo, 390pp., $27.50

ST JOHN-STEVAS, Norman, Law and Morals. NY, 1964, 8vo, 123pp., $18.50

STOCK, John, A Practical Treatise on the Law of Non Compotes Mentis; or, Persons of Unsound Mind. P, 1839, 8vo, later 1/2 linen, LL, $65.00

STONE, Harlan Fisk, Law & Its Administration. NY, 1915, 8vo, 232pp., first edition, $45.00

STORY, Joseph, Commentaries on the Law of Bailments with Illustrations from the Civil and the Foreign Law. 4th ed., rev. corr. & enl., roy8vo, 667pp., B, 1841, later linen, $95.00
"completely exhausts the whole learning on the subject....had he written no other work than this, his reputation....would have been secure." Marvin, 669.

982) STORY, Joseph, Commentaries on the Constitution of the United States; with a Preliminary View of the Constitutional History of the Colonies and States, Before the Adoption of the Constitution. Boston/Cambridge, 1833, roy8vo, 3vols., bound in contemp. roan, slightly rubbed and slightly scuffed in a few places, light sporadic foxing, a clean, crisp, handsome set, scarce; first edition. $2500.00

After the Federalist this is the single most important work on the American Constitution.Comparing it with the Federalist, James Kent wrote, "it is written in the same free and liberal spirit, with equal exactness and soundness of doctrine, and with great beauty and elegance of composition." (American Law,(1847), I, 241.) "The judicial station of the author, his opportunities for hearing constitutional questions mooted and settled, for the last quarter of a century, his habits of patient and thorough investigation, give a weight and value to Judge Story's writings upon Constitutional Law, which few similar works can claim. The disciple of Chief Justice Marshall, thus qualified, undertook the exposition of our Constitutional Law, commencing with the history of the colonies, their rights & pribileges, and tracing the progress of the Constitutional Law in America, down to the publication of his work. Whoever seeks for a complete history and exposition of this branch of our jurisprudence, will have recourse to the above work, which is written with great candor, and characterized by extended research, and a careful examination of the vital principles upon which our government reposes. Taking the Federalist as the basis of his Commentaries, he advocates a liberal construction of the palladium of our liberties, in order to attain a proper exercise of the functions of the government, ...The volumes of Judge Story were translated into German by Professor Buss of Frybourg, and have been repeatedly commended by learned foreigners, as well as by the author's own countrymen, as affording a most satisfactory and admirable explanation of the powers of the Federal Government of the United States. A late writer remarks, that "Cet ouvrage est regarde comme classique, non seulement en Amerique, mas aussi par toutes les personnes qui, en Europe, se sont ocupes de l'etude de la Constitution des Etats Unis." Marvin, 669; Story's reputation was high in Europe where he was esteemed by Savigny and regarded by Lord Campbell as "at the head of the jurists of the present age....greater than any law-writer of which England could boast, or which she could bring forward since the days of Blackstone." Sumner, The Scholar, the Jurist....

33) STORY, Jos., Commentaries on the Constitution of the United States, with a Preliminary View of the Constitutional History of the Colonies and States before the Adoption of the Constitution. 3rd ed. B, 1858, roy8vo, 2vols., later linen, (his original text with editorial notes indicated),$225.00

34) STORY, Jos., Commentaries on the Constitution of the United States....Abridged by the Author for the Use of Colleges and High Schools. B, 1833, roy8vo, 736pp., later liner, $150.00

35) STORY, Jos., A Familiar Exposition of the Constitution of the United States....Designed for the Use of School Libraries and General Readers. NY, 1852, 12mo, 372pp., $75.00

36),STORY, Jos., Miscellaneous Writings. B, 1835, roy8vo, 527pp., orig. cl., sl. wear, first edition,$150.0

37) STORY, Jos., Life & Letters, ed. by His Son, Wm. Story. B, 1851, roy8vo, 2vols., orig. cl., rebacked and spines expertly remounted, first edition, $175.00

38) STORY, Jos., Discourse Pronounced before the Phi Beta Kappa Society....B, 1826, 8vo, 58pp., later linen, first edition, $57.50

39) STORY, Jos., Discourse Pronounced upon the Inauguration of the Author as Dane Professor of Law in Harvard University. B, 1829, 8vo, 60pp., first edition, $75.00

)0) STORY, Jos., Discourse upon the Life, Character & Service of the Hon. John Marshall, Pronounced on the 15th Day of October, at the Request of the Suffolk Bar. B, 1835, 8vo, 74pp., first edition, $125.00

)1) STOWELL, Ellery, & MUNRO, H., International Cases: Arbitrations & Incidents Illustrative of International Law as Practiced by Independent States. B, 1916, roy8vo, 2vols., 1200pp, sl. soil,$37.50

)2) STRONG, C.F., Modern Political Constitutions: Introduction to the Comparative Study of Their History & Existing Form. L, 1952, 8vo, 383pp., few pp. underlined, $20.00

)3) STRONG, Theron, Landmarks of a Lawyer's Lifetime. NY, 1914, roy8vo, 552pp., $22.50

)4) STRONG, Theron, Joseph H. Choate....Lawyer, Ambassador. NY, 1917,roy8vo, 389pp., $22.50

)5) STUART, M.(oses), Conscience and the Constitution; with Remarks on the Recent Speech of Daniel Webster in the Senate on the Subject of Slavery. B, 1850, 8vo, 111pp., later linen, $35.00

)6) STUBBS, W., Select Charters & Other Illustrations of English Constitutional History. 8th ed., Oxford, 1895, 8vo, 554pp., $30.00

)7) STUBBS, W., & TALMASH, G., The Crown Circuit Companion, First American Edition into which has been Incorporated the Work formerly Published under the Name of the Crown Circuit Assistant; both Works have also been Carefully Revised and such Additions made thereto as Modern Statutes & Decisions Have Rendered Necessary. NY, 1816, roy8vo, 540pp., contmp. roan, hinge reinforced, $95.00

)8) SUGDEN, Sir Edward, A Practical Treatise of Powers, from the 6th London ed. P, 1837, 8vo, 2vols., later 1/2 linen, sporadic foxing, LL, $115.00 "second to no modern elementary law book," Marvin.

)9) SUGDEN, Sir EDw., A Series of Letters to a Man of Property, on Sales, Purchases, Mortgages, Leases, Settlements & Devises. P, 1834, 8vo, 54pp., later linen, LL, $47.50

)00)SULLIVAN, Wm., Dunne: Judge, Mayor, Governor. C, 1916, 4to, 848pp., $37.50

)01) SULLIVAN, Wm., Address to the Members of the Bar of Suffolk Mass, B, 1825, 8vo, 63pp., $27.50

)02) SUMNER, Chs., The Scholar, the Jurist, the Artist, the Philanthropist. B, 1846, 8vo, 72pp., later linen, (remarks on Story, the jurist), $45.00

03) SUTLIFFE,Rob., Impressions of an Average Juryman. NY, 1925, 8vo, 114pp., $17.50

04) SUTHERLAND, Arthur, The Law at Harvard: A History of Ideas & Men, 1817-1967. Harvard,1967,408p $17.50

05) SUTHERLAND, A., Constitutionalism in America: Origin & Evolution of Its Fundamental Ideas. NY, 1965, roy8vo, 618pp., $27.50

06) SWAN, Jos., A Manual for Executors & Administrators in the Settlement of the Estates of Deceased Persons. 5th ed., rev., with Notes by P. Matthews. Colombus, 1859, 8vo, 33ppp., linen, $45.00

07) SWINBURNE, Henry, A Treatise of Testaments and Last Wills, Compiled out of the Laws, Ecclesiastical, Civil & Canon, as also out of the Common Law, Customs & Statutes of this Realm. 7th ed., corr. & much enl., D, 1793, roy8vo, 2vols., contemp. roan, sl. scuffed, first published in 1590, the work was regarded as authoritative for almost two centuries. $150.00

)8) SWINDLER, Wm., Magna Carta: Legend & Legacy. Ind, 1965, 8vo, 379pp., $25.00

)9) SWISHER, Carl, Stephen J. Field: Craftsman of the Law. DC, 1930, roy8vo, 473pp., $27.50

10) SWISHER, Carl (ed.), Selected Papers of Homer Cummings, Attorney General of the U.S. 1933-39. NY, 1939, roy8vo, 316pp., inscribed by Cummings, $22.50

SZASZ, Thomas, Law, Liberty & Psychiatry. NY, 1963, roy8vo, 381pp., $22.50

TAFT, Henry, Witnesses in Court. NY, 1934, 8vo, 89pp., $17.50

TAFT, Wm. Howard, Ethics in Service. Yale, 1915, 8vo, 101pp., first edition, 1/1000, lectures on the ethics of the legal profession, scarce, $47.50

TANNER, J. R., Constitutional Documents of the Reign of James I. Cambridge, 1956, 8vo, 389pp., rear cov. sl. soiled, $25.00

TANNER, Thomas, Bibliothca Britannico-Hibernica Sive, de Scriptoribus qui in Anglia, Scotia, et Hibernica ad Saeculi XVII Initium flouerunt....L, 1748; Reprint: 1963, folio, 788pp., $95.00

TAYLOR, Albion, Labor Problems & Labor Law. NY, 1944, roy8vo, 663pp., $22.50

TAYLOR, Chs., Biographical Sketches & Review of the Bench & Bar of Indiana. 1895, roy8vo,848p.$65.00

TAYLOR, Hannis, The Science of Jurisprudence: A Treatise in Which the Growth of Positive Law is Unfolded by the Historical Method & Its Elements Classified & Defined by the Analytical. NY, 1908, roy8vo, 676pp., $35.00

TAYLOR, Hannis, The Origin & Growth of the English Constitution: An Historical Treatise. B, 1899, roy8vo, 2vols., 1300pp., $65.00

TAYLOR, John, A Treatise on the American Law of Landlord & Tenant. NY, 1844, roy8vo,500p, $47.50

THACHER, John, Charlecote: or, The Trial of William Shakespeare. NY, 1895, 8vo, 125pp,$25.00

THAYER, Wm. Roscoe, Life & Letters of John Hay. B, 1915, roy8vo, 2vols., $35.00

THOMPSON, Geo., & BRADY, G., Law in a Business Environment. Cal, 1963, roy8vo, 687pp., $22.50

THOMPSON, Pishey, Sampson's (Wm.) Discourse; and Correspondence with Various Learned Jurists upon the History of the Law, with the Addition of Several Essays, Tracts and Documents Relating to that Subject, Washington City, 1826, 8vo, 202pp., later linen, rare, $125.00
"Sampson was the first in America to fix public attention on the subject of legal reform....& he labored assiduously for many years with a more than Bentham zeal." Marvin, 627.

THOMSON, Chs., The Ordinances of the Mines of New Spain, trans. from the Original Spanish, with Observations upon the Mines & Mining Associations. L, 1825, 8vo, 76,196pp, linen, $95.00

THORELLI, Hans, Federal Anti-Trust Policy. Johns Hopkins, 1955, roy8vo, 658pp, ex lib, $27.50

TIDD, Wm., Practice of the Court of King's Bench in Personal Actions, with Reference to Cases of Practice in the Court of Common Pleas. 2nd American ed., with Adds. by a Gent. of the Bar. NY, 1807, 8vo, 2vols., later linen, "No practical treatise in modern times approaches nearer to judicial authority than this." Marvin, 691. $125.00

TIEDEMAN, Christopher, The Unwritten Constitution of the United States: A Philosophical Inquiry into the Fundamentals of American Constitutional Law. NY, 1890, 12mo, 165pp., sl.rubbed, $27.50

TIMASHEFF, NS., Introduction to the Sociology of Law. Harvard, 1939, 8vo, 418pp., $25.00

TOMPKINS, Dorothy, The Supreme Court of the U.S., A Bibliography. Univ. of Cal, 1959, 8vo,217p, $30.0

TOMPSON, Geo., Practical Suggestions & Instructions to Young Attornies & Attornies Clerks, Pointing Out Measures Best Calculated for Their Advantage, Errors into Which They May Easily Fall, & Proper Methods of Practice. 2nd ed. by Jos. Greaves. L, 1836, 12mo, 559pp., later linen, $75.00

TRACY, John, Hints on Entering the Practice of Law. Ann Arbor, 1933, roy8vo, 255pp., $22.50

The Treaties of Peace, 1919-1923. NY, Carnegie Endowment, 1924, 8vo, 2vols., sl. wear, $35.00

Trial of the Antichrist, Otherwise the Man of Sin, for High Treason Against the Son of God, Tried at the Sessions House of Truth, before the Rt. Hon. Divine Revelation, Lord Chief Justice of His Majesty's Court of Equity....taken in Short Hand by Rev. W.L.S.G., from the 2nd Dublin ed., Pittsburgh, 1830, 12mo, 187pp., contemp. roan, bit rubbed but sound, $37.50

The Trial of Daniel Isaac Eaton for Publishing a Supposed Libel, Intitled Politics for the People; or, Hog's Wash, at Justice Hall in the Old Bailey, Feb. 24, 1794. 2nd ed., L, n.d., 8vo, 62pp. later linen, $45.00

Trial of Augustin Boyle French, John F. Burke & Matthew Welch, for Conspiracy....taken in Short Hand by Wm. Gurney. L, 1819, 8vo, 412pp., later linen, $45.00

Trial of the Case of the Commonwealth versus David Lee Child for Publishing in the Massachussets Journal a Libel on the Hon. John Keyes, Before the Supreme Judicial Court, Reported by John W. Whitman. B, 1829, 8vo, 119pp., title soiled, $45.00

Trial of Joan of Arc, Being a Verbatim Report of the Proceedings from the Orleans Manuscript, with an Intro. & Notes by W. S. Scott. Conn, 1956, roy8vo, 173pp., $25.00

Trial of Prof. John White Webster. Intro. by Geo. Dilnot.NY, 1928, roy8vo, 224pp., $18.50

Trial of Wm. Codling, Mariner, John Reid, Mariner; Wm. McFarlane, Merchant, & Geo. Easterby, Merchant, for Willfully & Feloneously Destroying & Casting Away the Brig Adventure on the High Seas. L, 1803, 8vo, 260pp., later linen, $47.50

Trials of Patrick Maxwell Wallace & Michael Shaw Wallace for Wilfully Destroying the Brig Dryad Off Cuba, with Intentto Defraud the Marine Insurance Companies. L, 1841, 8vo, 294pp. linen,$45.00

The Third Trial of Jacob Barker for Conspiracy. NY, 1827, 8vo, 255pp., later linen, $37.50

The Trial of Colonel Quenten by a General Court Martial, by W. D. Gurney. L, 1814, 272p, lin, $45.00

TROLLER, Alois, Law & Order: An Introduction to Thinking About the Nature of Law. Leyden 1969, 8vo, 90pp., wrps, $15.00

TSIEN, Tche-hao, La Republique Populaire de Chine: Droit Constitutionnel et Institutions. P, 1970, roy8vo, 646pp., wrps, $30.00

TUCKER, Henry St. Geo., Lectures on Constitutional Law for the Use of Law Classes at the University of Virginia. Richmond, 1843, 8vo, 242pp., later linen, $57.50

TUCKER, Henry, Limitations on the Treaty Making Power under the Constitution ofthe United States. B, 1915, roy8vo, 444pp., $27.50

TURNER, Ralph, The King & His Courts: The Role of John & Henry III in the Administration of Justice, 1199-1240. Cornell, 1968, 8vo, 310pp., $20.00

TWISS, Benj., Lawyers & The Constitution: How Laissez Faire Came to the Supreme Court. Princeton, (1942) Rep: 1962, 8vo, 269pp., $22.50

TWISS, Horace, The Public & Private Life of Lord Chancellor Eldon,with Selections from His Correspondence. P, 1844, 8vo, 2vols., later linen, $75.00

1051) ULLMANN, Walter, The Medieval Idea of Law as Represented by Lucas de Penna. L, 1946, 8vo, 260pp., later linen, ex lib, $25.00

1052) U. S. Commissioner of Labor, 24th Annual Report: Workman's Insurance & Compensation Systems in Europe. DC, 1911, roy8vo, 2vols., 2750pp., $75.00

1053) U. S. Tariff Commission, Reciprocity & Commerical Treaties. DC, 1919, roy8vo, 535pp., $25.00

VALMAER (Ream, Michael,) Lawyer's Code of Ethics: A Satire. St. L., 1887, 12mo, 143pp., $35.00

VANDERBILDT, Arthur, The Challenge of Law Reform. Princeton, 1955, 8vo, 194pp., ex lib, $17.50

VAN HISE, Chs., Concentration & Control: A Solution of the Trust Problem. NY,1918, 8vo, 288p, $18.50

Sacrosanctum Oecumenicum Concilium Vaticanum II: Constitutiones, Declarationes. R., 1966, 4to, 1292pp; with this: Deretz & Nocent (eds.), Dictionary of the Council. 1968, 506pp., $37.50

VATTEL, J., The Law of Nations; or, The Principles of the Law of Nature Applied to the Conduct & Affais of Nations & Sovereigns. 7th American ed., from the New Ed. by Jos. Chitty. P, 1849, roy8vo, lxvi, 500pp., later linen, $95.00

VAUGHN, Maria, A Widow Against the Courts. Trenton, n.d. (1915), 8vo, 161pp., $22.50

VEICOPOULOS, Nicholas, Traite des Territories Dependentes. Geneve, 1960-71, 4to, 2vols,wrps, $45.00

VERHAEGEN, Jacques, La Protection Penal contre les Exces de Pouvoir et la Resistance Legitime a l'Authorite. Brux, 1969, roy8vo, 502pp., 1/2 morocco, $35.00

VIEILLE, Paul, & BANISADR, Abol-Hassan, Petrole et Violence: Terreur Blanche et Resistance en Iran. P, 1974, 8vo, 346pp., wrps, $22.50

VILLIAUME, N., L'Esprit de la Guerre. P, 1861, 8vo, 407pp., later linen, $45.00

VILLOT, Le Lt. Colonel, Moeurs, Coutumes et Institutions des Indigenes de l'Algerie. 3rd ed. Alger, 1888, sm8vo, 521pp., later linen, $37.50

VINOGRADOFF, Paul, English Society in the 11th Century.Oxford, 1908, roy8vo, 599pp., $25.00

VIOLETTE, Eugene, English Constitutional Documents Since 1832. NY, 1936, 8vo, 225pp., $17.50

The Virginia Report of 1799-1800, Touching the Alien & Sedition Laws, together with the Virginia Resolutions of 1798, the Debate & Proceedings Thereon in the House of Delegates of Virginia & Several Other Documents Illustrative of the Raports & Resolutions. Richmond, 1850, 8vo, 264pp., bds, rebacked, $57.50

VON HALLER, Sigmund, Encyclopädie der Bayerischen Gesetzgebung. Fürth, 1853, 8vo, 3vols., contemp. 1/2 calf, $75.00

VON HOLST, Hermann, The Constitutional & Political History of the United States, trans. by Lalor Mason. C, 1889, roy8vo, 8vols., $195.00

VON MEHREN, Arthur, The Civil Law System: Cases & Materials for the Comparative Study of Law. NJ, 1957, 4to, 922pp., $25.00

VON RANKE, Leopold, A History of England Principally in the 17th Century.Oxford, 1875, roy8vo, 6vols., $145.00

VON RAUMER, Friedrich, Geschichtliche Entwicklung der Begriffe von Recht, Staat u. Politik. (1861) Rep: 1971, 8vo, 308pp., $22.50

VON SCHUSCHNIGG, Kurt, International Law. Mil., 1959, roy8vo, 512pp., $27.50

WAIGHT, Leonard, History & Mechanism of the Exchange Equalization Account. Cambridge, 1939, 8vo, 91pp., $17.50

WALKER, Nigel, Crime & Punishment in Britain: An Analysis of the Penal System in Theory, Law & Practice. Edinburgh UP, 1965, roy8vo, 367pp., $25.00

WALSH, Wm., Outlines of the History of English & American Law. New York Univ. Pr, 1924, roy8vo, 531pp., $30.00

WALTER, Erich (ed.), Religion & the State University. Univ. of Michigan, 1958, roy8vo,321p, $25.00

WARBURTON, A.F., Trial of the Officers and Crew of the Privateer Savannah, on the Charge of Piracy in the U.S. Circuit Court for the So. Di_t. of N. Y. NY, 1862, roy8vo, 385pp., later lin, $65.00

WARD, Wm., A Treatise on Legacies or Bequests of Personal Property.P, 1837, 8vo, 222pp., later linen, LL, $45.00

WARNER, G. J., Means for the Preservation of Public Liberty: An Oration. NY, 1797, 8vo, 22pp., orig. ptd. wrps., $30.00

WARREN, Chs., The Supreme Court in United States History. rev. ed. B, 1947, roy8vo, 2vols., $57.50

WARREN, Cha., History of the American Bar.B, 1911, roy8vo, 586pp., faded, $22.50

WARREN, Edw., Spartan Education. B, 1942, 8vo, 164pp., (Harvard law prof.), $17.50

WARREN, Samuel, A Popular & Practical Introduction to Law Studies. from the London ed. P, 1836, 8vo, 241pp., later 1/2 linen, LL, $57.50 "stands at the head of all works of its class." Marvin.

WASHBURN, Emory, Lectures on the Study & Practice of the Law Delivered in the Law School of Harvard University. B, 1871, 8vo, 318pp., later linen, $30.00

WATERMAN, Th., The Justice's Manual: A Summary of the Powers & Duties of Justices of the Peace in the State of New York. 2nd ed. rev. Albany, 1829, 8vo, 294pp., contemp. roan, sl. scuffed, $57.50

WATKINS, Chs. Principles of Conveyancing, with an Introduction to the Study of That Branch of the Law....with very Considerable Adds. by Richard Preston. P, 1838, 8vo, 114pp, lat. lin, LL, $37.50

WATSON, Alan, Roman Private Law around 200 B.C. Edinburgh UP, 1971, 8vo, 187pp., $22.50

WATSON, Wm., A Treatise of the Law of Partnership, first American from the 2nd London ed., to which are Added Many New References to American Decisions. P, 1807, 8vo, 400pp., contemp. calf, front hinge very sl. cracked near crown, handso me copy, $75.00

WATSON, Wm., Practical Treatise on the Law Relating to Sheriff....P, 1834, 8vo, 370pp;. later 1/2 linen, sl. dpst. few leaves, LL, $45.00

WAUTERS, Alphonse, Les Libertes Communales: Essai sur leur Origine et Leurs Premiers Deveolppements en Belgique, dans le Nord de la France, et sur les Bords du Rhin. Brux, 1968, roy8vo,773pp,$37.50

WEBSTER, Daniel, Speeches & Forensic Arguments. B, 1838, roy8vo, 2vols., orig. cl. sl wear, $65.00

WEBSTER, Hutton, Rest Days: A Study in Early Law & Morality.NY, 1916, roy8vo, 325pp, $22.50

A) LIEBER, Francis, Legal & Political Hermeneutics. 3rd ed., rev. w/adds. by Wm. Hammond, St. L., 1880, roy8vo, 275pp., later linen, title in fine facsimile. $45.00

WATSON, Wm., The Clergy-Man' Law; Or, The Complete Incumbent, Collected from the 39 Articles, Canons, Decrees in Chancery, Exchequer, as All the Statutes & Common Law Cases Relating to the Church & Clergy of England, Digested Under Proper Heads for the Benefit of Patrons of Churches and Parochial Clergy; and Will be Found Useful to All Students & Practitioners of the Law. 4th ed., with Large Additions & Alterations. L, 1747, folio, 656pp., later linen, $175.00

WEBSTER, Ralph, Legal Medicine & Toxicology. P/L, 1930, roy8vo, 862pp., $27.50

WEDGWOOD, C. V., The Trial of Charles I. L, 1964, 8vo, 253pp., $20.00

WEDGWOOD, Prof. Wm., LL. D., The Government & Laws of the United States....A Complete & Comprehensive View of the Rise Progress....of the State & National Government. NY, 1866, roy8vo, 477p, lin.$48.50

WEISSER, Michael, Crime & Punishment in Early Modern Europe. NJ, 1979, 8vo, 193pp., $17.50

WELFORD, Richard, A Practical Treatise on Equity Pleadings, with Observations on the New Orders of 1841. P, 1846, 8vo, 271pp., later linen "a careful & methodical explanation." Marvin, 723.$45.00

(WELLMAN, Bert J.), The Legal Revolution of 1902, by a Law-Abiding Revolutionist. Chicago, Kerr, 1898, 8vo, 334pp., (political fiction, radical), scarce, $35.00

WELLMAN, Francis, Gentlemen of the Jury: Reminiscences of 30 Years at the Bar. NY, 1944, 298p. $20.00

WENTWORTH, John, A Complete System of Pleading: Comprehending the Most Approved Precedents & Forms, of Practice, Chiefly Consisting of Such as Have Never Before Been Printed, with an Index to the Principal Work, Incorporating it and Making it a Continuation of Townshend's and Cornwall's Tables to the Present Time. D, 1799, 8vo, 10vols., contemp. calf, bit rubbed, several front hinges cracked or wormed but all firm, one hinge expertly reinforced, $250.00

WESKETT, John, A Complete Digest of The Theory, Laws & Practice of Insurance; Compiled from the Best Authorities in Different Languages,...with a Preliminary Discourse Wherein are Deliniated the Very Great Disorders which Prevail in the Affairs of Insurance, their Principal Causes Explained, & Methods Proposed for better Regulation & Prevention. L, 1781, very tall folio, lxxxiv, 612pp., later 1/2 calf & bds, nice copy, scarce (mainly maritime law), $225.00

WEST, Raynard, Conscience & Society: A Study of the Psychological Prerequisites of Law & Order. NY, 1945, 8vo, 261pp., $22.50

WESTERMARCK, Eds., The History of Human Marriage. 5th ed., NY, 922, roy8vo, 3vols., $75.00

WESTIN, Alan, Privacy & Freedom. NY, 1967, roy8vo, 487pp., $25.00

WESTLAKE, John, Collected Papers on Public International Law, ed. J. Oppenheim, Cambridge, 1914, roy8vo, 705pp., rebacked, $45.00

WHARTON, Francis, A Treatise on the Criminal Law of the United States, Comprising a Digest of the Penal Statutes of the General Government, & of Mass, New York, Pa. & Virginia, with the Decisions on Cases Arising from those Statutes, and a General View of the Criminal Jurisprudence of the Common & Civil Law. 3rd ed., P, 1855, roy8vo, 1128pp., later linen, $125.00 (scarce)

WHEATON, Henry, An Address Pronounced at the Opening of the New York Athenaeum. NY, 1824, 8vo, 44pp., later linen, (Sup.Crt. reporter & authority on international law & its history), $37.50

WHEELER, Everett, Daniel Webster: Expounder of the Constitution. NY, 1905, 4to, 188pp.,$25.00

WHEELER-BENNETT, John, & LATIMER, H., Information on the Reparation Settlement, Being the Background & History of the Young Plan & the Hague Agreements, 1929-30. L, 1930, 8vo, 253pp, sl. wear,$25.00

WHITE, Albert, The Making of the English Constitution. NY, 1908, 8vo, 410pp., $20.00

WHITE, Edw., Legal Antiquities: A Collection of Essays Upon Ancient Laws & Customs. St.L., 1913, roy8vo, 349pp., $27.50

WHITE, E., The Law in the Scriptures with Explanations of the Law Terms & Legal References in Both the Old & New Testaments. St.L., 1935, roy8vo, 422pp., $30.00

WHITE, Edw., Commentaries on the Law in Shakespeare, with Explanations of the Legal Terms used in the Plays, & a Consideration of the Criminal Types Presented. St. L., 1913, roy8vo, 524p, $30.00

WHITE, Leonard, The Jacksonians: A Study in Administrative History, 1829-61. NY, 1954, 593p, $20.00

WHITMORE, Wm., The Colonial Laws of Massachussets, Reprinted from the Edition of 1672, with Supplements through 1686. B, 1887, 4to, 395pp., contemp. 1/2 morocco, sl. rubbed, $47.50

WHITNEY,,Simon, Anti-Trust Policies. NY, 1958, roy8vo, 2vols., $45.00

WIGMORE, John Henry, The Principles of Judicial Proof. 2nd ed. rev., B, 1931, roy8vo, 1056p, $45.00

WIGMORE, John, A Kaleidoscope of Justice: Containing Authentic Accounts of Trial Scenes from All Times & Climes. DC, 1941, roy8vo, 751pp., $35.00

WIGMORE, John & KOCOUREK, Alb. (eds.), The Rational Basis of Legal Institutions, Intro, by Oliver Wendell Holmes. NY, 1923, 8vo, 603pp., $30.00

(WIGMORE), KOCOUREK, Alb. (ed.), Celebration Legal Essays by Various Authors to Mark the 25th Year of Service of John Henry Wigmore. Northwestern, 1919, 4to, (contributors include Duguit, Freund, Goudy, Holdsworth, Pollock, Pound, Williston), sl. cover soil, $55.00

WIGRAM, Jas., Points in the Law of Discovery. P, 1838, 8vo, 102pp., later lin, LL,$47.50
"One of the most valuable contributions to juridical literature which has appeared for several years....learned, acute & discriminating." Jos. Story in Marvin, 733.

WILBOUR, Chs., Trial of Chs. M. Jefferds for the Murder of....NY, 1862, roy8vo, 324pp, lin,$45.00

WILCOX, Henry, Foibles of the Bench. C, 1906, 8vo, 144pp.,$22.50

WILKES, Geo., Shakespeare from an American Point of View, Including an Inquiry as to His Religious Faith & His Knowledge of Law,...L, 1877, roy8vo, 471pp., later linen, $30.00

WILKINS, David, Leges Anglo-Saxonicae, Ecclesiasticae & Civiles, Accedunt Leges Eduardi Latinae, Guilielmi Conquestoris Gallo-Normannicae, et Henrici I Latinae, Subjungitur Domini Henr. Spelmanni Codex Legum Veterum Statuorum Regni Angliae, quae ab Ingressu Guiliemi I usque ad Annum Nunum Henr III edita sunt; Toti Operi Praemittitur Disertatio Epistolaris Admodum Reverendi Dominis Guilielmi Nicolsoni Episcopi Derrensis, De Jue Feudali Veterum Saxonum. L, 1721, tall folio, xxiv, 434pp., later 1/2 calf & marbled boards, bit rubbed & scuffed, one of 49 subscribed large paper copies; appended is an excellent Glossarium; this is the first appearance of Spelman's Codex. $250.00

WILKINSON, Jas., The Practice in the Action of Replevin. P, 1834, 8vo, 102pp, linen, LL, $37.50

WILLARD, Jos., Half a Century of Judges & Lawyers. B, 1895, 8vo, 371pp; $25.00

1130) MONROE, James, A View of the Conduct of the Executive in Foreign Affairs of the United States, Connected with the Mission to the French Republic During the Years 1794, 5 & 6. Illustra ed by His Instructions & Correspondence and Other Authentic Documents. P, 1797, 8vo, lxvi, 407pp., contemp. roan, expertly re-backed in calf, slight trace of sporadic dampstain of first & last few leaves (which appears more as foxing), first edition, $350.00
Monroe was appointed minister to France in 1794; he was well received due to his well-known French sympathies. His avid Republicanism caused the Federalist administration to recall him in 1796; this is his defense of his actions.

WILLCOCK, J. W., The Office of Constable: Comprising the Laws Relating to High, Petty & Special Constables, Headbproughs, Tithingmen, Borsholders & Watchmen. P, 1840, 8vo, 88pp, LL, $45.00

WILLCOCK, J. W., The Law of Municipal Corporations; together with a Brief Sketch of their History and a Treatise on Mandamus & Quo Warranto. P, 1836, 8vo, 306pp., later linen, LL, $57.50

WILLIAMS, Montague, Later Leaves, Being the Further Reminiscences of....Queen's Counsel. L, 1891, roy8vo, 423pp., sl. wear, $22.50

WILLIAMS, Sydney, Forensic Facts & Fallacies. L, 1885, 12mo, 276pp., sl. wear, $25.00

WILLIS, John, A Practical Treatise on the Duties & Responsibilities of Trustees. P, 1835, 8vo, 129pp., later linen, $37.50 LL

WILLIS, Henry, The Federal Reserve System: Legislation, Organization, Operation. NY, 1923, 8vo, 1765pp., ($100.00), $60.00

WILLIS, John, Pleadings in Equity Illustrative of Lord Redesdale's Treatise on the Pleadings in Suits in the Court of Chancery. P, 1842, 8vo, 281pp., later 1/2 linen, LL, $47.50

WILLOUGHBY, Wm. et al., System of Financial Administration of Great Britain. NY, 1917, 361p, $22.50

WILLS, Wm., An Essay on the Rationale of Circumstantial Evidence, Illustrated by Numerous Cases. P, 1843, 8vo, 128pp., later linen, LL, $65.00
James Kent urged the publication of the American edition of this work which "contains the soundest information on the subject....executed in a most luminous & philosophical manner." Marvin.

WILSON, James, The Works of, ed. by Rob. McCloskey. Harvard, 1967, roy8vo, 2vols., $45.00

(WILSON), OBERING, Wm., The Philosophy of Law of James Wilson, Justice of the Supreme Court, 1789-1798: A Study in Comparative Jurisprudence. DC, n.d., roy8vo, 276pp., buck, $22.50

WILSON, John, A Treatise on Springing Uses & Other Limitations by Deed, Corresponding with Executory Devises....P, 1836, 8vo, 69pp., later linen, LL, $37.50

WILSON, Woodrow, Constitutional Government in the United States. NY, 1908, 8vo, 236p, 1st ed, $35.00

WINDEYER, W. J., Lectures on Legal History. Sydney, 1938, roy8vo, 280pp., $27.50

WINDOLPH, F. L., Reflections on Law in Literature. Univ. of Penn, 1956, 8vo, 82pp.,

WINSLOW, Forbes, The Plea of Insanity in Criminal Cases. P, 1843, 8vo, 42pp, later linen,LL, $57.50

WITT, John, Life in the Law. L, 1920, 8vo, 224pp., sl. faded, $22.50

WHITTINGHAM, Richard, Martial Justice: The Last Mass Execution in the US. C, 1971, 8vo, 281p, $18.50

OLFFE, B. P., The Royal Demesne in English History: The Crown Estate in the Governance of the Realm from the Conquest to 1509. Ohio State UP, 1971, roy8vo, 324pp., $25.00

The Wonderful Trial of Caroline Lohman, Alias Restell, NY, 1847, roy8vo, 38 pp., linen, $37.50

WOOD, Thomas, An Institute of the Laws of England: Or the Laws of England in Their Natural Order, According to Common Use. Published for the Direction of Young Beginners or Students in Law.... 10th edition, brought down to the Present Time, by Upwards of 1000 Additional Reference. L, 1772, folio, 637pp., later 1/2 calf & bds, $325.00
"Before the Commentaries of Blackstone were published, Wood's Institute was the only treatise that furnished a comprehensive view of the common law....according to Blackstone 'upon the whole, however, his work is a valuable performance; and great are the obligations of the student to him and his predecessor, Finch, for their happy progression reducing the elements of the law from their former chaos to a regular methodical science." quoted in Marvin, 744.

WOOD, Thomas, A New Institute of the Imperial or Civil Law, with Notes Shewing in Some Principal Cases amongst Other Observations, how the Canon Law, the Laws of England and the Laws and Customs of Other Nations Differ from It. 4th edition, corr., to which is Prefixed....A Treatise of the First Principles of Laws in General; of their Nature & Design, and of the Interpretation of Them. L, 1730, folio, 342pp., later 1/2 calf and bds, bit rubbed, $375.00

) WOOLRYCH, Humphrey, A Treatise on the Law of Ways, Including Highways, Turnpike Roads, Tolls, Private Rights of Way, Bridges, & Ferries. P, 1834, 8vo, 323pp., later linen, LL, $45.00

WOOLSEY, Theodore, Political Science: The State Theoretically & Practically Considered. NY, 1878, roy8vo, 2vols., $45.00

WORDSWORTH, Chs., The Law of Joint Stock Companies. P, 1843, 8vo, 334pp., later 1/2 linen,LL,$57.50

WORLD WAR I: An excellent collection of scarce & rare English language pamphlets relating mainly to the legal and political aspects of the war; dealing in particular with: Censorship, War Taxation & Finance, Belgium, German War Aims, British War Aims, Violations of International Law by Germany, Turkey, the Balkans & Near East, Economic & Industrial Problems, Navy Submarines, the Case of the Allies, Peace & the League of Nations. Details on Request.

WORTHINGTON, Geo., An Inquiry into the Power of Juries to Decide Incidentally Questions of Law. P, 1840, 8vo, 62pp., later linen, LL, $47.50

WRIGHT, Arnold, & SMITH, P., Parliament Past & Present: A Popular & Picturesque Account of a Thousand Years in the Palace of Westminster, the House of the Mother of Parliaments. with 643 illustrations & 18 color plates. L, 1903, 4to, 592pp., contemp. 1/2 morocco, $75.00

WRIGHT, Quincy, A Study of War. Univ.of Chicago, 1942.roy8vo, 2vols., 1552pp, the complete ed,$45.00

WU, John, The Fountain of Justice: A Study in the Natural Law. NY, 1955, 8vo, 287pp., $22.50

YNDHAM, Horace, Feminine Frailty. L, 1929, roy8vo, 352pp., $22.50

WYZANSKI, Chs., Whereas---A Judge's Premises: Essays in Judgment, Ethics & the Law. B, 1965, 8vo, 312pp., $22.50

) YERRINGTON, Jas., Report of the Case of Geo. Hersey, Indicted for the Murder of Betsy Tirrell before the Supreme Judicial Court of Massachusettes. B, 1862, roy8vo, 267pp. linen, $45.00

YOUNG, Arthur, The Single Tax Movement in the US. Princeton, 1916, 8vo, 340pp., $22.50

ZABEL, Max, The Patent Royalty Contract. NY, 1933, (w/1946sup.) roy8vo, 262pp., $25.00

CATALOGUE 38
LAW AND LEGAL HISTORY
(with Law Prints & Economics)
WITH AN ADDENDA OF VARIA

INCLUDING SCIENCE POLITICAL ECONOMY LITERATURE REFERENCE

RICHARD ADAMIAK
1545 EAST 60th St.
CHICAGO, ILL.60637
312-955-4571 (from 7AM to Noon

TERMS OF SALE: All titles are offered on a subject-to-prior-sale basis. Prices are net in US dollars; shipping charges extra. Deferred remittance for institutions. Past private clients are expected to remit upon receipt; new private clients may be asked to remit upon receipt of a pro-forma invoice. We will ship in the manner most appropriate to the order & destination. Air-freight (via KLM Royal Dutch Airlines available on request. All books, unless otherwise noted, are in very good condition; all significant defects are noted. Any book is returnable within five days of receipt only if deemed not as described. All cable and phone reserves must be confirmed in writing within seven days.

REFERENCES: Marvin, Legal Bibliography, 1847; Encyclopedia Britannica, Eleventh Edition (EBII); Encyclopedia of the Social Sciences, 1937 (ESS); where no reference is given the material is usually drawn from one or more of the following: Allgemeine Deutsche Biographie (1875); Grand Dictionnaire Universel (1875); Jöchers Allgemeines Gelehrten Lexikon (1750).

---

1) ABBOTT, Edith, Immigration: Select Documents & Case Records. Univ. of Chicago, 1924,roy8vo,809p, $30.00

2) ABBOTT, Austin, A Brief for the Trial of Criminal Cases. 3rd ed.,enl., Ro., 1925, roy8vo, 1176p. $30.00

3) ABBOTT, Nathan, (ed.), Brief-Making & the Use of Law Books. St. P, 1906, roy8vo, 472pp., $27.50

4) ACKERMAN, Bruce, Private Property & the Consitution. Yale, 1977, 8vo, 303pp., $20.00

5) ADAMES, Jonas, The Order of Keeping a Court Leet & Court Baron, with the Charges Appertaining to the Same. L, 1650, 8vo, 51pp., later 1/2 calf, $250.00

6) ADAMIAK, Richard, Justice & History in the Old Testament, with a Foreword by David Noel Freedman. Cl, 1982, 8vo, xiv, 103pp., $12.95

7) ADLOW, Elijah, The Genius of Lemuel Shaw: Expounder of the Common Law. Mass, 1962, roy8vo,388p, $25.00

8) ADVISORY COMMISSION ON THE REVIEW OF THE CONSTITUTION OF THE FEDERATION OF RHODESIA & NYASALAND: Report, Appendix VIII: Evidence, Northern Rhodesia, Written & Oral Evidence, Feb-Mar, 1960. London, 1960, folio, 5vols., orig. ptd. wrps. $75.00

9) AITKEN, Hugh (ed.), The State & Economic Growth. NY, 1959, roy8vo, 389pp., $22.50

10) ALFANGE, DEan, The Supreme Court & the National Will. NY, 1937, 8vo, 297pp., $22.50

11) ALLEN, Wm. & ALLEN, C. (eds.), Foreign Trade & Finance: Essays in Int'l Economic Equilibrium & Adjustment. NY, 1959, 8vo, 500pp., $22.50

12) ALTHUSIUS, The Politics of, An Abridged Translation of the 3rd ed. of the Politica Methodice Digesta trans. F. S. Carney, Pref. by Carl J. Friedrich. B, 1964, 8vo, xxxvi,232pp., important legal philosopher & early proponent of federalism, $25.00.

13) AMERICAN ARBITRATION ASSN, Suggestions for the Practice of Commercial Arbitration in the U.S. Oxford UP, 1928, roy8vo, 247pp., $27.50

14) AMES, Jas. Barr, A Selection of Cases in Equity Jurisdiction with Notes & Citations. Harvard UP, 1927, roy8vo, 2vols., $37.50

15) AMES, Andrew, The Great Oyer of Poisoning: the Trial of the Earl of Somerset for the Poisoning of Sir Thomas Overbury in the Tower of London....from contemp. MSS. L, 1846, 8vo, 551pp., linen, $75.00

16) AMOS, Sheldon, The Science of Law. NY, 1883, 8vo, 417pp., $30.00

17) ANDREWS, Wm., Bygone Punishments. L, 1899, 8vo, 311pp., ill., $35.00

18) ANGOFF, Chs., The Book of Libel: A Practical Guide for Editors & Authors. rev. ed., NY, 1966, 8vo, 452pp., $25.00

19) (ANSTEY, John), The Pleader's Guide, A Didactic Poem....with the Arguments of Counsellor Bother'um & Counsellor Bore'um.... L, 1796, 8vo, later linen, 2 parts as one, $87.50

20) ANTIEAU, Chester, Commentaries on the Constitution of the U.S. Buffalo, 1960, roy8vo, 416pp., $35.00

21) ARNOT, Hugo, A Collection & Abridgement of Celebrated Criminal Trials in Scotland from 1536 to 1784, with Historical & Critical Remarks. Glasgow, 1812, 8vo, 440pp, later linen, $75.00

22) ASHTON, Arthur (one of His Majesty's Counsel, Bencher of the Inner Temple,)As I Went on My Way. L, 1924, 8vo, 267pp., bit rubbed, $22.50

23) ATLAY, J.B. (ed.), The Trial of the Stauntons. L, 1911, 8vo, 332pp, (Notable Eng. Trials), $22.50

24) AYRES, Leonard, Turning Points in Business Cycles. NY, 1939, roy8vo, 214pp., $17.50

25) AUGUSTINUS (Agustin), Antonius, De Legibus et Senatus Consultis Liber, Adiunctis Legum Antiquarum et Senatusconsultorum fragmentis, cum Notis. Rome, 1583, small 4to, 339pp; contemp. vellum, sl. wear, light-moderate sporadic dampstain, sound, attractive copy, a rare work by a highly regarded Spanish authority (1516-1586) on Roman & Canon Law, Allgemeines Gelehrten Lexicon, I, 642, $275.00

26) AUSTIN, John, The Province of Jurisprudence Determined and The Uses of the Study of Jurisprudence with Intro. by H.L.A. Hart, NY, 1954, 8vo, 396pp., sl. soil.marg. 1st few leaves, $22.50

AUSTIN, John, Lectures on Jurisprudence or the Philosophy of Positive Law. NY, 1875, 8vo, 2vols., $75.00

AYMAR, Brandt & SAGARIN, E., A Pictorial History of the World's Great Trials from Socrates to Eichmann. NY, 1967, 4to, 373pp., $35.00

BAAR, Carl, Separate but Subservient: Court Budgeting in the American States. Mass, 1975, roy8vo, 210pp., $17.50

BACON, Francis, The Works of Lord Bacon, with an Introductory Essay & Portrait. L, 1871, small 4to, 2vols., contemp. 1/2 calf, nice set, $115.00

Another set, London, 1846, bound in later linen, $87.50

BACON, Francis, The Works of, A New Edition with a Life of the Author by Basil Montague. P, n.d. (c. 1850), 4to, 3vols., orig. cl., rebacked, nice set, $145.00

,BACON, Francis, The Works of, London, 1819, 8vo, 10vols., contemp. 1/2 calf and marbled boards, raised bands, spines heavily gilded, beautiful set, $500.00

BAILEY, Martin, National Income & the Price Level: A Study in Macrotheory. NY, 1962, 8vo, 304p, $20.00

BAKER, Chs., Monopolies & the People. NY, 1889, 8vo, 263pp., $25.00

BALDERSTON, C., Managerial Profit Sharing. NY, 1928, roy8vo, 127pp., $17,50.

BALDWIN, Roger & RANDALL, C., Civil Liberties & Industrial Conflict. Harvard, 1938,8vo, 137p,$22.50

BANCROFT, Hubert How, Popular Tribunals. SF, 1887, roy8vo, 2vols., laterlinen, $75.00

BANERJEE, D. N., Our Fundamental Rights: Their Nature & Extent, as Judicially Determined. Calcutta, 1960, 8vo, 477pp., $25.00

BARBER, Richard, The American Corporation: Its Power, Its Money, Its Politics. NY, 1970, 8vo,309p,$20.

BARBICHON, P. M., Dictionnaire Complet de Tous les Lieux de la France et des ses Colonies...... Paris, 1831, thick 8vo, 2vols., 2100pp., contemp. 1/2 calf, a very comprehensive work, $175.00

BARGER, Harold, Money, Banking & Public Policy. C, 1962, roy8vo, 714pp., $25.00

BARLOW, E. R., & WENDER, T., Foreign Investment & Taxation (Harvard Law School, Int'l Problems in Taxation), NJ, 1955, roy8vo, 481pp , $27.050

BARNARD, Chester, The Functions of the Executive. Harvard, 1948, 8vo, 334pp., $20.00

BARNES, Harry E., In Quest of Truth & Justice: De-Bunking the War Guilt Myth. C, 1928, roy8vo, 423pp., $25.00

BARNETT, Geo., State Banks & Trust Companies Since the Passage of the National Banking Act. DC,GPO, 1911, 8vo, 366pp., orig. ptd. wrps, $22.00

BARTON, Sir D. P. & BENHAM, C., The Story of the Inns of Court. B, 1928, 8vo, 320pp., $25.00

BAUMOL, Wm., Welfare Economics andthe Theory of the State, with a New Intro: Welfare & the State Revisited. Harvard, 1965, 8vo, 212pp., $20.00

BEALE, Joseph Henry, Cases on Legal Liability. Harvard, 1925, 4to, 883pp., $37.50

BEALE, Jos. Henry, A Selection of Cases & Other Authorities upon Criminal Law. 3rd ed., Harvard 1915, 4to, 1011pp.,sp'ne lettering faded, $35.00

BEARD, Charles A., American Government & Politics. new ed.,rev., NY, 1919, 8vo, 788pp., $27.50

BEARD, Chs. A., The Republic: Conversations on Fundamentals. NY, 1944, 8vo, 365pp., $25.00

BECKER, Carl., The Declaration of Independence: A Study in the Historey of Political Ideas. NY, 1942, 8vo, 286pp., $22.50

BELL, Philip, The Sterling Area in the Postwar World: Internal Mechanism & Cohesion, 1946-1952. Oxford UP, 1956, 8vo, 487pp., $22.50

BEMIS, Geo., Report of the Case of John Webster for theMurder of Geo. Parkman before the Supreme Judicial Court of Mass. & an Appendix Containing Several Interesting Matters Never Before Published. Detroit, 1897, 8vo, 394pp., $45.00

BENNETT,H., Trade Marks: Legal & Commercial Aspects. NY, 1949, 8vo, 479pp., $25.00

BENSON, Capt L., The Book of Remarkable Trials & Notorious Characters, with Numerous Illustrations by Phiz, L, n.d. (c. 1860), 8vo, 545pp., orig. cl., sl. wear, scarce, $47.50

BEHTHAM, Jeremy, The Correspondence of, ed. by Timothy Sprigge, Univ. of London, 1968, Vols. I & II, 1752-1780, roy8vo, 2vols., (List Price: $120.00), $60.00

BERKSON, Larry, & CARBON, S., The U.S. Circuit Judge Nominating Commission: Its Members, Procedures & Candidates. C, 1980, 8vo, 260pp., wrps, $10.00

BERLANSTEIN, Lenard, The Barristers of Tolouse in the 18th Century, 1740-1793. Johns Hopkins UP, 1975, 8vo, 210pp., $22.50

BEROLZHEIMER, Fritz, The World's Legal Philosophies. trans. Jastrow. B, 1912, 8vo, 490pp, $25.00

BEVERIDGE, Albert, The Life of John Marshall. B/NY, 1929, roy8vo, 4vols., $75.00

BEVERIDGE, Albert, Abraham Lincoln. NY, 1928, roy8vo, 4vols., excellent set, $85.00

BEVERIDGE, Albert, The State of the Nation. Ind, 1924, 8vo, 277pp., $22.50

BEVIS, Herman, Corporate Finaicial Reporting in a Competitive Economy. (Columbia Univ. Studies) NY, 1965, roy8vo, 212pp., $22.50

BIGELOW, Melville, The Law of Wills.B, 1898, 8vo, 398pp., $27.50

BIGELOW, Melville, The Law of Bills, Notes & Checques. 2ned, B, 1900, roy8vo, 349pp., $30.00

BIGGS, John, The Guilty Mind: Psychiatry & the Law of Evidence. NY, 1955, 8vo, 236pp., $22.50

BIRKENHEAD, Rt. Hon., Points of View. L, 1922, 8vo, 2vols., (learned essays), $45.00

BLACKSTONE, Sir William, Commentaries on the Laws of England in Four Books, with an Analysis of the Work, from the 19th London edition, with Notes by Christian, Chitty, Lee, Hovenden & Ryland, & also References to American Cases by a Member of the New York Bar. P, 1864, vols. bound as 2, later linen, nice set, $150.00

BLACKSTONE, Sir Wm., Commentaries on the Laws of England, from the Author's 8th Edition, 1778, edited for American Lawyers by William G. Hammond, with Copious Notes & References to All Comments on the Text in the American Reports, 1787-1890. SF, 1890, 12mo, 4vols., later linen, a scarce & valuable edition, $215.00

72) BLACKSTONE, Sir Wm., Commentaries on the Laws of England, with an Analysis of the Work, with the Last Corrections ofthe Author, and Notes, from the 21st London Edition, with Copious Notes Explaining the Changes in the Law Effected by Decision or Statute down to 1844; Vol. I ed. by J.F. Hargrave; vol. II by G. Sweet; vol. III by R. Couch; vol. IV by W. N. Welsby, together with Notes Adapting the Work to the American Student by John L. Wendell. NY, 1858, roy8vo, 4vols., bound in later linen, slight marginal dampstain of a few leaves in vol. 4; a very scarce and scholarly edition, $325.00

73) BLACKSTONE, Sir Wm., Commentaries o n the Laws of England, together with a Copious Analysis of the Contents & Notes with References to English & American Decisions & Statutes to Date which Illustrate or Change the Law of the Text....Also Containing some Considerations regarding the Study of the Law, by Thomas M. Cooley. 3rd ed., rev., C, 1884, roy8vo, 4vols. bound (as issued) as 2, later linen, $145.00

74) BLACKWELL, Th., College Law. DC, 1961, roy8vo, 347pp., $25.00

75) Blanc, Louis, The History of Ten Years. L, 1844, 8vo, 2vols., rebacked, $47.50

76) BLOUGH, Roy, The Federal Taxing Process. NY, 1952, roy8vo, 504pp., $27.50

77) BLUTWELL, Geo., A Manual of the Direct & Excise Tax System of the US. B, 1864, roy8vo, 498pp, $47.50

BOVEE, Marvin, Reasons for Abolishing Capital Punishment. C, 1878, 8vo, 328pp., later linen, $36.00

79) BOX, Muriel, The Trial of Marie Stopes. L, 1967, roy8vo, 392pp., $22.50

80) BRADSHAW, TF., Developing Men for Controllership. Harvard, 1950, 8vo, 231pp., $20.00

81) BRANDT, Irving, The Bill of Rights: Origin & Meaning. Ind., 1965, roy8vo, 567pp., $25.00

82) BRECKENRIDGE, Sophonsbia, Marriage & the Civil Rights of Women. Unvi. of Chicago, 1931, roy8vo, 158pp., $25.00

83) BRIGGS,Herb.(ed.), The Law of Nations: Cases & Documents.NY, 1947, roy8vo, 984pp., $30.00

84) British Year Book of Int'l Law, 1970, XLIV. Oxford UP, 1971, 4to, 314pp., $20.00

85) Britsh Yearbook of Int'l Law, 1968-69, XLIII, Oxford UP, 1970, 4to, 353pp. $22.50

86) British Yea book of Int'l Law, 1923-4. IV, Oxford UP, 4to, 264pp., $27.50

87) BROOKE, Michael, & REMMERS, H., The Strategies of Multinational Enterprise: Organization & Finace. L, 1970, roy8vo, 389pp., $25.00

88) BROWN, Esther, Lawyers & the Promotion of Justice. NY, 1938, 8vo, 302pp., $22.50

89) BROWN, Josephine, Public Relief, 1929-1939. NY, 1940, 8vo, 524pp., $22.50

90) BROWN, Ralph, Loyalty & Security: Employment Tests in the US. Yale UP, 1958, roy8vo, 524pp., (Yale Law School Studies #3), $27.50

91) BROWN, Samuel, The Life of Rufus Choate. 2nd ed, B, 1870, 8vo, 468pp., $35.00

92) BROWNE, Cynthia, State Constitutional Conventions from Independence to the Completion of the Present Union, 1776-1959: a Bibliography. Conn, 1973, roy8vo, 250pp., $22.50

93) BROWNE, Irving, Elements of the Law of Domestic Relations & of Employer & Employed. 2nd ed., rev. B, 1890, 8vo, 166p., $22.50

94) BROWNE, J. H., The Medical Jurisprudence of Insanity. L, 1871, 8vo, 341pp., scarce, $75.00

95) BROWNELL, Emery, Legal Aid in the US. Rochester, 1951, roy8vo, 333pp., $25.00

96) BRUERE, Henry, The New City Governm-nt: Municipal Administration based on a Survey of 10 Commission Governed Cities. NY, 1912, 8vo, 438pp., $22.50

97) BRYANT, Margaret, English in the Law Courts: The Part that Articles, Prepositions & Conjunctions Play in Legal Decisions. (1930), NY, 1970, 8vo, 316pp., $22.50

98) BRYCE, Jas., Studies in History & Jurisprudence. Oxford, 1900, 8vo, 2vols., sl. wear, $45.00

99) (Bryce), FISHER, H.A.L., James Bryce. NY, 1927, roy8vo, 2vols., $35.00

100)BUCKINGHAM, Walter, Theoretical Economic Systems: A Comparative Analysis. NY, 1958, 8vo, 518pp, $25.00

101)BUCKLAND, W. W., The Roman Law of Slavery. Cambridge UP, 1970 (1908), roy8vo, 735pp., $47.50

102)BUCKLAND, W. W., A Text Book of Roman Law. 3rded., rev. Peter Stein. Cambridge UP, 1963, roy8vo, 764pp., $57.50

103)BUCKLAND, W. W.. & MC NAIR, A., Roman Law & Common Law. 2nd ed., rev., by Lawson, Cambridge UP, 1965, 8vo, 439pp., $37.50

104)BUCKNILL, Rt. Hon. Sir Alfred, The Nature of Evidence. L, 1953, 8vo, 143pp., $22.50

105)BURGESS, John., The Sanctity of Law. NY, 1938, 8vo, 345pp., $25.00

106)BURGESS, W. R., The Reserve Banks & the Money Market. NY,1927, 8vo, 328pp., $20.00

107)BURN, Richard, The Justice of the Peace & Parish Officer. 13thed., L, 1776, 8vo, 4vols., contemp. calf, beautiful set, "the most useful bookever published on the law relating to the Justices of the Peace," Marvin, 163. $225.00

108)BURNS, Arthur & MITCHELL, Wesley, Measuring Business Cycles. NY, 1946, small folio, 560pp., $37.50

109)BURNABY, Evelyn, Memories of Famous Trials. L, 1907, roy8vo, 240pp., $25.00

110)BURNETT, Edmund, The Continental Congress. NY, 1941, roy8vo, 751pp., $30.00

111)BURNHAM, Jas., Congress & the American Tradition. C, 1965, roy8vo, 361pp., $25.00

112)BURTON, John, Narratives of Criminal Trials in Scotland. L, 1852, 8vo, 2vols in 1, 1/2 calf, $47.50

113)BUTTS, I. R., The New Business Man's Assistant & Ready Reckoner....Consisting of Legal Forms & Instructions....B, 1854, 132pp; bound with his: The Trader's Guide & Business Man's Legal Companion, Containing the Laws of Trade, Bills of Exchange & Notes, Contracts & Agreements.... B, 1854, 120pp; also bound with his: Improved Edition of the Landlord & Tenant's Assistant, Containing the Legal Rights, Duties & Liabilities....B, 1855, 108pp., 8vo, orig. cloth, $65.00

114)Byrnes, Thomas, Professional Criminals of America. NY, 1886, folio, 433pp., profus. illustrated with original photographs, later linen, very scarce & one of the first books of its kind in US, $95.00

115)CADY, Edwin, The Law of Insurance. Rochester, 1934, 4to, 427pp., $25.00

116)CAGAN, Phillip, Determinants & Effects of Changes in the Stock of Money, 1875-1960. Columbia UP, 1965, roy8vo, 380pp., $22.50

CALTHROP, Charles, The Relation Between the Lord of a Manor and the Copy-Holder His Tenant, Delivered in the Learned Readings of the Late, Excellent & Famous Lawyer Charles Calthrop, of the Honorable Society of Lincoln's Inn...2nd ed., much corr. & amended. L, 1650, 8vo, 76pp., later 1/2 calf, $250.00

CANNAN, Edwin, A History of the Theories of Production & Distribution in English Political Economy from 1776-1848. 3rd ed., L, 1953, 8vo, 336pp., $20.00

CAPPOLLETTI, Mario, The Italian Legal System. Stanford UP, 1967, roy8vo, 462pp., $27.50

CARDOZO, Benjamin, Law & Literature & Other Essays. NY, 1934, 8vo, 190pp., $22.50

CARSON, Hampton, The History of the Supreme Court of the United States, with Biographies of all the Chief & Assoc. Justices, Ill. with Steel Engravings of all the Justices.P, 1902, 4to,2vols,$125.00

The Cases of Polygamy, Concubinage, Adultery, Divorce, etc. Seriously & Learnedly Discussed, being a Complete Collection of all the Remarkable Tryals & Tracts which have been Written on these Important Subjects. L, 1732, 12mo, 240pp., later linen, $125.00

CASPER, Gerhard, &POSNER, Rich., The Workload of the Supreme Court. C, 1976, 118pp., wrps, $10.00

CASTBERG, Frede, Freedom of Speech in the West: A Comparative Study of Public Law in France, the US & Germany. Oslo UP, 1960, roy8vo, 475pp., $35.00

The Celebrated Trial of Madeline Pollard vs Breckinridge, The Most Noted Breach of Promise Suit in the History of Court Records. n.p. n.d. (c.1890), 8vo, 320pp., sl. worn, sl. embrowned, $30.00

Celtic Law Papers, Introductory to Welsh Medieval Law & Govt. Brux, 1973, roy8vo, 213pp., $22.50

A Century of Law Reform: Twelve Lectures on the Changes in the Law of England During the 19th Century, Delivered in the Old Hall, Lincoln's Inn. L, 1901, 8vo, 431pp., $45.00

CHADBOURN, Jas., Lynching & the Law. Univ. of No. Carolina, 1933, 8vo, 221pp., $22.50

CHANDLER & SALISBURY, Du Pont & the Making of the Modern Corporation. NY, 1971, roy8vo, 475pp, $25.00

CHAPMAN, John, Fiscal Functions of the Federal Reserve Banks. NY, 1923, 8vo, 213pp., $20.00

Report of the Trial of the Hon. Samuel Chase, One of the Associate Justices of the Supreme Court of the United States, Before the High Court of Impeachment Composed of the Senate of the United States, for Charges Exhibited Against Him by the House of Reps....with the Necessary Documents & Official Papers, from His Impeachment to Final Acquittal, Taken down in Short Hand by Chs. Evans & the Arguments of Counsel Revised by Them from His Manuscript. Balto, 1805, 268pp; bound with this: Impeachment of Samuel Chase, Esq....withthe Articles Exhibited Against Him by the House of Representatives....with His Answer & Pleas. Likewise the Replication of the House of Reps. Balto, 1805, 68pp., bound in later 1/2 calf & bds. $350.00

CHASE, Stuart, Men & Machines. NY, 1937, 8vo, 354pp., $12.50

(CHICAGO), Sullivan's Chicago Law Directory, 1924-25, An Official List of Members of the Bar, with full Information about the Courts, Officials & Rules of Practice. 48th Annual Ed., 8vo, 290pp., orig. ptd. cloth, $27.50

(CHICAGO), Gunthorp's Legal Directory of Chicago, 1928, 25th Annual Edition. 8vo, 408pp., $25.00

(CHICAGO), Sullivan's Chicago Law Directory, 1933-34, 57th Annual Edition, 8vo, 470pp., $25.00

CHOATE, Rufus, Addresses & Orations. B, 1879, 8vo, 529pp., $37.50

CHOUKROUN, Chs., Les Droits des Associes non Gerants dans les Societies a Responsabilite Limitee. P, 1957, roy8vo, 233pp., wrps, $22.50

CHRIMES, S. B., English Constitutional Ideas in the 15th Century. Camb. UP, 1936, roy8vo,415p. $35.00

CHRISTOPH, Jas., Capital Punishment & British Politics. Univ. of Chicago, 1962, 8vo, 202pp., $22.50

CHURCH, F. J., The Trial & Death of Socrates. L, 1880, 8vo, 190pp., $22.50

CHUTE, Marchette, The First Liberty: History of the Right to Vote in America, 1619-1850. NY, 1969, 8vo, 371pp., $22.50

Civil War Pamphlet Collection, 1852-1865, about 140 titles, price: $2500.00 details on request.

CLAPHAM, John, An Economic History of Modern Britain: III: Machines & National Rivalries, 1887-1914, with an Epilogue, 1914-1929. Camb, UP, 1963, roy8vo, 577pp., $25.00

CLARENDON, Edward Earl of, The History of the Rebellion & Civil Wars in England...written by the Rt. Hon. Late Lord High Chancellor of England. Oxford, 1702, tall folio, 3vols., contemp. calf, expertly rebacked, beautiful set, first edition, Grolier Club List of 100 Books Famous in English Literature, $575.00

CLARK, Roger, A UN High Commissioner for Human Rights. Hague, 1972, roy8vo, 186pp., $22.50

CLINTON, Henry Lauren, Extraordinary Cases.. NY, 1896, 8vo, 403pp., $27.50

COBDEN, Richard, Speeches on Questions of Public Policy. ed. by John Bright & Jas. T. Rogers, L, 1870, roy8vo, 2vols., very slight wear, first edition, $75.00

COCKBURN,Hanry, Circuit Journeys. Edinburgh, 1889, 8vo, 420pp., $22.50

COGLEY, John, & HUTCHINS, Rob., Natural Law & Modern Society. Cl., 1961, 8vo, 285pp., $22.50

COHEN, Edw., Ancient Athenian Maritime Courts. Princeton UP, 1973, 8vo, 233pp., $22.50

)COHEN, Morris & COHEN, F., Readings in Jurisprudence & Legal Philosophy. NY, 1951, 4to, 944p,$35.00

)COKE, Sir Edward, Certain Select Cases in Law....Translated out of a Manuscript Written in His Own Hand, Never Before Published. L, 1659, 4to, 72pp., bound in 18th century sheep, expertly rebacked, nice copy, rare, NUC reports only one copy in No. America, first edition, $750.00

)COLE-BETHEL, Lillian, Compendium & Question Book of Parliamentary Law. Co, 1892, 16mo, 68pp., $15.00

)COLLINGWOOD, R. G., & MYRES, J., Roman Britain & the English Settlements. 2nd ed., Oxford, 1937, 8vo, 515pp., $35.00

)Colonial Laws & Courts, with a Sketch of the Legal Systems of the World and Tables of Conditions of Appeal to the Privy Council, under the General Editorship of Alexander Renton & Geo. Phillmore, (Reprinted from Burge's Commentaries on Colonial & Foreign Laws). L, 1907, 4to, 420pp, $65.00

)COMMONS, John & ANDREWS, J., Principles of Labor Legislation. 4th ed., rev. NY, 1936, 8vo,606p $25.00

)Compilation of Senate Election Cases, 1789-1885, by Geo. Taft; Continued to1893 by Geo. Furber; Cont'd to 1903 by Geo. Buck. DC, GPO, 1903, roy8vo, 993pp., (Senate, 58th Cong, Sp. Ses, Doc 11), contemp. 1/2 morocco, $37.50

)The Computer & the Invasion of Privacy: Hearings before A Subcommittee on Govt. Operations, H.R. 89th Cong., 2nd Ses, roy8vo, 311pp., 1966, $22.50

159) COOLEY, Thomas, The General Principles of Constitutional Law of the U.S. 3rded., by Andrew McLaughlin, B, 1898, 8vo, 423pp., $30.00

160)COOPER, Frank, State Administrative Law. Ind., 1965, roy8vo, 2vols., $37.50

161) COULTON, G. G., Inquisition & Liberty. L, 1938, roy8vo, 354pp., scarce, $35.00

162) COX, Jos., The Recluse of Herald Square: Mystery of Ida Wood. NY, 1964, 8vo,246p,$17.50

163) CRAGG, Gerald, Freedom & Authority: A Study of English Thought in the Early 17th Century. P, 1975, roy8vo, 334pp., $22.50

CREECH, Margaret, Three Centuries of Poor Law Administration: A Study of Legislation in Rhode Island. Univ. oc Chicago Prrss, 1936, roy8vo, 331pp., $27.50

Crim. Con. Actions & Trials & Other Legal Proceedings Relating to Marriage Before the Passing of the Present Divorce Act. L, n.d. 8vo, 110pp., later linen, scarce $37.50

CROKE, J. G. (ed.), Poems of the Law. SF, 1885, 12mo, 311pp., $27.50

CROMWELL, Oliver, Writings & Speeches, with Intro., Notes, & Sketch of His Life by Wilbur Abbott. Harvard, 1937, roy8vo, 2vols., 1500pp., $75.00

CURRAN, Barbara, Trends in Consumer Credit Legislation. Univ. of Chicago, 1965, 4to, 394p, $25.00

CURTIS, Geo. Ticknor, Constitutional History of the United States from the Declaration of Independenc to the Close of the Civil War. NY, 1895, roy8vo, 2vols., classic work, $75.00

CURTIS, Geo. Ticknor, Life of Daniel Webster. 2nd ed.,NY,1870, roy8vo, 2vols., contemp. 1/2 morocco, sl. dpst. few leaves, $57.50

CZERNIN, Ferdinand, Versailles, 1919. NY, 1964, 8vo, 437pp., $20.00

DAINOW, Jos. (ed.), The Role of Judicial Decisions & Doctrines in Civil Law & in Mixed Jurisdictions. St. Louis Univ. Pr., 1974, roy8vo, 350pp., $22.50

DARROW, Clarence, The Story of My Life. NY, 1934. 8vo, 495pp., $30.00

DARROW, Cl., Verdicts Out of Court. ed. A. Weinberg, C, 1963, roy8vo, 448pp., $27.50

(DARROW), Attorney Clarence Darrow's Plea for Mercy and Prosecutor Robert E. Crowe's Demand for the Death Penalty in the Loeb-Leopold Case. C. n.d. (1926), 8vo, 164pp., orig. ptd. wrps, sl. stain, very scarce, $35.00

DARROW, Clarence, Farmington. NY, 1919, 8vo, 220pp., $25.00

DAVIDSON, Eugene, The Trial of the Germans: Nuremberg,1945-6. NY, 1966, roy8vo, 636pp., $27.50

DAVIS, Andrew, The Origin of the National Banking System. Dc, GPO, 1910, 8vo, 212pp., wrps, $22.50

DAVIS, H.W., England Under the Normans & Angevins. L, 1905, roy8vo, 577pp., $25.00

DAVIS, Jefferson, The Rise & Fall of the Confederate Government. L, 1881, roy8vo, 2v. lat. lin, $75.0

DAVIS, Kenneth C., Discretionary Justice. Louisiana St. UP, 1969, roy8vo, 233pp., $20.00

DAWES, Chs., A Journal of the Reparations. L, 1939, 8vo, 527pp., (Chairman of the First Committee of Experts, Reparation Commission, 1924), $27.50

DEAN, Arthur, William Nelson Cromwell, 1854-1948: An American Pioneer in Corporation, Comparative & International Law. NY, 1957, roy8vo, 237pp., $25.00

DEANS, R., Notable Trials: Romances of the Law Courts. L, n.d. (1906, 8vo, 349pp., $25.00

DE COULANGES, Fustel, The Ancient City: A Study in the Religion, Laws & Institutions of Greece & Rome. tr. W. Small, B, 1873, 8vo, 527pp., sl. cov. soil, $30.00

DE HAAS, Jacob, Louis D. Brandeis: A Biographical Sketch with Special Reference to His Contributions to Jewish & Zionist History. NY, 1929, 8vo, 296pp., $25.00

DE LOLME, J. L., The Constitution of England, or an Account of the English Government, in which it is Compared both with the Republican Form of Government, and the Other Monarchies of Europe. 4th ed., corr. & enl., L, 1784, 8vo, 540pp., later 1/2 calf, classic work, $125.00

DELUPIS, Imgard, International Law & the Independent State.L, 1974, roy8vo, 252pp., $22.50

DE MARTENS, Chs., Le Guide Diplomatique: Precis des Droits et des Fonctions des Agents Diplomatiques et Consulaires. 5thed., Leipzig, 1865, roy8vo, 2vols.as one, 1000pp., contemp. 1/2 mor, $115.00

DEWEY, Davis, State Banking Before the Civil War: bound with: CHADDOCK, Rob., The Safety Fund Banking System in New York, 1829-1866. DC, GPO, 1910, 8vo, 388pp., wrps., $25.00

DEWEY, Davis., Financial Historyof the US. 12th ed., NY, 1934, 8vo, 600pp., $25.00

DEWING, Arthur, The Financial Policy of Corporations. 4th ed. NY, 1941, roy8vo, 2vols., $37.50

DICEY, A. V., Lectures on the Relation Between Law & Public Opinion in England during the 19th Century. L, 1905, roy8vo, 503pp., $30.00

DICKINSON, J.C., The Great Charter: Translation with Intro. & Notes. L, 1968, 8vo, 31pp.,wrps, $15.00

DICKINSON, Z.C., Collective Wage Determination: Problems & Principles in Bargaining, Arbitration & Legislation. NY, 1941, 8vo, 640pp., $27.50

DIGBY, Kenelm, Introduction to the History of the Law of Real Property. 4th ed, Oxford,1892,$27.50

DILLON, John, The Laws & Jurisprudence of England & America. B, 1894, roy8vo, 431pp., $35.00

DIXON, Hepworth, John Howard & the Prison World of Europe, from Original & Authentic Documents. Mass, 1852, 8vo, 442pp., $37.50

DOUGLAS, David, William the Conqueror: The Norman Impact upon England. Univ. of Cal. Press, 1964, roy8vo, 476pp., $27.50

DOUGLAS, William O., North from Malaya: Adventure on Five Fronts. NY, 1953, 8vo, 352pp., first ed. scarce, $30.00

DUBLIN, Louis, & LOTKA, A.., The Money Value of a Man. rev.ed., NY, 1946, roy8vo, 214p., $22.50

DUER, Wm., A Course of Lectures on the Constitutional Jurisprudence of the US. 2nd ed., rev. & enl. B, 1856, 8vo, 545pp., rebacked, $65.00

DUNCAN, G. T. O., The High Court of Delegates. Cambridge UP, 1971, 8vo, 318pp., $27.50

DUNKEL, Wilbur, William Lambarde, Elizabethan Jurist, 1536-1601. Rutgers UP, 1965, 8vo,201p, $22.50

EAST, Edward Hyde, A Treatise of the Pleas of the Crown. P, 1806, 8vo, 2vols., later 1/2 calf & bds. The author spent 15 years on the work and "because he had access to private collections of cases, his treatise is the result of a most thorough examination and sifting of all the English Crown Law....still a standard work upon Criminal Law." Marvin, 286. $150.00

EBENSTEIN, Wm., The Pure Theory of Law. (1945), 1969, 8vo, 211pp., $17.50

EDWARDS, Corwin, The Price Discrimination Law. DC, 1959, roy8vo,698pp. $27.50

EDWARDS, Corwin, Trade Regulation Overseas: National Laws. NY, 1966, roy8vo,752pp, $25.00

EDWARDS, Rob., & MAGEE, J., Technical Analysis of Stock Trends. Mass, 1948, 8vo, 431pp., $20.00

ELLIOT, Mabel, Conflicting Penal Theories in Statutory Criminal Law. Unvi. of Chi,1931,8vo, $25.00

ELY, Richard, Taxation in American States & Cities. NY, 1888, 8vo, 544pp., $27.50

EMERSON, Th., The System of Freedom of Expression. NY, 1970, roy8vo, 754pp., $27.50

ENGBERG, Edw., The Spy in the Corporate Structure & the Right to Privacy. NY, 1967, roy8vo,274p,$25.00

ERNST, Morris, & SCHWARTZ, A., Censorship: Search for the Obscene. NY, 1964, 8vo, 287pp., $17.50

ESPINASSE, Isaac, A Digest of the Law of Actions & Trials at Nisi Prius. 3rd American from the 3rd London ed., Walpole, 1808, 8vo, 2vols., contemp. roan, sl. rubbed, nice set, $87.50

Every Day Ethics. Yale UP, (with a lengthy chapter on lawyer-client relations), 1910, 150pp, $17.50

FARRAND, Maxx, The Records of the Federal Convention of 1787. Yale UP,1911, 4to, 3vols., $75.00

FARRER, Jas., Crimes & Punishments, Including a New Translation of Beccaria's 'Dei Delitti e delle Pene.' L, 1880, 8vo, 251pp., $35.00

FARRAR, Timothy, Report of the Case of the Trustees of Dartmouth College against Wm. Woodward, Argued in the Superior Court of Judicature of the State of New Hampshire, Nov., 1817, and on Error, in the Supreme Court of the U.S., Feb. 1819. Portsmouth, (1819), roy8vo, 406pp., later linen, light sporadic foxing, uncut, first edition, still the major source for this seminal case, $125.00

FAWCETT, Sir Chs., The First Century of British Justice in India: An Account of the Court of Judicature at Bombay, established in 1672, and of Other Courts of Justice in Madras, Calcutta & Bombay, from 1661 to the Latter Part of the 18th Century. Oxford UP, 1934, roy8vo, 269pp., scarce, $37.50

The Federalist....also the Continentalist & other Papers by Alexander Hamilton. ed. by Jbbh C. Hamilton, P, 1904, roy8vo, 658pp., $27.50

The Federalist, ed. with Intro. & Notes by Jacob Cooke. Wesleyan UP, 1961, roy8vo, 672pp., $30.00

FELDMAN, Franklin, & WEIL, S., Art Works: Law, Policy & Practice. NY, 1974, roy8vo, 1240pp., $30.00

FELIX,David, Walter Rathenau & the Weimar Republic: The Polirics of Reparations. Johns Hopkins Univ. Pr., 1971, roy8vo, 210pp., $22.50

FENN, Dan (ed.), Management's Mission in a New Society. NY, 1959, 8vo, 345pp., $17/50

FENWICK, The Proceedings against Sir John Fenwick, Bar., Upon a Bill of Attainder for High Treason... L, 1702, 8vo, 348pp., conte mp. calf, sl. scuffed, front hinge cracked but firm, $75.00

FENWICK, Chs., Cases on International Law. 2nd ed., rev. & enl., C, 1951, 4to, 895pp., $35.00

FEUER, Mort., Personal Liabilities of Corporate Officers & Directors. NJ, 1961, 4to, 240pp., $25.00

FINLASON, W. F., Reeve's History of English Law from the Time of the Romans to the Reign of Queen Elizabeth, and an Introductory Dissertation on the Nature & Use of Legal History, the Rise & Progress of Our Laws, & the Influence of Roman Law in the Formation of Our Own. New American ed., P, 1880, 8vo, 5vols., orig. cl., sl. wear, $175.00

FINN, R. W., Domesday Studies: The Liber Exoniensis. L,1964, 8vo, 172pp., $22.50

FISHER, Irving, The Stock Market Crash& After. NY, 1930, 8vo, 286pp., new linen, $30.00

FISHER, Wm., The Forest of Essex: Its History, Laws,Administration & Ancient Customs. L, 1887, 4to, 446pp., later linen, $65.00

FLETA, Sue Commentarius Juris Anglicani, Sic Nuncupatus sub Edwardo Rege Primo, Seu Circa Annos Abhnic CCCXL ab Anonymo Conscriptus, atque e Codice Vteri, Autore ipso Aliquantilum recentiori, Nunc Primum Typis Editus, Accedit Tractatulus vetus de Agendi Excipiendai Formulis Gallicanus Fet Assavoir Dictus, Subjungitur etiam Joan. Seldeniad Fletam Dissertatio Historica. Editio Secunda, Multis Erroribus Purgata. L, 1685, small4to, 553pp., later 1/2 calf, sl. sporadic foxing & sl. trace embrowning, $275.00

FONER, Philip, The Fur & Leather Workers Union. Newark, 1950, roy8vo, 708pp., $20.00

FORBES, Russell, Governmental Purchasing. NY, 1929, roy8vo, 369pp., $27.50

FORD, Paul L. (ed.), Pamphlets on the Constitution of the U.S. Published during Its Discussion by the People, 1787-1788., with Notes & Bibliography.NY, 1888, roy8vo, 451pp., ex lib, $35.00

FORDHAM, Edw (ed.),Notable Cross-Examinations. L, 1951, 8vo, 202pp., $22.50

FORSYTH, W., Hortensius: An Historical Essay on the Office & Duties of an Advocate. 3rd ed., L, 1879, 8vo,431pp., $45.00

FOSS, Edw., Biographia Juridica: A Biographical Dictionary of the Judges of England from the Conquest to the Present Time. L, 1870, roy8vo, 792pp., later linen, $75.00

FOSS, Edw., Memories of Westminster Hall: A Collection of Interesting Incidents, Anecdotes & Historical Sketches Relating to Westminster Hall, Its Famous Judges & Lawyers & Its Great Trials, with an Historical Introduction. B, 1874, roy8vo, 2vols., $87.50

FOUILLEE, A. et al., Modern French Legal Philosophy. B, 1916, 8vo, 578pp., $25.00

FRANK, Jerome, A Man's Reach: The Philosophy of Judge Jerome Frank: Selected Writings. ed. B. Kristein. NY, 1965, roy8vo, 450pp., $25.00

FRANK, Judge Jerome & Barbara, Not Guilty. NY, 1957, 8vo, 249pp., $25.00

FRANKFURTER, Frlix, The Case of Sacco & Vanzetti. B, 1927, 8vo, 118pp., 1st ed, later issue, $35.00

FRANKFURTER, Felix & GREENE, Nathan, The Labor Injunction. NY, 1930, roy8vo, 343pp., 1st ed, $45.00

FRANKFURTER, Felix, A Selection of Cases Under the Interstate Commerce Act. 2nd ed., Harvard, 1922, roy8vo, 798pp., orig. cl., bit of underlining & marginalia, scarce, $75.00

FREEMAN, A. C., Treatise of the Law of Judgments. 5th ed., rev. & enl. SF, 1925, 4to, 3vols, $75.00

FRIEDLAENDER, Ann, Dilemma of Freight Transportation Regulation.DC, 1969, roy8vo, 216pp., $20.00

FRIEDRICH, Carl (ed.), Revolution:(Nomos, Yearbook of the American Society for Political & Legal Philosophy, Vol. VIII), NY, 1967, 8vo, 246pp., $22.50

GAIUS, The Institutes of, Text with Critical Notes, Translation & Commentary by F. de Zulueta. Oxford, 1953, 8vo, 2vols., $65.00

GALLOWAY, Geo., The Legislative Process in Congress. NY, 1964, 8vo, 687pp., $25.00

252) GAREIS, Karl, Introduction to the Science of Law; trans. Alber Kocourek, Intro. by Roscoe Pound. B, 1911, 8vo, 375pp., $27.50

253) GARVER, John, John William Sterling: Biographical Sketch. Yale UP, 1929, roy8vo, 113pp., scarce, (of Sherman & Sterling), $27.50

254) GELDART, W.T., Elements of English Law. L, 1910, 12mo, 256pp., $22.50

255) Geneva Convention of 12 August 1949: Commentary, III: Geneva Convention Relative to the Treatment of Prisoners of War, by Jean de Preux. 1960,roy8vo,764p, $25.00

Geneva Convention of 12 August 1949; Commentary, I: Geneva Convention for the Amelioration of the Wounded & Sick in Armed Forces in the Field. 1952, roy8vo, 466pp., $25.00

GETTYS, Luella, The Law of Citizenship in the US. C, 1934, 8vo, 221pp., $20.00

GIFFEN, Jas., Legal & Practical Aspects of Trade with the Soviet Union. NY, 1969, roy8vo,371p,$25.00

GILLETTE, Wm., The Right to Vote: Politics & the Passage of the 15th Amendment. Johns Hopkins Univ. Pr., 1965, roy8vo, 181pp., $22.50

GINNELL, Laurence, The Brehon Laws: A Legal Handbook. L, 1894, 8vo, 249pp., $35.00

GLANVILLE, De Legibus et Consuetudinibus Regni Angliae. ed. Geo. Woodbine, Yale UP, 1932, roy8vo, 306pp., $45.00

GLOVER, Edw., The Roots of Crime (Selected Papers on Psycho-Analysis, II), NY, 1960, roy8vo,422p,$22.50

GLUCKMAN, Max, The Judicial Process Among the Barotse of Northern Rhodesia. 2nd e.d, corr. Manchester UP, 1967, 8vo, 469pp., $27.50

GODLEY, Leon, Outline of Equity. 2nd ed., NY, 1931, roy8vo, 214pp., $22.50

GODWIN, Wm., Political Justice: A Reprint of the Essay on "Property" from the Original Edition. ed. H. S. Salt. L, 1890, 8vo, 155pp., $22.50

GOLDFARB, Ronald, The Contempt Power. Columbia UP, 1963, roy8vo, 366pp., $22.50

GRAHAM, Benj. & MC GOLRICK, C., The Interpretation of Financial Statements. 2nd ed., rev. NY, 1964, 8vo, 117pp., $17.50

GRAVEN, Jean, Le Difficile Progres du Regne de la Justice et de la Paix Internationales par le Droit, des Origines a la Societe des Nations. P, 1970, roy8vo, 602pp., $22.50

GRAVES, W. B. (ed.), Intergovernmental Relations in the US. NY, 1978, roy8vo,218pp., $22.50

GRAVESON, R. H., Law: An Outline for Intending Students. L, 1967, 8vo, 207pp., $22.50

GREELEY, Horace, & CLEVELAND, John, A Political Text-Book for 1860....also a History of the Struggle Respecting Slavery in the Territories and of the Action of Congress as to the Freedom ofthe Public Lands. NY, 1860, roy8vo, 248pp., $47.50

GREEN, Leon, Judge & Jury. KC, 1930, roy8vo, 429pp., $37.50

GREGORY, Chs., Labor & the Law. NY, 1946, 8vo, 467pp., $25.00

GRISEZ, Germain, Contraception & the Natural Law. Mil., 1964, 8vo, 245pp., $20.00

GROSECLOSE, Elgir, Money: The HumanConflict: A Survey of Monetary Experience. Univ. of Oklahoma, 1934, roy8vo, 304pp., $22.50

GROSS, Hanns, Empire & Sovereignty: A History of the Public Law Literature in the Holy Roman Empire 1599-1804. Univ. oc Chicago, 1973, 8vo, 541pp., wrps., $25.00

GROSS, Leo (ed.)., The Future of the Int'l Court of Justice. NY, 1976, roy8vo, 2vols., $35.00

GROTIUS, Hugo, De Imperio Summarum Potestatum Circa Sacra, Cui Accedunt: David Blondel, De Jure Plebis in Regimine Ecclesiastico, et de Officio Magustratus Christiani de Alius Autoris. (1690) Reprint: 1970, small4to, 315pp., $35.00

HAINES, Chs G., The American Doctrine of Judicial Supremacy. NY, 1914, 8vo, 365pp., $22.50

HALASZ, Nick., Captain Dreyfus: A Story of Mass Hysteria. NY, 1955, 8vo, 274pp., $22.50

HALE, Sir Matthew, The Historyof the Common Law of England. 3rd ed., Corm, London, 1739; bound with his: The Analysis of the Law: Being a Scheme or Abstract of the Several Titles & Partitions of the Law of England Digested into Method. 3rd ed., corr. L, 1739, 148pp., 8vo, bound in contemp. calf, expertly rehinged, nice copy, $250.00

HALL, Wm., Treatise on International Law. 7th ed. Oxford, 1917, roy8vo, 864pp., $30.00

HAMILTON, Earl, REES, Albert, & JOHNSON, Harry, (ed.s), Landmarks in Political Economy: Selected Articles from the Journal of Political Economy. Unvi. of Chicago, 1962, roy8vo, 622pp., (includes papers by Veblen, Pareto, Viner, Knight, Friedman & Schumpeter), $30.00

HAMMOND, Basil, Bodies Politic & Their Governments. Cambridge UP, 1915, 8vo,555ppp., $35.00

HAMPE, Theodor, Crime & Punishment in Germany, as Illustrated by the Nuremberg Malefactor's Book. translation with introduction by Malcolm Letts. L, 1929, 8vo, 175pp., $22.50

HANSEN, Altin, The Dollar & the Int'l Monetary System. NY, 1965, 8vo, 290pp., $20.00

HARDING, Arthur, Double Taxation of Property & Income. Harvard, 1933 (Harvard Studies in the Conflict of Laws, I), roy8vo, 326pp., $27.50

HARRIS, Richard, Mr. Bumpkin's Lawsuit: or, How to Win Your Opponent's Case. L, 1883, 8vo, 385pp., scarce, $35.00

HARRIS, Richard, Before & at Trial: What Should be Done by Counsellor, Solicitor. 1st American from the 2nd London ed., NY, 1890, 8vo, 399pp., $25.00

Harris, Richard, Hints on Advocacy intended for Practice in Any of the Courts. rev. & adapted from the2nd English edition by an American Lawyer. St.L, 1890, 8vo, 172pp., $27.50

HARRIS, Virgil, Ancient, Curious & Famous Wills. B, 1911, roy8vo, 472pp., $30.00

HARROD, R. F., Life of John Maynard Keynes. L, 1951, roy8vo, 674pp., later line, $25.00

Harvard Legal Essays, Written in Honor of and Presented to Jos. Henry Beale & Samuel Williston. Harvard UP, 1934 roy8vo, 553pp., $35.00

HARVEY, Peter, Reminiscences & Anecdotes of Daniel Webster. B, 1909, 8vo, 480pp., $22.50

HASKINS, Chs. H., The Normans in European History.(1915), 1970, 8vo, 258pp., $22.50

HAUSNER, Gideon, Justice in Jerusalem (Eichmann Trial)NY, 1966, roy8vo, 528pp., $25.00

HAY, Peter, Federalism & Supranational Organizations: Patterns for New Legal Structures. Univ. of Illinois Press, 1966, roy8vo, 335pp., $25.00

HAYASHI, Taizo, Guide to Japanese Taxes, 1973-74. T, 1973, 8vo, 727pp., $22.50

HAYES, Wm., Principles for Expounding Dispositions of Real Estate to Ancestor & Heirs in Tail, Parent & Issue. P, 1835, 8vo, 110pp., $37.50

HAYNES, Evan, The Selection & Tenure of Judges. 1944, roy8vo, 308pp., $25.00

HERBERT, Wm., The History of the Twelve Great Livery Companies of London. (1834) L, 1968, roy8vo, 2vols., $37.50

HICKS, Fred, Men & Books Famous in the Law. Ro., 1921, 8vo, 259pp., $22.50

HICKS, John, Capital & Growth. Oxford UP, 1965, 8vo, $22.50

HICKS, John, Value & Capital. 2nded., Oxford UP, 1965, 8vo, 340pp., $22.50

HILL, Frederick, Decisive Battles of the Law. NY, 1907, 8vo, 267pp., sl. dpst., $20.00

HILL, Fred., Lincoln the Lawyer. NY, 1906, 8vo, 332pp., $22.50

The History and Antiquities of the Four Inns of Court & the Nine Inns of Chancery....to which is Subjoined an Appendix, Containing Several Modern Orders, Made Up by the Society of Lincoln's Inn....and also a List of the Present Benchers of the Four Inns of Court. The Whole is Published by the Desire of Some Members of Paul, in Order to Point Out the Abuses in the Govt. of the Four Inns of Court & Chancery, and to Propose Such Expedients for Remedying Them & Regulating the Study & Practice of the Law by Act of Parliament as Shall be Judged Necessary.L, 1780, 8vo, xx,251pp., contemp. calf, rebacked, nice copy, $175.00

HOBBES, Thomas, A Dialogue Between a Philosopher & a Student of the Laws of England, ed.with Intro. by Jos. Cropsey. Univ. of Chicago, 1971, roy8vo, 168pp, $22.50

HOBMAN, J. B., (ed.), Palestine's Economic Future: A Review of Progress & Prospects. L, 1946, 4to, 309, cxpp., ill., $45.00

HOLBORN, Louise (ed.), War & Peace Aims of the UN, Sept. 1939 to Sept. 1945. B, World Peace Foundation, 1948, roy8vo, 2vols., 1300pp., $45.00

HOLDEN, Paul, Top Management Organization & Control. Harvard, 1941, roy8vo, 239pp., $20.00

HOLDSWORTH, Wm., Sources & Literature of English Law. Oxford UP, 1925, 8vo, 247pp., $27.50

HOLLAND, Th. E., Elements of Jurisprudence. 6th ed., Oxford UP, 1893, roy8vo, 395pp., $22.50

HOLMES-POLLOCK, The Correspondence of Mr. Justice Holmes & Sir Frederick Pollock, 1874-1932. Harvard UP, 1941, roy8vo,2vols., $45.00

HOLMES-LASKI, The Correspondence of Mr. Justice Holmes & Harold J. Laski, 1916-1935, ed. Mark de Wolfe Howe. Harvard, 1953, roy8vo, 2vols., $57.50

HOLYBAND, Claudius (Claude de Sainliens), The French Littleton, the Edition of 1609, with Intro. by M. C. Byrne. Cambridge UP, 1953, 8vo, xxxii,220pp., $30.00

HOMANS, Geo., English Villiages of the 13th Century. NY, 1960, roy8vo, 478pp., $25.00

HONNOLD, John, The Life of the Law: Readings in the Growth of Legal Institutions. Glencoe, 1964, roy8vo, 581pp., $30.00

HORVITZ, Paul, Monetary Policy & the Finaicial System. 2nd ed., NJ, 1969, 8vo, 525pp., $22.50

HOWARD, Chs., & SUMMERS, Rbb., Law: Its Nature, Functions & Limits. NJ, 1965, roy8vo, 466pp., few pp. underlined, $22.50

HOWE, Mark de Wolfe, Justice Oliver Wendell Holmes. Harvard, 1957-63, roy8vo, 2vols., $45.00

HURD, Richard, Principles of City Land Values. 2nd ed., NY, 1905, roy8vo, 159pp., $22.50

HUSKISSON, Wm., Speeches of, with a Biographical Memoir. L, 1831, 8vo, 3vols., bound in contemp. calf, slightly rubbed, beautiful set, first edition, $250.00

HUTCHINS, B. L., & HARRISON, A., History of Factory Legislation. 3rded., NY, 1966, 8vo,298pp,$20.00

Justinian, Institutionum, with Intro & Commentary by J.B. Moyle. Oxford, 1912, roy8vo,682pp,$47.50

Justinian, Institutes, with Notes by Th. Cooper. P, 1812, roy8vo, 714pp., roan, $65.00

The Irish Pound, 1797-1826: A Reprint of the Report of the Committee in the British House of Commons,..with Intro. by W. Fetter. Northwestern UP, 1955, 8vo, 134pp., $17.50

IRVING, H. B., The Life of Judge Jeffreys. NY, 1906, 8vo, 380pp., $30.00

JACKSON, R. M., The Machinery of Justice in England. Cambridge UP, 1940, 8vo, 342pp., $22.50

JACOBS, Clyde, Law Writers & the Law Courts: The Influence of Cooley, Tiedeman & Dillon upon American Constitutional Law. Univ. of Cal., 1954, 8vo, 223pp., $22.50

JAPAN: Laws, Ordinances & Other Regulations Concerning Foreign Exchange & Foreign Trade. T, 1969, 8vo, 925pp., $27.50

JAY, Cyrus, The Law: What I Have Seen, What I have Heard, What I have Known. L, 1868, 8vo, 351pp., $35.00

JEAFFRESON, John, Pleasantries about English Courts & Lawyers: A Book about Lawyers. NY, 1876, 8vo, 322pp., $37.50

JENKS, Edw., A Short History of English Law. B, 1913, 8vo, 390pp., $25.00

JENKS, Edw., Law & Politics in the Middle Ages. NY, 1905, roy8vo, 352p; $30.00

JENSEN, Andrew, The Trial of Chaplain Jensen. NY, 1974, 8vo, 288pp., $17.50

JEVONS, W. Stanley, The Theory of Political Economy, with Notes and an Extension of the Bibliography of Mathematical Economics by H. S. Jevons. 4th ed., L, 1924, roy8vo, 339pp., some pencil underlining, $35.00

JEVONS, W. Stanley, Methods of Social Reform and Other Papers. L, 1883, roy8vo, viii,383pp., orig. cloth, the very slightest trace of wear at crown, nice copy, first edition, $375.00

JEVONS, W. Stanley, Money and the Mechanism of Exchange. NY, 1887, 8vo, 349pp., rebacked, $35.00

JOHNSON, Arlien, Public Policy and Private Charities: A Study of Legislation in the US and of Administration in Illinois. Univ. of Chicago, 1931, roy8vo, 230pp., $25.00

JOHNSON, Harry G., Essays in Monetary Economics. 2nd ed, Harvard, 1969, 8vo, 332pp., $22.50

JOINER, Chs., Civil Justice & the Jury. NJ, 1962, 8vo, 238pp., $22.50

JOLIFFE, J.E., The Constitutional History of Medieval England. 3rded.,L, 1954, roy8vo,524p,$35.00

JOLOWICZ, H. F., Roman Foundations of Modern Law. Oxford, 1961, 8vo, 277pp., $30.00

345) JONES, Alfred, Life, Liberty & Property: A Story of Conflict & a Measure of Conflicting Rights. P, 1941, 8vo, 397pp., $22.50

346) JONES, A. H. M., Sparta. Harvard, 1967, 8vo, 189pp., $22.50

347) JONES, Wm., An Essay on the Law of Bailments. Dublin, 1790, 8vo, 100p, linen, $45.00

JONES, Lawrence, Investment Policies of Life Insurance Companies. Harvard, 1968, 8vo,568pp., $22.50

KATCHER, Leo, Earl Warren: A Political Biography. NY, 1967, roy8vo, 502pp., $27.50

KEIGWIN, Chs., Cases in Common Law Pleading, with Summaries of Doctrine upon Several Heads of that Subject. R, 1924, roy8vo, 777pp., some underlining, $25.00

KEIR, D.L., Constitutional History of Modern Britain, 1485-1937. NY, 1938, roy8vo, 568pp., $35.00

KEISER, Norman, Macroeconomics, Fiscal Policy & Economic Growth. NY, 1964, 8vo, 525pp., $22.50

KEMMERER, Edwin, & DONALD, The ABC of the Federal Reserve System. 12th ed. NY, 1950, 8vo,229p, $22.50

KENNEDY, John, Memoirs of the Life of William Wirt. new & rev. ed., P, 1850, 8vo, 2vols., $47.50

KENT, James, Memoirs & Letters of. B, 1898, 8vo, 341pp., $35.00

KENT, James, Commentaries on American Law, 12th edition, edited by Oliver Wendell Holmes; and 13th edition, edited by Chs. Barnes. B, 1884, roy8vo, 4vols., the best edition of this classic work, with the complete notes of Holmes and Barnes' addition of subsequent cases, new linen, $250.00

KENYON, J. P., The Stuart Constitution: Documents & Commentary, 1603-1688. Cambridge UP, 1966, roy8vo, 523pp., wrps., $ bit of underlining, $22.50

KEYNES, John Maynard, A Treatise on Money. London, Macmillan, 1930, 8vo, 2vols., fine set in the original cloth with the original dust jackets, first edition, $[illegible]

KILLINGSWORTH, Chs., State labor Relations Acts: a Study of Public Policy. Univ. of Chicago, 1948, 8vo, 327pp., $25.00

KING, F. H., Farmers of 40 Centuries: Permanent Agriculture in China, Korea & Japan. P, n.d. 1900, 8vo, 379pp., $25.00

KINLEY, David, The Independent Treasury of the US & Its Relations to the Banks of the Country. DC, GPO, 1910, 8vo, 370pp., wrps., $25.00

KIRBY, Jas., Selected Articles on Criminal Justice. NY, 1926, 8vo,314pp., $20.00

KISSINGER, Henry, The Troubled Partnership: Re-Appraisal of the Atlantic Alliance. NY, 1965, 8vo, 256pp., $22.50

KOEGEL, Otto, Walter S. Carter: Collector of Young Masters, or Progenitor of Many Law Firms. NY, 1953, roy8vo, 491pp., $25.00

KONEFSKY, Samuel, Chief Justice Stone & the Supreme Court. NY, 1945, 8vo, 290pp., $22.50

KONVITZ, Milton, Fundamental Liberties of a Free People. Cornell UP, 1957, roy8vo, 420pp., $22.50

KONVITZ, Milton, A Century of Civil Rights. NY, 1961, roy8vo, 293pp., $22.50

KORKUNOV, N., General Theory of Law. B, 1909, 8vo, 524pp., $25.00

LABAND, Paul, Die Vermögenrechtlichen Klagen nach den Sachsischen Rechtsquellen des Mittelalters. B, 1869, roy8vo, 406pp., $35.00

LADAS, Stephen, The International Protection of Literary & Artistic Property: Vol. I: International Copyright & Interamerican Copyright. NY, 1938, 8vo, 679pp., ex lib, $25.00

LAKE, Jas., Law & Mineral Wealth: The Legal Profile of the Wisconsin Mining Industry. Univ. of Wisconsin Press, 1962, 8vo, 219pp., $22.50

LANGEN, Eugen, Transnational Commercial Law. Leiden, 1973, roy8vo, 279pp., $25.00

LASKI, Harold, Reflections on the Constitution. NY, 1951, 8vo, 220pp., $25.00

LASKI, Harold, Liberty in the Modern State. NY, 1949, 8vo, 175pp., $22.50

The Laws of England, Being a Complete Statement of the Whole Law of England, by the Late Earl of Halsbury....& Other Lawyers; 3rd ed., edited by Lord Simmons. L, 1952ff., roy8vo, 39vols., plus 1vol. Table of Cases; 2vol. Index; 1vol. Table of Statutes; and 6vols. of supps (to 1972), together 49 vols in excellent condition, $875.00

LAWSON, F. H., Negligence in the Civil Law. Oxford, 1955, 8vo, 341pp., $30.00

LAWSON, John, Leading Cases Simplified: A Collection of the Leading Cases of the Common Law. St.L., 1882, roy8vo, 318pp., scarce, $37.50

LEA, Henry, Superstition & Force: Essays on the Wager of Law, the Wager of Battle, the Ordeal, Torture. 2nd ed., rev., P, 1870, 8vo, 480pp., contemp. 1/2 morocco, sl. wear, $35.00

LEAGE, R. W., Roman Private Law Founded on the Institutes of Gaius & Justinian. L, 1906, roy8vo, 429pp., $27.50

LEFFLER, Geo., The Stock Market. NY, 1951, roy8vo, 626p;., $20.00

LEFTWICH, Richard, The Price System & Resource Allocation. rev.ed., NY, 1964, 8vo, 381pp., $20.00

LEVINE, Louis, The Women Garment Workers Union. NY, 1924, 8vo, 608pp., $22.50

LEVY, Beryl, Cardozo & the Frontiers of Legal Thinking.Oxford, 1938, 8vo, 315pp., $22.50

LEVY, H.P., The Press Council: History, Procedure & Cases. L, 1967, roy8vo, 505pp., $30.00

LEVY, Isaac, & SMOLENS, B. (eds.), Court is in Session, foreword by Owen H. Roberts. NY, 1950, 8vo, 241pp., $22.50

LEVY, S. L., Nassau W. Senior, 1790-1864, Critical Essayist, Classical Economist & Advisor of Governments. L, 1970, roy8vo, 336pp., $25.00

LILLY, John, A Collection of Modern Entries, or Select Pleadings in the Courts of King's Bench Common Pleas & Exchequer, to which is Added a Collection of Writs in Most Cases Now in Practice. 5th ed., L, 1791, small4to, 2vols., later 1/2 calf, $150.00

LINDQUIST, Rob., The Bank & Its Publics: Philosophy & Technique of Bank Public Relations. NY, 1956, 8vo, 289pp., $17.50

LIVINGSTON, Edward, A System of Penal Law for the United States of America, Consisting of a Code of Crimes & Punishments; A Code of Procedure in Criminal Cases; A Code of Prison Discipline & a Book of Definitions, Prepared & Presented to the House of Representstives of the United States, by Edward Livingston. Washington, Gales & Seaton, 1828, folio, x,142,187,51,45pp., contemp. roan, slight trace of wear, sound, crisp copy, first edition, $1250.00

Livingston practiced law in New York City, rising rapidly to distinction. In Congress he led the opposition to Jay's Treaty & opposed the Alien & Sedition Laws. In a celebrated case he was opposed by John Marshall. In 1804 he moved to Louisiana where he prepared a provisional code of judicial procedure. As Secretary of State Under Jackson, he prepared a number of state papers, the most important being the famous anti-nullification proclamation of 1832.

In content & organization his System of Penal Law for the US, which was never adopted, follows the code of criminal law & procedure which he prepared for Louisiana in 1824, but which was not published in full until 1833. That code, known as the "Livingston Code," "foreshadowed nearly every reform in penology in the last half century." (ESS, IX,552)It attracted wide praise in America & Europe by its remarkable simplicity & vigor. Kent, Story, Madison, Marshall & Jefferson all expressed their admiration & enthusiasm for his work. The code was reprinted in England, translated into French, and German reviewers reproduced it almost in full in their notices. Bentham proposed that the whole work be printedfof the use of the English nation and Sir Henry Maine called Livingston "the first legal genius of modern times." EB11, XVI,811.

LLOYD, Henry Demarest, Wealth Against Commonwealth. NY, 1894, roy8vo, 563pp., 1sted, $35.00

LONG, Clarence, Building Cycles & the Theory of Investment. Princeton UP, 1940, 8vo,239p, $20.00

LONG, Geo., Reflections on Certain Parts of the Law of England, with Suggestions for the Improvement of the Same. L, 1827, 8vo, 148pp., $75.00

LORD LLOYD OF HAMPSTEAD, Introduction to Jurisprudence. 3rd ed., NY, 1972, roy8vo, 873pp., $35.00

LORD RUSSELL OF LI.ERPOOL, The Record: The Trial of Adolf Eichmann. NY, 1963, 8vo, 351pp, $27.50

LORE, Martin, How to Win a Tax Case. NY, 1955, roy8vo, 244pp., $27.50

LOYN, H. R., Anglo-Saxon England & the Norman Conquest. L, 1964, 8vo, 422p., $27.50

LUCAS, Arthur, The Legal Minimum Age in Massachusetts. P, 1927, 8vo, 84pp., $17.50

LUCIEN-GRAUX, Dr., Le Maroc Economique. P, 1928, 4to, 600pp., orig. ptd. wrps., $57.50

LYON, Hastings, The Constitution & the Men Who Made It. B, 1936, 8vo, 314pp., $22.50

MABLY, Gabriel de., Le Droit Publique de L'Europe. n.p., 1746, 8vo, 2vols., calf, rubbed, $175.00

MACAULAY, Setwart, Law & the Balance of Power: Automobile Manufacturers & Their Dealers. NY, 1966, 8vo, 224pp., $22.50

MACDONALD, Wm. (ed.), Select Charters & Other Documents Illustrative of American History, 1606-1775. NY, 1899, 8vo, 401pp., $25.00

MACE, Myles, Growth & Development of Executives. Harvard, 1950, 8vo, 200pp., $20.00

MACKINNON, F. B., Contingent Fees for Legal Services: C, 1964, roy8vo, 246pp., $22.50

MAGILL, Roswell, Taxable Income. rev. ed., NY, 1945, 8vo, 491pp., $25.00

MAINE, Sir Henry Sumner, Ancient Law, first American from the 2nd London edition, with an Intro. by Theodore Dwight. NY, 1864, roy8vo, LXIX, 400pp., orig. cl., rebacked, $125.00

MAINE, Henry Sumner, Ancient Law. Intro. by Theodore Dwight. NY, 1885, roy8vo, 400p., later lin,$35.00

MAINE, Hanry Sumner, Dissertations on Early Law & Custom. NY, 1886, roy8vo, 402pp., $30.00

MAINE, Henry Sumner, Lectures on the Early History of Institutions. L, 1875, roy8vo,412pp., $27.50

MAINE, Sir Henry, Popular Government. NY, 1886, roy8vo, 261pp., sl. marg. dpst., $27.50

MAITLAND, F. W. (ed.), Pleas of the Crown for the County of Gloucester, before the Abbot of Reading & His Fellow Justices Itinerant, in the Fifth Year of the Reign of King Henry III, & the Year of Grace, 1221. L, 1884, 8vo, LII,155pp., orig. cloth, nice copy of the first edition of the author's first book, rare, only one copy reported in No. America, $150.00

MAITLAND, F. W., Domesday Book & Beyond. Cambridge, 1897, roy8vo, 527pp., rebacked, 1st ed,$75.00

MAITLAND, F. W., The Letters of, ed. by C.H.S. Fifoot. Cambridge, 1965, roy8vo, 397pp., $35.00

MAITLAND, F. W., & MONTAGUE, F., A Sketch of English Legal History. NY, 1915, 8vo, 229p., $25.00

MALTHUS, T. R., An Essay on the Principle of Population, reprinted from the Last Edition Revised by the Author, with a Biography of the Author, Full Analysis & Critical Introduction, by G. T. Bettany. L, 1890, roy8vo, XL,614pp., rebacked, $37.50

MARCHAL, Jean, & LECAILLON, T., La Repartition du Revenue National: I: Les Salaries. P, 1958, roy8vo, 667pp., $22.50

MARJORIBANKS, Edw., Carson the Advocate. NY, 1932, roy8vo, 455pp., $22.50

MARKBY, Sir Wm., Elements of Law Considered with Reference to Principles of General Jurisprudence. Oxford, 1889, 8vo, 443pp., $35.00

MARNELL, W., The First Amendment: Religious Freedom in America. NY, 1964, 8vo, 247pp., $20.00

MARSHALL, Alfred, Official Papers. L, 1926, roy8vo, 428pp., $27.50

MARSHALL, Jas., Intention in Law & Society, foreword by Wm. O Douglas. NY, 1968, 8vo,237p, $22.50

MARSHALL, John, The Life of George Washington. Va, 1926, 8vo, 5vols., (Reprint Price: $247.50) $125.00

MARSHALL, John, The Life of George Washington, Intro. by Henry St. Geo. Tucker. NY, 1930, roy8vo, 2vols., sl. cov. soil, $87.50

)MASON, Alpheus, Harlan Fiske Stone: Pillar of the Law. NY, 1956, roy8vo, 914pp., $27.50

)MASON, Alpheus, Brandeis: A Free Man's Life.NY, 1946, roy8vo, 713pp., $25.00

) MASON, Alpheus, The Supreme Court from Taft to Warren. Louisiana, 1958, 8vo, 250pp., $22.50

) MASTERS, David, Crime of the High Seas. L, 1936, roy8vo, 280pp., $30.00

) MASTERSON, Wm., Jurisdiction in Marginal Seas. NY, 1919, roy8vo, 423pp., $30.00

MATHUR, Gauton, Planning for Steady Growth. Oxford, 1965, 8vo, 386pp., $20.00

MATTHEWS, Nathan, Municipal Charters. Harvard, 1914, roy8vo, 210pp., $27.50

MATTHEWS, R. C., The Business Cycle. Univ. of Chicago, 1959, 8vo, 300pp., $22.50

MAXWELL, Jas., The Fiscal Impact of Federalism in the US. Harvard, 1946, 8vo, 427pp., $25.00

MAY, Arthur, The Valuation of Residential Real Estate. 2nd ed., JN, 1953, 8vo, 286pp., $22.50

MAYERS, Lewis, The American Legal System. rev. ed., NY, 1964, roy8vo, 594pp., $27.50

---11--

435) MC DONALD, Forrest, E Pluribus Unum: The Formation of the American Republic, 1776-1790. B, 1965, 8vo, 326pp., $22.50

436) MC DONALD, Forrest, We the People: The Economic Origins of the Constitution. Univ. of Chicago, 1958, roy8vo, 436pp., $25.00

437) MC GOVNEY, Dudley, The American Suffrage Medley: The Need for a Uniform National Suffrage. Univ. of Chicago, 1949, roy8vo, 201pp., $22.50

MAIN, Chs. H., The High Court of Parliament & Its Supremacy.(1910), 1962, 8vo, 409pp., $30.00

MC KAY, Rob., Reapportionment: Law & Politics of Equal Representation. NY, 1965, 498pp., $25.00

MC LAUGHLIN, Andrew, Constitutional History of The US. NY, 1935, 8vo, 833p., $25.00

MC MICHAEL, Stanly, Appraising Manual. 3rd ed. enl., NY, 1944, 8vo, 715pp., $35.00

MC NUTT, John C. Catalogue of the Indiana State Law Library. 1898, roy8vo, 725pp., $75.00

MEMBERS OF THE FACULTY OF THE YALE LAW SCHOOL, Two Centuries Growth of American Law, 1701-1901. NY, 1901, roy8vo, 538pp., $37.50

Memorial Addresses on the Life & Character of Isaac Wilson, Wm. Barry, Eugen Canfield, Alonzo Searles & A. C. Mc Cole, Late Members of the Kane County Bar Assn. Elgin, Ill., 1892, 8vo, 46pp., $22.50

MIDGLEY, E. B. F., The Natural Law Tradition & the Theory of International Relations. NY, 1975, roy8vo, 588pp., $30.00

MILL, John Stuart, Principles of Political Economy, from the 5th London ed. NY, 1874, roy8vo, 2vols., orig. cl., sl. wear but sound, $27.50

MILLETT, John, Government & Public Administration. NY, 1959, roy8vo, 484pp., $25.00

Minutes of the Committee of the First Commission for Detecting & Defeating Conspiracies in the State of New York, Dec 11, 1776 to Sept 23, 1778, to which is Added Minutes of the Council of Appointment, Apr 2, 1778 - May 3, 1779, New York Hist. Soc., 1924, roy8vo, 2vols., $47.50

MIRAGLIA, Luigi, Comparative Legal Philosophy. Intro. Alb. Kocourek. B, 1912, 8vo, 793pp, $27.50

MITCHELL, Sidney, Taxation in Medieval England. ed. Painter, Yale, 1951, roy8vo, 413pp., $35.00

MITTAL, R. L., Public Library Law: International Survey. Delhi, 1971, 8vo, 624pp., $25.00

MOMMSEN, Theodor, Römisches Staatsrecht, (3rd ed, 1887), Rep: 1969, roy8vo, 5vols., $175.00 still the definitive work.

MONAGHAN, Jay (ed.), Lincoln Bibliography, 1839-1939. Springfield, 1943, roy8vo, 2vols. spines bit faded (Collections of the Ill. St. Hist. Lib., XXXI; Bibliogr. Ser, IV), $47.50

MOODY, J., The Credit Union Movement, 1850-1970. Univ. of Nebraska, 1971, roy8vo, 369pp.$22.50

MOORE, John Bassett, A Digest of International Law. DC, GPO, 1906, roy8vo, 8vols., sl. rubbed and some underlining, $125.00

MORAWETZ, Victor, Banking & Currency Problems in the US. NY , 1919, 8vo, 119p. $17.50

MORGAN, Edmund, Introduction to the Study of Law. C, 1926, 8vo, 187pp., $22.50

MORRIS, Homer,Parliamentary Franchise in England, 1885-1918. NY, 1921, 8vo, 209pp., $22.50

MORRIS, Wm., The Medieval English Sheriff, to 1300. Manchester UP, 1968, 8vo, 291pp., $27.50

MORSE, John, Treatise on the Law of Banks & Banking. 3rd ed., rev. & enl., B, 1888, roy8vo, 2vols., contemp. roan, nice set, $75.00

MUIRHEAD, Jas., Historical Introduction to the Private Law of Rome. 2nd ed., rev. by Goudy. L, 1899, roy8vo, 457pp., $30.00

MUNRO, Wm., Municipal Government & Administration. NY, 1923, 8vo, 2vols., $35.00

MURPHY, Bruce, The Brandeis Frankfurter Connection: The Secret Political Activities of Two Supreme Court Justices. Oxford, 1982, 8vo, 473pp., new copies, $18.95

MYRDAL, Gunnar, An American Dilemma: The Negro Problem & Modern Democracy. NY, 1944, roy8vo, 1483pp., $35.00 (relied on as evidence in civilrights cases)

NAGEL, Stuart (ed.), The Rights of the Accused in Law & Action. Ca, 1972, roy8vo,320pp., $25.00

NEARING, Scott, War: Organized Destruction & Mass Murder. NY, 1931, 8vo, 310pp., $22.50

NEILSON, Geo., Trial by Combat. NY, 1891, 8vo, 347pp., $35.00

NEISON, Ralph, Economic Factors in the Growth of Corporation Giving. NY, 1970, roy8vo,115p, $17.50

A New & Complete Collectionof the Most Remarkable Trials for Adultery from the Tme of Henry VIII to the Present Period. L, 1780, 8vo, 2vols., later linen, $85.00

NEWMAN, Jos., Motivation Research & Marketing Management. Harvard, 1957, 8vo, 525pp., $22.50

NICHOLS, John & BRUCE, J. (eds.), Wills from Doctor's Commons: A Selection from the Wills of Eminent Persons Proved in the Court of Canterbury, 1495-1695. Camden Soc., 1863, roy8vo, 175pp., $35.00

NIZER, Louis, My Life in Court. NY, 1961, roy8vl, 524pp., $20.00

NOKES, G. D, An Introduction to Evidence. L, 1952, roy8vo, 427pp., $25.00

NORTHRUP,,Herbert, Compulsory Arbitration & Government Arbitration in Labor Disputes. DC, 1966, roy8vo, 449pp., $25.00

NOY, William, The Grounds & Maxims, & also An Analysis of the English Laws, to which is Annexed a Treatise on Estates by Sir John Doderidge & Observations on a Deed of Feoffment, by T. H. with Notes & Adds. by Chs. Barton. L, 1806, 12mo, 160pp., later linen, $85.00

NOY, Sir Wm., The Complete Lawyer, or, A Treatise Concerning Tenures & Estates in Lands of Inheritance for Life & Other Hereditaments & Chattels, Real & Personal, & How any of them may be Conveyed in a Legal Form...together with Observations on the Authoris Life. L, 1665, 12mo, 127pp., later 1/2 calf, $275.00

(Nuremberg) OFFICE OF THE U.S. CHIEF COUNSEL FOR THE PROSECUTION OF AXIS CRIMINALITY, Nazi Conspiracy & Aggression. (trial Transcripts), DC, GPO, 1946-48, thickroy8vo, 11vols., $350.00

"O", Forensic Fables. L, 1961, 8vo, 456pp., $20.00

O'BRIEN, Pat., The Revolution in Egypt's Economic System: From Private Enterprise to Socialism, 1952-1965. Oxford, 1966, roy8vo, 354pp., $22.50

O'DONNELL, Bernard, The Old Bailey & Its Trials. NY, 1951, 8vo, 226pp., $20.00

OSBORNE, John, William Cobbett: His Thought & Times. Rutgers UP, 1966,8vo, 272pp., $20.00

OSBORNE, Th., Society & Prisons. Yale UP, 1916, 8vo, 246pp., $22.50

PARRY, Hon. Ed., The Drama of the Law. L, 1924, 8vo, 319pp., new linen, $20.00

PARRY, Leonard, Some Famous Medical Trials. NY, 1928, roy8vo, 326pp., $22.50

PARSONS, Theophilus, Memoir of Chief Justice of the Supreme Judicial Court of Massachusetts, with Notices of Some of His Contemporaries. B, 1861, 8vo, 476pp., $35.00

PARSONS, Theophilus, The Law of Contracts. 6th ed., B, 1873, roy8vo, 3vols., roan, $75.00

PASVOLSKY, Leo, The Economics of Communism with Special Reference to Russia's Experiment. NY, 1921, 8vo, 312pp., $22.50

PATON, W. A., Accountant's Handbook. 3rdedd., NY, 1944, 8vo, 1500pp., $27.50

PAULSEN, Monrad, Legal Institutions Today & Tomorrow: The Centennial Conference Volume of the Columbia Law School. Columbia UP, 1959, roy8vo, 346pp., $27.50

PEASE, Rob., & CHERRINGTON, H., Mortgage Banking. NY, 1953, roy8vo, 458pp., $22.50

PEASE, Theodore C., The Laws of the Northwest Territory, 1788-1800. Springfield, 1925, roy8vo, xxxvi,591pp., $37.50

PEEL, Geo., The Financial Crisis of France. L, 1925, 8vo, 322pp., $22.50

PELHAM, Camden, The Chronicles of Crime; or, The New Newgate Calendar; being a Series of Memoirs & Anecdotes of Notorious Characters who have Outraged the Laws of Great Britain from the Earliest Period to the Present Time, Including a Number of Curious Cases Never before Published. Embellished with 52 Steel Engravings from Original Drawings by "Phiz." L, 1841, roy8vo, 2vols., orig. cl., sl. wear of extremeties, $115.00

PERKINS, Dexter, Hands Off: History of the Monroe Doctrine. B, 1941, roy8vo, 455pp., $27.50

PETERS, Th., Criminal Law. NY, 1935, roy8vo, 224pp., $22.50

PHILBRICK, Francis (ed.), The Laws of the Indiana Territory, 1801-1809. Springfield, 1930, roy8vo, 734pp., (Colls. of the Ill. St. Hist. Lib, XXI, Law Ser, II), $37.50

PHILBRICK, Fred., Language & the Law: Semantics of Forensic Research. NY, 1949, 8vo, 254pp., $22.50

PHILLIPS, Geo., An Exposition of the Principles of Pleading under the Codes of Civil Procedure. C, 1896, roy8vo, 604pp., $35.00

PHILLIPSON, Coleman, Termination of War & Treaties of Peace. L, 1916,roy8vo, 486pp., $27.50

PINCUS, Wm., Clinical Education for Law Students. NY, 1980, roy8vo, 467pp., $10.00

POLANYI, Michael, The Logic of Liberty. Unvi. of Chicago, 1951, 8vo, 206pp., $22.50

POLE, J. R. Political Representation in England & the Origins of the American Republic. NY, 1966, roy8vo, 606pp., $25.00

Political Handbook of the World. Publishedfor the Council on Foreign Relations, NY, 1928, 1931, 1934, 1937, 1942, 1943, 1944. Reprint: 1971, 4to, 8vols., 57.50

POLLOCK, Sir Frederick, & MAITLAND, F.W., The History of English Law Before the Time of Edward I. Cambridge/Boston, 1895, 4to, 2vols., orig. cl., first edition, scarce, a very clean, tight set, $150.00

POLLOCK, Sir Frederick, Essays in Jurisprudence & Ethics. L, 1882, roy8vo, 383pp., $35.00

POLLOCK, Frederick, & WRIGHT, R., An Essay on Possession in the Common Law. Oxford, 1888, roy8vo, 244pp., $35.00

(POLLOCK, Frederick) Leading Cases done into English by An Apprentice of Lincoln's Inn. 2nd ed., L, 1876, 8vo, 64pp., $30.00

POLLOCK, Frederick, Leading Cases done into English & Other Diversions. L, 1892, 8vo, 98pp,$35.00

POLLOCK, Frederick, Oxford Lectures & Other Discourses. L, 1890, 8vo, 303pp., $35.00

POSNER, Louis, Liability of the Trustee under the Corporate Indenture. NY, 1929, 8vo,120p, $20.00

POUND, Roscoe, An Introduction to the Philosophy of Law. Yale, 1922, 8vo, 307pp, 1st ed, $37.50

POUND, Roscoe et al, Jubilee Law Lectures, 1889-1939. School of Law, Catholic University of America. DC, 1939, 8vo, 182pp., $25.00

POUND, Roscoe, Criminal Justice in America. NY, 1930, 8vo, 226pp., $27.50

POUND, Roscoe, Justice According to Law. Yale, 1952, 8vo, 98pp., $22.50

*********** LAW PRINTS---ALL FRAMED ***********

"An Amiable Judge," Original color lithograph by "Spy" (Leslie Ward) 8x13; framed 16x22, $125.00

"The Barrister" Original artist's proof dry point etching, #3 of 60 signed by the artist, 7½x12; framed: 14½x19½, by S. Van Abbe, $225.00

"Briefing Counsel," Original artist's proof dry point etching by S. Van Abbe, #5 of 60 signed by the artist, 12½x8½; framed: 19½x15½, $225.00

"Counsel's Opinion," Original artist's proof dry point etching by S. Van Abbe, #28 of 60 signed by the artist, 10½x11; framed: 16½x20, $225.00

"Cross Examination," Original artist's proof dry point etching by S. Van Abbe, #55 of 60 signed by the artist, 10½x11; framed: 16½x20, $225.00

"Evidence," Original artist's proof dry point etching by S. Van Abbe, #11 of 60 signed by the artist, 11x11½; framed: 17x20, $225.00

"The Gatehouse, Lincoln's Inn," by Sidney R. Jones, original artist's proof etching signed by the artist, 9x12; framed: 14½x19½, $150.00

"Gray's Inn, the Hall," Etching by Herbert Railton (1892), 9x7; framed: 10x14, $125.00

"The House of Commons," (1807) by Rowlandson & Pugin, aquatint in color, 10½x9; framed: 16½x15, $150.00

"The House of Lords," aquatint in color by Rowlandson & Pugin, 10½x9; framed: 16½x15, $150.00

---15---

525) "Inner Temple Lane, Fleet Street," by Sidney R. Jones, original artist's proof etching signed by the artist, 5½x13; framed: 14½x19½, $150.00

526) "The Inner Temple Library," etching by Herbert Railton, 7x11; framed, 10x14, $125.00

527) "Interior of Lincoln's Inn Hall," engraving by A. E. Pearce (1893); 7x9½; framed: 10x14, $125.00

528) "Interior of the Temple Church," etching by Herbert Railton (1892); 7x11; framed, 10x14, $125.00

529) "Judicial Light Weight," by "Spy," original color lithograph; 8½x14½; framed: 16x21½, $125.00

"The Law's Delay--A Corner in Barnard's Inn," etching by E. Stamp after W. F. Yeames (1891), 6½x8½; framed: 10x14, $125.00

"The Library, Middle Temple," etching by Herbert Railton (1892), 9x7; framed: 10x14, $125.00

"Lincoln's Inn," by Nathaniel Sparks, original artist's proof etching signed by the artist, 9x12; framed: 14½x19½, $150.00

"Lincoln's Inn Hall," etching by Herbert Railton, 7x10; framed: 10x14, $125.00

"Lord Rutheford," etching, artist not identified, n.d. 10x13; framed: 20½x26, $125.00

"Master's House from the Inner Temple," etching by Herbert Railton (1892), 7x10; framed:10x14, $125.00

"Middle Temple Hall," etching by Herbert Railton, (1892), 7x10; framed: 10x14, $125.00

"Middle Temple Hall & Fountain Court,"etching by Herbert Railton, 9½x7; framed: 10x14, $125.00

"Old Bailey Session House," original water color drawing by T. Hosmer Shepherd (1811), signed, 7½x5½; framed: 14x12½, $125.00

"Oxford Circuit," original color lithograph by Spy (1896), 8½x13; framed: 16x21½, $125.00

"A Point of Law," by S. Van Abbe, original artist's proof dry point etching, signed by the artist, #50 of 60; 11x11½; framed: 17x20, $225.00

"Prosecuting Counsel," by S. Van Abbe, original artist's proof dry point etching, #2 of 60 signed by the artist, 7½x12; framed: 14½x19½, $225.00

"Rufus," original color lithograph by Spy (1904), 8½x13; framed: 14½x19½, $125.00

"Rufus Choate," etching, artist not identified, 6½x8½; framed: 13x16, $65.00

"Sergeant's Inn, Chancery Lane," by T. Hosmer Shepherd, original water color (1810), 10½xx8; framed: 14½x14, $125.00

"Sergeant's Inn, Fleet Street," by Sidney R. Jnnes, original artit's proof etching signed by the artist, 7½x11½; framed: 14½x19½, $150.00

"Sir Lloyd Kenyon" by T. Fittler, steel engraving, (1783), 14x19; framed: 22x28, $150.00

"Slim," original color lithograph by Spy, (1904), 8½x13½; framed: 16x21½, $125.00

"Slow & Steady," original color lithograph by Spy, (1900), 8x13½; framed: 16x21½, $125.00

"Staple Inn, Holborn," by Sidney R. Jones, original artist's proof etching sighed by the artist, 5½x13; framed: 14½x19½, $150.00

"Staple Inn, " etching by Herbert Railton, (1892), 9½x7½; framed: 14x10, $125.00

"Summing Up," by S. Van Abbe, original artist's proof dry point etching, #32 of 60 signed by the artist, 10½x11; framed: 16½x20, $225.00

"The Temple Church," engraving by Herbert Railton, (1893), 6½x9½; framed: 10x14, $125.00

"Ulsterman, K. C.,", original calor lighograph by Spy, (1903), 8½x13; framed: 16x21½, $125.00

Proceedings in the Trial of Andrew Johnson, President of the United States, before the U.S. Senate on Articles of Impeachment Exhibited by the House of Reps, DC, 1868, roy8vo, 1090pp, $85.00

PROCHNOW, Herbert (ed.), Determining the Business Outlook. NY, 1954, 8vo, 445p., $20.00

PROFFATT, John, The Curiosities & Law of Wills. SF, 1877, 12mo, 216pp., $22.50

The Public Laws of the State of Illinois Passed at the 21st Session ofthe General Assembly. Chicago, D. B. Cooke & Co., Law Book Publishers, 1859, 4to, 280pp., contemp. roan, $85.00

PUFENDORF, Samuel, Of the Law of Nature & Nations. Done into English by Basil Kennett, 4th ed., L, 1729, folio, 878pp., later 1/2 calf, sl. marg. dpst, nice copy, $450.00

PURCELL, Theodore, Blue Collar Man: Patters of Dual Allegiance in Industry. Harvard, 1960, roy8vo, 300pp., $20.00

AN UNRECORDED FIRST EDITION

PURVES, J. A., Law Visions; or, Pills for Posterity. L, 1736, 12mo, 238pp., contemp. calf, expertly rehinged, nice copy, not in NUC; not in BMC; a caustic attack on the legal profession and the common law system, arguing for parliamentary regulation of the former and codification of the latter; $350.00

PUSEY, Merlo, Charles Evans Hughes. NY, 1952, roy8vo, 2vols., $37.50

PUTERBAUGH, Sabin, Illinois Pleading & Practice. 2nd ed., rev. & enl., Chicago, Callaghan & Cutler, 1867, roy8vo, 899pp., later linen, nice copy, $87.50 (pre-fire imprint)

QUELLER, Donald, The Office of Ambassador in the Middle Ages. Princeton, 1967, 8vo, 251p, $22.50

RAMSAY, Sir Jas., The Angevin Empire, or the Three Reigns of Henry II, Richard I & John. Oxford, 1903, roy8vo, 555pp., $35.00

RANTOUL, Rob. Jr., Memoirs, Speeches & Writings, ed. by Luther Hamilton, B, 1854, roy8vo, 864pp., orig. cl., important early 19th century American attorney, abolitionist, death penalty opponent, strict constitutional constructionist, scarce, $65.00

RAY, I., M.D., A Treatise on the Medical Jurisprudence of Insanity. 5thed, w/Adds., B, 1871, roy8vo, 658pp., contemp. roan, bit rubbed, $65.00

READ, Conyers (ed.), William Lambarde & Local Government: His "Ephemeris" and 29 Charges to Juries and Commissions. Cornell UP, 1962, 8vo, 189pp., $22.50

READ, Homer, Recognition & Enforcement of Foreign Judgments in the Common Law Courts ofthe British Commonwealth. Harvard, 1938, roy8vo, 371pp., $27.50 (Harvard Studies in the Conflict of Laws, II)

Records, Computers & the Rights of Citizens: Report of the Secretary's Advisory Committee on Automated Personal Data Systems. U.S. Dept. of Health, Education & Welfare. 1973, 8vo, 344p., $25.00

Recueil des Cours: Collected Courses of the Hague Academy of International Law. 1971. Vols. I & III, Leiden, 1971, 2vols., $25.00

REDDEN, Kenneth, An Introductory Survey of the Place of Law in Our Civilization. Charlottesville, 1946, roy8vo, 272pp., some pencil underlining, $22.50

REED, John, Practical Suggestions for the Management of Law Suits & Conduct of Litigation, both in & Out of Court. NY, 1875, 8vo, 392pp., scarce, $35.00

Report of the Director of the Mint upon the Production of Precious Metals in the U.S. During the Year 1893. DC, 1894, 8vo, 317pp., $22.50

Report of Cases in the Vice Admiralty of the Province of New York, & in the Admiralty Court of the State of New York, 1715-1788, with Historical Intro. & Appendix, by Chs. Hough. Yale UP, 1925, roy8vo, 350pp., $30.00

RHEA, Rob., The Dow Theory. NY, 1932, roy8vo, 252pp., $20.00

RICHARDS, John, Abraham Lincoln: the Lawyer Statesman. B, 1916, roy8vo, 260pp., $25.00

RIDDLE, N. G., The Investment Policy of Trust Institutions. C, 1934, roy8vo, 310pp., $17.50

RIDEAU, Joel (ed.), Legal Aspects of Ecomomic Integration. Leiden, 1972, roy8vo, 620pp., $27.50

ROBINSON, Gerald, Going Public: Successful Securities Underwriting. NY, 1961, roy8vo, 353pp., $25.00

ROBINSON, Roland, The Management of Bank Funds. 2nd ed., NY, 1962, roy8vo, 445pp., $22.50

ROBINSON, Wm., Elementary Law. rev & new ed., B, 1910, roy8vo, 762pp., $35.00

ROBITSCHER, Jas., Pursuit of Agreement: Psychiatry & the Law. P, 1966, roy8vo, 270pp., $22.50

ROCK, Ronald, Hospitalization & Discharge of the Mentally Ill. Unvi. of Chicago, 1968, roy8vo, 268pp., $25.00

ROGERS, R. V, The Law of the Road: Wrongs & Rights of a Traveller (Legal Recreations, IV), SF 1876, 12mo, 275pp., $25.00

ROMMEN, Heinrich, The Natural Law: A Study in Legal & Social History & Philosophy. trans. T. H. Hanley, St.L, 1955, roy8vo, 290pp., $25.00

ROSENHEIM, Marg (ed.), Justice for the Child. NY, 1962, 8vo, 240pp., $22.50

ROSENNE, Shabtai, The World Court. 3rd ed, Leiden, 1973, roy8vo, 252pp., $22.50

~~xxxxxxxxxxxxxxxxxxxxxxx~~ RUSSELL, Isaac, Outline Study of Law. 3rded, NY, 1900, 344pp, $35.00

RUSSELL, John, The Finance of Higher Education. Univ. of Chicago, 1954, roy8vo, 416pp, $22.50

SAULINIER, Raymond, Contemporary Monetary Theory: Studies of Some Recent Theories of Money, Prices & Production. NY, 1938, 8vo, 420pp., $22.50

SAYRE, Francis, A Selection of Cases in Criminal Law, with Intro. by Roscoe Pound. R, 1927, 4to, xxxix, 1135pp., $37.50

SAYERS, R. S. (ed.), Banking in Western Europe. Oxford, 1964, 8vo, 403pp., $22.50

SCHENK, Alan, The Value Added Tax in the UK. C, 1976, roy8vo, 300pp., $22.50

SCHERMERS, Hanry, International Institutional LawII: Functioning Legal Order. Leiden, 1972, roy8vo, 790pp., $20.00

SCHLATTER, Richard, Private Property: History of an Idea. Rutgers UP, 1951, 8vo, 283pp., $25.00

SCHLESINGER, Rudolf (ed.), Formation of Contracts: A Study ofthe Common Core of Legal Systems. DF/L, 1968, 1968, 4to, 2vols., $27.50

SCHNEIDER, David, History of Public Welfare in the State of New York, 1609-1866. Univ.of Chicago, 1938, 8vo, 395pp., $22.50

SCHOFIELD, Henry, Essays on Constitutional Law & Equity & Other Subjects. ed. by the Faculty of Law, Northwestern Univ., B, 1921, 4to, 2vols., $65.00

SCHULZ, Fritz, Classical Roman Law. Oxford, 1969, roy8vo 650pp., $45.00

SCHULZ, Fritz, History of Roman Legal Science. Oxford, 1946, 8vo, 358pp., $37.50

SCOTT, Henry, Distinguished American Lawyers with Their Struggles & Triumphs in the Forum. NY, 1891, 4to, 716pp., ill.with engraved plates, scarce, later linen, $87.50

SCOTT, Jas. Brown, (ed.), Instructions to the American Delegates to the Hague Peace Conferences & Their Official Reports. Oxford UP, 1916, 4to, 138pp., (Carnegie Endowment), $26.50

SCOTT, Jas. Brown (ed.), The Hague Court Reports. Oxford UP, 1916, 4to, cxi,664pp., small hole in spine, $45.00

SCOTT, Jas. Brown, (ed.), Cases on International Law, Principally Selected from Decisions of English & American Courts. St.P, 1922, 4to, 1196pp., $37.50

Secret Journals of the Acts & Proceedings of Congress from the First Meeting Thereof to the Dissolution of the Confederation by the Adoption of the Constitution. B, 1821, 8vo, 4vols., contemp. roan, sl. wear of extremeties, few hinges a bit cracked but all firm, new labels, first edition, $350.00

SEDGWICK, Theodore, A Treatise on the Measure of Damages. 9th ed., rev. & enl., NY, 1913, 4to, 4vols., $75.00

SEE, Henri, Modern Capitalism. NY, 1928, 8vo, 225pp., $17.50

SEIDMAN, Joel (ed.), Trade Union Government & Collective Bargaining. NY, 1970, roy8vo, 304p, $22.50

SELDEN, John, Titles of Honor. 3rd ed., Corr. L, 1672, folio, 756pp., old calf, rebacked, sporadic foxing & soil, $375.00

SELIGMAN, Edwin, The Shifting Incidence of Taxation. 4th ed.,rev, Columbia, 1921, roy8vo,431p,$30.00

SELLERS, Alvin, The Leopold-Loeb Case, with Excerptsfrom the Evidence of the Alienists. Brunswick, Ga., 1926, 8vo, 312pp., scarce, $30.00

SEN, S. R., The Economics of Sir James Steuart. Harvard, 1957, 8vo, 207pp., $20.00

~~xxxxxxxxx~~,613) SEYFARTH, SHAW, FAIRWEATHER, Labor Relations & the Law in W. Germany & the U.S. Unvi. of Michigan, 1969, roy8vo, 606pp., $22.50

614) SEYMOUR, S, M., Bantu Law in So. Africa, 3rd ed., Cape Town, 1970,roy8vo,429p,$27.50

615) SHERMAN, Chs., Roman Law in the Modern World. B, 1917, roy8vo, 3vols., $105.00

616) SHIEL, Rt. Hon. Richard, Sketches of the Irish Bar, with Memoir & Notes by R. S. Mackenzie. St.L., 1882, 8vo, 2vols. bound as one, nice copy, $45.00

617) SHINN, Glenn, Reasonable Freight Rates. DC, 1952, roy8vo, 195pp., $22.50

618) SHIPMAN, Benjamin, Handbook of Common Law Pleading. 3rd ed., St.P, 1923, 4to, 644pp., $27.50

SHULTZ, Birl, The Securities Market & How It Works. NY, 1946, roy8vo, 433p., $20.00

SHULTZ, Gladys, How Many More Victims? Society & the Sex Criminal. P, 1965, 8vo, 363pp., $22.50

SHULTZ, Wm., American Public Finance & Taxation. rev. ed., NY, 1936, roy8vo, 635pp., $27.50

SIDNEY, Algernon, Discourses Concerning Government, Published from an Original Manuscript of the Author. L, 1698, folio, 462pp., contemp. calf, skillfully rebacked, covers bit rubbed, new end sheets, forecorners a bit worn,nice copy, first edition, a classic work of republican political philosophy, the government of laws and not of men, $750.00

SIMON, Rita (ed.), The Sociology of Law: Interdisciplinary Readings. Pa, 1968, roy8vo, 688p, $27.50

SINDLINGER, Harvey & NELSON, G., Illinois Township Laws. C, 1940, roy8vo, 609pp., $27.50

SMITH, Geo., Elements of Right & of the Law, to which is Added an Historical & Critical Essay upon the Several Theories of Jurisprudence. 2nd ed., C, 1887, 8vo, 398pp., scarce, $30.00

SMITH, Reginald, Justice & the Poor" A Study ofthe Present Denial of Justice to the Poor with Particular Reference to Legal Aid Work in the US. NY, 1919, 4to, 271pp., $30.00

SMITH, Richard, Corporations in Crisis. NY, 1963, roy8vo, 214pp., $20.00

The Social Evil in Chicago: A Study of Existing Conditions with Recommendations by the Vice Commission of Chicago. C, 1911, roy8vo, 399pp., $27.50

SOHM, Rudolph, The Institute: A Textbook of the History & System of Roman Private Law. trans. Jas. Ledlie, 2nd ed., Oxford, 1901, roy8vo, 639pp., later linen, $37.50

SOLDAN-HEPPE, Geschichte der Hexenprozesse, neu Bearbeitet und Herausgegeben von Max Bauer. (History of the Witchcraft Trials), Hanau/M, 1968, 8vo, 2vols., 1000pp., $47.50

SOMBART, Werner, Die Juden und das Wirtschaftsleben. L, 1911, roy8vo, 476pp., orig. 1/2 vellum & bds, firstedition, $115.00

SPENCER, Wm., & GILLAM, C., Casebook of Law & Business. NY, 1953, 4to, 968pp., $25.00

SPRAGUE, O. M., History of Crises under the National Banking System. DC, 1910, 8vo, 484pp., wrps, sl. wear, $25.00

STAHL, David et al, The Community & Racial Crises. NY, Practicing Law Institute, 1966, 364p, $25.00

STANSBURY, Arthur, Report of the Trial of Jas. H. Peck, Judge of the U.S. Dist. Court for the Dist. of Missouri, before the Senate of the U.S., on an Impeachment....for High Misdemeanors in Office. B, 1833, roy8vo, 592pp., later linen, $75.00

The Statutes of Illinois: An Analytical Digest of All the General Laws in Force at the Present Time, from 1818 to 1868, ed. by Eugene L. Gross. Chicago, E. B. Myers & Co., Law Booksellers & Publishers, 1868, roy8vo, 1000pp., contemp. roan, sl. wear, $85.00

Statutes of Illinois, Embracing All of the General Laws of the State in Force Dec 1, 1857, with Marginal Notes Showing the Contents of Each Section, and a Reference to the Decisions of the Supreme Court upon the Construction of Each Statute, compiled by Samuel Treat, Walter Scates, & Rob. Blackwell. Chicago, D. B. Cooke & Co., 1858, 4to, 2vols., contemp. roan, $115.00

STEIN, Herbert, The Fiscal Revolution in America. Univ. of Chicago, 1969, roy8vo, 526pp., $25.00

STENTON, Doris, English Justice Between the Norman Conquest & the Great Charter. P, 1964, roy8vo, 238pp., $27.50

STENTON, F. M., The First Century of English Feudalism, 1066-1166. Oxford, 1954, 8vo, 311pp, $30.00

STENTON, Doris, After Runnymede: Magna Carta in the Middle Ages. Va, 1965, 8vo,54pp, wrps, $17.50

STEPHEN, Sir Geo., (also attributed to Sir Jas. Stephen and to Samuel Warren), Adventures of an Attorney in Search of Practice: A Delineation of Professional Life. 2nd ed., L, 1840, 8vo, 450pp., rebacked, $45.00

STEPHEN, Henry John, A Treatise on the Principles of Pleading in Civil Actions. 3rd American from the 3rd London ed., with Adds. by Fr. Troubat. P, 1837, roy8vo, 650pp., later linen, $36.50

STEPHEN, Sir Jas. F., A General View of the Criminal Law of England. 2nd ed., L, 1890,399p, $35.00

STEPHEN, Sir Jas. F., A Digest of the Law of Evidence. 2nd ed., St.L, 1876, 16mo, 226p, $25.00

STEPHEN, Sir Jas. F., A History of the Criminal Law of England. L, 1883, 8vo, 3vols., contemp. 1/2 calf, sl. rubbed, $75.00

STEPHEN, Leslie, The Life of Sir Jas. Fitzjames Stephen, A Judge of the High Court of Justice. L, 1895, roy8vo, 504pp., sl. wear, scarce, $35.00

ST. GERMAIN, Christopher, A Dialogue in English between a Doctor of Divinity & a Student in the Laws of England, Newly Corrected & Improved with Additions. (L), 1638, 12mo, 352pp., contemp. calf, sometime rebacked, black letter, sound, attractive copy, $225.00

ST GERMAIN, Christopher, Doctor & Student: or Dialogues Between a Doctor of Divinity & a Student in the Laws of England; Containing the Grounds of those Laws together with Questions & Cases Concerning the Equity & Conscience thereof; also Comparingthe Civil, Canon, Common & Statute Laws, & Shewing wherein they vary from One Another, the 16th Edition, to which are Now Restored & Added (by W. W.) Thirteen Chapters on the Power & Jurisdiction of the Parliament, etc. Omitted in All the Editions, since the Year 1531, except the Last. L, 1761, 8vo, 344pp., contemp. calf, rebacked, nice copy, $250.00

ST GERMAIN, Christopher, The Doctor & Student....rev. & corr. by Wm. Muchall, to which are Added Two Pieces Concerning Suits in Chancery by Subpoena. Cincinnati, 1874, roy8vo, 401pp., later linen, $65.00

,STOKES, Anthony, A View of the Constitution of the British Colonies in North America & the West Indies. (1783), Reprint: L, 1969, 8vo, 561pp., $35.00

STORY, Jos., Commentaries on the Law of Bailments with Illustrations from the Civil & Foreign Law. 5th ed., rev. corr. & enl., later linen, $75.00

) STORY, Jos., Life & Letters, ed. by His Son, Wm. Story. B, 1851, roy8vo, 2vols., orig. cl, first edition, $150.00

---16---

STOWELL, Ellery & MUNRO, H., International Cases. B, 1916, 8vo, 2vols., $27.50

STRONG, Theron, Landmarks of a Lawyer's Lifetime. NY, 1914, roy8vo, 552p, $20.00

STRONG, Thero, Jos. Hodges Choate: Lawyer, Ambassador. NY, 1917, roy8vo, 389p, $22.50

The Supreme Court of the United States, Its History by Hampton L. Carson, and Its Centennial Celebration (Feb. 1890). Prepared underthe Direction of the Judiciary Centennial Committee. P, 1894, folio, 2vols., later linen, with full page engravings of all the justices to that date, $125.00

SWIFT, Zepeniah, A Digest of the Laws of the State of Connecticut. NH, 1822, roy8vo, 2vols., bound in contemp. roan, nice set, $75.00

SWISHER, Carl, The Growth of Constitutional Power in the US. Univ. of Chicago, 1946, 8vo, 261p, $20.00

SWISHER, Carl, American Constitutional Development. 2nd ed., B, 1954, 4to, 1145pp., $37.50

SWISHER, Carl, Roger B. Taney. NY, 1935, roy8vo, 608pp., $30.00

TAYLOR, Hannis, The Science of Jurisprudence. NY, 1908, roy8vo, 676pp., $35.00

TAYLOR, Hannis, The Origin & Growth of the English Constitution. B, 1900, 8vo, 2vols., 1200pp., covers a bit spotted, $65.00

TERRE, Francis, L'Influence de la Volonte Individuelle sur les Qualifications. P, 1957, 599p, $20.00

THOMPSON, Faith, Magna Carta. Univ. of Minnesota, 1948, roy8vo, 410pp., $27.50

THOMSON, Geo., A Kind of Justice: Two Studies in Treason (Gowrie Conspiracy & Red Colin Campbell) L, 1970, 8vo, 220pp., $20.00

TIDD, Wm., The Practice of the Court of King's Bench in Personal Actions....2nd American ed., with Corrs. & Adds. by a Gent. of the Bar. NY, 1807, 8vo, 2vols., later linen, "No treatise in modern times approaches nearer judicial authority than this." Marvin, 691; $115.00

TILLOTSON, Lee, The Articles of War Annotated. 2nd ed., rev. Pa, 1943, roy8vo, 291pp., $22.50

TIMBS, John (ed.), A Book of Modern Legal Anecdotes, the Bar, Bench & Woolsack. L n.d.(1900), 12mo, 156pp., $22.50

TODD, John, The Mechanism of Exchange. Oxford, 1949, 8vo, 290pp., $20.00

TOLLES, N. A., The Origins of Modern Wage Theories. NJ, 1964, 8vo, 241pp., $20.00

TORIQUIAN, Shavarsh, The Armenian Question & International Law. Beirut, 1973, roy8vo, 330p, $25.00

TRACHTENBERG, Alex, History of Legislation for the Protection of Coal Miners in Pennsylvania. NY, 1942, 8vo, 239pp., $25.00

TREHARNE, R. F., The Baronial Plan of Reform, 1258-1263. Manchester UP, 1971, roy8vo, 478pp, $30.00

TUCKER, Geo., Your Will: How to Make It. B, 1895, 8vo, 113pp., $20.00

TURNER, Ralph, The King & His Courts: The Role of John & Henry III in the Administration of Justice. Cornell UP, 1968, 8vo, 310pp., $22.50

TYLER, Samuel, Memoir of Roger Brooke Taney. Balto, 1872, roy8vo, 659pp, sl. wear, $35.00

ULC, Otto, The Judge in a Communist State. Ohio UP, 1972, roy8vo, 307pp., $22.50

UMBREIT, Kenneth, Our Eleven Chief Justices: A History of the Supreme Court in Terms of Their Personalities. NY, 1938, roy8vo, 375pp., $30.00

UNITED STATES, 59th Congress, 1st Session, Senate, Document #243. Regulation of Railway Rates: Hearings before the Committee on Interstate Commerce....on Bills to Amend the Interstate Commerce Act. DC, GPO, 1906, thick roy8vo, 6vols., original 1/2 morocco, scarce, $175.00

UPHOFF, Walter, Kohler on Strike: 30 Years of Conflict. B, 1966, roy8vo, 449pp., $30.00

UPTON, Francis, The Law of Nations Affecting Commerce During War, with a Review of the Jurisdiction, Practices & Proceedings of Prize Courts. NY, 1861, roy8vo, 303pp., later buck, ex lib, $75.00

URCH, Erwin, The Evolution of the Inquisitorial Procedure in Roman Law. (1930), Rep: 1980, 8vo, 67pp., wrps., $10.00

VANDERBILDT, Arthur, Minimum Standards of Judicial Administration. NYU Pr, 1949, roy8vo, 752p, $27.50

VENN, J. A., The Foundations of Agricultural Economics, Together with an Economic History of British Agriculture During & After the Great War. Cambridge UP, 1933, roy8vo, 600pp., $37.50

VERNEY, Lady, Howthe Peasant Owner Lives in Parts of France, Germany, Italy & Russia. L 1888, 8vo, 234pp., $20.00

VERWEY, Wil., Economic Development, Peace & Int'l Law. Assen, 1972, roy8vo, 363pp., $25.00

VINOGRADOFF, Paul, Common Sense in Law. NY, n.d. (1910), 12mo, 256pp., $22.50

VINOGRADOFF, Paul, The Growth of the Manor. 2nd ed., rev. L, 1911, 8vo, 384pp., $30.00

VINOGRADOFF, Paul, Villainage in England. Oxford UP, 1968, roy8vo, 464pp., $35.00

VON BAR, Carl L., A History of Continental Criminal Law, trans. T. Belli, pref. by Wigmore. B, 1916, roy8vo, 561pp., spine lettering faded, $30.00

von HOLST, Hermann, The Constitutional & Political History of the U.S. trans. Lalor & Mason. C, 1889, roy8vo, 8vols., nice set, $175.00

von Jhering, Rudolf, Geist des Romischen Rechts auf den verschiedenen Stufen seiner Entwicklung. (Spirit of Roman Law in the Various Stages of Its Development), 10th ed., (1907), Rep: 1968, 8vo, 4vols., a classic, $125.00

von MEHREN, Arthur, The Civil Law System. NJ, 1957, 4to, 922pp., $22.50

von MISES, Ludwig, Theory & History. (Yale, 1957), Rep: 1969, 8vo, 384pp., $25.00

WAIGHT, Leonard, History & Mechanism of the Exchange Equalization Account. Cambridge UP, 1939, 8vo, 91pp., $17.50

WALKER, Nigel, Crime & Punishment in Britain: An Analysis of the Penal System in Theory, Law & Practice. rev. ed., Edinburgh UP, 1968, roy8vo, 373pp., wrps, $20.00

WALTER, Erich (ed.), Religion & the State University. Univ. of Michigan, 1958, roy8vo, 321p, $22.50

WALTERS, Raymond, Albert Gallatin: Jeffersonian Finaicier & Diplomat. NY, 1957, 8vo, 461p, $20.00

The Walworth Parracide: A Full Account of the Astounding Murder of Mansfield T. Walworth by His Son, with the Trial & Conviction.. n.p., n.d. (NY, 1876), 8vo, 50pp., $45.00

---17---

701) WAMBAUGH, Eugene, The Study of Cases. 2nd ed., B, 1894, 8vo, 333pp., $25.00

702) WANDER, Herb., & GRIENENBERGER, W. (eds.), Selected Articles on Federal Securities Law. C, 1968, roy8vo, 985pp., $27.50

703) WAR DEPT., OFFICE OF THE JUDGE ADVOCATE GENERAL, A Digest of Opinions of the Judge Advocates General of the Army. DC, 1912, roy8vo, 1171pp., $25.00

704) WARD, Robert, An Inquiry into the Foundation & History of the Law of Nations in Europe from the Time of the Greeks & Romans to the Age of Grotius. L, 1795, 8vo, 2vols., contemp. calf, beautiful set, $250.00

WARKOV, Seymour, Lawyers in the Making. C, 1965, 8vo, 180pp., $20.00

WARREN, Chs., Congress, the Constitution & the Supreme Court. B, 1935, roy8vo, 346pp, $25.00

WARREN, Chs., The Supreme Court in United States History. B, 1926, rev ed., 2vols., $65.00

WARREN, Jos., Select Cases & Other Authorities on the Law of Wills & Administration. Cambridge, Harvard, 1917, roy8vo, 879pp., $25.00

WARREN, Samuel, The Experiences of a Barrister & Confessions of an Attorney. B, 1881, 8vo, 376pp., sl.wear, $35.00

WARREN, W. L., Henry II. Univ. of California, 1973, roy8vo, 693pp., $25.00

WATERS, Jas., The Court of Missing Heirs. NY, 1941, 8vo, 281pp., $22.50

WATSON, Richard, & DOWNING, R., The Politics of Bench & Bar: Judicial Selection under the Missouri Non-Partisan Plan. NY, 1969, roy8vo, 393pp., $22.50

WATT, Francis, Terrors of theLaw, Being Portraits of Three Lawyers, "Bloody Jeffrieys," "Bluidy Advocate Mackenzie" and the Original Weir of Hermiston. L, 1902, 12mo, 129pp., $25.00

WATT, Francis, The Law's Lumber Room. L, 1906, 8vo, 139pp; bound with his: Second Series, 1908, 202pp., learned studies in legal history, $35.00

WEBB, Leicester (ed.), Legal Personality & Political Pluralism. Univ. of Melbourne, 1958, 8vo, 200pp., $22.50

WEBSTER, Daniel, Speeches & Forensic Arguments. B, 1846, roy8vo, 3vols., sl. wear, $75.00

WEDGWOOD, C. V., The King's Peace, 1637-1641. NY, 1956, 8vo, 510pp., $22.50

WEISSER, Michael, Crime & Punishment in Early Modern Europe. NJ, 1979, 8vo, 193p, $17.50

WELLMAN, Francis, Gentlemen of the Jury: Reminiscences of 30 Years. NY, 1944, roy8vo, 298pp, $20.00

WESKETT, John, A Complete Digest of the Theory, Laws & Practice of Insurance, Compiled from the Best Authorities in Different Languages....with a Preliminary Discourse Deliniating the Very Great Disorders which Prevail in the Affairs of Insurance, their Principal Causes Explained & Methods Proposed for better Regulation & Prevention. L, 1781, tall folio, 612pp., later 1/2 calf & bds, $250.00

WEST, B. B., Wills & How Not to Make Them, w/ a Selection of Leading Cases. L, 1893, 12mo, 186p, $25.00

WESTON, Alan, Privacy & Freedom. NY, 1967, roy8vo, 487pp., $22.50

WHARTON, Francis, & STILLE, F., Medical Jurisprudence. 4th ed., P, 1882, roy8vo, 3vols., roan, $125.00

WHEATON, Henry, A Digest of the Law of Maritime Captures & Prizes. NY, 1815, 8vo, 380pp., later linen, first edition, $150.00

WHEELER-BENNETT, John, & LATIMER, H., Information on the Reparation Settlement, Being the Background & History of the Young Plan & the Hague Agreements, 1929-1930. L, 1930, 8vo, 253pp., sl.wear, $20.00

WHITE, Albert, The Making of the English Constitution. NY, 1908, 8vo, 410pp., $22.50

WHITE, G. E., The American Judicial Tradition. Oxford UP, 1976, roy8vo, 441pp., $20.00

WHITE, John, Public & Private Property, with Reference to Several Decisions of the Supreme Court. Pa, 1935, 8vo, 312pp., $27.50

WHITMORE, Wm., The Colonial Laws of Massachusetts, Reprinted from the Edition of 1660, with the Supplements to 1672, Containing also the Body of Liberties of 1641. B, 1889, 4to, 312pp., plus 8pp. supp. laid in, contemp. 1/2 morocco, sl. rubbed, $57.50

WHITNEY, Henry C., Life on the Circuit with Lincoln, with Sketches of Generals Grant, Sherman & McClellan, Judge Davis....& Other Contemporaries. B, 1892, 4to, 601pp., orig. cl., ill., 67 plates, scarce, Howes W386 "aa", $75.00

WICKER, Elmus, Federal Reserve Monetary Policy, 1917-1933. NY, 1966, 8vo, 221pp., $20.00

WIGMORE, John Henry (Chairman), Committee of the Association of American Law Schools.(eds.), Select-Essays in Anglo-American Legal History, by Various Authors. B, 1907, roy8vo, 3vols., over 2500pp., best collection of its kind ever published, $125.00

WILKINSON, Th., The Urbanization of Japanese Labor, 1863-1955. Univ. of Mass, 1965, roy8vo, 243p, $20.00

WILLIAMS, Chs. R., Some Professional Recollections by a Former Member of the Council of the Incorporated Law Society. L, 1883, 8vo, 326pp., later linen, $30.00

WILLIAMSON, Harold (ed.), Growth of the American Economy. 2nd ed., NJ, 1951, roy8vo, 946p, $20.00

WILLIAMS, John, The Theory of Investment Value. Harvard, 1938, roy8vo, 613pp., $22.50

WILLIAMS, Joshua, Principles of the Law of Personal Property. 2nd American from the 2nd English ed., w/Notes to the Latest American Decisions by Gerhard & Wetherill. P, 1855, roy8vo, 484p, $65.00

WILLIS, Hugh, Introduction to Anglo-American Law, Covering Briefly Legal Philosophy, Legal History Legal Biography & Legal Bibliography. Indiana Univ. Stud, XIII, No. 69, (1926), 234pp, $30.00

WILLISTON, Samuel, The Law Governing the Sale of Goods at Common Law. 2nd ed. NY, 1924, 2vols, $47.50

WILSON, James, Works of. ed. McCloskey. Harvard, 1967, roy8vo, 2vols., $57.50

WINFIELD, Percy, Chief Sources of English Legal History. Harvard, 1925, 8vo, 374p, faded, $35.00

WINGFIELD, Marshall, An Old Virginia Court, Being a Transcript of the Records of the First Court of Franklin County, Virginia, 1786-1789, with Biographies of the Justices & Stories of Famous Cases. Memphis, 1948, roy8vo, 258pp., $37.50

WITT, John, Life in the Law. L, (1920), 8vo, 224pp., sp. sl. faded, $20.00

WOLFFE, B. B., The Royal Demesne in English History: The Crown Estate in the Governance of the Realm from the Conquest to 1509. Ohio UP, 1971, roy8vo, 324pp., $25.00

WOLFF, Hans, Roman Law: An Historical Introduction. Univ. of Oklahoma, 1951, 8vo, 260pp, $22.50

WOOD, Gordon, Creation of the American Republic, 1776-87. Univ. of No.Carolina Press, 1969, roy8vo, 653pp., $25.00

WOOD, Thomas, A New Institute of the Imperial or Civil Law, with Notes Shewing in Some Principal Cases amongst Other Observations, How the Canon Law, the Laws of England & the Laws & Customs of other Nations Differ from It, 4th ed., Corr., to which is Prefixed....A Treatise of the First Principles of Laws in General, of Their Nature & Design, & of the Interpretation of Them. L, 1730, folio, 342pp., later 1/2 calf & bds, bit rubbed & scuffed, nicecopy, $275.00

This is an author and title index. If an entry gives an author or editor on the title page it is indexed under that name. If no name is given it is indexed under title. Trials are partial exceptions. If no editor or reporter is given then the work is indexed under the last name of the first dedendant mentioned in the title. If none is mentioned, then the work is indexed by title. All "prints" "manuscripts" and "yearbooks" are indexed under those designations.

GIFFORD, John 3

HEINEMANN, 286
HELLMAN, Geo. 307

Richard Adamiak is a Chicago bookseller who has specialized in law materials for ten years. He is a doctoral candidate in the University of Chicago. He has contributed articles to the *Journal of Politics*, *Journal of the History of Ideas* and *Survey: A Journal of East and West Studies* and is the author of *Justice and History in the Old Testament* (Cleveland: 1982).